Also by Michael J. Weldon
The Psychotronic® Encyclopaedia of Film

Also from Titan Books
The Bare Facts Video Guide
Behind The Mask: The Secrets of Hollywood's Monster Makers
The Hellraiser Chronicles
Hong Kong Action Cinema
The Illustrated Dinosaur Movie Guide
The Illustrated Frankenstein Movie Guide
The Illustrated Vampire Movie Guide
The Illustrated Werewolf Movie Guide
Immoral Tales: Sex and Horror Cinema in Europe 1956-1984
Sacred Monsters: Behind the Mask of the Horror Actor
Sex and Zen & A Bullet in the Head
Shock: The Essential Guide to Exploitation Cinema

All Titan's film and TV titles are available through most good bookshops or direct from Titan Books' mail order service. For a free catalogue or to order, telephone 01536 763 631 or contact Titan Books Mail Order, PO Box 54, Desborough, Northants., quoting reference PVG/PB.

THE PSYCHOTRONIC VIDEO GUIDE

Michael J. Weldon

TITAN BOOKS

Dedicated to:
42nd Street

THE PSYCHOTRONIC VIDEO GUIDE
ISBN 1 85286 770 1

Published by
Titan Books
42-44 Dolben Street
London SE1 0UP

First Titan edition November 1996
1 3 5 7 9 10 8 6 4 2

Design by Junie Lee
Edited by Gordon Van Gelder
Cover design by Chris Teather

British Library Cataloguing-in-Publication Data. A catalogue record for this book is available from the British Library.

Photo permissions appear on page 638, which constitutes an extension of this copyright page.

Printed in Great Britain by Hartnolls Ltd, Bodmin, Cornwall.

Acknowledgments

Special thanks to Suh Mi Hwa (aka Mia Weldon), Akira Fitton, and Fred Brockman. This book and *Psychotronic® Video* magazine wouldn't exist without them. Same goes for Mathew Bialer, Gordon Van Gelder, Mary Louise Mooney, Michael J. Ford, Andrew J. Klyde, and Eileen Schlesinger Cotton.

Thanks to Dale Ashmun, Sean Axmaker, Lucas Balbo, Keith Bearden, Art Black, Richard Bojarski, Eric Caiden, Ken Carpenter, Paula Catarino, Dan Clowes, Larry Cohn, Nancy Coleman, Shane M. Dallman, Dennis Daniel, David Del Valle, John Donaldson, Gary Dumm, Craig Edwards, Joyce Faust, David F. Friedman, Drew Friedman, Lowell Goldman, Greg Goodsell, Rickard Gramfors, Rudolph Grey, Alan Handelman, Richard Henderson, Frank Henenlotter, Gary Hertz, John Holmstrom, Fred Hopkins, Peter Hughes, Justin Humphries, Mark Isted, Ian Johnston, Ed Kelleher, Charles Kilgore, J. D. King, Jim Knush, David Konow, Steve Latshaw, Johnny Legend, Kurt Loder, Jay Lorenz, Greg Luce, Mark Madenwald, Brett McCormick, Maitland McDonagh, Kevin McDonough, Brian McMahon, Harry Medved, Donald Metz, Vincent J. Mizzi, Barry Monush, Michael Murphy, Peter Orr, Louis Paul, Anthony Petkovich, Michael Price, Char Rao, Thomas C. Rainone, Johnny Ramone, Jim Ridenour, Cynthia Rose, Todd Rutt, Al Ryan, Gordon K. Smith, Audrey Sparkes, Frank Uhle, Tom Unterburger, Mike Vraney, Steve Voce, Mark Voger, Kevin Walsh, Bill Warren, Ken Weiner, Tom Weiser, Michael Will, and everyone else who worked on or contributed to *Psychotronic®* magazines, calendars, books, or our store, plus all you *Psychotronic®* readers throughout the world.

Thanks to Sally Eckhoff, Charlie Beesley, Christopher Cerf, Bob Martin, and everybody who helped get *Psychotronic®* started back in the East Village in the early eighties and Jim Ellis, John Morton, John Thompson, David Thomas, and everybody who first encouraged me to write about this stuff back in the seventies in Cleveland. And I wish Tom Allen, Mike Antel, Lester Bangs, Stiv Bators, Patti Dow, Bradly Fields, Berni Goodrich, Brian Hudson, Jim Hurley, Peter Laughner, Norman Petrie, George Scott, Alfred Sturdevant, and too many others were still around.

Foreword

What the Psychotronic® Video Guide Reviews

There are alphabetical reviews here of more than 3000 features (and select TV shows on video) that are considered Psychotronic®. That means horror, science fiction, fantasy, and exploitation movies. These are the releases that used to be called "B" features and were later popular in inner-city grindhouses, at drive-ins, and on local late-night TV. These days, you can see many of them at any time of the day on cable TV or whenever you want to on video. It doesn't matter when or where they were made, whether they're "good" or not, whether they cost a few thousand dollars or over $100 million. They can be barely released obscurities, acknowledged cult items, or over-hyped and over-merchandised household names. And unlike other movie guides, nothing is omitted because it's in bad taste. All of this stuff is out there. You should know about it.

I've included silent features now available on tape, serials that were previously only available in condensed TV release versions, and features from any time period that have been rediscovered thanks to video. I've included most seventies black action movies, many Italian westerns, women-in-prison movies, jd (juvenile delinquent) and rock and roll movies, select Asian and martial arts titles, mondo documentaries, biblical and historical epics, some WWII propaganda movies, various "underground" features, and many old (pre-porno) "adults only" movies. Roadshow movies covering once-forbidden themes like drugs, prostitution, and even childbirth are here along with nudist-colony features and vintage adult dramas and comedies that featured nudity as the main attraction.

Most movies are reviewed here for obvious reasons. Others are reviewed because of the companies that made or released them, the director, or the casts. You'll find releases by top quality directors of the past (Hitchcock, Lang, Buñuel . . .), the most Psychotronic® directors of the past (Corman, Castle, Browning . . .) and the most prolific of recent years (Franco, Ray, Santiago . . .). Anything that Roger Corman had anything to do with fits, as well as nearly anything from the companies he was involved with (AIP, New World, and Concorde). Other companies that have turned out appropriate stuff nonstop are Cannon, Charles Band's Full Moon (and before that Empire and Wizard), Troma, P.M., and the (unrelated) AIP video company. Name-brand video companies (RCA, Warner, Republic, MCA . . .) usually have little or nothing to do with the old companies of the same names and in no way guarantee any kind of high quality viewing.

Information Included

D: director	**A:** actor
S: screenwriter	**C:** cinematographer
P: producer	**M:** music
E: editor	

I provide director, screenwriter, and producer credits whenever possible. I only include running times when a title is especially long (say, over 2 hours) or short (under 70 minutes) or when it's worth noting that it is (or was) available in versions with different running times. Running times in guide books are notoriously inacurate and debatable. I'm not about to compete with time-obsessed fans who sit around with stop watches. Years are also debatable. I try and list the year of release, but if a movie was completed in 1985 and released in 1989, it's a 1985 movie. It doesn't matter when it was first screened in America, reviewed, or released on tape. Soundtrack information is included but whether or not a particular soundtrack is in print at this time or has been released on CD is information that changes monthly and is up to you to find out. And just what is the difference these days between a theatrical release, a made-for-cable or network TV movie, or a direct-to-video movie? Nobody really knows, most don't care, and don't believe what video boxes say.

Ratings

Movies released before November 1969 were not rated, although some of them were later rated for video release. With some exceptions, these movies were either considered all right for the general public or were denied a seal of approval and were considered "adults only." Most of the post-November 1969 movies in this book are rated R. I'll note if they were rated X (or later, NC-17), PG-13, PG, or in rare cases, G. The rating system becomes more meaningless every year. Some video releases are rated, many are not. Many older "adults only" movies would be rated R, PG, or even G (!) today. One movie rated PG in 1972 would get an R today, but so would another movie that was rated X in 1972.

Video Releases

Most, but not all, of the titles covered in this book have been or will be released on video. Titles already on tape include the most current release company name before the year. Just because your nearest video store doesn't stock them doesn't mean they're not out there, and there's a growing business in out-of-print tapes and mail-order sales and rentals (see page 637). The price of video tapes is unpredictable and senseless. One new hit is a "sell through" title at $20 while another new title is closer to $100. The price of one title will go up and down over the years as it goes in and out of print and is acquired by different companies. Also, beware of sell through tapes recorded at the LP (middle speed) or, even worse, at the EP speed. The viewing future will probably bring a major media push to convince you that you're old fashioned and out of it if you still use a VCR and watch tapes. Remember Beta!

Title Changes

Alternate American titles are cross referenced within the book. If you look up *Ator the Invincible* and it says See *Blade Master,* then that movie in reviewed in this book under *Blade Master.* If you see *Assault of the Rebel Girls = Cuban Rebel Girls,* that means that if you rent the video *Assault of the Rebel Girls* you'll really be seeing *Cuban Rebel Girls,* which was already reviewed in my earlier book (*The Psychotronic® Encyclopedia of Film*). Alternate or original foreign titles are only listed before the review. More features have been given more misleading new titles then ever before. There are movies available under three or four different titles at the same time! Have you even rented (or even bought) the same movie more than once because of deceptive titles? Thought so. The world of *Psychotronic®* video is a world of ripoffs and deceptions. Think P. T. Barnum at all times. There should be a law. There isn't.

Alternate Versions

Many features are available in different versions. Some movies have existed in various versions with different footage in theatres, on tape, on cable, and on commercial TV. That doesn't even include alternate versions for various countries and tapes available in versions with different ratings. Some things have improved, though. It wasn't long ago when you could see a movie in a theatre, then if was a safe enough title, it would show up on TV censored in many ways and cut to make room for commercials. Unless it was a major hit, it would air a few times then disappear, seemingly forever. Thousands of other features never played TV at all. Movies are still cut and censored on TV (and on some cable channels), but if you bother to look you might have choices on tapes. In some cases you can choose R or unrated versions, dubbed or subtitled versions, widescreen or panned-and-scanned versions, original or "director's cut" versions. Of course this is all just a huge scam to get more of your money and has nothing to do with artistic freedom.

Trends

Some types of features come and go in cycles. The eighties saw a revival of 3-D movies, anti-Communist movies, and end-of-the-world/post-nuke movies (a modern equivalent of westerns). These all originally flourished in the fifties. Anti-drug movies even made a comeback in the "just say no" Reagan years and *Alien* (and its first sequel) ushered in a deluge of fifties-inspired outer space monsters menacing small crews in closed quarters (spaceships, building, labs, or subs). By the late eighties, there were more martial arts or kickboxer movies than there were in early seventies and black-cast movies (of all types) made a major comeback. Since the seventies when expensive "blockbuster" hits recycled ideas and plots from old B movies and serials, many (most) of the biggest hits have been 100% Psychotronic®. Arnold Schwarzenegger is just Steve "Hercules" Reeves with bigger budgets and better agents. The *Batman* and *Raiders* movies are big-budget versions of old Saturday matinee serials with better special effects.

It took a while, but critics and media personalities were forced to adapt to covering and appreciating Psychotronic® movies, or lose their jobs. The types of movies that used to be ignored, condemned, and considered just for kids are now important major money makers and even award-winners. Who could have predicted a day when an actress (Kathy Bates) would win an Oscar for starring in a Stephen King adaptation (*Misery*, 1990), or that a serial-killer hit (*The Silence of the Lambs*, 1991) by a director who used to make drive-in movies for Roger Corman could sweep the Oscars (best film, director, actor, and actress)? And what about movies based on video games?

No More Underground

Every technique, theme, and idea formerly used in "underground" movies is now in rock videos, TV commercials, major productions, and on TV shows. I sometimes wonder how older viewers (especially ones who remember the days before TV) can stand to watch today's movies, TV shows, and commercials with all the hand-held "shakycam" work and fast editing. These techniques were used for many years to suggest intoxication, madness, and drug trips. Now they're used to sell products and to try to make the most ordinary feature or program seem "hip." Like it or not (and I know many who hated it), in some ways *Natural Born Killers,* directed by Oliver Stone (from a script by Quentin Tarantino) is the ultimate in-your-face nineties movie, throwing in our current obsession with serial killers, corrupt and inept officials, commercialism and media overkill, sex, drugs, and rock and roll, and horror and violence, using every existing underground movie and rock video cliché.

How We Watch Movies

Everybody used to say that movies were being killed off by TV, then it was by video, cable TV, or high ticket prices. Movies are still a national pastime in most countries, the industry still makes tons of money, and more people are interested in the behind-the-scenes details than ever. I miss inner-city grindhouses (a lot), drive-ins, and revival or "art" theatres, but there are more screens out there than there used to be. When I was a kid, I could ride my bike to several theatres, which was great, but as an adult, I can drive to several multiplexes and have a choice of over 20 movies. Of course most of them suck, but that's another matter. Cable TV and video releases help movies make even more money. Countless stations show new and old Psychotronic® movies. The only thing cable TV is killing off is network TV. We'll see even more specialized cable stations (and pay-per-view movies) until more people will start to watch TV like David Bowie did in *The Man Who Fell to Earth.* Lucky us.

Budgets

Some viewers used to think that making movies with budgets over $40 million was some kind of sin. Features are now going over $100 million. I'm glad that someone took the time and money to make *Blade Runner, Brazil,* and *Robocop.* I'm amazed that we've had the most expensive Dracula, Wolfman, Frankenstein, and Dr. Jekyll and Mr. Hyde movies of all time in recent years (although none of them touched the respective thirties versions). I like to see that money on

the screen, and I'll go out of my way to see an expensive feature on the largest screen available (admittedly, a serious problem for viewers in most areas these days). On the other hand, video and cable has helped low-budget releases flourish and young independent filmmakers, who at one time could show their features in a few specialized theatres, can reach a much larger audience and maybe even make a profit (!) by selling their efforts on tape. Even a terrible, amateur, shot-on-video horror movie has the potential to make profits. Some directors have made a decent living making and selling their extremely cheap (and often awful) homemade features. Except for the truly amateur homemade releases, most of today's low-budget movies at least look good . . . even if the acting, direction, and scripts are terrible. The days of visible boom mikes, flimsy sets, and laughable day-for-night shots are pretty much in the past. Today's lowest-budgeted features look slick and professional and can include special effects (FX) barely dreamed of a decade ago.

Where They're From

Outside of America, Italy has been the number one country for quantity of Psychotronic® movies since the sixties. Germany was very important in the silent days (and in the sixties for fun B movies), and England was important from the fifties through the seventies, but Italy is consistant.

Most American movies aren't made in Hollywood anymore, and that's a good thing. I'd much rather see anything made in New York, Chicago, or Pittsburgh, or better yet, somewhere in Texas, Florida, or Louisiana. We need more accents and fewer boring sunny L.A. streets. It's also useful to visit Canada and get used to Canadian accents, because sometimes it's the only way to tell which movies set in big American cities were really shot in Toronto or Vancouver.

Complaints

Some people (as usual) have been complaining about the amount of sex and violence on the screen. They should go back and check out some early seventies movies made shortly after the rating system went into effect or see what people accept in other countries. Others have complained about the rampant cynicism in recent features. They should check out some post-WWII "film noir" or simply take a look around at real life, which for most people on this planet is more horrifying than anything shown in movies. Still others worry about possible new censorship because certain people like to blame everything that's wrong with their country, their family, and their lives on movies and TV. Movie censorship has been abolished for the most part in this country for decades, and everyone with enough money has access to videos, cable TV, and computers, so it's too late to return now. Unless some future administration manages to turn back the entertainment clock to around the time of the early fifties (not an unthinkable possibility), everything is out there and you have to deal with it, like it or not. Meanwhile, you might as well stop complaining and enjoy what you like to watch. Go to your local middle-of-the-road video store and demand that they stock more of what you want to see, whether its thirties comedies, sixties biker movies, or seventies lesbian vampire movies. It doesn't matter if they won't stock X or NC-17 tapes and consider themselves a family store, your family deserves better than just the top-renting new releases.

Not Just Nostalgia

As much as I love golden-age horror, fifties juvenile delinquent, and science fiction movies from various "more innocent" times, I still look forward to what's new and what's next. I think it's important to see where Psychotronic® movies came from and where they're going. Unwatchable and boring junk has always been around along with classics, undiscovered gems, and just satisfying time-wasters. I am tired of too many horror comedies, too many sequels (even though many are sequels in name only), too many kickboxer movies, and too many lame "erotic thrillers," though. And why is it that in countless horror and action movies, the sole black character is always the first to die? It's interesting to watch the way stock WWII Axis villains were quickly replaced with years of Communist villains. By the early nineties, cliché villains were most likely to be Arabs, industrialists, lawyers, or ponytailed guys named Wolf. The same characters move through the same plots, year after year. Only the actors, settings, fashions, vehicles, and quality of special effects change. Watching the same plot remodeled to appeal to different tastes, political climates, or countries is part of what being a movie fan is all about. It's all part of history and before you know it, everything in this book will be twentieth-century history. Pretty scary, isn't it?

Psychotronic® History

The first movie reviews I wrote were at high school (in Lakewood, Ohio). This was during the time of the Vietnam War, assassinations, demonstrations, rock festivals, lots of drugs in the suburbs for the first time, and general chaos, fear, and confusion (like now . . . but the music was better). An assignment would be to review a book. I'd review a movie (any movie) and of course get a failing or the dreaded "incomplete" grade. I had been making "monster" scrapbooks since I was about ten and I continued to file away pictures, clippings, and information on the movies I cared about. My first published reviews were years later when I was working for an import and "punk rock" store in Cleveland Heights called the Drome (formally Hideo's Discodrome). I wrote a hand lettered, illustrated, movies-on-TV review column for *CLE* magazine, in between articles on Devo, The Dead Boys, and Destroy All Monsters (not the movie).

In New York, that column somehow mutated into the *Psychotronic® TV* guide, a crude, xeroxed, hand-lettered publication that came out every week for one exhaustive year (1980–81). That led to *The Psychotronic® Encyclopedia of Film* (Ballantine, 1983), written and researched with the help of several friends, long before I owned a VCR or had cable TV (or knew about AIDS or crack). The first book was followed by freelance writing and I hosted *Psychotronic®* film festivals around Northern Europe, America, and in Brazil.

Psychotronic® Video Magazine

is currently a 92-page quarterly consisting of reviews, career interviews with actors and directors, columns, articles, and rare illustrations. A 6-issue subscription is $25. A sample copy is $5. (Cash, check, Mastercard, Visa, or Amex accepted). Write for overseas rates. Send all orders, correspondence, and VHS feature review tapes to 3309 Rt. 97, Narrowsburg, NY, 12764.

ABBY

(Cinefear, 1974) **D/P:** William Girdler
S: G. Cornell Layne **P:** Mike Henry

Warner sued AIP, claiming that this movie (from Louisville, Kentucky) copied *The Exorcist* too closely (it doesn't), and it was withdrawn. A happy marriage counselor (Carol Speed) lives in a new house with her preacher husband (Terry Carter). Her father-in-law (William Marshall) studies the Yoruba religion in Nigeria, and Abby somehow becomes possessed. She has a deep, echoing voice, freaks out in the church choir, and

gives a white lady a heart attack. She kicks her husband in the crotch and starts picking up men in a bar and killing them. In the final confrontation, she floats, but a cross and some foreign words from Marshall stop her. With Juanita Moore, Austin Stoker, and Charles Kissinger. It's hard to take most of it seriously, but Marshall is good and it's good to finally see this rare feature.

ABCs OF LOVE

(SW, 1950s) **D:** "Lillian Hunt"

One of many dated b/w burlesque features, for those who want to experience what was once an adults-only show. Strippers who keep their tassels on alternate with comedians, and it ends with a singer named Gilda. William S. Thompson of Ed Wood Jr. movie fame shot it, and the narration is in rhyme.

THE ABDUCTION

(Media, 1975) **D:** Joseph Zito **S/P:** Kent E. Carroll

This exploitation curiosity item received some advance publicity as the first X-rated feature with name Hollywood stars, but it was released (years later) with an R rating, and nobody cared. Leif Erickson, Dorothy Malone, and Lawrence Tierney are the names. Some people figured *The Abduction* was about the Patty Hearst case, but it was based on a novel written before the kidnapping, although it wasn't released until 1981. Judith-Marie Bergan stars. Like many of the directors in this book, Zito started out directing porno movies.

THE ABDUCTORS

(Monterey, 1971) **D/S:** Don Schaim
P: Ralph T. Desiderio

Three cheerleaders (a blonde, brunette, and a redhead) are kidnapped by slavers who tie them up and sell them to businessmen. Some models are nabbed too, and blonde Cheri Chafaro (in her second film as the heroine, Ginger) is sent to rescue them, but they decide they like the slave life (!). The redheaded cheerleader is played by Jeramie Rain (also in *Last House on the Left*) who was Mrs. Richard Dreyfuss in real life. With Richard Smedley, Jennifer Brooks, and Patrick Wright. *Girls Are for Loving* was next in the violent and cheesy Ginger series.

THE ABOMINATION

(Donna Michelle, 1985) **D/P:** "Max Raven"/ Bret McCormick **S:** Bando Glutz

The Abomination is an ambitious, bloody, hungry-monster-in-a-kitchen movie from Texas. Young Cody keeps waking up and screaming. Scenes are repeated over and over. His narration is pretty relentless as he walks around in dark sunglasses killing people to feed his laughable monsters: "It's the abomination! I must get him food! Demon from Hell! You are the horror from Babylon, Mother!" His sick mom watches a TV evangelist, puts her hands on the TV, and coughs up a tumor. There's a chainsaw decapitation, slit throats, hands bit off, an exorcism, a cat in a toilet, and good ole fart humor. With Blue Thompson (the director's wife). "Raven" returned with more direct-to-tape horrors.

ABOVE SUSPICION

(MGM, 1943) **D:** Richard Thorpe **S:** Keith Winter, Melville Baker, Patricia Coleman **P:** Victor Saville

An American couple's honeymoon in London just before WWII turns into a spy mission. Joan Crawford and Fred MacMurray travel throughout Europe, especially in Germany. If Joan and Fred aren't enough of a draw, how about Conrad Veidt (who died before this was released) as a helpful count and Basil Rathbone as a Gestapo chief? The script was based on a novel by Helen MacInnes.

ABOVE THE LAW

(Warner, 1988) **D/S/P:** Andrew Davis **S:** Steven Pressfield, Ronald Shusett **P/A:** Steven Seagal

Nico, a brooding hero Nam vet and ex–CIA man, is now a Chicago cop. Pam Grier is his partner, who spends most of the movie in a coma, and Henry Silva is perfect as Zagon, a slimy CIA operative (also seen in Nam flashbacks) who uses heroin when torturing people. This was the acting debut for 6'4" Steven Seagal and is still his best feature to date. It was based on his (supposed) experiences as a CIA agent in Nam and is very much against the intelligence agency. Seagal was also an aikido martial-arts instructor and (supposedly) the first non-Asian to open a martial-arts school in Japan. It also helped that he taught studio head Mike Ovitz. Seagal went on to star in more violent action features (most with snappy three-word titles). With Sharon Stone, Thalmus Rasulala, and a brief barroom appearance by *Henry* star Michael Rooker.

ABRAXAS

(Prism, 1991) **D/S/P/A:** Damien Lee
P: David Mitchell, Curtis Peterson   Canada

An alien (Sven-Ole Thorsen) with a laser gun asks a woman, "Are you a birthing member of the human race?" Before she can answer, he impregnates her by touching her and she instantly has a baby. Five years later, a good alien (Jesse "the Body" Ventura) with a laser gun (and ponytail) falls for the woman and tries to protect her mute 5-year-old boy, who has mysterious powers. It all takes place in and around a small, snowy New York State town just before Christmas. Jim Belushi shows up as the school principal in this *Terminator* ripoff by the director of *Ski School*.

ABSOLUTE BEGINNERS

(HBO, 1986) **D:** Julian Temple **S:** Christopher Wicking, Richard Burridge, Don McPherson **P:** Stephen Wooley, Chris Brown   UK

Based on Colin MacInnes' novel set in 1958 London, *Absolute Beginners* is a unique, PG-13 musical look at the record-making biz by the director of *The Great Rock and Roll Swindle*. It also attempts to deal with the racial problems in England at the time. Eddie O'Connell stars as a photographer, and the cast includes Patsy Kensit, David Bowie as an ad man, James Fox, Terence Stamp, Steven Berkoff, Anita Morris, Ray Davies (as Arthur), Mandy Rice-Davies, Sade, Robbie Coltrane, Jess Conrad, Sandie Shaw, and the late Slim Gaillard. Gil Evans wrote the score, available on EMI. And look for *Expresso Bongo* (1960), which tells a similar story and was actually made at the time.

ABSOLUTION

(Bingo, 1978) **D/P:** Anthony Page
S: Anthony Shaffer **P:** Danny O'Donovan   UK

Richard Burton stars as Father Goddard, a strict Catholic priest teaching at a boys' school. Dominic Guard is the pet student who plays too many practical jokes on him. (Christopher Lee was once considered for the lead.) Shaffer had also written *The Wicker Man* and *Frenzy*. With Billy Connolly and Andrew Keir. It wasn't released in the US until 1988, four years after Burton died.

THE ABYSS

(Fox, 1989) **D/S:** James Cameron **P:** Gale Ann Hurd

The Abyss was a big PG-13 disappointment after Cameron's blockbuster hit *Aliens*. An oil-rig crew has to rescue a sunken American nuclear submarine. Ed Harris and Mary Elizabeth Mastrantonio star with Cameron regular Michael Biehn as the navy lieutenant who loses it and plans to nuke the Russians. Also with Leo Burmester, Todd Graff, and Chris Elliott. The great, innovative (but sparingly used) ILM FX received an Oscar, but the same techniques were put to better use in *Terminator II*. The underwater sequences were filmed at Earl Owensby's North Carolina studios, in an abandoned nuclear reactor tank. There's also a happy *E.T.* ending with heavenly voices that was a bit much for me. Cameron delivered a nearly

3-hour movie but the theatrical release was trimmed to 145 minutes. A long (very expensive) segment showing cities threatened by tidal waves was totally cut. This footage and more were put back for the 1993 "special edition" laserdisc release, running 171 minutes, available letterboxed or scanned, and including an additional one-hour (!) director interview/"making of" documentary disc. The roughly $50 million feature was a box-office washout, but before it was even released it had "inspired" many much cheaper underwater science-fiction adventures, including *DeepStar Six, Leviathan, Endless Descent,* and *Lords of the Deep.*

ACCESS CODE
(Prism, 1983) **D/P/E:** Mark Sobel **S:** Stanley Richards

A CIA agent (Michael Durrell), and then his sister try to save the US from nuclear destruction after villains infiltrate the nation's computer system. In a nearly senseless film pieced together from footage shot at various times, "guest stars" Martin Landau, Michael Ansara, and Macdonald Carey sit around talking for long stretches and whole scenes were obviously never even shot or completed.

ACCIDENTS
(1989) **D:** Gideon Amir **S:** John T. Eubank **P:** Elmo De Witt   Australia

A small, remote-controlled saucer called "the Scout" kills scientists. A research scientist (Edward Albert) teams up with a researcher (Leigh Taylor-Young) to investigate. With Jon Cypher.

ACCIÓN MUTANTE
(VSOM, 1992) **D/S:** Alex de la Iglesia **S:** Jorge Guerricaechevarria **P:** Agustín and Pedro Almodovar   Spain

Members of a terrorist group led by Antonio Resines end up on another planet in this violent action/horror/sci-fi comedy set in Spain in 2013. The group includes Siamese twins, a legless man on a flying disc, and a giant. There are shootouts, gore, a space monster, and heavy-metal music. Frédérique Feder is the kidnapped rich girl. The same French FX people did *Delicatessen.*

THE ACCURSED
(1957) **D:** Gilbert Gunn **D/S:** Michael McCarthy **P:** E. J. Fancey   UK (*The Traitor*)

Allied Artists released this mystery in 1960, capitalizing on the new horror fame of Christopher Lee. He plays a German-Jewish doctor, a former member of a WWII resistance group attending an annual reunion held at the home of a British colonel (Donald Wolfit). One of the men is a former Nazi who has been killing off the others. With Anton Diffring, Robert Bray, and Karel Stepanek. The plot is the same as *The Unholy Night* (1929).

ACE DRUMMOND
(Video Dimensions, Sinister, 1936) **D:** Ford Beebe, Cliff Smith **S:** Wyndham Gittens, Norman S. Hall, Ray Trame

Ace (John King), a pilot hero with atomic ray guns, battles "the Dragon" in Mongolia. It's a Universal 13-chapter serial based on the comic strip created by Eddie Rickenbacker. With Jean Rogers (from the same year's *Flash Gordon*), Noah Berry Jr., C. Montague Shaw, and Lon Chaney Jr. as Ivan. A mixture of Caucasian and Asian actors play the grand lama, Chang-Ho, and Kai-Chek. Beebe co-directed 25 serials in about 10 years.

ACE HIGH
(Paramount, 1967) **D/S:** Giuseppe Colizzi **S/P:** Bino Cicogna   Italy/Spain (*I Quattro dell'Ave Maria*)

The popular team of Terence Hill and Bud Spencer star as two con men out to rob a casino owned by Kevin McCarthy. They're joined by Eli Wallach, playing pretty much the same character as in *The Good, the Bad, and the Ugly,* and Brock Peters as a former slave turned acrobat. The long (137-minute) comic western was released at 122 minutes and rated M.

ACES: IRON EAGLE III
(New Line, 1991) **D:** John Glen **S:** Kevin Elders **P:** Ron Samuels

This time Chappy (Louis Gosset Jr.) gets together a group of flying war vets (and one comic relief ghetto kid) in Brownsville, Texas. They fly WWII planes to destroy a cocaine factory in Peru run by a former Nazi (Paul Freeman) and corrupt American soldiers. The cast includes Horst Buchholz from Germany, Sonny Chiba from Japan, and bodybuilder Rachel McLish, who is tied up several times. Also with future U. S. Senator Fred Thompson, Christopher Cazenove, Mitchell Ryan, and Ray Mancini. Glen also directed five James Bond movies.

ACE VENTURA, PET DETECTIVE
(Warner, 1993) **D/S:** Tom Shadyac **S:** Jack Bernstein **P:** James G. Robinson

Jim Carrey is a bumbling detective hired to find the kidnapped Miami Dolphins' dolphin mascot. Incredibly, this PG-13 comedy was a #1 box-office hit and made Carrey a big-bucks star, compared (by the critics who hated him) with Jerry Lewis. With Courtney Cox, Sean Young as a cop, Udu Kier as a mysterious millionaire, rapper Tone Loc, football star Dan Marino, and Rebecca Ferratti. Carrey's next was *The Mask. Ace Ventura: When Nature Calls* (1995) is the sequel.

THE ACID EATERS
(SW, 1968) **D/P:** B. Ron Elliot/Byron Mabe **S:** Carlos Monsoya/Monson

Four middle-class office-worker couples become weekend "bikers" in all-red clothes. They go for a (topless) swim, play strip poker, and "freak out" on (and in) "the White Pyramid." In fantasy segments, a guy has sex with his neighbor and a blonde dances topless while a black guy plays bongos. Comic actor Buck Kartalian dominates things as Arty and also shows up with a pitchfork as the devil, who shows the others how to smoke pot and gives them huge cubes of LSD. The dubbing of this silly adult sex-and-drug comedy is

awful, and the motorcycle scenes seem endless, but the flash-forward editing is effective, and the women look fine. David F. Friedman was the cinematographer for this 65-minute feature from his FPS Ventures. The tape is a very good color print.

ACROSS 110th STREET
(Key, 1972) **D:** Barry Shear **S:** Luthor Davis **P:** Fouad Said, Ralph Serpe

Anthony Quinn and Yaphet Kotto are cops after amateurs trying to rip off the Italian mob. Considered bloody, violent, and too depressing at the time it was released, this influential action hit from United Artists is a classic of its kind. Real locations were used for the story, based on a novel by Wally Ferris. Anthony Franciosa is a gangster's son who castrates a man, Richard Ward, Paul Benjamin, Antonio Fargas, and Burt Young costar, and Gloria Hendry made her film debut. The Bobby Womack songs are on the J. J. Johnson soundtrack from UA. Quinn was also an executive producer.

THE ACT
(Vestron, 1982) **D/P:** Sig Shore **S:** Robert Lipsy **P:** David Greene   (*Bless 'Em All*)

Action star Robert Ginty is a lawyer hired by a crooked union leader. With Sarah Langenfield, Eddie Albert, Pat Hingle, Jill St. John, and David Huddleston. Shore is known for producing the *Superfly* movies. From Film Ventures.

ACTING ON IMPULSE
(Academy, 1993) **D:** Sam Irvin **S:** Mark Pittman, Allan Moskowitz **P:** David Peters

A manic movie scream queen (Linda Fiorentino) wanted for the murder of a producer goes to a hotel during a sales convention where a psycho fan lurks. She seduces a married salesman (C. Thomas Howell) and takes him and a shoe saleswoman (Nancy Allen) bar-hopping. This PG safe-sex comedy is pretty mild and is barely saved by the many guest stars in small roles. With Mary Woronov as a slow-burn desk clerk, Isaac Hayes (also in the director's *Guilty as Charged*) as a detective, Paul Bartel as a director, Don Most (pretty lame) as a house detective, Adam Ant, Zelda Rubenstein, Judith Hoag, Tom Wright, Cassandra Peterson (Elvira), and plugs for *Femme Fatales* magazine. They say Peter Lupus, Kim McGuire, Miles O'Keeffe, Dick Sargent, and Brinke Stevens are in there somewhere too. It premiered on Showtime.

ACTION HEROES OF THE CLIFFHANGER SERIALS
(Goodtimes, 1992)

This is an entertaining introduction to the wonderful world of 30s through 50s serials. After a brief intro, nearly 60 fun (and funny) serial trailers (many from Universal and Columbia) make up this almost 2-hour compilation tape. Some of my favorites here are *King of the Rocketmen, The Phantom Empire, The Mysterious Dr. Satan, The Green Hornet, Captain Marvel, The Undersea Kingdom, Flash Gordon, Superman, The Perils of Nyoka,* and the *Batman* serial (as rereleased in the pop-art 60s). Many of the trailers are for lesser-known (and less worthy) serials or for re-issues, but I don't care. I wouldn't sit through the complete chapters of some of these unless a death ray were pointed at my head. My only complaint is a few too many lookalike western-serial trailers, but I'm glad I now know what John Wayne and Little Billy looked like in *Shadow of the Eagle*. It's worth it just to see the trailer for the obscure *Scouts to the Rescue*, with Indians talking backwards! Recommended.

ACTION JACKSON
(Warner, 1988) **D:** Craig R. Baxley
S: Robert Reneau **P:** Joel Silver

After too many *Rocky* movies, former Oakland Raiders star Carl Weathers enjoyed his first starring role as Action Jackson, a Detroit supercop with a law degree. It's similar to early 70s Jim Brown and Fred Williamson movies. Action's demoted for tearing the arm off the sexual-deviant son of Craig T. Nelson (a gangster industrialist, drug dealer, and wife killer). Vanity, as the drug addict girlfriend, sings "Undress Me." With Sharon Stone (she dies), Robert Davi, Nicholas Worth, Bill Duke, Ed O'Ross, Sonny Landham, and Melissa Prophet. Baxley had been the second unit/stunt director for TV shows like *The A Team*. Herbie Hancock and Michael Kamen provided the score, and there's a Lorimar soundtrack.

ACTION USA
(Imperial, 1988) **D/P:** John Stewart
S: David Reskin **P:** Susan Stewart

Mobsters murder a guy in Texas then go after his girlfriend (Barri Murphy). William Smith is an FBI chief and Ross Hagen (also the associate producer) is Drago, the guest villain. With Cameron Mitchell and Hoke Howell. The ending features comic outtakes.

ACT OF PIRACY
(Warner, 1987) **D:** John "Bud" Cardos
S: Hal Reed **P:** Igo Kantner S. Africa

A Nam vet (Gary Busey) and his family battle mercenaries on a yacht. Ray Sharkey overacts again as the gun-runner villain who hijacks them. With Belinda Bauer, Nancy Mulford, and Ken Gampu. The score by Morton Stevens, and his music for *The Great White*, were released on One World.

ACT OF VENGEANCE
(HBO, 1974) **D:** Bob Kelljan **S:** Betty
Conklin **P:** Buzz Feitsham (*Rape Squad*)

The director of *Count Yorga* made this AIP exploitation release. Five women team up and learn karate to avenge themselves against rapists, pimps, and abusive men in general. Peter Brown (*Foxy Brown*) wears an orange leisure suit and a hockey mask and forces his victims to sing "Jingle Bells." With Jo An Harris, Jennifer Lee (one-time wife of Richard Pryor), Lisa Moore, Connie Strickland, Anneka di Lorenzo, Patricia Estrin, Joan McCall, Cheryl Waters, and Ross Elliot. Lada Edmunds Jr. (formerly a frantic dancer on the *Hullabaloo* show) stars as a karate instructor. Most of the women have nude or topless scenes.

ADAM AND EVE
(SW, 1956) **D/S/P:** Alberto Gout
Mexico (*Adan y Eva*)

While other films of the time were banned and condemned by the Catholic Church because of nudity, this Eastmancolor movie was given an "A-3" rating because it was "based on the Bible"! We see lots of real scenes of Earth's beauty while a narrator quotes the Old Testament, then settle into an Eden set for the familiar story, ending with an earthquake. Eve (French one-time Miss Universe Christiane Martel) has long hair (covering vital parts) and Adam (Carlos Baena) wears an easy-to-see flesh-colored G-string. Adam has to teach her to walk, eat, and swim. David F. Friedman (who presents this tape) was one of the distributors. An all-naked premiere was held at a nudist colony, and miniature Bibles were sold at some showings. This was still being screened in the 60s. *The Sin of Adam and Eve* (Video Dimension, 1967), by Miguel Zacharias, was a remake that Dimension released in the early 70s.

ADAM AND SIX EVES
(1960) **D:** John Wallis **S:** Lawrence
Donner **P:** Robert Rico

An hour-long comic color nudie feature about an everyman type named Adam (Randy Brent) prospecting for gold with a donkey in the desert. Six nearly naked Eves are in his oasis mirage. It was filmed in 3-D but released flat in 1962. The names in the credits are pseudonyms.

ADAM LOST HIS APPLE
(SW, 1965) **D:** Earl Wainright
P: Harry Kerwin

A photographer discovers two shipwrecked women and a man living as nudists. This color release was filmed in Florida and the Bahamas. Gene Berk stars, with Mal Arnold and Bill Rogers.

THE ADDAMS FAMILY
(Worldvision series, 1964–66)

The best thing about the movie *The Addams Family* is that it prompted the video release of the original TV episodes (2 per tape). There's even a special Voyager laser disc with two episodes plus interviews and a history of the whole program. I was amazed by the outrageous and subversive situation comedy when I was a kid, and it's still great today. Who wouldn't want an eccentric, lovable, understanding, and extremely rich family like this? The entire cast was exceptional, with John Astin and Carolyn Jones as Gomez and Morticia, the only 60s TV couple who seemed to have sex on their minds (24 hours a day). Jackie Coogan as Uncle Fester, Blossom Rock as Grandmama, and Ted Cassidy as Lurch (look for his

rare "Do the Lurch" single) were all perfect. Lisa Loring as little Wednesday was a role model for some pretty interesting, now grown-up women, and even the enthusiastic Pugsley (Ken Weatherwax) was pretty cool. Unfortunately, out of the adult cast, only Astin is still alive. Episodes of the TV cartoon series (1973–75) are also on tape from Hanna Barbera.

THE ADDAMS FAMILY
(Paramount, 1991) **D:** Barry Sonnenfeld **S:** Larry Wilson, Caroline Thompson **P:** Scott Rudin

Making the first *Addams Family* movie turned out to be a capital idea, judging by the box-office receipts, but it couldn't touch the 60s TV series. Angelica Huston is disappointing as a dreamy Morticia, but Raul Julia is pretty good as a swashbuckling Gomez. The makers wanted everybody to know that it was based on Charles Addams' *New Yorker* cartoons and not the TV series. That was mostly a lie, of course, and also a problem, because the familiar elements from the series that they left out are missed. The plot has Christopher Lloyd as a fake, bungling Uncle Fester, set up to infiltrate and rob the rich family. Christina Ricci is great as little Wednesday. She and Pugsley (Jimmy Workman) put on a school *Hamlet* production with lots of blood, in a standout scene. Dan Hedeya and Elizabeth Wilson are the villains, and Carel Struycken (the giant from *Twin Peaks*) is Lurch. Thanks to modern FX, Thing now scurries around wherever it wants (and it's played by magician Christopher Hart). The first-time director was the innovative cinematographer for the Coen brothers' movies, but *The Addams Family* suffers from some very cheap-looking sets and an out-of-place fantasy-sculpture graveyard that seems left over from *Edward Scissorhands*. Also with Judith Malina as Granny, Dana Ivey, and Sally Jessy Raphael (as herself). The heavy promotion and

The real *Addams Family*.

tie-ins were inevitable, but M. C. Hammer's irritating end rap theme and tie-in rock video were both too much for me. *The Addams Family* (rated PG) made $55 million in US/Canada rentals, so a new TV cartoon series appeared, followed by a sequel. David Levey, the creator and executive producer of the TV series (who received no credit or payment for the feature), sued Paramount (with good reason).

ADDAMS FAMILY VALUES
(Paramount 1993) **D:** Barry Sonnenfeld
S: Paul Rudnick **P:** Scott Rudin

The same leads return, plus Joan Cusack as a cheerful but evil nanny for the new baby, Pubert. The baby (with a mustache) is there just to start off two plots that could have been two TV episodes. Fester marries the gold-digging nanny, and the kids are sent to summer camp. In comic scenes most unlike anything in the original cartoons, Wednesday ruins a camp play by being "politically correct." With Carol Kane as Grandmama, Peter MacNicol and Christine Baranski as camp counselors, and Peter Graves in a bit part. The set design is by Ken Adam (from the James Bond movies). Rudnick, who wrote the screenplay for this PG-13 release, is also the columnist "Libby Gelman-Waxner" in *Premiere* magazine. The Atlas soundtrack features remakes of 70s soul hits.

ADDICT: *See* BORN TO WIN

ADIOS AMIGO
(Vidmark, 1975) **D/S/P/A:** Fred Williamson

Fred Williamson (directing himself for the first of many times) and Richard Pryor play Big Ben and Sam Spade in a PG-rated comedy/western. They're arrested and put on a chain gang, then team up for adventures. With Thalmus Rasulala and former Tarzan Mike Henry. Pryor's lines were mostly ad-libbed. Pryor hated the results and publicly apologized for being in it, saying he had done it just for the money. Williamson's other westerns (*The Legend of Nigger Charley* and *The Soul of Nigger Charley*) were more violent. The music by the Blue Infernal Machine is on a London soundtrack LP. It was made in New Mexico.

ADIOS, SABATA
(United Artists, 1970) **D/S:** "Frank Kramer"/
Gianfranco Parolini **S:** Reanato Izzo **P:** Alberto
Grimaldi Italy (*Indio Black Sai Chi Ti Dico*)

Yul Brynner, dressed in black fringe, is hired to steal some gold from an Austrian commandant in Mexico for the revolution. His thief sidekick is played by Dean Reed (the late American folk singer famous for defecting to the USSR). An Indian acrobat and a guy with a gun in his banjo also help. Released as a sequel to *Sabata* (by the same director), it's really an unrelated western that has been retitled, with the leading character renamed in the dubbing.

THE ADULT VERSION OF JEKYLL AND HYDE
(SW, 1972) **D:** Lee Raymond **D/P:** Byron Mabe,
L. Ron Elliot **S:** Robert Birch **P:** David F. Friedman

A modern-day doctor, who already cheats on his fiancé and has killed a man, reads the handwritten diary of Dr. Jekyll. He drinks a potion and all of a sudden has a cape, cane, top hat, and limp as he ties up, rapes, and kills women. This color movie combines lots of full nudity and sex with brainless violence. There's an (offscreen) castration and a woman being beaten likes it. The only fun part is borrowed from *Dr. Jekyll and Sister Hyde* (1971). When the potion is too strong the doc becomes a blond woman, so he can seduce his nurse and fiancée. Rene Bond as the nurse is in several sex scenes. The music is bar-band rock and jazz fusion. It was advertised as being "Excruciating!" Mabe also directed *She Freak, Space Thing,* and many others. Bond was also in *The Jekyll and Hyde Portfolio* (1972).

ADVENTURE AT THE CENTER OF THE EARTH
(SW, 1963) **D:** Alfredo Crevana
S: J. M. Fernando Unsain **P:** Jesús Sotomayor
Mexico (*Aventura al Centro de la Tierra*)

Dinosaurs, a cyclops, a winged reptile, a bat creature, and rat-faced monsters are all in this Mexican wonder. It was filmed in real caverns. In Spanish only.

ADVENTURE ISLAND
(Sinister, 1947) **D:** Peter Stewart **S:** Maxwell
Shane **P:** William Pine, William Thomas

Rory Calhoun and Rhonda Fleming (with her much-publicized red hair) star in a Cinecolor version of Robert Louis Stevenson's story "Ebb Tide" from Paramount. It's about shipwrecked sailors

ADULTS ONLY

Because of video, thousands of old (mostly pre-porno) "adults-only" movies have been rediscovered by fans and collectors. Nudist-colony movies go back to the 30s, but they became common in the fifties, because as "documentaries" they could legally feature nudity. Eventually, laughable plots were added, and as restrictions changed, a whole industry of adult "nudie" movies flourished (from the late 50s to the early 70s). There were nudie dramas, comedies, musicals, horror movies, westerns, and fairy tales. Many were extemely cheap, were badly acted and directed, and fit into the "so bad it's good" category, but others (especially some of Russ Meyer's) are as good as any major studio features. Some are light in tone and inoffensive and others are as nasty and sick as they could get away with at the time. By the early 90s the first fanzines about these features were published, and more people were watching and even enjoying them. The various pseudonyms used in some credits are still being figured out. Here are the top 10 Adults-Only filmmakers. These people (all American) are worth looking into and have developed cult followings:

1. Russ Meyer
2. Radley Metzger (later aka Henry Paris)
3. Michael and Roberta Findlay
4. Doris Wishman
5. Herschell Gordon Lewis
6. Barry Mahon
7. David F. Friedman (producer)
8. Lee Frost
9. Harry Novak (producer)
10. A. C. Stevens

ACTUALLY FILMED IN A NUDIST COLONY

CLEAN—DECENT—WILL NOT OFFEND ANYONE— BEST NUDIST PICTURE MADE

and a madman (Alan Napier) who rules an island by making the local natives think he's a god. Anybody who disagrees ends up in his snake pit. With Paul Kelly and John Abbott. Only 66 minutes.

ADVENTURE OF THE ACTION HUNTERS

(Vestron, 1982) **D/S:** Lee Bonner
S: Leif Elsmo **P:** Mary Holland

In the 50s, Ronald Hunter and Sean Murphy search for hidden money and fight off gangsters (including John Waters regular George Stover). It was filmed in Baltimore and released in 1987 by Troma.

ADVENTURES IN DINOSAUR CITY

(Republic, 1992) **D:** Brett Thompson **S:** Willie Baronet, Lisa Morton **P:** Luigi Cingolani

The kids of a scientist are sucked into a TV screen and land in the Stone Age. They encounter comic cave people and dinos (puppets and people in masks). The John Criswell FX in this PG-rated bore are supposed to be "Animatronics." With Omri Katz, Shawn Hoffman, Irwin Keys, and Tiffanie Poston as the cute, blond teen daughter.

THE ADVENTURES OF BARON MUNCHAUSEN

(RCA/Columbia, 1988) **D:** Terry Gilliam **S:** Charles McKeown **P:** Thomas Shuhly   UK/W. Germany

After making the wonderful *Time Bandits* and the fascinating *Brazil*, former Monty Python member Gilliam made this epic, PG-rated $52-million, 126-minute fantasy. It ended up losing a lot of money. It's incredible to look at and made with impressive detail, but the endless raging battle with the Turks wore me out, and the best parts will suffer on the small screen. John Neville (Sherlock Holmes in the 1965 *A Study in Terror*) is the fabled 18th-century adventurer and liar who goes back and forth in time with a ten-year-old girl (Sarah Polley) and has a select group of followers with superpowers. Oliver Reed is great as Vulcan, king of the underworld, with a new ICBM missile. With Eric Idle, *Brazil* star Jonathan Pryce, Uma Thurman as Venus, Sting, unbilled Robin Williams as the king of the moon, and Jack Purvis (from *Time Bandits*). The production design is by Dante Ferretti, the 2nd-unit director was horror specialist Michele Soavi, and the music by Michael Kamen is on a Warner soundtrack. It was the second production of Python's Prominent Features (after *A Fish Called Wanda*). An illustrated screenplay was published. Clips from two earlier versions—*Baron Munchausen* (Germany, 1943) and *The Fabulous Baron Munchausen* (Czechoslovakia, 1962)—are included on the Criterion laserdisc version, along with commentary by the director.

THE ADVENTURES OF BRISCO COUNTY JR.

(Fox, 1993) **D:** Bryan Spencer
S/P: Jeffrey Boam, Carlton Cuse

This was a pilot for a western/fantasy TV series that was like the series *The Wild Wild West* meets *Indiana Jones*. Bruce Campbell (star of all the *Evil Dead* movies) is a university-educated adven-

turer who becomes involved with a mysterious floating orb. With Billy Drago as the villain, Anne Trenko, John Piper-Ferguson, Julius Carry, Stuart Whitman, John Astin as a scientist, and F. Lee Ermy as the sheriff father who is killed.

THE ADVENTURES OF BUCKAROO BANZAI ACROSS THE EIGHTH DIMENSION

(Vestron, 1984) **D/P:** W. D. Richter
S: Earl Mac Rauch **P:** Neil Canton

This PG-rated would-be cult film, intended as the first in a series, has become popular over the years on videotape and deserves a look. At least the filmmakers tried something original instead of the usual rehash of old serials and comic books. Peter Weller stars as a half-Japanese martial artist, neurosurgeon, nuclear physicist, and jet car driver with a New Jersey rock band and groupies. He's world famous and has a group of expert helpers called "the Hong Kong Cavaliers." A complicated plot about preventing WWIII and Lectroids who landed on earth on Halloween in 1939 involves John Lithgow as Dr. Lizardo, a mad scientist possessed by aliens. The cast includes Ellen Barkin, Jeff Goldblum, Lewis Smith, Rosalind Cash, Matt Clark, Clancy Brown, Robert Ito, Dan Hedaya and Vincent Schiavelli. The 103-minute feature was rated PG. Richter had written the remakes of *Invasion of the Body Snatchers* (1978) and *Dracula* (1979).

Vincent Schiavelli, John Lithgow, and Christopher Lloyd in *The Adventures of Buckaroo Banzai Across the Eighth Dimension*

ADVENTURES OF CAPTAIN AFRICA

(Stokey, 1955) **D:** Spencer Gordon Bennet
S: George H. Plympton **P:** Sam Katzman

One of the last (and cheapest) serials produced, this 15-chapter Columbia serial featured extensive stock footage from *The Phantom* (1943), so star John Hart was dressed to resemble Tom Tyler (and his stunt man) from the earlier serial. With June Howard, Rick Vallin, Ben Welden, and a man in a gorilla suit. Good for some laughs.

ADVENTURES OF CAPTAIN MARVEL

(Republic, 1941) **D:** William Witney, John English
S: Ronald Davidson, Norman S. Hall, Arch B. Heath, Joseph Poland, Sol Shore **P:** Hiram S. Brown

Most fans consider this 12-chapter serial one of the best ever made. My personal fave is *Flash*

Gordon, but the captain comes close. He had made his Fawcett comic-book debut only a year before this serial was released. In Thailand's "Lost Valley of the Kings," the ancient Shazam shows teen newsboy Billy Batson (Frank Coughlin Jr.) how to become the flying superhero (just say, "Shazam!"). Tom Tyler, who looked just right for the part, stars as the superman with a cape and a lightning bolt on his chest but stunt man Dave Sharpe has more screen time. He fights "the Scorpion" (the voice of Gerard Mohr) back in the LA area. The flying scenes are advanced for the time and unlike some other crime-fighters, Captain Marvel often killed villains by throwing them off cliffs or with machine guns. With Louise Currie and Billy Benedict. A feature version was called *The Return of Captain Marvel*. The serial was rereleased in 1953 and again in 1966 because of the popularity of the *Batman* TV series and all the camp hype. Also on laserdisc.

THE ADVENTURES OF CHARLIE CHAN

(IVE, 1956–57)

3 volumes from the syndicated half-hour TV series were released on tape. The show was filmed on location in Europe with the great character actor J. Carroll Naish as Charlie Chan and James Hong as his number 1 son. Many well-known British actors had guest-star roles (Honor Blackman is in Volume 3).

ADVENTURES OF EL FRENETICO AND GO GIRL

(1993) **D/S:** Pat Bishow **S:** Jon Sanborne **P:** Owen Cooper

El Frenerico (Charles Pellegrino), a drunken masked Santo type and the kung-fu fighting Go Girl (Francis Lee) battle the local Krazy Kakes snack food king (Jon Sanborne) when he kidnaps a lady reporter. He has a wax museum hideout, a henchwoman named Hilda, an assistant Gomar, and snacks that turn consumers into zombies. This fun, short film with (on-purpose) bad dubbing reminds me of *Shock! Shock! Shock!* and has 60s-style instrumental music. Lance Lurie was the art director and created the monster-head bugs. Bishow also made *Soul Tangler*.

THE ADVENTURES OF FORD FAIRLANE

(Fox, 1990) **D:** Renny Harlin **S:** Daniel Waters, James Cappe, David Arnott **P:** Joel Silver, Steve Perry

Controversial standup insult comic Andrew Dice Clay made his star debut as a rock detective in LA in this awkward comedy adventure. Clay's overhyped career stalled the year this was released to mass indifference. Priscilla Presley and Wayne Newton (as an evil rock manager) make fun of their old images again, but Lauren Holly and Maddie Corman are the real costars. With Robert (Freddy Krueger) Englund as a killer with a terrible British accent, Ed O'Neill, former Prince associates Sheila E. and Morris Day, Gilbert Gottfried, Vince Neil, Tone Loc, Delia Sheppard, MTV's Kurt Loder (as himself), and a cliffhanger ending on the top and sides of the Capitol Records building. The music is by Yello. Harlin made *Die Hard II* the same year and Clay returned in *Dice Rules.*

ADVENTURES OF FU MANCHU

(1956)

Two episodes of the syndicated series starring Glen Gordon as Sax Rohmer's villain and Lester Stevens as Sir Nayland Smith are available. With sexy Laurette Luez (from *Prehistoric Women*) as Lia. The directors were William Witney and Franklin Adreon, both veterans of many serials.

THE ADVENTURES OF HERCULES

(MGM, 1983) **D/S:** "Lewis Coates"/Luigi Cozzi
P: Alfred Pecoriello   Italy (*Hercules II*)

Lou Ferrigno returns as the musclebound hero and tries to stop the moon from crashing into earth. This bizarre, PG-rated kids' film uses lots of footage from the first Cozzi/Ferrigno *Hercules* (also from Cannon) and includes scenes copied from *Forbidden Planet, Clash of the Titans,* the original *King Kong,* and others. Cartoon special effects look like they were lifted from a video game. Ferrigno (whose voice was dubbed this time) made a better "Incredible Hulk." With Milly Carlucci and William Berger. The score is by Pino Donaggio.

THE ADVENTURES OF LUCKY PIERRE

(World's Sleaziest, 1961) **D/C:** Herschell Gordon Lewis **P:** David F. Friedman

Although it was released two years after Russ Meyer's *The Immoral Mr. Teas,* this similar, hour-long, shot-in-Chicago, (!) full-color comic nudie hit is more fun. The announcer is dragged away by hospital attendants after he announces that the film we're about to see has "a cast of thousands" and is "a pinnacle of achievement." Billy Falbo (a burlesque comic) sees naked women everywhere, in a series of short, silent skits. His shrink is naked; then an artist paints three naked models in the woods. A woman bathes while plumbers (Falbo and William Kerwin) try to work, a "bird-watcher" looks at sunbathers, and women pose in a photo studio. The best and longest part takes place at a drive-in showing *"I Was a Teenage Nudist* and 65 cartoons!" In a (partially b/w) short, *Picnic at the Playground,* happy naked women in high heels climb on the jungle gym, go down the slide, swing on the swings, and spin on a merry-go-round. The all-female drive-in staff is naked too in this surreal, sexy segment. The color is excellent. Sound by producer Friedman. Released on tape with a Joe Bob Briggs intro.

THE ADVENTURES OF ROBINSON CRUSOE

(1952) **D/S:** Luis Buñuel **S:** Philip Roll
P: Oscar Dancigers, Henry Ehrlich   Mexico

This Pathécolor version of the Daniel Defoe novel stars Dan O'Herlihy, who is alone on screen for two-thirds of the 90-minute running time. In this version he doubts his Christian faith and encounters cannibals. It was a surprising hit for Buñuel during his long Mexican period. O'Herlihy was nominated for an Oscar after the film's release in America by U. A. in 1954. Jaime Fernández is Friday.

ADVENTURES OF SHERLOCK HOLMES:
See SHERLOCK HOLMES

ADVENTURES OF SIR GALAHAD

(Stokey, 1949) **D:** Spencer G. Bennet **S:** George Plympton, Lewis Clay, David Mathews **P:** Sam Katzman

Characters can disappear in this 15-chapter Columbia serial starring George Reeves as the knight in armor busy looking for the sword of Excalibur. Charles King is a comic villain, and William Fawcett plays Merlin. In one scene "the Black Knight" is tripled. Reeves became Superman for the first time two years later.

ADVENTURES OF SMILIN' JACK

(VCI, 1943) **D:** Ray Taylor, Lewis D. Collins **S:** Morgan B. Cox

This 13-chapter Universal serial is based on a comic strip about an American flyer (Tom Brown) working for the Chinese army. The post–Pearl Harbor plot deals with Axis spies and takes place in Hawaii, Shanghai, and Hong Kong. With Marjorie Lord, Rose Hobart as the evil Fräulein von Treufel, Turhan Bey as the leader of "the Black Samurai," Keye Luke, Philip Ahn, and Sidney Toler.

ADVENTURES OF SUPERMAN

(Warner, 1948) **D:** Spencer Gordon Bennet, Thomas Carr **S:** Arthur Hoerl, Lewis Clay, Royal Cole **P:** Sam Katzman (*Superman; Superman: The Serial*)

Kirk Alyn stars in the first 15-chapter Columbia Superman serial. Noel Neill (who later was in the TV series) is Lois Lane, Tommy Bond is Jimmy Olsen, and Pierre Watkin is Perry White. The whole story is told, from the beginning on Krypton, and "the Man of Steel" eventually grows up and fights the blond "Spider Lady" (Carol Foreman), who is after "the reducer ray" and has an electric web. The strangest and most fun parts of this serial are the animated flying sequences. Alyn jumps up and becomes a cartoon streaking through the air. For some reason, Warner removed the opening chapter credits for the 2-volume video release, ruining it for collectors. *Atom Man vs. Superman* was the serial sequel. Also look for the earlier and better Dave Fleischer/Paramount *Superman* cartoons on tape compilations.

ADVENTURES OF SUPERMAN (TV series):
See TV'S GREATEST ADVENTURES OF SUPERMAN

ADVENTURES OF TARZAN

(Video Yesteryear, 1921) **D/S:** Robert F. Hill
S: Lillian Valentine

This 15-chapter silent serial (with a musical score) stars big Elmo Lincoln (real name Otto Elmo Linkenhelt, from Arkansas) with a long-hair wig. He had been the first screen Tarzan in *Tarzan and the Apes* (1917) and *The Romance of Tarzan* (1918) and had already starred in three other serials. The story was partially based on Edgar Rice Burroughs' "Tarzan and the Jewels of Opar" and featured the jealous queen of Opar and an evil Bolshevik. With 16-year-old Louise Lorraine as Jane, Numa the lion, Tantor the elephant, and a man in a bizarre chimp suit. The first Tarzan serial, a big hit in 1921 (ten years before Johnny Weissmuller), was rereleased in a shorter version with sound effects in 1928 and found a new life playing "underground" midnight shows in the late 60s. Now over 70 years old, it's a bit of history on video.

ADVENTURES OF THE FLYING CADETS

(Stokey, 1942) **D:** Ray Taylor, Lewis D. Collins **S:** Morgan B. Cox, George Plympton, Paul Huston **P:** Henry Macrae

A 12-chapter Universal serial with Johnny Downs, Bobby Jordan, and Billy Halop (from the East Side Kids movie series) as young flying cadets. They have to clear their names of a murder charge and fight "the Black Hangman," who plans to sell helium to the Nazis, and assorted WWII spies. With Jennifer Holt.

THE ADVENTURES OF TOPPER

(USA, 1953–55)

3 episodes of the CBS-TV series are on tape. Leo G. Carroll played the befuddled Cosmo Topper haunted by Marian and George Kirby, a friendly ghost couple (Anne Jeffreys and Robert Sterling), and their Saint Bernard, Neil. The show was based on the same Thorne Smith novel as the 1937, 1939, and 1941 movies produced by Hal Roach. The features are much better, of course, but *Topper* was pretty good for early-50s TV.

AD HOC ADVOCATED ADULT Amusement

YOU'LL SEE MORE AND LAUGH MORE THAN EVER BEFORE!

DELIGHTFUL, DELECTABLE, DESIRABLE, DELICIOUS DAMSELS DEVOID of Any and All Inhibitions!

Millions spent for actors, settings, and story! Not a penny for costumes!

THE ADVENTURES OF LUCKY PIERRE

FILMED IN FLESHTONE COLOR And SKINAMASCOPE Starring BILLY FALBO And PIERRE'S PLAYMATES

AELITA, QUEEN OF MARS

(Kino, 1924) **D:** Yakov Protazanov **S:** Fyodor Otsep, Alexei Faiko   USSR *(Revolt of the Robots; Aelita)*

This historic silent film, a science-fiction comedy based on a novel by Alexei Tolstoy, features a futuristic, "constructivist" version of Mars. A scientist shoots his wife and flees to Mars with a soldier and a detective. He become involved with Queen Aelita, and the soldier leads a revolution. *Aelita* played at international film festivals in 1993. The 113-minute video has a piano score and is a beautiful print. The original version ran two hours.

AENIGMA

(VSOM, 1986) **D/S:** Lucio Fulci **S:** Glorio Mariuzzo **P:** Ettore Spagnolo   Italy/Yugoslavia

In a plot similar to *Patrick*, a vengeful spirit enters a girl in coma (Lara Naszinski), and students at a Boston school for girls begin to die. With Jared Martin, Sabrina Siani, and a hard-to-believe death-by-snail scene.

AERODROME

(1983) **D:** Giles Foster **S:** Robin Chapman **P:** Kenith Trodd   UK

In a futuristic England, the fascist leaders build a mysterious aerodrome. This BBC TV production, based on Rex Warner's 1941 novel, is similar in some ways to the film *Things to Come* (1936). With Peter Firth, Richard Johnson, and Jill Bennett.

AFRAID OF THE DARK

(New Line, 1991) **D/S:** Mark Peploe **S:** Frederick Seidel **P:** Simon Bosanquet   UK/France

A kid (Ben Keyworth) in West London whose best friend is a dog wanders around, listens, peers, and spies with his telescope. He comes to suspect several local men (including a nudie photographer) of being the psycho who kills blind women. This was the first feature directed by Bertolucci's screenwriter (and brother-in-law) and has surprising reality shifts that might fascinate or infuriate you. It also shows the strong influence of Hitchcock and Michael Powell. With James Fox as the boy's cop dad and Fanny Ardant as his blind mom.

AFRICA BLOOD AND GUTS

(Shockwave, 1966) **D/S/E:** Gualtiero Jacopetti, Franco Prosperi **P:** Angelo Rizzoli   Italy *(Africa Addio)*

The original 138-minute (120 in the US) documentary by the makers of *Mondo Cane* is a very stark and serious look at revolution in Africa in the 60s and the results of colonialism. In 1970 it was rereleased by Jerry Gross' Cinemation with a new, stronger title and cut down to only 83 minutes. Most of the social commentary and historical background was removed, along with some of the stronger scenes. It's this version that became a notorious exploitation-circuit grossout hit and has been available on tape. Most viewers remember the circumcision rite. There was even an *Africa Addio* soundtrack on UA.

AFRICA EXPRESS

(1975) **D:** Michelle Lupo **S:** Mario Amendola, Bruno Corbucci   Italy/W. Germany

In the first of several films featuring Ursula Andress and Jack Palance, she's a secret agent and he's an American businessman. With Biba the chimp and Giulino Gemma. They all returned in *Safari Express* (1976). Americans know Ursula better from *Slave of the Cannibal God* (1977). She was taking her clothes off in all her films around that time.

AFRICAN RAGE

(MPI, 1976) **D:** Peter Collinson **P:** Alan Girney   *(Fatal Assassin; The Long Shot; Portrait of an Assassin)*

Simon Sabela is a tribal leader under the care of a hospital where Anthony Quinn works. With John Phillip Law as a hit man and Ken Gampu.

AFRICAN SAFARI

(1962) **D/S/P:** Ronald E. Shanin

This G-rated documentary was released in 1969. It features jungle animals, an erupting volcano, and "the Mountains of the Moon." From Crown International.

AFRICA SPEAKS

(Sinister, 1930) **D:** Walter Futter

The adventures of real-life explorer Paul Hoefler among the Wassara and Ubangi tribes of the Congo are narrated by Lowell Thomas. Thomas also narrated *The Blonde Captive* (1932) and *Mussolini Speaks* (1933) for Columbia. If this documentary looks at all familiar, it's because the Monogram studios later used extensive footage from it for all of their cheap Bomba the Jungle Boy movies, made from 1949 to 1955.

AFTER DARK, MY SWEET

(IVE, 1990) **D/S:** James Foley **S/P:** Robert Redlin **P:** Ric Kidney

Jason Patric is Kid Collie, an unshaven punch-drunk ex-boxer (recently escaped from a mental hospital) who knows a lot more than people think. He becomes the handyman and sometime lover of a conniving widow (Rachel Ward) in a desert town and also narrates this kidnapping-gone-wrong tale. Bruce Dern is perfect as the weasel ex-cop con man Uncle Bud. With George Dickerson and Jeanie Moore. It's based on a Jim Thompson novel and uses much of the original dialogue. Released the same year as two other Thompson adaptations, *The Grifters* and *The Kill-Off*.

AFTER HOURS

(Warner, 1985) **D:** Martin Scorsese **S:** Joseph Minion **P:** Amy Robinson, Griffin Dunne

This was Scorsese's "little" project after the commercial failure of *The King of Comedy* (1983). Griffin Dunne (who coproduced) stars as a Manhattan computer operator trapped without any money in Soho at night. The comic nightmare features a lot of interesting, troubled women and a surprising look at homophobia. It looks great, thanks to the cinematography by Michael Ballhaus (a Fassbinder regular) and includes several nods to Roger Corman's films (especially *A Bucket of Blood*). *After Hours* was voted best film at Cannes in 1986, but a lot of people seem to hate it, for some reason. I like it a lot. With Rosanna Arquette, Verna Bloom, Linda Fiorentino, Teri Garr, Catherine O'Hara, John Heard, Cheech and Chong, Dick Miller, Will Patton, Bronson Pinchot, and Rockets Redglare. Watch for the director in a punk-club scene.

Griffin Dunne and Catherine O'Hara in Martin Scorsese's *After Hours.*

AFTERMATH

(Prism, 1978) **D/S/P/A:** Steve Barkett

Post-nuke gang leader Sid Haig fights the director/star and his real-life son as astronauts. With appearances by Forrest J. Ackerman as the curator of the last museum on Earth, Eric Caidin (as a corpse), Jim Danforth, and the voice of Dick Miller. The castle home of coproducer Ted V. Mikels was used as a location. This very low-budget movie took a long time to get released. The Barketts returned with *Empire of the Dark* (1991).

AFTER MIDNIGHT

(CBS/Fox, 1989) **D/S/P:** Jim and Ken Wheat **P:** Richard Arlook, Peter Green

Three supposedly true horror tales are told by students of a crazed professor (Ramy Zada) who teaches a "Psychology of Fear" course. It's all inspired by the classic *Dead of Night* and includes a similar dream/reality cycle ending. The last and best story is about a mysterious phone caller, and there are a few excellent and surprising FX like an animated skeleton and a very convincing decapitated head. With Julian McWhirter, Marge Helgenberger, Pamela Segall, and Marc McClure. An unexpected MGM release by the makers of *Ewoks: The Battle for Endor.*

AFTER SCHOOL

(1989) **D/P:** William Olson **S/P:** Hugh Parks **S:** John Linde, Rod McBrien, Joe Tankersley   *(Before God; Return to Eden)*

A young priest (Sam Bottoms) debates an ex-priest (Robert Lansing) about the existence of God on *The Dick Cavett Show* and falls in love with Renee Coleman as September Lane. Coleman has a nude scene, and other women (including Page Hannah and Sherrie Rose) are topless in flashbacks showing the primitive world.

AFTERSHOCK

(Paramount, 1989) **D:** Frank Harris **S:** Michael Standing **P:** Roy McAree

An alien (Elizabeth Kaitan) visits during WWIII, learns to speak English by absorbing a dictionary, and meets good and bad earthlings. One-eyed Richard Lynch, John Saxon, Mathias Hues, and Michael Berryman (with lipstick and eye makeup) are villains, and Chris Mitchum and Russ Tamblyn have roles, but the real costars are two unknown guys who have a martial arts battle in front of the old mill where most of the nonplot takes place.

AFTER THE BALL WAS OVER

(SW, 1969)

A paranoid New York City woman (Alice Noland) tells a shrink about her "dreams." Their conversation is heard over the silent footage. In what turns out to be a plot to take her money, the husband sets her up to swap mates and takes nude photos of her after injecting her with drugs. Monster masks and makeup are seen during the drug sequence, and a dead body emerges from a tub as in *Diabolique.* The obscure b/w feature is just over an hour long and features nudity, some sex, and interesting music that sounds like Devo. It has no production credits.

AFTER THE FALL OF NEW YORK

(Vestron, 1984) **D/S:** "Martin Dolman"/ Sergio Martino **S:** Julian Berry, Gabriel Rossini **P:** Luciano Martino   Italy/France *(2019: Dopo la Caduta di New York)*

In one of the more violent Italian *Mad Max*–inspired movies, Michael Sopkiw as Parsifal is sent to Manhattan to rescue the only fertile woman left on earth so that the rat infested post-WWIII world can be repopulated (in New Jersey!). With Edmund Purdom as the president, George Eastman as Big Ape, rebels in the subway, midgets, torture, mutilation, and rape. It was originally rated X, then was cut for an R.

L'AGE D'OR

(Scorched Earth, 1930) **D/S/P/E:** Louis Buñuel **S:** Salvadore Dali **P:** The Vicomte de Noailles   France

A man throws a giraffe and a cardinal out of the window, the hero kicks a dog and knocks down blind people, a woman sucks the toe of a statue, and bishops turn into skeletons. Made two years after Buñuel and Dali's *Un Chien Andalu*, this unique, controversial feature ridicules the state,

the church, and the military, and uses anarchy, subversion, and nudity. The producer later became a devout Catholic and had the film withdrawn from circulation for years. It was banned for decades in many countries anyway. Only 63 minutes long, it has a classical music score.

AGENCY

(Vestron, 1979) **D:** George Kaczender **S:** Noel Hynde **P:** Robert Lantos, Stephen J. Roth Canada *(Mind Games)*

Robert Mitchum runs a major ad agency. He puts subliminal messages into TV commercials to brainwash the population so that he can easily enter politics. With Lee Majors and Valerie Perrine.

THE AGE OF INSECTS

(CD, 1990) **D/P:** Eric Maranno **S:** Andy Rees

A wealthy lingerie manufacturer pays to have his wayward punk son rehabilitated by a New York City (mad) doctor conducting hormone experiments. The doctor's East Indian assistant (Lisa Zane) falls for the young man while helping with his "rebirth," caused by rubbing on insect enzymes. *Age* features lots of impressive closeups of real insects, experimental video techniques, good hypnotic original music, and some good laughs.

When Lance awakes after the experiments a wonderful special effect makes his every move subject to LSD-type trails while everything else appears normal. If only this independent 8mm feature didn't have the endless irritating narration and so much overbearing dialogue it could almost pass as a classic comic/science-fiction/drug movie. Zane went on to costar in *Bad Influence, Freddy's Dead* and others. With Jack Ramey and Dallas Munroe.

AGUIRRE, THE WRATH OF GOD

(New Yorker, 1972) **D/S/P:** Werner Herzog W. Germany/Mexico/Peru *(Aguirre, der Zorn Gottes)*

Herzog's magnificent, hypnotic look at the 16th-century conquistadors was shot on location in the Amazon jungle. It was the international hit that made him and his star, the late Klaus Kinski, famous. Pizarro's men are after the fabled "Seven Cities of Gold," but Kinski, as Don Lope de Aguirre, doesn't even appear until near the end. Characters argue, fight, and kill each other, then starve and hallucinate, while Indians pick them off with arrows. The image of the defeated, mad Aguirre, with his dead daughter on an out-of-control raft covered with monkeys is unforgettable. With Helena Rojo and Ruy Guerra. Herzog also directed Kinski in *Nosferatu* and three other features. *Aguirre* was shot in German- and

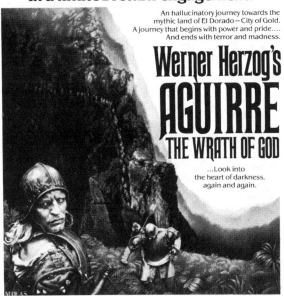

THE MOST EXCITING CULT EXPERIENCE OF ALL TIME
In a limited return engagement.

An hallucinatory journey towards the mythic land of El Dorado — City of Gold. A journey that begins with power and pride.... And ends with terror and madness.

Werner Herzog's AGUIRRE THE WRATH OF GOD

...Look into the heart of darkness, again and again.

English-language versions (as *Nosferatu* was). The excellent soundtrack is by Popul Voh. *Burden of Dreams* (1982) is about the making of the film (see entry).

A HAUNTING WE WILL GO
(1942) **D:** Alfred L. Werker **S:** Lou Breslow **P:** Sol M. Wurtzel

Nobody likes Laurel and Hardy's 40s features much, and with good reason, but this one features encounters with magicians, gangsters, coffins, and (fake) ghosts. With magicians Blackstone and Dante, plus Sheila Ryan, Willie Best and Elisha Cook Jr .The Fox feature is 69 minutes long.

AIP: FAST AND FURIOUS
(Trailers On Tape, 1985)

AIP was known for knowing how to sell a picture, so naturally their coming-attractions trailers were pretty great. This tape offers 33 trailers in 59 minutes. They range from the ultracheap *Phantom from 20,000 Leagues* (1955) to the big budget *Meteor* (1979), one of the movies that sank the company. They all are fun but unfortunately aren't programmed in any sensible way. You do get 5 Beach Party trailers and 6 for Roger Corman's movies. Some of my favorites are for Corman's *A Bucket of Blood (1959), Blood Bath (1966), The Brain That Wouldn't Die (1959)*, Edgar G. Ulmer's *The Amazing Transparent Man (1960)*, and *Squirm (1976)*, with an Ernie (Ghoulardi) Anderson voice-over. And look for *AIP: The Cool and the Crazy* (1986).

AIRHAWK
(Video City, 1984) **D/S/P:** Don Bellisario

This is the pilot for *Airwolf*, a TV series that copied the movie *Blue Thunder* and was trash/action TV at its dumbest. Jan-Michael Vin-

cent is the Nam-vet hero, a helicopter pilot. He and Ernest Borgnine work for Alex Cord and use the world's most sophisticated helicopter. An evil doctor (David Hemmings) steals another helicopter, and an agent (Belinda Bauer) poses as a belly dancer to infiltrate his operation. While making the series Vincent was going through a serious coke and alcohol binge. He emerged the burned-out direct-to-video exploitation star he is today.

AIRHEADS
(Fox, 1994) **D:** Michael Lehmann **S:** Rich Wilkes **P:** Robert Simmonds, Mark Burg, Michael Richards

A struggling heavy-metal band, the Lone Rangers, take over a radio station and take hostages in an attempt to get airplay. Steve Buscemi, Brendan Fraser, and Adam Sandler are the inept band members. With Joe Mantegna as a DJ, Michael McKean as a program director, Chris Farley and Ernie Hudson as cops, Amy Locane, Michael Richards, Judd Nelson, Nina Siemaszko, Harold Ramis and Kurt Loder. Rated PG-13. Lehmann also directed *Heathers*. With songs by the Ramones, Motorhead (Lemmy also appears), and Skid Row.

AIRPLANE II: THE SEQUEL
(Paramount, 1982) **D/S:** Ken Finkleman **P:** Howard W. Koch

*Airplane! (*1980) was a hilarious hit spoofing the *Airport* series (and the 1957 Dana Andrews movie *Zero Hour*). This really bad sequel about a space shuttle is not by the makers of the original. It even used old music from *Battlestar: Galactica*. The only possible reason to see it is for the guest stars: William Shatner, Sonny Bono, Raymond Burr, Chuck Connors, Rip Torn, John Vernon, Laurene Landon, Jack Jones, Richard Jaeckel, Sandahl Bergman, Hervé Villechaize, Kitten Natividad, and Chad Everett. Robert Hays, Julie Hagerty, Lloyd Bridges, Peter Graves, and the late Stephen Stucker all returned from the original.

AKIRA
(Orion, 1989) **D/S/P:** Katsuhiro Otomo **S:** Izo Hashimoto Japan

This was the best known Japanese animated feature in America at the time of its release. The impressive science fiction adventure takes place in the post-nuke 21st century and is based on Otomo's graphic novel. It features biker gangs and futuristic fascists. Otomo also directed the live action *World Apartment Horror*. Orion also

released other popular Japanese animated movies including *Vampire Hunter D*. Voyager released the laserdisc version (with audiotracks in Japanese and English).

AKIRA KUROSAWA'S DREAMS
(Warner, 1989) **D/S/E:** Akira Kurosawa **P:** Hisao Kurosawa, Mike Y. Inoue Japan

Dreams was the 28th feature by the 79-year-old director Akira Kurosawa. After the classic epics *Kagemusha* (1980), and *Ran* (1985), it was a very personal project that disappointed some viewers. Eight segments (in 119 minutes) include Akira Terao as "I," an observer. Some segments are beautiful and haunting, and several are based on familiar Asian ghost stories. The effects of war are seen when zombie warriors return, and a post-nuke segment has mutant plants and people. All of the master director's films after the 60s had foreign backing. This was "a Steven Spielberg presentation" and included some ILM FX (from George Lucas' company). Martin Scorsese even plays Van Gogh, painting frantically in a field. A note to *Godzilla* fans: the creative consultant was Ishiro Honda. Many thought this would be Kurosawa's swan song, but he returned with *Rhapsody in August* only a year later.

"I" (Akira Terao) meets a demon after a nuclear apocalypse in *Akira Kurosawa's Dreams*.

ALABAMA'S GHOST
(IVE, 1972) **D/S/P:** Frederic Hobbs

A black man (Christopher Brooks) discovers the belongings of magician "Carter The Great" in a secret catacomb under the club where he sweeps up. He tries on the costumes and soon becomes "Alabama, King of the Cosmos," a master magician who tours with a rock group. The very theatrical Brooks (who was "Jesus" in *The Mack*) plays Alabama with a deep, hearty laugh, looking like Screamin' Jay Hawkins. The movie is filled with actual, historical stage-magic props (especially a spirit cabinet) and old magic-show posters. It also features hash smoking, hippie dancing girls, a man playing a woman, voodoo ceremonies, a vampire woman, and a ghost with his heart on the outside. The theme is by the Turk Murphy (Dixieland) Jazz Band, who appear, as do the Loading Zone (also in *Roseland*). The tape has the unnecessary Elvira hosting. Who is Hobbs, and how could he have escaped attention for so long?!

ALADDIN

(Media, 1985) **D:** Sergio Corbucci **S:** Mario Amendola **P:** Ugo Yucci   Italy (*Super Fantagenio*)

A teen named Al Hadden finds a magic lamp. Bud Spencer is the genie. The Cannon feature was filmed in Miami and costars Janet Agren as the boy's mother. Spencer (real name Carlo Pedersoli), a big, bearded actor, is a major star in Europe and was a frequent costar with Terence Hill in comedy westerns.

ALADDIN AND HIS LAMP

(1952) **D:** Lew Landers **S:** Howard Dimsdale, Millard Kaufman **P:** Walter Wanger

A genie (Charles Horvath) can change his shape. John Sands stars, with Patricia Medina as Jasmine, Noreen Nash, and John Dehner. The film is only about an hour long. Landers directed at least seven features released in 1952.

ALADDIN AND HIS MAGIC LAMP

(United, 1967) **D:** B. Rytsarev **S:** V. Vitkovich, G. Yagdfeld   USSR

This live-action color and widescreen Arabian fantasy movie was filmed in "Storybook Color!" Some of the American video copies include new wraparound scenes produced by Jeffrey C. Hogue. Also look for *Aladdin and his Wonderful Lamp* (Fox, 1985), a 52-minute Faerie Tale Theatre presentation directed by Tim Burton.

ALAKAZAM THE GREAT

(1960) **D:** Lee Kresel, Teiji Yabushita, Daisaku Shirakawa **D/S:** Osamu Tezuka, Lou Rusoff   Japan (*Saiyu-ki*)

AIP released this Toei Studios feature-length cartoon fantasy about a magical singing monkey and Merlin the magician. It's based on a Chinese legend and was directed by the creator of *Astroboy*. They used Frankie Avalon, singer Dodie Stevens ("Pink Shoe Laces"), Jonathan Winters, Arnold Stang, and Sterling Holloway for the voices and added new Les Baxter music (released on Veejay). A marketing bonanza of licensed dolls, puzzles, puppets, and rings was planned. The fact that *Alakazam* was not a hit put a stop to plans for a series of AIP animated coproductions.

ALBINO

(Media, 1975) **D/P:** Jurgen Goslar **S:** Scot Finch   Rhodesia/W. Germany/UK/S. Africa (*Whispering Death; Night of the Askari*)

An ex-cop (James Faulkner) trails an albino terrorist, in a bloody movie about race problems. Christopher Lee is a police commissioner who pronounces the word "albeeno" and Trevor Howard (who was also in *Slavers*, by the same director) plays a corrupt plantation owner whose daughter (Sybil Danning with a wig) is raped and scalped by the albino and his followers. With Horst Frank (star of tbe 1959 film *The Head*).

AL CAPONE

(Fox, 1959) **D:** Richard Wilson **S:** Marvin Wald, Harry Greenberg **P:** John H. Burroughs

Rod Steiger is Capone in one of the best of the late-50s and early-60s gangster bios. Fay Spain costars with Martin Balsam, James Gregory, and Nehemiah Persoff. The director had started his career working with Orson Welles.

THE ALCHEMIST

(Ace, 1980) **D:** "James Amante"/Charles Band **S:** Alan J. Adler **P:** Lawrence Applebaum

A 19th-century magician puts a curse on a man (Robert Ginty) making him ageless. In 1955 North Carolina (it was filmed in California) he's still young, with a 90-year-old daughter, and a waitress (Lucinda Dooling) is the reincarnation of his wife. *The Alchemist* was over five years old before it was released. Watch the rubber demons from Hell and see why. The Richard Band soundtrack was released by Varese Sarabande and included his music for *Zone Troopers*.

ALEXANDER: THE OTHER SIDE OF DAWN

(American, 1977) **D:** John Erman **S:** Walter Dallenbach **P:** Wilford Lloyd Baumes

The NBC-TV sequel to the famous *Dawn: Portrait of a Teenage Runaway* (1976) stars Leigh J. McCloskey as a Hollywood street hustler. He wants to marry a teen hooker (Eve Plumb) but becomes involved with a gay football pro. With Earl Holliman, Juliet Mills, Jean Hagen, and Francis Faye. McCloskey, who also appeared in the earlier highly rated, then-controversial teen-exploitation TV movie, later showed up in Argento's *Inferno* and nonsense like *Fraternity Vacation* and *Hamburger: The Motion Picture*.

ALEX IN WONDERLAND

(1970) **D/S/A:** Paul Mazursky **S/P:** Larry Tucker

Mazursky had been an actor who helped develop the TV series *The Monkees*. After he directed his first feature, the hit *Bob and Carol and Ted and Alice*, MGM let him make this self-indulgent drug fantasy about a director (Donald Sutherland) who agonizes about what his next film should be, has fantasies about Fellini and his films, and takes LSD for inspiration. Fellini himself appears, and some Nino Rota music is used. With Ellen Burstyn, Michael Lerner, Jeanne Moreau (as herself), Richard Geary, and dwarf Angelo Rossitto (!) as Fellini number one. Laszlo Kovacs was the cinematographer. From MGM. Mazursky returned to the autobiographical theme with *The Pickle* (1993).

ALFRED HITCHCOCK TRAILERS

(Trailers on Tape, 1985)

Twenty Hitchcock movie trailers from *Rebecca* (1940) to *Topaz* (1969) are on this tape in chronological order. The best are the ones featuring Hitchcock himself: *Psycho* (the famous long tour of the set), *The Birds* (a great lecture about the history of the way people treat birds), and *Marnie* (where Hitch introduces each character in his new "sex mystery"). Some earlier ones are narrated by the stars like Joan Fontaine (*Suspicion*), Robert Cummings (*Saboteur*), and, best of all, James

Stewart (*Rope*). This tape includes Hitchcock's cameo appearance in *Spellbound*, Ingrid Bergman finding a shrunken head in the seldom-screened *Under Capricorn*, and Jerry Mathers in a space suit discovering a body in *The Trouble with Harry*. Sometimes the rerelease trailers are better than the originals, but the one for *Rear Window* (rereleased after *Psycho*) is disappointing and silly.

ALFRED HITCHCOCK PRESENTS

(MCA series) **D:** Alfred Hitchcock

Volume 1 (78 minutes long) from the long-running TV program was released in 1986, just after the revived Hitchcock TV series and consists of 3 episodes directed by the host: "The Case of Mr. Pelham" (1955) with Tom Ewell, the famous "Lamb to the Slaughter" (1958) with Barbara Bel Geddes, and "Banquo's Chair" (1959) with John Williams, made around the same time as *Psycho*. This tape is a valuable compilation and a great way to see what the master of suspense was doing on the small screen during one of his most creative periods.

ALFRED HITCHCOCK PRESENTS

(NBC, 1985) **D/S:** Joel Oliansky, Steve De Jarnatt, Randa Haines, Fred Walton

Four stories remade from the original series comprised the pilot for a new NBC series, introduced by a long dead and colorized (!) Alfred Hitchcock. I think it was sacrilege too, but it is interesting to see how these tales were modernized and the casting was good. In De Jarnatt's segment, "Man from the South," John Huston (who also narrates the whole film) stars with Steven Bauer, Kim Novak, and Melanie Griffith (plus her mother, Tippi Hedren, as a waitress). Ned Beatty, Lee Ving, Annette O'Toole, and Bruce Davidson are in the other stories. The series began in 1985 and these four were later shown separately in the revised series when it moved to the USA network (1987–89).

ALIAS THE CHAMP

(1949) **D:** George Blair **S:** Albert Demond **P:** Steven Auer

Gorgeous George, a wrestler who was famous at the time, thanks to TV, stars in this 60-minute feature. The mob frames him for a murder in the ring. Robert Rockwell is a cop, and Barbara Fuller sings. The other real wrestlers in the cast include Tor Johnson ("the Super Swedish Angel"), Sammy Menacker, and Bomber Kulkovitch, later known as actor Henry Kulky.

ALI BABA AND THE FORTY THIEVES

(MCA, 1944) **D:** Arthur Lubin **S:** Edmund L. Hartman **P:** Paul Mavern

Jon Hall (as ousted hero prince Ali) and Maria Montez, "the Queen of Technicolor," star in a Technicolor Universal fantasy/adventure. Turhan Bey costars as the knife-throwing Jamiel, Kurt Katch is the evil Mongolian Hulagu Khan, and Andy Devine is the comic Abdullah. This is a movie where the thieves are singing good guys

Tor Johnson ("The Super Swedish Angel") in *Alias the Champ.*

and they actually say, "Open, sesame" at the magic cavern. Also with Frank Puglia as Cassim, Ramsey Ames, Angelo Rossitto and Scotty Beckett. *Sword of Ali Baba* (1965) is a very cheap remake using much of the same footage.

ALI BABA GOES TO TOWN

(1937) **D:** David Butler **S:** Harry Tugend, Jack Yellen **P:** Darryl F. Zanuck

Eddie Cantor goes back in time and rides a flying carpet in this musical comedy. With Tony Martin, Roland Young, June Lang, John Carradine as Ashak and Louise Hovick (Gypsy Rose Lee.)

ALICE

(First Run, 1988) **D/S:** Jan Svankmajer
Switzerland/UK/W. Germany *(Neco z Alenky)*

Alice in Wonderland is told in a modern setting with horror, surrealistic, and erotic touches by a master Czech animator. A real actress (Kristyna Kohoutova) stars with animated scary creatures, skeleton birds and fish, and raw meat that moves. Also look for the compilation tape *Jan Svankmajer: Alchemist of the Surreal* (Kino, 1989).

ALICE

(Orion, 1990) **D/S:** Woody Allen **P:** Robert Greenhut

This unhappy Alice (Mia Farrow) visits a Chinese herbalist (Keye Luke in his last role), who sends her on a voyage to find herself. She meets the ghost of her first love (Alec Baldwin), has an affair, and becomes invisible, in a PG-13 movie that resembles Fellini's *Juliet of the Spirits.* Joe Mantegna costars with William Hurt, Judy Davis, Blythe Danner, Cybill Shepherd, Gwen Verdon, Julie Kavner, Bernadette Peters. Also with Patrick O'Neal, James Toback, Bob Babalan and Elle McPherson. Allen's next was *Shadows and Fog,* also with fantasy elements.

ALICE COOPER: PRIME CUTS

(Polydor, 1991) **D:** Neal Preston
P: Charles Murdock

Here's where 70s punk and heavy-metal rockers and David Bowie got a lot of ideas. Cooper, the king of horror rock (whose real name is Vincent Furnier) talks about being from Detroit, running track with the rest of his great trashy-sounding band, meeting Frank Zappa, the chicken incident, and doing a hologram with Salvador Dali. He says "Dead Babies" was an anti-child-abuse song. Most of the tape, though, is one great live or TV clip after another, including classic early stuff like "Ballad of Dwight Frye" and "Eighteen" and even parts of "Levity Ball," and "Black Ju Ju." Cooper enjoyed 10 top-40 hits during the 70s. He had parts in movies (see index) and tapes of concerts and other videos are available. Look for *Alice Cooper: Welcome to My Nightmare* (Rhino, 1975). Vincent Price was the host, and it was cowritten by Alan Rudolph and choreographed by David Winters (who later formed AIP video). Lester Bangs once wrote that these guys would be the next Rolling Stones. He was almost right.

ALICE IN ACIDLAND

(SW, 1969) **D/P:** "John Donne" **S:** "Gertrude Steen"

A psychiatrist begins narrating the sad tale of Alice Trenton, a nice college student who gets in with the wrong crowd. Alice starts narrating too, and after a while they alternate, explaining the silent b/w footage on the screen. Alice goes to a pool party given by her beautiful, smiling French teacher, Freda. Wearing a polka-dot bikini, Alice smokes her first cigarette ("I felt like a real kid!") and drinks. All of a sudden she and Freda are naked in a bathtub kissing and fondling each other. Later, they hop into a Volkswagen and go to the bathroom of a service station so they can change into hip clothes and smoke a joint. They walk on the Sunset Strip ("She'd now become a wild twilight hippie!") until they find another party. Animal fondles Alice on the floor ("Animal had pushed the right button!") while a sappy song about soft lips plays. The men have normal conservative haircuts and wear black slacks with

Alice Cooper on stage in *Alice Cooper: Prime Cuts.*

combs in their back pockets. During sex scenes, they leave their boxer shorts on. The sex scenes are pretty much adults-only. Most of the music is by a jazz trio.

At yet another party, where lots of pot is smoked, an "acid test" is announced and Alice swallows a sugar cube. ("I began to float, my temples were pounding!") The offscreen shrink informs us that Animal has driven Alice's best friend to suicide. The rest of the movie is completely unrelated, full-color, psychedelic footage showing Alice's trip. The music gets wilder, somebody recites some poetry and there's a frantic light-and-strobe show. ("Let me eat the flowers!") Women with painted eyes and paper flowers dance, strip, lie around naked, and pose. ("Take me! Love me!") The dead friend shows up. The last shot is Alice in a straitjacket in a padded cell. ("She's a mental vegetable!") The End.

ALICE IN WONDERLAND

(MGM, 1933) **D:** Norman McLeod
S: Joseph L. Mankiewicz, William Cameron Menzies **P:** Louis D. Lighton

Charlotte Henry (from *Babes in Toyland*) is Alice in an all-star Paramount film that's worth seeing for some bizarre casting. With W. C. Fields as Humpty Dumpty, Cary Grant as the Mock Turtle, Edward Everett Horton as the Mad Hatter, Richard Arlen, Gary Cooper, Jack Oakie, Charlie Ruggles, Sterling Holloway, Edna May Oliver, Lucien Littlefield, Mae Marsh, Louise Fazenda, Leon Erro, and Roscoe Ates. The next two versions of the story were released in 1948 (a British version with puppets) and 1951 (Disney animation).

ALICE IN WONDERLAND

(Edde, 1976) **D:** Bud Townsend
S: B. A. Fredericks **P:** Bill Osco

The musical/fantasy/sex comedy from the makers of *Flesh Gordon* (1972) stars Kristine DeBell as a virginal singing librarian who discovers a sexual wonderland with the usual Lewis Carroll characters. The costumes and makeup are terrible and the singing and dancing are irritating, but this was popular in theaters in a cut version. Later it was rereleased with hard-core scenes (some featuring DeBell, also in mainstream movies) restored. The X version (from Caballero) features lesbian, 69, and masturbation scenes. With Larry Gelman, Jason Williams, and porn stars Teri Hall and Bree Anthony. Producer Osco made *Mona* (1970), "the first porno feature." *Alice* is by the director of *Nightmare in Wax* and the father of actress Patrice Townsend (*Sitting Ducks*).

ALICE IN WONDERLAND

(1985) **D:** Harry Harris
S: Paul Zindel **P:** Irwin Allen

Little Alice goes to show-biz hell for 4 hours with ridiculous guest stars trashing a classic book. The CBS-TV movie by the late "master of disaster" cost a record $14 million. The appalling cast includes Steve Allen and Jayne Meadows, Scott Baio, Ernest Borgnine, Lloyd and Beau Bridges, Red Buttons, Sid Caesar and Imogene Coca, Carol Channing, Sammy Davis Jr., Patrick Duffy, George Gobel, Eydie Gorme, Merv Griffin, Sherman Hemsley, Ann Jillian, Arte Johnson, Harvey Korman, Steve Lawrence, Karl Malden, Roddy McDowall, Donna Mills, Pat Morita, Robert Morley, Anthony Newley, Louis Nye, Donald O'Connor, Martha Raye. Telly Savalas, John Stamos, Ringo Starr, Sally Struthers, Jack Warden, Jonathan Winters and Shelley Winters.

ALICE'S ADVENTURES IN WONDERLAND

(1972) **D/S:** William Sterling **P:** Derek Horne   UK

Fiona Fullerton (later in *A View to a Kill*) stars in a musical version of the famous story, with Michael Crawford as the White Rabbit, Peter Sellers as the March Hare, Ralph Richardson as the caterpillar, Michael Hordern, Spike Milligan, Flora Robson, Dudley Moore, and other famous guest stars. The John Barry soundtrack was released by Warner.

ALICE THROUGH THE LOOKING GLASS

(1966) **D:** Alan Hadley

This curiosity item is another example of how a classic children's tale is turned into a celebrity employment project. The NBC-TV special features Ricardo Montalban, Nanette Fabray, Agnes Moorehead, Jack Palance, Robert Coote, Jimmy Durante, Richard Denning, and the Smothers Brothers. RCA even released a soundtrack.

ALIENATOR

(Prism, 1989) **D:** Fred Olen Ray
S: Paul Garson **P/A:** Jeffrey C. Hogue

A female terminator (bodybuilder Teagan) is sent by a space warden (Jan-Michael Vincent) to go after an alien killer (Ross Hagen) who has escaped from a prison ship. Teagan looks real silly with her teased blond hair and scrap-metal bra. With John Phillip Law, P.J. Soles, Leo V. Gordon, Robert Clarke, Fox Harris, Robert Quarry, Donna Wildsmith, Jay Richardson, and Hoke Howell. Ray says it's his version of *The Astounding She Monster* (1958) which starred Clarke.

ALIEN ATTACK: *See* SPACE 1999

ALIEN FACTOR

(Media, 1978) **D/S/E:** Don Dohler

This 16mm made-in-Baltimore wonder shot in "Qualitycolor" was released to TV stations by Gold Key, and it still shows up at the oddest times. Three escaped alien monsters land in a small town during wintertime, followed by a good, human-appearing alien. The coverup plotline is from *Jaws*. The acting and the synth score are laughable, and the monsters are pretty pathetic but interesting considering the nonexistent budget. There's even a (transparent) animated dinosaur. Everything stops while a 60s-style long-

haired band plays in a bar. Near the end, a girl says, "Wait! Wait! It doesn't make any sense!" With Don Leifert, Dick Dyszel (Washington, DC TV horror host Count Gore DeVol) as the mayor, Johnny Walker (a local DJ) and George Stover. Ernest D. Farino is credited with FX.

ALIEN FROM LA

(Media, 1988) **D:** Albert Pyun **S:** Debra Ricci, Regina Davis **P:** Golan/Globus   S. Africa

Sports Illustrated model Kathy Ireland stars as a valley-girl cocktail waitress looking for her missing father in Africa. At one point she falls down a hole and ends up in Atlantis, where she's considered an alien. This PG-rated Cannon nonsense was made with footage from their *Journey to the Center of the Earth*. It was considered bad enough for *Mystery Science Theater 3000*. With Linda Kerridge (*Fade to Black*) in two roles, Thom Mathews, and Don Michael Paul.

ALIEN INTRUDER

(PM, 1992) **D:** Richard Jacques Gale
S: Nick Stone **P:** Merhi, Pepin

It's sad to see Billy Dee Williams in this cheap, stupid science-fiction tape (and his acting is pretty sad too). He picks prisoners (including Maxwell Caulfield) to go with him to a ship where a virtual-reality program helps create fantasies (copied from *Westworld*). Tracy Scoggins is the alien woman who invades the lame fantasy segments (which make up most of the movie) and turns the men against each other. There are biker, surfer, western, and detective sequences (the last two in b/w) and a nude shower scene. With Jeff Conaway in a very small part and Kevin Lowe.

ALIEN MASSACRE = WIZARD OF MARS

ALIEN NATION

(CBS/Fox, 1988) **D:** Graham Baker **S:** Rockne S. O'Bannon **P:** Gale Anne Hurd, Richard Kobritz

In this clever but flawed mismatched-cop science-fiction movie, James Caan stars as a clichéd divorced, alcoholic, racist LA cop in 1991. His black partner is killed and replaced by Mandy Patinkin as Sam Francisco, an alien "newcomer." He can get drunk on sour milk and has a head that looks like a piece of Sugar Pops cereal. The aliens are newly arrived victims of American racism, called "slags," and many live in a slum. Terence Stamp is an alien drug dealer who becomes a monster. The Stan Winston studio provided the FX. Several sequences were cut (when it was known as *Outer Heat*), and James Cameron did an uncredited rewrite before the film's release. It also became a short-lived TV series.

ALIEN NATION

(Fox, 1989) **D/S:** Kenneth Johnson
P: Tom Chehank, Arthur Seidel

Gary Graham and Eric Pierpoint (as detective George Francisco) are the mismatched human and alien cops who end up dealing with racism and AIDS. The alien even becomes pregnant. This

was the pilot for the Fox-TV series (1989–90) Many people thought that the series was more successful than the theatrical feature. With Terry Treas and Michelle Scarabelli. The Fox TV movie *Alien Nation: Dark Horizon* (1994) revived the characters.

ALIEN OUTLAW

(1985) **D/S/P:** Phil Smoot **P:** George B. Walker

This science-fiction movie shot in North Carolina with old-time B-western stars Lash La Rue, Sunset Carson, and Wild Bill Cody is a must-see in my book. At this time nobody has dared to release it. Things have a way of sneaking out on videotape though. Smoot (great name) also directed *Dark Power* (1984).

ALIEN PREDATOR

(TWE, 1984) **D/S/P:** Deran Sarafian **P:** Carlos Aured   US/Spain (*Cosmos Mortal; The Falling*)

A piece of Skylab with a briefly seen *Alien*-copy life form falls on young US tourists in dune buggies in Spain. Dennis Christopher, Martin Hewitt, and Lynn-Holly Johnson star. A mutilated cow and dog eat each other, and there are chestburster scenes. The Helen Sarlui production (called *Mutant II* in England) was to be released theatrically by Film Ventures, which went out of business.

ALIEN PREY

(Comet, 1977) **D:** Norman J. Warren **S:** Max Duff **P:** Terence Marcel, David Wimbury   UK (*Prey*)

This bad science-fiction/sex movie is (incredibly) a virtual remake of *The Fox* (1968) which was based on a D. H. Lawrence novella. A young man (Barry Stokes), really an alien on Earth for the first time, joins a lesbian couple in a secluded cottage. Animals (and policemen) are found mutilated and a lot of time is used up with soft-core sex scenes featuring Sally Faulkner (from *Vampyres*) and Glory Annan.

ALIEN PRIVATE EYE

(Raedon, 1987) **D/S/P/E:** Nik Rubenfeld

Nikki Fastinetti stars as alien hero Lemro in this laughable mess that has some similarities to *I Come in Peace* (made later). Lemro has a 30s-style private eye office, dances like Michael Jackson, fights like Bruce Lee, and has Mr. Spock ears. Aliens on earth battle over an addictive designer drug. The sound is so bad you can hear the creaking of leather jackets and traffic noise over the dialogue. With a cold-turkey scene, a Keith Richards reference, a terrible Peter Lorre imitation, topless sex, and a disco.

ALIENS

(CBS/Fox, 1986) **D/S:** James Cameron **S:** Walter Hill, David Giler **P:** Gale Anne Hurd

Aliens made $43,700,000 in North American box-office receipts (more than the original) and the bigger (and, most agree, even better) non-stop sequel to one of the most copied hits of the 70s is a must see. Sigourney Weaver (who received an Oscar nomination!) returns as Ripley and battles a hive of huge, horrible aliens at a terraforming colony on the planet Acheron while protecting a little girl named Newt. With Cameron regular Michael Biehn as the leader of the Marine group, Paul Reiser (corporate scum), Lance Henriksen (great android), Bill Paxton, Jenette Goldstein as the muscular female marine, and William Hope. The Stan Winston studio FX received an Oscar. The letterboxed laserdisc version restores 17 minutes and includes an interview with the director. The cassette and theatrical version is 137 minutes. The James Horner soundtrack was released on Varese Sarabande. An unrelated 1980 Italian movie was called *Alien #2* (or *Alien Terror*).

Ripley (Sigourney Weaver) and Newt (Carrie Henn) in *Aliens*.

ALIENS ARE COMING

(Worldvision, 1980) **D:** Harvey Hart
S: Robert W. Lenski **P:** Phillip Saltzman

Tom Mason starred in this failed NBC-TV pilot film from Quinn-Martin that recycled Larry Cohen's original concept from the old *Invaders* program. It's set at Hoover Dam. With Eric Braedon, Max Gail, Ed Harris, and Gerald McRaney.

ALIENS, DRAGONS, MONSTERS, AND ME

(Cerebus, 1986) **D:** Richard Jones

The career of stop-motion-animation genius Ray Harryhausen was given a London museum retrospective at the time that this one-hour documentary (originally on the Disney Channel) was shot. Clips from just about everything he worked on are included. Ray Bradbury is interviewed, Bradbury and Kerwin Mathews add commentary, and

Gary Owens narrates. The Lumivision disc version is longer. Harryhausen received a special Oscar in 1993.

ALIEN SEED

(AIP, 1989) **D/S:** Bob James
S: Douglas K. Grimm **P:** Mark Paglia

A science-fiction movie with a bad script, terrible action scenes, cheap special effects, too many chase scenes, and irritating slow-motion dreams might not sound very enticing, but Eric Estrada (!) is in it. The former *CHIPS* star, who was also an associate producer, was in at least 20 direct-to-video projects in the late 80s, so if you like this one, knock yourself out. The plot is about a close encounter and a government cover-up. Steven Blade and Heidi Payne star, and there are topless-bar scenes. It was filmed in Colorado.

ALIENS FROM SPACESHIP EARTH

(Video Gems, 1977) **D/P:** Don Como

Another dull pseudodocumentary from Gold Key about religious cults and "inner peace" groups. Dramatic reenactments try to prove that great men from the past were aliens. Lynda Day George and Leigh Taylor-Young are in it, and the music is by Donovan!

ALIENS RETURN = THE RETURN

ALIEN SPACE AVENGER

(AIP, 1988) **D/S:** Richard Haines
S: Lynwood Sawyer **P:** Ray Sundlin, Robert W. Harris   (*Space Avenger*)

Four aliens take over the bodies of two couples during the 30s, hide out in a space sphere, and emerge 50 years later in New York City, still wearing 30s clothes. A comic-book artist (Robert Prichard) bases a hit *Space Avenger* comic on their exploits and they go after him while trying to find plutonium so that they can return home and fight some human emotions. What might at first sound like a silly science-fiction comedy is really a very clever and well made, violent, action-packed movie with sex, gore, laughs, and good acting. In both time periods the aliens acquire guns and blast nearly everybody they encounter. When an alien's arm is shot off, it grows back. The stars includes Charity Staley and Angela Nicholas as aliens and Gina Mastrogiacomo as the cartoonist's girlfriend who is taken over by a puppet alien (and has the major nude scene). Porn star Jamie Gillis has a funny role, and clips from the original *Flash Gordon* are put to good use. The locations include Central Park, the Tunnel club, a Times Square video arcade, Washington Square Park, an elevated subway, and 42nd St., where *Vampire Hookers* and *Dolemite* are playing! Parts were filmed in

Peekskill, New York. With Billy Rae McQuade (from *Mother's Day*) and Char Rao. The director previously made Troma movies.

ALIEN TERROR

(MPI, Sony, 1968) **D/S:** Jack Hill **D:** Juan Ibanez **P:** Luis Enriquez Vergara   US/Mexico
(*Sinister Invasion; Invasion Siniestra*)

This wacky period science-fiction story (set in Europe) was the last of the four Boris Karloff movies made back-to-back in LA shortly before he died. In fact, it is the great horror star's last movie. Most of the scenes were filmed in Mexico, and the footage was later (badly) edited together. Some scenes have abrupt jumpy edits, and the illusion of Karloff acting with people filmed at another time in another country fails pretty often. Boris plays a kindly professor with a female assistant who has a badly scarred face. He creates a molecular ray that can blow up rocks. When the ray blasts a hole in the roof, it's seen by aliens who decide to kill everybody to save themselves. A curly-haired blond guy arrives in an antique flying saucer wearing a silver suit and takes over the mind of a local sex-crazed, psychotic killer in a top hat (the strange-looking Yerye Beirute). The alien life forces are passed in what resembles a transparent heart. The professor's mind is also taken over, so during the rest of the movie the alien/killer tries (in vain) to suppress his voyeuristic and killing tendencies, and the alien/professor tries to suppress his concern for his sexy, blond niece, played by Christa Linder (*Night of a Thousand Cats*). After more women in low-cut gowns are killed, angry villagers arrive, just like in old Universal horror movies. Boris destroys the alien force and his machine "so humanity can't commit suicide," and his house burns.

ALIEN³

(Fox, 1992) **D:** David Fincher **S/P:** David Giler, Walter Hill **S:** John Fasano **P:** Gordon Carroll

This grim, murky mess by a 29-year-old first-time-director known for Madonna videos cost over $50 million and made about half that much. It's up there with the third *Exorcist* and *Godfather* movies for being overall wrong. Sigourney Weaver returns (with shaved head) and encounters celibate, monklike prisoners. With Charles Dutton (a real-life ex-con) as the inmate leader, Charles Dance as the doctor, Paul McGann, Brian Glover, and Lance Henriksen (briefly). Some called it a daring AIDS allegory, but you could say that about dozens of cheaper science-fiction and horror movies. Before it was released, an *Aliens* video "triple pack" was released with the first two features and a 23-minute "making of" *Alien³* tape (also released separately). If it had told the full, true story of the troubled production (how much all the uncredited screenwriters were paid and how entire parts were reshot) it would have been more interesting than the feature itself. The last-minute suicide ending was filmed just before the release. The Elliot Goldenthal soundtrack is on MCA.

ALIEN WARRIOR

(Vestron, 1985) **D/S:** Ed Hunt **S:** Rueben Gordon, Steve Schonenberg **P:** Yakov Bentsvi   Canada (*King of the Streets*)

An alien vigilante (Brett Clarke) has to prove his bravery in this *Terminator* ripoff, so he fights drug dealers and pimps on Earth. With Talley Chanel (from the pages of *Penthouse*) and Pamela Saunders (from *Playboy*).

THE ALIEN WITHIN

(MNTEX, 1990) **D/S:** Ted Newsom, Kenneth Hall **P:** Peter Stewart

This is Hall's *Evil Spawn* (1986) with new scenes added by producer Fred Olen Ray (who had a feud with original director Hall). With most of the original cast plus Richard Harrison, Gordon Mitchell, Melissa Moore, Jay Richardson, and Suzanne Ager. Now you can experience a wonderfully awful movie in two different versions!

ALIEN WOMEN

(SW, 1969) **D/S:** Michael Cort **S:** Alastair McKenzie   UK (*Zeta One: The Love Factor*)

A spy (Robin Hawden) narrates this story after a game of strip poker (with Yutte Stensgaard) in his playboy pad. The plot is something about alien women wearing white boots and wigs who kidnap Earth women. Dawn Addams (in her last known feature) is Zeta, their leader. The spy convinces a stripper to infiltrate the aliens. With Brigitte Skay, Anna Gael, Valerie Leon, and James Robertson-Justice. With cheap psychedelic FX, compact picture phones, torture scenes, and lots of female warriors wearing pasties while they zap men in the woods. It's slow going, but some of you might want to check out the naked Hammer starlets. The Tygon film was based on a British comic strip.

ALISON'S BIRTHDAY

(Vestron, 1979) **D/S/A:** Ian Coughan **P:** David Hannay   Australia

During a seance, a dead father warns his daughter, Alison (Joanne Samuel), that she'll be possessed at 19. A cult that worships a female sorceress tries to make the prediction come true. This Filmways release copies ideas from *Rosemary's Baby* and *The Exorcist*. It's a David Hemmings production. The British actor produced a number of features in Australia and New Zealand in the 80s.

ALIVE

(Touchstone, 1992) **D:** Frank Marshall **S:** John Patrick Shanley **P:** Robert Watts, Kathleen Kennedy

Buena Vista/Touchstone released this long (123-minute) R-rated remake of Rene Cardona's *Survive!* (1976). A plane carrying a team of Uruguayan rugby players crashes in the snowy Andes (curtesy of ILM FX). Eventually survivors resort to eating their dead companions. Ethan Hawke stars, with Josh Hamilton and Vincent Spano.

John Malkovitch introduces the story as a passenger who remembers it all 20 years later. *Alive: 20 Years Later* (Touchstone, 1993) is a documentary about the real survivors (it's based on a real incident) and the making of this movie.

ALL AMERICAN MURDER

(Prism, 1991) **D:** Anson Williams **S:** Barry Sandler **P:** Bill Novoor

Christopher Walken is Detective Decker in this dumb but entertaining direct-to-video *Twin Peaks*–inspired feature. It was made in Tulsa, Oklahoma, by the guy who played Potsie on *Happy Days*. Arty (Charlie Schatter), a fast-talking, trouble-making, pyromaniac son of a judge, is enrolled at a fine college and told to straighten out or else. He immediately has sex with the dean's wife (Joanna Cassidy), falls for the perfect blond cheerleader, and is blamed when she goes up in slow-motion flames. Many more people die while the tough but intelligent and sympathetic maverick Decker and the frantic Artie try to discover who the killer might be. Incriminating sex photos appear, and a deaf handyman with a power drill adds some gore effects. The absurd end of this red-herring-filled mystery will leave you astounded (or angry as hell). With Josie Bissett (from *Melrose Place*). Sandler wrote *Crimes of Passion*.

ALLAN QUATERMAIN AND THE LOST CITY OF GOLD

(Media, 1986) **D:** Gary Nelson, Newt Arnold **S:** Gene Quintano **P:** Golan/Globus

Richard Chamberlain and Sharon Stone find a lost city of gold (and a lost race of Phoenicians) in this useless Cannon PG comedy/adventure sequel to its *King Solomon's Mines* remake from 1985. They were filmed at the same time to save $. James Earl Jones is the warrior Umslopogaas. Henry Silva as Agon and Cassandra Peterson (better known as Elvira) as an evil queen rule the lost city. It was filmed in Zimbabwe and includes Cleveland jokes and a spear-proof tunic. This feature is also a remake of Alvin Rakoff and Harry Alan Towers' 1977 *King Solomon's Treasure*.

ALLEY CAT

(Vestron, 1982) **D:** "Edward Victor"/Eduardo Palmos **S/P:** Robert E. Waters **P:** Victor Ordóñez   (*Dragon Fly*)

Karin Mani's grandparents are killed by a gang, but the sexy part-Asian star is sent to prison. When she's released, she fights back with martial arts. Like Tura Satana, Mani is supposed to be a mixture of Asian and Native American (and she takes her clothes off). The Film Ventures release also features Britt Helfer. By the director of *Fighting Back*.

ALLEY TRAMP

(SW, 1966) **D/C:** Herschell Gordon Lewis **S:** Allison Louise Down **P:** Tom Dowd

The credits of this b/w exploitation movie from Chicago were all fake. It's about a teenage girl who has sex with her cousin, then her mother's lover. While in the hospital for an abortion she

tries to rape an intern, and she ends up in an insane asylum. Down, the first lady of exploitation screenwriters, also wrote *Blood Feast* and many others directed by Lewis.

ALLIGATOR ALLEY = THE HOOKED GENERATION

ALLIGATOR EYES

(Academy, 1990) **D/S/P:** John Feldman **P:** Ken Schwenker

Annabell Larson stars as a mysterious blind hitchhiker with a talking computer. After three people on the way to Virginia Beach pick her up, she seduces both men (off screen) and they all argue and fight about her. They end up on Okrakoke Island on Halloween. This well-made film has interesting, believable characters and features flashbacks, narration by two different characters, some nudity, a shooting, and frequent Jim Jarmusch–inspired blackouts.

ALLIGATOR II: THE MUTATION

(RCA, 1991) **D:** Jon Hess **S:** Curtis Allen **P:** Brandon Chase

Joseph Bologna stars as a night shift cop in what's basically a PG-13 remake of the original John Sayles–scripted movie (1980). Bologna is good, and so are Richard Lynch as a knife-throwing Cajun gator hunter and Steve Railsback as a killer real-estate developer. The giant-gator attack carnival is OK, but too much time is spent on a rookie cop and his new love interest. Also with Brock Peters as a police chief, Dee Wallace-Stone as the lab technician wife, Bill Daily from *I Dream of Jeannie* as the corrupt mayor, Holly Gagnier, Professor Tanaga, Woody Brown, and Kane Holder. It was made for ABC-TV (where we saw it) but was picked up for distribution by New Line.

THE ALLNIGHTER

(MCA, 1987) **D/S/P:** Tamar Simon Hoffs **P:** Nancy Israel

Susanna Hoffs (from the Bangles) stars in a PG-13 teen movie made by her mom. Three high-school girls want sex on the eve of their graduation. With Dedee Pfeiffer, Joan Cusack, Michael Ontkean, John Terlesky, and Pam Grier as a cop. The Bangles were a great group (for a very short time).

ALL'S FAIR

(1989) **D:** Rocky Lane **S:** Randee Russell, John Finegan, Tom Rondinella, William Pace **P:** Jon Gordon

Here's yet another movie about weekend war games. Jennifer Edwards works for candy-bar manufacturer George Segal. Left out of the all-male company games, she forms an all-female team. With Sally Kellerman, Robert Carradine, and Lou Ferrigno.

ALL THAT JAZZ

(Fox, 1979) **D/S:** Bob Fosse **S/P:** Robert Alan Arthur

This dark, disturbing autobiographical musical with fantasy segments stars Roy Scheider as the pill-popping, womanizing, egomaniacal choreographer and director Joe Gideon (Fosse). People from Fosse's real life appear as "themselves," and he goes through graphic open-heart surgery. With Jessica Lange, Ann Reinking, Sandahl Bergman, Vicki Frederick, Ben Vereen, and John Lithgow. Fosse also choreographed (of course). The 123 minute feature was released by Columbia with 20th Century. A soundtrack was on Casablanca.

ALL THE KIND STRANGERS

(Fox, 1974) **D:** Burt Kennedy
S: Clyde Ware **P:** Roger Lewis

Stacy Keach and Samantha Eggar are held prisoner by seven backwoods orphans with vicious dogs in this TV movie. The kids kills people who refuse to stay and become their parents. With John Savage and Robby Benson (who sings the title song). It was filmed in Tennessee.

ALL THE LOVIN' KINFOLK

(SW, 1970) **D/S/P:** John Hayes **P:** Daniel Cady

Mady Maguire (from *Norma*) stars in a pretty senseless soft-X period backwoods-sex movie. With a square dance, barnyard sex, an old car to make you think its the 30s, and Uschi Digart. The original video box had porn star Taja Rae on the cover.

. . . ALL THE MARBLES

(MGM/UA, 1981) **D:** Robert Aldrich **S:** Mel Frohman
P: William Aldrich   (*The California Dolls*)

This ahead of its time women's-wrestling movie didn't really find an audience until it started playing on cable TV. It was the last film by Aldrich. A small-time hustler (Peter Falk) travels though the Midwest managing a female tag team and encounters gangsters and other troubles. Laurene Landon and Vicki Frederick are both perfect as the tall, beautiful fighters. With Burt Young, Richard Jaeckel, Mike Mazurki, Tracy Reed, Angela Aames, and Susan Mechsner. Brinke Stevens is an extra.

ALL THIS AND WORLD WAR II

(1976) **D:** Susan Winslow **P:** Sandy
Lieberson, Martin J. Machat

Some people still don't believe that this film was made and think it's just a two-record boxed set with a booklet and ads for T-shirts. The film is all old newsreel footage set to Beatles cover songs. The songs are by many artists, including Bryan Ferry, Tina Turner, Frankie Valli, Keith Moon, Peter Gabriel, and Roy Wood. Hear Helen Reddy and the Bee Gees sing while Hitler plans and Nazis march and kill. Amazing.

ALMOST AN ANGEL

(Paramount, 1990) **D/P:** John Cornell **S/A:** Paul Hogan

Paul Hogan is a minor LA thief who disguises himself as Willie Nelson, then Rod Stewart. He gets hit by a car, meets God (Charlton Heston), and becomes a good guy. After two *Crocodile Dundee* hits, nobody went to this PG feel-good fantasy. With Linda Kozlowski (Hogan's wife), Elias Koteas, Joe Dallesandro, and David Alan Grier.

ALMOST HUMAN

(Prism, 1974) **D:** Umberto Lenzi
S: Ernesto Gastaldi **P:** Luciano Martino
Italy (*Milano Odia: La Polizia Non Puo Sparare; The Kidnap of Mary Lou*)

Giulio (Tomas Milian), a demented criminal, kidnaps a rich man's daughter (Anita Strindberg). In the US, this violent, mean-spirited feature (complete with nudity, children murdered and forced male/male oral sex) was promoted (by Joseph Brenner) as if it were a horror movie. With Henry Silva as a cop, Ray Lovelock, and Laura Belli. Milian (from Cuba) returned in *Assault with a Deadly Weapon*.

ALMOST SUMMER

(1978) **D/S:** Martin Davidson **S:** Judith
Berg, Marc Eric Rubel **P:** Rob Cohen

Bruno Kirby, Lee Purcell, Tim Matheson, and Didi Conn are in this light, PG-rated tale of high-school elections that turns serious. Some then-new Beach Boys (and Brian Wilson) songs are on the MCA soundtrack and Mike Love is in the movie.

aloha, bobby and rose

(Media, 1975) **D/S:** Floyd Mutrux **P:** Fouad Said

An auto mechanic (Paul Le Mat from the *American Graffiti* movies) and his girl (Dianne Hull) hold up a liquor store and turn to a life of crime in this PG chase movie. With Robert Carradine, Edward James Olmos, and Tim McIntire.

ALOHA SUMMER

(Warner, 1988) **D:** Tommy Lee Wallace
S/P: Mike Greco **S:** Bob Benedetto

Six guys of different nationalities become surfing friends in Hawaii in 1959. With Chris Makepeace, Don Michael Paul, Tia Carrere, Yuji Okumoto, and Sho Koshugi. This PG feature is by the director of *Halloween III*.

ALONE AGAINST ROME

(Sinister, 1962) **D:** "Herbert Wise"/Luciano Ricci
S: Ennio Mancini, Gianni Astolfi, Gastad Green
P: Marco Vicario   Italy (*Solo Contra Roma*)

Rossanna Podesta (whose husband produced) is Fabiola, a self-sacrificing Christian, in a tale of gladiators. Lang Jeffries is the mighty Brenno. Riccardo Freda staged the gladiator-arena fight climax. With Philippe LeRoy and Gabrielle Tinti.

ALONE IN THE DARK

(RCA/Columbia, 1982) **D/S:** Jack Sholder **P:** Bob Shaye

Alone in the Dark is a classic horror movie with humor, a punk sensibility and a great overacting cast. It starts with a shocking nightmare scene in a diner. Some psychotic killers escape from a mental hospital during a power failure and go after a New Jersey family, but there's much more. Jack Palance is the scary war vet Frank Hawkes,

New York's the Sick Fucks on stage in *Alone in the Dark*.

Martin Landau is Preacher, and big Erland van Lidth de Jeude (from *The Wanderers*) joins them. Donald Pleasence is the weird, pot-smoking doctor who says the killers are just confused. Dwight Schultz (from *The A-Team*) is the doctor dad of the fractured family under siege and the Sick Fucks play "Chop up Your Mother." Sholder had been an editor of New Line trailers and also made the underrated *The Hidden*.

ALPHABET CITY

(CBS/Fox, 1984) **D/S:** Amos Poe
S: Gregory Heller **P:** Andrew Braunsberg

Vincent Spano is a Lower East Side drug dealer with a heavy New York accent who plans to retire and has to go on the run from mobsters. With Kate Vernon, Michael Winslow, Zohra Lampert, Jamie Gertz, and Raymond Serra. The music is by Nile Rogers. This was the first and last real movie by Poe, who had directed New York underground films like *Subway Riders* (1981).

THE ALPHA INCIDENT

(Media, 1976) **D/P:** Bill Rebane

The government tries to cover up a deadly organism from Mars in this PG-rated science fiction movie. People at a remote railroad depot managed by Ralph Meeker are terrorized. With John Alderman and George "Buck" Flower. It was made in Gleason, Wisconsin, where Rebane usually works. He was the director of *Monster a Go Go* and *The Giant Spider Invasion*, so you might known what to expect. Confused viewers in some cities saw it on a double bill with *Star Wars*!

ALWAYS

(MCA, 1989) **D/P:** Steven Spielberg **S:** Jerry Belson,
Ron Bass **P:** Frank Marshall, Kathleen Kennedy

This is a remake of the Spencer Tracy film, *A Guy Named Joe* (1943) with Yellowstone Park firefighters replacing the WWII pilots. Richard Dreyfuss dies and returns as a guardian angel who helps Holly Hunter. With John Goodman, Brad Johnson, Audrey Hepburn, Roberts Blossom, Marge Helgenberger, Keith David, and some ILM FX. The PG-rated film made money but was a flop in the big-bucks Spielberg world. The tape is letterboxed and runs 123 minutes. The John Williams soundtrack is on MCA.

THE AMATEUR

(Fox, 1982) **D:** Charles Jarrott **S:** Robert Littell, Diana Maddox **P:** Joel B. Michaels, Garth H. Drabinsky   Canada

John Savage stars as a computer expert out for revenge in East Berlin in this cold war spy thriller. With Christopher Plummer, Marthe Keller, Ed Lauter, John Marley, Arthur Hill, Graham Jarvis, Jan Rubes, and Nicholas Campbell. Producer Drabinsky started Cineplex Odeon and is responsible for raising ticket prices in North America, among other offenses.

THE AMAZING DR. G

(1965) **D:** G. Simonelli   Italy
(Due Mafiosi Contra Goldfinger)

This AIP TV release, a parody of the 1964 James Bond film *Goldfinger,* stars Franco Franchi and Ciccio Ingrassia, known as Francio and Chechio. AIP released another of the comedy team's movies, *Dr. Goldfoot and the Girl Bombs,* to theatres. Maybe they were funny in Italian, but their humor, based on dialects and puns, doesn't translate at all. Many Americans consider them the least funny comedians they've ever seen.

AMAZING GRACE

(1973) **D:** Stan Latham **S/P:** Matt Robinson

Jackie "Moms" Mabley stars as an old lady who involves herself in Baltimore politics in this G-rated comedy. Slappy White helps her try to get Moses Gunn elected mayor. With Rosalind Cash, Butterfly McQueen, and Stepin Fetchit. It was filmed in Philadelphia. Mabley also starred in *Boarding House Blues.*

AMAZING GRACE AND CHUCK

(HBO, 1987) **D:** Mike Newell
S/P: David Field   *(Silent Voice)*

Athletes save the world in a PG-rated Capraesque tale that has been called "embarrassing, inept, and simple." A kid (Joshua Zuehlke) convinces major sports figures on both sides of the Iron Curtain to refuse to play in order to protest nuclear weapons. The kids of the world join the protest. With Jamie Lee Curtis, Gregory Peck as the president, Alex English (a real Boston Celtics star), William L. Peterson, Dennis Lipscomb, and Lee Richardson. The year this came out, Peck attended a USSR peace conference and appeared in an anti–Bork for Supreme Court TV ad, angering President Reagan. This film was backed by "executive consultant" Ted Turner and CNN. Varèse Sarbande released the Elmer Bernstein soundtrack.

THE AMAZING MR. BLUNDEN

(1972) **D/S/A:** Lionel Jeffries **P:** Barry Levinson   UK

In a supernatural fairy tale set after WWI, a ghost (Jeffries) helps kids solve a 100-year-old mystery. Based on Antonia Barber's novel *The Ghost.* With Laurence Naismith, Lynne Frederick and Diana Dors. This G-rated feature was released by Hemisphere in 1974.

AMAZING STORIES, BOOK ONE

(MCA, 1985–86) **D:** Steven Spielberg, Danny DeVito **P:** David E. Vogel

Executive producer Spielberg made a deal with NBC-TV that they couldn't cancel his expensive anthology series (1985–87) even if the ratings were bad (which they were), so 44 episodes were filmed. In Europe one compilation was a theatrical release and the rest went straight to tape. The other producers for the series were Kathleen Kennedy and Frank Marshall. The first US tape release features two stories. "The Mission," a one-hour-long war story directed by Spielberg features Keifer Sutherland and Casey Siemaszko. "Wedding Ring," directed by and starring Danny DeVito, features Rhea Perlman (his wife) and Tracy Walter. The tapes are all in stereo.

AMAZING STORIES, BOOK TWO

(MCA, 1986–87) **D:** Robert Zemeckis, Brad Bird **P:** David E. Vogel

"Go to the Head of the Class" is a one-hour-long witchcraft story, directed by Zemeckis with heavy-metal rock. Mary Stuart Masterson and Christopher Lloyd star, and Stan Winston provided FX. "The Family Dog," by Bird (and designer Tim Burton) is an animated cartoon tale with the voices of Stan Freberg, Mercedes McCambridge and Annie Potts. It became an animated CBS series in 1993.

AMAZING STORIES, BOOK THREE

(MCA, 1985–86) **D:** Mick Garris, Lesli Linka Glatter, Peter Hyams **P:** David E. Vogel

"Life on Death Row," directed by Garris stars Patrick Swayze and Hector Elizondo. "The Amazing Falworth," directed by Hyams, features Gregory Hines and Richard Masur. The cast of "No Day at the Beach," directed by Glatter, includes Charlie Sheen and Ray "Boom Boom" Mancini.

AMAZING STORIES, BOOK FOUR

(MCA, 1985–87) **D:** Martin Scorsese, Paul Michael Glaser, Daniel Petrie **P:** David E. Vogel

Scorsese fans, this is the tape to look for. He directed *Mirror Mirror,* (written by Joseph Minion) which stars Sam Waterston as a horror movie director, Helen Shaver, Tim Robbins as the phantom, and Dick Cavett as himself. *Blue Man Down,* directed by Glaser, stars Max Gail. *Mr. Magic,* directed by Petrie, stars Sid Caesar and Leo Rossi.

AMAZING STORIES, BOOK FIVE

(MCA, 1985–86) **D:** Bob Balaban, Leslie Linka Glatter, Norman Reynolds **P:** David E. Vogel

The Pumpkin Competition, directed by Balaban, stars Polly Holliday and June Lockhart. *Without Diana,* directed by Glatter, features Billy Green Bush and Dianne Hull. *Fine Tuning,* directed by Reynolds, includes Mathew Laborteaux, Milton Berle, and Angelo Rossitto. Episodes directed by Joe Dante, Paul Bartel, Bob Clark, Clint Eastwood, and Tobe Hooper will eventually be released on tape too.

THE AMAZING TRANSPLANT

(SW, 1969) **D/S/P:** "Louis Silverman, Dawn Whitman" (Doris Wishman)

Wishman is known to some for directing the notorious Chesty Morgan movies *Double Agent 73* and *Deadly Weapons.* If you've seen either, you'll have an idea what to expect here. A naked woman plays a (badly dubbed) zither. Her boyfriend, Arthur (Juan Fernandez), arrives and says "Let's get married!" She agrees, but after an unsuccessful attempt at sex, says "Poor, sick Arthur," so he strangles her. He acts like a zombie when he sees gold earrings. He visits a doctor, who introduces him to the sexually active but dying Felix. Arthur becomes Felix's buddy, then blackmails the doctor into transplanting his now-dead friend's penis onto him. ("O, how I wanted to be like Felix!") Arthur talks during the operation. He kills more women. News-paper headlines (the kind anybody can order in Times Square) are constantly shown: ARTHUR BARON STILL MISSING! A radio newscaster says, "Campus Riots— and ARTHUR BARON STILL MISSING!" Arthur's uncle, a cop, searches for him, but only encounters other people's flashbacks of lesbian sex, throwing up, and rape. (One flashback star is early porn star Kim Pope.) This badly lit, shot-in-Brooklyn (?) nonsense has some scenes reversed, so that a box of crackers reads ZTIR (!). *The Amazing Transplant* is usually in the horror-movie section of video stores.

AMAZING WORLD OF PSYCHIC PHENOMENA

(Vid America, 1976) **D/S:** Robert Guenette

In between TV series, Raymond Burr narrated this G-rated semidocumentary look at psychic healers, scientists, and quacks, Edgar Cayce, and acupuncturists. With Uri Geller and Jeanne Dixon. It was a Sunn Classics release.

AMAZON

(Live, 1992) **D/S/P:** Mika Kaurismaki
S: Richard Reitinger

Kari Vaananen stars as a Finnish businessman in the Brazilian rain forest with his two daughters. He's being unjustly pursued by police and becomes involved in a search for diamonds and gold. The ecological-adventure features Robert Davi (who narrates and sings "The Lion Sleeps Tonight"!) as a drunken bush pilot and Rae Dawn Chong as a teacher. It's all narrated by a dead man.

AMAZONIA: *See* WHITE SLAVE

AMAZON JAIL

(Continental, 1985) **D/S:** Osualdo de Oliveira **S:** Larry Dolgin, Alfredo Palacios   Spain/Italy

Satanists in Brazil capture women who have escaped from a jungle prison and make them slaves. With lots of nudity, lesbian sex, and dance numbers. Elisabeth Hartman stars.

AMAZONS

(Westworld, 1984) **D:** Paul Michael Glaser
S: David Solomon **P:** Stuart Cohen

A doctor (Madeleine Stowe) discovers a secret organization of women plotting to take over the country and kill men. Tamara Dobson co-stars, with Stella Stevens, Jennifer Warren, Jack Scalia, Nicholas Pryor, and William Schallert, in this ABC-TV movie.

AMAZONS

(MGM/UA, 1986) **D:** Alex Sessa
S: Charles Saunders **P:** Hector Olivera

Female warriors battle each other, and a villainous leader has lightning bolt fingertips. Windsor Taylor Randolph (aka porno actress Lisa Berenger) stars, with Penelope Reed and Danitza Kingsley. A lion is transformed into a naked woman. There's nude swimming and sex. This Roger Corman/Concorde movie was filmed in Argentina.

AMAZON WOMEN = GOLD OF THE AMAZON WOMEN

AMAZON WOMEN ON THE MOON

(MCA, 1985) **D/P:** John Landis **D:** Joe Dante,
Carl Gottlieb, Peter Horton, Robert K. Weiss

This underrated *Kentucky Fried Movie* "sequel" wasn't released until it was two years old. It includes many hilarious segments (some in b/w) spoofing old horror, science-fiction, and exploitation movies and is full of in-jokes for fans. Ed Begley Jr. is the (naked) "Invisible Man." Henry Silva impersonates Jack Palance hosting *Bullshit or Not* and proves that Jack the Ripper was the Loch Ness Monster. Sybil Danning is an outer-space queen, and William Marshall is captain of "the video pirates." With Russ Meyer, Arsenio Hall, Monique Gabrielle (walking around naked on the street), Lou Jacobi, Michelle Pfeiffer, Griffin Dunne, Steve Forrest, Lana Clarkson, Steve Guttenberg, Rosanna Arquette, Belinda Belaski, Kelly Preston, Angel Tompkins, Corinne Wahl, Ralph Bellamy, Howard Hesseman, Andrew Dice Clay, Joey Travolta, Keenan Ivory Wayans, B. B. King and Forrest J. Ackerman (as the US president). Steve Allen hosts a celebrity funeral roast with Henny Youngman, Jackie Vernon, Rip Taylor, Slappy White, and Charlie Callas. It's all

Lou Jacobi is transported into a 50s science fiction movie in *Amazon Women on the Moon.*

crammed into 85 minutes and you can see whole different segments (like "The French Ventriloquist's Dummy," starring Dick Miller and Jenny Agutter) not on the tape or shown theatrically, in the TV version. Don't miss Carrie Fisher, Paul Bartel, and Mike Mazurki in the post-credits *Sex Madness* spoof.

THE AMBASSADOR

(MGM, 1984) **D:** J. Lee Thompson
S: Ronald M. Cohen **P:** Golan/Globus

Elmore Leonard's *52 Pick Up* (filmed under that title in 1986) was the basis for this story set against the Israeli-Palestinian crisis. Robert Mitchum stars, with Ellen Burstyn as his wife, Rock Hudson (in his last theatrical release), as a security officer), Donald Pleasence and Fabio Testi. The 50-something Burstyn has a topless scene.

AMBITION

(Media, 1991) **D/P:** Scott Goldstein
S/A: Lou Diamond Phillips

Phillips is an unlikable, long-haired LA book store owner researching "the Valentine's Day Massacre killer" (Clancy Brown). In order to be able to write a book about the newly paroled, well-known psycho, he hires him to work in the store, drugs him with speed, and generally messes with his mind. The absurd movie features Cecilia Peck, Grace Zabriskie, Chris Mulkey, and disco flashbacks.

THE AMBULANCE

(Columbia, 1989) **D/S:** Larry Cohen
P: Moctezuma Esparza, Robert Katz

The Ambulance has an effective but simple premise, good acting, lots of mean, sarcastic, and eccentric characters, great NYC location work, and some excellent action sequences. A mysterious old ambulance picks up people suffering from diabetes and takes them to a secret hospital that sells their bodies. A Marvel cartoonist (Eric Roberts) who witnessed the kidnapping of Janine Turner tries to convince some cops (James Earl Jones and Megan Gallagher) that he's not crazy. A feisty old *New York Post* reporter (Red Buttons, who is perfect in the role) helps. With Eric Braeden as the main villain doctor, Laureen Landon, Jill Gatsby (Cohen's daughter), Stan Lee (as himself), and stirring music by Jay Chattaway. The tape was finally released in 1993.

AMBUSH: *See* THE SCAVENGERS

AMBUSH AT CIMARRON PASS

(Fox, 1958) **D:** Jodie Copeland
S: Richard G. Tayor, John K. Butler
P: Herbert E. Mendelson

This low-budget, post–Civil War western with an Apache attack features Clint Eastwood in his biggest film role prior to the Italian westerns. He plays an ex–Confederate

Army soldier. The star is Scott Brady as a Union Army sergeant. With Margia Dean. 20th Century–Fox rereleased it in the 60s and gave Eastwood top billing in the ads.

AMERICA

(Sony, 1982) **D/S:** Robert Downey
P: Paul A. Leeman   *(Moonbeam)*

The signal of a New York cable TV station is accidentally bounced off the moon and broadcast throughout the world. With Zack Norman, Tammy Grimes, Michael J. Pollard, and Richard Belzer. It wasn't released until 1986 and nobody had much that was good to say about it then.

AMERICANA

(Vestron 1973) **D/P/A/E:** David Carradine
S: Richard Carr **P:** Skip Sherwood

In 1972, David Carradine was the star of the popular *Kung Fu* series and had just been in *Boxcar Bertha* with his common-law wife, Barbara Seagull (later Hershey). He directed one movie and starred in another with Hershey, but they were never finished or released. He also made this PG feature, which was finally released (by Crown) in 1981 after years of editing work. Carradine even made some personal appearances to introduce his film, in which he also sings. He shows up on foot wearing a cap and beard in the small town of Drury, Kansas (the real citizens play themselves), and simply says "I need a place to crash." He takes odd jobs, is harassed by the locals and the sheriff, and begins the slow, difficult restoration of an abandoned merry-go-round. We learn after a while that he's a Nam vet captain who reports for his disability payments only when everything else goes wrong. *Americana* is a well-made, nonexploitative movie that takes its time and manages to say a lot about unfortunate changes in the country. The quiet hero has troubled relationships with an ex-biker/vet (Michael Greene) who sponsors cockfights in the shell of a church, and Barbara Hershey, who wanders around barefoot in a white dress. *Americana* was a family affair. Hershey's father, Arnold Hertstein, plays the general-store owner. David's brother Bruce is the sheriff, and brother Robert was an assistant cameraman. Dan (*Grizzly Adams*) Haggerty was the set dresser and animal handler, and John Barrymore III (Drew's half brother) has a role.

AMERICAN ANGELS: BAPTISM IN BLOOD

(Paramount, 1989) **D/S/P:** Ferd and Beverly Sebastian

The couple who brought us *Gator Bait* and *Rocktober Blood* return with a ridiculous "behind the scenes" look at female wrestlers. It's the Magnificent Mimi vs. the Black Venus, and more. See whipped cream wrestling, comical dwarf-wrestling, the Luscious Lisa, (Jan Mackenzie from *Gator Bait II*) take a shower, and sex in the ring. You can buy this on laserdisc and hear lines like, "I'll poke out your eyes and piss in your brains!"

AMERICAN BEAUTY HOSTAGES: *See* EBONY, IVORY, AND JADE

AMERICAN BORN

(PM, 1991) **D/S:** Raymond Martino **S:** Addison Randall **P:** Richard Pepin, Joseph Merhi

Andrew Zeller is a New York City kid obsessed with gangster videos who thinks he's become a real-life gangster after his father is killed. Joey Travolta plays his uncle, and vintage film clips are used.

AMERICAN COMMANDOS

(Vestron, 1984) **D/S:** Bobby A. Suarez **S/A:** Ken Metcalf   (Hitman)

Nam vets in California, led by a former Green Beret (Chris Mitchum), are sent on an antidrug mission in Southeast Asia. They discover other American vets running drug factories in the Golden Triangle. With John Phillip Law, Franco Guerrero and Metcalf. It was filmed in the Philippines.

AMERICAN CYBORG: STEEL WARRIOR

(Warner, 1994) **D:** Boaz Davidson **S:** Brent Friedman, Bill Crounse, Don Pequingnot

In another post-nuke movie, Joe Lara (a TV Tarzan) is the long-haired hunk hero who protects Mary (Nicole Hansen) a blonde trying to save a rare live fetus. John Ryan is the indestructible *Blade Runner*–look bad-guy cyborg with black leather and short white hair. This one includes mutant face cannibals, a gang in drag, and scientist rebels. Much of the Cannon release, which was made in Israel, takes place in an old factory. The music copies the score from *The Last of the Mohicans*.

AN AMERICAN DREAM

(1966) **D:** Robert Gist **S:** Mann Rubin

Stuart Whitman stars as a TV talk-show host who may have killed his wife, in a movie based on Norman Mailer's novel. The police and gangsters are after him. With Janet Leigh (who sings), Eleanor Parker, Susan Denberg (from *Frankenstein Created Woman*), Barry Sullivan, Lloyd Nolan,

Wolfman Jack in *American Grafitti.*

Murray Hamilton, Les Crane, Paul Mantee, and George Takei. It includes some (at the time, daring) nudity and nightmare sequences. William Conrad was the executive producer.

AMERICAN DREAMER

(1971) **D/S/P:** Laurence Schiller **D/S:** L. M. Kit Carson **S/A:** Dennis Hopper

An ego-trip movie from Dennis Hopper, who is seen (with his brother) working on the at-the-time unreleased *The Last Movie*, at home in Taos, shooting guns, taking drugs, receiving visitors, and having a good time in a bathtub full of naked women. For Hopper completists only. There's a soundtrack LP too, on Mediart, featuring Gene Clark, the Hello People, and others.

AMERICAN DRIVE-IN

(Vestron, 1985) **D/S/P:** Krishna Shaw **S:** David Ball

A night at a drive-in, with a comedy/revenge plot. Scenes from *Hard Rock Zombies,* by the same people, are economically used.

THE AMERICAN FRIEND

(Pacific Arts, 1976) **D/S:** Wim Wenders US/France/Germany (*Der Amerikanische Freund*)

Dennis Hopper, as crooked art dealer Tom Ripley, travels around Europe trying to double-cross (and help) Bruno Ganz, who has been set up by international mobsters. They convince Ganz that he's terminally ill and should commit two murders. It's based on Patricia Highsmith's novel *Ripley's Game* and makes a fascinating, classic movie. Ganz sings the Kinks "Too Much on My Mind." With directors Nicholas Ray as an artist and Sam Fuller as a gangster, and singer David Blue. The film is 123 minutes and subtitled. Wenders also codirected *Lightning Over Water* (1980) with Ray, about his last days before dying.

AMERICAN GOTHIC

(Vidmark, 1987) **D:** John Hough **S:** Terry Lens **P:** John Quested   UK/Canada

Three young couples take a private plane to a Pacific Northwestern island to camp out and find themselves stranded. They're typical slasher-movie jerks who deserve to die. Only Sarah Torgov, as Cynthia, has a personality, because she was in an asylum after her baby drowned. They discover a family who live like it was still the 20s (sort of) and act very strict. Ma is Yvonne De Carlo and stern Pa is Rod Steiger: "No Devil's play in this house!" They have accents that don't seem to fit the region and three middle-aged "children" who kill people and store bodies in the basement. The daughter has a mummified baby. With the offscreen violence and attempts at humor, this movie could have been made in the early 70s. Michael J. Pollard, who was in *America* and *The American Way*

(*Riders of the Storm*) around the same time, is fun in *American Gothic* as Woody. He has the same baby face and funny puzzled smile as he did in the 60s. Pa whips the other brother "in the name of God" after he has sex with a dead female visitor (also offscreen, of course). With Mark Lindsay Chapman and Fiona Hutchison. British director Hough had done movies for Hammer and Disney.

AMERICAN GRAFFITI

(MCA, 1973) **D/S:** George Lucas **S:** Willard Huyuck, Gloria Katz **P:** Francis Ford Coppola

A brilliant nostalgia movie about one summer day and night in 1962 before the 50s had really ended for good. The cast of (then new) stars is excellent. With Richard Dreyfuss, Ronny Howard, Paul LeMat, Charles Martin Smith, Cindy Williams, Candy Clark, 12-year-old Mackenzie Phillips, Harrison Ford, Bo Hopkins, Wolfman Jack, Kathy Quinlan, Joe Spano, Debralee Scott, Kay Lenz, Suzanne Somers, and Flash Cadillac and the Continental Kids, who do "Louie Louie" and other songs. The cinematography is by Haskel Wexler and the choreography is by Toni Basil. The hit double-LP MCA soundtrack with the famous carhop cover was a great original oldies compilation (but Kenneth Anger and Martin Scorsese used the oldies idea first in the 60s). Some scenes were restored when *American Graffiti* was rereleased in 1979. The full version runs 112 minutes. The PG hit was nominated for five Oscars, made over $55 million, and taught mooning to new generations. It also spawned the popular but awful *Happy Days* TV series and the much-hated *More American Graffiti.*

AMERICAN HOT WAX

(Paramount, 1976) **D:** Floyd Mutrix **S:** John Kaye **P:** Art Linson

Alan Freed (Tim McIntire) arranges an anniversary show (his last) at the Brooklyn Paramount while being harassed by the authorities. It's a simple plot but a great recreation of what might have gone on at an all-star rock show before most of the major talent got busted or died. Real, still-great rockers (Chuck Berry, Jerry Lee Lewis) play themselves 20 years earlier, and typical but not "real" doo-wop and rock groups appear. With Laraine Newman as a Carole King character, Jay Leno, Fran Drescher, Jeff Altman, Cameron Crowe, Hamilton Camp, and Screamin' Jay Hawkins. The double soundtrack on A&M features good oldies and one LP of new live material from the film.

AMERICAN KICKBOXER

(Warner, 1992) **D:** Frans Nel **S:** Emil Kolbe **P:** Anant Singh

John Barrett stars as a wrongly imprisoned world champ who fights his way back to the top. With Keith Vitale and Brad Morris. The film was made in South Africa. *American Kickboxer II* (Vidmark, 1993) starred Dale "Apollo" Cook.

Screamin' Jay Hawkins in *American Hot Wax.*

AMERICAN NIGHTMARE

(Media, 1981) **D:** Don McBreart
S: John Sheppard **P:** Ray Sager

A man (Lawrence S. Day) searches for his runaway sister (as in *Hardcore*) in the red-light district, and there's a psycho killing strippers. Michael Ironside is a Toronto cop. There are lots of topless stripper scenes. With Lora Stanley, Claudia Udy, Alexandra Paul (*Christine*), and Leonore Zann.

AMERICAN NINJA

(MGM/UA, 1985) **D:** Sam Firstenberg
S: James R. Silke **P:** Golan/Globus

In the first of a series of movies about soldiers who use martial arts from Cannon, Michael Dudikoff (in his first starring role) is Joe Armstrong. He has amnesia but uncovers military-base corruption. Curtis Jackson (Steve James) is his fighting buddy. Black Star (Tadashi Yamashita/ Bronson Lee) works for an arms dealer and uses a laser ray. With Judie Aaronson. Filmed in and set in the Philippines.

AMERICAN NINJA II: THE CONFRONTATION

(Media, 1987) **D:** Sam Firstenberg **S:** Gary Conway, James Booth **P:** Golan/Globus

Dudikoff and James return to beat up more bad guys. The heroin-dealer villain (and co-scriptwriter) is *I Was A Teenage Frankenstein* star Gary Conway. He makes scientists create "super-killer ninjas" on a Caribbean island. There's lots of action.

AMERICAN NINJA III: BLOOD HUNT

(Warner, 1989) **D/S:** Cedric Sundstrom
P: Harry Alan Towers

David Bradley (who at least can fight) replaces series star Michael Dudikoff and is teamed with Steve James, back again as Curtis Jackson. Good old Marjoe Gortner, as Cobra, creates a germ weapon, and there's yet another *Enter the Dragon* style martial-arts tournament on an island. With Michele Chan. The Cannon release was filmed in South Africa.

AMERICAN NINJA IV: THE ANNIHILATION

(Warner,1991) **D:** Cedric Sundstrom
S: David Geeves **P:** Christopher Pearce

An Arab sheik with a compact nuclear weapon hires ninjas to fight for him in a small African country (it was filmed in South Africa). The heroes try to rescue commandos being held for ransom. Dudikoff (from the first two movies) returns with David Bradley. James Booth is the main villain, and also featured is South African Ken Gampu (from *The Gods Must Be Crazy*).

AMERICAN POP

(1981) **D:** Ralph Bakshi **S:** Ronni Kern **P:** Martin Ransohoff

Bakshi's animated story of the history of American pop music, from the turn of the century up to new wave and punk rock, is interesting and has some great rotoscope animation, but it's pretty one-sided. It centers on Jewish immigrants from Russia and their descendants, from the days of vaudeville and burlesque to beatniks, folk musicians, and hippies and drugs (a Janis Joplin type singer ODs), and ends with a Springsteen/Seeger/Presley combination superstar. I don't see how a history of American pop music could totally leave out black and country artists! Most of the songs are remakes, but Lou Reed is one of the various artists on the soundtrack released by MCA. With the voices of Ron Thompson, Roz Kelly, and Frank DeKova. From Columbia.

AMERICAN SAMURAI

(Warner, 1992) **D:** Sam Firstenberg
S: John Corcoran **P:** Allan Greenblatt

David Bradley (from the *American Ninja* movies) is an American reporter and martial arts expert with a yakuza drug-dealer half brother (Mark Dascascos). He ends up participating in "live blade" death battles against swordsmen from around the world in an arena in Turkey. With Valerie Trapp. The Cannon release was scripted by the editor of *Inside Kung-Fu* magazine.

THE AMERICAN SCREAM

(Innovid, 1988) **D/S/P:** Mitchell Linden

In this horror comedy, some kids kill adults during Christmas vacation in the Sierra Nevada mounains. With Kevin Kaye, Pons Maar, Jennifer Darling, and Edy Williams as a stripper.

AMERICAN SHAOLIN: KING OF THE KICKBOXERS II

(Academy, 1992) **D:** Lucas Lowe
S/P: Keith W. Strandberg

A guy from Ashbury Park New Jersey (Reese Madigan) studies martial arts in China, then re-turns to America to fight Trent Bushy. Most of the time is devoted to monks teaching martial arts. The Asian-backed feature is not a sequel.

AMERICAN TIGER

(Academy, 1989) **D/S:** "Martin Doleman"
Sergio Martino **S:** Roberto Leoni, Sauro Scandlini   Italy (*American Rickshaw; Riscio*)

A college student in Miami (Olympic gymnast Mitch Gaylord) is framed for the murder of an evangelist's son in this convoluted martial-arts fantasy. He befriends an ageless Asian witch (Michi Kobi) and teams up with a stripper (red-head Victoria Prouty) to find the real killer. With Donald Pleasence, as an evil reverend after a magical statue, and Sherrie Rose.

AMERICA'S DEADLIEST HOME VIDEOS

(Randum, 1992) **D/S:** Jack Perez **P/A:** Mick Wynhoff

Danny Bonaduce, a former *Partridge Family* child star, was a staple of scandal magazines when this video production shot on High 8 was made. He plays a guy recording his road trip with a camcorder, who is forced by a trio of criminals to document their robbery and killing spree. Most of the tape is seen from the camera's point of view. It was made in Wisconsin, and the FX are by Jeffrey Lyle Segal, who also worked on *Henry*.

AMERICA 3000

(MGM/UA, 1986) **D/S:** David Engelbach
P: Golan/Globus

Laurene Landon as a post-nuke barbarian warrior is the only reason to watch this *Road Warrior*–inspired movie. One guy makes himself president because he's found clothes and a ghetto blaster in a time capsule. Chuck Wagner leads a rebellion against the female characters, and there's a big ape-man monster and martial-arts battles. With Carmilla Sparv. The PG-13 Cannon feature was filmed in Israel.

AMERIKA

(1987) **D/S:** Donald Wrye **P:** Richard L. O'Connor

In the ultimate Reagan-era-fear-of-the-Evil Empire project, the USSR takes over the US without a war, declares martial law and puts citizens in labor camps! Kris Kristofferson stars as a presidential candidate who's sent to a political prison in this ABC-TV miniseries, first shown in seven parts. Most of it takes place in Nebraska. With Robert Urich, Sam Neill, Cindy Pickett, Mariel Hemingway, Christine Lahti, Wendy Hughes, Armin Mueller-Stahl, Ivan Dixon, and Lara Flynn Boyle. The series cost roughly $40 million to produce. The USSR protested vociferously.

AMIN: THE RISE AND FALL

(Thorn EMI, 1981) **D/P:** Sharad Patel
S: Wade Huie **P:** Christopher Sutton
UK/Kenya (*The Rise and Fall of Idi Amin*)

This Times Square classic stars Amin look-alike Joseph Olita as the notorious dictator who ruled Uganda from 1971 to 1978. It's bloody and exploitative, sure, but what do you expect in a movie about a mass killer who ate his enemies? The director is from India. And look for Barbet Schroeder's documentary *General Idi Amin Dada* (Warner, 1974) for the real thing.

THE AMITYVILLE CURSE

(Vidmark, 1989) **D:** Tom Berry **S/P:** Michael Kreuger **P:** Franco Battista   Canada

Yuppies buy a house where a priest has been murdered. They start fixing it up and die one by one. This has nothing to do with any other *Amityville* movies and is based on a novel by Hans Holzer. With Kim Coates, Jan Rubes, Helen Hughes, Damna Wightman and Cassandra Gava (*Conan*).

AMITYVILLE III

(Vestron, 1983) **D:** Richard Fleischer **S:** "William Wales"/David E. Ambrose **P:** Stephen F. Keston (*Amityville 3-D; Amityville: The Demon*)

This is not a sequel, the producers claimed. Whatever it is, it was rated PG (the first two films received R ratings), was from DEG, and has nothing new except for the good 3-D effects which you can't experience on tape anyway. Journalist Tony Roberts moves into the famous house and strange stuff happens. With Tess Harper, Candy Clark, Robert Joy as a parapsychologist, and John Beal. Lori Loughlin and Meg Ryan (who wants to have sex with a ghost) are the teens in the cast. The original *Amityville Horror* was an AIP release. Orion (which became AIP after several takeovers) released II and III, which were followed by even worse *Amityville* movies.

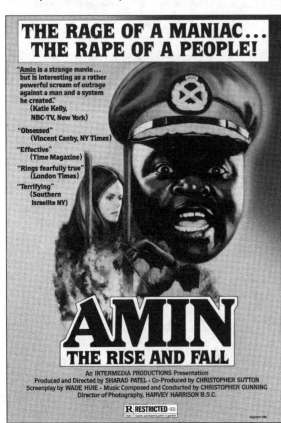

THE RAGE OF A MANIAC... THE RAPE OF A PEOPLE!

"Amin is a strange movie... but is interesting as a rather powerful scream of outrage against a man and a system he created." (Katie Kelly, NBC-TV, New York)

"Obsessed" (Vincent Canby, NY Times)

"Effective" (Time Magazine)

"Rings fearfully true" (London Times)

"Terrifying" (Southern Israelite NY)

AMIN THE RISE AND FALL

An INTERMEDIA PRODUCTIONS Presentation
Produced and Directed by SHARAD PATEL · Co-Produced by CHRISTOPHER SUTTON
Screenplay by WADE HUIE · Music Composed and Conducted by CHRISTOPHER GUNNING
Director of Photography, HARVEY HARRISON B.S.C.

R RESTRICTED

THE AMITYVILLE HORROR: THE EVIL ESCAPES, PART IV

(Vidmark, 1989) **D/S:** Sandor Stern **P:** Barry Bernardi   (*Amityville IV: The Evil Escapes*)

Originally made for NBC-TV, here's a sequel that seems determined to induce sleep. An ugly, possessed lamp purchased at an Amityville yard sale is sent to the California home of grandma Jane Wyman. Her widowed daughter (Patty Duke) and three kids move in and the trouble starts. A parakeet dies in a toaster oven, a hand is ground up in a garbage disposal, and a chainsaw goes out of control. An exorcist priest arrives from New York City to help. For some reason the video release of this TV movie is rated R. Stern wrote the original *Amityville Horror* (1979).

AMITYVILLE 92: IT'S ABOUT TIME

(Republic., 1992) **D:** Tony Randell **S/P:** Christopher DeFaria **S:** Antonio Toro

A haunted clock turns a sunny suburban house into a place where weird things happen. The architect dad (Stephen Macht) suffers from a bite from a rabid (phantom) dog. The nice daughter (Megan Ward) becomes a sex tease and helps her boyfriend sink into a pool of goo. The confused teen son is accused of painting swastikas on a neighbor's home. Only Nita Talbot understands what's going on and she's impaled by a giant penguin (!). Dick Miller has a bit part, and there's one good (but out of place) sex scene with one-time Miss Universe Shawn Weatherly. It's the 6th *Amityville* movie and there's no real reason to watch it.

AMITYVILLE: A NEW GENERATION

(Republic, 1993) **D:** John Murlowski **S/P:** Chris DeFaria **S:** Antonio M. Toro

Blond Lala Sloatman (formally billed as just Lala) stars as an artist who moves into a loft building. People see their deaths in a haunted mirror, and lengthy flashbacks to an asylum "explain" it all. With Ross Partridge, Terry O'Quinn as a police detective, Julia Nickson-Soul as an artist named Suki, David Naughton as the landlord, and Richard Roundtree as a bald artist. Lala and Julia have topless scenes.

AMONG THE LIVING DEAD: *See* ZOMBIE 4

THE AMOROUS SEX: *See* SWEET BEAT

AMSTERDAM KILL

(Columbia, 1977) **D/S:** Robert Clouse **S:** Gregory Tiefer **P:** Andre Morgan US/Hong Kong

Robert Mitchum is a retired narc lured to Hong Kong to help bust a drug ring. Bradford Dillman, Richard Egan, Leslie Nielsen, and Key Luke all show up in this adventure

by the director of *Enter the Dragon.* Raymond Chow was the executive producer. Clouse next made the obscure *Omega Connection* and *Game of Death,* using footage of the late Bruce Lee.

AMSTERDAMNED

(Vestron, 1988) **D/S/P/M:** Dick Mass **P:** Laurens Geels   Netherlands

A cop (Huub Stapel) is after a killer scuba diver scarred by toxic chemicals who hides in canals. There's an impressive speedboat chase (very similar to one in *Puppet on a Chain,* also filmed in Amsterdam), some intentional humor, and the *Jaws*-inspired theme of trying to keep the murders from hurting tourism. With Monique van de Ven (also in *The Lift* by the same director).

THE AMY FISHER STORY

(Capitol Cities, 1992) **D:** Andy Tennant **S:** Janet Brownell

This was just one of three (!) "Long Island Lolita" movies, part of a media phenomenon. Drew Barrymore stars as the real-life Amy who tries to kill the wife of her lover, mechanic Joey Buttafuoco (Anthony John Denison). Harley Jane Kozak costars as a (real) NYC newspaper reporter. The tape of the ABC-TV movie includes extra sex scenes featuring a body double. Other versions of the same overhyped story were CBS-TV's *Casualties of Love* with Alyssa Milano (and Lawrence Tierney) and NBC-TV's *Lethal Lolita: Amy Fisher—My Story* with Noelle Parker.

THE ANATOMIST

(Sinister, 1961) **D/S:** Leonard William **P:** Vincent Johnson   UK

This is one of many features based on the story of the Edinburgh grave-robbers Burke and Hare (among them is the 1945 Karloff film *The Body Snatcher*). It was made just after the better-known *Mania (The Flesh and the Fiends).* Alastair Sim stars as Dr. Knox, with Jill Bennett, Adrienne Corri, George Cole, and Michael Ripper. Harry Alan Towers and Richard Gordon were involved with the production.

ANATOMY OF A PSYCHO

(SW, 1961) **D/P:** "Brooke L. Peters"/ Boris Petroff **S:** Jane Mann, Larry Lee

The *Ohio Gazette* announces, MARCO DIES TONIGHT! The killer's obsessed brother, Chet (Darrell Howell), gets together a small "gang" in a messy shack hangout pad for revenge. Ronnie Burns (the son of George and Gracie!) is Micky, the boyfriend of Chet's sister and the son of the witness whose testimony sent Marco to the gas chamber. The gang (in hoods) beat the DA's son, fight the judge's son at a party and burn the judge's house. A detective (with terrible skin) finally gets the misguided "psycho" to break down and cry, "Help me!" With Pamela Lincoln (from *The Tingler*) and Judy Howard and Russ Bender (both from *The Ghost of Dragstrip Hollow*). Petroff also made *The Unearthly* (1957) with Tor Johnson and *Shotgun Wedding* (1963), which was written by Ed Wood Jr.

AND GOD SAID TO CAIN

(Unicorn, 1969) **D/S:** Anthony Dawson/Antonio Margheriti **S/P:** Giovanni Addessi   Italy/Germany (*Shoot Twice; E Dio Disse A Caino*)

Klaus Kinski stars as a man who is wrongly imprisoned for murder, is pardoned, and seeks vengeance. The post–Civil War western features Peter Carsten and Marcella Michelangelo. Margheriti also made many horror and science-fiction movies.

ANDROID

(Media, 1982) **D:** Aaron Lipstadt **S/A:** Don Opper **S:** James Reigle **P:** Mary Ann Fisher

Klaus Kinski, as Dr. Daniel, attempts to create the perfect female android (Brie Howard) on a space station. Don Opper is the bald Max 404, a sensitive clone who picks up human traits watching old movies. Three escaped convicts arrive to complicate matters. *Android* is one of many low-budget features filmed on the familiar sets from *Battle Beyond the Stars* (1980), but it's the best. The stars are perfect in their roles, and *Android* manages to be exciting, funny, and very charming. It was one of Roger Corman's last New World productions.

Klaus Kinski in *Android*.

AND THE WALLS CAME TUMBLING DOWN

(1984) **D:** Paul Annett **S:** Dennis Spooner, John Peacock   UK

Barbie Benton stars as a psychic American searching for salvageable historical landmarks for the British government. Flashbacks reveal that in the 15th century the church she's inspecting was used by Satanists, and a man was walled up alive. Modern-day characters are reincarnations, and a demolition worker is strangled by electric chords. Peter Wyngarde, Brian Deacon, and Carol Royl also appear in this TV movie.

ANDY AND THE AIRWAVE RANGERS

(RCA/Columbia 1989) **D/S:** Deborah Brock **S/P:** Jed Horovitz   (*Andy Coby's Incredible Video Adventure*)

An evil wizard imprisons kids inside a TV set, where they encounter lots of footage from *Space Rangers* and other Roger Corman productions. With "special appearances" by Bo Svenson, Vince

Edwards, Erik Estrada, and Richard Thomas. Corman was the executive producer of the PG-rated feature.

ANDY WARHOL'S FLESH, HEAT, TRASH: *See* FLESH, HEAT, TRASH

AND YOU THOUGHT YOUR PARENTS WERE WEIRD

(Vidmark, 1991) **D/S:** Tony Cookson **P:** Just Betzer

Young brothers (Joshua Miller and Edan Gross) invent a stumpy robot with a vacuum cleaner body to sell so the family can keep their house. During a Halloween-party séance, the spirit of their late scientist father (the voice of Alan Thicke) takes over. The PG fantasy comedy features Marcia Strassman from *Honey, I Shrunk the Kids* as the mom and Gustav Vintas as the bad guy.

ANGEL

(Starmaker, 1983) **D:** Robert Vincent O'Neil **S:** Joseph M. Cala **P:** Roy Watts, Donald P. Borchers

The first "in-house" production of New World after Roger Corman sold it was an exploitation hit. "High-school honor student by day, hooker by night!" claimed the effective ads. Innocent-looking Donna Wilkes is 15-year-old Molly, a Hollywood schoolgirl who calls herself Angel on the streets. Cliff Gorman is the police detective, and John Diehl (from *Miami Vice*) is the psycho killer he's after. The down-and-out characters Angel hangs out with help make the movie memorable: Susan Tyrrell as a lesbian, Dick Shawn as a transvestite named Mae, and Rory Calhoun as an old street cowboy. With Mel Carter, Elaine Giftos, and Ross Hagen. Andrew Davis was the cinematographer. *Avenging Angel* was the first sequel.

ANGEL III: THE FINAL CHAPTER

(Starmaker, 1988) **D/S:** Tom DeSimone **P:** Arnold Orgolini

Each *Angel* movie has a different actress playing the avenging teen hooker. This time, she's played by Mitzi Kapture (*Silk Stalkings*). After a gambling ship with topless waitresses is raided in New York City, Angel, a photographer, returns to LA. Her estranged mother reveals that Angel has a 14-year-old sister, Michelle, before being blown up. Star villainess Maud Adams says, "This is the United Fucking States of America. We don't car-bomb people here!" Angel goes undercover as a hooker and porno actress to find Michelle (Tawny Fere). The action involves drug smuggling and a slave market. Richard Roundtree plays a cop. Mark Blankfield plays "Spanky," a gay ex-street hustler who of course, is killed. Dick Miller, Toni Basil, Roxanne Kernohan, and Laura Albert also show up for a while. Maud Adams, once a Ford model, ends up frozen in Spanky's ice cream truck. A poster for director DeSimone's *Reform*

School Girls is on a wall. For all the in-jokes about the porno biz, you'd think this mediocre sequel was made by people who actually made porno movies. It was. The end theme is by Lou Rawls. Chris Spedding is credited with "additional guitar." From New World.

ANGEL IV: UNDERCOVER

(Live, 1994) **D:** George Axmith **S:** Dobe B. Levinson, Frank Chance **P:** Brad Southwick, Gary De Pew

This one has no connection with the other American *Angel* movies. It stars blond Darlene Vogel as a police photographer who investigates a friend's murder. With Roddy McDowall as a pill-popping former rock star and Mark DeCarlo (from the *Studs* TV show).

ANGEL

(World, 1986) **D/S:** Teresa Woo **D:** Raymond Leung **P:** Gary Chan, Amy Choi   Hong Kong (*Iron Angels*)

Martial-arts movies became more modern and international in the 80s. This action-packed epic takes place in Hong Kong, Bangkok, Tokyo, and the Philippines. It includes large-scale battles, bombs, machine guns, torture, lots of James Bond–style devices and excellent martial-arts fight scenes. The Angel organization is led by a Chinese-American man (Alex Fong) and includes two Chinese women— a singer (Elaine Lui) and a secretary (Moon Lee)—and a Japanese martial-arts master. They try to stop the awesome kung-fu-fighting drug lord Madame Yeoung (Yukari Oshima). She wears all black and cuts four fingers off a man's hand during a corporate board meeting. Then she whips a captive till he's bloody, laughs, and licks the blood. Some surprising FX must have been inspired by the *Evil Dead* movies. The exciting finale features the three female stars (after most of the men have been killed off) fighting in a factory. Subtitles are in English and Chinese. *Angel* was a big hit and spawned some official sequels and other series like the *Operation Pink Squad* movies, plus many more features trying to cash in by putting *Angel* in their titles.

ANGEL II

(World, 1988) **D/P:** Teresa Woo/ Raymund Leong **S:** William Hsu Hong Kong (*Hong Kong Police Madame II*)

Alex Fong, Moon Lee (now disguised as a businesswoman) and Elaine Lui return with a new angel (Kharina Isa). There's a Hitler-fan villain with a small army, transvestites, and jungle warfare. *Angel III* (World, 1989) with Fong Lee, and Kharina Isa featured terrorists led by a Qaddafi type in Thailand.

ANGEL COMES TO BROOKLYN

(1945) **D:** Leslie Goodwins **S:** Stanley Paley, June Carroll **P:** Armand Schaefer

Charles Kemper is an angel who puts on a Broadway show. Kaye Dowd, Robert Duke, and C. Montague Shaw star in this forgotten Republic B film by the director of *The Mummy's Curse*, featuring FX by Howard and Theodore Lydecker.

ANGEL EYES

(Atlantic, 1991) **D/S:** Gary Graver
P: Jeffrey B. Mallian, Steve Armogida

Angel (Monique Gabrielle) is a killer teen who tries to ruin the relationship her real estate developer stepfather (John Phillip Law) is having with Rachel Vickers (aka porn star Raven). The two women have many sex scenes (including one with each other) and a sub plot concerns a loan shark (Erik Estrada). Rachel Harrison, Suzanne Ager, and Hoke Howell are also in the "psycho erotic thriller" from executive producer Fred Olen Ray.

ANGELFIST

(New Horizons, 1992) **D/P:** Cirio H. Santiago
S: Anthony L. Greene

If you've seen *TNT Jackson* (1975) or *Firecracker* (1981), both by Santiago, you know the "American lady fighter avenges the death of her sister" routine right down to the topless kickboxing scene. Yes, executive producer Roger Corman had Santiago use the same script again. Cat (Catya) Sassoon (daughter of Vidal and actress Beverly Adams) stars in this version. She's very good doing backflips and high kicks and obviously had breast implants for nude scenes. Fights take place in an ice house (remember Bruce Lee), on a subway, and even in a ring, and there's a cockfight. Melissa Moore takes showers (there are lots of showers in this movie), is tied up, and also fights. Michael Shaner and Ken Metcalfe also appear. Made in the Philippines.

ANGEL HEART

(IVE, 1987) **D/S:** Alan Parker
P: Alan Marshall, Elliot Kastner

For a modern horror movie, this has a complex plot and great atmosphere, but it's no classic. It's based on the novel *Fallen Angel*, by William Hjortsberg. In 1955, Brooklyn detective Harry Angel (Mickey Rourke) goes to Harlem and New Orleans to find a missing singer. People he visits die (head in fan, drowned in gumbo). Lisa Bonet is Epiphany Proudfoot, daughter of a voodoo priestess. Because she was on the highly-rated *Cosby* TV series at the time, and there was a controversial sex-and-raining-blood scene in *Angel Heart*, it got a lot of publicity. Robert De Niro plays one of his eccentric supporting roles, with long nails and hair, as Louis Cyphre. With Charlotte Rampling, Brownie McGhee, and Kathleen Wilhoite. The video release restored 10 seconds missing from the theatrical version. The Trevor Jones soundtrack (featuring some good blues classics) is on Island.

ANGEL OF DEATH

(Starmaker, 1986) **D/S:** " Frank Drew White"/Andrew Bianchi **S:** Gregory Freed, Jesús Franco **S/P:** Daniel Lesou (*Commando Mengele*)

Christopher Mitchum stars in a movie about Nazi hunters tracking down Dr. Josef Mengele (Howard Vernon). With Franco regulars Jack Taylor, Robert Foster, and name star Fernando Rey, and Dora Doll. The Dr. Moreau–like experiments include a monkey man, but despite all the buildup we never get to see the mutants. There's lots of shooting, though. Filmed in Uruguay and released by New World.

ANGEL OF DESTRUCTION

(New Horizons, 1994) **D/S:** Charles Phillip Moore
P: Cirio H. Santiago

Maria Ford stars as a blond martial-arts-expert cop and former stripper in Honolulu who takes over a murder case after her undercover private-eye stepsister (Charlie Spradling) is killed. Jessica Mark plays a blond lesbian stripper and rock star who performs a topless S&M stage show with her female partner (Chandra). Both have silicone breasts and want to be "back on the cover of *Rolling Stone*." Her mob backer says he wants "more Peggy Lee and less Marquis de Sade." Meanwhile, a big, scary, dead-eyed mercenary psycho (Jimmy Broome) kills Asian hookers. There's lots of mindless stuff to enjoy here, including fights, shootings, explosions, crotch kicks, topless videos, severed fingers, and Ford in stripper, topless kung-fu, and slo-mo sex scenes. This Philippines production is a remake of *Black Belt*.

ANGEL OF H.E.A.T.

(Vestron, 1981) **D/P:** Meryl A. Schreiberman
S: Helen Sanford

Marilyn Chambers, as agent Angel Harmony, works for "Harmony's Elite Attack Team" and has to save the world from a mad scientist with the ultimate weapon and androids. The popularity of the *Charlie's Angels* series ensured success for many mediocre movies like this. Made by the creator of *Parts: The Clonus Horror* (1979), it was filmed in the Lake Tahoe region and features lots of nudity and comedy. It debuted on cable TV. Mary Woronov is a lesbian H.E.A.T. agent featured in a mud-wrestling scene. One-time porno star Chambers was also in David Cronenberg's *Rabid* (1977).

ANGEL ON MY SHOULDER

(Sinister, 1946) **D:** Archie Mayo **S:** Harry Segall, Roland Kibbee **P:** Charles R. Rogers

Mickey Rourke in Angel Heart.

Paul Muni as a murdered ex-con goes to Hell in an elevator with the Devil (Claude Rains), then is sent to earth as a respected judge. It's a good fantasy with serious overtones and includes an excellent Hell sequence. Anne Baxter, Onslow Stevens, Jonathan Hale, and Fritz Leiber are also in the U.A. release. The music is by Dimitri Tiomkin. Rains had also been in the somewhat similar *Here Comes Mr. Jordan* (1941), based on a play by Segall. A 1980 TV remake starred Peter Strauss.

ANGEL ON THE AMAZON

(1948) **D:** John Auer **S:** Lawrence Kimbal

Vera Hruba Ralston (whose husband, Herbert J. Yates, owned Republic Pictures) is a woman who becomes an ageless jungle queen because she kills a black panther. It doesn't make a whole lot of sense, but it's pretty bizarre. With George Brent, Brian Aherne, Richard Crane, and Walter Reed.

ANGELS

(New Pacific 1971) **D/S:** Joe Viola
S/P: Jonathan Demme   (*Angels Hard as They Come; Angels: Hell on Harleys*)

Scott Glenn stars as Long John, a sullen, bored, pill-dealing Hell's Angel. He arrives with a friend on *Easy Rider*–style bikes at Lost Cause, a ghost town where the Dragons, led by the sadistic "General" (Charles Dierkop wearing a WWI German helmet), party with terrified hippies. He saves a blonde (who had asked "What about Altamont?" and brought up Manson's name) from being raped. She dies from a stab wound, and he and two others are blamed, jailed, put on trial, found guilty, dragged behind bikes, and generally degraded. It all ends in a violent, all-out battle when fellow Angels arrive. This was the first feature credit for Demme, who admits the plot was lifted from Kurosawa's *Rashomon*. It was originally released by Corman's New World. Gary Busey, who plays a peaceful hippie, was once a sidekick to a Tulsa, Oklahoma, TV horror host. He probably got his first screen-acting job because he was the drummer for Carp (there's one LP on Epic), who did the soundtrack of OK instrumental rock. With James Iglehart, Janet Wood, Gary Littlejohn, and Sharon Peckinpah. Demme and Viola made *The Hot Box* next.

ANGELS BRIGADE

(Vestron, 1978) **D/S:** Greydon Clark **S:** Alvin L. Fast

Seven women led by a lounge singer (Susan Lynn Kiger) go after drug dealers (led by Peter Lawford). They wear bikinis and travel in a "super van." The veteran cast includes Jack Palance, Neville Brand, Jim Backus, Pat Buttram, Alan Hale Jr., and Arthur Godfrey (!). With Darby Hinton, Jacquelin Cole, and Sylvia Anderson. A PG-rated New World release.

ANGELS: HELL ON HARLEYS: *See* ANGELS

ANGELS IN THE OUTFIELD

(MGM, 1951) **D/P:** Clarence Brown
S: Dorothy Kingsley, George Wells

Paul Douglas, as the brawling Pittsburgh Pirates manager, promises an angel (the voice of James Whitmore) that he'll be good if his team gets heavenly help. Donna Corcoran is the orphan who can see the heavenly choir on the playing field and tells two reporters (Janet Leigh and Keenan Wynn). With Spring Byington and Ellen Corby as nuns, Lewis Stone, Bruce Bennett, and Marvin Kaplan. Guest stars include Bing Crosby, and Ty Cobb, Joe DiMaggio, and other baseball greats. Douglas was also in the baseball fantasy *It Happens Every Spring* (1949).

Charles Dierkop in *Angels*.

ANGELS IN THE OUTFIELD

(Walt Disney, 1994) **D:** William Dear **S:** Holly Goldberg Sloan **P:** Irby Smith, Joe Roth

Since *Field of Dreams* (1989) and other baseball movies became box-office winners, this PG remake made sense, but it's even sappier than the original and has more FX. Only a foster child (Gordon Levitt) can see angel Christopher Lloyd, who leads a group of angels helping a team to win. Danny Glover costars as the team manager, with Brenda Fricker, Tony Danza, and Ben Johnson. It was shot in Oakland Stadium.

ANGELS OF THE CITY

(Raedon, 1989) **D/S/A:** Lawrence Hilton-Jacobs **S/P:** Joseph Merhi **S:** Raymond Martino **P:** Richard Pepin

It's the first feature directed by the former *Welcome Back, Kotter* costar, who became an action-video star in the late 80s. LA coeds dressed as hookers for a sorority initiation are kidnapped by pimps. Hilton-Jacobs plays a police detective.

ANGELS WASH THEIR FACES

(1939) **D:** Ray Enright **S:** Michael Fessier, Niven Busch, Robert Buckner **P:** Hal B. Wallis

The adult stars of this vintage Warner Brothers juvenile-delinquent movie are Ronald Reagan as the district attorney and Ann Sheridan (from the first *Angels* film). Frankie Thomas is Sheridan's little brother, a good guy getting into trouble. Billy Halop (Billy), Leo Gorcey (Leo), Bobby Jordan (Bernie), Gabriel Dell (Luigi), Huntz Hall (Huntz), and Bernard Punsley (Sleepy) are the real stars, though. With Patrick Remsen, Bonita Granville, and Margaret Hamilton.

ANGELS WITH DIRTY FACES

(MGM, CBS/Fox, 1938) **D:** Michael Curtiz **S:** John Wexley, Warren Duff **P:** Samuel Bischoff

Lower East Side childhood buddies grow up and become a gangster (James Cagney) and a priest (Pat O'Brien) in a classic Warner Brothers jd and prison film. Humphrey Bogart (in his third film with the Dead End Kids) also stars, with Ann Sheridan and George Bancroft. The kids all had new names again—Billy Halop (Soapy), Bobby Jordan (Swing), Leo Gorcey (Bim), Gabriel Dell (Patsy), Huntz Hall (Crabface), and Bernard Punsley (Hunky)—and were billed as "the Crime School and Dead End Kids." Nobody forgets the great ending, when tough Cagney goes to the chair and turns "yellow," screaming and begging hysterically so the kids won't consider him a hero. Music by Max Steiner. The MGM video version is colorized.

ANGEL TOWN

(Imperial, 1990) **D/P:** Eric Karson **S:** S. Warren **P:** Ash R. Shaw

We didn't need another post–Jean-Claude Van Damme fighting star, but French kickboxer Oliver Gruner starred in this anyway. He's a fighting postgrad LA student who helps Theresa Saldana and her family in Watts because gangs have been attacking them. With Tony Valentino, Peter Kwong, and Mark Dacascos. Karson also directed *The Octagon,* with Chuck Norris.

ANGKOR—CAMBODIA EXPRESS

(Vestron, 1981) **D/P:** Lek Kitiparaporn **S:** Roger Crutchley, Kailan **P:** Richard Randall Italy/Thailand (*Kampuchea Express*)

Somebody had to make a Pol Pot/Cambodia massacre exploitation movie, so the producer of *The Wild Wild World of Jayne Mansfield* decided he was the man for the job. It seems like there would be more movies about the subject. Robert Walker Jr. stars with the late Christopher George, Woody Strode, and Nancy Kwan. At least they did it before *The Killing Fields.*

ANGST

(1984) **D/S:** Gerald Kargl **S/C:** Zbigniew Rybczynski Austria (*Fear*)

In one of the most effective and simple psycho killer movies around, a young man (Erwin Leder) is released from prison after ten years. He breaks into a suburban home and kills the inhabitants when they return home — and gets away with it. It was supposedly based on a true incident. Rybczynski was known for his interesting rock videos. You have to wonder whether John McNaughton managed to see this before making *Henry: Portrait of a Serial Killer.*

ANGUISH

(Fox, 1987) **D/S:** Bigas Luna **P:** Pepón Coromina Spain (*Angustia*)

If you like horror movies with cosmic overtones, look for this bizarre film within a film within a film. Michael Lerner is a psychotic Los Angeles lab technician who collects eyeballs and is dominated by his mother (irritating Zelda Rubenstein, from the *Poltergeist* movies). He watches the silent film *The Lost World* in a theater, but everything we've seen turns out to be a film called *The Mommy,* being watched in a theater. A man (Ángel José) watching it starts killing people in the theater. There's a warning about subliminal messages on the soundtrack, but even if that's a lie, *Anguish* is very disorienting, as intended.

ANIMAL INSTINCTS

(Academy, 1992) **D:** Gregory Hippolyte **S:** Georges des Essentes **P:** Andrew Garroni

This is based on an actual Florida case where a Florida voyeur cop (Maxwell Caulfield) managed his nympho hooker wife (Shannon Whirry, who narrates) and videotaped her sessions with other cops (and some women). With Delia Sheppard as a rich lesbian, Mitch Gaylord, Erika Nann, and name-value guest stars Jan-Michael Vincent as a mayoral candidate, John Saxon as a lawyer, and David Carradine as a blackmailing strip-club owner. It's available in R or unrated versions. Whirry, who had acted on stage and in *Out for Justice,* went on to star in more "erotic thrillers" by Hippolyte (aka Greg Dark of the Dark Brothers porno movie fame).

ANIMAL INSTINCTS 2

(Academy, 1994) **D:** Gregory Hippolyte **S:** Darryl Haney **P:** Andrew Garroni

Joanna (Shannon Whirry) returns, now divorced but still talking to the camera and narrating more flashbacks. Her new psycho/voyeur/security-expert suburban neighbor (Woody Brown) hides video cameras in her house. Meanwhile Joanna takes showers, poses nude for an artist, and joins in a threesome. This sequel doesn't have guest stars to take time away from the sex scenes. With Elizabeth Sandifer as the neighbor's wife and Jennifer Campbell. Available R or unrated.

Michael Lerner in *Anguish.*

ANNA TO THE INFINITE POWER

(RCA, 1982) **D/P:** Robert Weimer

A telekinetic 12-year-old girl with supernatural powers tries to find her clone sisters while spies pursue her. It's well-made science fiction aimed at kids, with Martha Byrne, Dina Merrill, Jack Gilford, and Donna Mitchell.

THE ANNIHILATOR

(1986) **D:** Michael Chapman **S:** Roderick and Bruce Taylor **P:** Alex Beaton

An NBC-TV series-pilot *Terminator* copy with Mark Lindsay Chapman as a reporter being chased by the police for killing his girlfriend (Catherine Mary Stewart). She was really a double, one of the evil aliens with radar vision trying to take over Earth. With Susan Blakely, Lisa Blount, Geoffrey Lewis, and Brion James.

THE ANNIHILATORS

(Starmaker, 1985) **D:** Charles E. Sellier Jr. **S:** Brian Russell **P:** Allan C. Pederson

Nam vets take back the streets of the Southpoint neighborhood of Atlanta. They battle horrible killer-rapist punks (led by Paul Koslo) with guns, meat cleavers, and hammers who take a busload of schoolkids hostage. Christopher Stone stars with Lawrence Hilton-Jacobs (from *Welcome Back, Kotter*) and one-time Brian DePalma regular Gerrit Graham. The director and cinematographer of this violent movie, Henning Schellerup, had made family films for Sun Classics. From New World.

ANOTHER CHANCE

(Republic, 1988) **D/S/A:** Jesse Vint **P:** Roger Camras

An actor (Bruce Greenwood) who dies is allowed to return to earth if he can stay faithful to one woman. Some scenes are set in Heaven and Hell, and there are dream sequences, temptresses, a demon, and people impersonating famous actors. With Vanessa Angel, Jeff East, Barbara Edwards, Brenda Bakke, Karen Witter, and Anne Ramsey.

ANOTHER DAY, ANOTHER MAN

(SW, 1966) **D/S/P/E:** Doris Wishman

Doris Wishman made more than two dozen unique (some say terrible) adults-only movies from the late 50s until the early 80s. Wishman film festivals were later held in Berlin and LA. This wonder opens with nice b/w stills and jazz music. Steve (Tony Gregory) and Ann (Barbi Kemp), happy newlyweds, walk in Central Park. She and her former roommate Tess undress and pose in their underwear. The camera closes in on the radio, then on a bra on the floor. She moves into a new furnished apartment with Steve, who says, "You're so good, so pure. I don't think you could do anything wrong." Burt, a sleazy pimp, visits Tess but falls asleep and dreams. He narrates his dream (a movie in itself) with a voice like a cartoon gangster. The dream features "twins" Dolly and Daisy, a new girl named Meg, and her hayseed boyfriend. The women shower, undress, and dance. The camera wanders to close in on a wastepaper basket, tilts to the ceiling, then back to the floor. Burt wakes: "I must have been dreaming!" Steve gets sick, Ann goes to work for Steve (wearing a mesh body stocking), Tess gets pregnant, and Steve recovers and surprises Ann at "work." The camera shows a potted plant. Steve stabs himself. Sometimes the actors look at the camera. The dialogue was all added later. It's a rare occurrence when a few words happen to match the lips. Great stuff!

ANOTHER 48 HOURS

(Paramount, 1990) **D:** Walter Hill **S:** John Fasano, Jeb Stuart, Larry Gross **P:** Lawrence Gordon, Robert D. Wachs

Eddie Murphy and Nick Nolte return in a stunt-filled action sequel, with bad bikers and drug dealers. A bus rolling over 17 times and then smashing into a semi is a highlight. With Brion James, Ed O'Ross, Bernie Casey, Andrew Divof, Kevin Tighe, Tisha Campbell, and Page Leong. Watch for a scene where cars crash though a movie screen with a giant Kitten Natividad on it.

ANOTHER SON OF SAM

(Neon, 1988) **D/S/P:** Dale A. Adams

There is nothing about New York City's "Son of Sam" killings in this dreary, no-star, regional movie about murder on a campus.

THE ANTICHRIST

(1991) **D/S:** Guy Bodart

The makeup, sound, and lighting for this indy horror movie are all substandard. I could live with that, if it weren't so slow-moving. Blond Lorelei Lanford is a woman in Vegas who is pursued by a POV camera. When possessed, she has long black fingernails and a white face, and yells, "Shut up, Bug off! Ha, ha, ha!" With flashbacks to Africa and Palestine and a dream sequence. Robert Berry is the friendly archaeologist/priest. The video box says "unrated," but it would be a PG-13, maybe. The director is from Belgium.

ANTI-CLOCK

(1980) **D/P:** Jack Bond **D/S:** Jane Arden   UK

An experimental video feature shot in b/w and color that played some US midnight bookings. It was called "a nuclear comedy." By the makers of *Separation* (1967), a film with music by Procol Harum.

ANTS = IT HAPPENED AT LAKEWOOD MANOR

ANY WHICH WAY YOU CAN

(Warner, 1980) **D:** Buddy Van Horn **S:** Stanford Sherman **P:** Fritz Manes

Clint Eastwood stars as bare-knuckles fighter Philo in the PG sequel to the hit action comedy *Every Which Way But Loose* (1978). Sondra Locke, Geoffrey Lewis, Ruth Gordon, and of course Clyde the chimp return. The highlight is an all-out bare-knuckles fight with Eastwood and William Smith that took a week to film. With gangsters, bikers, country music, Harry Guardino, Glen Campbell, Anne Ramsey, Kulie Brown, and Don Vadis. The Warner soundtrack features singing by Eastwood (with Ray Charles), Locke, and Campbell, and some oldies.

APACHE'S LAST BATTLE

(Sinister, 1964) **D:** Hugo Fregonese **S:** Robert A. Stemmle   France/Italy/W. Germany/Yugoslavia (*Shatterhand; Old Shatterhand*)

Doris Wishman's *Another Day, Another Man.*

Lex Barker stars in his deerskin fringes (but with someone else's dubbed-in drawl), and Pierre Brice is his blood brother, Winnetou, an Apache chief. In this entry in the popular series, booze-hungry Comanches kill for white renegades. It all ends in a big battle for a fort. With Daliah Lavi as a half-breed and Guy Madison as the bad cavalry officer. It was originally in Super Panorama 70 and was rleased in the US by Goldstone. The pan-and-scanned TV-print video is pretty worn out.

APACHE VENGEANCE

(Allison, 1970) **D:** Ron Joy **S/P:** Dick Bakalyan   (*The Animals*)

Michelle Carey plays an Apache woman tracking down the men who raped her. The writer/producer was a jd star who went on to act in Disney movies after making this western. Henry Silva is the main villain, and Keenan Wynn, Joseph Turkel, and John Anderson are in it too. Two years later, *Hannie Caulder*, a British production with Raquel Welch, used the same plot.

APARTMENT ZERO

(Academy, 1988) **D/S/P:** Martin Donovan **S/P:** David Koepp   UK

Colin Firth is a stuffy, paranoid British film fanatic who runs a revival theater in Argentina. Hart Bochner, his new bisexual American boarder, is also a psycho hitman responsible for a series of grisly deaths. In one scene they watch *Compulsion* together. Originally 124 minutes long, this complex psychological thriller was shortened by the director himself for the video version, which is 114 minutes. It was filmed in Buenos Aires.

THE APE CREATURE

(1968) **D:** Alfred Vohrer **S:** Alfred Greger W. Germany   (*Der Gorilla von Soho; Gorilla Gang*)

Edgar Wallace's *Dark Eyes of London* (1924) was first filmed in England in 1939, starring Bela Lugosi (it's also known as *The Human Monster*). This is the second German version (the first was in 1961) directed by Vohrer and the least known of the three. It was released in the US by Sam Sherman's Independent International. The plot, (Scotland Yard vs. a secret gang that drowns people for insurance money) is the same, but this time the setting is a reform school run by nuns, and there's more comedy. Characters are called Sergeant Pepper, Dr. Jekyll, and Mr. Sugar, and it's not due to American dubbing. A criminal known as "the Ape" is a man in a gorilla suit (pretty hard to take seriously but a fine film tradition). There's also more sex than in earlier Wallace features. A running gag concerns the bald old Sir Arthur and his many mistresses. There's a lesbian cat fight and a sex club with "a living wax museum." Horst Tappert stars as the chief investigator, with Uschi Glass and Herbert Fux. It's been on the USA network, among others.

APE MAN OF THE JUNGLE

(1962) **D:** "Charles Foster"/Carlo Veo Italy (*Tarzak Contra gli Uomini Leopardo*)

An AIP TV release with a Tarzan copy called Tarzak. He rescues a safari from a tribe of natives led by "the Leopard man."

APEX

(Republic, 1993) **D/S:** Phillip Roth **S:** Ronald Schmidt **P:** Gary Jude Burkett

Richard Keats stars as a scientist of the future who goes back through time to try and stop a robot from killing people in the Mojave Desert. Then he returns to an alternate future "old LA" where people he knew, including his wife, Natasha (Lisa Ann Russell), are now different characters and a war with *Robocop*-look robots is raging in the ruins. Mitchell Cox is a fighter with a blond buzz cut. This movie has nightmares, flashbacks, lots of explosions and red lights, and really good sound effects. From the makers of the darker *Prototype X29A*, also with Cox. It was shot in Nevada.

APHRODISIAC!

(Mondo, 1971) **D/S/P:** Dennis Van Zak **P/C:** Tom Parker   (*The Sexual Secret of Marijuana*)

This is a pro-pot (and anti-booze) documentary (narrated by a "doctor") with interesting b/w historical footage (NYC mayor Fiorello LaGuardia should be a hero to smokers everywhere) and real interviews with people on the streets of Hollywood. Plus—Whoa!—it's also an early color porno feature. "Real" people look into the camera and tell us about how marijuana changed their sex lives, and their narrated flashbacks prove it. Unlike some stuff from the time, the hard-core scenes are well shot, have good-looking women, and feature many positions. A businessman (John Holmes!) tells us how his secretary turns him on and claims that, after smoking "I felt like a superman!" A woman says, "It was as if I was transformed into a huge cunt!" They also manage to throw in a marijuana party ("a new American tradition"), a nude encounter group, pot-brownie eating, interracial sex (in the woods), silent-movie footage of cavemen, Nam soldiers getting high, car crashes—and Ruby killing Oswald! Incredible!

APOCALYPSE NOW

(Paramount,1979) **D/S/P:** Francis Ford Coppola **S:** John Milius

One of the best war films ever made was based on Joseph Conrad's *Heart Of Darkness*, once planned as Orson Welles' first feature. Playing the star role gave Martin Sheen a heart attack but assured him later voice-over work for endless TV commercials and narration of other Vietnam War–related projects. Marlon Brando got mixed reviews but a good percentage of the profits. Everything else aside, the leaping-tiger scene made me jump out of my theater seat, something that never happened during a horror movie. The excellent cast includes Robert Duvall and Dennis Hopper (both in top form), Frederic Forrest, Albert Hall, Sam Bottoms, 14-year-old Larry (now Lawrence) Fishburne, Scott Glenn, G.D.

Martin Sheen in *Apocalypse Now.*

Spradlin, Harrison Ford, Lee Ermy (later in *Full Metal Jacket),* and the late Bill Graham. Colleen Camp, Cyndi Wood, and Linda Carpenter are the *Playboy* Playmates. The Oscar-winning cinematography is by Vittorio Storaro. The production design is by Dean Tavoularis. Eddie Romero and John Ashley, who had been making movies in the Philippines for years, were associate producers. In 1992 the tape was rereleased, "remastered and enhanced," in regular or widescreen (letterboxed) versions running 153 minutes. The excellent double Elektra soundtrack album features the Doors' uncensored version of "The End," Micky Hart, Hendrix soundalike Randy Hansen, and some choice oldies and dialogue. See also *Hearts of Darkness,* a documentary about the filming of *Apocalypse Now.*

APOLOGY

(HBO, 1986) **D:** Robert Bierman **S:** Mark Medoff

In New York City, Soho sculptor Lesley Ann Warren requests phone confessions to use for an art project. A psycho caller who kills homosexuals is after her, and Peter Weller (just before *Robocop*) is a cop on the case. With John Glover, Christopher North, and Harvey Fierstein. From HBO cable.

THE APPLE

(Paragon, 1980) **D/S/P:** Menahem Golan **P:** Yoram Globus   US/W. Germany (*Star Rock*)

A record producer/Devil called Mr. Boogalow (Vladek Sheybal) takes over a young folk-singing duo in New York City of the future (1994). The new dance craze is called "the Bim." He uses sex and drugs to keep his stable of talent under his thumb, but God shows up at the end to help the kids out. Catherine Mary Stewart is top-billed in this ridiculous PG musical fantasy which steals ideas from *The Rocky Horror Picture Show.* Cannon also released a soundtrack album. Golan's next as director was *Enter the Ninja.*

THE APPLEGATES

(Media, 1989) **D/S:** Michael Lehman **S:** Redbeard Simmons **P:** Denise Di Novi   (*Meet the Applegates*)

Lehman's follow-up to his *Heathers* is a devastating and funny look at how modern life in the US can ruin and devolve even the closest family, disguised as a science-fiction comedy (or an "eco-comedy," as it was promoted). Like *Heathers*, it's set in suburban Ohio. Ed Begley Jr., Stockard Channing, and their family of giant, garbage-eating Brazilian cockroaches arrive near Akron on an important mission and disguise themselves as a "typical" American family. Almost immediately, they're seduced by TV, drugs, heavy-metal music, sex, and alcohol. The daughter (Camille Cooper) becomes a bitter, pregnant lesbian, and the mom becomes a credit-card junkie and shoplifter. They forget their mission and all secretly spin cocoons around tasty humans. *The Applegates* is a clever, bizarre movie, and the human-cockroach makeup and special effects are excellent. With Glenn Shadix and Dabney Coleman in drag (a bad idea).

APPLE PIE

(1975) **D/S/C:** Howard Goldberg

Tony Azito is a godfather type who narrates this (so far unreleased) NYC crime comedy in flashback. Brother Theodore plays his father, and Larry "Bud" Melman, Veronica Hamel, and Irene Cara appear.

THE APPOINTMENT

(1982) **D/S/P:** Lyndsey Vickers   UK

A family faces an evil force in a house, and Edward Woodward is cursed by his daughter (Jane Merrow).

APPOINTMENT WITH FEAR

(IVE, 1985) **D/S:** "Alan Smithee"/Razmi Thomas
S: Bruce Meade **P:** Tom Boutross

A detective (Douglas Rowe) goes after a psycho mental patient, under the influence of an Egyptian god named Attis, who kills LA high-school girls. The killer uses astral projection (as in *Psychic Killer*) to get around. With Deborah Vorhees, Michelle Little, and Dayton Allan (from the old *Steve Allen Show*) as a friendly bum. Moustapha Akkad was the executive producer and the cinematography is by Nicholas von Sternberg. The director "disowned" this odd New World release and had his name removed.

APPRENTICE TO MURDER

(Starmaker, 1987) **D:** R.L.Thomas
S: Alen Scott, Wesley Moore **P:** Howard K. Grossman   (*The Long Lost Friend*)

Donald Sutherland is a mystical country "Pow Wow" doctor who believes that an evil man (Knut Husebo) has put a hex on him. This PG-13 New World release was filmed in Norway but is set in Pennsylvania during the 20s. Chad Lowe, Mia Sara, and Rutanya Alda costar. It's pretty slow going. Sutherland also appeared in a Kate Bush video as bizarre Freudian Marxist Wilhelm Reich.

LES APPRENTIS SORCIERS

(1977) **D/S:** Edgardo Cozarinsky **S:** A. Tauman   France

You won't find this one in English, but it's one of several European productions that Dennis

Hopper was in around the time of *The American Friend* (1976). Cozarinsky, from Argentina, directed this humorous tale of Latin American exiles in Paris, radical politics, and avant-garde filmmaking. ZouZou stars, and Marie-France Pisier, Christian Marquand, and others make appearances. Hopper plays an American spy.

APRIL FOOL'S DAY

(Paramount, 1986) **D:** Fred Walton
S: Danilo Bach **P:** Frank Mancusco Jr.

The producer and studio that made the Friday the 13th movies backed and released this mediocre horror spoof. Heiress Deborah Foreman and her teen friends are killed off at a mansion on an island. The cast (including Griffin O'Neal) play jokes and pull pranks on each other, and there's a cheat ending. Made in British Columbia by the director of *When a Stranger Calls* (1979). The Charles Bernstein soundtrack is on Varèse Sarabande, and there was even a book based on the feature.

ARABIAN NIGHTS

(MCA, 1942) **D:** John Rawlins
S: Michael Hogan **P:** Walter Wanger

Maria Montez and Jon Hall acted together for the first time in this fun Universal Technicolor comic fantasy complete with torture-chamber sequences. She's Sheherazade and he's Harun ar-Rachid. With Sabu (in his first non-Korda feature) as an acrobat, Turhan Bey, Leif Erickson, Edgar Barrier as the grand vizier, John Carradine as a slave guard, Shemp Howard as a comic Sinbad(!), Billy Gilbert, Elyse Knox, John Qualen, and Acquanetta (Burnu Davenport) as a harem slave girl. Thomas Gomez relates the tale. Montez (born in the Dominican Republic to Spanish parents while her diplomat father was stationed there) went on to star in five more features with Hall. Ford L. Beebe was the second-unit director.

ARABIAN NIGHTS

(Water Bearer, 1974) **D/S:** Pier Paolo Pasolini
Italy/France (*Il Fiore delle Mille e una Notte*)

The third of Pasolini's medieval trilogy includes fantasy tales (and stories inside of stories) told by a black slave girl who is sold, kidnapped, mistaken for a man, and declared heir to a kingdom. This is nothing like a Hollywood movie! It was filmed on actual locations all over North Africa and the Middle East. The X rating for violence and casual nudity kept it from most American screens. With a red-haired flying demon, a man turned into a monkey, and castration. The music is by Ennio Morricone. The film was originally 155 minutes, but the letterboxed tape runs 130. United Artists released it after *The Decameron* (1970) and *The Canterbury Tales* (1971). The director's last film was the infamous *Salò* (1975).

ARACHNOPHOBIA

(Disney, 1990) **D:** Frank Marshall **S:** Don Jakoby,
Wesley Strick **P:** Kathleen Kennedy, Richard Vane

Jeff Daniels stars as a small-town doctor afraid of spiders who faces thousands of them breeding in

his barn. The story starts with Julian Sands in South America (parts were shot in Venezuela). In-joke scenes refer to *Aliens, Jaws,* and (yawn) *Psycho*. It was billed as a "thrillomedy" and cost much more than the total of all the other tarantula and spider movies ever made ($31 million). It was also probably the first feature with a disclaimer stating that no spiders had been harmed during filming. With John Goodman as the gung-ho exterminator, Harley Jane Kozak, Stuart Pankin, and Henry Jones. Steven Spielberg was the executive producer of this PG film from Buena Vista/Disney. The soundtrack on the Hollywood label is by Trevor Jones.

ARCADE

(Paramount, 1992) **D:** Albert Pyun
S: David S. Goyer **P:** Cathy Gesualdo

Teens play a virtual-reality game that feeds on their souls. The Full Moon production is like a cheap version of *Tron* and includes similar by-then-clichéd computer FX. Megan Ward and Peter Billingsley have to save their friends, and the computer brain (the voice of Jonathan Fuller) has Freddy Krueger–type lines. With John DeLancie, Sharon Farrell, and Seth Green. It was released in 1994.

ARCHANGEL

(VSOM, 1990) **D/S:** Guy Madden
S: George Toles **P:** Greg Klymkiw   Canada

In a bizarre b/w spoof of a 20s WWI movie, the main characters all suffer from amnesia. One Russian soldier uses his own intestines to strangle a Bolshevik. Kyle McCulloch (from Madden's better-known *Tales from Grimli Hospital*) stars as a Canadian soldier with an amputated leg helping Russians fight Germans.

THE ARCHER: FUGITIVE FROM THE EMPIRE

(MCA, 1981) **D/S/P:** Nick Corea **P:** Stephen P. Caldwell

Lane Caudell is Toran in this NBC-TV sword-and-sorcery series pilot. Belinda Bauer costars, with Victor Campos, Kabir Bedi, Priscilla Pointer, Richard Moll, Richard Dix Jr. (star of the Al Adamson movies), and George Kennedy as Brackus, the hero's dad.

ARENA

(1953) **D:** Richard Fleischer **S:** Harold
Jack Bloom **P:** Arthur M. Loew

Gig Young stars in this 3-D, Anscocolor movie filmed at Tucson's La Fiesta de los Vaqueros rodeo. It's not much of a story, but the 3-D rodeo action must have been pretty exciting at the time. With Jean Hagen, Polly Bergen, Harry Morgan, Barbara Lawrence, Lee Van Cleef, and Morris Ankrum. Fleischer directed *20,000 Leagues Under the Sea* next.

ARENA

(TWE, 1988) **D:** Peter Manoogian **S:** Danny
Bilson, Paul Demeo **P:** Irwin Yablans

If you liked TV shows like *Battlestar Galactica* you might make it through this juvenile, PG-13, science-fiction comedy from Charles Band. A blond hunk hero fights goofy-looking creatures in armor in front of a big crowds on a star station. The plot rips off a Fredric Brown short story that had already been done twice on *Star Trek* and once on *The Outer Limits*. With Claudia Christian, Shari Shattuck (*The Naked Cage*), who sings, Hamilton Camp (with four arms), Jack Carter as the fight commentator, and another *Star Wars* cantina spoof. John Buechler, Steve Wang, and Screaming Mad George worked on the many creatures. The unrelated 1973 Pam Grier movie called *The Arena* has been retitled *Naked Warriors* on tape.

ARE THESE OUR CHILDREN?

(1931) **D/S:** Howard Estabrook **P:** Louis Sareky

A nice kid (Eric Linden) goes bad, shoots an old man during a robbery, and ends up on death row in this early juvenile deliquent film that approaches *Reefer Madness* excess. With girls who use hooch. Rochelle Hudson costars, with Ben Alexander and Mary Kornman. Estabrook scripted hits like *Hell's Angels* (1930) and *David Copperfield* (1935).

ARE THESE OUR PARENTS?

(1944) **D:** William Nigh **S:** Michael Jacoby **P:** Jeffrey Bernerd

Noel Neill (later famous as Lois Lane on the *Superman* TV series) is a teen who goes wrong. Her mother (Helen Vinson) hangs out at roadhouses, and her boyfriend's father (Lyle Talbot) doesn't take his WWII defense job seriously. Nigh also made *Where Are Your Children?* at Monogram.

ARE YOU IN THE HOUSE ALONE?

(Worldvision, 1978) **D:** Walter Graumen **S:** Judith Parker **P:** Jay Benson

Kathleen Beller is a terrorized high-school student in this CBS-TV movie. With Blythe Danner, Tony Bill, Ellen Travolta, and Dennis Quaid. It was based on Richard Peck's novel.

ARIA

(Academy, 1987) **D/S:** Robert Altman, Bruce Beresford, Bill Bryden, Jean-Luc Godard, Derek Jarman, Fran Roddam, Nicolas Roeg, Ken Russell, Charles Sturridge, Julian Temple **P:** Don Boyd

In one of the stranger post-MTV features around, 10 opera arias are interpreted by 10 international directors as if they were rock videos. Everybody agrees it's a mess, but you might want to check out what Godard, Roeg, or Russell came up with. Beverly D'Angelo, Bridget Fonda (making her debut), John Hurt, Anita Morris, Theresa Russell (as King Zog), Buck Henry, and Julie Hagerty appear. The soundtrack is on RCA Red Seal.

ARISE! THE SUBGENIUS VIDEO

(PMV, 1969)

Bob Dobbs appears everywhere in this tape, which many saw on *Nightflight*. There are choice, well-edited snippets from old science-fiction movies and TV commercials, plus Bob songs, Bob rap, and footage of his 1984 onstage assassina-

tion. Altered footage, photos, and audiotracks (and Mark Mothersbaugh) help explain Church of the Subgenious theories on religion, politics, various conspiracies, and the end of the world.

ARIZONA HEAT

(Republic, 1988) **D/P:** John G. Thomas **S:** Daniel M. Colmerauer

Taking an idea from *The Enforcer*, a tough Arizona cop (Michael Parks) is teamed with a lesbian cop (Denise Crosby). They track down a serial killer who is after cops.

THE ARIZONA KID

(1971) **D/S:** Luciano B. Carlos **P:** Cirio H. Santiago   Italy/Philippines

A real rarity: Mamie Van Doren, after we thought she'd retired, costarring in a Filipino comedy/western. Comedian Chiquito stars, and Gordon Mitchell is the villain. Some parts are in English, but other parts are in Tagalog. It's not good or anything, but a dedicated Mamie completist might find a copy in a Filipino-owned video store in major US cities. Just don't confuse it with an old Roy Rogers movie of the same name. Mamie didn't show up in another feature until *Free Ride* (1986).

THE ARK OF THE SUN GOD

(TWE, 1983) **D:** "Anthony Dawson"/ Antonio Margheriti **S:** Giovanni Simonelli   Italy/Turkey (*I Soprawissuti della Citta Mortà*)

More *Raiders* fantasy/action stuff, with British actor David Warbeck as a James Bond–like safecracker in Istanbul. Some of the music was ripped off from *Battlestar Galactica*. With John Steiner and Allan Collins (whose real name is Luciano Pogozzi).

ARMED FOR ACTION

(AIP, 1992) **D/P:** "Max Raven"/Bret McCormick

Joe Estevez stars as a cop transporting a Mafia hitman across country. They're ambushed in a small town. With Rocky Paterson and David Harrold.

ARMED RESPONSE

(RCA/Columbia, 1986) **D/P:** Fred Olen Ray **S:** T. L. Langford **P:** Paul Hertzberg   (*Jade Jungle*)

Nam-vet ex-cop David Carradine owns a bar in LA's Chinatown, where his ex-cop dad (Lee Van Cleef in one of his last roles) drinks. Bad guys led by a yakuza named Akira (Mako), who is after a statue, kill Carradine's brother and torture another brother, so it's time for revenge, shooting, and exploding cars. Carradine has Nam flashbacks and nightmares. Michael Berryman wears a smile button, gives Mako fortune cookies, and has a slo-mo fight with Carradine. With Laureen Landon and Dick Miller together in a funny scene, Brent Huff, Lois Hamilton, Ross Hagen, Conan Lee, Fox Harris, Dawn Wildsmith, Michelle Bauer, Susan Stokey, Bobbie Bresse, the di-

rector, and a clip of Boris Karloff as Mr. Wong. The strangest parts are the many Carradine reaction shots in the bar scenes.

ARMOUR OF GOD

(1986) **D/S/A:** Jackie Chan   Hong Kong

International action superstar Jackie Chan fractured his skull making this, the most expensive Hong Kong film made up to that time ($15 million). His rock-star friend's girlfriend is kidnapped (and turned into a temporary zombie) in Europe. In an attempt to acquire all the pieces of the valuable "Armour of God," Jackie ends up battling a cult of martial-arts monks with machine guns who live in a vast cavern. A lot of time is spent on comedy and the relationships between the four major characters, but the stunts and fight scenes are great, as usual. The biggest surprise is when he's faced with a team of black lady kicking kung-fu killers in high heels and leather. The Golden Harvest release was the second-highest-grossing film in Hong Kong up to that time. It was shot in Spain, Morocco, Austria, the Philippines, and other locations.

ARMOUR OF GOD II: OPERATION CONDOR

(1990) **D/S/A:** Jackie Chan **S:** Edward Tang, Ma Mei-Ping **P:** Raymond Chow   Hong Kong (*Feiying Gaiwak*)

Chan returns as Condor, hired to find Nazi gold in the Sahara. He goes on the international adventure with three women and has to rescue the German one (Eva Cobo de Garcia) and the Chinese one (comedienne Carol Cheng) after they're kidnapped into slavery. Shoko Ikeda is the Japanese one. The sequel uses even more elements from *Raiders* films, including a Nazi fortress, and Chan does more amazing stunts. The most expensive feature made in Hong Kong up to that time, it took over two years to complete.

ARMY OF DARKNESS: EVIL DEAD III

(MCA, 1991) **D/S:** Sam Raimi **S:** Ivan Raimi **P:** Robert Tappert

Bruce Campbell returns as the sarcastic wiseguy Ash in a slapstick, medieval-fantasy-oriented, bigger-budget third *Evil Dead* feature. It starts with a brief recap of the first two movies (featuring Bridget Fonda), is filled with Three Stooges gags, and has a Monty Python look. Ash has a chainsaw arm, a Remington shotgun, and a '73 Oldsmobile. Animated swordfighting skeletons appear, and there's also an evil Ash to battle (in a scene inspired by *The Manster!*) and at one point many little Ashes. Parts were shot in Bronson Canyon. With Embeth Davidtz (later in *Schindler's List*), Marcus Gilbert as King Arthur, and cameos by Josh Becker, Harley Cokliss, William Lustig, Bernard Rose, Patricia Tallman, Bill Moseley, Theodore, and Sam Raimi. The music is by Danny Elfman. Universal held up the release until 1993, because of an unrelated rights battle over a *Silence of the Lambs* sequel with producer Dino De Laurentiis. It was cut to a brief 80 minutes, and the original downbeat post-nuke ending was replaced with a new ending. Some parts are too dark or blurry, too. A complete 96-minute version is on a Japanese laserdisc.

ARMY OF ONE
(Live, 1993) **D/P:** Vic Armstrong
S: Steven Pressfield **P:** Illana Diamond

Dolph Lundgren is an escaped con who was framed for murder by a corrupt detective (George Segal). He takes a female cop (Kristen Alfonso) hostage in a Ferrari in the desert and heads for LA. With Geoffrey Lewis, Michelle Phillips, Bert Remsen, and Ken Foree. R or unrated versions are available.

AROUND THE WORLD WITH FANNY HILL
(Kit Parker, 1973) **D/S:** Mac Ahlberg **P:** Tore Sjoberg

Shirley Corrigan stars in this sex comedy as the wife of a TV-commercial director who becomes a soft-core movie star. With Gaby Fuchs and Christina Lindberg. It was filmed on location around Europe by Mikael Alomon, who later lensed *Thelma and Louise,* and was presented by David F. Friedman. Ahlberg also made the unrelated *Fanny Hill* (1968).

AROUSED
(SW, 1966) **D/S:** Anton Holden **S/P:** Ray Jenkins

A Manhattan cop (Steve Hollister) searches for a psycho who kills hookers in this b/w adults-only feature. The killer is a bartender who keeps mannequins in his apartment. With a *Psycho* shower scene, a castration, Times Square footage, and a cosmic cyclical ending.

THE AROUSERS
(Embassy 1970) **D/S/P:** Curtis Hanson **P:** Tamera Asseyen   (*Sweet Kill; A Kiss from Eddie*)

Tab Hunter plays Eddie, a milk-drinking high-school gym teacher living at a beach house who is also a pathetic, impotent voyeur and a necrophiliac killer. After years as a blond-hunk pinup, this was his last major theatrical role until John Waters brought him back for *Polyester* (1981). This film wasn't released until 1972 (by Roger Corman's New World). In a by-now-clichéd scene, Eddie's mother (in a flashback) is seen as the likely cause of his problems. Most of the many murders aren't bloody, but the slow, moody music and Hunter's convincing acting make them very effective. After the first victim is killed, her roommate tells the LAPD about Eddie, but they bust her for pot instead! Isabel Jewell (a star in the 30s) plays a neighbor, Roberta Collins plays a hooker who dresses up for Eddie and pretends to be dead, and Sandy Kenyon (*Beyond the Doors*) is the TV newscaster. It's pretty disturbing. Asseyen produced *Norma Rae* (1979) and other major releases.

THE ARRIVAL
(Prism, 1990) **D/A:** David Schmoeller
S/P/A: Daniel Ljoka **P:** Ron Matonak

Max, an old man exposed to a meteor, "dies," but he returns and gets younger by killing a woman every two weeks. The old man (who sniffs for menstrual blood) is pretty strange. After a while he becomes Joseph Culp (Robert's son), an expressionless young man in black leather. In a sequence copied from *Five Easy Pieces,* he's picked up by a lesbian couple. After he kills them, he goes after his nurse from years earlier (Robin Frakes), and federal agent John Saxon tries to capture him. Michael J. Pollard, has a small role, and for some reason director Stuart Gordon and his wife show up. Nearly everything in this dull movie happens offscreen, but there is a sex-in-a-tub-of-blood dream.

THE ARROGANT
(1986) **D/S/P:** Philippe Blot   (*Sylvia Kristel's Desires*)

This pretentious road movie was shot in Nevada and debuted on the Playboy channel. A killer on a motorcycle who thinks he's God (Gary Graham) picks up a hitchhiking waitress (Sylvia Kristel), and fantasy sequences and sex scenes follow. Kristel was also in Cannon's *Lady Chatterley's Lover, Emmanuelle,* and *Mata Hari.*

ARTIST'S STUDIO SECRETS
(Video Dimensions, 1964) **D:** J. M. Kimbrough
P: Lou Campa

A Greenwich Village artist named Percy likes to see partially clothed women, so his wife makes sure his models take *all* their clothes off. A 70-minute b/w comedy from Boxoffice International. One of the two models is cross-eyed.

ART DECO DETECTIVE
(1993) **D/S/P:** Philippe Mora **P:** Bruce Critchley

John Dennis Johnson is Art Deco, a detective who is set up while investigating the murder of a movie star (Rene Riffel, who plays twins) in a conspiracy-movie satire by the director of the *Howling* sequels. With Stephen McHattie as a terrorist, Brion James, Mel Smith, and Joe Santos.

THE ART OF DYING
(PM, 1991) **D/A:** Wings Hauser
S/P: Joseph Merhi **P:** Richard Peppin

Actor Hauser directed and starred in three features made in quick succession for PM video. This is the most outrageous one. A killer (played by 6'6" Gary Wentz) and his male lover "talent scout" (Mitch Lara) make snuff films by recreating deaths from movies. There's another *Psycho* shower, a *Scarface* chainsaw killing, and a *Deer Hunter* Russian-roulette scene. Hauser is a troubled LA detective having an affair with Kathleen Kinmont, who is kidnapped. With Michael J. Pollard as a police psychiatrist, Sarah Douglas, Sidney Lassick, and Onna Zee.

THE ART OF MURDER
(1989) **D/S/P:** Milan Ziukovic

An American actor (Oliver Wright) in Belgrade is a suspect when the director of his new film is murdered. More people die as he tries to discover who the real killer is. From Concorde.

ASESINOS DE OTROS MUNDOS
(1971) **D:** Ruben Galindo **P:** Pedro
Galindo Aguilar   Mexico

This is one of many movies with Santo, a masked wrestling hero, and it was never dubbed into English. It's memorable because the skin-eating, killer-alien monster seems to be a dirty rubber sheet that makes the monster in the American film *The Creeping Terror* seem scary. It's controlled by a bad guy on a gold throne who threatens from TV screens. Gladiators fight, and the losers are shot. Santo, who usually wrestles, also mows down his opponents with a machine gun. See Santo running from the slow-moving monster and fighting bad guys to avant-garde jazz! See the exiting climax with even more rubber-sheet monsters!

AS NATURE INTENDED : *See* (NAKED) AS NATURE INTENDED

ASSASSIN
(1986) **D/S:** Sandor Stern **P:** Neil T. Maffeo

Robert Conrad is a retired CIA agent tracking down a right-wing killer named Golem (actually a robot) played by Robert Young. Karen Austin and Robert Webber costar in this TV movie.

ASSASSINATION
(Media, 1987) **D:** Peter Hunt
S: Richard Sale **P:** Pancho Kohner

Charles Bronson is a Secret Service agent in a tame (for him) PG-13 thriller. He protects the First Lady

---

"ART" MOVIES

Sleaze and horror fans: Don't discount so-called foreign "art" features just because you've met jerks who patronize them and condemn what you like. You don't have to wait in line to get into theaters full of uptight, snotty intellectuals anymore; you can watch at home on tape! Many of the most challenging or shocking movies that broke sex, nudity, and political taboos were foreign. Depending on your personal tastes (and ability to read subtitles), check out titles by Buñuel, Bergman, Fellini, Godard, Pasolini, Ferreri, Herzog, and, more recently, Pedro Almodovar or Peter Greenaway.

(Jill Ireland) from the assassins of a senator (Michael Ansara) who thinks the president will have a better chance of reelection as a widower. With Eric Stern (star of *The Love Butcher*!), Jan Gan Boyd, Randy Brooks, William Prince, and Peter Lupus. The music is by Valentine McCallum. Ireland was in 15 features with her (second) husband, Bronson. After this, she was in only one more film, *Caught* (1987), a Billy Graham production, before dying of cancer in 1990.

THE ASSASSINATION BUREAU

(Paramount, 1969) **D:** Basil Dearden
S/P: Michael Relph

Jack London wrote the story on which this turn-of-the-century adventure is based. Oliver Reed is Ivan Dragomiloff, leader of an all-male assassination organization. Diana Rigg, backed by Telly Savalas, infiltrates the bureau and hires Dragomiloff to have himself killed. It was filmed all over Europe, ends in a flaming zeppelin, and was rated M. With Curt Jurgens, Philippe Noiret, Clive Revill, George Couloris, and Milton Reid. Rigg and Savalas were in *On Her Majesty's Secret Service* the same year.

ASSASSIN OF YOUTH

(Hollywood Confidential, 1935)
D: Elmer Clifton   (*Marijuana*)

A high-school girl smokes the evil weed and is on the road to ruin. A reporter poses as a soda jerk to infiltrate the pot-smoking teens. Gangsters sell the drugs, kids have wild parties, girls skinny-dip, and joints fall from the sky! The original ads said, "Puff—Party—Tragedy!" The full version is 80 minutes long, but some tapes are much shorter. *Marijuana Menace* is the hilarious film within the film. Luana Walters (*The Corpse Vanishes*) costars with Arthur Gardner. The director also made *Captain America. Reefer Madness* was made around the same time.

ASSAULT = IN THE DEVIL'S GARDEN

ASSAULT OF THE KILLER BIMBOS

(Urban Classics, 1988) **D/P:** Anita Rosenberg
S: Ted Nicolau **P:** John Schouweiler

Go-go dancers named Lulu and Peaches (Elizabeth Kaitan and Christina Whitaker) are accused of murder and flee to a Mexican resort, in this road-movie/comedy/adventure. Tammara Souza is a truck-stop waitress who joins them. Nick Cassavetes and Griffin O'Neal are surf bums. With Eddie Deezen and Patti Astor. The song at the end is "Don't Call Me Bimbo." David DeCoteau was executive producer. Some people claim that the hit *Thelma and Louise* copied this movie. Rhino released the various artists soundtrack.

ASSAULT OF THE PARTY NERDS

(Prism, 1988) **D/S/P/A:** Richard Gabai
P: M. Alex Becker

A direct-to-video *Revenge of the Nerds* frat-house copy, with Michelle Bauer and Linnea Quigley as

Muffin and Bambi, Troy Donahue, Burt Ward, and Tantala. It was made in five days. David De-Coteau was the executive producer. Gabai also made *Assault of the Party Nerds II* (VCI, 1994) with Ward, Bauer, Quigley, Arte Johnson, and Rhonda Shear.

ASSAULT OF THE REBEL GIRLS = CUBAN REBEL GIRLS

ASSAULT WITH A DEADLY WEAPON

(USA, 1976) **D:** Umberto Lenzi **S:** Dardano Sacchetti
Italy (*Alt Roma a Mano Armata; Brutal Justice*)

A crime thriller sold as horror (with fake credits) by New York's Aquarius releasing company in 1982. Tomas Milian stars as a hunchbacked criminal (who defiantly pisses on the police-station floor) and Maurizio Merli is an obsessive cop. With token American name-star Arthur Kennedy and Ivan Rassimov. Sybil Danning hosts the tape.

ASSIGNMENT TO KILL

(1966) **D/S:** Sheldon Reynolds

Patrick O'Neal stars as a private eye in Switzerland who battles killers working for villain Herbert Lom. With Joan Hackett, John Gielgud, Peter Van Eyck, Oscar Homolka, and Kent Smith. William Conrad was the executive producer of the film, which was held up until 1969 and rated M.

ASTONISHED

(Leo, 1987) **D/S:** Jeff Kahn **D:** Travis
Preston **P:** William J. Taylor

This odd but interesting mixture of drama and comedy stars Liliana Komorowska as a European woman in an East Village apartment who is broke, has reality problems, and is accused of two murders. Characters from her dreams start to appear in her real life. A dead landlord/pimp shows up again. Several of the main characters (including the singer she falls for) are black. Komorowska (whoever she is) is very good in two roles (and has a topless scene). With music by Michael Urbaniak.

THE ASTRONAUT

(ABC, 1972) **D:** Robert Michael Lewis **S:** Gerald DiPego, Charles Kuenstle **P:** Harve Bennett

After an astronaut (Monte Markham) dies on Mars, a lookalike impersonates him in a government coverup scheme. Jackie Cooper, Susan Clark, Robert Lansing, and real astronaut Wally Schirra costar in this TV movie.

ASYLUM EROTICA = SLAUGHTER HOTEL

ASYLUM OF THE INSANE

(1971) **D:** Byron Mabe **D/S/P:** Donald E.
Davidson **S/P:** David F. Friedman

There were many phony 3-D features. This one was Friedman's remake of *Freaks*, called *She*

Freak (1966) with about three minutes of poor 3-D effects (including a guy demonstrating a yo-yo, as in *House of Wax*) added.

AT CLOSE RANGE

(Vestron, 1986) **D:** James Foley **S:** Nicholas
Kazan **P:** Ellliot Lewitt, Don Guest

A ruthless career criminal (Christopher Walken) returns to his Pennsylvania hometown in 1978. His adoring sons (real-life brothers Sean and Christopher Penn) want to join his gang but discover what he's really like. A violent, fascinating movie based on real incidents. With Mary Stuart Masterson, Eileen Ryan, Candy Clark, Tracey Walter, Crispin Glover, Kiefer Sutherland, Millie Perkins, and Stephen Geoffreys. It was shot in Tennessee. Director Foley made *After Dark, My Sweet* next.

ATLAS IN THE LAND OF THE CYCLOPS

(Sinister, 1961) **D:** Antonio Leonviola **S:** Oreste
Biancoli, Gino Mongini **P:** Ermanno Donati,
Luigi Carpentieri   Italy (*Maciste nella Terra dei Ciclopi*)

The one-eyed giant eats people, and evil Queen Capys (Chelo Alonso) does a lot of horrible things to the population of Sadok but falls in love with the muscular hero, Maciste (Gordon Mitchell). Mitchell went on to the more interesting *The Giant of Metropolis* (1962) and many other Italian features.

AT MIDNIGHT I TAKE YOUR SOUL

(SW, 1963) **D/S/A:** Jose Mojica Marins
Brazil (*A Mei Noite Levarei sua Alma*)

Marins is Ze do Caixo (or "Coffin Joe"). Ze makes his first screen appearance, bearded, in a black cape and top hat. He has intense eyes and introduces himself, speaking directly into the camera. During the credits, weird music plays, accompanied by howls, screams, maniacal laughter, and thunder. A second introduction is made by a Gypsy witch holding a skull. She also looks into the camera and her voice is heavily echoed. Ze is hateful and evil and relishes every contemptible thing he does, but he acts polite to the townspeople as long as they don't defy him. He scares, manipulates, and humiliates people whenever possible. He lives in a house with hands sticking out of the walls (good hat racks), smokes a skull-shaped pipe, and has servants. Except for cars seen in the background, the small town seems stuck in the 19th century. Ze spends a lot of time dropping by funerals, expressing his condolences to the grieving people, who know he's responsible for the high death rate.

In the local bar he approaches a table of men and breaks a wine bottle. He stares at one man (*White Zombie*/Lugosi–style eye closeups are cut in), then suddenly uses the bottle to cut off two of his fingers! Most of the special effects are pretty convincing. The guy sobs, while Ze chomps down on a big (turkey?) leg. A big, bald guy knocks him down. Ze jumps on the bar, kicks the man in the head, then brutally whips him until his face is streaming blood and he cries. He tapes a woman's mouth shut, and while she lies in bed in a negligée, he lets a huge tarantula crawl on her and bite her. One woman he desires bites him on the lip when he tries to kiss her. Later he kills her boyfriend by stabbing him, putting him in a bathtub, smashing his head on the side, filling the tub, then drowning him. Then he brings her a bird in a cage, beats her, rapes her (off screen), and drinks her blood. She hangs herself after he leaves laughing. He pokes a doctor's eyes out (Three Stooges style), leaving bloody sockets, then pours alcohol on him and lights a match. He takes the crown of thorns from a bust of Christ and smashes it into a man's face. Although he does all these horrible things, he rescues a little boy from an abusive father, and is disturbed by the fortune-telling witch, who mocks him. He seems to be tempting death by stealing gifts from graves and defiantly yelling in the graveyard. Ze fears "Inferno!!" Voices and the laughing, floating ghost of the suicide torment him, and he freaks out while scary music and screaming (which sounds like the Doors' "Horse Latitudes") is heard. The doctor's corpse, surrounded by an eerie glow, returns to light his pipe. In one scene shown in negative, he sees a procession of his dead victims carrying him in an open casket. In a tomb, the terrified, bloody Ze breaks open coffins and screams insanely when he sees corpses covered with maggots and spiders. The townspeople (with torches) find him and the camera closes in on his upside-down mutilated face as the clock strikes midnight. The tape is subtitled. *Tonight I'll Take Your Corpse* followed.

ATOMIC CITY

(1952) **D:** Jerry Hopper **S:** Sydney Boehem **P:** Joe Sistrom

An atomic scientist's son (Lee Aaker) is kidnapped by Russian agents who demand hydrogen-bomb secrets. This anti-Communist story is filmed documentary style, using the real Los Alamos atomic-energy laboratory as a location. It was the first feature for the former big-band singer Gene Barry, who plays the hero father. He was in *War of the Worlds* (also for Paramount) the next year. With Nancy Gates, Milburn Stone, Lydia Clark, and Bert Freed.

ATOM MAN VS. SUPERMAN

(Warner, 1950) **D:** Spencer Gordon Bennet **S:** George Plympton, Joseph F. Poland, David Mathews **P:** Sam Katzman

The 15-chapter Columbia sequel to *The Adventures of Superman* (1948) has mostly the same cast and more fun animated flying scenes. Lyle Talbot is the bald villain Lex Luthor, disguised as "the Atom Man" (with a wild, glittery, silver helmet and a cape). Superman (Kirk Alyn again) has more to do than in the first serial. With a heat ray, "the Phantom Zone," an animated flying saucer, Bronson Canyon, and the inevitable overuse of stock footage. Available on 2 cassettes. Just a year later George Reeves took over the role in a short feature (*Superman and the Mole Men*) that led to the famous TV series.

ATOR: THE FIGHTING EAGLE

(Thorn EMI, 1982) **D/S:** "David Hills"/A. Massaccesi **S:** Michele Soavi **P:** Alex Susmann   Italy

This was the first of several PG-rated lunkhead muscleman adventures made just after the first *Conan*. Miles O'Keeffe (Bo Derek's *Tarzan*) stars. It's pretty bad but not as bad as the sequels. With Edmund Purdom as Griba, blond beauty Sabrina Siani, Laura Gemser, Ritza Brown, a "tarantula man," and a visit to "the land of the walking dead." *The Blade Master*, *Iron Warrior*, and *Quest for the Mighty Sword* followed.

ATOR THE INVINCIBLE: *See* BLADE MASTER

ATROCITIES OF THE ORIENT

(Video Dimensions, 1959) **D:** William Jansen   Philippines

WWII Filipino freedom-fighters battle brutal Japanese occupiers in a serious, adults-only exploitation shocker. Crude but not funny, as some video boxes suggest, it includes real war-atrocity newsreel footage, musical segments, and a romantic subplot, and features some nudity. An ad promised, "See women tortured with unspeakable barbarity!" Linda Estrella stars. Some earlier features with the same theme were *Beasts of the East*, *Samurai*, and *Sins of the Orient*. This was first released in the US by Astor (they removed all the credits) and sometimes played on a bill with *Marijuana*.

ATTACK OF THE BEAST CREATURES

(Western World, 1983) **D/P:** Michael Stanley **S:** Robert A. Hutton **P:** William R. Szinsky   (*Hell Island*)

In 1920, survivors of an unseen sinking boat try to survive on an island that looks like a forest. They have problems, though, besides the usual hunting for food and bickering about what to do. The water in a stream is like acid, so a character trying to get a drink becomes a gory mess, then a skeleton. And the island is home to "hundreds" of killer dolls just like the one in the *Trilogy of Terror* TV movie with Karen Black! They drop from trees, make shrieking sounds, and attack like rats. You can easily imagine somebody off screen throwing them at people. The unknown actors must have had a great time pretending to fight them and running away. All those killer dolls are scary, I guess, but they move their arms up and down, have floppy hair, and make a hilarious fluttering sound when they run. In one classic scene, they all worship in front of a big (for them) wooden idol. This is my favorite movie from Connecticut since *Horror of Party Beach*! I wonder if the director is the former rock star from Cleveland. Nah, couldn't be.

ATTACK OF THE B MOVIE MONSTERS

(1985) **D:** Wayne Berwick **S/P:** Ted Newsom

In this mixture of stock footage and new comedy scenes, with a stop-motion monster from the director of *Microwave Massacre*, 50s science-fiction stars (John Agar, Kenneth Tobey, Les Tremayne, Anne Robinson, Gloria Talbott, Robert Clarke, and Robert Shayne) show up. Scenes were shot in Bronson Canyon, and Brinke Stevens and Forrest J. Ackerman are in it too. The director said the

one-hour tape was suposed to be expanded or reshot as a feature, but it never was. The tape was once available from *Filmfax* magazine.

ATTACK OF THE 50 FT. WOMAN

(HBO, 1993) **D:** Christopher Guest **S:** Joseph Dougherty **P:** Debra Hill

Daryl Hannah narrates and stars as Nancy Archer, the rich, unhappy wife who grows and seeks revenge against the men in her life, in this updated remake of the 1957 cult fave by the director of *The Big Picture*. The dialogue is more thoughtful, references to *Forbidden Planet*, *Tarantula*, and other films are added, and female aliens appear at the end. With Daniel Baldwin as the unfaithful husband, Christi Conaway in the Yvette Vickers role, William Windom as the father, Frances Fisher as the shrink, Victoria Hass (also in *Serial Mom*) as the deputy, Hamilton Camp, and Richard Edson. Not bad, but it didn't need to be 25 minutes longer than the original. Gene Warren Jr. FX. Scenes from the original film show up on a drive-in screen, and screenwriter Mark Hannah gets a "based on" credit.

ATTACK OF THE HIDEOPOID

(Demolition, 1989) **D/S/P/A/E:** Rick Werner Fahr **P:** Diana Robinette

This is an overlong, strange, homemade Seattle feature about an irritating, telepathic, hillbilly cannibal with Cronenberg-inspired growths. A running joke concerns the number of flashbacks and flashbacks inside of flashbacks, and there's plenty of filler band footage (the Young Fresh Fellows do "Go Go Gorilla"). The best parts involve computer-generated blue dots (a great effect), and some scenes are copied from *The Manster*. With seven local bands and Fred Hopkins.

ATTACK OF THE KILLER CAVE BABES: *See* ONE MILLION AC/DC

ATTACK OF THE ROBOTS

(SW, 1966) **D:** Jesús Franco **S:** Jean-Claude Carrière **P:** Michel Safra   Spain/France (*Cartes sur Table*)

This comic science-fiction/spy movie used to be on local TV (AIP released it) but it's b/w, so don't look for it there anymore. Eddie Constantine plays Al Peterson, playboy and James Bond–type ex-Interpol agent. Scientist Fernando Rey, working for Lady Cecilia (Francois Brion), creates kamikaze "robots," zombielike men with dark skin, in all-black clothes and glasses that change color when they're killed. Al is kidnapped and taken to an opium den in Asia, poses as a boxer from Brooklyn in Spain, and gets to romance Sophie Hardy. Carrière cowrote some of Buñuel's greatest screenplays. This has swinging music, great sunglasses, and some good moments. Franco (who appears as a pianist) did a remake in 1985 that's available only in Europe.

ATTACK OF THE SWAMP CREATURES = THE BLOOD WATERS OF DR. Z

AT THE MAX

(1991) **D:** Julian Temple, Christine
Stand **P:** Michael Cohl, André Picard

The Rolling Stones' 1990 Steel Wheels tour in Europe (with a giant *Blade Runner*–inspired set) was filmed in IMAX (images 10 times the size of 35mm) to be shown on screens that can be "8 stories high." The Stones are helped by the Uptown Horns and (too many) other sidemen. Haskell Wexler was the camera consultant. It's been screened at museums.

AT THE SLEAZIES

(Leoram, 1991) **D:** Herb Padilla Jr.
S: Paul Hugli **P:** Jeff Valencia

Rocky and Electra are the sleaze version of Siskel and Ebert. Rocky (Rob Nutt) is a funny-looking, beer-swilling, blond punk with shades, and Electra (Royce) is a sarcastic dominatrix with a ponytail and a riding crop. They introduce nine rare nudie-movie trailers, then review the films while insulting each other. The reviewer segments are actually funny, very well done (for a change), and the actors have no problem with the many big words. The real reason to own this tape, though, is to see the incredible trailers. Here are the original trailers for *Orgy of the Dead* and *Please Don't Eat My Mother!* More obscure ones are for *Dr. Sex* and *The Peeping Phantom* (he's a monster in a cape chasing strippers around a theater). Two of the best are for nudie/drug movies, *Smoke of Evil* and *Acid Dreams*. A bonus trailer is for a "European" book, *Stag Party Pictures* ("For he-men only"!). This book was sold in theaters along with 12 photos (in a plain envelope) for only $12! Selling books like this was common in 60s adult theaters. At the Roxy in Cleveland, the pitchman (a guy who looked like he'd escaped from a carnival) appeared in person. He also sold candy bars "with one—five—ten—or—more—dollar bills in them!'

THE ATTIC

(Unicorn, 1979) **D/S:** George Edwards
S: Tony Crechales

The Attic is an obscure but pretty good PG-rated modern gothic psychological drama filmed in Wichita, Kansas. Ray Milland is real nasty as the domineering father in a wheelchair. Carrie Snodgress is his mousy librarian daughter who has to take care of him. She imagines how to humiliate or kill him and spends time with her chimp, Dickie. With Rosemary Murphy, Ruth Cox, and Marjorie Eaton. Edwards produced Curtis Harrington movies. Gary Graver was the cinematographer.

ATTILA

(SW, 1954) **D:** Pietro Francisci **S:** Ennio De Concini, Primo Zeglio **P:** Carlo Ponti, Dino De Laurentiis
Italy/France (*Attila: Flagello di Dio*)

Anthony Quinn stars as Attila the Hun in a color spectacle considered pretty bloody in its day. With Sophia Loren as his woman, Irene Papas, Henri Vidal, and Eduardo Ciannelli. Joseph E. Levine released it in the US in 1958 to capitalize on Loren's fame. Quinn had also costarred in *Ulysses* for the same producers. Francisci also directed the famous first Steve Reeves *Hercules (1959).*

AUDITIONS

(Wizard, 1978) **D:** Harry Tampa/
Hurwitz **S/P:** Charles Band

A narrator claims that real people have been secretly filmed auditioning for *Fairytales II* on movie sets. An offscreen voice tells each person to strip and do various things. Several nude women masturbate for the camera, one with a skeleton foot. Linnea Quigley, as "an underage star-struck kid," does a wild nude dance in a dungeon, then has sex in various positions and is part of an "S&M fantasy." This almost-X, fake-documentary "comedy" has some awful *Gong Show*–type scenes and naked women (and men) talking endlessly. The cast includes porno stars Ronda Jo Petty, Rick Lutz, William Margold, and Jack Cassidy, plus Stumpy the Midget. The music is from producer Band's *Laserblast.* Quigley was also in *Fairytales.*

AUNTIE LEE'S MEAT PIES

(Columbia, 1991) **D/S:** J. F. Robertson **S/P:** Gerald Stein

Karen Black is a Satanist who sends out her four cheerful, beautiful nieces to lure men back so they can be killed, ground up, and sold as pies. Members of a heavy-metal band are the main victims. The humor is pretty odd, the FX are laughable, and Kristine Rose, Ava Fabian, Teri Weigel, and Pia Reyes (all from the pages of *Playboy*) do not have the expected nude scenes. Each one has her own "fantasy room," though, and there's also a full-grown female "baby." The cast includes Michael Berryman (in a larger than usual role) as a handyman, Pat Morita as the sherrif, Huntz Hall (!), and Kasha. The Mentors and Suicidal Tendencies are heard on the soundtrack. Robertson produced *The Crawling Hand* and later made many porno features as "Adele Robbins."

AURORA ENCOUNTER

(Starmaker, 1985) **D/P:** Jim McCullough Sr.
S/P: Jim McCullough Jr.

Jack Elam stars with Peter Brown in a family feature about a UFO in 1897 Texas. The odd cast includes the late country singer Dottie West, the late Spanky McFarland (from the *Our Gang/Little Rascals* series) as the governor, Carol Bagdasarian, and director Charles B. Pierce as a preacher. The alien is played by a dying, prematurely aged kid (Micky Hays) with progeria. It was shot outside Dallas at "the Big D ranch."

AUTOMAN

(1983) **D:** Lee H. Katzin **S/P:** Glen Larson

This is the pilot for a (very) short-lived ABC-TV series that copied the movie *Tron.* Desi Arnaz Jr. creates a holograph crime-fighter (Chuck Wagner) with a supercar and a talking computer-cursor helper. With Robert Lansing, Camilla Sparv, and Patrick Macnee as the villain. Larson was the guy responsible for series like *Buck Rogers, Battlestar Galactica,* and *Knightrider.*

AUTOPSIA DE UN FANTASMA

(Sinister, 1966) **D/P:** Ismael Rodriguez
S: Armando Crispini, Lucio Baitistrada
Mexico (*Autopsy of a Ghost*)

John Carradine was in quite a few south-of-the-border movies, but this slapstick comedy/horror oddity also stars Basil Rathbone and Cameron Mitchell! Despite the three English-speaking stars (who are all dubbed by others), *Autopsia* is available only in Spanish. It's a very goofy, sometimes funny color movie full of surprises. The credits are presented by great skeleton, witch, and devil marionettes in an old-fashioned circus-tent show. The story opens during a thunderstorm—it rains (actual) buckets! Rathbone is Canuto Pérez, a medieval ghost in a castle who talks to his own skeleton. He can disappear at will, sleeps in a coffin, and also has a talking tarantula. Mitchell is Moléculo, an absent-minded scientist wearing crooked bifocals. Best of all is Carradine as the Devil. He has a funny, deep voice, and a retractable tail he uses as a lasso, turns people into goats, and disguises himself as a mailman and an undertaker. His arms can lengthen (just like Freddy Krueger's) and in one scene he tells a little kid in an angel costume to jab a woman in the ass with a syringe. She turns into a robot with a skirt, a wig, and a Cousin Itt voice.

Bizarre Mexican comedians with impossibly high voices, looking like they've escaped from vaudeville, complicate matters. One guy dresses like a child, runs a torture chamber, and splashes everybody, including himself, in gasoline, before being banished to Hell. *Autopsia* has hippies, sexy women, a gorilla in a dog house, men in drag, classical music, instrumental rock, comic signs in English, and some fun special effects. Eventually, we discover that it's all a play directed by the Devil. *"Este es el fin!"* The stars look like they're having a good time. Carradine and Rathbone were also both in the American *Hillbillies in a Haunted House,* filmed around the same time (just before Rathbone died).

AUTOPSY

(Mogul, 1973) **D:** José M. Forque   Spain (*Tarot; Ángela*)

Sue Lyon marries blind old Fernando Rey but has sex with his valet. The maid and cook become involved in the murder-for-money plot. With Gloria Grahame. Not to be confused with the 1973 Spanish Mondo movie or the 1976 Italian movie with Mimsy Farmer (from *Prism*) with the same title.

AUTUMN BORN

(Monterey, 1979) **D/P:** Lloyd Simandl   Canada

Dorothy Stratton stars in her first feature, the one described in *Star 80* as "a traumatic bondage film." In it, she's a 17-year-old orphan about to inherit a financial empire. She's tied up, subjected to brainwashing, and whipped. It was released on video only after she was murdered in real life. Also with Roberta Bizeau. The same year, Stratton was in *Americathon* and *Skatetown, USA.*

AVALANCHE

(1994) **D:** Paul Shapiro **S:** Tim Redman
P: Jonathan Goodwill   Canada

Michael Gross and his teen daughter (Deanna Milligan) and young son are trapped in a snowbound house in the Canadian Rockies, also containing a seemingly indestructable killer diamond thief (David Hasselhoff). The Fox TV movie was filmed in British Columbia.

THE AVENGERS

(EMG series, 1961–69)

The wonderful original British spy/fantasy *The Avengers* series starred Patrick Macnee as John Steed, paired first with Ian Hendry, then with a series of very modern women who wore great clothes and knew martial arts: Honor Blackman as Catherine Gale (1962–64), Diana Rigg as Mrs. Emma Peel (1965–68), then Linda Thorson as Tara King (1968–69). Blackman quit and played Pussy Galore in *Goldfinger,* and Rigg quit and was in *On Her Majesty's Secret Service.* The Rigg episodes are the coolest, and many are now on tape. Some of the Blackman episodes (never shown in the US on TV) are also on tape and provide a fascinating look at how the series evolved. There are 65 53-minute episodes available. The first episode that was on tape was "A Touch of Brimestone" (1966), and it was sold in the S&M section of porno stores. There was also *The New Avengers* (1976–79) with Macnee and Joanna Lumley.

AVENGING ANGEL

(Starmaker, 1985) **D/S:** Robert Vincent O'Neil
S: Joseph M. Cala **P:** Sandy Howard, Keith Rubinstein

Betsy Russell takes over the Molly/Angel role in this sequel to *Angel* (1983). The former Hollywood teen hooker is now a law student packing a .357 Magnum who goes undercover as a hooker to avenge the death of her detective friend. Rory Calhoun and Susan Tyrrell return to lighten things up and are joined by a bag lady and transvestites, Ossie Davis, Ross Hagen as a hit man, Lynda Weismeier, Charlene Jones, Deborah Vorhees, Karen Mani, and Hoke Howell. Another actress took over for *Angel III.*

THE AVENGING CONSCIENCE

(Video Yesterday, 1914) **D/S/P:** D. W. Griffith

This is one of the oldest horror features available on tape and was a major all-star release in its day. It's based on Edgar Allan Poe's story "The Tell Tale Heart," with touches of the poem "Annabel Lee." The editing and double exposures were advanced at the time, and the film has Griffith's typical religious touches, not found in Poe. Henry B. Walthall stars as the killer who has visions of Christ and Moses before he kills his uncle and walls up the body "for the love of Annabel Lee" (Blanche Sweet). With Donald Crisp, Dorothy Gish, and Mae Marsh. Griffith made it at Reliance-Majestic. It's 78 minutes long. Many other silent Griffith films are available on tape, including his famous epics *Intolerance* (1915) and *The Birth of a Nation* (1916).

AVENGING FORCE

(Media, 1986) **D:** Sam Firstenberg
S/A: James Booth **P:** Golan/Globus

The martial-arts fighters from Firstenberg's *American Ninja* movies return as different characters. Michael Dudikoff is agent Matt Hunter, and Steve James is a kung-fu-fighting candidate for senator in Louisiana. Star villain John P. Ryan is the leader of "the Pentacle," a white supremacist group. Ryan dies at the end, but in the real world he might be David Duke. With James Booth, Bill "Superfoot" Wallace, a manhunt in the bayou, and the spectacle of lots of tourists being killed during Mardi Gras by ninjas.

AVENGING GODFATHER

(Active, Intergobal 1977) **D/S:** J. Robert Wagoner
P/A: Rudy Ray Moore **S:** Cliff Roquemore
(*Disco Godfather*)

Comedian Rudy Ray Moore, from Fort Smith, Arkansas, was famous for his X-rated "party albums" before he became a movie star in *Dolemite* (1975). This was his fifth movie, and it's an amazing, PG-rated, anti-drug, action movie/ musical. Active changed the title for the video because they don't realize that "disco" is now a profitable nostalgia word, just like "Hollywood" or "rock and roll." Moore plays Tucker Williams, "the Disco Godfather," at his own popular Blueberry Hill club. Every night he wears outrageous jumpsuits and commands the mixing boards, rapping to the house, "Put your weight on it! Put your weight on it!" His student basketball-star nephew Bucky shows up on PCP ("The newest psychedelic chemical of the 70s!") and promptly freaks out. Tucker starts a one-man "Attack the wack!" campaign, confronts pushers and criminal chemists, and visits a hospital ward where a PCP victim has a flashback to when she roasted and served her baby for dinner. As Tucker, Rudy is determined, likable, and believable (except when his double shows up for fight scenes). This movie is jammed with incredible freak-out sequences that could have been inspired by *Glen or Glenda.* A skeleton walks, eyes light up, a cartoon demon appears, and a witch cuts off Bucky's hands! There's an exorcism, a doctor prescribes shock treatments, and gangsters snort coke off the cover of the *Saturday Night Fever* soundtrack album! This movie has a soundtrack album too, and it's worth a whole lot more than copies of the album from that Travolta movie! With Carol Speed (the star of *Abby*). Watch this tape and find out what you've been missing!

AVENGING SPIRIT = DOMINIQUE

THE AWFUL DR. ORLOF

(SW, 1961) **D/S:** Jesús Franco **P:** Sergio Newman
Spain/France (*Gritos en la Noche*)

In 1912 the blind Morpho (Richard Valle) kidnaps women and takes them to a castle on an island. Dr. Orlof (Howard Vernon) just wants a new face for his disfigured daughter (Diana Lorys). A ballerina (also Lorys) goes undercover to help her police-inspector boyfriend catch the killer. Maria Silva is a cabaret dancer (she sings in Spanish), and Franco himself can be seen playing the piano. This b/w film has some impressive atmospheric shots, especially the ones with the bizarre Morpho. The Frank Henenlotter Sexy Shocker release is the dubbed American version released in 1964 by Sigma III. The subtitled French version from Video Search of Miami has some brief additional nudity. Franco returned to the Dr. Orlof(f) character many times.

AXE

(SW, 1974) **D/S/A:** Frederic R. Freidel **P:** J. G. "Pat" Paterson Jr.   (*California Axe Murders; Lisa Lisa*)

Three escaped cons attack a disturbed young girl (Lisa Lee) living on a farm with her catatonic grandfather. She knows how to decapitate chickens, and she's prepared to fight back with an axe and a razor. This is 65 minutes of dreary rural revenge produced in Charlotte, North Carolina by the man who made *Dr. Gore. Axe* was rereleased in 1983 and was once available on a tape with *Scream in the Streets.*

BABES IN TOYLAND

(Orion, 1986) **D:** Clive Donner **S:** Paul Zindel **P:** Tony Ford, Neil T. Maffeo

A pre-*femme fatale* Drew Barrymore stars with Keanu Reeves (!) in an overlong (150-minute) NBC-TV version of the Victor Herbert operetta filmed in Munich. With Richard Mulligan (who was soon to marry a porno star in real life) as Barnaby, Eileen Brennan, Jill Scholen, and Pat Morita. Leslie Bricusse wrote a new score. Zindel also wrote the 80s TV version of *Alice in Wonderland*. By the way, *Babes in Toyland* was also a great three-woman band from Minneapolis who most likely took their name from this version instead of the 1934 or even the 1961 version.

BABY CART series: *See* LIGHTNING SWORDS OF DEATH and LONE WOLF

BABY DOLL

(Warner, 1956) **D:** Elia Kazan **S/P:** Tennessee Williams

This atmospheric film set in the backwoods was condemned by the Legion of Decency and the Catholic Church and was banned in many areas. John Waters said it made him decide to be a director. Karl Malden burns the cotton mill of his rival, Sicilian Eli Wallach (in his film debut), who gets revenge by seducing Malden's young still-virginal wife (Carroll Baker, who was nominated for an Oscar). The acting of the entire cast (which includes Mildred Dunnock, Rip Torn, and Lonny Chapmen) is inspired. The great soundtrack by Kenyon Hopkins includes "Shame Shame Shame" by Smiley Lewis. It was filmed in Benoit, Mississippi.

THE BABY DOLL MURDERS

(Republic, 1992) **D/S/P:** Paul Leder **P:** Ralph Thornberg

Each time a psycho in a hooded sweatshirt is about to kill, we get to see the victim naked first (usually having sex). This "erotic thriller" is packed with comedy and sex scenes. Jeff Kober (a guy with a really strange face) and Bobby Di-Ciccio are LA police detectives who are after the killer. The suspects include a mechanic and a deaf man, but you'll probably figure out who's leaving those baby dolls by the bodies. With John Saxon as the top cop, Melanie Smith, Julie McCullough, and Eileen Seeley. The entire cast is proudly introduced at the end. Leder was in his 4th decade of turning out this stuff.

BABY FACE NELSON

(1957) **D:** Don Siegel **S:** Irving Shulman, Daniel Mainwaring **P:** Al Zimbalist

Mickey Rooney has one of his best 50s roles as the famous Depression-era gangster. Carolyn Jones costars as his girlfriend. With Leo Gordon (perfect as Dillinger), Ted De Corsia, Cedric Hardwicke, Anthony Caruso, Jack Elam, John Hoyt, and Elisha Cook Jr. Rooney was back playing short gangsters in *The Last Mile* and *The Big Operator* (both 1959).

BABYLON FIVE

(1993) **D:** Richard Compton **S:** J. Michael Straczynski **P:** Robert Latham Brown

The feature pilot for the TV series stars Michael O'Hare as the commander of a futuristic space ship whose huge station includes humans and members of four alien races. Jerry Dole costars as the security chief, with Mira Furlan as a bald alien, Tamlyn Tomita, Patricia Talman, and Johnny Sekka. With music by Stewart Copeland and computer FX. Straczynski was the executive producer and creator, and Harlan Ellison was a consultant. The recast, syndicated series (with regulars O'Hare, Dole, and Furlan, plus Claudia Christian, Peter Jurasik, Andreas Katsulas, Stephen Furst, and Bill Mumy) debuted in 1994 (at the same time as the very similar but more expensive *Star Trek* spinoff *Deep Space Nine*), with Miles Copeland as executive producer.

THE BABY MAKER

(Warner, 1970) **D/S:** James Bridges **P:** Richard Goldstone

In this controversial (at the time) Robert Wise production from short-lived National General, hippie Barbara Hershey agrees to conceive a baby with a suburban man for $500. Scott Glenn (in his first feature), as her boyfriend, plays the guitar, takes psychedelic drugs, and has an affair. He rides a motorcycle in this and his next two features (*Angels: Hard as They Come* and *Hex*). It's complete with dated clothes and music. With Sam Groom, Colin Wilcox-Horne, Jeannie Berlin, Phyllis Coates, and Brenda Sykes.

BABY: SECRET OF THE LOST LEGEND

(Touchstone, 1985) **D:** B. W. L. Norton **S:** Clifford and Ellen Green **P:** Jonathan T. Taplin (*Dinosaur: Secret of the Lost Legend*)

Paleontologists William Katt and Sean Young find an inflatable-looking, cute baby dinosaur in the jungles of the Ivory Coast. Its father is killed and its mother is kidnapped. Young is also kidnapped (by tribesmen). Patrick McGoohan is the leading scientist villain of this PG-rated *King Kong*-inspired Disney misfire.

THE BABYSITTER

(1969) **D:** Don Henderson **S/A:** James E. McLarty **P/A:** George E. Carey

A judge (Carey), about to sentence a motorcycle gang for a murder, is blackmailed with evidence of his affair with a teenage babysitter, Candy (Patricia Wymer). A counterframe is planned by planting marijuana on the bikers. With Kathy Williams and Robert Tessier. The music for this b/w, R-rated Crown International feature is by the Food. *Weekend with the Babysitter* was a follow-up.

THE BABYSITTER

(HBO, 1980) **D:** Peter Medak **S:** Jennifer Miller **P:** David Garcia

Stephanie Zimbalist stars as a psycho housekeeper who plays deadly mind games with the parents who hired her (William Shatner and Patty Duke). This ABC-TV movie also features John Houseman.

BABY SNAKES

(MPI, 1979) **D/P/A/M/E:** Frank Zappa

This part-live feature actually played theatrically. Originally 166 minutes, it was later trimmed to 91 minutes but is complete on tape. The concert is from Halloween 1977 in New York City and features lots of Zappa guitar work. With Adrien Belew, drummer Terry Bozzio, Roy Estrada, Peter Wolf, and Ron Delsener. If you're not a Zappa fanatic, the reason to watch *Baby Snakes* is the excellent clay animation by Bruce Brickford. *The Amazing Mr. Brickford* (MPI, 1987) is a solid hour of his animation (with Zappa's music).

BACHELOR PARTY

(Fox, 1984) **D/S:** Neal Israel **S:** Pat Proft **P:** Ron Moler, Bob Israel

The maker of *Tunnelvision* and *Americathon* were responsible for this teen hit featuring Tom Hanks and hookers at a wild party. Tawny Kitaen is his future bride, and don't miss the sight of the head of William Tepper on the naked body of Monique Gabrielle. With Adrian Zmed, Michael Dudikoff, George Grizzard, Brett Clark, John Bloom, Ji-Tu Cumbuka, Angela Aames and Roseanne Katon.

BACHELOR'S DREAM

(Rhino, 1967) **D/P:** A. C. Stevens/ Stephen C. Apostoloff **S:** Jason Underwood (*Bachelor Party*)

This feature, advertised as being "in loving color and gorgeous Astrovision," is a crudely made throwback to early nudies like *The Immoral Mr. Teas*. Funny-looking everyman Abner Bidle imagines himself alone in a theater watching strippers on stage. Most of the feature is tinted b/w footage that Stephens owned but did not film himself. Several new full-color scenes (a blonde taking a bubble bath, a woman dancing topless at home with a stuffed bunny, and a brief lesbian encounter) were added. It's hard to imagine grown men paying to watch this in a theater in 1967, but they did. The video version is subtitled *Naked Dream of the Naughty Nerd* (!). On Rhino's Saturday Night Sleazies (Volume II) with *Lady Godiva Meets Tom Jones*.

BACKBEAT

(Polydor, 1994) **D/S:** Iain Softley **S:** Stephen Ward, Michael Thomas, Stephen Woolley, Phinola Dwyer   UK

This is the best movie ever made about the Beatles, and it almost makes you forget all their later overblown experimentation and Paul McCartney's epic ballad hits. It's about the Beatles when they were a hardworking, hard-rocking, pill-popping bar band playing before strip acts in Hamburg in 1961. It centers on Stu Sutcliff (Stephen Dorff) as the artist and bass player falling for Astrid Kirchner (Sheryl Lee) and on the jealous John Lennon (Ian Hart, also in the 1992 film *The Hours and the Times*). Astrid comes up with the famous haircuts, and Stu suffers from a brain hemmorhage, possibly brought on by a fight Lennon started. With Gary Bakewell as McCartney and Chris O'Neill as George Harrison. The excellent Virgin soundtrack (all covers of covers) features members of Nirvana, REM, Sonic Youth, and others as the early Beatles and was produced by Don Was.

George Harrison (Chris O'Neill), Stu Sutcliff (Stephen Dorff), and John Lennon (Ian Hart) in *Backbeat*.

BACK DOOR TO HELL

(1964) **D:** Monte Hellman **S:** Richard A. Guttman **P:** Fred Ross   US/Philippines

Singer Jimmie Rodgers (whose hits had stopped coming), the still-struggling Jack Nicholson, and John Hackett star as Americans in this WWII story. They take back a town with the help of some Filipino freedom-fighters, but the Japanese threaten to execute one child per hour if the Americans don't give up. Nicholson gets drunk, worries, wonders, and is eventually shot. Conrad Maga and Annabelle Huggins are the Filipino stars. 20th Century–Fox released the Lippert production. Nicholson was in four Hellman movies in a row. This one was made back to back with *Flight to Fury* (1965).

BACKDRAFT

(MCA, 1991) **D:** Ron Howard **S:** Gregory Widen **P:** Brian Grazer, Pen Densham, John Watson

Howard made a more serious version of the kind of all-star 70s disaster movies Irwin Allen used to make but with the addition of expensive, state-of-the-art ILM FX. It's long (135 minutes). Kurt Russell and William Baldwin star as firemen brothers at odds with each other while fighting large, picturesque fires. Robert De Niro is the chief arson investigator. With Donald Sutherland, Scott Glenn, Jennifer Jason Leigh, Rebecca De Mornay,

Jason Gedrick, J. T. Walsh, David Crosby, and the director's brother Clint. The climactic fire in a chemical warehouse was the basis for a Universal Studios tour attraction. A letterboxed edition is available.

BACKFIRE

(Vidmark, 1987) **D:** Gilbert Cates **S:** Larry Brand, Rebecca Reynolds **P:** Danton Rissner   US/Canada

Karen Allen is married to a disturbed but rich Nam vet (Jeff Fahey) who has violent flashbacks. Keith Carradine is a mysterious drifter. The complex *film noir* drive-a-person-to-suicide plot includes the reliable blood-from-a-shower trick and Allen in topless scenes. With Bernie Casey and Dean Paul Martin, who died after production (in British Columbia). It debuted on Showtime.

BACK FROM HELL

(Kashmir, 1992) **D/S/P/C/M/E:** Matt Jaissle

A black priest (Shawn Scarbrough, who narrates) visits his old friend Jack (Larry DuBois), a young Hollywood star who is in hiding after selling his soul to the devil. Jack also confesses that he "smoked a doobie with a talk show host." The two guys encounter masked killers with axes, a possessed cop, zombies, gore, and spurting blood. A hand from a Bible grabs Father Aaron by the crotch and he eventually fights back with a chainsaw, yelling, "Tell Satan I said, kiss my black ass!" The all-male cast 16mm feature was shot in rural areas around Ann Arbor by the then 20-year-old director.

BACK IN ACTION

(MCA, 1994) **D:** Steve DeMarco **S:** Karl Schiffman **P:** George Flak

An LA detective (Roddy Piper) joins a former Special Forces agent and vigilante (Billy Banks) to battle bad guys and rescue Banks' sister (Bobbie Phillips) in Toronto. The SGE release is mostly fights and shooting, with some torture thrown in.

BACKSTAB

(1990) **D:** James Kaufman **S:** Steve Koval **P:** Tom Berry

James Brolin stars as an architect having an affair, in this *Fatal Attraction* copy, with Meg Foster, June Chadwick, and Isabelle Truchon (featured in the sex scenes).

BACKSTREET DREAMS

(Vidmark, 1990) **D:** Rupert Hitzig **D/S/A:** Jason O'Malley **P:** Lance H. Robbins

You don't want to see this Brooke Shields movie set in Hoboken, New Jersey, but you might want to know about it. O'Malley, the creator and star,

plays Dino, an Irish-Italian wrestler who doubles as an enforcer for gangsters and has a slutty young wife (Sherilyn Fenn) and an autistic little boy. Shields plays Stevie, a social worker who softens him up, tells him about Neal Cassidy, and teaches his son. Meanwhile, a drug deal in Newark with some black men gets violent, the boy is kidnapped, and the young stars fall in love. Filmed in Hoboken, Weehawken, and Union City (and in LA), this vanity production also features Burt Young, Anthony Franciosa, Nick Cassavetes, Joe Pantoliano, and Ray "Boom Boom" Mancini. Hitzig also directed *Night Visitor*.

BACK STREET JANE

(Scorched Earth, 1989) **D/S/P/C/M/E:** Ronnie Cramer

Cramer's first feature (in 16mm b/w) is a great-looking story of "blank generation" people who live for drugs. Two bored, unemployed friends, Diane (Monica McFarland) and Jane (Marlene Shapiro), sneak into a dealer's house to rip him off. They find him murdered, so they slowly and methodically track down the killers to blackmail them. Nicole, a Eurasian dragon lady (Sheila Ivy Traister), kills her male partner and gives half her coke stash to the blackmailers, after she puts arsenic in it. She goes to stay with two guys, gets high, and talks about monster movies before they all nod out. There's effective (offscreen) sex and violence and nonstop double-crosses and plot surprises in the tradition of movies like *The Killing*. The actors, who do fine, low-key work, have all been in plays or TV shows. Cramer, based in Denver, made excellent rock videos for his group, Alarming Trends, first.

BACK TO BACK

(MGM, 1989) **D:** John Kincade **S:** George Francis Skrow **P:** Brad Krevoy, Steven Stabler

Hitchhiker Apollonia joins the two sons of a disgraced armored-car driver on a search to find a lost fortune in the Nevada hills. With a good cast, including Bill Paxton, Ben Johnson, Susan Anspach, and Luke Askew. Apollonia was also in *Ministry of Vengeance* for Roger Corman's Concorde.

BACK TO THE BEACH

(Paramount, 1987) **D:** Lyndall Hobbs **S:** Peter Krikes, Steve Meerson, Christopher Thompson **P:** Frank Mancuso Jr.

Frankie Avalon and Annette Funicello (who were the executive producers) have settled down in Ohio, more than 20 years after their *Beach Party* movies. They go on a Hawaii beach vacation with their kids and encounter has-been 60s TV stars Connie Stevens, Don Adams, Bob Denver, Alan Hale, the surviving cast members of *Leave It to Beaver*, and Edd "Kookie" Byrnes. Dick Dale and the late Stevie Ray Vaughn play "Pipeline." With Lori Loughlin, Fishbone, and Pee-wee Herman (who sings "Surfin Bird"). This PG film was "based on characters created by Lou Russoff" back at AIP. The original movies had better guest stars.

BACK TO THE FUTURE

(MCA, 1985) **D/S:** Robert Zemeckis **S/P:** Bob Gale **P:** Neil Canton

Original star Eric Stoltz was fired well into production, so replacement Michael J. Fox (who had been starring in President Reagan's favorite TV program, *Family Ties*) became the time-traveling Marty McFly. This Steven Spielberg production from 20th Century-Fox made tons of money. Dr. Brown (Christopher Lloyd) and a nuclear-powered DeLorean take McFly back to the nostalgic and simpler 50s to help his own father (the always weird Crispin Glover) stand up to bullies and meet his mother (Lea Thompson). There's a near-incest theme with his mother in this PG-rated hit. A theater of the past (showing a Ronald Reagan western) that later became a porno theater is a message the president himself must have enjoyed. Huey Lewis and the News do "The Power of Love," a song we all got real sick of, and the scene where McFly invents rock and roll by showing a black band how to play is one of the most irritating of the decade. With Marc McClure, Casey Siemaszko, James Tolkan, Thomas F. Wilson, Elisabeth Shue, Billy Zane, and George "Buck" Flower as a bum. The ILM FX (used in the entire series) are typically great, and the soundtrack is on MCA.

BACK TO THE FUTURE, PART II

(MCA, 1989) **D:** Robert Zemeckis
S/P: Bob Gale **P:** Neil Canton

This one starts right where *Part I* left off. The limited talents of Michael J. Fox were spread a little thin playing three roles at once, and at nearly 30 he was a little too old for a teen. The sequel was a flop compared to the original. He travels to 2015 and plays his own son (and daughter), then goes back to 1985, then back to 1955. Lloyd, Thompson, Wilson (the villain), Siemaszko, Tolkan, Zane, and Shue all returned. Glover asked for too much money. Wilson steals the DeLorean time-machine car and goes back to 1955 to bet on sports events. With Joe Flaherty, Flea, Jason Scott Lee, and Buck Flower. Capra's classic but overquoted *It's a Wonderful Life* is the major plot inspiration. The end is just a setup for *Part III*, which was filmed at the same time, a practice that used to result in lawsuits and criticism but by the late 80s was accepted as just business as usual.

BACK TO THE FUTURE, PART III

(MCA, 1990) **D:** Robert Zemeckis
S/P: Bob Gale **P:** Neil Canton

Fox, Lloyd, Thompson, and Shue return again in a comedy/science-fiction/western set mostly in 1885. With Mary Steenburgen and western character actors Matt Clark, Pat Buttram, Harey Carey Jr., and Dub Taylor. The ILM FX are fine as usual, and the group ZZ Top shows up for a cameo. Crispin Glover sued over *Parts II and III* (where Jeffrey Weissman was given his role and copied his acting style). The diminishing financial returns made this the last stop for the overage teen time-traveler. There's also a *Secrets of the "Back to the Future" Trilogy* tape from MCA.

BACKTRACK

(Vestron, 1988) **D/S/A:** Dennis Hopper
S: Rachel Kronstadt **P:** Dick Clark, Dan Paulson   (*Do It the Hard Way; Catch Fire*)

Originally this movie was 3 hours long. Hopper had his name removed from a 98-minute version, but a 102-minute tape was released in 1992. It's an excellent road movie with gangsters, *penitentes* in New Mexico, action, and art arguments. Hopper plays a calm, sax-playing hitman named Milo who loves Charlie Parker's music. Jodie Foster plays the woman he's hired to kill, a successful LA artist who makes LCD sign art with thought-provoking messages (by real artist Jenny Holtzer). Milo claims he's given up his whole life for her, and she has no choice but to spend the rest of her life with him. The great cast of hoods includes Dean Stockwell, Vincent Price, John Turturro, and a ranting Joe Pesci. And there's Fred Ward and Sy Richardson as cops, Charlie Sheen, Julie Adams, Toni Basil, and Bob Dylan as a sculptor.

BACKWOODS

(Cinema Group, 1986) **D:** Dean Crow
S: Charles Joseph **P:** Maureen Sweeney   (*Geek!*)

A hillbilly father and his geek son terrorize and kill urban campers. It's from Indiana. *Luther the Geek* (from Illinois) covered some of the same territory.

BAD ATTITUDE

(Xenon, 1990) **D:** Bill Cummings
S: Crane Webster **P:** Bruce Clark

A demoted undercover drug cop (Leon, who resembles Jimmy Cliff in *The Harder They Come* on his custom-built chopper) battles local drug dealers. The tough bad guys are both overacting women in male drag (!) who never seem to leave their van. A tattooed Vietnamese woman in black leather (Gina Lim) works for a blind street preacher, but neither are what they seem. There isn't really enough action, violence, or sex, but Susan Finque is pretty outrageous as Mendez (she/he bites an ear off), and the ending (a shootout with female vigilantes) is worth seeing. Filmed in Seattle. Leon, later in big-budget movies and the star of *Cool Runnings*, was also associate producer.

BAD BLONDE

(1952) **D:** Reginald Le Borg **S:** Guy Elmes, Richard Landau **P:** Anthony Hinds   UK (*The Flanagan Boy*)

In this Hammer film (released by Lippert in the US), Barbara Payton plays Lorna, a scheming blonde who seduces a boxer (Tony Wright) and convinces him to murder her fight-manager husband (Frederick Valk). Payton was also in *The Four-Sided Triangle* (1953), a Hammer science-fiction movie. The company was capitalizing on the actress's many real-life scandals. In the early 60s she was arrested for prostitution.

BAD BLOOD

(1981) **D:** Mike Newell **S/P:** Andrew Brown   New Zealand/UK

During WWII a farmer (Jack Thompson) kills seven people and is hunted in the bush country. The film is based on a real incident.

BAD BLOOD

(Academy, 1989) **D/P:** Chuck Vincent
S: Craig Horrall   (*A Woman Obsessed*)

"Ruth Raymond" (aka 70s porno star Georgina Spelvin) stars in a Baby Jane-type role. She's an artist living in a Long Island mansion who imagines her dead husband has been reincarnated as her grandson. Various characters are killed. With Linda Blair as her daughter-in-law (who spends most of the movie in bed), Troy Donahue, Christina Veronica, and Jane Hamilton/Veronica Hart. It was one of many direct-to-video features made by Vincent and Horrall before both died of AIDS.

BAD BOY

(Allied Artists, 1949) **D:** Kurt Neuman
S: Robert Hardy Andrews **P:** Paul Short

"Danny is going straight—straight to the electric chair!" That's how they advertised the third feature with Audie Murphy, America's most decorated WWII soldier. It was his first starring role, as a 16-year-old Dallas juvenile delinquent named Danny Lester. He's sent to a boys' ranch to reform. Lloyd Nolan and Jane Wyatt are the adult stars, with James Gleason, Stanley Clements, Martha Vickers, former child stars James (Jimmy) Lydon and Dickie Moore, Selena Royle (later in *Robot Monster*), and Tommy Cook (later in *Missile to the Moon*).

THE BAD BUNCH

(VCI, 1973) **D/S/A:** Greydon Clark
S/P: Alvin L. Fast   (*Tom; Nigger Lover*)

A war vet (Clark) goes to the Watts area of LA to deliver a letter from a black friend who died in Nam. He encounters his friend's hostile younger brother Tom aka Makimba (Tom Johnigar), hippie girls, gangsters, and Aldo Ray and Jock Mahoney as hateful cops. (Former screen Tarzan Mahoney had a stroke shortly afterward.) Most viewers agree that the film is "depressing and racist." A scene at a pool party is an excuse for naked women (like Bambi Allen and Jacquelin Cole). The theme song is called "Nigger Lover," and the music is by Ed Cobb, once known for his psychedelic and garage-rock hits. It was rated GP, then R. Exploitation specialist Mohammed "Mardi" Rustam was the executive producer of this Dimension release and appears in the cast. It was filmed on location.

BAD CHANNELS

(Paramount, 1992) **D:** Ted Nicolaou
S: Jackson Barr **P:** Keith Rayson

A small-town DJ (Paul Hipp) is held hostage by aliens during a marathon. Nothing much happens in this boring, dumb comedy with terrible effects, but every once in a while a rock video wakes you up. One of them is a Devo takeoff, and one character imitates Crispin Glover. With Charlie Spradling, Martha Quinn as a reporter, Aaron Lustig, and Sonny Carl Davis. The box tries to lure renters with "music by Blue Oyster Cult." They (or what was left of them) do two forgettable songs. Nicolaou also made the (much better) *Subspecies* movies.

BAD DREAMS

(CBS/Fox, 1988) **D/S:** Andrew Fleming
S: Steven E. deSouza **P:** Gale Anne Hurd

Richard Lynch (with his real-life damaged face), is a Jim Jones type of cult leader who dies during a mass suicide in a fire in 1973. Somehow he returns years later to terrorize the lone survivor (Jennifer Rubin) when she comes out of a coma. Most of this unsuccessful horror movies takes place in an insane asylum for young people (as did the previous year's *Nightmare on Elm Street III*, also with Rubin). With Harris Yulin as a crazed shrink, Bruce Abbott, Dean Cameron, and Sy Richardson. The effects are by Michelle Burke. The soundtrack, on Varèse Sarabande, was composed by Jay Ferguson (from Spirit) and features the original "I Had Too Much to Dream" by the Electric Prunes and "The Time Has Come Today" by the Chambers Brothers.

BADGE OF THE ASSASSIN

(Vidmark, 1985) **D:** Mel Damski **S:** Lawrence Roman

A CBS-TV movies with James Woods playing a (real) DA chasing after three 70s cop-killers in Harlem, San Francisco, and New Orleans. Yaphet Kotto and Alex Rocco help him, and Pam Grier and Rae Dawn Chong are Black Liberation Army revolutionaries in the Bronx. It's based on a best-selling 1979 novel by Robert K. Tannenbaum. The music is by Tom Scott.

BAD GEORGIA ROAD

(VCI, 1977) **D/S/P:** John C. Broderick **S:** Jeffrey Bernini

Gary Lockwood and Carol Lynley star in this southern-appeal drive-in movie. With Royal Dano, Mary Woronov, and George "Buck" Flower in the solid exploitation cast.

BAD GIRLS (1974): *See* DELINQUENT SCHOOLGIRLS

BAD GIRLS

(Fox, 1994) **D:** Jonathan Kaplan **S:** Ken Friedman, Yolande Finch **P:** Linda Obst

Madeleine Stowe is the prostitute heroine sentenced to death for killing an abusive customer in this revenge western set in 19th-century Oregon. She teams up with Mary Stuart Masterson, Drew Barrymore, and Andie MacDowell, and they flee from Pinkerton detectives and battle bad guys led by James Russo. With James LeGros, Robert Loggia, and Dermot Mulroney as a good-guy gunslinger. Director Tamara Davis was fired after three weeks of production. The script was rewritten, and Kaplan, who made drive-in hits in the 70s, took over. Jerry Goldsmith provided the score. The unrated version on video includes three extra minutes.

BAD GIRLS DO CRY

(Sinister, 1954) **D:** Sid Melton **P:** Howard Freeman

David F. Friedman created the ad campaign for this road-show exploitation classic. It has no synced dialogue, and in some scenes two people just look at each other, not even opening their mouths, while voices are heard. It's the sad tale of

small-town blond beauty Sally Downs (Misty Ayers). She goes to a model agency ("Why not?"), is attacked by the typical slimeball guy with a little mustache ("What a cheap trick. And I fell for it!"), is shot up with drugs, and ends up a hooker and prisoner. Sally and the other women undress a lot, showing off garter belts and underwear, and there's a cat fight. Comedy relief is provided by an insurance man who can't get laid, a gay customer who doesn't respond to a sexy dance, the *Dean and Jean* radio soap opera, and an alcoholic madam who accidentally drinks milk and spits it out. I liked the part where a man hides behind a phone pole to avoid being shot. Believe it or not, this 63-minute wonder was released to theaters in 1965. Director Melton was an actor who played Uncle Charlie, the manager, on *The Danny Thomas Show* and Alf on *Green Acres*.

BAD GIRLS' DORMITORY

(Active, 1985) **D/S:** Tim Kincaid
P: Cynthia DePaula

This trashy women-in-prison movie was made in New York by a director who had been known as Joe Gage when making all-male X-rated features. It was the first of many R movies he made over several years for the video market, and it features sex, drugs, and rape. It stars Teresa Farley, Jennifer Delora, Francis Raines, and Marita. Ed French provided the FX.

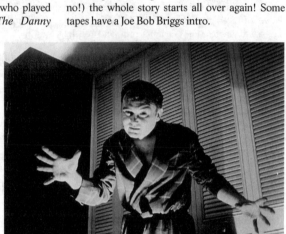

Doris Wishman's *Bad Girls Go to Hell*.

BAD GIRLS FROM MARS

(Vidmark, 1989) **D/S/P:** Fred Olen Ray **S:** Mark Thomas McGhee **P:** Grant Austin Waldman

The familiar plot of this one is about characters being killed off by a masked killer while making a grade-Z movie. Edy Williams stars as Emmanuelle, a famous madam who is turned on by the smell of garbage. She appears topless a lot (of course) and has a brief lesbian scene with Brinke Stevens. Also in the cast are Jay Richardson as a hammy actor and Jasae. Cinematographer Gary Graver, Ray, and Waldman all appear on camera, along with posters for other Ray features (a self-promotional device that Ed Wood Jr. used to use). The last line is "Will this movie ever end?" It was made in five days.

BAD GIRLS GO TO HELL

(Sleaziest, 1965)
D/S/P: "Dawn Whitman"/Doris Wishman

A b/w made-in-Manhattan marvel about the downfall of newlywed Meg Kelton (Gigi Darlene). After a happy shower with her businessman husband, he leaves, and she kills an attacking janitor in self-defense. Her voice-overs ask, "What have I done? Where can I go? I'll go to New York!" She arrives by bus at the Port Authority terminal (where we see closeups of lots of feet pounding the pavement) and heads for Central Park (where very loud bird-tweets are dubbed in). Now known as Ellen Green from Chicago, she goes home with a friendly guy who gets mad, chugs a bottle of

booze, and beats her with a belt. She escapes and moves in with Della, a lesbian. Ellen claims she's an acrobatic dancer and proves it by standing on her head in her underwear. Both women lounge around in bikini underwear while the camera goes to the left of the room, then to the right, then back again, and instrumental jazz and rock play. A newspaper XTRA! headline announces, POLICE SEEK BLONDE SUSPECT IN BOSTON MURDER CASE! After some (offscreen) lovemaking, she leaves and rents a room for $20 a week. The landlady's husband attacks her, so she takes a job as a companion to an older woman whose son turns out to be a detective on the Boston murder case! Meg is caught, but she wakes up screaming. It was all a dream! Then (oh no!) the whole story starts all over again! Some tapes have a Joe Bob Briggs intro.

BAD GIRLS IN THE MOVIES

(Vestron, 1986) **D/P:** Dominic Paris

This ill-conceived 56-minute compilation of uncredited scenes shows female delinquents and killers from various features. Some scenes are from *Satan's Sadists, Deadly Weapons*, and several other Doris Wishman movies. A "prison psychiatrist" stars in the wraparound sequences.

BAD GUYS

(IVE, 1985) **D:** Joel Silberg **S:** Brady W. Setwater, John Gillis **P:** John D. Backe, Myron A. Hyman

This dumb, PG-rated comedy about two suspended cops who become wrestlers features Adam Baldwin, James Booth, Ruth Buzzi, and lots of name wrestlers like Sergeant Slaughter. It was created by the talented, trend-following director of *Breakin'*, *Rappin'*, and *Lambada*.

BAD INFLUENCE

(RCA, 1990) **D:** Curtis Hanson
S: David Koepp **P:** Steve Tisch

Star Rob Lowe was in the news for his homemade sex video from Atlanta when this modernized *Strangers on a Train* variation was released. He plays a psycho in LA who befriends computer programmer James Spader, videotapes him having sex, and soon has him robbing liquor stores. With Lisa Zane, Joyce Meadows, Charisse Glen, and

Kathleen Wilhoite. The UCLA grad screenwriter went on to write scripts for films directed by Spielberg, De Palma, and others. There was a various artists soundtrack.

BADLANDS

(Warner, 1973) **D/S/P/A:** Terrence Malick

Martin Sheen and Sissy Spacek (who narrates) play the real Charles Starkweather and Caril Fugate in 1958. The infamous garbage collector turned killer starts by shooting his girlfriend's father (Warren Oates), and the couple flee through several states until they're captured. It's a great-looking film shot in Colorado (for an amazing $500,000), and it uses romantic pop songs coming from the radio instead of the expected rock and roll. This look at the boring 50s is more realistic than usual. Alan Vint, Gary Littlejohn, and Ramon Bieri are also in the cast. Malick has made only one other feature, *Days of Heaven* (1978). For other movies based on Starkweather, look for *The Sadist* and *Stark Raving Mad*.

BAD LIEUTENANT

(Live, 1992) **D/S:** Abel Ferrara **S/A:** Zoe Lund **P:** Edward Pressman, Mary Kane

Harvey Keitel goes all out as a nameless, corrupt, depraved, lapsed-Catholic New York City cop in serious debt. He's put on the case of a raped nun (Frankie Thorn) who forgives her attackers and refuses to name them. Keitel shoots, smokes, and snorts heroin and crack, drinks, sells drugs, gambles on Mets games, masturbates in front of some teen girls, and has sex with hookers. He also does a crying nude scene and has a vision of Christ (Paul Hipp) on the Cross. Screenwriter Lund, who plays his junkie girlfriend, was the star of Ferrara's *Ms. 45* (as Zoe Tamerlis). The music includes Scooly D rapping over Led Zeppelin riffs and the late Johnny Ace. An NC-17 and a shorter R-rated version are available. The video we saw had an anti-drug spot at the beginning. Ferrara made *Body Snatchers* next.

BAD LORD BYRON

(1949) **D:** David Mcdonald **S:** Terence Young, Anthony Thorne **P:** Aubrey Baring UK

Dennis Price, as the poet Lord Byron, faces a heavenly court that's reviewing his life. The cast includes Joan Greenwood, Mai Zetterling, and Ernest Thesiger.

BAD MANNERS

(HBO, 1984) **D/S:** Robert "Bobby" Houston **S:** Joseph Kwong **P:** Kim Jorgensen Canada (*Growing Pains*)

Some orphans spring a kid from a rich couple (Martin Mull and Karen Black) and totally trash the house. The orphanage is run by a sadistic nun (Anne DeSalvo) and her assistant, who uses cattle prods. With Kimmy Robertson and Edy Williams. At one time Disney was going to release this movie, but New World ended up with it. The director costarred in *The Hills Have Eyes*.

BAD MAN'S RIVER

(High Desert, 1971) **D/S:** Eugenio Martin **S:** Phillip Jordan Italy/Spain
(*E Continuavano a Fregarsi il Milione di Dollari*)

Lee Van Cleef leads an outlaw gang in a comic western. James Mason costars, with Gina Lollobrigida, Gianni Garko, and Diana Lorys. Scotia International released this with a PG rating in the US.

THE BAD SEED

(1985) **D:** Paul Wendkos **S/P:** George Eckstein

This is an ABC-TV remake of the 1956 feature (which is available from Warner). Both are based on Maxwell Anderson's play about an inherently evil little girl. Carrie Welles stars, with Blair Brown as her mother. David Carradine is creepy as Leroy, the handyman. With Lynn Redgrave and Richard Kiley.

BAD TASTE

(Magnum, 1987) **D/S/P/A/C/E:** Peter Jackson **S:** Tony Hiles, Ken Hammond New Zealand

Jackson (then in his 20s) took four years to make this unrated, 16-mm wonder, for which he also did the FX. It's a unique comic/action/gore/science-fiction movie. Government investigators on a small island discover that the entire population is missing. It turns out that aliens living in a house that's really a space ship have been using the people as junk food. Most of *Bad Taste* takes place in bright daylight near the ocean, so the outrageous (and well done) scenes of blood and dismemberment are all the more shocking. The down-under accents are pretty thick, and there are no females in the cast. The music by Michelle Scullion and the end theme by the Remnants are excellent. A picture disc soundtrack was released. Jackson returned with *The Feebles*.

BAD TIMING: A SENSUAL OBSESSION

(VSOM, 1980) **D:** Nicolas Roeg **S:** Yale Udoff **P:** Jeremy Thomas UK

A suicidal married woman (Theresa Russell) is involved with a hateful, womanizing psychiatrist (Art Garfunkel) in Vienna. Harvey Keitel is a detective who investigates her death, which is revealed in flashbacks. Strippers on a trampoline and a necrophiliac sex scene helped keep it from wide release. It was Roeg's first feature after *The Man Who Fell to Earth* (1976) and would have been called just *Obsession*, but Brian De Palma used the title first. Russell, who later married the director, starred in many more of his films. The uncut version runs 128 minutes and is available on a Japanese laserdisc (but with all pubic hair obscured!). With Denholm Elliott, Daniel Massey, Robert Walker Jr., and Dana Gillespie. The soundtrack features the Who (the irritating "Who Are You?"), Tom Waits, Keith Jarrett, Billie Holiday, and others. World Northal released a cut version of this Rank film in the US.

BAIL JUMPER

(Fox Lorber, 1990) **D/S:** Christian Faber **S/P:** Josephine Wallace

Eszter Balint stars as a Missouri shoplifter who heads for New York with her small-time crook boyfriend (B. J. Spalding). It's a road movie, a love story, and a disaster film with falling meteorites, floods, a swarm of locusts, an eclipse, a tidal wave, an earthquake, and tornadoes. With Joie Lee as a clairvoyant and Bo Brinkman.

BAIL OUT

(Vestron, 1988) **D/P/A:** Max Kleven **P/A:** David Hasselhoff **P:** Sanford Hampton (*W. B. Blue and the Bean*)

David Hasselhoff is WB (White Bread), a bail-bondsman who has to keep Linda Blair alive for a court appearance during a drug war (involving Iranians) in South America. She's kidnapped and tied up. This crime comedy is one of several direct-to-video releases starring the Hasselhoff/Blair team. John Vernon plays yet another villain in a Blair movie, and Debra Lamb and Buck Flower are in there too.

BALBOA

(Vestron, 1982) **D/S/P:** James Polakof

Tony Curtis is a tycoon with a real-estate scam in a condensed version of a *Dallas*-type miniseries that was never aired. Carol Lynley, Chuck Connors, Sonny Bono, Cassandra Peterson (Elvira), Lupita Ferrer, and Henry Jones are in the cast. Leo Sayer is on the soundtrack. Martine Beswick narrates, and some nude scenes were added years later for the video debut.

THE BALCONY

(Mystic Fire, 1963) **D/P:** Joseph Strick **S/P:** Ben Maddow

Shelley Winters is Madame Irma in this b/w adaptation of Jean Genet's allegorical play. Peter Falk is her police-chief lover. With Lee Grant, Ruby Dee, Jeff Corey, and Kent Smith. Leonard Nimoy (!), who plays the rebel leader, also starred in another Genet adaptation, *Deathwatch* (1966). Strick also filmed *Tropic of Cancer*.

LA BAMBA

(RCA, 1987) **D/S:** Luis Valdez **P:** Taylor Hackford, Bill Borden

Lou Diamond Phillips stars as 17-year-old singer Ritchie Valens (Valenzuela). He has premonitions of the 1959 plane crash that he died in. Esai Morales costars as his jealous brother. Phillips doesn't look anything like the real (heavier-set) Valens, and the movie deals more with his identity problems as a Mexican-American who speaks only English than with his brief career as a rock star, but it's pretty interesting. With Elizabeth Pena, Joe Pantoliano, Marshall Crenshaw as Buddy Holly, Stephen Lee as "the Big Bopper," Rick Dees, and Brian Setzer. Valens' singing voice is provided by David Hidalgo of Los Lobos. Valens' own songs and some Little Richard standards are performed. The theme song became a hit again and was used in commercials for many products. By the 90s Phillips was the star, and sometimes the director, of many direct-to-video movies, often playing Native Americans. This Columbia release is PG-13.

BAMBOO GODS AND IRON MEN

(1974) **D:** Cesare Gallardo **S:** Kenneth
Metcalfe **P:** Cirio H. Santiago   Philippines

James Iglehart stars in this kung-fu and boxing
action movie, with Shirley Washington, Ken Metcalf, Eddie Garcia, and Ciquito. Inglehart was the
boxer in *Beyond the Valley of the Dolls* and
starred in Santiago's *Savage!* (also from AIP).

THE BAMBOO HOUSE OF DOLLS

(VSOM, 1973) **D:** Kuei Chih Hung
P: Run Run Shaw   Hong Kong

Before *Ilsa: She Wolf of the SS*, this Asian version
of a similar tale was released. It features prisoners
(Chinese and American women, mostly) in a
Japanese WWII camp run by a sadistic female
warden with a whip. Lo Lieh plays a Chinese soldier who helps some of the women escape. Birte
Tove is top-billed as an American blonde. This exploitation movie seems aimed at Western audiences. Peppercorn Wormser released it in America.

BANDERA BANDITS

(TWE, 1972) **D/S:** Sergio Corbucci **S:** Sabatino
Ciuffini **P:** Roberto Loyola   Italy/W. Germany/Spain
(*Cronaca Criminale del Far West; Sonny and Jed*)

Tomas Milian and Susan George are *Bonnie and
Clyde*-type robbers being pursued by a lawman
(Telly Savalas). This western features Rossana
Yanni and Herbert Fux. The score is by Ennio
Morricone. K-Tel (the mail-order-record people)
released it in the US.

BAND OF THE HAND

(RCA, 1986) **D:** Paul Michael Glaser **S:** Leo
Garen, Jack Baran **P:** Michael Rauch

A Nam vet (Stephen Lang) trains five street
punks in the Everglades to battle drug dealers in
Miami. With John Cameron Mitchell, Larry (now
Lawrence) Fishburne, Lauren Holly, and James
Remar as a drug king. Michael Mann was the ex-
ecutive producer, and the *Miami Vice* influence is
obvious. Bob Dylan sings the title song with Tom
Petty. Soundtrack on MCA.

BANG BANG! YOU'RE DEAD!

(Ace, 1966) **D:** Don Sharp **S:** Peter Yeldham **P:** Harry
Alan Towers   UK (*Our Man in Marrakesh; Bang Bang!*)

This comedy stars Tony Randall as an American
who becomes involved with spies and gangsters in
Morocco. Senta Berger costars as a CIA agent.
With Herbert Lom, Terry-Thomas, and Klaus Kinski as Arabs, and Wilfrid Hyde-White. This AIP
release was filmed in Marrakesh. Sharp made *The
Brides of Fu Manchu* the same year.

THE BANKER

(MCEG/Virgin, 1989) **D/P:** William Webb
S: Dana Augustine

LA cop Robert Forster is after a musclebound
banker (Duncan Regehr) who paints his face like
a South American Indian and kills and mutilates
hookers with a laser-sight crossbow. The psycho

Klaus Kinski in *Bang, Bang, You're Dead.*

thinks he's collecting souls and is indestructible.
With Shanna Reed, Jeff Conaway and Leif Garrett
as pimps, Richard Roundtree as a police captain,
William Webb, Teri Weigel (in a sex scene), and
Deborah Richter.

BANZAI RUNNER

(Vidmark, 1987) **S/P:** John G. Thomas
S: Phillip L. Harange

Dean Stockwell stars as a California highway patrolman who goes after hit-and-run drivers. With
John Sheperd, Charles Dierkop, Billy Drago, and
lotsa car chases.

BARABBAS

(RCA, 1961) **D:** Richard Fleischer **S:** Christopher
Fry, Ivo Perilli **P:** Dino De Laurentiis

Anthony Quinn stars in a long (144-minute) biblical epic (released by Columbia in 70mm for some
engagements). Barabbas, a thief, is condemned,
then pardoned. Jesus dies in his place. Barabbas
becomes a slave and has to fight Jack Palance
(great as Torvald, the sadistic captain of the gladiators) in the arena. Barabbas is freed and captured
again, then crucified because he has become a
Christian. The international cast includes Silvana
Mangano, Arthur Kennedy as Pontius Pilate, Katy
Jurado, Harry Andrews, Vittorio Gassman, and
Ernest Borgnine as Lucius. Mangano's brother
(and the brother-in-law of De Laurentiis) plays
Christ. The film is based on the book by Par
Lagerkvist, previously filmed in Sweden in 1952.

BARBARIAN QUEEN

(Vestron, 1985) **D:** Hector Olivera **S:** Howard R.
Cohen **P:** Frank Isaac, Alex Sessa

In a typical Concorde/Corman movie filmed in
Argentina, Amethea (6-foot-tall Lana Clarkson)
and her friends seek revenge after her wedding is
disrupted by some torture and rape and killing.
There's lots of nudity in this 70-minute time-
waster. The topless Amethea is put on the rack.
She can castrate men during sex with her well-
developed muscles. With the future director Katt
Shea (Ruben) as her sidekick, Dawn Dunlap,
and Frank Zagarino. R and unrated videos are
available.

BARBARIAN QUEEN II: THE EMPRESS STRIKES BACK

(Live, 1989) **D:** Joe Finley **S:** Howard
Cohen, Lance Smith **P:** Alan Krone,
Anthony Norway

Lana Clarkson returns (this time
called Athelia) and is imprisoned by
the evil King Ankaris (several
times). She escapes and joins a
group of Amazons in leather bikinis. There's topless mud-wrestling,
swordfighting, and Lana, topless,
suspended over a bed of spikes.
With Rebecca Wood and Elizabeth
Jaeger. It was shot in Mexico.

BARBARIAN MASTER: *See* SWORD OF THE BARBARIANS

THE BARBARIANS

(Cannon, 1987) **D:** Ruggiero Deodato
S: James R. Silke **P:** John Thompson   Italy

This laughable movie stars David and Peter Paul
(known as "the Barbarian Brothers"!) as Kut-
chek and Gore. Richard Lynch, with long, braided
blond hair, is the evil Kadar, and appearances are
made by a dragon, reptile men, and a wolfman.
With Eva LaRue, Michael Berryman as "the Dirt-
master," and George Eastman. Pino Donnagio did
the soundtrack.

THE BARE HUNT

(Video Dimensions, 1963)   (*My Gun Is Jammed*)

A goofy-looking (and sounding) private detective
(Marv Watson) is on a big case. He investigates
characters in the nudie-movie business and meets
naked models and actresses like "the Boobsy
Twins." The figure models look pretty good. No
other credits are available.

BARE KNUCKLES

(TWE, 1977) **D/S/P:** Don Edmonds

This is the most violent movie I can remember
seeing on local TV in Cleveland in the late 70s.
Edmonds made it after his Ilsa films. It's about a
bounty hunter who's after a kung-fu killer. Sherry
Jackson, who used to be on *The Danny Thomas
Show*, costars with black action star Gloria Hen-
dry (in her last feature), Robert Viharo, and John
Daniels.

BARELY PROPER

(1975) **D/P/A:** Brad Grinter **S:** Manny Dietz

This rare Florida movie by the maker of *Blood
Freak* was a throwback to early–60s nudist
movies. It's about a teacher put on trial by the
school board for belonging to the Seminole Health
Club nudist colony. Ed Trostle and Carol Riccio
star. There's a play (also called *Barely Proper*)
within the film, starring Cindy Walker. Grinter,
who made *Never the Twain* next, was a nudist
himself.

BARFLY

(Warner, 1987) **D/P:** Barbet Schroeder
S: Charles Bukowski **P:** Tom Luddy, Fred Roos

Mickey Rourke temporarily redeemed himself and his career playing a drunken Los Angeles writer based on Bukowski. Faye Dunaway is pretty great too. With Jack Nance, Alice Krige, Frank Stallone, and veteran character actor Fritz Feld. Bukowski even makes a brief appearance. Francis Ford Coppola presented the Cannon feature. The music is good jazz and R&B, and the cinematography is by Robby Muller. It was the first American feature for the Swiss director, whose two-volume *The Charles Bukowski Tapes* (Lagoon) feature the late notorious writer himself.

BARN OF THE NAKED DEAD

(1973) **D/P:** Alan Rudolph **S:** Roman
Valenti, Ralph Harold   (*Terror Circus*)

Before he became Robert Altman's protegé, Rudolph was assistant director of *The Brady Bunch*. He made *Premonition* (1972) and this horror movie using a phony name. Three women on the way to Vegas in a beat-up station wagon are stranded in the desert. Andrew Prine (*Simon, King of the Witches*) shows up in a jeep and takes them home to add to his collection of women chained up in the barn. One says "He's like all other men. He wants to control us, and I hate him!" He dresses like a ringmaster, chains 12 of them together, and whips them in the desert. The women argue constantly about what to do. Sometimes he selects one, paints her with blood, lets her go, and releases a hungry cougar. He decides one woman is his mother. It all takes place on what was an H-bomb test site, and a long-haired mutant shows up. Except for some interesting experimental music, this movie has terrible sound and bad editing, and it's pretty dreary. With Jennifer Ashley (*Guyana: Cult of the Damned*). David Keith was a stunt man.

THE BARON

(Paragon, 1975) **D/S:** Philip Fentry   (*Black Cue*)

Calvin Lockhart plays an actor making a movie with an all-black cast. He has real-life trouble because he borrowed money from the mob. With Richard Lynch as a sadistic gangster, Joan Blondell, Raymond St. Jacques, Marlene Clark, and Gail Strickland. Fentry also wrote *Superfly*.

BARON BLOOD

(Redemption, 1972) **D:** Mario Bava **S:** Vincent
Forte **P:** Alfred Leone   Italy (*Gli Orrori del Castello di
Noremberga; The Torture Chamber of Baron Blood*)

Here's a nice-looking, 88-minute, letterboxed, British print of a movie that was released (cut) by AIP here. When the often hysterical Elke Sommer and Antonio Cantafora read a parchment in a huge (real) old castle in Austria, they unleash the spirit of the accursed, scar-faced, 16th-century baron who built it. The killer (of many characters) looks like Vincent Price in *House of Wax* but turns out to be a man named Alfred Becker, who buys the castle and restores it. The late Joseph Cotten,

who laughs and jokes a lot, is very good in the role, played mostly in a wheelchair. Some standout scenes show skewered bodies on the rooftop, the burning spirit of a witch, death by iron maiden, and bodies coming back to life. With little Nicole Elmi (in a larger role than in most of her 70s horror movies), Massimo Girotti, Rada Rassimov, and Alan Collins as the caretaker. It also has the original Stelvio Cipriano soundtrack, with some nice, typically 60s Italian electric-guitar and bongo passages.

BARON MÜNCHHAUSEN

(Video City, 1943) **D:** Josef von Baky **S:** Erich
Kästner   Germany (*Münchausens Abenteuer*)

The year 1943 was the 25th anniversary of Germany's famous UFA studios, the company that had produced *The Last Laugh*, *Metropolis*, and many other classics. Of course, by then, the studio and everything else was owned and run by the state. Propaganda Minister Josef Goebbels chose *Barön Münchhausen*, which had already been filmed in France, Italy, Germany, the US, the USSR, and Czechoslovakia, as the prestige color-epic anniversary release. I was amazed at how much Terry Gilliam's overblown and overbudgeted version, *The Adventures of Baron Munchausen* (1989), copied this one (available with subtitles on tape, running 110 minutes). It opens at a lavish 18th-century party. All of a sudden you notice an electric light, then a car, and realize it's a costume party. People talk about Rudolf Raspe's 18th-century book recounting the Baron's adventures and wonder whether he was real. This colorful fantasy is much more adult than Gilliam's version, with topless harem girls, a nude painting that comes to life, and a eunuch harem-keeper. The Baron has encounters with Catherine the Great, Count Cagliostro, and Casanova. He has a servant, Christian, who can run superfast. He rides a cannonball and is captured in a Turkish fort. They escape in a balloon and go to the moon, where one day equals an earth year. The man in the moon carries around his wife's head, and people grow from tree pods. There's a human clock, living clothes that bark, and an invisibility ring. The Baron in this version, played by Hans Albers (*Variety*; *The Blue Angel*) is ageless. It's interesting to note that Russians are mostly shown as drunks devouring piles of caviar. The comic bad-guy Arabs are shown mistreating black slaves. People in Nazi-occupied countries didn't want to see an expensive, showoff fantasy film backed by Nazis, and it certainly wasn't welcome in America at the time. The UFA studios disappeared just two years later. A fantasy film that could have been as famous as *The Wizard of Oz* and *The Thief of Bagdad* is unknown to most and pretty much lost in history. Von Baky, the Hungarian-born director, worked in West Germany until his death in 1966. His last film was a 1961 Edgar Wallace thriller, *The Strange Countess*.

BARRACUDA

(1978) **D/S/P/A:** Harry Kerwin
S/P/A: Wayne Crawford   (*The Lucifer Project*)

Florida river pollution affects fish and people. Wayne-David Crawford stars in this *Jaws*-inspired science-fiction obscurity with Jason Evers, Bert Freed, and William Kerwin. Kerwin also made adult titles like *My Third Wife George* (1968) and *Sweet Bird of Aquarius* (1970). The music is by the Frankfurt Radio Symphony Orchestra and Klaus Schulze (?!).

BARRY MCKENZIE HOLDS HIS OWN

(VSOM, 1974) **D/S/P:** Bruce Beresford
S/A: Barry Humphries   Australia

Barry Crocker plays six roles in this comedy sequel to *The Adventures of Barry Mckenzie*. Both features, based on a comic strip, are filled with anti-British gags, slang words, and lots of "booze and broads." Donald Pleasence as Count Plasma kidnaps Mckenzie's aunt (Crocker), thinking she's the queen of England, and siphons her blood to sell. A reverend (Crocker) saves the day with a cross made of beer cans. With Barry Humphries as Dame Edna Everage, Roy Kinnear as a kung-fu cook, and the real Australian prime minister. Beresford made more serious Hollywood movies later.

BARTON FINK

(Fox, 1991) **D/S:** Joel Coen
S/P: Ethan Coen **P:** Graham Place

John Turturro stars as a serious New York Jewish writer who's in Hollywood during WWII trying to write a screenplay for a Wallace Beery wrestling movie for "Capital Pictures" on his Underwood typewriter. While suffering from writer's block, he befriends a salesman living at the same hotel (John Goodman), who turns out to be a mass murderer of German descent. The film is funny for a while but turns into a nightmare, with *Eraserhead* ideas, dream sequences, a decapitated head, and great fire scenes in the hotel. Characters are partially based on Clifford Odets (Turturro), William Faulkner (John Mahoney), and Louis B. Mayer (Michael Lerner). With Judy Davis and Steve Buscemi. The screenplay was published with *Miller's Crossing*.

BASIC INSTINCT

(Live, 1992) **D:** Paul Verhoeven
S: Joe Eszterhas **P:** Alan Marshall

A rich bisexual novelist (Sharon Stone) is suspected of being a serial killer who uses icepicks to kill men during sex. The movie's first victim is a retired rock star named Johnny Boz. She seduces the ex-alcoholic, chain-smoking San Francisco detective nicknamed Shooter (Michael Douglas) who's on the case. With Jeanne Tripplehorn as his girlfriend and shrink, Leilani Sarelle (*Neon Maniacs*) as Stone's lover, George Dzundza as his detective partner, Wayne Knight, and Dorothy Malone. Eszterhas received a record $3 million for the script (which borrows from several Hitchcock features). Protests by gay groups during filming started a deluge of publicity, and the $40 million movie made many millions. Tri Star cut it for an R rating in the US. It was an even bigger hit (uncut) in Europe. The tape put 42 seconds back (R and unrated videos were released), and the Pioneer laserdisc version added a running commentary by the director. See the director's own earlier *The Fourth Man* for an interesting comparison. With a film clip from *Hellraiser*, Rob Bottin FX, and a Jerry Goldsmith score.

BASKET CASE 2

(SGE, 1990) **D/S:** Frank Henenlotter **P:** Edgar Ievins

Duane (Keven Van Hetenryck) and his mutant twin, Belilal, return in a "freaks' rights" sequel to the 1982 NYC cult classic. Both twins fall in love, and there's more comedy, but Henenlotter keeps a sick edge to things. Granny Ruth (famous singer turned actress Annie Ross) provides a refuge for freaks, and her Staten Island house is filled with bizarre, fantastic characters. The Tod Browning–inspired horror comedy actually suffers from latex-makeup overkill. Heather Rattray (from family movies like *Mountain Family Robinson*) is Duane's girl. Kathryn Meisle and Matt Mitler work for scandal-magazine editor Jason Evers (from *The Brain That Wouldn't Die!*). With a sideshow, Ted Sorel, and Beverly Bonner. It was filmed back to back (for SGE) with *Frankenhooker*, and the dual soundtrack by Joe Renzi is on SMI.

BASKET CASE 3: THE PROGENY

(SGE, 1991) **D/S:** Frank Henenlotter
S: Robert Martin **P:** Edgar Ievins

This time the now pretty insane Duane, Belilal, their protector Granny Ruth (Annie Ross), and all the freaks from *Part II* flee to Atlanta and stay in another house. This movie opens with highlights from the first two. The filmmakers, probably bored with the concept by then, practiced absurd extreme overkill in every way possible and added more comedy and even a musical number. Duane falls for the sheriff's daughter (Tina Louise Hilbert). When Belilal becomes a father, an endless stream of little monsters are born. In the best scene (inspired by *Aliens*), Belilal attacks a sheriff (Gilbert Roper) in an incredible custom-made metal apparatus. With the Morell twins.

THE BAT

(Sinister, 1925) **D/P:** Roland West **S:** Julien Josephson

For years *The Bat* was thought to be a lost film. (Roughly 50 percent of all films made before 1950 are lost.) The United Artists release was rediscov-

Belial returns in Frank Henenlotter's *Basket Case 2*.

ered and is now on tape with an orchestral score. It's an adaptation of Mary Roberts Rinehart's mystery novel and stage play about a notorious masked criminal with bat wings, big ears, and sharp teeth stalking an old, dark house being rented by a mystery writer. The story had first been filmed as *The Circular Staircase* in 1915. Jack Pickford stars, with Louise Fazenda as the comic maid, the mysterious Sojin as the butler, Tullio Carminati as the detective, and Emily Fitzroy as Cornelia Van Gorder. The huge room sets were designed by William Cameron Menzies. Roland West (from Cleveland) also made *The Monster* (1925), with Lon Chaney, and an even better remake of *The Bat* called *The Bat Whispers* (1931). Batman creator Bob Kane must have seen one of the versions, because the shadowy, threatening, almost supernatural Bat was an obvious inspiration for the hero Batman. The Scimitar version adds *Bat Clips*, a short film about the *Batman* TV show.

BATES MOTEL

(1987) **D/S:** Richard Rothstein
P: Ken Topolsky, George Linder

"Norman Bates may be gone, but the hotel lives on!" claimed NBC-TV when they aired this series pilot. A mental patient (Bud Cort) inherits the famous motel (right after the events of the original movie) and reopens it. The idea for the projected occult-theme anthology series was that each week would center on a different guest. Lori Petty, Jason Bateman, Gregg Henry, Moses Gunn, and Buck Flower were in the pilot too.

THE BATMAN

(Sony, 1943) **D:** Lambert Hillyer **S:** Victor McLeod, Leslie Swabacker, Harry Fraser **P:** Rudolph C. Flothow

The first 15-chapter Columbia serial based on the comic-book characters created by Bob Kane was the only serial directed by a B-western specialist. Lewis Wilson and Douglas Croft star as Batman and Robin. J. Carroll Naish as the Japanese Dr. Daka turns men into zombies with his machine. His headquarters are behind an amusement-park attraction showing Japanese atrocities. Some chapters of the WWII-era serial are "Slave of the Rising Sun," "A Nipponese Trap," and "The Doom of the Rising Sun." When Sony (Japanese-owned) issued the videotape of the serial, they altered all the dialogue that referred to the villain being Japanese (!). Some viewers probably didn't notice or care about this subversive tampering, but you should know about it. With Charles Middleton, Shirley Patterson, and stunt man Eddie Parker. In 1965 it

was rereleased to theaters as *An Evening with Batman and Robin*, lasting four hours. I sat through the whole damn thing in Cleveland, where it opened. Columbia also made *Batman and Robin* (1949), with different stars.

J. Carroll Naish as the evil Japanese Dr. Daka in the original *Batman* serial.

BATMAN

(Warner, 1989) **D:** Tim Burton **S:** Sam Hamm, Warren Skaaren **P:** Jon Peters, Peter Gruber **M:** Danny Elfman

This PG-13 movie has great sets and is a darker version of the hero than most people were used to. But the whole project seemed rushed, the ending was bad, and it was all kind of an overhyped mess, actually. Burton was only 28 when he directed *Batman*, his third feature. Michael Keaton stars, but Jack Nicholson got a record $50 million (maybe as much as $60 million!) for playing the Joker. Kim Basinger is Vicki Vale, Robert Wuhl is fun as a wisecracking reporter, Jack Palance as a corporate gang leader is killed off too soon, and British horror star Michael Gough plays Alfred, the butler (and pocketed some side cash by doing Diet Coke TV ads as the character). With Pat Hingle as Commissioner Gordon, Billy Dee Williams, Tracey Walter, and Jerry Hall. Danny Elfman did the (orchestral) soundtrack, and Prince provided (mediocre) songs and recorded "Scandalous Sex Suite 12" with Basinger. His complete "soundtrack" album is available. Batman runs 126 minutes. Not long after the film's release, script doctor Skaaren died, and production designer Anton Furst (who received an Oscar for his art direction) killed himself. *Batman* had a record number of licenses for merchandising (160 at the time of the record-breaking premiere) and the highest number of single openings (2,850 US screens on June 23, 1989). *Batman* is second only to *E.T.* in video sales. The hype worked. Both the Elfman score and an alternate Prince soundtrack were released.

BATMAN AND ROBIN

(Goodtimes, 1949) **D:** Spencer Gordon Bennet **S:** George Plympton, J. F. Poland, Royale K. Cole **P:** Sam Katzman

The second 15-chapter Columbia Batman serial is available on 2 cassettes. Part of the first chapter (usually longer than the others) is cut on the tape, though. Robert Lowry and John Duncan took over as Batman and Robin and had to battle the black-hooded Wizard, who has a machine that paralyzes traffic and who can become invisible. Jane Adams is Vicki Vale, and Lyle Talbot (who played Lex Luthor in a *Superman* serial) is Commissioner Gordon. With Ralph Graves and stunt man Eddie Parker doing most of the Bat fighting.

BATMAN: MASK OF THE PHANTASM

(Warner, 1993) **D/P:** Eric Radomski, Bruce W. Timm
S: Alan Burnett, Paul Dini, Martin Paso, Michael Reaves
P: Benjamin Melniker, Michael Uslan

After the animated Fox-TV series, this PG animated feature, which captures the feel of early comics, was released. Kevin Conroy (Batman), Stacy Keach (the Phantasm), Mark Hamill (the Joker), Dana Delaney, Hart Bochner, Efrem Zimbalist Jr. (Alfred), Abe Vigoda, John P. Ryan, and Dick Miller provide the voices.

BATMAN RETURNS

(Warner, 1992) **D/P:** Tim Burton
S: Dan Waters **P:** Denise DiNovi

Batman (Michael Keaton) becomes a supporting character in his own sequel, which takes a very dim view of government and media. It was shot on sets with a German-expressionist look, and many scenes take place in a copy of Rockefeller Center at Christmastime. Danny DeVito is the confused, grotesque Penguin (Stan Winston did the makeup), who discovers he's Oswald Cobblepot, runs for mayor, then tries to kidnap all the firstborn children of Gotham City. Christopher Walken is corrupt tycoon Max Schreck, the real villain. Michelle Pfeiffer is his pathetic secretary, who miraculously survives being pushed out of a window and emerges as a sexy, backflipping Catwoman with a tight black-leather outfit and a whip (kickboxer Kathy Long was her double). Some people in the Times Square audience yelled in outrage when Batman tore off his mask, unnecessarily revealing his identity to several characters. This long (126-minute) feature cost an estimated $80 million. It made lots of money, though, and megamerchandising (with companies like McDonald's) helped. All the penguins (real and created) are pretty great, though. With Michael Gough, Pat Hingle, Michael Murphy as the mayor, Vincent Schiavelli, Jan Hooks, Christy Conaway, Stuart Lancaster, and Paul Reubens as the Penguin's father. Danny Elfman did the score, and Steve Johnson worked on the FX. *Batman Forever* followed.

*batteries not included

(MCA, 1987) **D/S:** Mathew Robbins **S:** Brad Bird, Brent Maddock, S. S. Wilson **P:** Ronald L. Schwary

Steven Spielberg was an executive producer of this PG fantasy with Oscar-winning ILM FX. Hume Cronyn and Jessica Tandy (in between *Cocoon* movies) and their neighbors are being evicted from a Lower East Side tenement build-ing. Some friendly aliens arrive in two little flying saucers and help. It's almost the light side of *Liquid Sky*. With Elizabeth Pena, John Pankow, Wendy Schaal, and James LeGros. Filmed in the real East Village, where no aliens have shown up to help so far.

BATTLEFLAG

(1976) **D/P:** Ottokar Runze **S:** Herbert Asmodi   W. Germany/Spain (*Die Standard*)

Simon Ward stars as a cadet serving the Austro-Hungarian Empire at the end of WWI. This seldom-seen action movie/love story costars Siegfried Rauch, Jon Finch, Peter Cushing as Major Hackenberg, Wolfgang Preiss, Maria Perschy, and Lil Dagover (from the original silent version of *The Cabinet of Dr. Caligari*).

BATTLE FORCE

(Quality, 1978) **D/S:** "Humphrey Longan"/Umberto Lenzi, Cesare Frugoni   Italy/W. Germany/Yugoslavia (*The Great Battle; Il Grande Attacco*)

An all-star WWI movie by the same director who next made *Make Them Die Slowly*. It's about how the war affects the lives of members of an American family and a German family. With Helmut Berger, Samantha Eggar, Stacy Keach, Edwige Fenich, Henry Fonda, John Huston, Evelyn Stewart, and Giuliano Gemma. Orson Welles narrates some newsreel footage to fill up more time.

THE BATTLE OF AUSTERLITZ

(USA, 1959) **D/S:** Abel Gance **S:** Nelly Kaplan
P: Alexander Salkind   Italy/France/Yugoslavia/Liechtenstein (*Austerlitz*)

Gance directed the famous triple-split-screen 1927 epic *Napoléon* (which was rereleased to great acclaim in 1981). For his last film, Gance returned to the same subject, but by the time this all-star version made it to the US it was badly dubbed, and about 43 minutes (out of 166) were missing. Now it's commonly available on video and even found in Woolworth stores. The original (also on tape) is really impressive only on a wide screen in a theater. This version is fun for spotting some of the guest stars. With Claudia Cardinale, Martine Carol, Vittorio De Sica, Orson Welles, Jean Marais, Jack Palace, Michel Simon, Rosanno Brazzi, Leslie Caron, and Pierre Mondy as Napoléon. This money-losing epic cost around $4 million (a lot in the late 50s).

THE BATTLE OF LOVE'S RETURN

(1971) **D/S/P/A:** Lloyd Kaufman

Yes, Troma once made a G-rated feature. Lynn Lowry, who was usually in more daring projects (like *I Drink Your Blood*, from the same year) stars. Kaufman was also directing X-rated features (as Louis Su) at the time. The unknown Oliver Stone (!) acted in this obscurity, then was a producer for Troma's *Sugar Cookies* (also with Lowry).

THE BATTLE OF NERETVA

(Republic, 1971) **D:** Veliko Bulajic **S:** Ugo Pirro
P: Steve Previn   US/Italy/W. Germany/Yugoslavia (*Bitka na Neretvi*)

AIP released this 102-minute version of the nearly three-hour epic about the Nazi invasion of Yugoslavia (which was a timely topic again in the 90s). Yul Brynner stars, with Orson Welles, Sergei Bondarchuk, Curt Jurgens, Sylvia Koscina, Hardy Kruger, and Franco Nero. The music by Bernard Herrmann was left over from his rejected *Torn Curtain* score. The soundtrack is on Entacte.

BATTLE OF THE AMAZONS

(1973) **D:** "Al Bradley"/Alfonso Brescia **S:** Mario Amendola, Bruno Corbucci **P:** Riccardo Billi
Italy/Spain (*Amazzoni Donne d'Amore e di Guerra*)

Lucretia Love (from *The Arena*) stars in a violent, R-rated movie about female warriors on horseback. Eventually their male victims and some villagers defeat them with martial arts. The ads said, "Hell hath no fury like 10,000 women!"

BATTLE OF THE BOMBS

(Rhino, 1985)

Johnny Legend put together this 80-minute compilation of scenes and trailers from wonders like *Orgy of the Dead, I Changed My Sex, The Creeping Terror, The Terror of Tiny Town*, and *Eegah!* The tape is pretty much a long commercial for Rhino video, but it's totally entertaining and a great way to hook an unsuspecting, casual viewer into the dangerous and addictive habit of watching and appreciating "bad" movies. For a while there, Rhino was the number 1 company releasing 50s and 60s Psychotronic classics on video.

BATTLE OF THE COMMANDOS

(Republic, 1969) **D:** Umberto Lenzi **S:** Dario Argento, Rolf Griminger, Eduardo M. Brochero
Italy/Spain/W. Germany (*Legion of the Damned*)

A WWII movie starring Jack Palance as Colonel Anderson, whose commandos must destroy a German cannon. With Wolfgang Preiss, Curt Jurgens, Diana Lorys, and Thomas Hunter. This is of interest to some as one of the earliest features Dario Argento was involved with.

BATTLE OF THE MODS

(1966) **D:** Franco Montemurro **S:** Ennio De Concini, Adriano Bolzoni, Michael A. Scheiber **P:** Luigi Waldeitner   Italy/W. Germany (*La Battaglia dei Mods; Crazy Baby*)

Ricky (Ricky Shayne) is a mod guitar player in Liverpool. His girlfriend is killed in a rumble with some rockers, so he flees to London, then Paris, and ends up in decadent Rome, where he becomes involved with the sister of his rich businessman father's mistress. Joachim Fuchsberger is the dad. This color film wasn't released in the US until 1968, when mods and rockers were either unknown or forgotten.

BATTLESTAR GALACTICA
(MCA series, 1978–80)

At least 8 episodes of the ABC-TV copy of *Star Wars* are on tape and run 47 minutes each. These TV episodes were the most expensive ("$1 million each") produced up to that time. The series was pretty dumb and unoriginal when it was new but might be old enough for some laughs by now. The late Lorne Greene starred in the entire series, with Richard Hatch, Dirk Benedict, a robot dog, and Maren Jensen, who all left in 1979. Some actors who were around for just one season were Anne Lockhart, Robyn Douglas, and Richard Lynch as Xavier. One episode, "The Return of Starbuck," is on Goodtimes. The feature-length series pilot was released theatrically (and is on tape), and two episodes became a feature overseas, *Mission Galactica: Cyclon Attack*.

THE BAT WHISPERS
(Scorched Earth, 1931) **D/S/P:** Roland West **P:** Joseph M. Schenck

In this fascinating remake of West's *The Bat* (1925), a radio announcer warns about "that notorious madman, the mysterious criminal, the Bat!" and we see the jewel thief (or his huge, frightening bat shadow) in action in New York City. This opening segment is incredible, using advanced sweeping camera movements and an incredible scale model city. The story settles into the familiar secluded, old, dark mansion with secret rooms and many characters wondering who the Bat is. Chester Morris (with his pencil-thin mustache) is the detective hero, the wonderful Gustav von Seyffertitz is a doctor, and Grace Hampton is rich Mrs. Van Gorder (with her comedy-relief maid). This United Artists film features some very odd special effects that will have viewers rewinding for another look. The stage-bound surprise gimmick ending is worth waiting for and makes you promise not to reveal who the killer is, so I won't. The print of this rare film is excellent, but somebody managed to repeat a scene during the trans- fer. Astor rereleased it in the 40s. Another remake, *The Bat*, with Vincent Price, was released in 1959.

BAY OF BLOOD = TWITCH OF THE DEATH NERVE

Chester Morris in Roland West's *The Bat Whispers*.

BEACH BABES FROM BEYOND
(Paramount, 1993) **D:** "Ellen Cabot"/David DeCoteau **S:** Alexander Sachs **P:** Karen L. Spencer

This sex comedy has a 60s plot (AIP beach-party movies), 70s music (new wave), and lots of ready-for-cable nudity and slo-mo sex. Three blond alien "teens" (Sarah Bellomo, Tamara Landry, and Nicole Posey) arrive on the beach, where each of them has sex scenes (including one pretty explicit, oil-soaked, doggy-style fuck). With Linnea Quigley (as an adult for a change), Joe Estevez (as the Big Kahoona), Joey Travolta, and Burt Ward. Also with the briefly seen and incredibly ugly pair of "name" (!) stars Jaqueline Stallone and Don Swayze. It was shot in Mexico.

BEACH BALLS
(1988) **D:** Joe Ritter **S:** David Rocklin **P:** Matt Leipzig

Phillip Paley goes after dreamgirl Heidi Helmer. Girls in bikinis are featured in this Roger Corman/Concorde release. There was a various artists soundtrack.

THE BEACH BOYS: AN AMERICAN BAND
(Vestron, 1985) **D/S:** Malcolm Leo **P:** Leo Peterson, Bonnie Peterson

This authorized biographical documentary tells only part of the story, of course, but it's excellent for what it does show. The live and TV footage covers all phases of the band, but the only way to tell when unidentified, early, live performance footage changes is the size of the stripes on the shirts. Footage that was cut from the *TAMI Show* is here, plus fun scenes from *Girls on the Beach*. Highlights include an "In My Room" promo film, "Help Me, Rhonda" live, and Brian Wilson singing "Surf's Up" at home alone in 1966. Brian is interviewed from his bed (from a 1976 TV special), but probably had little to do with this tape. Excerpts from shows in Germany and Prague after the hits stopped in the late 60s are great, but the late Dennis Wilson singing "You Are So Beautiful" is painful. The Beach Boys deserve to be remembered for more than supplying themes for irritating car and soda commercials and the embarrassing public battle over who controls what's left of Brian Wilson. A later version of this tape is cut. Also look for *The Story of the Beach Boys* (1990).

THE BEACH GIRLS
(Paramount, 1982) **D:** Pat Townsend **S:** Patrick Duncan, Phil Groves **P:** Marilyn J. Tenser, Michael D. Castle

Deborah Blee, sharing her uncle's beach house with friends, throws a big party. With James Daughton, Corinne Bohrer, Jeane Tomasina (from *Playboy*), Adam Roarke, Catherine Mary Stewart as a "surfer girl," and music by Michael Lloyd. From Crown.

BEACH HOUSE
(Thorn EMI, 1982) **D/S:** John Gallagher **S/P:** Marino Amoruso (*Down the Shore*)

Italian teen slobs from Brooklyn go to the beach for a vacation and have problems with upper-class jocks from Philly. Kathy McNeil and Richard Duggan star in this minor release from New Line.

BEACH RED
(VSOM, 1967) **D/S/P/A:** Cornel Wilde **S:** Clint Johnston, Donald A. Peters, Jefferson Pascal

You've never seen a WWII movie like this. Wilde created a bizarre, brutal, antiwar movie using psychedelic editing to deal with memory and honor. He plays the leader of a US Marine battalion in the Philippines. Rip Torn is the sadistic sergeant. Wilde remembers the days with his wife (his real-life wife, Jean Wallace), while the Japanese captain (Genki Koyama) remembers his home life. Parts of it are daring and inspired, while others will have you shaking your head in disbelief. The United Artist release was filmed on location in the Philippines and Japan. Wilde next made *No Blade of Grass* (a post-nuke feature that *Road Warrior* borrowed a lot from).

BEAKS: THE MOVIE
(IVE, 1987) **D/S/P:** René Cardona Jr.   Mexico (*El Ataque de los Pájaros; Birds of Prey*)

The director of *Night of the Bloody Apes* made this gory *Birds* ripoff. Whole scenes are copied from Hitchcock, but these birds peck out eyes (in closeup), eat babies, and even bring down airplanes. The ending takes place on a bird-filled train. Christopher Atkins (from *The Blue Lagoon*) and Michelle Johnson star as a photographer and a reporter. With Italian exploitation regular Gabrielle Tinti.

BEAR ISLAND
(Starmaker, 1979) **D/S:** Don Sharp **S:** David Butler, Murray Smith **P:** Peter Snell   Canada/UK

This PG-rated Alistair MacLean adaptation, about ex-Nazis after gold in a sunken U-boat and a multi-national United Nations scientific expedition at the Arctic, was a big money-loser. Donald Sutherland stars as an American biologist, with Vanessa Redgrave, Richard Widmark (a Nazi), Christopher Lee (a Polish scientist), Barbara Parkins, and Lloyd Bridges. Filmed in British Columbia and Alaska, it was the most expensive Canadian feature ever made up to that time. Sharp, a former Hammer director, and Harry Alan Towers followed this with *What Waits Below* (1983).

THE BEAST = EQUINOX

BEASTMASTER 2: THROUGH THE PORTAL OF TIME
(Republic, 1991) **D/S/P:** Sylvio Tabet **S:** R. J. Robertson, Jim Wynorski, Ken (Wings) Hauser, Doug Miles

The 1982 Don Coscarelli movie *Beastmaster* became a hit on cable TV, so Marc Singer returned in his loincloth as the long-haired Dar in this PG-13 fantasy/comedy sequel. Wings Hauser is the villain with a leather mask covering half his face and a laser weapon. A beautiful witch (Sarah Douglas) tells him how he can rule the world by going through a time portal and stealing a neutron bomb. MTV VJ Kari Wuhrer is a rich LA girl who somehow drives her red Porsche through the portal. Eventually the parallel-world characters join her in the present, along with Dar's animal friends (a tiger, an eagle, and two ferrets). The dialogue is painful ("Chill out, Lord Dude"), and the ancient characters adapt to modern ways too fast, but it's okay light entertainment. Watch for the theater marquee announcing *Beastmaster II*. With Robert Z'Dar and Michael Berryman. Mark Damon was executive producer.

THE BEAST OF MOROCCO

(Sinister, 1966) **D:** Frederic Goode **S:** Bruce Stewart **P:** Harry Field   UK (*The Hand of Night*)

This feature has great opening credits, showing a bat and a skull with an eye, then proceeds with a nightmare inside of a nightmare. A depressed British architect (William Sylvester) who thinks he's losing his mind goes to Morocco, where a phantom woman (Alizia Gur) and her laughing old servant, Omar, appear. He goes to a castle, where a group of black dancing girls are all killed. Despite what some have written, this movie is in color, has a vampire, and is pretty good. Some parts were shot on location.

THE BEAST OF THE DEAD = BEAST OF BLOOD

BEASTS (1972) = THE TWILIGHT PEOPLE

BEASTS

(Prism, 1983) **D/P:** Don Hawks   Canada (*Claws*)

A killer grizzly menaces Tom Babson and Kathy Christopher.

THE BEASTS ARE IN THE STREET

(1978) **D:** Peter Hunt **S:** Lawrence Heath **P:** Harry S. Sherman

The wild animals from a park escape and terrorize a small town. Carol Lynley, Billy Green Bush, Dale Robinson, Philip Michael Thomas, and Bill Thurman costar. This Hanna-Barbera TV production was filmed in Texas.

THE BEAST THAT KILLED WOMEN

(SW, 1965) **D/P/C:** Barry Mahon **S:** Clelle Mahon

A story is told in flashback to a detective in a hospital. A couple at a nudist camp sleep in twin beds. The acting is bad even for a nudie movie. Women dance around a fire. Later, a gorilla starts grabbing and killing them, and the cops arrive. That's about it, except for the topless square-dancing (!) and a scene where two naked black women walk away from the camera. Byran Mabe was assistant director. The one-hour color feature was made in Miami Beach, and is presented by Frank Henenlotter.

THE BEAST WITH THE MAGIC SWORD

(VSOM, 1983) **D/S/P/A:** Jacinto Molina/Paul Naschy Spain/Japan (*La Bestia y la Espada Mágica*)

Naschy returns for his 10th time as el Hombre Lobo/Daninsky. Set in 16th-century Japan, then in Europe, where a Japanese woman who loves a werewolf puts him out of his misery, this movie looks like a deranged *Conan* copy. *The Beast* has lots of nudity, gore, and decapitations. With Gerald Tichy and Sergio Molina. One of several Naschy features that were coproduced by Japanese companies, it's two hours long and subtitled.

THE BEAT

(Vestron, 1987) **D/S:** Paul Mones **P:** Julia Phillips, Jon Lok, Nich Weschler   (*The Conjurer*)

David Jacobson plays an imaginative new kid in a New York City neighborhood full of street gangs. He ends up teaching them poetry. John Savage, David Glover, and Kara Glover costar.

THE BEATNIKS

(SW, 1959) **D/S:** Paul Frees **S:** Arthur Jullian **P:** Edward Heite

Four guys and a girl named Iris stage a robbery wearing skull masks. Their singing leader, Eddie (Tony Travis), is discovered in a Hollywood soda shop and makes a record the next day. The next night he's on the *Rocket to Stardom* TV show, and he falls for his agent's blond secretary (Joyce Terry) just as fast. The moody, jealous, jive-talking Moon (Peter Breck from *Shock Corridor*) ruins everything when he kills a bartender, then shows up to tell Eddie, "You're one of us. Are you hip?" Breck steals the whole show, laughing, ranting, and killing, dressed all in black. If you don't expect a "beatnik" movie, this is a lot of fun. Frees was one of the most famous voices in 50s science-fiction hits. He even cowrote the pop songs like "Sideburns Don't Need No Sympathy"! Kenneth Herts was production supervisor.

BEAT STREET

(Vestron, 1984) **D:** Stan Lathan **S:** Andy Davis, David Gilbert, Paul Golding **P:** David V. Picker, Harry Belafonte

Rae Dawn Chong and Guy Davis star in this PG breakdancing musical about ghetto kids making it in show biz. With Duane Jones (from *Night of the Living Dead*), the expected rapping from Melle Mel, Africa Bambaata, and Soul Sonic Force, and graffiti. The original story was by *High Times* editor Steven Hager. The soundtrack is on Atlantic.

THE BEAUTIES AND THE BEAST

(API, 1973) **D:** Ray Naneau **S:** Gaynor MacLaren **P:** Art Jacobs   (*The Beast and the Vixens*)

Here's the world's first nudie Bigfoot movie. A narrator crouching in the woods with binoculars tells about the giant footprints found in the Pacific Northwest. A woman rows a boat to shore, sunbathes topless, and is carried away by a man in a gorilla suit and a caveman mask—before the credits! The beast carries another woman (wearing go-go boots) to his cave. He brings another, played by a redhead who is now porno star Coleen Brenan. He watches a naked couple in the woods, scares the guy away, and grabs another woman for his cave collection. Meanwhile Uschi Digart ar-

rives at a cabin with another woman to "research a term paper." Soon they meet hippie campers, and they all strip and go swimming. A bearded guy sings "Gypsy Mountain Madness," and his jealous girlfriend has a dream about two women wearing only gun-belts facing off for a Wild West shoot-out!? She wakes in time for a long sex scene with her boyfriend. Two sadistic ex-cons with guns show up looking for a treasure and tie everybody up, then start to mess with the women. A bearded old hermit (and his rubber-masked beast-man friend) save the day! We never find out what happened to the women in the cave.

THE BEAUTIFUL, THE BLOODY, AND THE BARE

(SW, 1964) **D:** Sande N. Johnson **P:** Al C. Ruban

This one had credits on street signs. It's a color New York City movie about Peter, a photographer who comes to stay with an old friend who owns a life-drawing studio on Bleecker Street, in Greenwich Village. After we see lots of naked women posing for art students, we see lots of naked women posing for Peter. The problem is, when he sees red he goes crazy and strangles them. Lots of other red things (shirts, chairs) don't seem to affect him, though. The first woman dies in Central Park. At the end Peter is all bloody, "an inhuman demon, gurgling, screaming," chasing his friend's red-haired wife with a knife over rooftops. Jack Lowe stars, with Marlene Denes and Debra Page. It was rereleased by Boxoffice International.

BEAUTY AND THE BEAST

(Republic, 1987) **D:** Richard Franklin

Linda Hamilton (from the *Terminator* movies) stars as the New York City attorney who loves the gentle Beast, Vincent (Ron Perlman), who hides out beneath the city like *The Phantom of the Opera*. This series pilot also features Ray Wise and Ron O'Neal. Episodes of the romantic-fantasy CBS-TV series (1987–90) are on individual tapes lasting 52 minutes each. Laser versions have two per disc. The tapes were being released while the show was still being produced. The starring couple eventually had a baby on the show, and Hamilton's character was killed off and replaced by Jo Anderson.

BEAUTY AND THE BEAST

(1987) **D:** Eugene Marner **S:** Carole Lucia Satrina **P:** Golan/Globus

The G-rated version is really for kids. John Savage stars as the singing Beast and Rebecca De Mornay is the singing Beauty. Better yet, look for *Beauty and the Beast* (Fox, 1983), Roger Vadim's 52-minute long Faerie Tale Theatre version starring Klaus Kinski as the beast!

BECAUSE OF THE CATS

(Prism, 1972) **D:** Fons Rademakers **S:** Hugo Klaus   Netherlands/Belgium

Pre-*Emmanuelle* Sylvia Kristel costars in a story about cult murders, with Alexandra Stewart and Bryan Marshall. The director later received a best-foreign-film Oscar.

BEDROOM EYES

(Fox, 1984) **D:** William Fruet **S:** Michael Alan Eddy **P:** Robert Lantos, Stephen P. Roth   Canada

In this erotic mystery, Harry Ross (Kenneth Gilman), a voyeur stockbroker watches a bisexual redhead (Barbara Law), sees a murder, and becomes the number 1 suspect. *Rear Window* was the obvious influence, with added sex, violence, and flashbacks. With Dayle Haddon.

BEDROOM EYES II

(Vidmark, 1989) **D:** Chuck Vincent **S:** Gerard Cicoritti **P:** Arnant Singh

Wings Hauser is Harry Ross, the stockbroker framed for a murder, in this "sequel." He's married to Kathy Shower and is having an affair with Linda Blair (they were later married in real life). With Alan Rickman, Jennifer DeLora, Kimberly Taylor, and Jane Hamilton/Veronica Hart as a psycho.

BEDROOM WINDOW

(Vestron, 1987) **D/S:** Curtis Hanson **P:** Martha Schumaker

Steve Guttenberg witnesses a murder in Washington, DC, but can't tell anybody because he was with his boss's wife (Isabelle Huppert) at the time. This Hitchcock-type feature was based on a novel, *The Witness*, by Anne Holden. With Elizabeth McGovern, Wallace Shawn, and Paul Shenar. Robert Towne was the executive producer of the DEG release. Hanson did *Bad Influence* next.

BEETLEJUICE

(Warner, 1988) **D:** Tim Burton **S:** Michael McDowell, Warren Skaaren **P:** Michael Bender, Larry Wilson, Richard Hashimoto

Michael Keaton stars as the crude, funny, mumbling ghost Beetlejuice and plays him like a dirty-old-man used-car salesman in this surprise PG-rated horror/comedy hit. It launched the career of Winona Ryder (whose godfather is Timothy Leary), who plays the suicidal, punk-look girl. Her pretentious parents (Catherine O'Hara and Jeffrey Jones) try to cash in by exploiting the ghosts in their new Upstate New York house. Alec Baldwin and Geena Davis as the good ghost couple are secondary, surrounded by all the comedians, fun special effects (by Chuck Gaspar and Robert

Winona Ryder as Lydia in *Beetlejuice*.

Short), and ghoulish gags. With Gary Shadix, Robert Goulet, Dick Cavett, Annie McEnroe, and Harry Belafonte's calypso "Banana Boat Song." Sylvia Sidney, as the keeper of a way-station to Hell, has cigarette smoke coming out of her slit throat. The Danny Elfman score is from Warner. *Beetlejuice* also became a kids' TV cartoon series (also on Warner video). Burton directed Keaton in *Batman* next.

BEFORE DAWN

(1933) **D:** Irving Pichel **S:** Garrett Fort, Marian Dix **P:** Merian C. Cooper

This forgotten, one-hour-long RKO release was produced by the same man who (with Ernest B. Schoedsack) produced *King Kong* (1933), and like that hit, it was based on an Edgar Wallace novel. Warner Oland is a sinister Viennese doctor in New York City, Stuart Irwin is the comedy-relief police detective, and Dorothy Wilson is a clairvoyant. They all come together in a haunted-house setting. Also with Frank Reicher. Pichel had also directed Cooper and Schoedsack's production of *The Most Dangerous Game* (1932).

BEG!

(1994) **D/S:** Robert Golden **S/A:** Peta Lily **S:** David Glass **P:** Sandra Yarwood   UK

Lily, a mime, who directed the play this is based on, is the head of the women's ward at a private hospital where a murder is committed and a power struggle occurs. It's a black comedy.

BEGGARS IN ERMINE

(Sinister, 1934) **D:** Phil Rosen **S:** Tristram Tipper **P:** William T. Lackey

Lionel Atwill stars as a steel-mill manager who loses his legs because of an accident with molten lead and then is cheated out of his wife and his business. He manipulates the stock market and organizes a profitable society of cripples and beggars who help him seek vengeance. This Monogram film is very similar to some Lon Chaney Sr. movies. With Henry B. Walthall, Betty Furness, and George "Gabby" Hayes. Horror great Atwill rivaled Karloff and Lugosi for a short while and had already starred in *Dr. X, The Mystery of the Wax Museum, The Vampire Bat, Murders in the Zoo,* and others.

BEGINNER'S LUCK

(Starmaker, 1983) **D/S:** Frank Morris **S/P:** Caroline Morris

A virgin law student (Sam Rush) becomes involved in a comic *ménage à trois* with neighbors. From New World.

THE BEGUILED

(MCA, 1970) **D/P:** Don Siegel **S:** Irene Kamp, Albert Maltz, Claude Traverse

Clint Eastwood is a wounded Union Army corporal who seeks sanctuary in a southern girls' school run by Geraldine Page. He tries to take advantage of the situation but ends up helpless, with his leg amputated, and afraid for his life. Elizabeth Hartman and Jo Ann Harris costar, and Pamela Ferdin's turtle is killed. This grim historical horror film was shot in New Orleans. It was a box-office failure because most Eastwood fans probably didn't like seeing him at the mercy of women. The hits *Dirty Harry* and *Play Misty for Me* (with the hero terrorized by another woman) were released the same year. Screenwriters Kamp and Maltz (he had been jailed and blacklisted) used pseudonyms because they didn't like the ending of the finished film.

BEHAVE YOURSELF!

(United, 1951) **D/S:** George Beck **P:** Jerry Wald, Norman Krasna

Shelley Winters and Farley Granger adopt a stray dog that carries information some gangsters want. This RKO comedy features Lon Chaney Jr., Hans Conried, Francis L. Sullivan, William Demarest, Elisha Cook Jr., and Marvin Kaplan. Classic pinup artist Vargas painted the original poster.

BEHIND ENEMY LINES

(Monterey, 1988) **D:** Cirio H. Santiago **S:** Joe Mari Avellana   Philippines

Robert Patrick is a GI who returns to Nam on a mission to rescue POWs. There's a motorcycle escape, bad Russians, and Lydie Denier in a wet T-shirt. It's a sequel to *Eye of the Eagle*.

BEHIND LOCKED DOORS

(Best, 1976) **D/S/P:** Charles Romine **S:** Stanley H. Brasloff **P:** Harry Novak   S. Africa (*Anybody, Anyway*)

A sick tale of a scientist/rapist trying to create the perfect mate. His sister and an ugly necrophiliac servant help him torment some women whose car has run out of gas nearby. Released in the US by Box Office International.

BEHIND THAT CURTAIN

(1929) **D:** Irving Cummings **S:** Sonya Levien, Clarke Cummings

Warner Baxter and Lois Moran star in a creaky mystery featuring Boris Karloff and the first (brief) sound-film appearance of Charlie Chan (played by E. L. Parks). Karloff was in nine films in 1929. This was considered a lost film for years. It was originally released in silent and sound versions.

BEHIND THE CELLAR DOOR = TERROR FROM UNDER THE HOUSE

BEHIND THE WALL

(Hurricane, 1984) **D/S:** James Dearden **P:** Mark Forstater, Bob Weiss   UK (*The Cold Room*)

A college girl (Amanda Pays), visiting her writer father (George Segal) in East Berlin, somehow goes through a time warp to WWII. She becomes another person who is trying to smuggle out a Jewish woman (Renee Soutendijk) hidden in the next room. Based on a novel by Jeffrey Caine, it was filmed in England and Germany and had its US debut on HBO.

THE BEING

(HBO, 1980) **D/S:** Jackie Kong
P/A: William Osco *(Easter Sunday)*

A briefly seen killer-mutant kid is a result of nuclear waste. Osco stars, using the alias Rexx Coltrane, and surrounds himself with one of those oddball all-star casts: Martin Landau, José Ferrer, Dorothy Malone as the mother of the monster, Ruth Buzzi, Kinky Friedman, Murray Langston, and Marianne Gordon Rogers (Kenny Rogers' wife). Most of the stars appear briefly, then die. The narration attempts to make sense of it all.

THE BELIEVERS

(HBO, 1986) **D/P:** John Schlesinger **S:** Mark Frost **P:** Michael Childers, Beverly Camhe

Martin Sheen screams and yells a lot as a New York City police psychologist whose wife is mysteriously electrocuted by a coffeemaker. His son (Harley Cross) is chosen to be sacrificed by people from the Caribbean who practice Santería in Harlem. Helen Shaver develops a zit full of spiders in the most memorable scene in this upscale horror movie by the man who directed *Midnight Cowboy*. It was based on the novel *The Religion*, by Nicolas Conde, and photographed by Robby Muller. With Robert Loggia, Harris Yulin, Lee Richardson, Richard Masur, Jimmy Smits, and Trey Wilson. The soundtrack, on Varèse Sarabande, was composed by J. Peter Robinson.

BELL, BARE, AND BEAUTIFUL

(SW, 1963) **D/C:** Herschell G. Lewis
S: Leroy C. Griffith **P/A:** David F. Friedman

A young millionaire (William Kerwin) is obsessed by an unknown woman he dreams about. He goes to a shrink, places a sketch of the woman in a newspaper ad, and discovers that she's stripper Gina Adair (played by stripper Virginia "Ding Dong" Bell, "48–24–36"). They end up at a nudist camp (Spartan's Tropical Gardens in Miami). Bell, the main attraction of this Eastmancolor nudie movie, was four months pregnant at the time. Producer/actor Friedman also did the sound. With Jerry Eden and Sunny Dare. The title spoofs the title of the Broadway play and film *Bell, Book, and Candle*.

BELL, BOOK, AND CANDLE

(RCA, 1958) **D:** Richard Quine
S: Daniel Taradash **P:** Julian Blaustein

A Manhattan witch (Kim Novak) falls for a publisher (James Stewart), casts a spell on him, and loses her powers. Jack Lemmon is her warlock brother, Ernie Kovacs is an author, Janice Rule is the publisher's fiancé, and Elsa Lanchester and Hermione Gingold are witches. This comedy/fantasy from Columbia is based on the 1950 Broadway play by John Van Druten. James Wong Howe did the color cinematagraphy. A remake is planned.

BELLE DE JOUR

(Miramax, 1967) **D/S:** Luis Buñuel **S:** Jean-Claude Carrière **P:** Robert and Raymond Hakim   France/Italy

Catherine Deneuve (shortly after starring in Polanski's *Repulsion*) is the frigid new wife of a wealthy surgeon. She has S&M fantasies and starts spending her afternoons working in an expensive Paris brothel where all kinds of unspeakable things are implied. She seems to find happiness only after her husband (Jean Sorel) has been crippled. Buñuel uses dreams and flashbacks and typically plays around with the audience's expectations. Genevieve Page is the lesbian madam, and Pierre Clementi is the criminal customer with gold teeth. With Michel Piccoli, Francisco Rabal, George Marchal, Françoise Fabian, and a Japanese man with a mysterious box. Allied Artist released this controversial film in the US. Martin Scorsese arranged a theatrical rerelease in 1995.

THE BELLS

(Video Yesterday, 1926) **D/S:** James Young
P: I. E. Chadwick

Five years before *Frankenstein*, Boris Karloff plays one of his first important roles as a sideshow mesmerist in this silent rarity with an excellent cast, from Chadwick Pictures. A mean landlord (Gustav von Seyffertitz) wants money or the daughter of businessman Lionel Barrymore. On Christmas, a visiting Jew from Warsaw (with gold in his belt) is killed with an axe in the snow. Barrymore pays the landlord and becomes burgomaster but suffers from nightmares, sees a ghost, and goes mad from hearing sleigh bells. Karloff helps reveal who the killer is. He looks great (made up to resemble Dr. Caligari) and makes a woman float at the fair. *The Bells* had made English actor Sir Henry Irving famous in 1872. It had already been filmed four times, and three sound versions were made in the 30s in Europe. This version is 92 minutes long and includes music.

BELOVED INVADERS: THE VENTURES

(1965) **D/P:** George M. Reid **S:** Junko Terayama   Japan

The Ventures, from Tacoma, Washington, were one of the first American rock bands to become big in Japan. They toured there in the mid-60s, recorded some albums just for Japan, and even starred in this great b/w movie, part travel documentary, part concert-performance film. The print is excellent and letterboxed. The beginning is priceless. A narrator starts things off (in Japanese) as we see some scenes of everyday life in Tokyo. Then a teenager picks a selection from a jukebox ("Out of Limits," from the classic *Ventures in Space* album), and we see records being made at a pressing plant, then sold in stores. Lots of young guys are shown buying and practicing with electric guitars; then various homegrown rock groups play. One group is so amateurish that audience members cover their ears. The Ventures, four ordinary-looking Joes with 50s pompadours whose voices are dubbed into Japanese, are shown walking down a street and are identified (Nokie, Don, Bob, and Mel). Then, in an exhilarating scene, a couple dance wildly by the

seashore to a great, upbeat Ventures cut. Ventures mania has obviously arrived! The rest of the movie consists of the group sightseeing, signing autographs, eating noodles with chopsticks, and traveling around the country, with concert footage from each city shown. They even fly to Hiroshima, where they visit a crowded Pachinko parlor. If you're an instrumental-group fan you'll love this rare movie.

BELOW THE BELT

(1974) **D/S/P:** Robert Fowler **S:** Sherry Sonnet

Regina Baff is a New York waitress who becomes a female wrestler, "the Beautiful Boomerang." With "Terrible Tommy," Shirley Stoler, and the voices of the Firesign Theater. It was (finally) released in 1980.

BE MY GUEST

(1965) **D/P:** Lance Comfort **S:** Lyn Fairhurst   UK

David Hemmings and his rock band have a new place to play when his family inherits a seaside hotel. This is a follow-up to 1963's *Sing and Swing* (aka *Live It Up*). Guest artists include Jerry Lee Lewis, backed by the Nashville Teens, and some British groups you've never heard of. The late Small Faces/Humble Pie singer Steve Marriot is the drummer in Hemmings' band. A year later Hemmings was in *Blowup*.

BENEATH THE VALLEY OF THE ULTRAVIXENS

(RM, 1979) **D/P/C/E/A:** Russ Meyer

Lavonia (Francesca "Kitten" Natividad) and Lamar (Pat Wright) are a small-town couple who have exaggerated, wild sex with many other characters. Lavonia calls herself Lola when she strips at the Other Ball. He works for Junkyard Sal (June Mack). Stuart Lancaster is the narrator, and Henry Rowland is back as Martin Bormann. With Ann Marie (in two roles), Uschi Digart, Candy Samples, and Mary Gavin. Meyer throws in his usual comic violence, a chainsaw, an evangelist, and sex in a coffin, and shows up as himself. This is Meyer's last to date, and it's my least favorite of his 70s features. Others were funnier and sexier. Since then, Meyer has run his own video company and announced film, video, and book projects that never seem to get finished. Whenever he does finish something, a growing legion of fans will be waiting for it.

BERETTA'S ISLAND

(Live, 1994) **D:** Michael Preece
S/P/A: Franco Columbo

Franco Columbo, a short former Mr. Universe, stars as a musclebound Interpol agent (and winemaker) who goes home to Sardinia (and to Vegas) to battle drug dealers, led by Van Quattro. Columbo's real-life friend Arnold Schwarzenegger shows up for a few minutes in a workout scene. Elizabeth Kaitan and Jen Percheval costar.

BERKELEY SQUARE

(1943) **D:** Frank Lloyd **S:** Sonya Levien, John L. Balderston **P:** Jesse L. Lasky

Leslie Howard is an American who somehow goes back in time to 18th-century England and falls for Heather Angel. The cast also includes Samuel S. Hinds, Valerie Taylor, and Alan Mowbray. This romantic fantasy from 20th Century-Fox was remade as *I'll Never Forget You* (1951), using the same script. Balderston also scripted many early Universal horror classics.

THE BERLIN CONSPIRACY

(RCA, 1991) **D:** Terence H. Winkless **S:** Jackson Barr **P:** Kevin Reidy (*The Day the Wall Came Down*)

Executive producer Roger Corman, the first person to make a movie exploiting the 1958 Soviet Sputnik (*War of the Satellites*), was one of the first with a camera crew in Berlin when the wall came down. The trouble is, by the time he got this one onto video shelves it was old news. It's about two agents, former rivals, Klaus (Stephen Davies) and CIA man Harry (Marc Singer), trying to keep some canisters of deadly bacteria out of the hands of terrorists. They also both want Mary Crosby. There's one sex scene featuring extras and a comic fight. The sound is bad. I was wondering about the realities of shooting in Germany just after reunification. Except for some Berlin Wall footage, this was made in Sofia (Bulgaria) and LA. From Concorde and the director of *Bloodfist*.

BERMUDA TRIANGLE

(Lightning, 1978) **D:** Richard Friedenberg **S:** Stephen Lord **P:** Charles E. Sellier, James L. Conway

A G-rated pseudodocumentary with re-creations of supposed events, based on a book by Charles Berlitz. The narration is by Sunn Classics regular Brad Crandall and Thalmus Rasulala.

BERRY GORDY'S THE LAST DRAGON *See* THE LAST DRAGON

BERSERKER

(Starmaker, 1987) **D/S:** Jef Richard **P:** Jules Rivera

A Viking spirit in a bear mask possesses a man who kills teen campers. Buck Flower is the "name" in this silly slasher-in-the-woods movie. The cinematography is by Henning Schellerup. It was filmed in Utah.

BEST DEFENSE

(Paramount, 1984) **D/S:** Willard Huyck **S/P:** Gloria Katz

Dudley Moore is a failing inventor who is given the secret of the "DYP Giro" supertank weapon in this flop comedy. "Guest star" Eddie Murphy, as a US lieutenant, accidentally drives his tank into the middle of a war between Iraq and Kuwait, so at least they predicted that right. With Kate Capshaw as Moore's wife, George Dzundza, Tom Noonan, David Rasche, and Tracey Ross. It was shot in Hollywood and Israel.

THE BEST OF ALFRED HITCHCOCK PRESENTS: *See* ALFRED HITCHCOCK PRESENTS

THE BEST OF DARK SHADOWS: *See* DARK SHADOWS

THE BEST OF MARTIAL ARTS FILMS

(1992) **D/S:** Sandra Weintraub **P:** Fred Weintraub

John Saxon narrates this very entertaining look at modern martial-arts movies, which briefly covers the careers of Cynthia Rothrock, Angela Mao, Jackie Chan, Samo Hung, Yuen Baio, Jean-Claude Van Damme, Richard Norton, and Benny "the Jet" Urquidez using choice film clips. The Weintraubs made a documentary on Bruce Lee (using some of the same footage) at about the same time. This one debuted on Cinemax.

THE BEST OF SEX AND VIOLENCE

(Wizard, 1981) **D:** Ken Dixon

John Carradine hosts a compilation of 40 exploitation trailers. Carradine's sons David and Keith show up for a few seconds, but his segments are ill-conceived and embarrassing. Seek out this tape for the incredible Rudy Ray Moore trailers (*Dolemite; Disco Godfather*) and appearances by Cassandra (Elvira) Peterson (*Working Girls*), Vanity (*Tanya's Island*), Phyllis Davis (*Terminal Island*), Claudia Jennings, Uschi Digart, Edy Williams, Laura Gemser, and others. Angelo Rossitto also appears, and Brinke Stevens is on the video box.

BEST OF THE BEST

(SVS, 1989) **D:** Bob Radler **S:** Paul Levene **P/A:** Phillip Rhee **P:** Peter E. Strauss

James Earl Jones and "spiritual adviser" Sally Kirkland take an American taekwondo team to Korea to compete. Phillip Rhee stars in this PG-13 *Rocky*-style movie. He goes after the martial-arts-champ killer (his real-life brother Simon Rhee) of his brother in Korea. He got a lot of names to act in his movie, including Eric Roberts, Christopher Penn, and Louise Fletcher. With John P. Ryan and Kane Hodder too. From Taurus Films.

BEST OF THE BEST 2

(Fox, 1993) **D:** Robert Radler **S:** Max Strom, John Allen Nelson **P/A:** Phillip Rhee **P:** Peter E. Strauss

Phillip Rhee returns in a more exploitative and violent (R-rated) sequel, this time from a major studio. Christopher Penn is killed, and Rhee and Roberts fight gladiators in a hidden illegal-betting fight arena under a Las Vegas nightclub. They also train with Sonny Landham, as Rhee's alcoholic Native American stepbrother, in "the Valley of Fire." The bad guys are gladiator Ralph Moeller and Wayne Newton as Weldon, the MC. With Meg Foster, Edan Gross, and Simon Rhee. *Best of the Best 3* followed.

BEST SELLER

(Orion, 1987) **D:** John Flynn **S:** Larry Cohen **P:** Carter De Haven

A wired, psychotic corporate hitman (James Woods) teams up with an LA cop (Brian Dennehy) to help him write a book. The two stars are excellent, and the teaming of Flynn and Cohen was a great idea. With Victoria Tennant and Paul Shenar as the industrialist criminal threatened by the existence of Woods.

BETRAYAL

(Cinema Home, 1974) **D:** Gordon Hessler **S:** James M. Miller **P:** Gerald I. Isenberg

An ABC-TV movie starring Amanda Blake (from *Gunsmoke*) as a wealthy widow who advertises for a companion. The young girl who gets the job (Tisha Sterling) is a killer and extortionist working with a boyfriend. With sex star Rene Bond as a waitress. Not to be confused with several other tapes with the same title.

BETRAYAL OF THE DOVE

(Prism, 1992) **D:** Strathford Hamilton **S:** Robby Benson **P:** Ashrok Amritraj

Helen Slater is a single mom who goes on a blind date with a doctor (Billy Zane). Murders occur in this "Hitchcockian psychological thriller" and many characters are suspected. With David Lander as her lawyer boyfriend, Alan Thicke as her alky ex, Kelly LeBrock, Stuart Pankin, and Harvey Korman. Benson wrote the story with Karla DeVito.

BETRAYED

(1944) **D:** William Castle **S:** Philip Yordan, Dennis J. Cooper **P:** Maurice and Franklin King (*When Strangers Marry*)

A small-town girl (Kim Hunter, from *The Seventh Victim*) marries a stranger (Dean Jagger) and goes to Manhattan. An old boyfriend (Robert Mitchum) shows up, and a series of silk-stocking murders occur. The 67-minute Monogram release also features Neil Hamilton as a police detective and Milton Kibbee.

BETTER OFF DEAD

(Key, 1985) **D/S:** Savage Steve Holland **P:** Michael Jaffe

High-school student John Cusack loses Amanda Wyss to a jock. He becomes suicidal but eventually finds French exchange student Diane Franklin to replace her. The PG-rated teen comedy features animated singing hamburgers, an attack by newspaper boys, and other odd surprises. With Curtis Armstrong as the best friend, David Ogden Stiers and Kim Darby as the parents, and Vincent Schiavelli as a teacher. Holland also made *One Crazy Summer* and *How I Got into College*.

A BETTER TOMORROW

(Republic, 1986) **D/A:** John Woo **S:** Chan Hing-Kai, Leung Suk **P:** Tsui Hark Hong Kong

Ti Lung (an ex-con Triad gangster) and Leslie Cheug (a cop) play brothers in a violent, bloody, action-packed hit. Chow Yun-Fat costars as Mark, a now-derelict friend who has lost a leg. It features a shootout finale that later features had to try and top. With Emily Chu and Waise Lee. This was the biggest Hong Kong hit ever released at the time. Woo, Hark, and Chow Yun-Fat were all major forces in the new-look Hong Kong features of the 80s and 90s and helped gain international critical acclaim for the industry (and do away with old-style kung-fu movies).

A BETTER TOMORROW II

(1987) **D/S:** John Woo **S/P:** Tsui Hark   Hong Kong

The same cast returns in this popular sequel, but since Mark was killed in the first film, Chow Yun-Fat plays the character's twin brother. He teams with cop Leslie Cheung and reformed gangster Ti Lung to fight criminals. There's an exciting conclusion with a staggeringly high body count, and some scenes take place in America. Star Chow Yung-Fat was in the equally violent hit *The Killer* the next year.

A BETTER TOMORROW III: LOVE AND DEATH IN SAIGON

(1989) **D/S/P:** Tsui Hark   Hong Kong

Chow Yun-Fat and Tony Leung returned in this slower-paced, longer (130-minute), and more serious prequel to the first two films in the series. There's a major female character this time, Anita Mui as a businesswoman who becomes a warrior. It's partially set in Vietnam during the early 70s (the director was born there) and unlike the first two movies was not a major hit.

THE BEVERLY HILLBILLIES

(Fox, 1993) **D/P:** Penelope Spheeris
S: Lawrence Konner, Mark Lowenthal,
Jim Fisher, Jim Staal **P:** Ian Bryce

This PG-rated remake of the popular TV series (1962–71) stars Jim Varney as Jed, Cloris Leachman as Granny, Erika Eleniak as Ellie May, Diedrich Bader as Jethro, Lily Tomlin as Miss Hathaway, and Dabney Coleman as Mr. Drysdale. Lea Thompson is a gold digger who's after Jed (the same plot as *Addams Family Values*), and there are cameos by Zsa Zsa Gabor, Dolly Parton, and original star Buddy Ebsen.

BEVERLY HILLS BODYSNATCHERS

(SGE, 1989) **D:** John Mostow
S/P: P. K. Simonds Jr. **P:** John Mostow

A serum revives the dead in this black comedy. Vic Tayback (in his last role) is a mortician, and Frank Gorshin is a mad doctor. They run into trouble when they revive a gangster. With Art Metrano and Brooke Bundy.

BEVERLY HILLS BRATS

(Media, 1988) **D:** Dimitri Sotirakis
S: Linda Silverhorn **P/A:** Terry Moore

Terry Moore (still claiming to be Howard Hughes' widow) produced this PG-rated comedy. A boy (Peter Billingsley) arranges for Burt Young and Robert Tessier to kidnap him so he'll get more attention from his rich parents. Martin Sheen is the plastic-surgeon dad, and Moore is the mom. With Natalie Schafer, George Kirby, and Martin's son

Ramon Sheen. Janet Sheen was associate producer. Nobody liked it, but if you do, you can relive some of your favorite scenes while watching the outtakes at the end.

BEVERLY HILLS COP

(Paramount, 1984) **D:** Martin Brest **S:** Daniel Petrie Jr. **P:** Don Simpson, Jerry Bruckheimer

Eddie Murphy is at his best as Detroit cop Axel Foley in a role once planned for Sylvester Stallone. He joins Judge Reinhold and John Ashton as LA cops to bring down a British gangster (Steven Berkoff) who killed his partner (James Russo). With Lisa Eilbacher, Ronny Cox, Bronson Pinchot, Paul Reiser, and Karen Mayo Chandler. This action comedy was a huge hit, so sequels followed. The Danny Elfman soundtrack (with various artists) was also a big seller on MCA.

BEVERLY HILLS COP II

(Paramount, 1987) **D:** Tony Scott **S:** Larry Ferguson, Warren Skaaren **P:** Don Simpson, Jerry Bruckheimer

Eddie Murphy, Judge Reinhold, and John Ashton return in an inferior sequel with an interesting group of villains. Brigitte Nielsen, Jurgen Prochnow, and Dean Stockwell steal diamonds and use a rifle range as a front. With Allen Garfield as the police chief, Ronny Cox (bedridden), Paul Reiser (he stays in Detroit), Gilbert Gottfried, Chris Rock, and Carrie Leigh as herself. The sequel also features Hugh Hefner and many *Playboy* centerfolds and models as *Playboy* Playmates at a pool party: Rebecca Ferratti, Kymberly Herrin, Luanne Lee, Venice Kong, Kym Page, Ola Ray, Kari Whitman, and Alana Soares.

BEVERLY HILLS COP III

(Paramount, 1994) **D:** John Landis
S: Steven E. deSouza **P:** Robert Rehme

Detroit cop Axel Foley (Murphy) goes back to LA and is teamed with Judge Reinhold again, but few people cared anymore. Parts of this action comedy are set in a theme park, called Wonderworld, run by a Walt Disney type (Alan Young), and there are typical John Landis in-jokes. With Theresa Randle, Hector Elizondo, Stephen McHattie, John Saxon, Bronson Pinchot (again), Al Green as a minister, and Julie Strain. The score is by Nile Rogers. It cost roughly $50 million and was a commercial flop.

BEVERLY HILLS GIRLS

(Hideaway, 1985) **D/S:** Mike Hall

Michelle Bauer is a lesbian millionaire video producer, and Linnea Quigley (who sings) is the lesbian leader of a rock group. With Becky LeBeau. This soft-X film was shot on video. Bauer was also in *New Beverly Hills Girls*.

BEVERLY HILLS VAMP

(Vidmark, 1988) **D:** Fred Olen Ray
S: Ernest D. Farino **P:** Grant Austin Waldman

This comedy is loaded with Hollywood gags and references to director Ray's own career. Manic Eddie Deezen stars. He and his nice-guy friend Tim Conway Jr. are would-be filmmakers. They

visit a whorehouse run by Britt Ekland as Madame Cassandra, who has a gay butler and is actually a vampire. When her usually-naked vampire hookers (like Michelle Bauer, Jillian Kessner, and Debra Lamb) are having sex, the men leave their pants on like in old nudie movies. Deezen becomes an enthusiastic vampire-hunter with a cross on his underwear after his friend is bitten. Writer Farino used to do effects for S. F. Brownrigg movies in Texas. With Jay Richardson as the Ray-like director, Robert Quarry, Dawn Wildsmith, and Pat McCormick delivering an overlong intro.

BEWARE, MY LOVELY

(Republic, 1952) **D:** Harry Horner
S: Mel Dinelli **P:** Collier Young

Robert Ryan is a confused, unpredictable, frightening psycho who takes a job as a handyman at the home of a widow (Ida Lupino). This simple, underrated feature from RKO was based on Dinelli's play.

BEWARE OF CHILDREN

(1960) **D:** Gerald Thomas **S:** Norman Hudis,
Robert Estridge **P:** Peter Rogers   UK (*No Kidding*)

In this comedy, a couple (Leslie Phillips and Geraldine McEwan) inherit an old manor house and turn it into a vacation resort for rich kids. The international assortment of spoiled brats chop down trees, steal cars, and terrorize an alcoholic cook by dressing up as ghosts. AIP released the comedy in America.

BEWARE, SPOOKS!

(1939) **D:** Edward Sedgwick **S:** Richard Flournoy **P:** Robert Sparks

Joe E. Brown, the once-popular wide-mouthed comedy star, is a bumbling rookie detective who chases an escaped criminal (Marc Lawrence) in a Coney Island amusement park haunted house. With Mary Carlisle and Clarence Kolb. Just over an hour long, it was overshadowed by a bigger-budget crime comedy released the same year, Paramount's *The Cat and the Canary* (Bob Hope's first hit).

THE BEYOND: *See* SEVEN DOORS OF DEATH

BEYOND AND BACK

(1978) **D:** James L. Conway **S:** Stephen Lord **P:** Charles E. Sellier Jr.

See after-death experiences recreated in this pseudodocumentary based on a book by Ralph Wilkerson. Actors play Plato and Houdini's wife. Lots of people saw this at drive-ins. What a way to spend an evening! The narration is by Sunn Classics' familiar voice of Brad Crandall.

BEYOND A REASONABLE DOUBT

(VidAmerica, 1956) **D:** Fritz Lang
S: Douglas Morrow **P:** Bert Friedlob

Lang's last American feature stars Dana Andrews as a novelist who puts his life on the line to discredit capital punishment. After he lets himself

They went into the unknown and returned with startling revelations about life after death.

BEYOND AND BACK

Some will believe — others will not. DECIDE FOR YOURSELF!

G

Produced by **Charles E. Sellier, Jr.**
Directed by **James L. Conway** • Written by **Stephen Lord**
Narrated by **Brad Crandall** • Based in part on the book by **Ralph Wilkerson**
Color by **Technicolor**

Benjamin Dobbs, a psychology student whose parents are dead, dreams about a nonexistent younger brother and a (topless) woman with a scary voice. Some of the best nightmare images are a light bulb exploding in slow motion, a balloon filled with blood, and a janitor with no hands who approaches and says, "Shake." Benjamin writes down his dreams and shows them to his professor. Soon the man (and his house) disappear: "Nothing around here seems real! I can't feel anything!" There are zombies and a demonic red monster that mangles its victims. A female doctor is decapitated. The score is somber and menacing. It's hard to follow all the changing fragments of this interesting movie, but I guess that's the point. I think Woelfel could work wonders with a slightly bigger budget. He made this at Ohio State University in Columbus when he was 26 years old.

BEYOND JUSTICE

(Vidmark, 1990) **D:** Duccio Tesari **S:** Adriano Bolzoni, Sergio Donati, Luigi Montefiori Italy

CIA agent Rutger Hauer goes to the Moroccan desert to rescue Carol Alt's son. The rich-brat New York kid has been chosen by his Muslim grandfather (Omar Sharif) to lead his tribe. Kebir Bedi is Sharif's son. With Donald Sutherland and Elliott Gould, for name-value support, and Brett Halsey. Some missile and kung-fu fights occur. The score is by Ennio Morricone.

BEYOND MOMBASA

(1956) **D:** George Marshall **S:** Richard English **P:** Adrian Worker, Tony Owen UK/US

Cornel Wilde stars as the leader of a group searching for uranium in the African jungle. With Donna Reed, Christopher Lee as a French hunter, Leo Genn, and Ron Randell. They experience a Mau Mau attack, alligators, and leopard men. This color Columbia release was shot in British East Africa.

BEYOND REASON

(Media, 1977) **D/S/A:** Telly Savalas **P:** Howard Koch (*Mati*)

Bet you didn't know that Kojak directed a movie. He's Dr. Mati, a shrink who is seeing things and losing his mind, and who may even be a killer. Diana Muldaur costars with Laura Johnson and Melissa Prophet. Priscilla Barnes (who was the original star) was mostly cut out of this PG feature which was not released until 1982.

BEYOND THE CALL OF DUTY

(1991) **D/P:** Cirio H. Santiago **S:** T. C. McKelvey Philippines

Jan-Michael Vincent stars as a US Army commander who rescues some soldiers and a group of singing orphans at the end of the Vietnam war. Lots of Vietcong soldiers die, and things blow up. With Jillian McWhirter and Eb Lottimer. From Concorde.

BEYOND THE CELLAR DOOR = TERROR FROM UNDER THE HOUSE

BEYOND THE CURTAIN OF SPACE: *See* ROCKY JONES

BEYOND THE DOOR III

(RCA, 1989) **D:** Jeff Kwitny **S:** Sheila Goldberg Italy (*The Train*)

LA coeds go to the countryside to reenact an ancient ritual and encounter "the Prince of Darkness." The rest of the movie takes place on a train on a collision course. It was shot in Yugoslavia and has a surprisingly high-budget look. With Bo Svenson as a Serbian professor (!), Savina Gersak, Mary Kohnert, Victoria Zinny, and a dwarf. *Beyond the Door* (1975) was an *Exorcist* copy, and *Beyond the Door II* (1979) was an unrelated, retitled Mario Bava movie, so the three make up another fake "series." Ovidio Assonitis (who directed the original using the name Oliver Hellman) was the executive producer.

BEYOND THE DOORS

(Unicorn, 1983) **D/S/P:** Larry Buchanan (*Down on Us*)

See how a government assassin killed Jimi Hendrix, Janis Joplin, and Jim Morrison! Dallas-based Buchanan is a conspiracy buff who made *The Trial of Lee Harvey Oswald* (1964) years before a TV movie with the same name. It's not hard to imagine that maybe the American government was somehow behind the deaths of famous role-model rock stars. This was (finally) released with a new title to cash in on Oliver Stone's *The Doors*. A lot of time is spent showing actor clones of the rock stars live in concert. Each one of them performs three whole songs that sound sort of like songs made famous by the originals. You might recognize bits of familiar lyrics but not enough for Larry to have to pay any copyright fees. The only song he could get away with copying is "The Star Spangled Banner"! No matter who's supposed to be playing in whatever city, they always seem to be on the same stage in front of the same audience.

Jimi and Janis meet and sing drunken blues together backstage. Janis confronts Morrison in the ladies' room. You get to see Jimi pose with topless blondes for an LP cover, meet "the Plaster Casters," and watch a New York drag show. Morrison in Miami screams, "Wake up before the whole world goes into the atomic sewer!" and "How does it feel to be vermin?!" See Janis shoot up while watching Vietnam war footage on TV. Nixon is heard saying, "These voices must be still." The government assassin (Sandy Kenyon, who landed a short-lived role on *Knots Landing* after this) is shown at home breaking his son's records. He offs two of the stars, but Jim Morrison fakes his own death in Paris and hides out in a Spanish monastery (!), where he later dies anyway. Bu-

be tried (the trial is televised) and sentenced to death for a crime he didn't commit, the evidence that would free him is destroyed, and his fiancé (Joan Fontaine) has to save the day. The plot takes some surprising (and hard-to-believe) turns, and although the low budget of this RKO production sometimes shows, it's pretty dark and fascinating. With Sidney Blackmer, Barbara Nichols, Shepperd Strudwick, Arthur Franz, and Dan Seymour. Andrews had also been in Lang's *While the City Sleeps*, released the same year (it's also on video).

BEYOND DARKNESS

(Imperial, 1990) **D/S:** "Clyde Anderson"/ Claudio Fragasso **S:** Sarah Asproon Italy

A minister (Gene LeBrock) and his family move into an isolated house. *Amityville Horror* stuff happens, but the FX are minimal. An alcoholic expriest helps them, and there's something about a kid-killing woman on death row. From the maker of *Rats* and *Monster Dog*. Laura Gemser is credited with costume design, so Joe D'Amato was probably involved in this derivative bore.

BEYOND DEATH'S DOOR

(1979) **D:** Henning Schellerup **S:** Fenton Hobart Jr. **P:** Stan Siegel

If you loved *Beyond and Back*, here's another look at what happens when you die. With Tom Hallick as a doctor who believes, after two dying patients (a hooker and a skier) relate their cosmic, heart-stopping experiences. "Their experience could change your life—and death," said the ads. It was Schellerup's follow-up to *In Search of Historic Jesus*.

BEYOND DREAM'S DOOR

(VidAmerica, 1988) **D/S:** Jay Woelfel **P:** Dyrk Ashton

chanan's movie is eerily fascinating despite (or because of) being too long, too dark, and too cheap. Someday a director with money will tackle the same idea for a major company, and Larry will be able to say "I did it first" again. With Stuart Lancaster and Karen Mayo-Chandler.

BEYOND THE LAW

(Sinister, 1968) **D/S:** Giorgio Stegani
S: Fernando Di Lio   Italy/W. Germany
(*Al di la della Legge; The Good Die First; Bloodsilver*)

Lee Van Cleef is a thief who wanders the West with a preacher (Lionel Stander) and an ex-slave. He becomes a sheriff in order to rob a silver shipment before his former partner (Gordon Mitchell) can get to it. With Antonio Sabata, Ann Smyrner, Herbert Fux, and Bud Spencer.

BEYOND THE LAW

(Live, 1992) **D/S:** Larry Fergusson
P: John Fielder, Mark Tarlov

Bearded, long-haired Charlie Sheen is an Arizona cop who goes undercover in a gang of arms-dealing, murdering bikers. He also has flashbacks to the time he killed his abusive uncle. It's all based on a real case. Linda Fiorentino costars as a photographer, with Michael Madsen, Rip Torn, Leon Rippy, and Courtney B. Vance. It was released in 1994. Fergusson (one of the uncredited scriptwriters on *Alien³*) wrote a script that copies *Stone Cold*.

BEYOND THE LIVING = NURSE SHERRI

BEYOND THE LIVING DEAD: *See* THE HANGING WOMAN

BEYOND THE STARS

(1989) **D/S:** David Saperstein
P: Michael Plotkin   (*Personal Choice*)

Christian Slater, as a kid on vacation, meets an astronaut (Martin Sheen) who was on the moon and who reveals surprising secrets about his trip. With Robert Foxworth, Sharon Stone, Olivia D'Abo, and F. Murray Abraham.

BEYOND THE UNIVERSE

(1981) **D/S:** Robert Emenegger **S/P:** Allan Sadler

A scientist in the 21st century tries to save Earth from further destruction after two atomic wars. He makes contact with "God." With David Ladd, Jaqueline Ray, and Christopher Carey. Emenegger is a UFO specialist.

BEYOND TOMORROW

(Sinister 1940) **D:** A. Edward Sutherland
S: Adele Comandini **P:** Lee Garmes

The spirits of three rich New York City businessmen (Harry Carey, C. Aubrey Smith, and Charles Winninger) return to Earth on Christmas Eve to help a young couple (Richard Carlson, as a singing Texan, and Jean Parker). This romantic fantasy

from RKO is more serious than most. There's a murder, and some characters are sent to Hell. With Maria Ouspenskaya as an exiled Russian noblewoman and former silent-film star Rod LaRocque.

BIG

(CBS/Fox, 1988) **D:** Penny Marshall **S:** Gary Ross,
Anne Spielberg **P:** James L. Brooks, Robert Greenhut

A 12-year-old kid becomes Tom Hanks, and Elizabeth Perkins falls for the childish man. With John Heard, Robert Loggia, Jon Lovitz, and Mercedes Ruehl. This PG romantic fantasy/comedy hit was followed by many similar movies, such as *Vice Versa* and *18 Again*.

BIG BAD BOLD BOSS: *See* BOSS

BIG BAD JOHN

(Magnum, 1989) **D:** Burt Kennedy
S: Joseph Berry **P/A:** Red Steagall

Jimmy Dean stars as a retired sheriff living in a swamp cabin who goes after Big Bad John (football star Doug English). Mostly characters in "monster" trucks shoot at each other, but this PG-13 film ends like the song, in "that nameless pit." Dean's 1961 hit single of the same name is heard, but not his version. With Jack Elam, Ned Beatty, Bo Hopkins, Anne Lockhart, and Romy Windsor.

BIG BAD MAMA II

(MGM, 1987) **D/S:** Jim Wynorski
S: R. G. Robertson **P:** Roger Corman

Angie Dickinson returns as a Depression-era killer in Texas in this remake of and sequel to the 1974 original. She uses a body double this time for her nude scene (with costar Robert Culp), but young Danielle Brisebois (from *All in the Family* and *Archie Bunker's Place*) and Julie McCullough (from *Growing Pains* and the pages of *Playboy*) have topless scenes as her seductive daughters. With Bruce Glover as the evil candidate for governor, Kelly Maroney, Linda Shayne, and Harriet White Medin. The music is imitation Morricone. From Concorde.

THE BIG BET

(Cinema Group, 1986) **D/S/P:** Bert I. Gordon

Sylvia Kristel helps a teenager (Lance Sloane) seduce a schoolgirl. With Kim Everson, Elizabeth Cochrell, Stephanie Blake, Monique Gabrielle, speeded-up film, porno tapes, teen fantasies, and nudity. Gordon made another sex comedy, *Let's Do It*, next.

THE BIG BIRD CAGE

(Warner, 1972) **D/S:** Jack Hill **P:** Jane
Schaffer   (*Women's Penitentiary II*)

The comic New World sequel to the previous year's *The Big Doll House* features "women so hot with desire they melt the chains that enslave them!" Anitra Ford is kidnapped during a nightclub shootout and thrown in jail. The bamboo

"big bird cage" is a tall sugar mill. Blossom (Pam Grier), a mercenary, leads a prison break with the help of Sid Haig as Django. The women rape the gay prison guard (Vic Diaz), then smother him by sitting on his face. Drive-in cheap thrills with Roberta Collins, Teda Bracci as a lesbian, Carol Speed (from *Abby*), and Candice Roman.

THE BIG BRAWL

(Warner, 1980) **D/S:** Robert Clouse
P: Fred Weintraub

Jackie Chan starred in his first American film, by Bruce Lee's best-known director. Not enough people here knew who Chan was (the number 1 star in Asia), and not many were interested in a 30s gangster movie, set in Chicago, with martial-arts fighting. Mako is the old master who trains him. With Rosalind Chow, Kristine DeBell (from the X-rated *Alice in Wonderland*), José Ferrer, Lenny Montana, and H. B. Haggerty as a wrestler. Raymond Chow was the executive producer. The music is by Lalo Schifrin (who also scored *Enter the Dragon*).

THE BIG BUST OUT

(Embassy, 1973) **D/S/P:** "Richard Jackson"/
Sergio Garrone   Italy/W. Germany
(*La Mònaca tre Bastardi, e sette Peccatrici*)

Vonetta McGee (from *Hammer* and *Blacula*) and a group of prisoners (and a nun) escape from a Middle Eastern prison, are caught by slavers, and escape again. With Gordon Mitchell, Tony Kendall, and William Berger. This New World film features nudity, rape, lesbian scenes, and a sadistic dwarf. It was made by a director who later gained notoriety in Europe for a series of pretty vile Nazi-theme movies.

THE BIG CAGE

(1933) **D:** Kurt Newmann **S:** Edward
Anthony, Ferdinand Reyher

Clyde Beatty, in his film debut, stars as himself, a famous wild-animal trainer. In one memorable scene, 20 lions and 20 tigers escape from the same cage. Mickey Rooney is the kid who idolizes him, and Anita Page is the trapeze-artist love interest. With Andy Devine and Wallace Ford. The Universal feature was rereleased by Realart in 1950. The animal footage was used in countless other films over the years. Beatty returned in *The Lost Jungle* and *Darkest Africa*.

BIG CALIBRE

(Sinister, 1934) **D/S:** Robert North Bradbury
P/A: A.W. Hackel **C:** John Alton

This strange, gothic western stars Bob Steele (who was the director's son). A mad scientist (Perry Murdock) wearing a disguise kills the hero's father with a capsule of corrosive gas. The production was supervised by Sam Katzman and distributed by Bradbury. Steele, a B-western star since 1927, later became a character actor. He retired in the 70s after playing a regular role on the *F Troop* TV series.

THE BIG COMBO

(Prism, 1955) **D:** Joseph H. Lewis
S: Phillip Yordan **P:** Sidney Harmon

Cornel Wilde stars as a detective named Diamond in this *film noir*, sex-and-violence cult classic by the director of *Gun Crazy*. Diamond uses any means available to break up the operations of a mob financier (Richard Conte), whose motto is "First is first and second is nobody," and tries to get Jean Wallace (his real-life wife) away from him. Lee Van Cleef and Earl Holliman play Fante and Mongo, a homosexual pair of thugs, and Brian Donlevy is killed with his own hearing aid. John Hoyt, Ted De Corsia, Whit Bissell, and Robert Middleton also appear in this United Artists release.

THE BIG CRIMEWAVE

(Favorite, 1987) **D/S/A:** John Paizs
Canada (*Crimewave*)

A would-be crime novelist (Steven Penny) has writer's block. This surreal comedy with an evil Elvis was made over a three-year period.

BIG DADDY

(1965) **D/S/P:** Carl K. Hittleman   (*Paradise Road*)

Reed Sherman (the associate producer) falls for an illiterate swamp girl in the Florida Everglades. Victor Buono plays the title character. Gators and a voodoo witch doctor figure in the plot. M. A. Ripps (*Poor White Trash*) retitled and rereleased this indy feature (by the screenwriter of *Jesse James Meets Frankenstein's Daughter*) in 1969. With Joan Blondell, Chill Wills, Tisha Sterling, Billy Benedict, and Arline Hunter.

THE BIG DEADLY GAME

(1955) **D/S:** Daniel Birt **S/P:** Robert Dunbar
UK (*Third Party Risk*; *Deadly Game*)

In this Hammer film (released in the US by Lippert) Lloyd Bridges is an American on vacation in Spain who becomes involved with a smuggling ring. Simone Silva, Finlay Currie, and Ferdy Mayne are also in the cast.

THE BIG DOLL HOUSE

(Embassy, 1971) **D:** Jack Hill **S:** Don Spencer
P: Jane Shaffer   Philippines (*Women's Penitentiary*)

Eddie Romero and actor John Ashley were the executive producers of this first-of-its-kind women-in-prison drive-in classic. Red-haired Judy Brown is top-billed and has nude scenes. Pam Grier is a tough lesbian hooker named Grear and also sings the theme song, "Long Time Woman." It was her first major role after being in *Beyond the Valley of the Dolls*. With Roberta Collins, Sid Haig (in his first of six appearances with Grier), Kathryn Loder as a sadistic guard, Brooke Mills, and Pat Woodell. *The Big Bird Cage* was a follow-up with most of the same cast.

THE BIG FISHERMAN

(1959) **D:** Frank Borzage **S:** Howard
Estabrook **S/P:** Rowland V. Lee

Howard Keel stars as Saint Peter in a 180-minute religious epic based on the novel by Lloyd C. Douglas. With Susan Kohner, John Saxon, Martha Hyer, Herbert Lom as King Herod, Rhodes Reason, Henry Brandon, and Jonathan Harris (from *Lost in Space*). God strikes down an evil man, Christ appears, but the best miracles are the visible microphones and electric lights. This money-losing film cost $4 million and was originally shown in Panavision 70mm. It was the last film by Borzage, who had been a director since 1916. Buena Vista released but did not produce it.

BIGFOOT THE MYSTERIOUS MONSTERS

(1975) **D/S:** Robert Guenette

Peter Graves narrates a pseudodocumentary about Bigfoot, the Abominable Snowman, and the Loch Ness Monster. With scenes from *Land of the Yeti* (1964). *Bigfoot: Man or Beast?* (1971) was another similar documentary. *Bigfoot* (1987) was a Disney TV movie directed by John Huston's son Danny.

BIGGER THAN LIFE

(1956) **D:** Nicholas Ray **S:** Cyril Hume,
Richard Maibaum **P/A:** James Mason

James Mason is excellent as a grade-school teacher hooked on life-saving cortisone. He becomes a tense megalomaniac who insults and outrages everybody, eventually terrorizes his family, and intends to kill his wife (Barbara Rush) and son. Walter Matthau is a family friend who tries to get help. With Roland Winters. It was released (in Cinemascope) the year after *The Man with the Golden Arm*. The two films led to changes in censorship rules forbidding the depiction of drugs in films.

BIGGLES: ADVENTURE IN TIME

(Starmaker, 1985) **D:** John Hough **S/P:** Kent
Walwin **S:** John Groves **P:** Pom Oliver   UK

Peter Cushing (in his last film appearance) plays a retired Royal Air Force colonel in this PG-rated time-travel fantasy. A young American businessman (Alex Hyde-White in his first role) goes back in time to WWI and helps rescue his "time twin," a British pilot named Biggles (Neil Dickson), from the Germans. It's based on characters, created by Captain W. E. Johns, that were popular in the 20s. New World released it in the US. Cushing died in 1994.

THE BIG GUNDOWN

(Columbia, 1967) **D/S:** Sergio
Sollima **S:** Sergio Donati, Tulio
Demicheli **P:** Alberto Grimaldi
Italy (*La Resa dei Conti*)

Lee Van Cleef, just after costarring in Leone's *The Good, the Bad, and the Ugly*, stars as a Texas lawman chasing a Mexican outlaw (Tomas Milian) at the request of a wealthy railroad man. He eventually discovers that he's being used and that the man he's after is innocent. This serious political western was made by the screenwriter of *Burn!* and *The Battle of Algiers*. With Fernando Sancho and Walter Barnes. The music is by Ennio Morricone. The uncut European version runs 114 minutes, but Columbia cut it for the US and it was rated M. The ads said, "Mr. Ugly comes to town today!"

THE BIG HEAT

(RCA, 1953) **D:** Fritz Lang **S:** Sydney
Boehm **P:** Robert Arthur

Lang's best 50s film is a *film noir* classic starring Glenn Ford as a police detective investigating the suicide of his partner. He discovers that the chief of police works for the gangsters responsible and that most people are like "scared rabbits." Because he won't back down, his wife (Jocelyn Brando) is blown up in her car, and he becomes a determined vigilante. Lee Marvin as a sadistic gangster and Gloria Grahame as his moll both use hot coffee as a weapon. Scorsese called this Columbia release one of the most important American films of all time. It was based on a book by William P. McGivern. With Jeanette Nolan, Alexander Scourby, Carolyn Jones, and Dan Seymour. Ford and Grahame were teamed again in Lang's next film, *Human Deisre* (1954), a remake of Jean Renoir's *La Bete Humaine* (1938).

THE BIG HEAT

(1988) **D:** Andrew Kai, To Kei Kong
S: Gordon Chan **P:** Tsui Hark   Hong Kong

Waise Lee (*Bullet in the Head*) stars as a cop who leads a group against a crime boss to avenge the death of his partner (Kuo Choi). With Chu Kong as a crimelord importing drugs for the Russians, and lots of violence and blood.

BIG HOUSE, USA

(1955) **D:** Howard W. Koch
S: John C. Higgins **P:** Aubrey Schenck

Broderick Crawford and his prison gang make life Hell for new inmate Ralph Meeker, a kidnapper who has a fortune stashed away. Koch filmed in documentary style at Casabel Island Prison and in a Colorado national park. Considered excessively

Lon Chaney Jr. in *Big House, USA*.

violent when released, the film includes death by blowtorch and boiler vat. With William Talman, Lon Chaney Jr. as Alamo Smith, Charles Bronson as Benny Kelly, and Reed Hadley.

THE BIG HURT

(Magnum, 1986) **D/S:** Barry Peak
S: Sylvia Bradshaw   Australia

A reporter (David Bradshaw) for a Melbourne tabloid discovers a government-backed plot involving "pain/pleasure drugs" that were tested on hookers.

BIG MAN ON CAMPUS

(Vestron, 1989) **D:** Jeremy Kagan **S/A:** Allan Katz
P: Arnon Milchan   (*The Hunchback of UCLA*)

Katz is a comic hunchback living in the UCLA bell tower. He's put on trial and tested, but a doctor (Cindy Williams) falls for him, and he falls for Melora Hardin. Another doctor (Jessica Harper) wants to exploit him. With Corey Parker, Tom Skerritt, and Gerritt Graham as a TV host. This PG-13 film was a trial to sit through.

BIG MEAT EATER

(Media, 1982) **D/S:** Chris Windsor
S/P: Laurence Keane **S:** Phil Savath   Canada

Toy-robot aliens go after radioactive meat that forms in a septic tank below a butcher shop, in this unique would-be cult film set in the 50s, with some funny song-and-dance numbers. George Dawson, acting almost as nerdy and cheerful as Pee-wee Herman, stars, sings, and talks to the camera as the local butcher who has invented a new, universal language. He hires a singing-psycho janitor named Abdullah, played by Big Miller (a black Canadian jazz musician). Andrew Gillies plays the other main character, a member of an eccentric Moldavian family. New Line released it in 1984.

THE BIG NIGHT

(1960) **D:** Sidney Salkow **S:** Ric Hardman **P:** Vern Alves

Some teens find a lot of money and fight over it, resulting in death and "a nightmare of violence," as the ads promised. Randy Sparks (who later founded the New Christy Minstrels) stars with Venetia Stevenson (*Horror Hotel*). Sparks also sings the title song. Dick Foran, Jesse White, and Dick Contino also appear in this b/w film.

THE BIG NOISE

(Fox, 1944) **D:** Mal St. Clair **S:** Scott
Darling **P:** Sol M. Wurtzel

Laurel and Hardy, as janitors at a detective agency, deliver a secret "super bomb" in this bad WWII comedy. Stan plays "Marizy Doats" on an accordion, and they end up dropping the bomb on a Japanese submarine. With Arthur Space, Doris Merrick, Veda Ann Borg, Phil Van Zandt, and Jack Norton. The once-great comedy team appeared in only three more features.

THE BIG PAYOFF: *See* WIN, PLACE, OR STEAL

THE BIG PICTURE

(RCA, 1989) **D/S:** Christopher Guest
S/P: Michael Varhol

Kevin Bacon is an Ohio film student in Hollywood who discovers just who gets the money to make features, and why. He takes a phone-sales job and directs a rock video. This on-target comedy is filled with fantasy sequences, in-jokes, some excellent acting, and guest stars. With Emily Longstreth, Teri Hatcher, J. T. Walsh as a film executive, Jennifer Jason Leigh, Martin Short as a creepy agent, Kim Myori, John Cleese, Jason Gould, and Michael McKean (who acted with director Guest in *This Is Spinal Tap*).

THE BIG RED ONE

(Warner, 1980) **D/S:** Samuel Fuller **P:** Gene Corman

The last American feature that Fuller had control of after *The Naked Kiss* (1964) was based on his own WWII experiences. Lee Marvin stars as the weathered sergeant leading a group of very young soldiers as they land on the beaches. With Mark Hamill as Griff, Robert Carradine, Bobby Di Cicco, Perry Lang, Siegfried Rauch, and Stèphane Audran. The battle scenes are very convincing, there's a great asylum scene, and concentration-camp scenes were filmed in Israel with Israeli soldiers playing guards. Monte Hellman was the second-unit director. United Artists released it with a PG rating, but Fuller had more career setbacks when his next feature, *White Dog* (1982), was withdrawn by Paramount. A Dutch documentary, *Sam Fuller and the Big Red One* (1979) is narrated by the late Aldo Ray.

THE BIG SCORE

(Vestron, 1983) **D/A:** Fred Williamson **S:** Gail Morgan
Hickman **P:** Michael S. Landes, Albert Schwartz

This is the eighth feature Williamson made as director and star, and it's one of his best. The story is from scripts originally written for *Dirty Harry* movies. Williamson stars as Chicago narcotics cop Frank Hooks. Richard Roundtree and John Saxon are other cops. With Nancy Wilson (making her acting debut) as a nightclub singer and Ramsey Lewis, Ed Lauter, D'Urville Martin, Tony King, Michael Dante, and Bruce Glover as a hitman working for gangster Joe Spinell. The score is by Jay Chattaway, and the cinematography is by Joao Fernandes, who also shot *Deep Throat* and *The Devil in Miss Jones*. Harry Hurvitz was the executive producer.

THE BIG SLEEP

(IVE, 1978) **D/S/P:** Michael Winner
P: Elliott Kastner   UK

Robert Mitchum returns as Philip Marlowe in a modernized, R-rated remake (from United Artists) of the 1946 Bogart classic. It's also a follow-up to Mitchum's *Farewell, My Lovely* (1975). Candy Clark, Joan Collins, and Sarah Miles are the women who try to use and confuse the detective, and Oliver Reed is gangster Eddie Mars. With

Richard Boone as a hitman, Edward Fox, John Mills, Harry Andrews, Richard Todd, Colin Blakely, and even James Stewart.

THE BIG SNATCH

(SW, 1968) **D:** "Ronnie Runningboard"/B. Ron Elliot

A long-haired guy in a pickup truck, with trained dogs, kidnaps 5 women off the street. He insults them and makes them dance and call him master. They all do exercises topless in an empty pool. Momo, the servant, is whipped when he tries to mess with the women. It looks like it would be easy for them to escape, but finally Uschi Digart says, "Let's sock it to him, night and day," so they tie him up and they do. This color movie has lots of nudity and sex (outdoors, in the shower . . .) and fake credits. With Peggy Church (*All American Girl*). Newspapers in 1968 often changed the title to *The Big Catch*. Alan Rudolph's *Barn of the Naked Dead* (1973) had a similar plot, without so much sex.

THE BIG SWEAT

(AIP, 1990) **D:** Ulli Lommell **S:** Max
Bolt **P/A:** Joanne Watkins

The crash footage (nearly half the running time of this tape!) was lifted from *Gone in Sixty Seconds* (1974), by the late H. B. Halicki. Other footage was borrowed from Lommell's own *Cold Heat* (also 1990). Robert Z'Dar is the FBI-agent hero, and Steve Malone leads a gang of bank robbers.

THE BIG TNT SHOW

(1966) **D:** Larry Peerce **P/M:** Phil Spector

This excellent "electrovision" followup to the *TAMI Show* was taped in 1965 at the Lost Angeles Moulin Rouge club. David McCallum, star of the popular TV series *The Man from U.N.C.L.E.*, is the host. The musical stars (in order of importance, in my opinion) are Bo Diddley (with the Dutchess!), Ike and Tina Turner, Ray Charles, the Ronettes (with Spector's wife, Ronnie), the Byrds, Donovan, the Lovin' Spoonful, Petula Clark, Roger Miller, the Modern Folk Quartet, and Joan Baez. Spector was showing how much popular music was changing at the time, but no matter how good the newer hit-makers were, they couldn't really compete with the established R&B acts. Watch this to see Bo and Tina during their prime, work-til-you-drop days. You won't find better footage of either one. Peerce followed this with *The Incident*. Young Sky Saxon and Johnny Legend are in the studio audience. Parts of this movie are in the video release *That Was Rock*.

BIG TOP PEE-WEE

(Paramount, 1988) **D:** Randal Kleiser **S/P/A:** Paul
Reubens **S:** George McGrath **P:** Debra Hill

Pee-wee Herman invites a circus to set up on his land after local townspeople throw them out. His best friend is Vance the talking pig, but he falls for Valeria Golino, and they enjoy "the longest kiss in screen history." This PG movie ends with a farm-theme circus, and the stuffy locals become happy kids again. It seems as though the reason *Pee-wee's*

Big Adventure (1985) was so good had a lot to do with director Tim Burton. This follow-up was a flop, Pee-wee's once popular show ended in 1991, then a scandal resulted from an absurd arrest in a porno theatre in Florida. Anyway, in what will likely be the last Pee-wee Herman movie, he invents a hot-dog tree and giant vegetables. Kris Kristofferson keeps 6-inch-high Susan Tyrrell in his pocket. With Penelope Ann Miller, Kenneth Tobey, Kevin Peter Hall, and naturally tiny Michu. The Arista soundtrack features Danny Elfman's score, which copies Nino Rota.

THE BIG TOWN

(Vestron, 1987) **D:** Bem Bolt **S:** Robert Roy Pool **P:** Martin Ransohoff, Don Carmody

Matt Dillon is a small-town crapshooter in 50s Chicago, where he meets a stripper played by Diane Lane (her real-life mom was a *Playboy* centerfold). The film is based on the novel *The Arm* by Clark Howard. With Tommy Lee Jones, Suzy Amis, Bruce Dern, Lee Grant, Tom Skerritt, and Lolita Davidovich.

BIG TROUBLE IN LITTLE CHINA

(Fox, 1986) **D:** John Carpenter **S:** Garry Goldman, David Z. Weinstein **P:** Larry J. Franco **M:** John Carpenter, Alan Howarth

Kurt Russell is a wisecracking truck driver with a John Wayne voice in this PG-13 fantasy/adventure/comedy with martial arts, machine guns, lots of FX, and rubbery monsters. It has a lot in common with *The Golden Child*, released the same year, but is a lot more fun. Sue Francis (Suzee Pai, *Penthouse*'s January 1981 Pet, from Toledo) is kidnapped by an ancient magician (James Hong) in San Francisco, and Russell tries to rescue her. With Dennis Dun, Kim Cattrall, Victor Wong, Kate Burton, James Pax, and many other Asian actors (including Cary-Hiroyuki Tagawa and Jade Go). The soundtrack by the director and his usual collaborator, Alan Howarth, was on Enigma. This was the fourth Carpenter/Russell feature (after *Elvis*, *Escape from New York*, and *The Thing*). With FX by Steve Johnson.

BIG WEDNESDAY

(Warner, 1978) **D/S:** John Milius **S:** Dennis Aaberg **P:** Buzz Feitshans (*Summer of Innocence*)

James Hong and Suzee Pai in *Big Trouble in Little China*.

Jan-Michael Vincent, Gary Busey, and William Katt are legendary surfers in a widescreen, PG-rated feature that was overlooked when released. It cost $11 million to make (a very big budget at the time) and includes excellent surfing footage. The story takes place from the early 60s to the mid–70s and shows the changes that the Vietnam War brought. With Lee Purcell, Patty D'Arban-ville, Barbara Hale (Katt's real-life mother), Reb Brown, and Robert Englund. It's 126 minutes long (but a TV version is shorter). The soundtrack includes some choice oldies (including "Green Onions") and some classic authentic Hawaiian music. The director surfed in real life, which explains some of the dialogue in *Apocalypse Now* (written by Milius and Coppola).

BIKERS, BLONDES, AND BLOOD

(SW, 1994)

Johnny Legend introduces this compilation of around 40 trailers plus a 1966 US Navy social-etiquette short, *Blondes Prefer Gentlemen*. Some rare and outrageous trailer highlights are *Racers From Hell*, *Road Devils*, *The Undertaker and His Pals*, *Captive Girl* (Buster Crabbe and Johnny Weismuller), *Girl in Black Stockings*, *The Wild, Wild World of Jayne Mansfield*, *Queen of Blood*, *Teenage Tramp*, *Teenage Strangler*, and the 4-feature "Chiller Carnival of Blood" show. A few of these titles haven't been reviewed or listed anywhere yet.

BIKINI ISLAND

(Prism, 1991) **D/P:** Anthony Markes **S:** Emerson Bixby **P:** Zachary Matz

Five models are taken to a remote island for a *Swimwear Illustrated* shoot. An unknown psycho kills off the models and the photo crew members using arrows, strangulation, and a bathroom plunger. Most of the time is spent with the girls posing in bikinis or taking showers while rock songs are heard. A creepy handyman lurks, and somebody peeps through (huge) keyholes. This really stupid Mike Curb production at least looks good. Holly Floria is the top-billed survivor. A stuntman was killed making this.

BILL AND COO

(Video Yesterday, 1947) **D:** Dean Riesner **S:** Royal Foster, Dean Riesner **P/A:** Ken Murray

They don't make 'em like this anymore. "George Burton's Love Birds" star in this bizarre novelty movie from Republic. A whole town full of

Keanu Reeves, George Carlin, and Alex Winter in *Bill and Ted's Excellent Adventure*.

birds who act like humans is menaced by a black crow who attacks during a circus. Circus acts take up most of the 61-minute running time. Murray also narrates.

BILL AND TED'S EXCELLENT ADVENTURE

(Orion, 1987) **D:** Stephen Herek **S:** Chris Matheson, Ed Soloman **P:** Scott Krooft, Michael S. Murphy, Joel Soisson

Alex Winter and Keanu Reeves are Bill and Ted in this clever time-travel fantasy/comedy. A guy from the future named Rufus (George Carlin) helps the lovable lunkheads pass history class by taking them back in time in a phone booth (an idea from *Dr. Who*). They meet Billy the Kid (Dan Shor), Joan of Arc (the Go Gos' Jane Weidlin), Genghis Khan (Al Leong), "So Crates," Napoleon, Lincoln, and Sigmund "Frude." Before they can help out in the classroom, the confused famous characters experience a shopping mall. With Bernie Casey, Diane Franklin, Clarence Clemens, and Fee Waybill. After DEG made this PG film it was delayed for two years, but it became a hit when Orion released it. *Bill and Ted* became an animated TV show before it was sequelized, and inspired *Wayne's World*. Matheson is the son of the famous scriptwriter Richard Matheson. Not bogus.

BILL AND TED'S BOGUS JOURNEY

(Orion, 1991) **D:** Peter Hewitt **S:** Chris Matheson, Ed Soloman **P:** Scott Kroopf

Bill (Alex Winter) and Ted (Keanu Reeves) return, go to Heaven and Hell, meet martians, and beat the *Seventh Seal*–style Grim Reaper (William Sadler) at Clue and Twister. They also meet God, the Devil, Albert Einstein, and the Easter bunny! With evil robots of the heroes, Rufus (George Carlin), Amy Stock-Poynton, Sarah Trigger, Joss Ackland, Pam Grier, and Taj Mahal. The world is saved by Kiss playing "God Gave Rock and Roll to You." This PG sequel was to be (and should have been) called *Bill and Ted Go to Hell*. A terrible live-action Fox-TV series followed.

BILLY JACK

(Warner, 1971) **D/S/P/A:** Tom Laughlin
S/A: Dolores Taylor **P:** Mary Rose Solti

The half-breed karate expert and ex–Green Beret Nam hero from AIPs biker movie *Born Losers* (1967) returns. He saves horses from being used for dog food and protects an Arizona "freedom school" for runaways. Laughlin's real-life wife, Dolores Taylor, costars, with Bert Freed, Kenneth Tobey as the mean deputy sheriff, and the Committee comedy troupe (with Howard Hesseman). McLaughlin directed (as T. C. Frank), and he and his wife used fake names (Frank and Theresa Christina) for writing. The low-budget, PG movie was started at AIP but was moved to Fox and then to Warner. Laughlin took it back from Warner in 1973 and "four-walled" it into hundreds of theaters himself, using saturation advertising and making it a very profitable cult hit. It's a long 115 minutes. The Warner soundtrack features Coven doing the hit "One Tin Soldier." *The Trial of Billy Jack* (1974) was next.

BILLY JACK GOES TO WASHINGTON

(1977) **D/S/A:** Tom Laughlin
S/A: Dolores Taylor **P:** Frank Capra Jr.

After *The Trial of Billy Jack*, Laughlin returned in a talk-filled, anti-nuke remake of Frank Capra's

Tom Laughlin is *Billy Jack*.

classic *Mr. Smith Goes to Washington*. This was a very bad idea, and few people ever saw the results. Dolores Taylor costars, as usual, with Sam Wanamaker, Luci Arnaz, E. G. Marshall, Pat O'Brien, and Dick Gautier. It runs a long 155 minutes. By 1981 the former cult star was reduced to acting in *The Legend of the Lone Ranger*. He made the papers in 1986 while working on *The Return of Billy Jack* in Times Square, but the film was never finished. In 1991 Laughlin announced he was running for president. He might have had a chance 20 years earlier.

BIMBOS IN TIME

(Asylum, 1993) **D/P/A:** Todd Sheets **S:** Roger Williams

While this silly time-warp sci fi comedy was obviously made on an incredibly low budget, it's very ambitious, including many costumed extras in various time settings and some good location work. There's even a medieval battle scene with suits of armor. *Bimbos* (which would be rated PG) is loaded with this-is-a-movie in-jokes and also throws in animated dinos, a disco scene, robots on skateboards, some old rock hits, historical figures, and A-bomb footage. My favorite character is a comical older-lady villain (Cathy Metz) with a rolling pin. There are outtakes and interviews at the end. It's the last of a Kansas City video trilogy, following *Bimbos BC* and *Prehistoric Bimbos in Armageddon City*.

BIOHAZARD

(VGB, 1983) **D/S/P/A:** Fred Olen Ray

A small, face-ripping lizard monster from another dimension (played by the director's son) is unleashed at a desert lab, in this very low-budget *Alien* copy. The late Aldo Ray is a general, and the late Angelique Pettyjohn (who had been in hardcore features like *Body Talk* and *Titillation* in 1982) is a mind-reader. Also with an unrecognizable Carroll Borland (from Tod Browning's *Mark of the Vampire*) and Robin Schurtz. The end features plenty of outtakes of Pettyjohn naked and Johnny Legend singing. It was Ray's first 35-mm feature after the unreleased *Brain Leeches*, *The Alien Dead* (with Buster Crabbe), and *Scalps*. He went on to direct a record number of features, always with name stars from the past.

BIONIC SHOWDOWN: THE SIX MILLION DOLLAR MAN AND THE BIONIC WOMAN

(1989) **D:** Alan J. Levi **S:** Michael Sloan **P:** Nigel Watts

Lee Majors and Lindsay Wagner return and run around in slow motion again. New, younger bionic heroes join them, and they all try to capture a bionic spy. With old series regular Richard Anderson, Lee Majors II, and Robert Lansing.

This ABC-TV pilot was the network's attempt to create a spinoff series from the two lame 70s shows. The network wouldn't give up, so *Bionic Breakdown* (1994) followed.

BIRD OF PARADISE

(Video Yesterday, 1932) **D/P:** King Vidor **S:** Wells Root, Wanda Tuchock, Leonard Praskins

Dolores Del Rio is Luana, a native girl in a sarong. Joel McCrea falls in love with her, but she's chosen to be sacrificed to the volcano god. Lon Chaney Jr. plays his very first role. This RKO feature, based on a play by Walton Tully, was remade in 1951.

BIRD OF PARADISE

(1951) **D/S/P:** Delmer Daves

Debra Paget is Kalua, and Louis Jourdan is the outsider who loves her. This Technicolor remake was filmed in Hawaii. With Jeff Chandler, Everett Sloane, Jack Elam, and Maurice Schwartz as the big Kahuna. Water turns to blood, Paget walks on hot coals, and, in an ending viewers never forget, she sacrifices herself to save her people by leaping into the active volcano.

BIRD ON A WIRE

(MCA, 1990) **D:** John Badham **S:** Louis Venosta, Eric Lerner, David Seltzer **P:** Rob Cohen

Mel Gibson, who's in a witness-protection program, and his lawyer ex-girlfriend Goldie Hawn hide out from drug-dealer killers, in this PG-13 by-the-numbers adventure filmed in Canada. David Carradine had his first major theatrical-release role in years as the main villain. It all ends in a battle in a zoo/rain forest. With Joan Severance, Bill Duke, Jeff Corey, and Stephen Tobolowsky. The Neville Brothers sing the title song, written by Leonard Cohen, and Bob Dylan's "Blowin' in the Wind" is heard.

THE BIRDS II: LAND'S END

(MCA, 1994) **D:** "Allan Smithee"/Rich Rosenthal **S:** Jim and Ken Wheat **P:** Ted Kurdyla

Chelsea Field and Brad Johnson move to Gull Island somewhere on the East Coast with their daughters and soon are being attacked by seagulls. Local officials act like they're in *Jaws*. This 30-years-later sequel to Hitchcock's movie was shot in North Carolina and debuted on Showtime. With James Naughton, Jan Rubes, and original star Tippi Hedren as a shopkeeper. Animatronics and real birds were used.

BIRTH OF THE BEATLES

(1979) **D:** Richard Marquand **S:** John Kurland, Jacob Eskendar **P:** Tony Bishop   US/UK

The early days with Pete Best (consultant on the film) and Stu Sutcliffe are touched on, but this mostly looks at the mop-tops up until the first *Ed Sullivan Show* appearance. With lookalike actors and music by Rain. Members of the Beatles sued to stop this Dick Clark production but lost. It was made for ABC-TV but played theatrically in Europe. Two years later a film version of the plot-less stage play *Beatlemania* was released. See *Backbeat* instead.

THE BISHOP MURDER CASE

(1930) **D:** Nick Grinde, David Burton **S:** Lenore Coffee

Fourteen Philo Vance detective features were made by different studios with various stars from 1929 to 1947. They were all based on novels by S. S. Van Dine (Willard Huntington Wright). Here, Basil Rathbone stars as the upper-class Vance. (William Powell played the detective in the first Vance film, *The Canary Murder Case*, made by Paramount in 1929, and later starred in three more.) A deranged killer called "the Bishop" uses Mother Goose rhymes to plan his murders. With Leila Hyams (from *Island of Lost Souls*), Roland Young, and a crippled hunchback. It was nearly a decade before Rathbone became Sherlock Holmes.

THE BISHOP'S WIFE

(Samuel Goldwyn, 1947) **D:** Henry Koster **S:** Robert E. Sherwood **P:** Samuel Goldwyn

Watch this after you get sick of *It's a Wonderful Life*. Cary Grant stars as a charming angel in human form named Dudley who arrives just before Christmas to help a young Episcopal bishop (David Niven) and his wife (Loretta Young) build a new church and repair their marriage. With Monty Woolley, James Gleason, Elsa Lanchester, Regis Toomey, and some of the kids from *It's a Wonderful Life*. Billy Wilder and Charles Brackett (uncredited) wrote additional scenes. The RKO release was later colorized. A remake is planned.

THE BITCH

(Thorn EMI, 1979) **D/S:** Gerry O'Hara **P:** John Quested   UK

Joan Collins is "the bitch" in a disco/sex movie based on a story by her sister, Jackie Collins. She owns a disco and has Mafia problems. With Ian Hendry and Sue Lloyd. The soundtrack includes tunes by Blondie, the Stylistics, and Three Degrees. It was followed by a sequel, *The Stud*.

BITE ME, DARLING!

(1970) **D/S/P:** Helmut Foernbacher **S:** Martin Roda Becher, W. H. Riedl   Germany (*Beiss Mich, Liebling*)

This sex comedy about a stud mailman features a psychiatrist who becomes a vampire. With Eva Renzi, Brigitte Skay, and Barbara Valentin. *The Vampire Happening* was a more ambitious German vampire/sex comedy from the same year.

BITTER HARVEST

(Prism, 1993) **D:** Duane Clark **S:** Randall Fontana **P:** Steven Paul, Gary Binkow

Jim Kelly in *Blackbelt Jones*.

In an erotic thriller that copies *Bonnie and Clyde* (again), Patsy Kensit is a blond real-estate saleswoman who wants the estate of hick Stephen Bladwin, and Jennifer Rubin is a blond hitchhiker. The three of them end up robbing banks together. With M. Emmet Walsh and Adam Baldwin.

BITTER MOON

(New Line, 1992) **D/S/P:** Roman Polanski **S:** Gerard Brach, John Brownjohn

Oskar (Peter Coyote, who narrates) is a wealthy, egotistical American would-be writer in Paris who becomes involved with a beautiful waitress (Emmanuelle Seigner). The relationship goes downhill from love and lust to boredom, TV-watching, S&M games, abuse, cheating, hatred, and revenge. Seven years later he's crippled and in a wheelchair, telling it all to an embarrassed but fascinated Brit (Hugh Grant) on an ocean liner just before New Year's Eve. The depressing tale is based on a novel by philosopher Pascal Bruckner. With Kristen Scott Thomas. There's a clip from *Once Upon a Time in America*, a score by Vangelis, and appropriate older hit songs by Brian Ferry, the Eurythmics, and others. *Bitter Moon* was a hit in Europe, and Fine Line released it in America (in 1994) after NC-17 rating threats. Polanski had married Seigner in 1989. His next was *Death and the Maiden* (1994).

BITTER VICTORY

(1957) **D/S:** Nicholas Ray **S:** Rene Hardy, Gavin Lambert **P:** Paul Graetz   France/UK

A love triangle interferes during a British commando raid in North Africa during WWII. Richard Burton, Curt Jurgens, and Ruth Roman star, with Christopher Lee as a British sergeant and Nigel Green. The full British version of the film, shot in Libya and France, is 103 minutes long.

THE BLACK ABBOT

(Sinister, 1963) **D/S:** Franz Gottlieb **S:** Johannes Kai   W. Germany (*Der Schwartze Abt*)

Charles Regnier stars as Inspector Puddler in an Edgar Wallace mystery about a killer in a black cloak and hood and a family treasure. With Joachim Fuchsberger, Dieter Borsche, Eddi Arent, Werner Peters, and Klaus Kinski as Thomas, the butler. It was released to TV in the US.

BLACK ALLEY CATS

(SW, 1972) **D:** John Hayes **S:** Joseph Drury **P:** John Munchkin

Some private-school girls (two black, two white) want revenge for a rape attack by a gang. They take kung-fu lessons, learn to shoot, and wear masks and black-cat logos on their jackets. "The Alley Cats" rob corrupt businessmen and make everyone at a rich people's party strip (including Uschi Digart). They also attack and strip the new Jamaican student in the showers. She doesn't mind much and soon joins them. Marsha Jordon plays a lesbian who seduces her student babysitter while her rapist/doctor husband takes pictures. They are punished too, of course.

THE BLACK ARROW

(RCA, 1984) **D:** John Hough **S/P:** Harry Alan Towers   US/UK/Spain (*La Flecha Negra*)

Stephan Chase and Georgia Slowe star in an adventure based on a novel by Robert Louis Stevenson. With Oliver Reed as the landowner villain, Fernando Rey, and Donald Pleasence. (The story had also been filmed in 1948 with Louis Hayward.) It debuted on the Disney Channel but was a theatrical release in Europe. Towers was making movies for Playboy (*Frank and I, Black Venus, Christina*) and Disney at the same time.

BLACKBEARD'S GHOST

(Disney, 1967) **D:** Robert Stevenson
S: Bill Walsh **P:** Walt Disney

Peter Ustinov is the friendly ghost of a cursed 18th-century pirate who helps a modern-day college track team coach (Dean Jones) on the Carolina coast. He also saves an inn run by Elsa Lanchester from gangsters. This typical Disney fantasy/comedy features Suzanne Pleshette, Richard Deacon, silent-film star Betty Bronson, and Alan Carney as a bartender.

BLACK BELT

(New Horizons, 1992) **D/S:** Charles Phillip Moore
P: Cirio H. Santiago

Don "the Dragon" Wilson is an ex-cop who uses martial arts to protect a singer (Diedre Imershein) from a psycho Nam-vet serial killer (Mathias Hues). With Richard Beymer as a crooked record producer, Maria M. Ruiz, Brad Hefton, Ernest Simmons, and many real martial-arts fighters as bad guys. Roger Corman, who started Wilson's acting career with the *Bloodfist* series, was the executive producer. It was later remade as *Angel of Destruction. Blackbelt II: Fatal Force* (New Horizons, 1993) stars Blake Bahner.

BLACK BELT JONES

(Warner, 1974) **D:** Robert Clouse **S:** Oscar Williams **P:** Fred Weintraub, Paul Heller

"Black Belt" Jones (Jim Kelly) fights the Mafia to protect his martial-arts school in Watts. Gloria Hendry (*Live and Let Die*) is a fighter too, in this PG feature. With Scatman Crothers and Eric Laneuville. There's a big battle in a car wash at the end. By the makers of *Enter the Dragon*, which Kelly had also been in. Music by Dennis Coffey.

BLACK BIKERS FROM HELL = BLACK ANGELS

BLACK BRIGADE

(1969) **D:** George McGowan **S/P:** Aaron Spelling
S: David H. Kidd **P:** Danny Thomas   (*Carter's Army*)

This ABC-TV movie is about a redneck army captain from the South (Stephen Boyd) put in charge of black troops in 1944 on the road to Berlin. With Richard Pryor, Billy Dee Williams, Rosie Grier, Moses Gunn, Robert Hooks, Glyn Turman, and Paul Stewart. Susan Oliver is credited with "TVs first interracial kiss" (if you don't include *Star Trek*).

BLACK CAESAR

(Orion, 1973) **D/S/P:** Larry Cohen

This was Cohen's first film after *The Housewife*. Fred Williamson is at his best as Tommy Gibbs, a shoeshine boy who grows up to beat the Italian mob. The AIP hit includes Gloria Hendry,

D'Urville Martin as the (fake) Reverend Rufus, Julius W. Harris, Don Pedro Colley, James Dixon, Val Avery, and Art Lund as the racist cop who ends up having to shine Gibbs' shoes while singing "Mammy" in blackface. The amazing ending was shot on the streets of New York, with Gibbs being gunned down in front of Tiffany's. The music is by James Brown ("Down and Out in New York City"), Fred Wesley, and Lyn Collins and is on the Polydor soundtrack. *Hell Up in Harlem* is the sequel (1973). With makeup FX by Rick Baker.

BLACK CARRION

(1984) **D:** John Hough **S:** Don Houghton   UK

A satanic 60s rock band in a castle keep playing "Shakin' All Over." Season Hubley and Leigh Lawson are in this Hammer TV movie, shown on *Fox Mystery Theater*.

THE BLACK CAT

(Rhino, 1980) **D/S:** Lucio Fulci **S:** Sergio Salvati
P: Biagio Proietti   Italy (*Il Gatto Nero*)

Fulci fans used to his gory movies like *Zombie* and *Gates of Hell* were disappointed by this tamer effort, but it's pretty interesting. I can't think of a movie with more closeups of eyes. The widescreen image was cropped for video release, so sometimes when the edges are cut off all you see is the bridge of a person's nose! Mimsy Farmer, a blond 60s American teen star, in Europe ever since Barbet Schroeder's *More* (1969), plays an American photographer taking pictures in a crypt in a British village. Patrick Magee is Miles, a medium trying to contact the dead with electrical equipment. A lot of things happen that make no sense, but Miles' mysterious black cat seems to be causing various violent deaths. He tells the cat, "We need each other. We're bound together by hatred!" David Warbeck is a Scotland Yard inspector on a bike. Farmer is asked to photograph dead people and is attacked by bats. Magee drugs the cat and tries to hang it. It all ends with the familiar Poe cat-in-the-wall scene. This is one strange movie (it was filmed in Rome and England), and Magee and Farmer are better than Fulci deserves. With Dagmar Lassander. The music is by Pino Donaggio.

BLACK CAT

(1990) **D/S:** Luigi Cozzi   Italy
(*Edgar Allan Poe's Black Cat*)

Here's another horror movie about making a horror movie, full of Mario Bava/ Dario Argento movie references that fans will enjoy and lots of shock effects. An early line is: "That man is no director. He's a butcher!" Ann (Florence Guerin) is a pregnant actress whose husband, Mark, directs "spaghetti horror" movies. Another actress (Caroline Munro) lives with the screenwriter. Together they discuss Argento's *Suspiria* and plan to make *Out of the Depths*, about the witch Livana ("the third mother"), who shows up in various disguises to kill and manipulate. Brett Halsey appears as a

mean, wheelchair-bound producer in a haunted house. There are lots of confusing dream sequences and guts from a TV. Black cats are frequently shown to justify the title, lightning strikes a lot, and part of "Radar Love" is heard. The hard-to-believe cosmic Cozzi ending involves control of time and space (and *2001*). With Urbano Barbarini and Michele Soavi. From 21st Century.

BLACK CAT

(VSOM, 1991) **D/P:** Stephen Shin   Hong Kong

This is basically an uncredited remake of the French film *La Femme Nikita*. Like that very influential hit, it starts out really violent, spends time as a love story, then gets back to some outrageous action. Jade Leung stars as the young, harmonica-playing criminal who has a computer chip (called "the Black Cat") implanted in her head and becomes a government assassin in Hong Kong and eventually in Canada and Japan. Simon Yam is the CIA trainer. The tape is (badly) dubbed. A laserdisc version has multiple soundtracks (English, Mandarin, and Cantonese). *Black Cat II* (also with Leung) followed. This is better than the American version (*Point of No Return*).

BLACK CHARIOT

(1971) **D/S/P:** Robert L. Goodwin

Bernie Casey joins a Black Panther-type group, but they're betrayed by a member. This was promoted as "the first all-black feature" (it wasn't). Goodwin, a TV screenwriter, raised money door to door in LA, shot it partially on videotape, and released it himself.

BLACK CLUE = THE BEAST MUST DIE

BLACK COBRA

(Video Gems, 1976) **D/S:** "Joe D'Amato"/
Aristide Massaccesi   Italy (*Eva Nero; Erotic Eva*)

Judas, a rich playboy in Honk Kong (Jack Palance), is obsessed with snakes. He takes in Eva (Laura Gemser), who dances topless with cobras at a nightclub. The plot involves murders for money and features nudity (of course) and lesbian scenes. It was shot on location around Hong Kong. With Gabrielle Tinti. The uncut version runs 98 minutes.

BLACK COBRA

(Southgate, 1986) **D:** Stelvio Massi **S:** Danilo Massi **P:** Luciano Appignani   Italy

Fred Williamson is a New York City police detective who shoots it out with a gang of psycho bikers (led by a Schwarzenegger clone) and saves a witness (Eva Grimaldi). With Sabrina Siani as the police chief's daughter who is kidnapped. The title and theme were borrowed from Stallone's *Cobra*, and it was followed by three sequels.

BLACK CUE: *See* THE BARON

BLACK DEVIL DOLL FROM HELL

(Budget, 1984) **D/S/P/M:** Chester Novell Turner

Here's a hard-to-believe, low-budget, homemade film with an all-black cast. A churchgoing lady (Shirley L. Jones) is compelled to buy a doll at a magic shop. The possessed doll is actually a Jerry Mahoney mannequin (the kind you used to be able to buy) in blackface and a Rasta wig. The big-eyed doll watches the woman shower and soon becomes her secret lover, growling, "Beg for it, bitch!" Long sequences show the doll grunting and thrusting on top of her. She throws away her Bible, the doll leaves, and she picks up guys at discos and bars, but they just don't measure up. Do-it-all Turner also performs the (not bad) rock-and-roll theme song. If it sounds stupid, offensive, hateful, and crude, it is, but I swear that some of the doll's dialogue was copied in *Child's Play*. The tape runs 70 minutes (including 7 minutes of opening credits!).

THE BLACK DOLL

(1938) **D:** Otis Garrett **S:** Harold Buckley **P:** Irving Starr

A rich, corrupt businessman and several other characters are murdered. A Mexican voodoo doll is left with each body. The mystery takes place in an old, dark house by the sea, complete with secret tunnels. Donald Woods stars as a detective, and Edgar Kennedy is the irritating comic-relief sheriff. With Nan Grey, Holmes Herbert, and William Lundigan. Phil Karlson was the assistant director of this 66-minute film, the second in a series of seven Universal "Crime Club" B-movie mysteries based on stories from pulp magazines.

THE BLACK DUKE

(1963) **D:** Pino Mercanti **S:** Mario Amendola **P:** Tulio Bruschi   Italy/Spain (*Il Duco Nero*)

Cameron Mitchell plays the Italian Renaissance military conqueror and ladies' man Cesare Borgia. Caterina Sforza (Gloria Millan) tries to have him destroyed by sending spies and women to poison him. It was one of several Italian historical costume movies Mitchell starred in during the 60s.

BLACK EAGLE

(Imperial, 1988) **D:** Eric Karson **S:** A. E. Peters **P:** Shimon Arama

In a spy drama with martial arts, hero Sho Koshugi goes to Malta to recover a secret laser device from a downed American plane. Jean-Claude Van Damme is the unstoppable Soviet villain. With Bolo Yeung and Kane and Shane Koshugi.

BLACK ELIMINATOR: *See* DEATH DIMENSION

BLACK EMANUELLE

(1975) **D/S:** "Albert Thomas"/Alberto Albertini   Italy (*Emanuelle in Africa*)

Laura Gemser, in the first of a long series of "black Emanuelle" movies, is a photographer in Africa. She has dream sex with natives, sleepwalks in the nude, and becomes involved with Karin Schubert (who later did porno) and her boyfriend. The two female stars returned in *Emmanuelle Around the World*. There's also the unrelated *Black Emanuelle, White Emanuelle*, with Louisa Longo. "Thomas"/Albertini also made *Black Emanuelle 2* (with Sharon Lesley) and *Yellow Emanuelle* (with Chai Lee). Gemser was in *Emanuelle in Bangkok* next.

BLACK EVIL = GANJA AND HESS (cut version)

BLACK EYE

(1974) **D:** Jack Arnold **S:** Mark Haggard **P:** Pat Rooney

Fred Williamson is Shep Stone, a suspended California police detective turned private eye. He has to deal with a drug ring, porno movie producers, Jesus freaks, and murder. Teresa Graves (the star of the ABC-TV series *Get Christie Love*) is his bisexual girlfriend. With Richard Anderson, Rosemary Forsyth, Richard X. Slattery, and Bret Morrison (radio's "the Shadow"). Arnold also directed Williamson in *Boss*.

BLACK FORCE: *See* GANG WARS

BLACK FORCE II: *See* MAN ON THE RUN

BLACK GAUNTLET: *See* BLACK STARLET

THE BLACK GESTAPO

(Unicorn, 1975) **D/S/A:** Lee Frost **D/P/A:** Wes Bishop   (*Ghetto Warriors*)

This absurd, nasty movie has almost the same plot as *Bucktown* (from the same year). "The Black People's Party of Watts" is organized to fight white gangsters who sell drugs, take protection money, and rape local women. Gangsters are beaten, shot, thrown out of windows, and, in one case, castrated. The vigilante leader, Colonel Kojan (Charles P. Robinson), goes too far when he starts acting like the gangsters and his men start goosestepping ("Sieg heil" is dubbed in). Hero Rod Perry stops him. The directors play drug-dealer gangsters. With adult-movie regulars Dona Desmond and Uschi Digart as hookers. It opens with German Gestapo footage and includes some good microphone shadows. Frost did *Race with the Devil* (starring Peter Fonda) and The *Thing with Two Heads* (with Bruce Dern) next.

THE BLACK GLOVE

(1954) **D:** Terence Fisher **S:** Ernest Borneman **P:** Michael Carreras   UK (*Face the Music*)

This Hammer film was released by Lippert in the US. Alex Nicol stars as an American trumpet player who tries to find the killer of a British singer.

THE BLACK GODFATHER

(Magnum, 1974) **D/S/P:** John Evans

Rod Perry, as a black gangster, goes against the white mob. With heroin, kidnapping, and death by meat cleaver. Evans returned with *Blackjack* (1978). Perry went on to star in *Black Gestapo*. From Cinemation.

BLACK GUNN

(1972) **D:** Robert Hartford-Davis **S:** Robert Shearer **P:** John Heyman, Norman Priggen

Jim Brown stars as an LA nightclub owner out for revenge after the drug-dealing mob kills his revolutionary Nam-vet brother. He uses ex-cons and vets with guns to wipe out the gangsters. With Martin Landau as a used-car salesman who smuggles drugs in tires, Brenda Sykes (from *Ozzie's Girls*), Luciana Paluzzi, Keefe Brasselle, William Campbell, Bruce Glover, Stephen McNally, Bernie Casey, Gary Conway, Jeannie Bell (from *Playboy*), and some priceless haircuts. Brown starred in *Slaughter* the same year.

BLACKHAWK

(Stokey, 1952) **D:** Spencer Gordon Bennet, Fred F. Sears **S:** George Plympton, Royal K. Cole, Sherman L. Lowe

The year Eisenhower ran against Stevenson was the peak year for anti-Communist movies. This 15-chapter Columbia serial starring former Superman Kirk Alyn got the message across to kids. It was based on Will Eisner's comics, which were originally about a group of seven men fighting the Axis during WWII. The gadgets in the serial include a ray gun and a disintegrator, and the hero has a hawk's-head insignia on his military jacket. Carol Forman, who had also played evil women in *The Black Widow* (1947), *Brick Bradford* (1947), and *Superman* (1948), is Laska. With John Crawford.

BLACK HEART

(1994) **D/S/C/E:** Jim Exton

Two young guys hunt for a blood drinking serial rapist murderer (Don McCarrens, a security guard in real life) who does his thing in graveyards and lives in a van. A young woman (Shelli Wallace) invites the homeless killer into her home, and more deaths results. The slow moving movie (filmed in Memphis) has characters washing their faces, shaving, and just sitting around for long stretches of time, and Wallace (who has large breasts) takes a shower. The original punk music is instumentals and songs. The director is based in Durham, North Carolina.

BLACK HEAT: *See* THE MURDER GANG

BLACK HOOKER: *See* BLACK MAMA

BLACK ICE

(Prism, 1992) **D:** Neil Fearnley **S:** Arme Olson, John Alan Schwartz **P:** Vonnie von Helmolt   Canada

Joanna Pacula, on the run from a killer government agent (Michael Ironside), finds reluctant help from a cabdriver/writer (Michael Nouri) with a ponytail. It's a snowbound road/murder movie with one sex scene featuring Pacula's body double. The unrated version (I saw the R) must be an improvement. It was shot in Manitoba.

BLACKJACK

(1971) **D/P:** William T. Naud **S/P/A:** Dick Gautier
(*Wild in the Sky; God Bless the Bomb*)

Three anti-war activists hijack a B-52 bomber in a PG-rated comic adventure from AIP. It ends with Fort Knox being nuked. George Stanford Brown stars with Brandon De Wilde (in his last role), James Daly as the president, Keenan Wynn as a general, Tim O'Connor, Robert Lansing, Dub Taylor, Bernie Kopell, and Joseph Turkel.

BLACK JACK

(VSOM, 1981) **D/S/A:** Max Boulois   Spain

Peter Cushing receives top billing in this story about a casino robbery. Claudine Auger, Hugo Stiglitz, and Fernando Sancho are also in it, but it was barely released outside Spain.

BLACK LIZARD

(Cinevision, 1968) **D:** Kinji Fukasaku
S: Masashige Narusawa   Japan (*Kurotokage*)

A male actor (Akihiro Maruyama) stars as "the Black Lizard," a female jewel thief. She is a master of disguises (and wigs) and has an island hideaway where she collects "dolls" (naked people who are supposed to be dead). A detective tries to rescue the kidnapped Eurasian daughter of a jewel merchant. *Black Lizard* includes decapitated heads, a bloody hand cut off, a death couch, a midget, and some wild nightclub scenes. It's based on a play by the controversial writer Yukio Mishima (Paul Schrader later made a movie about him), who is also in the cast. This very 60s and uniquely Japanese movie from Shochiku had a successful run in Paris in 1984 and was revived in New York a few years later. Maruyama is a well-known transvestite entertainer in Japan. Fukasaku later made more mainstream science-fiction/disaster features like *The Green Slime, Message from Space*, and *Virus*. The tape is letterboxed.

BLACK LOLITA

(1974) **D/S/P:** Stephen Gibson
S: Mike Brown   (*Bad Lolita*)

In the only all-black 3-D film, Yoland Love is "foxier than Foxy Brown, deadlier than Cleopatra Jones." Love (Miss Black Galaxy) stars as a singer who returns home, puts together a team of fighters, and goes after gangsters. The shootout ending takes place on a merry-go-round.

BLACK LOVE

(1972) **D/P:** Herschell Gordon Lewis

Lewis shot this X-rated, soft-core obscurity in Chicago. It was made in three days. He made his last hillbilly and horror movies (*Year of the Yahoo* and *The Gore Gore Girls*) the same year, retired from filmmaking, and became wealthy writing mail-order books about advertising techniques.

BLACK MAGIC

(VLS, 1949) **D/P:** Gregory Ratoff **D/A:** Orson Welles **S:** Charles Bennett, Richard Schlayer

Welles stars as the 18th-century hypnotist Cagliostro in a feature based on a work by Alexandre Dumas père. Cagliostro, a Gypsy whose parents have been hanged, becomes a carnival magician, learns hypnotism from Dr. Mesmer, and uses his new powers for a complicated revenge against members of the court of Louis XV in France. With Nancy Guild as Marie Antoinette, Valentina Cortese, Harriet White Medin, and Akim Tamiroff as a Gypsy. Barry Kroeger, as Dumas, tells the story in flashback to his son, Alexandre Dumas *fils* (Raymond Burr!). Welles directed some sequences without credit. Screenwriter Bennett had written many Hitchcock classics. The Edward Small production was filmed in Italy (just before Welles appeared in *The Third Man*) and was released by United Artists.

BLACK MAGIC

(SB, 1977) **D:** Ho Meng-Hua
P: Run-Me Shaw   Hong Kong

A magician (Lo Lieh, the Indonesian-born star of *Five Fingers of Death, The Stranger and the Gunfighter*, and other films) makes a lot of money casting love spells for people but still lives in a remote shack. Spells require a finger and some teeth hidden under a bed, or prayers over a burning head. A man wants a rich woman who won't give him the time of day. He has a spell put on her. She has a spell put on a construction worker. She has to strip in a graveyard, help rob a grave, and provide some of her hair, blood, and milk. The man has to drink drool from a corpse's mouth. A bride finds worms under her skin. The magician decides he wants the woman himself. It's hard to keep track of who has spells on whom, but this tape never gets boring. A good magician (who looks like a Chinese Wilford Brimley) fights the bad magician at the construction site during the special-effects-filled ending. Filmed in Singapore. Star Ti Lung returned in the even more bizarre *Black Magic II* (known in the US as *Revenge of the Zombies* and *Black Magic III* (or *Queen of the Zombies*) by the same director. Ho Menga also made *The Flying Guillotine* (1975) and *Goliathon* (1977). The Shaw brothers later produced a similar black-magic feature, *Seeding of a Ghost* (1984), with even more blood, nudity, and maggots.

BLACK MAGIC

(MCA, 1992) **D/S:** Daniel Tapitz **P:** Dan Wigutow

Judge Reinhold is haunted by a dead cousin (Anthony LaPaglia) in a South Carolina town. He falls for the witch his cousin wants him to kill (Rachel Ward). Brion James is also featured in this PG-13 black comedy.

BLACK MAGIC TERROR: *See* QUEEN OF BLACK MAGIC

BLACK MAGIC WOMAN

(Vidmark, 1991) **D/P:** Deryn Warren
S: Gerry Daly **P:** Marc Springer

Mark Hamill stars in this boring video as a suburban art-gallery owner who needs an exorcism after a jealous witch casts a spell on him. A headless chicken shows up in his bed, he becomes impotent, and the already sick-looking actor (he had facial surgery after a car accident in real life) gets worse, thanks to makeup. Only the Hispanic characters understand what's happening, but they can't protect even themselves. Apollonia (Kotero) and Amanda Wyss costar, and Santana's original version of the title song is heard. With exploitation staples like sex in the shower and death by boiling water. After this, Hamill was in movies directed by Screaming Mad George and Jesús Franco!

BLACKMAIL

(Republic, 1929) **D/S:** Alfred Hitchcock **S:** Benn W. Levy, Charles Bennett **P:** John Maxwell   UK

Blackmail was the first feature-length sound film made in England. When production began (at Gainsborough Pictures) it was a silent film. Some scenes were reshot, but the characters don't speak until the second reel. (The first all-talking British film was *The Clue of the New Pin*, an Edgar Wallace adaptation released the same year.) The star, Czech actress Anny Ondra, was the first performer in films ever to be dubbed (by English actress Joan Barry, who starred in Hitchcock's *Rich and Strange* in 1932). The original posters for *Blackmail* said, "See it and hear it—our mother tongue as it should be spoken" (a dig at American sound films). Her boyfriend is the detective assigned to the case. There's an exciting chase in the British Museum, and the ending should satisfy modern viewers. Hitchcock had already directed nine features and would stay in England another ten years. You can spot him reading a newspaper on the subway. With Sara Allgood and Donald Calthrop. The Criterion laserdisc version includes an alternate audiotrack (featuring Charles Bennett, the then 92-year-old screenwriter) and a rare screen test.

BLACKMAIL

(Paramount, 1991) **D:** Ruben Preuss
S: Miguel Tejada-Flores

Dale Midkiff and Beth Toussaint are drifters who blackmail a gangster's wife (Susan Blakely). Mac Davis is a detective and John Saxon is the gangster, in this made-for-cable feature.

BLACK MAMA, WHITE MAMA

(1972) **D/P:** Eddie Romero **S:** H. R. Christian **P:** John Ashley   *(Women in Chains)*

This AIP release and *Savage Sister* were the last of many John Ashley films made in the Philippines. It was from a story by Jonathan Demme, who copied it from *The Defiant Ones*. Pam Grier, as a hooker, and Margaret Markov, as a revolutionary, escape from prison disguised as nuns. There are gun battles, cat fights, and a shower scene. Sid Haig is a bounty hunter in cowboy clothes. With Lynn Borden (who was a regular on the TV series *Hazel*) and Eddie Garcia as a drug-dealing pimp. The female stars returned in *The Arena*.

BLACK MOON

(Nightmare, 1975) **D/S/P:** Louis Malle **S:** Ghislain Uhry, Joyce Buñuel   France/W. Germany

Cathryn Harrison (Rex's daughter) flees the future, where men and women are at war against each other, to a fantasy world with talking animals and unicorns. Ex-Warhol star Joe Dallesandro and Alexandra Stewart (as brother and sister) are there too. *Black Moon* was shot in English around the director's own farm, with striking cinematography by Sven Nykvist. It was a flop, so Malle moved to America and made *Pretty Baby* (1978) and *Atlantic City* (1980).

BLACK MOON RISING

(Starmaker, 1985) **D:** Harvey Cokliss **S:** John Carpenter, Desmond Nakano **P:** Joel B. Michaels, Douglas Curtis

They took the title from a great song, but the movie doesn't come close. Killers are after government agent Tommy Lee Jones (in a jet-powered car). There's humor along with the action, and the cast includes Linda Hamilton (who steals the car for villain Robert Vaughn), Richard Jaeckel, Lee Ving, Bubba Smith, Dan Shor, William Sanderson, Keenan Wynn, Nick Cassavetes, and Don Opper. John Carpenter was executive producer of the New World release.

BLACK OAK CONSPIRACY

(Charter, 1977) **D:** Bob Kelljan **S/P/A:** Jesse Vint **S:** Hugh Smith **P:** Tom Clark

Jesse Vint has to fight the crooked sheriff in this New World drive-in movie. Karen Carlson, Albert Salmi, and Seymour Cassel costar.

BLACKOUT

(1955) **D:** Terence Fisher **S:** Richard Landau **P:** Michael Carreras UK *(Murder by Proxy)*

Dane Clark stars as an American war vet who recovers from a night of heavy drinking and thinks he might have murdered somebody. With Belinda Lee and Alfie Bass. This film was released in America by Lippert.

BLACKOUT

(1978) **D:** Eddy Matalon **S:** John C. Saxton **P:** Ivan Reitman   Canada/France

A group of criminals terrorize people in an apartment building during the 1977 New York City blackout. With Jim Mitchum, Robert Carradine, Belinda Montgomery, June Allyson, Ray Milland, and Jean-Pierre Aumont.

BLACKOUT

(Fox Hills, 1985) **D:** Douglas Hickox **S:** David Ambrose **P:** Richard Parks, Richard Smith, Les Alexander

After a car crash, Keith Carradine, suffering from amnesia, emerges from plastic surgery and marries Kathleen Quinlan. Richard Widmark thinks he's the masked mass murderer who killed his family. With Michael Beck. This HBO movie is set in Seattle but was filmed in Vancouver.

BLACKOUT

(Magnum, 1988) **D/P:** Doug Adams **S/P:** Joseph Stephano   *(The Attic)*

Gail O'Grady stars as a repressed virgin who returns to her family's old house and suffers from nightmares. Carol Lynley (who appears topless) is her unloving mother, and the father is missing. With Joanna Miles and death by screwdriver. The video box plays up the fact that Stephano wrote the screenplay for Hitchcock's *Psycho*.

BLACKOUT

(1992) **D/P:** Paulita Sedgwick **S:** Damian Wong   UK

Three young people go to the "Red Zone" of a futuristic London in this low-budget underground feature. Kali stars as a blond rocker, with Guy Beckett as her boyfriend and Abi Manox as his sister. With Ultra Violet, Eddie Tudor-Pole, and Angel Sedgewick.

BLACK OUT: THE MOMENT OF TERROR = GANJA AND HESS (cut version)

BLACK PARACHUTE

(1944) **D:** Lew Landers **S:** Clarence Upson Young **P:** Jack Fier

William Smith and Carol Speed in *Black Samson*.

John Carradine stars as a Nazi general occupying an unnamed European country. Hero Larry Parks is an American who disguises himself as a Nazi colonel. Osa Massen is a Nazi spy, and Jonathan Hale is the deposed king. Eight Landers pictures were released in 1944.

BLACK RAINBOW

(Media, 1989) **D/S:** Mike Hodges **P:** John Quested, Geoffrey Helman   UK

Rosanna Arquette, part of a phony traveling clairvoyant act with her drunken father (Jason Robards), discovers she can actually predict deaths. Tom Hulce is a reporter who gets involved. It was filmed in and set in North Carolina, complete with kudzu weeds. The US debut for this interesting feature was on Showtime.

THE BLACK ROOM

(Vestron, 1981) **D:** Elly Kennedy **D/S:** Norman Thaddeus Vane **P:** Aaron C. Butler

Stephan Knight and Cassandra Gaviola, as a brother and sister with a Beverly Hills house, lure people for sex games in a special back room, then drain their blood with an elaborate pump system. The blood spurts all over. The voyeur brother watches sex, and there are S&M scenes. It's not very good but is fascinating in a cheap-movie way. With the model from the cover of the Jefferson Starship *Spitfire* LP and Linnea Quigley in a small role.

THE BLACK ROSE

(1950) **D:** Henry Hathaway **S:** Talbot Jennings **P:** Louis D. Leighton

Orson Welles plays Bayon, a 13th-century Mongol conqueror, in this 2-hour Technicolor epic from 20th Century-Fox. Tyrone Power stars as a Saxon, with Cecile Aubry as "the Black Rose," Michael Rennie, Jack Hawkins, Herbert Lom, Finlay Currie, James Robertson Justice, Laurence Harvey, and Torin Thatcher. It was filmed by cinematographer Jack Cardiff in England and North Africa.

BLACK ROSES

(Imperial, 1988) **D/P/E:** John Fasano **S:** Cindy Sorrell **P:** Ray Van Dorn

Sal Vivano leads the heavy-metal group Black Roses. They arrive in a small town to play, and parents argue over whether it's a bad idea or not. Since the band has made a deal with the Devil, they turn kids into ugly zombie parent-killers. With Ken Swofford, Carmine Appice (from Vanilla Fudge), and Julie Adams. It was an SGE production that came in a 3-D video box. Various artists are featured on the Enigma soundtrack. Fasano had previously directed *Rock and Roll Nightmare*.

BLACK SAMSON

(1973) **D:** Charles Bail **S:** Warren Hamilton Jr. **P:** Daniel B. Cady

A bearded LA nightclub owner named Samson (Rockne Tarkington) has a pet lion and uses kung fu to fight white drug-dealing gangsters (like William Smith) and drug pushers. With Connie Strickland, Carol Speed, and John Alderman. The music is by Allen Toussaint. By the director of *Cleopatra and the Casino of Gold*. From Warner.

BLACK SAMURAI

(Continental, 1977) **D:** Al Adamson **S:** B. Radick **P:** Barbara Holden   (*Black Terminator*)

Jim Kelly is a rich, James Bond-type playboy, Nam vet, and government agent for D.R.A.G.O.N. His girlfriend (Essie Lin Chia) is kidnapped by "the Warlocks," drug-dealing, women-selling, voodoo-worshiping killers. Felix Silla (Cousin Itt on *The Addams Family*) is a midget Warlock. With Marilyn Joi and D'Urville Martin. It takes place in Hong Kong and Haiti. Kelly returned in *Death Dimension*, also directed by Adamson.

BLACK SHAMPOO

(VCI, 1976) **D/S:** Greydon Clark **S/P:** Alvin L. Fast

John Daniels stars as swinging hairdresser Jonathan Knight, who fights the mob. There's lots of R-rated sex, a pool cue goes through a man, there's death by chainsaw, and a gay assistant is beaten up. With Tanya Boyd. It's blaxploitation at its worst, from the director of *Satan's Cheerleaders*. From Dimension.

BLACK SISTER'S REVENGE

(Unicorn, 1975) **D/S/P:** Jamaa Fanaka   (*Emma Mae*)

Jerri Hayes stars as a short, southern country cousin who moves in with some suburban LA relatives. She's laughed at and called "that ol' hamhock broad," but she can fight ("C'mon, you doodlebug!") and ends up robbing a bank to raise bail for a guy on "fender benders" (reds) she likes. This entertaining piece of the 70s is loaded with afros, bell bottoms, good funky music, corrupt cops, a cat fight, lots of swearing, and a character named Big Daddy with a rifle and a turban who gives a speech about the evil white man. It was partially backed by AFI. Fanaka went on to make more outrageous movies, including the *Penitentiary* series.

THE BLACK SIX

(Unicorn, 1974) **D/P:** Matt Cimber/Matteo Ottaviano **P:** George Theakos

"Six times tougher than *Shaft*! Six times rougher than *Superfly*!" If you believe that ad line, you deserve to watch Jean Washington, Mercury Morris, "Mean" Joe Greene, and other NFL stars as friendly Nam-vet bikers avenging a brother's death in a southern city. They fight bad white bikers at the end, which is followed by the message, "Honky, look out!" From Cinemation.

BLACKSNAKE!

(1973) **D/S/P:** Russ Meyer **S:** Len Neubauer (*Sweet Suzy; Dutchess of Doom*)

After making films at 20th Century-Fox, Meyer filmed his only major flop in Barbados. Meyer himself seems to think it failed because it's the only feature he made with women with normal-sized breasts. Critics hated this story of a 19th-century slave revolt in the Caribbean and accused Meyer of trying to capitalize on the black-action craze. It has very little sex or nudity, but it has his great fast editing and lots of violence (whippings, a machete attack, a crucifixion). After all that, the movie has a comical happy ending. Anouska Hempel stars, and David Warbeck (usually in Italian horror movies) plays two roles. With Bernard Boston, Percy Herbert, and Dave Prowse (who played Darth Vader in the *Star Wars* series). When released in theaters, *Blacksnake!* included a trailer for *Viva Foxy*, starring Edy Williams, a film that was never made. The version I saw was in French.

BLACK STARLET

(Video Gems, 1974) **D:** Chris Munger **S:** Howard Ostroff **P:** Daniel B. Cady   (*Black Gauntlet*)

Juanita Brown (veteran of movies like *Caged Heat* and *Foxy Brown*) stars as Clara, who leaves Gary, Indiana, for Hollywood. She's robbed, arrested, lied to, used, and abused. She sleeps with a producer and even stars in a movie. With Rockne Tarkington, Nicolas Worth, and Al "Grandpa" Lewis (!) as Sam Sharp, a dry cleaner.

BLACK STREET FIGHTER

(1974) **D:** Timothy Galfas **S:** Tim Kelly **P:** Peter S. Traynor, William Larrabure   (*Black Fist*)

Richard Lawson stars as Leroy Fist, a street-fighter in Los Angeles who starts working for mobsters. Philip Michael Thomas costars, with Dabney Coleman as a crooked cop and Anazette Chase.

BLACK SUNDAY

(Paramount, 1977) **D:** John Frankenheimer **S:** Ernest Lehman, Kenneth Ross, Ivan Moffat **P:** Robert Evans

Terrorists plot to blow up the president during the Super Bowl game (Cowboys vs. Steelers), in this superior disaster thriller based on a novel by Thomas Harris (author of *The Silence of the Lambs*). Robert Shaw is the Israeli-commando hero, and Bruce Dern is the former Nam-POW terrorist in the Goodyear blimp. With Marthe Keller as a Palestinian terrorist, Stephen Keats, Fritz Weaver, Michael V. Gazzo, and William Daniels. Don't confuse it with the classic 1960 Mario Bava horror movie of the same name.

BLACK TRASH: *See* SOUL PATROL

BLACK VALOR: *See* SAVAGE!

BLACK VAMPIRE = GANJA AND HESS (cut version)

A BLACK VEIL FOR LISA

(1968) **D/S:** Massimo Dallamano **S:** Petri and Belli   Italy (*La Morte Non ha Sexo*)

John Mills stars as a narcotics cop with a beautiful, cheating, ex-criminal wife (Luciana Paluzzi). He hires a hitman (Robert Hoffmann) to kill her, and the anticipated double cross occurs.

BLACK VENGEANCE: *See* HEARTBREAK HOTEL

BLACK VENUS

(MGM, 1983) **D:** Claude Mulot **S/P:** Harry Alan Towers

Former Miss Bahamas Josephine Jacqueline Jones stars as Venus in a 19th-century erotic tale made for Playboy-TV. Most of it is a flashback about a guy obsessed with a statue of Venus. With Mandy Rice-Davies as the madam, Karin Schubert (also in Towers' *Christina*) as a lesbian, Florence Guerin, Helga Line, and red-haired Monique Gabrielle fucking a pirate. Mulot also made the bizarre *Blood Rose* (1969).

BLACK WATER

(Academy, 1994) **D/S:** Nicholas Gessner **S:** Laird Koening **P:** Bernard Lang, Peter-Christian Fueter

Julian Sands is a British tax attorney who is blamed for a murder while fishing in Tennessee. Stacey Dash (*Mo' Money*) is the black teen hitch-hiker he picks up. With Rod Steiger as a judge, Ned Beatty, Ed Lauter, Denise Crosby, Brian McNamara, and Johnny Cash in a cameo as himself. It was based on a novel by Hans Werner Kettenbach and made by the director of *The Little Girl Who Lives Down the Lane*.

BLACK WEREWOLF = THE BEAST MUST DIE

THE BLACK WIDOW

(Stokey, 1947) **D:** Spencer Gordon Bennett, Fred C. Bannon **S:** Franklyn Adreon, Basil Dickey, Jesse Duffy, Sol Shore

A 13-chapter Republic serial starring Bruce Edwards as hero Steve Colt and Carol Foreman as the evil, sexy (and supposedly Asian) Sombra, "the Black Widow." She wears a great-looking slit skirt with a jewel-encrusted front. A "matter transmitter" is the device everybody wants. With Theodore Gottlieb (later known as Brother Theodore) as Hitomu and Virginia Lindley. The 1966 feature version was *Sombra, the Spider Woman*.

THE BLACK WIDOW

(1951) **D:** Vernon Sewell **S:** Alan McKinnon **P:** Anthony Hines   UK

Christine Norden stars in this early Hammer feature, based on a BBC-TV serial. It's only 62 minutes long and costars Robert Ayers. Sewell made *Ghost Ship* the next year.

BLACK WIDOW

(Fox, 1987) **D:** Bob Rafelson **S:** Ronald Bass **P:** Harold Schneider

Justice Department agent Debra Winger puts her life on the line and goes after rich, seductive Theresa Russell, who kills her husbands and always gets away with it. With Sami Frey, Nicol

Williamson, Terry O'Quinn, Dennis Hopper, Mary Woronov, Diane Ladd, John Heard, Rutanya Alda, Leo Rossi, James Hong, and David Mamet.

THE BLACK WINDMILL

(MCA, 1974) **D/P:** Don Siegel **S:** Leigh Vance   UK

The young son of British agent Michael Caine is kidnapped and held for a ransom of diamonds. The agent discovers he can't even count on his own allies while on the trail of the kidnappers in London and Paris. With Donald Pleasence, Delphine Seyrig, John Vernon, Clive Revill, *Space 1999's* Catherine Schell, John Rhys-Davies, and Murray Brown. It's a Universal release.

BLADE IN THE DARK

(Lightning, 1982) **D/P:** Lamberto Bava
S: Elisa Briganti, Dardano Sacchetti Italy
(*La Casa con la Scala nel Buio*)

A composer (Andrea Occhipinti) working on a horror-movie score goes to an isolated, old, dark house to work. A phantom slasher kills in vicious ways similar to the murders in the film he's working on. Michelle Soavi (the assistant director) and Lara Naszinski costar in this shocking Dario Argento-inspired feature (with bad dubbing).

BLADE MASTER

(Media, 1982) **D/S:** "David Hills"/A. Massaccesi
P: John Newman   (*Ator, the Invincible*)

Miles O'Keeffe saves Earth from a superbomb, fights a giant snake, and hang-glides. This *Ator* sequel features visible sunglasses and tire tracks and a senseless atomic explosion at the end. With Lisa Raines/Foster (star of the 1981 *Fanny Hill*), Chen Wong, and David Cain Haughton as Zor. New Line released it.

BLADE OF THE RIPPER

(Regal, Saturn, 1970) **D:** Sergio Martino **S:** Eduardo Brochero, Ernesto Gastaldi   Italy/Spain (*Lo Strano Vizio della Signora Wardh; The Next Victim; Next!*)

Somebody is trying to drive Edwige Fenech mad, and she has nightmares about a slasher. With George Hilton, Alberto De Mendoza, and Ivan Rassimov. The video version, called *The Next Victim,* is missing most of the nudity and violence. It's set in Vienna.

BLADES

(Media, 1988) **D/S:** Thomas Rondinella
S/P: John P. Finegan **S:** William R. Pace

This *Jaws* parody features a possessed-killer power-mower at a golf course in Wildwood, New Jersey. The plot of the original *Jaws* is copied closely. From Troma.

BLAKE OF SCOTLAND YARD

(Stokey, 1937) **D/S:** Robert F. Hill
S: William Lord Wright

A 15-chapter Victory serial starring Ralph Byrd (better known as Dick Tracy) as Sir James Blake. The same director had made a 1927 serial version for Universal. A death-ray television is the futuris-tic weapon in the hands of "the Scorpion" (Lloyd Hughes). This was the last independent serial produced. The rest were all from three studios (Republic, Universal, and Columbia). A 70-minute condensed version is also available from Sinister.

BLAKE'S 7

(BFS series, 1978–81)   UK

Six futuristic outcasts and a computer named Zen battle "the Federation." Gareth Thomas stars with Sally Knyvette. 26 volumes of the series (105 minutes each) have been released.

BLANK GENERATION

(1979) **D/S:** Ulli Lommel **P:** Roger Deutsch

When German actor/director Lommel came to America he hooked into the New York underground scene. *Cocaine Cowboys* and this punk-rock spy story were his first American projects. It wasn't released until it showed up in England in 1991. Poet/rocker Richard Hell and Carole Bouquet (from *That Obscure Object of Desire*) star, and Andy Warhol shows up. Not to be confused with Amos Poe's live-at-CBGB *Blank Generation* (1976).

BLANKMAN

(Columbia, 1994) **D:** Mike Binder **S/A:** Damon Wayans **P:** Eric Gold, Doc Erickson

Wayans is a nerdy inventor turned no-power superhero and David Alan Grier is his older brother partner. The two stars (both from the *In Living Color* show) fight the mob and look like Rat Pfink and Boo Boo from Ray Dennis Steckler's 60s *Batman* spoof. Robin Givens costars as a TV news reporter with Christopher Lawford, Jon Polito, and Jason Alexander. The PG-13 comedy is a Columbia release.

BLASTFIGHTER

(Vestron, 1984) **D:** "John Old Jr."/Lamberto Bava **S:** Max Von Ryt, Luca Von Ryt   Italy (*First Blood*)

Michael Sopkiw stars as an ex-con called Tiger who becomes a Rambo-type crime-fighter. With George Eastman and Valerie Blake.

BLAST OFF

(HBO, 1967) **D:** Don Sharp **S:** Dave Freeman **P:** Harry Alan Towers   (*Those Fantastic Flying Fools*)

It's a Victorian-era race to the moon based on Jules Verne (the same story as *From the Earth to the Moon*). Burl Ives is P. T. Barnum, and Troy Donahue, Gert Frobe, Daliah Lavi, and Hermione Gingold costar. This AIP film is one of several (all with Terry-Thomas) that followed *Those Magnificent Men in Their Flying Machines* and *The Great Race* (both 1965).

BLAST-OFF GIRLS

(SW, 1967) **D/S/P:** Herschell Gordon Lewis

Attention: readers who are or were in bands should see this movie! It's a former lost classic about the rise and fall of the Big Blast, a teen garage band (played by a real, authentic, non-actor Chicago garage band, the Faded Blue) in Florida. Boojie Baker (Dan Conway) becomes their sleazy manager, and they have a hit called "Noise" (it's shown on the charts just after the Yardbirds). He provides new clothes, studio time, champagne, and women, but when the band rebels for lack of profits, he frames them on a pot bust. Then they go on TV high and sing "Go —— Yourself, My Friend." With Lewis regular Ray Sager as Boojie's assistant and Colonel Harlan Sanders (!), who shows up to offer fried chicken to the group for playing while little kids dance. The keyboard player sounds like Pigpen from the Grateful Dead! The ending is copied from the TV series *The Monkees*. Louise Downe was the assistant director. David Friedman later tackled the same topic with *Bummer!*

BLAST OF SILENCE

(1961) **D/S/A:** Allen Baron **P/C:** Merrill Brody

This fascinating, bleak tale about a paranoid hitman from Cleveland named Frank Bono was finally recognized at the 1991 Berlin Film Festival and went on to play the revival circuit. Frank arrives in New York City on Christmas Eve to kill a gangster. Everything is filmed on location in Harlem, on the Staten Island Ferry, in a Greenwich Village jazz club (where Dean Shelton sings a memorable song), and on streets filled with irritating holiday cheer. The distinctive voice of Lionel Stander provides (often unnecessary) narration throughout the film and begins by stating, "You were born with hate and anger built in. Took a slap on the backside to blast out the scream." With Molly McCarthy and Larry Tucker (*Shock Corridor*). Baron made another movie, *Terror in the City* (1963), starring Lee Grant, and directed many TV programs.

BLAZE STARR: THE ORIGINAL

(Blaze Video, 1960) **D/P/A:** Doris Wishman
S: Melvin Stanley   (*Blaze Starr Goes Nudist; Back to Nature; Nature Girl*)

Real-life big-breasted stripper Starr plays an actress who infuriates her fiancé/agent (with a drawn-on mustache) by spending weekends at a nudist camp and missing "press functions." When dressed, she wears a pointy bra, gold lamé pants, and gold high heels. Camp highlights include nude checkers and archery, and a nude underwater swimming sequence. The funniest character is Andy, the camp director, who always wears swim trunks, drinks Cokes, and plays the accordion. He's played by Ralph Young (of Sandler and Young) and also sings the theme song backed by Doc Severinson and his band! This vintage nudist-colony movie (in bright Eastmancolor) was retitled to cash in on the biographical movie *Blaze* (1989). Blaze herself had a small role in the story of her involvement with Louisiana governor Earl Long (played by Paul Newman). It was a Disney feature!

BLAZING STEWARDESSES

(VidAmerica, Marathon, 1975) **D:** Al Adamson
S/P: Sam Sherman **S:** John D'Amato
(*Texas Layover; Cathouse Callgirls; The Great Truck Robbery; Up Like a Shot*)

Regina Carroll and two other stewardesses go to a dude ranch in this sex comedy/western. Yvonne De Carlo runs a whorehouse (and sings). With old-time stars Don "Red" Barry, Bob Livingston, and Jimmy and Harry Ritz. There's a masked villain and sex-with-an-inflatable-doll, but not much nudity. It was sort of a sequel to *Naughty Stewardesses* (1973). Like most movies from Independent International, it was released over the years with different titles to confuse people.

BLIND DATE

(Vestron, 1983) **D/S/P:** Nico Mastorakis
S: Fred C. Perry   (*Deadly Seduction*)

Joseph Bottoms goes blind after seeing a murder in Athens. Keir Dullea is a doctor who can temporarily restore vision with a computer implant. This New Line film was shot in Greece. With Kirstie Alley, Marina Sirtis (from *Star Trek: The Next Generation*) as a hooker (topless), a pre-star Valeria Golino, James Daughton, and "introducing" Lana Clarkson (topless). The soundtrack by Stanley Myers is on Varese Sarabande. Not to be confused with the 1987 Kim Basinger movie from RCA.

BLIND FEAR

(Academy, 1989) **D:** Tom Berry **S:** Sergio Alteri
P: Pierre David, Franco Battista   Canada

Shelley Hack is a blind employee at a deserted Maine lodge. Three killer gangsters (including Kim Coates) arrive. It's like *Wait Until Dark* with some new twists. With Jan Rubes.

BLINDFOLD: ACTS OF OBSESSION

(Libra, 1993) **D/S:** Lawrence Simeone **P:** Ronnie Hadar

Shannon Doherty, a big-deal, "difficult" TV teen in tabloid news at the time, stars in her first "erotic thriller." She's a bored, rich married woman who gets involved with her shrink (Judd Nelson). Shannon (who will never receive an acting award) gets naked in slo-mo sex scenes. We also get a confusing plot about a Halloween killer who uses blindfolds and handcuffs, complete with nightmares and flashbacks. With Kristian Alfonso, Drew Snyder, and Michael Woods. It was shot in Dallas. A cut version debuted on the USA Network, and the video is R or unrated.

BLIND FURY

(Columbia, 1989) **D:** Philip Noyce **S:** Charles Robert Carner **P:** Daniel Grodnik, Tim Matheson

A blind Nam-vet swordsman (Rutger Hauer) who was missing in action (and has flashbacks) has to protect a kid (Brandon Call) from gangsters on the road from Miami to Reno. Hauer is good, as usual, in this pretty exciting and funny gimmick-action movie, based on a script for the Japanese *Zatoichi* series by Ryoza Kashahara, and filmed in Australia. With Terry O'Quinn, Meg Foster, Lisa Blount, villains Noble Willingham, Nick Cassavetes, and Randall "Tex" Cobb, Harriet White Medin, and, in the best fight scene, Sho Koshogi. The Australian Noyce made *Dead Calm* the same year. Look for the original *Zatoichi* movies from Ocean video.

BLINDMAN

(1971) **D:** Fernando Baldi **S/P/A:** Tony Anthony **S:** Piero Anchisi, Vincenzo Cerami **P:** Saul Swimmer   US/Italy

Tony Anthony is the philosophical hero Blindman, hired to deliver 50 mail-order brides (who have actually been sold into slavery and appear naked a lot). Ringo Starr is Candy, the overacting Mexican bandit who rapes and kills in what was intended to be a parody of Italian westerns. With Lloyd Batista and Magda Konopka. Shot in Spain, this was a hit practically everywhere but in the US (where it was released by 20th Century–Fox). It was a product of Allan Klein's Abcko company, which had also backed *El Topo*. Anthony later starred in the 3-D movies *Comin' at Ya!* (which reused the *Blindman* plot) and *Treasure of the Four Crowns*.

BLIND RAGE

(MGM, 1976) **D:** Efron C. Pinion **S/A:** Leo Fong **S:** Jerry O. Tirazona   Philippines

D'Urville Martin stars with Leo Fong and Tony Ferrer in an action movie about five blind criminals who rob a bank. Fred Williamson, who usually had Martin in his films, shows up as CIA agent Jesse Chowder.

BLIND VISION

(Worldvision, 1990) **D/S:** Shuki Levy
S: Winston Rickard **P:** Jonathan Braun

After appearing on *Twin Peaks*, Lenny Van Dohlen became a direct-to-video psycho specialist. Here he's an office-mail-room nerd and psycho voyeur obsessed with a blond coworker and neighbor played by the director's wife, Deborah Shelton. He talks to himself, visits a shrink, has nightmares, and watches her with a zoom lens in *Rear Window*–derived scenes. The guest stars all watch Shelton too. Robert Vaughn as her angry ex watches. Louise Fletcher as the landlady watches, and Ned Beatty as a police sergeant watches. This unrated, not very erotic thriller was shot in Norfolk, Virginia, and also features Stoney Jackson. Thelma Houston provides the theme song.

BLINK

(New Line, 1994) **D:** Michael Apted
S: Dana Stevens **P:** David Blocker

Shawnee Smith screams in a good remake, *The Blob.*

Madeleine Stowe stars as a blind musician who partially regains her sight after a corneal transplant and witnesses a murder. We see her unreliable point of view (thanks to computer FX). Aidan Quinn is the Chicago police detective she falls in love with. With Laurie Metcalf, James Remar, and Paul Dillon. The Celtic rock band she plays with is the Drovers. The score is by Brad Fiedel.

BLINK OF AN EYE

(Vidmark, 1991) **D:** Bob Misiorowski
S: Edward Kovach **P:** Jacob Kotzky

Michael Paré stars as a soldier who goes to a Turkish refugee camp to rescue the daughter (Janis Lee) of a CIA director. Terrorists plot to steal plutonium for a nuclear war, and Paré is temporarily blinded, but he's psychic, so he defeats the bad Arabs anyway. With Uri Gavriel as a helpful Kurd.

BLISS

(NW, 1985) **D/S:** Ray Lawrence **S:** Peter Carey **P:** Anthony Buckley   Australia

In a bizarre black comedy, Barry Otto plays a family man who dies from a heart attack, experiences Heaven, and is revived by paramedics. In a nightmare sequence, cockroaches crawl out of a woman. He decides that his wife and children are no good and that life on earth is Hell. With Helen Jones.

THE BLOB

(RCA, 1988) **D/S:** Chuck Russell **S:** Frank Darabont **P:** Jack H. Harris, Elliott Kastner

Thirty years after the original movie *The Blob* (also produced by Harris), this modernized version was released. I still like the original with Steve McQueen, but this is an excellent remake. Kevin Dillon is the juvenile-delinquent star who ends up with cheerleader Shawnee Smith while the mysterious blob (with tentacles) terrorizes a small town. Much of the simple plot is the same (and a few key scenes are copied), but there's a new government-conspiracy explanation. This version has more action, more tension, and better special effects. With Donovan Leitch (son of the singer), Del Close (who was also in *Beware the Blob!*) as the Reverend Meeker, Jack Nance, Candy Clark, Joe Seneca, Art La Fleur, Erika Eleniak, Charlie Spradling and Julie McCullough (from *Playboy*). The soundtrack by Michael Hoenig is on Cinedisc.

BLOBERMOUTH

(1990) **D/S:** Kent Skov **S:** Steven L. Rothman, Steve Pinto, Robert Bucholz **P:** Jack H. Harris

The LA Connection comedy group redubbed the original 1958 movie *The Blob.* Steve McQueen becomes a struggling standup comic. The Blob now talks with an animated mouth. The screenwriters provided the voices. The new comedy version received an R rating.

BLONDE ALIBI

(1946) **D:** Will James **S:** George Bricker **P:** Ben Pivar

Martha O'Driscoll is "the most beautiful clue that ever lured men to danger" in this one-hour Universal movie, costarring Tom Neal (who had just been in *Detour*) as a flyer accussed of murder. Also with Elisha Cook Jr., Robert Armstrong, and Donald MacBride. O'Driscoll (*House of Dracula; Ghost Catchers*) married a rich Chicago man and retired after this.

BLONDE BAIT

(1956) **D:** Elmo Williams **S:** Val Guest, Richard Landau **P:** Anthony Hinds   UK (*Women Without Men*)

Beverly Michaels (the star of Hugo Haas' *Pickup* and the women's-prison movie *Betrayed*) stars in her last movie. She's an American showgirl who breaks out of a British prison. With Joan Rice and Gordon Jackson. New scenes were added (with Jim Davis, Richard Travis, and Paul Cavanagh) to this Hammer film for the US release (by Associated). "I don't need a gun to catch a man!" was an ad line.

BLONDE EMANUELLE (IN 3-D)

(1978) **D:** Giorgio Ferreri **P:** Stephen Gibson   (*Disco Girls in Hotskin*)

Monique Fabergé plays Emanuelle in a ripoff 3-D sex movie made in California. It was promoted as being "European" and was rated NC-17 in 1990.

BLONDE FIST

(1991) **D/S:** Frank Clarke **P:** Joseph D'Morais, Christopher Figg   UK

Margi Clarke stars as a Liverpool mom who becomes a boxer managed by an ex-stripper (Carroll Baker). It was advertised as "*Thelma and Louise* meets *Rocky*."

BLONDE GODDESS

(Video X, 1982) **D:** Bill Eagle (Bill Milling) **P:** Bobby Bouchard

This X-rated, hard-core feature is a Walter Mitty takeoff. Star Jonathan Ford is a comic-book artist who imagines himself in several of his own stories and naturally gets to have plenty of sex. In a *Raiders of the Lost Ark*–inspired segment he rescues a woman from a goddess (Susanna Britton) in a Mexican temple. Other segments concern WWI flyers and a superman on another planet. A b/w segment is a Bogart takeoff. It's more imaginative than standard porno, but don't expect too much. With Jacqueline Lorians, Loni Sanders, and Ron Jeremy.

BLONDE ICE

(1948) **D:** Jack Bernard **S:** Kenneth Ganet, Raymond Schrock **P:** Martin Mooney

Leslie Brooks (who had been in Rita Hayworth musicals) stars as a "blond Svengali" in this forgotten bad-girl movie, with Robert Paige and Michael Whalen. Bernard also made *Unknown Island* the same year for the same company.

BLONDE ON A BUM TRIP

(SW, 1967) **D:** Ralph Mauro **P:** Jack Braverman, Ed Adlum

I love this 65-minute b/w sex/drugs/rock and roll movie filmed in New York City. Flashbacks related in a hospital by various characters show how Susan, a naive chemistry major with blond bangs, is used by her roommates and a guy named TJ to make LSD for them and ends up "caught in a whirlpool of life." Sugar cubes are passed out at a party. Everybody chants, "LSD's got a hold on me!" to bongo music. The freak-out scenes are clever, and there are several tasteful sex scenes. One stars a sexy black maid and another features a Nixon mask. The excellent and frequently heard theme ("Put the Clock Back on the Wall") is by Tower recording group the E-Types. They sound like the Electric Prunes to me. The Bit-a-Sweet (on MGM) are seen doing "Out of Sight, Out of Mind" at a discotheque, and the Vagrants (with Leslie West) are heard doing "I Love You, Yes I Do." The fashions, music, and editing are all top-notch (the dubbing isn't), and there's some welcome, intentionally hip humor. Mauro also made a nudie, *Girls in the Saddle* (1969). Braverman later produced *Voodoo Dolls* (in Canada), and Adlum made *Shriek of the Mutilated* and *Invasion of the Blood Farmers*!

BLONDE SAVAGE

(Sinister, 1947) **D:** S. K. Seeley **S:** Gordon Bache **P:** Lionel J. Toll

"Blonde ruler of a pagan paradise! Prize of thrill-hungry men!" This was the first release by Eagle Lion (formally PRC). Gale Sherwood is the blond Meelah, singing leader of an African tribe. Leif Erickson tells the whole *Tarzan*-inspired tale in flashback. A standout bizarre singing scene was later used in the compilation feature *It Came from Hollywood*. With Veda Ann Borg, Douglas Dumbrille, and Matt Willis. Sherwood later sang in nightclubs with Nelson Eddy.

BLOOD

(1971) **D/S:** Mario Caiano **S:** Antonio Saguera, Horst Hachler **P:** Nello Santi, Hans Pfluger Italy/W. Germany (*L'Occhio nel Labirinto*)

Rosemary Dexter dreams that her psychiatrist lover (Horst Frank) is a psycho killer. She goes to a castle on a beach where his mistress (Alida Valli) lives. With Sybil Danning and Adolfo Celi. This movie features flashbacks, LSD trips, a severed head, and a giant eyeball. It's by the director of *Nightmare Castle* (1965).

BLOOD AND CONCRETE: A LOVE STORY

(RCA, 1991) **D/S/E:** Jeffrey Reiner **S/P/E:** Richard LaBrie

This very cool and funny LA-punk-scene drug/crime movie has some of the same spirit as *Repo Man*. Billy Zane (*Dead Calm*) stars as a car thief accused of murder who moves in with Jennifer Beals, as a suicidal cabaret singer, after they meet in a graveyard. Darren McGavin is in top form as a determined older cop who doesn't get any respect, and Nicholas Worth (*Don't Answer the Phone*) is a

big, gay gangster pushing addictive "libido pills." With James LeGros as Worth's scary, violent lover and Harry Shearer. The music is by Nuclear Assault. Miles Copeland III was the executive producer for IRS. The video is letterboxed.

BLOOD AND GUNS

(1968) **D/S:** Giulio Petroni **S:** Sergio Solinas, Ivan Della Mea   Italy (*Tepepa; Viva la Revolución!*)

Tomas Milian stars as Tepepa, a Mexican revolutionary, in this political western. Orson Welles is Colonel Casscarro, the chief of police. With John Steiner and José Torres.

BLOOD AND GUTS

(IVE, 1978) **D:** Paul Lynch **S:** Joseph McBride, William Gray, John Hunter **P:** Peter O'Brian

William Smith is an aging, alcoholic wrestler with a young wrestling troupe in this PG-rated film. Lynch did *Prom Night* and *Humungus* next.

BLOOD AND SAND

(Vidmark, 1989) **D:** Javier Elorrieta **S:** Rafael Azcona, Ricardo Franco **P:** Jose Frade   Spain

Nude scenes of Sharon Stone and real Spanish bullfights were the selling points of this remake about a young married matador (Christopher Rydell) having an affair. With Ala Torrent, Aldo Sanbrell, and Simon Andreu. Earlier, more successful versions starred Rudolph Valentino (1922) and Tyrone Power (1941).

BLOOD AND STEEL

(Fox, 1959) **D:** Bernard Kowalski **S:** Joseph C. Gilette **P:** Gene Corman

John Lupton stars in this 62-minute b/w 20th Century–Fox film about a native girl (Ziva Rodann) who helps US Navy Seabees free island villagers from the Japanese during WWII. With Brett Halsey, black actor James Edwards (*Home of the Brave*), and James Hong. Floyd Crosby was the cinematographer.

BLOOD AT SUNDOWN

(Imperial, 1965) **D/S:** Duccio Tessari **P:** Luciano Ercole Italy/Spain (*Una Pistola para Ringo; A Pistol for Ringo*)

A professional killer ("Montgomery Wood"/Giuliano Gemma) is hired to free a ranch from Mexican bandits (led by Fernando Sánchez) who are holding hostages.

BLOODBATH

(21st Genesis, 1976) **D:** Silvio Narizzano **S/A:** Win Wells **P:** Andrés Vicente Gómez Spain (*The Sky Is Falling*)

Dennis Hopper is Chicken, a grisly-looking junkie poet who hallucinates a lot and has nightmares, religious visions, and frequent, disturbing childhood flashbacks. He mistreats his black girlfriend and says things like "Nothing is real. Everything is permitted." Treasure (Carroll Baker) is an alcoholic ex–Hollywood star who sings, throws parties, and shows off her scrapbook (with actual star photos of Carroll Baker). Richard Todd is an alcoholic pilot still wearing his WWII uniform, and Treasure's gay companion is played by the scriptwriter. They're in a Spanish village where kids are dying and funeral processions go by on Good Friday. All the main characters are self-destructive, miserable, and doomed and Narizzano makes you look at all kinds of *Mondo*-type ugliness. It's some serious weirdness from the director of *Die! Die! My Darling!* Not to be confused with the 1966 or 1976 *Bloodbath*.

BLOODBATH AT THE HOUSE OF DEATH

(Media, 1983) **D/S/P:** Ray Cameron
S: Barry Cryer **P:** John Downes   UK

Radio and TV star Kenny Everett and one-season *Saturday Night Live* regular Pamela Stephenson star as paranormal researchers who go to "Headstone Manor." Guest star Vincent Price is the leader of a group of Devil worshippers. With some animation, a killer teddy bear, *Carrie, Alien,* and *Star Wars* spoofs, lots of fart humor, and a man flushed down a toilet.

BLOODBEAT

(TWE, 1982) **D/S:** Fabrice-Ange Zaphiratos
P: Helen Boley, Henri Zaphiratos

A woman (Helen Benton) in deer-hunting country is possessed by a Japanese samurai warrior. This confusing movie was made in Wisconsin with French-backing. It includes dream sequences, magical powers, nudity, and blood. (For a change of pace, see *Ninja III*, in which a woman is possessed by a ninja.)

BLOOD BRIDE: *See* THE BRIDES WORE BLOOD

BLOOD CASTLE (1970) = SCREAM OF THE DEMON LOVER

BLOOD CASTLE (1972) = FEMALE BUTCHER

BLOOD CITY = WELCOME TO BLOOD CITY

BLOOD CLAN

(Monarch, 1990) **D:** Charles Wilkenson
S/P: Glynis Whiting   Canada

In Scotland in 1895, soldiers in kilts massacre an entire clan, living in caves, who have been accused of murder and cannibalism. A judge (Gordon Pinsett) rescues one little girl and emigrates to Canada. By 1910 the girl has grown into a strong-willed redhead (Michelle Little) living with her adopted family on a farm. Her awful stepmother hates her, and she has nightmares with a Stonehenge-like setting. A series of mutilation murders make the townspeople suspect her. *Blood Clan* is a suspenseful, well-made feature with surprising plot twists. It was filmed in Alberta.

BLOOD CULT

(VCI, 1985) **D:** Christopher Lewis
S: Stuart Rosenthal **P:** Linda Lewis

This was called "the first" shot-on-video horror release. It was shot with a Sony Betacam but wasn't really the first. Female students are being killed on campus, and (rubber) body parts are collected to assemble a new body for a blood sacrifice (to a dog god!). It features dismembered bodies and gore and a lame *Psycho* shower scene. It was directed in Tulsa, Oklahoma, by the son of Loretta Young (!), whose brother Peter was in the group Moby Grape. *Revenge* was a sequel.

BLOOD DELIRIUM

(1988) **D:** Sergio Bergonzelli
S/P: Raffaella Mertes   Italy

John Phillip Law stars as a deranged artist who belives he's the reincarnation of Van Gogh. He tries to make a musician (Brigitte Christensen) "become" his late wife (whose body sits at a piano) and paints with blood. Gordon Mitchell is his necrophiliac butler.

BLOOD DINER

(Vestron, 1987) **D/P:** Jackie Kong
S: Michael Sonye **P:** Jimmy Maslon

This is a very gory, dumb comedy/horror takeoff on Herschell Gordon Lewis' 1963 *Blood Feast* (it was planned as *Blood Feast II*), but it's bad in a way that the original wasn't. Two nephews of Uncle Anwar run a "health food" diner where they serve their victims. The late Rick Burks and Carl Crew star. *Blood Diner* features rock bands (Art Fein was the music consultant), topless aerobics, and low-riders.

BLOOD EVIL = DEMONS OF THE MIND

BLOOD FEAST: *See* NIGHT OF A THOUSAND CATS

BLOODFIST

(MGM, 1989) **D:** Terence H. Winkles
S: Robert King **P:** Roger Corman

World light-heavyweight kickboxing champion Don Wilson (in his first starring role) is Jake "the Dragon." He goes to Manila to avenge the death of his brother. *Bloodfist* copied *Blood Sport* and *Kickboxer* but was a major hit for Concorde, Corman's production company. With Riley Bowman, Joe Marie Avellana, and Filipino-movie regular Vic Diaz as a detective. Sequels followed with the Japanese-American Wilson.

BLOODFIST II

(MGM, 1991) **D:** Andy Blumenthal
S: Catherine Cyran **P:** Roger Corman

Don "the Dragon" Wilson returns as Jake the Dragon in a copy of *Enter the Dragon.* He goes to the Philippines again, to find a missing friend. Kidnapped along with other international fighters, he's taken to a secret island, where he's forced to battle superstrong fighters (created by a mad scientist using monkey glands) in a steel cage while rich people watch and make bets. There's some sex and an anti-drug lecture. Wes Craven received an "adviser" credit.

BLOODFIST III: FIRST TO FIGHT

(New Horizons, 1992) **D:** Oley Sassone **S:** Allison Burnett **P:** Roger Corman   *(Forced to Fight)*

Don "the Dragon" Wilson is Jimmy Boland this time, and he's in prison for a crime he didn't commit. He makes friends with Richard Roundtree and John Cardone, and becomes involved in racial battles between black and white inmates. This was the first release from Corman's own video division. It includes topless scenes from *TNT Jackson* being watched by inmates. With Rick Dean and Richard Joseph Paul.

BLOOD FREAK

(Simitar, 1971) **D/S/P:** Brad Grinter
S/A: Steve Hawkes   *(Blood Freaks)*

A man (Brad Grinter) sits behind a desk, smokes, looks down, and reads about "a pretty girl with a problem" and "a catalyst." Steve Hawkes, who conceived this moral tale, stars as Herschell, a big, muscular, strait-laced Nam-vet biker with wide sideburns. He offers a ride to Angel (a Bible-quoting Loretta Lynn clone with a flat tire) and ends up at her bad sister Ann's drug party. Angel lectures, "You know your body is a temple of the holy spirit. You shouldn't defile it!" When a girl comes on to Herschell, he calls her a tramp, so her boyfriend and Ann plot to make him an addict. The narrator reminds us that Herschell is conservative and responsible. The girl's scientist father, who owns a noisy turkey farm, offers him a maintenance job and a home. Ann, in her new bikini, offers him a joint. He smokes, laughs, and follows her to bed: "I'm not a coward!" The father uses him for a guinea pig, serving him a whole drugged turkey. He shakes and gets sick from withdrawal pains, then smokes more pot, *Reefer Madness*– style. After a while he becomes a turkey-headed monster with flared jeans, a turkey monster that gobbles! He shows a note to Ann, who's lounging on a leopard-skin water bed. She says, "You sure are ugly!" He goes after the drug dealers (who play 8-track tapes). In his nightmare, people eat him, and a (real) turkey is decapitated. He cuts the leg off a screaming dealer with a power saw. It looks like the actor has a wooden leg, making the bloody scene strangely effective. Angel, of course, cures Herschell with prayer. The narrator (Grinter) talks about "the human body as a mixing bowl," and in an unexpected instance of intentional comedy/ irony he has a coughing fit from smoking! Grinter was also responsible for the Hitler horror movie *Flesh Feast.* Hawkes owned some lions and also made and starred in some obscure Tarzan ripoffs. The acting, makeup, and rock-music soundtrack are all wonderfully horrible. The first time I saw this incredible made-in-Florida tale was in Paris. It was pretty interesting dubbed into French, but I missed dialogue like "Go ahead and become a Bible freak. I don't give a damn!"

BLOOD FRENZY

(Hollywood Family Entertainment, 1987)
D/P: Hal Freeman **S:** Ted Newsom

A maniac kills off a group of "troubled" teens during group encounter sessions held in the desert. "Pop Goes the Weasel" is heard during the murders. With Wendy MacDonald and grown-up Lisa Loring (who played Wednesday in the original *Addams Family*) as Dory. It was made by a porno director (he made the *Caught from Behind* series) but features blood, not sex.

BLOOD GAMES

(Epic, 1989) **D:** Tanya Rosenberg
S: Craig L. Clyde, James L. Hennessey, George P. Saunders **P:** Yakov Bentsui

"Babe and His Ball Girls" (manager Ross Hagen and a bunch of sexy young female baseball players) travel around in a bus for exhibition games. After they beat a bunch of unshaven, beer-drinking rednecks (including Buck Flower), the local survivalist boss's beloved son is shot, and Hagen is killed. The distraught father offers "$1000 per dead bitch!" and it's dumb, violent hillbillies vs. terrified women in the woods. Laura Albert stars as the pitcher. All the women are seen naked in a shower, and none of them ever wear bras. Several of them are killed, but the survivors are more devious than the backwoods attackers. Not as bad as it could have been, *Blood Games* suffers from too many slo-mo scenes, and the one black character is there just so that she can be an extra in the shower scene, then die.

BLOOD HARVEST

(UAV, 1986) **D:** Bill Rebane **S:** Ben Benson, Emil Joseph **P:** Luseszek Burzynski   (*The Marvelous Mervo*)

Here it is—the gory horror movie with Tiny Tim! He's the weird "Marvelous Mervo," always lurking around. He wears clown makeup and talks and sings to himself. He prays, sings, and cries in church. Jill (Itonia Salocheck) returns to her family's small-town farm, but nobody is there. Mervo is the "crazy" brother of her jealous childhood boyfriend. Characters are hung upside down, and their throats are cut so the blood can be collected in a bucket. Jill is knocked out, tied up in bed, and photographed. Rebane is the man who made *Monster A Go-Go*, *The Giant Spider Invasion*, and many more, all in Wisconsin. This is his only movie with lots of blood and nudity. Because of that fact (and Tiny Tim), it's his best by default.

BLOOD HOOK

(Prism, 1987) **D:** James Mallon **S:** Larry Edgerton, John Galligan **P:** David Herbert

Troma released this horror movie, made in backwoods Wisconsin and directed by a guy who later produced the *Mystery Science Theater* TV show. Teen fishermen and a family are killed off by a crazed war vet with a metal plate in his head. He sells his victims as bait, and many fish jokes are told. With Lisa Todd (from *Hee Haw*).

BLOOD HUNGER (1974) = VAMPYRES

BLOOD HUNGER

(Even Steven, 197?) **D/S/C:** Gary Graver
P: Ed DePriest

It's packaged like a horror movie, but it's a cheap nudie movie that opens with a (real) crushed cat.

A private eye narrates a story about women who are kidnapped and raped, but it's a comedy. Graver's reflection is visible on the side of a phone booth. With Antoinette Maynard, Walt Phillips, and Uschi Digart.

BLOOD HUNT = THE THIRSTY DEAD

BLOOD IN THE STREETS

(1972) **D/S:** Sergio Sollima **S:** Ardiono Maiuri, Massimo De Rita   Italy/France/ W. Germany (*The Revolver*)

This gangster movie stars Oliver Reed as an Italian official forced to release a prisoner (Fabio Testi) because his wife has been kidnapped. The pursuit of the kidnappers leads to Paris. With Agostina Belli and an Ennio Morricone score. From Independent International.

BLOOD ISLAND = THE SHUTTERED ROOM

BLOOD LINK

(Nelson, 1982) **D:** Alberto De Martino **S:** Theodore Apstein **P:** Robert Pagaggi   Italy (*The Link*)

Women are being killed in this convoluted sex-and-violence horror movie by the director of *Puma Man*. Michael Moriarty is a shrink who "sees" the murders. He thought his (Siamese!) twin brother had died in a fire. Some of the actors and an Ennio Morricone score make it worth seeing. With Penelope Milford, Cameron Mitchell as a punch-drunk boxer, Geraldine Fitzgerald, and Martha Smith (from *Playboy*).

BLOODLUST

(Top, 1981) **D/S:** Walerian Borowczyk
P: Robert Kupferberg, Jean-Pierre Labrande
France (*Dr. Jekyll et les Femmes; Dr. Jekyll and Miss Osbourne; Bloodbath of Dr. Jekyll*)

Dr. Jekyll (Udu Kier) uses transcendental medicine (and music) and becomes Dr. Hyde (played by a different actor without eyebrows). This whole movie takes place in the house where overnight guests have gathered for Jekyll's wedding to Fanny Osbourne (Marina Pierro). (Fanny Osbourne was the wife of Robert Louis Stevenson, author of *The Strange Case of Dr. Jekyll and Mr. Hyde*.) A woman is killed, so a general (Patrick Magee), who likes to whip women, takes charge. Fanny eventually bathes in Jekyll's solution, and after a destructive fit she kills too. Howard Vernon is a doubting doctor. The unique acting styles of Kier and Magee help make this deconstruction of a literary classic (in English) worthwhile. Set design by director Borowczyk. The Japanese laserdisc version is uncut (more sex and nudity) but is digitally censored.

BLOODLUST

(1992) **D/S/P:** Richard Wolstencroft
S: Jon Hewitt   Australia

Three modern-day vampires (two are female) go on a killing spree in a city armed with guns. Dumb cops, religious-cult members, and drug dealers are

after them. The feature has sex, blood, drugs, and punk-rock music. It made news when it was seized by customs officials in the UK.

BLOODLUST: SUBSPECIES III

(Paramount, 1993) **D/S:** Ted Nicolaou
P: Vlad and Oana Paunescu

The second sequel to *Subspecies* has the same characters as *Bloodstone* but offers nothing new. Anders Hove is Radu again, bringing (topless) female victims to vampire Denise Duff. Her sister (Melanie Shatner), Kevin Blair, and Jon Haiduc are still trying to save her. It's padded with flashbacks from the other features, and has a few seconds of stop-motion animation. The whole series was filmed in Romania.

BLOOD MASSACRE

(Star III, 1988) **D/S/P/E:** Don Dohler
S/P: Barry Gold, Dan Buehl

When you think of directors who live and work in Baltimore, you might come up with John Waters and Barry Levinson, but there's also Don Dohler. This effort is scratchy-looking and laughable, but it does have a few surprises. A group of demented Nam vets and a girlfriend drink Schaefer beer, kill somebody during a convenience-store holdup, then hold a family hostage in a remote house. They insult and abuse the horrified people, but the captives turn out to be not only cannibals (!) but rotted ghouls under their (synthetic?) skin. George Stover, a veteran of several Waters and Dohler films who looks like Karl Malden's brother, gets his first top billing as the mean Rizzo.

BLOODMATCH

(HBO, 1990) **D/S:** Albert Pyun

A pumped-up Hope Marie Carlton (from Andy Sidaris movies) fights and defeats men for revenge. Villain kickboxer Thom Mathews kidnaps and tortures fighters and makes them fight to the death in Las Vegas. With kickboxer Benny "the Jet" Orquidez.

BLOOD MOON (1970) = THE WEREWOLF VS. THE VAMPIRE WOMEN

BLOOD MOON

(IVE, 1989) **D:** Alec Mills **S:** Robert Brennan
P: Stanley O'Rourke   Australia

A psycho uses barbed wire to kill in the woods behind a Catholic girls' school. Lots of characters are involved in many subplots. There's a shower-room scene and a ridiculous glam-rock band, and there was a "Fright Break" in theaters. The Brian May soundtrack was released in Australia. The producer and director returned with *Dead Sleep*.

BLOOD OF A POET

(Home Vision, 1930) **D/S:** Jean Cocteau
France (*Le Sange d'un Poète*)

Four surrealistic segments (in 53 minutes) show the adventures of a young poet. The sight of his own blood drives him mad and causes visions. It was the first film by the famous director of *Beauty and the Beast*. A documentary, *Jean Cocteau: Autobiography of an Unknown* (Home Vision), is also available.

THE BLOOD OF HEROES

(HBO, 1989) **D/S:** David Peoples **P:** Brian Rosen   Australia (*Salute of the Jugger*)

You've probably seen all the post-nuke *Road Warrior* copies you can stand, but face it, they were the westerns of the 80s, and they're still around. This one's by the writer of the *Blade Runner* script, and it's one of the best, with a good cast. It doesn't feature hyped-up vehicles but centers on a ragged group who travel around to compete in a violent game that uses dog skulls on sticks. One-eyed Rutger Hauer stars, with Joan Chen, Vincent Phillip D'Onofrio, Hugh Keays-Byrne as Sir Vile, Max Fairchild, and fighter Richard Norton. They travel to more games, then reach the giant, underground league headquarters. The American version is 90 minutes long and is missing 12 minutes.

BLOOD OF JESUS

(Discount, 1941) **D/S/P/A:** Spencer Williams **P:** Alfred Sacks

Reggie Jackson (Williams), a small-town non-believer, accidentally shoots his Baptist wife. She dies and goes to a crossroads, where a laughing Devil (with horns and a tail) sends the handsome Judas to lead her astray in a juke joint. He wants to make her a hostess, but she runs away and wakes in bed at the end. There's a ladder to Heaven, a transparent lady angel, and a statue of Christ that talks. The music is all gospel until she takes the wrong road. Then jazzy swing music and some great slide-guitar truckin' blues music is heard. This incredible movie cost only $5,000! It was the first of seven made by Williams, the major black director after Oscar Micheaux (whose career was in the 20s and 30s). Williams made the similar *Go Down Death* (1944) and later starred as Amos on *Amos and Andy* on TV (1951–53).

BLOOD ON THE BADGE

(AIP, 1992) **D/S/P:** Bret McCormick **S:** John Cianetti

A pumped-up young cop (David Harrod) goes to a small Texas town with his new female partner (Desire LaFore) to avenge the death of his former (black) partner (Todd Everett), who appears in dreams to give helpful clues (!). The rich, racist, terrorist/survivalist villain, who owns a sausage company, is eaten by pigs at the end. With slo-mo deaths, motel sex with a maid, a guitar soundtrack, and machine guns that light up like firecrackers. "Name" star Joe Estevez is the cops' boss. Blue Thompson, who used to act in McCormick's Dallas-based movies, was the editor, and the audio is by Tony Brownrigg.

BLOOD QUEEN

(Video Search, 1972) **D/P:** Radley Metzger **S:** Brian Phelan   US/Yugoslavia (*Little Mother*)

Christiane Kruger stars as the ruthless Marina Pinares (based on Eva Perón), who rises from being an out-of-work actress sharing a cheap apartment to become the wife of the powerful leader (Siegfried Rauch) of "Argonia." Flashbacks reveal all the plotting, sex, media manipulation and killing that got her there. *Blood Queen* is a very well made feature with excellent editing and is very political. It was probably too serious for Metzger fans expecting just more stylish sex. Mark Damon (an ex–teen star) is her lover who turns against all the corruption. They have a sex scene on different sides of a shower door. With Ivan Desny as a general and Anton Diffring as the cardinal. The Audubon film was cut in America for an R rating. The letterboxed, subtitled, uncut version I saw features some full nudity and is in Finnish. Metzger made this and *Score* (1973), both in Yugoslavia, then became "Harry Paris" for a series of acclaimed hard-core features.

BLOODRAGE

(IVE, 1979) **D:** Joseph Bigwood **S:** Robert Jahn **P:** Joseph Zito, Alan M. Braverman   (*Never Pick Up a Stranger*)

Ian Scott is a psycho peeping Tom who kills hookers in Times Square. We hear his voiceover monologue. With James Johnson as a vigilante cop, Judith-Marie Bergen, Irwin Keyes, and Lawrence Tierney (also in *Abduction* and *The Prowler* by Zito).

BLOOD RAGE

(Paramount, 1984) **D:** John W. Grissmer **S:** "Richard Lamden"/Bruce Joel Rubin **P/A:** Marianne Kanter (*Nightmare at Shadow Woods*)

This was written by Bruce Joel Rubin (*Ghost*), which is really embarrassing for him. An evil twin (Mark Soper) keeps killing while his innocent brother (whose just escaped from the nuthouse) is blamed. Louise Lasser as the confused mom screams a lot on a phone and says *Mary Hartman*–style lines. The producer costars as a doctor from the asylum. Ted Raimi appears. A girl is cut in half, a head is split open, and somebody is decapitated, so if all you want is some gore, you've got it in this dumb horror movie shot in Jacksonville, Florida. Ed French did the FX. Grissmer also made *Scalpel* (1976).

BLOOD RECKONING: *See* DEATH RAGE

BLOOD RED

(Nelson, 1986) **D:** Peter Masterson **S:** Ron Cutler **P:** Judd Bernard, Patricia Casey

Sicilian grape farmers battle railroad men in the Napa Valley wine country during the 1850s. It's the only feature with Eric Roberts and his sister Julia (making her debut as his sister), but wasn't released until 1990. With Dennis Hopper as a corrupt railroad tycoon, Burt Young as a hired thug, Giancarlo Giannini, Susan Anspach, Marc Lawrence, Frank Campanella, Lara Harris, Horton Foote Jr., Charles Dierkop, and Aldo Ray as Father Stassio. The music is by Carmine Coppola.

BLOOD RELATIONS

(Nelson, 1987) **D:** Graeme Campbell **S:** Stephen Saylor **P:** Nicolas Stilliadis   Canada

Three generations of a family try to kill each other for a fortune. Ray Walston is the bedridden grandfather with a neurosurgeon son (Jan Rubes) and a spoiled, jet-setting grandson (Kevin Hicks) who brings his girlfriend (Canadian beauty Lydie Denier) to the family mansion. This movie has lots of blood, violence, and nudity and some plot surprises. With Carrie Leigh.

BLOOD RELATIVES

(United Artists, 1977) **D/S:** Claude Chabrol France/Canada (*Les Liens du Sang*)

Donald Sutherland is a Quebec police detective investigating the murder of a teen (Lisa Langlois). His character is based on Steve Carella in the 87th Precinct novels by Ed McBain. The plot involves incest. The cast includes Stéphane Audran, Donald Pleasence as a pedophile, and David Hemmings. Some other features by Chabrol

Joan Chen on a post-nuke sports team in *The Blood of Heroes*.

(sometimes called the French Hitchcock) available in the US on tape are *Bluebeard*, *Bad Girls*, and *Club Extinction*.

BLOOD SABBATH

(JLT, 1972) **D:** Brianne Murphy **S/P:** William A. Bairn **P:** Lisa Fluet   (*Yyalah*)

This is sort of a fairy tale for adults and is a must for the *General Hospital* fan in your life. Tony Geary is a hitchhiking Nam vet with an acoustic guitar, sandals, and sideburns. While he's sleeping in the woods of Mexico (?), five naked hippie women (including Uschi Digart) wake him and chase him. He hits his head on a rock, then is woken again, this time by some kind of nice sea goddess named Yyalah (Susan Damante with a terrible blond wig and too much eye makeup). The evil, topless Queen Alotta (Dyanne Thorne!) wears a crown, a red cape, and a black bikini bottom, but her female followers are always naked. Alotta plans to sacrifice a child. The tortured Geary just wants to spend a night with Yyalah, so he offers his soul and drinks blood. With baby-killing Nam flashbacks, topless dancing, the decapitation of a priest, a freak-out sequence, and weird music (theremin and flute). The female director (from England) was a cinematographer who later shot the *Little House on the Prairie* series. Hugo Grimaldi (*The Human Duplicators*) was the supervising editor.

BLOOD SALVAGE

(Magnum, 1990) **D/S:** Tucker Johnson **S:** Ken Sanders **P:** Martin J. Fischer   (*Mad Jake*)

Danny Nelson, known in the Atlanta area for Cates Pickles TV ads, plays Jake Pruitt, a Bible-quoting maniac surgeon in dirty overalls with a big smile and a great Ben Johnson–type voice. His sons, the dumb and mean Hiram and the stupid but friendly Roy, cause car accidents, tow the victims, then keep them artificially alive. The ridiculous barn/lab is filled with dead or alive mutilated and drugged bodies (including Elvis) hanging from the ceiling with life-support tubes sticking out. Jake sells body parts to Ray Walston, who bargains for better prices and says, "This place stinks!" Jake keeps a crippled beauty-contest winner named April (Lori Birdsong) locked up as a replacement for his dead daughter. John Saxon (who was also in *Cannibals in the Streets*, filmed in Atlanta) is her father. April is the only survivor in an ironic ending. This tasteless comic/horror movie is comparable in some ways to *Mansion of the Doomed* and *Motel Hell*, and is memorable for Nelson and the wheelchair-bound female lead. With boxer Evander Holyfield (an executive producer).

BLOOD SCREAMS

(Warner, 1986) **D/S/P:** Glenn Gebhardt **P:** Pedro Villa, Paul Gongaware

Russ Tamblyn was in his first feature in years, playing a magician in a plot about accursed 16th-century monks in modern Mexico. With Stacey Shaffer and Isela Vega as a witch. Shot in Mexico and released by Concorde. *Blood Screams* launched Tamblyn's direct-to-video career.

BLOODSHACK

(Sinister, 1971) **D/S/P/E/C:** "Wolfgang Schmidt"/Ray Dennis Steckler **S:** Christopher Edwards **S/A:** Ron Haydock **P:** Carol Flynn (*Chopper: Curse of the Evil Spirit*)

The director's wife, Carolyn Brandt (as herself), inherits a ranch possessed by an Indian spirit. One version of this very boring feature is padded with lots of rodeo footage. With the late Ron Haydock, who turns out to be the killer, and Steckler's kids. Haydock had been a rockabilly singer and edited the 60s magazine *Fantastic Monsters*. Sinister also offers a "director's cut."

BLOOD SHED: *See* CRAZED

BLOOD SIMPLE

(MCA, 1984) **D/S:** Joel Coen **S/P:** Ethan Coen

Blood Simple is a modern *film noir* classic inspired by James M. Cain, with horror ideas from Poe and a title from Dashiell Hammett. Frances McDormand (making her film debut) stars, with Dan Hedaya as her jealous bar-owner husband. M. Emmet Walsh is perfect as a sleazy detective in a yellow suit hired to kill the wife's lover (John Getz). Also with Samm-Art Williams. It has good plot twists, atmosphere, and innovative camerawork by Barry Sonnenfeld, and it was made in Texas for less than a million dollars. The soundtrack by Carter Burwell was released by Varèse Sarabande (on an album that includes music from *Raising Arizona*). Joel Coen started out working on *Fear No Evil* (1981) and with Sam Raimi on *The Evil Dead*. An illustrated screenplay was published after the brothers made *Raising Arizona*, *Miller's Crossing*, and *Barton Fink*.

BLOOD SISTERS

(Sony, 1986) **D/S/C:** Roberta Findlay **P:** Walter E. Sear

Sorority girls on a scavenger hunt are killed off while spending the night in an old mansion that used to be a whorehouse and was the site of a multiple killing. There are ghosts in mirrors, hazing hijinks, nudity, a lesbian scene, and a transvestite killer. With Amy Bretano, Maria Machart, John Fasano, Maitland McDonagh, and Ruth Collins.

BLOOD SONG

(Abacus, 1979) **D/S:** Alan J. Levi   (*Dreamslayer*)

Frankie Avalon (the same year as *Grease*) stars as a flute-playing axe murderer. He's telepathically linked to a blood donor. Donna Wilkes sees the killer in her nightmares. With Dane Clark and Richard Jaeckel. Filmed in Oregon.

BLOODSPELL

(Forum, 1987) **D:** Deryn Warren **S:** Gerry Daly **P:** Jessica Rains

A telekinetic teen (Anthony Jenkins) is sent to an asylum for young people, and people start dying in gory ways. He's possessed by the spirit of his dead sorcerer father. The same people made *Mirror of Death* the same year.

BLOOD SPLASH = NIGHTMARE

BLOODSPORT

(Warner, 1988) **D:** Newt Arnold **S:** Sheldon Leitch **P:** Mark DiSalle

Bloodsport, from Cannon, was based on the true story of Frank Dux, the first Westerner to win the secret Kumite martial-arts competition in Hong Kong. It was the first starring role for the Belgian Jean-Claude Van Damme (real name Van Varenberg). He's trained by Senzo "Tiger" Tanaka and has to fight Bolo Young (from *Enter the Dragon*) as the crooked, mean Korean contestant. With Forest Whitaker, Leah Ayers-Hamilton, and Michel Qissi. After a while, kickboxer movies were as common as post-nuke-survival movies.

BLOODSTALKERS

(Vidmark, 1975) **D/S/A:** Robert W. Morgan **P:** Ben Morse   (*The Night Daniel Died*)

Two New York couples vacationing in a shack in the Florida Everglades are killed by a (fake) creature. A psycho Nam vet is the real problem. This film copies *The Texas Chainsaw Massacre* in several ways and was filmed near Fort Lauderdale. Doug Hobart provided the bloody effects. Ads claimed it was "banned in 24 countries!" Former teen actor Kenny Miller stars. Several of the actors had appeared in *Mako: Jaws of Death*.

BLOODSTONE

(Forum, 1988) **D:** Dwight Little **S:** Curt Allen **P:** Nico Mastorakis

An ex-cop (Bret Stimely) and his heiress wife (Anna Nicholas) hunt for rubies in India, in this PG-13 *Raiders of the Lost Ark*. With Christopher Neame and Laura Albert as Kim Chi.

BLOODSTONE: SUBSPECIES II

(Paramount, 1993) **D/S:** Ted Nicolaou **P:** Vlad and Oana Paunescu

Surprise—this is one of the best vampire movies in recent years. Anders Hove returns as Radu, the ugly, creepy, long-haired *Nosferatu*-style vampire from *Subspecies*. Denise Duff becomes a vampire, and her sister (Melanie Shatner) arrives. With the Romanian Michael Dewish as a Dr. Van Helsing type, Pamela Gordon as Radu's sorceress "mummy," Jon Haiduc, and Kevin Blair. The Romanian location work is excellent, using an actual castle and an old theater, and the giant vampire shadows are very effective. Also with a nude shower scene (Duff) and some animated creatures from David Allen. Next in the series was *Bloodlust*.

BLOOD SUCKERS

(Virgin Vision, 1970) **D:** Robert Hartford-Davis **S:** Julian More **P:** Graham Harris   UK (*Incense for the Damned*)

A narrator relates the story of how "I was asked to investigate" the whereabouts of Richard, an Oxford student missing in Greece. He flies to Greece with Richard's fiancée and a school friend

(African actor Johnny Sekka). They're joined by an embassy official (Patrick Macnee, in between *The Avengers* series). It turns out that Richard is a masochistic virgin, an easy victim for a sadistic female "vampire" who has sex-and-drug orgies. Hartford-Davis also directed the swinging-London horror movie *Corruption* (1967), and this more serious effort is also padded with nudity and a long psychedelic-orgy sequence with lots of warped lead-guitar sounds and somebody singing, "Baby, don't flash your evil eyes at me!" Top-billed Peter Cushing actually has a supporting role as an Oxford professor but is in one great scene where Richard, back in England, almost causes a riot by giving an anti-academic speech. A surprisingly thin Edward Woodward has one scene as an expert who talks about how a person could achieve an orgasm having their neck sucked. Originally released in America on a double bill with *Blood Thirst*, it's based on the novel *Doctors Wear Scarlet*, by Simon Raven.

BLOODSUCKERS FROM OUTER SPACE

(Warner, 1984) **D/S:** Glenn Coburn
P: Gale Boyd Latham

Texas farmers become brainwashed bloodsuckers in this gore spoof with a photographer hero, a *Psycho* shower scene, lots of puking, and guest "star" Pat Paulsen as the president.

BLOODSUCKING (NAZI) ZOMBIES: *See* OASIS OF THE ZOMBIES

BLOODSUCKING PHAROS IN PITTSBURGH

(Paramount, 1990) **D/S:** "Alan Smithee"/Dean T. Schetter **P:** James A. Baffico, Laurence Barbara, Beverly Pewberthy (*Picking up the Pieces*)

This was announced as (yet another) remake of *Blood Feast*. Two cops and a detective's daughter pursue a chainsaw killer. Some of the humor is of the anything-goes *Airplane* variety, and some memorable black-humor gags make this a very anti-smoking feature. Although the killings take place off screen, Tom Savini provided the results. With a decapitation, a face ripped off, a wild cat fight, weird "twin" old-lady coroners, and despicable Arabs in "the Egyptian part of town." The surprise star is ex–porno star Veronica Hart (aka Jane Hamilton), enjoying her best role in an R-rated movie. Filmed in Pittsburgh.

BLOOD, SWEAT, AND BULLETS

(Cinetrust, 1990) **D/S:** Bob Cook

A hard-drinking army major (Phil Stallone) has to take seven female-killer prisoners (led by Heidi Payne) to Brazil so they can pose as hookers and kill some Cuban officers. It was filmed around Orlando, Florida.

BLOOD THIRST (1979) = 'SALEM'S LOT

BLOOD THIRST

(Sinister, 1965) **D/P:** Newt Arnold
S: N. I. P. Dennis   Philippines

A sex-crimes specialist from New York City named Adam Rourke (Robert Winston) arrives in the Philippines to go undercover as a writer and help his friend Captain Miguel (Vic Diaz) solve a series of murders. Women are discovered hung upside down with their blood drained. Adam is a fast-talking, wisecracking type who seems more interested in two living females, Serena, the belly dancer at the El Barrio club, and Miguel's adopted sister, Sylvia. We finally find out who the lumpy-faced monster (in a crypt) is at the end. This b/w film was released in the US in 1971 by Chevron, along with the British *Bloodsuckers*.

BLOODTHIRSTY EYES

(VSOM, 1971) **D:** Michio Yamamoto
S: Masura Takesue, Ai Ogawa **P:** Fumio Tanaka
Japan (*Chi o Suu Me; Lake of Dracula*)

Toho tried to copy Hammer with a series of vampire movies with Western ideas. Mori Kishida is the vampire, whose ancestors emigrated from Transylvania. He preys on some women staying at a lakeside house, and a doctor investigates. The widescreen feature is subtitled. Yamamoto made a trilogy, including *Night of the Vampire/The Vampire Doll* (1970) and *Evil of Dracula/The Vampire Rose* (1975).

BLOODTIDE

(1980) **D/S:** Richard Jeffries **S/P:** Nico Mastorakis, Donald Langdon   UK/Greece (*Red Tide*)

Treasure hunter James Earl Jones accidentally frees an (unconvincing) underwater monster that used to force the local people to sacrifice virgins. With José Ferrer, Lila Kedrova as a nun, and Mary Louise Weller, Deborah Shelton, and Martin Kove as visiting Americans. Filmed in Greece.

BLOOD TIES

(New Horizons, 1991) **D:** Jim McBride
S: Richard Shapiro **P:** Gene Corman

Jason Lendon is a Texas teen whose parents were staked and burned by a group of vampire hunters. He goes to Long Beach, California, and learns from a *Lost Boys*–type group of motorcycle-riding teen vampires, part of an empire-building Carpathian vampire clan (the heroes) led by Patrick Bauchau (from *Creepers*). Meanwhile, a Carpathian reporter (Harley Venton) who wants to lead a normal life has an affair with a DA (Kim Johnson-Ulrich). With Michelle Johnson, Michael C. Gwynne, Bo Hopkins, and Grace Zabriskie. Also with the same mansion exterior used in *House on Haunted Hill* and Donald Trump and Zsa Zsa Gabor on TV. This bloodless Fox-TV series pilot by the director of *Great Balls of Fire* was conceived while the "new" *Dark Shadows* looked like it might be a hit. The tape is slightly different from the original broadcast version.

BLOOD TRACKS

(Vista, 1985) **D:** Mats Olson **D/S:** Mike Jackson
S: Anna Wolf **P:** Tom Sjoberg   Sweden

Members of a rock group called Easy Action are at a remote mountain ski resort to make a video. They're killed off by members of a mutant cannibal family.

BLOOD WARRIORS

(Imperial, 1993) **D:** Sam Firstenberg **S:** Ram Alon, David Bradley **P:** Gope T. Samtani   Indonesia

Direct-to-video action star David Bradley is a former Marine from Texas who wears a cowboy hat, fights, plays guitar, and sings. With Jennifer Campbell and Frank Zagarino and Tanaka as fighting villains.

BLOODY BIRTHDAY

(Starmaker, 1980) **D/S:** Ed Hunt
S: Barry Pearson **P:** Gerald T. Olson

Three ten-year-old California kids use bats, arrows, and guns to kill townspeople and teachers. It turns out that they were all born simultaneously during a total solar eclipse (an idea from *Village of the Damned*). Susan Strasberg stars as a schoolteacher, and José Ferrer is a doctor. With Joe Penny, Michael Dudikoff, Julie Brown (who appears topless in a cemetery), and some voyeurism and sex. It was released in 1986. Olson later produced the hit *House Party*.

THE BLOODY BROOD

(SW, 1959) **S/P:** Julian Roffman **S:** Elwood Ullman, Ben Kerner, Des Hardman   Canada

Here's a must for fans of Peter Falk and beatnik movies. Nico (Falk) works for a crime boss and hangs out in a stylish basement club (there's a big skeleton hand in the background). His first line is: "There's no doubt about it. The world's falling apart." The normal, square hero in this anti-beatnik movie is the brother (Jack Betts) of an innocent delivery boy who's killed. Nico and his bored TV-director friend put ground glass in his hamburger at a party. The dialogue is priceless, and the punks in leather jackets are named Studs and Weasel. Roffman also made the 3-D classic *The Mask*.

BLOODY FRIDAY

(1973) **D/P:** Ferd, Beverly Sebastian
S: Ann Cawthorne   (*The Single Girls*)

Claudia Jennings stars in this drive-in murder movie. With Joan Prather, Greg Mullavey, Albert Popwell, and Mercy Rooney (from *Playboy*) as the killer. It was made after *Gator Bait*, also from Dimension and with Jennings.

BLOODY GIRL = MALENKA THE VAMPIRE

BLOODY MOON

(TWE, 1980) **D/A:** Jesús Franco
S: Rayo Casablanca **P:** Wolf C. Hartwig
W. Germany (*Die Säege des Todes*)

Olivia Pascal's friends are killed off by somebody with a scarred face and long hair who's escaped from an asylum. Her rich aunt in a wheelchair is burned, a woman is cut in half by a saw, and there's some nudity and disco music. Franco shows up as a doctor. A clip from this was used in Pedro Almodovar's *Matador*.

BLOODY NEW YEAR

(Academy, 1986) **D:** Norman J. Warren **S:** Frazier Pearce **P:** Hayden Pearce UK (*Time Warp Terror*)

Three young couples manage to strand themselves in an old hotel on an island that somehow (don't ask) has become stuck in the year 1959. Warren tells his convoluted teens-in-peril story using cost-effective special effects and ideas from *The Shining, The Evil Dead,* and *Nightmare on Elm Street*. There's a phantom rock band, a ghost maid, a possessed girl, and even a tablecloth monster, and a clip of the flying brains from *Fiend Without a Face* on TV that outshines everything else.

BLOODY PIT OF HORROR

(SW, 1965) **D:** "Max Hunter"/Massimo Pupillo **S:** Roberto Natale, Romano Migliorini **P:** Francesco Merli Italy (*Il Boia Scarlatto*)

A group of people break into an old castle to shoot sexy covers for horror novels. Mickey Hargitay (Jayne Mansfield's bodybuilder husband), believing he's the reincarnation of a 17th-century executioner in red tights and a mask, acts insane and very excited as he uses various devices (hot wax, hot coals, and ice water) to torture and kill the "sinning" women. Sharp spears cut into the clothes (and breasts) of four bound women as they go around in circles on a wooden S&M merry-go-round. *Bloody Pit* is laughable (awful dubbing), fascinating (Hargitay was Arnold Schwarzenegger's hero!), and very sick. With Walter Brandi (star of *Playgirls and the Vampire*) as the horror novelist and Femi Benussi (*Tarzana*). The production credits were all fake Anglicized names. This Frank Henenlotter Sexy Shocker release is a letter-boxed, uncut version (called both *Crimson Executioner* and *A Tale of Torture* on the print) with 10 minutes never before seen in this country. It was first released here (in "Psychovision") in 1967 (by Pacemaker). I saw it years later on an unforgettable Cleveland drive-in double bill with *Goke*.

BLOODY TRAIL

(Paragon, 1972) **D/P:** Richard Robinson **S:** Gale Robinson (*Monteego*)

Brad, an ex-soldier from Virginia, hops a train and is beaten and robbed. A black woman who nurses him turns out to be part of a group of renegade former slaves who have reverted to their tribal ways, complete with makeup and spears. The ending is extremely stupid, and it's all padded with real Civil War–era photos and sepia-tinted war footage from some other movie for flashbacks. It's a novel exploitation idea but is pretty slow going. Robert Mitchum's brother John and Rance Howard are lowlifes on the train. I imagine the video is cut, because except for a few brief scenes the expected sex and nudity are absent. Louis Sher (*The Stewardesses*) was the executive producer. Robinson explored racial problems again in his *Heartbreak Hotel*.

BLOODY WEDNESDAY

(Prism, 1984) **D/P:** Mark G. Gilhuis **S/P:** Philip Yordan (*The Great American Massacre*)

An auto-repair-shop worker (Raymond Elmendorf) who has lost his wife and job lives as a caretaker in an abandoned hotel. He imagines (or does he?) sex with his shrink, he talks to his teddy bear (the voice of Billy Curtis), and his bed sheet turns into a snake. Some mean punks give him a machine gun, and he uses it to kill everybody in a diner (in slow motion). It's an unpredictable movie inspired by the (real) California McDonald's massacre, with a moral message about what society can do to a person.

BLOWN AWAY

(Live, 1992) **D:** Brenton Spencer **S:** Robert C. Cooper **P:** Peter R. Simpson

Corey Haim is a ski-resort employee, and Nicole Eggert is the teen nympho who wants him to help kill her rich father. This "teen erotic thriller" also features Corey Feldman and Gary Farmer. It comes in R or unrated versions. Ray Sager was a producer.

BLOWN AWAY

(MGM, UA, 1994) **D:** Stephen Hopkins **S:** Joe Batteer, John Rice **P:** John Watson

This was the bomb movie that competed with *Speed*. It has a more complex plot and lots of flashbacks. Jeff Bridges stars as a Boston explosion-expert cop, Jimmy Dove. Tommy Lee Jones is a Northern Irish prison-escapee terrorist with a personal grudge who vows to kill Dove's violin-playing wife (Suzy Amis) and stepdaughter. With Forest Whitaker and Lloyd Bridges (then 81) as the uncle. It runs 121 minutes.

BLOWUP

(MGM, 1966) **D/S:** Michelangelo Antonioni **S:** Tonino Guerra **P:** Carlo Ponti UK/Italy

After his oblique trilogy *L'Avventura, La Notte,* and *Eclisse*, Antonioni went to England and created this international hit. David Hemmings is a rich, jaded London photographer who discovers he may have taken an incriminating picture of a murder. You might think about the Zapruder film of the Kennedy assassination as you watch Hemmings become obsessed with enlarging the photo to search for details. Vanessa Redgrave is top-billed, and the cast includes Sarah Miles, model Veruschka (as herself), Tsai Chin, and a rare look at the Yardbirds, with Jimmy Page and Jeff Beck. Jane Birkin and Gillian Hills (from *Beat Girl*) are in an "orgy" scene, and Birkin made it into the record books for being the first person in a major-release film to show pubic hair. MGM used a subsidiary called Premiere to release *Blowup* after it was denied a production-code seal. The rare MGM soundtrack features Herbie Hancock's music plus "Stroll On" by the Yardbirds. I saw a great-looking new print in Paris in the 80s and can recommend *Blowup* as thought-provoking, ahead-of-its-time entertainment (even if you don't like mimes).

BLUE COLLAR

(MCA, 1978) **D/S:** Paul Schrader **S:** Leonard Schrader **P:** Don Guest

The first film directed by Schrader, who had written *Taxi Driver* and *Rolling Thunder*, is a devastating look at how workers are kept in their place, written by Schrader's brother (who went on to make *The Killing of America*). Richard Pryor, Harvey Keitel, and Yaphet Kotto play Detroit auto-assembly-line workers who pull off a small union robbery and accidentally take an incriminating notebook. With Ed Begley Jr., Harry Bellaver, Cliff De Young, and Tracy Walter. The Ry Cooder soundtrack includes "Hard-Working Man," sung by Captain Beefheart. The film is from Universal.

BLUE DESERT

(Academy, 1990) **D/S:** Bradley Battersby **S:** Arthur Collins **P:** Joel Soisson, Michael Murphy

Craig Scheffer (*Nightbreed*) stars as a killer on a motorcycle in a small desert town. He and a cop (D. B. Sweeney) both want Courtney Cox.

THE BLUE GARDENIA

(Warner, 1953) **D:** Fritz Lang **S:** Charles Hoffman **P:** Alex Gottlieb

Anne Baxter thinks she's killed an artist (Raymond Burr) who made drunken advances to her. The police think she's guilty too, but a reporter (Richard Conte) attempts to prove her innocence. Based on a mystery by Vera Caspary (the author of *Laura*), it has a surprising ending. With Ann Sothern, George Reeves as a cop, and Nat "King" Cole (as himself, performing in a nightclub). Lang's next was *The Big Heat*. The next year Burr was the wife-killer in *Rear Window*.

THE BLUE IGUANA

(Paramount, 1988) **D/S:** John Lafia **P:** Steven Gold, Sigurjon Sighvatsson

Dylan McDermott stars in a bizarre detective/western spoof. He's hired by IRS agents Dean Stockwell and Tovah Feldshuh to go to El Diablo, Mexico, and recover millions of dollars. With Jessica Harper, Pamela Gidley, James Russo, and Flea. It was shot in Mexico.

THE BLUE LAGOON

(RCA, 1980) **D/P:** Randal Kleiser **S:** Douglas Day Stewart

Kleiser directed this remake of a 1949 British hit (which starred Jean Simmons) after he made *Grease*. Two little kids grow up together stranded on an island. After half an hour they become Brooke Shields and Christopher Atkins, making his film debut. (Atkins was in *Playgirl* the same year.) Nestor Almendros was the cinematographer. With Leo McKern and William Daniels. The copies were more exploitative. Sabrina Siani was in the Italian *Blue Island* (1981). Then Phoebe Cates starred in *Paradise* (1982). A sequel, *Return to the Blue Lagoon* (1991), starred Milla Jovovich and was a major flop.

BLUE MONKEY

(RCA, 1987) **D:** William Fruet **S:** George Goldsmith **P:** Martin Walters Canada (*Green Monkey; Insect*)

You could call this "Alien in a Hospital," but the slimy, fast-moving mutant "caterpillar" monster that can reproduce itself is pretty effective. The hospital it's in is filled with kids and drunken old ladies. Steve Railsback is the detective hero in this Sandy Howard production. With Gwynyth Walsh, Don Lake, Susan Anspach, John Vernon, and Joe Flaherty and Robin Duke (both from SCTV).

BLUE MOVIES

(Academy, 1986) **D/S:** Paul Koval, Ed Fitzgerald **P:** Maria Snyder

Two losers try to make a porno movie, and the mob moves in. This very cheaply made comedy features Lucinda Crosby (Cathy Lee's sister) as a porno star, Christopher Stone, Russell Johnson (from *Gilligan's Island*), Larry Linville (from *M*A*S*H*), and Don Calfa.

BLUE MURDERS

(1985) **D/S:** Charles Weiner **S:** Geoffrey Pico Canada (*The Porn Murders*)

A crime reporter searches for a psycho who kills people in the porno business. Made for TV and not very exciting.

BLUE PARADISE

(TWE, 1982) **D/S:** "John Wilder"/Luigi Russo **S:** Domenico Raffle **P:** Enzo Doria (*Adam and Eve; Adam and Eve Against the Cannibals*)

This wacked-out story features an erupting volcano and dinosaurs lifted from Ray Harryhausen's *One Million BC* (1966). The ancient couple (Mark Gregory and Andrea Goldman) also fight natives who roll a giant rock at them (just like in *Raiders of the Lost Ark*).

THE BLUES BROTHERS

(MCA, 1980) **D/S:** John Landis **S/A:** Dan Aykroyd **P:** Robert K. Weiss

John Belushi and Dan Aykroyd expanded their mediocre *Saturday Night Live* soul-men skits into a pretty fun movie full of car crashes. At least the musical-comedy/action film brought some of the original singers and musicians to a new audience. Watch for Cab Calloway ("Minnie the Moocher"), Ray Charles, Aretha Franklin (who does a killer version of "Think"), James Brown, and music by Steve Cropper and Donald "Duck" Dunn (of Booker T and the MGs), who appear as themselves. With John Candy, Henry Gibson as a Nazi, Charles Napier, Carrie Fisher, Kathleen Freeman, and bits by John Lee Hooker, Steven Spielberg, Steve Lawrence, Frank Oz, Twiggy, and Paul Reubens (Pee-wee Herman). More good R&B oldies are on the Atlantic soundtrack.

BLUE STEEL

(MGM, 1990) **D/S:** Kathryn Bigelow **S:** Eric Red **P:** Edward R. Pressman

This was disappointing, coming after Bigelow's *Near Dark*. Jamie Lee Curtis is a suspended New York City rookie cop blamed for murders committed by a schizo/psycho Wall Street commodities trader (Ron Silver). Silver overacts horribly, Curtis' character seems too thick sometimes, and it all gets too dumb pretty fast. With Elizabeth Pena, Louise Fletcher, Philip Bosco, Clancy Brown, and a wife-abuse subplot. There's a very violent street-chase shootout at the end. Bigelow married James Cameron the same year. Oliver Stone was an executive producer.

BLUE SUEDE SHOES

(1979) **D:** Curtis Clark **P:** Penny Clark UK

The first rock-and-roll weekend at the Great Yarmouth Holiday Camp is featured in a documentary. Rockers watch Ray Campi and others, and the late Bill Haley is seen in a 1978 London performance. Film clips of Gene Vincent, Eddie Cochran, and others are also shown.

BLUE THUNDER

(RCA/Columbia, 1983) **D:** John Badham **S:** Dan O'Bannon, Don Jakoby **P:** Gordon Carroll

A Nam-vet LA police pilot (Roy Scheider) who has flashbacks steals a deadly government surveillance/attack helicopter (developed for the 1984 Olympics), in an attempt to stop a right-wing, Nam-vet-pilot army colonel (Malcolm McDowell) whose conspiring to use the copter (also perfect for voyeurs) against LA ghetto residents. A super sky battle results. Warren Oates shows up too briefly (in his last role), and Candy Clark and Daniel Stern co-star. Badham made *War Games* the same year. There was an ABC-TV series based on *Blue Thunder* in 1984, and the more successful *Air Wolf* series was basically a copy of this movie.

BLUE VELVET

(Warner, 1986) **D/S:** David Lynch **P:** Fred Caruso

This one really took American audiences by surprise and got people to notice Dennis Hopper again. Lynch was even nominated for an Oscar! *Blue Velvet* is disturbing, long (2 hours), and fascinating even for the viewers who hated it. It was made by the ailing DEG movie studio run by Dino De Laurentiis, who had also backed *Dune*. Future *Twin Peaks* star Kyle McLachlan stars as Jeffrey Beaumont, in a town called Lumberville. Hopper is frightening as Frank Booth, and Isabella Rossellini is the victimized singer Dorothy. With Laura Dern (who went on to *Wild at Heart*), Dean Stockwell (who lip-syncs to Roy Orbison's "In Dreams"), Hope Lang, Priscilla Pointer, Brad Dourif, and Jack Nance. The soundtrack, composed by Angelo Badalamenti, is on Varèse Sarabande and includes Bobby Vinton's title hit from late 1963. You could also look for the animated *The Alphabet* and *The Grandmother*, Lynch's pre-*Eraserhead* shorts, on tape.

BOARDING HOUSE

(Paragon Classics, 1982) **D:** John Wintergate **S:** Jonema **P:** Peter Baahlu (*Housegeist*)

If you watch many horror tapes, you know that lots of them these days are (obviously) shot with video cameras (just like porno tapes). This historic, brain-damaged, overlong, bad LA horror movie with a synthesizer score was the first. It was transferred to 35mm, and in 1984 it actually played in theaters, advertised as being shot in "Horrorvision!" A long, hard-to-read computer scrawl, accompanied by loud, irritating beeps, informs us of the history of the cursed Hoffman house. We get solarized flashbacks, dreams, and flashforwards, along with a "ten years later" plot.

Jim (Hank Adly) is an irritating blow-dry blond with a gold earring, a tie-dyed muscle shirt, a cowboy hat, and leopard-skin briefs. He chants, "Om," and makes a bar of soap and a sock float. He buys the house and rents rooms to adoring young women. A laughable, "weird," limping, peeping-Tom, Nam-vet, punk gardener lurks. A doctor pulls his own guts out, a nurse hangs herself, a woman runs through a graveyard in a nightgown, another sees a (real) pig's head in the mirror, hands come out of a bed, and there's death by floating ice pick, electrocution by hair dryer, plus nudity—and a pie fight. Jonema, the scriptwriter, plays Victoria, lead singer of the 33 1/3 rock band. They play at a pool-side party. She gets *lots* of screen-time and closeups. When the killer female is revealed, she has an exorcist voice and

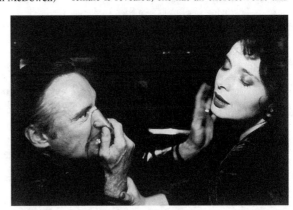

Dennis Hopper and Isabella Rossellini in *Blue Velvet*.

breathes steam. The end is a psychic battle between her and Jim: "Focus! White light! White light!" You can pick up a rerelease copy for under 10 bucks in better check-cashing stores.

BOARDINGHOUSE BLUES

(Fang, 1948) **D:** Josh Binney **S:** Hal Seeger **P:** E. M. Glucksman

You might remember Jackie "Moms" Mabley as an old-lady comic on network TV during the 60s. Here she is, years earlier, starring in an all-black musical-comedy vaudeville-revue featuring many acts. It's a real find—it's "prehysterical!" The bare plot is about Moms needing money to keep the evil landlord from evicting her and her assortment of show-biz tenants. Comedy routines that must go back to the turn of the century are mixed with novelty acts, dancing, and singing. There's an acrobatic guy in a monkey suit, an amazing dancer with one arm and one leg, tap-dancers Stump and Stumpy, a great band, singer Bull-moose Jackson, and comics who tell drug jokes. Moms impersonates a Gypsy fortune-teller, tap-dances, makes jokes about Cab Calloway, serves "hot cakes and rabbit stew" for dinner, and says, "Open the door, Richard!" at the film's end. Moms also starred in *Amazing Grace*.

BOARDING SCHOOL

(Vestron, 1976) **D:** André Farwagi **S:** Paul Nicholas
W. Germany (*Hotel der Leidenschaftlichen; Passion Flower Hotel; Preppy School Girls; Virgin on Campus*)

16-year-old Nastassja Kinski is an American girl at a Swiss boarding school during the 50s. She comes up with a plan for the students to pose as prostitutes to get boys from a nearby boys' school. With Fabiana Udenio and Kurt Raab, who was also the art director. This sex comedy was released several times to cash in on Kinski's fame. It was only her fourth role after Wim Wenders' *Wrong Move* (*Falsche Bewewgung*, 1974), the Hammer film *To the Devil, a Daughter* (1975), and *For Your Love Only* (1976), by Wolfgang Petersen.

BOB AND SALLY

(1948) **D:** Erle C. Kenton   (*The Story of Bob and Sally*)

This road-show presentation, *A Mom and Dad* (1947) imitation, from "Social Guidance," includes real scenes of a normal and a Cesarean birth. A horrifying (real) VD sequence is shown near the end, after the live talk presented by "hygiene commentator Roger T. Miles." It was still playing in the late 50s. Kenton had been the director of the horror classic *Island of Lost Souls* (1933). His last film was *One Too Many* (1950).

BOBBIE JO AND THE OUTLAW

(Vestron, 1976) **D/P:** Mark L. Lester
S: Vernon Zimmerman

Lynda Carter is a carhop and Marjoe Gortner is a bandit who thinks he's the reincarnation of Billy the Kid, in this *Bonnie and Clyde* copy from AIP. It takes place in modern-day New Mexico and features Belinda Belaski, Jesse Vint, Merrie Lynn Ross, Lynda Kimball, and a manic Gerrit Graham. Steve Brodie was the coproducer. Topless

scenes of Carter (TV's former "Wonder Woman") from this exploitation movie have appeared in countless men's magazines over the years.

BOCA

(Republic, 1994) **D:** Rene Manzor, Walter Avancini, Zalman King **S:** Ed Silverstein
P: Jeff Young, Joffre Rodriguez   US/Brazil

Executive producer Zalman King used footage from a 1990 Brazilian film, a Brazilian documentary, and his own *Wild Orchid* and added new (uncredited) scenes to create a soft core sex movie that's also an exposé about the problems of Brazilian street kids. Rae Dawn Chong stars and relates flashbacks as an American TV reporter with Tarcisio Meira in new and older scenes as Boca, a crime lord, Martin Kemp as a photographer and Martin Sheen. Sex and violence scenes are shown in slo-mo.

BOCCACCIO '70

(VSOM, 1962) **D/S:** Federico Fellini, Luchino Visconti **D:** Vittorio De Sica **S:** Cesare Zavattini
P: Carlo Ponti, Antonio Cervi   France/Italy

Multidirector anthologies like this used to be common in Europe. I wish somebody could get the rights to all of them, disassemble them and release short compilations of each director's work (all Fellini, all Godard, etc.). *Boccaccio '70* includes three stories. Visconti's stars Romy Schneider, and De Sica's stars Sophia Loren. (A fourth episode was cut from the US release.) Fellini was between *La Dolce Vita* and *8 1/2* when he created his episode, "The Temptation of Dr. Antonio," and it's the one you'll remember. A sexy woman on a billboard (Anita Ekberg) comes to life. She taunts and lifts up a moral crusader who has demanded that the poster be taken down. I wonder whether Fellini saw *Attack of the 50 Ft. Woman*.

THE BODY

(T.Z, 1967) **D:** Romolo Guerrieri **S:** Ernesto Gastaldi   Italy/France (*The Sweet Body of Deborah; Il Dolce Corpo di Deborah*)

Carroll Baker and Jean Sorel return to Geneva from their honeymoon. A man accuses the husband of causing the suicide of his girlfriend, played by Evelyn Stewart (real name Ida Galli). The "giallo" murder mystery has a double-twist ending. With George Hilton. This was the first of many features Baker made in Italy. Warner released it in the US.

BODY AND SOUL

(MGM, 1981) **D:** George Bowers **S/A:** Leon Isaac Kennedy **P:** Golan/Globus

In a remake of the 1947 John Garfield film, Leon Isaac Kennedy becomes a boxer to pay for his sister's operation. With Jayne Kennedy, Peter Lawford, Michael V. Gazzo, Perry Lang, Muhammed Ali (as himself), and Mel Welles. Lots of *Playboy* Playmates (Rosanne

Katon, Johari Azizi, Laurie Senit, and Ola Ray) are in one scene. Jayne and Leon posed in *Playboy*, then were divorced the next year. She became a TV hostess and said she had been born again. Bowers also made *The Hearse* and became an editor of major features.

BODY BAGS

(Republic, 1993) **D:** John Carpenter, Tobe Hooper
S: Dan Angel, Billy Brown **P:** Sandy King

Executive producer Carpenter is also the wise-cracking host, the Coroner, in this Showtime horror-anthology series pilot that's as good as *Tales from the Crypt*, which it copies. Alex Datcher works the night shift in "The Gas Station," with Robert Carradine, Sam Raimi, David Naughton, Buck Flower, and Wes Craven. "Hair" is a comic tale that has a sci-fi twist, with Stacy Keach, Sheena Easton, David Warner, Kim Alexis, and Deborah Harry. Mark Hamill receives the eye of a serial killer in "Eye," the lone segment by Hooper, with Twiggy, Charles Napier, and John Agar and Roger Corman (!) as doctors. KNB did FX, and Rick Baker did the special makeup.

BODY BEAUTIFUL

(1953) **D/P:** Max Nosseck **S:** Nat Tonchuck, Arnold Phillips   (*Miss Body Beautiful*)

Susan Morrow (*Cat Women of the Moon*) stars as a model, with Robert Clarke, Noreen Nash, and O. Z. Whitehead. Nosseck later made *The Garden of Eden*, set in a nudist colony (1957). A WWII refugee, he settled in Germany in the 50s and made two films there.

BODY CHEMISTRY

(RCA, 1990) **D:** Kristine Peterson
S: Jackson Barr **P:** Alida Camp

Corman/Concorde released this kinky *Fatal Attraction* copy set in a sex-research lab. Married Marc Singer has a wild affair with Lisa Pescia, but she won't let him go. They have sex at work, in a van in front of his house, and wherever and however she wants it. Pescia is pretty amazing as the crazed, jilted lover. She ends up threatening his wife and family. She also substitutes a tape of S&M sex featuring herself and Singer for his son's *Teenage Mutant Ninja Turtles* video. With Mary Crosby as the wife and Joseph Campanella.

BODY CHEMISTRY II: THE VOICE OF A STRANGER

(Columbia, 1991) **D:** Adam Simon **S:** Jackson Barr, Christopher Wooden **P:** Alida Camp

Gregory Harrison (one-time star of the *Trapper John, MD* TV series) stars as a suicidal ex-cop and sexual deviant who beats up women. He ends up being used by radio psychiatrist Lisa Pescia (from the first film) for sexual experiments. She's being blackmailed by the radio-station owner (Morton Downey Jr.). With Robin Riker, director John Landis as a shrink, Clint Howard, and, in flashback sequences (lifted from other Corman/Concorde productions), Maria Ford and Monique Gabrielle. Simon also made *Brain Dead*.

A giant Anita Ekberg in Fellini's *Boccaccio '70* segment.

BODY CHEMISTRY III: POINT OF SEDUCTION

(New Horizons, 1994) **D:** Jim Wynorski
S: Jackson Barr **P/A:** Andrew Stevens

Andrew Stevens is a big-deal TV producer who wants the rights to the story of the hostess of a cable sex show (Shari Shattuck) who has killed two of her lovers. They spend most of the movie fucking in places where they could easily be caught. Too bad either the sex scenes are too dark or Shattuck leaves her clothes on. When she's naked you can see her crotch cover. With Chick Vennera, Morgan Fairchild as Stevens' soap-opera-star wife, Robert Forster, Stella Stevens, Delia Sheppard, and Becky LeBeau. Followed by *Body Chemistry IV*.

BODY COUNT

(Midnight, 1986) **D:** Ruggiero Deodato
S: Alessandro Capone, Dardeno Sacchetti
P: Alessandro Fracassi   Italy (*Camping del Terror*)

Teens are killed in the woods again, but there's a good US/Italian exploitation cast. Mimsy Farmer is married to camp owner David Hess but loves the sheriff (Charles Napier). With Ivan Rassimov, Bruce Penhall (the motorcycle-racing champ formally on *CHIPs*), and John Steiner. The music is by Claudio Simonetti of Goblin.

BODY COUNT

(Forum, 1987) **D/S/P/E:** Paul Leder
(*The Eleventh Commandment*)

A dangerous psycho (Bernie White) breaks out of an asylum and goes after his uncle (Dick Sargent, from *Bewitched*). With Greg Mullavey, who had been acting in Leder movies since 1970 (*The Marigold Man*) and was in many more, including *I Dismember Mama* (1974).

THE BODY DISAPPEARS

(1941) **D:** D. Ross Lederman **S:** Erna
Lazarus, Scott Darling **P:** Bryan Foy

In this Warner Brothers comedy, a formula developed by Edward Everett Horton to bring back the dead makes people invisible instead, and soon half the cast is invisible. Jeffrey Lynn stars, with Jane Wyman (Ronald Reagan's wife at the time), Willie Best, Marguerite Chapman, Craig Stevens, and Natalie Schafer.

BODY DOUBLE

(RCA/Columbia, 1984) **D/S/P:** Brian De Palma
S: Robert J. Arrech

De Palma's worst showoff Hitchcock copy borrows shamelessly from *Rear Window* and *Vertigo*. A struggling actor who is a claustrophobic voyeur (the boring Craig Wasson) house-sits after being fired from a movie (*Vampire's Kiss*) and witnesses a murder committed by an "Indian" killer with a large electric drill. Melanie Griffith got the attention for playing porno star Holly Body. With Gregg Henry, Deborah Shelton, Dennis Franz, Barbara Crampton (in a sex scene), Brinke Stevens, Barbara Peckinpah, Alexandra Day, and porno actresses Annette Haven, Linda Shaw (as herself), and Windsor Taylor Randolph/Lisa Berenger.

Frankie Goes to Hollywood does "Relax" during one of the MTV-inspired sequences. The score is by Pino Danaggio.

BODY FEVER

(Sinister, 1968) **D/S/P/A:** Ray Dennis Steckler
S: William Edgar **P:** Keith A. Webster
(*Super Cool; The Last Original B Movie*)

Ray Dennis Steckler, who acts under the name Cash Flagg, is best known for *The Incredibly Strange Creatures That Stopped Living and Became Mixed-Up Zombies*. This is his Bogart tribute/spoof. Down-and-out private detective Charles Smith (Steckler), who has to hitchhike everywhere, narrates the story. He's hired to find a girl, played by Carolyn Brandt (his wife at the time). She wears Catwoman-style tight clothes during robberies. The music is a great mixture of rock, bongos, and a full orchestra. The plot includes strippers, junk, and a gangster called Big Mac. Posters for Ray's other movies are on the wall in a bar, where Liz Renay is seen briefly. It's a typical dumb-fun Steckler production with an oddball cast, including Gary Kent (a regular in biker movies), Herb Robbins (who directed *The Worm Eaters*), Coleman Francis (who directed *The Beast of Yucca Flats*), and rockabilly singer Ron Haydock. The big late-60s question is: "Are you a bird? Birds fly!"

BODY HEAT

(Warner, 1981) **D/S:** Lawrence Kasdan **P:** Fred T. Gallo

Kathleen Turner (very sexy in her first role) baits a Florida lawyer (William Hurt) into killing her husband (Richard Crenna). This hit looks back to 40s *film noir* and copies *Double Indemnity*, but it in turn influenced countless "erotic thrillers" produced later. With Ted Danson and Mickey Rourke.

BODY LANGUAGE

(Paramount, 1992) **D:** Arthur Allan Seidelman
S: D. Gurskis, Brian Ross **P:** Robert M. Rolsky

Linda Purl is a psycho secretary out to take the job of her executive boss (Heather Locklear). She imitates her, then kills with a knife and a paperweight. This USA Network TV movie copies *Single White Female*. It also features Edward Albert as the big boss, James Acheson, and Jeff Kizer.

BODY MELT

(Prism, 1993) **D/S/M:** Philip Brophy **S/P:** Rod
Bishop **P:** Daniel Scharf   Australia

Injected vitamins from a health farm cause hallucinations and cause people to mutate, crack open, and melt. Two Italian kids from a Melbourne suburb become lost in the outback and visit a seemingly retarded family. The kids (whose father developed the drug) kill a kangaroo and eat its glands. This odd gore movie, which borrows a lot from David Cronenberg's movies, features comedy, some disturbing scenes, and full nudity. A mutant woman collects ribs, musclebound workers create more vitamins, and a blobby creature emerges from a pregnant woman. Gerald Kennedy stars as a police detective.

BODY OF A FEMALE

(1965) **D/P:** J. Elsworth, Julian Marsh **S:** Francis Ellie

Future director Roberta Findlay (aka "Anna Riva") stars as a Cuban stripper named Cindy who works near Coney Island. She's drugged and taken to a mansion owned by Spencer, a rich, crazy man (future director Lem Amero) by a drifter named Bruno. Spencer whips her and hunts down Cindy and Bruno on a beach. This b/w nudie also features a very rare appearance by Betty Page.

BODY OF EVIDENCE

(MGM, 1992) **D:** Uli Edel **S:** Brad
Mirman **P:** Dino De Laurentiis

Did Madonna kill her millionaire record-biz lover with rough sex? Not many people cared, and they stayed away from this movie in droves. Willem Dafoe costars as the foolish defense lawyer who falls for her. With Joe Mantegna, Jurgen Prochnow, Anne Archer, and Julianne Moore. It's by the director of the much better *Last Exit to Brooklyn*. R and NC-17 tapes are available.

BODY OF INFLUENCE

(Academy, 1993) **D:** Gregory Hippolyte
S: David Schreiber **P:** Andrew Garoni

Blond Shannon Whirry (also in Gregory's *Animal Instincts* movies) seduces and ruins the life of a Beverly Hills shrink (Nick Cassavetes, who narrates). He videotapes sessions with "repressed" housewife patients who talk a lot and tell their dreams. Some sex scenes involve handcuffs, guns, and strangling, and there's talk about a serial killer. A detective (Richard Roundtree) says, "It wasn't difficult to figure out." I think I saw the tame R version. It was pretty boring. With Sandahl Bergman, Don Swayze, Sandra Margot (aka Tiffany Million), Monique Parent, and Anna Karin.

BODY PARTS

(Paramount, 1991) **D/S:** Eric Red **S:** Norman
Snider **P:** Frank Mancuso Jr.   Canada

The arm of a criminal psychologist (Jeff Fahey) is replaced by a brilliant but crazed woman doctor (Lindsay Duncan). Artist Brad Dourif (an acting high point) and an athlete receive other body parts that turn out to be from a condemned serial killer. Fahey starts losing control of his arm and is afraid he'll kill his own family. With Kim Delaney as his wife and Zakes Mokae (*The Serpent and the Rainbow*) as a perplexed cop. *Body Parts* seems pretty subdued until near the end, with car chases, gore effects (by Gordon Smith), and the fairly ridiculous mad doctor and her creation scene. It's full of plot implausibilities but has a standout car-accident scene. Just after its release, the Jeffrey Dahmer serial-killer story hit the news, and some theaters pulled the feature. The very good soundtrack on Varèse Sarabande is by Loek Dikker.

BODY PUZZLE

(Triboro, 1992) **D:** "Larry Louis"/
Lamberto Bava **S:** Bruce Martin   Italy

The body of the husband of Tracy, a wealthy widow and editor (Joanna Pacula), is stolen. Soon body parts (an ear, a hand) continue to turn up in surprising places in her remote home. It seems that her husband was a promiscuous bisexual, so there are many suspects. Although it seems she'd be in constant hysterics, Tracy finds time to act cheerful and fall in love even after a severed penis shows up in her pool! Tom Arana (*The Church*) and Gianni Garko are two thick cops who should be fired. This movie is as stupid as *Pieces* (from 10 years earlier) without the gore. With Erica Blanc as a shrink, Susanna Javicoli (*Suspiria*), and John Morghen. Classical music (Moussorgsky's "A Night on Bald Mountain") was added to the soundtrack of the US version.

BODY ROCK

(HBO, 1984) **D:** Marcelo Epstein **S:** Desmond Nakano **P:** Jeffrey Shechtman

Lorenzo Lamas goes big-time as a club emcee in this PG-13 breakdancing movie. Lamas (son of 50s stars Fernando Lamas and Arlene Dahl) later became a direct-to-video action star. With Vicki Frederick, Cameron Dye, Ray Sharkey, and Grace Zabriskie. It was shot by Robby Mueller and directed by a guy who had done rock videos.

THE BODY SHOP: *See* DOCTOR GORE

BODY SHOT

(Triboro, 1993) **D/P:** Dimitri Logothesis **S:** Robert Ian Strauss **P:** Gene Margolis

Robert Patrick (*Terminator II*) stars as a blond LA paparazzo who becomes the patsy when a reclusive Madonna-type singer called Chelsea is killed. Michelle Johnson as a Chelsea lookalike is featured in several (pretty tame) sex scenes. The plot is filled with improbable nonsense. With Jonathan Banks, Ray Wise, and Kim Miyori as a clever detective. Charles Napier, Kenneth Tobey, and Liz Torres have brief roles. There's a scene at the Griffith Park observatory, and a cheap nightmare sequence. By the director of *Slaughterhouse Rock*.

BODY SLAM

(Nelson, 1987) **D:** Hal Needham **S/P:** Shel . Lyton **S:** Steve Burkow **P:** Mike Curb

Dirk Benedict is a music promoter who gets into the wrestling world and takes a group of fighters on tour, in this comedy from DEG with Tanya Roberts, Billy Barty, John Astin, and Roddy Piper, Captain Lou Albano, the Wild Samoans, and other real wrestlers.

BODY SNATCHERS

(Warner, 1992) **D:** Abel Ferrara **S:** Stuart Gordon, Dennis Paoli, Nicholas St. John **P:** Robert H. Solo

This is the third version of Jack Finney's novel, this time with gun battles, explosions, and teen stars. The original was *Invasion of the Body Snatchers* (Republic, 1956). Tom Burman handled FX for this and the 1978 Philip Kaufman version (also produced by Solo). Gabrielle Anwar stars (and narrates) as a teen living on an Alabama army base with her parents when the pod people start taking over. Billy Wirth is her chopper-pilot boyfriend,

Christine Elise is the rebellious daughter of the base commander (R. Lee Ermey), Terry Kinney is her EPA-investigator father, Meg Tilly is her stepmother, and Forest Whitaker is a medical officer who tries to warn people. Larry Cohen has co–story credit. It was filmed at an abandoned Air Force base near Selma.

BODYWAVES

(New Horizons, 1991) **D:** P. J. Pesce **S:** B. Zenga **P:** Mike Elliot

Two LA tanning-lotion salesmen teach some teen nerds how to score. This dumb comedy features dreams and fantasy segments. With Sean'a Arthur, Sherrie Rose, Sandra Wild, Larry Linville, and Dick Miller.

BOG!

(Genesis, 1978) **D:** Don Keeslar **S:** Carl N. Kitt **P:** Michelle Marshall

A creature kills people and drains their blood in a swamp, in this PG-rated movie with veteran Hollywood stars. Gloria DeHaven plays the female lead and an old witch, Marshall Thompson is a doctor, and Aldo Ray is the sheriff. The man-in-a-rubber-suit monster is saved for the end. With Leo Gordon and lots of odd freeze frames. It was filmed in Wisconsin

BOGGY CREEK II

(Media, 1983) **D/S/P/A:** Charles B. Pierce

The official PG-rated sequel to Pierce's *The Legend of Boggy Creek* (1972) was released by Aquarius and played on 42nd Street as *The Barbaric Beast of Boggy Creek*. An Arkansas professor (Pierce) and his students (including Pierce's real-life son) camp out in Texarkana to obtain evidence of the beast (a man in a gorilla suit). Convincing locals are interviewed about what they saw.

BOILING POINT

(Warner, 1993) **D/S:** James B. Harris **P:** Marc Frydman

Wesley Snipes stars as a US Treasury agent in LA. His partner (Dan Hedaya) is killed, and he's about to be reassigned to Newark. Dennis Hopper (in another standout performance, as Red Diamond) and Viggo Mortensen are the psychotic-killer villains. Snipes and Hopper hunt each other amid crack addicts and whores. It's based on a novel by Gerald Petrievich. With Lolita Davidovich as a hooker, Seymour Cassel as a counterfeiter, Tony LoBionco as a Mafia loanshark, Valerie Perrine, and James Tolkan.

BOIN-N-G

(SW, 1963) **D/S:** Herschell Gordon Lewis **S/P:** David F. Friedman

One of five Lewis/Friedman features released in 1963 (the most famous was *Blood Feast*), this color comedy about making a nudie movie was shot in Barrington, Illinois. An inexperienced producer and director (not unlike Lewis and Friedman) hire a cameraman, audition naked women, and film them posing and walking around an

estate on a private lake. Everything goes wrong, but a distributor is happy to buy the finished product. William Kerwin (who was in five 1963 titles) stars, with Linda Cotten (*The Adventures of Lucky Pierre*), Thomas Sweetwood, Vickie Miles, and Laurence Wood. Producer/screenwriter David F. Friedman also did the sound.

BOLERO

(IVE, 1984) **D/S/C:** John Derek **P/A:** Bo Derek

In the Dereks' follow-up to *Tarzan*, Bo is Ayre McGilvary, a virgin in the Sahara Desert in the 20s. Bo rides a horse naked, is covered with honey, and has slo-mo sex scenes. Cannon generated a lot of publicity by releasing this film unrated. With George Kennedy, Olivia D'Abo (the teen daughter of the former singer for Manfred Mann), and Andrea Occhipinti as Angel, the bullfighter. Available in R or unrated versions. A (Menahem) Golan/(Yoram) Globus production.

THE BONEYARD

(Prism, 1990) **D/S:** James Cummins **P:** Richard F. Brophy

Here's a film with a difference. It's suspenseful, serious, and surprising but has some unexpected laughs too. The scary, slimy, mummylike little cannibal zombies in an old city morgue are Asian-style Kyoshe kids with tails. Star Deborah Rose plays the reluctant-psychic heroine, who just happens to weigh about 300 pounds. Former Corman regular Ed Nelson (*The Brain Eaters*) is a patient cop called Jersey, Phyllis Diller (without a wig) is a mean, nasty old woman who runs the morgue, and Norman Fell (!), with a ponytail and earring, is a mortician. You won't believe the Big Daddy Roth–like monster Diller becomes, or the giant-poodle monster!! Cummins also did the FX. Filmed in Statesville and Ashville, North Carolina.

BONNIE AND CLYDE: THE TRUE STORY

(1992) **D/S:** Gary Hoffman

Tracy Needham and Dana Ashbrook star as the young, real-life criminals in a TV movie that was shot in East Texas. With Doug Savant and Michael Brown.

BONNIE'S KIDS

(Forum, 1973) **D/S:** Arthur Marks **P:** Charles Stroud

Tiffany Bolling and Robin Mattson star as sisters in this road picture. They're on the run after having killed their abusive father. With Alex Rocco and Timothy Brown as hitmen who are after them, Scott Brady, Leo Gordon, Steve Sandor as a stud detective, and Sharon Gless as a waitress.

BOOB TUBE

(UA, 1975) **D/S:** Christopher Odin **P:** Jerry Adler, Al Burton

This X-rated, soft-core soap-opera spoof (with commercials) is more of a nudie movie than movies like *Tunnelvision*. With John Alderman and Sharon Kelly, both funny veterans of many adults-only movies, and Becky Sharpe. From Independent International. The unrelated *Boob Tube Strikes Back* (aka *The Fabulous Fanny*) (1978) was directed by Lee Frost.

THE BOOBY HATCH

(1975) **D/S/P:** Jack Russo **D/S/A:** Rudy Ricci **P:** Russell Steiner   (*The Liberation of Cherry Janowski; Dirty Book Store*)

Here's a sex comedy that some of the people behind the original *Night of the Living Dead* conjured up without George Romero. It was released by International Artists.

BOOGEYMAN II

(VCI, 1982) **D:** Bruce Starr **S/P/A:** Uli Lommel **S/A:** Suzanna Love

Former Fassbinder actor Uli Lommel plays Micky Lombard, a director filming the story of the lone survivor from *The Boogeyman* (Suzanna Love, his real-life wife). Lots of footage from the original feature (with John Carradine) is used in flashbacks. Lommel works out his hatred of Hollywood by showing how the director is forced to add sex and violence. Obnoxious show-biz types are killed at a pool party, and there's death by electric toothbrush. The video was banned in the UK. Lommel went on to direct many more horror and action features that usually went directly to video.

BOOK OF NUMBERS

(1973) **D/P/A:** Raymond St. Jacques **S:** Larry Spiegel

Raymond St. Jacques and Philip Michael Thomas star as waiters who become involved in a Depression-era numbers racket in Arkansas. With singer Freda Payne and D'Urville Martin. The music is by Sonny Terry and Brownie McGhee. There's a Brut soundtrack. It was filmed in Texas.

BOOM IN THE MOON

(USA, 1945) **D:** Jaime Salvador **S:** Victor Trivas **P:** Alexander Salkind   Mexico (*El Moderno Barba Azul*)

Buster Keaton, in his last starring role, is a WWII soldier who thinks he's landed in Japan but is in Mexico. Local authorities think he's the Bluebeard killer of local women and sentence him to death. He and another condemned man are pardoned so that they can be guinea pigs in a rocket to the moon. They land back in Mexico and think they're on the moon. This rare, dubbed comedy will probably disappoint fans of both science fiction and Keaton.

THE BOOST

(HBO, 1989) **D:** Harold Becker **S:** Darryl Ponicsan **P:** Daniel H. Blatt

New York couple Sean Young and James Woods move to LA (their first big mistake) so that he can sell tax shelters. He eventually becomes a bankrupt coke addict who steals from his boss. It was based on *Ludes*, by Benjamin Stein (the deadpan teacher from *Ferris Bueller's Day Off*). This drug-

hysteria movie is remembered by most because Woods sued Young for $6 million in 1989, charging harassment. The publicity didn't help either one of their careers. The executive producer was Julia Phillips (author of the memoir *You'll Never Eat Lunch in This Town Again*). With Amanda Blake and Grace Zabriske.

BOOT HILL MAMAS: *See* OUTLAW WOMEN

BOOTLEG

(AIP, 1988) **D/S/P:** John Prescott **P:** Trevor Hawkins   Australia

John Flaus is a detective involved with prostitutes, evil government agents, and anti-nuke terrorists.

BOOTLEGGERS

(1974) **D/P:** Charles B. Pierce **S:** Earl J. Smith   (*Bootlegger's Angel*)

Paul Koslo and his backwoods Arkansas cousin fool around, start fights, spend time in jail, and shoot the guys who killed their grandpa (Slim Pickens). With Jaclyn Smith as Sally Fannie. Pierce made the PG-rated Howco release after *The Legend of Boggy Creek* (1972).

BORA-BORA

(1968) **D/S:** Ugo Libertore **P:** Alfredo Bini   France/Italy

AIP released this R-rated tale of a man looking for his wife on some South Sea islands. He ends up with a 15-year-old native wife and a mistress. Haydee Politoff and Corrado Pani star. The music is by Lex Baxter.

BORDER RADIO

(Pacific Arts, 1984) **D/S:** Allison Anders, Dean Lent, Kurt Voss **P:** Marcus De Leon

Real-life rockers Chris D. (from the Flesh Eaters), John Doe (from X), and Dave Alvin (from the Blasters) take money owed them for a gig and run to Mexico. This semi-improvised b/w feature was made over a period of three years by UCLA students who had worked on Wenders' *Paris, Texas* (cowritten by Anders) and was released in 1987. With one-time Corman actress Luana Anders and Green on Red.

BORIS AND NATASHA

(Academy, 1988) **D/A:** Charles Martin Smith **S:** Charles Fradlin, Linda Favila **P:** Jonathan D. Krane

Dave Thomas and Sally Kellerman (the executive producer, who also sings the theme song) star in a live-action movie based on Jay Ward's Potsylvanian spy characters from the *Rocky and Bullwinkle* TV cartoon series. The narrated comedy plot is about a scientist with a time-reversal microchip. With Andrea Martin, John Candy, Alec Rocco, Sid Haig, Anthony Newley, Christopher Neame, Arye Gross, and John Travolta (as himself). MCEG, the company that produced the film, went bankrupt, and it debuted on Showtime in 1992.

B.O.R.N.

(Prism, 1988) **D/S/A:** Russ Hagen **S/A:** Hoke Howell **P/A:** Claire Hagen

The title stands for "Body Organ Replacement Network." William Smith and Russ Tamblyn are plastic-surgeon villains who sell human organs and kidnap Russ Hagen's three daughters. With P. J. Soles (who was also the coproducer), Debra Lamb, Amanda Blake (from *Gunsmoke*—this was her last role before she died of AIDS), Rance and Clint Howard, Dawn Wildsmith, Kelly Mullis, and Lorraine Michaels (from *Playboy*).

BORN AMERICAN

(Magnum, 1986) **D/S:** Renny Harlin **S/P:** Markus Selin   Finland/US

Three young Americans in Lapland cross the USSR border, go to jail, are tortured by the KGB, and escape. It stars Chuck Norris' son Mike, David Coburn, and Steve Durham, with Thalmus Rasulala and Albert Salmi. Harlin, from Helsinki, is really named Lauri Harjula. He went on to huge features like *Die Hard* II. This movie, from Concorde/Cinema Group, was banned in his native Finland, which still had a "special relationship" with its Soviet neighbor at the time.

BORN IN EAST LA

(MCA, 1987) **D/S/A:** Cheech Marin **P:** Peter MacGregor Scott

This comedy is based on a comedy record and video by Marin that was a spoof of a Bruce Springsteen hit. Despite that, it's pretty funny and was a great concept. Rudy Robles (Marin), a man in Los Angeles who can't speak Spanish, is rounded up with illegal aliens and deported to Mexico. With Daniel Stern, Paul Rodriguez, Jan-Michael Vincent, Jason Scott Lee, and Neith Hunter as the redhead. Cheech does a funny version of "Purple Haze." The movie is from Universal. The TV version is longer.

BORN IN FLAMES

(1983) **D/S/P:** Lizzie Bordon **S:** Hisa Tayo

In New York City of the future, a women's army plans to overthrow the government. This 16mm feminist feature took five years to complete. It ends with explosions at the World Trade Center. Honey stars, with singer Adele Bertei and Kathy Bigelow.

BORN INNOCENT

(Program Hunters/Westernworld, 1974) **D:** Donald Wrye **S:** Gerald DiPego **P:** Bruce Cohn Curtis

Linda Blair is a 14-year-old runaway in a harsh, realistic reformatory. The infamous rape-with-a-broomstick scene was cut in the US after a lawsuit against NBC-TV but remains in European- release versions. With Joanna Miles, Mary Murphy, and Janit Baldwin. Kim Hunter and Richard Jaeckel are the parents. It was one of three network-TV movies Blair made in between *Exorcist* movies. She later went back to jail in *Chained Heat* and *Red Heat*. It was filmed in New Mexico.

BORN KILLER

(AIP, 1988) **D:** Kimberly Casey **S/P:** David Prior **S/A:** Ted Prior **P:** David Winters

Two escaped cons attack some vacationing teenagers during a war game with paint guns. With Ty Hardin, Robert Z'Dar, Fritz Mathews, and Adam Tucker.

BORN OF FIRE

(Vidmark, 1986) **D/P:** Jamil Dehlavi **S:** Raficq Abdullah **P:** Therese Pickard   UK

Fans of *El Topo* may appreciate this beautifully filmed, confusing, and sometimes disturbing mystical tale. Peter Firth stars as a British concert flutist who goes to Turkey and has a musical duel with an evil-master fire-spirit magician (Oh-Tee). It's chock full of parallel events, paradoxes, symbolism, puzzles, hallucinations, and incredible visuals. A female astronomer (Susan Crowley) has sex with a (real) deformed dwarf and gives birth to an insect monster. A skull eclipses the moon, a man becomes a giant baboon, and there's lots of nudity, blood, snakes, and maggots. James Galway provided the flute-playing. It was filmed in Turkey.

BORN TO BE BAD

(1950) **D:** Nicholas Ray **S:** Charles Schnee **P:** Robert Sparks

Joan Fontaine is Christabel Caine, "Man-bait!" in this RKO release. In a plot like a Hugo Haas movie, she ruins the lives of both novelist Robert Ryan and millionaire Zachary Scott. Mel Ferrer and Joan Leslie are also in the cast. It followed Ray's *Knock on Any Door* (1949).

BORN TO BOOGIE

(MPI, 1972) **D/S/P:** Ringo Starr **S/A:** Marc Bolan

Find out what "TRexstasy" was all about. T. Rex concert footage ("Telegram Sam," "Jeepster") is mixed with staged sequences, including a surreal mad tea party and acoustic versions of some hits. Elton John and Ringo also appear in this 75-minute letterboxed Apple Films feature. The year it was released star Marc Bolan and T. Rex had five top-10 hits in England. It was a busy year for Starr too. He was in *Blindman* and *Concert for Bangladesh*. Bolan died in a car accident in 1977. A double soundtrack was released in England.

BORN TO KILL

(1947) **D:** Robert Wise **S:** Eve Green, Richard Macaulay **P:** Herman Schlom **M:** Constantin Bakaleinikoff

Lawrence Tierney is incredible as a sullen psycho killer who wants his wife's divorced sister (Claire Trevor). He also wants to "fix it so I can spit in everybody's eye." It's based on James Gunn's novel *Deadlier Than the Male* and is one of the darker movies of the 40s. With Walter Slezak, Elisha Cook Jr., Philip Terry, and Audrey Long, Tierney was also in *The Devil Thumbs a Ride* at RKO the same year.

THE BOSTON BLACKIE SERIES

Columbia released 14 features (1941–49), all starring Chester Morris as an ex-thief, con man, and part-time magician who solved crimes. Series regulars were Richard Lane as a police detective and George E. Stone as Blackie's friend Runt. Some were directed by big names like Robert Florey, Edward Dmytryk, and Budd Boetticher. *Chance of a Lifetime* (1943) was the first feature directed by William Castle. There was also a radio show, then a TV series starring Kent Taylor.

Morris also played the hypnotist in *The She Creature*.

BORN TO WIN

(MGM, 1971) **D:** Ivan Passer **S:** David Scott Milton **P:** Philip Langer   *(Addict)*

George Segal stars as a New York City junkie and thief, in this black comedy shot on location. It was Passer's first American feature. With Paula Prentiss, Karen Black as Parm, Hector Elizondo, Andy Robinson as a killer, and the then-unknown Robert De Niro in a small role as a cop.

THE BORROWER

(Cannon, 1989) **D:** John McNaughton **S:** Mason Nage, Richard Fire **P:** R. P. Sekon, Steven A. Jones

An alien is punished by being sent to Earth in human form but needs to replace its head every once in a while. It becomes a hunter (Tom Towles), than a homeless man (Antonio Fargas). The alien also retains (parts of) the memory of each victim. Meanwhile, a violent rapist is after cop Rae Dawn Chong. Most of *The Borrower* takes place in downtown LA, where a zombie-like, bloody man with women's sunglasses wouldn't cause alarm. This is an awkward, slow-moving mixture of a serious, gritty cop drama, a horror movie, and odd humor. It's a surprise when the alien uses a dog's head, but it doesn't really work as it should have. It's also irritating when the alien, who only changes heads, also has different-sized bodies. With Don Gordon, Pam Gordon, Bentley Mitchum, Madchen Amick videotaping a band, a *Henry* poster, a Cleveland joke, and the Goodyear blimp. This delayed second feature by the maker of *Henry* finally played some midnight dates in 1991, after the original distributor went bankrupt. *Sex, Drugs, and Rock and Roll* (1991) was McNaughton's third feature.

BOSS

(Magnum, 1974) **D/P:** Jack Arnold **S/P/A:** Fred Williamson   *(Boss Nigger; Black Bounty Hunter, Big Black Bold Boss)*

Williamson and D'Urville Martin star as bounty hunters in the 1870s. This comic action movie treats racial problems in a humorous way. They free a slave woman (Carmen Hayworth), and become the allies of some Mexicans. The cast includes R. G. Armstrong, William Smith (who had been in *Hammer* with Williamson) as a racist outlaw, Barbara Leigh, Don "Red" Barry, and Bruce Gordon. It was Arnold's last theatrical feature and was a PG-rated Dimension release. Williamson and Arnold had also made *Black Eye*.

THE BOSTON STRANGLER

(Fox, 1968) **D:** Richard Fleischer **S:** Edward Anhalt **P:** Robert Fyer

Tony Curtis is schizophrenic plumber Albert De Salvo in this serial-killer movie based on the bestseller by Gerold Frank. De Salvo was convicted of killing 13 women in the Boston area from 1962 to 1964. Henry Fonda plays the assistant DA who sets up the investigation to find the killer. A psychic is called in, and every known sex offender is questioned. With George Kennedy, Murray Hamilton, William Hickey as a pathetic suspect with a handbag fetish, Hurd Hatfield as a gay suspect, Sally Kellerman as an almost victim, William Marshall, Jeff Corey, James Brolin, and John Cameron Swayze. The long (two-hour) Fox film uses a multi-split-screen technique for some sequences, includes references to the JFK funeral, and was filmed mostly in Boston. Tony Curtis' voice was also used in *Rosemary's Baby* the same year.

BOULEVARD

(Live, 1994) **D:** Penelope Buitenhuis **S/A:** Rae Dawn Chong **P:** Peter Simpson, Ray Sager

Chong stars as a hooker who sees a pimp (long-haired Lou Diamond Phillips) commit a murder. She also tries to help a woman (Kari Wuhrer) fleeing from an abusive husband. With Joel Bissonette and Lance Henriksen as a cop. The music is by Ian Thomas.

BOULEVARD NIGHTS

(Warner, 1979) **D:** Michael Pressman **S:** Desmond Nakano **P:** Bill Benenson

Richard Yniguez and Danny De La Paz star as two Mexican-American brothers involved with street gangs. This serious anti-gang movie was filmed on location in LA, where Chicano groups protested the opening.

BOUND AND GAGGED: A LOVE STORY

(Triboro, 1993) **D/S:** Daniel Appleby

Ginger Lynn Allen cheats on her abusive husband (Chris Mulkey) with a woman (Elizabeth Saltarrelli). When they're discovered and the wife wants to end the relationship, the lover kidnaps her and takes her to a "deprogrammer" (Karen Black!). It's an unrated black comedy.

BOUND FOR GLORY
(MGM, 1976) **D:** Hal Ashby **S:** Robert Getchell
P: Robert F. Blumofe, Harold Leventhal

David Carradine is the young Woody Guthrie, hopping trains, hitchhiking, and singing during the years 1936–40. Songs include "Deportees" and "This Land Is Your Land." With Ronny Cox, Melinda Dillon as Guthrie's wife, Gail Strickland, Randy Quaid, M. Emmet Walsh, Ji-Tu Cumbuka, and James Hong. Haskell Wexler's cinematography received an Oscar (this was the first feature to be partially shot with a Steadycam). It's one of the best (and at 150 minutes, the longest) of all the films on the Depression and was nominated for several Oscars. The United Artists soundtrack includes cuts by Woody Guthrie, Arlo Guthrie, the Weavers, and others. Ashby made the hit *Coming Home* next. Carradine went on to Ingmar Bergman's *The Serpent's Egg*, then more drive-in movies.

THE BOUNTY HUNTER
(1954) **D:** André de Toth **S:** Winston Miller **P:** Samuel Bischoff

This Randolph Scott western was shot in 3-D but released flat by Warner Brothers. With Dolores Dorn, Marie Windsor, Ernest Borgnine, Dub Taylor, and Fess Parker. De Toth (who was blind in one eye) had already directed the 3-D features *House of Wax* (with Vincent Price) and *The Stranger Wore a Gun* (with Scott).

BOUNTY HUNTER
(AIP, 1989) **D/S/A:** Robert Ginty
S: Thomas Baldwin **P:** Fritz Mathews

A corrupt Oklahoma sheriff (Bo Hopkins) steals land from Indians. The plot was stolen from 1955's *Bad Day at Black Rock*. First-time director Robert Ginty stars as a man who returns home to avenge the death of his Nam-vet Indian buddy. With Loeta Waterdown and a score by Rita Coolidge.

BOUNTY TRACER
(Republic, 1992) **D:** Kurt Anderson
S: Caroline Olsen **P:** Pierre David

Lorenzo Lamas stars as a kickboxing bounty hunter whose brother has been killed. He teams up with some East LA homeboys to battle Mathias Hues and Cyndi Pass. Also with Anthony Peck and Whip Hubley.

BOXING BABES
(AIP, 1986) **D/P:** Stewart Dell   (*Foxy Boxing*)

In a Long Beach, California, club, girls in bikinis dance, then box (losing their tops in the process). This tape includes three fights and was reissued because one of the fighters is Traci Lords. Also with *Penthouse* Pet Ginger Miller.

BOXING HELENA
(Orion, 1992) **D/S:** Jennifer Chambers Lynch
P: Carl Mazzocone

Sherilyn Fenn is an accident victim who loses her legs. A rich and sick voyeur surgeon (Julian Sands) who has been obsessed with her removes her arms and keeps her captive on a pedestal in his mansion. It's a "metaphor" that has a cheat ending. The Fine Line release (originally planned to star Madonna) was the debut of the 24-year-old daughter of David Lynch. It gained publicity when Kim Basinger was sued for around $9 million for backing out of the leading role. Then the MPAA threatened an NC-17 rating. With Bill Paxton, Kurtwood Smith, Art Garfunkel, Betsy Clark, and Nicolette Scorsese. The music is by Graham Revell. The Orion laserdisc is a longer "director's cut" with audio commentary and other extras.

A BOY, A GIRL
(1969) **D/S/E:** John Derek
P: Jack Hanson   (*The Sun's Up*)

This is the only movie Derek directed that didn't star one of his wives, and it was shot in 16mm. Dean Martin's son Dino Jr. (from *Dino, Desi, and Billy*) stars with Airion Fromer. They're 15-year-olds who fall in love, but after a friend dies in a motorcycle crash, she goes away with a rich man who gives her a horse and he takes LSD with an older woman. With Karen Steele, Kerwin Mathews, Peggy Lipton, and Michael Nader. Cannon rereleased it in 1970 under a new title. Derek also wrote the songs sung by the Jamme, a group whose LP was produced by John Phillips.

THE BOWERY BOYS SERIES

Members of the Dead End Kids became the Bowery Boys at Monogram in 1946. Some of them stayed for 12 years and an incredible 48 features. When Monogram went upscale in 1953 and became Allied Artists, they kept making Bowery Boys movies (and Bomba movies). Sach (Huntz Hall) was in all 48 Bowery Boys titles. Slip (Leo Gorcey) quit in 1956, and was replaced by Stanley Clements. By 1958 Hall was 38 years old and had been playing basically the same "boy" since *Dead End* debuted on Broadway in 1936! A lot of the boys' adventures deal with fantasy, haunted houses, crazy experiments, ghosts, time travel, and even the Devil. While some hate these comedies, others collect them, and there's a book called *The Bowery Boys* (Citadel) if you need the details. Warner and Grapevine released some of them on tape starting in 1992. *Spook Busters* (1946), *Bowery Buckeroos* (1947), *Hard Boiled Mahoney* (1947), *Blues Busters* (1950), *Ghost Chasers* (1951), and *Clipped Wings* (1953) were released first. *The Bowery Boys Revisited* (Parade, 1991) is a good overview, with trailers, film clips, some outtakes, and interviews.

Bela Lugosi and Angelo Rossitto meet the East Side Kids in *Spooks Run Wild*.

THE BOYS

(1962) **D/P:** Sidney J. Furie **S:** Stuart Douglas   UK

A group of London teddy boys (and one girl) are accused of murdering an old man for his money. Richard Todd is the prosecuting attorney at their trial, and Robert Morley is the defense attorney. Dudley Sutton and Jess Conrad (*Horrors of the Black Museum*) are two of the accused. With Patrick Magee, Felix Aylmer, Ian Fleming, and Wilfrid Brambell and Roy Kinnear (both soon to show up in Beatles movies). The fine instrumental music in this 123-minute feature is by the Shadows (an EP was released in England). Furie made *The Leather Boys* next.

BOY SLAVES

(RKO, 1939) **D/P:** P. G. Wolfson
S: Albert Bein, Ben Orkow

Teen lawbreakers are exploited at a southern turpentine plant. Anne Shirley stars with James McCallion and Roger Daniel. This serious exposé was considered in bad taste in the US, and it received an "H certificate" in the UK.

THE BOYS NEXT DOOR

(Starmaker, 1985) **D:** Penelope Spheeris
S: Glen Morgan, James Wong **P:** Keith Rubenstein, Sandy Howard

Maxwell Caulfield and Charlie Sheen are Southern California high-school grads who go on a murder and rape spree on the way to LA. With Patti D'Arbanville, Moon Zappa, and Kenneth Cortland. It's a pretty violent film from New World.

BOYS' PRISON

(1954) **D/S:** Willis Goldbeck **S:** Jack Andrews
P: Ray Alcorn   (*Johnny Halliday*)

William Bendix stars as a retired calvary officer who rehabilitates a kid (Allen Martin). Astor advertised it as "the story of teenage terror!" when it was rereleased, but it was really more of an uplifting family feature filmed at the Indiana Boys' School in Bloomington. The original release, from United Artists, had a cross-promotion scheme involving Tootsie Rolls. With Hoagy Carmichael, who sings, and Stanley Clements.

THE BOY WHO COULD FLY

(Lorimar, 1986) **D/S/A:** Nick Castle **P:** Gary Adelson

An uplifting PG film that deals with serious subjects (like suicide), centering on an autistic boy (Jay Underwood) who maybe can fly. With Bonnie Bedelia, Fred Savage, Colleen Dewhurst, Fred Gwynne, Louise Fletcher, and Lucy Deakins, and bits by directors John Carpenter and Tommy Wallace.

THE BOY WHO CRIED BITCH

(1991) **D:** Juan López Campanella
S: Catherine Mary Levin **P:** Louis Tancredi

A disturbed 12-year-old (Harley Cross, from *The Believers*) is thrown out of prep school, then out

of a psychiatric hospital. He leads his younger brothers astray and threatens his mother (Karen Young) with an axe. It's a believable first effort by an NYU student from Argentina who said he wanted to see what "Manson, the Hillside strangler, and Jon Hinckley were like as children." With Jesse Bradford and Moira Kelly.

BOYZ IN THE HOOD

(Columbia, 1991) **D/S:** John Singleton
P: Steve Nicolaides

Real-life violence at openings of this serious look at life in urban LA gained it a lot of publicity. Lawrence Fishburne plays the strong single dad of Cuba Gooding Jr. Ice Cube costars as one of the local guys going nowhere fast. With Nia Long (from *The Guiding Light*), Angela Bassett, Tyra Ferrell, Regina King, and Morris Chestnut. Heard but unseen helicopters in South Central LA are a constant presence. The music is by Stanley Clarke. The 23-year-old director made *Poetic Justice* (1993) next.

BRADDOCK: MISSING IN ACTION III

(Media, 1988) **D:** Aaron Norris **S/A:** Chuck Norris
S: James Bruner **P:** Golan/Globus

Norris goes back to Nam again to look for his Vietnamese wife and son, and he rescues some Amerasian children and a priest while he's there. With Aki Aleong as a sadistic Vietnamese general and Miki King. Four Filipino soldiers died while working as extras. In 1988, Norris' autobiography, *The Secret of My Inner Strength*, was published, and he campaigned for George Bush.

THE BRAIN (1971) = BRAIN OF BLOOD

THE BRAIN

(IVE, 1988) **D:** Edward Hunt **S:** Barry Pearson
P: Anthony Kramreither   Canada

David Gale (Dr. Hill in *Reanimator*) is Dr. Blake, the local TV host of *Independent Thinkers* on Channel 9. He commands a giant killer brain and brainwashes the locals, causing them to hallucinate and commit murder and suicide. James (Tom Breznahan, from *Twice Dead*), a high-school troublemaker with a high IQ, is sent to the celebrity doctor by his parents. Mom says, "Dr. Blake wouldn't be on TV if he wasn't good!" James has electrodes attached to his head and imagines the female assistant topless. Soon he's hallucinating like crazy and on the run with his blond girlfriend (Cyndy Preston), who works at a 7–Eleven type of store, trying to warn the people busy watching Blake on TV. This movie borrows ideas from David Cronenberg's films (as did Hunt's 1977 *Plague*) and from *Invasion of the Body Snatchers, Strange Invaders, Nightmare on Elm Street*, and even *Fiend Without a Face*, but it's a fun, action-packed science-fiction/horror movie. Some of the low-budget special effects are well done, but others are laughable. The brain becomes a big, scary, floating face with movable teeth that eats people whole, people are decapitated, and characters have surprising hallucinations.

BRAIN DAMAGE (1971) = BRAIN OF BLOOD

BRAIN DAMAGE

(Paramount, 1987) **D/S/E:** Frank Henenlotter
P: Edgar Eivens

Rich Herbst (aka Rich Hearst, from *The Guiding Light*) stars as young Brian. Elmer is an animated, hallucination-inducing, eel-like parasite (with the voice of Zacherly!) that injects "juice" into Brian and sings in the bathtub. Brian tries to go "cold turkey" in a hotel room. "I don't get a brain, you don't get my juice," says Elmer. "We'll see who cracks first." This surprising drug-addiction/horror movie premiered at the Cine 42 on 42nd Street. It was cut even more than the R-rated theatrical version on tape but is available complete and uncut in the UK. With Beverly Bonner and Ari Roussimoff. Jim Muro operated the Steadycam, and Bob Martin wrote the novelization. This was Henenlotter's second feature (there's a *Basket Case* in-joke appearance on the subway) and is one of his best.

BRAIN DEAD

(MGM, 1990) **D/S:** Adam Simon
S: Charles Beaumont **P:** Julie Corman

Bill Pullman stars as neurologist Dr. Rex Martin. Bill Paxton, his corporate friend, blackmails him, making him go to a hospital to see Halsey, a crazy, devious, paranoid accountant who has slaughtered his own family but has valuable secrets locked in his mind. Bud Cort takes the bizarre-acting honors as the funny and scary Halsey. "Cosmetic" brain surgery and shock therapy lead to personality switches, horrible visions, dreams in dreams, nightmares, and flashbacks, making *Brain Dead* hard to follow but a good trip movie. The seriousness is ruined by characters running around with valuable, rare brains in jars, usually stored on insecure shelves you know will tip over, and a silly ending. With Nicholas Pryor as a doctor and a blood-spattered hitchhiker who keeps reappearing, Patricia Charbonneau, and George Kennedy. The script was written by Charles Beaumont (known for his *Twilight Zone* episodes), who died in 1967. The director was only 28.

BRAIN DONORS

(Paramount, 1992) **D:** Denis Duggan **S:** Pat Proft

You'd have to be crazy to remake a Marx Brothers comedy, but this is basically *A Night at the Opera*, with John Turturro as Groucho, Mel Smith as Chico, Bob Nelson as Harpo, Terri Copley, and Nancy Marchand. It opens with Will Vinton Claymation title sequences. Steve Johnson did the FX. Duggan also made *Problem Child*, which copied *The Bad Seed*. With music by Mark Mothersbaugh of Devo.

THE BRAIN MACHINE

(Paragon/Electric, 1972) **D/S:** Joy Houck Jr.
S: T. H. Phillips **P:** Stephen E. Burnham
(*Grey Matter; The E-Box*)

A preacher (James Best) makes people reveal their secrets. The military wants his invention. This was made in Mississippi and wasn't released until 1977. Gerald McRaney (*Major Dad*) is the star. McRaney was also in *Night of Bloody Horror* (1969) and *Women of Bloody Horror* (1970), by the Houcks (father and son).

BRAINSCAN

(Columbia, 1994) **D:** John Flynn **S:** Andrew Kevin Walker **P:** Michael Roy   Canada

Michael (Edward Furlong) is a limping horror-fan kid, a loner who plays a CD-ROM virtual-reality game that conjures up the heavy-metal-look Trickster (T. Ryder Smith). Michael ends up accused of a series of murders by a police detective (Frank Langella). Although it features Steve Johnson FX, lots of issues of *Fangoria*, and a Freddy Krueger–type character, this is a very anti–horror movie horror movie with an irritating cheat ending. With Amy Hargreaves, Jamie Marsh, and Zak the dog. The Triumph release was filmed in Montreal. The Columbia soundtrack features bands like the Butthole Surfers and Mudhoney.

BRAIN SMASHER: A LOVE STORY

(Vidmark, 1993) **D/S:** Albert Pyun **P:** Tom Karnowsky

A very toned-down Andrew Dice Clay is a niceguy bouncer in Portland, Oregon who helps a model (Teri Hatcher) battle acrobatic, blackmasked Chinese "Red Lotus Monk" villains who walk everywhere. Her martial-arts-fighting sister, a botanist, (Deborah Van Valkenburg), has a rare flower that can bring world domination. It's a fun enough movie, but Clay fans will miss the old Diceman. With Yuji Okumoto, Brian James, and Tim Thomerson as thick cops, Nicolas Guest, and Queen Kong. You see lots of Portland, where the streets seem to be empty at all times.

BRAINSTORM

(1965) **D/P:** William Conrad **S:** Mann Rubin

A research scientist (Jeffrey Hunter) wants to get rid of rich Dana Andrews and marry his suicidal wife (Anne Francis). Andrews convinces everybody that Hunter is insane and should be locked up. With Viveca Lindfors, Michael Pate, Strother Martin, and a surprising (unhappy) ending. Future *Jake and the Fatman* star Conrad directed it after *Two on a Guillotine* and *My Blood Runs Cold*.

BRAINSTORM

(MGM/UA, 1983) **D/P:** Douglas Trumbull **S:** Robert Stitzel, Phillip Frank Messina

Scientists Christopher Walken and Louise Fletcher develop a sensory-experience headset called Brainstorm, and the government steps in to use it as a weapon. Characters using the awkward looking headset experience heaven, death, and, in one case, extreme orgasms. With Cliff Robertson and Jordan Christopher. This PG film was originally planned to showcase Trumbull's 60-frame-persecond Showscan process, but MGM agreed only to let the dream sequences be shot in Super Panavision 70mm. Natalie Wood, who plays Walken's estranged wife, drowned in Catalina (while on a boat with Walken) in 1981, near the end of production. The feature was almost scrapped but was finally released, and it disappointed most who saw it. Trumbull did FX for *Candy, 2001, Close Encounters of the Third Kind*, and *Blade Runner*. *Silent Running* (1971) is his only other feature as a director.

THE BRAINSUCKER

(Raedon, 1988) **D/S/A:** Herb Robbins **P:** Dawn Middleman

If you wondered what happened to the guy who made and starred in *The Worm Eaters* (1977), I'm afraid he made this too. Jonathan Middleman stars as Max, a vagrant outcast who goes to a mad doctor and becomes a killer. He rants to the camera constantly as he goes around killing his enemies by putting a giant corkscrew into the backs of their heads (an awful effect). He poses as Dr. Suck, a shrink. A French cop and a Chicago cop (Herb Robbins) search for the killer. The whole embarrassing mess looks and sounds like an irritating, amateurish TV comedy skit. It was made in Santa Fe, New Mexico.

THE BRAIN THAT WOULDN'T DIE

(Chiller, 1959) **D/S:** Joseph Green **P:** Rex Carlton

This sleazy horror favorite about a doctor looking for a new, sexy body for his decapitated fiancée's head has been easy to see on tape for years because Warner and then Rhino released a 70-minute cut version. Other versions run up to 92 minutes. Filmed near Tarrytown, New York, in 1959, it was released by AIP. If you've seen this movie only on TV or on the cut tape, here are some things you may have missed: an exposed brain during an operation, a stripper fight, and the famous mutant-escapes-from-the-closet highlight. He (it) rips the arm off the doctor's assistant, who dies a very slow death, going up, then down, the stairs while wiping blood all over the wall with his shoulder. It takes a bite from the doctor's shoulder, holds up the bloody hunk of flesh, and throws it on the floor! The music, by the way, is great. One song goes, "Ooh wah ooh wah wah dig it dig it." There were 43 investors backing the project. Carlton planned to show the doc's head being bitten off during the last reel, which would have been in color. Scenes were shot with rats menacing the head. Carlton, who had promoted beauty contests and wrestling events, produced *C-Man* (1949), with John Carradine; *Mr. Universe* (1951), a wrestling movie; and *The Devil's Hand* (1958). In the late 60s he killed himself after borrowing mob money to finance more movies. Green (31 at the time) had made a burlesque film called *Sex Kittens*. Virginia Leith, from Cleveland (who was signed with Fox at the time), played Jan, the fiancée/head ("Ha ha ha ha hee hee hee"). One of the photographers in the "art" classes is Sammy Petrillo (from *Bela Lugosi Meets a Brooklyn Gorilla*). The mutant is played by 7'8" Eddie Carmel, who had been "Eleazer Carmel, the wrestling champion of Israel" and "the Happy Giant Clown" on TV(!). He was also the subject of Diane Arbus photos. The Rhino version has an Elvira intro.

BRAINWASH

(Media, 1981) **D:** Bobby Roth **S:** Beth Sullivan, Stephen Bello **P:** Gary L. Mehlman, Jeffrey White (*Deceit; Circle of Power; Naked Weekend*)

Yvette Mimieux runs therapy sessions for executives and their wives at an estate in the woods. The couples who attend suffer physical and mental abuse and humiliation. John Considine and Denny Miller help her. It's supposedly based on real executive-training sessions. With Christopher Allport, Cindy Pickett, Scott Marlowe, Julius Harris, and Terence Knox.

BRAINWAVES

(Embassy, 1982) **D/S/P:** Ulli Lommel **S/A:** Suzanna Love   (*Shadow of Death*)

A woman in a coma (Suzanna Love) receives brain waves from a murder victim and retains the victim's memory, so the killer is after her. Keir Dullea is her husband, and Tony Curtis is a mad doctor. With Corinne Wahl, who is electrocuted in a bubble bath, and Vera Miles. It was rated R, then PG.

BRAM STOKER'S DRACULA (1973) = DRACULA

BRAM STOKER'S DRACULA

(Columbia, 1992) **D/P:** Francis Ford Coppola **S:** Jim Hart **P:** Freed Fuchs, Charles Mulvehill

Instead of the expected state-of-the-art FX, Coppola used various ideas from the silent-movie days, which relied on sets and bizarre costumes. He also used too many narrators and added a prologue showing how the 15th-century prince Vlad the Impaler "became" Dracula. This romantic tale of the undead quickly became the biggest-grossing vampire movie of all time. Gary Oldman, as Dracula, has three distinct human looks (and hairstyles) and can become a batman, a wolfman, a mist, or rats. Winona Ryder costars as Mina, his lost love, Anthony Hopkins is a joking Dr. Van Helsing, and Keanu Reeves is a bland Jonathan Harker. With Sadie Frost, Tom Waits as Renfield, Richard E. Grant as Dr. Seward, Cary Elwes, and Bill Campbell. The film runs 123 minutes and was shot by Michael Ballhaus. Annie Lennox does the end theme, and Dracula's screaming voice is provided by Lux Interior. The Criterion widescreen laserdisc includes an alternate-track narration by the director, his son, Roman Coppola, and others. The Columbia "Special Edition" includes a half-hour HBO documentary on the film. The Columbia soundtrack is by Polish composer Wojciech Kilar.

BRAND OF SHAME

(1968) **D/P:** B. Ron Elliot **S/P:** David F. Friedman **S:** Gene Radford

A sex-and-violence "adult color western"/comedy about a schoolmarm (Samantha Scott) who arrives on a stagecoach with a map to a gold mine. A lesbian dance-hall owner (Martha Jordan) plots to steal the map.

BRAND X

(1970) **D/S/P:** Win Chamberlain

This is one of the first of several counterculture takeoffs on TV that were released in the early 70s. At the time, sex and drugs were taboo in television, and *Saturday Night Live* wasn't on yet, so *Brand X* is very dated. Taylor Mead stars in several roles, including the president of the US. The cast of this New Line release includes Sally Kirkland, Tally Brown, Abbie Hoffman, Ultra Violet (who sings), Candy Darling, Baby Jane Holzer, and Sam Shepard.

BRAZIL

(MCA, 1985) **D/S:** Terry Gilliam **S:** Tom Stoppard, Charles McKeown **P:** Arnon Michan

Brazil is Gilliam's best feature. It's a dazzling, frightening, and funny improvement on the *1984* theme, with great, heroic fantasy dream sequences and a fascinating, crumbling 40s industrial nightmare look. Jonathan Pryce is the clerk hero whose dreamgirl is Kim Greist. Katherine Helmond is wonderful as his plastic-surgery-obsessed mother. With Michael Palin, Bob Hoskins, Robert De Niro as a terrorist plumber, David Warner, Ian Holm, and Ian Richardson. There was a lot of publicity about the delay in the US release. Universal refused to release the film, and Gilliam refused to recut it, but he did eventually. It came out here at 131 minutes (the original is 142 minutes). The US and UK versions each contain some different scenes. The Japanese version is longer and letterboxed. Beware of the re-edited US TV version, with a false happy ending. The Michael Kamen soundtrack is on Milan. *The Battle of Brazil* is a book about the controversy. Gilliam tried to top this with *The Adventures of Baron Munchausen*.

BREAKER! BREAKER!

(Embassy, 1977) **D/P/M:** Don Hulette **S:** Terry Chambers

After retiring as world middleweight karate champ, Chuck Norris stars (for the first time) in a kung-fu road movie as a fighting trucker searching for his younger brother unjustly imprisoned in a redneck jail. This AIP film, rated PG, costars George Murdock and Terry O'Connor.

BREAKFAST AT MANCHESTER MORGUE

(VSOM, 1974) **D:** Jorge Grau **S:** Sandro Continenza, Marcello Cosia **P:** Edmondo Amanti Italy/Spain (*Non si Deve Profanane il Sonno dei Morti; Sleeping Corpses Lie; Don't Open the Window*)

Now you can see a widescreen, uncut version of the first notable, serious *Night of the Living Dead*–inspired zombie movie. Government agricultural research near a nuke plant causes bodies in a nearby old crypt, a morgue, and a hospital to rise. More zombies are created by touches of blood, and they eat people and rip apart a nurse in brief gore scenes. Arthur Kennedy is a tough, conservative cop (complete with Scottish accent) who arrests the long-haired, anti-establishment hero (Ray Lovelock) on a motorcycle. Also with Cristina Galbo. The tape is in English with Spanish subtitles.

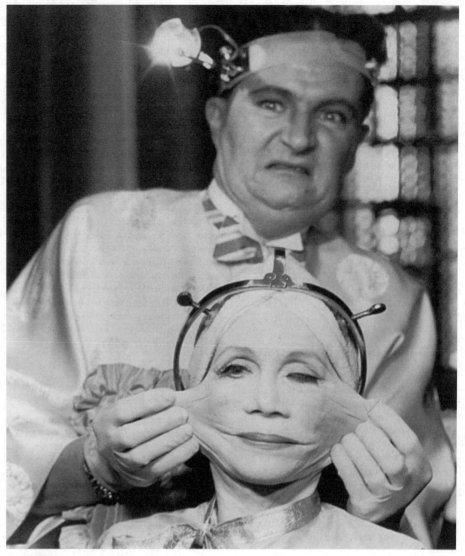

Katherine Helmond in *Brazil*.

BREAKFAST OF ALIENS

(Hemdale, 1989) **D/S/M:** David Lee Miller **S/A:** Vic Dunlop **P:** Brian James Ellis

Walter (Dunlop) is a childish overweight idiot who delivers pizza for a dwarf. He becomes a popular obnoxious (and loud) standup comedian after he swallows a tiny alien in his cereal. Walter also becomes an alcoholic coke addict who hallucinates and eventually he mutates into a slimy killer monster. I hated this movie until near the end. It's a pretty good look at the price of fame. With Deborah Hobart as a sexy blonde, Steve Franken as a gay neighbor, Donald Gibb, Johnny Dark, Murray Langston, and the band Haunted Garage. Wayne Toth provided the FX.

BREAKIN'

(MGM, 1984) **D:** Joel Silberg **S/P:** Allen DeBevoise **S:** Charles Parker **P:** David Zito

In this rush-released, PG, breakdance-exploitation *Flashdance* ripoff set in LA, Aldolfo "Shabba-Doo" Quinones and Michael "Boogaloo Shrimp" Chambers teach a white waitress (Lucinda Dickey) to dance so she can win a contest. With Ice T in a harmless role that makes his later contro-

versies very suspect. The soundtrack is on Polydor. Silberg also made the equally inane *Rappin'* and *Lambada* for Cannon.

BREAKIN' 2: ELECTRIC BOOGALOO

(MGM, 1984) **D:** Sam Firstenberg **S:** Jan Ventura, Julie Reichert **P:** Golan/Globus

In the tradition of *Don't Knock the Rock* and its sequel, and *Don't Knock the Twist* and its sequel, the same main cast returns in a plot about developers threatening an LA community recreation center run by Boogaloo and Shabba-Doo. They put on a show to raise money, just like in 30s musicals. With Susie Bono, Ice T doing a lame rap, and a Tor Johnson mask.

BREAKING GLASS

(Paramount, 1980) **D/S:** Brian Gibson **P:** Davina Belling, Clive Parsons   UK

Kate (Hazel O'Connor) becomes a new-wave star, leaving her punk band behind. With Phil Daniels (from *Quadrophenia*), Jon Finch, and Jonathan Pryce as a junkie sax player. Tony Visconti was the musical director, and the soundtrack is on A&M. In the US, the ending with Kate in an insane asylum (!) was deleted, and the film was rated PG.

BREAKING POINT

(Rep, 1994) **D:** Paul Ziller **S:** Michael Berlin, Eric Estrin **P:** Robert Vince   Canada

Gary Busey is a detective after the "Surgeon" (Jeff Griggs), a serial killer and male stripper in Seattle. With Darlanne Fluegel as his cop partner and Kim Cattrall as the killer's ex. A censored TV version has swear words like "mother freaker." Filmed in Vancouver.

BREAK IN THE CIRCLE

(1955) **D/S:** Val Guest
P: Michael Carreras   UK

Forrest Tucker stars as an adventurer hired by a German millionaire to help a Polish scientist escape to the West. This color Hammer film (released in the US in b/w by 20th Century–Fox) was filmed in London and Hamburg, and features Eva Bartok, Marius Goring, and Eric Pohlmann. Tucker was also in Hammer's *The Abominable Snowman* (1957), directed by Guest.

A BREED APART

(Thorn EMI, 1984) **D:** Philippe Mora **S:** Paul Wheeler **P:** John Daly, Derek Gibson

Donald Pleasence, as a crazed millionaire egg collector, wants an endangered bald eagle's eggs from a North Carolina island. Environmentalist Rutger Hauer owns the island and is pretty crazed himself. Mountain climber Powers Boothe is hired to steal the eggs. With Kathleen Turner, Brion James, and Jane Bentzen.

BREEDERS

(Lightning, 1986) **D/S:** Tim Kincaid **P:** Cynthia DePaula

Virgins are kept by green-insect rapist aliens living under the Empire State Building. The girls bathe in sperm. Teresa Farley stars as a doctor. With Frances Raines and Matt Mitler (who had both been in the off-Broadway play *Grindhouse*) and Amy Bretano. There's a mutant baby, bad acting, flubbed lines, and lotsa nudity. Ed French provided the FX (and he also acts).

BRENDA STARR

(1976) **D:** Mel Stuart **S:** George Kirgo **P:** Robert E. Larson

This ABC-TV series-pilot version of the 40s comic strip by Dale Messick stars Jill St. John. She goes to the Brazilian jungle and encounters voodoo. With Victor Buono, Torin Thatcher, Barbara Luna, Sorrell Brooke, and Marcia Strassman. *Brenda Starr, Reporter* (VCI, 1945) was a Columbia serial with Joan Woodbury.

BRENDA STARR

(Columbia, 1986) **D:** Robert Ellis Miller
S: Noreen Stone, James David Buchanan, Jenny Wolstone **P:** Myron A. Hyman

This much-delayed and pretty dull PG-film finally premiered (in Tokyo) in 1989, then opened in the US in 1992. An artist (Tony Peck, son of Gregory) enters his own comic strip, where Brooke Shields is the redheaded Brenda. With Timothy Dalton as Basil St. John, Diana Scarwid as Brenda's rival, Charles Durning, Eddie Albert, Kathleen Wilhoite, Ed Nelson as President Truman, and Henry Gibson as a former Nazi. With animated segments, Commies, and Amazon-crocodile attacks. The cinematographer was Freddie Francis (who had just shot *Dune*), and it was filmed in NYC and Puerto Rico. A Saudi prince who liked Brooke put $22 million into the project.

BREWSTER MCCLOUD

(MGM, 1970) **D:** Robert Altman
S: Nora William Cannon **P:** Lou Adler

Altman made this unique fantasy/comedy after the hit *M*A*S*H*. Bud Cort lives in a bomb shelter under the Houston Astrodome. He learns to fly in the Astrodome with self-made wings, while the police try to find out who's responsible for deaths caused by bird droppings. With Shelley Duvall (in her first film), Sally Kellerman as a protective angel in a trenchcoat, Michael Murphy, William Windom, Stacy Keach as a 120-year-old flying ace, Margaret Hamilton, René Auberjonois, Jennifer Salt, and Bert Remsen. John Phillips wrote and sings parts of the score, released by MGM. The premiere was held at the Astrodome, where a record 23,930 people saw a special 70mm print.

BRICK BRADFORD

(Stokey, 1947) **D:** Spencer Gordon Bennet, Thomas Carr **S:** George Plympton, Arthur Hoerl, Lewis Clay **P:** Sam Katzman

This 15-chapter Columbia serial, based on a comic strip, stars Kane Richmond. He and Linda Johnson travel back to the 18th century in a "time top" (a big, clunky-looking, upright metal ship), and they also use a professor's "crystal door" to go to the moon. Rick Vallin is Sandy, and Carol Forman is Queen Khana. The first chapter is called "Atomic Defense."

BRICK DOLL HOUSE

(SW, 1967) **D/P:** Tony Martinez,
David F. Friedman **S:** Joe Delg

Five women tell the police their own version of what happened before the murder of their exotic-dancer roommate, Min Lee. Martinez was known for starring in a road-company version of *Man of La Mancha*. He failed to complete this adult-only sex movie (it lasts only one hour), so Friedman took over.

THE BRIDE

(RCA/Columbia, 1985) **D:** Fran Roddam
S: Lloyd Fonvielle **P:** Victor Drai

Despite Sting as Dr. Charles Frankenstein and wide-eyed Jennifer Beals as the independent bride he creates, this film has some great sequences (the ones without the stars, mostly). The subplot, with Clancy Brown (from Urbana, Ohio) as the mon-

ster and his dwarf friend David Rappaport joining a Budapest circus, is the best part. With Geraldine Page, Quentin Crisp, Veruschka, Phil Daniels, Cary Elwes, and Guy Rolfe. The Maurice Jarre soundtrack is on Varese Sarabande. The PG-13 release was from Columbia.

THE BRIDE OF JOHNNY IN MONSTERLAND

(1992) **D/S/C/A:** Jonathan Morrill **S/A:** David Bishop

There's way too much talk in this long (100-minute), senseless fantasy/comedy that includes frequent nods to features like *Freaks*, *The Bride of Frankenstein*, *Carnival of Souls*, *Dr. Cyclops*, *The Wizard of Oz*, and others. It constantly goes from color to b/w, has solarized scenes, and is filled with dream and nightmare sequences. It was shot on tape in Provincetown.

BRIDE OF RE-ANIMATOR

(IVE, 1989) **D/P:** Brian Yuzna **S:** Woody Keith, Rick Fry

Jeffry Combs is Dr. Herbert West ("How dare you judge my work!"), and Bruce Abbott and David Gale also return from the 1985 hit. *Bride* has even more humor, outrageous Screaming Mad George and John Carl Buechler FX (arm/leg, eyeball/hand, bat head), and some Dave Allen animation. With Fabiana Udenio (from Argentina), Claude Earl Jones (son of James) as a police lieutenant, Kathleen Kinmont as the bride, and Johnny Legend. R and unrated tapes are around, but only the bootlegs are uncut. Silver Screen issued a Richard Band soundtrack that includes music from the first movie too. This film was copied by several Hong Kong productions.

BRIDES OF THE BEAST = BRIDES OF BLOOD

BRIDE OF THE KILLER NERD

(Riot, 1992) **D/S/P:** Mark Steven Bosko, Wayne A. Harold

Toby Radloff is back as Harold in the sequel to *Killer Nerd*. He's got a new data-processing job in a new state, but he's still a nerd, and even though he killed his mother in the first movie, she shows up (with an axe in her head) to torment him. He becomes suicidal, repeating, "I work, I eat, I sleep, I work," but falls for Thelma Crump (Heidi Lohr), a female student (with pimples and braces). After they're humiliated at a party (where everybody drinks Busch beer) they go on a bloody revenge spree together. It's a pretty good sick sequel with effective gore FX. There's an ill-conceived, irritating black-guy victim. And why does the girl in the *Psycho* shower scene have panties on? Parts were filmed in Cleveland's Public Square, and the Twistoffs, a great-sounding band with three horns, play at a party.

THE BRIDE WITH WHITE HAIR

(1993) **D/S:** Ronny Yu **S:** David Wu, Lam Ki To **P:** Michael and Raymond Wong   Hong Kong (*Jiang-Hu*)

There's a romance between a Ming-dynasty swordsman (Leslie Chung from *Rouge*), working for some united clans, and Wolf Girl (Brigitte Lin

Ching), a fighter for an underground rebel group. She's a beautiful witch with a whip who was raised by wolves. With bloody violence, some gore and sex scenes, and a supernatural male/female Siamese-twin villain. It was followed by *The Bride with White Hair II* (1993).

THE BRIDE WORE BLACK

(MGM, 1967) **D/S:** François Truffaut
S: Jean-Louis Richard **P:** Oscar Lewenstein
France/Italy (*La Mariée Était en Noir*)

Jeanne Moreau's husband is killed by a stray bullet on her wedding day. The obsessed woman goes after the five killers, in a Hitchcock-inspired feature complete with a Bernard Herrmann score. She uses various methods (poison, knife, bow and arrow). It was based on Cornell Woolrich's 1940 novel (so was Truffaut's next, *Mississippi Mermaid*). With Claude Rich, Michel Bouquet, Michel Lonsdale, Jean-Claude Brialy, Charles Denner, and Alexandra Stewart. The tape is subtitled.

THE BRIDES WORE BLOOD

(Regal, 197?) **D/P:** Robert R. Favorite
S: (there were 5 of them)   (*Blood Bride*)

Made in Jacksonville, Florida, this movie is slow, boring, and confusing. It involves a family curse, a psychic, and a plot by a vampire demon to impregnate an unsuspecting blonde (Dolores Heisel). Dreams, flashbacks, and a voiceover don't help matters much. Some actors flub their lines, there's a closeup of a needle going into a vein, and a dimwit mute has Beatle bangs and a snake. The death-by-sunlight transformation scene is one of the worst ever. The only good part is the large, ornate Casa De Lorca mansion.

BRIGADOON

(MGM/UA, 1954) **D:** Vincente Minnelli
S: Alan Jay Lerner **P:** Arthur Freed

A magical Scottish village reappears every 100 years. This MGM Cinemascope and Ansccolor musical was based on the 1947 Broadway hit by Lerner and Loewe (which was based on an old German story and later inspired Herschell Gordon Lewis' *2000 Maniacs* (1964)!). Gene Kelly and Cyd Charisse star, with Van Johnson, Barry Jones, and Elaine Stewart.

THE BRIGAND OF KANDAHAR

(1965) **D/S:** John Gilling **P:** Anthony Nelson-Keys   UK

Oliver Reed is Eli Khan, leader of the Gilzhais in 1850s India. He likes to torture members of the Bengal Lancers. Ronald Lewis is the hero, and Yvonne Romain is Ratina. The last of many Hammer appearances for Reed, this film uses footage from *Zarak* (1957). It was released in the US by Columbia.

A BRILLIANT DISGUISE

(Prism, 1994) **D/S/A:** Nick Vallelonga
P: David Andreole Corrigan

A sports writer (Anthony John Denison) falls for a nympho painter (Lysette Anthony) who seems to

have multiple personalities (including man-hating psycho and "12-year-old child"). Sex scenes (in studios, galleries, and bathrooms) and murder result. With Cathy Shower, Ray Shafer, Devin Devasquez, Corbin Bernsen as the shrink, and models Beverly Johnson and Elizabeth Nottoli.

BRIMSTONE AND TREACLE

(MGM, 1982) **D:** Richard Loncraine
S: Dennis Potter **P:** Kenith Trodd   UK

The script was first done as a BBC-TV movie in 1976, but it was not aired until after this theatrical version. Sting plays an irritating, mysterious drifter (the Devil?) who "cures" a nearly catatonic, handicapped young woman (Suzanna Hamilton, later in *1984*), by raping her. Denholm Elliott is her father, and Joan Plowright is her mother. For some theatrical bookings it was blown up to 70mm. United Artists released it in the US.

BRING ME A VAMPIRE

(SW, 1959) **D:** Alfredo E. Crevena
S: Alfredo Ruanova **P:** Mario García
Camberos   Mexico (*Écheme al Vampiro*)

Heirs gather in a haunted castle for the reading of the will, in this vampire comedy dubbed and released in America by K. Gordon Murray.

BRING ME THE HEAD OF ALFREDO GARCIA

(MGM, 1974) **D/S:** Sam Peckinpah **P:** Martin Baum

Peckinpah made this in Mexico as a reaction to the failure of his *Pat Garrett and Billy the Kid* (1973). You've heard how bad *Alfredo* is. Watch it and decide for yourself. Bennie, a piano player at a tourist bar in Mexico City (Warren Oates), talks to a rotting human head in a dirty sack covered with flies. He's become a bounty hunter determined to bring back the head of a corpse because a man has offered ten thousand dollars for it. Gig Young and Robert Webber are gay hitmen. A major scene takes place in an old cemetery, and the film ends with a gun pointing at the audience. With Isela Vega, Kris Kristofferson as a biker, and Helmut Dantine (who was the executive producer). The full, uncut video version runs 112 minutes.

BRITANNIA HOSPITAL

(HBO, 1982) **D:** Lindsay Anderson
S: David Sherwin **P:** Davina Belling   UK

A hospital during its 500th anniversary is the setting for this disturbing, bizarre satire. There's a head-transplanting mad professor and one horrifying look at a generic mutant. With Joan Plowright, Leonard Rossiter, Jill Bennett, Marsha Hunt, Alan Bates, Mark Hamill, Robbie Coltrane, Arthur Lowe, and Malcolm McDowell repeating his roles in Anderson's *If* (1969) and *O Lucky Man* (1973). United Artists released the film in the US.

THE BROKEN LAND

(1962) **D:** John Bushelman **S:** Edward J. Lasko **P:** Leonard A. Schwartz

Jack Nicholson is the misunderstood young son of an outlaw in this color western from 20th

Century–Fox. He's wrongly imprisoned by a corrupt, sadistic sheriff (top-billed Kent Taylor), escapes, gets into more trouble without even trying, and is killed. With Dianne Darrin and Jody McCrea as the romantic leads. This hour-long film was backed by Roger Corman and shot by Floyd Crosby. Bushelman had also directed *Wild Youth*, with Nicholson.

BROKEN TRUST

(Monarch, 1993) **D/P:** Ralph Portillo
S: James Elliot, Jeff Spielman

People try to drive an heiress (Kimberly Foster) to suicide in an "erotic thriller." With Nick Cassavetes as her husband, Kathryn Harris as the red-haired sister featured in most of the sex scenes, Edward Albert as a lawyer, Don Swayze as a cop, and Wendy McDonald.

BRONX EXECUTIONER

(Warner, 1989) **D:** "Bob Collins"/
Umberto Lenzi   Italy

Michael Dudikoff is the host of this movie about cyborgs fighting humans. With Gabrielle Gori and Woody Strode. From Cannon.

BRONX WAR

(Academy, 1989) **D/S/A:** Joseph B. Vasquez
P: Elizabeth Frankel

In this outrageous, unrated, extremely violent gang movie, Tito Sunshine (Vasquez with a ponytail) is the cool but naive owner of a Bronx strip bar with a loyal gang that deals coke and stolen credit cards. Rachel (Charmain Cruz), a bad sister, is his downfall when she comes to stay after escaping a drug-related slaughter. A war with vicious black gangsters kills off most of the cast. An arm is cut off in one blood-spurting scene. Fabio Urena costars as Tito's right-hand man.

THE BROTHER FROM ANOTHER PLANET

(Key, 1984) **D/S/A/E:** John Sayles
P: Peggy Rajski, Maggie Renzi

Joe Morton (*Terminator II*) is a mute, telepathic, three-toed escaped alien who lands on Ellis Island and goes to Harlem. He gets a job at a video arcade, where he easily "repairs" broken games, finds a girlfriend (Dee Dee Bridgewater), and stops a hard-drug dealer. In a nod to *Cyborg 2087* (1966), two alien bounty hunters (Sayles and David Strathairn) track him on foot. With Steve James as a bartender, Rosette Le Noire, Fisher Stevens, and Josh Mostel. Cinematographer Ernest Dickerson later worked for Spike Lee. Made for only $300,000, this is one of the best by the maverick, Hoboken-based director. A soundtrack is available.

BROTHERHOOD OF DEATH

(MPI, 1976) **D/S/P:** Bill Perry **P:** Richard Barker

"Watch these brothers stick it to the Klan!" Three Nam vets (played by former Washington Redskins) return home during the 60s. They help register voters, then have to fight the KKK.

THE BROTHERHOOD OF THE BELL

(1970) **D:** Paul Wendkos **S/P:** David Karp

This surprisingly paranoid ABC-TV movie is about conspiracies and how people become successful by joining secret societies. Glenn Ford stars as a professor whose life is in danger because he hasn't paid his bill from "the Brotherhood of the Bell." People around him die, and he goes on a TV talk show (hosted by William Conrad as a Joe Pyne type) to expose the corrupt, ruthless ruling elite. With Dean Jagger, Maurice Evans, Rosemary Forsyth, Will Geer, Eduard Franz, Dabney Coleman, and Robert Clarke.

BROTHER JOHN

(Columbia, 1971) **D:** James Goldstone
S: Ernest Kinoy **P:** Joel Glickman

A karate-fighting Messiah returns to a southern town with racial problems, and he's played by Sidney Poitier. Beverly Todd as a schoolteacher costars, with Will Geer as a doctor, Bradford Dillman as the DA, and Paul Winfield. The music is by Quincy Jones. The film is rated PG.

BROTHERLY LOVE

(1985) **D:** Jeff Bleckner **S:** Ernest Tidyman

Businessman Judd Hirsch is stalked by his psycho twin, just out of a mental hospital. A TV movie with George Dzundza, Barry Primus, and Karen Carlson.

BROTHER ON THE RUN: *See* MAN ON THE RUN

BROTHERS

(1977) **D:** Arthur Barron **S/P:** Edward Lewis **P:** Mildred Lewis

A serious prison movie with Bernie Casey, Vonetta McGee, Ron O'Neal, and Stu Gilliam. It's about (the real) black militant professor Angela Davis and San Quentin convict George Jackson (who was shot in 1971). He and his brother were known as the Soledad Brothers. The Jackson family sued. The music by Taj Mahal is on a Warner soundtrack. Filmed at the North Dakota State Penitentiary.

BROTHERS IN ARMS

(Republic, 1989) **D:** George Jay Bloom III **S:** Shane Kilpatrick **P:** Mark R. Gordon, Christopher Melendandri

Jack Starrett is the religious-fanatic father of inbred hillbilly killers who hunt humans in the Rockies, in another *Deliverance* copy. With lots of sex and humiliation scenes and DeDee Pfeiffer. Also with Todd Aleen and Mitch Pileggi.

BRUCE GENTRY

(Stokey, 1949) **D:** Spencer Gordon Bennet, Thomas Carr **S:** George Plympton, Joseph F. Poland, Lewis Clay **P:** Sam Katzman

A 15-chapter Columbia serial, based on a comic strip, starring Tom Neal (from *Detour*). With Judy Clark, Tris Coffin as Krendon, Jack Ingram, Eddie Parker, Dale Van Sickel, and flying discs.

BRUCE LEE: CURSE OF THE DRAGON

(Warner, 1993) **D/P:** Fred Weintraub, Tom Kuhn **S:** Davis Miller

This documentary, narrated by George Takei, was released after the film *Dragon* and the death of Brandon Lee. With scenes from Bruce Lee's films, candid scenes, and interviews with James Coburn, Chuck Norris, Kareem Abdul-Jabbar, and Brandon Lee. *The Real Bruce Lee* (Video Gems, 1979), the first Lee documentary, contains scenes from his childhood features. *Bruce Lee: The Legend* (Fox, 1984) is another documentary. The Arts and Entertainment network did a good documentary in 1994, part of the *Biography* series. *Bruce Lee and Kung Fu Mania* (Goodtimes, 1992) is a short on the making of *Enter the Dragon* and has many Shaw Brothers trailers.

BRUCE LEE FIGHTS BACK FROM THE GRAVE

(Media, 1978) **D/S:** Doo Yong Lee
P: Chong Huang Kuok

Many Bruce Lee ripoffs are around, but this is one of the worst. It opens with a tacked-on prologue with "Lee" (Bruce Lea/Jun Chong) bursting from a phony-looking grave. It was filmed in LA with an Italian and Chinese cast. There's no Lee footage at all, and the villain is called Marcus Welby! Some sources claim that Umberto Lenzi was involved with this. *The Dragon Dies Hard* (1975) and *Bruce Lee, Super Dragon* (1976) were both cash-in Allied Artists releases with actors playing Lee.

BRUTAL FURY

(AIP, 1988) **D/S/P:** Frederic P. Watkins
P: James A. Sullivan   (*Missy*)

Here's a Dallas-area exploitation movie with flashbacks and terrible fight scenes. Quiet, red-haired Missy (Lisa-Gabrielle Green) joins "the Sisterhood," a secret group of kickboxing, vigilante high-school students with skull masks and initiation rites. They start by beating other girls for their offenses ("That's for smoking pot in our rest room!" "That's for selling your body, bitch!") Missy, who was abused as a child and has a "dual personality," gets more serious ("I am the instrument of God's vengeance!") as she kills drug dealers and a lesbian gym teacher. Meanwhile, a young woman with a detective boyfriend goes undercover (with a punk look) at the school. Texas *is* a special place.

BRUTAL GLORY

(Quest, 1987) **D:** Koos Roets **S:** Tinus Grobler **P:** Philo Pieterse   S. Africa

Robert Vaughn is an Irish boxing promoter in 1918 New York City. He fights martial-arts actor James Ryan, then goes to Africa for a safari, has adventures, and meets Gor the bushman.

BRUTAL SORCERY

(Ocean Shores, 1984) **D:** Pam Ling
Hong Kong/Thailand

Here's another outrageous Southeast Asian horror title. A cabbie who picked up some ghosts becomes involved with black magic. Children become chickens, and there are the usual worms and maggots, severed pigs' heads, and good and evil sorcerers.

THE BRUTE

(Cinemateque, 1952) **D/S:** Luis Buñuel **S:** Luis Alcoriza **P:** Oscar Danciger   Mexico (*El Bruto*)

A slaughterhouse worker (Pedro Armendariz) falls for the daughter (Rosita Arenas) of a man he accidentally murdered while harassing tenants for a corrupt landlord boss. With Katy Jurado. Buñuel complained that he was forced to tone down the script too much. His *Robinson Crusoe* from the same year was more successful.

BULLDOG DRUMMOND

The crime-solving British gentleman Captain Hugh Drummond was created in 1919 by "Sapper" (Herman Cyril McNeile) for the first in a series of novels. The character first made it to the screen in 1922. *Bulldog Drummond* (Embassy, 1929), with Ronald Colman, was the first sound version, and Colman was also in a sequel, *Bulldog Drummond Strikes Back* (Goldwyn, 1934). A British film, *The Return of Bulldog Drummond* (1934), starred Ralph Richardson as Drummond. In *Bulldog Jack* (1935), British comedian Jack Hulbert takes the place of an ailing Drummond, and Richardson plays the French villain, Morrell. *Bulldog Drummond Escapes* (Paramount, 1937) starred Ray Milland. Paramount then produced a series of eight films (1937–39) starring John Howard, usually with John Barrymore, in his days of fading glory, as Inspector Neilson. (Most are available from Embassy Video or Sinister.) Later there were two with Ron Randell from Columbia in 1947 and two with Tom Conway from 20th Century–Fox in 1948. *Calling Bulldog Drummond* (1951) from MGM, with Walter Pidgeon, was a bigger-budget production. The Bond-influenced *Deadlier Than the Male* (1966) and *Some Girls Do* (1969) starred Richard Johnson. *Bullshot Crummond* (HBO, 1982) was a British spoof of the early films.

Fabian stars in Larry Buchanan's *A Bullet for Pretty Boy.*

THE BRUTE AND THE BEAST

(1966) **D:** Lucio Fulci **S:** Fernando Di Leo   Italy (*Tempo de Massacre*)

This violent western is about a prospector (Franco Nero) who has to battle a sadistic man and his son who have taken over the family ranch. With George Hilton.

BRUTES AND SAVAGES

(MPI, 1975) **D/P:** Arthur Davis

This travelogue/*Mondo* movie filmed in South America was advertised with the claim "After *Jaws* and *King Kong* comes another box-office blockbuster!" It mostly shows primitive tribes killing animals and includes a (fake) scene of a man being eaten alive by a "giant" crocodile. Davis also hosts. The backers were Japanese.

BUCK ROGERS

(UA, 1939) **D:** Ford Beebe, Ralph De Lacy **S:** Norman S. Hall, Ray Trampe

After the first two great *Flash Gordon* serials, Buster Crabbe became Buck Rogers. The 12-chapter Universal serial, based on novels and the comic strip by Phillip Francis Nowlan, is available in a two-tape set. After a dirigible crash, Buck and Buddy (Jackie Moran) spend 500 years in suspended animation, then take a spaceship to Saturn and have many adventures. Constance Moore costars as Wilma Deering. With C. Montague Shaw as Dr. Huer, Anthony Ward as Killer Kane, evil ruler of the world of the future, Henry Brandon as Captain Lasca, and Philson Ahn as the helpful Prince Tallon. The lumpy, zombielike Zuggs were my favorite characters when the serial was shown on the *Ghoulardi* show in Cleveland. The 50s feature versions were called *Planet Out-*

laws and *Destination Saturn* (also on video). *Buck Rogers* was rereleased after *Star Wars* as "the original interplanetary adventure."

BUCK ROGERS

(MCA, 1979–81)

Episodes of the lame NBC series *Buck Rogers in the 25th Century* (lasting 47 minutes each) are on tape. The irritating comedy-relief robot Twiki was played by Felix Silla (who was also Cousin Itt on the series *The Addams Family*) with Mel Blanc's voice ("be de be de be"). This series used props from the *Battlestar Galactica* series. Gil Gerard stars with Erin Gray, Tim O'Connor, sexy Pamela Hensley as Princess Ardala, and either Henry Silva or Michael Ansara as Killer Kane. One episode, "Ardala Returns," is on a Goodtimes video. There was also a 1950–51 *Buck Rogers* series on ABC.

BUCKSTONE COUNTY PRISON

(1977) **D:** Jimmy Huston **S:** Tom McIntyre **P/A:** Earl Owensby   (*Seabo*)

Earl plays Seabo, a bounty hunter in 1957 wrongly blamed for a murder. In prison, he's chained and tortured by the warden (Don "Red" Barry). A sheriff (Sunset Carson) helps get him out, and he teams up with real-life ex-con and country singer David Allan Coe (who also provides the music) to catch the real killer. Stunt coordinator Ed Parker also acts, and Craig T. Nelson is an inmate. Filmed in North Carolina.

BUCKTOWN

(Orion, 1975) **D:** Arthur Marks **S:** Bob Ellison **P:** Bernard Schwartz

Fred Williamson, as Duke Johnson, returns to his corrupt southern hometown of Buchanan to bury

his brother, a victim of the local police, led by Art Lund. Corrupt blacks and whites are everywhere. Pam Grier costars with Thalmus Rasulala, Bernie Hamilton, Tony King, and Carl Weathers. This AIP release was shot in Kansas City, Missouri.

BUDDY BUDDY

(MGM/UA, 1981) **D/S:** Billy Wilder **S:** I. A. L. Diamond

Suicidal Jack Lemmon is a big problem for hitman Walter Matthau. Paula Prentiss (who retired after this and *Saturday the 14th*) and Klaus Kinski as Dr. Hugo Zuckerbrot, Joan Shawlee, and Ed Begley Jr. costar in this remake of the French comedy *A Pain in the A—*. It was Wilder's last feature.

THE BUDDY HOLLY STORY

(RCA, 1978) **D:** Steve Rash **S:** Robert Gitler **P:** Fred Bauer

Gary Busey is good and does his own singing (not so good) as the young musical genius from Lubbock, Texas. This was Busey's big break after 7 years in films, and he received an Oscar nomination. It's a typical fact-bending music bio but worth catching. Charles Martin Smith, Don Stroud, and Busey all play their own instruments, and they made some personal appearances after the film's release. With Maria Richwine as Holly's Mexican wife, Albert Popwell, Conrad Janis, "Stymie" Beard, and Buddy Miles. See Little Richard's autobiography for another look at the "shy" Holly. The soundtrack is on MCA.

BUFFY THE VAMPIRE SLAYER

(Fox, 1992) **D:** Fran Rubel Kuzui **S:** Joss Whedon **P:** Kaz Kuzui, Howard Rosenman

Kristy Swanson stars as an athletic blond air-head valley girl cheerleader who learns from an endlessly reincarnated mystic (Donald Sutherland) that she's one of a long line of vampire hunters. He trains her and she goes after the pointy-eared, living-dead team of Rutger Hauer as Lothos (who plays the violin) and Paul Reubens (with goatee and long hair) using martial arts and a stake. Her boyfriend, Luke Perry (from *Beverly Hills 90210*), helps. The vampires crash a high-school prom. It's a lot better than the *Teen Wolf* movies. With Natasha Wagner, Mark DeCarlo, Sasha Jenson (*Dazed and Confused*), Michael Kopelow (*The Stoned Age*), Hilary Swank, Liz Smith, and Candy Clark. The PG-13 comedy was by the female director of *Tokyo Pop*. The soundtrack (mostly 60s covers) features Mathew Sweet, Ozzy Osbourne, the DiVinyls, and others.

A BULLET FOR BILLY THE KID

(1963) **D:** Raphael Baledon **S:** Raymond Oban **P:** Alfred Ripstein   Mexico

Jerry Warren recut and released this 61-minute color western in the US. It stars Gaston Sands, with Steve Brodie and Lloyd Nelson in new scenes.

A BULLET FOR THE GENERAL

(Nelson, 1966) **D:** Damiano Damiani **S:** Salvatore Laurani **P:** Bianco Manini   Italy/Spain (Quien Sabe?)

Gian-Maria Volontè is El Chucho, a guerrilla leader of the 1910 Mexican revolution. Klaus Kinski is his religious-fanatic brother, El Santo. With Lou Castel as an American mercenary with gold bullets and Martine Beswick. This 135-minute political western was released in a severely cut version by Avco Embassy.

A BULLET FOR PRETTY BOY

(1970) **D/P:** Larry Buchanan **S:** Henry Rosenblum

Fabian stars as Pretty Boy Floyd, seen first as an Oklahoma farmer who is forced into a fight at his own wedding. He accidentally kills a man and seems trapped in a life of crime. AIP released this GP-rated feature made in the Dallas area. With Adam Roarke, Jocelyn Lane, Camilla Carr, Bill Thurman, and Cynthia Rose. There's an AIP soundtrack album with music by Harley Hatcher and the Source. It's pretty bad but a must for Buchanan completists. Buchanan's previous feature had been the documentary *Sex and the Animals*.

A BULLET FROM GOD: *See* GOD'S GUN

BULLET IN THE HEAD

(Long Shong, 1990) **D/S/P:** John Woo **S:** Patrick Leung, Janet Chun   Hong Kong

Tony Leung, Jacky Cheung, and Waise Lee flee Hong Kong after a gang war in the late 60s. They go to Saigon and become involved with the wartime black market, and are tortured by the Vietcong. This very violent, long (135-minute), but intense and emotional action drama was made just after the Tiananmen Square massacre and has an anti-Communist theme. It's one of the all-around best from Woo. Simon Yam costars. Neil Diamond's "I'm a Believer" is on the soundtrack. The Cinema City laser version is drastically cut.

BULLETPROOF

(RCA, 1987) **D/S:** Steve Carver **S:** T. L. Lankford **P:** Paul Hertzberg

Gary Busey, as blond LA cop Frank "Bulletproof" McBain, tries to rescue a big silver supertank called Thunderblast from some Commies in New Mexico. He keeps all the bullets pulled out of him in a jar. With Darlanne Fluegel, Henry Silva as a Libyan colonel, William Smith as a Russian commander who blows up churches, L. Q. Jones, R. G. Armstrong, Thalmus Rasulala, Rene Enriquez, and Lydie Denier. The associate producer was Fred Olen Ray, who also cowrote the ridiculous story. Busey was in critical condition after his motorcycle crash in 1988. This was made before he announced he had sobered up.

BULLETPROOF HEART

(1994) **D:** Mark Malone **S:** Gordon Melbourne **P:** Robert Vince, William Vince   (Killer)

A hitman (Anthony LaPaglia) is hired to kill a woman (Mimi Rogers), but he falls for her. This familiar sounding *film noir* takes place during one night in NYC. With Matt Craven and Peter Boyle.

BULLIES

(MCA, 1985) **D:** Paul Lynch **S:** Bryan McCann, John Sheppard **P:** Peter Simpson   Canada

A moonshiner and his sadistic sons (the Cullins) terrorize a family led by a pacifist stepfather at a British Columbia ski resort. The ending is inspired by *Straw Dogs*. With Stephen B. Hunter, Olivia D'Abo (in a wet T-shirt) as the bad family's daughter, and Bill Croft. The production supervisor was Ray Sagar. Scenes from this were used on a *Donahue* show in 1993 to illustrate how films could incite real-life violence. Lynch was a guest.

BUMMER!

(Magnum, 1973) **D:** William Castleman **P/A:** David F. Friedman

The title's good, but you'll probably be disappointed by this look at a rock group. Stuart Whitman's son Kipp stars as Duke, lead singer of "the Group." The lesbian manager wants to fire the drunken, fat-slob, woman-hating bass player, who ends up going on a raping and killing spree. Carol Speed (from *Abby*), Connie Strickland, and Diane Lee Hart are the groupies. There's some sex, and Bob Cresse and producer Friedman show up as cops.

BUNNY O'HARE

(1972) **D/P:** Gerd Oswald **S:** Stanley Z. Cherry, Coslough Johnson

Bette Davis and Ernest Borgnine star as bank robbers disguised as hippies. AIP released this PG oddity, but Davis sued them (the suit was later dropped) because she claimed they had censored her dialogue and destroyed the film. With John Astin, Jack Cassidy, Jay Robinson, and Bruno ve Soto. The music is by Mike Curb, and Billy Strange and Full Circle do a song by Keith Richards. AIP released a soundtrack album.

The 'burbs

(MCA, 1989) **D:** Joe Dante **S:** Dana Olsen **P:** Larry Brezner, Michael Finnell

The weird Klopek family (Henry Gibson, Brother Theodore, and Courtney Gaines) are suspected of all kinds of horrible things in a nice suburban neighborhood. Bruce Dern is the shell-shocked Nam-vet neighbor of normal Tom Hanks and Carrie Fisher. With Corey Feldman, Gale Gordon, Dick Miller, Franklyn Ajay, Rance Howard, and Wendy Schaal. The effects are by ILM, and the score is by Jerry Goldsmith. Scenes from *The Exorcist* and *The Texas Chainsaw Massacre* are seen on TV. Dante blamed a writers' strike for production problems, but *The 'burbs* just isn't very successful, despite some funny moments. Ron Howard was a producer of this PG film.

BURDEN OF DREAMS

(Flower, 1982) **D/P:** Les Blank

Werner Herzog is shown trying to make his epic *Fitzcarraldo* in Ecuador over a period of several years. This fascinating documentary shows how the obsessive director treats the native actors, deals with setbacks, and pushes ahead despite incredible odds. Original costars Mick Jagger (who left because of other commitments) and Jason Robards (who became ill after five weeks of shooting) are shown in early footage. Jagger didn't act again in a real feature until *Freejack* (1992). Klaus Kinski, who remained to star in *Fitzcarraldo*, and Herzog had a public feud over making this feature. Kinski claimed to hate him and was said to have threatened his life.

THE BURGLAR

(1956) **D:** Paul Wendkos **S:** David Goodis **P:** Louis W. Kellerman

This is a serious feature written by David Goodis (whose novel *Down There* became Truffaut's *Shoot the Piano Player*) and based on his own novel. It was shot on location in Philadelphia and Atlantic City by first-time director Wendkos. *Burglar* opens with classic bad guy Dan Duryea in a theater watching an excellent (and convincing) newsreel about "Sister Sarah," a famous, rich, and fake spiritualist. He and his cronies (including Jayne Mansfield and Mickey Shaughnessy) rob the woman, hide out, and fight among themselves. They flee to Atlantic City, where they encounter a crooked killer cop and other serious problems. The film is filled with desperate, weary soul-searching characters and Cold War references, and was obviously patterned after several Orson Welles classics. The cinematography is excellent, the acting is fine all around (including Stewart Bradley and Martha Vickers), and Jayne wears a

BURLESQUE FEATURES

Many adults-only movies from the 30s through the 50s, usually plotless and in b/w, featured strippers and exotic dancers. A lot of them were simply filmed live stage shows (complete with baggy-pants comedians) featuring minimal nudity. Others added flimsy plots. These are just some of the many titles available on tape (most from SW): *ABC's of Love; Bagdad After Midnight; Burlesque in Harlem; Hollywood Burlesque; Kiss Me Baby; A Night at the Follies; Oriental Vanities; Strip Strip Hooray; Striptease Girl; Striptease Murder Case*, and *Tijuana After Midnight*.

THE BUSIEST AMERICAN ACTORS

In the video-boom era, if you ask some people which actors work the most, they might say Gene Hackman or Martin Sheen, but thanks to the miracle of video releases, these very Psychotronic character actors and B stars have them beat creditwise. These are some of the faces you're most likely to see (like it or not) when renting those secondary titles:

1. David Carradine (carrying on in the grand tradition of his father)
2. Karen Black
3. Shannon Tweed
4. Troy Donahue
5. William Smith
6. Linda Blair (who married Wings Hauser)
7. George Kennedy
8. Ned Beatty
9. M. Emmet Walsh

polka-dot bikini in one scene. *Burglar* is worth looking for just to see the diving horse and the old Steel Pier funhouse where mechanical ghouls repeat, "We, the dead, welcome you. We, the dead, welcome you." It was remade in France in 1972, with Jean-Paul Belmondo, as *The Burglars*.

BURGLAR FROM HELL

(Falcon, 1993) **D/S:** Chip Herman

A bunch of guys go to a rented house (in Rockaway Beach) for a vacation and some girls show up. A séance reanimates a big, laughing zombie (Bryant Sohl) in a Kool shirt and most of them (and some gang members who show up) are killed. This ambitious shot-on-video feature has nightmares, a sex fantasy, and a shower scene (featuring Nancy Felciano). It also has enough characters and character developement for several movies. They have arguements, fights, and racial discussions (some are black) before they die. The gore FX, makeup, and sound are all bad, and there's an obvious dummy, but I enjoyed it anyway. Barry Gaines stars with Angela Jackson as the medium girlfriend. The director works as a New York bus driver.

BURIAL GROUND

(Vestron, 1979) **D:** Andrea Bianchi **S:** Piero Regnoli   Italy (*Le Notte di Terror; Zombie III*)

Slow-moving zombies from a churchyard attack a country-club party. An eyeball is skewered, and a zombie kid bites his mother's nipple off. The very gory, badly dubbed feature was billed in Europe as if it were part of a series.

BURIED ALIVE

(Sinister, 1939) **D:** Victor Halperin
S: George Wicker **P:** Ben Judell

This was made (for PRC) by Halperin after *Torture Ship*. The current video cover makes it look like a horror movie. It's not, but so what! It is about electric chairs. A nurse (Beverly Roberts) falls for and helps Johnny (Robert Wilcox), a trustee prisoner who becomes the warden's chauffeur and is framed for the murder of a guard.

Ernie, the executioner, drinks after frying killer Joe Brzinski and gets into a bar fight. The dumb Big Bill (copied from *Of Mice and Men*) figures in the plot. Halperin made only one more feature, *Girls' Town* (1942).

BURIED ALIVE

(IVE, 1979) **D/C:** "Joe D'Amato"/Aristide Massaccesi **S:** Ottavio Fabri **P:** Marco Rossetti   Italy (*Buio Omega; Blue Holocaust; Beyond the Darkness*)

A young taxidermist orphan living in a mansion keeps his dead girlfriend around. He tortures and kills women and eats a heart. With actual autopsy and cremation scenes. The music is by Goblin. The gory, unrated release upset people even in 42nd Street audiences.

BURIED ALIVE

(RCA, 1988) **D:** Gerard Kikoine
S: Jake Clesi, Stuart Lee **P:** Harry Alan Towers   S. Africa

This modern mixture of several Poe stories, set in an American school for delinquent girls, is worth it only for the cast. Robert Vaughn stars as the celebrity doctor who runs the Ravenscroft Institute. Donald Pleasence is an eccentric, scene-stealing, junk-food-eating doctor in a gray wig and bow tie. Karen Witter (from *All My Children*) is the new blond teacher. Former porno star Ginger Lynn Allen is a tough, pot-smoking inmate. The script wastes elements of Poe's stories "The System of Dr. Tarr and Professor Feather," "The Black Cat," and "The Premature Burial." Guest star John Carradine (in his last role before he died in Milan in November 1988) is a surprise walled-up character. With a hand emerging from a toilet, death by electric mixer, and a student who says, "This asshole has his dick in your brains and you don't even know it!" Unlike Kikoine's

bizarre *Edge of Sanity*, this one doesn't have much sex. Girls in a shower scene even have panties on. Edgar Allan Poe's middle name is spelled "Allen" in the credits. With Nia Long and Arnold Vosloo. From Cannon.

BURIED ALIVE

(MCA, 1990) **D:** Frank Darabont **S:** Mark Patrick Carducci **P:** Nicki Marvin

This modern variation on Poe was made for the USA network. Jennifer Jason Leigh (good in an evil role) poisons her husband (Tim Matheson) and has him buried (in a cheap, damaged coffin without formaldehyde), but he's not really dead. He manages to dig his way out and plots his revenge by building a maze for his wife and her doctor/lover (William Atherton). With Hoyt Axton.

BURLESQUE IN HARLEM

(SW, 1949) **D:** William Alexander
P: Joseph Tully   (*Rock 'n Roll Burlesque*)

It's just a series of stage acts, but this is a treasure trove of black performers. Dick Barrow is the (big) MC and sings "I've Got a Juicy Baby." An equally big lady dances and sings "I'm Just a Big Gal Doin' the Best I Can." Top-billed comedian Pigmeat Markham is featured in several routines, and a lady comedian says "Honey, he had so many wrinkles on his forehead, they had to screw his hat on!" Gertrude "Baby" Banks dances several times, dressed in a bikini, and the acrobatic Taza steals the show. With Mabel Hunter, Vivian Harris, Jo Jo Adams, Hucklebuck Jones (there were a half dozen "Hucklebuck" songs on the R&B charts that year), and tap dancers Slip and Slide. The rock title was for a late 50s reissue. The TNT Pictures release, now a Roadshow Rarities video, is from a jumpy print.

Busiest American actor David Carradine is crucified on a train in Scorsese's *Boxcar Bertha.*

BURNDOWN

(MEG, 1989) **D:** James Allen
S: Anthony Barwick, Colin
Stewart **P:** Ed Fredericks   S. Africa

A southern nuclear boom town becomes a ghost town in this murder mystery with a radioactive rapist/ killer. Cathy Moriarty (from *Raging Bull*) is a reporter, Peter Firth is the sheriff, and Hal Orlandini discovers a group of disfigured, hooded men living in the closed plant.

THE BURNING COURT

(Sinister, 1961) **D/S:** Julien Duvivier **S:** Charles
Spaak **P:** Yvon Guezel   France/Italy/W. Germany
(*La Chambre Ardent*; *Curse of the Coffin*)

A group of people visit an eccentric old student of black arts who lives in an ancient, cursed castle. Characters die after a costume party. It was based on a novel by American mystery writer John Dickson Carr. With Jean-Claude Brialy, Nadja Tiller, and Edith Scob. The films of the French director, whose career spanned nearly 50 years, include *The Golem* (1936) and *Flesh and Fantasy* (1943).

THE BURNING CROSS

(Ace, 1974) **D:** Terence Young **S:** Sam Fuller, Millard
Kaufman **P:** William Alexander   (*The Klansman*)

Nobody liked this all-star race-problem movie from Paramount about civil-rights workers, the KKK, lynchings, rape, and vigilantes. Sam Fuller was set to direct but backed out. Lee Marvin is top-billed as the fair minded sheriff of Ellenton, Alabama, Cameron Mitchell is his racist, lynch-mob-leading deputy, and Richard Burton is a reclusive aristocrat. O. J. Simpson, as a black militant, kills off Klansmen. With Lola Falana, David Huddleston, Luciana Paluzzi, Linda Evans, Hoke Howell, and Jeanne Bell. The Staple Singers are on the soundtrack.

BURNING MOON

(Dead Alive, 1992) **D/S:** Olaf Ittenbach   Germany

After a violent gang fight, a teenage junkie tells three horror stories to his little sister. A decapitating escaped mass murderer dates an unsuspecting girl; in the 50s, a Satanic rapist priest chains up a woman; and, uh, I forget the third one. This grim relentless overlong movie has lots of extreme gore FX. Some are well done but the obvious dummy being run over is a problem. It was filmed in Munich and is subtitled except for frequent fuck-yous and OKs.

THE BUSHIDO BLADE

(HBO, 1979) **D:** Tom Katani
S: William Overgard **P:** Arthur Rankin Jr.
US/Japan (*The Bloody Bushido Blade*)

Richard Boone (in his last role) stars as Admiral Perry in this historical action movie about a steel samurai blade that is to be given to the Americans but is stolen. The impressive cast includes Toshiro Mifune, Sonny Chiba, James Earl Jones, Laura Gemser (*Emmanuelle*), and Mako, but Frank Converse is the star. Kotani also did *The Last Di-*

nosaur (1977) with Boone for Rankin/Bass, the team known for the annual *Rudolph the Red-Nosed Reindeer* TV cartoon special. Though some called *The Bushido Blade* an attempt to cash in on the *Shogun* miniseries (also with Mifune), it was made first.

THE BUSHWACKERS

(Sinister, 1952) **D/S:** Rod Amateau
S: Tom Gries **P:** Larry Finley

Lon Chaney Jr. is a crippled land baron, the villain of this western. John Ireland is the Confederate Army vet hero. With Dorothy Malone, Wayne Morris, Lawrence Tierney, and Jack Elam. It was a Jack Broder (*Bride of the Gorilla*) production.

THE BUS IS COMING

(1971) **D:** Wendell James Franklin
S: Robert H. Raff **S/P:** Horace Jackson

A black Nam vet (Mike Simms) returns home to LA and learns that his brother was killed by racist cops. He joins a militant group to get revenge. Franklin was an early black director who made this in LA and Cleveland before the black-action craze.

BUSTED UP

(MCA, 1986) **D:** Conrad E. Palmisano
S/P: Damien Lee **P:** David Mitchell   Canada

Paul Coufolos is a street-fighter who owns a gym in the ghetto but has to fight to keep it. Irene Cara, his girlfriend, sings "She Works Hard for the Money."

BUSTER'S BEDROOM

(Alliance, 1990) **D/S:** Rebecca Horn
S: Martin Mosebach **P:** Luciano Gloor
Canada/Germany/Portugal

A crazy doctor (Donald Sutherland) takes over the Nirvana House, a hospital where Buster Keaton supposedly once stayed. Amanda Ooms is the teen star of this absurdist comedy full of bizarre characters. Also with Valentina Cortese, Geraldine Chaplin, Mary Woronov, and Taylor Mead. It was shot by Sven Nykvist.

BUTTERFLY

(Vestron, 1981) **D/S/P:** "Matt Cimber"/Matteo
Ottaviano **S:** John Goff   US/Canada

Kady (Pia Zadora), a 17-year-old, drives her "father" (Stacy Keach) to plot a murder and tempts him with incest. Keach guards a silver mine for Ed McMahon and June Lockhart. With Orson Welles as a lecherous small-town judge, Stuart Whitman, Edward Albert Jr. (also in Cimber's *A Time to Die*), Lois Nettleton, James Franciscus, Paul Hampton, and Buck Flower. It was based on a James M. Cain story set in 1937 and is the best known of Cimber's many exploitation movies, thanks to Pia's publicity. She was also in Cimber's *Fake-Out* (1982) and posed for *Penthouse* in 1983.

BUTTERFLY MURDERS

(1979) **D:** Tsui Hark (Xu Ke) **S:** Lum
Chi-Ming   Hong Kong (*Tieh Pieni*)

Hark's first effort concerns a journalist trying to solve a mystery in "Martial World" with help from a master fighter and a woman called Green Breeze. They go to a mysterious castle, where they encounter poisonous butterflies and a killer in black leather armor. Lau Siu-Ming and Wong Shih-Tong star. It was a commercial flop when released but was rediscovered by fans later, after Hark became a major director and producer. He had studied film in Texas.

BUY AND CELL

(Starmaker, 1988) **D:** Robert Boris
S: Ken Krauss, Merrin Holt **P:** Frank Yablans

Wall Street investment broker Robert Carradine is unjustly sent to jail, where he plays the stock market. With Malcolm McDowell as the warden, Michael Winslow, Lise Cutter, Ben Vereen, Randall "Tex" Cobb, Rowdy Roddy Piper, Imogene Coca, and Fred Travalena. This comedy includes in-jokes about earlier prison movies. Charles Band was the executive producer of this New World release, shot in Italy.

BY DAWN'S EARLY LIGHT

(HBO, 1990) **D:** Jack Sholder **S:** Bruce
Gilbert **P:** Thomas M. Hammel

This Cold War thriller, based on the novel *Trinity's Child*, had the US and the USSR launching nuclear missiles at each other. Powers Boothe stars in this cable feature, with Rebecca De Mornay, James Earl Jones, Darren McGavin, Rip Torn, Martin Landau, and Peter MacNicol.

BYE BYE BIRDIE

(RCA, 1963) **D:** George Sidney
S: Irving Brecher **P:** Fred Kohlmar

This Technicolor light-rock musical from Columbia was based on the 1960 Broadway hit, which was inspired by Elvis being drafted in 1958. Conrad Birdie (Jesse Pearson), the Elvis/Conway Twitty character, visits a small town before beginning his stint in the army. Ann-Margret (who went on to act opposite the real Elvis in *Viva Las Vegas*) costars, with Bobby Rydell, Janet Leigh, Dick Van Dyke, and Paul Lynde. Van Dyke and Lynde had both been in the play. With Ed Sullivan and a scene where a turtle is given speed. The RCA soundtrack was a big seller.

BYE BYE MONKEY

(Nightmare, 1978) **D/S:** Marco Ferreri
S: Gérard Brach, Rafael Azcona   Italy/France

Gérard Depardieu and 70s porno star Abigail Clayton (also in the Joe Spinnell *Maniac*) adopt "baby Kong" (a chimp) found near the World Trade Center. With Marcello Mastroianni, James Coco, Mimsy Farmer, Geraldine Fitzgerald, and Clarence Muse. The giant, King Kong from the Dino De Laurentiis remake appears. The film was shot in English in New York City.

CABEZA DE VACA

(New Horizons, 1989) **D/S:** Nicolás Echevarría
S: Guillermo Sheridan **P:** Rafael Cruz,
Jorge Sanchez   Mexico

Geraldo Villareal, as the Spanish explorer Álvar Núñez Cabeza de Vaca, and Juan Diego, as the treasurer of the expedition, survive a storm in the New World in 1528. They're enslaved by a medicine man and develop mystical powers over a period of eight years. The 128-minute film, based on a true story, partially resembles *Aguirre* and *The Naked Prey.* It was released in the US by Roger Corman and can sometimes be seen on PBS.

CABIN BOY

(Touchstone, 1994) **D/S:** Adam Resnik
P: Tim Burton, Denise Di Novi

Chris Elliott stars as Nathaniel, a geeky, obnoxious, rich, British "fancy lad" who always asks for the trouble he gets in. He accidentally ends up on the fishing boat the *Filthy Whore.* This odd PG-13 fantasy/comedy, which seems to be set in several time periods at once, would never had been made if it hadn't been for the clout of Tim Burton. It costars Melora Walters, Brion James, Mike Starr, and Brian Doyle Murray. Ann Magnuson is the six-armed Kali, Russ Tamblyn is a half shark/half man, and Ricki Lake is the ship's figurehead. With some Harryhausen–type animation (such as an ice monster and a talking cupcake during a hallucination scene), Bob Elliott (the star's real-life father), and David Letterman.

THE CABINET OF DR. CALIGARI

(Republic, 1919) **D:** Robert Wiene **S:** Carl
Mayer, Hans Janowitz **P:** Erich Pommer
Germany (*Das Cabinet des Dr. Caligari*)

The very theatrical and influential *Caligari,* made shortly after WWI, is a must see for serious horror fans. It's famous for its incredible impressionistic sets. I first saw it in a revival theater as a kid with my grandfather (who was around and watching movies in 1919), and he said it looked more like it was made in 1900 to him. Conrad Veidt is the sleek, zombielike somnambulist Cesare, used by the fairground hypnotist Dr. Caligari (Werner Krauss) to kill. The entire story is told by a man who turns out to be an inmate in an asylum run by the doctor. Also in the cast are Lil Dagover, Friedrich Feher, Hans von Twardowski, and Rudolph Klein-Rogge. The Republic video version has a music score, is tinted (as when originally released), and runs 69 minutes. The original time was 82 minutes, and it's been listed at many different running times (most tapes run too fast). Wiene and Veidt reteamed in 1925 for the original version of *The Hands of Orlac.* Pommer also produced many early films by Fritz Lang, who had originally been asked to direct *Caligari.* Made by Decla-Bioscop (which was absorbed by UFA in 1923), it is said to have cost around $20,000! A

book of the original shooting script was released in 1988. Update/remake attempts were made in 1962 (*The Cabinet of Dr. Caligari*), 1989 (*Dr. Caligari*), and 1991 (*The Cabinet of Dr. Ramirez*).

THE CABINET OF DR. RAMIREZ

(1991) **D/S:** Peter Sellars **P:** Rainer
Mockert   US/Germany

Chicago theater director Sellars made a pretentious (silent) remake of *The Cabinet of Dr. Caligari* in New York City. David Lynch was the original executive producer but isn't in the credits. Characters die in various bloody ways, then show up in a clinic at end. Mikhail Baryshnikov (from Latvia) stars as Cesare, with Joan Cusack, Peter Gallagher, and Werner Klemperer. There's a symphonic score.

CABIRIA

(Kino, 1914) **D:** Giovanni Pastrone
S: Gabrielle D'Annunzio   Italy

This epic film (over 2 hours) is about a girl named Cabiria (Lidia Quaranta) who is saved by Maciste (Bartolomeo Pagano) from being sacrificed to a pagan god while Mount Etna erupts. Pagano returned as Maciste in other films. D. W. Griffith was influenced by it when he made the Babylonian sequence of *Intolerance,* and it was a predecessor of all later *Hercules*-type features.

CAESAR THE CONQUEROR

(1963) **D:** "Amerigo Anton"/Tanio Boccio
S: Arpad De Riso **P:** Roberto Capitano   Italy
(*Giulio Cesare il Conquistadore delle Gallie*)

Cameron Mitchell stars as Julius Caesar. Mitchell spent much of the 60s in Europe playing cowboys, Vikings, murder suspects, and villains.

CAFE FLESH

(VCA, 1982) **D/S/P:** "Rinse Dream"/Steven Sayadian
S: Herbert W. Day **P/C:** "F. X. Pope"/Joseph Robertson

In a dreary post-nuke future, "sex negatives" watch "sex positives" perform in a club with a *Cabaret*-type MC. The frequent closeups of leering voyeurs make this an anti-porno porno movie. Patrons who saw it when it opened in adult theaters probably hated it, but it became a cult feature for others, at midnight screenings. *Penthouse* July 1981 Pet Pia Snow costars as Lana. She was also in *Bad Girls* (1982), and a transsexual movie, *Shannon* (1983) before she became "scream queen" Michelle Bauer. With Becky Savage, Marie Sharp, Kevin Jay, and Ken Starbuck. The same guy made the unique *Nightdreams* (1981) and its later direct-to-video sequels and his own (non-porno) *Dr. Caligari* (1989).

CAGE

(Orion, 1989) **D/P:** Lang Elliott **S:** Hugh Kelly

Big Lou Ferrigno (who is nice, and dumb, and childlike after being shot in the head in battle) and Reb Brown are Nam buddies who run a bar. Fixed "human cockfights" make a lot of money in a secret LA Chinatown location, and gangsters trick Ferrigno into risking his life in the "cage." With

Michael Dante, James Shigeta, Marilyn Tokuda, and Al Leong. This violent movie has lots of ethnic slurs and delivers the goods for action fans. Elliot also made Tim Conway comedies. *Cage II: The Arena of Death* (1994) followed, with the same leads.

THE CAGE

(Magnum, 1977) **D:** Karen Arthur **S:** Don Chastain
P: Diana Young   (*The Mafu Cage; My Sister, My Love*)

You probably know that actress Carol Kane can be pretty interesting and funny, but you've never seen her like this. She plays a young woman who grew up in Africa and is obsessed with her "Mafu" (which turns out to be an orangutan). She lives with her astrologist sister (Lee Grant), who works at Griffith Park Observatory and is totally nuts. Kane is amazing—yelling, screaming, swearing, and doing frenzied native dances (to some excellent African-based music). She also keeps James Olson in a cage and does other disturbing things. Also with Will Geer. It's based on a play. The unheralded Arthur later made *Lady Beware* (1987) and other features.

CAGED DESIRES

(1970) **D/P:** Don Davis **S/A:** Barbara Peeters

This obscure, adults-only women-in-prison movie stars Peeters, who went on to direct movies for Roger Corman like *Bury Me an Angel* (1972) and *Humanoids from the Deep* (1980). Nudie director Davis had done production work on *Orgy of the Dead.*

CAGED FURY

(VBG, 1984) **D:** Cirio H. Santiago **S:** Bobby
Greenwood **P:** Emily Bass   Philippines

American women in a Vietnamese prison are brainwashed and given shock treatments to make them zombielike human bombs. Using an idea from *Telefon,* they kill when they hear a phrase over the phone. Ken Metcalf is the American hero. With Bernadette Williams, Taaffe O'Connell, and some nudity. The casting was by Jim Wynorski.

CAGED FURY

(RCA, 1989) **D/S:** Bill Milling **P:** Bob Gallagher

Roxanne Michaels, as a blond would-be actress in Hollywood, is sent to a secret women's prison. Erik Estrada is the Harley-riding hero in this movie with kung fu and bikers. With Paul Smith, James Hong, Michael Parks, Jack Carter, Melissa Moore, Blake Bahner, and porno stars, including Ron Jeremy (one of the producers), Ty Randolph, and Kascha. From 21st Century.

CAGED HEAT II: STRIPPED OF FREEDOM

(New Horizons, 1994) **D/P:** Cirio H. Santiago
S/P: Paul Ziller   (*Prisoners*)

This is more like Jack Hill's *The Big Doll House* (1971) than Jonathan Demme's *Caged Heat* (1974) and is very much like a vintage 70s drive-in action movie. Jewel Shepard stars as a CIA agent who goes undercover in a penitentiary to try and rescue a princess (Chanel Akiko Hirai) who had been kidnapped. In one scene, Jewel (who uses a Clint Eastwood–style delivery) is hung upside down by her hair for a long time and is whipped, but is basically fine afterwards. The women fight each othert a lot but I want to know why they wear pants in the showers. With Vic Diaz as the bald rapist warden, Pamella D'Pella as the tough, big-busted, black junkie gang leader, and Susan Harvey. It was made in the Philippines.

CAGED IN PARADISO
(Vidmark, 1989) **D:** Mike Snyder
S: Michele Thyne **P:** John G. Thomas

Women (including Irene Cara, whose husband produced) in an island prison are surrounded by deadly lasers. *Fame* star Cara was an exploitation movie regular by the mid-80s. Joseph Culp (son of Robert) plays a terrorist.

CAGED MEN PLUS ONE WOMAN
(1972) **D/S:** Edward J. Forsythe **S:** Jerry Thomas **P:** Avron M. Slutker   UK

A man is conned by a woman into committing a crime , and he ends up in prison, where a lot of violent things happen. Ross Stephanson and Maureen McGill star, with Abdullah the Butcher.

CAGED TERROR
(New World, 1972) **D/S/P:** Barry McLean, Kristen Weingartner   (*Golden Apples of the Sun*)

Percy Harkness and Elizabeth Suzuki are a hippie couple having a good time in the country until some folk-singing psycho Nam vets show up. The video debut came when the feature was 20 years old.

CAGED VIRGINS
(SW, 1971) **D/S:** Jean Rollin **P:** Sam Selsky   France (*Requiem pour un Vampire; The Virgins and the Vampires; Dungeons of Virgins; Crazed Vampire*)

Two pigtailed lesbians (a blonde and a redhead) dressed as clowns blow up a car after a chase and hide out in a cemetery. They go to a castle where a female vampire with 18th-century clothes and pointy teeth keeps brutal, ugly male slaves. The two crooks are tied up, pawed, and eventually used to lure more (male) victims. It's slow going, has very little dialogue, and features real bats. Marie-Pierre Castel and Mireille Dargent star. It was the 4th of Rollin's unique vampire movies. This is the dubbed Boxoffice International American-release version, originally rated X but looking like an R. *Dungeons of Terror* (Best) is a different video version, and an uncut, subtitled version is available too.

CAGED WOMEN
(Vestron, 1982) **D/E:** "Vincent Dawn"/ Bruno Mattei **S:** Palmanbroccio Molenti, Oliver Lemat   Italy (*Women's Penitentiary IV; Emanuelle: Reportage da un Carcere Femminile*)

Journalist Emanuelle (Laura Gemser) goes undercover as a prostitute/prisoner. This sick movie is filled with lesbians, gays who are beaten up and raped, and lotsa sadism. Full bedpans are thrown at guards, and rats attack prisoners in the "hole." Gabrielle Tinti plays a prison doctor. The husband/wife acting team of Gemser and Tinti had already been in around 20 films together. The same year, they were in a Michael Landon movie (!), *Passion and Valor*. The same cast returned in *Women's Prison Massacre*.

THE CALENDAR GIRL MURDERS
(Edde, 1984) **D:** William A. Graham **S:** Scott Swanton, Gregory S. Dinallo **P:** James O'Fallon

Tom Skerritt is a cop investigating serial-killer murders, in this ABC-TV movie. Sharon Stone costars, with Robert Culp as the calendar publisher. Also with Barbara Parkins, Robert Morse, Alan Thicke, Robert Beltran, and Claudia Christian, plus Rip Taylor, Meredith MacRae, and Peter Brown as themselves.

CALIFORNIA
(1963) **D/P:** Hamil Petroff **S:** James West

Revolutionaries fight Mexican troops in 1841 California. Jock Mahoney stars as Don Miguel, with Faith Domergue, Michael Pate, and Nester Paiva.

CALIFORNIA AXE MURDERS: *See* AXE

CALIFORNIA DREAMING
(1979) **D:** John Hancock **S/A:** Ned Wynn **P:** Christian Whitaker

Dennis Christopher stars as an uncool guy from the Midwest who desperately tries to fit in on the beach in California. With Glynis O'Connor, Seymour Cassel, Tanya Roberts, Jimmy Van Patten, Stacy Nelkin, Marshall Efron. AIP released it years after their 60s beach-party movies.

CALIGULA
(Vestron, 1980) **D:** Tinto Brass, Giancarlo Lui, Piernico Solinas **S:** Gore Vidal **P:** Bob Guccione, Franco Rossellini   US/Italy

Malcolm McDowell stars in this infamous X-rated historical movie from *Penthouse* magazine, which was most likely inspired by Pasolini's *Salò* (1977). It's an uneven exploitation movie, of course, but like it or not, it has the ability to shock. Seeing it during its X-rated 42nd Street run was a real experience. It was the only time I saw several (probably high as a kite) guys in the audience stand up and scream during a movie. The cast includes Peter O'Toole, Sir John Gielgud, Helen Mirren, Teresa Ann Savoy (from *Salò*) as Caligula's sister, John Steiner, Lori Wagner, and Anneka De Lorenzo. Some of the name stars later claimed they didn't know about the stronger scenes, and names were removed from the production credits. Vidal had his name removed too. *Caligula* features an incredible decapitation machine, blood-drinking, impalement, guts, a male fist-fuck, some hard-core sex, and gore. Marjorie Lee Thorson, 1975 Pet of the Year, later sued Guccione, claiming that her role had done "irreparable harm" to her acting career. She was awarded $4.06 in damages by the Supreme Court. The X version runs 148 minutes, but the uncut version is said to be 156 minutes. The R-rated reissue is 105 minutes. X and R tapes are available. *Penthouse* released a soundtrack album, and copy movies were made in Europe (*Caligula Erotica, Emperor Caligula, The Untold Story, Caligula's Slaves, Caligula and Messalina*). Some tapes were retitled. *Caligula: Funniest Home Videos* is actually the 1965 British comedy *Carry On Cleo*!

CALIGULA REINCARNATED AS HITLER: *See* THE GESTAPO'S LAST ORGY

CALIGULA REINCARNATED AS NERO
(Magnum, 1981) **D/S/E:** "Vincent Dawn"/Bruno Mattei **S:** Antonio Passalia   Italy (*Nerone e Poppea*)

Nero is portrayed as a dumb, comic character in this cheap movie with a lion played by a man in a suit. It was actually filmed in 70mm with Dolby sound.

CALIGULA: SINS OF ROME: *See* MESSALINA, MESSALINA

CALIGULA: THE UNTOLD STORY: *See* EMPEROR CALIGULA: THE UNTOLD STORY

THE CALLER
(TWE, 1987) **D:** Arthur Allan Seidelman **S:** Michael Sloane **P:** Frank Yablans

Malcolm McDowell terrorizes Madolyn Smith in a remote cabin. He turns out to be a robot covered with fake flesh, in a double-surprise ending. John Buechler did the FX for this claustrophobic Empire release, shot in Italy. Made by the director of Arnold Schwarzenegger's first film, *Hercules Goes Bananas*.

CALL ME
(Vestron, 1988) **D:** Sollace Mitchell **S:** Karyn Kay **P:** John E. Quill, Kenneth F. Martel

In New York, Patricia Charbonneau is turned on by an obscene phone call, in this "erotic thriller." She ends up involved with drugs and crooked cops. With Patti D'Arbanville, Stephen McHattie (who follows her around), and Steve Buscemi as Switchblade.

CALL OF THE JUNGLE
(1945) **D:** Phil Rosen **S:** George Callahan **P:** Philip N. Krasne

This was the last of three movies that stripper Ann Corio starred in at Monogram. The first two were musicals. All three run about an hour each. She's a South Seas native helping an American cop (James Bush) find sacred pearls in a temple. With I. Stanford Jolley and Phil Van Zandt.

CALL OF THE SAVAGE

(Stokey, 1935) **D:** Louis Friedlander **S:** Nate Gazert, George Plympton, Basil Dickey

This 12-chapter Universal serial stars Noah Berry Jr. as a Tarzan-like jungle man. In one sequence, a cure for polio is discovered in the jungle. With Dorothy Short and Bryant Washburn. It was based on *Jan of the Jungle,* by Otis Adelbert Kline. *The New Adventures of Tarzan,* another serial, was released the same year.

THE CALL OF THE WILD

(Warner, 1972) **D:** Ken Annakin **S:** Hubert Frank, Tibor Reeves **P:** Arthur Brauner Germany/Spain/France/Italy

Charlton Heston stars in this version of Jack London's novel set in Alaska, about a dog named Buck. Heston falls for Michele Mercier, as a barkeeper, and discovers gold. With George Eastman (*The Grim Reaper*) as Black Burton and Maria Rohm. It was filmed in Finland. Harry Alan Towers was the executive producer.

CALYPSO JOE

(1957) **D/S:** Edward Dein **S:** Mildred Dein **P:** William F. Broidy

Angie Dickinson, as a stewardess with beatnik/musician friends, plans to marry a South American millionaire. With Herb Jeffries and His Calypsomaniacs, Lord Flea, the Easy Riders, Ed Kemmer, and Laurie Mitchell. Dein made it after *Shack Out on 101.* This Allied Artist feature played on double bills with *Hot Rod Rumble.*

CAMERON'S CLOSET

(SVS, 1987) **D:** Armand Mastroianni **S:** Gary Brandner **P:** Luigi Cingolani

A scientist (Tab Hunter) tests the telekinetic abilities of his son, Cameron (Scott Curtis), but falls on a machete and loses his head in an early scene. Cameron moves in with his psychiatrist mom (Mel Harris) and her asshole actor boyfriend, and more people die. There's a 50s-style winged monster created by Carlo Rambaldi in the closet (another dimension, actually). Most of it is pretty boring. With Cotter Smith as a cop, Chuck McCann as a scientist, Leigh McCloskey, Kim Lankford, and Gary Hudson. The script was written by the author of *The Howling* and made by Marcello's cousin, who also directed many episodes of the *Friday the 13th* TV series. The music is by Henri Manfredini.

CAMILLE 2000

(Magnum, 1969) **D/P:** Radley Metzger **S:** Michael DeForrest

Danielle Gaubert, who has already "ruined many men," is the beautiful, spoiled, jet-set junkie mistress of a rich duke. She throws many wild champagne-and-pill parties at a villa. The most memorable has a prison theme complete with cells and handcuffs. It's a very stylish and colorful widescreen modernization of the Alexandre Du-

mas story, with imaginative erotic scenes. Nino Castelnuovo and Eleanora Rossi-Drago costar. It was filmed in English in Rome by American director Metzger, who made *The Lickerish Quartet* (1970) next. Gaubert died in 1970.

CAMPFIRE TALES

(K. Beech, 1990) **D/S/P:** Paul Talbot **D/S:** William Cooke

Original Leatherface Gunnar Hansen is a bearded bum who intrudes on three camping kids reading horror comics and tells them four scary stories. One is about a hook-hand killer. It's bloody and features a clip of Karloff from *The Terror.* One is about an evil young guy who is punished by "Satan" Claus at Christmas. Another is a period story about a pirate, an ex-slave, and zombies on an island. The oddest is a "just say no" tale about two guys who cop some killer pot, smoke it in bongs in their basement hangout, and mutate and eventually fall apart. It features more clips on TV (*Reefer Madness; Witchcraft Through the Ages*). It's a fun anthology with gore and effective rock music.

THE CAMP ON BLOOD ISLAND

(1958) **D/S:** Val Guest **S:** Jon Manchip White **P:** Anthony Hinds   UK

Hammer took a break from gothic horrors to make this bloody (for the time) look at the real-life horrors of a WWII Japanese prisoner-of-war camp. André Morell stars, with Carl Mohner, Barbara Shelley, and Michael Gwynn. Columbia released it in the US. Hammer returned to the same theme with *The Secret of Blood Island* (1965).

CAMPUS CORPSE

(Vestron, 1977) **D/P:** Douglas Curtis **S/P:** Bruce Shelley   (*The Hazing, The Curious Case of the Campus Corpse*)

This GP-rated obscurity about death resulting from hazing pranks has a cast that includes Jeff East, the late Brad Davis (in his first feature), and Charles Martin Smith (from the *American Graffiti* films). Curtis later directed *The Sleeping Car.*

CANADIAN BACON

(Polygram, 1994) **D/S/P:** Michael Moore **P:** David Brown

America and Canada go to war in a comedy by the maker of the documentary *Roger and Me.* The late John Candy stars, with Rhea Perlman, Alan Alda, Kevin J. O'Connor, Bill Nunn, G. D. Spradlin, Kevin Pollak, Wallace Shawn, and Steven Wright.

CANADIAN MOUNTIES VS. ATOMIC INVADERS

(Republic, 1953) **D:** Franklin Adreon **S:** Ronald Davidson

Bill Henry stars as a Mountie Sergeant who battles spies, in this Cold War Republic serial. With Sue Morrow, Arthur Space as Marlof, and Dale Van Sickle. A condensed TV version was called *Missile Base at Taniak.* Adreon directed all of the

last five Republic serials. The next two (*Man with the Steel Whip* and *Trader Tom of the China Seas*) are available from Stokey.

CANDYMAN

(Tri Star, 1992) **D/S:** Bernard Rose **P:** Steve Golin

A Chicago grad student (Virginia Madsen) investigates an urban legend about the "Candyman" in the Cabrini Green projects. Tony Todd (star of the *Night of the Living Dead* remake) is the spirit of an artist, the son of a slave who had been lynched (stung to death by bees) for being with a white woman. He has a hook hand for killing and wants Madsen, who ends up accused of the murder of the baby of Vanessa Williams (not the former Miss America). *Candy Man* is an uneasy mixture of real-life ghetto horrors and a half-assed supernatural story with mediocre FX. It was based on "The Forbidden," a short story by executive producer Clive Barker. His name was not used in the publicity, but the film proved to be the biggest Barker hit up to that time, and a sequel followed. With Kasi Lemmons and Carolyn Lowry. Phillip Glass provided the score.

CANDYMAN: FAREWELL TO THE FLESH

(Polygram, 1995) **D:** Bill Condon **S:** Rand Ravich **P:** Sigurjon Sighvatsson

The wealthy New Orleans family of Annie Tarrant (Kelly Rowan) seems to be cursed. We eventually find out that the supernatural Candyman (Tony Todd), who's back during Mardi Gras, is a family secret. Annie's brother (William O'Leary) is blamed for the killings. The 19th-century flashbacks of Candyman's torture and death (for being with a white woman) are disturbing. This sequel is more awkward than the original, the special effects are minor, the Phillip Glass score is sleep inducing and characters say the magical name Candyman many times, practically asking to die. Also with Timothy Carhart, Veronica Cartwright, Bill Nunn, and Matt Clark.

CANDY MOUNTAIN

(Republic, 1988) **D:** Robert Frank **D/S:** Rudy Wurlitzer **P:** Ruth Waldburger   Canada/France

Kevin J. O'Connor is an untalented would-be rock musician in New York City who is sent to find Elmore Silk (Harris Yulin), a legendary, reclusive guitar-maker. This pretty slow northbound road movie takes place mostly in Canada but picks up with some celebrity cameos. With Roberts Blossom, Bulle Ogier, David Johansen as a rock star, Tom Waits, Leon Redbone, Dr. John, Airto Lindsay, and Rockets Redglare.

CANDY SNATCHERS

(1973) **D:** Guerdon Trueblood **S/P:** Byron Gindoff

Here's a real find, an obscure and well-made exploitation movie that delivers and has clever, unexpected plot twists. Tiffany Bolling and two guys kidnap a young teen named Candy (Susan Sennett) and bury her alive, waiting for the ransom money from her wealthy parents. The plot flirts with rape, incest, drugs, dismemberment, and murder. The soundtrack is period "wacka wacka" guitar, and the theme song is "Money Is the Root of All Happiness." Tiffany Bolling was also in *Wicked Wicked*, *Centerfold Girls*, and *Kingdom of the Spiders*. Sennett (who has a topless scene) was one of *Ozzie's Girls* on TV the same year (!). This General Film Corp. movie (presented by Arthur Marks) has not been officially released on tape but can be found in mail-order catalogs.

Maria Rojo and Candice Rialson are two of the *Candy Stripe Nurses.*

CANDY STRIPE NURSES

(Nelson, 1974) **D/S:** Allan Holleb **P:** Roger Corman

The last of five nurse drive-in movies from New World is more of a comedy than the others, but it has the usual elements (three sexy women, topless scenes, guns, and some kind of political or feminist statement). Star Candice Rialson cures an impotent rock star, Robin Mattson has an affair with a basketball player, and Maria Rojo solves a gas-station holdup. With Dick Miller, plus Tom Baker and Sally Kirkland, who had both been in New York underground movies.

CANDY TANGERINE MAN

(Unicorn, 1975) **D/P:** "Matt Cimber"/ Matteo Ottaviano **S:** George Theakos

John Daniels stars as a suburban LA businessman who, unknown to his family, is also the "Black Baron," a Hollywood Boulevard massage-parlor owner and overdressed pimp. He battles Italian gangsters and eventually decides to give up his illegal life. With Angel (Tracy) King, C. D. Lefleur, Mikel Angel, Pat Wright, and "the actual hookers and blades of the Sunset Strip." This is the kind of black exploitation movie that's easy to condemn. It's a violent, nasty movie with a hand pushed in a garbage disposal and a hooker's breasts cut off. Daniels returned in *Black Shampoo* and *Getting Over*.

CAN HIERONYMUS MERKIN EVER FORGET MERCY HUMPPE AND FIND TRUE HAPPINESS?

(1969) **D/S/P/A:** Anthony Newley
S: Herman Raucher UK

Newley made this self-indulgent, Fellini-inspired autobiographical mess with his real-life wife, Joan

Collins (as Polyester Poontang). It's about a filmmaker who turns 40, chases after young girls, and meets the Devil. Collins and Newley were divorced shortly after the film's release. It received an X rating in America, and few people saw it. Connie Kreski (from the pages of *Playboy*) is Mercy. With Milton Berle, George Jessel (who sings), Stubby Kaye, Victor Spinetti, and Robert Hutton.

CANNIBAL: *See* JUNGLE HOLOCAUST

CANNIBAL APOCALYPSE = CANNIBALS IN THE STREETS

CANNIBAL CAMPOUT

(Intercoast, 1988) **D/P:** Tom Fisher
D/A: Jon McBride **S:** John Rayl

A toxic-waste drum is used for a still in this amateurish shot-on-video horror from New Jersey. The resulting cannibals attack and eat teens (and a fetus) in the woods.

CANNIBAL FEROUX: *See* MAKE THEM DIE SLOWLY

CANNIBAL HOLOCAUST

(Mogul, 1978) **D:** Ruggiero Deodato **S:** Gianfranco Clerici **P:** Franco Palaggi Italy (*Jungle Holocaust*)

The director of *The Last Survivor* (1976) returns with more exploitative cannibal atrocities. A search party finds footage shot by a *mondo*-documentary film crew in South America. The filmmakers had killed animals and raped a native woman. This incites the Amazonian natives to do even more horrible things (impale a naked woman, rip out a human fetus), and there's a piranha attack. R. Bolla (a.k.a. Robert Kerman) is a professor. The uncut 96-minute version (*Canibal Holocausto*) is out in Venezuela, in English with Spanish subtitles, for completists who can't get enough. This controversial movie, which included animals actually being killed, hasn't been topped

for disgusting scenes. It's also a very convincing, clever, subversive, and dishonest feature, pretending to condemn everything it shows.

CANNIBAL HOOKERS

(Camp, 1987) **D/S/P:** Donald Farmer
P/A: Gary J. Levinson

Hillary and Dee Dee, two sorority pledges, have to pose as hookers. They buy punk clothes at Hollywood Book and Poster (owner Eric Caidin makes an appearance). The guys watch footage from a (real) zombie-gore movie (*Curse of the Screaming Dead*) and talk about sex with pigs. The girls become zombie cannibals. A blonde chained in a dungeon has her Buckwheat shirt ripped off. With producer Levinson as Lobo, Mayra Grant, Sheila Best (from G.L.O.W.) as the head of the sorority, and Matt Borlenchi. It was shot (on video) in Ted V. Mikels' "castle." The sound is terrible, one girl keeps looking at the camera, and the FX consist of blood and boobs. The music, by Das Yahoos and Ben Vaughn ("She's a Real Scream") was issued on Skyclad. Farmer also made *Scream Dream*, *Demon Queen*, and *Vampire Cop*.

CANNIBAL ISLAND

(SW, 1956)

Publicity for this one-hour exploitation documentary about South Pacific pygmies proclaimed, "A telephoto lens was a necessary part in the making of this picture because closer contact with the natives would have meant certain death!" The videotape box claims that it was produced as a government training film. With topless Polynesian women and very racist narration.

CANNIBALS OF THE SOUTH SEAS

(1912)

This was the first of many films by the husband/wife team of Martin and Osa Johnson, originally backed by George Eastman. They used editing tricks and were accused of staging many scenes, but they continued to make popular documentaries in exotic locations until Martin's death in a plane crash in 1937.

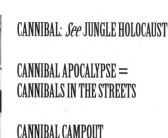

CANNON

This company was purchased by Menahem Golan and Goram Globus, two cousins from Israel, in 1979. It became the most prolific and publicized producer of features in the world for many years. They made some major releases, signed Charles Bronson and Chuck Norris to exclusive contracts, and turned out international action, horror, and exploitation movies like the ones AIP

used to. In one year they backed 44 features. Eventually the cousins stopped talking and split into Cannon and the rival 21st Century. This created the spectacle of the former partners making rival lambada and rap movies. More names changes followed. Golan, who also directs (*Delta Force*), once worked for Roger Corman.

CANNIBAL WOMEN IN THE AVOCADO JUNGLE OF DEATH

(Paramount, 1988) **D/S:** "J. D. Athens"/J. F. Lawton
P: Gary W. Goldstein (*Piranha Women*)

Shannon Tweed is a feminist college professor who goes to a Southern California jungle with a young, comic bimbo and an inept but macho mercenary (Bill Maher). This deadpan PG-13 *Indiana Jones* parody with feminist maneaters also features Barry Primus and Adrienne Barbeau as the empress. There's a lot of talk, but some of it is pretty funny. It was made by the scriptwriter of the hits *Pretty Woman* and *Under Siege*. Tweed is good as the tough feminist (she keeps her clothes on, for a change), but it's hard to forget that she dated Hugh Hefner and had breast surgery to get into the pages of *Playboy* magazine and start her career.

CANNONBALL RUN

(Vestron, 1980) **D:** Hal Needham
S: Brock Yates **P:** Albert S. Ruddy

This popular and nearly plotless action/comedy hit copied Corman's *Cannonball* and *The Gumball Rally* (both 1976). Burt Reynolds and his comic sidekick Dom DeLuise star with car crashes, more car crashes, and many guest stars. Jackie Chan (who helped make it a hit in Asia too) gets to beat on bikers played by Peter Fonda and Robert Tessier. With Adrienne Barbeau, Dean Martin and Sammy Davis Jr. as Catholic priests, Roger Moore (who thinks he's James Bond), Farrah Fawcett, Bert Convy, Jack Elam, Jamie Farr, Bianca Jagger, Johnny Yune, and Katt Shea. The outtakes at the end are now a common way to pad the running time of a feature. A Golden Harvest (Hong Kong) production.

CANNONBALL RUN II

(Warner, 1983) **D/S:** Hal Needham
S: Harvey Miller **P:** Albert S. Ruddy

Reynolds and DeLuise returned, and Raymond Chow and Golden Harvest were the backers again, bringing Jackie Chan with them. It's got more of the same lame gags and even more guest stars. Look for Jack Elam, Richard Kiel, Henry Silva, and actors from *The Andy Griffith Show* (Don Knotts, Jim Nabors, and George "Goober" Lindsay). Most of the "Rat Pack" show up, including Dean Martin and Frank Sinatra (both in their last feature film appearances to date) and Sammy Davis Jr. again. With Shirley MacLaine and Marilu Henner dressed as nuns, Ricardo Montalban and Jamie Farr as Arabs, Telly Savalas, Michael Gazzo, Doug McClure, Katt Shea, Louis Nye, Mel Tillis, Susan Anton, Catherine Bach, Sid Caesar, Tony Danza, Abe Vigoda, Tim Conway, Arte Johnson, and some Ralph Bakshi animation. The third in this painful series didn't feature Reynolds and was called *Speed Zone*.

CAN SHE BAKE A CHERRY PIE?

(Paramount, 1983) **D/S:** Henry Jaglom
P: M. H. Simonsons

Karen Black, in a rare, serious 80s feature, leaves her husband and ends up with Michael Emil. They talk a lot. Black and Jaglom had been off-Broadway actors together in the early 60s. With Michael Margotta (from *Drive, He Said,* also with Black).

THE CANTERBURY TALES

(Water Bearer, 1972) **D/S/A:** Pier Paolo Pasolini **P:** Alberto Grimaldi
Italy/France (*I Racconti di Canterbury*)

Four of Chaucer's 14th-century tales are told by Chaucer himself (Pasolini). The highlight is a visit to hell, where giant devils shit out friars. With Laura Betti, Hugh Griffith, Josephine Chaplin, Jenny Runacre, Tom Baker, Robin Askwith, and Ninetto Davoli. United Artists released this years after Pasolini was killed (1975), and it received an X rating. *The Arabian Nights* (1974) and *Salò* (1975) were next from the controversial director.

THE CANTERVILLE GHOST

(MGM, 1944) **D:** Jules Dassin **S:** Edwin Harvey Blum **P:** Arthur L. Fields

Charles Laughton stars as a cursed 17th-century ghost who had been walled up alive, in this lavish fantasy/comedy with a WWII background. A modern-day relative (Robert Young) has to perform a brave act to free him. It's (sort of) based on a story by Oscar Wilde, whose novel *The Picture of Dorian Gray* was filmed the next year. With Margaret O'Brien as a child who is not afraid of the ghost, William Gargan, Una O'Connor, Frank Faylen, Frank Reicher, Peter Lawford, and Mike Mazurki. Dassin was blacklisted in 1950 and settled in Europe. The RCA video version is a 1986 TV remake starring John Gielgud.

CAN'T STOP THE MUSIC

(HBO, 1980) **D:** Nancy Walker
S: Bronte Woodward **S/P:** Alan Carr
P: Jacques Morali, Henri Belolo

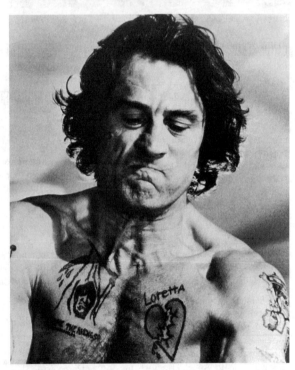

Two Roberts (Mitchum and De Niro) as Max Cady in two versions of *Cape Fear.*

Carr backed this PG-rated disaster after his success with *Grease*. A model (Valerie Perrine) tries to get Steve Guttenberg's songs recorded by the Village People (who play themselves). This 40s-style musical story of the rise of the once-popular group includes Busby Berkeley-style numbers featuring men in gyms, shower rooms, and swimming pools (at the YMCA) and ends with a big concert in San Francisco. With Olympic decathlon champ Bruce Jenner, Paul Sand, Tammy Grimes, June Havoc, Barbara Rush, Jack Weston, Leigh Taylor-Young, and various musicians, who are on the Casablanca soundtrack. The one-time director was best known for being in Bounty paper-towel TV commercials. By the time this $20 million flop came out, the Village People were no longer having top-40 hits. Carr returned with (what else?) *Grease II* (1982).

CANVAS: THE FINE ART OF CRIME

(Live, 1992) **D/S:** Alain Zaloum
S: Brenda Newman   Canada

Vittorio Rossi is a New York artist who becomes a criminal to save his brother. Gary Busey is a psycho criminal art dealer, John Rhys-Davies is a killer Greek thief, and Cary Lawrence is the girl. Filmed in Quebec.

THE CAPE CANAVERAL MONSTERS

(1960) **D/S:** Phil Tucker **P:** Richard Greer

Aliens (spots of light) take over two bodies from a car crash. Soon they've got a secret lab (at Bronson Canyon), where they take orders from a voice in a box. The armless male alien (Jason Johnson) runs around shooting down Earth rockets with a long, awkward bazooka. The scar-faced female alien, Nadja, (Katherine Victor, who was also in many Jerry Warren movies) shoots up a woman and puts her into a transmitter. The young scientist hero (Scott Peters) calls his girlfriend (Linda Connell) "Little Monkey." This has lots of science talk (like "electric-convulse shock therapy"), a German scientist, and enough bizarre and hilarious situations to be worthy of the famed director of *Robot Monster*.

CAPE FEAR

(MCA, 1961) **D:** J. Lee Thompson
S: James R. Webb **P:** Sy Bartlett

Robert Mitchum is pretty terrifying as Max Cady, the clever and relentless white-trash ex-con out to punish lawyer Gregory Peck and his family in this feature based on *The Executioners*, by John D. MacDonald. Polly Bergen is his wife, and Lori Martin is their daughter. With Martin Balsam, Telly Savalas, Barrie Chase, and Edward Platt. *Cape Fear* was filmed in Georgia in b/w, featured an unsettling Bernard Herrmann score, and was released by Universal. After seeing both versions, I think the original is still better. Scenes of Mitchum killing in the swamp and crushing an egg over Bergen top anything in the remake.

CAPE FEAR

(MCA, 1991) **D:** Martin Scorsese
S: Wesley Strick **P:** Barbara De Fina

This was Scorsese's biggest hit (to date) and could be considered his first horror movie. It was great to see Robert De Niro, as Max Cady, back working with Scorsese again, and it's easy to see why the modernized color and R-rated version was so popular. Some of the much-promoted scary parts come too close to *Friday the 13th* territory, and when Cady keeps fighting even after his face is burned off, horror fans will immediately think of Freddy Krueger. They made it longer (130 minutes), added more tension between the lawyer and his wife, and changed a few scenes and situations. (It seems as though Scorsese would rather have remade *The Night of the Hunter* (1955), in which Robert Mitchum plays a killer whose hands are tattooed with the words "love" and "hate"; De Niro's many tattoos include "truth" and "justice.") Scene-stealing Juliette Lewis (daughter of actor Geoffrey) plays the young daughter. Nods to the original include Peck, Mitchum, and Balsam all showing up in smaller roles, and Herrmann's original score was redone by Elmer Bernstein (and released on MCA). Nick Nolte and Jessica Lange are the troubled and terrified parents. With Joe Don Baker, Fred Thompson, and Illeana Douglas (granddaughter of Melvyn Douglas). The cinematographer was Freddie Francis, and Saul Bass created the title se-

quence. *Cape Fear* was filmed in Florida and was presented by Spielberg's Amblin Entertainment (Spielberg himself was originally set to direct).

THE CAPITOL HILL GIRLS

(1977) **S/P:** "William J. Condos"/
Bill Condon(*The Arab Connection;
Best Little House on Capitol Hill;
Capitol Hill: Behind Closed Doors*)

An X-rated 3-D movie in "Lazer Vision" partially filmed on location in Washington, DC, back in the days of Jimmy Carter. The cast includes Christine Burke and Alex Anders (probably fake names), and nobody took credit for directing.

CAPONE

(Vidmark, 1989) **D:** Michael Pressman **S:** Tracy Keenan Wynn **P:** Vicki Niemi-Gordon

Ray Sharkey stars as Al Capone, and Keith Carradine is a special FBI agent. This movie shows how the famous gangster continued to run the rackets from behind bars and also plotted the assassination of the mayor of Chicago. The same story was told on the original *Untouchables* TV show. Debrah Farentino and Charles Haid costar. Rod Steiger starred in *Al Capone*, (1959), Neville Brand in *The Scarface Mob* (1962), and Roger Corman produced a 1975 *Capone* starring Ben Gazzara.

CAPTAIN AMERICA

(Stokey, 1944) **D:** John English, Elmer Clifton
S: Royal Cole, Ronald Davidson, Basil Dickey

This 15-chapter Republic WWII serial stars Dick Purcell (who died after production) as assistant DA Grant Gardner, who is also the costumed hero Captain America. Lionel Atwill is Dr. Maldor (aka "the Scarab"), who uses "the purple death" to kill his enemies and can bring animals back to life. Lorna Grey is Gardner's assistant, Gail Richards. Dale Van Sickle is the captain in the many fight scenes. It was based on Jack Kirby and Joe Simon's comic-book character. *Captain America* and *Captain America II: Death Too Soon* (both 1979 and both on MCA) are TV movies about the original's son.

CAPTAIN AMERICA

(Columbia, 1989) **D:** Albert Pyun
S: James Tolkin **P:** Menahem Golan, Tom Karnowski

Matt Salinger (the 6'4" son of J. D. Salinger) stars as somebody's idea of a hero. He fakes being sick several times and doesn't even wear his costume in most of the movie. It starts out during WWII with a battle against "the Red Skull" (an Italian orphan transformed by Nazis). The Captain is frozen in Alaska, and

the Skull (Scott Paulin) goes on to do horrible things in the world with his evil daughter. Did you know that Martin Luther King, JFK, and John Lennon were killed by the Skull? Two kids from Ohio who saw the Captain once grow up to be the US president (Ronny Cox) and a newspaper editor (Ned Beatty). Beatty helps him thaw out, and Cox is kidnapped. With Darren McGavin as an evil US general, Melinda Dillon, Michael Nouri, and Billy Mumy. The PG-13 film was made in Yugoslavia by 21st Century and (finally) was released on tape in 1992.

CAPTAIN APACHE

(Prism, 1971) **D:** Alexander Singer
S/P: Milton Sperling **S:** Philip Yordan   UK

What seems like a "spaghetti western" was actually made in England by a British director. Lee Van Cleef is an Indian Confederate Army officer who stops landowner villain Stuart Whitman from starting an Indian war. Whitman's men dress up like Indians and also try to kill President Grant. With Carroll Baker and Percy Herbert. It has some great rock-style music and even hallucination scenes. It's rated PG.

CAPTAIN EO

(1986) **D:** Francis Ford Coppola **P:** Rusty Lemorande

Michael Jackson's 17-minute 70mm 3-D short was made to be shown only at Disney theme parks. It took over a year to make and cost a record $20 million, which mostly went to ILM FX. George Lucas was executive producer. With Dick Shawn and Angelica Huston as the Supreme Leader robot. It was a very commercial year for Coppola, who also made *Peggy Sue Got Married*.

Lionel Atwill is the Scarab in the *Captain America* serial.

CAPTAIN GALLANT OF THE FOREIGN LEGION

(Sinister, 1955–57)   (*Foreign Legionnaire*)

Buster Crabbe had starred in serials from 1932 (*Tarzan the Fearless*) until 1952 (*King of the Jungle*). He starred in this popular half-hour NBC-TV Saturday-morning kids' show with own son, Cullen (as Cuffey). Crabbe plays the commander of the French Foreign Legion's North African desert headquarters. The show, shot on location, was syndicated and rebroadcast for years. With Al "Fuzzy" Knight as the comic sidekick. Episodes were directed by Sam Newfield (*Nabonga*).

Serial hero Buster Crabbe became a TV hero as *Captain Gallant of the Foreign Legion.*

CAPTAIN MIDNIGHT

(Rhino series, 1955)

Richard Webb stars, with his Silver Dart plane, the all-kids secret squadron, comic sidekick Icky, and scientist Tut. The inspiration for this show was the success of the *Captain Video* TV series, but this is more anti-Communist. When it was syndicated it was renamed *Jet Jackson*. Three 60-minute volumes, with two episodes each, are available with the original TV commercials for Kix and Ovaltine. Not to be confused with the 1942 Columbia serial *Captain Midnight*.

CAPTAIN VIDEO, MASTER OF THE STRATOSPHERE

(Stokey, 1951) **D:** Spencer Gordon Bennet, Wallace A. Grissell **S:** Royal Cole, Sherman L. Lowe **P:** Sam Katzman

This 15-chapter Columbia serial was actually based on a TV show, a sure sign of the coming death of serials. The live TV series, *Captain Video and His Video Rangers*, began in 1949, starred Al Hodge, and ran until 1955. In an effort to make this serial special, scenes on different planets were tinted different colors. To make it appeal to the youngest kids possible, there wasn't even a female costar. Judd Holdren stars, wearing what looks like a very old football helmet. He flies around in cartoon rocket ships and fights some very old and familiar-looking clunky movie robots. With Larry Stewart as the young Video Ranger, Gene Roth as Vultura, leader of the planet Atoma,

Jack Ingram, I. Stanford Jolly, and Skelton Knaggs. *The Lost Planet* (1953) was a serial sequel, also with Holdren.

CAPTIVE

(Continental, 1987) **D/S:** Paul Mayersberg **P:** Don Boyd   UK/France

Irina Brook (daughter of British director Peter Brook and actress Natasha Parry) stars as the daughter of a rich man (Oliver Reed) who is kidnapped by fashion-model anarchists. The score, by the Edge (from U2) includes the debut of Sinead O'Connor. The director was a Nicolas Roeg collaborator, and his film (inspired by the Patty Hearst kidnapping) has been called "erotic, arty, and pretentious." Reed was also in Roeg's *Castaway* the same year.

CAPTIVE RAGE

(Forum, 1988) **D/S:** Cedric Sundstrom **S:** Rick Marx **P:** Harry Alan Towers, Barry Wood, Keith Rosenbaum S. Africa

Oliver Reed, as a crazed South American general, kidnaps American coeds as ransom for his drug-dealer son being held in the US. There's lots of torture and some rape. With Robert Vaughn and Claudia Udy.

CAPTIVE WOMAN

(TZ, 1980) **D/S:** Jesús Franco **S:** G. E. Derendor **P:** Erich Tomeck   W. Germany/Spain (*Die Nackten Superhexen von Rio Amore; Naked Superwitches of the Rio Amore; Orgia de los Nonformanas*)

Katja Bienert, who was raised in a convent, comes to Spain to search for her sister (Ursula Buchfellner), a prisoner in a whorehouse. There's nudity and S&M scenes. Raquel Evans and Robert Foster costar. The rest of the titles in this (at least) seven-volume video "series" are unrelated except for the obvious themes.

CAPTIVE WOMEN II: *See* SS EXPERIMENT

CAPTIVE WOMEN III: *See* SWEET SUGAR

CAPTIVE WOMEN IV: *See* FRÄULIEN DEVIL

CAPTIVE WOMEN V: *See* HELL TRAIN

CAPTURED IN CHINATOWN

(Sinister, 1935) **D/S:** Elmer Clifton **P:** Bert Sternbach

Rin Tin Tin was so popular in the early 30s that there were imitation hero-dog movie stars. This

Consolidated Pictures release was part of a rival series featuring Tarzan, a German-sheperd police dog. It's about a Chinese Tong war, a valuable necklace, murder, and a villain named Zamboni. Tarzan saves the day. With Charles Delaney and Marion Schilling.

THE CAPTURE OF BIGFOOT

(Active, 1979) **D/S/P:** Bill Rebane **S:** Ingrid Neumayer

George "Buck" Flower and Otis Young (from *The Last Detail*) are in this guaranteed bad movie (Troma picked it up for release) by the director of *The Giant Spider Invasion*.

CAPTURE THAT CAPSULE

(SW, 1961) **D/S/P:** Will Zens   (*Spy Squad*)

This absurd, slow-moving, boring b/w movie demonstrates that Communist spies in America are underfunded, unorganized, gullible, jive-talking sarcastic men who can't follow orders, say "comrade" and "the party" a lot, and will fight over a can of beer. The plot concerns a space capsule (it looks like a megaphone to me) that the Commies only think they have captured. The theme is played on an out-of-tune piano and drums. Some of the non-action takes place in the Marine World parking lot. Richard (not Dick) Miller stars. David Bradley (*They Saved Hitler's Brain*) was assistant director. Incredibly, Zens went on to direct at least 8 other features, including two starring Marty Robbins. Presented by Johnny Legend.

CARAVANS

(1978) **D:** James Fargo **S:** Nancy Voyles Crawford, Thomas A. McMahon, Lorraine Williams **P:** Elmo Williams   US/Iran

Anthony Quinn stars in this PG-rated James Michener adaptation filmed in Iran. Christopher Lee, as the powerful Sardar Khan, helps Michael Sarrazin search for Jennifer O'Neill, as the daughter of a US senator who has joined Quinn and his nomadic group. The plot is the same as *The Searchers*. Also featured are Joseph Cotten and Barry Sullivan, with an Iranian supporting cast. It was backed by the Shah of Iran during his last days in power and cost a reported $14 million. Fargo later made *Voyage of the Rock Aliens*. Quinn had also been in *The Message* (1970), backed by Quaddafi. There's an Epic soundtrack.

CAREER BED

(SW, 1969) **D/S:** Joel M. Reed **P:** Jeff Gold

This b/w adults-only drama is by the maker of *Bloodsucking Freaks*. Future porno star Jennifer Welles is Susan Potter, a "virgin" with a horrible stage mother (Honey Hunter) whom one character calls "a sewer." Mom seduces Susan's boyfriend, and a lesbian casting agent in a pants suit (Georgina Spelvin) seduces Susan. Reed's movie is more concerned with hateful dialogue and insults than with sex and nudity. In one scene, a bald gangster makes a photographer bark like a dog for money. It all leads to an ironic ending.

There's a Times Square tour sequence that's too dark to see well, and the editing is very bad. The rock music (by the Lost Children) sounds like it's from San Francisco.

CAREFUL!

(VSOM, 1993) **D/S:** Guy Madden   Canada

Madden's first feature in color is a comedy set in Tolzbad, an Alpine village where a sneeze can start an avalanche. Animals have their vocal chords cut. Madden regular Kyle McCulloch stars, with director Paul Cox and Jackie Burroughs.

THE CARELESS YEARS

(1957) **D:** Arthur Hiller **S/P:** Edward Lewis

Dean Stockwell stars in this mild teen drama. It was the first role in six years for the former child star. Natalie Trundy plays "a girl from the 'right' kind of home, stumbling into the 'wrong' kind of love!" as the United Artists ads claimed. The couple flee to Mexico but return and take their parents advice to wait until they finish school. With Barbara Billingsley (just before she became June Cleaver on TV), John Larch, and Virginia Christine. Stockwell was in the more serious *Compulsion* next.

CAR 54, WHERE ARE YOU?

(Orion, 1989) **D:** Bill Fishman **S:** Eric Tarloff, Ebbe Roe Smith **P:** Robert H. Solo   Canada

The guy who made *Tapeheads* also made this PG-13 feature based on the TV comedy series (1961–63). It was shelved, then released to horrible reviews in 1994. David Johansen (a long way from his New York Dolls days) stars as New York City police officer Gunter Toody. He and John McGinley, as Muldoon, protect a witness (Jeremy Piven). With Daniel Baldwin as a mobster, Fran Drescher, Rosie O'Donnell, and Nipsey Russell and Al Lewis from the original show. There's a rap score by Bernie Worrell, and the Ramones do "I Believe in Miracles" in a club.

THE CARHOPS

(1980) **D:** Peter Locke **S:** Paul Ross, Michael Blank **P:** Jim Buckley

Wes Craven was the editor of this teen sex comedy from NMD. It was made by porno people and features Kitty Carl and Lisa Farringer.

CARMILLA

(Cannon, 1989) **D:** Gabrielle Beaumont **S:** Jonathan Furst **P:** Bridget Terry

Sheridan Le Fanu's frequently filmed vampire novel is transplanted to the post–Civil war American South. Meg Tilly is the shape-shifting living/dead Carmilla, and Ione Skye (Leitch, daughter of singer Donovan) is the young girl she befriends and bites. Dogwood is used to ward off vampires. Roddy McDowall and Roy Dotrice costar. Linda Hunt narrates. This *Shelley Duvall's Nightmare Classics* Showtime presentation runs 52 minutes. By the female director of *The Godsend*.

CARNAGE = TWITCH OF THE DEATH NERVE

CARNAGE

(Media, 1983) **D/S/P/C:** Andy Milligan **P:** Louis Mishkin

The video box tries to convince you that "you'll scream with laughter!" but this scratchy-looking *Amityville Horror* copy, filmed on Staten Island, isn't a comedy and it isn't exactly funny. It is a typically senseless Milligan movie. Newlyweds move into an old house, the scene of an earlier murder/suicide. When a man taking a bath is electrocuted by a radio (playing harmonica music), you can see his underpants. When the husband's New York secretary shows up, a floating axe decapitates her obvious dummy head. A butcher knife flies into a priest's head. After all this, none of the dead people are missed, no police arrive, and the couple calmly worry about leaving: "I love this house so much!" Eventually the wife joins the laughing ghost couple with echo voices.

CARNIVAL MAGIC

(1981) **D:** Al Adamson **S:** Mark Weston, Bob Levine **P:** Elwin Feltner

Markov (Don Stewart) is a carnival magician working with Alex, an intelligent chimp. Alex is kidnapped and sold to a scientist. He tries to commit suicide, dies, and is brought back to life by the power of prayer! With Regina Carroll. It was followed by Adamson's *Lost* (1984), with Sandra Dee.

CARNIVAL OF FOOLS: *See* DEATH WISH CLUB

CARNIVAL OF SOULS

(VidAmerica, 1962) **D/P:** Herk Harvey **S:** John Clifford

After a successful 1989 theatrical rerelease with lots of press, good new reviews, and TV coverage, this low-budget cult film from Lawrence, Kansas, was officially released on tape. (Previous video versions were shorter.) This is "the director's full-length authorized version" (84 minutes), the best and most complete version we'll ever see. *Carnival of Souls* was originally released at 80 minutes, (but was listed as 91 before the Herts Lion 1962 release). There's a fun new b/w introduction by Harvey ("It may come back to haunt you"), and some whole scenes have been restored. Most of the new footage shows people talking (two men at the organ factory, a talk with a gas-station attendent). The new video version is a must, if only for the superior quality of the print. Watch Harvey's *Carnival of Souls* again and wonder about its influence on others. Think about *Night of the Living Dead* (zombies), *Blue Velvet* (birds), and *Eraserhead* (music), for example. Since the rerelease, scenes have even been copied for TV commercials.

CARNIVAL STORY

(1954) **D/S:** Kurt Neumann **S:** Hans Jacoby **P:** Maurice and Frank King W. Germany/US (*Rummelplatz der Liebe; Circus of Love*)

Carnival Story was filmed in Munich and Vienna, in color, simultaneously in English and in German. The German version (starring Eva Bartok, Curt Jurgens, Bernhard Wicki, and Adi Berber as Groppo) was released in 3-D. RKO released the English-language version (starring Anne Baxter, Steve Cochran, Lyle Bettger, George Nader, and Jay C. Flippen) in the US flat. All the actors appear in both versions. In one they star, in the other they're in the background. In 1958 the German version was dubbed into English and released in America too. In 1960 it was rereleased on a double bill with Herschell Gordon Lewis and David F. Friedman's first movie, *The Prime Time*! And for some reason, the first English version seemed to be the film most likely to show up on local TV stations at three in the morning during the 80s. So there's a good chance you've seen this drama!

CARNOSAUR

(New Horizons, 1993) **D/S:** Adam Simon **P:** Mike Elliott

Thanks to executive producer Roger Corman's timing and publicity, this gory *Jurassic Park* rip-off was a money maker. Unfortunately, the best part of the movie is a picture of Alfred E. Neuman. *Carnosaur* doesn't make much sense, the music is boring, there's too much talk, and the dinosaurs created by John Buechler are often laughable. Raphael Sbarge stars as a security guard, and Jennifer Runyon is his girlfriend from a commune. An evil, government-backed scientist (Diane Ladd) in an underground lab in upstate New York develops a virus in chicken eggs that makes women give birth to blood-hungry dinosaurs. This results in a stomach-bursting birth scene (a cliché used in many Corman productions). It's based on a novel by Harry Adam Knight (a pseudonym of John Brosnan). With Harrison Page as a sheriff, Ned Bellamy, Clint Howard, and a clip from Simon's *Brain Dead*. *Carnosaur II* followed.

CARNY

(Warner, 1980) **D:** Robert Kaylor **S/P/M/A:** Robbie Robertson **S:** Thomas Baum

Robertson, leader of The Band, backed and starred in this underrated carnival movie. He's a manager facing mobsters, Jody Foster is a 17-year-old runaway, and Gary Busey is Bozo the clown, who gets dunked in water daily for a living. With

Gary Busey as Bozo in *Carny*.

Meg Foster, Kenneth McMillan, Elisha Cook Jr., Bert Remsen, Craig Wasson, and Fred Ward. From United Artists. The Warner soundtrack is by Alex North.

CAROLINE AT MIDNIGHT

(New Horizons, 1993) **D:** Scott McGuinness
S: Travis Rink **P:** Mike Elliot

Clayton Rohner (from *I, Madman*) stars as Jack Lynch, investigative reporter, in an "erotic thriller" told in a series of flashbacks (and a nightmare collage). Mia Sara is married to killer drug-dealer cop Tim Daley, whose partner is/was Judd Nelson. In the R version, Sara has several unmemorable sex scenes. Some more of "the hippest stars" (according to the video box) are Virginia Madsen as a black-haired drug dealer, Paul LeMat as a gray-haired cop, and Stacy Travis, plus Zach Galligan and Thomas F. Wilson, who appear briefly as detectives.

THE CARPATHIAN EAGLE

(Thriller, 1980) **D/S:** Francis Megahy
S: Bernie Cooper UK

Elvira hosts this one-hour-long Hammer TV drama about a police detective trying to find out who's been killing people by cutting their hearts out. With Suzanne Danielle and Sian Phillips.

THE CARPENTER

(Republic, 1987) **D:** David Wellington
S: Doug Taylor **P:** Pierre Grise Canada

A woman (Lynne Adams) cuts up her husband's expensive suit while suffering from a nervous breakdown. In the mental hospital she has to share a room with a woman who keeps repeating "Knock on wood." Her husband, a teacher who puts his classes to sleep and is having an affair with a student, takes her from the hospital directly to their new house, still being renovated. She dreams and seems to be having hallucinations. Wings Hauser, acting very restrained and quiet, is a carpenter who works in the middle of the night without the other workers knowing. Although this movie could be seen as thoughtful, and even feminist at times, it's also part *Toolbox Massacre*, as Wings becomes the woman's secret protector, cutting off a would-be rapist's arms with a chainsaw, crushing hands in a vice, and using a nail gun to pin somebody to the floor. The old-fashioned Wings (a ghost?) goes on about what bad shape people are in today. While drilling a dead man's chest, he exclaims, "See what I mean? Soft!" It's available in R and unrated versions, but even in the unrated version I saw, most of the violence is off screen or pretty tame by today's standards. Made in Quebec, it was the first effort by a film-school graduate.

CARPET OF HORROR

(Sinister, 1962) **D:** Harald Reinl **S:** Felix Lutzkendorf, Giuseppe Mangione Germany/Italy/Spain (*Der Teppich des Grauens*)

Secret agents in London battle a master criminal who uses poison gas to kill. This is not an Edgar Wallace adaptation. With Joachim Fuchsberger, Karin Dor, and Eleonora Rossi-Drago.

THE CARRIER

(Magnum, 1987) **D/S:** Nathan White **P:** Jeffrey Dougherty

An outcast teenager carries a disease in an early 60s Michigan town cut off from the outside world during a flood. Flesh deteriorates as soon as he touches somebody, so everyone else wears protective plastic suits. Eventually they split into religious and nonbeliever groups and fight each other. This interesting, gory, no-budget, AIDS-inspired feature was filmed in Michigan. There's also a Bigfoot-like creature (it started the infection).

THE CARS THAT EAT PEOPLE

(RCA, 1973) **D/S:** Peter Weir **P:** Hal McElroy, James McElroy Australia (*The Cars That Ate Paris*)

The people of a small town in the outback cause accidents and rob the passengers. A doctor (Kevin Miles) turns the victims into living vegetables, and the cars are turned into spiked killing machines. Star Terry Camilleri's voice was dubbed in the 74-minute US version from New Line. The original runs 91 minutes. Weir's first feature is a black comedy and nothing like a *Mad Max* movie, despite the presence of Bruce Spence in the cast. Weir did *Picnic at Hanging Rock* next.

CARTEL

(Southgate, 1989) **D:** John Stewart
S: Moshe Hadar **P:** Ronnie Hadar

Don Stroud is a violent, out-of-control cokehead drug lord who terrorizes the family of pilot hero Miles O'Keeffe. Both of them end up in the same jail where William Smith is a corrupt guard. O'Keeffe sneaks out to kill the guys who killed his sister (Suzanne Slater), then sneaks back in. This violent SGE release also features Crystal Carson.

CAR WASH

(MCA, 1976) **D:** Michael Schultz **S:** Joel Schumacher **P:** Art Linson, Gary Stromberg

Franklin Ajaye receives top billing, but this nearly plotless, fun, PG-rated movie has many guest stars in top form. Richard Pryor is the phony preacher Daddy Rich, and Antonio Fargas is a militant gay character. With Tracy Reed, George Carlin, Professor Irwin Corey, Ivan Dixon, Bill Duke, Lorraine Gary, Melanie Mayron, Garrett Morris, Clarence Muse, the Pointer Sisters, and Brooke Adams. Schultz had directed *Cooley High*

They run on blood.

THE CARS THAT EAT PEOPLE

FROM **NEW LINE CINEMA** PG

Actor Richard Johnson was the co-producer of this Cannon release, adapted from Lucy Irvine's bestselling novel, which was based on a true story. Also with Virginia Hey. The soundtrack includes songs by British singer/songwriter Kate Bush.

THE "CARRY ON" SERIES

The British *Carry On* comedies started in 1958 with *Carry on Sergeant* and were still being made more than 20 years later. The original regulars were Sidney James, Kenneth Williams, and Kenneth Connor, and Gerald Thomas was the regular series director. Americans caught some of the very British comedies on late-night TV, but some had theatrical releases here too. Three—*Carry on Doctor* (1968), *Carry on Camping* (1970), and *Carry on Henry VIII* (1972) were released by AIP. The following have been on tape in America: *Carry on Ad-miral* (VCI, 1956), *Carry on Nurse* (HBO, 1958), *Carry on Cruising* (VSOM, 1962), *Carry on Cleo* (HBO, 1965), *Carry on Cowboy* (HBO, 1966), *Carry on Doctor* (1968), *Carry on at Your Convenience* (Axon, 1971), *Carry on Behind* (1975), and *Carry on Emmanuelle* (1978). Psychotronic fans should enjoy *Carry on Spying* (1964) and *Carry on Screaming* (1966), which can be found on tape if you look hard enough. A new title, *Carry on Columbus*, was produced in 1992.

the year before. The hit theme song and the hit double MCA soundtrack are by Rose Royce. A 1979 TV pilot based on this movie starred Danny Aiello.

CASABLANCA EXPRESS

(Trylon, 1990) **D:** Sergio Martino **S:** Ernesto Gustabi **P:** Pietro Innocenzi   Italy

Two sons of famous actors (Jason Connery and Francesco Quinn) have to save Churchill from the Nazis in North Africa. Donald Pleasence and Glenn Ford are Allied generals.

A CASE FOR MURDER

(MCA, 1993) **D/S:** Duncan Gibbons **S:** Pablo F. Fenjves **P:** Michael S. Murphy

Jennifer Grey is New York lawyer Kate Weldon, Peter Berg is a Chicago lawyer, and Belinda Bauer is his wife. It's "Hitchcockian."

THE CASEBOOK OF SHERLOCK HOLMES: *See* SHERLOCK HOLMES

THE CASE OF THE CAT PEOPLE = CAT PEOPLE (1942)

CASINO ROYALE

(1954) **D:** William H. Brown **S:** Anthony Ellis, Charles Bennett

The first James Bond adaptation was on the *CBS Climax!* live anthology show, eight years before *Dr. No.* Barry Nelson was an American "Jimmy" Bond, and Peter Lorre was Le Chiffre, the gambling villain. With Linda Christian and Michael Pate. The novel had just been published (in 1953), and it was later used as the basis for the 1967 Bond comedy of the same name. It's 55 minutes long.

CASSANDRA

(Virgin, 1987) **D/S:** Colin Eggleston **S:** John Ruane, Chris Fitchett **P:** Trevor Lucas   Australia

The daughter of a famous fashion photographer (Tessa Humphries) has nightmare visions of murders in a movie much like *The Eyes of Laura Mars* (1978). She discovers that her parents are brother and sister, and that her killer twin brother has just gotten out of a mental hospital. People are decapitated and throats are slashed. With Shane Briant. The music is by Trevor Lucas, formerly of Fairport Convention.

CAST A DEADLY SPELL

(HBO, 1991) **D:** Martin Campbell **S:** Joseph Dougherty **P:** Gale Ann Hurd

Mixing H. P. Lovecraft with Raymond Chandler is an intriguing idea, but I wish they had taken it a little more seriously and stuck to the original concept. The always-reliable Fred Ward stars as Philip Lovecraft, a detective in 1948 Los Angeles. It's a fantasy time when seemingly everybody (except Lovecraft) uses magic. Objects float in the air, his landlady is a witch, a man talks backwards, and gangsters use spells to kill. Gremlins in a car engine and traditional monsters in the city jail are just silly, and the black zombies (one looks like a dark Tor Johnson) are an awkward throwback to old Monogram movies. A rich man (David Warner) hires Lovecraft to bring back his copy of the *Necronomicon* and protect his daughter (Julianne Moore), a virgin who hunts unicorns. A stone gargoyle comes to life, one of the "old ones" is revived, and a major character spends the entire film in drag. With Clancy Brown and Arnetia Walker. It was followed in 1994 by *Witch Hunt*.

CASTAWAY

(Warner, 1986) **D:** Nicolas Roeg **S:** Allan Scott **P:** Rick McCallum

A wealthy publisher (Oliver Reed) advertises for a woman to spend a year with him on a deserted island. Amanda Donohoe (in her film debut) takes the job and spends much of the movie wearing little more than a belt with a knife, but she doesn't want any part of his sex fantasy. Reed develops nasty boils. Donohoe was also the best reason to see Ken Russell's *The Lair of the White Worm*.

THE CASTLE

(1968) **D/S:** Rudolph Noelte
P/A: Maximilian Schell **P:** Walter Reade Jr.
W. Germany/Switzerland (*Das Schloss*)

Schell is K., a land surveyor who arrives in a village where he has been hired by some rulers in a castle. Everybody in the village tries to keep him away from the castle, nobody inside will see him, and he becomes obsessed with doing what he was summoned to do. The film is based on an unfinished 1926 Kafka novel and was shot in Austria. K. died in the original ending, which was later altered. Schell was also in *Labyrinth* (1992), also adapted from Kafka.

CASTLE OF DEATH = DEVIL'S NIGHTMARE

CASTLE OF THE CREEPING FLESH

(Magnum, 1967) **D/S/P:** "Percy C. Parker"/Adrian Hoven **S:** Eric Martin Schnitzler   W. Germany (*Im Schloss der Blutigen Begierde; The Castle of Bloody Lust*)

This horror movie about a perverse count (Howard Vernon) has the same cast, crew, and locations of the Jesús Franco films (*Succubus* and *Kiss Me, Monster*) that Hoven (*Mark of the Devil*) also produced. With Janine Reynaud and some gory open-heart surgery.

CASTLE OF THE MONSTERS

(SW, 1957) **D:** Julián Soler **S:** Fernando Galiana **P:** Jesús Sotomayor   Mexico (*El Castillo de los Monstruos*)

Germán Robles (star of *The Vampire* and *The Vampire's Coffin*) is El Vampiro again in this horror comedy. Newlyweds in a haunted castle discover "Frentenstein," a werewolf, a mummy, a gorilla, and one American monster that Universal must have made legal threats about, "la Bestia de la Laguna Negra" (the Creature from the Black Lagoon). In Spanish.

CASTLE OF THE WALKING DEAD = BLOOD DEMON

CATACLYSM

(Genesis, 1979) **D:** Tom McGowan, Greg Tallas, Philip Marshak **S:** Philip Jordan **P:** Darryl A. Marshak (*The Nightmare Never Ends; Satan's Supper*)

To me, any movie available under four titles, and with three directors and Cameron Mitchell, is worth checking out. Naturally, this is an uneven, low-budget oddity under any title, but in a way it's an exploitation classic. The young Mr. Olivier is a decadent, ageless one-time Nazi who likes to hang out in discos and is actually Satan, with hooves. Marc Lawrence, as an old Nazi-hunter, is on to him, and tries to convince a cop (Mitchell). In this odd move, Lawrence, who used to play gangsters a lot, also shows up as Mitchell's partner. Meanwhile, *Night Court*'s Richard Moll (with hair) is

WILLIAM CASTLE

This prolific director and master showman produced or directed about 65 features. He started making B movies in the Boston Blackie, Crime Doctor, and Whistler series in the 40s, then made Techicolor period-adventure movies (some in 3-D). Starting with *Macabre* (1958), Castle became an onscreen celebrity, and each of his new horror movies had a great gimmick involving publicity and/or audience participation ("Emergo!," "the Fright Break," and "the Punishment Poll"). Thanks to John Waters (a fan), cable TV, and the reprinting of Castle's entertaining memoirs (*Step Right Up!*), Castle (who died in 1977) has a growing following.

---

the "Noble Prize–winning" author of the bestseller *God Is Dead*. His wife, a successful surgeon (Faith Cliff, a pretty terrible actress), has nightmares about Olivier's past atrocities and finds herself chosen to defeat him. The laughable scenes don't prepare you for the effective and shocking operating-room possession climax, which includes real open-heart surgery. Filmed in Salt Lake City and San Diego by the Marshaks, who also made *Dracula Sucks* (1979). This easy-to-find, multitabled feature is also available in an altered and condensed version as part of *Night Train to Terror* (plus animation scenes). The most complete version (92 minutes) is *Cataclysm*.

THE CATAMOUNT KILLING
(1976) **D:** Krzysztof Zanussi   W. Germany

Hallmark (AIP) released this film, made in Vermont by a Polish director. A banker with business and family problems is transferred to a town called Pittsville. He seduces an older woman, and they plan a payroll heist together. With Horst Buchholz, Ann Wedgeworth, Polly Holliday, and Chip Taylor.

THE CAT AND THE CANARY
(Video Yesteryear, Sinister, 1927) **D:** Paul Leni **S:** Robert F. Hill, Alfred A. Cohn **P:** Carl Laemmle

Look for this Universal film on tape. It's the ultimate old-dark-house mystery/comedy. Everything about the reading-of-the-will plot and an escaped madman was old even in 1927, but the camerawork and some then-new optical effects are still being studied and copied today. The atmospheric Upstate New York mansion sets are especially great. It was based on a popular play that debuted in 1922. Laura La Plante and Creighton Hale star as cousins, with Lucien Littlefield, Arthur Edmund Carewe, Tully Marshall, Flora Finch, Gertrude Astor, Forrest Stanley, and Martha Mattox as Mammy Pleasant. The tape is 70 minutes and features a newly recorded score, but the original running time was 86 minutes. Leni, an important German director and art director, directed only four films for Universal before dying of blood poisoning. This film was remade as *The Cat Creeps* (1930) in English and Spanish versions, as a Bob Hope comedy (1939), and as a British comedy directed by Radley Metzger in 1978.

THE CAT BURGLAR
(1961) **D:** William Witney **S:** Leo Gordon **P:** Gene Corman

June Kenny (*Attack of the Puppet People*) and Jack Hogan star in this 65-minute United Artist crime drama, written by an actor often in Roger Corman features and produced by Corman's brother. It's about foreign agents who kill for a secret formula. With Greg Palmer, Gene Roth, and Bruno Ve Sota. Daniel Haller was the art director.

CAT CHASER
(Vestron, 1989) **D:** Abel Ferrara **S:** Elmore Leonard, Jim Borrelli, Alan Sharp **P:** Peter Davis, William Panzer

Kelly McGillis is in love with Miami hotel owner Peter Weller but is married to Tomas Milian, the former head of the Santo Domingo secret police. This *film noir* love triangle is better than other Elmore Leonard adaptations (*Stick, 52 Pick-Up*) but went direct to video in the US. With Charles Durning and Frederic Forrest. The music is by Chick Corea. An R-rated version and a longer, unrated version (featuring some pretty shocking violence and nudity) are available.

CATCH MY SOUL
(1973) **D:** Patrick McGoohan **S/P:** Jack Good **P:** Richard Rosenbloom   (*Santa Fe Satan*)

The same year as *Godspell* and *Jesus Christ Superstar*, the star of the TV series *The Prisoner* directed singer Richie Havens as Othello in a hippie commune. The film, rated PG, got terrible reviews and disappeared. It's based on Jack Good's rock opera. With Season Hubley as Desdemona, Lance LeGault as Iago, Susan Tyrrell, Tony Joe White, and Delaney and Bonnie Bramlett. The British stage version had starred Jerry Lee Lewis (!) and P. J. Proby. The Cinerama release was rated PG.

CATCH THE HEAT
(Media, 1987) **D:** Joel Silberg **S:** Sterling Silliphant **P:** Don Van Atta

Mr. Hannibal (Rod Steiger), a talent agent in Buenos Aires, hires dancers and tells them they'll get important jobs in other countries if they have breast implants. They're taken to a well-armed secret base where a doctor hides heroin in their breasts. Later on they're killed for the drugs. Despite the exploitative (but nearly believable) premise, things are kept pretty light and comic. Tiana Alexander (real name Tiana Thi Thanh Nga, Silliphant's wife) stars as Checkers Goldberg, a San Francisco–based agent posing as dancer Cinderella Poo to expose Steiger. She's funny and pretty, and she can fight. Her bumbling, lovesick partner is David Dukes. Steiger's bouncers are a big black guy, wrestler Professor Toru Tanaka, and a skinny white guy. Lots of jokes are made about language differences. Most of the violence and blood is offscreen, but people swear a lot: "You're fuckin' dog meat!" Steiger, as usual, wears a hairpiece that looks ready to slide off at any minute, flashes his big grin once in a while, and spends the rest of the time slowly building to emotional explosions. The ending is a big battle with lots of heavy artillery. The screenplay was written by the same man who wrote the script for Steiger's Oscar-winning role in *In the Heat of the Night* (1967). Brian Thompson is also in the cast.

THE CAT FROM OUTER SPACE
(1978) **D/P:** Norman Tokar **S:** Ted Key

This G-rated Disney comedy about an alien cat (made the year after *Star Wars*) has a plot similar to *E.T.* (1982). It stars Ken Berry, Sandy Duncan, Harry Morgan, Roddy McDowall, McLean Stevenson, Jesse White, and Hans Conried.

CAT IN THE BRAIN
(Video Search, 1989) **D/S/A:** Lucio Fulci **S:** Giovanni Simonelli **P:** Luigi Nannerini, Antonio Lucidi   Italy (*Un Gatto nel Cervello; Nightmare Concert*)

Fulci, a balding guy with beard and glasses, plays a horror-movie director who goes to a shrink (who hypnotizes him) because he's disturbed by memories of his own films and seems to be a killer himself. "It's as if my brain were being eaten by a cat," he explains. Just about anything can trigger gory clips from (what else?) Fulci horror movies, which make up the bulk of this paste-up feature. If you like overkill, check out the many decapitations and cut-up bodies, a cannibalism scene, and a change-of-pace shower scene. Fulci also imagines his German backers as Nazis. With Melissa Longo and Bret Halsey (in a comic S&M sequence). It's dubbed into English.

CAT IN THE CAGE
(Genesis, 1978) **D/S/P:** Zarin Dast **S:** Richard Vasquez

A young man (Behrouz Wossoughi) returns to the LA-area family mansion from "the booby hatch." His rich father, Rachid Khan (Frank DeKova), has married his dead wife's nurse (Sybil Danning), who plots with her chauffeur lover to kill the old man for his fortune. She's deathly afraid of cats and likes being slapped. Meanwhile, the black housekeeper practices witchcraft on a cat. This nutty, mean-spirited movie features Danning nude, what seems to be a wolf man, and a laughable ending. With Colleen Camp (who sings the title song) and Mel Novak.

CAT MURKIL AND THE SILKS

(Seagull, 1976) **D:** John Bushelman
S/P: William C. Thomas

An obscure LA street-gang movie about a psychotic teen who kills the leader of his own gang and blames a rival gang. With Derrell Maury (*Massacre at Central High*), Rhodes Reason, Steve Bond, and Doodles Weaver. The director edited Bert I. Gordon movies.

CAT'S EYE

(MGM, 1985) **D:** Lewis Teague
S: Stephen King **P:** Martha Schumacher

Drew Barrymore, a cat, and a small troll (created by Carlo Rambaldi) are in "The General," written by King specifically for Barrymore, who had starred in his *Firestarter*. Two other stories in the PG-13 anthology from DEG were adapted by the writer from his short stories. James Woods stars in "Quitters Inc.," about extreme ways to stop smoking cigarettes, with Alan King. Kenneth McMillan and Robert Hays are in "The Ledge," about a deadly bet, with Candy Clark, James Naughton, and Patty LuPone. There's some animation and the song "96 Tears," and the *Christine* car and the *Cujo* dog also make in-joke appearances. It was one of several King/Dino De Laurentiis collaborations made in North Carolina. The cinematography was by Jack Cardiff, and Alan Silvestri provided the score, released on Varèse Sarabande.

CAT WOMEN OF THE MOON

(Rhino, 1953) **D:** Arthur Hilton
S: Roy Hamilton **P:** Al Zimbalist

There's too much talk and not enough action, but any movie with Marie Windsor (as Helen, the navigator) falling for (20-years-older) Victor Jory on the Moon, while alien women in black tights dance a ballet, has a lot going for it. And who can forget the great Sonny Tufts as the commander, the giant spiders, and the music by Elmer Bernstein? The gold-hungry guy on the space mission says, "You're too smart for me, baby. I like 'em stupid," before he's stabbed to death. Hilton, usually an editor, was British. Incredibly, this Astor release (later "presented" by Wade Williams), was remade as *Missile to the Moon* (1958). The (lousy) 3-D goes on and off throughout the tape. Rhino also released *Robot Monster* (also produced by Zimbalist, and with awful, partial 3-D) and *The Mask* (excellent partial 3-D with glasses).

CAVE GIRL

(RCA, 1985) **D/S/P/C:** David Oliver

A teen comedy with a nerd (Daniel Roebuck) who goes back in time and finds love, lions, and cannibals. It costars Cindy Ann Thompson, with Michelle Bauer and Jasae in small parts. From Crown International.

THE CAVERN

(1965) **D/P:** Edgar G. Ulmer **S:** Michael Pertwee, Jack Davies   Italy/W. Germany (*Sette Contro la Morte*)

This was Ulmer's last film and it's much better than his other 60s features. *The Cavern* is actually a fascinating allegorical tale. During WWII in Italy, a diverse group of four Allied servicemen, a German soldier, an Italian soldier, and his girlfriend are trapped in a cave after a bombing attack. They discover alcohol and dynamite, but no matter what they try they can't seem to get out. Brian Aherne is especially good, and the cast also includes John Saxon, Rosanna Schiaffino, Larry Hagman, and Peter Marshall. 20th Century–Fox released it in the US.

CAVE-IN!

(1979) **D:** George J. Fenady
S: Norman Katkov **P:** Irwin Allen

You know a movie is special when NBC-TV makes it, then doesn't air it for four years. Dennis Cole, Leslie Nielsen, Julie Sommars, Ray Milland, and James Olson are trapped in caverns, and two cave-ins occur. Allen made *Beyond the Poseidon Adventure* the same year.

CB4: THE MOVIE

(MCA, 1993) **D:** Tamara Davis **S/P:** Nelson George **S/A:** Chris Rock **S:** Robert LoCash

Chris Rock stars in a *This Is Spinal Tap*–like look at the ex-con Cell Block 4 rap trio, really nice suburban guys. With Alan Payne, Phil Hartman, Chris Elliott as a documentary filmmaker, Theresa Randle, and Charlie Murphy (Eddie's brother). Ice T, Ice Cube, and other real rap stars have cameos. MCA also released the soundtrack of this Universal feature. The independent *Fear of a Black Hat* from the same year used the same idea.

C. C. AND COMPANY

(1970) **D:** Seymour Robbie **S/P:** Roger Smith **P:** Allan Carr   (*Chrome Hearts*)

Joe Namath is pretty ridiculous as C. C. Ryder, a member of the Heads, led by William Smith as Moon. (Smith had already been in *Angels Die Hard*, *The Losers*, and *Run Angel Run*.) C. C. saves Ann-Margret from the rest of the gang when her limo breaks down. He leaves the free life to go to Vegas with her, but the gang kidnaps her. Sid Haig, Greg Mullavey, Bruce Glover, and Gary Littlejohn are bikers. With Teda Bracci as Pig and Jennifer Billingsley. Wayne Cochran and the C. C. Riders appear to do a number, and Mitch Rider is heard. Ann-Margret sings too, and they're all on the Avco Embassy soundtrack. Her husband produced and wrote this R (later PG) movie. Allan Carr and Smith had also produced *The First Time* (1969). Namath's acting career didn't go very far, but he was also in *Chattanooga Choo Choo* (1984).

CEASE FIRE

(1953) **D:** Owen Crump **S:** Walter Doniger **P:** Hal B. Wallace

This Korean War docudrama features real American and Korean servicemen in 3-D. It was filmed on location in South Korea. One of the soldier/actors is said to have actually died on screen. Cheong Yul Bak stars as Kim. The score is by Dimitri Tiomkin. From Paramount.

CEASE FIRE

(HBO, 1985) **D:** David Nutter **S:** George Fernandez **P:** William Grefe

Don Johnson stars as a shell-shocked Nam vet still having flashbacks. His friend commits suicide. The serious feature was made in Miami just before Johnson became a big name in the TV series *Miami Vice*, but it was shelved for several years. With Lisa Blount, Chris Noel, and William Kerwin. It was the first feature produced by Grefe since *Mako: The Jaws of Death* (1976).

CELEBRITY COMMERCIALS

(Good Times)

Around 40 commercials are on this one-hour tape. Some of the celebs making extra bucks are Boris Karloff, Ronald Reagan, Charles Laughton, Johnny Weissmuller, Ernie Kovacs, the Monkees, the Nelson family, and the Three Stooges. Some are characters (Captain Midnight, the Lone Ranger, the Cisco Kid, Sergeant Bilko), impersonations (Laurel and Hardy), cartoon characters or actors before they were known (Marilyn Monroe, Christopher George, Louise Lasser). Charlton Heston, Steve McQueen, Nick Adams, Humphrey Bogart, Jack Benny, Lucy and Desi, and Fred and Barney all hawk cigarettes. Also with the famous early-70s animated King Kong Volkswagen ad. Watch this tape and see why you are what you are today. Wouldn't you eat Shredded Wheat if Rin Tin Tin endorsed it? The sell though low-priced tape was purchased in a shopping mall.

CELIA, CHILD OF TERROR

(1988) **D/S:** Ann Turner **P:** Timothy White, Gordon Glenn   Australia

Rebecca Smart stars as 9-year-old Celia, who starts imagining fictional monsters after her grandmother dies in 1950s Australia. It's not a horror movie. With Nicholas Eadie and Mary Anne Fahey.

THE CELLAR

(Hemdale, 1990) **D:** Kevin Tenney
S/P: Patrick Wells **P:** Steven E. Berman

A young boy (Chris Miller) visiting his divorced father in the Arizona desert knows about an Indian spirit in the basement of the farmhouse. Nobody believes him, but many are killed by the monster (some kind of a mutant boar) in this PG-13 movie. With Patrick Kilpatrick, Suzanne Savoy, and Ford Rainey.

CELLAR DWELLER

(Starmaker, 1986) **D:** John Carl Buechler
S: Kit DuBois **P:** Bob Wynn

Jeffrey Combs is a horror-comic artist in the early 50s. His creations come to life, and he's killed by his own 8-foot-tall monster. Years later, a new female cartoonist (Deborah Mullowney) revives the creature in Combs' country house, now part of an artists' colony. With Pamela Bellwood, Yvonne De Carlo, Vince Edwards, and Cheryl Ann Wilson. This Empire feature was filmed in Italy and released by New World. Buechler also did the FX. Frank Brunner provided the comic art.

CELL BLOCK GIRLS: *See* THUNDER COUNTY

CEMETERY HIGH

(Unicorn, 1987) **D/S/P:** Gorman Bechard
P: Kristine Covello

The Scumbusters, high-school-grad-cheerleader vigilantes, wipe out "male slimeballs" with guns. You get jokes about vigilantes, gore, and a "gore gong and horror hooter" gimmick. Characters talk to the camera, and the onscreen narrator is killed! With Debi Thibeault, Karen Nielsen, and Ruth Collins. Made in Waterbury, Connecticut.

CEMETERY MASSACRE: *See* NORTHVILLE CEMETERY MASSACRE

CENSORED

(SW, 1965) **D/P:** Barry Mahon

A man (Sid Berry) who reminds me of Bud Abbott gives a long, serious, (and pretty factual) lecture about movie censorship. The various scenes he shows us that were cut from "art" and adult films were actually created for this b/w movie. If you like this kinda stuff, it's a brilliant concept, Mahon really knew how to photograph beautiful women, and parts are downright surreal. He was also an equal-opportunity employer (remember this was made in the early 60s). A black man portrays an artist and a black woman is the star of the outrageous nudist colony scenes (also in the *Shameless Shorts* compilation—*PV* magazine #16). Models pose naked, a naked woman talks on the phone, and women strip down for life in a nudists colony. The most suprising scenes copy the then-new adults only "roughie" features. There's some bondage, a Nazi woman torturer, and a hilarious H. G. Lewis–type movie scene takeoff. When a guy cuts a woman's (obviously wood) leg off there's no blood! The (excellent) editing was by Byron Mabe.

THE CENSUS TAKER

(1984) **D/S:** Bruce Cook **S:** Gordon
Smith **P:** Robert Bealmer

Greg Mullavey and Meredith MacRea (already an established team in obscure exploitation movies) kill a census taker (Garrett Morris) because he asked too many personal quesions and try to hide his body from a detective (Timothy Bottoms). It's a black comedy.

THE CENTERFOLD GIRLS

(Media, 1974) **D:** John Peyser **S:** Robert
Peete **P:** Charles Stroud

Models for *Bachelor* magazine go to an island mansion and are killed off. Andrew Prine is a psycho killer with wire-rimmed glasses. This very-low-budget movie (presented by Arthur Marks) has a drug subplot and a good exploitation cast, including Ray Danton, Francine York, Jeremy Slate, Aldo Ray as a rapist, Mike Mazurki, and Dan Seymour. Jennifer Ashley, Jamie Lyn Bauer, Tiffany Bolling as a stewardess, Connie Strickland, Teda Bracci, Janet Wood, and Anneka De Lorenzo (from

Penthouse, also in *Caligula*), Ruthy Ross (from *Playboy*), and others play centerfolds and are in the many topless scenes.

CENTER OF THE WEB

(AIP, 1992) **D:** David Prior **P:** Kimberly Casey

Charlene Tilton is an assistant DA whose acting-teacher boyfriend (Ted Prior) is kidnapped by gangsters, then recruited by the government to work undercover. There are lots of car crashes. With Robert Davi, Tony Curtis, Chuck Connors, Charles Napier, and Bo Hopkins. This played the Harris, on 42nd Street.

CENTIPEDE HORROR

(World, 1989) **D:** Keith Li **S:** Amy Chan, Suet
Ming **P:** Stephen C. K. Chan   Hong Kong

See characters puking up centipedes and scorpions! See an exorcism and reanimated flying-chicken skeletons! It's all the result of black-magic spells and a curse in Thailand, because somebody's father cheated on his wife years ago.

CERTAIN FURY

(Starmaker, 1985) **D:** Stephan Gyllenhaal
S: Michael Jacobs **P:** Gilbert Adler   US/Canada

There's nothing like an exploitation movie starring two young Oscar winners. Tatum O'Neal is Scar, a tough, illiterate hooker, and Irene Cara is innocent and middle-class. In a courtroom facing charges, they accidentally become part of a shootout/breakout and flee into the sewers and slums of a city. It's basically another *Defiant Ones* copy. Peter Fonda is a wealthy gangster, Moses Gunn is Cara's father, and Nicholas Campbell is a drug dealer/pornographer. Cara appears topless, is shot up with drugs, and gets raped. The director of this New World release later made *Paris Trout*.

A CERTAIN SACRIFICE

(Virgin, 1979) **D:** Stephen Jon Lewicki

Nobody would ever have cared about this 58-minute super-8 punk-attitude student film if it hadn't costarred future megastar Madonna. She did it in New York for "$100" several years before her first LP was released and later tried to sue to keep it unreleased. The grainy film with bad sound features Madonna as "bad girl" Bruna. She's naked, is smeared with blood, joins in (simulated) group sex, is raped, and eventually helps kill and eat her rapist. This was for sale in Kmarts for years.

CHA-CHA-CHA BOOM

(1956) **D:** Fred F. Sears **S:** James B.
Gordon **P:** Sam Katzman

A talent scout with his own record company looks for new Latin talent to sign. With Pérez Prado, the Mary Kay Trio, Alix Talton, and José González González. The songs include "Cuban Rock and Roll" and "Voodoo Suite." Sears directed *Rock Around the Clock* (also for Columbia) the same year.

CHAIN GANG

(1984) **D/S:** Worth Keeter **S:** Todd
Durham **P/A:** Earl Owensby

This is one of several 3-D adventure movies made at Owensby's EO studios in North Carolina. He stars as Rafe McPherson, and Al "Lash" La Rue is in the cast. The ads compared it to *The Wild Bunch*. Don't believe it.

CHAIN GANG WOMAN

(Academy, 1971) **D/S/A/C/E:** Lee Frost
P/A: Wes Bishop

A ripoff title disguises a drive-in movie about an all-male chain gang. An ad said, "The road from a chain gang to Hell is very short." Robert Lott is on a Georgia chain gang for a marijuana bust. He escapes with a "sex killer" (Michael Sterns), and they take over a farmhouse. With country music and split-screen chase sequences. From Crown International

CHAINED HEAT

(Vestron, 1983) **D:** "Paul Nicolas"/Lutz
Schaarwaechter **S:** Vincent Mongoi
P: Billy Fine   US/W. Germany

Chained Heat may be the ultimate modern WIP (women-in-prison) feature. Linda Blair (who went topless for the first time) is the innocent new inmate, Stella Stevens is the strict prison officer, Henry Silva is the coke dealer/pimp guard, and John Vernon is the warden, who deals in drugs and women (and videotapes his hot-tub orgies). Tamara Dobson (from the *Cleopatra Jones* movies), as Duchess, leads the black gang, and Sybil Danning, as Erika, leads the white gang. With Edy Williams, Monique Gabrielle in the hot tub, John Aprea, Jennifer Ashley, Louisa Moritz, Marcia Karr, Nita Talbot, Greta Blackburn, Michael Callan, and John Vernon's daughter, Kate, as a prisoner. This follow-up to *The Concrete Jungle* (1982) also includes some transvestites and some visible boom mikes.

CHAINED HEAT 2

(New Line, 1993) **D/P:** Lloyd Simandl
S: Chris Hyde **P:** John Curtis

Red-haired Brigitte Nielsen as Magda, the new warden, towers over the rest of the female cast in this "sequel" (actually a remake of *Red Heat*) set in (and shot in) Prague. She smokes drugs, snorts coke, and turns girls into expensive prostitutes at a castle for the corrupt US ambassador (Paul Koslo). Magda also likes to be whipped (off screen) by her laughing lesbian guard Rosa (Jana Suandova), who makes naked prisoners work in a coke factory at night and is like a younger version of Rosa in *From Russia with Love*. Kimberly Kates is the innocent tourist who was framed, and Kari Whitman is her sister, who wants her out. As far as women-in-prison movies go it's real tame. You do get shower scenes, but Brigitte keeps herself pretty much covered, and her acting hasn't improved. By the director of *Maniac Warriors*.

CHAIN OF DESIRE

(Prism, 1992) **D/S:** Temistocles Lopez **P:** Brian Cox

In another version of *La Ronde* (see *New York Nights*), interconnecting stories about sex are centered around a Manhattan nightclub. With Linda Fiorentino, Elias Koteas, Patrick Bauchau, Grace Zabriske as a dominatrix, Malcolm McDowell as her closet-case husband, and Seymour Cassel as a pedophile artist.

CHAIN REACTION

(1980) **D/S:** Ian Berry **P:** David Elfick   Australia

Nuke-plant officials want to kill a contaminated worker (Ross Thompson) before he can notify people about a cover-up concerning nuclear waste and a near meltdown that caused an earthquake. Steve Bisley and Anna-Maria Winchester are a vacationing couple. George Miller was the associate producer of this *China Syndrome*–inspired action thriller after he directed *Mad Max*.

CHAINS OF GOLD

(Academy, 1992) **D:** Rod Holcolmb **S:** John Petz, Linda Favila **P:** Jonathon D. Krane

John Travolta is a Miami-area social worker who goes beyond the call of duty to save a kid named Carlos (Benjamin Bratt). Gangs use kids to work their drug factory, put them in suspended cages, and kill the defectors. Travolta (who also cowrote this) falls down the side of a building and is kidnaped, shot at, and thrown in an alligator pit. His ex-wife (Marilu Henner) is a gang lawyer, and Bernie Casey and Hector Elizondo are cops. Also with Joey Lawrence and Conchita Ferrell.

THE CHAIR

(Imperial, 1986) **D:** Waldemar Korzeniowsky **S:** Carolyn Swartz **P:** Anthony Jones   (*Hot Seat*)

There were a lot of prison horror movies in the late 80s. None were very good, but this (possibly the first completed) is the worst. James Coco (who died shortly after filming) is corny, sentimental, and overbearing as a friendly doctor practicing primal therapy on a small group of inmates in an old, rundown prison that's haunted by electrical forces. The inmates include Stephen Geoffreys, a black drag queen, and *Stranger Than Paradise* star Richard Edson (in flashbacks). The only memorable parts involve an animated eyeball in a light bulb. With Trini Alvarado and the irritating Paul Benedict (from *The Jeffersons*). The theme song is sung by Lonette McKee. It was filmed by Angelika Films (the theater owners) at the old Essex County (New Jersey) jail and in New Paltz, New York, and released in 1989.

THE CHAIRMAN

(1969) **D:** J. Lee Thompson **S:** Ben Maddow **P:** Mort Abrahams   US/UK (*The Most Dangerous Man in the World*)

A transmitter (actually a bomb) is planted in the skull of a Nobel Prize–winning scientist (Gregory Peck) who is asked by the president to go to China to obtain a supergrowth enzyme. He's lied to and used by the Communists and his own government.

CHARLIE CHAN

The famous Chinese detective Charlie Chan was based on a character in books by Earl Derr Biggers (1884–1933). In 1926, only one year after the first novel (*The House Without a Key*) was published, a silent Pathé serial based on it was made, with Japanese actor George Kuwa as a comic Chan. Another Japanese actor, Kamiyama Sojin, played Chan in Paul Leni's *The Chinese Parrot* (Universal, 1928). A sound film, *Behind the Curtain* (Fox, 1929), had English actor E. L. Park playing Chan as a supporting character.

Fox then put Swedish actor Warner Oland (who had been starring in their Fu Manchu movies) into a series of 17 features that lasted from 1929 until the actor's death in 1938. They have the highest production values and the best plots and guest stars. Keye Luke often played Lee Chan, "number one son." *Charlie Chan in Paris* (1935), *Charlie Chan at the Opera*, with Boris Karloff (1936), and *Charlie Chan's Secret* (1936) are on video from Key.

Sidney Toler took over the role in 1938 and was in 11 Fox films until 1942. (Victor) Sen Young usually played Jimmy Chan, "number two son." George Zucco is in *Charlie Chan in Honolulu* (1938), and Lionel Atwill is in *Charlie Chan in Panama* (1940) and *Charlie Chan's Murder Case* (1940). In 1944 Monogram took over the series, and Toler was in 11 more until he died in 1947. These are the ones with Mantan Moreland as comic-relief chauffeur Birmingham Brown and Benson Fong as Tommy Chan, "number three son." More people are familiar with the Monogram entries because they've been on TV so much. Sen Young and Keye Luke showed up in some of the Monogram entries too. The movies got more predictable as the years went by and often had more comedy than crime-solving. *Charlie Chan at the Wax Museum* (1940), *Murder Over New York* (1940), *Charlie Chan in Rio* (1941), *Castle in the Desert* (1942), *Meeting at Midnight* (or *Black Magic*), *Charlie Chan in the Secret Service*, and *The Chinese Cat* (all 1944), and *The Jade Mask*, *The Shanghai Cobra*, and *The Scarlet Clue* (all 1945) are on video.

Roland Winters took over the role for the last six films (1947–1949). *The New Adventures of Charlie Chan* was a 1957 TV series starring J. Carroll Naish and James Hong. Tapes of these programs have been around. *The Return of Charlie Chan* (1971) was a TV-pilot feature with Ross Martin as Chan. Because of protests over the appearance of yet another Caucasian actor in the role, it wasn't aired for eight years.

Mantan Moreland as Birmingham Brown and Keye Luke in *The Jade Mask*.

JACKIE CHAN

For many years Chan was the biggest star in Asia. A former child actor and stunt man, he starred in many comic period martial-arts movies. Many of these early titles are available (dubbed) in the US (often from All Seasons) under various confusing and misleading titles. Some are: *Eagle's Shadow Fist* (1973), *All in the Family* (1975), *Hand of Death*, (1975), *Shaolin Wooden Men* (1976), *New Fists of Fury* (1976), *To Kill with Intrigue* (1977), *Dragon Fist* (1978), *Half a Loaf of Kung Fu* (1978), *Magnificent Bodyguard* (1978), *Snake and Crane Art of Shaolin* (1978), *Spiritual Kung Fu* (1978), *Eagle's Shadow* (1978), his first big hit, *Drunken Master* (1979), *Fearless Hyena* (1979), his first film as director, *Young Master* (1980), and *Fearless Hyena II* (1980). Some ripoff titles used new footage of doubles for Chan mixed with outtakes or old scenes. A 1980 US production, *The Big Brawl*, failed to make him a star here, but his Hong Kong hits continued to break box-office records. His biggest and best-known action features are *Police Story* (1987), *Project A* (1983), and *Armour of God* (1986). They all had sequels.

With Anne Heywood, Arthur Hill, Burt Kwouk, Keye Luke, and Conrad Yuma as Chairman Mao. Jerry Goldsmith wrote the score of this M-rated 20th Century–Fox release.

CHALLENGE

(Continental, 1974) **D:** Martin Beck **P/A:** Earl Owensby

This was the first of many movies that Owensby made in North Carolina. In the simple, PG-rated revenge plot, he blows away the guys who killed his wife. Owensby's movies were advertised as "clean, decent entertainment" and played exclusively in southern states until some became video releases.

THE CHALLENGE

(1970) **D:** "Alan Smithee" **S:** Marc Norman **P:** Jay Cipes, Ed Palmer

Darren McGavin and Mako are warriors who represent America and an unnamed Asian country in the future. They're sent to a deserted island to fight to the death as an alternative to WWIII. With Broderick Crawford, James Whitmore, Adolph Caesar, Skip Homeier, and Paul Lukas. It was made for ABC-TV. The director's real name is unavailable.

THE CHALLENGE

(Fox, 1982) **D:** John Frankenheimer **S:** John Sayles, Richard Maxwell, Ivan Moffat **P:** Robert L. Rosen, Ron Beckman

American boxer Scott Glenn, training in Kyoto, Japan, ends up eating food that moves and is buried up to his neck, in this odd movie filmed in Kyoto by Americans. Toshiro Mifune and Atsuo Nakamura are rival brothers after a family samurai sword. Mifune invades his brother's high-security corporation with a bow and arrows and a sword. With Donna Kei Benz. It was Sayles' first filmed script after *The Howling*. Steven Seagal was the fight coordinator. The music is by Jerry Goldsmith. A recut and retitled version was later shown on TV as *Sword of the Ninja*.

A CHALLENGE FOR ROBIN HOOD

(1968) **D:** C. M. Pennington-Richards **S:** Peter Bryan **P:** Clifford Parkes   UK

Barrie Ingham stars as Robin Hood in a typical tale of the merrie men of the forest, with a cast of actors unknown in the US (where it was released by 20th Century–Fox). Hammer had also made *Men of Sherwood Forest* (1954) and *Sword of Sherwood Forest* (1960), the latter with Richard Greene, who also starred in the TV series *The Adventures of Robin Hood* .

CHANCES ARE

(RCA, 1989) **D:** Emile Ardolino **S:** Perry Howze, Randy Howze **P:** Mike Lobell

Robert Downey Jr. is the reincarnated soul of the husband of Cybill Shepherd. With Mary Stuart Masterson as their daughter, Ryan O'Neal, Marc McClure, Mimi Kennedy, and Kathleen Freeman. Tri Star released this PG comedy with music by Maurice Jarre. Downey later starred in another body-switch comedy, 1993's *Heart and Soul*.

CHANEL SOLITAIRE

(1981) **D:** George Kaczender **S:** Julian Spangler **P:** Larry Spangler   US/France

Marie-France Pisier stars as Coco Chanel, who rises from poverty to conquer the fashion world. About $1 million was spent on costumes in this two-hour-long romantic biography. The international cast includes Timothy Dalton, Rutger Hauer, Karen Black, Brigitte Fossey, and Catherine Allegret as a lesbian.

CHANG

(Milestone, 1927) **D/P:** Merian C. Cooper **P:** Ernest B. Schoedsack

Roughly 50 percent of this extraordinary 67-minute documentary was staged or fake, making it an early "docudrama." The Paramount release was filmed in the jungles of Siam (now Thailand) and features a real farming family. Cooper and Schoed-sack's follow-up to *Grass* (1925) is famous for the long sequence of an elephant herd destroying a native village. Some scenes were later copied in the filmmakers' next project, *King Kong*. The restored video release includes a new orchestral score.

CHANGE OF MIND

(1969) **D:** Robert Stevens **S/P:** Seeleg Lester, Richard Wesson

The brain of a white district attorney is transplanted into a dead black man (Raymond St. Jacques). The DA tries to resume his life in the new body, but his family and colleagues shun him. He eventually goes for help to the woman (Janet MacLachlan) who was married to the dead man and ends up a hero in a court case involving a bigoted sheriff. With Susan Oliver and Leslie Nielsen. This R-rated movie, filmed in Toronto, features music composed and conducted by Duke Ellington. Don't expect another *The Thing with Two Heads*.

THE CHANNELER

(Magnum, 1990) **D/S/P/A:** Grant Austin Waldman

A group of people from LA go backpacking. One guy has visions of a miner. He becomes possessed, rolls his eyeballs back, and talks with a deep voice. A monster with limp rubber claws kills people, and everything is explained in a cave at the end. Jay Richardson plays a nice guy husband and is the best part of the movie. Dan Haggerty is a Nam vet doing research in the woods and Euro star Richard Harrison is a bar owner who comes to the rescue. *The Channeler* starts out better than average, but gets boring and stupid pretty fast. With Robin Sims, Cindy Brooks, and a from-the-neck-down-only nude shower scene. Fred Olen Ray was the executive consultant.

THE CHANT OF JIMMY BLACKSMITH

(1978) **D/S/P:** Fred Schepisi

At the turn of the century, a half-breed Aborigine (Tommy Lewis) raised by an English missionary (Jack Thompson) declares war on all whites after years of abuse. He starts by killing a family with an axe. The film was adapted from a novel by Thomas Keneally that was based on a true incident. Most US prints are cut. Schepisi later made *Iceman* in the US.

THE CHARGE AT FEATHER RIVER

(1953) **D:** Gordon Douglas **S:** James R. Webb **P:** David Weisbart

The Cavalry rescues two women being held by hostile Cheyenne Indians, in this 3-D Natural-vision and Warner Color feature. Guy Madison (TV's Wild Bill Hickok) stars, with Frank Lovejoy (who had just been in the 3-D horror hit *House of Wax*), Vera Miles, Steve Brodie, Helen Westcott, Onslow Stevens, Neville Brand, and Henry Kulky. Bullets, arrows, and even tobacco juice seemed to shoot or be spat out at the audience. The music is by Max Steiner.

CHARLEY AND THE ANGEL

(1973) **D:** Vincent McEveety
S: Roswell Rogers **P:** Bill Anderson

Harry Morgan is the angel in this G-rated Disney fantasy/comedy set in the Depression-era Midwest. Fred MacMurray (who had starred in several Disney hits a decade before) is Charlie, a store owner, and Cloris Leachman is his wife. The plot is mostly a light version of Capra's *It's a Wonderful Life*. Richard Bakalyan as a bootlegger, Edward Andrews, Barbara Nichols, and George Lindsay make it (almost) bearable for adults, and there are newcomers like Kurt Russell as a teen who likes Charlie's daughter, Vincent Van Patten, and Ed Begley Jr.

CHARLEY ONE-EYE

(1972) **D:** Don Chaffey **S:** Keith
Leonard **P:** James Swann   UK

Richard Roundtree (just after *Shaft*) is "the black man," a Union Army deserter who kills his commanding officer and flees to Mexico. He meets up with "the Indian" (Roy Thinnes), an outcast half-breed with a bad leg. Nigel Davenport is a sadistic bounty hunter. This allegory was produced by David Frost's British production company for Paramount.

CHARLIE BOY

(IVE, 1980) **D:** Francis Megahy **S:** Bernie
Cooper, Francis Megahy   UK

Elvira introduces this 60-minute Hammer TV production about a British couple and an African voodoo idol. She also appears during a break and at the end to remind you how dull it is. With Leigh Lawson and Marius Goring.

CHARLY

(Fox, 1968) **D/P/A:** Ralph Nelson **S:** Sterling Silliphant

A mentally retarded Boston man (Cliff Robertson) who works at a bakery undergoes an operation to accelerate his brain development. It succeeds, and he falls in love with a social worker (Claire Bloom). He becomes an awkward genius and runs away for a while to be a hippie, but his independence is temporary. Based on the novel *Flowers for Algernon*, by Daniel Keyes, the film includes split-screen hippie sequences and music by Ravi Shankar. The cast includes Dick Van Patten. Robertson first played the role on TV in 1961. He developed the script, secured the financing, and received an Oscar for his efforts. He has wanted to make a sequel for many years, but *Awakenings* (1991), with Robert De Niro, probably put an end to those plans.

THE CHASE

(Vidmark, 1991) **D:** Paul Wendkos
S: Guerdon Trueblood

Casey Siemaszko is an escaped psycho bank robber in Denver. With Barry Corbin as a cop, Ben Johnson, Megan Follows, and Ricki Lake. It was made for TV.

THE CHASE

(1994) **D/S:** Adam Rifkin **P:** Brad
Wyman, Cassian Elwes

Charlie Sheen (also an executive producer) is an escaped con (he was framed) who hijacks a BMW, takes heiress Kristy Swanson hostage, and drives from San Diego to Tijuana. The cops and the media follow. With Ray Wise as the millionaire father, Josh Mostel, Cary Elwes, Marshall Bell, and Claudia Christian. The soundtrack is heavy metal, and musicians Henry Rollins and Anthony Kiedis also act. This PG-13 film from 20th Century–Fox was shot in Texas by the director of *The Dark Backward*.

CHASERS

(Warner, 1994) **D/A:** Dennis Hopper **S:** Joe Batteer,
John Rice, Dan Gilroy **P:** James G. Robinson

Tom Berenger and William McNamara are seamen assigned to transport a court-martialed sailor who turns out to be sexy Erika Eleniak. She has nude scenes, and uses disguises to try to escape. Another little-seen project of Hopper's, it has Gary Busey, Frederic Forrest, Seymour Cassel, Crispin Glover, Dean Stockwell, Marilu Henner, and Hopper himself in small roles. The comic action takes place on the southern Atlantic coast.

CHASTITY

(1969) **D:** Alessio de Paola **S/P/M:** Sonny Bono

After *Good Times* (1967), with Sonny, Cher made her solo starring debut in this R-rated movie when she was in between top-40 hits. She runs away from home, hitchhikes, encounters hookers, lesbians, and prostitutes, smokes pot, steals a car, goes to Mexico, pretends to be a hooker, and rips off a young would-be customer's money. She also reveals that she was a victim of childhood incest. It was rated R, then PG. With Barbara London, Stephen Whittaker, and Tom Nolan. The soundtrack is on Atco. The film was a flop, but the famous couple named their kid after it anyway. Cher didn't act in a feature again until *Come Back to the Five and Dime, Jimmy Dean, Jimmy Dean* (1982).

CHATO'S LAND

(MGM, 1972) **D/P:** Michael Winner
S: Gerald Wilson UK/Spain

Winner directed Charles Bronson for the first of many times in this post–Civil War western shot in Spain. He plays an Apache half-breed who speaks only two lines of English in the entire movie. Bounty hunters are after him for killing a sheriff, but he ends up pursuing and killing them. It was violent for a PG rating, and, typically for Bronson movies of the time, was a hit in Europe but was ignored in the US (where United Artists released it). With Jack Palance, Richard Basehart, Jill Ireland (Bronson's real-life wife), James Whitmore, Simon Oakland, Richard Jordan, and Ralph Waite.

CHATTAHOOCHEE

(HBO, 1990) **D:** Mick Jackson
S: James Hicks **P:** Aaron Schwab

Gary Oldman, as a Korean War vet returning to the South as a hero in the early 50s, becomes suicidal, shoots up the town, and ends up in a brutal insane asylum called Chattahoochee. He receives shock treatments there but attempts to expose the horrible conditions. Dennis Hopper and M. Emmet Walsh are fellow patients. With Frances McDormand, Pamela Reed, and Ned Beatty.

CHATTERBOX!

(Vestron, 1977) **D:** Tom De Simone
S: Mark Rosin **P:** Bruce Cohn Curtis

The inspiration for this AIP release was probably a French porno film called *Pussytalk* (or an American one called *Angel Above, Devil Below*). They're both about talking (and, in this case, singing) vaginas. Don't you miss the 70s? Candice Rialson (remembered for some Roger Corman drive-in hits) works at a beauty parlor owned by Rip Taylor. Her new voice gets her into trouble, making wisecracks to a lesbian at work and to her shrink. She goes on a TV show hosted by Professor Irwin Corey, "sings" naked on stage, has a hit record ("Wang Dang Doodle"), goes on tour, stars in a musical feature with chicken men, and makes the cover of *Time* magazine. *Chatterbox* features discos, a clip from that famous old "talking frog" cartoon, and too many painfully bad gags for any sober viewer to endure. The new songs were written by Neil Sedaka (!). Also with Larry Gelman (from *The Bob Newhart Show*). De Simone also made gay porno titles like *Good Hot Stuff* and several Linda Blair movies.

CHE!

(1969) **D/P:** Richard Fleischer **S:** Michael
Wilson, David Karp **S/P:** Sy Bartlett

Omar Sharif stars as Dr. Ernesto Guevara, who became the revolutionary Che Guevara, in a biographical feature with a pretty odd cast. He helps Castro overthow Batista in Cuba, tries to start a revolution in Boliva, and is shot in 1967, just two years before 20th Century–Fox released this much-hated M-rated feature. Actors playing characters who knew Guevara tell the story, talking to the camera. It was advertised with lines like, "With a dream of justice, he created a nightmare of violence!" Jack Palance is Castro! With Cesare Danova, Robert Loggia, Woody Strode, Barbara Luna, Abraham Sofaer, Sid Haig, Perry Lopez, Adolph Caesar, and director Jesús Franco as Sergeant Terraza(!). It was filmed in Puerto Rico and Malibu and has music by Lalo Schifrin.

CHEECH AND CHONG'S NEXT MOVIE

(MCA, 1980) **D/S/A:** Thomas Chong
S/A: Cheech Marin **P:** Howard Brown

The comedy team's follow-up to *Up in Smoke* has even less of a plot. There's plenty of pot humor, though, plus Evelyn Guerrero, "Mousie" Gardner, Michael Winslow, Bob and Edie McClurg, Missy Cleveland, Rikki Marin, future *Saturday Night Live* regular Phil Hartman, and future Pee-wee Herman Paul Reubens as a desk clerk. From Universal.

CHEECH AND CHONG'S NICE DREAMS

(RCA, 1981) **D/S/A:** Thomas Chong
S/A: Cheech Marin **P:** Howard Brown

The third Cheech and Chong hit has them selling pot from an ice-cream truck. Stacy Keach is the Sarge (back from *Up in Smoke*), Evelyn Guerrero costars again, and this time Paul Reubens is Howie Hamburger. With Timothy Leary (as himself), Cheryl "Rainbeaux" Smith, and Linnea Quigley. The Columbia release was shot by Brianne Murphy, the only female union director of photography in Hollywood at the time.

Cheech Marin and Tommy Chong in *Cheech and Chong's Nice Dreams.*

CHEECH AND CHONG'S THE CORSICAN BROTHERS

(Vestron, 1984) **D/S/A:** Thomas Chong
S/A: Cheech Marin **P:** Peter MacGregor-Scott

Drugs were left out of the last Cheech and Chong movie, a PG-rated period comedy shot in France. They play Alexandre Dumas' Corsican Brothers, who can feel each other's pain. With Roy Dotrice, Sophie Favier, Edie McClurg, and family members Rikki Marin, Rae Dawn Chong, and Robbie Chong. The team had also been in the historical comedy *Yellowbeard* (1983). After this they appeared in *After Hours*, then went their separate ways after being a team since 1970. From Orion (formerly AIP).

CHEERLEADER CAMP

(Prism, 1987) **D/P:** John Quinn **S:** David Lee Fein, R. L. O'Keefe **P:** Jeffrey Prettyman (*Bloody Pom Poms*)

Cheerleader Betsy Russell has nightmares about murders at a summer camp. A guy videotapes embarrassing moments for comedy relief, and campers start dying in various gory ways. Leif Garrett is the hero, and Lucinda Dickey is a mascot in an alligator costume. With Buck Flower, Karen Russell, and Teri Weigel and Rebecca Ferratti (from *Playboy*).

CHEERLEADERS' WILD WEEKEND

(Vestron, 1979) **D:** Jeff Werner **S:** D. W. Gilbert, Jason Williams **P:** Chuck Russell

Jason Williams (who was also the associate producer) and Christine DeBelle star in this sex comedy from Dimension. A busful of cheerleaders are kidnapped. Williams had starred in *Flesh Gordon*, and DeBelle was Alice in the X-rated *Alice in Wonderland*. With Tracy Ann King.

CHERRY, HARRY, AND RAQUEL!

(RM, 1969) **D/S/P/C:** Russ Meyer
S: "Thomas J. McGowan"/Tom Wolfe

The same man who wrote *The Right Stuff* scripted this violent, early, X-rated Russ Meyer hit. Charles Napier is lecherous, corrupt sheriff Harry Sledge, who runs drugs, has sex with the pot-smoking female stars, and engages in a bloody battle with a rival Indian pot-smuggler. Linda Ashton is Nurse Cherry, and Larissa Ely is Raquel, the mistress of bedridden narcotics king Mr. Franklin (Franklin Bolger). Raquel has sex with Harry, Cherry, and the dead Mr. Franklin. With Bert Santos and Uschi Digart as Soul in inserted comic scenes. A lesbian sequence shot in Meyer's pool was also added to expand the running time. Napier was also in three other forgotten "nudies" released in 1969. A soundtrack LP was released on the Beverly Hills label. This was Meyer's last indy film before making the classic *Beyond the Valley of the Dolls* and the tame *The Seven Minutes* (both at 20th Century–Fox).

CHERRY 2000

(Orion, 1985) **D:** Steve DeJarnatt
S: Michael Almereyda **P:** Edward R. Pressman, Caldecot Chubb

Melanie Griffith is a tough female tracker with an old red Mustang in the post-nuke year 2017. David Andrews hires her to go to the dangerous Zone Z and get important parts for his love robot, Cherry 2000 (Pamela Gidley). This overlooked feature has some amazing stunts worthy of the best James Bond movies, a good cast, and some effective, intentional humor, and it's one of the few original post–*Mad Max* movies around. Ben Johnson is Six Finger Jake, running an underground ferryboat, Tim Thomerson leads a suburban barbecue cult, and Brion James is a crook. Also with Michael C. Gwynne, Harry Carey Jr., Robert Z'Dar, Larry Fishburne, and special guests Gort and Robby. *Cherry 2000* was shot near Las Vegas and at Hoover Dam. This PG-13 feature wasn't released (by Orion) until 1988. The scriptwriter directed *Twister* (1989).

CHESTY ANDERSON, USN

(Program Hunter, 1975) **D:** Ed Forsyth
S/P: Paul Pompian **S:** H. F. Green, Henning Schellerup (*Anderson's Angels*)

Shari Eubank (*Super Vixens*) wants revenge after her sister is killed in a garbage chopper. She, Rosanne Katon, and two other WAVES who know kung fu go after Ace Garbage boss Frank Campanella. His underling (scene-stealing Timothy Carey in a silver jacket) sings and rants ("Buck, buck, buck"). Scatman Crothers sings and plays pool. There's very little nudity (Katon has a topless scene), but there is a dwarf bartender and a man-eating plant,

and you can see the microphone. Also look for Fred Willard as a corrupt senator's aide, Dyanne Thorne as a nurse, Uschi Digart, Nell Carter, and Betty Thomas (from *Hill Street Blues*).

CHEVY VAN

(1976) **D:** Sam Grossman **S:** Celia Susan Cotelo, Rob Rosenthal **P:** Paul Lewis (*The Van*)

Stuart Getz stars as a kid impressing girls with his customized van, in this dumb teen-sex comedy. With Deborah White, Stephen Oliver, Michael Lloyd, and Danny DeVito, who nobody could have predicted would become famous.

CHEYENNE WARRIOR

(New Horizons, 1994) **D:** Mark Griffiths
S: Michael B. Drunman **P:** Mike Elliott

When westerns returned in a big way, executive producer Roger Corman (who had started directing low-budget westerns in the 50s) offered this PG-13 film. Kelly Preston stars as a pregnant woman who is taken in by an injured Indian (Pato Hoffman) after her husband is killed. They fall in love. With Bo Hopkins, Rick Dean, Clint Howard, and Dan Haggerty.

THE CHICKEN CHRONICLES

(Nelson, 1977) **D:** Francis Simon **S:** Paul Diamond **P:** Walter Shenson

Steve Guttenberg, one of the most overused actors of all time, made his debut in this passable PG teen comedy. He works at a fast-food joint in late-60s Beverly Hills. With Phil Silvers, Ed Lauter, Lisa Reeves, Meredith Baer, and lots of top-40 hits (mostly on the Imperial label).

UN CHIEN ANDALOU

(1928) **D/S/P:** Luis Buñuel, Salvador Dali France

There are more incredible images in this 24-minute short than in just about any feature you could name. It caused scandals when it was new. It's the one that begins with an eyeball being sliced with a razor blade. Classical music is heard while a man drags two priests, two grand pianos, and two

Charles Napier as Harry in Russ Meyer's *Cherry, Harry, and Raquel!*

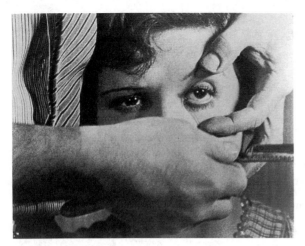

Buñuel's *Un Chien Andalou.*

dead donkeys. Some kids first saw it in the mid-70s when it was used to open David Bowie concerts. Buñuel and Dali (who later hated each other) also collaborated on *L'Age d'Or* (1930).

THE CHILD

(Best, 1977) **D:** Robert Voskanian
S: Ralph Luca **P:** Robert Dadashian
(*Kill and Go Hide!; Zombie Child*)

A little girl (Rosalie Cole) who lives in a remote home with her father can raise the dead and uses zombies from the nearby graveyard to kill the people she thinks killed her mother. Laurel Barnett is the new governess. The little girl dies with an axe in her head at the end. It was released by Boxoffice International.

CHILD BRIDE

(SW, 1937) **D:** Harry J. Revier
(*Child Bride of the Ozarks*)

In a backwards mountain community, the progressive schoolmarm, Miss Carol, crusades for a child-marriage law. Local men in hoods with torches tie her up and are about to tar and feather her during a weird lightning storm, but she's saved by the dwarf Angelo (Angelo Rossitto) and the simple-minded Happy, who work at a still. Meanwhile, Jake, the evil still owner, kills his partner and plans to marry the man's cute, very innocent, and very underage daughter, Jennie (Shirley Miles). All this would make a fine hillbilly exploitation movie, but this one goes an extra step further and includes a (still surprising) nude skinny-dipping sequence with Jennie, who looks maybe 12. The acting is awful, but I'm sure nobody complained. Revier also directed the serial *The Lost City* (1935) and the notorious *Lash of the Penitentes* (1936), which has scenes just like the teacher-in-peril scene here. *Child Bride* was a Kroger Babb presentation (presented on tape by David F. Friedman). Some sources claim it later played as *Dust to Dust*, with a reel showing the birth of a baby added. The tape includes two dozen choice trailers.

CHILD OF DARKNESS, CHILD OF LIGHT

(Paramount, 1991) **D:** Marinia Sargenti
S: Brian Taggert **P:** Paul Tucker

Two teenage girls (Sydney Penny and Kristin Datillo) mysteriously become pregnant. A Catholic priest says that one will have the son of God, the other the son of Satan. This USA Network movie is based on a novel by James Patterson. With Brad Davis, Paxton Whitehead, Viveca Lindfors, Sela Ward, and Anthony John Dension.

CHILD OF SATAN = TO THE DEVIL, A DAUGHTER

THE CHILDREN

(1990) **D:** Tony Palmer
S: Timberlake Wertenbaker **P:** Andrew Montgomery UK/W. Germany

What are exploitation greats Karen Black, Joe Don Baker, and Britt Ekland doing in this drama, based on a novel by Edith Wharton? Ben Kingsley stars as a man who has an affair with a teenage girl while planning to marry a widow (Kim Novak). With Geraldine Chaplin and Siri Neal. Filmed in Switzerland and Venice.

CHILDREN OF THE CORN

(New World, 1984) **D:** Fritz Kiersch **S:** George Goldsmith **P:** Donald Borchers, Terrence Kirby

I hated this senseless killer-kids movie, based on a Stephen King short story (from *Night Shift*). The only memorable scene is when the kids of a small Nebraska town slaughter all the adults after church one day. Peter Horton, as a doctor, and Linda Hamilton arrive in town several years later and have to fight for their lives. The kids sacrifice humans to some god in the fields, and something burrows under the dirt. John Franklin is the lead weird/scary kid, Isaac. With R. G. Armstrong and Courtney Gains. The Jonathan Elias soundtrack is on Varèse Sarabande. A better, student-made short version of the same story is available on the tape of *The Stephen King Night Shift Collection*.

CHILDREN OF THE CORN II: THE FINAL SACRIFICE

(Paramount, 1992) **D:** David Price **S:** A. L. Katz, Gilbert Adler **P:** Scott A. Stone, David G. Stanley

A kid (Paul Scherrer) and his divorced tabloid-journalist father (Terence Knox) go to a small town where "over 50" decomposed bodies have been discovered but the killer kids are free to stand around and stare. Kids attack a doctor with syringes and crush an old lady under a house, but the negative FX, POV stalking scenes, and computer-animation "void" scenes don't really cut it. Christie Clark and Rosalind Allen (also in Price's *Son of Darkness*) are the female love interests, Ryan Bollman is Micah (who eventually morphs into what looks like *The Hideous Sun Demon*), and Ned Romero is an American Indian anthropology professor who talks about Koyaanisqatsi (Hopi for "life out of balance"). It was shot in North Carolina. *Childen of the Corn III* followed.

CHILDREN OF THE FULL MOON

(Thriller, 1980) **D:** Tom Clegg **S:** Murray Smith UK

TV horror hostess Elvira introduces this one-hour Hammer "House of Horrors" TV production about a couple (Diana Dors and Robert Urquhart) whose car breaks down in the woods. They go to a mansion where the strange kids turn out to be werewolves.

CHILDREN OF THE NIGHT

(Columbia, 1991) **D:** Tony Randel **S:** Nicolas Falacci **P:** Christopher Webster

In a dark, dreary, misty, empty small town, a young priest keeps two female vampires (Karen Black and Maya McLaughlin) chained up in a room. They sleep covered with goo, eat leeches, and are controlled by a tall ex-priest/vampire with a mutant face (David Sawyer). The set of the submerged crypt under a church is interesting, but this movie is senseless and irritating. Top-billed Black gets to rant in her one scene. Ami Dolenz costars with Peter DeLuise, as a teacher. Garrett Morris drinks and preaches from a van with an electric cross on top. This Fangoria production was shot in Wisconsin and Michigan by the director of *Hellbound* (which didn't make any damn sense either). KNB handled the FX.

THE CHILDREN OF TIMES SQUARE

(Fries, 1986) **D/S:** Curtis Hanson **P:** Marcy Gross, Ann Weston

ABC-TV presented this exploitative look at Times Square runaways. With just a little swearing and nudity it could have played in Times Square, so I considered it a find on network TV. Howard Rollins Jr. is a coke dealer who leads kids astray, and Joanna Cassidy is a mother who arrives at the Port Authority bus terminal searching for her kid. With Griffin O'Neal, Joe Spinell, hookers, pornographers, and dealers.

CHILD'S PLAY

(MGM, 1988) **D/S:** Tom Holland **S:** Don Mancini, John Lafia **P:** David Kirschner

It's way too much like the old *Twilight Zone* episode "Talking Tina," but *Child's Play* caught on, thanks largely to a good TV ad campaign showing how much kids were scared by it and liked to yell ("Chucky! Chucky!"). Brad Dourif as murderer Charles Lee Ray doesn't last very long, but his soul and voice live on in a popular (and ugly) doll. All the kids want Good Guy dolls, and when Alex Vincent as six-year-old Andy gets the possessed one, the trouble stars. This doll talks, walks, kills, and makes wisecracks. Although sometimes a mechanical device, Chucky is mostly played by Ed Gale. The ending, with Catherine Hicks as the mom battling the seemingly indestructible evil-killer doll, is a lot like the doll segment of *Trilogy of Terror*. With Chris Sarandon as a Chicago cop and Dinah Manoff. Holland also directed *Fright Night*. Chucky merchandise was available for real kids to own, which seems even more demented than Freddy Krueger dolls. The producer is the head of Hanna Barbera cartoons(!).

CHILD'S PLAY 2

(MCA, 1990) **D:** John Lafia **S:** Dan Mancini **P:** David Kirschner

MGM/UA passed on making a sequel, so Universal got the rights. Little Alex Winter returns, trying in vain to warn people in Chicago about Chucky, the killer doll. Gerrit Graham and Jenny Agutter, as his foster parents, and Grace Zabriske all show up, just to be killed off. Busy Brad Dourif's voice is used for Chucky's wisecracks again. Scenes of the doll doing horrible things are either scary or pretty hilarious, depending on the mood of the viewer. The best part is a suspenseful end sequence set in an automated factory turning out more Chuckies.

CHILD'S PLAY 3

(MCA, 1991) **D:** Jack Binder **S:** Don Mancini, **P:** David Kirschner, Robert Latham Brown, Laura Moskowitz

Now 16 years old, Andy (Justin Whalin) is at military school, still haunted by what happened before. For some reason, a new Chucky doll tries to possess a tiny, childish black cadet (Jeremy Silvers). With Andrew Robinson as a military barber, and the voice of Brad Dourif. It was partially filmed in Missouri. A pretty good concept went downhill real fast. The ad line for this useless entry was "Don't fuck with the Chuck." In England in 1994, this tape was blamed for the real-life murder of a child by two older children.

CHILLER

(Edde, 1985) **D:** Wes Craven **S/P:** J. D. Feigelson

Michael Beck returns after being frozen for 10 years, but he's without a soul and does creepy things. With Beatrice Straight, Paul Sorvino, Laura Johnson, and Jill Schoelen. It was the third TV movie by the director of *The Last House on the Left* and debuted on CBS. Craven directed episodes of the revived *Twilight Zone* the same year. FX by Stan Winston.

CHILLERS

(Troma, 1988) **D/S/P/E:** Daniel Boyd

Five people miss their Ohio Valley bus and spend time at the station telling each other scary tales. It's a very well made, serious horror anthology filmed in South Charleston, West Virginia. A girl has an affair with a guy she met at an indoor pool (they have sex in the shower), but he's really a scary-looking ghost with white eyes and a deep head wound. In my favorite story, a kid tells about a camping trip where the wimpy adult leader turns out to be a scary, crazy killer. A woman has an encounter with a TV newsman/vampire. A young guy can wish dead people listed in newspaper memorials ads back to life. A professor tells about a female student who was possessed by an Indian spirit. The characters all come together in a fun, *Dead of Night*–inspired, bus-to-hell ending. All the stories have clever plot twists, and the music (some songs sound like Lou Reed) and FX are mostly top-notch. The 33-year-old director, from Martinsburg, West Virginia, previously

made documentaries and was a professor of communication at West Virginia State College. Troma picked this up for release.

THE CHILLING (1972) = DEATHDREAM

THE CHILLING

(Hemdale, 1989) **D:** Deland Nuse **D/S/P:** Jack A. Sunseri

This time Linda Blair assists a doctor (Troy Donahue) in a cryogenics lab in Kansas City. The intro asks, "Would God approve, or is this Satan's work?" Troy has been stealing organs from the frozen bodies to sell. On Halloween, lightning strikes each corpse separately at midnight, and green cannibal/zombies with glowing eyes start walking. The laughable zombies are wrapped in tin foil. Dan Haggerty is a heroic security guard. Subplots involve Linda's alcoholic boyfriend and a Nam vet holdup man who has sex in a shower with his girlfriend. The acting is unusually bad.

CHIMES AT MIDNIGHT

(1966) **D/S/A:** Orson Welles **P:** Emiliano Piedra, Angel Tasca   Spain/Switzerland (*Campanadas a Medianoche; Falstaff*)

Orson Welles is excellent as the large, corrupt Sir John Falstaff, in another of his neglected must-see classics. It's based on parts of five Shakespeare plays and was shot in b/w in Spain. The bloody scenes of senseless battles are some of the best ever shot and were done by second-unit director Jesús Franco. Keith Baxter is Prince Hal, with Sir John Gielgud as King Henry IV, Margaret Rutherford, Jeanne Moreau, and Fernando Rey. The narration is by Sir Ralph Richardson. The complete running time is 119 minutes. Sadly, it was Welles's last completed fictional feature.

CHINA GIRL

(Vestron, 1987) **D:** Abel Ferrara **S:** Nicholas St. John **P:** Michael Nozik

A Romeo and Juliet story set in New York City's Chinatown and Little Italy was a pretty good (if unrealistic) idea. *China Girl* has gangsters and good fight scenes staged in real streets (not on sets, like *Year of the Dragon*). Richard Panebianco and Sari Chang star as the young lovers, with James Russo, Russell Wong, James Hong, and David Caruso (later the star of *NYPD Blue*).

CHINA 9, LIBERTY 37

(VSOM, 1978) **D/P:** Monte Hellman **S:** Douglas Venturelli   Italy/Spain (*Clayton and Catherine*)

Fabio Testi stars in this western as Clayton Drumm, a gunman who is saved from hanging if he'll kill a landowner/gunman (Warren Oates) for the railroad. He invites himself in and takes off with Oates' young wife, Catherine (Jenny Agutter) instead. They join a midget at the circus and drink a cocaine remedy. With Helga Line and Sam Peckinpah, who shows up as a journalist. The score is by Pino Donaggio. Hellman's next was *Iguana* (1988).

CHINA O'BRIEN

(Imperial, 1988) **D/S:** Robert Clouse **P:** Fred and Sandra Weintraub

Blond 5'3" Cynthia Rothrock (from Scranton, Pennsylvania) became a high-kicking kung-fu star in Hong Kong before returning home to star in a series of features. Here she's an ex-cop/martial-arts teacher who returns to Utah to help her sheriff father battle drug-dealer gangsters. With Richard Norton as the secondary martial-arts fighter. In better days, Clouse had directed Bruce Lee, Jackie Chan, and Jim Kelly movies. Rothrock also made an instructional tape, *Defend Yourself*.

CHINA O'BRIEN II

(Imperial, 1989) **D:** Robert Clouse **S:** James Hennessy, Craig Clyde **P:** Fred and Sandra Weintraub

Small-town sheriff China O'Brien (Cynthia Rothrock) and Matt (Richard Norton) are after a drug lord (Harlow Marks) who escaped from prison. It was released directly to video in 1992.

THE CHINA SYNDROME

(RCA/Columbia, 1979) **D/S:** James Bridges **S:** T. S. Cook, Mike Gray **P/A:** Michael Douglas

Incredibly, this influential message thriller (without a music score) opened just before the Three Mile Island "Incident" in Pennsylvania. When the cooling system in a California nuke plant fails, there's a cover-up. A TV news reporter (Jane Fonda) and a cameraman (Michael Douglas) convince corporate-executive Jack Lemmon of the danger. Fonda and Lemmon received Oscar nominations. With Scott Brady, James Karen, and Wilford Brimley. By the director of *Colossus: The Forbin Project* (1979).

CHINATOWN

(Paramount, 1974) **D/A:** Roman Polanski **S:** Robert Towne **P:** Robert Evans

Polanski made only two American features, *Rosemary's Baby* and *Chinatown*. Both are classics, but this brilliant, complex, 131-minute thriller set in 30s LA is one of the best films of the 70s. Jack Nicholson, as J. J. Gittes, and Faye Dunaway, as Evelyn Mulray, both were nominated for Oscars. John Huston is very convincing as Noah Cross. With Perry Lopez, John Hillerman, Diane Ladd, Dick Bakalyan, Burt Young, Bruce Glover, and James Hong. Screenwriter Towne, who received an Oscar, had started with Roger Corman movies. He worked (uncredited) on *Bonnie and Clyde* and *The Godfather*. Set director Rube Levitt had worked on the TV series *The Addams Family*. Nicholson himself directed the much-delayed and unpopular sequel, *The Two Jakes* (1990), also written by Towne.

CHINATOWN AFTER DARK

(Sinister, 1931) **D:** Staurt Patton **S:** Betty Burbidge **P:** Ralph M. Link

Madame Ling Yu (Carmel Myers), a San Francisco Chinatown dragon lady, kills for a dagger with a valuable ruby on its handle. The hero is Rex Rease and the cast inludes Barbara Kent as Lotus and

Billy Gilbert as a comical police captain. This rare, short (59-minute), early-talkie mystery was made by Action Pictures.

CHINATOWN MURDERS: MAN AGAINST THE MOB

(Vidmark, 1989) **D/P:** Robert Pressman
S: Michael Petryn

George Peppard stars as an honest 40s LA cop, and Ursula Andress plays a whorehouse owner. The plot of this TV movie concerns waterfront gangs and "white slavery." With Charles Haid, Richard Bradford, Jason Beghe, Joe Tornatore, Julia Nickson, and James Pax.

THE CHINESE CONNECTION

(Fox, 1971) **D/S/A:** Lo Wei   Hong Kong (*Fist of Fury*)

In 1908, when Shanghai is occupied by the Japanese, Bruce Lee seeks revenge (and uses disguises) after his teacher is killed. He beats a whole school of Japanese fighters and one Russian villain. In a famous scene, Lee kicks apart a sign reading, "No dogs or Chinese allowed." It was Lee's second starring feature and broke records in Hong Kong. Nora Miao costars. The dubbing was done in England. The importers of this film somehow switched titles with his first one and called it *Fists of Fury*. By the time most Americans saw the film, the screen's first international kung-fu star was dead at 33. *New Fists of Fury* (1976), a sequel with some of the same actors, starred Jackie Chan.

A CHINESE GHOST STORY

(1987) **D:** Ching Siu-Tung **S:** Yuen
Kai Chi **P:** Claudie Chung

Look for this atmospheric medieval-fantasy hit with brilliant camera work. Ning (Leslie Cheung) is a bumbling monk in love with the ghost Sian (Wang Tsu Hsien/Joey Wang). To please her he has to face decapitated heads, sceaming skulls, and an androgynous tree-spirit demon that becomes a giant life-sucking tongue. Tsui Hark was the executive producer. Only the UK version has English subtitles. As with most hits, there were sequels and many ripoffs.

CHINESE GHOST STORY II

(1990) **D:** Ching Siu-Tung **S:** Lau
Tai-Mok, Kan Keito **P:** Tsui Hark

A monk (Leslie Cheung) is jailed, then teams up with a Taoist magician (Jacky Cheung) to battle a rock demon. Joey Wang is a reincarnation of the original ghost. It was the biggest hit in Asia at the time and has even more slapstick and action and FX than the first movie. It opens with scenes from the original.

A CHINESE GHOST STORY III

(1991) **D:** Ching Siu-Tung **S/P:** Tsui Hark

The story is the same as in *I* but takes place 100 years later. This time Tony Leung is the comic young Buddhist monk, with Joey Wang as the female ghost. The tree demon also returns. Jacky Cheung plays a different role. As in all these features, there are a lot of FX.

CHITTY CHITTY BANG BANG

(1968) **D/S:** Ken Hughes **S:** Roald
Dahl **P:** Albert Broccoli   UK/US

This 145-minute, Super Panavision 70mm, G-rated musical fantasy based on a novel by Ian Fleming was a commercial flop but remains a favorite of some people who saw it as kids. Dick Van Dyke stars, with his flying car, and Sally Ann Howes is Truly Scrumptious. Also with Lionel Jeffries, Gert Frobe, Anna Quayle, and Benny Hill. This UA release was filmed in Britain, France and West Germany.

THE CHOCOLATE WAR

(Forum, 1988) **D/S:** Keith Gordon
P: Jonathan D. Krane

The star of *Christine* directs for the first time. John Glover plays the dictatorial headmaster of an all-boys Catholic high school with a secret society called the Vigils. This black-comedy/drama, based on Robert Cormier's novel, features Ilan Mitchell-Smith, Bud Cort, Adam Baldwin, and Jenny Wright.

A CHOICE OF WEAPONS

(Paragon, 1975) **D:** Kevin Connor **S:** Julian Bond,
Steve Rossen **P:** Fred Weintraub, Paul Heller
UK (*Trial by Combat; A Dirty Knight's Work*)

In a film with a plot much like an *Avengers* episode, David Birney investigates the murder of his father (Peter Cushing) with the help of a retired police commissioner (John Mills). Cushing had been the leader of the Order of Avalon, modern-day knights in armor, taken over by Donald Pleasence, who has them execute escaped criminals. The cast includes Barbara Hershey, Margaret Leighton, and Brian Glover. Pleasence and Cushing were also in *Land of the Minotaur* the same year.

CHOKE CANYON

(Media, 1986) **D:** Chuck Bail
S/P: Ovidio G. Assonitis **S:** Sheila
Goldberg, Alfonso Brescia
(*On Dangerous Ground*)

Stephen Collins is a cowboy/physicist fighting a corrupt industrialist dumping nuclear waste. To save the planet, he has to conduct sound/energy experiments in a canyon at the exact time that Haley's comet passes. With Lance Henriksen, Bo Svenson, and Nicholas Pryor. The PG movie, filmed in Utah, has lots of action and great stuntwork but is pretty silly.

CHOPPER CHICKS IN ZOMBIETOWN

(RCA, 1988) **D/S:** Dan Hoskins
P: Maria Snyder   (*Chrome Hearts*)

The plot of this one is female bikers vs. zombies, and it's a good horror spoof. Don Calfa (from *Return of the Living Dead*) as a mad doctor/funeral director turns townspeople into cannibal zombies with the reluctant assistance of a tiny dwarf (Ed Gale, who could be the Michael Dunn of the 90s). The biker heroines include Catherine Carlen (who's great and also sings), Jamie Rose (from *Falcon Crest*), and Vicki Frederick. They save a bus full of cynical, blind orphans who help them knock the heads off the attacking zombies and lure them into a church with raw meat. Martha Quinn (from MTV) plays a local woman. Ed French provided the FX. The hip soundtrack features Alex Chilton, Camper Van Beethoven, and the Panther Burns. The great title song at the end is by the DBs. Released by Troma.

THE CHOPPERS

(Fang, 1961) **D:** Leigh Jason **S/P/A:** Arch Hall Sr.

Five jive-talking teens ride in a poultry truck and totally strip down cars. All (including Torch and Flip) are introduced by the narrator (Arch Hall) at the beginning. Jack "Cruiser" Bryan (16-year-old Arch Hall Jr., making his debut) the leader, sings the classic "Kongo Joe," "Monkey in My Hat Band," and other songs. The gang even steals hubcaps in broad daylight while a couple makes out in their car at the Chick-a-Dolly Drive-In ("Tacos 15¢"). A cop and an insurance agent are after them, and it all ends with a shootout at the junkyard. Hall also narrated. The gorgeous Marianne Gaba (*Playboy*'s Miss September, 1959) is Liz, the insurance man's helpful assistant. Bruno Ve Sota is the comic-relief stolen-parts dealer Big Moose (he had played a similar role in *Hot Car Girl*). Arch's last line is "We had a ball!" He returned in *Wild Guitar* and *The Sadist*. All of them are highly recommended!

CHOPPING MALL

(Vestron, 1986) **D/S:** Jim Wynorski **S:** Steve
Mitchell **P:** Julie Corman   (*Kilbots; R.O.B.O.T*)

Overage "teens" partying in a shopping mall at night are trapped inside and picked off by three out-of-control robot guards with killer laser beams. The movie features brief in-joke cameos from Roger Corman actors like Dick Miller, Paul Bartel, Mary Woronov, and Mel Welles and topless scenes by the female stars, Kelli Maroney, Barbara Crampton, and Suzanne Slater. With John Terlesky, Gerrit Graham, and Angela Aames (who died in 1988). From Concorde.

Roman Polanski about to slice Jack Nicholson's nose open in *Chinatown*.

THE CHRISTIAN LICORICE STORE

(1969) **D:** James Frawley **S/P:** Floyd Mutrix

Beau Bridges is a tennis champ who becomes corrupted in Hollywood. With Maud Adams and Cindy Williams in their first roles, veteran actor Gilbert Roland, Allen Arbus, McLean Stevenson, Barbara Leigh, Talia Shire, Greg Mullavey, Anne Randall, and the late Tim Buckley performing the incredible "Pleasant Street" (the film's title comes from the lyrics). Directors Monte Hellman, James B. Harris, and Theodore J. Flicker also appear. It was the first film by Frawley and was released (with sex scenes cut out) in 1971 by National General. Mutrix also wrote *Two-Lane Blacktop*.

CHRISTIANE F.

(Media, 1981) **D:** Ulrich Edel **S:** Hermann Weigel **P:** Bernd Eichinger, Hans Weth   W. Germany

Corman's New World released this excellent drug movie in the US. It stars Nadja Brunkhorst as the (real) Christiane F., a West Berlin girl who turns to prostitution to support her junk habit. It's pretty grim and long (124 minutes), but since the girl is a Bowie fan, his music (which had been recorded in Berlin) is put to good use, and he appears in some concert footage. The excellent all-Bowie soundtrack is on RCA. One effective scene has a mostly wasted audience in a theater showing *Night of the Living Dead*. Dubbed and subtitled versions played in American theatres. The same team later made *Last Exit to Brooklyn*.

CHRISTINE

(RCA, 1983) **D:** John Carpenter **S:** Bill Phillips **P:** Richard Kobritz

Keith Gordon plays Arnie, a misfit student in a small California town whose possessed 1958 red Plymouth Fury, named Christine, plays only old rock hits. The car somehow makes him cool, kills his enemies, and can reassemble itself. It was one of three movies based on Stephen King books that were released in 1983. With John Stockwell, Alexandra Paul, Harry Dean Stanton, Roberts Blossom, Robert Prosky, and Kelly Preston. The special effects and the music of this Columbia release are better than the story. The soundtrack is on Motown.

THE CHRISTINE JORGENSEN STORY

(VSOM, 1970) **D:** Irving Rapper **S:** Robert E. Kent **P:** Edward Small

United Artists released this melodramatic R-rated biography of George Stevenson Jr., who went to Denmark and became Christine Jorgensen (who was also the inspiration for *Glen or Glenda*). Most viewers agree that star John Hansen seems more like a drag queen than a transsexual. The cast includes young Pamelyn Ferdin (later in *The Toolbox Massacre*), Stuart Erwin, Joyce Meadows, and Svetlana (later a porno director). It was written by the same man who gave us *The Fastest Guitar Alive* and *Hot Rods to Hell*. In 1991 it was part of a clever cable-TV double bill with *Homicidal*.

A CHRISTMAS CAROL

(MGM, 1938) **D:** Edwin L Marin **S:** Hugo Butler **P:** Joseph L. Mankiewicz

Dickens' famous tale had been filmed many times, but this was the first American sound version. Reginald Owen (a one-time Sherlock Holmes) stars as Scrooge, with Leo G. Carroll as Marley's ghost, Ann Rutherford as the ghost of Christmas present, Gene Lockhart as Bob Cratchit, Kathleen Lockhart as Mrs. Cratchit, and their real-life daughter June as their daughter. The MGM release (which was rereleased every Christmas for years) is only 69 minutes long. It was later colorized.

A CHRISTMAS CAROL

(United, 1951) **D/P:** Brian Desmond-Hurst **S:** Noel Langley   UK (*Scrooge*)

Nearly everyone agrees that this is the best, darkest version of the famous story. Alastair Sim stars as Scrooge, with George Cole as young Scrooge, Michael Hordern as Marley's ghost, Mervyn Johns as Bob Cratchit, Hermione Baddeley as Mrs. Cratchit, Kathleen Harrison, Jack Warner, Miles Malleson, Ernest Thesiger, Peter Bull (who also narrates), and Patrick Macnee as young Marley. United Artists released it in the US. It was later colorized.

A CHRISTMAS CAROL

(1984) **D:** Clive Donner **S:** Roger Hirson **P:** William Storke, Alfred Kelman   UK

George C. Scott stars as Scrooge in this atmospheric version of the Dickens classic. The British cast includes Frank Finlay as Marley's ghost, David Warner and Susannah York as the Cratchits, Angela Pleasence as the ghost of Christmas past, Edward Woodward as the ghost of Christmas present, Michael Carter as the ghost of Christmas future, and Lucy Gutteridge. It debuted on CBS-TV. *An American Christmas Carol* (1979) is an updated version from ABC-TV starring Henry Winkler. A British musical version is called *Scrooge* (1970).

CHRISTMAS EVIL

(Genesis, 1980) **D/S:** Lewis Jackson **P:** Burt Kleiner, Peter Kameron
(*You Better Watch Out; Terror In Toyland*)

A toy-factory asembly-line boss (Brandon Maggart) thinks he is Santa. He's been obsessed with Christmas and Christmas things since he saw his mom having sex with "Santa" as a kid. The madman even keeps lists of the neighbor kids who are naughty and nice, and he kills while dressed as Santa, humming "Santa Claus Is Coming to Town." It's very cheap but better than the later *Silent Night, Deadly Night*. A police lineup of Santas is one memorable image. It was rereleased in 1983.

A CHRISTMAS STORY

(MGM, 1983) **D/S/P:** Bob Clark **S:** Leigh Brown, Jean Sheperd **P:** Rene Dupont   Canada

Even if you hate Christmas movies (and with a few exceptions, you should) this one, based on part of Jean Shepherd's *In God We Trust, All Others Pay Cash*, (and narrated by the author) is a must. It's irreverent, funny, rude, and nostalgic. Ralphie (Peter Billingsley), growing up in an American city in the 40s (parts were filmed in Cleveland), wants a Red Ryder BB gun for Christmas. All the confusing and scary events are seen through his eyes, including a nightmarelike visit to a department-store Santa (Jeff Gillen). Another memorable scene shows a schoolkid whose tongue gets stuck on a frozen pole. Darren McGavin is great as "the old man," and Melinda Dillon is the mother. Clark made *Porky's II* the same year, but don't let that stop you.

CHROME AND HOT LEATHER

(Orion, 1971) **D:** Lee Frost **S:** Michael Allen Haynes, David Neibel, Don Tair **P:** Wes Bishop

Tony Young stars as a Green Beret out to get the bikers who killed his fiancé. He gets help from his Special Services friends, including Motown great Marvin Gaye (in his first and last acting role) as a soldier with an ascot who rides a motorcycle. Biker-movie veterans William Smith and Peter Brown costar (both had been in the *Laredo* TV series). With screenwriter Haynes

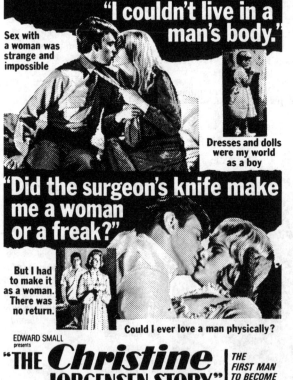

Sex with a woman was strange and impossible

"I couldn't live in a man's body."

Dresses and dolls were my world as a boy

"Did the surgeon's knife make me a woman or a freak?"

But I had to make it as a woman. There was no return.

Could I ever love a man physically?

EDWARD SMALL presents
"THE *Christine* JORGENSEN STORY" | THE FIRST MAN TO BECOME A WOMAN

introducing JOHN HANSEN Screenplay by ROBERT E. KENT and ELLIS ST. JOSEPH
Based on the book by CHRISTINE JORGENSEN Directed by IRVING RAPPER Produced by EDWARD SMALL

(a stuntman who later became the Marlboro Man) and Larry Bishop (Joey's son). And look for Cheryl Ladd, Dan Haggerty, and Erik Estrada. The AIP release was rated PG.

CHROME HEARTS: *See* C. C. AND COMPANY

CHROME SOLDIERS
(Paramount, 1992) **D:** Thomas J. Wright
S: Nick Ranall **P:** Derek Kavanaugh

In a clichéd 70s plot, three Nam-vet buddies (the late Ray Sharkey, Yaphet Kotto, and Nicholas Guest) join Desert Storm vet Gary Busey in small-town Oregon to avenge the murder of his brother. They all ride motorcycles (with helmets) and uncover a deadly marijuana-business plot. William Atherton is the sheriff. The movie debuted on the USA Network.

CHUCK BERRY: HAIL! HAIL! ROCK 'N' ROLL
(MCA, 1987) **D:** Taylor Hackford **P:** Stephanie Bennett

A special St. Louis Fox Theater concert in 1986 (just before Berry's 60th birthday) is shown in this two-hour film, along with interviews (Little Richard, Bo Diddley, Jerry Lee Lewis, Roy Orbison, the Everly Brothers) and backstage problems. The excellent concert, produced by Keith Richards, features a band led by Richards (who was trying to pay back the difficult Berry for ripping off all his guitar licks) and Etta James, Eric Clapton, Robert Cray, Linda Rondstadt, and Julian Lennon. Universal released the film and the soundtrack album. Chuck Berry also hosts *Born To Rock* (Music Media, 1984), a condensed version of *The TAMI Show* and *The Big TNT Show*.

CHUCK'S CHOICE CUTS
(Admit One)   Canada

If you can find a copy of this ahead-of-its-time tape, you'll be glad. Chuck was an early-80s Toronto cable-TV host who pretended to be a security guard playing parts of the station's vast collection of trash-culture tapes after hours. This compilation features some amazing 60s juke-box videos, choice trailers, and film scenes.

C.H.U.D.
(Media, 1984) **D:** Douglas Cheek
S: Parnell Hall **P:** Andrew Bonhime

Homeless people living in the sewers of New York City have become monsters (Cannibalistic Humanoid Underground Dwellers) because of toxic waste. This attempt to do something a bit different was shot on location, but it doesn't work and has below-par FX (by Ed French and John Gaglione). John Heard stars as a photographer. Daniel Stern overacts as a minister running a soup kitchen. With Laurie Mattos and Kim Greist (*Brazil*). New World (and Tony Randall) messed with it a lot by adding humorous narration and cutting out nearly 20 minutes, including a massacre in a diner that was later restored in the TV version. John Goodman is in the TV version only.

C.H.U.D. II: BUD THE CHUD
(Vestron, 1989) **D:** David Irving
S: Ed Naha **P:** Jonathan Krane

This teen-zombie comedy takes place on Halloween and has no relation to the first film at all. Students steal the corpse of zombie-cannibal Bud (Gerrit Graham), created by the army. More zombies, created by bites, invade a small town and a Halloween party. The young heroes somehow manage to freeze the zombies in a swimming pool. Many guest stars show up briefly, and most become zombies too. With Robert Vaughn, Tricia Leigh Fisher, Bianca Jagger, June Lockhart, Norman Fell, Rich Hall, Jack Riley, Clive Revill, Priscilla Pointer (the director's mother), Rich Hall, Larry Linville, and Robert Englund.

THE CHURCH
(Southgate, 1988) **D:** Michele Soavi **S/P:** Dario Argento **S:** Franco Ferrini **P:** Mario and Vittorio Cecchi Gori   Italy (*La Chiesa*)

Originally planned as *Demons III*, this film starts with an interesting historical prologue showing Teutonic knights slaughtering "witches" in a pit sealed with a big cross, where a huge Gothic cathedral will later stand. As in the *Demons* movies, most of the action takes place in one haunted location where people are trapped and killed, but *Church* is a lot slower, more serious, and (at 102 minutes) maybe too long. The church, filled with tourists, priests, and a fashion-magazine camera crew, seals itself (as in *Land of the Pharoahs*). Argento's daughter Asia stars as Lotte, the caretaker's young daughter, the only character who knows how to escape. The cast also includes John Richardson. The dead rise again, a demon is seen briefly (in a *Rosemary's Baby*–inspired scene), and other things that don't necessarily make any sense happen, but it all looks impressive. Wish we could have seen it in a theater. The cinematography, art direction, and music (by Keith Emerson and Goblin, with themes written by Philip Glass) are all typically excellent. Filmed in Rome, Hamburg and Budapest, it's available in an unrated and a slightly edited R-rated letterboxed version. Argento and 33-year-old Soavi made *The Devil's Daughter* next.

CIA: CODE NAME ALEXA
(PM, 1992) **S/P:** Joseph Merhi **P:** Richard Pepin

Lorenzo Lamas stars as a CIA agent who works out of a sewage plant where kung-fu teams are trained. His real-life wife, Kathleen Kinmont, plays a kickboxing international terrorist (called "a Rambo bitch") who becomes his lover and helps stop her psycho boss (Alex Cord) from achieving world conquest. O. J. Simpson plays an LA police detective, which gave this movie a rental boost in 1994.

CIA II: TARGET ALEXA
(PM, 1994) **D/A:** Lorenzo Lamas
P: Richard Pepin, Joseph Merhi

Lamas and Kinmont team up to stop John Savage from selling a nuclear guidance system to North Korea. The two stars were divorced in 1994, but continued to act together. With Pamela Dixon and John Ryan. Kinmont returned in *C.I.A. 3: Nation Under Siege* (1994).

CINDERELLA
(Vestron, 1977) **D:** Michael Pataki
S: Frank Ray Perill **P:** Charles Band

This X-rated sex/musical comedy at least is better than most similar 70s movies. Cheryl "Rainbeaux" Smith stars, with Sy Richardson as the "fairy" godmother, Kirk Scott, Mariwin Roberts, and Linda Gildersleeve. The video is (or was) available in R or unrated versions. Pataki, usually an actor, had directed *Mansion of the Doomed* (1975). Al Adamson's awful *Cinderella 2000* was released the same year.

CINDY AND DONNA
(1970) **D/P:** Robert J. Anderson
S: Barry Clark **P:** Terry Anderson

Crown International didn't usually release X-rated movies, but this one received the dreaded rating. Debbie Osborne and Nancy Ison star as suburban teenage half-sisters who experience sex, drugs, and more sex.

CINEMACABRE TV TRAILERS
(Cinemacabre)

Since we all spent more time watching TV than sitting in theaters, these two tapes bring back more memories than theatrical-trailer tapes. They cram in dozens of collectible spots for sci-fi and horror movies, always different from the ones seen in theaters and lasting from 20 to 60 seconds. Many have silent endings, so that the local-station voice-over could tell you where the movie was playing. Some are reissues (especially kid-appeal fantasy movies from MGM). The all-b/w tape (50s/60s) runs 84 minutes It features lots of Hammer, Toho, AIP, Corman, Castle, and K. Gordon Murray titles. "See *Them!*" and "*Psycho* is back!" (rated M) are two great campaigns. The all-color tape (some 60s, lots of 70s) runs 110 minutes. It includes some great Bava, Argento, Harryhausen, and Hitchcock hits, Amicus and Hammer double bills, and more major-studio releases than the b/w tape. With *Barbarella*, *Spirits of the Dead*, *The Ghost and Mr. Chicken*, *Chamber of Horrors*, *Deranged*, and *Flesh Gordon* and *Witchcraft '70* (two X-rated features!).

CIRCLE OF FEAR
(1989) **D:** Clark Henderson **S:** Frederic Bailey **P:** Isabel Sumayo   Philippines

Patrick Dollaghan (imitating Michael Douglas) stars as a Nam vet who searches for his kidnapped daughter and finds out that she's been sold as a sex slave in Manila. With Wesley Pfenning and Vernon Wells. A Concorde release.

CIRCUITRY MAN

(RCA, 1990) **D/S:** Steven Lovy **S:** Robert Lovy **P:** Steven Reich, John Schouweiler

In the near future, a tough bodyguard turned clothing designer named Lori (Dana Wheeler-Nicholson) ends up on the run with Danner (Jim Meltzer), a handsome, suicidal pleasure-droid with a ponytail. They attempt to drive from LA to New York in a 1964 Galaxy, mostly through an underground-garage tunnel. They're pursued by or betrayed by the lurking, bald Plughead (Vernon Wells, from *Road Warrior*, who is excellent); Juice (Lu Leonard), a big, ugly female gangster; Yo-Yo, a tough blonde with two goons; a pair of bumbling cops; Leech (Dennis Christopher), a filthy mechanic from New Jersey; and Japanese biker bandits. Topside, they need oxygen tubes and visit the Last Gasp Cafe, an air stop. Sure, some of this sounds silly or derivative, but *Circuitry Man* is a clever, sometimes funny, well-made science-fiction adventure (and love story). The cinematography, acting, and special effects are all top-notch, the plot moves are not predictable, and the tape is letterboxed. It's a lot more fun than *Hardware*, for instance, or *Total Recall*. The songs are sung by Deborah Holland. The executive producer was Miles Copeland (IRS Records), who at least did something worthwhile with all that Police money.

CIRCUITRY MAN II

(Columbia, 1994) **D/S:** Steve Lovy **S:** Robert Lovy **P:** Stephen Reich

The leads return in an almost plotless, sometimes funny comedy sequel from I. R. S. An FBI agent (Deborah Shelton, who has a topless scene) forces Danner the droid (Jim Melzler, who has flashbacks) to go with her to a desert work camp to stop Plughead (Vernon Wells) from more killing. Leech (Dennis Christopher) and an idiot mute

Vernon Wells as Plughead in *Circuitry Man*.

(Nicholas Worth) escape together. With a pair of stupid bounty hunters, Buck Flower as a guard, Judy Tenuta, and Traci Lords (as a scientist named Norma). Worth gets the last laugh.

CISCO PIKE

(1972) **D/S:** Bill L. Norton **P:** Gerald Ayers

Singer Kris Kristofferson, in his first acting role, stars as a rocker forced to deal heroin by a crooked cop (Gene Hackman). Karen Black costars, with Harry Dean Stanton, Allen Arbus, Roscoe Lee Browne, Antonio Fargas, and Severn Darden. In one scene Kristofferson goes to bed with Joy Bang and Viva. The Sir Douglas Quintet and Sonny Terry are heard on the soundtrack.

CITIZENS BAND

(Paramount,1977) **D:** Jonathan Demme **S:** Paul Brickman **P:** Shep Fields   (*Handle with Care*)

Spider (Paul Le Mat), runs a southwestern CB shop and emergency-rescue service. Many subplots and interesting characters helped make this PG comedy a critical favorite. With Candy Clark, Marcia Rodd, Ann Wedgeworth, Bruce McGill, Demme regular Charles Napier (funny as "the Chrome Angel"), Roberts Blossom, and Ed Begley Jr. Paramount cut, retitled, and rereleased it in an attempt to reach a larger audience. Songs by Richie Havens, Joe Cocker, and others are heard.

CITIZEN TANYA

(Provisional, 198?) **D/S/P:** Raymond Pettibon **D/A:** Dave Markey

This seemingly endless (it's 87 minutes) talk-filled tape stars Shannon Smith as Patty Hearst. She's kidnapped and becomes revolutionized. Markey (*Desperate Teenage Love Dolls*) also directed *1991—The Year Punk Broke*.

CITIZEN X

(HBO, 1995) **D/S:** Chris Gerolmo

With all the movies about real and fictional serial killers, none could top the real story of Chikatilo (Jeffrey DeMunn) the former schoolteacher who killed and mutilated a record number (52) of young boys and girls in the Soviet Union. This made-for-cable movie shows how serious government corruption and backward police procedures made it possible for him to keep on killing for over eight years. It's one of the most effective looks at life during the final years of the USSR. Stephen Rea stars as the forensic expert who persists in his nearly impossible job to find the killer. With Donald Sutherland as his military superior, Max Von Sydow as a psychiatrist, Radu Amzulrescu, John Wood and Joss Ackland. It was based on the book *The Killer Department* by Robert Cullen and was shot in Hungary.

CITY HUNTER

(1993) **D:** Wong Ching   Hong Kong

Jackie Chan stars as womanizing P.I. Mung Bo, hired by a Japanese tycoon to find his daughter (Kumiko Goto). Characters magically appear in a video game. This slapstick comedy/action movie with FX and in-jokes was based on Japanese comics (and the *Streetfighter II* video game). Joey Wang costars, with Richard Norton and Gary Daniels as terrorists on a cruise ship. A scene from *Game of Death* is used. It was shot in Hong Kong and Japan.

CITY IN FEAR (1972): *See* A PLACE CALLED TODAY

CITY IN FEAR

(Vestron, 1980) **D:** "Allan Smithee"/Jud Taylor **S:** Albert Ruben **P:** Ronald Lyon   (*Panic on Page One*)

David Janssen (in his last role) stars as an alcoholic columnist. The story is loosely based on the "Son of Sam" murders, and Mickey Rourke is the serial killer. With Robert Vaughn as the newspaper publisher, Susan Sullivan, William Prince, Perry King, William Daniels, and M. Emmet Walsh. It debuted on NBC-TV.

CITY LIMITS

(Vestron, 1984) **D:** Aaron Lipstadt **S:** Don Opper **P:** Rupert Harvey, Barry Opper

A post-plague city in the year 2003 is the scene of rival kid-biker-gang battles after most adults have died. John Stockwell stars, with Kim Cattrall, Rae Dawn Chong as Yogi, James Earl Jones (who also narrates), Robby Benson, producer Don Opper, and John Diehl. The film (from the makers of *Android*) was later ridiculed on *Mystery Science Theater 3000*.

CITY OF BLOOD

(Magnum, 1983) **D/S:** Darrell Roodt **P:** Anant Singh   S.Africa

An anti-apartheid medical examiner investigates the ceremonial killings of white prostitutes. (Their hands and feet are chopped off and the bodies burned.) "Spirit warriors" in the city are blamed. It's a confused mixture of horror and politics. With Ken Gampu (later in *The Gods Must Be Crazy*).

CITY OF FEAR

(1965) **D:** Peter Bezencenet **S/P:** Harry Alan Towers **P:** Sandy Howard, Arthur Steloff   UK

Paul Maxwell stars as a Canadian reporter, in this Cold War drama. He falls for Terry Moore in Budapest. Marisa Mell is a spy. With Pinkas Braun and Albert Lieven. It was filmed in Austria and Hungary. Moore's other 60s spy movie was *A Man Called Dagger* (1966)

CITY OF SHADOWS

(Starmaker, 1986) **D/P:** David Mitchell **S/P:** Damian Lee **P/A:** John P. Ryan

Paul Coufos and John P. Ryan are rival brothers in the near future. Ryan is a rebel cop, and Coufos is a maniac who kidnaps and kills young boys. New World released this offbeat movie, filmed in Canada. The soundtrack is by Tangerine Dream.

CITY OF THE WALKING DEAD

(Continental, 1980) **D:** Umberto Lenzi
S: Piero Regnoli, Antonio Corti, Luis María Delgado
P: Diego Alchimede, Luis Mendez   Italy/Spain
(*Incubo sulla Città Contaminata; Nightmare City*)

Mexican star Hugo Stiglitz is a reporter in this story of a nuclear spill that causes people to become fast-moving, bloodsucking zombies carrying knives and axes. Some of them arrive in an airplane and attack a disco and an amusement park. Guest star Mel Ferrer as a general ("Aim for the brain!") was featured in newspapers ads as "star of *Falcon Crest!*" With Francisco Rabal and Laura Trotter. The zombies aren't very impressive-looking.

CLAIRVOYANT: *See* THE KILLING HOUR

THE CLAN OF THE CAVE BEAR

(Fox, 1986) **D:** Michael Chapman
S: John Sayles **P:** Gerald I. Isenberg

Daryl Hannah is Ayla, an "ugly" outcast orphan who becomes a warrior in this flop based on the best-selling novels by Jean M. Auel. Neanderthals think the Cro-Magnon girl is an evil spirit. With Pamela Reed, James Remar, and Nicole Eggert. There are subtitles for the made-up language. It was filmed in Canada by Chapman, a cinematographer. Mark Damon was the executive producer.

CLARENCE

(Republic, 1990) **D:** Eric Till **S:** Lorne Cameron, David Hoselton **P:** Seaton McLean

Robert Carradine is Clarence the angel (from *It's a Wonderful Life*) in this comic fantasy. He helps a widow (Kate Trotter) and her kids. It was filmed in Toronto and debuted on the Family Channel.

CLASS

(Vestron, 1983) **D:** Lewis John Carlino **S:** Jim Kouf, David Greenwalt **P:** Martin Ransohoff

In one of the many older-woman/teenage-boy sex comedies of the 80s, wealthy but bored Jaqueline Bisset seduces innocent young Andrew McCarthy (in his film debut), and his roommate, her son (Rob Lowe), finds out. AT&T spokesman Cliff Robertson is her husband. With John Cusack, Lolita Davidovich, Casey Siemaszko, Virginia Madsen (making her debut), and Stuart Margolin. It was released by Orion (formerly AIP).

CLASS OF 1999

(Vestron, 1988) **D/P:** Mark L. Lester
S: C. Courtney Joyner

Lester made this worthy follow-up to his own *Class of 1984* (1981). Kennedy High School in Seattle of the future is the setting, and the plot is inspired by *Robocop*. The school is heavily armed and guarded, and principal Malcolm McDowell brings in an outside firm with supereffective android teachers. Stacy Keach acts pretty strange as an albino. Pam Grier, John P. Ryan, and Patrick Kilpatrick are all good as the android teachers who go out of control. Some of the FX and action sequences are excellent. Bradley Gregg stars, with Traci Lind as the principal's daughter. With Joshua Miller (*Near Dark*), Darren E. Burrows, and Jill Gatsby. R and unrated versions are available.

CLASS OF 1999 II

(Vidmark, 1994) **D:** Spiro Razatos
S: Mark Sevi **P:** Russell Markowitz

Sasha Mitchell is pretty bizarre as the last of the kickboxing "battle-droids," working as an emotionless substitute teacher who beats, blows up, and kills delinquent students (and is a voyeur). Unlike *Class of 1984* and *Class of 1999* (both very good action-packed exploitation movies) this boring sequel takes place almost entirely in the woods and resembles a cheap war movie. Nick Cassavetes and Caitlin West, as teachers, are featured in a sex scene. Non-star scenes from *Class of 1999* are reused to fill up time and save more money.

THE CLASS OF MISS MacMICHAEL

(1978) **D:** Silvio Narizzano **S/P:** Judd Bernard   UK/US

Glenda Jackson stars in this comic update of *The Blackboard Jungle*. With Oliver Reed, Michael Murphy, Rosalind Cash, and Phil Daniels (*Quadrophenia*). By the director of *Why Shoot the Teacher?* (1977).

CLASS OF NUKE 'EM HIGH

(Media, 1986) **D/S:** "Samuel Weil"/Richard W. Haines **D/S/P:** Lloyd Kaufman **S:** Mark Rudnitsky, Stuart Strutin **P:** Michael Herz

Radioactive "atomic high" pot causes a nice teen couple to give birth to a mutant creature who helps fight the ridiculous Cretins gang. R. I. Ryan is in this typically stupid Troma movie, set in New Jersey. By the director of *Splatter University*. Even their *Toxic High* movies are better, but two sequels followed anyway.

CLASS OF NUKE 'EM HIGH II: SUBHUMAN MELTDOWN

(Media, 1991) **D/S:** Eric Louzil **S/P:** Lloyd Kaufman **S:** Carl Morano, Marcus Roling, Jeffrey W. Sass, Matt Unger **P:** Michael Herz

Brick Bronsky, a musclebound blond, stars as a reporter who narrates this tale of how much things have mutated at school, in another overkill Troma comedy. The mad Professor Holt (Lisa Gaye with a 2-foot-high beehive hairdo) creates topless drone workers with mouths in their belly buttons and some other animated mutants. An animated giant Godzilla/squirrel stomps some model buildings. With lots of girls in bikinis, scenes from the first movie (including the Smithereens), and porno stars Sharon Mitchell and Trinity Loren. *Class Of Nuke 'Em High, Part III: The Good, The Bad, and the Subhuman* (1991) was made at the same time. Both had Japanese investors (who probably have deep regrets).

CLASS REUNION

(Private Screenings, 1970) **D/P:** "A. C. Stevens"/Stephen Apostoloff **S:** Ed Wood Jr.

Wood had written *Orgy of the Dead* for Stevens back in 1965 and went on to write several more 70s adult-only soft-core features for him. Wood rarely received any credit for these films. Some say Stevens didn't even pay him. By then porno films were becoming common, so Stevens no longer had to make the men leave their boxer shorts on during sex scenes, but he stopped just short of making hard-core porno. Stevens has been quoted as saying, "I don't make smoot!" *Class Reunion* has a surprising gay sex scene that must have sent typical adult-movie theater goers running for the exit doors. It also features tinted b/w footage from Stevens' *College Girls*. At one point a woman called Fluff says to a guy called Wimpy, "I'm always ready, willing, and I hate to use the word 'able,' but for lack of a better word, able." The press book said: "*Class Reunion* is a strong film in the tradition of sex and what sex stands for, and if the antiquated missionary position is impossible for some, then they must seek out and investigate other ways. *Class Reunion* investigates most of those other ways. Some will love this story while others turn purple, but all will leave the theater with something new in their minds . . . and there is little doubt but what they have learned something about their own welfare." With Terry Johnson, Foreman Shane, and Marsha Jordan, plus Rick Lutz and the late Rene Bond (a real-life couple who were also in *Please Don't Eat My Mother* and many nudie and porno movies).

CLASS REUNION MASSACRE = THE REDEEMER

CLAWS

(Video Gems, 1977) **D:** Richard Banslach, Robert E. Pierson **S/P:** Chuck D. Keen

A "spirit" bear kills people in a national park, in this *Jaws*-inspired horror movie made after the similar *Grizzly* (1976). With Jason Evers, Ken Gampu, Myron Healy, veteran actor Leon Ames, and Anthony Caruso. It was filmed in Alaska.

CLAY PIGEON

(VCL, 1971) **D/P/A:** Tom Stern, Lane Slate **S:** Ronald Buck, Buddy Ruskin, Jack Gross   (*Trip to Kill*)

Stern stars as a decorated Nam vet who is set up by Telly Savalas and the FBI and becomes an LA narc disguised as a hippie. Other Nam vets are involved in the drug-dealing and violence. It's supposedly based on a true story. With Marlene Clark, Robert Vaughn, Burgess Meredith, Ivan Dixon, Jeff Corey, John Marley, and Peter Lawford. It features music by Arlo Guthrie, Kris Kristofferson, and others. From MGM.

CLEAN AND SOBER

(Warner, 1988) **D:** Glen Gordon Caron **S:** Tod Carroll **P:** Tony Ganz, Debra Blum, Jay Daniel

Michael Keaton is a fast-talking real-estate salesman, in debt and with a drinking and cocaine problem, who goes to a drug clinic to avoid embezzlement (and possibly murder) charges. He falls for Kathy Baker there and really does straighten out. With Morgan Freeman, M. Emmet Walsh, Claudia Christian, Brian Benben, Harley Jane Kozak, and Luca Bercovici (*Ghoulies*). The film showed the serious side of Keaton. The next year he played the title role in *Batman* (and had a publicized affair with porno star Rachel Ryan, who played a corpse). This was one of many late 80s horrors-of-coke movies. Ron Howard was the executive producer.

CLEAN, SHAVEN

(Fox Lorber, 1993) **D/S/P:** Lodge H. Kerrigan

This film fest award-winning indy feature is about a possible child serial killer (Peter Green, later in *Pulp Fiction*). The schizophrenic man hears voices and is searching for his lost daughter. Some women fainted when this was screened at the Sundance Film Festival. It was shot on an island off New Brunswick and on Long Island. The director is from Brooklyn.

CLEAR AND PRESENT DANGER

(Paramount, 1994) **D:** Philip Noyce **S:** John Milius, Donald Stewart, Steven Zaillian **P:** Mace Neufeld, Robert G. Rehme

Harrison Ford returns as Jack Ryan in the sequel to *Patriot Games*. Willem Dafoe costars as a mercenary in Colombia. Anne Archer is back, and the cast also includes Harris Yulin, Miguel Sandoval as a drug lord, and James Earl Jones. Donald Moffat is a Bush-like president. Also with Henry Czerny, Ann Magnusun, Dean Jones, Thora Birch, and Hope Lange. This major action/adventure movie was shot in Mexico.

THE CLEARING

(1991) **D/S/P:** Vladimir Alenikov   USSR

In the 8th century, a woman is killed during a pagan ritual. Some blame a local medicine woman, but the village chieftain (George Segal!) thinks it's the work of a werewolf. With nightmare sequences, blood, and nudity. Available on Canadian video.

CLEO/LEO

(Starmaker, 1985) **D/S/P/E:** Chuck Vincent

A sexist businessman drowns and is reincarnated as a woman (Jane Hamilton/Veronica Hart). The mostly porno-star cast of this New World release includes Ginger Lynn Allen, Ruth Collins, Jennifer DeLora, and Kimberly Taylor (from *Penthouse*). Hart was in more than 20 films by the late Vincent. For the same plot, check out 1991's *Switch*, starring Ellen Barkin and Jimmy Smits.

CLEOPATRA JONES

(Warner, 1973) **D:** Jack Starrett **S:** Max Julien, Sheldon Keller **P:** William Tennant

The 6'2" Tamara Dobson stars as the kung-fu-fighting CIA narcotics agent, in this PG-rated, comic-book-style black action-movie hit. She drives a customized black Corvette and orders the napalming of Turkish opium fields. Shelley Winters, as a butch LA gang leader/drug dealer called Mommy, plants dope in a halfway house. Winters wears black leather and overacts even more than usual. With Antonio Fargas as drug dealer Doodlebug, Bernie Casey, Brenda Sykes, Esther Rolle, Albert Popwell, Paul Koslo, and John Alderman. The popular Warners soundtrack by J. J. Johnson features Joe Simon, Millie Jackson, and jazz. Writer Julien (who also co-produced) starred in *The Mack* the same year. Dobson returned in a sequel.

Tamara Dobson stars in *Cleopatra Jones*.

CLEOPATRA JONES AND THE CASINO OF GOLD

(Warner, 1975) **D:** Chuck Bail **S/P:** William Tennant   US/Hong Kong

Tamara Dobson returns, this time in Hong Kong and with even more silver eye shadow. Stella Stevens is Bianco Jovan, the drug-dealing dragon lady of Macao. With Albert Popwell, Norman Fell, and Asian actress Tanny as Cleopatra's private-eye friend Mi Ling, who has motorcycle-riding helpers. A Run Run Shaw coproduction.

CLIFFHANGER

(Columbia, 1993) **D/P:** Renny Harlin **S:** Michael France **P:** Alan Marshall

After several comedy flops, Stallone plays a Rocky Mountain rescue expert who goes after fugitive criminals who have robbed a Treasury Department jet and survived a plane crash. Much of the high-up action takes place during a storm. John Lithgow is a psychotic British thief, and Michael Rooker (*Henry*) is Sly's former buddy on the rescue team. With Janine Turner (from the TV series *Northern Exposure*) as his helicopter pilot girlfriend, Ralph Waite, Paul Winfield, and Rex Linn. The Tri Star release, set in Colorado but shot in the Italian Alps, reportedly cost $65 million and was made by the director of *Die Hard II*. The

score is by Trevor Jones. *K2* and Herzog's *Scream of Stone* were other early-90s mountain-peril features.

CLOAK AND DAGGER

(Republic, 1946) **D:** Fritz Lang **S:** Albert Maltz, Ring Lardner Jr. **P:** Milton Sperling

Lang's first post-WWII film is about the last days of the war and the development of the atomic bomb. A professor (Gary Copper) becomes a secret OSS agent. He has to rescue a female scientist from Nazis in Switzerland, then another nuclear scientist (Vladimir Sokoloff) in Italy. With Lilli Palmer, Robert Alda, Dan Seymour, and Marc Lawrence. Warner Brothers removed some of the anti-bomb dialogue before releasing the film. In 1947, Maltz and Lardner were blacklisted and jailed.

CLOAK AND DAGGER

(MCA, 1984) **D:** Richard Franklin **S:** Tom Holland **P:** Alan Carr

Nobody believes Henry Thomas (after *E.T.*) when he witnesses an espionage-related murder. Dabney Coleman plays both his father and a make-believe hero, Jack Flack. It was (loosely) based on "The Boy Who Cried Murder," by Cornell Woolrich (first filmed as *The Window* in 1949). With Michael Murphy, John McIntire, Jeanette Nolan, Robey, and Christine Nigra. Holland wrote *Fright Night, Class of '84*, and others. From Universal.

THE CLONING OF JOANNA MAY

(1992) **D:** Philippe Saville **S:** Ted Whitehead **P:** Gub Neal   UK

In the near future, an industrialist (Brian Cox) has his wife's lovers murdered. She (Patricia Hodge) leaves, so he uses a DNA sample to have her cloned. This black comedy/fantasy about the war of the sexes is based on a story by Fay Weldon (as was *She Devil*). With Billie Whitelaw and Siri Neal. It debuted on the Arts and Entertainment Network.

CLOSET LAND

(Fox, 1991) **D/S:** Radha Bharadwaj **P:** Brian Grazer, Ron Howard

In the near future, an author of children's books (Madeleine Stowe) is interrogated by a representative of a totalitarian government (Alan Rickman). This is basically a two-character play.

CLOUDBURST

(1950) **D/S:** Francis Searle **S:** Leo Marks **P:** Anthony Hinds   UK

Robert Preston stars as a WWII vet, working for the British Foreign Office, who must hunt for his wife's killer. With Elizabeth Sellars, Harold Lang, and Noel Howlett. This b/w Hammer film was released in the US by United Artists.

CLOUD DANCER

(Prism, 1978) **D/P:** Barry Brown **S:** William Goodheart

David Carradine and Joseph Bottoms (who has a drug problem) are competing daredevil flyers in this PG-rated drama with lots of good stunt work. Jennifer O'Neill has Carradine's baby. With Colleen Camp, Albert Salmi as the simple-minded brother, Salome Jens, Nina Van Pallandt, and Hoyt Axton.

CLOUDS OVER ISRAEL

(1962) **D:** Ivan Lengyel **S:** Moshe Hadar **P:** Mati Raz   Israel (*Sinaia*)

Hemisphere was known for releasing horror and action movies, often from the Philippines. This film, set during the 1956 Arab-Israeli war, was different. A young pilot (Yiftah Spector) has to bail out of his plane in Egypt, where he helps an injured Bedouin woman who is in shock. In 1965 Hemisphere released this film and the more typical *Psycho a Go-Go* and *Blood Creature*.

CLOWNHOUSE

(RCA, 1988) **D/S/P:** Victor Salva **P:** Michael Danty, Robin Mortarotti

Here's proof that clowns are scary. Just before Halloween, three kid brothers, alone in a big, old, isolated house, have to defend themselves against three escaped mental patients. The relentless killers are dressed as Cheezo, Bippo, and Dippo, the traveling circus clowns they murdered. This serious, atmospheric, and old fashioned horror movie takes its time introducing the very different and believable brothers and has a great suspenseful score by Michael Becker, a scary one-eyed fortune teller and (mostly offscreen) murders. I don't really know why it's rated R, but *Clown House* is a good one for young horror fans or older ones who aren't looking for sex and blood. The executive in charge of production was Roman Coppola, post production was done at the Zoetrope studios, a poster for *The Outsiders* is on a wall, and the brothers watch *Dementia 13* on TV!

THE CLOWN MURDERS

(TWE, 1975) **D/S:** Martyn Burke **P:** Christopher Dalton   Canada

A fake kidnapping takes place at a rich people's Halloween party. Stephen Young stars, with Al Waxman and Susan Keller. A pre-SCTV John Candy plays Ollie, which is the only reason this tape was released in the US.

THE CLUB

(Image, 1993) **D:** Brenton Spencer **S:** Robert C. Cooper **P:** Ilana Frank   Canada

The Devil is released at a senior prom held in an old house, and after midnight only five kids are left trapped inside. Joel Wyner (the demon) replaced Corey Haim after several days of shooting, which only partially explains why this movie is so senseless. It's full of false scares, and for the cosmic ending, the film goes backwards at fast speed. Wyner does an imitation of Jack Nicholson in *The Witches of Eastwick*. With Kim Coates as a rapist

guidance counselor who beats a kid to death in the men's room, blond Andrea Roth (also in *The Psychic*), and Kelly Taylor. There's one morphing scene in a tape that copies the *Prom Night* series (also from Canada).

CLUB DEAD = TERROR AT RED WOLF INN

CLUB EXTINCTION

(Prism, 1989) **D:** Claude Chabrol **S:** Solace Mitchell **P:** Ingrid Windisch   W. Germany/France/Italy (*Dr. M*)

Chabrol made this ill-conceived coproduction, filmed in English. It was "inspired" by Fritz Lang's 1922 silent *Dr. Mabuse, der Spieler* but was instantly dated when the Berlin Wall came down. Alan Bates stars as Dr. Marssfeldt, whose subliminal messages on his 21st-century West Berlin TV station cause suicides. Jennifer Beals, who works for him, is on billboards and screens everywhere telling people that it's "time to go." H-bomb footage is screened in a disco, and there's a sinister New Age retreat in the desert. Hanns Zischler (*Kings of the Road*) is the unshaven police lieutenant who investigates. With William Berger, Wolfgang Preiss (who played Mabuse in more enjoyable 60s movies), and Andrew McCarthy in a bit part. Mekong Delta performs a song.

CLUB FED

(Prism, 1990) **D:** Nathaniel Christian **S:** Jordan Rush **P:** Norman Stevens

Judy Landers, as a gangster's girl, is framed and sent to a minimum-security prison, in this PG-13 in-joke-filled comedy. With Burt Young as the warden, Karen Black as an inmate, Joseph Campanella as an FBI agent, Mary Woronov, Lyle Alzado, and Wally George. Both Allen Garfield and Sherman Hemsley appear in drag. Judy Landers' mother was the executive producer. She also produced *California Casanova* for sister Audrey Landers.

CLUB LIFE

(Starmaker, 1985) **D/S/P:** Norman Thaddeus Vane

Tony Curtis owns a neon-lit New York City disco. Tom Parsekian stars as a biker who becomes the bouncer but flees after Curtis and an older bouncer (Michael Parks) are killed by the mob. With Jamie Barrett, Dee Wallace Stone as a drug-addict singer, Pat Ast as Butch, Kristine DeBell, D.W. Stone, and lots of martial arts. Curtis was in *Midnight* for the same director. This was a Troma release.

CLUE

(Paramount, 1985) **D/S:** Jonathan Lynn **P:** Debra Hill

A silly murder mystery/comedy based on a story by co-executive producer John Landis and on the Parker Brothers board game. With Eileen Brennan, Tim Curry, Madeline Kahn, Michael McKean, Martin Mull, Lesley Ann Warren, Colleen Camp, Howard Hesseman, Lee Ving, and Jane Weidlin (from the Go Gos). The original gimmick was that three endings were filmed, and you didn't know

which you were going to see. Very few people cared enough to pay to see it more than once, and now all three endings are on the video.

THE CLUTCHING HAND

(Stokey, 1936) **D:** Albert Herman **S:** Leon D'Usseau, Dallas Fitzgerald **P:** Louis Weiss

Jack Mulhall stars as Craig Kennedy, a scientific detective, in a 15-chapter Stage and Screen serial (one of only three from the indy company). The same character had been in *The Exploits of Elaine* (1915) and other silent serials. The hooded villain has a formula for synthetic gold, and there are many television monitors. With Marion Schilling, William Farnum, Yakima Canutt, Robert Frazer, Mae Busch, Gail Patrick, and Jon Hall. A feature version is available from Sinister.

C-MAN

(Dark Dreams, 1949) **D/S/P:** Joseph Lerner **S:** Bernie Giler

Dean Jagger is Cliff, a US customs agent posing as a private eye, in this violent Film Classics release, shot on location in New York City. The star, who narrates, was 46 and balding, but he's supposed to be 35. He gets beaten up a lot. John Carradine, as Doc, is forced by ruthless international jewel thieves to knock out a woman in the bathroom of an airplane, then inject her with something to keep her out. A nightclub scene includes a great drunk sing-along, "Do it Now!" The tape of this rare film has some sound problems. Lerner directed *Studs Lonigan* (1960), with Jack Nicholson, and executive producer Rex Carlton went on to produce *The Brain That Wouldn't Die*.

COACH

(Media, 1978) **D:** Bud Townsend **S:** Stephen Bruce Rose **P:** Mark Tenser

Cathy Lee Crosby is a high-school basketball coach in this PG teen movie from Crown International, with Keenan Wynn, Michael Biehn, Rosanne Katon, and Brent Huff. Townsend also made *Alice in Wonderland*.

COAST OF SKELETONS

(1965) **D:** Robert Lynn **S/P:** Harry Alan Towers **S:** Anthony Scott Veitch   UK/W. Germany

Richard Todd stars as Sanders in Towers' sequel to his remake of Edgar Wallace's *Sanders of the River* (previously filmed in 1935, starring Paul Robeson as Bosembo and Leslie Banks as Sanders). It's about a search for diamonds in Africa, murder, double crosses, and gold. Heinz Drache costars with Marianne Koch and Dale Robertson. The US debut of this American Seven Arts release was in Cincinnati.

THE COBRA

(Unicorn, 1967) **D:** Mario Sequi **S:** Gumersindo Mollo **P:** Fulvio Luccisano   Italy/Spain (*Il Cobra*)

The Chinese Communists are smuggling opium into America by hiding it in Arab oil tankers. Dana Andrews is the retired agent called upon by the

Secret Service to stop the operation. With Anita Ekberg as a helpful addict and Peter Martell. This AIP release was filmed in the Middle East.

COBRA

(Warner, 1986) **D:** George P. Cosmatos
S/A: Sylvester Stallone **P:** Golan/Globus

LA cop Mario Cobretti (Stallone) is after "the night slasher" (Brian Thompson). The serial killer uses an axe in this one, and there are lots of product plugs. With Brigitte Nielsen, Andrew Robinson, Val Avery, and Art Le Fleur. That perfect couple, Sly and Brigitte, were also in *Rocky V* together but divorced in 1987. A Cannon release.

COBRA VERDE

(VSOM, 1988) **D:** Werner Herzog **S:** Peter Green

The late, great Klaus Kinski (with long blond hair) stars in his last (and least seen) of 5 Herzog features, as the brooding Francisco Manuel Da Silva (called Cobra Verde), a barefoot 19th-century Brazilian bandit. A sugarcane-plantation owner hires him to keep his slaves in line, but Verde has children with all of the man's illegitimate black daughters. As punishment, he's sent alone to Africa, at the risk of his life, to reopen the slave trade. He survives, trains an all-female (topless) army, is appointed viceroy, and has 62 more children! Based on *The Viceroy of Ouidah*, by Bruce Chatwin, the film concludes when slavery is finally abolished in Brazil, in 1888. This ironic tall tale features bats, crabs, heads on poles, a cross-eyed prince, an insane king, and some extreme (real) cripples. The music is by Popol Vuh. The West German production was shot in Dahomey and Bahai, Brazil, and was backed by DEG. The tape (in English) has Spanish subtitles.

THE COBWEB

(1955) **D:** Vincente Minnelli **S:** John Paxton **P:** John Houseman

Technicolor weirdness, with Richard Widmark as the head of an asylum, Gloria Grahame as his wife, John Kerr as a patient obsessed with Van Gogh, Lauren Bacall, Charles Boyer, Susan Strasberg, Paul Stewart, Fay Wray, Lillian Gish, Virginia Christine, Tommy Rettig, and Oscar Levant, who sings. Patients make drapes as therapy.

COCAINE COWBOYS

(New Pacific, 1979) **D/S:** Ulli Lommel
P: Christopher Francis Gierke

A drug-smuggling, horse-riding rock group on Long Island is the subject of this boring film. Jack Palance is their manager, and Andy Warhol appears because it was filmed at his Montauk summer home. With Tom Sullivan, Suzanna Love, and the Cowboy Island Band. Watch for visible boom mikes. Lommel, from Germany, made *Blank Generation* around the same time.

THE COCAINE FIENDS

(Video Dimensions, 1936) **D:** William A. O'Connor, Norton S. Parker   (*The Pace that Kills; Girls of the Street; What Price Ignorance?*)

Eddie and Jane (Lois January) are a brother and sister working at a roadside restaurant. She takes dope-pusher Nick's "headache powders" and runs away to the big city, where she goes to the Dead Rat Cafe (complete with rats painted on the wall). Eddie follows her, takes "a sleigh ride with some show birds," and ends up an addict with a pregnant hooker girlfriend. They finally meet again in an opium den, but Eddie drowns himself. One of the most entertaining of the old anti-drug movies, it's a remake of a 1928 film, *The Pace that Kills* (Video Yesterday), in which a farm boy (Owen Gorin) goes to the big city. It runs 68 minutes (some copies are 60).

COCAINE WARS

(Media, 1984) **D:** Hector Olivera **S:** Steven M. Krauzer **P:** Roger Corman, Alex Sessa   (*Vice Wars*)

John Schneider (from the TV series *The Dukes of Hazzard*) becomes a Rambo type to destroy a coke factory run by ex-Nazis. With Kathey Witt and Royal Dano. This Concorde release was shot in Mexico.

THE COCKEYED MIRACLE

(1946) **D:** S. Sylvan Simon **S:** Karen DeWolf **P:** Irving Starr

Frank Morgan is a turn-of-the-century Maine shipbuilder who dies but is allowed to return as a ghost and help his family. Keenan Wynn is his ghost father (who had died in his 30s). With Audrey Totter and Marshall Thompson as Morgan's kids, Cecil Kellaway, Richard Quine, Leon Ames, Morris Ankrum, and Arthur Space. This comic fantasy was based on a play by George Seaton.

COCKFIGHTER

(Platinum, 1974) **D:** Monte Hellman **S/A:** Charles Willeford **P:** Roger Corman   (*Born to Kill*)

Warren Oates (who narrates) makes a vow of silence after losing a cockfight. This was the first feature based on a novel by Charles Willeford and was filmed in Georgia by Nestor Almendros. With Harry Dean Stanton, Richard B. Shull, Millie Perkins, Laurie Bird (from *Two-Lane Blacktop*), and Troy Donahue. Ed Begley Jr. and Steve Railsback have standout scenes as young hicks. It was a flop, so Corman (who had added a dream sequence) tried again with another title. He also had Joe Dante edit in some car crash and sex scenes from *Night Call Nurses*. Willeford became "cool" years later, so the video is the original version. The year 1974 was a good one for Oates, who was also in the cult films *Bring Me the Head of Alfredo Garcia*, *White Dawn*, and *Badlands*. Hellman's next was to be the Hammer/Hong Kong movie *Shatter*, but he was replaced.

COCKSUCKER BLUES

(1972–76) **D:** Robert Frank, Daniel Seymour **P:** Marshall Chess   (*CS Blues*)

This famous 16-mm Rolling Stones tour documentary received an X rating, was withdrawn by the band, and was shown legally only at some special screenings beginning in 1979. While roadies are shown shooting up and snorting things, scenes of band members (mostly Keith Richards) using drugs were removed. It's a (mostly boring) backstage look at the group's 1972 American tour, with some songs. Keith does throw a TV set out of a hotel window, though. With Stevie Wonder, Tina Turner (also in *Gimme Shelter*), and the jet set: Andy Warhol, Dick Cavett, Truman Capote, and Terry Southern. Robert Frank took the "Exile on Main Street" photos. Bootleg tapes are around, of course, but even they are often cut. *Ladies and Gentlemen, the Rolling Stones* (1974) is a more standard concert film from the same tour.

THE COCKTAIL HOSTESS

(1972) **D/P:** "A. C. Stevens"/ Stephen C. Apostoloff **S:** Ed Wood Jr.

"You pay for the drinks. They do the rest!" Set at Club 69, this is pretty graphic, with threesomes, orgies, and a rape. This cast includes Rene Bond, Rick Lutz, Terri Johnson, and Lynn Harris. It was shot back to back with *Snow Bunnies*. This was one of Stevens' many features written by Ed Wood Jr.

COCOON

(Fox, 1985) **D:** Ron Howard **S:** Tom Benedek
P: Richard D. Zanuck, David Brown, Lili Fini Zanuck

Don Ameche, Wilford Brimley, and Hume Cronyn star as Florida retirees who are accidentally "revitalized" by aliens when they swim in treated water. Their wives (Jessica Tandy, Gwen Verdon, and Maureen Stapleton) go for a swim too, so all three old couples can breakdance. Brian Dennehy leads the aliens (including Tahnee Welch and Tyrone Power Jr.). Everyone leaves for another planet forever (or until the sequel) at the end. With Steve Guttenberg, Jack Gilford, and Clint Howard. Ameche received a best-supporting-actor Oscar. The ILM FX also got an Oscar. It was released by 20th Century–Fox and rated PG-13.

COCOON II: THE RETURN

(Fox, 1988) **D:** Daniel Petrie **S:** Stephen McPherson **P:** Richard D. Zanuck, David Brown, Lili Fini Zanuck

The old couples return from space to visit with friends and families in this PG sequel. It features lots of outtakes from the original. Ameche, Guttenberg, Cronyn, Tandy, Stapleton, Gilford, Welch, and more ILM FX return. With Elaine Stritch and Courteney Cox.

C.O.D.

(Vestron, 1982) **D/S/P:** Chuck Vincent **S:** Rick Marx, Jonathan Hannah   US/W. Germany

Rival executives have to come up with an ad campaign for the Beaver Bra Company (sounds like the Arch Hall movie *What's Up Front?*). Chris Lemmon stars, with Olivia Pascal, Corinne Alphen, Marilyn Joi, Teresa Ganzel, and Samantha Fox.

CODE NAME: VENGEANCE

(AIP, 1986) **D/P:** David Winters
S: Anthony Palmer   S. Africa

Ex-CIA agent Robert Ginty is sent to North Africa to rescue a Middle Eastern magnate's wife and son. With Shannon Tweed, Cameron Mitchell as Dutch, Don Gordon, James Ryan, and Kevin Brophy.

CODENAME: WILD GEESE

(Starmaker, 1984) **D:** "Anthony Dawson"/ Antonio Margheriti **S:** Tito Carpi, Gianfranco Couyoumdjian **P:** Edwin C. Dietrich W. Germany/Italy (*Geheimcode Wildgänse*)

They called it "third in the series," but this movie has no relation to the others. Mercenaries fight a Burmese opium warlord in the Golden Triangle. Lewis Collins stars, with Lee Van Cleef as China, Mimsy Farmer, Klaus Kinski, and Ernest Borgnine. There's a Morricone score. Collins and Kinski were back in *Commando Leopard*, by the same director, the next year.

CODE NAME ZEBRA

(TWE, 1986) **D:** Joe Tornatore **S:** Robert Leone **P:** Joe Kaufman

A group of Nam vets (all played by sons of famous actors) form an international anti-crime unit. This sequel to the same director's *Zebra Force* (1976) stars Jim Mitchum, Timmy Brown (son of Jim), Lindsay Crosby, and Frank Sinatra Jr. (!), with Mike Lane as a hitman villain, Charles Dierkop as Crazy, and Deanna Jurgens.

CODE OF SILENCE

(HBO, 1985) **D:** Andy Davis **S:** Michael Butler **P:** Raymond Wagner

Chuck Norris, as a Chicago cop posing as a sanitation worker, is after drug lord Henry Silva, and there's a police cover-up. This is one of Chuck's best. The screenplay was originally written for a Dirty Harry movie. With Dennis Farina and Bert Remsen. Davis later directed Steven Seagal's first film, *Above the Law*, also with Silva and set in Chicago. From Orion. Soundtrack on Easy Street records.

COFFIN JOE'S VISIONS OF TERROR

(SW, 1994)

This tape consists of 14 outrageous, hype-filled (and subtitled!) trailers (1963–86) for a series of

bizarre Brazilian movies directed by and/or starring Joe Mojica Marins. They feature shocking horror and sex, in color and b/w.

COFFY

(Orion, 1973) **D/S:** Jack Hill **P:** Robert A. Papazian

"She's the godmother of them all, the baddest one-chick hit squad that ever hit town!" Pam Grier, in her first starring role, is a nurse named Coffin in this popular AIP movie. She pretends to be a junkie and infiltrates the mob as revenge for her little sister, who is catatonic from drugs. She seduces the pusher, then blows his head off. There's surprising nudity and gore in the scene (often cut out). Sid Haig is the bald henchman of mob boss Allen Arbus (who had been in Robert Downey movies). With cat fights, plenty of action, topless scenes, razors in afros, and a man shot in the crotch. The cast includes Booker Bradshaw, Robert DoQui, and Linda Haynes. The Polydor soundtrack is by Roy Ayers.

COHEN AND TATE

(Nelson, 1989) **D/S:** Eric Red **P:** Antony Rufus Isaacs

Roy Scheider and a wired punk (Adam Baldwin) are hitmen who hate each other. They kidnap a kid (Harley Cross) whose parents they have murdered. This suspenseful Texas road movie is by the screenwriter of *The Hitcher*. Red's first (obscure) feature was *Gunman's Blues* (1981).

COLD COMFORT

(Republic, 1989) **D:** Vic Sarin **S:** Richard Beattie, L. Elliot Simms **P:** Ilana Frank, Ray Sager   Canada

A crazed gas-station owner (Maury Chaykin) on the Manitoba prairies kidnaps a traveling salesman (Paul Gross) as a birthday present for his young daughter (Margaret Langrick). With Jayne Eastwood. This was originally a play.

COLD FEET

(IVE, 1989) **D:** Robert Dornhelm **S:** Tom McGuane, Jim Harrison **P:** Cassian Elwes

Keith Carradine, Sally Kirkland, and a pretty crazed Tom Waits star in an odd movie about smuggling jewels into the US from Mexico in a horse. With Bill Pullman, Rip Torn, Kathleen York, Vincent Schiavelli, Jeff Bridges (who was in McGuane's *Rancho Deluxe*) as a bartender, and Chuck Woollery as himself. Dornhelm also made *Echo Park*.

COLDFIRE

(PM, 1990) **D/A:** Wings Hauser **S:** Joe Hart **P:** Richard Pepin, Joseph Merhi

Two young California cops go undercover to bust dealers pushing

Henry Silva in *Code of Silence*.

coldfire, a new Soviet designer drug. This was the first film directed by Hauser, who plays an older cop. With Darcy De Moss and Nancy Locke (Hauser). Hauser directed two more films soon afterward.

COLD HEAT

(AIP, 1989) **D/S:** Ulli Lommel

This story involves child abuse, kidnapping, and mercenaries. John Phillip Law, Britt Ekland, and Robert Sacchi star.

COLD HEAVEN

(Hemdale, 1990) **D:** Nicolas Roeg **S/P:** Allan Scott **P:** Jonathan D. Krane

Theresa Russell wants to get out of her marriage. Her pathologist husband (Mark Harmon) dies in a boating accident in Mexico but reappears in California sick and confused, with a bashed-in skull. She relates flashbacks and dreams and has a vision of the Virgin Mary. With James Russo as her lover, Julie Carmen as his wife, Will Patton as a priest, Talia Shire as a nun, and Seymour Cassel. The script (based on a novel by Brian Moore) is by the screenwriter of Roeg's much better *Don't Look Now*. Hemdale waited two years to release this slow-moving, angst-filled movie.

COLD JUSTICE

(RCA, 1989) **D/S:** Terry Green **P/A:** Dennis Waterman

Roger Daltrey stars as a poor former British boxer, known as "Keith the thief," who lives in Chicago with his fighting pit-bull dog. After lots of working-class local color (bowling, shots and beers, minority squabbles and fights, an illegal boxing match, and a suicide) a drinking "priest of the people" (Waterman, who was in *Scars of Dracula*) is crucified. I didn't get it either. Penelope Milford costars.

COLD STEEL

(RCA, 1987) **D:** Dorothy Ann Puzo **S:** Michael Sonye, Moe Quigley **P:** Lisa M. Hansen

Brad Davis is an LA cop out to avenge the Christmas Eve murder of his father. Iceman, the killer (Jonathan Banks), is an ex-cop with bad scars who has to talk with a voice box and who blames

Ernest Borgnine, Mimsy Farmer, and Lee Van Cleef, three American stars in Europe, in *Codename Wildgeese*.

Pam Grier is *Coffy*.

Davis for his problems. Adam Ant is his sadistic sidekick. With Sharon Stone, Eddie Egan, and Sy Richardson.

COLD SWEAT

(Paramount, 1993) **D:** Gail Harvey **S:** Richard Beattie **P:** Peter R. Simpson   Canada

With Shannon Tweed on the video box, this is presented as yet another "erotic thriller." Actually, it's a pretty funny over-the-top spoof (with two R-rated Tweed sex scenes) that's played seriously. Ben Cross is a family man who is secretly a contract killer. A grouchy Toronto real estate agent (SCTV's Dave Thomas) has a coke dealer (Adam Baldwin) contact Cross to off his business partner (Henry Czerny). Thomas's wife (Tweed) is having affairs with the dealer and the partner and the various hateful characters all double- and triple-cross each other. Meanwhile, the ghost (Lenore Zann) of an innocent witness that Cross killed shows up in a graveyard, then in his house and even his bathtub. He has nightmares and flashbacks and says, "I shot you, alright? It happens." The theme song by Chris Rea is very good. Ray Sagar was co-producer and it debuted (cut) on the USA Network.

A COLD WIND IN AUGUST

(1961) **D:** Alexander Singer **S:** Burton Wohl **P:** Philip Hazelton

Scott Marlowe (*The Cool and the Crazy*), as an underage New York City janitor's son, is seduced by a stripper (Lola Albright). He later discovers to his horror what she does for a living. With Herschel Bernardi and Joe De Santis. It was filmed by Floyd Crosby in b/w. The first cult film condemned by the Catholic Church's Legion of Decency, it's one of John Waters' "guilty pleasures."

THE COLLECTOR

(RCA, 1965) **D:** William Wyler **S/P:** John Kohn **S:** Stanley Mann **P:** Jud Kinberg   US/UK

Terence Stamp is a neurotic London bank clerk who wins a football pool, buys an estate, and devotes his time to collecting and studying butterflies. He abducts an art student (Samantha Eggar) and keeps her prisoner in a basement apartment, waiting for her to start loving him. This creepy psycho movie is better than most, thanks to Wyler and Stamp, who received a best-actor award at the Cannes Film Festival, but it's also long (2 hours).

COLLEGE GIRL CONFIDENTIAL

(Rhino, 1968) **D/P:** "A. C. Stevens"/ Stephen C. Apostoloff   (*College Girls*)

The guys at the LSD fraternity have a wild toga party with a table loaded with drugs and a folk singer. This entertaining nudie movie also has a lesbian scene, flashbacks, a Jayne Mansfield painting on a wall, a gay cheerleader who loves the school showers, and an anti-drug message at the end. In the scene everybody remembers, Harvey Shane takes too many pills and jumps off a balcony. Costar Marsha Jordan (real name Kopete) was in five of Stevens' films, and Shane was in even more. On *Saturday Night Sleazies*, Volume I.

THE COLLEGE GIRL MURDERS

(1967) **D:** Alfred Voher **S:** Alex Berg W. Germany (*Der Monk mit der Peitsche*)

A 1928 American film, *The Terror* (from a novel by Edgar Wallace), was the first sound horror film. It was remade in the US as *Return of the Terror* in 1934. The novel was also the basis for a British film, *The Terror*, made in 1938. A West German version, *Der Unheimliche Monk*, was filmed in 1965. This sequel to that version is the only one in color and can sometimes be seen on American TV. The German title means "the monk with the whip." The killer wears a red robe with a pointed hood and emerges from a blue fog with a white whip. College girls are killed with an acid gas dispensed from a Bible. Joachim Fuchsberger stars as Inspector Higgins, with Uschi Glas, Siegfried Schurenberg, and Jan Hendricks.

COLLEGE SCANDAL

(1935) **D:** Elliott Nugent **S:** Frank Partes, Charles Brackett

Characters are killed for revenge after a hazing accident. The plot was reused in many later horror movies, but this is also a musical. Arline Judge, Johnny Downs, and Wendy Barrie are in this Paramount release. It was remade as *Sweater Girl* (1942).

COLLISION COURSE

(HBO, 1987) **D:** Lewis Teague **S:** Frank Darius Namei **P:** Robert Court, Ted Field

Future *Tonight Show* host Jay Leno is a Detroit cop teamed with a Japanese detective (Pat Morita) in this PG action comedy, which rips off *Red Heat*. With Tom Noonan, Susan Sarandon, Ernie Hudson, Al Waxman, Soon-Teck Oh, and Randall "Tex" Cobb. It was filmed in Detroit by DEG (which went bankrupt) and wasn't released until 1992.

COLONEL MARCH OF SCOTLAND YARD

(Sinster series, 1953–54)   UK

Boris Karloff stars as a pipe-smoking police detective with an eye patch, in this British TV series. It was syndicated in the US. Of the 26 episodes filmed, 6 volumes with 2 episodes each are available. Titles include "The Abominable Snowman," "The New Invisible Man," "The Talking Head," and "The Sorcerer." Some were directed by Hammer regular Terence Fisher.

COLOR OF LOVE = LORD SHANGO

COLOR OF NIGHT

(Hollywood, 1994) **D:** Richard Rush **S:** Mathew Chapman, Billy Ray **P:** Buzz Feitshans

Bruce Willis stars as a troubled New York City shrink who moves into the home of his best friend, an L.A. shrink (Scott Bakula) who was murdered. He takes over his friend's group therapy sessions,

COLORIZATION

Many older psychotronic movies have been colorized. This is done for purely economic reasons, because polls have shown that many more people will rent, buy, or watch a feature if it's in color, which is sad but probably true. If you disapprove, you can (hopefully) turn the color off on your TV set. If you don't like this practice, Ted Turner is the main villain. The worst job of coloring I've seen (so far) is *The Absent Minded Professor* (Disney, 1961).

sleeps with his girlfriend (Jane March from *The Lover*), and tries to figure out who the mystery killer is while being closely watched by comical cop (Rueben Blades). March is the youngest-looking lover of a middle aged man in an American movie in many years and this trashy, over the top, often funny feature has sex, nudity, gore, *Vertigo* scenes, and lots of nutty patients. Brad Dourif is an obsessive lawyer, Lance Henriksen is a cop whose family was killed, Kevin J. O'Connor is an artist, Lesley Ann Warren is the nympho, and there's this odd young boy. Also with Jeff Corey, Shirley Knight, and Kathleen Wilhoite. Music by Dominic Frontiere. Rush made AIP movies in the 60s. It was just over two hours long in theatres. The 15 minutes longer "director's cut" video includes scenes of Willis naked which had been removed to avoid an NC-17 rating. The uncut tape was rated R anyway.

COLORS

(Orion, 1988) **D:** Dennis Hopper **S:** Michael Schiffer **P:** Robert H. Solo, Paul Lewis

Sean Penn and Robert Duvall are cop partners at odds with each other while dealing with gangs in LA. It was Hopper's biggest hit as director, and cuts from the popular soundtrack were being heard from cars and boom boxes for years after. Herbie Hancock composed parts of the soundtrack, which features Ice T's hit title track and some select oldies by groups like War. With Maria Conchita Alonso, Sy Richardson, Jack Nance, Seymour Cassel, Richard Rust, Damon Wayans, and Tony Todd. Trinidad Silva (who died in a traffic accident in 1988) is great as Frog. The cinematography is by Haskell Wexler. Real gang members were cast in supporting roles, and the street slang is pretty convincing. The tape (127 minutes) is seven minutes longer than the theatrical version.

THE COLOSSUS OF RHODES

(1960) **D/S:** Sergio Leone **S:** Ennio De Concini **P:** Michele Scaglione Italy/France/Spain (*Il Colosso di Rodi*)

This was the first feature credited to Leone, who had also codirected the biblical epic *Sodom and Gomorrah* and had been the assistant director on several big biblical epics. American Rory Calhoun stars as Dario, a Greek captain who tries to destroy the gigantic bronze statue of Colossus on the island of Rhodes. He has to fight in the arena and an earthquake topples the statue at the end. From MGM. Leone's next as director was *A Fistful of Dollars*. The French-language version is on tape.

COMBAT SHOCK

(Troma, 1984) **D/S/P/E:** Buddy Giovinazzo (*American Nightmare*)

Frankie (Ricky Giovinazzo), an unemployed, addicted Nam vet, has gory, horrifying war nightmares and flashbacks. He owes money to a drug dealer, who has him beaten. He and his miserable, starving, pregnant wife and their sick, deformed baby are about to be evicted from their slum apartment. The baby wails and cries constantly. The wife stares at a broken TV set. Frankie thinks, "I can no longer tell where one torture ends and the next begins." His junkie friend ODs by putting drugs directly into an open wound. Little-girl hookers walk the streets, people wait in unemployment lines, other people rip each other off, and Frankie wanders aimlessly. During one of his mental breakdowns, Nam footage is projected onto his face, a great effect previously used in 60s drug movies. The editing and FX are excellent, making it all a little hard for many viewers to take. It ends in a bloodbath of killing (and worst of all, he drinks a carton of very sour milk). This depressing but well-made 16mm $40,000 film was made in Port Richmond, Staten Island, by a former College of Staten Island student. His younger brother stars and composed the impressive synthesizer score. Despite the horror-movie overtones, Buddy Giovinazzo interviewed Nam vets and researched the subject before writing the script, and his dedication shows. He's an admitted fan of *Eraserhead* and *Taxi Driver*, two movies you might think about while watching this. The 85-minute video release of this hard-to-sell item tries to pass it off as a war film! The original uncut version (*American Nightmare*) is 100 minutes long.

COMEBACK

(MGM, 1981) **D/S:** Christel Buschmann **P:** Joachim von Vietinghoff   W. Germany

In this almost plotless movie, Eric Burden is Rocco, a rock star in black leather pants who owes money, has a junkie wife (Julie Carmen), and hates the way rock has become big business. Bailed out of jail in LA after a coke bust, he goes to W. Berlin. He sings at a whorehouse there, with Louisiana Red playing steel guitar, and is attacked by a jealous German and an American debt collector. In one scene Rocco yells, "I'm dead. You're all dead!" on stage then attacks his manager. The new songs performed on stage (including the punk attempt "Who Gives a Fuck") are pretty bad, but when Burden gets back to older blues classics he sounds great. With Michael Cavanaugh and John Amprea. Burden also appeared in *Gibbi* (1979) by the same director.

COME BACK, CHARLESTON BLUE

(1972) **D:** Mark Warren **S:** Ernest Kinoy **P:** Samuel Goldwyn Jr. **M:** Donny Hathaway

This comic sequel to *Cotton Comes to Harlem*, is based on the novel *The Heat's On,* by Chester Himes. The director had worked on the TV series *Rowan and Martin's Laugh-In.* Godfrey Cambridge and Raymond St. Jacques return as Gravedigger Jones and Coffin Ed Johnson. Drugs are smuggled in Thanksgiving turkeys in Harlem. With Peter DeAnda and Marcia McBroom.

COME BACK TO THE 5 AND DIME, JIMMY DEAN, JIMMY DEAN

(Sultan, 1982) **D:** Robert Altman **S:** Ed Graczyk **P:** Scott Bushell

In this filmed version of Graczyk's Broadway play, five small-town Texas women, who started a James Dean fan club when he was filming *Giant* nearby, gather at Woolworth's 20 years later. All of them are neurotic. Sandy Dennis even thinks Dean was the father of her child. Cher (in her "serious" film debut) costars, with Karen Black as a transsexual, Kathy Bates, Sudie Bond, and Marta Heflin.

THE COMEBACK TRAIL

(1971) **D/S/P:** Harry Hurvitz

Chuck McCann and a partner put an old star (Buster Crabbe) in a western, hoping he will die so that they can collect the insurance. With Ina Balin, Henny Youngman, Professor Irwin Corey, Hugh Hefner, Joe Franklin, and Monte Rock III. It was based on a story cowritten by Roy Frumkes (*Street Trash*) and may have been released in 1982. McCann and Balin were also in Hurvitz's *The Projectionist*. Crabbe's only other post-60s role was in Fred Olen Ray's *Alien Dead* (1980).

THE COMIC

(Magnum, 1985) **D/S/P:** Richard Driscoll   UK

Set "in another time, in another place," this arty, foggy movie is about Sam Coxe (Stevie Munro), an untalented guy with dyed orange hair who wants to be "the king of comedy." In order to get a standup job at a music hall, he kills the resident comedian and buries him. One of the dream sequences is in b/w, with only his hair in color. The director must have liked *Rumblefish* and *Cafe Flesh*, because he borrowed ideas from both of those cult movies. There's a rock-video sex scene, a jazz band, a ponderous organ-music soundtrack, and some goose-stepping guards with ponytails. The endless dialogue is often obscured by wind noise, and several slow-motion scenes seem to go on forever. Chris Tucker (*The Elephant Man; Quest for Fire*) provided some forgettable FX.

COMIC BOOK CONFIDENTIAL

(Pacific Arts, 1988) **D/S/P:** Ron Mann **P:** Martin Harbury, Don Haig   Canada

This documentary covers the history of comics, including the Senate hearings on horror comics in the 50s, DC Comics, and EC Comics. *Mad* is well represented by the late William M. Gaines (seen defending comics before a Senate subcommittee), the late Harvey Kurtzman, and Al Feldstein. R. Crumb, Harvey Pekar, Bill Griffith, Will Eisner, Art Spiegelman, Stan Lee, and many other artists and writers are interviewed, and some narrate their own strips. Dr. John does the theme song. It's also available on CD-ROM with additional footage and lists of the artists' works.

COMING SOON

(MCA, 1983) **D:** John Landis **S:** Mick Garris

Jamie Lee Curtis hosts this 55-minute made-for-TV look at Universal horror classics. Most of it consists of classic trailers, including the great 8-minute *Psycho* trailer starring Hitchcock. There are some interviews and behind-the-scenes segments. It also wastes time promoting new (in 1983) Universal releases by Spielberg and others.

THE COMMANDER

(1988) **D:** "Anthony M. Dawson"/Antonio Margheretti **S:** Arne Elsholtz, Titi Carpi **P:** Edwin C. Dietrich Italy/Philippines

Lewis Collins, Lee Van Cleef, Donald Pleasence, John Steiner, and Brett Halsey star in this WWII movie.

COMMANDO

(1963) **D/S:** Frank Wisbar **S:** Arturo Tofanelli Italy/Belgium/Spain/W. Germany (*Marcia o Crepa*)

Stewart Granger stars as a captain in the French Foreign Legion in 1961, near the end of the Algerian war. Dorian Gray costars. This was the last film by the German-born maker of *Strangler of the Swamp* (1945). An AIP release.

COMMANDO

(Fox, 1985) **D:** Mark L. Lester **S:** Steven E. De Souza **P:** Joel Silver

Arnold Schwarzenegger, as ex-commando Colonel John Matrix, is forced to lead a mission in S. America after his daughter (Alyssa Milano) is kidnapped by a dictator (Dan Hedaya). This violent 20th Century–Fox film is funny on purpose. With Rae Dawn Chong as a stewardess, Vernon Wells as a gay Marine, Bill Paxton, Bill Duke, David Patrick Kelly, Chelsea Field, and Ava Cadell.

COMMANDO CODY, SKY MARSHAL OF THE UNIVERSE

(Stokey, 1953) **D:** Fred C. Bannon, Harry Keller, Franklin Adreon **S:** Ronald Davidson, Barry Shipman

Republic had released two Commando Cody serials, *Radar Men from the Moon* and *Zombies of the Stratosphere*. Since the days of theatrical serials were nearly over, they decided to make a series of 12 half-hour TV adventures (without cliffhanger endings). The episodes aired on NBC first, then ended up playing in theaters after all. Judd Holdren (from *Zombies*) was Cody again, and Aline Towne again costarred. Gregory Gaye was Retik, from the Moon, and the cast also included Lyle Talbot (who had been in the Batman and Superman serials at Columbia), Richard Crane, William Schallert, Denver Pyle, and John Crawford. This was the last gasp for the overused rocket-pack flying-man scenes, which were first filmed for *King of the Rocket Men* (1949) and were later the inspiration for *The Rocketeer* (1991)

COMMANDO GIRLS: *See* HELL SQUAD

COMMANDO LEOPARD

(1985) **D:** "Anthony M. Dawson"/Antonio Margheretti **S:** Roy Nelson **P:** Edwin C. Dietrich Switzerland/W. Germany/Italy

Lewis Collins, Klaus Kinski, and John Steiner star in this war movie, made in the Philippines. It's about rebels in a fictitious South American country and was made after Margheretti's *Codename: Wild Geese* (with part of the same cast).

An outer-space lab of the future! From *Commando Cody*.

COMMANDO SQUAD

(TWE, 1987) **D/P:** Fred Olen Ray **S:** David A. Jackson, James Saad, Tom Riparetti, Steve Le Gassick **P:** Alan Amiel

Playboy Playmate Kathy Shower makes her debut in a black wig as a government drug-enforcement agent in Mexico. She poses as a hooker (but keeps her clothes on) to rescue her partner, Brian Thompson (from *Cobra*). There are a lot of car chases and guest stars, including villains William Smith, Sid Haig (as Iggy), and Ross Hagen. With Robert Quarry, Mel Welles, Dawn Wildsmith, Russ Tamblyn as a biker (like in *Satan's Sadists*), and the director himself. Marie Windsor is seen running the Hollywood Book and Poster Store. Scenes were filmed at Bronson Canyon.

COMMERCIAL MANIA

(Rhino)

Johnny Legend compiled 60 minutes of choice American TV commercials from the 50s through the early 70s. The ones for beer and cigarettes are especially interesting. Many celebrity ads are included, with the Three Stooges, Harpo Marx, Lucy and Desi, Ronald Reagan, and others. *Commercial Mania: The Special Edition* is a half-hour version.

THE COMMIES ARE COMING! THE COMMIES ARE COMING!: *See* RED NIGHTMARE

COMMITTED

(Media, 1987) **D:** William A. Levy **S:** Simon Last, Paul Mason S. Africa

Jennifer O'Neill arrives as a nurse and becomes an abused inmate in an asylum run by William Windom. Narration helps hold together this disjointed variation on the much-used "lunatics taking over the asylum" plot (the film was once abandoned as unfinished). By the director of *Wham, Bam, Thank You, Space Man* (1973). With Robert Forster, Sidney Lassick, and Ron Paillo.

THE COMMITMENTS

(CBS, 1990) **D:** Alan Parker **S:** Dick Clement, Ian La Fresnais, Roddy Doyle **P:** Roger Randall-Cutler, Lynda Myles

A struggling Dublin soul cover band (they consider the Irish "the blacks of Europe") disintegrates just when they could be making it on records. Based on a 1990 book by Roddy Doyle, this film makes statements about slum life and Ireland itself. Andrew Strong is the lead singer, and Robert Akins is the determined guy who gets the musicians together. With Michael Aherne, Bronagh Gallagher, Angela Ball, and Maria Doyle. The "group" actually played some dates in America after the film was released. 20th Century–Fox also released *The Making of "The Commitments."*

COMMON BONDS

(Academy, 1991) **D:** Allan Goldstein **S:** Alan Aylward, Michael Ironside **P:** Richard Davis Canada (*Chaindance*)

Michael Ironside (who also was the executive producer and cowrote this comedy/drama) is a prisoner handcuffed to a cerebral-palsy victim in a wheelchair (Brad Dourif) as part of a demented reform program. He has to care for him, but they hate each other. With Rae Dawn Chong, as the social worker responsible for the plan, and Bruce Glover.

COMMON-LAW CABIN

(RM, 1967) **D/P/C/E:** Russ Meyer **S:** John E. Moran, **P:** Eve Meyer

Meyer's first color movie with a plot has the same rural setting as his previous hits *Lorna* and *Mudhoney* and lots of outdoor go-go dancing. It's an outrageous crime-and-sex melodrama with Jack Moran, Babette Bardot, Adele Rein, Alaina Capri (star of *Good Morning and Goodbye!*), Ken Swofford (later a regular on the TV series *Fame*), and Franklin Bolger. It sometimes played as *How Much Loving Does a Normal Couple Need?*

COMMON-LAW WIFE

(SW, 1963) **D:** Eric Sayers **S:** Grace Nolan **P:** Fred A. Kadane

M. A. Ripps (*Poor White Trash*) presented this b/w feature, made in Texas. It's similar in some ways to the rural dramas Russ Meyer was about to make, with good dialogue (written in this case by a woman) but minus the comedy. A rich, corrupt old man throws out his live-in lover, Linda (Annabelle Lee), and asks his gold-digging niece, Baby Doll (Lacy Kelly), to move in. Kelly (also in Irving Klaw's *Nature's Sweethearts*) is great as the sarcastic, wild beauty who uses the (married) sheriff and Bull out in the swamp to get what she wants and plots murder. Linda fights back, and the ending is outrageous! I liked all the twisting in the club too. Mike shadows are visible. Lee went on to act in S. F. Brownrigg movies like *Don't Look in the Basement*. I want to see Sayers' other movie, *The Garbage Man!*

COMMUNION

(MCEG, 1989) **D/P:** Philippe Mora **S/P:** Whitley Strieber **P:** Dan Allingham

Christopher Walken as Whitley Strieber (*The Hunger; Wolfen*) recalls under hypnosis how he encountered skinny ETs ("little blue fuckers") in his Upstate New York cabin. Lindsay Crouse is his wife, and Frances Sternhagen is his psychiatrist. It's based on Strieber's 1987 book and is 110 mostly boring minutes with group-encounter sessions and Eric Clapton theme music. Another tape, *Close Encounters of the Fourth Kind*, is an hour of interviews with Strieber, hosted by Roddy McDowall.

COMPAÑEROS

(1970) **D/S:** Sergio Corbucci **S:** Dino Mauri, Massimo De Rita   Italy/Spain/W. Germany (*Vamos a Matar, Compañeros!*)

Franco Nero is a Swedish mercenary who helps a Mexican revolutionary (Tomas Milian). Jack Palance steals the show as a character with a wooden hand (he had been nailed to a cross) and a pet hawk named America to which he feeds chunks of his victims. With Fernando Rey and Karin Schubert. It's a long (121-minute) sequel to *Professional Gun* (1968), by the same director, also with Palance and Nero. Ennio Morricone composed the score.

THE COMPANY OF WOLVES

(Vestron, 1984) **D/S:** Neil Jordan **S:** Angela Carter **P:** Chris Brown   UK

Sarah Patterson stars as a Little Red Riding Hood type in a slow-moving but fascinating black-comedy/allegory based on stories by Angela Carter. Angela Lansbury as Granny tells the fantasy/horror stories, and there are dreams inside of dreams. With David Warner, Brian Glover, Danielle Dax, Stephen Rea, and an unbilled Terence Stamp. Chris Tucker created the transformation FX, including a wolf that actually emerges from a human. It was all filmed in a studio, with production design by Anton Furst. The George Fenton score is on Varese Sarabande.

THE COMPLEAT BEATLES

(MGM/UA, 1982) **D:** Patrick Montgomery

Malcolm McDowell narrates this nearly 2-hour unauthorized biography (which received limited theatrical release). It's the best overall look at the Fab Four (so far). The early days are the most interesting. Stu Sutcliff and Pete Best are covered, and there's some good live footage of Tony Sheridan (who is interviewed). The Beatles are seen playing in Hamburg and at the Cavern in Liverpool ("Some Other Guy"), then on international Beatlemania tours. After the "Penny Lane" promo film, things go downhill fast. Long, ponderous versions of "Let It Be," "Hey Jude," and other later epics waste way too much time as the group is seen dissolving. George Martin, Marianne Faithfull, Gerry Marsden, and others are also interviewed. Watch it on a double bill with *The Rutles*. Also check out *The Beatles' First US Visit* (MPI, 1990), which was directed by Albert Maysles for British TV. There are also many other Beatles tapes and others just on Lennon or McCartney.

COMPLEX WORLD

(Hemdale, 1989) **D/S:** James Wolpaw **P:** Geoff Adams, Rich Lupo, Dennis Maloney

An evil presidential candidate wants to close the Heartbreak Hotel nightclub/bar, owned by his son (Dan Welch), so he hires terrorists to blow it up. Stanley Mathis stars as Morris, a folk-singing terrorist who does a funny anti–New Jersey song. This amusing indy film from Providence, Rhode Island, features NRBQ playing briefly, band member Tom Ardolino geting high and talking to Elvis on the phone, Captain Lou Albano as a biker, and the Young Adults (featuring Dave Hanson) doing comic songs on stage.

COMPULSION

(Fox, 1959) **D:** Richard Fleischer **S:** Richard Murphy **P:** Richard D. Zanuck

Adapted from the book by Meyer Levin, this film is based on the real Leopold-Loeb case, which also inspired Hitchcock's *Rope* (1948) and *Swoon* (1992). Two very intelligent young men from wealthy Chicago families, fascinated by the writings of Nietzsche and involved in an excessively close (possibly sexual) relationship, kidnapped and killed a14-year-old cousin of one of them. It was "the crime of the century" in the 20s. Dean Stockwell and Bradford Dillman star, with Orson Welles as an anti-death-penalty defense attorney patterned on Clarence Darrow. The three stars shared the best-actor award at Cannes. Welles' 15-minute summation speech was even released on a record. With E. G. Marshall as the prosecuting attorney, Diane Varsi (in her last feature for nearly a decade), Martin Milner, and Richard Anderson.

COMPUTER BEACH PARTY

(Vestron, 1985) **D/S/P/E:** Gary Troy

In this beach-party comedy made in Galveston, Texas, a computer expert tries to stop beach property from becoming a tourist attraction.

THE COMPUTER WORE TENNIS SHOES

(Walt Disney, 1970) **D:** Robert Butler **S:** Joseph L. McEveety **P:** Bill Anderson

In the first of three Disney fantasy/comedies starring Kurt Russell, he's Dexter, a student with a computer in his brain, pursued by gangsters. With Cesar Romero, Joe Flynn, William Schallert, Richard Bakalyan, and Fritz Feld. Russell had been in Disney films since *The Absent Minded Professor* (1960), was still in them in 1975 (*The Strongest Man in the World*), and finally made a career change by starring as Elvis on TV in 1979. He returned as Dexter in *The Barefoot Executive* (1971) and *Now You See Him, Now You Don't* (1972). Disney remade *Computer . . .* as a TV movie in 1995.

COMRADES IN ARMS

(Republic, 1991) **D/S/P:** J. Christian Ingvordsen **S/P/A:** Steven Kaman, John Weiner   Canada

Rick Washburn stars as Bone, an ex–Green Beret, in this awful, senseless "action" movie made in Ontario. It has something to do with KGB agents helping to battle a drug cartel in the Colombian jungle. Boring dialogue scenes alternate with explosions and generic battles. Lance Henriksen is wasted as a CIA chief, and the late Lyle Alzado is laughable as a Russian general. Ingvordsen also made several movies starring Jake LaMotta. Henriksen was also in his movie *The Outfit*.

CONAN THE DESTROYER

(MCA, 1984) **D:** Richard Fleischer **S:** Stanley Mann **P:** Raffaella De Laurentiis

There's more comedy in this PG sequel to the R-rated *Conan the Barbarian* (1982). Arnold Schwarzenegger protects a virgin princess (Olivia D'Abo) on a quest for a magic gem. With scene-stealing Grace Jones as Zula, Wilt Chamberlain, Mako as a wizard, Tracey Walter, Sarah Douglas, Jeff Corey, and Ferdy Mayne. Carlo Rambaldi created the Dagoth monster. It was filmed in Mexico. Fleischer did *Red Sonja* (1985) with Arnold next. This was the star's first film after his *Shape Up with Arnold* tape (1983). A more embarrassing tape is *Carnival in Rio* (After Dark, 1983), a Playboy TV special, with Arnold as the leering host.

COMMUNISM

Anti-Communist features flourished in America in the early 50s. Even if you agree with the message, most of them are pretty ridiculous, and some are hilarious. Around the same time, generic villains with German names and accents became generic villains with Russian names and accents in serials, spy movies, science fiction movies, and TV adventure shows. The villains stayed around, but specific anti-Communist movies were rare in the 60s (except for a few about Cuba) and the 70s. As soon as Reagan was elected, they returned. The 80s revival reached a peak with several Stallone hits. After the fall of Communism in Europe, generic movie villains started having German names and accents again, or were Arabs. *Better Dead Than Red* (1992) is a good book about the whole phenomenon.

Arnold Schwarzenegger in *Conan the Destroyer*.

CONCORDE AFFAIR '79

(VSOM, 1978) **D:** Ruggero Deodato
S: Ernesto Gastaldi, Renzo Genta   Italy

Remember *The Concorde: Airport '79*, the last of the *Airport* movie series? Well, it did better business in Europe than here, so this spy movie ripped off the title. James Franciscus leads the name cast, with Americans-in-exile Mimsy Farmer, Joseph Cotten, Van Johnson, and Edmund Purdom. Deodato's next film was *Cannibal Holocaust*.

CONCRETE ANGELS

(Academy, 1987) **D/P:** Carlo Liconti **S:** Jim Purdy **P:** Anthony Kramreither   Canada

A battle-of-the-bands contest is held in 1964 Toronto to select one to open for the Beatles. Joseph Dinambro stars

THE CONCRETE JUNGLE

(1960) **D:** Joseph Losey **S:** Alun Owen
P: Jack Greenwood   UK (*The Criminal*)

Stanley Baker stars as an ex-con in this grim story of a racetrack robbery. He's sent back to prison but won't tell the other cons where the loot is stashed, so he's tortured and his girlfriend is kidnapped. With Sam Wanamaker, Patrick Magee, Nigel Green, Jill Bennett, Patrick Wymark, and Edward Judd. It's based on a story by Jimmy Sangster. Losey's next film was *These Are the Damned*, made for Hammer.

THE CONCRETE JUNGLE

(RCA/Columbia, 1982) **D:** Tom DeSimone
S: Alan J. Adler **P:** Billy Fine

Skier Tracy Bregman is Cherry, set up by her boyfriend, busted for coke, and sent to women-in-prison Hell. Jill St. John (in her last theatrical feature to date) is Warden Fletcher. There's lots of the expected torture and humiliation. With exploitation veteran Peter Brown, Sondra Currie, Barbara Luna as a killer lesbian known as "the Cat," Aimee Eccles, Camille Keaton, Nita Talbot as a social worker, Marcia Karr, Greta Blackburn, and Carol Conners. Producer Fine returned with *Chained Heat* (1983).

CONDEMNED TO HELL

(TWE, 1982) **D/S:** Anibal Di Salvo   Italy

A typical innocent young woman (Leonor Benedetto) is sent to a typical movie-world women's prison. After the showers, scenes of lesbian sex, and beatings by guards, she gets revenge.

CONDEMNED TO LIVE

(Sinister, 1935) **D:** Frank Strayer
S: Karen DeWolf **P:** Maury M. Cohen

Ralph Morgan stars as a kindly professor who seems to become a vampire during the full moon and terrorizes a European village. It turns out that he had been bitten by a vampire bat in an African cave (actually Bronson Canyon) as a child. With Mischa Auer as Zan, the hunchbacked servant who dumps bodies at Bronson Canyon, Pedro De Cordoba as a Dr. Van Helsing type, and Maxine Doyle. It uses the same music and Universal sets as the Lionel Atwill movie *The Vampire Bat* (1933), with a similar plot and by the same director. Made by an independent studio, Invincible Pictures, it's only 65 minutes long.

CONDEMNED WOMEN

(1938) **D:** Lew Landers **S:** Lionel
Houser **P:** Robert F. Sisk

Made a dozen years before the better-known *Caged* (1950), this tough women-in-prison movie shows that the clichés were already in place. Anne Shirley takes the rap for her boyfriend and ends up at the state penal institution for women. Louis Hayward is the reform-minded prison psychiatrist, Esther Dale is the sadistic matron. With Sally Eilers, Lee Patrick (also in *Caged*), and Jack Carson. Shirley was also in *Boy Slaves*.

CONDOR

(1986) **D:** Virgil L. Vogel **S:** Len Janson,
Chuck Menville **P:** Peter Nelson

In this ABC-TV series pilot, set in the future of the 1990s, a secret agent (Ray Wise) and his *Robocop*-like android partner (Wendy Kilbourne) work for an agency run by Craig Stevens.

CONDORMAN

(Disney, 1981) **D:** Charles Jarrott **S:** Marc Stirdivant,
Glen Caron, Mickey Rose **P:** Jan Williams

Jill St. John oversees prisoner abuse in *The Concrete Jungle*.

Michael Crawford stars in this PG-rated spy spoof as an American cartoonist in Paris whose cartoon character helps in the adventure. Oliver Reed is the evil Sergei, and Barbara Carrera is Natasha.

CONEHEADS

(Paramount, 1993) **D:** Steve Barron **S:** Tom
Davis, Dan Aykroyd **P:** Lorne Michaels

Dan Aykroyd and Jane Curtin are pointy-headed aliens posing as a middle-class "French" couple in Queens, where he works as a cabdriver. They move up to Paramus, New Jersey, and eventually return home. It was made 15 years after the skits on *Saturday Night Live*, but this PG comedy has its moments, and the final scenes on their native planet are very impressive. With Michelle Burke (also in *Dazed and Confused*) as their sexy (and bald) daughter, Chris Farley as her boyfriend, Michael McKean as a government immigration official, Dave Thomas as the alien high master, Adam Sandler, Sinbad, Laraine Newman, Jason Alexander, Michael Richards, Tom Arnold, Phil Hartman, Chris Rock, Jon Lovitz, Jan Hooks, Garrett Morris, and many other (mostly) former SNL cast members. The movie contains plugs for Subway sandwiches and Pepsi.

CONFESSIONS OF A BLUE MOVIE STAR

(Cinematheque, 1975) **D/S/C:** Richard R. Rimmel,
Andrzej Kostenko (and Wes Craven)
W. Germany (*The Evolution of Snuff*)

An interesting post–Manson murders Roman Polanski interview is intercut (out of context) into this documentary supposedly made by a student of the director. A narrator tells us the story behind the headline-making suicide of a part-Polish, Nietzsche-reading medical student who killed herself after a brief career as a sex-film star in Munich. Behind-the-scenes segments show auditions for simulated sex roles, and actors, would-be actors, and a first-time director are interviewed and shown at work. Anybody who can stay interested should wait until after the *End* for an added segment showing "a director of snuff films," talking with a paper bag over his head (!), who proceeds to show footage from his "real snuff film," actually gory footage (usually missing from prints) from *The Last House on the Left* (!).

CONFESSIONS OF A HITMAN

(Hemdale, 1991) **D/S:** Larry Leahy
S/P: Tony Cinciripini

James Remar stars as a Mafia hitman, dying from a brain tumor, who robs the mob and heads for Vegas in a limo. With Emily Longstreth as a hitchhiker and Michael Wright as the driver. The score by Billy Talbot (of Crazy Horse) includes Neil Young. Bill Murray and Steven Paul were executive producers.

CONFESSIONS OF A PEEPING TOM:
See HI, MOM!

CONFESSIONS OF A SERIAL KILLER

(New Horizons, 1985) **D/S:** Mark Blair
P: Cecyle Osgood Rexrode

Robert Burns, the production designer for *The Texas Chainsaw Massacre, The Hills Have Eyes, Reanimator,* and other horror hits, stars as killer Daniel Ray Hawkins, a forgettable nobody with glasses and a mustache. The character is based on real serial killer Henry Lee Lucas, and this excellent film follows what really happened much more accurately than *Henry* did. Daniel is seen at 15, with a crippled father and a slutty mother. His hooker sister (Eleese Lester) helps him kill, and they move around Texas and Louisiana with Ol' Moon, a "queer." They take Polaroids of victims. Daniel Ray's last words in a local jailhouse are "Can I get another chocolate milkshake?" The music by William Penn is excellent. Roger Corman released this low-budget movie, made in Austin, Texas, in 1992 with ad art that made it look like *The Silence of the Lambs*!

CONFESSIONS OF A SORORITY GIRL

(1994) **D:** Uli Edel **S/P:** Debra Hill **S:** Gigi Vorgan

This Showtime Rebel Highway movie is a remake of Corman's *Sorority Girl* (1957), which was itself a teen remake of *The Strange One* (also 1957) which was based on a novel by Calder Willimgham. Jamie Luner stars as the new sorority member who ruins the lives of other students. With Alyssa Milano. By the German director of *Last Exit to Brooklyn*.

CONFESSIONS OF A VICE BARON

(Fang, Hollywood Confidential, 1937)   *(Skid Row)*

Reusing old footage is a Hollywood tradition, but this road-show classic (without any credits) went to new extremes. Apparently Willy Castelo was typecast playing oily con men in 30s movies (just as Timothy Farrell was in the 50s). Here he stars as Lucky Lombardo, death-row inmate #1452, telling his story to the warden, who tells him, "Make it snappy!" The rest of the movie is scene after scene from *Mad Youth, Smashing the Vice Trust, The Wages of Sin,* and other earlier features that all starred or featured Castelo! If you didn't recognize, say, the hard-to-forget Dead Rat Cafe scene from *The Cocaine Fiends*, you'd probably never figure out the flashback editing scam, because Willy always looked pretty much the same. His snappy confession reveals that he posed as a count, ran an escort service (there's a bit of nudity in this segment), posed as a doctor, performed illegal abortions, sold babies, posed as a respectable businessman, kidnapped schoolgirls, was named "king of the red lights," and fell in love. After he tells all, he gives a warning speech directly to *You* before going to the chair. Wonderful stuff, originally presented by Real Life Dramas.

CONFESSIONS OF TOM HARRIS

(UAV, 1966) **D:** David Nelson **D/C:** John Derek
S/P/A: Don Murray   *(Childish Things; Tale of the Cock)*

Don Murray (who also narrates) is a no-good, alky Nam vet who tries amateur boxing in Vegas, then takes a job collecting debts for gangsters. Eventually he's born again, after he rapes Linda Evans (offscreen), then follows her to her father's sanctuary for alcoholics, where he's cast as Judas at a Last Supper picnic. The inspired cast includes David Brian, Logan Ramsey, Gary Clarke, future porno actress Angelique Pettyjohn, Gypsy Boots talking in rhyme, and former teen star Rod Lauren (*The Crawling Hand*) as himself. Evans, who was Derek's pre-Bo wife, gets a lot of closeups. Jonathan Haze was the production manager, and yes, the codirector was Ricky's brother. This Hollywood misfire was first released in 1969 then again in 1972. Murray went on to *It Won't Rub Off, Baby* and *The Viking Queen*. He was also in *The Cross and the Switchblade* (1970) and other religious redemption features.

CONFIDENTIAL REPORT

(Criterion, 1955) **D/S/P/A:** Orson Welles
UK (*Mr. Arkadin*)

In a film with obvious *Citizen Kane* touches, the wealthy Gregory Arkadin (Orson Welles) hires an American cigarette smuggler (Robert Arden) to reconstruct his life before 1927. Arden talks to odd characters all over the world who are always killed afterwards. The cast includes Paola Mori, Michael Redgrave, Patricia Medina, Akim Tamiroff, and Mischa Auer. It was filmed all over Europe and in Mexico. The first US release was in 1962 (cut), and it was released on laserdisc in 1992.

THE CONQUERED CITY

(1962) **D:** Joseph Anthony **S:** Guy Elmes, Eric Bercovici, Marc Brabdel   Italy (*La Citta à Prigioniera*)

AIP released this WWII drama, set in Greece during the Nazi retreat. David Niven stars, with Lea Massari, Ben Gazzara, Michael Craig, and Martin Balsam.

THE CONQUEROR

(MCA, 1956) **D/P:** Dick Powell **S:** Oscar Millard

John Wayne is Genghis Khan in this RKO/Howard Hughes $6 million fiasco that's fascinating on several levels. The script and the miscast Wayne make the 110-minute Cinemascope and Technicolor epic great for laughs, but no other film has had such a horrible and long-lasting effect. It was shot in Utah, in an area still contaminated by atomic tests conducted in 1953 at Yucca Flats, Nevada. Then sand from the location was brought back to the studio to be used in retakes and additional scenes. In the years since the production, at least 91 members of the cast and crew have contracted cancer, and at least 46 have died of it. Besides Wayne and director Powell, the following actors died of cancer: Susan Hayward (who played a red-haired Tartar princess), Agnes Moorehead, Lee Van Cleef, Thomas Gomez, John Hoyt, Ted De Corsia, and William Conrad. Pedro Armendariz committed suicide after hearing the diagnosis. Leo Gordon, Billy Barty, and at least some of the 300 American Indians who played Tartar horsemen are still with us. Hughes later paid $12 million to buy back the rights to this film (and *Jet Pilot*), and kept it out of circulation until 1974.

CONQUEST

(Media, 1984) **D:** Lucio Fulci **S:** Gino Capone, José Antonio de la Loma **P:** Giovanni Di Clemente
Italy/Spain/Mexico (*El Bárbaro*)

Jorge Rivero stars in a gory *Conan* copy. He fights his own double, an ape man, zombies, killer bats, and "mummy men." Sabrina Siani (from *Ator*) is the evil, brain-eating queen. She wears a gold mask and sleeps covered with snakes, wearing only a spiked G-string. With Andrea Occipinti (*Bolero*), lifesaving dolphins, and music by Claudio Simonetti (of Goblin). Much of the gore was cut from the US version. The most complete version is available on tape in Venezuela.

CONQUEST OF THE EARTH

(MCA, 1980) **D:** Sidney Hayers, Sigmund Neufeld Jr., Barry Crane **S:** Glen A. Larson
P: Jeff Frelich, Frank Lupo, Gary B. Winters

This feature version (made for overseas theatrical release) of the "new" *Battlestar Galactica* TV series (*Battlestar 1980*) is about another Cyclon attack. With series star Lorne Greene, Kent McCord, Barry Van Dyke, Robyn Douglas, Robert Reed, and Wolfman Jack (as himself).

CONRAD BROOKS MEETS THE WEREWOLF

(1993) **D/A:** David "The Rock" Nelson

Everything about this tape is terrible, but watching three Brooks (Biedrzycki) brothers (they all appeared in *Jailbait*) is an experience. Henry is 84 and Ted also appeared in *Female Trouble*. In Baltimore, Conrad chases a werewolf (the overbearing director) through a Jewish cemetery. He says "This gun don't have no effect," then repeatedly runs over a werewolf dummy with a car while laughing and repeating the same lines. All the bad takes are left in and still more outtakes are at the end. With interviews (complete with multiple bad takes).

CONSUMING PASSIONS

(1987) **D:** Giles Foster **S:** Paul D. Zimmerman **P:** William P. Cartlidge   UK

This black comedy was based on the play *Secrets*, by Michael Palin and Terry Jones of Monty Python. Tyler Butterworth accidentally knocks three workers into a vat of chocolate, and chocolate sales soar. Jonathan Pryce is the evil candy-company manager. With Vanessa Redgrave (overacting), Sammi Davis, and Freddie Jones.

CONTAGION

(Sony, 1988) **D:** Karl Zwicky **S/P:** Ken Methold **P:** Leo Barretto   Australia

In a film influenced by *The Shining*, a young traveling salesman (John Doyle), trapped in a mansion overnight, is offered immortality and wealth if he kills for the mysterious owner.

CONTAMINATION: *See* ALIEN CONTAMINATION

CONTEMPT

(Embassy, 1963) **D/S/A:** Jean-Luc Godard
P: Carlo Ponti   France/Italy (*Le Mépris*)

This is the Godard film most likely to show up on American TV, so watch for it. Its "about" the planning of a film version of Homer's epic *The Odyssey* to be made in Rome and it shows what Godard thought about mainstream producers like the ones who backed this fascinating film. *The Odyssey* is to be produced by a crude American (Jack Palance) and directed by the great Fritz Lang, who plays himself. Brigitte Bardot and her screenwriter husband (Michel Piccoli) are invited to the producer's villa on the Riviera. The characters planning to make the troubled international production all speak in various languages. The movie was condemned by the Catholic Church's Legion of Decency. The 103-minute feature, shot in color and Cinemascope, is available subtitled or dubbed.

CONTROL

(1987) **D:** Giuliano Montaldo
Italy/Canada/France (*The Waiting Room*)

Burt Lancaster stars in this nuclear-disaster movie, whose plot was rewritten after Chernobyl. With Ben Gazzara, Kate Nelligan, Andrea Occhipinti, Erland Josephson, Zeudi Araya, Ingrid Thulin, and Kate Reid. It was an HBO debut in America.

CONVICTED WOMAN

(1940) **D:** Nick Grinde **S:** Joseph
Carole **P:** Ralph Cohn

A Columbia studios women-in-prison movie with extortion and suicide. Rochelle Hudson is the innocent women who is sent up. Glenn Ford is the reporter who exposes the corruption. With Freda Inescort and Lola Lane.

CONVICT WOMEN

(SW, 1970) **D:** John Hayes **S:** Edward M.
Kingfield **P:** C. Roger Hiller   (*Bust Out*)

A very wimpy devout Christian takes his wife and four young women on a picnic. Rene Bond constantly sneaks off to run around naked in the woods and have sex with her boyfriend. In one scene she crosses a log bridge naked on her knees. Two killer escaped cons show up saying they're geologists, and all the girls have sex in the woods. Later on, the wife is raped (in a ghost town) but likes it, and the tied-up husband has to watch. This brainless movie has lots of pretty imaginative (very near porno) sex.

THE COOK, THE THIEF, HIS WIFE, AND HER LOVER

(Vidmark, 1989) **D/S:** Peter Greenaway
P: Kees Kasander, Dennis Wigman
C: Sacha Vierney Holland/France

Four (!) video versions of this controversial film were released: uncut, NC-17, 123 minutes; letterboxed, uncut but cropped, 95 minutes; R-rated version; and R-rated and letterboxed. During a week at La Hollandaise, a restaurant owned by a loud, brutal London gangster (Michael Gambon), there's sex, violence, and (unrealistic) cannibalism. Helen Mirren is the wife, Richard Bohringer is the cook, and Alan Howard is the book-reading lover. With Tim Roth and Ian Dury. Various rooms are in different colors like in Corman's *Masque of the Red Death*.

THE COOL AND THE CRAZY

(1994) **D/S:** Ralph Bakshi
P: Lou Arkoff, Debra Hill

Alicia Silverstone (star of *The Crush* and some popular rock videos) is a bored young wife who has an affair with a hoodlum (Matthew Flint). This Showtime cable Rebel Highway series movie takes its name from the classic 1958 teen/drug movie of the same name. Maybe Bakshi was hired to make this because he had recently directed *Cool World*. With Christine Harnos and Jared Leto.

COOL AS ICE

(MCA, 1991) **D:** David Kellogg
S: David Stenn **P:** Carolyn Pfeiffer

In one of the more embarrassing results of the rap craze, Vanilla Ice, stars as a musician/student with a motor scooter who falls for an honor student (Kristen Minter) in a new town. With Candy Clark and Michael Gros as the parents, Sidney Lassick, Dody Goodman, and Naomi Campbell. Universal released this PG flop.

COOL BREEZE

(1972) **D/S:** Barry Pollack **P:** Gene Corman

This is a remake of John Huston's classic *The Asphalt Jungle* (1950), which had already been remade as a western *Badlanders*, (1958) and as *Cairo* (1962). Thalmus Rasulala stars as an ex-con who plans a diamond heist, with Jim Watkins, Judy Pace, Margaret Avery in the Marilyn Monroe role, Paula Kelly, Raymond St. Jacques, Pam Grier as Mona, and Robert Shayne. Solomon Burke is heard on the MGM soundtrack.

COOLEY HIGH

(Orion, 1975) **D:** Michael Schultz
S: Eric Monte **P:** Steve Krantz

This is a sort of more serious black *American Graffiti* (it even tells what happened to all the main characters at the end) set on the South Side of Chicago in 1964. Glynn Turman (*JD's Revenge*) as Preach and Lawrence Hilton-Jacobs as Cochise join two others and steal a car for joyriding. The results are tragic, but the movie has comedy and great music and is a classic of its kind. With Garrett Morris as an understanding teacher, Cynthia Davis, and future director Robert Townsend in a small part. Great Motown oldies fill the soundtrack. Writer Monte later created the *Good Times* TV series. The TV show *What's Happening!!* was loosely based on this movie. Schultz did *Car Wash* (1976) next. The film was released by AIP.

THE COOL ONES

(1967) **D:** Gene Nelson **S:** Joyce
Geller **P:** William Conrad

This show-biz comedy features Roddy McDowall, doing a parody of Phil Spector, as a young, self-made rock millionaire who tries to create and manipulate a new hit singing duo. He arranges for a young has-been pop star (Gil Peterson) to have a public affair with a go-go dancer (Debbie Watson) while both are on *Wiz Bam*, a *Shindig*-type TV show. The film could have been much better but it's still a fun piece of the 60s by the director of several mediocre Elvis movies. Watch for appearances by the Leaves (who do "Dr. Stone"), Mrs. Miller, Glen Campbell, and the Bantams. The choreography is by Toni Basil, the music is by Billy Strange and Ernie Freeman, and the songs were written by Lee Hazelwood. With Nita Talbot, Phil Harris, and Robert Coote.

COOL WORLD

(Paramount., 1992) **D:** Ralph Bakshi **S:** Michael
Grais, Mark Victor **P:** Frank Mancuso Jr.

Gabriel Byrne stars as a confused cartoonist (painfully) transported to a parallel "toon" world that he created. Sex with "doodles" is forbidden there, so most of the plot is whether he'll do it with Holli Wood, a sexy blond toon (the voice of Kim Basinger). They do (it's PG-13 rated), and she becomes human for the real-world ending. Brad Pitt costars as an ageless live-action WWII vet trapped as a detective. The best characters, though, are the hyperactive, violent cartoon fig-

Gil Peterson is one of *The Cool Ones*.

ures who constantly intrude. The film is packed with mind-blowing 30s-style cartoon effects, background details, and gags, but the interaction between live and animated chacters should have been better. With Frank Sinatra Jr. (as himself) and Carrie Hamilton. David Bowie provided the end theme. It was Bakshi's first in over 9 years, his 12th feature in all.

COOTIE GARAGES

(1990) **D/S/P:** Marcy Hedy Lynn

Cootie Garages (the title is explained at the end) is an excellent color-coordinated/comedy/fantasy/horror film by a filmmaker from Detroit. It's about wigs that change ordinary people into exotic characters. Parts are inspired by the grave-robbers Burke and Hare, H. G. Lewis' *The Gruesome Twosome,* and *The Gorgon.* Other reference points are early John Waters (but better-looking) and Devo videos. The effects (animation, decapitation, bugs 'n' blood) are good, and the soundtrack is perfect. It's 54 minutes long and was made in New York City.

COP

(Paramount, 1988) **D/S/P:** James B. Harris **P/A:** James Woods   (*Blood on the Moon*)

Woods is a cop with marriage problems who goes after a serial killer, in this surprising movie based on the novel *Blood on the Moon,* by James Ellroy. Lesley Ann Warren costars as a feminist bookstore owner, with Charles Durning, Charles Haid, and Randi Brooks. It was the first film from one-time Kubrick partner Harris since *Fast Walking* (also with Woods).

COP IN BLUE JEANS

(VSOM, 1975) **D/S:** Bruno Corbucci **S:** Mario Amendola   Italy (*Squadra Antiscioppo*)

Tomas Milian stars as Nico, an undercover cop who's after a gangster (Jack Palance), in this violent action crime movie.

COP KILLER: *See* CORRUPT

COP KILLERS

(TWE, 1973) **D:** Walter Cichy **P/A:** Bill Osco **P:** Howard Ziehm   Canada

Jason Williams and Bill Osco (both of *Flesh Gordon* fame) star as guys who botch a coke deal, which leads to a kidnapping and a murder spree on the road.

CORNBREAD, EARL, AND ME

(HBO, 1975) **D/P:** Joe Manduke **S:** Leonard Lamendorf

This drama about Chicago ghetto kids is based on the novel *Hog Butcher,* by Ronald Fair. Larry (Lawrence) Fishbourne is the real star, as the 12-year-old "me" of the title, who is traumatized by the murder of his friend, Cornbread, a basketball player (former UCLA star Keith Wilkes). Tierre Turner is Earl. With Moses Gunn, Rosalind Cash, Bernie Casey, Antonio Fargas as One Eye, Logan Ramsey, Thalmus Rasulala, and the Blackbyrds. The film was released by AIP and rated PG.

ROGER CORMAN

Corman is the number one psychotronic producer of all time. With one exception (*Frankenstein Unbound*), he stopped directing in 1971. At that time he left AIP and formed his own New World, the drive-in movie company of the 70s. The company staggered on without him after he sold it in 1981 and formed Concorde and later New Horizons video. Several books have been published about Corman and his movies, and his autobiography, *How I Made a Hundred Movies in Hollywood and Never Lost a Dime,* was published in 1990.

These are my top 10 personal favorites among all the movies directed by Corman:
1. The Masque of the Red Death (1964)
2. Bucket of Blood (1959)
3. Not of This Earth (1956)
4. Bloody Mama (1970)
5. The Little Shop of Horrors (1960)
6. The Intruder (1962)
7. The Trip (1967)
8. The Wild Angels (1966)
9. Attack of the Crab Monsters (1957)
10. It Conquered the World (1956)

CORRUPT

(HBO, 1981) **D/S:** Roberto Faenza **S:** Ennio De Concini, Hugh Fleetwood **P:** Elda Ferri   Italy (*Cop Killer; Order of Death*)

Harvey Keitel stars as a corrupt New York City cop with a very expensive empty apartment who keeps Leo Smith (John Lydon) prisoner. He beats and humiliates him, but the strange young man ends up breaking him down. Veteran actress Sylvia Sidney plays Lydon's mom. The film is based on *Order of Death,* by Hugh Fleetwood. This was the only acting role for former Sex Pistols lead singer Johnny Rotten (John Lydon). Ennio Morricone wrote the score. The 113 minute film had 15 minutes cut by New Line for its 1983 US release.

THE CORRUPTION OF CHRIS MILLER

(1972) **D:** Juan Antonio Bardem **S:** Santiago Moncada **P:** Xavier Armet   Spain (*Behind the Shutters*)

Jean Seberg is the stepmother of a traumatized young woman (Marisol). They take in a drifter, they both fall in love with him, and then they kill him. Meanwhile, a killer dressed as a monk with a sickle terrorizes the countryside. With Barry Stokes and Gerard Tichy.

THE CORRUPT ONES

(Nelson, 1966) **D:** Bill Catching **S:** Brian Clemens **P:** Arthur Brauner France/Italy/W. Germany (*Il Signo di Pechino*)

Robert Stack is a photographer in Macao who becomes involved in murder and a search for treasure in an underground tomb. Nancy Kwan is the evil Tong leader Tina, and Elke Sommer is a widow who is kidnapped. Christian Marquand is also featured. Dusty Springfield sings the theme song. Clemens was a major writer for the TV series *The Avengers.*

CORVETTE SUMMER

(1978) **D/S:** Mathew Robbins Hal Barwood **E:** Amy Jones

Mark Hamill, in his first movie after *Star Wars,* goes after Las Vegas car thieves who have his Corvette. Annie Potts is a hooker who helps him in this PG comedy. With Danny Bonaduce, Brion James, and Dick Miller.

THE COSMIC MAN

(Rhino, 1958) **D:** Herman Green **S:** Arthur C. Pierce **P:** Robert A. Terry

This talky pro-science movie is full of good terms like "photon chamber," "anti-gravity," "cyclotron," and "sonic boom." It also stars John Carradine as a chess-playing phantom alien who arrives in what looks like a big, floating golf ball. Bruce Bennett, who began his career as a star of 30s serials (*Tarzan, The Lone Ranger*), is Dr. Carl Sorenson, a famous physicist who was responsible for the A bomb. His opponent is an air force colonel who wants to blow things up. Sorenson says, "There's only one team now, ever since Hiroshima." Lyn Osborne (*Space Patrol*) looks miserable as an enlisted man. They all go to a lodge owned by a blond widow whose crippled genius son, Kenny, only has 6 months to live. It takes Kenny and his mom forever to figure out that the mysterious guest with weird glasses and a hat is really the alien, even though they both speak with the unmistakable Carradine voice! Kenny says, "Sure looks bad for Dr. Sorenson and the cosmic man, doesn't it, Mom?" Pierce went on to write lots of silly but fun science-fiction movies, including *The Human Duplicators, Women of the Prehistoric Planet* (which he also directed), and *Dimension Five.*

COSMIC SLOP

(HBO, 1994) **D:** Reginald Hudlin, Warrington Hudlin, Kevin Rodney Sullivan **S:** Trey Ellis **P:** Ernest Johnson

You could call this thought-provoking fantasy trilogy by the makers of the *House Party* movies a black *Twilight Zone* but it's no imitation. In "Space Invaders" an alien (who looks like Ronald Reagan) make a deal with the government to take all the black people away. "The First Commandment" involves voodoo and a living female saint. "Tang" is based on a Chester Himes story. With Robert

Guillaume, Michele Lamar Richards, Jason Bernard, Brock Peters, Kasey Kasem, Nicholas Turturro, Paula Jai Parker, and Chi McBride. The HBO movie hosted by a three-eyed George Clinton was shown both as a feature and in three separate parts.

COSMOS: WAR OF THE PLANETS

(1977) **D:** "Al Bradley"/Alfonso Brescia
Italy (*Cosmo 2000; L'Invasion degli Extracorpi*)

John Richardson stars in another cheap Italian space movie. A spaceship investigates an out-of-control planet, finding a robot and an underground civilization. The heroes help the inhabitants destroy a computer.

COTTON CANDY

(1978) **D/S:** Ron Howard **S/A:** Clint
Howard **P:** John Thomas Lenox

This NBC-TV movie is about a 60s garage band. Too bad it's so damn light. Charles Martin Smith stars, with Clint Howard, Manuel Padilla Jr., and Alvy Moore. The Howards' dad, Rance, coproduced and acted too.

COTTON COMES TO HARLEM

(MGM, 1970) **D/S:** Ossie Davis **P:** Samuel Goldwyn Jr.

The "first really successful black action feature" was based on a pretty complicated novel by Chester Himes, who grew up in Cleveland and spent time in jail. (His novels were first published in France.) Gravedigger Jones (Godfrey Cambridge) and Coffin Ed Johnson (Raymond St. Jacques) are plainclothes Harlem cops investigating a "back to Africa" preacher (Calvin Lockhart) who is really out for money (which is hidden in a bale of cotten). With Judy Pace, Redd Foxx as Uncle Bud, Cleavon Little, and Lou Jacobi. It was shot in Harlem. The soundtrack is on UA. *Come Back, Charleston Blue* (1972) is the sequel. *A Rage in Harlem* (1990) is also based on a novel by Himes.

COTTONPICKIN' CHICKENPICKERS

(SW, 1967) **D/S/P:** Larry E. Jackson
S: Robert Baron **P:** Dick Randall

Country singers Del Reeves and Hugh X. Lewis star as two guys who get caught stealing chickens on the way to Miami and have to do road-clean-up-duty. This dumb, overlong hillbilly-moonshine musical has terrible editing, mixed day/night shots, and visible mike shadows. Guest stars include Tom Noonan and Mel Tillis (who sings "You Dirty Ol' Egg-Suckin' Dog") as copter pilots, Greta Thyssen as herself (in a polka-dot bikini), Sonny Tufts as a drunk telling jokes, Maxie Rosenbloom as a mailman, and Lila Lee (from the original *Blood and Sand*). My favorite song is "Comin' on Strong," sung by the big David Wilkins. The associate producer was David Puttnam (*Chariots of Fire*). Jackson also made *Las Vegas Hillbillies*. The color tape is presented by Johnny Legend.

THE COUNTERFEIT TRAITOR

(Paramount, 1962) **D/S:** George Seaton
P: William Perlberg

William Holden stars in a long (140-minute) but rewarding feature about an American-born Swedish citizen who sees nothing wrong with selling oil to the Nazi government in Germany during the war. He's forced to work as a double agent for the British, is branded a traitor by his anti-Nazi friends, and eventually learns just what is going on after he falls in love with a German woman active in the underground (Lilli Palmer). With Hugh Griffith, Eva Dahlbeck, Wolfgang Preiss, and Klaus Kinski (who spends part of the movie as a corpse). Based on a true story and shot on location in Europe, it's available on two cassettes.

COUNTERFORCE

(IVE, 1987) **D:** Anthony Loma **S:** Douglas
Burton **P:** Carlos Vasallo

A special-mission team is hired to protect a Middle Eastern leader (Louis Jourdan) from a dictator (Robert Forster). The international guest stars include George Rivero, George Kennedy, Andrew Stevens, Isaac Hayes, Hugo Stiglitz, and Kabir Bedi.

THE COUNT OF MONTE CRISTO

(1974) **D:** David Green **S:** Sidney
Caroll **P:** Norman Rosemont

Richard Chamberlain stars in a version (at least the seventh) of the famous Alexandre Dumas story. It was made for TV but played in theaters in Europe. With Tony Curtis as the evil Mondego, Trevor Howard, Louis Jourdan, Donald Pleasence, Kate Nelligan, and Taryn Power.

COVERGIRL

(1981) **D:** Jean-Claude Lord **S:** Charles Dennis
P: Claude Heroux   Canada (*Dreamworld*)

Jeff Conaway (from *Taxi*) tries to make model Irena Ferris "the face of the 80s." This New World release about the fashion industry was shot in Toronto but is set in NYC. The cast also includes Michele Scarabelli.

COVER GIRLS

(1977) **D:** Jerry London **S:** Mark
Rodgers **P:** David Gerber

In this NBC series pilot, Jayne Kennedy and Cornelia Sharpe are secret agents who are also fashion models. With George Lazenby, Vince Edwards, Don Johnson, and Ellen Travolta.

COVER ME, BABE

(1970) **D:** Noel Black **S:** George Wells
P: Lester Linsk   (*Run Shadow Run*)

Robert Forster is a student filmmaker in LA who stops at nothing in this R-rated film (later rated PG-13) from 20th Century–Fox about underground filmmaking. He makes a documentary on human depravity and is rejected by his live-in girlfriend (Sondra Locke) and the studio. With Sam Waterston, Michael Margotta, Floyd Mutrux, Jeff Corey, Regis Toomey, and Susanne Benton. Some of the music is by Bread, a bad sign. Forster had just starred in *Medium Cool*, and Black had directed *Pretty Poison*

COVER UP

(IVE, 1990) **D:** Mannu Coto **S:** William
Tannen **P:** Jacob Kotzky, Sharon Harel

The US government blames fictitous Iraqi terrorists as an excuse to go to war against Iraq. Dolph Lundgren stars as a journalist in Tel Aviv. With Lou Gossett Jr. and missing chemicals that kill in seconds. This timely release went directly to video.

CRACKDOWN

(MNTEX, Front Row, 1975) **D:** Barry Shear
S: Roger O Hirson **P:** Philip D'Antonio,
Barry Weitz   (*Strike Force, Crack*)

Joe Spinell is the bad guy in this NBC-TV pilot for a New York City cop show about drug busts. Cliff Gorman stars, but costar Richard Gere is featured on the video box.

CRACKDOWN

(1990) **D:** Louis Morneau **S:** Ross
Bell, Daryl Haney **P:** Luis Llosa

Cliff DeYoung stars as a wired US drug enforcer, and Robert Beltran (from *Eating Raoul*) is a Peruvian cop after a major South American dealer. With Jamie Rose. This *Lethal Weapon* copy (from executive producer Roger Corman) was filmed in Peru.

CRACK HOUSE

(Warner, 1989) **D:** Michael Fischa **S:** Blake
Schaefer **P:** Jim Silverman, Joan Weidman

Cheryl Kaye becomes an addicted hooker after her boyfriend goes to jail. Top-billed Jim Brown is a woman-beating drug kingpin, Anthony Geary is a school guidance-counseler/dealer, Richard Roundtree is a cop, and Angel Tompkins is Kaye's alcoholic mom. This downbeat tale of black and Chicano gangs includes a SWAT tank attack.

CRACKING UP

(1977) **D:** Rowby Goren, Chuck Staley
S: The cast **P:** C. D. Taylor, Rick Murray

AIP released this improv comedy movie about TV coverage of a California earthquake (including spoofs of commercials), was written by stars Phil Proctor, Peter Bergman, the Ace Trucking Company, the Credibilty Gap, and Neal Israel. With Fred Willard, Harry Shearer, and the Tubes performing their hits. Not to be confused with the 1983 Jerry Lewis movie of the same name (from Warner).

CRASH AND BURN

(Paramount, 1990) **D:** Charles Band **S:** J.S. Cardone
P: David DeCoteau, John Schouweiler

In 2030 a giant robot is killing people stuck at Ralph Waite's local TV station (sounds like *The Slime People*). The characters include two porno stars. David Allen's FX are the only reason to watch. With Paul Ganas as the hero, Megan Ward as the teen granddaughter, and Bill Moseley.

THE CRAVING

(Vestron, 1980) **D/S/A:** "Jacinto Molina"/
Paul Naschy **P:** Modesto Pérez Redondo
Spain (*El Returno del Hombre Lobo*)

Horror star Paul Naschy directed himself as "el Hombre Lobo" (a role he had played many times) in this retread of *The Werewolf vs. the Vampire Women* from 10 years earlier. The werewolf fights vampires in the 16th century, in this good-looking movie with some gore and nudity. Silvia Aguilar is Countess Bathory. The film was not successful in Spain, and Naschy had to seek funding in Japan for future projects.

CRAWLERS

(Columbia/Tri Star, 1990) **D/S:** "Martin Newlin"/
Fabrizio Laurenti, "David Hills"/Aristide
Massaccessi **S:** Daniel Steele, Albert Lawrence
Italy (*Troll III; Contamination Point 7*)

Radiation in Alaska causes killer vines. Tentacles plunge through a dummy head and clichéd fast POV shots abound. The awful, phonetic line readings of the Italian actors make it even worse. The costumes are by Laura Gemser.

THE CRAWLING HAND

(Video Gems, Rhino, 1963) **D/S/E:** Herbert L.
Strock **S:** William Edelson **P:** Joseph F. Robertson

This is the movie that introduced "The Bird," by the Rivingtons, so it's historically important, besides being a classic of its kind. In Florida an astronaut returning from the moon is seen on a TV monitor yelling, "Kill! Kill!" The scientists (Peter Breck and Kent Taylor) push a button and blow him up. Their secretary is Allison Hayes. Meanwhile, in Palms, California, the owner of a malt shop talks about a meteor and tells his teen customers, "Eat, drink, and be merry. Tomorrow you die!" (three times) but warns them not to dance. When "The Bird" plays on the jukebox, they can't help themselves. Paul (Rod Lauren), a handsome young "lone wolf" medical student, takes a beautiful Swedish exchange student (Sirry Stephan) to the beach. She changes into a bikini, them screams when she spots the astronaut's arm in the sand. At night Paul takes the arm home and hides it in the fridge. It slithers out, hides under the pillow of Mrs. Hotchkiss, the landlady, and strangles her. It also attacks Paul. He wakes up next to Mrs. Hotchkiss' corpse in an ambulance. The arm takes over Paul's mind, making him into a teen *Hands of Orlac* killer with blackened eyes. He confesses to his portable tape recorder. The sheriff is played by pre–*Gilligan's Island* Alan Hale Jr. Incredibly, the fingerprints from the scene of the crime match the blown-up astronaut's, so the Florida cops show up to investigate. My favorite scene is when Paul attacks the malt-shop owner at night. He pushes him against the jukebox and strangles him while strobe lights go on and off and "The Bird" plays ("Tweet! Tweet!"). Some cats in a junkyard eat the flesh off the arm at the end. Strock is best known for *I Was a Teenage Frankenstein*. This one's better.

CRAWLSPACE

(Vestron, 1986) **D/S:** David Schmoeller
P: Roberto Bessi

Ex-Nazi voyeur Karl Gunther (a very intense Klaus Kinski) takes in female boarders. His home is equiped with secret passageways and rooms, torture devices, and killing contraptions. He works on his memoirs every night and plays Russian roulette. One woman, kept in a cage, has no tongue. With Talia Balsam, Barbara Whinnery, and Sally Brown. The music by Pino Donaggio is on Varese Sarabande. The Empire production was filmed in Italy. (*Crawlspace* is also the name of an LA band.)

CRAZY FAT ETHEL II

(Video City, 1987) **D/S/P/E:** "Nick Phillips"/
Steve Millard **P:** Frances Millard

This unbelievable 70-minute sequel to *Criminally Insane* (1974) includes lots (about 50 percent) of gory footage from the original feature used as flashbacks. It was shot on video. The laughing, always-eating Priscilla Alden is released from the asylum and goes to a halfway house. *Death Nurse*, produced the same year, is even more of the same.

CRAZY JOE

(1974) **D:** Carlo Lizzani **S:** Lewis John
Carlino **P:** Dino De Laurentiis   US/Italy

Peter Boyle stars as the (real) New York gangster Crazy Joe Gallo. He makes friends with black inmates while in prison and is eventually gunned down in a Little Italy clam house. Fred Williamson costars, with Paula Prentiss, Rip Torn, Luther Adler, Eli Wallach, Henry Winkler, Sam Coppola, and Hervé Villechaize as Samson. The Columbia release was based on a story by Nicolas Cage.

CRAZY JOE

(1992) **D:** Steve Carver **S:** Stephen
Peters **P:** Menaham Golan, Ami Artzi

Justin Lazard is a street-killer forcefully retrained by a black-belt fighter (Rachel York) working for the government. With Krista Shook, Eb Lottimer, David Carradine (who had been directed by Carver several times in the past), and R. G. Armstrong. From 21st Century.

THE CRAZY RAY

(Sinister, 1923) **D/S/E:** René Clair   France
(*Paris Qui Dort; Le Rayon Invisible; At 3:25*)

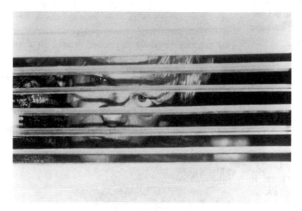

Klaus Kinski peeking out of his *Crawlspace*.

A mad scientist, Dr. Bardon, uses a ray to immobilize the people of Paris. Only six people in an airplane and on the Eiffel Tower, remain normal. This rare silent film is 61 minutes long. It was the first film made by the great director.

CRAZY SAFARI

(VSOM, 1990) **D:** Lo Weng-Tung **S:** Barry Wong
P: Charles Leung, Jimmy Leung   Hong Kong/S. Africa

The two *The Gods Must Be Crazy* movies were international hits and "hopping vampire" movies had been popular in Asia for years, so someone decided to combine both concepts. A Chinese magician/priest (Lam Ching Ying, from the Mr. Vampire series) and his young assistant buy the mummy of a Chinese vampire in London. On the way back their plane goes down in Africa and the vampire becomes a god to local natives. Nixau (from the *Gods* movies) plays a native chief who fights the slave-trader villains with the help of the spirit of Bruce Lee (!). With lots of animal comedy, a Lugosi film clip, pretty racist dialogue, and Coke plugs. The silly letterboxed, dubbed feature is in several languages.

CRAZY WILD AND CRAZY

(SW, 1965) **D/P:** Barry Mahon

Bob Meyer (the cinematographer) introduces himself and talks about shooting nudes, while showing us his short films. With topless baseball (in fast motion), naked women walking (in slow motion), multiple image "mistakes," and lots of nudist-colony scenes (volleyball, topless diving, and nude aerobics). It's all accompanied by comic piano and xylophone music and sound FX and is a pretty clever way to make a feature from pieces of film. It's in color and is 65 minutes.

CREATED TO KILL = EMBRYO

CREATOR

(HBO, 1985) **D:** Ivan Passer **S:** Jeremy
Leven **P:** Stephen Friedman

An eccentric scientist (Peter O'Toole) tries to clone his wife, who has been dead for 30 years, in this comedy. With Mariel Hemingway as a nymphomaniac, Vincent Spano as Boris, the lab assistant, Virginia Madsen, Rance Howard, Ellen Geer, Jeff Corey, John Dehner, Ian Wolfe, and David Ogden Stiers. From Universal.

CREATURE

(Media, 1984) **D/S/P:** William Malone
S: Alan Reed **P:** William G. Dunn
(*Titan Fiend*)

In this *Alien* copy set on an American spaceship, Klaus Kinski shows up as strange astronaut Hans Rudy Hofner from the rival West German spaceship. Stan Ivar, Lyman Ward, Wendy Schaal, Marie Laurin, and

Diane Salinger costar. Victims of the cannibal monster become zombie slaves with mind-control blobs on the backs of their necks. There's some nudity and exploding heads.

CREEPAZOIDS
(Urban Classics, 1987) **D/S/P:** David DeCouteau **S:** Buford Hauser **P:** John Schouweiler

It's 1998, post-nuke teen time, again, as five army deserters wander around in the acid rain until they settle in an abandoned building, complete with everything they need. An *Alien*-style creature and a pretty bad giant-rat puppet terrorize them. The fifth-wheel computer guy dies first, Lianna has a nude shower-sex scene, and characters run down endless corridors. At the end an effective baby monster (copied from *It's Alive*) is the only scary part. DeCouteau is another director who started at Corman's old New World studios, and had, at 26, already directed a half-dozen features. This one, from Empire, is only 71 minutes. With porno star Ashlyn Gere.

THE CREEPER
(1978) **D/A:** Peter Carter **S:** Ian Sutherland **P/A:** Lawrence Dane   Canada (*Rituals*)

Hal Holbrook stars in another *Deliverance* copy. Some doctors rough it on vacation, and the expected things happen.

THE CREEPERS (1971) = IN THE DEVIL'S GARDEN

CREEPERS
(Media, 1983) **D/S/P:** Dario Argento **S:** Franco Ferrini **P:** Angelo Jacono   Italy (*Phenomena*)

American Jennifer Connelly enrolls at an expensive private school in Zurich. The plot is similar in some ways to Argento's *Suspiria*, but this time the girl star solves a series of grisly murders with the help of a crippled scientist (Donald Pleasence), his intelligent chimp, and insects that she can communicate with. With Dario Nicoldi, Dalila Di Lazzaro (*Andy Warhol's "Frankenstein"*), Patrick Bauchau, and Argento's daughter Fiore as a victim. Michele Soavi was assistant director and appears in the film. It was made in Switzerland. The heavy-metal soundtrack (Bill Wyman, Iron-Maiden, Motorhead) is on Enigma. New Line released a cut version in 1985. Even the cut version remains a well-made, unique horror movie full of surprises. The 82-minute tape is missing 20 minutes. A longer version is on Japanese laserdisc. Argento's next was *Terror at the Opera*.

CREEPSHOW 2
(Starmaker, 1987) **D:** Michael Gornick **S:** George A. Romero **P:** David Ball

This is a pretty bad sequel to Romero's 1982 film. Animated segments are inserted between the three Stephen King stories (with Tom Savini and the voice of Joe Silver playing "the Creep"). In "Old Chief Wood'nhead" a cigar-store Indian avenges the deaths of general-store owners George Kennedy and Dorothy Lamour. Lois Chiles is terrorized by a dead hitchhiker who keeps saying, "Thanks for the ride, lady!" in "The Hitchhiker," with Stephen King as a truck driver. Pot-smoking students are attacked by a living oil slick in "The Raft," with Page Hannah. The director was Romero's cinematographer. From New World.

CREEPY CLASSICS
(Fox, 1987) **D:** Pamela Page

Vincent Price, in a movie theater, hosts a half-hour of trailers and scenes from many AIP horror movies, including the original *Night of the Living Dead*, and *Invasion of the Body Snatchers* (1956).

Jennifer Connelly in Argento's Creepers

CRIME AND PASSSION
(Vestron, 1976) **D:** Ivan Passer **S:** Jesse Lasky Jr., Pat Silver **P:** Robert L. Abrams   (*Ace Up Your Sleeve*)

Omar Sharif convinces his secretary/mistress Karen Black to marry the vengeful tycoon (Bernhard Wicki) to whom he's heavily in debt. This comedy drama from AIP costars Joseph Bottoms. Black had also been in Passer's films *Born to Win* and *Law and Disorder* .

CRIME AND PUNISHMENT, USA
(1959) **D:** Dennis Sanders **S:** Walter Newman **P:** Terry Sanders

George Hamilton made an impressive debut in this modern version of the Dostoevsky classic with a beatnik setting. He's a law student in Santa Monica who has gotten away with a murder and is hounded by a police detective (Frank Silvera, who is excellent). With Mary Murphy (from *The Wild One*) and Barry Atwater. Roger Corman was the executive producer for Allied Artists. Sanders later made *Elvis: That's the Way It Is* and *Invasion of the Bee Girls*. There have been at least ten film versions of *Crime and Punishment* made in various countries. A 1935 American version starring Peter Lorre was directed by Josef von Sternberg. A 1946 low-budget American version is called *Fear*.

CRIMELORDS
(Academy, 1991) **D/S:** Wayne Crawford **S:** Rand Ravich, Gregory Small **P:** Arthur Payne, Frank Notaro   South Africa

Crawford is Elmo, a burned-out cop, and Martin Hewitt (*Endless Love*) is his Cockney partner. The action is set in LA and Hong Kong. With James Hong as a crook and Susan Byun (from *Sgt. Kabukiman NYPD*). It's all pretty ridiculous, but the action is pretty good.

CRIME OF CRIMES
(VCI, 1988) **D/S/P:** Alfred Zacharias

Richard Yniguez (*Boulevard Knights*) stars as a poor family man new to LA. He's blamed for a murder and arrested, his pregnant wife passes out and ends up in a hospital, and his little girl is kidnapped. Aldo Ray (!) is a child-molester who drives an ice-cream truck so that he can lure children and deliver them to doctors for body parts. The whole thing seems to be a nightmare for Hispanics in America. This is "A David Carradine Presentation," but he spends most of the time in an office as a cop. Also with Al Adamson movie regular Kent Osborne. The soundtrack is good. By the Mexican maker of *Demonoid*. Anthony Cardoza (*The Beast of Yucca Flats*) was the executive producer.

THE CRIME OF DR. CRESPI
(Sinister, Silvermine, 1935) **D/P:** John H. Auer **S:** Lewis Graham, Edwin Olmstead

Erich von Stroheim was a great director and a fascinating personality. I'd watch anything he was involved in at least once. Liberty Pictures made this 63-minute movie in one week, in the Bronx, only a few years after his directing career had been destroyed (he continued to act and write screenplays until his death in 1957). Republic released it. Poe's story "The Premature Burial" was the inspiration. Stroheim, as Dr. André Crespi, spends most of the movie behind a desk smoking and yelling at people. He's glad when his former assistant (who married the woman he's obsessed with) has a car crash. When the man is brought to his clinic, Crespi drugs him so that he appears dead and has him buried alive. The only humor is about an Italian man finding out that his wife has had quintuplets (a reference to the famous Dionne quintuplets). It's fun to see Dwight Frye as a good-guy doctor, but after the opening there's no music and the print is pretty jumpy. The director (from Budapest) went on to make lots of movies for Republic and RKO. Silvermine video put this into their ill-conceived two-for-one "Worst of Hollywood" series with *Fugitive Road* (1934), starring Stroheim. The box claims *Crespi* is hilarious. It might be a bargain, except that the tape wasn't long enough for two features! I was watching *Crespi*, trying to stay awake, dozed for a few seconds, and was startled awake by the whirring of the VCR rewinding. I've read that the ending is the best part. It's not on the damn tape, though.

CRIMES AT THE DARK HOUSE
(Sinister, 1940) **D/P:** George King   UK

Warner Baxter starred as Dr. Robert Ordway in 10 Columbia features (1943–49) based on a popular radio program. The medical detective, who had once been a criminal, had lapses of amnesia. He used his knowledge of psychiatry to capture killers. William Castle directed *Crime Doctor's Warning* (1945), *Crime Doctor's Manhunt* (1946), *Just Before Dawn* (1946), and *Crime Doctor's Gamble* (1947). *Shadows in the Night* (1944) was about a ghost and featured George Zucco.

Tod Slaughter stars as a maniac who impersonates Sir Percival Glyde and manages to claim an inheritance from a mysterious mansion. He's haunted by the rightful heiress, whom he put into an asylum. The dialogue includes lines like "Betray me and I'll feed your entrails to the pigs!" This 61-minute film, based on Wilkie Collins' novel *The Woman in White* (also filmed in 1929, and in 1948 with Sydney Greenstreet), was released in the US by Exploitation Pictures. Many scenes were copied from earlier Slaughter melodramas (all of which he first starred in on the British stage).

CRIME SCHOOL

(1938) **D:** Lewis Seiler **S:** Crane
Wilbur, Vincent Sherman

This Warner Brothers follow-up to United Artists' hit *Dead End* (1937) is actually a remake of the James Cagney movie *The Mayor of Hell* (1933). Humphrey Bogart is a social worker who becomes the warden of a reform school and puts a stop to beatings and bad food. The Dead End kids (all with new names), sent there for stealing, are Billy Halop (Frankie), Bobby Jordan (Squirt), Leo Gorcey (Spike), Huntz Hall (Goofy), Bernard Punsley (Fats), and Gabriel Dell (Bugs). With Gale Page and Milburn Stone. The music is by Max Steiner. *Angels with Dirty Faces* was next.

CRIME SMASHER

(United American, 1943) **D:** James Tingling
S: Michael L. Simmons, Walter Gering
P: Lindsay Parsons

Professor Cosmo Jones (Frank Graham) is an inept amateur detective who does voice impersonations. When an heiress is kidnapped during a crime wave, Jones and a janitor (Mantan Moreland) try to help. As usual, Moreland steals his scenes and says things like "Well, dog my cat!" With Edgar Kennedy as the comical police captain leading bumbling Irish cops, Richard Cromwell, Gale Storm, Herbert Rawlinson, and Tristam Coffin. The Monogram release, just over one hour, was based on a CBS radio program.

THE CRIMES OF DR. MABUSE: *See* THE TESTAMENT OF DR. MABUSE

CRIMES OF PASSSION

(Starmaker, 1984) **D:** Ken Russell **S/P:** Barry
Sandler **P:** Donald P. Borchers

Russell's first movie after *Altered States* (1980) had critics scratching their heads. Kathleen Turner stars as a fashion designer who spends her nights as China Blue, an expensive hooker. Anthony Perkins goes over the top again as the psychotic reverend who sings "Get Happy." With Annie Potts, Bruce Davison, Louise Sorel, and John Laughlin. The music is by Rick Wakeman. Released by New World, it's available in an R-rated or unrated, uncut version (with the cop and nightstick scene). Russell explored some of the same themes in *Whore* (1991).

THE CRIMES OF STEPHEN HAWKE

(Sinister, 1936) **D/P:** George King
UK (*Strangler's Morgue*)

Tod Slaughter, in his third feature, plays a mad killer, "the Spine-breaker," and also a kind moneylender who helps his foster daughter. With Marjorie Taylor and Eric Portman. Slaughter appears as himself in the intro to this 65-minute film.

CRIMES OF THE BLACK CAT

(VSOM, 1972) **D/S:** Sergio Pastore
S: Sandro Continenza, Gianni Simonelli
Italy (*Sette Scialli di Seta Gialla*)

A maniac uses the poisoned claws of a black cat to kill models. Sylva Koscina stars, and Anthony Stephen is a blind composer whose girlfriend was a victim. With Giacomo Rossi-Stuart. If you've seen Bava's *Blood and Black Lace* (1964) you can probably guess who the killer is.

CRIMES OF THE FUTURE

(Nightmare, 1970) **D/S/P/C/E:** David Cronenberg

Only men are left in the world, and there's an attempt to develop new means of sexual release at the House of Skin and the Institute of Neo-Venereal Disease. A young physician narrates. People bleed colored liquids. Cronenberg's second film is 63 minutes and cost only $20,000. It's on tape with *Stereo*, his first, featuring many of the same actors.

CRIME STORY

(1993) **D:** (Kirk) Wong Che Keung **S:** Cheun
Tin-nam, Chan Man-keung **P:** Leonard K. C. Ho
Hong Kong (*Chung On Tsuo; Police Story IV*)

Jackie Chan stars as a burned-out cop hired to protect a millionaire real-estate developer who is kidnapped. This is a more serious John Woo–influenced movie with lots of gunshot action, set in Hong Kong and Taiwan. Ken Cheong costars as a bad cop.

CRIMEWAVE

(Charter, 1985) **D/S:** Sam Raimi **S:** Joel
and Ethan Coen **P:** Robert Tapert
(*XYZ Murders; Broken Hearts and Noses*)

Brion James and Paul L. Smith are hilarious as Coddish and Crush, crazed rat exterminators with cartoonish voices who are hired to kill people. The colorful, hard-to-classify PG-13 comedy with cartoon sound effects, wild action scenes, and Three Stooges gags was filmed in Detroit. It's the only major collaboration by the then not-too-well-known Sam Raimi and the Coen brothers. They all seem to hate it but you might like it as I do. Reed Birney is sort of the star as an idiot about to go to the electric chair. With Louise Lasser, Bruce Campbell as the Heel, Edward R. Pressman, Emil Sitka, and Ted Raimi. James used his own voice by the way. Not to be confused with a 1986 Canadian film of the same name. The next time the Coens and Raimi made a movie together was *The Hudsucker Proxy* (1994).

CRIME ZONE

(MGM, 1988) **D/P:** Luis Llosa **S:** Daryl Haney

In a smoky, post-WWIII world of darkness, cigar-smoking David Carradine (also the associate producer) is a US goverment agent. He gives young "subgrade" lovers Sherilyn Fenn and Peter Nelson a chance to escape if they do certain tasks for him. It's a futuristic *Bonnie and Clyde,* made in Peru, from Roger Corman's Concorde. The plot includes televised executions and a rejuvenation center.

CRIMINAL ACT

(Prism, 1988) **D:** Mark Byers
S/P: Daniel Yost   (*Tunnels*)

Catherine Bach and Charlene Dallas are a newspaper reporter and photographer who discover that a greedy real-estate developer is killing homeless people. With Nicholas Guest, John Saxon, and Vic Tayback as an exterminator of giant rats (which never show up).

CRIMINAL LAW

(1989) **D:** Martin Campbell **S:** Mark
Kasdan **P:** John Daley, Derek Gibson

Gary Oldman, playing an American attorney in Boston, is after a very disturbed serial killer who turns out to be his client (Kevin Bacon). With Karen Young, Joe Don Baker, Tess Harper, and Elizabeth Sheppard. The confrontation scenes at the end of this outrageous feature are pretty amazing. Jerry Goldsmith wrote the score. Campbell is also the director of *Cast a Deadly Spell.*

THE CRIMINAL LIFE OF ARCHIBALDO DE LA CRUZ

(Water Bearer,1955) **D/S:** Luis Buñuel
S: Eduardo Ugarte **P:** Alfonso Patino
Gómez Mexico (*Ensayo de un Crimen*)

The rich Archibaldo de la Cruz (Ernesto Alonso) is a would-be serial killer. Because of memories of a childhood incident that a music box brings back, he thinks he's destined to kill women. Every time he tries to kill one, she dies, but from other causes. He becomes obsessed with a model for store dummies (Miroslava Stern). When he tries confessing to the police, they're uninterested. With Rita Macedo and Adriadna Welter (*The Brainiac*). Watch this black comedy if you liked Jodorowsky's *Sante Sangre*. The film was released in the US in 1962. It's subtitled.

CRIMINALLY INSANE

(World, 1973) **D/S:** "Nick Phillips"/
Steve Millard **P:** Frances Millard

Priscilla Alden is Ethel, a 250-pound compulsive eater with a bad temper, in this one-hour 16mm horror oddity influenced by John Waters. Ethel is let out of the asylum to live with her grandma. She kills her, but her hooker sister shows up. The producer is the director's mother and the wife of showman S. S. "Steamship" Millard. This was released on a homemade double bill with Millard's *Satan's Black Wedding*. Incredibly, Alden returned 14 years later in *Crazy Fat Ethel II* and *Death Nurse*.

CRIMSON

(TWE, Wizard, 1974) **D/S/FX:** "John Fortune"/
Juan Fortuny **S/A:** Paul Naschy Spain/France
(*Las Ratas no Duermen de Noche*)

Despite the title and video-box art, this is a gangster movie. Paul Naschy is a jewel thief who is shot and spends most of the movie in a coma. He receives a brain transplant and another gangster, called "the Sadist," is decapitated by a train. In France, porno inserts were added.

THE CRIMSON GHOST

(Republic, 1946) **D:** William Witney, Fred C. Bannon
S: Albert Demond, Basil Dickey, Jesse Duffy, Sol Shore

This 12-chapter Republic serial stars Charles Quigley as the criminologist hero and Linda Stirling as his assistant. The Crimson Ghost (I. Stanford Jolley provided the voice) steals the cyclotrode, a device that can short-circuit all electricity. He also has control collars for his henchmen. When the collars are pulled off they're killed by an electric shock. The ghost is one of the greatest serial images, a mystery man in a cape with a skull face and glaring eyeballs. An 80s New York City band, the Misfits, used the ghost as their symbol. With Clayton Moore, Keene Duncan, and Eddie Parker. The 1966 condensed feature version is called *Cyclotrode X*. On cable TV it's been shown colorized and cut.

CRIPPLED MASTERS

(Ocean Shores, 1984) **D:** Ho Wang Muri   Hong Kong

An evil medieval king has the arms chopped off one man and the legs cut off another. His victims join together (one on the other's shoulders) for revenge, and an old master trains them to fight. It's a sequel to *Crippled Heroes* (1983). Anthony Quinn once starred in a western called *Deaf Smith and Johnny Ears* (1972), about a deaf and blind gunfighter team, but these movies use real armless and legless men! Unique thrills for jaded viewers.

CRISIS IN THE KREMLIN

(New Horizons, 1992) **D:** Jonathan Winfrey
S: Jonathan Fernandez, Daryl Haney
P: Steven Rabiner   (*Red Target*)

Executive producer Roger Corman made use of some actual footage of the failed Soviet coup in this exploitation/action movie. Robert Rusler stars as a CIA agent in Vilnius, Lithuania, who stops a plot to kill Gorbachev. With Denise Bixley, Stephen Danilov, and Theodore Bikel. It was shot in Russia, Bulgaria (mostly), and Germany. From Concorde.

CRITTERS

(RCA, 1985) **D/S:** Stephen Herek
S: Dominic Muir, Don Opper
P: Rupert Harvey

This science-fiction story, set in a farming community called Grover's Bend, Kansas, is exciting, funny, and imaginative. Alien bounty-hunters arrive and assume human form. One looks like a rock star (Terrence Mann) and the other takes over various bodies. They're after Krites, lethal, rolling fur-ball aliens with sharp teeth. Scott Grimes is Brad, the farm-kid hero, and Dee Wallace Stone and Billy Green Bush are his parents. With M. Emmet Walsh as the sheriff, Billy Zane, and Don Opper. It's from the makers of *Android*. Herek went on to direct *Bill And Ted's Excellent*

Adventure. The David Newman soundtrack is on Enigma. This film and its sequels, all from New Line, are rated PG-13.

CRITTERS 2: THE MAIN COURSE

(RCA, 1988) **D/S:** Mick Garris
S: D.T. Twohy **P/A:** Barry Opper

The alien Krites come back on Easter Sunday, and there's more comedy. Scott Grimes returns as Brad, and Don Opper (as Charlie, a character who was taken over by a bounty-hunter in the first movie) and two other aliens show up. With Liane Curtis, Barry Corbin, Eddie Deezen, and Roxanne Kernohan. The FX for all the *Critters* movies are by the Chiodo Brothers (*Killer Klowns from Outer Space*).

CRITTERS 3: YOU ARE WHAT THEY EAT

(RCA/Columbia, 1991) **D:** Kristine Peterson
S: David S. Schow **P:** Barry Opper, Rupert Harvey

This entry sucks. It looks good only next to a *Ghoulies* sequel. Most of it takes place in an apartment where some people are trapped, and features the supposedly funny, furry, rubbery monsters. They kill off a few characters and eat beans and fart. The stars are cute preteens. Charlie (Don Opper) is back (too briefly), and there's a long, confused "best of" flashback to Part 1. With Leonardo DiCaprio.

CRITTERS 4

(New Line, 1991) **D/P:** Rupert Harvey
P/A: Don Opper **S:** Joseph Lyle, David J. Schow

This time it's Critters in space, and it's a huge improvement over the previous entry. The dim-witted but fun bounty-hunter Charlie (series regular Opper) ends up (with critter eggs) on an abandoned futuristic space station with the

One of the scariest-looking serial villains, *The Crimson Ghost.*

small crew of a salvage ship. Gum-chewing Brad Dourif, as the thoughtful and intelligent Al Bert, stars, with the soon-to-be-famous Angela Bassett as a tough, intelligent, and sexy black woman, Anders Hove (from the *Subspecies* movies) as a mean, stupid captain with a Neil Young look, Eric DaRae, who's after a stash of drugs, a teen boy stowaway, Terrence Mann (from the first two movies) as the now evil Og, and Martine Beswick as the voice of the computer. This was shot back to back with Part 3.

CRO-MAGNON

(1974) **D:** Richard A. Colla
S: Lane Slate **P:** George Eckstein

A Cro-Magnon family battles Neanderthals during the last Ice Age. Some people thought this TV pilot with Victor French and Henry Wilcoxon (star and coproducer of several Cecil B. DeMille epics) would become a hit series.

CRONOS

(Vidmark, 1993) **D/S:** Guillermo del Toro
P: Bertha Navarro, Arthur Gorson   Mexico

Federico Luppi (from Argentina) stars as Jesús, an old antique-store owner who discovers a mechanized gold object (with an insect inside) created by a 16th-century alchemist. It restores youth, but the user needs blood to survive. A sadistic American named Angel (Ron Perlman) is sent by his dying industrialist uncle (Claudio Brook, from Buñuel's *Simon of the Desert*) to steal the object. With Margarita Isabel, and Tamara Shanath as the little grandaughter. The 29-year-old director first made short films, studied makeup with Dick Smith, and did FX for other Mexican productions. This was an expensive feature by Mexican standards and won awards there. Available dubbed or subtitled.

THE CROOKED CIRCLE

(Sinister, 1932) **D:** H. Bruce Humberstone
S: Ralph Spence **P:** William Sistrom

ZaSu Pitts is the housekeeper of an old dark house with a phantom violinist, secret passageways, skeletons, and a Hindu mystic named Yoganda. The Sphinx Club, a group of amateur detectives, try to expose the Crooked Circle, a hooded occult sect. This comic mystery was scripted by the writer of *The Gorilla* (a popular play that had been filmed twice) and was made by the independent World Wide company. Ben Lyon co-stars, with James Gleason as a cop, Irene Purcell, Raymond Hatton, and Roscoe Karns. This is one of the most atmospheric of the many "forgotten horrors" that have resurfaced on videotape. Early horror/mystery/comedy talkies were common on local TV stations in the 50s, and I can barely remember watching several with ZaSu Pitts in my pre–elementary school days.

THE CROSS AND THE SWITCHBLADE

(Vanguard, 1970) **D/S:** Don Murray
S: James Bonnet **P:** Dick Ross

Pat Boone is (real) ghetto preacher David Wilkinson, from Pennsylvania. Erik Estrada (in his film debut) is (real) Mau Mau gang member and junkie Nicky Cruz. This inspirational PG film, made on location in New York City, includes scenes of preparing a heroin fix and shooting up. Though laughable to many, it played at church-backed drive-in shows for many years, and the real Cruz gave lectures around the world. The soundtrack on Light records features the Young People singing and Bible readings by Boone. Don Murray continued acting, and in 1977 he directed an unreleased movie about Father Damien, "the leper priest" (not to be confused with the 1980 TV movie). By the late 80s, former TV star Estrada was appearing in four or five direct-to-video action and horror titles a year. This was Boone's last film. Later he was a GM spokesman, did Japanese ads for toupees, campaigned for Bush, and released an exercise video.

CROSS COUNTRY

(Charter, 1983) **D:** Paul Lynch **S:** Logan N. Danforth, William Gray **P:** Pieter Kroonenberg   Canada

Richard Beymer stars as a psycho killer ad executive on a road trip with a topless dancer (Nina Axelrod) and a musician (Brent Carver). Michael Ironside is the corrupt cop after him. It's based on a novel by Herbert Kastle.

CROSSED SWORDS

(1978) **D:** Richard Fleischer **S:** George MacDonald Fraser **P:** Pierre Spangler   (*The Prince and the Pauper*)

Mark Lester stars in this comic all-star version of Mark Twain's famous novel, with Oliver Reed, Racquel Welch, Ernest Borgnine, George C. Scott, Rex Harrison, David Hemmings, Harry Andrews, and Charlton Heston as King Henry VIII. Sybil Danning is the top-billed female! Several of the cast members had been in the popular films *The Three Musketeers* and *The Four Musketeers*, which obviously inspired this, and Lester and Reed had starred in *Oliver!* together. This Warners release runs 121-minutes and was shot by Jack Cardiff. (A 1954 Errol Flynn movie made in Italy has the same title.)

CROSSING THE LINE

(RCA, 1990) **D:** Gary Graver **S:** Rick Marcus **P:** Jonathan R. Vanger   S. Africa

Teen dirt-bike racing doesn't sound very interesting, but at least this movie has a solid exploitation cast, inlcuding Paul L. Smith, Vernon Wells, Cameron Mitchell, and John Saxon.

CROSS OF THE DEVIL

(VSOM, 1970) **D/S:** John Gilling **S:** Jaquinto Molina   Spain (*La Cruz del Diablo*)

A British novelist (Ramiro Oliveras) travels to Spain and finds out that his sister has been killed by a gang of robbers called the Devil's Cross. He smokes hashish while experiencing writer's block and has visions of a woman (Emma Cohen) from the past. Based on *Leyendas* (legends), written by the 19th-century Spanish poet and novelist Gustavo Adolfo Bécquer, this was the last film by the British director. The letterboxed tape is subtitled.

CROSSROADS

(RCA, 1986) **D:** Walter Hill
S: John Fusco **P:** Mark Carliner

Ralph Macchio (*The Karate Kid*) is a teen guitar prodigy who stops an old bluesman friend (Joe Seneca) of the legendary Robert Johnson from making a deal with the Devil. With Jami Gertz and music by Ry Cooder, Steve Vai, and Sonny Terry.

CROSSROADS AVENGER

(Sinister, 1953) **D/S/A:** Ed Wood Jr.

This 25-minute color TV western pilot made the same year as Woods *Glen or Glenda*, stars Tom Keene. The series was to be called *The Adventures of the Tucson Kid* and a second pilot was reportedly shot too. With Tom Tyler, Lyle Talbot, Keene Duncan, and Wood himself as a Pony Express rider. The tape adds a short with Keene Duncan demonstrating trick rifle shots plus trailers.

THE CROW

(Mirimax, 1994) **D:** Alex Proyas **S:** David J. Chow, John Shirley **P:** Edward R. Pressman

28-year-old Brandon Lee stars as Eric Draven, a rock musician who returns from the grave as a ghoulish superhero out for revenge. This dark, uncompromising fantasy based on comics by James O'Barr is filled with bad weather, drugs, and hopelessness. It takes place on Devil's Night in what's left of Detroit (actually elaborate sets in North Carolina). Michael Wincott is the long-haired villain with a sadistic sister/lover (Bai Ling). With Ernie Hudson as a cop and Rochelle Davis as the little girl. Made by an Australian video director, this could have been a hit even if Lee hadn't died (March 31, 1993) during production. The scene in which Lee was actually shot was removed, the script was reworked (Michael Berryman's Skull Cowboy character was cut out), and convincing state-of-the art computer technology was used to put Lee in scenes that were filmed after his death. His face was even put on another actor's body. It's a major contrast to the way his father Bruce Lee's after-death movie *Game of Death* was handled. The hit Atlantic rock soundtrack features Helmet, Nine Inch Nails, My Life With the Thrill Kill Kult, Henry Rollins and others. Varèse Sarabande released the Graeme Revill score. Paramount made *The Crow* but Miramax (which had recently been purchased by Disney) released it. The video also includes Lee's last interview.

CRUISING

(Warner, 1980) **D/S:** William Friedkin
P: Jerry Weintraub

Al Pacino goes underground looking for a homosexual killer and maybe discovers his own homosexuality and becomes a killer in the ambiguous ending. There were protests while it was being filmed in New York's Greenwich Village and more protests at the opening, but not too many people bothered to see it. The extras in a leather bar are real. The actors include Paul Sorvino as the police chief, Karen Allen, Richard Cox, Joe Spinell,

James Remar, Barton Heyman, Powers Boothe, and Don Scardino (from *Squirm*). The Jack Nitzsche soundtrack is on UA. Friedkin also made *The Boys in the Band*.

THE CRUSH

(Warner, 1993) **D/S:** Alan Shapiro
P: James G. Robinson

A 14-year old blonde (15-year-old Alicia Silverstone) falls bad for a magazine writer (Cary Elwes) who rents the guestroom of her parents's mansion. She secretly helps him with his writing but when he rejects her she turns wasps loose on his girlfriend (Jennifer Rubin) and cleverly ruins his relationship, credit, job, and even his chance to move. The younger-cast *Fatal Attraction*–type movie is pretty frightening. Kurtwood Smith and Gwynyth Walsh are the oblivious parents. The score is by Graeme Revill (*Hand that Rocks the Cradle*). The Warners release was filmed in Vancouver. Not to be confused with *Crush* (1994) from New Zealand.

CRY-BABY

(MCA, 1990) **D/S:** John Waters **P:** Rachel Talalay

Johnny Depp, a kid from the wrong side of the tracks, falls for Amy Locane, goes to jail, wins a chicken run, and sings. The PG-13 musical follow-up to Waters' *Hairspray* is set in 1954 Baltimore, where the squares battle the "drapes." Susan Tyrrell and Iggy Pop are Cry-Baby's white-trash parents. Ricki Lake, Traci Lords, and Kim McGuire as Hatchetface are drape girls. With Willem Dafoe (just after playing Jesus) as a prison guard and Polly Bergen as the rich grandmother. Susan Lowe and Mary Vivian Pearce are still around from the old days. And check out these odd couples: Patti Hearst and David Nelson, Joe Dallesandro and Joey Heatherton and Troy Donahue and Mink Stole. The Elvis-style dance numbers were choreographed by Lori Eastside. This Waters film, his most mainstream and least effective, was from Universal, and Ron Howard (!) was an executive producer. Rachel Sweet is on the soundtrack. The tape is letterboxed.

CRY BLOOD, APACHE

(UAV, 1970) **D/A:** Jack Starrett **S:** Sean McGregor
P/A: Jody McCrea **P:** Harold Roberts

This R-rated hippie western features Joel McCrea (who coproduced with his actor son) in his next-to-last film. Jody McCrea and other prospectors slaughter a group of Indians to steal some gold. The surviving Indians track and kill all but one of the prospectors (Joel, playing Jody's character years later), who tells the story in flashback. With Don Henley and Robert Tessier, who was also the second-unit director. Starrett directed after *Run, Angel, Run* and *The Losers*.

A CRY IN THE NIGHT

(Republic, 1992) **D/S/P:** Robin Spry
P: Jamie Brown   Canada

Carol Higgins Clark stars in this PG-13 movie based on a modern-gothic novel by her mother, Mary. A woman leaves New York City to marry a rich, eccentric artist (Perry King) in Montreal, then has nightmares about a serial killer and the death of her baby. It has too many false scares and an ending all too familiar to *Psycho* fans. With Annie Girardot as a crazy servant and Chris Wiggins (from the *Friday the 13th* TV series).

CRYSTAL FORCE

(Vista, 1990) **D:** Laura Keats **S:** Jerry
Daly, Jared Brady **P:** Craig Suttle

A girl (Katherine McCall) buys a crystal from an antique dealer (the Devil himself) that unleashes a soul-collecting demon (a man in a monster suit). This no-star obscurity is available in R and unrated versions.

CRYSTAL HEART

(1987) **D:** Gil Bettman **S:** Linda
Shayne **P:** Carlos Vassallo   US/Spain

Tawny Kitaen is a rock singer who falls for a wealthy young Spaniard (Lee Curreri) who makes music while confined to a controlled environment because of a rare, fatal illness. With Lloyd Bochner and Marina Saura. There's some sex and a nightmare sequence.

CRY TOUGH

(1959) **D:** Paul Stanley **S/P:** Harry Kleiner

A young Puerto Rican ex-con (John Saxon) tries to go straight but gets involved with his former gang in this downbeat teen-crime movie. Saxon and Linda Cristal, as his girlfriend, were advertised as "the hottest teen stars on the screen today!" In Europe the film had a sex scene, and photos ended up in American men's magazines, creating lots more publicity. Saxon, who had been playing teens since *Running Wild* (1955) and was about to graduate to more adult roles, tries to act like Brando. Joseph Calleia, Don Gordon, Perry Lopez, and Harry Townes costar.

CRY UNCLE!

(Troma, 1971) **D/E:** John Avildsen
S: David Odell **P:** David Jay Disick

Ricki Lake, Johnny Depp, and Traci Lords in John Waters' *Cry-Baby*.

THE CRUSH

Donald Pleasence in Polanski's *Cul-de-Sac*.

Avildsen made this sex-and-bad-taste comedy for Cambist after the success of *Joe*. Allen Garfield, as a slob New York City detective, is hired by a man being blackmailed by the women he acted with in a porno movie. With Madeline de le Roux, Debbi Morgan, Paul Sorvino, and a necrophilia scene that people were talking about. Lloyd Kaufman acts and was the production manager, and his company, Troma, later became the distributor. Garfield/Goorwitz had been in other adults-only movies like *Orgy Girls* and *Roommates* (both 1969).

CRY WILDERNESS

(1987) **D/P:** Jay Schlossberg-Cohen **S/P:** Philip Yordan

A Bigfoot creature (an actor in an ape suit) befriends a student. His father, an Indian, and a big-game hunter think the creature is an escaped tiger. With Faith Cliff from *Cataclysm*. The often out-of-focus PG release is very low-budget.

CTHULHU MANSION

(Republic, 1990) **D/S/P:** Juan Piquer Simón
P: José G. Maesso   Spain

This is supposed to be based on H. P. Lovecraft, but don't be fooled again. Frank Finlay stars as Chandu, a stage illusionist whose assistant is his daughter (Marcia Layton). A group of obnoxious, drug-dealing delinquents (including Melanie Shatner) hold them hostage in their own remote house and the captors die in various supernatural ways. It all has something to do with Chandu's wife, his former assistant, who burned to death during a show. Her demise is shown in b/w several times. You can see the microphone and watch for continuity problems to pass the time.

CUJO

(Warner, 1983) **D:** Lewis Teague
S: Don Carlos Dunaway, Lauren Currier
P: Daniel H. Blatt, Robert Singer

A killer-dog Stephen King adaptation that starts like a long soap opera. Eventually a woman who has been having an affair (Dee Wallace after *E.T.*) and her kid (Danny Pintauro) are in a car being attacked by a vicious, rabid Saint Bernard. The dog had been bitten by vampire bats. The dog FX are excellent (they used several mechanical and real dogs). With Christopher Stone and Ed Lauter. Teague followed this with King's *Cat's Eye* (1985)

CUL-DE-SAC

(Nightmare, 1966) **D/S:** Roman Polanski
S: Gerard Brach **P:** Gene Gutowsky

Look for this odd early Polanski comedy/drama, his last in b/w. Donald Pleasence is a retired businessman living in a castle on a remote island with his bored French wife (Françoise Dorleac). Two wounded gangsters (Lionel Stander and Jack MacGowran) arrive by car during the low tide and insist on waiting for an important phone call. Former model Jacqueline Bisset has her first speaking role. Original prints run 111 minutes. Polanski had already directed Dorleac's sister, Catherine Deneuve, in *Repulsion* (1965), which was also co-scripted by Brach and backed by Tony Tenser of Tygon Films.

CULT OF THE DAMNED

(1969) **D/S:** Robert Thom **P:** Jerome F. Katzman   (*Angel, Angel, Down We Go*)

This very 60s movie (full of flashbacks, flashforwards, collages, dream sequences, and in-jokes) partially copies Pasolini's *Teorema* (1968) but

with a Hollywood setting. It would make a good double bill with *Beyond the Valley of the Dolls*. Jordan Christopher is a singer in black leather named Bogart (he looks like Jim Morrison) who seduces all the members of a rich, decadent family, causing their destruction. Future lesbian folk singer Holly Near (who also narrates) is Tara, the "fat and dopey," suicidal, Christina Crawford-like daughter. Top-billed Jennifer Jones is the former-movie-star mother, and Charles Aidman is the Howard Hughes–like bisexual masochist father. Bogart's new group includes Lou Rawls and Roddy McDowall. The music is mostly pretty lightweight, and the lyrics are stupid, but my favorite scene is Bogart doing a gospel-inspired number while breaking glass. Thom also wrote *Wild in the Streets* and *Bloody Mama*, and both are better than this. AIP retitled this from *Cult of the Damned* to cash in on the Manson murders. Tower released the soundtrack by Mann/Weill. This has been shown (cut) on the USA Network.

CULT OF THE DEAD

(MPI, Unicorn, 1968) **D/P:** Juan Ibáñez **D/S:** Jack Hill
S/P: Luis Enríquez Vergara   US/Mexico (*La Muerte Viviente; Snake People; Isle of the Snake People*)

Boris Karloff is Count Carl von Molder who dresses like Colonel Sanders and owns a sugarcane plantation on an island off Haiti in this period voodoo/zombie movie. Molder's servant has a *Bride of Frankenstein* streak in her hair, can start fires with her eyes, and does some wild snake dances. His niece (Juliassa) arrives from the mainland with a sadistic French captain intent on enforcing law and order, against the wishes of a local soldier (Carlos East). When questioned about voodoo and murders, Molder says, "Zombies? Oh, really!" Meanwhile, his niece dreams that she wakes in a coffin next to a duplicate of herself. The identical women kiss each other. Rafael Múñoz (aka Santanón), a dwarf actor (who had been in *Puss n Boots* and three *Little Red Riding Hood* movies distributed by K. Gordon Murray), has flowers painted on his bald head and a walking stick with a shrunken head on the end. He brutally whips a woman to death. Molder later beats his foreman with his cane because the man fell in love with a black zombie (and was trying to have sex with her). Other female zombies attack soldiers and drink their blood. Eventually we discover that Molder is the mysterious, Satanic, cigar-smoking priest Damballa! Karloff/Molder/Damballa is played by a double most of the time but is a good horror character. At the end, explosions kill most of the cast. This is, overall, the best of the four Mexican features Boris was in. It has good music, a pretty coherent plot, and effective voodoo-ceremony scenes. The Unicorn video box "guarantees an orgy of terrifying images!"

CULT PEOPLE

(Cine Phile, 1989) **P:** David Del Valle, Kevin M. Glover

This is a one-hour tape of interviews in which seven actors and directors discuss their psychotronic credits. It looks like a (very professional) public access cable-TV show on a simple studio set. All the interviews are interesting, but most are too short! The best is with Cameron Mitchell, who has a great memory and a good sense of humor about his career. He says interesting and very flattering things about Mario Bava and talks about how he was typecast as a rapist in many features. Film clips are used for his segment only, and posters for his movies are on the wall. Other actors on the tape are James Karen (who talks about doing Shakespeare with John Carradine and shows a photo of himself with Marilyn Monroe) and Patrick Macnee (who discusses *The Avengers* and says, "Most of my friends are dead"). Michael Sarne talks about *Myra Breckenridge* and Waris Hussein (from India) talks about the 1963 *Dr. Who* TV pilot he directed. Curtis Harrington discusses working with Dennis Hopper and Simone Signoret. Russ Meyer tells a story about Fritz Lang pretending to marry Miriam Hopkins! Producers DelValle and Glover compiled the material and DelValle hosts.

CURB SERVICE

(Majestic, 1978) **D:** Barbara Peeters **S:** Dallas Meredith **P:** John B. Kelly, Robert D. Frintzman   (*Starhops*)

Three carhops try to save a failing drive-in theater. Dorothy Burnham and Jillian Kesner costar with Dick Miller. Stephanie Rothman was going to direct (she wrote the script but received no credit). Peeters, one of the only women making drive-in movies, directed only one more, *Humanoids from the Deep*.

CURFEW

(Starmaker, 1988) **D:** Gary Winick **S:** Kevin Kennedy **P:** Julia Phillips

Wendell Wellman and John Putch are deranged brothers who escape from death row, take the DA's family hostage, and employ mental and physical torture. Kyle Richards is the daughter. From New World.

CURFEW BREAKERS

(SW, 1956) **D/S:** Alexander Wells **P:** Charles E. King   (*Narcotics Squad*)

A 17-year-old heroin addict commits a holdup murder and goes cold turkey ("ten days' torment") in a cell. A cop narrates and tells us about police procedures. One undercover narc works as a carhop. At the Melody Mill, a band with an upright bass, a sax, and a standup female drummer (!) plays. The female lead scat-sings ("Baby, baby"). It's a great scene. Alex Wells and Sheila Urban are the young stars. Most of the actors have southern accents and use hip lingo (cat, pad, dig; cops are called rag-pickers). Paul Kelly (who died after production) is the top-billed police lieutenant and Regis Toomey is a concerned school coach. Cathy Downs (*The She Creature*; *The Amazing Colossal Man*) is the aunt, and Byron Foulger has one scene. This must have been produced just after *The Man with the Golden Arm* (1955) broke the drug taboo in films. The tape is hosted by Johnny Legend.

THE CURIOUS DR. HUMPP

(SW, 1967/70) **D/S:** Emilio Vieyra **P:** Orestes Trucco   Argentina (*La Venganza del Sexo*)

You won't believe this bizarre b/w horror/sex movie. A mad scientist (Aldo Barbero) has women kidnapped, gives them aphrodisiac shots, and watches the results ("veritable screwing machines") on closed-circuit TV with his blond assistant. The kidnapper is a black-faced monster with a light in its head, and the scientist takes orders from a talking brain (from Italy). Some added sex scenes were shot in New York City (for the 1970 US version), but the original ones are the best. In one sequence we hear strange, hypnotic music and see a pretty explicit lesbian scene. The camera sweeps around the misty grounds as zombielike patients roam around, reveals that the bizarre monster is playing the music, then returns to the bedroom. There's a reporter hero, strippers, drugs, burning bodies, and a decapitation. It's a Frank Henenlotter Sexy Shocker release.

THE CURIOUS FEMALE

(SW, 1969) **D/P:** Paul Rapp **S:** Winston R. Paul

In the year 2177 everything in LA is run by a master computer that encourages promiscuous sex. 20th-century sex movies are banned because they show relationships (!). A couple break the law by watching a film from 1969 called *The Three Virgins*. Angelique Pettyjohn, in her only top-billed appearance, is one of the virgins. Jazz musician Slim Gaillard plays. This soft-core sex comedy with orgy and lesbian scenes was from Fanfare.

CURIOSITY KILLS

(MCA, 1990) **D:** Colin Bucksey **S:** Joe Batteer, John Rice **P:** Alan Barnette

C. Thomas Howell, as an apartment-house handyman and a photographer, suspects a tenant has been killed when Jeff Fahey moves into a loft. This USA network movie "in the Hitchcock tradition" features Rae Dawn Chong as a sculptor, Courteney Cox, and Paul Guilfoyle.

THE CURSE

(Media, 1987) **D:** David Keith **S:** David Chaskin **P:** Olividio G. Assonitis   (*The Farm*)

Strange growths and maggots appear on an isolated Tenesseee farm after a meteor falls. The locals become mutant, pus-filled killers. It's based on the same H. P. Lovecraft story as *Die, Monster, Die* (1965). Wil Wheaton and his real-life sister Amy star, with Claude Akins as their religious-fanatic stepfather, John Schneider, and Cooper Huckabee. Director Keith (usually an actor) has a bit part. It was partially filmed in Rome. Lucio Fulci was the associate producer.

CURSE II: THE BITE

(TWE, 1988) **D/S:** "Fred Goodwin"/Federico Prosperi **S:** Susan Zelouf **P:** Ovidio G. Assonitis, Kenichi Tominaga   Italy/Japan (*The Bite*)

Because of an incorrect injection after a snake bite, J. Eddie Peck's hand mutates into a giant snake head and he vomits snakes. When he cuts the snake off, it grows back. This retitled feature has no relation to *The Curse* but is much better. It's a surprising horror/road movie set in New Mexico. Some Asian horror ideas are used, and Screaming Mad George provided the FX. Jill Schoelen is the horrified girlfriend. With Savina Gersak, Jamie Farr, Bo Svenson as a sheriff, and Sydney Lassick. It was filmed in New Mexico.

CURSE III: BLOOD SACRIFICE

(RCA, 1990) **D/S:** Sean Barton **S:** John Hunt **P:** Christopher Coy   S. Africa (*Panga*)

The business of unrelated "sequels" has gone too far. This movie was called *Panga*. Review copies were even circulated using that title. Some genius decided at the last minute to retitle it, so now it's part of a "series." By any name, it sucks. It's set in East Africa in 1950 and concerns a pregnant American woman (Jenilee Harrison) who's cursed by a witch doctor. It's full of irritating false scares, offscreen killings, plot inconsistencies, and scenes that are too dark to make out. A briefly seen monster (created by Chris Wallas) looks suspiciously like the fish man from *Screamers*. One black character who seems like a hero for a few seconds is immediately decapitated. The positive parts are (I guess) gray-haired Christopher Lee as a doctor in a white suit who knows more than he lets on, a topless scene, and some bloody bodies.

CURSE IV: THE ULTIMATE SACRIFICE

(Columbia, 1988) **D:** David Schmoeller **S:** Giovanni DiMarco, R. Barker Prince **P:** Hope Perello   (*Catacombs*)

This long-shelved Empire feature, made in Italy, was later sold as a "sequel." It's better than average, with interesting characters and dialogue. "The Beast," a muscular guy with long white hair who was locked in a cell in an abbey in 1506, comes back to life. There are nightmares, flashbacks, and several standout scenes. A crucified Christ statue comes to life, pulls out the nails, and kills a monk. One possessed character walks on the ceiling. Jeremy West stars as the very strict new brother superior, with Laura Schaefer as a visiting American Catholic-school teacher, and Timothy Van Patten as a young monk who's losing his faith. The soundtrack is by Pino Donaggio.

THE CURSED MEDALLION = NIGHT CHILL

CURSE OF DEMON MOUNTAIN: *See* SHADOW OF CHIKARA

THE CURSE OF HER FLESH

(SW, 1968) **D/S/P:** Julian Marsh **P/C:** "Anna Riva"/ Roberta Findly

In the twisted b/w immediate sequel to *The Touch of Her Flesh* (1967), the one-eyed Richard Jennings (Robert West) is now posing as the owner of a strip club. He uses a sword, an arrow, a switchblade, and poison ropes to kill people (mostly strippers). Eventually he kills his late wife's actor lover in an open-top truck with a machete. With topless dancers, a nude S&M lesbian stage show ("the red-hot scandal of 1968") with whips, a stag film called *Squash Crazy,* and lots of talk about how fucked up the world is. The end titles say, "Has this ended the bloody career of Richard Jennings? Don't fail to see *The Kiss of Her Flesh,* coming soon to this theatre."

CURSE OF THE BLUE LIGHT

(Magnum, 1988) **D/S/P:** John H. Johnson

In this amateur-looking Lovecraft-inspired movie shot in Colorado, teens battle oozing zombies and creatures that live underneath a graveyard. They were only trying to resurrect an ancient stone creature. Available in R and unrated versions.

CURSE OF THE CRYSTAL EYE

(New Horizons, 1989) **D:** Joe Tornatore **S:** Mikel Angel **P:** Robert Patterson, Maurice Smith

Jameson Parker searches for the treasure of Ali Baba in Bombay, in the desert, and in some caverns. He also falls for an ambassador's daughter (Cynthia Rhodes, who smiles a *lot*). The light adventure features lots of extras and horses, and since it's a Corman production those scenes are mostly likely from another movie. Also with a ridiculous and useless floating carpet, unconvincing quicksand, and Parker in blackface. Mike Lane is Hashim. It was filmed in Mauritius.

CURSE OF THE EVIL SPIRIT: *See* BLOOD SHACK

CURSE OF THE HEADLESS HORSEMAN

(VSOM, 1971) **D/S/P:** "John Kirkland"/ Leonard Kirkman

This was made back to back with the awful *Carnival of Blood.* It's set at a western theme park. Ultra Violet has a bit part. Kirkman also directed porn movies as Leon Gucci.

CURSE OF THE HIDDEN VAULT

(1964) **D/S:** F. J. Gottlieb **S:** R. A. Stemmle W. Germany (*Die Gruft mit dem Ratselschoss*)

Based on Edgar Wallace's *Angel Esquire,* which had been filmed in England in 1919. With Judith Dornys, Harold Leipnitz, Werner Peters, and Klaus Kinski as George. It was released directly to American TV.

CURSE OF THE LIVING DEAD: *See* NIGHTSTALKER

CURSE OF THE PINK PANTHER

(MGM, 1983) **D/S/P:** Blake Edwards **S:** Geoffrey Edwards **P:** Tony Adams

The *Plan 9* of detective comedies, part II. This film consists of outtakes from *Trail of the Pink Panther* (1982) made at the same time and also featuring Peter Sellers (who had died in 1980), combined with new footage. David Niven's voice, weakened by the disease he died of in 1984, was dubbed by impressionist Rich Little. Herbert Lom, as Inspector Dreyfus, hires a New York cop (Ted Wass, the real star), who talks to Niven, Ca-

pucine, and Robert Wagner. At the end, Clouseau turns out to be Roger Moore "after plastic surgery" (!). With Bert Kwouk, Joanna Lumley, Robert Loggia, and Harvey Korman. Yet another *Pink Panther* movie was made in 1992.

CURSE OF THE QUEERWOLF

(Raedon, 1987) **D/S/P/E:** Michael Pirro

This pun-filled Super 8 *Wolfman* parody, filmed in Santa Monica, is more silly than offensive and has some funny moments. It makes fun of gays and also homophobic, macho bachelors. Larry Smallbutt (Michael Palazzolo) becomes a queerwolf (or dickanthrope) after being bitten on the ass by a woman he picked up in a bar (who turns out to be a man but is played by an actress). After the transformation, Larry suddenly has an earring, limp wrists, and a red hanky in his back pocket. He wakes up in a gay bathhouse. All the werewolf clichés (the full moon, the Gypsy,) are here, but this Larry has to be killed by a silver dildo. *Deliverance, The Beverly Hillbillies, The Exorcist,* and John Wayne are also parodied. Forrest J. Ackerman has his strangest bit part so far as a patient who is force-fed alcohol until he expands and explodes, and Ed Wood Jr. regular Conrad Brooks is also in the cast. Pirro also made (and starred in) *A Polish Vampire in Burbank* (1983) and *Death Row Gameshow* (1987).

CURSE OF THE SCREAMING DEAD

(Mogul, 1982) **D/P:** Tony Malinowsky **S:** Lon Huber

Hunters and their girlfriends find a diary that brings back Confederate-soldier zombie cannibals. This was shot in Maryland and has some gore and some bad makeup.

CURSE OF THE YELLOW SNAKE

(Video Yesteryear, 1963) **D/S:** Franz-Josef Gottlieb **S:** Janne Furch   W. Germany (*Der Fluch der Gelben Schlange*)

Joachim Fuchsberger is a millionaire who owns a legendary ancient artifact called "the Yellow Snake." His evil part-Asian brother, Fing Tsu (Pinkus Braun), wants it and uses a Chinese terrorist gang to steal it. The odd camera angles and lighting make this one to look for. It's based on a novel by Edgar Wallace.

CURTAINS

(Vestron, 1982) **D:** "Jonathan Stryker"/Richard Ciupka **S:** Robert Guza Jr. **P:** Peter R. Simpson   Canada

Samantha Eggar goes undercover in an asylum to research a film role but her director husband (John Vernon) arranges for her to stay there. Then he brings six young actresses to his country estate for auditions to replace his wife in film. Somebody in a mask starts killing them off. With Linda Thorsen and Maury Chaykin. The director of the film within the film has the same name as the one that the real director hides behind in the credits.

CUT AND RUN

(Starmaker, 1984) **D:** Ruggiero Deodato **S:** Cesare Frugoni **P:** Alessandro Fracassi   Italy (*Amazonia: La Jungle Blanche; Amazon: Savage Adventure*)

This New World release, shot in Venezuela and Miami, concerns the missing son of a rich American and a jungle cocaine factory. Lisa Blount and Leonard Mann star as a Miami reporter and a student cameraman. Richard Lynch is the drug-dealing ex–Green Beret colonel who was behind the Jonestown massacre (!), seen in flashbacks. Michael Berryman, as the scary, bald Indian leader Quecho, attacks with a group of (real) Indians using blowguns and machetes. The beautiful Valentina Forte costars, with Willie Aames (*Eight Is Enough*), Gabriele Tinti, John Steiner, and the briefly seen Karen Black. The music by Claudio Simonetti (of Goblin) is excellent. The American release was drastically cut for an R rating, but *Inferno in Direta* (Video Search of Miami) is an uncut, dubbed version (in French) featuring Quecho decapitating nude women and some more gore.

CUTTER

(1972) **D:** Richard Irving **S/P:** Dean Hargrove

Peter De Anda (*Come Back, Charleston Blue*) stars as a post-*Shaft* black private eye in Chicago looking for a missing quarterback. With Barbara Rush, Stepin Fetchit, Cameron Mitchell as a coach, Gabriel Dell, and Robert Webber. From NBC.

CUTTER'S WAY

(MGM, 1981) **D:** Ivan Passer **S:** Jeffrey Alan Fiskin **P:** Paul R. Gurian   (*Cutter and Bone*)

Two forgotten lowlifes expose the corrupt rich. Jeff Bridges is gigolo and beach bum Bone. John Heard is crippled, alcoholic, one-eyed Nam vet Cutter, who sees a a wealthy man dump the body of a high-school cheerleader in the trash. With Lisa Eichhorn as Mo, Stephen Elliot, Ann Dusenberry, and Nina Van Pallandt. It's based on the novel by Newton Thornburg and was shot in Santa Barbara. The music is by Jack Nitzsche. From United Artists.

THE CUTTHROATS

(American, 1969) **D/S/P:** John Hayes **P:** Daniel Cady   (*She Devils of the SS; SS Cutthroats*)

This one starts like a western, with a theme song "The Ballad of Jimmy Johnson," but Jimmy turns out to be a cowboy/soldier in Germany (looking an awful lot like Southern California) at the end of WWII. The first scene is a roadside rape (this seems to be common in Hayes' movies). Six soldiers kill a bunch of Germans (on a golf course!) and end up with (surprise!) six remaining fräuleins, who put on a silly burlesque show. Everybody has (faked) sex (in a steam room, in a room with a swastika bedspread), plots against each other, and fights over jewels. Uschi Digart (*Supervixens*) in a military uniform, strips and pours wine over her breasts to celebrate the end of the war. This played on 42nd Street in 1984(!).

CUTTHROATS NINE

(Liberty, 1973) **D/S:** Joaquín Romero Marchent
Spain/Italy (*Condenadores a Vivir*)

In possibly the most violent Eurowestern ever made, seven chained prisoners are escorted by a cavalry guard (Robert Hundar) and his daughter (Emma Cohen). When this played in some American theaters, "terror masks" were given to patrons so that they could hide their eyes during brutal scenes.

CUTTING CLASS

(Republic, 1989) **D:** Rospo Pallenberg **S:** Steve Slavkin, **P:** Rudy Cohen, Donald R. Beck

Donovan Lietch (the son of the singer) was in an asylum because he was blamed for axe murders. Now in school, he wants A student Jill Schoelen. An art teacher is baked in a kiln, a head is smashed in a vise, and there's death by Xerox machine and power tools, in this better-than-average slasher spoof from a director who wrote John Boorman films. Wall of Voodoo provides some music. With Roddy McDowall as the principal, future star Brad Pitt, Martin Mull, and Dirk Blocker (son of Dan).

CYBER C.H.I.C.

(Hemdale, 1990) **D:** Ed Hansen **D/S:** Jeff Mandel **P:** Mark Paglia, Douglas Grimm (*Roboc.h.i.c*)

Playboy Playmate Kathy Shower was associate producer of this overlong dumb comedy but she quit after the shooting started and the credited director was replaced too. Another woman was called in to impersonate Shower for most of the movie. The show must go on. . . . Without the awful gags, and pimp/hooker biker/drug dealer subplot it could have been an OK kids movie. She acts like Data on *Star Trek* as a heroic robot with curly blonde hair. She wears a body stocking for a brief "nude" scene. Burt (Robin) Ward is embarassing as a pudgy, nerdy, nervous terrorist and so are Jack Carter as a mad scientist in a wheelchair and the Firesign Theatre's Phil Proctor (fast becoming a regular in bad movies) as the police chief.

CYBEREDEN

(VSOM, 1993) **D/S/P:** Mario Orfini **S:** Grazia Giardiello, Roberto Iannone Italy (*Jackpot*)

Adriano Celentano (a comedian and rock singer) stars as a gardener who helps rescue a kid from a computer-generated world. Kate Verson costars, with Christopher Lee and Carroll Baker. It was a major release in Italy.

CYBERNATOR

(Vista, 1991) **D/S/A:** Robert Rundle
S/P/A: Edward Sanchez

Lonnie Schuler is a hero cop in LA of the future. His (black) partner is killed, and he uncovers a conspiracy concerning cyborgs. His blond stripper girlfriend (Christina Peralta) looks a lot like Hillary Clinton, and she makes some hilarious faces while trying to act. Most of the time is taken up with talking, shooting, strippers in a bar, and

some out-of-focus sex. With Michael Foley (*Divine Enforcer*) as a white-faced martial-arts-fighting cyborg with tubes in his head, William Smith (with hair), Jay Richardson, and an obese belly dancer.

CYBERTRACKER

(Image, 1993) **D/P:** Richard Pepin
S: Jacobsen Hart **P:** Richard Merhi

Don "the Dragon" Wilson stars as a futuristic secret-service agent who is framed for murder. He's pursued by cyborgs and joins the rebels. With Richard Norton, Stacie Foster, Steve Burton, John Aprea, and Jim Maniaci.

CYBORG

(Warner, 1988) **D:** Albert Pyun
S: Kitty Chalmers **P:** Golan/Globus

Jean-Claude Van Damme stars as Gibson, who goes from futuristic Atlanta to New York with a cure for the plague. This *Mad Max* copy was made with remains of the unfinished *Masters of the Universe II*. There's a revenge plot, flashbacks, torture, crucifixion, and lots of action, but it was cut for an R. With Deborah Richter (Miss California 1975), Dayle Haddon as Pearl Prophet, a robot, Rolf Muller, and Vincent Klyn as the leader of the Flesh Pirates gang. Characters are named after electric guitars (Fender, Rickenbacker). It was filmed at the DEG studios in Wilmington, North Carolina, by Cannon

CYBORG II

(Vidmark, 1993) **D/S:** Michael Schroeder
S: Ron Yanover, Mark Goodman **P:** Raju Patel, Alain Silver (*Glass Shadow*)

An impressive copy of the city in *Blade Runner* shows us that this is the future. Elias Koteas falls for the very nice-looking Angelina Jolie, an acrobatic, kung-fu-fighting creation of corporate bad guys, and they go on the run "topside." Some parts are slow or corny, but this is an impressive-looking movie with a fun cast. Jack Palance hovers over everything as the loud, helpful, philosophical Mercy. He narrates ("I am the voice of God Almighty!"), his mouth shows up on TV screens, and during a sex scene he watches and cries. Billy Drago is memorable as a pale drug-addict killer who loses it when his face is destroyed, Karen Shepard is a torturing villainess, and a gray-bearded Allen Garfield is a corporate villain. With Tracey Walter, Renée Ammann, and a brief flashback of *Cyborg* star Jean-Claude Van Damme. Peter Allen wrote the music. The FX are by KNB. *Cyborg III*, by the same director, followed.

CYBORG COP

(Vidmark, 1993) **D:** Sam Firstenberg
S: Greg Latter **P:** Danny Lerner

David Bradley stars as a former cop who goes to the Caribbean and finds that his former partner (Todd Jensen) is now a cyborg. With John Rhys-Davies and Alonna Shaw (topless). It was shot in South Africa.

CYBORG COP II

(Vidmark, 1994) **D:** Sam Firstenberg
S/P: Danny Learner

David Bradley returns, and this time a psycho killer named Starkraven (Morgan Hunter) becomes a cyborg. Jill Pierce costars. *Cyborg Cop III* (without Bradley) and *Cyborg Soldier* (with Bradley) followed, both by Firstenberg.

CYBORG: THE SIX MILLION DOLLAR MAN = THE SIX MILLION DOLLAR MAN

CYCLE PSYCHO: *See* SAVAGE ABDUCTION

CYCLE VIXENS

(Simitar, 1977) **D/P:** Peter Perry **D/S:** John Arnoldoy **C:** Ron Garcia (*Young Cycle Girls*)

Three bored, underage Colorado girls in cutoffs decide to ride their motorcycles to California. The bearded dad of two of them actually says okay. Their friend has to sneak out. After some comedy hijinks and riding in their bikinis for a while, they meet a drugged-out couple. This leads to rape and stolen bikes. They recover, determined to make it to the Coast, but once they get there they are all shot dead! Now, that's exploitation. Lorraine Ferris is top-billed. It's a cut version. Cinematographer Garcia shot Coppola's *One From the Heart* not long after this.

CYCLONE

(RCA, 1986) **D/A:** Fred Olen Ray **S:** Paul Garson, T. L. Langford **P:** Paul Hertzberg

Secret agents are after a supercharged motorcycle. Heather Thomas (*The Fall Guy*) stars, with Jeffrey Combs as her brainy boyfriend and Martin Landau as the main villain. There are lots of chase scenes. With Martine Beswick, Robert Quarry, Huntz Hall, Troy Donahue, Russ Tamblyn, Dawn Wildsmith, Michael Reagan (the ex-president's adopted son!), and Tim Conway Jr. Also with Ashley Ferrare, Michelle Bauer, and Pamela Gilbert in a shower, and Ray himself.

CZECH MATE

(1984) **D:** John Hough **S:** Jeremy Burnham UK

The first of 13 Hammer "House of Mystery and Suspense" TV movies. Susan George and her former husband (Patrick Mower) go to Prague, he disappears and she's arrested as a spy. It was filmed in Vienna.

DADDY-O

(RCA, 1958) **D:** Lou Place **S:** David Moessinger
P: Elmer Rhoden Jr.   (*Out on Probation*)

Singer Dick Contino is hired by gangsters to drive a getaway car. Sandra Giles costars in this AIP teen movie, originally released on a double bill with *Road Racers*. With Bruno Ve Sota and Gloria Victor. The music is by John Williams, who went on to become the most successful film composer in the business.

DADDY'S BOYS

(RCA, 1987) **D:** Joe Minion **S/A:** Daryl
Haney **P:** Roger Corman

A psychotic widower (Raymond J. Barry) and his three sons go on a crime spree. Jimmy (Daryl Haney) joins up with a hooker (Laura Burkett), and they become "Adam and Eve" criminals. With Dan Shor and Linda Shayne. Minion, who wrote Scorsese's *After Hours*, was given one week's notice by Corman to shoot this in a matter of days on sets left over from *Big Bad Mama II*. From Concorde.

DADDY'S DEADLY DARLINGS

(Paragon, 1972) **D/S/P/A:** Marc Lawrence   (*Pigs*)

A psychotic woman (Toni Lawrence) takes a job as a hired hand at a pig farm. She lures men to their death (and castrates them with a razor). Zambrini (Marc Lawrence), her boss, feeds the bodies to his pigs. Jesse Vint is the sheriff. Aquarius released this odd (and too dark-looking) family project made by character actor Lawrence (whose real name is Max Goldsmith) in 1984.

DAGGER EYES

(VSOM, 1983) **D/S:** Carlo Vanzina
S: Enrico Vanzina   Italy

Assassins try to kill a hooker (Carole Bouquet) for a lighter containing negatives showing a politician's assassination. With Janet Angren as another hooker, John Steiner, and Gabrille Tinti.

DALI

(1989) **D:** Antonio Ribas **S:** Miguel Sanz, Enrico Goma, Temistocles López **P:** Vito, Ricardo Di Bari   Spain/Italy

Lorenzo Quinn (Anthony's son) stars as Dali, and Sarah Douglas is his muse, Gala. The film centers on their much-publicized time in New York in 1940. Flashbacks show the eccentric, self-promoting artist's early days in Spain and his work with Buñuel on films. Some easier-to-find documentary tapes are *Salvador Dali: A Self-Portrait* (Pacific Arts), narrated by Orson Welles, and *The Definite Dali* (Kulture).

THE DALTON GIRLS

(Fang, 1957) **D:** Reginald LeBorg
S: Maurice Tombragel **P:** Howard Koch

The late-50s teen explosion affected every kind of movie. This is a juvenile-delinquent western with female gunslingers. When the Dalton gang is killed off, their female relatives take over. Merry Anders is the leader. With John Russell, Lisa Davis, and Penny Edwards. LeBorg also directed *Voodoo Island* at United Artists the same year.

DAMAGED GOODS

(SW, 1937) **D:** Phil Stone
S: Upton Sinclair **P:** Irving Starr

The script (by the author of the famous exposé *The Jungle*) is based on the 1903 play about venereal disease by Eugène Brieux. Pedro De Cordoba plays a doctor.

DAMAGED GOODS

(T&A, 1961) **D/S:** Haile Chace **P:** Sid Davis   (*VD*)

This movie about high-school seniors in trouble borrows an old title and features a five-minute US Public Health Service documentary on the evils of venereal disease at the end. The school's star athlete gets VD after a drunken night with a hooker in a seaside town. The instrumental theme song is by the Ventures. The video box makes this tame film appear to be a porno movie.

DAMAGED LIVES

(1933) **D/S:** Edgar G. Ulmer **S:** Don Davis

This "adults-only" VD movie was Ulmer's first film in the US. The 70-minute drama about the dangers of fooling around was made for the Canadian Social Health Council by Columbia. It was originally followed by a filmed 10-minute lecture on venereal disease (one for men and a different one for women) presented by a doctor (actor Murray Kinnell, the carnival barker in *Freaks*). The actors include Diana Sinclair, Lyman Williams, and Jason Robards Sr. The feature was from the Weldon Picture company.

DAMNED RIVER

(Fox, 1989) **D:** Michael Schroeder **S:** John Crowther, Bayard Johnson **P:** Lance Hool

Deliverance strikes again. Stephen Shellen is a very psychotic killer who guides a group of yuppies on a river adventure in Africa. With John Terlesky. Schroeder also made *Out of the Dark*.

DAMSELVIS

(Big Broad, 1994) **D/S/P:** John Michael McCarthy

This one-hour underground-style (altered video footage, b/w/color) feature shows a rural schoolgirl (Sherry Lynn Garris) who is killed, then reborn, on a motorcycle wearing white leather fringe. Others follow her to a pyramid in Tupelo, where a monster Elvis fights a black Jesus. It's pretty interesting, with some gore and the star and her killer (Ghetty Chasum) are both naked in the woods. The music is mostly one guitar with some feedback. Hugh Gallagher, who made *Gorotica* with some of the same cast (also in Memphis), was the cameraman. McCarthy, a cartoon-ist, also created a *fumetti* (Italian photo comic strip) version.

DANCE HALL RACKET

(Hollywood Confidential, 1953) **D:** Phil Tucker
S/A: Lenny Bruce **P:** George Weiss

The ill-fated standup comedian and social commentator Lenny Bruce appears in his only feature as Vinnie, a murdering bouncer with a switchblade at Scali's Dance Emporium. The racket is run by Ed Wood Jr. movie regular Timothy Farrell as Umberto Scali. The cast includes Honey Harlowe (Bruce's real-life stripper wife) and Sally Marr (his mother), who does the Charleston. The adults-only feature, by the director of *Robot Monster* (1953) and the producer of *Glen or Glenda*, features a little nudity. It's only 55 minutes long. Farrell played basically the same character in *The Devil's Sleep* and *Pin Down Girls*. Bruce had also written the script for *The Rocket Man* (1954), an RKO film about a boy with a space gun that makes crooked people honest.

DANCE MACABRE

(Columbia, 1991) **D/S/A:** Greydon Clarke
P: Menahem Golan

Argento fans might get a few laughs out of this stupid *Suspiria* ripoff filmed in Saint Petersburg (!) Robert Englund (with a beard and facial scar) stars as an American choreographer at a Russian dancing school. He also plays a ridiculous-looking crippled lady ballerina. Englund in drag (with a fake nose) speaking with a voice box is not a pretty (or convincing) sight. Blond Michelle Zeitlin (from *Lambada*) does not look anything like a ballerina, and her acting is worse than Englund's. Of course there are murders, flashbacks, dreams, nude scenes, and that surprise (!) ending. All I could think of was what the Russian actors thought of their new freedom to act in international junk like this. Harry Alan Towers backed the 21st Century release, which was called *Phantom of the Opera II* in some countries.

DANCE OF DEATH

(MPI, Unicorn, 1968) **D:** Juan Ibáñez
D/S: Jack Hill **S/P:** Luis Enríquez Vergara
US/Mexico (*Macabre Serenade; House of Evil*)

In 1900 in Europe Boris Karloff (with mutton-chop whiskers) plays spooky music on a pipe organ in his mansion. He cheerfully insults all his relatives (including Julissa), who arrive for the reading of a will, and talks of his brother Hugo, who plucked out his eyes after "his brain shrank." Boris dies early in the movie, and Hugo's diabolical "toys" begin killing people. One is shot by a toy cannon, another by a suit of armor, others by jerky, life-size dolls. At the end we discover that Boris is still alive (!), playing a special hidden organ that shoots flames, and everything burns up. The worst of the last four Karloff movies, both boring and senseless, this wasn't released until 1978!

DANCE OF THE DAMNED

(Virgin, 1988) **D/S:** Katt Shea Ruben **S/P:** Andy Ruben

This vampire movie uses the same Venice, California, sets used in *Stripped to Kill II*, also by executive producer Roger Corman and Ruben. At

Cafe Paradise, where topless dancers seem to be in *Flashdance* outtakes, Cyril O'Reilly, a young, ultrahip long-haired vampire (who sees everything in monochrome), watches a very thin stripper (Starr Andreef). He offers the suicidal young woman $1000 to talk. They take a bus, go to the beach, then go to his pad. The caring vampire, who has an exercise bike and hates cigarette smoke, cries and talks about his bitter life. She says her best friend as a child was her Barbie Doll. Except for scenes of bullets popping out of his chest and a skinhead attack on the bus, this is actionless and bloodless. With Maria Ford. Corman had it remade as *To Sleep with a Vampire*.

DANCE OR DIE

(City Lights, 1987) **D/S:** Richard Munchin
P: Richard Pepin, Joseph Meri

This was called a horror movie, but it's a story about a guy (Ray Kieffer) trying to stay away from drugs while he choreographs a musical in Las Vegas. Lots of people are shot.

DANCE WITH DEATH

(HBO, 1990) **D:** Charles Philip Moore
S: Daryl Haney **P:** Mike Elliot

Roger Corman and his Concorde company reuse everything. This is a remake of *Stripped to Kill*, from only four years earlier, based on the story (and film) by Katt Shea Ruben and Andy Ruben. It uses some of the music from Corman's *Naked Obsession* and *In the Heat of Passion*. A reporter (Barbara Alyn Jones) goes undercover as a stripper to find the serial killer who preys on the dancers. With Maxwell Caulfield as the prime suspect, Martin Mull as the strip-club owner, Catya Sassoon as a lesbian, Maria Ford, and Kelly Crosby.

DANGER MAN

(MPI series, 1961) UK

Patrick McGoohan stars as security investigator John Drake in a b/w series filmed on location around the world. 4 half-hour volumes are available. McGoohan later returned as Drake twice, in two better-known series, *Secret Agent* and *The Prisoner*. The star, often considered British, was born in New York City.

THE DANGEROUS

(Orion, 1994) **D/S:** Rod Hewitt
P: David Winters   (*Divine Wind*)

This revenge thriller received attention because its costar, Paula Barbieri, was O. J. Simpson's girlfriend. The cast includes Robert Davi, Michael Pare, Joel Grey, John Savage, Cary-Hiroyuki Tagawa, and Elliott Gould. It was shot in New Orleans.

A DANGEROUS AGE

(Sinister, 1959) **D/S:** Sidney J. Furie   Canada

An underage girl runs away from boarding school to be with her lover. It's pretty boring. With Ann Pearson, Ben Piazza, and Kate Reid. This was the first film by Furie, who later worked in England (*Dr. Blood's Coffin*, *The Snake Woman*, *The Ipcress File*) and the US.

DANGEROUS ASSIGNMENT

(Sinister series, 1952)

Brian Donlevy stars as secret agent Steve Mitchell in a syndicated series filmed on location around the world. Donlevy, who also starred in the radio version, went on to play Professor Quatermass in two Hammer films. 17 volumes, each containing 2 half-hour shows, are available.

DANGEROUS GAME

(Academy, 1988) **D:** Stephen Hopkins **S:** Peter West **P:** Judith Est, Basil Appleby   Australia

A psychotic Irish cop (Steven Grives) on suspension stalks punk-look teens who break into a department store. With Kathryn Walker and Miles Buchanan. Similarities to *Die Hard* were played up on the video box. Hopkins went on to direct *Nightmare V*, *Predator II*, and others in the US.

DANGEROUS GAME

(MGM, 1993) **D:** Abel Ferrara **S:** Nicholas St. John **P:** Mary Kane   (*Snake Eyes*)

Harvey Keitel (who had just starred in Ferrara's *Bad Lieutenant*) is Eddie Israel, a Ferrara-like New York director. He goes to LA to make a movie called *Mother of Mirrors*, starring an acting couple (Madonna and James Russo). The director and his female star have an affair. Ferrara's real-life wife plays Israel's wife. Both of the falling-apart relationships are affected by the characters in the movie being made (and lots of drugs are taken). There's a clip from *Burden of Dreams*, with Werner Herzog. Like most movies with Madonna, this was a commercial flop. R and unrated versions are available.

DANGEROUS HEART

(MCA, 1994) **D:** Michael Scott
S: Patrick Cirillo **P:** Harvey Frand

Tim Daly stars as a drug-dealing killer who pretends to be a businessman and has an affair with a cop's wife (Lauren Holly). Joe Pantoliano costars.

DANGEROUS LOVE

(Media, 1988) **D/S:** Marty Ollstein
P: Brad Krevoy, Steven Stabler

Women using a video dating service are killed by a psycho who videotapes the murders. A detective (Elliott Gould) is on the case. With Lawrence Monoson, Brenda Bakke, Teri Austin, and soap-opera star Anthony Geary. From Roger Corman/Concorde.

DANGEROUSLY CLOSE

(Media, 1986) **D:** Albert Pyun **S/A:** John Stockwell **S:** Scott Field **P:** Harold Sobel

In another inferior copy of *Massacre at Central High*, a Nazi-like gang of psycho yuppies called the Sentinels (led by John Stockwell) scare poor kids at school. Violence and death result. The hero is J. Eddie Peck, and the cast includes Carey Lowell, Dedee Pfeiffer, Angel Tompkins, and Karen Witter. The various artists soundtrack is on Enigma.

DANGEROUS OBSESSION

(AIP, 1986) **D/S:** Lucio Fulci **S/P:** Vincenzo Salviani **S:** Ludovica Marineo, Jesús Balcazar Italy (*Il Miele del Diavolo*; *Devil's Honey*)

This erotic revenge movie copies *9 1/2 Weeks* and even has a sax-player character who tries to look like Mickey Rourke. The star, though, is Bianca Marsillach, as Jessica, who takes her clothes off at every possible opportunity. Her boyfriend, an abusive, kinky, bisexual, exhibitionist musician, dies on the operating table after a motorcycle accident. She blames Dr. Simpson (Brett Halsey), a surgeon who is turned on by the color red and cheats on his wife (Corinne Clery) with hookers in the office. Jessica kidnaps the doc, smashes his car with an axe, and keeps him tied up naked at a beach house, feeding him dog food, while she walks around naked and recites poetry ("the Devil's honey pot"). She also drops molten wax on him and says, "My name is fear!" All the while, we see on/off flashbacks showing how the sax man messed with her mind and got her pregnant. Halsey, the star of *The Return of the Fly* (1959), moved to Europe in the 60s and married actress Luciana Paluzzi. The US video is cut (of course).

DANGEROUS TO KNOW

(1938) **D:** Robert Florey **S:** William R. Lipman, Horace McCoy

In this adaptation of *On the Spot*, by Edgar Wallace, Anna May Wong (who had been in a Broadway version) stars as Madame Lan Ling, the mistress of a wealthy crime boss (Akim Tamiroff). She seeks revenge when he gets interested in another woman (Gail Patrick). With Lloyd Nolan, Anthony Quinn, Roscoe Karns, and Hedda Hopper.

DANGER WOMAN

(1946) **D:** Lewis D. Collins **S:** Joseph Michael **P:** Morgan B. Cox

Don Porter stars as a scientist working on atomic energy. His long-missing wife (Patricia Morison) shows up with some crooks out to steal his formula. Brenda Joyce costars, with Milburn Stone and Samuel S. Hinds. This 59-minute Universal B movie was part of the original TV "Shock" (horror films) package in the 50s.

DANGER ZONE

(MGM, 1986) **D:** Henry Vernon **S/P/A:** Jason Williams **S/P:** Tom Friedman **S:** Karen Levitt

Flesh Gordon star Jason Williams is Wade Olson, undercover narc. The Reaper (Robert Canada) and his coke-dealing biker gang terrorize the Skirts, a female rock band, in the desert outside Las Vegas. With Michael Wayne (son of John and producer of *The Green Berets*) and Suzanne Tara.

DANGER ZONE II: REAPER'S REVENGE

(M.C.E.G., 1988) **D:** Geoffrey G. Bowers **P/A:** Jason Williams **S:** Dulaney Ross Williams **P:** Tom Friedman

In this western-on-motorcycles sequel, the Reaper is released from prison and kidnaps the girlfriend (Jane Higgenson) of hero Wade Olson (Jason Williams).

DANGER ZONE III: STEEL HORSE WAR

(Premiere, 1990) **D:** Douglas Bronco **S/P/A:** Jason Williams **S:** Gregory Poirier

Jason Williams returns again as a bike-riding ex-cop whose girlfriend was killed by the Reaper (Robert Canada) in Part II. *Danger Zone IV: Bad Girls, Mad Girls* followed on cable TV, and *Death Riders* (Monarch, 1993) featured the same characters.

DANTE'S INFERNO

(1924) **D:** Henry Otto **S:** Cyrus Wood, Edmund Goulding

Ralph Lewis is a mean slumlord and businessman who drives a man to suicide. He's tried for murder and executed, but demons take him to Hell (represented by red-tinted footage from the Italian silent film *Dante's Inferno*). At the end it's all revealed to have been a dream. The 20th Century–Fox film is one hour long. A better-known 1935 version (with the same great silent footage) starred Spencer Tracy. In 1937, Dan Sonney used the Italian footage again for his roadshow movie *Hellavision*!

THE DAREDEVIL

(1972) **D:** Robert W. Stringer **P:** K. Gordon Murray

George Montgomery stars as a race-car driver who works for drug dealers on the side. Terry Moore and Gay Perkins costar, and Cyril Poitier is the (black) mortician villain. It was the last production of 60s showman Murray. The music is by the Brooklyn Bridge.

DAREDEVILS OF THE RED CIRCLE

(Stokey, 1939) **D:** William Witney, John English **S:** Barry Shipman, Franklyn Adreon, Rex Taylor

This action-packed 12-chapter Republic serial stars Charles Quigley, Herman Brix (in 1940 he became Bruce Bennett), Dave Sharp, and Carole Landis. Charles Middleton is the crazy ex-con #39013 who uses poison gas and other means to try to kill off the members of the Daredevils, a trio of athletes who perform at an amusement center when not battling bad guys. Mysterious messages from the Red Circle help the Daredevils (who wear big zeros on their chests). With Miles Mander and C. Montague Shaw. Snowflake, a Stepin Fetchit type of comedian, appears as himself.

DARIO ARGENTO: MASTER OF HORROR

(VSOM, 1991) **D/S:** Luigi Cozzi   Italy

Argento's more recent features are examined behind the scenes in this 80-minute sequel to *Dario Argento's World of Horror* (1985). Pino Donaggio, Michelle Soavi, Cozzi, and of course Argento are interviewed. You see how the bullet FX were achieved in *Opera* and how melons and meat are stabbed for sound effects. Argento poses at Poe's grave in Baltimore and says that producers "are like rampaging demons born in my brain but raised by someone else." *Two Evil Eyes, The Church*, and *Devil's Daughter* are also covered. The Italian-language tape has been subtitled in English.

DARIO ARGENTO'S WORLD OF HORROR

(Vidmark, 1985) **D/S:** Michelle Soavi   Italy

This excellent documentary includes interviews with Argento (the man loves violence) and behind-the-scenes footage of the making of every feature he directed from *The Bird with the Crystal Plumage* (1970) to *Creepers* (1985). Films he produced (*Dawn of the Dead* and *Demons*) are covered too. Viewers who have seen only the US versions of Argento's movies will be amazed by the many uncut scenes revealed here. This tape is easier to find than some of the films themselves and is a good introduction to Europe's premier horror perfectionist.

THE DARK

(Imperial, 1993) **D:** Craig Pryce **S:** Robert C. Cooper **P:** Robert Bregman, Craig Pryce   Canada

A barely seen carnivorous rodent lives in dark tunnels under a graveyard and pulls victims under (as in *Blood Beach*). Stephen McHattie stars as a brooding widower scientist in leather on a motorcycle. He picks up a small-town blond waitress (Cynthia Belliveau) and later has himself buried alive (with no air supply!) as bait for the creature. Brion James is a sadistic cop, Jaimz Woolvett is a young gravedigger, and Neve Campbell is a pretty deputy sheriff. It was made in Ontario and at least is better than the director's awful *Revenge of the Radioactive Reporter*. It could be rated PG.

DARK AGE

(Charter, 1986) **D:** Arch Nicholson **S:** Sonia Borg **P:** Basil Appleby   Australia

A giant killer crocodile is loose in Queensland, and poachers are after it. John Jarratt and Nicki Coghill star, and David Gulpilil (*The Last Wave*) leads a crocodile cult.

DARK ANGEL: THE ASCENT

(Paramount, 1993) **D:** Linda Hassani **S:** Mathew Bright **P:** Vlad Paunescu, Oana Paunescu

Before it turns into a love story, this unique Full Moon feature is pretty good. It's impressive and laughable at the same time. Veronica (Angela Featherstone), a pretty she-devil with wings and horns (and boots and a miniskirt), argues with her sweaty, slobbering devil father (Nicholas Worth!), who works cutting out tongues and torturing the damned in Hell (great sets!). She runs away and emerges (naked) from a sewer on a city street. The now normal-looking and clothed Veronica hypnotizes a young doctor (Daniel Markel) but gets depressed watching TV news, so she goes out for some vigilante work. She hangs a rapist and rips the spine from another, and she and her German Shepherd partially eat another. The film is supposed to be set in America but was obviously made in Romania. Charlotte Stewart is the demon mom. Bright also wrote the Drew Barrymore film *Gun Crazy*.

THE DARK BACKWARD

(RCA/Columbia, 1991) **D/S:** Adam Rifkin **P:** Brad Wyman, Cassian Elwes

The influence of John Waters and David Lynch on young directors (this one was 24) becomes more apparent every year. The fact that this got made (and released in some theaters) can only be due to the name stars who were brave (or desperate) enough to be in it. Judd Nelson stars as a greasy, sweaty garbage man who becomes "Desi, the three-armed wonder comic," in this warped post-everything show-biz fable. Bill Paxton takes the acting honors as his always cheerful accordion-playing partner, Gus. Wayne Newton is a riot as a small-time agent, and King Moody (who was in *Teenagers from Outer Space*) is pretty great as the host of *The Twinkle Doodle Show*. There's an incredible b/w cat-and-mouse gore cartoon, a human xylophone, and a hard-to-believe sex scene with Paxton and three of the largest women imaginable. Also in the cast are James Caan, Lara Flynn Boyle, Claudia Christian, and Rob Lowe. Producer Elwes (brother of actor Cary Elwes) also backed *Jack's Back* and *White of the Eye*. The signs for Blimps products (Weaselroni, Pork Juice) seen everywhere in the film were confusing people all over New York City in 1990, when they were posted as teaser ads. As odd as this movie is, those signs intruding into real life were even more effective.

THE DARK CRYSTAL

(Buena Vista, 1982) **D/P:** Jim Henson **D:** Frank Oz **S:** David Odell **P:** Gary Kurtz   UK

In a fantasy world ruled by flesh-eating Skeksis, two remaining Geflings try to mend a magic crystal that will restore peace. This dark PG fantasy with ILM FX was made by Henson and Oz between their Muppet movies. British actress Billie Whitelaw provides one of the voices, Jim Henson and Frank Oz provide others.

DARKER THAN AMBER

(Chiron, 1970) **D:** Robert Clouse **S:** Ed Waters **P:** Walter Seltzer, Jack Reeves

This was the first of a planned series based on the Travis McGee books, by John D. MacDonald (who also wrote *Cape Fear*). Rod Taylor (the same year as *Zabriske Point*) stars. Bill Smith is a psychotic blond bodybuilder, and they have an incredible arm-breaking fight on a ship, done without stuntmen. Some say that Bruce Lee chose Clouse to direct his *Enter the Dragon* after seeing it (the scene is censored in the TV and video version). The plot concerns prostitution and drug smuggling in the Florida Keys and the Caribbean. With Suzy Kendall (*The Bird with the Crystal Plumage*), Theodore Bikel, Ahna Capri, Chris Robinson, and Jane Russell (in her last role) as a hooker called the Alabama Tigress. From National General Pictures.

Sam Elliott played McGee in a 1983 ABC-TV movie. Smith was also in Clouse's *Ultimate Warrior* (1975).

DARKEST AFRICA

(Republic, 1936) **D:** B. Reeves Eason, Joseph Kane **S:** John Rathmell **P:** Nat Levine

This was the very first of 66 Republic serials. The 15 chapters star real-life animal trainer Clyde Beatty as himself. In some ways it resembles *Flash Gordon*, from the same year. There are cool flying bat men from the lost city of Joba, tiger men, a large gorilla, and a giant lizard. With blond Elaine Shepard and the strange looking Manuel King ("the world's youngest animal trainer") as Baru, the jungle boy. Stuntman Ray Corrigan plays a bat man and a gorilla. Parts were filmed at Jungleland, a tourist park owned by King's father near Brownsville, Texas. Curly-haired Beatty, who did not look like a leading man, had already been in *The Lost Jungle* (1934) produced by Levine. *King of Jungleland* and *Bat Men of Africa* are condensed feature versions of this serial. The same team made Republic's second serial, *The Undersea Kingdom*, too.

DARK FORCES = HARLEQUIN

THE DARK HALF

(Orion, 1991) **D/S:** George A. Romero **P:** Declan Baldwin

Timothy Hutton stars as a writer using the pseudonym George Stark for his best-selling slasher novels. When he's blackmailed, his alter ego emerges and kills with a razor. The writer is blamed for the killings, and his wife (Amy Madigan) and a local sheriff (Michael Rooker) try to help clear him. Hutton's characters are obviously inspired by Stephen King and (an evil) Elvis. The 50s jd–look Stark wears all black and whistles, "Are You Lonesome Tonight?" Twins are important to the plot. With Julie Harris as a helpful, pipe-smoking professor, Robert Joy as a blackmailer, Rutanya Alda as the publisher, Royal Dano (in his last role) as a gravedigger, and "4,500" soul-transferring sparrows. It's based on King's 1989 book, set in Maine, but was shot around Pittsburgh. Romero's best film in years, it is (like his others) too long (122 minutes). The Orion release was delayed until 1993. The soundtrack is by Christopher Young.

DARK HERITAGE

(Cornerstone, 1989) **D/P:** David McCormick

After some campers are killed, some guys spend the night in an old mansion to try to videotape something. Later on some other guys dig a tunnel and discover the killers, people in tights and masks who jump around like monkeys. There are a few good laughs if you can stay awake through all the talk and scenes leading nowhere. A b/w dream sequence was inspired by *Carnival of Souls*. Filmed in Atlanta, Baton Rouge, and Geismar, Louisiana.

DARK HORSE

(Live, 1992) **D:** David Hemmings **S:** J. E. MacLean **P/A:** Tab Hunter

This is the uplifting story of a girl (Ari Meyers) in the Rockies and her horse. It's here simply because of the producer (who also wrote the story) and the cast. With Ed Begley Jr., Mimi Rogers, Donovan Leitch, and Samantha Eggar.

THE DARK HOUR

(Sinister, 1936) **D:** Charles Lamont **S:** Ewaet Adamson **P:** George R. Batcheller

Ray Walker stars as a detective in this old-dark-house murder mystery from the independent Chesterfield company. The cast includes Irene Ware (from *The Raven*, 1935), Hedda Hopper, E. E. Clive, William V. Mong, and Miki Morita as Choong, the butler. The 64-minute film ends with the surprise that the killer is a man in drag, a traditional cheat ending that filmmakers continue to use.

DARK INTRUDER

(Shocktoons, 1965) **D:** Harvey Hart **S:** Barre Lyndon **P:** Jack Laird

This atmospheric 59-minute period horror movie was a TV pilot for a projected series to be called *The Black Cloak* but was released to theaters by Universal instead. Another TV pilot shown in theaters, *Chamber of Horrors* (1966), used the same idea of a turn-of-the-century crime-solver with a dwarf assistant. They simply changed the San Francisco location to Baltimore and had the detective own a wax museum instead of being unemployed and rich. Leslie Nielsen isn't really very good as the man of leisure with a secret crime lab, but *Dark Intruder* has a great plot and lacks a typical happy ending. It's about a growling, hunchbacked Sumerian demon and features misty scenes in Chinatown and in a graveyard. A plot twist about an evil, deformed Siamese twin will surprise fans of *Basket Case*. Werner Klemperer is Professor Malaki.

DARKMAN

(MCA, 1990) **D/S:** Sam Raimi **S:** Chuck Pfarrer, Ivan Raimi, Daniel Goldin, Joshua Goldin **P:** Robert Tapert

Raimi's *Phantom of the Opera*–derived, comic-book-type movie was more successful than the more expensive *Batman* or *Dick Tracy* (both released first) in many ways. Irish actor (and future Oscar nominee) Liam Neeson is very good as the tragic scientist who develops

synthetic skin that lasts only 100 minutes. After mobsters destroy his face and lab, he becomes Darkman, with a new secret headquarters. Frances McDormand (from the Coen brothers' films) is his lawyer girlfriend, and the LA mobsters are led by Larry Drake (who collects severed fingers). With Nicholas Worth, Colin Friels as a corporate villain, and Professor Tanaka. Bit parts went to John Landis and Jenny Agutter (seen briefly as doctors), Theodore Raimi, and Bruce Campbell. The stunt work is excellent, the very good FX are by Tony Gardner and Larry Hamlon, and it has another Danny Elfman score (available on MCA).

THE MOST DIABOLIC SHOCKER EVER TO STUN THE SCREEN

YOU'LL BE POSSESSED BY THE DARK INTRUDER ....TILL YOU SCREAM WITH SUSPENSE! starring LESLIE NIELSEN JUDI MEREDITH MARK RICHMAN Written by BARRE LYNDON Directed by HARVEY HART Produced by JACK LAIRD A UNIVERSAL PICTURE

Liam Neeson, star of *Darkman*, with Nicholas Worth.

There were two direct-to-video MCA sequels, *Darkman II: The Return of Durant* and *Die Darkman Die*, both starring Arnold Vosloo.

DARK MANSIONS

(1986) **D/P:** Jerry London **S:** Robert L. McCullough

This TV pilot is a modern-gothic drama about a haunted estate near Seattle. Linda Purl moves there to write about the family. With Joan Fontaine, Michael York, Paul Shenar, Lois Chiles, Raymond St. Jacques, Dan O'Herlihy, Nicollette Sheridan, and Melissa Sue Anderson.

THE DARK MIRROR

(Republic, 1946) **D:** Robert Siodmak
S/P: Nunnally Johnson

Olivia De Havilland stars as twins Terry and Ruth Collins (one is evil) in this psychological murder mystery released by Universal, with Lew Ayres as a psychiatrist who specializes in twins (and uses ink-blot tests), Thomas Mitchell as a cop, and Richard Long. Siodmak had just made *The Spiral Staircase*. De Havilland returned in *The Snake Pit*. Jane Seymour starred in a 1984 TV remake.

DARK MISSION

(Media, 1988) **D/S:** Jesús Franco
P: Daniel Lesoeur   France

The plot involves opium harvesting and smuggling. The stars are Christopher Lee, Brigitte Lahaie, Christopher Mitchum, and Richard Harrison. It was filmed in Portugal. Lahaie and Mitchum are also in Franco's *Faceless*.

DARKNESS

(Film Threat, 1992) **D/S/P:** Leif Jonker

Zombies (that can run) show up in a convenience store, an abandoned house, and a car wash (!) and kill local teens. Guns, a chainsaw, the sun, and holy water in a soda bottle are all used as weapons. The hero (Gary Miller) is also credited with the bloody FX. The scene of mass zombie deaths is the best. There's a synthesizer score with some heavy-metal and punk music added. The Super 8, all-teen-cast, Wichita production took 3 years to complete. Jonker claims he sold his own blood to pay the bills. That's impressive, and it's a good start, but *Darkness* (most of it is too dark to see) is really not as outstanding as some would have you believe.

DARK NIGHT OF THE SCARECROW

(Fox, 1981) **D:** Frank De Felitta
S: J. D. Feigelson **P:** Bobbi Frank

This CBS-TV movie is often shown on Halloween. A small-town postman (Charles Durning) reluctantly leads a vigilante group stalking a harmless retarded man (Larry Drake) blamed for the killing of a young girl. His ghost returns. With Claude Earl Jones, Lane Smith, and Jocelyn Brando. The director is a horror novelist.

DARK OBSESSION

(Prism, 1989) **D:** Nicholas Broomfield **S:** Tim Rose
Price **P:** Tim Bevan   UK (*Diamond Skulls*)

Amanda Donohoe and Gabriel Byrne star in a murder mystery with sex scenes and plot twists. With Michael Hordern and Sadie Frost (*Bram Stoker's Dracula*). R and NC-17 tapes are available. The director usually made documentaries (including *Chicken Ranch*).

DARK OF THE NIGHT

(Vestron, 1985) **D/S/P:** Gaylene Preston
S: Geoff Murphy, Graeme Tetley
New Zealand (*Mr. Wrong*)

A single working woman (Heather Bolton) buys a used Jaguar haunted by the ghost of the previous owner, a woman who was murdered. The ghost eventually saves her from a psycho hitchhiker, in this feminist ghost story.

THE DARK POWER

(Magnum, 1985) **D/S/P:** Phil Smoot

Toltec Indians, an extinct Mexican tribe, attack some college students in a house. Lash La Rue stars as the friendly, bearded ranger who eventually saves the day with his trademark whip: "Feel my whip, son of a bitch!" This fun obscurity, set in the Southwest (but made in North Carolina), includes nudity, some extreme (laughable) gore, a fat janitor who farts, and racist jocks who die while a black student lives. The tall Indian spirits have scary monster faces, but they mostly just stand around and shoot arrows. It's stupid and has a bit too much comedy, but I liked it. Great accents, several likable characters, and Lash (a star of low-budget 40s westerns) is cool. I need to see his earlier movies, directed by Ron Ormond! Lash was also in Smoot's *Alien Outlaws*.

DARK RIDER

(AIP, 1991) **D/S:** Bob Ivy **S/A:** Chuck Williams

Doug Shanklin stars as a small-town, motorcycle-riding Nevada sheriff who breaks the law to catch toxic-waste-spilling mobsters led by Joe Estevez. With Heidi Floria.

DARK ROMANCES, Volume I

(1986) **D/S/P/C:** Mark Shepard **P:** Patricia Miller

If you enjoy horror-anthology movies but find them too tame (or too silly), these low-budget tapes offer sex, drugs, and violence. "The Black Veil" opens with a quote from *She* and is about Justine (Julie Carson), star of the Grand Guignol theater in Paris. Her friend Meg tells the slow, somber, talky story from an asylum. Several characters become addicted to drinking a mixture of opium and alcohol, and the film attempts to illustrate their altered states. There are lots of optical effects, clips from Méliès films, flashbacks within flashbacks, an exorcism, and a slimy puppet monster. Nearly everything is filmed in closeup. A standout FX scene shows the skin being cut off a woman's face. The shorter tale on this tape is "Listen to Midnight," about an incubus. After a surprising quote from JFK's diary, it's narrated by a hateful, drunken young LA photographer. At one point he watches Corman's *The Little Shop of Horrors* in a bar. The lasting images here include a dragonfly tattoo, nipple rings, and big breasts. With Dawn Wildsmith. Both stories feature Brinke Stevens.

DARK ROMANCES, Volume II

(1986) **D/P:** Mark Shepard and others
P: Patricia Miller

This tape offers 5 stories by different directors. "Scream queen" Brinke Stevens is in nearly every one. In the comic horror tale "She's Bad, She's Blonde, She's Lunch" (by Shepard) the late, great Fox Harris recreates his weird-atomic-scientist role from *Repo Man*. A busty blonde and her dumb boyfriend go on a convenience-store robbery and murder spree (for rent money) and make the mistake of trying to hustle Dr. Howard in a lovers' lane. My second-favorite episode, it features shocking violence, sex, gore, and great special effects. "Cardinal Sin" (by Bryan Moore) is a clever look at religious repression at home and the dangers of masturbating. A young guy keeps a copy of *Hustler* hidden in his drawer and becomes obsessed with Brazilian porno star Elle Rio (who plays her own mean-eyed, snarling, sexy self). His mother makes him read at Bible meetings and forces him to kneel and pray at home. He's very distracted by visions of sex with Elle. The ending is shocking and surprising. This is the most unique and memorable segment. "Pet Shop of the Month" (by Rodd Matsui) is about a pathetic man who is a slave to his mean blond wife, a large woman in S&M garb. This comic episode features clips of Lugosi in *The Devil Bat*, a fast punk version of "Time Has Come Today," and another puppet monster. Matsui did the makeup for all seven stories. "Last Love" (by John Strysik) involves a ghost and a female psychiatrist. It has a freak-out sequence with lots of white light, some sex, a monster, and hypodermic needles. It didn't make too much sense to me. "What Goes Around" (by Patricia Miller), in black and white, features a divorced, ex-alcoholic piano-bar musician whose family died in a car crash. He's picked up by a blonde (Stevens) who collects art (and artists). He becomes happy and starts writing serious music again but has to pay a price.

DARK SANITY

(Prism, 1978) **D:** Martin Green **S:** Philip Pine, Larry Hilbran **P:**Ben Brothers (*Straitjacket*)

A newly married alcoholic woman has visions of severed body parts. A retired cop (Aldo Ray) tells her he had the same visions when he was investigating an axe murder. There's gore and a clichéd, Poe-inspired black cat. A lawsuit charged the Cinevid company with "selling or losing" the film.

DARK SHADOWS

(MPI series, 1966–71)

It's strange to think that a daytime horror soap opera set in three time periods was so popular. You have to like (or be able to tolerate) soap operas to enjoy it, because it's slow, and very cheap-looking. Talk about video overkill—196 (!) volumes of 5 episodes each are available. The series was created by Dan Curtis and taped in New York City. You can also find *The Resurrection of Barnabas Collins*, two "best of" tapes (30 minutes each), *Dark Shadows: The 25th Anniversary* (with interviews and Jonathan Frid reading Poe's "The Tell Tale Heart"), and the ridiculous *Dark Shadows Music Videos* tape. The stars were Jonathan Frid as vampire Barnabas Collins, Joan Bennett, Grayson Hall, Kathryn Leigh Scott, David Selby, John Karlen, Kate Jackson, Thayer David, and many others who came and went over the years.

DARK SHADOWS BLOOPERS

(MPI, 1993)

This is the perfect tape for those who never liked the original daily *Dark Shadows* much (including me). Countless embarrassing and funny mistakes (which have been seen for years in syndication and on tape) are crammed into 45 minutes. Actors trip, hit their heads, and try to ignore flies on their faces. Stagehands, cameras, and microphones intrude everywhere. Visual and audio FX go wrong in every possible way. You can hear directors feeding lines to confused actors. Kid actors and the many real candles used provide endless problems. Doors refuse to open, and walls and gravestones move. It's no wonder that so many characters' names were mangled, since many actors played as many as 5 (!) different people in alternate time periods. The tape is very well edited and includes footage from the early b/w years. Recommended!

DARK SHADOWS

(MPI, 1991) **D/S/P:** Dan Curtis **S:** Hall Powell, Bill Taub, Steve Feke

After making the most expensive miniseries in history (*The Winds of War* and *War and Remembrance*), Curtis returned to his first concept. This was the NBC-TV pilot for a prime-time series that was canceled after only two months. It was a lot better-looking and much sexier than the original. Barbara Steele (in her first major acting role in many years) is Dr. Julia Hoffman, trying to cure vampire Barnabas Collins (Ben Cross). The series borrowed some ideas from the then-current *Twin Peaks*. With Jean Simmons, Roy Thinnes, Joanna

Going, Lysette Anthony, Barbara Blackburn, Ely Pouget as a psychic, and Jim Fyfe as Willie Loomis. The tape has 15 additional minutes. The other 11 episodes were often preempted by the Gulf War, but they're all on tape.

DARKSIDE

(Vidmark, 1987) **D/P:** Constantino Magnatta **S:** Alan Magee, Matt Black **P:** Philip Good   Canada

A Toronto cabdriver (Tony Galeti) picks up a porno star (Cyndy Preston) who has filmed proof that the people she works for are making snuff films. With David Hewlett. The video box compares it to the previous year's *Blue Velvet*.

THE DARK SIDE OF MIDNIGHT

(Prism, 1984) **D/S/P/A:** Wes Olsen

Cops hunt for the "Detroit Creeper," a long-haired serial killer, in Fort Smith, Arkansas. The high point is a kid wearing a Tor Johnson mask. A Troma release.

DARK SIDE OF THE MOON

(Vidmark, 1989) **D/P:** D. J. Webster **S:** Carey W. Hayes, Chad Hayes

An *Alien* copy about an evil presence that rips its way through humans on a spacecraft orbiting the moon in the year 2002. It has some gut-busting gore and zombies and an explanation for the Bermuda Triangle. With Will Bledsoe as the hero, Wendy McDonald as the Sigourney Weaver character, John Diehl, Camilla Moore as a humanoid, and Joseph Turkel as the science officer.

DARK TIDE

(Vidmark, 1993) **D:** Luca Bercovici **S/P:** Sam Bernard **S:** Robert L. Levy **P:** Nathan Zahavi

Brigitte Bako is a woman who goes to an island, where they worship snakes, with an unhappy snake expert (Chris Sarandon). She has sex with him, makes a local girl dance with her in public (which leads to an offscreen rape), then has sex in an underground pool with a beefy local half-breed (Richard Tyson). A lot of this forgettable unrated tape looks like outtakes from a Jacques Cousteau special. The two lesser-known stars were both in Zalman King movies. The director (*Ghoulies*) often acts in bad movies too.

DARK TOWER

(Forum, 1987) **D:** "Ken Barnett"/Freddie Francis and Ken Weiderhorn **S:** Robert J. Averech, Ken Blackwell, Ken Weiderhorn **P:** John R. Bowey, David M. Witz   Spain

A supernatural force kills people in a new high-rise in Barcelona. Jenny Agutter, as the architect of the Único Plaza, claims that an invisible force threw a

window washer to his death. An elevator kills people. Michael Moriarty investigates and discovers a ghost with no eyes. With Carol Lynley, Theodore Bikel, Kevin McCarthy, and Anne Lockhart. Weiderhorn replaced director Francis on this troubled Sandy Howard production, filmed in Barcelona.

DARKTOWN STRUTTERS

(Charter, 1975) **D:** William Witney **S:** George Armitage **P:** Gene Corman   (*Get Down and Boogie*)

This musical comedy/action movie set in the LA ghetto used to astound unprepared viewers on late-night TV. Trina Parks (from *Diamonds Are Forever*) stars as Syreena, leader of a group of singing biker women. The main villain is a double for Colonel Harlan Sanders. He sells overpriced rib dinners, wears a Devil costume, and clones black leaders in his dungeon. The wild 70s costumes alone are enough to make this worth

SUPER SISTERS ON CYCLES

BETTER MOVE YOUR BUTT WHEN THESE LADIES STRUT!

SINGIN' DANCIN' STRUTTIN'

DARKTOWN STRUTTERS

watching. With Edna Richardson, Bettye Sweet, Shirley Washington, Roger E. Mosley (later on *Magnum, P.I.*), Frankie Crocker, and Dick Miller as one of the stupid racist cops. It was the last feature by the veteran director of 23 (!) serials (and *The Cool and the Crazy*) and was scripted by the writer of Roger Corman's *Gassss*. The Dramatics do "What You See Is What You Get" in a jail cell. From Corman's New World.

DARK UNIVERSE

(Curb, 1993) **D/P** Steve Latshaw **S/P/A:** Pat Moran

This movie, made in Orlando, is a sort of remake of *First Man into Space* (1959). An astronaut crashes in the swamp and mutates (some morphing FX are used) into a T. Rex–look monster. Blake Pickett stars as a reporter, Bentley Tittle is a guide for a group of archaeologists, and Joe Estevez (mostly heard and not seen) is the guy who backed the space flight. With Cherrie Scott, Steve Barkett, and William Grefe. Fred Olen Ray and Jim Wynorski were the executive producers and Ray did the 2nd-unit directing and scored a *Carnosaur* prop for the monster. Jim Danforth provided some matte paintings. Latshaw did better on his own (*Vampire Trailer Park*).

DARK WATERS

(VSOM, 1994) **D:** Mariano Baino
S: Andy Bark   UK/Italy

Louise Salter is a British girl who discovers a cult on an island. This was made in Russia and in the Ukraine on the Black Sea, by Italian and British filmmakers.

D.A.R.Y.L.

(Paramount, 1985) **D:** Simon Wincer
S: David Ambrose, Allan Scott, Jeffrey Ellis
P: John Heyman, Burt Harris, Gabrille Kelly

Ten-year-old Daryl (Barret Oliver) is adopted by Mary Beth Hurt and Michael McKean after surviving a bad accident. He turns out to be a perfect son but is really a government-developed robot scheduled to be terminated. With Colleen Camp. Rated PG.

DATE WITH AN ANGEL

(HBO, 1987) **D/S:** Tom McLoughlin
P: Martha Schumacher

In this PG comedy/fantasy, a beautiful angel (French actress Emmanuelle Beart) breaks her wing on an earthly mission and ends up falling for the dying young musician she was sent to help (Michael E. Knight). His rich fiancée (Phoebe Cates) doesn't understand. With David Dukes and Bibi Besch. It was one of the last features from DEG.

DAUGHTER OF DARKNESS

(Vidmark, 1989) **D:** Stuart Gordon
S: Andrew Laskos **P:** Andras Hamori

Mia Sara goes to Bucharest, Romania, and uncovers a group of vampires led by Anthony Perkins as Anton Crainiac. These vampires have strange split tongues. This CBS-TV movie invents new and different vampire lore. It was filmed in Hungary and was hardly worth the expense. With Jack Coleman.

DAUGHTER OF DEATH

(Raja, 1982) **D:** Paul Nicholas/ Lutz Schaarwaechter **S:** Maurice Schmidt   W. Germany/US (*Julie Darling*; *Bad Blood*)

A 14 year-old-girl (Isabelle Mejias) feeds rats to her pet snake and has sex dreams featuring her father (Anthony Franciosa). She sees a delivery man kill her mother, so she blackmails him, then plots to kill her new stepmother (Sybil Danning, who has an expected nude scene) and her young stepbrother. Mejias (also in the 1979 movie *Girls*, with Anne Parillaud) is pretty good. By the director of *Chained Heat*.

DAUGHTER OF DRACULA

(Nightmare, 1972) **D/S/A:** Jesús Franco France/Portugal (*La Fille de Dracula*)

Britt Nichols is Luisa Karlstein and Daniel J. White is Max Karlstein, in a horror movie set on the coast of Portugal. It's a remake of a movie Franco had done ten years earlier, with vampires added. With Howard Vernon as Dracula (a role he also played in *The Screaming Dead*), Anne Libert, Fernando Bilbao, and Lina Romay.

DAUGHTER OF SHANGHAI

(1937) **D:** Robert Florey **S:** Gladys Unger

Anna May Wong as Lan Ying Lin searches for the mobsters who killed her father. She poses as a dancer in a Central America dive run by Charles Bickford and is helped by a federal agent (Philip Ahn). This 67-minute Paramount film features J. Carrol Naish, Buster Crabbe, and Anthony Quinn as villains who smuggle illegal aliens, Paul Fix, and Mae Busch. Quinn was in six features with Wong. Next was *Dangerous to Know*, also by Florey.

DAUGHTER OF THE DRAGON

(Joe Franklin's Collectibles, 1931) **D/S:** Lloyd Corrigan **S:** Monte M. Katterjohn, Sidney Buchman

The last of three Paramount features with Warner Oland as Fu Manchu, this actually stars Anna May Wong (who was also in Von Sternberg's *Shanghai Express* with Oland in 1932). What makes it a true Hollywood rarity is that Japanese Sessue Hayakawa, early Hollywood's only male

Asian star, plays a Chinese detective who falls in love with the Chinese-American Wong, early Hollywood's only female Asian star. As usual, Fu is after the Petrie family in London. While dying from a bullet wound, he summons his daughter, dancer Princess Ling Moy, and makes her swear to avenge him. He calls her his "man-daughter," and she quickly learns to be an evil dragon lady vowing, "I will be your son!" Throughout the movie, Fu's mysterious voice reminds her, "You must kill!" She loves Bramwell Fletcher (who was also in *The Mummy* and *Svengali* at about the same time) but must kill him. Hayakawa (who uses some martial-arts moves) loves her, until he discovers the diabolical plot. Paramount features from the early 30s always look impressive and usually have a special edge to them. This one has sliding doors, a zombie, a comic-relief gay secretary, and acid thrown in a woman's face. Great stuff, even though they got Chinese, Japanese, and Korean names mixed up!

DAUGHTER OF THE JUNGLE

(1949) **D:** George Blair **S:** William Lively **P:** Franklin Adreon

A plane with two cops escorting two gangsters goes down in the African jungle. A white jungle goddess named Tokoora (Lois Hall) saves them from hostile natives. This ridiculous Republic movie uses scenes from *Jungle Girl* (1941), features Caucasian actors speaking cartoon broken English as the natives, a man in a gorilla suit, and a witch doctor. James Cardwell is the hero, and Sheldon Leonard is the main gangster. By the director of *The Hypnotic Eye* (1959).

DAUGHTER OF THE SUN!

(SW, 1962) **D/C:** Herschell Gordon Lewis **P:** David F. Friedman

This was Friedman and Lewis' first Miami movie. Rusty Allen stars as teacher Pamela Walker. She defends herself during an emergency school-board meeting (in a suburban living room) convened

'DAUGHTER OF THE DRAGON'

ANNA MAY WONG · WARNER OLAND and SESSUE HAYAKAWA

because she posed for *Nudist Life Magazine*. One impressed younger teacher (Jerry Eden) joins her at the Sunshine Nature Camp, where there's "no immorality or lewdness," and the b/w movie miraculously turns to full color. Pamela strips in a room (but leaves her high heels on), then introduces him to other nudists, who play volleyball, and lounge on rubber rafts. They fall in love and play golf (with clothes on). Back at the camp, they shower, swim, and play volleyball in the water. After she learns that she can continue teaching, keep him, and stay a nudist, everything turns to full color again. Friedman, who also did the sound, says Allen was a gorgeous 17-year-old lesbian brought to him by famous photographer Bunny Yeager.

DAUGHTER OF THE SUN GOD
(1962) **D/S:** Kenneth Herts **P:** Edward A. Biery

Explorers encounter quicksand, snakes, crocodiles, and an Inca godess (Juanita Llosa) in this color feature from the original distributors of *Carnival of Souls*. William Holmes stars, with Lisa Montell (from *World Without End* and *She Gods from Shark Reef*). Partially shot in Brazil and Peru, it features music by Les Baxter.

DAUGHTERS OF THE FRESH FLESH
(Video Search, 1974) **D/S:** "Michel Gentil"/Jean Rollin **S:** Natalie Perrey   France (*Bacchanales Sexuelles*)

Females in tights and masks kidnap blonde Sophie from a friend's Paris apartment and take her to a mansion where the blonde High Priestess Medina smokes a hookah. Sophie is tied up and whipped in a torture chamber while a couple fuck. With maids fighting, a lesbian scene (to avant garde jazz), and a threesome. Eventually a masked ceremony becomes an orgy. Joelle Couer, Marie-France Morel, and Anne Brilland star in the (soft core) sex movie and posters for Rollin's horror movies are on a wall. It's letterboxed and subtitled.

DAVID CRONENBERG: LONG LIVE THE NEW FLESH
(1986) **D:** Laurens C. Postma **P:** Chris Rodney   UK

Great clips are used in this 50-minute documentary on Canada's most famous director. Cronenberg is heard ("A virus is only doing its job"), Stephen

Lisa Montell in *Daughter of the Sun God*.

King is interviewed, and Scorsese says, "Cronenberg is late 20th century." Critic Robin Ward says his movies are "unpleasant, distasteful, and totally negative." Cronenberg says, "An artist has no social responsibility whatsoever." Everything from *They Came from Within* to *The Fly* is covered, with special attention given to *Videodrome*.

DAWN: PORTRAIT OF A TEENAGE RUNAWAY
(1976) **D:** Randal Kleiser **S:** Darlene Young **P:** Douglas S. Cramer

The drive-in comes to America's living rooms in this NBC-TV movie. Eve Plumb (from *The Brady Bunch*) is 15-year-old Dawn, who runs away to the big city and ends up working as a hooker. With Leigh McCloskey as Alexander, Lynn Carlin, Joan Prather, William Schallert, Anne Seymour, Anne Ramsey, and Bo Hopkins as Swan. Shaun Cassidy is on the soundtrack, and the Runaways are heard doing "Cherry Bomb." *Alexander: The Other Side of Dawn* (1977) was the sequel.

THE DAY AFTER
(Embassy, 1983) **D:** Nicholas Meyer **S:** Edward Hume **P:** Robert A. Papazian

The Day After is (and will probably remain) the top-rated TV movie of all time. Over 100 million viewers tuned in to ABC on November 20, 1983, and saw Lawrence, Kansas (where *Carnival of Souls* was filmed!) nuked. Various residents are seen before and after the bombing. The Reagan White House had Secretary of State George Shultz go on TV afterward and assure the country that no war was planned. Jason Robards stars, with JoBeth Williams, Steve Guttenberg, John Lithgow, Bibi Besch, Amy Madigan, Dennis Lipscomb, Stephen Furst, and Arliss Howard. The score, by David Raksin, includes Virgil Thomson's *The River*. The film received 11 Emmy nominations. It was 135 minutes when first shown but was cut down for reruns and overseas theatrical release.

DAY DREAM
(1966) **D/S:** Tetsuji Takechi, Joseph Green **P:** Toyojiro Nagashima   Japan (*Hakujitsumo*)

Joseph Green, who made *The Brain That Wouldn't Die*, created color dream sequences and added them to a controversial b/w 1964 Japanese movie, which he then released. An art student has dreams involving naked women in masks and a vampire, while under sedation in a dentist's office. One scene has a naked woman going through a car wash.

THE DAY IT CAME TO EARTH
(Paragon, 1977) **D:** Harry Z. Thomason **S:** Saul J. Fisk **P:** John Braden

In the 50s a meteor reactivates a corpse in a lake. The growling, skull-faced zombie kills the gangsters who dumped him there and goes after the glowing meteorite some kids took. This fun movie from Little Rock is filled with fake

50s rock ballads, but the monster is scary and the college-kid stars are likable. The girls are played by blond Delight De Bruine and Rita Wilson (who later married Tom Hanks). Former TV comedian George Gobel is a professor who helps investigate the meteorite. Some scenes take place in a haunted house and a movie theater. Thomason also made *Visions of Evil* (1973), *Encounters with the Unknown* (1975), and *Revenge of Bigfoot* (1979). He and his wife, Linda Bloodworth-Thomason, later became TV producers and helped their friend Bill Clinton win the presidential election.

A DAY OF JUDGMENT
(HBO, 1980) **D:** C.D.H. Reynolds **S:** Tom McIntyre **P:** Earl Owensby

Red-eyed Death (complete with a scythe) arrives in a North Carolina town during the 30s and sends sinners to Hell. He also decapitates some of them. At the end, it all turns out to have been a dream, so the sinners can reform. William T. Hicks and Harris Bloodworth star in this southern drive-in movie.

DAY OF THE DEAD
(Media, 1985) **D/S:** George A. Romero **P:** Richard A. Rubinstein

After *Night of the Living Dead* (1968) and *Dawn of the Dead* (1979) Romero returned for another, less satisfying look at flesh-eating zombies, this time set in an underground missile silo in Florida where some of the last humans study the undead. Lori Cardille stars as Sarah, a scientist who has to fight macho army men and zombies (she's the daughter of Pittsburgh horror host Chilly Billy, who had played a TV reporter in *NOTLD*). *Day* has some good shocks and some spirited acting, and it delivers the gore, but it has too much talk. With Joseph Pilato as a frantic commando who is disembowled, Howard Sherman as a likable zombie named Bub who's being studied and trained, Terry Alexander, Richard Liberty, John Amplas, and many writers (including Bob Martin) and musicians (made up by Tom Savini and his crew) as zombie extras. It's 102 minutes long. The John Harrison soundtrack is on Saturn. The original plot had the mind-control zombies fighting the normal zombies, but Romero couldn't raise the budget to film the whole script.

DAY OF THE DOLPHIN
(Nelson, 1973) **D:** Mike Nichols **S:** Buck Henry **P:** Robert E. Relyea

George C. Scott studies dolphins that are being used in an attempt to assassinate the president. The dolphins eventually talk to him (using the voice of Buck Henry). Scott's character is based on the life of the real Dr. John Lilly, who developed the Sensory Deprivation Tank. (*Altered States* was also inspired by him.) With Trish Van Devere, Paul Sorvino, Edward Herrmann, Severn Darden, and Phyllis Davis. The Avco Embassy release was a financial flop but has many fans.

George Romero and zombies from his *Day of the Dead.*

DAY OF THE LOCUST

(Paramount, 1975) **D:** John Schlesinger
S: Waldo Salt **P:** Jerome Hellman

This incredible movie, based on Nathanael West's book, looks at various losers in 30s Hollywood. Karen Black stars as Faye Greener, "part-time whore" and star. With Donald Sutherland, William Atherton, Burgess Meredith (who was nominated for an Oscar), Geraldine Page, Bo Hopkins, Billy Barty, Nita Talbot, Paul Jabara, Richard Dysart, and William Castle as a director (he also played one in *Shampoo* the next year). It's 144 minutes long.

DAY OF THE MANIAC: *See* THEY'RE COMING TO GET YOU

DAY OF THE NIGHTMARE

(SW, 1965) **D:** John Bushelman
S: Leonard Goldstein **P:** Leon Bleiberg

Jonathan Crain (Cliff Fields) is an artist who ties up his model "my way" and whips her after she dances topless for him. Later on, he pays to watch a lesbian couple, has a blurry flashback of his mother having sex with a stranger, and cries, "Whip me, Mama!" His shrink father (John Hart) has his own flashback. Oh, yeah—Jonathan (who has a split personality) likes to kill women while in (extremely unconvincing) drag. There's also a sequence with blindfolded swingers. John Ireland (who was a regular on *Rawhide* at the time!) is top-billed as the police detective who says, "Every day people go crazy." Also with Elena Verdugo (from *The House of Frankenstein*), an unbilled Liz Renay, and Foreman Shane. Ted V. Mikels was the cinematographer. Bushelman usually worked as an editor for Bert I. Gordon. This movie (originally from Herts Lion) was featured in a 1974 *Adam Film World* magazine, making me think that much of the nudity was added years later to spice up this incredible (if overlong) movie. The b/w tape is presented by Frank Henenlotter.

DAY OF THE PANTHER

(1987) **D:** Brian Trenchard-Smith
S: Peter West **P:** Damien Parer   Australia

Edward John Stazak is Jason Blade, a martial-arts hero in Hong Kong and Perth. He was trained by a Chinese cult, "the Panthers," and battles a drug kingpin. Blade returned in *Fists of Blood* (1989), by the same director.

DAY OF THE TRIFFIDS

(1981) **D:** Ken Hannam
S: Douglas Livingston **P:** David Maloney   Australia

Most readers familiar with John Wyndham's 1951 novel about killer plants didn't much like the 1963 film version (available on UAV). This 290-minute BBC-TV production tries to be truer to the source. Killer plants attack after nearly everyone has been blinded during a meteor shower. John Duttine and Emma Relph star. It was shown on PBS in three parts in 1987.

DAY OF WRATH

(Sinister, 1943) **D/S/P:** Carl Theodor Dreyer
S: Poul Knudsen, Mogens Skot-Hansen
Denmark (*Vredens Tag*)

A 17th-century minister is cursed by a woman before she's burned as a witch. His young wife falls in love with his son, the minister dies of a stroke, and she's condemned as a witch. Religious fanaticism, repressed sexuality, and witchcraft are the themes of this dark film, made during the German occupation by the director of *Vampyr*. There are long silent segments. It was 110 minutes long when first released. US prints are subtitled.

DAY OF WRATH

(Imperial, 1967) **D/S:** Tonino Valerii
S: Ernesto Gestaldi, Renzo Genta
P: Alfonso Sansone   Italy/W. Germany
(*Day of Anger; I Giorni Dell'ira*)

Young Giuliano Gemma follows gunfighter Lee Van Cleef on a donkey, becomes his apprentice, and eventually is better than the master. With Walter Rilla, Crista Linder, and Yvonne Sanson. It was filmed in Spain. Valerii later directed *My Name Is Nobody* (1973), produced by Sergio Leone. The original rating for the National General release was M.

THE DAY THAT SHOOK THE WORLD

(VidAmerica, 1977) **D:** Vejiko Bulajic
S: Paul Jarrico   Yugoslavia

This AIP release attempts to show how WWI was started. Christopher Plummer stars as Archduke Franz Ferdinand, assassinated in Sarajevo. With Florinda Bolkan and Maximilian Schell. The screenwriter was blacklisted in 1951, settled in France, and never worked in the US again.

DAYS OF FURY

(1979) **D/S:** Fred Warshofsky
P: Doro Vlado Hreljanovic

Vincent Price is the onscreen host and narrator of this documentary look at disasters both natural (fires, volcanoes, floods) and not (plane crashes, sports deaths).

DAZED AND CONFUSED

(MCA, 1993) **D/S/P:** Richard Linklater
P: Jim Jacks, Sean Daniel

Jason London stars as Randall "Pink" Floyd, a pot-smoking quarterback who refuses to sign the coach's no-drug pledge. It's the last day (and night) of the school year at a suburban high school in 1976 in Austin, and this movie does an excellent job of recreating the feel and look of the period. It's very funny, nostalgic, and scary in ways that *American Graffiti* was not. The $6 million Universal film was made by the 31-year-old director of *Slacker*. Rights to the original 70s hits on the soundtrack (Kiss, Alice Cooper, Foghat, Sweet, Black Oak Arkansas) took up one-sixth of the budget. 30 characters have recurring roles. With Wiley Wiggins as the kid who is initiated, Rory Cochrane, Sasha Jenson, Michelle Burke, Parker Posey, and Milla Jovovich (who had starred in *Return to the Blue Lagoon*).

D.C. CAB

(MCA, 1983) **D/S:** Joel Schumacher **P:** Topper Carew, Cassius Vernon Weathersby

Adam Baldwin and his cabdriver friends save the kids of an ambassador from kidnappers in Washington. With Max Gail as the Nam vet who owns the cab company, Mr. T. as Samson, Timothy Carey as the Angel of Death (!), Paul Rodriguez, Charlie Barnett, John Diehl, the Barbarian Brothers, Jill Schoelen, and Irene Cara (as herself). The Universal comedy has a Giorgio Moroder score. The various artists is soundtrack on MCA.

DEAD AGAIN

(Paramount, 1991) **D/A:** Kenneth Branagh **S:** Scott Frank **P:** Lindsay Doran, Charles H. Maguire

This romantic, gothic mystery thriller with a reincarnation theme gets frantic and gory, with scissor stabbings at the end. It borrows a lot from Hitchcock (especially *Rebecca*) and from *Citizen Kane* and is full of plot twists. In LA, amnesiac Emma Thompson is tormented by memories of a concert pianist (also Thompson) who was murdered in the 40s. A private detective (Branagh) and an eccentric antique dealer/hypnotist (Derek Jacobi) become involved. The 40s sequences are b/w. This box-office hit was advertised as a horror film (with great posters). With Robin Williams, Andy Garcia, Hanna Schygulla, and Campbell Scott.

Lee Van Cleef in *Day of Wrath*

The Patrick Doyle soundtrack is on Varèse Sarabande. Branagh and Thompson (*The Tall Guy*), who were married in real life, starred in Branagh's productions of *Much Ado About Nothing* and *Henry V*.

DEAD AIR

(MCA, 1994) D: Fred Walton **S:** David Amman **P:** Oscar L. Costa

Gregory Hines is a small-town late-night radio dj whose girlfriend has been murdered. More characters die in this mystery by the maker of the *When a Stranger Calls* movies. Debrah Farentino co-stars with Beau Starr, Gloria Reuben, and Laura Herrington. It debuted on Showtime.

DEAD ALIVE

(Vidmark, 1992) D/S: Peter Jackson **S:** Stephen Sinclair, Frances Walsh **P:** Jim Booth New Zealand (*Brain Dead*)

After *The Feebles*, thirty-year-old Jackson returned with live actors in this very outrageous and gory horror comedy about zombies in 1957. Lionel (Timothy Balme) is the nerdy hero whose awful mother is bitten by an (animated) rat/monkey from Sumatra. Soon the zombism spreads and there's a house full of zombies, including a kung-fu zombie priest and a zombie baby. The unending, over-the-top, comic carnage includes decapitations, gut-munching, and Lionel's incredible power-lawn-mower defense. An unrated version or a 12-minute-shorter R version is available on tape.

DEAD-BANG

(Warner, 1989) D: John Frankenheimer **S:** Robert Foster **P:** Steve Roth

Alcoholic LA police detective Don Johnson goes after black bikers who have killed a cop but ends up teaming up with a black deputy sheriff (Tim Reid) for a violent confrontation with well-organized white supremacists who plan to cause race riots and take over the country. In one scene Johnson throws up on a suspect. With Frank Military, Penelope Ann Miller, William Forsythe as a Christian FBI agent, Bob Balaban, Danielle Quinn, and Ron Jeremy. It's supposed to be based on real events.

DEAD BEAT

(Live, 1994) D/S: Adam Dubov **S:** Janice Shapiro **P:** George Moffly, Christopher Lambert

In mid-60s New Mexico, Bruce Ramsey is Kit, a limping, Elvis-look con man and womanizer who is convinced to go on a murder spree by a rich girl (Natasha Wagner). It's loosely based on a real serial killer who some say inspired Manson. A follower (Balthazar Getty) tells the story. With Meredith Salinger, Deborah Harry, Sara Gilbert, and Alex Cox. It was shot in Arizona.

DEADBEAT AT DAWN

(Ketchum, 1987) D/S/A: Jim Van Beeber **P/C:** Mike King

Jim Van Beeber is Goose, leader of the Ravens. Paul Harper is the psychotic leader of the Spiders.

Goose quits his own gang and plans to settle down after he's made enough money selling junk. When his Ouija-board-using girlfriend (Megan Murphy) is beaten to death by Ravens with golf clubs, he hides out with his crazed junkie father in a derelict apartment. After the rival gangs combine to attempt an armored Brinks-truck robbery, Goose is reduced to taking orders, while seeking revenge. The nothing-to-lose young people in this movie are mostly very believable. They wear ripped jeans and boots and have long, messy hair. They smoke pot, drink beer, take pills, snort coke, and drink hard liquor, sometimes all in one night, then make big plans. An especially dumb one called Bonecrusher does Rush and yells, "I don't give a shit about nuthin'!" There are graveyard knife and gun battles, some martial-arts fighting, stolen motorcycles, fingers bitten off, a decapitation, the bloody ghost of the dead girlfriend, some pretty warped music, and a man ordering breakfast for himself and God. I could have done without some of the kaleidoscopic segues and red lights, but otherwise this is one of the most downbeat, unpretentious, independent action movies I've seen. It was made by talented film school guys based in Cincinnati.

DEADBOLT

(New Line, 1992) D: Douglas Jackson **S:** Frank Rehwaldt, Maria Trafficant **P:** Pierre David, Thomas Berry Canada

Justine Bateman is a divorced medical student who lets a man (Adam Baldwin) move into her condo with her. He turns out to be a manipulating psycho who holds her captive. With Michelle Scarabelli and Chris Mulkey. The same people made *The Paperboy* next.

DEAD BOYS CAN'T FLY

(VCI, 1992) D/P: Howard Winters **S:** Anne Wolfe

A trio of guys terrorize, rob, rape, and kill people working in a New York City office building on a holiday. Goose (Brad Friedman) is a crazed blond in drag who says, "I'm a sociopath lady!" The others are the quieter psycho Buzz (Jason Stein) and Jojo (Daniel L. Johnson). A (way too young) grizzled Nam-vet janitor (David John) tries to stop them. There's some good cinematography, actual Nam footage, and heavy-metal music, but a lot of this is more laughable than disturbing. Bennett Theissen (director of the early 80s New York play *Grind House*) plays a suicidal lawyer. With Ruth Collins (in a Marilyn imitation scene), Delia Sheppard, Sheila Kennedy, and Jennifer Delora. It's available in R and unrated versions.

DEAD CALM

(Warner, 1989) D: Philip Noyce **S/P:** Terry Hayes **P:** George Miller, Doug Mitchell Australia

After a shocking car crash at the start, this settles into a suspensful, three-character, psycho-on-a-boat movie. Nicole Kidman and Sam Neill have to fight for their lives when the intense Billy Zane shows up. It's a great-looking, clever movie with good horror elements and a nude scene that helped Kidman become a star in the US. The film is adapted from a novel by Charles Williams that

was also the basis of an unfinished Orson Welles film (*The Deep*). Producer Miller also directed the second unit scenes.

DEAD CERTAIN

(Hemdale, 1990) D/S/P: Anders Palm **P:** Mark Cutforti Canada

Anthony Quinn's dull son Francisco stars as a divorced, unshaven, sweaty Toronto cop (who uses hookers and junk) looking for a psycho killer. Brad Dourif, who lives in a big loft with banks of TVs tuned to static, is the prime suspect. Karen Russell is the cop's ex-wife. Despite flashbacks, flashforwards, and arty cinematography, it's still boring. The music by Charlie Mole is good.

DEAD CONNECTION

(Polygram, 1993) D/M: Nigel Dick **S:** Larry Golin **P:** Steve Golin, Gregg Fineberg (*Final Combination*)

Michael Madsen is a (blond) LA police detective who teams up with a freelance reporter (Lisa Bonet) to catch a British necrophiliac serial killer named Welton (Gary Stretch). The killer tells his victims that he's a rock manager, uses the names of real boxers, and calls phone-sex lines. This moody film attempts to be like a 40s film noir detective movie. Dick also made *Deadly Intent* (1988).

DEAD END

(Embassy, 1937) D: William Wyler **S:** Lillian Hellman **P:** Samuel Goldwyn

One of the great social-problem films, this Warner Brothers production is based on Sidney Kingsley's play. An early juvenile-delinquent movie, it was the launching pad for the Dead End Kids/Bowery Boys. Sylvia Sidney and Joel McCrea star, with Humphrey Bogart as Baby Face Martin, Allen Jenkins as Hunk, and Claire Trevor. The kids are Billy Halop as Tommy (the leader), Leo Gorcey as Spit, Bobby Jordan as Angel, Gabriel Dell as T. B., Huntz Hall as Dippy, and Bernard Punsley as Milty. They had been in the play since it opened in 1935. The great sets recreate NYC's Sutton Place as luxury housing was going up next to slums. The cinematography is by Gregg Toland. Alfred Newman wrote the music. Bogart and most of the gang returned the next year in *Crime School*.

DEAD END

(1992) D/P/E: Robert Tiffe **S/P/A:** Martin King

In a very effective supernatural road movie, Frank (Martin King), a big, long-haired killer, dominates his sometimes reluctant partner, Harold (Robert Restaino), from back East. They pay for their acts of senseless violence on a seemingly endless desert road going through an Indian reservation, as victims show up in different forms to torment them. The two stars, who have a lot of dialogue, are very convincing. There are b/w sex/murder flashbacks, some freak-out editing, and some great-looking women. There's a good rock theme, and the soundtrack by Legal Weapon is on Triple XXX.

DEAD END CITY

(AIP, 1989) D/S/P: Peter Yuval **S:** Michael Bogart

Dennis Cole (from the 60s TV series *Felony Squad*) is the police chief, and Robert Z'Dar is a street-gang leader. It's about vigilantes, corrupt cops, and a government conspiracy.

DEAD-END DRIVE-IN

(Starmaker, 1986) **D:** Brian Trenchard-Smith
S: Peter Smalley **P:** Andrew Williams   Australia

In the near-future world of 1990, young people are tricked into a government drive-in/prison camp that shows kung-fu and exploitation movies. Most of the trapped teens enjoy the movies and junk food, but they can't leave. Ned Manning as Crabs (who has a red-and-white '56 Chevy convertible) tries to escape with his girlfriend (Natalie McCurry). New World released the film in the US. Trenchard-Smith made *Escape 2000*, also set in a futuristic concentration camp.

DEADFALL

(Vidmark, 1993) **D/S:** Christopher Coppola
S: Nick Vallelonga **P:** Ted Fox

This *Grifters*-inspired, all-star *film noir* attempt is a mess but will be talked about for years. Michael Biehn stars as a con man (and narrates his flashbacks), but Coppola's brother Nicholas Cage (in a laughable wig) steals the movie (acting as out of control as he did in *Vampire's Kiss*) until his face is pushed into boiling grease. James Coburn does his best, considering (in two roles), and blond Sarah Trigger is around for sex scenes. Charlie Sheen has his own pool-hustler scene, and Angus Scrimm (with a metal arm and claw hand), Peter Fonda, Michael Constantine, Micky Dolenz teamed with Clarence Williams III (!), and Renee Estevez show up. Coppola, who also made *Dracula's Widow*, managed to find roles for relatives Talia Shire and Marc Coppola too.

DEAD FLOWERS

(1992) **D/S:** Peter Ily Huemer   Austria

Alex (Thierry Van Werveke), a pest exterminator who lives with his grandmother, picks up a stranded woman (Kate Valk) who claims to be the American daughter of a spy. She turns out to be a ghost, and a messenger of death takes her back. Alex takes a ferryboat to the underworld (a warehouse) to try and find her. Obviously inspired by recent Wim Wenders movies, this is a well-made romantic fantasy. Music includes Brian Ferry's "In Your Mind" and some American 60s garage rock from Pebbles albums. In German with subtitles.

DEAD GIRLS

(Raedon, 1990) **D:** Dennis Devine
S: Steve Jarvis **P:** Eugene James

The Ozzy Osbourne "Suicide" song controversy probably inspired this teen horror movie. A Dead Girls song ("Life is a total bummer, death ends all") inspires a wrist-slashing group suicide. The sister of band member Birtha Beirut (or Gina) is the only survivor. The group (four girls and Marky the drummer) go to a remote cabin with the recovering sister to rest and avoid bad publicity. The cast is killed off by a person in a rubber skull mask, from Gina's lyrics. There's also a pushy Oriental manager, a bodyguard, a nurse, Elmo, a retarded, stuttering handyman, a weird female groupie, and a hostile black sheriff: "I burned my daughter's collection of your albums!" Gina has nightmares. Characters are killed with a nail gun, by stabbing, fire, axe—all the things that Gina wrote about! This film holds some kind of record for false endings.

DEAD HEAT

(Starmaker, 1988) **D:** Mark Goldblatt **S:** Terry Black **P:** Michael Meltzer, David Helpern

Treat Williams is LA cop Roger Mortis and musclebound Joe Piscopo is his wisecracking partner, in a horror-gore comedy so bad that the video tries to pass it off as a serious action movie! The plot concerns a conspiracy to keep old rich people alive. Williams becomes a zombie cop, there's a zombie biker, and in one scene meat in a butcher shop comes to life. The FX are by Steve Johnson. With Lindsay Frost, Darren McGavin as a corrupt coroner, a tired-looking Vincent Price (wasted in a nothing role), and Keye Luke, Professor Tanaka, and Martha Quinn. The Ernest Troost soundtrack is on Varese Sarabande. *Blue Jean Monster* (1990) was a Hong Kong copy of this feature.

DEAD IS DEAD

(Tempe, 1992) **D/S/P/E/A:** Mike Stanley

Eric, a coke addict with a beard and a dumb-looking Renaissance haircut, is given a life-restoring drug and goes on a vengeance spree that takes him to Manhattan. Others use the drug and keep returning to life. Needles go into arms in slow motion. There are lines like "You look like a penis with the dry heaves," a boring synthesizer score, and really bad FX. It was shot (on tape) in Michigan (where the creator/star produced a local TV show), with a few New York location shots added.

DEAD KIDS = STRANGE BEHAVIOR

THE DEADLIEST ART: THE BEST OF MARTIAL ART FILMS

(Fox, 1990) **D:** Sandra Weintraub
P: Fred Weintraub   US/Hong Kong

John Saxon hosts a letterboxed documentary about features from Hong Kong's Golden Harvest company. Samu Hung, Jackie Chan, Yuen Biao, and Cynthia Rothrock are interviewed, and many action clips are shown. There's also a look at Bruce Lee (of course). Weintraub produced *Enter the Dragon*.

DEADLINE FOR MURDER: *See* THE NAKED FLAME

DEADLOCK

(Fox, 1991) **D:** Lewis Teague **S:** Broderick Miller **P:** Bramko Lustin   (*Wedlock*)

In a change-of-pace role, Rutger Hauer is strong and intelligent but not a tough guy. In the near future, he's framed by his girlfriend (Joan Chen) and James Remar after planning a diamond robbery with them. He's sent to Camp Holiday, a prison where inmates can wander around. The problem is that they're linked electrically with unknown other prisoners, and if they stray too far from each other they blow up. Several head-exploding scenes are as good as in the *Scanners* movies. Hauer is tortured by the corrupt warden (Stephen Tobolowsky) and escapes with Mimi Rogers, in a mixture of *The Defiant Ones* and a revenge plot. It's pretty good, but for some reason *Graffiti Bridge* is still showing at a theater in "the future." With Basil Wallace. Hauer and Chen were also in *Blood of Heroes*.

THE DEADLY AND THE BEAUTIFUL = WONDER WOMEN

DEADLY BET

(PM, 1992) **D:** Richard W. Munchkin **S/P:** Joseph Merhi **S:** Robert Tiffe **P:** Richard Pepin

Jeff Wincott bets his girlfriend (Charlene Tilton) in a kickboxing match in Las Vegas and loses. He has to stop drinking, train hard, and win her back from the bad guy (Steven Vincent Leigh). With Sherrie Rose, Gary Daniels, and Ray Mancini.

DEADLY BREED

(Raedon, 1989) **D/S:** Charles T. Kanganis **P:** Richard Pepin, Joseph Merhi

A racist police captain (William Smith) secretly uses a gang of skinheads to kill minorities. A parole officer (Blake Bahner) discovers the plot. With Allison Randall and Rhonda Grey.

DEADLY COMPANION

(Ace, 1979) **D:** George Bloomfield
P: Jerome Simon, David Main **S:** Thomas Headley, Jr.   Canada (*Double Negative*)

A mental patient (Michael Sarrazin) tries to solves his wife's murder. Anthony Perkins seems to be responsible. With Susan Clark, Howard Duff, Kate Reid, John Candy (featured on the video box), and Pita Oliver.

DEADLY DAPHNE'S REVENGE

(AIP, 197?) **D/S:** Richard Gardner **S:** Tim Bennett **P:** Dick Horton, Mark Castor

Cindy (Laurie Tait Partridge) is a blond hitchhiker who goes to a lawyer after being picked up and raped by some weekend hunters at a summer lodge. This movie shows how the lives of the hunters are ruined before the trial even happens. In the laughable ending, Charlie, the racist trucking-company owner who egged the others on (he looks like Kenny Rogers), is killed by Daphne, a black woman who escaped from an asylum. Everyone wears bellbottoms and has bad haircuts. Troma picked up this 70s movie, had it copyrighted, and retitled it in 1987.

DEADLY DREAMS

(1988) **D:** Kristine Peterson
S/A: Thom Babbes **P:** Matt Leipzig

A writer (Mitchell Anderson) whose parents were killed by a psycho dreams that the killer is after him. With Juliette Cummins, Stacy Travis, and Beach Dickerson. The director started out with Roger Corman.

DEADLY EMBRACE

(Prism, 1989) **D/S/P:** "Ellen Cabot"/
David DeCoteau **S/P:** Richard Gabai

In a flashback-filled *film noir* attempt made in five days, a rich Beverly Hills woman (Ty Randolph aka Windsor Taylor Randolph) hires a young handyman (Ken Abraham) while her husband is away and is killed. Jan-Michael Vincent is the spying husband. With Jack Carter, Albert Popwell, Ruth Collins, and Linnea Quigley for topless scenes. Michelle Bauer (in the spirit of old Russ Meyer movies) is "the female spirit of sex."

DEADLY EXPOSURE

(Atlantic, 1993) **D/P:** Lawrence Mortorff
S/A: Asher Brauner

After a man leaves a synagogue he's lynched in an LA park by a gang of masked white supremacists. His unemployable, alcoholic, formally famous journalist son (a bearded, still young-looking Robby Benson in all-black clothes) investigates. Benson takes time out to have sex scenes with a reporter who's a fan of his work (Laura Johnson) and to read *Answer Me!* magazine. The neo-Nazi group turns out to be a cover for an assassination attempt, but we learn that "Nazis were into psychedelics, sacrifices, the whole nine yards." With 70s drive-in star Andrew Prine as the leader of the Brotherhood, Isaac Hayes as a police lieutenant, Paul Hampton (*They Came from Within*) as a senator, Jeff East, and Bentley Mitchum. The executive producer was Steven Paul (*Slapstick of Another Kind*).

DEADLY EYES

(Warner, 1982) **D:** Robert Clouse **S:** Charles Eglee
P: Jeffrey Schectman, Paul Kahert   (*The Rats*)

Sam Groom, Sara Botsford, Scatman Crothers, and Lisa Langlois are all in a movie about giant, intelligent rats in New York City. The rats even attack a baby in a baby chair. The problem is, they're really dogs (just like in *Attack of the Killer Shrews*). I liked *Of Unknown Origin* (1983) better, as far as 80s giant-rat movies go. The Golden Harvest production was based on a James Herbert novel.

DEADLY FORCE

(Nelson, 1983) **D:** Paul Aaron **S:** Ken Barnett,
Barry Schneider **P:** Sandy Howard

An LA psycho working for a guru with a past kills girls and carves Xs on their foreheads. Sadistic, on the edge, ex–New York City cop Stoney Cooper (Wings Hauser, just after *Vice Squad*) is called in to catch him. With Joyce Ingalls as Stoney's ex-wife, a TV reporter, and Paul Shenar.

Marilyn Chambers is seen on a TV screen. At one point Sam Peckinpah was supposed to direct, and Embassy even planned a series.

DEADLY FRIEND

(Warner, 1986) **D:** Wes Craven **S:** Bruce Joel
Rubin **P:** Robert M. Sherman, Robert Crawford

A kid scientist (Matthew Laborteaux) puts the microchip brain of his robot into the pretty girl next door (Kristy Swanson) after her drunken father beats her to death. The strong robot girl goes out for vengeance and even kills some bikers. With Anne Ramsey. A bloody scene with a head smashed by a basketball was added by the producers. The Charles Bernstein soundtrack is on Varèse Sarabande. The film is based on the novel *Friend*, by Rubin, who went on to write the hit *Ghost*.

DEADLY GAME

(Paramount, 1991) **D:** Thomas J. Wright
S: Wes Claridge **P:** Johanna Persons

A mysterious masked millionaire with a group of black and Asian hunters and killer dogs watches seven people on his misty island with video cameras as they're killed off. Each character's background and crime is revealed through flashbacks that keep things interesting. Michael Beck and Jenny Seagrove star, with Marc Singer. Soon-Tech Oh as a tattooed yakuza has the best flashback, with multiple decapitations. With Roddy McDowall, Mitchell Ryan, and Professor Tanaka. The USA Network movie was filmed near Mount Hood, in Oregon. The ending is a hoot.

DEADLY GAMES

(Fires, 1980) **D/S:** Scott Mansfield   Canada

A black-gloved stranger kills in a small town while characters talk and play a horror board game. Alexandra Morgan stars, with Sam Groom as a cop, Jo Ann Harris as a reporter, Steve Railsback, Colleen Camp, Dick Butkus, June Lockhart, and Denise Galik.

DEADLY ILLUSION

(RCA, 1987) **D/S:** Larry Cohen **D:** William
Tannen **P:** Irwin Meyer   (*Love You to Death*)

Cohen, who was replaced as director, wrote this as a Mike Hammer movie. He had purchased the rights to several Mickey Spillane novels for a possible series, but it fell through after the failure of the *I, the Jury* remake (1982). Billy Dee Williams is Hamburger, a wisecracking New York City private detective who causes a lot of accidental deaths while unraveling a double-cross plot. Cohen's trademark locations (the Rockefeller Center ice-skating rink at Christmas, Shea Stadium, Times Square) are put to good use in some amazing action scenes. Joe Spinell opens this comic action movie with a shootout in a gun-permit line. Vanity is Rina, the sexy Velda substitute. With Morgan Fairchild, Joe Cortese, John Beck, and Michael Wilding Jr. (son of Elizabeth Taylor) as the main villain.

DEADLY IMPACT

(Vestron, 1983) **D/S/P:** "Larry Ludman"/
Fabrizio De Angelis **S:** David Parker Jr.   Italy

Fred Williamson is a helicopter pilot, and Bo Svenson is a cop investigating a mob murder in Vegas. A couple have been scamming the slot machines using a computer. With John Morghen and Marcia Clingan. Filmed at the Golden Nugget, in Las Vegas, and in Phoenix.

DEADLY INNOCENCE

(Quest, 1988) **D/S/P:** Hugh Parks **D:** John D.
Patterson **S:** Joseph Tankersley

Amanda Wyss plays Andy, a sad girl who runs a remote gas station. Her best friend is Pee Wee, a nice retarded girl, and she has eyes for the local sheriff (busy Andrew Stevens). After her strict, religious father (John Anderson) dies, leaving her confused and alone, a strange woman (Mary Crosby, who shot J. R.) shows up and moves in. Wyss has the nude scene, but Crosby really gets to show off, playing a devious, seductive, schizophrenic man-killer on the run who has crazed conversations with her other self. This odd, low-key psycho movie (filmed in Florida) is pretty good until the dumb ending.

DEADLY INTENT

(Fries, 1988) **D:** Nigel Dick **S:** John Goff
P: Thomas Fries, Jackelyn Giroux

After an archaeologist is murdered, various characters go after his widow for the jewels he brought back. With Lisa Eilbacher, Steve Railsback, Maud Adams, Lance Henriksen, Fred Williamson, and Persis Khambatta.

DEADLY LOVE

(Complete, 1987) **D/S:** Michael O'Rourke
P: Sally Smith

One of the worst. Nothing is right about this idiotic horror movie. It's loaded with confused flashbacks, closeups, dreary synthesizer music, and POV camera shots. A young woman inherits the house where her aunt, Crazy Annie, committed suicide. Lots of people are killed by a crazed caretaker, or a biker ghost from the 60s, or a blackmailing imposter. Who cares? Filmed in Utah (I think).

DEADLY MESSAGES

(1985) **D:** Jack Bender **S:** William
Bleich **P:** Paul Pompian

Kathleen Beller receives deadly messages from a Ouija board, and a murder is commited. This ABC-TV movie features Michael Brandon, Dennis Franz, Kurtwood Smith, and a clip from *The Tingler*.

DEADLY NEIGHBORS

(VCI, 80) **D/S/E:** Don Dohler   (*Fiend*)

Mr. Longfellow (Don Leifert, from *Alien Factor*), a suburban music teacher who teaches in his bare basement, is really a resurrected corpse! The large, sweaty, bug-eyed, rude man with a mustache and all-black clothes makes the neighbors suspicious as he kills off local women (and even a little girl). He sometimes glows red, and he talks to his cat and Mr. Frye (George Stover), manager of the music academy. They constantly say "Mr. Longfellow" and "Mr. Frye." There are several plugs for Dohler's *Film Magic* book. This was filmed in Milford, Delaware.

DEADLY OBSESSION

(Republic, 1987) **D/S:** Jeno Hodi **S:** Paul Wolansky, Brian Cox **P:** Anant Singh

John Doe (Joe Paradise), an animal-rights activist and college janitor, threatens to kill coeds if he doesn't receive a million dollars. He lives in tunnels, puts rat poison in ice cream, and stalks Darnell Martin. It doesn't make a whole lot of sense.

DEADLY POSSESSION

(Vestron, 1988) **D/S:** Craig Lahiff **S/P:** Jerry Jennings   Australia

Two female students in Adelaide try to find out who the masked psycho killer on campus is. Penny Cook and Anna-Maria Winchester star. Some parts are copied from older horror classics.

DEADLY PREY

(Sony, 1987) **D/S:** David A. Prior **P:** Peter Yuval

Ted Prior is the Nam-vet hero in a ripoff of *The Most Dangerous Game* set in a secret California mercenary camp. Prior (brother of the director) rips off a man's arm and beats him with it. With name guest stars Cameron Mitchell and Troy Donahue, Fritz Mathews, William Zipp, and Suzanne Tara.

DEADLY REACTOR

(AIP, 1989) **D/S/A:** David Heavner **P:** Fritz Mathews   (*Reactor*)

David Heavner stars as Cody, a gunslinger and preacher in the futuristic Wild West. He's made sheriff and battles post-nuke bikers. It all copies Eastwood westerns. With Alyson Davis and Stuart Whitman as Duke.

DEADLY RIVALS

(MCA, 1992) **D/P/C:** James Datson **S:** Redge Mahaffrey

Andrew Stevens is a government laser weapons expert in Miami in this story about spies (including Margaux Hemingway), gangsters (Joseph Bologna and Francisco Quinn, who narrates), torture, and rival sisters. With Cela Wise, Randi Inmgerman, and Richard Roundtree as an FBI agent.

DEADLY SANCTUARY = JUSTINE

THE DEADLY SECRET

(AIP, 1994) **D/P:** Jason Hammond **S/A:** Douglas Stalgren **P/M:** Erik Hansen

A rich real-estate man who helped kill a girl when he was a college student is blackmailed. With Joe Estevez, Tracy Spalding, and Reggie Cale.

DEADLY SPAWN: *See* RETURN OF THE ALIENS: DEADLY SPAWN

DEADLY SPY GAMES

(Unicorn, 1989) **D/S/P/A:** Jack Sell **S/P:** Adrianne Richmond

Jack Sell is a government agent who can prevent WWIII in this James Bond spoof. With Tippi Hedren, Troy Donahue as Python, and footage from Sell's *Outtakes*.

DEADLY STRANGERS

(Paragon, 1974) **D:** Sidney Hayers **S:** Philip Levine **P:** Peter Miller   UK

Hayley Mills picks up a hitchhiker (Simon Ward), and they go to a town where an asylum inmate is loose. With Sterling Hayden. Mills has one of her first topless scenes.

DEADLY SURVEILLANCE

(Republic, 1989) **D/S:** Paul Ziller **S:** Hal Salwen

Susan Almgren is a psychotic hooker who kills cops, and Michael Ironside is the tough cop after her. With Christopher Bundy as her boyfriend, Michael McGill as a junkie, David Carradine in a small role as a cop, drug smugglers, and violence. It was made for cable TV.

DEADLY TRACKERS

(Warner, 1972) **D:** Barry Shear, Samuel Fuller **S:** Lukas Heller **P:** Fouad Said

Richard Harris (after *A Man Called Horse* and *Man in the Wilderness*) stars as a sheriff who tracks bank robber Rod Taylor to Mexico after his wife and son are killed. With William Smith as a retarded muscleman, Isela Vega, and Neville Brand. Fuller, the original director, also wrote the story. He started shooting in Spain but didn't get along with Harris, so the film was reshot in Mexico. Some of the music was from *The Wild Bunch* (1969).

DEADLY TREASURES OF THE PIRANHA = KILLER FISH

DEADLY TWINS

(Prism, 1985) **D/S/P:** Joe Oaks

Judy and Audrey Landers (real-life sisters, but not twins) are twin singers who are raped and beaten in Cologne by the son of a mob boss. It's revenge time.

DEADLY VENGEANCE

(Active, 1970) **D/P/E/C:** Amin Chaudhri **S:** Joel O'Brien   (*Sweet Vengeance*)

This tape, claiming to star Grace Jones, is a New York City crime/sex movie originally rated X. The story concerns a woman who goes after gangster Big Mike after he kills her boyfriend. She lets a gay photographer paint her body and take her picture (for *Freakout* magazine) in exchange for martial-arts lessons in Central Park. She poses as a hooker, slits some gangsters' throats, then dies in flames after her car crashes. The producers must have decided to try to deceive black action movie fans a few years later, because they added several scenes with *Shaft*-style music, two black characters, and more explicit (soft-core) sex. Near the beginning, a very young-looking Grace Jones (with short natural hair) greets her boyfriend, Slick Jones. They have almost-porno sex, ruined by the cameraman, who usually focuses on the guy's butt. Slick leaves and does it with Big Mike's woman, then gets shot in the head when they're discovered. No more Grace, on with the "real" movie. By the director of *Tiger Warsaw* (1987).

DEADLY VISION

(Elecktra, 1979) **D:** Ivan Nagy **S:** Robert Carrington **P:** Jay Benson (*Mind over Murder; Are You Alone Tonight?*)

A psycho killer who blows up planes is mentally in touch with housewife Deborah Raffin. With Andrew Prine, Bruce Davison, and Robert Englund.

DEADLY WEAPON

(TWE, 1987) **D/S:** Michael Miner **P:** Peter Manoogian

Rodney Eastman (*Nightmare on Elm Street III*) stars as an Arizona kid who thinks he's from outer space. He finds an antimatter gun and blasts his enemies and his father until the army shows up to stop him. Kim Walker (*Heathers*) is his girlfriend. With Gary Frank, Michael Horse, William Sanderson, and Ed Nelson. Miner cowrote *Robocop*, but this Empire release sounds a lot like *Laserblast*, a 1978 Charles Band production

DEADLY WEAPONS

(SW, 1973) **D/P:** Doris Wishman **S:** Judy J. Kushner

"See the mob get busted when Chesty takes her revenge." "73-32-36" Chesty Morgan stars as Zsa Zsa in her first movie, and with Doris Wishman directing you know it's at least unique. I can't think of a worse actress. She literally smothers bad guys with her enormous breasts. Porno star Harry Reems (*Deep Throat*) costars. Some of the music was stolen from an Italian western. Chesty (really Lillian Wilczkowsky, born in Poland) returned in the slightly better-known *Double Agent '73*. *Deadly Weapons* was released by Hallmark (an AIP offshoot) in 1975, and those who saw it will never forget the experience. Earlier tapes include a Joe Bob intro.

DEAD MAN'S REVENGE

(MCA, 1994) **D:** Alan J. Levi **S:** Jim Byrnes, David Chisolm **P:** Ed Lahti

Bruce Dern is an evil railroad baron who kills the family of a homesteader (Michael Ironside) and frames him. This western features Keith Coulouris and singer Randy Travis.

DEAD MAN WALKING

(Republic, 1987) **D/P:** Gregory Brown **S:** John Weidner, Rick Marx **P:** John Thurman Suttle

"Zero men" with a life expectancy of only a few years track each other across a wasteland in plague-ridden 1997. A chauffeur (Jeffrey Combes) hires a a bounty hunter (Wings Hauser) to help rescue an heiress (Pamela Ludwig). With Brion James as the crazed, orange-haired maniac villain, Sy Richardson, and Nancy Locke (Hauser). This action satire includes chainsaw Russian roulette and a human torch nightclub act at Cafe Death. From one of "the Dark Brothers" of *New Wave Hookers* fame. The same main cast was also in his *Street Asylum*.

DEAD MATE

(Prism, 1988) **D/S:** Straw Weisman **P:** Lew Mishkin

An ex-hooker working as a truck-stop waitress (Elizabeth Mannino) has nightmares and impulsively marries a rich man. Her new mortician husband turns out to be a necrophiliac who killed his other wives. Everyone else in the small town likes dead bodies too. The director started out working on Andy Milligan movies.

DEAD MEN DON'T DIE

(Academy, 1990) **D/S:** Malcolm Marmostein **P:** Wayne Marmostein

Elliott Gould is a TV newscaster who is shot by drug dealers and revived by a voodoo priestess and cleaning lady (Mabel King). She announces, "I be his manager." He continues to deliver the news on the air, but she magically reads the copy to him, which he says in her broken English. Hilarious! Gould spends part of the movie as a zombie in a dress. With Melissa Anderson and George "Buck" Flower. Marmostein wrote some of the other movies that helped destroy Gould's career (*Whiffs* and *S*P*Y*S*). This actually played in New York City theaters!

THE DEAD NEXT DOOR

(Electro, 1989) **D/S/P/A/E/M:** J. R. Bookwalter

This one, from Akron, has been called "the most expensive Super 8 feature ever made." It cost nearly $100,000 and took the then teenage Bookwalter almost 4 years to complete. Basically it's a gory, plotless, blatant copy of Romero's *Living Dead* sequels, with in-joke character names. Zombie Squad cops use rifles and machetes to battle the fast-moving zombies (first seen in a video store). The zombie-rights protest group is a funny idea. Some brief scenes were shot near famous buildings in Washington, DC. Scott Spiegel appears as a cop, some of the dialogue was dubbed by Bruce Campbell, an *Evil Dead* clip is used, and it was partially financed by Sam Raimi, who "disowned" it. Bookwalter later made many shot-on-video features.

DEAD OF NIGHT

(1987) **D:** Deryn Warren **S:** Gerry Daly **P:** Jessica Rains

Sara (Julie Merrill), a repressed woman abused by her boyfriend, performs a ritual and is pos-sessed by Sura, an evil sorceress. Now sexy, she picks up men, takes them home for sex, and rips their throats out. There's nudity and gore. Not to be confused with the classic British horror anthology of the same name (available from HBO).

DEAD OF WINTER

(MGM, 1987) **D:** Arthur Penn **S/P:** Marc Shmuger **S:** Mark Malone **P:** John Bloomgarden

In a plot based on a B movie, *My Name Is Julie Ross* (1945), Mary Steenburgen is an actress hired by Roddy McDowall for a movie to be filmed in his old mansion. She's held prisoner there, and thanks to flashbacks and a multiple plot twist we discover that she's really . . . (It's not a great movie, but it's suspenseful enough that you should find out for yourself.) With Jan Rubes.

DEAD ON

(Orion, 1993) **D:** Ralph Hemecker **S:** April Wayne **P:** Stu Segall

Strangers on a Train provides the plot of this "erotic thriller." Shari Shattuck is a blond painter married to an attorney (David Ackroyd). Matt McCoy is a pilot who hates his rich wife (Tracy Scoggins) and wants her killed. R and unrated versions are available.

DEAD ON SIGHT

(Paramount, 1994) **D:** Ruben Preuss **S:** Lewis Green **P:** Roxanne Messina Captor

Jennifer Beals is a college student who has nightmares and premonitions about a serial killer in a ski mask. Daniel Baldwin costars, with Kurtwood Smith and William H. Macy.

DEAD PIGEON ON BEETHOVEN STREET

(VSOM, 1972) **D/S:** Sam Fuller **P:** Joachim von Mengershausen   W. Germany
(*Tote Taube in der Beethovenstrasse*)

Glenn Corbett goes to Germany to avenge the killing of his partner and encounters drugs, blackmail, and porno. With Christa Lang (Fuller's wife), Anton Diffring, Stephane Audran, Alex D'Arcy, Barry Jones, and Fuller himself as an American senator. The music is by Can. Little seen outside of Germany, it was the first feature that Fuller had control of after *The Naked Kiss*. The title was similar to Fuller's *Pickup on South Street*, from twenty years earlier.

DEAD PIT

(Imperial Entertainment, 1988) **D/S/P/E:** Gimel Everett **S/E:** Brett Leonard

"Jane Doe" (Cheryl Lawson) is in a dark, smoggy asylum full of clichéd wackos because she can't remember her identity. She usually wears the standard patient clothes, bikini panties and a short undershirt. She dreams about a nurse spraying her with a hose while she's hung by her wrists topless. Top-billed Jeremy Slate (a 60s biker-movie regular) is Swan, the gray-haired doctor who hypnotizes her, causing frightening flashbacks. A spiral staircase leads to "the dead pit," where a mad young doctor sticks syringes into victims' heads and performs lobotomies. A patient gets a dental drill stuck in his eye, a head is thrown into Jane's room, and the mad doctor possesses her. The doc's victims (lots of spastic, bloody, brain-eating zombies) all emerge from the pit (like in *The Sentinal*) and attack. A British patient tries to help ("For dead people they sure are smart!"), and the ending is pretty good. There's typical sleep-inducing synthesizer music. This tape has a great box with green eyes that glow when you push it in the right spot. Porno star Shauna McCullough was used for the topless scene.

THE DEAD POOL

(Warner, 1988) **D:** Buddy Van Horn **S:** Steve Sharon **P:** David Valdes

Dirty Harry movie number 5 is an anti–horror movie movie. San Francisco cop Harry Callahan (Clint Eastwood) is teamed with a Chinese partner (Evan C. Kim) who, of course, dies. He then (reluctantly at first, of course) works with a TV reporter (Patricia Clarkson). Liam Neeson is a low-budget horror-movie director making *Hotel Satan* and is a prime suspect when actors, celebrities, and a film critic on a hit list are killed by a psycho serial-killer horror-movie fan (and writer). Film clips from *It's Alive III*, *Cujo*, and *Time After Time* are used. Also with Jim Carrey. Eastwood was mayor of Carmel at the time. The year this was released, Eastwood directed *Bird*, did anti-drug TV ads, and campaigned for George Bush.

DEAD RINGERS

(Media, 1988) **D/S/P/A:** David Cronenberg **S:** Norman Snider **P:** Marc Boyman   Canada

After his remake of *The Fly* became a mainstream hit, Cronenberg turned to a more believable and upsetting story. It was adapted from the novel *Twins*, by Bari Wood and Jack Geasland, which was based on the true story of twin New York City doctors who died in 1975. Jeremy Irons is incredible playing both twins. Brilliant and eccentric Toronto gynecologists Beverly and Elliot Mantle conduct fertility experiments and trade women.

Jeremy Irons in Cronenberg's *Dead Ringers*.

When one falls for a movie star (Genevieve Bujold) their routine falls apart, and things get very disturbing. With Stephen Lack and some amazing gynecologist's tools. It's 116 minutes long. Cronenberg returned with *Naked Lunch* (1991).

DEAD SLEEP

(Vestron, 1990) **D:** Alec Mills **S:** Michael Rymer, **P:** Stanley O'Toole   Australia

Linda Blair is Maggie, an American nurse on the night shift in a Brisbane mental hospital. The head doctor (Tony Bonner) uses electroshock treatments, lets patients die, and has (offscreen) sex with female patients. He keeps a special ward of topless patients prisoner. Linda quits, then returns to expose the electronic sleep/drug treatment deaths. A subplot involves Linda's catatonic ex-boyfriend, a bad artist. The director was a cinematographer. The music is by Brian May. The movie is dull.

DEAD SPACE

(RCA, 1990) **D:** Fred Gallo
S: Catherine Cyran **P:** Mike Elliott

This is a cheap, boring, mild remake of Corman's *Forbidden World* (1982), itself an *Alien* copy, with more music and FX taken from *Battle Beyond the Stars* (1980). Marc Singer is the hero, with an awful wisecracking robot sidekick. A mutant creature enters a woman's nose. It grows and goes into the vents of the foggy spaceship. The full-grown creature is really bad! Laura Tate costars. From Concorde, the recycling champ of the film business.

THE DEAD TALK BACK

(Sinister, 1957) **D/S/P:** Merle S. Gold

Henry Krasger (Aldo Farnese, with pretty fake-looking hair and beard) looks into the camera and says, "My philosophy is metaphysics." He (and a police lieutenant) narrate the "true" story of how Henry helped solve a murder case. Rene (Laura Brock), a model who sits around in her negligée, is pinned to a wall with a crossbow at the rooming house where she, Henry, and the various suspects live. Henry has a radio that can communicate with the dead, and during a spooky séance items float around and Rene, dead in a tank, talks! The Headliner production, filmed in Hollywood, features a jazz band and a brief look at a 50s record store. The supernatural part is a cheat, but it's a sort of charming, low-budget feature and is a welcome release after being shelved for 36 (!) years. There's also a great *Carnival of Souls* trailer.

DEADTIME STORIES

(Cinema Group, 1985) **D/S:** Jeffrey Delman
S: Charles F. Shelton, J. Edward Kiernam
P: William Paul   (*Freaky Fairy Tales*)

Three comic-horror versions of fairy tales are told to a kid by a babysitting uncle. There's a killer witch, a werewolf version of Little Red Riding Hood, and Cathryn de Prume as Goldi Lox. Ed French created the (pretty good) gore FX. It was filmed from 1982 to 1985 and released in 1987.

With Scott Valentine, Melissa Leo (*Streetwalkin'*), and Matt Mittler as the werewolf. Executive producer William Links also backed *Deep Throat*.

DEAD WOMEN IN LINGERIE

(Monarch, 1990) **D/S/P:** Erica Fox **S/A:** John Romo

An LA private eye (John Romo) is hired to track down a serial killer who preys on mistreated immigrant garment workers. Maura Tierney costars, with Jerry Orbach, Dennis Christopher, June Lockhart, and Lyle Waggoner. It played in LA theaters after the video came out.

THE DEAD ZONE

(Paramount, 1983) **D:** David Cronenberg
S: Jeffrey Boam **P:** Debra Hill   Canada

One of the few really good Stephen King adaptations deals with political assassination and the possible end of the world. Christopher Walken awakens from a coma with psychic powers. He can save lives and predict the future, and he has a clear apocalyptic vision. Martin Sheen is the dangerous political candidate Greg Stillson ("the voice of the people"). With Brooke Adams, Tom Skerritt, Herbert Lom, Anthony Zerbe, and Colleen Dewhurst as the mother of deranged killer Nicholas Campbell. The flashback and flash-forward scenes are powerful, and the acting is excellent (especially Walken and Dewhurst). The music is by Michael Kamen and is on Milan Records. Released the same year as *Cujo* and *Christine,* it was a Dino De Laurentiis production.

DEAF SMITH AND JOHNNY EARS

(VSOM, 1973) **D/S:** Paolo Cavara **S:** Harry Essex, Oscar Saul **P:** Joseph Jani   Italy (*Los Amigos*)

Anthony Quinn is a Civil War hero and gunfighter who is a deaf-mute. Franco Nero is his partner, Johnny Ears. They're sent to the republic of Texas by the president to stop a colonel who plans to become dictator. This "spaghetti western" costars Pamela Tiffin as a whore and Ira Fürstenberg. Rated PG.

DEALING: OR THE BERKELEY-TO-BOSTON FORTY-BRICK LOST-BAG BLUES

(1972) **D/S:** Paul Williams **S:** David Odell **P:** Edward R. Pressman

A Harvard grad (Robert E. Lyons) takes a load of grass to Berkeley, in this counterculture comedy. Barbara Hershey flies to Boston with 40 kilos and is busted. A cop takes half of it and sells it himself. With John Lithgow as a dealer, Charles Durning, Joy Bang, and Buzzy Linhart. It was based on a novel by Michael Crichton (*Westworld, Looker, Jurassic Park*) and was barely released by Warner. Williams also made *Out of It* and *The Revolutionary*.

DEAL OF THE CENTURY

(Warner, 1983) **D:** William Friedkin
S: Paul Brickman **P:** Bud Yorkin

Chevy Chase and Sigourney Weaver star in a failed black comedy about international arms dealers.

Chase sells a secret superweapon to a South American dictator. With Gregory Hines, Vince Edwards, Graham Jarvis, and Wallace Shawn.

DEATH BECOMES HER

(MCA, 1992) **D/P:** Robert Zemeckis
S: Martin Donovan, David Koepp

In Beverly Hills, an aging actress (Meryl Streep) and an author (Goldie Hawn) both want a plastic surgeon (Bruce Willis). They both drink an eternal-life drug obtained from a priestess (Isabella Rossellini), return from the dead, and go after each other with shovels in this dark comic fantasy about greed and vanity. It includes advanced ILM FX, an old castle, and lots of exaggerated thunder and lightning. The doctor becomes an alcoholic "mortician to the stars." In surprising scenes, Streep walks around with her head on backwards and Hawn appears extremely fat or with a giant hole through her stomach. With Sydney Pollack, Ian Ogilvy, Michelle Johnson, and Kathy Long. Warhol, Elvis, and Marilyn also appear. Alan Silvestri provided the score. The FX are by ILM and Dick Smith. The ending of this very expensive PG-13 Universal release was reshot at the last minute.

DEATH BEFORE DISHONOR

(Starmaker, 1986) **D:** Terry Leonard
S/P: Lawrence Kubik **S:** John Catliff

Fred Dryer (former LA Rams football player and *Hunter* TV series star) is a Rambo-type marine sergeant fighting evil, torturing, kidnapping Arabs. With Joanna Pacula, Sasha Mitchell, Brian Keith, and Paul Winfield. The director is a stuntman. The co–executive producer of the New World release was Frank Capra Jr.

DEATH BY DIALOGUE

(City Lights, 1988) **D/S:** Tom Dewile
P: Richard Pepin, Joseph Merhi

This one's about a haunted movie script. A guy and four friends visit his crippled taxidermist uncle and his harsh housekeeper, who live next to a movie set. People start to die according to the script, so finally some of the survivors try to rewrite the script to save themselves (a good idea that is dropped). Some of the dream sequences are memorable, if pointless. A heavy-metal band appears playing outside and a head is smashed with a guitar. A topless girl decapitates some guy. Other parts are botched, like a man on fire, obviously a stuntman in an asbestos suit. The black kid is a typical clichéd third wheel hanging out with two couples, but as the soundtrack reminds us, "Party down and lose control!"

DEATH CAR ON THE FREEWAY

(1979) **D/A:** Hal Needham
S: William Wood **P:** Stan Shpetner

A maniac on the LA freeway attacks women in cars with his van. A TV reporter (Shelley Hack) tracks him down. This CBS-TV movie also features George Hamilton, Frank Gorshin, Peter Graves, Dinah Shore, Harriet Nelson, Barbara Rush, Abe Vigoda, Morgan Brittany, Sid Haig, and director Needham.

DEATH CHASE

(AIP, 1988) **D/S:** David A. Prior **S:** James L. Hennessy Jr.,
Craig L. Hyde **P:** Peter Yuval, Yakov Bentsvi

William Zipp stars as a guy caught up in a corrupt
businessman's game of death. With Paul Smith
and Jack Starrett.

DEATH COLLECTOR

(Raedon, 1988) **D/P:** Tom Gniazowski
S: John McLaughlin **P:** Jean Bodon, Paul
Falcone, Leopard Wurm   (*Tin Star Void*)

This was made in New Haven by an NYU grad. In
the future, a directionless, grinning, muscular
singer in a cowboy hat (Daniel Chapman) goes to
prison when his sheriff brother is murdered. After
being released, he battles bad guys in a high-
security building. Characters drive 50s cars in this
pretty dry attempt at mixing science fiction and
westerns. With horror novelist Philip Nutman as
the villain's right-hand man, Ruth Collins, and
Debi Thibeault. The star was in *Exquisite Corpses*
and some Chuck Vincent movies. Apparently he
died of AIDS.

DEATH DIMENSION

(Movietime, 1978) **D:** Al Adamson **S/P:** Harry Hope
(*Black Eliminator; Kill Factor; Freeze Bomb; Icy Death*)

Jim Kelly (from Paris, Kentucky) became the first
black martial-arts star, in *Enter the Dragon*. Later
he starred in movies made in Italy and Hong
Kong and, worst of all, two in America, directed
by Adamson. The first was called *Black Samurai*.
This was the second, and you can find it under at
least four different names from different video
companies. You might even rent it several times
by mistake, and that should make you pretty
damn mad. Almost worth seeing for the crazed
cast, this typical Adamson mismash has bad
sound and is too dark (thank cinematographer
Gary Graver) but has some pretty good music.
As Detective Ash, Kelly teaches kung-fu kicking
and drinks malt liquor, "the black man's beer."
His police-captain boss is one-time James Bond
George Lazenby. A doctor on an island is forced
to develop and demonstrate a "freeze bomb."
Four men forced to stand by the bomb when it
detonates are covered with snow and die. The
doc implants a microdot with the formula under
the scalp of his female assistant, then kills himself. Guest-star villains who are after the valuable
dot include a very angry Aldo Ray and Harold
Sakata (from *Goldfinger*) as the Pig. Another
guest star, Terry Moore, says, "Oh, God, if you
just knew how cruel the Pig was!" Kelly and
Myron Bruce Lee (!) are the heroes with
nunchucks. A "Haitian" villain who hides out at
an LA whorehouse threatens people with a big,
ugly snapping turtle. Some scenes were filmed in
Las Vegas, a favorite location of the director. One
of the executive producers was Dick Randall. My
favorite scene is a long closeup of the turtle eating grapes.

DEATH DREAMS

(New Line, 1991) **D:** Martin Donovan
S: Robert Glass **P:** Roni Weisberg

Marg Helgenberger, the wife of Christopher
Reeve, sees the ghost of their dead child. With
Cec Verrell and Fionnula Flanagan. Dick Clark
was the executive producer of this movie.

DEATH DRUG

(Academy, 1978) **D:** Oscar Williams **S:** Roland S.
Jefferson, M.D. **P:** Demetrius Johnson

Philip Michael Thomas is an LA musician who
makes a good living installing heating systems.
Suddenly he's signed to a record label and told,
"You'll be as big as Donna Summer!" He's also
given a free joint ("Stick with the kick! The tower
of power!") which immediately leads to angel-
dust use and paranoid, hostile, violent, wack behavior. He hallucinates (his hairbrush becomes an
alligator!), freaks out in a PCP ward, and sees
monster masks in slow motion. His funeral is televised! With Rosalind Cash as a doctor, Vernee
Watson as the scared wife, DJ Frankie Crocker,
and the Gap Band doing some funk tunes. When
this PG-13 film was released on tape to cash in on
Miami Vice, an even more overblown Venice
Beach angel-dust freak-out attack prologue and
Thomas music videos were added. Williams also
made *The Final Comedown* (1972).

DEATH FEUD

(Southgate, 1987) **D/S/A:** Carl Monsoon
P: Mardi Rustam

This story of white slavery and revenge stars Frank
Stallone as a merchant seaman in love with a drug-
addicted hooker (Karen Mayo-Chandler). With
Anthony Caruso as the main villain, Christopher
Mitchum, Lisa Loring (Wednesday on the TV se-
ries *The Addams Family*) as a helpful hooker,
Greta Blackburn as a topless dancer, Nicholas
Worth, Gail Thackray, and Charles Dierkop. Mon-
soon, who plays a gay motel clerk, made *Please
Don't Eat My Mother*. Rustam backed many other
exploitation wonders.

DEATH FROM A DISTANCE

(Sinister, 1936) **D:** Frank R. Strayer
S: John M. Kraft **P:** Maury M. Cohen

Invincible Pictures used props from Universal's
The Invisible Ray for this 68-minute murder mystery with a science-fiction theme, set at an astro-
nomical observatory. Ted Mallory stars as a police
detective, with Russell Hopton, Lola Lane, and
Wheeler Oakman. There's a weird scientist, a psycho killer, and a "ghost."

DEATH GAME

(United, 1974) **D/P:** Peter Traynor
S: Anthony Overman, Michael Ronald
Ross **P:** Larry Spiegel   (*The Seducers*)

A San Francisco architect (Seymour Cassel)
whose family is away on his birthday lets two girls
into his home during a thunderstorm. Colleen
Camp and Sondra Locke, who claim to be underage, seduce him in the bathtub (a scene worth the
rental), then tie him up. They eat like pigs, put on
grotesque makeup, scream, have food fights,
smash furniture, and kill a delivery boy. Much of

the action is captured with a hand-held camera.
The cast is excellent, and both female stars have
nude scenes, a rarity for the underrated Camp (recently in *Sliver*). It's better than any recent "erotic
thriller," and the end is priceless! The only part I
didn't like was the overused, irritating "My Dad"
song. This claims to be based on a true story!
Sissy Spacek (who was also involved with *Phantom of the Paradise* and *Eraserhead*) was one of
the art directors.

DEATH HOUSE

(AIP, 1988) **D/A:** John Saxon **S:** William Selby,
David S. Freeman, Kate Whitcomb **P:** Nick Marino

So, after being in movies since 1955, Saxon got to
direct a prison/horror movie! He stars as an evil
government man using behavior-modification
drugs in a botched attempt to create an army of
superstrong fighters. It's pretty dumb, but it has
its moments. Inmates become killer zombies, and
there's some gore, a topless dream sequence, and
a Dead Kennedys song, and it all ends at Bronson
Canyon! Dennis Cole is the blond hero, a Nam-
vet chauffeur who is set up and sent to prison,
where he teams up with Tane McClure, a blond
nurse. Anthony Franciosa is a gangster whose gay
brother (Michael Pataki) is also in prison. Ron
O'Neal shows up for one scene. Fred Olen Ray
(who helped direct) and David DeCoteau are
thanked in the credits.

DEATH JOURNEY

(Unicorn, 1976) **D/P/A:** Fred Williamson **S:** Abel Jones

In a follow-up to his *No Way Back*, Fred
Williamson is rich LA playboy and detective Jesse
Crowder. He's hired to transport a criminal witness (Bernard Kuby) to New York City. They
manage to pass through Kansas City, Saint Louis,
and Chicago while gangsters try to kill them. With
D'Urville Martin and Sam Coppola.

DEATH MACHINE

(Vidmark, 1994) **D/S:** Steve Norrigton
P: Dominic Anciano   UK

Brad Dourif is Jack Dante, a crazy scientist working for a big corporation in the future who creates
a killer robot. With former model Ely Pouget and
William Hootkins. The first-time director, known
for doing makeup in the *Aliens* sequels, was 29.
The producer had backed *Reflecting Skin*.

DEATH MAGIC

(Domino Theatre, 1992) **D/S/P:** Paul Clinco

Time jumps from 1875 to the present and back in
this ambitious first-effort horror movie. Five
young people who are followers of a Satanist
manage to conjure up a laughing 19th-century
killer corporal with a saber. Hanged for leading a
massacre, he always appears in a red light. Parts
are laughable, but you get guts and lots of nudity
during various ceremonies. A naked couple are
skewered and blood spurts during a decapitation.
The lady police captain is a nice touch. It was
made in Tucson.

DEATHMASK

(Prism, 1983) **D/S:** Richard Friedman **S:** Jeffrey Goldenberg **P:** Louis K. Sher   (*Unknown*)

Farley Granger is a grim New York City medical investigator trying to identify a dead four-year-old boy. This depressing movie features Ruth Warrick as a psychic, Danny Aiello as a cop, and some porno people: Veronica Hart, Kelly Nichols, and R. Bolla. Friedman (then an NYU student) went on to make *Scared Stiff*, *Doom Asylum*, and other 80s horror obscurities.

DEATH MATCH

(Monarch, 1994) **D:** Joe Coppoletta **S:** Curtis Gleaves, Robert Wyatt **P:** Mike Meyer

A former kickboxing champ (Ian Jacklin) and a reporter (Renee Ammann) look for a missing man and encounter illegal matches run by an arms dealer. With Martin Kove, Richard Lynch, and many martial-arts champs like Matthias Hues, Benny Urquidez, Danny Lopez, Jorge Rivera, and Nick Hill.

DEATH MERCHANT

(AIP, 1990) **D:** Jim Winburn **S:** Karl Holman

Ivan J. Rado and Andrew Singleton star in this cheap, plot-heavy film about a stolen missile-guidance microchip. With Lawrence Tierney as an arms dealer and Martina Castle.

DEATHMOON

(Media, 1978) **D:** Bruce Kessler **S:** George Schenck **P:** Jay Benson

An executive (Robert Foxworth) has a recurring nightmare about a wolf man. He goes to Hawaii to forget and becomes involved with France Nuyen, but a native curse interferes. This CBS-TV movie features Joe Penny, Debralee Scott, and Charles Haid. It's by the director of *Simon, King of the Witches*.

DEATH NURSE

(Video City, 1987) **D/S:** "Nick Phillips"/ Steve Millard **P:** Frances Millard

This shot-on-video marvel was made at the same time and in the same house as *Crazy Fat Ethel II*. It has the same star (Priscilla Alden) and uses footage from that film. It also reuses footage from *Criminally Insane*, showing the same axe-murder scene (now a "dream") twice! As a matter of fact, the credits on all three films are identical. Alden, as nurse Edith Mortley, runs a charity hospital with her brother. She kills people, then feds them to rats in the basement. The patients are all old and/or ugly. Does your video store stock these titles!?

DEATH OF A CENTERFOLD: THE DOROTHY STRATTEN STORY

(1981) **D:** Gabrielle Beaumont **S:** Donald L. Stewart **P:** Paul Pompian

Jamie Lee Curtis stars in this NBC-TV movie, televised more than a year before *Star 80* was released. After a half-dozen horror movies, it was a career move for Curtis (who doesn't look anything like Stratten). With Bruce Weitz as her killer husband, Mitchell Ryan as Hugh Hefner, Robert Reed as the Bogdanovich character, Tracy Reed, Bibi Besch, and Luca Bercovici.

THE DEATH OF OCEAN VIEW PARK

(1979) **D:** E. W. Swackhamer **S:** John Furia Jr., Barry Oringer **P:** Michael Trikilis

An amusement park is demolished by a hurricane during the 4th of July weekend in this cut-rate disaster movie, a Playboy production for ABC-TV. The real 80-year-old Ocean View Park in Norfolk, Virginia, set for demolition, was actually destroyed. Mike Connors stars, with Diana Canova, Perry Lang, Mare Winningham, Martin Landau, and Mel Welles.

DEATH PROMISE

(Paragon, 1977) **D:** Robert Warmflash **S:** Norbert Albertson Jr. **P:** Serafim Karalexis

"Charles Bonet" stars as a Hispanic kung-fu master who battles evil New York City slumlords after his boxer father is killed. His buddies are a black guy and an Oriental guy. The fights are pretty hilarious, and everyone yells a lot. Boom mikes are visible, and when the characters go to China the scene is filmed in a backyard.

DEATH RAGE

(VidAmerica, 1976) **D:** Antonio Margheretti **S:** Guy Casals   Italy (*Blood Reckoning, Con la Rabbia Agli Occhi*)

Yul Brynner is an American hitman in Naples. Barbara Bouchet and Martin Balsam costar in this crime film.

DEATH RIDES A HORSE

(High Desert, 1967) **D:** Giulio Petroni **S:** Luciano Vincenzoni **P:** Alfonso Sansone Italy (*Da Uomo a Uomo*).

John Phillip Law, whose family was massacred by outlaws, spends his childhood planning revenge. He eventually teams up with an ex-con gunfighter (Lee Van Cleef) who is after the same outlaws (his former partners) because they framed him. The score is by Ennio Morricone. The violent 2 hour film was rated M when released by United Artists. It was popular (in Europe, anyway) and was remade as *Viva Django* (1971).

DEATH RIDES TO OSAKA

(United, 1983) **D:** Jonathan Kaplan **S:** Carole and Michael Raschella **P:** Claude Binyon Jr.   (*Girls of the White Orchid*)

Jennifer Jason-Leigh, a singer in a Tokyo nighclub, is sold into slavery by the yakuza. With Mako, Soon-Teck Oh, Ann Jillian, and Leslie Wing. It's one of the movies Kaplan made after the box-office failure of *Over the Edge*, and it debuted on NBC-TV. The video, cable, and overseas theatrical versions had added nudity.

DEATH RING

(New Line, 1992) **D:** Robert J. Kizer **S:** George T. LeBrun **P:** Gary M. Bettman

Mike Norris stars as a Nam-vet hero whose girlfriend (Isabel Glasser) is kidnapped and taken to an island. The millionaire villain (Billy Drago) holds private manhunts for rich men. The softspoken, long-haired Drago, who never looked more like Michael Jackson, is the reason to watch, as he kicks a man to death after stabbing hin with a fork. His assistant is Miss Ling (Elizabeth Fong Sung), and other relatives of famous actors (Chad McQueen and Don Swayze) are in the movie too. Parts were fimed at Bronson Canyon, and there are a few good gore FX. Kizer also made *Hell Comes to Frogtown* (1987).

DEATHROW GAMESHOW

(Media, 1987) **D/S:** Mark Piro **P:** Brian J. Smith

On the *Live or Die* show, condemned prisoners have a chance to compete and live. This *Running Man*–inspired low comedy from Crown includes a *Blue Velvet* parody, sex, religion, and fart humor. With John McCafferty as the host, "Beano," and Debra Lamb eating fire.

DEATH SCENES

(1989) **D/S/P:** Nick Bougas

Dr. Anton Lavey shows LA-area-true-crime photos from the 30s and 40s and tells the stories behind various grisly murders. The deaths of actors and criminals are also covered. Ray Atherton was the executive producer.

DEATH SCENES II

(Wavelength, 1992) **D/S/P:** Nick Bougas

This disgusting tape features actual footage of people dying, including wars, mass murders and the helicopter crash that occurred during the production of *Twilight Zone: The Movie*. There are also stills from the scene of the Manson murders and *Signal 30* car-crash footage. Unlike many *Mondo* movies, this is all too real.

DEATH'S ECSTASY = THE BEAST

THE DEATH'S HEAD VIRGIN

(1972) **D:** Norman Foster **S:** Ward Gaynor **P/A:** Larry Ward, Jock Gaynor   Philippines

A treasure-hunting diver (Ward Gaynor) removes an amulet from a skeleton and unleashes a skull-faced sea siren who uses him for revenge. He looks for women to scalp on an island. The story is told to the man's wife (Diane McBain) by a cop (Vic Diaz).

DEATH SPA

(MPI, 1987) **D:** Michael Fischa **S:** James Bartruff, Mitch Paradise **P:** James Beardley-Jones

Another stupid, bloody gore movie, this time set at a computerized health spa. The late Merritt Butrick stars (sometimes in drag), with Rosalind Cash (*The Omega Man*) as a police sergeant, a wasted Ken Foree, Brenda Bakke, Shari Shattuck, Alexa Hamilton, and Chelsea Field. Characters are killed by excessive steam, flying shower tiles, exercise machines, and a locker. It's filled with false scares, and a big party is thrown after count-less characters have been killed. Beatles com-pletists: a scene from *A Hard Day's Night* is on a TV screen. Available in R and unrated versions.

DEATHSTALK

(World, 1974) **D:** Robert Day **S:** Stephen Kandel, John W. Bloch **P:** Richard Caffey

Convicts escape, kidnap two married women, and take off on rubber rafts. Vic Morrow, Vince Ed-wards, Carol Lynley, Anjanette Comer, Neville Brand, and Norman Fell are in this NBC-TV movie.

DEATHSTALKER

(Vestron, 1983) **D:** John Watson
S: Howard R. Cohen **P:** James Sbardellati

Self-centered blond hunk Richard Hill is Death-stalker, and Barbi Benton is a kidnapped princess. There's lots of nudity, raping, blood, mud-wrest-ling, decapitations, dwarfs, and an ugly, boar-headed beast man. The villain magically turns into Barbi at one point, and Lana Clarkson has a top-less swordfighting scene. Benton, former *Playboy* model and country singer, was last seen doing half-hour how-to-play-the-piano "infotainment" com-mercials. This entertaining New World release was filmed in Argentina. Sequels followed.

Barbi Benton and the boar man in *Deathstalker*.

DEATHSTALKER II: DUEL OF THE TITANS

(Vestron, 1987) **D:** Jim Wynorski
S: Neil Ruttenberg **P:** Frank Asaac Jr.

This sword-and-sorcery parody is full of in-jokes and references (to Hammer films, James Bond, Conan, and executive producer Roger Corman). It's also padded with footage and outtakes from the first film, scenes from Corman's *The Terror*, and even bloopers at the end. John Terlesky is Deathstalker this time. *Penthouse* Pet Monique Gabrielle is the princess (and her vampire clone) and John La Zar (from *Beyond the Valley of the Dolls*) is an evil sorcerer. The evil twin drinks the blood of peasant boys. With Maria Socas, Toni Naples as Sultana, wrestler Queen Kong/Deanna Booher, a mandolin-playing dwarf, and topless scenes (of course!). It was filmed in Argentina and released by Concorde.

DEATHSTALKER III: THE WARRIORS FROM HELL

(Vestron, 1988) **D/P:** Alfonso Corona
S: Howard R. Cohen **P:** Antonio de Noriega

After the outrageous first movie and the ridicu-lous-on-purpose second one, this is pretty dull. John Allan Nelson is Deathstalker, and Thom Christopher is the evil wizard with a zombie army. With Carla Herd as the princess (and her twin sis-ter) and Terri Treas. The Mexican director of the Concorde release also made *World of the Vam-pires* (1960).

DEATHSTALKER IV: MATCH OF TITANS

(Vestron, 1990) **D/S:** Howard R. Cohen
P: Steven Rabiner

Richard Hill (who had been away making bad movies in the Philippines) returns from the first movie, and many warriors arrive for a tourna-ment. With Maria Ford, Brett Baxter, Michelle Moffet, and Brett Clark.

DEATH: THE ULTIMATE MYSTERY

(1975) **D/S/P:** Robert Emenegger,
Allan Sadler

A bearded man driving a car hosts this documen-tary look at death, with shocking footage and many experts (doctors, gurus, museum curators) interviewed. Cameron Mitchell's voice was used for the narration, and the filmmakers try to make you think it's him onscreen too. It was part of the *Gamma Chronicles* se-ries and was later copied by the more famous *Faces of Death*.

DEATH WARMED UP

(Vestron, 1984) **D/S:** David Blyth
S: Michael Heath **P:** Murray Newey
New Zealand (*Death Warmed Over*)

The hero (Michael Hurst) killed his parents on the orders of a mad hyp-notist/brain surgeon (Gary Day). He's released from the asylum and goes to the island hospital where the doc is creating a race of mutant warriors. With motorcycles, zom-bies. nudity, gore FX, and Bruno Lawrence as a hunchback.

DEATH WARRANT

(Warner, 1990) **D:** Deran Sarafian
S: David S. Goyer **P:** Mark DiSalle

Jean-Claude Van Damme stars as a Canadian un-dercover mountie/kickboxer in prison. A psycho called Sandman (Patrick Kilpatrick) is killing con-victs, and an organ-selling scam is uncovered. With Robert Guillaume (TV's *Benson*), Cynthia Gibb, Art LaFleur, and Joshua Miller.

DEATH WATCH

(1966) **D/S/P:** Vic Morrow **P/A:** Leonard Nimoy

Years before *Poison* (1991), Vic Morrow and Leonard Nimoy made this arty (of course), low-

budget Jean Genet adaptation while one was star-ring in the *Combat* TV series and the other was about to become Mr. Spock. Nimoy, Michael For-est, and Paul Mazursky play prisoners who spend the whole movie talking in a French prison cell. The ads promised "homosexual outlaws on a ram-page." With Gavin McLeod (from *The Love Boat*).

DEATHWATCH

(Embassy, 1979) **D/S/P:** Bertrand Tavernier **S:** David Rayfiel   France/W. Germany (*La Morte en Direct*)

In the near future, a reporter (Harvey Keitel) with a camera implanted in his brain is sent by an ex-ploitative TV station to film a terminally ill woman (Romy Schneider). This sad (and long) film was shot around Glasgow (in English) and was based on a novel by David Guy Compton. It also features Harry Dean Stanton, Max von Sydow, Bernhard Wicki, and Robbie Coltrane. Schneider did die soon after (in 1982).

DEATH WISH

(Paramount, 1974) **D:** Michael Winner
S: Wendell Mayes **P:** Hal Landers, Bobby Roberts

After years of being the biggest box-office draw in the world (except for America), it took this con-troversial revenge movie to finally make Charles Bronson a star in his own country. He's Paul Kersey, a liberal Manhattan architect who turns vigilante after his daughter is raped and his wife is killed. A typically intense Jeff Goldblum (in his film debut) is the main killer/rapist. With Hope Lange as Bronson's wife, Vincent Gardenia, Chris-topher Guest, Olympia Dukakis, and Kathleen Quinlan. The Herbie Hancock soundtrack is on Columbia. Dino De Laurentiis was the executive producer. Winner had already directed Bronson in *Chato's Land*, *The Mechanic*, and *The Stone Killer*.

DEATH WISH II

(Warner, 1982) **D:** Michael Winner
S: David Englebach **P:** Golan/Globus

This more violent sequel, made eight years later, is set in LA. Bronson's daughter (in a coma from the first movie) is raped (again), then impaled on an iron fence. With Jill Ireland, Anthony Franciosa, Silvana Galardo, Roberta Collins, and the return of Vincent Gardenia. The hit film was released by Filmways (formerly AIP), which became Orion in 1982.

DEATH WISH III

(MGM, 1985) **D:** Michael Winner
S: Michael Edmonds **P:** Golan/Globus

Kersey (Charles Bronson) is back in New York City. This ridiculous sequel has gay bikers and a multiracial street-punk gang (led by Gavan O'Her-lihy) who terrorize an apartment complex. Bron-son himself is busted, but he gets out and helps old people, using machine guns and rocket launchers. With Martin Balsam, Deborah Raffin as Bronson's new girlfriend, Ed Lauter, Marina Sirtis, and Alex Winter. It was cut for an R rating. The music by Jimmy Page (!) was issued as a soundtrack album, and a "making of" tape was produced.

DEATH WISH IV: THE CRACKDOWN

(Media, 1987) **D:** J. Lee Thompson **S:** Gail
Morgan Hickman **P:** Pancho Kohner

Bronson is the architect crusader again, in the
least violent sequel. He pits rival crack-dealing LA
gangs against each other. With Kay Lenz, John P.
Ryan as the millionaire who backs him and turns
out to be the drug kingpin, Perry Lopez, and
Soon-Teck Oh. It features a roller-rink gun battle
and lots of drugs. This Cannon release was the
seventh Bronson movie directed by Thompson.

DEATH WISH V: THE FACE OF DEATH

(Warner, 1993) **D/S:** Allan A. Goldstein **P:** Damien Lee

Bronson, now 72 years old (!), is in love with fashion designer Lesley-Anne Down, who is (surprise!) killed. There's death by acid, shrink wrap
and poisoned cannoli. Michael Parks is a killer
garment-district mobster (and the ex-husband of
Down), Robert Joy is his transvestite right-hand
man, and Saul Rubinek is the DA. The 21st Century production is set in Manhattan but was shot
in Toronto.

DEATH WISH CLUB

(Regal, "1983") **D:** John Carr **S:** Philip Yordan
P: Edmund J. Bodine   (*Carnival of Fools*)

Greta (Meredith Haze), a woman who sells popcorn at a carnival, leaves with a decadent millionaire. A student (Rick Narnes) at a frat party falls
in love with her while watching her in a stag film
(she wanted to be an actress). He finds her, and
they both end up in her mentor's "death club"
where variations of Russian Roulette are played.
People die in imaginative ways—crushed by a
contruction ball, burned to a crisp by a computer,
and strangest of all, stung to death by a giant
(badly animated) winged beetle. Screenwriter
Yordan also shows up as a man in a porno theater.
The *Carnival of Fools* tape uses *Carnival of Souls*
ad art! This very odd feature includes nudity and
is also part of the trilogy *Night Train to Terror*.

THE DECAMERON

(Water Bearer, 1970) **D/S/A:** Pier Paolo Pasolini
Italy/France/W. Germany (*Il Decamerone*)

Eight of Boccaccio's bawdy tales are told in this
film, the first part of a trilogy. Several are fantasy-
oriented, concerning ghosts, a miracle, heaven and
hell, and a woman turned into a donkey. It was
rated X in the US but was an art-house hit anyway.
With Silvana Mangano as the Madonna, Monique
Van Vooren, and an Ennio Morricone score. It was
a commercial hit in Europe, and "sequels" were
made in Italy. *Decameron III* (1973), for instance,
was directed by Antonio Margheretti. United
Artists also released Pasolini's *The Canterbury
Tales* (1971) and *Arabian Nights* (1974).

DECEIT

(Columbia, 1989) **D:** Albert Pyun
S: Kitty Chalmers **P:** Tom Karnowski

This is the most irritating, pretentious, and cheap
movie from a major distributor in years. It might
appeal to those who like off-Broadway plays,

though. A man (Norbert Weisser) who claims he's
"an alien sex fiend" spends most of the movie in a
room talking to an unimpressed captive woman
(Samantha Phillips) in her underwear. He plans to
blow up the world, but fails to get her to take the
rest of her clothes off. Another "alien" shows up,
and they all talk and yell.

THE DECEIVERS

(Warner, 1988) **D:** Nicholas Meyer **S:** Michael Hirst
P: Ismail Merchant, Tim Van Rellim   UK/India

Pierce Brosnan as a British officer goes undercover
in 1825 India to catch thugee-cult killers. It was
based on a novel by John Masters but is similar to
the notorious Hammer film *The Stranglers of Bombay* (1959). The killers worship Kali and fill mass
graves with wealthy travelers. With Saeed Jaffrey,
Shashi Kapoor, and Helena Mitchell. The John
Scott soundtrack is on RCA. It's PG-13.

THE DECLINE OF WESTERN CIVILIZATION

(Media, 1981) **D:** Penelope Spheeris
P: Gordon Brown, Jeff Pettyman

This documentary (with one of the best titles
ever) takes an unflinching look at the LA punk
scene. It includes band performances and interviews with Lee Ving, the late Darby Crash (of the
Germs), Billy Zoom, and others. Black Flag, Circle Jerks, Bags, Fear, and X perform. It all looks
even more ridiculous with age. Spheeris had acted
in *Naked Angels* and went on to direct *Wayne's
World* (1992).

THE DECLINE OF WESTERN CIVILIZATION PART II: THE METAL YEARS

(Columbia, 1988) **D:** Penelope Spheeris
S/P: Jonathan Dayton, Valerie Faris

This documentary makes a perfect double bill
with *This Is Spinal Tap*. Many music celebs and
would-be celebs are interviewed, some play onstage, and the editing is great. Alice Cooper, Kiss,
Ozzy Osbourne, Poison, Megadeth, and Lemmy
(from the mighty Motorhead) are featured. Steve
Tyler of Aerosmith says, "Millions went up my
nose." Common themes are money, groupies,
booze, drugs, rehab, and musicians as prostitutes.
With Teri Weigel. New Line released the Miles
Copeland III production, and the soundtrack is on
Capitol. Spheeris followed with *Thunder and
Mud* (1989) about professional wrestling.

DEEP COVER

(New Line, 1992) **D:** Bill Duke **S:** Michael
Tolkin **S/P:** Henry Bean **P:** Pierre David

Lawrence Fishburne stars as an honest LA undercover cop who poses as a pusher and gets way too
involved with sex, drugs, easy money, and killing.
Jeff Goldblum is an attorney who is also a coke-
snorting, drug-dealing psycho, Gregory Sierra is a
sadistic dealer, and Sydney Lassick is his flunky.
The government drug agents are useless or worse.
With Victoria Dillard, Charles Martin Smith as
the DEA director, Clarence Williams III as a born-
again cop, Kamala Lopez, and Glynn Turman.
Duke made this action-packed film after *A Rage
in Harlem*.

DEEP END

(VSOM, 1970) **D/S:** Jerzy Skolimowski **S:** J. Gruza,
B. Sulik **P:** Helmut Jedele   UK/W. Germany

John Moulder-Brown stars as Mike, an unexperi-
enced London teen working in a public bath.
Things go from light and funny to perverse as he
becomes obsessed with, fantasizes about, and accidentally kills Jane Asher, an "older" red-haired
coworker. The music is by Can and Cat Stevens.
Also with Diana Dors. Paramount released this
strange feature on a double bill with the unbearable preteen movie *Friends*. The director later
made *The Shout*.

DEEP RED

(MCA, 1994) **D:** Craig R. Baxley
S: D. Brent Note **P:** Timothy Marx

Michael Biehn as a PI with a clichéd 40s-look
office narrates a movie with killer milkmen. His
ex-wife, also a detective (Joanna Pacula), is protecting a little girl whose blood heals and reverses
the aging process (thanks to a close encounter).
John De Lancie is a shape-shifting (morphing) evil
scientist. With Michael Des Barres and a rare pro-
smoking plot device. Baxley's *I Come in Peace* was
much better than this film with its unoriginal
name, which debuted on the Sci-Fi Channel.

DEEP SPACE

(TWE, 1987) **D/S/P:** Fred Olen Ray
S: T. L. Lankford **P:** Alan Amiel

In another *Alien*-inspired movie from Ray (*Bio-
hazard*), monsters escape from a space lab on
earth. Cops Charles Napier and Ron Glass (from
Barney Miller) go after a man-eating space bug in
California. Napier eventually battles a monster
with a chainsaw. With Ann Turkel, James Booth,
Bo Svenson, Anthony Eisley, Julie Newmar, and
Peter Palmer (both from *L'il Abner*), Fox Harris,
Elizabeth Brooks, and Dawn Wildsmith. It was
Ray's most expensive feature as director (at $1.5
million), and he appears in it too.

DEEPSTAR SIX

(IVE, 1988) **D/P:** Sean Cunningham **S:** Lewis
Abernathy, Geof Miller **P:** Patrick Markey

This was made to beat the big-budget *Abyss* to the
nation's screens. Neither one is too great. Greg
Evigan stars, with Miguel Ferrer (who is pretty
good when he loses it), Nancy Everhard, Taurean
Blacque, Nia Peeples, and Cindy Pickett. There's a
barely seen Chris Walas and a mutant crab monster designed by Mark Shostrom and Walas. The
score is by Harry Manfredini.

DEF BY TEMPTATION

(Southgate, 1990) **D/S/P/A:** J. James Bond III

Bond stars as a very naive divinity student from
the South visiting his brother (Kadeem Hardison)
in New York. He falls for Cynthia Bond as the
"temptress" who kills men during sex. This was
the first all-black horror movie in many years.
Bond had acted in Spike Lee movies and used
Lee's cinematographer, Ernest Dickerson, for this
film. With Bill Nunn (*Do the Right Thing*), Melba

Kadeem Hardison and Bill Nunn in *Def by Temptation*.

Moore, Samuel L. Jackson, a man-eating TV set, and stockings that put themselves on. It was released by Troma. The soundtrack, featuring various artists, is on Orpheus.

DEF-CON 4

(Starmaker, 1983) **D/S/P:** Paul Donovan
P: Maura O'Connell, Michael Donovan   Canada

Three astronauts return to post-nuke Earth. The only survivor (Tim Choate) fights off cannibal mutants, survivalists, and *Mad Max* punks from a slave-labor camp. With Kate Lynch, John Walsch, Lenore Zann, Maury Chaykin. Tony Randall was the film "doctor" for this New World release, filmed in Nova Scotia.

DEFENDING YOUR LIFE

(Warner, 1991) **D/S/A:** Albert Brooks **P:** Michael Grillo

After an ad exec (Brooks) dies in a car crash he arrives in Judgment City. Rip Torn counsels him on how to defend himself, and then selected, mostly embarrassing parts of his life are evaluated. He falls for Meryl Streep, who seems to have been perfect. With Lee Grant, Buck Henry, and Shirley MacLaine in an appropriate bit part. This PG comedy was Brooks' fourth film as director and star, after *Real Life*, *Modern Romance* and *Lost in America*.

DEFENSE PLAY

(TWE, 1988) **D/A:** Monte Markham **S:** Aubrey Soloman, Steven Greenberg **P:** Wolf Schmidt

A couple of teens just out of high school (David Oliver and Susan Ursitti) battle Commie agents. A killer infiltrator is trying to stop the Star Wars program. The federal budget and common sense were probably what stopped Star Wars in real life.

DEFIANCE

(Vestron, 1980) **D:** John Flynn **S:** Thomas Michael Donnelly **P:** William S. Gilmore

Blue-collar worker Jan-Michael Vincent takes on New York City street gangs. Theresa Saldana costars, with Art Carney, Fernando Lopez, Rudy Ramos, Danny Aiello, Lenny Montana, Sonny Landham, and Fred Lincoln. The PG-rated film "caused" an obsessive fan to stab Saldana in real life, and she went on to play herself in a TV movie based on the incident, *Victims for Victims: The Theresa Saldana Story* (1984). This was one of the last AIP releases before it briefly became Filmways.

THE DEFIANT ONES

(MGM, 1958) **D/P:** Stanley Kramer
S: Nathan E. Douglas, Harold Jacob Smith

This maverick b/w prison-break movie about race relations has been imitated many times in exploitation movies. Tony Curtis and Sidney Poitier were both nominated for Oscars as the handcuffed prisoners on the lam. Cara Williams is a white-trash widow, Theodore Bikel is the sheriff who has to hear rock and roll during the chase, and Lon Chaney Jr. (in a good role) is a former chain-gang prisoner who helps them. Also with Charles McGraw, Whit Bissel, Claude Akins, Kevin Coughlin, and Carl "Alfalfa" Switzer (shortly before he was killed). Kramer's next was *On the Beach*. "Nathan E. Douglas" was the pseudonym of blacklisted screenwriter Nedrick Young.

THE DEFIANT ONES

(1986) **D:** David Lowell Rich **S:** James Lee Barrett **P:** Robert Lovenheim

This updated but unnecessary TV remake is based on the original script. Robert Urich and Carl Weathers star and were coproducers. With Laurie O'Brien, Barry Corbin, Ed Lauter, and Thalmus Rasulala.

THE DEFILERS

(SW, 1965) **D/C:** Lee Frost **S/P:** David F. Friedman

This b/w variation of *The Collector* was considered the first of the "roughies," adults-only movies that added violence to the nudity and/or soft core sex. Byron Mabe (who later directed *She Freak* and others for Friedman) and Jerome Eden (from Friedman's nudist colony movies) are two guys bored by beach parties, beer, pot, and sex. They kidnap a woman (Mai Jansson) and keep her in the basement. The way-too-young actor playing Mabe's father wears a fake mustache. From Sonney Amusements.

THE DEGENERATES

(1967) **D/S/P:** Andy Milligan

Before making a series of low-budget horror movies, Milligan made this b/w post-nuke obscurity. In the year 2000 three surviving guys (one is called Go-Go) intrude on five sisters (one is insane) in a farmhouse. Some of the women fight back, and characters are killed by fire and a pitchfork through the chest. Other Milligan titles from the same period are *The Depraved!*, *Kiss Me Kiss Me*, and *Tricks of the Trade*.

DÉJA VU

(MGM, 1984) **D:** Anthony Richmond
S: Ezra D. Rappaport **P:** Golan/Globus   UK

Jaclyn Smith and Nigel Terry are reincarnations of a couple who died in a fire 50 years earlier. This Cannon release, directed by Smith's husband, is also a murder mystery. Smith plays two roles. With Shelley Winters and Claire Bloom.

THE DELICATE DELINQUENT

(Paramount, 1957) **D/S:** Don McGuire
P/A: Jerry Lewis

Jerry Lewis stars in his first movie without Dean Martin. It's a spoof (based on the Damon and Pythias story) of all the 50s juvenile-delinquent films. Jerry is a janitor arrested along with a group of slum teens. Darren McGavin (in a role planned for Dean Martin) is a friendly rookie cop. With Martha Hyer and Horace McMahon. It was a box-office hit for Paramount, which released *Mr. Rock and Roll* and Elvis in *Loving You* the same year.

DELICATESSEN

(Paramount, 1991) **D/S:** Marc Caro, Jean-Pierre Jeunet **S:** Giles Adrien   France

This stylish post-nuke cannibal black comedy ("presented" by Terry Gilliam) was a cult hit in France and played midnights in New York. Dominique Pinon (from *Diva*) is a once-famous clown who becomes a handyman at a deli in an apartment building where transients end up in the soup. Vegetarian terrorists live in the sewers below. With Marie-Laure Dougnac, Jean-Claude Dreyfus as her butcher father, Sylvie Laguna as a woman who can't seem to commit suicide, Howard Vernon (who eats snails), and Chick Ortega. The filmmakers had prieviously made short features and cartoons.

DELINQUENT DAUGHTERS

(Sinister, 1944) **D/P:** Albert Herman
S: Arthur St. Claire **P:** Donald C. McKean

In this PRC release, the crooked owner of a cafe forces some teenagers who were involved in a hit-and-run accident to commit crimes for him. With June Carlson and Fifi D'Orsay (from *Nabonga*).

DELINQUENT SCHOOLGIRLS

(Vestron, 1974) **D/S:** Gregory Coratio
S/P: Maurice Smith **S:** John Lamb
(*Bad Girls*; *Carnal Madness*)

In this sex/action comedy, three escaped lunatics invade a school where John Alderman is the principal. Michael Pataki goes over the top, using different bizarre voices throughout the film. His companions are Stephen Stucker (from the *Airplane* movies) as a former dress designer and a black guy (Bob Minor, from *Coffy*) who always talks about being horny. With Sharon Kelly as a student who knows karate and Buck Flower.

DELIRIOUS

(MGM, 1992) **D:** Tom Mankiewicz **S/P:** Lawrence D. Cohen, Fred Freeman **P:** Doug Claybourne

John Candy is the head writer for a soap opera who is magically transported to the fictional small town he created. While trapped as a Wall Street villain character he uses his typewriter to alter events and try to win the girl (Mariel Hemingway). With Emma Samms (in a dual role), Raymond Burr, Charles Rocket, David Rasche, Jerry Orbach, Renee Taylor, Marvin Kaplan, and Robert Wagner (as himself). It's rated PG.

DELIRIUM

(Academy, 1979) **D/S:** Peter Maris
S: Richard Yalem **P:** Sunny Vest

An impotent Nam-vet killer (Nick Panouzis) is hired for vigilante work by local-government right-wingers to clean up criminals and street scum. He flips out and starts killing everybody. This 16mm film includes Nam flashbacks.

DELIVERANCE

(Warner, 1972) **P/ D:** John Boorman
S/A: James Dickey

Although it was a hit, it took a while for this story of modern man out of his element to become the effective but much-copied cliché it is now. When today's exploitation filmmakers need action ideas they often look to this or *Straw Dogs* (1971). Jon Voight stars, with Burt Reynolds and Ned Beatty (who has to squeal like a pig in his film debut), as Atlanta businessmen on a canoe trip. Ronnie Cox plays the guitar on the hit "Dueling Banjos." With Billy McKinney, Ed O'Neill, and Charley Boorman. It was based on Dickey's 1970 novel and was filmed on location in Georgia by Vilmos Zsigmond. The soundtrack is on Warner. Boorman did *Zardoz* next.

DELIVERY BOYS

(1984) **D/S:** Ken Handler **P:** Craig Horall, Per Sjosted

Pizza delivery boys enter a breakdancing contest in this sex comedy. Joss Marcano, Jim Soriero, and Tom Sierchio star. Mario Van Peebles has a small role. With porno stars Samantha Fox, Veronica Hart, Taija Rae, and Kelly Nichols.

THE DELPHI BUREAU

(1972) **D:** Paul Wendkos **S/P:** Sam H. Rolfe

Laurence Luckinbill stars as a government agent with a photographic memory, in this TV pilot for a short-lived series. He has to find a fleet of Air Force planes that vanished. With Celeste Holm, Dean Jagger, Cameron Mitchell, Bradford Dillman, Bob Crane, Joanna Pettet, Dub Taylor, and Pamelyn Ferdin.

THE DELTA FACTOR

(1970) **D/S/P:** Tay Garnett

Mickey Spillane himself backed this adaptation of his then-recent novel. Christopher George stars as an international thief forced by the CIA to marry an agent (Yvette Mimieux), pose as a drug dealer, and rescue a scientist from a Caribbean fortress. With Diane McBain, Yvonne De Carlo, Sheri Spillane (from all those Mike Hammer book covers), Ralph Taeger, Ted De Corsia, and an animated sequence from Hanna Barbera. The original rating was R. Spillane also starred in one movie, *The Girl Hunters* (1963). Garnett, who had begun as a screenwriter in silent movies, died in 1977.

THE DELTA FORCE

(Media, 1986) **D/S/P:** Menahem Golan
S: James Bruner **P:** Yoram Globus

This starts as an accurate re-creation of the actual TWA highjacking in Athens, then becomes a laughable all-star disaster movie (and what a group of stars!). Chuck Norris (with a customized James Bond–style motorcycle) and Lee Marvin (in his last role) star as the hero commandos. The evil Arabs are led by Robert Forster as Abdul. With *Airport* series vet George Kennedy as a Catholic priest, Shelley Winters, Martin Balsam, Joey Bishop, Lainie Kazan, Susan Strasberg, Bo Svenson, Robert Vaughn, Hanna Schygulla as the German stewardess, Steve James, and Kim Delaney. It was filmed in Israel. In 1987 *Chuck Norris Karate Commandos*, a cartoon series, debuted on Saturday-morning TV. The soundtrack is on Enigma.

Chuck Norris in the all-star *Delta Force*.

DELTA FORCE II: OPERATION STRANGLEHOLD

(Media, 1990) **D:** Aaron Norris **S:** Lee Reynolds
P: Yoram Globus, Christopher Pearce

Five people died in a helicopter crash while making this feature in the Philippines (and see *Braddock: Missing in Action III*). The scene they died for was left in the film. Chuck Norris and US Marines battle the Medellín drug cartel in Colombia. Billy Drago (who rapes a woman, then kills her husband and baby) is the main villain. With John P. Ryan, Richard Jaeckel, and those great skydiving sequences.

DELTA FORCE III: THE KILLING GAME

(Warner, 1991) **D:** Sam Firstenberg
S/P: Boaz Davidson **S:** Greg Latter
P: Christopher Pearce   (*Young Commandos*)

Evil Arabs plan to blow up America with some missing nukes, so lots of sons of famous actors (and one director) save us. With Mike Norris, Nick Cassavetes, Eric Douglas, Matthew Penn, and John P. Ryan (from *Delta Force II*) as Sergei. Harry Alan Towers was the executive producer of this Cannon release.

DELTA FORCE COMMANDO

(Vista, 1987) **D:** "Frank Valenti"/ Pierluigi Ciriaci
S: David Parker Jr. **P:** Alfred Nicolaj   Italy

Brett Clark is the hero out for vengeance. It's set in Nicaragua (where the heroes destroy the Sandinista government) but was shot in Nevada and Wisconsin. With Fred Williamson, Bo Svenson (also in the real *Delta Force*), and Mark Gregory. *Delta Force Commando II* (Live, 1991) followed, with Williamson, Richard Hatch, and Van Johnson.

DELTA FOX

(1975) **D/S/P:** Ferd and Beverly Sebastian

Priscilla Barnes is kidnapped by an antihero hitman (Richard Lynch) who discovers that he's the target of another hitman. Barnes goes topless, and Lynch shows his (real) badly scarred neck and chest. With Stuart Whitman, Richard Jaeckel, and John Ireland. The film wasn't released until 1983.

DELTA HEAT

(Academy, 1991) **D:** Michael Fischa
S: Sam Scribner **P:** Richard L. Albert

Lance Henriksen as an ex-cop who helps LA cop Anthony Edwards solves a series of drug-related killings in New Orleans, in this action comedy. With Betsy Russell, swamp scenes, and a Rockin Doopsie soundtrack.

DELUSION

(RCA, 1991) **D/S:** Carl Colpaert
S: Kurt Voss **P:** Daniel Hassid   (*Mirage*)

Jim Meltzer embezzles money, then picks up a Vegas showgirl (Jennifer Rubin) and her hitman boyfriend while driving through the desert. With Jerry Orbach, Tracey Walter, and a pet lizard. I.R.S. produced this Lynch-like feature by the director of *In the Aftermath*.

DEMENTED

(Media, 1980) **D:** Arthur Jeffries **S:** Alex Rebar **P:** Arthur Jeffries, Mike Smith

Sally Elyse leaves a mental hospital where she's been a patient since being raped. Her husband (Bruce Gilchrist, aka Harry Reems) cheats on her, she hallucinates, and some boys put on masks to scare her. She fights back, torturing and killing with a meat cleaver. In one scene a man's balls are sliced off with a wire. Written by the star of *The Incredible Melting Man*.

DEMENTED DEATH FARM MASSACRE: THE MOVIE

(Troma, 1986) **D:** Donn Davison
D/P: Fred Olen Ray

John Carradine as the judge of Hell watches damned people. Most of this sad project is footage from the unreleased *Shantytown Honeymoon* (1972), by Davison, a magician, spook-show promoter, and hustler. Ray bought the film for around $5000, added some new scenes with Carradine, and sold it to Troma.

DEMETRIUS AND THE GLADIATORS

(Fox, 1954) **D:** Delmer Daves
S: Philip Dunne **P:** Frank Ross

The sequel to *The Robe* (1953) is a lot like a big-budget Hercules movie. Victor Mature stars as a freed slave who hides the holy robe of Christ and is forced to become a gladiator. With blonde Debra Paget, Michael Rennie, William Marshall as a Nubian gladiator, Susan Hayward as Messalina, Richard Egan, Ernest Borgnine, and Jay Robinson as Caligula. Franz Waxman wrote the score. The video is letterboxed.

DEMOLITION MAN

(Warner, 1993) **D:** Marco Brambilla
S: Daniel Waters, Robert Reneau, Peter M.
Lenkov **P:** Joel Silver, Michael Levy

Sylvester Stallone is John Spartan, a cop in 1996 LA who's after a laughing, blond psycho killer (Wesley Snipes). Both are sent to a Cryoprison and frozen, only to unthaw in sterile, "perfect," clean 2032, and the chase continues. Sex, violence, alcohol, swearing, and caffeine are all outlawed, and people of the future listen to old TV jingles instead of songs. This movie has enough violent action, though, and works pretty well as a social comedy. Spartan has virtual-reality sex with a future cop (Sandra Bullock) who is fascinated by 20th-century culture. Eventually he helps the underground fighters (led by Denis Leary) against the corrupt rulers. Many were fired (some behind the camera and the original female lead) before this expensive ("$70 million") movie was finished. The director had made TV commercials in Europe. The title is from a Police tune.

THE DEMON

(VidAmerica, 1981) **D/S/P:** Percival Rubens   S. Africa

Cameron Mitchell stars with Jennifer Holmes in this horror mystery. A maniac with steel claws on his gloves kills some sexy nursery-school teachers. Mitchell plays a psychic investigator with ESP and gets to act out of control again, providing the only memorable scenes.

DEMON COP

(AIP, 1990) **D/S:** Rocco Karege
D: Hal Miles **D/P:** Fred Olen Ray

Another unreleased feature (*The Curse of Something Bestial*) with new footage by Ray. Cameron Mitchell stars.

DEMON HUNTER

(Camp, 1965) **D/S:** Massey Cramer
P: Bob Hadley **S:** Bob Corley   (*Blood Demon; The Legend of Blood Mountain*)

When's the last time you saw a horror comedy from Georgia about a troglodyte? George Ellis plays Bestoink Dooley, an overage, balding copyboy who resembles a burlesque comic, with a dumb haircut and spats on his shoes. He tries to get promoted by writing a scoop about a monster. In a scene that seems to last for hours, Bestoink eats cookies in bed, then has a long, silent dream with two elegant women catering to him. The monster is a man with a mask and big teeth, very white skin, patches of hair, two tails, and a big, awkward ass. He's supposed to be funny, I guess. I've seen a lot of stupid creatures in movies but almost fell off my chair when this one appeared. The women have beehive hairdos (courtesy of the Decatur University of Cosmetology), there's a bikini beach party at a lake (where a teen who was warned about the creature says, "Bad scene if this cat's for real!"), and the local accents are great. It all ends with a long comic chase scene. It's a must for fans of movies like *The Creeping Terror*, and it features Erin Fleming (Groucho Marx's controversial 70s companion) and Kenny Rogers' wife!

DEMONIAC

(Wizard, 1974) **D/S/A:** Jesús Franco
Spain/France/Belgium (*Exorcism; The Ripper of Notre Dame*)

A religious maniac cuts the "impurity" out of women in Paris and writes about his exploits for *Dagger and Garter* magazine. A European hardcore sex version is called *Exorcism et Messes Noir*. It was also released with new footage and a different plot as *Il Sadico di Notre Dame*. The US video is the most cut version.

DEMONIC TOYS

(Paramount, 1992) **D:** Peter Manoogian
S: David S. Goyer **P:** Anne Kelly

After a police shootout, characters are trapped in a warehouse by a shape-shifting little boy with an echo voice. He can possess others, cause hallucinations (like Kristine Rose as a big-chested blonde who strips), and make toys with big, ugly teeth kill. A bear bites off fingers, there's a robot, and there's one "good" toy, an animated soldier (actually another kid). An absurd flashback shows a woman giving the dead body of the demon baby to unsuspecting trick-or-treaters. There's some gore, lots of swearing, and dumb wisecracks. When a killer baby doll burns it says, "Oh, you're getting me hot, you prick!" Tracy Scoggins stars as an undercover cop, and Bently Mitchum is a young chicken deliveryman. *Dollman vs. Demonic Toys* was a sequel.

A DEMON IN MY VIEW

(Vidmark, 1992) **D/S:** Petra Hafter
P: Theo Hinz   Germany

Anthony Perkins is a mysterious lodger in London who watches the other tenants. He also dresses up a mannequin in the basement. Through flashbacks we learn that he was brought up as a girl by his aunt and probably strangled two women 20 years earlier. When his beloved mannequin is burned on Guy Fawkes Day he flips out again. With Sophie Ward and Uwe Bohm. The music is by Pino Donaggio. Perkins made only one more film, *In the Deep Woods*.

DEMON KEEPER

(New Horizons, 1993) **D/P/E:** Joe Tornatore
S: Mikel Angel **P:** Cheryl Latimer

Attention, fans of *Grotesque*. Tornatore is back with more inept but entertaining nonsense! Dirk Benedict is pretty funny trying to play an English supernatural expert with a goatee. He attends a séance given near New Haven by a con artist (Edward Albert). While ten people are "trapped" by a storm, a horned, winged demon (Mike Lane) that looks like it belongs onstage with Gwar is conjured up and possesses them. Dirk's advice to the survivors is to "avoid vice and passion." Some of his dialogue is completely missing! Narrated flashbacks try to sort things out, and the demon (who I suspect is also the screenwriter) has a scene with the naked and extremely large-breasted 1992 Pet of the Year, Katrina Maltby. The FX are by David Hewitt. It was filmed in Zimbabwe!

DEMON MASTER=CRAZE

DEMON MOUNTAIN: *See* SHADOW OF THE CHIKARA

THE DEMON MURDER CASE

(1982) **D:** William Hale **S:** William Kelly **P:** Len Steckler

A boy (Charlie Fields) is possessed. With Cloris Leachman as a psychic, Andy Griffith as a demonologist, Eddie Albert as a priest, Kevin Bacon, Joyce Van Patten, and the voice of Harvey Fierstein as the demon. Dick Clark was the executive producer of this NBC-TV movie, filmed in Newport.

DEMON OF PARADISE

(Warner, 1987) **D/P:** Cirio H. Santiago
S: Frederick Bailey

A fake-looking man in a sea-lizard suit kills people in Hawaii. The plot copies *Jaws* (or maybe *Piranha*), but it's a remake of Corman's *Up from the Depths* (Vestron, 1979). With Leslie Huntley and Kathryn Witt as a herpetologist. From Roger Corman's Concorde.

DEMON OF THE LAKE: *See* CREATURE FROM BLACK LAKE

DEMON POSSESSED

(AIP, 1989) **D/P:** Christopher Webster **S:** Julian Weaver

An old woman in the future narrates this horror movie about couples in an isolated, snowbound cabin, remembering "the nightmare back in the 1990s." A Ouija board conjures up a hooded Satanist (seen in shadows), and a guy in a coma becomes possessed. There are very discreet sex scenes and an icicle through an eyeball. It was made in Chicago.

DEMON QUEEN

(All American, Mogul, 1987) **D/S/P:** Donald Farmer
P: David Reed

This is similar to Fred Olen Ray's *The Tomb* but with more nudity, jokes, and blood, and it's much cheaper. It's a very bad first new release from Jeffrey C. Hogue, who started by marketing old bad films. With Mary Fanaro.

THE DEMONS

(Unicorn, 1972) **D/S:** "Clifford Brown"/ Jesús Franco **P:** Victor de Costa

This is sort of a sequel to Franco's *Night of the Blood Monster* (1969). A witch-killing noblemen is cursed by a sorceress burned at the stake. Her two daughters become nuns and tempt other nuns with lesbianism at a castle. Their death kiss turns men into skeletons. There's lots of torture, rape, suicide, masturbation, and nudity. Howard Vernon stars, with Anne Lipert, Britt Nicols, and John Foster as the witch-torturer. The soundtrack is heavy-metal music! It was released (cut) in the US by Hemisphere.

DEMONS

(Starmaker, 1985) **D/S:** Lamberto Bava **S/P:** Dario Argento **S:** Dardano Sacchetti, Franco Ferrini   Italy (*Demoni*)

In Munich people receive free tickets to watch what seems to be a teen version of *Black Sunday* at the large Metropol theater. Echoing events in the movie on the screen, characters in the theater become infected and mutate into pus-oozing, cannibalistic zombies. Nobody can get out of the theater. While the patrons panic or kill each other some stoned teens try to get in, and, incredibly, a heliocopter crashes through the roof of the building. A hooker and her black pimp are the best characters in this silly but wild gorefest. With Urbano Barberini, Nicoletta Elmi, Michelle Soavi, and a heavy-metal soundtrack (Billy Idol, Motley Crue). New World released it in the US.

Zombies in a movie theater from *Demons.*

DEMONS 2

(Imperial, 1986) **D/S:** Lamberto Bava **S/P:** Dario Argento **S:** Franco Ferrini, Dardano Sacchetti   Italy (*Demoni 2: L'Incubo Retorna*)

This time zombies emerge from a TV set in an apartment during a teen birthday party, and everyone is trapped in the building. It's a virtual remake of the original, also filmed in Munich, with a new setting. Some of the same actors even show up in different roles. Acid blood goes through floors, and there's a zombie dog and zombie bodybuilders. With David Knight and Asia Argento. Six minutes were cut for an R rating, and it was released directly to tape in the US. The title

Demons 3 was used for a Bava movie (*The Ogre*) in 1988 and an Umberto Lenzi movie (*Black Demons*) in 1991. *Demons 4* is *The Church* and *Demons 5* is *La Maschera del Demonio.*

THE DEMONS OF LUDLOW

(TWE, 1983) **D/P/C:** Bill Rebane **S:** William Arthur, Alan Ross

A haunted harmonium causes bloody deaths during the bicentennial of a New England town. The town's founder, whose hands had been cut off, appears and kills. It was filmed in Wisconsin at about the same time as *The Devonsville Terror*, which had a similar plot and some of the same production people. Cheri Cafaro was an associate producer.

DEMONSTONE

(Fries, 1989) **D:** Andrew Prowse **S:** John Trayne, David Phillips, Frederick Bailey **P:** Andrew Prowse   Philippines (*Heartstone*)

Flashbacks show how the descendants of some bandits were cursed hundreds of years ago by a Chinese priest. An American reporter (Nancy Everhard) goes to an archeological dig but doesn't realize she's become possessed. Her eyes glow, the image goes negative when she kills, and victims' hearts are "half-eaten." A former captain called Andy Buck (Jan-Michael Vincent, who narrates) is blamed. This one has political intrigue, lots of battles, chases, machine-gun fire, and even spearfighting and swordfighting. The location work is great. With Lee Ermey as a foul-mouthed Marine major ("I support half the whores in Manila!") and Peter Brown. Brian Trenchard-Smith was the executive producer.

DEMONWARP

(Vidmark, 1987) **D:** Emmett Alston **S:** Jim Bertges, Bruce Akiyama **P:** Richard L. Albert

A Bigfoot monster controlled by aliens attacks camping teens in Demon Woods. The creature decapitates people, the aliens rip out hearts, and zombies show up. There's plenty of gore and topless scenes from starlets like Pamela Gilbert and Michelle Bauer. George Kennedy is the dad of a victim, and Shannon Kennedy is in the cast. John Buechler created the monster. From the director of *New Year's Evil* and *Nine Deaths of the Ninja.*

DEMON WIND

(Prism, 1990) **D/S:** Charles Philip Moore **P:** Paul Hunt, Michael Bennett

If you loved the *Evil Dead* movies, you might sit through this movie filled with flashbacks, dreams, and altered reality problems. A bunch of teens go to an old, isolated, farmhouse. Corey (Eric Larson) has been dreaming about the house, where his demon-worshiping ancestors lived. Only one wall is left, but when they pass through the door it's a whole house. One guy is an obnoxious blond

asshole, another is a showoff karate-kicking magician. The females (including X star Tiffany Million) have no character, but they know how to appear topless. When one girl is suddenly turned into a doll nobody seems to care, and they continue to argue about unrelated personal problems. A tongue from a cow skull kills one girl, wet, lumpy-faced demons with echo voices show up, and various cast members become *Night of the Living Dead*–type zombies and attack the house. When one zombie is stabbed by a magic dagger it becomes younger, a baby, then a dove. In the comic-book ending all the zombies become one big demon monster, Corey turns into a creature that looks like an extra from *Alienation*, and they fight. It comes in a 3-D box.

THE DEMON WITHIN = THE MIND SNATCHERS

DERANGED

(Moore, 1973) **D/S:** Alan Ormsby **D:** Jeff Gillen **P:** Tom Karr, Bob Clark   Canada

This uncut version of a movie once released by AIP is worth checking out. It remains the most realistic feature based on the famous Wisconsin farmer who was a grave-robber and cannibal, Ed Gein, here called Ezra Cobb (the wonderful Roberts Blossom). *Deranged* is a very strong (and very funny) ghoulish horror classic. During a séance, Ezra hears that he "misses the carnal aspects of marriage." He says, "Carnival?" Restored scenes show Cobb opening the head of a Sunday-school teacher and spooning out the brains. This and other impressive FX scenes were created by Tom Savini. The country music is by Stompin' Tom Connors. Bob Clark (who did not codirect) had his name removed. The tape includes a very good Wisconsin TV 26-minute documentary, *Ed Gein: American Maniac* (1981). Gein, the inspiration for *Psycho, The Texas Chainsaw Massacre,* and other films, died in a minimum security prison hospital in 1984. Karr also offers a new *Making of Deranged* tape and the original shooting script.

DERANGED

(Republic, 1987) **D/P:** Chuck Vincent **S:** Craig Horrall

Vincent made many films (porno and sex comedies) but this disturbing *Repulsion* copy shot in New York City has one of those pretentious reality-vs.-fantasy plots that allow the director to get away with all kinds of nonsense. A pregnant woman (Jane Hamilton, aka Veronica Hart) is attacked by a burglar in her apartment and has a miscarriage. She hides the body, puts a pillow under her dress, and pretends nothing happened. Visitors, real and imagined, arrive, the body stinks, and her father (Jamie Gillis), who committed suicide, keeps showing up in the bathtub. It's pretty unwatchable. With a porno-star cast, including Jennifer Delora and Jerry Butler.

LE DERNIER COMBAT

(RCA/Columbia, 1982) **D/S/P:** Luc Besson **S/P/A:** Pierre Jolivet   France

The director of *Subway* and *La Femme Nikita* made this stark, nearly silent b/w post-nuke

A bad dream from Chuck Vincent's *Deranged*.

movie. There's only one word of dialogue. A nice guy (Jolivet) and a big brute are survivors. There's a rain shower of fish.

DE SADE
(Nightmare, 1969) **D:** Cy Endfield, Roger Corman, Gordon Hessler **S:** Richard Matheson, Peter Berg   US/W. Germany (*Das Ausschweifende Leben des Marquis de Sade*)

Few people have seen this interesting, ambitious "head" movie, branded with an X when first released in America (by AIP offshoot Trans Continental). It wasn't released in England at all. Sam Arkoff said it was "AIP's biggest flop until *Meteor*." Young Michael Reeves (*The Conqueror Worm*) was set to direct, but after he died Cy Endfield was hired. Endfield soon ended up in the hospital with flu, so executive producer Louis M. Heyward got Hessler and Corman to film most of *De Sade* without credit. Cleveland-born star Keir Dullea had just been in *2001*, and *De Sade* was obviously conceived as a lavish major international production, sort of a combination of *The Trip* and the Poe movies Matheson had scripted. You're never sure if what you see is part of a play, "real," or a (false?) memory. It all tries to show how your mind is a prison. John Huston, perfect as de Sade's uncle, hovers over everything as he manipulates characters. *De Sade* is a fascinating 60s artifact, with music by Billy "Batman" Strange and the Berlin Symphony, a Bond-like theme, and bongo music (the soundtrack was on Tower). De Sade's downfall is told out of sequence, in flashbacks. The frequent scenes of whipping probably bothered reviewers more than the tame sex scenes shot with distorted, tinted lenses. The interesting cast includes Senta Berger, Lilli Palmer, and Anna Massey (*Peeping Tom*). The German uncut, original version ran 113 minutes.

DE SADE '70
(Video Search, 1970) **D/S/C/A:** Jesús Franco **P:** Karl-Heinz Mannchen Liechtenstein   (*Eugenie*)

Soledad Miranda stars as a Berlin teen in love with her widowed writer father (Paul Muller), who is a secret voyeur and sadist. They eventually kidnap models and hookers together, but she falls for a jazz musician. Franco appears in this softcore movie as a director. It's subtitled.

DESERT KICKBOXER
(1992) **D/S:** Isaac Florentine **S:** Jim Lofti **P:** William G. Dunn Jr.   (*Desert Hawk*)

John Haymes Newton (the original star of the *Superboy* TV series) is Hawk, a part-Indian ex-cop and kickboxer who battles coke smugglers in Arizona, led by Paul L. Smith. With Judie Aaronson, Sam DeFrancisco, and Michael M. Foley.

DESERT WARRIOR
(Prism, 1988) **D/P:** Jim Goldman **S:** Bob Davies, Carl Kuntze Philippines (*Sand Wars*)

Zerak (Lou Ferrigno) has sword battles in cages, gets radiation poisoning, and rides a motor tricycle, in this PG-13 post-WWIII action movie. Shari Shattuck costars.

DESIRE AND HELL AT SUNSET MOTEL
(Fox, 1990) **D/S:** Allen Castle **P:** Donald P. Borchers

Here's an odd, comic film *noir* attempt set in the early 60s at a three-story pink California motel with a pool. Characters insult and plot against each other endlessly. It's hard to second-guess what exactly is going on, because several times someone wakes up and "it was all a dream." Flashbacks explain everything at the end, after amnesia drops are used! Sherilyn Fenn is married to a jerk salesman (Whip Hubley) and becomes involved in various ways with David Johansen and David Hewlett as a bop-talking beatnik. Paul Bartel is the voyeur motel owner, and Kenneth Tobey is a cop. There's lots of talk about Commies and the bomb. Pierre David was an executive producer.

DESPERADOS
(Private Screenings, 1969) **D/S:** Lee Frost **P:** R. W. Cresse   (*Hot Spur*)

A Mexican named Carlo is the hero out for revenge in this S&M sex western with Virginia Gordon, Wes Bishop, and John Alderman.

THE DESPERADOS
(RCA, 1969) **D:** Henry Levin **S:** Walter Brough, Clarke Reynolds **P:** Irving Allen

Jack Palance shines as crazed parson Josiah Galt, who seeks vengeance for the death of his Indian wife by killing and looting with his three sons. This post–Civil War western stars Vince Edwards as the son who rebels against the violence, George Maharis, Neville Brand, Sylvia Sims, and Kate O'Mara.

THE DESPERADO TRAIL
(1965) **D:** Harold Reinl **S:** Harold G. Peterson, Joachim Bartsch **P:** Horst Wendlandt   W. Germany/Yugoslavia (*Winnetou III*)

Lex Barker and Pierre Brice return as Old Shatterhand and his Apache friend, Winnetou. Winnetou (a very popular character in Germany) dies in this installment, about an Indian war instigated by white men. With Rik Battaglia and Sophie Hardy. The characters were created by the popular late-19th-century writer Karl May.

DESPERATE CRIMES
(AIP, 1991) **D/S:** Andreas Marfori **S:** Billy Damota **P:** Agnese Fontana Italy (*Il Ritmo del Silenzio; Mafia Docks*)

Van Quattro is the dull and moody hero from New Jersey in this grim, flashback-filled movie. He wants to know who killed his nice girlfriend (Elizabeth Kaitan, star of the flashbacks) and ends up falling for a German whorehouse owner (Rena Niehaus) and trying to get information from a hooker with spike heels (Denise Crosby). Most of the sex scenes involve minor characters (a couple in a shower, two lesbian hookers). Meanwhile, a sadistic black man and a creepy, skinny guy with a ponytail kill for a musclebound crime boss (Franco Columbu). Traci Lords (featured on the video box) is seen briefly as a junkie hooker who dies.

THE DESPERATE HOURS
(MGM, 1990) **D/P:** Michael Cimino **S:** Lawrence Kohner **P:** Dino De Laurentiis

Mickey Rourke plays the Bogart role in this remake of the 1955 movie (adapted from a novel and play by Joseph Hayes, and based on an actual incident). Three escaped convicts invade a house and take hostages. Anthony Hopkins is the wealthy Nam-vet lawyer with an underage daughter (Shawnee Smith), Mimi Rogers is his estranged wife, Kelly Lynch is his lawyer girlfriend, Lindsay Crouse is the hostage negotiator, and David Morse and Elias Koteas are thugs. *Year of the Dragon* is a better Cimino/Rourke movie.

DESPERATE LIVES
(USA, 1982) **D:** Robert Michael Lewis **S/P:** Lew Hunter

CBS-TV brought us this "just say no" movie about students and drugs. A brother and sister (Doug

Keir Dullea stars in *De Sade*.

McKeon and Helen Hunt) score from Sam Bottoms. Their student counselor (Diana Scarwid) tries to help, but paralysis and death occur anyway. Diane Ladd and Tom Atkins are the parents. With William Windom, Art Hindle, and Dr. Joyce Brothers. Rick Springfield sings the title song.

DESPERATE LIVING
(New Line, 1977) **D/S/P/C:** John Waters

Waters' first film without Divine had a self-imposed X rating and was a financial flop. It's a grim fantasy with cannibalism, revolution, and sex changes, filmed mostly on weird-looking sets. Mink Stole and her black maid, Grizelda ("400-pound" Jean Hill), flee town after Grizelda kills her husband by sitting on him. They end up in Mortville, a land for criminals ruled by Edith Massey as wicked Queen Carlotta. Waters hired Liz Renay (who had a mobster boyfriend, had been in jail, had been a stripper, and had written two amazing books) to costar as Muffy. Renay had also acted for Ray Dennis Steckler and A. C. Stevens and had been in some X features. The cast also includes Waters regulars Susan Lowe, Mary Vivian Pierce, Cookie Mueller, and George Stover. The screenplay was published in 1988 as part of the book *Trash Trio*. Waters didn't direct again until *Polyester* (New Line, 1981).

Mink Stole in John Waters' *Desperate Living.*

DESPERATELY SEEKING SUSAN
(HBO, 1985) **D:** Susan Seidelman
S: Leora Barish **P:** Sarah Pillsbury

Rosanna Arquette stars as a bored suburban New Jersey housewife who has a Manhattan adventure when she's mistaken for a hip con woman (Madonna). It's the only Madonna movie that's good, and she's only in parts of it. With Anne Carlisle, Ann Magnuson, Aidan Quinn, Robert Joy, Mark Blum, Laurie Metcalf, John Turturro, Airto Lindsay, and Rockets Redglare. Many actual location are used, including Love Saves the Day on 2nd Avenue.

DESPERATE TEENAGE LOVE DOLLS
(Hollywood Home Theatre, 1984) **D/S/P:** Dave Markey **S/P/A:** Jordan Schwartz **S/A:** Jennifer Schwartz

Filmed in and near Hollywood, this is the story of the rise and fall of Bunny (Hilary Rubens), Kitty (Jennifer Schwartz, the producer's sister), and

Patch, a likable female gang/rock group who record a hit single ("Come on Up to Me") but end up killing several people. An original member, Alexandria, escapes from a mental hospital after killing her doctor with a a guitar, starts shooting up, and has to be replaced. The She Devils, a murdering rival gang led by Tanya Hearst (Tracy Lea), cause trouble, and the Love Dolls drug their sleazy manager (Steve McDonald of Redd Kross), who has a bad trip and is attacked by Felix the Cat. One of the best lines is "Gee, thanks for killing my mom!" The original soundtrack apparently included lots of actual famous records by Blue Cheer, Sweet, the Seeds (singer Sky Saxon also acts), and others. Nobody bothered to pay for the right to use them, so the records were replaced by other new songs (or cover versions), but many of the familiar original intros remain, a great disorienting (accidental) concept. A soundtrack album (on SST) features Redd Kross (their theme song is a classic!), who also back the Love Dolls, Black Flag, and others. The original cost of this hour-long, do-it-yourself, 8mm-to-videotape movie was said to be $250! The sequel was *Lovedoll Superstar*.

DESTINATION FURY
(1961) **D:** Giorgio Bianchi **S:** Clarence Weff
France/Italy *(Mani in Alto)*

AIP-TV released this Eddie Constantine spy-adventure spoof. He stars as Eddie, an international narc in Paris. The American-born star was in dozens of similar European films. With Renato Rascel and Dorian Gray.

DESTINATION MOONBASE ALPHA:
See SPACE 1999

DESTINY
(Video Yesterday, 1921) **D/S:** Fritz Lang
S: Thea von Harbou   Germany
(Der Müde Tod)

In this silent fantasy set in the early 19th century, a woman (Lil Dagover, from *The Cabinet of Dr. Caligari*) drinks poison and visits Death (Bernard Götzke), begging him to spare the life of her lover. She's given three opportunities to save a life (each is represented by a burning candle) in three different periods of history. First she's reincarnated as a caliph's sisiter in 9th-century Bagdad, then in Renaissance Italy, and finally in ancient China, where she's the daughter of a court magician. The cast includes Rudolf Klein-Rogge (later in *Metropolis*). This 80-minute film, produced by Decla-Bioscop, was Lang's seventh, and it was his most ambitious work up to that time. Buñuel said that it inspired him to direct. Lang continued to top himself, with *Dr. Mabuse* (1922), *The Nibelungen* (*Part I: Siegfried; Part II: Kriemhild's Revenge*, both 1924), and *Metropolis* (1926).

DESTINY TO ORDER
(Off Hollywood, 1988) **D/S:** Jim Purdy **P:** Seaton McClean, Jonathan Goodwill, John Kramer   Canada

A young writer meets (and becomes) his own creations, in this droll hip fantasy. Stephen Ouimette stars as the everyman writer J. D. and narrates in the pulp *noir* style. *Destiny* goes all over the place, since the studded-leather-jacket-wearing villain (the great Michael Ironside, from *Scanners*) steals the computer disc containing a detective novel and controls J. D.'s life. The confused guy "becomes" an alcoholic detective, a skateboard kid, and even a hooker. Ironside makes him/her rap. The model of his dreams (Alberta Watson) becomes a stripper, and a big, menacing biker sings opera. Some characters speak French (which is normal, since this movie is set in Montreal). It could have been better, but it's different enough to be fun. With Victoria Snow and Michelle Bauer.

DESTROYER
(Virgin, 1987) **D:** Robert Kirk
S/P: Rex Hauck, Peter Garrity

Lyle Alzado (who died of steroid abuse in 1992) is Ivan Moser, a mass murderer on death row. He goes to the chair during a prison riot. A director (Anthony Perkins) shows up months later to make *Death House Dolls* in the now-closed prison. Deborah Foreman, as a movie stunt woman, has nightmares, and Ivan, now a ghost, kills again. This prison/horror movie has imaginative murders, dream sequences, a film within the film, nudity, and another *Psycho* nod. With Jim Turner, Katt Shea, and Lannie Garrett. It was followed by *The Chair* (which was made first) *Prison, Shocker, Horror Show, Ernest Goes to Jail* and *Guilty as Charged*, all horror movies with electric chairs.

THE DESTRUCTORS
(Vestron, 1974) **D:** Robert Parrish
S/P: Judd Bernard   *(The Marseille Contract)*

Michael Caine stars as a hitman in this drug-smuggling thriller. Anthony Quinn is a drug agent, and James Mason is an international drug dealer. With Catherine Rouvel and former presidential press secretary Pierre Salinger. It was filmed in Paris and released by AIP.

DETONATOR
(New Line, 1992) **D/S:** David S. Jackson
P: Peter Snell   *(Death Train)*

This is an excellent action movie that should have been released theatrically. Ted Levine (*The Silence of the Lambs*) is a ruthless American terrorist who hijacks a train in Germany full of plutonium for a renegade Russian general (Christopher Lee in his best role in a long time) who plans to rebuild the Soviet Union. An egotistical special agent (star Pierce Brosnan) is brought in by a UN official (Patrick Stewart) and teamed with a markswoman and translator (Alexandra Paul). Characters have language problems (subtitles are used) as the train barrels through Europe headed for Iraq. It's based on Alistair MacLean's novel *Death Train* and was shot in Slovenia and in a Zagreb, Croatia, studio. The music is by Trevor Jones.

DETOUR

(Video Dimensions, 1945)
D: Edgar G. Ulmer **S:** Martin
Goldsmith **P:** Leon Fromkess

PRC released this all-time cult favorite just after WWII ended. It was
based on Goldsmith's 1938 novel.
Tom Neal stars as down-and-out
nightclub pianist Al Roberts. He
hitches from New York to LA to be
with his waitress girlfriend (Claudia
Drake). The things that happen to
him (in only 69 minutes) will amaze
any viewer ("Whichever way you
turn, fate sticks out a foot to trip
you"), and you won't believe Ann
Savage as Vera. This public-domain
film, available from many video
companies, was the first "poverty-row" movie chosen by the Library of Congress for preservation (in 1993). In
real life, Neal made headlines in 1951 when he
beat up actor Franchot Tone over starlet Barbara
Payton (who later became a hooker). The incident
ended Neal's film career. In 1965 he went to jail
for six years for shooting his third wife. He died
soon after his release. Ulmer made 11 features for
PRC in five years, including *Girls in Chains*
(1943) and *Bluebeard* (1944). *Detour* is said to
have been made in four days for $20,000.

DETOUR

(1989) **D:** Wade Williams
S: Roger Hull **P:** Bennett Mossman

Tom Neal Jr. (who resembles his late father) stars
in this obsessive but bad remake featuring terrible
acting. It was shot with the same-model 40s camera and obsolete Cinecolor. It also uses the same
Arizona road with the same '41 Lincoln convertible! The original script is followed, and subplots
from the novel that Ulmer didn't have time or
money to shoot are included. With Lea Lavish in
the Ann Savage role, Susanna Foster, and Ann
Robinson. Williams also created much-publicized
altered versions of *Rocket Ship X-M* and *The
Hideous Sun Demon* that few people ever saw.

DETROIT 9000

(HBO, 1973) **D/P:** Arthur Marks **S:** Orville Hampton

The ads said, "It's the murder capital of the
world—Motortown, where the honkies are the
minority race." Hari Rhoades, as the detective-
sergeant hero, is paired with a white detective
(Alex Rocco) to solve the robbery of a black congressman. With Vonetta McGee as a hooker, Ella
Edwards, Scatman Crothers, June Fairchild, and
Detroit police commisioner John Nichols (as himself). Holland, Dozier, Holland wrote the songs.

THE DEVASTATOR

(MGM, 1985) **D/P:** Cirio H. Santiago
S: Joseph Sugarman   (*The Destroyers*)

Pot farmers battle a Nam vet (Richard Hill) who
has nightmares. Future director Katt Shea Ruben
is his gas-station-attendant girfriend. From Concorde.

THE DEVASTATOR (1988): *See* HOSTILE TAKEOVER

THE DEVIL

(Video City, 1981) **D:** Chang Jen Chieh **S:** Luk Pak
Sang **P:** C.H. Wong, Mao Hung Chi   Hong Kong

A witch cures a screaming possessed man covered
with boils by cutting open his chest and letting all
the (real) snakes, worms, and centipedes out. He
pukes up lots of snakes. She warns him, "No
drinking for three days and no women for seven
weeks." He drinks and starts puking up green
slime, pus, and more snakes and insects. Meanwhile Ding Dong, a meddling little kid/bellboy,
coaches a young man in how to impress Miss
Chang. The man marries her and laughs as he
takes her money and sells the family hotel. A
woman he killed, now a green-faced floating ghost
in a white robe with a half-mutated face, is after
him. She does impressive somersaults and leaps
while weird singing that sounds like Yoko Ono is
heard. When the ghost catches up with him he
cuts off his own hand and pukes snakes, worms,
and bugs right into the camera. There's a suprise
ending. The dubbing was (obviously) done in
England. During a bar scene Billy Joel Muzak
plays.

DEVIL GIRL FROM MARS

(Rhino, 1954) **D:** David MacDonald
S: John C. Mather, James Eastwood
P: Edward and Harry Lee Danziger   UK

People will tell you how terrible this science fiction invasion movie is. Watch it anyway! A diverse group of people at the remote Bonnie Prince
Charlie Inn in the Scottish Highlands are terrorized by the mean, sexy, indestructible alien Naya
(Patricia Laffan) and her clunky robot, Chani
(with a built-in death ray). Naya lands in a loud,
spinning flying saucer ("It's white hot!") looking
for some strong Earthmen to help repopulate her
planet. She resembles a model in an incredible
black leather outfit with a cape. She can blur and
disappear (into the 4th dimension), puts an invisible wall around the inn, and has a paralyzer ray.
She even blasts a cripple ("a hopeless specimen").
Hazel Court is gorgeous, in an early role, as a
woman from London. Adrienne Corri works at
the inn and is the girlfriend of an escaped killer.
The score is very emotional, and everything is
played very serious and very British: "While we're

still alive, we might as well have a cup of tea." It
was based on a play. The Danzigers were known
in England for their many low-budget features.

DEVIL IN THE HOUSE OF EXORCISM = HOUSE OF EXORCISM

THE DEVIL MASTER

(Regal, 1976) **D/S/P:** Donald Jackson,
Jerry Younkins   (*The Demon Lover*)

This is really a gem of its kind. Big, long-haired
Levol Blessing (Chris Robbins) is a martial-arts
student and devil-worshipper who has booze and
dance parties at his "castle" and tries to get the
kids to help with his ceremonies. He actually conjures up an impressive horned, red-eyed demon.
Pamela, a blonde, rebels ("I'm not doing anything
so disgusting") and is later found dead. A kid
says, "It's a dead body, just like on TV!" A detective in plaid pants investigates the deaths and
says, "I'm talking about blood city, ghoul." Almost everybody has flares and long hair. The look
and some of the dialogue can be excused by the
time and the place (Detroit). One guy looks like
Frank Zappa, and a "geeky" one does the bump.
Gunner Hansen (*The Texas Chainsaw Massacre,
Leatherface*) plays Professor Peckinpah, and
Howard the Duck cartoonist Val Mayerik plays
Damian. *The Demon Lover Diary* was an (unflattering) documentary about making this. Jackson
still directs.

THE DEVIL MONSTER

(Sinister, 1946) **D/S:** Edward Graham
P/E: Adrian Weiss

A man (Barry Norton) goes out on a fishing boat
to search for a missing sailor on a Pacific island.
It's only one hour long, and that's mostly narrated
stock footage of sea animals and men fishing.
Scenes of topless native women made this a (very
cheap) adults-only road-show release. An octopus
vs. eel fight is pretty good but was obviously shot
in a tank. In one scene all the natives pass out
from drinking. The "monster" is a manta ray
that's harpooned at the end.

THE DEVIL ON WHEELS

(Loonic, 1947) **D/S:** Crane Wilbur **P:** Ben Stoloff

This postwar teens-in-trouble movie from P.R.C.
is a classic of its kind. Daryl Hickman stars as a
teen who likes to race his hopped-up car. Extreme
tragedy results. The parents are to blame. Terry
Moore (then known as Jan Ford) costars with
Noreen Nash and James Cardwell. Only 67 minutes long. Wilbur had a long and incredible career
as an actor in silent films, a screenwriter as early
as *The Monster* (1925), and a director of features
going back to *Tomorrow's Children* (1934).

DEVIL RIDER!

(VSOM, 1970) **D/S/P:** Brad Grinter **S/P:** Charles G.
Ward **S:** Carol McGowan   (*Master's Revenge*)

Kathy, a young blonde (Sharon Mahon), leaves the
beach with a biker gang ("Why not?" she says),
smokes a "happiness bomb," and becomes their

The FANTASTIC Night Of TERROR That Menaced The Fate Of The World!

INVASION FROM OUTER SPACE!... SIGHTS TOO WEIRD TO IMAGINE! DESTRUCTION TOO MONSTROUS TO ESCAPE!

"DEVIL GIRL" FROM MARS

starring Hugh McDermott · Hazel Court · Peter Reynolds · Adrienne Corri · Joseph Tomelty · Sophie Stewart · John Laurie · Patricia Laffan · Directed by David MacDonald · Produced by Edward J. Danziger & Harry Lee Danziger · A Spartan Release

captive. Her mother hires a detective, who finds her older alcoholic hooker sister. She proceeds to narrate a flashback about how bikers raped her. The middle-aged detective then goes undercover (with a wig!), and Kathy's karate-teacher boyfriend comes to the rescue before she becomes a "mama." The bikers wear ponchos and vests, and the acting is laughable. There's a cat fight to the death ("I think this chick is snuffed out!"), a snake's head bitten off, and some brief nudity. The hippie/garage band seen playing is called Heroes of Cranberry Farm. Mahon is the daughter of director Barry Mahon, who shot this in Florida. The tape has Spanish subtitles. Grinter went on to make the incredibly bad *Blood Freak* (1972).

DEVIL'S AGENT

(1961) **D/S:** John Paddy Carstairs
S: Robert Westerby **P:** Emmett Dalton
UK/W. Germany/Ireland (*Im Namen des Teufels*)

Peter Van Eyck stars as a double agent who falls for an escapee from Hungary (Marianne Koch). This spy story takes place mostly on an East German estate but was filmed in Dublin. With Christopher Lee as Baron von Staub, Macdonald Carey, Billie Whitelaw, and Niall MacGinnis. Peter Cushing played a role too but was cut out before the film's release.

DEVIL'S CANYON

(1953) **D:** Alfred L. Werker **S:** Frederick
Hazlitt Brennar **P:** Edmund Grainger

A 3-D western with Stephen McNally as a psychotic killer who breaks out of an Arizona jail and goes after Dale Robertson. Virginia Mayo is an outlaw's girlfriend. With Arthur Hunnicutt, Jay C. Flippen, Whit Bissell, Morris Ankrum, Earl Holliman, Paul Fix, and Glenn Strange. The film was released about a year before Howard Hughes sold RKO.

DEVIL'S COMMANDMENT

(Dark Dreams, 1956) **D/S:** Riccardo
Freda **S:** Piero Regnoli Italy (*I Vampiri*)

Mario Bava shot this early Cinemascope European horror film (and supposedly directed some scenes). Headlines say, ANOTHER BLOODLESS CORPSE! after a woman's body is found in the river Seine (in modern-day Paris). Antoine Balpetre is the professor with a crippled assistant, but the duchess Giselle (Gianna Maria Canale) turns out to be the ageless vampire who needs blood to survive. Her transformation scene is very good, and this movie has lots of skulls. Wandisa Guida costars, and Paul Muller (later in Franco movies) is the journalist hero. Canale is better known for *Hercules* and *Goliath and the Vampires*. The tape is letterboxed. In the US it was released as an adults-only film because of the opening bath scene.

THE DEVIL'S DAUGHTER

(Reel Images, 1939) **D/P:** Arthur Leonard
S: George Terwilliger (*Pocomania*)

This very rare 65-minute black-cast zombie movie, filmed in Jamaica, is a remake. Terwilliger directed the original 1935 version, called *Ouanga* (or *Crime of Voodoo*). Miss Isabel feels cheated out of a banana plantation, so she uses drugs and superstition to put the owner in a trance. This movie has lots of dancing and singing as well as dice-shooting ("put and pay"), a cockfight, and a voodoo ceremony with a "blood dance" ("Come forth, omnipotent one!"). There's a tough, handsome black hero, a weak white villain, and comedy relief from New York City ("I lived in Harlem, on Sugar Hill, for 25 years. Don't pull that jive on me!"). One character thinks his soul has been transferred into a piglet that others want to eat. Nina Mae McKinney (star of the 1929 *Hallelujah*, the first black-cast Hollywood film, and once billed as "the black Garbo") stars, with Hamtree Harrington. An old Capitol Film 16mm rental catalog I found in Richmond, Virginia, offered this as well as 39 other "all-Negro" titles, including *She Devil*, *Murder with Music*, and *Son of Ingagi*.

DEVIL'S DAUGHTER

(Republic, 1990) **D/S:** Michele Soavi **S/P:** Dario
Argento Italy (*La Setta; Demons 4*)

After a massacre by bikers and "the faceless ones," Satanists in 70s California ("A Horse with No Name" is heard), this slow-moving horror/fantasy movie settles into a present-day house in Frankfurt. A teacher (Kelly Curtis, Jamie Lee's stepsister) with pet rabbits meets Herbert Lom, who puts a scarab in her nose. It lives in her brain, making her dream of a poppy field. She discovers a gate to Hell in the basement, and hooks in skin pull a face off (like in *Hellraiser*). In the confusing cosmic ending, a giant pelican rapes her, and an egg is hatched. With Daria Nicoldi. Pino Donaggio wrote the score.

DEVIL'S 8

(1969) **D/P:** Burt Topper **S:** James Gordon
White, Willard Huyck, John Milius

A federal agent (Christopher George) goes undercover as a southern road-gang convict. He plans an escape and leads the convicts in an attack on a moonshine operation run by Ralph Meeker. With Ross Hagen, Fabian, Tom Nardini, Leslie Parrish, Cliff Osmond, Joseph Turkel, and Lana Edmund Jr. Mike Curb provided the music. The film was rated M. Topper's AIP days went back to movies like *Diary of a High School Bride* (1959). It was the first credit for Milius and Huyck, who went on to work with George Lucas.

DEVIL'S FEMALE

(CIC, 1974) **D:** Michael Walter **S:** August Rieger
W. Germany (*Magdalena von Teufel Besessen*)

A cheerful blond orphan (Dagmar Hedrich) at a boarding school is possessed by an invisible demon. The loud sound of flies is heard when she has her "seizures," sometimes furniture flies around, and she says things like "You dirty nun fucker!" Psychiatrists hypnotize her. She speaks in many voices, and eventually she throws up snakes and is okay. The star, a former model, is naked a lot and is extremely enthusiastic in the role. It was produced the same year as *The Tempter, Beyond the Door, Demon Witch Child,* and other possession movies and played (as *Beyond the Darkness*) in US theaters. The out-of-print tape is from Canada.

THE DEVIL'S HAIRPIN

(1957) **D/S/P/A:** Cornel Wilde **S:** James Edmiston

Cornel Wilde is Nick, a tyrannical retired racing champ who runs a restaurant but returns for one last race after the death of his brother. Wilde's real-life wife, Jean Wallace, costars, with Mary Astor, Paul Fix, and Arthur Franz. There's pretty good 50s-car footage. It's been called an uncredited remake of Howard Hawks' *The Crowd Roars* (1932), which was officially remade as *Indianapolis Speedway* (1939).

THE DEVIL'S HAND

(1942) **D/S:** Maurice Tourneur **S:** Jean-Paul le Chanois
France (*La Main du Diable; Carnival of Sinners*)

Pierre Fresnay is a poor painter who sells his soul to the devil. A withered living hand is a symbol of the contract. Previous owners of the hand (from various time periods) show up in masks and tell their stories. The film, made during the German occupation, was released in the US in 1947. Maurice Tourneur worked in the US from 1911 to 1926. His son, Jacques Tourneur, spent most of his career in the US. Both are considered masters of fantasy, mystery, and horror.

THE DEVIL'S HAND

(SW, 1959) **D:** William Hole Jr.
S: Jo Heims **P:** Alvis K. Bubis

Robert Alda has frequent dreams of a woman (Linda Christian) dancing on clouds. Neil Hamilton (Commisioner Gordon in the *Batman* TV series) is "the high executioner" with a mute Tibetan servant. He runs a doll shop, a front for voodoo dancing and ceremonies in the basement. The dream girl convinces the hero to join in. A wheel of swords is used for a sacrifice. He says, "You're a she devil, evil, but beautiful, fascinating!" Soon his luck increases. With Bruno Ve Sota. The instrumental rock theme is pretty good. Crown International released the film.

DEVIL'S HARVEST

(Hollywood Confidential, 1942) **D:** Ray Test

Satan is superimposed whenever "reefer" is shown in this WWII-era anti-drug movie. An investigator goes after pushers for 52 minutes.

DEVIL'S ISLAND

(Sinister, 1926) **D:** Frank O'Connor **S:** Leah Baird

Richard Tucker is Jean Valyon, a Paris surgeon serving time in a brutal penal colony. Pauline Frederick, Marian Nixon, and George Lewis are also in this rare prison movie from the independent Chadwick company. It was remade with Boris Karloff in 1940.

THE DEVIL'S JOINT

(SW, 1969)

This pro-pot documentary features unidentified scenes from many old drug-scare movies and newsreel clips. The narrator talks of the early anti-drug "propaganda war" and explains how prohibition created more drug use. Some old drug songs and comic title cards are added. It's interesting but seems too long to endure. Trailers for some classic exploitation movies are at the end of the tape.

THE DEVIL'S MESSENGER

(SW, 1962) **D/S:** Curt Siodmak **D:** Herbert L. Strock
S: Leo Guild **P:** Kenneth Herts   Sweden

Lon Chaney Jr. as the Devil links 3 episodes of a pretty good Swedish TV horror-anthology program Siodmak made in 1959, called *Number 13 Demon Street*. In Hell, Chaney looks in a rotary file and says, "Next!" as he sends his messenger, Satanya (Karen Kadler), to participate in the supernatural tales. The first (and by far the best) concerns a fashion photographer (John Crawford). He kills a woman, but she shows up in photos and in his studio to haunt him. In the other eposodes, a miner discovers a woman frozen in a

block of ice, and a fortune-teller convinces a man he will die at midnight. At the end Lon points at the camera and a 500-megaton bomb goes off, destroying the world! The "new" footage is by Strock, whose next project was *The Crawling Hand*.

THE DEVIL'S MISTRESS

(Sinister, 1966) **D/S:** Orville Wanzer
P/A: Wes Moreland

In this odd 66-minute color horror/western, four cowboys on the run go to a cabin, kill the religious husband, and rape his half-Indian wife, Liah (Joan Stapleton). The men all die in mysterious ways, and the husband is still alive. It was filmed in New Mexico.

THE DEVIL'S PET

(1994) **D/S/P/C:** Donald Jackson
S: Mark Williams **P:** Michael Miller

Gini Dante and Jeff Conaway star as low-budget horror directors eating in a restaurant (actually in Hell). With Julie Strain.

THE DEVIL'S POSSESSED

(All Seasons, 1974) **D:** Leon Klimovsky **S/A:** Paul Naschy   Spain/Argentina (*El Mariscal del Infierno*)

Paul Naschy is Field Marshal de Lancre, in 13th-century France, who goes mad seeking the magical "philosopher's stone." An alchemist who needs virgin blood to make gold teams with the marshal's evil wife. There are swordfights, a peasant revolt, torture scenes, and a chopped-off head that talks.

THE DEVIL'S SLEEP

(Sinister, 1949) **D:** W. Merle Connell

Umberto Scali (Timothy Farrell) uses his health spa for "fat society dames" as a front for his illegal drug ring. He cleverly blackmails a philosophical female judge (Lita Grey-Chaplin) with naked photos of her daughter (Tracy Lynne). There's a long comic scene with a cute overweight woman named Tessie Tesse. Scali's comic assistant says "Those blimps really line your pockets!" Hopped up high school kids take "goofies" and "bennies." With a laughable fight, characters tied up, some near nudity, and a doctor talking about "hypnotics." William Thomason is the hero police sergeant and George Eiferman (Mr. America 1948) is "Mr. America." Grey had been Charlie Chaplin's "child bride." John Mitchum (just after his brother Robert was busted!) is also in the "brilliant cast." William C. Thompson was the cinematographer. The print is jumpy (and may be cut in some spots) but is still an exploitation must. Scali and his perfect pencil thin mustache returned in *Pin Down Girls*.

THE DEVIL'S SON-IN-LAW

(Interglobal, Active, 1977) **D/S:** Cliff Roquemore
(*Petey Wheatstraw; The Devil's Son-in-Law*)

After Petey Wheatstraw (comedian Rudy Ray Moore) is born (full grown) on a stormy night in a shack, he beats up his father for disturbing his

sleep. Later Petey becomes a nightclub comedian and dies when evil Mr. White blasts a funeral. He goes to Hell (a red spotlight is the special effect) and meets Satan. If he marries the Devil's ugly daughter he can return to Earth for revenge. You won't believe it! His magic cane can turn men into dogs and make fat people thin. With Leroy and Skillet as rival comics and Sy Richardson. There was even a soundtrack album (on Magic Disc), featuring Nat Dove and the Devils. Roquemore directed Rudy in *The Human Tornado* too. Leroy and Skillet were also real nightclub comedians and "party album" stars.

THE DEVIL'S UNDEAD = NOTHING BUT THE NIGHT

THE DEVIL TIMES FIVE

(Sinister, 1974) **D:** Sean McGregor **S:** John Durrea **P:** Dylan Jones, Michael Blowitz (*People Toys; Horrible House on the Hill*)

Five psychotic kids (one disguised as a nun!) escape from a mental hospital and terrorize and kill people at a remote mountain ski lodge. Lengthy slo-mo, b/w scenes of kids killing with hammers, chains, and a piranha are pretty memorable. They burn a woman alive and put a man inside a snowman. Future teen idol Leif Garrett kills with an axe. With a cat fight, brief sex scenes, a Lenny-like worker who likes rabbits, and bizarre synthesizer music. Gene Evans stars as the mean, bearded Papa Doc, and Sorrell Booke is a pathetic doctor. From Jerry Gross' Cinemation.

THE DEVIL WALKS AT MIDNIGHT = THE DEVIL'S NIGHTMARE

DEVIL WOMAN

(SW, 1970) **D:** Albert Yu, Felix Villar
S/P: Jimmy L. Pascual   Philippines

A girl (Rosemarie Gil) born during a thunderstorm can control snakes and has snake hair (!) hidden under a scarf. Villagers kill her parents, so she grows up seeking revenge. She lives in a cave and uses a local gang to help. A new Chinese doctor (Alex Fang Lee) becomes a reluctant kung-fu hero. There are lots of fight scenes, some involving snakes and fireballs. American military music is played at a boxing match, since this takes place in the 19th century. Other sources give different credits. The music (probably lifted from another movie) is good. The color tape is letterboxed.

THE DEVONSVILLE TERROR

(Nelson, 1982) **D/S/P/C:** Ulli Lommel
S: George T. Lindsay

Three women arrive in a New England town on the 300th anniversary of the burning of three witches. One, the new schoolteacher (Suzanna Love, Lommel's real-life wife), says that God is a woman and is accused of witchcraft. After some unusual deaths, the town reenacts its past. The best effects are worms coming out of the face of Donald Pleasence as a cursed doctor. With Robert Walker Jr. The FX are by David L. Hewitt. The associate producer was Bill Rebane. It was filmed in Wisconsin.

DIAGNOSIS: MURDER

(1974) **D:** Sydney Hayers **S:** Philip Levene **P:** Peter Miller   UK

Christopher Lee as a psychiatrist, Dr. Haywood, plots to kill his wife so that he can be with his mistress (Judy Geeson). Then his wife disappears. With Jon Finch, Jane Merrow, and Dilys Hamlett. This British TV movie also played in some theaters.

DIAL HELP

(Prism, 1988) **D/S:** Ruggiero Deodato **S:** Joseph Cavara and Mary Cavara **P:** Galiano Juso, Giovanni Bertolucci   Italy (*Ragno Gelido*)

Charlotte Lewis (after *Pirates* and *The Golden Child*) stars as a sexy model with a possessed phone. There's also a killer ceiling fan and other household appliances, and many people die. The music is by Claudio Simonetti. William Berger costars.

DIAL M FOR MURDER

(1981) **D:** Boris Sagal **S:** John Gay **P:** Peter Katz

Angie Dickinson plays the Grace Kelly role in this NBC-TV remake. Frederick Knott's play became a Hitchcock film, and there were two TV versions before this one. Christopher Plummer has the Ray Milland role, and the cast includes Michael Parks, Anthony Quayle, and Ron Moody. Sagal (father of actress Katey Sagal) later died in a helicopter accident.

THE DIAMOND TRAP

(Vidmark, 1988) **D:** Don Taylor **S:** David Peckinpah **P:** Neil T. Maffeo

Brooke Shields stars in this TV comedy movie. Howard Hesseman is a New York City detective who follows her to London. With Darren McGavin and Ed Marinaro. Taylor, an actor (*Battleground*, *Stalag 17*), began directing in 1961.

THE DIAMOND WIZARD

(1953) **D/A:** Dennis O'Keefe **D:** Montgomery Tully **P:** Steven Pallos   UK

O'Keefe is a US Treasury agent helping Scotland Yard find a missing atomic scientist. This is the only 3-D film made in England in the 50s. It was released here by United Artists. With Margaret Sheridan and Philip Friend.

DIARY OF A BACHELOR

(1964) **D/P:** Sandy Howard **S:** Ken Barnett

William Traylor stars in a b/w AIP comedy about a fiancée finding her future husband's diary. With Dagne Crane, Joe Silver, Dom DeLuise, Arlene Golonka, Paula Stewart, and, at the end of the cast, Nai Bonet. It was filmed on location in New York City. Howard, who still produces exploitation movies, is best known for *A Man Called Horse* (1970).

DIARY OF A CHAMBERMAID

(Cinematheque, 1964) **D/S:** Luis Buñuel **S/A:** Jean-Claude Carrière   France/Italy (*Le Journal d'une Femme de Chambre*)

Jeanne Moreau stars as a servant, Célestine, who works for a decadent family on a Normandy estate in 1928. The father (Michel Piccoli) has a shoe fetish, and the brutal, fascist gamekeeper seems to be a child-murderer. This unsettling b/w film has no music and is subtitled. An earlier version of Octave Mirbeau's novel had been directed by Jean Renoir in 1946 (available from Republic Video).

DIARY OF A HITMAN

(Columbia, 1990) **D:** Roy London **S:** Kenneth Pressman **P:** Amin Q. Chaudhri

Forest Whitaker stars as a hitman on his last job. He's supposed to kill Sherilyn Fenn (and her new baby). This was advertised in 1992 as being a new Sharon Stone feature (after *Basic Instinct* was a hit). She has only a small role, and most of it is like a bad play. With James Belushi and Lois Chiles.

DIARY OF A MAD HOUSEWIFE

(MCA, 1970) **D/P:** Frank Perry **S:** Eleanor Perry

Carrie Snodgress has an affair with an author (Frank Langella) while her attorney husband (Richard Benjamin) climbs the Manhattan ladder of success. It's pretty dreary, but the original Alice Cooper band plays at a party and Peter Boyle has a very small role.

DIARY OF A NUDIST

(SW, 1961) **D/P:** Doris Wishman **S:** Melvin Stanley   (*Nature Camp Confidential*)

An angry newspaper editor ("This is outrageous, and I'm going to do something about it!") sends Stacy, a blond reporter (Davee Decker), to a nudist camp to write an exposé. Instead of telling how sinful it is she writes about how great it is. He eventually shows up at the camp (in his shorts) after firing her, and they fall in love. All the naked women walk with strategically placed towels, purses, or papers. During a volleyball game, the team facing the camera wear shorts! The lounging nudists look like the Eloi in *The Time Machine*. The underwater swimming scenes were also in Wishman's *Blaze Starr: The Original*. This timid color nudist feature was shot at the Sunny Palms Lodge in Homestead, Florida, and in Palmerton, Pennsylvania. (the different footage is obvious). Decker was also in *Orgy at Lil's Place* (1963). The Joe Bob intro version went out of print real fast.

DIARY OF FORBIDDEN DREAMS

(TWE, 1972) **D/S/A:** Roman Polanski **S:** Gerald Brach **P:** Carlo Ponti   Italy (*Che?; What?*)

Sydne Rome (from Ohio) stars as an innocent, unquestioning young woman who finds herself at an Italian mansion owned by an eccentric millionaire (Marcello Mastroianni) who likes to be whipped and claims to have been a pimp. She writes in her diary and spends most of the movie walking around naked, which is why this movie wasn't shown much in the US. Hugh Griffith is a dying old man, and Polanski is Mosquito, a character with a spear gun. Polanski made this odd, rarely seen comic *Alice in Wonderland* for adults between *Macbeth* and *Chinatown*. The dubbed 112-minute film was cut to 94 minutes in the US.

DICK AND JANE DROP ACID

(Surf Reality, 1991) **D/A:** Matt Mitler **S/A:** Jeff Eyres **P:** Robert Pritchard

In the tradition of old road-show movies, this opens with an anti-LSD lecture, has flashbacks, and shows how innocents are led astray. Longhairs smoke pot in a basement, and electric Kool-Aid is served at a "cube" party. Undercover cops get high and freak out. The British pusher/villain has to deliver three new addicts a month. The music is by a Thousand Tiny Fingers. It was shot on tape in the East Village. Mitler was in *Basket Case 2*, *Spring Break*, and others.

DICK BARTON, SPECIAL AGENT

(Sinister, 1948) **D:** Alfred Goulding **S:** Alan Stranks **P:** Henry Halstead   UK (*Dick Barton, Detective*)

A mad scientist plans to destroy London with germ warfare, in this early Hammer film. Don Stannard is Dick Barton. This was the first of a series of films based on a BBC radio series.

DICK BARTON STRIKES BACK

(Sinister, 1949) **D:** Godfrey Grayson **S:** Ambrose Grayson   UK

Don Stannard returns, only to be thrown into a cage of poisonous snakes. Sebastian Cabot is one of the criminals with an atomic device that can destroy cities. *Dick Barton at Bay* (1950) followed. It was the last of this Hammer series, because the star died in a car crash.

DICK TRACY

(Rhino, Sinister 1937) **D:** Ray Taylor, Alan James **S:** Barry Shipman, Winston Miller **P:** Nat Levine

Chester Gould's newspaper comic strip (which debuted in 1931) was the basis for this 15 chapter Republic serial, one of the best serials ever made. Ralph Byrd stars as the FBI agent fighting the Spider Gang. The "Lame One" has a very modern and impressive futuristic flying wing and a hunchbacked mad scientist assistant named Moloch. They kidnap Tracy's brother, operate on him, and make him a mindless slave. With Kay Hughes as Gwen, Smiley Burnette, Francis X. Bushman, and Lee Van Atta as Junior (the only other character used from the comic strip). Byrd, who also debuted as Tracy on radio in 1937, returned as Tracy in three more Republic serials and two forties features. He was still playing Tracy in an early fifties TV series until he died in 1952. The old Dick Tracy movies and serials were on sale everywhere while the Beatty version was in release.

DICK TRACY

(Touchstone, 1990) **D/P/A:** Warren Beatty **S:** Bo Goldman, Jim Cash, Jack Epps Jr.

This was supposed to be as big a hit as *Batman*, but it didn't help that Beatty had been in only the commercial flops *Reds* (1981) and *Ishtar* (1987) in the 80s and that costar Madonna can't act. Al Pacino (better than in *The Godfather III*, from the same year!) is Big Boy Caprice and Dustin Hoffman is funny as Mumbles. The cast includes

Glenne Headly, Charlie Korsmo, and an amazing arena of underused villains (in extreme makeup) and guest stars: William Forsythe as Flattop, R. G. Armstrong as Pruneface, Charles Durning, Paul Sorvino, Mandy Patinkin, Seymour Cassel, Dick Van Dyke, Mary Woronov, Kathy Bates, Henry Jones, Catherine O'Hara, Henry Silva, James Caan, Estelle Parsons, Alan Garfield, Michael J. Pollard, Mike Mazurki, James Tolkan, and Hamilton Camp. Even Luann Lee and Rebekka Armstrong from *Playboy* are in it. The cinematography is by Vittorio Storaro (*The Last Emperor*, *Reds*). It was the first feature made in digital sound, and Danny Elfman wrote the score. Chester Gould had died in 1985, so he didn't live to see his creation looking confused in a yellow raincoat.

William Forsythe is Flattop in *Dick Tracy*.

DICK TRACY'S G-MEN

(VCI, 1939) **D:** William Witney, John English **S:** Barry Shipman, Franklin Adreon, Donald Davidson

In the third Dick Tracy serial from Republic, Ralph Byrd has to battle Irving Pichel as Zarnoff, head of a spy ring. This time Gwen and Junior are absent. With Phyllis Isley (later known as Jennifer Jones). The 15 chapters are 270 minutes.

DICK TRACY RETURNS

(VCI, 1938) **D:** William Whitney, John English **S:** Barry Shipman, Franklin Adreon, Donald Davidson

Ralph Byrd returns in the second Dick Tracy serial from Republic. It has the extra attraction of Charles Middleton (from the *Flash Gordon* serials) as the villain, Pa Stark, head of a notorious criminal family. With Lynne Roberts as Gwen and Jerry Tucker as Junior. The 15 chapters are 260 minutes.

DICK TRACY VS. CRIME INC.

(VCI, 1941) **D:** William Witney, John English **S:** Donald Davidson, Norman S. Hall, William Lively

Ralph Byrd, in the fourth and final Dick Tracy serial, battles "the Ghost," a criminal who wears a great immobile, full-head mask. This time New York City is destroyed, thanks to footage from the movie *Deluge* (1933). Byrd later returned in the 1947 features *Dick Tracy's Dilemma* and *Dick Tracy Meets Gruesome*. This 15-chapter Republic serial runs 270 minutes.

DIE HARD

(Fox, 1988) **D:** John McTiernan **S:** Jeb Stuart, Steven de Souza **P:** Lawrence Golden, Joel Silver

As far as action/disaster movies go, this one delivers and has been copied many times. A 40-story LA high-rise office building is destroyed while German terrorists take it over during a Christmas party and hold everybody for ransom. A wise-cracking New York City cop named John McClane (Bruce Willis) battles the terrorists (Alan Rickman and Alexander Godunov). With Bonnie Bedelia, Reginald VelJohnson, William Atherton, James Shigeta, Robert Davi, Hart Bochner, and Terri Lynn Doss and Kim Malin (from *Playboy*). It's 131 minutes.

DIE HARD 2: DIE HARDER

(Fox, 1990) **D:** Renny Harlin **S:** Doug Richardson, Steven de Souza **P:** Lawrence Gordon, Joel Silver

Here's a very expensive, all-out sequel that made much more than the original. This time Willis is in a Washington, DC airport, and new terrorists have to be stopped. With Bonnie Bedelia and William Atherton from the original, Franco Nero, John Amos, William Sadler, Dennis Franz (providing unwanted comedy relief), John Leguizamo, Art Evans, Robert Patrick, and Watergate lawyer Fred D. Thompson. It copies Bond films in many ways and was cited as having a record number of "acts of violence" (200). A whole planeload of Brits is blown up in midair. Some of the ILM FX are awesome, but knowledgeable viewers can still spot models. Harlin, director of *Prison* and *Nightmare on Elm Street IV*, did *The Adventures of Ford Fairlane* the same year. *Die Hard: With a Ven-geance* followed in 1995.

DIE LAUGHING

(Warner, 1980) **D:** Jeff Werner **S/P/A:** Robby Benson **S:** Jerry Segal **P:** Mark Canton

Cabdriver Robbie Benson is accused of killing a scientist who made a bomb out of nuclear waste. Russian spies are also involved in this failed black comedy. With Charles Durning, Peter Coyote, Elsa Lanchester (in her last role), Bud Cort, and Linda Grovenor. Benson later turned director with *White Hot* (1988).

DIEN BIEN PHU

(1992) **D/S/P:** Pierre Schoendorffer **P:** Jacques Kerschner   France

Donald Pleasence stars as an American reporter during the 57-day battle that drove the French from Vietnam in 1954. The film was made in Tonkin. The director was an army cameraman and prisoner of war in real life. It's considered historically important and was very expensive. Schoendorffer also narrates.

DIE, SISTER, DIE!

(MPI, 1978) **D/P:** Randall Hood **S:** Tony Sawyer   (*The Companion*)

Jack Ging plots to kill his sister for money. Antoinette Bower (*Superbeast*) is his nurse accomplice. This obscure movie features Hollywood veterans Edith Atwater and Kent Smith (they were married in real life, and this is his last known role) and Richard Emhardt. There's a dream sequence in a pool of blood.

DIE WATCHING

(Triboro, 1992) **D:** Charles Davis **S:** Kenneth J. Hall **P:** Nanda Rao

Christopher Atkins stars as Michael (instead of Mark) in a very blatant ripoff of *Peeping Tom*. He videotapes a series of women with oversize, inflated breasts, then ties them up and kills them. It's complete with disturbing childhood flashbacks and strip sequences to rock songs sung by a Jim Morrison imitator. Vali Ashton (also a producer) costars as the artist neighbor who loves and trusts him. Tim Thomerson is an LA police detective. This New World release was written by the guy who made *Evil Spawn* (1987).

DIGGIN' UP BUSINESS

(Monarch, 1989) **D/P/A:** Tom Pardew **D:** Mark Byers **S:** Tim Minear **P:** Rick Eye

Lynn Holly Johnson works in a mortuary. She devises gimmicky funerals (a corpse shot out of a cannon, a dead stripper in a cake) to make money, in this PG comedy. With Murray Langston ("the Unknown Comic"), Billy Barty, Yvonne Craig, Linnea Quigley, and Dawn Wildsmith, plus Ruth Buzzi and Gary Owens from *Laugh-In*.

DIGITAL DREAMS

(Media, 1983) **D:** Robert Dornhelm **S/A:** Richard O'Brien **P/A:** Bill and Astrid Wyman   UK

Wyman (who quit the Rolling Stones in 1992) made this 16mm, 72-minute film for TV. James Coburn plays several characters, and Wyman's (now former) Swedish wife complains a lot. Some animation and Stones concert footage are used, and Wyman visits his neighbor Marc Chagall. He also plays a song with Muddy Waters, Buddy Guy, and Junior Wells.

Ralph Morgan is the Ghost in *Dick Tracy vs. Crime, Inc.*

DIKA: MURDER CITY

(Moore, 1995) **D:** Michael Moore

Dika Newlin is a woman in her 70s who performs in several different styles. She sounds awful backed by a rock band in a club singing Elvis songs in black-leather male drag. She's very strange doing rambling originals and playing a keyboard and is charming and funny doing her songs (and playing kazoo) with just a guy playing acoustic guitar. Dika is interviewed and also meows one whole song. This documentary from Richmond, Virginia, includes a NOTLD scene.

DILLINGER

(Key, 1945) **D:** Max Nosseck **S:** Philip Yordan **P:** Maurice and Franklin King

This was the biggest hit Monogram ever made. It was considered brutal and controversial when released (just before WWII ended in Europe) and was banned in Chicago! It made Lawrence Tierney a star. The robbery sequence was "borrowed" from Fritz Lang's *You Only Live Once.* The cast was great for a Monogram film: Edmund Lowe, Anne Jeffreys as "the lady in red," Eduardo Ciannelli, Elisha Cook Jr., and Marc Lawrence. Nosseck (born in Poland) also directed Tierney (who was in and out of jail a lot in real life) in *Shakedown* and *The Hoodlum.* Tierney also had a small role in a mediocre 1991 TV version of *Dillinger.*

DILLINGER

(Vestron, 1973) **D/S:** John Milius **P:** Buzz Feitshans

Warren Oates looks perfect for the title role in this version of the Dillinger legend, released by AIP. The supporting cast is even better than in the 1945 version: Ben Johnson as Melvin Purvis, Michelle Phillips, Cloris Leachman, Richard Dreyfuss (as Baby Face Nelson), Harry Dean Stanton, Geoffrey Lewis, John Ryan, and Steve Kanaly. It was the first movie directed by Milius and was filmed in Oklahoma. The Barry Devorzon soundtrack is on MCA. Corman's New World later made *The Lady in Red* (1979), with Robert Conrad as Dillinger.

LA DINASTIA DRACULA

(Eagle, 1978) **D:** Alfredo B. Crevenna   Mexico

Fabian as Dracula in 18th-century Mexico doesn't sound very promising, but I saw this in an Upper West Side Manhattan theater (now long gone, of course) and was very impressed. It had a bigger budget than most Mexican horror movies. There's an impressive cavern hideout, and Fabian (dubbed into Spanish) isn't bad at all.

DINOSAUR ISLAND

(New Horizons, 1993) **D/P:** Jim Wynorski, Fred Olen Ray **S/A:** Bob Sheridan, Christopher Wooden

Warren Oates stars in *Dillinger,* with Harry Dean Stanton, Geoffrey Lewis, and John Ryan.

This is like a 50s lost-world movie, plus some nudity and outdoor sex. A group of comic enlisted men (led by Ross Hagen) encounter an often topless female tribe (led by Toni Naples) on an island. Blond Antonia Dorian is the main attraction in her standout sex scene, and Naples fights Michelle Bauer. With Richard Gabai, Becky LeBeau, Steve Barkett, and Peter Spellos as Turbo. Oh, yeah, there's also a pretty good triceratops, the busy *Carnosaur* prop monster, some awful puppet dinos, and scenes filmed at Bronson Canyon. Gary Graver (*One Million AC/DC*) shot it. The longer Image laserdisc has both directors commenting on their 12-day feature.

DINOSAUR MOVIES

(Simitar, 1993) **D:** Donald F. Glut

Glut hosts a 2-tape compilation set with Forrest J. Ackerman, Ray Harryhausen, and Jim Danforth talking and lots of rare clips going back to the silents. With the cartoon *Gertie the Dinosaur* (1914) and Willis O'Brien's short *The Dinosaur and the Missing Link* (1915).

THE DION BROTHERS

(1973) **D/A:** Jack Starrett **S:** Bill Kerby, Terrence Malik **P:** Jonathan T. Taplin (*The Gravy Train*)

Stacy Keach and Frederic Forrest are West Virginia brothers who become criminals, in this comic action movie. With Margot Kidder, Barry

Primus, Denny Miller, and Richard Romanus. Starrett (who had just done *Cleopatra Jones*) replaced the original director, Malik.

DIPLOMATIC IMMUNITY

(Fries, 1991) **D/P:** Peter Maris **S:** Randall Frakes, Jim Trombetta, Richard Donn

The daughter of Bruce Boxleitner is raped and killed by a German psycho who the police release. He goes to Paraguay, where his evil dominatrix mother (Meg Foster) rules from an island fortress. The dad goes after him with help from Robert Forster as a CIA agent and Billy Drago as an arms dealer. With Fabiano Udenio as a hooker and Christopher Neame.

DIRECT HIT

(PM, 1994) **D/P:** Joseph Merhi **S:** Jacobsen Hart **P:** Richard Pepin

William Forsythe is a hitman in Hollywood with one last assignment, to kill exotic dancer Jo Champa. He decides to protect her instead. With Richard Norton as a bad assassin, John Amprea as a corrupt politician, George Segal as the boss, Juliet Landau, and Steve Garvey.

DIRECTING MOVIES FROM ACTION TO RAP

(1993)

Ted V. Mikels discusses making 11 features, and trailers (or film clips) are shown for each one, in this amusing self-promotion tape. Mikels, a jolly, likable eccentric who sometimes acts in his own creations, really seems to love making his low-budget features. Shanti (or Dr. Wendy Altamura), Mikels's stern-looking British-accented companion, pretends she doesn't know the answers to the (scripted) questions she asks, and a bored-looking guy (said to be a writer) is there mostly to stop the star from talking too long and ask, "Do you like being called a cult hero?" It's kind of like Mikels took over *The Joe Franklin Show.* Features covered go back to the b/w *Black Klansman* and *Strike Me Deadly* and include *Astro Zombies, The Corpse Grinders* (he's planning a sequel!), *The Doll Squad* ("total entertainment for all ages!"), and more recent (and less interesting) direct-to-video action movies that are "coming to a theater near you soon!" He even discusses producing *The Worm Eaters.*

THE DIRT BIKE KID

(Nelson, 1986) **D:** Hoite C. Caston **S:** David Brandes, Lewis Collick **P:** Julie Corman

Peter Billingsley with his Yamaha bike that flies, fights bikers and an evil banker (Stuart Pankin). This PG film, "inspired" by parts of *E.T.* is from Roger Corman's Concorde.

THE DIRT GANG

(MPI, 1972) **D:** Jerry Jameson **S:** William Mercer, Michael C. Healy **P:** Joseph E. Bishop

One of AIP's later biker movies stars Paul Carr, Michael Forest, and Michael Pataki. A biker encounters a film crew in the desert. This Roger Corman production, by the director of *Airport '77*, features typical sex (Uschi Digart is in it) and violence.

DIRTIEST GAME IN THE WORLD

(1975) **D:** James Bryan

Titus Moore (Titus Moody) is a candidate for California state representative. He wants the hippie vote, so he runs on a legalize-marijuana platform and checks out their life-style. This leads to pot-smoking and lots of sex and nudity. After an outdoor lesbian sex scene, his alky wife loses it and starts whipping the hippies during an orgy. This is followed by an extremely bloody and gross suicide scene. Then most of the characters are shot. The acting is awful. This sick "soft-core" sex movie has several surprisingly extreme scenes. Jean Stone costars with Coleman Francis (*The Beast of Yucca Flats*). Moody filmed new wraparound sequences on Hollywood Boulevard. He assures us that this is "a cult classic" and ends by saying he was Sam Peckinpah's roommate.

THE DIRTY GAME

(1965) **D:** Terence Young, Christian-Jacque, Carlo Lizzani **S:** Jo Eisinger
France/Italy/W. Germany (*Guerre Secrete*)

AIP released this b/w Cold War spy drama. Robert Ryan as the US intelligence chief in Europe recalls three past operations he supervised. Henry Fonda, Vittorio Gassman, Annie Girardot, Bourvil, and Peter Van Eyck are in the cast. A soundtrack recording was released on Laurie.

DIRTY GAMES

(AIP, 1989) **D/S:** Greg Hofmeyr
P: Albie Venter, Roy Sargeant   S. Africa

Valentina Vargas, in Africa to avenge the death of her scientist father, blames her ex-lover Jan-Michael Vincent, a molecular scientist. The confusing, boring "thriller" is totally without merit.

DIRTY HARRY

(Warner, 1971) **D/P:** Don Siegel **S:** Harry Julian Fink, Rita M. Fink, Dean Reiser

Clint Eastwood as San Francisco police inspector Harry Callahan goes after Andrew Robinson as Scorpio in a ski mask. The maniac killer was inspired by the real San Francisco Zodiac killer. He demands ransom money or he'll commit a murder a day. He buries a girl alive and hijacks a school-bus full of kids. The cast includes Reni Santoni, Harry Guardino, John Vernon, and Debralee Scott as a nude corpse. This is one of the best action/cop movies ever made. It was a big hit and was called "fascist" by the *New York Times*. The star was originally supposedly to be Paul Newman, then Frank Sinatra. Eastwood returned as Harry in *Magnum Force* (1973) and more sequels, all from Warner.

DIRTY MARY, CRAZY LARRY

(Magnetic, 1974) **D:** John Hough **S:** Leigh Chapman, Antonio Santean **P:** Norman T. Herman

Peter Fonda is a former stock-car driver who turns to crime with his mechanic (Adam Roarke) and Susan George. A sheriff in a helicopter (Vic Morrow) pursues them. With Roddy McDowall, William Campbell, Kenneth Tobey, and Lynn Borden. There's some excellent stunt work. The 20th Century release was to have been produced by James Nicholson (who had just left AIP), but he died.

DIRTY O'NEIL

(1974) **D/S:** Howard Freen **D:** Lewis Teague **P:** John C. Broderick

AIP released this feature about the sex life of a small-town California cop. It stars Morgan Paul, with Art Metrano, Pat Anderson, and Liv Lindeland. Teague made *The Lady in Red* (1979) and *Alligator* (1979) next.

DISASTER AT SILO 7

(Triboro, 1988) **D:** Larry Elikann
S: Douglas Lloyd McIntosh **P:** Julian Krainin

Michael O'Keefe is an Air Force technician who prevents an apocalypse. This TV movie is based on a 1980 Titan II missile accident near Little Rock and was filmed in an actual Titan II silo. With Peter Boyle, Patricia Charbonneau, Perry King, and Joe Spano.

DISCONNECTED

(Active, 1978) **D/S/P:** Gorman Bechard
S: Virginia Gilroy

A shy psycho (Mark Walker) makes silent phone calls, and a detective investigates. Frances Raines has a double role as good and bad twins. One works in a video store. This was filmed in Waterbury, Connecticut, by the maker of *Psychos in Love*.

DISCREET CHARM OF THE BOURGEOISIE

(Cinematheque, 1972) **D/S:** Luis Buñuel
S: Jean-Claude Carrière **P:** Serge Silberman   France

In a twist on the "plot" of Buñuel's *The Exterminating Angel*, some people try to enjoy a planned dinner that is always interrupted. Rich, powerful characters have disturbing dreams and always end up walking endlessly on a road while remaining oblivious to the chaos around them. One dream about a dead man is better than most entire horror movies. This movie is in a class of its own and will make you forget most other obvious "anti-establishment" movies you might have seen. The South American ambassador (star Fernando Rey) carries a cocaine stash in his diplomatic pouch. With Delphine Seyrig, Jean-Pierre Cassel, Stephane Audran, and Bulle Ogier. It's subtitled. The film received an Oscar as best foreign film. Buñuel said it was his last, but went on to make *The Phantom of Liberty* (1974) and *That Obscure Object of Desire* (1977).

DISORDERLIES

(Warner, 1987) **D/P:** Michael Schultz **S:** Mark Feldberg, Mitchell Klebanoff **P:** George Jackson, Mitchell Jaffe

Andrew Robinson is Scorpio in *Dirty Harry*.

Kool Rock, Buffy, and Markie (the Fat Boys) are hired by evil Anthony Geary to care for his elderly, rich uncle (Ralph Bellamy) who hopes the situation will kill him. The Fat Boys do rap remakes of songs like "Louie Louie," "The Twist," and "Wipeout." Bellamy received an honorary Oscar the year this was released. The soundtrack is on Polydor.

DISTORTIONS

(Academy, 1987) **D:** Armand Mastroianni **S:** John Goff **P:** Jackelyn Giroux

Piper Laurie stars as an evil aunt in an old mansion who drugs her recently widowed niece (Olivia Hussey). This *Diabolique* copy has double and triple crosses, flashbacks, and a society of lesbians. With Steve Railsback, June Chadwick, Edward Albert, Rita Gam, and Terence Knox.

DISTURBANCE

(1989) **D/P:** Cliff Guest **S:** Laura Radford **P:** Ron Cerasuola

Timothy Greeson stars as a psycho who kills women.

DISTURBED

(Live, 1990) **D/S:** Charles Winkler **P:** Brad Wyman **S:** Emerson Bixby

Dr. Russell (white-haired Malcolm McDowell) runs a mental hospital where he occasionally drugs and rapes female patients. A new patient, Sandy (model Pamela Gidley), is an angry, suicidal ex-model who doesn't like him much ("You lousy, motherfucking, cocksucking prick!"), With the help of a faithful patient (the always good Geoffrey Lewis) he kills her, but she seems to come back and haunt him. McDowell has his moments: an impressive, spinning freak-out scene and a great sex nightmare, where the naked woman on top has no head! Some *Evil Dead*–style tricks (like a hypodermic needle flying through the air) and good cinematography help, but this movie is filled with clichéd nuts (and, of course, a midget) and has an ending that doesn't make sense. Clint Howard plays a crazy, bearded, comic-relief flasher, and the head nurse is played by Amy Irving's mother, Priscilla Pointer (Steven Spielberg's former mother-in-law). Director Charles Winkler, the son of *Rocky* producer Irvin Winkler, made the film in Colorado. The irritating "it's only a movie" ending features the director's voice yelling, "Cut it!"

THE DIVINE ENFORCER

(Prism, 1991) **D/S:** Robert Rundle **S:** Tanya York **P:** Scott Pfeiffer

Here's an all-star classic of bad filmmaking. Father Daniel (Michael Foley), a new LA priest, is also a limb-breaking kickboxer vigilante with psychic powers. A very disturbing Don Stroud (who looks awful) is Otis, a psychotic "vampire" serial killer who drains the blood of his (topless) female victims. Skulls light up and talk to him: "Kill the bitch!" He rants and cries and goes to confession naked. A psychic girl (Carrie Chambers) has visions of Otis (and of sex with her father). Erik Estrada and Jan-Michael Vincent are priests who sit at a dinner table looking bored while being

served by Judy Landers in a miniskirt. Jim Brown and Robert Z'Dar show up (briefly) as drug dealers, and a singer named Hiroko imitates Madonna. The avenging priest says, "Open the gates of Hell, for I am the right hand of God!" It ends with a rap theme. Don't miss this!

THE DIVORCEE

(Nite Flight, 1969) **D/S/P/A:** A. C. Stevens/Steven Apostoloff (*Frustrations*)

Bett Brent (Marsha Jordan), "a free woman," has sexual adventures, talks to her doll (Orphan Annie), and drinks too much. One man whips her with branches in a sauna. She makes another bark like a dog. She confesses all during a psychodrama session at a party that soon becomes an orgy. She ends up clutching her doll, and sobbing for help. One of the actors, Bill Williams, was also in *Tickle Me* and *Rio Lobo*. *The Divorcee* and *Lady Godiva Rides* both star Jordan (who was in *Count Yorga* at around the same time) and feature Liz Renay (*Desperate Living*), plus many of the same cast members.

DIXIE DYNAMITE

(VCI, 1976) **D/S:** Lee Frost **S/P:** Wes Bishop

Jane Anne Johnstone and Kathy McHaley are southern sisters whose moonshiner father is killed by a stupid deputy. Warren Oates is a car racer and their only friend, in this PG rural action movie. Christopher George and R. G. Armstrong costar, but the real surprise is (an unbilled) Steve McQueen. The music is by Duane Eddy, Dorsey Burnette, and the Mike Curb Congregation. From Dimension and the makers of lots of sleazy adult movies (and *The Thing with Two Heads*).

DJANGO

(Magnum, 1965) **D/S:** Sergio Corbucci **S:** Bruno Corbucci, Franco Rossetti **P:** Manola Bolognini   Italy/Spain

Franco Nero stars as the gunfighter Django in a bizarre, violent, comic western that was as influential as *A Fistful of Dollars* (at least in Europe). He keeps a machine gun in a coffin and battles KKK members in a cemetery. A man is forced to eat his own ear. The widescreen film, shot in Eastmancolor, was banned in some countries but spawned sequels and countless imitations and ripoffs. *With Django Came Death* (1967) also stars Nero and features Klaus Kinski.

DJANGO KILL

(VSOM, 1967) **D/S/P:** Giulio Quest **S:** Franco Arcalli   Italy (*Sei Sei Vivi, Spara!*)

In one of the strangest and most violent westerns ever made, Django (Tomas Milian) and two Indians battle two rival groups in a western town.

ADULTS ONLY x   IN EASTMAN COLOR

DO DIVORCEE'S HAVE MORE FUN? ...SEE FOR YOURSELF

THE DIVORCEE

AN A-A PRODUCTION STARRING MARSHA JORDAN

One man is shot with gold bullets, so gang members tear him apart for the gold. A man is roasted on a spit and a talking parrot comments on the action. *Viva Django* (1968) starred Terence Hill.

DJANGO STRIKES AGAIN

(1987) **D/S:** "Ted Archer"/Nello Rossatti **S:** Franco Reggiani **P:** Spartaco Pizzi Italy/Spain/W. Germany (*Djangos Rückkehr*)

More than 20 years after the original film, the name Django still sold tickets (or tapes) in Europe. Franco Nero returned in this late sequel, with Donald Pleasence, William Berger, and the late Chris Connelly.

D.O.A.

(Roach, VCI, 1949) **D:** Rudolph Maté **S:** Russell Rouse, Clarence Greene **P:** Harry M. Popkin

Businessman Edmond O'Brien reports his own murder to the cops at the beginning of this *film noir* classic and tells the rest in flashback. He searches San Francisco and LA for the person who slipped him a slow poison. With Pamela Britton, Neville Brand (in his first film) as a psycho killer, Luther Adler, Beverly Garland, and Lurette Luez (from *Prehistoric Women*). The music is by Dimitri Tiomkin. Most of this United Artists film was shot on location. Maté was the cinematographer of *Vampyr* (1932). Few people realize that *D.O.A.* was based on a 1931 German film, *Der Mann der Seinen Mördet Sucht*, directed by Robert Siodmak, who later specialized in *film noir* in America. The Hal Roach video is colorized.

D.O.A. II

(1969) **D/P:** Eddie Davis **S:** Russell Rouse, Clarence Greene   Australia (*Color Me Dead*)

Nobody seems to remember this R-rated remake filmed in Sidney using the original *D.O.A.* script (uncredited), but it showed up on tape in the US, retitled, after the 1988 remake was released. Tom Tryon stars as Frank Bigelow, with Carolyn Jones and Rick Jason.

D.O.A.

(TVH, 1988) **D:** Rocky Morton, Annabel Jankel **S:** Charles Edward Pogue **P:** Ian Saunder, Laura Ziskin

You know things have changed when Disney (!) makes a remake of a downbeat 40s classic about a dying man. It was written by the guy who wrote the remake of *The Fly* and *Psycho III*. The directors (husband and wife) created *Max Headroom*. Dennis Quaid stars as a professor poisoned in New Orleans. Meg Ryan is the student who reluctantly helps him. There's a nail-gun murder and people get stuck together with Crazy Glue. Charlotte Rampling, Daniel Stern, Jane Kaczmarek, Brion James, and Christopher Neame are in the cast. Look for the 1949 version. It's ten times better (and cheaper to buy). This is actually the fourth version of *D.O.A.* I guess we can expect another version in about 2008.

D.O.A.: A RIGHT OF PASSAGE

(Lightning, 1981) **D/P:** Lech Kowalski

The Sex Pistols are seen playing and self-destructing on their 1978 US tour. There are lots of interviews and footage of other bands playing in England. With the Clash, Dead Boys (with Stiv Bators), X-Ray Specs, Generation X (with Billy Idol), and Sham 69. The most memorable interview is with that fun, soon-to-be-dead couple Nancy Spungen and Sid Vicious, later recreated in *Sid and Nancy*.

THE DOBERMAN GANG

(Fox, 1972) **D:** Byron Chudnow **P:** David Chudnow

Trained Doberman pinscher dogs rob banks in the first of a PG series. Byron Mabe (who directed nudie movies for David F. Friedman), Hal Reed, and Julie Parrish star. *The Daring Dobermans* (1973), also from Dimension, and *The Amazing Dobermans* (1976), with Fred Astaire (!), followed, all by Chudnow.

DR. ALIEN!

(Paramount, 1988) **D/P:** David DeCoteau **S:** Kenneth J. Hall **P:** John Schouweiler
(*I Was a Teenage Sex Mutant*)

A professor (Judy Landers) who is really an alien makes a college-student nerd (Billy Jacobi) irresistible to women, in this pretty ridiculous sex comedy. A snakelike gland grows out of his fore-

head. There are lots of topless scenes and lots of "scream queens." With Troy Donahue, Edy Williams, Olivia Barash, Michelle Bauer, Julie Gray, Elizabeth Kaitan, and Karen Russell. Ginger Lynn Allen, Laura Albert, and Linnea Quigley all show up in a dream sequence.

THE DOCTOR AND THE DEVILS

(Fox, 1985) **D:** Freddie Francis **S:** Ronald Harwood **P:** Jonathan Sanger   UK

The first film directed by former Hammer and Amicus regular Francis since 1975 is historical horror based on a 40s screenplay by poet Dylan Thomas. It's about the 19th-century grave-robbers Burke and Hare and is similar in many ways to *Mania/The Flesh and the Fiends* (1960). It had been performed as a play, and Fritz Lang, then Nicholas Ray, had planned to film it. Mel Brooks was the executive producer (Francis had shot his production *The Elephant Man* in 1980). Timothy Dalton stars as Dr. Rock, and Jonathan Pryce and Stephen Rea are Fallon and Broom, the body-snatchers. The film shows blood-splattered operations and the hopeless squalor of the lower classes. With Twiggy (very good as a prostitute), Julian Sands, Beryl Reid, and Sian Phillips. 20th Century–Fox barely released it in the US.

DOCTOR BLOODBATH = HORROR HOSPITAL

DR. CALIGARI

(Southgate, 1989) **D/S:** Stephan Sayadian **S:** Jerry Stahl **P:** Joseph F. Robertson

Some of the images (a giant tongue, a woman masturbating in front of a TV, people eating sheep's legs, yellow and pink clothes) in this drug-and-dream filled "remake" are inspired, but it all resembles a dreary, pretentious off-Broadway play. A very sexy Laura Albert stars as Mrs. Van Houten, with the scene-stealing late Fox Harris (the film is dedicated to him) and Jennifer Miro (former lead singer of the San Francisco group the Nuns). Madeleine Reynal is Dr. Caligari's granddaughter. The film is different. Sayadian is the guy who made the post-nuke porno movie *Cafe Flesh*. Robertson produced *The Crawling Hand*.

DR. CRIPPEN

(1962) **D:** Robert Lynn **S:** Leigh Vance **P:** John Clein   UK

Donald Pleasence stars as the real Dr. Hawley Harvey Crippen, a London physician charged in 1910 with murdering his wife with an overdose of tranquilizers. During the trial he tells how his unfaithful and alcoholic wife (Coral Browne) was blackmailing him and how he accidentally killed her, then dismembered the body. He and his mistress (Samantha Eggar), disguised as a boy, then tried to escape to Canada. Donald Wolfit is the crown prosecutor. Earlier versions of the story

had been filmed in 1942 and 1957. Nicolas Roeg was the director of photography. Warner released the b/w feature in America.

DOCTOR DEATH, SEEKER OF SOULS

(Prism, 1972) **D/P:** Eddie Saeta **S:** Sal Ponti

Fred (Barry Coe), a guy with thick sideburns, wants his wife, Laura (who died in a car crash), back. He goes to a fake séance. He visits the Society of the Dead, but they're crazy. Then he answers an ad about reincarnation and meets Tanya, an expert (Florence Marley, from *Queen of Blood*). She sends him to Dr. Death (John Considine with a beard), who practices "selective reincarnation." During his stage act he asks for a volunteer, and gray-haired Moe Howard (!!) comes up to confirm that there is a dead body onstage. Moe gives the body the once-over: "Why, certainly, she's dead, all right!" Dr. Death then saws a woman with a horribly burned face in half, and her soul (a dancing ghost in a dress) enters the dead woman. During the rest of the movie Dr. Death fails to bring back Fred's wife, but he is obsessed with his failure and refuses to give up. Considine, later a regular in Robert Altman and Alan Rudolph movies, gives an all-out performance, killing one woman after another with help from his assistant, Thor, and screaming, "Enter that body! Why do you resist these beautiful souls?" When somebody stabs him blood, spurts from the doctor's body into the face of the attacker, who disintegrates, then bursts! A bloody head with guts attached is delivered in a box. *Dr. Death* is a very strange movie. Also in the cast are Cheryl Miller (from the *Daktari* TV series) and West Coast TV horror host Seymour.

DOCTOR DOLITTLE

(Fox, 1967) **D:** Richard Fleischer **S/M:** Leslie Bricusse **P:** Arthur P. Jacobs

Rex Harrison stars in this animal-rights musical fantasy. It lost so much money that 20th Century–Fox was almost ruined. Samantha Eggar costars, with Anthony Newley, Richard Attenborough, Peter Bull, and Geoffrey Holder. It's based on novels by Hugh Lofting. Filmed partially in the British West Indies, it was shot in Todd-AO and was originally 152 minutes long. Jacobs did better with his next animal-theme film, *Planet of the Apes*.

DR. DRACULA

(1981) **D/S:** Paul Aratov **D:** Al Adamson **S:** Cecil Brown, Gary Reathman **P:** Lou Sorkin

A magician/hypnotist/author with a pointy beard (Larry Hankin) is the reincarnation of Svengali. His evil publisher (who is also reincarnated) tells him what to do. This is a reworked version of a feature called *Lucifer's Women* (1975), with the addition of a vampire/psychiatrist (Geoffrey Land). It's a real effort to make sense of it all, but there are some bizarre and interesting things going on. After an exorcism two identical Svengalis discuss life. With John Carradine as a Satanist, Donald Berry as a worried father, Jane Bruntel Cohen as "a pure soul," and Regina Carrol. Anton Lavey (!) was the technical adviser for the Black Mass scenes (complete with animal noises). Sam Sherman provided additional dialogue, and Gary Graver has a cinematography credit. The film has been on the USA Network, and the tape was released in Europe.

DOCTOR FRANKEN

(1980) **D:** Jeff Lieberman, Marvin J. Chomsky
S: Lee Thomas **P:** Robert Berger

Robert Vaughn stars as a modern-day descendant of Dr. Frankenstein in New York City who creates John Doe (Robert Perrault) from body parts. John seeks out various people who have lost limbs and organs, an idea later used in *Body Parts* (1991). This TV series pilot also features David Selby and Teri Garr.

DR. FRANKENSTEIN'S CASTLE OF FREAKS = HOUSE OF FREAKS

DR. GIGGLES

(MCA, 1992) **D/S:** Manny Coto
S: Graeme Whifler **P:** Stuart Besser

Larry Drake (from *Darkman*) stars as the son of a doctor who was lynched for cutting victims' hearts out. He escapes from a mental hospital and returns to his small-town family home. He makes silly remarks and giggles while killing stupid teens. In one absurd, sick flashback a little boy breaks out of his naked mother's corpse (KNB did the bloody FX). Holly Marie Combs (from the TV series *Picket Fences*) costars as a young girl with a heart problem. With Keith Diamond as a cop, Glenn Quinn, Cliff DeYoung, John Schuck, Sara Melson, and Michelle Johnson. The music is by Brian May. This Universal release, based on a Darkhorse comic series, was filmed outside Portland, Oregon.

DR. GORE

(United, 1972) **D/S/P/FX/A:** J. G. "Pat" Patterson
(*The Body Shop*)

Dr. Brandon (Patterson), a plastic surgeon whose wife has died, creates a tall blonde for himself. The operation scenes, with severed body parts, are very gory. Paterson also did the makeup. He makes the new woman's mind "a complete blank," but after endless, clichéd scenes (without dialogue) showing their "perfect" love, she (Jenny Driggers) comes on to his grunting, mute, hunchbacked servant and takes to the road in a bikini in search of more men. The doc ends up in an asylum, where he has flashbacks of this entire hard-to-endure, slow-moving movie. Bill Hicks and the Rainbows play in a club. Patterson (who died in 1974) had worked for Herschell Gordon Lewis, was a Charlotte, North Carolina, TV horror host for a while, and presented live spook shows (which much of this movie resembles). The late William Girdler is credited with the awful, irritating music and sound. In the 80s a very serious intro by Lewis was added to the tape, replacing the title song.

DR. HACKENSTEIN

(Forum, 1987) **D/S:** Richard Clark
P: Renza Mizbani, Megan Barnett

During the 20s a pleasant-seeming but mad young doctor (David Muir) keeps his wife's head alive at his remote home. Two bitchy sisters who drink, a voyeuristic kid brother, and a nice female cousin crash a Model T nearby and end up spending the night. The doc cuts off various body parts from the girls for his wife after they try to seduce him. The cast includes Stacey Travis and Phyllis Diller, who has one comic scene as the mother, reporting the missing kids to the police. Hollywood odd couple Logan Ramsey and his late wife, Anne, are graverobbers. Anne Ramsey died after receiving an Oscar nomination for *Throw Momma from the Train*. Her tongue cancer was so bad that you can't understand her at all in this misfire horror comedy. Nobody seems to mention that her career took off only after part of her tongue was removed. I think her last-minute fame is in the tradition of Rondo Hatton. The high point of comedy here is a deaf maid who uses signs to communicate.

DR. JEKYLL AND MR. HYDE

(Sinister, Video Yesterday, 1920) **P:** Louis Meyer

This rare film, set in contemporary New York City, was made to compete with the John Barrymore version. The whole story is revealed as a nightmare. Star Sheldon Lewis was a villain in silent serials too. It's 40 minutes long, with the original organ score recreated on the tape (from Video Yesterday). Nobody even knows who directed it. An even earlier Universal version (Sinister, 1913) stars King Baggot. The 26-minute tape of that film is missing some footage. Robert Louis Stevenson's famous story had already been filmed many times.

DR. JEKYLL AND MR. HYDE

(Kino, Republic, Goodtimes,1920) **D:** John S. Robertson **S:** Clara S. Bernanger **P:** Adolph Zukor

John Barrymore stars in the classic American silent version. The same year two illegal, unauthorized versions were made, one in the US by Louis Meyer (see above) and one in Germany (*Der Januskopf*) by Murnau, which is lost. This was filmed at Paramount's Long Island studios. Barrymore appears in one scene as a giant spider. With Nita Naldi, Brandon Hurst (as a character borrowed from *The Picture of Dorian Gray*), and Louis Wolheim. The Republic and Kino versions are tinted, and the Kino tape also includes the rare 10-minute 1912 James Cruze version, directed by Lucius Henderson. Various video versions have different organ scores, some different scenes, and various running times (65 minutes is the most complete). Other silent Barrymore films that are available include *Beau Brummel* (1924) and *Don Juan* (1926).

DR. JEKYLL AND MR. HYDE

(Sony, 1973) **D/P:** David Winters
S: Sherman Yellin   UK

Kirk Douglas, in his first dramatic TV role, is a *singing* Jekyll and Hyde! Originally aired on NBC as a Timex special, this was filmed in England and has a solid Brittish cast, including Michael Redgrave, Donald Pleasence, Susan George, Susan Hampshire, and Stanley Holloway. Winters (Weizer) went on to direct *The Last Horror Film* (1981)

with Joe Spinnell, produce *Linda Lovelace for President* (1976), and create AIP (one of the most prolific and trashiest direct-to-video companies).

DR. JEKYLL'S DUNGEON OF DEATH

(Magnum, 1979) **D/P/E/C:** James Wood
S/A: James Mathers

This obscurity turns out to be a martial-arts/horror movie. Always ranting ("Love is painful!") and laughing, the bearded great-grandson of the famous doctor injects people (kidnapped by his mute black assistant, Boris) with a "rage serum," then films them beating each other up. The rest of the mimimal plot concerns a lobotomized sister and an outraged professor. Headlines say, "Citizens in terror!" It's supposed to be the 50s, but everything has a 19th-century look, except for the flared pants and afros! Five fights (two black guys, two women, a black woman and a white woman) in a room take up much of the time. Made in San Francisco with actual black-belt fighters.

DR. LAMB

(VSOM, 1992) **D/A:** Danny Lee
S: Law Kam Fai   Hong Kong

Simon Yam stars as a cabdriver who's a necrophiliac serial killer. Danny Lee is the detective who arrests him. When the killer finally confesses, the last half of the movie is flashbacks. The man kills "bad" women, photographs their naked bodies, then dismembers them. Lee was also in *The Killer*.

DR. MABUSE, THE GAMBLER

(Sinister, 1922) **D/S:** Fritz Lang **S:** Thea von Harbou   Germany (*Dr. Mabuse, der Spieler*)

The first (two-part) silent Mabuse film mirrors the decay of post-WWI German society. It uses some expressionistic and cubist sets and deals with cocaine addiction, occultism, and jazz. Rudolf Klein-Rogge is Dr. Mabuse, a criminal, hypnotist, and master of disguises. He kidnaps a countess and ruins her millionaire husband while the prosecutor, Wenk (Bernhard Goetzke), tries to track him down. The total running time is 165 minutes (the original total time was 242 minutes). It's also available as *The Fatal Passion of Dr. Mabuse*, an 88-minute version. Lang returned to the character in *The Testament of Dr. Mabuse* (1933) and *The Thousand Eyes of Dr. Mabuse* (1960).

DR. MABUSE VS. SCOTLAND YARD

(Sinister, 1963) **D:** Paul Ostramayer
S: Ladislav Foder **P:** Arthur Breymer
W. Germany (*Scotland Yard Jagt Dr. Mabuse*)

The new Dr. Mabuse (the original one transfers his soul to new bodies every once in a while) plans to control mankind with a stolen telepathy ray. The ray gun (disguised as a camera), which turns the film negative while it's on, makes one man into an instant violin virtuoso, a friendly postman into a killer zombie, a hangman hang himself, and a duke steal Princess Diana's (!) jewels. Peter Van Eyck plays Major Turn of Scotland Yard. He lives with his cigar-smoking mystery-fan mother when not traveling back and forth between Munich and London. Klaus Kinski (who was appearing in as many as ten films a year back then) is Joe Right (!), a British inspector who seems pretty dull until Dr. Mabuse turns the ray on him and he becomes a double-agent killer. Since the ray's effects last only 24 hours, Kinski gets to snap out of it a few times. The 5th in a series of 6, this Mabuse film was based on the writings of Bryan Edgar Wallace, son of the famous mystery writer.

DR. MINX

(Continental, Wizard, 1975) **D/S/P:** Hikmet Avedis

Edy Williams (famous for Russ Meyer films and for posing on the beach at Cannes) stars as a rich doctor who becomes involved with a young boy. William Smith, Randy Boone, and Alvy Moore costar. It's a sex comedy with a tragic ending. Marlene Schmidt is in the cast and was also the executive producer for Dimension. The music is by Shorty Rogers.

DOCTOR MORDRID

(Paramount, 1991) **D/P:** Albert and Charles Band **S:** C. Courtney Joyner

Jeffrey Combs stars as a 4th-dimensional fighter in a blue suit and cape who poses as a wealthy New York City man who has a huge apartment with a wall of TV monitors and a raven named Edgar. The animated dinosaur fight in a museum (created by David Allen) is cool, but "the demons from the other side" are glimpsed for only a few seconds. The half-assed film rips off *Dr. Strange* comics, *Highlander*, and *Warlock*. Like many other Band features, it seems aimed at young kids but includes nudity (Julie Michaels) and characters saying stuff like "Don't fuck with me, lady, I'm on a mission for the master!" Yvette Nipar is a police-consultant neighbor, and Brian Thompson is a long-haired bad guy.

DR. OTTO AND THE RIDDLE OF THE GLOOM BEAM

(KnowhutIMean, 1985) **D/S/P:** Don Cherry **S/P:** Coke Sams

Jim Varney plays Dr. Otto and four other roles, including his own aunt, in his first feature. Varney later had some success in his Ernest movies (also by Cherry), but this independently produced mad-doctor spoof remains pretty obscure.

DR. SEX

(SW, 1964) **D/S/P/A:** "Theo Mikacecci"/Ted V. Mikels **S/P:** "Juan Rogero"/Wayne Rogers

Dr. Ludwig von Sex (Victor Sandor), a psychiatrist with a thick Bela Lugosi–type accent, relates five strange cases, for his new book, to his assistants. This bizarre fantasy/sex comedy, in color, has some good-looking naked women, a jazz music score, and flashbacks inside of flashbacks. For some reason, the opening titles are in Spanish. One patient tuns out to be a dog, a psychiatrist turns into a mannequin, and there's a house "haunted" by naked women (including Marsha Jordan) doing household chores. Parts of this tape are scratchy, and a brief part in the middle is missing, but it's still a worthwhile and rare find for

fans of "nudie cutie" movies. Actor Wayne Rogers (from the *M*A*S*H* TV series) also wrote *Astro Zombies* (1968)!

DR. WHO

(CBS/Fox series, 1963–88) UK

This series was a TV phenomenon, outlasting changing times and stars. It debuted on November 23, 1963 (the day after JFK died). It looks even cheaper than the American series *Dark Shadows*, but has a certain charm (and a great theme tune). At least 40 volumes (92 minutes each), featuring Patrick Troughton (1966–70), Jon Pertwee (1970–74), and Tom Baker (1974–81) as the doctor, are available, and more are being released. *The Five Doctors* (Image, 1983) was a 90-minute special on the program's 20th anniversary. *Dr. Who: The Tom Baker Years* (Fox) is another documentary. William Hartnell was the first (1963–66) doctor and Peter Davison was the fifth (1981–84). Peter Cushing played him in two 60s features, and two other doctors followed in the 80s; the show lasted until 1988.

DOCUMENT OF THE DEAD

(Studio Entertainment, 1989) **D/S/P:** Roy Frumkes

Back when Romero was filming his first *Night of the Living Dead* sequel, *Dawn of the Dead*, in a Pittsburgh-area shopping mall, film student Roy Frumkes arrived from New York with a School of Visual Arts crew. He interviewed Romero and filmed him (and Tom Savini) working, cut in scenes from other Romero projects, and got Susan Tyrrell to narrate the finished documentary. For various reasons, Frumkes (who went on to produce and write *Street Trash*) couldn't get *Document of the Dead* distributed or shown in public. Ten years later he went to the set of *Two Evil Eyes*, and the complete results are a must for Romero and Savini fans and those interested in special effects and low-budget film production. In the older footage the very friendly and thoughtful Romero discusses rating problems, says Hawks' *The Thing* was a major influence, and explains that they could shoot *Dawn* in the mall only from 11 P.M. until 7 A.M. Savini is shown applying makeup and doing stunt work. A rare highlight is a *Fantastic Voyage* takeoff advertising Calgon soap that Romero's company made. In the new footage the director wears the same plaid scarf and explains that his yo-yo is "a nicotine substitute." There are also scenes from *Martin* and *Monkey Shines*.

DOG EAT DOG

(Sinister 1963) **D:** Ray Nazarro, Gustav Gavrin, Albert Zugsmith **S:** Robert Hill, Michael Elkins **P:** Ernst Beuback, Carl Szokol   Italy/W. Germany (*Einer Frist den Anderen; La Morte Vestita di Dollari*)

In my opinion, any movie with Jayne Mansfield is worth watching, and one with her and Cameron Mitchell is essential. This grim b/w crime film made in Yugoslavia is not disappointing. It opens with Darlene (Mansfield) writhing in bed as paper money falls on her. She bites and kisses the bills, kicks her legs, then gets up and dances. Meanwhile, her laughing goon husband chases Corbet (Mitchell) in a car, gets out, kicks him in the face

and pushes him over a cliff. Despite all the cash, Darlene, who calls everybody Crackers, says, "Right now, I'd settle for a fresh lipstick and panties in Teaneck, New Jersey!" The manager of the hotel and his girlfriend (whom he calls his sister) find out about the stolen loot. All of them end up on a remote island where a crazy, dying madam lives in her ex-bordello villa with a scheming, bald servant (Pinkas Braun). Everybody plots against everybody else, and they have violent fights. Jayne does the twist. After a few murders, Corbet, who spends the whole movie with a bloody face, cracks up, yelling, "No gas, no money, no gas, no money!" and starts tearing up all the furniture. At the end, only Darlene is left, drowning in the ocean while grabbing at bills.

DOGS OF HELL

(Media, 1983) **D:** Worth Keeler III **S:** Tim McIntyre **P/A:** Earl Owensby   (*Rottweiler*)

Earl Owensby stars as the sheriff in this 3-D movie about vicious killer dogs trained by the army that escape in a mountain retreat. It was the first of several 3-D films from the EO studios in North Carolina. The 3-D FX are pretty good, and other FX were done by Fred Olen Ray.

DOIN' IT: *See* THE FIRST TIME

DOIN' TIME ON PLANET EARTH

(Warner, 1987) **D:** Charles Matthau **S:** Darren Star **P:** Golan/Globus

The 23-year-old son of Walter Matthau directed this PG comedy about an alienated teen (Nicholas Strouse) who thinks he's from another planet. Adam West and Candice Azzara believe him and encourage him to help other aliens return to their home planet. With Hugh O'Brian, Maureen Stapleton, and Roddy McDowall as a minister.

DOLEMITE

(Xenon, 1974) **D/A:** D'Urville Martin **S:** Jerry Jones **P/A:** Rudy Ray Moore

Rudy Ray Moore's first film was a phenomenon in inner-city theaters. The flashback-filled movie (from Dimension) had to be cut to avoid an X rating. Dolemite (Moore), a club owner who usually talks in rhyme (and likes to call people things like "rat-soup-eatin' honky muthafucka!") is set up by his evil, drug-dealing rival Willie Green (Martin). Say what? He gets out of jail with the help of whorehouse madam Queen Bee (Lady Reed) and recruits an all-ho kung-fu "army" to seek revenge and clear his name. Right on! Dolemite raps two funny stories, one about the Titanic and one about the monkey and the lion. Moore's influence on many current rappers and comedians is obvious. Can ya dig it? Rudy's fight double is obvious, and mike shadows are visible, but you won't care. Lady Reed toured with Moore and recorded her own Black Angel party records. James Ingram sings.

DOLLMAN

(Paramount, 1991) **D:** Albert Pyun **S:** Chris Roghair **P:** Cathy Gesuald

Tim Thomerson (from the *Trancers* movies) is blond Brick Bardo, a futuristic *Dirty Harry* clone who takes a space ship to the Bronx. On Earth he and his ship are tiny, so most of the movie is filled with laughable sub–Bert I. Gordon optical FX. A little kid brings him home, but he has to fight an ugly talking head who blows people up. With Kamala Lopez, Nicholas Guest, and Jackie Earl Haley (*Damnation Alley*) as a killer punk. I fell asleep. The opening hostage scene is the best part. Pyun used to work for Cannon, and his best was probably *The Sword and the Sorcerer* (1982).

DOLLMAN VS. DEMONIC TOYS

(Paramount, 1993) **D/P:** Charles Band
S: Craig Hamann

Here's a new low in sequels, using scenes from *Demonic Toys*, *Dollman*, and *Bad Channels* as time-killing narrated flashbacks. Tiny alien cop Tim Thomerson teams up with Ginger (Melissa Behr), an incredibly shrunken blonde in a polka-dot bikini. The main new part features the demonic baby doll (who looks and sounds like Uncle Fester on speed) saying things like "Split him a new asshole!" The doll ties up the tiny Ginger in a bed and threatens to rape her and also has a flashback! Also with Tracy Scoggins, Full Moon's resident dwarf, Phil Fondacaro, and songs by Quiet Riot.

DOLLS

(Vestron, 1986) **D:** Stuart Gordon
S: Ed Naha **P:** Brian Yuzna

An elderly couple (Guy Rolfe and Hillary Mason) judge unwanted visitors to their remote London mansion. When obnoxious teens and a hateful couple arrive, dolls attack them. Most of them obviously deserve to die. Carrie Lorraine is the innocent little girl who dreams of a giant killer teddy bear. Carolyn Purdy-Gordon is the very wicked stepmother. There's some stop-motion animation. It was the second feature by Gordon but wasn't released until after *From Beyond*. The killer-doll idea was later reused for Band's *Puppetmaster* series.

DOLLY DEAREST

(Vidmark, 1991) **D/S:** Maria Lease **P:** Daniel Cady

Sam Bottoms, Denise Crosby, and their kids move to Mexico to reopen a doll factory. Spirits released by an archaeologist (Rip Torn) possess the dolls. A girl doll comes alive and controls their cute little girl. The child has a demon voice, and the killer dolls have scary faces and can run. The father is really dense, and my fave line, spoken by Crosby is "I'm not losing my daughter to a goddamn 900-year-old goat head!" It's a lot better than *Child's Play III*. The director was the wife of producer Cady (an adults-only vet). Lee Frost was the production manager. Pierre David was an executive producer.

DOMO ARIGATO

(1972) **D/S/P:** Arch Oboler Japan

It seems impossible to see, but this G-rated boy-meets-girl movie was shot in 3-D Spacevision

(like Oboler's *The Bubble*). It was filmed in Japan and stars Bonnie Sher, whose parents ran Sherpix, the company that released *The Stewardesses*. It's said to have some of the finest 3-D effects ever filmed.

DON QUIXOTE

(1955) **D/S/A:** Orson Welles **P:** Oscar Dansigers, Alessandro Tasca, Francisco Lara Spain

Welles started this film in 1955 and worked on it for many years, but only 40 minutes were finished. In 1992 Jesse Franco did postproduction and editing and added new dubbing by Spanish actors. The results were shown at film festivals. Welles relates the famous tale to little Patty McCormack (*The Bad Seed*). Francisco Reiguera stars, with Akim Tamiroff as Sancho Panza. Franco also did second-unit work on Welles' *Chimes at Midnight* (1966) and *Treasure Island* (unfinished).

DON'T BOTHER TO KNOCK

(1952) **D:** Roy Ward Baker
S: Daniel Taradash **P:** Julian Blaustein

Here's Marilyn Monroe in an early dramatic starring role as a psychotic babysitter in a NYC hotel. It's based on a novel by Charlotte Armstrong. Richard Widmark costars with Anne Bancroft (in her film debut), Jeanne Cagney, Donna Corcoran, Elisha Cook Jr., and Jim Backus. 20th Century–Fox had put Monroe under contract (for the second time) in 1950 and was steadily enlarging her roles. A 1991 Fox-TV remake was called *The Sitter*.

DON'T GO IN THE WOODS (ALONE)

(Vestron, 1979) **D/P:** James Bryan **S:** Garth Eliasson **P:** Roberto and Suzette Gomez

In Utah a survivalist mountain man in a Viking costume rips people's arms off. He uses a machete, hooks, or an axe. There's lots of gore and Buck Carradine in a very cheap production. It was banned on tape in England. The end theme is "The Teddy Bear's Picnic."

DON'T GO NEAR THE PARK

(Direct, 1979) **D/S/P:** Lawrence D. Foldes **S:** Linwood Chase (*Nightstalker; Curse of the Living Dead*)

A brother and sister are cursed by their hag mother "12,000 years ago" (at Bronson Canyon). Then, "16 years ago," the brother still looks young because he kills kids (by ripping open their chests). He rents a room from, hypnotizes, then marries Linnea Quigley (who has a shower scene). They have a baby girl named Bondie who grows up and runs away when she (Tamara Taylor) turns 16. Bondie has a magic amulet, so she can blow up a van full of rapists, and she ends up at a ghost town with other runaways and a strange woman with an eye patch (her ancient cave aunt!). Dad plans to sacrifice Bondie to break the curse. This absurd movie has many flashbacks, nightmares, gore, zombies, laser-ray eyes, transformation scenes, and pot-smoking. All this, and Aldo Ray appears as a writer studying "the Griffith Park curse." The acting, lighting, FX,

and editing are all awful. It was "based on actual occurrences"! Caution: Do not watch this one while intoxicated!

DON'T GO TO SLEEP

(Unicorn, 1982) **D:** Richard Lang
S/A: Ned Wynn **P:** Richard Lang

A girl killed in a car crash returns from the grave to take her family with her. With Ruth Gordon, Dennis Weaver, Valerie Harper, and Robert Webber. This ABC-TV movie, which copies *Poltergeist*, was written by the son of actor Keenan Wynn.

DON'T LOOK BACK

(Warner, 1967) **D:** D.A. Pennebaker
P: Albert Grossman, Don Court

Bob Dylan is seen in his 24-year-old-prime, during his 1965 British tour, in a fascinating b/w 16mm. documentary. People try to interview him, and behind-the-scenes plans and confrontations are shown. The performance footage is excellent, and there's a great early "rock video" for "Subterranean Homesick Blues." With Joan Baez, Alan Price, Donovan, and Allen Ginsberg. Dylan had the film withdrawn during the mid 70s. Another Dylan documentary, *Eat the Document* (covering his 1966 European tour), was also directed by Pennebaker. It was shot as a TV special but was seen only in underground movie theaters in the early 70s.

DON'T LOOK IN THE ATTIC

(Mogul, 1981) **D/S/P:** Charles Austin
P: Michael Peyers Italy

Jean-Pierre Aumont stars in this story of a cursed house in Turin where people are after an inheritance. A killer's face changes. It's letterboxed.

DON'T MAKE WAVES

(1967) **D:** Alexander Mackendrick **S:** Ira Wallace, George Kirgo **P:** John Calley, Martin Ransohoff

Tony Curtis is a con man having an affair with Claudia Cardinale by the California shore. The last film by the director of *Sweet Smell of Success* does a good job of making fun of LA life-styles. Sharon Tate plays Malibu, a surfer and skydiver, and the cast also includes Robert Webber, Joanna Barnes, Mort Sahl, Jim Backus (as himself), and Edgar Bergen as a female astrologer. The Byrds do the title song, which was available on an MGM soundtrack recording.

DON'T MESS WITH MY SISTER!

(VidAmerica, 1984) **D/S/P/E:** Meir Zarchi
(*American Junkyard*)

Steve (Joe Perce) works for his brother-in-law at a car parts junkyard, lives on West 101st Street in Manhattan, and takes accounting classes at night school. After a surprise birthday party thrown by his wife, he becomes involved with the paid entertainment, Anika, a beautiful but intellectual blond belly dancer (Jeannine LeMay). Trying to defend her one evening leads to murder. His wife finds out about the affair and runs to her Italian goon brothers, and Steve gets beaten up a lot. Zarchi directed the controversial *I Spit on Your Grave*, but this is closer to a New York Scorsese movie, especially *After Hours*. It's very well made, with good unknown local actors, and has surprising plot twists, humor, violence, and an ironic non-ending. It was released in 1988.

DON'T OPEN 'TIL CHRISTMAS

(Vestron, 1983) **D/A:** Edmund Purdom **S:** Derek Ford **P:** Dick Randall, Steve Minasian   UK

Somebody in London is killing department store Santas. Turns out it's a masked psycho newspaper reporter who saw his mom killed by a Santa when he was a kid. Star Alan Lake was once the real-life husband of Diana Dors. With Edmund Purdom as a Scotland Yard inspector, Belinda Mayne, and Caroline Munro, who has a small part as a rock singer. This movie has topless scenes (Pat Astley). Santas are dismembered, strangled, burned, and slashed, and one Santa is castrated in a public toilet.

DON'T PANIC: *See* SATAN'S BLOOD

DON'T TELL DADDY

(Fries, 1972) **D:** Franz Antel **S:** Hans Billian, Greta Lowinger   W. Germany/Swiss (*Blutjüng und Liebeshungrig*; *Naughty Nymphs*; *Spanish Fly*; *Passion Pill Swingers*)

In a typical 70s European sex comedy, two experienced sisters try to get their virgin sister (Sybil Danning) on the pill. When aphrodisiac sleeping pills are given to patients at a hospital, everybody (except two gay guys) chases the nurses. The dumbest characters are Italian. Danning (who isn't even billed on the video box) has a nude swim and a nude run through the woods. Meanwhile, an aunt has sex outdoors a lot. Eva Garden costars.

DON'T TORTURE THE DUCKLING

(Nightmare, 1972) **D/S:** Lucio Fulci **S:** Roberto Gianviti, Gianfranco Clerici **P:** Renato Laboni   Italy (*Non si Sevizia un Paperino*; *The Long Night of Exorcism*)

Young boys are found mutilated and killed in a Sicilian mountain village. Many locals are suspects. With Tomas Milian as a reporter, Barbara Bouchet as a hooker, Florinda Bolkan as a Gypsy witch, and Irene Papas. The movie shows eyeless children and decapitated animals.

DON'T WORRY, WE'LL THINK OF A TITLE

(1966) **D:** Harmon Jones **S:** John Hart **S/P/A:** Morey Amsterdam

This plotless b/w spy comedy (barely) released by UA is filled with Ernie Kovacs–type visual gags, slapstick, backwards and slo-mo scenes, and even Chinese subtitles. Morey Amsterdam is mistaken for a defecting cosmonaut, or something like that. Mr. Big is played by a midget.

Rose Marie costars, and Richard Deacon and Carl Reiner show up too (*The Dick Van Dyke Show* ended the year this was made). Whichever TV stars and comedians happened to be around at the time show up in brief gag scenes. In one scene that borders on subversive, Moe Howard has a totally serious role as a lawyer! Also with January Jones as Magda, Joey Adams, Percy Helton, Nick Adams, Steve Allen, Milton Berle, Forrest Tucker, Maxie Rosenbloom, Cliff Arquette, and Arlene Hunter. Irene Ryan even shows up as Granny in the Clampett truck.

DOOM ASYLUM

(Academy, 1987) **D/S:** Richard Friedman **S:** Rick Marx **P:** Steve Menkin

A couple drinking and driving while listening to a bad version of "The House of the Rising Sun" crash. Badly burned and thought to be dead, the guy kills the autopsy doctor and "ten years later" the rotting, lovesick killer makes dumb Freddy-type wisecracks while killing teens (usually off-screen) in an abandoned asylum. Made in New Jersey, this horror/comedy has a few laughs and interesting characters. Tina and the Tots, a female band in leather skirts, play tape loop/scream/noise music in the old building. Tina is Ruth Collins. Patty Mullen is the best band member, though. She's a vicious fighter, and has an incredible laugh (and a topless scene). Both of them were in *Playboy* or *Penthouse*, a fact pointed out on the video box. The contrasting victims include a shrink's daughter, a baseball-card-collecting nerd, and an indecisive guy. The movie must have been less than an hour long before they added repeated slo-mo shots of the black band member's romantic fantasy and scenes from Tod Slaughter movies on a TV. Slaughter was a unique, old-fashioned British horror star of the 30s and 40s. Some of his movies are out on Rhino tapes, but if you want a good sampler this movie includes long clips (the best scenes) from five of his movies!

DO OR DIE

(RCA/Columbia, 1990) **D/S:** Andy Sidaris **P:** Arlene Sidaris

Pat Morita is the bald crime lord trying to take over the world (he even has a sex scene with Carolyn Liu). In a plot like *The Most Dangerous Game*, he hires teams of assassins to chase former centerfolds Dona Spier (in her *fifth* Sidaris movie) and Roberta Vasquez. The chase continues with helicopters, dune buggies, boats, and bikes from Hawaii through Texas, Las Vegas, and the Louisiana Bayou and ends with ninja fights in the woods. Erik Estrada (also in *Guns*) is the hero. There are fake comic Cajuns, lots of changing-clothes scenes, hot-tub scenes, sex in the water, and some *huge* tits. Bruce Penhall costars, with Cynthia Brimhall, Ava Cadall, and Stephanie Schick.

THE DOORS

(LIVE, 1991) **D:** Oliver Stone **S:** J. Randall Johnson **P:** Sasha Harari

Stone, responding to understandable fascination with the 60s, made this fantasy bio in between the more serious *Born on the Fourth of July* and *JFK*. Unlike most rock bios, it deals with politics, change, and drugs (in a positive way). The music (original and recreated) sounds great, and the visual ideas are good (some of the ILM FX are similar to those in Ken Russell's *Altered States*). Even the unrealistic concert footage is impressive. Val Kilmer is okay as the late Jim Morrison, but the facts are twisted and the actors picked to play the band (Kyle MacLachlan, Kevin Dillon, and Frank Whaley) just seem ridiculous, as does Meg Ryan as a girlfriend. Some of the best scenes involve Kathleen Quinlan as a "witch" who does a daring nude scene and Wes Studi as an Indian spirit. It's also fun to see actors trying to play people like Warhol (Crispin Glover!), Edie Sedgwick (Jennifer Rubin), Ed Sullivan (Will Jordan), and Nico (Kristina Fulton). With Michael Madsen, Mimi Rogers, Billy Idol, Paul Williams, William Kunstler, Eric Burden, Annie McEnroe, Bill Graham (also a producer), Charlie Spradling, Debi Mazur, and Delia Sheppard. The Pioneer laser version includes interviews and behind-the-scenes footage. Real Doors videos are around, including *The Doors: Soft Parade, Dance on Fire*, and *Live at the Hollywood Bowl* (all from MCA). Ron Howard was an executive producer.

THE DOORS TO SILENCE

(VSOM, 1991) **D/S:** "H. Simon Kittay"/ Lucio Fulci **P:** "Joe D'Amato"/Aristede Massaccesi   Italy (*Le Porte del Silenzio*)

John Savage is a man in Louisiana who discovers that he's actually dead (*Carnival of Souls* style) from a car crash. It was shot on location in the swamp.

DOPEMANIA

(Rhino, 1987)

Newsreel footage, film clips, school films, and a silent-serial chapter (*The Weed of Death*) are combined in a fascinating 60-minute look at how America exploited, lied to, or tried to educate people about drugs. It was compiled by Johnny Legend. Rhino's *Guide to Safe Sex* is a companion release.

DOPPELGANGER

(Fox, 1992) **D/S:** Avi Nesher **S:** Donald Borchers

Pat Morita and Dona Spier in *Do or Die*

Drew Barrymore stars as Holly Goodis, who may have killed her mother in New York City. She goes to LA and becomes the roommate of a struggling writer (George Newborn), has sex with him, then says she didn't. Barrymore is crucified in a nightmare sequence and is seen naked in a blood shower. Newborn and Leslie Hope (as his girlfriend) are very good, and Drew is better than expected. The mysterious double plot and the surprise (!) ending (complete with bloody KNB FX monsters) almost make this worth seeing just to find out how stupid movies can be. Postproduction tampering can't explain it all away, either. Dennis Christopher is pretty bad here, and the mostly wasted guest stars are Dan Shor, Sally Kellerman, George Maharis, Nicole Hansen, and Luana Anders. The ITC production premiered (cut) on the Sci-Fi Channel. The director also made *Time Bomb*.

THE DORM THAT DRIPPED BLOOD

(Media, 1981) **D/S/P:** Jeff Obrow **D/S:** Stephen Carpenter **S:** Stacy Giachino   (*Pranks; Death Dorm*)

This forgettable *Friday the 13th* copy was made by UCLA students for $90,000. It's a teen slasher movie about the last students in a condemned 7-story dorm. Daphne Zuniga appears in a small role, having her head crushed under a car. A Chris Young soundtrack was issued on Citadel. Obrow and Carpenter got better and followed this with *The Power* and *The Kindred*.

DOUBLE AGENT 73

(Strand, 1974) **D/S/P:** Doris Wishman

Chesty Morgan stars in a follow-up to *Deadly Weapons*. This one is even worse but is more unique and fascinating in a depressing, unpleasant kind of way. A camera implanted in her (73-inch!) chest will explode if she doesn't do a spy job. All through the movie she undresses, lifts her breasts, and a loud, exaggerated shutter click is heard as she photographs somebody. She looks miserable and has to wear ugly platform shoes. There are no sex scenes, despite the presence of porno star Harry Reems. Chesty does oil herself, though. Joe Bob introduces some copies of the tape. Chesty was also in *Fellini's Casanova* (1976), in a scene with Donald Sutherland.

DOUBLE BLAST

(Vidmark, 1993) **D:** Tim Springs **S:** Paul Joseph Gulino **P:** David Hunter   Philippines

Two kid kickboxers go after two crooks who have kidnapped a professor (Linda Blair) and are trying to grab a treasure. With Dale "Apollo" Cook as the kids' father, Ron Hall, Robert Z'Dar, and Joe Estevez. This PG-rated comedy copies the popular *Three Ninjas* movies.

DOUBLE-CROSSED

(HBO, 1991) **D/S:** Roger Young **P:** Albert J. Saltzer

Dennis Hopper stars as Barry Seal, a Louisiana drug-smuggling pilot who turns informer against Medellín drug cartel members for the DEA. With Robert Carradine as the agent, Edward Edwards as Oliver North, Richard Jenkins, and Adrienne Barbeau as Seal's wife. This HBO movie is based on a true story and does a good job of exposing the Reagan/Bush support for the Contras in Nicaragua.

DOUBLE DOOR

(1934) **D:** Charles Vidor **S:** Gladys Lehman, Jack Cunningham

This rare old-dark-house mystery, based on a Broadway play, is set in a 5th Avenue mansion complete with a hidden torture chamber. Mary Morris is a wealthy old woman who threatens to put her sister (Ann Revere) back into the secret chamber, and she also ruins the lives of relatives she doesn't like. The two female leads were also in the play. With Kent Taylor and Evelyn Venable. From Paramount.

DOUBLE DRAGON

(MCA, 1994) **D:** Jim Yukich **S:** Michael Davis, Peter Gould **P:** Alan Schecter

Orphan brother heros (Hawaiian-born part-Asian Mark Dacascos and Scott Wolf) have half of an ancient Chinese talisman medallion. This PG-13 action/fantasy/comedy is based on a series of video games set in post-nuke, partially underwater 21st-century Hollywood. With Robert Patrick as the bearded villain, Julia Nickson as their mentor and guardian, and Alyssa Milano (with short hair) as a gang leader. Also with Kristina Malandro Wagner, Al Leong, and bits with Vanna White, George Hamilton, and Gilbert Gottfried. The Jay Ferguson soundtrack (Milan) features various rock artists. Yukich was known for his Phil Collins and Whitney Houston videos.

DOUBLE EXPOSURE

(Vestron, 1982) **D/S/P:** Byron Hellman (*The Photographer*)

Models are being killed, and a photographer (Michael Callan), who dreams of the killings, is the prime suspect. With James Stacy (who lost an arm and leg in a 1973 motorcycle crash) as his brother, a former stuntman. The rest of the cast is impressive, considering the low budget: Pamela Hensley as a cop, Joanna Pettet, Cleavon Little, Seymour Cassel, Robert Tessier, Sally Kirkland, Terry Moore, Misty Rowe, Victoria Jackson (later on *Saturday Night Live*), Kathy Shower, and Jeana Tomasino from *Playboy*. The Crown International release also features some mud-wrestling.

DOUBLE EXPOSURE

(Prism, 1993) **D/S:** Claudia Hoover **S:** Christine Colfer, Bridget Hoffman **P:** Joanne Watkins

Ian Buchanan is a businessman who hires a PI (Ron Perlman) to kill the lover of his wife (Jennifer Gatti). With Dedee Pfeiffer.

DOUBLE FACE

(Unicorn, 1969) **D/S:** "Robert Hampto"/ Riccardo Freda **S:** Paul Hengge   Italy/W. Germany (*La Doppa Faccia; Lis and Helen*)

A wealthy industrialist (Klaus Kinski, who also narrates) learns that his wife (Margaret Lee) is having a secret lesbian affair. She dies when a bomb goes off in her Jaguar, and he becomes involved with a mysterious blonde (Christiane Kruger) who takes him to swinging LSD parties and shows him a porno movie that seems to costar his late wife. Lucio Fulci worked on the screenplay. The cast also includes Sidney Chaplin. Most of the nudity was removed for TV screenings in the US and has not been restored to the video. In the mid-70s new sex footage was added in Europe (featuring Jesse Franco star Alice Arno), and the film was rereleased as *Chaleur et Jouissance*. Based on an Edgar Wallace novel filmed previously in England as *The Diamond Man* (1924) and *The Malpas Mystery* (1960), it was the last Wallace adaptation for Kinski, who had played memorable supporting roles in many made in the early 60s.

DOUBLE IMPACT

(RCA, 1991) **D/S:** Sheldon Lettich **S/P/A:** Jean-Claude Van Damme **P:** Ashok Amritraj

Van Damme stars as twins whose parents were shot. The mean smuggler brother with a cigar was raised in Hong Kong, and the strong-but-naive one was raised in Hollywood by a bald Geoffrey Lewis. They hate each other but team up in Hong Kong for revenge. They fight evil, drug-dealing gangsters and fight each other over a blonde (Alonna Shaw). With Bolo Yeung as a powerful bodyguard with a scar, Corey Everson, Julie Strain, and Simon Rhee. This movie has too many explosions, guns, and slow-motion scenes and not enough martial arts. It ends with a rap song and was made for Michael Douglas's production company.

DOUBLE JEOPARDY

(Fox, 1993) **D:** Lawrence Schiller **S:** Craig Tepper

Bruce Boxleitner is a married Salt Lake City private-school headmaster. An ex-lover (Rachel Ward) hires his attorney wife (Sela Ward), seduces him, and sets him up for a murder. Sally Kirkland plays a police detective. It was made for Showtime.

THE DOUBLE McGUFFIN

(1977) **D/S/P:** Joe Camp

Michael Gerard and Vincent Spano are teens who discover an assassination plot, in this PG movie. Orson Welles explains the Hitchcock-derived title, and Elke Sommer, Ernest Borgnine, George Kennedy, and Ed "Too Tall" Jones appear.

DOUBLE OBSESSION

(Columbia, 1992) **D/S:** Eduardo Montes

Margaux Hemingway is a psycho killer who kidnaps Beth Fisher. She's seen from 1980, as a college student, to the present day. With Frederic Forrest, Maryam D'Abo as her college roommate, and Scott Valentine.

DOUBLE-O KID

(Prism, 1992) **D/S:** Duncan McLachlan **S:** Andrea Buck **P:** Steven Paul

Corey Feldman (who also narrates) becomes a teen spy for the CIA on a courier mission in LA in this forgettable PG-13 comic adventure. The villains, led by Brigitte Nielsen, who uses various disguises, are after a computer key-card. Feldman falls for Nicole Eggert. With Wallace Shawn, John Rhys-Davies, Anne Francis, Basil Hoffman, and Karen Black as the mother. The director also made *Scavengers* (1988).

DOUBLE REVENGE

(Republic, 1988) **D:** Armand Mastroianni **S:** Brian Tobin, John Sharkey **P:** T. J. Castronolo, John S. Curran

Survivors of a bungled bank robbery seek revenge. Joe Dallesandro (20 years after his underground/Warhol days) stars, with Theresa Saldana, Leigh McCloskey, Richard Rush, and Nancy Everhard.

DOUBLE TARGET

(VSOM, 1987) **D/E:** "Vincent Dawn"/Bruno Mattei **S:** Claudio Fragasso **P:** Franco Guadenza   Italy

Former *Ator*-series star Miles O'Keeffe is in this Vietnam adventure movie, with busy Donald Pleasence, Bo Svenson, Alan Collins, and Kristine Erlandsson.

DOUBLE THREAT

(AIP, 1992) **D/S:** David S. Prior **P:** Kimberly Casey

Sally Kirkland stars as an aging movie star who becomes violent when her new leading man (Andrew Stevens) has an affair with her body double (Sherrie Rose). This "erotic thriller," presented by David Winters, was filmed in Mobile, Alabama. It features movie in-jokes and Kirkland fondling her large silicone breasts and masturbating while watching Stevens pump up. Richard Lynch costars as a cop. With Anthony Franciosa, Chick Vennera, and Ted Prior. Available in R and unrated versions.

DOUBLE TROUBLE

(RCA, 1992) **D:** Joe Paragon **S:** Jeffrey Kerns, Kurt Wimmer **P:** Brad Krevoy, Steve Stabler

This comedy stars the Barbarian Brothers (Peter and David Paul) as identical twins Peter and David. One is a cop, the other is a long-lost playboy and thief. Both have shaggy hair. They're teamed up by the police chief (James Doohan) to expose an LA smuggling ring led by Roddy McDowall. With Bill Mumy (!) as a hitman, Collin Berensen as an FBI agent, Steve Kanaly, Troy Donahue, and David Carradine.

Renfield in the Spanish version of *Dracula*

DOUBLE VISION

(Republic, 1992) **D:** Robert Knights **S:** Tony Grisoni **P:** Steve Walsh   UK/Canada

Kim Cattrall stars as an American who goes to London, where she has nightmares and flashbacks concerning her sister drowning as a little girl. Meanwhile, her missing identical twin (also Cattrall) is the mistress of Christopher Lee and is also having an affair with an Indian cabdriver. When the wild sister really is killed, the quiet, nice one impersonates her to capture the killer. This slow-moving mystery is based on a Mary Higgins Clark novel, *The Anastasia Syndrome*.

DOWN THE DRAIN

(RCA, 1989) **D:** Robert C. Hughes **S:** Moche Hadar **P:** Ronnie Hadar

This heist comedy stars Andrew Stevens as a lawyer who plans to rob a bank. With Teri Copley (who has a memorable nude scene, possibly using a double), Don Stroud as a villain, Stevens' real-life mom Stella, John Matuszak, Joseph Campanella, Ken Forree, Buck Flowers, Pedro Gonzalez-Gonzalez, Benny "the Jet" Urquidez, and the former Beaver, Jerry Mathers.

DOWN TO EARTH

(Columbia, 1947) **D:** Alexander Hall **S/P:** Don Hartman **S:** Edwin Blum

Rita Hayworth stars as Terpsichore, the muse of song and dance, who comes down to Earth because a producer (Larry Parks) is planning a jazz musical about her and the other eight muses. This color musical from Columbia is a semi-sequel to their *Here Comes Mr. Jordan* (1941) and features James Gleason and Edward Everett Horton repeating their roles from the earlier fantasy hit. Also with Roland Culver as Mr. Jordan, George Macready, and Adele Jergens. It was later remade as *Xanadu* (1980).

DRACULA

(MCA, 1931) **D:** George Melford **S:** Garrett Ford, Dudley Murphy **P:** Carl Laemmle Jr.

In the days of early talkies some films were shot several times with different actors using the same script for foreign markets (with silent films, only the intertitles had needed to be changed). This *Dracula* was shot in Spanish during 22 nights at Universal. Melford used the same sets as the Lugosi version but redressed and relit them. He incorporated some unused footage shot by Tod Browning (even a long shot of Lugosi), but everything else is his. This *Dracula* is familiar but also very different, 29 minutes longer (104 minutes), and occasionally better. When Dracula (Carlos Villarias) strangles Renfield ("Si, Maestro! No, Maestro! Por favór!") he throws him off the high stairs. When Dr. Van Helsing pounds in a very long stake, the vampire groans a lot. Eva (Lucy) was played by a teenage Lupita Tovar, who had also

been in Medford's Spanish-language version of *The Cat Creeps*. (She later married agent Paul Kohner and became the mother of Susan Kohner.) The actors are from Spain, Mexico, and other countries, so the accents vary quite a bit. The film was still playing in Spanish-language theaters in the 50s. A complete print was discovered in Cuba and was released on tape (with an intro by Tovar) in 1992. "Yo no bebo . . . vino."

DRACULA BLOWS HIS COOL

(Private Screenings, 1979) **D/S:** Carlo Ombra **S:** Grunbach and Rosenthal   W. Germany
(*Graf Dracula Beisst Jetzt in Oberbayern*)

A men's-magazine photographer and his models go to a Bavarian castle. Gianni Garko stars as both the hero and the vampire count. It's a comedy, inspired by *Love at First Bite*, but with lots of nudity.

DRACULA CINEMATIC SCRAPBOOK

(Rhino, 1991) **D/S:** Ted Newsom

This is one of a series of trailer compilations with (rather blandly read) historical narration plus select scenes. Only a collector who has everything could complain about the contents. There's every Universal and Hammer vampire trailer, plus scenes from the original *Nosferatu* and more. My faves are the *Mark of the Vampire* trailer in which Lugosi speaks to the audience, a scene from *Uncle Was a Vampire* with Christopher Lee, and trailers from *Blacula*, *The Seven Brothers Meet Dracula*, the *Billy the Kid/Jesse James* horror double bill, and *One More Time*, with Christopher Lee. There are just too many vampire movies for any compilation to attempt to be complete (the tape goes only to the early 70s, a wise move), but I did miss Mexican vampires and *The Vampire* (1957). *Dracula: Fact or Fiction* (Worldvision, 1993) is a 40-minute TV program with film clips and interviews, and *Dracula in the Movies* (Goodtimes, 1992) is mostly trailers.

DRACULA EXOTICA

(TVX, 1980) **D:** Warren Evans **P:** Ken Schwartz

Jamie Gillis (from *Dracula Sucks*) returns as the count in his second porno vampire movie. For some reason this one is set in the future (1990) and Dracula is in New York City, where Samantha Fox is an FBI agent who thinks he's a Communist. She becomes a vampire on a train, and so does Vanessa Del Rio, so there's blood with the sex again. With Erik Edwards and Bobby Astyr.

DRACULA RISING

(New Horizons, 1992) **D:** Fred Gallo **S:** Rodman Flender, Daniella Purcell **P:** Roger Corman

Christopher Atkins is extremely bland as Vlad the vampire in this slow, romantic horror movie (with funny love songs). Long flashbacks reveal that he was a monk during the plague. He was tempted by a woman (Stacy Travis) who was burned as a witch. She's reincarnated as an LA art restorer (Travis again, of course). Doug Wert is the bad former monk/vampire who used to whip him. It's nice to see Travis (*Hardware*) in something else, but a body double was used for her underwater sex scene.

DRACULA SUCKS

(Unicorn, 1978) **D/S:** Philip Marshak
S/P: Daryl Marshak   (*Lust at First Bite*)

This porno vampire movie used to be pretty easy to find (Media put out a cut, soft-core version), so a lot of people must have seen it. It's set in an asylum and is really pretty horrifying. Jamie Gillis is pretty good as a red-eyed Dracula, and Reggie Nalder (usually in "real" movies) plays a dried-up-looking Dr. Van Helsing. The mixture of mostly bad acting, comedy, sex, blood, and semen doesn't really work. Even in the "soft" version you see the late John Holmes' penis being bitten, and somebody plays Hitler. The all-star porno cast includes Annette Haven as Mina, Serena as Lucy, Seka, Kay Parker, Pat Manning, Nancy Hoffman, John Leslie, Paul Thomas, and Bill Margold. A theater was busted for showing the R-rated version in Edmonton, Alberta, Canada. Gillis returned as a vampire in *Dracula Exotica* (1980) and *Princess of the Night* (1990).

DRACULA'S VIRGIN LOVERS = DRACULA'S GREAT LOVE

DRACULA'S WIDOW

(HBO, 1988) **D/S:** Christopher Coppola
S: Kathryn Ann Thomas **P:** Stephen Traxler

A few years before Francis Ford Coppola made his *Dracula*, two of his nephews made vampire movies (*Vampire's Kiss* was the other one). A young guy (Lenny Van Dohlen) runs a wax museum on Hollywood Boulevard and spends his spare time watching an 8mm. print of the silent *Nosferatu*. Sylvia Kristel (the original star of the *Emmanuelle* films) plays the vampire lady (with a black wig) who is delivered (just like in *Abbott and Costello Meet Frankenstein*), wakes, and bites him to use as a servant: "Who's your husband?" "Dracula, you fool!" Usually she just kills people, becoming an ugly-faced monster ripping bodies apart, and sometimes she becomes a bat. They go to a Satanic Mass (which looks too much like some gay S&M ritual), and she slaughters everybody. A cop (Josef Sommer, who also narrates), his dumb assistant (Marc Coppola), and an old man named Helsing hunt for the killer. The film has very somber music, some gore, a strange mechanical bat, and too many trendy blue and red lights. With George Stover. It was made for Dino De Laurentiis just before his company went bust.

DRACULA: THE BLOODLINE CONTINUES

(All Seasons, 1972) **D:** Leon Klimovsky
S: Lazarus Kaplan **P:** José Pérez Giner   Spain
(*La Saga de los Dracula*; *Saga of Dracula*)

A pregnant woman and her new blond-hunk husband go to Transylvania to visit her grandfather, Vlad Tepes. The whole family turn out to be vampires who drink blood in wine glasses, and the baby is to be the family heir. The woman has dreams of an outrageous bat face, but they put a little too much Vaseline on the camera lens. The vampire women always take their tops off before they bite somebody. The baby vampire drinks blood from his mom (a scene duplicated in *Grave of the Vampire*, an American movie from the same year). The most memorable character is a mutant hunchback boy with one huge eye (!) locked in the attic. Klimovsky is known for making movies starring Paul Naschy. The year 1972 was a big one for vampire movies (over a dozen).

DRACULA THE DIRTY OLD MAN

(SW, 1969) **D/S/P:** William Edwards

Alucard (Vince Kelly) is a bearded vampire living in a cave (Bronson Canyon). He goes through walls and can become a bat (on a wire), but he needs help, so he hypnotizes a reporter (Bill Whitton) who becomes Irving Jeckleman, a werewolf. The same awful mask and three-clawed paws were used in *The Mummy and the Curse of the Jackal*! He kidnaps women, and the vampire ties them up in his cave and magically zaps their clothes off. It's a crude movie with some surprising gore and a necrophilia scene, made worse by dubbed-in "funny" Yiddish accents. The reporter's red-haired girlfriend (Ann Hollis) runs all over the cave naked, but pants are left on during sex scenes. It was presented by Whit Boyd.

DRACULA VS. FRANKENSTEIN: *See* ASSIGNMENT TERROR

DRAGNET

(MCA, 1987) **D/S:** Tom Mankiewicz **S/A:** Dan Aykroyd
S: Alan Zweibel **P:** David Permut, Robert K. Weiss

Aykroyd doing an impersonation of Jack Webb as Sergeant Joe Friday led to this comedy about a pagan cult led by an evangelist (Christopher Plummer). He wears a goat head, virgins are sacrificed, and there's a giant snake. I'd like it better if it weren't also a spoof of the real *Dragnet*. Aykroyd is supposed to be Friday's cop nephew. With Tom Hanks, Alexandra Paul, Jack O'Halloran, Elizabeth Ashley, Dabney Coleman, and Harry Morgan as Captain Bill Gannon. From Universal. MCA released the soundtrack.

DRAGON AGAINST VAMPIRE

(Saturn, 1985) **D:** Lionel Leung   Hong Kong

Some bored Brits partially ruined this one with smart-ass dubbing, calling characters Elton, Martin, or Fanny. It's a comic horror movie that starts out with three Chinese stooges as starving graverobbers. They eat a dog. When a character is scared by a vampire he wets his pants (as a person would do in real life but seldom in Western movies). After the two dumber ones are dead the hero battles a vampire with the help of an old teacher in an underground cave who practices Shaolin sorcery. A restaurant owner is decapitated and his daughter is possessed, talking with a man's voice and drinking chicken blood. A Buddhist symbol (the one that the swastika was copied from) is protection against vampires. The vampire sometimes behaves and looks like the European model but has his secrets tattooed on his back. It's too bad the print is so dark. You can hardly see the dream sequences. The soundtrack is all "borrowed" Tangerine Dream music.

DRAGON AND THE COBRA: *See* FIST OF FEAR, TOUCH OF DEATH

DRAGONARD

(Warner, 1987) **D:** Gerald Kikoine **S:** Rick Marx **S/P:** Harry Alan Towers   S. Africa

This has the same setting as Russ Meyer's *Blacksnake*. Patric Warburton stars as a slave in the 18th-century Caribbean. Eartha Kitt (who was also in *Uncle Tom's Cabin*) runs a brothel. Oliver Reed is the Scottish Captain Shanks. Dragonard is a whipping post. Kikoine made dozens of French porno movies and later did the incredible *Edge of Sanity*. With Claudia Udy and Annabel Schofield. *Master of Dragonard Hill* was the sequel.

DRAGON FIGHT

(WB, 1990) **D/A:** Warren Stevens
S: Budd Lewis **P:** Kenneth Dalton

This stinker, filmed mostly in the Arizona desert, debuted on HBO. Paul Coufus (who looks like a mutant Harrison Ford) is a tortured corporate-backed fighter who doesn't want to fight. His opponent, Robert Z'Dar (in silly-looking medieval armor) will kill anybody and has "a magic lady" (Fawna MacLaren, *Playboy*'s 35th-anniversary Playmate) around to heal him. Meanwhile, Michael Pare, James Hong, and Joe Cortese somehow watch all that happens (not much) on TV monitors in an office. George "Buck" Flower provides narration, even after his character dies! Also with Alexa Hamilton (from *Death Spa*), Charles Napier as a ranger, and Aki Leong. The only good part is the guitar soundtrack.

DRAGON FIRE

(New Horizons, 1993) **D:** Rick Jacobson
S: Bentley Gray, Kevin Ingram **P:** Mike Elliot

This film has lots of good fights and good fighters. Dominic Labanca is the (*Blade Runner*–look) 21st-century LA martial-arts hero whose brother's death must be avenged. Battles to the death take place in "the Pit," for money, and frequent trips to a bar showcase some good nude dancers. The best character is Eddie (Harold Hazledine), a laughing, long-haired hippie/con-man/fighter. Eddie's blonde stripper sister (Pamela Rund) proves that they're still using silicone in the future. Michael Blanks (brother of Billy) has an echo voice and is supposed to be the scariest fighter. Space footage is from Corman's *Battle from Beyond the Stars*. The video box copies the ad art for the Bruce Lee biopic *Dragon* very closely.

DRAGONFLY: *See* ONE SUMMER LOVE

DRAGONFLY SQUADRON

(Sony, 1953) **D:** Lesley Selander **S/P:** John Champion

Bet you didn't know Monogram ever made a 3-D movie. The company (called Allied Artists by then) didn't bother to release it in 3-D, even though they had made it that way. John Hodiak stars in this Korean War story, with Barbara Britton, Bruce Bennett, Gerald Mohr, Harry Lauter, Benson Fong, Fess Parker, Chuck Connors, and Pamela Duncan.

DRAGON INN

(Long Shore, 1992) **D:** Raymond Lee **S/P:** Tsui Hark **S:** Carbon Cheung, Xiao Wu   Hong Kong

This historical action fantasy, set during the Ming dynasty, features a swordfighting couple (Tony Leung Fai, from *The Lover*, and Brigitte Lin/Ching Hsia) who have to protect two royal children from the eunuch villains who have seized power. Donnie Yen is an evil acrobatic eunuch, and Maggie Cheung runs the inn in the desert where much of the action takes place. It's filled with secret passages, and pastries made with human flesh are served there. This is a remake of *Dragon Gate Inn* (1966).

DRAGONS FOREVER

(1986) **D/A:** Samo Hung   Hong Kong

In this all-star film, a gangster uses a chemical factory to process illegal drugs. A widow (Pauline Yeung) whose lake is being polluted hires a lawyer (Jackie Chan) to sue. He falls for her cousin (Deanie Yip), and eventually Chan, Hung and their crazy friend (Yuen Baio) are battling the gangsters. The male stars of this action comedy were all members of the Peking Opera school as children.

DRAGON: THE BRUCE LEE STORY

(MCA, 1993) **D/S:** Rob Cohen **S:** Edward Khmara, John Raffo **P:** Raffaella De Laurentiis

This biopic is very good, but it sanitizes Bruce Lee's life and totally leaves out his childhood acting career. Jason Scott ("no relation") Lee (from Hawaii) stars as the legendary Lee. The film was inspired by his widow Linda Lee's book *The Bruce Lee Story*. Lauren Holly plays blond Linda. The couple faced racial prejudice, and Lee is seen having nightmares about a huge demon. One good early-60s fight scene is backed by "Green Onions." Lee is shown on the TV series *The Green Hornet* (Van Williams plays the director). The cast also includes Robert Wagner as a producer, Nancy Kwan, Michael Learned, Paul Mantee and a *Breakfast at Tiffany's* clip with Mickey Rooney as a stereotyped "oriental." John Badham was the executive producer of this PG-13 Universal film, shot partially in Hong Kong and Macao. The soundtrack, released by MCA, is by Randy Edelman. Brandon Lee (portrayed as a little kid here) died just before this was released. The laserdisc includes audio commentary by the director and Lee's widow.

DRAGON WORLD

(Paramount, 1994) **D:** Ted Nicolaou **S:** Suzanne Glazener Naha **P:** Charles Band

Sam Mackenzie stars as an American orphan who grows up in a castle in Scotland. He befriends a (Dave Allen–animated) friendly dragon as a kid and later has to defend him from money-hungry

bad guys as a teen. Brittany Powell costars with John Calvin and Andrew Kier. The PG-rated fantasy was shot in Romania.

DRAGSTRIP GIRL

(1994) **D:** Mary Lambert **S:** Jerome Gary **P:** Lou Arkoff, Debra Hill

Natasha Gregson Wagner (the daughter of Natalie Wood) falls for Mark Dacascos, who steals cars. This Showtime remake also features Traci Lords and Anthony Edwards. The original 1957 AIP movie is available from RCA/Columbia, but this is more a copy of *West Side Story*.

DREAM A LITTLE DREAM

(Live, 1989) **D:** Marc Rocco **S:** Daniel Jay Franklin **P:** D. E. Eisenberg

Corey Feldman and Jason Robards Jr. somehow switch bodies. Meredith Salinger is the object of the teen's affection. With Corey Haim, Piper Laurie, Harry Dean Stanton, Alex Rocco, Victoria Jackson, and Susan Blakely. The music for this PG-13 comedy is by John Williams. *Dream a Little Dream 2* (Columbia, 1995) with the two Coreys followed.

DREAMANIAC

(Wizard, 1986) **D/P:** David DeCoteau **S:** Helen Robinson

Frat teens are killed by a succubus who makes Freddy Krueger–inspired wisecracks. With Kim McKamy and Thomas Burns. This was the first non-porno feature by a director who went on to make many direct-to-video releases.

DREAMCHILD

(Warner, 1985) **D:** Gavin Millar **S:** Dennis Potter **P:** Rick McCallum, Kenith Trodd

Coral Browne (Mrs. Vincent Price, in her last role) stars as Alice Liddell Hargreaves, the inspiration and model for *Alice in Wonderland*. She's 80 years old and is in NYC in 1932 for the Lewis Carroll centennial celebration. Troubling flashbacks and memories of her odd childhood are brought on by a pushy reporter (Peter Gallagher). It's a great idea and is very well done. Ian Holm is a tormented, stuttering Lewis Carroll. Jim Henson created the dream sequences, which include *Alice in Wonderland* characters. With Amelia Shankley as little Alice, Jane Asher as her mother, and Imogene Boorman.

Jason Scott Lee as Bruce Lee, in *Dragon*.

DREAM DEMON

(Warner, 1988) **D/S:** Harvey Cokliss **S:** Christopher Wicking **P:** Jonathan Olsberg, Nik Powell, Peter Watson-Wood, Timothy Woolford   UK

Jemma Redgrave is an English socialite with narcoleptic dreams about people dying. Then they really do. Kathleen Wilhoite is her American punk friend. There are lots of "is it real?" fantasy FX and music by Bill Nelson (from BeBop Deluxe) in this movie, which seems to have been inspired by *Nightmare on Elm Street*. Tim Spall and Jimmy Nail costar. The US release wasn't until 1993.

DREAMER OF OZ: THE L. FRANK BAUM STORY

(1990) **D:** Jack Bender **S:** Richard Matheson **P:** Erv Zavada

John Ritter is the struggling writer L. Frank Baum. The true story of his attempt to support his family is interspersed with fantasy scenes from his Oz books. With Annette O'Toole, Rue McClanahan, Courtney Barilla as Dorothy, and Charles Haid as the Cowardly Lion. This was a TV movie.

DREAM LOVER

(MGM, 1986) **D/P:** Alan J. Pakula **S/P:** Jon Boorstein

Kristy McNichol is treated by a New York dream researcher (Ben Masters) in an attempt to stop her recurring nightmare. With Gayle Hunnicutt, Paul Shenar, Matthew Penn, and Joseph Culp. It was shot in London by Sven Nykvist. *Dream Lover* was also the name of a 1986 Chow Yun Fat movie made in Hong Kong.

THE DREAM MACHINE

(Live, 1989) **D:** Lyman Dayton **S:** Eric Hendershot **P:** Fenton Terry, Michael Wergler

Corey Haim has a dead body in the trunk of his Porsche turbo car, and the killer stalks him on a college campus. With Evan Richards and Jeremy Slate. It's PG.

DREAM NO EVIL

(Star Classics, 1971) **D/S/P:** John Hayes **P:** Daniel Cady   (*Now I Lay Me Down to Die*)

Brooke Mills (*The Big Doll House*), who dives off 30-foot towers as part of a traveling revival show, wants to find her father (Edmond O'Brien). He's dead, but he rises from an embalming table and resumes being a loud, hard-drinking, squeeze-box-playing Irishman. She starts killing people (with a knife, an axe, a scythe). The story is held together by constant overkill narration. Some parts are like a play, but it's pretty creepy. Marc Lawrence is a pimp/undertaker, Michael Pataki is a theatrical faith-healer, and Arthur Franz is a shrink who explains things in a *Psycho*-inspired ending. It's from Boxoffice International. Hayes made *Garden of the Dead* and *Grave of the Vampire* next.

DREAMSCAPE

(HBO, 1984) **D/S:** Joseph Ruben **S:** Chuck Russell, David Loughery **P:** Bruce Cohn Curtis

Telepathic Dennis Quaid is part of an experiment to project psychics into people's dreams. It's really part of a plot to assassinate the president (Eddie Albert). This movie has some great stop-motion FX in nightmare segments. The president has nuclear-war nightmares, there's a dragon, and zombies are on a subway. With Kate Capshaw, Max von Sydow, Christopher Plummer, and George Wendt. The Maurice Jarre soundtrack is on Sonic Atmospheres. For the record, this was the first film rated PG-13.

DREAMSLAYER: *See* BLOOD SONG

DRESSED FOR DEATH = STRAIGHT ON TILL MORNING

THE DRIFTER

(MGM, 1988) **D/S/A:** Larry Brand **P:** Ken Stein

Fashion designer Kim Delaney is married to Timothy Bottoms but has a one-night stand at a motel with a mysterious hitchhiker (Miles O'Keeffe). People in her apartment building are killed, several psychos are suspects, and she takes her clothes off. It was inspired by *Fatal Attraction.* Roger Corman was the executive producer of this Concorde release.

DRIVE, HE SAID

(1970) **D/S/P:** Jack Nicholson **S:** Jeremy Larner **P:** Steve Blauner

Jack Nicholson directs for the first time. The script was based on Larner's novel about college roommates in the early 60s but was updated to the very different late 60s. William Tepper is an Ohio college basketball player, and Michael Margotta is a student activist and draft dodger. With Bruce Dern (also in *Psych-Out* and *The Trip,* which Nicholson wrote) as a basketball coach, Karen Black (*Easy Rider*) as his wife, Robert Towne, Henry Jaglom, June Fairchild, and Mike Warren (later a *Hill Street Blues* regular). Some sex scenes and surprising male locker-room nudity resulted in an X rating, later changed to an R. It's from BBS (the same year as *Five Easy Pieces*), also with Black.

DRIVE-IN

(RCA, 1976) **D:** Rod Amateau **S:** Bob Peete **P:** Tamara Asseyev, Alex Rose

A Texas drive-in is the setting as star Lisa Lemole leaves her gangster boyfriend for a nice guy (Glenn Morshower) and other subplots unfold. The fun part of this comedy is the lengthy scenes from (the fictional) movie hit *Disaster '76,* featuring an earthquake, a tidal wave, and ship and planes disasters. Also with Trey Wilson and Ashley Cox from *Playboy.* Allthough little remembered today, this low budget PG Columbia feature

made over four million dollars in North American rentals. *Drive-In Massacre* was released the same year. The director's next was *Seniors.*

DRIVE-IN FOLLIES

(Audubon, 1989)

Radley Metzger himself compiled and narrates this compilation of more than 30 trailers for most of his own classy European sex movies, various Audubon adults-only releases from Europe with stars like Elke Sommer, Essy Persson, and Agnes Laurent, and several from Japan. Some trailers are letterboxed, and one is in French. You won't find a lot of these elsewhere. My faves are *Vibration, I Spit on Your Grave, Lickerish Quartet,* and *The Artful Penetration of Barbara.*

DRIVE-IN MADNESS!

(Imagine Inc., 1987) **D/S/P:** Tim Ferrante

Most of the trailers here are from the dregs of the exploitation business, but they're rare and outrageous. A lot of them were made by producer Sam Sherman for Hemisphere (the Bloodorama Shock Festival is incredible!) or his own Independent International (*Girls for Rent, Satan's Sadists, Horror of the Blood Monsters,* with the voice of Brother Theodore). Others are from Charles Band's Empire (*From Beyond, Psychos in Love*). Some favorites are the *Queen of Blood/Bloodbath* double bill, *The Green Slime,* and *Vampyres.* You also get on-camera interviews with James Karen, Sherman, Forrest J. Ackerman, Bobbie Bresee, Linnea Quigley, George Romero and Tom Savini, and John Russo and Russell Steiner from *Night of the Living Dead* (plus its original trailer). A 38-minute version is called *Screen Scaries* (Simitar).

THE DRIVER'S SEAT

(Embassy, 1973) **D:** Giuseppe Patroni Griffi **S:** Muriel Spark **P:** Franco Rossellini   Italy (*Identikit; Psychotic*)

Elizabeth Taylor stars in her weirdest movie as Lisa, a suicidal woman who goes to Rome and has a series of encounters. It's probably the only feature where Taylor is tied up and raped. Rumor has it that Liz tried to keep it from circulation, but it's out on tape now under several names. With Ian Bannen, Mona Washbourne, and Andy Warhol. The screenwriter wrote *The Prime of Miss Jean Brodie.* The cinematographer was Vittorio Storaro. Liz's next stop was the USSR, where she starred in *The Blue Bird* (1976).

DRIVING FORCE

(Academy, 1988) **D:** A. J. Prowse **S:** Patrick Edgeworth **P:** Howard Grigsby, Rod Confessor   Australia

In the post-nuke near future, rival tow-truck drivers cause fatal pileups to get business. With Americans Sam Jones, Catherine Bach, Don Swayze (who leads the Black Knights), and Billy Blanks.

Drive-in

DRIVING ME CRAZY

(RCA/Columbia, 1992) **D/S:** Jon Turtletaub **S:** David Tausik, John London **P:** Brad Kevoy, Steven Stabler   (*Trabi Goes to Hollywood*)

Comic Thomas Gottschalk stars as an eccentric East German inventor trying to sell his turnip-fueled Trabant car (Trabi for short). He goes to LA, where gangsters (Dom DeLuise and James Tolkan) steal it. He hires Billy Dee Williams to get it back. With Michelle Johnson, Steve Kanaly, George Kennedy, Milton Berle, Celeste Yarnall, Richard Moll, Starr Andreef, Tiny Lester Jr., and Morton Downey Jr. as a spiritualist.

DROP DEAD FRED

(IVE, 1991) **D:** Ate De Jong **S:** Carlos Davis, Anthony Fingleton **P:** Paul Webster

Phoebe Cates, divorced and living with her mom, is visited by her imaginary childhood friend (British comedian Rik Mayall, from the TV series *The Young Ones*). The fantasy character helps her deal with life again. With Marsha Mason, Carrie Fisher, Tim Matheson, and (an uncredited) Bridget Fonda. The director of this PG-13 comedy also made six features in Holland and *Highway to Hell.*

DROP DEAD, GORGEOUS

(1991) **D:** Paul Lynch **S:** Thomas Baum **P:** Julian Marks

Somebody is trying to kill a model (Jennifer Rubin). With Peter Outerbridge, Sally Kellerman, and Michael Ironside. This was a cable-TV movie.

DROP ZONE

(Paramount, 1994) **D:** John Badham **S:** Peter Barsocchini **P:** D. J. Caruso, Wallis Nicita

Wesley Snipes (back in planes after *Passenger 57*) stars as a U.S. marshal who goes undercover to capture drug cartel members who escape from a 747 with parachutes in Florida. The major action scenes involve freefalling. With Gary Busey (also in the skydiving movie *Point Break*) as the main bad guy and Yancy Butler (*Hard Target*) as a skydiving ex-con who teaches Snipes to parachute. Also with Claire Stansfield, Grace Zabriskie, Lyle Secor, Malcolm-Jamal Warner, Michael Jeter, Corin Nemec, and Luca Bercovici.

DRUGSTORE COWBOY

(IVE, 1989) **D/S:** Gus Van Sant **S:** Daniel Yost **P:** Nick Wechsler, Karen Murphy

Matt Dillon, his wife (Kelly Lynch), and his best friend (James LeGros) and his girlfriend (Heather Graham) rob pharmacies to get drugs in the early 70s, in Portland, Oregon. With James Remar as a cop, Grace Zabriske, and William Burroughs as Tom, an addicted priest. It's an excellent, believable movie showing the junkie life-style. The good oldies soundtrack (on Novus) is perfect and features a great use of "Psychotic Reaction." Van Sant's first feature was *Mala Noche*, and he followed this one with *My Own Private Idaho*.

DRUM

(Vestron, 1976) **D:** Steve Carver **S:** Norman Wexler **P:** Ralph Serpe

Ken Norton returns in a 20-years-later sequel to *Mandingo* (1975). Warren Oates buys him from bordello madam Isela Vega. With Pam Grier, Brenda Sykes (also in *Mandingo*), Paula Kelly as a lesbian maid, Cheryl "Rainbeaux" Smith, Fiona Lewis, Roger Mosley, and Royal Dano. Norton and Yaphet Kotto are hung upside down naked and whipped, but they revolt at the end. Original director Burt Kennedy was replaced by the maker of the exploitation hits *The Arena* and *Big Bad Mama*. United Artists released the Dino De Laurentiis production after Paramount refused to. Originally given an X rating (thanks to nudity, whipping, and castration), it was later heavily edited.

DRUMS OF FU MANCHU

(Stokey, 1940) **D:** William Witney, John English **S:** Franklyn Adreon, Morgan B. Cox, Ronald Davidson

Henry Brandon is the bald Dr. Fu Manchu in LA's Chinatown, and William Royle is Sir Nayland Smith in this 15-chapter Republic serial. Most serials were named after heroes. This was one of the few where the villain isn't even captured or killed. There are some imaginative torture scenes and some pretty scary-looking henchmen. Even the titles are great: "Satan's Surgeon," "Revolt!" and "The Pendulum of Doom," for example. With Gloria Franklin as Fah Lo Suee, Philip Ahn, Luana Walters, and Dwight Frye. Fu Manchu later returned as a TV series from Republic (1955–56) and a series of 60s features starring Christopher Lee.

DRUMS OF JEOPARDY

(Sinister, 1931) **D:** George B. Seitz **S:** Florence Ryerson

This rare independent production from the old Tiffany studios is a remake of a 1923 silent movie and is based on a novel of the same name. Warner Oland plays a Czarist Russian scientist named Boris Karlov, which, believe it or not, was also the character's name in the original and was not used to capitalize on the then new star Boris Karloff. Oland is first seen looking scary in a typically atmospheric mad-lab setting, but we soon discover he's a good guy—until his daughter commits suicide over a playboy prince and his mind snaps. He vows to destroy the whole Petrov family. After the

Revolution, Karlov and his assistant (Mischa Auer) follow the Petrov sons to New York and, using disguises, spies, and the small drums on a cursed necklace as a warning, proceed to kill them. This film has no music and has awkwardly dubbed sound effects, but Oland is great as the cool, relentless, ingenious killer, and it's fun to see the serial-style perils, like the secret room filling up with water, and speeded-up fight scenes.

DRUMS OF TAHITI

(1953) **D:** William Castle **S:** Douglas Hayes, Robert Ekert **P:** Sam Katzman

Dennis O'Keefe (also in the 3-D *The Diamond Wizard*) stars with Patricia Medina. The 3-D highlights include a volcano and a hurricane. From Columbia.

DRUMS O' VOODOO

(Sinister, 1934) **D:** Arthur Hoerl **S/A:** J. Augustus Smith **P:** Louis Weiss   (*She Devil*)

An all-black cast stars in this rare feature, adapted from a short-lived Broadway play, *Louisiana*, by J. Augustus Smith and featuring the stage performers. Actress and singer Laura Bowman stars as old Aunt Hagar, a voodoo priestess who puts a spell on a pimp who "works for Satan" and runs a juke joint. The evil one is struck by lightning and dies in quicksand. With Lionel Monages and Edna Barr. The 70-minute Sinister print is full of splices.

DRUNKEN MASTER II

(VSOM, 1994) **D:** Lau Kar-leung **D/A:** Jackie Chan **S:** Tseng King-Sang, Yun Kai-chi   Hong Kong (*Tsui Kun II*)

After years of modern-day gangster hits, Hong Kong started a revival of the kind of comic period kung-fu movies that were so popular in the 70s. Chan stars as Wong Fei-hong in a more elaborate "sequel" to his 1979 hit, complete with early-20th-century British bad guys, comedy, and a plot about smuggling ginseng (with a jade seal hidden inside). Action highlights are a fight on a train and an encounter with a large gang with axes. With Ti Lung as the father, singer Anita Mui as the stepmother, and Ho Sung Pak. Chan replaced the original director.

du-BEAT-e-o

(Fox Hills, 1984) **D/S/P:** Alan Sachs

In 1979 Joan Jett (and some substitute Runaways) starred in a movie, *We're All Crazy Now*. It was never released, but here is where the footage ended up. The late Ray Sharkey (who says he was a junkie at the time) stars (and narrates) as an in-your-face director in hock to gangsters. He holes up in a studio to finish a feature starring Joan Jett. He forces his editor (Derf Scratch, from Fear) to work around the clock at gunpoint while he has sex with an innocent blonde (Nora Gaye). He rants over the Jett concert footage, so you can't hear the songs. That's the whole plot. You also get lots of real fast editing, Gary Panter art, *Mondo* death footage, WWII propaganda, puking, gore, Joanna Went performance art (presented as a nightmare), and onscreen songs by Tex and the

Horseheads and the Mentors. One song is by Rainbeaux Smith (seen in the old footage). This thing is nuts! It played in theaters!

DUDES

(IVE, 1987) **D:** Penelope Spheeris **S:** J. Randal Johnson **P:** Herb Jaffe, Miguel Tejada-Flores

NYC punk rockers on the way to LA battle redneck killers in the Utah desert. With Jon Cryer dressed as a cowboy, Daniel Roebuck dressed as an Indian, Catherine Mary Stewart, Lee Ving as a biker, Pamela Gidley, and Flea from the Red Hot Chili Peppers. The heavy metal soundtrack is on MCA.

THE DUMMY TALKS

(Sinister, 1943) **D:** Oswald Mitchell **S:** Michael Barringer **P:** Wallace Orton   UK

Jack Warner stars in this murder mystery, with stage variety acts taking up most of the running time. The best part is the séance at the end, where a dummy lying on a table (actually a midget) gets up and walks out the door.

DUNE

(MCA, 1984) **D/S:** David Lynch **S:** Eric Bergren, Christopher De Vore **P:** Raffaella De Laurentiis

Giant sandworms produce a mind-expanding spice that prolongs life, and good and evil families battle for control of a desert planet. Jodorowsky started directing the epic novel by Frank Herbert in 1975, but the production was closed down. Ridley Scott was going to make it too. Lynch eventually made it, and the audience scratched their heads (or stayed away). The 140-minute PG-13 film was first shown in 70mm. Many more people saw it on network TV in 1989. The two-part TV version, by "Allan Smithee" (it was disowned by the director), has 50 extra minutes, is missing 10 from the theatrical version, and has different narration. More viewers will discover the drug-induced industrial look of the confusing epic in days to come. It was shot in Mexico by Freddie Francis (who had also shot *The Elephant Man*). The music is by Toto (and Eno and Daniel Lanois), and Carlo Rambaldi was in charge of FX. Kenneth McMillan is memorable as floating, pus-filled Baron Harkonnen, who pops his zits. This character (and others) were actually marketed as plastic dolls! It's easy to forget the cast, but Kyle MacLachlan stars (in his film debut), and some of the others are Sean Young, Jack Nance, Virginia Madsen, Patrick Stewart, Francesca Annis (from Polanski's *Macbeth*), Brad Dourif, José Ferrer, Dean Stockwell, Max von Sydow, Linda Hunt, Freddie Jones, Richard Jordan, Silvana Mangano, Sian Phillips, Jurgen Prochnow, Paul Smith, Sting, and Everett McGill.

DUNE WARRIORS

(RCA/Columbia, 1991) **D/P:** Cirio H. Santiago **S:** T. C. McKelvey **P:** Christopher R. Santiago

David Carradine stars as the wise, older wandering warrior Michael in yet another *Road Warrior* copy (from the Philippines), set in "New California, 2040 A.D." Luke Askew is William, leader of the heavily armed bad guys who want the water that the peaceful desert villagers have. Jillian McWhirter (nice but determined village woman) and Isabel Lopez (Oriental warrior) show up for brief topless and nude scenes. Characters fight with swords and/or guns, and lots of things blow up. I wondered why the director would bother to hire dozens of dwarfs just to have them run through one unimportant scene, then realized the scene was simply taken from his earlier *Stryker* (1983). The music score is awful, and Carradine's martial-arts fight scenes must have been edited by a blind man. It's a Roger Corman/Concorde production.

THE DUNGEONMASTER

(Lightning, 1984) **D/P:** Charles Band **D:** Rose Marie Turko, John Buechler, David Allen, Stephen Ford, Peter Manoogian, Ted Nicolaou **S:** "Allen Actor" (*Ragewar*)

An evil wizard wanders the galaxy and holds a girl hostage. For some reason, seven directors were assigned to various segments, making it a monumental mess. The Dungeons and Dragons game was the plot inspiration. With Jeffrey Byron, Leslie Wing, Richard Moll, the band W.A.S.P., and some David Allen animation.

DUNGEON OF TERROR = CAGED VIRGINS

DUPLICATES

(Paramount, 1992) **D:** Steven Sandor **S:** Andrew Neiderman

Gregory Harrison and Kim Griest see duplicates of their lost son and his uncle. Cicely Tyson and Kevin McCarthy are the scientists behind the confusing plot. This USA Network movie is by the makers of *Pin*.

DUST DEVIL

(Paramount, 1992) **D/S:** Richard Stanley **P:** Joanne Sellar

Chelsea Field is a South African woman taking an aimless journey in her Volkswagen over desert highways after leaving her husband. She picks up a supernatural killer (Robert Burke) "from the other side of the mirror." He photographs and has sex with his female victims, removes fingers, paints walls with blood, and nails a heart to a door. This serious, atmospheric horror movie has well-done gore, sex, some surreal scenes, an effective feeling of dread, and excellent music by Simon Boswell. Zakes Mokae (*The Serpent and the Rainbow*) is a cop suffering from nightmares (inside of nightmares), and Marianne Sagebrecht has a small role as a coroner. This 87-minute US version of the UK production was redubbed and has a new voiceover. Miramax did a really good job. The British theatrical version was 108 minutes, and the film was originally 125 minutes. It was shot in Namibia and South Africa. Stanley (from South Africa) also made *Hardware* and is planning a Dr. Moreau remake.

DUSTY AND SWEETS McGEE

(1971) **D/S/P:** Floyd Mutrux

This pseudo-documentary look at a straight LA couple who become heroin addicts includes interviews with dealers, junkies, and hustlers. The couple commit suicide at the end. Billy Gray (from the *Father Knows Best* (!) TV series) shows up as a dealer. The Warner soundtrack consists of good oldies and Van Morrison's "Into the Mystic."

THE DYBBUK

(Ergo, 1937) **D:** Michael Waszynsky **S/P:** Alter Kacyzne, Andrzej Marek   Poland

Here's a real rarity, featuring the first screen exorcism. Shot in Yiddish in Warsaw, it was rediscoved and restored to 122 minutes, and new subtitles were added, for screenings in 1989. It's adapted from a play that was based on a Yiddish legend. A bride (Lilli Liliana) is possessed by the soul of a young man who secretly dabbled in Cabala (a mystical form of Judaism) before he died.

Dune

DYING TRUTH

(Cornerstone, 1984) **D:** John Hough **S:** Martin Woth **P:** Roy Skeggs   UK (*A Distant Scream*)

A photographer (David Carradine) takes his married lover (Stephanie Beacham) to an old British seaside hotel. She sees a mysterious old man (also Carradine) lurking around. He can predict what will happen and turns out to be a convicted killer from the future. Carradine even gets to talk to himself. This interesting, moody Hammer TV movie has a twist ending.

DYNAMITE BROTHERS

(1973) **D:** Al Adamson **S:** John D'Armato **P:** Jim Rein, Marvin Lagunoff   (*Stud Brown*)

Former football star Timothy Brown is hero Stud Brown, who teams up with a Chinese kung-fu expert (James Hong) to fight a drug lord (Alan Tang) in LA. Carol Speed is a mute. The Charles Earland jazz score was released on Prestige. Cinemation made it but went bankrupt, so it was released by Independent International. They actually used ad lines like "He has what every woman wants—he packs the biggest rod in town!"

DYNAMITE CHICKEN

(Monterey, 1969) **D/S/P:** Ernest Pintoff

Comedy material by the Ace Trucking Company and Richard Pryor is edited around a collage of footage of media and rock people. The very dated feature includes frustrating, brief glimpses (or just the sounds) of Jimi Hendrix, Muddy Waters, John and Yoko, Allen Ginsberg, The Velvet Underground, and Lenny Bruce, mixed with some animation, newsreel footage, and lots of naked women (including some bondage) scenes. Leonard Cohen recites a poem. It was rereleased in the 80s to capitalize on Pryor's fame.

DYNASTY

(Best, 1976) **D:** Mei Chung Chang **S:** Liu Kuo Hioung **P:** Frank Wong   Hong Kong (*Sora Tobu Jujiken*)

Mike Findlay (*Snuff*) was the 3-D supervisor of this bloody martial-arts hit, in "Real-a-Rama and Super 3-D!" and originally with quadraphonic sound. Bobby Ming stars and battles an evil warlord. Everything protruded from the screen: horses, swords, arrows, spears, and decapitated heads. The TV version is very cut and will make you wish you had caught it in a theater. It was shot in Taiwan.

THE EAGLE HAS LANDED

(1977) **D:** John Sturges **S:** Tom Mankiewicz
P: David Niven Jr., Jack Winer   UK

Nazis plot to kidnap Churchill. Michael Caine stars, with Donald Sutherland, Robert Duvall, Jenny Agutter, Donald Pleasence as Heinrich Himmler, Anthony Quayle, Jean Marsh, Judy Geeson, Treat Williams, Larry Hagman, and Siegfried Rauch. It was based on Jack Higgins' bestseller. AIP released a cut (123-minute) version of the 134-minute film.

EARTH ANGEL

(1991) **D:** Joe Napolitano **S:** Nina
Shengold **P:** Ron Gilbert

Cathy Podewell star as Angela, an airhead-blonde high-school prom queen who dies in a car crash in 1962, and returns 20 years later as an angel to do good deeds. With Rainbow Harvest, Dustin Nygren, Roddy McDowall as the angel who assigns her, Mark Hamill, Cindy Williams, Garrett Morris, Alan Young, and Erik Estrada. Some of them appear in both the 60s and 90s scenes. It's an ABC-TV movie full of former TV stars.

EARTHBOUND

(1940) **D:** Irving Pichel **S:** John
Howard Lawson **P:** Sol Wurtzel

Warner Baxter is murdered in Europe and returns as a ghost to help the man who is blamed (Henry Wilcoxon). Andrea Leds is his helpful wife, and Lynn Bari is the jealous former girlfriend who killed him. The 67-minute 20th–Century Fox release was a remake of a 1920 movie.

EARTHBOUND

(1979) **D:** James L. Conway **S/P:** Michael Fisher

The Sunn Classics people invaded network TV (NBC) with this series pilot (it was also screened in theaters). Burl Ives and his grandson befriend Christopher Connelly, Meredith MacRae, and their alien family. Conway also made *Hangar 18*.

EARTH GIRLS ARE EASY

(Vestron, 1988) **D:** Julien Temple **S/A:** Julie Brown
S: Charlie Coffey, Terrence E. McNally **P:** Tony Garnett

After *Absolute Beginners* and lots of rock videos, Temple made this PG-rated MTV-style science-fiction musical comedy. Three brightly colored hairy and horny aliens in LA learn English, lose their hair, and become California guys. Geena Davis and Jeff Goldblum star, and Damon Wayans and Jim Carrey are the other aliens. With Michael McKean, Julie Brown, Charles Rocket, Larry Linville, and Angelyne. It was one of several features with Goldblum and Davis, who were married at the time. Nile Rodgers wrote the score, and Brown wrote and sings " 'Cause I'm a Blonde." The movie is based on her song of the same name. It was made for DEG.

THE EARTHLING

(Vestron, 1980) **D:** Peter Collinson **S:** Lanny Cotler
P: Elliot Schick, John Strong   Australia

After AIP became Filmways, Sam Arkoff presented this PG drama. William Holden stars as a terminally ill man who teaches an orphan (Ricky Schroder) to survive in the bush country. With Jack Thompson.

EARTH'S FINAL FURY = WHEN TIME RAN OUT

EASTERN CONDORS

(Paragon, 1986) **D/A:** Samo Hung
Hong Kong

This large-scale, subtitled action movie shot in the Philippines, borrows ideas from *The Dirty Dozen*, *The Deer Hunter*, *The Guns of Navarone*, and even *Dr. No*, so there's a lot going on. Set in 1976, it's about a Chinese/American S.Q.U.A.T. team (led by the director, a comic costar of some of Jackie Chan's best movies) sent to destroy a secret US arsenal left behind in Vietnam before the Vietcong can use it. They take their pick of prisoners, then team up with three Cambodian female guerrillas, led by Joyce Godenzi (a former Miss Hong Kong). Yuen Biao, an impishly handsome, comical young fighting star, is a black-market hero who defects and joins them. Biao (and others) use martial arts, but most of the fighting is with machine guns and explosives. The Oscar-winning Haing S. Ngor (*The Killing Fields*) plays a shell-shocked local. My favorite of many insults is "Nonsense, masturbator!" and there's some surprising (anti-US) political humor.

EASY WHEELS

(Fries, 1988) **D/S:** David O'Malley **S:** Ivan Raimi, Celia
Abrams **P:** Dimitri Villard   (*Women on Wheels*)

Eileen Davidson (from *The Young and the Restless*) is She Wolf. Raised by wolves as a baby, she leads a tough, man-hating group of female bikers who steal babies to be raised by wolves. A group of bikers, led by Paul Le Mat, are the heroes, and they can sing doo-wop gospel. With Barry Livingston (from *My Three Sons*) as a reporter who rides with the bikers, Karen Russell, Roberta Vasquez (from *Playboy*), Ted Raimi as a bartender, and George Plimpton. Bruce Campbell was an executive producer of this odd comedy.

EAT AND RUN

(Starmaker, 1984) **D/S:** Christopher Hart
S: Stan Hart **P:** Jack Briggs   (*Mangia*)

Ron Silver is a 40s-style New York City detective narrating a comic tale of a 300-pound alien named Murray (R.L. Ryan from *The Toxic Avenger*). Murray eats Italians in New Jersey. From New World.

EATEN ALIVE = DOOMED TO DIE

EATING RAOUL

(Fox, 1982) **D/S/A:** Paul Bartel
S: Richard Blackburn **P:** Anne Kimmel

Paul Bartel and Mary Woronov star as Paul and Mary Bland, squares who start advertising in sex papers and killing the obnoxious people who show up. Raoul (Robert Beltran) muscles in on their racket by selling the bodies to a fast-food restaurant. It's a very funny social comedy with a cult following. Bartel presented an off-Broadway stage version in 1992. With Buck Henry, Ed Begley Jr. as

Robert Beltran and Ed Begley Jr. in *Eating Raoul.*

a fake hippie, and Billy Curtis. A soundtrack was released, including a great Spanish version of "Devil with a Blue Dress." Bartel and Woronov (who some assumed were married in real life) went on to play variations of the same couple as guest stars in several other features.

EAT MY DUST!

(1976) **D/S:** Charles B. Griffith **P:** Roger Corman

Ron Howard is Hoover Niebold, who steals a racing car to impress his girlfriend (Christopher Norris). This PG drive-in hit also features Dave Madden, Corbin Bernsen, Paul Bartel, and Ron's dad and brother, Rance and Clint Howard. Barbara Peeters was the second-unit director and the score is by David Grisman. It was one of the top-grossing features from Roger Corman's New World, so Howard got to direct himself the next year in the similar *Grand Theft Auto*.

EAT THE DOCUMENT

(1972) **D/P/A:** Bob Dylan
D: D. A. Pennebaker **P:** Howard Alk

This rare, 55-minute "anti-documentary" of Dylan's 1966 European tour has become a bootleg-tape favorite. It features some great Royal Albert Hall live electric concert footage of Dylan, the Band, and (for one song) Johnny Cash. Best of all, though, are long scenes of a nearly incoherent Dylan in the backseat of a car with John Lennon. Both are pretty out of it, and Dylan keeps threatening to puke. Young Robbie Robertson occasionally adds to the rambling conversation from the front seat.

EAT THE RICH

(RCA/Columbia, 1988) **D/S:** Peter Richardson
S: Pete Richens **P:** Tim Van Pellin   UK

After being fired from a restaurant where they serve fried baby panda, a transsexual (Lanah Pellay) takes it over and puts rich people on the menu. This cannibal comedy features Robbie Coltrane, Angie Bowie, Koo Stark, Fiona Richmond, Miranda Richardson, Rik Mayall, Bill Wyman, Paul and Linda McCartney, and Nosher Powell. Lemmy and Motorhead appear in the film and play the theme song, which shoulda been a hit.

EBB TIDE

(Paramount, 1994) **D/P:** Craig Lahiff
S: Robert Ellis, Peter Goldsworthy
P: Paul Davies, Helen Leake   Australia

Harry Hamlin is a lawyer who falls for a murder suspect (Judy McIntosh). This "erotic thriller" also features John Waters and Sue Lyons.

EBONY, IVORY, AND JADE

(VCI, 1976) **D/P:** Cirio H. Santiago
S: Henry Barnes Philippines (*Foxforce; Foxfire; American Beauty Hostage; She Devils in Chains*)

This PG adventure is about three American women in Hong Kong for Olympic track games who are stalked by killers, then kidnapped by slavers and held for ransom. President Ford is quoted more than once about his concern. Colleen Camp plays a stuck-up heiress, and Roseanne Katon (also in Santiago's *The Muthers*) gets some pretty good flips in during martial-arts fights. Sylvia Anderson is a tall, bitter black runner. The title and ad art are misleading, because Jade, the Asian woman, dies early. "Ebony, Ivory, and Ebony" would be more accurate. There's a battle in an old, aboveground cemetery. Unfortunately, the sound stinks, the photography is too dark, and nobody bothered to dub long conversations in the Tagalog language! It was originally released by Dimension.

EBONY, IVORY, AND JADE

(1979) **D:** John Llewellyn Moxey **D/P:** Jimmy Sangster

Sangster (a crime novelist who worked on many Hammer films) copied both the 1976 film of the same name and *Charlie's Angels* for this CBS-TV pilot film. A Las Vegas dance team, Debbie Allen (Ebony) and *Playboy* centerfold Martha Smith (Ivory), work for Nick Jade (Bert Convy) as secret agents on a case in the Middle East, protecting scientist Nina Foch and her fomula for a deadly new explosive. With Claude Akins, Ji-Tu Cumbuka, David Brenner, and Frankie Valli (as himself).

ECCO

(SW, 1963) **D:** Gianni Proia **P:** Francesco Mazzei Italy (*Mondo di Notte Tre*)

The condescending narration read by George Sanders gives this mondo documentary a special edge. Some highlights of the "sequel" to *World By Night* are the last performance of the famous Grand Guignol theater in Paris, complete with gore FX and a man who sticks long needles through his body (he was featured in the ads). Also with karate, twisting, lesbians, strippers, juvenile delinquents, artificial insemination, and reindeer castration. Presented by Dick Randall. It was one

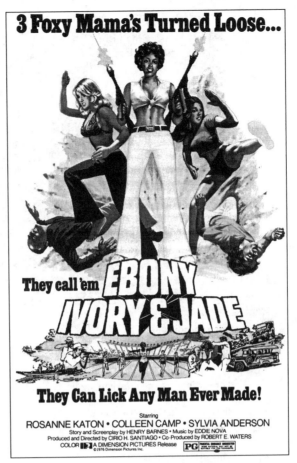

3 Foxy Mama's Turned Loose...

They call 'em **EBONY IVORY & JADE**

They Can Lick Any Man Ever Made!

Starring
ROSANNE KATON • COLLEEN CAMP • SYLVIA ANDERSON
Story and Screenplay by HENRY BARNES • Music by EDDIE NOVA
Produced and Directed by CIRIO H. SANTIAGO • Co-Produced by ROBERT E. WATERS
COLOR A DIMENSION PICTURES Release **PG**
©1976 Dimension Pictures Inc.

of only three features shot in "Panorama" wide screen (the video is letterboxed). R.W. Cresse re-edited and wrote a new script for the 1965 American release. The original *World By Night* (1960), from the same producer, was released in America by Warners.

ECHOES

(VidAmerica, 1980) **D:** Arthur Allan Seidelman
S: Richard J. Anthony **P:** George R. Nice

A New York City art student (Richard Alfieri) has nightmares about his evil unborn twin and thinks he's reincarnated. Mercedes McCambridge (in her last role) is an art-gallery owner, Gale Sondergaard (in her last known role) is a psychiatrist, and Ruth Roman is his mother. The plot was ripped off for *Dead Again* and *Deja Vu*.

ECHO PARK

(Kartes, 1986) **D:** Robert Dornheim **S:** Michael Ventura **P:** Walter Shenson   US/Austria

Susan Dey is an actress (and single mother) working as a Strip-o-gram girl. Tom Hulce is her songwriter roommate working as a pizza delivery man. Various characters in a bad part of LA want to be in show biz. With Cheech Marin, Cassandra Peterson (Elvira) as his wife, Michael Bowen as a would-be Arnold Schwarzenegger, and Timothy Carey.

THE ECSTASIES OF WOMAN

(1969) **D/C:** Herschell Gordon Lewis
P: Thomas D. Dowd

Lewis made this nudie movie in Hollywood using pseudonyms. On the eve of his wedding, a guy enjoys his all-night bachelor party on a yacht. During the party he remembers past conquests. It was advertised as "a total experience in shameless pleasure." Walter Camp, Bonnie Clark, and Forman Shane are featured.

ED AND HIS DEAD MOTHER

(Fox, 1992) **D:** Jonathan Wacks
S: Chuck Hughes **P:** William Christopher Gorog
(*Bon Appetite, Mama*)

Steve Buscemi (*Reservoir Dogs*) stars as a depressed guy running a small-town hardware store. He pays a devious cryogenics salesman (John Glover with white hair) to resurrect his late mother (Miriam Margolyes). She sleeps in the refrigerator, eats live bugs to keep alive, and eventually needs human flesh. The PG-13 black comedy doesn't exactly "work," but I can't hate a movie starring Buscemi and Glover, and Sam Jenkins as a very sexy neighbor is another plus. With Ned Beatty as the voyeur uncle, Rance Howard as a homicidal preacher, and Gary Farmer. KNB provided the FX (including a chainsaw decapitation in a graveyard and a talking head), and the Golden Palominos and They Might Be Giants did some of the songs. Wacks also made *Powwow Highway* and *Mystery Date*.

EDDIE AND THE CRUISERS

(Avid, 1983) **D/S:** Martin Davidson **S:** Arlene Davidson **P:** Joseph Brooks, Robert K. Lifton

Reporter Ellen Barkin tries to find out what happened to members of a 60s New Jersey rock band, in a movie that takes place in two time periods. Michael Paré (making his debut) is the group's leader, Eddie Wilson, whose body was never found after a 1964 car accident. Tom Berenger is the real star as the songwriter. With Joe Pantoliano, John Stockwell, and Helen Schneider. John Cafferty and the Beaver Brown Band provided the (too polished and modern) music. This PG-13 movie was popular on cable TV, so a sequel was made. Davidson also directed *The Lords of Flatbush*.

EDDIE AND THE CRUISERS II: EDDIE LIVES!

(IVE, 1989) **D:** Jean-Claude Lord **S:** Charles Zev Cohen **P:** Stephane Reichel   Canada

Michael Paré returns as Eddie Wilson. It seems he's been working on a construction job in Montreal for 18 years. With Marina Orsini, Kate Lynch, and bits by Larry King, Bo Diddley, and Martha Quinn (as themselves). The Beaver Brown Band did the music for this PG-13 sequel.

EDDIE PRESLEY: A TRIBUTE TO THE KING

(1992) **D:** Jeff Burr **S/A:** Duane Whitaker **P:** Bill Burr

An overweight Hollywood security guard and former Elvis impersonator living in a van has flashbacks of his life and a mental breakdown. It's based on a play by star Duane Whitaker. Stacie Bourgeois costars, and a number of cult names appear: Roscoe Lee Browne, Clu Gulagher, Lawrence Tierney, Daniel Roebuck, Willard Pugh, Ted Raimi, Ian Ogilvy, Quentin Tarantino, Tim Thomerson, John Lazar, and Kitten Natividad. Burr made the 16mm independent film after his *Leatherface* was cut beyond recognition by New Line.

THE EDGE

(1989) **D/S:** Nicholas Kazan **D:** Carl Shenkel, Luis Mandoki **S:** Alan Sharp **P:** Christopher Morgan

A better-than-average anthology is hosted by a face called the Watcher. The 3 dark stories about sex and death debuted on HBO. The stars are Brad Davis and Kelly Lynch, Rutger Hauer and Michael Rooker, and Christian Slater and Bridget Fonda.

EDGE OF HONOR

(1991) **D/S:** Michael Spence **S:** Mark Rosenbaum **P:** Jay B. Davis, Peter Garrity

Corey Feldman stars in a story about Boy Scouts in the Pacific Northwest who fight the Mafia and redneck killers in the woods over some rocket launchers. With Scott Reeves, Meredith Salinger, Don Swayze, and Christopher Neame.

EDGE OF SANITY

(Virgin, 1989) **D:** Gérard Kikoine **S/P:** Harry Alan Towers **S:** Ron Raley, Ewars Simons **P:** Edward Simons   UK/Hungary

A little kid watches a couple having sex in a barn. The woman watches the kid. The man spanks the kid, then the woman dies. It's only a childhood trauma relived by Dr. Jekyll, played this time by Anthony Perkins. The rich doctor, limping and using a cane, becomes Hyde after experiments with anesthesia. Hyde looks like an 80s Iggy Pop punk, turns green when he smokes cocaine from a glass pipe, and is obsessed by bare asses. He announces himself, "Hi, Jack Hyde!" He humiliates people (and himself) and kills women, usually by slitting their throats. He masturbates while watching a black pimp and a hooker have sex, then keeps the pair as slaves. Meanwhile, his selfless wife (Glynis Barber) helps hookers at a church. Perkins has never acted stranger or more out of control (and that's saying a lot). His laughing, nervous, psychotic behavior is unbelievable. This movie looks like a sleazier-than-usual Ken Russell version of the Jack the Ripper story. Cameras tilt and circle around while everything turns pink. An interesting continuity error occurs when Hyde cuts off a woman's panties and they magically reappear. With Sarah Maur-Thorp and Claudia Udy. The director made many French porno movies, then erotic movies for Playboy TV for Harry Alan Towers. This is available in an R and an unrated version. There is also a sell through *Making of Edge of Sanity* (UAV) which was sold in Woolworth stores!

DOUBLE THE TERROR. DOUBLE THE FUN.

ANTHONY PERKINS *is Henry Jekyll*   ANTHONY PERKINS *is Jack Hyde*

EDGE OF SANITY

A ripping good time.

EDWARD SIMONS Presents AN ALLIED VISION PRODUCTION ANTHONY PERKINS as DR. JEKYLL & MR. HYDE "EDGE OF SANITY" ANTHONY PERKINS · GLYNIS BARBER · DAVID LODGE · SARAH MAUR-THORP · BEN COLE · LISA DAVIS Edited by MALCOLM COOKE Music composed and conducted by FREDRIC TALGORN Screenplay by J.P. FELIX · RON RALEY Executive Producer PETER A. McRAE Produced by EDWARD SIMONS · HARRY ALAN TOWERS Directed by GERARD KIKOINE MILLIMETER FILMS

EDGE OF THE AXE

(Forum, 1987) **D:** "Joseph Braunstein"/ José Larraz **S:** Joaquin Amichatis, Javier Morrieta   Spain

Former inmates of an asylum are being killed in Paddock, Texas. Some are decapitated or have fingers cut off. Patty Shepard and Jack Taylor (also both in the director's *Rest in Pieces*) costar.

EDIE IN CIAO! MANHATTAN

(Pacific Arts, 1971) **D:** John Palmer, David Weissman

Edie Sedgwick pretty much plays herself as a speed-freak heiress living in a tent in an empty pool. Allen Ginsberg is in this near-documentary underground film, and Roger Vadim shows up as a doctor when she gets sex and shock treatments. Flashbacks are from a b/w 1967 film with Viva. Richie Havens, John Phillips, and Skip Battin from the Byrds are on the soundtrack. Edie, a marginal Andy Warhol "superstar," died at 28, three months after filming, and was later the topic of a best-selling book. This played in the 80s, with newer footage added. Weissman also put together *Shogun Assassin*.

EDWARD SCISSORHANDS

(Fox, 1990) **D/P:** Tim Burton **S:** Caroline Thompson **P:** Denise di Novi

Edward Scissorhands (Johnny Depp) is created in a great spooky old mansion sitting at the edge of a fantasy 60s-style suburb with brightly colored houses. The kindly mad doctor (Vincent Price) dies before he's finished, and the awkward boy with large scissors for hands and all-black clothes is taken home by suburban Avon lady Dianne Wiest. A blond Winona Ryder is her daughter, and Alan Arkin is her husband. With Kathy Baker, Anthony Michael Hall, Stuart Lancaster, Robert Oliveri, and Conchata Ferrell. They painted real houses in Florida for this PG-13 modern fairy-tale comedy. Stan Winston was in charge of FX. 20th Century–Fox threatened the makers of *Edward Penishands*, a porno parody, which was supposedly withdrawn.

ED WOOD

(Touchstone, 1994) **D/P:** Tim Burton **S:** Scott Alexander, Larry Karaszewski **P:** Denise di Novi

Be glad that Burton had the clout to make this wonderful look at the late and ridiculed cult figure Ed Wood Jr. and to do it in b/w. Johnny Depp stars (he's better than you'd think) as the eager young eccentric dress-wearing director, and Martin Landau is great as Bela Lugosi, down and out and addicted but always a pro. Wood works on three of his 1950s movies (*Glen or Glenda*, *Bride of the Monster*, and *Plan 9 from Outer Space*), and we see loving recreations of scenes from each one. With Patricia Arquette as Kathy Wood, Sarah Jessica Parker as girlfriend Dolores Fuller, Jeffrey Jones as Criswell, Bill Murray as Bunny Breckinridge, Lisa Marie as Vampira, Ed Starr as producer George Weiss, and George "the Animal" Steele as Tor Johnson. Also with G. D. Spradlin, Juliet Landau, Conrad Brooks, and Vincent D'Onofrio as Orson Welles. The old Brown Derby restaurant was remodeled for scenes. Partially based on Rudolph Grey's *Nightmare of Ecstasy* book, the Touchstone release runs 124 minutes. The score by Howard Shore is on Hollywood Records.

ED WOOD: LOOK BACK IN ANGORA

(Rhino, 1994) **D/S/P:** Ted Newsom

This documentary uses scenes from movies Wood directed and wrote plus interviews with his sad widow Kathy Wood, WWII friend and director Joe Robertson, Steven Apostoloff, Conrad Brooks, and Dolores Fuller. Color footage from the unfinished *Crossroads Avenger*; a behind-the-scenes clip of the *Orgy of the Dead* set (note T.V. Mikels), and the revelation that Fred Olen Ray's unfinished *Beach Blanket Bloodbath* used a script by Wood are high points. The many lines of dialog used out of context to comment ironically on Wood's life are too much like (irritating) current TV series promo spots. The 50 minute running time is padded with non-Wood Lugosi clips and some ill-advised "facsimile footage" scenes and for some reason there are no scenes from *Night of the Ghouls* (a Rhino release!). I enjoyed hearing the familiar voice of narrator Gary Owens recommending *Psychotronic* magazine at the end. *The Haunted World of Ed Wood* was another 1994 documentary.

THE ED WOOD STORY: THE PLAN NINE COMPANION

(MPI, 1992) **D/S/P:** Marck Carducci *(Flying Saucers over Hollywood)*

This tribute to Ed Wood Jr. and his "anti-masterpiece" *Plan 9 from Outer Space* has lots of interviews (and lots of toupées) and covers most of the bases. *Plan 9* fans won't be disappointed. Vampira, Paul Marcos, Valda Hanson, Gregory Walcott, and Stephen Apostoloff are here, along with fans and experts like Drew Friedman, Rudolph Grey, Harry Medved, Joe Dante, Sam Raimi, Scott Spiegel,

Vincent Price creates *Edward Scissorhands*.

FJA, and Eric Caidin. Conrad Brooks leads a tour of the old Quality studios. Also with a tribute to Tor, a look at the Don Post studios, silent footage of Wood directing, and the Chiller Theatre animation opening. At 111 minutes, it's 32 minutes longer than the feature it documents.

EERIE MIDNIGHT HORROR SHOW = THE TORMENTED

18 AGAIN!
(Starmaker, 1988) **D:** Paul Flaherty **S:** Josh Goldstein, Jonathan Prince **P:** Walter Colblenz

George Burns (92 but playing an 81-year-old) somehow becomes his own 18-year-old grandson (star Charlie Schlatter). This PG body-switch comedy costars Miriam Flynn and features Tony Roberts, Anita Morris, Jennifer Runyon, Red Buttons, George DiCenzo, and Pauly Shore.

800 LEAGUES DOWN THE AMAZON
(New Horizons, 1993) **D/P:** Luis Llosa **S:** Laura Schiff, Jackson Barr

Daphne Zuniga travels downriver in Brazil with a "river rat" bounty hunter (Adam Baldwin), her father (Barry Bostwick), her doctor fiancé (Tom Verica), and a comedy-relief singing servant. Her father is accused of murder so there's a race to prove his innocence and save his life. With an *Aguirre*-inspired Indian attack and gators and piranha. Roger Corman was executive producer of this PG-13 Jules Verne adaptation.

8 MILLION WAYS TO DIE
(Fox, 1986) **D:** Hal Ashby **S:** Oliver Stone, David Lee Henry **P:** Steve Roth

Jeff Bridges is an alcoholic ex-cop involved with drugs. Rosanna Arquette is his high-priced call-girl girlfriend. This adaptation of a novel by Lawrence Block was Stone's last script for another director's film. Robert Towne worked on it too. With Andy Garcia as the sadistic pimp, Alexandra Paul, and Randy Brooks.

EL
(Hen's Tooth, 1952) **D/S:** Luis Buñuel **S:** Luis Alcoriza **P:** Oscar Dancigers Mexico (*This Strange Passion*)

Francisco Arturo De Córdova, a wealthy and religious man, lives alone with his servants in his art-nouveau villa. He finds his dream woman in a church, marries her, but becomes insanely jealous and even has visions of strangling a priest. Eventually he has a breakdown and enters a monastery. The Cannes Film Festival jury called this a bad B movie. Not to be confused with Buñuel's *El Bruto*, made the same year.

EL CONDOR
(Warner, 1970) **D:** John Guillermin **S:** Larry Cohen, Steven Carabatsos **P:** André De Toth

Jim Brown and Lee Van Cleef (as Jaroo) escape from a chain gang, join up with some Apache Indians (led by Iron Eyes Cody), and attack the Mexican fort El Condor for the gold inside. This R-rated National General release included some nudity during love scenes with Marianna Hill and Brown. The cast also includes Patrick O'Neal and Elisha Cook Jr. The music is by Maurice Jarre.

ELECTRA GLIDE IN BLUE
(MGM, 1973) **D/P:** James William Guercio **S:** Robert Boris

Robert Blake plays a naive Nam-vet motorcycle cop involved in a murder investigation, in this downbeat film with hippie murder suspects and an ending "borrowed" from *Easy Rider*. With Mitchell Ryan, Jeannine Riley, Billy Green Bush, Royal Dano, and Elisha Cook Jr. Madura, the Marcels, and Chicago are seen in concert footage. Director Guercio was the manager, the producer, and a writer for Chicago, so their long song "Tell Me" is heard in its entirety, and Terry Kath (who later killed himself playing Russian roulette in real life) is the killer. A double United Artists soundtrack was released.

ELECTRA LOVE 2000
(1994) **D/S/E:** Jay Raskin **P:** Vicky Prodromidou

Robin O'Dell stars as a hooker in "a modern version of the Greek classic" by the director of *I Married a Vampire*. It features Gregory Pitts and Susie Owens.

THE ELECTRIC CHAIR
(SW, 1972) **D/S/P/FX/A:** J. G. "Pat" Patterson

After a young married minister and the woman he was having an affair with are found bloody and dead ("The tongue was ripped out of her head!") this very entertaining North Carolina movie becomes a courtroom drama with detailed exploitable scenes of people in the electric chair. Mose Cooper (Patterson), a religious fanatic, is found guilty and sent to the chair but is reprieved at the last minute. Just when you think it's all over, the sheriff arrests

---

80s FAVES
(TOP 25, IN ALPHABETICAL ORDER)

1. *Basket Case* (1982)
2. *Blade Runner* (1982)
3. *The Blob* (1988)
4. *Brazil* (1985)
5. *The Dead Zone* (1983)
6. *The Evil Dead* (1983)
7. *Flesh + Blood* (1985)
8. *Hellraiser* (1987)
9. *The Hitcher* (1986)
10. *The Lair of the White Worm* (1988)
11. *Near Dark* (1988)
12. *A Nightmare on Elm Street* (1984)
13. *Reanimator* (1985)
14. *Repo Man* (1984)
15. *The Road Warrior* (1981)
16. *Robocop* (1987)
17. *Rumblefish* (1983)
18. *Sonny Boy* (1987)
19. *The Stepfather* (1987)
20. *Street Trash* (1987)
21. *The Terminator* (1984)
22. *They Live* (1988)
23. *The Thing* (1982)
24. *Videodrome* (1982)
25. *White of the Eye* (1987)

The early 80s saw a new wave of anti-Communist and 3-D movies. It all had something to do with having an ex-actor president who managed to use mass hypnosis on a national scale. After a while, a record number of end-of-the-world and post-nuke movies were being made all over the world. *E.T.* (1982) was (and probably still is) far and away the top-grossing film of all time. It was the first to break over $200 million in US/Canada rentals and is also the top selling video of all time. Spielberg gets "$5 per tape" (!). Sears paid $40 million to show it on network TV in 1991, then offered it cheap in their stores. It was uplifting family science fiction, but at least "Papa Oom Mow Mow" was used in it. Nine other features earned over a hundred million. They are (in descending order) *Return of the Jedi*, *Batman*, *Home Alone*, *Ghostbusters*, *Raiders of the Lost Ark* (followed by its two sequels), *Beverly Hills Cop*, and *Back to the Future*. These are the movies that the most people watched as the country faced the horrors of AIDS, crack, and rising crime.

ELLERY QUEEN

The writer and master detective was created by Frederic Dannay and Manfred Bennington Lee, two Brooklyn cousins who used the pen name Ellery Queen, and gave the same name to their fictional detective. On the screen, Donald Cook starred as Ellery Queen in *The Spanish Cape Mystery* (1935), and Eddie Quillan starred in *The Mandarin Mystery* (1937), both for Republic. A popular radio series led to a series of four Columbia films (1940–41) starring Ralph Bellamy as a comic crime-solver, with Charley Grapewin as his inspector father. William Gargan took over the role for three films more in 1942. Some guest stars were Anna May Wong (*Ellery Queen's Penthouse Mystery*), George Zucco (*Ellery Queen and the Murder Ring*), and Gale Sondergaard (*Enemy Agents Meet Ellery Queen*). The TV series *The Adventures of Ellery Queen* (1975–76), starring Jim Hutton and David Wayne, was better than most of the movies.

Crazy Billy, a new trial begins, more flashbacks are shown, and it all gets wilder than you'd expect. There are visual shocks (no gore, though), nudity (in a black club), Patterson's scary-looking real-life wife, local accents, and some decent experimental music. If that isn't enough, you get some flubbed lines and unintentional humor, and the soft-rock background music includes a cover of the Pretty Things' "I Can See You" (!). Patterson and future director Worth Keeter worked on the makeup. It's a Frank Henenlotter Sexy Shocker release. Akira Fitton created the 1975 ad campaign.

ELECTRIC DREAMS
(MGM/UA, 1984) **D:** Steve Barron
S/P: Rusty Lemorande **P:** Larry DeWaay

Lenny Von Dohlen stars as a guy in San Francisco who loves his neighbor (Virginia Masden). The big trouble is his sophisticated computer (Bud Cort's voice), which is in love with the same girl and sabotages everything. This PG fantasy includes scenes from movies like *Madame Satan, The Giant Claw,* and *Forbidden Planet*. Giorgio Moroder scored the soundtrack. Maxwell Caulfield and Koo Stark are also featured. Barron made rock videos for Michael Jackson and Fleetwood Mac and later directed *Teenage Mutant Ninja Turtles*.

THE ELEMENT OF CRIME
(Unicorn, 1984) **D/S/A:** Lars von Triers **S:** Niels Voersel Denmark (*Forbrydelsen Element*)

A cop is hypnotized to help solve a series of murders in a sepia-tone post-nuke Europe where dead horses float in a river. The cast includes Me Me Lei (from cannibal movies) as a hooker. It was filmed in English. The director returned with *Zentropa*.

ELIMINATORS
(Fox, 1986) **D:** Peter Manoogian **S:** Paul De Meo, Danny Bilson **P:** Charles Band

A vengeful "mandroid" is played by R.J. Reynolds tobacco heir Patrick Reynolds. This PG movie throws in everything: a lesbian river queen, a flying robot, a prehistoric tribe, kung fu. Andrew Prine as a riverboat pilot costars with Denise Crosby as a scientist and Conan Lee as Ninja. It was shot in Spain but is set in South America.

ELLIE
(Vestron, 1984) **D:** Peter Wittman
S: Glen Allen Smith **P:** Francine Rudine

Shelley Winters and her three sons kill off her wealthy husbands, in this black comedy. The daughter of one of the victims (played by *Penthouse* Pet of the Year Sheila Kennedy, who has nude scenes) seeks revenge. With Edward Albert, George Gobel as a preacher, and Pat Paulsen as a sheriff. Wittman also made *Play Dead*.

ELSTREE CALLING
(1930) **D:** Adrian Brunel, Alfred Hitchcock, André Charlot, Jack Hulbert, Paul Murray **S:** Val Valentine **P:** Walter C. Mycroft UK

A variety of unrelated sketches make up this early talkie, the first British musical-comedy film. In one segment, a family tries to watch the first broadcast on television (a concept then still five years in the future). Alfred Hichcock directed Anna May Wong and Donald Calthrop in a broadly comic rendition of a scene from Shakespeare's *The Taming of the Shrew*.

ELVES
(AIP, 1989) **D/S:** Jeff Mandel **S:** Mark Griffith, Bruce Taylor **P:** Mark Paglia

A young fast-food waitress in an old department store (Julie Austin) is chosen to be mated with an elf as part of a Nazi plan. She discovers that her grandfather is an ex-Nazi and that he's really her father: "I impregnated my own daughter to create an offspring who would be suitable to mate with an elf!" Her hateful, cat-killing mother (Deanna Lund, from the *Land of the Giants* show) is busy being naked in the tub when an elf throws in an electric radio. A lecherous, coke-sniffing store Santa is castrated by elves and replaced by a chain-smoking, homeless ex-detective (Dan Haggerty). A professor trying to explain the Nazi master-elf plan says, "If you could ignore their brutality, they were just crackpots." Besides the choice bad and hateful dialogue, the seldom-shown elf faces are pretty effective and spooky, but it's too bad we mostly see their rubber hands and feet. This tape is too dark, most of the FX (and the accents) are awful, and the blurry point-of-view "monster vision" is headache-inducing. It was filmed in Colorado.

ELVIRA, MISTRESS OF THE DARK
(Starmaker, 1988) **D:** James Signorelli
S: Sam Egan, John Paragon, Cassandra Peterson **P:** Eric Gardner, Marc Pierson

TV horror-movie hostess Cassandra Peterson/Elvira stars as a TV horror-movie hostess who inherits a haunted house in the old fashioned New England town of Falwell. This comedy has a strong anti-moralistic message and is filled with dumb sex jokes, silly FX, and one-liners. *It Conquered the World* and *Attack of the Killer Tomatoes* clips are also thrown in. The movie didn't do much business, but I liked Elvira on the big screen a lot more than on the small screen making fun of other movies. She's sexy and funny. Edie McClurg and Jeff Conaway are also in this New World release. Cassandra Peterson has also hosted other video releases from various companies over the years.

ELVIS AND THE BEAUTY QUEEN
(1981) **D:** Gus Trikonis **S:** Julia Cameron **P:** Charles B. Fitzsimons

Cassandra Peterson as *Elvira, Mistress of the Dark*.

Linda Thompson of Memphis was NBC's "program consultant" for this, the second Elvis TV movie, and Stephanie Zimbalist plays her. Thompson was a post-Priscilla girlfriend. Don Johnson (!?) plays Elvis. With Ann Dusenberry, Ruta Lee, and Ken Foree. Ronnie McDowell did the dubbed-in singing. In the future, every Elvis girlfriend, date, and pickup will have a TV movie based on her experiences.

ELVIS AND THE COLONEL

(1993) **D:** William A. Graham **S:** Phil Penningroth **P:** Daniel A. Sherkow

NBC aired this around the time of the much-publicized Elvis postage stamp. Beau Bridges stars as "Colonel" Tom Parker, shown to be vulgar but not a villain. Rob Youngblood as Elvis narrates from beyond the grave. It's considered the worst of the Elvis TV movies.

ELVIS IN HOLLYWOOD

(BMG, 1993) **D:** Frank Martin **P:** Jerry Schilling

Elvis's pre-musical and pre-army acting period (*Love Me Tender, Loving You, Jailhouse Rock,* and *King Creole*) is explored with home movies, film clips, and interviews. The 65-minute tape was authorized by his estate.

ELVIS IN THE MOVIES

(Goodtimes)

I bought this at a shopping mall, and I'm glad I did. It's a complete compilation, with trailers for all 33 movies (1956–72). Plugs for soundtracks end many of them, and some are letterboxed. It shows

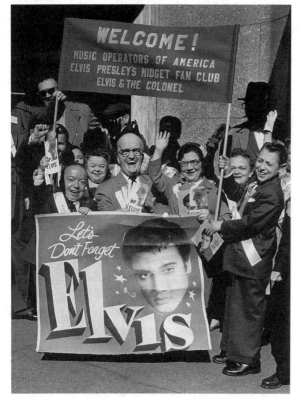

Elvis in Hollywood

EMANUELLE

The first Emmanuelle movie was such an international hit that, along with its sequels, a long-running "fake series" of soft-core sex adventures was created with star Laura Gemser. Gemser (or Moira Chen), a dark-skinned beauty from Java, was a major box-office draw in much of the world in the 70s. Although none of these movies did much theatrical business in the US, many are on tape under various titles. Because the Italian "Joe D'Amato" was the most frequent director, many of them are extremely twisted. There were also non-Gemser ripoffs, spoofs, and unrelated features with *Emanuelle* added to the titles. (And see *Black Emanuelle, Caged Women, Daughter of Emanuelle, Trap Them and Kill Them,* and *Women's Prison Massacre.*)

how the King's acting career paralleled Godzilla's (going from threatening tough guy to nice guy who hung out with little kids) and just how ridiculous his Sam Katzman movies were.

ELVIS ON TOUR

(MGM, 1972) **D/S/P:** Robert J. Abel, Pierre Adidge

The King performs 29 songs in his rhinestone jumpsuit during his 1971 cross-country tour. With spilt-screen effects and Dolby sound, plus some early *Ed Sullivan Show* clips. James Burton plays and The Sweet Inspirations provide backup vocals. Martin Scorsese was an editor and "montage supervisor." Shortly after it was released Elvis was divorced. He spent the rest of his life doing live shows and getting more out of touch with reality. This was the last Elvis movie released during his lifetime.

ELVIS STORIES

(Rhino, 1987) **D:** Ben Stiller

It's a half-hour spoof of tabloid Elvis stories, with the King being spotted in a supermarket and a writer claiming that Lennon and Elvis were the same person. The *Elvis Is Everywhere* video by Mojo Nixon is the best part. With John Cusack and Mike Myers. The director (son of Anne Meara and Jerry Stiller) later made *Reality Bites*.

ELVIS: THAT'S THE WAY IT IS

(MGM, 1970) **D:** Denis Sanders **P:** Herbert F. Solow

Elvis performs 27 songs (everything from "Little Sister" to "Polk Salad Annie") at the International Hotel in Las Vegas at the beginning of his first tour since 1957. The Sweet Inspirations provide the backup vocals. Some celebs shown in his audience include Cary Grant, Sammy Davis Jr., and Xavier Cugat. The year this was released, Elvis received his special-drug enforcement badge from President

Nixon. Elvis' last film as an actor, the ridiculous *Change of Habit*, was released the same month (November). The next Elvis feature, *Elvis on Tour*, was live too. Sanders did *Soul to Soul* next.

EMANON

(Nelson, 1986) **D/S/A:** Stuart Paul **P:** Dorothy Koster Paul, Hank Paul

The Messiah (Stuart Paul) arrives in New York City wearing rags and lives with homeless people. A crippled boy asks him for a miracle to help his mom's dress business. Read the title backwards. With Cheryl M. Lynn. Paul also made and starred in *Fate* (1990) with Lynn. The Paul family seems to have a (confused) mission. They also produce movies directed by Steven Paul (like *Eternity*). Their movies might be considered a cross between those of Frank Capra, Tom Laughlin, and Ed Wood Jr.

EMANUELLE IN AMERICA

(VSOM, 1976) **D:** Joe D'Amato/Aristide Massaccesi **S:** Maria Pia Fusco   Italy

Laura Gemser is a photographer who goes from New York City to California, DC, Venice, and the Carribbean, where she visits a millionaire's mansion with a harem and uses her secret camera. This movie is so extreme that David Cronenberg was inspired by it to make *Videodrome*. The original 100-minute uncut version (available from Venezuela with Spanish subtitles) features *Mondo* and snuff movie footage (all incredible fakes), gore, hardcore sex (with extras), and horse masturbation. With Paola Senatore and Gabrielle Tinti. Gemser returned in *Emanuelle Around the World, Emanuelle and the White Slave Trade*, and the infamous *Trap Them and Kill Them* (all 1977, all by D'Amato).

EMANUELLE IN BANKOK

(VidAmerica, 1976) **D/C:** "Joe D'Amato"/ Aristide Massaccesi **S:** Maria Pia Fusco   Italy (*Black Emanuelle Goes East; Black Emanuelle II*)

This one features the usual sex and orgies, and a snake and a muskrat fight. With Debra Berger, Ivan Rassimov as Prince Sanit, and Gabrielle Tinti. Alan Shackleton released it in America.

EMMANUELLE

(RCA, 1973) **D:** Just Jaeckin
S: Jean-Louis Richard   France

Sylvia Kristel stars in this international erotic hit based on the autobiographical book by Emmanuelle Arson (who was in *The Sand Pebbles* with Steve McQueen). The liberated jet-setter has sex in an airplane, in an opium den, on a squash court with a woman, and with a couple. The character was first played by Erica Blanc in 1971, but this is the hit. It cost under a half-million and grossed more than $100 million worldwide. The biggest hit in France when it was first released, it played in one Paris cinema until 1985! It spawned an official series and even more parallel copy movies and they're still making them! Columbia released it here ("X was never like this!"), and it made nearly $5 million in North American rentals. Guitarist Fripp sued over use of his music and won. With Marika Green and Alain Cuny.

EMMANUELLE IV

(MGM, 1984) **D:** Francis Giacobetti **S:** Francis Leroy, Iris Letans **P:** Alain Siritzky   France

Seven years after *Goodbye Emmanuelle*, Sylvia Kristel goes to Brazil for an operation and becomes 23-year-old Swedish model Mia Nygren, and she's in 3-D! The same ridiculous plot was used in *The Resurrection of Eve* (1973), a Marilyn Chambers porno movie. With Christian Marquand and Sophie Berger. It was from Cannon, but Roger Corman's Concorde added new dream scenes (including Brinke Stevens) and released it to US theaters in 2-D. Various versions were filmed, with different amounts of sex, for TV, video, and foreign markets.

EMMANUELLE V

(New Horizons, 1986/92) **D/S:** Walerian Borowczyk **D:** Steve Barnett **S:** Alex Cunningham, Howard R. Cohen

American beauty Monique Gabrielle stars in another "sequel." She's a (very popular) movie star who is abducted from her yacht by an Arab sheik while promoting her new hit, *Love Express*. Producer Roger Corman again added new and different footage for the US version and cut much of the sex (and most of the black characters) out. Heidi Payne, Michelle Burger, and Roxanna Michaels are members of the topless harem. The French version is uncut. It was filmed on the African island of Réunion. Borowczyk directed *Immoral Tales* (1980).

EMMANUELLE VI

(1988) **D:** Bruno Zincone **S:** Jean Rollin **P:** Alain Siritzk

Natalie Uher stars in this one, set in the Amazon jungle. It was made in Venezuela. Jean Rollin shot additional scenes. Sylvia Kristel returned again in *Emmanuelle VII* (1992), directed by Francis Leroy. A French *Emmanuelle* TV series starring Marcela Walerstein debuted in 1994 on Cinemax. Sylvia Kristel related sexual flashbacks filmed in various exotic locations.

EMMANUELLE, THE JOYS OF A WOMAN

(Paramount, 1975) **D/S:** Francis Giacobetti
S: Robert Elia   France   (*Emmanuelle II*)

Sylvia Kristel stars in the first legitimate sequel, with Umberto Orsini, Catherine Rivet, and Laura Gemser who became "Black Emanuelle" in her own series as a masseuse. The music is by Francis Lai. It was rerated NC-17 in 1991. The next in the series was *Goodbye, Emmanuelle*, a title as believable as *Friday the 13th: The Final Chapter*.

EMMA MAE: *See* BLACK SISTER'S REVENGE

THE EMERALD JUNGLE

(Continental, 1980) **D:** Umberto Lenzi
S: Rederico Zanni **P:** Antonio Crescenzi   Italy
(*Mangiati Vivi!*; *Doomed to Die*; *Eaten Alive*)

A blowgun assassin in New York City leaves behind an atrocity film. Janet Angren (who spends time walking around 42nd Street) and Nam deserter R. Bolla/Robert Kerman (also in *Make Them Die Slowly*) search for her lost sister (Paola Senatore). They go to New Guinea, where a Jim Jones type (Ivan Rassimov) lives in a village surrounded by a jungle with cannibals. He even conducts a Kool-Aid mass suicide. Animal slaughter, nudity, castration, and rape are all shown in this movie, which "borrows" scenes from Lenzi's own *Man from Deep River* and Deodato's *Jungle Holocaust*. With Me Me Lai and Mel Ferrer in a small role as a New York City professor. It was filmed in Sri Lanka. The US video title is a ripoff of John Boorman's *The Emerald Forest*.

(EMPEROR) CALIGULA: THE UNTOLD STORY

(TWE, 1981) **D/S:** "David Hills"/ Aristide Massaccesi
S: Richard Franks **P:** Alexander Sussman   Italy

This is an attempt to outgross the more expensive *Caligula* (1980). Tongues are ripped out, swords go up asses, and there are many sex scenes. Laura Gemser wants to kill Caligula (David Cain Haughton) for causing the death of her girlfriend but falls for him. With Gabrielle Tinti. Michele Soavi worked on the script. An uncut hard-core version includes sex with a horse.

THE EMPEROR JONES

(Sinister, VY 1933)
D: Dudley Murphy **S:** Dubose Heyward **P:** John Krimsky-Gifford

This is Paul Robeson's second film. He plays Pullman Porter Brutus Jones, a fugitive from a chain gang who shoots dice, sings spirituals, and manages to become a Haitian ruler. He convinces the locals that he's indestructable, and becomes an emperor in a mirrored palace, surrounded by fawning courtiers. Ultimately he has to flee to a swamp filled with ghosts, where he goes mad and is killed by a silver bullet. The film is based on Eugene O'Neill's (1920) Broadway play, which had starred Robeson. The

cast includes Dudley Digges, Fredi Washington, Frank Wilson, and Jackie "Moms" Mabley in a bit part! It was filmed on Long Island. Murphy had cowritten the script for *Dracula* (1931). Herman Rosse designed the sets for this film, *Dracula,* and other Universal horror classics.

ENCINO MAN

(Hollywood, 1992) **D:** Les Mayfield
S: Shawn Schepps **P:** George Zaloom

Sean Astin discovers a Cro-Magnon man (Brendan Fraser) frozen in ice while digging a swimming pool. He and a friend (MTV's Pauly Shore) clean him up and try to pass him off as a transfer student at school, and the "cool" caveman is a hit with the girls. Shore, playing a character at least ten years younger than he was at the time, is the real star. I understand the appeal of Jim Carrey, Jim Varney, Pee-wee Herman, and *Wayne's World*, but not Shore. The dumb PG teen comedy from Buena Vista features Megan Ward, Robin Tunney, Renee Ammann, Michael DeLuise, Mariette Hartley, and Richard Masur.

ENCORE = THE COMEBACK

ENCOUNTER AT RAVEN'S GATE

(Hemdale, 1987) **D/S:** Rolf De Heer
S/P: Marc Rosenberg   Australia
(*Incident at Raven's Gate*)

Although the video box says "the best since *Mad Max*," this odd, unique movie is nothing like that action classic. During a drought in the outback, the red sky rains dead birds, family pets attack, ghosts are seen, and people go mad. The star is a blond punk-look guy living with his older brother and his sexy sister-in-law. An asshole opera-fanatic cop becomes a killer, and a short nuclear scientist snoops around. The clever, obscure script never explains anything, but it seems as though unseen aliens are to blame. The cinematography is excellent, and things get real strange when characters start talking in speeded-up voices. The Easybeats' "Friday on My Mind" is used twice. Check it out.

ENCOUNTERS OF THE SPOOKY KIND

(VSOM, 1981) **D:** Samo Hung **P:** Raymond Chow
Hong Kong

The world is ending in Australia again—*Encounter at Raven's Gate.*

A man invokes spirits (and the monkey king) when his wife cheats on him. Ten years later Hung directed and starred in *Encounters of the Spooky Kind II* (1990) about the ghost of a little girl.

ENDANGERED

(Academy, 1994) **D/S:** Nick Kellis **P:** Frank Kostenko Jr.

While camping, Sandra Hess is raped by four drug runners. She escapes and seeks revenge. With Rick Aiello, Martin Kove, and Rene Estevez.

ENDANGERED SPECIES

(MGM/UA, 1982) **D/S:** Alan Rudolph **S:** Joel Bender **P:** Carolyn Pfeiffer

The CIA (not UFOs) turns out to be behind germ-warfare experiments responsible for cattle mutilation. Robert Urich stars as a New York detective, with JoBeth Williams, Paul Dooley, Hoyt Axton, Peter Coyote, Dan Hedaya, Harry Carey Jr., John Considine, and Heather Menzies. Zalman King was executive producer.

ENDGAME

(Media, 1983) **D/S:** "Steven Benson"/Aristide Massaccesi **S:** Alex Carver   Italy (*Bronx Lotta Finale*)

In this *Mad Max* copy, the hero helps a group of telepathic people fight bikers. With Moira Chen/Laura Gemser as a telepathic mutant, Pier Luigi Conti/Al Cliver as the warrior hero, Luigi Montefiori/George Eastman, and Gordon Mitchell. Michele Soavi was the assistant director and appears in the film.

ENDLESS DESCENT

(LIVE, 1989) **D/S/P:** Juan Piquer Simón **P:** José Escriva, Francesca De Laurentiis   Spain/US (*The Rift*)

In another *Abyss* ripoff, a near-future nuclear sub searches for a lost sub. They discover an air-filled world under the ocean with mutant eels, fish, and bug monsters caused by genetic experiments. Jack Scalia is the hero, Ray Wise is the villain, and R. Lee Ermy is the captain. With Deborah Adair, Ely Pouget, and Edmund Purdom.

ENDLESS LOVE

(MCA, 1981) **D:** Franco Zeffirelli **S:** Judith Rascoe **P:** Dyson Lovell

Martin Hewitt is obsessed with Brooke Shields (who used a body double for love scenes), and he likes to start fires. Shirley Knight and Don Murray play her concerned parents. This pretty hilarious troubled-teen movie, based on a novel by Scott Spencer, has some interesting cast members: with James Spader (in his debut) as her brother, Tom Cruise (in his debut) as an arsonist, Jami Gertz, Richard Kiley, Beatrice Straight, and Penelope Milford. The theme is by Lionel Richie singing duet with Diana Ross. Hewitt later became a minor direct-to-video star.

THE ENDLESS SUMMER

(1966) **D/S/P/E/C:** Bruce Brown

Three surfers search for the perfect wave in this 16mm low-budget documentary shot in Australia, New Zealand, Tahiti, Nigeria, and Hawaii in 1963–64. They find what they're looking for in South Africa. The PG film made "$30 million" and helped spread the sport of surfing. Brown also narrates. The Sandals provided the music, and an album was released on World Pacific. Brown also made the motorcycle-racing film *On Any Sunday* (1971).

ENDLESS SUMMER II

(New Line, 1994) **D/S/E:** Bruce Brown **S/E:** Dana Brown **P:** Ron Moler, Roger Riddell

Surfers Pat O'Connell (who uses a short board) and Robert "Wingnut" Weaver (who uses a long board) hit the big waves in Alaska, France, Fiji, Java, and Bali, in this PG sequel. Brown also narrates.

THE END OF AUGUST AT THE HOTEL OZONE

(1967) **D:** Jan Schmidt **S:** Pavel Juracek Czechoslovakia (*Konec Sprna v Hotelu Ozon*)

A group of survivalist women on horseback roam the post-nuke world. The only man they find is an old guy with a hotel, a phonograph, and one record of "The Beer Barrel Polka." Some actual animal-slaughter scenes are included. New Line released this minor cult film in 1970. It's subtitled.

END OF THE ROAD

(Fox, 1970) **D/S/A:** Aram Avakian **S/P:** Terry Southern **S:** Dennis McGuire **P:** Stephen F. Kesten

An English teacher (Stacy Keach) loses his mind at the clinic of Dr. D. (James Earl Jones). Inmates are encouraged to live out fantasies, and one man has sex with a chicken. With Harris Yulin, Dorothy Tristan, Grayson Hall, James Coco, Graham Jarvis, and M. Emmet Walsh. The Allied Artists release, based on a 1958 novel by John Barth, received an X rating, which is why you probably never saw it.

END OF THE WORLD

(SW, 1930/34) **D/S/A:** Abel Gance **S:** Andre Lang **P:** Ivanoff   France (*La Fin Du Monde*)

Martial Novalic (Victor Francen, who later starred in *J'Acusse*) predicts a comet will destroy earth. He has an observatory and a large staff and arranges a meeting of scientists from various countries to plan a better future world. Meanwhile there's a stock market panic, martial law is declared, and Novalic is charged with treason. The common man either prays a lot or panics while the filthy rich have drunken parties. In the end, not all is lost but we get to see creative montages of mass destruction. Gance's 105-minute 1930 epic was cut to only 54 minutes and played on the American roadshow circuit in 1934 as *Paris After Dark*. This is the condensed verion, leaving out the main character of Novalic's Christ-like brother (played by Gance himself) and the more revealing orgy scenes. America was spared the nudity, serious politics, and blasphemous crucifixion scene, but got to see a new, long stage-bound introduction (very much like the one used for the 1930 *Dracula*) by Dr. Clyde Fisher. This is a real rarity.

ENEMY AGENT

(1940) **D:** Lew Landers **S:** Sam Robins, Edmund L. Hartmann **P:** Ben Pivar

Richard Cromwell stars as a draftsman mistaken for a spy. G-men are trying to recover some stolen security plans. This one-hour Universal B movie features footage from *Radio Patrol*, a 1937 serial, and was part of the original Shock TV package. With Helen Vinson, Robert Armstrong, Marjorie Reynolds, Jack Arnold, and Jack LaRue.

ENEMY GOLD

(Prism, 1993) **D/P:** Drew Sidaris **S:** Wess Rahn, Christine Sidaris

Suzi Simpson stars (with a high-tech crossbow), and Bruce Penhall and Mark Barriere are federal agents. Hitwoman Jewel Panther (Julie Strain) and some Bolivian drug dealers are after a stash of Confederate gold in East Texas and Louisiana. With Tai Collins. There are lots of topless scenes, guns, and bikinis. It was a family affair. Parents Andy and Arlene Sidaris were the executive producers.

ENEMY MINE

(CBS/Fox, 1985) **D:** Wolfgang Petersen **S:** Edward Khmara **P:** Stephen Friedman

Remember *Robinson Crusoe on Mars*? Well, here's an expensive version of the same idea with elements from *The Mole People* and modern ILM FX. Dennis Quaid and Lou Gossett Jr. (as a hermaphrodite "Drac") are both stranded on a barren planet. Gossett (with amazing makeup by Chris Walas) has escaped from space slave traders. With Brion James and Lance Kerwin. The film (based on a story by Barry B. Longyear) was started by Richard Loncrane, who shot millions of dollars worth of footage. It was all scrapped, the locations were changed, and Petersen was hired. The $33 million cost includes all of the footage shot.

ENEMY TERRITORY

(Empire, 1987) **D:** Peter Manoogian **S:** Stuart Kaminsky, Bobby Liddell **P:** Cynthia DePaula, Tim Kincaid

Insurance agent Gary Frank is sent to the worst possible Bronx housing project, where he faces the Vampires, a black street gang. The NAACP prevented the screening of this movie in NYC, calling it racist. With Stacy Dash, Jan-Michael Vincent as a wheelchair-bound psycho Nam vet, singer Ray Parker Jr., and Tony Todd as the Count. Guest star Vincent was in the middle of his worst drug-and-alcohol abuse when he appeared.

ENEMY UNSEEN

(AIP, 1991) **D/P:** Elmo De Witt **S/A:** Greg Latter **P:** Desiree Markgraaf   S. Africa

Vernon Wells and a multi-racial mercenary group save Roxy (Angela O'Neill) the daughter of a wealthy American industrialist from a black tribe that worships crocodiles. They sacrifice women to the croc and have subtitles when they talk. Most of the time is spent on an *Apocalypse Now*–style river journey. With Stack Pierce and Ken Gampu.

THE ENEMY WITHIN

(HBO, 1994) **D:** Jonathon Kirby **S:** Darryl Ponnnicssan, Ron Bass **P:** Robert Papazian

Forest Whitaker stars in a cable TV remake of *Seven Days in May* (1964) which was scripted by Rod Serling. It's about a military coup in America led by Jason Robards. With Sam Waterston and Dana Delaney.

THE ENFORCER

(Warner, 1976) **D:** James Fargo **S:** Dean Reiser, Sterling Silliphant **P:** Robert Daley

In the third Dirty Harry movie, Clint Eastwood is teamed with a female cop (Tyne Daly) in San Francisco. They argue and go after an underground terrorist group of Nam vets who kidnap the mayor and bomb police headquarters. With Harry Guardino, Bradford Dillman, Albert Popwell, and John Mitchum. Not to be confused with the 1951 Bogart film of the same name.

ENFORCER FROM DEATH ROW

(Lightning, 1978) **D:** Efron C. Pinon, Marshall M. Bordon **P:** Michael Badway, Michael Sullivan **C:** Frank Harris Philippines (*Ninja Nightmare; Ninja Assassins*)

Leo Fong is a kung fu fighter on death row, who is released to save the world from bad guys with a deadly bacteria in the Philippines. With bad ninjas, torture scenes, and expolsions. Cameron Mitchell has a small role. Mitchell and Fong were also in *Kill Point* and *Low Blow,* both by this feature's cinematographer.

ENTER THE DEVIL = THE TORMENTED

ENTER THE DRAGON

(Warner, 1973) **D:** Robert Clouse **S:** Michael Allin **P:** Fred Weintraub, Paul Heller

Bruce Lee stars in his last real movie (as Lee). It was a huge international hit, was released the year he died, and made more than $11 1/2 million in North American rentals alone. This is the most famous, most copied, and most spoofed of all kungfu hits. It has some of the best fight scenes of all time. Many of its stars launched careers by appearing in it. John Saxon as Roper and Jim Kelly as Williams are the costars, forced to fight at a secret island fortress. Kelly spends too much time with women and is beaten and tortured. With martial-arts star Angela Mao (Ying), Shih Kien/Master Bong Soo Han (with a lethal hand attachment), Anha Capri, and Marlene Clark. Samo Hung, Jackie Chan, and other future martial-arts stars are seen briefly. Yang Sze (later billed as Bolo Yeung or "the Chinese Hercules") was still playing bad guys in martial-arts movies in the 90s. The Lalo Schifrin soundtrack is on Warner.

ENTER THE NINJA

(MGM/UA, 1981) **D/S:** Menahem Golan **S/P:** Judd Bernard **S:** Dick Desmond **P:** Yoram Globus

Franco Nero as Cole goes to the Philippines to help his friend Alex Courtney save his plantation. Susan George costars, Sho Kosugi is the bad ninja, and

Christopher George is the main villain. People scoffed at Nero as a martial-arts fighter (this was years after he starred in Italian westerns) and this movie is pretty silly, but it was popular, and Kosugi (not Nero) returned in more Cannon ninja movies.

THE ENTITY

(CBS/Fox, 1982) **D:** Sidney J. Furie **S:** Frank De Felitta **P:** Harold Schneider

Barbara Hershey stars as a suburban single mom who is repeatedly raped by an invisible demon. Nobody believes her, of course, until she's isolated at a university and the supernatural being shows up and is frozen. Scenes of Hershey naked and being molested were done with special effects and fake body parts (by Stan Winston). The 42nd Street audience went wild. With Ron Silver, Alex Rocco, and Jacqueline Brooks. It was adapted from De Felitta's novel, which was supposedly based on an actual case (!?). He also wrote *Audrey Rose.* It was released by 20th Century–Fox.

EPITAPH

(City Lights, 1987) **D/S/P:** Joseph Merhi **P:** Richard Pepin

An LA detective (Jim Williams) covers up the murders committed by his wife (Delores Nascar). She uses many imaginative, sick ways to kill (mostly) men.

EQUALIZER 2000

(MGM/UA, 1986) **D:** Cirio H. Santiago **S/A:** Frederick Bailey **P:** Leonard Hermes   Philippines

The title refers to a gun. This is a dumb *Mad Max* clone set in Alaska "100 years after the nuclear winter." *Penthouse* Pet of the Year Corinne Alphen (later Wahl) was Miss Nude Massachusetts of 1987. She stars with the bearded Australian Richard Norton as Slade, who lives in a cave equipped with a metalworking shop. With Robert Patrick and Filipino character actor Vic Diaz.

Jim Kelly, John Saxon and Bruce Lee in *Enter The Dragon.*

EQUINOX

(Columbia, 1993) **D/S:** Alan Rudolph **P:** David Blocker

Identical twins (both Matthew Modine) in the near-future city of Empire live parallel lives. One is a

gangster, one is a shy garage mechanic. Sometimes Rudolph tries to make easy-to-follow hits. This isn't one of them. With Tyra Ferrell as a morgue attendent trying to solve a mystery, Marisa Tomei, Lara Flynn Boyle, Lori Singer, Fred Ward, M. Emmet Walsh, Kevin J. O'Connor, and Tate Donovan. Not to be confused with the 1967 film of the same name.

ERIKA'S HOT SUMMER

(SW, 1970) **D/P/C:** Gary Graver **P:** Paul Hunt

A playboy photographer takes nude shots of a woman outdoors, goes to a hippie dance where the strobe lights never stop, and has sex with another woman. All the while, he remembers the one who got away (*Vixen* star Erica Gavin). Erica is the reason this Box Office International release did business. She strips and runs on the beach naked, falls in love, and frolics with the photographer in frequent flashbacks. The soft-rock music and romantic tone make it seem like an attempt at a "couples movie." The ending is memorable.

ERIK THE VIKING

(Orion, 1989) **D/S/A:** Terry Jones **P:** John Goldstone   UK

Tim Robbins (a few years before audiences realized who he was) stars as the dumb but sensitive Erik, at the battle of Ragnarok. He sails to the end of the world (and to Atlantis, to Hell, and over the rainbow). This PG-13 comedy from the co-director of *Monty Python and the Holy Grail* features Mickey Rooney as the grandfather, John Cleese as Halfdan the Black, Eartha Kitt, Freddie Jones, and a dragon. The Norse gods are revealed to be little kids. It was filmed in Norway and Malta. The music is by Neil Innes.

ERNEST GOES TO CAMP

(Touchstone, 1987) **D/S:** John Cherry **S:** Coke Sams **P:** Stacy Williams

A lot of stars do commercials, but this is a case of a guy who did successful (local) TV commercials becoming a movie star (for a while at least) because of them. Jim Varney (from Lexington, Kentucky) had been on *Fernwood 2-night* and other TV shows since 1976. Cherry had directed nearly 4,000 Ernest P. Worrell commercials (compiled on the *Ernest Film Festival* and *Hey, Vern! It's My Family Album* videos) and the obscure *Dr. Otto and the Riddle of the Gloom Beam.* This PG comedy hit was filmed in Nashville. Ernest is a very dumb janitor put in charge of summer-camp misfits. With John Vernon, Iron Eyes Cody, and Lyle Alzado. It made nearly $10 million in North American rentals, so sequels followed, from Disney's Touchstone.

ERNEST GOES TO JAIL

(Touchstone, 1990) **D/S:** John Cherry **P:** Stacy Williams

ENGLAND

The country that revitalized the horror market (thanks mostly to Hammer) and the rock-music business, and gave us James Bond in the 60s, seemed to be in a creative (and economic) slide by the 80s. Sure, there were some classic 80s films, but it's been a long time since we looked to the UK for reliable shocks (or decent music). The prolific studios are gone, the best directors are dead or retired, and no new horror stars have emerged to replace Cushing and Lee. But there are many older features to rediscover and enjoy.

There were so many prison/horror/electric-chair movies in the late 80s that this PG parody was inevitable. Jim Varney as Ernest P. Worrell ends up in jail. Varney plays Ernest and his evil lookalike too. With Charles Napier as the warden, Randall "Tex" Cobb, and the actress with the topical name, Barbara Bush.

ERNEST RIDES AGAIN

(Monarch, 1993) **D/S:** John Cherry
S: Wiliam A. Akers **P:** Stacy Williams   Canada

Ernest helps a Virginia college professor (Ron K. James) find a Revolutionary War cannon with the British crown jewels hidden inside. This *Indiana Jones*–inspired PG chase comedy was shot in British Columbia by an independent production company. *Ernest Goes to School* (Monarch), by a different director, followed.

ERNEST SAVES CHRISTMAS

(Touchstone, 1988) **D:** John Cherry **S:** B. Kline, Ed Turner **P:** Stacy Williams, Doug Claybourne

Christmas movies have always been a sure box-office bet. Enough people will always send their kids to watch them. Jim Varney as Ernest, a Florida cabdriver, picks up Santa, who is looking for a successor. With Douglas Seale, Oliver Clark, and Billie Bird.

ERNEST SCARED STUPID

(Touchstone, 1991) **D/S:** John Cherry **P:** Stacy Williams

In the fourth and last of the PG series made by Disney's Touchstone, a witch accidentally releases an indestructible, evil, giant troll in Missouri on Halloween. It turns kids into wooden voodoo dolls and unleashes other trolls and monsters. Jim Varney (who plays several characters) stars, with Eartha Kitt and a truck-driving dog.

EROTICA

(1961) **D/S/P/C/E/A:** Russ Meyer **P:** Peter D. Cenzie

This rare, early Russ Meyer film is nothing but a series of six shorts presented by an onscreen film editor. They have names like *Bikini Busters* and *Nudists on the High Seas*. It's 65 minutes.

THE EROTIC ADVENTURES OF PINOCCHIO

(American, 1971) **D/S:** Corey Allen **S/P:** Chris Warfield

A fairy godmother (blond Dyanne Thorne, looking great) strips and introduces this dumb sex-comedy version of the familiar children's story, which should have been on a double bill with *Lady Frankenstein*. Cepeta (nudie regular Monica Gayle) works naked, carving "the perfect man" (Alex Roma). The naive "wooden" man is led astray by Jojo and ends up satisfying all the women at a whorehouse. In a lesbian scene Uschi Digart and her friend have dubbed-in male voices. Pinocchio even performs in a live sex show. His penis (never shown without covering) grows "three feet" long. Women throw wreaths on it, walk on it, and ride it. A running gag is that Thorne waves her magic wand and accidentally makes her clothes disappear. This was the first film by former teen actor Corey Allen, from Cleveland (*Rebel Without a Cause*), who went on to direct *Avalanche* (1978) and TV's *Star Trek: The Next Generation* (1987). Ray Dennis Steckler was the cinematographer, and his wife Carolyn Brandt has a small role watching the sex show. Back in 1971, *Adam Film World* magazine put out a *Pinocchio* photo comic (just like the great *Horror of Party Beach* magazine) for $1. Try and find a copy now!

EROTIC ADVENTURES OF SUPERKNIGHT

(Academy, 1976) **D/S/P:** Raphael Nussbaum   *(The Amorous Adventures of Don Quixote and Sancho Panza)*

This unique R-rated American musical/sex comedy set in Spain has good (dubbed) singing and some pretty outrageous and funny lyrics (a woman sings "You Come Too Soon," for instance). With Patrick Wright and Haji, from Russ Meyer films. It almost seems like an attempt at making a period rock musical with lots of nudity. The assistant director was Henning Schellerup (*In Search of Historic Jesus*).

THE EROTIC ADVENTURES OF ZORRO

(SW, 1971) **D:** Robert Freeman **S/P:** David F. Friedman

After a nice photo-comic-book come-to-life credit sequence, a narrator takes us back to LA 150 years ago. It's the usual Zorro story with lots of dumb gags and jokes plus sex and full nudity. The sex-in-the-straw scene is pretty hot, and there are the expected lesbian and whipping scenes and masturbation by foot. Douglas Frey stars as Don Diego/Zorro, who puts on a gay act. Costar Robyn Whiting (real name Jackie Giroux) later married Steve Railsback. With John Alderman as Esteban and Bob Cresse as Sergeant Phil Latio. It was filmed on the old Selznick lot used for *Duel in the Sun* and has high production values. French and German producers put up two-thirds of the money (about $75,000 total!). The color print is very good. There was also *The Erotic Adventures of the Three Musketeers,* from West Germany, the same year.

EROTIC EVE: *See* BLACK COBRA

EROTIC ILLUSION: *See* THE LICKERISH QUARTET

EROTIC INSTINCT: *See* THE LICKERISH QUARTET

EROTIC NIGHTS OF THE LIVING DEAD

(VSOM, 1980) **D/C:** "Joe D'Amato"/Aristide Massaccesi   Italy (*Le Notte Erotiche dei Morte Viventi*)

A man buys the supposedly uninhabited tropical cat island and goes there with a woman and the owner of a boat. A mysterious woman (*Black Emanuelle* series star Laura Gemser) is there with her grandfather (who can't be photographed), lots of cats (seen in frequent closeups), and (finally) slow-moving maggot-faced zombies in rags. Meanwhile, the main part of this movie is one (unfinished) sex scene after another (on a boat, in the water, on the beach) and some nude dancing. The sex-crazed survivor (George Eastman) is seen in a mental hospital at the beginning and end of the movie, which has been subtitled in English for the first time. *Porno Holocaust* is the same movie with hard-core inserts. The full-length Italian version runs 103 minutes.

THE EROTIC RITES OF FRANKENSTEIN

(Nightmare, 1972) **D/S:** Jesús Franco
P: Victor de Costa   Spain/France
(*La Maldición de Frankenstein*)

Cagliostro (Howard Vernon) has Dr. Frankenstein killed and kidnaps his daughter, Vera (blond Britt Nichols), and the monster (Fernando Bilbo). He keeps her chained in the basement, holds a coven with masked, naked zombie women, and creates a (naked) woman. In the most outrageous scene Vera and a man are tied up (naked) back to back over poison spikes while the monster flogs them. Anne Lipert plays an interesting (naked) bird woman with blue feathers, lethal claws, and psychic powers. Vernon's fake goatees change from scene to scene. Dennis Price appears in one scene as the doctor, and Franco is his assistant. This ridiculous (but imaginative) movie has some jazz on the soundtrack. It was made in Portugal. Letterboxed copies are around. They same cast appeared in Franco's *The Screaming Dead* the same year.

EROTIC TALES

(1994) **D/S:** Bob Rafelson, Susan Seidelman, Ken Russell, Melvin Van Peebles, Paul Cox, Mani Kaul

6 mostly comic stories make up this international compilation film, much like similar ones from Europe in the 60s but with more nudity. Rafelson's stars Arliss Howard and Cynda Williams.

Seidelman's is a fantasy with a woman who enters the world of a Dutch painting and Van Peebles's features a motorcycle that becomes a woman.

THE EROTIC TOUCH OF HOT SKIN

(Video Dimensions, 1964) **D/S:** Max Pecas
S: Maurice Cury, Robert Torolt

A young couple become involved with a murder (and a younger woman). Fabienne Dali (later in *Kill, Baby, Kill*), Sophie Hardy (who strips her clothes off several times), and Jean Valmont star in this b/w dark, adult crime film. Radley Metzger shot and added new footage in America, and his Audubon company released the film in the US. Several strip sequences seem to have been added.

EROTIKILL

(Force, 1973) **D/S/A:** "J. P. Johnson"/
Jesús Franco **S:** Gerard Brissard **P:** Marius
Lesoeur France (*La Comtesse Noir*;
The Bare-Breasted Countess; *The Loves of Irina*)

Lina Romay stars as (the mute) Countess Irina Karlstein, a cursed vampire who can become a bat. She falls for a poet (Jack Taylor). Franco plays a forensic surgeon, and Dr. Orloff shows up as a blind hippie. With Monica Swinn and Alice Arno. *Erotikill* is the 72-minute horror version. *The Loves of Irina* (Private Screenings) is a much longer sex/horror version without the vampire angle. A European version includes hard-core deep-throat sex scenes. It was shot on a Portuguese island. Video Search of Miami offers the ultimate subtitled composite version for Franco collectors.

ESCAPADE IN JAPAN

(1957) **D/P:** Arthur Lubin **S:** Winston Miller

Jon Provost (from *Lassie*) and Roger Nakagawa are the kid stars of this light Technicolor film made on location in Japan. Cameron Mitchell and Teresa Wright are the parents, and Clint Eastwood is Dumbo, a helpful American pilot. Eastwood was in three earlier Arthur Lubin films: *Francis in the Navy*, *Lady Godiva*, and *The First Traveling Saleslady*. This was made by RKO but released by Universal after Howard Hughes sold his studio.

THE ESCAPE ARTIST

(Vestron, 1980) **D:** Caleb Deschanel
S: Melissa Mathison, Stephen Zito
P: Doug Claybourne, Buck Houghton

Griffin O'Neal stars as the son of a magician killed by corrupt local politicians. He investigates on his own and does some Houdini-inspired escapes. Francis Ford Coppola was the executive producer. The director had shot *The Right Stuff* and *Being There*. Mathison cowrote *E.T.* (and married Harrison Ford). Few people saw the film when it was finally released by Orion in 1982. I liked it for the cast, the fact that it was partially shot in Cleveland, and a scene in a magic store owned by Jackie (Uncle Fester) Coogan (in his last role). The store's walls are covered with rare items from the collection of magician Bill Weldon (my father). With Raul Julia, Desi Arnaz (in his last role) as the mayor, Teri Garr,

Joan Hackett (in her last role), John P. Ryan, M. Emmet Walsh, Huntz Hall, and Gabriel Dell.

ESCAPE FROM BLOOD PLANTATION

(Marathon, 1982)
D/S/A: Kurt Raab W. Germany
(*Insel der Blutigen Plantage*)

"Bloody Olga" runs a Philippine island prison with the help of three horny dwarfs. With spiders, voodoo, and female inmates. Udo Kier and Barbara Valentine star, with the director. All of them had been in Fassbinder features, so don't expect action. The theme song is *The Island of the Bloody Plantation*.

ESCAPE FROM CELL BLOCK 3: *See* WOMEN UNCHAINED

ESCAPE FROM HELL: *See* SAVAGE ISLAND

ESCAPE FROM PLANET EARTH = DOOMSDAY

ESCAPE FROM SAFEHAVEN

(Sony, 1988) **D/S:** Brian Thomas Jones,
James McCalmont **P:** Steven Mackler

A punk-look post-nuke NYC bomb shelter is the setting. The villains are British, and there's a topless blond dominatrix. It was shot in Brooklyn by the makers of *Rejuvenator*.

ESCAPE FROM SURVIVAL ZONE

(AIP, 1990) **D:** Chris Jones **S:** Mark Talbot-Butler
P: Geoff Griffiths, John E. Eyres

Terence Ford (brother of Harrison) stars as an alcoholic news photographer who discovers a scandal at a survivalist training camp.

ESCAPE FROM TERROR

(1960) **D:** George Coogan **D/A:** Jackie
Coogan **S/P:** Egon C. Nielsen

"It's Yankee ingenuity vs. ruthless red-agent cunning!" The future Uncle Fester (Coogan) stars as MVD agent Petrov (and directs!). Mona Knox and Mike Stokey escape from the Baltics to Copenhagen. Gabriel Dell and Lynn Merrick also appear. The Coogan Film production is in b/w and color. Coogan was in *Sex Kittens Go to College* the same year.

ESCAPE FROM THE BRONX

(Media, 1983) **D:** Enzo G. Castellari
S: Dardana Sachetti Italy (*Fuga dal Bronx*)

Mark Gregory returns as Trash in a violent post-nuke sequel to *1990: The Bronx Warriors*. With Henry Silva as the head of the goverment extermination squad and Timothy Brent.

ESCAPE FROM WOMEN'S PRISON

(VGB, Lettuce, Continental, 1974) **D:** Conrad Buegnel
S: Giovanni Brusatori **S/P:** Bruno Fontana **P:** Aldo
Baglietta Italy (*Mujer Contra Mujer*)

Four women on the run (including a revolutionary and a lesbian drug addict) hijack a bus full of tennis players. They hold them hostage and abuse them in a mansion. A Dick Randall presentation, it was on a tape with *Sweet Sugar*.

ESCAPES

(Prism, 1986) **D/S/P:** David Steensland
P: Angela Sanders

Vincent Price, as a mailman, introduces 6 mediocre *Twilight Zone*–type short stories. At the beginning, he delivers an *Escapes* tape to a kid, who then watches it. The end concept is copied from *Dead of Night*. With John Mitchum. Price wasn't choosing his projects with much care at this point.

ESCAPE 2000

(Nelson, 1980) **D:** Brian Trenchard-Smith
S: Jon George, Neill Hicks **P:** Anthony I. Ginane,
William Fayman Australia (*Turkey Shoot*)

In the future (1995), a fascist government puts rebel "deviants" in a concentration camp. Star Steve Railsback is tortured in a cage. Olivia Hussey takes showers and is nearly gang-raped. Michael Craig runs the camp, where prisoners are allowed to escape, then are tracked down. Australian critics chose it as the worst movie ever made in their country. With Lynda Stoner, Carmen Duncan, and a killer female midget. The extreme violence (and some nudity) was cut for the 77-minute New World US release, but there were rating problems anyway. Brian May provided the soundtrack.

ESMERALDA BAY

(VSOM, 1989) **D/S/A:** Jesús Franco **S/P:** Daniel Lesoeúr   France/Spain (*La Bahia Esmeralda*)

A corrupt colonel, Madero (Brett Halsey), runs the Central American republic of Puerto Santo. This spy story features Robert Foster as a rebel leader, Fernando Rey as the president, George Kennedy as a rich arms dealer, Ramón Sheen (Estevez), and Lina Romay.

ETERNAL EVIL

(Vestron, 1985) **D:** George Mihalka **S:** Robert Geoffrin **P:** Pieter Kroonenburg   Canada (*A Blue Man*)

Winston Rekert stars as a TV commercial director who sees killings in his sleep. The story involves astral projection and ancient couples who inhabit young bodies. The disorienting special effects, from an out-of-body-experience point of view, and some erotic scenes make this pretty interesting. With Karen Black as a lesbian and Lois Maxwell (from James Bond movies). By the director of *My Bloody Valentine*.

ETERNITY

(Academy, 1989) **D/S/A:** Stephen Paul **S/A:** Jon Voight **S:** Dorothy Kostner Paul   (*Avator*)

It's hard to figure why, after years away from the screen, Oscar winner Jon Voight would cowrite and star in this preachy, illogical, flashback-filled feelgood fantasy movie, which tries to be the new *Billy Jack*. I'd consider the concept of reincarnation, but all the characters in the medieval British scenes somehow show up in modern-day America reincarnated as similar characters. Voight plays an honest, cosmic morning-TV host and studio owner. He's a friend to the Indians, rides a white horse, and says, "Let's live in peace and harmony." At one point his old self gets to comfort and advise his modern self. Armand Assante and John P. Ryan are the villains. Voight's reincarnated true love (Eileen Davidson) is naked in the flashbacks and has sex standing up (with her clothes on) with Assante. It all ends with religious imagery as the whole country rises up against rampant corruption. The oddball cast includes Wilford Brimley ("It's the right thing to do"), Kaye Ballard, Lainie Kazan, Charles Dierkof, Frankie Valli as Guido, and Jilly Rizzo. Young do-it-all Paul also made *Slapstick of Another Kind* (1982), starring Jerry Lewis. His parents back movies made by him and his brother, Stuart.

EUREKA

(MGM, 1983) **D:** Nicolas Roeg **S:** Paul Mayersberg **P:** Jeremy Thomas   UK

Gene Hackman stars as a prospector who, after many years, strikes gold. He buys a tropical island, but gangsters show up and want it for a gambling resort. As his life and family fall apart, a voodoo ceremony/orgy takes place (resembling some scenes from the later *Angel Heart*). It all ends in a trial for murder and *Citizen Kane*–inspired flash-

backs. This complex, troubled, 129-minute film was (barely) released in theaters by United Artists. Theresa Russell costars as the daughter, with Rutger Hauer, Ed Lauter, Joe Pesci, and Mickey Rourke.

EUROPE IN THE RAW

(1963) **D/P/C:** Russ Meyer

You may never see this early *Mondo*-style sex documentary by Meyer, because he later used footage from it, featuring Denise Duvall, Heidi Richter, and other beauties, for his *Mondo Topless* (1966). Strippers and prostitutes are shown in various European cities.

EVE AND THE HANDYMAN

(RM, 1960) **D/S/P/C/E:** Russ Meyer

Meyer's second feature stars his wife, Eve, in all the major female roles. She also narrates. Dressed as a detective, she follows the comic handyman (Anthony James-Ryan) as he encounters artists, hitchhikers, and nude sunbathers. The 65-minute film, shot in San Francisco, was shown with a 10-minute Meyer short called *The Naked Camera*. Meyer released this on tape for the first time in 1992. He did not direct *Eve and the Merman*, a 1965 nudie.

EVEL KNIEVEL

(1971) **D:** Marvin Chomsky **S:** John Milius, Allan Caillou **P/A:** George Hamilton

When you think of George Hamilton's hits, there's *Love at First Bite* (1979) and this one. He plays the real-life motorcycle daredevil and 70s media star, and there's lots of stunt work. With Vic Tayback, Dub Taylor, Sue Lyon, Bert Freed, Judy Baldwin, Rod Cameron, and Cheryl "Rainbeaux" Smith. The real Evel was in *Viva Knievel! (1978)*. Milius also cowrote *The Devil's Eight* (1969).

EVEN COWGIRLS GET THE BLUES

(New Line, 1993) **D/S:** Gus Van Sant **P:** Lauir Parker

This rambling feminist fantasy road movie was based on Tom Robbins' "unfilmable" 1976 novel. Uma Thurman (who narrates) stars as the wide-eyed hitchhiking virgin model Cissy Hamkshaw (with extra large thumbs). In 1973, Countess (John Hurt) sends her to the Rubber Rose Ranch where she meets a band of renegade lesbian cowgirls who use peyote. With Rain Phoenix as Jellybean, and Lorraine Bracco. Keanu Reeves is an Indian, Pat Morita is a wise man in a cave, and Buck Henry is a doctor. Other small roles are played by Angie Dickinson, Sean Young paired with Crispin Glover, Ed Begley Jr. paired with Carol Kane, Udo Kier, Roseanne Arnold, Ken Kesey, and singer Victoria Williams. William Burroughs is seen crossing a street. The U.S Fine Line premiere was delayed for the director to reedit and the narration by Robbins was added. k.d. lang is on the hit soundtrack. The FX are by Steve Johnson.

EVEN DWARFS STARTED SMALL

(1969) **D/S/P/M:** Werner Herzog   W. Germany (*Auch Zwerge Haben Klein Angefangen*)

Of all of Herzog's unusual films, this might be his most extreme statement. It's also the first movie since *The Terror of Tiny Town* with a cast of "little people." Some of the dwarfs and midgets who are inmates at the "institution" stage a revolt, trash the place, torment other (blind) dwarfs and midgets, fight one another for power, and crucify a monkey.

EVEN HITLER HAD A GIRLFRIEND

(Scorched Earth, 1991) **D/S/M:** Ronnie Cramer

A soft-spoken depressed, voyeuristic security guard eats beef jerky and watches cable TV in his underwear. He also narrates and/or thinks out loud throughout the whole film. He worries that he looks like a serial killer, and his father shows up on TV to criticize him. He starts calling for hookers (and bargains them down on the phone), gets a video camera, and tapes the paid-for sex. He also catches crab lice and has even more problems. The music (by Cramer's Alarming Trends) is fine, and most the the movie is pretty believable, but it sure isn't much fun to watch. Star Andy Scott was later shot to death while working at a convience store. It was made in Omaha. A sequel is *The Hitler Tapes*.

EVE OF DESTRUCTION

(Nelson, 1991) **D/S:** Duncan Gibbons **S:** Yale Udoff **P:** David Madden

Dutch actress Renee Soutendijk stars as Dr. Eve Simmons and her lookalike android creation, Eve VIII. The lethal robot (with a nuclear device) escapes and lives out some of her divorced creator's fantasies. She kills whenever a man calls her a bitch and picks up a guy in a bar and bites off his cock (offscreen). Gregory Hines as an antiterrorist specialist tries to stop the confused, out-of-control robo-woman. With Kevin McCarthy as the abusive father, Michael Greene, and Nancy Locke. It starts in San Francisco, moves to a small town, and has a senseless ending involving a baby in a New York City subway station. It's not very good. The Philip Sarde soundtrack is on Colossal. It's from Orion.

EVERYBODY LOVES IT

(SW, 1964) **D:** Phillip Mark **S/P:** Edward Everitt

Alfred E. Newman, Hitler, and Ben Casey show up in this color nudie comedy. A comic voice narrates, and a TV-studio janitor is the main character. The topless and nearly nude scenes were the selling points, but the comedy dominates. *Combat, The Naked City*, and Marlboro cigarette TV ads are other targets of spoofs. In the best scenes women do the twist outdoors. With Little Jack Little (from *Not Tonight, Henry*) as the Dr. Zorba character.

EVERY BREATH

(Columbia, 1992) **D/S:** Steve Bing **S/A:** Judd Nelson **S:** Andrew Fleming **P:** Steve Stabler, Brad Kevoy

Nelson is pretty uninteresting as a broke, unemployed actor who is beaten up twice in one day. He follows Joanna Pacula to a lesbian club, then to her home. She's afraid of her rich arms-dealer husband (Patric Bachau), who likes to bury people alive and watch them on a wall of TVs. It all turns out to be dangerous game-playing by the bored couple. John Pyper Ferguson costars in this dull movie. The music is by Nils Lofgren.

EVERY MAN FOR HIMSELF AND GOD AGAINST ALL

(1974) **D/S/P:** Werner Herzog (*Jeder, Fur Sich und Gott Gegen Alle; The Mystery of Kaspar Hauser*)

A wild boy (Bruno S.) found in the 1820s near Nuremberg learns to read and write quickly. He claims he was kept in a hole for 16 years and some think he's the heir to the Dukedom of Baden. Hauser was later murdered. One of Herzog's greatest films, it's based on a German legend/mystery. A new version was made in 1993.

EVIL ALTAR

(Southgate, 1988) **D:** Jim Winburn
S: Bred Friedman **P:** Robert A. Miller

Now, here's a plot. In the small town of Red Rock, big and bald William Smith is Reed Weller, a (French?) Satanist wearing all-black clothes and Chinese slippers. He orders "the collector," his one assistant, "Bring me 103 victims. The last must be a virgin, and they must not be from this town." 30 years later, the collector, looking like a demented bum in mirror sunglasses and a stocking cap, is still at it, stuffing bodies in a dirty sack. Weller also changes the future for locals who cooperate with him. Robert Z'Dar (from *Maniac Cop*), a strange-looking actor nearly as big as Smith, plays an asshole cop who helps cover up the disappearances of all the missing children. At one point the collector dies, then shows up on a TV set. A floating killer baseball threatens a young girl. This ridiculous movie has lots of nonsense dialogue and some serious continuity problems. The synthesizer score goes, "Aahhhhh!"

THE EVIL BELOW

(Raedon, 1989) **D:** Jean-Claude Dubois **S:** Art Payne **P:** Barrie Saint Claire   South Africa

Wayne Crawford, as Max Cash, and June Chadwick dive for sunken treasure. There are shark attacks, a cursed island, and lots of nightmare scenes.

EVIL CLUTCH

(Rhino, 1988) **D/S:** Andreas Marfori
P: Agnes Fontana   Italy (*Notte nel Bosco*)

A young couple on vacation in a small town are warned of danger by a strange man on a motorcycle who talks with a voice box. A young woman who asks them for help is really some kind of demon. The filmakers must have seen the *Evil Dead* movies a few times, because the rest of the movie is nonsense dismemberment, chainsaws, and gore, taken to absurd extremes. There's a lot of pointless and irritating POV camera work. The title is from an early scene, where a guy's crotch is clawed. It was made in Italy (in and around a nice-looking old town) but everyone speaks English with very strong accents. The director returned with *Desperate Crimes*.

EVIL COME, EVIL GO

(Luna, 1972) **D/S:** Walt Davis **P:** Robert C. Chin

Sister Sarah Jane Butler (Cleo O'Hara, using a hillbilly accent) has her own religion on the streets of LA. She sings hymns, plays an accordion, and preaches against "pleasurable sex" and "love-generation men" in front of Grauman's Chinese Theater. Penny (Sandra Harrison) takes her in ("I'm a lesbian, but I'll stop it") and becomes her disciple and servant, luring men to be killed, robbed, then buried in the yard. This odd adult movie has some bloody scenes, some (near-X) sex scenes (lesbian and straight), and comic sound effects. In the non-ending, a folksinging hippie, seen in the background earlier, follows the women. O'Hara is pretty convincing. With porno stars Rick Cassidy and John Holmes (playing pool!). Chin directed some of Holmes' best-known features, and Holmes was the assistant director of this one!

THE EVIL DEAD

(HBO, 1982) **D/S:** Sam Raimi **P:** Robert G. Tapert

This first-time, low-budget horror movie not only led to a successful career for its creator but was one of the most original features of the 80s. It was started in 1979 (as *Book of the Dead*), shot in 16mm in Tennessee. Effects shots were added in Franklin, Michigan. It was eventually completed for $90,000. That money came from Detroit-area dentists and doctors (who got a 350 percent return on their investment). It hit in the UK first, and a Stephen King quote helped spread the word. New Line released it in the US in 1983. The whole cast, five students in a remote cabin, open a book they shouldn't, are possessed, mutate, and attack one another. The plot is the same as *Equinox* (1967), itself a recommended cult film. The innovative "shakycam" camerawork has been imitated a lot (especially in Hong Kong). Future director Joel Coen was the assistant editor. Bruce Campbell stars as Ash. Two not-so-cheap sequels followed. The Joseph DeLuca soundtrack was released on Varèse Sarabande.

Bruce Campbell is Ash in *The Evil Dead*.

EVIL DEAD II: DEAD BY DAWN

(Vestron, 1987) **D/S:** Sam Raimi
S: Scott Spiegel **P:** Robert G. Tapert

Raimi got more money and made a more gory, outrageous, and relentless comedy remake of *The Evil Dead*. It starts with a refilmed, condensed recap of the first film, covering the whole plot in ten minutes. It was backed by De Laurentiis and DEG,

who released it unrated. Steve Wang designed some of the mind-boggling FX. Bruce Campbell returns as Ash, and Sarah Berry is the daughter of the archeologist who originally unleashed the demons. Ash battles his own hand (which laughs at him), and there's the incredible flying eyeball (!). Some of the humor is Three Stooges–inspired, and the surprise cosmic ending set the scene for *Army of Darkness* (1992). The cast includes Theodore Raimi. The Joseph DeLuca soundtrack was released on Varese Sarabande.

EVIL DEAD TRAP

(VSOM, 1991) **D:** Seishu Ikeda
Japan (*Shiryo No Wana*)

The TV-hostess star (Miyuki Ono) of *Nami's Late Night* receives a snuff video in the mail. She and four young female coworkers and one guy go to what seems to be an abandoned former American army base to investigate and most of them (and a nearby rapist) are killed (decapitation, impalement). The influence of Dario Argento is strong in this nearly plotless gore movie, and the music even sounds like Goblin. The mystery killer, in a touch of *Peeping Tom*, listens to tapes of his mother's accusing voice. A few scenes are impressive, but there are way too many false scares. The letter-boxed tape is subtitled. The Japanese title means "creation of a ghost." *Hideki: Evil Dead Trap II* (1993), directed by Isou Hashimoto, features a haunted female movie projectionist. More sequels followed.

EVIL IN THE SWAMP

(Chivron, 1974) **D:** Burt Kennedy **S:** Clyde Ware
P: Roger Lewis   (*All the Kind Strangers*)

Seven orphans, in a remote farm house with killer dogs, trap people to be their new parents. Stacy Keach and Samantha Eggar star, with John Savage, Robby Benson (who also sings the theme song), and Arlene Farber. It was filmed in Tennessee and it debuted on ABC-TV.

EVIL JUDGMENT

(Media, 1984) **D/S/P:** Claudio Castravele **S:** Victor Montesana
P: George Amssellem   Italy

A waitress (Pamela Collyer) joins her hooker friend (Nanette Workman) at a secluded mansion to be with a rich old man. Meanwhile, a psycho slasher who has escaped from an asylum shows up. This bloody movie was filmed in Canada.

THE EVIL OF DRACULA

(Paramount, 1975) **D:** Michio Yamamoto **S:** Ei Ogawa, Masaru Takasue   Japan (*Chio o Suu Bara*)

Like some then-recent Hammer vampire movies, this is set at a remote girls' school. Toshio Kurosawa stars as a new professor who is bitten by the vampire wife of the vampire principal. Flashbacks to 200 years earlier show how a European sailor arrived and spread the terror because he had been forced to renounce Christianity. The third and last of Toho's western-style vampire movies by the same director, it was released to TV in the US. *The Vampire Doll* (1970) and *The Lake Of Dracula* (1971) were the others.

EVIL ROY SLADE

(1972) **D/A:** Jerry Paris **S/P:** Garry Marshall, Jerry Belson

John Astin stars as a man who was raised by wolves in a western comedy pilot for a series (*Sheriff Who?*) that would have shown good guy guest stars being killed every week. The villains would be the regulars. The series never happened, but the NBC pilot (actually two episodes) developed a small cult following and Salvador Dali reportedly said it was his favorite film. With Mickey Rooney, Dick Shawn, Pam Austin, and Dom DeLuise. Also with Milton Berle, Henry Gibson, Edie Adams, Luana Anders, Pat Morita, Penny Marshall, and John Ritter.

EVILS OF THE NIGHT

(Lightning, 1983) **D/S/P:** Mardi Rustam **S:** Philip Dennis Connors

If you want a good example of inept filmmaking created just to supply product and like to see once-popular stars degraded, this is for you! A "space vampire" doctor (John Carradine) is seeking blood for his dying planet. The all-star cast of this mind-numbing movie from the Rustam brothers, Mardi and Mohammed (*Psychic Killer, Eaten Alive*), is outstanding. The plot is recycled from Rustam's *Evil Town*. Julie "Catwoman" Newmar and Tina Louise are the doc's assistants. Louise ("the movie star" on *Gilligan's Island*) replaced Newmar as Stupefyin' Jones in *Lil' Abner* on Broadway back in the 50s. Here they are together! The dumb and sadistic garage mechanics are played by Aldo Ray and Neville Brand (!), who were both in Rustam's production *The Psychic Killer* (1975) and died in the early 90s. Brand also starred in Tobe Hooper's amazing *Eaten Alive* (1976), produced by Mardi, but this was his last known role. The fourth most decorated soldier in America's history unfortunately developed a very bad drug and drinking problem. You might wonder how this tape managed to avoid an X rating, especially the parts with porno stars Amber Lynn, Jerry Butler, and Crystal Breeze. The cast also includes Dawn Wildsmith.

EVIL SPAWN

(Camp, 1986) **D/S:** Kenneth J. Hall **P:** Anthony Brewster, Frank Bresee

Bobbie Bresee (*Mausoleum*) is a faded blond star who injects a youth serum that backfires and turns her into an insect monster, all because she wants the lead in *Savage Goddess*. John Carradine appears for a few minutes. He's the feeble Dr. Zeitman, who tells crazy, evil Donna Shock (Dawn Wildsmith, with really stiff hair), "Carry on with my plan." Bresee has an eye-catching nude shower scene, then looks pretty funny when her teeth grow and her eyes turn red and later when she has a rubber face. She dreams that she wins an Oscar. Forrest J. Ackerman, who helped make Bobbie Bresee a "cult figure," is seen cleaning a pool. This movie

has laughable special effects, lots of nudity, and a script obsessed with the making of cheap movies. Choice bad dialogue is repeated over and over in the deranged actress's mind. Despite everything, *Evil Spawn* is nonstop fun in a sort of desperate way. The best part is when stunning Pamela Gilbert, as the monster woman's secretary, goes for a nude swim. Uncredited executive producer Fred Olen Ray shot the Carradine footage, did rewrites, and shot additional footage. He later prepared a new version called *The Alien Within* (1990).

EVIL SPIRITS

(Prism, 1990) **D/C:** Gary Graver **S/A:** Michael Angel **P:** Sidney Niekerk

Deranged Karen Black owns a boardinghouse where tenants die. She cashes their government checks, turns them into meat loaf, and talks to her husband's mummified corpse. The *Psycho*-derived horror comedy features Arte Johnson, Michael Berryman, Martine Beswick, Robert Quarry, Anthony Eisley, Bert Remsen, and Debra Lamb (who dances naked). Virginia Mayo and Yvette Vickers make their first appearances in many years. Graver also shot many Fred Olen Ray movies with many of the same actors.

EVIL STALKS THIS HOUSE

(1981) **D:** Gordon Hessler **S:** Deke Heyward   (*A Tale Of Evil*)

Jack Palance stars in a cheap-looking TV pilot for a series that never happened called *Tales of the Haunted*. The host is Christopher Lee.

THE EVIL THAT MEN DO

(RCA/Columbia, 1984) **D:** J. Lee Thompson **S:** David Lee Henry, John Crowther **P:** Pancho Kohner

Charles Bronson is a retired hitman living on a tropical-paradise island. He's hired to eliminate a British doctor (Joseph Maher) who tortures his victims and uses shock treatments. This movie, featuring beatings and rape, was Bronson's most depraved. With Theresa Saldana, José Ferrer, John Glover, and Raymond St. Jacques.

EVIL TOONS

(Prism, 1990) **D/S/P:** Fred Olen Ray **P:** Victoria Till

Four young women are hired (by Dick Miller) to clean up an old house. There's a cartoon monster (designed by Chas Balun) that looks like the Tasmanian Devil from Warner cartoons, but it appears only briefly, so don't be tricked into thinking this is a horror version of *Who Framed Roger Rabbit*. The real star is gorgeous Monique Gabrielle, playing the "shy" one with glasses. She has the best topless-in-front-of-a-mirror scene in recent memory. Madison Stone (usually in porno movies) "becomes" the monster after a while. David Carradine is a long-haired ghost with an evil (but silly-looking) talking book who lurks around just like Lugosi in some old Monogram movie. Miller sits down and watches a long clip from *A Bucket of Blood* on TV, and Michelle Bauer shows up as his wife. With Susanne Ager, porno star Barbara Dare,

and Arte Johnson. Mike Curb, former lieutenant governor of California, was one of the producers.

EVIL TOWN

(TWE, 1984) **D:** Edward Collins **D/S/P:** Peter S. Traynor **D/S:** Larry Spiegel **D/P:** Mardi Rustam, William D. Sklar **S:** Richard Benson

As you can see from the confusing credits, this is a paste-up job of old and older footage, from as far back as 1972, finished in 1984, and released to an unsuspecting public in 1987. It's mostly a film called *God Damn Dr. Shagetz,* starring old Dean Jagger as a mad scientist who experiments on young people to keep a small town's old people alive forever. Two couples camping out are the starring victims. James Keach is the hero. Robert Walker Jr. (around the time he starred in *Son of the Blob*) is the other name camper. Familiar-looking older actors (including Regis Toomey) drug the unsuspecting visitors. A lot of time is spent showing newer, more exploitative scenes with two idiot garage mechanics terrorizing female teens before delivering them to the secret clinic. The cast also includes action star Jillian Kessner (*Firecracker*) and a topless Lynda Wiesmeier from *Playboy* in scenes added later. One of the directors, Mardi Rustam, liked the story so much that he remade it on his own as *Evils In The Night*!

EVIL WITHIN

(A-pix, 1989) **D/S:** Alain Robak **P:** Ariel Zeitoun   France (*Baby Blood*)

Bianca (Emmanuelle Escourrou, who is naked a lot), a sexy gap-toothed woman with a French circus in Africa, returns home and becomes a waitress. She has a wisecracking unborn baby in her womb that commands her to "Feed me with blood!" Its comments about men make her laugh. People are stabbed and decapitated and a blood bank truck is stolen. She has a nightmare of the baby's birth and when it finally arrives, it resembles an octopus. The feature is pretty amusing, but I think the director must have seen *Brain Damage* a few times. We saw it subtitled (from Video Search) but it's available now dubbed. The soft voice used in the dubbed version is Gary Oldman!

THE EWOK ADVENTURE

(MGM, 1984) **D:** John Korty **S:** Bob Carrau **P:** Thomas G. Smith

This *Return of the Jedi* TV spinoff features the furry Ewoks, with Emmy-winning ILM FX, and is narrated by Burl Ives. Warwick Davis is Wicket. With Fionnula Flanagan, Guy Boyd, Dan Fishman, and Debbie Carrington. In Europe it played theatrically (as *Caravan of Courage*), but we got it on ABC. George Lucas was the executive producer.

EWOKS: THE BATTLE FOR ENDOR

(MGM, 1985) **D/S:** Jim and Ken Wheat **P:** Thomas G. Smith

Wilford Brimley stars as a hermit, Sian Phillips is a witch, and Warwick Davis returns as Wicket. There are a cave monster and giants. George Lucas was the executive producer of this ABC-TV movie. The ILM FX received another Emmy.

EXCESSIVE FORCE

(New Line, 1993) **D:** John Hess **S/P/A:** Thomas Ian Griffith **P:** Erwin Stoff, Oscar L. Costo

Thomas Ian Griffith, a 6'4" black belt (from *Karate Kid III*) stars as a kickboxing, jazz-piano-playing Chicago cop out for vengeance. With Lance Henriksen as his mean boss, Charlotte Lewis as his ex-girlfriend, Burt Young as a sadistic, drug-dealing gangster, James Earl Jones as the owner of a jazz club, and Tony Todd. This violent movie was made in Chicago. A sequel followed.

THE EXECUTIONER

(Video Gems, 1974) **D/S/A:** "Dominic Micell"/Duke Mitchell *(Mafia Massacre; Like Father, Like Son)*

Mitchell's semi-autobiographical gangster movie is more like a crude *Goodfellas* than like *The Godfather*. At least it's just as violent. After everyone in an office is gunned down, the crippled boss is electrocuted in a urinal. A finger is sent through the mail ("That's his finger, all right—I've seen it a million times"), a black pimp is crucified, a man is impaled on a meat hook (through his eye), a porno movie is made on a boat, a poodle is served to its owner, and more bloody shootouts occur at a funeral and at a dinner party. A headline says, 13 LA BOOKMAKERS AND PROCURERS SLAIN! Mitchell also narrated and provided Barney Rubble's singing voice! Matt Cimber distributed this for a while.

THE EXECUTIONER, PART II

(Marquis, 1980) **D:** James Bryant **S/P/A:** Renee Harmon

Christopher Mitchum as an LA cop and Renee Harmon as a reporter go after a mysterious hooded Nam-vet vigilante killer. Aldo Ray has a small role as the police commisioner. This has no relation to *The Executioner* or to the *Exterminator* movies, but the deceptive title fooled a lot of people when it was released by 21st Century. It was on a tape with *Frozen Scream*, also produced by and starring Harmon.

EXECUTIVE ACTION

(Warner, 1973) **D:** David Miller **S:** Dalton Trumbo **P:** Edward Lewis

Nearly 20 years before Oliver Stone's *JFK* made headlines, this movie (with an original screenplay by Mark Lane and Donald Freed) was ignored at the box office and by the media. It uses actual footage and reenactments (just like *JFK*) and was initially developed by Donald Sutherland (who's in *JFK*). Burt Lancaster, Robert Ryan (in his last role), and Will Geer star as the very convincing, influential right-wing conspirators. The film shows how a team of disposable assassins could have been trained, while Oswald was chosen to take the rap, and also explains why the president was killed, using actual speeches by Kennedy. The original newspaper ads for the National General release featured an incredible list of all the people connected with the assasination who had mysteriously died in the years since (the list is much longer now). With John Anderson, Paul Carr, Ed Lauter, and Dick Miller.

EXILED IN AMERICA

(Prism, 1990) **D/S/P:** Paul Leder **P:** Ralph Thornberg

Edward Albert plays a Central American freedom-fighter hiding out in the US and pretending to have died. Maxwell Caulfield falls for his wife (Kamala Lopez), who works at a diner owned by Stella Stevens. Wings Hauser is a sheriff.

EXORCISM

(All Seasons, 1974) **D/S:** Juan Bosch **S/A:** Paul Naschy   Spain *(Exorcismo)*

Paul Naschy plays the exorcist priest in this early *Exorcist* copy (Naschy said this was written first). A young woman possessed by the ghost of her father does all the Linda Blair moves and even twists heads off. Naschy tries to put the bad spirit into a German shepherd. With Maria Perschy, Grace Mills, and lots of badly dubbed talking.

EXORCIST III: LEGION

(CBS/Fox, 1990) **D/S:** William Peter Blatty **P:** Carter DeHaven Jr.

The original 1973 feature remains the highest-grossing horror movie of all time, so despite the first flop sequel (which is ignored here) Part III was made. There's more talk about God and evil than anything the audience expected and wanted to see. Members of the first-night Times Square audience yelled, "Don't waste your money!" to people in line outside. I agree. This movie is nuts! It was adapted from Blatty's novel *Legion* (1983), which was based on the real zodiac killer. It shouldn't even have been called an *Exorcist* movie. Parts were reshot in a futile attempt to make it more commercial and easier to understand. It's set 15 years after the original. George C. Scott replaces Lee J. Cobb as the atheist Jewish cop who goes to see *It's a Wonderful Life* a lot. Brad Dourif as the Gemini killer explains the confusing plot in a long, intense ranting scene in an asylum. Jason Miller is "patient X." With Nicol Williamson (in added scenes, as an exorcist), Scott Wilson, Viveca Lindfors, Ed Flanders as a priest, George DiCenzo, Samuel L. Jackson, Don Gordon, Harry Carey Jr., and Zohra Lampert. One bizarre scene has an old woman on a ceiling. Black people are murdered, and a kid is decapitated and crucified. There's a (literal) heaven scene with a black angel. It even features an in-joke plug for the *Child's Play* movies. The Ennio Morricone soundtrack is on Warners.

THE EXOTIC ONES

(1968) **D/S/P/A:** Ron Ormond **P:** June Ormond *(The Monster and the Stripper)*

The Ormonds' last pre-Jesus movie is one of the most amazing exploitation movies ever made. Because of problems with the lab that processed the prints, it was withdrawn from distribution shortly after its release and remained unseen for nearly 20 years. This one has it all: nudity, gore, drugs, a monster, music, comedy, and impossible-to-duplicate 60s New Orleans local atmosphere. The introduction (spoken by Ron Ormond) is a *Mondo*-style look at Bourbon Street nightclubs. Ron plays Nemo, a drug-dealing gangster who runs one of the clubs. He has amazing hair with bangs, always wears dark sunglasses, and smokes cigars. A pretty tough character, he orders his men to dump the full contents of a large spitoon down the throat of a double-crosser. June is Bunny, the most cheerful ("Okey-dokey!"), sweetest, hip grand-mother type imaginable, usually seen in solo close-ups wearing wild glasses and hats while auditioning new strip acts. She even does an act of her own with an LSD reference. Sleepy LaBeef, a huge 50s rockabilly singer from Smackover, Arkansas, who once toured with Elvis and still records and tours, makes his acting debut as "the swamp thing," snorting and grunting while wearing a loin-cloth, fake teeth, a fright wig, and some hair pasted on his chest (sometimes). Nemo has him captured and makes him a *Mighty Joe Young* type of attraction. The "monster" tears off a man's arm and beats him to death with it, rips off a dancer's breast (off-

George C. Scott fails to notice an old lady on the ceiling in *Exorcist III*.

screen) and, as part of the stage show, actually geeks a (real, live) chicken and drinks its blood: "The screams from these living animals will make the strongest man vomit!" Tim Ormond plays Tim, a backwoods boy who becomes the monster's trainer, and sings a hard-to-forget prerecorded song ("The hurt goes on and on and on and on and on and on") in a double-tracked voice. The monster falls for the nice girl singer ("Some idiot dame trying to break into this crazy rat race they call show business!"), who does an excellent job lip-syncing to a very soulful song (actually by a high-pitched black singer). The best of the many bizarre and entertaining strip acts is Titania, a mean-looking wild woman with lots of eye makeup who does an incredible acrobatic act (twirling flaming tassels), eats fire, and dances. She also starts a good cat fight backstage. More fun characters, like an undercover cop in a straw hat, and great dialogue ("That big peckerwood!") help make *The Exotic Ones* a must-see item by the incredible Ormonds. It was shot (partially) on location in New Orleans and in the Okefenokee Swamp. The interiors were shot in the same Nashville studio where Elvis recorded "Heartbreak Hotel," owned at the time by the United Methodist Church!

EXPLOITATION CLASSICS
(Sinister)

This compilation consists of 22 trailers in almost chronological order. The early exploitation trailers for adults-only movies like *Maniac* ("There is chills!"), *Assassination of Youth* ("Tragic orgies!"), and *Slaves in Bondage* are long, badly edited, and without the music and hyper announcers' voices that later became common, but they're fascinating to watch. The tape continues with *Striporama* (with Betty Page in a bubble bath), *She Shoulda Said No!*, 50s juvenile-delinquent movies, and 70s drive-in classics (*Switchblade Sisters!*, *Bury Me an Angel!*). You also get great trailers for classics like *Freaks* (a reissue with jazz music) and Ed Wood's *Glen or Glenda*.

EXPLORERS
(Paramount, 1985) **D:** Joe Dante **S:** Eric Luke **P:** Edward S. Feldman, David Bombyk

Some kids blast off in their own spaceship. Ethan Hawke, River Phoenix (making his film debut), and Jason Presson create the spaceship from a rebuilt carnival-ride car. They meet funny aliens who watch Earth TV and sing TV commercials and series theme songs. With Amanda Peterson, Dick Miller, Brooke Bundy, and Bradley Gregg. This PG science-fiction comedy has Rob Bottin FX. Dante also supervised the special video and TV versions.

EXPLOSION
(1969) **D/S:** Jules Bricken **S:** Alene Brickman **P:** Julian Roffman   Canada

Don Stroud stars as a hippie who teams up with a draft dodger (Gordon Thomson). They steal a car and head for British Columbia. By the time they get to Vancouver, the draft dodger, upset over his brother's death in Vietnam, has killed several cops. Stroud was also in *Bloody Mama, Angel Unchained,* and others released by AIP.

EXPOSED
(MGM, 1983) **D/S/P/A:** James Toback

Nastassja Kinski stars as a small-town American girl who becomes a model in Paris and gets involved with Rudolf Nureyev. He's a concert violinist plotting to kill an Argentinian terrorist (Harvey Keitel). With Bibi Andersson, Ian McShane, Pierre Clementi, Ron Randell, James Russo, and Iman. Toback made this after *Fingers* (starring Keitel) and *Love and Money* (with Klaus Kinski).

EXPOSURE
(HBO, 1991) **D:** Walter Salles Jr. **S:** Rubem Fonsea **P:** Albert Flaksman   (*High Art*)

Peter Coyote stars as a photographer in Rio who specializes in scenes of death. When a hooker he befriended is killed by a ponytailed coke and arms dealer, he takes extensive knife-fighting lessons from a mysterious specialist (Tcheky Karyo, from *La Femme Nikita*). Obsessed with seeking revenge, he alienates his girlfriend (Amanda Pays) and takes a train to Bolivia and back. This Mira-max release is based on a novel by the screenwriter. It has some great cinematography, excellent South American location work, some music by Peter Glass, a dream sequence, and a dwarf.

EXQUISITE CORPSES
(Monarch, 1988) **D/S/P:** Temistocles Lopez **P:** Ken Schwenker

An East Village murder and spies are featured in this arty indy comedy with musical numbers, starring Gary Knox as a trombone player from Oklahoma who makes it in transvestite nightclubs. With Zoe Tamerlaine Lund (Tamerlis) from *Ms. 45* as a hooker and Ruth Collins. Lopez made *Chain of Desire* (1992) next.

EXQUISITE TENDERNESS
(1994) **D:** Carl Shenkel **S:** Bernard Sloane, Patrick Cirillo **P:** Alan Beattie, Chris Chesser   Canada

Isabelle Glasser stars as an assistant head of surgery who is blamed for a death caused by a doctor (Malcolm McDowell). James Remar helps her investigate. With Charles Dance and Peter Boyle. It was filmed in an actual Vancouver mental hospital. Steve Johnson did the FX.

EXTERMINATING ANGEL
(Hen's Tooth, 1962) **D/S:** Luis Buñuel **P:** Gustavo Alatriste   Mexico (*El ángel Exterminador*)

Silvia Pinal (from *Viridiana*) stars in this brilliant and disorienting social allegory with repeating and overlapping sequences. After the servants leave the house, the guests at a fancy dinner party find that they can't leave. Characters fight, make love, cook a sheep, die, kill themselves, and even practice witchcraft and plan a sacrifice in order to get out. Buñuel made his next film, *Diary of a Chambermaid* (1964), in Europe and then made one more film in Mexico (*Simon of the Desert*, 1965) before ending his long exile and returning to Europe permanently.

THE EXTERMINATOR
(Nelson, 1980) **D/S:** James Glickenhaus **P:** Mark Buntzman

This made $4 million in North American rentals, a lot for a lowly exploitation movie at the time. Nam vet Robert Ginty becomes a vigilante in New York and uses a flamethrower to kill. He also has flashbacks. Characters die in many various ways, but the gangster-in-a-meat-grinder scene is a highlight. Christopher George is a police detective with a hot dog grill on his desk. With Steve James as the Nam-vet friend who dies and Samantha Eggar. Stan Winston did the FX. An Avco Embassy release.

EXTERMINATOR II
(MGM/UA, 1984) **D/S/P:** Mark Buntzman, William Sachs

Robert Ginty returns with his flamethrower. Armored-garbage-truck attacks are the highlight of this inferior sequel. With Deborah Gefner as the erotic dancer girlfriend, Mario Van Peebles as "X," leader of a multiracial gang, and Irwin Keyes. John Turturro and Ayre Gross have early roles. From Cannon.

EXTERMINATORS OF THE YEAR 3000
(HBO, 1983) **D:** "Jules Harrison"/Giuliano Carnimeo **S:** Elisa Briganti, Dardano Sacchetti **P:** Camillo Teti   Italy/Spain (*Gli Sterminadori dell'Anno 3000*)

Alan Collins (real name Luciano Pigozzi) and Fred Harris (real name Fernando Bilbo) star with Beryl Cunningham in yet another Italian *Mad Max/Road Warrior* copy.

THE EXTRAORDINARY SEAMAN
(1967) **D:** John Frankenheimer **S:** Rock Dresner **P:** Edward Lewis

David Niven is a failed British WWI lieutenant who returns as a ghost to redeem himself in the Pacific in WWII. Eventually he and his old gunboat ram a Japanese ship during a peace-treaty signing, and he has to wait for another war to prove himself again. Faye Dunaway costars in this anti-war comedy, with Alan Alda, Mickey Rooney, Jack Carter, and Juano Hernandez. The MGM release (which includes WWII-era news footage of famous people) was shelved for two years and was a critical and commercial disaster.

EXTREME JUSTICE
(Vidmark, 1993) **D:** Mark Lester **S/P:** Frank Sachs **S:** Robert Boris

An LA cop (Lou Diamond Phillips) joins his former partner (Scott Glenn) in a secret police hit squad to eliminate dangerous criminals. The group has been corrupted by Glenn and also kills innocent people. The film is said to be based on fact. With Chelsea Field and Yaphet Kotto. It premiered on HBO.

EXTREME PREJUDICE
(Avid, 1987) **D:** Walter Hill **S:** John Milius **P:** Buzz Feitshans

Nick Nolte, a Texas Ranger, goes after his former best friend, Powers Boothe, a coked-up drug lord with a private Mexican army. Michael Ironside is a corrupt CIA man, Maria Conchita Alonso is Nolte's woman, who used to be with Boothe, and Rip Torn is Nolte's sheriff friend, who is killed off early. With William Forsythe, Clancy Brown, and Tiny Lister. There's lots of action, Nam-vet commandos, and a violent end that rips off *The Wild Bunch*. Jerry Goldsmith did the soundtrack.

EXTREME VENGEANCE
(AIP, 1994) **D/S/M:** Roger Zahr **P:** Sam Rose

David A. Cox (who resembles Charles Bronson a bit) stars as an ex-cop who's after some Hollywood gangsters who killed his son, in this bad *Death Wish copy*. Tanya George costars. This was probably produced years before the video-release date.

EYEBALL

(Prism, 1974) **D/S:** Umberto Lenzi
S: Felix Tusell   Italy/Spain (*Gatti Rossi nell'un Labirinto di Vetro; The Devil's Eye*)

A psycho in a red cape kills women and takes their eyes. The flashback-filled *giallo* (whodunit) stars John Richardson and Martine Brochard.

AN EYE FOR AN EYE

(Embassy, 1981) **D:** Steve Carver **S:** William Gray, James Bruner **P:** Frank Capra Jr.

Chuck Norris as San Francisco cop Sean Kane quits the force after his partner is killed by drug dealers and takes revenge. With villain Christopher Lee, Richard Roundtree, Matt Clark, Mako, Maggie Cooper, Terry Kiser, Richard Norton, and Rosalind Chao. There's lots of slo-mo kicking.

EYE OF THE DEMON

(Vidmark, 1987) **D:** Carl Schenkel
S: R. Timothy Kring **P:** Michael Rhodes

Bay Coven was a boring, made-for-TV occult movie that also played on TV as *Strangers in Town*. Now it has another title, and you can pay to see it! There's a witch conspiracy against Pamela Sue Martin after she and her husband move to an island off the shore of Massachusetts (obviously California). Barbara Billingsley is really 300 years old. With your other favorite TV stars, Woody Harrelson and Jeff Conaway. A church blows up. You'll fall asleep. The executive producers were Jon Peters and Peter Guber.

EYE OF THE DRAGON

(1988) **D:** Leo Fong **S:** James Bellamesari **P:** George Chung

Blond Cynthia Rothrock (from Pennsylvania) stars in her first feature shot in the US, with Richard Norton, Troy Donahue, and Bill "Superfoot" Wallace. Rothrock started her martial-arts acting in Hong Kong. Director Fong starred in his own martial-arts movies.

EYE OF THE EAGLE

(MGM, 1987) **D/P:** Cirio H. Santiago
S: Leonard Hermes   Philippines

Santiago made yet another bad Nam adventure movie for executive producer Roger Corman. It's about a Special Forces team fighting the North Vietnamese. Robert Patrick stars, with Brett Clark and Cec Verrell. Patrick returned in a sequel, *Behind Enemy Lines*.

EYE OF THE EAGLE II: INSIDE THE ENEMY

(MGM, 1989) **D/S:** Carl Franklin **S:** Dan Gagliasso **P:** Catherine Santiago

The survivor of an ambush falls for a Vietnamese girl, but she's sold into prostitution by a drug-dealing American officer. With Todd Field, William Field, and Andy Wood. Cirio H. Santiago was the executive producer.

EYE OF THE STORM

(New Line, 1992) **D/S:** Yuri Zeltser **S:** Michael Stewart
P: Carsten H. W. Lorenz, Oliver Eberle   US/Germany

A blind teen (Bradley Gregg, star of *Class of 1999*) is protected by his older brother (long-haired Craig Sheffer). They live at a remote motel in the desert, where their parents were murdered ten years earlier. The customers are usually killed, and Sheffer sells their cars. A wild, hard-drinker (Dennis Hopper) and his trashy young wife (Lara Flynn Boyle) show up when their car breaks down on the way to Vegas. Boyle comes on to the older brother, and Hopper gets the young one drunk and lets him drive his car. It's more of a dreary character study than a horror movie, but Hopper, as usual, brightens things up when he's onscreen. Roland Emmerich was an executive producer.

EYE OF THE STRANGER

(Monarch, 1993) **D/P/A:** David Heavner

Do-it-all Heavner is a black-leather stranger out for revenge (patterned after Clint Eastwood in Italian westerns) who arrives in a modern-day small town run by a corrupt mayor (Martin Landau). Sally Kirkland costars, with Joe Estevez as the drunken sheriff, Don Swayze, Stella Stevens, Sy Richardson, and Sydney Lassick. Not to be confused with *Eyes of a Stranger* (1981), with Jennifer Jason Leigh.

EYE OF THE TIGER

(Avid, 1986) **D:** Richard Sarafian
S: Michael Montgomery **P:** Tony Scott

Ex-con Nam vet Buck (Gary Busey) is framed by the sheriff and unjustly jailed. Later he goes home to fight small-town drug-dealer bikers led by Blade (William Smith). He uses a customized armored RV with cannons, and friend Yaphet Kotto drops grenades from a plane. Bikers are decapitated by wires (an idea copied from *She Devils on Wheels!*). Bikers dig up Busey's dead wife and put her on his doorstep. A biker gets TNT up his ass. With Seymour Cassel, Bert Remsen, and Denise Galik. By the director of *Vanishing Point*. The title song from *Rocky III* (!) is used again.

EYES OF FIRE

(Vestron, 1983) **D/S:** Avery Crouse
P: Philip J. Spinelli   (*Crying Blue Sky*)

This extraordinary movie, set in 1750 in the French territories of North America, is a slow but fascinating and unique horror fantasy. Demons, Shawnee Indians, and possessed characters live in the wilderness. Souls are trapped in trees and in the land itself. Dennis Lipscomb stars as a preacher who survives a lynching, and Karlene Crocket is Lean, a character with special powers (and nude scenes). Some call it too arty, others criticize the optical effects. I love it. Made in Missouri with a $1 million budget, it was 106 minutes. 16 minutes were cut by Aquarius, which released it to puzzled Times Square moviegoers.

EYES OF THE BEHOLDER

(Columbia, 1992) **D/S/E:** Lawrence L. Simeon
P: David Henderson

Lenny Von Dohlen is an artist who escapes from a (clichéd) mental asylum and shows up to terrorize his rich doctor at a remote house during a raging thunder-and-lightning storm. He rants, smashes things, and shoots, punches, and humiliates his captives. Flashbacks reveal his experimental surgery. Joanna Pacula (whose body double takes a shower), Matt McCoy (who is forced to walk on broken glass), blond Australian Kylie Travis (who has a topless scene), and one-time Aussie James Bond star George Lazenby (!) are the victims. Charles Napier is a police detective and Vivian Schilling has a small role as a cop. The Greg Turner score copies Bernard Herrmann.

EYES OF THE JUNGLE

(1953) **D:** Paul Landres **S:** Barry Shipman, Sherman L. Lowe **P:** Rudolph Flothow

Jon Hall stars in this Columbia film, based on his TV series *Ramar of the Jungle*. He and his assistant go to India and stop a slave-trading ring that deals in women. There's a plant that causes "wasting sickness." With Edgar Barrier, Robert Shayne, Raymond Montgomery, and lots of stock footage.

EYES OF THE SERPENT

(Academy, 1992) **D/C:** Ricardo Jacques Gale
S: Stewart Chapin **P:** Stephen Lieb
(*In the Time of the Barbarians II*)

This is a medieval story of an evil woman (Lenore Andriel) after some magic swords. Her good blond sister (Lisa Toothman) has a good daughter (Diana Frank, the star), and the bad cousin (Carlton Lynx) uses a whip. If you're in the right mood it's pretty funny, especially when the scholar's hand is cut off by an electric zap. Tom Schultz costars as Galen, the musclebound swordsman with an eye patch who calls a bad guy with a helmet "spitoonhead." With a topless dance, a romantic sex scene, and idiot Siamese twins. Most of it takes place in the woods, where filming is cheap.

EYEWITNESS TO MURDER

(New Horizons, 1992) **D/E:** Jag Mundhra
S: Michael Potts **P:** Ashok Amritraj

Andrew Stevens is an angry LA cop whose wife was blown up trying to protect an artist (Sherilyn Wolter, from *General Hospital*) blinded by a drug dealer (with a junkie assistant) at an art opening. Stevens falls for her at a remote artists'-colony hideout. With Adrian Zmed as his partner, Carl Strano as a killer, and even Karen Elise Baldwin (who cowrote the story) as a kickboxing nurse. This is boring!

THE FABULOUS ADVENTURES OF BARON MUNCHAUSEN

(American Video, 1961) **D/S:** Karel Zeman
S: Joseph Kainar   Czechoslovakia (*Baron Prasil; The Original Fabulous Adventures of Baron Munchausen; The Fabulous Baron Munchausen*)

Animation and glass paintings based on Gustave Doré's etchings from a 19th-century edition of the novel are used in this classic fantasy. It opens with the history of flight, as an astronaut lands on the moon and discovers that the Baron (and other historical figures) have already been there. The Baron (Milos Kopecky) calls the astronaut Moonman and takes him to earth on a nautical ship drawn by flying horses. There's a battle against the Turks, a giant fish that eats ships, a beautiful princess, and some anti-government messages. This influenced Terry Gilliam's film *The Adventures of Baron Munchausen* (1989).

THE FACE AT THE WINDOW

(Kino, 1939) **D/P:** George King   UK

This is an adaptation of a play (by F. Brooke Warren) that had been the basis of two silent films and a 1932 film starring Raymond Massey. Tod Slaughter stars as the devious, lecherous, and wealthy Chevalier del Gardo, in 1880 Paris. In the outrageous ending, a crazed scientist uses his invention to probe the brain of a dead victim and discover who the killer, called the Wolf (the face at the window), is.

FACE IN THE FOG

(Sinister, 1936) **D:** Robert Hill **P:** Sam Katzman

A mad hunchback called the Fiend murders members of the cast of a play called *Satan's Bride*, using bullets made of "frozen poison." This very rare and cheap forgotten horror from the independent Victory Pictures features June Collyer and Lloyd Hughes.

FACE OF MARBLE

(Fang, 1946) **D:** William Beaudine
S: Michael Jacoby **P:** Jeffrey Bernard

John Carradine stars as a kindly brain surgeon trying to revive the dead in this convoluted Monogram film. He brings Brutus, a great Dane, back to life, and the dog becomes a vampire/zombie/ghost that can walk through walls and that "drains the blood of livestock" (offscreen). Then he turns his young wife (Claudia Drake) into a transparent companion for the dog. Half the movie seems to consist of Carradine and his assistant, Robert Shayne, sitting at a table by a picture of the ocean outside the window. Willie Best is wasted as Shadrach, "the boy," and the voodoo-priestess maid is totally from left field. At the end Carradine contemplates suicide, the maid kills herself, and the wife and the dog kill themselves.

FACE OF THE FROG

(1959) **D:** Harold Reinl **S:** Trygve Larsen, J. Joachim Bartsch   W. Germany (*Der Frosch mit der Maske*)

A killer wears a hood over a bizarre frog mask with big, protruding eyeballs. This film is based on Edgar Wallace's *The Fellowship of the Frog*, which had previously been filmed as an American serial (*The Mark of the Frog*, 1928) and a British feature (*The Frog*, 1937). With Siegfried Lowitz, series regular Joachim Fuchsberger, and veteran actor Fritz Rasp (*Metropolis, Spies, Emil and the Detectives*).

FACELESS

(Nightmare, 1988) **D/S:** Jesús Franco
S: Pierre Ripert, Jean Mazaril
S/P: René Chateau   France
(*Predateurs de la Nuit*)

In some ways this is the ultimate Franco film, and it was shot in English. It has an all-star cast, is gory, absurd, very sleazy, and tasteless, and is full of multilayered references to earlier Euro-horror hits, especially Franco's own *The Awful Dr. Orloff*. Helmut Berger (*Dorian Gray*, 1970) stars as Dr. Flamond, a voyeur trying to restore the beauty of his sister, Ingrid, which was destroyed when a scarred woman threw acid in her face. His big clinic in Paris, where he treats silly, rich, vain older women, has TV monitors everywhere (as in *The Thousand Eyes of Dr. Mabuse*). One patient (Stephane Audran) has a long syringe thrust into her eye. Telly Savalas (in New York) hires a Nam-vet private eye (Christopher Mitchum) to find his kidnapped daughter, a coke-sniffing model (Caroline Munro), who's being held in one of the clinic's padded cells. The doc visits Professor Orloff (Howard Vernon), who sends him to a former SS officer and war criminal (Anton Diffring, in his last role) for professional advice. The doc has a threesome with his nurse (the beautiful former porno star Brigitte Lahaie) and a hooker picked up in Pigalle. Lahaie has lines comparing actresses with hookers. A facial-skin-peel scene is a direct copy of a scene in *Eyes Without a Face* taken to absurd extremes. A rapist servant decapitates somebody with a chainsaw, then kisses the head. Others are killed with scissors and a power drill. Mitchum fights a gay fashion designer and his muscle-bound boyfriend, Do Do. After an irritating non-ending, we hear the theme song (it was a 45rpm record in France). Nobody else shoots sex scenes through a fish tank like this. Totally incredible! The Canadian video version is cut, the French one is not.

FACE OF TERROR

(1962) **D:** Isidoro Martínez Ferry, William Hole Jr. **S:** Monroe Manning **P:** Gustavo Quintano   Spain (*La Cara del Terror*)

An escaped mental patient (Lisa Gaye, later in *Castle of Evil*) has her disfigured face restored by a plastic surgeon (Fernando Rey). Unlike many other 60s European restored-face horror movies, the doctor is the victim and the woman is a crazed killer who has to keep using a special solution so that her face doesn't disintegrate. She takes a job in a hotel and almost gets married, but of course things go wrong. New footage was shot for the American release.

FACE OF THE SCREAMING WEREWOLF

(Sinister, 1959) **D/S:** Gilberto Martínez Solarz
S/P: Fernando de Fuentes **S:** Juan Garcia
D/P: Jerry Warren   (*La Casa del Terror*)

Three doctors hypnotize Miss Ann Taylor with a revolving swirl on a fan. Her flashbacks ("I can see an ancient land") reveal her leading a Mayan ceremony in a pyramid. A doctor takes her to Yucatán, bringing on another (much longer) flashback, with dancing, a sacrificial-altar stabbing, and impressive Yma Sumac–style singing. Lon Chaney Jr., as the traditional Universal-look mummy, is seen briefly. A completely different growling Mexican mummy is shot. Back in civilization, the two mummies are presented to an audience, the lights go out, the doctor is shot, and Chaney disappears, only to show up in a lab (inside a wax museum?!), trapped in a pressure chamber. A mad doctor (Yerye Beirute, later in the Mexican Karloff movies) puts poor Chaney into a big, spinning machine. Later on, lightning strikes, wax figures are shown in closeup, the full moon shines, and the unbandaged Lon (looking as he did in *The Indestructible Man*) turns into the wolf man (!) (thanks to time-lapse photography) and kills a man. The other skinny mummy with a scary face kidnaps his reincarnated princess. Newspaper headlines scream: ANN TAYLOR KILLED! MUMMY DESTROYED! The werewolf escapes from the operating table, kills more doctors, and is put in a cage. His first line of dialogue is "No!" When he escapes (again), he climbs all the way up the outside of a building with a woman on his back, then carries her down the stairs! After a chase scene with jazz music he returns to the lab, bites a doctor on the neck, then passes out—and dies in a fire! One of the cops says, "He was just an ordinary guy." In most of the scenes, it's pretty obvious that the monster is a double. Most of the original dialogue footage was cut, and a radio announcer's voice informs us (in English) of what's going on. Mexican comedy star Tin Tan (real name Germán Valdez) as the wax-museum caretaker was also trimmed for the 1965 US release. Some parts don't make much sense, but it's short (an hour), is fairly bloody (for the time), and must be the best mummy-in-a-wax-museum-that's-really-a-werewolf movie ever made.

FACES OF DEATH

(MPI, 1978) **D:** "Conan Le Cilaire"
S: Alan Black **P:** Roselyn T. Scott

This mondo movie was a hit in Japan first, was released here by Aquarius, then later became a video rental hit and spawned sequels. Michael Carr appears as the narrator, Dr. Francis B. Gross. The Make-up Effects Lab (MEL) in Hollywood created many of the "real" scenes, including an electric-chair electrocution, a Middle Eastern beheading, a San Francisco cannibal cult, alligator and bear attacks, and monkey-brain eating. Scenes of natural disasters, airplane crashes, and autopsies are real.

FACES OF DEATH II

(MPI, 1981)

All volumes have the same phony credits and host. Unlike the others in the series, this features mostly real news footage of accidental deaths, a fatal-boxing match, and Libyan firing squads. Much of *Faces of Death III* (MPI, 1985) is faked, and there's even a statement at the end of the credits admitting that. In the mid-80s these tapes made the news because they were renting so well and college fraternities were reportedly using them in hazing rituals. More sequels and copies followed. *The Worst of Faces of Death* (Gorgon, 1989) is an hour-long tape, mostly from *I* and *III*, with a narrator ("Dr. Louis Flellis"). It was blamed for a California kid's suicide in a 1994 lawsuit.

FACES OF DEATH IV

(1990)

A new, comical narrator ("Dr. Louis Flellis") shows us worn-out duplicated footage and faked footage. This was a midnight hit in theaters in Florida and Arkansas (in 1993) but was banned in Germany, where even more unrelated sequels appeared: *Faces of Death V* and *VI* (by the makers of *Faces of Torture*).

FACES OF HORROR

(Fantasy, 1989)

Anything with a title like this was renting in the late 80s. Somebody took three public-domain films (all once distributed by AIP) and threw in ten minutes of one here, ten minutes of another there, and so on, then put out a tape with a skull on the box. The random scenes are from *Queen of Blood* (1966), *Yog, Monster from Space* (1970) and *The Thing with Two Heads* (1972)! The lazy crooks who sold this figured out how to dupe people vainly searching for more gross-out *Mondo* thrills. Somebody laughed all the way to the bank. It's funny to imagine a video-renter, hoping to see real people killed and tortured, getting home and seeing Dennis Hopper feeding a space-vampire woman, a giant Japanese octopus, and Bruce Dern creating a two-headed man. Along the same lines, *Facing All Death* (DeGregory) was a "series" of 8 unrelated, often retitled, feature films.

FAIR GAME

(Imperial, 1982) **D/S:** Christopher Fitchett **S:** Ellery Ryan **P:** David Barclay, Terry Gore   Australia

Three private-school girls are in a desolate resort town controlled by a psycho killer. With Carrie Mack and Kim Trengrove. A different Australian *Fair Game* (Nelson, 1985) stars Cassandra Delaney as a woman running an animal sanctuary in the outback. Three psycho poachers kill her animals and tie her topless to the front of a truck. She eventually gets revenge. Mario Andreacchio was the director.

FAIR GAME

(Vidmark, 1987) **D/S/P:** Mario Orfini, Lidia Ravena   Italy (*Mamba*)

Greg Henry (from *Body Double*) is a technical wizard who terrifies his estranged wife, Trudie Styler (she's married to Sting in real life), by locking her inside a big, computerized LA house with a poisonous snake that he controls. He watches her from his van outside. There are lots of snake-point-of-view shots, and Styler screams a lot. With Bill Moseley (from *The Texas Chainsaw Massacre II*). Giorgio Moroder scored the music.

FAIRYTALES

(Media, 1978) **D:** "Harry Tampa"/ Harry Hurwitz **P:** Charles Band

This is another example of the 70s trend of making adult sex versions of children's stories. It's an X-rated fantasy and is also a musical. It's real silly, of course, but has some clever moments. With Angela Aames as Little Bo Peep, Nai Bonet and Sy Richardson (both in *Nocturna*, by the same director), a young Linnea Quigley, Angelo Rossitto (again typecast as a dwarf), and Evelyn Guerrero.

FAKE-OUT

(HBO, 1982) **D/S/P/A:** "Matt Cimber"/ Mateo Ottaviano   (*Nevada Heat*)

Right after Pia Zadora mania started with the publicity for *Butterfly*, she starred in this gangster comedy by the same director, "presented by" Meshulam Riklis, her multimillionaire husband. It's virtually a comedy remake of Cimber's *Lady Cocoa* (1975). Pia, as a Vegas singer and dancer, does her stuff onstage, then is arrested by Telly Savalas and his real-life brother George, both making Kojak in-jokes. She takes the rap for her Italian hood boyfriend and goes to prison, where she cheerfully leads an exercise class. After a shower attack and more women-in-prison clichés, Pia says, "I'll talk!" and is put under the protective custody of Savalas and Desi Arnaz Jr. (!) at a casino. Cimber, as a hitman, tries to kill her, Larry Storch is a loudmouth drug dealer/talent agent, and Buck Flower is a cowboy. Most of the time is used up with car chases and stupid car stunts. Pia is fun to watch—for a while. Too bad this plays like a boring TV movie.

FALL OF THE EAGLES

(1990) **D:** Jesús Franco **S:** Ilona Kunseova **P:** Daniel Lesoeur   France (*La Chute des Aigles*)

Mark Hamill (in a career low) is a German Nazi in 1939. He and an anti-Nazi (Ramon Sheen) both have to join the army. Meanwhile, a Berlin cabaret singer (Alexandra Erlich) who is also the daughter of a banker (Christopher Lee) is sent to the Russian front. This romantic-triangle drama uses stock footage from a 70s Italian WWII movie.

THE FALL OF THE HOUSE OF USHER

(Sinister, 1928) **D/S:** Jean Epstein
France (*La Chute de la Maison Usher*)

Luis Buñuel was the assistant director of this avant-garde film based on two stories by Edgar Allan Poe ("The Fall of the House of Usher" and "The Oval Portrait"), but he quit because of artistic differences. The cast includes Marguerite Gance (wife of director Abel Gance) and Jean Debucourt. There's a scene of copulating toads. It's available on a 55-minute tape, with a musical score, along with a forgotten American silent 1928 version, directed by James Sibley Watson.

THE FALL OF THE HOUSE OF USHER

(Sinister, 1948) **D/P/C:** Ivan Barnett
S: Kenneth Thompson, Dorothy Catt   UK

This 70-minute independent British film is said to be pretty dull, although it received an H (horrific) certificate when released in the UK. Later versions were Corman's hit *The House of Usher* (1960) with Vincent Price, a Sunn Classics version (1980), and a 1989 version.

FAMOUS T AND A

(Wizard, 1982) **P:** Charles Band

Sybil Danning hosts this long-out-of-print compilation, which simply shows nude or topless scenes of famous or good-looking actresses from various movies that were in release from Charles Band's Wizard video at the time. New footage of Danning was shot. With Cassandra Peterson (*Working Girls*), Vanity (*Tanya's Island*), Ursula Andress (*Slave of the Cannibal God*), Phyllis Davis in scenes cut from *Terminal Island* and *Sweet Sugar*, Edy Williams, Claudia Jennings, Uschi Digart, Laura Gemser, Brigitte Bardot, and Jacqueline Bisset. This was released after *The Best of Sex and Violence*, from the same company, and includes

---

THE FALCON series

Michael Arlen (a British novelist born Dikran Kuyumjian in Armenia) created the adventurer and crime-solver Gay Stanhope (the Falcon) in a short story. George Sanders (who had previously played the Saint) played the Falcon in four features at RKO (1941–42), then quit and was replaced by his real-life brother, Tom Conway, in nine more (1943–46). Most of these had too many comic characters and not enough mystery. *The Falcon Takes Over* (1942) was based on Raymond Chandler's novel *Farewell My Lovely*. John Calvert was in three low-budget quickies (1948–49) from the independent Film Craft company. Many actors played the character on the radio, and Charles McGraw was the Falcon in a syndicated TV series (1954–55). *The Falcon's Adventure* (1947) is the only video available at this time (from Turner).

some of the same scenes. Home-video and cable-TV watchers with lots of spare time created their own similar compilations. Some even sold them through the mail.

THE FAN

(Paramount, 1981) **D:** Edward Bianchi
S: John Hartwell, Priscilla Chapman
P: Robert Stigwood

A Broadway star (Lauren Bacall) is stalked by a psycho with a razor. Young Michael Biehn plays the obsessed nut case who works at the (real) Record City store on Broadway and 8th Street in Manhattan. Just before this film was made I worked at that (excellent, now long gone) store, and Biehn works at my station doing my job. Dick Smith gore FX were added later. Costar James Garner blasted the film and producer Stigwood in print, saying that he had only appeared in it because Bacall had asked him to. Maybe he objected to the scene in a gay bar where a throat is slit during a blow job, or lines like "How would you like to be fucked with a meat cleaver!?" With Maureen Stapleton and Hector Elizondo. Pino Donaggio wrote the score, and tunes by James Brown, Junior Walker, the Specials, and others are included. It was released by Filmways (which had been AIP a few months earlier) just after the John Lennon assassination.

FANDO AND LIS

(VSOM, 1968) **D/S:** Alexandro Jodorowsky
S: Fernando Arrabal **P:** Juan López Moctezuma
Mexico (*Fando y Lis*)

Jodorowsky's first (b/w) feature is based on an avant-garde play by Arrabal that he had directed. On the way to the imaginary, enchanted city of Tar, a man (Fando) pushes a paralyzed woman (Lis) in a cart. The miserable, sobbing couple remember their horrifying childhoods and encounter women in bikinis with whips, men in drag, and bodies emerging from graves. With many flashbacks, fast editing, film running backwards or burning, and many bizarre scenes, it's not an easy movie to like or even watch. It was released (cut and subtitled) by Cannon in 1970. Jodorowsky's *El Topo* and Arrabal's own *Viva la Muerte* followed in 1971.

FANGS

(UAV, 1974) **D/S/P:** Arthur A. Names **S:** John T. Wilson
(*Snakes; Holy Wednesday*)

Familiar character actor Les Tremayne plays Snakey Bender, an eccentric old small-town guy who raises snakes. Every Wednesday he has a John Philip Sousa march party with a friend. When the friend gets married and the townspeople turn on Snakey, it's time for revenge. But there's more. A seemingly normal lady teacher gets off on snakes ("Put that naughty little boy around my neck!"), and the town is full of strange, perverted characters. With Richard Kennedy (from the *Ilsa* films), Bruce Kimball, Marvin Kaplan as a preacher, the warden from *Switchblade Sisters*, and nudity. Another *Fangs!* (Pagan, 1992) is a one-hour vampire documentary by Bruce G. Hallenbeck featuring Veronica Carlson, clips, and Hammer trailers.

FANNY HILL

(Central Park Media, 1968) **D/S:** Mac Ahlberg
P: Tore Sjoberg   Sweden

Redhead Diana Kjaer stars in a version of the famous 1749 erotic novel, this time set in Stockholm. It was presented in the US by Jerry Gross' Cinemation. Ahlberg later came here and became a very busy cinematographer. *Around the World with Fanny Hill* was a "sequel." The videos were from David F. Friedman.

FANNY HILL

(MGM, 1979) **D:** Gerry O'Hara **S:** Stephen Chesley
P: Harry Benn   UK (*Sex, Lies, and Renaissance*)

Lisa Raines Foster (who has many nude scenes) stars in yet another adaptation of *Fanny Hill*, this time from the director of *The Bitch*. Shelley Winters runs a whore house. With Oliver Reed as a lawyer and Wilfred Hyde-White. International deal-maker Harry Alan Towers was the executive producer for Playboy.

FANNY HILL MEETS DR. EROTICO

(1967) **D/P:** Barry Mahon

Sue Evans stars in this nudie movie set in a castle. She goes to work for a doctor, and his Frankenstein monster falls in love with her. It all ends with locals carrying torches burning the monster. It was a sequel (!) to *Fanny Hill Meets Lady Chatterley* and was followed by *Fanny Hill Meets the Red Baron*. Both were by Mahon and starred Evans.

FANTASIES

(Fox, 1973) **D/S/C:** John Derek **P:** Kevin Casselman   (*And Once Upon a Love*)

The 16-year-old Kathleen Collins (aka Bo Derek) and Peter Hooten star as a brother and sister who fall in love on a Greek island. Eventually they find out that they aren't really related, so it's not really an incest movie, but Bo is naked a lot. It was shot in Greece and wasn't released until 1981 (after the Dereks' *Tarzan*). Derek made the X-rated *Love You* (1978) next.

FANTASM

(VSOM, 1976) **D:** "Richard Bruce"/Richard Franklin
S: Ross Dimsey **P:** Anthony I. Ginnane   Australia

A comic doctor and a woman narrate this dated, episodic, mostly unerotic soft-core sex movie, made for the Australian market (and shot partially in LA). Uschi Digart is in a lesbian-steam-bath sequence, and the late John Holmes (from Ashville, Ohio) is in a pool with an Asian woman. I guess they tried to appeal to everyone. The Rene Bond and Serena sequences both involve rape, and others feature a Black Mass, black men, whipping, incest, cross-dressing, and shaving. Also with Mary Gavin/Candy Samples, Sue Deloria, and Bill Margold. Franklin later directed *Psycho II*, *F/X II*, and some episodes of the *Beauty and the Beast* TV series!

FANTASM COMES AGAIN

(VSOM, 1977) **D:** "Eric Ram"/Colin Eggleston
S: Ross Dimsey **P:** Anthony I. Ginnane   Australia

This time a man preparing a sex-help column reads letters, and we see the writers' (soft core) fantasies. Cheryl "Rainbeaux" Smith has sex at a drive-in (showing *Phantasm*), Serena has sex in a church, and Uschi Digart is a lesbian cowgirl. With sex (a threesome) in an elevator, under water, and on a trampoline. Candy Samples, John Holmes, Rick Cassidy, Bill Margold, and Tom Thumb are all in it too, and yes, that's Johnny Legend reading in a library. Eggleston directed many other features, including *Casandra* and *The Wicked*. Australians have their own real porno movies now.

THE FANTASIST

(Republic, 1986) **D/S:** Robin Hardy
P: Mark Forsater   Ireland

Moira Harris stars as a country girl in Dublin. A killer starts calling her on the phone. The main suspects are Christopher Cazenove as a policeman, Timothy Bottoms as a neurotic writer, and John Kavanagh. By the director of the acclaimed *The Wicker Man* (1973).

THE FANTASTIC FOUR

(1993) **D:** Oley Sassone **S:** Greg Nevius **P:** Steve Rabiner

Mister Fantastic (Alex Hyde-White), the Invisible Girl (Rebecca Staab), the Human Torch (Jay Underwood), and the Thing (a stuntman) go into space and battle Doctor Doom (Joseph Culp). The (very) low budget Roger Corman production was made because German executive producer Bernd Eichinger had to back a quick feature to retain the rights to the Marvel Comics characters. It was promoted, then shelved (bootlegs are available). Eichinger then planned to back a much bigger budgeted Fantastic Four movie at Fox. Sassone and the stars said they knew nothing of the behind-the-scenes manipulations.

FANTASTIC PLANET

(Embassy, 1973) **D:** Rene Laloux   France/Czechoslovakia (*Planet of Fantastic Creatures*)

Tiny, humanoid Ohms rebel against their zombie Drog masters. The limited but strange animation in this PG film, based on drawings by Roland Topor, is highly regarded by science fiction fans. Corman's New World released it in the US.

THE FANTASTIC PLASTIC MACHINE

(1969) **D/S/P:** Eric Blum, Lowell Blum

This G-rated documentary is about an American surfing team competing in Australia. They also surf in Fiji, Hawaii, and New Zealand. The "plastic machine" is a new kind of surf board. From Crown International.

THE FANTASY FILM WORLD OF GEORGE PAL

(Starmaker, 1985) **D/S/P:** Arnold Leibovit

This welcome one-hour documentary covers all aspects of the professional life of the late George Pal. Born in Hungary, he designed sets for UFA in Berlin, then had his own studio producing animated-puppet commercials in Holland. He came to the US in 1940 and made Puppetoon shorts for Paramount. (They're available from Loonic Video. *The Puppetoon Movie* is a 1987 compilation.) From 1950 to 1968 he produced and/or directed and did special effects for 13 science-fiction or fantasy features. *The War of the Worlds* (1953) and *The Time Machine* (1960) are two of the best. Choice scenes from most of his feature films and many of his shorts, and even some of his European commercials, are included here, and there are onscreen interviews with Ray Harryhausen, Ray Bradbury, Russ Tamblyn, Tony Curtis, Rod Taylor, Joe Dante, and others. It's narrated by the familiar voice of Paul Frees.

FANTASY ISLAND
(1977) **D:** Richard Lang **S:** Gene Levitt
P: Aaron Spelling, Leonard Goldberg

Ricardo Montalban as Roarke and Hervé Villechaize as Tattoo first started taking $50,000 a head to fufill rich people's fantasies in this ABC-TV series pilot. The long-running series was inspired by the success of the long-running *Love Boat*, from the same producers, and had the same awesome number of guest stars. Sandra Dee, Peter Lawford, Bill Bixby, Carol Lynley, Hugh O'Brian, Eleanor Parker, Victoria Principal, and Dick Sargent had the honor of being the first guests. *Return to Fantasy Island* followed.

FANTASY MISSION FORCE
(1983) **D:** Chu Yen Ping
P: Shen Hsiao Yin   Hong Kong

One of the strangest kung-fu comedies ever, this involves generals from various countries being held captive by Japanese villains. It's impossible to tell in which century it takes place. A captain (Jimmy Wang Yu) with a commando squad is sent to rescue them and encounters many odd characters on the way. The film has a haunted mansion, ghosts, singing, dancing, and martial-arts fights. Jackie Chan, who is not the star, and Lin Ching Hsia play a pair of robbers.

FARAWAY, SO CLOSE!
(Fox, 1992) **D/S/P:** Wim Wenders **S:** Ulrich Ziegler   Germany (*In Weiter Fernem so Nah!*)

Otto Sander returns as the angel Cassiel from *Wings of Desire.* He becomes human and turns to drinking and crime in reunited Berlin. Nastassja Kinski is his angel companion this time, and Bruno Ganz, Solveig Dommartin, and Peter Falk (as himself) return from the first film. Also with Horst Buchholz, Lou Reed (who sings), Willem Dafoe as Emit Flesti (say it backwards), and Mikhail Gorbachev (!), who talks of the need for harmony in the world. This 164-minute PG-13 film (140 minutes in the US) is in English, with subtitles for some dialogue, and is partially b/w. The soundtrack features U2, Johnny Cash, and others.

FAREWELL, MY LOVELY
(IVE, 1975) **D:** Dick Richards **S:** David Zelag Goodman
P: Jerry Bruckheimer, George Pappas   UK

Robert Mitchum stars as Philip Marlowe in this excellent remake of Raymond Chandler's novel (filmed as *The Falcon Takes Over* in 1942. Charlotte Rampling costars as Velma, with John Ireland, Sylvia Miles, Jack O'Halloran, Anthony Zerbe, Harry Dean Stanton, Cheryl "Rainbeaux" Smith (who has a nude scene), Sylvester Stallone, and Joe Spinnell.

FAREWELL, UNCLE TOM
(VSOM, 1971) **D/S/A:** Gualtiero Jacopetti, Franco Prosperi   Italy

The ads said, "300 years of hate explodes today!" and claimed that this was all based on truth. The filmmakers (whose previous feature was *Africa Addio*) appear as modern-day filmmakers who somehow take a helicopter back in time to the old South, where they interview people and show torture, rape, and branding. It's an extremely tasteless, over-the-top exploitation feature that ends with modern-day American blacks imagining slaughtering the white population. It's pretty strong stuff and received an X rating. It was filmed in Haiti and the US. The original version was 130 minutes.

FAR FROM HOME
(Vestron, 1989) **D:** Meiert Avis **S:** Tommy Lee Wallace **P:** Donald P. Borchers

Drew Barrymore (who also narrates), is 13-year-old Joleen. She's stuck at a run-down trailer park in Banco, Nevada, near a nuclear dump, with her writer father (Matt Frewer). Two boys (Andras Jones, from *Nightmare 4*, and Anthony Rapp, later in *Dazed and Confused*) are interested in Joleen (who wears bikinis), and meanwhile a psycho killer is on the loose. This movie has great atmosphere, a cast of interesting characters, an effective electronic soundtrack, and frequent closeups of a bug zapper. I like it a lot. Susan Tyrrell is the mean trailer-park owner (she gets electrocuted in a bathtub), Richard Masur is a Nam-vet gas-station owner, and Dick Miller is the sheriff. Also featured are Jennifer Tilly, Karen Austin, and Teri Weigel. It's based on a story by Theodore Gershuny. This was Drew Barrymore's first teen role (after she was in an alcohol-abuse clinic, at 13), and it's one of her best films.

THE FARMER
(1975) **D:** David Berlansky **S:** George Fargo, Janice Colson-Dodge **P/A:** Gary Conway   (*Killer Farmer*)

After WWII, a war-vet Georgia farmer (Gary Conway) does some work for the local mob. He later seeks vengeance after his ranch hand is killed, his barn is burned, and his girlfriend (Angel Tompkins) is raped. This sick drive-in movie had to be cut to receive an R rating. With Michael Dante (who is blinded with acid) and Ken Reynard (a black man who is burned alive). Columbia released the indy production. The late Gene Clark is heard on the soundtrack. Conway had been the star of the *Land of the Giants* TV series.

FAR OUT MAN
(RCA, 1989) **D/S/A:** Tommy Chong **P:** Lisa M. Hansen

After the popular Cheech and Chong comedy team split up, Cheech had a pretty good acting career for a while. Chong, meanwhile, made this "home movie," playing a burnout looking for his kid and one-time old lady (his real-life wife, Shelby). The cast includes Rae Dawn Chong, C. Thomas Howell (her then real-life husband), Cheech Marin and Judd Nelson (as themselves), various Chong kids, Martin Mull as a crazy shrink, Paul Bartel, and Bobby Taylor (of the Vancouvers). One scene is repeated several times.

THE FAR PAVILIONS
(HBO, 1984) **D:** Peter Duffell
S: Julian Bond **P:** Geoffrey Reeve

This HBO miniseries is based on M. M. Kaye's novel set in 19th-century colonial India. Ben Cross stars, with Amy Irving, Omar Sharif, John Gielgud, Christopher Lee as Kakaji Rao, Rosanno Brazzi, Robert Hardy, and a primarily Indian supporting cast.

FASCINATION
(VSOM, 1979) **D/S:** Jean Rollin **P:** Joe de Lara   France

In 1916 a blond guy who has stolen some gold hides out in a castle. Eva and Elizabeth, two beautiful women staying there (Brigette Lahaie and

Franca Mai), mock, deceive, and seduce him. His enemies arrive with guns, but after having sex with one of them Eva puts on a cape, picks up a scythe (very cool scene), and kills them. More women arrive during a storm for a midnight blood-drinking ceremony, and the ending is a surprise. Some of this doesn't make much sense, but the female leads are excellent, and there are plenty of sex scenes, lesbian and otherwise. Lahaie (who was also in Franco and Kikoine movies and was a major porno star for years) is fascinating. The film is subtitled.

FAST CHARLIE, THE MOONBEAM RIDER

(1979) **D:** Steve Carver **S:** Michael Gleason
P: Roger Corman, Saul Klugman

David Carradine stars as a WWI deserter competing in the first long-distance motorcycle race. Brenda Vaccaro is his fan/girlfriend, and the cast includes L. Q. Jones, R. G. Armstrong, Jesse Vint, and Noble Willingham. The film is PG.

FAST COMPANY

(Admit One, 1978) **D/S:** David Cronenberg
S/P: Courtney Smith **P:** Michael Lebowitz,
Peter O'Brian, S. Phil Savan   Canada

Articles on Cronenberg always neglect this car-racing film. It took a while to find a copy, and while it's no *They Came from Within*, it's interesting enough and has a solid exploitation cast. The title refers to Fasco, a big oil company that sponsors famous racer Lonny "Lucky Man" Johnson (William Smith). He travels around western Canada and the northwestern US in the back of a fully equipped office-apartment/truck and races custom-built cars that run on Nitro fuel. John Saxon, as the weasely Amercian Fasco representative, makes Johnson drive funny cars (an embarrassing setback) and will resort to murder for profit. The sport of racing is shown as dangerous, overcommercialized show biz, with drivers manipulated by their sponsors. Cars explode, drivers burn. The rock soundtrack is Springsteen-influenced. Claudia Jennings, 70s B-movie queen, doesn't have a lot to do as Johnson's girlfriend in this, her last film. She died in a car crash the next year.

THE FASTEST GUITAR ALIVE

(MGM, 1967) **D:** Michael Moore
S: Robert E. Kent **P:** Sam Katzman

By 1967 the late Roy Orbison had stopped having hits and was recording inferior albums for MGM. Sam Katzman had already produced Elvis' *Kissin' Cousins* and *Harum Scarum*. Michael Moore had already directed Elvis in *Paradise Hawaiian Style*. I guess they figured this comedy would make the big O a movie star too. His acting is terrible, and boy, does he look weird with that shiny black hair! In his only acting role Roy is Johnny, a Confederate spy. He's also a womanizing singer, a master of disguises, is part of a Dr. Long's Elixir traveling medicine show (complete with six sexy chorus dancers), and is planning to rob the San Francisco mint. Nobody dies during the Wild West action, but Roy sings seven songs (yes, there was a soundtrack album). His singing is great, as usual, but most of the songs are forgettable or silly. During the "Medicine Man" song he plays a drum while four "Indian"

women dance onstage. The dumbest song, by the chorus girls (led by Joan Freeman), is "Snuggle as a Buggle in a Ruggle." Roy's special guitar gun is just a comic prop: "I can kill you and play your funeral march at the same time." The comic Indians (led by Iron Eyes Cody) use "new, impressionistic war paint." Sam the Sham (another MGM recording artist) has a small role.

FAST FOOD

(Fries, 1989) **D/P:** Michael A. Simpson
S: Clark Brandon, Lanny Horn
P: Stan Wakefield

Tracy Griffith (Melanie's half-sister) stars as Sam, a cute tomboy who owns a gas station turned burger stand. Jim Varney (who usually plays Ernest) is corrupt fast-food tycoon Wrangler Bob, who wants the business for himself at any cost. Formula 9, an aphrodisiac, is added to the burger sauce, making business boom as customers get turned on. There isn't much sex in this PG-13 teen comedy with a plot that could have been used for a porno movie, but it's good dumb fun. Too many characters use catchphrases like "I'm history" and "Read my lips," though. Traci Lords guest-stars as Dixie Love, Pamela Springsteen is a sorority leader, Michael J. Pollard works at the gas station, and Kevin McCarthy is a judge. It's by the director of the *Sleepaway Camp* sequels.

FAST GETAWAY

(RCA/Columbia, 1990) **D:** Spiro Razatos
S: James Dixon **P:** Paul Hertzberg

Corey Haim and Leo Rossi are son and father bank robbers who have to face a kickboxing ex-partner (Cynthia Rothrock). The cast also features Marcia Strassman. The director of this PG-13 New Line release is a stunt coordinator and stuntman.

FAST GETAWAY II

(Live, 1994) **D:** Oley Sassone
S: Mark Sevi **P:** Russell D. Markowitz

Corey Haim returns as a former robber now running an insurance business with his girlfriend (Sarah G. Buxton). Kickboxer Cynthia Rothrock frames him for a break-in, and when his father (Leo Rossi) gets out of prison they go after her again. This PG-13 sequel was shot in Arizona.

FAST TIMES AT RIDGEMONT HIGH

(MCA, 1982) **D:** Amy Heckerling **S:** Cameron
Crowe **P:** Art Linson, Irving Azoff

This influential California-teen hit is adapted from Crowe's book, which was based on his own experiences as an undercover high-school student. The believable characters deal with peer presure, boredom, minimum-wage jobs, and sex. Many teen stars got their start here. Sean Penn is excellent as the drugged-out Spicoli, a model for many others in the years to come. Phoebe Cates misinforms Jennifer

Jennifer Jason Leigh and Phoebe Cates in *Fast Times at Ridgemont High*.

Jason Leigh about sex. With Judge Reinhold, Tom Nolan, Forest Whitaker, Richard Romanus, Amanda Wyss, Anthony Edwards, Eric Stoltz, Kelli Maroney, James Russo, Lori Sutton, Pamela Springsteen, Nicolas Coppola (later Cage) in his debut, Lana Clarkson, Ava Lazar, and Ray Walston and Vincent Schiavelli (who were also in the 1986 CBS-TV *Fast Times* series, also directed by Heckerling). Crowe produced *The Wild Life*, a sequel. Asylum released a various artists double soundtrack.

FAST-WALKING

(Key, 1980) **D/S/P:** James B. Harris

James Woods stars as Fast-Walking Miniver, a corrupt, pot-smoking guard in an overcrowded southwestern prison. This barely released gem, based on *The Rap* by Ernest Brawley, has enough black humor, nudity, hookers, violence, and drugs to surprise the most jaded viewer. With Kay Lenz, Tim McIntire, M. Emmet Walsh, Susan Tyrrell (who runs a whorehouse), Robert Hooks (as a black militant), Timothy Carey, and Sidney Lassick. Harris had directed *The Bedford Incident* and *Some Call It Loving* and teamed up with Woods again for *Cop*.

FATAL ASSASSIN: *See* AFRICAN RAGE

FATAL ATTRACTION

(Paramount, 1987) **D:** Adrian Lyne **S:** James
Dearden **P:** Stanley R. Jaffe, Sherry Lansing

It copied a lot from Eastwood's *Play Misty for Me*, but this glossy lady-psycho movie was based on *Diversion*, a short 1979 film by scriptwriter Dearden. It made $70 million at the box office and was one of the most talked-about (and copied) films in years. Michael Douglas is a New York lawyer who has a one-night stand with publishing executive Glenn Close at her loft in the meat-packing district. After he rejects her, she goes to his suburban home and boils the family's pet rabbit, tries to blow up his car, and kidnaps his kid. Both Close and Anne Archer (who plays his wife) were nominated for Oscars. Ellen Foley and Fred Gwynne are also in the cast. In the letterboxed "director's series" video, the original ending (seen outside the US) is tacked onto the US ending, along with outtakes and an interview with Lyne. In the original ending, which Paramount changed for the US release, Douglas goes to jail for Close's murder/suicide. The Maurice Jarre soundtrack is on GNP. *Fatal Attraction* (1981) is a retitled Canadian movie (*Head On*) with Sally Kellerman.

FATAL BEAUTY

(MGM, 1987) **D:** Tom Holland **S:** Hillary Henkin, Dean Riesner **P:** Leonard Kroll

Some people don't think that comedienne Whoopi Goldberg should have starred in this violent movie, which had to be cut to receive an R rating, but that's show biz. The video version has been further cut, eliminating an interracial love scene. She's a police detective who uses disguises to go after drug dealers, Sam Elliott is a security expert, Harris Yulin is the main drug pusher, Ruben Blades is her partner, and Brad Dourif and Mike Jolly are ex-cons who shoot up a shopping mall. The cast also includes Jennifer Warren, Cheech Marin, John P. Ryan, James LeGros, Belinda Mayne, and Celeste Yarnall. It's by the director of *Child's Play* and *Fright Night*. The various artists soundtrack is on Atlantic.

FATAL BOND

(1992) **D:** Vince Monton **S/P:** Phil Avalon   Australia

Linda Blair falls for a guy (Jerome Ehlers) who tells her he's wanted for parking tickets. He's really a serial killer. They go to a beach motel. He seduces and then kills a surfer girl. Her religious father searches for the killer.

FATAL CHARM

(Academy, 1989) **D:** "Alan Smithee"/ Fritz Kiersch **S:** Nicholas Niciphor **P:** Bruce Cohn Curtis, Jonathan D. Krane

Christopher Atkins is a "sexy and charming" guy accused of the rape and murder of six women. He's convicted, encounters violent homosexuals in San Quentin, and escapes. In disguise (sunglasses!), he looks for the high-school student (Amanda Peterson) who has been writing to him. She sent him a photo of her girlfriend, though. Peterson has frequent, blurry erotic dreams where Traci Dali has sex on her knees in a van. With Mary Frann (from *Newhart*), Andrew Robinson, James Remar, Peggy Lipton, Robert Walker Jr., Lar Park Lincoln, and Ken Foree as a convict who threatens to cut Atkins' dick off. It premiered on Showtime.

FATAL EXPOSURE

(Tapeworm, 1989) **S/P:** Peter B. Good **S:** Chris Painter

A Herschell Gordon Lewis fan made this one in Alabama. The killer, a young blood-drinking photographer in an old mansion, talks to the camera. He decapitates a man, then has his church-lady wife pose for negligée bondage shots before he injects

her with acid. He buries bodies in an old graveyard and finds a girl to help him recruit models to kill. The characters are all incredibly stupid, and so is the script, but the cinematography is very good, there's a pretty surprising sex scene and a nightmare sequence, and everyone has very real accents.

FATAL GAMES

(1982) **D:** Michael Elliot **P:** Chris Mankiewicz

A killer using a javelin stalks schoolgirls at the Olympics. With Sally Kirkland as a transsexual killer, Melissa Prophet, Angela Bennett, Teal Roberts, and Linnea Quigley and Brinke Stevens (they're seen in a shower). It's unrated.

FATAL INSTINCT

(MGM, 1993) **D/A:** Carl Reiner **S:** David O'Malley **P:** Katie Jacobs, Pierce Gardner

Armand Assante stars as a cop who is also a lawyer in this mostly unfunny PG-13 spoof of *Fatal Attraction*. Sean Young is blond Lola Cain, Kate Nelligan is the wife trying to have him killed, and Sherilyn Fenn is his secretary. With James Remar, Tony Randall as a lawyer, and Eartha Kitt. There are on-screen sax solos by Clarence Clemons. It also spoofs *Double Indemnity*, *Body Heat*, *Cape Fear* (the remake), *Sleeping with the Enemy*, and others.

FATAL JUSTICE

(AIP, 1992) **D/C:** Gerald Cain **S:** Bret McCormick **P:** Denis Dodson

Suzanne Agar (also a coproducer) stars as a hit lady in a bikini. She's ordered to "retire" Mars (Joe Estevez), who turns out to be her father. Fred Olen Ray was an executive producer, and it was filmed in Texas and Louisiana.

FATAL MISSION

(Media, 1989) **D/S:** George Rowe **S/P:** Chosei Funahara **S/A:** Peter Fonda **S:** Anthony and John Gentile   US/Japan

Peter Fonda stars as a CIA assassin posing as a French journalist on a mission in North Vietnam. This action movie, which was shot in the Philippines, costars Tia Carrere (*Wayne's World*) as a Chinese guerilla assassin, Jim Mitchum, and Mako.

THE FATAL PASSION OF DR. MABUSE: *See* DR. MABUSE, THE GAMBLER

FATAL PULSE

(Celebrity, 1987) **D/P:** Anthony Christopher **S:** James Hundhausen

This sorority-house-slasher movie has blood, sex, lots of ridiculous suspects, and death by LP. Martin Sheen's brother Joe Phelan/Estevez owns the frat house. With Michelle McCormick, Ken Roberts, Roxanne Kernohan, and porno star Hershall Savage as a cop.

FATAL PURSUIT: *See* I SPIT ON YOUR CORPSE

FATAL SECRET

(Studio, 1987) **D/S:** Andrew Nelson, Mats Helge **P:** Roger Lundgren   Sweden (*Animal Protector*)

David Carradine stars as a drug and arms dealer in one of several films he made in Sweden. This spy story costars Camille Lunden.

FATAL SKIES

(AIP, 1989) **D/S:** Thomas C. Dugan **P:** Peter Yuval

Timothy Leary, who had done guest-star bits in other movies, stars as the villain behind toxic-waste dumping who has to battle heroic skydiving teens. The ads said, "Strap in, climb on, drop out!" With Jay Richardson, Veronica Carothers, and Melissa Anne Moore. It was made by a USC graduate.

THE FAT BLACK PUSSYCAT

(SW, 1963) **D/S:** Harold Lea **P:** Arnold Panken

This slow-moving New York City beatnik movie has a plot that's hard to follow. It starts with a head-line, SHOES OF NUDE MURDER VICTIM MISSING! A jazz quartet plays (for a long time), and there's lots of beat poetry. Frank Janus stars as a nice-guy detective, but the surprise cast members are Geoffrey Lewis (father of Juliette), in Washington Square Park, Hector Elizondo, and poet Hugh Romney, later known as Wavy Gravy of Woodstock fame. The Pussycat was a real cafe and theater in Greenwich Village. M. A. Ripps wrote the story. It's a Frank Henenlotter Sexy Shocker release.

FAT GUY GOES NUTZOID!

(Prism, 1983) **D/S:** John Golden **S:** Richard Golden **P:** Emily Dillon

Troma released this low comedy (originally titled *Zeisters*). Peter Linari is a pathetic, 300-pound deaf-mute with a mohawk who's called the Mooka. He makes friends with two nerds, farts, pukes, and hides in a car. Retarded kids at summer camp start a riot, and there are Quaaludes jokes. Some parts take place in Manhattan. The guitar score is by Leo Kottke!

FATHERLAND

(Warner, 1994) **D:** Christopher Menaul **S:** Stanley Weiser, Ron Hutchinson **P:** Frederic Muller, Llene Kahn

The premise that Germany won WWII and Hitler still rules Europe in 1964 provides a fascinating background for what starts out as a murder mystery. We learn that the fighting with Stalin's USSR still goes on and Joseph Kennedy is the president of America, but other events stay the same (Hiroshima stopped Japan and the Beatles are an international hit). Rutger Hauer stars as an SS detective and single dad in Berlin who teams up with an American reporter (Miranda Richardson) and finds out about the big secret (the Holocaust) closely guarded by the Gestapo. This happens just when the American president arrives to resume relations with Germany on Hitler's 75th birthday. Also with Rory Jennings as the detective's son, Peter Vaughn, Jean Marsh, and Rudolph Fleischer as Hitler. The HBO alternate-history movie is based on Robert Harris' best selling book. It was shot in Prague.

FATHERS AND SONS

(SVS, 1991) **D/S:** Paul Mones **P:** Jon Kilik

Jeff Goldblum is Max Fish, an alienated, alcoholic, formerly famous movie director and widower who owns a book store and directs plays in Asbury Park, NJ, while trying to keep his teen son (Rory Cochrane, who narrates) out of trouble. Meanwhile, the mysterious "Shore Killer" is on the loose, and the local kids party and take a new drug called "chew." It's more about characters relating to each other than what the (telepathic) serial killer does, but the Jersey shore locations are a pleasant change. With Ellen Greene *(Little Shop of Horrors)*, Famke Janssen, Spike Lee's sister Joie, and Rosanna Arquette in a very small role as a fortune teller.

FAUST

(Video Yesterday, 1926) **D:** F. W. Murnau **S:** Hans Kyser **P:** Erich Pommer   Germany

The most famous version of the old legend (the basis of at least 17 other films made before and after this one) about a man who sells his soul to the Devil stars Emil Jannings as Mephistopheles and Gosta Ekman as Faust. The 90-minute tape of this silent film, made by UFA, features the original organ score. The German intertitles are subtitled in English. The cast includes director William Dieterle, who made an American version *(All That Money Can Buy/The Devil and Daniel Webster)* in 1941. (Faust was later the name of a pioneering West German 70s noise band.) Murnau went to the US in 1927, made four films, and died in a car accident in 1931, at the age of 42. Jannings, considered one of the greatest actors in the world at the time, also starred in Murnau and Pommer's *The Last Laugh* (1924). He remained in Germany during the Nazi era, was made head of the company that produced his films, and was honored as an "artist of the State."

FEAR

(Wizard, 1980) **D/S:** Riccardo Freda **S:** Fabio Piccioni, Cesare Antonio Corti   Italy/France
(L'ossessione Che Uccide; Murder Obsession)

An actor takes his girlfriend and part of his cast and crew home to visit his mother (Anita Strindberg), and people die. Laura *(Emanuelle)* Gemser, John Richardson, and Stefano Patrizi costar. This *giallo* mystery has nudity, nightmares, a sick ending, a bat attack, and a giant spider. The American tape is missing some scenes.

FEAR

(Virgin, 1988) **D:** Robert A. Ferretti **S:** Rick Scarry, Kathryn Connell **P:** Lisa M. Hansen

Nam vet Cliff De Young, his wife (Kay Lenz), and their kids are at an isolated cabin. He has disturbing flashbacks. Some escaped cons, led by Nam-vet mass murderer Frank Stallone and Robert Factor, take hostages, and the family fights back. This bloody movie features a cock in a rat trap.

FEAR

(Vestron, 1989) **D/S:** Rockne O'Bannon **P:** Richard Kobritz

Ally Sheedy is a South Carolina girl with ESP who "sees" a killer (played by John Agar!) so the police can show up and shoot him. Years later she's an author in LA who ends up working for the police (who don't believe in her powers) to track "the ShadowMan." This serial killer, who writes "Fear Me" on a wall with blood, talks to her and taunts her inside her head while he kills. With Lauren Hutton as her manager, Michael O'Keeffe as the guy next door, and Dina Merrill. The worst part of this mediocre movie is the constant use of irritating "Blur-o-vision." It debuted on Showtime.

FEAR CITY

(HBO, 1984) **D:** Abel Ferrara **S:** Nicholas St. John **P:** Bruce Cohn Curtis

After the indy *Driller Killer* and *Ms. 45*, Ferrara made this for 20th Century-Fox. There was way too much nudity, drugs, and violence for them, so it ended up being released by the exploitation specialists at Aquarius. Tom Berenger stars as an ex-boxer working as an agent for strippers in New York City. His clients are being killed by a psycho-killer karate expert, and gangsters cause more trouble. Billy Dee Williams is a cop. Melanie Griffith, as a drug-addicted stripper having an affair with Rae Dawn Chong, does an entire routine onstage wearing just a G string. With Jack Scalia, Rossano Brazzi, Michael V. Gazzo, Jan Murray, Ola Ray, Maria Conchita Alonso (in her first US movie), Emilia Crow, Lori Eastside, and Tracy Griffith (Melanie's half-sister). The theme song is by David Johansen.

THE FEAR INSIDE

(Fox, 1991) **D:** Leon Ichaso **S:** David Birke **P:** John Broderick

An agoraphobic woman (Christine Lahti) rents rooms in her mansion to crazed killer Dylan McDermott and neurotic Jennifer Rubin. David Ackroyd is her husband. This made-for-cable movie is like *Lady in a Cage* (1964).

FEAR IN THE NIGHT

(Sinister, 1946) **D/S:** Maxwell Shane **P:** William H. Pine, William C. Thomas

Years before he was Bones on *Star Trek*, DeForest Kelley dreams that he has committed a murder. His brother-in-law (Paul Kelly) discovers that it's a frame-up involving a mansion and hypnosis. The movie, based on a Cornell Woolrich story called "Nightmare," features some great dream and flashback sequences. With Ann Doran and Robert Emmett Keane. Ten years later the same director remade it as *Nightmare*, starring Kevin McCarthy and Edward G. Robinson. The original was screened at several film festivals in 1992.

FEARLESS TIGER

(Imperial, 1990) **D/S:** Ron Hulme **P/A:** Jalal Merhi   Canada *(Black Pearls)*

Jalal Merhi leaves his father's Toronto shopping-cart business to go to Hong Kong, learn martial arts, and avenge the drug death of his brother.

Lazar Rockwood is the evil nirvana dealer. With Monika Schnarre, Jamie Farr as the father, and Bolo Yeung.

FEAR OF A BLACK HAT

(Fox, 1993) **D/S/A:** Rusty Cundlieff **P:** Darin Scott

Look for this hilarious, on-target spoof of rap music. The story of the rise and fall of the (fictional) NWH (Niggaz with Hats) rap group is told by a sociologist and filmmaker (Kasi Lemmons). The trio is leader Ice Cold (Rusty Cundlieff), Tasty Taste (Larry B. Scott, from the *Revenge of the Nerds* movies), and DJ Tone Def (Mark Christopher Lawrence). They record a "Kill Whitey" LP, and we see perfect videos for "Booty Juice" and "Fuck the Security Guards." The film began as a short. It's better than the similar, higher-budgeted *CB4*. Kurt Loder plays himself. Also with Monique Gabrielle.

FEAST OF FLESH

(1968) **D:** Emilio Vieyra **S:** Antonio Rosso **P:** Ortestes A. Trucco   Spain

A masked killer sticks syringes into women at a resort. A police inspector and his girlfriend solve the mystery. A 66-minute version played on a double bill in the US with the Mexican film *Night of the Bloody Apes*.

FEDERAL FOLLIES

(Vid City series)

Here are 8 60-minute volumes presenting some of the short educational films made by the US government over the years. Many (well, all) of them are obviously designed to misinform and manipulate the population, for various reasons. These are some highlights: "Duck and Cover" (1), "Our Job in Japan" (2), "Trip To Where?" and "Your Job in Germany" (3), "Jap Zero," with Ronald Reagan! (4), "Code of Conduct," with Jack Webb (5), a Disney hygiene film (6), "Defense Against the Spy" (7), and "The More We Get Together," with Robbie Benson as a teen drunk (8).

THE FEEBLES

(MTI, 1989) **D/S/P/C:** Peter Jackson NZ *(Meet the Feebles)*

Most viewers will find this a bit much, but if you can dig it, it's really well done—sort of a mean-spirited, X-rated, bad-taste "Spluppets" musical. It's complete with sex, suicide, drugs, and body fluids. Like the Muppets, these characters are a mixture of puppets, marionettes, and people in animal suits. It's a backstage story starring "Wobert," a shy hedgehog. There's an amazing *Deer Hunter*–copy Nam flashback, a rat (with a Peter Lorre voice) who makes S&M porno movies, and a fly reporter who eats shit. It's funny to see a huge walrus, an even bigger crab monster, and all the tiny creatures trying to cheat, abuse, or have sex with each other, but not everybody will laugh at the rabbit with AIDS. The Michelle Scullion music was released on a picturedisc. There was an earlier American feature by Gerard Damiano called *Let My Puppets Come*, and the French *Marquis* (also released in 1989) also had puppets, sex, and violence.

FEELIN' GOOD

(1966) **D/S/P:** James A. Pike **S:** Mildred Maffei

Actual color footage of a 1966 Boston Jaycees battle of the bands was used in this independent teen drama filmed in color. The director's son, Travis Pike, stars as a ex-GI who returns to Boston, his girlfriend, and their musician friends. With the Brattle Steet East, the Montclairs, and others. Pike was a local TV director.

FELLINI SATYRICON

(MGM, 1969) **D/S:** Federico Fellini
P: Alberto Grimaldi Italy/France

Fellini's most shocking film shows what life might have been like in decadent, ancient Rome. Very impressive-looking, it mixes Fellini's always in-credible real human faces, sex (with just about anybody or anything that moves), and magic, and is the first place many people saw (or even thought about) a hermaphrodite. Martin Potter stars, with Hiram Keller, Capucine, and Alain Cuny. It was Fellini's first film after *Juliet of the Spirits* (1966). The subtitled United Artists release is over two hours long, and the tape is letterboxed. The ex-cellent Nino Rota soundtrack is also on United Artists. Tina Aumont starred in an Italian ripoff, *Satyricon* (1970) by Gian Luigi Polidoro.

FEMALE ANIMAL

(SW, 1970) **D:** Juan Carlo Grinella **S:** Octavio Bellini, Marcello Lazarini Italy/Spain
(*La Mujer del Gato; Teenagers for Sale*)

Arlene Tiger stars as Angelique, a woman from a fishing village who becomes a maid in a mansion, where she has affairs with a count and his son. She also takes LSD, has sex with the stableboy and the count's mistress, and ends up as a hooker servicing a priest. Filmed in Puerto Rico, it was rated X when released by Jerry Gross' Cinemation company and was rereleased in 1978 by Sam Sher-man's Independent International.

THE FEMALE BUNCH

(Imperial, IVC, 1969) **D:** Al Adamson **S:** Jale Lockwood, Brent Nimrod **P:** Raphael Nussbaum

Five women on horseback (and a small plane) track a couple hiding in a cave. He asks, "How did you get into this mess?" The line is repeated over and over with a heavy echo until Sandy begins to narrate her incredible feature-length flashback. She was a suicidal Vegas waitress with a rotten singer boyfriend (wearing a silver lamé jacket). Her friend Libby (the director's wife, Regina Car-rol, with incredible piled-up hair) takes her to a se-cret ranch with no men: "We don't give a damn about society here! It takes guts to be free!" The fascist-bitch leader (Jennifer Bishop) buries one woman alive in a coffin to test her. Lon Chaney Jr. plays Lonnie, a grizzled, hard-drinking, friendly, lovesick former stuntman who tends the horses. He has lines, but his voice is in pretty bad shape. After Bishop shoots up, there's a psychedelic les-bian scene. In Mexico the women abuse locals: "Wetback! Greaser! Don't drink the water! Ha, ha!" Russ Tamblyn (with a droopy mustache) is first seen taking a piss. He has his face branded,

bites a woman on her breast, and gets stuck with a pitchfork. Lon is brained with a hammer and dragged by a horse, but he saves the day at the end! This is sort of a terrible (and too dark) night-mare mixture of *The Wild Bunch* and *Faster, Pus-sycat! Kill! Kill!* with sex, drugs, nudity, and violence. It was shot at the notorious Spahn Ranch, not very long before the Manson-family murders. The executive producer was Mardi Rus-tam, and the assistant director was John "Bud" Cardos, so you can't blame just Adamson. Cha-ney's last movie (he died in 1973), it didn't come out until 1971, when it was promoted by stressing the Manson connection!

THE FEMALE JUNGLE

(RCA, 1954) **D/S/A:** Bruno Ve Sota
S/P/A: Burt Kaiser (*The Hangover*)

This low-budget crime film was directed by actor Bruno Ve Sota just after he was in *Dementia/ Daughter of Horror*. Burt Kaiser, the unfamous pro-ducer/star, sold his movie to ARC (pre-AIP) which put it on a 1956 double bill with Corman's *Okla-homa Woman*. Actress Monica Madison has been strangled, and drunken off-duty police lieutenant Jack Stevens (Lawrence Tierney), whose only friend is a very observant young black janitor, is a suspect. The plot jumps from character to character and in-cludes flashbacks (at the Hollywood Can Can Club) as the story unfolds. Alex (Kaiser), an alcoholic, un-employed artist with a waitress wife (Kathleen Crowley), is having an affair with Candy Price (Jayne Mansfield, in her film debut). Candy is very serious and bitter, and she talks a lot: "You're trouble, Al. You always will be. But I've come around to give you a touch of your own medicine." John Carradine has a good role as a mysterious, menacing, rich gossip columnist who escorted the

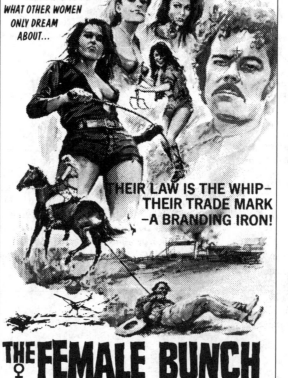

THEY DARE TO DO WHAT OTHER WOMEN ONLY DREAM ABOUT...

THEIR LAW IS THE WHIP—
THEIR TRADE MARK
—A BRANDING IRON!

THE FEMALE BUNCH

dead actress to a premiere. He wears glasses and plays classical music very loud. Watching this shad-owy, dark film about desperate and doomed charac-ters makes me think that maybe Bruno really did direct the amazing *Dementia/Daughter of Horror* (1953). His next job as director was *The Brain Eat-ers* (1959). Jayne Mansfield was paid $150 for act-ing in *The Female Jungle,* then returned to her job selling popcorn at a movie theater.

FEMALE NEO NINJAS

(VSOM, 1993) **D:** Tomoyuki Kasai Japan

This wild fantasy features three nice, acrobatic, fighting teen girls in cool black-leather clothes who live with their grandfather/teacher. A confused young man arrives from the past (and in flash-backs) with a magic scroll, and they help him out. It sounds and looks like a Saturday-morning kids' show with mediocre but fun FX, but about half-way through, when there's a closeup of one girl's ass as she crawls away from some new threat, it becomes something you wouldn't see on TV (at least not in this country). One girl is tied up and whipped while wearing a see-through net top, then tied up topless with a snake on her body. After some more sexy S&M scenes there's a corrupt poli-tician who parties with topless women and wants ultimate power from aliens with a flying saucer. The subtitled print is excellent.

FEMALE ON THE BEACH

(Universal, 1955) **D:** Joseph Pevney **P:** Albert Zugsmith

Middle-aged Joan Crawford, a former Vegas dancer, is a rich widow who falls for stud Jeff Chandler after she discovers him making breakfast in her beach house. He has already romanced (and may have killed) her former tenant. She reads the dead woman's diary but decides to marry him anyway. With Jan Sterling, Judith Evelyn, Charles Drake, Cecil Kellaway, and Natalie Schafer. This was the Craw-ford movie after *Johnny Guitar*.

FEMALE PLASMA SUCKERS = BLOOD ORGY OF THE SHE DEVILS

FEMALES FOR HIRE

(1968) **D/S:** Rolf Olsen W. Germany
(*Der Arzt von Saint Paul; Sidewalk Doctor; Shock Treatment; Bedroom Stewardesses*)

Curt Jurgens starred as a St. Pauli–area doctor in Hamburg, and Chris-tine Rucker is a prostitute. The US version (called *The Bedroom*) with new scenes shot by Al Adamson in the US, was released in 1976 for people suckered into drive-in sex-movie triple bills. From Independent International.

FEMALE SPACE INVADERS = STARCRASH

Lawrence Tierney and John Carradine in *The Female Jungle*.

FEMALE TROUBLE

(Continental, Cinema Group, 1974)
D/S/P: John Waters

"Crime equals beauty" is the motto of Dawn Davenport (Divine) in Waters' follow-up to *Pink Flamingos*. First seen as a teen, she grows up, becomes famous, shoots the audience during her trampoline act, and goes to the electric chair for murder. It's Waters at his best, filled with very funny scenes and memorable lines. Mink Stole is Taffy, Dawn's illegitimate daughter, who plays car crash and joins the Hare Krishnas. Edith Massey is incredible as the "fag hag" aunt bulging out of leather bondage clothes. With David Lochary and Mary Vivian Pearce as the Dashers, Michael Potter as Gator, Cookie Mueller, and George Stover. In one scene, Divine (playing Dawn and Earl) rapes herself. It was Divine's last Waters film until *Polyester* (1981). *Female Trouble* debuted in Baltimore and was distributed by New Line. Sadly, nearly all of the stars are now dead.

FEMME FATALE

(Republic, 1990) **D:** André Gutfreund **S:** Michael Ferris, John D. Brancato **P:** Andrew Lane, Nancy Rae Stone

Lisa Zane (from *Bad Influence*) has multiple personalities. One is underground actress Maura Sade. Colin Firth is her forest-ranger husband, Lisa Blount is an LA lesbian S&M movie director, Billy Zane (the star's real-life brother) is a painter, Scott Wilson is a doctor, and Suzanne Snyder is a model with a bag on her head.

FEMME FONTAINE: KILLER BABE FOR THE CIA

(Troma, 1994) **D/S/P/A:** Margot Hope

An assassin (Hope) looking for her father, who disapeared in South America, discovers a porno scam in Chinatown and a neo-Nazi group. James Hong is a martial-arts master, and Catherine Dao is a dragon lady. Gary Graver was the editor and cinematographer of this comedy adventure.

LA FEMME NIKITA

(Vidmark, 1989) **D/S:** Luc Besson   France (*Nikita*)

This was one of the most influential features of the late 80s. Anne Parillaud is a junkie punk-gang member who is arrested for killing a cop during a holdup and goes to prison. She's forced to go through a long government reprogramming period and is let out to commit political assassinations in a tight black skirt. Her trainers are a detatched government agent (Tcheky Karyo) and a fashion consultant (Jeanne Moreau). She blows away a lot of people and is allowed to live on her own, but she falls in love with a supermarket clerk, Jean-Hughes Anglade. The begining is very violent, but it settles into a relationship movie with spy touches. Parillaud is excellent, especially before she's "reformed." The title was changed in America, so people wouldn't think it was Russian! A Hong Kong version is *Black Cat* (1991). The US remake (with Bridget Fonda) is *Point of No Return*.

FEROCIOUS FEMALE FREEDOM FIGHTERS

(Media, 1982) **D:** Yuri Burman

The LA Connection comedy group redubbed a Hong Kong film with new dialogue, dialects, and sound effects (like Woody Allen years earlier with *What's Up, Tiger Lily?*). It includes female wrestlers. Troma released it (and a sequel).

THE FERTILICHROME CHEERLEADER MASSACRE

(Stimco, 1989) **D/S/P:** Patric Shawn O'Neill
P: Sam Albright

If you like slow science fiction with some good "trip" sequences this b/w feature from Seattle might do the trick. It concerns a guard at a remote nuclear power station, usually out protecting the glowing orbs in the desert. He cooks a rabbit, snake, and beer stew for dinner. A mad scientist (in a smoking jacket) and his teen gang kidnap the guard's cheerleader daughter for "fertilichrome" experiments that cause women to have one baby a month. Some of the sound effects are interesting, but the music made me pretty sleepy. With members of the Screaming Trees.

ffolkes

(MCA, 1980) **D:** Andrew V. McLaglen **S:** Jack Davies
P: Elliot Kastner   UK (*North Sea Hijack*; *Assault Force*)

Roger Moore stars as a cat-loving, woman-hating mercenary hired to stop crazed (of course) terrrorist Anthony Perkins and his gang from blowing up oil rigs after they hijack a ship in the North Sea for ransom. With James Mason, Michael Parks, David Hedison, and Jeremy Clyde.

F FOR FAKE

(Home Vision, 1973) **D/A:** Orson Welles **P:** Dominique Antoine, François Reichenbach

The last film completed by Welles is a humorous, playful, fascinating documentary. Welles ("I am a char-latan") added much new footage to a French TV show (shot by Reichenbach) about art forger Elmyr de Hory. The topics explored include Welles' "War of the Worlds" radio broadcast, Clifford Irving (who wrote a fake autobiography of Howard Hughes), and deceptions and fakery in general. Nina Van Pallandt, Oja Kodar, Joseph Cotten, Laurence Harvey, and Peter Bogdanovich appear as themselves. Cinematographer Gary Graver also worked on Welles' unfinished *The Other Side of Midnight* (from 1970–76).

FIELD OF FIRE

(HBO, 1990) **D/P:** Cirio H. Santiago
Philippines (*Battle Gear*)

David Carradine stars as an American general leading a squadron behind enemy lines in Cambodia on a rescue mission. It was released by Concorde.

THE FIEND = BEWARE THE BRETHREN

THE FIEND WHO WALKED THE WEST

(1958) **D:** Gordon Douglas **S:** Harry Brown, Philip Yordan **P:** Herbert B. Swope Jr.

Here's a remake of *Kiss of Death* (1947), this time as a western. Hugh O'Brian is Hardy, a bank robber serving time, and future producer Robert Evans is the sadistic, giggling, psycho inmate with a mother complex (played by Richard Widmark in the original) who terrorizes Hardy's wife (Linda Cristal) and kills his friends. With Dolores Michaels, Stephen McNally, June Blair, Edward Andrews, and Ron Ely. This 20th Century–Fox release has music by Les Baxter.

FIERCE: *See* FIGHTING MAD

THE FIFTH MISSILE

D: Larry Peerce **S:** Eric Bercovici **P:** Arthur Fellows

Robert Conrad and Sam Waterston star as naval commanders during war games on an atomic submarine. They almost cause WWIII. With Richard Roundtree, Art LaFleur, Yvette Mimieux, and David Soul. This NBC-TV movie was filmed in Italy and on Malta.

Anne Parillaud stars in *La Femme Nikita*.

THE FIFTH MUSKETEER

(RCA, 1977) **D:** Ken Annakin **S:** David Ambrose
P: Ted Richmond   Austria (*Behind the Iron Mask*)

This version of Dumas' novel *The Man in the Iron
Mask* was titled to make people think it was a sequel to Richard Lester's *The Four Musketeers*
(1975). Beau Bridges stars as King Louis XIV and
his brother who goes to prison. The musketeers (all
old men this time) are Lloyd Bridges, Alan Hale Jr.,
José Ferrer, Cornel Wilde, and Rex Harrison. With
Sylvia Kristel, Ursula Andress, Olivia de Havilland
(it was her last film), Ian McShane, and Helmut
Dantine. It was filmed in Austria and released by
Columbia. James Whale directed *The Man in the
Iron Mask* (1939). Richard Chamberlain starred in
a TV-movie version that debuted in 1977.

52 PICK-UP

(1986) **D:** John Frankenheimer **S:** Elmore
Leonard, John Steppling **P:** Menahem Golan

A wealthy businessman (Roy Scheider) has a brief
affair with a nude model. She's videotaped being
killed, and he's framed and blackmailed by sleazy
John Glover with help from a crazed Clarence Williams III. They also force him to watch the snuff
film they made. With Ann-Margret as his wife,
Vanity, Kelly Preston, and Doug McClure. Jamie
Gillis, Ron Jeremy, and other porno stars are in
sex-club scenes. The same Elmore Leonard novel
had been filmed as *The Ambassador* in 1984.

FIGHT FOR YOUR LIFE

(After Hours, 1977) **D:** Robert A Endelson **S:** Straw
Weisman **P:** William Mishkin   (*Held Hostage; Stayin'
Alive; Getting Even; Bloodbath at 1313; Fury Road*)

A racist hillbilly (William Sanderson, from the
Newhart show) and two other sadistic prison escapees (one Chinese and one Mexican) terrorize a
black minister and his family. The victims fight
back and eventually take a bloody revenge. The
plot steals from *The Desperate Hours* (1957). It
was filmed in upstate New York. Most viewers find
this movie beneath contempt, but it was released
many times under various titles by Mishkin. Sometimes it was double-billed with *Snuff* or a kung-fu
movie, and sometimes it was advertised to make it
look more like a horror movie.

FIGHTING BACK

(Paramount, 1982) **D:** Lewis Teague **S:** Tom Headley,
David Z. Goodman **P:** Dino De Laurentiis

Tom Skerritt is an Italian-deli owner in South
Philadelphia. During one day his best friend is
shot, his mother's finger is cut off, and his wife has
a miscarriage. So he organizes a vigilante group
and seeks revenge. He also becomes a media celebrity. This movie shows the negative aspects of
vigilantism while exploiting it. With Michael Sarrazin, Patti LuPone, Yaphet Kotto, David Rasche,
and Pat Cooper. It was made between the director's
Alligator and *Cujo*.

FIGHTING DEVIL DOGS

(Republic, 1938) **D:** William Witney, John English
S: Barry Shipman, Franklyn Adreon, Ronald Davidson

Lee Powell stars as a Marine-lieutenant hero in this
12-chapter Republic serial (in real life he was
killed in action in WWII). A mad scientist called
the Lightning (Hugh Sothern) uses deadly electronic "fire bolts" to battle the Marines from his fu-

turistic Wing plane. The villain wears a cool black
cape and mask and has some impressive weapons.
With Herman Brix (later Bruce Bennett), Eleanor
Stewart, and Montague Love. The 1966 feature
version was called *The Torpedo of Doom*.

FIGHTING FISTS OF SHANGHAI JOE

(TWE, 1973) **D:** Mario Caiano **P:** Renato
Angiolini, Roberto Bessi   Italy (*Il Mio
Nome E' Shanghai Joe; Shanghai Joe*)

Here's a western ripoff of the *Kung Fu* TV series.
Chen Lee stars as a Chinese martial-arts fighter
who helps transport slave labor before fighting
back. Klaus Kinski is a villain whose coat is lined
with knives. With Gordon Mitchell and Giacomo
Rossi-Stuart. Kinski was in *Aguirre* the same year.

FIGHTING MAD

(1976) **D/S:** Jonathan Demme **P:** Roger
Corman **E:** Monte Hellman

Peter Fonda is an Arkansas farmer who uses a bow
and arrow to fight a powerful, corrupt real-estate-
development company that caused the deaths of
his father and brother (Scott Glenn) while conducting illegal strip mining. With Lynn Lowry
(from *I Drink Your Blood*), Philip Carey, John
Doucette, and Nobel Willingham. It was one
of several features Corman produced for 20th
Century–Fox. Demme had directed *Caged Heat*
and *Crazy Mama* at New World.

FIGHTING MAD

(Continental, 1977) **D/S:** Cirio H. Santiago
US/Philippines (*Fierce; Death Force*)

James Ingleheart is a soldier left behind while fighting in Vietnam. His partners leave him for dead
while smuggling gold and Japanese soldiers who
don't know WWII is over (!) capture him, then
train him as a samurai swordsman. He seeks revenge. Jayne Kennedy and Leon Isaac Kennedy costar. Leon Isaac, a Cleveland DJ known as Leon the
Lover, married former Miss Ohio Jayne Kennedy
and took her last name. Both had been in movies
(in supporting roles) since 1972. They were also in
Body and Soul together. The film was produced by
New World, then rereleased to capitalize on their
later careers.

FILMGORE

(Wizard, 1983) **D:** Ken Dixon **P:** Charles Band

Elvira (Cassandra Peterson) hosts a compilation of
film clips, all from the same (now defunct) video
company. Her *Movie Macabre* program started on
KHJ-TV in 1981. There are scenes from *The Texas
Chainsaw Massacre*, *Snuff*, and several Herschell
Gordon Lewis gore movies.

FILMHOUSE FEVER

(1986) **D:** Dominic Paris

This is an hour-long compilation of old trailers (including some good and rare ones), plus typical silly
comedy skits, by the director of *Dracula's Last
Rites* (1980).

FIFTIES FAVES
TOP 10, IN ALPHABETICAL ORDER

1. *The Beast from 20,000 Fathoms* (1953)
2. *Black Sunday* (1960; available in different US, UK, or Italian versions)
3. *Dementia* (1953; available with or without the added narration by Ed McMahon)
4. *Horror of Dracula* (1959)
5. *Invasion of the Body Snatchers* (1956; available colorized)
6. *Night of the Demon* (1957; now available in the uncut British version or colorized)
7. *Peeping Tom* (1960; reissued theatrically in 1979, with Martin Scorsese's backing, and available in the complete 101-minute version)
8. *Psycho* (1960)
9. *Seventh Voyage of Sinbad* (1958)
10. *The Thing* (1951; finally available uncut, on Criterion laserdisc)

The 50s was the first time when "teenager" meant
something. Great, fun movies and classic rock
songs were created just for teens. The launching
of Sputnik in the USSR helped start a boom in
science-fiction movies, and the "threat" of TV led
to Cinemascope and 3-D movies. It was also the
time when TV horror hosts (and newsstand monster magazines) first showed up and the last serials were produced. Postwar *film noir* movies were
still common, and a parallel world of adults-only
and road-show movies was going strong. The 50s
films that grossed more than $10 million include
many Cinemascope epics, *The Shaggy Dog*, *20,000
Leagues Under the Sea*, and *Psycho* (yes, it's technically a 50s movie). Cecil B. De Mille's *Ten Commandments* 1956 remake of his 1923 silent version
of *The Ten Commandments* cost $43 million and
was the top-grossing film, followed by 2 Disney
animated movies.

FILLMORE

(1972) **D:** Richard T. Heffron **P:** Herbert F. Decker

A dozen rock groups are shown playing concerts in 1972, the final days of the Fillmore West in San Francisco, using split-screen techniques. The bands include the Grateful Dead, Santana, Jefferson Airplane, Hot Tuna, Quicksilver Messenger Service, Boz Scaggs, It's a Beautiful Day, the Rowan Brothers, and Cold Blood. Some of the groups were already way past their prime and had suffered personnel changes. Too bad the movie wasn't made in 1967. The late Bill Graham is interviewed throughout.

FINAL ALLIANCE

(RCA, 1988) **D:** Mario De Lio **S/P:** Harel Goldstein **S:** John T. Eubank **P:** Ami Artzi   S.Africa

David Hasselhoff and a cougar go on a vengeance spree. With Jeanie Moore, Bo Hopkins, and John Saxon as Ghost, albino leader of the Vipers bikers. It's set in Texas.

THE FINAL ANALYSIS

(Warner, 1992) **D:** Phil Joanou **S:** Wesley Strick **P:** Charles Roven, Paul Junger Witt, Tony Thomas

Richard Gere (also a producer) stars as a San Francisco psychiatrist who becomes involved with two sisters (Uma Thurman and Kim Basinger). The plot copies *Vertigo* and several 40s crime movies. Eric Roberts is Basinger's jealous Greek gangster husband. She goes nuts if she has one drink just like her character in the comedy *Blind Date*. With Keith David and Harris Yulin. Dean Tavouris was the production designer. It was the first screenplay by the writer of the *Cape Fear* remake and *Batman Returns*.

FINAL APPROACH

(Vidmark, 1991) **D/S/P:** Eric Steven Stahl **S:** Gerald Laurence

You know something is wrong when a movie had to be promoted as having "the world's first all-digital sound." It's basically a two-character *Twilight Zone*–type cosmic science fiction story. A dazed and confused Air Force pilot with amnesia (James B. Sikking) is involved in a top-secret project. A psychiatrist (Hector Elizondo) questions him in a room. The flashback-filled story is complete with altered-reality scenes, computer graphics, and *2001*-style aerial shots. It would make a good drug movie on the big screen. With Kevin McCarthy and Madolyn Smith.

THE FINAL COMEDOWN

(Bingo, 1972) **D:** Alan Arkush **D/S/P:** Oscar Williams   (*Blast*)

Billy Dee Williams stars as an electronics expert who becomes an angry revolutionary. Flashbacks show why, in this violent but serious social-commentary film. Raymond St. Jacques is Imir, a militant leader. With Pamela Jones, D'Urville Martin, and R. G. Armstrong. When New World re-released it as *Blast* in 1977, Roger Corman had a half-hour of new action scenes (including Paul Bartel) added. It was originally partially backed by the American Film Institute. Director Williams, from the Virgin Islands, made the family comedy *Five on the Black Hand Side* (1973) next.

FINAL EMBRACE

(New Horizons, 1991) **D:** Oley Sassone **S:** R. J. Robertson, Jim Wynorski **P:** Roger Corman

A psycho kills a female video star (Nancy Vale), and her twin sister (also Vale) shows up. An LA cop (Robert Rusler) starts sleeping with the sister, who's a suspect, but his friendly partner and father (Dick Van Patten!) disapprove. There are many other suspects (a director, record producer, crazed fan, coked-up rival singer) and many false scares. A lot of time is spent showing video scenes, and there are several R sex scenes.

FINAL IMPACT

(PM, 1992) **D/P:** Joseph Merhi **D/S:** Stephen Smoke **P:** Richard Pepin

Lorenzo Lamas and Kathleen Kinmont (his then real-life wife) star in a *Rocky*-inspired movie set in Las Vegas. An ex-champ fighter running a bar, he trains kickboxer Michael Worth, who wants his title back. With Jeff Langton as a bad-guy fighter, Mimi Lesseos, and Gary Daniels. Lamas and Kinmont were also in *Snake Eater* and other action films.

FINAL JUSTICE

(Vestron, 1984) **D/S/P:** Greydon Clark

Joe Don Baker (in his third Clark feature) is a rural Dallas-area cop kicked off the force. He patrols the Mexican border, then has to escort a Mafia boss (Rossano Brazzi) to Rome.

FINAL ROUND

(Worldvision, 1992) **D:** George Erschbamer **S:** Arne Olsen **P:** Robert Vince

Lorenzo Lamas is a kickboxing mechanic who is kidnapped and becomes a human target being hunted by killers, in another variation on *The Most Dangerous Game*. With (his then real-life wife) Kathleen Kinmont, Anthony De Longis, Isabelle Johnson, and Clark Johnson.

THE FINAL SANCTIONS

(AIP, 1990) **D/S:** David A. Prior **P:** David Marriot

In the future (which looks just like today), after a nuclear strike, William Smith is a Russian general who trains Sergei (Robert Z'Dar) and gives him psychological tests. Meanwhile, a prisoner in America (Ted Prior) is chosen by his government to battle Z'Dar Rambo-style in the Virginia woods. After a long, not too exciting battle Smith and a US general arrive and blow them both up, proving that the whole world is really run by one big, corrupt government and that you've been tricked into seeing another lousy AIP video release. It was filmed near Mobile, Alabama.

THE FINAL TERROR

(Vestron, 1980) **D:** Andrew Davis **S:** Jon George, Neill Hicks, Ronald Schusett **P:** Joe Roth   (*Campsite Massacre; Forest Primevil*)

Former AIP president Samuel Arkoff presented this horror movie, but it was also released in 1983 by Aquarius. A female psycho and her son kill campers and their ranger boyfriends. The surprising cast includes Rachel Ward, Daryl Hannah (who was in *The Fury* next), Adrian Zmed, Lewis Smith, and Joe Pantoliano as Eggar, a sinister handyman/killer in a bear suit. The director later went on to Chuck Norris and Steven Seagal movies. The music features guitar feedback.

FINDERS KEEPERS

(1966) **D:** Sidney Hayers **S:** Michael Pertwee **P:** George H. Brown

Cliff Richard and his backup group, the Shadows, are hired to play at a Spanish resort, but all the tourists have gone because the US has lost a "mighty mini" bomb in the ocean. A foreign power has bugged the hotel, and the musicians are thrown into jail. Robert Morley is Colonel Roberts, and Robert Hutton is a naval commander. It was Richard's last movie with the Shadows.

FINDERS KEEPERS, LOVERS WEEPERS!

(RM, 1968) **D/P/A/C/E:** Russ Meyer **S:** Richard Zachary

Paul Lockwood owns a Sunset Strip topless go-go club. His lover (Lavelle Roby) plans to rob his club, and his wife (Anne Chapman) has an affair with the bartender. The sex-in-a-pool scene is intercut with demolition-derby footage. This crime story was the first Meyer film to be booked into a first-run, legitimate theater (in Philadelphia).

FINGERS

(Turner, 1977) **D/S/P:** James Toback **P:** George Barrie

Harvey Keitel is Jimmy Fingers, a New York City concert pianist who collects gambling bets for his gangster father (Michael V. Gazzo). He's obsessed with the irritating 60s song "Summertime Summertime" (by the Jamies) and has proctological problems. The cast of this very unnerving movie includes Tisa Farrow, Tanya Roberts (raped in a public bathroom), Danny Aiello, Zack Norman, and Lenny Montana. Jim Brown exploits his real-life violent-bad-guy reputation by cracking two women's heads together. First-time director Toback also cowrote Brown's first book. He personally hosted the screening I saw at the old St. Marks Theatre in the East Village and criticized Brut Films for not releasing it properly.

FINISHING TOUCH

(Columbia, 1991) **D:** Fred Gallo **S:** Anthony L. Greene **P:** Steve Rabiner

An LA video artist (Arnold Vosloo, also in *Hard Target*) with short white hair seems to be a snuff filmmaker who kills patrons of a nightclub. Michael Nader (with his deep whisper voice) is a jealous detective. His clichéd ex-wife, Shelley Hack (who uses a body double for sex scenes), is a cop who becomes involved with the suspect. It all has an irritating twist ending. Ted Raimi is a comic cop and Art Evans is the lieutenant. By the director of *Dead Space*.

FIRE AND ICE

(RCA, 1983) **D/P:** Ralph Bakshi **S:** Roy Thomas, Gerry Conway **P:** Frank Frazetta

A battle beween good and evil (the sorcerer Necron) rages in mystical prehistoric times. Bakshi used live models as the basis for the animation, which was inspired by Frank Frazetta's art. The voices include those of Steve Sandor, Leo Gordon, and Susan Tyrrell. It was released by 20th Century–Fox. Bakshi did some TV work (including the new *Mighty Mouse*) and a Rolling Stones video before his next film, *Cool World* (1992).

FIRE AND ICE

(Nelson, 1987) **D/S/P/C:** Willy Bogner

Suzy Chafee (from Chapstick commercials) and French-Canadian skier John Eaves star in this fantasy love story. It's narrated by John Denver, who must have needed the money badly. It was a PG release from Roger Corman's Concorde.

FIREBALL JUNGLE

(Dark Dreams, 1968) **D:** Joseph P. Mawra **S:** Harry Whittington **P:** G. B. Roberts

The star of this violent, wacked-out car-racing movie is the crazy, hotheaded stock-car racer Cateye Mears, who looks sorta like Link Wray. Cateye and his buddies ride motorcycles, beat people, put out cigarettes on faces, use switchblades and broken bottles in fights, and steal women. An R&B crooner sings at an imitation Playboy Club, girls fight on the beach to instrumental surf music (the loser is dragged by her hair behind a motorcycle), and there's a (real) elimination race with 67 cars! A long, amazing, comedy-filler sequence is in a bizarre club where gay men and women sit on toilet seats at the bar and beer comes from a urinal. One woman has a painted-on dress, another has eyes painted on her eyelids (a great shock effect). A Tiny Tim imitator (!) with a howling dog entertains. All that, plus the nice, lame, fake-hippie group Mercy singing their real-life hit single "Love Can Make You Happy"(!) at the Have-a-Joint Club. A sign on the wall says, "LSD for lunch bunch." The soul theme song goes, "It's a fireball jungle we're living in." The video is pretty washed out, but who cares! It probably always looked that way. John Russell, who looks like a 20s villain, is Mr. Nero, a playboy gangster who likes golf. Lon Chaney Jr. plays Sammy, the unshaven, beer-drinking, Lenny-like junk-car-lot manager who talks to his dog, Herman. Joseph P. Mawra/Joseph Prieto/José Priete, who made this in Tampa, also directed the 60s *Olga* movies and *Shanty Tramp*!

FIREBIRD 2015 A.D.

(1980) **D:** David Robertson **S:** Barry Pearson, Biff McGuire, Maurice Hurley **P:** Merritt White

Cars are banned in the 21st century, and a government agent assigned to destroy them starts destroying their owners too. Darren McGavin and Doug McClure star.

FIRECRACKER!

(Monterey, 1981) **D/S:** Cirio H. Santiago **S/A:** Ken Metcalf **P:** Syed Kechico

Santiago remade his own *TNT Jackson* (1975), this time with blond Jillian Kessner as a karate fighter in the Philippines whose sister is murdered. With Ken Metcalfe and Darby Hinton, as mobsters, and Vic Diaz. Publicity claimed Kessner was "the winner of the 1981 North American Black Belt Olympics" (all a lie). Her one naked fight is a highlight.

FIREFOX

(Warner, 1982) **D/P/A:** Clint Eastwood **S:** Alex Lasker, Wendell Wellman

Eastwood is an American pilot who comes out of retirement to sneak into the USSR and steal a top-secret MIG-31 warplane that can be mind-controlled. He has Nam flashbacks of a napalmed girl, and there's a subplot about Soviet Jews. With Freddie Jones, David Huffman, Warren Clarke, and Ronald Lacey. This PG box-office disappointment features John Dykstra FX and originally ran a long 137 minutes. In the real world, the year this was released Eastwood financed a "military excursion" into Laos to rescue MIAs. He returned the next year in a much cheaper sure thing, *Sudden Impact*.

FIREHEAD

(AIP, 1990) **D/S/P:** Peter Yuval **S:** Jeff Mandel

Chris Lemmon (impersonating his father, Jack, more than ever) stars as a nice-guy scientist teamed with a brilliant CIA beauty (Gretchen Becker). A Soviet defector named Ivan (Brett Porter) has deadly laser-ray eyes, can "move molecules," and has been destroying US defense contractor's factories. Christopher Plummer is a government bureaucrat who also runs the Secret Order, a group that wants all-out war. He keeps a photo of Mussolini on the wall and plans to kill the president. Martin Landau is a retired admiral who tells Lemmon to beware. This movie has more guns and explosions than science fiction, but it's okay. Becker also sings the ridiculous theme song. A prologue is set in Estonia, but it was all filmed in Mobile, Alabama.

FIRE IN THE SKY

(Paramount, 1993) **D:** Robert Lieberman **S:** Tracy Torme **P:** Joe Wizan, Todd Black

From the trailers I thought this would be a boring, 70s-style speculation movie, but it's real good. It's based on Travis Walton's "true" book, embellished by screenwriter Torme (son of Mel). In 1975 everybody in a small town thinks that a group of young lumberjacks have killed the missing Travis (D. B. Sweeney), but the lumberjacks say that they saw him ascending into a space ship. James Garner is the out-of-town sheriff who tries to make them confess, as UFO buffs and reporters arrive from around the world. The nightmarish scenes of aliens experimenting on their captive in a huge, gooey, no-gravity spaceship are excellent, thanks to ILM FX. Robert Patrick (*Terminator II*) is the real star as Travis' best friend Mike. With Craig Sheffer, Peter Berg, Henry Thomas, Bradley Gregg, Noble Willingham, and Kathleen Wilhoite. The Neville Brothers do the excellent end theme, "Sons and Daughters" (available on the Varése Sarabande soundtrack). This PG-13 film was made in Oregon.

FIRE MONSTERS AGAINST THE SON OF HERCULES

(Sinister, 1962) **D/P:** Giorgio Marzelli **S:** Arpad De Riso **P:** Alfio Quanttrini   Italy (*Maciste Contra i Monstri*)

Reg Lewis as Maciste battles a Hydra, cave men, and a sea monster during the Ice Age. With Margaret Lee.

THE FIRE NEXT TIME

(Cabin Fever, 1992) **D:** Tom McLoughlin **S:** James Henerson **P:** Edwin Self

This made-for-TV future disaster/road movie is long (180 minutes) but worth your time. It borrows some ideas from *The Grapes of Wrath* and has the interesting notion that after a series of devastating events (fires, hurricanes, global warming) Americans will become refugees and fight to cross the closed and guarded Canadian border. Signs say, YANKEE STAY OUT! Craig T. Nelson stars as a Louisiana shrimp-boat captain who tries to keep his family together. Bonnie Bedelia costars. With Richard Farnsworth, Justin Whalen, Ashley Jones as the daughter who joins a commune, Jurgen Prochnow's "perfect" upstate New York community, Charles Haid, a bearded John Vernon in Nova Scotia, an uncredited Louise Fletcher, and singer Odetta. McLoughlin also made *Sometimes They Come Back* (1991), probably the best Stephen King TV movie.

FIREPOWER

(PM, 1993) **D/P:** Richard Pepin **S:** Michael January **P:** Joseph Merhi

Long-haired Gary Daniels and Chad McQueen are cop partners in the "Hellzone" of the L.A. of the future (2007) who go undercover as arena fighters. Joseph Ruskin runs a death ring in a smoky nightclub behind a movie theater and makes and sells a fake AIDS vaccine. More time is spent on car chases, explosions, police brutality, and shootouts than one-on-one fighting and it all gets pretty dull. With Jim Hellwig (a wrestler, known as the "Ultimate Warrior") as the silly looking, long-haired, medieval-look swordsman and Alisha Das.

FIRESTARTER

(MCA, 1984) **D:** Mark Lester **S:** Stanley Mann **P:** Frank Capra Jr.

Drew Barrymore has special mental powers because her parents were part of a government experiment. A lot of fire FX are used as she ignites objects (and people) at will. The cast of this Stephen King adaptation includes George C. Scott as an Indian with a ponytail, Martin Sheen and Moses Gunn as government bad guys, David Keith and Heather Locklear (making her film debut) as her parents, Art Carney, Louise Fletcher, and Freddie Jones. It was filmed at the DEG studios an North Carolina and is almost 2 hours long. The Tangerine Dream soundtrack is on MCA. *Firestarter* was originally slated to be directed by John Carpenter and to star Burt Lancaster. The later *Spontaneous Combustion* has a similar plot.

FIREWALKER

(Image, 1986) **D:** J. Lee Thompson **S:** Robert Gosnell **P:** Menahem Golan

206

Chuck Norris and Lou Gossett star as fortune hunters in this PG *Raiders of the Lost Ark*–copy comic action movie. Melody Anderson has a treasure map, so they go to Guatemala to look inside a Maya temple. With Will Sampson, Sonny Landham as the leader of a cult tribe, and John Rhys-Davies. Norris is not funny. It's a Golan/Globus production.

FIRST BLOOD

(IVE, 1981) **D:** Ted Kotcheff **S:** Michael Kozoll, William Sackheim **P:** Buzz Feitshans

Even *Rambo*-sequel haters should check out this superior action movie. Stallone stars (in his first non-*Rocky* hit) as Nam-vet Green Beret hero John Rambo, a man of few words. He's arrested in Hope, Oregon, for vagrancy, escapes, has flashbacks, and battles the local cops and the National Guard. With Richard Crenna as Rambo's former commander, Brian Dennehy as the sheriff, David Caruso, Jack Starrett, and Suzee Pai. Jerry Goldsmith wrote the score. It was the first real hit from Orion (formerly AIP). In real life, a man who killed his boss claimed he did it after watching *First Blood* 20 times. He was declared insane.

FIRSTBORN

(Paramount, 1984) **D:** Michael Apted **S:** Ron Koslow **P:** Paul Junger Witt, Tony Thomas

Two kids have to save their divorced mom from her demented druggie boyfriend, who moves in with them. Teri Garr stars, and Peter Weller is the drifter who uses and sells coke. Christopher Collet and Corey Haim are the sons who are on to his ways. With Sarah Jessica Parker and Robert Downey Jr. One of the executive producers of this PG-13 film was Sherry Lansing. Apted's great documentary *28 Up* was released the same year. EMI released the soundtrack.

THE FIRST DEADLY SIN

(Warner, 1980) **D:** Brian G. Hutton **S:** Mann Ruben **P:** George Pappas

Roman Polanski was slated to direct this adaptation of Lawrence Sanders' novel. Frank Sinatra stars as a police lieutenant who's after a psycho killer. Faye Dunaway spends most of the movie in bed as his hospitalized wife. With David Dukes, Brenda Vaccaro, James Whitmore, Anthony Zerbe, and Joe Spinell as a doorman. To date, this is Sinatra's only starring role in a theatrical film since 1970. It was released by Filmways, which had been AIP a few months earlier.

THE FIRST NUDIE MUSICAL

(Chiron, 1976) **D/S/M/A:** Bruce Kimmel **D:** Mark Haggard **P:** Jack Reeves

A dying studio is saved by making a porno musical. Cindy Williams (just before the *Laverne and Shirley* TV series) stars. She's not naked, but some others are. With Stephen Nathan as the director, Susan Stewart (*Mantis in Lace*), Leslie Ackerman, Diana Canova, and Alexandra Morgan. Williams was also in the unfunny *Spaceship* (1981), by the same director. The video box says that this film stars Ron Howard!

THE FIRST POWER

(Nelson, 1990) **D/S:** Robert Resnikoff **P:** David Madden

Lou Diamond Phillips stars as a very young LA police detective. Tracy Griffith (as a psychic) helps him track a Satanist killer (Jeff Kober) who inhabits other bodies (or does he just make people think he does?). A nun comes to the rescue in the end, and there are hallucination scenes. It's all confusing and unsatisfying. There aren't many FX, but there is one amazing leap from a tall building. With Dennis Lipscomb, Mykel T. Williamson, David Gale, and Melanie Shatner. Stuart Copeland did the music for this Orion release.

FIRST STRIKE

(Video City, 1984) **D/S:** Allen Kuskowski **S/P:** Dave Hanson **P:** Bob Nudo

The Soviets plan WWIII, in what's been called the first shot-on-video feature. Stuart Whitman stars as the captain of the submarine *USS Cobra*. With Persis Khambata as a double agent, Paul Mantee, Leon Askin, and Robert Clarke. It was made in West Germany and San Diego.

THE FIRST TIME

(1981) **D/S:** Charles Loventhal **S:** Susan Weiser-Finley, W. Franklin Finley **P:** Sam Irvin   (*Doin' It*)

Tim Choate stars as a college-freshman film student. This comedy was directed by a 22-year-old who had studied with Brian De Palma (who appears in the film). With Marshall Efron, Jane Badler, Wallace Shawn as a film professor, Krista Errickson, and Wendie Jo Sperber.

THE FIRST TURN ON!

(Vestron, 1983) **D/S/P:** Michael Herz, Lloyd Kaufman **S:** Stuart Strutin, Mark Torgl, Georgia Harrell

Overage kids on a camping trip with their professor are stuck in a cave, so they tell each other sex stories. Supposedly Madonna tried out for this and was turned down by the producers. With Sheila Kennedy (from *Penthouse*) and Professor Irwin Corey. R and unrated versions of the Troma production are available on tape.

THE FISHER KING

(TriStar, 1991) **D:** Terry Gilliam **S:** Richard LaGravenese **P:** Debra Hill, Lyda Obst

In this overlong (137-minute) fantasy/comedy morality tale, a homeless former professor (Robin Williams) thinks he's a knight searching for the Holy Grail in New York City. A shock radio personality (Jeff Bridges) feels responsible when a listener goes into a bar with a machine gun and kills a "yuppie scum." Bridges quits his job, drinks, then gets a job at a video store run by Mercedes Ruehl. Key scenes take place in Grand Central Station and Central Park, where Williams is pursued by a red knight on horseback.

With Amanda Plummer, Michael Jeter, Harry Shearer, Bradley Gregg, and Tom Waits. The film won four Oscars, and the screenplay was published. The laserdisc version includes outtakes, trailers, and an extra commentary track by Gilliam.

FISTFIGHTER

(Avid, 1989) **D:** Frank Zuniga **S:** Max Bloom **P:** Carlos Vasallo

George (or Jorge) Rivero stars as C. J. Thunderbird, a bare-knuckle boxer in Bolivia who ends up in jail and seeks revenge. With villain Mike Connors, Edward Albert Jr., and Matthias Hues.

A FISTFUL OF DEATH

(TWE, 1970) **D:** Demofilio Fidani **S:** Domenico Fadani   Italy (*Giù la Testa, Hombre!*)

This is a real bottom-of-the-barrel western with Hunt Powers, Gordon Mitchell, and Klaus Kinski as Reverend Cotton.

A FISTFUL OF DOLLARS

(MGM, 1964) **D:** Sergio Leone **S:** Duccio Tessari **P:** Arrigo Columbo, Giorgio Papi

This was not the first modern European western, but it was the first international hit. The plot was lifted from Akira Kurosawa's *Yojimbo* (1961). Leone wanted Lee Marvin or James Coburn to star. Clint Eastwood was on a break from the *Rawhide* TV series when he got the role of "the man with no name." This influential "spaghetti western" wasn't even released in the US until 1967 (by United Artists), with fake English-sounding credits. Leone was "Bob Robertson." With Gian Maria Volonte and Marianne Koch. The score, on RCA, is by Ennio Morricone. Harry Dean Stanton is in new scenes added by Monte Hellman for the ABC-TV version. Eastwood returned immediately in *For a Few Dollars More* (1965).

A FISTFUL OF DYNAMITE

(MGM, 1971) **D/S:** Sergio Leone **S:** Luciano Vincenzoni, Sergio Donati Italy (*Giù la Testa; Duck, You Sucker!*)

This was the least successful of Leone's westerns in the US (it was released by United Artists). It's also the most political. The original version opens with

James Coburn in *A Fistful of Dynamite*.

a quote from Mao! James Coburn is an Irish revolutionary who has flashbacks of his early days. He joins up with a Mexican peasant/bandit (Rod Steiger) for a robbery. They end up being heroes of the revolution in 1913. Coburn's specialty is using dynamite and nitroglycerin, and he rides a motorcycle. Steiger's acting is pretty out of control. There's a Nazi-style German commander and a record number of dead bodies. Morricone provided another excellent score. Antonio Marheriti did FX work. It was originally 158 minutes in Italy, but the longest US prints and the video are 138.

FIST OF FEAR, TOUCH OF DEATH

(Edde, 1980) **D:** Matthew Mallinson **S/A:** Ron Harvey **P:** Terry Levine   (*Dragon and the Cobra*)

Bruce Lee is seen in some film clips talking about martial arts, Fred Williamson appears for a few minutes as a fight promoter, and Ron Van Clief is shown training. A lot of the footage of this paste-up ripoff is from a movie called *Forced to Fight* and from real Madison Square Garden martial-arts shows. The late Adolph Caesar also appears. He narrated many of the trailers for Aquarius, which was responsible for this.

FIST OF HONOR

(PM, 1993) **D:** Richard Pepin **S:** Charles Kanganis **P:** Scott McAboy

Sam Jones stars as a martial-arts boxer who gets involved in a Mafia feud in LA while collecting debts. Joey House, as his lounge-singer girlfriend, is featured in sex scenes, Harry Guardino and Abe Vigoda are rival mobsters, and Bubba Smith is a corrupt cop.

FIST OF STEEL

(AIP, 1991) **D:** Irvin Johnson **S:** Anthony Jesu **P:** David Hunt   (*Eternal Fist*)

This post-nuke martial-arts movie copies *The Blood of Heroes* a lot. Cynthia Khan (not to be confused with Michelle Khan, whom she "replaced" in several Hong Kong sequels) stars (in two roles). Dale "Apollo" Cook (who resembles Cash Flagg!) is a skinhead kickboxer. The mass-murdering bad guys, led by Main Frame, ride dune buggies and fight over water. The fight scenes are pretty good, and Khan, as Wild, a vengeance-seeking former Christian in black, makes it worthwhile. In one scene Cook is crucified. In the next scene the holes in his hands are gone. With loud kung-fu-movie-style sound effects, flashbacks, and an H-bomb opening. I'm not sure where it was filmed, but many of the names in the credits are Spanish. Not to be confused with *Fists of Steel* (1989).

FISTS OF FURY

(Fox, 1972) **D/S:** Lo Wei   Hong Kong (*Big Boss*)

Bruce Lee is a very naive country guy who goes to Bangkok and works at an ice factory run by the evil Big Boss (Han Ying Chieh). The boss is dealing drugs, and Lee's friend is found packed in ice. There's a big assault on all the bad guys at the end. Nora Miao costars. Just before Bruce Lee starred in this, his first, worst-dubbed, and crudest kung-fu

movie, he was a regular on the short-lived TV series *Longstreet* and an instructor to the stars in Hollywood. His next was *The Chinese Connection* (the real *Fists of Fury*—the titles were switched in the US), which was released here first. This film is available letterboxed on laserdisc.

FISTS OF STEEL

(PDS, 1989) **D/S/P:** Jerry Schaefer

Real-life boxers Carlos Palomino and Alexis Arguello battle terrorist Henry Silva in Hawaii. This comic action movie features drugs, a transvestite character, a robot, and Soviet and Arab villains. With Marianne Marks, Robert Tessier, and Rockne Tarkington. The line producer was actor Rory Calhoun.

FIT TO KILL

(Columbia, 1993) **D/S:** Andy Sidaris **P:** Arlene Sidaris

Dona Spier and Roberta Vasquez are hired to protect a Chinese dignitary and "the Alexa stone," a diamond that was stolen by the Nazis, in the 8th Sidaris generic tits-and-guns series. With Bruce Penhall, Mark Barriere, Cynthia Brimhall, Julie Strain, Ava Cadell, Sandra Wild, Carolyn Liu, and villain R. J. Moore (returning from *Hard Hunted*). The next Sidaris movie, *Enemy Gold*, was by Drew Sidaris.

FITZCARRALDO

(Warner, 1982) **D/S/P:** Werner Herzog **P:** Lucki Stipetic   W. Germany

Klaus Kinski stars as Brian Sweeney Fitzgerald, who wants to build an opera house in the middle of the Amazon jungle and then bring Caruso there to sing. He has an entire ship hauled over a mountain and must fight off hostile natives. The cast includes Claudia Cardinale. It's the fourth Kinski/Herzog film and, like *Aguirre*, features Popol Vuh's music. New World released it with subtitles, and Corman put Kinski into *Android* the same year. If you watch all 157 minutes of *Fitzcarraldo*, you have to see *Burden of Dreams*, by Les Blank, too. It's about the many problems encountered in the making of this movie.

FIVE BOLD WOMEN

(1959) **S:** Mortimer Braus, Jack Pollexfen **P:** Jim Ross

Merry Anders, Irish McCalla (from the TV series *Sheena, Queen of the Jungle*) as Big Pearl, Kathy Malone, and two others "used a weapon no bad-man could—sex!" They also take baths in a river. Jeff Morrow and Jim Ross are the male stars in this bad-girl western. Anders was also in *The Dalton Girls*. From Criterian Films.

FIVE CAME BACK

(Turner, 1939) **D:** John Farrow **S:** Dalton Trumbo, Nathanael West, Jerry Cady **P:** Robert Fisk

Although we never actually see them, this is the first major movie with cannibals, and it's a good one. A passenger plane crashes in the South American jungle, and the 12 survivors have to choose which 5 will be rescued by a tiny plane be-

fore the headhunters attack. With Lucille Ball, Chester Morris, C. Aubrey Smith, John Carradine, Kent Taylor, Patric Knowles, Allen Jenkins, and Joseph Calleia as a political prisoner. Farrow remade this as *Back from Eternity* (1956), also for RKO. West died in a car accident in 1940. Trumbo served a 10-month sentence in 1950 for refusing to "cooperate" with the House Un-American Activities Committee. He was blacklisted until 1960.

FIVE CORNERS

(Edde, 1986) **D/P:** Tony Bill **S:** John Patrick Shanley **P:** Forrest Murray   US/UK

You'll be surprised by this drama set in the Bronx in the early 60s. The overlapping plots follow various characters who all interact at some point. Jodie Foster is afraid of an unpredictable psycho (John Turturro) who just got out of jail. She goes to Tim Robbins for help, but he wants to be in a southern freedom march and has decided to be nonviolent. Two German guys pick up some girls and play death-defying games in elevator shafts. A teacher is killed, an old lady is thrown out of a window, and a penguin in the zoo is beaten to death. It's funny, violent, and thought-provoking. With Elizabeth Berridge and Todd Graff. George Harrison was an executive producer, and the theme is the Beatles' "In My Life."

FIVE DAYS OF MILAN

(Nightmare, 1973) **D/S:** Dario Argento **S:** Nanni Balestrini   Italy (*Le Cinque Giornate*)

Argento's fourth film is set in 1848, when the people of Milan revolted against the Austrian occupation. It's a serious film with some comedy, starring Adriano Celentano as a young thief who becomes caught up in the revolution. Marilu Tolo costars. It's available only in Italian.

FIVE DOLLS FOR AN AUGUST MOON

(Nightmare, 1970) **D:** Mario Bava **S:** Mario Di Nardo **P:** Luigi Alessi   Italy (*Cinque Bambole per la Luna d'Agostino*)

A group of people who have come to a castle on a Mediterranean island to see an inventor's new creation are killed off, and the bodies are stored in a walk-in freezer. It's based (uncredited) on Agatha Christie's *Ten Little Indians* and was never released in the US. With Ira Furstenberg, Edwige Fenech, and William Berger.

FIVE EASY PIECES

(RCA, 1970) **D/P:** Bob Rafelson **S:** Carol Eastman **P:** Richard Wechsler **C:** Laslo Kovacs

Jack Nicholson stars as Bobby, an oil-field worker and classical musician. He lives in a trailer with Rayette (Karen Black). After 12 years of acting, it was Nicholson's first lead in a major film. He and Black were both nominated for Oscars. The only things Rafelson had directed previously were episodes of *The Monkees* and *Head*. With Susan Anspach, Billy Green Bush, Ralph Waite, Fanny Flagg, Sally Struthers, and Toni Basil. The soundtrack features classical music and "Stand by Your Man." Cinematographer Kovacs had also shot *Easy Rider*. From Columbia.

FIVE FINGERS OF DEATH

(VSOM, 1972) **D:** Cheng Chang Ho
S/A: Lo Lieh **P:** Raymond Shaw, Run
Run Shaw   Hong Kong (*King Boxer*)

This was the first kung-fu hit in the US and made more money here than any other non–Bruce Lee 70s martial-arts film. Warner Brothers gave it a major release and devised an effective ad campaign. Lo Lieh stars as Chao Chi-Hao, a medieval martial-arts student who learns the secret of "the iron fist." Lieh later starred in many other films including *The Stranger and the Gunfighter,* with Lee Van Cleef.

555

(King, 1988) **D/P:** Wally Koz **S:** Roy M. Koz

This amateurish, shot-on-video family project (from Chicago) received some attention when it was released because it was so gory (and bad). It features a bearded-hippie killer, gore, nudity, and necrophilia.

FIVE FOR HELL

(Video Treasures, 1969) **D:** "Frank Kramer"/
Gianfranco Parolini **S:** Renato Izzo **P:** Paolo Moffa,
Aldo Addobbati   Italy (*Cinque per L'Inferno*)

Klaus Kinski is Captain Muller in this WWII adventure. With John Garko and Margaret Lee.

THE FIVE HEARTBEATS

(CBS/Fox,1992) **D/S/P/A:** Robert Townsend
S: Keenan Ivory Wayans

The rise and fall of the five members of a Temptations-like group with gangster managers is the theme of this underrated film, which is very much based on real events and singers. Townsend stars as Donald "Duck" Matthews, with Michael Wright, Leon, Diahann Carroll, Harold Nicholas, and Theresa Randle. The music is by Stanley Clarke.

FIVE LOOSE WOMEN: *See* FUGITIVE GIRLS

THE FIVE MAN ARMY

(VSOM, 1969) **D:** Don Taylor **S:** Dario Argento,
Marc Richards   Italy (*Un Esercito di Cinque Uomini*)

Horror great Argento cowrote this serious western about the Mexican revolution. Peter Graves stars as a Dutchman who (behaving much as he did on the then-current *Mission: Impossible* TV series) assembles a group of specialists and explains a gold-robbery plan. With James Daly as a dynamite expert, big Bud Spencer, Tetsuro Tambe as a silent, knife-throwing Japanese samurai, Marc Lawrence, Giacomo Rossi-Stuart, and Daniela Gioroam (Miss Italy 1967). Ennio Morricone wrote the score. Argento had also cowritten the great *Once upon a Time in the West.*

FIVE MINUTES TO LOVE

(Sinister, 1963) **D:** John Hayes **S/P/A:** Paul Leder
S: William Norton   (*The Rotten Apple*)

If a pretentious, downbeat off-Broadway play filmed in a junkyard sounds good to you, watch this one. The bullying junkyard owner, Harry (Paul Leder), talks nonstop. Blowhard (King Moody), a dummy who works for him, smokes pot. A corrupt cop beats people up. Rue McClanahan (from *The Golden Girls!*) is Pooch, "a crazy whore." Characters, each in their own world, rant, quote Nietzsche, and talk about lesbians and underage sex. The normal characters are an unhappy couple (Will Gregory and the very pretty Gaye Gordon) living in a '48 Ford with their baby. One spinning-camera scene (featuring Rue) is very impressive. The print of this b/w Headliner production is very good. Something Weird offers a version that includes a personal prologue by Leder.

THE FLAMING FRONTIER

(VSOM, 1965) **D:** Alfred Voher **S:** Fred Denger,
Eberhard Keindorf **P:** Wolfgang Kuhnlenz
W. Germany/Yugoslavia (*Old Surehand*)

Stewart Granger is Old Surehand in one of a series of westerns based on books by the 19th-century German writer Karl May. The plot concerns a gold mine and a train robbery. Pierre Brice as the Apache blood brother Winnetou became the real star of the popular series. With Leticia Roman and Terence Hill. The dubbing is terrible.

THE FLAMING SIGNAL

(Sinister, 1933) **D:** C. E. Roberts,
George Jeske **P:** William Berke

A flyer (John David Horsely) and his German shepherd, Flash the wonder dog, are stranded on a jungle island with missionaries and bad guys after pearls. The natives hold a sacrificial ritual, and Manu, a dead witch doctor (Mischa Auer), seems to return from the grave. This 64-minute independent production also features Henry B. Walthall and Noah Beery Sr.

THE FLAMING TEEN AGE

(Sinister, 1957) **D/P:** Irvin S. Yeaworth Jr. **D:** Charles
Edwards **S:** Jean Yeaworth, Ethel Barrett

A narrator relates a tale about a teen who drinks. The characters have strong southern accents. This soon evolves into a flashback inside of a flashback, the real movie, which has nothing to do with teens! (And, judging from a Times Square marquee seen in the film, it was made in 1945!) It's a convoluted tale (also with flashbacks inside of flashbacks!) of Fred Garland (Noel Rayburn), a no-account guy from Roanoke, Virginia, who moves to New York City and, with no experience, manages to produce a play. Booze and gambling catch up with him,

though, and he drinks iodine, goes to jail, shoots up, finds God, and lectures others about the paths of evil. I think the original movie was called *Twice Convicted.* Yeaworth (who later made *The Blob*) must have been quite a hustler to sell a 12-year-old movie as the "true, unvarnished confession of a juvenile delinquent!" He also later made *Way Out* (1966), filmed in the Bronx, which starred real drug addicts.

THE FLASH

(Warner, 1990) **D:** Robert Iscore **S:** Danny
Bilson, Paul DeMeo **P:** Steven Long
Mitchell, Craig W. Van Sickle

John Wesley Shipp stars as the police chemist who secretly becomes the superfast costumed crimefighter, in this film based on the DC comic-book character. With Amanda Pays, M. Emmet Walsh, Paula Marshall, Robert Hooks, Richard Belzer, Tim Thomerson, Michael Nader, and Priscilla Pointer. This CBS-TV series pilot led to a better-than-average series (staring Shipp and Pays) that lasted only one season. *Flash II: The Trickster* was also released.

FLASHBACK

(Paramount, 1990) **D:** Franco Amurri
S: David Loughert **P:** Marvin Worth

Dennis Hopper stars as Huey Walker, a 60s radical who is still wanted for disrupting a Spiro T. Agnew rally (!). Kiefer Sutherland, the young FBI agent trying to bring him in, is the embarrassed son of hippies. Hopper is great, and the movie is funny. With Carol Kane, Cliff De Young, Paul Dooley, and Richard Masur and Michael McKean as former activists. Walker has a best-selling book at the end. The soundtrack is by Barry Goldberg, with music by Jefferson Airplane, Steppenwolf, REM, and others.

FLASH GORDON

(Stokey, 1936) **D/S:** Frederick Stephani
S: George Plympton, Basil Dickey, Ella O'Neill

Flash Gordon is the most expensive serial ever made, and the best, as far as I'm concerned. It might not have the best stunts, but it does have the most interesting characters and perils, great costumes, and weird monsters. The 13-chapter Universal serial, based on Alex Raymond's comic strip, stars Buster Crabbe as Flash, Jean Rogers as Dale Arden, and Frank Shannon as Dr. Zarkov. Charles Middleton is the ultimate serial villain, Ming the Merciless, and Priscilla Lawson is his evil, sexy daughter, Aura. The main plot line is: Ming wants Dale, Aura wants Flash. Other important characters are Prince Barin (John Alexander) and the winged Vultan of Sky City (John Lipson). There are robots, shark men, lion men, monkey men, and a dragon monster (Glen Strange). Sets and props were borrowed from earlier Universal horror classics and from the film *Just Imagine* (1930). I first saw the serial (and loved every minute) on the *Ghoulardi* show in Cleveland. There are two sequels, condensed

Buster Crabbe and Priscilla Lawson in *Flash Gordon*.

feature versions (including *Rocket Ship* and *Spaceship to the Unknown*), an X-rated spoof (*Flesh Gordon*), and a 1980 remake.

FLASH GORDON

(Sinister series, 1953)

Steve Holland starred in this unique-looking syndicated TV series, produced in West Germany. Irene Champlin was Dale Arden. Although 39 episodes were filmed, only 4 volumes with 2 episodes each are available. Some titles are "Micro-Men Menace" and "Death in the Negative."

FLASH GORDON CONQUERS THE UNIVERSE

(Stokey, United American, Sinister, 1940)
D: Ford Beebe, Ray Taylor **S:** George Plympton, Basil Dickey, Barry Shipman

The original screenwriters were brought back for the third and last serial. Flash goes back to Mongo to save Earth. Carol Hughes plays Dale Arden, Frank Shannon is Zarkov (as always), and Happy is (thankfully) gone. Charles Middleton is back as Ming, Anne Gwynne is the evil Sonia, and Roland Drew plays Prince Barin. There are rock men, the Robin Hood men, and new costumes for everybody. Sinister also offers the feature version of this 12-chapter Universal serial.

FLASH GORDON'S TRIP TO MARS

(Stokey, 1938) **D:** Ford Beebe, Robert Hill **S:** Ray Trampe, Norman S. Hall, Wyndham Gittens **P:** Barney Sarecky

This 15-chapter sequel to the Universal serial is great but not quite as good as the first. The same main stars return, but this time Beatrice Roberts plays Queen Azura, Donald Kerr is added as the unnecessary comic relief Happy Hapgood, and Dale's hair isn't blond anymore. Ming tries to take over Mars, and Prince Barin helps Flash again. My favorite new characters are the ugly clay men (led by C. Montague Shaw), who can magically fade into cavern walls. The tree men are pretty good too. There was originally a tinted sequence. *Mars Attacks the World* is a condensed feature version. Crabbe played Buck Rogers (in 1939) before returning as Flash one last time.

FLATLINERS

(RCA, 1990) **D:** Joel Schumacher **S:** Peter Filardi **P:** Michael Douglas, Rick Bieber

Ticket buyers expecting a fun fantasy movie most have been surprised by this one, adapted from a novel by Dean Koontz. It has very serious themes (suicide, racism, sexism). Medical students haunted by past events and indiscretions take turns letting each other "die" so that they can have after-death experiences. It's pretty heavy stuff, and it doesn't really work. Some humor helps, but why does the university lab look like a museum (or a set from some Fritz Lang silent movie), and why doesn't anyone interfere? The "shakycam" work gets irritating after a while too. Kiefer Sutherland (also in *The Lost Boys* by Schumacher) stars, with Oliver Platt, Kevin Bacon, and William Baldwin, who secretly videotapes sex. It was a modest hit because of overhyped costar Julia Roberts. Columbia made it before, but released it after, *Pretty Woman*.

FLAVIA THE HERETIC

(VSOM, 1974) **D/S/P:** Gianfranco Mingozzi **S:** Raniero di Giovanbattista, Sergio Tau, Francesca Vietri, Fabrizio Onofri, Bruno de Geronimo   Italy (*The Rebel Nun*; *Flavia*; *Priestess of Violence*; *La Monaca Musulmana*)

Flavia (Florinda Bolkan) is sent to a 13th-century Portuguese nunnery where torture is common and a crazy tarantula cult appears. She wonders why God is a man and runs away with a Jew named Abraham. She's coached by an older rebel nun, then joins her new Muslim lover, who leads an invading army and punishes rapists. She hallucinates a female Christ, a dead nun rising, and women crawling out of a cow's carcass! Flavia is skinned alive (offscreen) at the end. Some scenes feature full nudity, whipping, castration, impaling, and torture. It's pretty strong and amazing stuff with some historical basis and feminist themes. The great music helps too. The director was known for making documentaries. The Brazilian-born star claims to have been JFK's last lover. Think about that while you watch this. It's subtitled.

FLESH

(Paramount, 1968) **D/S/P/C:** Paul Morrissey **P:** Andy Warhol (*Andy Warhol's Flesh*)

Joe Dallesandro stars as Joe, a hustler providing for his wife and kid on New York's Lower East Side by having sex with men. His ex-girlfriend, a topless dancer (Geri Mil-ler), lives with transvestites Candy Darling and Jackie Curtis. With Geraldine Smith, Barry Brown, and Patti D'Arbanville (said to have been 14). Made after *Lonesome Cowboys* and followed by *Trash* and *Heat* (all starring Dallesandro), it was a midnight-movie hit (and deserved to be).

FLESH + BLOOD

(Vestron, 1985) **D/S:** Paul Verhoeven **S:** Gerard Soetman **P:** Gys Versluys (*The Rose and the Sword*)

After years of "Hollywood" history, it's great to see a movie like this. It's the tale of a kidnapped 16th-century princess (Jennifer Jason Leigh), but there's nothing nice or simple about it. Verhoeven has plenty to say about religion and politics while telling a great story with humor, violence, sex, plot surprises, and maybe some magic. Most of the characters either are really stupid and hateful or have to debase themselves to survive. Events are complicated by the plague. A diseased dog carcass is pretty effective for germ warfare. Rutger Hauer costars as Martin, an ex-soldier with a ragged crew of looters and killers. With Tom Burlinson, Jack Thompson, Susan Tyrrell, Brion James, and Blanca Marsillach. Orion barely bothered to release it. It was the first film in English for the Dutch Verhoeven. He made *Robocop* next. Two classics in a row!

Brion James follows Rutger Hauer in *Flesh + Blood*.

FLESH AND BLOOD

(Video Yesteryear, Sinister, 1922) **D/P:** Irving Cummings

Lon Chaney stars as a lawyer in Chinatown who pretends to be a cripple to get even with a businessman who framed him and sent him to prison. He discovers that his daughter is in love with his enemy. This 74-minute silent film has a musical score.

FLESH AND BLOOD

(Oooomm Films, 1990) **D/S/P/E:** Jeff Mentges

After Ohio-born porno legend John Curtis Holmes died of AIDS in 1988, *Rolling Stone* printed a feature article about his drug problems and his arrest on suspicion of murder (he was involved but was acquitted). Eric Roberts and Christopher Walken said they wanted to play him in a movie (Andrew Prine would be perfect!), but meanwhile Mentges, a film student from the Baltimore/DC area, managed to make *Flesh and Blood* for only $15,000. The mostly b/w film plays around with facts and time (of course), but it's fun to watch, has an original jazz score and an intro by a "doctor," and is a worthy exploitation accomplishment with enough drugs and violence (but no onscreen sex). Breon stars as the pathetic part-time pimp, drug-delivery man, and thief Johnny Wade. Everybody treats him like shit, and after too much freebasing (he carries a suitcase with the works) he can't even do what he's famous for anymore. My main question is: During the brief "porno" scenes (in color), where are the camera and light people? Watching the film, I realized that these color scenes resemble Ray Dennis Steckler's 60s comedies, and that the balding Breon resembles Steckler! Coincidence?

FLESH AND BULLETS

(1985) **D/S/P:** Carlos Tobalina

This crime movie, with Cornel Wilde, Cesar Romero, Yvonne De Carlo, Aldo Ray, and Sharon Kelly/Colleen Brennan, is by a porno director (*Mai Lin vs. Serena*). It didn't play in many theaters. Maybe it's good. It was the last role for Wilde, who died in 1988. Ray was also in the X-rated *Sweet Savage* (1977) and was the first actor ever expelled from the Screen Actors Guild (in 1986), for acting in so many nonunion features.

FLESHBURN

(1983) **D/S:** George Gage **S:** Beth Gaso

Former porno star Sonny Landham stars as an Indian Nam vet who escapes from an asylum. He kidnaps four psychiatrists, takes them out into the desert, and leaves them there. He also uses witchcraft. From Crown International.

FLESH-EATING MOTHERS

(Academy, 1988) **D/S/P:** James Aviles Martin **S:** Zev Shlasinger **P:** Miljan Peter Ilich

A sexually transmitted virus creates suburban-housewife cannibals. A corrupt cop is eaten alive. Cheating husbands and kids are victims, and a wife-beater is tortured, then eaten. This cheap gore comedy starring Grace Gawthrop is available in R and unrated versions.

FLESH FEAST

(World Video, 1970) **D/S/P:** Brad F. Ginter **S:** Thomas Casey **P/A:** Veronica Lake

Brooklyn-born Veronica Lake (Constance Ockelman) was a star in the 40s (*Sullivan's Travels*, *This Gun for Hire*, *I Married a Witch*, *The Blue Dahlia*). Her career ended in 1951, with *Stronghold*, except for the obscure Canadian *Footsteps in the Snow* (1967) and this R-rated horror movie made in Miami Beach. As Dr. Elaine Fredericks, Lake conducts "anti-aging" experiments at her home. Carl Shuman arrives from South Africa on a secret mission and begins working with her. A South American tough guy and his two hoods arrive. The one named José gets involved with one of the live-in nurses. A newspaper editor whose reporter has been killed at the airport arranges for his female assistant to pose as a nurse to investigate. Everybody waits for the mysterious Max Bauer (Bill Rogers) to arrive. Anyway, as you probably know, it's part of a plot to disguise the exiled Hitler and keep him young, but Lake is really just waiting so that she can have a chance to kill him with maggots. Psychedelic lights are used every time the magical larvae are shown, and weird music is heard. "I know it seems crazy, but so does this whole case!" Bodies are stolen for experiments (the undercover nurse helps). Body parts hang in a freezer: "This whole thing is bizarre, crazy!" This "crazy" movie is tedious and badly dubbed. Actors flub lines, and the editing is terrible. With Chris

Martel (*Scream, Baby, Scream*). In 1989 Missouri governor John Ashcroft signed a "slasher-movie" law making "films that portray murders, sexual mutilation, cannibalism, and nudity off-limits to persons under 17." A title that cropped up in the debate was *Flesh Feast*!

FLESH GORDON AND THE COSMIC CHEERLEADERS

(New Horizons, 1989) **D/S:** Howard Ziehm **S:** Douglas Frisby **P:** Maurice Smith   Canada

Blond kickboxer Vince Murdocco stars in this very cheap-looking sequel that resembles the worst of Troma. Like the original, it's a sex-comedy parody of the old serials, but this time the animation is almost nonexistent and the nudity is minimal. "Naked" women even wear G strings. If you have to see singing turd people, a farting asteroid, and a homosexual dickhead monster, I guess they're the selling points here. The 1972 *Flesh Gordon* (also by Ziehm) is still around on tape, so why bother with this? It was filmed in Detroit and Canada.

FLESHPOT ON 42ND STREET

(SW, 1973) **D/S/C:** Andy Milligan **P:** William Mishkin

I liked this color drama better than most of Milligan's horror movies. The acting isn't bad, parts are funny, and, incredibly, the tape is letter-boxed (!). It almost has the feel of one of Paul Morrissey's Warhol movies from the period. Diana Lewis (who is naked a lot) stars as a cheerful young woman who robs her live-in lover after he kicks her out. She moves in with a friendly drag queen (who has most of the best lines) in the East Village and starts charging for sex, but she falls for a man (porno star Harry Reems) who lives on Staten Island. There's more dialogue than sex: "We'll go to a double bill at the Lyric, *Torture Dungeon* and *Bloodthirsty Butcher*." "If Nixon gets in again, it'll probably be a police state anyway!" Milligan shot it himself with a hand-held camera and left in a few good microphone shots. Fred Lincoln is in it too.

FLESHTONE

(Prism, 1994) **D/S:** Harry Hurwitz **P:** David Sheldon

Martin Kemp (from *The Krays*) stars as an LA artist hooked on phone sex who is framed for a murder. Lise Cutter costars, with Tim Thomerson and Suanne Braun. By the director of *Nocturna*, it's available in R and unrated versions.

FLICKS

(Media, 1981) **D/S:** Peter Winograd **S:** Larry Arnstein, David Hurwitz, Lane Sarasohn **P:** Bert Kamerman   (*Loose Joints*)

This plotless film consists of parodies of old movies. The cartoon of violent, brawling cats in a retirement home is a high point. There are coming-attractions trailers, a science-fiction serial (*Lost Heroes of the Milky Way*), newsreels, and a horror-movie spoof (*House of the Living Corpse*). With Pamela Sue Martin, Joan Hackett, Martin Mull, Richard Belzer, George "Buck" Flower, and the voice of Harry Shearer. Bill Paxton was a set designer. The Chiodo Brothers created the alien masks. It's not very funny and wasn't released until 1987.

FLIGHT OF BLACK ANGEL

(1991) **D:** Jonathan Mostow **S:** Henry Dominic **P:** Daniel Doty, Michael C. Green

Peter Strauss is a fighter-pilot instructor. One of his students decides that he's "the angel of the Lord," uses real missiles during maneuvers, and plans to destroy Las Vegas. With William O'Leary and James O'Sullivan. From TV.

FLIGHT OF THE LOST BALLOON

(1961) **D/S:** Nathan Juran **P:** Bernard Woolner

Marshall Thompson takes Mala Powers (from *The Unknown Terror*) and "a Hindu" to Egypt in a hot-air balloon to search for a lost explorer and a treasure. The trio are attacked by giant condors and cannibals, and Mala is tortured on a stretching rack. This color film, produced by Woolner Brothers (released by AIP), was shot in Puerto Rico, in "Spectrascope."

FLIGHT OF THE NAVIGATOR

(Disney, 1986) **D:** Randal Kleiser **S:** Michael Burton, Douglas Day Stewart **P:** Robby Wald, Dimitri Villard

A kid (Joey Cramer) helps some friendly aliens. Later he falls and loses consciousness. When he wakes up (eight years later) he hasn't aged and has special navigational powers. With Veronica Cartright, Cliff De Young, Sarah Jessica Parker, Howard Hesseman, and the voice of Paul Reubens (Pee-wee Herman).

FLIGHT OF THE SPRUCE GOOSE

(1986) **D/S:** Lech Majewski **S:** Chris Burdza **P:** Michael Hausman

This is an obscure "action adventure" made in Pittsburgh. The cast includes Karen Black, Dennis Christopher, director George Romero, Jennifer Runyan, Betsy Blair, and Dan O'Shea.

THE FLIGHT THAT DISAPPEARED

(1961) **D:** Reginald LeBorg **S:** Ralph Hart, Judith Hart, Owen Harris **P:** Robert E. Kent

Three American scientists flying to Washington to discuss their new "beta thermonuclear warhead" end up on a mysterious plateau. They have to face a jury representing the people of the future. Instead of stranding them in time, "the Sage" shows them future destruction and allows them to return to Earth, where they destroy their plans. This b/w United Artists film stars Craig Hill, Paula Raymond, and Dayton Lummis. LeBorg made *Diary of a Madman* next.

FLIGHT TO FURY

(Warner, 1964) **D:** Monte Hellman **S/A:** Jack Nicholson **P:** Fred Ross   US/Philippines

What kind of role would future star Jack Nicholson write for himself, back when he had nothing to lose? Here he is (with a mustache) as a psychotic diamond smuggler. After gambling in Manila he and his gang crash-land a plane in the jungle. They turn against one another and fight bandits over some stolen jewels. He kills himself at the end.

Dewey Martin stars as the hero, with Fay Spain and Vic Diaz. Made in the Philippines as part of a two-picture deal (with *Back Door to Hell*), it originally ran 80 minutes but was 62 when first released (by Lippert). The video is 76 minutes.

FLIGHT TO NOWHERE

(Sinister, 1946) **D:** William Rowland **P:** William B. David

This early fear-of-the-bomb movie has a plot that involves a stolen map of uranium deposits. The posters said, "Franco threatens with atomic energy!" and "The atom bomb may be used on America!" The low-budget production stars Evelyn Ankers, Alan Curtis, Jerome Cowan, former cowboy star Hoot Gibson, and Jack Holt.

FLIGHT TO TANGIER

(1953) **D/S:** Charles Marquis Warren **M:** Paul Sawtell **P:** Nat Holt

Passengers bound for Tangier are after a letter of memo worth millions. Jack Palance (billed as "that *Shane*-shooting man") and Joan Fontaine star, with Corinne Calvet and Jeff Morrow. It was a 3-D release from Paramount.

THE FLINTSONES

(MCA, 1994) **D:** Brian Levant **S:** Tom S. Parker, Jim Jennewein, Steven de Souza **P:** Bruce Cohen

At least 32 (!) writers worked on the anti-big business plot, but the countless merchandising tie-ins made the message hard to take. ILM created great dinosaurs, though. The stone-age Honeymooners are John Goodman as Fred, Rick Moranis as Barney, Elizabeth Perkins as Wilma, and Rosie O'Donnell as a plump Betty. Kyle MacLachlan is Fred's embezzler boss, Halle Berry integrates Bedrock as his sexy secretary, and Elizabeth Taylor (!) is Fred's mother-in-law. The cast also includes Richard Moll, Irwin Keyes, Jonathan Winters, the voice of Harvey Korman, and Jay Leno. The Jim Henson workshop provided the FX. The B-52's play the theme song and appear; other songs are by various rock groups. Steven Spielberg was the executive producer of this expensive PG hit.

THE FLORIDA CONNECTION

(Unicorn, 1978) **D/S:** Robert J. Emery **S:** Bill Whitlock **S/P:** Massey Creamer

Bad, corrupt cops cheat good marijuana dealers in the Everglades. June Wilkinson (!) is a big-chested platinum-blond charter pilot with an English accent. She's hired by a hunk dope smuggler in bellbottoms (played by her husband at the time, football star Dan Pastorini). There are air-boat rides, a dog race, chases, shootouts, a comic drunk, and a (surprise!) ending. It's pretty slow going. Bill Thurman, from Larry Buchanan movies, spies for the cops. The producer also made *The Legend of Blood Mountain*.

FLOUNDERING

(A-Pix, 1993) **D/S:** Peter McCarthy

James LeGros has a nervous breakdown, tries to kill the chief of police, and kidnaps his next-door neighbor (Maritza Rivera). Revolution occurs in post-riot LA. With Steve Buscemi, John Cusack, Ethan Hawke, Kim Wayans, Lisa Zane, Alex Cox, Dave Navarro (from Jane's Addiction), Exene Cervenka, Sy Richardson, and Olivia Barash. This was made in 16mm by the producer of *Repo Man, Sid and Nancy, I'm Gonna Git You, Sucka*, and other notable films. Caroline released the various artists soundtrack.

FLOWERS IN THE ATTIC

(Starmaker, 1987) **D/S:** Jeffrey Bloom **P:** Sy Levin, Thomas Fries

New World released this toned-down adaptation of V. C. Andrews's novel by the director of *Blood Beach*. Sex and incest were cut out for a PG-13 rating. Victoria Tennant (at that time Mrs. Steve Martin in real life) keeps her four kids (whom grandma calls "the Devil's spawn") hidden in the attic so that she can find a rich husband. She also puts poison into their cookies. Kristy Swanson costars, with Louise Fletcher as the Bible-quoting grandma. It was originally slated to be directed by Wes Craven. Andrews, (who has a bit role as a maid) died in 1986, but new books by a ghost-writer continue to be released.

Jeff Goldblum and Geena Davis in David Cronenberg's *The Fly*.

THE FLY

(Fox, 1986) **D/S/A:** David Cronenberg **S:** Charles Edward Pogue **P:** Stuart Cornfield

Cronenberg added incredible strength, a heightened sex drive, and increased mental powers to the original concept. This "remake" of the 1958 film was his biggest hit (it was actually the fourth *Fly* movie). Jeff Goldblum stars as the brilliant, intense Seth Brundle, who mutates so much that by the end he's a Chris Walas special effect. There's an inside-out baboon and other disgusting things, but an arm-wrestling scene is the most shocking. With Geena Davis, John Getz, and Joy Boushel. Walas and his crew received an FX Oscar. The director is seen as a gynecologist in a dream sequence about an abortion. The Howard Shore soundtrack is on Varese Sarabande. Brian Ferry sings "Help Me."

THE FLY II

(CBS/Fox, 1989) **D:** Chris Walas **S:** Mick Garris, Jim Wheat, Ken Wheat **P:** Steven Charles Jaffe

This should have been called *Son of the Fly*. Talk about disappointing sequels! Eric Stoltz stars as Martin Brundle, son of the Jeff Goldblum character. He grows up superfast and is a genius. He's also a prisoner in a secret corporate lab and sometimes becomes a monster who roars. With Daphne Zuniga (*Spaceballs*), Lee Richardson, and Harley Cross. John Getz returns from *The Fly*. FX expert Walas directs for the first time. It's a Brooksfilm production. The Christopher Young soundtrack is on Varese Sarabande.

THE FLYING DISC MAN FROM MARS

(Republic, 1950) **D:** Fred C. Brannon **S:** Ronald Davidson **P:** Franklin Adreon

Mota (spell it backwards) the Martian (Gregory Gay, with a German accent) arrives in a flying saucer with a "thermal disintegrator" to destroy Earth. Mota had also been in *The Purple Monster Strikes* (1945). Walter Reed stars as the flying hero with a jet pack, with Lois Collier, James Craven, and the usual ace Republic stuntmen. The flying scenes were lifted from *King of the Rocket Men* (1949). This 12-chapter serial was also released as *Missile Monsters*, a feature version.

THE FLYING GUILLOTINE

(1975) **D:** Ho Meng Hua **P:** Raymond Shaw, Run Run Shaw

There were so many kung-fu movies in the 70s that some inner-city theaters showed nothing but Chinese martial arts. Many were bad or forgettable, but this one (by the director of *Infra Man* and the *Black Magic* movies) stands out. The concept is absurd but entertaining. It really features a flying guillotine that lands on a person's head and decapitates him! There's also *The Flying Guillotine II* and *Master of the Flying Guillotine*.

FLYING SAUCER

(Rhino, 1950) **D/S/P/A:** Mikel Conrad **S:** Howard Irving Young

Sam B. (Mikel) Conrad was an actor and self-promoter from Columbus, Ohio, who had been in PRC and Lippert westerns. After small roles in *Abbott and Costello Meet the Killer* and *Francis* (both 1949) he decided to make his own film. The result (the world's only anti-Communist flying-saucer movie) is a unique experience, shot partially on location in scenic Alaska. Conrad plays Mike Trent, a millionaire Manhattan playboy/sportsman/two-fisted drinker/war vet who reluctantly goes undercover to his native Alaska with a blond "nurse" to find out about a rumored saucer before the Commies can get hold of it. He falls in love, thinks an obvious spy is really the new caretaker, and gets drunk, beaten up, and shot in Juneau. The briefly-seen saucer is a film first. It makes a roaring sound as it speeds through the sky but turns out to be from Earth, and it's piloted by Denver Pyle (!). In 1949 the movie had an advance world premiere in Columbus, and it went on to play in theaters for several years. After *Untamed Women* and *Hoodlum Empire* (both 1952) Conrad's acting career ended.

FLY NOW, PAY LATER

(SW, 1969) **D/P:** B. H. Dial **S:** Gillian Vastlake

Charlotte Rouse stars as Sally, a sexy blond stewardess taken hostage by international drug smugglers. There are b/w fantasy and dream sequences, snakes, lesbians, and S&M scenes. It was made in and around New York City.

FM

(MCA, 1978) **D:** John A. Alonzo
S: Ezra Sachs **P:** Rand Holston

DJs at a progressive-rock station in LA go on strike when they're forced to use a playlist of conservative hits. The concept will be hard to follow for anybody who didn't live through the late 60s. Too bad they didn't set this PG comedy in the late 60s and use some decent music! Michael Brandon stars, with Eileen Brennan, Alex Karras, Martin Mull, Cleavon Little, Cassie Yates, Norman Lloyd, and James Keach. Tom Petty, Linda Rondstadt, REO Speedwagon, and others appear as themselves and perform songs. The hit-filled MCA double soundtrack was more popular than the movie. Alonzo shot *Chinatown* and *Close Encounters*.

FOLDS OF THE FLESH

(VSOM, 1970) **D/S/P:** Sergio Bergonzelli
S: Fabio de Agostini   Italy

Pier Angeli and Eleonora Rossi Drago star as mother-and-daughter slashers. This movie features decapitation, Nazis, nudity, and rape. Angeli committed suicide while making her next film, *Octaman*. She had once thought she'd marry James Dean.

FOOD OF THE GODS II

(Avid, 1989) **D/P:** Damien Lee **S:** Richard
Bennett **P:** David Mitchell   Canada (*Gnaw*)

Nobody wanted a sequel to the 1976 AIP film directed by Bert I. Gordon, but Roger Corman and Concorde produced one anyway. A female doctor uses synthetic growth hormones. Some student radicals release lab animals, and giant rats attack teens on campus. There's a giant boy, a big (rubber-looking) hand, and a sex-while-growing dream scene (!). With Paul Coufos, Roy Dotrice, and Lisa Schrage.

THE FOOL KILLER

(Republic Collectibles, 1963) **D:** Servando
Gonzalez **S:** Morton Fine **S/P:** David Friedkin
Mexican/US (*El Asesino de Tontos*)

This high-quality movie (filmed around Knoxville, Tennessee) features Anthony Perkins in one of his most interesting roles. George, a post–Civil War orphan (12-year-old Edward Albert Jr., in his first role), runs away from his mean, strict foster parents and roams the countryside meeting various characters. He narrates his story and sometimes talks to the camera. Henry Hull (*The Werewolf of London*) is an eccentric widower known as Dirty who talks about the notorious eight-foot-tall "fool killer." He calls George a fool for trying to clean up his filthy shack. Perkins is a reclusive, unpredictable, shell-shocked ex-soldier with amnesia and a dead man's name, Milo Bogardus. He first appears in the woods

in a series of jarring closeups accompanied by scary music. He plays a flute, takes George for a nude swim in the river, and has some choice lines: "The first thing I knew was pain." "It's like two armies in my head." "I can feel the grass grow beneath me!" Milo is against organized religion, says he's a faith healer, and in one amazing scene freaks out and yells, "I seen God!" After a scary hellfire sermon at a revival meeting, the excited, impressionable George is nearly born again ("Save me! Save me! Glory!"), passes out, and wakes to find Milo gone and the preacher dead, with an axe in his back. This great-looking b/w film has excellent cinematography, editing, and acting. It was released to theaters in 1965 and again, reedited, in 1969, gaining a (very small) cult following. Friedkin and Fine also wrote *The Pawnbroker*.

FOR A FEW DOLLARS LESS

(VSOM, 1966) **D/S:** Sergio Corbucci
S: Bruno Corbucci, Mario Guerra **P:** Franco
Palaggi   Italy (*Per Qualche Dollari in Meno*)

Although this has a ripoff title, Corbucci had already made six westerns. Lando Buzzanca and Raimondo Vianello star, which is why nobody bothered to release this in the US.

FOR A FEW DOLLARS MORE

(MGM, 1965) **D:** Sergio Leone **S:** Luciano Vincenzoni
P: Alberto Grimaldi   Italy (*Per Qualche Dollari in Piu*)

After the sucess of *A Fistful of Dollars* (nearly everywhere but in the US) Eastwood returned in a bigger and better sequel. It cost $600,000 (said to be three times what the first film cost), runs 130 minutes, and is in Techniscope and Technicolor. Gian Maria Volante costars as Indio, with the late Lee Van Cleef as Colonel Mortimer and the late Klaus Kinski as "the hunchback." Van Cleef had been playing villains since 1952. Eastwood and Van Cleef returned in *The Good, the Bad, and the Ugly*. All three were released here in 1967 (by United Artists). The Ennio Morricone soundtrack (on UA) is on only one side. The other side is music from other films.

THE FORBIDDEN DANCE

(Epic, 1990) **D:** Greydon Clark **S:** Roy
Langsdon, John Platt **P:** Marc S. Fischer

Menahem Golan's 21st Century made this quickie PG-13 lambada movie, which fought it out at the

Anthony Perkins in *The Fool Killer*.

box office with several other lambada movies. This one is the most absurd, has the best cast, and teaches valuable lessons about the rain forest and the ozone layer. Nisa (Laura Herring, a former Miss USA) is a Brazilian jungle princess who goes to Beverly Hills to stop a big corporation from destroying her land. She becomes a maid, has safe sex with her employers' son, teaches the lambada at a disco, becomes Xtasy, the star attraction at a fantasy whorehouse, is kidnapped by corporate villain Richard Lynch (who wears a cowboy hat and dances), and wins an audition to dance on Kid Creole's TV show. Sid Haig is hilarious as a big, ugly witch doctor who dances in his loincloth and yells, "Yi yi ya ya ya!" a lot. He also roars like a lion and follows Nisa to LA. Kid Creole and the Coconuts (who should definitely be in better movies) do two songs. The Kid's right-on closing message on TV is "Boycott their ass!"

FORBIDDEN ISLAND

(Columbia, 1959) **D/S/P:** Charles B. Griffith

Griffith was on a brief break from writing Roger Corman movies when he made this 66-minute b/w adventure. A skin diver is hired to recover a lost emerald from a sunken ship. Jon Hall stars, with John Farrow, Jonathan Haze, and Nan Adams.

FORBIDDEN MOON: *See* ROCKY JONES

FORBIDDEN SUN

(Academy, 1989) **D:** Zelda Baron **S:** Robin
Hardy, Jesse Lasky Jr., Pat Silver **P:** Peter
Watson-Wood   UK (*Bulldance*)

Lauren Hutton stars in this rape-revenge movie set on the isle of Crete, where women are training for the Olympics. Viveca Davis does an ancient dance, flipping over a bull's horns. With Cliff De Young, Samantha Mathis, Renee Estevez, and Robert Beltran.

FORBIDDEN ZONE

(Media, 1980) **D/S/P:** Richard Elfman
S: Matthew Bright, Martin W. Nicholson

It didn't quite make it as a cult hit when new, but this is the strangest musical imaginable. Shot in b/w, it copies the look of the Fleischer brothers' 30s cartoons and includes animation. The dynamic screen team of Susan Tyrrell and Hervé Villechaize are the king and queen of the Sixth Dimension. They make out on a table, torture people, and have sex with zombielike beings. Marie-Pascal Elfman stars, with Viva, Joe Spinnell, and the Kipper Kids. It has the first soundtrack music by the director's brother, Danny Elfman (who plays the Devil) and his group, Oingo Boingo.

FORCED ENTRY

(Vestron, 1975) **D/S/P:** "Jim Sotos"/
Dimitri Sotirakis **S/P:** Henry Scarpelli
(*The Last Victim; The Night Killer*)

An impotent, schizoid killer-rapist/gas-station attendant narrates (à la *Taxi Driver*) this low-key exploitation movie. Tanya Roberts is a housewife he terrorizes. Nancy Allen has a topless scene as a hitchhiking victim who is decapitated after giving the killer a blow job. Some slow-motion killings are repeated. Made in New Jersey and on Staten Island, it was reedited and released in 1980 because of the name stars. The title was also used for a 70s porno movie about a Nam-vet rapist.

FORCED ENTRY

(Subversive Propaganda, 1988)
D/S/P: Norm Orschorschki

This 45-minute parody set in Lynchburg, Virginia (the home of Jerry Falwell), is about the NVC (Neighborhood Vigilance Committee), a fundamentalist, right-wing community-action group fighting "degenerates, dope, and the Devil." To illustrate what would happen if you didn't support the NVC, a girl ("Imagine your own teen daughter!") is kidnapped by masked "dope-crazed punks running amok." The entire segment is seen from her point of view ("Victivision") as she's driven away, poked with a cattle prod, and drugged (there's a pretty amusing drug sequence). Jim "Stonewall" Jackson interrupts often to go on about Commies, homosexuals, and others who "virtually annihilate social behavior." Locals, who swear by guns, Budweiser, and Confederate flags, are seen catching mutant catfish in a nuclear-plant drainage canal. The tape is in "Shock-a-Rama," which simply means that once in a while a photo of Popeye (the freak-show attraction seen in the movie *Mutations*, not the sailor) is flashed on the screen and a very loud buzz is heard.

FORCED TO FIGHT: *See* BLOODFIST III: FIRST TO FIGHT

FORCED TO KILL

(PM, 1994) **D:** Russell Solberg
S/P/A: Corey Michael Eubanks

Eubanks (a former stuntman and the son of TV host Bob Eubanks) stars as a multitalented kickboxing repo man captured by a backwoods Arizona family who make him fight in bare-fist battles. With Michael Ironside as a psycho country sheriff, Don Swayze, Clint and Rance Howard, Kari Whitman, Mickey Jones, Bridget Butler, and Cynthia Blessington.

FORCED VENGEANCE

(MGM, 1982) **D/S:** James Fargo **S:** Franklin Thompson **P:** John W. Bennett

Nam vet Chuck Norris goes to Hong Kong and works at a casino. He takes on Michael Cavanaugh and the Asian underworld while protecting the daughter of the casino owner. Mary Louise Weller and Richard Norton costar, and Mike Norris has a small role. Fargo had directed several Clint Eastwood movies.

FORCE: FIVE

(Media, 1981) **D/S:** Robert Clouse **P:** Fred Weintraub

Joe Lewis (*Jaguar Lives*) leads a team of mercenaries to rescue a senator's daughter (Pam Huntington) from the island of cult leader Master Bong Soo Han. This martial-arts movie is from the director of *Enter the Dragon* (which featured Han in a similar role) and is a remake of *Hot Potato* (1976). With Richard Norton and Benny "the Jet" Urquidez.

FORCE OF IMPULSE

(Sinister, 1961) **D:** Saul Swimmer
S: Francis Swann **P/A:** Tony Anthony

Toby (Tony Anthony) is a 17-year-old high-school football player in love with rich, blond Bunny (Teri Hope, *Playboy*'s Miss September 1958). The mumbling, defensive Toby robs his own grocer father (J. Carrol Naish) so that he can take her out. With Jody McCrea (in a standout scene when drunken gang members "take him for a ride"), Robert Alda (father of Alan) as Bunny's dad, Christina Crawford (!), and Lionel Hampton as his vibes-playing self. It was filmed in Miami Beach. Anthony (real name Roger Tony Petitto) later starred in spaghetti westerns (*A Stranger in Town, The Stranger Returns*), and Hope was in *Pajama Party* and two Elvis movies. Swimmer also directed *Mrs. Brown, You've Got a Lovely Daughter* (1968).

A FORCE OF ONE

(Media, 1979) **D:** Paul Aaron
S: Ernest Tidyman **P:** Alan Belkin

Chuck Norris is a Nam vet who fights cop-killing drug dealers in a California town. The karate fighter has a good supporting cast for this one: Jennifer O'Neill, Clu Gulager, Ron O'Neal, James Whitmore Jr., Bill Wallace, and Mike Norris. It was a follow-up to *Good Guys Wear Black*. Tidyman wrote *Shaft* and *Shaft's Big Score!*

FORCE 10 FROM NAVARONE

(Warner, 1978) **D:** Guy Hamilton **S:** S. Robin Chapman **P:** Oliver A. Unger   UK

AIP released this Alistair MacLean adaptation, starring Robert Shaw (who died in 1978). It's an inferior sequel to *The Guns of Navarone* (1961) about an attempt to blow up a bridge the Nazis plan on using. With Harrison Ford, Edward Fox, Barbara Bach, Franco Nero, Carl Weathers, and Richard Kiel.

Richard Norton, Benny "the Jet" Urquidez, Pam Huntington, Ron Hayden, and Sonny Barnes in *Force: Five*.

FOREIGN CORRESPONDENT

(Warner, 1940) **D:** Alfred Hitchcock **S:** Charles Bennett, Joan Harrison **P:** Walter Wanger

Hitchcock's second American film and his first with a WWII theme stars Joel McCrea as an American reporter in England and Holland in 1939. Nazis kidnap Van Meer, a Dutch diplomat (the great German actor Albert Basserman, who had fled Nazi Germany in 1933), and some interesting things happen in a remote Dutch windmill. The war begins and seems to follow the reporter around. A meek hitman (Edmund Gwenn) tries to push him off Westminster Cathedral. The passenger plane he's on is shot down over the Atlantic. At the end, while London is being bombed, he broadcasts a stirring speech telling Americans to prepare for war. With Laraine Day, Herbert Marshall, Eduardo Ciannelli, Martin Kosleck, Harry Davenport, and George Sanders and Robert Benchley as reporters (Benchley and novelist/screenwriter James Hilton contributed additional dialogue). William Cameron Menzies was the production designer. This was the most expensive (and at 120 minutes the longest) Hitchcock film up to that time. It received six Oscar nominations. It was produced by Selznick International and released by United Artists. Hitchcock's next film was a comedy, *Mr. and Mrs. Smith*, followed by *Suspicion* (both 1941).

THE FOREST

(Starmaker, 1981) **D/P/A:** Don Jones
S: Evan Jones   (*Terror in the Forest*)

A cannibal hermit (Michael Brody) living in a cave kills campers in the woods. The ghosts of his dead kids try to help the campers! This slasher movie is by the director of *The Love Butcher*. It's too dark to see very well.

FOREVER

(Prism, 1992) **D/S:** Thomas Palmer Jr.
S/P: Jackelyn Giroux

A rock-video director (Keith Coogan) moves into the Hollywood mansion where silent-film director William Desmond Taylor (Steve Railsback) was murdered. Ghosts of silent stars emerge from a Moviola, and he falls for actress Mary Miles Minter (Sean Young). With Sally Kirkland as his agent and lover, Diane Ladd as actress Mabel Normand, Terence Knox as actor Wallace Reid, Nicholas Guest, and Renee Taylor.

FOREVER DARLING

(1956) **D:** Alexander Hall **S:** Helen Deutsch **P/A:** Desi Arnaz

James Mason is a guardian angel sent to help the "perfect" marriage of a socialite (Lucille Ball) and a research scientist (Desi Arnaz) who has invented a new insecticide (and sings). Lucy thinks she's losing her mind when she first sees him, but soon she learns to help and respect her husband. With Louis Calhern, John Emery, John Hoyt, Natalie Schafer, and Nancy Kulp. In real life no angel helped the failing marriage of the famous TV-star couple, who also starred in the more popular film *The Long, Long Trailer* (1954), also in color and from MGM. Hall had also directed the fantasies *Here Comes Mr. Jordan* (1941), *Once Upon a Time* (1944), and *Down to Earth* (1947).

FOREVER EVIL

(United, 1987) **D:** Roger Evans **S:** Freeman Williams **P:** Jill Clark, Hal Payne

Here's one from Houston, an attempt to copy *The Evil Dead* shot on video. At least it has great opening credits. A bunch of young people in a house are killed off in a variety of ways by a demon unleashed by a Lovecraft-inspired book. It mixes fantasy elements, gore, and a hard-to-believe attack by amateur Rambo/ghostbusters. One FX scene stands out from the rest of this overlong tape, and it's a "dream sequence." A girl rips a monster baby out of her stomach. Pretty disturbing, but it'll wake you up.

FOREVER, LULU

(Columbia, 1987) **D/S/P/A:** Amos Kollek

Hanna Schygulla stars as a writer in New York City who gets involved in a murder and drug deals. This comedy (by the son of the mayor of Tel Aviv) copies *Desperately Seeking Susan* (Deborah Harry plays the Madonna role). With Dr. Ruth Westheimer, Alec Baldwin (making his debut) as a cop, and Annie Golden. Kollek plays Schygulla's agent.

FOREVER YOUNG

(Warner, 1992) **D:** Steve Miner **S:** Jeffrey Abrahams **P:** Bruce Davey

Mel Gibson is a test pilot in 1939 who is supposed to be frozen for a year to test cryogenics, but ends up forgotten in a military warehouse for years. Two kids thaw him out in 1992, and he falls for their single mom (Jamie Lee Curtis). This PG romantic fantasy features Elijah Wood, George Wendt, Joe Morton, and Ava Lazar. The makeup is by Dick Smith. Jerry Goldsmith wrote the score. It was a step up for the director of two *Friday the 13th* movies.

FORGER OF LONDON

(Sinister, 1961) **D:** Harald Reinl **S:** Johannes Kai W. Germany (*Der Falscher von London*)

This is an adaptation of an Edgar Wallace story first filmed in England in 1928. An amnesiac playboy is suspected of leading a ring of counterfeiters. With Karin Dor, Hellmut Lange, and Walter Rilla. It was released directly to TV in the US.

THE FORGOTTEN ONE

(Academy, 1989) **D/S:** Philip Badgel **P:** Peter Garrity

The always excellent Terry O'Quinn stars as a widowed novelist who moves into a big old empty (and haunted) house in Denver. He has nightmares and becomes terrified and confused as a 19th cen-

tury female ghost decides he's her eternal lover. Neighbor Kristy McNichol (also a writer) narrates. Although it's basically an old fashioned gothic romance, *The Forgotten One* features some modern nudity and an excellent scene with the ghost rising from water. With Elizabeth Brooks (*The Howling*). It was made in Colorado.

FORGOTTEN WOMEN

(1949) **D:** William Beaudine **S:** Scott Darling **P:** Jeffrey Bernard

Elyse Knox, Theodora Lynch, and Veda Ann Borg are the forgotten women (they drink too much) in this Monogram feature. With Edward Norris, Noel Neill (from the *Superman* TV series), and Robert Shayne. Knox (*The Mummy's Tomb*) soon afterward married football star Tom Harmon, retired, and had a son, actor Mark Harmon.

FOR HEAVEN'S SAKE

(1950) **D/S:** George Seaton **P:** William Perlberg

Two angels (Clifton Webb and Edmund Gwenn) are sent to Earth to help a little angel (Gigi Perreau) who has been waiting years to be born. Her future parents are a director (Robert Cummings) and his actress wife (Joan Bennett). Webb takes the form of a rich Texas rancher, and Joan Blondell is supposed to romance him so that he'll back a play. This pro-family 20th Century–Fox fantasy/comedy also features Jack LaRue, Whit Bissell, and Tommy Rettig (from *Lassie*) as another unborn child. Seaton and Perlberg also made *Miracle on 34th Street* (1947).

FOR LOVE OR MONEY

(SW, 1967) **D/P:** Don Davis **S:** James Rogers

This film is about a gang of female sex spies who work for Instant Secretaries, Inc. It was adapted from Ed Wood Jr.'s novel *The Sexecutives* (published as an adults-only photo-novel in 1968 by Private Editions and sold for $1.50). The plot involves blackmail photos, LSD, and body-painting. It's from Crest Films. Davis had worked on *Orgy of the Dead* and directed *Gun Runners* (1969) with a script by Wood.

FOR LOVE OR MURDER: *See* KEMEK

FOR MEMBERS ONLY

(SW, 1959) **D:** Ramsey Herrington **S:** Norman Armstrong **P:** John P. Wyler UK (*The Nudist Story*)

A girl (Shelley Martin) inherits a nudist colony. It was produced by The Danzigers (Edward and Harry) who made *Devil Girl from Mars*.

FOR MEN ONLY

(1952) **D/P/A:** Paul Henreid **S:** Lou Morheim   (*The Tall Lie*)

Some UCLA fraternity pledges kill a dog, and a professor (Henreid) exposes their hazing practices. The Lippert release features Margaret Field, Kathleen Hughes, Vera Miles (in her second film), Douglas Kennedy, and Russell Johnson. Henreid directed two other films about teens in trouble (*Live Fast, Die Young* and *Girls on the Loose*, both 1958) and *Dead Ringer* (1962).

FOR MEN ONLY

(SW, 1967) **D/S/P:** Peter Walker   UK (*I Like Birds; Hot Girls for Men Only*)

This was the first film by Walker, who later switched from nudie movies to horror (*House of Whipcord*). A London fashion columnist with a rich, jealous fiancé takes a job with a small-town moral crusader and publisher who is really a Hugh Hefner type (with a gay photographer). This silly color comedy features five screaming, naked "birds" tied up in a barn. Their nude escape scene (with bongo music) is the movie's highlight. At the end, they make their voyeur kidnappers pull a car like horses. Supposedly 18 more minutes (probably concerning two naked women in an agent's office) were added for the US release, bringing the length to 61 minutes. Note the poster for the Walker Brothers and Roy Orbison.

THE FORMULA

(MGM, 1980) **D:** John G. Avildsen **S/P:** Steve Shagan

This commercial flop was based on Shagan's novel about a formula for synthetic oil and international conspiracies. George C. Scott stars as an LA policeman who's after the killer of his friend. Marlon Brando (who was paid $3 million for three scenes) costars, with Marthe Keller, John Gielgud, Beatrice Straight, G. D. Spradlin, Marshall Thompson, and Richard Lynch in a dual role.

42ND STREET

Every major American city had a movie district where double bills of all kinds could be enjoyed in large, ornate, old movie palaces. By the 70s many shopping-mall theaters had been built, and audiences had changed. Kung fu, black action, and porno joined horror, *Mondo*, exploitation, and action movies from around the world. Like other fans, I saw many incredible features in these inner-city theaters (in Cleveland, then New York), but they're almost all gone now. The theaters on 42nd Street, in the Times Square area, were victims of real-estate developers, corrupt politicians, and crack. If these theaters had been left alone, they'd be doing fine today.

FORTIES FAVES
TOP 10, IN ALPHABETICAL ORDER

1. *Arsenic and Old Lace* (CBS/Fox, 1941. This Frank Capra classic from Columbia has been colorized, so it's on TV more, which is great, but it's also been reedited and cut. They even took out the Brooklyn Dodgers intro to make more time for commercials!)
2. *The Beast with Five Fingers* (1946)
3. *Beauty and the Beast* (1946)
4. *Cat People* (1942)
5. *Dead of Night* (1945)
6. *The Devil and Daniel Webster* (Criterion, 1941. Made by RKO and also known as *All That Money Can Buy*, it's available in a fully restored 109-minute version on laserdisc, with the addition of 22 missing minutes and commentary.)
7. *Mighty Joe Young* (Turner, 1949. Made by RKO, it's been colorized by Turner but is available on laserdisc in b/w with the Technicolor fire sequence restored.)
8. *The Picture of Dorian Gray* (1945)
9. *Strangler of the Swamp* (1946)
10. *The Wolf Man* (1941)

FORT APACHE, THE BRONX
(Warner, 1981) **D:** Daniel Petrie **S:** Heywood Gould **P:** Martin Richards

Paul Newman is an Irish street cop in a surprisingly downbeat and violent movie (compared to others he's been in). Ken Wahl is his partner. It was based on the real experiences of two cops. With Edward Asner, Pam Grier, Danny Aiello, Kathleen Beller, and Rachel Ticotin. It runs 125 minutes.

FOR THE LOVE OF IT
(SW, 1969) **D/S:** Will Tremper   W. Germany
(*How Did a Nice Girl Like You Get into This Business?*; *Nice Girl*; *Naughty Cheerleaders*)

Barbi Benton (from *Playboy*) stars in this German sex comedy (shot in Florida) about a naive girl who becomes a "playgirl." With Klaus Kinski, Clyde Ventura, and Broderick Crawford. Independent International released it in the US as *Naughty Cheerleaders* in 1975.

FORTRESS
(HBO, 1985) **D:** Arch Nicholson **S:** Everett De Roche **P:** Raymond Menmuir   Australia

A teacher (Rachel Ward) and her students are kidnapped by a gang in the outback. They escape and seek revenge in this violent movie, which debuted on HBO.

FORTRESS
(Live, 1992) **D:** Stuart Gordon **S:** Steve Feinberg, Troy Neighbors, Terry Curtis Fox **P:** John Davis, John Flock   Australia/US

This is one of the best by Gordon. A futuristic, computer-automated, underground American prison uses robots and lasers to control the male and female inmates, who also have implants that can cause extreme pain (and explosions). A married couple (Christopher Lambert and Loryn Locklin) are imprisoned because she became pregnant a second time (a felony). Poe (Kurtwood Smith) runs the prison. Tom Towles and Vernon Wells are prisoners, Jeffrey Combs is a computer whiz, and Carolyn Purdy-Gordon is the voice of the computer. Originally planned for Schwarzenegger, it was filmed at the Warner studios in Queensland, Australia, and was released in Europe first. A sequel is planned.

FORTRESS OF AMERIKKKA
(Imperial, 1989) **D/S:** Eric Louzil **P:** Lloyd Kaufman, Michael Herz   (*The Mercenaries*)

Gene LeBrock stars as a half-Indian ex-con who wants revenge for the murder of his brother. He fights female mercenaries in the woods (and at Bronson Canyon). With porno star Kasha (Le Priol) as a missing hiker and François Papilion. This senseless Troma release was filmed in California by the director of *Lust for Freedom*.

FORT TI
(1953) **D:** William Castle **S:** Robert E. Kent **P:** Sam Katzman

George Montgomery stars as a captain during the French and Indian War. This is the first 3-D film in which an actor spits at the audience (*The Charge at Feather River*, released a few months later, has a similar scene). The Columbia release also used the first 3-D matte paintings, and spears, muskets, cannons, and tomahawks seem to fly out of the screen. It's not a great western but has some of the best 3-D effects. Joan Vohs costars. The Three Stooges' 3-D short *Spooks* originally played on the same bill.

FORTUNE AND MEN'S EYES
(MGM, 1971) **D:** Harvey Hart, Jules Scherwin **S:** John Herbert **P:** Lester Persky, Lewis Allen   Canada

Wendell Burton stars as a guy imprisoned for possession. He becomes the sexual slave of Zooey Hall (*I Dismember Mama*) to protect himself from other cellmates. Michael Greer (from *The Gay Deceivers*) is Queenie. It's based on an off-Broadway play (once revived with Sal Mineo), but was toned down a lot for the screen. Hart replaced Schwerin, the original director, after nine weeks of shooting in a Quebec prison.

FORTUNE DANE
(Vidmark, 1986) **D:** Nicholas Sgarro, Charles Correll **S:** Ronald M. Cohen **P:** Thomas Kane

Carl Weathers stars as a football star turned cop. His small friend David Rappaport is killed. This ABC-series pilot (shown in theaters in Europe) features Joe Dallesandro as Perfect Tommy, Adolph Caesar, and Sonny Landham. Weathers and Dallesandro were in the series, which lasted exactly a month.

FORTY-ACRE FEUD
(Madhouse, 1965) **D:** Ron Ormond **S/P:** Bil Packman

Del Reeves stars as Del Culpepper in this 16mm Nashville hillbilly comedy with country music. There's a plot about electing a state representative from a town called Shagbottom and some Romeo and Juliet lovers. It's mostly a valuable piece of the 60s for country fans. With Jan Moore, Ferlin Husky as Simon Crumb and as himself, and Minnie Pearl. George Jones, Ray Price, Bill Anderson, Skeeter Davis, and Loretta Lynn are just some of the stars who sing the "25 country hits."

FORTY DEUCE
(1982) **D:** Paul Morrissey **S:** Alan Browne **P:** Jean-Jacques Fourgeaud

Kevin Bacon stars as a male prostitute in New York City trying to sell a runaway boy to Orson Bean to get money for a drug deal. With Esai Morales. The music is by Manu Dibango. It was based on an off-Broadway play. This and Morrissey's *Madame Wang's* (1979) had little or no release.

THE 40S

More B movies were made during the war than at any other time. WWII themes showed up everywhere, and after the development of the atom bomb and the end of the war, *film noir* flourished. The Poverty Row studios were at their peak, and serials, detective-series movies, and horror movies were released every week. Films that made more than $10 million include three Disney cartoon features (the top three of the decade), followed by the long-running road-show hit *Mom and Dad* (!) and Cecil B. DeMille's *Samson and Delilah*.

216

FORT APACHE, THE BRONX

Renee Soutendijk and Jeroen Krabbe in *The 4th Man*.

FOR YOUR HEIGHT ONLY

(HQV, 1979) **D:** Raymond Jury   Philippines

One of the ultimate spy spoofs stars 2'9" dwarf Weng Wang as Agent 00. He uses James Bond–type gadgets and martial arts to battle the bad guys, and he gets the girl. In real life (according to *Guinness*, "the shortest actor to play a leading role in films") he was a paratrooper and black belt. He also starred in *Agent 00* (1981). The bad English dubbing adds unintentional humor.

FOUL PLAY

(1974) **D/S:** Gus Trikonis **S/P/A:** Ross Hagen Philippines (*Superchicken; Supercock*)

Ross Hagen stars as a cowboy involved with cockfighting. Nancy Kwan costars (she was also in *Wonder Women* and *Night Creature* with Hagen). This was made the same year as *Cockfighter*.

FOUR BOYS AND A GUN

(1957) **D/P:** William Berke
S: Philip Yordan, Leo Townsend

The ads said, "These kids are going straight—to the electric chair!" Some teens attempt to hold up a fight arena and are wrongly accused of killing a cop. With Frank Sutton, James Franciscus (in his first role), and Terry Green. Berke also directed some of the Jungle Jim movies. This played on a double bill with *The Wild Party*.

THE FOUR DEUCES

(HBO, 1975) **D:** William H. Bushnell Jr.
S: C. Lester Franklin, Don Martin
P: Menahem Golan

Jack Palance stars as a Prohibition-era ganglord, in a Golan/Globus movie that mixes violence, sex, and humor. With Carol Lynley, Warren Berlinger, Adam Roarke, H. B. Haggerty, and Martin Kove.

THE 4th MAN

(Cinematheque, 1979) **D:** Paul Verhoeven
S: Gerard Setman **P:** Rob Houwer   Netherlands

A bisexual writer (Jeroen Krabbe) sleeps with a blond hairdresser (Renee Soutendijk) to get to her boyfriend. Her three previous husbands all died mysteriously. This bizarre horror comedy features nightmares, hallucinations, castration, voyeurism,

near-X sex, and nudity (some in a graveyard). A subtitled version is also available from Tamarelle. Verhoeven was the leading Dutch director at the time. This was made before his *Spetters* (1980) but not released in the US until 1984.

FOXES

(Key, 1980) **D:** Adrian Lyne
S/P: Gerald Ayers **P:** David Puttnam

Four suburban-LA teen girls face the problems of sex, drugs, and bad parents. Jodie Foster stars with Cherie Currie (from the Runaways) as a doomed party girl, Marilyn Kagan, Kandice Stroh, Sally Kellerman, Randy Quaid, Scott Baio, Adam Faith, and (in a small role) Laura Dern. The ads for this R-rated United Artists film said, "Daring to do it!" The Giorgio Moroder Casablanca soundtrack features Donna Summer's hit "On the Radio." *Phoxes* was a play based on this movie, starring men in drag.

FOXFIRE: *See* EBONY, IVORY, AND JADE

FOXFORCE: *See* EBONY, IVORY, AND JADE

FOXTRAP

(Orion, 1985) **D/P/A:** Fred Williamson
S: Aubrey K. Rattan   Italy

Chris Connelly hires Thomas Fox (Fred Williamson), a cigar-smoking LA playboy/detective, to find his heiress niece (Donna Owen), who's missing in Europe. Fox goes to Venice and Rome, walks around the (real) Cannes Film Festival, and then returns to LA. There's a subplot about porno videos and drugs. A gay man sacrifices his life to help Fox. During the big shootout at the end, everybody but Fox dies. With Beatrice Palme and Arlene Golonka.

FOXY BROWN

(Orion, 1974) **D/S:** Jack Hill
P: Buzz Feitshans

Pam Grier stars in her fourth and last film by director Hill. She poses as a hooker for the mob to get the guys who killed her cop lover (Terry Carter). It's pretty outrageous, with decapitation by plane propeller, castration, rape, drugs, bondage, gay and lesbian characters, and lots of wigs. Actually, Grier is abused too much in this one and doesn't spend enough time kicking ass. 8 minutes had to be cut out for the UK release. With Antonio Fargas (a standout) as her drug-dealer brother Link, Sid Haig as a bearded pilot, Juanita Brown as a captive hooker, and Peter Brown. The Motown soundtrack is by Willie Hutch. It's from AIP. Feit-

shans went on to produce Arnold Schwarzenegger movies, including *Total Recall*.

FP 1 DOESN'T ANSWER

(Sinister, 1932) **D:** Karl Hartl **S:** Walter Reisch, Robert Stevenson, Peter MacFarlane **P:** Eberhard Klagemann Germany (*FP1 Antwortet Nicht*)

This big-budget film about a flying ace and a giant mid-Atlantic floating platform (FP 1) is based on a novel by Curt Siodmak. Three versions (in German, English, and French) were shot simultaneously on a Baltic island. The English-language version (which is available on tape) stars Conrad Veidt and Jill Esmond. The German version (also on tape) stars Hans Albers and Sybille Schmitz and features Peter Lorre as a journalist. The French version stars Charles Boyer. Erich Pommer, executive producer for UFA, fled Nazi Germany the year after this was released, as did Veidt, Lorre, Siodmak, and screenwriter Reisch.

FRAGMENT OF FEAR

(1971) **D:** Richard C. Sarafian **S:** Paul Dehn
P: John R. Sloan **C:** Oswald Morris

David Hemmings is a reformed drug addict in Pompeii who wants to know who killed his aunt (Flora Robson). The mystery is complicated by

Foxy's in town,
... so gather 'round and watch a real shake down. 'Cause she's got drive and that ain't jive. She don't bother to bring 'em back alive!

Don't mess aroun' with...

Foxy Brown

PAM GRIER AS **FOXY BROWN**

Also starring PETER BROWN · TERRY CARTER as Michael
Co-starring KATHRYN LODER · HARRY HOLCOMBE · Produced by BUZZ FEITSHANS
Written and Directed by JACK HILL · COLOR by Movielab · An AMERICAN INTERNATIONAL Picture

Original Music Score and Songs
Performed by WILLIE HUTCH
Soundtrack Album available on Motown Records

© 1974 American International Pictures Inc.

hallucinations. Gayle Hunnicutt co-stars, with Wilfrid Hyde-White, Adolfo Celi, Mona Washbourne, Daniel Massey, Roland Culver, and Zakes Mokae. This Columbia PG film is based on a novel by John Bingham. The director made *Vanishing Point*.

FRAMED

(Paramount, 1974) **D:** Phil Karlson **S/P:** Mort Briskin **S:** Joel Briskin

The people who made *Walking Tall* returned with another revenge tale. This time Joe Don Baker, a gambler, is set up and goes to jail, where he befriends a cockroach. When released, Baker beats people up, drags a man by his nose, and shoots his ear off. It was the last feature by Karlson, veteran of many Monogram and Columbia B movies. With Conny Van Dyke (Dick's sister), Gabriel Dell (from the Dead End Kids/Bowery Boys) as a hitman, John Marley as a Mafia boss, Brock Peters, Paul Mantee, and Hoke Howell.

FRAMEUP

(Republic, 1990) **D/S/P:** Paul Leder **S:** Reuben Leder

Wings Hauser is small-town sheriff who tries to find a boy's killer. Frances Fisher is a helpful police dispatcher and Dick Sargent is the main bad guy. With Heather Fairfield and Bobby Diciccio. A sequel followed.

FRAMEUP II: THE COVER-UP

(Republic, 1992) **D/S/P:** Paul Leder

John Saxon is a corrupt, murderous S&L president in a small California town. He kidnaps the wife (Frances Fisher) and daughter of the sheriff (Wings Hauser). With Margaux Hemingway as his coke-addict wife, Patti D'Arbanville, and Peter Kwong.

FRANK AND I

(MGM, 1984) **D:** Gerard Kikoine **S/P:** Harry Alan Towers France (*Liberated Lady*)

This is one of many erotic TV movies Towers made for Playboy. Jennifer Inch stars, with Sophie Favier.

FRANKENHOOKER

(Southgate, 1990) **D/S:** Frank Henenlotter **S:** Robert Martin **P:** Edgar Ievens

James Lorinz stars as Jeffrey, a young New Jersey inventor who lives with his mom (Louise Lasser). When his girlfriend is chopped up by a power lawn mower that he invented, he looks for body parts to remake her. He also develops "Supercrack," which makes hookers who smoke it blow up, and sticks a power drill into his head to clear his mind. Lorintz

A phantasmagoria of fright.

COLUMBIA PICTURES Presents
DAVID HEMMINGS
GAYLE HUNNICUTT in

FRAGMENT OF FEAR

is a one-man show, saying funny lines (usually to himself) all through the movie, and this is one of Henenlotter's best movies. Patty Mullen is Elizabeth, who becomes an awkward, pieced-together monster with a hooker's memory. With Shirley Stoler, Beverly Bonner, Zacherle (as a TV weatherman), Jennifer Delora, Heather Hunter (later star of a porno tape called *Frankenhunter*), Charlotte Helmcamp, Kimberly Taylor, and Susan Napoli. The original video box says, "Wanna date?" when a button is pushed. Although the horror and violence are obviously cartoonlike, this got an X, but was released with a self-appointed "A." It's available as an R or unrated tape. The soundtrack by Joe Renzetti (with *Basket Case II* music) is on SMI.

FRANKENSTEIN

(Lightning, 1984) **D:** Jeremy Bear **S:** Victor Gialanella UK

This British TV movie, shot on tape, is based on the flop Broadway play. The US debut was on Showtime. The tape is hosted by Elvira. With John Gielgud as the blind hermit, Robert Powell as Dr. Frankenstein, Carrie Fisher, and David Warner as the monster.

FRANKENSTEIN

(Turner, 1992) **D/S/P:** David Wickes UK

Billed as the most faithful adaptation (I think it is, so far), this is a

very good version, with Dr. Frankenstein (Patrick Bergin) duplicating his own body in a vat. The result is an angry, unfinished creature (Randy Quaid) who demands a mate and kills lots of people before Frankenstein confronts the monster by the Bering Sea. The frantic creator feels the monster's pain while everybody he cares about dies. The tale is told in flashback to a ship's captain. With Fiona Gillies as Eizabeth, Sir John Mills as the blind hermit, Lambert Wilson, and Michael Gothard (in his last role). The only weak part is a crude-looking mutant animal. It was filmed in Poland and debuted here on TNT. By the director of *Jack the Ripper* (1988) and *Jekyll and Hyde* (1990).

FRANKENSTEIN: A CINEMATIC SCRAPBOOK

(Rhino, 1991) **D/S:** Ted Newsom

Here you have every trailer in the Universal and Hammer series, plus other 50s and 60s American Frankenstein movies and *Lady Frankenstein*. Some rare scenes include Karloff in his monster makeup for a celebrity baseball game in 1941 and Glen Strange on an *Abbott and Costello* TV show in 1954. Trailers for the monsterthon movies *House of Frankenstein*, *House of Dracula*, and *Abbott and Costello Meet Frankenstein* show up here and in *Dracula: A Cinematic Scrapbook* and *The Wolf Man Chronicles*, other 60-minute compilations from Rhino.

FRANKENSTEIN '80

(MPI, 1973) **D:** Mario Mancini **S:** Fernando di Leone **P:** Benedetto Graziani Italy

John Richardson stars, with Gordon Mitchell as Otto. A monster called Mosaico kills strippers, hookers, and bums. This ridiculous movie features sex, gore, nudity, and decapitation. Carlo Rambaldi provided the FX. *Lady Frankenstein* (1971) and *Frankenstein's Castle of Freaks* are other Italian sex/monster movies from the same period.

FRANKENSTEIN GENERAL HOSPITAL

(New Star, 1988) **D:** Deborah Roberts **S:** Michael Kelly, Robert Deel **P:** Dimitri Villard

Mark Blankfield stars as Dr. Frankenstein's great-grandson, with an assistant named Iggy, in this unfunny comedy follow-up to *Jekyll and Hyde . . . Together Again*, also with Blankfield. The lab scenes are b/w. With Irwin Keyes as the monster, Kathy Shower, and Bobby "Boris" Pickett.

James Lorinz stars in *Frankenhooker*.

FRANKENSTEIN'S CASTLE OF FREAKS

(Magnun, 1973) **D/S:** "Robert H. Oliver"/
Dick Randall **S:** Mario Francini Italy
(*House of Freaks; Il Castello della Paura*)

Billed as a Frankenstein movie, this is really a pretty warped and funny cave man movie with lots of nudity. It was released in the US by Harry Novak and his adults-only Boxoffice International. Michael Dunn is the dwarf Genz, the lonely, misunderstood, vengeful necrophiliac/rapist/voyeur assistant of Count Frankenstein (*South Pacific* star Rossano Brazzi). After being mistreated and thrown out, he teams up with a short, ugly Neanderthal man named Ook (played by "Boris Lugosi"). Ook lives in a cave and says, "Ook, ook, ook." Meanwhile, the doctor's sexy daughter and her friend bathe in milk and strip in Ook's cave to enjoy the convenient hot springs every time things threaten to get dull. The doctor works on Goliath, a big Neanderthal man with Bozo-the-Clown hair. There's lots of thunder and lightning. Igor, a hunchbacked servant (Gordon Mitchell), beats a maid, Edmund Purdom shows up as the law, the "monsters" fight over a kidnapped girl, and the villagers assemble with torches. The 3'4" Dunn, an excellent actor (whose voice was dubbed by somebody else in England), died in 1974, a possible suicide. He had been nominated for an Oscar in 1965 for his film debut, in *Ship of Fools*.

FRANKENSTEIN'S GREAT AUNT TILLIE

(Video City, 1983) **D/S/P:** Myron G. Gold Mexico

Here's an unfunny period comedy set in Transylvania but filmed by an American director on a set in Mexico. Although it seems to go on forever, this is a short version of what apparently was once a miniseries! After editing, costar Zsa Zsa Gabor is seen only in a silent flashback for a few seconds. If you enjoy hearing Donald Pleasence (as Victor Frankenstein, in a stupid wig) mumble for an eternity, this tape's for you. Yvonne Furneaux (the sister in *Repulsion*) is Aunt Tillie, and she talks too much too. June Wilkinson (*Macumba Love*) is Victor's wife. Aldo Ray is the burgormaster. A blue monster in suspenders eventually shows up for some sub–*Young Frankenstein* yuks, Pleasence is shown in drag playing a flute, and village women hold an ERA rally. If you manage to watch till the end, you'll be rewarded with lots of outtakes from the long version. The music is by Ronald Stein, who used to score a lot of AIP movies.

FRANKENSTEIN ISLAND

(Monterey, 1981) **D/P:** Jerry Warren
S: Jacques Lacouter

Jerry Warren, who died in 1988, directed hard-to-believe movies like *Teenage Zombies* and *Man Beast*. This, his last ridiculous effort, is a treasure for fans of really desperate low-budget filmmaking. Four balloonists land on an island and meet characters who must have escaped from Z-movie heaven. A tribe of jungle women in leopard-skin bikinis are actually aliens. Warren regular Katherine Victor (in a great silver/white wig) is a mad doctor married to the 200-year-old, bedridden assistant to Dr. Frankenstein. John Carradine, as the ghost of Dr. Frankenstein, shows up once in a while, superimposed over the action, spouting

meaningless dialogue ("The power! The power! The power!"), just like Lugosi in *Plan 9 from Outer Space*. Cameron Mitchell, as a sea captain, is kept in a cell to supply blood and is the father of an alien girl. A group of servant zombies wear sunglasses, sweatshirts, and black knit hats. Robert Clarke (*The Hideous Sun Demon*) is the hero, alongside B-movie vet Steve Brodie. At the end, the Frankenstein monster shows up, and Andrew Duggan as a military officer thinks the whole story is crazy. As one character says, "So much has happened, the mind can't catalog it!"

FRANKENSTEIN'S PLANET OF MONSTERS

(Nomad, 1993) **D/P/E/C:** Brad Anderson
S/P/E/A: Mike Brunelle

Three female astronauts and their floating cyborg head are tricked into landing on a barren planet run by a Frankenstein monster (Mike Brunelle, in good makeup). They befriend a wolf man, are chained up in a dungeon, and are attacked by an army of monsters (people in masks). Models are used for the castle and the spaceship, and there's some animation. This 45-minute tape from Somerville, Massachusetts, is fun and would be rated G.

FRANKENSTEIN: THE COLLEGE YEARS

(1991) **D:** Tom Shadyac **S:** Bryant
Christ, John Trevor Wolff **P:** Richard E.
Johnson, Scott D. Goldstein

William Ragsdale and Christopher Daniel Barnes star as premed students who bring a professor's creation (Vincent Hammond) to life. He becomes a football hero and defender of justice. An evil professor (Larry Miller) and his assistant try to kidnap the monster. There are lots of bad-taste jokes in this comedy, which debuted on Fox-TV.

FRANKENSTEIN UNBOUND

(Fox, 1990) **D/S/P:** Roger Corman **S:** F. X.
Feeney **P:** Thom Mount, Kabi Jaeger

Roger Corman directed for the first time in 20 years, but his film, based on a novel by Brian Aldiss, received only a token theatrical release from 20th Century–Fox, which cut out 20 minutes. John Hurt stars as an LA scientist in in 2031. He causes a time slip and ends up in 1817 Geneva, Switzerland (with a talking car). The late Raul Julia is Dr. Frankenstein, who creates a bride for his monster (Nick Brimble). Mary Shelley and people who were close to her when she wrote the novel *Frankenstein* mix with characters from the novel and the man from the future. It's all kind of awkward, with several dreams and out-of-place fantasy sequences. Nobody from the past seems to notice the car! With Bridget Fonda as Mary Shelley, Jason Patric as Lord Byron, Michael Hutchence (from INXS) as Percy Bysshe Shelley, Catherine Corman, and the voice of Terri Treas. There was no reason for this movie to have an R rating.

It's 82 minutes long. Julia went on to play Gomez in *The Addams Family* and *Addams Family Values*, and Corman probably shelved any further plans to direct.

FRANKENWEENIE

(Buena Vista, 1984) **D:** Tim Burton
S: Lenny Ripps **P:** Julie Hickson

Burton made this 27-minute b/w short while he was with Disney. Disney declined to release the PG-rated short even though it had cost a million dollars to produce, claiming that it was too scary for kids to see in theaters, as had been planned. It was worth the wait. Burton was 25 when he made it. It's a great-looking, cute, and clever comedy mixing the Frankenstein story with the visual style of *Bride of Frankenstein* (and the original *Invaders from Mars*). Barrett Oliver (*The NeverEnding Story*) is Victor, a kid who brings his dog, Sparky, back to life. Paul Bartel is a science teacher, and Shelley Duvall and Daniel Stern are the parents. Burton also made *Vincent* (1983), an animated b/w short, while with Disney. It's about a boy who imitates his idol, Vincent Price (who narrates). Disney let Burton go, and in a few years he was one of the most successful directors around.

FRANK HENENLOTTER'S SEXY SHOCKER REEL

(SW, 1994)

Select scenes from 31 films made in various countries (mostly in the 60s) and released as part of the Sexy Shocker series are in this mind-blowing 100 minute sampler. Some highlights are scenes from *The Awful Dr. Orloff*, *The Bloody Pit of Horror*, *The Curious Dr. Humpe*, *Horrors of Spider Island*, *Mondo Balardo*, *Mondo Pazzo*, and *Sexy Prohibitismo*. Since most of you wouldn't want (or couldn't afford) all 31, this is a great idea, but be prepared, because comic and/or sexy scenes with strippers, monsters, and mad doctors are mixed with disturbing *Mondo* scenes and some pretty strong and sick torture and rape scenes.

THE POWER IS 7,000,000 VOLTS!

IT'S ALIVE!

BEWARE the jolt at

FRANKENSTEIN ISLAND

PG

starring JOHN CARRADINE · CAMERON MITCHELL · STEVE BRODIE · ROBERT CLARKE
EASTMAN COLOR CHRISWAR pictures

FRANTIC

(Warner, 1988) **D/S:** Roman Polanski
S: Gerard Brach **P:** Thom Mount   France

An American doctor (Harrison Ford) and his wife (Betty Buckley) go to Paris. She disappears, and he becomes involved with Emmanuelle Seigner and political intrigue. Ford is dull, and this Hitchcockian thriller is way too long (120 minutes). A miniature Statue of Liberty is an interesting touch. Ennio Morricone wrote the score. Alexandra Stewart is in the cast, and Polanski plays a bit part. Seigner, his 21-year-old girlfriend at the time, married him and returned in his *Bitter Moon* (1992).

FRATERNITY VACATION

(Starmaker, 1985) **D:** James Frawley
S: Lindsay Harrison **P:** Robert C. Peeters

Stephen Geoffreys stars as Wendell, an awkward guy who becomes "cool," in this movie about Palm Springs teens trying to get laid. His friends (Cameron Dye and a pre-star Tim Robbins) are the victims of a memorable frat-joke scene with nude Kathleen Kinmont and Barbara Crampton. With Sheree J. Wilson (from *Dallas*), Leigh McCloskey, Amanda Bearse, Britt Ekland, Max Wright, Franklyn Ajaye, John Vernon as the police chief, and Nita Talbot as his wife. The soundtrack features various rock artists. Denise di Novi (*Batman Returns*) was an executive producer of this New World release.

FRÄULEIN DEVIL

(Wizard, 1977) **D:** "Mark Stern"/Patrice
Rhom   Italy (*Captive Woman 4*)

Melissa Longo is a hooker-turned-colonel running a WWII Nazi brothel on a train. With Pamela Stanford and Lisa Lynn Montiel. Longo was in Tinto Brass' *Salon Kitty* (1975), which this copies, and played a similar role in *Helga, She Wolf of Spilberg*.

FREAKED

(Fox, 1993) **D/S/A:** Alex Winter **D/S:** Tom
Stern **S:** Tim Burns **P:** Harry and Mary Jane
Ufland   (*Hideous Mutant Freekz*)

Alex Winter is Ricky Coogan, star of the fictitious *Ghost Dude* series who's helping to promote poison fertilizer. He and his friend Ernie (Michael Stoyanov) go to South America and encounter a bearded sideshow owner (Randy Quaid) with a freak-making machine. Megan Ward is joined with Ernie, and Ricky's face is mutated. This fun, wacky comedy spoofs everything, from *The Twilight Zone*, *Hollywood Squares*, and *Gumby* to the Harryhausen cyclops. Even a hammer has a flashback. With Alex Zuckerman as Ricky's number one fan, William Sadler as a corporate villain, an unrecognizable Keanu Reeves as the dog-faced boy, Mr. T as a bearded lady, Brooke Shields, Larry "Bud" Melman, Gibby Haynes, and the voice of Bobcat Goldthwait. Steve Johnson, Screaming Mad George, the Chiodo Brothers, and David Allen all provided FX, under the supervision of Tom Rainone (who also appears). It's PG-13 and was released by 20th Century–Fox. The directors had done the *Idiot Box* series for MTV.

THE FREAKMAKER = THE MUTATIONS

FREAKSHOW

(1989) **D:** Constantino Magnatta
S: Bob Farmer **P:** Anthony
Kramreither   Canada

Four very bad horror stories are told. Audrey Landers stars as a TV newscaster in linking segments.

FREAKY FRIDAY

(Disney, 1976) **D:** Gary Nelson
S: Mary Rodgers **P:** Ron Miller

A teen (Jodie Foster) and her mom (Barbara Harris) switch personalities for a day, in this G-rated body-switch movie that's very much ahead of its time. With John Astin, Patsy Kelly, Ruth Buzzi, Marc McClure, Marvin Kaplan, Dick Van Patten, Sorrell Booke, Kay Ballard, and Charlene Tilton. The basic plot was reused in countless 80s films. Nelson went on to direct the expensive Disney flop *The Black Hole*.

FREDDY'S DEAD: THE FINAL NIGHTMARE

(RCA, 1991) **D:** Rachel Talalay **S:** Michael
DeLuca **P:** Robert Shaye, Aaron Warner

Robert Englund stars as supernatural killer Freddy Krueger for the "last" time. This awkward movie is set in a small Ohio town in the future, when all the children have been killed off. Shon Greenblatt has amnesia and nightmares. Teen-runaway-shelter worker Lisa Zane is Freddy's daughter. Yaphet Kotto is a doctor who uses dream therapy (and 3-D glasses). Lezlie Deane fights Freddy with martial arts. The small cast mostly acts in a cramped old-house set. The disappointing 15-minute last reel is in 3-D. The look of the film is similar to *The Mask* (also distributed by New Line). There are nods to *The Wizard of Oz* and *The Twilight Zone*, and useless bit parts by Johnny Depp, Alice Cooper, Rosanne Barr, and New Line president Shaye don't help. The 32-year-old director was an accounting assistant for Roger Corman and a production assistant for John Waters, then produced two Waters and two *Nightmare* movies. A soundtrack with various rock artists is on Metal Blade, and the Brian May score is on Varèse Sarabande. The 6th and "final" movie in the series, this made more than $17 million and was followed by *Wes Craven's New Nightmare*.

FREDDY'S NIGHTMARES

(1988–90)

This syndicated horror-anthology series was hosted by Robert Englund as wisecracking Freddy Krueger. It was a lame attempt to cash in on the popular movies, and episodes were awkwardly filmed so that they could be syndicated as hour or half-hour shows. The show could be pretty violent for TV. The scripts were awful. It's set in Springwood.

Barbara Harris and Jodie Foster switch personalities in *Freaky Friday*.

Some directors were Tom De Simone, Ken Weiderhorn, and William Malone. Five tapes lasting 47 minutes each are available. *No More Mr. Nice Guy* is the feature-length pilot, directed by Tobe Hooper. From Warner.

FREE FALL

(Vidmark, 1993) **D:** John Irvin
S/P: David Zito, Les Weldon

A wildlife photographer in Africa (Pamela Gidley) has an affair with a sportsman (Eric Roberts) who claims to be an Interpol agent assigned to protect her. Jeff Fahey is her publisher fiancé. It was shot in Venezuela (not Africa), and the video box makes you think it's like *Cliffhanger* (which it isn't). A USA cable debut.

FREEJACK

(Warner, 1992) **D:** Geoff Murphy **S/P:** Ronald
Shussett **S:** Steven Pressfield **P:** Stuart Oken

Emilio Estevez plays a race-car driver who crashes and is somehow transported to New York City in 2009. His body is to be taken over by a rich, dying man during "psychic surgery." It's a *Blade Runner*–look movie filled with car crashes, shootouts, and old ideas. Mick Jagger (in his first role since *Ned Kelly*) is Vacendak, a grim-faced bounty hunter out to capture Estevez. Anthony Hopkins shows up once in a while on a TV screen. Rene Russo and David Johansen are characters from 1991 who somehow haven't aged at all in 20 years. With Jonathan Banks, John Shea, Vincent Schiavelli, Esai Morales, Jerry Hall (Jagger's real-life wife) as a TV reporter, and Amanda Plummer as a comic nun with a gun. There's a computer-animated ending with a theme by John Lydon. Loosely based on a novel by Robert Shekley, it was made in Atlanta by the New Zealand–born director of *Uta* and *The Quiet Earth* (who, you might say, sold out with this and *Young Guns II*). New York audiences even laughed at the trailer.

FREE RIDE
(IVE, 1985) **D:** Tom Trbovich **S:** Ronald Z. Wang, Lee Fulkerson **P:** Tom Boutross   (*Boarding School*)

Teens borrow a car with mob money in it. This prep-school comedy stars Gary Herschberger (later on *Twin Peaks*). With Peter DeLuise, Frank Campanella as a gangster, Warren Berlinger, Dawn Schneider, Tally Channel, and porno star Krista Lane. Mamie Van Doren, in her only post-60s film, is the head nurse at Monroe College. Her husband, the dean (Brian MacGregor), is named Dean Stockwell. Moustapha Akkad was the executive producer.

FREEWAY
(Starmaker, 1988) **D/S:** Francis Delia **S:** Darrell Fetty **P:** Peter S. Davis, William Panzer

Exploiting headlines about real 1987 shootings on the LA Freeway was a natural idea, so New World did it. A nurse (Darlanne Fluegel) wants to find the man who killed her husband. James Russo is a bounty hunter, Richard Belzer is a radio-talk-show host, and Billy Drago is a psycho, Bible-quoting ex-priest waiting for Armageddon who calls the show. With Michael Callan, Kenneth Tobey, and Clint Howard. Delia had done exceptional videos for Wall of Voodoo ("Mexican Radio") and the Ramones ("Psychotherapy").

FREEWAY MANIAC
(Media, 1987) **D/S/P:** Paul Winters **S:** Gahan Wilson

Despite the then-topical title, this is a parody about a mad killer who escapes from an asylum and ends up on the set of a low-budget science-fiction movie in the desert. Loren Winters stars.

FREE, WHITE, AND 21
(All Season, 1962) **D/S/E:** Larry Buchanan **S/P:** "Hal Dwain"/Harold Hoffman **S:** Cliff Pope

Greta (Annalena Lund), a 22-year-old blonde from Stockholm who worked with CORE to help integrate the South, accuses Ernest Jones (Frederick O'Neal), a black Dallas businessman, of rape. In court, testimony is given, and we see her flashbacks, then his flashbacks, of what happened. He admits to having sex with her but says that she consented. In one scene she does the hobo twist in an all-black club while Joe Johnson and his orchestra play. After the closing statements, all you see for a long time is a ticking clock (this is when ushers handed out cards in the theater so that the audience could vote). Buchanan said that when the clock was shown at drive-ins, people threw things at the screen. The acting is good, especially by O'Neal (who had been in the all-black version of *Anna Lucasta* (1958) and was later in *Cotton Comes to Harlem*). It's all handled very tastefully and has a nice, unexpected ending. It was made in a Dallas studio, reportedly for $35,000, and was very profitable for AIP. The b/w print is excellent.

The cast includes Bill McGhee (from *Don't Look in the Basement*). Buchanan directed *Under Age*, another courtroom drama, next.

FREEZE BOMB: *See* DEATH DIMENSION

THE FRENCH LINE
(Turner, 1954) **D:** Lloyd Bacon **S:** Mary Loos, Richard Sale **P:** Edmund Grainger

Jane Russell stars in this 3-D musical hit as a Texas oil heiress who sails to Paris (it was all shot in the studio). Incredibly, this film from Howard Hughes' RKO was denied an MPAA seal of approval and was censored in some towns. Maybe it was the ads: "J.R. in 3-D. It'll knock both your eyes out!" With Gilbert Roland, Mary McCarty, Arthur Hunnicutt, Paula Corday, and Craig Stevens.

FRENCHMAN'S FARM
(Magnum, 1986) **D/S:** Ron Way **S/P:** Larry Fishburn, Matt White   Australia (*Frenchman's Death Farm*)

A college student drives on a back road to avoid brushfires. She sees a 1944 decapitation murder happen. The ghost of an executioner is guarding a treasure. Ray Barrett and Norman Kaye star.

THE FRENCH REVOLUTION
(1989) **D/S:** Robert Enrico, Richard Heffron **S:** David Ambrose, Daniel Boulanger **P:** Alexandre Mnouchkine   France/W. Germany/Italy/Canada

This epic, a 2-part 337-minute miniseries, cost a whopping $50 million and was never shown in the US. Christopher Lee is the chief executioner, miniseries queen Jane Seymour is Marie Antoinette, and Klaus Maria Brandauer is Danton. Peter Ustinov, Sam Neill, Claudia Cardinale, and many, many others are also in the cast.

FRESH AIR: *See* NAUGHTY STEWARDESSES

FRESH KILL
(City Lights, 1987) **D/S/P:** Joseph Merhi **P:** Richard Pepin

A would-be Hollywood actor working in a meat market becomes involved with gangsters, drugs, and revenge, in this violent, senseless movie. With Robert Z'Dar.

FRESH LIVE CREAM
(Polydor, 1993) **D/P:** Martin Baker **P:** Jenne Baker

This 75-minute documentary combines new interviews with members of the short-lived 60s "supergroup" Cream and footage from their 1967–68 performances (mostly live). While their legendary jamming on blues classics seems boring and plodding, some lesser-known originals sound great (especially "We're Going Wrong"). During the interviews, the still-famous Eric Clapton seems pretty humorless, and drummer Ginger Baker is the most egotistical but the most fun to watch. Lead singer and writer Jack Bruce (who's gained a

lot of weight) is the forgotten talent of the group. They're all embarrassed by the comic clip of them lip-syncing to "Anyone for Tennis" on American TV. Some of the live footage is from an easy-to-find tape, *The Farewell Concert*. We also see a pre-Cream Baker in *Gonks Go Beat*!

FRIDAY FOSTER
(Orion, 1975) **D/P:** Arthur Marks **S:** Orville Hampton

Pam Grier is Friday Foster, a fashion photographer (the character is based on a syndicated comic strip). This was a change from the sex-and-violence mov-ies she had starred in, and it failed at the box office. Yaphet Kotto is her private-detective boyfriend, Thalmus Rasulala is a billionaire targeted for an assassination, Godfrey Cambridge is a gay dress designer, and Jim Backus is a racist villain. With Eartha Kitt, Scatman Crothers, Ted Lange, Carl Weathers, and Jack Baker. Marks (son of Groucho Marx) also directed Grier in *Bucktown*. It was released by AIP.

FRIDAY THE 13TH: THE FINAL CHAPTER
(Paramount, 1984) **D:** Joseph Zito **S:** Barney Cohen **P:** Frank Mancuso

There were more victims but less blood in the 4th movie in this money-making slasher series. It made more money than the previous three and featured some actors who actually had careers. With Crispin Glover (!) as Jimmy, Kimberly Beck, Corey Feldman as Tommy (the kid who kills Jason), Judie Aronson, Joan Freeman (*Panic in the Year Zero*), Peter Barton (from *The Young and the Restless*), twins Camilla and Carey More, and Ted White as Jason. Tom Savini provided the FX, and one character is a monster-makeup fanatic. Despite the hopeful title there were many more in the series.

FRIDAY THE 13TH, PART V: A NEW BEGINNING
(Paramount, 1985) **D:** Danny Steinmann **S:** Martin Kitrosser **P:** Timothy Silver

This had even less blood than *The Final Chapter*, to avoid rating problems (and save money). John Shepard stars as the now-teen Tommy (played by Corey Feldman in flashbacks). He's released from a mental hospital and seems to have "become" Jason (who is played by Dick Wieand). With Juliette Cummins and Deborah Vorhees.

FRIDAY THE 13TH, PART VI: JASON LIVES
(Paramount, 1986) **D/S:** Tom McLoughlin **P:** Don Behrns

Offscreen killings are the best this diluted entry can offer. The director was a former mime who directed *Date with an Angel* next. Ron Palillo and a friend dig up a grave. Lightning revives "maggothead" Jason (C. J. Graham). Thom Mathews as Tommy Jarvis (a survivor from the last time) and the sheriff's daughter (Jennifer Cooke) are the main characters. This has more intentional humor, in-jokes, and an Alice Cooper theme, "He's Back." *Friday the 13th*, an unrelated syndicated TV series (also from Paramount), debuted in 1987 and lasted until 1990.

Pam Grier stars in *Friday Foster*.

FRIDAY THE 13TH, PART VII: THE NEW BLOOD

(Paramount, 1988) **D:** John Carl Buechler
S: Daryl Haney **P:** Lain Paterso

A telekinetic girl (Lar Park Lincoln) goes to Crystal Lake with her mother and her irritating shrink (Terry Kiser). She accidentally releases Jason from his watery grave, and they have a confrontation at the end. Other characters are killed off. It starts with film clips of death scenes from the first 6 movies. Jason (Kane Hodder) has his hockey mask off this time. With Elizabeth Kaiten and Heidi Kozak. The director is a makeup expert.

FRIDAY THE 13TH, PART VIII: JASON TAKES MANHATTAN

(Paramount, 1989) **D/S:** Rob Hedden
P: Randolph Cheveldave

They just kept getting worse. A cheat ad campaign made people think it took place in a horrifying midtown Manhattan. It's actually set on a cruise ship taking high-school grads to NYC. The subway scenes were filmed in Canada. Most of the characters are killed before the boat docks. One kid videotapes everything. With Jensen Daggett, Scott Reeves (from *The Young and the Restless*), and Kane Hodder as Jason again, this time revived by

an electric current. It was the lowest-grossing of the series but was followed by yet another one, *Jason Goes to Hell: The Final Friday*.

FRIGID WIFE

(SW, 1962) **D:** Paul Landres, Ben Parker
S/P: "John Kenlo"/Julius Weinstein **S:** Sam Roeca, George Wallace Sayre **P:** David Diamond

A doctor introduces several patients who have flashbacks about emotional disorders and impotence. This was made by Parker and "Kenlo." Then the real story begins. It was originally a 1950 Monogram movie called *Modern Marriage*. A newlywed (Margaret Field) runs away from her husband (Robert Clarke) on their wedding night and attempts suicide. She goes to a rest home and has a flashback to the 40s. This is followed by her husband's flashback, then her mother's (!) flashback. Reed Hadley (with his little mustache) plays a doctor. Clarke and Field (Sally's mother, known as Maggie Mahoney after she married actor Jock Mahoney) were also in *The Man from Planet X* (1951). Landres later directed *The Vampire* (1957) and *The Return of Dracula* (1958).

FRIGHT HOUSE

(Studio Entertainment, 1989) **D/S/P:** Len Anthony

Al Lewis (living off his Grandpa role from *The Munsters*) hosts this paste-up double-bill video. *Fright House* is about witches. In *Abandon*, a woman never ages. With Duane Jones and Jennifer Delora.

FRIGHTMARE

(Vestron, 1981) **D/S:** Norman T. Vane
P: Patrick Wright, Tallie Wright
(*The Horror Star; Upon a Frightmare*)

Members of a teen horror-film society kidnap the body of Conrad Ragzoff (Ferdy Mayne), an actor who starred in horror movies. His widow holds a séance, and the reanimated corpse kills off the obnoxious kids in an old house. It's a good idea but a bad movie. With Luca Bercovici, Nita Talbot, Jeffrey Combs, and Leon Askin.

FRIGHTMARE II = FRIGHTMARE (1974)

FRIGHT NIGHT

(RCA/Columbia, 1985) **D/S:** Tom Holland **P:** Herb Jaffe

Vampire Chris Sarandon and some followers move in next door to a teen (William Ragsdale) who tries to warn people in vain. Roddy McDowall as TV-horror-movie host Peter Vincent believes him and becomes a real-life Van Helsing type. The overacting but memorable Stephen Geoffreys is his friend Evil Ed, who becomes a vampire. With Amanda Bearse (later a regular on *Married . . . with Children*), who becomes a sexy vampire, and Heidi Sorenson. The first movie directed by the writer of *The Beast Within* and *Psycho II* has some good FX (by Steve Johnson) and includes clips from *Scars of Dracula* and *Octaman* (and a scene from *Children Shouldn't Play with Dead Things*, later cut out). The TV studio is the old Monogram studio. It was a hit, and a sequel followed. The soundtrack, featuring various artists, is on CBA.

FRIGHT NIGHT PART II

(IVE, 1988) **D/S:** Tommy Lee Wallace
S: Tim Metcalfe, Miguel Tejada-Flores
P: Herb Jaffe, Mort Engelberg

Roddy McDowall and William Ragsdale return as vampire hunters in a sequel that played in theaters after its video release. The vampires include a gay black guy and a muscleman. The Gene Warren FX borrowed some Chinese ideas (like bugs and maggots from bodies). With Julie Carmen as the vampire sister of the vampire from the first movie, Traci Lin, Brian Thompson, and Merritt Butrick.

FRITZ THE CAT

(1972) **D/S:** Ralph Bakshi **P:** Steve Krantz

Cinemation released the first X-rated cartoon feature, then AIP picked it up. Based on the 60s underground comic strip by R. Crumb (who did not like the results), it takes place in the East Village, Harlem, and LA, and features pigs as cops, crows as blacks, Hell's Angels, sex, drugs, and revolution. The music includes hits by Bo Diddley, Billie Holiday, and others. Bakshi had worked on Terrytoons and did the "new" *Mighty Mouse* TV cartoons in the 80s. A sequel, *The Nine Lives of Fritz the Cat*, was by another director.

FROGTOWN II

(York, 1994) **D/C:** Donald Jackson **P:** Scott Pfeiffer

Robert Z'Dar is a bad substitute for Roddy Piper as Sam Hell in this PG-13 sequel that has little of the charm of the original, *Hell Comes to Frogtown*. He and Denice Duff (from the *Subspecies* sequels) are sent by the Texas rocketeer captain (Charles Napier) to rescue Lou Ferrigno, who spends most of the movie lying around turning green. With Brion James (using his cartoon voice in two roles), Don Stroud, and Rhonda Shear. It's got bad puppets, dumb songs, a lame western-town setting, and a waste of the *Rocketeer*-inspired flying concept.

FROM BEYOND

(Vestron, 1986) **D/S:** Stuart Gordon
S: Dennis Paoli **S/P:** Brian Yuzna

After the gross-out hit *Re-Animator*, Gordon reassembled some of the same cast for another wild movie "based on Lovecraft." It's a daring mixture of horror, science fiction, and S&M sex. A "sonic resonator" is created by the brilliant and deranged Dr. Pretorious (Ted Sorel), who wants "to see more than any man has ever seen." He unleashes 4-D demons and becomes a mutated creature who can be seen only by someone who has developed a "third eye." Jeffrey Combs has one, a pineal gland sticking out of his forehead. With the very sexy Barbara Crampton, Ken Foree, and Carolyn Purdy-Gordon. Parts of the film are amazing, but some of the special effects are shown too long and look kind of rubbery. It was shot in Rome and cut for an R rating in the US. The Richard Band soundtrack is on Enigma.

FROM HELL TO VICTORY

(UAV, 1979) **D/S:** "Hank Milestone"/ Umberto Lenzi
S: Gianfranco Clerici, Anthony Fritz, José Luis Martínez
Italy/France/Spain (*Contro Quattro Bandieri*)

Fright Night

Old friends from various countries meet once a year in Paris. In 1939 they're torn apart by WWII. George Peppard stars in this PG film, made up of 6 individual segments showing the experiences of the main characters. With George Hamilton, Horst Buchholz, Capucine, Howard Vernon as an SS officer, Sam Wanamaker, Jean-Pierre Cassel, Raymond Lovelock, and Anny Duperey.

FROM THE DEAD OF NIGHT

(AIP, 1989) **D:** Paul Wendkos **S:** William Bleich

Lindsay Wagner is a fashion designer who drowns, floats through a tunnel of light (this entire sequence is shown twice), then revived. In Mexico, on the Day of the Dead, death figures appear to her, and people around her start to die. Back in LA she joins an encounter group and learns about the "walkers" (the name of the Gary Brandner novel this is based on), who are trying to finish her off. This NBC-TV miniseries is too long (200 minutes) but has some good moments, including a body in the morgue coming to life and a zombie kid on a skateboard. There's also a love triangle. With Bruce Boxleitner, Robin Thomas, Robert Prosky, Merritt Butrick (who died the year this was shown), and Diahann Carroll.

FRONTIER HELLCAT

(VSOM, 1964) **D:** Alfred Vohrer **S:** Eberhard Keinhard, Johannes Sibelius **P:** Horst Wendlandt
W. Germany/Italy/France/Yugoslavia
(*Unter Geiern; Among Vultures*)

Stewart Granger is Old Surehand (replacing usual series star Lex Barker) in this western, part of a series based on novels by the 19th-century German writer Karl May. The Vultures, a gang of robbers, disguise themselves as Indians and kidnap Elke Sommer. Pierre Brice is Winnetou the Indian, as usual, and Terence Hill has a small part. Most of the cast returned in *Rampage at Apache Wells*, and Granger was also in *Flaming Frontier*.

FROSTBITER: WRATH OF WENDIGO

(1991) **D/S/P:** Tom Chaney

Hunters unleash a demon (an animated reindeer) on a northern Michigan island. Ron Asheton (from the Stooges!) is a doctor on a hunting trip. There's a rock soundtrack and a comic-book version of this *Evil Dead* copy.

FROZEN SCREAM

(Platinum, 1980) **D:** Frank Roach **S:** Doug Ferrin, Michael Soney, Celeste Hammond **P/A:** Rene Harmon

A doctor and his nurse (Harmon) freeze people and turn them into zombies. Voiceovers try to make sense of it all. Harmon also produced *The Execution, Part II*.

FROZEN TERROR

(Vestron, 1980) **D/S:** Lamberto Bava
S: Pupi Avati, Roberto Gandus **P:** Gianni Minervi, Antonio Avati   Italy (*Macabro*)

A girl sees her mother (Bernice Stegers) having sex, so she tries to drown her brother in the bathtub. On the way to the hospital the car crashes, and the mother's lover is decapitated. The mother ends up in a mental ward. Later she's released, but she's obsessed with the head of her lover, which she keeps in the freezer but takes to bed at night. Her psychotic daughter bothers her too. The first film by Mario Bava's son is "based on a true story" and is set in New Orleans. You won't believe the ending.

FRUITS OF PASSION: *See* THE STORY OF O, Part II

FRUSTRATION: *See* THE DIVORCEE

FTA

(1972) **D/P:** Francine Parker **S:** Robin Menken, Michael Alimo, Rita Martinson, Holly Near, Len Chandler, Pamela Donegan, Dalton Trumbo
S/P/A: Jane Fonda, Donald Sutherland

AIP released this period-piece documentary, which very few people saw. Fonda and Sutherland (who lived together at the time) and Holly Near went to towns near Army bases presenting an anti–Vietnam War show called *Free* (or *Fuck*) *the Army*. Fonda and her IPC (Indochina Peace Campaign) company produced the film. The same year Fonda was in Godard's *Tout Va Bien*. She and Sutherland returned in *Steelyard Blues* (1973).

FUEGO

(1968) **D/S/P/A:** Amando Bo   Argentina

Isabel Sarli (who is incredible) stars as the insatiable Laura in this crazed South American sex movie, which did good business in the US. She marries a rich man but ends up in bed with other men, like the phone repairman. She goes to a shrink, decides it's all hopeless, and drives her car over a cliff. The theme song, "Fuego" (fire), is heard during scenes like the one where she reveals that she's wearing only a fur coat in the snow. This is probably the first X-rated movie I ever saw (at the Westwood Art Theatre, in Lakewood, Ohio). Bo also directed Sarli in *Put Up or Shut Up* (1959), *Heat* (1960), *Woman and Temptation* (1966), *Mohair* (1967), and *Tropical Extasy* (1970).

FUGITIVE GIRLS

(VEC, 1973) **D/P:** "A. C. Stevens"/Stephen C. Apostolof **S/A:** Ed Wood Jr.   (*Five Loose Women; Hot on the Trail; Women's Penitentiary VIII*)

Cult figure Ed Wood Jr. (a forgotten man at the time) worked (often uncredited) on nudie films made by Stevens. He wrote this one and appears as Pop, who runs a remote gas station, and as a sheriff. The film was rated X and has soft-core sex scenes. An R-rated, softer version is called *Five Loose Women*. After a sex scene with badly dubbed-in "Oooh, aah, ooh, aah," the guy (with long thick sideburns) decides to hold up a liquor store, shoots the owner, and leaves the clichéd women's-prison-movie victim/star (Jabie Abercrombie) to take the rap. Her cellmates at the minimum- security work farm are nudie star Rene Bond as a bank embezzler with a thick southern accent ("There's only two things worthwhile for a girl—men and money!"), Cap, a manic, short-haired dyke who killed her husband ("His mistake was, he turned me on to women, and I dug it!"), and a black woman (Donna Desmond) who trades insults with the southerner ("dirty white trash!"). Cap says, "I'm getting sick and tired of this rainbow trip!" After she forces Dee into a long lesbian scene, they all escape and stay with organic hippies in the woods until Cap says, "They all smell like freaks!" A hippie says, "Good Christ, a lesbian!" and a chain fight starts. In a scene Ed borrowed from his script for *The Violent Years* (1956) the women steal a guy's car and rape him ("Leave me alone!"). They also ambush some bikers, fight them using martial arts, then take over the home of a paralyzed Nam vet. *Fugitive Girls* has a funny, recurring Hammond-organ theme and enough Wood touches to make it a must for his fans, who can't get enough (he was the assistant director). The cast includes Foreman Shane.

FULL CONTACT

(VSOM, 1992) **D/P:** Ringo Lam **S:** Nam Yin   Hong Kong

Chow Yun Fat stars as a nightclub bouncer who gets mixed up with a gang of Thai killers. Ann Bridgewater is his dancer girlfriend, and Simon Yam is the gay ganglord in Bangkok.

FULL ECLIPSE

(HBO, 1993) **D:** Anthony Hickox **S:** Richard Christian Matheson Jr., Michael Reaves **P:** Peter Abrams, Robert Levy

After a John Woo–style shootout in a club, a cop who was shot (Anthony Michael Denison) is revived as a supercop ("Dirty Harry on crack"). It turns out that Garou (Bruce Payne) is an ageless werewolf who uses injections to turn other cops into members of his vigilante crime-fighting "pack." Top-billed Mario Van Peebles is tricked into joining them by Patsy Kensit. They all mutate, with beast faces and long claws that come out of their knuckles (a bad idea), and go into a frenzy while killing lots of criminals. This is pretty good for a TV horror movie. R and unrated versions are available.

Vincent D'Onofrio as "Gomer" Pyle and Lee Ermey in Stanley Kubrick's *Full Metal Jacket*.

FULL FATHOM FIVE

(MGM/UA, 1990) **D/A:** Carl Franklin **S:** Bart Davis **P:** Luis Llosa

Just what we needed from Roger Corman—a cheap, boring, dated, PG-rated ripoff of *The Hunt for Red October* set just before the invasion of Panama. Michael Moriarty, as a US submarine captain, gets to play the piano and sing, and even seduce a Panamanian rebel (Maria Rangel). Rebels capture a Soviet nuclear submarine and assign a Cuban captain, who decides to sink a Saudi tanker and announces that he'll destroy Houston. Moriarty must have been happy to be in a successful (and good) TV series (*Law And Order*) after this. It was made in Peru.

FULL METAL JACKET

(Warner, 1987) **D/S/P:** Stanley Kubrick **S:** Michael Herr, Gustav Hasford   UK

Kubrick's first film since *The Shining* is a major antiwar movie (and it includes the ultimate use of "Surfin' Bird"!). Matthew Modine stars and narrates as Private Joker, who becomes a *Stars and Stripes* reporter in Vietnam. The incredible first 44 minutes take place at a basic-training camp, with Lee Ermey as the gunnery sergeant and Vincent D'Onofrio as big, bald Private "Gomer" Pyle. If you want to know what military training is like, look at this movie. The second part takes place in Nam and features the earth-shattering, complete "Papa Oom Mow Mow" end of the Trashmen's classic. With Adam Baldwin as Animal Mother and Arliss Howard. In real life Ermey was a Marine drill instructor who served in Vietnam. It was all filmed in England, using lots of 360-degree camera panning. The production design is by Anton Furst. It's based on *The Short Timers*, by the late Gustav Hasford.

FUN

(1994) **D/P:** Rafal Zielinski **S:** James Bosley

Alicia Witt and Renee Humphrey are California teens who meet on the road and commit a senseless murder. The story is told from the juvenile-detention center. This serious color and b/w film, by the Polish-born director of teen comedies like *Screwballs* and *Spellcaster*, is based on a play.

FUNERAL HOME

(Paragon, 1980) **D/P:** William Fruet **S:** Ida Nelson   Canada (*Cries in the Night*)

A teen (Lesleh Donaldson) goes to stay with her nice but disturbed grandmother (Kay Hawtrey) at her hotel (formerly a funeral home). People begin to disappear. Barry Morse costars in this PG-rated MPM release.

FUNLAND

(Vestron, 1987) **D/S:** William Vanderkloot **S:** Bonnie Turner, Terry Turner **P:** Michael A. Simpson

David Lander (from *Laverne and Shirley*) stars in this offbeat PG-13 action comedy about an amusement park. William Windom is a clown who fights against the new mob owners. With Robert Sacchi and Jan Hooks. It was scripted by *Saturday Night Live* writers.

THE FUNNIEST SHOW ON EARTH

(1954) **D/S:** Mario Mattoli **P:** Carlo Ponti, Dino De Laurentiis   Italy (*Il Piu Comico Spettacolo del Mondo*)

Popular comedian Toto stars in a spoof of Cecil B. De Mille's then-new *The Greatest Show on Earth*. With Marc Lawrence, May Britt, and Anthony Quinn and Silvana Mangano in bit parts.

THE FUNNY MAN

(1994) **D/S:** Simon Sprackling **P:** Nigel Odell   UK

Tim James stars as an athletic, wisecracking, supernatural killer, in this low-budget horror comedy set in a haunted house. The house is won from Christopher Lee in a poker game. With Benny Young and Paula Chan. It's an expanded version of a short called *Hand of Fate*. The filmmakers are former members of a punk band, and the impressive FX are by Neill Gordon (*Nightbreed*).

THE FURTHER ADVENTURES OF TENNESSEE BUCK

(Media, 1987) **D/A**: David Keith **S**: Barry Jocobs, Stuart Jacobs **P**: Gideon Amir

David Keith stars as Buck Malone in this R-rated *Raiders of the Lost Ark* copy set in Borneo. He's an alcoholic no-good, but women can't keep away from him. Kathy Shower (from *Playboy*) costars, with Sydney Lassick. There are cannibals, gore, naked native women, and lots of racist and sexist jokes. It was shot in Sri Lanka.

FURY

(MGM, 1936) **D**: Fritz Lang **S**: Bartlett Cormack **P**: Joseph L. Mankiewicz

One day in 1933, after making *The Testament of Dr. Mabuse* (which the Nazis banned), Fritz Lang was summoned by Propaganda Minister Josef Goebbels and told that Hitler wanted him to head UFA and make Nazi films. That evening Lang fled to France. Spencer Tracy stars in Lang's first American film, as a man wrongly arrested in a small Illinois town for a kidnapping. An angry crowd sets fire to his jail cell. The bitter man survives but hides, pretending to be dead, so that the townspeople can be tried for his death. It was a strong start for Lang's new career in exile. Sylvia Sidney costars as Tracy's fiancée, with Bruce Cabot, Walter Abel, Edward Ellis, and Walter Brennan. Sidney returned in Lang's *You Only Live Once* (1937) and *You and Me* (1938).

THE FURY OF HERCULES

(Sinister, 1961) **D**: Gianfranco Parolini **S**: P. Parloni, Giorgio C. Simonelli   Italy/France (*La Furia di Ercole*)

Brad Harris stars as superstrong Hercules, with Brigitte Corey, Alan Steele, and the late Serge Gainsbourg.

FUTURE FORCE

(AIP, 1989) **D/S**: David A. Prior **P**: Kimberly Case

John Tucker (David Carradine) is an LA bounty hunter working with COPS (Civilian Operated Police Systems) in the near future. He communicates with a crippled guy on his car monitor. Corporate villains put a price on his head and send out the late Robert Tessier to kill him. After a lot of driving around, the best part is a junkyard shootout, followed by a punchout battle with big, bald Tessier. Carradine makes his remote-controlled bionic hand (copied from the movie *The Glove*) fly through the air to punch and choke the unstoppable villain. With William Zipp and Dawn Wildsmith. Carradine and his wife, Gail Jenson, were the associate producers.

FUTURE HUNTERS

(Vestron, 1986) **D**: Cirio H. Santiago **S**: J. L. Thompson **P**: Anthony Maharaj Philippines (*The Spear of Destiny*)

Richard Norton is a warrior from 2025, who travels back to the present to find a spear "that killed Jesus." He saves Robert Patrick (later in *Terminator II*) and Linda Carol from bikers, but is killed, so they take up the spear and battle the bad guys. With kung fu, explosions, pygmies, Amazon women, and Mongols. It's a bad mixture of *Mad Max, Indiana Jones,* and many others. With Bruce Li.

FUTURE KICK

(Concorde, 1990) **D/S**: Damian Klaus **P**: Roger Corman

Don "the Dragon" Wilson is a kickboxing cyborg bounty hunter ("All you get from feelings is dead") in the future. Meg Foster is a wealthy housewife on the Moon who goes to LA to investigate the death of her husband. Ed Lottimer is Heinz, a killer who uses a triple knife to cut out his victims' organs. Christopher Penn turns out to be a machine. There are some surprising decapitations, an exploding head, and strippers hanging on poles in a topless bar (just like in a dozen other recent Corman productions). Parts of the plot copy *Total Recall*, the strip scenes were lifted from *Stripped to Kill II*, and it all turns out to be a dream (!).

FUTURE KILL

(Vestron, 1984) **D/S**: Ronald W. Moore **P**: Greg Unterberger, John H. Best

The best thing about this science-fiction/action movie made in Dallas was the poster by Giger. In the future, some frat teens break into mutant territory to rescue their leader. Two *Texas Chainsaw Massacre* stars are in the cast, Marilyn Burns and Ed Neal as a burned mutant in a metal mask called Splatter. He has an altered voice and steel claws. The director was 25.

FUTURE SCHLOCK

(1984) **D/S/P**: Barry Peak, Chris Kiely   Australia

Conservatives put nonconformists into a walled-up ghetto in the post-nuke 21st century. This comedy stars Maryanne Fahey and Michael Bishop.

FUTURE SHOCK

(Hemdale, 1993) **D/S**: Oley Sassone, Matt Reeves **D/S/A**: Vivian Schilling **D/P/A**: Eric Parkinson

This anthology is similar to *Terror Eyes*, in that Vivian Schilling wrote her own segment and the other two are by UCLA students. Despite the very misleading video box, it's worth seeing, if only for Sassone's comedy "The Roommate" (made in 1988), starring Bill Paxton, in top form as a smiling, ponytailed con man who moves in with a morgue attendant (Scott Thompson). It's letter-boxed (!) and also features James Karen and Rick Rossovich. In "Jenny Porter," Schilling has nightmares and paranoid visions in a high-security house. Brion James and Sydney Lassick appear, and scenes from *Howling II* and *Return of the Living Dead* are on TV. "Mr. Petrified Forest," by Reeves, is a comic tale about a photographer (Sam

Clay) who worries about earthquakes and imagines different deaths. Amanda Foreman costars. In the framing sequences a shrink (Martin Kovel) hears the tales from his patients. Julie Strain plays a stripper in the stupid intro. It's available in unrated and PG-13 versions.

FUTURE WOMAN

(Sinister, 1968) **D**: Jesús Franco **S/P**: Harry Alan Towers   Spain/W. Germany/USA (*La Ciudad Sin Hombres; Rio 70; The Girl from Rio*)

Shirley Eaton stars and gets to wear many strange plastic outfits as the evil man-hating Sumuro (or Sumitra) in a sequel to *The Million Eyes of Su-Muru* (1967). The Spanish detective hero (Richard Wyler) is hired by a rich banker (Walter Rilla) to go to the Amazon and rescue his daughter. With George Sanders torturing Maria Rohm. It was shot in Brazil and Spain, and AIP released a cut version direct to TV in America. Both features were loosely based on Sax Rohmer novels.

FUTURE ZONE

(AIP, 1989) **D/S**: David A. Prior **P**: David Winters, Gail Jenson   (*Future Force II*)

Ted Prior is the son of the COPS bounty hunter played by David Carradine in *Future Force*. He arrives from the future to save his own parents (or something like that). Charles Napier is the police-captain corporate villain. Carradine lives with his (real-life) wife, Gail Jenson, in a small suburban house. He wipes out drug dealers ("You have a right to die"), battles a whole gang with two guns, and puts on his bionic hand when things get really rough. The car wrecks are good, and Carradine seems to be having a good time with the role.

F/X

(HBO, 1986) **D**: Robert Mandel **S**: Robert T. Megginson, Gregory Fleeman **P**: Dodi Fayed, Jack Weiner

There's a conspiracy plot and good New York City action in this movie about a special-effects expert (Bryan Brown) who's hired by the Justice Department to fake the death of a government-witness mobster (Jerry Orbach). Since he works on horror movies, there's Carl Fullerton makeup and *I Dismember Mama* jokes. Brian Dennehy costars as a cop. With Cliff De Young, Trey Wilson, Tom Noonan, Diane Venora, Angela Bassett, and Mason Adams. The movie did well on tape.

F/X 2: THE DEADLY ART OF ILLUSION

(Orion, 1991) **D**: Richard Franklin **S**: Bill Condon **P**: Dodi Weiner, Jack Weiner

This tamer (PG-13) retread/sequel has more comedy and lots of plot turns. There's a complex conspiracy involving the Vatican, New York City police, psycho killers, and major corporations. Bryan Brown as the FX-expert hero and Brian Dennehy as a cop return. With Rachel Ticotin, Joanna Gleason, Philip Bosco, Kevin J. O'Connor, and James Stacy as a cyborg. There's a robot clown.

GABRIEL OVER THE WHITE HOUSE

(MGM, 1933) **D:** Gregory La Cava
S: Carey Wilson **P:** Walter Wanger

Do not miss this amazing political fantasy, released at the height of the Depression. Walter Huston stars as Judson E. Hammond, an uninvolved, uninformed, corrupt, do-nothing bachelor president. After he suffers a near-fatal concussion, a heavenly presence takes over. The divinely inspired leader initiates Roosevelt-type emergency measures to help the American people, declares martial law and vows to have gangsters (including his former cronies) shot by firing squad, collects foreign debts, and gathers world leaders (including Germans and Japanese) to witness a show of force meant to convince them not to start wars. Franchot Tone is the president's secretary, and Karen Morley is his mistress. With Dickie Moore (from the Our Gang comedies), C. Henry Gordon, Mischa Auer, and Akim Tamiroff. Not a typical MGM feature (it was backed by William Randolph Hearst), it was based on a novel.

GABRIELLA

(SW, 1970) **D:** Mack Bing **S/P/A:** Jack Mattis **P/M:** Louis Yule Brown

This peace-and-love movie about "the bullshit this society puts you through" features full nudity, softcore sex, and lame light rock. First we see how hateful the out-of-it parents of young Gabriella (Gabrielle Caron) are. Then a friendly couple making a sex documentary chose Gabriella and her boyfriend to "be themselves" for the camera. This means sex in a Garden of Eden setting, which is contrasted with scenes of hate, racism, and war. Then the people of the world (or at least the ones on some block in LA) are freed to dance naked and make love in the streets. Also with a slo-mo topless dancer, an onstage sex show, an interview with a gay man (Mattis), and a funk band at Gazzarri's. Producer Brown usually did the music for Jerry Lewis movies!

GALACTIC GIGOLO

(Tempe, 1987) **D/P/C:** Gorman Bechard
S/A: Carmine Capobianco **P:** Kris Covello   (Club Earth)

Carmine Capobianco is an alien broccoli who arrives in Prospect, Connecticut, disguised as Elvis and uses hypnotic powers to seduce local women. Husbands fight back, and Italian mobsters want him to join the mob. This comedy features naked women. With Debi Thibeault and Ruth Collins.

THE GALAXY INVADER

(VCI, 1985) **D/S/E:** Don Dohler

An alien with a laser weapon lands on earth and is stalked by a group of rednecks. This PG film was shot on video in Baltimore and stars Richard Ruxton, Don Leifert, George Stover, and Dohler's relatives and neighbors.

GALAXY OF DINOSAURS

(CVH, 1992) **D/C:** Lance Randas
S: Jon Killough **P:** J. R. Bookwalter

If you've ever wanted to see James K. Shea's *Planet of the Dinosaurs* (1978) here's your chance. Bookwalter used all of that film's excellent animated dinosaur footage and shot new stuff as cheaply as possible on video in some woods in Mogadore, Ohio. Five human "aliens" with no costumes or anything materialize and walk around. They try to interact with and react to the older footage, get high from mushrooms, and meet a cave man who says "Ug." The comic fat guy faints, pukes, and eats a dinosaur, the black guy turns out to be gay, and the end rips off *Planet of the Apes.*

GALLERY OF HORROR = DR. TERROR'S GALLERY OF HORROR

THE GAMBLER AND THE LADY

(1953) **D:** Patrick Jenkins, Sam Newfield **P:** Anthony Hinds   UK

Dane Clark plays an American gambler who falls in love and tries to reform in England. Kathleen Byron and Naomi Chance costar. Lippert added new scenes to the Hammer film for the US release.

GAMBLING WITH SOULS

(Video Dimensions, 1936) **D:** Elmer Clifton
S/P: J. D. Kennis

A young blonde marries a hardworking student and turns to prostitution for extra income. There's a cat fight and lots of women in their underwear. Tragedy follows. Scenes from this 68-minute road-show hit were later used in *Teenage* (1944).

THE GAME

(TWE, 1982) **D:** Bill Rebane **S:** Larry Dreyfus, William Arthur **P:** Alan Rainier, Barbara Rebane

Bored millionaires bring people to an isolated resort and try to scare them away. Whoever stays gets a million dollars. They start dying, though (shot, hanged, eaten by rats), and we're supposed to figure out who the killer is. Could it be the scarred hunchback? There's a clip from *Giant Spider Invasion*, which (like this) was made in Wisconsin.

THE GAME

(1988) **D:** Cole McKay **S:** Peter Summers **P:** Tom B. Jenssen

Joseph Campanella stars in another *Most Dangerous Game* copy. He infiltrates a group of rich killers to avenge the death of his family. With Craig Alan and Tadashi Yamashita.

GAMERA VS. BARUGAN = WAR OF THE MONSTERS

GAMERA VS. GAOS = RETURN OF THE GIANT MONSTERS

GAMERA VS. GIGER = GAMERA VS. MONSTER X

GAMERA VS. GUIRON = ATTACK OF THE MONSTERS

GAMERA VS. VIRAS = DESTROY ALL PLANETS

GAMERA VS. ZIGRA

(1971) **D:** Noriaki Yuasa **S:** Fumi Takahashi **P:** Yoshihiko Manabe   Japan
(*Gamera Tai Shinkai Kaiju Jigara*)

In the last of the original seven flying-turtle movies, Zigra, the bad sea monster, has flippers, a beak, and a shark head. Two kids are the stars and there's a female alien and lots of animal tricks at a Sea World park. Gamera returned in *Supermonster* (1980) which was mostly stock footage. Most of the movies were released directly to TV in the US but later came out (retitled) on video. *Gamera the Invincible* (1965), the first in the series, was released to US theaters with additional footage featuring Albert Dekker and Brian Donlevy. The Celebrity video version lacks that footage. This was the only time the turtle was the villain. Daiei was purchased by its rival Toho in 1994, and they announced a new Gamera movie.

GANG BUSTERS

(Classic Cliffhangers, 1942)
D: Ray Taylor, Noel Smith **S:** Morgan Cox, Al Martin, Vic McLeod, George Plympton **P:** Ford Beebee

Kent Taylor stars in this 13-chapter Universal serial based on a radio program. The evil Professor Mortis (Ralph Morgan) uses a death-simulating drug to make his gang members appear to be zombies. Robert Armstrong and Irene Harvey costar.

GANG JUSTICE

(AIP, 1993) **D/S:** Richard W. Park **S:** Simon Blake Hong **P:** Moshe and Simon Bibyan

Joon B. Kim stars as an Asian immigrant who has to battle racism and has a crippled, alcoholic stepfather (Erik Estrada). Jonathan Gorman is his half-brother.

THE GANGSTER

(Fox, 1947) **D:** Gordon Wiles **S:** Daniel Fuchs **P:** Maurice King, Frank King

Barry Sullivan is a paranoid Brooklyn racketeer. English skating star Belita is his lounge-singer girlfriend. This *film noir* has a more impressive cast than most Allied Artists productions: Joan Lorring, Sheldon Leonard, Akim Tamiroff, John Ireland, Harry Morgan, Elisha Cook Jr., Leif Erickson, Fifi D'Orsay, Virginia Christine, Jeff Corey, Billy Gray, and in an early role, Shelley Winters. Wiles was a former art director, and this is filmed on painted sets.

GANGSTERS' LAW

(TWE, 1969) **D:** Siro Marcellini **S:** Piero Regnoli
Italy (*Quintero; La Legge dei Gangsters*)

Maurice Poli, Susy Anderson, and Klaus Kinski star in a movie about Italian bank robbers.

GANG WARS

(Sun, 1975) **D/S:** Barry Rosen **S/P:** Niki Patton **P:** Steve Madoff   (*Black Force; Devil's Express*)

This black-action/kung-fu/horror movie, made in New York City, has bad sound, bad lighting, and lifeless fight scenes, but it has a Chinese zombie killing people in subway tunnels, so it can't be all bad. War Hawk Tanzania plays See-Fu, a tall, cop-hating martial-arts teacher with an Afro. He takes Rodan, a Hispanic student, with him to Hong Kong. Rodan disturbs an ancient burial site (this is shown in a flashback), and unseen zombies attack a Chinese businessman, causing him to grow Ping-Pong-ball eyes. He takes a boat to Manhattan and mutates at the 135th Street subway station, killing people after luring them into dark passages by yelling, "Please help me! It's dark in here! I'm scared!" Meanwhile black and Chinese street gangs fight each other, coke deals go down, a woman wins a bar fight, and Brother Theodore (!) preaches outside the subway station: "Listen to those rats underground! Rats! Rats! Rats!" After an impossible-to-see slow-motion fight in the subway, we get to see "the demon," a guy in a monster suit and mask.

GANJASAURUS REX

(Rhino, 1987) **D:** Ursi Reynolds

Rhino rescued this homemade 100-minute comedy with a doll-like dinosaur that craves huge California marijuana plants. It was written by the entire cast and includes drug humor.

THE GARBAGE PAIL KIDS MOVIE

(Paramount, 1987) **D/S/P:** Rod Amateau **S:** Melinda Palmer

Topps Chewing Gum produced this PG movie to cash in some more on the success of their bad-taste bubble-gum trading cards. There's a prison for the ugly midget monsters and characters like Valerie Vomit and Foul Phil. Anthony Newley stars as a magician, with MacKenzie Astin, Phil Fondacaro as Greaser Greg, and Leo V. Gordon.

THE GARDEN

(1976) **D:** Victor Noru **S:** Yosef Avisar **P:** Isaac Shani, Yosef Diamant   Canada/Israel

An old man (Shai K. Ophir) with an Eden-like garden in Jerusalem thinks mute Melanie Griffith is an angel. She flees from some bikers and helps him stand up to real-estate developers. She's also naked a lot. The director was from the USSR.

THE GARDEN OF EDEN

(SW, 1954) **D/S:** Max Nosseck **S:** Nat Tanchuck, Arch W. Johnson **P:** Walter Bibo

It's historically important that this color nudist-colony film from Excelsior was the first to pass the New York Board of Censors in 1960, five years after being banned. The Supreme Court had ruled that nudity "per se" was not obscene, allowing *Garden of Eden* to be legally shown and opening the door to other nudist "documentaries." Within a few years there were dozens of them, directed by people like Russ Meyer, Herschell Gordon Lewis,

and Doris Wishman. This was the last American movie by the Polish-born director of *Dillinger* (1945), who settled in Germany in the late 50s. The cast includes character actor R. G. Armstrong (with a mustache and clothes), Mickey Knox, and Jamie O'Hara. It was "endorsed by the American Sunbathers Association."

GAS FOOD LODGING

(Columbia, 1992) **D/S:** Allison Anders **P:** Daniel Hassid

Fairuza Balk (from *Return to Oz*) and Ione Skye are the daughters of a truck-stop waitress (Brooke Adams). They live in a New Mexico trailer park and experience problems with men. Balk spends time watching old Mexican movies. With James Brolin as the absent father, Donovan Leitch (Skye's real-life brother), and Chris Mulkey. The IRS production is based on *Don't Look and It Won't Hurt*, by Richard Peck. The music is by J. Mascis of Dinosaur Jr. Anders, the red-haired, tattooed director, made *Mi Vida Loca/My Crazy Life* (1994), about a girl gang, next.

GASLIGHT

(MGM, 1944) **D:** George Cukor **S:** John Van Druten, Walter Reisch, John Balderston **P:** Arthur Hornblow Jr.

This gothic thriller is a remake of a 1940 British film. Both are based on *Angel Street*, a play by Patrick Hamilton. Ingrid Bergman (who received an Oscar) stars as the wife of crazed jewel-thief Charles Boyer. He does a good job trying to drive her insane, though modern audiences find her naiveté a little hard to take. With Joseph Cotten as a Scotland Yard detective, Dame May Whitty, and 19-year-old Angela Lansbury (making her film debut) as a maid. Lansbury was in *The Picture of Dorian Gray*, also from MGM, the next year. The negative of the 1940 *Gaslight* (directed by Thorold Dickinson and starring Diana Wynyard and Anton Walbrook) was destroyed by MGM, but several prints turned up in the 50s. It is sometimes called *Angel Street*.

GAS PUMP GIRLS

(1978) **D:** Joel Bender **S/P:** David A. Davies

A group of sexy girls help Uncle Joe (Huntz Hall, from the Dead End Kids/Bowery Boys) with his gas station after he suffers a heart attack. Joe E. Ross and Mike Mazurki are sent by a corporate-owned gas station to rob them. With Kirsten Baker and Sandy Johnson (from *Playboy*). Bender later made *The Retuning* and *The Immortalizer*.

THE GATE

(Vestron, 1987) **D:** Tibor Takacs **S:** Michael Nankin **P:** John Kemeny   Canada

Some kids whose parents are away learn a spell from a booklet that comes with a heavy-metal record. They dig a hole in a suburban backyard, and slimy *Gremlins*-type trolls emerge. The excellent, surreal stop-motion creatures make this PG-13 movie worth looking for. With Stephen Dorff and Louis Tripp.

GATE II

(Columbia/Tristar, 1989) **D:** Tibor Takacs **S:** Michael Nankin **P:** Andreas Harvey   Canada

This senseless, R-rated sequel (filmed in Toronto) stars Louis Tripp (from the original) as a kid who mixes his computer knowledge with an ancient ceremony and conjures up a small, animated "minion." Soon wishes can come true, but the false material goods requested by thick-headed teens turn to shit (literally), and the tough guys turn into monsters. Eventually the hero also becomes a monster in another dimension and dies, but everything is back to normal at the end. With Pamela Segall. It finally got a limited US theatrical release after sitting around for a few years. *I, Madman*, by the same director, was a lot better.

GATES OF HEAVEN

(RCA, 1978) **D/P/E:** Errol Morris

Yes, there is a feature-length documentary about a pet cemetery, and it's devastating. The pet owners and the cemetery owners are interviewed. Morris later made *The Thin Blue Line*.

GATES OF HELL

(Paragon, 1980) **D/S/P:** Lucio Fulci **S:** Danny Sacchetti **P:** Giovanni Masini   Italy (*Paura nella Citta dei Morti; Frayeurs; City of the Living Dead*)

Zombies rise in Dunwich (in "New England"). This has the famous power-drill-through-a-head scene. It's one of the goriest, maggot-filled zombie movies of the period. Christopher George stars as a reporter. Katherine McColl is a psychic. Janet Angren helps to try to close the gates before All Saints' Day, but she's killed and comes back from the dead. John Morghen is Bob, the village idiot.

GATOR BAIT

(Paramount, 1973) **D/S/P/M:** Beverly Sebastian **D/P/C/M:** Ferd Sebastian

The late Claudia Jennings stars as Desiree, a Cajun poacher blamed for a murder after her sister (Janit Baldwin) is killed. She hides out in the swamp and kills men with her pump-action shotgun. This violent drive-in hit from Dimension was one of the best to star Jennings, who wears really skimpy clothes. It was filmed in the Thibodaux area of Louisiana. With Clyde Ventura and Bill Thurman. The Sebastians had previously made the sex films *I Need* (1967), *The Love Clinic* (1968), and *Marital Fulfillment* (1970). Beverly is from Atlanta, and Ferd is from Houston.

GATOR BAIT II: CAJUN JUSTICE

(Paramount, 1986) **D/S/P:** Ferd Sebastian, Beverly Sebastian

In this sequel/remake, a Cajun wedding is disrupted by scummy backwoods villains. The husband (Tray Loren) is killed, and Angelique, the bride (red-haired Jan Mackenzie) is kidnapped and raped. She escapes, which leads to boat chases and revenge. Mackenzie was aka Lucious Lisa when wrestling for G.L.O.W.

The late Claudia Jennings in *Gator Bait*.

THE GAY DECEIVERS

(VSOM, 1969) **D:** Bruce Kessler
S: Jerome Wish **P:** Joe Soloman

Two guys who don't want to be drafted into the army decide to pretend they're gay. They move into an apartment in a gay neighborhood together, and although they continue to see their girlfriends, soon everybody believes that the've come out of the closet. Kevin Coughlin (*Maryjane*) and Lawrence Casey (*The Student Nurses*) star in this timely comedy, with Brooke Bundy, Jo Ann Harris, and Jack Starrett as the colonel. The music is by Stu Phillips.

THE GEEK

(Class X, 1981)

Here's an abominable-snowman movie you probably missed. A cultured-sounding narrator tells us about the three couples in a van who plan to camp out. After two (unflattering) hard-core sex scenes, a hairy monster (you can see the sleeves of the suit) arrives and fucks the third (best-looking) woman doggy style. She doesn't seem to mind. He rapes another one, and the men fight. The End. It was shot in Oregon, Washington, and Alberta. There are no credits.

GEEK MAGGOT BINGO

(Penetration, 1983) **D/S/P/E:** Nick Zedd

Zedd's second feature (after *They Eat Scum*) takes place entirely on purposely cheap-looking sets (a cardboard phone, drawn-on dungeon walls). There's some kind of comic mad-doctor-and-vampire plot, with some nudity from a woman who acts brain damaged (Brenda Bergman) and simulated sex thrown in. The lighting, editing, acting, and sound are all terrible, but where else could you see Richard Hell as a drunk cowboy, *Fangoria* editor Bob Martin as a salesman, and Zacherle (seen falling

asleep during breaks). With Donna Death. It was shot in 16mm. Ed French created a pretty good two-headed creature.

GEISHA GIRL

(Sinister, 1952) **D/S/P:** Ray Stahl
D/P: George Breakston

Rocky (William Andrews) and comic nerd Archie are privates on leave in Tokyo. Spies are after Archie because he unknowingly has some pills that are "stronger than the A bomb." Martha Hyer is a stewardess who becomes a spy. There's a con-man/magician called Zorro, Cold War jokes, MPs, a geisha school, and a long floor show. The music is by Albert Glasser. Breakston made *The Manster*, also with Tetsu Nakamura.

GENERATION

(1985) **D:** Michael Tuchner
S/P: Gerald Di Pego

Richard Beymer (*West Side Story*) is Alan Breed, an inventor and father in the year 2000. His brother is a gladiator in a Rollerball-type sport. This unusual failed pilot aired on ABC-TV. With Cristina Raines, Bert Remsen, Kim Myori, and Priscilla Pointer.

THE GENIE

(1957) **D:** Lance Comfort **S:** Doreen
Montgomery **P/A:** Douglas Fairbanks Jr.   UK

Fairbanks is a genie in one of the 3 stories in this trilogy, with Yvonne Furneaux (*The Mummy*, 1959) and Martin Milner. This is from the *Douglas Fairbanks Presents* TV series.

THE GENIUS

(1975) **D/S:** Damian Damiani **S:** Fulvio Morsella,
Ernesto Gastaldi **P:** Sergio Leone   Italy/France/
W. Germany (*Un Genio, Due Compari, e un Pollo*)

Despite the interesting cast and the fact that Leone produced it, this comic western is not available in America. Terence Hill stars as a prank-playing rogue, with Miou-Miou, Klaus Kinski (in his last western), Patrick McGoohan, and Robert Charebois. It's 126 minutes long and features an Ennio Morricone score.

GENTLEMEN PREFER NATURE GIRLS

(SW, 1963) **D/P:** Doris Wishman **S:** Marvin Stanley

In a typical nudist-colony-movie plot, the non-believer decides that the nudist life is just right for him (and his business) at the end. In this case the troublemaker owns a real-estate agency and fires Tom, who is a nudist. He doesn't know that Tom is happily married to Ann, also a nudist, who also works for him. Meanwhile we get to see lots of nice, naked ladies at the Sunny Palms Lodge in Homestead, Florida.

GENUINE RISK

(RCA, 1989) **D/S:** Kurt Voss **P:** Larry
Ratner, Guy Louthan, William Ewart

Peter Berg and Michelle Johnson star in a 40s-style crime story with a love triangle. It's pretty dumb but features Terence Stamp in a rare major role in the 80s. It also has violence, nudity, comedy, and Sid Haig. Voss also made *Border Radio*. An IRS production.

THE GEORGIA PEACHES

(1980) **D:** Daniel Haller **S:** Mick Benderoth,
Monte David Stettin **P:** James Sbardellati,
Thomas M. Hammell

Roger Corman was the executive producer of this New World/CBS-TV series pilot. Country singer Tanya Tucker stars as a southerner running a car-repair shop. She and two girlfriends are forced to become government agents. With Dirk Benedict, Terri Nunn, and Sally Kirkland.

GERMANY NINE ZERO

(1991) **D/S/E:** Jean-Luc Godard **P:** Nicole
Ruelle   France (*Allemagne Neuf Zero*)

After 26 years, Eddie Constantine returns as Lemmy Caution. He's looking for a missing girl, this time in reunified Germany. Only 62 minutes, (in French and German), it's sort of a sequel to Godard's *Alphaville*. Constantine, an American who died in 1993, had been a star in Europe since the 50s. He played Caution in several films.

GESTAPO'S LAST ORGY

(Video City, 1977) **D:** Cesare Canevani
S: Antonio Luaarella   Italy (*Caligula Reincarnated
as Hitler; The Last Orgy of the Third Reich*)

In a *Night Porter*–copy exploitation movie, the commandant of a concentration camp returns to the ruins years later and has flashbacks of women set on fire, whipped, and lowered into a vat of acid. Some American video company tried to pass this off as a "Caligula" movie.

THE GETAWAY

(1972) **D:** Sam Peckinpah **S:** Walter Hill
P: David Foster, Mitchell Brower

Steve McQueen is Doc McCoy, just out of a Texas prison, and Ali McGraw is his wife, Carol, in a violent (but PG-rated) bank-heist movie based on Jim Thompson's novel. With Al Lettieri and a typical Peckinpah lineup: Ben Johnson, Dub Taylor, Slim Pickens, and Bo Hopkins. Sally Struthers is kidnapped. McQueen was also in the director's less interesting *Junior Bonner* the same year. It was filmed in San Antonio and other southern Texas locations and released by National General.

THE GETAWAY

(MCA, 1994) **D:** Roger Donaldson
S: Walter Hill, Amy Jones **P:** David Foster

Alec Baldwin and Kim Basinger are the safecracking McCoys in this very close remake set in Ari-

GERMANY

It's easy to divide German film production into four periods. Many of the silent epics and expressionist classics that you've heard about are now on tape. Germany at the time led the film world with its horror and fantasy films. Fritz Lang was the top director. Films made after the Nazis took over and production was nationalized are either hateful propaganda or trivial musicals, comedies, and melodramas. Only historians and film scholars watch these today. There was a postwar B-movie boom, and West Germany produced Dr. Mabuse sequels, many adaptations of Edgar Wallace thrillers, some juvenile-delinquent movies, westerns, and horror movies. By the 70s a new wave of serious directors (Herzog, Wenders, Fassbinder) provided most of the country's exports.

zona. Doc is released from a Mexican prison and hired by crimelord James Woods. With Michael Madsen as the former partner, Richard Farnsworth in the Slim Pickens role, Burton Gilliam, and Jennifer Tilly (who is kidnapped). The sharpshooter wife is stronger than in Peckinpah's film, and there's more sex. R, unrated, and widescreen laserdisc versions are available.

GET CHRISTIE LOVE!
(Xenon, 1974) **D:** William A. Graham
S: George Kirgo **P:** Peter Nelson

After the success of several Pam Grier movies, ABC-TV made this series pilot, starring Teresa Graves as an LA cop who goes undercover to trap drug dealers. It's worth seeing for Graves, who is sexy, funny, and sarcastic. She wears an Afro and uses martial arts and jive talk when necessary. The gangsters talk about Japan, watch samurai movies, and smuggle heroin in reels of Japanese films. With Harry Guardino as her boss and Louise Sorel. The series, based on a novel by Dorothy Uhnak, lasted for only one season. Graves, who was also in *Trouble Man* and *Black Eye*, later became religious and retired from acting. Our loss.

GET CRAZY
(Nelson, 1983) **D:** Allan Arkush **S:** Danny Opatoshu, Henry Rosenblum **P:** Hunt Lowery

The Fillmore East (called the Saturn here) is the setting for this fun, underrated comedy. Lots of things go wrong before and during a big New Year's Eve show. Daniel Stern stars, with Stacy Nelkin, Allen Garfield as the Bill Graham character, and Malcolm McDowell doing a Mick Jagger takeoff. Fabian and Bobby Sherman are comic bad guys. With Ed Begley Jr., Howard Kaylan, Lou Reed (who does a great song at the end), Mary Woronov, Paul Bartel, Fred Willard, Dick Miller, Lee Ving, Clint Howard, Denise Galik, Lori Eastside, and Andy Hernandez. Arkush (*Rock 'n' Roll High School*) had worked on the light shows at the real Fillmore. He retreated to TV after *Get Crazy* failed at the box office and to date has directed only one more film, *Caddyshack II* (1988).

GET SMART AGAIN!
(Worldvision, 1989) **D:** Gary Nelson
S: Leonard Stern **P:** Burton Nodella

Don Adams and Barbara Feldon are now married former agents brought out of retirement to stop K.A.O.S. from using a weather machine (shamelessly copied from *In Like Flint*). With John De Lancie as a double agent, Kenneth Mars, and series semi-regulars Bernie Kopell, Dick Gautier, and King Moody. This pretty dull TV movie is the second reunion feature for the very funny 60s series. The other was *The Nude Bomb* (1980). A new *Get Smart* series aired briefly on Fox in 1995.

GETTING EVEN
(Vestron, 1986) **D:** Dwight H. Little **S:** M. Phil Senini, Eddy Desmond **P:** J. Michael Liddle   (*Hostage: Dallas*)

Industrialist Joe Don Baker steals a deadly gas that melts flesh and threatens to kill off the population of Dallas if he doesn't receive $50 million. Edward Albert and Audrey Landers are government agents trying to stop him. There are lots of helicopter stunts in this movie, made in Texas.

GETTING LUCKY
(Raedon, 1990) **D/S:** Michael Paul Girard
P: Gerald Feiffer, Tony Miller

A leprechaun in a beer bottle grants wishes to a teen. He becomes an inch tall and gets into girls' underwear. Steven Cooke stars.

GETTING OVER
(Unicorn, 1976) **D/S:** Bernie Rollins
P/A: John R. Daniels

Malcolm McDowell as a rock star and Stacy Nelkin in *Get Crazy*.

Daniels, star of *Black Shampoo* and *Candy Tangerine Man*, produced this one. He takes a job as head of Impossibly Funky Records owned by a big record company run by racist mobsters. His group the Heavenly Sisters (played by the Love Machine) becomes a hit, and he falls for the lead singer.

GETTING STRAIGHT
(RCA, 1970) **D/P:** Richard Rush
S: Robert Kaufman

Elliott Gould stars as a Nam vet who becomes a graduate student and English instructor. He has affairs with students, becomes involved in demonstrations, and gives up the academic life for the cause. With Candice Bergen, Cecil Kellaway, Max Julien, Jeff Corey, Jeannie Berlin, Brenda Sykes, Gregory Sierra, Billie Bird, and Harrison Ford. Laszlo Kovacs was the cinematographer. The Colgems soundtrack LP featured the New Establishment. This Columbia release, by the director of AIP's *Psych-Out* and *The Savage Seven*, was a box-office flop.

GHETTO BLASTER
(Prism, 1989) **D:** Alan Stewart **S:** Clay McBride
P: David DeCoteau, John Schouweiler

A young man (Richard Hatch) returns to his violent neighborhood, finds out that his father has been killed, and goes on a one-man vengeance spree using martial arts. With R. G. Armstrong, Richard Jaeckel, and Rose Marie.

GHOST
(Paramount, 1990) **D:** Jerry Zucker
S: Bruce Joel Rubin **P:** Lisa Weinstein

Patrick Swayze stars as the ghost of a banker who was shot in Tribeca. He contacts his girlfiend (Demi Moore) through a comic medium (Oscar-winning Whoopi Goldberg). He can punch villains, but he can't touch Demi. Some of the best scenes concern Vincent Schiavelli as a ghost on the subway. With Rick Aviles and Tony Goldwyn. This PG-13 romantic fantasy (with ILM FX) was a theatrical hit and an even bigger, record-breaking video hit. The music by Maurice Jarre is on Varèse Sarabande. The use of the song "Unchained Melody" on the soundtrack started a mini-revival of the Righteous Brothers' music.

THE GHOST AND THE GUEST
(Sinister, 1944) **D:** William Nigh
S: Morey Amsterdam **P:** Arthur Alexander, Alfred Stern

James Dunn and Florence Rice are newlyweds from New York City spending their honeymoon in a haunted farmhouse. Gangsters show up looking for hidden diamonds, and there's a hangman ghost. This 59-minute PRC comedy was written by a future costar of *The Dick Van Dyke Show*.

GHOSTBUSTERS

(Columbia, 1984) **D/P:** Ivan Reitman **S/A:** Dan Aykroyd, Harold Ramis **C:** Laszlo Kovacs

This PG comedy was Columbia's biggest hit up to that time. John Belushi was originally supposed to star. It was copied a lot (especially in Asia) and spawned many products, two rival TV cartoon shows, and a sequel. It's nothing more than a cleverly scripted, big-budget, high-tech version of old comedies like *Ghost Catchers* (1944), *Spook Busters* (1946), or *Ghost Chasers* (1951). The giant marshmallow man threatening New York City is a high point. Bill Murray and writers Dan Aykroyd and Harold Ramis are paranormal investigators using an old fire house as their headquarters. Sigourney Weaver and Rick Moranis become possessed. With Annie Potts, Ernie Hudson as the fourth ghostbuster (with almost nothing to do), William Atherton, Joe Franklin, Kimberly Herrin (from *Playboy*), and porno star Ron Jeremy in a crowd scene. The FX are by ILM. The score by Elmer Bernstein (*Robot Monster*) and the hit title song by Ray Parker Jr. are on Arista. Reitman had directed *Meatballs* (1979) and *Stripes* (1981), both starring Murray.

GHOSTBUSTERS II

(RCA/Columbia, 1989) **D/P:** Ivan Reitman **S/A:** Harold Ramis, Dan Aykroyd

One of the least satisfying sequels in memory is another cute-baby movie (there were lots of them at the time). All the stars repeat their roles, and there are more ILM FX (including the return of the *Titanic* and moving the Statue of Liberty). Peter MacNicol is irritating while possessed by a 17th-century painting. *Cannibal Girls* (an earlier Reitman production) is on a marquee. With Christopher Neame, Harris Yulin, Page Leong, and Janet Margolin, Cheech Marin, Chloe Webb, Phoebe Legere, and Brian Doyle Murray in bit parts. The soundtrack is on MCA. Columbia released this PG box-office disappointment.

GHOST CHASE

(Virgin, 1988) **D/S:** Ronald Emmerich **S:** Roland Kubisch   Germany/US

Roger Corman released this PG film made in Hollywood. It's about a movie mogul who's after some teen filmmakers for the magical trinkets they have. With Jill Whitlow, Jason Lively, and Dana Ashbrook. Corman also released Emmerich's *Making Contact*.

GHOST DAD

(MCA, 1990) **D:** Sidney Poitier **S:** Brent Maddock, S. S. Wilson **P:** Terry Nelson **M:** Henry Mancini

In this PG comedy made the same year as *Ghost*, Bill Cosby plays a widowed father of three, who dies in an accident. He returns as a ghost who can fly and go through objects to help his family. Despite his enormous TV fame, Cosby's movies around this time always flopped. This PG comedy costars Denise Nicholas, Kimberly Russell, Ian Bannen, Barry Corbin, Dana Ashbrook, and Arnold Stang.

GHOST FEVER

(Nelson, 1985) **D:** "Alan Smithee"/ Lee Madden **S/P:** Ron Rich **S:** Oscar Brodny, Richard Egan **P:** Edward Coe

Sherman Hemsley and Luis Avalos star as comical Georgia cops sent to a haunted house where they meet two female spirits. This 40s-style PG comedy includes ethnic humor and the evil ghost of a slave owner (Pepper Martin). With Myron Healey and Joe Frazier. Hemsley (from the TV series *The Jeffersons*) also plays the ghost of a slave. The film copies ideas from *Lucky Ghost* (1941). The director had his name removed after scenes were reshot for a 1987 release.

THE GHOST GOES WILD

(1947) **D:** George Blair **S:** Randall Faye

A Manhattan playboy/cartoonist (James Ellison), his fiancée (Anne Gwynne), and his butler (Edward Everett Horton) go to his haunted Connecticut farmhouse and hold a séance. Ellison later pretends to be a ghost, but a real one (Lloyd Corrigan) shows up. There's also a courtroom subplot. This Republic comedy features Ruth Donnelly, Jonathan Hale, and Holmes Herbert.

GHOSTHOUSE

(Imperial, 1988) **D:** "Humphrey Humbert"/Umberto Lenzi **S:** Cynthia McGavin, Sheila Goldberg **P:** Aristide Massaccesi   Italy (*La Casa; Ghost House*)

A psychic little girl kills her parents. Twenty years later teens die in a haunted house. There's death by hatchet, fan, glass, acid, and guillotine, a maggot face, and a killer puppet. Lara Wendel and Greg Scott star. It was filmed in Boston.

A GHOST IN MONTE CARLO

(1990) **D:** John Hough **S:** Torence Feely   UK

Sarah Miles, Oliver Reed, and Christopher Plummer star in this adaptation of a gothic romance by Barbara Cartland. The cast also includes Samantha Eggar, Fiona Fullerton, Lysette Anthony, and Ron Moody. It debuted in the US on TNT.

GHOST IN THE MACHINE

(Fox, 1993) **D:** Rachel Talalay **S:** William Davies, William Osborne **P:** Paul Schiff

A Cleveland computer-store worker (Ted Marcoux) who is also "the Address-book killer" dies in a car wreck and somehow becomes electricity. He terrorizes a single mom (Karen Allen) and her son (Wil Horneff) by entering computers, phone lines, and household appliances. Chris Mulkey is a computer hacker who tries to help. There's a crematorium nightmare and a room that becomes a microwave, but the FX segments are sparse. It should have been rated PG. With Jessica Walter. Graeme Revell wrote the music. Talalay made Freddy Krueger movies.

GHOST KEEPER

(New World, 1980) **D/S:** James Makichuk **S:** Douglas MacLeod   Canada

Some people riding snowmobiles go to an abandoned inn. An old lady, her slasher son, and an unseen creature are there.

GHOSTMASTERS

(Cinemacabre, 1991)

Magician Mark Walker presents this high-quality 23-minute compilation of rare spook-show trailers. You get to see Francisco, Raymond ("He sleeps in his own coffin"), Donn Davison, Kara-Kum, Dr. Silkini, and several for Joe Karsten and Philip Morris. One trailer (for *Dr. Evil*) is in color. Added titles give the real names of the stars. Walker also wrote an excellent book called *Ghostmasters*.

GHOST OF A CHANCE

(1987) **D:** Don Taylor **S:** Hank Bradford **P:** Sam Strangis

Redd Foxx is a jazz pianist who is accidentally killed by a New York City police detective (Dick Van Dyke) and returns to haunt him and to help his own grandson. With Geoffrey Holder as a heavenly mesenger who gives a tour of Hell and Richard Romanus. This TV movie, which debuted on CBS, copies parts of *Here Comes Mr. Jordan* (1941).

THE GHOST OF RASHOMON HALL

(Sinister, 1947) **D:** Denis Kavanagh **S:** Pat Dixon **P:** Harold Baim   UK (*The Night Comes Too Soon*)

Some aristocrats try to scare each other with stories. In one, a doctor rids a house of ghosts. This 59-minute film is based on a play. With Valentine Dyall and Anne Howard.

GHOST OF THE CHINA SEA

(1958) **D:** Fred F. Sears **S/A:** David Brian **S/P:** Charles B. Griffith

David Brian, Lynn Bernay, and Jonathan Haze star in this WWII story set in the Philippines. Griffith directed *Forbidden Island* (1959), also at Columbia.

GHOST PATROL

(Sinister, 1936) **D/P:** Sam Newfield **S:** Joseph O'Donnell **P:** Leslie Simmonds

Tim McCoy is a G-man hero who rides horses and flies a plane, in this science-fiction western released a year after the *Phantom Empire* serial. Villains kidnap a scientist and his "radium-tube" ray machine, which can blow airplanes out of the sky. With Claudia Dell and Wheeler Oakman. It was from Puritan Pictures and runs less than an hour.

GHOST RIDERS

(Prism, 1987) **D:** Alan L. Stewart **S:** Clay McBride, James J. Desmarais

The ghosts of some outlaws hanged in Texas 100 years earlier return. With Bill Shaw and Jim Peters. Not to be confused with *Ghost Rider* (1935), a Rex Lease western.

GHOSTS CAN'T DO IT

(RCA, 1990) **D/S/C:** John Derek **P/A:** Bo Derek

Anthony Quinn plays Scotty, the cantankerous billionaire husband of 5'4" Bo Derek. He's her "great one," "the great Scott." After Scotty has a heart attack, then shoots himself, he constantly shows up as a ghost. The problem is that there's no connection whatsoever between Quinn, reacting, laughing, coaching on a bare set covered by clear plastic bags, and Bo, constantly talking to nobody (and taking her clothes off a lot). A gangster forces Bo to take sleeping pills while she's naked in a pool. She plans to kill Fausto (Leo Damien) so that Scotty can take over his body. Julie Newmar shows up a few times as an angel to talk to Quinn, and Donald Trump, the world's most hated millionaire, plays himself. The dialogue is indescribable. Few people realize that this is the eighth film that former actor John Derek has directed, and only half of them star Bo, who was once a model for Kellogg's Corn Flakes boxes. Derek also directed obscure movies starring Ursula Andress, Linda Evans, and Annette Haven, and he was married to only two of them. This was the third Derek movie for Don Murray, who plays Bo's friend. It was filmed in Sri Lanka, the Maldive Islands, Wyoming, and Hong Kong, and I'm sure everybody involved had a nice time.

THE GHOST SHIP

(Fang, 1943) **D:** Mark Robson **S:** Donald Henderson Clarke **P:** Val Lewton

Crew members on a small boat on the way to Mexico are dying, and the new third officer (Russell Wade) thinks he knows who the killer is. Richard Dix is the soft-spoken captain who's losing his mind, Skelton Knaggs is a deaf-mute who thinks out loud, and Lawrence Tierney is a wise-guy lieutenant who is crushed by a giant anchor chain. Sir Lancelot provides calypso music during a bloody knife fight. This remains one of the hardest to see of Lewton's RKO productions.

GHOST SHIP

(VCI, Sinister, 1951) **D/S/P:** Vernon Sewell   UK

A young Canadian couple (Hazel Court and Dermot Walsh) buy a haunted pleasure boat. A medium is consulted, and flashbacks show why the ghosts are there. The same director used the same plot, based on a French play (but set in a house), in five (!) films. The others are *The Medium* (1934), *The Latin Quarter* (1945), *Ghosts of Berkeley Square* (1947), and *House of Mystery* (1961). This was released by Lippert in the US.

THE GHOSTS OF HANLEY HOUSE

(Sinister, 1964) **D/S:** Louise Sherrill **P:** Joseph Durkin Jr.

Five people play blackjack and drink tall ones while spending the night in a haunted house. They have a séance, then attempt to leave. Hank, the lead, has too much eye makeup (and too many closeups) and a picture of lightning is used! The movie actually pays off, though, with a glowing-orb spirit, axe-murder flashbacks, and decapitated heads. I'm guessing (from the "y'alls") that this was filmed in Texas somewhere just after *The Haunting* (which it copies), and that the rambling, fuzzy guitar and organ instrumental music was added around 1968. This rare find was never released before the tape but played on Comedy Central's *Mystery Science Theater 3000*, where the writers told you where to laugh.

GHOSTS . . . OF THE CIVIL DEAD

(1988) **D:** John Hillcoat **S/A:** Nick Cave **S:** Gene Conkie **P:** Evan English   Australia

This disturbing movie, set in the near future, is about an all-male prison in the middle of a desert where porno videos, gay sex, and drugs are tolerated. The corrupt authorities, who monitor everything, encourage violence, and a rebellion occurs. Many real ex-cons are in the cast. Cave, singer for the Bad Seeds, shows up late as a manic new inmate. The director had previously done rock videos.

GHOST STORY: *See* MADHOUSE MANSION

GHOST STORIES: GRAVEYARD THRILLER

(Vestron, 1986) **D:** Lynn Silver

This 60-minute tape is listed so that you won't make a mistake and rent it. An actor on a cemetery set tells a few stories. Nothing is shown.

THE GHOST TALKS

(1929) **D:** Lewis Seiler **S:** Frederick Brennan

An heiress (Helen Twelvetrees, who was in *The Cat Creeps* the next year) and an amateur detective (Charles Eaton) go to a haunted house looking for her late uncle's bonds. Crooks are after the bonds too. Stepin Fetchit is the comic caretaker. This early Twentieth Century–Fox talkie, based on a play, is only an hour long.

GHOSTS THAT STILL WALK

(VCI, 1977) **D/P:** James T. Flocker

A boy is possessed by an Indian spirit in Death Valley. His grandparents take him to a psychic, and boulders smash their home. This PG movie is from Gold Key.

GHOST TOWN

(Starmaker, 1988) **D:** Richard Governor **S:** Duke Sandefur **P:** Timothy D. Tennant

Franc Luz stars as a modern-day deputy sherriff looking for Catherine Hickland. Devlin (Jimmie F. Skaggs) and his men rule the zombies in a ghost town in a different dimension. With Bruce Glover. It's based on a story by David Schmoeller. One of the last productions from Charles Band's Empire, it was filmed in Old Tucson, Arizona (a movie-set replica). It was cut for an R rating and released by New World.

THE GHOST TRAIN

(Sinister, 1941) **D:** Walter Forde **S:** Sidney Gilliat   UK

Comedian Arthur Askey stars in a story about gun-runners during a haunted train during WWII. People are trapped in a station and told they'll die if they look at the train. Nazi agents are revealed. It's based on a play filmed as a silent and again in 1931.

THE GHOST WALKS

(Sinister, 1934) **D:** Frank Strayer **S:** Charles S. Belden **P:** Maury M. Cohen

Some people go to an old mansion where an insane woman comunicates with the dead. It turns out to be part of a new play, but somebody is really killed, and a madman is loose in the house. John Miljan stars, with June Collyer, and Johnny Arthur. This hour-long film from Chesterfield was by the director of *The Vampire Bat* and *Condemned to Live*.

GHOST WARRIOR

(Vestron, 1986) **D:** Larry Carroll **S:** Tim Curnen **P:** Charles Band   (*Swordkill*)

A frozen, 400-year-old samurai warrior (Hiroshi Fujioka) is found in a Japanese cave. He's brought to life by scientists in LA and fights again.

GHOST WRITER

(Prism, 1989) **D/S:** Kenneth J. Hall **P:** David De Coteau, John Schouweiler

Judy Landers is the ghost of a murdered 60s movie star in this PG comedy by the maker of *Evil Spawn*. She haunts a beach house and convinces a tabloid writer (Audrey Landers) to help reveal the killer. Joey Travolta, David Doyle, and Jeff Conaway costar. Lots of guest stars show up: Anthony Franciosa, John Matuszak, Dick Miller, Pedro Gonzalez-Gonzalez, George "Buck" Flower, the Barbarian Brothers, and Kenneth Tobey and Nels Van Patten as cops. It ends in the Hollywood Wax Museum. It's "presented by" Ruth Landers (the stars' mom) and both sisters sing.

GHOULIES

(Vestron, 1984) **D/S:** Luca Bercovici **S/P:** Jeffrey Levy

The same year as *Gremlins* we got *Ghoulies*, but we don't actually see much of them. A young guy (Peter Liapis) in the basement of an old mansion conjures up some puppet monsters, two dwarfs, and his Satanist father. Some LA teens die. With Lisa Pelikan, Michael Des Barres, Jack Nance, Mariska Hargitay, Bobbie Bresee, Jason Scott Lee, and the late Tamara De Treaux (who played E.T.) as a satanic midget. The John Carl Buechler FX are mediocre. The ads for this PG-13 movie featured a ghoulie in a toilet. This was the first feature I saw being filmed on a set (I had seen too many being filmed on the streets of Manhattan). It was made at Roger Corman's lumberyard studio in Venice. I thought having been there would make the results more interesting to me, but it didn't work that way.

GHOULIES II

(Vestron, 1988) **D/P:** Albert Band **S:** Charlie Dolan, Dennis Paoli

The puppets from *Ghoulies* return in "Stan's Den," a traveling carnival's spook show. This PG-13 comedy has heavy-metal music. Damon Martin stars, with Royal Dano as Uncle Ned, Kerry Remsen, dwarf Phil Fondacaro, and Starr Andreef.

GHOULIES III: GHOULIES GO TO COLLEGE

(Vestron, 1990) **D:** John Carl Buechler **S:** Brent Olson **P:** Ian Patterson **M:** Michael Lloyd

Lots of topless or naked girls and a little light bondage are the only memorable special effects in this lame fraternity/horror comedy (rated R). Those puppets come out of a toilet again, there's a *Psycho* shower scene, and Kevin McCarthy really hams it up as a professor who tries to control the creatures. In-jokes include a copy of the Re/Search *Pranks* book. With Hope Marie Carlton, Griffin O'Neal, and Marcia Wallace (from *The Bob Newhart Show*).

GHOULIES IV

(Columbia, 1993) **D:** Jim Wynorski **S:** Mack Sevi **P:** Gary Schoeler

A sexy, blond Satanist killer (Stacie Randall, from *Trancers IV*) in black leather sacrifices victims in an attempt to please a hooded demon. Peter Liapis returns from the first *Ghoulies* as a detective and also plays the demon. Barbara Alyn Woods and Bobby Di Ciccio are other cops. Two comic, wise-cracking ghoulies (dwarfs in masks) have nothing to do with the plot but at least are better than the usual puppets. There's an Art Carney/Ed Norton imitator, flashbacks from the first movie, lots of hookers, and talk about sex. It's pretty bad, but the 60s-sound theme music is good. Expect more sequels.

GHOUL SCHOOL

(CVH, 1990) **D/S/P:** Timothy O'Rawe

Toxic gas released in a high-school boiler room turns members of the swimming team into running blue zombies with fangs. A rock band (the Blood-Sucking Ghouls) and two nerdy horror fans are trapped in an auditorium (like in *Demons*). There's lots of (amateur) gore, but the best (?) part is Joe Franklin (!) in his office talking on the phone and with Jackie "the Joke Man." There's a buildup for Franklin to become a zombie too, but it never happens. The guy who plays the principal is one of the worst actors in memory. With porno star Savannah. David DeCoteau was the executive producer. It was made in Wayne, New Jersey.

THE GIANT OF THUNDER MOUNTAIN

(1990) **D:** James Roberson **S/A:** Richard Kiel **S:** Tony Lozito **P:** Joseph Raffill

Real-life giant Kiel (who was also an executive producer) stars as a legendary friendly giant hermit, in this family adventure. In a plot similar in some ways to *Eegah!* (in which he starred back in 1963), he's discovered by kids, shaves his beard, and comes out of hiding. With Jack Elam as a crooked carny man, Marianne Rogers, William Sanderson, Foster Brooks, George "Buck" Flower, and Bart the Bear.

THE GIANTS OF THESSALY

(Sinister, 1960) **D/S:** Riccardo Freda **S:** Giuseppe Masini, Mario Rossetti **P:** Virgilio De Blasi   Italy
(*I Giganti della Thessalia*)

Jason and Orpheus seek the Golden Fleece and encounter a witch who turns men into monsters. Roland Carey stars, with Ziva Rodann and Massimo Girotti.

GIDGET GOES HAWAIIAN

(1961) **D:** Paul Wendkos **S:** Ruth Brooks Flippen **P:** Jerry Bresler

Only James Darren returned from the original *Gidget* (1959), but red-haired Deborah Walley (later a regular at AIP) makes her debut in the starring role, and Carl Reiner plays her dad. It's a tame romantic comedy, of course, with Michael Callan, Peggy Cass, and Darren singing bad songs like "Wild About the Girl." From Columbia. The same director/producer/ writer team returned with *Gidget Goes to Rome* (1963), an even lamer entry starring Cindy Carol and James Darren. Then *Gidget* became a TV series (1965–66) with Sally Field. There were TV movies: *Gidget Grows Up* (1970), with Karen Valentine; *Gidget Gets Married* (1972), with Monie Ellis; and *Gidget's Summer Vacation* (1985), with Caryn Richman. Finally (?) there was *The New Gidget* (1986–88), a series with Caryn Richman. Jonathan Demme once made a short called *Gidget Goes to Hell*.

G.I. EXECUTIONER

(1971) **D/S:** Joel Reed **P:** Marvin Farkas   (*Dragon Lady; Wits' End*)

Tom Keena stars as a Nam-vet nightclub owner hired by mercenaries in Singapore. With Angelique Pettyjohn as a stripper, Janet Wood, and a Chinese villain. This warped James Bond–type adventure includes lots of drugs, gay stuff, nudity, and gore. It's by the director of *Bloodsucking Freaks*. Troma released it in 1985.

GILDERSLEEVE'S GHOST

(1944) **D:** Gordon Douglas **S:** Robert E. Kent **P:** Herman Schlom

This was the last of four movies based on *The Great Gildersleeve*, a once popular, now forgotten 40s radio comedy show. Throckmorton P. Gildersleeve (Harold Peary) is a small-town water commissioner who is helped in a political campaign by two ghosts (both played by Peary), two mad scientists who make a sexy blonde (Marion Martin) invisible, and a gorilla (Charles Gemora). With scared black servants (Nicodemus Stewart as a chauffeur and Lillian Randolph as a maid), Frank Reicher, Jack Norton as a drunk, and many radio actors who were famous at the time. This RKO release film is 63 minutes.

GIMME AN "F"

(1981) **D:** Paul Justman **P:** Martin Poll   (*T&A Academy 2*)

This teen movie is about a cheerleading competition. With Jennifer C. Cooke, Daphne Ashbrook, John Karlen, and Beth Miller. By the director of several Cars and J. Geils videos.

Cheri Caffaro stars in *Ginger*.

GIMME SHELTER

(Abkco, 1970) **D:** David Maysles, Albert Maysles, Charlotte Zwerin **P:** Ronald Schneider

This amazing 16mm rock-concert documentary would make a good double bill with *Night of the Living Dead*. The part before and after a man (Meredith Hunter) in the crowd of 300,000 is killed by Hell's Angels hired to patrol the stage area is devastating. The Rolling Stones do "Under My Thumb" and "Sympathy for the Devil" as the cameras zoom in on horrified, confused, stoned, and sad faces in the audience. Some bikers onstage look as if they'd like to kill the band. The film is effectively speeded up or slowed down slightly during these scenes. The footage is later replayed and discussed. Sonny Barger (on the radio) says, "I am not no peace creep." Somebody says that the people going to the Altamont Speedway for the free concert (in December 1969) are "like lemmings going to the sea." Jefferson Airplane, Ike and Tina Turner, and the Flying Burrito Brothers do only one song each. Marty Balin is knocked out by bikers, and Jerry Garcia says, "Oh, bummer." The Stones, also seen at some Madison Square Garden concerts, do seven songs in all. Another great part is "Love in Vain" with slow-motion visuals. The movie was shot by George Lucas (!), Haskell Wexler, Robert Elfstrom, and others.

GINGER

(Monterey, 1970) **D/S:** Don Schain **P:** Ralph T. Desiderio, Anthony J. Desiderio

Cheri Caffaro, a blonde with a serious tan, stars in the first of a drive-in hit series as Ginger McCallister, "the female James Bond." Hired to bust a sex-and-drug ring operating on the New Jersey shore, she has nude and bondage scenes and strangles, shoots, and castrates villains. Caffaro, who won *Life* magazine's Bardot-lookalike contest as a teen, was married to the director. This was followed by *The Abductors* and *Girls Are for Loving*.

THE GIRL

(Starmaker, 1986) **D/P:** Arne Mattsson **S:** Ernest Hotch   UK

A 14-year-old girl (Clare Powney, who was really 23) seduces a married attorney (Franco Nero). They go to a private island but are followed by a reporter (Frank Brennan). Blackmail, a double-cross, and murder result. With Bernice Stegers and Christopher Lee in a small role. In the US New World released this erotic thriller by a Swedish director.

GIRLFRIEND FROM HELL

(IVE, 1989) **D/S/P:** Daniel M. Peterson **P:** Alberto Lensi

If you like low humor, happy endings, and bad rock soundtracks, you might go for this teen comedy. Lezlie Deane, a painfully shy girl (who keeps puking at a party), is possessed by a troublemaking demon from Purgatory (Liane Curtis). All of a sudden she has Elvira-style hair, insults everybody, and keeps talking about how "this is getting so boring." She chugs booze and has sex with guys at a party who dry up and and die afterward. Dana Ashbrook (from *Twin Peaks*) is a confused-looking "chaser" with a ray gun who tries to get rid of the demon. The girls at the party spend a lot of time punching people in the face. A special-effects highlight is a lobster in a restaurant coming alive. With James Karen in a small role as a slob father, James Daughton, and Christina Veronica. This played some midnight shows after the video release.

GIRLFRIENDS

(Riot, 1994) **D/S/P:** Wayne Harold **D/P:** Mark Bosko

Nina Angeloff and Lori Scarlett star as Wanda and Pearl, lesbian serial killers. This comedy was made by the Ravenna, Ohio, creators of the *Killer Nerd* movies.

THE GIRL FROM S.I.N.

(SW, 1966) **D/S/A:** C. Davis Smith **S:** Rick Kuehn

Agent 0069, who uses karate, is first seen stripping and sucking on a man's toes before offing him with an icepick. Dr. Sexus (a fake Oriental) has female servants and big, Tor-like guards in an apartment. A photographer (seen shooting a nude model drinking milk) is drugged and tortured. A blonde named Karen takes some invisibility pills developed by her professor boss (Smith) to spy on Sexus but reappears naked and is tied up. A narrator with a comic voice tells us that this is all happening in Chinatown. There is no dialogue. Smith was the cinematographer for many Doris Wishman moves. This 67-minute b/w film, made in New York City, is a Frank Henenlotter Sexy Shocker release.

THE GIRL FROM TOBACCO ROW

(Ormond, 1966) **D/S/P:** Ron Ormond **P:** June Ormond

The Ormonds made three 60s country movies in Nashville. Country superstar Tex Ritter is the strict Reverend Bolton. His cute daughter, Nadine (Rachel Romen), becomes involved with an escaped con (Earl "Snake" Richards) who isn't a bad guy. Her fiddle-playing hunk-cop boyfriend objects. Gangster "Vic Naro"/Ron Ormond shows up looking for some stolen loot and tortures a guy just the way he did in *The Exotic Ones*: "Tic, tac, toe. Where'd ya stash the dough?" Most of the cast members sing. The older sister sings "Will the Circle Be Unbroken?" while playing an autoharp,

the theme song, "Run, Bit, Run," is pretty great, and there's more (giant-sized) harmonica-playing, including "The Flight of the Bumblebee." It all ends in a big barn fight. Tim Ormond, who plays little brother Tim, later marketed these tapes himself.

THE GIRL-GETTERS

(1964) **D:** Michael Winner **S:** Peter Draper **P:** Kenneth Shipman UK (*The System*)

Oliver Reed picks up women by taking their photographs at the beach, Jane Merrow is a model he falls for. With Barbara Ferris, Julia Foster, Harry Andrews, and David Hemmings. The Searchers do the (very good) theme song. AIP released this in the US. Reed was also in two comedies by Winner, *The Jokers* and *I'll Never Forget What's 'is Name*.

THE GIRL IN A SWING

(HBO, 1988) **D/S:** Gordon Hessler **P:** Just Betzer, Benni Korzen UK/US

In a supernatural romance, Meg Tilly stars as a mysterious German girl in Denmark who marries a wealthy British antique dealer (Rupert Frazer). She hallucinates and takes her clothes off a lot. The film is based on the novel by Richard Adams and was made in Denmark. The title refers to a rare ceramic sculpture. Originally 2½ hours long, it was cut in England, then cut even more for the US release.

THE GIRL IN BLACK STOCKINGS

(Shock Toons, 1957) **D:** Howard W. Koch **S:** Richard Landon

Obviously David Lynch caught this on late-night TV and planned *Twin Peaks* the next morning. What a movie! What hateful dialogue! It's set at a Utah resort hotel. The sheriff (John Dehner) announces, "A girl was slaughtered and cut up like a side of beef tonight!" There's an Indian deputy with one arm. Everybody seems to have been involved in some way with the dead girl, and they say she was evil. An outside investigator shows up. The suspects keep changing, and more people are murdered. A man is killed by a lumber machine. The cast of this United Artists release includes Anne Bancroft, Lex Barker, Marie Windsor, and Mamie Van Doren. She also starred in *Untamed Youth* and *Born Reckless*, by director Koch, and is fine as the sexy young mistress of a washed-up movie star. Stuart Whitman and Dan "Hoss" Blocker (before *Bonanza*) have small roles. Ron Randell (from Australia) takes the acting honors as the incredibly bitter, paralyzed rich man who owns the hotel.

GIRL IN HIS POCKET

(Sinister, 1957) **D:** Pierre Kast **S:** Franco Roche France (*Un Amour de Poche*)

Jean Marais stars as a man who shrinks his mistress (Genevieve Page) to doll size. Her nude scenes were the selling point when this was released in the US in 1960. With Jean-Claude Brialy and Agnes Laurent.

THE GIRL IN LOVERS' LANE

(Screen Gems, 1960) **D:** Charles R. Rondeau **S:** Jo Heims **P:** Robert Roark

A runaway (Lowell Brown) is helped by a guy named Bix (Brett Halsey) after he's robbed by small-town juvenile delinquents. They both get jobs at a diner. A lynch mob forms after a rapist (famous bad guy Jack Elam) causes the death of Joyce Meadows. Ronald Stein provided the jazzy score. This b/w Filmgroup production (by the director of *The Devil's Partner*) played on a double bill with *The Wild Ride* (with Jack Nicholson).

THE GIRL IN ROOM 2A

(Prism, 1976) **D/S:** William Rose Italy (*La Casa della Paura*)

Women are trapped and killed in a mansion by an old lady and her demented son. Raf Vallone leads a cult of red-hooded killers. With Rosalba Neri (star of *Lady Frankenstein*), Brad Harris, Daniela Giordano, and Karin Schubert. There's nudity and torture. The plot makes very little sense.

GIRL ON A CHAIN GANG

(Sinister, 1965) **D/S/P:** Jerry Gross

Three Freedom Rider college students (a black man, a white man, and a white woman, Julie Ange) are arrested by redneck cops. The men are killed. She's raped and put on an all-black, all-male chain gang. This b/w exploitation feature was made just a year after civil-rights workers were killed in Mississippi. There's no nudity but plenty of uneasy violence. Gross directed *Teenage Mother* next, then concentrated on distribution.

GIRLS ARE FOR LOVING

(Fries, 1973) **D/S:** Don Schain **P:** Ralph P. Desiderio

Cheri Caffaro returns in the third (and most outrageous) movie about Ginger McCallister, a martial-arts-fighting spy. There are several nude scenes. Men are castrated by a piano wire and shot in the balls. With Timothy Brown (from the *Dynamite Brothers*) as her partner/lover and Jocelyn Peters as the villainess with a group of muscular black henchmen. It was filmed in the Virgin Islands.

GIRLS COME TOO!

(SW, 1968) **D:** Larry Wolk **P:** Irving Klaw   (*How I Became a Nudist*)

Maria Stinger, a (real) model with a platinum wig, stars and narrates. She starts by showing her scrapbook ("My picture has appeared in *Tab, Eye, Frolic, Vue*") and plugging her book. The owner of a horse ranch (where she and her model friends ride topless) takes her to Eden Sunland Paradise. Endless pro-nudity talk fades into the background as we see naked women playing volleyball, jumping rope, swimming, etc. Unlike most nudist movies, everybody is completely exposed in some scenes, including the men. Some of the men like to show off by doing back flips. Other memorable moments are two naked women on a motorcycle, naked men smoking (the healthy life!), and a fashion show where the women wear only fur coats! A clothed guard protects the furs, and a local furrier is credited at the end (so is a wigmaker). The more revealing footage was added to *Nature's Sweethearts*, a 1963 film made by Irving Klaw of Betty Page fame. Photographer Bunny Yeager was the technical coordinator and Joseph P. Mawra was an editor.

GIRLS IN CHAINS

(Sinister, 1943) **D:** Edgar G. Ulmer **S:** Albert Reich **P:** Peter Van Duinen

A new counselor at a girls' reformatory (Arline Judge) tries to bring reforms despite the corrupt superintendent and head matron. The plot involves kidnapping and murder. Ulmer had been directing Yiddish and all-black features since making *The Black Cat* (1934). This was the first of 11 films he made at PRC in four years (including *Bluebeard* and *Detour*).

GIRLS IN PRISON

(1994) **D:** John McNaughton **S:** Samuel Fuller, Christa Lang Fuller **P:** Lou Arkoff, Debra Hill

The director of *Henry* and the director of *Shock Corridor* collaborated on this Showtime Rebel Highway movie and nobody even seemed to notice. Missy Crider is framed for murder and sent to a prison where Ione Skye is a lesbian convict. It's a remake (in name only) of Edward Cahn's 1956 AIP movie and includes the expected shower scenes. With Anne Heche, Bahni Turpin, and Nicolette Scorsese.

GIRLS IN THE NIGHT

(1953) **D:** Jack Arnold **S:** Ray Buffam **P:** Albert J. Cohen

A family moves to New York's Lower East Side and their teen kids get into trouble. The son (Harvey Lembeck, who later played Eric von Zipper in beach movies) robs a (phony) blind man who is later found dead. Patricia Hardy is his sister, and Glenda Farrell and Anthony Ross are their parents. With Joyce Holden and Don Gordon. Universal promoted this as a follow-up to *City Across the River*. Arnold directed *It Came from Outer Space* the same year. His major juvenile-delinquent film was *High School Confidential* (1958).

GIRLS' NIGHT OUT

(HBO, 1982) **D:** Robert Deubel **S/P:** Andrew N. Gurvis **S:** Gil Spencer Jr., Joe Bolster, Kevin Kurgi   (*The Scaremaker*)

A psycho-killer basketball-team mascot in a bear costume (!) knifes sorority girls on the Ohio State University campus at Columbus. With Rutanya Alda, Julie Montgomery, Hal Holbrook as a security guard trying to solve the murders, and his son David Holbrook as a suspect. Oldies are used on the soundtrack.

GIRLS OF THE BIG HOUSE

(1945) **D:** George Archainbaud **S:** Houston Branch

Lynne Roberts is an innocent girl who goes to prison, escapes, and finally clears her name in this Republic release. Virginia Christine and Adele Martin costar. There are several musical numbers (performed in a nightclub and in the prison rec room).

GIRLS ON PROBATION

(1938) **D:** William McGann, Harry Seymour **S:** Crane Wilbur **P:** Bryan Foy

This 63-minute Warner Brothers B movie costars Ronald Reagan as an assistant DA (he was in eight Warner films in 1938). Jane Bryan, a young ex-con on parole, goes to work for him, and they fall in love. She was framed for the theft of a dress from the dry-cleaning shop she worked at, and now the girl who got her into trouble shows up with a blackmail scheme. With Susan Hayward (in her fifth feature), and Sig Rumann. It was rereleased in 1956 to cash in on the then-famous Hayward, even though she had only a small role. Reagan's film career was nearly over by then.

GIRLS ON THE ROAD

(Unicorn, 1972) **D:** Thomas J. Schmidt **S:** Larry Bischof, Michel Levesque, Gloria Goldsmith

This obscure film from executive producer Joe Soloman opens with the credits on signs (and on the towel being used by Uschi Digart). Future *Twin Peaks* sheriff Michael Ontkean stars as a manic-depressive Nam vet who suffers from (way too many) b/w war flashbacks. Still other flashbacks are in blurred color. Two nice, rich, straight virgin girls take a vacation in Monterey "to be free," encounter Ontkean, and come to the conclusion that he's a psycho killer. Ralph Waite (from *The Waltons*) runs a seaside hippie village where his followers are being murdered. It's pretty tame for a Fanfare movie but good for some dated laughs.

GIRLS' SCHOOL SCREAMERS

(Vestron, 1984) **D/S/P:** John P. Finegan **P:** Pierce J. Keating, James W. Finegan Jr.   (*The Portrait*)

Catholic-school girls hold a séance in a haunted house in Philadelphia. There are flashbacks and a ghost. Mollie O'Mara stars. Troma released it because nobody else would.

THE GIRLS THAT DO

(SW, 1967) **D/S/P:** Sidney Knight   (*Some Girls Do*)

Ruth (Joanne Fair) arrives in NYC for the first time, walks around a lot, then moves in with two women who tell her, "The Village is a groovy place. You'll have a ball!" Gigi, a topless waitress, narrates her flashback, and Sylvia, a divorcée, narrates hers (about how her husband got her involved with whips). Ruth is conned out of her clothes on her first modeling job. After being tricked and abused by men, the angry women decide to teach one a lesson, so they drug his drink, tie him up, and make him watch them play strip poker. This b/w movie features a lesbian scene, sex with underwear still on, and bad acting, all backed by free-form San Francisco–style rock instumental music by The Lusty Four.

GIRLS TOWN

(1942) **D:** Victor Hugo Halperin **S:** Gene Kerr, Victor McLeod **P:** Lou Brock, Jack Schwartz

A beauty-contest winner (June Storey) and her ugly-duckling sister (Edith Fellows) go to Hollywood to become actresses. They find trouble. With Anna Q. Nilsson, Warren Hymer, and Paul Dubov. This PRC release was the last film by the director of *White Zombie*.

THE GIRL, THE BODY, AND THE PILL

(SW, 1967) **D/P:** Herschell Gordon Lewis **S:** Allison Louise Down   (*The Body and the Pill*)

After a silly theme song with a baby crying and an intro by Mr. Price (a high-school principal who speaks directly to the camera), this becomes a soap-opera-style look at the problems Miss Barrington (Pamela Rhea), a well-meaning blonde teacher (with a red convertible), faces trying to inform her students about contraception. Her classes are cancelled, she's suspended, and she's attacked by a student. A tough "bad girl" replaces her mother's birth-control pills with saccharine pills, which results in an illegal abortion. Most of the students look as if they're over 30. With *Taste of Blood* star Bill Rogers and Ray Sager. A garage band called the Fly-by-Nights plays at a party. Mr. Price returns for two more serious talks. Rhea is a better actress than in most Lewis films, and this isn't really bad, just much tamer than you'd expect, even though it received an R rating.

THE GIRL, THE GOLD WATCH, AND DYNAMITE

(1981) **D:** Hy Averback **S:** George Zateslo **P:** John Cutts

This syndicated TV movie, a sequel to *The Girl, the Gold Watch, and Everything*, stars Lee Purcell and Philip MacHale. Zohra Lampert returns, and the cast includes Jack Elam, Gary Lockwood, Jerry Mathers, Richie Havens, Lyle Alzado, Tom Poston, Gene Barry, Morgan Fairchild, Larry Linville, and Carol Lawrence.

THE GIRL, THE GOLD WATCH, AND EVERYTHING

(1980) **D:** William Wiard **S:** George Zateslo **P:** Myrl A. Schreiberman

Robert Hays and Pam Dawber star in this syndicated TV movie about a magic watch that can stop time, with Zohra Lampert, Ed Nelson, Maurice Evans, MacDonald Carey, and Jill Ireland. It's based on a fantasy by John D. MacDonald.

THE GIRL WHO KNEW TOO MUCH

(1969) **D**: Francis D. Lyon **S**: Charles A. Wallace **P**: Earle Lyon

Adam West (in his first post-*Batman* role) stars as Johnny Cain, a retired CIA agent. This R-rated spy movie costars Nancy Kwan as his ex-mistress, now working for a gangster, with Robert Alda, Nehemiah Persoff, Buddy Greco, and bad Communist characters. Lyon also directed jaw-droppers like *Castle of Evil*, *Cyborg 2087* (which *The Terminator* ripped off), and *Destination Inner Space*.

GIRL WITH AN ITCH

(SW, 1957) **D/P**: Ronnie Ashcroft **S**: E. Shaylor Heats, Jay M. Kude **P/A**: Peter Perry Jr.

A sexy, gold-digging blonde (Kathy Marlow) in a very low-cut dress and high heels shows up with an empty suitcase for some "fruit trampin'" work and immediately comes between the orchard's owner (Robert Armstrong) and his son, Orey (Robert Clarke). The theme song is about "that devil Mari Lou." There's a roll in the hay, a cat fight in water, frequent harmonica solos, and an earthquake. This enjoyable Howco production is one of three Ashcroft movies Clarke starred in (*The Astounding She Monster* is the best known). The Roadshow Rarities video is an excellent print.

THE GIRL WITH HUNGRY EYES

(SW, 1966) **D/S/P/A/E**: William Rotsler

Kitty (Vicky Dee), a girl with pigtails, is in the woods with her abusive boyfriend. Tiger Cat (Cathy Crowfoot) shows up and kills him with a rock. Kitty moves in with the jealous Hollywood lesbian but thinks, "She doesn't own me." There are flashbacks, cat fights, a whipping, Kitty's shower, and Pat Barrington dancing and stripping to rock instrumentals. The dubbed-in sound is bad, and there's too much "blurovision" for the sex scenes. It's from Boxoffice International.

GIVE MY REGARDS TO BROAD STREET

(Fox, 1984) **D**: Peter Webb **S/A/M**: Paul McCartney **P**: Andros Epaminondas

Paul McCartney stars in this story about the search for the missing master tapes of his new album videos. There are lots of musical segments. The cast includes Bryan Brown, Linda McCartney, Ringo Starr (as himself), his wife, Barbara Bach (they were better in *Caveman*), Tracey Ullman, and Ralph Richardson (in one of his last appearances). This PG ego trip didn't do too well at the box office.

THE GLADIATOR

(Starmaker, 1986) **D**: Abel Ferrara **S/P**: Bill Bleich **P**: Robert Lovenheim

Ken Wahl stars as a California vigilante with a souped-up tow truck who goes after reckless and drunk drivers after his brother is killed in a hit-and-run accident. With Nancy Allen as a talk-radio

host, Robert Culp, Rosemary Forsyth, Rick Dees, and Linda Thorson. This New World production (by the director of *Driller Killer* and *Ms. 45*) was a failed ABC-TV pilot.

GLADIATOR

(Columbia, 1992) **D**: Rowdy Herrington **S**: Lyle Kessler, Robert Kamen **P**: Frank Price

James Marshall and Cuba Gooding Jr. star as young boxers and friends. Marshall resorts to illegal boxing matches in a warehouse stadium to pay off his father's gambling debts. This movie has lots of fights. With Brian Dennehy as a bad-guy promoter, Robert Loggia, Ossie Davis, and John Heard (who had his name removed from the theatrical credits).

GLADIATOR OF ROME

(Sinister, 1962) **D**: Mario Costa **S**: Gian Paolo Callegari **P**: Giorgio Agliani   Italy (*Il Gladiatore di Roma*)

Former Tarzan Gordon Scott was in at least a dozen Italian movies. This time he's Marcus, a gladiator who saves some Christian slaves. With Wandisa Guida as a slave who's really a princess and Roberto Risso.

THE GLADIATORS

(Media, 1969) **D**: Peter Watkins **S**: Nicholas Gosling **P**: Goran Lindgren   Sweden (*Gladiatorerna*)

In the future (1994) soldiers from various countries compete in a televised "Peace Game." This semi-documentary science-fiction movie was released by New Line (it opened in Yellow Springs, Ohio). It was the first film by British director Watkins after his excellent movie about a rock star in a fascist state, *Privilege*.

THE GLASS SHIELD

(Buena Vista, 1994) **D/S**: Charles Burnett **P**: Tom Byrnes, Carolyn Schroder

Michael Boatman stars as the first black cop in a bad section of LA, in this film about racism and police corruption. Lori Petty is the only female cop there. Ice Cube is arrested for the murder of Elliott Gould's wife. With Michael Ironside, Richard Anderson, M. Emmet Walsh, Bernie Casey, and Sy Richardson. It's by the director of *To Sleep with Anger*.

THE GLASS SPHINX

(1967) **D**: Luigi Scattini **S**: Adalberto Bolzoni **P**: Fulvio Lucisano   Italy/Spain/Egypt (*La Sfinge di Cristallo*)

AIP released this Egyptian-tomb movie starring Robert Taylor and Anita Ekberg. People kill each other over a life-sustaining elixir. With Giacomo Rossi-Stuart (Jack Stuart). The US version, released by AIP, has music by Les Baxter. Ekberg was in *Fangs of the Living Dead* the same year.

THE GLASS TOMB

(1955) **D**: Montgomery Tully **S**: Richard Landau **P**: Anthony Hinds   UK (*The Glass Cage*)

Eric Pohlmann has the key to solving a murder, but he's been "buried alive" for a carnival publicity

stunt. John Ireland and Honor Blackman star, with Sidney James, Geoffrey Keene, and Ferdy Mayne. Lippert released this 59-minute Hammer mystery in the US.

GLEAMING THE CUBE

(Vestron, 1988) **D**: Graeme Clifford **S**: Michael Tolkin **P**: Lawrence Turman, David Foster

Christian Slater and Steven Bauer star in this PG-13 skateboard movie with a subplot about Vietnamese mobsters and the death of an adopted Vietnamese boy. With Richard Herd, Ed Lauter, Jack Riley, and a lot of Vietnamese kids. Tolkin made *The Rapture* and wrote the novel *The Player*. Clifford directed several *Faerie Tale Theatre* episodes.

GLITCH!

(Academy, 1988) **D/S/P**: Nico Mastorakis

Dick Gautier is planning a low-budget movie called *Sex and Violence*. Two comic burglars, posing as the producer and director, check out the auditioning bathing beauties (including Teri Weigel, Laura Albert, and Debra Lamb). With Julia Nickson and Ted Lange.

GLITTER GODDESS OF SUNSET STRIP

(1991) **D**: Dick Campbell **S/P/A**: Llana Lloyd

This fascinating, mind-numbing, feature-length video deserves a cult following. In real life, Lloyd, a California blonde who worked as a model and a reporter, grew up with a proud lesbian mother who drove in demolition derbies (!) and a schizo father. She later hit the TV-talk-show circuit (sometimes with her mom) to talk about her life. This video has all of her TV appearances (including *Oprah* and *Phil Donahue*) and actual color home movies, plus recent reenactments of events in her life. Lloyd plays herself at various ages and her own mother! Lloyd's daughter plays her as a little girl. The video looks at the lesbian underworld of the 50s with compassion, passes through the drugged-out 60s, then tries to recreate the glam-rock 70s in Hollywood. Angela Bowie appears as herself, and some guy lamely pretends to be Alice Cooper ("my mentor"). Various Ed Wood Jr. and Larry Buchanan movies came to my mind while watching this flawed but sincere tape.

THE GLOVE

(Media, 1978) **D**: Ross Hagen **S/P**: Julian Roffman **S**: Hubert Smith   (*Blood Mad; The Glove: Lethal Terminator*)

Rosey Grier is an escaped convict who kills with a custom-built steel glove that was attached to his hand by his jailers. He can smash people (or solid metal) with ease but isn't really a bad guy. He wants to help a tenement-rebuilding project (and he plays the guitar and sings!). John Saxon is an ex-cop bounty hunter who's after him. The all-star cast of this bad but strangely entertaining and ahead-of-its-time science fiction/action movie includes Joanna Cassidy, Jack Carter, Keenan Wynn, Joan Blondell, Aldo Ray, Nicholas Worth, and Michael Pataki. Roffman directed the classic Canadian 3-D movie *The Mask*. Hagen, an actor, had produced films in the Philippines and became a Fred Olen Ray regular in the 80s. This is the last film with Grier (he campaigned for Pat Robertson in 1987).

G-MEN NEVER FORGET
(Republic, 1947) **D:** Fred Brannon, Yakima Canutt
S: Franklin Adreon, Basil Dickey, Jesse Duffy

Future *Lone Ranger* star Clayton Moore is the government-man hero of this 12-chapter Republic serial. Roy Barcroft is the villain, Murkland, and the plot concerns turning people into exact duplicates with plastic surgery. With Drew Allen, Ramsay Ames, and the usual expert stuntmen.

G-MEN VS. THE BLACK DRAGON
(Republic, 1942) **D/S:** William Witney **S:** Ronald Davidson, Joseph O'Donnell, Joseph Poland

Rod Cameron is an American agent named Rex, Constance Worth is a British agent named Vivian, and Roland Got is Chang of the Chinese Secret Service. The trio of Allied heroes in this 15-chapter Republic wartime serial battle the Japanese Black Dragon Society, led by Haruchi (played by Nino Pipitone!), which smuggles enemy agents into the US disguised as mummies. Some chapter titles are "The Yellow Peril," "Beast of Tokyo," and "Democracy in Action." C. Montague Shaw is a professor. There are robot planes that sink ships, a torture chamber, death by buzz saw, exploding paint, a raven with a poison beak, and lots of exploding miniatures. The 1943 feature version is *Black Dragon of Manzanar*.

THE GNOME-MOBILE
(1967) **D:** Robert Stevenson
S: Ellis Kadison **P:** James Algar

Walter Brennan and D. J. Mulrooney are gnomes in a redwood forest who are helped by the niece and nephew of a lumber baron (also played by Brennan), in a movie similar to the earlier *Darby O'Gill and the Little People* (by the same director). With Matthew Garber and Karen Dotrice (the kids in *Mary Poppins*), Ed Wynn (also from *Mary Poppins*, in his last film role), and Richard Deacon. This live-action fantasy was completed just after Walt Disney's death. It's based on a children's story written decades earlier by the radical author Upton Sinclair.

A GNOME NAMED GNORM
(Polygram, 1988) **D/FX:** Stan Winston
S/P: Pen Densham **S:** John Watson
P: Robert Q. Cort, Scott Kroopf *(Upworld)*

If you liked *Ratboy* you might go for this slight, PG-rated story about a hairy gnome from under the Earth who witnesses a killing. Ugly, depressed Gnorm likes big breasts and hits bad guys in the crotch. Anthony Michael Hall stars as a young cop, with Claudia Christian as his partner, Jerry Orbach as their corrupt boss, and Robert Z'Dar. A Vestron production, it was finally released in the US in 1994.

John Saxon in *The Glove*.

GO ASK ALICE
(1973) **D:** John Korty **S:** Ellen M. Violet
P: Gerald I. Isenberg

Teenage Alice (Jamie Smith-Jackson) freaks out from LSD on ABC. William Shatner and Ruth Roman (who were in the exploitation classic *Wanna Ride, Little Girl?/Impulse* around the same time) star in this favorite of fans of 70s TV movies. It features Julie Adams, Andy Griffith, Robert Carradine, Mackenzie Phillips, Charles Martin Smith, and characters identified only as pushers and sadists. From the published diary of an anonymous addict who OD'd.

GODDESS OF LOVE
(1988) **D:** Jim Drake **S/P:** Don Segall **P:** Phil Margo

Vanna White, for those of you who have forgotten, became a celebrity by turning letters on *Wheel of Fortune*. She had been in early-80s movies like *Graduation Day, Looker,* and *Gypsy Angels*. She stars in this fantasy TV movie as Venus. David Naughton falls for her. The cast includes John Rhys-Davies as Zeus, Amanda Bearse, Betsy Palmer (from *Friday the 13th*), Sid Haig, and Little Richard. Watch for it.

GOD FORGIVES, I DON'T
(VSOM, 1967) **D/S:** Giuseppe Colizzi
S: Gumersindo Mollo **P:** Enzo D'Ambrosio
Italy/Spain *(Dio Perdona, Io No)*

This is the first western starring the once very popular team of blond Terence Hill (real name Mario Girotti) and big Bud Spencer (real name Carlo Pederzoli). They play a gunfighter and an insurance detective after money from a train robbery. Frank Wolff is gang leader Bill San Antonio. AIP released it in the US.

GOD'S BLOODY ACRE
(TWE, 1975) **D:** Harry Kerwin **S/P/A:** Wayne Crawford **S/P:** Andrew Lane

Three hillbillies living in a lean-to in the forest attack a bulldozer (with rocks) and somehow manage to cut the driver in half. Then they go on a killing spree, attacking two vacationing couples. Thomas Wood is Monroe, the father figure ("This time we ain't leavin'."). Billy has puffed-out hair,

and Ezra is the dumbest of the brain-dead group. From a distance they look like the rock group Cream! They beat, rape, and hang other characters. Wayne Crawford is an anti-violence dropout from an office job who heads out on the road on a motorcycle. Crawford (*Barracuda, Crime Lords*) is one of my favorite bad actors. In most movies he looks like he's in extreme pain while trying to do a Robert De Niro impersonation. This exploitation anti-classic has many flashbacks, false scares, violence, some gore, some "ramblin'" folk music, bad black dudes in a Cadillac, and some clever editing. One flashback is triggered by a Busch can.

GOD'S GUN
(Warner, 1975) **D/S:** "Frank Kramer"/
Gianfranco Parolini **P:** Menahem Golan
Italy/Israel *(A Bullet from God)*

Lee Van Cleef plays both a retired gunfighter and his preacher twin in this western, shot in Israel. Jack Palance costars as a gang leader, with Leif Garrett, Richard Boone, Sybil Danning, Dody Palance, and Cody Palance. Produced by Golan/Globus, it was cut in the US. The next year Van Cleef and Garrett returned in *Kid Vengeance* for Cannon.

GOD'S LITTLE ACRE
(UAV, 1958) **D:** Anthony Mann
S: Philip Yordan **P:** Sidney Harmon

This film about Depression-era southern white trash is based on Erskine Caldwell's controversial, best-selling novel. Robert Ryan stars as Ty Ty Walden, a man of God searching for gold on his land. His sons are Jack Lord and Vic Morrow. With Aldo Ray as his son-in-law, Tina Louise (in her film debut) as Griselda, Buddy Hackett as the sheriff, Fay Spain as Darlin' Lil, Gloria Talbott, Rex Ingram, and Michael Landon as an albino. The cast is one to ponder, and the movie itself is an excellent mixture of sex, violence, and humor. In the late 60s this still played drive-ins, billed with *Little Mother*.

GODZILLA
(Zontarian, 1954) **D/S:** Inoshiro Honda
S: Takeo Murata **P:** Tomoyuki Tanaka   *(Gojira)*

You've all probably seen the recut and dubbed Americanized version, but this is the real thing (from Toho), running the full 98 minutes and subtitled for the first time. Horacio Higuchi translated the dialogue and the complete credits, and Jan Arthur Johnson (from *Zontar* magazine!) created the easy-to-read subtitles. It's a better movie (without Raymond Burr), and the subtitles and restored footage drive home the point that this is a scary, somber postwar movie about the H bomb. It was made less than nine years after Hiroshima and Nagasaki were bombed and Japan surrendered. It's easy to see the giant, unstoppable radioactive monster ("illegitimate child of the bomb") as a symbol of the bomb (or even America). Dr. Serizaw (Akira Takarada) gets more screen time. He's a brilliant, tragic war hero (with an eye patch) whose true love (Momoko Kochi), a survivor of the Nagasaki bomb, loves another. The ending is a plea to stop nuclear testing.

GODZILLA 1985

(Starmaker, 1984) **D:** Kohji Hashimoto, R. J. Kizer **S:** Hidekazu Nagahara   Japan

This was the first Godzilla movie in ten years, so it was some kind of event. In the US the people at New World added footage of Raymond Burr just as Warner Brothers had done with the first *Godzilla*, back in 1956! They also added some really bad humor (Tony Randall was the script doctor) with the dubbing and pretty much wrecked it. The Cold War plot has Godzilla destroying a Soviet submarine and almost triggering a nuclear holocaust. Tokyo is nearly destroyed again. With Keiju Kobayashi, Ken Tanaka, and Yasuka Sawaguchi. There are clips from the original film. The Burr-less Japanese original from Toho runs 20 minutes longer. The US theatrical release was a flop, and this was the last Godzilla movie (to date) to play American theaters.

GODZILLA RAIDS AGAIN = GIGANTIS, THE FIRE MONSTER

GODZILLA VS. BIOLANTE

(HBO, 1990) **D/S:** Kazuki Omori **P:** Tomoyuki Tanaka   Japan (*Gojira Tai Biolante*)

The second of Toho's "new" Godzilla movies looks better than most and has some great, almost poetic scenes. This time scientists create a giant, scary-looking plant monster (using Godzilla's cells) that mutates, grows, sprouts vines (each has a mouth with sharp teeth), and spews green acid. The two

Godzilla 1985

monsters go to Osaka, but some of the most impressive scenes are not of mass destruction. The human characters are a scientist and his daughter (Megumi Odaka), a girl with ESP who can communicate with Godzilla and evil Arabs. The effective soundtrack uses the original theme and a "disco" version. There's a Godzilla-memorial cocktail lounge. The great-looking tape is letterboxed and dubbed. Godzilla returned to battle old foes (Ghidrah, Mechagodzilla, and Mothra) in the next three movies, which have not been officially released in the US.

GODZILLA VS. GIGAN = GODZILLA ON MONSTER ISLAND

GODZILLA VS. KING GHIDRAH

(VSOM, 1991) **D/S:** Kazuki Omori **P:** Tomoyuki Tanaka   (*Gojira Tai Hingu Gidora*)

Years after Godzilla became a comical defender of Japan (and little kids) the original concept creature is back. Kazuki Omori has rewritten the character with a fascinating, confusing, and political new creation story that starts in 2204 and goes back to 1992, 1954, and 1944! During the war a "normal" dinosaur scares away invading Americans in the South Pacific, saving Japanese soldiers. In 1954 an H-bomb test turns the dino into Godzilla. In 1992 a new Godzilla wins a big battle with the three-headed Ghidrah, so aliens from the future create Mechaghidrah. They want Godzilla destroyed to stop a future when Japan will buy all other nations (!). One character says, "History has no room for sentimentality." There's also a superfast human-size American (?) robot and more unlikely plot twists. The stirring original Godzilla theme music is used, and the battle scenes are the best in many years. This movie made the US news for being "anti-American." Copies with English subtitles are around. A "making of" film was also released.

GODZILLA VS. MECHAGODZILLA

(VSOM, 1994) **D:** Takao Okawara **S:** Wataru Mimura

The fifth in the revived series was released in Japan as a 40th-anniversary film. It features lots of battles, including Rodan vs. Godzilla in the Bering Strait. A cute baby Godzilla hatches, and big Godzilla wants it back. The UN Godzilla Counter-measure Center creates and sends a flying Mechagodzilla. Megumi Odaka returns once again as a psychic. This was followed by *Godzilla vs. Space Godzilla*.

GODZILLA VS. MONSTER ZERO = MONSTER ZERO

GODZILLA VS. MOTHRA = GODZILLA VS. THE THING

GODZILLA VS. QUEEN MOTHRA

(VSOM, 1992) **D:** Takao Okawara **S:** Kazuki Omori

This has the same basic plot as *Godzilla vs. the Thing* (1962) and was a big hit for Toho in Japan. The twins from Infant Island (now called the Cosmos) sing a Mothra song, and Godzilla battles Mothra and the winged Battra in Tokyo at the end. The stars are Kobayashi Satomi and Bessho Tetsuya. Megumi Odaka returns as the psychic from the previous two Godzilla films. I liked the original and the recent *Biolante* and *Ghidrah* movies a lot better. This is subtitled.

GO! GO! GO! WORLD

(Video Yesteryear, 1964) **D:** Renato Marvi **D/S/P:** "Marco Vicario"/Antonio Margheriti   Italy (*Il Pelo nel Mondo*)

"We didn't make the world. We only photographed it!" Margheriti, using another pseudonym, codirected this *Mondo* movie in between Barbara Steele and Christopher Lee movies. It features Bowery bums, female mud-wrestling in Germany, judo, dog-eating, Italian hookers, New Guinea child brides, Cannes bikini fashions, chastity-belt stores, strippers, snake charmers, bitchy narration, and laughable sound effects. The soundtrack was on Musicor.

GOIN' COCOANUTS

(1978) **D:** Howard Morris **S:** Raymond Harvey **P:** John Cutts

Donny and Marie Osmond star in their first (and last) movie. Bad guys are after Marie's necklace in Hawaii. Get the supporting cast: Ted Cassidy (in his last role), Harold "Oddjob" Sakata, Marc Lawrence, Kenneth Mars, and Herb Edelman. When it was released, the singing Mormons still had their own TV show, but their hit-making days were over. Little Jimmy Osmond starred in *The Great Brain*, based on John D. Fitzgeralds books, the same year. Both were backed by the Osmond family.

GOING BERSERK

(MCA, 1983) **D/S:** David Steinberg **S:** Dana Olson **P:** Claude Heroux   Canada

In this SCTV spinoff, limousine driver and rock drummer John Candy is kidnapped by a religious sect and brainwashed to kill his future father-in-law, a congressman. It's not very funny. With Joe Flaherty, Eugene Levy, Pat Hingle, Paul Dooley, Richard Libertini, Ernie Hudson, and Dixie Carter. *Strange Brew* was the other SCTV feature in 1983.

GOING STEADY

(1958) **D:** Fred F. Sears **S:** Budd Grossman **P:** Sam Katzman

Molly Bee and Alan Reed Jr. are high school students who are secretly married in this Columbia release. She gets pregnant and their parents get worried. With Irene Hervey and Byron Foulger. In the 60s Bee (who recorded for MGM) was in *The Young Swingers* and *Hillbillys in a Haunted House*.

GOLD

(LS Video, 1934) **D:** Karl Hartl **S:** Rolf E.
Vanloo **P:** Alfred Zeisler   Germany

Hans Albers (*Münchhausen*) and Friedrich Kayss-
ler are scientists trying to create gold with a huge
atomic reactor. Brigitte Helm (*Metropolis*) and
Lien Deyers (*Spies*) costar. Hartl directed the German version of *FP 1 Doesn't Answer* (1932), starring Albers. Originally two hours long, *Gold* was a
major UFA production made in German and
French versions with different male leads. Scenes
of the reactor were later used in the American film
The Magnetic Monster (1953), directed by Curt
Siodmak (who wrote the novel on which *FP 1* was
based and with his brother, director Robert Siodmak, fled Nazi Germany in 1933).

THE GOLDEN CHILD

(Paramount, 1986) **D:** Michael Ritchie
S: Dennis Feldman **P:** Edward S. Feldman,
Robert D. Wachs

Big Trouble in Little China and this film were both
Hollywood action/fantasy/comedy movies with
Asian themes from the same year. Eddie Murphy
stars as a detective who looks for missing children.
Charles Dance (who works for the Devil) kidnaps
the magical Tibetan "golden child" (who can make
a Pepsi can dance). The boy is played by J. L.
Reate, a girl. Kee Nang (Charlotte Lewis) recruits
Murphy, who gets some help from a magic sword
and a parrot. With James Hong and Victor Wong
(both were also in *Big Trouble*, which is better),
Randall "Tex" Cobb, and Eric Douglas. There are
ILM FX and a score by Michel Columbier, which
replaced one by John Barry, for some reason.

GOLDEN NEEDLES

(1974) **D:** Robert Clouse **S:** S. Lee Pogostin,
Sylvia Schneble **P:** Fred Weintraub

Joe Don Baker stars in a tale about a golden statue
containing magical acupuncture needles that can
restore youth. The *Maltese Falcon*–derived plot
takes place in Hong Kong and LA. Jim Kelly costars (for kung-fu fighting), with Elizabeth Ashley,
Ann Sothern as a madam, and Burgess Meredith.
Wayne Wang (*Chan Is Missing*, *Slamdance*) was
the assistant director. Baker was also in *The Pack*,
directed by Clouse.

GOLDEN YEARS

(Worldvision, 1991) **D:** Ken Fink **S:** Stephen
King **P:** Mitchell Galin, Peter McIntosh
(*Stephen King's "Golden Years"*)

Keith Szarabajka and Frances Sternhagen are cus-
todians at a secret government lab run by a mad
scientist (Bill Raymond). Szarabajka gets younger
because of an explosion and has to flee federal
agents. The cast also includes Felicity Huffman and
Ed Lauter. The credits are for the 2-hour CBS-TV
series pilot. King also wrote the first 4 of the 6 episodes in the summer series, and he and Richard
Rubenstein were the executive producers. The
4-hour double cassette has a new (happy) ending
not seen on TV. Dick Smith did the old-age makeup. David Bowie's song of the same name is the
theme.

GOLDILOCKS AND THE THREE BARES

(1963) **D:** Herschell Gordon Lewis
P: David F. Friedman, Tom Dowd

This was planned as *Singing in the Sun*, a nudist
musical, but most of the music was cut. It's set in a
Roaring Twenties nightclub in Miami where a
singer (Rex Marlow) and a comedian (William
Kerwin) work. They date Vicki Miles (aka Allison
Downe), and Netta Malina but can't figure out why
they're never available on weekends. It's because
they're nudists, and instead of just the usual nudist-
camp footage this Eastman Color wonder features
naked women on a yacht. With boxer Joey Maxim
(as himself) and *Blood Feast* star Mal Arnold.

THE GOLEM

(Sinister, 1920) **D/S/A:** Paul Wegener
D: Carl Boese **S:** Heinrich Galeen
(*Der Golem: Wie Er in die Welt Kam*)

Paul Wegener plays the legendary clay statue the
Golem in this silent German classic filmed at UFA
using twisted, expressionist sets and clay miniatures representing the medieval Prague ghetto.
Both the Golem and a knight of the emperor (Ernst
Deutsch) fall in love with the rabbi's daughter
(Lyda Salmonova, Wegener's real-life wife). To
protect the Jewish people, Rabbi Loew (Albert
Steinrück) brings the Golem to life with alchemy
and magic. A servant later sends the creature on a
rampage. The best scenes are when the mean-faced
Golem starts fires, kills people, and drags a woman
by the hair. The spirit of Ashtaroth is a great special
effect, a floating head that forms letters with steam
from its mouth. Ernst Lubitsch was the supervising
director, Carl Freund was the cinematographer, and
Edgar G. Ulmer was the assistant cameraman. Wegener and Galeen had codirected and Galeen had
scripted *Der Golem* (1914), and Wegener had directed *Der Golem und die Tanzerin* (1917). Both
starred Wegener. No prints of either film have survived. (Wegener remained in Nazi Germany and
was honored as an "artist of the state." Galeen fled
to the US in 1933, but nothing is known of his life
or work after he came here. He had directed and/or
scripted many expressionist classics of horror and
fantasy, including *Nosferatu*, *Waxworks*, and *The
Student of Prague*.) This impressive epic originally
ran 118 minutes and was released by Paramount in
the US. It's 70 minutes now and has an organ score.
Two movies about the Golem were made in France
in 1937 and 1966. In a modern-day version, *It*
(1966), a museum employee (Roddy McDowall)
brings the Golem to life again.

LE GOLEM

(Ergo, 1935) **D:** Julien Duvivier **S:** André-Paul
Antoine **P:** Josef Stern   France/Czechoslovakia
(*The Legend of Prague*)

The Golem is under the control of Rabbi Jakob
(Charles Dorat), but the creature is taken away by
King Rudolf II (Harry Baur) and chained in a cell.
The king's spiteful mistress (Germaine Aussey) releases the Golem, which destroys the palace and
kills everyone in it. This version, based on a 1916
novel by the German writer Gustav Meyrinck, was
filmed in Prague. It runs 96 minutes (originally
100) and has subtitles.

GOLDFACE, THE FANTASTIC SUPERMAN

(SW, 1967) **D:** Adalberto Albertini **S/P:** P. C. Balcazar
Italy (*Goldface, il Fantastico Superman*)

A masked wrestling hero named Goldface (Spartaco B. Antoni) battles a criminal organization.
This movie manages to copy Mexican wrestling
movies and James Bond films at the same time.

GOLIATH AGAINST THE GIANTS

(Sinister, 1962) **D:** Guido Malatesta
S: Gianfranco Parolini **P:** Cesare Seccia
Italy (*Goliath Contro i Giganti*)

Brad Harris has to resist amazons and battle a
sea creature before he can defeat the evil Bokan
(Fernando Rey). With Gloria Milland and Barbara
Carroll.

GONE IN 60 SECONDS

(Media, 1974) **D/S/P/A:** H. B. Halicki

"See 93 cars demolished!" Halicki was a stunt man
who made his own movies for drive-ins. This PG
car-crash movie was popular enough for him to
make *The Junkman* (1982). Years later he made
Gone in Sixty Seconds II (1989) and died while
doing a car stunt. The action scenes from the first
movie were reused in *The Big Sweat* (1990).

GONKS GO BEAT

(1965) **D/P:** Robert Hartford-Davis
S: Jimmy Watson **P:** Peter Newbrook   UK

An alien from Gonk is sent to Earth to stop the
battle between the island of Beatland and the island of Ballad. Most of the screen time is devoted
to musical acts on cheap sets, and there's a Romeo
and Juliet subplot. The Nashville Teens and Lulu
and the Lovers (who also do the title song) represent Beatland. Mike Leander arranged a drum-
battle sequence with two rows of competing
drummers (including Ginger Baker, then with the
Graham Bond Organization), and the two groups
go to war, with guitars instead of guns, at the end.
Jazz music is used for a dream sequence. With
Kenneth Connor (from the *Carry On* films) and
Gillian French. By the director of *Corruption*.

GOOD AGAINST EVIL

(1977) **D:** Paul Wendkos **S:** Jimmy Sangster

This ABC-TV series pilot stars Dack Rambo as a
writer who teams up with an exorcist (Dan
O'Herlihy) to battle the evil Rimmin (Richard
Lynch) and his group of Devil worshippers. With
Elyssa Davalos and Kim Cattrall. Wendkos also di-
rected *The Mephisto Waltz* (1971).

GOODBYE, EMMANUELLE

(Thorn EMI, 1977) **D/S:** François Leterrier
S: Monique Lange   France

The third in the Sylvia Kristel series was the last
she starred in (but not the last she appeared in).
With Umberto Orsini, Alexandra Stewart, and
Olga Georges-Picot. The music is by Serge Gainsbourg. Kristel returned in *Emmanuelle IV* but
turned into another actress through the miracle of
plastic surgery.

GOODBYE, NORMA JEAN

(HBO, 1975) **D/S/P:** Larry Buchanan **S:** Lynn Shubert

"This is the way it was," claims the intro, and if Larry Buchanan says so, you can believe every word. Former *Hee Haw* regular Misty Rowe stars as the young Marilyn Monroe. In 1942 she goes to see *Citizen Kane*. After her guardian throws her out, she works at a munitions factory, is raped by a cop, becomes "Miss Whammo-Ammo," and at 16 gets married in Mexico to a munitions worker. After he's drafted she poses for scandalous pulp magazine photos while men pay to watch through holes in a wall. At one session she's bound and gagged. She gets raped several more times but knows "I'm going somewhere!" and gets down on her knees for the head of "Rampant Studios." She has flashbacks and visions of her crazy mother. A man showing stag films announces that a snuff film will be next: "If you vomit your guts out, you still have to pay!" She demands a screen test, attempts suicide, and is taken under the wing of star "Al James." After they finally have sex he dies. It ends with her screen test. The sound is bad, and the tape jumps in some places. Russ Meyer regular Stuart Lancaster has a role. Now-famous producer Debra Hill was the script supervisor! The movie was despised by critics but made money. The long-awaited "sequel" was *Goodnight, Sweet Marilyn* (1989).

GOODFELLAS

(Warner, 1990) **D/S:** Martin Scorsese
S: Nicholas Pileggi **P:** Irwin Winkler

Longtime fans of Scorsese's earlier, lesser-known *Who's That Knocking at My Door?* and *Mean Streets* were rewarded with this hit. It has similar great performances, great period rock music, humor, violence, and lots of drugs. Ray Liotta stars and narrates as the young Irish/Italian guy who eventually turns state's evidence against killer mobsters Robert De Niro, Joe Pesci (who received an Oscar), and Paul Sorvino. The frantic cocaine sequence is one of many highlights. With Lorraine Bracco, Gina Mastrogiacomo, Debi Mazar, Samuel L. Jackson, Henny Youngman and Jerry Vale (as themselves), and Chuck Low as Morrie the wig-maker. A key scene with Pesci was filmed in New York's (now long gone) Hawaii Kai nightclub. It all ends with Sid Vicious' "My Way." Based on Nicholas Pileggi's 1985 book about real-life mobster Henry Hill, *Wiseguy* (that title had been used for another movie), the film is 146 minutes long.

GOOD GUYS WEAR BLACK

(Vestron, 1979) **D:** Ted Post
S: Bruce Cohn **P:** Allan F. Bodah

Chuck Norris, in his second movie as a star, gets in a few good kicks as an ex–Green Beret trying to stop an assassination plot, but this PG political-corruption "thriller" isn't very exciting, and neither is Chuck's acting. With Anne Archer, Lloyd Haynes, James Franciscus, Dana Andrews as an evil politician, and Jim Backus as a bellboy. Post also directed several Clint Eastwood movies. Chuck returned in *A Force of One*.

GOOD IDEA!

(Edde, 1975) **D/S:** John Trent **S:** David
Main **P:** David Perlmutter   Canada
(*It Seemed Like a Good Idea at the Time*)

John Candy is all over the video box for this PG comedy, but he plays only a supporting role as a cop. Anthony Newley is the star, trying to win back his wife (Stefanie Powers). With Isaac Hayes as a sculptor, Yvonne De Carlo, Lloyd Bochner, and Lawrence Dane. Candy and Dane starred as the same cop characters in *Find the Lady* (1976), by the same director.

GOOD MORNING AND GOODBYE!

(RM, 1967) **D/P/C/E:** Russ Meyer **S:** John E. Moran

In one of Meyer's best sex/comedy/morality tales (this time in color) Angel (Alaina Capri) cheats on and humiliates her rich farmer husband Burt (Stuart Lancaster). Stone, a constuction worker (Patrick Wright), has affairs with Angel and Burt's young daughter. Everything turns out all right after Burt is revitalized in the woods by a sorceress (Haji). The only nudity is a woman running in a field (shown at the beginning and the end). Moran also wrote *Faster, Pussycat! Kill! Kill!* Joe Perrin, who narrates this and several other Meyer films, was also the control voice in the TV series *The Outer Limits*. Eve Meyer was the associate producer.

GOODNIGHT GOD BLESS

(Magnum, 1987) **D:** John Eyers **S:** Ed Ancoats
P: Geoff Griffith, Zafar Malik   UK

A priest stabs and guns down five kids and their teacher in a schoolyard. New York City cop Joe Vanovitch is on the case and dating the mother of a little girl who was almost a victim. This movie is filled with false leads, doesn't bother to show any of the killings, has a very irritating false ending, but includes a possession (featured on the video box), so it can be classified as a horror movie.

GOODNIGHT, SWEET MARILYN

(Off Hollywood, 1989) **D/S/P:** Larry Buchanan

More than an hour of this movie (Marilyn's flashbacks from her deathbed) is footage from Buchanan's already flashback-filled *Goodbye, Norma Jean*! The new footage (all 30-some minutes of it) stars impersonator Paula Lane as Marilyn and Phyllis Coates (Lois Lane in the *Superman* TV series) as the ghost of her mother (!). One-time biker-movie star Jeremy Slate plays a fictional character who "took her life to save her" and tells how he did it in flashbacks. Misty Rowe is Marilyn in the older footage. Incredible.

THE GOOD SON

(Fox, 1993) **D/P:** Joseph Ruben
S: Ian McEwan **P:** Mary Anne Page

Macaulay Culkin (that *Home Alone* kid) stars as a psycho who tries to corrupt his cousin (Elijah Wood), who's staying with Culkin's family in Maine (great scenery) after the death of his mother. Culkin had drowned his baby brother. Now he tries to kill his little sister (Quinn Culkin), and even his mother

(Wendy Crewson) is in peril. Despite the Culkin backlash, this is a very good *Bad Seed* type movie (even though Wood is a better actor than the star). Elmer Bernstein wrote the music. Culkin's father blackmailed 20th Century–Fox into giving his son this role (Jesse Bradford was slated to play it) by delaying his okay for *Home Alone II*. This film was to have been directed by Michael Lehmann, but the director of *The Stepfather* got the job.

THE GOOD, THE BAD, AND THE UGLY

(MGM, 1967) **D/S:** Sergio Leone **S:** Luciano Vincenzoni
M: Ennio Morricone   Italy (*Il Buono, il Bruto, il Cattivo*)

Clint Eastwood stars as Joe in his third, best, and last "spaghetti western." He shares screen time with scene-stealing Eli Wallach as Tuco and Lee Van Cleef as Setenza. This awesome tale of a search for gold buried in a graveyard includes a trip to a prisoner-of-war camp and a vast Civil War battle. The 180-degree camera moves in the graveyard-shootout ending are lost on TV. The incredible Morricone soundtrack (featuring his best use of distorted electric guitar and voices as instruments) is on United Artists, but Hugo Montenegro had the hit cover version of the theme. With Victor Israel, Chelo Alonso, and Rada Rassimov. The double tape runs 162 minutes, but the original time was 181 minutes. United Artists released all three Leone/Eastwood movies in 1967. The next year Eastwood returned home for *Hang 'Em High*, and Leone topped himself again with *Once Upon a Time in the West*.

GOOD TIMES WITH A BAD GIRL

(Video Dimensions, 1967) **D/S:** Barry Mahon

A conservative millionaire is forced to land his private jet in Las Vegas. While his wife is at a garden exhibit he has an affair with Sue, a young "nymphomaniac." It's in b/w (when most films were already in color).

THE GOONIES

(Warner, 1985) **D/P:** Richard Donner
S: Chris Columbus **P:** Harvey Bernhard

Some kids from a small town find a treasure map and go on an adventure. This is based on a story by Steven Spielberg (an executive producer), who borrowed some ideas from a favorite Our Gang short, *Mama's Little Pirates* (1934). He also borrowed Max Steiner's music from *Adventures of Don Juan* (1948) and a clip from *Captain Blood* (1935). With Sean Astin, Josh Brolin, Corey Feldman, Ke Huy Quan, Martha Plimpton, Anne Ramsey as the evil Mama Fratelli, Joe Pantoliano, and John Matuszak as a mutant. ILM provided the FX. Cyndi Lauper sang the theme song. In one scene the kids read *Mad* magazine. The film is 114 minutes long.

GOR

(Warner, 1987) **D:** Fritz Kiersch **S:** Rick
Marx **S/P:** Harry Alan Towers

A 20th-century American professor (Urbano Barberini), magically transported to the planet of Gor, helps to battle barbarians (led by Oliver Reed) who have taken the "life stones" from a peaceful group. With sword duels, a female dwarf, and torture. The cast of this fantasy, shot in South Africa and Mauritius, includes Paul L. Smith, Larry Taylor, and Rebecca Ferratti. New villain Jack Palance shows up at the end to introduce the sequel, *Outlaw of Gor*. Both films are based on books by John Norman.

GORDON'S WAR

(Fox, 1973) **D:** Ossie Davis **S:** Howard Friedlander, Ed Spielman **P:** Robert L. Schaffel

Paul Winfield is a Nam-vet Green Beret back in Harlem whose addict wife has died. He recruits three war buddies and they fight the drug dealers, who all work for a white man seen only on TV screens. This violent action movie from 20th Century–Fox features Carl Lee, David Downing, Tony King, and Grace Jones. The Buddha soundtrack features New Birth, Barbara Mason, and others. This is one of six films by actor/director Davis, who was later a regular in Spike Lee's movies.

GORE-MET ZOMBIE CHIEF FROM HELL

(Tempe, 1986) **D/S/P/C/M:** Don Swan **S:** Jeff Baughn, William Highsmith

A 14th-century priest is still around eating flesh and running a beach-front deli. You can judge this Super 8 gore comedy by its cover (and title).

GORGASM

(1991) **D/S/P:** Hugh Gallagher   (*Main Force*)

Gabriella (a biker-magazine centerfold) stars as a woman who kills men after they answer her personal ads. A detective (Rik Bullock) investigates by visiting a porno store (it charges a browsing fee) and a sleazy publisher. He has a slow-motion nightmare and watches a spanking tape. She strips for her victims before stabbing or decapitating them and also whips a dummy. He loses his mind at the end. Gallagher, who edits *Draculina* magazine, made *Gorotica* next.

GORGON VIDEO, VOLUME I

(MPI, 1989) **P:** Stuart Shapiro, Waleed Ali

Michael Berryman hosts this 69-minute magazine-format tape, complete with gore and nudity. It features interviews with Wes Craven ("I'm a working-class kid from Cleveland"), Linnea Quigley, Troma's Lloyd Kaufman, the KNB FX crew, and reviewer Rick Sullivan, who recommends *Bad Taste* and *Henry*. There are film clips, a big Sinister Cinema plug, trailers, the band Gwar, and an anti-censorship message. Alex Winter directed one segment. Volume II in the planned series was made (with Stuart Gordon and Penn and Teller) but never released.

GOROTICA

(Ill-Tec, 1992) **D/S/P:** Hugh Gallagher (*Wake of the Dead*)

Carrie (Ghetty Chasun), a necrophiliac dominatrix with a multipierced body, watches the *Death Scenes* tape, masturbates with a skull, and in two (soft-core) scenes has sex with a body. Yes, this is the result of letting the German *Nekromantic* into the US of A. This film actually has its own clever (very) bad-taste subplots concerning a young thief

(Dingo Jones), a valuable jewel, and a necro guy. Carrie says, "You're dying of AIDS, you're fucking dead people, and you want me to beat you!" There's effective music by Drain and White Slug. This 60-minute tape, by the editor of *Draculina* magazine, was shot in Memphis in five days. Donald Farmer was also involved. Gallagher made *Gore Whore* next.

GORP

(HBO, 1980) **D:** Joseph Ruben **S/P:** Jeffrey Konvitz **P:** Louis S. Arkoff

Michael Lembeck stars as a waiter in this movie, which copies *Meatballs*' summer-camp and has quaaludes gags. With Dennis Quaid, Fran Drescher, David Huddleston, and Rosanna Arquette in a small role. Ruben had directed *The Pom-Pom Girls* and *Joyride*. AIP became Filmways in 1980. This was one of their last releases.

GOTHAM

(Warner, 1988) **D/S:** Lloyd Fonvielle **P:** Gerald I. Isenberg, Keith Addis

Tommy Lee Jones is Eddie Mallard, a small-time private detective hired by a rich man (Frederic Forrest) who wants his wife (Virginia Madsen) to stop bothering him. Murdered 13 years earlier, she's now a ghost. Madsen has nude scenes, including one in a refrigerator. This attempt at a sexy, supernatural *film noir* debuted on Showtime.

GOTHIC

(Vestron, 1986) **D:** Ken Russell **S:** Stephen Volk **P:** Penny Corke   UK

Here's what might have happened at a villa in Switzerland during the summer of 1816 to inspire Mary Shelley to write the novel *Frankenstein*. It's like a feature-length version of the opening scene of *Bride of Frankenstein*, done in typical Russell fashion. The characters hold a séance, have nightmares, take opium, and drink laudanum. In one vision Miriam Cyr has breasts with eyes, and a demonic dwarf makes a brief appearance. Gabriel Byrne is Lord Byron, Julian Sands is Percy Bysshe Shelley, Timothy Spall is Dr. John Polidori, and Natasha Richardson makes her screen debut as Mary Shelley. The Thomas Dolby soundtrack is on Virgin. *Haunted Summer* (1988) tells the same story in a more conventional fashion.

GRAFFITI BRIDGE

(Warner, 1990) **D/S/A:** Prince **P:** Arnold Stiefel, Randy Phillips

In this PG-13 sequel to the hit *Purple Rain* (1984) singers Prince and Morris Day fight for control of the Grand Slam, a Minneapolis nightclub. With Ingrid Chavez as the poetry-writing girlfriend, Jerome Benton, George Clinton, Mavis Staples, and Day's reunited group, the Time. It was the third movie directed by Prince.

THE GRAND DUEL

(Sinister, 1972) **D:** Giancarlo Santi **S:** Ernesto Gastaldi   Italy/Monaco (*Il Grande Duelo*; *The Big Showdown; Storm Rider*)

Lee Van Cleef is an ex-sheriff who saves an innocent young fugitive (Horst Frank) from bounty hunters several times. An effeminate killer in all-white clothes is the brother of the sheriff. What happens doesn't make much sense, but there are b/w flashbacks, a machine-gun massacre, and kung fu movie–style leaps in the air. This is a panned and scanned cut version.

GRANDMA'S HOUSE

(Academy, 1988) **D:** Peter Rader **S:** Peter Jensen **P:** Nico Mastorakis

A recently orphaned teen (Kim Valentine) and her younger brother (Eric Foster) are sent to live with their grandparents in a farmhouse surrounded by an orange grove. They discover that the kindly but strange old folks are really killers. A woman lurking outdoors (Brinke Stevens) turns out to be their mother, who has been in an asylum. Rader also made *Hired to Kill* (1990).

THE GRAND SILENCE

(1968) **D/S/P:** Sergio Corbucci **S:** Vittoriano Petrilli, Mario Amendola **M:** Ennio Morricone Italy/France (*Il Grande Silenzio*)

Jean-Louis Trintignant stars as the mute gunfighter Silence in a western that takes place entirely in the snow. It's considered one of the best European westerns but had no official US release. Klaus Kinski costars as Tiger, an evil bounty hunter, with Americans Vonetta McGee and Frank Wolff.

GRAND THEFT AUTO

(Warner, 1977) **D/A:** Ron Howard **S/A:** Rance Howard **P:** Jon Davison

Roger Corman let 22-year-old Ron Howard (from Duncan, Oklahoma) direct for the first time after he had starred in *Eat My Dust!* (1976), a drive-in hit. Howard and Nancy Morgan elope in her father's Rolls Royce, and he chases them from LA to Las Vegas. This teen comedy is another excuse to smash up a lot of cars. Marion Ross (from the then-current *Happy Days* TV series, which starred Howard), Dick Miller, Hoke Howell, Rance Howard, Paul Bartel, and Clint Howard are also in this PG New World release. Gary Graver was the cinematographer, Joe Dante was the editor and is credited with montage, and Allan Arkush was the assistant director. Howard did some TV movies, then *Night Shift* (1982).

GRAND TOUR

(Academy, 1992) **D/S:** David Twohy **P:** John O'Connor   (*Disaster in Time; Timescape*)

A contractor (Jeff Daniels) who has been blamed for his wife's death fixes up an old house as a hotel. A group of very odd "tourists" check in to watch "spectacles." I don't want to give away what happens, but it involves a meteor, time travel, and hallucination-causing tea. It's set in a small Ohio town but was filmed in Oregon. Twohy wrote *Alien III*, but don't let that stop you from watching this very clever and well made science-fiction movie. With Emilia Crow, Ariana Richards, and Nicholas Guest. It debuted on the USA Network under an alternate title.

GRASS: A NATION'S BATTLE FOR LIFE

(Milestone, 1925) **D/S/P/C:** Merian C. Cooper, Ernest B. Schoedsack

The men who made *King Kong* started out making documentaries. This one, from Paramount, was their first. It shows 50,000 members of a nomadic Iranian ethnic group, the Bakhtiari, migrating (barefoot) through snow-covered mountains, with their livestock to get to seasonal grazing lands. The 70-minute video has a new score. The team made *Chang* (1927) next.

GRAVE SECRETS

(Southgate, 1989) **D:** Donald Borchers **S:** Jeffrey Polman, Lendre Wright **P:** Michael Alan Shores

Paul Le Mat, a professor who lectures on "innocent" ghosts, discovers a headless female ghost at a remote bed-and-breakfast owned by Renee Soutendijk (who should have stayed in the Netherlands if this was her best offer). They try to find the head so that the pathetic ghost can rest in peace (Wasn't that the plot of *The Headless Ghost* back in 1959?). It's not scary, and the minimal FX are pretty lousy. With David Warner, Olivia Barash, and Lee Ving.

GRAVE SECRETS: THE LEGACY OF HILLTOP DRIVE

(Worldvision, 1992) **D:** John Patterson **S/P:** Gregory Goodell

This overcomplicated *Poltergeist*-inspired TV movie is about a new suburban house where everything malfunctions and screaming, floating faces appear. It turns out that it was built on a slave graveyard. The credits claim it's a true story. Patty Duke (*Amityville IV*) stars, with Kirsten Warren, David Soul, and David Selby.

THE GRAVEYARD = PERSECUTION

GRAVEYARD SHIFT

(Virgin, 1986) **D/S:** Gerard Ciccoritti **P:** Michael Bockner   Canada

The production crew from *Psycho Girls* returned with this one about a vampire cabdriver. Silvio Oliviero (he was in *Psycho Girls* and looks kind of like

Chris Sarandon) stars in what is supposed to be Manhattan. His love interest/victim (Helen Papas) is a terminally ill TV director. In this movie vampirism is a cure for cancer. The gore was cut to avoid an X rating, but lots of nudity remains. Some may be unhappy with the rock-video-style scenes (the director started out doing TV commercials), but they helped make it a video hit, and there's a sequel, *The Understudy*.

GRAVEYARD SHIFT

(Paramount, 1990) **D/P:** Ralph S. Singleton **S:** John Esposito **P:** William J. Dunn

"The 19th adaptation for film or TV of a King novel or short story" was one of the all-time worst. David Andrews stars as a guy who gets a night job in a Maine textile mill. It's all too dark, the accents are awful, and the monster is nearly nonexistent. Stephen Macht as the mean boss has the worst accent. Brad Dourif as a Nam-vet rat catcher is the only good part. With Kelly Wolf and Andrew Divoff.

GRAYEAGLE

(1977) **D/S/P/A:** Charles B. Pierce

AIP released this PG western, basically a low-budget, uncredited remake of John Ford's *The Searchers* (1956). Ben Johnson, a veteran of several Ford westerns, stars (in the John Wayne role), with Iron Eyes Cody, Lana Wood (who was in *The Searchers*), Jack Elam, Alex Cord, and Paul Fix. AIP released four of Pierce's films.

GRAY LADY DOWN

(MCA, 1978) **D:** David Greene **S:** James Whitaker (and 6 others!) **P:** Walter Mirisch

Universal made this PG adventure, a box-office flop. Charlton Heston stars as the captain of a sunken nuclear submarine. David Carradine has a good role as the inventor of the Snark, an experimental diving vessel. With Stacy Keach, Ned Beatty, Stephen McHattie, Christopher Reeve (the same year as *Superman*), Ronny Cox, Rosemary Forsyth, and Priscilla Pointer.

GREASE

(Paramount, 1978) **D:** Randal Kleiser **S:** Bronte Woodward **P:** Alan Carr, Robert Stigwood

Carr produced this PG nostalgia musical after presenting the Mexican cannibal hit *Survive!* (1977). Both were released by Paramount, the *Friday the 13th* company. It's based on a Broadway show and includes hit songs by Olivia Newton-John and Frankie Valli. John Travolta (after *Saturday Night Fever*) costars with Newton-John. The supporting cast includes Stockard Channing, Eve Arden, Joan Blondell, Dody Goodman, Sid Caesar, Alice Ghostley, Fannie Flagg, and even Frankie Avalon and Edd Byrnes. The newcomers are Jeff Conaway, Didi Conn, Eddie

Deezen, Dinah Manoff, Michael Tucci, Ellen Travolta, and Lorenzo Lamas. Sha-Na-Na, who had been redoing 50s rock since the 60s (they performed at Woodstock), play Johnny Casino and the Gamblers. The film was a major hit.

GREASE 2

(Paramount, 1982) **D:** Patricia Birch **S:** Ken Finkleman **P:** Robert Stigwood, Alan Carr

The choreographer of *Grease* directed the flop sequel. Maxwell Caulfield and Michelle Pfeiffer play the leads. She became a star anyway, and he ended up in direct-to-video horror movies. With Pamela Segall, Tab Hunter, Connie Stevens, Adrian Zmed, Lorna Luft, and twins Liz and Jean Sagal. Eve Arden, Sid Caesar, Dody Goodman, Didi Conn, and Eddie Deezen returned.

GREASED LIGHTNING

(Warner, 1977) **D:** Michael Schultz **S:** Kenneth Vose, Lawrence DuKore, Melvin Van Peebles **P:** Hannah Weinstein

Richard Pryor plays Wendell Scott, the (real) first black championship racing-car driver. After serving in WWII he drives moonshine shipments for bootleggers in Virginia, goes to jail, and faces racism while trying to make it on the southern racing circuit. Melvin Van Peebles was replaced by Schultz as director. Pam Grier (who was engaged to Pryor at the time) plays his wife. With Beau Bridges, Cleavon Little, Richie Havens, Vincent Gardenia, Noble Willingham, and Julian Bond. It's PG.

GREASER'S PALACE

(1972) **D/S:** Robert Downey **P:** Cyma Rubin **M:** Jack Nitzsche

Allan Arbus stars as a Christlike drifter who parachutes into the Old West in a zoot suit, walks on water, and heals people. This underground western parody features Luana Anders, Hervé Villechaize, Toni Basil, and Don Calfa. It was Downey's last film until *Up the Academy* (1980).

GREAT ACTORS OF THE 20th CENTURY, Volume II

(Rhino)

This compilation consists of 3 half-hour TV dramas with horror stars. Boris Karloff stars in "The Vestris" (1958) as a ghost who warns a sea captain's wife. Vincent Price stars in "The Brainwashing of John Hayes" (1955) set in Communist China. Lon Chaney Jr. stars in "The Golden Junkman" (1956). They're all from forgotten b/w TV anthology shows.

THE GREAT ADVENTURE

(Media, 1974) **D:** Gianfranco Baldanello **S:** Juan Logar, Jesús Rodríguez   Italy/Spain (*Il Richiamo del Lupo*)

Jack Palance stars as town boss "Bet a Million" Bates in this adaptation of a Jack London story about a boy and his dog (played by Buck) in Alaska. Joan Collins is a dance-hall girl.

See the greatest cars in the world destroyed!

GRAND THEFT AUTO

RON HOWARD IS FUNNIER AND FASTER HE'S A HIGH SPEED DISASTER!

METROCOLOR
A NEW WORLD PICTURE
PG PARENTAL GUIDANCE SUGGESTED

THE GREAT ALASKAN MYSTERY

(Classic Cliffhangers, 1944) **D:** Ray Taylor, Lewis D. Collins **S:** Maurice Tombragel, George H. Plympton

Milburn Stone (later in *Gunsmoke*) stars in this 13-chapter Universal serial. Axis spies want to steal scientist Ralph Morgan's "perpetron," a matter-transmitting machine. With Marjorie Weaver, Fuzzy Knight, Martin Kosleck, Jack Ingram, and Jay Novello.

GREAT BALLS OF FIRE!

(Orion, 1989) **D/S:** Jim McBride **S:** Jack Baran **P:** Adam Fields

Making a movie about Jerry Lee Lewis was a great idea, but Dennis Quaid just doesn't cut it as the wild, southern piano-pounder. He seems too innocent. Winona Ryder costars as Lewis' 13-year-old second cousin (and third wife), Myra Gale. The PG-13 film ends in 1958, when the marriage scandal temporarily derailed his career. With Trey Wilson (who died in 1989) as Sam Phillips, Alec Baldwin as Lewis' cousin Jimmy Swaggart, Stephen Tobolowsky, Steve Allen (as himself), Lisa Blount, Joe Bob Briggs, and Tav Falco. Jimmy Vaughn, Mojo Nixon, and John Doe are Jerry Lee's band, and Michael St. Gerard shows up as Elvis. Actors play Alan Freed, Chuck Berry, Big Maybelle, and other real people. It was based on Myra Gale's book. Lewis himself recorded new versions of his old songs (including the hits and "Real Wild Child"). Look for the real thing on the tape *Shindig Presents Jerry Lee Lewis* (Rhino).

THE GREATEST STORY EVER TOLD

(MGM, 1965) **D:** David Lean, Jean Negulesco (both uncredited) **D/S/P:** George Stevens **S:** James Lee Barrett

The greatest Ultra Panavision 70/Cinerama and Technicolor epic ever filmed took five years to finish. It was originally 260 minutes, was cut to 195 minutes when it flopped, then was cut again, to 141 minutes. Charlton Heston is John the Baptist, and Dorothy McGuire is the Virgin Mary. Watching it for the cameo appearances by guest stars can be very rewarding. Check out Telly Savalas as Pontius Pilate, Donald Pleasence as the Devil, and John Wayne (!) as a Roman centurion. Some of the others are Claude Rains, Robert Loggia, Robert Blake, John Considine, Pat Boone, Shelley Winters, Sidney Poitier, Van Heflin, Carroll Baker, Ed Wynn, José Ferrer, Roddy McDowall, David McCallum, Victor Buono, Richard Conte, Sal Mineo, Angela Lansbury, and of course Max von Sydow as Jesus Christ. United Artists released it. Who would have thought that Martin Scorsese would try to top this over 20 years later?

THE GREAT FLAMARION

(Sinister, 1946) **D:** Anthony Mann **S:** Anne Wigton, Heintz Herald, Richard Well **P:** William Wilder

Erich von Stroheim stars as Flamarion, a sharpshooter in a vaudeville act. His assistant (Mary Beth Hughes) pretends to be in love with him, tricks him into killing her husband, then goes off

with another man (Dan Duryea). This was one of several low-budget Republic features von Stroheim starred in before leaving the US for France.

THE GREAT IMPERSONATION

(1935) **D:** Alan Crosland **S:** Frank Wead, Eve Greene

Edward Lowe plays a disgraced Austrian baron in Africa who kills a wealthy, alcoholic Britisher (also played by Lowe), assumes the dead man's identity, and moves to his ancestral home in England, where a "ghost" screams and spies plot. Universal promoted this 64-minute film as a horror movie. Sets from *The Old Dark House* and *Bride of Frankenstein* are reused, and parts of the plot are borrowed from *The Hound of the Baskervilles*. The story had first been filmed in 1920 and was remade again (with Ralph Bellamy) in 1942. With Dwight Frye as a bearded madman of the bog, young Valerie Hobson as the disturbed wife (she was in *The Mystery of Edwin Drood*, *The Werewolf of London*, and *Bride of Frankenstein* the same year), Brandon Hurst as the butler, Spring Byington, and Nan Grey.

THE GREAT JESSE JAMES RAID

(1953) **D:** Reginald LeBorg **S:** Richard Landau **P:** Robert L. Lippert

The cast includes Willard Parker as Jesse James, with Jim Bannon and Wallace Ford, but this B western from Lippert is notable because it features Barbara Payton and Tom Neal. In 1951 Neal had beaten Payton's boyfriend at the time, actor Franchot Tone, giving him a concussion and a broken nose. She married Tone, but left him a few months later for Neal. That relationship didn't last. She made only one more film. In 1963 she wrote her autobiography, *I'm Not Ashamed*. She died in 1967, at 40. This was Neal's last film. In 1965 he was sentenced to six years in prison for manslaughter after shooting his third wife. Less than a year after his release he died.

THE GREAT LOS ANGELES EARTHQUAKE

(Vidmark, 1990) **D:** Larry Elikann **S:** William Bast, Paul Hudson **P:** Stratton Leopold   (*The Big One*)

A scientist (Joanna Kerns) knows the big one is coming, but politicians cover up her report. A news leak causes mass panic, and tremors create a disaster (and the threat of a nuclear meltdown). With Dan Lauria, Joe Spano, Richard Masur, and Ed Begley Jr. This 2-part TV movie aired just months after a major San Francisco earthquake.

THE GREAT ROCK AND ROLL SWINDLE

(Warner, 1980) **D/S:** Julien Temple **P:** Jeremy Thomas, Don Boyd   UK

Russ Meyer was set to direct *Who Shot Bambi?* (with Marianne Faithfull as Sid's mum!). He worked only four days, the Sex Pistols fell apart, and Sid Vicious died. Jonathan Kaplan was hired and fired next. The Sex Pistols' manager, Malcolm McLaren, had this put together anyway. It's "held together" by his series of "lessons" about manipulating and exploiting a band, the press, and the public. The essential parts feature Johnny Rotten and are live: "Anarchy" (with Glen Matlock),

"God Save" on a boat, an excellent "Pretty Vacant," and the last song at the last show (in San Francisco), "No Fun." Another highlight is Vicious doing "My Way" onstage in Paris (it had already been seen in *Mr. Mike's Mondo Video* and was later recreated in *Sid and Nancy*). The rest is other people doing Pistols songs, Sid doing Eddie Cochran, cartoon animation, comic bits, and way too much McLaren. With train robber Ronnie Biggs in Brazil, Jess Conrad (*Horrors of the Black Museum*), James Aubrey (*Lord of the Flies*), and Nancy Spungen and Mary Millington (both now dead). Some performance footage was shot by Derek Jarman. The film was (finally) released in the US in 1992.

GREAT SCOUT AND CATHOUSE THURSDAY

(Vestron, 1974) **D:** Don Taylor **S:** Richard Shapiro **P:** Jules Buck, David Korda

Lee Marvin stars in this wacky, PG-rated western comedy about a whorehouse in 1908 Colorado, from AIP. With Oliver Reed as an Indian, Robert Culp, Elizabeth Ashley, Kay Lenz, Strother Martin, and Sylvia Miles. Former actor Taylor also directed sequels to *Planet of the Apes* and *The Omen*.

THE GREAT SKYCOPTER RESCUE

(MGM, 1981) **D/P:** Lawrence D. Foldes (*Skycopter Summer*)

Evil bikers take over a California town. A local DJ quits his job to become a pilot hero. Aldo Ray appears as the corrupt sheriff. With William Marshall and Russell Johnson. It was the last release from Dimension, a company co-founded in 1971 by Laurence Woolner, who had helped Roger Corman start New World.

THE GREAT SMOKEY ROADBLOCK

(1978) **D/S:** John Leone **P:** Allan F. Bodoh (*The Last of the Cowboys*)

Henry Fonda stars as an aging driver whose truck is repossessed while he's in the hospital. He steals it back and goes on a last cross-country run with a bunch of hookers. This PG drive-in movie features Eileen Brennan, Susan Sarandon (who coproduced it), Melanie Mayron, Robert Englund, and John Byner as a DJ. This has an unusually strong cast, compared to other films from Dimension.

THE GREAT SPY CHASE

(1964) **D/P:** George Lautner **S:** Michel Audiard, Albert Simonin   Italy (*Les Barbouzes*)

AIP released this Cold War spy comedy. Agents from various countries, wearing disguises, try to get a scientist's secrets from his stripper widow (Mireille Darc). Lino Ventura is the French spy, and Bernard Blier costars.

THE GREAT TEXAS DYNAMITE CHASE

(1977) **D:** Michael Pressman **S:** David Kirpatrick **P:** David Irving

Claudia Jennings and Jocelyn Jones star as Candy and Ellie Jo, "the dynamite women," bank robbers (in cut-off jeans) on the run in this New World release. The gimmick (besides some R-rated nudity) is that they blow up a lot of things with big packs of dynamite. With former *Rifleman* TV series son Johnny Crawford (he's also in *The Naked Ape*) as Slim, a shoplifter who joins them, and Tara Strohmeier. The director later made *Teenage Mutant Ninja Turtles II*.

THE GREED OF WILLIAM HART

(Sinister, 1948) **D:** Oswald Mitchell **S:** John Gilling **P:** Gilbert Church   (*Horror Maniacs*)

Tod Slaughter, the first horror star in England, ended his feature-film career with this version of the legend of Burke and Hare, the Edinburgh body snatchers. This cut version preserves only 53 minutes of the original 79 minutes. It played in the US in 1953 under the great exploitation title *Horror Maniacs*. Slaughter went on to appear in some shorts and on TV, and he returned to the stage, where he had begun. He died in 1956, just before British horror movies became big business.

The Greed of William Hart, aka Horror Maniacs

THE GREEN ARCHER

(Stokey, 1940) **D:** James W. Horne **S:** Morgan B. Cox, John Cutting, Jesse A. Duffy **P:** Larry Darmour

This 15-chapter Columbia serial is based on an Edgar Wallace novel. Other versions were made in 1925 by Pathé and in 1960 in West Germany. It's about murders around an old castle and a ghostly archer. Victor Jory stars, with Iris Meredith and James Craven.

THE GREEN ARCHER

(Sinister, 1960) **D:** Jürgen Roland **S:** Wolfgang Menge, Wolfgang Schnitzler W. Germany (*Der Grüne Bogenschütze*)

Gert Frobe and Karin Dor star in this murder mystery. It's part of a series of Edgar Wallace adaptations.

THE GREEN BERETS

(Warner, 1968) **D:** Ray Kellogg, Mervyn LeRoy **D/A:** John Wayne **S:** James Lee Barrett **P:** Michael Wayne

This is the only major film made during the Vietnam War that supported US involvement. Military officials and equipment were made available for the production. David Janssen is the liberal antiwar reporter set straight by Colonel Mike Kirby (John Wayne) in the combat zone. The film was released just after Robert Kennedy was shot and just

before Nixon and Agnew were picked to run on the Republican ticket. Even if you are a lifelong Republican who loves Wayne, it's too long (133 minutes) and filled with clichés. Besides Wayne and Janssen, Aldo Ray, Jim Hutton, Bruce Cabot, Raymond St. Jacques, and Jack Soo have since died (a conspiracy?). Also in the cast are Luke Askew, Irene Tsu, Jason Evers, and Richard Pryor (!?). Co-director Kellogg also made *The Killer Shrews* and *The Giant Gila Monster*! Barrett also wrote *The Greatest Story Ever Told* (which Wayne was in).

THE GREEN-EYED BLONDE

(1957) **D:** Bernard Girard **S:** Sally Stubblefield **P:** Martin Melcher

Sexy blonde Susan Oliver was 19 and making her screen debut in this "story of a teenage firebomb" from Warner Brothers. It takes place at a detention home for girls, and the plot concerns car theft, murder, and an illegitimate baby. Cornelius Gunter (from the Coasters) sings the theme song, and the score is by Leith Stevens. The producer was married to Doris Day.

THE GREEN HORNET

(Stokey, 1940) **D:** Ford Beebe, Ray Taylor **S:** George H. Plympton, Basil Dickey, Morrison C. Wood

This 13-chapter Universal serial based on a popular radio series is from the producers of the *Flash Gordon* serials. Gordon Jones stars as newspaper publisher Britt Reid, but the radio-series Hornet (Al Hodge) provides the voice of his masked crime-fighting alter ego. Keye Luke is Kato (a role played on TV years later by Bruce Lee), and Anne Nagel is Lenore. They have a superfast car and a gas gun. Some chapters are "Flying Coffins," "Bullets and Ballots," and "Panic in the Zoo." Anne Gwynne and Alan Ladd have small parts. It's available on two cassettes. The immediate sequel, *The Green Hornet Strikes Again* (1940), stars Warren Hull as Reid, with the same major cast members, but is not available on tape.

THE GREEN MAN

(Fox, 1990) **D:** Elijah Moshinsky **S:** Malcolm Bradbury **P:** David Snodin   UK

The owner of an English inn (Albert Finney), who drinks too much, has sex with his doctor's wife (Sarah Berger) on his 53rd birthday, after his senile father (Michael Hordern) dies. He also starts seeing ghosts, and it turns out that the inn is haunted by an evil 17th-century minister (Michael Culver). There are bat attacks, a living tree, an exorcism, and nightmares inside of nightmares. This 3-hour BBC movie debuted in the US on the Arts and Entertainment Network. It's based on a Kingsley Amis novel. With Linda Marlowe as Finney's wife, Nicky Hensen, and Nickolas Grace.

GREEN MANSIONS

(MGM, 1959) **D:** Mel Ferrer **S:** Dorothy Kingsley **P:** Edmund Grainger

Audrey Hepburn stars as Rima, "the bird girl," who can communicate with the creatures of the Amazon jungle. Anthony Perkins is her confused lover. This odd romantic fantasy is based on W. H. Hudson's novel. With Lee J. Cobb, Sessue Hayakawa, Henry Silva, Michael Pate, and Nehemiah Persoff. Ferrer and Hepburn were married when they made this MGM color production. After the failure of this movie and the marriage, Ferrer relocated to Europe, where he continued to act and direct.

THE GREEN PASTURES

(MGM, 1936) **D:** William Keighley **D/S:** Marc Connelly

Racial stereotypes abound as the Old Testament is seen through the eyes of southern black children. The cast includes Rex Ingram in three roles, Eddie "Rochester" Anderson, and Oscar Polk. Based on Connelly's Pulitzer Prize–winning Broadway play, this Warner Brothers production was the first film with an all-black cast made by a major studio since *Hallelujah* (1929). The next ones were *Cabin in the Sky*, a musical fantasy about good and evil, and *Stormy Weather*, a backstage musical (both 1943).

GREEN SNAKE

(Long Shore, 1993) **D/P:** Tsui Hark **S:** Lilian Lee **P:** Ng See Yuen   Hong Kong

Maggie Cheung and Joey Wang star as snakelike shape-shifters who decide to become sexy human women and get involved with men. A monk tries to destroy them. During a battle one becomes a giant flying snake and fights a flying dragon created from the monk's tattoo. Based on a Chinese novel already filmed several times, this was a commercial flop.

GREETINGS

(Vidmark, 1968) **D/E:** Brian De Palma **S/P:** Charles Hirsch

Nobody cared about De Niro or De Palma when this New York City underground comedy about draft dodging was released. Jonathan Warden makes a stag movie, Robert De Niro is a peeping Tom, Gerrit Graham is obsessed with the JFK assassination and conspiracy theories, and Allen Garfield is "the smut peddler." De Niro is the one who ends up being drafted and sent to Nam. There's an actual LBJ speech. It was rated X when first released by Sigma III. De Palma's sequel, *Hi, Mom!*, features many of the same actors and was also written by Hirsch.

GREMLINS

(Warner, 1984) **D:** Joe Dante **S:** Chris Columbus **P:** Mike Finnell **M:** Jerry Goldsmith

This PG-13 horror fantasy, full of in-jokes and irreverent comedy, was an unexpected hit. It takes place at Christmastime in a perfect looking old-fashioned American small town. Inventor Hoyt Axton buys a mysterious furry pet from Asian antique-shop owner Keye Luke for his son. When Luke's strict warnings are ignored, the cuddly creature spawns rude reptilian demons (sort of a cat/frog mixture) who trash the town and mock everything sacred to the locals. Zach Galligan and Phoebe Cates are the teen stars, with Polly Holliday, Scott Brady (in his last role), Harry Carey Jr., Dick Miller, Jackie Joseph, Corey Feldman, Judge Reinhold, Kenneth Tobey, William Schallert, and Don Steele. There are Chris Wallas FX, scenes from *Invasion of the Body Snatchers* and *Snow White and the Seven Dwarfs*, and references to *It's a Wonderful Life*. The Goldsmith score is on Geffen. Columbus and Wallas both became directors themselves. Steven Spielberg was an executive producer and appears briefly. The hit movie spawned many imitations and a sequel.

GREMLINS 2: THE NEW BATCH

(Warner, 1990) **D:** Joe Dante
S: Charles Haas **P:** Mile Finnell

After six years, Dante returned with a bigger, wilder PG-13 sequel set in New York City. The trouble is that it made less than half of its $50 million cost. I guess it was just too much entertainment for the average viewer. Or maybe the anti–greed/big business message was hard to take from executive producer Spielberg. The new mutant Gremlins fly, talk, sing, and take over a high-rise. Galligan and Cates star again. John Glover is funny as a Donald Trump/Ted Turner composite character, and Robert Prosky is a TV horror host made up to look like Grandpa Munster. Christopher Lee is a scientist (it was promoted as his "203rd film role"), and Dick Miller and Jackie Joseph have larger roles. With Haviland Morris as Marla, Gedde Watanabe, Keye Luke, and Kathleen Freeman, and bits by John Astin, Henry Gibson, Paul Bartel, Kenneth Tobey, Page Hannah, Leonard Maltin, Belinda Balaski, Tony Randall, and Howie Mandel. Hulk Hogan, Dick Butkus, and Bubba Smith play themselves, and Bugs Bunny and Daffy Duck appear. Rick Baker and Steve Wang were in charge of the FX. There are clips from *Octoman*, *The Beast From 20,000 Fathoms*, and a nudist-colony movie. The Jerry Goldsmith score is on Varèse Sarabande. *Hellzapoppin*-style film-breaks gags were replaced by different scenes for the video.

GREY MATTER: *See* THE BRAIN MACHINE

GREYSTOKE: THE LEGEND OF TARZAN, LORD OF THE APES

(Warner, 1984) **D/P:** Hugh Hudson, Robert Towne, Michael Austin **S:** "P. H. Vazak"/ Robert Towne **P:** Stanley S. Canter

Christopher Lee as Dr. Catheter in *Gremlins II: The New Batch.*

The most expensive Tarzan movie of all time, filmed in Super Techniscope, was a troubled production and a box-office flop. It's long (130 minutes) and flawed, but it does have some awesome scenes and is closest to Edgar Rice Burroughs' books. It was filmed in Cameroon and Britain. Christopher Lambert stars (for the first time in the US), and Andie MacDowell (dubbed by Glenn Close) is Jane. The supporting cast includes Ian Holm as a Belgian explorer, Sir Ralph Richardson (he's great in his last role, and he has a memorable death scene), James Fox (his second role since the 1970 film *Performance*), Cheryl Campbell, Ian Charleson, and Nigel Davenport. Rick Baker created the excellent apes. Robert Towne, who had written the script in 1976, wanted to direct. He used his dog's name for his screenwriting credit. The dog was nominated for an Oscar.

GRIEF

(Academy, 1993) **D/S:** Richard Galtzer
P: Ruth Charney

The Love Judge, a syndicated TV series, is filmed in a hotel formerly used by prostitutes. Craig Chester stars as the suicidal head writer whose partner has died of AIDS. Much of this comedy/drama is flashbacks. With Illeana Douglas, Lucy Gutteridge, and (in the fictitious TV series) Joanna Went, Paul Bartel, and Mary Woronov.

GRIEVOUS BODILY HARM

(Fries, 1988) **D:** Mark Joffe **S:** Warwick Hind **P:** Richard Brennan   Australia

Colin Friels stars as a police detective who searches for his missing wife and goes after a psycho killer. With John Waters (not the director), Bruno Lawrence, and Shane Briant. It's 136 minutes long.

THE GRIFTERS

(HBO, 1990) **D:** Stephen Frears **S:** Donald E. Westlake **P:** Martin Scorsese, Robert A. Harris **M:** Elmer Bernstein

Everybody cons everybody, the acting is fine, and there's some surprising sex and violence in this adaptation of a Jim Thompson novel. It concerns a bleached-blond con woman (Anjelica Huston), her estranged con-man son (John Cusack), and his new lover/partner (Annette Bening). With Pat Hingle (in a scary performance) as Bobo Justus, Stephen Tobolowsky, Sandy Baron, Henry Jones, J. T. Walsh, Jeremy Piven, and Charles Napier as a businessman who becomes a victim of one of the many no-lose scams. The soundtrack is on Varèse Sarabande.

GRIM PRAIRIE TALES

(Academy, 1990) **D/S:** Wayne Coe
P: Richard Hahn

The always interesting Brad Dourif is a 19th-century city slicker on the prairie at night who runs into a strange, loudmouthed trapper (James Earl Jones) with a dead man on his horse. They tell stories

around a campfire. One is about disrupting a sacred Indian burial ground. Another is about a racist settler and a lynch mob. A bizarre tale concerns some kind of succubus. The last story, about a gunfighter, features a surprise cartoon nightmare (and a character wearing very out-of-place modern briefs). The biggest problem is that the scenes around the campfire are more interesting and have more tension than the stories themselves. With William Atherton, Lisa Eichhorn, and Marc McClure.

GRINDHOUSE HORRORS

(Ecco, 1992)

Most of the more than 40 trailers on this 100-minute compilation tape are from the late 60s to the early 80s. You get horror, exploitation, mondo, and kung-fu, and many are trailers you probably have not seen. Some highlights are *Sweden, Heaven and Hell, Savage Island, Shogun Assassin, Deep Red, Virgin Witch, Deranged, Street Trash, The Doll Squad, Chinese Hercules,* and *Jungle Warriors*.

THE GRISSOM GANG

(1971) **D/P:** Robert Aldrich **S:** Leon Griffiths

Although it fits in with *Bloody Mama* and other violent 70s movies about rural family crime in the 20s, this was an adaptation of *No Orchids for Miss Blandish*, a novel by James Hadley Chase, which had been filmed under that name in England in 1948. Kim Darby is a rich girl kidnapped by Ma Grissom (Irene Dailey) and her psycho sons. Scott Wilson is especially demented. With Tony Musante, Robert Lansing, Ralph Waite, Wesley Addy, and Connie Stevens. It was produced by the short-lived Cinerama.

THE GROOVE ROOM

(TZ, 1973) **D/S/P:** Vernon C. Becker
S: Barry E. Downes   UK (*Champagne Gallop; A Man with a Maid; What the Swedish Butler Saw; Tickled Pink; Teenage Tickle Girls*)

This 3-D period sex comedy has been released many times with different titles over the years by AIP, Independent International, and even Troma. It has also been shown in 3-D on cable TV, so a lot of people have seen it. Ollie Soltdoft stars as Ole, a photographer and inventor in an ornate turn-of-the-century whorehouse. He seduces various women and uses some light bondage and some kind of orgasm contraption. Some of the (soft-core) sex scenes are pretty good. Diana Dors co-stars as Madame Helga, with Sue Longhurst. Jack the Ripper even shows up. It was filmed in Sweden.

THE GROOVE TUBE

(Media, 1972) **D/S/P/A:** Ken Shapiro **S:** Lane Sarasohn

Like *Tunnelvision* (1976), this is a sex comedy with unrelated spoofs of TV shows and commercials. It was originally rated X. Both movies were semi-underground hits before the concept became common on TV itself, with *Saturday Night Live*. Chevy Chase (also in *Tunnelvision*) has a small role (his first) as a character married to (porno star) Jennifer Welles. With Richard Belzer and Buzzy Linhart. Shapiro was later behind *Night Flite*, on the USA Network.

GROTESQUE

(Media, 1987) **D/A:** Joseph Tornatore **S/A:** Mikel Angel **P:** Mike Lane, Chuck Morrell

I saw it, but I still don't know if it's supposed to be funny or not. A group of violent, laughing, overacting psycho "punkers" kill Linda Blair's vacationing family in an isolated vacation house in the mountains. Linda escapes in the snow, but meanwhile a rubbery-faced mutant/retard/hunchback brother (who cries, "Mama! Papa! Mama! Papa!") pursues the killers. A plastic-surgeon uncle (Tab Hunter) shows up for the (huh!?) ending. With Guy Stockwell as the horror-movie makeup-expert father, Donna Wilkes (*Angel*), Charles Dierkop, Luana Patten, Nels Van Patten, and Robert Z'Dar (with spike hair). Blair was also the coproducer. By the director of *Zebra Force*.

GROUNDHOG DAY

(Columbia, 1993) **D/S/P/A:** Harold Ramis **S:** Danny Rubin **P:** Trevor Albert

Bill Murray stars as a cynical Pittsburgh TV weatherman who has to repeat the same day endlessly in a small Pennsylvania town. He discovers that he can do whatever he wants (and can't die) but still has romantic trouble with his producer (Andie McDowell). The experience eventually makes him a better person. This PG comic fantasy features Chris Elliott as the cameraman, Stephen Tobolowsky, Robin Duke, and Brian Doyle-Murray. Sonny and Cher's "I Got You Babe" is heard many times. The soundtrack is on Epic.

GROUND ZERO

(IVE, 1987) **D/P:** Michael Pattinson, Bruce Myles **S:** Mac Gudgeon, Jan Jardi Australia

Colin Friels stars as a TV cameraman investigating the death of his father, also a cameraman, who may have filmed too much during 50s A-bomb tests conducted by the British government in Australia. With Donald Pleasence as a crippled test survivor and Jack Thompson. This PG Columbia release is based on real events.

GROUPIES

(1970) **D/P:** Robert Dorfman, Peter Nevard **P:** Robert Weiner

The Filmore East and West provided the setting for this 16mm documentary. The Chicago Plaster Casters, Miss Pamela, and others are interviewed, along with Joe Cocker, Ten Years After, Spooky Tooth, Terry Reid, and others, who all do appropriate songs ("Good Morning, Little Schoolgirl," "Bang Bang"). It was rated X when released by Maron.

GROUP MARRIAGE

(1972) **D/S:** Stephanie Rothman **S/P:** Charles S. Swartz **S:** Richard Walter

There's humor and nudity in this drive-in sex comedy about a communal house. With Claudia Jennings (in her first costarring role) Victoria Vetri, Jayne Kennedy (Miss Ohio of 1970), Aimee Eccles, Zack Taylor, Jeff Pomerantz, Solomon Sturges (son of director Preston Sturges), and Milt Kamen.

The music is by John Sebastian! Dimension was run by a married director and producer. Rothman had directed *It's a Bikini World* (1967), *Student Nurses* (1970), and *Velvet Vampire* (1971).

GROWING PAINS

(Thriller, 1980) **D:** Francis Megahy **S:** Nicholas Palmer UK

Elvira hosts this 60-minute Hammer TV movie. Barbara Kellermann and Gary Bond star as a couple who adopt a "bad seed" after their son dies.

GRUNT! THE WRESTLING MOVIE

(Starmaker, 1985) **D:** Allan Holzman **S:** Roger D. Manning **P:** Anthony Ranel

Greg "Magic" Schwartz as Mad Dog Joe is the star of this comedy documentary about wrestling. With Robert Glaudini, Lydie Denier, Wally George, and midgets. From New World and the director of *Forbidden World*.

THE GUARDIAN

(MCA, 1989) **D/S:** William Friedkin **S:** Steven Volk, Dan Greenburg **P:** Joe Wizan

A Druid spirit named Camilla (Jenny Seagrove) poses as a nanny so that she can sacrifice babies. She's hired by an unsuspecting wealthy young couple (Carey Lowell and Dwier Brown). There's a vicious wolf attack and a tree that kills would-be rapist bikers. When the dad attacks the tree with a chainsaw, it spews blood and screams (Steve Johnson provided the FX). It made me think of *From Hell It Came*. With Miguel Ferrer and Brad Hall. There are some nude-nanny scenes. This followed Friedkin's then unreleased *Rampage* (1987).

GUARDIAN OF HELL

(1980) **D:** Stefan Oblowsky **P:** John L. Chamblis Italy (*The Other Hell*)

Nuns in a convent become possessed. There's also a telekinetic baby and a mirror leading to Hell.

GUARDIAN OF THE ABYSS

(Thriller, 1980) **D:** Don Sharp **S:** Anthony Read UK

Elvira hosts this 60-minute Hammer TV program. Rosalyn Landor and Ray Lonnen star in a tale about an antique mirror that leads to Hell.

GUESS WHAT WE LEARNED IN SCHOOL TODAY?

(VGB, 1970) **D/S/C/E:** John G. Avildsen **S:** Eugene Price **P:** David Gil

Suburban high-school sex education is the theme of this comedy by the man who later made *Rocky*. The woman who wants the classes is named Mrs Lillywhitehorn. The vice-squad cop who tries to stop her is called Roger Manly. Meanwhile, frustrated wives of conservative community leaders smoke pot and have lesbian affairs. Lieutenant Manly ends up getting arrested for having sex with a black male cop who was in drag. Avildsen made this forgotten R-rated satire and the hit *Joe* for Cannon.

GUILTY AS CHARGED

(Columbia, 1991) **D:** Sam Irvin **S:** Charles Gale **P:** Randolph Gale

In this black comedy/drama, Rod Steiger is a religious fanatic whose family has been killed. He kidnaps criminals who managed to escape the death penalty, takes them to his Chicago meat-packing warehouse, and with "the will of God" kills them with his own winged, art-deco electric chair. It's an awkward concept that flirts with political issues, but Steiger must have liked the role, because he really acts (unlike some of his recent performances). A few of the condemned prisoners cry before going to the chair. Steiger's assistant and organist is Isaac Hayes, Lauren Hutton is the wife of a corrupt congressman (he's also a killer), and Heather Graham is a parole officer. With Lyman Ward, Irwin Keyes, Zelda Rubinstein, and Mitch Pileggi (from *Shocker*). Irwin edited an impressive horror-movie fanzine called *Bizarre* in the 70s. This is from IRS.

Rod Steiger in his electric chair, in *Guilty as Charged*.

GUILTY AS SIN

(Hollywood, 1993) **D:** Sidney Lumet
S: Larry Cohen **P:** Don Carmody

Don Johnson stars as a sexist, psycho gigolo accused of throwing his wife out of a window in their Chicago penthouse. He has an affair with his defense attorney (Rebecca De Mornay). With Stephen Lang, Jack Warden as a detective, Tom McComus, Dana Ivey, and Robert Kennedy. Who would have expected the director of *The Pawnbroker* to use a script by the director of *It's Alive III*?! This Buena Vista release was filmed in Toronto.

GUILTY PARENTS

(SW, 1933) **D/S:** Jack Townley

Helen (Jean Lacy) is a 20-year-old blond "on the threshold of womanhood." She's on trial in Ohio for "exterminating a vile creature." Flashbacks show how she reluctantly was initiated (stripped behind a curtain) into the drunken Fraternal Order of the Pink Elephant. Soon her boyfriend is shot during a holdup. She gives up her baby in New York City, becomes a chorus girl, and is blackmailed into setting up a dancing school to provide girls for gangsters. Helen's puritanical mother is blamed, and Helen jumps out of the courtroom window! By the director of *Mummy's Boys*. This vintage J. D. Kendis exploitation tape is presented here by David F. Friedman.

GUMS

(AVA, 1976) **D/S/P:** Robert J. Kaplan
S: Paul and Sam Cohen **P:** Isaac Roberts

This is a senseless, tasteless, crude porno parody of *Jaws* with terrible dubbing, but Brother Theodore as Captain Clitoris, the Quint character, gets to dress like a Nazi and rant uncontrollably: "Yuckata- yuckata-yuck. Cool it, you castrates! Unspeakable filth!" He also talks to his pet vulture, who has a giant spurting cock. R. Bolla, a porno actor in Italian cannibal movies, has the Richard Dreyfuss role. Instead of a shark there's a killer cocksucker mermaid, played by 70s porno star Terri Hall. Unappealing hard-core scenes last only a few seconds. Two men have sex with an inflatable doll, and two dogs are shown fucking. Hall swims around in a swimming pool/set, and in the only long sex scene she gets it on with an "Indian" woman on the beach after some abstract nude dancing. Just when you think it couldn't get any dumber, puppet characters show up, have sex, and sing (!). It was filmed in Florida and New York.

GUN BLAST

(197?) **D/S:** Nick Millard **P:** Irmgard Millard

Mr. Grant, a tough but basically nice ex-con (who looks kinda like Eddie Constantine mixed with Morley Safer), is talked into pulling off a drug heist by a woman. It takes place in Mexico and LA, and every scene has a title announcing the date and place. This is like a very low-budget *film noir* with a breast fetish. During sex scenes Grant kisses his new partner's breasts, and during a sex-show scene Uschi Digart massages and licks her own. This scene is supposed to be on a stage, but it looks as if Millard simply edited in a sex loop.

The soundtrack is mostly flamenco guitar (just like in Ed Wood's *Jailbait*) plus a singer who sounds a lot like Yoko Ono. We also see a woman applying blue eye shadow and hear some very uncinematic-sounding gunshots. By the makers of *Crazy Fat Ethel II*.

GUN CRAZY

(Fox, 1949) **D:** Joseph H. Lewis **S:** Millard Kaufman, MacKinlay Kantor, Dalton Trumbo (uncredited)
P: Frank King, Maurice King   (*Deadly Is the Female*)

This ahead-of-its-time sex-and-guns cult classic was inspired by the real Bonnie and Clyde and based on Kantor's story in the *Saturday Evening Post*. John Dall stars as Bart Tare, a small-town marksman who meets Annie Laurie Starr (Peggy Cummins) at a carnival shooting gallery. They marry, and she encourages their life of crime: "I want action!" With Berry Kroeger, Annabel Shaw, Morris Carnovsky, and Russ Tamblyn as the young, revolver-stealing Bart. The United Artists release includes some impressive, advanced camera work and dialogue like "We go together like guns and ammunition." Lewis later matched *Gun Crazy* with the obsessive *The Big Combo* (1954).

GUNCRAZY

(Academy, 1992) **D:** Tamra Davis **S:** Matthew Bright **P:** Zane W. Levitt, Diane Firestone

Drew Barrymore has her best role so far as Anita, a sympathetic 16-year-old "class slut" who lives in a rural California trailer with her absent hooker mom's boyfriend, Rooney (Joe Dallesandro). She corresponds with Howard (James LeGros), an impotent convict, and learns to shoot. Anita kills and burns Rooney (good gore FX) to stop the forced (offscreen) sex and says, "Here lies a pig. May he rot in hell!" Howard gets out of Chino, and the doomed couple end up on the road in a disastrous crime and accidental-murder spree. With Billy Drago as a long-haired, snake-handling preacher,

Peggy Cummins and John Dall in *Gun Crazy*.

Michael Ironside as a parole officer, Ione Skye, and Tracey Walter. It borrows from the 1949 film of the same name, but it's not a remake and stands up just fine on its own. *Guncrazy* debuted on Showtime, then played some theaters. The director (in her late 20s), who had done rock videos, made the rap comedy *CB4: The Movie* next.

GUNFIRE

(Bongo, 1978) **D:** Monte Hellman **S:** Jerry Harvey, Douglas Venturelli **P:** Gianni Bozzacchi, Valerio De Paolis   Italy (*China 9, Liberty 37*)

Railroad barons save a condemned man (Warren Oates) so that he can kill a gunman for them. With Fabio Testi, Jenny Agutter, and Sam Peckinpah. It was Hellman's last film for ten years and his fourth with Oates. The music is by Pino Donaggio. The original title refers to a traffic sign.

GUN FURY

(1953) **D:** Raoul Walsh **S:** Irving Wallace, Roy Huggins
P: Lewis J. Rachmil **M:** Mischa Bakaleinikoff

This 3-D Columbia western stars Rock Hudson as a rancher whose fiancée (Donna Reed) has been abducted. With Phil Carey, Leo Gordon, Neville Brand, and Lee Marvin as Blinky. Walsh, like Andre De Toth, had only one good eye, but he knew how to make a good western.

GUN GIRLS

(SW, 1953) **D/S/E:** Robert C. Dertano
P: Edward Frank **C:** William C. Thompson

A narrator tells us all about "the new teenage problem." Teddy, a (too old-looking) wise-ass blond teen ("I'm hip"), robs a guy in the alley with her friend Dora. Her boyfriend is the brother of the probation officer (who gives a speech). Joe (Timothy Ferrell) buys the stolen goods ("I'm a businessman") and plans a warehouse heist. His big mistake is dumping the beautiful blond Joy, who becomes pregnant. Obviously filmed in LA, it's supposed to be set in New York. There are lots of news headlines and a cat fight. This Eros production is very similar to *The Violent Years* (1956), written by Ed Wood Jr. Ferrell returned as the same character in Dertano's much wilder hard drug movie *Girl Gang* (SW, 1954).

GUNMEN

(Live, 1994) **D:** Deran Sarafian
S: Stephen Sommers **P:** Laurence Mark, John Davis, John Flock

An illiterate outlaw (Christopher Lambert) is busted out of a South American jail by a New York City special-forces agent (Mario Van Peebles) and they go after a missing drug-money fortune. Denis Leary is the killer hired by crippled drug lord Patrick Stewart to off them. This over-the-top film copies *The Good, the Bad, and the Ugly*. With Brenda

Bakke (who has a sex scene), Kadeem Hardison, Sally Kirkland, and rapper Big Daddy Kane. It's from Miramax. The two stars were also in *Highlander III*.

GUNS

(RCA, 1990) **D/S:** Andy Sidaris **P:** Arlene Sidaris

Erik Estrada is a South American drug smuggler/gunrunner in Hawaii. The fifth in a series of brainless Sidaris sex-and-spy movies, this features "six *Playboy* playmates," nude oil-wrestling, and transvestite hitmen. Dona Speir costars (in her fourth Sidaris movie), with Roberta and Devin Vasquez, Cynthia Brimhall, Phyllis Elizabeth Davis (from *Terminal Island*), Michael Shayne, Kym Malin, Liv Lindeland, Donna Spangler, former TV-kid-show host Chuck McCann, Tony Curtis' daughter Allegra, and boxer Chu Chu Malave. Filmed in Hawaii, in Las Vegas, and at London Bridge (it's in Arizona).

GUNSLINGER

(Duravision, 1956) **D/P:** Roger Corman
S: Charles Griffith

When Roger Corman started his career as a director he wasn't making science-fiction or horror movies. His first film was *Five Guns West* (1955), and he made three more wacky westerns for ARC (the company that became AIP) in 18 months. This is his last western. It was made in 7 days (1 day over schedule) and is in color. It borrows a lot from Nicholas Ray's *Johnny Guitar* (1954), but then so does *Once Upon a Time in the West*. It opens with arty, modern 50s titles and jazz music! If you're a Corman fan who likes to see his regular troupe of actors in anything (like me), you'll love it. If you're looking for a good western, forget it! Rose Hood (Beverly Garland) becomes marshal after her husband (William Schallert) is gunned down. She guns down the killers during the funeral and sleeps in a jail cell. Erica Page (Allison Hayes) runs the local bar and uses her pathetic, lovesick barkeep (Jonathan Haze) to murder people who get in the way of her plan to get rich when the railroad arrives. "Little man, you're too stupid!" she tells him many times. Erica also hires Cane (John Ireland), a brooding killer who wears only black, and orders him to kill Rose, whom he's in love with. Rose, whom Cane calls "that chesty marshal," gets to punch out Erica during a cat fight. The set looks like a ghost town, and the cast is minimal. When three dancing girls do the same act several times we see two tables with spectators but hear what sound like hundreds of loud people. Dick Miller is with the pony express, and Bruno Ve Sota plays a businessman. Garland starred in five early Corman movies. From 1969 to 1972 she was the stepmother in the TV series *My Three Sons*. She owns two hotels in California.

GUNS OF THE BLACK WITCH

(Sinister, 1961) **D/P:** Domenico Paolella
S: Luciano Martino, Ugo Guerra   Italy
(*Il Terrore dei Mari*)

Don Megowan stars as Jean, a heroic 17th-century French pirate who battles the evil Spanish rulers of a Caribbean island. With Silvana Pampanini and Emma Daniel. AIP released it.

THE GUTTER GIRLS

(1963) **D/P:** Robert Hartford-Davis **S:** Derek Ford
UK (*The Thrill Seekers; The Yellow Teddybears*)

Linda (Annette Whiteley), a boarding-school girl, becomes pregnant by a window cleaner/pop singer named Kinky. The school girls have an anti-virgin club and party with a prostitute friend who suggests that Linda go to work for her to earn money for an abortion. Hartford-Davis later made *Corruption* and *The Bloodsuckers*, both with Peter Cushing.

A GUY NAMED JOE

(MGM, 1943) **D:** Victor Fleming
S: Dalton Trumbo **P:** Everett Riskin

Spencer Tracy is a daredevil American pilot in England during WWII who's shot down and goes to Heaven, a giant military flying field run by Lionel Barrymore. His ghost is sent back to Earth to help another pilot (Van Johnson). This 2-hour MGM fantasy costars Irene Dunne and features Ward Bond, James Gleason, Barry Nelson, and Esther Williams. *Happy Land* and *The Human Comedy* are other uplifting WWII dramas from the same year. Fleming, used to big projects, had already directed *The Wizard of Oz* and *Gone with the Wind* (both 1939) and *Dr. Jekyll and Mr. Hyde*, with Tracy (1941). This film was remade by Steven Spielberg as *Always* (1989).

THE GUYVER

(New Line, 1991) **D/FX:** Screaming Mad George, Steve Wang **S:** John Purdy **P:** Brian Yuzna   (*Mutronics*)

A college student (Jack Armstrong) becomes an Inframan-type armor-plated hero and fights lots of bad guys turned into monsters. This is a fun American movie based on a popular Japanese comic book by Yoshiki Takaya. Vivian Wu costars as a scientist's daughter, and Mark Hamill is a CIA agent who becomes a cockroach (!) monster. The scientist villain (the late David Gale) turns into a giant dino-monster in his underground lab for one of the many fight scenes. Michael Berryman, Jimmy Walker (who raps), Spice Williams (who also does stunts), and Peter Spollos all become monsters too. Also with Jeffrey Combs, Linnea Quigley, and first assistant director/second-unit director Tom Rainone in a fun gag scene. Wang also made *Kung Fu Rascals*. Episodes of the Japanese *Guyver* TV cartoon show are also on tape (from US Renditions).

GUYVER II: DARK HERO

(New Line, 1994) **D/P/E:** Steve Wang **S:** Nathan Long

David Hayter stars, with Kathy Christopherson as a scientist's daughter, Christopher Michael, Ann George, Veronica Reed, and lots of fighting women. Wang also directed the popular *Mighty Morphin Power Rangers* TV show.

GWAR LIVE FROM ANTARCTICA

(Warner, 1990) **P:** Ivan Purvis

Gwar is the ultimate post-nuke show band, with a monster alien singer, bloody slave roadies, and mutant *Conan*-type band members who engage in simulated sex, rape, and dismemberment while playing music that sounds to me like a hard-core punk Black Sabbath. One monster "comes" on the audience. It's all pretty dumb, and I don't even like the music, but I still recommend seeing Gwar, and this hour-long tape is the safe way to do it. They do 14 songs live onstage and are seen in a video for "Sick of You." It's from Metal Blade, a division of Warner Brothers!

GWAR—PHALLUS IN WONDERLAND

(Metal Blade, 1992) **D:** Distortion Wells

Gwar ("from Antarctica") has gotten more musical but no less juvenile and outrageous. This is a planned production with seven new songs and lots of fantasy segments. Some of them are clever, shocking, and funny. Others aren't. You get lots of monsters, guts, puke, dismemberment, and bad taste. A kid kills his mom with a skateboard. Gwar cereal comes with a crack pipe. A court case decides whether something is a fish or a penis. A TV evangelist is punished for raping boys. There's even political commentary (!) and Corporal Punishment, a comical symbol of the US.

GYMKATA

(MGM, 1985) **D:** Robert Clouse
S: Charlie Carner **P:** Fred Weintraub

A martial-arts fighter (Olympic champ Kurt Thomas) participates in an obstacle-course death game in a mythical kingdom. With Richard Norton, Conan Lee, Tadashi Yamashita, and Buck Kartalian as the khan. There are bad ninjas, a giant Viking, crazy, toothless fighters with scythes, and lots of blood. This bizarre film was made in Yugoslavia by the director of *Enter the Dragon*.

GYPSY ANGELS

(Vidmark, 1981) **D:** "Alan Smithee"

Vanna White is an Atlanta stripper (she keeps her top and G string on) who falls for a barnstorming stunt pilot (Gene Bicknell, who was an executive producer). He crashes and has amnesia. There are lots of stunt-flying scenes. With Lyle Waggoner as a Vegas preacher, Richard Roundtree as a doctor, Elizabeth Ashley, the late Peter Lawford, and Tige Andrews (who narrates the flashbacks). This was filmed in Missouri (with backing from a Pizza Hut franchise owner) and was finally released in 1994. The director hid behind a generic pseudonym.

GYPSY MOON: *See* ROCKY JONES

HACK 'EM HIGH

(Urban Classic, 1987) **D/S/P:** Gorman Bechard
S: Carmine Capobianco **P:** Kris Covello

If you liked *Psychos in Love*, this is another horror spoof by the same people from Connecticut. With Debi Thibeault and Ruth Collins.

HAIL, CAESAR

(Prism, 1993) **D/A:** Anthony Michael Hall **S:** Robert Mittenthal **P:** Steven Paul, Barry Collier

Hall (looking ridiculous with short yellow hair) narrates the story of how he tries to impress Buffer (Bobbie Phillips), the bitchy daughter of a secret arms dealer (Nicholas Pryor), becomes the manager of the millionaire's eraser factory, and goes to jail. There's also some nonsense about his rock trio. The only bright spot in this mild PG comedy is Robert Downey Jr.'s standout manic scene. Also with Samuel L. Jackson as the mailman, Frank Gorshin, Judd Nelson, and Robert Downey Sr. as a butler. It's supposedly based on a Mark Twain novel.

HAIR

(MGM, 1979) **D:** Milos Forman
S: Michael Weller **P:** Lester
Persky, Michael Butler

This tame PG film adaptation of the 1967 antiwar, "age of Aquarius" Broadway musical hit is filled with familiar songs (sounding stronger than the 60s versions by lightweights like the Cowsills and the Fifth Dimension) and excellent dancing (choreographed by Twyla Tharp). John Savage stars as the Oklahoma boy who goes to Manhattan before being drafted. With Treat Williams (awkward-looking in long hair), Beverly D'Angelo, Nicholas Ray as the general, Charlotte Rae, and Annie Golden. The Czech Forman had directed *Taking Off* (1971) and *One Flew over the Cuckoo's Nest* (1975) in the US. This United Artists release is 122 minutes long. RCA released a double soundtrack album.

HAIRSPRAY

(New Line, 1988) **D/S/A:** John Waters **P:** Rachel Talalay

Waters' first feature since *Polyester* (1981) is a great PG (!) comedy about rock-and-roll dancing (and integration) in 1962 Baltimore. The kids all want to appear on the local (segregated) Corny Collins show (which is based on a real program). Ricki Lake stars as Tracy Turnblad, a smaller version of her huge housewife mother. Divine (who died after the premiere) plays both the mom and a male racist TV station owner. Jerry Stiller is the gag-shop-owner dad. With Sonny Bono (who became mayor of Palm Springs in 1988, then a Congressman in 1994) and Debbie Harry as the parents of Tracy's rival and Michael St. Gerard (star of the brief *Elvis* TV series) as her new boyfriend. Characters do the bug, read *Mad* magazine, and pop zits. With Ruth Brown as Motormouth Maybelle, owner of an R&B record store,

Mink Stole, Pia Zadora and Ric Ocasek as beatniks, and Waters himself as a crazed shrink. The excellent soundtrack is on MCA (and includes Rachel Sweet's theme song), but some of the best dance oldies are missing (like the one by Bunker Hill!). This was Waters' last film for New Line. His next film was *Cry-Baby*.

HALF HUMAN

(Rhino, 1955) **D:** Inoshiro Honda, Kenneth G. Crane **S:** Takeo Murata **P:** Tomoyuki Tanaka
Japan (*Jujin Yukiotoko*)

This Toho film was Honda's follow-up to *Godzilla* and features two of that film's stars, Akira Takarada and Momoko Kochi. It borrows ideas from *King Kong* and *Tarzan Escapes*. Villagers pray to a big "Peking man" who lives in a huge cave filled with stalactites and bats. A beautiful mountain girl wearing a miniskirt has to offer him food. A rescue party and scientists show up after some skiers disappear. The snowman ties one man up and hangs him over the side of a cliff. Evil circus people capture the monster and his son. When the kid is shot daddy goes on a rampage, destroying the village. The independent DCA company got US-release rights in 1958 and did a miserable job trying to Americanize this film as Warner Brothers had done with *Godzilla*. They cut out all the dialogue and maybe half the movie, substituting John Carradine as a scientist who sits in a room and tells the story. Every time things get interesting we're back in that room with John telling us what's already happened and even trying to psychoanalyze the creature. Morris Ankrum does an autopsy on the body of the little creature. The real movie ends in a volcano (just like *The Manster*, also codirected by Crane). Much as I like Carradine, this frustrating version makes me want to see the original without him. *The Snow Creature* (1954) and *Man Beast* (1955) are less interesting American abominable-snowman movies made around the same time.

HALF-MAN, HALF-BEAST but **ALL MONSTER!**

HALF HUMAN

starring **JOHN CARRADINE**

with RUSS THORSON · ROBERT KARNES · MORRIS ANKRUM

produced by TOMOYUKI TANAKA

directed by KENNETH G. CRANE

From the wild frozen wastes of the world comes
The MURDERING MONSTER that moves like man!

HALFWAY TO HELL

(SW, 1954) **D:** Robert Snyder **S:** Quentin Reynolds **P:** Kroeger Babb

Although many anti-Communist movies now seem laughable, this 62-minute documentary is a very

well made, expertly edited history lesson with lots of excellent news footage mixed with some scenes from movies. It traces the history of modern Germany back to Kaiser Wilhelm II and WWI, and the history of the USSR back to the 1917 revolution, convincingly comparing Hitler and Stalin, Fascists and Communists, and showing how the population of both countries became "robots." There's footage of Czar Nicholas II, Trotsky (speaking in English), Mussolini (meeting Hitler and later hanging upside down), concentration-camp survivors, and mass graves in Poland. A theremin is heard on the soundtrack, and Reynolds also narrates. Hallmark Pictures double-billed this with *Karamaja*, so a lot of people saw it. The video is a David Friedman Roadshow Rarity. It's followed by a long trailer for *Seeds of Destruction*, with Kent Taylor as a Commie posing as a minister!

HALL OF THE MOUNTAIN KING = NIGHT OF THE HOWLING BEAST

HALLOWEEN 4: THE RETURN OF MICHAEL MYERS

(RCA/Columbia, 1988) **D:** Dwight H. Little
S: Alan B. McElroy **P:** Paul Freeman

Donald Pleasence (as a scarred Dr. Loomis) returns in what should have been called Part 3. Michael Myers, who has been in and out of a coma for 10 years, is after the daughter of the original Jamie Lee Curtis character. With Ellie Cornell, Danielle Harris, Michael Pataki, Kathleen Kinmont, Beau Starr, and Sasha Jensen. John Carl Buechler did the makeup. Alan Howarth's reused score was issued on Varèse Sarabande. You'd be better off looking for *Halloween* (Media, 1978), *Halloween II* (MCA, 1981), or even the unrelated *Halloween III: Season of the Witch* (MCA, 1982). Executive producer Moustaka Akkad received all the rights to the *Halloween* series in court. John Carpenter (who directed or produced the first three) urged people not to see the others. Michael Myers, by the way, was the name of the British distributor who helped make John Carpenter's *Assault on Precinct 13* a hit in the UK.

HALLOWEEN 5: THE REVENGE OF MICHAEL MYERS

(CBS/Fox, 1989) **D/S:** Dominique Othenin-Gerard **S:** Michael Jacobs
P: Ramsey Thomas

In the direct sequel to Part 4, Danielle Harris stars as a 9-year-old niece of Michael Myers, who has seizures whenever he's about to kill. Donald Pleasence captures the masked killer in chains. The characters and situations are pretty stupid. With Wendy Kaplan, Donald L. Shanks, Jeffrey Landman, and Ellie Cornell and Beau Starr from Part 4. There's another Alan Howarth score and a safe-sex scene. The ending is a setup for another sequel—*Halloween 6: The Curse of Michael Myers* (1995), which turned out to be Donald Pleasence's last film.

HALLOWEEN NIGHT

(Atlas, 1988) **D/E:** Jag Mundra **S:** Carla Robinson
P: Raj Mehrotra   (*Hack O'Lantern*)

Two brothers and a sister have a Satanist grand-father who delivers pumpkins every Halloween. The good brother is a rookie cop. The bad one lives in the basement, lifts weights, and follows the grandfather (who killed their father). The sister has a nude bath scene. Three different hot blondes have nude scenes. I think one of them is porno star Jeannie Fine. She gets a pitchfork through her head. During a dream sequence a heavy-metal band with a female singer plays a whole song while a black girl with six arms, a dot on her forehead, and death-ray eyes dances around. (It's not as good as it sounds.) At a party a guy does a standup comedy act about centerfolds. The Mercenaries and DC La Croix play. Mayra Grant (from *Star Slammer*) gets stabbed. The grandfather is very strange, thanks partially to a deep, dubbed-in voice that sounds like Harvey Fierstein. Like many 80s West Coast horror videos it seems like a series of auditions for the filmmaker's friends and neighbors, who are all musicians, actors, or models.

HALLUCINATIONS IN A DERANGED MIND

(SW, 1977) **D/S/P/A:** Jose Mojica Marins
Brazil (*Delirios de um Anormal*)

This amazing overkill movie includes scenes from "10" earlier movies by Marins as nightmares and flashbacks and is a good sampler of his unique ca-reer. Marins plays himself, a famous filmmaker, and his fictional character Ze de Caixo (or Coffin Joe). Tania is his perfect woman, and a shrink con-sults Marins for help. It turns out that Ze kills when Mojica blacks out. It includes the excellent Hell scenes from *This Night I Will Possess Your Corpse*, gory cannibalism scenes, acid in the face, whipping, nudity, laughing skulls, bodies used for stairs, frogs on breasts, bell-bottom pants, a draw-ing of Boris Karloff, and much, much more. Some b/w scenes are tinted. It's subtitled.

HAMBURGER: THE MOTION PICTURE

(Media, 1986) **D:** Mike Marvin **S:** Donald Ross
P: Edward S. Feldman, Charles R. Meeker

Teens work at a fast-food restaurant. One guy has problems with an inheritance. This comedy stars Leigh McCloskey, with Dick Butkus, Chuck Mc-Cann, Debra Blee, Randi Brooks, Karen Mayo-Chandler, and Roberta Vasquez (from *Playboy*). It's by the director of *The Wraith*.

HAMMER

(1972) **D:** Bruce Clark **S:** Charles
Johnson **P:** Al Adamson

Fred Williamson (in his first starring role) is B. J. Hammer, a dock worker turned boxer. His drug-dealing Mafia manager, Big Sid (Charles Lamp-kin), manipulates his career, then tells him to take a dive. Vonetta McGee (she was in *Blacula* the same year) is the gangster's secretary who becomes Hammer's girlfriend and is kidnapped. William Smith is a sadistic hitman. It takes Hammer a long time to wise up, take action, and listen to good LA cop Bernie Hamilton. With D'Urville Martin, Tracy

King, and Leon Isaac (later Kennedy). The score is by Solomon Burke. This UA release is by the New Zealander director of *Naked Angels*.

HAMMERHEAD

(1968) **D:** David Miller **S:** William E. Bast,
Herbert Baker **P:** Irving Allen   UK

Vince Edwards is American secret agent Charlie Hood in this James Bond copy. Hammerhead (Peter Vaughn), the villain, collects old and valu-able pornography. He's also after nuclear secrets. With Judy Geeson as a nightclub entertainer, Bev-erly Adams and Diana Dors as Hammerhead's mis-tresses, Michael Bates, Douglas Wilmer, Veronica Carlson, and Tracy Reed. A London "happening" includes a topless cellist. The Colgems soundtrack features Madeline Bell. A Columbia release.

HAMMER HORRORS

(*Trailers on Tape*)

This is the kind of compilation I'd like to see more of. It sticks to one theme (films made by England's Hammer studios from 1955 to 1974) and is com-plete and chronological when presenting trailers for movies in a series. It's 75 minutes long and con-sists of an intro and 28 trailers. There are trailers for all 7 Frankenstein movies, the 3 Quatermass science-fiction movies, the 4 Mummy movies, and, best of all, the 14 vampire movies (half of them star Christopher Lee). They also added trailers for *The Hound of the Baskervilles*, *The Gorgon*, and *The Phantom of the Opera*. Kate Bush's theme "Hammer Horror" is heard during the well-edited intros. Although all the movies were from one stu-dio, these are American trailers made by the vari-ous companies (large and small) that released the features here.

HAMMER: THE STUDIO THAT DRIPPED BLOOD!

(BBC, 1987)

This hour-long TV documentary is a must for fans of the British studio that revitalized the horror movie in the late 50s with worldwide hits like *The Curse of Frankenstein* and *Horror of Dracula*. Nar-rated by Charles Gray, it includes interviews with Hammer stars Peter Cushing and Christopher Lee, and with many of the behind-the-scenes talents (such as producers Anthony Hinds, Michael Car-reras, and Aida Young, writer Jimmy Sangster, and director Don Sharp). Bette Davis is shown drown-ing a child in a bathtub (*The Nanny*), Ingrid Pitt is decapitated, and Lee is shown at the New York premiere of *Horror of Dracula*. The only non-Hammer person interviewed is Martin Scorsese, a fan, who saw *The Curse of the Werewolf* at the New York Paramount. The tightly run company was at its best before it moved out of the Bray stu-dios (actually an old house) in 1967. Eventually they seemed to run out of ideas, and production standards dropped. In 1968 the people who were once condemned for adding full-color blood and severed limbs to gothic horror received an industry award from the Queen. By the early 70s they had added nudity to horror movies, but Americans saw heavily cut versions that were badly distributed. By the 80s Bray was being used for TV commercials and rock videos.

HAMMETT

(Warner, 1982) **D:** Wim Wenders **S:** Ross
Thomas, Dennis O'Flaherty, Thomas Pope
P: Fred Roos, Ronald Colby, Don Guest

Frederic Forrest stars as the alcoholic mystery writer Dashiell Hammett, who's drawn into a mur-der case and a political conspiracy (involving Chi-natown and porno movies) in 30s San Francisco. Nicolas Roeg wanted to direct this film (based on a novel by Joe Gores), but Wenders made a great-looking film (his first in the US) despite serious production problems. With Peter Boyle as a Pink-erton man, Lydia Lei, Marilu Henner, Roy Kinnear, Elisha Cook Jr., R. G. Armstrong, Sylvia Sidney, Samuel Fuller, Royal Dano, Jack Nance, Fox Har-ris, and Hank Worden. Wenders made *The State of Things* while this was on hold. Francis Ford Cop-pola was the executive producer for Orion, but it was finally released by Warner Brothers. It's PG. The same idea of a real-life author as a character in his own fiction was later used in *Kafka* and *Naked Lunch*.

HANDGUN

(Triboro, 1994) **D/S:** Whitney Ransick **P:** Bob Gosse

Treat Williams is a violent thief whose father (Sey-mour Cassell) is hiding out in a crummy New York apartment with a payroll fortune. Williams and his con man brother (Paul Shulze), the cops, and other gangsters search for him. The low-budget di-rectoral debut is in the tradition of *Reservoir Dogs*, complete with choice oldies used for ironic effect on the soundtrack. With Michael Rappaport, Anna Thompson, and Angel Caban.

THE HANDMAID'S TALE

(HBO, 1989) **D:** Volker Schlöndorff **S:** Harold
Pinter **P:** Danny Wilson **M:** Ryuichi Sakamoto

Women have no rights in the fascist America of the near future (called Gilead). The Old Testament rules, minorities are deported to "homelands," and gays are hanged. The remaining fertile women are rounded up, and assigned to wealthy child-less couples. Natasha Richardson is a "handmaid" (breeder) to a hypocritical, self-righteous security chief (Robert Duvall) and his infertile wife (Faye Dunaway). It's based on Margaret Atwood's 1985 novel. With Aidan Quinn, Elizabeth McGovern (as a lesbian hooker), Victoria Tennant (as Aunt Lydia, who trains handmaids), Traci Lind, Blanche Baker, and David Dukes.

HANDS OF DEATH = NURSE SHERRI

THE HANDS OF ORLAC

(Sinister, 1960) **D/S:** Edmond T. Greville
S: John Baines **P:** Steven Pallos, Donald
Taylor **M:** Claude Bolling   UK/France

This third version of the story about a brilliant pi-anist with the hands of an executed murderer was shot on the French Riviera. It adds new subplots and characters and is much better than you might expect. Mel Ferrer stars as the tormented Orlac, and Christopher Lee is in top form as Neron, a sin-ister magician. Dany Carrel is Li-Lang, Neron's very cute assistant. During a stage illusion, her dress disappears, and she sings in French wearing a bikini. Neron puts swords through a girl in a coffin and has devil puppets. The best scene (as in *Mad Love*) is when Lee masquerades as the dead killer with hook hands ("Give me back my hands!"), but there are many good moments and some excellent cinematography. Donald Pleasence, David Peel (as a pilot), and Donald Wolfit (as a surgeon) are all seen briefly. Greville had just directed the teen classic *Beat Girl* (also with Lee). Ferrer was in Vadim's *Blood and Roses* next. A 105-minute French-language version with several different actors was made at the same time. The British version is 95 minutes, and the US version is only 87.

HANDS OF STEEL

(Vestron, 1986) **D/S:** "Martin Dolman"/
Sergio Martino **S:** Elisabeth Parker, Saul
Sasha   Italy (*Vendetta dal Futuro*)

In 1997 in America, a muscular renegade cyborg who knows martial arts (Daniel Greene) is hiding out with the owner of a bar in the desert (Janet Angren). John Saxon is a mercenary-leader villain, and George Eastman is an arm-wrestling (!) villain. It was filmed in Arizona. The music is by Claudio Simonetti (from Goblin).

THE HAND THAT ROCKS THE CRADLE

(Disney, 1992) **D:** Curtis Hanson **S:** Amanda
Silver **P:** David Madden **M:** Graeme Revell

Calculating, devious Rebecca De Mornay poses as a nanny and is hired to care for the newborn son and five-year-old daughter of a Seattle couple. She wants to destroy them because she had a miscarriage after her creepy gynecologist husband (John De Lancie) killed himself. She blames her employer (Annabella Sciorra), who reported that he sexually molested her. With Ernie Hudson as a mentally handicapped handyman, Matt McCoy as the husband, Madeline Zima as the daughter, and Julianne Moore as a friend. There's a clip from *White Zombie*. Despite some serious holes in the plot, this was a hit. The script (a USC master's thesis) was probably inspired by *Fatal Attraction* but also has some similarities to *The Guardian*. The soundtrack is on Hollywood Records. Hanson also directed *Bad Influence* and *The Bedroom Window*.

THE HANGED MAN

(1974) **D:** Michael Caffey **S:** Ken
Trevey **P:** Andrew J. Fenady

Steve Forrest is a gunslinger who survives his hanging and becomes a mystical hero in the Old West. This ABC-TV movie, a Bing Crosby production, features Cameron Mitchell, Sharon Acker, Dean Jagger, Will Geer, Barbara Luna, and Rafael Campos.

HANG 'EM HIGH

(MGM, 1968) **D:** Ted Post **S/P:** Leonard Freeman
S: Mel Goldberg **M:** Dominic Frontiere

The year after the three Eastwood/Leone westerns were released in the US, Eastwood starred in this home-grown imitation. Many thought it was Italian too. It's good, but Post (who had directed Eastwood in episodes of *Rawhide*) is no Leone. A judge (Pat Hingle) saves Jed Cooper (Eastwood) from hanging and makes him a deputy, but he goes after the men who tried to lynch him. Inger Stevens costars with Ed Begley, Arlene Golonka, James MacArthur, Charles McGraw, L. Q. Jones, Alan Hale Jr., veteran cowboy star Bob Steele, Bruce Dern, and Dennis Hopper (who loses it in a prison). The soundtrack is on UA.

HANGFIRE

(RCA, 1991) **D:** Peter Maris **S:** Brian D.
Jeffries **P:** Brad Krevon, Steve Stabler

A serial killer, a rapist, and other cons escape on a bus from a New Mexico prison and hold a village hostage. This was advertised as being about the Gulf War! Jan-Michael Vincent as a National Guard commander and Brad Davis as a sheriff are both Nam vets. With Kim Delaney, James Tolkan as Patch, Ken Foree, George Kennedy as the warden, and Yaphet Kotto. Big, strong guys (Lou Ferrigno, Lyle Alzado, and Peter Lupis) show up too.

HANGING BY A THREAD

(1979) **D:** Georg Fenady **S:** Adrian Spies **P:** Irwin Allen

In one of Allen's many disaster movies (this was made for NBC-TV), sightseers have flashbacks of their lives as their train dangles over a mountain gorge. Patty Duke and Sam Groom star, with Donna Mills, Bert Convy, Cameron Mitchell, Roger Perry, and Deanna Lund.

THE HANGING OF JAKE ELLIS

(1969) **D/S/P:** J. Van Hearn   (*The Calico Queen*)

Square-jawed future Russ Meyer regular Charles Napier stars as a cattle driver (and sings the theme song!) in this nudie western. With Deborah Downey (*Lady Godiva Rides*) and Bambi Allen. Napier also starred in *House Near the Prado* by Van Hearn.

THE HANGING WOMAN

(Neon, 1972) **D/S:** Jose Luis Merino **S:** Enrico Columbi
P: Ramona Plana   Spain/Italy (*La Orgia de los Muertos*;
Return of the Zombies; Beyond the Living Dead)

Serge (Stelvio Rossi), the long-haired blond nephew of a count, arrives in a 19th-century village to inherit a villa. The count's widow (Dianik Zurakowska) practices black magic and conjures up a ghost, a scientist (Gerard Tichy) in the basement tries to raise the dead with electricity, and Igor (Paul Naschy) is a laughing, lurking necro voyeur who keeps ladies' underwear in his hut. Reanimated zombies eventually show up in the catacombs, and the end of this fun horror movie copies Roman Polanski's *The Fearless Vampire Killers*. There's some nudity, a bloody decapitation, and an autopsy scene. This version was dubbed in the UK.

HANGIN' WITH THE HOMEBOYS

(New Line, 1990) **D/S:** Joseph B. Vasquez
P: Richard Brice

Vasquez's third feature was his first hit, thanks to some excellent actors (and some ideas borrowed from *American Graffiti*). After crashing a party, four very distinct characters from the South Bronx decide to drive to unfamiliar territory, Manhattan ("The Bronx is wack tonight"), for a long, aimless Friday night. They talk, drink, argue, crash a car, are arrested as subway-fare beaters, visit Show World, and feel out of place after sneaking into a pretentious downtown nightclub to try to pick up girls. The night is a turning point in the lives of some of them. John Leguizamo stars, with Doug E. Doug as a guy worried about his future, Nestor Serrano as a Puerto Rican who pretends to be Italian, and Mario Joyner as an actor. The theme is the hit "I Got the Power."

HANGMEN ALSO DIE

(1943) **D/P:** Fritz Lang **S:** John Wexley,
Bertolt Brecht (uncredited)

Brian Donlevy stars as Dr. Svoboda, a Czech patriot who kills (the real) Nazi official Reinhard Heydrich in Prague in 1942. The Nazis threaten to kill 400 people unless he gives himself up. (In real life, the entire male population of the town of Lidice was killed.) James Wong Howe was the cinematographer. With Walter Brennan, Anna Lee, Gene Lockhart, Dennis O'Keefe, Jonathan Hale, and Lionel Stander. Douglas Sirk's version of the same events, *Hitler's Madman*, with John Carradine as Heydrich, was released the same year.

THE HANG-UP

(SW, 1969) **D/S:** John Hayes

Sebastian Gregory (*Help Wanted Female*) stars as a neurotic undercover vice cop. He goes to strip clubs, gay bars, and swingers' clubs and falls for a hippie (Sharon Matt).

HANNAH LEE

(1953) **D/P:** John Ireland, Lee Garmes **S:** McKinlay
Kantor, Alfred "Rip" Von Ronkle   (*Outlaw Territory*)

It's ranch owners vs. homesteaders in a 3-D and stereo western released by Realart. MacDonald Carey stars, with Joanne Dru and John Ireland (who were married at the time). The couple sued executive producer Jack Broder for not paying them. They were also in the 3-D *Southwest Passage*.

HANNIBAL BROOKS

(1969) **D/P:** Michael Winner **S:** Dick Clement,
Ian La Frenais **M:** Frances Lai   UK

Oliver Reed stars in this WWII action comedy. He and Michael J. Pollard are prisoners of war who somehow escape from Munich to Switzerland over the Alps with an elephant named Lucy. It features Karin Baal, Wolfgang Preiss, and a mostly German cast. It was Pollard's biggest role until he starred in *Dirty Little Billy* (1972). UA released the soundtrack.

HANSEL AND GRETEL

(UAV, 1954) **D:** Walter Janssen **S:** Gerhard F.
Hummell   W. Germany/Italy

Childhood Productions released this fairy-tale movie in the US in the 60s and sold a tie-in record. The Americanized version includes new songs and narration by Paul Tripp. There's a 1985 *Faerie Tale Theatre* version (from Fox), with Ricky Schroeder and Joan Collins, and a Cannon film made in Israel (Warner, 1987), with David Warner and Cloris Leachman as the witch.

HANUSSEN
(1955) **D/A:** O. W. Fischer **D:** George Marischka W. Germany

This film isn't available in the US. It's about a well-known clairvoyant who collaborates with the Nazis. Klaus Kinski costars. It's also known as *Hitler's Astrologer*. Another version, directed by Istvan Szabo and starring Klaus Maria Brandauer, was made in 1988 and has the same title.

THE HAPPENING
(1967) **D:** Elliot Silverstein **S:** Frank R. Pierson, James D. Buchanan, Ronald Austin **P:** Jud Kinberg

The Supremes' theme song made it to number 1, but this is a very out-of-it comedy about hippie beach-bum crooks who accidentally kidnap a Florida gangster (Anthony Quinn). George Maharis as Taurus, an overacting Michael Parks, Robert Walker Jr., and Faye Dunaway (in her film debut) as a coed are the kidnappers. With Martha Hyer in bed with Milton Berle, Oscar Homolka, Clifton James, Jack Kruschen, and Luke Askew. Presented by Sam Spiegel. The soundtrack is on Colgems. The same plot was used for *The Biggest Bundle of Them All* (made the same year in Europe), with Raquel Welch.

HAPPY HELL NIGHT
(1992) **D/S:** Brian Owens **S:** Ron Peterson **P:** Leslie Sunshine Canada/Yugoslavia

Darren McGavin saw eight teens killed during a fraternity-pledge night in 1965 when they resurrected the corpse of an evil priest named Zachary. McGavin's sons and two other guys, now in the same fraternity, break into the asylum where Zachary has been for 25 years. The creepy, bald, Nosferatu-look supernatural priest escapes and starts killing again with an ice axe. Characters go to Hell, a statue of Jesus comes alive, and there's some nudity and gore.

THE HAPPY HOOKER
(Warner, 1974) **D:** Nicholas Sgarro **S:** William Richert **P:** Fred Caruso

Lynn Redgrave stars as Xaviera Hollander in this tame (R-rated) comedy version of the bestselling memoirs of the famous New York madam. With Jean-Pierre Aumont, Tom Poston, Richard Lynch as a corporate crook, Nicholas Pryor, Anita Morris (seen topless), and Denise Galik. Hollander herself starred in *My Pleasure Is My Business* (MPI, 1974), and Samantha McClaren played her in the hard-core *The Life and Times of Xaviera Hollander* (1974).

THE HAPPY HOOKER GOES HOLLYWOOD
(Warner, 1979) **D:** Alan Roberts **S:** Devi Goldenberg **P:** Menaham Golan

Martine Beswick, looking great, is Xaviera Hollander in the third and last of the "series," which is probably the funniest. She finances her own film by setting up a whorehouse with fantasy rooms in Los Angeles. Adam West costars, with Phil Silvers, Richard Deacon, Edie Adams as a Rona Barrett type, Chris Lemmon, Dick Miller, Army Archerd, Lindsay Bloom, Tanya Boyd, Susan Lynn Kiger (from *Playboy*), and K. C. Winkler. West and Deacon have a scene in drag. The Cannon release was called *Hollywood Blue* in the UK.

THE HAPPY HOOKER GOES TO WASHINGTON
(Warner, 1977) **D/P:** William A. Levey **S:** Robert Kaufman

Joey Heatherton takes over as Xaviera Hollander, the famous madam, in a sequel by the director of *Blackenstein* and *Slumber Party '57*. She's ordered to Washington to testify before Congress. Cannon put together a pretty crazed cast. George Hamilton costars, with Ray Walston, Jack Carter, Phil Foster, Marilyn Joi, Louisa Moritz, Billy Barty, Joyce Jilson (as herself), K. C. Winkler, Pamela Zinszer (from *Playboy*), Lisa London, and Raven De La Croix. It was one of the few starring roles for Heatherton, whose next appearence (in a movie that was released) was in John Waters' *Cry-Baby*. Kaufman also wrote the hit *Love at First Bite*, starring Hamilton.

Joey Heatherton and George Hamilton in *The Happy Hooker Goes to Washington*.

HAPPY HOUR
(Avid, 1987) **D/P:** John De Bello **S/P:** J. Stephen Peace **S:** Constance Dillon

Rich Little (the favorite impressionist of several US presidents) and Jamie Farr (from *M*A*S*H*) are each hired by rival beer companies to obtain a special formula that makes beer addictive. Tawny Kitaen works with Farr, and Eddie Deezen also has a role in this dumb comedy. Little is awful. Devo did the theme song. Add *Strange Brew* (1983) and *Beer* (1985) for a beer-comedy triple bill. De Bello also made the Killer Tomatoes movies (three of them).

HARDBODIES
(RCA, 1984) **D/S:** Mark Griffiths **S:** Steve Green, Eric Alter **P:** Jeff Begun, Ken Dalton

Some middle-aged guys at the beach hire a young guy to help them score with many (often topless)

girls. Originally made for Playboy TV, it was released by Columbia. With Roberta Collins as Lana, Courtney Gaines, Joyce Jameson, Elizabeth Kaitan, and Kathleen Kinmont.

HARDBODIES II
(1986) **D/S:** Mark Griffiths **S:** Curtis Wilmot **P:** Jeff Begun, Ken Solomon

Some Americans are making a movie on a Greek island. There's less nudity than in the first one, but it's just as dumb. With Roberta Collins, Fabiana Udenio (*Bride of Re-Animator*), Brenda Bakke, and James Karen. More sequels followed.

HARD-BOILED
(Fox Lorber, 1992) **D:** John Woo **S:** Barry Wong **P:** Linda Kuk, Terence Chang Hong Kong

Chow Yun-Fat stars as a cop called Tequila who likes jazz. Tony Leung is an emotionally scarred hitman who's really an undercover cop. There's an incredible long, nonstop, high-body-count shootout at a large hospital, the secret headquarters of an arms-smuggling operation in the near future (1997). The killers are all dressed as cops, and the heroes are disguised as gangsters. Another shootout is in a restaurant. The American tape is 127 minutes (the film was originally 130) and is dubbed or subtitled. The Criterion laserdisc includes audio commentary by Woo. Woo went to New Orleans to make *Hard Target* next.

HARDCASE AND FIST
(Forum, 1988) **D/S/P:** Tony Zarindast **S:** Bud Fleischer

Ted Prior is a Nam-vet LA cop who goes undercover in prison to get mobsters. He also has combat flashbacks. With Carter Wong as a martial-arts fighter and Debra Lamb.

HARD CONTRACT
(Fox, 1969) **D/S:** S. Lee Pogostin **P:** Marvin Schwartz

James Coburn stars in a drama about a hired assassin in Europe who has sex only with prostitutes, until a socialite (Lee Remick) poses as a hooker, has an affair with him, and disrupts his routine. With Burgess Meredith, Sterling Hayden, Patrick Magee, Karen Black, and Lilli Palmer. It was shot on location in Europe and released by 20th Century–Fox.

HARDCORE
(Columbia, 1978) **D/S:** Paul Schrader **P:** Buzz Feitshams

George C. Scott stars as Van Dorn, a strict Calvinist from Grand Rapids, Michigan, who searches for his runaway daughter, now appearing in porno movies (like *Slave of Love*) in California. He hires a detective (Peter Boyle), then teams up with a young hooker (Season Hubley) who has met his daughter. Van Dorn investigates the porno business on various levels and even pays $100 to sit through a snuff film. At one point he puts on a phony beard and mustache, poses as a porno producer, and auditions male actors in an attempt to find the one who was in a photograph. *Hardcore* is interesting but laughable at times. X-rated-movie magazines went out of their way to condemn it and point out that the snuff connection was farfetched. Schrader himself was raised as a Calvinist in Grand Rapids. His next film was *American Gigolo*. With Dick Sargent (from *Bewitched*), Leonard Gaines, Ed Begley Jr., Leslie Ackerman, Bibi Besch, and Serena. John Milius was the executive producer. The Jack Nitzsche soundtrack includes cuts by CSNY, Mink De Ville, and Byron Berline.

HARD DRIVIN' = THUNDER IN CAROLINA

THE HARDER THEY COME

(HBO, 1973) **D/S/P:** Perry Henzell **S:** Trevor Rhone

Roger Corman's New World picked up this Jamaican film (the first), added subtitles, and released it first to inner-city theaters. Later it became a midnight movie-cult favorite and helped popularize reggae in the US. Singer Jimmy Cliff stars as Ivan, a reggae star in Kingston. He receives only $20 for his record, starts working in the ganja business to make some money, is set up, kills some cops, and becomes a martyr. By this time his record is a big hit. Much of the story is based on Cliff's real life, and it was also inspired by Italian westerns and American black-action films. The famous Mango soundtrack LP includes many hits by Cliff, Toots and the Maytals, Desmond Dekker, and others. Some other reggae films are *Rockers* (1978), and *Reggae Sunsplash* (1980). Cliff plays a role in the comedy *Club Paradise* (1986) and performs several songs.

Jimmy Cliff in *The Harder They Come*.

HARD HUNTED

(Columbia, 1992) **D/S:** Andy Sidaris **P:** Arlene Sidaris

Tony Peck (son of Gregory), who had costarred in *Brenda Starr*, probably never expected to be in a spy adventure full of *Playboy* Playmates and cellular-phone conversations, but here he is. R. J. Moore (son of Roger) is the young villain, who's after an atomic device in a jade Buddha. Carolyn

Liu and Al Leong assist him. With Donna Spier (in her sixth Sidaris movie), Roberta Vasquez, Ava Cadall as the host of a radio sex show, Becky Mullen, and Claudia Brimhall (who sings). They all wear bikinis or nothing at all. The seventh in a series, it was partially filmed in Hawaii and Arizona.

THE HARD RIDE

(Orion, 1971) **D/S:** Burt Topper **P:** Charles Hanawalt

Robert Fuller (from *The Wagon Train* TV series) stars as a Nam vet returning home with his (black) friend's body, in this AIP biker movie with a message. Sherry Bain costars with William Bonner, Robert Tessier, and Marshall Reed. It features the last of the Davie Allen and the Arrows soundtracks (on Paramount), with additional songs by Bill Medley and others.

HARD ROAD

(SW, 1970) **D/C/E:** Gary Graver
S: Richard Stetson **P:** Ed De Priest

Connie Nelson (from *Angels Die Hard!*) stars as a 17-year-old drop-out mom who becomes a receptionist for an LA rock promoter (Gary Kent), smokes pot with a rock star, has (offscreen) sex, graduates to dropping bennies and snorting crystal (cue freakout sequence), dates lots of men, and moves in with a heroin addict (John Alderman) and his girlfriend. He makes her become a hooker, and she winds up in jail and goes cold turkey. But the final, worst, most destructive thing of all is that she takes LSD! This depressing, narrated, road-to-ruin movie (in color) crams in everything from similar films from all previous decades. A doctor introduces a birth-of-a-baby sequence, and there's a VD talk with gruesome visual warnings. With Liz Renay as the platinum-blond mother in mink, William Bonner, and Mike Weldon. It's a Johnny Legend video release.

HARD-ROCK ZOMBIES

(Vestron, 1983) **D/S/P:** Krishna Shaw
S: David Ball

Members of a heavy-metal band are murdered by a Hitler cult, return as zombies, and attack anti-rock locals, in this horror spoof. With Annabelle Larson and Lisa Toothman.

HARD TARGET

(MCA, 1993) **D:** John Woo
S/A: Chuck Pfarrer **P:** Rob Tapert

Jean-Claude Van Damme stars as Cajun merchant seaman Chance Boudreaux in Hong Kong director Woo's first film in English. Lance Henriksen is Fouchon, a rich villain who arranges hunts (in the style of *The Most Dangerous Game*) with ex-servicemen as the targets. Yancy Butler is Natasha (she plays the role using a single facial expression). New Orleans is portrayed as a lawless city full of homeless people and rampant crime. The action includes chase scenes on boats, motorcycles, and horseback, and there's an impressive ending in a

warehouse full of Mardi Gras floats. With Arnold Vosloo as the short-haired right-hand man of the villain, Wilford Brimley as an old Cajun, and Kasi Lemmons as a cop. Sam Raimi was the executive producer, Ted Raimi has a cameo, and Dale Ashmun is an extra. This Universal release was cut for an R rating. It has a score by Graeme Revell.

HARD TICKET TO HAWAII

(Warner, 1987) **D/S:** Andy Sidaris **P:** Arlene Sidaris

Soap-opera star Ron Moss stars in this spy story with *Playboy* centerfolds who take their clothes off. Blondes Dona Spier and Hope Marie Carlton battle a drug ring, and there are sumo wrestlers, transvestite spies, and a cancer-infected snake. With Cynthia Brimhall and Patty Duffek. The next Sidaris movie was *Picasso Trigger*.

HARD TO DIE

(New Horizons, 1990) **D/P:** "Arch Stanton"/Jim Wynorski **S:** Mark McGee, James B. Rogers   (*Tower of Terror*)

Melissa Moore, Gail Harris, and Bridget Carney (plus Lindsay Taylor and Debra Dare) arrive at a closed office building for an inventory job at Acme Lingerie. They take showers, try on underwear, move boxes upstairs, and walk around until one (Taylor, who is one of the best-looking women in these movies) becomes possessed. There's a gun shop in the building too, so you get women in lingerie shooting each other with machine guns. Orville Ketchum seems to be a killer zombie, and Forry Ackerman has one of his largest roles ever as a professor, although he never leaves his office. Posters for Wynorski movies are on a wall. It's fun and has lots of brainless action. The video box compares it to *Die Hard!* This 76-minute Concorde release was filmed back to back with *Sorority House Massacre II* (which had much of the same cast) and has flashback footage from *Slumber Party Massacre*.

HARD TO KILL

(Warner, 1989) **D:** Bruce Malmuth **S:** Steve McKay **P:** Lee Rich, Michael Rachmill

Steven Seagal is a cop who awakens from a 7-year coma and wants revenge. His family was killed and he was left for dead after he uncovered political corruption involving an evil senator. Seagal's real-life wife, Kelly LeBrock, costars as a nurse. With Bill Sadler and Frederick Coffin. Mamuth also directed *Nighthawks*.

HARD TRAIL

(1969) **D/S:** Greg Coratio **P:** Maurice Smith

In his only 60s film, Lash La Rue stars as Slade, leader of the Hard Bunch gang. Gary Graver shot this nasty-sounding adult western, which is said to exist in two versions, one with more sex and nudity. With Donna Bradley, John Bloom, and Monica Gayle.

THE HARD TRUTH

(Live, 1994) **D:** Kristine Peterson
S: Jonathan Tydor **P:** Brad Southwick

Eric Roberts is an electronic expert who's blackmailed into helping to steal some mob money by a suspended cop (Michael Rooker) and his girlfriend (Lysette Anthony). It's by the director of *Body Chemistry*.

HARDWARE

(HBO, 1990) **D/S:** Richard Stanley
P: Joanne Steller, Paul Trybit   UK

Dylan McDermott and John Lynch are zone-tripper scavengers in post-nuke NYC. The head of a Mark 13 killer robot they find rebuilds itself in the bunker-style loft of Stacy Travis (as a dope-smoking red-haired artist). This impressive-looking movie has good FX and was made by a 24-year-old video director. It copies ideas from many earlier movies, but the creators of a 1981 *Shok* comic book sued over similarities. Travis has nude scenes and is watched by a voyeur. There's Iggy Pop's voice as Angry Bob on the radio, a dwarf junk dealer, Lemmy from Motorhead as a cabdriver, and segments from Mark Pauline and Gwar videos. To avoid an X rating in theaters 12 seconds were cut. R and unrated versions are available. The Simon Boswell soundtrack is on Varèse Sarabande.

Stacy Travis in *Hardware*.

THE HARD WAY

(MCA, 1991) **D:** John Badham **S:** Daniel Pyne,
Lem Dobbs **P:** Rob Cohen, William Sackheim

Michael J. Fox stars as a movie star tagging along with tough NYC cop James Woods who is after an unstoppable serial killer (Stephen Lang). The climax takes place in a theater (showing a movie with Fox on screen) and on an impressive giant moveable sign that was actually erected in Times Square. With Annabel Sciorra, LL Cool J, Christina Ricci, and Penny Marshall. From Universal.

THE HARLEM GLOBETROTTERS ON GILLIGAN'S ISLAND

(1981) **D:** Peter Baldwin **S/P:** Elroy Schwartz
S: Sherwood Schwartz **P:** Hap Wyman

All of the original cast returned for this NBC-TV movie, except that Constance Forslund plays Ginger. With Martin Landau as a mad scientist who creates robots of the famous basketball-playing Globetrotters, Barbara Bain, Scatman Crothers, and Rosalind Chao. It followed *Rescue from Gilligan's Island* (1978) and *The Castaways on Gilli-*

gan's Island (1979). Since these films were made, stars Alan Hale Jr., Jim Backus, and Natalie Schafer have all died.

HARLEM ON THE PRAIRIE

(1938) **D:** Sam Newfield **S:** Fred Myton **P:** Jed Buell

Herb Jeffries (a onetime singer with the Duke Ellington orchestra) is the singing-cowboy hero of the first all-black western. The contemporary story is about a search for gold. With Connie Harris, Maceo Sheffield, Spencer Williams, and comedians F. E. Miller and Mantan Moreland. The 55-minute film, from Associated Features, was one of 17 (!) Newfield films released that year. (Another one was *The Terror of Tiny Town*, an all-midget western.) *Harlem Rides the Range* (1939) also stars Jeffries.

HARLEY DAVIDSON: THE AMERICAN MOTORCYCLE

(Cabin Fever, 1993)

The Harley company endorsed this tape commemorating their 90th anniversary. It has movie clips, news footage, interviews, and a soundtrack by Robby Kreiger of the Doors. Hoyt Axton narrates, and James Caan, Peter Fonda, David Crosby, Larry Hagman, Lou Reed, and some country stars appear as special hosts. It's 73 minutes long.

HARLEY DAVIDSON AND THE MARLBORO MAN

(MGM, 1991) **D:** Simon Wincer
S: Don Michael Paul **P:** Jere Henshaw

Mickey Rourke is Harley, a broken-down biker in near-future LA (1996). He teams up with "the Marlboro Man," a bearded rodeo cowboy (Don Johnson), and they rob a corrupt bank president who's responsible for their favorite bar being shut down. But they end up with a stash of an addictive new drug called crystal dream, instead of money. The critically hated comic adventure features Tom Sizemore, Chelsea Field, Vanessa Williams, Tia Carrere, Daniel Baldwin, Giancarlo Esposito, Robert Ginty, and Julius Harris. From MGM.

HARLEY'S ANGELS: *See* NORTHVILLE CEMETERY MASSACRE

HAROLD AND MAUDE

(Paramount, 1972) **D:** Hal Ashby
S/P: Colin Higgins **P:** Charles Mulvehill

Harold (Bud Cort), a rich 14-year-old with a Cadillac hearse, falls for 79-year-old Maude (Ruth Gordon), who lives in an old railroad car. This black comedy became an early cult movie. (Maude was partially based on actor Peter Lawford's mother.) In some of the best scenes, Harold fakes his death in various ways to shock his family. The authority and military figures are cartoonish. Vivian Pickles costars, with Cyril Cusack, Charles Tyner, and

Ellen Geer. The music by Cat Stevens is from his first LP for A&M. Ashby did *The Last Detail* next. In 1993 Cort directed himself in *Ted and Venus*.

THE HARRAD EXPERIMENT

(Wizard, 1973) **D:** Ted Post **S:** Ted Cassidy,
Michael Werner **P:** Mel Sokolow

This R-rated Cinerama adaptation of Robert Rimmer's bestselling novel about free love at a coed college was pretty boring when new but is an interesting period piece today. It stars James Whitmore, with Tippi Hedren as a "human values" teacher. Don Johnson (in his third film), Laurie Walters, Victoria Thompson, Michael Greene, Gregory Harrison, and Bruno Kirby appear naked, and Johnson has an outdoor scene where he attempts to seduce Hedren, the mother of his future real-life wife, Melanie Griffith (who is an extra here). The improvisational group Ace Trucking Company appear as themselves. Walters and Thompson both returned in the sequel, *Harrad Summer* (1974), available on tape as *Student Union* (Wizard). The soundtracks of both films are on Capitol.

HARRY AND THE HENDERSONS

(MCA, 1987) **D/S/P:** William Dear **S:** William E. Martin

Spielberg's Amblin company backed this PG friendly-Bigfoot comedy with an anti-gun message. A family rescues the monster, then keeps it at home. With John Lithgow, Melinda Dillon, Lainie Kazan, Don Ameche, and M. Emmet Walsh. The FX by Rick Baker and ILM received an Oscar. The soundtrack is on MCA. Harry (the late Kevin Peter Hall) watches *The Addams Family* on TV. Hall also starred in the *Harry and the Hendersons* TV series and in *Misfits of Science*.

HARRY NOVAK'S BOX OFFICE BONANZA OF SEXPLOITATION TRAILERS, Volumes I and II

(SW)

Boxoffice International was one of the most prolific companies producing and releasing soft-core adult movies. They later branched out and acquired some horror and action movies from various countries. Volume I features 60s movies like *Kiss Me Quick, The Touchables, The Bloody and the Bare, Mondo Mod, Cool It, Baby, Venus in Furs,* and *Mantis in Lace*. Volume II features 70s movies, including *Please Don't Eat My Mother, The Dirty Mind of Young Sally, When Women Played Ding Dong,* and *The Concubines*. Each tape is 100 minutes.

THE HARVEST

(Columbia, 1992) **D/S:** David Marconi

Miguel Ferrer (who narrates) stars as a Prozac-popping American screenwriter who investigates an unsolved murder in a Mexican beach town. He meets a blonde (Leilani Sarelle, his real-life wife) in a gay bar but wakes up missing his valuables and a kidney. With Anthony John Denison as the blond bartender/killer, Henry Silva as the local police chief, Harvey Fierstein as the producer, Tim Thomerson, and Matt Clark. With flashbacks, flashforwards, hallucinations, slo-mo sex, some bloody killings, and a surprise ending. It's not great, but it's interesting to see Ferrer in a leading role and Silva as a good guy.

HARVEY

(MCA, 1951) **D:** Henry Koster **S:** Mary Chase, Oscar Brodney **P:** John Beck

James Stewart stars in this adaptation of Mary Chase's Pulitzer prize–winning comedy about a gentle alcoholic named Elwood P. Dowd who talks to a 6-foot-tall, invisible rabbit. Josephine Hull as his sister (she received an Oscar), Victoria Horne, and Jesse White (great as an asylum guard) had been in the Broadway production. The cast also includes Cecil Kellaway, Peggy Dow, Wallace Ford, and Charles Drake. It's similar to some of the classic Capra films. Universal released it.

THE HAUNTED

(VC2, 1976) **D/S/P:** Michael De Gaetano **P:** Nicholas P. Nizich

An Indian woman (Anne Michelle) is accused of witchcraft during the Civil War, put on a horse (naked), and sent to die in the desert. Makes sense, right? About 100 years later the descendants of her persecutors in an Arizona ghost town think they're cursed. Aldo Ray lives with his blind, widowed sister-in-law (Virginia Mayo) and his two nephews. One of them (Jim Negele) sings sappy folk songs and falls for a British woman (Michelle, of course) who gets stuck there until her red convertible is repaired. Mayo has tasteful sex flashbacks to "when he eased into me." A phone booth is installed in the cemetery (!?), and Aldo (the real star) gets meaner and crazier. The soundtrack (!) is on Midland. The dialogue is pretentious and depressing. This is by the director of *UFO: Target Earth*.

THE HAUNTED

(1991) **D:** Robert Mandel **S:** Darrah Cloud **P:** Daniel Schneider

A Catholic wife (Sally Kirkland) is the only member of her family to notice strange things in their new house. She consults experts on demons and ghosts, as well as a priest. In one scene she floats in her bedroom. It's "based on a real story." Jeffrey De Munn, Louise Latham, Stephen Markle, Diane Baker, and Joyce Van Patten are also in this Fox-TV movie.

THE HAUNTED CASTLE

(Video Yesterday, 1921) **D:** F. W. Murnau **S:** Carl Mayer, Berthold Viertel   Germany (*Schloss Vogelöd*)

Paul Hartmann stars in this crime story as a nobleman who entertains guests amid strange happenings. A dream sequence features a phantom bird. This silent film is 75 minutes long and has English intertitles. Murnau, who had directed a version of *Dr. Jekyll and Mr. Hyde* called *Der Januskopf* in 1920, made *Nosferatu* next.

HAUNTED HONEYMOON

(HBO, 1986) **D/S/A:** Gene Wilder **S:** Terence Marsh **P:** Susan Ruskin

Wilder and his real-life wife Gilda Radner star in a horror comedy patterned on those of the 30s and 40s. He plays a 30s radio actor (like Red Skelton in his *Whistling* series). With Dom DeLuise as a woman, Jonathan Pryce, and Paul L. Smith. There's a werewolf and sets that copy the silent film *The Cat and the Canary*. It's not very funny, but it is strange to see Radner (before she died in real life) appear as a ghost. This PG Orion release was filmed in England (as was the 1940 movie of the same name, starring Robert Montgomery).

THE HAUNTED HOUSE

(1928) **D:** Benjamin Christensen **S:** Richard Bee, Lajos Biro **P:** Wid Gunning

Four possible heirs to a fortune go to an old family house where they find a weird caretaker (William V. Mong), a mad doctor (Montague Love), a nurse (Thelma Todd), and a sleepwalking woman who sings. The ghosts turn out to be fake. This horror comedy, based on a play, also features Chester Conklin and Flora Finch. Cornell Woolrich wrote the intertitles. First National released it in silent and partial-sound versions. All prints are now lost. The Danish Christensen (spelled Christiansen in the US) also made *Seven Footprints to Satan* and *The House of Horror* (both 1929) with Mong and Todd. He was a director, screenwriter, and actor whose best-known film is *Häxan* (*Witchcraft Through the Ages*), made in Sweden in 1922.

HAUNTED SUMMER

(Media, 1988) **D:** Ivan Passer **S:** Lewis John Carlino **P:** Martin Poll   UK

This movie, based on a novel by Anne Edwards, shows the young free-love-and-drugs crowd Mary Shelley (Alice Krige) was part of when she created the novel *Frankenstein* at a villa in Switzerland during the summer of 1816. With Philip Anglim as a bisexual Lord Byron, Eric Stoltz as Percy Bysshe Shelley, Laura Dern, Rupert Everett, and Alex Winter as Dr. John Polidori. It's from Cannon. Ken Russell's *Gothic* (1986) tells the same story.

HAUNTING FEAR

(Rhino, 1989) **D/S/P:** Fred Olen Ray

Brinke Stevens stars as a wife who has nightmares and is afraid of being buried alive, in this movie "based on" Poe's story "The Premature Burial." Her husband (Jay Richardson) has (almost-X) sex with his secretary (Delia Sheppard), and they plot to get rid of her. She returns from being "dead" in the basement, laughing while she kills. With guest stars Jan-Michael Vincent as a cop who sits in his car, Karen Black as a hypnotist, Robert Clarke as a doctor, Robert Quarry, Michael Berryman, and Hoke Howell. And talk about unholy alliances! It's a Fred Olen Ray movie acquired by Troma and released by Rhino.

THE HAUNTING OF M

(1979) **D/S/P:** Anna Thomas

Shelagh Gilbey is Marianna, a spinster haunted by the ghost of a young man from Victorian times. Her actress sister (Nina Pitt) helps to figure out who the ghost is and why he's there. This low-budget film was made in Scotland by a UCLA graduate.

THE HAUNTING OF MORELLA

(New Horizons, 1990) **D:** Jim Wynorski **S:** R. J. Robertson **P:** Roger Corman

It's bad but still pretty entertaining for a lesbian-sex/horror movie based on Poe. The tale of Lenora, possessed by her father's late wife, Morella, had previously been told in Corman's *Tales of Terror* (1962). Nicole Eggert (from the *T. J. Hooker* TV series) is Lenora (and Morella). A lesbian scene in a waterfall with tall Lana Clarkson and Maria Ford is pretty memorable. And check out the bikini underwear. With an unshaven David McCallum in dark shades as the reclusive New England father, Deborah Dutch, and Gail Thackray.

THE HAUNTING OF SARAH HARDY

(Paramount, 1989) **D:** Jerry London **S:** Thomas Baum **P:** Richard Rothschild

Newlywed Sela Ward is haunted by her late mother (a suicide) in the family mansion. It all turns out to involve deception and blackmail. With Morgan Fairchild as her soap-opera-actress friend, Polly Bergen as the housekeeper, Roscoe Born, and Michael Woods. It was made on the coast of Oregon and debuted on the USA Network.

THE HAUNTING OF SEACLIFF INN

(1994) **D/S:** Walter Klenhard **S:** Tom Walla **P:** Timothy Marx

Ally Sheedy and William R. Moses are a couple that move into an old Mendicino home to open a bed-and-breakfast. They discover that murders had occurred there a century ago and ghosts of the victims appear. With Lucinda Weist and Louise Fletcher. From USA cable.

THE HAUNTING PASSION

(1983) **D:** John Korty **S:** Michael Berk, Douglas Schwartz **P:** Paul Radin

Jane Seymour, married to sportscaster Gerald McRaney (from *Major Dad*) and living near a bayou, finds herself interested in a sexy ghost. The NBC-TV movie was billed as "an erotic ghost story." With Millie Perkins.

THE HAWK

(Academy, 1993) **D:** David Hayman **S:** Peter Ransley   UK

Helen Mirren is a woman with a history of depression who suspects that her husband (George Costigan) is a serial killer who gouges eyes out. Mirren is best known in the US for her starring role as a police detective in the British series *Prime Suspect* and its sequels, shown on PBS.

HAWKEN'S BREED

(Starmaker, 1986) **D/S/P:** Charles B. Pierce **P:** Sandy Garrison

Peter Fonda is a frontier trapper who helps an Indian woman avenge the murder of her husband

and son. (Fonda says that this movie was never finished, but it showed up on tape anyway.) With Serene Headin, Jack Elam, Sue Ane Langdon, and Bill Thurman. From the maker of the Boggy Creek movies.

HEAD

(Rhino, 1968) **D/S/P:** Bob Rafelson **S/P:** Jack Nicholson

The Monkees (Peter Tork, Micky Dolenz, Davy Jones, and Michael Nesmith) were in only one movie, released several months after their *Help*-inspired TV show was cancelled by NBC. It confused their young fans with its plotless, anti-establishment, drug-influenced, musical-comedy segments, as the foursome search for the meaning of life and sing about how phony the Monkees concept is! Now it's a visually fascinating period piece full of Hollywood in-jokes, fringe celebrities, clips from old movies, and Vietnam War footage. The band is seen as dandruff on Victor Mature's head. Their music is criticized by Frank Zappa. Davy is KO'd by Sonny Liston. They encounter topless dancer Carol Doda, Annette Funicello, and Terry (later Teri) Garr. A news clip of a very mean-looking California governor Ronald Reagan is pretty chilling. Also look for clips from *The Black Cat* and for wrestler Tiger Joe Marsh, who looks like Tor Johnson. Nicholson had just written the script for Roger Corman's *The Trip*. He worked on *Head* with Rafelson the year before he was recognized as star material in *Easy Rider*. Nicholson, Dennis Hopper, and Rafelson are all in *Head*, taking part in behind-the-scenes "it's only a movie" gags. Kubrick fans might want to see it for its references to *Dr. Strangelove*'s Coke machine and the *2001* monolith, plus early Kubrick regular Timothy Carey, who takes acting honors in a memorable schizo-scary recurring role. This would make an interesting video double bill with *The Trip*, for the scenes of Mike Nesmith's bad drug trip, which are similar to Peter Fonda's horror/acid visions. It includes some beautiful solarized color photography, imaginative FX, and musical segments that would make great rock videos on their own. Monte Hellman was the editor. The songs are some of the group's best and can also be heard on Rhino's reissued soundtrack album. Rhino has also released episodes of the TV show on tape.

THE HEAD

(Sinister, 1959) **D/S:** Victor Trivas **P:** Wolf C. Hartwig W. Germany (*Die Nackte und der Satan*)

This is the movie that obviously inspired the American film *The Brain That Wouldn't Die*. Dr. Abel (French actor Michel Simon) can keep a dog's head alive using his Serum Z. The mysterious Dr. Ood (Horst Frank) arrives at the (very modern) clinic, picks up a turtle, notices the crippled, hunchbacked nurse, and quickly takes over. When Abel dies of heart disease, Ood saves his head, keeps it hooked up to tubes on a table, and makes him help in experiments to give the nurse a new body! As in the American movie, the crazed scientist wants a really sexy body, so naturally he goes to the Tam-Tam Sex Club to check some out. Seconds after the successful operation Ood offers the surprised stripper/nurse a cigarette and starts kissing her. The only reason that the respected Michel

Simon agreed to play a head in a German exploitation movie was that his body and face had temporarily been partially paralyzed after he used some tainted makeup. Unable to find work, he took this undemanding role for the money, hoping the movie wouldn't cross the border. It also features Barbara Valentin, sort of a German Diana Dors, whom some will remember from Fassbinder films. When it was released in Cleveland in 1961, shrunken heads were given away free to patrons at the Hippodrome.

HEADHUNTER

(Academy, 1988) **D:** Francis Schaeffer **S:** Len Spinelli **P:** Jay Davidson   S. Africa

After *The Believers*, *Angel Heart*, and *The Serpent and the Rainbow*, all fairly big-budget voodoo movies, we got low-budget voodoo movies like this. Wayne Crawford, an exploitation star since *Barracuda* (1978), looks sort of like Frank Zappa's lost brother. He plays a brooding, drinking Miami cop whose wife (June Chadwick) has a female lover: "My wife is a muff diver!" Soon he's sleeping with his sympathetic partner, Kay Lenz (who should be in better movies). Meanwhile, a tribe in Nigeria is attacked by an unseen force, and a witch doctor in Miami is decapitated. More people are decapitated by a "chameleon demon" while *The Hideous Sun Demon* plays on TV. After a lot of boring talk the ending is absurd enough to wake you up. Crawford's possessed wife (with an *Exorcist* voice) rips off his car door. The sight of him driving wildly to get away with no door is hilarious. The ending involves a chainsaw fight intercut with more *Sun Demon* footage and a demon who looks an awful lot like the one in *The Unnameable*. If the "Nigerian community" of Miami looks strangely unfamiliar, it's because the movie was really shot in South Africa.

HEADLESS EYES

(Wizard, 1971) **D/S:** Ken Bateman **P:** Ronald Sullivan

A starving artist (Bo Brundin) has his eye popped out with a spoon when he tries to burglarize a Manhattan apartment. He kills people, scoops their eyes out, and makes sculptures and mobiles with them. The very low-budget oddity, made in New York City, was released in 1983. Sullivan was later known as porno director Henri Pachard.

HEADS

(Republic, 1993) **D:** Paul Shapiro **S:** Jay Stapleton **P:** Jonathan Goodwill, Derek Mazur   Canada

Jon Cryer (who narrates) is a young proofreader on a small-town newspaper who's trying to solve a series of decapitation murders. He reluctantly gets involved with the wild, estranged daughter (Jennifer Tilly) of his editor boss (Edward Asner) and also becomes the prime suspect. With Roddy McDowall, Earl Pastko (from *Route 66*) as Lloyd, and Shawn Alex Thompson. This R-rated black comedy with eccentric characters doesn't really work, but the many well-done scenes of heads and headless bodies are kind of surprising (and there's a nightmare sequence). It was made for Showtime in Manitoba.

HEALER

(1994) **D/P:** John G. Thomas **S:** Russ Reina

Tyrone Power Jr. is an ex-con working as a paramedic who learns the value of life. John R. Johnson costars. David McCallum is a drifter called the Jackal, and Turhan Bey is an old Russian immigrant.

HEAR NO EVIL

(1982) **D:** Harry Falk **S:** Tom Lazarus **P:** Paul Pompian

This pilot for a CBS-TV series about a San Francisco cop (Gil Gerard) who becomes deaf in a fight is no big deal, but the subplot about drug-dealing bikers is pretty good. Wings Hauser and Brion James are the main bikers, and Raven De La Croix (!) is one of their women. They have a huge, *Wild Angels*–style funeral procession. With Bernie Casey and Mimi Rogers.

HEAR NO EVIL

(Fox, 1992) **D:** Robert Greenwald **S:** R. M. Badat **P:** Davis Matalon

In a plot that copies *Wait Until Dark*, Marlee Matlin is a deaf woman whose life is in danger because she unknowingly has a valuable stolen coin. D. B. Sweeney falls for her while trying to help, which leads to scenes showing how to relate to deaf people and a brief topless shot of Matlin. Martin Sheen is the corrupt police lieutenant (a role his brother Joe Estevez could have handled), and Mickey O'Malley (giving the best performance) is a reporter. Marge Redmond (from *The Flying Nun*) is in one scene. It's by the director of *Xanadu*.

HEART AND SOULS

(MCA, 1993) **D:** Ron Underwood **S:** Brent Maddock, S. S. Wilson **P:** Nancy Roberts, Sean Daniel

In the most complex of the many soul-transfer movies, the souls of four people who died in a San Francisco bus crash in 1959 all end up entering the body of a yuppie bankruptcy lawyer (Robert Downey Jr.), born at the instant of the crash. They take him over one at a time to complete unfinished tasks. Downey has an acting challenge as he adapts the characteristics of the various spirits. With Charles Grodin, Tom Sizemore, Alfre Woodard, and Kyra Sedgwick as the souls, and Elisabeth Shue. This PG-13 Universal release is by the director of *Tremors*.

HEARTBREAK HOTEL

(Vid America, 1973) **D:** Richard Robinson **S:** B. W. Sandefur **P/A:** Michael Christian (*Black Vengeance*; *Redneck County*; *Poor Pretty Eddie*)

Shelley Winters has been in so many obscure movies that it's no wonder few people remember this all-star disaster, made somewhere in between the more famous *Cleopatra Jones* and *Tentacles*. Producer Christian stars as Eddie, a gigolo would-be Elvis impersonator. Shelley is Birtha, a mean, alcoholic, racist, vain, jealous ex-stripper who owns a backwoods motel. Her faithful servant is big Ted Cassidy (with a facial scar). Slim Pickens is pretty funny as the yokel sheriff ("Hot dayam!") with a retarded nephew. Dub Taylor is a bartender/justice of the peace ("Goddamn Yankees are like hemorrhoids!"). They're all a living nightmare for star Leslie Uggams, as a famous TV singer unfortunate enough to have her car break down nearby. Eddie, who seems harmless at first, attempts rape. Then the terrorized woman is locked up, accused of stealing a jeep, and put on trial. If that's not distasteful enough for you, Shelley does her strip act. You've been warned. Uggams had been a regular on the TV show *Sing Along with Mitch*. The director made *Thunder County* next, followed by *Women's Prison Escape* (both 1974). This one is available under various titles, sometimes in boxes that might make you think it's a horror movie.

Ted "Lurch" Cassidy in *Heartbreak Hotel*.

HEARTBREAK HOTEL
(Touchstone, 1988) **D/S:** Chris Columbus
P: Debra Hill, Linda Obst

Elvis (David Keith) is kidnapped by an Ohio teen (Charlie Schlatter) in 1972. He cheers up the kid's family, and they help him return to his roots. Tuesday Weld (from *Wild in the Country*) is the divorced mom. Flashbacks from Elvis movies are used (the Presley estate cooperated). I worked in a Cleveland record store with a good stock of Elvis LPs at the time this movie takes place and can testify that many diehard Elvis fanatics in Ohio would have been capable of kidnapping him, no matter what the cost. Many people thought Elvis could literally perform miracles. Many still do.

HEART CONDITION
(Columbia, 1990) **D/S:** James D. Perriott
P: Robert Shaye

Bob Hoskins and Denzel Washington star in this action/fantasy comedy whose plot is similar to the plot of *The Thing with Two Heads*. A racist LA cop (Hoskins) receives a heart transplant from a murdered black lawyer (Washington) who shows up as a ghost and makes him help find the killer. With Chloe Webb, Roger E. Mosley, and Ja'net Du Bois. It's by the director of *Misfits of Science*. From New Line.

HEART OF DARKNESS
(Turner, 1993) **D:** Nicolas Roeg **S:** Benedict
Fitzgerald **P:** Bob Christiansen, Rick Rosenberg

Nicolas Roeg decided to film Joseph Conrad's 1902 novel with the original setting. It's interesting to compare this with *Apocalypse Now*. Tim Roth stars as Marlow, who tells his story in flashback. He's sent by a Belgian trading company on a journey up the Congo River in a leaky steamboat to find Kurtz (John Malkovich), an ivory trader who has become a mad prophet and king. With Morten Faldaas (in the Dennis Hopper role), James Fox, and Iman. It was filmed in Belize and debuted on TNT. Marlow is also the narrator of Conrad's *Lord Jim*, filmed in 1965.

HEART OF JUSTICE
(1992) **D:** Bruno Barreto **S:** Keith
Reddin **P:** Donald P. Borchers

A novelist (Dennis Hopper) is gunned down by the man (Dermot Mulroney) he based his last novel on. The cast of this *film noir* includes Eric Stoltz, Jennifer Connelly, and the late Vincent Price. Price and Connelly were also in movies that Hopper directed around the same time. This was made for TNT by the director of *Dona Flor and Her Two Husbands*.

HEART OF MIDNIGHT
(Virgin, 1988) **D/S:** Mathew Chapman
P: Andrew Gaty

Jennifer Jason Leigh stars as a troubled young woman who inherits a closed-down warehouse club from her uncle, who died of AIDS. It turns out to have been an S&M sex club with red walls, secret passages, and theme rooms. A guy who seems to be a cop (Peter Coyote) keeps showing up. This confused movie has many attempts at surrealism, lots of flashbacks, and a girl in a rubber dress chained up. With Frank Stallone as a singing cop, Steve Buscemi, and Brenda Vaccaro as the mother. It was filmed in Charleston, South Carolina. Chapman also made *Strangers Kiss*, a tribute to Stanley Kubrick.

HEARTS OF DARKNESS: A FILMMAKER'S JOURNEY
(Paramount, 1991) **D/S:** Fax Bahr, George
Hickenlooper **P:** George Laloom, Les Mayfield

Orson Welles planned to film Joseph Conrad's *Heart of Darkness* in 1939. George Lucas was going to direct a contemporary version, *Apocalypse Now*, in 1969. Coppola started it in 1976, and it wasn't released until 1979. This excellent documentary, partially based on behind-the-scenes footage shot by Eleanor Coppola, tells the whole story of the production: filming during a civil war in the Philippines, dealing with President Marcos, using a real local tribe, Harvey Keitel being fired after one week, and Martin Sheen's heart attack. We see how they filmed the tiger scene and the decapitated heads, how the script was changed often, and how the actors improvised (including 14-year-old Larry (now Laurence) Fishburne). The Coppola kids (Sophia, Gio, and Roman) appear, and there are scenes on a French plantation never seen before and *Mondo*-like segments of the (actual) rit-

ual killing of animals. It debuted on Showtime, then was shown in theaters.

HEARTS OF FIRE
(Lorimar, 1987) **D/P:** Richard Marquand
S: Scott Richardson, Joe Esterhaus **P:** Jennifer
Miller, Jennifer Alward   UK/Canada

Bob Dylan is retired rock star Billy Parker on his chicken farm near Pittsburgh. His 18-year-old singing girlfriend, Molly McGuire (one-hit singer Fiona Flanagan), leaves him (and her tollbooth job) and goes to the estate of British rock star James Colt (Rupert Everett). Billy follows, so we get to see Dylan jump into a crowd of jeering punks and throw a TV (and a bed) out of a window, in this really embarrassing love-triangle story. Everett sings "Tainted Love," and a blind female fan blows her brains out during a show. With Julian Glover as a butler named Alfred, Richie Havens (who sings), Ron Wood, and Ian Dury. Marquand, the director of *Return of the Jedi*, died during production. The soundtrack is on Columbia.

HEARTSTOPPER
(Tempe, 1989) **D/S:** John Russo **P:** Charles A. Gelini

Kevin Kindlin stars as a physician who is hanged as a vampire at Fort Pitt during the American Revolution and is resurrected in modern times. He confesses his story (in flashback) to a priest, kills members of a multiracial gang with a razor (as in *Martin*), and falls for Lenora (Moon Zappa!). A descendant turns out to be a masked serial killer who wants to be a vampire. Tom Savini is a cop who has flashbacks, cries, and is shown pumping up. Savini also provided the FX (surgery and autopsy scenes, an arm that grows back). Michael J. Pollard is an odd vampire expert. The constant time changes are disorienting, and the sappy love themes are a bit much, but it's an interesting enough vampire movie. Russo based the film (made in Pittsburgh) on his novel *The Awakening*. The vocals are by Michael J. Weldon.

HEAT
(Paramount, 1972) **D/S/C:** Paul Morrissey
S: John Howell **P:** Andy Warhol **M:** John Cale
(*Andy Warhol's Heat*)

Joe Dallesandro stars as a former child actor who's now a hustler, and Sylvia Miles is a fading minor movie star, in Morrissey's *Sunset Boulevard* parody. With Pat Ast, Andrea Feldman, and Ray Vestal. It was the third (and most commercial) of Morrissey's underground Dallesandro "trilogy," which includes *Flesh* and *Trash*.

HEATHERS
(Starmaker, 1989) **D:** Michael Lehmann
S: Daniel Waters **P:** Denise Di Novi

"This is Ohio. If you don't have a brewski in your hand, you might as well be wearing a dress." Winona Ryder and Christian Slater star in this great teen movie, a black comedy and murder story set in Westerburg, Ohio. Although parts are like *Massacre at Central High*, this has realistic teen dialogue and is right on target about peer pressure, sports, and class horrors. Shannen Doherty, Lisanne Falk, and Kim Walker are the Heathers, a trio of bitchy, perfect, have-it-all girls whom Veronica (Ryder) hangs out with until she meets the devious (and crazy) J.D. (Slater). With Penelope Milford, Glenn Shadix as a preacher, and Rene Estevez. Lehmann followed this with *The Applegates*. It's from New World. David Newman's soundtrack is on Varèse Sarabande.

HEAT OF PASSION

(1991) **D/S/P:** Rodman Flender

A young actor living in a crummy apartment (Nick Corri) falls for a psychotherapist (Sally Kirkland). He plays a rapist in a TV docudrama series (hosted by Jack Carter). There's lots of nudity and sex in this "erotic thriller" by the director of *The Unborn*.

HEAT STREET

(City Lights, 1987) **D/S/P:** Joseph Merhi
P: Richard Pepin

In this violent, direct-to-tape release, a black boxing coach (Quincy Adams), whose daughter was killed by bikers, and a white repo man (Del Zamora) team up to battle LA gangs.

HEAT WAVE

(Sinister, 1954) **D/S:** Ken Hughes **P:** Anthony Hinds   UK (*The House Across the Lake*)

Hillary Brooke stars as a blond murderess in this early Hammer mystery, with Alex Nicol as a novelist, Paul Carpenter, and Sidney James. Lippert released this 68-minute film in the US.

HEAVEN

(Pacific Arts, 1987) **D:** Diane Keaton **P:** Joe Kelly

Here's an example of what an Oscar-winning actress can do with spare time and money. "100" people are asked what they think about Heaven, and lots of good (unidentified) old (public-domain) film clips are seen. In this unique PG-13 documentary, many of the people interviewed are very serious about what they hope to find in Heaven, but most of the clips are funny (because they're from old comedies or are just so absurd). Clips from various church and evangelist films are also used. With Don King and clips from Ron Ormond movies. I was a consultant on this movie, and I didn't get it either. Keaton also directed a Belinda Carlisle video in 1987.

HEAVEN AND EARTH

(Live, 1992) **D/S:** Haruki Kadokawa **S:** Toshido Kamata, Isao Yoshihara **P:** Yutaka Okada   Japan

This imitation of a Kurosawa epic is about 16th-century samurai-warlord brothers. One (Takaai Enoki) is spiritual and celibate. The other (Masahiko Tsugawa) is ruthless and wants more territory. Huge battle scenes with thousands of extras are the main attraction. It's narrated by Stuart Whitman and was filmed (for $42 million) in western Canada. It's been shown (subtitled and letterboxed) on cable TV.

HEAVEN BECOMES HELL

(1989) **D/S:** Mickey Nivelli **P:** Lotte Nivelli   (*Jealous*)

Two actors start a religion to raise the money to make an action movie. James Davies stars, with Michael Walker (as himself), Ruth Collins, and a West Indian supporting cast. This movie was made in New York City on a very low budget.

HEAVEN CAN WAIT

(Fox, 1943) **D/P:** Ernst Lubitsch **S:** Samson Raphaelson

A late-19th-century man who is considered a sinner (Don Ameche) recalls his life as he waits to enter Hell. With Gene Tierney, Laird Cregar as the Devil, Spring Byington, Marjorie Main, Charles Coburn, Allyn Joslyn, Signe Hasso, Florence Bates, Eugene Pallette, Louis Calhern, Scotty Beckett, and Dickie Moore. This 20th Century–Fox color production is based on a play by Laszlo Bus-Fekete. *Defending Your Life* (1991) used the same idea.

HEAVEN CAN WAIT

(Paramount, 1978) **D/S/A:** Warren Beatty
D/A: Buck Henry **S:** Elaine May

Warren Beatty stars as an LA Rams quarterback who goes to Heaven ahead of schedule and is allowed to return in the body of a murdered millionaire, in this updated remake of *Here Comes Mr. Jordan* (1941). This PG comedy hit was nominated for a lot of Oscars and was probably the inspiration for the many angel, ghost, and body-switch movies that followed. It was also Beatty's last hit until *Bugsy* (1992). With James Mason as Mr. Jordan, Julie Christie, Dyan Cannon as the unfaithful wife, Charles Grodin as her lover, Vincent Gardenia as the coach, Buck Henry, R. G. Armstrong, Hamilton Camp, and Keene Curtis.

HEAVEN HELP US

(HBO, 1985) **D:** Michael Dinner **S:** Charles Purpura **P:** Dan Wigutow, Mark Carliner

Kids in a Brooklyn Catholic school in 1963 are constantly threatened with Purgatory for venial sins. This comedy stars Andrew McCarthy, Kevin Dillon, Brad Dourif, Patrick Dempsey, Mary Stuart Masterson, Stephen Geoffreys, John Heard, and Wallace Shawn and Donald Sutherland as priests.

HEAVENLY BODIES!

(RM, 1963) **D/S/P/A/C/E:** Russ Meyer

This was the last of Meyer's plotless color nudie movies. It's only 62 minutes and played with Meyer's 10-minute short *Skyscrapers and Brassieres*. Both star Rochelle Kennedy. (Beware of a 1985 teen comedy with the same name, available on tape.) *Lorna*, Meyer's breakthrough hit, was next.

HEAVENLY CREATURES

(Mirimax, 1994) **D/S:** Peter Jackson **S:** Frances Walsh **P:** Jim Booth   New Zealand

Pauline, a shy, impressionable New Zealand schoolgirl (Melanie Lynsky, who narrates from a diary) is greatly influenced by Juliet, an imaginative, wealthy, blond English schoolgirl (Kate Winslet), and they eventually commit a murder. This unique movie is based on a real case from the 1950s. Orson Welles is a major character in the girls' fantasy dream world, as one of many clay models that come to life, in clips from *The Third Man*, and portrayed by an actor. The Juliet character grew up to be best-selling mystery novelist Anne Perry, a fact not known until this movie was released. The director's fourth feature was an arthouse hit (the acting is excellent) and was the first to receive attention outside of horror fanzines in America.

THE HEAVENLY KID

(HBO, 1985) **D/S:** Gary Medoway
S: Martin Copeland **P:** Mort Engleberg

A 60s juvenile delinquent (Lewis Smith) dies in a chicken race, then is brought back 17 years later as a guardian angel for a suicidal teen wimp (Jason Gedrick). This PG-13 teen comedy from Orion features a subway Purgatory, an angel on a motorcycle, and characters taking escalators to Heaven. With Jane Kaczmarek, Richard Mulligan, and Nancy Valen. Elektra released the soundtrack, featuring various artists.

HEAVEN ONLY KNOWS

(1947) **D:** Albert S. Rogell **S:** Art Arthur, Rowland Leigh **P:** Seymour Nebenzel   (*Montana Mike*)

Robert Cummings is an angel named Mike who's sent to the Old West to help a Montana saloon keeper and gambler (Brian Donlevy) save his soul. Mike isn't allowed to work any miracles, though. Marjorie Reynolds costars in this UA comedy/fantasy, with Stuart Irwin, John Litel, Edgar Kennedy, and Gerald Mohr.

HEAVEN WITH A GUN

(1969) **D:** Lee H. Katzin **S:** Richard Carr **P:** Frank King

Glenn Ford stars as a western preacher who is forced to reach for his guns. This is the first of several films with Barbara Hershey and David Carradine. She's Leloopa, an Indian whose father is hanged by Coke (Carradine), the henchman of evil John Anderson. The plot involves farmers vs. sheepmen. With Carolyn Jones, Noah Beery, Virginia Gregg, and Angelique Pettyjohn.

HEAVY METAL

(1981) **D:** Gerald Potterton **S:** Dan Goldberg, Len Blum **P:** Ivan Reitman

These 8 animated episodes based on comic strips from Heavy Metal comics are linked by an evil green monolith. A favorite segment (the first) concerns a cabdriver in New York City of the future. The science-fiction and fantasy episodes were made in various styles by animators in various countries. Reitman hired fellow Canadians John Vernon, Harold Ramis, Joe Flaherty, John Candy, and Eugene Levy for the voices. The music by Blue Oyster Cult (a great theme song), Devo ("Working in a Coal Mine"), Grand Funk, and others is on the hit Asylum soundtrack recording.

HEAVY PETTING

(Academy, 1989) **D:** Josh Waletzky
D/P: Obie Benz **S:** Pierce Rafferty

Sex in the 50s is the topic of this comic documentary. The many clips (from features and sex-ed films) are great, but only certain viewers will enjoy the semi-underground stars who are interviewed. They include David Byrne, William S. Burroughs, Allan Ginsberg, Sandra Bernhard, Ann Magnuson, Zoe Tamerlis/Lund, Josh Mostel, Spalding Gray, Laurie Anderson, and the late Abbie Hoffman. They all discuss dating and growing up in the 50s (even though some seem to have been born a little late for it). Rafferty codirected *The Atomic Cafe*. Rick Prelinger supplied the great archival footage.

HEAVY TRAFFIC

(AIP, 1973) **D/S:** Ralph Bakshi **P:** Steve Kranz

Bakshi's follow-up to *Fritz the Cat* was an X-rated (later R) AIP release mixing live action with rotoscope animation. An Italian/Jewish artist unleashes his personal furies and ends up in a cartoon. New York City is seen as a pinball machine with gangsters. The music consists of rock hits, plus some jazz and classical music. The voices were provided by Joseph Kaufman, Beverly Hope Atkinson, Jamie Farr, and Frank De Kova. Bakshi later used the same concept for *Cool World*.

HEIMWEH NACH ST. PAULI

(Fright, 1963) **D:** Werner Jacobs **S:** Gustav
Kampendonk **P:** Rapid-Constantin
Germany (*Homesick for St. Paul*)

This is in German, and Jayne Mansfield's not in it enough, but it's pretty amusing. Freddie Quinn (a short singing star) is Jimmy Jones, "the lonesome star." His first number (in a New York TV studio) is incredible. Wearing a silver suit and surrounded by dancing girls, he sings (in English), "I've got everything—suede shoes, diamond ring, golden guitar. They're callin' me the lonesome star!" Then he does a plug for Pam macaroni. Jayne, as "Sexy Hexy"/Evelyn, sings (dubbed in German) while holding a long cigarette holder. It's all a setup for a sentimental anti-showbiz musical, though, as Jimmy hides out from comical agents who want him to do Vegas, returns home to his flower-selling family, and enjoys drinking with his buddies on the Reeperbahn. First he walks around the pier in Hoboken and sings the theme ballad. In Hamburg guest star Jayne sings about Jimmy ("I've seen sailors, whalers") and does the twist. Quinn starred in about a dozen movies.

HE KILLS NIGHT AFTER NIGHT AFTER NIGHT

(1969) **D:** "Lewis J. Force"/Lindsay Shonteff
S: Dail Amber **P:** James Mellor
UK (*Night Slasher; Night After Night*)

A ripper kills women in London. A cross-dressing judge is the culprit. With Jack May and Linda Marlowe.

HELGA

(1967) **D/S:** Erich F. Bender, Terry
Van Tell **P:** Karl-Ludwig Ruppel, Vers
Salvatore Billitteri   W. Germany

Mom and Dad, the most famous old road-show childbirth film, was still playing when this more modern color version of the same idea was released. Helga (Ruth Gassman) becomes pregnant and has a baby boy. That's the plot, but the attraction was the actual childbirth scene. The US version contains some new footage and a prologue. AIP also released the sequel, *Michael and Helga* (1968).

HE LIVES

(Camp, 1967) **D:** Joseph Kane **S:** Don Fearheighly
P: E. Stanley Williamson   (*The Search for the Evil One*)

I expected this obscure Hitler horror movie to be terrible, like *Flesh Feast* or *They Saved Hitler's Brain*. It's no classic, but it's not exactly "camp" either. Flashbacks reveal that Hitler's double took poison in the bunker. The dictator and his faithful Martin Bormann (the late Henry Brandon) hide out in Madrid, Buenos Aires, and finally a castle in the Andes. Lee Paterson (later a regular on *One Life to Live*) is the Jewish hero, Anton Becker, who survived the Holocaust as a child. He's summoned to Israel, then sent by the OAS to work undercover in the Andes. He makes up with a hateful ex-girlfriend whose father is one of the Nazis. Another (nice) ex-girlfriend turns out to be a local doctor and accidentally ruins his cover. The crazed, gray-haired Hitler gives a speech about the Fourth Reich, then passes out. Bormann hunts Becker with German shepherds, in the style of *The Most Dangerous Game*. Armed OAS agents hide nearby, ready to attack. There are some disorienting editing mistakes and jumps, and absurd plot turns, but the color is good, and the movie is otherwise very professionally made. Don't rent it expecting cheap laughs. It's one of the last films by Kane, whose directing career goes back to 1935 and includes hundreds of Republic westerns (many with Gene Autry and Roy Rogers), serials (*The Undersea Kingdom*), and episodes of *Bonanza*.

HELL

(1960) **D/S/P:** Nonuo Nakagawa **S/P:** Ichiro
Miyagawa   (*Jigoku; Sinner to Hell*)

All that stuff about Herschell Gordon Lewis making the first gore movies is nonsense. Here's (amazing) proof that extreme gore was done elsewhere, earlier, and better. This whole nightmarish movie is extremely well made, surreal, and sometimes beautiful. The plot concerns a student with an evil friend (the young characters all wear sunglasses) who causes a hit-and-run death, families dramatically falling apart, and revenge. Lengthy, epic scenes in Hell show crowds of screaming people drowning in blood, rows of bodies, severed hands and heads, snakes, tridents, a ring of fire, and, incredibly, a man sawed in half while his guts spill out! There's also a contrasting reincarnation sequence with a baby floating in a river and a WWII flashback. The opening credits of this Shintoho production feature sexy women (just as in James Bond credits). The music is cool jazz, plus some theremin sounds. Shigeru Amachi and Yoichi Numata star. The letterboxed color laserdisc has been released in Japan. It's not translated. Recommended!

THE HELLBENDERS

(New Line, 1966) **D:** Sergio Corbucci **S:** Ugo
Liberatore, Jose G. Maesso **S/P:** Albert Band
M: Ennio Morricone   Italy/Spain (*I Crudeli*)

Joseph Cotten stars as a greedy Confederate general trying to escort a coffin full of cash out of enemy territory with his sons. This violent western features Aldo Sanbrell, Norma Bengell, and Julian Mateos. Morricone used a pseudonym. Ruggiero Deodato was the second-unit director.

HELLBENT

(Raedon, 1988) **D/S:** Richard Casey **P:** Louise Jaffe

Lemmy (Phil Ward), the leader of an LA garage band called Faust, makes a deal with a bar owner/Devil named Tanas. He starts drinking cough syrup, gets into fights with the audience, drinks alcohol, takes pills, has nightmares about his girlfriend, Angel, whipping him, shoots some people, becomes involved in plans to make a snuff movie, and ends up blind, singing folk music. It's pretty amusing. A Santa on a motorcycle shoots people, and a guy wearing a derby sings "Black Betty." The music, by Trotsky Icepick, Angry Samoans, Angst, and others, is on SST.

HELLBOUND: HELLRAISER II

(Starmaker, 1988) **D:** Tony Randel **S:** Peter Atkins
P: Christopher Figg **M:** Christopher Young   UK/US

"Two hours" after the end of *Hellraiser* (1987) Kristy (Ashley Laurence) wakes from a coma in an asylum. Clare Higgins also returns as the skinless wicked stepmother. Pinhead and other creatures appear, and characters climb surreal M. C. Escher–style stairs. This sequel is an interesting attempt to make a druggy horror movie, but my reaction is "Huh!?!" It features wide-eyed Imogene Boorman and scenes from *Hellraiser*. Clive Barker was an executive producer. It was cut for an R, but R and unrated video versions are available. New World went all out in their attempt to merchandise the various Cenobites. The score is on GNP Crescendo. *Hellraiser III* was next.

HELL COMES TO FROGTOWN

(Starmaker, 1987) **D:** Robert J. Kizer
D/S/P: Donald G. Jackson **S/P:** Randall Frakes

Pro wrestler "Rowdy" Roddy Piper stars as Sam Hell, chosen by females to help repopulate the post-nuke world. He's put into an exploding chastity belt and led by a scientist (Sandahl Bergman). They encounter mutant frog people in a bar (one is Nicholas Worth), William Smith as Count Sodom, and Rory Calhoun. This fun action comedy even includes Three Stooges gags. With Cec Verrill, Suzanne Solari, and Kristi Sommers. It's by the director of the notorious *Demon Lover* (1976). The FX are by Steve Wang (*Predator*). *Frogtown II* was the unworthy sequel.

HELL DRIVERS

(1957) **D/P:** Cy Endfield **P:** John Kruse   UK

Stanley Baker stars as an ex-con who takes a job driving a truck for crooks, in this all-star movie that borrows ideas from *The Wages of Fear*. Herbert Lom costars, with Peggy Cummins (*Gun Crazy*). The cast also includes future spies and a future Dr. Who: Patrick McGoohan, Sean Connery, Jill Ireland (later married to Charles Bronson), David McCallum (married to Ireland at the time), William Hartnell (the first Dr. Who), Gordon Jackson, and Sidney James.

HELL FIRE (1972): *See* INVASION FROM INNER EARTH

HELLFIRE
(1986) **D/S:** William Murray **P:** Howard Foulkrod

Kenneth McGregor and Sharon Mason star in a post-nuke movie filmed in New York City and Pennsylvania. This was Mickey Shaunessy's last role.

HELLFIRE ON ICE: *See* SWEET SUGAR

HELLFIRE ON ICE, PART II: ESCAPE FROM HELL: *See* SAVAGE ISLAND

HELLGATE
(Vidmark, 1989) **D:** William Levey
S: Michael O'Rourke **P:** Anant Singh

Ron Palillo (from *Welcome Back, Kotter*), who was nearly 40 at the time, stars in this awful, irritating teen horror movie. See it if you want to see Horshack naked. Set in a tourist ghost town, it features zombies, a plastic bat on a wire, a monster goldfish, hateful and stupid sex jokes, naked girls with silicone breasts, a can-can show, and another *Carnival of Souls* ripoff. There are also lots of false scares, fog, and slow-motion scenes. Did I mention the killer with metal strips on his face due to turtle bites? Palillo was also in Levey's *Committed*.

HELL HIGH
(Prism, 1985) **D/S/P:** Douglas Grossman **S:** Leo Evans **P:** David Steinman   (*Raging Fury*)

A biology teacher (Maureen Mooney) who witnessed a murder as a child is left for dead by student "pranksters" who drug her and force her into lesbian acts. She becomes a mystery killer on a vengeance spree. With Christopher Stryker and Karen Russell. This pretty sick movie was made in Westchester, New York.

HELLHOLE
(RCA/Columbia, 1985) **D:** Pierre De Mora
S: Vincent Mongol **P:** Billy Fine, Louis Arkoff

"Samuel Z. Arkoff presents" Judy Landers as an abused mental-hospital inmate with amnesia. Ray Sharkey is Silk, a psycho killer in leather posing as a prison aide. (Sharkey later said that he was a junkie at the time.) Mary Woronov is Dr. Fletcher, the necrophiliac-lesbian head of the hospital. Marjoe Gortner (!) is a lobotomizing doctor. With Edy Williams, Dyanne Thorne, 40s star Terry Moore (who posed in *Playboy* that year!), Lynn Borden

A burning stunt double in *Hello, Mary Lou: Prom Night II.*

and Robert Z'Dar. With the incredible cast, showers, catfights, mud fights, and glue sniffing, this should have been a sleaze classic. It's not.

HELLHOLE WOMEN
(CIC, 1980) **D/S/A:** "Robert Griffin"/ Jesús Franco
S: Gunther Ebert **P:** Lulio Poura   W. Germany/Spain
(*Sadomania; Holle der Lust*)

Ajita Wilson (a black woman who some claim used to be a man and who was a box-office draw in Europe) is Magda, the lesbian warden of a women's penitentiary. She and Robert Forster abuse inmates, feed them to crocodiles, and have organized manhunts. Ursula Buchfellner costars in this sadistic *Ilsa*-style movie.

HELL IS A CITY
(1960) **D/S:** Val Guest **P:** Michael Carreras   UK

Stanley Baker stars as a Manchester police inspector in this Hammer film, with John Crawford as an escaped-con jewel thief and killer, Donald Pleasence, and Billie Whitelaw.

HELLMASTER
(AIP, 1990) **D/S/P:** Douglas Schulze **P:** David J. Dalton

John Saxon is a crazy professor who performs deadly government drug experiments on students on a campus in 1969. 20 years later he offers "the reward" (special drugs) to a group of deformed "soulless freaks" with crosses on their foreheads who drive around in a bus and call him Papa. A (very) small group of students end up confronting the creatures on the empty campus. Amy Raasch stars as a psychic girl. The others students are a nice guy who likes her, an asshole jock (who uses a whip!), and a crippled guy who moves around awkwardly (like Everett Sloane in *The Lady from Shanghai*). Luckily, this was made around Detroit so that Ron Ashton, the guitarist from the Stooges (and Destroy All Monsters) could be in it! He

plays a mutant nun (!) who growls and shuffles along like a mummy! The violence is offscreen, and Saxon has only a few scenes, but some of the makeup is good (especially some mutant kids), and a few hallucination scenes are fun. I liked the coffin with a corpse in it chasing a kid down the hall. It was partially filmed (as *Them*) at a mental institution in Pontiac, Michigan.

HELLO, MARY LOU: PROM NIGHT II
(Virgin, 1987) **D:** Bruce Pittman **S:** Ron Oliver **P:** Peter Simpson   Canada
(*The Haunting of Hamilton High*)

This is much better than *Prom Night* (1980), Jamie Lee Curtis' worst horror movie. It's not even a real sequel. They just changed the title in the US. The "30 years later" revenge plot has Wendy Lyon possessed by Mary Lou (Lisa Schrage). There are lots of clever FX and nods to other horror movies: "It's Linda Blairsville!" Michael Ironside is the school principal. More *Prom Night* movies followed. An executive producer, Ray Sager, starred in *The Wizard of Gore*!

HELL ON THE BATTLEGROUND
(AIP, 1988) **D/S:** David A. Prior **P/A:** Fritz Matthews

William Smith (with his shaved head) appears with the director's brother, Ted Prior, in another forgettable adventure movie.

HELL RAIDERS
(1967) **D:** Larry Buchanan

John Agar is in WWII Italy (actually Texas), and a demolition squad has to destroy Allied records before the Germans arrive. With Richard Webb, Joan Huntington, and Bill Thurman. It's the "missing" non-science-fiction movie in the 8-movie package Buchanan made for AIP-TV. Agar was also in *Zontar, the Thing from Venus*. *Hell Raiders* was also the name of a bad movie made in the Philippines by Ferde Grofe Jr.

HELLRAISER
(Starmaker, 1987) **D/S:** Clive Barker
P: Christopher Figg **M:** Christopher Young

Horror author Barker directed this after hating the other adaptations of his books. It's a classic, the first bloody S&M fantasy/horror hit. Four Cenobites devoted to sensual pleasure can be released from another dimension by a carved puzzle box. They disfigure themselves and tear flesh with large hooks. Uncle Frank (Sean Chapman), now a withered skeleton, unleashed them. Now he uses his sister-in-law/former lover (Clare Higgins) to revive him. She picks up men and sucks them dry. Andrew Robinson is her husband, Ashley Laurence is her stepdaughter, and Doug Bradley is Pinhead. New World had this dubbed into "American." The video is 5 minutes longer than the R-rated theatrical version. It includes an ad for merchandise (shirts, mugs . . .). The Young score is on Pro-Arte. An alternate score (not used) by the group Coil is also available. *Hellbound: Hellraiser II* (1988) was the first sequel.

Clive Barker and his Pinhead creation from *Hellraiser*.

HELLRAISER III: HELL ON EARTH

(Paramount, 1992) **D:** Anthony Hickox
S: Bradley Atkins **P:** Lawrence Mortoff

Terry Farrell stars as a novice New York City TV reporter trying to cover some local murders. The ghost of a British WWI captain (Doug Bradley) shows up in her gory front-line nightmares (as does her father, who died in Vietnam). Bradley, with his cultured English voice, is also Pinhead (a relief from Freddy Krueger), who is freed from a strange, sculptured cube. Pinhead slaughters a whole nightclub full of people. Other new Cenobites with individual gimmicks also appear. This S&M horror sequel was shot in Highpoint, North Carolina, obviously not Manhattan. With Paula Marshall and Kevin Bernhardt. Motorhead does the end theme. Tony Randel (*Hellbound*) was to direct but was replaced. Barker sold off the film rights but was executive producer of this Miramax release. The tape is available in R and unrated versions. Some copies come with the documentary *Clive Barker: The Art of Horror* (Paramount). *Hellraiser: Bloodline* (1996) followed.

HELLRIDERS

(TWE, 1974) **D/S:** James Bryant
S/P/A: Renee Harmon

Here's a biker movie with Batman and Ginger. Snake (Russ Alexander) leads a biker gang so horrible that other bikers shun them. They're always fighting, and a Bible-quoting guy with one hand keeps a naked girl on a chain at all times. When they invade a "ghost town," the only person to stand up to them is a jogging doctor (Adam West). Tina Louise (in cowgirl clothes) is in peril when her car breaks down. As usual, cycle-riding scenes take up a lot of the time. Harmon (who plays a biker woman) is (I think) Dutch. She and Bryant also made *The Executioner Part 2* and she starred in *Frozen Scream*.

HELLROLLER

(Hollywood International, 1992)
D/C: G. J. Levinson **P:** Stuart Wall

A wheelchair-bound serial killer goes after women. There's nudity and gore. The cast includes Ruth Collins, Elizabeth Kaitan, Mary Woronov, Michelle Bauer, Johnny Legend, Eric Caidin, and porno star Hyapatia Lee.

HELL'S ANGELS FOREVER

(Media, 1983) **D:** Kevin Keating
D/S/P: Richard Chase **D/P:** Leon Gast
S: Sandy Alexander **P:** Peterson Tooke

Incredibly, this Hell's Angels propaganda documentary played in theaters and made $2 million. It was started in 1973 and took nearly 10 years to finish, with help from Jerry Garcia (an executive producer). The historical part is pretty interesting. The Angels say that the government framed Sonny Barger (who served time at Folsom Prison on drug charges) and that the Angels do not deal drugs. Biker movies are dismissed as nonsense, and real Angels are seen on the road, at their East Village headquarters, and at a party on a boat circling Manhattan. There are appearances by the Cleveland Breed, Bo Diddley, Willie Nelson, Johnny Paycheck, and Garcia. *The Greatful Dead Movie* is by the same filmmakers.

HELL'S BRIGADE

(1969) **D:** Leon Klimovsky **S:** José Luis
Merino, Manuel Sebares Italy/Spain
(*L'Urlo dei Giganti*; *A Bullet for Rommel*)

Jack Palance stars in this WWII adventure about a commando raid on Germany.

HELL'S KITCHEN

(1939) **D:** Lewis Seiler **S:** Carne Wilbur,
Fred Niblo Jr. **P:** Mark Hellinger

Ronald Reagan was the first adult star to be billed below the Dead End Kids. They were Billy Hallop (Tony), Leo Gorcey (Gyp), Bobby Jordan (Joey, who dies in a freezer), Huntz Hall (Bongo), Gabriel Dell (Ace), and Bernard Punsley (Ouch). Reagan plays Jim Donahue, a good-guy lawyer, and the title refers to a reform school, not the neighborhood in Manhattan. The film is a follow-up to *Crime School* (1938). It received an H (horrific) certificate in England. The cast includes Grant Mitchell, Stanley Fields, and Margaret Lindsay. Reagan and the kids returned in *Angels Wash Their Faces*, released just a month after this.

HELL SQUAD

(1958) **D/S/P:** Burt Topper

During WWII, five American soldiers in North Africa meet a German patrol wearing uniforms taken from dead Americans. With Wally Campo and Brandon Carroll. This was the first film by Topper, who was still working for AIP in the 70s.

HELL SQUAD

(Genesis, 1984) **D/S/P:** Kenneth Hartford
(*Commando Squad*; *Commando Girls*)

To rescue the kidnapped son of a diplomat, nine Las Vegas showgirls become commandos in the Middle East. With Glen Hartford, Tina Lederman, Bainbridge Scott, and Marvin Miller as the sheik. This Cannon release is memorably bad. It has lots of nudity and blood.

HELL UP IN HARLEM

(Orion, 1973) **D/S/P:** Larry Cohen

Even though he died in *Black Caesar*, Fred Williamson returns as gangster Tommy Gibbs in this quickly made sequel. This time his widower father (Julius W. Harris) joins in the action, becoming a high-living gangster with women and machine guns. Italian gangsters kidnap Gibbs' ex-wife (Gloria Hendry). The action locations include Coney Island, and there's a scuba-diving scene in the Florida Keys. It ends with Gibbs lynching the corrupt white district attorney. With D'Urville Martin (returning as the Reverend Rufus), Margaret Avery (who has a sex scene with Williamson), and Tony King. Edwin Starr sings on the Motown soundtrack and the Stylistics play at the Apollo. This AIP release ends with a setup for another sequel, which never happened.

HELP WANTED FEMALE

(SW, 1968) **D:** Harold Perkins

This b/w adult movie is sexy, creepy, cosmic, and funny. Jo Jo (in a wig) lures a businessman home, and after (offscreen) sex she karate-chops and robs him. Her blond roommate, Wanda, does a long, slow strip for Mr. Gregory (Jack Vorno), a paying customer in a smoking jacket with a pipe. After he takes LSD sugar cubes she asks, "You won't go ape on me, will ya, daddy?" Instead he narrates an amazing story about how he and Barbara, a blonde who likes S&M, pretend to photograph a nude model, then kill her. Later Barbara sneaks off with a college boy, so he kills her and takes her body to the beach with him to cut it up. Wanda and Jo Jo realize his story is true. Then Mr. Gregory wakes. Strange.

HELTER SKELTER

(CBS/Fox, 1976) **D/P:** Tom Gries **S:** J. P. Miller

The most famous Manson movie stars Steve Railsback, who is excellent. It's based on the book by Vincent Bugliosi (played here by George Di Cenzo) and centers on the trial. With Nancy Wolfe as Susan Atkins, Marilyn Burns (*The Texas Chainsaw Massacre*), Skip Homeier, Paul Mantee, and actors playing Charles "Tex" Watson, George Spahn, and other real people. It was 194 minutes (not counting commericals) when it debuted in 2 parts on CBS-TV. The tape is 119. There are fake Beatles songs. It's called *Massacre in Hollywood* in Europe.

THE HELTER SKELTER MURDERS

(1969) **D/C/E:** Frank Howard
S: J. J. Wilke Jr. **P:** Wade Williams

Most of this rare, fact-based, documentary-style film is b/w. No real names are used, but the real Manson is heard singing (from his ESP label album *Lie*), and his crazed vision of the future is dramatized. Flashbacks of the drug-devouring Manson family are seen during the courtroom proceedings.

THE HENDERSON MONSTER

(IVE, 1979) **D:** Waris Hussein **S:** Ernest Kinoy **P:** Robert "Buzz" Berger

Jason Miller stars as a Nobel prize–winning scientist who, while doing DNA research, develops a monster. With Christine Lahti as his assistant, Stephen Collins as her alcoholic science-fiction-writer husband, Larry Gates, David Spielberg, and Nehemiah Persoff. It was made for CBS-TV.

HENNESSY

(Cannon, 1975) **D:** Don Sharp
S: John Gay **P:** Peter Snell

Rod Steiger stars as an Irishman who plans to bomb the British Parliament on opening day, when the royal family attends, because his wife and child have been killed in Belfast. Lee Remick costars, with Richard Johnson, Trevor Howard, Peter Egan, and Eric Porter. The real Queen Elizabeth is seen in news footage. This is an AIP release by a Hammer director.

HENRY: PORTRAIT OF A SERIAL KILLER

(MPI, 1986) **D/S/P:** John McNaughton **S:** Richard Fire **P:** Lisa Dedmond, Steve Jones

This is excellent, one of the most disturbing and well-made films I've ever seen, and it was shot in 16mm in Chicago. The chilling but all too believable story is (loosely) based on real-life killer Henry Lee Lucas. The only film that you could maybe compare it to is *In Cold Blood* (1967), but the killer is never caught. The MPAA gave it an X rating, not for sex or violence (it includes both), but for "general tone." The much-delayed video is unrated. Henry (Michael Rooker) is a curly-haired, emotionless, illiterate, part-time exterminator who killed his mother and lives by the motto "It's either you or them." He's addicted to killing, knows it's easy to get away with, and carefully plans the murders, using different methods each time: "It's always the same and it's always different." His roommate is a dense, crude, impressionable drug-dealing TV addict named Ottis (Tom Towles). Both are ex-cons. Ottis' blue-eyed blond sister, Becky (Tracy Arnold) ("Did you really kill your mama?"), leaves her husband and moves in with the deadly duo, landing a job as a shampoo girl. In a film loaded with shocking scenes, the most disturbing to me was the killers watching themselves at work, repeatedly and in slow motion on video. Talk about violence as pornography! The music, cinematography, dialogue, acting, direction, and FX are all top-notch. Only the inclusion of the great song "Psycho" by the Sonics seemed a little too obvious. Since playing Henry so convincingly, Rooker has acted in major films like *Mississippi Burning* and *JFK*, and Towles

became a horror-movie regular (*Night of the Living Dead*, 1990). McNaughton's only previous credit was a gangster documentary, *Dealers in Death* (MPI), narrated by Broderick Crawford.

HENRY'S NIGHT IN

(SW, 1969)

I saw this b/w invisible-man sex comedy at the Standard in Cleveland when it was still pretty new, and I still don't know who made it (there are no credits). Forman Shane, a funny guy from all those A. C. Stevens movies, stars as Henry. He obtains a magic book, mixes a formula, and becomes invisible whenever he sneezes. Spooky harp and theremin music plays whenever this happens. He leaves his nagging wife at home and spies on women neighbors, then starts having sex with them (it's dark, and they keep their eyes closed and think he's their husband or boyfriend). It's all just a clever, silly way to show naked women caressing and kissing nobody. The blonde on an exercise bike is the best. Barbara Kline costars. If this were remade today it would be about teens, would be rated R, and would debut on cable TV.

HERCULES

(MGM/UA, 1983) **D/S:** "Lewis Coates"/ Luigi Cozzi **P:** Menahem Golan

Seeing this on 42nd Street was an early-80s highlight of living in New York. Nobody in the audience could believe they had paid for what they were seeing. Lou Ferrigno (dubbed) plays *Hercules*. It's an amazing, hilarious, cheap-looking fantasy with cut-rate *Star Wars*–style FX. Hercules goes into space and down to Hell, and fights monsters, robots, and a bear! Sybil Danning is the sexy Circe! With Mirella Dangelo, Ingrid Anderson, William Berger, Brad Harris, and Rosana Podesta. Pino Donaggio did the soundtrack. Ferrigno returned in *The Adventures of Hercules*. Sam Raimi executive-produced a series of Hercules TV movies, followed by a weekly syndicated series, starting in 1994, starring Kevin Sorbo and featuring cameos by Anthony Quinn as Zeus.

HERCULES II: *See* THE ADVENTURES OF HERCULES

HERCULES AGAINST MOLOCH = THE CONQUEST OF MYCENAE

HERCULES IN NEW YORK

(MPI, 1970) **D:** Arthur Allan Seidelman
S/P: Aubrey Wisberg

Arnold Schwarzenegger (using the name Arnold Strong) stars in his very first film, a corny comedy for kids shot on location (mostly in Central Park). His voice had to be dubbed. After arriving on Earth from Mount Olympus, Hercules teams up with a pretzel salesman (Arnold Stang). They're both broke but suddenly have tailored suits when they meet a professor (James Karen). Taina Elg is sent by the gods to punish him. Hercules fights a man in a bear suit, wrestles for gangsters, visits the Automat, and even goes to Hell. In the best scene he rides a chariot through Times Square (where

Easy Rider is playing). It took 12 years for Arnold to land another starring role (*Conan*). Seidelman later directed *The Caller*.

HERCULES IN THE HAUNTED WORLD

(Rhino, Hollywood's Best, 1961)
D/S/C: Mario Bava **S:** Alessandro Continenza, Duccio Tessari, Franco Prosperi **P:** Achille Piazzi
Italy (*Ercole al Centro Della Terra*)

Unless you're a fan of Italian muscleman movies, they probably all seem alike. This was Mario Bava's first feature after *Black Sunday*, and it's great compared to most Hercules movies, much more colorful and imaginative. A masked goddess narrates the tale of "the fiendish Lichas, a diabolical vampire" (Christopher Lee with someone else's voice). He emerges from a coffin, and the titles are shown over a revolving spiral. Lichas, who has become king, keeps his niece, Deianira, (Leonora Ruffo) in a trance. She rises from a coffin and floats. Hercules (former Mr. Universe Reg Park) and his small comic-relief friend sail to bring back a magic apple in a giant tree (guarded by condemned women in eternal darkness) to cure his love, Deianira. A talking rock monster tortures his friend. They go to Hades, where a naked woman in chains tricks them and vines scream when they bleed. There's an eclipse, and Hercules throws giant rocks when flying corpses attack. This Cinemascope film was scanned for TV.

HERCULES RETURNS

(1992) **D:** David Parker **S:** Des Mangan
P: Philip Jaroslow   Australia

This is Georgio Capitani's Italian *Hercules, Samson, Maciste, and Ursus Are Invincible* (1964) with new (adult) comic dialogue, plus new framing footage about a revival theater when Bruce Spence is the projectionist. Alan Steel plays Hercules.

HERE COMES MR. JORDAN

(RCA, 1941) **D:** Alexander Hall **S:** Sidney Buchman, Seton I. Miller **P:** Everett Riskin

Robert Montgomery stars as a boxer who also plays the saxophone and flies. When his plane crashes he's sent to Heaven, but it turns out that he wasn't meant to die yet. A heavenly official, Mr. Jordan (Claude Rains), gets him a new body, that of a millionaire about to be murdered by his wife (Rita Johnson) and her boyfriend (John Emery). This Columbia release, one of Hollywood's best fantasies, was nominated for seven Oscars. The cast includes Edward Everett Horton as Messenger 3014, Evelyn Keyes, and James Gleason. Horton and Gleason returned as similar characters (with Roland Culver as Mr. Jordan) in Columbia's color musical fantasy *Down to Earth* (1948). *Heaven Can Wait* (1978) was a remake.

HERE COMES SANTA CLAUS

(Starmaker, 1984) **D/S/P:** Christian Gion **S:** Didier Kaminka   France (*J'ai Rencontre le Père Noël*)

New World released this G-rated film before the big flop *Santa Claus* (1985) came out. It was shot in 3-D but shown flat. A girl and boy visit Santa's magic kingdom, where elves work and there's an ugly ogre. It was filmed in France, Finland, and Senegal.

HERE COME THE TIGERS

(UAV, 1979) **D/P:** Sean Cunningham **S:** Arch McCoy **P:** Stephen Miner   (*Manny's Orphans*)

Before making *Friday the 13th* Cunningham made this PG *Bad News Bears* ripoff. It stars Richard Lincoln, James Zvanut, and Fred Lincoln (from Cunningham's *Last House on the Left*). This was released by AIP, then by UA.

HERE WE GO ROUND THE MULBERRY BUSH

(1968) **D/P:** Clive Donner **S:** Hunter Davies **P:** Larry Kramer   UK

Barry Evans is a 17-year-old virgin, and Judy Geeson is the girl of his dreams. His comic adventures consist of not scoring with various girls. The cast includes Angela Scoular, Sheila White, Denholm Elliott, and Angela Pleasence. Traffic and the Spencer Davis Group provide music, produced by Simon Napier-Bell, and the SDG appear in this "mod" movie, which was considered daring at the time. The UA soundtrack has Traffic/Stevie Winwood tracks not available elsewhere. Davies wrote the book *The Beatles*.

THE HERITAGE OF CALIGULA: AN ORGY OF SICK MINDS = BLOODSUCKING FREAKS

HERO AND THE TERROR

(Media, 1988) **D:** William Tannen **S:** Michael Blodgett, Dennis Shryack **P:** Ray Wagner

Chuck Norris is "the hero" and Jack O'Halloran is 6'6" Moon, "the terror." The terror escapes from an insane asylum and hides in the vents of an LA movie theater. He snaps women's necks and keeps the bodies in a seaside restaurant. The movie is based on a novel by former actor Michael Blodgett (from *Beyond the Valley of the Dolls*). There's a subplot about the hero's pregnant wife (Brynn Thayer). With Steve James as the hero's partner, Billy Drago, Ron O'Neal as the mayor, Heather Blodgett, and Karen Witter (from *Playboy*). Cannon released it.

HER ODD TASTES

(SW, 1969) **D:** Don Davis **S/P:** Jerry Wilder

Years before *Emmanuelle*, Marsha Jordan stars as Capri, roaming the world to do sexual research. She talks to the camera and narrates what happened in Hong Kong (a woman shoots her up before their lesbian scene), South Africa (she's drugged and becomes the center of a Satanic orgy), Nairobi (sex at a hunting camp), and Jordan (an oily three way). At the end she admits, "Yes, I am depraved!" before fucking her bald publisher to death! This laughable soft-core movie has lots of stock footage of boats and jungle animals. It also features Asian and black women, not at all common in nudie movies. Henning Schellerup was the cinematographer. This and *The Muthers* are from Crest Films. Davis and Jordan returned with *Marsha, the Erotic Housewife*.

HEROES IN HELL

(Vestron, 1974) **D/S:** "Michael Wotruba"/ Aristide Massaccesi   Italy (*Eroi al Inferno*)

Klaus Kinski (in a small role) plays a German general kidnapped by partisans. This WWII movie has a prison in a castle, gory closeups of operations, and flashbacks and dream sequences. Kinski was in the strange *Death Smiles on a Murderer*, by the same director, the same year.

HEROES SHED NO TEARS

(Rainbow, 1985) **D/S:** John Woo **P:** Peter Chan Hong Kong (*A John Woo Film, Sunset Warrior*)

Soldiers of fortune are hired by the Thai government to bring back a drug-smuggling general from the Vietnam jungle. A mercenary and his son are the main characters. This gory adventure includes torture scenes and a tribe of cannibals. Woo had been directing since the early 70s, but this was one of his first films to gain international recognition.

HEROES STAND ALONE

(MGM, 1989) **D:** Mark Griffiths **S:** Thomas McKelvey Cleaver **P:** Luis Llosa

Central American mercenaries, not-so-bad *glasnost* Soviet agents, and Cubans are all involved in this spy movie. Chad Everett is a CIA mercenary, and Bradford Dillman is the villain, a former CIA agent turned gunrunner. With Elsa Olivero, Wayne Grace, and Rick Dean. It's a pretty boring Concorde release.

HEROIC TRIO

(VSOM, 1992) **D/P:** Ching Siu Tung, Johnny To **S:** Sandy Shaw, Susanne Chan   Hong Kong

A trio of Hong Kong superheroines are the main characters in this comic/action/fantasy/adventure movie. Anita Mui as Wonder Woman, Maggie Cheung as motorcycle-riding Thief Catcher, and Michelle Yeoh/Khan as Invisible Woman battle an evil cult leader who is reduced to a fighting skeleton at the end. The plot concerns baby kidnapping and cannibalism, and a flying guillotine even appears. The stars all returned in the post-nuke film *The Executioners/Heroic Trio II* (1993).

HE WALKED BY NIGHT

(1948) **D:** Alfred L. Werker, Anthony Mann (uncredited) **S:** John C. Higgins, Crane Wilbur **P:** Robert Kane

Richard Basehart is Morgan, an intelligent but psycho cop killer and thief who hides out in sewers. Scott Brady is the Hollywood cop obsessed with catching him. This Eagle Lion release is based on a true story and has *Dragnet*-style voice-over narration. Jack Webb even has a role (as a lab technician), and the film may have helped to inspire him to create *Dragnet* in 1949. The cast also includes Whit Bissell and Roy Roberts. John Alton is responsible for the impressive, documentary-style b/w cinematography. Anthony Mann directed parts of the film (without credit). It's available on Lumivision laserdisc.

HEXED

(Columbia, 1992) **D/S:** Alan Spencer **P:** Marc S. Fischer, Louis G. Friedman

Arye Gross stars as a hotel clerk who lies well (a lot) and lives in a fantasy world. He connives to have sex with a famous French model, Hedina (Claudia Christian), but she turns out to be a crazed (American) psycho killer who is being blackmailed. With lots of gags and some bad-taste humor (including a Rodney King–like beating by police). With Adrienne Shelly, R. Lee Ermey, Ray Baker, and Norman Fell. Christian has several nude scenes but used a body double.

HEY FOLKS, IT'S INTERMISSION TIME, VOLUMES I AND II

(SW)

These tapes, 100 minutes each, are the ultimate compilations for drive-in fans. They're from the 50s through the 70s and include ads for snack bars and food (Pepsi, hot dogs, Tommy's potato chips), local businesses and churches (Lancaster, Ohio; McCallister, Oklahoma), and, best of all, spook shows ("Man buried alive!"). There are also many variations on intermission countdowns, holiday greetings (with Father Time and a baby), and ads urging us to vote, fight against pay TV, or resist daylight-savings-time changes.

THE HIDDEN

(Media, 1987) **D:** Jack Sholder **S:** "Bob Hunt"/ Jim Kouf **P:** Robert Shaye, Gerald T. Olson

It wasn't a box-office hit, but this is a superior science-fiction/action movie. It's violent, funny, and even sentimental, and has some good stunt work. Kyle MacLachlan stars as an odd FBI agent who is really an alien sent to stop a bad alien who can assume any form (like a stripper, a dog, or a cop). Michael Nouri is the LA cop assigned to work with the agent. With Clu Gulager, Claudia Christian, and a scene in Bleecker Bob's record store. The Michael Convertino score is on Varese Sarabande.

THE HIDDEN II: THE SPAWNING

(New Line, 1993) **D/S:** Seth Pinsker **P:** Michael Meltzer, David Helperin

This crummy, talky "15 years later" sequel uses lots of the best footage from the (very good) original. Raphael Sbarge (also in *Carnosaur*) stars as a new good alien who finds the daughter (Kate Hodge) of the Michael Nouri character to help defeat the shape-shifting killer alien. They fall in love, and she teaches him to brush his teeth. The comic scenes of the alien as a bum slaughtering black teens are very unlike anything in the original, and the end really sucks. With (another) Michael Weldon as Beck. It debuted on the Sci-Fi Channel.

HIDDEN OBSESSION

(MCA, 1993) **D:** John Stewart **S:** David Reshan **P:** Tom Bradshaw, David C. Glasser   (*Rage*)

Heather Thomas is a divorced TV-news anchor on vacation in her isolated country home. A psycho is killing strippers and is after her now. Could it be the comic-relief boss, the Elvis impersonator, or the escaped con? Or could it be Jan-Michael Vincent, the friendly deputy sheriff with a ponytail? The false scares, exaggerated thunder, lame POV stalking scenes, and romantic music help make this one to avoid, but there is a certain fascination in looking at the reconstructed faces of the two stars. It's by the director of *Cartel* (1989).

HIDE AND GO SHRIEK

(New Star, 1987) **D:** Skip Schoolnik
S: Michael Kelly **P:** Dimitri Villard

A psycho kills off eight teens spending the night in a furniture store for a graduation party. An escaped con is a suspect, but the killer turns out to be a transvestite. With Rebunkah Jones and Donna Baltron. R and unrated video versions of this blood-and-sex movie were released.

HIDEAWAY

(Columbia, 1995) **D:** Brett Leonard
S: Andrew Kevin Walker, Neil Jimenez
P: Jerry Baerwitz, Agatha Hanczakowski

Jeff Goldblum stars as an antique dealer who is brought back to life after a car accident. Even his family thinks he's going crazy because he has a mental link to the spirit of a young Satanist serial killer (Jeremy Sisto) who died by suicide. The adaptation of Dean R. Koontz's novel features some great sounds during the "tunnel of light" sequences. Alicia Silverstone is the teen daughter in peril and Christine Lahti is the wife. The entertaining and over-the-top ending takes place underneath an amusement park and involves major good vs. evil fantasy FX. With Alfred Molina as the doctor and Rae Dawn Chong as a psychic. The score is by Trevor Jones. It was shot in British Columbia.

HIDEOUT IN THE SUN

(1960) **D:** Lazarus L. Wolk **S:** Doris
Chasnik **P:** Doris Wishman

Two brothers rob a bank and force a girl nudist to take them to a nudist colony. With Dolores Carlos and Carol Little. The first of many Wishman movies, it was made in Florida in Eastmancolor and released by Astor. Wishman was a cousin of Max Rosenberg, who cofounded Amicus in England.

HIDER IN THE HOUSE

(Vestron, 1989) **D:** Matthew Patrick **S:** Lem
Dodds **P:** Edward Teets, Michael Taylor

Remember a 1974 TV movie called *Bad Ronald*? This somewhat similar movie stars blond Gary Busey. He killed his abusive parents as a child, escaped from an institution, and sometimes hides in a secret attic space in a new home. A naive voyeur, he bothers neighbor Mimi Rogers and sees her family as his own. He also kills their dog. With Michael McKean as the husband, Bruce Glover, and Rebecca Armstrong. It went directly to video in the US, but the soundtrack by Christopher Young was issued on Intrada.

HIGH ANXIETY

(Fox, 1978) **D/S/P/A:** Mel Brooks **S:** Ron
Clark, Rudy De Luca, Barry Levinson

Brooks should have waited a while to make his Hitchcock spoof. Everybody got the *Psycho* and *Birds* gags, but many of the movies he parodied hadn't been in release for years and were not available on tape yet. He plays Dr. Richard Thorndyke, the new head of a private mental hospital. With Madeline Kahn, Cloris Leachman, Harvey Korman, Howard Morris, Dick Van Patten, Jack Riley, Charlie Callas, and future director Barry Levinson as the bellboy. The Asylum soundtrack includes music from Brooks' five earlier films.

HIGH-BALLIN'

(Vestron, 1979) **D:** Peter Carter **S:** Paul
Edward **P:** John Slan   US/Canada

Peter Fonda and Jerry Reed star as truckdriver friends in a PG-rated AIP action movie. Helen Shaver is a lady trucker. They all fight off villains hired to stop their operation.

HIGH DESERT KILL

(MCA, 1988) **D:** Harry Falk **S:** T. S. Cook **P:** Jon Epstein

Aliens arrive in New Mexico and take over some hunters. The odd feature, made for the USA Network, stars Marc Singer, Anthony Geary, Chuck Connors, and Micah Grant. Cook also wrote *The China Syndrome*.

HIGHLANDER

(HBO, 1986) **D:** Russell Mulcahy **S:** Gregory
Widen, Peter Bellwood, Larry Ferguson
P: Peter S. Davis, William Panzer

A NYC SoHo antique dealer (Christopher Lambert), is really one of the last of a breed of immortal warriors. He has to decapitate others to gain their powers. He's shown in 16th-century Scotland learning from the immortal Ramirez (Sean Connery). Connery's voice is heard throughout this confusing fantasy, but he appears only in flashback. With Beaty Edney, Alan North, Roxanne Hart, and Clancy Brown. Queen's music is on the soundtrack, and their songs from the movie appear on their album *A Kind of Magic*. Stephen Hopkins was the assistant director. 20th Century–Fox cut 17 minutes before releasing it in the US, where it did poor business. It was a big hit in Europe.

HIGHLANDER II: THE QUICKENING

(RCA, 1991) **D:** Russell Mulcahy **S:** Peter
Bellwood **P:** Peter S. Davis, William Panzer

This sequel has amazing, huge, *Blade Runner*–inspired sets and looks as if it must have cost more than *Terminator II*. (It was filmed in Argentina.) A big hit in Europe, it was released here by a tiny independent, Seymour Borde. Even if you're a fan of the original, this doesn't make any sense. (Brian Clemens cowrote the story.) It starts with absurd timeshifts and something about the rules of the planet Zeist, where a mammoth, *Dune*-inspired battle takes place. The plot involves Earth's ozone-layer problem. Christopher Lambert and Sean Connery return, but Lambert spends too much

time as a very unconvincing old man. Virginia Madsen is an "environmental terrorist," and Michael Ironside is an enthusiastic assassin who takes over a speeding subway full of people, in the most impressive action/disaster scene. The heroes have to decapitate the villains, and all of them have long hair. Some scenes are awesome, but overall it's a mess. Even the music by Stewart Copeland (*Rumble Fish*) is mediocre. The tape is letterboxed. A syndicated TV series and third movie followed.

HIGHLANDER: THE FINAL DIMENSION

(Miramax, 1994) **D:** Andy Morahan **S:** Paul
Ohl **P:** Claude Leger   Canada/France/UK

In this second sequel to *Highlander*, MacLeod (Christopher Lambert) battles the warrior Kane (Mario Van Peebles with a nose ring), who is discovered inside a mountain in Japan by an American archaeologist (Deborah Unger, who has two roles). The sword-fighting and decapitating action shifts to the Moroccan desert, NYC, and Scotland and there are the expected time switches and flashbacks. It was filmed in five countries. Also with Mako and Raoul Trujillo. The video is a "director's cut."

HIGHLANDER: THE GATHERING

(Hemdale, 1993) **D:** Thomas J. Wright,
Ray Austin **S:** Dan Gordon, Lorain Despres
P: Gary Goodman, Barry Rosen

Despite what the video box tries to make you think, this is just 2 episodes of the dull *Highlander* syndicated TV series, starring Adrian Paul as 400-year-old Duncan MacLeod. A kid (Stan Kirsch) and Alexander Vandernoot costar (she takes a blurry PG-13 shower). The guest villains are Richard Moll (with a metal mask) and Vanity. Christopher Lambert does appear in the first episode, and the Queen theme song is used.

HIGH NOON, PART II

(Fries, 1980) **D:** Jerry Jameson **S:** Elmore Leonard
P: Edward J. Monatgue   (*The Return of Will Kane*)

Lee Majors stars (in the Gary Cooper role) in this "sequel" made for TV. With David Carradine as a drifter, Pernell Roberts as a bounty hunter, M. Emmet Walsh, Katherine Cannon, Tracey Walter, and Michael Pataki. The original 1952 classic is available from Republic.

HIGHPOINT

(1984) **D:** Peter Carter **S:** Richard A.
Guttman **P:** Daniel Fine   Canada

An unemployed accountant (Richard Harris) becomes a chauffeur for a rich family and gets involved with the CIA and murder. The climax takes place on top of Toronto's CN tower. With Christopher Plummer, Beverly D'Angelo, Kate Reid, Peter Donat, Saul Rubinek, and Maury Chaikin.

HIGH SCHOOL U. S. A.

(KVC, 1983) **D:** Rod Amateau
S: Alan Eisenstock, Larry B. Mintz

Michael J. Fox stars in this NBC-TV comedy-series pilot with lots of other 60s TV stars. See Christian Glover as the nerd son of Bob Denver! Dwayne

Hickman is a lech teacher, Tony Dow is the principal, and David Nelson is the janitor. The older this gets, the more fun it is to watch. Nancy McKeon, Todd Bridges, and Anthony Edwards are the other young stars. With Angela Cartwright, Elinor Donahue, Lauri Hendler, Dana Plato, Steve Franken, Dawn Wells, and Barry Livingston.

HIGH SPIRITS
(Media, 1988) **D/S:** Neil Jordan
P: Stephen Wooley, David Saunders

Peter O'Toole (who looks like a ghost but isn't) stars as a drunken Irish nobleman who fakes a haunting to attract American tourists to his run-down castle. Real ghosts (Daryl Hannah and Liam Neeson) are already there, repeating their wedding-night murder. This clumsy PG comedy/fantasy also features Steve Guttenberg, Beverly D'Angelo, Jennifer Tilly, Peter Gallagher, Donal McCann, and Ray McAnally. Mark Damon was the executive producer. It was drastically recut by Tri-Star for the US release.

HIGH STAKES
(Vidmark, 1989) **D/S/P:** Amos Kollek   (*Melanie Rose*)

Sally Kirkland (with her inflated breasts) stars as a New York hooker named Bambi who tries to keep her daughter away from mobsters. Richard Lynch is her pimp, and Robert LuPone is a Wall Street stockbroker who wants her. With Maia Danziger and Kathy Bates.

HIGHWAY HELL
(Scorched Earth, 1937) **P:** Patrick Carlyle
(*Honky Tonk Girl*)

A Highway Patrol officer introduces this look at "the age of speed." Tough, whiskey-drinking women work for a fast-talking pimp named Mr. Slavik. He looks into the camera and tells us "how to pimp." They hang out at the bar of the Wagon Wheel motel and find men by standing in the road and saying, "Going my way mister?" A nude scene at a picnic is awkwardly edited into this road-show movie. Blackmail, innocent love, and drugged champagne lead to murder. Characters say, "You tart!" and "This is the modern age! Speed! Fast!" Another character (the philosophical Pop) talks to us at the end, saying, "Keep our highways clean." If you like vintage adults-only movies, this one is a must.

HIGHWAY PATROLMAN
(1992) **D:** Alex Cox **S:** Lorenzo O'Brien   Mexico

Roberto Sosas stars as Officer Rojas, a new highway cop stationed in the desert. He can't fight the system. He becomes disillusioned, then corrupt, and his best friend is killed. With Bruno Bichir and Vanessa Bauche as a junkie hooker. It's in Spanish with English subtitles. The British director made *Repo Man*.

HIGHWAY 61
(Paramount, 1992) **D/P:** Bruce McDonald
S/A: Don McKeller **P:** Don Colin
Brunton   Canada

A naive young barber (Don McKeller) living in a small town near Thunder Bay (northern Ontario) discovers a frozen body and ends up on a harrowing road trip to New Orleans with a lying, cheating, drug-dealing woman (Valerie Buhagiar) to deliver the drug-filled corpse. Meanwhile, "the Devil" (Earl Pastko) takes photos of people's souls and has them sign contracts in blood. This surefire cult movie is very funny, very cool, and full of satisfying surprises. The leads all have very theatrical, unusual faces. Pastko looks like the son of Jack Elam, and rugged-looking Peter Breck is great as a man with three singing and dancing daughters. The journey is full of real rock references and goes through St. Louis and Memphis. With sex in a graveyard, bikers, and a BTO tribute band. Jello Biafra is a border guard, and Tav Falco is a biker. A comic-book version has been published, and there's a soundtrack by Nash the Slash and others. McDonald also made *Roadkill*.

HIGHWAY TO HELL
(Raedon, 1989) **D:** B. A. Jenkins
S: Gary Kennamer **P:** "Max Raven"/
Brett McCormick

Nothing is shown in this boring tale of a mass murderer and rapist (Benton Jennings) who escapes from prison and goes on a killing spree. He yells and laughs hysterically, kills lots of people, and runs over a little girl. He makes a photographer (Blue Thompson, from *Ozone*) drive him around. Richard Henderson (usually in Italian movies) sits behind a desk most of the time, talks, and relates slow-motion flashbacks. S. F. Brownrigg is thanked at the end. It was filmed near Dallas.

HIGHWAY TO HELL
(HBO, 1990) **D:** Ate De Jong **S:** Brian Helgeland **P:** Mary Ann Page

In this oddball horror comedy made in Arizona, Chad Lowe is going to elope with Kristy Swanson, but a mutant "Hell cop" grabs her and takes her to another dimension in the desert. Some of the Steve Johnson FX are top-notch, including an animated three-headed dog and literal "hand" cuffs. There's also a naked, ugly female demon, bikers, a race with all Volkswagens, and a crowd of Andy Warhols. Patrick Bergin is the "satanic mechanic," and the cast includes Richard Farnsworth, Pam Gidley, Jerry Stiller and Anne Meara (and their kids, Ben and Amy), Gilbert Gottfried, Lita Ford, Kevin Peter Hall, and Jarrett Lennon (the kid from *Servants of Twilight*). The Tangerine Dream music is lifted from *Miracle Mile*. Hemdale released it in 1992. The director's next was *Drop Dead Fred*.

HIGH YELLOW
(1965) **D/S:** Larry Buchanan

Cindy (Cynthia Hull), a light-skinned black teen, gets a job as a maid for the dysfunctional family of

an oblivious Hollywood producer. She keeps a diary and befriends the wild, jive-talking teen daughter, Judy (Kay Taylor) whose brother was kicked out of the military for being a "queer boy." The Major (Bill Thurman) is a crazy, sadistic, alcoholic war-vet gardener, and Joseph (William McGhee) is a friendly servant. The depressed mother (Anne McAdams, from *Common-Law Wife*) stays in bed. This Dallas production shows how good Buchanan was before those AIP-TV movies. The characters are interesting and/or sympathetic, the acting is good, and the plot (including a murder) works on several levels. The instrumental theme is great, and I love the scenes at the Disco A-Go-Go, where Jody Daniels sings and the Rowdees do "Pushover." It's hard to find (thanks to the director) but recommended.

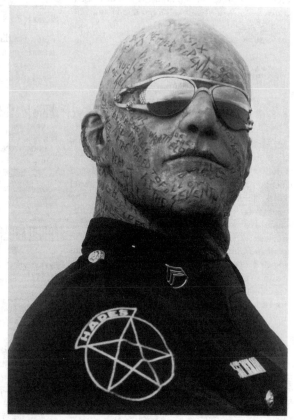
Highway to Hell

HI, HONEY! I'M DEAD
(1991) **D:** Alan Meyeson **S:** Carl Kleinschmitt **P:** Paula Rudnick

A successful, handsome Chicago building developer dies and a guardian angel (Paul Rodriguez) arranges to have him return as a better person who's a penniless nobody (Curtis Armstrong, from the *Revenge of the Nerds* movies). He ends up being a housekeeper for his own wife (Catherine Hicks). This is a Fox-TV movie.

THE HILLS HAVE EYES, PART II
(HBO, 1983) **D/S:** Wes Craven
P: Barry Cahn, Peter Locke

This terrible sequel spent three years in the can. A group of young motorcycle racers (including Robert Houston as Bobby) and a blind woman

(Tamara Stafford) are stranded in the desert and attacked by a cannibal family. It features lots of flashbacks to the classic 1977 original (available from Starmaker). Every surviving character has flashbacks (even Beast, the dog!). With Michael Berryman as Pluto, Janus Blythe as Ruby (who was trying to lead a normal life), James Whitworth as Jupiter, John Bloom (from *Brain of Blood*) as the Reaper, and the voice of Nicholas Worth. A longer "director's cut" has been sold by collectors. *The Hills Have Eyes, Part III* is planned (with a different director).

HI, MOM!

(American, 1970) **D/S:** Brian De Palma **P/E:** Charles Hirsch   (*Confessions of a Peeping Tom*)

Robert De Niro returns as Nam vet Jon Rubin in this R-rated sequel to De Palma's *Greetings* (1969). He rents a room on New York's Lower East Side and photographs people from his window (De Palma was already starting to use *Rear Window* ideas). Allen Garfield hires him to make a voyeur porno movie, but everything goes wrong (including his attempt to seduce Jennifer Salt), so he joins an underground acting group and plays the cop in a production of *Be Black, Baby*, where the white audience members are submitted to humiliation, searches, beatings, and arrests. He gets married, becomes an insurance saleman, and tries to settle down in a high-rise, but he can't take it and dynamites the laundry room. With Charles Durning, Paul Bartel, and Gerrit Graham. De Palma used b/w sequences, a split screen, and other "underground" techniques for his final independent political comedy. His next, *Get to Know Your Rabbit*, sat on the shelf at Warner Brothers for two years. This was the last of four De Niro/De Palma collaborations. It was cut years ago, after its brief theatrical run.

THE HIRED HAND

(Kartes, 1971) **D/A:** Peter Fonda
S: Alan Sharp **P:** William Hayward

After *Easy Rider*, Peter Fonda directed this great-looking, arty western shot by Vilmos Zsigmond. He and Warren Oates (the same year as *Two-Lane Blacktop*) are drifters. Each has an unusual relationship with Verna Bloom. With Severn Darden and Robert Pratt. Fonda made *Idaho Transfer* next.

HIRED TO KILL

(Paramount, 1989) **D/S:** Nico Mastorakis
D/P: Peter Rader

A soldier of fortune (Brian Thompson) and seven beautiful models go to a South American island fortress to liberate "the Brother" (José Ferrer). Oliver Reed is a sadistic secret-police chief. With George Kennedy, Michelle Moffett, and Penelope Reed. A stuntman was killed in a helicopter crash. It was filmed in Greece.

HIS NAME WAS KING

(All Seasons, 1971) **D:** Giancarlo Romitelli
S: Renato Savino   Italy (*Lo Chiamavano King*)

Richard Harrison stars in this western as a man who goes after the gang who killed his brother and raped his wife. With Anne Puskin and Klaus Kinski as Ryan, the sheriff.

HIT!

(Paramount, 1973) **D:** Sidney J. Furie **S:** Alan R. Trustman **P:** Harry Korshak   Canada

Billy Dee Williams is a federal agent out to destroy a French heroin ring after his teen daughter dies of an OD. He recruits a varied group of people who have suffered because of the drug trade and trains them in British Columbia. They all go to Marseilles to kill the gangsters. With Richard Pryor, Paul Hampton (*They Came from Within*), and Gwen Welles. The original release is a long 134 minutes. Williams and Pryor had been in *Lady Sings the Blues*, also directed by Furie.

THE HITCHCOCK CLASSICS COLLECTION

(Trailers on Tape, 1985)

Here are trailers for 20 of Alfred Hitchcock's films, from *Rebecca* (1940) to *Topaz* (1969), in chronological order. The best are the ones featuring Hitchcock himself: for *Psycho* (the famous long tour of the set), *The Birds* (a great lecture about the history of the way people treat birds), and *Marnie* (Hitchcock introduces each character in his new "sex mystery"). Some earlier ones are narrated by the stars, like Joan Fontaine (*Suspicion*), Robert Cummings (*Saboteur*), and, best of all, James Stewart (*Rope*). This tape includes Hitchcock's cameo appearance in *Spellbound*, Ingrid Bergman finding a shrunken head in the seldom-screened *Under Capricorn*, and Jerry Mathers in a space suit discovering a body in *The Trouble with Harry*. Sometimes the rerelease trailers are better than the originals, but the one for *Rear Window* (rereleased after *Psycho*) is disappointing and silly. Of course this is a must for Hitchcock fans.

THE HITCHER

(HBO, 1986) **D:** Robert Harmon **S:** Eric Red **P:** David Bombyk, Kip Ohman

C. Thomas Howell, delivering a drive-away Seville car, picks up a hitchhiker called John Ryder (Rutger Hauer) in Texas, and his life becomes a relentless nightmare. Hauer is terrifying as the seemingly supernatural killer who tells the kid, "I want you to stop me." A lot of cops are killed, and Howell is blamed and jailed. With Jennifer Jason Leigh as a waitress, Jeffrey De Munn, and Billy Green Bush. John Seale was the cinematographer. The Mark Isham soundtrack is on Silva. Red also wrote *Near Dark*, another excellent horror/road movie. *Return of the Hitcher* (1990) is an unrelated Italian movie by Umberto Lenzi.

HITCHHIKE!

(1974) **D:** Gordon Hesler
S: Yale M. Udoff **P:** Jay Benson

Cloris Leachman picks up a killer hitchhiker. Michael Brandon, Cameron Mitchell, Sherry Jackson, and Henry Darrow are featured in this ABC-TV movie. An Italian movie called *Hitchhike* stars David Hess as a psycho sadist.

THE HITCH-HIKER

(WPI, Sinister, 1952) **D/S:** Ida Lupino **S/P:** Collier Young

Ida Lupino was the only woman directing features in America when she made this story of a dangerous psycho (William Talman, later the DA in the *Perry Mason* TV series) who holds two vacationing businessmen captive in New Mexico. Frank Lovejoy and Edmond O'Brien are the men who just wanted to go fishing. Lupino also directed O'Brien in *The Bigamist* (1953). She and Young had been married (1948–50).

THE HITCHHIKER

(Lorimar series, 1984–91)

This HBO series, created by Lewis Chesler, was the first "R-rated" cable series. Each story of mystery or the supernatural is introduced by a hitchhiker (Nicholas Campbell) and has some nudity. Some of the better-known directors involved over the years were Paul Verhoeven, Phillip Noyce, Roger Vadim, and Mai Zetterling. Each 90-minute tape has three episodes. More tapes were released in Europe. Here are some stars of the tapes released in the US: Volume I: Harry Hamlin, Gary Busey, Karen Black, Geraldine Page; Volume II: Susan Anspach, Darren McGavin, Peter Coyote, Margot Kidder; Volume III: Willem Dafoe, Ornelia Muti, Tom Skerritt; Volume IV: Robert Vaughn, Sybil Danning, Michael O'Keefe.

THE HITCHHIKERS

(1971) **D/S/P:** Ferd and Beverly Sebastian

Hitchhiking movies were common in the 70s. There were also quite a few movies inspired by the Manson family. This drive-in wonder combines both. Misty Rowe (a regular on *Hee Haw*) is Maggie, a blond runaway who shoplifts and is raped by security guards. She ends up as a member of a Manson-type hippie cult. The leader (Noman Klar) makes the girls hitchhike and lead the drivers to others who rob them. The Sebastians did *Gator Bait* next.

C. Thomas Howell and Rutger Hauer in *The Hitcher*.

Misty Rowe in *The Hitchhikers*.

THE HITCHHIKER'S GUIDE TO THE GALAXY

(CBS/Fox, 1981) **D/P:** Alan J. W. Bell
S: Douglas Adams   UK

Simon Jones stars as Arthur Dent, a Londoner who's hitchhiking around in space and time (wearing his bathrobe) with Ford Prefect, an alien (David Dixon) and Marvin, "the paranoid android." They discover the origin of mankind and the meaning of life after Earth is destroyed. This 6-part BBC science-fiction/comedy series, based on the books by Douglas Adams, is on two tapes. Hannibal released the soundtrack.

HITCHHIKE TO HELL

(Best, 1967) **D/P:** Irv Berwick **S:** John Buckley

Howard (Robert Gribbin) is a normal-looking mama's-boy psycho who picks up hitchhikers in a red laundry van and strangles (and rapes) them. The victims are mostly teen girls whom he tries to talk out of running away, but one is a gay guy and a near victim is an 11-year-old girl. At other times Howard has flashbacks, assembles model cars, and drinks lots of root beer. Despite the theme, nothing is shown. Gribbin is very convincing in his role, and there's the added attraction of Russell Johnson (yes, the professor in *Gilligan's Island*) as a Crescent City cop who just can't understand today's uncaring parents. With Dorothy Bennett as the mother and John Harmon as the boss. Boxoffice International released this when it was several years old.

HIT LADY

(Prism, 1974) **D:** Tracy Keenan Wynn **S/A:** Yvette Mimieux **P:** Aaron Spelling, Leonard Goldberg

Yvette Mimieux is an artist who moonlights as a syndicate killer in a bikini. With Clu Gulager, Dack Rambo, and Keenan Wynn (whose son directed). The plot of this ABC-TV movie is basically the same as the plot of Al Adamson's *I Spit on Your Corpse* (from the same year). Mimieux's next notable film was *Jackson County Jail*.

HITLER, DEAD OR ALIVE

(Good Times, 1942) **D:** Nick Grinde
S: Karl Brown, Sam Neumann
P: Ben Judell

A trio of American ex-cons go to Germany to kill Hitler for a million dollars. A scientist who offered the money tells the whole story in flashback. Ward Bond is the leader (he speaks German), Paul Fix is the brains, and Warren Hymer is the dumb one. But the Nazis are even dumber. The unlikely heroes hijack a plane, then drive a beer truck to the Dachau prison where they pretend to be guards. Eventually, after Hitler's mustache has been shaved off, he (Bob Watson) is shot by his own men, who don't recognize him! The movie is silly but serious as "dames and kids" are killed. Watson also played *der Führer* in *The Devil with Hitler* (1942), *The Hitler Gang* (1944), and other films. This States Rights release was produced by the founder of PRC and received a lot of publicity when first released. Judell also produced *Hitler, Beast of Berlin* (1939). Grinde made several Karloff movies at Columbia.

HITLER'S DAUGHTER

(Paramount, 1990) **D:** James A. Contner
S: Christopher Cannon, Sherman Gray
P: Richard Luke Rothschild

The daughter of Hitler, backed by modern-day Nazis, plans to start the Fourth Reich in America. She rises to power in Washington, DC. This "hard to believe they made it" USA Network movie features Kay Lenz, Veronica Cartwright, Melody Anderson, and Patrick Cassidy.

HITLER'S SON

(1977) **D:** Rod Amateau **S:** Lukas Heller, Burkhardt Driest **P:** Dr. Gerd Göring

The leader of a right-wing German political party (Peter Cushing) and his chauffeur (Leo Gordon) discover that Willi, an illiterate young Munich woodcarver (Bud Cort), is the son of *der Führer*. They eventually have to kidnap him from a mental institution, then try to prepare him to lead a new reich. Nobody wanted to release this comedy when it was new, and it's still unavailable. The cast includes Felicity Dean and Anton Diffring. It was filmed in Munich by the (American) director of *The Statue* (1971), *High School USA* (1983), and *The Garbage Pail Kids Movie* (1987).

THE HITLER TAPES

(Scorched Earth, 1994) **D/M:** Ronnie Cramer
S: David Manning **P:** Phillip Koss

The late Andrew Scott had his second and last leading role in this sequel to Cramer's *Even Hitler Had a Girlfriend* (1991). Marcus Templeton (Scott) is a hopeless voyeur who can't get it up anymore but uses phone-sex lines. He also videotapes women, then sends the tapes to the current object of his obsessions (Karen Zaczkowsky). She watches them with a mixture of disgust and fascination before she finally throws them away. There are two shower scenes and a woman with huge breasts and guns. The Alarming Trends provide the music and are seen playing outdoors. It features Sheila Ivy Traister and was made in Omaha.

THE HIT LIST

(RCA, 1988) **D:** William Lustig **S:** John Goff, Peter Brosnan **P:** Paul Hertzberg

Jan-Michael Vincent's child is kidnapped by mistake. Lance Henriksen is a ninja-like assassin working for mob boss Rip Torn who kills the wrong family. This violent action movie features Charles Napier as a cop and Leo Rossi. Lustig also made the Maniac Cop movies.

THE HIT LIST

(Columbia, 1993) **D/P:** William Webb **S:** Reed Steiner

Jeff Fahey stars as a former government assassin turned hitman who is hired by a lawyer (James Coburn) to protect a rich widow (Yancy Butler, who used a body double). This *film noir* attempt is by the director of *The Banker*. With Michael Beach and Randy Oglesby as cops and Jeff Korber.

HIT MAN

(1972) **D/S:** George Armitage **P:** Gene Corman

Bernie Casey stars in this remake of the Michael Caine movie *Get Carter* (1971). An LA criminal lawyer (in a red leisure suit) whose brother has been murdered gets involved with gangsters and the world of sex movies. Pam Grier costars as Gozeldo, who wants to become a porno star but ends up thrown into a cage with a tiger. With Lisa Moore, Tracy King, Rudy Challenger, and Don Diamond. There's a scene at the Watts Tower. The director made New World's *Private Duty Nurses*.

THE HITMAN

(Cannon, 1990) **D:** Aaron Norris **S:** Robert Geoffrion **S/P:** Don Carmody   Canada

A cop (Chuck Norris) is the victim of a hit. He "comes back from the dead" on the operating table, takes a new identity, and goes undercover (with a beard) to expose Italian, French-Canadian, and Iranian drug gangs in Seattle and Vancouver. The (fake) bad guy Norris uses a sawed-off shotgun. With Michael Parks as the ex-cop villain who "kills" him, Al Waxman as a gangster, Alberta Watson, and Norris' kids. Harry Alan Towers was the executive producer for Cannon.

THE HITTER

(1979) **D/S/P:** Christopher Leitch
S: Ben Harris **P:** Gary Herman

Ron O'Neal is Otis, an ex-boxer in Baltimore who teams up with a washed-up promoter (Adolph Caesar) and starts fighting again. He had quit years before after accidentally killing a man in the ring.

With Sheila Frazier and Bill Cobbs. It was the last leading role for the former *Superfly* star. Gloria Jones and Taste of Honey are on the Capitol soundtrack.

HIT THE DUTCHMAN
(Vidmark, 1992) **D/P:** Menahem Golan
S: Joseph Goldman   US/Russia

After the release of period gangster movies like *Bugsy*, *Mobsters*, and *Billy Bathgate*, the Israel-based 21st Century made this ridiculous movie in the former Soviet Union. Bruce Nozick stars as Prohibition-era gangster Dutch Schultz. Sally Kirkland costars as his mother, Will Kemp is Legs Diamond, and Jennifer Miller is around for sex scenes. This "borrows" elements from *The Godfather*, James Bond movies, and even Italian westerns. Nozick plays the same character in *Killer Instinct*, which was filmed back to back with this. R and unrated versions are available.

HIT THE ROAD RUNNING
(1984) **D:** Worth Keeter III **S:** Thom L. McIntyre **P:** Earl Owensby

Bill Bribble stars as a deputy sheriff in this 3-D action movie made in North Carolina. When Owensby stopped making movies Keeter made more in Hollywood.

HITZ
(Vidmark, 1988) **D/S:** William Sachs
P: Oscar L. Costo   (*Judgment*)

Emilia Crow stars as a juvenile-court judge dealing with LA-barrio gangs in this violent mixture of social commentary, comedy, and action by the man who made *Galaxina* and *The Incredible Melting Man*. Karen Black shoots up a courtroom with a machine gun in a scene that's a highlight. With Francesco Quinn, Elliott Gould as a corrupt judge, Thalmus Rasulala, Ed Lauter, Sydney Lassick, and Cuba Gooding Jr. (*Boyz n the Hood*). When it was released (in 1992) new rap music was added to the soundtrack.

THE H-MAN
(RCA, 1958) **D:** Jnishiro Honda
S: Takeshi Kimura **P:** Tomoyuki Tanaka
Japan (*Uomini H*; *Bijyo to Ekitai Ningen*)

This welcome, easy-to-find release is a color, cinemascope science-fiction/gangster classic. It opens with an H-bomb blast. A drug dealer, outside in the rain, disappears. Only his suit and shoes are left. Flashbacks show how a ship got too close to the nuclear test. Police try to figure out what's going on, and a scientist dissolves a frog, while boiling and bubbling red-and-blue "slime monsters" kill more people. The *Tokyo Star's* headlines are "STRANGE MONSTER DISSOLVES HUMANS!" and "CITY MENACED BY H-MAN MONSTER!" Fun nightclub scenes feature a Julie London–type singer who sings "The Magic Begins" and "So Deep Is My Love" in English, some wild jazz, and chorus girls. It all ends in a sewer, where the crooks had hidden a bag of heroin and a terrorized woman cowers in her slip. The FX are imaginative and well done.

When Columbia released this in the US, audience members were given free "H-Man sponges." *The Blob* was released the same year. This was followed in 1960 by *Secret of the Telegian* (Sinister) and *The Human Vapor* (Video Gems), other Toho mutant-men movies.

HOBGOBLINS
(TWE, 1988) **D/S/P:** Rick Sloane

Teens fight off mutant hand-puppet creatures in this terrible *Gremlins* ripoff by the director of the Vice Academy series. Tom Bartlett and Paige Sullivan star.

HOCUS POCUS
(Disney, 1993) **D:** Kenny Ortega **S:** Mick Garris, Neil Cumbert **P:** David Kirschner, Steven Haft

Bette Midler, Sarah Jessica Parker, and Kathy Najimy are goofy 17th-century witch sisters in modern-day Salem, Massachusetts. The witches, who speak in unison, go after the teens who resurrected them in a museum on Halloween. Omri Katz, Thora Birch, and Vanessa Shaw are the kids. A boy who caused their hanging returns as a talking cat, and zombies appear. This PG comedy was a box-office flop but has good FX.

HOG WILD
(Nelson, 1980) **D:** Les Rose **S:** Andrew Peter Martin **P:** Claude Heroux   Canada

Michael Biehn and Patti D'Arbanville star in this action comedy about nerds victimized by bikers, with Matt Craven and Tony Rosato as Bull. It's by the director of *Gas*.

HOLD ME, THRILL ME, KISS ME
(Live, 1992) **D/S:** Joel Hershman **P:** Travis Swords

Bud (Max Parrish) hides out in an El Monte trailer park after shooting his scheming new wife (Sean Young) and encounters strange and comic characters there. Adrienne Shelly (from Hal Hartley movies) is Danny, a nice girl who lives with her crazy-bitch sister, Saber, a dancer (porno actress Andrea Naschak, perfect for the part). There's a former Hungarian opera star and her no-good son, flashbacks, and the top-billed Young (who doesn't have much screen time) returning as a vengeful

The H-Man

ghost. Also with Diane Ladd, and Timothy Leary (who's pretty good in a real role). The soundtrack includes tunes by the Cramps, the Pixies, the Violent Femmes, and others. The first-time director went to NYU's film school. R and unrated versions are available.

HOLLOWGATE
(City Lights, 1988) **D/S:** Ron Dizazzo
P: Richard Pepin, Joseph Merhi

A kid is nearly killed by his drunken father at a Halloween party, and ten years later he goes on a killing spree. Addison Randall and Katrina Avery star.

HOLLYWOOD AFTER DARK
(Sinister, 1961)   (*The Unholy Choice*)

Tony (Jack Vorno, from *Help Wanted Female*) is a weary, sarcastic, tortured former underwater-demolition expert who now runs a junkyard. He falls for a burlesque stripper (Rue McClanahan), accidentally kills a man, and totally botches a payroll robbery. Like *Five Minutes to Love*, also from Headliner Productions (and also with McClanahan), this has pretentious, serious dialogue and eccentric characters. Things are livened up by several strippers (especially a black one in pasties) and McClanahan's topless scene. There are no credits. McClanahan (Blanche in the TV series *The Golden Girls*) is also in *How to Succeed with Girls*. She's from Oklahoma.

HOLLYWOOD BABYLON
(Neon, 1971) **D/P:** Van Guylder **S/P:** L. K. Farbella

This unique but silly adults-only movie is a ripoff of Kenneth Anger's book and pretends to be a documentary about early scandals in "the sin capitol of the universe." A cheery narrator gives historical information and introduces color re-creations (with people playing famous actors) mixed with vintage public-domain silent-movie scenes. Some of the scenes are hilarious. Uschi Digart plays a lesbian Marlene Dietrich (!), Valentino is a voyeur, von Stroheim stages a real orgy, and Clara Bow does it with five football players. There's lots of sex, drugs, and nudity. The script is very sympathetic to the victims of scandals. With Jim Gentry, Ashley Phillips, and Myron Griffin. Guylder also directed David F. Friedman's *Ramrodder* (1969).

HOLLYWOOD BOULEVARD II
(MGM, 1989) **D:** Steve Barnett
S: Michael Sloane, Don Pugsley, Scott Narrie **P:** Chris Beckman, Tom Merchant

Joe Dante and Allan Arkush's 1976 *Hollywood Boulevard* was clever, funny, and cheap. This sequel is cheap. Ginger Lynn Allen (star of a million porno movies, she had a bit in *Young Guns II*) stars as the innocent Candy, who replaces the murdered star of a low-budget movie. Eddie Deezen watches Ginger/ Candy have R-rated sex with a screenwriter in front of a movie screen, in the only memorable scene. With Michelle Moffett, Maria Socas, Robert Patrick, Windsor Taylor Randolph, and Penelope Reed. Joe Bob Briggs shows up for a second, there are a lot of great explosions from other movies, and a heavy-metal band plays. Lots of past and present Corman directors (whom only a Concorde employee could maybe identify with the freeze-frame control) are in the useless ending (inspired by the great ending of the movie *Candy*).

HOLLYWOOD CHAINSAW HOOKERS

(Camp, 1987) **D/S/P:** Fred Olen Ray **S:** T. L. Langford

Hookers Linnea Quigley and Michelle Bauer kill the customers and duel with chainsaws in this un-rated detective/horror spoof. Jay Richardson as Chandler narrates. The best joke is when a hooker covers her velvet Elvis painting so that blood won't splatter on it. With Gunnar Hansen (from *The Texas Chainsaw Massacre*) as the blood-cult leader, Fox Harris, and Dawn Wildsmith. The music is by the Fugitive Kind. Ray basically re-made it as *Beverly Hills Vamp*.

HOLLYWOOD CHRONICLES

(MPI series)

Jackie Cooper narrates 13 50-minute documentary tapes. Some of special interest are: Censorship: The Unseen Cinema; The Futurists/Wizards of the FX; Poverty Row/The New Rebels; Scandal/Mysteries and Secrets; The Nightmare Factory; and Stereotypes and Minorities.

HOLLYWOOD CONFIDENTIAL

(Fang, 1948) **D/P:** Klayton W. Kirby
(*Sidestreets of Hollywood*)

Dorothy Abbott (who looks a bit like Lucille Ball) plays Dorothy Sloan, "a virgin in Hollywood" who's been sent there by her boss, the editor of a small-town newspaper, to write an exposé. She goes to a "haunted castle" where models pose in bikinis (one has a demon mask) and watches strip-pers dance in a club. She decides to pose, does some runway lingerie modeling, and answers some personal ads. There are flashbacks inside of flash-backs, a guy in drag who uses his falsies as an ash-tray, a catfight, and lines like "Did you ever feel as if you'd swallowed an electric vibrator?" Abbott narrates, then another actress starts reading her notes and takes over the narration. This road-show movie is based on Sloan's "amazing book." The 1953 rerelease (*Virgin in Hollywood*) contains a 3-D sequence.

HOLLYWOOD COP

(Celebrity, 1986) **D/S:** Amir Shervan
P: Moshe Bibiyan, Simon Bibiyan

David Goss tries to get a kidnapped kid back from mobsters. Meanwhile we see female oil-wrestling, bikers, crazed Arabs, kung-fu fighting, and car chases. Jim Mitchum is the gang boss, Aldo Ray is Fong, the Chinese (!) owner of a health club/whorehouse, and Cameron Mitchell and Troy Donahue are cops.

HOLLYWOOD DINOSAUR CHRONICLES

(Rhino, 1987)

Doug McClure hosts this 42-minute documentary with clips from *King Kong*, *The Lost World*, and other movies with dinosaurs.

THE HOLLYWOOD GAME

(Marathon, 1977) **D/S/P:** David Neil Gottlieb (*Game Show Models*; *The Hollywood Dream*; *Teenage Models*)

Independent International released this drive-in comedy with disco music. John Vickery stars, with singer Thelma Houston, Sid Melton, Willie Bobo (who also did the soundtrack), and Dick Miller.

HOLLYWOOD GHOST STORIES

(Castle Hill, 1986) **D:** James Forsher

John Carradine hosts a mixture of film clips and in-terviews about real ghosts with William Peter Blatty, Elke Sommer, Susan Strasberg, and Robert Bloch. Also included are a 1927 interview with Sir Arthur Conan Doyle, parts of *The Mystic Circle Mystery* (1936), with Houdini's wife, Bess, and a music-video ending, with Carradine.

HOLLYWOOD HARRY

(Media, 1985) **D/P/A:** Robert Forster **S:** Curt Allen
P: Branimar Arandjelovich (*Harry's Machine*)

Robert Forster stars as a clichéd divorced, alco-holic detective in this corny action comedy. His niece (his real-life daughter, Katherine) comes to live with him, and he has to find a runaway who was in a porno movie. He has a cartoon dream. Joe Spinell plays his friend Max, and Shannon Wilcox (his real-life wife at the time) also appears.

HOLLYWOOD HOT TUBS

(Vestron, 1984) **D:** Chuck Vincent
S: Craig McDonnell **S/P:** Mark Borde

A Hollywood guy gets a job repairing hot tubs. With Jewel Shepard as valley girl Crystal, future di-rector Katt Shea as Dee Dee, Edy Williams (also in the X-rated *Lady Lust* the same year) as Desire, and Becky Le Beau. Shepard returned in *Holly-wood Hot Tubs II* (IVE, 1989), with Tally Chanel, Spice Williams, and Michael Pataki.

HOLLYWOOD KNIGHTS

(Active, 1980) **D/S:** Floyd Mutrux **P:** Richard Lederer

This *American Graffiti* copy (by the maker of *American Hot Wax*) is set on Halloween night in 1965. Some teens seek revenge for the closing of Tubbies, a drive-in restaurant where they hung out. There are very dumb cops and jokes about tits, farts, and pigs. Only the black guys have pot. The cast includes Tony Danza, Fran Drescher, Robert Wuhl (who is very funny), Michelle Pfeif-fer as Suzy Q, Stuart Pankin, Otis Young, Art La Fleur, Debra Feuer, and *Playboy* Playmate Michelle Drake. It was the first time around for Danza, Wuhl, and Pfeiffer. This Columbia release has a 60s-oldies soundtrack (on Casablanca). The only problem is that it includes some hits from 1966.

HOLLYWOOD MAN

(1976) **D:** Jack Starrett **S/P/A:** William Smith (*Death Threat*)

William Smith stars as a movie star and former biker who uses money from the mob to make his own biker movie. This semi-autobiographical movie features Smith's real-life wife, Michelle Mar-ley, Mary Woronov as his girlfriend, Don Stroud as a stuntman, John Alderman, and Jennifer Billings-ley. Smith had just found new fame as Falconetti on TV in *Rich Man, Poor Man*.

HOLLYWOOD SCREAM QUEEN HOT TUB PARTY

(Tempe, 1992) **D:** Jim Wynorski, Fred Olen Ray

This 50-minute compilation of movie clips fea-tures Brinke Stevens, Monique Gabrielle, Michelle Bauer, Roxanne Kernohan, Kelly Maroney, and others. Scenes are from *Slumber Party Massacre*, *Sorority House Massacre II*, *Hollywood Chainsaw Hookers*, *Evil Toons*, and *Emmanuelle V*.

HOLLYWOOD SHUFFLE

(Image, 1987) **D/S/P/A:** Robert Townsend
S/A: Keenan Ivory Wayans

Townsend basically plays himself, a black actor faced with being stereotyped in Hollywood movies. He imagines himself in scenes from movies like *A Bat in Our House* and *Night of the Street Pimps* and spoofs *Rambo* and *Mandingo*. The commer-cial for "Black Acting School" shows (white) in-structors teaching black actors how to walk funky and speak jive. Wayans, who later used some of the same ideas for his *In Living Color* TV series, plays several roles. Wayans gave Townsend a cameo in his blaxploitation parody *I'm Gonna Get You Sucka!* (1988). With Anne-Marie Johnson, Star-letta DuPois, Damon Wayans, and Steve James. Townsend followed with *Eddie Murphy Raw* (1987) and *The Five Heartbeats* (1991).

HOLLYWOOD'S NEW BLOOD

(Raedon, 1988) **D/S:** James Shyman **P:** Ron Forster

A family whose house was blown up for a movie seek revenge during a seminar at a lake. Bobby Johnson and Francine Lapensee star.

THE HOLLYWOOD STRANGLER MEETS THE SKID ROW SLASHER

(Sinister, 1973) **D/C/E:** "Wolfgang Schmidt"/ Ray Dennis Steckler **S:** Christopher Edwards
P: Carol Flynn (*Model Killer*)

A horny photographer (Pierre Agostino) kills mod-els. Narrator Steckler's echoing voice is heard say-ing things like "Die, garbage, die!" Carolyn Brandt (Steckler's real-life wife) is the bookstore owner who kills bums with a switchblade. The "story" goes back and forth between the two killers. Then they meet and fall in love. There's no dialogue but lots of blood and nudity (especially in *Model Killer*, a longer version). Steckler, who made his cult clas-sics in the 60s, used a handheld 16mm camera for this one. Agostino returned in *Las Vegas Serial Killer*.

HOLLYWOOD UNCENSORED

(IVE, 1987) **D/S:** James Forsher **S:** Leith Adams, Barbara Myers, Beverly Stanley **P:** Julian Schlossberg

This light but fun documentary about censorship is divided into 2 parts. The hosts are the sons of more famous stars. A cheerful Douglas Fairbanks Jr. (last seen in *Ghost Story*) covers the 30s through the 50s. Peter Fonda (whose daughter Bridget is a bigger star these days) takes us up to the 80s and covers drug films. Early highlights are three great *King Kong* scenes that were unseen for decades, amazing (for the time) topless scenes from the European version of *High School Confidential*, and Ronald Reagan with Jayne Mansfield at an awards ceremony. Trailers for *The Love Life of a Gorilla* and *Sex Madness* are included, along with surprising pre-Code scenes with Barbara Stanwyck, Mae West, W. C. Fields, and tiny Shirley Temple playing a sexy adult singer. Jane Russell, Don Murray (who has made religious films and wants restrictions), Mamie Van Doren (also seen in *Girls Town*), and Sheree North reminisce. North is shown in a wild rock-dance segment and a famous 1953 bikini-dance short later sold through the mail. These scenes, and North herself (last seen in *Maniac Cop*), show why she should be better known and work more often. Fonda is seen on Hollywood Boulevard (and coping in *Easy Rider*). There are trailers for *Cocaine Fiends*, *Reefer Madness*, and *Silent Night, Deadly Night* (versions with and without Santa). Carroll Baker and Eli Wallach discuss *Baby Doll* ("the dirtiest film ever!"), and Martin Scorsese talks about *Taxi Driver* and *Peeping Tom*, which he first saw, uncut at New York's Fright Night show. While showing scenes from *Blood Feast*, Fonda yells, "Cut! Cut!" and looks away in disgust. Some of the public-domain footage may be overly familiar, but this is a very entertaining tape you'll probably wish was longer.

HOLLYWOOD VICE SQUAD

(Hollywood Home, 1986) **D:** Penelope Spheeris **S:** James J. Dogherty **P:** Arnold Orgolono, Sandy Howard

In this dumb action comedy from the director of *Suburbia*, various teams of LA cops encounter crimes. Ronny Cox, Leon Isaac Kennedy, and H. B. Haggerty are cops, Frank Gorshin is a comic gangster, Trish Van Devere is a mom looking for her hooker daughter, and Carrie Fisher busts an underage porno shoot. Robin Wright, Ben Frank, and Joey Travolta are also in the cast. It's from Roger Corman's Concorde and the producer of *Vice Squad*. Chris Spedding is on the soundtrack.

HOLLYWOOD ZAP

(Troma, 1986) **D/S:** David Cohen **P:** Bobbi Frank, Ben Frank

A southerner is in Hollywood searching for his father, and a former Wall Street stockbroker is searching for the ultimate video game. Ben Frank and Ivan E. Roth star in this comedy from Troma.

THE HOLY MOUNTAIN

(VSOM, 1973)
D/S/A/M: Alexandro Jodorowsky   Mexico

In Jodorowsky's "mescaline movie," nine disciples are on a quest to a mountain to discover the secret of immortality. They meet a master (the director) who shows them seven narrated tales of power, greed, and sex and teaches them to "destroy your illusions." This film looks more dated than the classic *El Topo* but has many similar images. Laughing children crucify Christ (Horacio Salinas), lots of tarantulas crawl over a screaming man, people are disemboweled, and a circus features toads playing conquistadors (a great scene). Dennis Hopper was originally cast but had a fight with the director. Jodorowsky had problems shooting in Mexico and had to finish it in America. It was an expensive flop midnight movie release (from Alan Klein's Abcko). For a while Klein would rent it only on a double bill with *El Topo*. Then both were withdrawn, only to show up years later on eagerly purchased bootleg videos. It's also available letterboxed on a Japanese laserdisc (with censorship dots for frontal nudity).

HOLY TERROR = ALICE, SWEET ALICE

HOLY WEDNESDAY: *See* FANGS

HOME BEFORE MIDNIGHT

(Lorimar, 1978) **D/S/P:** Peter Walker   UK

A songwriter (James Aubrey, from *Lord of the Flies*) for a band called Bad Accident is falsely accused of raping a 14-year-old girl (Allison Elliot, who has a shower scene), and his life is ruined by her parents and the court system. Richard Todd is an attorney, and Mick Jagger's lookalike brother Chris is the lead singer. The music is by the real band Jigsaw. Walker made the horror film *The Comeback* (with Jack Jones) the same year.

HOMEBOYS II: CRACK CITY

(AIP, 1989) **D/S:** Daniel Matmor **P:** Joe Paradise, H. Richard Garcia, Karen Burns

Brian Paul Stewart stars as David, a nice suburban guy who's forced to live with relatives in West Harlem, where he starts selling coke with his Mohawk-hair cousin. Parts of this movie are extremely ridiculous, but it's not boring. Characters are complex (a serious black radical, a killer American Indian priest, a Fagin-like Hispanic criminal). At one point David pretends to be gay to catch a leather-clad killer, and Delia Sheppard shows up as a dominatrix in a topless S&M nightclub. It all ends with homeless people fighting back and a quote from President Reagan. The music by Yuval Ron is very interesting and uses lots of phasing. This film has nothing to do with *Homeboy* (1988), *Homeboys* (1992), or even *Homeboyz* (1992). It may have been shot in Boston.

HOME FOR THE HOLIDAYS

(Vidmark, 1972) **D:** John Llewellyn Moxey **S:** Joseph Stefano **P:** Paul Junger Witt

A dying man (Walter Brennan, in his last role) summons his four daughters, who blame him for the death of their mother, and tells them that his second wife (Julie Harris) is trying to poison him. The dreary, cheap-looking old-dark-house murder mystery set at Christmas is an ABC-TV movie. It's like a mixture of *Dark Shadows* and Bergman's *Cries and Whispers*, with excess thunder and lightning and zoom-lens "shocks." Jessica Walter, Sally Field, Jill Hayworth, and Eleanor Parker are the daughters. It has no relation to the 1995 Jodie Foster movie.

HOME MOVIES

(Vestron, 1979) **D/P:** Brian De Palma **S:** Robert Harders **P:** Jack Temchin, Gil Adler   (*The Maestro*)

De Palma was teaching a film class at Sarah Lawrence when he made this comedy about filmmaking written by students, who also served as crew members and acted. Top-billed Kirk Douglas (who had been in De Palma's *The Fury*) guest stars as "the Maestro," a film instructor who encourages Keith Gordon to make a film. With Nancy Allen, Gerrit Graham, Vincent Gardenia, and Captain Haggerty. The Pino Donaggio soundtrack was released by Varèse Sarabande. De Palma married Allen in 1979 (it didn't last). Gordon took his role seriously. He went on to write *Static* and direct *The Chocolate War*. United Artists released this.

HOMER

(1970) **D:** John Trent **S:** Claude Harz **P:** Terence Dene

Don Scardino (later in *Squirm* and *Cruising*) stars as a Wisconsin farmboy with a motorcycle and a rock band. His parents try to make him cut his hair, he wrecks his father's car, he loses his virginity (with Tisa Farrow), and his best friend dies in Nam. Eventually he leaves town with some hippies. Alex Nicol is also in this GP-rated National General release. The Cotillion soundtrack features tracks by the Byrds, Cream, Led Zeppelin, and Buffalo Springfield.

HOME SWEET HOME

(1980) **D:** Nettie Pena **S:** Thomas Bush

Bodybuilder Jake Steinfeld plays a psycho bodybuilder who escapes from an asylum on Thanksgiving. He laughs while he kills people in an isolated house. Steinfeld is known as "the trainer to the stars." The soundtrack was on MSR.

HOMETOWN USA

(Vestron, 1979) **D:** Max Baer Jr. **S/P:** Jesse Vint **P:** Roger Cameras

The last of three movies directed by Baer (Jethro in the TV series *The Beverly Hillbillies*) is a teen comedy set in the late 50s. It copies *American Graffiti* and stars Gary Springer, Brian Kerwin, and Sally Kirkland.

HOMEWORK

(Kit Parker, 1979) **D/P:** James Beshears **S:** Maurice Peterson, Don Safran   (*Growing Pains*)

Joan Collins has an affair with her son's 16-year-old friend (Michael Morgan). With Lee Purcell, Wings Hauser as Rock, a coke-sniffing rock star, Carrie Snodgress, Betty Thomas, and Mel Wells. It was released in 1982 by Jensen Farley, who added new scenes and a nude body double for Collins. Annie Ample, Michelle Bauer, and Barbara Peckinpaugh appear topless in dream or nightmare scenes.

HOMEWRECKER

(Paramount, 1991) **D/S:** Fred Walton **S:** Eric Harlacher **P:** Robert M. Rolsky   (*Programmed for Murder*)

Robby Benson is not convincing as a brilliant, troubled scientist who develops a Star Wars–type defense-system robot. He retreats to his remote, high-tech vacation home, reprograms the computer (with the voice of Kate Jackson), and calls it Lucy. The jealous Lucy, with threatening mobile metal arms and hands, falls for the childlike scientist and eventually tries to kill his wife (Sydney Walsh, from *To Die For*) and little girl (Sarah Rose Karr) with knives, scissors, and gas. The first movie to debut on the Sci-Fi Channel, it was filmed around Portland, Oregon, by the director of *April Fool's Day*.

HOMICIDAL IMPULSE

(LIVE, 1992) **D/S:** David Tausik

Scott Valentine stars as an assistant DA who is seduced by his intern (Vanessa Angel) and drugged. Her uncle is the corrupt DA (Charles Napier). This R or unrated "erotic thriller" from Concorde features murder by acid, electric knife, and poker. Talia Shire is also in the cast.

HONDO

(1952) **D:** John Farrow **S:** James Edward Grant **P:** Robert Fellows

John Wayne stars as a cavalry scout in this 3-D Warner Brothers film, adapted from a story by Louis L'Amour. He was also the executive producer. The cast includes Geraldine Page (in her film debut), Ward Bond, Michael Pate, James Arness, Rodolfo Acosta, Lee Aaker, and Leo Gordon. The film was shot in Carmargo, Mexico. A 1967 TV series was based on it.

HONEYBABY

(UAV, 1974) **D:** Michael Schultz **S:** Brian Phelan **P:** Jack Jordan   (*Honeybaby, Honeybaby*)

Diana Sands is Laura Lewis, a UN interpreter who wins a trip on a TV game show and unknowingly transports a microdot with secret information to Beruit. Calvin Lockhart costars as a soldier of fortune. Cabaret star Bricktop also appears. Apparently this comic/action/spy movie wasn't completed as planned, so a prologue was added with a teen cousin smoking pot and telling the story. By the time it was released Sands had died of cancer.

HONEY, I BLEW UP THE KID

(Disney, 1992) **D:** Randal Kleiser **S:** Thom Eberhardt, Peter Elbling, Garry Goodrow **P:** Dawn Steel, Edward S. Feldman

I never thought Disney would rip off *The Amazing Colossal Man*, substituting a baby, but this PG comedy sequel to *Honey, I Shrunk the Kids* even includes scenes in Las Vegas, as in that 50s AIP hit. The FX are a lot better than Bert I. Gordon's, though. A two-year-old (played by the identical twins Daniel and Joshua Shalikar) becomes 7 feet tall, then a towering giant, because of his absent-minded inventor dad (Rick Moranis). Bad-guy scientist John Shea wants the baby for experiments. With Marcia Strassman, Robert Oliveri, Keri Russell as a babysitter, Lloyd Bridges, Kenneth Tobey, and Tom Rainone's hands. Novelist Kit Reed won a settlement because of the script's similarity to her story "The Attack of the Giant Baby" (1975).

HONEY, I SHRUNK THE KIDS

(Disney, 1989) **D:** Joe Johnson **S:** Ed Naha, Tom Schulman **P:** Penny Finkelman Cox

This hit PG fantasy is based on a story by horror directors Stuart Gordon and Brian Yuzna. Yuzna was an executive producer. Rick Moranis invents a shrinking-ray machine that accidentally makes his kids (Amy O'Neill and Robert Oliveri) and two neighbor kids smaller than ants. They end up in the backyard fighting scary giant bugs and tame an ant to help them. With Marcia Strassman, Matt Frewer, Kimmy Robertson (from *Twin Peaks*), and Kristine Sutherland. Filmed in Mexico. A sequel followed.

HONEYMOON ACADEMY

(HBO, 1988) **D/S:** Gene Quintano **S:** Jerry Lazarus **P:** Tony Anthony   (*For Better or for Worse*)

The title has nothing to do with this PG-13 *Romancing the Stone*–inspired comic adventure starring Kim Cattrall as a secret agent in Spain. With Robert Hays, Christopher Lee (in a small role), and Leigh Taylor-Young.

HONEYMOON IN VEGAS

(New Line, 1992) **D/S:** Andrew Bergman **P:** Mike Lobell

Card shark James Caan wins Sarah Jessica Parker from private eye Nicolas Cage in a poker game just as they're about to get married. This romantic comedy features a whole convention of Elvis impersonators, many Elvis songs, and a troupe of skydiving Elvises. Part of the film takes place in Hawaii. Some scenes parody James Bond movies, *Chinatown*, and *Wild at Heart*. Noriyuki "Pat" Morita, Anne Bancroft, Seymour Cassel, and Peter Boyle are also in the cast. Rob Reiner was the executive producer. The Epic soundtrack consists of cover versions of Elvis hits.

HONEYMOON MURDERS and HONEYMOON MURDERS II

(Cinevue/Postal, 1990) **D/S/P:** Steve Postal **S/P:** Gail Postal

The Postals churned out 10 (!) features in Bostwick, Florida, in 6 months! Each is overlong and talk-filled. In these two, Maurice S. Postal stars as a silly-looking monster who kills newlyweds. The Postals sold them by mail order. They never paid for their ad in *Psychotronic Video* magazine.

HONEYMOON OF TERROR

(SW, 1961) **D/S/P:** Peter Perry **P:** Basil C. Bradbury

A happy, playful honeymoon couple go to Vegas, then to deserted Thunder Island. He stupidly leaves cute, blond Marion (Dwan Marlow) alone and goes for supplies. She thinks about swimming ("Heck, yes!"), then sunbathes topless, attracting a club-footed logger who "went loco" and "lives like an animal." He chases her around (to bongo music) for the rest of the movie. This short (less than an hour) b/w film is from Sonney Amusement. The tape is a Frank Henenlotter Sexy Shocker. Perry also made *Mondo Mod* (1967) and edited Al Adamson movies.

HONKY

(Unicorn, 1971) **D:** William A. Graham **S/P:** Will Chaney **P:** Ron Roth

Brenda Sykes (*Cleopatra Jones*, *Black Gunn*) a midwestern high-school student from a well-off black family, has a romance with a poor white guy (John Nielson) with racist parents. After everybody criticizes them they sell some pot (and smoke it) to raise money to leave for California, which leads to a life of crime and disastrous results. With William Marshall as her doctor father, Marion Ross as his mother, John Hillerman, Matt Clark, Lincoln Kilpatrick, and Maia Danziger. Quincy Jones wrote the score, and Billy Preston sings. It was filmed in Kansas City and released by Jack A. Harris (*The Blob*).

HONKY TONK NIGHTS

(Tapeworm, 1978) **D:** Charles Webb **S/P:** Arthur Chang

Carol Doda is famous (at least to tourists in San Francisco) for being a top-heavy topless dancer and owning her own club. In this movie without an audience she plays a small-time Dolly Parton–inspired country singer billed as "Belle Barnes and Her 44s." When she shows up at a club run by a depressed Georgina Spelvin, the drunken patrons just yell, "Take it off!" Her guitarist/lover (Ramblin' Jack Elliot) writes a new arrangement for her song "You've Got to Change to Be a Star" ("nobody wants you the way you are"), and she is finally taken seriously as a singer. A rival singer, played by Serena (a better actress than Doda), gets to lip-sync "One More Drunk for the Road" and stab a lecherous old man in the face with a fork. Subplots fill up time with chase scenes, fights, and racing motorcycles. Spelvin and Serena, both major porno movie stars at the time, have brief nude scenes. So does Chris Cassidy, a lesser-known porno actress. The only real sex scene is performed outdoors by unknowns. Ramblin' Jack Elliot, a disciple of Woody Guthrie, was a pretty popular folk star until Bob Dylan came along. He should have done more acting in better movies. The biggest surprise for me, in this pretty dull movie, was an appearance by the wonderful San Francisco–based Hot Licks (without Dan Hicks) doing a number.

HONOR AND GLORY

(Imperial, 1992) **D/P:** "Godfrey Hall"/ Godfrey Ho **S:** Herb Borkland

Donna Jason stars as a TV reporter trying to expose a psycho martial-arts master and corporate criminal (John Miller) who's after the key to a nuclear arsenal. Her kickboxing FBI-agent sister (Cynthia Rothrock) helps. With Chuck Jeffries, Gerald Klein, and Richard Yuen.

THE HOODLUM

(Sinister, 1951) **D:** Max Nosseck **S:** Sam Neuman, Nat Tanchuck **P:** Maurice Kosloff

Lawrence Tierney stars as Vincent Lubeck, a hateful ex-con whose life begins and ends in the city dump. He causes the suicide of his brother's fiancée, worries his mother to death, and escapes in a hearse after a bank heist. With Allene Roberts, Marjorie Riordan, Lisa Golm, Gene Roth, and Edward Tierney (Lawrence's brother) as the brother. This Eagle Lion production (released by United Artists) is very cheap-looking, but Tierney, who later was frequently in trouble with the law, is fascinating. Nosseck also directed Tierney in *Kill or Be Killed*.

THE HOODLUM PRIEST

(1961) **D:** Irvin Kershner **S/P/A:** Don Murray **S:** Joseph Landon **P:** Walter Wood

Murray plays (real) St. Louis priest Father Charles Dismas Clark. He tries to help a young ex-con (Keir Dullea, in his film debut) reform, but he's fired from his job, shoots a man during a robbery, and goes to the gas chamber. With Larry Gates, Cindi Wood (the producer's wife), and Logan Ramsey. Kershner had directed *Stakeout on Dope Street* (1958) and *The Young Captives* (1959). Haskell Wexler was the cinematographer. Murray returned to the same theme when he directed *The Cross and the Switchblade* in 1972.

HOODLUMS: *See* GANGSTERS

HOOK

(RCA, 1991) **D:** Steven Spielberg **S:** Jim V. Hart, Malia Scotch Marmo **P:** Kathleen Kennedy, Frank Marshall, Gerald R. Molen

It's reassuring to know that everything Spielberg makes isn't a smash hit. This "$80 million" PG movie based on J. M. Barrie's play and book was a box-office flop. Robin Williams stars as a corporate raider who can't remember his childhood. When his children are kidnapped he must go to Never-Never Land, remember his past, and "become" Peter Pan again to rescue them. Charlie Korsmo (from *Dick Tracy*) and Caroline Goodall are the kids. The cast includes Dustin Hoffman as Captain Hook, Julia Roberts as Tinkerbell, Bob Hoskins, Maggie Smith, Phil Collins, and David Crosby and Glenn Close as pirates. There's a theatrical-looking pirate ship and mermaids. "The Lost Boys" have hip haircuts and use skateboards. ILM did the FX. John Williams wrote the score. This TriStar release is 142 minutes long and is rated PG.

THE HOOKER CULT MURDERS = THE PYX

HOORAY FOR HORRORWOOD!

(Dynacomm, 1990) **D:** Ray Ferry

Famous Monsters of Filmland magazine editor Forrest J. Ackerman takes us on a tour of his Holly-wood "Ackermansion" with its incredible collection of movie memorabilia, shows some classic movie clips, sings, and tells bad jokes and puns. The guests are Ray Bradbury, John Zacherle, Robert Englund, Bobbie Bresee, Linnea Quigley, and Tony Timpone. It's 75 minutes long.

THE HORN BLOWS AT MIDNIGHT

(1945) **D:** Raoul Walsh **S:** Sam Hellerman, James V. Kern **P:** Mark Hellinger

This is the fantasy/comedy that Jack Benny always joked about on his TV show. He's a trumpeter with a New York City radio orchestra who becomes an angel and is ordered to arrive on Earth at midnight and herald the end of the planet. Alexis Smith, Allyn Joslyn, John Alexander, and Guy Kibbee are angels too. It all turns out to be a dream. The cast also includes Dolores Moran, Reginald Gardiner, Franklin Pangborn, Margaret Dumont, Mike Mazurki, Jack Norton, and little Robert Blake. Franz Waxman wrote the music for this Warner Brothers film.

HORRIBLE HONEYS

(Trailers on Tape, 1988)

Every trailer on this 78-minute tape is for a horror or exploitation movie starring a woman. Some are grouped according to key words in titles, like *Bride, Daughter, Girl, Woman* (*Voodoo, Wasp, Leech, Snake, Cobra, 50 Ft.*) and *She* (*Creature, Freak, Monster, Demons*). Those are followed by female juvenile-delinquent, horror/science-fiction, and exploitation trailers. Besides the many obvious titles, some highlights are *Devil Girl from Mars*, *Female Jungle* (Mansfield and Tierney), *Berserk* (with a spike in Michael Gough's head), a road-show exploitation-release trailer for Ingmar Bergman's film *Monika*, here called *Monika: The Story of a Bad Girl* (music by Les Baxter), Ultra Violet in *Dinah East!* (a transsexual movie), and *Night of the Cobra Woman's* Marlene Clark naked. There are also some great special spots for *Blood-a-Rama* and *The Screaming Mee-Mee Show*.

HORRIBLE HORROR

(Goodtimes, 1986) **D:** David Bergman

John Zacherle, the famous TV horror host from Philadelphia (and New York City) recreates his funny 50s character on an interesting dungeon set and shows a pretty great public-domain selection of choice trailers, scenes from old horror and science-fiction movies, bloopers, outtakes, and rare 50s TV clips. Some titles are *King of the Zombies*, *Spider Baby*, *Flash Gordon* (the TV series), *Tales of Frankenstein* (a Brit-ish TV series), *Killers from Space*, and *Abbott and Costello Meet Frankenstein*. It's 110 minutes.

HORROR FARM: *See* DADDY'S DEADLY DARLINGS

HORROR HOUSE ON HIGHWAY 5

(Simitar, 1985) **D/S:** Richard Casey

First of all, this obscure video made around Holly-wood is stupid, very bad, and boring. A guy in a Nixon mask kills people, and a "Dr. Mabuse" (who thinks maggots are in his brain) and a retarded guy kidnap and drug female students. Characters wander endlessly through hallways in a house and discover bodies. The only reason somebody out there might want to see it is that writer Richard Meltzer (in a standout performance) plays a drunk driver who dies in a fight.

THE HORROR OF IT ALL

(MPI, 1983) **D/S/P:** Gene Feldman **S/P:** Suzette Winter

José Ferrer hosts this 60-minute history of pre-70s horror movies, which uses interviews, stills, and public-domain film clips. Directors Roger Corman, Rouben Mamoulian, Curtis Harrington, and

Lawrence Tierney and Gene Roth in *The Hoodlum*.

Herman Cohen, writer Robert Bloch, and actors John Carradine, Dana Andrews, Gloria Stuart, and Martine Beswick are heard and/or seen in new interviews.

THE HORROR SHOW

(MGM, 1989) **D:** James Isaac **S:** Allyn Warner, Leslie Bohem **P:** Sean S. Cunningham

Brion James stars as laughing Max Jenke, a mass murderer who's sent to the electric chair but returns to terrorize the cop (Lance Henriksen) who captured him. This failed attempt to create another Freddy Krueger was copied in the same year's *Shocker* by Cunningham's former partner Wes Craven. James and Henriksen are fine, but many of the FX, which try to outdo those in Nightmare on Elm Street movies, are mediocre or stupid (like the turkey scene). With Rita Taggart, Dedee Pfeiffer, Matt Clark, Alvy Moore, and Lawrence Tierney as the warden. This was known as *House III* in Europe (where it's longer), but it's better than any of the movies in the series. *The Horror Show* (1979) is a compilation tape, with Anthony Perkins looking at "60 years of Universal movie monsters."

THE HORRORS OF BURKE AND HARE

(Starmaker, 1971) **D:** Vernon Sewell **S:** Ernie Bradford **P:** Guido Coen   UK (*Burke and Hare*)

Grave-robbers Burke and Hare do their thing in Edinburgh. The story had already been filmed many times. Harry Andrews stars as Dr. Knox, with Derren Nesbit, Yootha Joyce, and Yutte Stensgaard. It's a black comedy with sex and nudity. The theme is by the Scaffold. New World released it in the US.

HORRORS OF SPIDER ISLAND

(SW, 1959) **D/S:** "Jamie Nolan"/Fritz Bottger **P:** Wolfgang Hatwig   W. Germany (*Ein Toter Hing im Netz*)

A plane full of American dancers (one has a southern accent) crashes (offscreen), and they end up on an island. Some men arrive, the women dance in flower bikinis, love blossoms, and jealousy results in a catfight. Meanwhile, their talent scout (Alex D'Arcy, or his double) is bitten by a spider and becomes a monster with a hairy face and claws. The closeups of his face are scary, but the editing is awful and the whole movie is confusing. With Barbara Valentin as Babs: "Her legs are worth their weight in gold." This print is called *It's Hot in Paradise*, the original Pacemaker US-release title. I first saw this famous rarity in Paris. The French-dubbed version had closeup scenes of all the women skinny-dipping (seen here only in a brief long shot). It was filmed in Yugoslavia and is part of the Frank Henenlotter Sexy Shocker series.

HORRORS OF THE RED PLANET = THE WIZARD OF MARS

THE HORSEPLAYER

(Republic, 1990) **D/S:** Kurt Voss **S/P:** Larry Ratner **S:** David Birke

Brad Dourif stars as Bud, an on-the-edge, reclusive racetrack fanatic who's on parole. He works nights for Vic Tayback (in his last role) in a liquor store's walk-in refrigerator (wearing a fur coat and ski mask). Sammi Davis seduces him, and her sarcastic, alcoholic artist "brother" (Michael Harris) chooses him to model for a series of violent paintings. Bud hates art (for good reason), though. Parts of this low-budget movie are like *A Bucket of Blood*. Davis and Voss (*Border Radio*) were married in real life. He also made *Genuine Risk*. The soundtrack is by the Pixies.

HOSPITAL OF HORROR = NURSE SHERRI

HOSTAGE

(RCA, 1987) **D:** Hanro Mohr, Percival Rubens **S:** Norman Winski, Michael Leighton **P:** Thys Heyns, Paul Raleigh S. Africa (*Colt; Flight 802*)

Wings Hauser, as the Nam-vet mercenary-commando hero, saves kidnapped Nancy Locke, as his girlfriend. This *Delta Force* copy is set on a train in Uganda taken over by Arab terrorists. With Karen Black as a porno star with a gay agent and Kevin McCarthy.

HOSTAGE TOWER

(Embassy, 1980) **D:** Claudio Guzman **S:** Robert Carrington **P:** Burt Nodella, Peter Snell

Peter Fonda stars in this CBS-TV adaptation of an Alistair MacLean tale about a master criminal (Keir Dullea) who captures the Eiffel Tower and holds hostages there, including the US president's mother. With Billy Dee Williams, Rachel Roberts (in her last role), Maud Adams, Celia Johnson, Douglas Fairbanks Jr., and Britt Ekland. It was made (partially in Paris) by the director of *Linda Lovelace for President*.

HOSTILE TAKEOVER

(IVE, 1988) **D:** George Mihalka **S:** Stephen Zoller, Michael A. Gilbert **P:** George Flak   Canada (*Office Party*)

In this black comedy, a hydroelectric-plant worker (David Warner) snaps and takes hostages. With Michael Ironside, Kate Vernon, and Jayne Eastwood.

THE HOT BOX

(VGB, 1972) **D:** Joe Viola **S/P:** Jonathon Demme

Four Peace Corps nurses are kidnapped and jailed in the Philippines. In a typical 70s drive-in plot, they become jungle revolutionaries fighting against the corrupt government. Margaret Markov stars, with Andrea Cagan, Charles Dierkop, and Laurie Rose. This New World release has lots of topless scenes. Viola and Demme also made *Angels, Hard as They Come*.

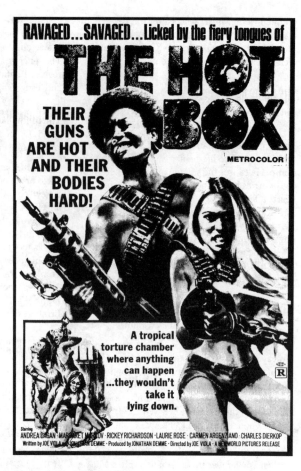

HOT CAR GIRL

(1958) **D:** Bernard Kowalski **S:** Leo Gordon **P:** Gene Corman

Duke (Richard Bakalyan) hates cops, steals car parts, drinks too much, talks jive, and ends up wanted for murder and hiding out at Bronson Canyon. Peg (June Kenny) is the tough girl who helps the juvenile delinquents strip cars. Janice (Jana Lund) is the rich girl who races in her convertible and goes to jail after a motorcycle cop is killed. This is pretty strong for a 50s teen movie. Characters are bashed, smashed, and killed, and sex is implied. Bruno Ve Sota runs the junkyard, and Ed Nelson is a cop. There's a jazzy Cal Tjader score. Roger Corman was the executive producer. Kowalski made *Night of the Blood Beast* the same year.

HOT CHILD IN THE CITY

(Paramount, 1987) **D:** John Florea **S:** George Goldsmith **P:** Giovanna Nigro-Chacon

Leah Ayres-Hamilton stars as the younger sister of Shari Shattuck, a Hollywood record-company executive who is murdered. She begins to assume her sister's personality as she searches for the killer. The music is by Billy Idol, Nick Glider, Lou Reed, and Fun Boy Three.

HOT CHOCOLATE

(Live, 1992) **D:** Josée Dayan **S:** Ginny Cerrella, Maryedith Burrell

Bo Derek, a rich Texan who's in France to buy a chocolate factory, falls for the owner's assistant

(Robert Hays). Bo keeps her clothes on in this "romantic comedy." It features Howard Hesseman and a midget bartender.

HOT DOG: THE MOVIE

(1984) **D:** Peter Markle **S:** Mike Marvin **P:** Edward S. Feldman

David Naughton is a "Manhattan punk" in this ski comedy with Shannon Tweed, *Playboy* Playmate Crystal Smith, and a slasher. "Hot-dogging" is choreographed skiing. This was followed by *Hamburger*.

HOTEL EROTICA = SLAUGHTER HOTEL (minus 21 minutes!)

THE HOTEL NEW HAMPSHIRE

(1984) **D/S:** Tony Richardson **P:** Neil Hartley

A very odd family manage to get by, in this adaptation of John Irving's novel set in Vienna, New York City, and New England. Jodie Foster, Nastassja Kinski (who wears a bear suit), and Rob Lowe are the older kids, and there's a little sister who doesn't grow. Rape and incest figure in this comedy/drama. Beau Bridges and Lisa Banes are the parents. With Amanda Plummer, Seth Green, Joely Richardson, Wallace Shawn as Freud (*not* Sigmund), Matthew Modine, Wilford Brimley, and Anita Morris. Orion released it to confused audiences.

HOTEL OKLAHOMA

(1990) **D/S:** Bobby Houston **S:** Lisa Sutton **P:** Terry Kahn, Ed Elbert, Gregory Vanger

This is a women's-prison movie with comedy and a lesbian-love-triangle murder. There's no nudity, but all the usual clichés are here. Kristen Cloke is the innocent sent up. With David Keith, Ray Sharkey, Karen Black (who was also in Houston's *Bad Manners*) as a crazy inmate, and Deborah May as the warden. It was filmed at the Oklahoma State Penitentiary.

HOTEL ROOM

(Worldvision, 1992) **D:** David Lynch, James Signorelli **S:** Barry Gifford, Jay McInerney **P:** Deepak Nayar

Lynch was the executive producer of this limited (and limited-appeal) HBO series. Each of the 3 odd stories takes place in a different year in the same room of a New York City hotel. They move very slowly and don't have much of a payoff, but what would you expect from Lynch? In 1969 Harry Dean Stanton and Freddie Jones (who doesn't show up in a mirror) are in the room with a hooker (Glenne Headly). Chelsea Field, Deborah Unger, and Mariska Hargitay are all former conquests of a director (Griffin Dunne) in Signorelli's contemporary segment. Crispin Glover (naturally) dominates Lynch's 1936 story, and Alicia Witt plays his wife.

HOT HEIR

(1984) **D:** Worth Keeter III **S:** Thom McIntyre **P:** Earl Owensby   (*The Great Balloon Chase*)

Diane Beatty and Ron Campbell star in this adventure movie about hot-air balloons, filmed in Shelby, North Carolina.

HOT ICE

(Night Flite, 1977) **D/S/P/A:** "A. C. Stevens"/ Stephen Apostolof **S:** Ed Wood Jr.

Ed Wood Jr. was the assistant director of this, the last of A. C. Stevens' nudie movies. Wood died in 1978, was rediscovered for his earlier films like *Plan 9 from Outer Space* and *Glen or Glenda*, and, incredibly, was the subject of a major motion picture, Tim Burton's *Ed Wood* (1994).

HOT MOVES

(Vestron, 1984) **D/P:** Jim Sotos **S:** Larry Anderson, Peter Foldy

An overweight virgin uses a telescope to watch girls on the beach, in another *Animal House* copy. He sees Jill Schoelen, Monique Gabrielle, and Deborah Richter.

HOT ON THE TRAIL: *See* FUGITIVE GIRLS

HOT POTATO

(Warner, 1976) **D/S:** Oscar Williams **P:** Fred Weintraub, Paul Heller

Jim Kelly (*Enter the Dragon*) is a martial-arts fighter who tries to rescue an ambassador's daughter in Thailand. With Irene Tsu, Sam Hiona, and George Memmoli. Producer Weintraub later had this remade as *Force: Five* (1981). Williams had directed *The Final Comedown*.

H.O.T.S.

(Vestron, 1979) **D:** Gerald Seth Sindell **S:** Cheri Caffaro, Joan Buchanan **P:** W. Terry Davis, Don Schain, Gerald Seth Sindell   (*T&A Academy*)

The title of this sex comedy (written by the star of the Ginger movies!) means "Honey, O'Hara, Teri, and Sam." With Susan Lynn Kiger and K. C. Winkler (from *Playboy*), Lindsay Bloom, Sandy John-

son, Pamela Jean Bryant, Angela Aames, Lisa London, Danny Bonaduce, and Dick Bakalyan. It has topless football, topless parachuters, and topless chess games. Other *H.O.T.S.* tapes are unrelated, retitled films.

H.O.T.S. II: *See* SWINGING CHEERLEADERS

HOT SHOTS!

(Fox, 1991) **D/S:** Jim Abrahams **S:** Pat Proft **P:** Bill Badalato

Charlie Sheen is ace flyer "Topper" Harley, in this PG-13 spoof of *Top Gun* (and the Reagan era). Cary Elwes costars, with Valeria Golino, Lloyd Bridges, Jon Cryer, Kristy Swanson, and Efrem Zimbalist Jr. Other movies, including *9½ Weeks*, *An Officer and a Gentleman*, *The Fabulous Baker Boys*, and *Dances with Wolves*, are ridiculed too, and actors play Elvis, the Pope, Saddam Hussein, Liberace, and Bogart. This was released just after *Naked Gun 2½*, by Abrahams' ex-partner David Zucker. It was a big hit.

HOT SHOTS! PART DEUX

(Fox, 1993) **D/S:** Jim Abrahams **S:** Pat Proft **P:** Bill Badalato

The same main cast (Sheen, Bridges, Golino) return in a pretty stupid spoof of *Rambo* movies and others, including *Star Wars* and *The Wizard of Oz*. Sheen is sent to Iraq with CIA agent Golino to rescue hostages from Saddam Hussein. With *Rambo* regular Richard Crenna, Brenda Bakke, and Miguel Ferrer. Martin Sheen shows up in an *Apocalypse Now* spoof, the president (Bridges) throws up in the lap of the Japanese prime minister, and they even make fun of Buddhist monks. 20th Century–Fox released this PG-13 film.

THE HOT SPOT

(Orion, 1990) **D:** Dennis Hopper **S:** Nona Tyson, Charles Williams **P:** Paul Lewis

The third movie directed by Hopper in three years is based on a 1952 novel *Hell Hath No Fury*, by Williams. Don Johnson stars as a con man and

H.O.T.S.

drifter working as a car salesman in Taylor, Texas. He becomes involved with his boss's wife (Virginia Madsen, who used a body double) and Jennifer Connelly (who has a topless scene). It's way too long (130 minutes), but some parts are inspired by David Lynch and are fairly extreme for an R rating. With Charles Martin Smith, Jack Nance, Barry Corbin, William Sadler, and Debra Cole. The Jack Nitzsche blues soundtrack (on Antilles) includes Miles Davis, John Lee Hooker, Taj Mahal, and others.

HOT TARGET

(1985) **D/S:** Denis Lewiston **P:** John Barnett, Brian Cook   New Zealand (*Restless*)

Rich, blond Simone Griffeth, the wife of a British tycoon, is seduced by a thief who's planning to rob her home. This *film noir* copies *Body Heat* and has some nudity. A Crown International release.

HOTTER AFTER DARK

(SW, 1967)

A voyeur detective named Mike Mallonen narrates this really cheap-looking adult movie with some of the worst acting ever. He "watches" sex scenes with dubbed-in groans (the men keep their underwear on) from a closet. In one scene he starts making out with a maid who turns out to be a man in drag. When a woman takes a shower her panties appear. There are no production credits for this b/w film.

HOT TO TROT!

(Warner, 1988) **D:** Michael Dinner **S:** Stephen Neigher, Hugh Gilbert **P:** Steve Tisch

Bobcat Goldthwait stars opposite a talking horse (with the voice of John Candy). Who would have thought that the Francis the Talking Mule/Mr. Ed idea would resurface yet again? Goldthwait hated this PG comedy so much that he directed himself in *Shakes the Clown*. With Dabney Coleman, Virginia Madsen, Jim Meltzer, Cindy Pickett, Mary Gross, and the voice of Burgess Meredith.

HOT UNDER THE COLLAR

(HBO, 1992) **D/P/A:** Richard Gabai

Richard Gabai disguises himself as a nun to save his hypnotized girlfriend (Angela Visser) from a convent. With Burt Ward. By the director of *Virgin High*.

THE HOUND OF THE BASKERVILLES

(Paramount, 1983) **D:** Douglas Hickox **S:** Charles Pogue **P:** Otto Plaschkes   UK

Ian Richardson stars as Sherlock Holmes, and Donald Churchill is Dr. John Watson, in this British TV movie shown on HBO. The cast includes Denholm Elliott, Brian Blessed, Ronald Lacey, Eleanor Bron, and Edward Judd. Nicholas Clay plays three roles. Richardson was also in *The Sign of the Four* the same year. A 1982 BBC version of *The Hound of the Baskervilles* stars Tom Baker. A 1988 version stars Jeremy Brett and is part of the Granada TV Sherlock Holmes series. Earlier versions starred Basil Rathbone (1941), Peter Cushing (1959), Stewart Granger (1972), and Peter Cook (1977).

HOUR OF THE ASSASSIN

(MGM, 1986) **D/P:** Luis Llosa **S:** Matt Leipzig

Ex–Green Beret Erik Estrada is in South America, hired by the military for an assassination plot. Robert Vaughn is the CIA man trying to stop him. Released by Corman's Concorde, it was filmed in Peru.

HOUR OF THE PIG

(1993) **D/S:** Leslie Megahey **P:** David M. Thompson   France/UK

In medieval Europe even animals could be accused of crimes and tried in court. Colin Firth stars as a Parisian defense lawyer working in a village who defends a pig owned by Gypsies that is accused of killing a boy. With Donald Pleasence as a local prosecuting attorney, Amina Annabi, Ian Holm, Nicol Williamson, Lysette Anthony, and Michael Gough.

HOUR OF THE WOLF

(MGM/UA, 1967) **D/S:** Ingmar Bergman Sweden (*Vargtimmen*)

Max von Sydow stars as a brooding artist on a secluded island haunted by demons in his imagination that become real. There's a bird man, and a woman's face comes off. Liv Ullmann is his wife, and Ingrid Thulin is his mistress. This moody film was copied by Oliver Stone for his first movie, *Seizure*. The cinematography is by Sven Nykvist. It's the second film in a Bergman trilogy starting with *Persona* (1966) and ending with *Shame* (1968).

THE HOURS AND TIMES

(Fox Lorber, 1991) **D/S:** Christopher Munch   UK

This 'what if' story shows John Lennon (Ian Hart) and the Beatles' homosexual manager, Brian Epstein (David Angus), on a 1963 vacation together in Barcelona. It's b/w and less than an hour long. Hart returned as Lennon in *Backbeat*.

HOUSE

(Starmaker, 1986) **D:** Steve Miner **S:** Ethan Wiley **P:** Sean S. Cunningham

A Nam-vet horror writer (William Katt) moves into a haunted house that he has inherited and works on a book about his war experiences. He has to arm himself to kill a slime monster, a zombie fish, zombies, and various rubber creatures. With George Wendt, Richard Moll as a tortured Nam-vet ghost, and Kay Lenz. This silly *Poltergeist* parody is based on a story by Fred Dekker. Miner had been working with Cunningham as an editor since *Last House on the Left*. This New World release includes a clip from *Don't Look in the Basement*.

HOUSE II: THE SECOND STORY

(Starmaker, 1987) **D/S:** Ethan Wiley **P:** Sean S. Cunningham

Arye Gross and Lar Park Lincoln move into a house once owned by their great-great-grandfather. They dig up the 170-year-old corpse (Royal Dano) and are sent to a ghost town, then to a primeval jungle to face a baby dino and a caterpillar/dog. With Gregory Walcott, Mitzi Kapture, and Devin Devasquez (from *Playboy*). A Varèse Sarabande album was released, with Harry Manfredini's score for both films. *House III* became *Horror Show* in the US. New World released this.

HOUSE IV: HOME DEADLY HOME

(New Line, 1990) **D:** Lewis Abernathy **S:** Geoff Miller, Deidre Higgens **P:** Sean S. Cunningham

Terry Treas inherits an isolated haunted house from her husband (played by William Katt, from the first movie) after a car crash kills him and cripples their daughter. Treas sees blood everywhere and is naked in a blood shower. Bungling comic villains work for an evil dwarf who runs a toxic-waste plant. Flashback dreams (with Katt) are repeated. There's too much talking, not enough sense, and bad, silly FX. With Denny Dillon, Ned Romero, and Kane Hodder.

HOUSEBOAT HORROR

(1987) **D:** Kendal Flanigan **D/S/P:** Ollie Martin   Australia

People making rock videos near a remote lake are killed off by a scarred, bald psycho who was burned on a movie set. Alan Dale and Christine Jeston star. The cast is mostly Australian TV soap stars. It was shot with a Betacam and was Australia's first direct-to-video slasher movie.

THE HOUSE BY THE CEMETERY

(Vestron, 1981) **D/S:** Lucio Fulci **S:** Dardano Sacchetti, Giorgio Mariuzzo **P:** Fabrizio De Angelis Italy (*Quella Villa Accanto al Cimitero*)

A family moves into a house near Boston. Dr. Freudstein, an ancient cannibal, is in the basement, and there's a little-girl ghost who tries to warn the family. Fulci regular Catriona/Katherine MacColl stars as the mom. With Dagmar Lassander and Paolo Malco. This unrated movie has gore, blood, decapitations, a giant bat, and maggots. It's pretty entertaining. The son character is copied from *The Shining*. It was partially shot on location in the US.

THE HOUSE BY THE RIVER

(1950) **D:** Fritz Lang **S:** Mel Dinelli **P:** Howard Welsch

Louis Hayward is a wealthy unpublished author who lives with his wife (Jane Wyatt) in an old mansion by a river. He accidentally kills the maid (Dorothy Patrick) while making unwanted sexual advances, throws the body into the river, and implicates his crippled brother, an accountant (Lee Bowman), in the maid's disappearance. The corpse resurfaces, and he imagines that his victim is in the house strangling him. One very contemporary touch has the killer capitalizing on the tragedy by writing a bestseller about it! This low-budget Republic release was based on a 1921 novel and is one of Lang's forgotten gems. The music is by George Antheil. Lang next made a Technicolor war movie, *American Guerrilla in the Philippines* (1950), the classic Technicolor western *Rancho Notorious* (1952), and the disturbing drama *Clash by Night* (1952).

HOUSEGEIST: *See* BOARDING HOUSE

THE HOUSE IN MARSH ROAD

(Sinister, 1960) **D:** Montgomery Tully **S/P:** Maurice J. Wilson UK (*The Invisible Creature*)

A poltergeist in an old house interferes when a man (Tony Wright) decides to murder his wife (Patricia Dainton).

HOUSE IN NIGHTMARE PARK = NIGHT OF THE LAUGHING DEAD

A HOUSE IN THE HILLS

(Live, 1993) **D/S/P/A:** Ken Wiederhorn **S:** Miguel Tejada-Flores **P:** Patricia Foulkrod

A would-be actress (Helen Slater) practices role-playing while house-sitting in Hollywood. A man pretending to be an exterminator (Michael Madsen) shows up for revenge and ties her up. Nobody is who they claim to be in this interesting film. It could have been a five-character play but is filled with clever plot twists, good acting, and some comic moments. With Jeffrey Tambor, Elyssa Davalos, and James Laurenson. Incredibly, most of this was shot in Luxembург! It's by the director of *Shock Waves* and *Eyes of a Stranger*.

THE HOUSEKEEPER

(Warner, 1987) **D:** Ousama Rawi **S:** Elaine Waisglass **P:** Harve Sherman UK/Canada (*A Judgement in Stone*)

Rita Tushingham (from Liverpool) is an illiterate British psycho housekeeper working for a New England family. Her friendship with a religious fanatic (Jackie Burroughs) leads her to use a shotgun on them. It's based on *A Judgement in Stone*, a novel by Ruth Rendell.

HOUSE NEAR THE PRADO

(1969) **D/S/P:** J. Van Hearn

Charles Napier and Marsha Jordan star in a tale of sex and assassination in South America. He's an American businessman who spends time in a whorehouse. It's adults-only.

HOUSE OF DARKNESS

(Sinister, 1947) **D:** Oswald Mitchell **S:** John Gilling **P:** Harry Reynolds UK

A ghost seeks vengeance on the stepbrother who killed him. With Laurence Harvey (in his first movie) and Leslie Osmond.

HOUSE OF DEATH

(Virgin Vision, 1981) **D:** David Nelson **S:** Paul C. Elliot **P:** Chuck Ison (*Death Screams*)

A psycho with a machete kills coeds at a party. Susan Lynn Kiger (from the pages of *Playboy*) stars. David Nelson (Ricky's brother) made and appeared in a 1984 Christian anti-porno TV special featuring President Reagan.

HOUSE OF DREAMS

(LS Video, 1964) **D/S/P/A:** Robert Berry

Berry is a writer who suffers from headaches and has nightmares. This 16mm b/w obscurity was made in Indiana and features some *Carnival of Souls*–type scenes. With Pauline Elliott as the alcoholic wife, Charlene Bradley, Lance Bird, and David Goodnow (later a CNN anchor).

HOUSE OF EVIL = THE EVIL

THE HOUSE OF HORROR

(1929) **D:** Benjamin Christensen **S:** Richard Bee **P:** Richard A. Rowland

A bachelor (former silent comic Chester Conklin) and his sister from Ohio (Louise Frazenda) go to see an uncle. Various characters are after diamonds, in this haunted-house comedy. The cast includes Thelma Todd and William V. Mong. Cornell Woolrich wrote the intertitles for this 65-minute First National silent film with sound effects and music. Much of the same cast had appeared in Christensen's *The Haunted House* (1928). Both movies are lost. *House of Horrors* is a 1946 movie with deformed actor Rondo Hatton.

HOUSE OF MYSTERY

(1934) **D:** William Nigh **S:** Albert De Mond **P:** Paul Malvern

A group of people are summoned to an old English country house owned by a man who was cursed in India. A gorilla starts killing them off. Ed Lowry stars in this Monogram movie, which is just over an hour. With Verna Hillie, George "Gabby" Hayes, Irving Bacon, and Brandon Hurst as a Hindu priest. It's by the director of *The Ape* (1940) and *Black Dragons* (1942). The same title was used for two British films (1941, 1961).

HOUSE OF 1000 DOLLS

(Orion, 1967) **D:** Jeremy Summers **S/P:** Harry Alan Towers W. Germany/Spain (*Das Haus der Tausend Freuden*)

I never expected this forgotten Vincent Price movie to have a major release, but here it is, from Orion. He does a telepathic stage act with Martha Hyer in Tangiers. The confused plot is about an international slave ring. Price makes the wife of a criminal pathologist (George Nader) vanish onstage, and she really disappears. An evil woman runs a whorehouse with a torture chamber. There are women in coffins, women wrestling in mud, women in underwear being flogged, and a surprise (!) ending. The cast includes Maria Rohm and Herbert Fux. It was filmed in Spain and played on an AIP double bill with *Mary Jane* (!). Summers directed *The Face of Evil* and *The Vengeance of Fu Manchu* for Towers too.

HOUSE OF SHADOWS

(Media, 1976) **D:** Richard Wulicher **S/P:** Ricky T. Tudela Argentina (*La Casa de los Sombras*)

Yvonne De Carlo stars as a rich woman whose hired companion has nightmares about murders committed years before. The cast includes John Gavin (soon to become US ambassador to Mexico) and Leonor Manso.

HOUSE OF TERROR (1972): *See* KIDNAPPED CO-ED

HOUSE OF TERROR

(TWE, 1972) **D:** Sergei Goncharoff **S:** Tony Crecharles **P:** George J. Gade (*The Five at the Funeral*)

A nurse (Jennifer Bishop) is hired to care for a rich, neurotic woman. Blackmail and murder result. Bishop was also in *Jaws of Death* and *Impulse*. The director was an editor for Al Adamson. John Bud Cardos was the second-unit director. With Arell Blanton and Mitchell Gregg. It's PG.

HOUSE OF THE BLACK DEATH

(Loonic, 1965) **D:** Harold Daniels, Reginald Le Borg, Jerry Warren **S:** Richard Mahoney **P:** William White, Richard Shotwell

John Carradine is André de Sade ("The word insanity does not apply to the de Sades!") in this talky b/w witch movie. His brother, Belial de Sade (a confused-looking Lon Chaney Jr.), has cloven feet and horns hidden by a hood. Belial leads a local group of witches who want André's power. Dolores Faith (*The Human Duplicators*) is their sister. A younger brother is a werewolf. In his one and only brief monster scene he wears a gorilla mask! Scenes with Katherine Victor as the witch Lila were added by Jerry Warren. Doctors, played by Andrea King (*The Beast with Five Fingers*) and Tom Drake (*The Cyclops*), spend the night. Two women fight over who killed a dog. Carradine and Chaney have no scenes together, but John eventually turns Lon into a skull. The most striking thing about this mess is that the story stops five times while women in revealing costumes do slow, sexy dances in a graveyard set complete with headstones and an altar!—in front of the Chaney Devil! Did Ed Wood see this before he wrote *Orgy of the Dead*?! The video copy has bad sound and is way too dark. This may also have been known as *Blood of the Man Devil*, *Night of the Beast*, and *Blood of the Man Beast*.

HOUSE OF THE DAMNED

(1963) **D/P:** Maury Dexter **S:** Harry Spaulding

This odd little haunted-house movie takes a while to get interesting, but there is a bizarre payoff. An architect (Ronald Foster) and his wife (Merry Anders) go to an empty California castle and are joined by a lawyer (Richard Crane) and his unhappy wife (Erica Peters). They all get spooked after a (real) half-man steals the keys and a headless woman is seen. Eventually a group of (real) carnival freaks (including a fat lady and giant Richard Kiel) are discovered living in the basement. This b/w 20th Century–Fox movie is by the maker of *The Day Mars Invaded Earth*.

HOUSE OF THE LONG SHADOWS

(MGM, 1982) **D:** Peter Walker **S:** Mitchell Armstrong **P:** Menahem Golan UK

Every review seemed to condemn this all-star horror/mystery for being clichéd and old-fashioned. It's based on the novel *Seven Keys to Bald-*

pate, by Charlie Chan–creator Earl Derr Biggers, and the Broadway play by George M. Cohan, filmed under the original title in 1917 and 1925 and three times by RKO (in 1930, 1935, and 1947). I never saw any of these movies and had never even heard of them, but I was pleasantly surprised to finally see the only movie that will ever be made with Christopher Lee, Peter Cushing, Vincent Price, and John Carradine. A successful writer (Desi Arnaz Jr.) bets his agent (Richard Todd) that he can write a gothic horror novel in 24 hours in an old Welsh house, Baldpate Manor. The caretakers are Carradine ("What are you doing he-ah!?") and his daughter (!) (Sheila Keith), a regular in Peter Walker's movies, who sings. Cushing arrives "seeking shelter." He sounds very strange because of a speech impediment. Price has the best dramatic entrance: "I have returned!" Lee shows up to purchase the house, empty since 1939. People are killed as the always-changing plot about the murderous, missing brother Roderick (who ate rats) unfolds. Cushing says, "We were going to fwee him!" Nothing is what it seems. On the negative side, the movie has too many false scares and Desi Jr. All the horror stars are great and in top form, the music is good, some parts are funny, and Lee and Price have a memorable axe fight.

THE HOUSE OF USHER

(RCA, 1988) **D:** Alan Birkinshaw **S:** Michael J. Murray **P:** Harry Alan Towers   S. Africa

This version has more going on than Roger Corman's 1960 movie, but that doesn't make it any good. Oliver Reed whispers and gets nauseated a lot as the modern-day Roderick Usher, living in his castle in England. Donald Pleasence plays his crazy, scene-stealing, decrepit, hunchbacked sculptor brother. Usher wants American Romy Windsor (*The Howling IV*), to help him carry on the Usher line, so he drugs her, rapes her, and marries her (in slow motion), surrounded by severed body parts. A butler (who resembles Timothy Leary) ties up a naked man and puts a hungry rat on his dick. When the castle crumbles you can see the wires as obvious doubles for Reed and Pleasence fight. Towers and Birkinshaw made their version of *The Masque of the Red Death* around the same time.

HOUSE OF WOMEN

(1961) **D:** Walter Doniger **D/S:** Crane Wilbur **P:** Bryan Foy

Shirley Knight is a pregnant woman sent to prison, in this unofficial remake of the famous *Caged* (1950). Andrew Duggan is the sadistic warden. With Constance Ford, Jeanne Cooper, Barbara Nichols as stripper Candy Kane, Virginia Gregg, and Jason Evers as a doctor. Wilbur codirected (uncredited). It's from Warner Brothers.

THE HOUSE ON BARE MOUNTAIN

(SW, 1962) **D:** R. L. Frost **S:** Denver Scott **P/A:** Bob Cresse

Granny Good (Cresse in old-lady drag, imitating Jonathan Winters) narrates this color "adult" comedy (about an hour long) set in a girls' school. A giant wolf man (with makeup by Harry Thomas) runs a still in the basement, and people dressed as

Dracula and the Frankenstein monster spike the punch at a costume party. There are a few laughs and plenty of topless or naked women. They undress, shower, sunbathe, exercise, and run up and down stairs one by one. I like the opening collage set to rock music, the trailer at the end, and the fact that the whole cast gets drunk. As far as nudie horror movies go, this rates after *Orgy of the Dead* and *Kiss Me Quick*, but it was first. It's a Frank Henenlotter Sexy Shocker release.

THE HOUSE ON SORORITY ROW

(UAV, 1982) **D/S/P:** Mark Rosman **P:** John G. Clark   (*House of Evil*)

A girl has a mutant baby. Then, 20 years later, she opens a sorority house and (surprise) there's a

slasher in the attic! Lots of poles and other things go through victims. With Eileen Davidson, Harley Jane Kozak, and Kate McNeil. The director worked with De Palma. Richard Band wrote the score.

THE HOUSE ON STRAW HILL

(New World, 1975) **D/S:** James Kenneth Clarke **P:** Brian Smedley-Aston   UK (*Trauma; Exposé*)

If you liked blond starlet Linda Hayden in *The Blood on Satan's Claw, Taste the Blood of Dracula,* or other movies, this is her ultimate starring role. It's an erotic horror/mystery with Udu Kier (fresh from his Morrissey Dracula and Frankenstein movies) as Paul Martin, a rich, stuffy, emotionless writer with a nice country house (and a great red typewriter). He occasionally freaks out while having bloody flashbacks (and flashforwards) and wears rubber gloves during sex. Hayden arrives as a typist for his new sex novel and spends a lot of time masturbating (in her room, in a field). She has a lesbian scene with Martin's visiting girlfriend (Fiona Richmond), kills the housekeeper, and blows away two rapists with a shotgun. The blood is unconvincing, and after a violent thunderstorm everything is suddenly sunny and dry, but the ending is a surprise, and the video print is excellent. Smedley-Aston produced *Vampyres* (1974), also with lots of nudity and blood. This was originally 117 minutes.

HOUSE ON THE EDGE OF THE PARK

(Vestron, 1979) **D:** "Roger D. Franklin"/Ruggiero Deodato **S:** Gianfranco Clerici, Vincenzo Mannino Italy (*La Casa Sperduta nel Parco*)

This is one sick movie. Psycho mechanics (David Hess from *Last House on the Left*, and John Morghen) go to a fancy party. Some of the rich people make fun of them, so they terrorize everyone (with rape, pissing, castration). Anne Belle costars.

THE HOUSE ON TOMBSTONE HILL

(AIP, 1987) **D/S/P:** James Riffel **P:** Melisse Lewis (*The Dead Come Home; Dead Dudes in the House*)

Young people trapped in an isolated old house are attacked by a laughing-old-woman ghost (Douglas E. Gibson) with scissors. Some of them become zombies. There's also a little-girl ghost and a whistling zombie. A hand is cut off, and one guy is cut in half. Ed French did the FX. This creepy 16mm *Evil Dead*–inspired Troma release was shot in Cherry Valley, New York, by a 28-year-old NYU graduate.

HOUSE PARTY

(RCA, 1990) **D/S:** Reginald Hudlin
P: Warrington Hudlin

Rappers Kid (Christopher Reid) 'n' Play (Christopher Martin) star in their first movie. Kid (who has *Eraserhead* hair) tries to attend Play's all-night party and has problems with Full Force as bad guys, the late Robin Harris as his father, dogs, and cops. The cast includes Tisha Campbell, Martin Lawrence, and George Clinton. Motown released the soundtrack. New Line made millions on this low-budget hit, so two lesser sequels and a Saturday-morning cartoon series followed. Kid 'n' Play also starred in *Class Act* (1992).

THE HOUSE THAT BLED TO DEATH

(Thriller, 1980) **D:** Tom Clegg **S:** David Lloyd UK

Elvira hosts this hour-long Hammer TV movie. Nicholas Ball and Rachel Davies star.

THE HOUSE THAT CRIED MURDER

(Creature Features, 1973) **D/S:** Jean-Marie Pelissie **S/P:** John Grissmer (*The Bride*)

The bride (soap opera star Robin Strasser) runs away after a violent fight with her cheating new husband (Arthur Roberts) during their elaborate wedding. He and his live-in girlfriend have nightmares. She sees a skull with a wedding dress and discovers a chicken head in bed. John Beal (star of *The Vampire*) has a good role as the bride's father. The disorienting, multi-surprise ending involves an axe and ghosts and the soundtrack features loud guitar blasts. It's a pretty interesting obscurity. Grissmer also made *Scalpel* (1977).

THE HOUSE WHERE DEATH LIVES

(1980) **D/P:** Alan Beattie **S:** Jack Viertel
P: Peter Shanaberg (*Delusion*)

A nurse (red-haired Patricia Pearcy) goes to a house to care for a crippled old man named Ivar (Joseph Cotten, in his last role). People are killed by being smashed in the head with table legs. It's all told in flashback. Simone Griffeth is also in the cast.

HOUSEWIFE

(New World, 1972) **D/S/P:** Larry Cohen
(*Bone; Dial Rat for Terror; Beverly Hills Nightmare*)

Cohen's first movie is a talk-filled black comedy. It was fraudulently promoted as an action-and-sex movie by Jack Harris. Yaphet Kotto is a thief who invades the Beverly Hills home of a white couple who are unhappily married and in debt. He holds the wife (Joyce Van Patten) hostage while the husband (Andrew Duggan) goes to the bank for money, but the husband has sex with a hippie (Jeannie Berlin) instead. Cohen (who made this in his own house) directed *Black Caesar* next. Rick Baker did the FX for both.

HOUSEWIFE FROM HELL

(Triboro, 1993) **D/S/P/M:** James Lane
D/S/P/E: Donald Jones

This "erotic comedy" is a like a cheap 60s nudie movie. If it had been made in the 60s I'd be impressed. A man (Gregg Bullock, who narrates) kills his wife (Lisa Comshaw) by throwing a hair dryer in the tub and immediately has sex with a neighbor. Then he has a series of sexual encounters with some pretty good-looking women. The wife, now a ghost, watches and a police detective (Ron Jeremy, imitating Peter Falk in *Columbo*) keeps showing up. Strippers with chainsaws say, "Time to die," some serious silicone strippers dance at a pool party, and it all ends in Heaven. With Marcia Gray, Jacqueline St. Clare, and Jennifer Peace (aka porno star Devon Shire), a girlfriend of O. J. Simpson. From Crown International.

HOWARD THE DUCK

(MCA, 1986) **D/S:** Willard Huyck
S/P: Gloria Katz

One of the most hated films of the 80s was based on a short-lived (1976–79) cult Marvel comic book set in Cleveland. It was obviously made in LA and suffers from long, boring chase scenes. Howard, who lives in a parallel world, finds himself in Cleveland, where he stays with Lea Thompson, who has a rock band called the Cherry Bombs. The reactions to the duck man are inconsistent. Some laugh, some scream, some think he's a short person, and others attack him. Jeffrey Jones is a doctor possessed by "the Dark Overlords." Fireballs form in his eyes, a snake emerges from his mouth, and he beams down a scary, giant animated scorpion/lobster monster. The ILM FX in these sequences are great. Howard works in a sex club and also encounters punk rockers and bikers. The cast includes Holly Robinson, Tim Robbins, and eight people credited as Howard. Thomas Dolby is on the MCA soundtrack. It was a major flop from executive producer George Lucas.

HOW I WON THE WAR

(MGM, 1967) **D/P:** Richard Lester
S: Charles Wood UK

Michael Crawford stars and narrates as Goodbody, an inept British officer who survives while all his men are killed off in North Africa during WWII. John Lennon (in his first and only solo acting role) costars as Gripweed, a Cockney soldier who once belonged to the British Union of Fascists. This antiwar satire uses real tinted newsreel footage and manages to refer to Vietnam. Dead soldiers return as different-colored ghosts and continue to fight. The accents are too thick for most Americans to understand, and even Lennon couldn't bring many people into the theaters. The cast includes Roy Kinnear, Jack MacGowran, Ronald Lacey, Alexander Knox, and Michael Hordern. It was released by United Artists.

HOWLING II: YOUR SISTER IS A WEREWOLF

(HBO, 1984) **D:** Philippe Mora **S:** Robert Sarno, Gary Brandner **P:** Steven Lane

This was the first of a series of inferior "sequels" to the 1981 hit. They all were based on novels by Gary Brandner and were made in different countries (this was filmed in Czechoslovakia). Christopher Lee stars as an occult investigator helping a cop (Reb Brown) investigate his sister's death. Sybil Danning is Stirba, the wolf queen (her topless scene is repeated many times). The cast includes Marsha A. Hunt (who had a baby with Mick Jagger in real life), Annie McEnroe, Ferdinand Mayne, midgets, and a punk group called Babel. The cable and syndicated TV versions are different from the video. Steve Johnson did the FX. The Steve Parsons score is on Filmtrax. The original Joe Dante movie is available too, of course (from Nelson).

HOWLING III: THE MARSUPIALS

(Vista, 1987) **D/S/P:** Philippe Mora
P: Charles Waterstreet Australia

Sympathetic werewolves live in a commune. An outcast wolf woman (Imogen Annesley) goes to Sydney and lands a job in a horror movie (*Shape-Shifters, Part 8*). Werewolves dressed as nuns come after her. With Barry Otto as a professor and Michael Pate. It's different. Steve Johnson did the FX.

HOWLING IV: THE ORIGINAL NIGHTMARE

(IVE, 1988) **D:** John Hough **S:** Clive Trevor, Freddie Rowles **P:** Harry Alan Towers S.Africa

Romy Windsor as a bestselling novelist has disturbing visions. She goes on vacation in California and encounters a female werewolf (Lamya Derval). Susanne Severeid, Michael T. Weiss, and Antony Hamilton are also in the cast. There's too much talking. Steve Johnson did the FX.

HOWLING V: THE REBIRTH
(IVE, 1989) **D:** Neil Sundstrom
S: Freddie Rose **S/P:** Clive Turner

A count summons eight people to his castle in Budapest. The plot is just like the plot of *The Beast Must Die*, which was another ripoff of *Ten Little Indians*. Philip Davis, Elisabeth Shue, and Mary Stavin are in the cast. It was filmed in Hungary.

HOWLING VI: THE FREAKS
(IVE, 1991) **D:** Hope Perello
S: Kevin Rock **P:** Robert Pringle

Brendan Hughes (*To Die For*) is a nice young British (?) drifter/werewolf who's staying with a preacher in a small town. Harker (Bruce Martyn Payne), who owns a traveling freak show, is really an evil, demon-faced vampire. Antonio Fargas plays a mean clown/geek, and there's an alligator boy, an East Indian dwarf with three arms, and a half-man, half-woman. Carol Lynley has a bit part. The werewolf transformations (the FX are by Steve Johnson) are long and painful. *The Howling: New Moon Rising* followed.

HOWL OF THE DEVIL
(Video Search, 1988) **D/S/A:** "Jacinto Molino"/ Paul Naschy **S:** Salvador Sainz (uncredited) Spain (*El Aullido del Diablo*)

Alex (Paul Naschy), a rich, reclusive horror star, died (a suicide) in 1981. His lonely son (Naschy's son, Sergio) now lives with Hector, Alex's nasty twin, an unsuccessful actor (Naschy), a servant, Eric (Howard Vernon), and a cook, Carmen (Caroline Munro, but sometimes a double). Hector dresses up as Rasputin, Fu Manchu, or Bluebeard and fools around with hookers, who are later found dead. The son watches his father's movies on TV, and various characters show up in real life. A friendly Frankenstein monster, Mr. Hyde, the Wolf Man, Quasimodo, and the Phantom (all Naschy) appear. Meanwhile, Hector and a local priest lust after Carmen. This nutty Naschy-overkill movie has nudity, some gore, a zombie, and the Devil himself! As Eric says, "He was a great actor!" The print (from Spanish TV) has been subtitled in English.

HOW TO GET AHEAD IN ADVERTISING
(1988) **D/S:** Bruce Robinson **P:** George Harrison, Dennis O'Brien   UK

Richard E. Grant stars as an ad man working on a campaign for pimple cream. He gets a boil on his neck, which develops (*Manster*-like) into an entire head that talks and starts taking over. This satire also stars Rachel Ward and Richard Wilson. Robinson later made *Jennifer 8* in the US.

HOW TO GET REVENGE
(Starmaster, 1989) **D:** Bob Logan

Hostess Linda Blair interviews real "top professionals in the revenge field" (cops and detectives),

who tell us how to harass people on the phone and through the mail, and even how to wreck somebody's marriage. They explain things like putting sugar in gas tanks, running a hose through a mail slot, and putting a man's name into gay ads. Another helpful tip is to report members of minorities to the immigration authorities. Linda makes wisecracks and quotes the Bible. A warning says that this 45-minute $10 video is "for entertainment purposes only!" I think enough people know how to do those things already. It's by the director of *Up Your Alley* and *Repossessed*, both with Blair.

HOW TO MAKE A DOLL
(SW, 1968) **D/S/P:** Herschell Gordon Lewis
S: Bert Ray

This was made primarily in a Miami theater and seems like a bad, overlong, talk-filled local-TV comedy skit. It's pretty unwatchable. After a serious voice-over intro, we meet Dr. Percy Corly (Robert Wood), a virgin sex-education teacher who lives with his mom, and a professor with a supercomputer that laughs and snorts. The professor makes a rabbit appear, then accidentally creates a gay man. After some more work he makes a blonde in a bikini and high heels: "I—am—programmed—to—love—only—Dr.—Corly." The professor also makes another woman for himself. He and the women disappear, and the computer talks with his voice. Corly puts on a hair-dryer dream machine (kinda like in *Total Recall*) and imagines being a playboy surrounded by bikini babes at the beach. Then zombie-like women say, "Per—cy—we—love—you" before vanishing. He falls for a shy egghead wearing glasses, and she turns into the first blonde, now with bunny ears. With Brad Grinter.

HOW TO SUCCEED WITH GIRLS
(SW, 1964) **D:** Edward A. Biery
S/P: William Norton **P/A:** Paul Leder

A narrator contrasts Pete, an asshole poet (Paul Leder), to Harvey, a timid daydreamer. Color dream sequences (the rest is b/w) are set in a mad lab (with monster masks) and a harem. The acting is awful, there's no nudity, and the silent-movie-style gags aren't funny. There is an "Ahab the A-rab" in-joke, though. With Marissa Mathes (*Blood Bath*), Rue McClanahan (also in Leder's *Five Minutes to Love*), and Cathy Crowfoot. Beach Dickerson was the production manager. Norton later wrote *I Dismember Mama* for Leder. He also wrote John Wayne and Burt Reynolds movies!

HUDSON HAWK
(RCA, 1991) **D:** Michael Lehman
S: Steven E. de Souza **P:** Joel Silver

Critics compared this much-hated, overexpensive parody to *Heaven's Gate*, even *Howard the Duck*. It's a buddy/musical-comedy/action/fantasy movie with Bruce Willis as a cat burglar and Danny Aiello as his partner. They both sing, which is the main problem. Sandra Bernhard and Richard E. Grant blackmail Willis and make him steal priceless Da Vinci artifacts in Italy in order to rebuild an alchemy machine and turn water into gold (impressive ILM FX are used). The Vatican seems like a pretty evil place in this movie. With Andie Mac-

Dowell as a nun, James Coburn, David Caruso, and Frank Stallone. William Conrad narrates. De Souza also wrote the *Die Hard* movies. The score is by Michael Kamen.

HUGHES AND HARLOW: ANGELS IN HELL
(Monterey, 1977) **D/S/P:** Larry Buchanan
S: Lynn Schubert

Howard Hughes (Victor Holchak) comes to Hollywood from Texas and meets Jean Harlow (Lindsay Bloom), a taxi dancer, on the set of a Laurel and Hardy short. They swear a lot, call each other a lot of nicknames, and have sex in a plane. A lot of this movie (told in flashbacks) consists of film screenings, old footage, and b/w re-creations of flying scenes. It's not as interesting as Buchanan's bios of Monroe and some rock stars. Adam Roarke is Howard Hawks, and the late Royal Dano is Will Hays.

HUGH HEFNER: ONCE UPON A TIME
(Uni, 1992) **D/S/P:** Robert Heath
S/P: Gary H. Grossman **S:** Michael Gross

Hefner (raised as a Methodist in Chicago) cooperated in the making of this documentary about his life and *Playboy* magazine. This is not a movie with Playmates. It shows scenes from *Return of the Dead*, a horror movie Hefner made and starred in at 16, and the original *Flash Gordon* serial, which he says was an early influence. It explores his onetime Dexedrene problem, the suicide of his longtime secretary, the Dorothy Stratten murder, the making of Polanski's *Macbeth*, the fall of the Playboy clubs, and Hefner's claims of being set up and persecuted by the government. James Coburn narrates. The executive producers of this IRS release were Mark Frost and David Lynch.

HUMAN BEASTS
(All Seasons, 1980) **D/S/P/A:** Paul Naschy
Spain/Japan (*El Carnaval de las Bestias*)

In Naschy's first Japanese film, he plays Bruno, a mercenary fighter. In Japan he double-crosses his lover (Eiko Nagashima) for some jewels, then kills her gangster brother and all of his henchmen. Back in Spain the wounded killer hides out in a home where two beautiful daughters fight over him. He has sex with both of them while their father whips the black maid (she likes it). Meanwhile, Eiko hires local crooks to spy on him. This crazed film has flashbacks, dream sequences, a ghost, religious (and fart) humor, nudity, drugs, S&M, slaughtered pigs, Italian-western music, big guns, cannibalism, and Naschy dressed as Napoleon.

HUMAN GORILLA
(Rhino, 1948) **D:** Budd Boetticher **S/P:** Eugene Ling **S:** Malvin Wald   (*Behind Locked Doors*)

Richard Carlson stars as a private eye who has himself committed to a private sanitarium to investigate a crooked judge. This is considered a *film noir* mystery, not a horror movie. In one scene, though, the hero is thrown into a padded cell with a crazed wrestler (Tor Johnson!). Lucille Bremer (in her last film) is a newspaperwoman, and Douglas Fowley is a sadistic guard. Made by Eagle Lion, a "Poverty Row" studio. The retitled Rhino tape also includes *Man Beast* (1956).

HUMAN HIGHWAY

(Warner, 1982) **D/S/A:** Dean Stockwell
D/A: "Bernard Shakey"/Neil Young **P:** L. A. Johnson

Neil Young and Russ Tamblyn are Lionel and Fred, a comic team of likable idiots working at a gas station near a nuclear plant during some indefinite 50s/60s time period. Their new boss (Stockwell) also owns the truck-stop restaurant next door where Dennis Hopper is the cook, and Sally Kirkland and Charlotte Stewart are waitresses. Devo appear in glowing red suits, singing while they haul radioactive material. In the most incredible part, Lionel has a dream (within a dream) that he's a famous rock star, "Frank Fontaine," on tour. Neil/Lionel/Frank and Devo do "Hey Hey My My" (!), and Devo do "Come Back, Jonee." At the end the whole cast sings "It Takes a Worried Man" (this was also a video), then climb stairs to Heaven (Stockwell is God) as the Earth blows up. Only Boojie Boy (Mark Mothersbaugh) is left to sing "Blowin' in the Wind"! A strange version of "Mr. Soul" and Skeeter Davis are also heard. Obvious models of reactors and trains are featured (*Reactor* and *Trains* were Young's latest LPs). This would make a great double bill with *Head*.

HUMANOIDS FROM ATLANTIS

(Tempe, 1992) **D/P/A/E:** J. R. Bookwalter
S: Lloyd Turner

This made-in-small-town-Ohio spoof goes out of its way to resemble one of the Larry Buchanan AIP-TV movies and is overloaded with self-promoting in-jokes and references. A would-be filmmaker (James L. Edwards) and his girlfriend find a man-in-a-suit sea monster. Although it seems even cheaper than Bookwalter's "serious" shot-on-video

releases, the characters are likeable and I actually sorta enjoyed watching it. David DeCoteau was the executive producer.

THE HUMAN SHIELD

(Cannon, 1992) **D:** Ted Post **S:** Mann Rubin
P: Christopher Pearce, Elie Cohn

Michael Dudikoff stars as a former US Marine who helped train Iraqi soldiers to fight Iran. Now with the CIA, the Ramboesque kickboxer hero returns to Iraq after the Gulf War to rescue his diabetic brother (Tommy Hinkley) from a Nazi-like general (Steve Inwood) who resembles Saddam Hussein. Hana Azulay-Hasfari is the love interest. This Cannon release was filmed in Israel.

HUMAN TARGET

(1992) **D:** Max Tash **S:** Danny Bislon,
Paul De Meo **P:** Michael O. Gallant

In this ABC-TV series pilot Rick Springfield stars as the DC Comics hero Christopher Chance, a Nam vet in a plane with a team of helpers. He takes on the identities of people in danger. Scott Paulin costars. The series aired on Saturday mornings.

THE HUMAN TORNADO

(Xenon, 1976) **D:** Cliff Roquemore
S/A: Jerry Jones   (*Dolemite II*)

Dolemite (Rudy Ray Moore) does his comedy act onstage. Then the plot begins. When he's caught in bed with the wife of a redneck Alabama sheriff, he jumps out of the window and rolls down a hill naked. Later he and nightclub owner Queen Bee (Lady Reed) fight white gangsters who run a massage parlor in California by training hookers to be karate fighters. The gangsters kidnap women and have an old lady in a basement who torments them with snakes, rats, hand grenades, and spikes over their heads. A gangster's mistress has a sex-dream sequence with naked musclemen going down a

playground slide. There are also musical numbers, car chases, and speeded-up fight scenes. The cast includes Jimmy Lynch as Mr. Motion, Ernie Hudson (*Ghostbusters*), and drag queen Lord Java. Moore was also the executive producer of this cartoonish Dimension release.

HUNCHBACK = THE HUNCHBACK OF NOTRE DAME

THE HUNCHBACK OF NOTRE DAME

(Republic, Vestron, Sinister, 1923) **D:** Wallace
Worsley **S:** Perely Poore Sheehan

Lon Chaney stars in one of his greatest roles, as Quasimodo, a bell-ringer in 15th-century Paris. Universal spent over a million dollars filming this adaptation of Victor Hugo's novel, and the role made Chaney a real star (after ten years of film acting). Patsy Ruth Miller costars as Esmeralda, with Brandon Hurst as the villain, Norman Kerry as the hero, Raymond Hatton, Ernest Torrence, Tully Marshall, Nigel De Brulier, and Joe Bonomo (stunts). William Wyler was one of the assistant directors. The 94-minute tape includes a musical score. The Republic video version is tinted. The first remakes include the wonderful RKO version, with Charles Laughton (1939), now colorized on tape (Turner), the mostly forgotten French version, with Anthony Quinn (1959), and the British TV version, with Anthony Hopkins (1982).

HUNDRA

(Media, 1983) **D/S/P:** "Matteo Ottaviano"/Matt
Cimber **M:** Ennio Morricone   US/Spain

After two Pia Zadora movies Cimber made two Laureen Landon movies. Here she stars as the blond survivor of a raid by evil Vikings. It has nudity and decapitations. The score was issued by Macola. Landon was Christian Brando's girlfriend for many years. Film Ventures released this. Cimber made it in Spain, back to back with *Yellow Hair and the Fortress of Gold*.

THE HUNGER

(MGM, 1983) **D:** Tony Scott **S:** Ivan Davis,
Michael Thomas **P:** Richard A. Shepard

Catherine Deneuve and David Bowie play ageless vampires in New York City. She keeps her dead lovers in the attic, and he's ill after 300 years and aging fast. It's based on a novel by Whitley Strieber. Susan Sarandon costars as the scientist they make help them, and she has a love scene with Deneuve. With Cliff De Young, Ann Magnuson, Dan Hedaya, Bessie Love, John Pankow, Beth Ehlers, and Willem Dafoe (in a phone booth). Bauhaus perform "Bela Lugosi's Dead" in a disco. The FX are by Dick Smith and Carl Fullerton. Varèse Sarabande released the score by Michel Rubini and Denny Jaeger. Scott was known as a director of Pepsi commercials at the time.

HUNK

(RCA, 1987) **D/S:** Lawrence Bassoff **P:** Marilyn Tenser

A computer nerd (John Allen Nelson) gets a new body from the Devil/Mr. D (James Coco). Robert Morse, Deborah Shelton, and Avery Schreiber are also in this Crown International comedy.

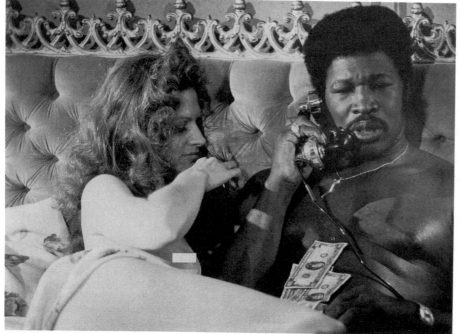

Rudy Ray Moore stars in *The Human Tornado*.

THE HUNTED

(MCA, 1995) **D/S:** J. F. Lawton
P: John Davis, Gary W. Goldstein

Christopher Lambert (*Highlander*) is an American businessman in Japan who must become a modern warrior when he becomes the prime target of a group of ninja assassins led by John Lone. Many people die while a centuries-old feud continues. Joan Chen is the love interest who dies early but shows up in flashbacks, Yoshido Harada is a samurai, and Yoko Shimada (from *Shogun*) is his wife. Director Lawton also wrote *Under Siege*. The Universal release was shot in Vancouver.

HUNTER'S BLOOD

(Embassy, 1987) **D:** Robert C. Hughes
S: Emmett Alston **P:** Myrl A. Schriebman

Deer hunters from the city (including Sam Bottoms, Clu Gulager, Joey Travolta, and Ken Swofford) go to the Arkansas woods. Crazed cannibal hillbilly poachers named Bubba, Snake, and Woody attack. Characters are decapitated and gutted and have their heads blown off. Billy Drago and Bruce Glover are the main redneck psychos. Also with Kim Delaney. Concorde/Corman released this obvious *Deliverance* copy, and it was on tape days after playing in theaters.

HUNTERS OF THE GOLDEN COBRA

(Vestron, 1982) **D:** "Anthony M. Dawson"/
Antonio Margheriti **S:** Tito Carpi **P:** Gianfranco
Couyoumdjian Italy (*I Cacciatori del Cobra d'Oro;
Raiders of the Golden Cobra*)

This WWII jungle adventure with evil Japanese, snakes, and a white jungle queen was made in the Philippines. David Warbeck stars, with John Steiner and Alan Collins. The same cast was also in *Ark of the Sun God*, by the the same director.

THE HUNT FOR RED OCTOBER

(Paramount, 1990) **D:** John McTiernan **S:** Larry
Ferguson, Donald Stewart **P:** Mace Neufeld

Alec Baldwin stars as former CIA man Jack Ryan in this pre-*glasnost* thriller based on the novel by Tom Clancy. Sean Connery is a Soviet submarine commander, and Scott Glenn is a US captain. With Sam Neill, Richard Jordan, James Earl Jones, Joss Ackland, Peter Firth, Tim Curry, future Tennessee Senator Fred Thompson, and Jeffrey Jones. ILM provided the FX. It's by the director of *Predator* and *Die Hard*. This was a big hit. *Patriot Games* (1992) and *Clear and Present Danger* (1994) were follow-ups starring Harrison Ford as Ryan.

THE HUNTING PARTY

(1971) **D:** Don Medford **S:** Gilbert Alexander,
William Norton **S/P:** Lou Morheim

A sadistic 19th-century Texas cattle baron (Gene Hackman) takes a hunting trip on his private train (with a bordello car). Outlaw Oliver Reed kidnaps his schoolteacher wife (Candice Bergen) because he wants to learn to read. She's raped (this was just after she starred in *Soldier Blue*), and the hunters go after Reed and his gang. This violent, hateful

Peckinpah ripoff features L. Q. Jones, Simon Oakland, G. D. Spradlin, and Mitchell Ryan. The UA release was filmed in Spain.

LAS HURDES

(1932) **D/S/E:** Luis Buñuel **S:** Pierre Unik **P:** Ramón
Acín   Spain (*Terre sans Pain; Land Without Bread*)

People suffer from hunger, disease, poverty, and superstition. The Catholic Church asks them for money. Disturbing images are shown while a matter-of-fact narration and Brahms' music are heard on the soundtrack. This 27-minute documentary about the poorest region in Spain was banned by the Spanish government. Buñuel dubbed American films in France and Spain; was the executive producer of four Spanish films; contributed to a documentary in Spain and one in France; went to America, where he worked for the Film Department of the Museum of Modern Art and then supervised foreign versions of Warner Brothers films; and in 1947 went to Mexico, where he began directing films again.

HURRICANE

(1937) **D:** John Ford **S:** Dudley Nichols, Oliver H. P.
Garrett **P:** Samuel Goldwyn **M:** Alfred Newman

Dorothy Lamour (in her sarong) and Jon Hall are Polynesian lovers separated when she's jailed for hitting a white man. Raymond Massey is the cruel governor, Mary Astor is his wife, John Carradine is a sadistic guard, and Thomas Mitchell is a drunken doctor (he was nominated for an Oscar). With C. Aubrey Smith and Jerome Cowan. It all ends with a spectacular typhoon. Stuart Heisler was the second-unit director. This UA hit was remade in 1979.

HURRICANE

(Paramount, 1979) **D:** Jan Troell **S:** Lorenzo
Temple Jr. **P:** Dino De Laurentiis

Roman Polanski was set to direct this absurd, big-flop remake of the 1937 movie, until he was charged with rape. Mia Farrow (after the flop *Avalanche*) and Dayton Kane star. With Jason Robards as her military father, Max von Sydow, Trevor Howard as a priest, Timothy Bottoms, and James Keach. Sven Nykvist was the cinematographer. Elektra released the Nino Rota soundtrack.

HURRICANE SMITH

(Warner, 1990) **D:** Colin Budds **S:** Peter
Klinoch **P:** Stanley O'Toole   Australia

Carl Weathers is a Texas tough guy looking for his missing sister on the Australian coast. With Jürgen Prochnow as a gangster dealing in drugs and women, Cassandra Delaney, and Tony Bonner.

THE HUSTLER OF MUSCLE BEACH

(1980) **D:** Jonathan Kaplan **S:** David S.
Milow **P:** Neil T. Maffeo

Richard Hatch stars as a promoter in this ABC-TV movie about bodybuilding in Venice, California. Kay Lenz costars, and the cast includes Jeannette Nolan, Kenneth McMillan, Jack Carter, Paul Bar-

tel, Bobby Van, Kames Hong, and bodybuilders Franco Columbo, Lisa Lyons (subject of the Robert Mapplethorpe photo book *Lady*), and others who went on to acting careers.

HYDRA = BLOOD WATERS OF DR. Z

HYPER SAPIEN: PEOPLE FROM ANOTHER STAR

(Warner, 1985) **D:** Peter Hunt **S:** Christopher
Adcock, Christopher Blue, Marnie Page
P: Jack Schwartzman, Ariel Levy   Canada

Three "cute," hairy aliens with three eyes and three legs appear in Wyoming. Ricky Paull Goldin stars as a farm boy called Dirt, with Keenan Wynn (in his last role), Gail Strickland, Sydney Penny, Peter Jason, Talia Shire, and Army Archerd. It's from Shire's production company, Taliafilm (she did *Rad* next), is PG, and was originally to be directed by Michael Wadleigh (*Wolfen*).

HYSTERICAL

(Magnum, 1982) **D:** Chris Bearde **S/A:** William and
Mark Hudson **S:** Trace Johnson **P:** Gene Levy

The Hudson brothers, William, Mark, and Brett (who borrow from the Three Stooges), are not funny, but they starred in this PG horror comedy anyway. It spoofs *The Shining, Jaws, The Exorcist, Taxi Driver . . .* and (badly) copies a zombie scene from *Carnival of Souls*. Richard Kiel is a 19th-century lighthouse keeper who was killed by his mistress (Julie Newmar). Murray Hamilton and Clint Walker become singing, dancing zombies. Also with Cindy Pickett, Bud Cort, Franklyn Ajaye, Keenan Wynn, Gary Owens, John Larroquette, Natalie Cole, Paul "Mousie" Gardner, and Charlie Callas as Dracula. It debuted on HBO in 1985. The brothers (from Portland) briefly had their own TV show and had some minor 70s hits as singers.

I ACCUSE MY PARENTS

(Loonic, Sinister, 1944) **D:** Sam Newfield **S:** Harry Fraser **P:** Max Alexander

A young man goes to work for a gangster to impress his nightclub-singer girlfriend. This early PRC jd movie opens with his trial for murder, where he says the film's title. The rest is a disappointing flashback. With Mary Beth Hughes, Robert Lowell, and John Miljan.

I AM A GROUPIE

(1970) **D/S:** Derek Ford **P:** Stanley Long, Barry Jacobs   UK

Trans America (a branch of AIP) released this R-rated story of a groupie named Sally (Esme Long) on the road with a group called the Orange Butterfly. After a van crash causes the lead singer's death she moves on to another group, Sweaty Betty. In a scene copied from the Rolling Stones' Redlands bust she's caught (naked) in a drug raid at their country estate. Eventually she leaves the wild bands for a folk singer who "genuinely cares."

I AM LEGEND

(SW, 1994)

John Zacherle introduces a compilation of things with the long-bearded Johnny Legend. He's seen on various TV programs, including the British *Beyond the Groove* and *The Dr. Shock Show* (the horror host seems like another imitation of Ghoulardi), and in films (*Bride of Re-Animator* and *Severed Ties*). He plays rock music live (and with the Legendary Stardust Cowboy), and appears with wrestlers and with Timothy Carey and Pia Zadora. Musical highlights are "Pencil Neck Geek" and the theme from *2000 Maniacs*. Parts of this feature were previously on a tape called *Mondo Legend* (1991).

I BOUGHT A VAMPIRE MOTORCYCLE

(1991) **D:** Dirk Campbell **S/P:** Mycal Miller, John Wolskel   UK

In this horror comedy, Neal Morrissey buys a possessed cycle in Birmingham. It runs on blood and decapitates people. With Amanda Noar, Anthony Daniels, and Burt Kwouk (spoofing his character from the *Pink Panther* series).

ICE

(PM, 1994) **D:** Brook Yeaton **S:** Sean Dash **P:** Joseph Merhi, Richard Pepin

Traci Lords and Phillip Troy are married thieves out to steal diamonds from a mobster (Jorge Rivero) for an insurance company. When the husband is killed the wife seeks revenge. Zach Galligan plays her double-crossing brother. There's a gunfight during a hockey game, and lots of shooting and explosions, but this is a very bad movie. Yeaton is married to Lords, who sings (with a dubbed-in voice) and fights, but doesn't even take her clothes off in the shower.

THE ICEBOX MURDERS

(Mogul, 1981) **D:** Francis R. Gordillo **S:** F. Ariza, F. Próspero   Spain (*El Cepo*)

Jack Taylor is a strange doctor in a mansion near Paris. Two women arrive, decapitatation murders occur on a boat, and everybody talks too much.

ICE CREAM MAN

(A Pix, 1994) **D/P:** Norman Apstein **S:** David Dobkin

Geeky looking Clint Howard is the wisecracking childlike psycho killer ice cream truck man. He does cartoonish things like putting a decapitated head on a giant cone. The amusing, hard-working all-star cast includes Jan-Michael Vincent as a cop, David Naughton, David Warner, Olivia Hussey, Sandahl Bergman, Lee Majors III, and Steve Garvey. It was the first starring role for Howard since *Evilspeak* (1982).

ICED

(Prism, 1987) **D:** Jeff Kwitny **S:** Joseph Alan Johnson **P:** Robert Seibert   (*Blizzard of Blood*)

Lisa Loring (grown-up little Wednesday from the TV series *The Addams Family*) gets naked in this horror movie by the director of *Beyond the Door III*. She's also electrocuted in a hot tub. A psycho at a ski resort kills people he holds responsible for a ski-accident death. It was made in Utah. Loring was also in *Blood Frenzy*.

ICEMAN

(MCA, 1984) **D:** Fred Schepisi **S:** Chip Proser, John Dimmer **P:** Patrick Palmer, Norman Jewison

John Lone (star of *The Last Emperor*) is a 40,000-year-old Neanderthal man called Charlie by the scientists who study him. He's kept in an artificial jungle in the Arctic and sings Neil Young's "Heart of Gold." Some of the scientists want to kill him. Lindsay Crouse and Timothy Hutton costar, with Danny Glover, Josef Sommer, and David Strathairn. The soundtrack is on Southern Cross.

THE ICEMAN COMETH

(1989) **D:** Clarence Fok Yiu Leung **S:** Stephen Shiu **P:** Johnny Mack   Hong Kong

Yuen Biao is Ching, a Ming-dynasty guard who's after a killer/rapist (Yeun Wah). Both are frozen (thanks to a statue of Buddha), then discovered 300 years later and taken to modern-day Hong Kong. Maggie Cheung is a prostitute kidnapped by the killer. This action fantasy uses ideas from *Time After Time* and *Highlander*.

THE ICE PIRATES

(MGM, 1984) **D/S:** Stewart Raffill **S:** Stanford Sherman **P:** John Foreman

TV star Robert Urich is the antihero in a *Star Wars* spoof about buccaneer spacemen with swords who are after giant ice cubes. Mary Crosby is a blackmailing princess, and Anjelica Huston (with a metallic bra) is the evil Maida. With John Matuszak, Ron Perlman, and John Carradine as the Supreme Commander. Raffill had directed G-rated family films. At least this was made before Mel Brooks' *Spaceballs*.

ICE STATION ZEBRA

(MGM, 1968) **D:** John Sturges **S:** Douglas Heyes **P:** Martin Ransohoff, John Calley

Rock Hudson stars as a US Navy submarine commander ordered to go to the North Pole. This Cold War thriller is about recovering a capsule from a Soviet space satellite. With Patrick McGoohan, Jim Brown, Ernest Borgnine as Boris Vaslov (a bad guy, maybe?), Tony Bill, Lloyd Nolan, and Alf Kjellin. This 152-minute MGM release, based on an Alistair MacLean novel, was shot in 70mm and was presented in Cinerama in some theaters. It was reportedly the favorite film of the reclusive billionaire Howard Hughes. MGM released the Michel Legrand soundtrack.

I COME IN PEACE

(Media, 1989) **D:** Craig R. Baxley **S:** Jonathan Tydor, Leonard Mass **P:** Jeff Young **M:** Jan Hammer   (*Dark Angel*)

Swedish muscleman, karate champ, and MIT alum Dolph Lundgren (*Rocky IV*) first got publicity as Grace Jones' boyfriend. He could have been as popular as Steven Seagal (or at least Jean-Claude Van Damme), but some of his movies were barely released to theaters. This one has a terrible title (in the US), but it's really entertaining and well made. A tall, albino alien in a duster (Matthias Hues) siphons endorphins out of humans and injects them with lethal doses of heroin, which he rips off from local gangsters. His space gun fires deadly, throat-slashing, spinning CDs (really). A dark-haired alien cop is sent to stop the scary space junkie (whose only dialogue is the title of the movie). Meanwhile, Jack Caine, a no-nonsense cop (Lundgren) with a coroner girlfriend, is put on the case, paired with a comic relief, by-the-books FBI agent (Brian Benben, star of the *Dream On* TV series). Michael J. Pollard and Jesse Vint have small but memorable roles. Former actor Mark Damon (*The House of Usher*) was one of the executive producers. Baxley (*Action Jackson*) filmed this in Houston.

I CONFESS

(Warner, 1953) **D/P:** Alfred Hitchcock **S:** George Tabori, William Archibald

Montgomery Clift is a Catholic priest who hears a confession of murder and finds himself on trial for the killing. He won't reveal the real killer and even faces a lynch mob. Anne Baxter is a woman he loved before he became a priest, Karl Malden is the prosecutor, and Brian Aherne is the defense lawyer. This b/w Warner Brothers film was based on a 1902 play by Paul Anthelme and filmed on location in Quebec. It was one of Hitchcock's least popular films but was followed by the hits *Dial M for Murder* and *Rear Window* (both 1954).

ICY DEATH: *See* DEATH DIMENSION

IDAHO TRANSFER

(MPI, 1971) **D:** Peter Fonda **S:** Thomas Mattieson **P:** Leland Hayward

The second film directed by Fonda is an ecological science-fiction story. A group of young volunteers travel to the future and backpack across a barren landscape, passing through three time zones. It was shot on location in Idaho but was barely released (Cinemation, the distributor, went bankrupt). It features only one name actor, Keith Carradine. Many ecology movies were released in 1971, including *Silent Running*, *Zero Population Growth* (from England), and *Godzilla vs. the Smog Monster* (from Japan). The video has an added (1988) intro in which Fonda talks about environmental awareness.

IDENTITY CRISIS

(Command, 1985) **D:** Bruce Pittman **S:** Peter Colley, John Shepard **P:** Anthony Kramreither   Canada (*Mark of Cain*)

A couple live in an old isolated mansion. The husband's twin escapes from an asylum. Authorities recapture the wrong twin and the wife is stuck with the killer. Robin Ward plays both men.

IDENTITY CRISIS

(Academy, 1989) **D/P:** Melvin Van Peebles **S/A:** Mario Van Peebles

A French fashion designer is poisoned, and a witch has him reincarnated as New York rap star Chilly D. Mario Van Peebles stars in this fantasy comedy featuring Ilan Mitchell-Smith and Shelly Burch. It was the end of a directing career for Van Peebles Sr., but his son went on to direct *New Jack City* and *Posse*.

I, DESIRE

(1982) **D:** John Llewellyn Moxey **S:** Robert Foster **P:** Audrey Blasdel-Goddard

David Naughton (who had just been in *An American Werewolf in London*) stars as an LA student working as a coroner's aide who meets a vampire hooker (Barbara Stock). This ABC-TV romantic horror movie features Brad Dourif and Dorian Harewood.

THE IDOLMAKER

(MGM, 1980) **D:** Taylor Hackford **S:** Edward Di Lorenzo **P:** Gene Kirkwood, Howard W. Koch **M:** Jeff Barry

This movie is based on the careers of rock promoter Bob Marcucci and his late-50s Philly singers Frankie Avalon and Fabian. Unfortunately, the songs sound too modern. Ray Sharkey stars as the Bronx songwriter turned manager who makes stars out of talentless Peter Gallagher (in his feature debut) and Paul Land. With Tovah Feldshuh as a teen-mag editor (based on Gloria Stavers), Joe Pantoliano, Maureen McCormick, John Amprea, and Olympia Dukakis. The score is on A&M. United Artists released the film. Marcucci sued.

I ESCAPED FROM DEVIL'S ISLAND

(1973) **D:** William Witney **S:** Richard L. Adams **P:** Roger Corman, Gene Corman

Jim Brown, Christopher George, Rick Ely as a gay prisoner, and James Luis as his lover escape from Devil's Island in 1918 on a raft and hide in the jungle. This attempt to cash in on *Papillon* was directed by a veteran of many serials. It features alligators, a shark attack, hostile Amazon natives, a leper colony, and lots of shooting and death. With Jan Merlin and Richard Rust. The music is by Les Baxter. This UA release was shot in the Philippines.

if...

(VSOM, 1969) **D/P:** Lindsay Anderson **S:** David Sherwin **P:** Michael Medwin   UK

Years before *Massacre at Central High*, *Class of 1984*, and others, this incredible film ends with British boarding-school boys setting fire to a lecture hall and shooting faculty members as they flee. Malcolm McDowell (the year before *A Clockwork Orange*) stars as Mick Travers. He and his friends are publicly flogged after they steal a motorcycle and enjoy some sex in town. With David Wood, Robert Swann, Christine Noonan, Arthur Lowe, Mona Washbourne, Simon Ward, and Robin Askwith. This color Paramount release was rated X (because of a tinted sex-fantasy scene), then cut for an R. Anderson's *O Lucky Man!* (1973) and *Brittania Hospital* (1982) feature McDowell as the same character.

IF LOOKS COULD KILL

(Republic, 1986) **D/S/P:** Chuck Vincent **S:** Craig Horrall

Tim Gail stars as a photographer who spies on a woman who embezzled money from a bank. This Hitchcock ripoff about voyeurs has a porno-star cast (Sheri St. Claire, Jamie Gillis, and Veronica Hart).

IF LOOKS COULD KILL

(Warner, 1991) **D:** William Dear **S:** Darren Star **P:** Craig Zadan, Neil Meron

Richard Grieco stars in this PG-13 Warner Brothers film as a high-school student on a trip to France who is mistaken for a secret agent. With Linda Hunt, Roger Rees, Gabrielle Anwar, and Roger Daltrey as a villain called Blade. The story is by Fred Dekker.

IGOR AND THE LUNATICS

(Troma, 1985) **D/S/P:** Billy Parolini **S/P:** Jocelyn Beard **S:** Tom Doran, Brendan Faulkner

A Manson-type group is released from prison and takes revenge on a town in New York State. People are cut in half, beaten, gutted, and killed with arrows and pitchforks. This Troma release (filmed in Carmel, New York) must have been left unfinished. The characters' names and the actors change (an interesting effect for bad-movie fans).

IGUANA

(Imperial, 1988) **D/S:** Monte Hellman   Switzerland

Everett McGill stars as Oberlus, an abandoned early-19th-century sailor with a deformed face who becomes king of an island in the Galapagos and declares war on mankind. He cuts off the fingers or heads of those who disobey but falls in love with Maru Valdivielso. Based on a novel by Alberto Vásquez Figueroa and filmed in the Canary Islands, it was Hellman's first film in 10 years but was seen by very few people.

I HATE YOUR GUTS!

(Independent Legend, 1962) **D/P:** Roger Corman **S:** Charles Beaumont

Here's a film that proves what Corman was capable of at one time. It was a flop when released in 1962 as *The Intruder*, was rereleased in 1966 as *Shame* (on an exploitation double bill with *Poor White Trash*), then was given another try as *I Hate Your Guts!* Charles Beaumont (known at the time for his work on *The Twilight Zone*) wrote the perceptive screenplay, based on his 1959 novel *The Intruder*, which was inspired by actual 1957 news reports of an "outside agitator." William Shatner is Adam Cramer, a devious, smiling, seductive "social worker" from "the Patrick Henry Society." He arrives in a Mississippi town in a white suit and dark sunglasses to convince the whites to fight the court-ordered integration of black students into the all-white high school. He assures them that "the NAACP is a Communist front headed by Jews who hate America!" and vows to keep the country "free, white, and American!" Mob hysteria soon takes over. A preacher dies when his church is bombed, a family is attacked, the newspaper editor is beaten, a cross is burned by the KKK, and a young man is nearly lynched. Meanwhile, Cramer amuses himself with an underage girl (Beverly Lunsford) and a married woman (Jeanne Cooper). This great-looking b/w film was made on location in Charleston, Missouri, with unprofessional locals playing most of the roles. Shatner is better than you would imagine, and the other leads are excellent. Robert Emhardt (the mob leader in *Underworld USA*) is a hateful local rich man allied with Cramer. Frank Maxwell (who was in several Corman films) is the brave editor. Charles Barnes (in his only known role) is a student accused of rape. Best of all is Leo Gordon as Sam Griffith, a big, loud, lusty carnival pitchman. His emotion-packed scenes are the film's highlights. Forget movies like *Mississippi Burning* or *Betrayed* and look for this.

ILLEGAL ENTRY: FORMULA FOR FEAR

(PM, 1993) **D:** Henri Charr **S:** John B. Pfeifer **P:** Jess Mancilla

Blonde Trace (Sabryn Gene't) flees from the people who killed her parents to get a secret formula. Ninjas, death by acid, and nude swimming are featured. With Barbara Lee Alexander.

ILLICIT BEHAVIOR

(Prism, 1991) **D:** Worth Keefer **S:** Michael Potts **P:** Ashok Amritras, Steve Beswick

Yes, it's another "erotic thriller," complete with a double-cross (and triple-cross) greed plot. Robert Davi is a divorced internal-affairs officer investigating a shooting at Griffith Park Observatory. Joan Severance is married to cop Jack Scalia and says she's afraid of her brother (her childhood lover). Severance has sex scenes in a kitchen and a car. Sometimes she's naked, at other times it's her body double. With James Russo, Jenilee Harrison, Sondra Currie, and Kent McCord. It's available in R and unrated versions. Keeter was a regular director for Earl Owensby and also made *LA Bounty*.

ILL MET BY MOONLIGHT

(1994) **D/S/P/M:** S. P. Somtow

A Midsummer Night's Dream is set in modern-day LA, but the characters speak Shakespeare's dialogue. The story still works, but I really could have done without the songs. Puck, one of the skateboarding street-kid fairies, gives love-potion drops to the wrong characters. Lysander, who was once in love with Hermia (Heidi Blose) and Demitrius both lust after the confused Helena (Judy Fei-Wing). Titania, the queen of the fairies (Rachel I. Sita Raine), jumps into bed with the comical Bottom (Ron Ford), whose face has been transformed into an ass (*not* a donkey's head, but . . .). One of the most notable aspects of this low-budget fantasy/comedy is that three of the four actresses are Asian. There's a happy ending (a Buddhist wedding) followed by an overlong presentation of a play, with Bottom doing Elvis. With novelist Tim Sullivan as Oberon, Timothy Bottoms as Hermia's father, and big Robert Z'Dar as the duke. It's pretty strange seeing Z'Dar, who usually plays brutal killers, spouting Shakespearian dialogue! Various other writers and random names also appear, including Bill Warren. Somtow, a novelist from Thailand, also directed *The Laughing Dead*. This film is letterboxed.

I'LL NEVER FORGET WHAT'S 'IS NAME

(1967) **D/P:** Michael Winner **S:** Peter Draper   UK

Oliver Reed stars in a counterculture comedy as a man who makes TV commercials and has a wife and two mistresses. He smashes his office with an axe one day and tries to go back to editing a literary magazine, but his former boss (Orson Welles) buys it. With Harry Andrews, Michael Hordern, Frank Finlay, Edward Fox, Carol White, and Marianne Faithfull (who got into the record books by saying "fuck" onscreen "for the first time"). Because of the word (and an oral-sex scene) the film was denied a production-code seal in the US, but it was released by a subsidiary of Universal. It's one of the films that led to a new US ratings system. Decca released the Francis Lai soundtrack.

I'LL NEVER FORGET YOU

(1951) **D:** Roy Baker **S:** John Balderston
P: Sol C. Siegel   UK (*The House on the Square*)

20th Century–Fox's remake of the 1933 romantic fantasy *Berkeley Square* uses the same script. Tyrone Power is an American working in London who goes back in time to the 18th century and falls in love with Ann Blyth. With Michael Rennie, Dennis Price, and Beatrice Campbell.

ILLUSIONS

(Prism, 1992) **D:** Victor Kulle **S:** Peter Colley
P: Steven Paul, Michael Canale, Gary Preisler

Robert Carradine and his wife (Heather Locklear), who has had a nervous breakdown, move to a new home. Carradine seems to be involved with

his visiting sister (Emma Samms), and Locklear starts to lose it again. Ned Beatty costars as the landlord.

I LOVE TO KILL = IMPULSE

ILSA, HAREM KEEPER OF THE OIL SHEIKS

(CIC, 1976) **D:** Don Edmunds **S:** Langton Stafford **P:** William J. Brody   Canada

Dyanne Thorne returns in the second Ilsa movie. It's not as offensive as the first but is still pretty strong stuff for viewers used to more standard exploitation movies. This time Ilsa runs a slave ring and tortures more people in the Middle East. There's an exploding-penis machine, more men are castrated, and topless black lesbians wrestle. Lepers attack the evil Ilsa at the end, then she's buried alive in shit. With Ivan Rassimov as the Sheik, Tanya Boyd and Marilyn Joi as the wrestlers, nudie regular Sharon Kelly, and Haji (from Russ Meyer movies). The convincing FX are by Joe Blasco. The Cinepix version is edited.

ILSA, SHE WOLF OF THE SS

(CIC, 1974) **D:** Don Edmunds **S:** Jonah Riyston
P/A: "Herman Traeger"/David F. Friedman

Friedman appears in this, the original Ilsa movie. He says that it's the only film he's not proud of. It certainly worked as a sick cult film, though, and spawned several sequels. Once whispered about by the few who would admit to watching it in a theater, this is now a common video rental and has been written about in mainstream magazines. Star Dyanne Thorne makes autograph-signing appearances at horror conventions, where some fans are disappointed that she seems so normal and friendly. She stars as Ilsa, commandant of Medical Camp 9. Ilsa says, "Once a prisoner has slept with me, he'll never sleep with another woman!" and castrates her lovers the next morning. Gregory Knoph is an American general who can do it all night, so she lets him live, which leads to her destruction. Female inmates are tortured and killed in various ways. Some are boiled alive, maggots are put into wounds, and death is caused by exploding diaphragms and superspeed dildos. There's plenty of nudity and some intentional (sick) humor. And, yes, the sets from *Hogan's Heroes* were used for the week-long shoot. Joe Blasco provided the grisly and effective FX. Blasco had done makeup for *The Lawrence Welk Show* (!) and the ABC Network and went on to open a popular FX studio in Hollywood. Director Edmunds had acted in movies like *Gidget Goes Hawaiian* and *Beach Ball*! The Cinepix version is edited.

ILSA, THE ABSOLUTE POWER: *See* ILSA, THE WICKED WARDEN

ILSA, TIGRESS OF SIBERIA

(American, 1977) **D:** Jean Lafleur **S:** Marvin McGara **P:** Julian Parnell   Canada

In the third Ilsa movie (this time by a different director), she runs Gulag 14 in Siberia during the Korean War but flees when Stalin dies in 1953, goes to Montreal, and runs a whorehouse/dungeon. The action takes place during the 1976 Olympics. KGB agents invade at the end. Dyanne Thorne stars again, and her real-life husband, Howard Mauer, is in the cast. There's plenty of outrageous sex and torture deaths and a man-eating tiger. It's also available in a cut version (as *Tigress*), minus the chainsaw/arm-wrestling scene. It was supposedly released by New World. A fourth Ilsa movie was advertised in *Variety* ("Ilsa meets Bruce Lee in the Bermuda Triangle"!) but was not actually made.

ILSA, THE WICKED WARDEN

(CIC, 1977) **D/S/A:** Jesús Franco **S/P:** Edwin C. Dietrich   Switzerland/W. Germany (*Greta; Haus Ohne Mannen; Ilsa, The Absolute Power; Greta, the Mad Torturer; Greta, the Sadist; Wanda, the Wicked Warden*)

This is one of four vile, humorless women-in-prison movies Franco made in succession for the same producer. It's *not* an Ilsa movie, but does copy them and was retitled in 1983 to cash in on their video popularity. Greta (Dyanne Thorne) runs a political prison in a South American jungle. An Amnesty International agent infiltrates it in search of her sister. There's lots of nudity, violence, and showers, a naked cat fight, lesbian scenes, snuff movies, acid injections, pins in breasts, and cannibalism. Greta is torn apart by the inmates at the end. With Tania Busselier as Abby, Lina Romay, and Howard Mauer. It uses the same sets as *Barbed Wire Dolls*. Cut and uncut versions are around.

Dyanne Thorne returns in *Ilsa, Tigress of Siberia.*

I, MADMAN

(Media, 1988) **D:** Tibor Takacs **S:** David
Chaskin **P:** Rafael Eisenman (*Hardcover*)

A young actress (Jenny Wright, from *Near Dark*)
with a cop boyfriend works at a used-book store.
She's fascinated by the horror novels of a dead author, Malcolm Brand, who "makes Stephen King
read like Mother Goose." In 40s period scenes,
Brand, a creepy, bald, lovesick doctor and poet,
slices off parts of his face to impress an actress,
also played by Wright. After a while the whole
front of his face is gone. He scalps another actress
and wears her hair. Randall William Cook, who
plays the bizarre killer, devised his own makeup
and did the stop-motion animation. An impressive
animated animal monster eats people (offscreen)
and has a climactic fight in the store. After being
cut in half, Cook resembles Johnny Eck in *Freaks*.
At the end both creatures turn into pages of a
book and float away. Although parts are boring
and a bit confusing, this movie is more interesting
than most dream/reality supernatural-killer movies
and includes some fun references to Hitchcock
and Tod Browning classics. Takacs also directed
The Gate movies.

IMAGES

(1972) **D/S:** Robert Altman
P: Tommy Thompson   UK/US

After his excellent *McCabe and Mrs. Miller*, Altman made this little-known *Repulsion*-type movie.
Susannah York is a children's-book writer living in
an isolated house in Ireland. She hallucinates a lot
and may be schizophrenic. Her evil double and her
dead lover appear, and characters are murdered.
René Auberjonois is her husband. Vilmos Zsigmond shot the film in Ireland. John Williams wrote
the score (on CIF) which includes "sounds" by
Stomu Yamashta. It's a Columbia release.

IMAGINE: JOHN LENNON

(RCA, 1988) **D/P:** Andrew Solt **P:** David L. Wolper

Yoko Ono helped make this documentary about
her late husband and is interviewed in it. Andy
Warhol, Jack Palance, Dick Cavett, and other celebs also appear. With footage of Lennon, the Plastic Ono Band, and the Beatles. Capitol released a
soundtrack LP. The original 1971 *Imagine* (Sony)
is a video album (the world's first) featuring all 10
songs from the Lennon album of the same name.
The two *Imagine* tapes share some footage.

I-MAN

(1986) **D:** Corey Allen **S/P:** Howard
Friedlander, Ken Peragine **P:** Richard Briggs

Scott Bakula is a cabdriver who becomes indestructible (along with his son and dog) because of
a mysterious gas. This Disney movie was the pilot
for an ABC-TV series that never made it, but
Bakula went on to star in the popular *Quantum
Leap* series. With John Anderson and Herschel
Bernardi.

I MARRIED A VAMPIRE

(Starmaker, 1983) **D/S:** Jay Raskin **P:** Vicky Prodomidov

Russ Meyer's first film was *The Immoral Mr. Teas*.

A country girl (Rachel Gordon) meets and marries
a 100-year-old vampire named Robespierre (Brendan Hickey) in the big city. Troma released this
16mm comedy in 1986.

I MARRIED A WITCH

(Warner, 1942) **D/P:** René Clair
S: Robert Pirosh, Marc Connelly

A witch (Veronica Lake) and her wizard father
(Cecil Kellaway) are burned in Salem, Massachusetts, in 1692. Centuries later, lightning frees their
spirits from being imprisoned in a tree. She plans
to curse a descendant (Fredric March) of the family that condemned them but falls in love with him.
He's running for governor and is engaged to Susan
Hayward. With Robert Benchley, Chester Conklin,
and Monte Blue. (MGM countered with *I Married
an Angel* the same year.) This charming fantasy/
comedy from UA was the inspiration for the 60s
TV show *Bewitched*. The famous French director
who made *The Ghost Goes West* (1935) in England, directed *It Happened Tomorrow* (1944) and

And Then There Were None (1945) in Hollywood
before returning to France after WWII.

I'M DANGEROUS TONIGHT

(MCA, 1990) **D:** Tobe Hooper **S/P:** Bruce
Lansbury **S:** Phillip John Taylor

A cursed Aztec cloak, made into a red dress, unleashes passion and hatred in a college town. This
film is based on a 1937 Cornel Woolrich story.
Madchen Amick (from *Twin Peaks*) stars as a shy
Cinderella type who makes the dress, then becomes known as a slut. With Anthony Perkins as a
suspicious professor, Natalie Schafer as the grandmother, Corey Parker, Dee Wallace Stone, R. Lee
Ermey, and William Berger. It debuted on the USA
Network.

I'M GONNA GIT YOU, SUCKA

(MGM/UA, 1988) **D/S/A:** Keenen Ivory Wayans
P: Peter McCarthy, Carl Craig

All the clichés of early-70s black-action movies are
revived in this often hilarious comedy. Wayans

stars as nice-guy Nam-vet Jack Spade in "Any Ghetto, USA," Bernie Casey is John Slade, Isaac Hayes is Hammer, and Jim Brown is Slammer. There's even a spoof of the black exorcist movie *Abby*. With Antonio Fargas as Flyguy, Steve James, Ja'net DuBois, Damon Wayans, Chris Rock, Clarence Williams III, Eve Plumb (from *The Brady Bunch*), Anne-Marie Johnson, Becky LeBeau, and John Vernon as Mr. Big. The Arista soundtrack features the Gap Band, Curtis Mayfield, and others. Wayans went on to create the TV series *In Living Color* and tried to do a *Hammer and Slammer* series, but there was only a pilot.

THE IMMORAL MR. TEAS
(RM, 1959) **D/S/C/E:** Russ Meyer

This was the first "nudie cutie" hit. Some viewers will notice right away that it's a pretty close copy of the French "Mr. Hulot" movies, with nudity added. It was Russ Meyer's first film and was shot in five days for $24,000. Meyer was a *Playboy* photographer at the time. This 63-minute Eastmancolor film was a big hit and inspired "150 imitations within one year" (!). It's the only one of Meyer's pre-*Lorna* movies that he has released on tape (five others remain nearly impossible to see). Bill Teas stars as a deliveryman who imagines that women's clothes disappear. There's music but no words. June Wilkinson appears (uncredited), and there's a shot of the director in an audience.

THE IMMORAL THREE
(SW, 1972) **D/P:** Doris Wishman
S: Robert Jahn   (*Hotter Than Hell*)

Three sisters (Sandy, Ginny, and Nancy) meet for the first time. They all stand to inherit a fortune and a luxury suburban house. Flashbacks reveal that their mom was "Agent 73," a big-breasted secret agent in Moscow who "used the only weapon she had." This color movie has lots of blood as characters die from a pitchfork, stabbings, and slashings. When not dying or killing, the various women take nude swims, suck on a banana, have sex, and do a sexy drunken aerobic dance. The music is *Shaft*-inspired "wah wah" guitar. Parts were filmed in New York City and Las Vegas. With Al Levitsky, a porno actor (also in *Martin*). The parts about the mother obviously inspired the Chesty Morgan movies Wishman made next. This was (briefly) a Joe Bob video release.

IMMORTAL COMBAT
(A-Pix, 1993) **D/S/P:** Daniel A. Niera **S:** Robert Crabtree   US/Mexico (*Resort to Kill*)

Roddy Piper and Sonny Chiba are fighting LA-based federal agents. Eventually they both end up on a Caribbean island where drugs are used to bring back the dead and a half-assed *Most Dangerous Game*–type hunt occurs. The main opponent is a crazy, growling, long-haired, musclebound revived serial killer. A series of many narrated flashbacks (and visions) help confuse everything. Ninjas appear. The best action is when Chiba (who had starred in the Japanese *Invasion of the Neptune Men* 32 years earlier!) has sword fights. With

Kim Morgan Greene as a photographer who is kidnapped, Meg Foster as the main villain, and big Tiny Lister, who cries. The music is overphrased rock.

THE IMMORTALIZER
(RCA, 1988) **D:** Joel Bender **S:** Mark M. Nelson **P:** Frederick Wolcott

Two couples are knocked out and kidnapped by ugly, growling, strong, lumpy-faced mutants. Big, bearded, laughing Dr. Devine (Ron Ray) transplants bloody young brains into old bodies in a hospital/house. Two derelict assistants (paid with booze) handle the mutants (kept in a pit) with cattle prods and feed them useless corpses, after they've gone through a *Corpse Grinder*–type machine. A cynical new criminal/doctor arrives to help, and the nurse wants both docs. The nurse is played by Melody Patterson (or Santangelo), Wrangler Jane from *F Troop* and the real-life wife of *Hawaii Five-O*'s James MacArthur! After a transplant, she runs around naked with a new body (but the same voice). One of the assistants feels up a drugged, naked teenage girl (*Playboy* Playmate Rebekka Armstrong). "A new female monster" is thrown in the pit, and all the monsters fight. If Jerry Warren (*Frankenstein's Island*, *Teenage Zombies*) were still alive, and had slightly better production values and actors, I'd swear that he directed this stupid movie.

IMMORTAL SINS
(New Horizons, 1991) **D:** Herve Hachuel **S:** Tom Cleaver, Beverly Gray **P:** Roger Corman, Alida Camp

Maryam D'Abo marries Cliff De Young, the cursed heir to a Spanish castle. A succubus (Shari Shattuck, who has the sex scenes) tries to break up the marriage. It was filmed in Spain.

I, MOBSTER
(SW, 1958) **D/P:** Roger Corman
S: Steve Fisher **P:** Gene Corman

Joe Santi (Steve Cochran) narrates this story of how he moved up in (the real) Murder Incorporated, carried out hits, did time, and had to appear before a congressional hearing. Flashbacks to his childhood are remarkably like those in Scorsese's *Goodfellas*. With Lita Milan (*Poor White Trash*), Robert Strauss, Celia Lovsky as the mother, and Lili St. Cyr (as herself). Smaller roles are played by Yvette Vickers, Robert Shayne, Ed Nelson, and Bruno Ve Sota. Floyd Crosby was the cinematographer. The music is jazzy. This b/w Cinemascope 20th Century–Fox release is more expensive-looking than other Corman films of the period. The tape (from TV) is panned and scanned.

IMPACT VIDEO MAGAZINE
(MPI, 1989) **P:** Stuart Shapiro, Waleed Ali

Alex Winter (*Bill and Ted's Excellent Adventure*) hosts videos by Public Enemy, Jane's Addiction, Butthole Surfers, and others. There are mondo-type sections with artist Robert Williams, SRL (Survival Research Laboratories), and Michael Musto in New York City. Also included is the car-

toon *Bambi Meets Godzilla*. The 80-minute tape is from the makers of *Mondo New York* (and the *Night Flight* cable-TV program).

THE "IMP" PROBABLE MR. WEE GEE
(1966) **D/S/P:** Sherman Price

Wee Gee, the famous crime photographer, stars in this color nudie comedy as himself (somebody else provided his voice). He falls for a store-window dummy and follows her when she's shipped to London, where he meets a sexy ghost in a haunted house, and to Paris, where he's chased on the Eiffel Tower. Wee Gee also worked on *Shangri-La* (1961).

IMPROPER CONDUCT
(Monarch, 1994) **D/S/P:** Jag Mundhra
S: Carl Austin **P:** Victor Bhalla

Tahnee Welch is an employee at an LA ad agency who is assaulted by a coworker (John Laughlin). Steven Bauer represents her in court, but she loses the case, then dies in a car crash. Her sister (Lee Anne Beeman, the real star) goes undercover at the agency to expose the guilty. With Kathy Shower as the daughter of boss Stuart Whitman, Nia Peeples, and Adrian Zmed. This movie about sexual harassment is full of sex and shower scenes featuring Welch, Beeman, and Shower. R and unrated versions are available.

IMPULSE
(I.V.E., 1974) **D:** William Grefe **S:** Tony Grechales **P:** Socrates Ballis   (*Want a Ride, Little Girl?*)

What a find! William Shatner is Matthew Stone, a creepy, lying, seductive, psycho gigolo/hustler with sideburns, a scar, and white flare pants. A perfect, clichéd b/w flashback shows how as a kid he defended his mother by running a samurai sword through a tattooed drunk (William Kerwin!). Another flashback shows him crying while strangling a woman, then sinking her car. He seduces a widow (Jennifer Bishop, from Al Adamson movies and *Hee Haw*) whose best friend is played by Ruth Roman (who was in *The Baby* the same year). Only the woman's bratty, precocious little blond daughter (Kim Nicholas, who is perfect in the role) knows what a creep he is. Shatner/Stone runs over a dog, hangs Harold ("Oddjob") Sakata, and says things like "People like you should be ground up and made into dog food!" The video print is scratchy, but *Impulse* has excellent, clever cinematography and editing and is the most enjoyable of Grefe's made-in-Florida movies. It's a sleaze classic.

IMPULSE
(Vestron, 1984) **D:** Graham Baker **S:** Nicholas Kazan, Don Carlos Dunaway **P:** Tim Zimmerman

A toxic spill contaminates the milk in a small farming town after a mild earthquake. People start acting strange, then everyone goes crazy, doing bizarre and destructive things. Tim Matheson stars as a doctor, with Meg Tilly, Hume Cronyn, Jeff Fahey, Bill Paxton, Sheri Stoner, John Karlen, and Claude Earl Jones. The director also made *Alien Nation*. This is from 20th Century–Fox.

IMPULSE

(Warner, 1990) **D:** Sondra Locke **S:** John De Marco, Leigh Chapman **P:** Albert S. Ruddy, Andre Morgan

Theresa Russell stars as an LA narcotics cop who goes undercover as a hooker and gets lost in corruption and crime. With Jeff Fahey, George Dzundza, and Alan Rosenburg. Russell (who is good, as usual) played a "real" hooker in her next film, *Whore.* This was the second film directed by Locke, who had just sued Clint Eastwood for palimony.

IMPURE THOUGHTS

(Nelson, 1985) **D/S/P:** Michael A. Simpson **S:** Michael J. Malloy **P:** William Vander Kloot

After four men die and are sent to Purgatory for forgotten, minor offenses against the Church, they remember their days as Catholic-school students together when JFK was shot. Brad Dourif stars in this PG comic fantasy, with Lane Davies, John Putch, and Terry Beaver. Dame Judith Anderson narrates. Simpson also made the *Sleepaway Camp* horror sequels.

IN ADVANCE OF THE LANDING

(1991) **D/P:** Dan Curtis   Canada

North American people talk about their close-encounter experiences in this documentary, and UFO cults are seen as religion. With Betty Hill and John Shepard Hill (their story was told in the movie *The UFO Incident*), 90-year-old cult leader Archangel Uriel, old b/w news footage, and many 50s sci-fi-movie scenes and trailers. Actress Sherrie Rose is seen in one of the "real" on-the-street interviews. This16mm documentary is based on a book. It's not by the Dan Curtis who directed *Dark Shadows.*

IN A GLASS CAGE

(Cinevista, 1986) **D/S:** Agustín Villaronga Spain (*Tras el Cristal*)

A Nazi doctor (Gunter Meisner) wanted for war crimes hides out in a Spanish villa during the 50s. His family is unaware of his vampirelike experiments on boys. When he falls and has to stay in an iron lung, a former victim (David Sust) arrives to be his nurse. Saying, "I love death," he uses blackmail and violence to take over. This has been called one of the most disturbing features ever made, by writers who should know. It was banned in Australia. It's subtitled.

IN A MOMENT OF PASSION

(Hemdale, 1992) **D/S/P:** Zbigniew Kaminski **S:** Charles Haigh

Maxwell Caulfield is a psycho German-movie stand-in who kills, then somehow impersonates, a German-movie star (Jeff Conaway!) at a stud farm where a stunt woman from Texas named Pammy (Chase Masterson, who looks like Talia Shire) is learning to ride for an acting role. She falls for the impersonator while he kills off the cast and has sex with Conaway's large-breasted girlfriend in the dark (so she won't notice the difference!). Pammy also gets drunk and goes topless in a beer hall. Viv-

ian Schilling shows up and sings (!) at a horse auction run by Joe Estevez. Julie Araskog is a blond lesbian, and Robert Z'Dar is Fritz. Wait till you hear the accents and the rap song. It's stupid! It's hilarious! It was shot in Lodz, Poland!

INCHON

(1981) **D:** Terence Young **S:** Robin Moore, Laird Koenig **P:** Mitsuharu Ishii   S. Korea/US

Reverend Sung Myung Moon backed this One Way production, which took four years (and a reported $48 million) to make and ran 140 minutes when released by MGM/UA. If you've ever wondered what happened to the money that all those Church of Unification kids used to collect on American streets, here's one possible answer. Moon is credited as "spiritual adviser." Jacqueline Bisset and Ben Gazzara star in this anti-Communist epic about the Korean War, with Toshiro Mifune (also in Young's *Red Sun*), Richard Roundtree, *Green Berets* star David Janssen (in his last role), Rex Reed, Gordon Mitchell, and Laurence Olivier as a very old-looking General Douglas MacArthur. It features big battle scenes with real American troops as extras and some astounding continuity errors. It was shot in South Korea. The Jerry Goldsmith score was issued by Regency. Moon was convicted of tax fraud in 1982.

THE INCIDENT

(Fox, 1967) **D:** Larry Peerce **S:** Nicholas E. Baehr **P:** Monroe Sachson

Tony Musante and Martin Sheen (in his first film) star as Joe and Artie. They mug an old man, then terrorize people on the subway. All the characters are introduced before they board the train. Beau Bridges is a soldier with a broken arm who finally stands up to them. With Brock Peters, Ruby Dee, Jack Gilford, Thelma Ritter, Jan Sterling, Gary Merrill, Donna Mills (in her film debut), and Ed McMahon (who is good). This 20th Century–Fox movie was filmed in b/w in NYC. It's based on *Ride to Terror,* a 1963 TV drama. Don't miss the opening instrumental theme by Terry Knight. I saw this movie in a high-school assembly, thought it was depressing and scary, but later moved to New York anyway.

IN COLD BLOOD

(RCA, 1967) **D/S/P:** Richard Brooks

In 1959 two ex-cons (played convincingly by Robert Blake and Scott Wilson) rob and kill a

family in Kansas. They're later caught, convicted, and hanged. The execution is depicted in graphic detail. This 134-minute film (told partially in flashbacks) is based on Truman Capote's 1966 novel. It's still the best true-crime movie around, not at all the typical Hollywood product. With John Forsythe as a cop, Paul Stewart as a reporter who narrates it, Jeff Corey, and Will Geer. It was shot on location in b/w by Conrad Hall in five states and Mexico. The Quincy Jones soundtrack is on Colgems. Brooks had directed *Blackboard Jungle* and *Elmer Gantry,* among many other important films.

Lou Ferrigno, on a break from starring in *The Incredible Hulk,* promotes the Movieland Wax Museum.

THE INCREDIBLE HULK RETURNS

(Starmaker, 1988) **D/S:** Nicholas Corea **P:** Daniel McPhee

Star Bill Bixby was an executive producer of this NBC-TV Hulk revival series pilot from New World. Lou Ferrigno returns as the Hulk, but the idea was to introduce another Marvel character, Thor. Also with Lee Purcell, Tim Thomerson, and Charles Napier as a Cajun villain. *The Trial of the Incredible*

Hulk, featuring Rex Smith as Daredevil (1989) and *The Death of the Incredible Hulk* (1990) followed. Bixby (who died in 1994) even directed those. The original series ran from 1978 to 1982.

THE INCREDIBLE SEX REVOLUTION

(1965) **D/S/P:** Albert Zugsmith

Lee Gladden (as himself) explains problems of the sexual revolution in this b/w "sex education" film. He hears stories from patients, Adam and Eve appear, and motel sex is illustrated. The only name in the cast is Alex D'Arcy. It was the first of Zugsmith's independent Famous Players adult films. He returned with *Movie Star American Style* (1966).

THE INCREDIBLY STRANGE FILM SHOW

(1988–89)   UK

These well-made, high-quality 45-minute (or less) documentaries were made by Channel X in London and hosted by Jonathan Ross. My only complaint is that they play down the more shocking and subversive elements of many of the films covered. I guess they had to do it that way for television. The programs were broadcast in the US on the Discovery Channel in 1990 (except for the Russ Meyer segment) and have been widely circulated on tape since. The show took its name from a book from Re/Search in San Francisco, which has taken it from Ray Dennis Steckler's movie *The Incredibly Strange Creatures Who Stopped Living and Became Mixed-Up Zombies.* The first is on American cult directors Herschell Gordon Lewis, Russ Meyer, Ted V. Mikels, Ray Dennis Steckler, John Waters, and Ed Wood Jr. The second series covers directors in Hong Kong (Jackie Chan and Tsui Hark) and Mexico (Santo), and includes segments on George Romero, Stuart Gordon, Sam Raimi, Fred Olen Ray, Tom Savini, and Doris Wishman. A third, higher-brow follow-up series, called *For One Week Only* (1990), includes directors Aki Kaurismaki from Finland, Pedro Almodovar from Spain, Alexandro Jodorowsky, and David Lynch.

INDECENCY

(MCA, 1992) **D:** Marisa Silver **S:** Amy Holden Jones, Holly Goldberg Sloan, Alan Ormsby **P:** Harvey Frand

Jennifer Beals goes to work at an ad agency after a mental breakdown. Her boss (Barbara Williams) is murdered. This PG mystery features drugs, sex, suicide, and embezzlement. With Sammi Davis-Voss and James Remar. Silver also directed *Vital Signs, Permanent Record,* and other films.

INDECENT BEHAVIOR

(WEA, 1993) **D:** Lawrence Lanoff
S: Rosalind Robinson **P:** Michael Cain

Gary Hudson stars as a detective on a case of murder by designer drug who falls for a sex therapist who's a suspect (Shannon Tweed). With Jan-Michael Vincent as her husband, Brandy Sanders (from *Penthouse*) as her niece, Michelle Moffat as a sex-surrogate, and Lawrence Hilton-Jacobs. R and unrated videos are available. *Indecent Behavior II* followed.

INDECENT DESIRES

(SW, 1967) **D/S/P:** Doris Wishman

A young guy with wire frames and salt-and-pepper hair finds a magic voodoo doll. Whatever he does to the doll (feels it up, undresses it, whips it . . .), Ann (blonde Sharon Kent) feels. She thinks she's losing her mind. After he sees her with her fiancé, he breaks the doll's neck. Ann has nude scenes and her friend Babs gets dressed, strips, then exercises. It's one of the last b/w New York movies by Wishman (who used the names "Louis Silverman" and "Dawn Whitman"), the hardest working woman in adults-only features.

INDIANA JONES AND THE LAST CRUSADE

(Paramount, 1989) **D:** Steven Spielberg **S:** Jeffrey Boam **P:** Robert Watts **M:** John Williams

In 1938 Harrison Ford as Indiana Jones and Sean Connery as his missing archaeologist father search for the Holy Grail, and become involved with Nazi Alison Doody. They face lots of rats and Nazis, and ride in a dirigible. Denholm Elliott and John Rhys-Davies return from *Raiders of the Lost Ark,* and River Phoenix is young Indy in the opening flashback. With Julian Glover and Alex Hyde-White. The ILM FX received Oscars again. This $115 million PG-13 hit from executive producer George Lucas includes many outrageous continuity errors. In 1991 all three Indiana Jones tapes were being sold as part of a promotional tie-in at McDonald's for around $5 each. The next stop for the concept (based on old serials) was the *Young Indiana Jones* TV series.

INDIANA JONES AND THE TEMPLE OF DOOM

(Paramount, 1984) **D:** Steven Spielberg **S:** Willard Huyck, Gloria Katz **P:** Robert Watts **M:** John Williams

This is a prequel to *Raiders of the Lost Ark,* set in 1935 Shanghai and India. Harrison Ford stars, with 12-year-old Ke Huy Quan as Short Round and Kate Capshaw. Dan Aykroyd has a bit part. There is a banquet featuring monkey brains and eyeballs, and a heart is ripped out. The ILM FX received an Oscar, but complaints about some of the effects in this PG "family" movie helped lead to the creation of the PG-13 rating. Complaints about the old-fashioned racism didn't change anything. It was shot in Sri Lanka and made $109 million. By the time this came out, we had already been offered three (!) TV rip-offs: *The Quest, Bring 'Em Back Alive,* and *Tales of the Gold Monkey.* Polydor released the soundtrack.

INDIAN PAINT

(1965) **D/S:** Norman Foster **P:** Gene Goree

Johnny Crawford (from the TV series *The Rifleman)* stars as 15-year-old Arikara, and Jay Silverheels (from *The Lone Ranger)* is his Commanche-chief father. Crawford sings, rides his horse, and participates in tribal rites. Floyd Crosby was the cinematographer of this Crown release, filmed in Texas.

INDIAN RAID, INDIAN MAID

(SW, 1969) **D/P:** Bob Favorite **S:** Bruce Kerr

This very dumb slapstick sex comedy features a bumbling secret agent, clichéd hillbillies, and "Indians." Long soft-core sex scenes take place in a car and a bathtub. It also includes fire breathing, strip poker, and silicone star Morgana's "devil dance."

THE INDIAN RUNNER

(MGM, 1991) **D/S:** Sean Penn **P:** Don Phillips

A small-town highway patrolman (David Morse) and his violent, out-of-control Nam-vet younger brother (Viggo Mortensen) are the main characters in this movie, based on the Bruce Springsteen song, "Highway Patrolman." With Valeria Golino, Charles Bronson as the father, Sandy Dennis (in her last role), Dennis Hopper as a bartender, Patricia Arquette, and Eileen Ryan (Penn's real-life mother). This 127-minute MGM release is set in Nebraska during the late 60s and includes many flashbacks.

THE INDIAN SCARF

(Sinister, 1963) **D:** Alfred Vohrer **S:** Georg Hurdalek, H. G. Peterson   W. Germany (*Das Indische Tuch*)

A black-gloved mystery man kills off people trapped in a castle for the reading of a will. Heinz Drache is the attorney. Klaus Kinski as Peter Ross terrorizes women with lit cigarettes and a tarantula. With Elizabeth Flickenschild and Ady Berber. It's based on Edgar Wallace's *The Case of the Frightened Lady,* which had been a play and was previously filmed in 1932 and 1940 in England. This version went directly to TV in the US.

INDIO

(Media, 1988) **D:** "Anthony Dawson"/ Antonio Marghereti **S/P:** Filiberto Bandini **M:** Pino Donaggio   Italy

In this environmentally correct action movie, Francesco Quinn stars as a half-Indian ex-Marine who becomes a Rambo-style fighter in the South American rain forest, waging a one-man war against corporate villain Brian Dennehy, a former Army colonel. With "Marvelous" Marvin Hagler. It was filmed in the Philippines, Borneo, Brazil, and Argentina.

INDIO II: THE REVOLT

(IVE, 1990) **D:** Antonio Marghereti **S/P:** Filiberto Bandini **S:** Gianfranco Bucceri   Italy

Former boxing champ "Marvelous" Marvin Hagler stars as Sergeant Iron. He leads Indians against the South American villains who destroy the rain forest and enslave the Indians. With Charles Napier as an evil highway builder and *Indio* star Francesco Quinn (who is killed at the begining). There's plenty of blood, mud, and explosions and a slave revolt in this sequel, probably filmed back to back with the original.

INDUSTRIAL SYMPHONY No. 1

(Warner, 1990) **D:** David Lynch

Singer Julee Cruise (from Iowa) sang on the *Blue Velvet* soundtrack, then appeared in the TV series *Twin Peaks.* She's in this strange, jazzy "opera" about a broken love affair in an industrial waste-land, with Laura Dern and Nicolas Cage (both in Lynch's *Wild at Heart* the same year). It's 43 minutes long. Cruise became a replacement member of the B-52's in 1992.

I NEVER PROMISED YOU A ROSE GARDEN
(1977) **D:** Anthony Page **S:** Lewis John Carlino, Gavin Lambert **P:** Terence F. Deane, Daniel H. Blatt, Michael Hausman

Kathleen Quinlan stars as a schizophrenic teen who hallucinates in a mental hospital. The people she hallucinates are played by a modern-dance troupe. Bergman star Bibi Andersson is a helpful psychiatrist. With Susan Tyrrell, Signe Hasso, Diane Varsi, Sylvia Sidney, Lorraine Gary, Barbara Steele, Reni Santoni, Dennis Quaid, and Jeff Conaway. Roger Corman was the executive producer of this unusually serious New World release, based on Hannah Green's memoir.

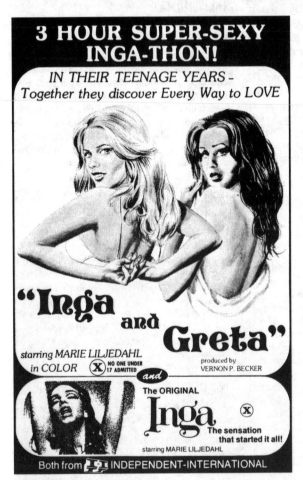

INEVITABLE GRACE
(1993) **D/S:** Alex Canawati **P:** Christian Capobianco

A Beverly Hills millionaire (Maxwell Caulfield), obsessed with Grace Kelly, blackmails a woman into "becoming" her. Jennifer Nicholson (Jack's red-headed daughter) stars as the woman who rushes out of a revival-movie theater and ends up in an asylum under the care of a doctor (Stephanie Knights). With Tippi Hedren as the director of the asylum, Samantha Eggar, Sandra Knight (Nichol-

son's former wife and his costar in *The Terror*), Victoria Sellers (daughter of Peter), and Taylor Negron. This Hitchcock-inspired low-budget debut by a USC film-school graduate was based on his 1989 student short.

INFERNO
(Fox, 1978) **D/S:** Dario Argento **P:** Claudio Argento **C:** Mario Bava   Italy

A gothic mansion in New York City overlooking Central Park is the setting for this confusing but atmospheric and memorable movie about "the mother of darkness." It's sort of a sequel to *Suspiria*. There are lots of rats, a bag of cats, and an amazing underwater chamber filled with corpses, Leigh McCloskey (from *Dallas*) stars, with Alida Valli, Daria Nicolodi, and Irene Miracle. Lamberto Bava was the assistant director. Cinematographer Bava (who died in 1980) is credited with the FX. Keith Emerson did the score. 20th Century–Fox, the company that had released *Suspiria* (1977), was supposed to release *Inferno*, but didn't. The uncut version runs 106 minutes. Argento's next, *Unsane*, wasn't released in American theaters either.

INGA
(VSOM, 1968) **D/S:** Joseph W. Sarno **P:** Donald C. Dennis   US/Sweden (*Jag en Oskuld*)

Marie Liljedahl stars as a 17-year-old sent to live with a scheming aunt who wants her to become a rich neighbor's mistress. She falls for a young man instead. This adult hit was released by Jerry Gross' Cinemation and later rereleased by Independent International on an X-rated double bill with *Inga and Greta* (also starring Liljedahl), advertised as "a 3 hour super-sexy Inga-thon!" Liljedahl is also in more bizarre movies, like *Eugenie* (1969) and *Dorian Gray* (1970), both from producer Harry Alan Towers, and *Grimm's Fairy Tales for Adults* (1970).

INGAGI
(1930)

This notorious exploitation hit was supposedly a documentary of "Sir Hubert Winstead's" expedition into the Belgian Congo. The footage of wild animals is from the silent film *Heart of Africa*. The ending features naked native women offering one of their own as human sacrifice to Ingagi the gorilla. This payoff segment was filmed in California with local women as natives and a man in a gorilla costume. *Ingagi* was so well known in the 30s that it was the topic of a joke in an Our Gang comedy. It was banned in Ohio and (for a while) in New York, played for years on the exploitation-film circuit, and was imitated many times by other films, including *Forbidden Adventure* (also called *The Love Life of a Gorilla*) and *Ankor*.

IN GOLD WE TRUST
(AIP, 1990) **D/P:** Chalong Pakdeevichit **S:** Tony S. Suvat, Buncherd Dhawee   Thailand (*Gold of the Samurai*)

Jan-Michael Vincent is an ex–Green Beret in Laos to track down some MIAs who have a stash of stolen gold. Sherrie Rose joins him, and Sam Jones is the psycho who leads the killer ex-soldiers. The plot (which copies parts of *Apocalypse Now*) includes local freedom fighters and some Japanese soldiers left over from WWII.

THE INITIATION
(HBO, 1984) **D:** Larry Stewart **S:** Charles Pratt Jr. **P:** Scott Winant

Daphne Zuniga (in her first role) stars as a sorority sister who has amnesia about her childhood and is hooked up to a "dream machine" to get rid of a recurring nightmare. She joins other young people in her father's department store at night, and they're decapitated (offscreen), axed, shot by arrows, or stabbed with garden tools. This bad-taste *A Nightmare on Elm Street*–inspired movie has a nude shower scene, a rape, and ridiculous multiple-surprise endings. A "repressed desires" costume party has teens dressed as hookers and in S&M gear. Vera Miles and Clu Gulager are the rich parents. This New World release was filmed in the Fort Worth area.

INNER SANCTUM
(Sinister, 1948) **D:** Lew Landers **S:** Jerome Todd Golland **P:** Samuel Rheiner, Walter Shenson

A Gypsy fortuneteller predicts disaster for a girl on a train, and a murder occurs. Charles Russell stars, with Mary Beth Hughes, Nana Bryant, Lee Patrick (*The Maltese Falcon*), and Fritz Leiber. This Film Classics release was based on the famous radio program, as were six earlier Universal features (all with Lon Chaney Jr.).

INNER SANCTUM
(RCA, 1991) **D/P:** Fred Olen Ray **S:** Mark Thomas McGhee **P:** Alam Amiel

This has nothing to do with the old Universal series or the radio program. It's a senseless "erotic gothic thriller" whose plot is similar to the plot of Ray's *The Haunting Fear*. Sadistic Joseph Bottoms has a wealthy wife in a wheelchair (Valerie Wildman) but wants to be with Margaux Hemingway (who is body-doubled by Michelle Bauer). Tanya Roberts (from *Charlie's Angels*) plays the blond live-in nurse, who has other ideas and most of the nude sex scenes. With Russ Tamblyn, Jay Robinson, Brett Clark, and Suzanne Ager. Ray used the same house for *Evil Toons* and *Spirits*. R and unrated versions are available. Mark Damon was the executive producer of this New Line release.

INNER SANCTUM 2
(Columbia, 1994) **D/S:** Fred Olen Ray **S:** Steve Armogida **P:** Alan Amiel

In between various nightmares, hallucinations, nightmares-inside-of-nightmares, and sex scenes there's some kind of plot here about Michael Nouri coming to stay with his late brother-in-law's traumatized wife (Sandahl Bergman) and people being decapitated. Blond Jennifer Reed (replacing Tanya Roberts as the nurse from the first movie) is the main visual attraction in and out of her mini-skirt. Bergman dances in a graveyard with her dead husband (Kato Kaelin in ghoul makeup) and there's a sex-with-a-rotting-corpse scene. With David Warner (doctor), Joe Estevez (cop), Robert Quarry (lawyer), Suzanne Ager, John Blythe Barrymore, and Margaux Hemingway lingering from *Inner Sanctum*. This was the unrated version.

INNERSPACE

(Warner, 1987) **D:** Joe Dante **S:** Jeffrey Boam, Chip Proser **P:** Michael Finnell

A Navy test pilot (Dennis Quaid) is miniaturized in a lab experiment, then accidentally injected into the body of a supermarket cashier (Martin Short). Spies chase after the confused Short. Although it's partially a comedic version of *Fantastic Voyage* (1966) it has typical Dante guest stars and gags. Meg Ryan costars with Kevin McCarthy, Fiona Lewis as Dr. Canker, Vernon Wells, William Schallert, Henry Gibson, Orson Bean, Kathleen Freeman, Dick Miller, Kenneth Tobey, Wendy Schaal, Joe Flaherty, and Andrea Martin. The FX by ILM and Rob Boltin received an Oscar. It was the first major video released letterboxed, which is great, but it includes a Pepsi commercial, which isn't. Geffen released the Jerry Goldsmith soundtrack, which includes various rock artists. Steven Spielberg was an executive producer.

INNOCENT BLOOD

(Warner, 1992) **D:** John Landis **S:** Michael Wolk **P:** Lee Rich, Leslie Belzberg

Anne Parillaud (the French star of *La Femme Nikita*) stars as Marie, a sexy vampire, in what could have been called *A French Vampire in Pittsburgh*. This horror comedy is actually better than Landis' *An American Werewolf in London* (1981), and Parillaud has several memorable nude scenes. Anthony La Paglia is an undercover cop who falls for her, Robert Loggia is a gangster who becomes a bloodsucker, and Don Rickles is a lawyer (he has the best death scene). Snowy Pittsburgh looks more interesting than it really does, thanks to added neon. Many vintage film clips (showing Hitchcock, Lugosi, and others) are glimpsed on TV sets, and Sinatra standards are used on the soundtrack. Small roles and bit parts are played by Angela Bassett, Tom Savini, Kim Coates, Linnea Quigley (in a cameo with her husband, Steve Johnson, who also did the FX), Teri Weigel, Sam Raimi, Sherrie Rose, Forrest J. Ackerman, Dario Argento, and Frank Oz. Dan Quayle appears in a clip.

INNOCENT PREY

(SVS, 1984) **D/S:** Colin Eggleston **P:** Ron McLean   Australia

If you missed P. J. Soles (*Halloween, Rock 'n' Roll High School*), here she is in a mediocre psycho-killer movie. In Dallas her con-man husband from New Zealand is captured after killing hookers, breaks out of prison, and murders a bunch of cops (he decapitates one). She flees to Sydney and stays

in a house owned by a young millionaire voyeur who monitors everything she does. More people start to die, and I fell asleep. Martin Balsam is a friendly sheriff from back home. The music is by Brian May.

INNOCENT SALLY

(Private Screenings, 1973) **D:** Bethel G. Buckalew (*The Dirty Mind of Young Sally*)

Red-haired Sharon Kelly (later billed as Colleen Brennan in X flms) is at her perky best starring in this sex comedy. She runs and stars on an illegal pirate radio station from a van, playing "music to ball by" and turning on listeners with her voice, backed by bongos and flute music. She takes calls and offers herself as the prize in a contest. George "Buck" Flower is Toby, her hick engineer, who says things like "Jumpin' Jehoshaphat!" Both have legit jobs at a real station, and comic cops are after them. The many sex scenes, featuring couples on a beach, in cars, at the station, and Kelly herself, border on (and briefly cross into) hard X. With Robyn Whitting.

INNOCENTS FROM HELL: *See* SISTERS OF SATAN

INN OF THE DAMNED

(Paragon, 1974) **D/S/P:** Terry Bourke **P:** Rod Hay   Australia

A German woman (Judith Anderson) runs a stage-coach inn in the late-19th-century outback. She and her husband kill lodgers because their children were killed by an escaped lunatic. With Alex Cord as an American lawman, Tony Bonner, and Michael Craig. It's more than two hours long.

THE INN ON THE RIVER

(Sinister, 1962) **D:** Alfred Vohrer **S:** Trygve Larsen, H. G. Peterson   W. Germany (*Das Gasthaus an der Themse*)

Joachim Fuchsberger, as Inspector Wade of Scotland Yard, tries to catch "the Shark," a killer in a scuba-diving suit. With Brigitte Grothum (who sings the theme song) and Klaus Kinski (with a mustache) as Gregor Gubanow, and Richard Much. There's some twist music. It's based on Edgar Wallace's *The India Rubber Men,* filmed as *The Return of the Frog* in 1938 in England.

IN 'N' OUT

(Starmaker, 1984) **D/S:** Richard Franco **S:** Eileen Kesend **P:** Michael James Egan US/Mexico (*Gringo Mojado*)

Divorced and suicidal Sam Bottoms goes to Mexico to claim an inheritance. This PG comedy costars Isela Vega.

IN POSSESSION

(1984) **D:** Val Guest **S:** Michael J. Bird   UK

An American (Carol Lynley) and her British husband (Christopher Cazenove) see visions of a mur-

der and a ghost couple while on vacation. Back in the city more strange things happen, and there's a trick ending. It's a Hammer TV movie.

THE INQUIRY

(1987) **D/S:** Damiano Damiani **S:** Vittorio Boniocelli   Italy (*L'Inchiesta*)

Keith Carradine is a Roman looking for the body of Christ several years after the Crucifixion. He disguises himself as a Jew and is mistaken for Christ by some lepers. A magician spins a man's head around. Harvey Keitel (soon to play Judas in *The Last Temptation of Christ*) is Pontius Pilate. It's by the director of *Amityville II*.

INQUISITION

(Vid City, 1976) **D/S/A:** "Jacinto Molina"/ Paul Naschy   Spain

Naschy is a witch-hunting judge in 16th-century France, during an outbreak of plague. He falls for a woman, is seduced and tricked, and ends up being burned as a warlock. Naschy also plays Satan. This was the first of many times that the horror star directed himself. He added lots of nudity, violence, and torture, and borrowed ideas from *Mark of the Devil* (1970).

IN SEARCH OF DR. SEUSS

(Turner, 1994) **D:** Vincent Paterson **S:** Keith R. Clarke **P:** Joni Levin

The children's-book characters of the late Dr. Seuss (Theodore Geisel) come to life in this mixture of fact-based biography and fantasy, using both live action and animation. Kathy Najimy is a reporter who is given a tour of the Seuss fantasy world by The Cat In The Hat (Matt Frewer). Various characters are played by Robin Williams, Christopher Lloyd, Billy Crystal, Howie Mandel, Eileen Brennan, Graham Jarvis, and Patrick Stewart. Also with a look at Seuss's Oscar-winning WWII short *Hitler Lives*(!). From TNT.

IN SEARCH OF HISTORIC JESUS

(Vestron, 1979) **D:** Henning Schellerup **S:** Marvin Wald, Jack Jacobs **P:** Charles Sellier Jr.

This G-rated Sunn Classics docudrama (from the same people who were in search of UFOs and various monsters) recreates events in the life of Christ (John Rubinstein) and wonders about "the Shroud of Turin." It reuses footage from *In Search of Noah's Ark*, but the cast includes some good character actors. With Royal Dano as the prophet, Nehemiah Persoff, John Anderson, John Hoyt, and Morgan Brittany. Brad Crandall narrates.

IN SEARCH OF NOAH'S ARK

(Vestron, 1976) **D/S:** James L. Conway **S/P:** Charles Sellier Jr.

The biblical re-creations, shot in Utah (standing in for Turkey), are out of focus and grainy, but this G-rated speculation movie was a hit. It's narrated by Brad Crandall. It was the most profitable of the many popular Sunn/Taft family releases, which included *Grizzly Adams* (1975), *Chariots of the Gods?*(1974), and *Beyond and Back* (1978).

INSERTS
(Paramount, 1976) **D/S:** John Byrum
P: Davina Belling   UK

Richard Dreyfuss stars as "the Boy Wonder," a manic, once-promising 30s Hollywood director who now makes illegal 16mm stag films in the mansion he refuses to leave. The unique theatrical feature takes place in the 30s. With Jessica Harper, Veronica Cartwright (who has surprising, energetic sex scenes) as a drug-addicted actress, and Bob Hoskins as Big Mac. Some have suggested that the (impotent) Dreyfuss character was based on Ed Wood Jr! Others suggest Tod Browning. United Artists released it.

THE INSIDE MAN
(Bingo, 1984) **D:** Tom Clegg **S:** Alan Plater **P:** Ingemar Ejve, Calvin Floyd, Bjorn Henricson   Sweden

Dennis Hopper is a CIA agent in Sweden who makes a young Marine (Gosta Ekman) go undercover to find a laser search device from a Soviet submarine. Hopper is only a guest star. With Hardy Kruger and Cory Molder. Clegg also directed Hammer TV movies in England.

INSIDE MONKEY ZETTERLAND
(Prism, 1992) **D:** Jeffrey Levy **S/P/A:** Steve Antin **P:** Chuck Grile, Tani Cohen

A young LA screenwriter (Steve Antin) who's in therapy and still lives with his dysfunctional family narrates (in various comical voices) his flashbacks and daydreams. His soap-opera-star mother (Katherine Helmond) rents a room to a terrorist couple (Martha Plimpton and Rupert Everett). Other recognizable actors show up in this "wacky" comedy, several as gay characters. With Patricia Arquette as the lesbian sister, Debi Mazar, Sofia Coppola, Sandra Bernhard, Ricki Lake, Luca Bercovici, Bo Hopkins as the biker father, and Lance Loud as a shrink. It's from IRS.

INSIDE OUT
(Playboy, 1992) **D:** Lizzie Borden, Adam Friedman, Linda Hossani, Alexander Payne, Tony Randel, Jeff Reiner, Richard Shepard **S:** Larry Golin, Robert Karstadt (+10 more) **P:** Alan Poul
(*Tales of the Unexpected*)

These 9 short "erotic tales of the unexpected" were part of a cable-TV series. One of the two by Randel stars Sherrie Rose as a woman in space with a romantic computer. One of Borden's (who also did two) stars Joe Dallesandro and Neith Hunter. One tale is about astral projection, and another features a man having sex with his female "better half" from a mirror world. Others star Cec Verrell and porno actress Rachel Ryan. A few are funny, sexy, or thought-provoking, and some might surprise you, but if you're looking for nudity you'll be disappointed. This tape seems designed for couples. At the price they're asking, each short will cost you around $8.

The Greatest Discovery of Our Time

In search of Noah's Ark

High atop a mountain in Eastern Turkey is a giant 5,000 year old wooden ship containing hundreds of stalls and cages.

IS IT NOAH'S ARK?

G

with BRAD CRANDALL
Technical Advisor/Historian DAVID BALSIGER   Directed By JAMES L. CONWAY
Copyright Sun Classic Pictures, Inc. © 1976   Produced By CHARLES E. SELLIER, JR.

INSIDE OUT II
(Playboy, 1992) **D:** 8 of 'em **P:** Alan Poul

The best segment is Yuri Sivo's hilarious and well-made takeoff on Woody Allan's *Zelig*, starring Kitten Natividad as a sex star. Bruce Glover is in a good segment by Nicholas Brandt. Most of the others are forgettable, and Tony Randel's b/w short about masked aliens is especially pretentious. The cast includes Jack Carter, George "Buck" Flower, and Lisa London. *Inside Out III* and *IV* (1992) followed.

THE INSIDERS: *See* POLICEWOMAN

INSIDE THE GOLDMINE
(1994) **D/S/A:** Josh Evans **S:** Uri Zighelboim **P:** Adam Stern

Alan Marshall stars with Josh Evans (son of Robert Evans and Ali McGraw) in this story about spoiled, bored Hollywood rich kids and the murder of a young woman. With Alicia Tully Jensen, Charlie Spradling, Natasha Wagner, Drew Barrymore, and many nonprofessional actors.

INSIGNIFICANCE
(Warner, 1985) **D:** Nicolas Roeg
S: Terry Johnson **P:** Jeremy Thomas

Famous people all show up in a New York City hotel in 1954. Marilyn Monroe (Theresa Russell) explains the theory of relativity to Albert Einstein (Michael Emil). It's based on Terry Johnson's play. No real names are used, but Tony Curtis seems to be Joseph McCarthy, and Gary Busey resembles Joe DiMaggio. The cast also includes Will Sampson. A theater marquee advertises *The Creature from the Black Lagoon*.

INSTANT JUSTICE
(Warner, 1987) **D:** Dennis Amar
D/S/P: Craig T. Rumar   (*Marine Issue*)

Michael Paré stars as a Marine sergeant named Youngblood who searches for his sister's killers, with help from a hooker (Tawny Kitaen). Charles Napier is Major Davis. It was filmed in Gibraltar.

INSTANT KARMA
(MGM, 1990) **D:** Roderick Taylor **S:** Bruce A. Taylor **P:** Dale Rosenblum, Bruce A. Taylor

Craig Sheffer stars in this comedy as a TV-network consultant looking for love. William Smith and David Cassidy are the stars of the fictitious *Rock 'n' Roll P.I.* series. They ride motorcycles and sing a duet. With Chelsea Noble, Orson Bean, Marty Engels, and Rebekka Armstrong.

INTENT TO KILL
(PM, 1992) **D/S:** Charles T. Kanagis
P: Richard Pepin, Joseph Merhi

Traci Lords returns in another action movie, this time as a cop who battles South American drug dealers led by Angelo Tiffe. There are feminist themes (she teaches self-defense to women, beats rapists, and throws out the cop she lives with for cheating). It also has lots of shooting, slo-mo explosions, car chases, and crashes (resulting in an NC-17 rating) and still manages to be kind of boring. The classical music doesn't help. The cast includes Yaphet Kotto as the captain, Michael Foley, and Elena Sahagan as a hooker. Kanagis also directed Lords in *A Time to Die*.

INTERCEPTOR
(Vidmark, 1992) **D:** Michael Cohn **S:** John Brancato, Michael Ferris **P:** Mark Armin, Frank Kostenko Jr.

Andrew Divoff is a Stealth Bomber pilot fighting killer terrorists led by Jürgen Prochnow. The villains are after two jets with virtual-reality guidance systems. The plot is basically the same as the plot of *Under Siege*. Also with Elizabeth Morehead.

INTERNATIONAL STEWARDESSES

(1974) **D/S/P:** Alf Silliman **P:** Chris J. Condon
(Supersonic Supergirls; The Stewardesses, Part II)

This 3-D X-rated sequel to *The Stewardesses* is by the same director. It was filmed around the world.

INTERVIEW WITH THE VAMPIRE

(Warner 1994) **D/S:** Neil Jordan **S:** Anne Rice **P:** Stephen Wolley **M:** Elliot Goldenthal

Brad Pitt stars as Louis, a 1790s New Orleans plantation owner and slave owner who becomes an ageless vampire searching for the meaning of it all. The story, which mostly shifts between 1870s Paris (where vampires stage horror plays) and modern times, is told from his point of view. Tom Cruise (in lift shoes) is the tall, blond Lestat. With Kirsten Dunst (who was 11 years old) as the little girl vampire, and Antonio Banderas as Armand. It's a great-looking movie and is much better than Coppola's *Dracula*. The only part I hated was the Guns 'n Roses remake of "Sympathy for the Devil" at the end. Anne Rice's 1976 novel had sold five million copies. The 122-minute David Geffen production was 17 years in development and was a hit for Jordan (just after his *The Crying Game*). It cost over $50 million and was shot in New Orleans, San Francisco, and Paris. Some of the Stan Winston gore FX were cut pre-release, but there's still a body-cut-in-half scene that's pretty strong for such a major release. Also with Stephen Rea and Christian Slater (who replaced the late River Phoenix) as the reporter. The score is on Geffen Records.

INTERZONE

(TWE, 1986) **D:** Deran Sarafian
S: James Edwards **P:** David Hills

A peaceful group turns to a warrior named Swan to save them from a post-nuke tribe. He's killed for failing and then brought back to life. With Bruce Abbott and female bodybuilder Tegan Clive.

IN THE AFTERMATH

(Starmaker, 1988) **D/S:** Carl Colpaert **S:** Mamoru Oshii   US/Japan *(Angels Never Sleep)*

An angel brings a magic egg to post-nuke Earth in animated scenes, and two survivors (Tony Markes and Rainbow Dolan) appear in live-action scenes. The director is from Belgium. Anthony Moore wrote the music.

IN THE COLD OF THE NIGHT

(Republic, 1989) **D/P:** Nico Mastorakis
S: Frank C. Perry

A musclebound Malibu beach gigolo/photographer (Jeff Lester) has dreams of killing women he had sex with. Adrienne Sachs is his dream-girl, a model with a motorcycle. It's about mind-control experiments and features lots of sex. With Shannon Tweed, Marc Singer, Brian Thompson, David Soul as a shrink, John Beck, and Tippi Hedren in one scene as a mom afraid of birds. Scenes are repeated, and clips of other Mastorakis films are watched on TV. It runs a long 113 minutes and is available in R and NC-17 versions.

IN THE DEEP WOODS

(Atlantic, 1992) **D:** Charles Correll **S:** Robert Nathan, Robert Rosenblum **P:** Frederic Golchan

Anthony Perkins played his last role in this NBC-TV movie, and it's a typically weird one. He's a man who follows a children's-book illustrator (Rosanna Arquette) while a psycho is killing successful women after torturing them with burns and pliers. It turns out that Perkins is after the "Deep Woods" serial killer, who murdered his daughter. The cast includes Will Patton as an FBI man, Chris Rydell as Arquette's strange brother, D. W. Moffat as her lover, and Kimberly Beck. It's based on the novel by Nicholas Conde.

IN THE EYE OF THE SNAKE

(AIP, 1994) **D:** Max Reid **S:** Efrem Camerin **S/P:** Jacques Sandoz   Switzerland

Marc (Jason Cairns) is a snake-expert teen who works at a museum in Geneva. He owns many snakes and even sleeps with and bathes with his pet python. He falls for Malenka (Sidney Penny), the assistant/mistress of a snake-expert professor (Malcolm McDowell) who turns out to be a fraud, a coward, and a dangerous psycho who seduced Marc's mother (Lois Chiles). Howard Vernon appears in flashbacks filmed in Burundi. The music is by Patrick Moraz. It could be rated PG. Reid also directed *Wild Thing* (1987), written by John Sayles.

IN THE HEAT OF PASSION

(RCA, 1992) **D/S/P:** Rodman Felder

Nick Corri stars as a part-time actor (named Charley Bronson) cast as a rapist on a reality TV program (hosted by Jack Carter). He's mistaken for the real wanted guy he portrayed and has an affair with an older, married psychiatrist (48-year-old Sally Kirkland), who shows up in various disguises to fool her rich husband and is frequently topless. There's sex and a murder. This Concorde release by the director of *The Unborn* is available in R and unrated versions. *In the Heat of Passion II: The Unfaithful* (1994) had an entirely different cast.

IN THE LINE OF DUTY: THE SIEGE OF WACO

(Republic, 1993) **D/P:** Dick Lowry **S:** Phil Penningroth

NBC-TV debuted this 84 days after the siege in which 86 cult members died in flames. It was being filmed while the events were happening. Now, that's exploitation! Tim Daly stars as would-be rock star turned cult leader David Koresh (he looks just like him), with Dan Lauria and William O'Leary. It was filmed outside Tulsa. Penningroth also wrote the TV movie *The Amy Fisher Story*.

IN THE LINE OF FIRE

(Columbia,1994) **D:** Wolfgang Peterson
S: Jeff Maguire **P:** Jeff Apple

Clint Eastwood stars as a secret service agent (called an old dinosaur) who was in Dallas on November 22, 1963, and regrets not having done more to save the president. John Malkovich (who received an Oscar nomination) is a relentless, intel-

ligent psycho after the current president. With Rene Russo, Dylan McDermott, John Mahoney, and Steve Railsback. It's 127 minutes long.

IN THE MOUTH OF MADNESS

(New Line, 1995) **D:** John Carpenter
S: Michael De Luca **P:** Sandy King

An insurance investigator (Sam Neill) is hired to search for a missing bestselling horror writer Sutter Kane (Jurgen Prochnow) whose book drives people crazy. His tale is told from an asylum. Most of this takes place in one of those typical Stephen King–style small mysterious New England towns. Neill is good and there are a few inspired reality-vs.-fantasy scenes, but other scenes should have been in another movie and a lot of it just doesn't make much sense. Still, it was Carpenter's best in years and has a great scene in a movie theater. The screenwriter is a young New Line executive. KNB created the Lovecraft-inspired mutant creatures. With Julie Carmen, pretty forgettable as a NYC book editor working for Charlton Heston, David Warner, Bernie Casey, and John Glover. It was shot in Toronto.

IN THE SHADOW OF KILIMANJARO

(IVE, 1984) **D:** Raju Patel **S/P:** Jeffrey M. Sneller **P:** Gautam Das

"Thousands" of hungry baboons (we see a few dozen) go on the rampage during a drought in Africa. It gets gory when natives eat baboons and baboons eat people. Timothy Bottoms stars, with Irene Miracle, John Rhys-Davies, and Michele Carey. Some animation was used. It's "based on a true story" and was filmed in Kenya.

IN THE SPIRIT

(Academy, 1990) **D:** Sandra Seacat **S:** Jeannie Berlin, Laurie Jones **P:** Julian Schlossberg

A Beverly Hills couple move to New York City, where they meet a mystic and have to hide from a killer. The cast of this black comedy includes Elaine May, Marlo Thomas, Jeannie Berlin, (May's real-life daughter), Peter Falk, and Melanie Griffith in a bit part.

INTIMATE DELUSIONS

(1992) **D/S:** Ron Oliver **P:** Ray Sager   Canada

David Keith and Shannon Tweed get married at Niagara Falls. Christopher Plummer and Joseph Bottons costar in this comedy, which features clowns and midgets. The director made *Prom Night III*.

INTIMATE STRANGER

(Paramount, 1991) **D:** Allan Holzman **S:** Rob Fresno **P:** Yoram Pelman, J. J. Lichauco Pelman

"She just turned on the wrong guy!" Deborah Harry stars as a cynical bar singer who takes a phone-sex job to make some money. Tim Thomerson calls her and kills a prostitute while she listens. The cast includes James Russo as the only cop who believes her, Grace Zabriskie, and Tia Carrere. It was made for cable TV by the director of *Forbidden World* (1982).

INTO THE BADLANDS

(MCA, 1991) **D:** Sam Pillsbury **S:** Dick Bebe, Gordon Davison, Marjorie Davis **P:** Harvey Friend

It's hard to believe that *Grim Prairie Tales* spawned another western horror anthology, but here it is. Bruce Dern is an eccentric bounty hunter who narrates the tale and stars in one. Dylan McDermott, Helen Hunt, and Andy Robinson are in the first one. Mariel Hemingway (looking more unreal than ever) is a religious prairie woman who faces a wolf attack. In Dern's tale he cuts his own toe off and talks to the rotting corpse he's trying to deliver. They all have twist endings, but they're pretty slow going and feature odd guitar music. The director, from New Zealand, also made *Zandalee* (with Nicolas Cage). Also with Lisa Pelikan. This was made in New Mexico for the USA Network.

INTO THE FIRE

(Vestron, 1987) **D:** Graeme Campbell **S:** Jesse Ballard **P:** Nicholas Stillada   Canada (*Legend of Wolf Lodge*)

Art Hindle and his rich wife (Susan Anspach) own a northwest estate. A young musician (Lee Montgomery) and his waitress girlfriend (Olivia D'Abo) show up. There's a confused seduction/murder/scam plot (with nudity), and they die at the end.

INTO THE NIGHT

(MCA, 1985) **D:** John Landis **S/P:** Ron Koslow **P:** George Folsey Jr.

Jeff Goldblum is an engineer with insomnia who ends up helping Michelle Pfeiffer, who's being chased by mobsters and SAVAK (Iranian secret police) because she has some smuggled emeralds. This adventure comedy features Kathyrn Harrold, Richard Farnsworth, David Bowie, Vera Miles, Irene Papas, Jake Steinfeld, and Dan Aykroyd. A lot of directors have cameos, including Jack Arnold, Paul Bartel, David Cronenberg, Jonathan Demme, Don Siegel, Richard Franklin, Jim Henson, Roger Vadim, and Amy Heckerling, and so does Forry Ackerman. Landis' *Spies Like Us* (1985) had director cameos too. I guess it was a show of support after *The Twilight Zone* deaths. The (out of print) MCA soundtrack is mostly cuts by blues and soul artists, including Marvin Gaye and B. B. King, who did the incidental music.

INTO THE SUN

(Vidmark, 1992) **D:** Fritz Kiersch **S:** John Brancato, Michael Ferris **P:** Kevin Kallberg, Oliver Hess

This action comedy has the same plot as *The Hard Way* (1991). Anthony Michael Hall is an actor who hangs out with Air Force flying ace Michael Paré to prepare for a role and ends up fighting Arabs in the desert. The cast includes Terry Kiser and Deborah Maria Moore. It's by the director of *Gor* and *Tuff Turf.*

INTRUDER

(Paramount, 1988) **D/S:** Scott Spiegel **P:** Laurence Bender   (*Night Crew*)

Teens working at night to prepare for a sale in a supermarket are killed by a pyscho. This extremely gory film was heavily cut to get an R rating for the US video release, but the Belgian and Japanese versions are complete. With Elizabeth Cox, Renee Estevez, Alvy Moore, Bruce Campbell, Sam and Ted Raimi, and Emil Sitka. Spiegel cowrote *Evil Dead II.*

INTRUDERS

(Fox, 1992) **D:** Dan Curtis **S:** Barry Oringer, Tracy Torme **P:** Banki Lustig

After the failure of the revived TV series *Dark Shadows* Curtis made this (originally 2-part) CBS-TV movie. Richard Crenna is an LA psychiatrist at a mental hospital who uses regressive hypnotism on people who have had "close encounters of the third kind." Aliens arrive and impregnate Dana Ashbrook. Mare Winningham is "chosen" as a child. Susan Blakely is her sister. Inmate Ben Vereen has disturbing flashbacks. Despite a few good scenes, this goes on way too long (163 minutes) and is pretty dull. With Daphne Ashbrook, Steven Berkoff, Rosalind Chao, and G. D. Spradlin.

INVADER

(Vidmark, 1992) **D/S:** Phillip S. Cook **P:** John R. Ellis

A pushy scandal-magazine reporter (Hans Bachman) discovers that "aliens" in dark sunglasses disguised as soldiers have taken over the Clarksburg Air Force base. He teams up with a (black) guy from the Defense Department (A. Thomas Smith), and they steal a superjet for an impressive air battle. A talking animated robot (like in *Robocop*) is the only other worthwhile thing in the film. This 21st Century production, made in Virginia, is aimed at kids and includes some comedy and lots of explosions. The cast includes Rick Foucheux and George Stover in one scene. Cook directed *Beyond the Rising Moon* (1988).

THE INVADERS (1961) = ERIK THE CONQUEROR

THE INVADERS

(Goodtimes series, 1967–68)

Roy Thinnes starred as architect David Vincent in the ABC-TV series created by Larry Cohen. Until he convinced several others, he was the only person who realized that aliens disguised as humans were taking over. The only way to identify the aliens was by their bent little fingers. Kent Smith was a regular, and many name stars were guests. Thinnes also appeared in a 1995 2-part revival attempt TV pilot, *The Invaders* (Republic).

INVADERS FROM MARS

(Nostalgia Merchant, 1953) **D:** William Cameron Menzies **S:** Richard Blake **P:** Edward L. Alperson

This is one of the most fondly remembered cult science-fiction hits of the 50s. Director Menzies (*Things to Come*) was also his own set designer. His brilliantly surreal, minimal sets, offbeat pacing, and "Is it a dream?" ending make this a unique, nightmarish experience. When little David tries to tell people that his parents have disappeared into a sand pit and become cold and zombie-like because of neck implants from Martians who landed near their backyard, only a lady doctor believes him. He has to escape his once loving parents ("Please don't let my father get me!"), and because everything is seen from David's point of view, the film is like Kafka for kids. (Menzies was once a children's book writer.) The parents (Leif Erickson and Hillary Brooke) are scary. Dad even smacks his son across the room. The doctor (Helena Carter) is understanding, reassuring, and great to look at, with flaming red hair and lips, a white dress, and stockings with seams. Jimmy Hunt plays David as an intelligent but frightened little kid. There's a good flying saucer, a memorable alien head in a round tank, silly but great mutant slaves, and cost-saving military stock footage. From 20th Century–Fox.

INVADERS FROM MARS

(Media, 1986) **D:** Tobe Hooper **S:** Dan O'Bannon, Don Jakoby **P:** Golan/Globus **M:** Christopher Young

The remake isn't a revisionist effort (like the 80s versions of *The Fly, The Thing,* or *Cat People*). It copies the original pretty closely but still gets practically everything wrong. Karen Black as the doctor seems frazzled and a bit crazy. Hunter Carson (Black's real-life son) is bland and most of the time seems either bored or blubbery. The parents (Timothy Bottoms and Laraine Newman) are fine in the beginning, but after being "taken over" they just do weird things, like eating raw hamburger. Money was obviously spent on state-of-the-art effects by John Dykstra and Stan Winston, but the more elaborate spaceship and monster aliens merely look like less effective leftovers from *Dune*. Attempts to modernize the dialogue and make it funny are pretty dismal. Jimmy Hunt (from the original) shows up as the police chief. The score is on Enigma. Watching both tapes together makes for a fascinating comparison between durably effective, low-budget creativity and today's trashing of old movies for quick remake profits. The Image Laser version includes "making of" shorts on this and *Lifeforce*. After doing three Cannon movies in a row, Hooper directed an episode of *The Equalizer*, the pilot for the *Freddy's Nightmares* TV series, and a Cars rock video. Newman hosted the syndicated *Canned Film Festival* on TV, presenting "bad" movies, the same year.

INVASION EARTH: THE ALIENS ARE HERE!

(Starmaker, 1987) **D:** George Maitland **S:** Miller Drake **P:** Max J. Rosenberg

Despite the misleading video box, this is a mixture of new scenes and endless, great film clips from dozens of 50s and 60s science-fiction movies. The clever, disorienting opening has people in a theater watching the scene in *The Blob* where people in a theater watch *Daughter of Horror*. Mel Welles (acting pretty much like Gravis in *The Little Shop of Horrors*) is the manager of the theater, but it's invaded by bug-man aliens and their brain/head leader, and he becomes a bug man too. They zap the projectionist, discuss *Plan 9 from Outer Space,* and start editing and showing alien and monster film clips. They use pods to replace people, who end up tied up in their underwear behind the screen. Meanwhile, some kids sneak around trying to stop the invasion, and we're subjected to some pretty forced humor and treated to great clips from big hits like *War of the Worlds*, *Them*, and *The Thing*, and cheapo faves like *The Brain from Planet Arous*, *Invasion of the Saucer Men*, and *The Giant Claw*, plus random scenes by Harryhausen, Corman, and Bert I. Gordon. Near the end the clips get better and the editing gets faster. The parts from *The Crawling Eye* and *Fiend Without a Face* are amazing. I forgot how bloody and squishy those flying brains with spinal cords were! Producer Rosenberg used be one of the heads of the British Amicus company and must have had the connections to get the rights to use all the clips. It's from New World.

INVASION FORCE = HANGAR 18

INVASION FORCE

(AIP, 1990) **D:** David Prior **S:** David Winters **P:** David Marriott

A film crew and actors with props battle real terrorists taking over an American city. Richard Lynch stars in this ripoff of *Invasion USA* (which Lynch is also in), with Renee Cline, Walter Cox, and David Shark.

INVASION FROM INNER EARTH

(API, 1972) **D/P:** Bill Rebane **S:** Barbara J. Rebane (*Hell Fire; They*)

A DJ in Manitoba is the star of a UFO talk show. Unseen aliens take over, and he thinks he's the last survivor. Characters hide out in a remote snow-bound farmhouse and discuss what could have happened. Paul Bentzen and Debbie Pick star in this very slow-moving feature. It was made (in Wisconsin) before Rebane's *The Giant Spider Invasion* but released in 1977.

INVASION OF PRIVACY

(Prism, 1992) **D/S:** Kevin Meyer **P:** Ashok Amritraj

Robby Benson stars as a psycho ex-con obsessed with a reporter (Jennifer O'Neill). She hires him to help with a prison story, and he has an affair with her daughter (Lydie Denier). The cast also includes Ian Ogilvy. R and unrated versions of this "erotic thriller" are available.

INVASION OF THE GIRL SNATCHERS

(VCI, 1973) **D:** Lee Jones **S:** Phineas T. Pinkham, Carla Rueckert (*The Hidan of Mount Bienjow*)

This seriously awful comedy from Arkansas was released (by Jeffrey Hogue) because of a bet that it couldn't make any money. It's about a cop going after human-looking aliens who kidnap women and take over their bodies.

INVASION OF THE SCREAM QUEENS

(See More Video, 1992) **D:** Donald Farmer

It could have used some more editing, but many actresses are interviewed on this tape, and movie scenes and trailers (lots of David DeCoteau) are included. The ones we'd expect (Brinke Stevens, who says she "looked like a werewolf" as a kid, Michelle Bauer, and Melissa Moore, who talks a lot) are here, along with actresses from Mark Pirro movies, Janus Blythe, Vivian Schilling, Elizabeth Kaitan (way too long), Martine Beswick, and Monique Gabrielle (bad takes and all). The best of all, though, is Mary Woronov, who talks about (and shows) some of her paintings and remembers working for Warhol, Corman, and others. A whole tape of just her talking would be interesting.

INVASION OF THE SPACE PREACHERS

(Rhino, 1990) **D/S/P:** Daniel Boyd **P:** David Wohl (*The Strangest Dreams*)

This ambitious, unpredictable science-fiction comedy is from West Virginia. Walter, a sensitive dentist (Jim Wolfe), and Rick, a yuppie accountant (Guy Nelson) set out for a cabin in the country. They insult each other by calling each other "'mo"s. On the way they stop at a gas-station tourist attraction, the House of Dung, then find a reptile-like alien who has crashed in a spaceship. The alien splits open, revealing Nova (Eliska Hahn), a pretty blond. Nova has a ray gun and chugs Coors. Johnny Angel, a (very good) rockabilly singer with female backup singers, does some numbers, and Jimmy Walker, an older country singer, does a song. The meandering plot includes a survivalist, pot-harvesting hippie commune and the Reverend Lash, a corrupt preacher who issues mind-control ear plugs to his followers and can make heads explode. Despite some nudity (swimming and sun-bathing) and drugs that nobody uses, it's a pretty innocent and fun movie with an excellent title sequence.

INVASION USA

(Sinister, 1952) **D:** Alfred E. Green **S/P:** Robert Smith **P:** Albert Zugsmith

Dan O'Herlihy hypnotizes a group of people in a NYC bar with his brandy glass, and they experience what could happen because "we don't have a strong enough Army." Soldiers in American uniforms attack through Alaska and take Washington State, then San Francisco. Eventually the (un-named) enemy destroys Boulder Dam, nukes military bases, shoots senators in DC, and drops the big one on New York City! Peggy Castle jumps out of a window to avoid the crude, drunken, lecherous (obviously Soviet) soldiers. There are lots of WWII references and stock footage of battles, plus some nice miniature work by Jack Rabin. Gerald Mohr stars as TV commentator Vince Potter, with William Schallert and two Lois Lanes (Phyllis Coates and Noel Neill). Columbia released this just as Eisenhower was becoming president. Amazing!

INVASION USA

(MGM, 1985) **D:** Joseph Zito **S/A:** Chuck Norris **S:** James Bruner **P:** Menahem Golan, Yoram Globus **M:** Jay Chattaway

Chuck Norris as ex–CIA agent Matt Hunter lives in the Everglades with an armadillo. When the Communists invade Miami and Atlanta he comes out of retirement and kicks ass. The ads said, "America wasn't ready, but he was!" Richard Lynch is the evil Rostov. With Melissa Prophet, Billy Drago, and James Pax. The Commies blow up a church, invade the suburbs on Christmas, try to blow up a full schoolbus, and even invade a mall! They kill Cuban boat people too. The story was by Aaron Norris. Tom Savini did the FX. The soundtrack was released by Varèse Sarabande.

INVINCIBLE BARBARIAN

(ANE, 1985) **D:** Franco Prosperi **S:** Peter Lombard   Italy

A warrior named Zucan who was raised by Amazons joins with a breeder slave (Sabrina Siani) to fight the oppressors. A narrator explains the be-

Richard Lynch is a Commie invader in *Invasion USA*.

ginning of the world, and some stock-footage dino-saurs are seen. Siani, who specializes in dumb movies like this, takes her clothes off again.

INVINCIBLE GLADIATOR

(Sinister, 1961) **D:** Antonio Momplet, Frank Gregory **S:** Francisco De Feo **P:** Cleto Fontini, Alberto De Martino   Spain/Italy (*Il Gladiatore Invincible*)

Richard Harrison stars in this Technicolor arena-fight movie, with Isabel Corey as Princess Sira.

THE INVISIBLE AVENGER

(Sinister, 1958) **D:** James Wong Howe, John Sledge **S:** George Bellak, Betty Jeffries **P:** Eric Sayers, Emanuel Demby   (*Bourbon Street Shadows*)

The famed Chinese-born cinematographer James Wong Howe directed two films, *Go, Man, Go!* (1954) starring the Harlem Globetrotters, and this odd crime movie, (actually episodes of a planned TV series) filmed in New Orleans, based on the famous radio series *The Shadow*. The dialogue and the plot, about an exiled South American leader and his evil twin, are on the level of a serial or Saturday-morning TV show. Richard Derr is La-mont Cranston, "the Shadow," who uses telepathy and hypnotism to "cloud men's minds" and laughs like a maniac every time he seems to disappear. Jogrendra (Mark Daniels) is his Asian-looking, cultured, philosophical, and mystical teacher, com-panion, and live-in assistant. They wear robes and meditate in their hotel room while they investigate the murder of a New Orleans musician and gang-sters plot to kill the Shadow. In a club, the Famous Door, Cranston says, "That last chorus went clear out of space!" Somebody plays "St. James Infir-mary." A "real" execution is broadcast on TV, and there's an on-location car chase through a ceme-tery. In 1962 this Republic film was rereleased with some new footage in a more "adult" version. "Who knows what evil lurks in the hearts of men?"

THE INVISIBLE DEAD

(Wizard, 1970) **D/S:** Pierre Chevalier **S:** Juan Fortuny Spain/France (*Orloff y el Hombre Invisible; The Love Life of the Invisible Man*)

Howard Vernon plays Dr. Orloff again, in this period horror film featuring an ape man and sex with an invisible man. Some versions have more nudity than others.

THE INVISIBLE KID

(Media, 1988) **D/S:** Avery Crounse **P:** Philip J. Spinelli

Nerd Jay Underwood becomes invisible and can wander into the girls' locker room at school. This teen comedy is like *Zapped!* Karen Black (who was also in *Zapped Again!)* is a dizzy mom who watches Brother Theodore's TV call-in show. The cast includes Michelle Phillips' daughter Chynna (from the Wilson Phillips group). It's by the di-rector of *Eyes of Fire*.

THE INVISIBLE KILLER

(Sinister, 1940) **D:** "Sherman Scott"/Sam Neufield **S:** Joseph O'Connell **P:** Sigmund Neufield

Sonic murders are caused by telephones (an idea later used in *Murder by Phone*). Grace Bradley stars, with Roland Drew as a detective. This 61-minute time-waster is from PRC.

THE INVISIBLE MANIAC

(Republic, 1989) **D/S:** "Rif Coogan"/Adam Rifkin **S/P:** Anthony Marks **S:** "Matt Devlin"/Brett McCormick

In this sex/horror comedy(?) Dr. Kevin Dornwin-kle (Noel Peters), a crazed, woman-hating, voyeur/killer scientist, escapes from an asylum and be-comes a substitute high-school physics teacher. He dreams of naked schoolgirls and finally perfects his serum and injects himself so that he can watch them in showers. He cracks up after students make fun of him and starts slaughtering them while laughing hysterically. The mute janitor is also a voyeur (so are most of the male students), and the principal blackmails students into having sex with her. The females (including Melissa Anne Moore, Debra Lamb, and the late porno star Savannah) look great, but Peters' irritating acting, the bad FX, and the stupid script will make you wish they were in a different movie. Producer Marks returned with *Bikini Island*.

THE INVISIBLE MENACE

(SW, 1937) **D:** John Farrow **S:** Crane Wilbur   (*Without Warning*)

Characters on a foggy Navy-base island are killed and tortured. Mr. Jeffries (Boris Karloff), an ex-con who was once an engineer in US-occupied Haiti, is the obvious suspect. Flashbacks show how his wife cheated on him and how he was framed. There's also a voodoo dance. With Marie Wilson as a dumb-seeming but observant new bride, Eddie Craven, and Regis Toomey as the officer of the guard. This 56-minute Warner Brothers film is based on a play. *Murder on the Waterfront* (1943) is a remake.

THE INVISIBLE MONSTER

(Stokey, 1950) **D:** Frank Brannon **S:** Ronald Davidson

Richard Webb stars as the hero of this 12-chapter Republic serial with an "invisible" villain. Aline Towne costars, with Stanley Price as "the Phantom Ruler," John Crawford, and Republic's fine stunt men. The feature version was *Slaves of the Invis-ible Monster*. Webb went on to star in the TV se-ries *Captain Midnight*.

THE INVISIBLE STRANGLER

(TWE, 1976) **D:** John Florea **S:** Arthur C. Pierce **P:** Earle Lyon   (*Astral Factor*)

A young psycho killer on death row learns an an-cient Buddhist technique for becoming invisible and goes on a murder spree. The plot is pretty similar to the plot of *Psychic Killer* (1975). Robert Foxworth stars as a cop, and the all-star cast in-cludes Stefanie Powers, Elke Sommer, Sue Lyon, Leslie Parrish, Marianne Hill, and Cesare Danova. It was released in 1984.

INVISIBLE: THE CHRONICLES OF BENJAMIN KNIGHT

(Paramount, 1994) **D:** Jack Ersgard **S:** Earl Kenton **P:** Vlad and Dana Paunesco

This is a (senseless) sequel to *Mandroid*. They were both shot in Bucharest, Romania. Michael Dellafemina somehow becomes invisible and the metal masked Drago (Curt Lowens) sends a comic group of insane peasants to kidnap girls in the woods. This involves (offscreen) gang rapes. Blonde beauty Jennifer Nash (taking over the role of a late scientist's daughter) proves to be the best special effect during her on-top fuck scene. This movie has lots of bad guys and slo-mo b/w flash-backs. With Brian Cousin returning as the scientist in a wheelchair who controls the remote robot.

THE INVISIBLE WOMAN

(1983) **D/P:** Alan J. Levi **S:** Sherwood Schwartz, Lloyd J. Schwartz

Alexa Hamilton is an invisible reporter in this NBC-TV series pilot about a museum robbery. Bob Denver, David Doyle, George Gobel, Harvey Kor-man, Art La Fleur, Garrett Morris, and Ron Palillo round out the comic cast.

INVITATION TO HELL

(Sony, 1984) **D:** Wes Craven **S:** Richard Rothstein **P:** Robert M. Sertner

Soap-opera star Susan Lucci is the Devil, and her country club is a gateway to Hell! This ABC-TV movie sounds a lot better than it is. Robert Urich and Joanna Cassidy are the unsuspecting new couple in town. The cast also includes Kevin McCarthy, Nicholas Worth, Joe Regalbuto, Soleil Moon Frye, Patty McCormack, and Michael Berry-man in a bit part.

IN YOUR FACE

(Video Vault, 1977) **D:** Frank Packard **S:** James Smalley **P:** J. P. Joshua   (*Abar, the Black Superman*)

This previously unknown wonder is a very ambi-tious and political curiosity item. A nice, middle-class black family moves to the suburbs and encounters insults, screaming, and worse from garbage-throwing whites. A black biker gang rid-ing Harleys comes to their rescue. Their leader, Abar (Tobar Mayo), is a militant, bald, kung-fu-fighting admirer of Malcolm X. He has political de-bates with the doctor dad (J. Walter Smith), who prefers Martin Luther King Jr. After the death of his kid, the doctor convinces Abar to drink a serum that has already made a rabbit indestruct-ible. Abar develops psychic powers, makes a hooker beat her pimp, then makes corrupt cops fight each other (near the Watts Tower). He has a vision of Christ, causes a storm, and creates rats and snakes to attack racist whites. This movie uses imitation *Shaft* music and is very low-budget (a hand-held microphone is visible in one scene), but the serious script makes it more of an admirable morale-booster than an exploitation movie. The doomed little boy even has a happy dream se-quence, with Abar appearing as a cowboy hero.

IRAN ANGELS: *See* ANGEL

IRON AND SILK

(1990) **D/P:** Shirley Sun
S/A: Mark Salzman   Canada

Mark Salzman stars as himself in this adaptation of his book about his experiences in China. He goes there in 1982 to teach English, learns kung-fu, and falls for a Chinese girl (Vivian Wu). His teacher is Pan Quingfu (also playing himself). Much of this PG film shows kung-fu training. It was shot in Canada.

THE IRON CLAW

(Stokey, 1941) **D:** James W. Horne **S:** Basil Dickey, George Plympton, Jesse A. Duffy **P:** Larry Darmour

This 15-chapter Columbia serial has a villain with a steel-hook hand. Charles Quigley stars, with Joyce Bryant and Forrest Taylor.

IRON EAGLE

(Fox, 1986) **D/S:** Sidney J. Furie **S:** Kevin Elders **P:** Ron Samuels, Joe Wizan

Jason Gedrick is an 18-year-old who flies a stolen fighter jet to the Middle East to rescue his father (Tim Thomerson), who has been sentenced to hang. He's helped by Louis Gossett Jr. as a renegade Air Force colonel named Chappy. Real Israeli Air Force planes were used for the impressive air-fight scenes. This PG-13 Tristar hit was released the same year as *Top Gun*. The rock soundtrack with various artists, including Queen and Dio, is on Capitol.

IRON EAGLE II

(IVE, 1988) **D:** Sidney J. Furie **S:** Kevin Elders **P:** Jacob Kotzky, Sharon Harel   Canada/Israel

Louis Gossett Jr. returns as Chappy. He leads a joint US/Soviet mission of teens to destroy Middle Eastern nuclear weapons. The cast includes Mark Humphrey and Stuart Margolin. This PG movie reportedly sold $21 million worth of tapes, so another sequel, *Aces,* was produced. The rock soundtrack with various artists is on Epic.

IRON HEART

(Imperial, 1991) **D:** Robert Clouse
S: Lawrence Riggins **P/A:** Britton Lee

Master Lee stars as an LA cop after killer drug dealer Richard Norton. With Bolo Yeung as Ice and Karman Kruschke.

IRONMASTER

(ANE, 1982) **D:** Umberto Lenzi **S:** Alberto Cavallone, Dardano Sacchetti, Lea Martino, Gabriel Rossini   Italy (*La Guerra del Ferro*)

William Berger and George Eastman (real name: Luigi Montefiore) star in this prehistoric action movie.

IRON MAZE

(1991) **D:** Hiroaki Yoshida **S:** Tim Metcalfe **P:** Ilona Herzberg, Hidenori Ueki   US/Japan

A Japanese businessman (Hiroaki Murakami) buys a shut-down steel plant in a small Pennsylvania town and plans to build an amusement park. His lonely American wife (Bridget Fonda) has an affair with the hotel bellboy (Jeff Fahey), and the businessman is nearly murdered at the plant. This event is seen from several points of view in the style of Kurosawa's *Rashomon*. The cast includes John Randolph and J. T. Walsh as a local cop. Oliver Stone was an executive producer.

IRON WARRIOR

(Media, 1985) **D:** "Al Bradley"/Alfonso Brescia **S:** Steven Luotto **P:** Ovidio G. Assonitis   Italy (*Echoes of Wizardry*)

Miles O'Keefe plays an imitation Conan called Ator (for the third time) and his own evil twin. He battles an evil sorceress and her silver-skulled "iron warrior" and helps a princess in a see-through blouse (Savina Gersak). It was filmed in Malta.

I SAW WHAT YOU DID

(1988) **D:** Fred Walton **S:** Cynthia Cidre **P:** Barry Greenfield

A pair of teen girls making prank phone calls unknowingly call a psycho killer and say, "I saw what you did!" Shawnee Smith (*The Blob*) and Tammy Lauren star, with Candace Cameron, Robert Carradine, and David Carradine (who was also in the TV remake of *The Bad Seed*). This TV remake of William Castle's 1965 movie is by the director of *April Fool's Day*.

THE ISLAND AT THE TOP OF THE WORLD

(Disney, 1974) **D:** Robert Stevenson **S:** John Whedon **P:** Winston Hibler **M:** Maurice Jarre

Adventurers in a big dirigible discover a lost world and a Viking civilization at the Arctic circle, in this Jules Verne–type fantasy/adventure from Disney. David Hartman stars, with Donald Sinden and Mako as the Eskimo guide Oomiak. The soundtrack was released by Disneyland Records.

ISLAND CLAWS

(Vestron, 1980) **D:** Hernán Cárdenas **S:** Jack Cowden, Ricou Browning **P:** Ted Swanson   (*Night of the Claw*)

Marine biologists discover a giant man-eating crab on an island off Florida. With Barry Nelson, Robert Lansing, and Nita Talbot. The crab (caused by a nuclear accident) doesn't appear until the very end. Roger Corman did it better in the 50s.

ISLAND FURY

(AIP, 1989) **D:** Henri Charr **S:** John B. Pfeifer **P:** Jess Mancilla, Marcus Robertson

Mardi Rustam was the executive producer, so as usual this is an unfinished (?) movie with new scenes added. After a lengthy part about two teen girls being kidnapped from some Chinatown, we get the big flashback (the older footage) set on a remote island. The late Hank Worden is Jedediah,

an old man living with his wife, their little grandson, and the mute, retarded Junior. The friendly-seeming old hicks are really crazy killers. They poison visitors' tea, blow up a boat ("It done blowed up higher 'n a kite!"), and keep bloody naked bodies (obvious mannequins!) hanging in the barn. The fight scenes are awful, and the action is interrupted by an earthquake. Michael Wayne is Repo.

ISLAND MONSTER = MONSTER OF THE ISLAND

ISLAND OF BLOOD

(Applause, 1982) **D/S/P:** Bill Naud   (*Whodunit?*)

Actors and a director making a movie on an island are murdered in various ways by a mystery killer. Tapes of rock songs describing the murders (by chainsaw, acid, spear) are left near the bodies. Rick Dean is in this obscure *Ten Little Indians* ripoff.

ISLAND OF LOST GIRLS

(SW, 1968) **D:** Roberto Mauri **S:** James Brewer, Robert F. Atkinson, Manfred R. Kohler **P:** Theodore Werner, Ralph Zucker   Italy/W. Germany (*Kommissar X; Drei Goldene Schlangen*)

Tony Kendall (real name Luciano Stella) stars as Joe Walker, aka Kommissar X, a muscular playboy/detective hired by a rich American tourist to find her daughter in Bangkok. Madame Kim So keeps topless young women in an opium-induced zombie state on her island and sells them as prostitutes. Brad Harris is Walker's friend Captain Roland. This was filmed on location and includes a crocodile farm, a cockfight, and a comic black midget. It was released by Hampton International, then International Artists in the 70s. The video print is faded and lacks credits. The Kommissar X series includes *Kiss Kiss, Kill Kill* (1965) and at least five others, all based on novels by Atkinson, and filmed in various countries.

ISLAND OF THE LOST

(Republic, 1968) **D:** John Florea, Ricou Browning **S:** Richard Carlson **S/P:** Ivan Tors

An anthropologist (Richard Greene) and his family are shipwrecked in the South Seas. With Luke Halpin (from the *Flipper* TV series), Robin Mattson, and Irene Tsu. Browning played the creature in *The Creature from the Black Lagoon,* and Richard Carlson (who cowrote this film) was the scientist hero.

ISLAND WOMEN

(Private Screenings, 1980) **D:** Jesús Franco **P:** Edwin C. Dietrich   (*Gefangenfrauen; Women's Penitentiary VII*)

Women are locked up in the Central American Tago Mago prison. French porno star Brigitte Lahaie stars, with Karine Ganbier as the warden. Nude fights and sex (8 minutes) were cut from the US-release video.

ISLE OF FORGOTTEN SINS

(Sinister, 1943) **D:** Edgar G. Ulmer
S: Raymond L. Schrock **P:** Peter
Van Duinen   (*Monsoon*)

John Carradine stars as a deep-sea pearl diver
searching for gold in a sunken ship, with Gale Sondergaard, Sidney Toler, Veda Ann Borg, and Frank
Fenton. Carradine starred in Ulmer's better-known
Bluebeard, also from PRC.

I SPIT ON YOUR CORPSE

(Super, Marathon, 1974) **D:** Al Adamson
S: John D'Amato **P:** Sam Sherman
(*Girls for Rent; Fatal Pursuit*)

Porno star Georgina Spelvin is a laughing, psycho
hitwoman in the desert who has been set up. Rosalind Miles and Susan McGiver are the women
sent to kill her. Parts of this R-rated drive-in movie
resemble Adamson's *Satan's Sadists*, with Spelvin
in the Russ Tamblyn role. The cast also includes
Robert Livingston, Barbara Bourbon, and veteran
Hollywood actor Kent Taylor in his sixth Adamson
film. Spelvin was in X films from the early 70s
until 1984, when she was in the first *Police Academy* movie.

I SPIT ON YOUR GRAVE

(Vid America, 1978) **D/S/P:** Meir Zarchi
P: Joseph Zbeda   (*Day of the Woman*)

After *Last House on the Left* (1972) this is the best-
known and most controversial American revenge
exploitation movie. Camille Keaton goes to an Upstate New York summer cottage to write. Four local
guys (one is retarded) rape her repeatedly. They
think she's dead, but two weeks later the nearly
catatonic woman lures them back and gets revenge
by killing them in various ways (using an axe,
castration, hanging, etc.). There's no background
music, making it even more unbearable for some
viewers. Keaton was also in Italian exploitation
movies. Siskel and Ebert blasted it on TV, helping
to make it notorious. The complete version is 101
minutes. R and unrated versions are available on
tape. The original *I Spit on Your Grave* was a 1959
French movie retitled by producer Radley Metzger.

IS THERE SEX AFTER DEATH?

(Spencer, 1971) **D/S/P:** Alan and Jeanne Abel

Alan Abel, a professional prankster, made and released this comic parody of a documentary, and he
appears in it as Dr. Rogers, the host and narrator.
Buck Henry is Dr. Manos, a breast expert, Marshall Efron plays a porno director, and Jim Dixon
impersonates President Nixon. There's an X-rated
magic show, dancing and singing at a nudist camp,
and a "sex bowl" competition. The cast also
includes Holly Woodlawn and Robert Downey.
Rated X but later cut for an R, it played midnight
and college shows for years. A paperback version
was published.

I STILL DREAM OF JEANNIE

(1991) **D:** Joseph Scanlan **S:** April Kelly **P:** Joan Carson

Barbara Eden returned as Jeannie in this TV movie
based on the popular NBC fantasy/comedy series
(1965–70). Bill Daily also returned, but since they
couldn't get Larry Hagman, Christopher Bolton
played astronaut Tony Nelson. Al Waxman and
Peter Breck are also in the cast.

IT

(Warner, 1990) **D/S:** Tommy Lee Wallace
S: Lawrence D. Cohen

Some small-town Maine kids encounter Pennywise
(Tim Curry), a magical, evil clown with sharp
teeth, and 30 years later they return as troubled
adults to face their fears again. It's based on Stephen King's thick 1986 novel (which borrows
ideas from Ray Bradbury's novel *Something
Wicked This Way Comes,* filmed in 1983). The
parts with the group of outcast kids are the best.
The shape-shifting clown appears as a werewolf, a
mummy, and finally a stop-motion spider. The cast
includes Richard Thomas, Tim Reid, Harry Anderson, Annette O'Toole, John Ritter, Richard Masur,
Dennis Christopher, and Olivia Hussey. Cohen also
wrote the screenplay for *Carrie.* This 240-minute
ABC-TV miniseries was shot in Vancouver. The
tape is 193 minutes.

ITALIAN STALLION

(GWN, 1970) **D/P:** Morton Lewis
(*Party at Kitty and Stud's Place*)

Sylvester Stallone plays Stud. He has sex with several women. A woman flashes him in the park, and
he gets upset and smashes a window. It all ends

when a black woman does a striptease at a party
and people smoke pot, which leads to an orgy. The
future star from New York was reportedly paid
$200 for acting in this cheap, hour-long, soft-core
adult movie, and 20 years later he was the highest-
paid star in show biz. His next role was a bit in
Woody Allen's *Bananas.*

IT CAME FROM SOMEWHERE ELSE

(Platinum, 1988) **D:** Howard Hassler
S: Patrick V. Johnson

It was promoted as "the worst film ever made," so
beware. This *Plan 9 from Outer Space* spoof was
made in Minnesota and is mostly b/w.

IT COULDN'T HAPPEN HERE

(RCA, 1991) **D/S/P:** Jack Bond **S:** James Dillon   UK

You'd have to really like the pop duo the Pet Shop
Boys (I don't!) to enjoy this pretentious, plotless,
slow movie full of their dreary songs. Partially set
at a seaside carnival, it's complete with WWII
scenes and attempts at surrealism. Joss Ackland is
a blind priest who helps kids. The big hit is "Western Town."

IT GROWS ON TREES

(1952) **D:** Arthur Lubin **S:** Leonard Praskins,
Barney Slater **P:** Leonard Goldstein

Irene Dunne (in her last film) and Dean Jagger discover that $10 bills grow on the trees in their back-
yard. The cast includes Les Tremayne, Joan Evans,
and Richard Crenna. Universal released this fan-
tasy/comedy by the director of most of the movies
in the Francis the Talking Mule series.

IT HAPPENED AT NIGHTMARE INN

(Sinister, 1973) **D/S:** Eugenio Martín **S:** Antonio
Fos **P:** José López Moreno   Spain (*Un Vela para
el Diablo; Nightmare Hotel*)

People disappear at a hotel owned by two sisters.
The dominant, religious-maniac sister kills women
who have "bad morals" with an axe or knives and
keeps the cut-up bodies in the basement, which
causes food poisoning. Judy Geeson arrives looking for her sister. The version on video is cut to 67
minutes. Martin also made *Horror Express.*

IT HAPPENED HERE

(Lippert, 1964) **D/S/P:** Kevin Brownlow,
Andrew Mollo   UK

Hitler's army occupies Great Britain in 1940, and
by 1944 it's a fascist state. An underground movement fights back. A nurse (Pauline Murray) pretends to be a fascist in order to continue her work,
but she's caught, and is forced to give injections to
foreign prisoners.This documentary-style film was
started in 1956 as an amateur production, was finished in 1964, and was a major release in 1966. It's
b/w, and some parts are 16mm. It was released in
the US by Lippert. It's available on tape with *Red
Nightmare.*

ITALY

Since the 50s, Italy has remained the country producing the most Psychotronic movies. Countless
western, spy, muscleman, horror, science-fiction,
and sex movies are made there, with actors from
all over the world speaking their own languages
and later dubbed for other markets. Italy's quality

movie directors (such as Federico Fellini) may have
periods of inactivity, but the exploitation directors
never stop. Some of the most prolific are "Anthony
M. Dawson," "Joe D'Amato," and Lucio Fulci. Mario
Bava (1914–80) and Dario Argento are the most
respected horror specialists.

IT HAPPENED TOMORROW

(1944) **D/S:** Rene Clair **S:** Dudley Nichols **P:** Arnold Pressburger

Dick Powell is an elderly newspaper reporter remembering what happened to him at the turn of the century. In flashback, he meets an old man who can magically show him newspapers for the next day. He gets all the important scoops, then reads of his own death. This fantasy comedy from UA features Linda Darnell, Jackie Oakie as a fake mystic, Edgar Kennedy, and Sig Ruman. Clair had just directed *I Married a Witch* (1942).

IT'S ALIVE III: ISLAND OF THE ALIVE

(Warner, 1986) **D/S:** Larry Cohen **P:** Paul Sadler

After his 1974 and 1978 *It's Alive* films, Cohen returned with the last one. Michael Moriarty, as the father of a mutant killer baby, goes to court to save his child. After five of the killer babies are sent to a remote island, they reproduce, escape to Florida, and fight bikers. There are some intentional laughs and outrageous scenes. The cast includes Laureen Landon, Karen Black as the mother of the mutant leader, Gerrit Graham, Neal Israel, Macdonald Carey, and Dawn Wildsmith. There's some animation. Rick Baker did the baby FX for all three films in the series, but the adult mutants are seen more in this one.

IT'S A MAD, MAD, MAD, MAD WORLD

(MGM, 1963) **D/P:** Stanley Kramer **S:** William Rose, Tania Rose

I can't believe that as a kid I sat through this whole epic, all-star, Cinerama road/chase movie about greed at a matinee (at the Detroit in Lakewood, Ohio). At the time I thought Dick Shawn was the funniest character. Spencer Tracy stars as a police chief trying to recover stolen money, but the cast is mostly comedians, led by Milton Berle, Sid Caesar, Buddy Hackett, Mickey Rooney, Jonathan Winters, and Terry-Thomas. Edie Adams and Dorothy Provine are wives, and Ethel Merman is a mother-in-law. Some of the many others from the past are Eddie "Rochester" Anderson, Alan Carney, Leo Gorcey, Joe E. Brown, Sterling Holloway, ZaSu Pitts, William Demarest, Edward Everett Horton, Buster Keaton, Andy Devine, Doodles Weaver, Arnold Stang, Marvin Kaplan, and Jimmy Durante. The Three Stooges are stop-motion-animated firemen. Seen briefly are Jerry Lewis, Carl Reiner, Jack Benny, and Peter Falk. It was 3 1/4 hours, but United Artists cut it to 2 1/2 after the premiere. On laserdisc it's 175 minutes plus a "making of" documentary. The UA soundtrack includes songs by the Shirelles.

ITS A SMALL WORLD

(SW, 1950) **D:** William Castle **S:** Otto Schreiber **P:** Peter Scully

Paul Dale stars as Harry, a sad-faced midget whose story is told in three parts. He's hidden away as a child, leaves his rural home at 21, and has to escape from a carnival. While working as a shoeshine boy in the big city, he drinks and falls for a sexy woman (Lorraine Miller) who lures him into being a pickpocket. Harry eventually finds happiness and a woman his own size at the Cole Brothers circus in Florida. Will Geer is Harry's father, Margaret Field is a childhood friend, and Steve Brody is a bootblack. This unique, sympathetic movie, one of Castle's most interesting, was released by Eagle Lion. Karl Struss shot it in b/w, often in actual locations.

IT'S A WONDERFUL LIFE

(Republic, 1946) **D/P:** Frank Capra **S:** Frances Goodrich, Albert Hackett

For many years this Christmas perennial from RKO was the most famous PD (public-domain) tape, and scenes from it showed up (at no charge) in other films. It's also been the inspiration for parodies and copies and has been colorized. As everybody knows, James Stewart stars as George Bailey, a suicidal small-town family man who gets another chance thanks to an angel (Henry Travers) who shows him how things would have been if he hadn't been born. The cast includes Donna Reed, Lionel Barrymore, Thomas Mitchell, Beulah Bondi, Frank Faylen, Ward Bond, H. B. Warner, Gloria Grahame, and Sheldon Leonard. The film received five Oscar nominations but was not a box-office hit in 1946. The 1992 Deluxe Collectors Edition includes a "making of" documentary, the original trailer, a hardcover book, and reproductions of a poster and a lobby card. *It Happened One Christmas* (1977) and *Clarence* (1990) are TV remakes. In 1988 Telarc released a soundtrack recording that also includes music from *A Christmas Carol* (1938) and *Miracle on 34th Street* (1947).

IT'S CALLED MURDER, BABY

(Vestron, 1982) **D:** Anthony Spinelli **P:** Billy Thornberg (*Dixie Ray, Hollywood Star*)

Guest star Cameron Mitchell plays a gangster in this porno movie (also released in an R-rated version). He plays virtually the same role in the MGM hit *My Favorite Year* from the same year. In the 40s, former movie star Dixie Ray (Lisa De Leew) hires a detective (John Leslie) to retrieve some compromising photos. He has sex with her and with Veronica Hart, Samantha Fox, Kelly Nichols, Jane Hamilton, and Juliet "Aunt Peg" Anderson.

IT'S ONLY A MOVIE!

(Cinema Images, 1990) **D/S/A:** Joseph Zaso **S/C:** V. C. Siegfried

A film crew goes to a haunted house, in this very amateurish b/w spoof. Brian Dixon is Madman Malone.

IT'S YOUR THING

(1970) **D:** Mike Gargiulo **P:** The Isley Brothers

A Yankee Stadium concert from June 21, 1969 was filmed on videotape and released to theaters. Tina Turner, the Isley Brothers, Moms Mabley, the Edwin Hawkins Singers ("Oh Happy Day"), the Brooklyn Bridge, Patti Austin, the Five Stairsteps and Cubie, and others perform. It was made three years before the better-known *Wattstax* (1973), by the Isleys, who had recently launched their own T-Neck label.

IT TAKES A THIEF

(Video Vault, 1959) **D/S:** John Gilling **P:** John Temple-Smith UK (*The Challenge*)

After her first stardom in America, Jayne Mansfield made two films in England in 1959. *Too Hot to Handle* is better known. In this crime story she

Frank Lovejoy stars in *I Was a Communist for the FBI*.

acts against type as Billy, a dark-haired, tough schemer. She plans a heist, enlists a group of men, and announces, "I'm the boss!" She's also the driver, and after her lover, Jim (Anthony Quayle), takes the fall before revealing where the stolen loot was stashed, she leads the rest of the gang on a headline-making crime spree. The story centers on Jim (a widower) after his five years in jail. Gang members beat his mother and kidnap his son. A cop (Edward Judd) tails and harasses him. Billy, now a blonde, runs a nightclub but lets her new man call the shots. Descriptions in books reveal that this is a cut American version. It's great to be able to see this rare Mansfield movie, with jazzy music and a good ironic ending, but the tape has a hum on the soundtrack, the reel changes weren't removed, and 2 reels are mixed up!

THE IVORY APE

(1980) **D:** Tom Kotani **S:** William Overgard **P:** Arthur Rankin Jr.

Jack Palance captures a rare white gorilla in Africa and smuggles it to Bermuda. Cindy Pickett and Steven Keats try to save it. This ABC-TV movie is by the director of *The Bushido Blade*.

I WANNA HOLD YOUR HAND

(Warner, 1978) **D/S:** Robert Zemeckis **S:** Bob Gale **P:** Tamara Asseyev, Alex Rose

When the Beatles arrive in New York for the taping of *The Ed Sullivan Show*, some New Jersey girls arrive in a hearse and try and get close to their new heroes. This PG comedy is the best Beatles movie without the Beatles (although 16 real Beatles songs are heard). Nancy Allen stars, with Theresa Saldana, Wendie Jo Sperber, Bobby Di Cicco, Marc McClure, Eddie Deezen (who swings over the audience at the show), Claude Earl Jones, Dick Miller, and Will Jordan as Sullivan. It makes a good companion piece to *The Beatles: The First US Visit* (MPI). Steven Spielberg was the executive producer of this film and *Used Cars* (1980) by Zemeckis. Neither one made much money, but they're both better than the *Back to the Future* movies the team made later.

I WANT TO LIVE!

(MGM, 1958) **D:** Robert Wise **S:** Nelson Gidding, Don Mankiewicz **P:** Walter Wanger

Barbara Graham, a former San Francisco hooker, went to the gas chamber in 1955, even though she insisted that she wasn't guilty of murder. The highly publicized case is dramatized in this 2-hour-long anti–death penalty feature from UA, starring Susan Hayward (who received an Oscar). Wise was allowed to witness an actual death by gas while preparing to direct it. The cast includes Simon Okland, Theodore Bikel, Philip Coolidge as one of the real killers, John Marley, Gavin McLeod, Peter Breck, and Jack Weston. Shelley Manne and other jazz musicians heard on the Johnny Mandel soundtrack are seen playing in a club. A 1983 ABC-TV remake stars Lindsay Wagner. *Why Must I Die?* (1960) is an AIP ripoff, with Terry Moore.

I WANT WHAT I WANT — TO BE A WOMAN

(Prism, 1972) **D:** John Dexter **S:** Gillian Freeman   UK

A man who wants a sex change falls in love. Anne Heywood (who seemed to go out of her way to be in controversial movies) stars, with Harry Andrews and Jill Bennett.

I WAS A BURLESQUE QUEEN

(1953) **D:** Frank McDonald **D/S/P:** Sidney Pink **S:** Leslie Vale, George Halasz **P:** Matty Kemp

Pink took a 1947 PRC movie called *Linda Be Good* and added some 3-D scenes with chorus girls. It was released as a new "adult" movie at the height of 3-D mania. The cast includes Elyse Knox, Marie Wilson, Jack Norton, Alan Nixon, Professor Lambertini, and Sir Lancelot (as himself). Pink also worked with Arch Oboler on the first major 3-D film, *Bwana Devil*.

I WAS A COMMUNIST FOR THE FBI

(1951) **D:** Gordon Douglas **S:** Crane Wilbur **P:** Byran Foy

Frank Lovejoy stars as (the real) Matt Cvetic, posing as a Pittsburgh steel worker in order to infiltrate Communists plotting to take over the US. Dorothy Hart, Philip Carey, and Richard Webb are also in this documentary-style film. Cvetic's exploits had been described in a *Saturday Evening Post* article and in a radio series. This Warner Brothers film was somehow nominated for the best-documentary Oscar! Lovejoy returned for more of the same in *Shack Out on 101*. Douglas went on to direct *Them!*, *In Like Flint*, and several Frank Sinatra movies.

I WAS A GROUPIE

(1970) **D:** "Fred William"/Jack Hill **S:** Manfred Gregor **P:** Erwin C. Dietrich   W. Germany (*Ich, ein Groupie*)

Blond Ingrid Steeger stars in this movie about sex, drugs, and rock and roll. She was in a series of sex comedies by Dietrich. Roger Corman was originally supposed to be involved, and it was advertised in Europe using his name. Hill (whose name was removed by the producer) went to the Philippines and made *The Big Doll House* next. This is not to be confused with *Groupies* or *I Am a Groupie*, both from the same year.

I WAS A TEENAGE MUMMY

(Ghost Limb, 1991) **D/P:** Christopher C. Frieri **S:** Diane Reinhardt

After three early-60s greasers beat up an Egyptian kid (wearing a fez) in a school bathroom, their victim gets his revenge by turning a schoolgirl (Joan Devitt) into a killer mummy, and a private eye who talks to himself investigates. A couple take a motorcycle ride to a graveyard, where they have a philosophical discussion before the mummy kills them, ripping off an arm and a head. There's some good editing, atmospheric lighting and camera work, and some stop-motion effects in this b/w horror spoof. I would have liked more of the

mummy and less of the out-of-control Turhan Bey clone. The A Bones play "Mum's the World" (a bird song) at a dance (and isn't that *Psychotronic Video* columnist Dale Ashman dancing?). All of the music is excellent (and some is backwards). There's a soundtrack on Norton. Frieri also made *The Orbitrons*.

I WAS A TEENAGE SERIAL KILLER

(1992) **D/S/C/E:** Sarah Jacobson

Kristin Calabrese (who resembles a young Barbara Hershey with a nose ring) stars as Mary, a woman on the road who kills men, usually for what they say to her (comments like "Great ass!" or "You need to have kids!"). She briefly finds love with a (male) killer, and the mood successfully changes from comic to serious. Despite the "feminist" theme, even the kind of guy she kills could enjoy the murders, the humor, and her nude sex scene. The 21-year-old director of this very well made 27-minute b/w 16mm movie is from Minneapolis and was a student of George Kuchar.

I WAS A TEENAGE TV TERRORIST

(Vestron, 1984) **D/S:** Stanford Singer **S/A:** Kevin McDonough **P:** Susan Kaufman   (*Amateur Hour*)

A high-school student (Adam Nathan) is sent to live with his father, who puts him to work as a stock boy at his right-wing Romance Entertainment cable-TV station in Jersey City. The son and his girlfriend (Julie Hanlon) plot against the station using harmless "terrorism," but he's blackmailed by his female boss. Joel von Ornsteiner is also in this Troma comedy.

I WAS A TEENAGE ZOMBIE

(Nelson, 1986) **D/P:** John Elias Michalakias **S:** James Martin

A dope dealer named Mussolini sells toxic pot, becomes a toxic zombie, and fights teens. This comedy includes a nod to Troma films. The cast includes Alan Rickman (*Shock! Shock! Shock!*). The Enigma soundtrack album is better than the 16mm film, which is too long at 90 minutes. The Fleshtones do the theme song, and there are songs by the Ben Vaughn Group, Dream Syndicate, Smithereens, the Waitresses, Violent Femmes, Los Lobos, Alex Chilton, db's and others.

JABBERWOCKY

(RCA/Columbia, 1977) **D/S/A:** Terry Gilliam
S: Charles Alverson **P:** Sandy Lieberson   UK

Michael Palin stars as a medieval barrel-maker's son who has to battle the man-eating Jabberwocky monster (a giant bird/dragon). He loves big Griselda Fishfinger instead of the princess (Deborah Fallender), daughter of King Bruno the Questionable. The cast includes Max Wall, Eric Idle, Neil Innes, Terry Jones, and David Prowse. This fantasy/comedy was the first solo film by the American-born Monty Python member, who went on to make *Brazil*. This film and *Monty Python and the Holy Grail* (1975) make a good double bill.

J'ACCUSE

(Sinister, 1937) **D/S:** Abel Gance
France (*I Accuse; That They May Live*)

Here's a powerful antiwar classic with great editing and visuals by the maker of the famous epic *Napoléon* (1927). Made just before WWII, it's a remake of Gance's 1919 silent film. Victor Francen (*The Beast with Five Fingers*) stars as Jean Diaz, a veteran of WWI who's obsessed with the horrors of war. When a new war begins he calls on dead soldiers to rise from their graves at Verdun and march. French veterans maimed and disfigured in WWI portray the horrifying zombie soldiers. Gance reused actual WWI footage from the silent version, plus some scenes from his film *The End of the World* (1929). The film was released (cut) on the American road-show circuit and advertised as a horror movie (which it is, in a sense) that was "banned in Europe." A restored and subtitled version was first screened in the US in 1979. Sinister offers the cut version. The complete (125 minute) uncut version is available from Connoisseur.

THE JACKALS

(Rawhide, 1967) **D/P:** Robert D. Webb
S: Lamar Trotti, Harold Medford   S. Africa

Five bandits in the late 1800s wastelands of Transvaal discover a ghost town and Opa, an eccentric old gold prospector (Vincent Price), living nearby with his angry gun-toting blond daughter (Diana Ivarson). She eventually falls for the gang's leader (Robert Gunner) and the Shanga tribe shows up at the end. Price is the main attraction. He's very good in a rare serious 60s non-horror role, but sometimes seems like a laughing Andy Griffith. It's a remake of *Yellow Sky* (1948) based on a book by W. R. Burnett (he also wrote *High Sierra*). Both borrow from Shakespeare's *The Tempest* (so did *Forbidden Planet*).

JACK BE NIMBLE

(Triboro, 1992) **D/S:** Garth Maxwell
P: Jonathan Dowling   New Zealand

Jack (Alexis Arquette) and Dora (Sarah Smuts-Kennedy) are a brother and sister who have a psychic link, despite being raised by different adoptive parents. Jack gets revenge on his abusive adoptive parents by hypnotizing them with a machine he made at school and forcing them to kill themselves. Dora and her older boyfriend (Bruno Law-

rence) search for Jack, and his weird, mean stepsisters seek revenge. This highly original disturbing, unpredictable film is by a 30-year-old director.

JACKER

(Falcon, 1993) **D:** Benjamin Stansky **S:** Chip Herman

Mike (Phillip Herman) is a creepy young guy who eats cereal with his own blood, kidnaps and kills people, and steals their cars. Jackson (Patric Jackson) is the black police detective after him, especially after his sister is killed. Nancy Felciano has a shower scene, a (toy) car is set on fire, and one actor plays twins. Some of the same people appeared in *Burglar from Hell*. From Rockaway Beach, N.Y.

JACK OF DIAMONDS

(1967) **D:** Don Taylor **S/P:** Sandy Howard **S:** Jack De Witt **P:** Helmut Jedele   US/W. Germany

George Hamilton, a jewel thief, moves from one country to another and robs guest stars Zsa Zsa Gabor, Carroll Baker, and Lilli Palmer (playing themselves). Marie Laforet is his new partner in Paris, and Joseph Cotten is his mentor, "the Ace of Diamonds." The cast also includes Maurice Evans and Wolfgang Preiss. This MGM release was filmed on location in several countries.

JACK'S BACK

(Paramount, 1988) **D/S:** Rowdy Herrington
P: Tim Moore

An LA serial killer celebrates the centennial of Jack the Ripper's murders by committing similar ones. James Spader stars as a doctor at a free clinic who becomes a suspect. This suspenseful movie involves telepathy and includes some good shocks and great plot twists. The cast includes Cynthia Gibb, Rod Loomis, and Chris Mulkey. Forget all the mediocre teen movies with Spader as a hateful yuppie. This is good. The original title was *Red Rain*.

JACKSON COUNTY JAIL

(Warner, 1975) **D:** Michael Miller **S:** Donald Stewart **P:** Jeff Begun, Roger Corman

Yvette Mimieux stars as an LA ad executive driving through the South on her way to New York. Drug-addict hitchhikers (one is Robert Carradine) beat and rob her, she's jailed on vagrancy charges, she's raped by a psycho deputy (Frederic Cook), and she escapes with Tommy Lee Jones. The fact that she fights back, kills the rapist, and becomes a real outlaw helped make this movie a hit for New World. It surprised people expecting a more exploitative treatment. Howard Hesseman, Severn Darden, Betty Thomas, Mary Woronov, and Patrice Rohmer are also in the cast. *Outside Chance* (Charter, 1978) was an unofficial remake, also starring Mimieux.

THE JACKSONS: AN AMERICAN DREAM

(ABC, 1992) **D:** Karen Arthur **S:** Joyce Eliason
P: Jermaine Jackson, Margaret Maldonado Jackson

Someday, somebody will make an incredible, reality-based movie about Michael Jackson. Meanwhile, this 4-hour ABC-TV miniseries, backed by the Jackson clan, will have to do. It tells the story of the musical family from Gary, Indiana, until the 1984 Victory tour, with 20 kids portraying the Jackson 5 at various ages. Their real hits are heard. Billy Dee Williams is Berry Gordy, Lawrence Hilton-Jacobs is the father, Angela Bassett is the mother, Holly Robinson is Diana Ross, and Vanessa Williams is the woman who discovered the Jackson 5. The cast also includes Margaret Avery, Wylie Draper, and Angel Vargas.

JACK THE RIPPER

(Sinister, 1959) **D/P/C:** Robert Baker,
Monty Berman **S:** Jimmy Sangster   UK

Many are suspected of being the killer who strangles and stabs women, in this atmospheric version of the familiar story. Much time is spent in a hospital morgue, and there's a scarred, mute hunchback, can-can dancing, and a cat fight. A New York City cop (Lee Patterson) helps Scotland Yard. The cast includes Betty McDowall and Eddie Byrne. In the shock ending of this b/w movie, the killer is crushed in an elevator and red blood oozes out. The modern, jazzy score is out of place but sounds great. Joseph E. Levine released the film in the US. The RCA soundtrack features narration by Cedric Hardwicke. Baker and Berman returned with a grave-robbing tale, *Flesh and the Fiends/Mania* (1960), which is even better.

JACK THE RIPPER

(1988) **D/S/P:** David Wickes **S:** Derek Marlowe   UK

Michael Caine stars as the Scotland Yard inspector who conducted the original investigation and later discovers the identity of the killer. Wickes did extensive research for this 200-minute British TV

Yvette Mimieux is in the *Jackson County Jail*.

movie, shown in 2 parts on CBS. With Armand Assante, Ray McAnally, Susan George, Jane Seymour, Harry Andrews (who died in 1989), Lysette Anthony (from the revived TV series *Dark Shadows*), Lewis Collins, Edward Judd, Ken Bones, and Michael Gothard. The year 1988 was the centennial of the Ripper's crimes and documentaries were also released, including *Jack the Ripper: The Final Solution* and *Jack the Ripper*. Caine returned in *Jekyll and Hyde*, by the same director.

JACOB'S LADDER

(Live, 1990) **D:** Adrian Lyne **S:** Bruce Joel Rubin **P:** Alan Marshall **M:** Maurice Jarre

This irritating, $40 million, bad-acid-flashback/ghost movie has a plot twist that copies "An Occurrence at Owl Creek Bridge." Tim Robbins as a troubled Nam vet working at the post office in New York City either is suffering as a result of drug experiments on soldiers and/or is dead and trying to get into Heaven. Robbins is good, and there are some pretty horrifying hospital scenes. It was made because the writer had just done *Ghost* and the director had just done *Fatal Attraction*, and nobody wanted to say no to them. It might make an interesting 1990-big-studio-death double bill someday with *Flatliners*. Elizabeth Pena costars, with Danny Aiello as a chiropractor, Perry Lang, Matt Craven, Jason Alexander, and Macaulay Culkin as the dead son. The Pioneer laserdisc adds 15 minutes. The soundtrack is on Varèse Sarabande. The illustrated sceenplay has been published.

JACOB TWO-TWO MEETS THE HOODED FANG

(VSOM, 1977) **D/S:** Theodore J. Flicker **P:** Harry Gulkin

A kid who says everything twice (Stephen Rosenberg) enters a fantasy world where he's put on trial for insulting an adult. He's jailed and tortured along with other kids. The masked, wrestling warden is Alex Karras. It's based on a children's book by Mordecai Richler. Flicker directed *The President's Analyst*.

JADED

(1989) **D/S/P/A:** Oja Kodar **P:** Gary Graver

This violent, underground-type film about lowlifes (a transvestite, a wife beater, a bisexual) in Venice, California, features Randall Brady, Elizabeth Brooks (*The Howling*), Jillian Kesner, and Kelli Maroney. The Yugoslavian director was Orson Welles' companion for many years before his death. She was in his *F for Fake* and several of his unfinished films.

JAIL BAIT

(SW, 1955) **D/S/P:** Edward D. Wood Jr. **S:** Alex Gordon (*The Hidden Face*)

Don (Clancy Malone), just released from jail, works for bad guy Vic Brady (Timothy Farrell), who has a beautiful, *Vogue*-model moll (Theodora Thurman). During a blackface minstrel show (starring Cotton Watts and Chick) Don botches a holdup and kills two cops: "They bleed just like anybody else." He goes to his kindly old goateed plastic-surgeon father (Herbert Rawlinson, who

died the day after his scenes were shot) and demands a new face. Wood's second film has flubbed lines and laughable parts, but the surprise ending is a worthwhile payoff. Dolores Fuller (Wood's girlfriend) is the concerned sister, Lyle Talbot is the inspector, and future Hercules Steve Reeves bares his chest. Wood fans can also spot Mona McKinnon, Conrad Brooks, and other familiar faces. The minstrel footage is from Ron Ormond's *Yes, Sir, Mr. Bones* (1951), and the irritating guitar and piano music by Hoyt Kurtin (who later wrote the music for *The Jetsons*) is from Ormond's *Mesa of Lost Women* (1952). This video version ends with Johnny Legend and Rudolph Grey talking on 42nd Street. The Rhino "director's cut" version runs 72 minutes and includes stripper footage (not by Wood) in place of the minstrel show.

JAILBIRD ROCK

(TWE, 1988) **D:** Phillip Schuman **S:** Carole Stanley, Edward Kovach **P:** J. C. Crespo

A dancer (Robin Antin) goes to prison for defending her mother by shooting her abusive stepfather. The inmates put on a show to cover an escape, in this PG women-in-prison musical. Ronald Lacey is the warden.

JAILBREAKERS

(1994) **D:** William Friedkin **P:** Lou Arkoff, Debra Hill

Shannen Doherty becomes involved with a young hoodlum (Antonio Sabata, Jr.) in a Showtime Rebel Highway movie. It uses the title only of an obscure 1959 AIP release.

JAKE SPEED

(Star Maker, 1986) **D/S/P:** Andrew Lane **S/P/A:** Wayne Crawford **P:** William Ivey

Wayne Crawford stars as a pulp hero come to life in this *Raiders of the Lost Ark* copy about white slavers (led by John Hurt, in probably his worst role) in Africa. Dennis Christopher costars as Remo, the hero's sidekick, with Donna Pescow, Barry Primus, Monte Markham, and veteran actor Leon Ames. New World released it.

JAMAICA INN

(Video Yesterday, 1939) **D:** Alfred Hitchcock **S:** Sydney Gilliat, Joan Harrison **P:** Erich Pommer, Charles Laughton   UK

Hitchcock's last British film before relocating to America is based on a novel by Daphne Du Maurier. Charles Laughton stars as the Squire of a Cornish village who is really a pirate leader. His men lure ships to their destruction, steal the cargoes, and kill the crew. The cast includes 19-year-old Maureen O'Hara, Leslie Banks, Emlyn Williams, Mervyn Johns, and Robert Newton. Laughton and Hitchcock often disagreed, and the results didn't please anyone. Hitchcock's next film was the hit *Rebecca* (1940), also adapted from a Du Maurier novel. Laughton and O'Hara costarred in *The Hunchback of Notre Dame* (1939) and *This Land Is Mine* (1944).

JAMAICA INN

(Starmaker, 1985) **D:** Lawrence Gordon Clark **S:** Derek Marlowe **P:** Peter Gordon Scott   UK

Patrick McGoohan is the villain in this four-hour remake from BBC-TV. Jane Seymour stars, with Trevor Eve, John McEnery, and Billie Whitelaw. It was syndicated on American TV.

JAMES BOND AT THE MOVIES

(Amwest)

This compilation of trailers ends with *A View to a Kill* (1985), so the Timothy Dalton movies are missing. Still, it's fascinating to see all the European costars, and the *Dr. No* trailer (the longest) is especially great. Sid Haig is in the *Diamonds Are Forever* trailer, and Roger Moore's painfully obvious double is in the one for *Live and Let Die*.

JAMES DEAN, A LEGEND IN HIS OWN TIME

(Starmaker, 1976) **D:** Robert Butler **S/P:** William Bast **P:** John Forbes   (*The Legend*)

Stephen McHattie is James Dean, and Michael Brandon is his early-50s roommate William Bast. Candy Clark, Meg Foster, Jayne Meadows, Katherine Helmond, Heather Menzies, Amy Irving, Brooke Adams, and Dane Clark are also in this NBC-TV movie. For the real Dean look for the documentaries *The James Dean Story* (Pacific Arts, 1957), directed by Robert Altman; *James Dean, the First American Teenager* (1975); and *Forever James Dean* (Warner, 1988).

JAMES DEAN, THE FIRST AMERICAN TEENAGER

(1975) **D/S:** Ray Connolly   UK

This documentary includes film clips and interviews with Carroll Baker, Dennis Hopper, Nicholas Ray, Vampira(!), Sammy Davis Jr., and others. Music from the 70s by Elton John, David Bowie, Lou Reed, and the Eagles is used, making it pretty dated. Stacy Keach narrates.

JAN AND DEAN: DEAD MAN'S CURVE

(Interglobal, 1978) **D:** Richard Compton **S:** Daleen Young **P:** Pat Rooney

Richard Hatch is Jan Berry, and Bruce Davison is Dean Torrence. The 1966 accident that left Jan in a near-vegetable state is the major event in this look at the popular West Coast singing duo Jan and Dean. It's based on a *Rolling Stone* article and was made by the director of *Angels Die Hard*. The cast includes Pamela Bellwood, plus Mike Love and Bruce Johnson of the Beach Boys, Wolfman Jack, and Dick Clark as themselves.

JANE AND THE LOST CITY

(Starmaker, 1987) **D:** Terry Marcel **S:** Mervyn Haisman **P:** Harry Robertson   UK

Blond Kristen Hughes stars as Jane in this PG *Raiders of the Lost Ark*–style adventure comedy, based on a British comic strip that began in 1932. Maud Adams is the evil German Lola Pagola, and

Japanese movies that played in America were either dubbed and cut Godzilla (or other giant-monster) bashes, or subtitled historical dramas, often starring Toshiro Mifune and directed by Akira Kurosawa. Many of these are great and should be seen. Japan has also produced a lot of exploitation movies with shocking sex, bondage, and violence that rival anything on Western screens (at least in the 60s). A recommended historical series that can be found on tape is the Baby Cart, or Lone Wolf, series.

Sam J. Jones is Jack Buck, an American. It was filmed in Mauritius. *The Adventures of Jane* (1949) is an earlier adaptation.

JANE EYRE

(Sinister, 1934) **D:** Christy Cabanne
S: Adele Comandini

The first sound version of Charlotte Brontë's gothic novel is considered one of the best 30s "poverty row" films. Colin Clive (best known as Dr. Frankenstein) is Edward Rochester, an English country squire, and Virginia Bruce is Jane Eyre, an orphan who becomes a governess. The cast includes Claire Dubrey as the mad wife locked in a secret wing of the mansion, Beryl Mercer, Aileen Pringle, Jameson Thomas, Lionel Belmore (also in *Frankenstein*), Jean Rogers, and future director Richard Quine. This Monogram release is 62 minutes long.

JANE EYRE

(Fox, 1942) **D/S:** Robert Stevenson **S:** Aldous Huxley, John Houseman **P:** William Goetz

This famous version of Charlotte Brontë's novel, from 20th Century–Fox, was made after the success of *Wuthering Heights* (1939) and *Rebecca* (1940), other gothic romances. Orson Welles, in his second starring role (after his *Citizen Kane*), is Edward Rochester. Joan Fontaine (also in *Rebecca*) is Jane Eyre. Peggy Ann Garner is Jane as a child, sent to an orphanage by Henry Daniell and Agnes Moorehead. Her friend there (played by 12-year-old Elizabeth Taylor) dies after being punished in the cold rain. The cast also includes Edith Barrett (in real life, Vincent Price's first wife), Margaret O'Brien, and John Abbott. Bernard Herrmann wrote the score. Stevenson went on to become a very successful director for Disney.

JANE EYRE

(1971) **D:** Delbert Mann **S:** Jack Pulman **P:** Frederick Brogger   UK

This version of the famous novel is an NBC-TV movie filmed in England. George C. Scott and Susannah York star, with Ian Bannen, Jack Hawkins, Jean Marsh, and Nyree Dawn Porter (who was in *The House That Dripped Blood* and several other early-70s horror movies). The John Williams score (on Capitol) received an Emmy. A 1983 BBC-TV version with Timothy Dalton is also available (from CBS/Fox). Another version was released theatrically in 1996, starring William Hurt.

JANIS

(MCA, 1975) **D/P:** Howard Alk, Seaton Findlay

Most of this documentary is live concert footage of the late Janis Joplin, sometimes with her original, underrated psych/garage band, Big Brother and the Holding Company. It includes her appearance on *The Dick Cavett Show* and her Texas high-school reunion. She can also be seen in *Monterey Pop*.

THE JAR

(Magnum, 1984) **D:** Bruce Toscano
S: George Bradley   (*Carrion*)

This very strange movie from Denver has effective touches in the style of *Carnival of Souls*. The music, camera work (parts are in b/w), lighting, and sound effects are all designed to make it disorienting. A man (Gary Wallace) has serious hallucinations after he brings home an old man he hit with his car. His tub fills with blood, he tries (in vain) to get rid of a demon baby in a jar, and he becomes involved with a very patient, concerned neighbor (Karen Sjoberg).

JASON GOES TO HELL: THE FINAL FRIDAY

(New Line, 1993) **D:** Adam Marcus
S: Dean Lorey, Jay Huguely-Cass
P: Sean Cunningham **M:** Harry Manfredini

New Line hired a 25-year-old NYU student to direct the ninth in the series. Since it bombed at the box office, maybe it really will be final. Jason is blown apart by the National Guard, but a black coroner in Ohio eats his brain (?!) and is possessed. The "spirit" (it looks like a lump of shit) inhabits other characters (like in *The Hidden*). John D. Lemay (from the *Friday the 13th* TV series) and Kari Keegan are the young stars. A crazy, sadistic black bounty hunter (Steven Williams, from *21 Jump Street*) tracks the killer back to Camp Crystal Lake. This brain-dead sequel features a shower scene and a girl split in half after R-rated sex. In the most tasteless scene, a creature enters Erin Gray between her legs. Also in the cast are Steven Culp as an asshole TV reporter, Billy

Green Bush as a sheriff, Allison Smith, and Julie Michaels. Kane Hodder is Jason for the third time. The video is the gorier "unrated director's cut." KNB did the FX.

JAWS OF SATAN

(1980) **D:** Bob Claver **S:** Gerry Holland
P: Bill Wilson   (*King Cobra*)

Fritz Weaver stars as a preacher whose ancestors were Druids. He has a big battle with Satan in the form of a snake. Gretchen Corbett and Christina Applegate are also in the cast.

JAWS OF THE ALIEN = THE HUMAN DUPLICATORS

JAWS 3 (-D)

(MCA, 1983) **D:** Joe Alves **S:** Richard Matheson, Carl Gottlieb **P:** Rupert Hitzig **M:** Alan Parker

The original plan was to make the third *Jaws* movie an all-out comedy (called *Jaws 3, People 0*), but they went 3-D and "serious" instead. The director was the production designer on the first two films in the series. Dennis Quaid stars as the son of sheriff Brody, who was killed in *Jaws II*. He works at the Undersea Kingdom in Florida and trains dolphins to help him fight the mythical shark. This PG sequel features Bess Armstrong, Louis Gossett, Jr. as the owner of the tourist attraction, Simon McCorkindale, Lea Thompson (making her debut), Barbara Eden (in a bit part), and Shamu the killer whale. MCA released the soundtrack.

Lisa Maurer, Louis Gossett Jr., Dennis Quaid, and Bess Armstrong react to something in *Jaws 3-D*.

JAWS: THE REVENGE

(MCA, 1987) **D/P:** Joseph Sargent
S: Michael de Guzman

The story in this inferior PG-13 sequel, the fourth in the series, picks up right after the second. Lorraine Gary (the wife of Universal chairman Sidney Steinberg) stars as the widow of Sheriff Brody. The same shark follows her and her son (Lance Guest) when they go to the Bahamas. Mario Van Peebles (with dreadlocks), Michael Caine (the busiest major name in movies at the time), and Karen Young are also in the cast. The video has three more minutes of shark attacks.

JEKYLL AND HYDE

(Vidmark, 1990) **D/S:** David Wickes **P:** Patricia Carr

Michael Caine stars as the good doctor and a lumpy-faced Hyde in this ABC-TV version filmed in England. Cheryl Ladd costars, with Joss Ackland and Lionel Jeffries. Weeks also directed Caine in *Jack the Ripper*.

JEKYLL AND HYDE: PACT WITH THE DEVIL

(VSOM, 1968) **D:** Jaime Salvador **S:** Ramón Obón, Aldolfo Torres Portillo **P:** Luis Enrique Vergara   Mexico (*Pacto Diabólico*)

John Carradine stars as Dr. Halback, a former colleague of the late Dr. Jekyll. He drinks a youth potion and poses as his own nephew (Miguel Ángel Álvarez). The young man goes to a burlesque house, gouges people's eyes out, and goes after a house guest (Regina Torne) who is the daughter of Dr. Jekyll. The cast also includes Isela Vega. The director made *La Señora Muerte* (also with Carradine). It's subtitled.

THE JEKYLL AND HYDE PORTFOLIO

(1972) **D/P:** Eric Jeffrey Haims **D:** Don Greer   (*Jekyll and Hyde Unleashed*)

Women are killed at a nursing school. Gray Daniels stars with nudie movie vets Mady McQuire, Terry Johnson, and Rene Bond. The *Adult Version of Jekyll and Hyde* was released the same year as this soft-core-sex version.

JEKYLL AND HYDE… TOGETHER AGAIN

(Paramount, 1982) **D/S:** Jerry Belson **S:** Monica Johnson, Harvey Miller, Michael Lesson

Comedian Mark Blankfield stars as a nerdy scientist who snorts a coke-like chemical and becomes "cool" (gold chains, punk hair). This dumb comedy features Bess Armstrong, George Chakiris, Krista Erickson, Tim Thomerson, George Wendt, and Cassandra Peterson as "a busty nurse." Blankfield (from the *Fridays* TV series) returned in *Frankenstein's General Hospital*.

JENNIE: WIFE, CHILD

(SW, 1968) **D:** James Landis, Robert Carl Cohen **P:** James Enochs   (*Albert Peckinpah's Revenge*)

Russ Meyer's *Lorna* (1964) was the obvious inspiration for this b/w rural sex comedy, complete with silly silent-movie intertitles. Albert, an old farmer, marries Jennie, a 20-year-old blonde (Beverly Lunsford, from *The Crawling Hand*). After she seduces Mario, a young farmhand, Albert drugs them and chains them up in his cellar. Jennie sings, "How'd You Like Me in My Birthday Suit?" before her nude swim, and another woman rides a motorcycle topless. Most of it was filmed (by cinematographer Vilmos Zsigmond) in 1965 as *Tender Grass*. The producer added footage of Davie Allan and the Arrows doing a new country-sound theme song in a club. The several Arrows instrumentals are typically good, but Allan and his double-necked guitar is mostly avoided by whoever shot the disappointing live footage. A Tower soundtrack was even released. Landis also directed *The Sadist*.

JENNIFER 8

(Paramount, 1992) **D/S:** Bruce Robinson **P:** Gary Luccesi **C:** Conrad Hall

Andy Garcia stars as a troubled, divorced big-city cop relocated to a small Northern California town. He investigates serial killings after a hand (and other body parts) are found at the city dump just before Christmas. He also falls for Uma Thurman, a blind woman who is the chief witness. Lance Henriksen is his partner and brother-in-law, and Kathy Baker is his sister. John Malkovich has a showoff role as an FBI interrogator. Also in the cast are Lenny Von Dohlen and Perry Lang. The British director had made *Withnail and I* and *How to Get Ahead in Advertising*, and his first American film is better than the plot suggests. It's 124 minutes long.

JESSE JAMES VS. THE DALTONS

(Columbia, 1954) **D:** William Castle **S:** Robert E. Kent **P:** Sam Katzman

Torches, guns, and lots more are hurled at the audience in this 3-D Technicolor Columbia western. Brett King stars as Joe Branch, who might be the son of Jesse James. Barbara Lawrence costars. It's only 65 minutes long.

JESSIE'S GIRLS

(Monterey, 1976) **D/P:** Al Adamson **S:** Budd Donnelly **P:** Michael F. Goodman   (*Wanted Women*)

Sondra Currie, as a Mormon widow, frees three female outlaws in this sex-and-revenge western. One of the outlaws is Regina Carroll (the director's wife) as a hooker. Rod Cameron has a bit part. It copies the Raquel Welch movie *Hannie Caulder* (1972).

JESUS OF NAZARETH

(Fox, 1976) **D/S:** Franco Zeffirelli **S:** Anthony Burgess, Suso Cecchi D'Amico **P:** Vincenzo La Bella

Robert Powell is Jesus in this 8-hour, star-studded miniseries, with Anne Bancroft, Claudia Cardinale, James Farentino, James Earl Jones, Stacy Keach, Tony Lo Bianco, James Mason, Ian McShane, Laurence Olivier, Ernest Borgnine and Anthony Quinn (both also in *Barabbas*), Donald Pleasence (also in *The Passover Plot*), Christopher Plummer, Fernando Rey, Ralph Richardson, Rod Steiger as Pontius Pilate, Peter Ustinov, Michael York, Ian Holm, and Olivia Hussey as the Virgin Mary. Zeffirelli later publicly criticized *The Last Temptation of Christ*.

THE JESUS TRIP

(Unicorn, 1971) **D:** Russ Mayberry **S:** Dick Poston **P:** Joseph Feury   (*Under Hot Leather*)

Heroin-dealing bikers kidnap a nun named Sister Anne (Tippy Walker), and she falls for their leader, Waco (Robert Porter). Billy "Green" Bush is a sadistic, corrupt cop, and Robert Tessier (who was also the second-unit director) is another cop. This no-action PG film is "an Eve Meyer presentation." The second wife of Russ Meyer died in 1977.

THE JEWEL OF THE NILE

(Fox, 1985) **D:** Lewis Teague **S:** Mark Rosenthal, Laurence Konner **P/A:** Michael Douglas **M:** Jack Nitzsche

Michael Douglas, Kathleen Turner, and Danny DeVito return in this PG sequel to 20th Century–Fox's *Romancing the Stone*, set in the Mideast. Teague, a former director of Corman films, had just done two Stephen King movies. The score is on Arista.

JEZEBEL'S KISS

(RCA, 1990) **D/S:** Harvey Keith **P:** Eric F. Sheffer

Katherine Barres stars (and has many nude scenes) as a young woman who goes after the killer of her grandfather. Also in the cast are Malcolm McDowell, Meg Foster, Everett McGill, Meredith Baxter, and Bert Remsen. It's by the director of *Mondo New York*.

JFK

(Warner, 1992) **D/S/P:** Oliver Stone **S:** Zachary Sklar **P:** A. Kitman Ho

Stone upset a lot of people with this dazzling dissection of American history centering on the New Orleans district attorney, Jim Garrison (Kevin Costner), who tried to disprove the Warren Commision. The film is fascinating even if you don't buy all (or any) of the conspiracy theories. It's based on books by Garrison and Jim Marrs. Gary Oldman is Oswald, Brian Doyle Murray is Ruby, and Sissy Spacek is Mrs. Garrison. Bizarre, supposedly real gay characters are played by Joe Pesci (!), Tommy Lee Jones, and Kevin Bacon. The cast also includes Michael Rooker, Wayne Knight, Laurie Metcalf, Vincent D'Onofrio, John Candy (with a great accent), Sally Kirkland, Lolita Davidovich, and Frank Whaley. Ed Asner, Jack Lemmon, and Walter Matthau all have memorable scenes. Garrison plays Chief Justice Earl Warren. Martin Sheen narrates the intro. Donald Sutherland's Agent X character says that the assassination was a coup d'état. The Kennedy autopsy scenes rival anything in a horror movie. The Warner Brothers release is 189 minutes long. The director's-cut video adds another 17.

JIGSAW

(1968) **D:** James Goldstone **S/P:** Ranald MacDougall

Remember a Gregory Peck movie called *Mirage* (1965)? Well, this is a remake, also from Universal, with fast editing, a Quincy Jones score, and LSD added to the plot. Bradford Dillman, as a scientist, accidentally manages to drink some coffee with LSD sugar cubes. He wakes up with amnesia in a strange apartment with a dead woman in the tub. He hires a detective (Harry Guardino), who is forced to take LSD by some hippies, and the scientist takes more LSD so that he can remember what happened! With Hope Lange, Pat Hingle, Diana Hyland, Victor Jory, Susan Saint James, James Doohan, and Michael J. Pollard. It was made for NBC-TV but was first shown theatrically.

JIGSAW MURDERS

(MGM, 1988) **D:** Jag Mundhra
S: Allen B. Ury **P:** Victor Bhalla

Cops in LA search for a psycho killer who leaves tattooed body parts around. There's a bachelor party with strippers and lots of nude modeling going on too (which is where Brinke Stevens and Laura Albert come in). Chad Everett stars as a cop, with Michelle Johnson, Yaphet Kotto as Dr. Fillmore, and Michelle Bauer. The director made *Open House*. It's from Concorde.

JIMI HENDRIX

(Warner, 1973) **D/P:** Gary Weis, Joe Boyd, John Head

Lots of good live and interview footage is used in this documentary. Pete Townsend and many non-famous people who knew Hendrix before the fame are featured. Hendrix is also the star of *Rainbow Bridge* (Rhino, 1971), and you can see him perform in *Monterey Pop* and *Woodstock*.

JIMMY THE KID

(SW, 1982) **D:** Gary Nelson **S:** Sam Brobrick **P:** Ronald Jacobs

Diff'rent Strokes star Gary Coleman is kidnapped by two crooks in this PG adventure comedy from New World that borrows the plot of O. Henry's "The Ransom of Red Chief." Paul Le Mat, Ruth Gordon, and Dee Wallace Stone team up to kidnap the bratty little kid (who was really 14 at the time). Also in the cast are Don Adams as a detective, Cleavon Little, Avery Schreiber, and Pat Morita.

JIMMY, THE WONDER BOY

(SW, 1966) **D:** Herschell Gordon Lewis **P:** Hal Berg

Lewis made this, his first kiddie movie (it's a musical), shortly after *Color Me Blood Red*. The acting is so bad, and the whole thing is so lame and ridiculous, that it's well worth watching. Little Jimmy Jay makes a reckless wish, and everybody stops moving. Aurora, a wizard's daughter (Nancy Berg, the producer's wife perhaps, who resembles Kathy Bates in *Misery*), takes him on a journey to "the world's end" to restart "the great clock." A Devil character called Mr. Figg (with incredible eyebrows) causes trouble by turning everything red and sings songs like "Think Big" and "Beans." The beans rain on a tribe of green Indians. To stretch the running time, there's a long slow-motion scene, and Aurora tells a story (a very badly dubbed European cartoon about a magic globe) that lasts for 20 minutes! This warped film was shot in Florida, at the same Coral Castles park as *Nude on the Moon*. The makeup was by *Nature's Playmates* star Louise Downs. Try to imagine being dropped off at a Saturday matinee to watch this when you were about nine years old. Around the same time Lewis directed additional scenes for the British *Sin, Suffer, and Repent*, a venereal-disease movie.

THE JIM ROSE CIRCUS SIDESHOW

(American Visuals, 1993) **D:** Jonathan Dayton, Valerie Faris

Rose, a very animated and loud MC, has taken some traditional sideshow attractions to new extremes by presenting this impressive traveling gross-out show for jaded young people at an old (packed) theater in Seattle. You might have seen sword swallowing, spikes up the nose, or worm and glass eating before, but how about a guy who has beer pumped in through his nose (too much coke?), or Mr. Lifto, who hangs heavy weights from his nipples and his dick!? Rose's show was also on the Lollapalooza tour.

THE JITTERS

(Prism, 1988) **D/P/E:** John Fasano **S:** Jeff McKay, Sonoko Kondo   US/Japan

This is a comedy with hopping vampires, which are popular in Asia. It's not as good as the better 80s Asian horror movies, but it's amusing enough. A small, multiracial gang led by Leech kills Uncle Lee, a rich Chinatown merchant. James Hong and his assistant/son mix a potion that revives the man as a vampire with Mr. Spock ears. Eventually, all the vampires (who can be stopped only by papers with symbols on them) defeat the gang. Some good FX show vampires exposed to a mirror sparking, melting, and then bursting, and when a head splits open there's a muscular, snake-tongued monster man inside. My favorite line is "I'm terrified beyond the capacity for reasonable thought." It was filmed in Toronto but is set in LA. Fasano also directed *Black Roses* and *Rock and Roll Nightmare*.

JIVE JUNCTION

(1943) **D:** Edgar G. Ulmer **S:** Irving Wallace **P:** Leon Fromkes

Are you ready for an Edgar G. Ulmer PRC musical? An all-girl swing band, organized by Dickie Moore (formerly in Our Gang comedies) and other teens, plays jitterbug music for soldiers in a barn. Tina Thayer and Gerra Young costar in this 62-minute WWII movie.

J-MEN FOREVER!

(Lightning, 1979) **D:** Richard Patterson **S:** Philip Proctor, Peter Bergman **P:** William Howard

Members of the Firesign Theatre (who were still funny at the time) provided the new comedy dialogue added to *Fighting Devil Dogs* and parts of other old serials cut together with new scenes. A DJ from outer space plans to take over Earth with rock music. The heroes fight back with Lawrence Welk tunes. It features Philip Proctor, Peter Bergman, Leonard Nimoy, and the voice of Michael Gwynne. Akira Fitton did the credits and poster for this 75-minute film.

JOCKS

(RCA, 1984) **D:** Steve Carver **S:** Michael Lanahanm, David Oas **P:** Ahmet Yasa   (*Road Trip*)

Scott Strader stars in this comedy about college tennis players in Las Vegas. Richard Roundtree costars as the coach who has to create a winning team, with Perry Lang, Christopher Lee as the college president, Mariska Hargitay, R. G. Armstrong, and Trinidad Silva. Crown International released it.

JOE

(Cannon, 1970) **D/C:** John D. Avildsen **S:** Norman Wexler **P:** David Gil

Peter Boyle is excellent as a hippie-hating New York City construction worker. He first blackmails and then makes an alliance with a rich executive (Dennis Patrick) who killed his daughter's drug-dealer boyfriend after she disappeared into the East Village drug scene. The WWII vets check out the scene together, get high, get laid, then massacre everybody in a commune. It's not a typical anti-establishment movie of the time but is a must-see. Susan Sarandon makes her acting debut as the daughter, blitzed on speed. Lloyd Kaufman (later with Troma) was the production manager. Jerry Butler and Exhuma are heard on the Mercury soundtrack. Mercury also released an album of dialogue called *Joe Speaks*. The ads for the film featured a hippie with a target on his face and the line "Keep America beautiful." Avildsen did *Guess What We Did in School Today* for Cannon the same year. A *Joe* sequel was promised for many years.

Dennis Patrick and Peter Boyle in *Joe*.

JOE VERSUS THE VOLCANO

(Warner, 1990) **D/S:** John Patrick Shanley **P:** Teri Schwartz

Tom Hanks stars as a dying nerd who is offered 6 months of paradise as an island king as long as he jumps into a volcano when his time is up. This fantasy/comedy features Meg Ryan in three roles, Lloyd Bridges, Robert Stack, Abe Vigoda as the Waponi chief, Dan Hedaya, Ossie Davis, Amanda Plummer, and Carol Kane. Steven Spielberg was an executive producer.

JOHN AND YOKO: A LOVE STORY

(SVS, 1985) **D/S:** Sandor Stern **P:** Aida Young

The lives of John Lennon (Mark McGann, from Liverpool) and Yoko Ono (Kim Miyori) from 1966 to Lennon's death are examined. It's pretty weak, considering what they had to work with. Actors play the other Beatles, Brian Epstein, Lennon's kids, Allen Klein, Linda Eastman

McCartney, Phil Spector, and May Pang. Lennon and Beatles songs are used on the soundtrack. Stern also wrote *The Amityville Horror*. Many real Lennon videos are available, including *Imagine* (Warner, 1988).

JOHN LENNON

(HBO, 1972) **D:** D.A. Pennebacker

This is a cut (56-minute) version of *Sweet Toronto*. The 12-hour September 13, 1969, Toronto festival was organized by and starred John Lennon, just after Woodstock. The first part is a classic lineup of people who influenced him: Chuck Berry, Bo Diddley, Jerry Lee Lewis, and Little Richard, all still in prime rockin' form. They have one song each on the tape. Then comes the Plastic Ono Band (with Lennon, Yoko, Eric Clapton, and Klaus Voorman). The *Live Peace in Toronto* LP is exactly what you see here. Yoko spends part of the time in a bag screaming, Clapton feeds back a lot, and they do the entire "Don't Worry, Kyoko." It's a wonder that the oldies fans didn't riot. All in all, it's a great concert movie as well as a major confrontation with and statement from the bearded Lennon.

JOHNNY CASH! THE MAN, HIS WORLD, HIS MUSIC

(Goodtimes, 1969) **D/S/C:** Robert Elfstrom
P: Arthur Barron

Johnny Cash was enjoying a pop-chart comeback with his "Folsom Prison Blues" when this concert documentary was made. He and June Carter Cash and her family sing and play lots of songs on tour. Carl Perkins was his guitarist at the time. Bob Dylan, whose new album was *Nashville Skyline* (his weakest up to that time), is seen in the studio with the man in black and sings "One Too Many Mornings." This film debuted on Nashville Entertainment TV. Elfstrom also made *The Nashville Sound* (1970) and *The Gospel Road* (1973), both with Cash.

JOHNNY FIRECLOUD

(Prism, 1974) **D/P:** William A. Castleman
S: Wilton Denmark **P:** David Friedman,
Peter B. Good, Anton Wickremasighe
(*The Revenge of Johnny Firecloud*)

If you crossed *Billy Jack* with *2000 Maniacs* you might come up with this story of the martial-arts-fighting Nam-vet Indian Johnny Firecloud (played by Puerto Rican Victor Mohica). Local Indians are humiliated, raped, and even lynched, until Johnny scalps a man, plants an axe in a skull, lights dynamite tied to a man's crotch, buries another man up to his neck (and pokes his eyes out), and hangs and whips Ralph Meeker, as the hateful, corrupt guy who runs the small town. The shocking, gory effects are by Joe Blasco (he also did *Ilsa*), who now runs an FX school in Hollywood. Scene-stealing Frank De Kova is the pathetic, alcoholic grandfather. *All My Children* star David Canary is the good cop. Christina Hart (*The Stewardesses*) is Johnny's ex-girlfriend. The only real American Indian in the cast (most of them look Italian) is Marlon Brando's friend Sacheen Littlefeather (of 1972 Academy Awards fame). She seems to have used a lot of silicone.

JOHNNY GOT HIS GUN

(Media, 1971) **D/S:** Dalton Trumbo
P: Bruce Post Campbell

Timothy Bottoms stars as a WWI soldier who is a deaf, mute, blind quadruple amputee after a bomb explosion. He remembers, dreams, and fantasizes in his hospital bed. The cast includes Diane Varsi (in her last role for many years) as a nurse, Jason Robards, Kathy Fields, Marsha Hunt, Eduard Franz, David Soul, and Anthony Geary. Donald Sutherland is Christ, and Tom Tryon (who was also an executive producer) has his last acting role. This Cinemation PG film is partially in b/w. It's based on Trumbo's 1939 anti-war novel (which was presented as a radio drama, with James Cagney playing Johnny). Trumbo was jailed for 10 months in 1950–51 and blacklisted until 1960 for refusing to testify before the House Un-American Activities Committee.

JOHNNY GUITAR

(Republic, 1954) **D:** Nicholas Ray
S: Philip Yordan **P:** Herbert Yates

Joan Crawford, dressed in black, stars as Vienna, in one of the oddest westerns of all time. She builds a saloon and gambling house on Arizona land that the railroad wants. She uses the Dancin' Kid (Scott Brady) but falls for Johnny Guitar (Sterling Hayden). The big showdown is between Vienna and cattle queen Emma Small (the awesome Mercedes McCambridge). The film has been called political satire and "Freudian feminism." Ward Bond, Ernest Borgnine, John Carradine as Old Tom, Royal Dano, Ben Cooper, and Paul Fix are also in the cast. Peggy Lee sings the theme song. Citadel released the soundtrack in 1981. Ray made *Rebel Without a Cause* the next year. Gene Corman was his agent.

JOHNNY HANDSOME

(IVE, 1989) **D:** Walter Hill **S:** Ken Friedman
P: Charles Roven **M:** Ry Cooder

Lance Henriksen and Ellen Barkin double-cross petty criminal Mickey Rourke in New Orleans. Mickey looks like "the Elephant Man" but has extensive plastic surgery in prison. With Elizabeth McGovern, Morgan Freeman, Forest Whitaker as the plastic surgeon, and Scott Wilson. It's based on a novel by John Godey. The soundtrack is on Warner.

JOHNNY RENO

(1965) **D:** R. G. Springsteen
S: Steve Fisher **P:** A. C. Lyles

Dana Andrews stars as a US marshal in this old-fashioned color western about a town in Kansas where an Indian chief's son is murdered. The cast includes Jane Russell, Lon Chaney Jr. (who was in eight Lyles westerns at Paramount), and John Agar (who was in five). Tom Drake and Dale Van Sickle are the bad-guy brothers.

JOHNNY SUEDE

(Paramount, 1991) **D/S:** Tom DiCillo
P: Yoram Mandel, Ruth Waldburger

Johnny Suede (Brad Pitt) is an immature, unemployed liar and would-be pop star with a giant pompadour. He lives in a crummy apartment in an unnamed city. His band lasts through one practice, and he has humorous girlfriend problems (with Catherine Keener and Alison Moir). Some of the surreal hallucinations and dream sequences (featuring an iguana and midgets) are top-notch. The cast includes Tina Louise, Calvin Levels, Samuel L. Jackson, and Nick Cave as rock star Freak Storm. There's a clip from *The Terror of Tiny Town*. The new music by Link Wray is great, and some old Ricky Nelson hits are heard too. DiCillo, a cameraman on Jim Jarmusch movies, filmed this in New York City neighborhoods. It was made with a Sundance Institute grant. Miramax released it on tape after Pitt had gone on to fame and bigger films.

JO JO DANCER, YOUR LIFE IS CALLING

(Columbia, 1986) **D/S/P/A:** Richard Pryor
S: Rocco Urbisci, Paul Mooney

Pyror stars as Jo Jo (himself) and his "alter ego." He's seen growing up in a whorehouse, becoming a nightclub comic, and getting married over and over. His 1980 freebasing coke accident (the first time many heard of smoking crack) is shown as a turning point in his life. It's not very good, but it is interesting to see a living talent in charge of presenting his own version of his story. The cast includes Debbie Allen, Fay Hauser, Carmen McRae, Billy Eckstine, Diahnne Abbott, Wings Hauser, Tanya Boyd (*Ilsa, Harem Keeper of the Oil Sheiks*), Paula Kelly (from *Playboy*), and Barbara Williams. Warner released the soundtrack, featuring various artists.

THE JOKERS

(1967) **D:** Michael Winner **S:** Dick Clement,
Ian La Frenais **P:** Maurice Foster   UK

Two upper-class brothers (Michael Crawford and Oliver Reed) make plans to steal the crown jewels from the Tower of London and then to return them. This crime comedy also features Harry Andrews, Daniel Massey, Michael Hordern, Frank Finlay, James Donald, and Edward Fox. Universal released it in the US.

JONATHAN OF THE BEARS

(1993) **D/S:** Enzo C. Casterelli **S:** Lorenzo De Luca
P/A: Franco Nero **P:** Vittorio Noia, Gabriel Sefarian
Italy/Russia (*Jonathan degli Orsi*)

In the first "borscht western" flashbacks tell the story of Jonathan, a kid who sees his parents murdered. He befriends a bear and later an Indian chief (Floyd "Red Crow" Westerman). Grown-up, vengeance-seeking Jonathan (Franco Nero) is a legend among Indians, but the chief's son (Knifewing Segura) is his rival. With John Saxon as a bad-guy oil man who has Jonathan crucified, Melody Robertson as a mute Indian, Bobby Rhodes, and David Hess. It was shot on Army bases in Russia.

JOSHUA

(Rhino, 1976) **D/P:** Larry Spangler **S/A:** Fred
Williamson   (*Joshua: The Black Rider*)

In an imitation of Clint Eastwood's Italian westerns, Williamson stars as a former Union Army soldier out for vengeance after his wife is kidnapped and his mother is killed. Mexican star Isela Vega costars.

JOURNEY BENEATH THE DESERT

(Sinister, 1961) **D:** Edgar G. Ulmer, Frank Borzage **S:** Ugo Liberatore, Remigio Del Grosso Italy/France (*Antinea; Della Citta Sepolta*)

A helicopter (an obvious toy in long shots) crashes during a storm in the restricted "atomic-explosion area" of a desert and ends up in the underground city of Atlantis, where the evil Queen Antinea (Haya Harareet) in a sexy costume makes one of the visitors a mindless zombie slave. Jean-Louis Trintignant stars, with Rod Fulton as a playboy looking for diamonds, Georges Riviere, and Jean Maria Volonte as a helpful blond Arab. There are dream sequences, evil Arabs, a torture chamber, a snake dance, a slave revolt, machine-gun battles, and an A-bomb explosion. This movie (released directly to TV in America) is crazy (and the washed-out Technicolor print seems to be missing scenes). Veteran director Frank Borzage started it (he died in 1962) and was replaced by Ulmer. The same story had been filmed in France (1922), Germany (1932), and as the Maria Montez movie *Siren of Atlantis* (1948).

JOURNEY INTO FEAR

(Turner, 1942) **D:** Norman Foster **S/P/A:** Orson Welles **S/A:** Joseph Cotten

After making *Citizen Kane* and *The Magnificent Ambersons*, Welles took a supporting role in this film as Turkish police chief Colonel Haki. It was his second film as an actor and the third (and, unfortunately, the last) of his Mercury Productions for RKO. Joseph Cotten stars in this entertaining WWII spy thriller, based on an Eric Ambler novel, with Dolores Del Rio, Ruth Warrick, Agnes Moorehead, Everett Sloane, and Hans Conreid as Oo Lang Sang the magician. It was remade in 1974 in Canada.

JOURNEY INTO THE BEYOND

(VCII, 1977) **D:** Rolf Olson **S:** Paul Ross **P:** Rudolph Kalmowicz W. Germany

John Carradine narrates this 104-minute documentary on psychic surgery, voodoo, exorcism, ghosts, and levitation. Many real experts appear.

JOURNEY OF HONOR

(MCA, 1990) **D:** Gordon Hessler **S:** Nelson Gidding **P/A:** Sho Kosugi US/Japan (*Shogun Mayeda*)

Lord Mayeda (Sho Kosugi) is the samurai protector of the son (Kane Kosugi) of a warring shogun (Toshiro Mifune, who was also an executive producer). They're sent to Spain to buy guns for the 17th-century civil war in Japan. The cast includes Polly Walker, David Essex as an evil duke, Christopher Lee as King Philip, and John Rhys-Davies as the sultan of Morroco. Martial-arts star Kosugi planned and produced this old-fashioned PG-13 epic after spending years in American ninja-action movies.

JOURNEY TO FREEDOM

(1957) **D:** Robert C. Dertano **S:** Herbert F. Nichols **P:** Stephen C. Apostolof

Jacques Scott stars as an Eastern European who escapes to America, where Communist agents continue to track him. Producer Apostolof, who had fled Bulgaria, later directed Ed Wood scripts as A. C. Stevens. Tor Johnson (from Ed Wood movies) has a major fight scene. Genevieve Aumont costars. The anti-communism feature is from Republic.

JOURNEY TO THE CENTER OF THE EARTH

(Warner, 1986) **D/S:** Rusty Lemorande **S:** Debra Ricci, Regina Davis, Kitty Chalmers **P:** Golan/Globus

Young people exploring a cave in Hawaii fall into a hole, and this barely released PG adventure in the lost city of Atlantis begins. With Kathy Ireland, Emo Phillips, and Sam Raimi. Ireland also fell into a pit in *Alien from LA* (1983), also from Cannon. Don't confuse this with the much better 1959 movie.

JOURNEY TO THE CENTER OF THE EARTH

(1993) **D:** William Dear **S/P:** Robert Gunter **S:** David Mickey Evans **P:** Marvin Miller

This TV movie remake was backed by producer John Ashley. Jeffrey Nording stars, with Farrah Forke, John Neville, F. Murray Abraham, Carel Struycken, Fabiana Udenio, and Kim Miyori.

JOYRIDE

(Vestron, 1977) **D/S:** Joseph Ruben **S:** Peter Rainer **P:** Bruce Cohn Curtis

A pair of teen couples leave LA, drive north, and end up breaking into a summer home in Alaska. All the stars of this AIP release are the children of actors. They're Robert Carradine, Melanie Griffith, Desi Arnaz Jr., and Anne Lockhart. Melanie and Anne have topless scenes. Much of the music on the United Artists soundtrack is by the Electric Light Orchestra.

THE JOYS OF JEZEBEL

(SW, 1967) **D/P:** A. P. Stootsberry **S:** Maurice Smith

Hell is the setting of this soft-core-sex comedy/fantasy, a good way for the filmmakers to get away with lots of scandalous things. The comic Devil (Christopher Stone, but not the actor in *The Howling*) lets Jezebel (Christine Murray, also in *Trader Hornee*) return to earth so that she can deliver the soul of a busty blond virgin named Rachel (Dixie Donovan) by taking over her body. The orgies in Hell are hard to see because of all the red filters on the lights. The sex action usually centers on breast-kissing. Goliath and Solomon are other characters. The dubbed soundtrack has rock guitar, voices, and parts that are backwards.

JOYSTICKS

(Vestron, 1983) **D/P:** Greydon Clark **S:** Al Gomez, Mickey Epps, Curtis Burch (*Video Madness*)

Joe Don Baker wants to shut down River City's video-game parlor, and the Pac Man kids fight back. Scott McGinnis stars, with Anne Ramsey, Corinne Bohrer, Becky Le Beau, and Kym Malin and Lynda Wiesmeier (from *Playboy*). Clark also directed *Wacko* (also with Baker and McGinnis), released by the same company (Jensen Farley).

JUBILEE

(Mystic Fire, 1977) **D/S:** Derek Jarman **P:** Howard Manlin, James Whaley UK

Queen Elizabeth I is transported to post-WWIII England and is horrified by punks, anarchy, and lesbians. This punk fantasy/musical features Jenny Runacre as Bod, Little Nell (Campbell) as Crabs, Richard O'Brien, Toyah Wilcox as Mad, Ian Charleson, and Adam Ant. The music is by Brian Eno, plus Adam and the Ants, Siouxsie and the Banshees, Wayne County, The Slits, Chelsea, and others. Jarman (who died in 1994) started as a set designer for Ken Russell. Eno did the music for his *Sebastiane* (1976) too.

JUD

(Prism, 1971) **D/S:** Gunther Collins **P:** Igo Kantor

A Nam vet (Joseph Kaufman) returns to LA at Christmastime and experiences dejection and misery. Claudia Jennings has a small role as Sunny. The Ampex soundtrack features music by the American Breed, Crow, John Hartford, and others.

JUDGE DEE AND THE MONASTERY MURDER

(1974) **D:** Jeremy Paul Kagan **S:** Nicholas Meyer **P:** Gerald I. Isenberg (*The Haunted Monastery*)

This was the first all-Asian-American TV movie. It's a bit like *The Name of the Rose*. The hero of Robert Van Gulick's series of novels is based on a real 7th-century Chinese judge. Khigh Dhiegh (from the TV series *Hawaii Five-0*) stars as the crime-solving judge, with Mako, Soon-Taik Oh, Irene Tsu, James Hong, and Keye Luke. There's a chamber of horrors and a killer bear. This was aired as a series pilot on ABC-TV at the same time as their *Kung Fu* series was at the height of its popularity. It's too bad it didn't become a series.

JUDGMENT DAY

(Magnum, 1989) **D/S/P:** Ferde Grofe Jr. **P:** Keith Lawrence

This teens-in-Hell horror/fantasy about a cursed Mexican village has some strong similarities to *The Laughing Dead*. When their tour bus has a flat tire, two American guys follow an old lady in black: "We could be following this hag into a trip to Hell!" Of course they do. Monte Markham is a friendly but worried American who runs a restaurant. He warns them to leave town. They end up at the 17th-century home of Cesar Romero, who has a mysterious, beautiful daughter and a black slave. Things get pretty strange when hooded monks on horseback start horsewhipping Monte. He really suffers: "Ohh! Ohh! Ohh! A-a-ahhhh!" Some very impressive and surprising scenes feature a crowd of people in chains being whipped while walking up a huge staircase. Monte and a topless woman are crucified. The Devil is pretty good too, with horns and three arms. In the 60s Grofe wrote or directed action movies made in the Philippines, like *Walls of Hell* and *The Steel Claw*. His company specializes in generic combat videos (they have 100 to choose from) and has done videos for *US News and World Report* and *CBS Video*. His father, Ferde Grofe, was a well-known composer who also wrote music for *Rocket Ship X-M* and other films.

JUDGMENT NIGHT

(MCA, 1993) **D:** Stephen Hopkins
S: Lewis Colec **P:** Gene Levy

Four young suburbanites in a giant rented RV take a detour on the way to a boxing match. They hit a kid who was shot by a gang and have to flee for their lives on foot into the projects. This urban *Deliverance* clone is set in Chicago. Emilio Estevez stars, with Cuba Gooding Jr., Peter Greene, Jeremy Piven, and Stephen Dorff. Onetime MTV comedian Denis Leary is the main villain. Violence was reported in movie theaters (again) when this Universal film opened. The soundtrack mixes rap (Run-DMC) and rock (Pearl Jam, Sonic Youth). Hopkins made *Blown Away* next.

JUGULAR WINE

(Pagan, 1993) **D/S/P/E:** Blair Murphy

A young anthropologist (Shaun Irons) narrates his journey. He was bitten by a female vampire on a ship in Alaska, then traveled around while slowly changing ("Even the very air hurts"), searching for answers. The ambitious, arty feature was filmed on location (in Philadelphia, New Orleans, LA, and even Alaska) and features brief flashbacks, b/w and sped up segments, lite rock, some nudity, a heart being eaten, and some excellent drug-like freak-out scenes. Also with Monica Packer, Lisa Malkiewicz, Aki Aleong, Henry Rollins (he says three words), Stan Lee, *Nosferatu* clips, and a black dwarf. The director grew up in his family's New Jersey funeral home.

JULIA AND JULIA

(Fox, 1987) **D/P:** Peter Del Monte **S:** Silvia Napolitano **M:** Maurice Jarre Italy

Kathleen Turner finds her dead husband (Gabriel Byrne) in another dimension and lives there with him and their children. In the real world (?) she has a relationship with a photographer (Sting). This is the first film shot in high-definition video.

JULIET OF THE SPIRITS

(Conoisseur, 1965) **D/S:** Federico Fellini
S: Tullio Pinelli, Ennio Flaiano **P:** Angelo Rizzoli
Italy (*Giulietta degli Spiriti*)

Fellini's wife, Giulietta Masina, stars as a rich woman who thinks her husband is cheating on her, in this surrealistic fantasy. She calls up spirits during a séance, consults a mystic, and hires a detective to follow her husband. It was Fellini's next film after *8 1/2* (1963), and he claims to have taken LSD to prepare for making it. Sylva Koscina is Juliet's sister, and Sandra Milo plays three roles. Nino Rota wrote the score. The film is 148 minutes long and in color.

JUNGLE ASSAULT

(AIP, 1989) **D/S:** David Prior **P:** Fritz Matthews

The daughter of a retired American general (William Smith) is rescued from terrorists in South America by Nam vets. This typically lame AIP action movie features Ted Prior, William Zipp, and Maria Rosado.

THE JUNGLE BOOK

(Hal Roach, Spotlite, 1942) **D:** Zoltan Korda
S: Laurence Stallings **P:** Alexander Korda

Sabu stars as Mowgli, a boy raised by wolves, in this classic color adaptation of Rudyard Kipling's famous novel set in India. He talks with animals, including a giant talking cobra (a great special effect). The cast includes Joseph Calleia, Rosemary De Camp, Frank Puglia, Patricia O'Rourke, John Qualen, Ralph Byrd, and Noble Johnson. Sabu had just been in *The Thief of Bagdad* (1940). The Miklos Rozsa scores for both Korda productions were released on a single LP by RCA in 1960. Disney made an animated version in 1967, and Jason Scott Lee starred in a 1994 version shot in India.

JUNGLE BRIDE

(Video Yesterday, Sinister, 1933) **D:** Harry O. Hoyt, Albert Kelly **S:** Leah Baird **P:** I. E. Chadwick

A shipwreck off the African coast leaves four people stranded in the jungle. This 63-minute Monogram film stars Charles Starrett as a murderer, blond Anita Page, Kenneth Thompson, and Eddie Borden.

JUNGLE DRUMS OF AFRICA

(1953) **D:** Fred C. Bannon **S:** Ronald Davidson

Clayton Moore stars as Alan King in his last serial. Phyllis Coates costars, with Roy Glenn as Naganto. Some of the 12 chapters in this Republic serial are "The Beast-Fiend" and "Voodoo Vengeance." Moore (the Lone Ranger) and Coates (Lois Lane) were better known as TV stars at the time.

JUNGLE GIRL

(Stokey, 1941) **D:** William Witney, John English
S: Ronald Davidson, Norman S. Hall, William Lively

Francis Gifford stars as Nyoka in this 15-chapter Republic serial adapted from a radio series (which was based on the title of an Edgar Rice Burroughs book). Tom Neal costars with a man in a gorilla suit and Frank Lackteen as Shamba, the evil (white) witch doctor. Bad guys like to tie Nyoka up. Also in the cast are Eddie Acuff as the comic-relief character, Gerarld Mohr as a gangster, Tommy Cook as Kimbu, and stunt people like Helen Thurston, Yakima Canutt, and Tom Steel. Kay Aldridge took over the role in a 1942 sequel, *Nyoka and the Tiger Man* (also called *The Perils of Nyoka*). Gifford went on to *Tarzan Triumphs* (1943).

THE JUNGLE GIRL AND THE SLAVER

(SW, 1957) **D:** Hermann Leitner **S:** Ernst von Saloman
W. Germany/Italy (*Liane, die Weisse Sklavin*)

The sequel to *Liane, Jungle Goddess*, was also released in the US (in 1960) and features brief topless scenes. Marianne Michael returns as the girl who grew up in the jungle. She encounters her rich Hamburg relatives again but is kidnapped by slave traders. The cast includes Hardy Kruger and Adrian Hoven.

JUNGLE HEAT

(Transworld, 1983) **D:** Gus Trikonis **S:** Gregory Weston King, Larry Johnson, Michael Vilner
Philippines (*Dance of the Dwarfs*)

Peter Fonda is a drunken helicoptor pilot hired by an anthropologist (Deborah Raffin). A jungle queen and some short, reptilian monsters are found at the end. John Amos is also in this PG movie, which copies *The African Queen* a lot.

JUNGLE HELL

(Dark Dreams, 1956) **D/S/P:** Norman Cerf

Much of this very cheap movie is narrated stock footage of India. Some of the elephant scenes are awesome, but they have nothing to do with the plot about a radioactive rock and a bogus holy man. Eventually we discover that a flying saucer (hilarious FX!) has been causing planes to crash and animals to attack. Sabu stars as a 29-year-old

CAN THIS MODERN MAN SURVIVE IN A STONE AGE WORLD?
Robert Harper planewrecked in an unexplored jungle hell,
THIS IS HIS TRUE STORY!
THE LAST SURVIVOR
R

aka *Jungle Holocaust*

"jungle boy." David Bruce is a doctor who fights a stuffed jaguar, K. T. Stevens is a blond doctor who arrives from London, and George E. Stone is an elephant hunter. The makeup is by Harry Thomas.

JUNGLE HOLOCAUST

(Video City, 1976) **D:** Ruggero Deodato **S:** Tito Carpi, Gianfranco Clerici, Renzo Genta, Giancarlo Rossi   Italy (*Cannibal; The Last Survivor; The Last Cannibal World; Il Ultimo Mondo Cannibale*)

A plane-crash survivor is captured by a primitive tribe. They hang him up (naked), thinking he can fly, but he falls and dies. Little kids piss on another prisoner in a cage, but a native woman (Me Me Lay) becomes "devoted" to him and brings him food (while romantic music plays). He escapes for some wild jungle sex, but she's captured, killed, sliced open, and filled with hot coals. An alligator is gutted, and a snake eats a lizard. The cast includes Massimo Foschi and Ivan Rassimov. It was shot in Malaysia and the Philippines. AIP released it in 1978 and it was rated X in 1984. Various versions (with more or less violence) have been released on tape. The sex is more surprising than the gore in the letterboxed version I saw. Me Me Lay looks great naked, but her eye makeup distracts from the stark realism (and do primitive natives have breast implants?). Deodato, a former assistant to Roberto Rossellini, worked on seven films by the Italian neorealist director. Lamberto Bava was the assistant director. Me Me and Ivan are also in *The Man from Deep River* (1972).

JUNGLE MASTER

(Force, 1970) **D/S:** Miles Deem **S:** M. Vitelli   Italy (*Kazan, il Favoloso Uomo della Giungla*)

Kazan and his mate, Sheeran, are played by "Johnny Kismuller" and "Simone Blondell." She's captured by a safari. There's lots of stock footage and a man in a gorilla suit. Yes, it's very bad.

THE JUNGLE QUEEN

(Stokey, 1944) **D:** Ray Taylor **D/S:** Morgan B. Cox **S:** George H. Plympton, André Lamb

Ruth Roman is Lothel, the magical guardian of a tribe. She can disappear and walk through fire. In this 13-chapter Universal serial Nazi agents in Africa try to use the tribe to fight the Allies. The cast includes Lois Collen, Edward Norris, Eddie Quillan, Douglas Dumbrille, and Clarence Muse as Kyba. It's one of the dumbest serials I've ever sat through.

JUNGLE RAIDERS

(Stokey, 1945) **D:** Lesley Selander **S:** André Lamb, George H. Plympton **P:** Sam Katzman

Kane Richmond stars in this 15-chapter Columbia serial. The plot involves a fungus that's a miracle cure. Some chapter titles are "Witch Doctor's Treachery" and "Valley of Destruction." Carol Hughes costars as Zara, with Eddie Quillan, Veda Ann Borg, and Janet Shaw. Selander made *Vampire's Ghost* the same year.

JUNGLE RAIDERS

(MGM/UA, 1984) **D:** "Anthony M. Dawson"/ Antonio Marghereti **S:** Giovanni Simonelli **P:** Luciano Appignani   Italy (*La Leggenda del Rubino Malese; Captain Yankee*)

It's another *Raiders of the Lost Ark* copy. In this PG action fantasy Christopher Connelly, Lee Van Cleef, and Alan Collins are after a ruby in Malaysia.

JUNGLE SIREN

(Sinister, 1942) **D:** Sam Newfield **S:** George Wallace Sayre, Sam Robins **P:** Sigmund Neufield

Buster Crabbe stars in this PRC movie with burlesque star Ann Corio as Kuhlaya, a woman raised in the jungle, and Greco the chimp. They outwit Nazis trying to start a native uprising. Buster was back in the PRC jungle, with Julie London, in *Nabonga* two years later.

JUNGLE STREET GIRLS

(1961) **D:** Charles Saunders **S:** Alexander Dore **P:** Guido Coen   UK (*Jungle Street*)

David McCallum stars as a young criminal who hangs out at the Adam and Eve strip club. He mugs an old man for money, double-crosses a guy who helps him rob the club's safe, and kidnaps a stripper (Jill Ireland, who was married to McCallum at the time). This was an adults-only release (from Ajay Films) in the US. It was the last of McCallum's juvenile-delinquent roles and Ireland's last film appearance until she started acting with Charles Bronson (whom she married in 1968).

JUNGLE WARRIORS

(Media, 1983) **D/S/P:** Ernst von Theumer **S:** Robert Collector US/W. Germany/Mexico

When seven sexy models crash-land in Peru, they're abducted by coke dealers. Sybil Danning stars as Angel (she tortures people), with Nina Van Pallandt, Paul L. Smith, John Vernon, Marjoe Gortner, Woody Strode, Alex Cord, Kai Wulff, Louisa Moritz, and Ava Cadell. This is the movie (it was filmed in Mexico) that Dennis Hopper was fired from for wandering around naked. He straightened out afterward. Gortner replaced him. Original director Billy Fine was replaced too.

JUNIOR

(Prism, 1984) **D:** Jim Hanley **S/P:** Don Carmody **S:** John Maxwell   (*A Cut Above*)

Two female ex-cons in bikinis flee to a redneck town. The corrupt sheriff, a musclebound young psycho, and his mother (played by a man in drag) torment them. They wreak a violent revenge.

JUNIOR G-MEN

(Stokey, Rhino, 1940) **D:** Ford Beebe, John Rawlins **S:** George Plympton, Basil Dicky, Rex Taylor

This is the first of three Universal WWII serials starring "the Dead End Kids and the Little Tough Guys." In this case it's four of the six Warner Brothers Dead End Kids: Billy Halop (Billy), Huntz Hall (Gyp), Gabriel Dell (Terry), and Bernard Punsley (Lug). They join with the FBI to find Billy's scientist grandfather, who has been kidnapped by the Flaming Torch group. Rather than "12 chapters of superthrills," this serial is said to be pretty awful and has little to do with planes. At least the sequel has a good villain.

JUNIOR G-MEN OF THE AIR

(Rhino, 1942) **D:** Ray Taylor, Lewis D. Collins **S:** Paul Huston

This 12-chapter sequel to the Universal serial *Junior G-Men* is available on two videos. Billy Halop (Ace) and his gang fight the Black Dragon group, led by a Japanese spy called the Baron (Lionel Atwill). Huntz Hall (Bolts), Gabriel Dell (Stick), and Bernard Punsley (Greaseball) costar, with Frankie Darro, Turhan Bey, and Jack Arnold. It's also in the *Saturday Night Serials* series (Rhino) with three other serials.

JUNIOR HIGH SCHOOL

(Tapeworm, 1977) **D/S:** Michael Nankin, David Wechter **S/E:** Steve Jacobson, Helyn Spears

Before she was well-known, 14-year-old singer Paula Abdul was fifth-billed in this light musical set in a California school. She gives a party. Kids dance and sing in class. It's impressive for a film by unknowns, but it looks like a play. Julius Wechter (of Baja Marimba Band fame) orchestrated the music. The movie was partially backed by the American Film Institute.

JUNKMAN

(TWE, 1982) **D/S/P/C/A:** H. B. Halicki

Halicki (with a terrible long haircut and sideburns) plays widowed movie star, stunt driver (and toy collector) Harlan Holis. This outrageous, PG-rated ego trip is filled with expert footage of car chases and car and plane crashes. There's a conspiracy to kill the hero and his daughter (Susan Shaw), the Hollywood premiere of *Gone in Sixty Seconds* (Halicki's 1974 drive-in hit), and the Goodyear Blimp. The newsreel opening resembles *Citizen Kane.* The ads promised, "Over 150 cars destroyed!" Hoyt Axton (who also provided some good music) plays himself. The cast also includes Lang Jeffries, Christopher Stone, Lynda Day George, custom-car king George Barris, Freddie Cannon and the Belmonts (at "a James Dean festival"), and Jewel Shepard. Halicki died filming car stunts in 1990.

JURASSIC PARK

(MCA, 1993) **D:** Steven Spielberg **S:** Michael Crichton, David Koepp **P:** Kathleen Kennedy, Gerald R. Molen **M:** John Williams

"The most successful worldwide theatrical release in history" is a lot like a $65 million version of *The Land Unknown* (MCA, 1957). This PG-13 Universal megahit based on Michael Crichton's novel had cross-promotions with a reported 100 companies. Sam Neill stars, with Laura Dern, Jeff Goldblum, and Sir Richard Attenborough as a Scottish millionaire who keeps genetically cloned dinosaurs on an island. The main victims are a lawyer, a fat guy, and a black guy. The cast also includes Wayne Knight, B. D. Wong, Samuel L. Jackson, Ariana Richards, and the voice of Richard Kiley. There's a *Mr. DNA* cartoon and a can of Barbasol. Stan Winston and ILM created the awesome, Oscar-winning FX. It's the second-highest domestic grossing film of all time (after Spielberg's *E.T.*). It was partially filmed in Hawaii during a hurricane. The score is on MCA. MCA also released *The Making of Jurassic Park.*

JUST A GIGOLO

(Water Bearer, 1978) **D/A:** David Hemmings **S:** Ennio de Concini, Joshua Sinclair   W. Germany (*Schöner Gigolo, Armer Gigolo*)

This was the most expensive movie made in Germany up to that time, but it's not very good. David Bowie stars as a Prussian WWI hero in early-30s Berlin. He works as a walking billboard and a servant, then becomes a gigolo. The cast includes Sydne Rome, Kim Novak, Curt Jurgens, and Maria Schell. Marlene Dietrich, who came out of retirement for a guest-star role, was filmed in Paris, but the editing makes her seem to be with Bowie in Berlin. The original running time was 147 minutes.

JUST BEFORE DAWN

(1980) **D:** Jeff Lieberman **S:** Mark Arywitz, Gregg Irving **P:** David Sheldon, Doro Vlado Hreljanovic

A group of young people become stranded in the Oregon forest. They were too dumb to listen to a ranger (George Kennedy), so they're killed off by mutant twins with machetes. The cast includes Chris Lemmon and Jamie Rose (from *All My Children*). In one scene a woman kills her attacker by thrusting her whole arm down his throat. Lieberman made this after *Squirm* and *Blue Sunshine*.

JUST FOR THE HELL OF IT

(SW, 1968) **D/P:** Herschell Gordon Lewis **S:** Allison Louise Downe

Except for some bikers, movie teenagers just didn't act like this until maybe *The Class of 1984.* A group of normal-looking, middle-class "gang" members smash up a house, a cafeteria, a club, and an office, pour paint on people, start fires, torment a blind man, attack little kids playing softball, put a baby into a garbage can, and enjoy every minute of it. They lure schoolgirls to a party by telling them that a singing star called Rocky Reeves will be there, then drug their drinks. Newspapers with headlines about the violence are shown being burned, stabbed, splattered with paint, and axed. It's overlong and crude, with strange jazz music in some scenes and some long scenes totally silent. Lewis throws in a very small amount of nudity and blood but mostly shows *destruction.* Frequent fade-outs were probably used for the same reason that Jim Jarmusch used them in *Stranger Than Paradise*, to hold together leftover film stock. Ray Sager, who went on to star in Lewis' *The Wizard of Gore*, plays gang leader Dexter as if he wishes he were Bruce Dern. Nancy Lee Noble is Mitzi, his wild, sadistic, cute, blond girlfriend. Lewis himself wrote "Destruction Inc.",

the great folk theme song: "Get in off the street or you're bound to meet . . . Destruction!" This Miami marvel was filmed back to back with the better-known *She-Devils on Wheels* and includes many of the same cast members. "They're the coming generation. They're coming from the zoo!"

JUST ONE OF THE GUYS

(RCA, 1985) **D:** Lisa Gottlieb **S:** Dennis Feldman, Jeff Franklin **P:** Andrew Fogelson

Joyce Hyser disguises herself as a boy so that she'll be taken seriously as a high-school journalist. Sherilyn Fenn is attracted to her. With Clayton Rohmer, Billy Jacoby, Leigh McCloskey, Arye Gross, and Rebecca Ferratti. Similar cross-dressing teen comedies followed, including *Little Sister*, *Nobody's Perfect,* and *Just One of the Girls.*

JUST THE TWO OF US

(SW, 1970) **D:** Jacques Deerson **D/S:** Barbara Peters   (*The Dark Side of Tomorrow*)

Two Army wives start hanging out together while their husbands ignore them. Eventually dark-haired Denise (Elizabeth Plumb) seduces blond Adrian (Alicia Courtney). Adrian later decides to have an affair with a guy, but the jealous Denise wants only her. John Aprea (*Savage Beach*, *Godfather III*) costars. Characters talk a lot and the sex scenes are very brief and intercut with other scenes. Some of the soft-rock songs played by a band with female backup singers at a beach pot party are really good. A psychedelic band plays at a club, and people dance to a cover version of a Big Brother and the Holding Company instrumental. Box Office International released this in 1973. Peters, one of the very first female exploitation directors, later made *Bury Me an Angel* (1972), *Summer School Teachers* (1976), and others for Roger Corman.

Florida juvenile delinquents in Herschell Gordon Lewis' *Just for the Hell of It.*

K-2

(Paramount, 1992) **D:** Franc Roddam
S: Peter Meyers, Scott Roberts   UK

A Seattle attorney (Michael Biehn) and a physicist (Matt Craven) decide to climb a treacherous mountain in Kashmir. This movie, based on a play by Meyers, has excellent stunts and cinematography (by Bagriel Beristain) but still gets pretty dull. With Patricia Charbonneau, Julia Nickson-Soul, and Luca Bercovici. *Cliffhanger* (1993), also about mountain-climbing, was a bigger hit.

KAFKA

(Paramount, 1991) **D:** Steven Soderberg **S:** Lem Dobbs **P:** Stuart Cornfield   US/France

This is an attempt (by the director of *sex, lies, and videotape*) to make an expressionistic film combining elements of Kafka's life and his writings. Jeremy Irons plays Kafka, an insurance clerk in 1919 Prague who also writes fiction on the side with his Remington. Trying to find a missing friend, he has to go to a castle with a bomb in a briefcase, and there are horror-movie overtones. The cast is great: Theresa Russell as a terrorist, Armin Mueller-Stahl as a police inspector, Joel Grey as a nosy office worker, Alec Guinness as Kafka's boss, Ian Holm as the mad Dr. Murnau, who's creating the perfect drone worker, Jeroen Krabbe, Brian Glover, and Robert Flemyng (from *The Horrible Dr. Hitchcock*). Filmed in b/w by Walt Lloyd in Prague, with a color sequence in the castle, it's rated PG-13. Barry Levinson was the executive producer. The soundtrack by Cliff Martinez was issued by Virgin. Other Kafka movies are *The Trial, The Castle, Metamorphosis, The Labyrinth, The Insurance Man,* and *Shadows and Fog.*

KALIFORNIA

(Polygram, 1993) **D:** Dominic Sena **S:** Tim Metcalfe **P:** Steve Golin, Aris McGarry, Joni Sighvatsson

A Pittsburgh magazine writer (David Duchovny) researching serial killers for a book, and his photographer girlfriend (Michelle Forbes), share a ride in their Lincoln convertible from Kentucky to California. Brad Pitt is Early Grayce, a beer-drinking psycho killer on the road with his childlike trailer-park girlfriend (Juliette Lewis, who has her first topless scenes). This was released at the same time as another killer-teen road movie, *True Romance* (with Pitt in a small role) and was followed by *Natural Born Killers* (starring Lewis). Patricia Talman is also in the cast. Pere Ubu is heard on a jukebox. It's R or unrated.

KAMA SUTRA

(1969) **D:** Kobi Jaeger **S:** George Wilson **P/C:** Richard Reuven Rimmel   W. Germany
(Kama Sutra: Vollendung der Leibe)

AIP took this sex documentary, deleted some footage, and added more about middle-class Americans taking drugs, swapping wives, and painting their bodies. It was rereleased by Transamerica in 1972.

KAMIKAZE

(1986) **D/S/P:** Luc Besson
D/S: Didier Grousset   France

A man (Michel Galabru) fired from his electronics job invents a video shooting device with which he can kill anyone appearing on TV just by aiming at the screen. A detective (Richard Bohringer) searches for the killer, who eventually loses it and starts killing in person too, dressed as a Japanese warrior.

KAMIKAZE 1989

(MGM, 1982) **D:** Wolf Gremm
S: Robert Katz   Germany

The director Rainer Werner Fassbinder stars as a chubby, bearded police detective who wears a leopard-skin suit. This futuristic spy thriller is about a fascist, media-controlled land and bomb threats. Fassbinder died before it was released. Also with Gunther Hoffmann and Franco Nero. The soundtrack is by Edgar Froese of Tangerine Dream. It's subtitled.

KANDYLAND

(New World, 1988) **D/S:** Robert Schnitzer **S:** Toni Serritello **P:** Rick Blumenthal

A stripper named Harlow Divine (Sandahl Bergman) teaches a new stripper (Kim Evenson, from *Playboy*) the tricks of the trade. Nothing very exciting or surprising happens, but there is a psycho bartender. With Catlyn Day. It's by the director of *Rebel* (1973), an early Stallone film.

KANSAS CITY BOMBER

(1972) **D:** Jerrold Freedman **S:** Calvin Clemens, Thomas Rickman **P:** Marty Elkfland

Raquel Welch stars as K.C., a roller derby star who tries to replace the current star (Helena Kallianiotes). With Jodie Foster, Kevin McCarthy, Mary Kay Place, Norman Alden, and Cornelia Sharpe. *The Unholy Rollers* (an AIP ripoff of this PG-rated MGM release), with Claudia Jennings, was more popular.

KARAMOJA

(SW, 1954) **D:** Dr. and Mrs. Truetle

A major gross-out Technicolor road-show hit in its day, this narrated documentary was filmed (in 16mm) by a California dentist and his wife. Kroger Babb released it and let everyone know it was hot stuff. ("See it all! Uncut! Uncensored! Unclothed! Unashamed!") Scenes feature naked natives drinking animal urine and blood from cows. They smear on animal shit and participate in coming-of-age rites. Front teeth are knocked out, and the main attraction is a circumcision. An earlier feature, *Slash of the Knife God*, had also featured circumcision footage. *Karamoja* was later cut to 66 minutes and billed with *Halfway to Hell*. David F. Friedman helped promote and distribute the double bill.

KARATE COP (1973): *See* SLAUGHTER IN SAN FRANCISCO

KARATE COP

(Imperial, 1993) **D:** Alan Roberts **S:** Denny Grayson, Bill Zide **S/P/A:** Ron Marchini **P:** Garrick Huey

Ron Marchini returns as John Travis, "the last cop on Earth" in the future, in this sequel to *Omega Cop*. It's got even more sub-*Road Warrior* villains and gladiator battles. The cast includes Carrie Chambers as the scientist he saves, David Carradine, and Michael M. Foley.

KARATE: THE HAND OF DEATH

(SW, 1964) **D/P/A:** Joel Holt **S:** David Hill

Joel Holt stars as Matt Carver, a cranky, short-tempered American karate black belt in Japan. He has WWII flashbacks ("I think I killed over 100 men") with theremin music. While he searches for the sister (Reiko Okada) of his teacher and friend (Akira Shiga), a really bad actor playing a Sydney Greenstreet type is after a coin stolen from a Nazi war criminal. Much time is spent on the history of karate, and there's a demonstration. Joseph Brenner released this ahead-of-its-time movie, filmed in Tokyo. Holt also coproduced *Primitive Love*, with Jayne Mansfield, and narrated *Mondo Oscenità*. This b/w feature is letterboxed and includes a Johnny Legend intro.

THE KEEP

(Paramount, 1983)
D/S: Michael Mann **P:** Gene Kirkwood, Howard Koch Jr.

German soldiers in the mountains of Romania during WWII use an ancient stone fortress as their headquarters. The Nazis are eaten alive by an unseen force. Scott Glenn stars as a mysterious hero named Glaeken Trismegistus, and Jurgen Prochnow is a good-guy German soldier. A professor and his daughter (Alberta Watson) are brought from a concentration camp to help. The cast also includes Ian McKellen and Gabriel Byrne. There's a monster (which looks like it's from a superhero comic book) at the end. This murky, confusing movie with dreary Tangerine Dream music is supposedly based on the legend of the Golem.

KEEP MY GRAVE OPEN

(Unicorn, 1979) **D/P:** S. F. Brownrigg **S:** F. Amos Powell

A crazy woman living in an old mansion thinks she's with her brother/lover, who lures victims to her. Bodies are hidden in an old car. This Texas movie by the director of *Don't Look in the Basement* is slow but creepy. Camilla Carr (now a novelist) stars, with Gene Ross as her shrink, Stephen Tobolowsky (who went on to many major productions), and Bill Thurman.

KEEP OFF MY GRASS!

(1971) **D:** Shelley Bedman **S/P:** Austin Kalish, Irma Kalish **P:** Albert J. Saltzer

Micky Dolenz stars as "the local Casanova" in this PG obscurity filmed in New Orleans. Marcus J. Grapes costars, with Christina Hart and Gary

Wood. The Monkees drummer and singer also starred in *Night of the Strangler*, also made in New Orleans. Neither were mentioned in his autobiography.

KEIKO MASK

(VSOM, 1993) **D:** Tomo Akiyama   Japan

A high school is run by a fascist costumed Jester with an army, whose only opposition is Keiko Mask, a mysterious super heroine who wears a red hood and cape—but nothing else! The naked woman flies through the air and kills by landing on a bad guy and wrapping her legs around his face. The Jester suspects all female teachers and students of being Keiko, so has them stripped and tied up for comparison. Much is made about typical Japanese movie censorship and the "fogging" of sexual organs. Oversized pink censor dots cover penises in a shower scene and a character who sees Keiko says "I can't function. She showed her vagina!" This action fantasy is funny, sexy, and works as a social satire. I've never seen anything quite like it. Keiko is played by "unknown." *Keiko Mask* must have been successful because there were two sequels. Threat Video offers *Keiko Mask 3* (as *Super Naked and Power Pussy*) without subtitles.

KEMEK

(Genesis, 1970) **D/S:** Theodore Gershuny, Don Patterson **S/P:** Harry Millaro **P:** Jack McCallum W. Germany/Canada/Italy (*For Love or Murder*)

Most of this confusing movie is an on/off flashback. There's a nightmare in a flashback and a b/w flashback within a flashback. Star Mary Woronov said it was "unfinished," so that explains things, sort of. A man (Cal Haynes) and a detective (Charles Mitchell, from *Porky's*) visit Mary Wonderly (Woronov) and get drunk as she relates flashbacks, set in Naples, about an experimental pleasure drug and how Marisa Love (Alexandra Stewart) died. Mary (who wears different clothes in nearly every scene) works for a blond guy (Helmut Schneider), and David Hedison is an unshaven writer whose friend is killed. Hedison has a bad-trip scene, and a futuristic (?) videotape looks suspiciously like an 8-track tape. It was filmed in Canada and Italy. The music is by the Modern Jazz Quartet, and the original "Nowhere to Run" is the theme song.

KENT STATE

(1981) **D:** James Goldstone **S:** Gerald Green, Richard Kramer **P:** Lin Ephraim

Various characters are seen during the four days of anti-war protests that led up to the May 4, 1970, killing of four students in Ohio. Jane Fleiss and Charley Lang star, with Talia Balsam, Keith Gordon, John Getz, Shepperd Strudwick, and, in small roles, Will Patton, Lenny Von Dohlen, and Ellen Barkin as a campus agitator. It was filmed on an Alabama college campus. Wes Craven was one of the producers. Originally 180 minutes long on NBC-TV, it's now as short as 120. The RCA soundtrack features appropriate 60s artists.

KENTUCKY FRIED MOVIE

(Media, 1977) **D:** John Landis **S:** David Zucker, Jim Abrahams, Jerry Zucker **P:** Robert K. Weiss

Before *Airplane* (1980), the Zucker/Abrahams comedy-writing team (from Milwaukee) ran the Kentucky Fried Theater satirical group in Madison, then wrote this film version with "110 bits and cameos." It's pretty funny. I especially like the ad for the JFK game and the spoof of *Enter the Dragon* with Evan Kim and Master Bong Soo Han. The cast includes Marilyn Joi as a Cleopatra Jones type, Uschi Digart, Felix Silla in *Catholic School Girls in Trouble* (cut from TV prints), Donald Sutherland, Bill Bixby, George Lazenby, Henry Gibson, Tony Dow, Tara Stromeir, Forry Ackerman, Simon Rhee, and Jack Baker. Rick Baker did the FX and appears as a gorilla. There's a disaster-movie spoof, too. Landis next made his first big hit, *Animal House*.

KENTUCKY JUBILEE

(Loonic, 1951) **D/S/P:** Ron Ormond **S:** Maurice Tombragel

Jerry Colonna stars in this 67-minute Lippert musical comedy by the director of *The Exotic Ones*. Jean Porter, James Ellison, and Fritz Feld costar, and acts like the McQuaig Twins, "Carrot Top" Anderson, Buck and Chickie, and the Y-Knot Twirlers appear.

KEOMA

(MNTEX, 1975) **D/S:** Enzo G. Castellari **S:** Nino Roli, Nico Ducci, Luigi Montefiori **P:** Manolo Bolognini   Italy (*Desperado*)

Franco Nero stars as a half-breed who returns home and has to fight his corrupt stepbrothers. This highly regarded western costars William Berger, Woody Strode, and Gabriella Giorgelli. It features a strange musical score. The director and star reteamed years later for the similar *Jonathan of the Bears*.

KEYHOLES ARE FOR PEEPING

(American Electric, 1972) **D/S/P:** Doris Wishman **S:** Lou Burdi   (*Or Is There Life After Marriage?*)

Jerry Lewis imitator Sammy Petrillo stars in this amazing adults-only artifact filmed in the director's NYC apartment. A woman reads *Everything You Always Wanted to Know About Sex* in bed but can't get any action out of her husband. She has an arty dream of her husband and another woman, wakes up, and beats him with the book! After the titles we meet manic "schmuck" Stanley Bebble (Petrillo), a mail-order-diploma marriage counselor who lives in a New York high-rise. Stanley has long greasy hair, wears ugly leisure suits, and sweats a lot. He does eye-popping double takes and the Lewis laugh, and even plays his own stereotyped Jewish mother, with a dubbed-in voice. The burlesque-style comedy includes sound effects like "Boinnng!!" after a joke, a slide whistle when pants fall down, and a nagging wife's voice speeded up. During a group-therapy session various couples' flashbacks show a wife stripping in front of a husband who won't take his eyes off the

football game on TV, a nagging mother-in-law played by a man, and long scenes of a belly dancer and Hawaiian dancers. Every once in a while Manuel, the Puerto Rican peeping-Tom janitor, looks through keyholes to watch unrelated sex scenes that range from very tame to almost porno. Usually the faces are obscured. Some segments are in color, some in b/w or tinted sepia, and one is shown entirely in negative. It's another Wishman movie to lose your mind to. Petrillo was supposed to star in Doris's next feature too, but she got sidetracked making Chesty Morgan movies.

KEY WITNESS

(1960) **D:** Phil Karlson **S:** Alfred Brenner **P:** Pandro S. Berman, Kathryn Hereford

Jeffrey Hunter stars as an LA businessman who witnesses a murder. Nobody else on the scene will testify, and he and his family are threatened by the jd killer, Cowboy (Dennis Hopper). The other gang members are singer Johnny Nash, Susan Harrison, Joby Baker and Corey Allen (also in *Rebel Without a Cause* with Hopper). With Pat Crowley, Frank Silvera, and Bruce Gordon. There's good hip dialogue and pot-smoking, and it was filmed on location.

KGB: THE SECRET WAR

(Magnum, 1985) **D:** Dwight Little **S:** Sandra K. Bailey **P:** Sandy Howard

KGB agents in LA plan to kill one of their own, and the CIA wants him to defect. The girlfriend of the man on the run says, "So much is happening that I don't understand!" Michael Billington stars, with Denise DuBarry, Michael Ansara, and Sally Kellerman. It's from Corman's Concorde.

KICKBOXER

(HBO, 1989) **D:** David Worth **D/P:** Mark DiSalle **S:** Glenn A. Bruce

Belgian-born Jean-Claude Van Damme cowrote the story and was also the fight choreographer for this tale of vengeance. He's after the people who killed his brother in Thailand. Dennis Chan trains him. With fighter Tong Po as himself and Benny "the Jet" Urquidez. Van Damme, who went on to much bigger-budgeted starring roles, was not in the sequels.

KICKBOXER 2: THE ROAD BACK

(HBO, 1991) **D:** Albert Pyun **S:** David Goyr **P:** Steve Friedman

Sasha Mitchell (*Spike of Bensonhurst*) stars as the tattooed younger brother of the original star, and he's out for revenge and kicking the bad guys. With Peter Boyle, Cary-Hiroyuki Tagawa, Matthias Hues, John Diehl, Dale Jacoby, and Dennis Chan (*Kickboxer*). Mark Damon was the executive producer.

KICKBOXER 3: THE ART OF WAR

(Live, 1992) **D:** Rick King **S:** Dennis Pratt **P:** Michael Pariser

Sasha Mitchell returns as kickboxing champ Sloan, who goes to Rio for a tournament. While there he

Michel Qissi and Cary Hiroyuki Tagawa in *Kickboxer 2*.

saves the sister (Althea Miranda) of a street kid from evil whoremongers. With series regular Dennis Chan and Ian Jacklin. It was filmed in Brazil. *Kickboxer 4* and 5 followed, both with Mitchell.

KICKBOXER FROM HELL

(Magnum, "1991") **D:** Alton Cheung
P: Joseph Lai   (*Zodiac America III*)

Someone took a pretty entertaining (70s?) Asian movie, about a vengeful ghost who possesses living people to get back at her cheating killer husband, and added some of the worst new footage I've ever seen. The new "star" is a beefy dyed blond (Mark Houghton) "working undercover against Lucifer," and the confused, unrelated new plot features kung-fu-fighting Satanists, a nun (Sooni Shroff), and a sledgehammer fight. The music is all stolen from various soundtracks by John Carpenter, Tangerine Dream, and Richard Band.

KICK FIGHTER

(AIP, 1988) **D:** Anthony Maharaj
S: Noah Blough   Philippines

Richard Norton stars as a man who is released from prison in Bangkok, takes fighting lessons from a blind, homeless martial-arts master, and goes to the Philippines to battle Benny "the Jet" Urquidez in a cage. It's all to make money for his sister's operation. There's also a cockfight.

KICK OR DIE

(AIP, 1987) **D/S:** "Charles Norton"/
Hanro Mohr **P:** Chris Davies, Lionel A.
Ephraim   S. Africa (*No Hard Feelings*)

Kevin Bernhardt (an American soap-opera star) is a martial-arts fighter protecting college girls from a killer/rapist who disguises himself as a black man. With Holaday Mason as a singer, Tim Wallace, and Mike Stone.

KIDNAPPED

(1971) **D:** Delbert Mann **S:** Jack Pulman
P: Frederick H. Brogger   UK

Michael Caine stars as Alan Breck, with Trevor Howard, Jack Hawkins, and Donald Pleasence, in this version of Robert Louis Stevenson's famous story. This G-rated movie was released by AIP and the soundtrack includes songs by Mary Hopkin. Earlier versions were made in 1948 (with Roddy McDowall) and in 1960 (from Disney).

KIDNAPPED

(Virgin, 1986) **D/S:** Hikmet Avedis
P: Marlene Schmidt

LA gangsters drug women and force them to be in porno movies. It's the *Hardcore* plot with nudity and humor added. Barbara Crampton teams up with a cop (David Naughton) to find her sister (Kim Evenson, from *Playboy*). With Charles Napier and Jimmy Walker. "Howard" Avedis had been making drive-in movies since the early 70s (*Stepmother*, *The Teacher*, *Dr. Minx*). The Sandy Howard production went directly to video.

KIDNAPPED COED

(SW, 1972) **D/S/P:** Frederick R. Friedel
(*House of Terror*)

This was made in North Carolina by the director of *Axe* and released by Boxoffice International. Jack Cannon and Leslie Ann Rivers star in this tasteless story of a red-headed woman living in a boardinghouse who is kidnapped for money by a small-time criminal. Others break in and rape her, and the kidnapper turns hero and kills them. It was first on tape with *Hitchhike to Hell*.

THE KIDNAPPERS

(1964) **D:** Eddie Romero **S:** Harry Harber
P: Cirio H. Santiago   Philippines (*Man on the Run*)

Burgess Meredith stars as an American in Manila, with a Filipino wife (Olivia Cenizal), whose son has been kidnapped. Romero, a major director in the Philippines, later specialized in horror movies like *Mad Doctor of Blood Island*.

THE KIDS ARE ALRIGHT: SPECIAL EDITION

(BMG, 1979) **D:** Jeff Stein **P:** Bill
Curbishley, Tony Klinger

Pete Townshend and John Entwistle helped with this excellent official Who documentary (without narration). It uses great footage from TV, concerts, interviews, and home movies. Early bits include "Shout and Shimmy" (in b/w) and parts of "Substitute" and "Pictures of Lily." The Who play at Monterey, at Woodstock, on the very last *Shindig* show, and on the Smothers Brothers' show. The Rock and Roll Circus version of "A Quick One" is a rare highlight. They know they were best in the beginning, so most of the footage is from the 60s. Keith Moon sings "Barbara Ann" and gives an S&M interview. Entwistle skeet-shoots gold records. The guest stars include Ringo Starr and Steve Martin. New World released it in theaters the same year as *Quadrophenia*. The double soundtrack is on MCA.

KID VENGEANCE

(Warner, 1976) **D:** Joe Manduke **S:** Bud
Robbins, Jay Telfer, Ken Globus **P:** Frank
Johnson   Italy/Israel (*Vengeance Vendetta*)

A prospector (Jim Brown) whose gold has been stolen teams up with a kid (Leif Garrett) whose parents have been killed and his sister kidnapped. Lee Van Cleef is the killer they're both after. With John Marley, Matt Clark, and Glynnis O'Connor. Brown and Van Cleef were also in *El Condor* (1970) and *Take a Hard Ride* (1975). This was the last movie Brown starred in for many years, and it was Van Cleef's last western. It was filmed in Israel and released by Cannon.

KILL

(USA, 1972) **D/S/P:** Romain Gary **P:** Alexander Salkind
France/W. Germany/Italy/Spain (*KILL! KILL! KILL!*)

Jean Seberg was a 19-year-old small-town Iowa girl when she was chosen after a massive talent hunt to star in Otto Preminger's flop *Saint Joan* (1957). After the international hit *Breathless* (1960) she stayed in France and was a major star there. Her second husband, novelist Romain Gary, starred her in two of his obsessive do-it-all movies, *Birds of Peru* (1968) and this strange anti-drug film. She plays the wife of a grouchy international cop (a bearded James Mason) who is a drug smuggler on the side. She's first seen wearing an Afro wig and listening to African music. Mason says, "You want to save the world, don't you!" Stephen Boyd steals the show as an unhinged but effectively brutal anti-drug agent. He spends the whole movie barechested, unshaven, and sweaty, wearing brown leather, shouting lines like "I'm a psycho!" and "You're my kind of bitch!" Seberg and Boyd have an affair (a body double is used for her nude scenes), and after a lot of violence all three stars join in a laughable, dreamlike machine-gun execution of dealers. Soul singer Doris Troy sings the theme song, and blues great Memphis Slim performs "Kill" at the piano in a steamy private club, surrounded by mannequins, naked women in cages, slave traders, and heroin dealers. To make sure the anti-drug message gets across, real footage of a 12-year-old junkie is shown. The cast also includes Curt Jurgens, Victor Israel, and Daniel Emilfork. In real life Seberg was the victim of a smear campaign by the FBI because of her involvement with the Black Panthers and suffered an emotional breakdown that led to her tragic death. Gary later killed himself. Boyd narrated the official Dianetics induction film (featuring Karen Black) before dying in 1977. Mason and Jurgens are gone too. Was 1972 really that long ago?

KILL A DRAGON

(1967) **D:** Michael Moore **S:** George Schenck, William Marks **P:** Hal Klein

Jack Palance stars as a soldier of fortune hired by Chinese villagers on an island to get rid of a gangster (Fernando Lamas), who threatens to blow them all up with a junk packed with nitroglycerin. With a team of karate experts, Aldo Ray as a tourist guide, Alizia Gur, and Kam Tong. The U. A. release was filmed in Hong Kong, Macao, and Kowloon.

KILL AND GO HIDE: *See* THE CHILD

KILL AND KILL AGAIN

(Film Ventures, 1981) **D:** Ivan Hall **S:** John Crowther **P:** Igo Kantor US/S. Africa

In a sequel to *Kill or Be Killed*, James Ryan stars as karate champ Steve Chase, who has mystic abilities. He, a scientist's daughter (Anneline Kriel), and a team of four rescue a captive scientist from an evil scientist named Marduk (who dresses like an old serial villain) in New Babylonia. A character called the Fly can levitate, and Marduk uses mind-control drugs to create zombie-like slaves. It all ends in an *Enter the Dragon*–style battle in an arena. Also with Ken Gampu. Part of it was filmed at the famous Sun City.

KILL CASTRO

(1978) **D/S:** Chuck Workman **S:** Robin Swicord **P:** Peter J. Barton US/W. Germany (*Cuba Crossing; Sweet Dirty Tony; Assignment: Kill Castro; The Mercenaries*)

Stuart Whitman stars as a soldier of fortune involved in a plot to kill Castro. This little-known feature also stars Robert Vaughn, Raymond St. Jacques, Woody Strode, Sybil Danning, Albert Salmi, Michael Gazzo, Caren Kaye, and Monti Rock III (!). It was filmed in Key West, Florida, and has been released under many names. Workman also directed *Stoogemania*.

KILL CRAZY

(Media, 1990) **D/S/A:** David Heavner **P:** Arthur Boris Leon

Bruce Glover and a right-wing survivalist group use David Heavner (who suffers from combat shock) and other camping Nam vets for *The Most Dangerous Game*–style hunting. Danielle Brisbois

(*Big Bad Mama II*) shows up for a nude swim but is attacked and killed. Also with Burt Ward as a mute, Gary Owens, and Lawrence Hilton-Jacobs. Anybody can direct features these days.

KILL CRUISE

(MCA, 1990) **D/S:** Peter Keglevic

Patsy Kensit and Elizabeth Hurley are British cabaret singers in Malta who meet an alcoholic yacht captain (Jurgen Prochnow). They all head for Barbados. Kensit becomes convinced he's a murderer and drug addict (he's actually diabetic), and Hurley has an affair with him. Tense but slow-moving (there's lots of lying around in bikinis), it has a surprise ending. It was made for cable TV.

THE KILLER: *See* DADDY'S DEADLY DARLING

THE KILLER

(Fox, 1989) **D/S:** John Woo **P:** Tsui Hark   Hong Kong

John Woo is the number-one action director in Hong Kong, and this very violent, nonstop-gunfire action movie shows why. Parts of the plot might be laughable to Western viewers, but the action sequences will leave you breathless. Woo said it was a tribute to the French films of Jean-Pierre Melville. Chow Yun-Fat stars as a harmonica-playing hitman who accidentally blinds a singer (Sally Yeh) in a shootout. He tries to help her while fighting his former close friend, a cop (Danny Lee), and other hitmen. Countless characters die in blazes of gunfire. The originally 136-minute, subtitled, NC-17 film was a surprise art-house hit in America. Subtitled or dubbed versions and R or unrated versions are available, and the letterboxed unrated Voyager laserdisc includes trailers from other Woo films.

KILLER

(Fox Lorber, 1989) **D/P:** Tony Ellwood **S:** Mark Kim Ray **P/A:** Tony Locklear

A brutal, unshaven serial killer (Duke Ernsberger) wears dark glasses and stays pretty cool while he slaughters lots of people. A clichéd flashback shows how he killed his mother while she was in bed with an abusive cop. Ash (Andy Boswell) is a friendly orphan who works at his uncle's gas station. He gets wise to the stranger, who then kills his uncle and kidnaps his girlfriend. Ash and a reluctant friend tail him during an all-night car chase. The killer says that doctors cut his soul out: "Without a soul you can never go to Heaven. But you can't go to Hell either." He puts out cigarettes on his hands and proves how he can't lose at Russian roulette. There's plenty of action and blood, and the acting and script are better than average too. The lighting isn't very good, but it was filmed around Charlotte, North Carolina in Super 8 for under $10,000. *Killer* is a good, serious horror movie. The 28-year-old director started out doing special effects for *Evil Dead II*.

THE KILLER ELITE

(MGM, 1975) **D:** Sam Peckinpah **S:** Marc Norman, Sterling Silliphant **P:** Martin Baum, Arthur Lewis

A crippled CIA agent (James Caan) is after his ex-friend, a gangster (Robert Duvall) who's planning to kill a liberal politician from Taiwan (Mako). This over-the-top movie is pretty violent for a PG rating and features some samurai sword battles. With Arthur Hill, Gig Young, Bo Hopkins, Burt Young, Helmut Dantine, Uschi Digart in a party scene, and Tiana. Monte Hellman edited the fight sequences.

KILLER FORCE

(Vestron, 1975) **D/S:** Val Guest **S:** Michael Winner, Gerald Sanford **P:** Nat Wachsberger, Patrick Wachsberger US/S. Africa (*Diamond Mercenaries*)

This diamond-heist movie stars Telly Savalas as the chief of security at a vault. The crooks are played by an odd assortment: Peter Fonda, Hugh O'Brian, Christopher Lee, O. J. Simpson, and Maud Adams. It was filmed in Namibia and Ireland and released by AIP. The soundtrack is on Audio Fidelity.

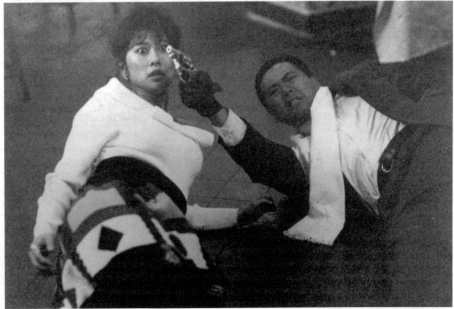

Sally Yeh and Chow Yun-Fat in John Woo's *The Killer*.

KILLER IMAGE

(Paramount, 1991) **D/S/P:** David Winning
S: Stan Edmonds **P:** Rudy Barichello,
Bruce Harvey   Canada

John Pyper-Ferguson stars as a photographer who has incriminating photos of a senator (M. Emmet Walsh). The senator's brother, Luthor (Michael Ironside with a ponytail), is a relentless, clever psycho killer who frames the hero for several murders. The headlines say, "PHOTO KILLER AT LARGE!" This violent movie includes teen gangs, a corpse on a rollercoaster, and frequent nightmares and flashbacks. It's full of plot holes and was obviously made in Canada (Calgary). Krista Errickson costars.

KILLER INSTINCT

(VEC, 1984) **D:** William Fruet **S:** John Beaird   Canada

Nicholas Campbell is a law student who doesn't believe in killing until he and some friends go to the hills of Tennessee and see Henry Silva and his backwoods friends kill somebody. Danone Camden has nude scenes.

KILLER INSTINCT

(Vidmark, 1992) **D:** Greydon Clark, Ken Stein
S: Neil Ruttenberg **P:** Menahem Golan   US/Russia

Christopher Bradley stars as Mad Dog Coll and Bruce Nozick is Dutch Schultz, in this Prohibition-era gangster movie. Rachel York costars as a speakeasy singer. This 21st Century feature is set in New York City, but was filmed in Moscow! It was made back to back with *Hit the Dutchman*, also with Nozick as Schultz. *Mad Dog Coll* (1961) was a lot better.

KILLER KLOWNS FROM OUTER SPACE

(Media, 1987) **D/S/P:** Stephen Chiodo
S/P: Charles Chiodo **P:** Edward Chiodo

This oddball, PG-13 takeoff on 50s drive-in science fiction movies starts with a comet landing in the woods. It turns out to be a circus tent. The interior resembles a set from the *Lost in Space* TV series, and it's filled with alien clowns of all sizes, with ray guns and electronic voices, who spin cotton-candy cocoons around their human victims. As in *The Blob*, teens can't convince the local authorities to act. Even though this movie drags in spots, it has a great concept, good special effects, and some inspired moments. A tiny clown on a bike is harassed by bikers and knocks the leader's head off, and a giant, scary clown attacks. Some goofy comedy-relief brothers in an ice-cream truck come to the rescue. Royal Dano is a backwoods victim, and sleaze great John Vernon plays the hateful Officer Mooney. The unique California group the Dickies provide a great theme song, and after the end credits they do it again in a rock video. The Chiodo brothers created the aliens in *Critters*.

KILLER NERD

(Tempe, 1991) **D/S/P:** Mark Steven Bosko,
Wayne A. Harold

Toby Radloff worked as a file clerk with comic-book writer Harvey Pekar at the VA hospital in Cleveland. Pekar put Toby into some issues of his *American Splendor* comics, which led to some MTV spots. In his film debut, Toby is Harold Hunkle, a comic-book collector with a possessive mother. When somebody tells him to "accentuate the positive," Harold says, "There's—not—one—iota—of—positive—to—accentuate." (Toby talks creepy and slow like that in real life.) Harold dreams of becoming cool and being with a stripper, but in real life everybody ridicules and torments him. After getting a punk haircut and going to a dance he gets beaten up (again) by drug dealers. He cracks up, yelling, "Nerd! Nerd! Nerd!" He kills people with acid and dynamite, decapitates a drug dealer, and punches his mom, then buries an axe in her head, laughing all the time. The end is bloody and shocking because you get the unsettling feeling that Toby is doing exactly what he might like to do in real life. Alan Mothersbaugh plays a bartender. It was filmed in Ravenna, Ohio. *Bride of the Killer Nerd* followed.

KILLER NUN

(Redemption, 1977) **D/S:** Giulio Berruti **S:** Alberto Torallo **P:** Enzo Gallo   Italy (*Suor' Omicidi*)

Anita Ekberg is Sister Gertrude, a modern-day nun working in an asylum. She becomes addicted to morphine, has nightmares, and is obviously losing her mind. She stomps on a patient's dentures, steals, and picks up men. She also has an affair with a younger nun (Paola Morra) and seems to be killing patients. The character is more confused and pathetic than scary or hateful. Morra has nude scenes. Alida Valli is the mother superior, Joe Dallesandro is a doctor, and Lou Castel is a crippled painter. This is a letterboxed British version.

KILLER PARTY

(Fox, 1984) **D:** William Fruet **S:** Barney
Cohen **P:** Michael Lepiner

Students are killed in old house on April Fools' Day during some frat hazing. The killer wears a diver's suit. There's some comedy, zombies, and a film-within-a-film opening. Joanna Johnson (from the TV series *The Bold and the Beautiful*) becomes possessed and hangs from the ceiling. With Martin Hewitt (*Endless Love*) and Paul Bartel (*Eating Raoul*) as a professor.

THE KILLERS

(1984) **D/S/P:** Patrick Roth

A former insurance man and a thief plan to rob a house. Murder and rape result. It's based on "Short Story" by Charles Bukowski, who appears as "the author." Jack Kehoe and Raymond Mayo star, with Anne Ramsey and Susan Tyrrell as "ragpickers."

KILLER'S CURSE = NURSE SHERRI

THE KILLER'S EDGE

(PM, 1990) **D/S/P:** Joseph Merhi
P: Richard Pepin   (*Blood Money*)

Wings Hauser stars as an LA Nam-vet cop who teams up with an FBI agent (Karen Black) to catch a Nam-vet counterfeiter (Robert Z'Dar) who has big guns.

KILLER'S KISS

(MGM, 1955) **D/S/P/C/E:** Stanley Kubrick
S: Howard O. Sackler **P:** Morris Bousel

United Artists released Kubrick's second feature but added a happy ending. This much-copied NYC crime film is only 67 minutes long. Bousel, the co-producer, was a Bronx chemist. The cast was from TV. Jamie Smith stars as a boxer, and Irene Kane (aka Chris Chase) is a nightclub dancer. The owner (Frank Silvera) of the Times Square club where she works tries to rape her and then holds her hostage in a warehouse full of mannequins. It's worth seeing just for the location work. Kubrick's next film was the even better *The Killing* (1956). Matthew Chapman's *Strangers Kiss* (1984) is about making this film.

KILLER'S MOON

(CIC, 1978) **D/S/P:** Alan Birkinshaw
P: Gordon Keymer   UK

Mental-hospital patients treated with LSD escape and kill camping schoolgirls and some of their boyfriends. It's gory and dumb, and includes rape scenes. The director later made bad movies for Harry Alan Towers.

KILLER SNAKES

(SW, 1972) **D:** Kuei Chi-Hung **P:** Raymond Shaw, Run-Run Shaw   Hong Kong

From the same year as William Grefe's *Stanley*, this more violent movie is about a pitiful young man named Keto (Kan Kuo-Liang) who uses snakes for revenge. This Shaw brothers production was released in America by Mahler Films. It features "1001 killer snakes."

KILLER TOMATOES EAT FRANCE

(Fox, 1991) **D/S/P:** John DeBello **S:** Constantine Dillon **S/P:** J. Stephen Peace

The gag-filled fourth in a series from New World (all directed by DeBello) is very silly and is aimed at kids. John Astin returns as Professor Gangrene. The tomatoes are hand puppets. The plot has something to do with Nostradamus's prophecies and a young couple (Angela Vissier and Marc Price). Most of the action takes place in a French château/hotel. A car chase was actually shot in Paris, and some WWII footage is used as filler.

KILLER TOMATOES STRIKE BACK

(Fox, 1991) **D/S/P/A:** John DeBello
S: Constantine Dillon, Rick Rockwell
P: J. Stephen Peace

John Astin returns as Professor Gangrene, who poses as a TV talk show host. Rick Rockwell is detective Lance Boyle, Crystal Carson solves tomato murders, and Steve Linquist is Igor. It followed *Return of the Killer Tomatoes* (1988).

KILLER WORKOUT

(Academy, 1987) **D/S/P:** David A. Prior
P: Peter Yuval   (*Aerobicide*)

Who is stabbing customers at a health spa? The same idea was used in *Death Spa*, and both movies are bad. Ted Prior, Fritz Matthews, and Marcia Karr are in the cast.

THE KILL FACTOR: *See* DEATH DIMENSIONS

THE KILLING

(MGM, 1956) **D/S:** Stanley Kubrick **P:** James B. Harris

Sterling Hayden stars as Johnny Clay, an ex-con from Kentucky, in this influential, b/w, narrated, documentary-style heist classic. The excellent cast includes Coleen Gray, scene-stealing Timothy Carey, Marie Windsor and Elisha Cook Jr. as a married couple, Joseph Sawyer, Jay C. Flippen, Vince Edwards, Ted De Corsia, and Joseph Turkel. Jim Thompson wrote the original screenplay, based on *Clean Break*, by Lionel White, but was credited only for "original dialogue." Thompson also wrote *Paths of Glory* for Kubrick. It was a U.A. release.

KILLING CARS

(Vidmark, 1985) **D/S:** Michael Verhoeven
W. Germany

Jurgen Prochnow stars as a car designer in Berlin who develops a nonpolluting "worldcar" that doesn't need gas. Arab oil interests try to suppress it. The cast also includes Senta Berger (the director's wife), Bernhard Wicki, and William Conrad as an American businessman.

THE KILLING EDGE

(1986) **D:** Lindsay Shonteff **S:** Robert
Bauer **P:** Elizabeth Gray   UK

A man (Bill French) searches for his family in a nuclear wasteland with terminators.

THE KILLING GAME

(City Lights, 1988) **D/S/P:** Joseph Merhi
P: Richard Pepin

Chad Howard stars as a hitman being blackmailed, with big Robert Z'Dar. The low-budget filmmakers later created the PM Video company.

KILLING HEAT

(1981) **D/S:** Michael Raeburn **P:** Mark Forstater
UK/Sweden (*The Grass Is Singing*)

Karen Black stars as a city woman who marries a farmer (John Thaw) and tries to adjust to rural life. John Moulder-Brown, John Kani, and Patrick Mynhardt are also in the cast. Black has a nude shower scene. This adaptation of Doris Lessing's novel was filmed in Zambia.

A KILLING IN A SMALL TOWN

(Vidmark, 1990) **D:** Stephen Gyllenhaal
S: Cynthia Ciore, Stephen Gyllenhaal
P: Dan Witt, Courtney Pledger

A married Sunday-school teacher (Barbara Hershey) has an affair with her best friend's churchgoing husband (John Terry). He calls it off, so she kills his wife with an axe. This is an adaptation of the novel *Evidence of Love*, by Jim Atkinson and John Bloom (aka Joe Bob Briggs!), which was based on an actual 1980 case near Dallas. Brian Dennehy is her attorney, and Hal Holbrook is a psychiatrist.

THE KILLING KIND

(American, 1973) **D:** Curtis Harrington
P: George Edwards **S:** Lenny Crechalon

Harrington (*Night Tide*) effectively ended his theatrical directing career with this tale of a young psycho killer (John Savage) just out of prison, where he has served two years for rape (he was forced to join in a gang bang). He insults and humiliates women, including his mother, Thelma (Ann Sothern), her boardinghouse tenants, a librarian, Louise (Luana Anders), and Cindy Williams. Sue Bernard (*Faster, Pussycat! Kill! Kill!*), the girl who cried rape, is his first victim, killed in an arranged car crash. His lawyer (Ruth Roman) is forced to get drunk, then is tied up and burned to death, while her client laughs. In a dream he's in a crib surrounded by women. An older tenant has a stairway elevator like the one in *Homicidal*. Harrington went on to lighter TV movies like *The Killer Bees* and *Devil Dog, Hound from Hell*. In real life Savage had already had two kids, acted in two obscure nudie movies, and joined SDS by the time this filmed-in-Malibu movie was made.

KILLING MACHINE

(Thriller, 1983) **D/S:** José Antonio Loma
P: Carlos Vasallo   Spain/Mexico

A Spanish truckdriver and demolition expert (Jorge Rivero) battles French farmers in a border area, as well as corrupt cops and gangsters. The cast includes Lee Van Cleef as a lawyer, Margaux Hemingway as a French aerobics instructor, Willie Ames, Richard Jaeckel, and Hugo Stiglitz. It was filmed in Spain and France. The tape has a Sybil Danning intro.

KILLING OBSESSION

(Triboro, 1994) **D/S/P:** Paul Leder

John Savage (see *The Killing Kind*) is a serial killer, released from a mental institution after 20 years, who has hallucinations and kills women from the phone book named Annie Smith. John Saxon is the doctor who reluctantly released him. Incredibly, it's a remake of Leder's notorious 1972 movie *I Dismember Mama* (aka *Poor Albert and Little Annie*). With Kimberly Chase as the now-grown-up Annie, Bobby DiCicco as a pimp, and porn star Hyapatia Lee as a hooker. The cast members are all shown again for the end credits. Saxon and DiCicco were also in Leder's *The Baby Doll Murders*.

THE KILLING OF A CHINESE BOOKIE

(Touchstone, 1976) **D/S:** John Cassavettes
P/A: Al Ruban

Cosmo (Ben Gazzara), who runs the Crazy Horse West, a sleazy Sunset Strip strip club, is forced to kill a bookie to pay off gambling debts to mobsters. Also in the cast are Morgan Woodward as a gangster, Timothy Carey and Seymour Cassel as his henchmen, Azizi Johari, and Haji as herself (although she was mostly cut out). Cassavettes made it the way he wanted to (pretty strange) for his own Faces company. The tape is 17 minutes shorter than the theatrical release.

THE KILLING OF AMERICA

(VSOM, 1981) **D:** David Weisman **S/P:** Leonard Schrader   Japan (*Violence in America*)

Paul Schrader's brother planned this chilling documentary look at "the land of a million murders and a hundred million guns." Famous serial killers are discussed or interviewed, political assassinations are covered (and the Zapruder film is shown), and the endless, normal, everyday big-city murders are tallied. John Lennon's death and the attempt on Ronald Reagan's life were recent events. It was made for the Japanese market and was never officially released in America but was a hit in Australia and other countries. Seeing it for the first time when it was 10 years old, I was struck by how much American *Hard Copy*–style TV shows resemble this grim movie and how much worse everything had gotten in those 10 years.

THE KILLING OF SATAN

(Paragon, 1974) **D:** Efrón C. Pinión **S:** José Maria Avilana **P:** Pio C. Lee   Philippines

A man (Ramón Revilla) is chosen by his dead uncle Miguel to battle evil forces. "The prince of magic" can hypnotize people, shoot rays from his hands, and make heads spin, but he and his men use guns when convenient. A Devil in a red suit keeps naked women caged in his cave. A snake becomes a man in a jockstrap. A giant boulder crushes a man into a bloody pulp. This fun movie throws in every low-budget effect the filmmakers could come up with. It includes *Penitentes* whipping themselves and ends with a major battle of magic.

KILLINGS AT OUTPOST ZETA

(United, 1981) **D/P:** Allan Sandler,
Robert Emenegger **S:** Peter Dawson

A rock-like creature that feeds on blood is discovered on the planet Zeta in the year 2002. Gordon Devol and Jacqueline Ray star in this very cheap direct-to-TV Gold Key feature.

KILLING SPREE

(Twisted Illusions, 1987) **D/S:** Tim Ritter **P:** Al Nicolosi

A jealous mechanic imagines his wife is having affairs, so he slaughters men with various tools. Red lights flash, followed by lots of extreme gore. The victims return as zombies. It was shot on video in Florida and directed by the 21-year-old who made *Truth or Dare*. His next film was *Wicked Games*.

THE KILLING TIME

(Starmaker, 1987) **D:** Rick King **S:** Don Bohlinger, James Nathan, Bruce Franklin **P:** Peter Abrams, Robert L. Levy   (*A Perfect Stranger*)

Beau Bridges is a small-town California deputy sheriff plotting to kill his mistress's husband. The convoluted *Body Heat*–inspired plot also involves Kiefer Sutherland, Wayne Rogers, Joe Don Baker, Harriet White Medin, and Camilla Kath. It's from New World.

KILLING ZOË
(Live, 1994) **D/S:** Roger Avary   France

Zed (Eric Stolz), a long-haired American safe-cracker in Paris, and a crazed local (Jean-Hughes Anglade, from *La Femme Nikita*) shoot heroin and botch a bank heist. This violent, partially subtitled movie features Julie Delpy as part-time hooker Zoë, and Gary Kemp. Quentin Tarantino was the executive producer. The 29-year-old Canadian director worked on *Reservoir Dogs*, *True Romance*, and *Pulp Fiction*. Tom Savini did the FX.

THE KILLING ZONE
(PM, 1991) **D/S:** Addison Randall **P:** Charla Driver

Big Daron McBee (from the *American Gladiators* TV show) stars as a convict recruited from a chain gang to capture a Mexican drug lord (James Dalesandro). The cast also includes Armando Silvestre as his crippled drug-agent uncle and Melissa Moore, who has a shower scene during a break in slow-motion fights.

KILL LINE
(Hemdale, 1988) **D/S:** Richard H. Kim
P/A: Robert W. Kim

Bobby Kim (*The Manchurian Avenger*) stars as Bone Crusher Bronson in this martial-arts revenge tale. A corrupt sheriff sends him to jail, and his family is murdered. The Korean star has also made features in Korea and Hong Kong. This one was filmed in Denver. With Peter Johnson and several of the stars from *Backstreet Jane*.

KILL ME AGAIN
(MGM, 1989) **D/S:** John R. Dahl **S:** David Warfield

Val Kilmer stars as a Reno private investigator who owes money to the mob. A woman (Joanne Whalley-Kilmer, his real-life wife at the time) who has robbed the mob wants him to fake her murder so that she can escape her psycho ex-husband (Michael Madsen), who wants to kill her. Also in the cast are Jonathan Gries and Bibi Besch. The director later made the hits *Red Rock West* and *The Last Seduction*.

KILL OR BE KILLED
(1950) **D/S:** Max Nosseck **S:** Arnold Phillips,
Lawrence Goldman **P:** Walter Jurmann

Lawrence Tierney is a man accused of a murder he didn't commit hiding out in the South American jungle. With Marissa O'Brien, George Coulouris as a plantation owner, and Rudolph Anders. From Eagle Lion. Tierney returned in *The Hoodlum* (1951) and *Singing in the Dark* (1956), also directed by Nosseck, who had launched his career with *Dillinger*.

KILL OR BE KILLED
(Media, 1980) **D:** Ivan Hall **S:** C. F.
Beyers-Boshoff **P:** Ben Volk   S. Africa

James Ryan (a dancer in real life) stars as a mystical kung-fu hero who battles a Nazi general/karate coach. The cast includes Charlotte Michelle and Norman Combes. This PG Cinemation release did well, so there was a sequel, *Kill and Kill Again*.

KILLPOINT
(Vestron, 1982) **D/S/P/E:** Frank Harris
P: Diane Stevenett

Leo Fong stars as an LA karate-fighting cop who avenges the rape and murder of his wife and teams up with an FBI man (Richard Roundtree). Cameron Mitchell is the sadistic psycho leader of a gang of gunrunners who raided a National Guard armory. With Stack Pierce and Hope Holliday. Harris was a former California TV news reporter. *Killpoint* was released by Crown International on its 25th anniversary. Fong and Mitchell returned in *Low Blow*.

KILL SQUAD
(Edde, 1982)
D/S/P: Patrick G. Donahue
P: Michael D. Lee   Philippines

Six martial-arts-fighting Nam vets of various nationalities battle Dutch (Cameron Mitchell) and his band of burglars. Among the fighters are Jean Glaudé, Jeff Risk, and Francisco Ramírez. Some characters are decapitated by axes.

KILL ZONE
(1985) **D/S:** David A. Prior
S/P: Jack Marino

Fritz Matthews is a deranged Nam vet who thinks he's back in the jungle during some war games. With Ted Prior and Melissa Moore. This is one of Prior's first (of way too many) direct-to-video features.

KILL ZONE
(New Horizons, 1991) **D/P:** Cirio H. Santiago
S: Frederick Bailey

Most of this Nam War film consists of endless shooting and explosions. Tony Dorsett (of the Dallas Cowboys) is sort of the star. He falls for a guerrilla fighter (Vivian Velez) with a designer black-leather bra. David Carradine is the "unconventional," racist, cigar-chomping Colonel Wiggins, who has people murdered and orders an illegal incursion into Cambodia. Carradine fans should check it out for the scene where he freaks out and yells, "Year of the fuckin' monkey!" while mowing down innocent villagers with a machine gun, and for his stupid return-from-the-dead scene. It was

12 Hands...
12 Feet...
24 Reasons
to Die!
After a Death for a Death
The price goes up!

PATRICK G. DONAHUE'S **KILL SQUAD**

JEAN **GLAUDÉ** · JEFF **RISK** · JERRY **JOHNSON** · BILL **CAMBRA** · FRANCISCO **RAMIREZ**

MARC **SABIN** · GARY **FUNG** · ALAN **MARCUS** · CAMERON **MITCHELL**

executive producer **LADD RUCKER** · director of photography **CHRISTOPHER W. STRATTAN** · stunt coordinators **MIKE DONAHUE · LARRY JACKSON**

produced by **MICHAEL D. LEE** · written, produced & directed by **PATRICK G. DONAHUE**   Summa Vista Pictures release

R RESTRICTED
Under 17 requires accompanying Parent or Adult Guardian

filmed in the Philippines. The local actors and extras do not look Vietnamese.

KILMA, QUEEN OF THE AMAZONS
(All Seasons, 1975) **D/S:** Manuel Iglesias Bonns
S: Miguel Cusso   Spain

During a 19th(?)–century pirate mutiny, Robinson, the navigator (with thinning blond hair and black eyebrows), escapes to an island. He sees an Easter Island statue and natives with bows who look suspiciously like Spaniards. Then a group of female warriors with spears and lots of eye makeup show up on horseback. In a temple they vow, "We shall always fight against men!" After Kilma (Eva Miller) is saved from snakebite death by the hero she falls for him. Other Amazons, with leather bondage belts, become upset. Although packaged like a daring, adults-only sex-adventure tape, this silly tale could be shown to kids on Saturday-morning TV without causing any trouble. It's by the director of *Night of the Howling Beast* (1976), starring Paul Naschy.

KINDER, MUTTER, UND EIN GENERAL

(1954) **D:** Laslo Benedek **P:** Erich Pommer   W. Germany

A group of German mothers set out to find their teenage sons, soldiers on the Eastern Front, in 1945. Hilde Krahl stars, with Bernhard Wicki, Maximilian Schell, and Klaus Kinski (who had been a teenage soldier himself). The Hungarian-born Benedek had already directed *The Wild One* (1954) in America.

THE KINDRED

(Vestron, 1987) **D/S/P:** Jeffrey Obrow **D/S/C:** Steven Carpenter **S:** John Penney, Earl Ghaffari

David Allen Brooks inherits his mom's lab in an isolated house and shows up there with his teen friends. Her gene-splicing experiments resulted in monsters. Rod Steiger costars as a mad scientist who revives a mutant cat, and Amanda Pays turns into an amphibian. With Talia Balsam and Kim Hunter, who dies early in the film. Joseph Stefano worked on the script. The David Newman soundtrack is on Varese Sarabande. Steiger was in *American Gothic* and *Feel the Heat* around the same time. Obrow spent the next few years directing rock videos, then made *Servants of the Twilight*.

THE KINGDOM

(1994) **D/S:** Lars von Trier **S:** Tomas Gislason **P:** Ole Riem   Denmark (*Riget*)

A hospital in Copenhagen is the setting for brain operations, ghosts, voodoo, organ transplants, severed heads, a monster baby, and rock and roll music. The very strange, comic four part, nearly four-and-a-half-hour movie was shot on video for TV by the acclaimed director of *The Element of Crime* (1984) and *Zentropa* (1990). Ernest Hugo Jaregard stars with Kristen Rolffes and Udo Kier.

KINGDOM OF THE VAMPIRES

(CVH, 1991) **D/P/E:** J. R. Bookwalter **S/A/M:** Matthew Jason Walsh **P:** Scott P. Plummer

A long-haired convenience-store worker is a very reluctant vampire whose horrible mother demands, "Kill for me!" Matthew Jason Walsh (who also stars in *Midnight II*) gives his all as he talks, cries, screams, begs, and finally panics and kills her. The trouble is that this shot-on-video release has no FX and moves at a snail's pace. It was made in Medina County, Ohio.

KING DONG

(Selectatape, 1984) **D/S/P/A:** Yancy Hendrieth **P:** Ben Yoman   (*Lost on Adventure Island*)

It's hard to believe that this fantasy/adventure *King Kong* ripoff/porno movie exists, but it does.

Made in Honolulu, it has some pretty good stop-motion animation, OK special effects, and amusing matte paintings but strictly amateur sex scenes. Crystal Holland, who had a short-lived porno career (*Surrender in Paradise*) after this, joins some people on a sailboat, which crashes. She and some actor using a fake name survive on an island where they see a long-necked, animated dinosaur, a normal-sized gorilla with impossibly long arms (played by the director), and a brown, animated, almost perfect copy of King Kong. The island also has female warriors on horseback, a T. Rex, black cannibals, and a big, floppy balloon hand for Kong to pick people up with. This would have made an amusing short, but most of the time is filled with badly lit, unappealing, hard-core fuck scenes. The only native who gets any is (surprise) the only white one. The hero does it doggy style with three handcuffed women at swordpoint. Holland has a lesbian scene with the island's queen. It was a real family project: Dee Hendrieth, another producer, did the costumes and plays two roles. At the end Crystal wakes up in a hospital where a terrible actor plays Dr. Cronenberg, and you hope it really was just a dream.

KING KONG LIVES!

(Lorimar, 1986) **D:** John Guillermin **S:** Ronald Shusset, Steven Pressfield **P:** Martha Schumacher **M:** John Scott

DEG produced this dumb flop sequel to the awful 1976 remake. Linda Hamilton leads a surgical team that gives Kong (who had fallen off the World Trade Center) an artificial heart. Brian Kerwin brings him a female Kong (with breasts), and the giant gorillas have a cute baby. The giant-heart-transplant scene does have a certain unique quality. This was made in North Carolina and features Carlo Rambaldi FX. The score is on MCA.

KING KUNG FU

(American, 1976) **D/S/A:** Lance D. Hayes **P:** Bob Walterscheid

This silly, dated spoof is filled with sight gags and jokes derived from the then-current De Laurentiis *King Kong* and the *Kung Fu* TV show. The newscaster hero (named Beau Bridges) looks like De Niro in *The King of Comedy*. There's a dream sequence, a gorilla's flashback, some animation, and even jokes about Ronald Reagan. Actually, it's pretty impressive for a movie made in Wichita and has some good gags. Postproduction was by Herbert Strock.

KING LEAR

(Xenon, 1987) **D/S/A:** Jean-Luc Godard **P:** Golan/Globus   US/Switzerland

Peter Sellars stars as Shakespeare's descendant in a postnuke hotel in Switzerland. In this experimental film are Burgess Meredith as a Mafioso, Molly Ringwald as his daughter, Woody Allen as Mr. Alien, and Quentin Tarantino, years before anybody heard of him. Norman and Kate Mailer show up as themselves. This Cannon feature was rated PG.

THE KING OF COMEDY

(RCA, 1981) **D:** Martin Scorsese **S:** Paul D. Zimmerman **P:** Arnon Milchan

Robert De Niro stars as Rupert Pupkin, an off-balance fan and would-be standup comic living with his mom in New Jersey. He decides to kidnap a network-TV talk-show host (Jerry Lewis!) so that he can bring his act to the public. This chilling, disturbing black comedy was not a box-office hit, but says volumes about "fame" and show biz. With Sandra Bernhard, Diahnne Abbott, Ed Herlihy, Shelley Hack, Tony Randall, Dr. Joyce Brothers, Victor Borge, the Clash, and *Tonight* show producer Fred De Cordova. Scorsese's mom plays Rupert's mom, and the director has a bit part as a TV director. It was filmed in 1981, after *Raging Bull*, but released in 1983. The various artists soundtrack is excellent (typical for a Scorsese movie) and a recording was issued by United Artists.

KING OF HEARTS

(MGM, 1966) **D/P:** Philippe De Broca **S:** Daniel Boulanger   France/UK (*Le Roi de Coeur*)

During WWI a Scottish soldier (Alan Bates) walks into a French town inhabited only by inmates of an asylum. He's there to defuse a bomb left by the Germans, but the carefree residents crown him king and arrange a wedding with an acrobat (Genevieve Bujold). With Pierre Brasseur, Jean-Claude Brialy, Micheline Presle, and Adolfo Celi. It became a cult hit when it was rereleased in America (by United Artists) and played revival houses for years. A soundtrack was also issued by UA. It's subtitled.

KING OF KINGS

(MGM, 1961) **D:** Nicholas Ray **S:** Philip Yordan **P:** Samuel Bronston **M:** Miklos Rozsa

Jeffrey Hunter is Christ and Siobhan McKenna is Mary, in a movie some critics at the time called *I Was a Teenage Jesus* (even though Hunter was in his mid–30s). Also in the cast are Hurd Hatfield as Pontius Pilate, Robert Ryan as John the Baptist, Rip Torn as Judas. Also with Ron Randell, Viveca Lindfors, Rita Gam, Harry Guardino, Guy Rolf, Royal Dano, and George Coulouris. Future horror star Paul Naschy was an extra. Narration read by Orson Welles and written by Ray Bradbury was added after MGM had the film cut. Like *The Last Temptation of Christ* (1988), it was denounced as blasphemous, and like Bronston and Ray's next epic, *55 Days at Peking*, this Super Techirama 70 movie is long (originally 168 minutes) and expensive, has a cast of thousands, and was filmed in Spain. The box-office failure of the two features ended Ray's career. Playing the son of God didn't help Hunter much either. MCA released the soundtrack.

KING OF KONG ISLAND

(Sinister, 1968) **D:** Robert Morris **S/P:** "Ralph Zucker"/Mario Pupillo **P:** Walter Brandt   Italy/Spain (*Kong Island; Eve; La Venere selvaggio*)

Esmeralda Barros is a woman brought up by (normal-sized) apes. A mad scientist (American actor Marc Lawrence) controls the robot-like apes, and Brad Harris is the hero.

KING OF NEW YORK

(Live, 1989) **D:** Abel Ferrara **S:** Nicholas St. John **P:** Augusto Caminito

Gangster Frank White (Christopher Walken) gets out of jail and sets up headquarters at the Plaza Hotel in NYC, with female bodyguards. He and a group of loyal black drug dealers battle the Mafia and Chinese and Colombian gangsters. He backs the building of a hospital, thinks of running for mayor, and becomes a hero to many. Lawrence (Larry) Fishburne costars as the "posse" leader, and Wesley Snipes and David Caruso are cops. This violent, outrageous action movie almost got an X rating. There are some great scenes on the subway and an unbelievable Times Square ending. It was booed at the New York Film Festival. The idea of a drug dealer as hero/politician was close to what really happened a few years later in Chicago. With Victor Argo, Joey Chin, Giancarlo Esposito, Steve Buscemi, James Lorinz, Phoebe Legere, Zoe Tamerlis, and Ariane. There's a clip from *Nosferatu*.

KING OF THE CARNIVAL

(1955) **D:** Franklin Adreon **S:** Ronald Davidson

The very last Republic serial stars Harry Lauter and Fran Bennett. They played circus acrobats and had to dress in some some very old-fashioned-looking costumes (with skull and crossbones insignias) to match all the footage from *Circus Girl* (1937). One of the supporting players is a young Stuart Whitman.

KING OF THE CONGO

(Stokey, 1952) **D:** Spencer Gordon Bennett, Wallace A. Grissell **S:** George Plympton, Royal K. Cole, Arthur Hoerl **P:** Sam Katzman

Buster Crabbe stars in his last (and worst) serial as Thunda, a jungle hero based on the hero of a comic book. A US Air Force captain searches for missing microfilm. The 15-chapter serial, from Columbia,

has men in gorilla suits, cavemen, magic rocks, and a man-eating plant. Gloria Dea as "Pha," Leonard Penn as Boris, and Jack Ingram co-star.

KING OF THE KONGO

(Stokey, 1929) **D:** Richard Thorpe **P:** Nat Levine

Boris Karloff plays Scarface Macklin, a gang leader, in this rare 10-chapter Mascot serial. It was released in silent and part-talkie versions (a first). Walter Miller stars as a Secret Service agent searching for his brother with Jacqueline Logan and there's a gorilla. Karloff also played villains in *The Hope Diamond Mystery* (1921), *Vultures of the Sea* (1928), and *The Fatal Warning* (1929), all silent serials. He and Miller returned in *King of the Wild* (1930).

KING OF THE MOUNTAIN

(1981) **D:** Noel Nosseck **S:** H. R. Christian **P:** Jack Frost Sanders

Garage mechanic Harry Hamlin and his beer-drinking friends race cars on the streets of LA. Dennis Hopper is the burned-out Cal, the former "king" of Mulholland Drive, and Sid Haig is a mechanic. This PG release based on a magazine article by Dave Berry, also features Joseph Bottoms, Deborah Van Valkenburgh, Dan Haggerty, and Seymour Cassel. Nosseck also made *Las Vegas Lady* and TV movies.

KING OF THE ROCKET MEN

(Republic, 1949) **D:** Fred Brannon **S:** Royal Cole, William Lively, Sol Shore

This 12-chapter Republic serial may have inspired *The Rocketeer* (1991). And if anything else looks familiar, it's because lots of stock footage from this serial was used in the other Republic flying-men serials: *Flying Disc Man from Mars* (1951), *Radar Men from the Moon* (1952), and *Zombies of the Stratosphere* (1952). Tristram Coffin stars as Jeff

King, who flies around wearing a leather jacket, a metal helmet, and a rocket-propelled backpack. The controls on his chest read: slow, fast, up, down, on, off. Mae Clarke is a photographer for *Miracle Science* magazine, and I. Stanford Jolley is the evil Dr. Vulcan. In the last chapter he destroys NYC with a tidal wave (there's stunning footage from the 1933 film *Deluge*). With Dave Sharpe, Tom Steele, and Eddie Parker (the busy stunt men). The 1951 feature version is called *Lost Planet Airmen*.

KING OF THE WILD

(Stokey, 1930) **D:** Reeves Eason **S:** Wyndham Gittens, Ford Beebe

Boris Karloff plays a villainous sheik in the last of his five serials. This Mascot jungle tale is about a bizarre-looking, ape-like creature. Walter Miller stars, with Nora Lane and Dorothy Christy.

KINGS AND DESPERATE MEN

(Magnum, 1977) **D/S/P/A/C/E:** Alexis Kanner **S:** Edward Ward   Canada

Patrick McGoohan is John Kingsley, an arrogant Montreal radio-talk-show host taken hostage on Christmas Eve by a political-extremist history professor (Alexis Kanner). Andrea Marcovicci is his shotgun-carrying accomplice. Meanwhile, a judge is kidnapped, the prime minister's wife (Margaret Trudeau!) and her child are held captive in an apartment, and the whole building is wired to explode. SWAT teams stand by, and Kingsley holds a phone-in trial on the radio. The ending is great. Kanner was Number 2 on the TV series *The Prisoner*, also starring McGoohan.

KING SOLOMON'S MINES

(Sinister, 1937) **D:** Robert Stevenson **S:** Michael Hogan, Roland Pertwee   UK

Cedric Hardwicke stars as Allan Quatermain in the first (and best) sound version of H. Rider Haggard's novel. Paul Robeson steals the show (and sings) as King Umbopa. With Roland Young, Anna Lee, and John Loder. In one scene, a female witch doctor puts a curse on some warriors and causes a volcano to erupt. Some of the battle scenes were shot on location. The next version was in 1950 with Stewart Granger.

KING SOLOMON'S MINES

(MGM/UA, 1985) **D:** J. Lee Thompson **S:** Gene Quintano, James R. Silke **P:** Golan/Globus

Richard Chamberlain is a bearded Allan Quatermain in this PG-13 "H. Rider Haggard meets Indiana Jones" movie with cannibals, bad Germans and Turks, an elephant stampede, and giant spiders. Sharon Stone costars, with Herbert Lom, John Rhys-Davies, and Ken Gampu. This comic Cannon feature "started the production boom in South Africa." The Jerry Goldsmith score was released by Restless. The sequel, *Allan Quatermain and the Lost City of Gold* (1987), was filmed at the same time.

King of the Rocket Men, the first serial with jet-pack-flying heroes.

KING SOLOMON'S TREASURE

(United, 1976) **D/P:** Alvin Rakoff
S: Allan Prior, Colin Turner   UK/Canada

David McCallum (who stutters for comic effect), Patrick Macnee, and John Colicos star as a trio of adventurers in Africa. This film, based on H. Rider Haggard's Allan Quatermain books, also features Britt Ekland as a Phoenician queen, Wilfrid Hyde-White, and Ken Gampu. Harry Alan Towers was executive producer. From Gold Key.

KINJITE: FORBIDDEN SUBJECTS

(Warner, 1989) **D:** J. Lee Thompson
S: Harold Nebenzal **P:** Pancho Kohner

Charles Bronson is an LA vice detective with a 15-year-old daughter, who teams up with a Japanese businessman (James Pax) whose daughter has been kidnapped. They go after a pimp (Juan Fernandez) who uses underage girls for porno shoots. There are some shocking scenes. With Perry Lopez, Peggy Lipton, Sy Richardson, Nicole Eggert, and Alex Hyde-White. It was Thompson's ninth Bronson feature. Parts of the Cannon release were filmed in Tokyo.

KIPLING'S WOMEN

(SW, 1963) **D/S/P:** Larry Smith **D/S:** Fred Hudson **P:** Harry Smith   UK

A retired British Army officer (who sings and recites poetry) remembers, dreams, and fantasizes about women. A Burmese woman bathes in a river, and a jealous, naked woman with a pet tiger stabs photos of a rival (a memorable image). It's "based on" Kipling's poem "The Ladies" and was mostly shot outdoors, featuring pinup models Margie Sutton, Lisa Gordon, and Virginia Rogers. Kroger Babb distributed this color adults-only film in America.

THE KISS

(RCA, 1988) **D/P:** Pen Densham **S:** Stephen Volk, Tom Ropelewski   Canada

Joanna Pacula is some kind of witch who comes to stay with her sister. After her sister dies, she seduces her brother-in-law and kills anybody who threatens her plans. Meredith Salenger is the niece who figures out what's going on. A flashback set in "the Belgian Congo, 1963" shows how it all started. There are Chris Walas FX, death by escalator, and some odd, senseless, threatening garden hoses and tools. Volk also wrote *Gothic* and *The Guardian*.

A KISS BEFORE DYING

(1956) **D:** Gerd Oswald **S:** Laurence Roman **P:** Robert L. Jacks

A smooth-talking psycho (Robert Wagner) pushes his pregnant college girlfriend (Joanne Woodward) off a roof and writes her suicide note. Later he goes after her rich sister (Virginia Leith, star of *The Brain That Wouldn't Die*). Jeffrey Hunter investigates. Mary Astor is Wagner's devoted mom. Also with George Macready and Robert Quarry. This underrated U.A. release is based on a novel by Ira Levin (*Rosemary's Baby*), and was shot in Cinema-scope and Deluxe Color. It was remade in 1991. The German-born Oswald followed with *Screaming Mimi* (1958).

A KISS BEFORE DYING

(MCA, 1991) **D/S:** James Dearden
P: Robert Lawrence

Matt Dillon throws Sean Young through a skylight. Later he goes after her social-worker sister (also played by Young). This inferior R-rated remake co-stars Diane Ladd, James Russo, Max von Sydow as the industrialist father of the sisters, and Adam Horovitz. The entire ending was reshot by Universal after it tested badly. There's a clip from *Vertigo*.

KISS DADDY GOODBYE

(Academy, 1980) **D/S/A:** Patrick Regan **S:** Alain Silver, Ron Abrahams, Mary Stewart   (*Revenge of the Zombies*; *The Vengeful Dead*)

Two little blond telekinetic twins (played by the director's kids) revive their dad (the director) after bikers kill him. They use the zombie to drive them around in a black car, and when they're done with him they make him dig his own grave (!). They also cause the deaths of the killers. Fabian (pretty laid back in one of his last roles) stars as the new deputy sheriff of a California seaside town. Marilyn Burns (*Texas Chainsaw*) is good as a concerned social worker who checks up on the kids. It's pretty strange, and Nell and Patrick Regan are quite effective. I wonder what they're doing these days.

KISS DADDY GOODNIGHT

(Academy, 1987) **D/S:** Peter Ily Huemer **S:** Michael Gabrieli **P:** Maureen O'Brien, William Ripka

Uma Thurman (in her film debut) stars as a girl in a blond wig who does coke and robs several men. She leads on an older man (Paul Richards), who then has her followed. This was made in Manhattan by first-time filmmakers with a low budget. Also in the cast are Paul Dillon, Steve Buscemi, Annabelle Gurwitch, and Arto Lindsay.

KISS ME A KILLER

(1992) **D/S:** Marcus De Leon **S:** Christopher Wooden **P:** Catherine Cyran

Julie Carmen is married to the violent Guy Boyd, owner of an East LA bar. A singer/guitarist (Robert Beltran) arrives, boosts business, and seduces her. Executive producer Roger Corman had this Concorde release remade with a country-music background as *Saturday Night Special*.

KISS ME, BABY

(SW, 1957) **D:** Lillian Hunt

Six beautiful strippers who go down to their pasties are featured in this filmed stage-show, along with long comedy segments. "Miss Dublin 1954" does a comic dance and sings. The headliner (she has the biggest chest) is Taffy O'Niel, "the Candy Kid." Merle Connell was the cinematographer, Phil Tucker (*Robot Monster*) was the editor, and Harry Thomas (*Frankenstein's Daughter*) did the make-up. They all worked on Ed Wood movies. The print of this b/w David Freidman Roadshow Rarity is excellent. It's followed by *Striptease Revealed*, a color short with Tempest Storm. Hunt (if that's a real name) directed a lot of nudie burlesque movies.

KISS ME KATE

(MGM, 1953) **D:** George Sidney **S:** Dorothy Kingsley **P:** Jack Cummings

Cole Porter's musical, based on Shakespeare's comedy *The Taming of the Shrew*, was filmed in 3-D by MGM. Kathryn Grayson and Howard Keel (*The Day of the Triffids*) star, with Ann Miller, Keenan Wynn, Bobby Van, James Whitmore, Ron Randell, Kurt Kaszner, Tommy Rall, Carol Haney, and future director Bob Fosse.

KISS ME, KILL ME

(Paragon, 1973) **D/S:** Corrado Farina
P: Simone Allouche   Italy (*Baba Yaga*)

Isabelle De Funes stars as a photographer, Valentina, a character based on a 60s Italian S&M comic strip by Guido Crepax. Carroll Baker is the aristocratic witch Baba Yaga, who captures Valentina in her castle with a dungeon and a bottomless pit. With George Eastman (Luigi Montefiori). It's a unique but dated allegorical sex fantasy. *Valentina* was also a 1987 Italian TV series.

KISS ME, MONSTER

(Redemption, 1967) **D/S/A:** Jesús Franco **S:** B. G. Hoffman **P:** Pier A. Caminecci, Adrian Hoven Spain/W. Germany (*Bésame, Monstruo*)

Janine Reynaud and Rossana Yanni are "the Red Lips," spies disguised as nightclub strippers. They encounter lesbian killers and mutant body-builders in an island castle where strange experiments are being conducted. The cast also includes Michel Lemoine and Adrian Hoven. The same cast and characters were in Franco's *Sadisterotica*, and husband and wife Lemoine and Reynaud were in *Succubus* the same year. This was first released on video in the US by Joseph Green.

KISS ME QUICK

(SW, 1964) **D:** Pete Perry, Max Gardens
(*Emmanuelle Meets Frankenstein*)

Russ Meyer had nothing to do with this Boxoffice International release (his name has been attached to it for years), but it's a clever color horror nudie movie comparable to *Orgy of the Dead*, except that the laughs are on purpose and it's sexier. A Peter Lorre voice sets up the "plot," about an effeminate alien named Sterilox (Fred Coe, doing a passable Stan Laurel imitation) visiting the castle of Dr. Breedlove, a mad doctor (with a Lugosi voice) to find some women for his planet. All the horror clichés are used (thunder and lightning, the mad doctor in his lab), and the Frankenstein monster (also Coe), a comic Dracula, and a weird female mummy appear. The sets are cheap, but the monster makeup is good and little extras (a skull says, "Cool it, baby") show up like in *Mad* magazine. Best of all, *Kiss Me Quick* is very sexy (and ass-obsessed) and was expertly shot by Lazlo Kovacs

(*Close Encounters...*). A blonde strips very slowly on an operating table. Women dance wildly to garage-rock instrumentals. In an exercise dungeon (!) naked women ride bikes, swing on a swing, and use a vibrating belt. In the best scene, which is surprisingly revealing for the time, three women strip and frolic in a small wading pool. The title is a takeoff on Billy Wilder's *Kiss Me, Stupid*, released the same year.

KISS OF DEATH (1968) = KISS AND KILL

KISS OF THE BEAST: *See* MERIDIAN

KITTEN WITH A WHIP
(VSOM, 1964) **D/S:** Douglas Heyes **P:** Harry Keller

Ann-Margret (the same year as *Viva Las Vegas*) stars in this surprising b/w feature as Judy Dvorak, a wild, sexy, anything-goes, jive-talking delinquent. She knifes a matron at a detention home, sets the place on fire, escapes, and breaks into the home of a San Francisco politician (John Forsythe). She blackmails him, holds a drinking party at his house, then forces him to drive her and another delinquent (Peter Brown) to Tijuana to have his knife wound treated. With Richard Anderson, Doodles Weaver, and Hal Hopper. This has played on *Mystery Science Theater 3000*. From Universal. Heyes also wrote *Ice Station Zebra*.

KNIGHT MOVES
(Republic, 1992) **D:** Carl Schenkel **S:** Brad Mirman **P:** Ziad al-Khoury, Jean-Luc Defait   US/Germany (*Face to Face*)

Christopher Lambert stars as a grand master competing in a chess tournament in Washington State. A woman he has spent the night with bleeds to death, and bloody messages are left on the wall. An electronic voice calls to brag about the killings. Many women die, and this world-famous guy is the prime suspect. I want to know where the media is?! Lambert's real-life wife, Diane Lane, is a police psychologist working on the case (they have slo-mo sex). Tom Skerritt (much better in the TV series *Picket Fences*) and Daniel Baldwin are cops, and Ferdinand Mayne is a blind man. A stakeout in a flooded basement is the visual highlight. With bodies as chess pieces, b/w flashbacks, and "I Put a Spell on You" on the soundtrack. It was filmed in Vancouver. Mirman also wrote the Madonna movie *Body of Evidence*. The tape is 12 minutes shorter than the version that played in Europe.

KNIGHTS
(Paramount, 1993) **D/S:** Albert Pyun **P:** Tom Karnowsky

Kathy Long is the futuristic kickboxing Nea, and Kris Kristofferson is Gabriel, a robot (!) programmed to kill cyborgs, who spends part of this very bad movie cut in half. They had a lot of nerve releasing this at all, since it's obviously unfinished and has no ending! It all takes place in the desert (of Utah), and characters dress in biblical garb. With Lance Henriksen as Job, ruler of the vampirish cyborgs, Scott Paulin, Gary Daniels, and Tim Thomerson in a bit part.

KNIGHTS OF THE CITY
(Star Maker, 1984) **D:** Dominic Orlando **S/P/A:** Leon Isaac Kennedy **P:** John C. Strong   (*Cry of the City*)

The Royals, a South Florida gang, are also a rap group, so there's lots of music and breakdancing in this action movie. Overage Leon Isaac Kennedy stars as the gang's leader, Troy, with Nicholas Campbell, Michael Ansara as an alcoholic who owns a record company, Janine Turner, Stoney Jackson, Smokey Robinson, the Fat Boys (who do "Jailhouse Rap"), K.C. (from the Sunshine Band), Cleveland's own Jeff Kutash as a dance instructor named Flash, and early rapper Kurtis Blow. Sammy Davis Jr. was in this mess at one time too, but luckily for him his part was cut out. Michael Franzese, the executive producer, was charged with racketeering and laundering money, and he went to jail. The credits are padded with the names of dialogue coaches and a psychiatrist. Private I released a soundtrack.

KNOCK ON ANY DOOR
(1949) **D:** Nicholas Ray **S:** Daniel Taradash, John Monks Jr. **P:** Robert Lord **M:** George Anthiel

Humphrey Bogart's Santana production company backed this early, serious jd movie. Bogart stars as a lawyer defending John Derek, who is accused of killing a cop. Flashbacks show the life of the troubled teen. With George Macready as the prosecutor, Allene Roberts, Mickey Knox, and Cara Williams. Columbia released this the same year as two other postwar juvenile-delinquency classics, *Gun Crazy* and *City Across the River*. *Let No Man Write My Epitaph* (1960) is supposed to be the sequel.

KONGO
(Shock Toon, 1932) **D:** William Cowan **S:** Leon Gordon

The silent Lon Chaney movie *West of Zanzibar* was remade, starring Walter Huston as the magician King Deadlegs Flint (he had also played the role onstage). This version is equally mind-boggling. If the native-sacrifice and "evolution" scenes look familiar, it's because MGM simply reused some of director Tod Browning's best footage from the original. I won't describe the sadistic, perverse, hate-driven plot, but some of the highlights are a decapitation trick with a talking head on a table, a chimp attack, and a twitchy, drug-addicted doctor (Conrad Nagel) buried up to his neck in a swamp full of leeches for a painful "cure." Virginia Bruce is a pure, blonde victim of Flint's sick revenge plan, and sexy Lupe Velez (sounding like Charo) is Tula, a new character. C. Henry Gordon plays a bad guy (as usual). This movie shows people being whipped, starved, and humiliated, and all the "ooga booga" native dialogue makes it even more racist than the original.

KOYAANISQATSI: LIFE OUT OF BALANCE
(Pacific Arts, 1983) **D/S/P:** Godfrey Reggio **S:** Ron Fricke, Michael Hoenig **M:** Philip Glass

Don't miss this unique documentary (without narration) directed and photographed by a Buñuel fan who was a monk for 14 years. The title means "life out of balance" in the Hopi Indian language. Speeded-up and time-lapse photography is used to contrast the natural beauty of America with the results of industrialization and modernization. There are excellent segments on Manhattan and on fast-food production. The look of this film and the score (on Antilles) was very influential, mostly on TV commercials. The score was performed live at Lincoln Center screenings. It's the first of a planned trilogy and was "presented" by Francis Ford Coppola. *Powaqqatsi* (1988) followed.

THE KRAYS
(RCA, 1990) **D:** Peter Medak **S:** Philip Ridley
P: Dominic Anciano, Ray Burdis   UK

Gary and Martin Kemp (from the 80s rock group Spandau Ballet) star as the real-life identical-twin psycho gangsters (one is gay) who terrorized the East End of London in the 60s. Their lives are seen from birth to death. Women are shown as important driving forces. The family helps while they run protection rackets. Billie Whitelaw is their doting mother. The cast also includes Charlotte Cornwell, Alfred Molina, Susan Fleetwood, and Tom Bell. The twins are still in jail. Screenwriter Ridley went on to direct *The Reflecting Skin*. Gary Kemp was later in *The Bodyguard*.

THE KREMLIN LETTER
(1970) **D/S/A:** John Huston **S:** Gladys Hill
P: Carter De Haven, Sam Wiesenthal

This complicated and violent all-star Cold War spy movie from 20th Century–Fox was universally panned, but it has its moments. Richard Boone and Dean Jagger lead a team of agents looking for a secret document that says the US and the USSR will attack China. The cast also includes Patrick O'Neal, Orson Welles, Max von Sydow, Bibi Andersson, Raf Vallone, Barbara Parkins, Lila Kedrova, Vonetta McGee, Nigel Green, and Marc Lawrence. George Sanders is memorable as "the Warlock," a San Francisco drag queen.

KRIEMHILD'S REVENGE: *See* SIEGFRIED

KRULL
(RCA, 1982) **D:** Peter Yates **S:** Stanford Sherman
P: Ted Mann, Ron Silverman **M:** James Horner   UK

Ken Marshall stars as a prince who rescues his fiancée (Lysette Anthony) from a beast and has to endure many other fantastic challenges. This film cost Columbia $27 million and lost money. It copies some ideas from *Star Wars* and *The Magic Sword* and has lots of FX. The giant animated spider is worth seeing, the Horner score is good, and there's a cyclops who's actually a good guy under a curse. Also in the cast are Liam Neeson, Freddie Jones, Francesca Annis, and Belinda Mayne. The score is on Southern Cross.

KRUSH GROOVE
(Warner, 1986) **D/P:** Michael Schultz
S: Ralph Farquhar **P:** Doug McHenry

Real-life violence at New York City screenings created publicity and helped make this rap musical a hit. It's based on the career of Russell Simmons. Blair Underwood (an *LA Law* regular) stars, with Eron Tabor, Sheila E., Run DMC (also in *Tougher Than Leather*), the Fat Boys, New Edition, Kurtis Blow, L. L. Cool J, and Rick Rubin. The soundtrack, featuring various artists, is on Warner.

KUNG FU FROM BEYOND THE GRAVE
(Ocean Shores, 1979) **D:** Li Zhoa **S:** Lu Feng
P: Bao Meng, Shao Weiying   Hong Kong (*Yin Ji*)

Rival ghost gangs and good and bad magicians fight humans who are after a magic book. Billy Chong stars, and Lo Lieh is a villain. This movie has an early example of *gyonsi* (hopping vampires), later a cliché in Asian horror movies. They can be destroyed only by menstrual blood from virgins.

KUNG FU RASCALS
(1990) **D/S/P/A:** Steve Wang **S/A:** Johnny Saiko

An animated living statue called "the Bamboo Man" (similar to Majin, from 60s Japanese movies) is the main villain in this Super 8 animated action movie with ninjas, mutants, and a witch (Marion Paras). Steve Wang leads a comic trio of heroes. The comedy is mostly piss and fart jokes. Wang did special effects for major features like *Batman* and *Predator* and later directed *The Guyver* movies.

KUNG FU: THE MOVIE
(Warner, 1986) **D:** Richard Lang **S:** Durrell Royce Crays **P:** Slip Ward, David Carradine

This pretty good attempt at reviving Carradine's Kwai Chang Caine character is set in the 1880s. It features Bruce Lee's son, Brandon Lee, as a bald assassin, Mako as an opium dealer, Keye Luke as Master Po (in flashbacks), Benson Fong, Martin Landau, Luke Askew, Ellen Geer, Calista Carradine, and John Alderman. It was a CBS-TV pilot. The *Kung Fu* series concept would not die. The next year a 60-minute pilot was made, set in modern times, with Lee but not Carradine. Then, in 1993, a successful syndicated series, *Kung Fu: The Legend Continues*, appeared, also set in modern times, with Carradine but not Lee.

KUNG FU ZOMBIE
(Ocean Shores, 1981) **D/S:** Hwa I. Hung
P: Pal Ming   Hong Kong

Billy Chong fights evil zombies and vampires. This comic horror movie features an exorcism, characters who eat dogs, magic, priests, and the dead leaping out of graves.

KURONEKO
(SW, 1968) **D/S:** Kaneto Shindo   Japan
(*Yabu no Naka no Kuroneko; The Black Cat*)

In the 12th century, samurai rape and kill an old woman and her daughter-in-law. The women return as "ghost cats," trapping and killing warriors. This chilling tale is from the Toho studios and the director of the classic ghost movie *Onibaba*.

KURT VONNEGUT'S "MONKEY HOUSE"
(Pacific Arts, 1991) **D:** Paul Shapiro, Gilbert Shelton, Allan King **S:** Jeremy Hole, Jeffrey Cohen, Stan Daniels **P:** Jonathan Goodwill, Gordon Mark

This Showtime series pilot, introduced by the author, dramatizes 3 short stories with ironic endings. The cast includes Len Cariou, Frank Langella, and Miguel Fernandez.

KWAHERI
(1964) **D:** Mr. and Mrs. Nikki Carter
P: David Chudnow, Thor Brooks

Forbidden African rituals, witch doctors, snake swallowers, blood drinkers, animal poachers, a virgin sacrifice, and marijuana are all parts of this color mondo documentary from Unusual Films. It opens with a snake swallowing a calf. Les Tremayne narrates. This was a hit thanks to promotion by Kroger Babb, who wrote all of the ad copy himself: "Forget Anything and Everything You've Seen Before!"; "Tell No One What You See!" Chudnow also produced several H. G. Lewis sex comedies.

L.A. BAD

(Starmaker, 1985) **D/S:** Gary Kent **P:** Tomi Barrett *(Rainy Day Friends)*

Esai Morales *(La Bamba)* stars in this drama about street kids, with Janice Rule, Carrie Snodgress, and John Phillip Law. The director had acted in many movies by Richard Rush, Al Adamson, and Ray Dennis Steckler.

LABORATORY

(1980) **D/S/P:** Allan Sandler **S:** Steve Marshall III

Aliens experiment on a group of humans, including a priest. There's a zombie and a decapitation in this low-budget obscurity. The associate producer was Anne Spielberg.

L.A. BOUNTY

(IVE, 1989) **D:** Worth Keeter **S/P:** Michael W. Leighton **P/A:** Sybil Danning

Sybil Danning, a former model, has been in all kinds of exploitation movies since the late 60s. After hitting a bit of a career low (acting for Chuck Vincent and Fred Olen Ray), she decided to produce her own project. She plays Ruger, a silent, vengeful ex-cop in jeans, sunglasses, and a black leather jacket. She lives in a trailer, smokes small cigars, and uses extremely large guns. Her evil rival is Cavanagh, a fast-talking, coke-dealing, crazed, earring-wearing killer artist played by a laughing, out-of-control Wings Hauser. All of his scenes were shot on a single set (his studio/headquarters), where he rants ("Life and death, life and death, life IS death!"), kills, and paints a female model. This ludicrous movie has lots of car chases, unrealistic dreamlike flashbacks, boring rock music, a western-style shootout (conveniently staged on a real studio backlot), and an overlong *Road Runner*–inspired battle at the end with lots of dynamite and the William Tell Overture! You just might like it. With Robert Quarry.

LABYRINTH

(Embassy, 1986) **D:** Jim Henson **S:** Terry Jones **P:** Eric Rattray

George Lucas was the executive producer of this fantasy, written by a former member of Monty Python. Jennifer Connelly, with the help of a troll, tries to rescue her little stepbrother, who has been taken away by goblins. David Bowie is Jareth, the goblin king (he sings). The many surprising creatures (some are elaborate Muppets) and the ILM FX in the maze-like fantasy world make it worth watching. With Kenny Baker and Toby Froud.

L.A. CRACKDOWN

(City Lights, 1987) **D/S/P:** Joseph Merhi **P:** Richard Pepin

A policewoman (Pamela Dixon) tries to reform two teenage girls who are crack addicts, with disastrous results. Then she goes after some dealers and kills them. Dixon returned in *L.A. Crackdown II* (1988), by the same filmmakers.

LADIES AND GENTLEMEN, THE FABULOUS STAINS

(1981) **D:** Lou Adler **S:** Rob Morton **P:** Joe Roth

Diane Lane (playing a 15-year-old) forms a band with her sister and cousin (Laura Dern). They have "skunk" hair and wear see-through tops. They go on a bus tour with a British punk band featuring Cook and Jones of the Sex Pistols and Paul Simeon of the Clash. The Stains become a media sensation with a following of rebellious young girls, but Lane is criticized for selling out, and it all falls apart. Some of the songs and music are pretty good (the ex-Pistols also wrote the songs), parts are funny, and Lane has a nude sex scene in the shower. It's too bad about the happy ending, though. Also in the cast are Christine Lahti, Peter Donat, Cynthia Sykes, and Fee Waybill (of the Tubes) as the washed-up leader of the Metal Corpses. Adler ran Ode records and produced Cheech and Chong movies.

THE LADIES' CLUB

(Media, 1984) **D:** "A. K. Allen"/Janet Greek **S/P:** Paul Mason **P:** Nick Mileti *(The Violated)*

A policewoman and rape victims plot revenge against rapists. Characters are kidnapped, drugged, and castrated. The director (who also made *Spellbinder,* a horror movie) had her name removed. Diana Scarwid stars, with Arliss Howard, Bruce Davison, and Karen Austin.

LADIES IN RETIREMENT

(1941) **D:** Charles Vidor **S:** Denham Fort, Garrett Fort **P:** Lester Cowan

In this gothic melodrama, a retired British actress (Isobel Elsom) lives in an isolated old house. The maid (Ida Lupino) invites her deranged sisters (Elsa Lanchester and Edith Barrett) to visit and kills people in ovens to keep them out of an institution. With Louis Hayward and Evelyn Keyes. The Columbia release, based on a Broadway hit, was remade as *The Mad Room* (1969), with Shelley Winters and Stella Stevens.

LADIES OF THE BIG HOUSE

(1932) **D:** Marion Gering **S:** Louis Weitzenkorn

Sylvia Sidney stars in this pre-Code women-in-prison movie from Paramount as an innocent woman sent up for a murder committed by a gangster (Earl Foxe). Gene Raymond costars, and Louise Beavers is one of the inmates. The story was by Ernest Booth, an ex-con himself.

LADIES THEY TALK ABOUT

(1933) **D:** Howard Bretherton, William Keighley **S:** Sidney Sutherland, Brown Holmes **P:** Ray Griffith

Barbara Stanwyck stars in this adaptation of the play *Women in Prison.* She's Nan, a small-town deacon's daughter who goes to reform school, then becomes part of a gang and is sent to San Quentin for a bank robbery. This pre-Code film is known for its tough dialogue. With Preston Foster, Lyle Talbot, Dorothy Burgess, Lillian Roth (who sings), Helen Ware, and Madame Sul-Te-Wan.

LADY AVENGER

(South Gate, 1986) **D/P:** David De Coteau **S:** Will Schmitz, Keith Kaczorek **P:** John Schwouweiler

Peggy Sanders escapes from prison and goes after the gang that murdered her brother. With Michelle Bauer. It was released in 1989.

LADY BEWARE

(IVE, 1987) **D:** Karen Arthur **S:** Charles Zev Cohen **P:** Toni Scotti, Larry Mortorff

Diane Lane stars as a window dresser named Katya in Pittsburgh (where this was filmed). Her controversial, sexy windows affect an X-ray technician (Michael Woods) who's a peeping Tom. He starts making obscene phone calls and harassing her, and even breaks into the giant loft where she lives alone. When nobody else really helps much, she fights back in a clever, nonviolent way. With Cotter Smith and Viveca Lindfors. Lane restarted her acting career with this film and *The Big Town* (also 1987), and has memorable nude scenes in both. Arthur also directed *The Mafu Cage/My Sister, My Love* (1978).

LADY BLUE

(1985) **D:** Gene Nelson **S:** Robert Vincent O'Neill **P:** Herb Wallerstein

Jamie Rose stars as a red-haired Chicago detective with a magnum who's after drug dealers in this pilot for a short-lived ABC-TV series. The character is like a female Dirty Harry, and the series was considered pretty violent for network TV at the time. With series regular Danny Aiello, Katy Jurado, Bibi Besch, Jim Brown, and Tony LoBianco.

LADY CHATTERLEY'S LOVER

(Pearl, 1981) **D:** Just Jaeckin **S:** Christopher Wicking **P:** Golan/Globus UK/France

Sylvia Kristel stars in this version of the D. H. Lawrence novel, with Ann Michelle, Nicholas Clay, former Miss Universe Emparo Múñoz, and former Hammer horror star Shane Briant. It's by the director of her Emmanuelle movies.

LADY COCOA

(Unicorn, 1974) **D/P:** "Matt Cimber"/ Matteo Ottaviano **S:** George Theakos

In a plot that must have been inspired by the real-life exploits of actress Liz Renay, "Lady Cocoa" (Lola Falana) is in prison for refusing to testify against her gangster boyfriend. She's allowed out in Lake Tahoe under the protective custody of two detectives (Gene Washington and Alex Dreier) because she promises to talk. Gangsters try to kill her and cars crash into a casino. Falana sings and has a topless scene. With Mean Joe Greene, Buck Flower, and Millie Perkins as a cross-dressing hitwoman. Cimber later remade this Dimension release as *Fake Out,* with Pia Zadora! Falana also starred in the Italian film *Black Tigress* (1968).

LADY DRACULA

(VSOM, 1975) **D:** Franz Josef Gottlieb
S: Redis Rada   W. Germany

Dracula (Stephen Boy) is killed by villagers in 1876. When a blonde (Evelyn Kraft, from *Goliathon*) he bit is unearthed in Vienna 100 years later, she starts killing. With Brad Harris as a cop and Eddi Arent.

LADY DRAGON 2

(Imperial, 1993) **D/C:** David Worth
S: Clifford Mohr **P:** Gope T. Samtani

Cynthia Rothrock is raped by Billy Drago's gang of diamond thieves, and her soccer-star husband is crippled. She seeks kickboxing revenge. The cast also includes Sam (*Flash Gordon*) Jones. This unrelated "sequel" to *Lady Dragon* (1991) was shot in Jakarta, Indonesia. The original stars Rothrock and Richard Norton.

THE LADY FROM SHANGHAI

(RCA, 1948) **D/S/P/A:** Orson Welles

In his first do-it-all movie after *Citizen Kane,* Welles stars and narrates (with a brogue) as an Irish seaman, Michael O'Hara, caught up in a murder mystery. The Columbia release was a flop at the time, some say because he had his wife Rita Hayworth's hair cut short and bleached blond for her role as Elsa Bannister. Now it's considered a *film noir* classic. With Everett Sloane as the crippled Arthur Bannister, Glenn Anders as Grisby, and Ted De Corsia. The famous shootout ending in a Chinatown fun house lined with mirrors has been copied countless times. Some scenes were filmed on Errol Flynn's yacht. William Castle was an uncredited on-location producer. The stars' marriage ended before the film's release. Elements of the plot were used in *The Come-On* (1956), with Sterling Hayden and Anne Baxter.

LADY GREY

(1980) **D:** Worth Keeter **S:** Tom McIntyre **P:** Earl Owensby

Ginger Alden stars as a country singer, and David Allan Coe is Black Jack Donovan. Alden was also in Owensby's *Living Legend,* about Elvis, her former boyfriend. This was shot in North Carolina.

LADYHAWKE

(Warner, 1985) **D/P:** Richard Donner
S: Edward Khmara, Michael Thomas, Tom Mankiewicz **P:** Lauren Shuler

A 13th-century knight (Rutger Hauer) and his true love (Michelle Pfeiffer) have been enchanted by an evil bishop. He becomes a wolf at night, and she is a hawk by day. A pickpocket (Matthew Broderick) and an old priest (Leo McKern) help to break the curse. Vittorio Storaro was the cinematographer of this 121-minute, PG-13 romantic fantasy. Alan Parsons did the rock soundtrack. Donner's *The Goonies* was released the same year.

THE LADY IN THE CAR WITH GLASSES AND A GUN

(1970) **D:** Anatole Litvak **S:** Richard Harris
P: Raymond Danan   US/France

In this psychological thriller a secretary in Paris (Samantha Eggar) has memory loss and encounters strangers who claim they know her. She picks up a hitchhiker (John McEnery) on the way to the Riviera, and he steals a car with a body in the trunk. Oliver Reed is her advertising-agency boss. This was the last feature by the Russian-born director of *Sorry, Wrong Number* (1948) and *The Snake Pit* (1949).

LADY IN THE DEATH HOUSE

(1944) **D:** Steve Sekely **S:** Harry O. Hoyt **P:** Jack Schwartz

Lionel Atwill stars as a criminologist investigating the case of a woman (Jean Parker) wrongly convicted of murder and sentenced to die in the electric chair. The executioner (Douglas Fowley) is also a scientist experimenting with reviving the dead. Most of the plot of this 56-minute PRC feature is told in flashback. The director had done *Revenge of the Zombies* the year before.

THE LADY IN WHITE

(Virgin, 1988) **D/S/P/M:** Frank Laloggia
P: Andrew G. La Marca

Big-eyed Lukas Haas is a boy named Frankie in the second feature by the young director of *Fear No Evil.* This nostalgic, PG-13 ghost story takes place on Halloween in 1962, in picturesque Willows Point, and is narrated by a grown-up Frankie, a Stephen King–type character. The ghost of a little girl haunts the school. Her dead angel/ghost mother wanders around looking for her, and her nearly catatonic aunt (Katherine Helmond) is considered a local nut case. An unknown serial killer tries to make little Frankie victim number 11. Alex Rocco costars as a member of Frankie's emotional Italian-American family. The film has excellent period detail and cinematography but stumbles when trying to copy *To Kill a Mockingbird* with a subplot about racism. With FX by Gene Warren, Ernest Farino, and others. It was filmed near Rochester, New York. The soundtrack is on Varèse Sarabande.

LADYKILLER

(MCA, 1992) **D:** Michael Scott
S: Shelley Evans **P:** Gordon Wolf

Mimi Rogers stars as a police photographer who meets wealthy John Shea through a dating service. People are killed, and he may be the murderer. With Tom Irwin, Bert Remsen, and Alice Krige.

THE LADYKILLERS

(Prism, 1988) **D:** Robert Lewis
S: Greg Dinallo **P:** Andrew Hill

In a reversal of a worn-out cliché, men who dance and strip at an LA club for women are being killed. Marilu Henner stars, with Susan Blakely and Lesley-Anne Down. It debuted on ABC-TV.

LADY STAY DEAD

(Video City, 1981) **D/S/P:** Terry Bourke   Australia

A bearded young gardener who's a psycho voyeur/rapist (Chad Hayward) has sex with an inflatable doll, works for a pop singer, and kills female employees.

LADY TERMINATOR

(Studio, 1988) **D:** Jalil Jackson **S:** Karr Kruinowz **P:** Ram Soraya   Indonesia
(*Nasty Hunter; Shooting Star*)

Somebody crossed *The Terminator* with a typical Southeast Asian black-magic/revenge story and came up with this amazing, violent, action-and-sex-filled movie. Since it has a Western star, it even played (unrated) in American theaters. In 1889, in a great-looking castle on a South Seas island, a magic queen with female servants has loud, sweaty sex surrounded by fog and candles but complains, "Is there any man who can satisfy me?!" Her 100th husband tricks her by pulling a snake (the essence of her magic) from between her legs. The snake becomes a knife, lightning flashes, and she walks into the sea vowing revenge on his granddaughter. Tanya, an anthropologist (star Barbara Anne Constable, who also receives a makeup credit), goes scuba-diving near the island 100 years later while researching the legendary queen. A tidal wave appears, and suddenly she's tied spread-eagle to a bed while an animated snake enters her. She emerges from the ocean naked near a city and confronts a group of drunken guys laughing and pissing. They each die, blood spurting in their faces, while having sex with her. She gets clothes (black leather) and a room (which she mostly destroys with telekinetic powers) and starts blowing away people with a machine gun. She kills lots of people on the street, in huge malls, and in a disco, stopping only to have sex with the bellboy. She's indestructible, but bullets can slow her down. She smashes up a police station where the cops are talking about bodies with "the cocks bitten off." Erica, a rock singer with a cop boyfriend, is the granddaughter the reincarnated queen is looking for, and her great-uncle is a good magician. But the dubious heroes are a couple of clichéd bonehead American guys ("Fuckin' A!"; "I'm outa here!") who show up for the final scenes of car and tank crashes and big explosions. You won't believe it.

THE LADY VANISHES

(MPI, Diamond, 1938) **D:** Alfred Hitchcock **S:** Sidney Gilliat, Frank Launder **P:** Edward Black   UK

This comedy/mystery classic has been copied countless times. A young woman (Margaret Lockwood) meets a kindly governess (May Whitty) as they're boarding a train in Europe. When the older woman mysteriously disappears, a musicologist (Michael Redgrave) helps her to sort it all out, while everybody on the train claims that the missing woman never existed. Also in the cast are Paul Lukas as a sinister brain surgeon, Mary Clare as a countess, Googie Withers, and the comic pair Basil Radford and Naunton Wayne (they were later teamed in *Night Train to Munich, Dead of Night,* and other films). A book containing the screenplay has been published. It was based on a novel by Ethel Lina White, as were *The Unseen* (1945) and *The Spiral Staircase* (1946). The film was produced by Gainsborough.

THE LADY VANISHES

(1979) **D:** Anthony Page **S:** George Axelrod **P:** Tom Sachs   UK

Cybill Shepherd and Elliott Gould star in a comic remake of Hitchcock's film, with Angela Lansbury as a spy who disappears on a train, Herbert Lom, Arthur Lowe, Ian Carmichael, and Jenny Runacre. This unsuccessful Rank/Hammer coproduction is one of the features that helped put Hammer out of business.

LAFAYETTE ESCADRILLE

(1958) **D/P:** William A. Wellman **S:** A. S. Fleischman

Tab Hunter stars in this WWI Foreign Legion movie, with Etchika Choreau, Clint Eastwood (in his last role before TV fame in the series *Rawhide*), Tom Laughlin (years before *Billy Jack*), David Janssen, Marcel Dalio, William Wellman Jr., Joel McCrea, and Brett Halsey. It was a flop and was the last feature by the man who had directed the first Oscar-winning film, *Wings* (1927). From Warner Brothers.

L.A. GODDESS

(Prism, 1993) **D:** Jag Mundhra **S:** Jerry Davis **P:** Michael Criscione, Bruce Mulhearn

Kathy Shower is a would-be scriptwriter and a stunt double for the star of an erotic western called *Frontier Foxes*. Studio head David Heavener falls for her and takes her to his mansion, but she says, "Sorry, Mr. Mogul, My script and my body are not for sale." With Wendy McDonald as the "sex-crazed" alcoholic movie star, Jeff Conaway as the director, Tally Chanel, Joe Estevez, and James Hong as the butler. Both the R and unrated versions feature showers and sex backed by romantic ballads.

L.A. HEAT

(PM, 1989) **D/P:** Joseph Merhi **S:** Charles T. Kanganis **P:** Richard Pepin

Lawrence Hilton-Jacobs stars as a detective who dreams of being a cowboy hero, with Jim Brown as the police captain, Pat Johnson, Gretchen Becker, and the usual strippers. This violent movie about drugs had a sequel, *L.A. Vice*.

THE LAIR OF THE WHITE WORM

(Vestron, 1988) **D/S/P:** Ken Russell   UK

Irish novelist Bram Stoker was suffering from Brights disease (which he died of the next year) when he wrote his last novel in 1911. It's a fantastic, fevered tale of pagan snake worshippers, virgin sacrifices, and a vampire-like snake-woman. Russell made a great comic movie from it, adding mind-blowing hallucination sequences and incredible, nightmarish, sacrilegious visions. One shows the crucifixion of Christ, a serpent, and impaled nuns. Amanda Donohoe stars as Lady Sylvia Marsh, a viciously funny, sexy, seductive (and often naked), venom-spewing snake-woman with a giant, *Dune*-like snake in her castle. Hugh Grant is the young lord whose ancestors slew a dragon. He and archaeologist Peter Capaldi try to help two lower class orphaned sisters (Catherine Oxenberg and Sammi Davis). Everyone has strong Scottish accents. There's a George Méliès clip, a *Citizen Kane* reference, and much more.

LAMBADA

(Warner, 1990) **D/S:** Joel Silberg **S:** Sheldon Renan **P:** Peter Shepard

J. Eddie Peck (*Curse II*) stars as a math teacher called Blade who hangs out with barrio kids at night and falls for Melora Hardin. Adolpho "Shabba-Doo" Quinones (*Breakin' I* and *II*) costars and was the choreographer. With Keene Curtis and Thalmus Rasulala. Executive producer Yoram Globus released this PG film at the same time as his cousin and former Cannon partner, Menahem Golan, released a wilder lambada movie, *The Forbidden Dance*.

THE LAND OF FARAWAY

(Starmaker, 1987) **D:** Vladimir Grammatikov **S:** William Aldridge **P:** Ingemar Ejve   Sweden/USSR/Norway (*Mio in the Land of Faraway*)

Nicholas Pickard and Christian Bale (from Spielberg's *Empire of the Sun*) star in this fantasy, based on books by Astrid Lindgren, with Christopher Lee as "the Black Knight," Timothy Bottoms as a medieval king, and Susannah York. It was filmed in the Crimea, at a Moscow studio, and in Scotland.

THE LAND OF NO RETURN

(1981) **D/S/P:** Ken Bateman **S:** Frank Ray Perilli   (*Snowman; Challenge to Survive*)

Mel Torme and William Shatner (what a pair!) star in a G-rated tale of a TV animal trainer whose plane crashes in Utah. Bateman also directed the obscure horror movie *Headless Eyes*!

LAND RAIDERS

(VSOM, 1970) **D:** Nathan Juran **S:** Ken Pettus **P:** Roy Rowland

Telly Savalas kills people and blames Apaches, which starts an Indian war. His brother (George Maharis) is the hero. Arlene Dahl is also in this western (filmed in Spain and Budapest), with Jocelyn Lane, George Coulouris, and Guy Rolfe. It was Dahl's last film until she appeared in several in the 90s with her son Lorenzo Lamas. Juran made only one more, *The Boy Who Cried Werewolf* (1973).

LANSKY'S ROAD

(1985) **D/S/P:** Richard Farr

A couple are abducted by flying saucers. The guy goes to a hospital, where media hysteria results. Officials pursuing the secrets he learned drug him and blame him for terrorist bombings. It was shot on video in Grand Junction, Colorado and is filled with bad camera zooms and slo-mo.

LASER MAN

(VSOM, 1988) **D/S/P/A:** Peter Wang US/Hong Kong

A philosophical NYC police captain (Peter Wang) narrates a rambling story about Arthur (Mark Hayashi), a laser scientist and friend of the family who is supposed to assassinate somebody with his invention. Arthur has a Jewish mother and girlfriend problems, so most of this comic movie deals with cultural clashes. Maryann Urbano costars, and Sally Yeh is the guest star. There's some Chinese dialogue, which is subtitled. Tsui Hark was the associate producer. Wang also made *The Great Wall*.

LASER MISSION

(Turner, 1989) **D:** Beau Davis **S:** Philip Gutteridge **P:** Hans Kuhle   W. Germany

Bruce Lee's son, Brandon, plays Michael Gold, an American mercenary who escapes from jail in a South American Communist country. He's handsome and he's cool, and this movie has lots of car chases, explosions, and guns, but it's not what you would expect from the son of the world's best martial-arts star. He helps Melissa (Debi Monahan), a blonde with a very high voice who's stranded in a desert wearing high heels and a low-cut dress. Her father is a professor (Ernest Borgnine, whose accent changes several times). An Austrian soldier of fortune (Werner Pochath) with a room full of heads is after a laser weapon developed by the professor and kidnaps her. Black slave laborers and comic Cubans work in a diamond mine. This was filmed in South Africa. Lee had also been in *Legacy of Rage* (1987).

LASER MOON

(Hemdale, 1991) **D/S/A:** Douglas K. Grimm **P:** Mark Paglia

A black-masked killer with a pen lite laser kills women after they have sex, then photographs their bodies. Someone starts confessing to the bored host of a late-night radio talk show (Harrison Le Duke). Traci Lords is Barbara Fleck, the new partner of a cop who watches TV in his car. At one point she says, "This movie sucks." It sure does. If the radio host's voice doesn't put you to sleep, the boring soft music will. Avoid this worse-than-usual video, made in Colorado Springs.

LASH OF LUST

(1968) **D:** "George Sheafer"/Al Adamson **S:** Sam Sherman **P:** Mardi Rustam

Bambi Allen and other women are kidnapped, in this adults-only sex western shot on the Spahn Ranch. Adamson later said that he had to have Charles Manson and some of his followers thrown off the set. He also directed other, tamer westerns (*Five Bloody Graves* and *The Female Bunch*) around the same time. This one wasn't released until 1974.

THE LASH OF THE PENITENTES

(Sinister, 1936) **D:** Harry Revier,
Roland C. Price **S:** Zelma Carroll
(*The Penitente Murder Case*)

Penitentes—Catholic religious fanatics who whip themselves—have existed in many parts of the world for hundreds of years. Some were active in New Mexico in the 30s. Filming was strictly forbidden, but Roland C. Price shot silent footage of them, Harry Revier shot exploitative new footage about a murder (including a tied-up, naked woman being whipped), and a road-show classic was born. Marie de Forest stars as Raquel. A 70-minute English version and a longer Spanish version were available for many years. Video versions are as short as 35 minutes. *The Penitentes* (1915), by D. W. Griffith, is an earlier look at the same cult.

LAST ACTION HERO

(Columbia, 1993) **D/P:** John McTiernan
S: Shane Black, David Arnott, William
Goldman (uncredited) **P:** Steve Roth

The original script for this expensive (probably over $100 milion!), long (122-minute) PG-13 commercial flop, with industry in-jokes, shameless plugs, and intentional continuity errors, was written by a pair of novices in their mid-20s, Zak Penn and Adam Leff. The incredible prepublicity included a giant, inflatable Arnold Schwarzenegger with dynamite (just after the World Trade Center bombing) in Times Square and a logo on a NASA rocket. Austin O'Brien is a kid with a magic movie ticket who enters a film, *Jack Slade IV*, that's set in LA of the future. Schwarzenegger is Slade, the fictional hero, and appears as himself with his wife, Maria Shriver. Slade and a British villain (Charles Dance) also enter real-life Manhattan. With Tom Noonan as "the Ripper," Robert Prosky as a Times Square projectionist, Mercedes Ruehl, Anthony Quinn, F. Murray Abraham, Art Carney, Michael Gazzo, Colleen Camp, Professor Tanaka, Tina Turner as the mayor, and a cartoon cat. Some of the briefly seen guest stars are Sharon Stone, Jean-Claude Van Damme, Damon Wayans, Melvin Van Peebles, Joan Plowright, Tony Curtis, Little Richard, Adam Ant, Hammer, Chris Connelly, James Belushi, and Chevy Chase. The soundtrack by Michael Kamen (on Columbia) includes tracks by Alice in Chains, AC/DC, Megadeath, and Aerosmith (a "Dream On" remake). The widescreen laserdisc runs 131 minutes. The video has ads for the soundtrack, the video game, and an Arnold fitness video. Slade's favorite line is "Big mistake."

THE LAST AMERICAN HERO

(1973) **D:** Lamont Johnson **S:** William Roberts
P: John Cutts, William Roberts   (*Hard Driver*)

Jeff Bridges stars as Junior Jackson, a North Carolina moonshiner who becomes a stock-car racer. With Gary Busey as his brother, William Smith as a rival driver, Valerie Perrine, Geraldine Fitzgerald, Ned Beatty, Art Lund, Ed Lauter, and *Plan 9 from Outer Space* star Gregory Walcott.

THE LAST AMERICAN VIRGIN

(MGM, 1982) **D/S:** Boaz Davidson **P:** Golan/Globus

A couple of guys (Steve Antin and Joe Rubbo) try to find a girl for their friend (Lawrence Monoson). The cast also includes Diane Franklin (in her debut), Brian Peck, Kimmy Robertson, and Louisa Moritz as the Mexican hooker they take him too. Davidson also directed the similar Israeli *Lemon Popsicle* series of teen comedies. The new-wave-hits soundtrack (on Columbia) is the best thing about this.

THE LAST BOY SCOUT

(Warner, 1991) **D:** Tony Scott **S:** Shane
Black **P:** Joel Silver, Michael Levy

Damon Wayans is a former football star with a drug problem teamed up with a sleazy former Secret Service agent (Bruce Willis). The plot, in there somewhere with lots of action and explosions, involves football corruption, and it all ends at a big game. With Chelsea Field, Noble Willingham, Halle Berry (a former Miss World from Cleveland), Kim Coates, Billy Blanks, Dick Butkus, and Sara Suzanne Brown. Black, who wrote *Lethal Weapon,* received $1.75 million for the script. Wayans' only other major film role had been in *Earth Girls Are Easy.* Michael Kamen did the soundtrack.

LAST CALL

(Prism, 1990) **D:** Jag Mundhra **S:** Steven
Lyama **P:** Ashok Amritraj

Shannon Tweed is a stripper who throws knives at teddy bears as part of her act, in this "erotic thriller." William Katt hires her to get back at some mobsters who cheated him in a real-estate deal. Tweed takes it off in sex and dance scenes. With Joseph Campanella as a gangster and Stella Stevens. There are b/w flashbacks and a Kiss pinball machine. It's available in R and unrated versions.

LAST CONTRACT: *See* PORTRAIT OF A HITMAN

THE LAST DANCE

(Prism, 1991) **D/P:** Anthony Marks **S:** Emerson Bixby

Dancers appearing on the *Miss Dance* TV show are being killed. The ads said, "Only the Sexy Die Young." With Erica Ringstrom, Cynthia Bassinet, Elaine Hendrix, and "Marci Brickhouse." The Seeds (!) and Savoy Brown are heard on the soundtrack. It's from Mike Curb's company and the makers of *Bikini Island.*

THE LAST DAYS OF POMPEII

(1984) **D:** Peter Hunt **S:** Carmen Culver
P: Richard Irving, William Hill   UK/Italy

NBC aired this 7-hour all-star mini-series with a disaster-movie ending. Olivia Hussey and Nicholas Clay star, with Ned Beatty, Brian Blessed, Ernest Borgnine, Lesley-Anne Down, Franco Nero, Anthony Quayle, Linda Purl, Laurence Olivier, and Marilu Tolo. Jack Cardiff was the cinematographer for this expensive project. The 1935 and 1960 versions were a lot shorter.

THE LAST DRAGON

(CBS/Fox, 1985) **D:** Michael Schultz **S:** Louis Venosta
P: Rupert Hitzig   (*Berry Gordy's "The Last Dragon"*)

Taimak stars as a Harlem teenager who is obsessed with martial arts and even dresses Chinese. He has to save a TV rock-video hostess (Vanity) from the outrageous Sho Nuff, "the shogun of Harlem" (Julius J. Carry III). This Motown production is a fun, cartoonish musical/action comedy. There's a gang fight in a movie theater showing *Enter the Dragon.* Vanity (D. D. Winters) was originally going to co-star with Prince in *Purple Rain.* Schultz directed *Krush Groove* the same year.

THE LAST EMBRACE

(Fox, 1979) **D:** Jonathan Demme **S:** David Shaber
P: Michael Taylor, Dan Wigutow **M:** Miklos Rozsa

Roy Scheider is an undercover government agent who has a nervous breakdown and becomes involved in a Hitchcock-type adventure involving Janet Margolin and rabbis in New York. The climax takes place at Niagara Falls. With John Glover, Charles Napier, Christopher Walken, and Mandy Patinkin. From United Artists. The score, released by Varèse Sarabande, was performed by the Nuremberg Symphony Orchestra. The director's next was *Melvin and Howard.*

THE LAST FIGHT

(Thorn EMI, 1983) **D/S/A:** Fred Williamson
P: Jerry Masucci **M:** Jay Chattaway

Panamanian-born Ruben Blades (making his American debut) stars as a salsa singer with gambling debts who turns to boxing for money. Fred Williamson, who appears as detective Jesse Crowder again, put together an impressive cast from the world of boxing, salsa music, and exploitation movies, including Willie Colon as a nightclub owner and gangster, Joe Spinell, Darlanne Fluegel, Nereida Mercado, Don King, boxer Salvador Sanchez, and José Torres. It was produced by the head of Fania Records.

THE LAST FRONTIER

(Stokey, 1932) **D:** Spencer Gordon Bennett,
Thomas L. Story **S:** George Plympton, Robert F. Hill

In one of his first roles, Lon Chaney Jr. stars as a western hero who doubles as a mysterious, Zorro-type masked man and as an Indian. Dorothy Gulliver co-stars. This 12-chapter serial is the only one RKO made. *Black Ghost* is the feature version.

THE LAST GLORY OF TROY = THE AVENGER

THE LAST HIT

(MCA, 1993) **D:** Jan Egleson **S:** Walter
Klenhard, Alan Sharpe **P:** Rob Christiansen

Bryan Brown is a former CIA assassin who settles down in New Mexico and falls for Brooke Adams. Her father (Harris Yulin) turns out to be the target of his unfinished assignment. It's by the director of *A Shock to the System.*

THE LAST HORROR FILM

(VCI, Media, 1981) **D/S/P/A:** David Winters
S/P/A: Judd Hamilton **S:** Tom Classen

American taxi driver Vinny Durand (Joe Spinell) dreams of making *The Loves of Dracula* while in Cannes for the 1981 film festival. He's a mother-dominated psycho who sweats, whimpers, and cries and is obsessed with actress Jana Bates. Caroline Munro plays the horror star whose streaked hair changes from scene to scene. Her real-life husband, Judd Hamilton, plays her director. Vinny also seems to be committing chainsaw decapitation murders. This amazingly silly movie was inspired by *Taxi Driver* (which Spinell had a small part in) and the attempt on President Reagan's life (Robin Leach shows up and asks about John Hinkley Jr.). It wasn't released until 1984. Spinell's real mom, Mary Spinell, plays his pot-smoking mother. Karen Black, Isabelle Adjani, and others show up in festival footage, and marquees announce *Polyester* and *Cannibal Holocaust*. The movie features June Chadwick, rock songs, some nudity and gore, and topless sunbathers (including Annie Ample). It also includes the then unthinkable idea that a woman could win a major award for acting in a horror movie. Spinell starred in the more disturbing *Maniac*. He and Munro were also in *Starcrash*.

THE LAST HOUR

(Academy, 1990) **D:** William Sachs
S: Jim Byrnes (*Concrete War*)

Michael Paré stars as an ex-cop with an Uzi, trying to rescue his ex-wife (Shannon Tweed) from gangsters in a skyscraper. Her stockbroker husband scammed the mob, so Bobby DiCicco kidnapped her. This *Die Hard* copy features a lot of slo-mo shooting scenes.

THE LAST HUNTER

(Vestron, 1980) **D:** "Anthony Dawson"/
Antonio Margheriti **S:** Dardano Sacchetti
P: Gianfranco Couyoumdjian Italy
(*L'Ultimo Cacciatore; Hunter of the Apocalypse*)

David Warbeck (a regular Dawson star) is a soldier behind enemy lines in Vietnam. This movie copies parts of *Apocalypse Now* and *The Deer Hunter*. The cast also includes Tisa Farrow (*Zombie*), John Steiner, and Alan Collins.

THE LAST MOVIE

(United American, 1970) **D/A:** Dennis Hopper
S: Stewart Stern **P:** Paul Lewis **C:** Laszlo
Kovacs **M:** Kris Kristofferson

Hopper stars as Kansas, a stunt man for a western being made in Chinchero, Peru. He stays behind after the production and the locals decide to copy the filmmakers with bamboo cameras and real bullets. Despite what you've heard, it's pretty damn interesting. Stella Garcia is his prostitute girlfriend, who wants lots of consumer goods. Hopper invited friends to Peru for the long shoot. Some play actors in the movie being shot. Don

Gordon and Julie Adams are good in major roles, Thomas Milian is a priest, and director Samuel Fuller plays himself. Look closely for Peter Fonda, John Phillip Law, Dean Stockwell, Russ Tamblyn, John Alderman, Toni Basil, Rod Cameron, Sylvia Miles, Michelle Phillips (she was married to the star for 8 days), Richard Rust, Kris Kristofferson (he wrote the music and makes his movie debut), Severn Darden, and Tom Baker. Kovacs also shot *Easy Rider*. The film shares the record for the longest pre-credits sequence (30 minutes). The Universal release was backed by Bob Rafelson and BBS after *Easy Rider* and was a major flop, ending Hopper's directing career for a long time. Phil Spector was going to produce but had a falling-out with Hopper. Hopper also made *American Dreamer* (1971), a companion documentary, while slowly editing *The Last Movie* down to 110 minutes.

THE LAST NINJA

(1983) **D:** William A. Graham **S:** Edward
Spielman **P:** Anthony Spinner

Michael Beck stars as Ken Sakura, an art dealer who was raised by a Japanese-American family (including Nancy Kwan and Mako) and is secretly a hero ninja. He rescues some scientists held hostage in a Dallas skyscraper. This ABC-TV series pilot also features Richard Lynch as the evil Professor Norden and John Larroquette.

LAST OF THE AMERICAN HOBOS

(1969) **D/S/P/C/A:** Titus Moody

This flashback-filled 16mm semidocumentary took four years to finish. It explores the history of hobos back to the Great Depression, using interviews with real 'bos in the 60s, folk songs, and historical reenactments. Moody talks to real characters like Slow Motion Shorty and Boxcar Myrtle, learns about hobo etiquette and life on the back roads and railroads, and shows what an actual flophouse is like. A man living in a cave tells how he lost his leg. One 'bo says "There's more after every war. We're even kids from Vietnam now." An annual hobo convention is held in Britt, Iowa. Tiger Joe Marsh, Bruno Ve Sota, and director Coleman Francis are in there somewhere too.

Julie Adams and Dennis Hopper in *The Last Movie*.

LAST OF THE FINEST

(Orion, 1990) **D:** John MacKenzie **S:** George
Armitage, Thomas Lee Wright **P:** John A. Davis

When three members of a suspended LA undercover narcotics cop team look for the killers of their partner, they discover a conspiracy. Brian Dennehy stars, with Bill Paxton, Joe Pantoliano, Michael C. Gwynne, and Pamela Gidley.

LAST OF THE RENEGADES

(VSOM, 1964) **D:** Harold Reinl **S:** Harold G.
Petersson **P:** Horst Wendlandt W. Germany/
France/Italy/Yugoslavia (*Winnetou II*)

Lex Barker returns as Old Shatterhand, and Pierre Brice is Winnetou again, in another film in a series, based on Karl May's western stories, that was very popular in Europe. Anthony Steel and Klaus Kinski are the villainous oilmen who try to start an Indian war. With Karin Dor and Terence Hill.

LAST OF THE WARRIORS

(AIP, 1989) **D/P:** Lloyd Simandl **D:** Michael Mazo
S: Chris Maruna Canada (*Empire of the Ash II*)

Melanie Kilgour (*Maniac Warriors*) joins a futuristic warrior (Ken Farmer) as they battle William Smith and his bad warriors. The film has lots of battle scenes, Kilgour taking a shower, Nancy Pataki as a lesbian priestess, and mutant cannibal zombies.

LAST PLANE OUT

(Fox, 1983) **D/P:** David Nelson
S: Ernest Tidyman **P:** Jack Cox

Jan-Michael Vincent stars as a Texas journalist in Nicaragua who falls for a Sandinista rebel (Julie Carmen). This political thriller is based on the journalistic experiences of producer Jack Cox. With Mary Crosby and William Windom. It's a PG-rated New World release.

THE LAST PORNO FLICK

(Abacus, 1974) **D:** Ray Marsh **S:** Larry Ditillio
P: Steve Bond (*The Mad Movie Makers*)

This comedy about making porno movies includes a *Deep Throat* parody but is rated PG because it doesn't show much. The cast includes Marianna Hill, Michael Pataki, Mike Kellin, and Anthony Carbone.

THE LAST REBEL

(1971) **D:** Denys McCoy **S:** Warren
Kiefer **P:** Larry G. Spangler

Joe Namath stars as a pool hustler, in this PG post–Civil War western set in Missouri but filmed in Spain. A sheriff (Ty Hardin) is after Namath, Jack Elam, and Woody Strode. The one-time football hero also starred in the biker movie *C.C. and Company* (1970) but later settled for doing TV commercials.

THE LAST REBEL

325

LAST RESORT

(Vestron, 1985) **D/A:** Zane Buzby
S: Steve Zacharias **P:** Julie Corman

Unemployed Charles Grodin takes his family on a Club Med vacation, in this sex comedy from Concorde with Mario Van Peebles, Gerrit Graham, Jon Lovitz, and Brenda Bakke.

THE LAST RIDE

(AIP, 1991) **D:** Karl Krogstad **S:** Ted Prior

In this close copy of *The Hitcher*, Daniel Ranger is a paroled inmate stalked by a psycho (Michael Regis) with a truck. Amy Newhavic is his waitress girlfriend.

THE LAST RIDER

(PM, 1990) **D/S/P:** Joseph Merhi **S:** Addison Randall, Ray Garmon **P:** Richard Pepin

A biker quits the Slavers gang, and his ex-buddies turn against him and kill his family. Erik Estrada stars in this revenge tale set in Las Vegas. With Mimi Lesseos, William Smith, Angeko Tiffe, and Kathrin Lautner.

THE LAST ROMAN

(1968) **D:** Robert Siodmak **S:** Ladislas Fodor
P: Arthur Brauner   W. Germany/Romania
(*Der Kampf um Rom*)

This two-part Roman Empire epic, more than three hours long and shot in Techniscope and Eastmancolor, was released in America cut down to 92 minutes. Laurence Harvey stars, with Orson Welles, Sylva Koscina, Honor Blackman, Harriet Andersson, Michael Dunn, and Lang Jeffries. It was based on a best-selling German novel by Felix Dann and was the last film by the director of *Phantom Lady* (1944) and *The Killers* (1946).

THE LAST SEDUCTION

(Polygram, 1994) **D:** John Dahl **S:** Steve Barancik **P:** Jonathan Shestack

Linda Fiorentino stars as a manipulative NYC woman who cons her husband (Bill Pullman), a medical student, into pulling off a big drug deal. Then she takes off with the money. On the way to Chicago she seduces a man (Peter Berg) in a small, upstate New York town and tries to trick him into murdering her husband. The cast also includes J. T. Walsh (also in Dahl's *Red Rock West*) as her lawyer and Bill Nunn. It debuted on HBO, was a critical smash, then did well in theaters.

THE LAST SHARK = THE GREAT WHITE

THE LAST SLUMBER PARTY

(United, 1987) **D/S/A:** Stephen Tyler
P: Bill F. Blair, Betty S. Scott

A killer slits the throats of some boring teens. This was released the same year as *Slumber Party Massacre II*.

THE LAST STARFIGHTER

(MCA, 1984) **D:** Nick Castle **S:** Jonathan Beutel
P: Gary Adelson, Edward O. Denault

Lance Guest is a kid living in a trailer park who becomes part of a video game. Robert Preston (in his last film) recruits him to join the Starfighters and battle the evil lizard-man Grig (Dan O'Herlihy, with maxiumum makeup). The impressive FX for this PG film were all done on computers. With Catherine Mary Stewart, Wil Wheaton, Cameron Dye, and Owen Bush.

THE LAST SUNDOWN

(Even Steven, 1971) **D:** Mike Bennett **S:** Mike Angel
P: Edward De Priest   (*Six Guns for Six Women*)

A couple of sadistic cattlemen take six dance-hall girls (including Marsha Jordan) to prison in this adults-only western.

THE LAST SURVIVOR: *See* JUNGLE HOLOCAUST

THE LAST TEMPTATION OF CHRIST

(MCA, 1988) **D:** Martin Scorsese **S:** Paul Schrader
P: Barbara De Fina **M:** Peter Gabriel

This retelling of the story of Christ is pretty interesting, but the protesters outside the Ziegfeld Theater in NYC were more memorable. It's a lot more believable than any of the older Hollywood Christ features, but like them it suffers from an "all-star" cast. Several people in the audience yelled out "It's David Bowie!" when Pontius Pilate appeared. Willem Dafoe stars as the flawed savior, and Barbara Hershey (who had her lips enlarged for the role) is Mary. With Harvey Keitel as Judas, Harry Dean Stanton, Verna Bloom, Roberts Blossom, Barry Miller, André Gregory, and Irvin Kershner. The soundtrack is excellent, and the ILM FX are put to good use. It's based on Nikos Kazantzakis' novel, which David Carradine says he gave to the director during the filming of *Boxcar Bertha*.

LAST VIDEO AND TESTAMENT

(1984) **D:** Peter Sasdy **S:** Roy Russell   UK

Deborah Raffin is having an affair with Oliver Tobias. Her international-businessman husband (David Langton) accidentally videotapes them, fakes his own death, and plots revenge by "haunting" them, using scientific methods. It's a Hammer TV movie.

THE LAST WALTZ

(United Artists, 1978) **D:** Martin Scorsese
P: Robbie Robertson

The Band perform at their "last" show, on Thanksgiving 1976, at the Winterland. They also play on an MGM soundstage. Guest stars include Bob Dylan, Van Morrison, Neil Young, the Staples Singers, Ronnie Hawkins, Muddy Waters, Dr. John, and Ringo Starr. Scorsese (a friend of Robbie Robertson) conducts the interviews with the group. Bill Graham sponsored the show. The cinematographers included Laszlo Kovacs and Vilmos Zsigmond, and U.A. released it. Scorsese made the

classy concert film in between *New York, New York* (1977) and *Raging Bull* (1980). The Band later got back together without Robertson.

THE LAST WARNING

(1929) **D:** Paul Leni **S:** Alfred A. Cohn **P:** Carl Laemmle

Universal reteamed director Paul Leni and actress Laura La Plante, from the hit *The Cat and the Canary* (1927), in this horror comedy set in a theater. A director (Montague Love) restages a play that was a hit until a real murder occurred, but the new production seems to be haunted by the ghost of the original leading man. (The sets from *The Phantom of the Opera* were used.) Roy D'Arcy costars, with Margaret Livingston and John Boles. This was released in silent and part-sound versions. It was remade as *House of Fear* (1939).

THE LAST WAVE

(Rhino, 1977) **D:** Peter Weir **S:** Tony Morphett, Petro Popescu   Australia

A lawyer (Richard Chamberlain) defending an Aborigine (David Gulpilil, from *Walkabout*) accused of murder has hallucinations of apocalyptic events and ancient tribal rituals. This was Weir's third feature and was released by United Artists.

LAS VEGAS BLOODBATH

(S.K.M.D., 1989) **D/S/P:** David Schwartz **P/A:** Ari Levin

This is a sick gore movie with terrible acting and endless scenes of cars. A young businessman named Sammy (Ari Levin) cracks after he finds his wife (a blond hair hopper) with the doorman: "I'll get even with them all!" He walks and drives around with his wife's head and shows it to a hooker before he knifes her in broad daylight, then ties her legs to his car and pulls them off. He talks to the head (shades of *Bring Me the Head of Alfredo Garcia*) and takes it to a bar. When a driver gives him the finger he shoots it off. He invades a house full of female "oil wrestlers" (we see their show on TV) and proceeds to slaughter them. He ties up and kills the pregnant one, cuts the baby out, and throws it against the wall. As I've said elsewhere, I don't make these things up; people send them for review. The FX are by a guy who does Vegas haunted-house shows. I don't know whether this video ever made it out of the Vegas area (there's a story about nobody being paid), which is just as well.

LAS VEGAS LADY

(1976) **D:** Noel Nosseck **S:** Walter Dallenbach
P: Joseph Zappala, Gene Slott

Stella Stevens stars in a Crown International release about a casino hostess who plans a robbery, with Stuart Whitman, Lynn Moody, George DiCenzo, Jesse White, and her son, Andrew Stevens.

LAS VEGAS SERIAL KILLER

(Sinister, 1985) **D/S/C/E:** "Wolfgang Schmidt"/
Ray Dennis Steckler **P:** Katharine Steckler

Killer Jonathan Glick (the 50-something Pierre Agostino) is paroled and stars killing again. Meanwhile, some crooks walk around. It's narrated by a reporter, but this awful movie still makes no sense and has no ending. Parades, a rodeo, signs, models posing—anything is thrown in to fill up the time. There's the silicone body of Miss World Burlesque, porno star Jeannie Pepper as a model, and a Smurf doll. It's sort of a sequel to *The Hollywood Strangler Meets the Skid Row Slasher*, also with Agostino. Steckler also directed many hard-X films (*Teenage Hustler, Las Vegas Erotica, Sex Rink*) using fake credits, and opened video stores in Vegas.

LAS VEGAS WEEKEND

(1985) **D/S/P:** Dale Trevillion

This is a comedy about a computer nerd (Barry Hickey) winning in Vegas and getting the girl. Cult director Ray Dennis Steckler is in the cast. The director made *One Man Force*.

LATE FOR DINNER

(SVS, 1991) **D/P:** W. D. Richter
S: Mark Andrus **P:** Dan Lupovitz

Two friends on the lam (Brian Wimmer and Peter Berg) are put into a deep freeze by a doctor in 1962. When they wake up in LA in 1991, Wimmer has to deal with his older, remarried wife and grown-up daughter. With Marcia Gay Harden, Colleen Flynn, and Peter Gallagher. This little-seen PG fantasy was Richter's first film after *Buckaroo Banzai*.

THE LATE NANCY IRVING

(1984) **D:** Peter Sasdy **S:** David Fisher   UK

Christina Raines is a diabetic golf pro in England who has a rare blood type. Marius Goring is a wealthy sadist with pet scorpions who needs her blood to stay alive, so he has her death faked. This Hammer TV movie copies *Coma*.

THE LATHE OF HEAVEN

(1980) **D/P:** David R. Loxton, Fred Barzyk
S: Roger E. Swaybill, Diane English

Bruce Davison stars as George Orr, who lives in Portland, Oregon, in the near future. His dreams affect the weather and the past, present, and future. He nearly ODs from drugs and is sent to a psychiatrist (Kevin Conway) who drugs him and uses him in an attempt to control overpopulation. As a result, millions die from a plague, racial problems get worse, everybody turns gray, and turtle-like aliens arrive. Margaret Avery costars as a lawyer. Filmed in Dallas using real futuristic-looking buildings, this highly praised PBS-TV production is based on Ursula K. Le Guin's novel. It's been much requested on video.

LATIN QUARTER

(Sinister, 1945) **D/S:** Vernon Sewell
P/A: Derrick De Marney   UK (*Frenzy*)

A Paris artist kills his wife and covers her in plaster. During a séance the killer is revealed. Derrick De Marney stars, with Joan Greenwood, Frederick Valk, and Valentine Dyall. So that's where the idea for *A Bucket of Blood* came from.

LAUGH, CLOWN, LAUGH

(Fright, 1928) **D:** Herbert Brenon **S:** Elizabeth Meehan **P:** Irving G. Thalberg

Tito (Lon Chaney) and Simon (Bernard Siegel) are Italian clowns who take in an abandoned girl named Simonetta. As she grows up (played by Loretta Young, who was 15 at the time), the clowns become big stars as Flik (lovesick and miserable) and Flok (now just a straight man). The plot, involving a count (Nils Asther) who suffers from "spells of uncontrollable laughter," is pretty contrived. It's an adaptation of a play by David Belasco and Tom Cushing, based on an Italian play (John Barrymore had starred in the Broadway version). Parts are remarkably similar to *The Man Who Laughs* (both are basically tragic stories of unrequited love). The attraction, of course, is Chaney, who does an incredible death-defying slide over an opera-house audience on a wire—on his head (!)—and has an unforgettable death scene. This rare MGM release was shot by James Wong Howe and has a musical score. The video I saw was taped from a theater screen.

THE LAUGHING DEAD

(1989) **D/S/M/A:** "S. P. Somtow"/Somtow Sucharitkul **P:** Lex Nakashima

The first directing effort of Somtow, a novelist from Thailand, is a wild tale, shot on location, of present-day Maya Indian sacrifice. This low-budget film has excellent music and cinematography, and an interesting plot. A busload of tourists from Tucson, Arizona, go to Oaxaca, Mexico, to see "the Festival of the Dead." Tim Sullivan, (a writer who was also the associate producer) plays the troubled Father O'Sullivan of the Sacred Heart Catholic Church, the guide for the trip. Also along are his secret lover (an ex-nun) and their son ("It's all your fuckin' fault, preacher dude!"), a New Age couple complete with crystals, an Oriental girl escaping from her brutal father, a hippie bus driver, and a jerk in a yellow suit who tells dirty jokes. Dr. Um Tzeck (Somtow), a professor with a computer who plays classical music, leads the Maya in their pagan sacrifices. Hearts are cut out, heads chopped off or crushed, and a ripped-off arm is shoved down somebody's throat. There's a cave of zombies and shocking dreams, and some characters turn into big, reptilian monsters. Some of the FX (by busy John Buechler and his crew) are shocking and well done, while a few are shown too long or are unconvincing. I was disappointed when Somtow switched to all-out comedy, after a great, serious buildup, but I'm sure others will love it that way. I didn't recognize him, but Forry Ackerman plays a corpse. This has only been released overseas.

THE LAUGHING, LEERING LURES OF DAVID FRIEDMAN

(SW, 1992)

This is a compilation of 18 trailers (most in color) for 60s and 70s adults-only films from "America's fearless young showman." Some are very funny, filled with puns, in-jokes and purposely overdone hard-sell. *The Lustful Turk* is a pretty hilarious "making of" short (a few of the trailers are nearly 10 minutes long). Most have lots of nudity, and some have spanking, whipping, rape, some near-X sex, and even a bit of hard-core. Marsha Jordan is featured in several, and Rene Bond, Kathy Williams, and Uschi Digart also appear. Some other titles are *Brick Doll House, Space Thing, Brand of Shame, The Adult Version of Jekyll and Hyde,* and *Ramrodder*.

L.A. VICE

(PM, 1989) **D/P:** Joseph Merhi **S:** Charles T. Kanganis **P:** Richard Pepin

Detective Jon Chance (Lawrence Hilton-Jacobs) and his American Indian partner are on a kidnapping case. William Smith is the retired captain who helps them. This is a sequel to *L.A. Heat*.

THE LAWLESS LAND

(MGM, 1988) **D:** Jon Hess **S/P:** Tony Cinciripini, Larry Leahy

Nick Corri and Amanda Peterson are pursued by a gang led by "Road Kill" (Leon Berkeley) in the near future. This *Mad Max* copy from Concorde was filmed in Chile. Hess also made *Watchers*.

THE LAWLESS RIDER

(1952) **D:** Yakima Canutt **S:** Edward D. Wood Jr.

Just before Ed Wood made his directorial debut with *Glen or Glenda*, he scripted this obscure western. The famous stuntman Yakima Canutt directed it, and it stars Johnny Carpenter (also a stuntman), with Frankie Darro, Douglas Dumbrille, Noel Neill, and Kenne Duncan. The 62-minute feature was released by UA in 1954. Duncan and Carpenter were later in Wood's *Night of the Ghouls*.

THE LAWNMOWER MAN

(New Line, 1992) **D/S:** Brett Leonard
S/P: Gimel Everett

Jeff Fahey stars as a grown man with the mind of a child (and a bad blond wig). Scientist Pierce Brosnan experiments on him, and he becomes an unstoppable madman who ODs from virtual reality, sees God, and faces evil military men. The plot is *Charly* mixed with *Brain Waves, Tron,* and *Man with the X-Ray Eyes*. The computer animation includes a (brief) sex scene. With Jenny Wright, Geoffrey Lewis, and Jeremy Slate as a priest. It's available in an R or an unrated "director's cut" with 32 (!) minutes of extra footage. (At least we didn't get a director's cut of Leonard's *The Dead Pit*.) Milton Subotsky is credited as the coproducer. He owned the film rights to Stephen King's short story "Nightshift." King successfully sued to have his name removed from this mediocre movie, and New Line was found to be in contempt of court in 1994 for leaving his name on the video. *Lawnmower Man II* followed.

LAW OF THE JUNGLE

(Sinister, 1942) **D:** Jean Yarborough
S: George Brickner **P:** Lindsay Parsons

An explorer (John "Dusty" King) and a singer (Arline Judge) on a jungle island encounter Nazis who are after a scientist. Mantan Moreland, Arthur O'Connell, and C. Montague Shaw are also in this 61-minute Monogram release.

LAW OF THE LAWLESS

(1964) **D:** William F. Claxton
S: Steve Fisher **P:** A. C. Lyles

Dale Robertson stars in this color Paramount western as a circuit-riding judge who arrives in a Kansas town to try a killer (John Agar). William Bendix is the sheriff, and Yvonne De Carlo is a dance-hall girl. Also with Bruce Cabot, Barton Mc-Laine, Richard Arlen, Kent Taylor, Lon Chaney Jr., Don Barry, Jody McCrea, and Rod Lauren.

LAWS OF GRAVITY

(Triboro, 1991) **D/S:** Nick Gomez **P:** Bob Gorse

Peter Greene (*Judgment Night*) stars in this very-low-budget *Mean Streets* type of story, concerning small-time thieves and stolen guns. It was filmed in Brooklyn. The soundtrack uses rap music.

THE LEATHER BOYS

(1963) **D:** Sidney J. Furie **S:** Gillian
Freeman **P:** Raymond Stross   UK

Mechanic Reggie (Colin Campbell) is married to Dot (Rita Tushingham), but he finds himself drawn into a relationship with another motorcycle racer (Dudley Sutton). The now tame gay theme of this movie made it controversial when it was released. All of the main characters race to Edinburgh. Furie also directed an American film about motorcycle racing, *Little Fauss and Big Halsy* (1970).

LEATHERFACE: THE TEXAS CHAINSAW MASSACRE 3

(RCA/Columbia, 1990) **D:** Jeff Burr
S: David J. Schow **P:** Robert Engleman

After Cannon made the first sequel, New Line took over the *Chainsaw* characters for a series. They blew it by firing Burr and cutting the movie drastically for an R rating. New scenes and a new ending were even filmed by second-unit directors. This second "sequel" ignores the first one and pretty much recycles the script of the original movie. Leatherface and a new cannibal clan with seven members (including a little blond girl killer) attack a vacationing couple. Kate Hodge (star of the *She Wolf of London* TV series) is the screaming main victim. A seemingly indestructible survivalist (Ken Foree) comes to the rescue. Viggo Mortensen is Tex. The uncut version was shown in other countries and later made it to bootleg tapes in the U.S.A. *Return of the Texas Chainsaw Massacre* was next.

LEATHER JACKETS

(Epic, 1990) **D/S:** Lee Drysdale **P:** Cassian Elwes

Cary Elwes, Bridget Fonda, D. B. Sweeney, and Christopher Penn hit the road after a botched, violent attempt to rip off a Vietnamese gang. This very downbeat action movie went directly to video after two years on the shelf, and critics hated it. It has a great cast of teen stars, and Fonda is especially good. Also in the cast are Craig Ng, James LeGros, Marshall Bell, and porno stars Ginger Lynn and Viper.

THE LEFT SIDE OF MY BRAIN

(1992) **D/S/E/A:** Jonathan Morrill **D/S:** Gary Wortzel

The ambitious 90-minute film, told mostly in flashbacks, was taped and filmed, in color and b/w, in NYC and Boston. It spans 16 years in the life of Raymond Salzberg, a naive would-be artist from New Jersey who eventually makes it. It has good locations and period changes and was obviously made by people who know the art scene. There's a flashback nightmare, a *Twilight Zone* type of structure (beginning = ending), original rock music, and a live appearance by the Smithereens. Morrill also made the less coherent *Bride of Johnny in Monsterland.*

LEGACY OF HORROR = LEGACY OF BLOOD

LEGACY OF SATAN

(Abacus, 1973) **D/S/P/E:** Gerard Damiano
P: Lou Parrish

Here's a forgotten 70s movie, and it should stay that way. An evil doctor and his blood-drinking followers worship "Lord Rakish." They lure people to a costume party where some are killed (and everyone talks a lot) and a woman (Lisa Christian) becomes the new "queen." The master says things like "You pitiful worm under my feet!" and mutates at the end. This slow movie has an irritating, buzzing synthesizer score that sounds like ELP outtakes. Damiano is better known for his many porno movies, including *The Devil in Miss Jones.*

LEGAL TENDER

(Prism, 1990) **D:** Jag Mundhra **S:** Barry
Roberts **P:** Ashok Amritraj

Robert Davi stars as a motorcycle-riding private eye. Blond Tanya Roberts owns a bar and poker joint. Morton Downey Jr. (!) is a Texas S&L executive and coke dealer who takes bubble baths with his women (including porno star Savannah) and kills a man with a meat cleaver. It's another "erotic thriller," and this time Roberts used a body double for the nude scenes. Wendy McDonald is also in this movie, which is from the director of *Night Eyes.*

THE LEGEND: *See* JAMES DEAN

LEGEND

(MCA, 1985) **D:** Ridley Scott **S:** William Hjortsberg
P: Arnon Milchan, Tim Hampton   UK

Tom Cruise and Mia Sara (aka Sara Pocciello) star in this PG fantasy for kids with elves and unicorns. Tim Curry is impressive as the demon Darkness. Billy Barty is also in the cast. It's pretty disappointing after Scott's *Blade Runner,* but the Rob Bottin makeup FX are good. Jerry Goldsmith's score was replaced by Tangerine Dream's for the 89-minute American release. The original, uncut 120-minute version is on video in Germany (dubbed).

THE LEGEND OF BLOOD CASTLE

(VSOM, 1972) **D/S:** Jorge Grau **S:** Juan Tebor
P: José María González Sinde   Spain/Italy
(*Ceremonia Sangrienta; Blood Castle; Female Butcher*)

A version of the Countess Elizabeth Báthory vampire legend set in Central Europe in 1857, this movie has many interesting images, torture scenes, real bats, and good makeup FX. It's much better than the Hammer versions. Bread is baked with blood, a corpse is put on trial, and a naked virgin boy is sent on a white horse to locate the tomb of a vampire. Elizabeth (Lucia Bose) bathes in blood, her living-dead husband, Karl (Esperanto Santoni), helps, and Ewa Aulin (*Candy*) is Marina, the star victim. Grau also made *Don't Open the Window/The Living Dead at Manchester Morgue.*

LEGEND OF DOLEMITE

(Xenon, 1994) **D:** Foster Gordon
S: Duane Ladage **S/P:** Leigh Savidge

A lot of this tape is comedian Rudy Ray Moore in a then-recent club appearance, but he's also seen on the Arsenio Hall show and talks about his party albums and his two *Dolemite* movies. Film clips (not always the best ones) are used. There are

CHRISTOPHER LEE

After years as a character actor in British films, Lee became a major international horror star after playing Dracula, the Frankenstein Monster, and the Mummy for Hammer studios in the late 50s. Throughout the 60s, horror fans looked forward to seeing just about anything he was in. After a few big money features (like *The Man with the Golden Gun* and *Airport '77*), Lee stopped doing horror movies but still acted a lot and did voices for some animated features. After the deaths of John Carradine, Vincent Price, and Lee's frequent costar Peter Cushing (who retired in 1986), he was the only well-known living horror star, and the tall, dark, and gruesome actor became a frequent narrator and spokesman for anything about horror. His appearances are still always welcome.

interviews with Lady Reed and LaWanda Page and appearances by Ice-T and Mike D. from the Beastie Boys.

THE LEGEND OF FRENCHIE KING

(1971) **D:** Christian-Jaque **D/S:** Guy Casaril **S:** Daniel Boulanger, Marie-Ange Anies **P:** Raymond Erger   Italy/France/Spain/UK (*Le Pistolere; Les Pétroleuses; Petroleum Girls*)

Brigitte Bardot and Claudia Cardinale are rival gang leaders in this almost all-female western/comedy set in the French settlement of Bougival Junction, New Mexico. Bardot had been in a similar western, *Viva Maria!* (1965). This was among her last films. Also in the cast are the mugging Michael J. Pollard as the sheriff, Emma Cohen, Patty Shepard and Teresa Gimpera as Frenchie's sisters, and Micheline Presle. K-Tel released it in America. It was shot in Spain.

THE LEGEND OF HILLBILLY JOHN

(R&G, 1973) **D:** John Newland **S:** Melvin Levy **P:** Barney Rosenzweig   (*Who Fears the Devil; My Name Is John*)

Hedges Capers stars as a young, wandering Appalachian ballad singer who encounters an ugly, animated bird creature (FX by Gene Warren) and goes back in time. This odd, G-rated fantasy about the Devil's work was filmed in North Carolina. Narrator Severn Darden looks into the camera, and when a character dies the film breaks. Denver Pyle, who plays the grandfather, talks/sings the theme, written by Hoyt Axton. Also with Sharon Henesy as the pretty girlfriend, Susan Strasberg as an old witch, Harris Yulin as an undertaker, R. G. Armstrong, Alfred Ryder, and Val Avery. Jack Harris released this film, directed by the host of the TV series *One Step Beyond*.

THE LEGEND OF LYLAH CLARE

(1968) **D/P:** Robert Aldrich **S:** Hugo Butler, Jean Rouvel

Kim Novak is an unknown actress (with vertigo) hired to play Lylah Clare, a famous actress. She seems to become possessed by the star, who died mysteriously on her wedding night, and the director (Peter Finch), who was married to Lylah, falls for her. Rosella Falk (*Modesty Blaise*) is a drug-addict and lesbian. Coral Browne is a famous gossip columnist. With Ernest Borgnine, Valentina Cortese, Lee Meriwether, Michael Murphy, and Ellen Corby. You won't believe how this long (130-minute) MGM movie ends. It's based on a TV play by Robert Thom. *The Blonde* (1980) is an uncredited porno remake starring Annette Haven.

THE LEGEND OF NIGGER CHARLEY

(1972) **D:** Martin Goldman **S/P:** Larry Spangler

Just after the release of *Buck and the Preacher*, Fred Williamson starred in this similar western set in the 1850s. He escapes from a Virginia plantation with D'Urville Martin and Don Pedro Colley after killing sadistic overseer John P. Ryan. A bounty hunter goes after them as they head west. With Tricia O'Neil as a half-Indian woman, Gertrude Jeanette, and Marcia McBroom. The theme song is by Lloyd Price. *The Soul of Nigger Charley* (1973) followed.

THE LEGEND OF SLEEPY HOLLOW

(Starmaker, 1979) **D:** Henning Schellerup **S:** Malvin Wald, Jack Jacobs, Tom Chapman **P:** James L. Conway

The Sunn Classics people made this adaptation of Washington Irving's famous story about the 17th-century headless horseman. It debuted on Halloween on NBC-TV and was aimed at kids. Jeff Goldblum stars as the Hudson Valley schoolmaster Ichabod Crane, with Dick Butkus, Meg Foster, and Paul Sand. It was filmed in Utah.

LEGEND OF THE SEA WOLF

(Simitar, 1975) **D:** Giuseppe Vari **P:** Joseph Green   Italy (*Wolf Larsen*)

Chuck Connors stars as the sadistic sea captain, in another version of Jack London's novel *The Sea Wolf*. The cast also includes Barbara Bach as a shipwrecked woman, Ivan Rassimov, Alan Collins, and Rick Battaglia.

THE LEGEND OF WOLF MOUNTAIN

(Hemdale, 1991) **D/S:** Craig Clyde **S:** James Hennessy **P:** Bryce Fillmore

Nicole Lund and two other kids in Utah are kidnapped by escaped prisoners (Robert Z'Dar and David Shark), in this PG adventure movie. Bo Hopkins and Mickey Rooney are forest rangers. A legendary Indian warrior (Don Shanks) helps with the rescue mission and becomes a wolf in a dream sequence. Vivian Schilling is the older sister.

LEGENDS

(Fox Lorber, 1994) **D:** Ilana Bar-Din

This excellent, all true 54-minute documentary is about the Las Vegas *Legends in Concert* show, featuring impersonators of Marilyn Monroe, Elvis Presley, and Judy Garland. Elvis (who goes on and on about his fans) and Marilyn fall in love, defect, and start their own show. Judy (who sounds *very* insane) eventually dies of cancer. The show's egotistical manager is seen rehearsing his new attraction, a Sammy Davis Jr. clone.

LENA'S HOLIDAY

(Prism, 1991) **D:** Michael Keusch **S:** Deborah Tilton **P:** Marilyn Jacons Tenser

Felicity Waterman stars as a blond East German tourist in LA who's obsessed with James Dean. Her bags are switched with those of a murder victim. This comedy takes place around the time the Berlin Wall fell. The cast, better than usual for Crown International, includes Chris Lemmon, Nick Mancuso, Michael Sarrazin, Pat Morita, Bill Dana, Susan Anton, and Liz Torres.

LENINGRAD COWBOYS GO AMERICA

(Orion, 1990) **D/S/P:** Aki Kaurismaki **P:** Klas Olofsson, Katinka Farago   Finland

A Finnish rock group with exaggerated pomps are considered bad in their homeland, so they go to America. After stopping in NYC they go on a tour of small towns and play at a Mexican wedding. The cast includes Nicky Tesco, Duke Robillard, and director Jim Jarmusch as a car dealer. This PG-13 comedy was backed by the Swedish Film Institute. The Cowboys returned in other features.

LEONARD PART 6

(RCA, 1987) **D:** Paul Weiland **S:** Jonathan Reynolds **P/A:** Bill Cosby

Even though Bill Cosby was starring in the top TV series at the time, this PG movie was a box-office flop. He plays a multimillionaire former secret agent trying to catch Medusa (Gloria Foster), who plans to make the animals of the world kill off the humans. There's a scene in which Leonard rides an ostrich and stops an attack by lobsters. Tom Courtenay is his butler, who narrates the story, and Joe Don Baker is a CIA man. Also with Moses Gunn, Grace Zabriskie, and Jane Fonda (as herself, doing aerobics). Cosby (who received a story credit) urged people not to see this, then followed it with the flop *Ghost Dad*.

LEOPARD IN THE SNOW

(1978) **D:** Gerry O'Hara **S:** Anne Mather, Jill Hyem **P:** John Quested   Canada/UK

This PG release from Roger Corman's New World was a Harlequin Romance production. A woman (Susan Penhaligon) has to abandon her car in a town called Cumberland Falls, in northern England, and meets a strange man (Keir Dullea) who lives in a remote house and has a leopard. With Billie Whitelaw, Jeremy Kemp, and Kenneth More.

LEPKE

(1975) **D/P:** Menahem Golan **S:** Wesley Thau, Tamar Hoffs   US/Israel

Tony Curtis is Louis "Lepke" Buchalter, head of "Murder Inc.," in this *Godfather*-inspired gangster epic set in the 30s and 40s. Anjanette Comer and Michael Callan costar. Vic Tayback is Lucky Luciano, and former JFK impersonator Vaughn Meader is Walter Winchell. Also with Warren Berlinger, Milton Berle, and Mary Wilcox. Cannon founder Golan had already directed more than a dozen features. Future director Andrew Davis was the cinematographer. Warner released it.

LEPRECHAUN

(Vidmark, 1992) **D/S:** Mark Jones **P:** Jeffrey B. Mallian

Warwick Davis (*Willow*) is a killer leprechaun with red hair and a green suit. He's after the American who stole his pot of gold, and he torments a man and his daughter (Jennifer Aniston of *Friends*) who have just moved into the house he was imprisoned in. Ken Olandt, Robert Gorman, and Mark Holton are painters who become involved. The makeup is good, but the mixture of gags, fantasy, horror, and gore is an uneasy one. This Trimark release was a surprise money-maker in theaters.

LEPRECHAUN 2

(Vidmark, 1994) **D:** Rodman Flender **S:** Turi
Meyer, Al Septien **P:** Donald Borchers

After a prelude in ancient Ireland, the talkative leprechaun (Warwick Davis) arrives in modern-day
LA. He kidnaps a blonde teen (Shevonne Durkin),
brings her to his maze of caves, and informs her
that she'll be "bearing my wee ones soon." Meanwhile, characters die by fan and espresso machine.
Charlie Heath is the nice-guy boyfriend who hosts
a Hollywood death tour for his alcoholic uncle
(Sandy Baron). With Clint Howard and Kimmy
Robertson. There are lots of dwarfs in a scene that
parodies *Freaks.* The FX are by Gabe Z. Bartolos
(*Frankenhooker*). In England this movie is called
One Wedding and Lots of Funerals (!).

LES PATTERSON SAVES THE WORLD

(Southgate, 1987) **D:** George Miller **S:** Barry
Humphries, Diane Millstead   Australia

Barry Humphries (aka Dame Edna Everidge) stars
as the ambassador to a fictional Middle Eastern kingdom. A colonel is planning to infect the
world with a deadly virus (called H.E.L.P.). Victims ooze pus. Joan Rivers plays the US president.
The music is by Tim Finn. This offensive, lowbrow
comedy is not by the same George Miller who directed *Mad Max.*

LETHAL GAMES

(AIP, 1991) **D:** John Bowen **S:** Danny
King **P:** Joseph R. Donato, Ron Lavery

Frank Stallone helps a small community fight a
gang hired by the mob. With Brenda Vaccaro,
Heidi Paine, and Karen Russell.

LETHAL WEAPON

(Warner, 1987) **D/S:** Richard Donner
S: Shane Black **P:** Joel Silver

The "lethal weapon" is Martin Riggs (Mel Gibson),
a deranged, suicidal cop whose wife has been
killed. He's teamed with his Nam-vet friend Danny
Glover, whose daughter is kidnapped by Nam-
vet villains. The military-style bad guys are led
by blond Gary Busey as a psycho hitman/drug
dealer and Mitchell Ryan. Gibson has a pro-pot-
legalization scene. With Tom Atkins, Darlene Love
(a singer on many classic 60s records that Phil
Spector produced), Cheryl Baker, Renee Estevez,
Traci Wolfe, Al Leong, Don Gordon, Damon
Hines, and Jackie Swanson and Terri Lynn Doss in
a shower. The soundtrack (on Warner) is by Michael Kamen (once leader of the New York Rock
and Roll Ensemble) and features Eric Clapton.
This was only a modest hit, but sequels added
more comedy and were much more successful at
the box office.

LETHAL WEAPON 2

(Warner, 1989) **D/P:** Richard Donner
S: Jeffrey Boam **P:** Joel Silver

Gibson and Glover return, and this time they're
after racist South African villains, led by Joss Ackland, who are laundering money and dealing

drugs. Joe Pesci, as an accountant who needs witness protection, steals scenes. There's more comedy with the violent action this time. Gibson even
does Three Stooges imitations. With Patsy Kensit,
Darlene Love, Traci Wolfe, and Buck Flower. I saw
this in a big, old theater in São Paulo, Brazil, with
Portuguese subtitles. They kept the sound low, so
it was kind of hard to hear. The Michael Kamen
soundtrack (on Warner) features Eric Clapton,
George Harrison, and Bob Dylan's "Knockin' on
Heaven's Door."

LETHAL WEAPON 3

(Warner, 1992) **D/P:** Richard Donner **S:** Jeffrey
Boam, Robert Mark Kamen **P:** Joel Silver

Mel Gibson, Danny Glover, and Joe Pesci return
again. Model Rene Russo (*Freejack*) is an internal-
affairs cop who's a kickboxer. The plot's about a
psychotic ex-cop (Stuart Wilson) running a gun
racket, but the slapstick gags take over the movie.
The old Orlando, Florida, city hall building was
blown up. Also in the cast are Darlene Love and
Damon Hines. The soundtrack (on Warner) is by
Michael Kamen, with contributions from Eric
Clapton, David Sanborn, and Sting, who warbles
the title song. It's rare for the same director to make
so many movies in a major series and even rarer for
each to make more money than the previous entry.

LETHAL WOMAN

(Vid America, 1988) **D:** Christian Marnham
S: Michael Olson, Gabe Ellis **P:** John Kaire
S. Africa (*The Most Dangerous Woman Alive*)

In a flashback, a soldier (Merete Van Kamp) in
Florida is the victim of an army coverup after she's
raped by a colonel. Later, rapists are lured to a fantasy island for an "erotic vacation," as women wait
to take revenge with their crossbows. After a big
feast the men are let loose in the woods, and it's
Most Dangerous Game time again. Topless women
writhe by a fire, a man's head is displayed on a
pole, and more heads hang in a room. Shannon
Tweed costars. There are nude scenes, lots of flashbacks, a midget, and some laughable dialogue.

LET IT BE

(Magnetic, 1970) **D:** Michael Lindsay-Hogg
P: Neil Aspinal

See the world's most famous pop group self-
destructing. The Beatles rehearse songs, record at
the Apple studios, then play a concert on the Apple
rooftop (1/30/69). It was the last time the group
played in public (surprising passersby on the street
below). Yoko Ono and Billy Preston also appear.
UA released this 16mm film. By the time the album
came out (more than 15 months later) it had been
reworked by Phil Spector, and the Beatles were
history. Skip this and watch *The Rutles: All You
Need Is Cash* (Pacific Arts, 1978).

LET IT ROCK

(Media, 1981) **D/S/P:** Roland Klick
W. Germany (*White Star*)

After directing *Out of the Blue,* Dennis Hopper
went to Germany to play a hyper American rock
agent who talks a lot about "the colonel" and Brian

Epstein. If you like manic Hopper, he's here nonstop, probably ad-libbing most of the time. He tries
to promote a guy who plays some kind of techno-
pop, giving him the name "White Star," to a punk
audience ("This is the future. What do you know
about music, punks?"). He hires David Hess (!) to
break store windows and start a riot for publicity
purposes, and plans an assassination attempt that
results in the death of an innocent girl. White Star
does not become a major act. Roger Corman retitled the movie for its US release and added footage of T.S.O.L. from *Suburbia.* Klick also made
Deadlock (1970), with music by Can.

LET'S DO IT! (1982): *See* DOING IT

LET'S DO IT

(Best, 1984) **D/S/P/E:** Bert I. Gordon

One of Mr. BIG's worst is a comedy starring Greg
Bradford as Freddie, a blond Hollywood virgin
with a serious mother complex. No woman can
seem to seduce him. A scene with giant breasts is
similar to the one in Bert's earlier *Village of the
Giants.* Freddie has a dream of naked women on a
trampoline, and his girlfriend has a dream that's
actual footage from the original *King Kong* (what,
no lawsuits?!). With Betsy Russell (*Private School*)
and (I think) Brinke Stevens. Gordon also made
two other sex comedies, *How to Succeed with Sex*
(1970) and *The Big Bet* (1986).

LET'S GET HARRY

(1986) **D:** "Alan Smithee"/Stuart Rosenberg
S: Charles Robert Carner, Samuel Fuller
P: Daniel H. Blatt   (*The Rescue*)

A soldier of fortune named Smilin' Jack (Gary
Busey) is hired to help rescue a pipeline worker
(Mark Harmon) and an ambassador kidnapped by
South American drug dealers. With Glenn Frey,
Robert Duvall, Rick Rossovich, Ben Johnson, Matt
Clark, Gregory Sierra, and David Hess. The di-
rector had his name removed and it was barely re-
leased.

LET THE GOOD TIMES ROLL

(1973) **D/S:** Robert J. Abel, Sidney
Levin **P:** Gerald I. Isenberg

Highlights from 1972 "oldies" stage shows, presented by Richard Nader, make up most of this
concert film. The artists are Fats Domino, Little
Richard, Bo Diddley, Chuck Berry, Bill Haley and
the Comets, the Shirelles, and Chubby Checker. If
the classic songs the stars do here were oldies in
1973, what are they now!? There are also choice
clips from 50s TV shows, newsreels, and films.

LEVIATHAN

(MGM, 1989) **D:** George Pan Cosmatos **S:** David
Peoples, Jeb Stuart **P:** Luigi De Laurentiis

At an underwater mining camp, infected vodka
from a Russian submarine turns Daniel Stern into
a fish monster. Peter Weller stars with Amanda
Pays (in the Sigourney Weaver *Alien* role), Richard
Crenna, Ernie Hudson, Lisa Eilbacher, Hector Elizondo, Michael Carmine, and Meg Foster. It was

shot in Rome. Ron Cobb was the production designer for this film (and *Alien*). Jerry Goldsmith wrote the score for this film (and *Alien*). Stan Winston did the FX for this film (and *Aliens*). Hmmm.

LIANE, THE JUNGLE GODDESS

(SW, 1956) **D:** Edward von Borsody
S: Ernst von Salomon **P:** Helmut Volmer
W. Germany (*Liane, die Weiss Sklavin*)

This sex-tease jungle-woman movie (in wonderful Pathé color) was released in America by DCA. Marion Michaels plays a beautiful, blond jungle girl living in an African tree house who saves a photographer (Hardy Kruger) from a native attack. In the early scenes Liane is topless and carefree (although she has red lipstick and mascara). Eventually her long hair is cut by a jealous lady doctor and she's kidnapped. Tonga, a faithful native warrior, and Simba the lion join her in Germany, where she wears sexy nightgowns and a bikini. Liane is called "you little Devil," "little savage," "little brat," and "pretty little bubblehead" by various characters. Reggie Nalder (*Salem's Lot*) is the evil Mr. Goering, a Hamburg shipbuilder who's after her inheritance. There's plenty of *National Geographic*–style topless native footage and out-of-place jazzy big-band music. *Liane* is exploitative, silly, and insulting, but very entertaining. A sequel was called *Nature Girl and the Slavers* in America.

LIARS' CLUB

(New Horizons, 1993) **D:** Jeffrey Porter
S: Jeff Yonis **P:** Mike Elliot

Although it shamelessly copies major parts of *River's Edge*, this is a very good movie that stands on its own. A high school girl is raped at a party by a football jock (Brian Krause). A big, blond guy called Jimbo (Michael Cudlitz) accidentally kills her while trying to shut her up and save his friend's future, which leads to a coverup by the other kids. Wil Wheaton stars as the nice-guy mechanic who reluctantly gets involved. There is no Dennis Hopper character, but there's a pot-selling little kid named Buzzard. With Soleil Moon Frye and Bruce Weitz.

LIAR'S EDGE

(New Line, 1993) **D:** Ron Oliver
P: Ray Sagar, Llana Frank   Canada

Shannon Tweed (who leaves her clothes on) is a divorced mother in a mobile home on the Canadian side of Niagara Falls with a teen kid (Nick Shields). Her new husband (David Keith) brings home his deranged brother (Joseph Bottoms) to live with them, and murder results. Christopher Plummer is Detective Weldon. It debuted on Showtime.

LIAR'S MOON

(Vestron, 1982) **D/S:** David Fisher **P:** Don P. Behrns

A poor kid (Matt Dillon) elopes with a banker's daughter (Cindy Fisher). With Susan Tyrrell, Hoyt Axton, Yvonne De Carlo, and Broderick Crawford.

This PG-rated Crown International film was released with alternate endings in which the girl either dies from an abortion or survives.

LIBERTY AND BASH

(Fries, 1990) **D:** Myrl A. Schreibman
S: Tina Plakinger **P:** Doug Forsythe

The people who made this comedy must have figured that *Tango and Cash* was going to be a big hit. It's about two muscular Nam vets (Miles O'Keeffe and Lou Ferrigno) who battle drug dealers in Miami. With Mitzi Kapture, Gary Conway, and Charles Dierkop. It's from the director of *Angel of HEAT.*

LICENSE TO KILL

(Sinister, 1964) **D:** Henri Decoin **S:** Jean Marcillac, André Haguet, André Legrand
France/Italy (*Nick Carter Va Tout Casser*)

Whether Eddie Constantine is playing Lemmy Caution, Nick Carter, or just Eddie, he's pretty much the same. He's cool, he's comical, and he kicks ass. Here, as Nick Carter, he battles Asian spies who are after a secret weapon. Daphne Dayle costars.

LICENSE TO KILL

(MGM/UA, 1989) **D:** John Glen **S:** Richard Maibaum
P: Albert C. Broccoli, Michael G. Wilson

After *The Living Daylights*, Timothy Dalton was James Bond for the second and last time. This is one of the most violent of the series. Carey Lowell costars, with Robert Davi as a South American drug dealer who cuts hearts out, Talisa Soto as Davi's woman, Anthony Zerbe, Don Stroud, Priscilla Barnes, Everett McGill, Cary-Hiroyuki Tagawa, Diane Lee-Hsu, and Wayne Newton as Professor Joe Butcher. David Hedison is back as Felix, and a very old-looking Desmond Llewelyn is Q again. Gladys Knight sings the title song. It was to be called *Licence Revoked*, but United Artists decided that Americans wouldn't understand that. The score is by Michael Kamen. It's 133 minutes and rated PG-13.

THE LICKERISH QUARTET

(Magnum, 1970) **D/P:** Radley Metzger
S: Michael De Forrest   US/Italy/W. Germany
(*Erotic Illusions*; *Erotic Instinct*)

I saw this stylish, pretentious, X-rated fantasy at the Detroit in Lakewood, Ohio, when it opened, and I'll never forget it. A bored couple living in an incredible castle in Italy go to a carnival with their teen son (who has seen a vision of the Virgin Mary). They see "the girl" (blond Erika Remberg) riding a motorcycle in a wall-of-death act, decide that she's the star of a stag film they like to watch at home, and bring her back to the castle. "The girl" has sex with "the boy" on the castle grounds, with "the man" in his erotic library, and with "the woman" while they watch, and then magically appear in, the stag film (which takes place during WWII). Frank Wolff (a 50s Corman actor) is "the man." This movie is sort of like an *Outer Limits* epsiode with sex and nudity. Metzger made *Little Mother* (1972) next.

LIEBESTRAUM

(MGM, 1991) **D/S/M:** Mike Figgis **P:** Eric Fellner

Kevin Anderson stars as an architect. Bill Pullman is his college friend, married to Pam Gidley. Their love triangle mirrors a double murder that occurred 40 years earlier in a creepy, condemned building. Characters have dream sequences. Also in the cast are Kim Novak (on her deathbed, throughout the movie), Catherine Hicks, and Taina Elg. The title theme is performed by Earl Bostic. The film is available in R or unrated versions with 7 extra minutes of sex.

LIES

(Key, 1983) **D/S/P:** Ken Wheat,
Jim Wheat **P:** Shelley Hermann

Ann Dusenberry is an out-of-work actress hired to play the lead in a movie being filmed in a mental hospital. Gail Strickland and Clu Gulager are behind the project, actually a scam to cheat an heiress out of her money. The actress ends up being prepared for electroshock treatments. The cast also includes Bruce Davison, Terence Knox, Bert Remsen, and Dick Miller.

LIES OF THE TWINS

(MCA, 1991) **D:** Tim Hunter **S:** Mel Frohman,
Walter Klenhard **P:** Tim Zinnemann

A model (Isabella Rossellini) becomes involved with her therapist (Aidan Quinn). She thinks she sees him with another woman, but he has an evil twin, also a psychiatrist. The film is based on a novel by Joyce Carol Oates and was made for the USA Network. With Iman, Claudia Christian, Hurd Hatfield, and Richard Harrison.

LIFEBOAT

(Fox, 1943) **D:** Alfred Hitchcock **S:** Jo Swerling **P:** Kenneth MacGowan

This technically innovative film takes place in a lifeboat containing nine people, after a freighter is sunk by a German submarine during World War II. They argue, fall in love, and starve while sharks circle. It was an effective WWII-time experimental feature with a strong message against trusting Nazis. Tallulah Bankhead stars with William Bendix, Walter Slezak as the Nazi on board, Mary Anderson, John Hodiak, Henry Hull, Heather Angel, Hume Cronyn, and Canada Lee. The director is seen in a newspaper floating by. The film is based on a story by John Steinbeck (who also worked on the script) and was released by 20th Century–Fox. It was remade as *Lifepod.*

LIFEFORCE

(Vestron, 1985) **D:** Tobe Hooper **S:** Dan O'Bannon,
Don Jakoby **P:** Golan/Globus **M:** Henry Mancini   UK

A spaceship inside Halley's comet brings a beautiful, lifeforce-sucking zombie (Mathilda May) to London. This is similar to the Professor Quatermass movie *Five Million Years to Earth* but more outrageous. Steve Railsback stars as a frantic American astronaut who tries to save the world from a plaugue of zombies, with Peter Firth, Frank Finlay, a pre–*Star Trek* Patrick Stewart, and

Michael Gothard. May spends most of the movie walking around naked (unless you see it on a commercial TV station, of course). She and other alien forces make characters disintegrate and turn all of London into a hysterical shambles. It's based on Colin Wilson's novel *The Space Vampires* and was first planned by Dino De Laurentiis, then by Cannon, to be filmed in 3-D. The soundtrack is on Varèse Sarabande. The Image laserdisc includes a 60-minute "making of" documentary about this and Hooper's *Invaders from Mars*.

THE LIFEFORCE EXPERIMENT

(1994) **D:** Piers Haggard **S:** Mike Hodges, Gerald MacDonald **P:** Nicholas Clermont   Canada

Donald Sutherland stars as a bearded scientist in Newfoundland trying to capture human energy at the point of death. Mimi Kuzyk, as a CIA agent working undercover, tries to stop him. The cast also includes Corin Nemec. First shown on the Sci-Fi channel, it's based on a Daphne Du Maurier story and was filmed in Montreal and Nova Scotia.

LIFE IS A CIRCUS

(1958) **D/S:** Val Guest **P:** E. M. Smedley-Aston   UK

Shirley Eaton stars (and sings) in this comedy/fantasy about rival circus owners. A genie (Lionel Jeffries) from a lamp uses magic to save her father's circus. With Eric Pohlman and Michael Holliday. Allied Artists released this b/w film in 1962.

LIFEPOD

(United, 1980) **D/S:** Bruce Bryant **S:** Carol Johnson

Gold Key TV made this *2001* copy. A talking pleasure computer rebels and threatens passengers on a space flight. With Kristine DeBell, Joe Penny, and Sandy Kenyon.

LIFEPOD

(Cabin Fever, 1993) **D/A:** Ron Silver **S:** Pen Densham **S/P:** M. Jay Roach

Looking at the short list of Hitchcock movies that hadn't been remade, Fox TV came up with *Lifeboat* (1944). In this version the survivors of a space-liner explosion in 2169 drift in a space pod. They argue, starve, suffocate, develop radiation scars, freeze, and die. Jessica Tuck is a reporter who videotapes what happens and narrates. One of them is a terrorist (it was a Nazi in the original). Ron Silver directs (he's no Hitchcock) and stars as a blind man. Also in the cast are Robert Loggia as a politician, Stan Shaw, CCH Pounder, Adam Storke, and Ed Gale as the best character, a dwarf mechanic with a cyborg arm.

LIFE RETURNS

(LSVideo, 1935) **D:** Eugene Frenke **S:** Arthur Horman, John F. Goodrich **P:** Lou Ostrow

This slow-moving hour-long, exploitation oddity from Universal is based on a real-life experiment conducted at the University of Southern California in 1934, in which scientists claimed that they had brought a dead dog back to life. After a lot of plot,

disgraced scientist Onslow Stevens' son's dog, Scooter, is grabbed by the dogcatcher and gassed. The actual USC footage is edited in as the dog is brought back to life. With George Breakston as the son, Valerie Hobson (from *Bride of Frankenstein*) as the wife, Frank Reicher, and Richard Quine. One of the actual USC scientists (Robert E. Cornish) and silent-film star Lois Wilson play scientists. The director sued Universal for not releasing the film properly, and a company called Scientart Pictures rereleased it in 1938. It was banned in Great Britain.

LIFESPAN

(Vestron, 1974) **D/S:** Alexander Whitlaw **S:** Judith Roscow, Alva Ruben **M:** Terry Riley US/UK/Netherlands

Hiram Keller is a young scientist trying to unlock the secret of a formula that stops the aging process. He falls for the widow (Tina Aumont) of the man who developed it, who committed suicide. Klaus Kinski is a sinister industrialist. This slow but interesting film was shot in Amsterdam.

LIFESTYLES OF THE RAMONES

(Warner, 1990) **D/P:** George Seminara **P:** Allen B. Goldman

12 Ramones videos are great to have on one tape, but this also features Johnny (at Yankee Stadium), Joey (in his living room), and Marky (working on a car) talking in between. Other celebs talk about the tremendous influence the Ramones have had since their first album changed the music world back in 1976. The videos prove how good, and how much fun, this band still is. My faves are "I Wanna Be Sedated" (what a song!), the mini-horror-movie "Psychotherapy" video (which was banned on MTV), their remake of "Time Has Come Today" (set in a church), and "Howling at the Moon." This tape introduces the new ex-Marine bass player, and past Ramones Tommy and Dee Dee aren't forgotten either.

THE LIFT

(Media, 1983) **D/S/M:** Dick Maas **P:** Matthijs Van Heijningen   Netherlands

A repairman (Huub Stapel) teams up with a reporter (Willeke Van Ammelrooy) to investigate a killer elevator in an office building. The American ads said, "For God's sake, take the stairs!" The elevator decapitates or suffocates people. Maas followed with *Amsterdamned*.

THE LIGHT AT THE EDGE OF THE WORLD

(UAV, 1971) **D:** Kevin Billington **S:** Tom Rowe **P/A:** Kirk Douglas   Spain/Liechtenstein

Kirk Douglas stars as a lighthouse keeper, in this adaptation of a Jules Verne novel. It was filmed in Spain but is set at Cape Horn, the southern tip of Argentina, in 1865. Yul Brynner leads the vicious killer pirates who are after the lighthouse. Also in the cast are Samantha Eggar as a shipwreck victim, Fernando Rey, and Victor Israel. It was originally over 2 hours long. Douglas had also been in the more successful Verne movie *20,000 Leagues Under the Sea* (1954).

LIGHT IN THE JUNGLE: THE STORY OF DR. ALBERT SCHWEITZER

(IVE, 1990) **D:** Grey Hofmyer **S:** Michel Potts **P:** Ashok Amritraj   (*Schweitzer, Out of Darkness*)

Malcolm McDowell stars as the famous humanitarian doctor in the French Congo in the late 40s. With Susan Strasberg as his wife, Andrew Davis, and John Carson. The serious PG Concorde release from executive producer Roger Corman was shot in Zimbabwe and the Ivory Coast. McDowell was usually playing psychos and madmen around the time.

LIGHTNING BOLT

(Sinister, 1965) **D:** "Anthony M. Dawson"/ Antonio Margheriti **S:** José López de la Loma **S/P:** Alfonso Balcazar   Italy/Spain (*Operazione Goldman*)

American Anthony Eisley (with dyed red hair) narrates and stars as a spy who goes undercover in Florida as a playboy to stop the sabotage of a NASA moon project. The villain with an underground city also owns a beer factory. This very 60s-looking adventure features serial-type near-death scenes, suspended animation, lots of fights and explosions, obvious models, and blurry stock footage. With Wandissa Leigh and Diana Lorys. Woolner released it in America.

THE LIGHTNING INCIDENT

(Paramount, 1991) **D:** Michael Switzer **S:** Michael Murray **P:** O. B. Weiss

The baby of a psychic Santa Fe sculptor (Nancy McKeon) living in an isolated house is kidnapped by a Hispanic cult of Devil worshippers for a sacrifice. After her husband and other people are killed with voodoo and reptiles, she goes to "the City of Lost Souls" in Central America (alone), where a blind sculptor teaches her to use her psychic power during a lightning storm. With Polly Bergen as her depressed mother, Elpidia Carrillo, Tantoo Cardinal, Tim Ryan, and Gary Clarke. This cable-TV movie, filmed in Arizona, doesn't rate high in the sense department.

LIGHTNING SWORDS OF DEATH

(VSOM, 1972) **D:** Kenji Misumi **P:** Shintaro Katsu **S:** Kazuo Koike, Gohseki Kojima   Japan (*Baby Cart: Lend a Child, Lend an Arm*)

The video poster for this one claims, "Adventures in butchery along a trail of gore!!" It's the first of a series that will be surprising to novice Western viewers. (We found the JA video version, *Lupin Wolf*, in our favorite Korean video store, dubbed into English.) Tomisaburo Wakayama is Ito Ogami, "the Lone Wolf," a master swordsman who roams the countryside with his baby in a specially rigged killer carriage. Mercenary samurai ambush and rape some women. When Ito arrives an honorable samurai who hated the others kills the women (they would have been too ashamed to live) and, despite asking to die, is spared by Ito. Then he protects a female slave who bit off the tongue of the man who bought her. The original owner, a female gang leader, wants her back and submits Ito to a hard-to-watch ceremonial punishment. After being hung upside down, beaten, and dunked under water, he doesn't even cry out, and she's so impressed that she hires him to help avenge her father's death. Everything ends in an amazing, large-scale battle with Ito and his child against a massive army fighting with martial arts, swords, and even guns. He, of course, also has to face the humiliated samurai he spared. It's hard to follow the strict codes and mixed allegiances, but the Lone Wolf movies are gorier than most horror movies and more complex than most martial arts movies, and they have more action than any modern cop movie. Part II, *Baby Cart in the Land of Demons/Baby Cart at the River Styx* (1972), by the same director, was released in America as *Shogun Assassin* (in 1982), with scenes from Part I added. These and the four other sequels are all available (subtitled) from Video Search. They are: Part III, *Flying on the Wind of Death in a Baby Cart/Baby Cart to Hades* (l972); Part IV, *Heart of a Parent, Heart of a Child* (1972); Part V, *Tread Lightly on the Path to Hell* (1973); and Part VI, *Daigoro, We're Going into Hell!* (1973). Comic books were translated and released in America too. (See also *Lone Wolf and Child: Final Conflict.*)

LIGHT OF DAY

(Vestron, 1987) **D/S:** Paul Schrader
P: Rob Cohen, Keith Barish

Rocker Joan Jett stars as a bar-band leader who wants to tour and get out of Cleveland. Michael J. Fox (as her brother) and Michael McKean are also in the band. The group has equipment problems and personality clashes and falls apart while staying in crummy motels. Gena Rowlands is their dying, religious mother. With Jason Miller and Del Close as a doctor. Bruce Springsteen wrote the title song. Most of this PG-13 film was shot in Chicago. CBS released the soundtrack.

THE LIGHT OF FAITH

(Sinister, 1922) **D/S:** Clarence Brown **S:** William Dudley Pelley   (*The Light in the Dark*)

Lon Chaney stars in this 33-minute silent film, which was shown (in an edited version) to religious groups in the 30s. Hope Hampton costars, with E. K. Lincoln. The screenwriter founded a fascist organization, the Silver Shirts.

LIGHTS OUT!

(Goodtimes)

Only 2 episodes of this live NBC-TV anthology series (1949–52) are on tape. The series was based on Arch Oboler's famous radio show.

LIKE FATHER, LIKE SON

(RCA, 1987) **D:** Rod Daniel **S:** Lorne Cameron, Steven L. Bloom **P:** Brian Grazer

In yet another of those never-too-funny 80s bodyswitch comedies, an Indian drug causes a heart surgeon (Dudley Moore) and his teen son (Kirk

Leslie Parrish, Jerry Lewis, and Julie Newmar in *Li'l Abner*.

Cameron) to exchange personalities. With Catherine Hicks, Patrick O'Neal, Sean Astin, and Cami Cooper. Daniel also directed the awful *Teen Wolf* and *K-9*.

LIKE IT IS

(SW, 1968) **D/S/C:** William Rotsler **P:** Chris Warfield

This hippie mondo movie with lots of drugs and complete nudity is made up of 72 minutes of b/w and color 16mm mail-order adults-only shorts that Rotsler had made. Narration was added.

L'IL ABNER

(Viking, 1940) **D:** Albert S. Rogell
S: Charles Kerr, Tyler Johnson

Granville Owen is L'il Abner and Martha O'Driscoll is Daisy Mae, in this hillbilly comedy based on Al Capp's comic strip. It's not very good, but it has a very odd cast of comedians, including Buster Keaton as Lonesome Polecat, Edgar Kennedy as Cornelius Cornpone, Chester Conklin, Lucien Littlefield, Johnny Arthur, Mickey Daniels, Al

"Fuzzy" St. John, and Doodles Weaver. The theme song was cowritten by Milton Berle. This RKO release was later picked up by Astor and played in small towns as late as the 50s. Columbia made five L'il Abner cartoons in 1944. Cut versions are on tape.

L'IL ABNER

(Paramount, 1959) **D:** Melvin Frank
S/P: Norman Panama

Dogpatch is chosen by the government for A-bomb tests, in this Technicolor version of the 1956 musical by Johnny Mercer and Gene De Paul, based on Al Capp's characters. Most of the Broadway cast are in the film, including Peter Palmer as L'il Abner, Leslie Parrish as Daisy Mae, Julie Newmar as Stupefyin' Jones, Stella Stevens as Appassionata Von Climax (Tina Louise played the role on the stage), and Stubby Kaye as Marryin' Sam. The women look great, the songs are good, and the plot is surprisingly anti-government. Mammy Yokum has visions, and Evil-Eye Fleagle puts the whammy on people. Jerry Lewis is a guest star.

LILIOM

(Sinister, 1934) **D/S:** Fritz Lang **P:** Erich
Pommer **M:** Rudolph Maté

When Fritz Lang fled Germany in 1933, he first
went to France where he made this version of Ferenc Molnár's play. The same story had been filmed
in Hollywood by director Frank Borzage (1930)
and was later turned into the Rodgers and Ham-
merstein musical *Carousel* (1956). Charles Boyer
stars as Liliom, a carnival barker who is fired,
turns to a life of crime, and kills himself to avoid
capture by the police. He stands trial in Heaven,
where his misdeeds are shown to him repeatedly
(on film). After 16 years in Purgatory he's allowed
to return to Earth to do a good deed, and he meets
his grown-up daughter. The film is in French. It
was originally 2 hours long, but the video available
in the US is 85 minutes. Lang, producer Erich
Pommer (also a German refugee), and Boyer all
went to Hollywood in 1934. The Polish-born Maté
arrived in 1935.

LIMIT UP

(Virgin, 1989) **D/S/A:** Richard Martini
S/A: Luana Anders **P:** Jonathan D. Krane

A Chicago Board of Trade worker (Nancy Allen)
makes a deal with an emissary of the Devil (Dani-
tra Vance). This PG-13 comedy also features Dean
Stockwell, Brad Hall, Ray Charles (as God!),
Rance Howard, Luana Anders (billed as Lu), Sally
Kellerman, and Ava Fabian.

THE LINCOLN CONSPIRACY

(1977) **D:** James L. Conway
S: Jonathan Cobbler **P:** Charles E.
Sellier Jr., Raymond D. Jensen

Bradford Dillman is John Wilkes Booth, in this
G-rated "speculative fiction" feature from Sunn
Classics. It was advertised as depicting "the true
facts, which were covered up for 110 years!"
Booth doesn't die in a fire but escapes to Canada.
John Anderson costars as Lincoln, with Robert
Middleton, John Dehner, and Whit Bissell.

LINDA AND ABILENE

(1969) **D:** "Mark Hansen"/Herschell G.
Lewis **P:** Thomas J. Dowd

This western about incest was filmed on the famous Spahn ranch. Sharon Matt and Kip Marsh
are an orphaned brother and sister, and Roxanne
Jones is a bar girl. It's similar to David Friedman's
The Ramrodder, from the same year.

LINDA LOVELACE FOR PRESIDENT

(Selectatape, 1976) **D:** Claudio Guzman **S:** Jack
Margolis **P:** David Winters, Charles Stroud

Yes, this is a real movie, filmed partially in Kansas
City and once available in X, R, or PG versions.
It's a silly, anything-goes comedy that insults every
known minority and is filled with endless sex
jokes, nudity, sex, kung fu, a dwarf, a talking
chimp, H-bomb footage, and guest stars. Scatman
Crothers does an all-rhyming routine in a pool
hall. Ex-Monkee Micky Dolenz acts goofy and is

Anne Carlisle as Jimmy in *Liquid Sky.*

seen with a naked girl. Joe E. Ross (from the TV
series *Car 54, Where Are You?*) is teamed with
Louis Quinn (from *77 Sunset Strip*), and Chuck
McCann plays two roles. There's also Marty Ingels
(*I'm Dickens, He's Fenster*), Robbie Lee (*Switchblade Sisters*), and former JFK impressionist
Vaughn Meader having sex with Lovelace and
singing "Nearer My God to Thee." Surprisingly,
some of this mess is funny. Lovelace, the original
porno star, is likable in the comic role and sexy in
the soft-core scenes. Producer Winters was married to Lovelace at the time. He formed AIP video
in 1986. Executive producer Arthur Marks directed Pam Grier and Fred Williamson hits. Dolenz was later in the Monkees reunion, and he
recorded a children's album in 1992.

LINE OF FIRE: *See* THE SWAP

THE LINGUINI INCIDENT

(Academy, 1991) **D/S:** Richard Shepard
S: Tamar Brott **P:** Arnold Orgolini

Rosanna Arquette stars in this NYC comedy with
Desperately Seeking Susan touches. She's a
waitress who's obsessed with Houdini and plans a
robbery. With David Bowie (looking old) as a bartender, Eszter Balint, Marlee Matlin, Buck Henry,
Viveca Lindfors, André Gregory, Julian Lennon,
and Iman.

LINK

(HBO, 1986) **D/P:** Richard Franklin
S: Everett De Roche **M:** Jerry Goldsmith

Terence Stamp is a scientist working in an isolated
mansion in Scotland. Elisabeth Shue is the student
caretaker. Link, one of three trained chimps (actually an orangutan), discovers he's going to die for
science, so he takes over, killing anyone in his way.
The score is on Varèse Sarabande, and the Kinks'
"Apeman" is heard.

LIONHEART

(Warner, 1987) **D:** Franklin J. Schaffner
S: Menno Meyjes, Richard Outten **P:** Stanley
O'Toole, Talia Shire **M:** Jerry Goldsmith

In the 12th century, a group of kids search for King
Richard I. Eric Stoltz stars, with Gabriel Byrne
as the evil "Black Prince," Deborah Barrymore,
Nicholas Clay, and Sammi Davis. This PG adventure was the last Taliafilm from Shire.

LIONHEART

(MCA, 1990) **D/S:** Shelton Lettich
S/A: Jean-Claude Van Damme **P:** Ash R. Shaw,
Eric Karson   (*A.W.O.L.; The Wrong Bet*)

Jean-Claude Van Damme is a Foreign Legionnaire
who deserts and becomes a professional bare-
knuckle streetfighter to save his brother. Harrison
Page costars, with Deborah Rennard (daughter of
Roger Moore), Lisa Pelikan, Jeff Speakman, and
Billy Blanks. It's from Universal.

LION OF THE DESERT

(1979) **D/P:** Moustapha Akkad
S: H. A. L. Craig   Libya/UK

Anthony Quinn stars as the real-life Omar Mukh-
tar, the leader of Libyan rebels who fought the
Italians from 1911 to 1931. Rod Steiger plays
Mussolini (as he did in the 1977 Italian film
The Last Four Days). This 162-minute Khaddafy-
backed production, filmed in Libya, features Oliver Reed, John Gielgud, Irene Papas, and Raf
Vallone. Akkad also made *The Message* (1976)
with Quinn and Pappas and backed the *Halloween*
movies in America. Maurice Jarre wrote the score.

LIPSTICK

(Paramount, 1976) **D:** Lamont Johnson
S: David Rayfiel **P:** Freddie Fields

A model (Margaux Hemingway) goes through a courtroom ordeal after being raped. The music teacher perp (Chris Sarandon) is acquitted and later rapes her younger sister (Mariel Hemingway), so Margaux shoots him in the crotch with a shotgun (as in dozens of other revenge movies). This Dino De Laurentiis production received publicity because it was the acting debut of Margaux (a former model) and Mariel. The ads said, "It isn't always an invitation to a kiss." With Perry King and Anne Bancroft as the prosecuting attorney.

LIPSTICK CAMERA

(Triboro, 1993) **D/S:** Mike Bonifer
S: L. G. Weaver **P:** Victoria Maxwell

A cute, innocent-looking pushy young woman (Ele Keats) wants to work in TV news. She borrows a tiny camera from her frustrated video-nut friend (bearded Corey Feldman) and obtains incriminating photos that two killers, former East German Stasi spies (Terry O'Quinn and Sandahl Bergman) are after. The cast also includes Brian Wimmer as a cameraman, Richard Portnow, and Charlotte Lewis. Billed as an "erotic thriller," it has no nudity, but Keats is very good.

THE LIQUIDATOR

(1966) **D:** Jack Cardiff **S:** Peter
Yeldham **P:** Jon Penington   UK

Rod Taylor stars as a war vet who hates bloodshed. Hired by Trevor Howard to be a James Bond type of assassin, he's supplied with a penthouse, cars, and women, and takes Jill St. John (who turns out to be a master spy) to the Riviera. Also with Wilfrid Hyde-White, Akim Tamiroff, Daniel Emilfork, and Suzy Kendall. Shirley Bassey (*Goldfinger*) sings the theme song.

LIQUID DREAMS

(Academy, 1991) **D:** Mark Manos
S: Zack Davis **P:** Zane W. Levitt

There are elements of *Twin Peaks, The Atomic Cafe,* and *Videodrome* in this would-be cult film. Candice Daly goes undercover as a stripper at the Twilight Club to investigate the murder of her sister. The strippers have to live in an apartment complex where TV screens show endless sex videos with subliminal messages. Some characters are "endorphin junkies." The R-rated version I saw has no nudity. Maybe the unrated version is better, but this film is badly written and directed, and is pretty boring. With Richard Steinmetz as a detective, Tracey Walter, and John Waters regular Mink Stole. John Doe and Paul Bartel have a scene each. Cassian Elwes was the executive producer.

LIQUID SKY

(Media, 1982) **D/S/P:** Slava Tsukerman
S/A: Anne Carlisle **S:** Nina V. Kerova

Tiny aliens land on a windowsill and live off an addictive substance produced by human brains during orgasm. It all takes place around the downtown NYC art and fashion scenes. Anne Carlisle stars as a bisexual punk model, Margaret, and a gay male model, Jimmy. The double role is in the spirit of

Homicidal and is very well done. With Paula E. Sheppard (*Alice, Sweet Alice*). The first American film by the Russian director was a midnight cult hit in NYC and a soundtrack was released.

LISA

(CBS/Fox, 1990) **D/S:** Gary Sherman
S: Karen Clark **P:** Frank Yablans

A 14-year-old (Staci Keanan) phones a stranger and poses as an older woman. Her phone suitor (D. W. Moffett) turns out to be "the candlelight killer." With Cheryl Ladd as her mom, Jeffrey Tambor, Edan Gross, and Elizabeth Gracen. This PG-13 United Artists release is mostly talk.

LISETTE

(1961) **D/S/P:** John Hough

John Agar is a married newspaperman who falls for a "Eurasian beauty" (Greta Chi) imported as a publicity gimmick. This obscure drama was made in Florida. Agar also sings the theme song, written by Les Baxter.

LISZTOMANIA

(Warner, 1975) **D/S:** Ken Russell **P:** Roy Baird   UK

After the hit musical *Tommy,* Russell returned to his series of irreverent, loony biographies. Roger Daltry (of The Who) is the 19th-century Hungarian composer and pianist Franz Liszt. The film includes his active love life and his relationship with his son-in-law Richard Wagner (Paul Nicholas). There are typical Russell dream sequences and Hitler references. This was the first film with a Dolby stereo soundtrack. With Sara Kestelman, Fiona Lewis, Ringo Starr (as the Pope!), Rick Wakeman (who wrote the score), Anulka Dzubinski (*Vampyres*), Nell Campbell, and Karen Mayo-Chandler. Russell's next film was another biography, *Valentino* (1977).

LITTLE ANGEL

(1957) **D/S:** Roberto Rodríguez **D:** Ken
Smith **S:** José Luis Celis, Rafael García
Travesi   Mexico (*La Sonrisa de la Virgen*)

K. Gordon Murray imported this drama about a miracle and added new scenes and narration by Hugh Downs, host of the TV show *Concentration* at the time (1962). After Marita (María García), a poor farm girl, talks to a statue of the Virgin, her cow gives birth. Rodríguez also directed the *Little Red Riding Hood* series, also starring Garcia.

LITTLE CIGARS

(1974) **D:** Chris Christenberry **S:** Louis
Garfinkle, Frank Ray Perilli **P:** Albert Band

Blond Angel Tompkins, the former mistress of a gangster (Joe De Santis), leads a gang of dwarf robbers. The little guys have a medicine show. Some do slapstick comedy while others steal cars. Tompkins and Billy Curtis have an affair in San Francisco and plot bank, casino, and movie-theater jobs. The other stars are Jerry Meren, Angelo Rossitto, Frank Delfino, Felix Silla, and Emory Souza. AIP released the unique PG-rated feature.

LITTLE DARLINGS

(Paramount, 1980) **D:** Ronald F. Maxwell **S:** Kimi
Peck, Darlene Young **P:** Stephen J. Friedman

This was Paramount's rival to United Artists's *Foxes,* from the same year. Will rich kid Ferris (Tatum O'Neal) or Angel (Kristy McNichol) lose her virginity first? That's the big question in this summer-camp movie with Armand Assante, Matt Dillon, Cynthia Nixon, and Nicolas Coster. With songs by Blondie, John Lennon, and others.

LITTLE DEVILS

(1991) **D/P:** Fred Olen Ray **S:** Mark Thomas McGee

Veronica Carothers plays twin roles in this horror comedy. Also in the cast are Robert Vaughn as the Devil, Priscilla Barnes, Suzanne Ager, Ruth Collins, Michelle Bauer, and Jay Richardson. Vaughn worked mostly in South Africa during the 80s and did hour-long TV infomercials for the "Helsinki formula" baldness remedy.

THE LITTLE DRAGONS

(Active, 1980) **D/P:** Curtis Hanson **S:** Harvey
Applebaum, Louis G. Atlee, Rudolph Borchert,
Alan Ormsby **P:** Hannah Hempstead

Karate experts rescue a girl kidnapped by Ann Sothern and her sons (Joe Spinell and John Chandler), who live together in a car. With Master Bong Soon Han, Charles Lane, and Chris Petersen. Tony Bill was an executive producer of this PG action comedy and also appears. Martial-arts movies for kids didn't really catch on until the 90s.

THE LITTLE DRUMMER GIRL

(Warner, 1983) **D:** George Roy Hill
S: Loring Mandel **P:** Robert L. Crawford

Diane Keaton stars as a pro-Palestinian American actress recruited by an Israeli counterintelligence offficer (Klaus Kinski) to trap a terrorist. This long (130-minute) movie is based on John Le Carré's bestselling novel (and he has an acting role). Also with Sami Frey, Thorley Walters, and Anna Massey. It was filmed in Israel, Greece, Lebanon, and other countries.

LITTLE LAURA AND BIG JOHN

(United, 1972) **D/S:** Luke Moberly,
Bob Woodburn **P:** Lou Wiethes

Karen Black and Fabian star in a *Bonnie and Clyde* copy about the turn-of-the-century Ashley gang in Florida (where this low-budget feature was made). Fabian had just starred in another period gangster movie, *A Bullet for Pretty Boy* (made in Texas).

LITTLE MONSTERS

(MGM/UA, 1989) **D:** Richard Alan Greenberg
S: Terry Rossio, Ted Elliot **P:** Jeffrey Mueller

Howie Mandel is a monster under a bed in this PG *Beetlejuice* copy. A kid (Fred Savage) living with his family in an old house finds him on Halloween and meets other creatures. With Daniel Stern, Margaret Whitton, and Frank Whaley.

LITTLE NEMO: ADVENTURES IN SLUMBERLAND

(Hemdale, 1992) **D:** Masami Hata, William T. Hurtz **S:** Chris Columbus, Richard Outten **P:** Yutaka Fujioka   Japan

Winsor McCay's incredible comic strip from the early 1900s becomes an expensive, G-rated animated musical with a new character, Nemo's flying-squirrel companion. The confused credits say that it's based on a story by (French comic-book artist) Moebius and Fujioka and derived from a concept by Ray Bradbury, who was advised by story consultants including Robert Towne. The main voices are supplied by Gabriel Damon as Nemo, Mickey Rooney as Flip, and René Auberjonois as Professor Genuis.

LITTLE NOISES

(Prism, 1991) **D/S:** Jane Spencer **S:** Jon Zeiderman **P:** Michael Spielberg

Crispin Glover completely dominates this odd comedy as a down-and-out NYC writer living in Hoboken who wants to impress his friend (Tatum O'Neal) with a book of poems. The small role was her first in many years. With Rik Mayall as his agent, John C. McGinley, Steven Schub, and Tate Donovan.

THE LITTLE PRINCE

(1974) **D/P:** Stanley Donen **S:** Alan Jay Lerner   UK

Paramount released this G-rated musical fantasy based on the story by Antoine de Saint Exupéry. Stephen Warner is the prince from a faraway star and Richard Kiley is the aviator who guides him. With Bob Fosse as the snake, Gene Wilder as the fox, Joss Ackland, Clive Revill, and Victor Spinetti.

LITTLE RED RIDING HOOD

(UAV, 1959) **D:** Roberto Rodríguez **S:** Fernando Morales Ortiz, Ricardo Garibay   Mexico (*La Caperucita Roja*)

K. Gordon Murray released this musical fantasy in America. Manuel "Loco" Valdez is a nasty wolf with a long tongue, teamed with Stinky the Skunk. María García stars. Sequels are *Little Red Riding Hood and Her Friends* (1959), *Little Red Riding Hood and the Monsters* (1960), and *Caperuceta Sus Tres Amigos*, the only one not dubbed into English. There are also German versions of this fairy tale made in the early 50s and an 80s Faerie Tale Theatre version (Fox).

LITTLE SHOP OF HORRORS

(Warner, 1986) **D:** Frank Oz **S:** Howard Ashman **M:** Alan Menken **P:** David Geffen

This PG-13 musical comedy, set in 60s NYC, is adapted from the 1982 off-Broadway musical, which was based on the 1960 Roger Corman cult movie. Incredibly, no credit is given to the original scriptwriter, Charles B. Griffith! Rick Moranis stars as Seymour Krelborn, a nerd who raises a man-eating plant in the flower shop where he works. He loves Audrey (Ellen Greene, from the stage production), who also works there. Also in the cast are Vincent Gardenia as Mushnik the flor-

ist, Steve Martin as Audrey's sadistic dentist/biker boyfriend, Jim Belushi, John Candy, Christopher Guest, Bill Murray, and a singing trio (featuring Tisha Campbell) named Crystal, Chiffon, and Ronette. Levi Stubbs (of the Four Tops) provides the voice of the plant, Audrey Jr. The soundtrack is on Geffen. An expensive sequence showing the giant plant attacking Manhattan at the end was deleted before the film's release. Lyricist Howard Ashman died of AIDS.

LIVE A LITTLE, STEAL A LOT

(1975) **D:** Marvin Chomsky **S:** E. Arthur Kean **P:** J. Skeet Wilson   (*Murph the Surf; You Can't Steal Love*)

Robert Conrad and Don Stroud star in an AIP movie based on real-life Florida beach bums who became jewel thieves and stole the Star of India. Also with Donna Mills, Luther Adler, Burt Young, and Paul Stewart. Motown released the soundtrack. Stroud was in many AIP films at the time. Conrad was in *Sudden Death* next.

LIVE BY THE FIST

(New Horizons, 1993) **D/P:** Cirio H. Santiago **S:** Charles Philip Moore   Philippines

In executive producer Roger Corman's remake of his *Forced to Fight*, kickboxer Jerry Trimble stars as a navy vet framed and thrown into prison on an island. George Takei is a wise prison inmate who teaches him non-violence, and Laura Albert is an Amnesty International worker.

LIVE! FROM DEATH ROW

(ABC, 1991) **D/S:** Patrick Duncan **P:** Julie Bilson Ahlberg

A TV tabloid-show hostess (Joanna Cassidy) is taken hostage while interviewing a serial killer (Bruce Davison) condemned to the electric chair. This ABC-TV movie costars Art LaFleur.

THE LIVELY SET

(1964) **D:** Jack Arnold **S:** Mel Goldberg, William Wood **P:** William Alland

James Darren stars as a race-car builder and driver who falls for Pamela Tiffin, in this comedy/drama with Doug McClure, Joanie Sommers, Marilyn Maxwell, Ross Elliot, and Greg Morris. Bobby Darin sings on the soundtrack, and the Surfaris sing "Boss Barracuda."

LIVE WIRE

(New Line, 1992) **D:** Christian Duguay **S:** Bart Baker **P:** Suzanne Todd, David Willis   Canada

Pierce Brosnan stars as an FBI explosives expert in Washington where politicians are blowing up after drinking liquid explosives. Ben Cross is the brains behind it all, and Ron Silver is a corrupt congressman making time with Brosnan's ex-wife (Lisa Eilbacher). With pretty good FX, exploding clowns, real scenes of international terrorism, and a clip from *Reefer Madness*. Al Waxman, Michael St. Gerard, Tony Plana, Tracy Tweed, and Nels Van

Patten are also in the cast. It's by the director of the *Scanners* sequels. It was filmed in Canada and debuted on HBO. R and unrated versions are available.

THE LIVING DAYLIGHTS

(MGM/UA, 1987) **D:** John Glen **S:** Richard Maibaum **P:** Albert R. Broccoli, Michael G. Wilson

When Timothy Dalton played James Bond for the first time, it was a nice change after too many Roger Moore movies. This was released on the 25th anniversary of the first Bond film, *Dr. No.* The plot concerns good and bad KGB agents. Maryam D'Abo (who was in a typical *Playboy* tie-in shoot) costars as Kara, with Jeroen Krabbe as a good-guy villain, Joe Don Baker, John Rhys-Davies, Virginia Hey (*Road Warrior*), and Catherine Rabett. There's a safe-sex scene. This 130-minute PG movie was shot in Gibraltar, Morocco, America, Italy, and Austria. *25 Years of James Bond*, a compilation soundtrack album, was released by Bainbridge the same year.

THE LIVING DEAD

(1932) **D:** Richard Oswald **P:** Gabriel Pascal Germany (*Fünf Unheimliche Geschichten; Unholy Tales*)

Paul Wegener is a mad scientist who kills his wife and walls her up. He goes on the run, followed by a reporter, and turns up in other adaptations of tales by Poe and Stevenson, including "The Black Cat," "Dr. Tarr and Professor Feather," and "The Suicide Club." This rare horror anthology wasn't released in America until 1940, in a badly dubbed and edited version. Scenes were used in *Dr. Terror's House of Horrors* (1943). Oswald and Pascal fled Germany in 1934.

THE LIVING DEAD

(Sinister, 1934) **D:** Thomas Bentley **S:** Frank Miller   UK

An evil doctor puts people into a death-like state. The famous stage actor Gerald Du Maurier stars, with George Curzon. It's based on a play.

LIVING DOLL

(1989) **D:** Peter Litten, George Dugdale **S:** Bob Greenberg **P:** Dick Randall   UK

Mark Jax stars as a lonely medical student working in a NYC morgue. He has a shrine to the hospital flower seller he loves. She shows up dead in the morgue, and after she's buried he digs up her moldy body and takes it home. Eartha Kitt plays his landlady. It's by the makers of *Slaughter High* (1986).

THE LIVING IDOL

(1957) **D/S/P:** Albert Lewin **P:** Gregorio Walterstein

Steve Forrest stars in this tale about a reincarnated Maya princess (Liliane Montevecchi) and a jaguar god. Also with James Robertson-Justice. René Cardona Sr. was an associate director of this color MGM release film, shot in Mexico. It's based on a novel by Lewin, who directed *The Picture of Dorian Gray* (1942).

LIVING TO DIE

(PM, 1990) **D/A:** Wings Hauser **S:** Stephen Smoke **P:** Richard Pepin, Joseph Merhi

Wings Hauser stars as a burned-out Las Vegas private eye involved in a blackmail plot, with Darcy Demoss as a "dead" hooker, Wendy MacDonald as a cop, and Asher Brauner. There's lots of nudity and blood.

LIVING VENUS

(SW, 1960) **D/P:** Herschell Gordon Lewis

William Kerwin stars as a Hugh Hefner type who starts a magazine called *Pagan* with a photographer (Harvey Korman, in his film debut). The new publisher leaves his fiancée, marries his star model, Peggy, and angers his partner, who quits. Later the magazine fails, and Peggy commits suicide. Danica D'Hont (a French Canadian) is the main attraction as Peggy. With Linne Nanette Ahlstrand (who was in *Playboy* and *Beast from the Haunted Cave*) and Billy Falbo. It was made in Chicago (home of *Playboy*). Joe Bob introduces some video-release prints. Lewis added nudity to his next feature, *The Adventures of Lucky Pierre* (1961) and had a hit.

LOADED GUNS

(1974) **D/S:** Fernando di Leo   Italy (*Colpo di Canna*)

Ursula Andress stars as an airline stewardess and secret agent who's after drug traffickers, with Marc Porel and Woody Strode as a gangland enforcer. This action film was cut for a PG rating in America, so Ursula's nude scenes are missing.

LOBSTER MAN FROM MARS

(I.V.E., 1989) **D:** Stanley Sheef **S:** Bob Greenburg **P:** Eyal Rimmon, Steven S. Greene

A young amateur filmmaker shows his movie to a producer (Tony Curtis), who decides to release it as a tax loss (as in *The Producers*). The film within a film is a fun, in-joke-filled nod to *Teenagers from Outer Space, Robot Monster,* and *It Conquered the World*. Deborah Foreman and Anthony Hickox (a young director in real life) star, with Patrick Macnee, Billy Barty, Phil Proctor, Bobby "Boris" Pickett (as the king of Mars), Skip Young (Wally from the TV series *Ozzie and Harriet)*, Ava Fabian, and the voice of Dr. Demento. They even used Bronson Canyon for a location. But the *Robot Monster* clone is way too skinny! The movie opens with a remake of the B-52's "Rock Lobster."

THE LOCH NESS HORROR

(Monterey, 1982) **D/S/P:** Larry Buchanan **S:** Lynn Schubert   (*Nessie*)

Characters spend a lot of time talking, and when the Loch Ness monster shows up it's really unconvincing. With Sandy Kenyon and Stuart Lancaster. The executive producer was Jane Buchanan, and Barry Buchanan acts. The Texas filmmakers' next was *Beyond the Doors*.

LOCK AND LOAD

(AIP, 1990) **D/S:** David Prior **S:** John Cianetti **P:** Kimberly Casey

It's boring, it's filled with talk, and it rips off *Telefon.* Jack Vogel (who is way too young for the role) stars as a Nam vet who has nightmares with bloody-faced zombies. Hypnotic suggestions are given to soldiers on the phone so that they'll commit crimes and then kill themselves. A bag of money in a car that blows up is removed intact. The cops don't notice. With Renee Cline and Jeffrey Smith. It was filmed in Denver.

LOCK UP

(IVE, 1989) **D:** John Flynn **S:** Richard Smith, Jeb Stuart, Henry Rosenblum **P:** Lawrence Golden, Charles Golden

Sylvester Stallone is a convict about to be paroled who is transfered to a high-security prison. He's such a good guy that he was first arrested for helping an old man who was being beaten up, and he escapes from prison to visit his dying father, then returns. Donald Sutherland is the sadistic warden who makes life hell for him. With John Amos, Sonny Landham (in his biggest non-porno role), and Darlanne Fluegel. Real inmates of New Jersey's Rahway State Prison play inmates. The Tri-Star release was a box-office flop.

THE LODGER

(Video Yesteryear, 1926) **D/S:** Alfred Hitchcock **S:** Eliot Stannard **P:** Michael Balcon   UK

Ivor Novello plays a mysterious stranger who may be Jack the Ripper. Hitchcock's first suspense thriller (it was his third film) uses advanced visual tricks like a see-through glass floor. A jealous detective (Malcolm Keen) accuses the lodger of being a killer, and a bloodthirsty mob attacks the man at the end. This silent film is based on a novel by Marie Belloc-Lowndes. It was remade in Britain in 1932 (again with Novello) and in America in 1944 (with Laird Cregar) and 1954 (with Jack Palance), as *Man in the Attic.*

LOIS AND CLARK: THE NEW ADVENTURES OF SUPERMAN

(1993) **D:** Robert Butler **S:** Deborah Le Vine **P:** Mel Efros, Thania St. John

Dean Cain and Teri Hatcher star as young Superman and sexy Lois Lane, with John Shea as Lex Luthor, Lane Smith as editor Perry White, and Tracy Scoggins. This is the pilot for an ABC-TV series stressing romance and light comedy over science fiction and crime.

LOLA

(1970) **D:** Richard Donner **S:** Norman Thaddeus Vane **P:** Clive Sharp   UK/Italy (*Twinky*)

Charles Bronson, in his first film after the magnificent *Once Upon a Time in the West,* is a 38-year-old American novelist who marries a 16-year-old English schoolgirl named Twinky (Susan George). The movie shows how their families take it. Bronson looked (and was) 49, and no major American company wanted it, so AIP released it in 1971 with a new title chosen to make people think of *Lolita*. The cast also includes Michael Craig, Trevor Howard, Jack Hawkins, Honor Blackman, Lionel Jeffries, Robert Morley, Paul Ford, Kay Medford, and Orson Bean.

LOLITA

(Voyager, 1962) **D:** Stanley Kubrick **S:** Vladimir Nabokov **P:** James B. Harris   UK

James Mason is British professor Humbert Humbert, who becomes obsessed with teen "nymphet" Dolores "Lolita" Haze (Sue Lyon) and marries her mother (Shelley Winters). Peter Sellers is devious playwright Clare Quilty, a master of disguises. Based on Vladimir Nabokov's 1955 novel, the film is told in flashbacks and is set in New Hampshire and Ohio. This b/w classic is visually impressive (of course) and very funny. Kubrick next made the more challenging films *Dr. Strangelove* (1963, also with Sellers), *2001* (1969), and *A Clockwork*

Sue Lyon is *Lolita.*

Orange (1971), all filmed in England. *Lolita* is 152 minutes long and is available on video and on Criterion laserdisc.

LONDON KILLS ME

(Live, 1991) **D/S:** Hanif Kureishi **P:** Tim Bevan   UK

A group of young people crash in an apartment above a meditation center, sell drugs, and rip off tourists. Justin Chadwick stars as the pathetic Clint, with Steven Mackintosh (who looks like Brian Jones) as Muffdiver, Emer McCourt as the heroin-addict girlfriend they share, Fiona Shaw, and Brad Dourif. There's an Elvis-impersonator stepfather. Kureishi wrote the screenplays for *My Beautiful Laundrette* (1985) and *Sammy and Rosie Get Laid* (1987).

LONELY HEARTS

(Live, 1991) **D/S/P:** Andrew Lane **S:** R. E. Daniels **P:** Robert Kenner

Eric Roberts stars as a con man who seduces women for their money. Beverly D'Angelo is conned by him and then helps him with his schemes. Joanna Cassidy is a private eye who's after him. Also with Charles Napier, Robert Ginty, Bibi Besch, Sharon Farrell (who has a topless scene), and Rebecca Street. It was made for cable TV.

THE LONELY HEARTS BANDITS

(1950) **D:** George Blair **S:** Gene Lewis

It's nowhere near as good, but this obscure Republic movie is based on the same actual events as *The Honeymoon Killers* (1970). John Eldredge and Dorothy Patrick are two grifters who join forces, posing as brother and sister. He marries widows, and then they kill them for their money. With Ann Doran, William Schallert, Kathleen Freeman, and Barbara Fuller. Eldredge played supporting roles in many films, including the 40s horror movies *The Black Cat* and *The Mad Doctor of Market Street*.

THE LONELY LADY

(MCA, 1983) **D:** Peter Sasdy **S:** John Kershaw, Shawn Robbins **P:** Robert R. Weston

Pia Zadora is a would-be screenwriter who goes to bed with nasty Hollywood men (and women) to get where she wants to go. She's even raped by a garden hose. This trashy movie is based on a Harold Robbins novel and was shot in Italy. With Jared Martin, Lloyd Bochner, Bibi Besch, and Ray Liotta. The Universal movie was the only Pia vehicle to receive a major release. Sasdy also directed Hammer horror movies.

THE LONELY MAN

(1957) **D:** Henry Levin **S:** Harry Essex, Robert Smith

Jack Palance stars as a gunfighter trying to reform, and his son is played by Anthony Perkins! If that isn't enough, the cast also includes Neville Brand, Lee Van Cleef, Elisha Cook Jr., Claude Akins, and Robert Middleton. From Paramount.

THE LONELY SEX

(SW, 1959) **D/S/P/C:** Richard L. Hilliard

A childish, depressed guy who wears only black and lives in a shack dreams that he kills (I think) and kidnaps a girl. Meanwhile, a balding, bearded voyeur boarder in the house where she lives is a killer who watches a stripper undress (twice). This minimal b/w film has very little dialogue and some arty shots and acting that make it resemble a 20s silent movie. It was released by Joseph Brenner and is by the director of *Psychomania* (1963).

THE LONE RANGER

(1938) **D:** William Witney, John English **S:** Barry Shipman, Franklyn Adreon, Ronald Davidson

Chief Thundercloud (a real American Indian) is Tonto, and an unbilled Lee Powell is the masked man of mystery with silver bullets. The screen's first Lone Ranger has a veil on his mask that covers his mouth. The serial's gimmick was that you didn't know which of the rangers was the hero until the end. The enduring legend started on a radio program in 1933. Also in the cast are Herman Brix (star of Tarzan serials and later known as Bruce Bennett), George Montgomery, and William Farnum. The first of the 15 chapters of this serial is "Heigh-Yo Silver!" (also the name of a feature version). Robert Livingston starred in a sequel serial, *The Lone Ranger Rides Again* (1939).

THE LONE RANGER

(1956) **S:** Stuart Heisler **S:** Herb Meadows **P:** Willis Goldbeck

Clayton Moore, who had been in serials for years, and Jay Silverheels (a real American Indian) were the Lone Ranger and Tonto on TV from 1949 to 1957 (except for a season when Moore was replaced). This color feature version from Warners is about a plot to steal silver from Indian land. With Lyle Bettger and Bonita Granville. Tapes of the TV series, with 2 episodes each, are available from Rhino.

THE LONE RANGER AND THE LOST CITY OF GOLD

(1958) **D:** Lesley Selander **S:** Robert Schaefer, Eric Freiwald **P:** Sherman A. Harris

The Lone Ranger (Clayton Moore) and Tonto (Jay Silverheels) expose a secret society of hooded villains in a color sequel from UA. With Douglas Kennedy and Noreen Nash. The characters didn't reappear until the flop *The Legend of the Lone Ranger* (1981).

THE LONERS

(Vid America, 1972) **D:** Sutton Roley **S:** John Lawrence **P:** Jerry Katzman

Dean Stockwell stars as a half-Navaho, hippie motorcycle racer with a bandanna who's blamed for the death of a patrolman. He teams up with a runaway (Pat Stich, who does the nude scenes) and a disturbed guy (Todd Susman), and they go on the run in the Southwest on cycles, committing robberies. With Gloria Grahame, Scott Brady as a cop, and Tim Rooney. Sam Katzman was the executive producer of the Fanfare release.

THE LONE RUNNER

(TWE, 1986) **D:** Ruggero Deodato **S:** Chris Trainor, Steven Luotto **P:** Maurizio Maggi   Italy/US

Miles O'Keeffe takes his explosive arrows on a mission to rescue an heiress (Savina Gersak) being held for ransom in the Moroccan desert. John Steiner, Ronald Lacey, and Michael Aronin are also in this ridiculous Ovidio Assonitis production, which is rated PG.

LONESOME COWBOYS

(1968) **D/S/P:** Andy Warhol **D/C/E:** Paul Morrissey

This gay western comedy was a hit on the underground midnight-movie circuit. It was rated X, but would barely rate an R today. Louis Waldren stars, with Viva, Taylor Mead as a nurse who does the Lupe Velez twist, and Joe Dallesandro as Little Joe. It was filmed around Tucson. Dallesandro was still acting in the 90s. Morrissey went on to direct nearly all of the Warhol movies. *Flesh* was his next project.

LONE WOLF

(Prism, 1987) **D:** John Callas **S:** Michael Krueger **P:** Sarah Liles

---

LONE WOLF Series

Michael Laynard was raised to be a criminal in Paris, and became a gentleman jewel thief. The character is based on novels by Louis Joseph Vance (starting in 1914). Several silent features were made and Columbia produced a series (1926–30) with Bert Lytell. After *The Lone Wolf Returns* (1935) starring Melvyn Douglas and *The Lone Wolf in Paris* (1938), starring Francis Lederer, a new Columbia series of nine features (1939–47) starred Warren William as a reformed Wolf and Eric Blore as a comic sidekick. Directors included Roy William Neill, Sidney Salkow, and Edward Dmytryk. Then Gerard Mohr was in *The Lone Wolf in London* (1947) and Ron Randell was in *The Lone Wolf and His Lady* (1949). There was a radio version, and a syndicated TV series starred Louis Hayward in 1955.

Small-town computer-hacker teens track down a killer werewolf, in this gory horror movie with Dyann Brown and Kevin Hart. The same people in Denver made *Mind Killer* and *Night Vision*.

LONE WOLF AND CHILD: FINAL CONFLICT

(VSOM, 1993) **D:** Shou Inoue   Japan

Years after the bloody 1972–73 Baby Cart series a second series of 10 features appeared, starring Kinosuke Nishikawa. Apparently they were edited from a TV series. This big-budget version retells the whole story. Masakazu Tamura stars, with Yushi Shibata as Diagaro. There's no gore or baby cart. See the entry for *Lightning Swords of Death*.

LONE WOLF McQUADE

(Vestron, 1983) **D/P:** Steve Carver **S:** B. J. Nelson **P:** Yoram Bel-Ami

Chuck Norris stars as J. J. McQuade, a Texas Ranger with a truck, in one of his better movies, a modern western. David Carradine as illegal arms dealer Rawley Wilkes is the main villain. With Barbara Carrera, Leon Isaac Kennedy, L. Q. Jones, Robert Beltran, and William Sanderson. It's from Orion (formerly AIP).

THE LONG GOODBYE

(1973) **D:** Robert Altman **S:** Leigh Brackett **P:** Jerry Bick

Elliott Gould is a very out-of-it modern-day Philip Marlowe in this satirical Raymond Chandler adaptation. Sterling Hayden and Nina Van Pallandt costar, with Henry Gibson, Mark Rydell, Warren Berlinger, Jack Riley, and Rutanya Alda. Look quickly for Arnold Schwarzenegger as a muscleman and David Carradine as a prisoner. The cinematography is by Vilmos Zsigmond, and the music is by John Williams. A U.A. release.

THE LONG HAIR OF DEATH

(Sinister, 1964) **D:** "Anthony M. Dawson"/Antonio Margheriti **S:** Bruno Valeri, Ernesto Gastaldi **P:** Felice Testa Gay   Italy (*I Lunghi Capelli della Morte*)

This was the rarest Barbara Steele horror movie in America until it showed up on video (letterboxed) in the early 90s. In the 15th century she's accused of murder, burned as a witch, and buried. Later, during a plague, lightning revives her (a great scene). She returns as a woman named Mary and prevents her daughter (Elizabeth Karnstein) from marrying Kurt, the count's son, who was the real killer. There's a lot of plot, and the castle intrigue gets kind of confusing, but Steele is in top form ("You're going to die!"), and there are many good parts. Kurt is eventually burned in a giant skull effigy (as in *The Wicker Man*). Margheriti also made *Castle of Blood* with Steele.

THE LONG RIDERS

(United Artists, 1980) **D:** Walter Hill **S:** Bill Bryden, Steven Phillips, Stacy Keach, James Keach **P:** Tim Zimmerman **M:** Ry Cooder

This superior western about the real Northfield, Minnesota, raid has the extra attraction of real actor brothers as stars. David, Keith, and Robert Carradine are the Younger brothers, Stacy and James Keach (also the executive producers) are the James brothers, Randy and Dennis Quaid are the Millers, and Christopher and Nicolas Guest are the Fords. Also with Pamela Reed as Belle Starr, Harry Carey Jr., and James Whitmore. A scene with John Carradine was deleted. The very good score was released by Warner. This is much better than the later *Young Guns* movies.

THE LONGSHOT

(1986) **D:** Paul Bartel **S/A:** Tim Conway **P:** Lang Elliot

Gangsters are after four losers who borrowed money to bet on horses and then lost. Tim Conway (in his only movie that's not for kids) stars, with Jack Weston, Harvey Korman, Ted Wass, Jonathan Winters, Anne Meara, Stella Stevens, and George DiCenzo. Mike Nichols was the executive producer of this PG-13 comedy.

LOOPING

(VSOM, 1980) **D:** Walter Bockmayer **S:** Bea Fröhlich   W. Germany

An old couple who dream of flying a looping plane are murdered. Hans-Christian Blech and Shelley Winters star, with Ingrid Caven, Sydne Rome, and Adrian Hoven. The music is by Brian Ferry and Roxy Music.

LOOSE SCREWS

(Lightning, 1984) **D:** Rafal Zielinski **S:** Michael Cory **P:** Maurice Smith   Canada

This stupid teen comedy, a sequel to *Screwballs,* is from Corman's Concorde. With Linda Shayne and Bryan Genesse.

LOOSE SHOES

(Key, 1977) **D:** Ira Miller **S:** Varley Smith **P:** Joel Chernoff   (*Coming Attractions; Quackers*)

Lots of performers have small roles in this plotless spoof of trailers for movies like *Skateboarders from Hell*, including Bill Murray (in his film debut), Jaye P. Morgan, Louisa Moritz, Misty Rowe, Betty Thomas, Howard Hesseman, Buddy Hackett (as himself), Ed Lauter, and Susan Tyrrell. Made by Mel Brooks' Brooksfilms, it was released in 1980.

LORD OF THE FLIES

(Public Media, 1961) **D/S:** Peter Brook **P:** Lewis Allen   UK

During a war in the near future, English schoolboys are evacuated from London in a plane that crashes in the South Pacific. They think that the body of the pilot is a mythical beast and kill a wild pig as a sacrifice. Ralph (James Aubrey) and Jack, the main bully (Tom Chapin), become the leaders of warring groups. This chilling b/w film is based on William Golding's 1954 novel. At one time it was to be directed by Luis Buñuel. It was filmed in Puerto Rico. The Criterion laserdisc includes auditions, outtakes, clips from the film's 1963 Cannes screening, commentary by Brook, and Golding reading from his novel.

LORD OF THE FLIES

(Nelson, 1990) **D/E:** Harry Hook **S:** "Sarah Schiff"/Jay Presson Allen **P:** Ross Miloy

The executive producers backed this updated color remake for the same reason that George Romero backed a remake of his *Night of the Living Dead* (they had lost the rights and profits from the superior original). The boys are American this time. With Balthazar Getty and Chris Furrh.

THE LORDS OF FLATBUSH

(RCA, 1974) **D/S/P:** Stephen F. Verona **D/S:** Martin Davidson **S:** Gayle Glecker **M:** Joe Brooks

Juvenile delinquents with leather jackets in 1957 Brooklyn have comic adventures. Perry King stars, with Sylvester Stallone (in his first billed role in a major release) and Henry Winkler (as a pre–*Happy Days* Fonz type). With Susan Blakely, Paul Jabara, Ray Sharkey, and Armand Assante in small roles. Davidson later made *Eddie and the Cruisers*. This Columbia release is rated PG. The soundtrack is on ABC.

LORDS OF MAGICK

(Prism, 1988) **D/S/P/E:** Davis Marsh **S:** Sherman Hirsch

A pair of sorcerer brothers from 10th-century England show up in modern-day California. In this shot-on-video film, which copies *Highlander*, a wizard possesses a street gang, rotting corpses have laser-beam eyes, and there are topless scenes.

LORDS OF THE DEEP

(MGM, 1989) **D:** Mary Ann Fisher **S:** Howard Cohen, Daryl Haney **P/A:** Roger Corman

A psycho commander (Bradford Dillman) kills his crew, in this cheap-looking PG-13 environmental-warning movie. Priscilla Barnes has LSD visions, and the monsters turn out to be cute, friendly *E.T.*-type aliens. Also with Daryl Haney and Eb Lottimer. Producer Corman himself shows up as a corporate executive.

LORNA

(RM, 1964) **D/P/C/E:** Russ Meyer **S:** James Griffith

This gothic melodrama was the first Russ Meyer film to have a plot. It was also his first in b/w. It opens with a fire-and-brimstone preacher (James Griffith, who narrates) in the middle of a road. His tale is about Lorna Maitland, a backwoods wife who finds satisfaction with an escaped con. Maitland's large, strange-shaped breasts and nude scenes helped make *Lorna* a hit, but the characters and plot also make it worth seeing. Death even appears with a scythe. With Hal Hopper, Mark Bradley, and Franklin Bolger. Meyer's other 1964 release was a disastrous collaboration with Albert Zugsmith in Europe, *Fanny Hill*.

LORNA THE EXORCIST

(VSOM, 1974) **D/S/A:** "Clifford Brown"/Jesús Franco   (*Les Possedées du Diable*)

A wealthy French businessman on vacation with his family is visited by Lorna, an ageless devil (Pamela Stafford) with lots of eye makeup. She's back to claim the soul of his daughter (Lina Romay) when she turns 18. Howard Vernon and Franco have small roles, and there's lots of sex. It's subtitled.

LOSIN' IT
(Embassy, 1981) **D:** Curtis Hanson **S:** B. W. L. Norton **P:** Bryan Gindoff, Hannah Hempstead   US/Canada

Jackie Earle Haley, Tom Cruise, and John Stockwell are three teens who go to Tijuana in this comedy with strippers, nudity, and Spanish fly. Shelley Long is a waitress who goes with them, and Joe Spinnell is a border guard.

LOST BATTALION
(1961) **D/S/P:** Eddie Romero **S:** César Amigo   US/Philippines

Leopold Salcedo as Ramón, a WWII Philippines guerrilla leader, and some Americans try to avoid the Japanese invaders and make it to safety in a submarine. With Diane Jergens. Kane Lynn was the executive producer of the AIP release.

THE LOST BOYS
(Warner, 1987) **D:** Joel Schumacher **S:** Janice Fischer, James Jeremias, Jeffrey Boam **P:** Harvey Bernhard

This teen horror hit has an MTV look and way too much POV camera work, and it copies ideas from 'Salem's Lot and Rebel Without a Cause. Jason Patric (son of Jason Miller) is a new kid in a California town that features an amusement park. Corey Haim is his worried kid brother. The Rambo/Van Helsing kids (Corey Feldman and Jamison Newlander) are the best part. Kiefer Sutherland, Jami Gertz, and Alex Winter are Peter Pan–style vampires. The adults include Dianne Wiest, Edward Herrmann, and Barnard Hughes as the eccentric taxidermist grandfather. There's fake Doors music and many Jim Morrison references. The INXS do the Easybeats' "Good Time Tonight" on the Atlantic soundtrack, featuring various artists. Mark Damon was the executive producer.

THE LOST CITY
(Stokey, Foothill, 1935) **D:** Harry Revier **S:** Pereley Poor Sheehan, Eddie Graneman, Leon d'Usseau **P:** Sherman L. Krellberg

Look for this 12-chapter independent Krellberg serial. It's even weirder than The Phantom Empire (from the same year). When it played in NYC in 1953 the TV station received a record number of complaints and took it off the air. It's bad, stupid, racist, and non-stop "Huh!?!" Kane Richmond stars as hero Bruce Gordon, who goes to Africa to trace the origin of earthquakes, hurricanes, and storms that have been threatening the world. William "Stage" Boyd wears lightning bolts as the mad Zolok, last of the Lemurians. He has turned the natives into towering zombies who grunt, and he can also turn black people white. Also in the cast are Claudia Dell as the blond daughter of a kidnapped scientist, George "Gabby" Hayes, Billy Bletcher as a hunchback, and "500 others." The electrical effects are by Kenneth Strickfadden. It was originally available as a complete serial, a feature, or a feature plus 8 chapters.

THE LOST CITY OF ATLANTIS
(1978) **D/P:** Richard Martin

Herbert L. Strock was the editor of this pseudo-documentary with narration. Excavations on the island of Thera, in the Aegean Sea, lead to questions. Were the ancient people there from Atlantis? Were they Egyptians, Maya, Etruscans, or aliens!?!

LOST CITY OF THE JUNGLE
(Stokey, Video Dimensions, 1946) **D:** Ray Taylor, Lewis D. Collins **S:** Joseph F. Poland, Paul Houston, Tom Gibson

Russell Hayden stars as a "United Peace Foundation" investigator in this 13-chapter Universal jungle-adventure serial. Sir Eric Hazarias (Lionel Atwill) steals Meteorium 245, a secret defense against the atomic bomb, and plans to start WWIII. The jungle is supposed to be in the Himalayas. Atwill became ill, had to quit, and died from pneumonia, but since the show must go on, a double (George Sorel) filled in for him in many scenes. Action scenes were lifted from Lost Horizon and the Maria Montez movie White Savage. With Jane Adams, Keye Luke, Gene Roth, and Arthur Space. Chapter titles include "Fire Jet Torture" and "Booby Trap Rendezvous." Universal made only one more serial.

THE LOST CONTINENT
(Fang, 1951) **D:** Sam Newfield **S:** Richard H. Landau **P:** Sigmund Neufeld

A search party climbs and climbs and climbs a taboo sacred mountain on a South Sea island to find a missing atomic rocket. They seem to go around in circles for hours but finally see animated dinosaurs in the jungle at the top. Cesar Romero stars as a playboy air-force major. The others are Hugh Beaumont, Whit Bissell, John Hoyt as a Russian who talks about concentration camps, and Sid Melton as a comic sergeant. They all smoke a lot. Hillary Brook and Acquanetta, the only women in this almost surreal all-star Lippert cheapie, have one scene each.

THE LOST EMPIRE
(Lightning, 1983) **D/S/P:** Jim Wynorski **M:** Alan Howarth

In a plot taken from The Game of Death, three fighting women go to a secret training island and battle the followers of the evil Dr. Sindu, gladiator style. After a good pre-credit sequence with ninjas in Chinatown and some plot about valuable jewels, Angel (Melanie Vincz), a blond supercop, enlists the others for a journey to avenge her brother's death. Raven De La Croix (a professional stripper who starred in Russ Meyer's Up) is White Star, a mystical Indian. She was also the associate producer. Angela Aames, a gum-chewing, shower-taking blond prisoner, wins a fight with Angelique Pettyjohn before she's paroled to go along. Pettyjohn (a sometime porno star) has the best (brief) part in the movie, wearing black leather boots and a bikini while she attacks with a whip. Angus Scrimm is the evil doctor, whose real face is a black skull. Howarth usually does John Carpenter scores.

(When he was in the 60s Cleveland band the Tree Stumps, he used to rise from a coffin onstage.) The special effects (good considering the budget) are by Ernie Farino. Also in the cast are Kenneth Tobey as a cop, grown-up Lassie star Tommy Rettig, Robert Tessier, Linda Shayne, a gorilla, and porno star Stacey Adams. It was originally announced as a 3-D film.

LOST IN SPACE pilots
(Columbia House, 1965) **D/S/P:** Irwin Allen **S:** Simon Winclerberd

The never-aired b/w pilot (No Place To Hide—The Space Family Robinson) for the ridiculous CBS series shows how the Robinson family were in suspended animation before landing on a mysterious planet. The dad (Guy Williams) has a jet pack and narrates. Their land rover is attacked by a giant cyclops (it was sold as a plastic model). Familiar Bernard Herrmann music was borrowed for the theme. In the second plot (The Reluctant Stowaway), which did air, Doctor Smith (Jonathan Harris) is added and the robot is a bad guy. Some low points are the obvious models, the stupid pet monkey with a headpiece that moves, "freezing" characters that sweat, and Billy Mumy singing. Also with June Lockhart, Marta Kristen, Angela Cartwright, and Mark Goddard. The series (later in color) lasted until 1968.

THE LOST JUNGLE
(Stokey, 1934) **D/S:** Armand Schaefer, David Howard **S:** Barney Sarecky, Wyndham Gittens

Famous animal trainer Clyde Beatty stars as himself in this 12-chapter Mascot serial. A dirigible carrying an expedition collecting animals for a circus crashes on an uncharted island where a killer gorilla guards a buried city. Some chapters are "Nature in the Raw," "Gorilla Warfare," and "Human Hyenas." With Cecilia Parker, Wheeler Oakman, and little Mickey Rooney. Beatty from Ohio, returned in Darkest Africa (1934).

LOST, LONELY, AND VICIOUS
(Sinister, 1959) **D:** Frank Myers **S:** Norman Graham **P:** Charles Casarelli

Ken Clayton stars as a death-obsessed (and James Dean–inspired) actor in Hollywood. Barbara Wilson is a drugstore clerk. Howco International promoted this as a "documentary." There's lots of talk.

THE LOST PLANET
(Stokey, 1953) **D:** Spencer Gordon Bennett **S:** George Plympton, Arthur Hoerl **P:** Sam Katzman

Judd Holdren stars as Rex Barrow and Captain Video in this 15-chapter sequel to the Columbia serial Captain Video (1951). It was the last science-fiction serial produced. The captain has a pretty female partner (Vivian Mason) this time, instead of a kid, and a new suit with a lightning bolt on the front. Dr. Grood (Michael Fox) uses mind-control helmets to turn people on the planet Ergo into robots. Gene Roth is the villain, Reckov. With scenes filmed at Bronson Canyon.

THE LOST PLATOON

(AIP, 1989) **D/S:** David A. Prior
S: Ted Prior **P:** Kimberly Casey

A WWII-vet reporter covering the war in Nicaragua discovers that four soldiers are really ageless vampires who drink only the blood of dying soldiers. Peasants are mass-murdered by an evil government general who turns out to be a vampire too. His mistress spins to death. William Knight stars. This silly film includes dialogue about the bad Soviets and fast-motion POV shots. It was filmed in Alabama.

THE LOST PROPHET

(1992) **D/S/C/M:** Michael De Avila **S:** Drew Morone, Larry O'Neil, Shannon Goldman

Jim Burton stars as an unstable guy who goes to an empty mansion for the summer and encounters punks, a serial killer, and a New Age witch. This narrated, arty b/w movie was filmed at and set at Lake George, New York (a great vacation spot).

THE LOST WEEKEND

(MCA, 1945) **D/S:** Billy Wilder **S/P:** Charles Brackett

Writers who drink, beware of this movie! Ray Milland (who received and deserved an Oscar) drinks, goes to pawnshops, drinks, and tries to write. He meets a hip-talking bar girl, thinks he sees a bat kill a mouse in a hole in his apartment, and wakes up in the (real) alky ward of a hospital. The film ends when he doesn't kill himself. The theremin music (later used in so many science-fiction movies) is by Miklos Rozsa. The film, shot on location in NYC in b/w, is based on a novel by Charles Jackson. With Jane Wyman, Phillip Terry, Doris Dowling, Howard Da Silva, and Frank Faylen. From Paramount.

THE LOST WORLD

(Milestone, 1925) **D:** Harry Hoyt **S:** Marion Fairfax
P: Earl Hudson, Watterson R. Rockacker

It may look a little crude now, but this adaptation of Sir Arthur Conan Doyle's novel was a big hit in its day. The plot is similar to *King Kong*. Professor Challenger (Wallace Beery) brings a brontosaurus to London. It escapes at the end and swims away. There's also an ape man (Bull Montana) and dinosaur battles. Willis O'Brien was responsible for the stop-motion animation FX. Bessie Love and Lewis Stone costar. It was the first movie shown on a passenger flight (Imperial Airways from London to Europe). Both the restored, tinted, 90-minute laserdisc version from Lumnivision and the Milestone video include a musical score, more than half an hour of historical material, missing scenes, the original trailer, and more. The worst and shortest version is from Goodtimes. It was originally 106 minutes. It was remade in 1960 by Irwin Allen (using real lizards) then by Harry Alan Towers (1992).

THE LOST WORLD

(Worldvision, 1992) **D:** Timothy Bond **S:** "Peter Welbeck"/Harry Alan Towers **P:** Frank Agrama, Norman Siderow   UK/Canada

Professor Challenger (John Rhys-Davies) and a rival (David Warner) go on an expedition to Africa in 1912, and bring back a cute baby pterodactyl. A Canadian reporter (Eric McCormack) narrates. With Nathania Stanford as an Acquanetta-look native and Tamara Gorski. This childish version of Sir Arthur Conan Doyle's novel may appeal to kids. It was filmed in Zimbabwe, along with a sequel, *Return to the Lost World*. Henry Alan Towers was the executive producer.

LOUISIANA TERRITORY

(1953) **D/C:** Harry W. Smith **S:** Jerome Bronfield **P:** Jay Bonafield, Douglas Travers

Howard Hughes presented this RKO 3-D story about the Louisiana Purchase, starring Val Winter as Robert Livingston. There's a travelogue section and Mardi Gras footage. It's only 65 minutes.

LOVE AND A .45

(Vidmark, 1994) **D/S:** C. M. Talkington **P:** Darin Scott

Gil Bellows (*The Shawshank Redemption*) is a non-violent Texas stick-up artist, Renee Zelwegger is his girlfriend, and Rory Cochrane is his crazed partner in crime. After a botched hold-up results in a series of murders, the couple becomes famous and the partner (now bald) seeks revenge. Also with Jeffrey Combs, Jack Nance, and Wiley Wiggins. Peter Fonda and Anne Wedgeworth play hippie parents. Several of the actors were also in *Dazed and Confused,* also made in Texas. The Sony soundtrack to the Trimark release was scored by Tom Verlaine. It features The Butthole Surfers, Jesus And Mary Chain, The Meat Puppets, and Johnny Cash.

LOVE AND MONEY

(1980) **D/S/P:** James Toback

Ray Sharkey is hired by billionaire businessman Klaus Kinski to influence a South American dictator (Armand Assante). He has an affair with Kinski's beautiful wife (Ornelia Muti). Veteran director King Vidor has an acting role as Sharkey's grandfather. It was released in 1982. Toback returned with *Exposed* (1983).

LOVE AND MURDER

(Coyote, 1988) **D/S/P:** Steven Hilliard Stern

Todd Waring stars as a photographer who takes sneak photos of women in their apartments with his zoom lens in another *Rear Window* ripoff. He accidentally photographs a murder, and a transvestite psycho goes after him. With Kathleen Lasky, Ron White, and Wayne Robson as the janitor who's suspected.

LOVE AND MIDNIGHT AUTO SUPPLY

(1978) **D/S/P:** James Polakof   (*Midnight Auto Supply*)

Michael Parks stars as the leader of a stolen auto-parts gang, in this PG action comedy with Scott Jacoby, Linda Crystal, Colleen Camp, and Monica Gayle. Rory Calhoun, Rod Cameron, and John Ireland are guest stars. It's by the director of *Slashed Dreams* (1974).

LOVE AT STAKE

(Nelson, 1987) **D:** John Moffitt **S:** Terrence Sweeney **P:** Michael Gruskoff   (*Burnin' Love*)

Kelly Preston is accused during the 1692 Salem witch trials, in this Mel Brooks–style comedy. Barbara Carrera is a real witch (who mutates into Anne Ramsey!), and Dave Thomas and Stuart Pankin are corrupt officials. With Patrick Cassidy, Bud Cort, Annie Golden, and Dr. Joyce Brothers (as herself). "Louie Louie" is played at a Thanksgiving dinner with Indians. This R-rated movie has nudity and drug jokes. It was filmed in Canada.

THE LOVE CAMP

(Active, 1980) **D/S/P/M/A:** "Christian Anders"/ Ilias Milonakos   W. Germany/Greece
(*Die Todesgottin des Liebscamps; Love Cult*)

Laura Gemser is the leader of the Children of Light cult in Greece. This is a musical (!) sex movie with several *Hair*-style songs and lots of nudity, sex, and lesbian scenes featuring Gemser. Cult members chant "The Divine One is everything and I am nothing." Those who disobey are thrown into a pit by a musclebound servant or are flogged while tied up naked and everybody is blown up with dynamite after a mass orgy at the end. Anders is Dorian, a blond cult leader who seduces a rich American Senator's blond daughter. Also with Gabrille Tinti.

LOVE CAMP 7

(SW, 1968) **D:** Lee Frost **S:** Wesdon Bishop
P/A: R. W. Cresse   (*Living Nightmare*)

Two WACs go undercover in a Nazi prison to get vital information from a scientist being held there. A scar-faced dyke doctor tortures prisoners. This adults-only "roughie" was rated X but is tame compared to many later features with similar themes. It features unconvincing accents and a narrator who relates everything in flashback and claims that it's all true. Kathy Williams costars, R. W. Cresse is the commandant, and David F. Friedman plays a general. It was a hit in Canada, so Friedman was hired to produce the first *Ilsa* film there.

LOVE, CHEAT, AND STEAL

(Columbia, 1994) **D/S:** William Curran
P: Brad Krevoy **E:** Monte Hellman

In this *film noir* attempt, killer Eric Roberts breaks out of prison, convinces the banker husband (John Lithgow) of his ex-wife and partner (Madchen Amick) that he's her brother, and forces her to help him rob her husband's bank. Also with Richard Edson, Dan O'Herlihy, David Ackroyd, and Donald Moffatt. It debuted on Showtime.

THE LOVE CLINIC

(1968) **D/P:** Ferd Sebastian **S:** Ann Cawthorne

A woman goes to a clinic and learns about fulfillment from a computer. Her husband gets jealous and angry. This sex comedy was from Boxoffice International. Beverly Sebastian was executive producer. The Sebastians also made *I Need* (1967) and *Marital Fulfillment* (1970). They went on to drive-in hits like *Gator*.

LOVE COMMUNE

(SW, 1970) **D/S:** Robert J. Emery **S:** John Pappas
P: George B. Roberts, Paul Rubenstein
(*Sign of Aquarius; Ghetto Freaks*)

Despite the video box, this embarrassing, plotless hippie/drug movie with imitation *Hair* songs was filmed entirely in Cleveland during a snowy winter. Much of the stoned dialogue seems to be improvised, man. The main characters are named Sonny, Stringbean, and Cleaver. A Tom Jones–type singer in fringes sings, "My name is Mousy. I feel lousy." Another song goes, "We cannot comprehend the straight way of life." There's a freak-out, a trip/fuck, a murder by a drug dealer, and downtown Public Square panhandling scenes. The nude dancing was choreographed by Jeff Kutash, from the local *Upbeat* show! A runaway girl's father is played by Bob Wells, who as Hoolihan cohosted what had been the *Ghoulardi* show! This obscure wonder opened (in Cleveland) as *Sign of Aquarius* and was later reissued, with ads featuring minor black characters, as *Ghetto Freaks*! It's from the producer of *Fireball Jungle* and *The Weird World of LSD*! Believe it or not, as a teen I wasted an afternoon going to a publicity-stunt casting call for this movie. I failed the "audition" for *Ghetto Freaks!*

LOVE CRIMES

(HBO, 1991) **D/P:** Lizzie Borden
S: Allan Moyle **P:** Rudy Langlais

Sean Young stars as an assistant DA who's after a con man and rapist (Patrick Bergin) posing as a photographer. With James Read and Arnetia Walker. R and unrated versions (complete with a spanking scene and Young nude) are available. It's by the director of *Working Girls*.

THE LOVE CULT

(SW, 1966) **D:** T. A. Dee **S:** Russell Fore

The Great Eric is a TV magician and hypnotist who decides to create a sex cult with the help of his supportive assistant and wife. He becomes Brother Eros and makes money from cult members in robes who chant, "Love is all that counts" and have orgies at his house. Rape, jealousy, blackmail, and murder result. The sex is very tame or offscreen. This 65-minute b/w movie is narrated by someone with a serious, Rod Serling type of voice.

LOVE DOLLS SUPERSTAR

(SST, 1986) **D/S/P:** David Markey **S:** Jennifer Schwartz, McDonald Brothers

In this welcome sequel to *Desperate Teenage Love Dolls* the Love Dolls reform and "climb back from the bottom." Tracy Lea shows up as the mother of Tanya, who was killed in the first film, and Steve McDonald (of Redd Kross) as a "freedom school" hippie attempts to avenge the death of his brother. Plotwise, things get a lot more out there than in the original. Bunny returns as a ghost, Alexandria is a hooker, Bruce Springsteen is assassinated by a guy possessed by a Kiss doll(!), Patch starts a new religion, and the Love Dolls massacre their own fans

Jonestown style (at Bronson Canyon), then head for outer space! There's also a funny hard-core punk-band takeoff. The SST soundtrack uses the same great groups again, plus Sonic Youth and others. Any rock movie that mixes references to Billy Jack, Charles Manson, and Jim Jones is all right with me. Markey also made the documentary *1991: The Year Punk Broke.*

THE LOVED ONE

(MGM, 1965) **D:** Tony Richardson **S:** Terry Southern, Christopher Isherwood **P:** John Calley, Haskell Wexler

If you haven't seen this, what are you waiting for? It was promoted by MGM as "the movie to offend everyone." Based on a 1948 novel by Evelyn Waugh, this black comedy about the funeral business in California is the closest thing to a John Waters movie ever made by a major studio, and in 1965! Luis Buñuel wanted to direct it once, but Tony Richardson got to make it because he had done the hit *Tom Jones*. Robert Morse stars as a British poet who comes to Hollywood after his art-director uncle (John Gielgud) hangs himself. Jonathan Winters (playing two brothers) runs Whispering Glades (a parody of the real Los Angeles cemetery Forest Lawn) and the Happy Hunting Grounds pet cemetery, Anjanette Comer is an embalmer, and Rod Steiger is incredible as Mr. Joyboy. There are hookers in coffins, and Joyboy's mom eats whole pigs and dies when the refrigerator falls on her during an eating binge. With Dana Andrews, Milton Berle, James Coburn, Tab Hunter, Liberace, Lionel Stander, Robert Morley, Margaret Leighton, Alan Napier, Elizabeth Ann Roberts (from *Playboy*), and singer Paul Williams as a kid who invents a rocket to send bodies into space. It was shot by Haskell Wexler. Even at 122 minutes, some parts were cut (including scenes with Jayne Mansfield and Barbara Nichols).

THE LOVE FACTOR: *See* ZETA ONE

LOVE FEAST

(SW, 1969) **D/P:** Joseph F. Robertson
S/A: Edward Wood Jr.   (*The Photographer*)

Lost Ed Wood Jr. movies keep turning up. In this 65-minute color sex comedy he stars (with a Shemp Howard haircut) as Mr. Murphy. He speaks to the camera: "Now I love girls! Girls! Girls! Girls!" He calls a model agency for women. He helps one undress. She gets into bed with the second one. More and more women arrive and strip, and some guys stop by too, creating a cartoonish pile of naked bodies on a bed. The big joke is that Wood is always interrupted and can't join them: "I'm gonna cry!" He makes distorted faces and goes outside and drinks several times. Eventually some women force him to wear a dog collar, put on a nightie, crawl on his knees bare-assed, and lick their boots. Wood was also in *The Sensuous Wife*, by Robertson.

LOVE FROM A STRANGER

(Sinister, 1936) **D:** Rowland V. Lee **S:** Frances Marion **P:** Max Schach   (*Night of Terror*)

Basil Rathbone is in top form as Gerald Lovell, a poetic ladies' man who is really a psychotic killer. He meets blond Ann Harding in France and marries her for her lottery money. They move into an isolated house in Kent, and he gets stranger as time passes. He fondles scarves that belonged to his previous wife, makes his new wife play the piano very fast, and listens to "In the Hall of the Mountain King" in his secret basement darkroom. Binnie Hale is a comic-relief aunt, and Joan Hickson (later Miss Marple on TV) is a simpleminded maid. This United Artists film, made in England, is adapted from a play by Frank Vosper, based on an Agatha Christie story. It was remade in 1947 in America. Lee also directed Rathbone in *Son of Frankenstein, The Sun Never Sets,* and *Tower of London*.

LOVE FROM A STRANGER

(Starmaker, 1947) **D:** Richard Whorf
S: Philip MacDonald

John Hodiak is a psycho who marries Sylvia Sidney, in this Eagle Lion remake of the 1936 film, this time set in 1901. It was Sidney's last film for years. John Howard and Ann Richards costar.

LOVE IN A GOLDFISH BOWL

(1961) **D/S:** Jack Sher **P:** Martin Jurow

Toby Michaels and Tommy Sands are college students who try to run away together, but their boat capsizes. She ends up being rescued by Giussepe (Fabian) and the Coast Guard. Tommy Sands and Fabian both sing in this lame teen comedy. With Jan Sterling, Edward Andrews, John McGiver, Majel Barrett, Denny Miller, and Toby Michaels.

LOVE IN 3-D

(1972) **D:** Walter Boos **S:** Florian Vollmer
P: Wolfgang C. Hartwig   W. Germany
(*Liebe in Drei Dimensionen*)

This 3-D soft-X film consists of 7 short segments. Dimension, then Monarch, released it in America, and it was advertised as being "filmed in 70mm," which was true, but they showed a 35mm version! It was still being booked in the 80s! Ingrid Steeger and Christine Lindberg star.

LOVE KILLS

(1991) **D:** Brian Grant **S:** Michael J. Murray **P:** Bob Roe

Virginia Madsen is an heiress and photographer in Salt Lake City whose psychologist husband (Jim Metzler) has interviewed serial killers for a book. A hitman on the run (Lenny Von Dohlen) hires her to take some pictures. Many plot twists follow. Kate Hodge is also in this USA Network movie.

THE LOVELESS

(Media, 1981) **D/S:** Kathryn Bigelow,
Monty Montgomery **P:** Grafton Nunes

In the 50s some bikers on the way to Daytona for races stop in a small southern town, wait for repairs, and mess with some local women. Don Ferguson and Monty Montgomery star with then unknown Willem Dafoe and rockabilly singer Robert Gordon. It's pretty slow going, but everybody looks cool and there's lots of rockabilly on the soundtrack. With Tina L'Hotsky and cartoonist J. D. King.

LOVE LETTERS

(Vestron, 1983) **D/S:** Amy Jones
P: Roger Corman   *(Passion Play)*

A disc jockey (Jamie Lee Curtis) has an affair with an older married man (James Keach). With Amy Madigan, Matt Clark, Bud Cort, Rance Howard, and Sally Kirkland as a hippie. Jones directed this serious New World film after making *Slumber Party Massacre*.

LOVE LETTERS OF A PORTUGUESE NUN

(VSOM, 1976) **D/S:** Jesús Franco
S/P: Erwin C. Dietrich **P:** Max Dora
Switzerland/W. Germany

Innocent 16-year-old María (Susan Hemingway) is forced to enter a convent (a beautiful real location) secretly run by Satanists. She's put in isolation, tortured, forced into sexual situations with men, women, and even a horned Devil (Herbert Fux), and told that it was all dreams. When she escapes inquisitors make her confess (on the rack) and decide to burn her in public. This is one of Franco's best, a well-made, lush-looking feature that transcends the obvious exploitation angles. William Berger is very good as the father confessor. The dubbed video has Dutch subtitles. The same story was filmed in Spain by Jorge Grau in 1978.

LOVE, LIES, AND MURDER

(Republic, 1992) **D:** Robert Markowitz
S: Daniel Hill **P:** Jay Bernsen, Danielle Hill

A businessman (Clancy Brown) convinces his daughter (Moira Kelly) and his sister-in-law (Sheryl Lee) to kill his wife. He sets up his daughter, marries his sister-in-law, and collects the life insurance. John Ashton is the insurance investigator. It's based on a true story. This TV movie is more than 3 hours long.

LOVELY BUT DEADLY

(Vestron, 1982) **D/S/P:** David Sheldon
S: Patricia Joyce **P:** Doro Vlado Hreljanovic

Lucinda Dooling is Lovely, a martial-arts-fighting cheerleader who goes undercover as a junkie to fight drug dealers because her brother OD'd and other cheerleaders are hooked. The plot is the same as *Coffy*. Also with Marie Windsor as her aunt, John Randolph, and Mel Novak.

THE LOVE MACHINE

(RCA, 1971) **D:** Jack Haley Jr. **S:** Samuel
Taylor **P:** Michael J. Frankovich

This trashy, funny adaptation of a Jacqueline Susann novel stars John Phillip Law as a TV newscaster who has an affair with the wife (Dyan Cannon) of a network executive (Robert Ryan) to get a promotion. With David Hemmings, Jackie Cooper, Shecky Greene, Sharon Farrell, Alexandra Hay, twins Madeleine and Mary Collinson in a shower, Gayle Hunnicutt, and Claudia Jennings. From Columbia. The soundtrack (on Scepter) features Dionne Warwicke.

LOVE ME DEADLY

(Video Gems, 1972) **D/S:** Jacques La Certe
P: Buck Edwards

It's hard to believe that this serious and disturbing necromaniac movie was made and probably played drive-ins. Mary Wilcox stars as Lindsay, a blond heiress. Her boyfriend (Christopher Stone) is tired of her not putting out. She falls for and eventually marries an art-gallery owner (Lyle Waggoner) but won't sleep with him either. A persistent mortician named Fred (Timothy Scott), who leads a secret cult of hooded necros, recognizes that she's obsessed by the dead, and eventually she's naked on top of a corpse. Fred also picks up prostitutes (male and female) to kill and drain. The movie has bad 70s hair, long romantic parts, love songs, flashbacks, and nightmares. H. B. Halicki was an associate producer. Wilcox was also in *Beast of the Yellow Night* and *Lepke*.

LOVE ME LIKE I DO

(1969) **D/S/P:** J. Van Hearn

Peter Carpenter and Dyanne Thorne (from the *Ilsa* movies) star as a married couple in this X-rated comedy about cheating and swapping in Las Vegas. The music is by the Mongolian Horse. Both stars were also in *Point of Terror*.

THE LOVE PIRATE

(1971) **D/S:** Barry Mahon

Florida schlock director Brad Grinter (*Blood Freak*) stars as pirate Captain Fu, with an all-female crew, in this nudie adventure. Doug Hobart was the set designer. It was filmed in North Miami Beach.

LOVE POTION NO. 9

(Fox, 1992) **D/S/P:** Dale Launer

Tate Donovan and Sandra Bullock are young lab workers who get mixed up with a love spray in this silly but nice PG-13 romantic comedy. She goes from being a nerd to having an English prince as a boyfriend. With Dale Midkiff and Anne Bancroft as a Gypsy.

LOVE SCENES

(MGM, 1983) **D:** Bud Townsend **S:** C. Panning Master
P: Vernon C. Becker   *(Ecstasy; Love Secrets)*

Tiffany Bolling stars with Franc Luz in this soap opera about the making of a sex movie. With Julie Newmar, Jack Carter, Britt Ekland, Monique Gabrielle, and Daniel Pilon. Bolling, Gabrielle, and others are naked a lot. This Harry Alan Towers Playboy production debuted on Playboy TV.

THE LOVES OF IRINA: *See* EROTIKILL

LOVE, STRANGE LOVE

(Vestron, 1982) **D/S:** Walter Hugo
Khouri **P:** Anibal Massanineto   Brazil

A boy named Hugo is sent to live in a large, ornate Brazilian whorehouse with his mother (Vera Fischer) during WWII. He gets an eyeful of sex, orgies, and political intrigue. The adult Hugo (now an old politician) magically wanders around the house remembering what happened. The reason to watch this is third-billed Xuxa (Meneghel), now the host of an incredibly popular children's show produced in Portuguese, Spanish, and English. If she were American this movie (released dubbed here) would be a *National Enquirer/Hard Copy* standby. She plays Tampa, a young whore who poses as "a German virgin from the South" and strips off her white teddy-bear costume while Dixieland jazz plays. She also attempts to seduce Hugo, who later has sex with his mom.

THE LOVE THRILL MURDERS

(Troma, 1971) **D/P:** Robert L. Roberts
S: Matt Cavanagh   *(Sweet Savior)*

Troy Donahue (looking like Leon Russell) is Moon, a Bible-quoting "chemical messiah," in this suitably sick, soft-core Manson movie set in NYC. Moon and his "family" live, sing (about plastic people), and have sex in a small apartment. The "freaks" are invited to help liven up a suburban swinger party. Moon gives a reluctant woman a popper and she screams, "Screw me, now!" His followers eventually kill everybody, including a pregnant actress (Renay Granville). Moon has nightmares of his childhood ("No, Papa!"), and we see flashbacks and flashforward glimpses of the slaughter. Bull is tricked into having sex with a comic transsexual named Spitzi. Scenes of Moon on his cycle riding through Times Square are shown twice. The soft-rock theme, written and sung by Jeff Barry (who created the Archies), is excellent and could have been a hit (really). Lloyd Kaufman was the production manager. This was later retitled and re-released by Troma. The video seems to be cut. The director later made *Patty* (1975).

LOVE WANGA

(SW, 1935) **D/S/P:** George Terwilliger   *(Ouanga; The Crime of Voodoo; Drums of the Jungle)*

This rare road-show horror movie "filmed entirely in the West Indies" (Haiti and Jamaica) was thought to be lost forever. The print is from Canada. A lot goes on in 56 minutes. Cleely (Fredi Washington), who owns a plantation on Paradise Island, is furious when her white plantation-owner lover, Adam, returns from NYC engaged to a white woman. "You belong with your kind," she says. "I'll show you what a black girl can do!" She uses voodoo to revive two bodies and to have the fiancée (Marie Paxton) kidnapped. The movie has a documentary intro, servants from Harlem dancing and gambling, voodoo ceremonies, and Sheldon Leonard as a threatening, evil overseer. The script was later reworked as *The Devil's Daughter* (1939). Terwilliger had written scripts for D. W. Griffith. Washington (who died in 1994) costarred in *Imitation of Life* (1934) and was in shorts with Duke Ellington and Cab Calloway.

BELA LUGOSI
(1882-1956)

Lugosi, a Hungarian star of stage and screen, becomes more of a cult figure every year. After attaining stardom in America in Dracula, he was in some Universal horror classics but was also in many more, cheaper, "poverty row" horror movies and serials. That's why he's a king of public-domain videotapes. Many Lugosi 30s and 40s titles from Monogram, P.R.C., and lesser studios are easy to find at low prices. People are fascinated by Lugosi: he played the screen's most famous vampire, he was in many low-budget oddities (including three

Ed Wood Jr. movies), he's seen as a tragic rival to Karloff, and the end of his life was so pathetic (he was broke and addicted to pain killers). Several tapes compile Lugosi interviews, TV appearances, and trailers and scenes from features. Most of these "documentaries" share some of the same (public domain) clips and interviews: *Bela Lugosi: The Forgotten King* (MPI), hosted by Forrest J. Ackerman, *Mondo Lugosi* (Rhino), *Bela Lugosi: Then and Now!* (Tempe), and several tapes about Ed Wood.

LOVE YOU TILL TUESDAY

(Polygram, 1969) **D:** Malcolm J. Thompson

This half-hour rarity is probably the earliest footage you'll find of David Bowie. He does the title song, a different version of "Space Oddity," the excellent "Let Me Sleep Beside You," and others (some never released), usually against a white background and with unseen orchestral backing. Hermione and Hutch also sing with Bowie in the background (the short-lived trio was called Feathers). Bowie wears an unfortunate-looking wig because his hair was short for his first movie role (*The Virgin Soldiers*). WARNING: Contains mime routines.

LOW BLOW

(Vestron, 1986) **D/C:** Frank Harris
S/P/A: Leo Fong   (*Savage Sunday*)

Leo Fong stars as ex-cop Leo Wong. Cameron Mitchell is a blind religious-cult leader, Yurakunda (!), and Akosa Busia is his black henchwoman, Karma. Troy Donahue wants his daughter back, so he hires Wong, who has martial-arts battles. This started Donahue's full-time exploitation-movie comeback. It's by the makers of *Killpoint*.

LOW DOWN DIRTY SHAME

(Hollywood, 1994) **D/S/A:** Keenen Ivory Wayans
P: Joel Roth, Roger Birnbaum

Wayans (in his first feature after *I'm Gonna Git You Sucka*) is Andre Shame, a cop turned private eye in a 70s-style action movie with comedy. The main action takes place in a shopping mall. Jada Pinkett and Salli Richardson are the women in Shame's life and Charles S. Dutton and Andrew Divoff are drug-dealing villains. Also with Corwin Hawkins and Gregory Sierra. The soundtrack is on Hollywood.

LOWER LEVEL

(Republic, 1991) **D:** Kristine Peterson **S:** Joel
Soisson **P:** W. K. Border, Michael Leahy

An architect (Elizabeth Gracen) in a computer-controlled high-rise that she designed is trapped at night by a psychotic, lovesick, voyeur security guard (David Bradley, from the *American Ninja* movies). It's pretty suspenseful and has one good erotic scene in a parking garage. She and her boyfriend (Jeff Yagher) strip and have sex in a car (while the guard watches on closed-circuit TV); then the water sprinklers go on. In a continuity error, the killer changes clothes and then changes back again. Also with Shari Shattuck. Peterson made *Body Chemistry* and *Deadly Dreams*. Elizabeth Gracen (or Ward) claimed she had an affair with President Clinton when he was governor and she was Miss Arkansas. Her character is named Hillary.

LSD PSYCHEDELIC FREAKOUT, Vol. I

(SW, 1994)

These 2 hours of unidentified clips from various 60s adults-only movies feature lots of naked dancers, strobe lights, hallucinations, and bongo music. Some choice clips are from *Alice in Acidland*, *Mantis in Lace*, *Acid Eaters*, *The Worst Crime of Them All*, *Wanda the Sadistic Hypnotist*, and *The Wild World of LSD*. There's also an *Acid Dreams* short.

THE LUCIFER COMPLEX

(VCI, 1976) **D/S:** David L. Hewitt
D: Kenneth Hartford **S:** Dale
Skillicorn **P:** David E. Jackson

After "the great war" of 1986 a survivor in a cave on a Hawaiian island (William Lanning) sits and watches "every document of mankind" (including old war footage, a band at a rock festival, and the bulk of this pathetic movie). An agent (Robert Vaughn) watches a belly dancer, then goes to a Nazi prison camp (in Florida) where naked people are kept in suspended animation. Aldo Ray is a German guard there ("Ya, ya"). Vaughn and a female inmate (Merrie Lynn Ross) attempt to escape with other women with machine guns, but he's cloned and has to fight himself! Oh yeah, Hit-

ler (with gray hair and big ears) is still alive! He can disappear like a ghost (?) and is going to take over the world with his clones! Also with Keenan Wynn, Leo Gordon, and Victoria Carroll. Some of the footage was left over from Hewitt's unfinished *Women of Stalag 13/Hitler's Wild Women*. This Gold Key production went directly to TV in 1979!

LUCKY GHOST

(Discount, 1941) **D:** William X. Crowley
S: Lex Neal, Vernon Smith **D:** Jed Buell

A comedy team billed as Miller and Mantan star in this amazing all-black comedy not found in any reference book. Jefferson (F. E. Miller) and Washington (Mantan Moreland) are hungry, homeless, and on the road. Miller is the more sensible one, but Mantan gets the laughs. After being caught stealing chickens they win the car, chauffeur, and clothes of two rich man by shooting dice. They go to a sanitarium being used as an illegal, posh nightclub for dining, dancing, and gambling. The owner becomes murderously jealous when Mantan dances with his sexy hostess girlfriend (Florence O'Brien). All of a sudden the ghosts of the original owners meet in a cemetery and decide to scare everyone and stop all the noise. An invisible man walks around, a skeleton plays the piano, and a ghost possesses Mantan, making him do a wild "gator" on the floor. If you've seen him only in Charlie Chan movies you won't be prepared for all-out Mantan. For some unknown reason a lone character who appears only outside the sanitarium is a white man in blackface! This was part of a series that included *Mr. Washington Goes to Town* (1940) and *Professor Creeps* (1941).

LUCKY STIFF

(RCA/Columbia, 1988) **D:** Anthony Perkins
S: Pat Proft **P:** Gerald T. Olson

Perkins' PG cannibal comedy was going to be called *My Christmas Dinner*. Donna Dixon stars as a beautiful woman who is part of an inbred cannibal family. She chooses a big guy (Joe Alaskey) to bring home for dinner. With Jeff Kober, Fran Ryan, and Leigh McCloskey. Perkins also directed *Psycho III*.

LUCKY THE INSCRUTABLE

(VSOM, 1967) **D/S/A:** Jesús Franco **S:** José
Luis Martínez Molla **P:** José Luis Jerez
Spain/W. Germany (*Lucky; El Intrépido*)

American Roy Danton stars as a comical Bond-like secret agent who goes to Rome and Albania to stop counterfeiters. The influence of the *Batman* TV series is obvious when comic-book balloons and panels are used. With Rosabla Neri as a sexy Albanian police commissioner and Dante Posani. This went directly to TV in America.

LUGOSI: THE FORGOTTEN KING

(1985) **D:** Mark S. Gilman, Dave Stuckey

Clips of many public-domain Lugosi movies are shown, along with interviews with Carol Borland

(*Mark of the Vampire*), Forrest J. Ackerman, John Carradine (*The Black Cat* and *Return of the Ape Man*), Alex Gordon, Ralph Bellamy (*The Wolf Man* and *The Ghost of Frankenstein*), and others.

LULU

(VSOM, 198?) **D/S:** Bigas Luna   Spain

A woman named Lulu (Francesca Neri) narrates her own flashbacks (some in b/w) of her descent into a life of dangerous sex for money in Madrid. This bizarre movie has transvestite hookers, incest, and live sex shows. Lulu is saved just in time before starring in a show with a dog. Music includes "Walk on the Wild Side" and "The Peter Gunn Theme." Luna, known to horror fans for his *Anguish* (its star, Ángel José, is in this too), is an arthouse hero because of films like *Jamón, Jamón* (1993).

LUNATICS: A LOVE STORY

(RCA, 1990) **D/S:** Josh Becker **P/A:** Bruce Campbell

Theodore Raimi (Sam's brother) is a delusional paranoic on medication who writes poetry in his LA apartment. He hallucinates like crazy and nearly becomes a psycho killer, but instead he becomes a hero to Deborah Foreman by defeating street-gang members. This unique romantic comedy/fantasy has some great scenes with animated spiders on Raimi's brain. The first time he gets up the courage to leave his apartment he thinks there's an earthquake, and a garbage truck appears as a giant spider. Campbell plays several roles, including Edgar Allan Poe (on a book cover). There's a "Nervous Breakdown" rap sequence and jazz background music. This Sam Raimi/Robert Tapert production was shot in Pontiac Hills, Michigan, in 1989.

LUNCHMEAT

(Tapeworm, 1986) **D/S/P:** Kirk Alex **P:** Mark Flynn

The original, large-size display box for this low-budget super-8 horror movie is pretty eye-catching (look for it). *Lunchmeat* isn't very original, and it's crude, but I liked it. A group of six yuppie-type teens from LA (and one nonconformist punk girl) end up lost in the woods and are killed off by a demented hillbilly family. Pa and his two sons sell human meat to a burger stand. A third son (the one on the box) is a big, retarded cannibal kept on a chain and whipped when he misbehaves. It's not really very gory for an 80s horror movie but is somehow disturbing and effective despite continuity problems and a weak ending.

LUNCH WAGON GIRLS

(Media, 1980) **D:** Ernest Pintoff **S:** Leon Phillips, Marshall Harvey **P:** Mark Borde
(*Lunch Wagon; Come and Get It*)

Three young women sell food at a construction site, and their rivals are gangsters. This drive-in comedy is similar to *Porky's*. Rosanne Katon, Pamela Jean Bryant, and Candy Moore star, with Rick Podell, Louisa Moritz, Chuck McCann, Rose Marie, Nels, Dick, and James Van Patton.

LURKERS

(Media, 1988) **D/C/E:** Roberta Findlay **S:** Ed Kelleher, Harriet Vidal **P:** Walter E. Sears

A cello-playing woman has conflicting flashbacks. Her dead mom haunts her, and dead people float. Christine Moore stars, with Gary Warner, Ruth Collins, Debbie Rochon, and writer Maitland McDonagh.

LURKING FEAR

(Paramount, 1994) **D/S:** C. Courtney Joyner **P:** Vlad Paunescu, Dana Paunescu

An ex-con (Blake Bailey, who narrates his own flashback) is after money buried in a Massachusetts graveyard. Most of the story (supposedly based on a work by H. P. Lovecraft) takes place in a church where characters argue and fight. A hard-drinking doctor (Jeffrey Combs) and his assistant (Ashley Lauren, from the *Hellraiser* movies) try to dynamite everything. Ghouls that look like the ones in EC comics emerge from tunnels, Lauren and Allison Mackie have a mud fight, and a heart is pulled out. Jon Finch (*Frenzy*) is a gangster, Paul Mantee is a priest, Vincent Schiavelli is a mortician, and Michael Todd is a zombie. Originally slated to be directed by Stuart Gordon, it was filmed in Romania.

LUST AT FIRST BITE: *See* DRACULA SUCKS

LUST FOR FREEDOM

(AIP, 1987) **D/S/P:** Eric Louzil **S:** Craig Kusaba

Blond Melanie Coll (who narrates) stars as a karate-fighting ex-cop framed and put into a desert prison. Troma bought an unreleased 70s (note the Jimmy Carter photo) women's-prison movie (*Georgia County Lockup*) filmed in Nevada and added new narration, a heavy-metal soundtrack by Grim Reaper, and more scenes of sex and violence. With some gore, whippings, rape, Deana Booher/Queen Kong, Michelle Bauer, and porno star Crystal Breeze in a lesbian scene.

THE LUSTFUL TURK

(SW, 1968) **D/P:** Ron Elliot **S:** David F. Friedman

After two Englishwomen and a female servant are kidnapped by Algerian pirates, they're given to a Sheik Ali. But they all fall for the pirate captain (who gets castrated at the end). With Michelle Triola (the actress who sued Lee Marvin for palimony), Abbe Rentz, Foreman Shane, and Kathy Williams. There's an animated sequence.

LUST IN THE DUST

(Star Maker, 1985) **D:** Paul Bartel **S:** Philip John Taylor **P:** Allan Glaser, Tab Hunter

Tab Hunter stars in a Clint Eastwood type of role, in this western comedy from New World. The title comes from what some critics had nicknamed *Duel in the Sun* (1946). Treasure maps are tattooed on the asses of Divine and Lainie Kazan. With Geoffrey Lewis, Henry Silva, Cesar Romero, Woody Strode, Courtney Gains, and a dwarf.

Divine's other non–John Waters appearances are in the West German documentary *Tally Brown, NY* (1979), a drag documentary from England called *The Alternate Miss World* (1980), *Trouble in Mind* (1985), and *Out of the Dark* (1989).

A LUST TO KILL

(SW, 1957) **D:** Oliver Drake **S:** Sam Roeca, Thomas Hubbard **P:** A. R. Milton, Patrick Betz

Jim Davis is kind-hearted Marshal Clint in this obscure indy western. Allison Hayes helps Don Megowan as one of the Holland boys gang escape from jail. A scene of naked women swimming (shown from the back) made it exploitable in the 50s. It opens and closes with the biblical quotes that became the Pete Seeger song "Turn, Turn, Turn," later sung by the Byrds. Hayes was in *The Disembodied, The Unearthly,* and *The Zombies of Mora Tau,* all released the same year. Drake later directed *The Mummy and the Curse of the Jackal.*

LUTHER THE GEEK

(Quest, 1989) **D:** Carlton J. Albright **S:** Whitey Styles **P:** David Platt

Luther Watts (Edward Terry), a repulsive, balding, blond maniac with metal teeth who makes chicken noises and crows like a rooster, is paroled after 20 years in prison. He had been strongly affected by seeing a real circus geek as a kid in 1938 (shown in an excellent prologue). Luther eats raw eggs in a supermarket and bites an old lady on the neck before heading for a remote farm where he ties up the young widow who lives there. Her oblivious, big-breasted daughter (Stacy Haiduk, who played Lana Lang in the *Superboy* TV series) shows up for a shower (then bed) sex scene with her boyfriend. When she finds her mother (Joan Roth) tied up she cries and leaves her there! Luther leaves the farm, kills people, returns, guts the boyfriend, bites the stupid sheriff's finger off, and stalks the determined mother, who triumphs in a bizarre, ridiculous, but oddly effective and memorable ending. It was directed in Iowa and Illinois by the same who wrote and produced *The Children* (1980).

MACABRO

(1965) **D:** Romolo Marcellini **S:** Giancarlo Del Re **P:** Guido Giambartolomei Italy (*Mondo Macabro; Tabu No. 2*)

Tribal circumcision rites, male geishas, snake-eating, Brazilian headhunters, and "railway roulette" are some topics explored in this mondo documentary narrated by Marvin Miller. Trans-American, the AIP offshoot that released it, originally planned to call this *It's a Sick, Sick World.*

MAC AND ME

(Orion, 1988) **D/S:** Stewart Raffill **S:** Steve Feke **P:** R. J. Lewis

In this subversive, PG-rated *E.T.* copy, aliens are revived by Coca-Cola and there's a musical number at a McDonald's (!). Many McDonald's plugs are included, and Ronald McDonald "himself" appears. The plot is: A kid in a wheelchair befriends a lost alien kid. The message is: Eat More Overpriced Junk Food, Kids! Christine Ebersole is the mom. Mark Damon (star of *The Devil's Wedding Night*) was the executive producer.

MACBETH

(Republic, 1948) **D/S/P/A:** Orson Welles

The first sound version of Shakespeare's play was made as cheaply as possible, in b/w, in about 21 days for Republic. Orson Welles is Macbeth, Jeanette Nolan is Lady Macbeth, and Dan O'Herlihy is Macduff. With Edgar Barrier, Roddy McDowall, Alan Napier, and William Alland, all using Scottish accents. Welles and O'Herlihy designed the simple, very theatrical sets. It was originally 105 minutes long but was sometimes shown cut at 89 minutes. It was released "restored" on laserdisc in 1992 with an additional audiotrack essay. Welles's next movie as a director was *Othello* (1951). Other features based on Shakespeare's *MacBeth* are *Joe Macbeth* (1955), a comedy about a modern-day American gangster, and Akira Kurosawa's *Throne of Blood* (1957), which has a samurai-era setting.

THE MACHINE

(1994) **D/S:** François Dupeyron **P:** René Gleitman France/Germany (*La Machine*)

A respected psychiatrist (Gérard Depardieu) uses a machine to trade minds and bodies with a psycho killer (Didier Bourbon). This serious horror movie was a major release in Europe. With Nathalie Baye as his wife, Natalia Woerner as his mistress, and Claude Berri. It's based on a novel by René Belletto.

MACHO CALLAHAN

(1970) **D/P:** Bernard Kowalski **S:** Clifford Newton Gould **P:** Martin C. Shute

"Macho" Callahan (David Janssen) escapes from a deadly Confederate prison camp and goes on a personal mission to kill the man who put him there (Lee J. Cobb). In Texas he accidentally kills a one-armed soldier (David Carradine). The widow (Jean Seberg) offers a reward. Later he rapes her, but she falls in love with him. With James Booth, Bo Hopkins, Diane Ladd, Pedro Armendariz Jr., and Matt Clark. This violent Avco Embassy western was filmed in Mexico. Seberg and Janssen later died tragically, within months of each other.

MACISTE IN HELL = THE WITCHES' CURSE

THE MACK

(Nelson, 1973) **D:** Michael Campus **S:** Robert J. Poole **P:** Harvey Bernhard

This outrageous black-action classic could still pack the house on 42nd Street 10 years after it was made. Max Julien stars as Goldie, a pimp in Oakland who is named "player" of the year before his violent downfall. Richard Pryor is his often hilarious buddy Slim. The dialogue is great, and characters die from rats, Drano, battery acid in veins, and dynamite in the mouth. With Roger E. Mosley as Goldie's militant brother, Juanita Moore as his mom, Don Gordon as a racist cop, Carol Speed, and Anazette Chase. The screenwriter was an ex-con and pimp in real life. The director also made *The Passover Plot.* Music by Willie Hutch and others is on the Motown soundtrack, but some video versions have a different 80s rerelease soundtrack. It was a Cinerama release.

Max Julien and Richard Pryor in *The Mack.*

MACON COUNTY LINE

(Embassy, 1974) **D/S:** Richard Compton **S/P/A:** Max Baer, Jr.

Accused of a murder they had nothing to do with, three Yankee kids are hunted by the law in Georgia in the 1950s. This AIP drive-in classic was the first feature produced by Max Baer, Jr. (Jethro in the TV series *The Beverly Hillbillies*), who also plays the sheriff. With Geoffrey Lewis, Joan Blackman, Cheryl Waters, Leif Garrett, Jesse Vint, and Alan Vint. Bobbie Gentry sings the theme song. *Return to Macon County* (1975) is the sequel.

MACON COUNTY WAR

(AIP, 1991) **D/S/P:** Bret McCormick

A man returns home to help out with a feud between families. Dan Haggerty stars. Fred Olen Ray was the executive producer. This has nothing to do with the 70s Macon County movies, but some video renters won't know that.

MAD AT THE MOON

(Republic, 1992) **D:** Martin Donovan **S:** Richard Pelusi **P:** Michael Kastenbaum, Matt Devlin

Mary Stuart Masterson stars in this slow-moving fairy tale/western as a woman who has an arranged marriage and discovers that her awkward, bearded farmer husband (Stephen Blake) suffers from "moon sickness." The pathetic man howls and roars in pain during his "transformations." She loves Hart Bochner (also in the director's *Apartment Zero*) as a mysterious gambler who likes bar girls like Cec Verrell. With Fionnula Flanagan and Daphne Zuniga in a flashback.

MAD AT THE WORLD

(Fang, 1955) **D/S:** Harry Essex **P:** Collier Young

This little-known but very cool b/w crime/jd movie from Ida Lupino's Filmmakers company was shot on location in Chicago. Keefe Brasselle is Sam, a Korean War vet who becomes a depressed vigilante after his baby is killed by a bottle thrown by a "wolfpack." The small gang (led by Paul Dubov) hangs out at the Hijackers social club, and a white bebop group plays. Frank Lovejoy (who narrates) costars as the helpful police captain, and Cathy O'Donnell and Karen Sharpe are the women in Sam's life. The supporting cast is priceless. Stanley Clements (from the Bowery Boys) and Joseph Turkel (later a Stanley Kubrick regular) are Ignatz and Pete, jds who drink, beat, rob, and kill. Young Aaron Spelling (!) is a wide-eyed suspect from the slums, and Joe Besser (!) is a gas jockey with useful information. The jazzy score is by Leith Stevens (*The Wild One*). Harry Essex, a well-known screenwriter, also directed *I, the Jury* (1953) in 3-D.

THE MAD DEATH

(Prime, 1983) **D:** Robert Young **S:** Sean Hignett **P:** Robert McIntosh UK

It all starts like a *Cujo* copy but escalates until the entire Scottish countryside is threatened by packs of rabid dogs. A mass dog hunt with S.W.A.T. teams is organized, and the hero is a veterinarian. Some people become rabid (pronounced "ray-bid"). They hallucinate and have nightmares about water. This was originally a TV miniseries. It's really pretty boring.

MAD DOG AND GLORY

(MCA, 1993) **D:** John McNaughton **S:** Richard Price **P:** Barbara De Fina, Martin Scorsese **C:** Robby Muller **M:** Elmer Bernstein

Martin Scorsese and Robert De Niro hired the director of *Henry: Portrait of a Serial Killer* to make this black comedy with some violent scenes. A mild-mannered Chicago police photographer (De Niro, trying to change his image) saves the life of a mobster (Bill Murray). As a reward he receives a woman called Glory (Uma Thurman) for a week, and they fall in love. Also with David Caruso, Tom Towles (*Henry*), Kathy Baker, and Richard Belzer. This Universal release is from De Niro's Tribeca company.

MAD DOG COLL

(1961) **D:** Burt Balaban **S/P:** Edward Schreiber

John Davis Chandler stars as Vincent Coll, a crazed young 20s gangster in NYC who challenges bootlegger Dutch Schultz (Vincent Gardenia). With Kay Doubleday as his stripper mistress, Brooke Hayward, Jerry Orbach, Telly Savalas, and Gene Hackman (in his first role) as a cop. It's in b/w. Chandler was in *The Young Savages* the same year. *Killer Instinct* (1992) is also about Coll.

MAD DOGS AND ENGLISHMEN

(1971) **D/P:** Pierre Adidge **P:** Harry Marks, Robert Abel   UK (*Joe Cocker: Mad Dogs and Englishman*)

Joe Cocker toured America in 1970 with a troupe of 42 musicians, including Leon Russell, Claudia Linnear, and Rita Coolidge, plus various girlfriends and kids. Adidge filmed 62 hours of footage and cut it down to 117 minutes for an MGM release. The A&M album was only Cocker's third.

MADE IN HEAVEN

(Warner, 1987) **D:** Alan Rudolph **S/P:** Bruce A. Evans, Raynold Gideon **P:** David Blocker

This romantic déjà-vu hippie movie may interest Neil Young fans. He appears and wrote the theme song, Buffalo Springfield songs are heard, and star Timothy Hutton even resembles Young after he's reincarnated. Hutton drowns saving some kids in the 40s (shown in b/w) and meets an unborn soul (Kelly McGillis) in heaven. Later they have to find each other on Earth with no memory of meeting before. A lot of time is spent explaining the rules of re-incarnation and heavenly teleportation, and some scenes take place in Heaven, with wings and everything. With Maureen Stapleton as a dead aunt, Don Murray, Amanda Plummer, and Ellen Barkin. There are bits by Tom Petty, Ric Ocasek, Mare Winningham, John Considine, and Debra Winger in drag as God. Lorimar released this PG feature, which was made in Georgia and South Carolina.

THE MAD EXECUTIONERS

(Sinister, 1963) **D:** Edwin Zbonek
S: Robert A. Stemmle **P:** Arthur Brauner
W. Germany (*Der Henker von London*)

This b/w horror mystery, based on a novel by Bryan Edger Wallace (son of Edgar Wallace), has enough happening for two movies. Criminals are being sentenced and hanged by a secret court of hooded judges who drive horse-drawn carriages and use coffins for tables. A Scotland Yard inspector (Hansjorg Felmy) and an amateur detective who uses disguises check up on the many

suspects. Meanwhile, a "fake" execution group appears, a body is sold to a museum as an ancient mummy (?!), and a mad surgeon/sex killer in a secret lab decapitates women and keeps their heads on an artificial body (this, unfortunately, is not shown). With Wolfgang Preiss and Maria Perschy. Some of the slow, Duane Eddy–type music is pretty great. The tape is letterboxed and includes trailers (good) but is also pretty worn out (bad).

MADHOUSE

(Virgin, 1980) **D/S/P:** "Oliver Hellman"/
Ovidio G. Assonitis **S:** Stephen Blakely,
Peter Shepard, Robert Gandus
Italy (*Scared to Death*)

The deformed identical-twin sister of a teacher at a school for the deaf (Trish Everly) escapes from an asylum and moves into an old mansion. She kills people with the help of her priest uncle and her trained Rottweiler. Dead bodies are arranged around a table for a birthday party. This gory movie by the director of *Beyond the Door* (1975) was filmed in Savannah, Georgia. The video was banned in England.

MADHOUSE MANSION

(Comet, 1974) **D/S/P:** Stephen Weeks
S: Philip Norman, Rosemary Sutcliff
M: Ron Geeson   UK (*Ghost Story*)

Naked Under Leather was a lot more fun, but here's another movie with singer Marianne Faithfull. It's a slow-moving story of three very different 20s British men vacationing at a huge estate. A doll becomes a little girl, and an old asylum is filled with ghosts. The dreams, nightmares, and bad memories of Miss Sophie (Faithfull) explain the restless spirits. Barbara Shelley plays two parts. The cinematography is good, but there are no notable special effects. It was shot in India. Stephen Weeks also directed Christopher Lee in *I, Monster*.

MADIGAN'S MILLIONS

(Video Treasures, 1966) **D/S:** Dan Ash
D: Stanley Prager, Giorgio Gentili
S: Jim Henaghen, José Luis Bayonas
P: Sidney Pink   Italy/Spain
(*Un Dollaro per Sette Vigliacchi*)

By 1969, when AIP released this unfunny G-rated comedy, its star, Dustin Hoffman, had been nominated for two Oscars. He plays an IRS agent sent to Rome to recover money hidden by a murdered gangster (Cesar Romero). When he meets the gangster's daughter (Elsa Martinelli) he thinks she's his mistress. With George Raft, Gustavo Rojo, and Gérard Tichy.

MAD JACK: *See* BLOOD SALVAGE

MAD MAX BEYOND THUNDERDOME

(Warner, 1985) **D:** George Ogilvie
D/S/P: George Miller **S/P:** Terry Hayes

After the awesome *Road Warrior*, this third and final Mad Max movie was a big disappointment. Mel Gibson (who did his own stunts) and Bruce Spence return. Max leads the post-nuke feral children at the end. Instead of hyperspeed chase scenes in costumized vehicles Max has to battle some guy while hanging from big rubber bands in a makeshift arena. Aunty Entity (Tina Turner) runs Barter Town and famous dwarf actor Angelo Rossitto enjoys his ultimate role as "the Master," always on the shoulders of "Blaster." This Columbia release was rated PG-13 (the first two were rated R).

MAD MISSION III

(Vestron, 1984) **D:** Tsui Hark **S:** Raymond Wong **P:** Karl Mak, Dean Shek   Hong Kong
(*Aces Go Places III: Our Man in Bond Street*)

This is part of a series of six (so far) silly action comedies that spoof James Bond movies, all very popular in Asia. Series star Samuel Hui is a master thief named King Kong who's hired to steal some jewels. Sylvia Chang and bald Carl Maka are the hero's police-couple friends. This entry features Richard Kiel reprising his *Jaws* role again as Big G, Tsunehara Sugiyama as Oddjob, and Peter Graves in a brief *Mission Impossible*–inspired scene. Doubles for James Bond and Queen Elizabeth steal the "Star of Fortune." The first two in the series, *Mad Mission* (1981) and *Mad Mission II* (1983), were directed by Eric Tsang and are available in America on video. *Aces Go Places IV: You Never Die Twice* (1986) was directed by Cheung Kuen. *Aces Go Places V: The Terracotta Hit* (1989) was directed by Lau Karl Leung.

Angelo Rossitto as "the Master" in *Mad Max Beyond Thunderdome*.

MADONNA: A CASE OF BLOOD AMBITION

(Atlas, 1990) **D:** Alain Zaloum **S:** Brenda
Newman **P:** Roger Racine   Canada

A woman (Deborah Mansy) kills the jurors who
convicted her father of the rape and murder of a
child after he is beaten to death in prison. She carefully plans each murder, seducing some of the victims. The film is based on a novel by Ed Kelleher
and Hariette Vidal.

THE MAD PLUMBER: *See* THE PLUMBER

MAD RON'S PREVIEWS FROM HELL

(Off the Wall, 1987) **D:** Jim Monaco
P: Ron Roccia, Jim Murray

A projectionist (Mad Ron Roccia), a ventriloquist
(Ron Pawlow), and a zombie dummy host an 82-
minute movie-trailer compilation made in Lands-
downe, Pennsylvania. Everyone agrees that the
comic bits in between are a problem, but the 45
theatrical-preview trailers shown make this a must
for hard-core gore-and-exploitation fans. Some of
the most notorious and disgusting movies ever
made are represented, often with scenes later cut
out of the actual films. Some titles are *I Drink Your
Blood, Africa, Blood and Guts, Man from Deep
River, Deep Red.* There are also trailers for the Ilsa
series and H. G. Lewis movies. The real mondo-
movie scenes are somehow even more shocking
when mixed with all the faked horror.

THE MAESTRO: *See* HOME MOVIES

THE MAFU CAGE: *See* THE CAGE

MAGICAL MYSTERY TOUR

(MPI, 1967) **D/P/A:** The Beatles   UK

The Beatles made this 60-minute fantasy, first
shown on TV in England, as a follow-up project to
the *Sergeant Pepper* album. It was criticized by
nearly everyone at the time, but I think it's improved with age. John, Paul, George, and Ringo
appear as wizards and as themselves in various
drug-induced scenes. Some highlights are "I Am
the Walrus" performed with animal masks, and
George and Paul at a burlesque show. With the
Bonzo Dog Band, Victor Spinetti (*Help!*), Ivor
Cutler, Mal Evans, and Mike McGear (Paul's
brother). A deluxe EP with six songs was issued in
England. A Capitol album, which added five older
hits, was released in America in time for Christmas
and made it to number 1.

THE MAGIC CRANE

(1993) **D:** Benny Chan **P:** Tsui Hark   Hong Kong

This period martial-arts/fantasy/adventure includes
some gore, sex, cannibalism, a swarm of bats, and a
giant crane and turtle. Tony Leung stars, with Chiu
Wai, Anita Mui, and Rosamund Kwan as lady magicians and Lawrence Ng as the main villain.

THE MAGIC FOUNTAIN

(Sinister, 1961) **D/P:** Allan David **S:** John Lehmann

Prince Alfred (Peter Nestler) searches for a magic
fountain in an enchanted castle to restore the health
of his dying father. When his two evil brothers
cause trouble, a dwarf turns them into ravens. This
Brothers Grimm fairy tale was filmed in the Black
Forest of Bavaria. The voices of Buddy Baer and
Hans Conried are heard, Steve Allen sings the title
song, and Cedric Hardwicke narrates the film and
plays the king in footage added in 1964. Weegee is
credited with (added) special effects.

THE MAGIC GARDEN OF STANLEY SWEETHEART

(1970) **D:** Leonard Horn **S:** Robert T.
Westbrook **P:** Martin Poll

Don Johnson (in his movie debut) stars as a Co-
lumbia University student who makes an underground sex film (called *Headless*) starring Holly
Near (she was also in *Angel, Angel Down We Go!*
and later became a feminist folk singer). He also
gets high and joins in body-painting and group sex.
With Linda Gillin, Michael Greer, and Dianne
Hull. Mike Curb was the musical supervisor, and
MCA released the soundtrack, featuring Davie
Allen, Richie Havens, Crow, Eric Burdon and War,
and others. This R-rated adaptation of Robert T.
Westbrook's novel was not popular. Johnson returned in other counterculture misfires like *Zach-
ariah* and *The Harrad Experiment.*

THE MAGICIAN

(Fright, 1926) **D/S/P:** Rex Ingram

The great German star Paul Wegener is Oliver
Haddo, a caped alchemist and hypnotist in France.
He has a remote castle known as "the sorcerer's
tower" with an elaborate mad lab and a dwarf assistant. Haddo needs "the blood of a maiden"
(Alice Terry) to create life, so he takes her over
Svengali style. In an incredible scene she's transported to Hell, where he appears as the Devil and
nearly naked horned men dance. Villagers attack
and blow up the castle at the end. The film is based
on a novel by Somerset Maugham that was inspired
by the real-life Aleister Crowley. The first two Universal Frankenstein movies borrowed a lot from
this ambitious horror/fantasy silent. An expensive
and impressive-looking MGM production, it was
filmed at Rex Ingram's studio in Nice, on location
in Paris and on the Riviera. Scenes are tinted in
various colors. It was unpopular when released and
called "tasteless and horrible" by reviewers. The
maiden is played by the American wife of the Irish
director. His assistant was the future British filmmaker Michael Powell (who also acts in the film).

THE MAGICIAN OF LUBLIN

(1979) **D/S/P:** Menahem Golan **S:** Irving S. White
P: Yoram Globus   Israel/W. Germany/Canada

Alan Arkin stars as a depressed Jewish traveling
magician in turn-of-the-century Poland. It's based
on a novel by Isaac Bashevis Singer, and features
Louise Fletcher, Shelley Winters (she was in several Golan pictures), Valerie Perrine, Maia Danziger, Lou Jacobi, and Warren Berlinger. Golan returned with more typical Cannon features like *The
Apple* (1980) and *Enter the Ninja* (1981).

THE MAGIC KID

(PM, 1993) **D/P:** Joseph Merhi **S:** Stephen
Smoke **P:** Richard Pepin   (*Ninja Dragons*)

Ted Jan Roberts (a black belt at 13) stars as a mar-
tial-artist kid who gets to meet his hero, Don "the
Dragon" Wilson, in LA. With Stephen Furst as his
uncle, an alcoholic professional clown in debt to a
mob boss (Joseph Campanella), Shonda Whipple,
Lauren Tewes, Pamela Dixon, and Chris Mitchum.
This PG film from guys known for R action movies
copies *Sidekicks* and *Three Ninjas.*

THE MAGIC KID II

(PM, 1994) **D/S/A:** Stephen Furst **S:** Nick
Stone **P:** Richard Pepin and Joseph Merhi

Flounder from *National Lampoon's Animal House*
made this PG sequel. The star (Ted Jan Roberts) of
the "Ninja Boy" movies leaves the Hollywood life
for school, but bad-guy studio executives plot to
lure him back to make them more money. With Allyce Beasley, Wil Shriner, and cameos by former
St. Elsewhere regulars William Daniels, Howie
Mandel, and David Morse.

THE MAGIC SERPENT

(VSOM, 1966) **D:** Tetsui Yamaguchi **S:** Marasu Igami
P: Shigeru Okawa   Japan (*Kai Tatsu Daikessen*)

This Toei fantasy features giant monsters (men in
suits), ninjas, a spider woman, and decapitations
and spurting blood. When ghosts appear the color
film changes to b/w. A prince (Hiroki Matsukata)
who is a student of a wizard is the hero. AIP released this (badly dubbed) directly to TV, while
some less intersting Japanese sci-fi movies played
in theaters.

THE MAGIC WEAVER

(United, 1960) **D/P:** Alexander Rou **S:** Eugene
Schwartz   USSR (*Mariya Iskusnitsa*)

The director of this color fairy tale made many fantasy films in the USSR, at the Maxim Gorky studios. It has lots of special effects, fantasy sets, and
excellent animal footage. A happy, singing soldier
helps a kid rescue his mother, a weaver, from a
wizard king with an underwater kingdom. She
says, "Freedom or slavery, it is all one." I like the
frog man and the pirates who sing in Russian. Allied Artists released it in America in 1965. Then
Jeffrey C. Hogue put it on video.

MAGNUM FORCE

(Warner, 1973) **D:** Ted Post **S:** John
Milius, Michael Cimino **P:** Robert Daly

It's not as good as *Dirty Harry* (1971), but Clint
Eastwood ("Do You Feel Lucky?") returns as San
Francisco cop Harry Callahan for the second time.
He discovers killers in the police department.
David Soul, Robert Urich, and Kip Niven (*Bummer!*) are cops who have become "executioners."
The cast also includes Hal Holbrook, Tim Matheson, Richard Devon, and Suzanne Somers (shot
dead in a pool). *The Enforcer* was next in the
series. In real life, two killer hold-up men claimed
they were inspired by this movie to force five of
their victims to drink Drano.

THE MAGUS

(1968) **D:** Guy Green **S:** John Fowles
P: John Kohn, Jud Kinberg   UK

Michael Caine takes a teaching job at a boys' school on a Greek island, replacing a man who killed himself. He visits the villa/asylum of Conchis, the god-like "Magus" (Anthony Quinn), where he's forced to play various games, is told to whip Candice Bergen (whom he has seen in a porno movie), and is put on trial. He discovers that Conchis was responsible for helping to arrange Nazi atrocities during the war (seen in flashbacks). With Anna Karina and Julian Glover. This confusing, reality-shifting feature was shot in Spain and released by 20th Century–Fox. It would make a good Quinn double bill with *The Visit* (1964).

MAHOGANY

(Paramount, 1975) **D:** Berry Gordy, Tony Richardson **S:** John Byrum **P:** Rob Cohen, Jack Ballard

Diana Ross is a poor girl who becomes a famous fashion designer in Europe. Billy Dee Williams loves her, but it's Tony Perkins as Sean, her psychotic photographer, who ruins her life and steals all his scenes. Motown president Berry Gordy (who was romantically involved with Ross) fired the director and made most of it himself (a big mistake). Perkins fans shouldn't miss it. With Jean-Pierre Aumont, Nina Foch, and Marisa Mell. The soundtrack is on Motown (of course). Ross' next film, the last of three (all for Motown), was *The Wiz*.

MAIDEN QUEST

(Private Screenings, 1970) **D:** Adrian Hoven **S:** Fred Denger **D/S/P:** David F. Friedman   W. Germany (*Siegfried und das Sägenhafte Liebesleben der Nibelungen; The Long Swift Sword of Siegfried*)

This comic sex remake of Fritz Lang's classic 1924 epic *Die Nibelungen* copies the original script pretty closely and was a hit in Germany. While it was being shot, *Cabaret* was being made on the next sound stage. Friedman "Americanized" it with dubbing. Russ Meyer regular Stuart Lancaster is the voice of the king. Star Raymond Harmstorf (known in Germany for playing Jack London on TV) became "Lance Boyle" in the US credits. Although there's no dragon, the story includes a magic cap of invisibility, a wall of fire, a trip to Iceland, a torture chamber, and the insatiable

Anthony Perkins in Berry Gordy's *Mahogany*.

Brunhild and her all-female army wearing *Barbarella*-type costumes. Although it's a well-produced costume film, it's a sex movie, and there's lots of nudity and very energetic sex. There's an orgy, topless dancers, voyeurs, and (best of all) sex with an invisible man. This is the first look Americans got of Sybelle Denninger (later Sybil Danning) as the king's sister, Kriemhild (pronounced "Cream-held"). She has pretty wild eyelashes and a surprising lesbian scene. The soundtrack uses music by Richard Wagner and some funny, out-of-place rock with electric-guitar leads. Director Hoven also produced *Succubus* and *Mark of the Devil*.

MAÎTRESSE

(Warner, 1976) **D/S:** Barbet Schroeder
S: Paul Voujargol   France

A thief (Gérard Depardieu) falls for a dominatrix (Bulle Ogier, who later married the director) after he and a partner break into her house. She dresses in black leather and operates a well-stocked torture chamber. Some real dominatrix customers were used for the strong torture scenes. This often shocking feature (in one scene, a penis is nailed to a board) received an X rating in America and was a surprise (and uncut) release by Warner Video in 1992.

THE MAJORETTES!

(Tempe, 1986) **D:** Bill Hinzman
S/P: John Russo   (*One by One*)

A psycho in a hood kills suburban high-school girls. A Devil-worshipping, drug-dealing biker gang is thrown in, along with many other suspects. It's based on John Russo's novel and was directed (badly) by a *Night of the Living Dead* zombie in Pittsburgh. With Russ Streiner, and cameos by Russo and Hinzman.

MAKE THEM DIE SLOWLY

(IVE, 1980) **D/S:** Umberto Lenzi **P:** Antonia Crescenzi   Italy (*Cannibal Feroux*)

Ads for this unrated shocker (falsely) claimed, "Banned in 31 countries." It's one of the stronger fake lost-civilization films talked about in reverent tones by "fans" and condemned by others (who usually haven't seen it). College students in Colombia encounter Indians who fight back after being abused by drug dealers. Meanwhile, a police lieutenant (Richard Bolla) searches for a dealer in NYC. There are fake scenes of severed limbs, brain and gut eating, castration, and torture. A woman is strung up in *A Man Called Horse*–style by her chest. If that isn't enough, a crocodile and turtle are actually killed. John Morghen is the sadistic drug dealer Mike. Women about to die sing "Red River Valley." It was made in South America and NYC. Aquarius released it in 1983, rated X.

MAKING CONTACT

(Starmaker, 1985) **D/P:** Roland Emmerich   W. Germany (*Joey*)

A kid (Joshua Morrell) talks to his dead dad on a magic phone, and an evil spirit is in a ventriloquist doll. This Spielberg-like PG fantasy is set in Virginia Beach but was filmed near Stutgart. New World released it. The director later made big-budget titles like *Universal Soldier* and *Stargate*.

MAKING MR. RIGHT

(HBO, 1987) **D:** Susan Seidelman **S:** Floyd Byars, Laurie Frank **P:** Mike Wise

John Malkovich stars as an anti-social scientist and his friendly lookalike, a robot creation called Ulysses. Ann Magnuson is Frankie Stone, a Miami publicist engaged to a congressman (Hart Bochner). She's supposed to sell Ulysses to the public but falls in love with him. With Glenne Headly, Laurie Metcalf, Ben Masters, and Polly Bergen. This Orion fantasy/comedy is rated PG-13.

MALAMONDO

(1964) **D/S:** Paolo Cavara **S:** Ugo Gregoretti, Zanetti **P:** Goffredo Lombardo   Italy (*I Malamondo*)

"Bizarre activities of European youth" are explored in this mondo movie. It features Swiss students who ski naked, Italians butchering a pig, a Paris "happening," female impersonators, an orgy in a graveyard, rock and roll in Italy, suicide, and miscegenation. The Ennio Morricone soundtrack is on Epic. The narration is by Marvin Miller, and Jane Morgan and Catherine Spaak sing.

MALIBU BEACH

(Starmaker, 1978) **D/S:** Robert J. Rosenthal **S:** Celia Susan Cotelo **P:** Marilyn J. Tenser

Kim Lankford stars as a lifeguard in this teen beach comedy with Stephen Oliver, James Daughton, Susan Player-Jareau, Tara Stromeir, and Rebecca Ferratti (from *Playboy*). It's from Crown International and the director of *Zapped!*

THE MALIBU BIKINI SHOP

(Fox, 1985) **D/S:** David Wechter **P:** Gary Mehlman, J. Rotcop, Leo Leichter   (*The Bikini Shop*)

College-grad brothers (Michael David Wright and Bruce Greenwood) inherit a bikini store from their aunt (the then-newsworthy Rita Jenrette). This sex comedy features Debra Blee, Jay Robinson, Kathleen Freeman, and hot tubs.

MALIBU EXPRESS

(MCA, 1984) **D/S/P:** Andy Sidaris

Former child actor Darby Hinton stars as a millionaire private eye, in this remake of the director's *Stacy!* (1973), which was a cable-TV staple for years. It features four *Playboy* playmates (Barbara Edwards, Lorraine Michaels, Lynda Wiesmeier, and Kimberly McArthur), lots of nudity, and a transvestite bar scene. With Art Metrano and, in small roles, Regis and Joy Philbin, porno star Shauna McCulloch, and Sybil Danning as a countess. Playboy magazine put up half the budget. *Hard Ticket to Hawaii* was the next by Sidaris, who went on to make many more interchangeable sex/action movies.

MALIBU HIGH

(1979) **D:** Irv Berwick **S:** John Buckley,
Tom Singer **P:** Lawrence D. Foldes

A girl (Jill Lansing) becomes a teen hooker who
gives a school teacher a heart attack by stripping
for him. It's by the director of *The Monster of Piedras Blancas*. The sequel to this sleazy Crown release was *Young Warriors*.

MALICE

(New Line, 1993) **D/P:** Harold Becker
S: Aaron Sorkin, Scott Frank **P:** Rachel Pfeffer,
Charles Mulvehill **M:** Jerry Goldsmith

A serial killer/rapist is loose on a New England
campus. Alec Baldwin stars as a supersurgeon ("I
am God") who rooms at the house of the college
dean and performs emergency surgery on the
man's wife (Nicole Kidman). This slick Columbia
feature has many plot holes and borrows ideas
from *Marnie*. Bill Pullman costars as the dean,
with Peter Gallagher as a lawyer, George C. Scott,
and Anne Bancroft.

MALPERTUIS

(VSOM, 1972) **D:** Harry Kumel **S:** Jean Ferry
P: Paul Laffargue   Belgium/France/W. Germany

The dying, god-like Cassavius (Orson Welles)
"captures" some Greek gods in his huge island
home and has them "sewn" into human skins by a
taxidermist. This adaptation of a novel by Jean Ray
is by the director of the cult vampire movie *Daughters of Darkness*. Mathieu Carriere is a sailor who
falls in love with Gorgon (Susan Hampshire, who
plays three roles) and becomes a statue. With Jean-
Pierre Cassel, Sylvie Varton, Daniel Pilon, and
Walter Rilla. A 124-minute English-language version exists, but it's been cut down to as short as 96
minutes.

MAMA'S DIRTY GIRLS

(TWE, 1974) **D/C:** John Hayes **P:** Ed
Carlin, Gil Lasky   (*Jessie's Girls*)

"Sultry sisters in sin—they fight dirty—they love
dirty!" Gloria Grahame marries for money, and
Candice Rialson and Sondra Currie are her money-
hungry daughters. This Premiere release was made
after Hayes' *Grave of the Vampire*.

MAN AND WIFE

(1969) **D/S:** "Matt Cimber"/Matteo Ottaviano

Cimber, who had married Jayne Mansfield and directed her last film (*Single Room Furnished*), made
this and other early porno movies. They were allowed to be screened because they were disguised
as documentaries. This has been called "the first
theatrical hard-core feature," and it was said to include 49 positions. Cimber later made black-action
and Pia Zadora movies.

MAN BAIT

(1952) **D:** Terence Fisher **S:** Frederick Knott
P: Anthony Hinds   UK (*The Last Page*)

Sexy Diana Dors was introduced to American audiences in this Hammer film released by Lippert. In
one of his last films, American star
George Brent plays a book dealer
who gets involved in blackmail and
murder. Marguerite Chapman, another
American, costars. Fisher's next was
Stolen Face.

MAN BEHIND THE SUN

(World Video, 1987) **D:** Xeng Le Law
S: Mou Wen Yuan, Teng Dun Jing,
Liu Mei Fei **P:** Fu Chi   Hong Kong
(*Hei Tai Yang 731; Black Sun 731*)

This unflinching, fact-based movie,
with convincing FX, about WWII
Japanese medical atrocities was produced the same year as *The Last
Emperor*. It shocked even the most
jaded viewers when it played in some American
theaters and was a hit in parts of Asia. In 1945
General Ishi takes over as director of the notorious
731 Squadron in Manchukuo (Manchuria), where
"3,000 Chinese, Korean, and Russian people
died." Japanese kids receive brutal training and
learn to hate Chinese and consider them less than
human. Prisoners are used for horrifying experiments and live autopsies. The ending explains that
the guilty escaped to Pusan, where they were
spared by the Americans, and that the results of
Ishi's germ-warfare experiments were used on our
side in the Korean War! The video is letterboxed.
The Japanese dialogue is dubbed into English,
but the Chinese dialogue is not. *Man Behind the
Sun 2: Laboratory of the Devil* (1991) and *Man Behind the Sun 3: Narrow Escape* (1994) followed.

MAN BITES DOG

(Fox Lorber, 1992) **D/S/P/A:** Rémy Belvaux
D/S/P/A/C: André Bonzel **D/P/A:** Benoît
Poelvoorde **S:** Vincent Tarvier   Belgium
(*C'est Arrivé près de chez Vous*)

A film crew follows a friendly, cultured, poetry-
spouting, racist, homophobic psycho killer (Benoît
Poelvoorde) who never stops talking while he's
busy at "work." The three-man crew eventually
joins him in committing crimes. This documentary-
style black comedy is disturbing (a gang rape and
guts are shown), too long, and more irritating than
anything else. It was shot in 16mm b/w by guys in
their 20s. Real relatives of the leads play themselves. It won several European awards. It's available as an NC-17 or unrated (cut) video (both are
in French with English subtitles). The complete
Criterion laserdisc includes an interview. The
lesser-known *America's Deadliest Home Videos*,
from the same year, used the same idea.

A MAN CALLED HORSE

(Fox, 1970) **D:** Elliot Silverstein
S: Jack De Witt **P:** Sandy Howard

In the early 19th century an Englishman, Lord
Morgan (Richard Harris), is captured by Sioux
Indians and becomes a slave. He learns their language and customs and falls in love with Running
Deer (Corinna Tsopei), the chief's daughter. Before
they can marry he has to prove himself by enduring the "sun vow" torture. The famous shock-

Richard Harris is *A Man Called Horse*.

ing scenes of Harris hanging from hooks stuck
through the skin on his chest inspired more tasteless imitations in European cannibal movies. Famous stuntman Yakima Canutt was the second-
unit director. With Judith Anderson, Dub Taylor,
Iron Eyes Cody, Manuel Padilla, and many real
American Indians. It was filmed in Mexico and released by National General. The Leonard Rosenman score is on Columbia. Harris returned in *Return of a Man Called Horse* and *Triumphs of a
Man Called Horse*.

A MAN CALLED RAINBO

(Section Eight, 1989) **D:** Lesser Pismo **D/S/P:** Robert
Schnitzer **S:** Scott Altizer **P:** Jeffrey Hilton

This is a reedited and redubbed version of *Rebel*
(1969) starring Sylvester Stallone. This time he's a
Nam-deserter hippy who has to help start WWIII.
The humor consists mostly of sex, drug, and shit
jokes.

A MAN CALLED SLEDGE

(VSOM, 1970) **D/S:** Vic Morrow **S:** Frank
Kowalski **P:** Dino De Laurentiis

James Garner stars as Sledge, a wanted man who
goes after a gold shipment with his gang (including Dennis Weaver and Claude Akins) and some
maximum-security prisoners they help to escape.
Laura Antonelli is his woman. This downbeat Columbia western, filmed in Spain and Italy, features
John Marley and Ken Clark. Morrow also directed
Deathwatch.

THE MANCHU EAGLE MURDER CAPER MYSTERY

(United Artists, 1973) **D/S:** Dean Hargrove
S/A: Gabriel Dell **P:** Edward K. Dobbs

This PG spoof of 40s private-eye films was barely
released, but check out the cast. Former Dead End
Kid Gabriel Dell stars as an amateur detective who
raises chickens. He tries to solve the murder of a
milkman (Dick Gautier). With Will Geer, Joyce
Van Patten, Anjanette Comer, Nita Talbot, Vincent
Gardenia, Barbara Harris, Sorrell Brooke, Jackie
Coogan, and Huntz Hall. Made by United Artists.

MANCHURIAN AVENGER

(HBO, 1984) **D:** Ed Warnick **S:** Pat Hamilton, Timothy
Stephenson **P:** Robyn Bensinger   (*Shanghai Joe*)

Bobby Kim, Bill "Sugarfoot" Wallace, and Michael Stuart star in this martial-arts western set in a Colorado gold-rush town.

THE MANCHURIAN CANDIDATE

(MGM, 1962) **D:** John Frankenheimer
S: George Axelrod **P:** Howard Koch

Frank Sinatra has nightmares of when he was a prisoner during the Korean War. He tries to stop brainwashed, zombie-like Laurence Harvey from assassinating a presidential candidate at Madison Square Garden. Harvey was programmed in Manchuria to obey orders whenever he sees a Queen of Diamonds. His mother (Angela Lansbury, who was nominated for an Oscar) is behind the plot to have her vice-presidential-nominee husband (James Gregory) become president. The flashback/nightmare brainwashing scenes are excellent, and Sinatra and Henry Silva (playing a Korean) have an early (for the US) martial-arts battle. With Janet Leigh, Leslie Parrish, Khigh Diegh, John McGiver, Whit Bissell, and Reggie Nalder. This 126-minute UA release was kept out of circulation for years (so was *Suddenly,* the other Sinatra assassination movie). It was rereleased theatrically in 1987. The video includes interviews with Sinatra, director John Frankenheimer, and others.

MAN CRAZY

(1953) **D:** Irving Lerner **S/P:** Sidney
Harmon **S:** Philip Yordan

Neville Brand is top billed as a Hollywood villain in this story about three women who want to be in the movies. The ads said, "It's Bold! Blunt! Brutal!" Christine White, Irene Anders, and Coleen Miller are the aspiring actresses. With Joe Turkel, Karen Steele, and Jack Larson. It's from 20th Century–Fox.

MANDINGO

(Paramount, 1975) **D:** Richard Fleischer
S: Norman Wexler **P:** Dino De Laurentiis

James Mason is a southern slave-owner in 1840. His daughter (Susan George) messes with a bare-knuckles-fighting slave (Ken Norton). This long (more than two hours), big-budget exploitation movie was condemned by the Catholic Church. It features Perry King, Ben Masters, Ji-Tu Cumbuka, Brenda Sykes, Debbi Morgan, and Laura Misch (from *Playboy*). Mason uses kids for footstools, there's male nudity, and characters are pitchforked and boiled alive. Norton returned in a sequel, *Drum*. Both features were based on books by Kyle Onstott (supposedly a pseudonym for a black French Quarter queen).

MANDINGO MANHUNTER: *See* MAN HUNTER

MANDRAKE THE MAGICIAN

(Stokey, 1939) **D:** Sam Nelson, Norman Deming
S: Joseph F. Poland, Basil Dickey, Ned Dandy **P:** Jack Fier

This 12-chapter Columbia serial stars Warren Hull (who also played the Green Hornet) as Mandrake, who has the power to cloud men's minds. The

character is based on the comic strip by Lee Falk. Al Kikume is his African sidekick, Lothar, and Doris Weston is Betty. The Wasp, the masked villain, has a deadly radium machine. There was also a 1954 TV series and a 1979 TV movie.

MANDROID

(Paramount, 1993) **D:** Jack Ersgard **S:** Earl Kenton, Jackson Barr **P:** Vlad Paunesco, Dana Paunesco

In Eastern Europe the masked Dr. Drago takes over a powerful, all-black, remote-control *Robocop*-look robot. The action high point is a shootout in an old building. This is another movie aimed at kids that for some reason ends with the bad guy in bed with a topless hooker. There's also a lame setup for a sequel called *Invisible*. Brian Cousins is the American hero, and Jane Caldwell is the blond daughter of a good scientist. It was made in Romania by a Swedish director.

MAN-EATER: *See* SHARK!

MAN-EATER OF HYDRA

(Sinister, 1965) **D:** Mel Welles **S:** Stephen Schmidt
P: George Ferrer   Spain/W. Germany (*Das Geheimnis der Todesinsel; Island of the Doomed*)

Six tourists visit the villa of botanist Baron von Weiser (Cameron Mitchell), and several are killed. The baron's menacing, dead servant seems to return to life, and his special hybrid tree has blood-sucking tubes. Mitchell plays it cool until near the (very bloody) end, when he sobs to his creation, "My darling, my pet, my baby!" and attacks with an axe. Elisa Montes is blond Beth, and Kay Fischer is red-haired Carla. Sylvia Miles dubbed the voice of the old lady with the camera. The soundtrack is cool jazz and some zither music. Allied Artists released it in America. Welles (an American actor known for early Roger Corman movies) also directed *Lady Frankenstein* (1972).

THE MANEATERS ARE LOOSE!

(1978) **D:** Timothy Galfas **S:** Robert W. Lenski **P:** Bill Finnegan

Tom Skerritt, Steve Forrest, Harry Morgan, and G. D. Spradlin star in this story about killer tigers unleashed near a California town. Diana Muldaur and Dabney Coleman are also in this CBS-TV movie.

MAN FACING SOUTHEAST

(Starmaker, 1986) **D/S:** Elisio Subiela
P: Lujan Pflaum   Argentina

A man mysteriously appears in a Buenos Aires mental hospital, claims to be an alien, and seems to have supernatural powers. A psychiatrist tries to figure him out. The cast includes Lorenzo Quinteros, Hugo Soto, and Ines Verengo. New World released this serious film (in Spanish with English subtitles) in America.

THE MAN FROM BEYOND

(Sinister, 1921) **D:** Burton King **S:** Coolidge
Streeter **P/A:** Harry Houdini

Houdini (who also wrote the story) stars as a man encased in Arctic ice who's thawed out and searches for the reincarnation of the woman he loved 100 years before. There's lots of magic and a cimactic battle on the edge of Niagara Falls. I saw this with my father and a hall full of other magicians when I was a kid. The famous escape artist and illusionist (born in Hungary and raised in Wisconsin) also starred in a serial, *The Master Mystery* (1918), and several other silent features.

MAN FROM DEEP RIVER

(Prism, 1972) **D:** Umberto Lenzi **S:** Francesco Barilli, Massimo D'Avaci **P:** M. G. Rossi   Italy (*Il Paese del Sesso Selvaggio; Deep River Savages*)

A macho British photographer (Ivan Rassimov) is captured by a tribe in Thailand while snorkeling, and he eventually marries the cannibal chief's daughter (Me Me Lai). With cannibals, torture scenes, a *Man Called Horse*–style hanging scene, monkey-brain eating, and nudity. It was the first of its kind and was shot on location in the Thai jungle. Both stars returned in the even stronger *Jungle Holocaust* (1976), by Ruggero Deodato. An uncut version with Spanish subtitles is available from VGV.

THE MAN FROM HONG KONG

(1975) **D:** Brian Trenchard-Smith **P:** Raymond Chow   Hong Kong/Australia

Jimmy Wang Yu (*The One-Armed Swordsman*) is a police inspector who goes to Sydney, Australia, and uses kung fu to battle drug dealers led by George Lazenby. Lazenby, who played James Bond once, was in other 70s Chinese features too.

THE MAN FROM O.R.G.Y.

(1970) **D:** James A. Hill **P:** Sidney Pink

Robert Walker Jr. searches for three prostitutes who have gopher tattoos on their asses, to inform them that they've inherited a uranium mine. A midget helps him, and some Mafia agents try to stop him. With Steve Rossi, Slappy White, Louisa Moritz, and Lynn Carter. This R-rated Cinemation sex comedy was filmed in NYC and Puerto Rico. Walker also starred in *Son of Blob!*

THE MAN FROM S.E.X.

(Catalina, 1979) **D:** Lindsay Shontoff
S: Jeremy Lee Francis **P:** Elizabeth Gray
UK (*Licensed to Love and Kill*)

Gareth Hunt is agent Charles Bind, in this boring movie with bad puns and exaggerated sound FX. The hero is cloned, a midget in bell bottoms uses a whip, people are thrown into a pool of acid, and a man plays Madame Wang. The oddest scene has a stripper twirling razor-blade tassels. This is part of a series of spy spoofs by the Canadian-born director.

THE MAN FROM U.N.C.L.E.

(MGM series)

This NBC-TV spy series lasted from 1964 (the same year as *Goldfinger*) to 1968. It was so popular that MGM released theatrical features made from TV episodes. Robert Vaughn is Napoleon Solo, and David McCallum is Illya Kuryakin. The only other regular cast member was Leo G. Carroll as Mr. Waverly. So far, 22 volumes are available, with 2 episodes on each 104-minute video. Some of the directors were Richard Donner, John Newland, and Barry Shear, and a list of interesting guest villains would be very long.

THE MANGLER

(New Line, 1993) **D/S:** Tobe Hooper **S:** Stephen Brooks **P:** Anant Singh   U.S./Israel/S. Africa

This Stephen King adaptation is a lot like *Graveyard Shift*: it's set in a small New England town and it's dark, dreary, and very confusing. King's *Night Shift* story was only twenty pages long. Ted Levine stars as a depressed cop trying to find out how and why a big old industrial laundry pressing machine is grinding up local workers. With gore scenes, an animated creature, a psychic (Daniel Martmor), and a possessed refrigerator. Robert Englund (looking like Dr. Strangelove in old-age makeup) is the heartless crippled sweatshop owner with a voice box and an eye patch. Also with Vanessa Pike and Lisa Morris. Harry Alan Towers was executive producer. Englund was also in Hooper's *Night Terrors,* shot around the same time.

MANHATTAN BABY

(Lightning, 1982) **D/A:** Lucio Fulci **S:** Elisa Livia Brigante, Dardano Sacchetti **P:** Fabrizio De Angelis   Italy
(*L'Occhio del Male; Eye of the Evil Dead; The Possessed*)

Christopher Connelly desecrates a tomb and is blinded by a cursed Egyptian medallion. Back in NYC his daughter (Martha Taylor) is possessed and goes on a bloody killing spree. With Cinzia De Ponti (Miss Italy 1979) and some horror-movie in-jokes. Fulci did *New York Ripper* the same year.

THE MANHATTAN PROJECT

(HBO, 1986) **D/S/P:** Marshall Brickman **S:** Thomas Baum **P:** Jennifer Ogden

A high-school kid (Christopher Collet) whose father is working on the Star Wars project steals some plutonium with help from his girlfriend (Cynthia Nixon) and builds his own nuclear reactor, nearly blowing up the world. This Columbia comedy/thriller was released after *War Games*. With John Lithgow, Jill Eikenberry, and John Mahoney. Brickman also made *Simon* (1980).

MAN HUNT

(Fox, 1941) **D:** Fritz Lang **S:** Dudley Nichols **P:** Kenneth MacGowan

Walter Pidgeon stars as Captain Thorndike, a British big-game hunter who fails in his first attempt to kill Hitler. He's arrested, escapes to London with Nazis in pursuit, and as the movie ends is ready to try again. With Joan Bennett, George Sanders and John Carradine as Nazis, and young Roddy McDowall. This 20th Century–Fox film is based on the novel *Rogue Male*, by Geoffrey Household. It was made after Lang's two westerns, *The Return of Frank James* and *Western Union*. Other Lang films with anti-Nazi themes are *Hangmen Also Die*

M·G·M presents **to trap a spy**

starring
ROBERT VAUGHN
with (as "MR. SOLO")
PATRICIA CROWLEY
Fritz Weaver · William Marshall · Will Kuluva
David McCallum · Ivan Dixon
written by   produced by   directed by
Sam Rolfe · Norman Felton · Don Medford
in **METROCOLOR**
Special Guest Star
LUCIANA PALUZZI

A feature version of the TV series *The Man from U.N.C.L.E.*

(1943), *Ministry of Fear* (1945), and *Cloak and Dagger* (1946). *Rogue Male* (1976) is a color BBC-TV remake starring Peter O'Toole.

MANHUNT

(VSOM, 1973) **D/S:** Fernando Di Leo **S:** Augusto Finocchi, Ingo Hermess Italy (*The Italian Connection*)

Henry Silva battles the mob, and there's a major heroin heist. With Woody Strode, Luciana Paluzzi, Sylva Koscina, Mario Adorf, and Aldolfo Celi.

THE MANHUNT

(Media, 1984) **D/S/P:** Fabrizio De Angelis   Italy

John Ethan Wayne is a horse trainer framed as a horse thief and hunted by the authorities. With Henry Silva, Bo Svenson, and Ernest Borgnine. It was filmed in Arizona and has fake production credits.

MAN HUNTER

(TWE, 1980) **D/S/M:** "Cliford Brown"/Jesús Franco **S/P:** Julian Estevez Goman   Italy/Spain/W. Germany (*Il Cacciatore di Uomini; Mandingo Manhunter*)

A blond movie starlet (Ursula Fellner) is kidnapped for ransom by gangsters and taken to an island where she is chained up. With Nam-vet cannibals, sacrifices in the jungle, and a huge black zombie with Ping-Pong-ball eyes, known as "the Devil," who rapes women and then eats them.

Notice the very unconvincing natives and bad makeup. With Al Cliver and Robert Forster.

MANHUNTER

(1974) **D:** Martin Beck **S:** Greg Lynellee **P/A:** Earl Owensby

Owensby made his first million sell8 ing pneumatic tools. He opened his own studio in Shelby, North Carolina, and produced action movies for distribution in the South. "The Confederate Clint Eastwood" starred in a reported 16 movies before selling his studio in 1990. He's Frank Challenge, superspy, in this *Walking Tall* ripoff, his first.

MANHUNTER

(Warner, 1986) **D/S:** Michael Mann **P:** Richard Roth   (*Red Dragon: The Search for Hannibal Lecter*)

William L. Petersen stars as a southern FBI agent who attempts to get into the mind of a serial killer in order to capture him. It's based on the Thomas Harris novel *Red Dragon* (1981). *The Silence of the Lambs* later used some of the same characters. The acting is great, and it's a very stylish, intense feature. Brian Cox is Dr. Lecter, and Tom Noonan is "the Tooth Fairy," who kills families during the full moon with a stocking on his head. With Kim Greist, Joan Allen, and Dennis Farina. Dino De Laurentiis backed the film. After the other Lecter movie became a hit NBC retitled this for TV to make people think it was a sequel.

MANHUNT IN SPACE: *See* ROCKY JONES

MANHUNT OF MYSTERY ISLAND

(Republic, 1945) **D:** Spencer Gordon Bennet, Wallace A. Grissell, Yakima Cannut **S:** Albert Demond, Basil Dickey, Alan James

A modern villain "becomes" the 200-year-old pirate Mephisto (Roy Barcroft) with the "transformation chair." He's after the "radio-atomic power transmitter." This 15-chapter Republic serial stars Richard Bailey as criminologist Lance Reardon and Linda Sterling as the daughter of a kidnapped scientist. The overworked stuntmen are Dale Van Sickel, Eddie Parker, and Tom Steele. The 1966 feature version is *Captain Mephisto and the Transformation Machine.*

MANIAC COP

(TWE, 1987) **D:** William Lustig **S/P:** Larry Cohen

When NYC cop Bruce Campbell's wife is killed he's blamed, and undercover vice cop Laurene Landon helps him escape and catch the real killer. Robert Z'Dar is Matt Cordell, the rarely seen, badly scarred, almost supernatural killer, a big former cop who was framed and sent to prison. In one scene he destroys a police station. It's a superior action movie with a horror subplot and some humor. With Tom Atkins as the cop on the case, Richard Roundtree, William Smith, Sheree North as a crippled policewoman, and Sam Raimi in a cameo appearance. Jay Chattaway wrote the score, which was released by Pho records, and David Carradine sings. Some uncovincing LA locations almost ruin the ending. It's from SGE.

MANIAC COP 2

(IVE, 1990) **D:** William Lustig **S/P:** Larry Cohen

This sequel is better than the original. The scary-looking killer cop (Robert Z'Dar) teams up with a hairy Times Square serial killer (Leo Rossi). Robert Davi stars as the detective hero, with Claudia Christian as a police psychologist, Michael Lerner, Clarence Williams III, Charles Napier, Claude Earl Jones, and Paula Tricky as a stripper. Bruce Campbell and Laurene Landon from *Maniac Cop* show up briefly. The action and fire scenes are excellent, as is the Jay Chattaway score.

MANIAC COP 3: BADGE OF SILENCE

(Academy, 1992) **D/P:** Joel Soisson **D:** William Lustig **S:** Larry Cohen **P:** Michael Leahy

The first two in this series are recommended, but this (which debuted on HBO) is not. Cohen and Lustig both walked before it was finished. Matt Cordell (Robert Z'Dar again) has a face that's seldom shown but even uglier, and he wants to get married. For some reason there's a church in a basement under a hospital, and Julius Harris is a voodoo medicine man there. Robert Davi returns from part 2 as a detective, Gretchen Becker is a cop called Maniac Kate, and Caitlin Dulany is a nurse. They try to top the first two movies (which we see clips from) with overdone scenes of flaming people and a *Road Warrior*–inspired chase. Also in the cast are an unbilled Robert Forster, Jackie Earl Haley, Paul Gleason, and Bobby DiCicco. The music is by Jerry Goldsmith. KNB did the FX.

MANIAC WARRIORS

(AIP, 1989) **D:** Michael Mazo **D/P:** Lloyd A. Simandl **S:** John Ogis **P:** John A. Curtis Canada (*Empire of the Ash*)

In the post-nuke "New Idaho" forest, littered with bodies, warriors fight each other. The ones with white hoods attack on horseback or on motorcycles. The ones in black have cars and tanks and follow a preacher. A lone warrior with a Clint Eastwood voice (Thom Schioler) teams up with a sexy, short-haired girl (Melanie Kilgour) who's searching for her sister. There are lots of women in black leather with machine guns, and Kilgour has a topless shower. Some fun bits from the past are thrown in (a Jane Fonda dartboard, nude Madonna pics, and a copy of *Steppenwolf Live!*), and there's an OK rock score. It was made in Vancouver for Canadian TV. Kilgour returned in *Last of the Warriors*.

MAN IN HIDING

(Hammer, 1952) **D/S:** Terence Fisher **S:** Paul Tabori **P:** Michael Carreras, Alexander Paal UK (*Mantrap*)

Paul Henreid stars in this Hammer mystery about a private detective who's after a killer. Lois Maxwell (later in James Bond movies), Kieron Moore, and Hugh Sinclair costar. United Artists released it in America.

MAN IN THE SHADOW

(1957) **D:** Jack Arnold **S:** Gene L. Coon **P:** Albert Zugsmith

Albert Zugsmith agreed to back Orson Welles' *Touch of Evil* (1958) if Welles would appear in this film. Both deal with murder and racism against Mexicans. Jeff Chandler is a morally committed sheriff investigating the death of a migrant worker. Welles is the rancher who covers things up. Also in the cast are Colleen Miller, Ben Alexander, Barbara Lawrence, Royal Dano, James Gleason, and William Schallert. Universal made the Cinemascope feature. Chandler starred in *The Tattered Dress*, another Cinemascope film by Zugsmith and Arnold, the same year.

THE MANIPULATOR

(Vestron, 1971) **D/S:** Yabo Yablonsky **P:** Chuck Brent (*B. J. Lang Presents*)

This is an incredible, disorienting, irritating, grotesque movie. Mickey Rooney stars, in his ultimate role, as an in-your-face, insane Hollywood makeup man with a gray beard. He rants, sweats, talks to mannequins, dances, puts on lipstick, and ties Luana Anders to a chair and feeds her baby food after she repeats "I'm hungry, Mr. Lang" over and over. It all takes place in a warehouse full of props and in a slaughterhouse. I don't know what the hell it's all about, and it's too much Mickey for any sane person to endure, but the cinematography is excellent, and the LSD-inspired flashbacks, subliminal flashes, and freak-out sequences (some with laughing, naked people in white makeup) are on a par with *The Trip* or *Easy Rider* (which both also feature Anders, by the way). Keenan Wynn shows up as a wino. The music is by Gil Melle.

MANKILLERS

(Sony, 1987) **D/S:** David A. Prior **P:** Peter Yuval (*Twelve Wild Women*)

Blond Lynda Aldon is assigned by the CIA to lead an all-female, *Dirty Dozen*–type group of prisoners in Colombia. They have to stop a renegade agent. William Zipp costars, with Edd Byrnes, Gail Fisher (from the *Mannix* TV series), and Edy Williams as the woman who trains them. Pretty boring.

MANNEQUIN

(Media, 1987) **D/S:** Michael Gottlieb **S:** Edward Rugoff **P:** Art Levinson

A department-store-window designer (Andrew McCarthy) falls in love with a mannequin (Kim Cattrall) who's inhabited by an ancient Egyptian spirit and sometimes comes to life. This PG movie was inspired by *One Touch of Venus* (1948). With James Spader as the villain, Estelle Getty, and Meshach Taylor as a black, gay decorator. The music is by Starship. It's from 20th Century–Fox.

MANNEQUIN II: ON THE MOVE

(1991) **D:** Stewart Raffill **S:** David Isaacs, Ken Levine, Betsy Israel **S/P:** Edward Rugoff

Blond Kristy Swanson is a cursed Bavarian peasant girl who's now a mannequin. William Ragsdale, who works at a Philadelphia department store, resembles a prince. Terry Kiser is the evil descendant of a sorcerer, and Meshach Taylor returns from the first film. 20th Century–Fox released this PG sequel.

MAN'S BEST FRIEND

(New Line 1993) **D/S:** John Lafia **P:** Bob Engelman

Lance Henriksen creates a DNA-altered killer dog called Max. Ally Sheedy is a San Reno, California TV reporter who steals the animal from a lab to save it, but Max kills and buries a mailman, swallows a cat whole, and pisses acid. Real and mechanical dogs were used, and some of the FX (by Kevin Yagher) are pretty good. The problem is that the killings are offscreen, and the light, comic music helps take away any suspense. Also with William Sanderson. It's by the director of *Child's Play 2*.

MANSON

(1972) **D/S/P:** Lawrence Merrick **S:** Joan Huntington

This often-banned and seldom-seen documentary features Manson's real-life followers at the Spahn ranch. Most of the footage, filmed before the famous murders, shows the communal free-love and drug life-style of the future killers. Manson himself is heard singing and is seen in some courtroom footage. District attorney Vincent Bugliosi, Jerry Rubin, and others are interviewed. AIP picked it up for a limited release.

THE MANSTER

(Sinister, 1959) **D:** Kenneth B. Crane **D/P:** George P. Breakstone **S:** Walter J. Sheldon Japan/US

Originally released in America by Lippert on an incredible double bill with *The Horror Chamber of Dr. Faustus* in 1962, this is the ultimate split-personality movie. A man in a skinny gorilla suit kills some women in a bath. Blood splatters on the wall. Up in the mountains, in a remote cave full of giant mushrooms and plants, we discover that he's a mutant. Dr. Suzuki (Satoshi Nakamura) says, "You were my brother. You were an experiment that didn't work out. I'm sorry!" and shoots him. An ugly, bug-eyed mutant screeching in a cage is his wife. Meanwhile, Larry Stanford, an American journalist (Peter Dyneley) shows up. His drink is drugged, and the doctor jabs a hypo into his shoulder. Back in Tokyo he gets drunk on sake, goes behind closed doors with four geishas, and misses his flight home. Suzuki sends his beautiful, obedient assistant, Tara (Terri Zimmern), to further corrupt him in a mineral bath. Unshaven and hung over, the reporter ignores his worried, pleading wife (Jane Hylton), who arrives from New York. A priest is killed in a temple by a werewolf-type hand and two women are murdered on the street. In his room Stanford sees an eyeball on his shoulder!!! (a high point of screen surrealism). Soon a small, scary extra head grows there. Both of his heads

become uglier, with big teeth and bulging eyes. He kills a psychiatrist. The climax takes place near a volcano. Behind a tree the Manster painfully splits into Stanford and another skinny ape man. They fight, and both fall into the volcano! See *Army of Darkness* for a tribute to this movie.

MANTIS

(1994) **D:** Eric Laneuville **S:** Sam Hamm
P: David Eick, Steve Ecclestine

Carl Lumbly stars as a brilliant, rich, wheelchair-bound neurosurgeon who is secretly a superhero with a space ship that lowers him from cables. He doesn't kill, he just temporarily paralyzes people, leaving a small praying mantis behind. Gina Torres is a pathologist, and Steve James (in his last role) is a bad guy working for the corrupt mayor. Sam Raimi (who also appears) and Sam Hamm (*Batman* movies) were the executive producers, and some parts are similar to Raimi's *Darkman*. It became a Fox-TV series with a new secret, underwater headquarters, but two white assistants were added and the mostly black cast of the series pilot was mostly gone.

MANTIS IN LACE

(SW, 1968) **D:** William Rotsler **S/P:** Sanford
White **C:** Laszlo Kovacs   (*Lila*)

Susan Stewart stars as Lila, a sexy topless dancer. She takes LSD, lures men to a secret warehouse, has sex with them while hallucinating, and kills them. The LA cops are dumbfounded. Great plot! A normal-looking guy with a big, dangling earring turns her on first: "You look hep, baby! What's your bag? Maybe we should groove together!" A

closeup shows a Capitol LP playing, but we hear the Lila theme (again). His face becomes other men's faces. Loud, echoing laughter and backwards music and dialogue are heard: "Oh, wow ! Oh, wild!" His head becomes a bunch of bananas, and she stabs him with a screwdriver. Russ Meyer star Stuart Lancaster plays Ackerman, a psychologist who tries to analyze her. She dances for him in a see-through nightie. During sex he turns into a mad surgeon with a syringe (the fast editing is excellent). A voice says, "Do as I say. Eat raw vegetables." Later she has flashbacks while dancing at the club and sees a submarine sandwich turn into a hand being sliced off. The next victim is an aggressive, drunken slob who gets chopped with a cleaver. Outside, marquees announce, "Topless, bottomless LSD revue" and Procol Harum! Among the strippers is Pat Barrington (*Orgy of the Dead*). The interesting cinematography by Kovacs is shortly before he did *Easy Rider*. The camera goes behind the strippers and back and forth in the audience. Most of the dialogue is corny and dated, but there are a lot of good, sarcastic lines. The strippers dance to rock music lifted from *Mondo Mod*. The makeup is by Michael Weldon, a guy who did lots of jobs behind (and in front of) the camera in adults-only and porno movies. This Box-office International film was released in 2 different versions with different amounts of nudity.

THE MAN WHO FELL TO EARTH

(1987) **D:** Robert J. Roth **S:** Richard
Kletter **P:** David Gerber

Believe it or not, this ABC-TV pilot, with Lewis Smith in the David Bowie role, could have become a series. He lands in NYC and decides to make money so that he can build a spaceship to return home. Meanwhile, he falls for single mom Beverly D'Angelo. With Wil Wheaton as her son and Annie Potts. The Burman studios provided the FX. The original 1976 Nicolas Roeg film is now available on video, uncut (145 minutes) and in stereo, from RCA. Both films are based on a novel by Walter Tevis.

THE MAN WHO FINALLY DIED

(1962) **D:** Quentin Lawrence **S:** Lewis
Greifer **P:** Norman Williams   UK

Stanley Baker goes to Bavaria when he learns that his father, who was believed killed in WWII, had been a POW in the Soviet Union who escaped to Germany after the war. He had lived at the home of a doctor (Peter Cushing) and married a woman (Mai Zetterling) before actually dying. Everything turns out to be part of an elaborate spy-and-scientist plot. This b/w film is based on a British TV serial. With Eric Portman, Niall MacGinnis, and Nigel Green.

THE MAN WHO KNEW TOO MUCH

(MCA, 1956) **D/P:** Alfred Hitchcock
S: John Michael Hayes, Angus McPhail

Hitchcock's only remake of one of his own features is a 2-hour Technicolor and Vistavision version of the 1934 b/w film (now a public-domain video). James Stewart and Doris Day (who sings "Que Será Será") star as the vacationing Americans whose son is kidnapped in Morocco. With Daniel Gelin, Bernard Miles, Hillary Brooke, Caroline Jones, Leo Gordon, and Reggie Nalder as Rien, the assassin. Hitchcock shows up in the marketplace. Bernard Herrmann wrote the score. Paramount re-released it to theaters in 1984. This "family film" was followed by the much more adult *The Wrong Man* and *Vertigo*.

THE MAN WHO LAUGHS

(Midnight, 1927) **D:** Paul Leni **S:** Charles E. Whittaker, Marion Ward, May McLean **P:** Carl Laemmle

I was surprised by the expensive look and epic scope of this impressive historical fairy tale based on Victor Hugo's novel. Gwynplaine (Conrad Veidt), actually an heir to the British throne, is sold to Gypsies as a child, and his face is carved into a permanent, wide grin. As an adult he travels with a carnival, first as a freak and then as a famous clown. Later he becomes a pawn in court intrigue. Mary Philbin (*The Phantom of the Opera*) is the blind Dea, Olga Baclanova (*Freaks*) is the king's sister, and Brandon Hurst (*The Hunchback of Notre Dame*) is the evil court jester. Both Veidt (who is excellent and also appears as his own father) and Leni had arrived in Hollywood from Germany in 1927. Universal added music, crowd noises, and sound effects, delaying the film's release. Leni died from blood poisoning in 1929. Bob Kane and William Castle both copied Veidt's face (for the Joker in the *Batman* comic strip and *Mr. Sardonicus*). The video I saw was of mediocre quality, but the film is well worth seeing. There was a European remake in 1965.

THE MAN WHO WAGGED HIS TALE

(Sinister, 1957) **D/P:** Ladislao Vajda **S:** István Bekeffi
Italy/Spain (*Un Angelo e Scesso a Brooklyn*)

Peter Ustinov stars as a cruel Brooklyn slumlord who is cursed and becomes a homeless dog. The dog does some good deeds and is eventually restored to normal. This was filmed in Madrid and Brooklyn. It wasn't released in America until 1961.

THE MAN WHO WASN'T THERE

(Paramount, 1983) **D/A:** Bruce Malmuth
S: Stanford Sherman **P:** Frank Mancuso Jr.

Steve Guttenberg becomes invisible and is chased by Soviet and American agents. This R-rated 3-D flop was originally supposed to have been directed by Larry Cohen. Also with Lisa Langlois, Art Hindle, Bill Forsythe, Jeffrey Tambor, Don Calfa, and Miguel Ferrer. When the invisible man goes into a shower room, Brinke Stevens, Michelle Bauer, and Linnea Quigley are seen showering in 3-D. The movie was partially filmed in Washington, D C.

THE MAN WITH A CLOAK

(1951) **D:** Fletcher Markle **S:** Frank
Fenton **P:** Stephen James

Joseph Cotten is a mysterious, drunken poet in
NYC of the 1840s who becomes involved in a
murder investigation. He turns out to be Edgar
Allan Poe, and a raven steals a will. Barbara Stanwyck is the villainess, working as a housekeeper
for a rich man (Louis Calhern). With Leslie Caron,
Margaret Wycherly, and Jim Backus. This is an
adaptation of a John Dickson Carr novel.

A MAN WITH A MAID: *See* THE GROOVE ROOM

THE MAN WITH BOGART'S FACE

(Fox, 1980) **D:** Robert Day **S/P:** Andrew J.
Fenady   (*Sam Marlowe, Private Eye*)

Robert Sacchi has plastic surgery, becomes Detective Sam Marlowe, and solves a *Maltese Falcon*
type of case in this PG spoof of *film noir* detective
movies. The cast is filled with name actors from
various eras: Franco Nero, Michelle Phillips, Olivia
Hussey, Victor Buono, Herbert Lom, Misty Rowe,
George Raft (it was his last film), Yvonne De
Carlo, Sybil Danning, Mike Mazurki, Victor Sen
Young, Martin Kosleck, Henry Wilcoxon, Dick Bakalyan, Buck Kartalian, Greg Palmer, and Jay Robinson. Some scenes were shot at Bronson Canyon.

THE MAN WITH ICY EYES

(VSOM, 1970) **D:** Alberto De Martino
S: Massimo De Rota, Arduino Mauri
Italy (*L'Uomo dagli Occhi di Ghiaccio*)

Antonio Sabato stars as a reporter looking into the
assassination of a senator. Barbara Bouchet costars, with Americans Victor Buono, Faith Domergue, and Keenan Wynn. It was made in New
Mexico. Domergue was also in the Italian film *One
on Top of the Other* at about the same time.

THE MAN WITH THE GOLDEN ARM

(UAV, 1955) **D/P:** Otto Preminger **S:** Walter
Newman, Lewis Meltzer **M:** Elmer Bernstein

The MPAA refused a seal for this feature because
it shows drug addiction. UA released it anyway,
and the production code was changed within a
year, allowing movies to deal with drugs, kidnapping, abortion, and prostitution. Frank Sinatra
stars as a junkie, gambler, and jazz drummer in
Chicago, with Kim Novak, Arnold Stang as his
buddy, Eleanor Parker as his crippled wife, and
Darren McGavin as a pusher. There are cold-
turkey scenes and a doctor using ultraviolet light
for healing. It's based on a novel by Nelson Algren.
The Decca soundtrack features Shelly Manne,
Shorty Rogers, and Bud Shank.

THE MAN WITH TWO BRAINS

(Warner, 1983) **D/S:** Carl Reiner **S:** Steve Martin,
George Gipe **P:** David V. Picker, William E. McEuen

Brain surgeon Steve Martin (back when he was
funny) marries sexy but evil Kathleen Turner and
falls in love with a brain in his laboratory. This

R-rated horror comedy costars David Warner
as Dr. Necessiter, Paul Benedict, Jeffrey Combs,
Randi Brooks, Merv Griffin as himself, and Sissy
Spacek as the voice of the brain. A clip of Nancy
Davis (Reagan) in *Donovan's Brain* is seen. Reiner
also made *Dead Men Don't Wear Plaid* and *All of
Me*, both with Martin.

THE MAN WITH TWO LIVES

(Sinister, 1942) **D:** Phil Rosen
S: Joseph Hoffman **P:** A. W. Hacker

A dog's heart is kept alive in a clichéd mad lab.
After the doctor's assistant (Edward Norris) dies in
a car crash he's brought back to life at midnight,
the same time that a gangster named Wolf is executed. Now a "ghostly freak" with no memory, he
takes over Wolf's gang and girlfriend and becomes
a killer while his friends and fiancée wonder what
to do. The ending of this 65-minute Monogram release reveals that it was all a dream (!), which has
kept it out of most horror-movie reference books.
It has some interesting camera zooms, and I like
the way the men wear their hats inside. Rosen also
directed *Spooks Run Wild* (1941) and *Return of
the Ape Man* (1944). Norris was also in *The Gorilla* (1939) and *Jungle Queen* (1945).

MARAT/SADE

(Water Bearer, 1966) **D:** Peter Brook **S:** Adrian
Mitchell **P:** Michael Birkett   UK (*The Persecution
and Assassination of Jean-Paul Marat as Performed
by the Inmates of the Asylum of Charenton Under
the Direction of the Marquis de Sade*)

Members of the Royal Shakespeare Company perform Peter Weiss' play, showing the singing inmates of an insane asylum being directed by the
Marquis de Sade. This historical, political horror/
musical is well worth searching for. Glenda Jackson (in her screen debut) as Charlotte Corday and
Patrick Magee as de Sade are both incredible. With
Ian Richardson as Marat, Freddie Jones, and John
Steiner (later a regular in Italian horror movies).
United Artists released the film and the excellent
soundtrack album.

MARCO POLO

(Prism, 1962) **D:** Hugo Fregonese **S:** Oreste Biancoli,
Duccio Tessari, Piero Pierotti, Antoinette Pellevant
P: Ermanno Donati, Luigi Carpenter   France/Italy

AIP released this small epic with former cowboy
star Rory Calhoun as the Italian explorer. He rescues Princess Amurroy (Yoko Tani), daughter of
Kublai Khan, meets a hermit who has invented
gunpowder, and builds a cannon.

MARCO THE MAGNIFICENT

(1964) **D:** Noel Howard **D/P:** Raoul Levy
S: Denys de la Patelliere   France/Italy
(*La Fabuleuse Aventure de Marco Polo*)

This epic 115-minute version of the Marco Polo
legend stars Horst Buchholz. It was shot on and off
by two directors. With Anthony Quinn as Kublai
Khan (looking like Ming the Merciless), Elsa Martinelli (looking great with her whip and sexy
clothes), Omar Sharif, Orson Welles (who was

working on his own film, *Chimes at Midnight*, at
the time and did this role to raise money), Akim
Tamiroff, and Robert Hossein. This was filmed in
Yugoslavia, Africa, and Asia. Jerry Vale sings the
theme. Columbia released the soundtrack.

MARDI GRAS FOR THE DEVIL

(Prism, 1992) **D/S:** David A. Prior
P: Jill Silverthorne   (*Night Trap*)

Here's another half-assed dud wasting several
name stars. Robert Davi is a cop in New Orleans.
He's after a bearded and ponytailed Satanist (Michael Ironside) who kills hookers and can leap out
of windows and over cars. Lesley-Anne Down has
little to do as Davi's ex, Lydie Denier has a topless
scene, Margaret Avery is one of those token black
characters who know about voodoo-type stuff, and
John Amos is the police captain. Mike Starr as
Davi's new partner has the best accent. The ending
is senseless. Besides some location work, most of
this was filmed in Mobile, Alabama, and LA.

MARDI GRAS MASSACRE

(VCI, 1978) **D/S/P/C:** Jack Weis

Dumb, corrupt cops investigate ritual murders in
New Orleans. A lounge-lizard psycho in a mask
and silly cape kills prostitutes for some unseen
goddess. He slices open a bound, nude woman and
removes her heart (she has no rib cage!). This
same scene (which ensured an X rating) is repeated for each different woman he kills. It's good
for the ridiculous dialogue and the locations and
locals, though. With Laura Misch (from *Playboy*)
and disco music provided by Westbound records.
It played on 42nd Street.

EL MARIACHI

(Columbia, 1992) **D/S/C/E:** Robert Rodriguez
S/P/A: Carlos Gallardo

Carlos Gallardo stars as a traveling guitar player.
After his guitar case is switched with one that has
a machine gun inside, he's mistaken for a gangster.
This excellent action comedy spoofs Italian westerns. It has dream sequences in a cemetery and a
Road Warrior type of ending. The cast also includes Consuelo Gomez as Domino and Peter
Marquardt. It was made for a reported $7,000 in
Mexico for the Spanish-language video market but
was picked up by Columbia. They blew it up from
16mm and subtitled it. After great reviews and
profits the 23-year-old director signed a multipicture deal (he had raised money by being a
drug guinea pig in Austin, Texas). He did a remake of *Road Racers* (1959) for cable TV and
then *Desperado* (1995), a remake of *El Mariachi*.

MARIHUANA

(SW, 1935) **D/P:** Dwain Esper   (*The Weed with
Roots in Hell*; "*Marijuana*"—*The Devil's Weed*)

See "the truth about the smoke from Hell!" from
the director of *Maniac/Sex Maniac* (1934). A
reporter goes undercover to investigate drug sales
by Tony the pusher. Characters smoke "the soul-
destroying reefer," scream, dance, hallucinate,
get pregnant, and kill themselves, but the skinny-

NAME: NANCY DANCER
MEASUREMENTS: 08/24/36 12/21/58
BORN: GARY, IND. 2/13/78
DIED: N.O., LA. 2/13/78

...and that was only the Beginning

MardiGras MASSACRE

Starring CURT DAWSON & GWEN ARMENT
Also Starring BILL METZO with
LAURA MISCH • CATHRYN LACEY • NANCY DANCER • BUTCH BENIT • WAYNE MACK and RONALD TANET
Assistant Producer JOHN STIMAC, Jr. • Cinematography by JACK McGOWAN • Produced and Directed by J. WEIS
IN COLOR • FROM OMNI CAPITAL RELEASING

WARNING • DUE TO SHOCKING SCENES OF EXTREME VIOLENCE
• WE RECOMMEND NO ONE UNDER 17 BE ADMITTED.

dipping scenes were the main attraction. Beethoven's Egmont Overture is used on the soundtrack. Esper also made *Narcotic, Reefer Madness, The Seventh Commandment,* and an early birth-of-a-baby movie, *Modern Motherhood.*

THE MARIHUANA STORY

(SW, 1951) **D:** Leon Klimowsky
S: Alfredo Jiménez   Mexico

Pablo, a respected surgeon (Pedro López Lager), experiences the underground, nightmare-world drug scene after his wife, a marijuana addict, is killed at a nightclub. He tells his story (including flashbacks inside of flashbacks) to the cops. He becomes hooked, is beaten and blackmailed, and has some bad-trip scenes (similar to the ones in *Dementia,* 1953) complete with laughing, distorted faces and a dwarf. A very sexy bikini-clad dancer helped make this a hot exploitation item. Tanny Navarro is Quiroga, a woman who tries to help him. This subtitled version (released by Dan Sonney) has a narrated intro and tries to make you think it all takes place in America. The video is a Johnny Legend presentation. Klimowsky directed *Witchcraft* (1954) in Argentina and later made many horror movies in Spain (often starring Paul Naschy).

THE MARILYN DIARIES

(Private Screenings, 1990) **D:** Eric Drake
S: Don Shiffrin **P:** Gary P. Connor

Marilyn Chambers stars as Marilyn, the mysterious author of an erotic diary. A magazine reporter tries to find her. This soft-core sex movie features Tara Buckman and Michael Rose. Chambers' first role

had been 20 years earlier in *The Owl and the Pussycat.*

MARJOE

(RCA, 1972) **D/P:** Howard Smith, Sarah Kernochan

Marjoe Gortner, later an exploitation-movie star (*Jungle Warriors, Hellhole,* and others), was once a popular but fake boy faith healer and evangelist. This fascinating documentary by a former *Village Voice* columnist shows the whole incredible story. The soundtrack on Warner includes dialogue and gospel music by André Crouch.

MARKED FOR DEATH

(Fox, 1990) **D:** Dwight H. Little
S/P: Michael Grais **S/P:** Mark
Victor **P/A:** Steven Seagal

Jamaican drug dealers, decapitations, and voodoo are major elements of this violent action hit. Steven Seagal is a former DEA agent in LA whose family is threatened. Keith David is his sidekick in killing off crazed Jamaican killers. Basil Wallace is pretty impressive as Screwface (the production title), who seems to have power over death. With Elizabeth Gracen, Jo-anna Pacula as a voodoo expert, Danielle Harris, Jimmy Cliff as himself, Al Israel, Elana Sahagun, and Teri Weigel. Part of the film takes place in Kingston, and reggae music is heard on the soundtrack. A disclaimer says that not all Jamaicans are criminals.

MARKED FOR MURDER

(Vidmark, 1989) **D/S/P:** Rick Sloane

Top-billed Wings Hauser is a crooked TV executive. Ken Abraham and Renee Estevez are his employees, sent to retrieve a videotape. Renee's dad, Martin Sheen, has a bit part (a new low for the former star). Also with Jim Mitchum as an FBI agent, Ross Hagen, and Jay Richardson.

MARK OF THE BEAST

(Rhino, 1990) **D/S:** Jeff Hathcoch **P:** Art Jacobs
(*Fertilize the Blaspheming Bombshell*)

A blonde (Sheila Cann) from Brooklyn is menaced by Satanists on her way to Las Vegas to find out what happened to her twin sister. It starts like *Orgy of the Living Dead* but goes downhill from there. Everything is too dark, there are several very long car chases in the desert, and the star takes two showers. She ends up running around in her underwear killing off Satanists. Rick Hill is a gas-station attendant with a 666 tattoo, Bo Hopkins is a sheriff, and Robert Tessier is a devil-master who says things like "You irreverent bitch! You pious slut!"

MARK OF THE DEVIL, PART 3: *See* SISTERS OF SATAN

MARK OF THE WITCH

(1970) **D/P:** Tom Moore **S/P:** Mary Davis **S:** Martha Peters

Jill, a college student who works at the campus bookstore, goes to a séance involving "the red book" and becomes possessed by a woman hanged as a witch in England (seen in the prologue). She says, "One acquires an almighty thirst in 300 years!" in her irritating new/old British accent. The new Jill kills her professor's dog, makes a bird fry, and has to ask what a phone is. She drugs a student's drink, brands him, makes him a servant, then leaves him dead in the woods. At the climax she splits in two and the professor, a cursed descendant of her killers, hangs himself. This PG feature was made in Dallas. Very tame considering the subject matter, it's filled with nice kids who wear bangs, miniskirts, and beads and who listen to lite music (by Sean Bonniwell of the Music Machine).

MARLEY'S REVENGE: THE MONSTER MOVIE

(Electro, 1989) **D/S/P/E:** Jet Elle **S/A:** Donnie Broom

Two guys with CB radios go on an adventure. The white guy is a nerd who idolizes a fictional hero. The black guy has relatives who are involved with voodoo. They're kidnapped by killer redneck drug smugglers and taken to the woods on an island. After the voodoo aunt is shot, Marley makes cannibal zombies crawl out of the ground and attack. It was filmed in Charlotte, North Carolina. Some local DJs show up at the end and joke about how bad the horror movie is, then eat themselves.

MARLOWE

(MGM, 1969) **D:** Paul Bogart **S:** Sterling Silliphant **P:** Gabriel Katzka

James Garner stars in a modern-day version of Raymond Chandler's novel *The Little Sister.* It's not the best private-eye movie but is worth catching for the cast. Gayle Hunnicutt costars, with Rita Moreno as a stripper, Carroll O'Connor as a police lieutenant, Sharon Farrell, Jackie Coogan, and Kenneth Tobey. Bruce Lee (as Winslow Wong) has two good action scenes. Orpheus (from Boston) do the title song. It was rated M.

MARRIED TOO YOUNG

(Sinister, 1961) **D:** George Moskov **S:** Nathaniel Tanchuck, Edward D. Wood Jr.

Apparently, while Ed Wood was making *Sinister Urge* for Headliner Productions they had him co-write this very dated movie about overage "teens." Harold Lloyd Jr. stars as too-nice Tommy, a high school student, race-car driver, and mechanic who marries Helen (Jana Lund, from *Don't Knock the Rock*). A local gangster named Lech (Anthony Dexter) leads the broke Tommy into a brief life of crime and hot cars. A judge blames it all on their parents, and Helen has a flashback. Marianna Hill (real name Schwarzkoff) is the sexy Marla, who dances and says things like "Daddy-o, so be a rectangle!" The video includes several good trailers. You can also check out Lloyd's acting talent in *Frankenstein's Daughter* (1958) and *Mutiny in Outer Space* (1964).

MARRIED TO THE MOB

(Orion, 1988) **D:** Jonathan Demme **S:** Barry Strugartz, Mark R. Burns **P:** Kenneth Utt

Michelle Pfeiffer plays the wife of a murdered Long Island hitman who hides out in the Lower East Side and falls for the FBI agent who's following her (Matthew Modine). This funny black comedy restarted the career of Dean Stockwell, who was nominated for an Oscar for playing Tony "the Tiger" Russo, and introduced audiences to Mercedes Ruehl as his wife. With Alec Baldwin, Joan Cusack, Trey Wilson, Charles Napier as a hairdresser, Tracey Walter, Al Lewis, Nancy Travis, David Johansen, Chris Isaak, Ellen Foley, and O-Lan Jones. Demme got serious with *The Silence of the Lambs,* his next feature. David Byrne scored the soundtrack, which features many interesting artists. It's on Reprise.

MARTIAL LAW

(Media, 1990) **D:** S. E. Cohen **S:** Richard Brandes **P:** Kurt Anderson

Chad McQueen (Steve's son) stars as an undercover cop called Martial Law who doesn't play by the rules. He's teamed with blond martial-arts star Cynthia Rothrock. David Carradine is the gun-running, car-stealing villain, who wears nice suits, runs a martials-arts school, and deals with Oriental gangsters. He hires the hero's brother and the trouble starts. With Professor Tanaka. Rothrock returned in *Martial Law 2: Undercover* (MCA, 1992).

MARTIAL OUTLAW

(Republic, 1993) **D:** Kurt Anderson **S:** Thomas Ritz **P:** Pierre David   Canada

Jeff Wincott is a kung-fu-fighting DEA agent, and Gary Hudson is his corrupt LAPD brother. They battle Russian drug smugglers. With Krista Errickson, Liliana Komorowska, and Richard Jaeckel as the alkie father.

MARTIANS GO HOME!

(IVE, 1990) **D:** David Odell **S:** Charlie Haas **P:** Michael D. Pariser

Randy Quaid stars in another almost-good odd movie. He's Marc Devereaux, a composer of music for TV shows, who narrates the tale of how irritating, green-faced, standup-comic Martians took over the world. Quaid is arrested, interrogated, and put into a mental hospital because he knows what's going on, but he saves the world in the end. Anita Morris plays a talk-show hostess, Ronny Cox is the president, and Gerrit Graham has a small role. The Martians sing "Martian Hop," "Green Tambourine," "They're Coming to Take Me Away, Ha-Ha," and "In the Year 2525." Pretty silly and rated PG-13, it's based on a script written in 1953, from Fredric Brown's novel.

MARTIN'S DAY

(Fox, 1985) **D:** Alan Gibson **S:** Allan Scott, Chris Bryant **P:** Richard F. Dalton   Canada

Richard Harris is a convict who kidnaps Justin Henry but becomes his friend. This PG family film, with Lindsay Wagner, James Coburn, and Karen Black, was an MGM release.

MARY SHELLEY'S "FRANKENSTEIN"

(Columbia, 1994) **D/A:** Kenneth Branagh **S:** Steph Lady, Frank Darabont **P:** Francis Ford Coppola, James V. Hart

Bram Stoker's "Dracula" was a big hit, so Francis Ford Coppola backed this obvious follow-up, the most expensive ($50 million) Frankenstein movie ever made. Kenneth Branagh stars as a long-haired, soul-searching, Victorian Dr. Victor Frankenstein who recreates a hanged beggar (Robert De Niro) in a brass tub. The movie looks impressive, but De Niro as the mangled, introspective, sobbing monster was a bad idea. Helena Bonham Carter is the doctor's adopted sister and fiancée, Elizabeth, who is attacked and briefly becomes a grotesque-looking female "monster" too (this is not in the novel). With Tom Hulce as a medical-school friend, John Cleese (excellent in a rare serious role) as the doctor who supplies the brain, Ian Holm as Victor's father, Robert Hardy, and Cherie Lunghi. The over-two-hour-long tale is told in flashback to a ship's captain (Aidan Quinn). It was shot in England and the Swiss Alps.

MASCARA

(Warner, 1987) **D/S:** Patrick Conrad **S:** Hugo Claus, Pierre Drouot   US/Germany/France

Murders are committed at a sex club, in this confusing movie about a brother and sister (Michael Sarrazin and Charlotte Rampling). Somebody is a transsexual.

LA MASCHERA DEL DEMONIO

(VSOM, 1990) **D/S:** Lamberto Bava **S:** Andrea Piazzesi Spain/Germany/France/Portugal (*Demons 5*)

After eight young skiers fall into a crevasse and land in a hidden crypt, they become possessed. A blind, white-haired priest is there, and a seemingly normal couple (Debora Kinski from *Paganini* and Giovanni Guidelli) try to survive. Promoted as a remake of his father's famous *Black Sunday/Mask of Satan,* it's really part of Lamberto's *Demons* series, complete with topless females chained up. I guess Eva Grimaldi as Anibas the witch has the Barbara Steele role. The sets, camera work, and music (by Simon Boswell) are all top-notch, but the hateful teen characters are too much like the ones in a *Friday the 13th* movie. Director Michele Soavi is also in the cast. The subtitled video is dubbed into Spanish.

THE MASK

(New Line, 1994) **D:** Chuck Russell **S:** Mike Werb **P:** Bob Engelman

Stanley Ipkis, a nerdy bank clerk (Jim Carrey), becomes a magic, comic, vengeance-seeking, green-faced guy in a 40s suit when he puts on an ancient mask. This PG-13 hit costars blond model Cameron Diaz as a nightclub singer, with Peter Riegert as a cop, Peter Green as a gangster, Amy Yasbeck,

Richard Jeni, and Max as Milo the dog (who's also transformed). The fun ILM FX make characters resemble Tex Avery cartoons. There are also music and dance segments, like "Cuban Pete." It's based on the Dark Horse comic book of the same name but borrows plot ideas from the 1961 3-D Canadian cult movie *The Mask,* which was also distributed by New Line. Columbia released the soundtrack featuring various artists. Sequels will follow.

THE MASKED MARVEL

(Stokey, 1943) **D:** Spencer Gordon Bennet **S:** Royal K. Cole, Ronald Davidson, Basil Dickey

This Republic 12-chapter WWII serial stars William Forrest (usually stunt man Tom Steel) as a masked insurance investigator who battles the evil Sakima (Johnny Arthur). The villain tries to destroy America's war industries and wants a new secret explosive. With Louise Currie. A 1966 feature version is *Sakima and the Masked Marvel.*

MASKS OF DEATH

(Lorimar, 1984) **D:** Roy Ward Baker **S:** N. J. Crisp **P:** Norman Pridgen   UK (*Sherlock Holmes and the Masks of Death*)

Peter Cushing stars as Sherlock Holmes again (he had been in *The Hound of the Baskervilles* in 1959), and John Mills is Dr. Watson. They help stop a war between England and Germany at the turn of the century. Also in the cast are Anne Baxter, Ray Milland as the home secretary, Anton Diffring as a German diplomat, Gordon Jackson, and Susan Penhaligon. This Tyburn production was a 2-part episode of the 1968–69 *Sherlock Holmes* BBC series, which had originally starred Douglas Wilmer.

THE MASQUE OF THE RED DEATH

(RCA/Columbia, 1988) **D:** Alan Birkinshaw **S:** Michael J. Murray **P:** Harry Alan Towers   S. Africa

A photographer from NYC (Michelle McBride) narrates this lame story about a modern-day masquerade party in a Bavarian castle. Somebody in a red mask is killing people and nobody can leave, but they have a Fabergé egg hunt anyway. Most of the characters are sarcastic, mean, and vain, so of course they deserve their silly deaths. Herbert Lom stars as Ludwig, Brenda Vaccaro is a foul-mouthed soap-opera star, and Frank Stallone (!) is Duke. There's a silly disco-pop band with a guitar player hanging from a wire. Not to be confused with producer Roger Corman's 1989 remake, this uses the same sets as 21st Century's *The House of Usher* (1988), by the same director. Since Poe's stories are in the public domain, anybody can make films from them anytime.

MASQUE OF THE RED DEATH

(MGM/UA, 1989) **D/S:** Larry Brand **S/A:** Daryl Haney **P:** Roger Corman

Young Adrian Paul plays Vincent Price's role as Prospero in Roger Corman's small-scale, quickie remake of his own 1964 classic. Patrick Macnee is

Machiavel and "the Red Death." He's seen briefly, then played by a masked double. Tracy Reiner (daughter of Rob Reiner and Penny Marshall) is Prospero's sister and lover. Also with Clare Hoak and Maria Ford. It played in theaters as *Edgar Allan Poe's "Masque of the Red Death"* to avoid confusion with the inferior rival version made in 1988. Forget both and go for the original, from Orion.

MASQUERADE

(Fox, 1988) **D:** Bob Swaim
S: Dick Wolf **P:** Michael I. Levy

This is an uncredited teen remake of *Suspicion*, which had already been remade as a TV movie. Meg Tilly is an heiress who marries Rob Lowe, who may be trying to kill her. With Kim Cattrall, John Glover, Dana Delany, and Barton Heyman. From MGM.

MASSACRE AT CENTRAL HIGH

(MPI, 1976) **D/S:** Renee Daalder **P:** Harold Sobel

A new kid at a California high school (Derrel Maury) seeks revenge after jock gang members push a car over his leg. At the end he blows up the whole school (a popular idea later used in *Rock 'n' Roll High School*). TV exposure over the years has made this a cult film. It doesn't live up to its title, but it's well worth seeing. With Andrew Stevens, Robert Carradine, Kimberly Beck, Roy Underwood, Brad Davis, Lani O'Grady (from the TV series *Eight Is Enough*), and Cheryl "Rainbeaux" Smith. The director later designed digital effects for movies like *Robocop*.

MASSACRE AT FORT HOLMAN

(Video Gems, 1972) **D/S:** Tonino Valerii
S: Ernesto Gastaldi **P:** Michael Billingsley
Italy/France/ W. Germany/Spain (*Una Ragione per Vivere e una per Morire;
A Reason to Live, a Reason to Die*)

A Union Army colonel (James Coburn) leads seven condemned men against a brutal Confederate major (Telly Savalas) who's protecting a fort full of gold. With Bud Spencer and Robert Burton. K-Tel released it. Valerii also made *My Name Is Nobody*.

MASSACRE AT GRAND CANYON

(1963) **D/S:** Sergio Corbucci **S/P:** Albert Band   Italy (*Massacro al Grande Canyon*)

James Mitchum (son of Robert) stars in this early spaghetti western, with Giorgio Ardisson and Giacomo Rossi-Stuart.

MASSACRE IN DINOSAUR VALLEY

(Lighting, 1985) **D:** Michele Tarantini
S: Lemick Tarantini   Italy

Here's one made in Brazil. I saw it in Sweden. It's about a group of typically diverse people stranded in the jungle after a plane crash. An archaeologist finds some dinosaur prints but no dinosaurs. They're attacked by killer Indians, and then the survivors are captured and put into a slave-labor camp run by drug dealers. There's nudity, comedy, and typical Italian gore, but nothing very memorable.

MASSACRE OF PLEASURE

(SW, 1966) **D:** "Jean-Loup Grosard"
France (*Massacre for an Orgy*)

A detective is involved with gangsters, white slavery, and drugs. This confusing b/w adult movie was released with dubbed narration, fake credits, and out-of-place sound FX by Bob Cresse.

MASSARATI AND THE BRAIN

(1982) **D:** Harvey Hart **S:** George Kirgo **P:** Charles B. FitzSimons

Peter Billingsley (*A Christmas Story*) is a 12-year-old genius who helps his soldier-of-fortune uncle (Christopher Hewett) retrieve a stolen treasure from a Nazi (Christopher Lee). This ABC-TV movie also features Daniel Pilon, Ann Turkel, Camilla Sparv, Markie Post, Heather O'Rourke, and Greta Blackburn.

THE MASTER

(1984)

All the episodes of this short-lived NBC-TV series are on 7 tapes. Lee Van Cleef is a WWII vet who became a ninja master in Japan. Back in America he travels in a van, searching for his lost daughter, with Timothy Van Patten. Sho Kosugi is Osaka, a bad ninja, who's always after them.

MASTERBLASTER

(Prism, 1986) **D/S:** Glenn R. Wilder
S/P: Randy Grinter **S/A:** Jeff Moldovan

Tom Laughlin stars in *The Master Gunfighter.*

A Nam vet (Moldovan) is involved in a mock killing tournament in which participants are really being killed. With Tracey E. Hutchinson and Kari Whitman. William Grefe was the executive producer of this film, made in Florida. Some other movies with similar plots are *Tag, Gotcha,* and *The Zero Boys.*

MASTER DEMON

(1991) **D/S:** Samuel Oldham
D: Art Camacho **P/A:** Eric Lee

A kung-fu expert (Lee), a lowly private eye (Steve Nave, who narates), and a cop (Sid Campbell) battle evil forces for a stolen talisman (a hand) in and around Hollywood. A bald demon (Gerard Okamura) conjures up a musclebound killer in leather with teased hair called Medusa (Kay Baxter Young, who died in 1988). The best gag is when she hits a building and it collapses. This low-budget comic martial-arts fantasy also features Ava Cadell and the World Wrestling Federation's "the Viking." The makeup (including a face being ripped off) is by Rodd Matsui. Oldham also codirected *Dark Romances* and *Zombie Party.*

THE MASTER GUNFIGHTER

(1975) **D/A:** Tom Laughlin **S:** Harold Lapland **P:** Philip L. Parslow

After playing Billy Jack three times, Laughlin tried out a new samurai-cowboy character, in this sometimes laughable PG remake of the Japanese film *Goyokin* (1966). He uses guns and swords to kill a lot of characters (often in slow motion) and wears hats that are too big. Injustice to Indians is a major part of the flashback-filled plot. With Barbara Carrera, Ron O'Neal (after the *Superfly* movies), Angelo Rossitto, and Victor Campos. Narration by Burgess Meredith was added, in an attempt to make sense of it all. The credited director, Frank Laughlin, is Tom Laughlin's son (nine years old at the time!). Laughlin spent lots of his own money for ads blasting critics who ridiculed his movie, which he distributed himself. He finished only one more feature, *Billy Jack Goes to Washington.*

THE MASTER KEY

(Stokey, 1945) **D:** Ray Taylor, Lewis D. Collins **S:** Joseph O'Donnell, George H. Plympton **P:** Morgan Cox

Milburn Stone stars as federal investigator Tom Brant, in this 13-chapter Universal serial. Nazis are after the "orotron," a machine developed by scientist Byron Foulger that extracts gold from sea water. With Jan Wiley, Dennis Moore, Maris Wrixon, Gene Roth, and Al "Lash" La Rue.

THE MASTER OF DRAGONARD HILL

(Media, 1987) **D:** Gerard Kikoine **S:** Rick Marx **S/P:** Harry Alan Towers   S. Africa

Kimberly Sissons and Patrick Warburton star in this sequel to *Drago-*

nard. Oliver Reed is the mean new governor, mistreating Caribbean slaves. With Herbert Lom as a pirate, Claudia Udy, and Eartha Kitt. It's from Cannon. Kitt and Lom had also been in *Uncle Tom's Cabin* (1965).

MASTER OF EVIL: *See* THE DEMON LOVER

MASTER OF THE FLYING GUILLOTINE

(Sinister, 1976) **D/S/A:** Jimmy Wang Yu
P: Wong Chuck Hon   Hong Kong

Fung, a blind man disguised as a priest, vows to kill a one-armed boxer (Wang Yu), the leader of a martial arts school. Fung's weapon resembles a red felt hat on a long chain with a circular saw blade inside and yes, incredibly, it decapitates people (and some chickens). This is a wild period kung fu fantasy with a tournament and many fights. There's a female eagle claw technique specialist, a bad Japanese fighter who joins Fung, and an Indian fighter with extending arms (an idea copied in *Nightmare on Elm Street*). The excellent soundtrack consists of stolen music by German bands Kraftwerk, Neu, and Tangerine Dream! The print is worn.

MASTERS OF MENACE

(RCA, 1990) **D:** Daniel Raskov
S/P: Tino Insana **P:** Lisa M. Hansen

David Rasche is a biker-gang leader, and Catherine Bach is his pregnant wife, in this PG-13 comedy with dumb gags. With Teri Copley as a topless dancer, George "Buck" Flower, and Lee Ving. There are bits by slumming comedians Dan Aykroyd, John Candy, and James Belushi. It's from New Line.

MASTERS OF THE CONGO JUNGLE

(Video Dimensions, 1959) **D/S:** Heinz Seilman
Belgium (*Les Seigneurs de la Forêt*)

Orson Welles hosts and narrates this documentary, shot in the Belgian Congo. It features wild animals, local customs, and human sacrifice. 20th Century–Fox released it.

MASTERS OF THE UNIVERSE

(Warner, 1987) **D:** Gary Goddard
S: David Odell **P:** Golan/Globus

Conan meets *Star Wars*. This whole movie is based on a line of Mattel toys. Despite that fact, it's not bad as mindless, PG-rated entertainment. Dolph Lundgren (in his first starring role) is He-Man, Frank Langella is unrecognizable as Skeletor, and Meg Foster (with her naturally glowing eyes) is Evil-Lyn. With Billy Barty as a wizard/inventor, Courteney Cox, James Tolkan, Jon Cypher, Chelsea Field, Christina Pickles, and Barry Livingston. A big laser battle in a used-record store is my favorite scene. Bill Conti did the soundtrack. The *Secret of the Sword* (1985) is an animated He-Man adventure.

MASTERS OF VENUS

(Sinister, 1962) **D:** Ernest Morris
S: Michael Barnes   UK

Two kids stow away on a spaceship to Venus. They discover survivors of the lost city of Atlantis and "the thing in the pit." This 8-part serial made for kids runs more than 2 hours.

THE MASTER'S REVENGE: *See* DEVIL RIDER!

MATA HARI

(MGM, 1984) **D:** Curtis Harrington
S: Joel Ziskin **P:** Golan/Globus

Curtis Harrington's last film to date stars Sylvia Kristel as the famous WWI spy. There's topless swordfighting, opium smoking, and nudity. Christopher Cazenove and Oliver Tobias costar. This Cannon release was cut for American distribution.

MATILDA

(1978) **D:** Daniel Mann **S/P:** Timothy Galfas **P:** Albert S. Ruddy

Elliott Gould and Robert Mitchum star in a misfire comedy about a boxing kangaroo (a man in a suit). Everybody thought it was really terrible, but Gould went on to many worse movies. With Harry Guardino, Clive Revill, Lionel Stander, Karen Carlson, and Roberta Collins. Andy Sidaris worked on this G-rated AIP feature.

MATINEE

(Malofilm, 1989) **D/S:** Richard Martin
P: Kim Steer, Cal Shumacher   Canada

Young people are killed while watching horror movies during a film festival, in this horror comedy set in small town. *Murder Camp* is the slasher movie being screened. Others are spoofs of *The Texas Chainsaw Massacre*, *The Cabinet of Dr. Caligari*, and a vampire movie. The same idea was used for *Popcorn*. The theater manager (Don Davis) has posters on his wall from real movies produced by Malofilm (including *Pin*). Ron White and Gillian Barber star.

MATINEE

(MCA, 1993) **D:** Joe Dante **S:** Charles Haas
P: Michael Finnell **M:** Jerry Goldsmith

Joe Dante manages to recapture the joy of attending an overhyped gimmick movie and the mood during the 1962 Cuban missile crisis, in this funny and nostalgic comedy. It spoofs fear of the end of the world, fallout shelters, and hucksterism. Simon Fenton stars as a kid in Key West, Florida. John Goodman is Laurence Woolsey, a William Castle type of showman and director who arrives to premiere his new movie, *Mant!* (shot in "Atomo-Vision"). Cathy Moriarty is Ruth Corday, his star, companion, and "nurse." With John Sayles and Dick Miller as phony protesters, Lisa Jakub, Robert Picardo, Jesse White, and Forry Ackerman. We see parts of the comical

b/w science-fiction movie within the movie. William Schallert, Kevin McCarthy, and Robert Cornthwaite (*The Thing*) are in it. There's even a spoof of a dumb Disney fantasy. The script is by the writer of *Over the Edge*. This PG-rated Universal release was shot in Florida. The soundtrack is on Varèse Sarabande. The laserdisc has extra *Mant!* footage and a complete *Mant!* trailer.

A MATTER OF DEGREES

(Prism, 1990) **D/S:** W. T. Morgan **S/P:** Randall
Poster **S:** Jack Mason **P:** Roy Kissin

Arye Gross stars as a college student living in a communal home who doesn't want to go on to Columbia Law School. He smokes pot, has fantasies about his dream girl, and decides to disrupt the graduation ceremonies after a corporation takes over campus radio station WXOX. This is like a milder version of an early-70s campus-protest movie without much left to protest. With Judith Hoag, Tom Sizemore, John Doe as a DJ, Fred and Kate of the B-52s, and John Kennedy Jr. in a party scene. It was shot at Brown University, in Providence. The director also made *The Unheard Music*, featuring X. The soundtrack, on Atlantic, includes music by the Minutemen, Pére Ubu, the Dream Syndicate, and others. A Twentieth Century release.

MAU MAU

(SW, 1954) **D:** Elwood G. Price
S: Dave Shepperd **P:** Joe Rock

News anchorman Chet Huntley (!) introduces and narrates this color documentary, less than an hour long, about the "growing unrest in white man's rule" in British East Africa. Most of the film is a historical look at the origins of the black rebellion in Kenya, led by Oxford-educated Jomo Kenyatta. White judges in wigs are shown sentencing black men to prison camps or the gallows, and the Mau Mau are said to be "patterned after Communists." Staged attacks are shown, with naked or topless "African" women running, then being killed by men with machetes. This is described as "an orgy of insane fury" and is followed by shots of actual dead bodies. One of the women was featured in the ads, and these scenes, of course, were why this was an exploitation hit. Did this film help Huntley get his job at NBC the next year!? The video, presented by David F. Friedman, includes dozens of trailers for jungle-theme movies.

John Goodman as the William Castle–inspired director in *Matinee*.

MAUSOLEUM

(Embassy, 1981) **D:** Michael Dugan
S/P: Robert Barich, Robert Madero

Evil Spawn star Bobbie Bresee made her debut in this equally ridiculous and fun low-budget horror movie about a family curse. Her rich husband is Marjoe Gortner. Bresee, who has the widest mouth in showbiz, makes a car blow up, an art dealer float, and her aunt's chest rip open, and in the film's most outrageous scene her toothy killer breasts attack Marjoe! Other highlights are Bresee's nude and topless scenes and her dancing to disco music with her ex-evangelist costar. Her eyes glow green, and sometimes she turns into a monster with a scary voice. Lawanda Page (Aunt Esther on *Sanford and Son*) is Elsie the maid. When she sees mysterious green smoke she says, "No more grievin'. I'm leavin'!" A weird Mexican gardener spends his time reading and sleeping. Bits of dialogue are badly edited in, and some parts make no sense at all. For those who love flashbacks (and who out there doesn't?) there are pointless flashbacks of nearly everything we've already seen. Whose flashbacks they are I don't know. The music is pretty good, but the love song at the end is a bit much.

MAX HEADROOM

(Warner, 1986) **D:** Rocky Morton, Annabel Jankel
S: Steve Roberts, George Stone **P:** Peter Wagg   UK

This is the original, hour-long innovative British TV program, first aired on Cinemax in America. It's about "blipverts," TV ads in the grim future that make viewers explode. Matt Frewer is the computer-generated star modeled after the brainwaves of a reporter (also Frewer), and Amanda Pays is his producer. Cinemax had the character do an interview show for a while, then the original show was remade for ABC-TV as the first part of a 14-episode 1987 series with different directors and writers. The cool, anti-establishment character was then ruined by being used to sell Coke and other products.

MAXIE

(Warner, 1985) **D:** Paul Aaron **S:** Patricia
Resnick **P:** Carter DeHaven

The ghost of a 20s flapper (Glenn Close) takes over the body of a modern-day woman (also Close) in San Francisco and tries to become a movie star by appearing in a remake of *Cleopatra*. This romantic fantasy costars Mandy Patinkin, with Ruth Gordon (in her last role), Barnard Hughes, Valerie Curtin, Leeza Gibbons, Harry Hamlin, and clips of Carole Lombard.

MAXIMUM BREAKOUT

(AIP, 1991) **D:** Tracy Lynch Britton **S:** Michelle J. Carl

Sydney Coale Phillips stars as a wealthy woman who is kidnapped. A group of guys try to get her out of prison. There's a white-slavery plot but no nudity.

MAXIMUM FORCE

(PM, 1992) **D/P:** Joseph Merhi **S:** John
Weidner, Ken Lamplugh **P:** Richard Pepin

Sam Jones (*Flash Gordon*), Jason Lively, and Sherrie Rose are renegade cops working for John Saxon. They go undercover to infiltrate the hookers and drug dealers led by Richard Lynch. Rose does some kung-fu fighting. With Mickey Rooney (who has been acting in movies since 1926!) as a corrupt police chief in a limo, Andrew Stevens, and Sonny Landham.

MAXIMUM OVERDRIVE

(Lorimar, 1986) **D/S:** Stephen King
P: Martha Schumacher

This slow-moving and slow-witted tale of what happens when a comet causes machines to attack people in Wilmington, North Carolina, is based on Stephen King's short story "Trucks" (in the *Night Shift* collection). Emilio Estevez plays a young cook at the Dixie Boy truck stop, run by cruel Pat Hingle. Laura Harrington is good as a pretty, independent-minded hitchhiker who keeps changing from skirts to pants while driverless semis circle the Dixie Boy and terrorize the stupid characters trapped inside. It takes them forever to find the weapons (in the basement!) and make their escape. Originally given an X rating by the MPAA, *Overdrive* was heavily edited before its theatrical release, removing most of the gore scenes that might have given it a reason to exist. Deaths caused by a steamroller and by soft-drink cans are supposed to be funny. Another hoot is a character staring into the end of a malfunctioning gas hose and getting an unleaded flood in his face. The only black actor in the cast, Giancarlo Esposito, is a looter. Marla Maples (!) is a victim. This is one of the movies, along with *King Kong Lives!* and *The Million Dollar Mystery*, that put Dino De Laurentiis' American-based DEG company out of business. King (who makes a cameo appearance) said, "I may have made the modern version of *Plan 9 from Outer Space*." Actually, Ed Wood's famous "bad" movie is funny, fascinating, and unique. This one is none of these things. Fans of AC/DC should know that only parts of the band's songs can be heard during the movie. Look for the great soundtrack album, *Who Made Who*, though.

MAXIM XUL

(Magnum, 1989) **D/S/P:** Arthur Egeli
S: Charles E. Rickard **P:** John Halvorsen

Jefferson Leinberger is a Baltimore cop investigating a series of brutal ripper deaths. The victims were all witnesses at a trial, and some are decapitated. Only Adam West, as a brooding professor with a goatee, knows all about the evil "Sumerian" demon. He fights it with medieval weapons at the end. Billie Shaeffer is a rich lawyer, and Mary Shaeffer is a reporter. The synthesizer music is by Micky Rat. The name Xul came from *Ghostbusters*.

MAYHEM

(City Lights, 1986) **D/S/P:** Joseph Merhi
P: Richard Pepin

Here's a violent, direct-to-video tale of pimps, hustlers, and kiddie porn with time-wasting slo-mo deaths. City Lights later became PM, named after the producers.

MAYUMI VIRGIN TERRORIST

(1990) **D:** Sang Ook Sheen **S:** Bong Sung
Shin **P:** Myung Gil Shin   S. Korea

You may think that George Kennedy is in too many American movies, but he works in other countries all the time too. Suh Ra Kim stars in this story, based on a real-life incident in which a Korean plane was blown up by a terrorist bomb.

MAZES AND MONSTERS

(Edde, 1982) **D:** Steven Hilliard Stern **S:** Tom
Lazarus **P:** Richard A. Briggs   Canada
(*Rona Jaffe's "Mazes and Monsters"*)

Some college students (including Tom Hanks and Chris Makepeace) play a Dungeons and Dragons type of fantasy video game and "flip into it." With Anne Francis, Vera Miles, Susan Strasberg, Lloyd Bochner, Murray Hamilton, and Kevin Peter Hall. This CBS-TV movie is based on a Rona Jaffe book.

McBAIN

(MCA, 1991) **D/S/A:** James Glickenhaus
P: J. Boyce Harman Jr.

McBain (Christopher Walken) and his Nam-vet friends help Maria Conchita Alonso overthrow a Colombian drug-cartel dictator. With Michael Ironside, Steve James, and Luis Guzman. This violent, cartoonish action movie has many good stunts and lots of explosions. It was made in the Philippines.

THE McGUFFIN

(1985) **D:** Colin Bucksey **S:** Michael
Thomas **P:** Kenneth Trodd   UK

In this homage to Alfred Hitchcock and *Rear Window*, Charles Dance stars as a film critic who watches some neighbors and becomes involved in a murder and a government cover-up plot. With Ritza Brown, Brian Glover, Jerry Stiller, Anna Massey (*Frenzy*), and Ann Todd (*The Paradine Case*).

THE McMASTERS

(Xenon, 1970) **D:** Alf Kjellin **S:** Harold
Jacobson **P:** Monroe Sachson

Brock Peters stars as Benji, a former slave and Union Army soldier who tries to return home and start a new life. His former master (Burl Ives) gives him a ranch, and a cattle-stealing Indian (David Carradine) gives his sister (Nancy Kwan) to him. Trouble comes from L. Q. Jones and one-armed former slave owner Jack Palance. When Benji is inside his house, surrounded by enemies, it seems like a scene from *Night of the Living Dead*. I like the realistic 19th-century western table manners (loud burps). With John Carradine as a preacher, R. G. Armstrong, and Alan Vint. It was made by a Swedish director working for a British company in New Mexico. The two versions that were released have varying amounts of violence and different endings. Peters was also in the Italian western *Aces High* (1968).

ME AND HIM

(RCA, 1988) **D/S:** Dorris Dörrie **S:** Warren D. Leight,
Michael Juckner **P:** Bernd Eichinger   W. Germany

Griffin Dunne is a NYC architect whose penis talks to him (in the voice of Mark Linn-Baker). Carey Lowell (who married Dunne in real life) costars, with Ellen Greene, Craig T. Nelson, Kara Glover, and David Alan Grier. This comedy, based on a novel by Alberto Moravia, is by the director of *Men*. Both were hits in West Germany.

MEAN DOG BLUES

(Vestron, 1978) **D:** Mel Stuart **S/P:** George Lefferts **P:** Charles A. Pratt

Gregg Henry stars as Paul, a country musician hitchhiking to Nashville. A corrupt, drunk politician (William Windom) and his wife (Tina Louise) pick him up, run over a kid, and blame him. Captain Omar Kinsman (George Kennedy) runs the prison work farm with help from killer dogs. Paul is whipped, abused, and pursued by the warden's underage daughter (Christina Hart) and by prisoners with names like Mary. With Kay Lenz as his girlfriend on the outside, Scatman Crothers, Gregory Sierra, James Wainwright, Logan Ramsey, Ian Wolfe, and Felton Perry. Bing Crosby was the executive producer of this AIP release (he worked on it until his death in 1977).

MEAN FRANK AND CRAZY TONY

(IVE, 1973) **D:** Michele Lupo **P:** Dino De Laurentiis Italy (*Dio, Sei un Padreterno!*)

Tony LoBianco wants to be like Lee Van Cleef, in this comic gangster movie. Simon Nuchtern added new footage for the American release. Sybil Danning introduces the tape.

MEAN JOHNNY BARROWS

(Unicorn, 1974) **D/P/A:** Fred Williamson **S:** Charles Walker, Jolevett Cato

Nam vet Johhny Barrows (Fred Williamson) is unjustly thrown out of the service and ends up as a gas-station janitor in LA. A gangster (Stuart Whitman) wants to hire him as a hitman. He finally agrees, with disastrous results. With Luther Adler, R. G. Armstrong, Anthony Caruso, Leon Isaac Kennedy, Roddy McDowall as a gay drug dealer running a flower shop, and Elliott Gould in a bit part as a dropout street person. From Dimension.

MEAN MACHINE = CAULDRON OF DEATH

MEAN STREETS

(Warner, 1973) **D/S:** Martin Scorsese **S:** Mardik Martin **P:** Jonathan T. Taplin

Martin Scorsese's brilliant movie about small-time Catholic gangsters in NYC's Little Italy is one of the best of the 70s. Harvey Keitel stars as Charlie, and Robert De Niro is Johnny Boy. It's packed with great acting and memorable scenes. I like the scene where Charlie spins around drunk to "Rubber Biscuit" (by the Chips) and the bizarre bar shootout where Robert Carradine walks in, lets his long hair down, and blasts a very drunk David Carradine. At one point Charlie and Johnny Boy go to a theater and watch Roger Corman's *Tomb of Ligeia*. Some of their improvised scenes were inspired by Abbott and Costello. The car-shootout ending (Scorsese is

the killer) is orchestrated to a blast of live Cream. With Amy Robinson (later a producer), Richard Romanus, Cesare Danova, and Jeannie Bell as a topless dancer. Corman wanted Scorsese to make it as a black-action movie! This could be considered the second part of a series that started with *Who's That Knocking at My Door* (1968), starring Keitel, and continued with *Good Fellas* (1990) and *Casino* (1995), both with De Niro. All have wonderful soundtracks consisting of classic and obscure (mostly) rock songs.

MEATBALLS

(1979) **D:** Ivan Reitman **S/P:** Dan Goldberg **S:** Janis Allen, Len Blum, Harold Ramis **M:** Elmer Bernstein Canada

In his first starring role, Bill Murray is a summer-camp counselor. Ivan Reitman and Harold Ramis had made *National Lampoon's Animal House* the previous year. This popular PG comedy was copied many times and spawned unrelated "sequels." With Chris Makepeace, Kristine DeBell, Kate Lynch, Rick Dees, Terry Black, and David Naughton (who sings the hit "Makin' It"). The soundtrack is on RSO.

MEATBALLS PART II

(RCA, 1984) **D:** Ken Wiederhorn **S:** Bruce Singer **P:** Tony Bishop, Stephen Poe (*Space Kid*)

John Mengatti stars as a camp counselor. A boxing match between opposing camps is the main event in this unrelated sequel from Tri-Star, and there's an alien kid who levitates people. With Kim Richards, Archie Hahn, Richard Mulligan, Hamilton Camp, John Larroquette, Paul Reubens (Pee-wee Herman), Felix Silla (Cousin Itt), Elayne Boosler, and Misty Rowe. Weiderhorn also made *King Frat*.

MEATBALLS III

(Avid, 1987) **D:** George Mendeluk **S:** Michel Paseornek, Bradley Kesden **P:** Don Carmody, John Dunning Canada

Roxy Du Jour (Sally Kellerman), the ghost of a dead porno star, has to get 14-year-old Patrick Dempsey laid. Al Waxman is Saint Peter, and Shannon Tweed is the love goddess. It was the first in the "series" to get an R rating.

MEATBALLS 4

(HBO, 1992) **D/S:** Bob Logan **P:** Donald P. Borchers

Corey Feldman stars as a skier hired by Jack Nance to be the recreation director at his Lakeside water-skiing summer camp. Evil Sarah Douglas, owner of the rival Twin Oaks camp, tries to take over Lakeside to sell it for real-estate development. Feldman sings and says, "I was in *Goonies*!" Characters play strip charades and take showers in this very stupid R-rated comedy. With Deborah Tucker, Kristie Ducati, Paige French, Christy Thom, Johnnny Cocktails, and Bentley Mitchum.

THE MEATEATER

(Active, 1978) **D/S:** Derek Savage **P:** Richard Tasse

A scarred cannibal who likes Jean Harlow haunts an abandoned movie theater. A family reopens the

place, and people die. *The Phantom of the Opera* copy includes old film clips. The cast includes Arch Jaboulian, Diane Davis, and Emily Spendler.

THE MECHANIC

(MGM, 1972) **D:** Michael Winner **S/P:** Lewis John Carlino **P:** Robert Chartoff, Irwin Winkler

In his first American film in many years, Charles Bronson stars as a hitman. Jan-Michael Vincent costars as his young protegé, with Keenan Wynn, Frank De Kova, Jill Ireland as a prostitute, and Lindsay Crosby. The plot concerns karate and hippies. This PG-rated United Artists release was partially filmed in Italy.

MEDICINE BALL CARAVAN

(1971) **D:** François Reichenbach **P:** François Reichenbach, Tom Donahue US/France

DJ Tom Donahue selected 150 people to go across the country on buses in the summer of 1970. The concert footage features B. B. King, Doug Kershaw, the original Alice Cooper group, Delaney and Bonnie, Sal Valentino (formerly of the Beau Brummels), and others. The associate producer and supervising editor was Martin Scorsese (after working on *Woodstock*). Joy Boyd was the musical supervisor. Warner released the soundtrack.

MEDIUM COOL

(Paramount, 1969) **D/S/P/C:** Haskell Wexler **P:** Jerrold Wexler

Robert Forster stars as a detached TV cameraman covering Robert Kennedy's assassination, the "Resurrection City" protest in Washington, DC, and the 1968 Chicago Democratic Convention riots. He becomes involved with a Nam widow (Verna Bloom) from West Virginia and loses his job. Shot on location, this film includes some incredible footage and has a powerful ending. With Marianna Hill, Peter Bonerz, Peter Boyle, and China Lee. Mike Bloomfield wrote the score. Paul Butterfield, the Mothers of Invention, and Wildman Fischer are heard on the soundtrack. Future director Andrew Davis was the assistant cinematographer. It received an X rating for some nudity (and probably for its politics).

MEDUSA AGAINST THE SON OF HERCULES

(Sinister, 1962) **D/S:** Alberto De Matino **S:** Mario Guerra, Luciano Martino **P:** Elmo Bistolfi Italy (*Perseo L'Invincibile*)

Richard Harrison battles Medusa (a walking tree with one eye), her stone men and a dragon. Carlo Rambaldi created the monsters. With Anna Ranalli and Arturo Dominici.

MEET MR. KRINGLE

(1956) **D:** Robert Stevenson **S:** John Monks Jr. **P:** Jules Bricken (*Miracle on 34th Street*)

Thomas Mitchell stars as Santa, with Teresa Wright, MacDonald Carey, Hans Conried, and Ray Collins. This 56-minute 20th Century–Fox remake of the 1947 classic was made for TV but released theatrically overseas.

MEET MR. LUCIFER

(1953) **D:** Anthony Pelissier
S: Monja Danischevsky   UK

The Devil (Stanley Holloway) uses a man (also Holloway) to help him with a plan to use TV broadcasts to ruin people's lives. Also in the cast are Peggy Cummins (*Curse of the Demon*), Kay Kendall, Gordon Jackson, and Ernest Thesiger. The same year, in America, Arch Oboler's anti-TV fantasy *The Twonky* was released. Both films were obviously ahead of their time and should be seen today.

MEET THE APPLEGATES: *See* THE APPLEGATES

MEET THE FEEBLES: *See* THE FEEBLES

MEET THE HOLLOWHEADS

(Media, 1989) **D/S/A:** Tom Burman **S:** Lisa Morton **P:** Joseph Grace   (*Life on the Edge*)

I can't believe somebody financed this "Huh!?" movie directed by a special-effects expert, but I'm sort of glad they did. It's a PG-13 post-nuke family/black comedy patterned in part on the *Jetsons* cartoons, on sets that look like leftovers from *Peewee's Playhouse*. An optimistic, hardworking dad (John Glover) brings his obnoxious, slimy boss home for dinner. His cheerful wife (Nancy Mette) serves mutant-frog snacks to the kids and works overtime preparing blue and green food. Everything comes from plastic tubes, including edible tentacles. Grandpa is fed with a giant syringe. The only scene not in the bizarre home is in some kind of void and features Logan Ramsey and his wife, Anne (who speaks with subtitles). With Juliette Lewis (before she was well known), Joshua Miller, and Bobcat Goldthwait. There's a rap theme. Ron Cobb was the "visual consultant."

MEGAVILLE

(Live, 1990) **D/S:** Peter Lehner **S:** Gordon Chavis **P:** Christina Schmidlin

It's pretty boring as science fiction, but this is about media addiction in the (40s-look) future. Raymond (Billy Zane with an Eddie Munster haircut) has flashbacks, flashforwards, and blackouts due to a malfunctioning computer-chip implant. A drug sold on TV makes ears bleed. The president is killed on TV, and Raymond goes on the run with a woman (Kristen Cloke). With Grace Zabriskie as his mother, Daniel J. Travanti as a crippled media mogul, Stefan Gierasch as a mad doctor, and Hamilton Camp.

MELINDA

(1972) **D:** Hugh A. Robertson
S: Lonne Elder III **P:** Pervis Atkins

Calvin Lockhart stars as a popular disc jockey and playboy named Frankie Parker. When Melinda (Vonetta McGee) is killed in his apartment he becomes the target of gangsters and the police. With Rosalind Cash, Paul Stevens, Rockne Tarkington, Ross Hagen, Jeanne Bell, and Jim Kelly as his karate instructor. The director of this violent black-action movie had edited *Midnight Cowboy* and *Shaft*. Jerry Butler provided music for the MGM release.

MELVIN AND HOWARD

(MCA, 1980) **D:** Jonathan Demme **S:** Bo Goldman **P:** Art Linson, Don Phillips

Melvin E. Dummar (Paul Le Mat) meets Howard Hughes (Jason Robards), and his life is changed even though he never gets any money from Hughes' will. Mary Steenburgen (who received an Oscar) costars as Melvin's wife, with Michael J. Pollard, Pamela Reed, Dabney Coleman, John Glover, Gloria Grahame, Martine Beswicke, Sonny Carl Davis, Denise Galik, and Cheryl "Rainbeaux" Smith. Charles Napier delivers the will. The script is based on the real claims of Dummar (who has a bit part) and it's one of Demme's best films.

MEMED MY HAWK

(1984) **D/S/A:** Peter Ustinov
P: Fuad Kavur   UK/Yugoslavia

Peter Ustinov stars as Abdi Aga, a local dictator in Turkey in the 50s. With Herbert Lom, Denis Quilley, Siobhan McKenna, and Michael Gough. Freddie Francis was the cinematographer. It's based on a novel by Yashar Kemal. Ustinov directed at least eight features.

MEMOIRS OF AN INVISIBLE MAN

(MCA, 1991) **D:** John Carpenter **S:** Robert Collector, Dana Olsen, William Goldman **P:** Bruce Bodner, Dan Kolsrud **M:** Shirley Walker

Chevy Chase is a stock analyst in San Francisco who becomes invisible because of a freak accident and is used by the CIA. His clothes also disappear, but the food he eats does not. The ILM computer-animation FX are good, and we get to "see" an invisible man puke. Advance publicity tried in vain to convince people that this was a new, "serious" Chevy Chase, and the expensive Warner release was a box-office flop. With Daryl Hannah, Sam Neill as an invisible agent, Michael McKean, Stephen Tobolowsky, and Rosalind Chao. The soundtrack was released by Varèse Sarabande. The script is based on a novel by H. F. Saint.

MEMOIRS OF A SURVIVOR

(1981) **D/S:** David Gladwell **S:** Kerry Crabbe **P:** Michael Medwin, Penny Clark   UK

A woman (Julie Christie) and a teenage girl (Leonie Mellinger) are survivors in a post-nuke society. The woman remembers her past. The film is an adaptation of a novel by Doris Lessing.

MEMORIAL VALLEY MASSACRE

(Nelson, 1988) **D/S:** Robert C. Hughes **S:** George Francis Skrow **P:** Brad Krevoy, Steven Stabler

A psycho kills camping bikers and some obnoxious teens. This horror parody features overworked video stars Cameron Mitchell and William Smith.

MEMORIES OF MURDER

(Prism, 1990) **D/P:** Robert Lewis **S:** John Kent Harrison, Nevin Schreiner

Nancy Allen has amnesia and visions of killing in flashbacks set in Seattle. A psycho killer turns out to be Vanity. With Robin Thomas, Olivia Brown, and Don Davis. The first film made by the Lifetime cable-TV network, it shows the influence of *Fatal Attraction*.

THE MEMORY OF EVA RYKER

(1980) **D:** Walter Grauman
S: Lawrence Heath **P:** Irwin Allen

Natalie Wood plays a dual role as a woman who died on a luxury liner torpedoed during WWII and as her daughter. Like most Irwin Allen productions, this CBS-TV movie has disaster scenes and many name stars, including Ralph Bellamy, Robert Foxworth, Bradford Dillman, Roddy McDowall, Peter Graves, Mel Ferrer, Jean-Pierre Aumont, Morgan Fairchild, and Vince Edwards.

MENACE FROM OUTER SPACE: *See* ROCKY JONES

MENACE II SOCIETY

(New Line, 1993) **D/S:** Allen and Albert Hughes **S/A:** Tyrin Turner **P:** Darin Scott

This violent inner-city action movie, inspired by *Mean Streets* and *Goodfellas*, was the first effort by talented 21-year-old twin brothers who had done many rap videos. It will not be enjoyed by Korean grocers. Tyrin Turner stars and narrates as Caine, a high-school graduate growing up in South Central LA. He and his wired friend with dreadlocks, O-Dog (Laranz Tate), sell drugs and steal cars. With Jada Pinkett, Vonte Sweet, Charles S. Dutton, Bill Duke, and Arnold Johnson (*Putney Swope*). Both the theatrical and video releases were cut for R ratings. The Voyager laserdisc, which is letterboxed and uncut, includes a short student film and alternate audio tracks about the making of *Menace*. The various artists rap soundtrack was also popular.

MEN OF SHERWOOD FOREST

(Sinister, 1954) **D:** Val Guest **S:** Allan Mackinnon **P:** Michael Carreras   UK

Don Taylor is Robin Hood in this early color Hammer film released by Astor in America. With Eileen Moore, Douglas Wilmer, and Reginald Beckwith. Hammer's other Robin Hood movies are *Sword of Sherwood Forest* (1960) and *A Challenge for Robin Hood* (1967).

MEN OF THE DRAGON

(1974) **D:** Harry Falk **S:** Denne Bart Petitclerc **P:** Barney Rosenzweig

A brother and sister (Jared Martin and Katie Salor) open a martial-arts school in Hong Kong with Robert Ito. Joseph Wiseman (*Dr. No*) is the main villain. This *Enter the Dragon* ripoff was aired by ABC-TV as a series pilot while *Kung Fu* was still on.

MERCENARIES: *See* CUBA CROSSING

THE MERCENARY: *See* A PROFESSIONAL GUN

MERCENARY FIGHTERS

(Media, 1986) **D:** Riki Shelach **S:** Bud Schaetzle, Dean Techetter **P:** Golan/Globus S. Africa (*Freedom Fighters*)

Peter Fonda and Reb Brown are soldiers of fortune hired to drive a tribe off their land so that a dam can be built. Brown sympathizes with them and changes sides. With Ron O'Neal and Jim Mitchum.

MERIDIAN

(Paramount, 1990) **D/P:** Charles Band **S:** Dennis Paoli (*Kiss of the Beast; Phantoms*)

The *Beauty and the Beast* TV series was probably the inspiration for this stupid but sexy romantic fairy tale filmed in Italy, but parts of it were obviously copied from the Italian Christopher Lee movie *Castle of the Living Dead* (1963). There's a traveling performance troupe with a dwarf, a fire eater, and a strongman and those same great, old caves with scary faces are shown. Charlie (Spradling) plays an American painter restoring a cursed 15th-century painting. Her best friend (Sherilyn Fenn), a sculptor, comes to stay with her in a castle, and they invite the performers to dinner. Now comes the real reason for this devious movie. After a slow-motion "trip" collage, good and bad twins from the troupe have slow-motion, breast-bouncing sex with the naked, drugged girls, then trade them off. Charlie and Sherilyn are both naked a lot, and Fenn has sex with the good and sensitive twin when he becomes a hairy beast too. When the naked man is transformed during a cheap-looking time-lapse sequence he becomes an animal man with pants on! There's also some nonsense about female ghosts, and characters cry about love and how unfair it all is. Fenn is from Detroit and her mother was in the Pleasure Seekers with her aunt, Suzi Quatro! You might want to play "48 Crash" while you watch Fenn's sex scenes. The Pino Donaggio soundtrack is on Moonstone.

MERLIN

(Hemdale, 1992) **D/P:** Paul Hunt **S:** Nick McCarty **P:** Peter Collins (*October 32nd*)

A reporter (Nadia Cameron) discovers that she's the reincarnation of the lost love of a medieval knight (Peter Phelps). This confusing PG-13 romantic action fantasy jumps from ancient times to an 1800s western town to present-day SF and features people with bows and arrows fighting people with machine guns. James Hong is a magician who protects her and Richard Lynch is the evil Pendragon. Desmond Llewelyn (Q in the James Bond films) has a scene as an astrologer. It was shot by Gary Graver (who also directed additional scenes) in Bratislava, Czechoslovakia.

MERLIN AND THE SWORD

(Vestron, 1982) **D:** Clive Donner **S:** J. David Wyles **P:** Martin Poll (*Arthur the King*)

Dyan Cannon visits Stonehenge and falls down a hole into Camelot where Malcolm McDowell is King Arthur. It's pretty ridiculous and was shelved for years, before debuting on CBS. With Candice Bergen, Edward Woodward, Rupert Everett, Liam Neeson, Michael Gough, Maryam D'Abo, and Terry Torday (*Tower of the Screaming Virgins*) as "the enchanted queen." It was originally 180 minutes long.

MESMERIZED

(Vestron, 1984) **D/S:** Michael Laughlin **P:** Anthony I. Ginnane UK/New Zealand/Australia (*Shocked*)

This gothic melodrama, based on a novel by Polish director, writer, and actor Jerzy Skolimowski, is set in New Zealand in the 1880s. It's told in flashback by Victoria (Jodie Foster), an orphan, while she's on trial for murder. A creepy rich businessman with a serious rat problem (John Lithgow) marries her, watches her through a hole in her bedroom wall, makes her trim his nose hairs, has his servant spy on her, and worse. Skolimowski (*The Shout*) based his novel on a real-life case. Harry Andrews is Victoria's stern father-in-law, Michael Murphy is a pastor who uses "the revolutionary new science" of hypnotism, and Dan Shor is her brother. This is much more serious and a lot less fun than Laughlin's *Dead Kids/Strange Behavior* (1980), also with Murphy and Shor, or his *Strange Invaders* (1983), with Shor. Foster also coproduced it. The video opens with an ad for Joyce Jilson, "White House astrologer"!

MESSALINA

(1960) **D:** Vittorio Cottafavi **S:** Ennio De Concini, Mario Guerra

Belinda Lee stars as the famous empress, in a feature that AIP released directly to TV. She also starred in *The Nights of Lucretia Borgia* and other European costume epics before dying young in a 1961 car crash.

MESSALINA AGAINST THE SON OF HERCULES

(Sinister, 1963) **D:** Umberto Lenzi **S:** Gian Paolo Callegari, Albert Valentin Italy (*Gladiatore di Messalina*)

Richard Harrison is Glaucus, a gladiator from Britain, and Lis Gastoni is Messalina, wife of Claudius. This movie, which has nothing to do with Hercules, features Marilou Tolo. Embassy released it.

MESSALINA, MESSALINA

(Video City, 1981) **D/S:** Bruno Corbucci **S:** Mario Amendola Italy (*Caligula: Sins of Rome*)

The impressive, massive sets from *Caligula* (1980) were used for this bizarre, slapstick sex comedy, which was badly dubbed in America. Empress Messalina (Anneka Di Lorewenzo) has men lined up to have sex with her (she's always on top to show off her silicone breasts). Tomas Milian is Baba, a crippled, curly-haired con man. Claudius is stupid and impotent, and he stutters. Theremin music is heard. Some more explicit sex scenes were badly inserted. At the end soldiers invade an orgy and start decapitating everyone in sight. Bodies are cut in half, and there's so much blood spurting everywhere that everyone slips in it. The incredible slapstick gore scene makes you forget the rest of this dumb comedy, and it features NYC underground star Taylor Mead!

THE MESSENGER

(Orion, 1987) **D/P/A:** Fred Williamson **S:** Brian Johnson, Conchita Lee, Anthony Wisdom US/Italy

Fred Williamson stars as a cat burglar who's a former Green Beret and an ex-con. Seeking vengeance for his addicted wife's death, he kills many drug-dealing mobsters in LA, Chicago, Las Vegas, and Italy. Chris Connelly and Cameron Mitchell are cops, and Joe Spinell (in his fifth Williamson movie) is a drug dealer. With Michael Dante, Val Avery, and Sandy Cummings.

MESSENGER OF DEATH

(Media, 1988) **D:** J. Lee Thompson **S:** Paul Jarrico, Richard Sale **P:** Pancho Kohner

Charles Bronson is a newspaper crime reporter investigating some "avenging angel" murders. He uncovers a Mormon religious feud involving brothers (Jeff Corey and John Ireland). With Trish Van Devere, Marilyn Hassett, Laurence Luckinbill, and Charles Dierkop. This was the eighth Bronson/Thompson project. From Cannon.

METALLICA

(1978) **D/S:** "Al Bradley"/Alfonso Brescia Italy (*Star Odyssey; Sette Uomini d'Oro nello Spazio*)

Friendly aliens help Earth prevent a takeover. A robot is named Jeeves. With Yanti Somer, Gianni Garko, and Mellissa Long.

METALSTORM: THE DESTRUCTION OF JARED-SYN

(MCA, 1983) **D/P:** Charles Band **S/P:** Alan J. Adler (*Metalstorm*)

Charles Band made this PG-rated 3-D flop after his 3-D *Parasite* (1982). Jeffrey Byron stars as a space ranger in the post-nuke future, with Kelly Preston, Mike Preston as the evil magician Jared-Syn, Richard Moll as Hurok, and Tim Thomerson. It was filmed at Bronson Canyon and features cyborgs. A sequel was planned but not made.

METAMORPHOSIS

(Imperial, 1989) **D/S:** "George Eastman"/ Luigi Montefiori Italy

A doctor (Gene LeBrock) trying to prolong life with DNA experiments, injects himself in the eye. He ages 50 years, then mutates into a reptile monster and kills. This *The Fly* copy was filmed in Norfolk, Virginia. Laura Gemser has a small role as a prostitute (and has a credit for costumes). The director was the star of *The Grim Reaper*. Some videos came in 3-D boxes with sound effects.

METAMORPHOSIS: THE ALIEN FACTOR

(Vidmark, 1990) **D/S:** Glen Takajian **P:** Ted A. Bohus, Scott Morette (*Return of the Aliens: Deadly Spawn*)

A research scientist (Marcus Powell) creates a wall-eyed mutant amphibian that bites him, and he becomes a red monster (in great pain) with tentacles and killer parasites. Teen sisters (Tara Leigh and Dianne Flaherty) arrive with a boyfriend (Tony Gigante) to investigate their father's death. It's all told in flashback and uses limited stop-motion FX and Animatronics. With Alan Rickman. This independent New Jersey production ran out of funds in 1988, was resumed later, and was released in 1993. It was planned as a sequel to the much better *Aliens: The Deadly Spawn* (1982), a personal fave.

METEOR MAN
(MGM, 1993) **D/S/A:** Robert Townsend
P: Loretha C. Jones

A nice, inner-city Washington, DC, teacher gains limited superpowers from a meteorite. He rallies the neighborhood to help fight crime and the peroxide-haired Golden Lords gang. Some ILM FX are used. With Marla Gibbs as the mother who makes his costume, James Earl Jones, Robert Guillaume, Bill Cosby, Nancy Wilson, Frank Gorshin, Stephanie Williams, Sinbad, Big Daddy Kane, and other rappers as villains. Michael Jackson sings the theme. Some of the name stars worked for minimal pay. This PG film was shot in Baltimore. Townsend also appeared as a superman in his *Hollywood Shuffle. Blankman* (1994) is a more sucessful black-superhero comedy.

METROPOLIS
(Cable, 1926) **D/S:** Fritz Lang **S:** Thea von Harbou **P:** Erich Pommer **C:** Karl Freund

The most expensive feature made in Germany up to that time, this was the biggest project of the famous UFA studios. It was two years in production, and although it's considered a classic now, it lost money. In 1989 an original two-sheet poster sold for $21,100 at an auction in Paris. The many wonders of *Metropolis* make it a must-see for anybody who cares about robots (the female robot is beautiful), science fiction, fantasy, horror, or politics. Much credit should go to the cinematography. A scene with 1,000 bald men (made to look like 6,000) in the Tower of Babel sequence is just a flashback. With Brigitte Helm (in her film debut) as Maria and the robot, Alfred Abel, Fritz Rasp, and Rudolf Klein-Rogge. The original American version was drastically cut, but the full version was 139 minutes. Video versions run up to 131 minutes and include a music score. A book containing the screenplay is available.

METROPOLIS
(Vestron, 1984) **D/S:** Fritz Lang **S:** Thea von Harbou **P:** Erich Pommer

Purists hate it for a number of reasons, but this shortened and modernized version of Lang's classic played theatrically. Luring teens in to see a nearly 60-year-old silent movie is no small accomplishment. It runs 87 minutes, is tinted, and has a Giorgio Moroder score that features cuts by Freddie Mercury, Adam Ant, Loverboy, Jon Anderson (I can't go on!). Just rent it, turn the sound off, and add some more appropriate music of your own choice, OK? Some scenes were restored with lost footage and still photos.

MEXICO IN FLAMES
(1981) **D/S:** Sergei Bondarchuk **S:** Ricardo Garibay, Carlos Ortiz Tejeda   Italy/Mexico/USSR (*Campanas Rojas*)

This was the first of a 4-part TV miniseries about American Communist writer John Reed (Franco Nero) during the Mexican Revolution. It was made at the same time as *Reds* and features epic battle scenes. With Ursula Andress as a wealthy girlfriend (she has a nude scene), Jorge Luke as Zapata, Jorge Reynoso as Pancho Villa, and Blanca Guerra.

MIAMI BEACH COPS
(AIP, 1992) **D:** James B. Winburn **S:** John Lindsey-Moulos (and 4 other jokers)

A pair of nice young Desert Storm vets working as deputy sheriffs in St. Cloud, Florida, go after a pair of killer holdup men on motorcycles working for a mystery man whose face is hidden. There's a boat chase, slow dancing to country music, and another corrupt police sergeant.

MIAMI BLUES
(Orion, 1990) **D/S:** George Armitage **P:** Jonathan Demme

Alec Baldwin stars as Junior, a redneck, psycho, and thief who breaks the finger of a Hare Krishna in an airport during the opening scene. He cons a lot of people and poses as a cop. It retains the sick humor of the Charles Willeford novel it's based on, and has nudity and violence. Jennifer Jason Leigh costars as a naive young hooker, and Fred Ward is a big surprise as Sergeant Hoke Moseley (he loses his dentures several times). With Charles Napier as a police sergeant, Shirley Stoler (her fingers are cut off), and Martine Beswicke. It was the first theatrical release by George Armitage since *Vigilante Force* (1979). Ward was also an executive producer.

MIAMI CONNECTION
(1986) **D:** Richard Park **S:** Joseph Diamond **P/A:** Y. K. Kim

Dragon Sound is a multiracial band made up of orphaned martial-arts students. A rival band hires real bikers to beat them up, and ninjas attack drug dealers. There's a decapitation, hands cut off, spurting blood, Koreans vs. Japanese, and a tae-kwondo demonstration. Vincent Hirsch is an Israeli band member. It was made in Orlando, where Kim teaches martial arts.

MIAMI HORROR
(Panther, 1985) **D:** Alberto Martino **S:** Rita Herbert, Frank Clark **P:** George Salvini   Italy (*Miami Golem*)

In this Italian movie shot in Florida, a German scientist at a university creates a generic something-or-other. John Ireland and his men go around killing people, and David Warbeck is a TV reporter who investigates. Laura Trotter, a psychic, takes a long shower. Some of the special effects are pretty funny (you could create them at home with an old 8mm projector), and during "a timeless moment" Warbeck faces his alien double. The best parts are the hydroboat chases, filmed in the Everglades. If you make it to the end you'll see the mutant-baby monster they call a Golem in a water tank. A whole long scene showing a corrosive liquid going through animal carcasses is accidentally repeated twice (!) on the video.

MIAMI SUPERCOPS: *See* SUPER FUZZ

MICHAEL JACKSON: MAKING MICHAEL JACKSON'S "THRILLER"
(Vestron, 1983) **D:** John Landis (*The Making of "Thriller"*)

The 14-minute "Thriller" video cost $2 million. The song is from the world's best-selling LP of all time, released in time for Xmas 1982. Remember how sick of hearing it you got? Jackson sings, dances, and becomes a werewolf, and zombies crawl out of their graves and dance. The Rick Baker FX are top-notch, Vincent Price's familiar voice helps, and Jackson's girlfriend is played by Ola Ray, a *Playboy* centerfold. Forry Ackerman even appears. Landis made it after *An American Werewolf in London* (1981). Lots of people paid for this hour-long tape to see how it was all done.

MICHAEL JACKSON'S "MOON WALKER"
(SMV, 1988) **D:** Colin Chivers **S:** David Newman **P:** Dennis E. Jones

This plotless, 93-minute film is partly a history of Michael Jackson the superstar. It features six Michael Jackson segments, vintage Jackson Five footage, animation, and live action. Journalists are seen as dogs chasing the star as a rabbit. There are lots of kids, Sean Lennon, Joe Pesci, and Bubbles the monkey. The centerpiece is a 22-minute version of "Smooth Criminal." Warner released it.

MICKEY ONE
(1965) **D/P:** Arthur Penn **S:** Alan M. Surgal

MEXICO

South-of-the-border horror and wrestling hero movies were common at Saturday matinees in America in the 60s. Many are on tape if you look hard enough, and many other good titles are available that are not dubbed. Fans can collect dozens of features starring the late great Santo, The Blue Demon, Neutron, and various wrestling women, vampires, and monsters. Mexico's *Psychotronic* movie era ended in the 70s. A good look at the wrestling hero phenomena is the *Incredibly Strange Film Show* segment with Johnny Legend.

This is probably the best movie Warren Beatty ever starred in, and it's still pretty unknown. He plays a confused comic from Detroit who tries to find nightclub work in Chicago while avoiding gangsters. It's a unique nightmare/paranoia movie, filmed on location. With Alexandra Stewart, Hurd Hatfield, Franchot Tone, Jeff Corey, and Donna Michelle. Columbia released this b/w film, and MGM released the Stan Getz soundtrack. Penn, of course, also directed *Bonnie and Clyde*.

MICKEY SPILLANE'S MIKE HAMMER: MURDER ME, MURDER YOU

(1983) **D:** Gary Nelson **S:** William Stratton **P:** Lew Gallo

The year after *I, the Jury* played in theaters, CBS-TV aired this first pilot for its series, starring Stacy Keach as a modern-day Mike Hammer. Keach is good (he also narrates), and the theme song ("Harlem Nocturne") is great. The series seems to have been aimed at fans of Russ Meyer movies. I don't think any network series had as many large-chested women in low-cut dresses. With Tanya Roberts as Velda, Michelle Phillips, Don Stroud (a series regular as Captain Pat Chambers), Lisa Blount, Delta Burke, Tom Atkins, and Eddie Egan. There was a syndicated Mike Hammer series with Darren McGavin (1957–59), and CBS had first tried to start a series in 1981 with *Mickey Spillane's "Margin for Murder,"* starring Kevin Dobson.

MICKEY SPILLANE'S MIKE HAMMER: MORE THAN MURDER

(1984) **D:** Gary Nelson **S:** William Stratton, Stephen Downing **P:** Lew Gallo

The second pilot feature for the CBS-TV series stars regulars Stacy Keach, Lindsay Bloom, and Don Stroud. The series seemed to run out of steam pretty fast, and the constant use of LA locations to stand in for NYC was too obvious. In 1985 Keach was busted for drugs in England and had to serve a six-month sentence. Tabloids shouted, "Hammer in the slammer!" The series was halted and then resumed as the watered-down *The Return of Mickey Spillane's Mike Hammer* (1986–87). Stroud had his own real-life drinking and drug problems too. With Lynn-Holly Johnson, Robyn Douglas, and Denny Miller. CBS later tried again with *Come Die with Me*, a 1994 series pilot starring Rob Estes and Pamela Anderson.

MICROWAVE MASSACRE

(Rhino, 1979) **D:** Wayne Berwick **S/P:** Thomas Singer, Craig Muckler

Comedian Jackie Vernon stars as a henpecked construction worker who kills his wife (Claire Ginsberg), keeps pieces of her in the refrigerator, and has his neighbors eating flesh. He brings home hookers and hitchhikers and kills them during sex. It was directed by the son of the man who made *The Monster of Piedras Blancas*. A talking video box with a light was used for the 1991 rerelease.

MIDNIGHT

(Vidmark, 1980) **D/S:** John Russo **P:** Donald Redinger   (*Backwoods Massacre*)

A girl (Melanie Verlin) runs away from home and her abusive cop stepfather (Lawrence Tierney). She and two guys who pick her up become victims of backwoods Satanists. This low-budget Pittsburgh production features a racial subplot and brief Tom Savini FX. The ending is a suprise, and Tierney is great as the dad. John Amplas is Abraham. Sam Sherman was the executive producer of this Independent International release, based on John Russo's novel.

MIDNIGHT

(SVS, 1988) **D/S/P:** Norman Thaddeus Vane **P:** Gloria J. Morrison

Lynn Redgrave is Midnight, a rich, Elvira-style TV horror hostess. Murders occur after her show is cancelled. This spoof of *Sunset Boulevard* features Frank Gorshin, Tony Curtis, Karen Witter, Rita Gam, Kathleen Kinmont, Gustav Vintas, Wolfman Jack as himself, and Tiny Lester and other pro wrestlers. The soundtrack was released by Traq. There was an attempt to make it a midnight movie in NYC.

MIDNIGHT 2: SEX, DEATH, AND VIDEOTAPE

(Tempe, 1993) **D/S:** John Russo **P/E:** J. R. Bookwalter

Matthew Jason Walsh stars as Abraham, a surviving member of the Satanist family from the original feature. He narrates and walks around with a camcorder taping his female victims, whom he kills during sex. A woman goes to a detective to ask him to find her missing friend. If you liked the original 1980 Pittsburgh feature, a lot of it is used here as flashbacks (including scenes with Lawrence Tierney). As a matter of fact, there are flashbacks inside of flashbacks. The new footage, which is disturbing and effective in spots, was taped in Akron, Ohio, for a reported $14,000. The most irritating part is the star constantly talking to the camera. That was a bad idea.

MIDNIGHT AT MADAME'S TUSSAUD'S

(Sinister, 1936) **D:** George Pearson **S:** Roger MacDougall, Kim Peacock **P:** Steven Edwards UK (*Midnight at the Wax Museum*)

A man (James Carew) bets that he can spend the night in a wax museum's chamber of horrors. Charles Oliver, Lucille Lisle, Bernard Miles, and William Hartnell are also in the cast of this 62-minute thriller.

MIDNIGHT CABARET

(Warner, 1988) **D/S:** Pece Dingo **S:** Lori Gloede **P:** Nicki Marvin

Michael Des Barres puts on a decadent "concept" Broadway play with a Devil character. Characters have nightmares, and things in the play really happen. Laura Herrington costars, with Lisa Hart Carroll and Lydie Denier.

MIDNIGHT CHILD

(Prism, 1992) **D:** Colin Bucksey **S:** David Chaskin **P:** Kimberly Meyers

Olivia D'Abo stars as a Satan-worshipping nanny who wants a girl to be the Devil's bride. With Marcy Walker and Cotter Smith. Victoria Principal was the executive producer of this cable-TV movie.

MIDNIGHT COP

(Vidmark, 1988) **D/S:** Peter Patzak **S:** Paul Nicholas, Julia Kent   W. Germany

Armin Mueller-Stahl stars as an eccentric, aging, Polish-born West Berlin chief inspector of police who's after a serial killer. He beats suspects and has an affair with a hooker (Morgan Fairchild). The killer shoots up women with heroin and hides bodies in a meat locker. With Julia Kent as the chief inspector's new partner, Michael York, Frank Stallone, and Allegra Curtis (daughter of Tony Curtis and Christine Kaufmann). The East German–born Mueller-Stahl, then known for some Rainer Werner Fassbinder movies, isn't even mentioned on the video box, but he makes this whole movie worth seeing. Director Peter Patzak is Austrian. York and Mueller-Stahl were also in his *Lethal Obsession*.

MIDNIGHT EXPRESS

(1978) **D:** Alan Parker **S:** Oliver Stone **P:** David Puttnam, Alan Marshall **M:** Giorgio Moroder   UK

Here's a real horror story for travelers, based on a true story. Brad Davis stars as Billy Hayes, an American college student arrested in Istanbul in 1970 for smuggling hashish and thrown into a hellhole jail. With Randy Quaid, John Hurt, Bo Hopkins, Irene Miracle, and Mike Kellin. Most viewers remember Paul Smith as Hamidou, a rapist guard. It was shot in Malta. Oliver Stone's script, based on the book by William Hayes, received an Oscar. Stone directed *The Hand* (1981) next. The soundtrack (on Casablanca) also received an Oscar.

MIDNIGHT FACES

(Sinister, 1926) **D/S:** Bennett Cohen

No reference books seem to include this cheap-looking, cliché-ridden, haunted-house/reading-of-the-will silent movie from the Goodwill company. It's complete with a caped figure in a wide-brimmed hat, lurking in a mansion on an island in the Florida bayou, and a comic scared black servant (even the title cards are racist). The many creepy suspects include the hired help, a "Chinese" man (played by Benihana founder Rocky Aoki, a Japanese-American), and a paralyzed man. The best part is a fight on the rooftop. Francis X. Bushman stars, with Kathryn McGuire (*Sherlock Jr.*) and Jack Perrin. It's a pretty good 55-minute print and includes a menacing musical score.

MIDNIGHT FEAR

(Rhino, 1990) **D/S:** Bill Crain **S:** Craig Hughes, Craig Wasson

David Carradine stars as a sheriff after a killer who skinned a woman alive. A man and his deaf-mute brother are the prime suspects. With Craig Wasson and August West. From New World.

MIDNIGHT GIRL

(Video Yesterday, 1925) **D/S:** Wilfred Noy
S: Jean Conover

Bela Lugosi was still pretty unknown in 1925, but he had already been in films since 1915, starting in his native Hungary. Lila Lee stars as a Russian opera singer in America. In this rare silent film from Chadwick Pictures, Lugosi (with a goatee) is her suitor. Lee went on to star in several old-dark-house movies and *The Unholy Three* (1930). It's 84 minutes, and new music has been added.

THE MIDNIGHT HOUR

(Vidmark, 1985) **D:** Jack Bender
S: Bill Bleich **P:** Ervin Zavada

This ABC-TV horror/comedy was made to cash in on the popularity of Michael Jackson's "Thriller." It's a good example of just how much horror became accepted, mixed up, and tamed by the mainstream. In a small Massachusetts town on Halloween a group of students (who all look too old for their parts) accidentally unleash Lucinda, a black witch/vampire hanged in the 18th century, and a graveyard full of zombies. It all happens because these "nice" kids decide to break into a museum and "borrow" some authentic costumes for a party. Graves explode, and the living dead emerge *Thriller* style. One perfectly preserved blond 50s cheerleader provides the love interest and makes comments about how things have changed for the worse. The makeup and special effects by the Tom Burman studios are typically good. Several scenes are rock-video style. The star, Shari Belafonte-Harper, dances and sings "Let's Get Dead" after becoming a vampire. The best scene is when she's bitten in the wine cellar. Wine spurts all over in slow motion, while "How Soon Is Now?" by the Smiths plays(!). The soundtrack has mostly old hits like "Little Red Riding Hood" by Sam the Sham and the Pharaohs and the great but overused "Bad Moon Rising." With LeVar Burton (who becomes a vampire), Kevin McCarthy (who becomes a zombie), Dick Van Patten, Lee H. Montgomery, Kurtwood Smith, Mark Blankfield, and Dedee Pfeiffer. There's a werewolf, a midget zombie, and the voice of Wolfman Jack.

MIDNIGHT KISS

(Academy, 1992) **D:** Joel Bender **S:** John Weidner
P: Manette Marion Zola   (*In the Midnight Hour*)

Michelle Owens stars as a Hollywood rape-crisis-squad cop who is bitten by a long-haired, blond vampire, priest, and serial killer (Gregory A. Greer) who says, "You shouldn't fuck with a man of God!" She has a trick dream-within-a-dream and becames a superstrong vampire herself so that she can throw criminals around. The male cops are all extreme assholes in this movie, which features some imaginative violence and an attack of vampire victims in a morgue. With Celeste Yarnall and Gabriel Dell Jr. as "Punk Number One." It's by the director of *Gas Pump Girls* (1978).

MIDNIGHT MADNESS

(1980) **D/S:** Michael Nankin,
David Wechter **P:** Ron Miller

Back in 1980 a PG movie from Disney was a surprise. This was the studio's first, and it's about an all-night scavenger hunt by LA college students. With David Naughton, Eddie Deezen, Stephen Furst, and a then unknown 18-year-old Michael J. Fox playing a 12-year-old.

MIDNIGHT MOVIE MASSACRE

(VCI, 1986) **D/S:** Mark Stock, Larry
Jacobs **S/P:** Wade Williams

Wade Williams was smart enough to go around securing the rights to some old science-fiction movies when video first caught on, but he wasn't smart enough to resist the temptation to make his own movie. It's set in a 50s theater and is overloaded with lame overeating, tit, nerd, and snot humor. Real trailers are used for filler, and a very unconvincing b/w re-creation of a serial wastes guest stars Robert Clarke and Anne Robinson (*War of the Worlds*). That footage is from an earlier, unreleased Williams project called *Space Patrol*. If you can stay awake until the end, there's an inspired scene with lots of old-fashioned tin-can robots who dance. It was shelved for four years.

MIDNIGHT WARRIOR

(PM, 1989) **D/P:** Joseph Merhi
S: Charles T. Kanganis **P:** Richard Pepin

Kevin Bernhardt is an LA TV-news cameraman who eventually sells out. This direct-to-video action movie features Lilly Melgar, Kevin Bernhardt, and Heidi Payne. It's by the director of *Night of the Wilding* and *Fresh Kill*.

A MIDSUMMER NIGHT'S DREAM

(1933) **D/P:** Max Reinhardt **D:** William Dieterle
S: Charles Kenyon, Mary McCall Jr.

Olivia De Havilland (in her screen debut) and Dick Powell star in this Shakespeare comedy/fantasy, but watch it for the all-star supporting cast, including James Cagney as Bottom, young Mickey Rooney as Puck, Victor Jory as Oberon, Anita Louise as Titania, Joe E. Brown, Arthur Treacher, Frank McHugh, Hugh Herbert, and Ian Hunter. Even little Kenneth Anger is in it. Cinematographer Hal Mohr won an Oscar. Erich Wolfgang Korngold arranged the Mendelssohn music. This prestigious Warner Brothers version of Max Reinhardt's stage production runs 132 minutes. There are silent films based on the play, including several made in Germany. Some later versions are dance films, cartoons, and TV movies. Diana Rigg and David Warner starred in a Royal Shakespeare Company version in 1969. *Ill Met by Moonlight* is a 90s modernized adaptation.

THE MIGHTY GORGA

(Cinema Concepts, 1969) **D/P:** David Hewitt
P: Robert V. O'Neil, Joan Hewitt, David Prentiss

Gorga is the worst *King Kong* copy ever made, anywhere, anytime. Mark Remington (Anthony Eisley) owns a small circus that needs a new attraction to keep the creditors away. He goes on a "safari" with two black bearers. They encounter a ridiculous lost white tribe who dress like Indians, keep skulls on poles, and worship "the Mighty

Gorga." The cast includes Scott Brady as a villain, Kent Taylor as the missing Congo Jack, Gary Kent, and future directors Greydon Clark and Gary Graver (who was also the cinematographer). You could say it was made for kids, but even in 1969 most kids would try to destroy a theater when confronted by *Gorga's* special effects. A man in an immobile gorilla mask is one thing, but this movie uses plastic toy dinosaurs. There's a lava flow (stock footage), a brief animated shot of a dragon (from another movie), and a "chamber of death" (Bronson Canyon). Even the cheapest movies use a blue screen to combine the actors with supposedly giant creatures. This time the actors are in an out-of-focus film shown on a normal screen. The man in a gorilla suit stands in front of the screen. At one point he carries a doll around. Hewitt also made *The Wizard of Mars* (1964) and others. Producer Robert V. O'Neil went on to direct the first two *Angel* movies.

THE MIGHTY JUNGLE

(Paragon, 1964) **D/S:** Ismael Rodríguez, Arnold
Belgarde **D/A:** David Da Lie   US/Mexico

Parade films took a Mexican movie, *La Ciudad Sagrada* (1959), and added two sets of new scenes (and music by Les Baxter) to make this incoherent, paste-up, near-mondo entertainment with much narration and animal footage. Marshall Thompson goes alone and unarmed to the Congo and befriends a tribe of real, naked pygmies. Meanwhile, his "partner" (Da Lie) goes off to the Amazon where he has adventures. In the weirdest (the Mexican) part, Da Lie eats some "forbidden fruit." He freaks out ("This can only be a hallucination!"), everything changes to negative, and he imagines climbing a pyramid where natives perform a human sacrifice. Back in the "real" world the movie ends with the number two hero killed by a crocodile and a naked woman (Rosenda Monteros) taking a shower! Thompson directed and starred in *A Yank in Vietnam* the same year.

THE MIGHTY URSUS

(1961) **D:** Carlo Campogalliani **S:** Giuliano Carmineo,
Giuseppe Mangione   Italy/Spain (*Ursus*)

Ursus (Ed Fury) has to rescue Attea (Maria Orfei) from an evil priest on an island. But she's been turned into an evil princess, so he's thrown into the arena, where he fights a bull, then leads a slave revolt. Sets left over from *King of Kings* were used. Fury returned in more Ursus movies.

MIKEY

(Imperial, 1992) **D:** Dennis Dimster-Denk
S: Jonathan Glasser **P:** Peter Abrams, Robert
Levy, Natan Zahavi

In a twist on *The Stepfather*, an adopted boy (Brian Bonsall, from the TV series *Family Ties*) kills off his entire suburban family, then moves on to another one, and keeps a videotape of the killings to watch. Mikey remains polite and cheerful but makes scary drawings, which concern his fourth-grade teacher, the (traditional) character who can't convince anyone else that something is seriously wrong. Mikey falls for his friend's older sister (Ashley Lawrence, from *Hellraiser*) and kills her boyfriend, along with more people. With John Diehl, Mimi Craven, Josie Bisset, and Lyman Ward. It was made in Arizona.

THE MILKY WAY

(Cinematheque, 1969) **D/S:** Luis Buñuel
S/A: Jean-Claude Carrière **P:** Serge Silberman
France /Italy (*La Voie Lactée*)

This may be the ultimate religious film. Anyone who can cope with subtitles might enjoy it, but so would open-minded biblical scholars. Two beggars on the road leading to a shrine have many surprising, often comic, dream-like encounters. They meet the Devil (Pierre Clementi), nuns are crucified, and the pope goes before a firing squad. With Michel Piccoli as de Sade, Edith Scob as the Virgin Mary, Alain Cuny, Claudio Brook, and Delphine Seyrig.

MILLENNIUM

(IVE, 1989) **D:** Michael Anderson **S:** John Varley **P:** Douglas Leiterman Canada

Kris Kristofferson investigates a midair plane explosion and discovers that the plane was hijacked to the future. Cheryl Ladd (with weird blond hair and space clothes) is Louise Baltimore, a leader of women commandos from 2000 years in the future. This long (108-minute), PG-13 time-travel/love story is based on Varley's 1983 story "Air Raid." It's set in a grim future when people can't reproduce and some are mutants. One whole section of the movie is repeated. With Daniel J. Travanti, Robert Joy, Lloyd Bochner, and Al Waxman.

MILLER'S CROSSING

(Fox, 1990) **D/S:** Joel Coen **S/P:** Ethan Coen **C:** Barry Sonnenfeld

This period gangster movie about a corrupt politician (Albert Finney) and his henchman (Gabriel Byrne) involved with the same woman (Marcia Gay Harden) is basically a remake of *The Glass Key* (1942) set in the late 20s. The 20th Century–Fox release has many good performances and typically odd Coen touches. With John Turturro, J. E. Freeman as the Dane, Jon Polito, Steve Buscemi, and bits by Sam Raimi and Frances McDormand. The Coen brothers made *Barton Fink* next.

THE MILLION DOLLAR DUCK

(1971) **D:** Vincent McEveety **S:** Roswell Rogers **P:** Bill Anderson

An atomic duck lays golden eggs, causing a worldwide economic crisis. Dean Jones and Sandy Duncan star in this light comedy, with Joe Flynn, Tony Roberts, James Gregory, Jack Kruschen, and Edward Andrews. In the 70s Disney movies got exceptionally lame. This one copies British director Val Guest's *Mr. Drake's Duck* (1951).

MILLION DOLLAR MYSTERY

(HBO, 1987) **D/P:** Richard Fleischer
S: Tim Metcalfe, Michael Tejada-Flores, Rudy De Luca **P:** Stephen F. Kesten

Back in 1914 *The Million Dollar Mystery* was a hit serial because a press agent cooked up a fake missing-heiress story. A 1927 version with Lila Lee is set in an old, dark house (and is available from Sinister). This version, released by DEG, stars Eddie Deezen(!). It copies *It's a Mad Mad Mad Mad World,* and it lost millions. Another press agent came up with the bright idea of awarding a million to a real person in a contest sponsored by Glad Bags. It was the last nail in DEG's coffin. Tom Bosley is a government agent who dies, with Kevin Pollak, Tawny Fere, and Rich Hall. MRC released the soundtrack. It was Fleischer's last film.

MILLIONS

(Prism, 1990) **D:** Carlo Vanzini **S:** Enrico Vanzina, Carol Vanzina **P:** Enrico Cecchigori, Vittorio Cecchigori

Billy Zane is a lying, scheming nephew in an international business family. He has an affair with his sister-in-law (Alexandra Paul, who has topless scenes). His uncle, in a coma after a helicopter crash, is married to Lauren Hutton, who fights Zane for power. With model Carol Alt as a swinging, drug-addicted cousin, Donald Pleasence (also in the director's *Nothing Underneath*) as a whispering banker, Jean Sorel, John Stockwell, and Florinda Bolkan.

A MILLION TO JUAN

(1994) **D/A:** Paul Rodriguez **S:** Francisca Matos, Robert Grasmere **P:** Steven Paul, Barry Collier

In this comedy based on a Mark Twain story, Edward James Olmos is an angel. Cheech Marin costars, with Ruben Blades, Polly Draper, Tony Plana, Paul Williams, Pepe Serna, and David Rasche. It's from the Samuel Goldwyn Company.

THE MILPITAS MONSTER

(VCI, 1975) **D:** Robert L. Burrill

A giant, animated, flying, garbage-eating Godzilla-type monster stars in this PG-rated amateur film made by a high-school teacher. The "proceeds went to his local high school." It has a *King Kong*–type ending and was made in the same city where the murder that inspired *River's Edge* occurred. Paul Frees narrates.

MINDBENDERS, VOLUMES I AND II

(SW, 1968–71)

These are 60s and early-70s documentary shorts, most made by the US Navy and local police departments. "Acid" (1971) is from the *Encyclopedia Brittanica*, "LSD: Insight or Insanity" (1968) is narrated by Sal Mineo, and "LSD: Trip to Where?" (1968) includes interviews with actor Richard Lynch and Timothy Leary.

MIND, BODY, AND SOUL

(AIP, 1992) **D/S/P:** Rick Sloan

After being in countless porno tapes, Ginger Lynn (Allen), a short blonde with very blue eyes, has acted in R-rated movies since 1988. She stars in this serious but very bad horror movie as a girl who is jailed for innocently attending a Satanic sacrifice with her boyfriend. The masked coven leader has a distorted voice, but it's obviously co-star Wings Hauser, who plays an attorney. Ginger is raped before being released from jail. She goes on a TV talk show to expose the Satanists and debates a "priestess." There's some nudity, car chases, and a "surprise" ending. Tami Bakke is a friend from jail, and Jay Richardson is a cop.

MINDFIELD

(Magnum, 1989) **D:** Jean-Claude Lord
S: William Deverall **P:** Tom Berry, Franco Battista Canada

Michael Ironside is a troubled, divorced Montreal man with memories of shock treatments. Christopher Plummer (the John Carradine of Canada) is Gregory, a Hungarian doctor who, under instructions from the CIA, experimented on people and "hit them up with LSD and burned their brains" to make them killers. The search for the truth leads to sex with a lawyer (Lisa Langlois), suicide, an undercover porno shop, a junkie artist, and gangsters who kill a man by pushing his eyeballs in with their thumbs. It all ends in a huge auditorium where hundreds of striking cops come to the rescue, followed by a reference to Lee Harvey Oswald. The LSD idea is wasted by not having any interesting visuals. Director Lord also made *Visiting Hours* with Ironside.

MIND GAMES: *See* AGENCY

MINDGAMES

(Fox, 1989) **D:** Bob Yari **S:** Kenneth Dorward **P:** Mary Apick

A couple (Edward Albert and Shawn Weatherly) and their kid (Matt Norero) pick up a mysterious stranger (Maxwell Caulfield) while traveling through the Southwest. He's a psychiatry student who manipulates them to prove some theory.

MINDKILLER

(Prism, 1987) **D/S:** Michael Krueger **S:** Dave Sipos, Curtis Hannum **P:** Sarah H. Liles (*The Brain Creature*)

This PG-13 comedy was shot on video in Denver. A horny-nerd librarian (Joe McDonald) uses mind control to get to girls, but a "brain monster" takes over one of his new girlfriends.

MIND OVER MURDER

(LD, 1979) **D:** Ivan Nagy **S:** Robert Carrington **P:** Jay Benson (*Are You Alone Tonight?*)

A serial killer is after a woman (Deborah Raffin) with psychic powers who is helping to solve a plane-crash mystery. This CBS-TV movie features David Ackroyd, Bruce Davison, Andrew Prine, and Robert Englund.

THE MIND SNATCHERS

(Prism, 1972) **D:** Bernard Girard
S: Ron Whyte **P:** George Goodman
(*The Demon Within; The Happiness Cage*)

Christopher Walken stars as a cynical, sarcastic, troublemaking private stationed in Frankfurt. He's arrested by MPs and taken to a remote mental hospital where scientists conduct pain-and-pleasure experiments. With a young-looking Ronny Cox as a manic patient who laughs a lot, Ralph Meeker as an officer, and Joss Ackland. Walken didn't become well known until *The Deer Hunter* seven years later. This PG-rated Cinerama release (based on the novel *The Happiness Cage*) was filmed in Denmark and backed by Joseph Papp.

MIND TRAP
(AMI, 1989) **D:** Eames Demetrios
S: Jay Sri, Bill Hart **P:** Vinay Shrivastava

Here we have your basic revenge plot with terrible acting and accents, awful dialogue, laughable fight scenes, and Dan Haggerty as Sergei, a director in red suspenders. We also have a mind-control-room plot and reel vs. real surprises as a movie is being made during the "action." There's too much talk, pointless topless scenes, blond villains, a comic S&M scene, a poster for *Rampage*, and references to Cat Stevens and *The Satanic Verses*. Bad movies fans might love it. The family of Sheena (Martha Kincare), an actress, is killed, and her zombie-like father passes on a valuable secret. Sheena sings "Soul Possession" at a party, and Lyle Waggoner (!) has a small, one-scene role: "You have ten seconds to contemplate the completeness of your failing!"

MIND TWISTER
(AIP, 1992) **D:** Fred Olen Ray **S:** Mark Thomas McGee **P/A:** Luigi Cingolani

This senseless "erotic thriller" was a sad way for Telly Savalas to end his long career. He's a police lieutenant who hears too many jokes about how old he is. The female patients of a swinger shrink (Gary Hudson) are being killed. To help catch the killers a blond would-be actress named Heather (top-billed Suzanne Slater) agrees to be videotaped making love to Hudson's Tura Satana–look wife (Erika Nann, who is featured in several sex scenes) but eventually stops and says, "My mind is expanded as far as it will go." With Angel Ashley as a blond cop, Maria Ford, and Nels Van Patten, and bit parts played by Richard Roundtree, Robert Quarry, Paula Raymond (*The Beast from 20,000 Fathoms*), director Ray, and John Blythe Barrymore as a pizza delivery boy. Gary Graver was the cinematographer. R and unrated tapes are available. I saw the R.

MINDWARP
(RCA, 1991) **D:** Steve Barnett **S:** Henry Dominick **P:** Christopher Webster

This was the first of the movies produced by *Fangoria* magazine. It's a mixture of ideas from *Road Warrior* (a post-nuke scavenger hero played by Bruce Campbell), *The Mole People* (underground mutant slaves), *Total Recall* (the lead character dreaming the whole thing), and even *West of Zanzibar* (the villain is really the heroine's father), so it can't be all bad. Most of it takes place in dark, misty tunnels, but they deliver with violent effects, and spurting blood and guts, and there's a pretty good sadistic blond torturer. Angus Scrimm stands out as the underground bad guy with claws. He pulls the eyes out of a young innocent girl, pushes

her in a giant meat grinder, and drinks her blood from skulls! Barnett also directed the useless *Hollywood Boulevard II*.

THE MINES OF KILIMANJARO
(Imperial, 1985) **D/S:** Mino Guerrini
P: Augustino Caminito   Italy (*Afrikanter*)

More *Raiders of the Lost Ark* stuff. Pre-WWII Nazis use a lost tribe in Africa for diamond mining. Tobias Hoels and Elena Pompei star, with Christopher Connelly, Gordon Mitchell, and Al Cliver.

MINISTRY OF FEAR
(1945) **D:** Fritz Lang **S/P:** Seton I. Miller

Ray Milland stars in this excellent WWII espionage thriller, based on a Graham Greene novel. He's released from an asylum and is mistaken for a Nazi agent at a carnival where he's given a cake containing microfilm. During a séance his dead wife accuses him of murder. Then Scotland Yard accuses him of another murder. With Marjorie Reynolds, Dan Duryea, Carl Esmond, Hillary Brooke, and Alan Napier. It was a great year for Milland, who also starred in *The Lost Weekend*. From Paramount.

MINISTRY OF VENGEANCE
(Media, 1989) **D:** Peter Maris **S:** Brian D. Jeffries, Mervyn Emrys, Ann Narcus
P: Brad Krevoy, Steven Stabler

John Schneider (from the TV series *The Dukes of Hazzard*) stars as a Nam-vet minister whose family is killed in Rome. He goes on a vengeance spree fighting Arab terrorists in Lebanon, but everything is eventually blamed on the CIA. This absurd Concorde release features torture scenes. With Ned Beatty, Yaphet Kotto, George Kennedy, Apollonia Kotero, and James Tolkan.

MINNESOTA CLAY
(1965) **D/S:** Sergio Corbucci **S:** Adriano Bolzoni
P: Danilo Marciani   Italy/France/Spain

Cameron Mitchell stars as a gunman who is going blind, in this widescreen, Technicolor Italian western made about the same time as *A Fistful of Dollars*. He escapes from prison (he was framed) and goes to a Mexican town where two gangs are trying to kill each other off. With Georges Riviere, Ethel Rojo, and Fernando Sánchez.

A MINUTE TO PRAY, A SECOND TO DIE
(1967) **D:** Franco Giraldi **S:** Ugo Liberatore, Louis Garfinkle **P:** Albert Band   US/Italy (*Escondido*)

Alec Cord stars as a wanted gunman in New Mexico who has epileptic fits. With Arthur Kennedy as a marshal, Nicoletta Machiavelli, and Robert Ryan in a small role as the governor. Cinerama released a cut version.

THE MINX
(SW, 1969) **D/S/P:** Raymond Jacobs
S/P: Herbert Jaffey

Three businesslike call girls are hired by a power-hungry NYC businessman (Robert Rodan) for a corporate party at a hunting lodge set up with hidden cameras. There are long, tasteful, out-of-focus sex scenes (backed by music that starts out like Duane Eddy and ends up sounding like the Rolling Stones' *Their Satanic Majesties Request* LP), voyeurism, and (offscreen) masturbation. It was the last film for blond 50s star Jan Sterling, who has a small role as the wealthy but unloved wife. The music is by the Cyrkle ("Red Rubber Ball") who are seen playing at Harlow's discotheque wearing *Sergeant Pepper's Lonely Hearts Club Band* uniforms. Cambist released this lame attempt at a "with it" movie. The video print is worn, but it includes some good trailers.

MIRACLE MILE
(HBO, 1988) **D/S:** Steve De Jarnatt **P:** John Daly, Derek Gibson **M:** Tangerine Dream

Anthony Edwards and Mare Winningham meet at the La Brea tar pits. He later answers a pay-phone call and discovers that an all-out nuclear war is about to start. At first everybody thinks he's nuts, then everybody starts fighting to evacuate the city. It's unique and underrated and, like De Jarnatt's *Cherry 2000,* few people saw it. With John Agar, Denise Crosby, Mykel T. Williamson, Brian Thompson, and Claude Earl Jones. A Columbia release.

MIRACLE ON 34th STREET
(Fox, 1947) **D/S:** George Seaton **P:** William Perlberg

Edmund Gwenn is Kris Kringle, a Macy's department-store Santa who goes to court to prove he's the real thing and not insane. Little Natalie Wood is the skeptical daughter of divorced mom Maureen O'Hara, who also works at Macy's. 20th Century–Fox originally released this film in June (a bad move), but later it became a seasonal favorite on TV every Christmas. With John Payne as a lawyer who loves O'Hara, Gene Lockhart, Jerome Cowan, William Frawley, Jack Albertson, Porter Hall, and Thelma Ritter (in her screen debut). Gimbels, Macy's New York rival at the time, is featured too. It's available colorized. *Meet Mr. Kringle* (1956) and a 1973 version starring Sebastian Cabot were both made for TV.

MIRACLE ON 34th STREET
(Fox, 1994) **D:** Les Mayfield **S/P:** John Hughes

This second updated remake (also from 20th Century–Fox) stars Mara Wilson as a lisping little girl, Richard Attenborough as a less-lovable Santa, Elizabeth Perkins as a depressed single mom, and Dylan McDermott as her lawyer boyfriend. Macy's refused permission to use its name this time. Also with Robert Prosky as a judge, J. T. Walsh, James Remar, and William Windom. This PG film is by the director of *Encino Man*.

MIRACLES FOR SALE
(1939) **D:** Tod Browning **S:** James Edward Grant, Marion Parsonnett, Harry Ruskin

Browning's last film is based on "Death from a Top Hat," a Great Merlini novel by Clayton Rawson, a magician from Ohio. Robert Young stars as Morgan, a magician/detective in Manhattan who sells and creates stage illusions. The shocking WWII-theme opening illusion features a woman put in a small coffin and machine-gunned by Japanese soldiers. Morgan solves a murder and debunks fake spiritualists. There's a séance, a ghostly head, and a new invention called "invisible spectacles" (contact lenses). Some illusions are explained, but others (optical effects) are not. Henry Hull has two roles, as Morgan's father and a radio-star professor with a Karloff-type voice. The MGM cast also includes Florence Rice, Frank Craven, William Demarest as a cop, and Gloria Holden as a European mystic.

MIRAGE

(1965) **D:** Edward Dmytryk **S:** Peter Stone **P:** Harry Keller **M:** Quincy Jones

Gregory Peck is a nuclear scientist who has amnesia after seeing his best friend fall from a 27th-floor window. He has discovered a way to neutralize radioactivity, and agents are after him. Also in the cast are Walter Matthau as a private eye, Diane Baker, Kevin McCarthy, Jack Weston, Leif Erickson, and George Kennedy. The Universal release was shot on location in NYC. The soundtrack was released by Mercury. *Jigsaw* is a remake.

MIRROR IMAGES

(Academy, 1991) **D:** Gregory Hippolyte **P:** Andrew Garoni

Delia Sheppard stars as twins in this "erotic thriller" with a psycho lover and murder. She takes showers and is in sex scenes (including a lesbian scene). With Jeff Conaway (*Taxi*), Julie Strain, Kee Anne Beaman, Nels Van Patten, and George "Buck" Flower as Wolfman. R and unrated tapes are available.

MIRROR IMAGES II

(Academy, 1993) **D:** Gregory Hippolyte **S:** Daryl Hanley **P:** Andrew Garoni

Shannon Whirry gets to play identical sisters (a vengeful whore and a traumatized, rich housewife). She also plays one of them as a teenager in b/w sex flashbacks and later gets to watch "herself" in action. The whole flashback-filled tale of murder and double-crosses is told to a sexy shrink (Kristine Kelly) who says, "There are ethical questions" before a hot lesbian session with her patient begins. This direct-to-video movie has many, varied, almost nonstop sex scenes. Shannon in the pool is a highlight. The cast also includes Luca Bercovici as the corrupt-cop husband (who does it with both Shannons), Sara Suzanne Brown, and Eva LaRue.

MIRROR, MIRROR

(Academy, 1989) **D/S:** Marina Sargenti **S:** Annette Cascone, Gina Cascone, Yuri Zeltser **P/M:** Jimmy Lifton

Rainbow Harvest (made up to resemble Winona Ryder in *Beetlejuice*) stars as a neurotic, out-of-place student who acquires supernatural powers from a bleeding, haunted mirror. This modernized

Carrie clone uses *Psycho* music to underscore the many death scenes. Characters die by steam, garbage disposal, etc. Karen Black (in a blond wig) is the ditzy mom, William Sanderson (with a ponytail) is a Nam-vet pet-cemetery owner, and Yvonne De Carlo is a real-estate broker. Charlie Spradling is also in the cast. The video box has a nice pseudo-3-D hologram cover.

MIRROR, MIRROR II: RAVEN DANCE

(Orphan, 1993) **D/S/P/M:** Jimmy Lifton **S:** Virginia Perfili

Tracy Welles (from the TV series *Mr. Belvedere*) is an orphaned teen sent to a remote Catholic school along with her violin-playing little brother. A demon from a mirror helps her kill off characters who are after her inheritance, like Roddy McDowall as a shrink and Sally Kellerman (who ages 120 years) as an evil half-sister. With Mark Rufallo, Lois Nettleton and Veronica Cartwright as nuns (Cartwright is a blind seer), William Sanderson (in a different role than the first movie) as a handyman, and Sarah Douglas.

MIRROR OF DEATH

(Sony, 1987) **D:** Deryn Warren **S:** Gerry Daly **P:** Jessica Rains

Empress Sura (Julie Merrill), a succubus from a mirror, takes over a battered girl. She becomes beautiful, picks up men, and kills them by cutting out their hearts, their eyes, etc.

MIRRORS

(1974) **D:** Noel Black **S:** Sidney L. Stebel **P:** John T. Parker   (*Bad Dreams; Marianne*)

Kitty Winn has nightmares in New Orleans, and someone is murdered. The cast also includes Peter Donat and William Svetland. First on video in Europe, it wasn't released in America until 1984.

MISERY

(RCA, 1990) **D/P:** Rob Reiner **S:** William Goldman **P:** Andrew Scheinman

Kathy Bates won the first best-actress Oscar for a horror movie. It was the most successful Stephen King adaptation at the box office and the second King movie by Reiner (after *Stand by Me*). James Caan is the captive romance writer who ends up using his typewriter as a weapon. Bates is his psychotic, lonely "number-one fan." Most of it takes place in a house in one room, but it manages to be suspenseful and scary. With Richard Farnsworth, Frances Sternhagen, Lauren Bacall, Graham Jarvis, and J. T. Walsh. The Marc Shalman soundtrack is on Bay Cities. Barry Sonnenfeld was the cinematographer and second-unit director. Bates returned to star in another King adaptation, *Dolores Claiborne* (1995).

THE MISFIT BRIGADE

(TWE, 1987) **D:** Gordon Hessler **S:** Nelson Gidding **P:** Just Betzer, Benni Korzen   US/UK (*Wheels of Terror*)

Anti-Nazi German prisoners are forced to fight the Red Army in 1943. This WWII action comedy, based on Sven Hassel's novel, features David Car-

radine as the mean Colonel von Weisshagen, Bruce Davison, Oliver Reed in a small part as a general, D. W. Moffett, and Svetlana.

MISSILES FROM HELL

(1958) **D:** Vernon Sewell **S:** Jack Hanley, Eryck Wlodek **P:** George Maynard   UK (*The Battle of the VI*)

Michael Rennie and Patricia Medina star in this WWII story (based on true incidents) about the British working with Polish partisans. A pre-star Christopher Lee plays Brunner, an SS officer.

THE MISSING GUEST

(1938) **D:** John Rawlins **S:** Charles Martin, Paul Perez

This comedy/mystery is a remake of *The Secret of the Blue Room* (1933). Scoop Hanlon (Paul Kelly), a reporter assigned to attend a masquerade party and spend the night in an old, haunted mansion on Long Island, pretends to be a psychic. Characters disappear, are murdered, and are frightened by (fake) ghosts. With Constance Moore, Selmer Jackson, and William Lundigan. It was remade again as *Murder in the Blue Room* (1944).

MISSING IN ACTION

(MGM, 1984) **D:** Joseph Zito **S:** James Bruner **P:** Golan/Globus

Chuck Norris, as a former POW, Colonel James Braddock, frees some MIAs in Nam. This *Rambo* clone, made in the Philippines by the director of *Friday the 13th: The Final Chapter*, features M. Emmet Walsh, Lenore Kasdorf, and James Hong. A prequel followed.

MISSING IN ACTION 2: THE BEGINNING

(MGM, 1985) **D:** Lance Hool **S:** Arthur Silver, Larry Levinson, Steve Bing **P:** Golan/Globus

This prequel was actually shot before the "first" movie (in Mexico and St. Kitts). The setting is a slave-labor opium operation in postwar Vietnam. Chuck Norris is hung upside-down with a rat, so he bites its head off. Soon-Teck Oh is the evil torturer Colonel Yin. The cast also includes Professor Tanaka. There was even a "making of" tape (on UA video), followed by *Braddock: Missing in Action III* (1988).

MISSING LINK

(J2, 1988) **D/S/C:** David and Carol Hughes **P:** Dennis D. Kane

The last ape man (Peter Elliot) wanders the plains of Africa after men have killed off his family. Typically excellent Rick Baker makeup FX are used for the ape man. This documentary-style PG film from Universal has no dialogue but is narrated by British actor Michael Gambon.

MISSION IN MOROCCO

(Republic, 1959) **D:** Anthony Squire **S:** Brian Clemens **P:** Sergio Newman   UK/Spain

Lex Barker stars as an oil-company executive in Morocco who investigates the death of a colleague. Juli Reding (*Tormented*) is his daughter, and Fernando Rey is a prince.

MISSION KILL

(Media, 1985) **D/S/P:** David Winters **S:** Maria Dante

Nam-vet demolition expert Robert Ginty joins the rebels in a South American revolution to get revenge after a friend is murdered. With Cameron Mitchell, Olivia D'Abo, Brooke Bundy, Sandy Baron, and Merete Van Kamp. Winters formed his own company, AIP Video, the next year.

MISSION MARS

(Unicorn, 1968) **D:** Nicholas Webster **S:** Michael St. Clair **P:** Everett Rosenthal

After a lot of time is spent introducing three astronauts and their girlfriends, the men are sent to Mars where they discover a frozen Soviet astronaut and a talking orb. Darren McGavin stars. Nick Adams is a geologist who brings a pastrami sandwich on board. The instrumental rock-music soundtrack (like a San Francisco bar band) helps set it in the late 60s, but the characters are more like they're from the early 50s. There's a nightmare sequence, NASA stock footage, and an obvious model space ship. The story is by Aubrey Wisberg. It was the first feature filmed at Miami's Studio City complex. Adams died of a drug overdose the year this was released by Allied Artists.

MISSION OF JUSTICE

(Republic, 1992) **D:** Steve Barnett **S:** George Saunders **P:** Pierre David, Kurt Anderson

Jeff Wincott stars as a martial-arts-fighting ex-cop who infiltrates a criminal organization. The Mission of Justice, a gang of ninja assassins disguised as a Guardian Angels type of group, is backed by mayoral candidate Brigitte Nielsen. Karen Sheperd is the hero's ex-partner. Also with Matthias Hues and Luca Bercovici.

MISS NYMPHET'S ZAP-IN

(1970) **D/P:** "Sheldon Seymour"/ Herschell Gordon Lewis

The Laugh-In show was still popular on TV when Lewis made this adults-only takeoff. It's a series of comic sketches featuring topless go-go dancers, painted breasts, and a hunter captured by black native women. It was filmed in California.

MISS RIGHT

(Sony, 1980) **D:** Paul Williams **S/A:** William Tepper **P:** Ibrahim Moussa   Italy

William Tepper, who starred in Jack Nicholson's *Drive, He Said* (1972), is an American reporter in Rome who tries to say goodbye to several girlfriends in one evening during separate dinners at his apartment. Karen Black and Marie-France Pisier have topless scenes. The international cast of beauties includes Margot Kidder, Clio Goldsmith, Virna Lisi, Dalila Di Lazzaro, and Jenny Agutter (who appears for only a few seconds). This comedy wasn't released in America until it came out on video in 1989.

MISS SADIE THOMPSON

(1953) **D:** Curtis Bernhardt **S:** Harry Kleiner **P:** Jerry Wald

This 3-D, color, stereophonic musical version of W. Somerset Maugham's *Rain*, filmed in Hawaii, stars Rita Hayworth as a singer (not a prostitute). In Memphis her dance scene was removed by censors. José Ferrer is Reverend Davidson, and Aldo Ray and Charles Buchinsky (Charles Bronson) are sailors. The Columbia remake was a hit. Other versions are the silent film *Sadie Thompson* (1928) with Gloria Swanson, *Rain* (1932) with Joan Crawford, and the version I'd like to see, *Dirty Gertie from Harlem* (1946).

MR. ARKADIN

(1955) **D/S/P/A:** Orson Welles
Spain/France (*Confidential Report*)

Orson Welles (with heavy makeup) stars as a mysterious millionare, in a film with *Citizen Kane* touches. Based on his novel, it was shot all over Europe, in Spanish-language and English-language versions. Welles married costar Paola Mori after filming was over. Also with Akim Tamiroff, Patricia Medina, Michael Redgrave, Mischa Auer, Katina Paxinon, Peter Van Eyck, Suzanne Flon, and Robert Arden. It was released, and pretty much ignored, in England in 1955 and in America in 1962. Welles said that recutting had made it the most butchered of all his films. His next film as director, also ignored at the time, was *Touch of Evil.*

MR. BILLION

(Fox, 1976) **D:** Jonathan Kaplan
S/P: Ken Friedman **P:** Stephen Bach

Italian superstar Terence Hill, in a rare American feature, plays a mechanic who heads across the country to San Francisco to claim an inheritance. This PG comedy costars Jackie Gleason and Valerie Perrine as swindlers, Slim Pickens, Chill Wills, R. G. Armstrong, Leo Rossi, and Dick Miller.

MR. DESTINY

(Touchstone, 1990) **D/S/P:** James Orr
S/P: Jim Cruickshank

This PG-13 movie copies *It's a Wonderful Life* (and *Peggy Sue Got Married*). James Belushi goes back to 1970 to relive a baseball game. This time he hits a homer, marries the prom queen (Rene Russo), and goes on to live in a North Carolina mansion. He eventually wants his middle-class life and real wife (Linda Hamilton) back. Michael Caine is the angel figure, a magical bartender. Also in the cast are Jon Lovitz, Hart Bochner, and Kathy Ireland.

MR. FROST

(SVS, 1990) **D/S:** Philip Setbon **S:** Brad Lynch **P:** Xavier Gelin   UK/France

Mr. Frost (Jeff Goldblum), who claims to be the Devil, says that he tortured and murdered 24 people, then buried them in a garden. Kathy Baker (from the TV series *Picket Fences*) is the psychiatrist he chooses to talk to after years of silence in a mental hospital. An inmate under his control goes on a shooting spree, killing religious leaders. The police inspector (Alan Bates) who captured him is the only one to realize who the manipulative, steely-eyed Frost really is. With Jean-Pierre Cassel as a cop, Daniel Gelin, Charlie Boorman, and Vincent Schiavelli. This British production (filmed in France) has similarities to *Exorcist III*. It includes a flashback, a nightmare, and maybe too much talking, but Goldblum and Baker are good.

MR. HORN

(1979) **D/A:** Jack Starrett **S:** William Goldman **P:** Robert L. Jacks, Elliot Kastner

David Carradine stars as the western folk hero Tom Horn in a 2-part CBS-TV movie set in the 1880s, with Richard Widmark, Karen Black, Enrique Lucero as Geronimo, Richard Masur, Jeremy Slate, Pat McCormick, and John Alderman. Steve McQueen plays the same role in *Tom Horn* (1980).

MR. MEAN

(Rhino, 1977) **D/P/A:** Fred Williamson **S:** Jeff Williamson   Italy

A gangster in Rome hires Mr. Mean (Williamson), an ex-cop from LA, to kill Lou Castel. Meanwhile gangsters try to kill Mean. He chases a car on foot and says, "Just call me Mean." His life is saved by his gold chain. It's pretty dull. Crippy Yocardo is his model girlfriend. The Ohio Players do the theme song and are seen playing in a club.

MR. MIKE'S MONDO VIDEO

(1979) **D/S/P:** Michael O'Donaghue **S:** Mitchell Glazer, Emily Praeger, Dirk Wittenborn

This 70-minute, comic, pseudo–mondo movie was shot on video for NBC-TV, was rejected for airing, then was released theatrically by New Line. It features Japanese women bathing in dolphin blood, Gig Young's groceries, Sid Vicious doing "My Way," and appearances by Carrie Fisher, Teri Garr, Joan Hackett, Deborah Harry, Margot Kidder, Klaus Naomi, and *Saturday Night Live* regulars Dan Aykroyd, Jane Curtin, Bill Murray, Gilda Radner, and Paul Shaffer.

MR. PAYBACK

(1995) **D/S:** Bob Gale

If you wasted your money seeing this silly and mean spirited PG-13 25-minute interactive movie in a theater (like I did), you got to choose various "plot" advancements by pushing one of three colored buttons on a joy stick attached to your seat. Advertised as "from the makers of the *Back to the Future*" movies, it's filled with bad taste gags, torture, and humiliation. Billy Warlock stars as some kind of android who helps people seek revenge. I imagine some parents who took their kids had second thoughts when the dominatrix school teacher was forced to get on her knees in bondage gear and act like a dog. In another version, a racist boss (Christopher Lloyd) appears in drag and blackface. Sony released the gimmick film in its own theaters. The picture quality is also substandard. Hopefully this technology will be used for better things in the future.

MR. PEEK-A-BOO'S PLAYMATES

(1962) **D/P:** Ronny Ashcroft
P: Lorraine Ashcroft   (*Like Wow!*)

A man finds magic glasses and sees naked women in a copy of *Paradisio* (1961). It's by the director of *The Astounding She Monster*.

MR. PETERS' PETS

(SW, 1962) **D/P:** Dick Crane

A balding Irish guy orders "animal ambrosia" that magically turns him into various animals so that he can watch women. A blonde takes a bubble bath (he's a cat), a woman sunbathes naked on a beach (he's a fish), three women strip on cliffs (he's a duck). There are also topless harem dancers. It's all silent color footage with narration and thinking out loud. Althea Currier (*Kiss Me Quick*) and Denise Daniels star. This 70-minute comedy is from Sonney Amusements.

MR. RICCO

(1975) **D:** Paul Bogart **S:** Robert
Hoban **P:** Douglas Netter

In his last starring role Dean Martin plays a San Francisco attorney hired to defend black militant Thalmus Rasulala, who's accused of murder. Also with Denise Nicholas, Cindy Williams, Geraldine Brooks, Philip Michael Thomas, and Ella Edwards. From MGM.

MR. VAMPIRE

(VSOM, 1984) **D:** Ricky Lau **S:** Wong
Ying, Szeto Cheuk Hon **P:** Leonard
K. C. Ho, Samo Hung   Hong Kong

The first in a very popular and much-copied period comic-horror series from Golden Harvest stars Lam Ching Ying (*Fists of Fury*) as "the one eyebrow priest." He's hired by a landowner to control his father, now a hopping, kung-fu-fighting vampire corpse. Also in the cast are Lu Nan Chung and Moon Lee. *Mr. Vampire 2* (1985) and #3 (1987) feature Yuen Biao. #4 (1987) stars Wu Ma as the priest. All were produced by Samo Hung and directed by Ricky Lau. There were the inevitable copies and ripoffs (some also with Lam Ching Ying), *Mr. Vampire V* and *VI* (1988 and 1989), and *Mr. Vampire 92*. Cool hopping-vampire puppets can be purchased in American Chinatowns.

MISTER ZEHN PROZENT

(1967) **D:** Guido Zurli **S:** Arpad De Riso,
Werner Hauff   W. Germany/Italy

A mystery man called Sigpress captures thieves and hands them over to Scotland Yard after taking 10 percent of what they stole for himself. George Martin stars, with Klaus Kinski and Ingrid Schoeller.

MITCHELL

(Rhino, 1975) **D:** Andrew V. McLaglen
S: Ian Kennedy Martin **P:** R. Ben Ephraim

Joe Don Baker stars as a detective who's after bigtime drug dealers Martin Balsam and John Saxon. The Allied Artists release is considered bad by some people mostly because of Baker's tough-guy acting. It's only available on tape in the *Mystery Science Theater 3000* version, with robot viewers making jokes. With Linda Evans as a call girl and Harold J. Stone.

MIXED BLOOD

(Media, 1984) **D/S:** Paul Morrissey **S:** Alan
Brown **P:** Antoine Gannage, Steven Fierberg

Brazilian actress Marilia Pera (*Pixote*) stars as Rita La Punta, a mom and ruthless drug dealer in NYC's "Alphabet City." Morrissey's sense of humor really shows, and this is one of his best. A scene in a (real) *Menudo* shop is a high point. The violent characters and situations are pretty believable and funny. Also with Richard Ulacia as Rita's son, Angel David, and Linda Kerridge.

MOANA

(1926) **D/S:** Robert Flaherty

This silent classic about Polynesian tribal life was the first feature called a "documentary" (in a review in the *New York Sun*). Paramount promoted it as "the love life of a South Seas siren!" and many people bought tickets to see the topless female natives being tattooed.

MOB BOSS

(Vidmark, 1990) **D/P:** Fred Olen Ray **S:** T. L. Lankford

In the same year as *GoodFellas* and *Godfather III*, Ray made this gangster comedy. Eddie Deezen stars as the idiot son of dying mobster William Hickey, with Morgan Fairchild, Stuart Whitman, Don Stroud, Brinke Stevens, Debra Lamb, Karen Russell, Jay Richardson, Leo V. Gordon, Dick Miller, Robert Quarry, Jasae, and Teagan. Also with Mike Mazurki (in his last role) and Jack O'Halloran, who both played Moose Malloy in different versions of *Murder, My Sweet*.

MOB BUSTERS

(1986) **D:** Winston Richard
P: Frank Wong   Hong Kong

Americans Richard Kiel (from the James Bond movies) and Misty Rowe (from *Goodbye, Norma Jean*) went to Asia and starred in this kung-fu comedy. Kiel was also in *War of the Wizards* and *Mad Mission III*, both made in Hong Kong.

MOBSTERS

(MCA, 1991) **D:** Michael Karbelnikoff **S:** Michael
Mahern, Nicholas Kazan **P:** Steve Roth

Universal released this misfire teen-appeal epic about young 20s gangsters after the success of *Young Guns* and its sequel. Christian Slater stars as Lucky Luciano, with Patrick Dempsey as Meyer Lansky, Richard Grieco as Bugsy Siegel, and Costas Mandylor as Frank Costello. Michael Gambon,

Anthony Quinn, and F. Murray Abraham show up as older gangsters. Also with Lara Flynn Boyle (and her body double), Christopher Penn, Nicholas Sandler, Seymour Cassel, Robert Z'Dar, Karen Russell, and Ava Fabian.

MOB STORY

(Shapiro, 1989) **D/S:** Jan Carlo, Gabriel Markiw
S: David Flaherty **P:** Anthony Kramreither   Canada

Kate Vernon stars, with her father, John Vernon, Al Waxman, and Margot Kidder, in this PG-13 "dark romantic comedy" about a mob boss training his nephew to be a criminal. It was filmed in Winnipeg.

MOBY DICK

(MGM, 1956) **D/S/P:** John Huston **S:** Ray Bradbury

It opens with a young seaman (Richard Basehart) who introduces himself and then narrates the story. He has to spend the night with Queequeg (Friedrich Ledebur) a harpooner from a tribe of tattooed headhunters. Before embarking he hears a sermon by Father Mapple (Orson Welles, who had once planned to direct his own version). John Huston's version of Herman Melville's difficult novel was not popular when it was released but it looks great, has some fine acting and special effects, and is well worth watching. Gregory Peck is the obsessed, one-legged Captain Ahab of the *Pequod*. The whale-hunting scenes are excellent (and were later copied in *Dune*). With Leo Genn as Starbuck, Harry Andrews, Mervyn Johns, Bernard Miles, James Robertson-Justice, and Royal Dano as the figure of doom. This Warner Brothers Technicolor release runs 116 minutes. The novel had been filmed twice with John Barrymore, in 1926 as a silent film, *The Sea Beast*, and in 1930.

MODEL BY DAY

(Academy, 1993) **D:** Christian Duguay **S:** Joseph
Loeb III, Mathew Weisman **P:** Kent Cord   Canada

A famous NYC model (Famke Janssen) becomes a kickboxing crime-stopper known as Lady X. She wears a lavender helmet, a bra, and boots, does back flips, and battles punks, carjackers, and the Russian Mafia. Meanwhile an imposter kills people. It's a fun movie with some good fight scenes. Steven Shellan is the cop she falls for, Kim Coates is a bad-guy nightclub owner, Shannon Tweed is a kung-fu teacher, and Sean Young has one scene. By the director of the *Scanners* sequels, it was filmed in Toronto.

THE MODEL KILLER: *See* HOLLYWOOD STRANGLER MEETS THE HILLSIDE SLASHER

MODEL MASSACRE = COLOR ME BLOOD RED

MODELS, INC.

(1952) **D:** Reginald LeBorg **S:** Harry
Essex, Paul Yawitz **P:** Hal E. Chester

Coleen Gray becomes involved in a racket in which models marry for money. Howard Duff is the hero, and John Howard is the bad guy. From Mutual Productions. Gray later became *The Leech Woman*. LeBorg's next was *Bad Blonde*.

MODERN PROBLEMS

(Fox, 1981) **D/S:** Ken Shapiro **S:** Tom Sherohman, Arthur Sellers **P:** Alan Greisman

Chevy Chase is an air-traffic controller who's exposed to nuclear waste and acquires telekinetic powers. This PG comedy by the director of *The Groove Tube* features Patti D'Arbanville, Dabney Coleman, Mary Kay Place, and Nell Carter.

MOHAMMAD, THE MESSENGER OF GOD

(1976) **D/P:** Moustapha Akkad **S:** H. A. L. Craig   (*The Message*)

In 1977 a Muslim sect took 100 hostages in Washington DC, and showings of this film were cancelled, all 180 minutes of it. Mohammad himself is never shown (that's forbidden) in this story of the birth of the Muslim religion, but there's a lot of action, and Anthony Quinn stars as his uncle. It's from the maker of the Kadafy-backed *Lion of the Desert* (also with Quinn) and the producer of the Halloween series. With Irene Papas, Michael Ansara, Johnny Sekka, Michael Forest, and André Morell.

MOLLY AND GINA

(A-Pix, 1994) **D/S/P:** Paul Leder **S:** Reuben Leder **P:** Ralph Tornberg

Frances Fisher (who narrates) is the secretary and mistress of an LA private eye who is killed. She teams up with a would-be actress (Natasha Gregson Wagner) whose boyfriend was killed at the same time. They search for a missing woman and try to find the killers. This comic movie has Fisher constantly mentioning Wagner's green hair and Wagner dropping the name of an earlier Leder film, *I Dismember Mama*. With Bruce Weitz as an asshole police sergeant, Stella Stevens as a rich alcoholic, long-haired Peter Fonda, Penny Johnson, and Leder regular Greg Mullavey. Fisher was also in Leder's *Frame Up* and *Frame Up II*.

MOM

(TWE, 1989) **D/S:** Patrick Rand **P:** Leon Dudevoir

A blind man (Brion James with a ponytail) who rents a room in LA turns out to be a cannibal/vampire monster who bites his elderly landlady. The life of her TV-newsman son (Mark Thomas Miller) is ruined when he finds her feeding in a back alley ("Mom!") and tries to keep her locked up at home. Jeanne Bates (*Silent Night, Deadly Night IV*) is great as the vampire mom. The sight of this gray-haired lady (wearing shades) on a relentless search for victims is pretty outrageous. Most of the killing is offscreen, but after a while she mutates, acquires a man's voice, and starts throwing people around. Stella Stevens (in her mid–50s) shows up as a sexy, drunk hooker, and Claudia Christian is a victim. James is also good, with his creepy, dark voice, but disappears too soon.

MOM AND DAD

(SW, 1944) **D:** William Beaudine **S:** Mildred Horn **P:** Kroger Babb, J. S. Jossey

Incredibly, this adults-only road-show movie grossed $16 million, making it the 4th-highest moneymaker of the 40s, behind three animated Disney films! It received a C (condemned) rating from the Catholic Church's Legion of Decency and was banned in many cities. The biggest hit from Kroger Babb, a former carnival barker from Wilmington, Ohio, it was still showing in the late 50s. His wife wrote the screenplay. It was presented (in person) by "Elliot Forbes, the eminent hygiene commentator." Forbes (who could be any fast talker) showed up in many towns at once. For a while, Olympic track star Jesse Owens (!) was the pitchman in black theaters. Nurses were in attendance, and the books *Man and Boy* and *Woman and Girl* (also written by Babb's wife) were sold. Screenings were for men only or women only and would begin with a *Star-Spangled Banner* singalong. In the film itself, puritanical parents don't tell their daughter about "personal hygiene," she becomes pregnant, her boyfriend dies, and the parents are blamed. The high-school teacher who wanted sex-education classes then gets to show (onscreen interruption for Forbes' talk) the birth-of-a-baby reel (both natural and cesarean births) plus what VD can do. David F. Friedman and Joe Solomon were distributors in later days. *Mom and Dad* was followed by imitators like (*The Story of*) *Bob and Sally*, *Because of Eve*, and *Street Corner*. The prolific Beaudine also directed the road-show family hit *Prince of Peace* (1949).

MOM AND DAD SAVE THE WORLD

(HBO, 1992) **D:** Greg Beeman **S:** Chris Matheson, Edward Solomon **P:** Michael Phillips

Parents Teri Garr and Jeffrey Jones are transported in their station wagon to another world where men are part dog and women are part fish. This PG comedy has a *Flash Gordon* serial look and rubbery creatures. Jon Lovitz is the evil but dumb emperor who's in love with Garr, and Eric Idle is an imprisoned king. Thalmus Rasulala and Wallace Shawn work for the emperor. With Kathy Ireland and Dwier Brown. This Warner release is by the same writers as the Bill and Ted movies.

MOMMIE DEAREST

(Paramount, 1981) **D:** Frank Perry **S:** Tracy Hotchner, Robert Getchell **S/P:** Frank Yablans

Audiences started laughing in the wrong places, and this Joan Crawford exposé/biography soon became some kind of cult movie. Paramount changed the ads to say, "The biggest mother of them all!" and mentioned the wire hangers. It's based on Christina Crawford's book about the horrors of living with her adoptive mother (who died in 1977). Faye Dunaway stars. After this film, *Wicked Lady*, and *Supergirl*, nobody took her seriously again until *Barfly*. Diana Scarwid costars as Christina, with Howard Da Silva as Louis B. Mayer and Steve Forrest, Rutanya Alda, and Jocelyn Brando as various reality-based characters. I can't wait for movies about Bette Davis and Bing Crosby.

MONACO FOREVER

(BRI, 1984) **D/P:** William A. Levey **S:** C. William Pitt

This is an obscure 48-minute comedy short set in France in the 50s with Charles Pitt as an American tourist (actually a jewel thief) who encounters various characters. They include Martha Farris, Sidney Lassick (as himself), and Jean-Claude Van Damme (in his first role) as a French-speaking homosexual karate fighter. Van Damme is featured on the cover of the video box. By the director of *Slumber Party '57*.

MONA'S PLACE

(American, 1970) **S/P/E:** John Hayes **P/C:** Paul Hipp   (*Fandango*)

James Whitworth (Papa Jup in *The Hills Have Eyes*) stars in this western with sex as Dan Murphy, leader of a lonely group of gold miners. He has lots of tattoos, a beard, and a big (real) nose. He takes Busby and Sissy Sam to Fandango to arrange for Mona (big-breasted Shawn Devereaux, from Russ Meyer's *The Seven Minutes*) to bring back her dance-hall girls to their camp. It's all kinda like a grade-Z version of Robert Altman's *McCabe and Mrs. Miller*, which was probably being filmed at the same time. The Irish villain, Muck Mulligan, is copied from Lee Marvin in *Cat Ballou*, with a patch on his half nose. The cowboys all sing "Oh, Susanna" in bathtubs, everybody has faked sex, all the women are forced to strip outside, there's a gang rape, and in the end the women kill the bad guys with hat pins.

MONDO MOVIES

The history of documentary movies designed to shock viewers goes back to (at least) 1903, when Edison released *An Execution by Hanging* and *Electrocution of an Elephant*. Documentaries showing strange cultures were popular major releases in the 20s. Some were more studious and honest than others, but many were partially (or totally) faked exploitation movies. Features showing naked natives, blood, and violence were roadshow adults-only staples for years. Some were called "Goona Goona" movies in the trade. In the early 60s, the Italian movie *Mondo Cane* created a worldwide sensation and many copies were released. By the 70s, some of these "mondo" movies had become extremely shocking and disturbing. These days many of these features are on tape and many more are made just for video release (see *Faces of Death*).

DOUBLE SHOCKER SHOCK!
YOU WON'T BELIEVE YOUR EYES!
THE MOST SENSATIONAL EXPOSE OF THE FREAK SIDE OF LIFE

MONDO CANE NO. 1 — **MONDO CANE NO. 2**

JERRY GROSS Presents

TOGETHER FOR THE FIRST TIME ...ONE BIG SUPER-SHOW!

THE "WITH-IT" SEX HIGHS!
SEE THE CHICKEN THAT SMOKES!
NAKED WITCHCRAFT MURDERS!
CO-ED ORGY BATHS!
TODAY'S CANNIBALISM!
SEE PRIESTS ON FIRE!

Directed by GUALTIERO JACOPETTI & FRANCO PROSPERI • Produced by MARRIO MAFFEI & GIORGIO CECCHINI • in TECHNICOLOR
A RIZZOLI FILM • Distributed by CINEMATION INDUSTRIES
R

MONDO BALARDO

(SW, 1963) **D:** Roberto Bianchi Montero **S:** Albert T. Viola   Italy

Much of this aimless mondo movie is staged, but the friendly, familiar voice of Boris Karloff narrating gives it a special edge. Several of the many, many scenes involve a bondage photo shoot in Hong Kong, sea turtles being decapitated, an opium den, lesbians, strippers, modern art, strange religious rites, and a behind-the-scenes look at the making of a Hercules movie. Many segments are set in West Germany, including escapes through the then recently completed Berlin Wall. Franz Drago, a midget who lip-synces to "I Ain't Got Nobody," is in the most unique part. The Karloff narration, written by Albert T. Viola, was added in 1967 for Crown International's release of the American version, advertised as "filmed in Stereorama." The video is a Frank Henenlotter release.

MONDO CANE

(Video Dimensions, 1962) **D/S/P:** Gualtiero Jacopetti   Italy (*Mondo Cane No. 1*)

This is the documentary that started it all. Gualtiero Jacopetti (who narrates) was a journalist and newsreel maker. He doesn't just show gross scenes. There's sense and irony in everything. The film made audiences think while shocking them. Scenes at a Hollywood pet cemetery, for instance, are followed by a look at an Asian restaurant where dogs are served. Other segments concerns sharks, bulls, Hawaiian tourists, drunken Germans, and nude body painting. Although it's very tame by today's standards it's still better than most of the later mondo movies. It was a worldwide hit, and so was the theme song, "More," which is now often played at weddings! Times Films released it, then Cine-

mation, which also released *Mondo Pazzo/Mondo Cane No. 2*. The hit LP is on UA.

MONDO FREUDO

(SW, 1966) **D:** R. L. Frost **P:** Bob Cresse

"Hidden cameras" capture various (mostly staged) scenes of London hookers, beatnik artists, a slave auction in Mexico, a Puerto Rican black mass in NYC, mud wrestling in Germany, and an S&M club in Japan. The filmmakers also appear and interview hookers in NYC.

MONDO HOLLYWOOD

(1967) **D/S/P:** Robert Carl Cohen

This narrated "documentary" is a series of many very brief (and pretty mundane) segments about "the city of dreams," shot too often with an out-of-control zoom lens. We see surfing, skateboarding, parachuting, war protests, an LSD lecture, body painting, topless waitresses, and lots of famous movie stars (like Zsa Zsa Gabor, Dean Martin, and Nancy Sinatra) in footage of a parade. A vegetarian lives in a garage with a monkey, and a hairdresser has some great wigs and hairpieces. There's a priceless bit with Governor Ronald Reagan, a photo from *The Mask* is shown, and Alfred Hitchcock is seen making *Torn Curtain*. Bobby Jamison, who had been a promising singer a few years earlier, is seen as a bearded hippie. The Mothers of Invention were cut out for legal reasons, but you can still see Frank Zappa and Jimmy Carl Black at a "freakout." Mike Curb put the soundtrack (on Tower) together, and the Arrows do a long instrumental.

MONDO KEYHOLE

(SW, 1966) **D/P:** John Lamb **D/S/C/E:** Jack Hill **P:** Ronald Graham   (*The Worst Crime of Them All!*)

This is a rape-revenge movie, but it's not what you'd expect. Howard (Nick Moriarty, who narrates) runs Art Products, a mail-order sex business offering nudist magazines, films, and albums like *Punishment in Hi Fi.* Cathy Crowfoot (who was Lamb's girlfriend) is a lesbian karate expert with a whip and leather bondage gear. At a Hollywood-models costume ball Dracula announces that the punch has LSD in it. The movie is filled with well-done, mind-altering camera FX (including flaming skulls and watches) and features elaborate bondage and S&M scenes, a naked woman underwater (Lamb also made *Mermaids of Tiberon*), and a heroin-addict wife. It's a 70-minute b/w Frank Hennenlotter Sexy Shocker.

MONDO MOD

(SW, 1967) **D/P/E:** Peter Perry **S:** Sherman Greene

DJ Humble Harve narrates this look at teens in LA in the wonderful year of 1966. It's a very entertaining mixture of real and obviously staged scenes. We see "the Group" (kids with acne) and a terrible white soul singer playing at the Whiskey à Go-Go, and we learn that teenagers spend up to $10 a month (!) on records. Long (very good) scenes show surfing and the Sunset Strip demonstrations. Pot and LSD use is explored and bikers attack a cameraman. Instrumental covers heard include "Can't Explain" (Love), "Feel a Whole Lot Better" (the Byrds) and "You Make Me Feel Good" (the Zombies). Laszlo Kovacs and Vilmos Zsigmond were the cinematographers (assisted by Ed De Priest), and Jack Starrett was the assistant director. This Timely Films release was backed by Harry Novak, who is interviewed by Johnny Legend at the end of the video. They talk about the late surfer Mike Weldon (seen in the film) and confirm that he doesn't edit *Psychotronic.* The video is available with *Pot Party Playgirls* (love that title!), an alternate topless-dancing version of the climactic party scene, released as a short.

MONDO NEW YORK

(MPI, 1987) **D/S:** Harvey Keith **S:** David Silver **P:** Stuart Shapiro

This late entry in the mondo craze is a look at various "underground" and performance-art stars and would-be stars in Manhattan as seen by a young woman (Joey Arias). Some of them are Rick Aviles, Joe Coleman, Phoebe Legere (who sings), Lydia Lunch, Ann Magnuson (who reads poetry), John Sex, and Annie Sprinkle.

MONDO PAZZO

(SW, 1963) **D/S:** Gualtiero Jacopetti **D/S:** Franco Prosperi **P:** Mario Maffei, Giorgio Cecchini   Italy (*Mondo Cane II*)

This sequel (also narrated by Gualtiero Jacopetti) features the Mexican "Day of the Dead," insect eating, American cops in drag, slave markets, a Buddhist monk burning himself to protest the war in Vietnam, and many more scenes (mostly authentic) of strange customs around the world. It was released in America (cut by 20 minutes) by Rizzoli, then Cinemation. The soundtrack is on 20th Century–Fox. Steve Rossi sings the theme song. Unrelated 80s European videos pretending to be part of a series go up to at least *Mondo Cane V.*

Ann Magnuson beats a dead horse in *Mondo New York.*

MONDO TOPLESS

(RM, 1966) **D/P/C/E:** Russ Meyer

After the box-office failure of *Faster, Pussycat! Kill! Kill!* this short (62-minute) color "documentary" was a momentary step back for Meyer, but it was a drive-in hit and is a hilarious classic of its kind. It includes footage from *Europe in the Raw* (1963) and Lorna Maitland's screen test for *Lorna*. Most of it is nonstop wild dancing by topheavy topless women, usually outdoors with a radio blasting. Their voiceovers explain their plans and goals. With Babette Bardot (who starred in *Common-Law Cabin*) and Pat Barringer. The music is by the Aladdins.

MONDO TRASHO

(Cinema Group, 1969) **D/S/P/C/E:** John Waters

Waters's first (and, at 95 minutes, longest) feature was made in 16mm and b/w, with no dialogue, for $2,000. Mary Vivian Pearce experiences a series of bizarre adventures. She meets a shrimper, sees a miracle in a laundromat, is run over by Divine, and is put into an asylum run by a mad doctor (David Lochary). Mink Stole tap dances. Pearce had been in Waters's shorts as far back as 1964 (*Hag in a Black Leather Jacket*). The other cast members had been in his *Roman Candles* (1966) and *Eat Your Makeup* (1968). Old hits are heard on the soundtrack. This was later distributed by New Line. Waters returned with *Multiple Maniacs* (1970).

MONDO VIOLENCE

(T-Z, 1977) **D/S:** Mario Morra, Antonio Climati   Italy

This consists mostly of narrated travelogue footage with animal-death scenes added. It includes real and fake footage and supposed alligators in the NYC sewer system. "Banned in 40 countries," says the video box. It's by a *Mondo Cane* cameraman.

MONEY FROM HOME

(1954) **D:** George Marshall
S: Hal Kanter **P:** Hal B. Wallis

Jerry Lewis as Virgil Yokum and Dean Martin as Honeytalk Nelson star in their only 3-D movie. It's based on a Damon Runyon story and involves gangsters, steeplechase racing, and an Arab sheik's harem. With Marjie Millar and Pat Crowley. From Paramount.

MONEY TO BURN

(New Line, 1994) **D/S:** John Sijogren **S/P:** Scott Ziehl

Chad McQueen and Don Swayze (stars of *Death Ring*) obtain a suitcase full of stolen money. This action movie features Joe Estevez, Julie Strain, and Sydney Lassick. Note the three relatives of more famous stars.

THE MONEY TREE

(Black Sheep, 1990) **D:** Alan Dienstag
P/A: Christopher Dienstag

Christopher Dienstag (an acting teacher and the director's son) stars as a Marin County pot grower.

This pro-NORML film deals with the details of growing, the personal problems of growers, drug-seeking helicopters, and wild pigs. It has improvised dialogue and a jazz score.

THE MONGOLS

(Sinister, 1960) **D:** André De Toth, Riccardo Freda
S: Ugo Guerra, Luciano Martino, Ottavio Alessi
P: Guido Giambartolomei   Italy/France (*I Mongoli*)

Genghis Khan's son Ogatai (Jack Palance) and his Mongol hordes invade Poland. Anita Ekberg (!) costars as his conniving mistress, Hulina. She looks great but not at all Mongolian. It's in Cinemascope and Eastmancolor.

Anita Ekberg in *The Mongols*.

MONGREL

(Paragon, 1982) **D/S:** Bob Burns

A practical joke at a boardinghouse leads to death, and a young tenant is afraid of dogs. Terry Evans stars, with Aldo Ray as the landlord and Mitch Pileggi (*Shocker*). This early direct-to-video feature comes in a very misleading monster-dog box and was shot in Austin, Texas. Bob Burns did the art direction for *The Texas Chainsaw Massacre* and starred in *Confession of a Serial Killer*.

MONIKA: THE STORY OF A BAD GIRL

(1952) **D/S:** Ingmar Bergman **S:** P.A. Fogelström   Sweden (*Sommaren med Monika; Summer with Monika; Monika*)

Kroger Babb cut Ingmar Bergman's 97-minute b/w film to 62 minutes, dubbed it into "American" English, added a new score by Les Baxter, and distributed it on the exploitation/road-show circuit in 1955, playing up the nude swimming scenes with star Harriet Andersson. It was advertised as "a picture for wide screens and broad minds!" (copy written by David F. Friedman) and played at drive-ins. Bergman's *Illicit Interlude* (1950) and *The Naked Night/Sawdust and Tinsel* (1953) had already been art-house hits, but more people saw this than any other Bergman film (until Roger Corman released some in the 70s).

THE MONK

(Video Search, 1972) **D/S:** Ado Kyrou **S:** Luis Buñuel, Jean-Claude Carriere **P:** Henri Lange **M:** Ennio Morricone   France (*Le Moine*)

This fascinating film, based on Matthew Gregory Lewis' 1796 novel, was to have been directed by Luis Buñuel and has been unjustly criticized because it wasn't. During the inquisition a Spanish Capuchin abbot, Father Ambrosio (Franco Nero), preaches chastity and is considered "the reincarnation of one of the apostles." He falls in love with a monk who's actually a female witch (Nathalie Delon). She leads him into a life of "fornication, sorcery, and murder." A decadent duke (Nicol Williamson) who has girls kidnapped and abuses orphans becomes his benefactor. When Ambrosio confesses the priest is so shocked that he dies. Inquisitors with skulls and crossbones condemn him, but he signs away his soul in blood to avoid paying for his sins. Unlike in most movies, this act is completely successful! The video has English subtitles added to Danish (?) subtitles. A 1991 Spanish remake stars Sophie Ward.

MONKEY BOY

(Prism, 1990) **D:** Lawrence Gordon Clark **S:** Stephen Gallagher **P:** Nick Gillott   UK (*Chimera*)

A pretty horrible-looking, super-strong mutant boy born in a lab is destined for vivisection. He escapes and murders a scientist and many other people, and the police search for him. It's based on the novel *Chimera*, by Stephen Gallagher. John Lynch stars, with Christine Kavanaugh and Kenneth Cranham. This 4-part TV mini-series had its American debut on the Arts and Entertainment Network and then was condensed for video release.

MONKEY HUSTLE

(Orion, 1976) **D/P:** Arthur Marks **S:** Charles Johnson

A new highway threatens a Chicago neighborhood, so the locals throw a big block party as a protest. Yaphet Kotto as Daddy Foxx and a toned-down Rudy Ray Moore are small-time gangsters. This PG comedy also features Rosalind Cash, Randy Brooks, Debbi Morgan, and Kirk Calloway. This AIP release was the last directed by the son of Groucho Marx, who also made the 70s black-cast features *Detroit 9000, Bucktown, Friday Foster*, and *JD's Revenge*.

MONKEY ON MY BACK

(1957) **D:** André De Toth **S:** Crane Wilbur, Anthony Veiller, Paul Dudley **P:** Edward Small

Cameron Mitchell, in probably his best dramatic starring role, is the real-life WWII hero and champion welterweight boxer Barney Ross, who became addicted to morphine. This and *The Man with the Golden Arm* (also from UA) were the first major studio releases to deal openly with drug addiction. A scene of Ross shooting up was cut in order to get an MPAA seal but was used in ads. For many years this movie was shown to patients in government-run addiction programs. With Dianne Foster as Ross' wife and Jack Albertson.

MONKEY SHINES: AN EXPERIMENT IN FEAR

(Orion, 1988) **D/S:** George Romero
P: Charles Evans   (*Ella*)

A quadriplegic Boston law student (Jason Beghe) develops a mind link with Ella, a superintelligent experimental monkey who's there to help him get through each difficult day. Ella carries out his subconscious wishes, and people are attacked and killed. With John Pankow as a scientist friend, Patricia Tallman, Joyce Van Patten, Janine Turner, and an irritating bird. The nurse is played by George Romero's wife, Kate McNeil. Tom Savini provided the FX. It's a long 115 minutes.

THE MONOCLE

(1964) **D:** Georges Lautner **S:** G. Rémy,
Jacques Robert   France

Oliver Despax stars as a French agent who goes after a gang of Asian terrorists who plan to destroy an American nuclear carrier. Barbara Steele costars in this b/w comedy/thriller.

MONOLITH

(MCA, 1993) **D/P:** John Eyres
S: Steven Lister **P:** Geoff Griffiths

Bill Paxton and Lindsay Frost (*Dead Heat*) star as mismatched, arguing LA cops. He has b/w flashbacks of his wife being shot. A Russian woman tries to kill a kid, and an indestructible alien with death-ray eyes changes bodies. This movie has lots of shooting, explosions, and burning men, but not much of a script. Guest stars John Hurt and Lou Gossett Jr. both get to yell a lot. The end of this SGE release copies *Predator II* (also with Paxton), as the heroes discover and, in a ridiculous climax, ride on top of (?!) a large flying saucer.

MONSIEUR VERDOUX

(Fox, 1947) **D/S/P/A:** Charles Chaplin

Chaplin stars as a Depression-era Bluebeard. The American Legion's threat to boycott theaters showing this 123-minute, pacifist-themed black comedy (which condemns war with statements like "One murder makes a villain, millions a hero. Numbers sanctify.") plus generally bad reviews, doomed the original release. It was kept out of release in America until 1964! Based on an idea by Orson Welles, it seems extremely tame today. Martha Raye costars, with Isobel Elsom, William Frawley, Marilyn Nash, and Fritz Leiber. The laserdisc version (from Image) includes script excerpts and commentary. When Chaplin left the country in 1952 to attend the English premiere of what turned out to be his last American film, *Limelight,* the US attorney general revoked his reentry visa.

THE MONSTER

(Dark Dreams, 1925) **D/P:** Roland West
S: Willard Mack, Albert Kenyon

Seeing just how far back horror clichés go is a good idea. Here's a Lon Chaney horror comedy made over 70 years ago. Dr. Ziska, a mad surgeon, runs a former sanitarium with trap doors, tunnels, and an electric chair in the hidden basement. His killer slave, a zombie-like ghoul man in a cape, and a guy who rolls invisible cigarettes use mirrors to cause car wrecks during thunder-storms, assuring new victims. A naive, lovesick, backwoods amateur detective (Johnny Arthur) shows up trying to find a missing person. Before being electrocuted himself, Chaney acts friendly in a smoking jacket, then demented in a lab coat, as he straps Gertrude Olmsted to his operating table: "At last the fools have brought me a woman! I shall transfer your soul into her body! Don't you dare call me mad!" A standout comic/action scene has the nervous hero escaping on a phone wire. The original comic intertitles are almost impossible to read, but after a while they're replaced by newer typed ones. A monotonous piano score is on the soundtrack, but you could supply your own (better) music. This was released the same year as the more famous Chaney hits *The Phantom of the Opera* and *The Unholy Three*. Johnny Arthur was Spanky's dad in the Our Gang short *Anniversary Trouble* (1935).

MONSTER

(Premiere, 1978) **D/S:** Herbert L. Strock
S/P: Kenneth Herts, Walter Robert Schmidt,
Garland Scott   (*Monstroid; Toxic Monster*)

The credits (and even the cast) for this all-star, PG, too-dark, ecology-minded movie are wrong in most books (including my first *Psychotronic* book). It was a 1975 promo reel first. An intro claims that what you are about to see is true and that it happened in 1971 in Colombia (where the creature scenes created by David Hewitt were shot). It was made later, though, in New Mexico. An American cement corporation (led by Phil Carey) has polluted a lake, creating a Loch Ness type of monster. The villagers stone and then burn a woman (whose husband had been killed by the monster) for being a witch. Carey sends tough guy Jim Mitchum to stop the bad news from leaking out, and he has problems with a pushy American lady reporter. Anthony Eisley is the foreman, messing around with the corrupt mayor's daughter. His blond ex-girlfriend has her legs bitten off after a nude swim. John Carradine is a priest who's against "the foreign polluters." The creature is seen as a big claw or as a silly puppet head with floppy jowls. Herbert L. Strock directed *I Was a Teenage Frankenstein* (1957). Kenneth Hartford/Herts directed *The Lucifer Complex* (1978).

THE MONSTER AND THE APE

(Stokey, 1945) **D:** Howard Bretherton **S:** Sherman Lowe, Royal K. Cole **P:** Rudolph C. Flothow

This Columbia serial features a man in a gorilla suit and an excellent, mean-faced robot (or metalogen). Robert Lowery (who also played Batman) stars, with Carole Mathews and Ralph Moran. George McCready is the mad-professor villain.

THE MONSTER AND THE STRIPPER: *See* THE EXOTIC ONES

MONSTER AT CAMP SUNSHINE

(SW, 1964) **D/S:** "Ferenc Leroget"
P: Gene Kearney

Chemicals used by a doctor in NYC make lab rats attack, so he simply tosses a bottle of the toxic waste into the river. In an upstate nudist camp, Hugo, a dumb, fat gardener, becomes a "monster" and attacks with an axe. Clare, a model, narrates the tale of what happened to her nudist-nurse roommate, Martha. The pretty female leads are seen topless at a nighttime birthday party and, in my favorite scene, modeling topless bathing suits on a NYC tenement roof. Nearly everybody has flashbacks and smokes a lot. It all starts with Monty Python–style montages, includes silent movie intitles, and ends with actual war footage to suggest the battle with Hugo. This b/w tape is presented by Frank Henenlotter.

MONSTER DOG

(TWE, 1984) **D:** "Clyde Anderson"/Claudio Fragasso
S/P: Carlos Aured   (*Los Perros de la Muerte; The Bite*)

American rock star Alice Cooper (real name Vince Furnier) stars as Vincent Raven, a rock star visiting his home town with a video crew. People die (his father was killed by a werewolf). With Victoria Vera. It's by the maker of *Rats.*

MONSTER HIGH

(RCA, 1988) **D:** Rudiger Poe **S:** Roy Langdon, John Platt **P:** Eric Bernt

Mr. Armageddon (David Marriott), an alien in human form, shows up to retrieve a doomsday device at a high school. There are comic aliens, rap songs, gore, and students playing a basketball game against monsters to save the world. The movie is narrated.

MONSTER HUNTER

(Wizard, 1977) **D/P:** "Peter Newton"/Aristide Massaccesi **S:** John Cart **P:** Donatella Donati Italy (*Anthropophagus II; Absurd*)

George Eastman (Luigi Montefiore) returns as the mutant killer cannibal in this gory immediate sequel to *The Grim Reaper* (1981). It has a plot like *Halloween* and takes place in small-town America during the Super Bowl. A priest (Edmond Purdom) and a cop search for the killer. The cast also includes Katya Berger as the bedridden main victim, Laura Gemser, and Annie Belle. *The Grim Reaper* (heavily cut in America) is on tape from Monterey.

MONSTER IN THE CLOSET

(Troma, 1983) **D/S:** Bob Dahlin
P: David Levy, Peter L. Bergquist

Donald Grant stars as a newspaper reporter who teams up with a teacher (Denise DuBarry) to try to defeat a 50s-style man-in-a-suit monster (Kevin

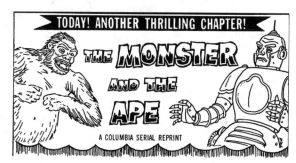

Peter Hall) who's literally in a closet. Stella Stevens and Paul Dooley own the house. This PG science-fiction parody set in San Francisco also features guest stars, including John Carradine as a blind man, Howard Duff, Henry Gibson, Claude Akins, Jesse White, and Donald Moffatt. Troma released it in 1986.

MONSTERS
(Lorimar, 1988–91) **D:** Michael Gornick, Ted Gershuny, Frank De Palma, Richard Friedman, Debra Hill, Ernest Farino, Bette Gordon, Sara Driver, and others **P:** George Romero

This light, low-budget weekly syndicated half-hour horror series was from the same people (especially Richard Rubinstein) who created the *Tales from the Darkside* show. Episodes were produced in studios in NYC and LA. Some corny and clichéd episodes are sure to make you groan, but many of the directors went on to features. Most episodes have at least one name actor. Some were David McCallum, Robert Lansing, Mary Woronov, Frank Gorshin, Linda Blair, Farley Granger, and Pam Grier. Each video has 2 episodes. Some shows were dedicated to Tom Allen, a creative force in NYC who died while the show was in production.

MONSTERS AND MANIACS
(Filmfax, 1988) **D:** Ted Newsom

Brinke Stevens hosts and narrates this 110-minute compilation of horror-movie scenes, trailers, and behind-the-scenes footage. It includes a tribute to 50s monster creator Paul Blaisdell.

MONSTERS CRASH PAJAMA PARTY
(Sinister, 1964) **D/S/P:** David L. Hewitt **S:** Jay Lister

This fascinating short (33-minute) artifact is the closest thing you'll ever see to an actual old, live spook show. It was shown at midnight, following David L. Hewitt's *Time Travelers*. After a very long narrated comic intro with a gorilla director, laughter, and screams, this clichéd horror comedy shows 10 teens going to an old, dark house for an initiation. The wisecracking guys leave the girls (now in nighties), not knowing about the mad doctor (Nick McGhee) with a Vampira-like assistant, a gorilla, and a hunchback. One girl is "turned into" a gorilla on an operating table, and they're all chained up in the dungeon. Then comes the "blackout," lightning, screams, and next the monsters would run out into the theater audience! Great stuff, and it's followed by a trailer for *Monster Crash* ("In fantastic horror vision!") and three live spook shows (*Dr. Sin, Houston's Hallucinations,* and *Dr. Rome the Ghostmaker*).

MONSTER SHARK
(1986) **D:** "John Old Jr."/ Lamberto Bava **S:** Gianfranco Clerici **P:** Mino Loy   Italy/France (*Red Ocean*)

The cells of a giant shark/octopus off the Florida coast can reproduce. Michael Sopkiw stars, with William Berger, Gianni Garko, and Dagmar Lassander. Based on a story by Luigi Cozzi and Sergio Martino, it includes some nudity and played on 42nd Street.

MONSTERS, MADMEN, AND MACHINES
(RKO, 1984) **D:** Daniel Helfgott, Alan Adler

Gil Gerard hosts 57 minutes of clips from 38 science-fiction movies, mostly from the 50s, divided into pointless sections like "The Beast," "The Girl," and "The Future."

THE MONSTER SQUAD
(Vestron, 1987) **D/S:** Fred Dekker **S:** Shane Black **P:** Jonathan A. Zimbert

Andre Gower and other kids in a monster-movie fan club encounter the old Universal monsters, in this fun PG-13 feature. Tom Noonan is a friendly Frankenstein monster, and Duncan Regehr is Dracula. Stan Winston and Steve Wang created the monsters (including the wolf man and the gill man) and FX. With Robby Kiger, Stephen Macht, Mary Ellen Trainor, and Randi Brooks. Black also wrote *Lethal Weapon*. A Tri Star release.

MONSTROSITY
(VSOM, 1988) **D:** Andy Milligan **P:** Lew Mishkin

Haal Borske stars as Frankie, a comic, lovesick creature with "the "brain of a child and the body of a giant." He was created by a guy whose girlfriend was killed by a gang in Hollywood. Andy Milligan made *Weirdo* next.

MONTEZUMA'S LOST GOLD
(1978) **D/P:** John Burrud, Milas Henshaw

This docudrama recreates the quest of 1860 murderer John Bodeen's 20-year search for gold hidden by the conquistadors. John Burrud (who later produced the Faces of Death series) narrates.

MONTY PYTHON AND THE HOLY GRAIL
(RCA/Columbia, 1974) **D/S:** Terry Gilliam, Terry Jones **P:** Michael White, John Goldstone   UK

"It makes *Ben-Hur* look like an epic!" said the ads. This version of the King Arthur legend is really a series of funny gags. It's remembered by some for the very gory scene of a knight who refuses to stop fighting even after his arms, legs, etc., are hacked off. All of the Python members contributed to the screenplay and appear in many roles, and Graham Chapman is King Arthur. The letterboxed laserdisc version from Voyager is the best-looking and includes alternate soundtrack commentary by the directors, some missing footage, and the Japanese-dubbed soundtrack. There are also 22 volumes (60 minutes each) of the TV series *Monty Python's Flying Circus*, as well as *Monty Python Live at the Hollywood Bowl* and the 20th-anniversary videos *Life of Python*, a BBC documentary with interviews, and *Parrot Sketch Not Included*, a "best of" compilation (all from Paramount).

MONTY PYTHON'S LIFE OF BRIAN
(Warner, 1979) **D/S/A:** Terry Jones **P:** John Goldstein   (*Life of Brian*)

Graham Chapman stars as Brian, born at the same time as Christ. He has a parallel life, is mistaken for the Savior, and is persecuted by the Romans. The finale is "Always Look on the Bright Side of Life," sung by dozens of crucified men. (It reentered the British charts in the early 90s.) George Harrison backed this irreverent comedy. Chapman and costars John Cleese, Terry Gilliam, Eric Idle, and Michael Palin all contributed to the screenplay. Spike Milligan is also in the cast, and there's animation by Gilliam.

MONTY PYTHON'S THE MEANING OF LIFE
(MCA, 1983) **D/S/A:** Terry Jones **P:** John Goldstone

The last and in many ways the most outrageous Python movie is a series of elaborate and expensive-looking sketches, some featuring blood and gore. Musical production numbers include "Every Sperm Is Sacred." A huge Terry Jones pukes up food at a restaurant. Cast members Graham Chapman, John Cleese, Terry Gilliam, Eric Idle, and Michael Palin all contributed to the screenplay. Gilliam directed the epic "Crimson Permanent Insurance" intro segment.

MOONCHILD
(1971) **D/S:** Alan Gadney **P:** Dick Alexander   (*Full Moon*)

An art student (Mark Travis) arrives at an old California mission being used as a hotel. He experiences many flashforwards and meets bizarre characters who argue about life. A mysterious blonde (Janet Landgard) is the daughter of an alchemist. John Carradine is the bearded Mr. Walker, "a keeper of words," and Victor Buono ends up presiding over an Inquisition-like trial. Hooded figures run around, and there's a one-eyed idiot hunchback, b/w dream sequences, and a (real) pig's head being ripped apart. This interesting, disorienting USC student film is not officially on video but has been recorded from a Boston TV station. Carradine and Buono both have lots of dialogue and must have enjoyed their roles (they couldn't have done this for the money). The wah-wah guitar theme dates it.

The Monster Squad

MOONFLEET

(1955) **D:** Fritz Lang **S:** Jan Lustig,
Margaret Fitts **P:** John Houseman

Jon Whiteley stars as an 18th-century boy put into the care of a renegade gentleman (Stewart Granger) who only wants his inheritance. The story involves smugglers, underground passageways, and a cemetery, and it would still be pretty scary for a kid to watch. With George Sanders, Joan Greenwood, Viveca Lindfors, Liliane Montevecchi, Alan Napier, John Hoyt, Jack Elam, Dan Seymour, Ian Wolfe, and Skelton Knaggs. The MGM release was in color and Cinemascope. In Jean-Luc Godard's *Contempt*, Fritz Lang says that Cinemascope is "good only for funerals and snakes."

MOON 44

(Live, 1990) **D/P:** Roland Emmerich **S:** Oliver Eberle
S/P: Dean Heyde **M:** Joel Goldsmith   W. Germany

The plot of this prison movie set in futuristic, industrial space is basically intelligent boys vs. musclebound lunkheads. Everything is very sweaty, smoky, and claustrophobic. Michael Paré plays Stone, an expressionless undercover agent and helicopter pilot who smokes and reads a lot. One boy hangs himself after being raped in the shower (off-screen). Malcolm McDowell is the suspicious Major Lee, Lisa Eichhorn is the only female on board, Stephen Geoffreys sells drugs, and Roscoe Lee Browne stays on Earth. Also with Dean Devlin, Leon Rippy, and Brian Thompson. The soundtrack is on One World. This expensive production went directly to video in America.

MOON IN SCORPIO

(TWE, 1987) **D:** Gary Graver
S: Robert S. Aiken **P:** Alan Amiel

Voiceovers and narration by a crazy woman were added to try to make sense out of footage shot at three different times. The plot is Nam vets on a yachting trip vs. supernatural victims of a massacre. The confusing feature stars John Phillip Law as a Nam vet, Britt Ekland as his bride, Robert Quarry, William Smith, James Booth, Donna Kei Benz, Jillian Kesner, and April Wayne. Fred Olen Ray was the coproducer.

THE MOONLIGHTER

(1953) **D:** Roy Rowland **S:** Niven
Busch **P:** Joseph Bernhard

Barbara Stanwyck and Fred MacMurray star in this 3-D tale of cattle rustlers, from Warners. With Ward Bond, Morris Ankrum, and Jack Elam.

MOONSHINE MOUNTAIN

(SW, 1964) **D/P/C:** Herschell Gordon Lewis
S/A: Charles Glore

Doug Martin, a country-music star (screenwriter Charles Glore, aka Chuck Scott) returns to mountain country to research "folk music." He encounters moonshiners with a giant still, a white gospel-singing family, a new girlfriend (Bonnie Hinson), and murder. *Color Me Blood Red* star

Adam Sorg is the psycho killer-rapist sheriff, and you'll recognize actors from *2000 Maniacs*. This crude movie, shot in South Carolina, features every inbred-hillbilly cliché imaginable and rape scenes, but from the jokey credits you can see that it isn't supposed to be taken seriously. "White Lightnin'" sung at a barn dance is the musical highlight. Pat Patterson was the assistant director and acts. The print is jumpy, the color is washed out, and the sound is bad.

MOONTRAP

(SGE, 1988) **D/P:** Robert Dyke **S:** Tex Ragsdale

Walter Koenig (in a rare non–*Star Trek* role) stars as Colonel Grant, in this story about the first manned moon mission in decades. Bruce Campbell is the copilot, and Leigh Lombardi is an alien woman. Killer robots are assembled from spare metal (and human) parts. There's some good stop-motion animation. It was made in Troy, Michigan.

MORE

(Warner Brothers, 1969) **D/S/P:** Barbet Schroeder
S: Paul Gegpuff   Luxembourg

Swiss-born Barbet Schroeder made this, his first feature, in France and on the beautiful Spanish island of Ibiza. Most of the dialogue is in English, but various characters speak untranslated French, German, and Spanish. Klaus Gruber stars as Stephen, a blank and directionless German guy who's hitchhiking to Morocco and has the mixed fortune of hooking up with a beautiful, uninhibited American girl (Mimsy Farmer). He smokes pot for the first time with her (while Pink Floyd's "Cymbaline" plays). They seem to be alone in paradise on Ibiza, but she's also involved with an ex-Nazi and hard drugs. He gets confused, hooked, and strung out, takes LSD, meditates, gets mad, goes into debt, and ends up in a wooden box. This unique time-piece made former AIP starlet Farmer (who spends half of the movie naked) a star in Europe. You may see this as a depressing but erotic version of *The Blue Lagoon* (also shot by Nestor Almendros) mixed with a modern version of *Reefer Madness* ("Fix me!"), but you won't forget it. Schroeder's movies can work on many levels, and there's a lot to read into this one if you want to. Parts of the famous Pink Floyd soundtrack are heard coming from a jukebox, a radio, records, and tapes. Floyd fans should know that there's also some good stuff not on the LP, originally released on Tower. (The group also scored Schroeder's *The Valley*.)

MORE AMERICAN GRAFFITI

(MCA, 1979) **D/S:** B. W. L. Norton
P: Howard Kazanjian

After the original hit, this was a box-office washout. Audiences didn't like what they were seeing. The film deals with changes in sex, drugs, rock and roll, and politics, often with humor. It has an ambitious if awkward structure (the segments go back and forth) and takes place on several different New Years Eves from 1964 to 1967. Characters go to Vietnam, protest, and become stoned, disillusioned, and even dead. With Candy Clark, Bo Hopkins, Ron Howard, Paul Le Mat (who is excellent), Mackenzie Phillips, Charles Martin Smith,

Cindy Williams, Scott Glenn, Mary Kay Place, Doug Sahm, Wolfman Jack, Country Joe and the Fish, and even Rosanna Arquette. Another great double MCA soundtrack includes hits by the Byrds, Hendrix, and Dylan, and "Fingertips," "Woolly Bully," and "96 Tears." George Lucas was the executive producer.

MORONS FROM OUTER SPACE

(Warner, 1985) **D:** Mike Hodges **S/A:** Griff
Rhys Jones, Mel Smith **P:** Barry Hanson   UK

After three stupid aliens land in England, scientists and military men study them. With Jimmy Nail, Dinsdale Landen, Joanne Pearce, Paul Brown, and James B. Sikking. By the director of the *Flash Gordon* remake. Smith and Jones have starred in and written comedy shows for British TV, including *Alas Smith and Jones* and *Not the Nine O'Clock News*. Smith directed *The Tall Guy*.

MORTAL PASSIONS

(Fox, 1989) **D:** Andrew Lane
S: Alan Moskowitz **P:** Gwen Field

Krista Errickson is married to suicidal Zach Galligan, and they live in a mansion. This unpredictable sex-and-murder story features David Warner, Michael Bowen, and Luca Bercovici. Wayne Crawford was an executive producer. Lane and Crawford have been making wacky, low-budget features since the early 70s.

MORTAL THOUGHTS

(RCA, 1991) **D:** Alan Rudolph **S:** William Reilly,
Claude Kerven **P:** John Fielder, Mark Tarlov

Demi Moore (who was also a coproducer) and Glenne Headly run a beauty shop in New Jersey. Headly's abusive husband (a bearded Bruce Willis) is killed "accidentally," and they cover it up. Harvey Keitel is the detective who demands even more flashbacks. With Billie Neal and John Pankow. It was a Columbia release.

MORTUARY

(Vestron, 1981) **D/S/P:** Hikmet Avedis
S/P: Marlene Schmidt

Christopher George (in one of his last features) and his real-life wife, Lynda Day George, are top billed in this movie about a killer who uses embalming tools (large needles through the chest). Mary McDonough (from *The Waltons*) is the real star, and a young Bill Paxton has the best role. Also with Alvy Moore and Michael Berryman. It was a Crown International release by the director of *The Fifth Floor*.

MORTUARY ACADEMY

(RCA, 1988) **D:** Michael Schroeder
S: William Kelman **P:** Dennis Winfrey

The Grimm brothers (Christopher Atkins and Perry Lang) inherit a mortuary but have to take classes there. Paul Bartel is the necrophiliac manager. Mary Woronov is a teacher who plays dead for him. He falls in love with the corpse of a cheerleader, but she's gang-banged on a beach (?!). This not-too-funny, very-bad-taste comedy is also loaded with ethnic jokes. Tracey Walter reanimates a heavy-metal bar-mitzvah band managed by Wolfman Jack. With Cesar Romero, Stoney Jackson, Anthony James, James Daughton, Dona Speir, Karen Witter, and Rebekka Armstrong. The theme is a remake of "Be True to Your School."

MOSQUITO

(Hemdale, 1994) **D/S:** Gary Jones **S:** Steve Hodge **P:** Dave Thiry   (*Blood Fever; Nightswarm*)

A giant killer mosquito from a space ship attacks campers. With Rachel Loiselle as the park ranger, Gunnar Hansen as an escaped bank robber with a chainsaw, Ron Ashton (from the Stooges), and Josh Becker. It was directed by an FX guy who had worked on Sam Raimi's movies. It was made near Detroit the same year as the similar *Skeeter* and *Ticks.*

MOTEL CONFIDENTIAL!

(Rhino, 1967) **D/P:** A. C. Stevens **S:** Mark Del Monde

A comedy-relief Italian runs the eight-dollar-a-night Quickie motel. For each couple who check in there's a story and a sex scene. One segment features a guy in drag. This episodic, adults-only movie is strangely similar to the later *Pink Motel.* It's also available on the tape *Saturday Night Sleazies, Volume III.*

MOTHER

(VSOM, 1970) **D/S/P:** Don Joslyn
(*Up Your Teddy Bear*)

There's a minimal plot here about Julie Newmar ordering the huge, childlike Skippy (Victor Buono) to convince the tiny, lovesick Clyde (Wally Cox) to work for her toy company. This bizarre comedy resembles a bad nudie movie, as Skippy sends one hooker after another to try to seduce Clyde. We also get endless fat gags involving Buono (who appears in drag), Cox in fantasy sequences following women, dancing, singing, and yodeling, Newmar in a black bikini, Angelique Pettyjohn naked in a steamroom, and many closeups of asses. With Claire Kelly, Thordis Brandt, and Valora Noland. The music is by Quincy Jones. Cox, a longtime friend of Marlon Brando (and the voice of Underdog), died in 1973. This R-rated release is from Gemeni, the company that released Ted V. Mikels' movies.

MOTHER'S BOYS

(Miramax, 1993) **D:** Yves Simoneau **S:** Barry Schneider, Richard Hawley **P:** Jack E. Freedman

Jude (Jamie Lee Curtis), a mom who ran off, returns after three years determined to get her husband (Peter Gallagher) and three sons back. She uses lies and emotional blackmail and nearly kills all of them. She lets her 12-year-old-son (Luke Edwards) drive a car and see her naked. It was the first horror role for Curtis since *Halloween II* and *Road Games,* back in 1981. With Joanne Whalley-Kilmer as the schoolteacher her husband now loves, Vanessa Redgrave as the rich grandmother who knows what a psycho her daughter is, and Joss Ackland. It's based on a novel by Bernard Taylor.

MOTORAMA

(Columbia, Tristar, 1992) **D:** Barry Shils **S:** Joseph Minion **P:** Donald P. Borchers **M:** Andy Summers

A determined 10-year-old named Gus (Jordan Christopher Michael) steals a '65 Mustang and goes on the road through mythical states in the Southwest, trying to collect enough letters to win a gas-station card game. Gus runs into many odd characters, in this unique and pretty great black comedy by the guy who wrote *After Hours.* Mary Woronov and Sandy Baron punch Gus' eye out, Drew Barrymore is in a nightmare, Susan Tyrrell is in a wig, Meat Loaf is a biker, Vince Edwards is a doctor, and Michael J. Pollard and Garrett Morris run a gas station. The cast also includes Flea, Jack Nance, Dick Miller, Martha Quinn, Robin Duke, Allyce Beasley, Shelley Berman, and John Diehl.

MOTORCYCLE GANG

(1994) **D:** John Milius **S:** Kent Anderson **P:** Lou Arkoff, Debra Hill

Gerald McRaney is a retired soldier who defends his family from bikers led by Jake (son of Gary) Busey. With Carla Gugino as the daughter and Elan Oberon. This Showtime Rebel Highways series movie and *Road Racer* (1993) both copy *Hot Rods to Hell* (1967). Ed Cahn's 1957 AIP movie *Motorcycle Gang* (available on Columbia video) is about illegal street racing.

MOTORPSYCHO!

(RM, 1965) **D/S/P/C/E:** Russ Meyer

A three-man gang led by the crazed Brahman (Stephen Oliver) harass a fisherman and his wife, then go after a country veterinarian (Alex Rocco) and rape his wife. Rocco teams with Cajun Ruby (Haji) for revenge. The bikers look just like any guys on Japanese bikes, but Oliver plays an early example of a deranged Nam vet. He went on to *Angels from Hell* (1968), *The Naked Zoo* (1969), *Savage Abduction* (1972), and others. Surf rock is heard coming from a transistor radio. With Coleman Francis. This b/w companion film to the more famous *Faster, Pussycat! Kill! Kill!* was very rare before its video release in 1992. I saw it dubbed into German. Meyer appears as the sheriff.

MOUNTAINTOP MOTEL MASSACRE

(Starmaker, 1983) **D/P:** Jim McCullough Sr. **S/P:** Jim McCullough Jr.

Evelyn (Anna Chappell), the heavyweight proprietor of a motel, kills with a scythe and hides in tunnels. She also puts snakes and rats in rooms. The ads said, "Please do not disturb Evelyn. She already is." Larry Buchanan regular Bill Thurman is the local reverend. New World released it in 1986.

THE MOUSE ON THE MOON

(1963) **D:** Richard Lester **S:** Michael Pertwee **P:** Walter Shenson   UK

The small, poor Duchy of Grand Fenwick convinces the world that it's entering the space race (great idea), so the USA, the USSR, and the UK all send financial aid. They use local wine for fuel and eventually really make it to the moon. Bernard Cribbins stars in this Cold War comedy, with Margaret Rutherford as the grand duchess, Ron Moody, Terry-Thomas, Michael Crawford, and June Ritchie as a beatnik. It's a sequel to *The Mouse That Roared* (1957). Both are based on novels by Leonard Wibberley.

MOVIE HOUSE MASSACRE

(Active, 1984) **D/S/P/A:** Alice Raley

When a Beverly Hills theater is reopened a psycho kills cheerleaders there. This amateur film features Mary Woronov as the owner's assistant.

THE MOVING FINGER

(Audubon, 1963) **D/S:** Larry Moyer

This previously unreleased b/w obscurity is set in NYC's Greenwich Village. Lionel Stander owns an espresso bar with a basement where pot smoking beatniks crash along with a wounded bank robber. With Barbara London (later in *Psychout*), Art Smith, and the famous street musician Moondog. The music is twist instrumentals. Stander's next appearance was in *The Loved One* (1965).

MOVING TARGET

(Southgate, 1989) **D/S:** Marius Mattei **S/P:** Josi W. Konski   Italy

Linda Blair fans, beware! In this made-in-Miami movie she has a useless role as a jilted doctor. The real star is Janine Linde, a young blonde who takes her clothes off at every possible opportunity. She has amnesia after her boyfriend is blown away by a mysterious killer biker wearing black. So she moves in with and seduces a tennis champ who she thinks is her father. A gangster (Stuart Whitman) is after her for a key to a fortune that she unknowingly has. Captain Morrison (Ernest Borgnine) investigates all the killings, and a (badly dubbed) female news reporter seems to be everywhere. This movie has lots of car chases and smashups, a slow-motion topless run on a beach, a disco scene, a great falling-off-a-balcony scene, plenty of dead people, and ridiculous (surprise!) plot twists. The cinematography is much better than necessary.

MOVING VIOLATION

(Fox, 1976) **D:** Charles S. Dubin
S: David Osterhout **P:** Julie Corman

Stephan McHattie and Kay Lenz star as a couple being pursued by a redneck sheriff, with Eddie Albert, Will Geer, Fred Willard, and Dick Miller. Roger Corman was the executive producer of this PG car-chase movie, and Barbara Peeters was the second-unit director.

MOZAMBIQUE

(1965) **D:** Robert Lynn **S:** Peter Yeldham **P:** Harry Alan Towers   UK

Steve Cochran stars as an American pilot forced to fly a colonel into Mozambique. He has lots of adventures and encounters a killer dwarf and drug dealers. With Hildegard Neff, Paul Hubschmid, and Vivi Bach.

M 3-D! THE MOVIE

(1976) **D:** "Stephen Gibson"
(*Lollipop Girls in Hard Candy*)

This 3-D sex movie with fake credits was advertised as being in "widescreen, color 3-dimension, super 70mm stereo" but was really in 35mm with mono sound. R, X, and hard-core versions were released, all with John Holmes, John Seeman, and William Margold. It played in West Coast art houses for years and was rereleased in 1991 as a midnight movie. It may have also been released in 1983 as *Scoring!*

MUDHONEY

(RM, 1965) **D/P/E/A:** Russ Meyer **S:** Raymond Friday Locke, William E. Sprague **P:** George Costello

Russ Meyer's follow-up to his hit *Lorna* is another b/w rural drama, set in Spooner, Missouri, during the Depression. An ex-con (John Furlough) finds work (and sex) at the Brenshaw farm, and Hannah Brenshaw eventually faces a lynch mob. Hal Hopper and Antoinette Cristiani star as the Brenshaws, with Stuart Lancaster as an uncle, Rena Horton as a deaf-mute, Franklin Bolger as a fire-and-brimstone preacher, and Lorna Maitland, this time as Clara Belle. It played in some towns as *Rope of Flesh* and was followed by *Motorpsycho!* (1965) and Meyer's by-now most famous feature, *Faster, Pussycat! Kill! Kill!* (1966). You should demand all of them at your local video store.

MUGSY'S GIRLS

(Vestron, 1985) **D/S/P:** Kevin Brodie
P: Leonard Shapiro   (*Delta Pi*)

Ruth Gordon, in one of her last movies, is a sorority house mother who enters her girls in a mud-wrestling contest. With Laura Branigan (who wrestles Annie Ample), Queen Kong (who wrestles Gordon!), Estrelita, and Eddie Deezen.

MULTIPLE MANIACS

(Cinema Group, 1970)
D/S/P/C/E: John Waters

Divine and Mr. David (David Lochary) run the Calvacade of Perversions, a traveling freak show featuring junkies, homosexuals, and pornographers. Suburban costumers are robbed and killed by their gang of drug-crazed killers. Mink Stole gives Divine a rosary job in a church, where she narrates her visions of Jesus. Divine also is raped by a giant lobster, eats a human heart, and is gunned down by the National Guard at the end. This 16mm b/w hit is one of Waters' best. With Mary Vivian Pearce, Cookie Muller as Divine's daughter, Susan Lowe, and Edith Massey (in her film debut). They all returned in *Pink Flamingos* (1972), Waters' most famous feature. All early Waters features were later distributed by New Line.

THE MUMMY AND THE CURSE OF THE JACKAL

(Academy, 1969) **D:** Oliver Drake
S/P: William C. Edwards

It's exciting for me to find a tape this old that was never shown theatrically or even on TV. It was released on tape in 1985 and has been mostly ignored since. The short-lived Vega International produced three movies in 1969. *Ride a Wild Stud* (a sex western) and *Dracula, the Dirty Old Man* (a sex/horror movie) were released, but this one, probably featuring the same jackal head as in *Dracula, the Dirty Old Man*, remained a rumor in the filmographies of costar John Carradine. Busy Anthony Eisley, also in *The Mighty Gorga, The Witchmaker*, and *Dracula vs. Frankenstein* (all made the same year), stars as David, a guy who talks about Atlantis and theories that will make him famous. He has himself locked in a house overnight with the body of an odd-looking, perfectly preserved ancient princess and becomes a very hairy, cartoonish werewolf with three big claws on each hand. The frequent, long, awkward time-lapse transformations are worth renting this for, but you also get an overweight, bug-eyed male mummy who fights the jackal on the streets of Las Vegas (as pedestrians look on in disbelief or even laugh) and in a badly lit casino. The mummy also kills a stripper and a belly dancer onstage. Several of the monster's victims cross their eyes before they die. An extremely long silent flashback, similar to the one in *Blood Feast*, is narrated by Eisley and shows us how mummies were prepared and placed in the tomb. The princess, who uses a hypnotic ring, is visited by "Mother Isis" (with horns), who tells her what to do. Carradine shows up as a professor and spends

Russ Meyer's Mudhoney.

a long time trying to explain things. The cinematography, by the same guy who filmed *The Slime People* and *She Freak,* is terrible, but the music is great. The theme song sounds like the Ventures doing music from *The Munsters.* Music by a jazz combo with bongos is edited with Booker T and the MGs–style rock and sitar music. Eisley later said that the director was senile. One of the four assistant directors was Wyatt Ordung (he wrote *Robot Monster*). The tape has an R rating, which is ridiculous. It's a G.

MUMMY'S BOYS

(Image, 1936) **D:** Fred Guiol **S:** Jack Townley, Philip G. Epstein, Charles Roberts **P:** Lee Marcus

Tired of the Three Stooges? Seen everything by the Marx Brothers? Try Wheeler and Woolsey! They starred in 21 comedies at RKO, until Woolsey died in 1938. Bert Wheeler is wide-eyed, baby-faced, and naive. Robert Woolsey is sort of an offbeat mixture of George Burns, Groucho Marx, and Shemp Howard. This time they go to Cairo to investigate a curse. They take along Catfish (Willie Best) because he's from Cairo (Illinois). Wheeler suffers from amnesia, so in the strangest scene Woolsey has him strung up and a map is tattooed on his back. There's a tomb, bats, a bizarre laughing hyena, the stars in drag, and a (fake) mummy with a deadly syringe. With Barbara Pepper, Frank Lackteen, and (I think) Noble Johnson. The print quality is excellent, and it's only 68 minutes long.

MUNCHIE

(New Horizons, 1992) **D/S:** Jim Wynorski
S: R. J. Robertson **P:** Mike Elliott

In this PG sequel (in name only) to *Muchies*, Munchie, a large, smiling puppet creature (with the voice of Dom DeLuise) helps a kid (Jamie McEnnan) fight school bullies and grants him wishes. Loni Anderson is his mom. She dates Andrew Stevens. The cast also includes Arte Johnson, Jay Richardson, Angus Scrimm, Toni Naples, Raven De La Croix, Becky LeBeau, Linda Shayne, and George "Buck" Flower, and Brinke Stevens, Monique Gabrielle, and Fred Olen Ray in a party scene. Roger Corman was the executive producer. *Munchie Strikes Back* (1993) followed.

MUNCHIES

(MGM, 1987) **D:** Bettina Hirsch
S: Lance Smith **P:** Roger Corman

The editor of *Gremlins* made this PG comedy about a junk-food-eating, *Gremlins*-style (puppet) creature who regenerates and duplicates himself. With Harvey Korman (in two roles), Paul Bartel, Nadine Van Der Velde, and Robert Picardo. Ads for this Concorde release said, "From the creators of *Little Shop of Horrors*." Roger Corman was the executive producer. Two "sequels" followed.

MUNDO DEPRAVADOS

(SW, 1967) **D/S:** Herb Jeffries **P:** Leroy C. Griffith   (*World of the Depraved*)

Johnny Decker and Larry Reed are leering, comedian police detectives who are after a black-masked "sex monster." They do awful impressions of Ed Sullivan and Topo Gigio. Meanwhile several voyeur characters eye the strippers, and famous stripper Tempest Storm demonstates how terrible her acting is. Also with Bunny Ware. David F. Friedman was the production manager for this b/w Boxoffice International release with a misleading name. The video is a Frank Henenlotter presentation.

THE MUPPET CHRISTMAS CAROL

(1992) **D/P:** Brian Henson **S:** Jerry Juhl

Michael Caine is Scrooge, and Kermit the frog is Bob Cratchit. This G-rated post–Jim Henson title from Buena Vista features Paul Williams' songs. Frank Oz was the executive producer.

THE MUPPET MOVIE

(Fox, 1979) **D:** James Frawley **S:** Jerry Juhl, Jack Burns **P:** Jim Henson

Sir Lew Lord (Orson Welles) signs Kermit when he finally arrives in Hollywood to become a star. Charles Durning is the villain who sells fried frogs' legs in his restaurant chain. The cast of this comic road movie also includes James Coburn, Carol Kane, Telly Savalas, Richard Pryor, Bob Hope, Paul Williams, Steve Martin, Edgar Bergen, Milton Berle, Mel Brooks, Elliott Gould, and Cloris Leachman. The voices are by Jim Henson and Frank Oz. *The Great Muppets Caper* (1981) and *The Muppets Take Manhattan* (1984) followed, with less interesting guests.

MURDER!

(Republic, 1930) **D:** Alfred Hitchcock
S: Alma Reville **P:** John Maxwell   UK

Herbert Marshall stars as a famous actor serving on a jury who tries to help a young actress (Nora Baring) on trial for murder. The killer turns out to be a "half-caste" transvestite (Esmé Percy). With Edward Chapman, Phyllis Constam, and Miles Mander. The film is adapted from a play, *Enter Sir John*, by Helen Simpson and Clemence Dane. It was also released in a German-language version called *Mary*. The director appears on a street in the second of his many cameos (the first had been in *The Lodger*, 1926).

MURDER À LA MODE

(1968) **D/S/E:** Brian De Palma

De Palma's first solo feature is a comedy/mystery set in NYC. Margo Norton falls for a filmmaker (Jared Martin) who is making a porno movie. She's murdered by an ice pick, and three characters tell their versions of what happened (*Rashomon* style). With De Palma regulars William Finley as Otto and Jennifer Salt.

MURDER AT THE BASKERVILLES

(Foothill, 1937) **D:** Thomas Bentley **S:** H. Fowler Mear **P:** Julius Hagan   UK (*Silver Blaze*)

Arthur Wontner is Sherlock Holmes for the fifth and final time, in this tale of a murdered groom and a missing racehorse. Ian Fleming is Dr. Watson, and Lyn Harding is Professor Moriarty. This and a German film from the same year were the last Holmes films made before Basil Rathbone began to play the role. It was released in America in 1941, retitled to make people think it was related to the first Rathbone film, *The Hound of the Baskervilles* (1939). Sir Henry Baskerville is a character.

MURDER BY CONTRACT

(1958) **D:** Irving Lerner **S:** Ben Sincoe **P:** Leon Chooluck

Vince Edwards stars as an unemotional hitman and college student hired by gangsters to kill a wealthy woman on the West Coast. Also in the cast are Herschel Bernardi, Philip Pine, and Caprice Toriel. This Columbia *film noir* is said to have influenced *Taxi Driver*.

MURDER BY MOONLIGHT

(Vidmark, 1989) **D:** Michael Lindsay-Hogg
S: Carla Jean Wagner **P:** Tamara Asseyev
UK (*Murder in Space*)

In 2015 the Americans and Soviets are mining on the moon. Brigitte Nielson, as a NASA agent, investigates the murder of a security chief with Julian Sands, a Russian major who interrogates suspects. They fight, then fall in love, and catch a transsexual terrorist. With Gerald McRaney, Jane Lapotaire, and Brian Cox. This PG-13 film debuted on British TV and then on CBS-TV. Trevor Jones wrote the score.

MURDER BY NATURAL CAUSES

(Lorimar, 1979) **D:** Robert Day **S:** Richard Levinson, William Link **P:** Robert A. Papazian

Katharine Ross plots to kill her husband (Hal Holbrook), a famous mentalist, with help from her lover (Barry Bostwick). With Richard Anderson and Victoria Carroll. Robert Day had directed horror and science-fiction movies in England, and the writers had created the *Columbo* TV series.

MURDER BY NUMBERS

(Magnum, 1989) **D/S/P:** Paul Leder **P:** Ralph Tornberg

Shari Belafonte-Harper and Sam Behrens (married in real life) star in this flashback-filled murder mystery. He's hired to investigate the death of a married man who had AIDS. Also with Jayne Meadows as the man's mother, Ronee Blakley, Dick Sargent, and Cleavon Little (who both died several years later).

MURDER BY PHONE

(Warner, 1980) **D:** Michael Anderson **S:** Michael Butler, Dennis Shyrack, John Kent Harrison **P:** Robert Cooper   UK (*The Bells*)

Richard Chamberlain stars as a teacher who investigates the mysterious death of a student (she shakes, bleeds, and dies after answering a phone in a subway station). While attending a conference, he's staying in NYC with an old friend (John Houseman) who works for the phone company. With Sara Botsford and Barry Morse. This is a cut (79-minute) version of *The Bells* (94 minutes).

THE MURDER GANG

(Super, 1976) **D/P:** Al Adamson **S:** John D'Amato, Sheldon Lee, Budd Donnelly
(*Black Heat; US Vice; Girls' Hotel*)

Timothy Brown (*The Dynamite Brothers*) stars as Las Vegas cop Kicks Carter. His TV-news-photographer girlfriend, Tanya Boyd (*Black Shampoo*), has the featured sex scene. Russ Tamblyn (in the last of his four Adamson movies) plays Ziggy, a loan shark and club owner who gets to smash a car up, beat a man to death with a hammer, then run him over. With Jana Bellan as Ziggy's lesbian boss, bald J. C. Wells as an arms dealer and gangster, Regina Carrol as a lounge singer (she sings a whole song), Geoffrey Land, and Al Adamson playing blackjack. There's a hand cut off, a tasteless gang rape, and lots of chases and shootouts. The soundtrack is all groove and funk music. Gary Graver shot it in Nevada, and Calvin Flood was the executive producer. Independent International used different titles (and different-length versions) for inner-city (black) theaters, drive-ins, video, and Canada!

MURDER IN HIGH PLACES

(1991) **D/S:** John Byrum **P:** Marvin Miller

An eccentric writer and former hippie (Ted Levine) is elected mayor of a town called Zenith. The body of his former wife (Traci Lords!) is dropped from a plane and crashes through a skylight. Adam Baldwin, Joyce Hyser, James Keach, James Sheridan, Miguel Ferrer, and Spice Williams are also in this murder mystery. It was shot in Aspen and debuted on NBC-TV.

MURDER IN SPACE

(Vidmark, 1985) **D:** Steven Hilliard Stern **S:** Richard Levinson, William Link **P:** Robert Cooper

Members of a multinational space probe are being murdered. With Wilford Brimley, Michael Ironside, Martin Balsam, Arthur Hill, Kate Lynch, and Richard Blackburn. When this was first broadcast Showtime didn't air the ending and offered cash prizes to viewers who could name the killer.

MURDER IN THE BLUE ROOM

(1944) **D:** Leslie Goodwins
S: I. A. L. Diamond, Stanley Davis

This WWII-era comedy/mystery was Universal's third version of the same story, made first as *Secret of the Blue Room* (1933) and then as *The Missing Guest* (1938). A party is thrown at a haunted mansion. The Three Jazzybelles, a female comedy trio created to replace the Ritz Brothers (who were originally slated to star), sing and dance and react to scary things. A comic ghost shows up, characters die, and a man who spends the night in the dreaded "blue room" disappears. Anne Gwynne stars, with Donald Cook, John Litel, Regis Toomey, and Ian Wolfe. Screenwriter I. A. L. Diamond later wrote many classics directed by Billy Wilder.

MURDER IN THE HEARTLAND

(1993) **D:** Robert Markowitz **S:** Michael O'Hara **P:** S. Bryan Hickox **C:** Ron Garcia

Tim Roth and Fairuza Balk star as mass killer Charles Starkweather and his 14-year-old girlfriend, Caril Ann Fugate, in this above average 2-part, fact-based ABC-TV movie, set in 1958. The second half is their trial, and the killings are seen again as Starkweather descibes them. Brian Dennehy is her attorney, and Randy Quaid is the trial prosecutor. Also with Miles O'Shea, Kate Reid, and Roberts Blossom. Period rock tunes are on the soundtrack.

MURDER IN THE RED BARN

(Sinister, 1935) **D:** Milton Rosmer
S: Randall Faye   UK (*Maria Marten*)

The 50-year-old actor Tod Slaughter makes his film debut as the evil squire Corder, a role he had played onstage for years. He impregnates a young woman, kills her, and frames her Gypsy boyfriend. The film opens like a play, introducing the players (including Sophie Stewart and Eric Portman), and runs only 67 minutes. This old melodrama (based on a real 1820 case) had been filmed three times previously. *Sweeney Todd, Demon Barber of Fleet Street* (1936) was Slaughter's next film.

MURDER LUST

(Prism, 1985) **D:** Donald Jones **S/P/M:** James Lane

An impotent security guard who teaches Sunday school (Eli Rich) picks up and kills hookers. The man, labeled "the Mojave murderer," is shown to be a schizo who is a good guy during the day. He buries bodies in a mass grave, which he likes to piss on. By the maker of *The Love Butcher*. With Ashley St. John.

MURDEROCK

(Domo, 1983) **D/S/A:** Lucio Fulci **S:** Gianfranco Clerici, Vincenzo Mannino **P:** Augusto Caminito Italy (*The Demon Is Loose; Uccide a Passo di Danza*)

Dancers auditioning for a show at "the New York Center for Performing Arts" are being killed with a needle. A detective investigates, and a dance teacher (Olga Karlatos) has nightmares. Also with Ray Lovelock, Al Cliver, and the director in a bit part. Keith Emerson provided the disco-music score, and there's a breakdancing sequence.

MURDER ONE

(Nelson, 1988) **D:** Graeme Campbell
S: Fleming "Tex" Fuller **P:** Nicolas Stiliadis

Brothers James Wilder and Stephen Shellan escape from a Maryland prison and kill a family of six, in this *In Cold Blood*–type of story based on a real 1973 Georgia case. Henry Thomas is the younger brother, who mostly watches. Patsy Cline's "Crazy" plays during a rape and murder. The director did *Psycho IV* next.

MURDEROUS VISION

(Paramount, 1991) **D/P:** Gary Sherman
S: Paul Joseph Gulino

A detective (Bruce Boxleitner) and a psychic (Laura Johnson) go after a serial killer (Joseph D'Angerio) who takes the skin off victims' faces. This USA Network movie copies *The Silence of the Lambs* and has faces in jars. With Robert Culp and Beau Starr.

MURDERS IN THE RUE MORGUE

(Vidmark, 1986) **D:** Jeannot Szwarc
S: Devis Epstein **P:** Robert Halmi

George C. Scott stars as Edgar Allan Poe's 19th-century French detective C. Auguste Dupin. Rebecca De Mornay costars, with Ian McShane and Val Kilmer. This CBS-TV movie was filmed in Paris. The director had just made *Santa Claus: The Motion Picture*. Earlier versions were made in 1914, with Bela Lugosi in 1932 (MCA), with Karl Malden in 1954, and with Jason Robards in 1971 (Vestron).

MURDER STORY

(Academy, 1988) **D:** Eddie Arno, Markus Innocent **P:** Tom Reeve   Netherlands

Christopher Lee is Willard Hope, the famous author of *Bloodbath,* who lives in Amsterdam. Tony (Bruce Boa), a young, would-be novelist, collects newspaper clippings for plot inspiration. Lee (with gray hair and black eyebrows) decides to help Tony investigate the real murder of a scientist. Even though he has a new girlfriend, Tony's mom thinks he's gay because he keeps talking about Hope. The conspiracy plot involves a feminist anti-porno demonstration, two men who resemble Orson Welles, and secret agents. Lee is fine in this sympathetic role, and his character is missed when he's killed off.

MURDER WEAPON

(Cinema Home, 1989) **D:** "Ellen Cabot"/ David DeCoteau **S:** Ross A. Perron
P/A: Linnea Quigley **P:** Fred Kenwamer

Disturbed inmates Karen Russell and Linnea Quigley escape from an asylum, throw a party, and kill men. Linnea is naked a lot. Lyle Waggoner is a shrink. There's a reused *Nightmare Sisters* scene with Michelle Bauer and Brinke Stevens on a TV screen.

MURPHY'S LAW

(Media, 1986) **D:** J. Lee Thompson **S:** Gail Morgan Hickman **P:** Pancho Kohner

Charles Bronson is an alcoholic detective framed for the death of his ex-wife. He likes to say, "Don't fuck with Jack Murphy." He escapes, handcuffed to a foul-mouthed 14-year-old shoplifter (Kathleen Wilhoite). This nutty movie features Carrie Snodgress as a killer with a crossbow in the Bradley Building, Richard Romanus, Angel Tompkins as a stripper, Lawrence Tierney, Leigh Lombardi, and Teri Lynn Peake (from *Penthouse*). Jill Ireland was

Bronson and Kathleen Wilhoite in *Murphy's Law*.

the coproducer. I saw this one in a theater in Copenhagen. It made me proud to be an American. *Murphy's Law* was also a band from Queens.

MUSIC OF THE SPHERES

(1984) **D/S/P:** G. Philip Jackson
S: Ganrille de Montmollin   Canada

A supercomputer called "the Beast" rules the 21st century. With Anne Dansereau and Peter Brikmanis.

MUTANT

(Vestron, 1983) **D:** John "Bud" Cardos
S: Peter Z. Orton, Michael Jones, John C. Kruize **P:** Igo Kantner   (*Night Shadows*)

Toxic waste creates blue-faced, oozing zombies in a small southern town. Wings Hauser is the visiting hero, Lee Harcourt Montgomery is his brother, and Bo Hopkins is the drunken sheriff. This talk-filled film also features Jody Medford and a "special appearance" by Jennifer Warren as the town's doctor. Film Ventures released it.

MUTANT HUNT

(Wizard, 1986) **D/S:** Tim Kincaid **P:** Cynthia De Paula

Cyborgs kill New Yorkers in the future. Rick Gianasi stars as hero Matt Riker. The villains are called Z and Domina. There's some gore and comedy. With Mary-Anne Fahey and Joel von Ornsteiner. Ed French created the FX. The music from *Breeders* is used.

MUTANT MASSACRE 2

(Daily Video, 1981) **D/S/P/A:** Carl J. Sukenick

This amateur Hollywood sci-fi movie, shot on video, is about aliens who turn people into mutants. It has narration and a clay-animation opening.

MUTANT ON THE BOUNTY

(Southgate, 1988) **D/P:** Robert Torrance
S/P: Martin Lopez

A droid (John Roarke) is the main character in this silly PG-13 sci-fi comedy set in 2048 on a spaceship. It's from the producer of the Killer Tomato series. Max (Kyle T. Heffner) is a mutant sax player (he has a ringing phone lodged in his skull), and there's a psycho killer on board. With Deborah Benson and Fox Harris.

MUTANTS IN PARADISE

(TWE, 1984) **D/S:** Scott Apostoulo **P:** William Moses

A scientist experiments on a nerdy student (Brad Greenquist) to create a nuke-proof man. This 16mm sci-fi spoof, made by a University of Virginia film student, has guest stars Eddie "the Egg Lady" Massey and Ray "Boom Boom" Mancini.

MUTATOR

(Prism, 1989) **D:** John R. Bowey **S:** Lynn Rose Higgins
P: Russell D. Markowitz   S. Africa (*Time of the Beast*)

Brion James, a great screen villain, is a dull screen hero in this boring, slow-paced movie about a

barely seen monster (created by the Burman studios) in a tightly sealed research institute. James goes undercover as a night-shift guard. *Wolfen*-style polarized POV shots waste a lot of time, but the monster does have a scary cat face. It's pretty similar to *Syngenor*, which is much better.

THE MUTHERS

(SW, 1968) **D/P:** Don Davis **S:** Jason Hunter

Will suburban-LA teen Suzy (Kathy Williams) witness her mother, Sally (Marsha Jordan), having sex with some guy at a "picnic"? That's the plot of this nudie. The cheating mothers hang out at the Pink Swan bar, the kids smoke pot at pool parties, the men leave their shorts on during sex, and a cat fight turns into a lesbian scene. Also with Virginia Gordon.

THE MUTHERS

(VEC, 1976) **D/P:** Cirio H. Santiago **S:** Cyril St. James

You'll wonder what century we're in as Jeanne Bell (who has a shower scene) and Rosanne Katon (both former *Playboy* models) lead "the Muthers," a group of pirates on a gunboat who use backflips and kung fu and give to the poor. The heroines go undercover in a prison camp on a coffee plantation to rescue Bell's sister, Marcy (Trina Parks, from *Diamonds Are Forever* and *Darktown Strutters*). Eventually Serena (Jayne Kennedy), the whip-wielding mistress of the sadistic warden, leads a breakout. It's basically just another tropical women-in-prison movie, but how many movies of any kind star four beautiful black women? Some of the dialogue in this Dimension release is in Spanish.

THE MUTILATOR (1979) = THE DARK

THE MUTILATOR

(Vestron, 1983) **D/S/P:** Buddy Cooper
D: John S. Douglass   (*Fall Break*)

Some college students are killed off while staying at a remote condo. This gory, unrated movie features NYC-area actors but was filmed in South Carolina. With Matt Mitler, Ruth Martinez, and Frances Raines.

MY BEST FRIEND IS A VAMPIRE

(HBO, 1988) **D:** Jimmy Huston
S: Tab Murphy **P:** Dennis Murphy

This comic, PG-rated horror movie is a variation on the plot of the later *Buffy the Vampire Slayer*. A teen delivery boy (Robert Sean Leonard) becomes a good-guy vampire. René Auberjonois is the vampire who teaches him, and David Warner is a vampire killer. With Evan Mirand, Cheryl Pollak, Cecilia Peck (daughter of Gregory Peck), and Fannie Flagg. Timbuk 3, Blondie, and others are heard on the soundtrack. It was filmed in Houston by the director of *Final Exam*.

MY BOYFRIEND'S BACK

(Touchstone, 1993) **D:** Bob Balaban **S:** Dean
Lorey **P:** Sean Cunningham   (*Johnnie Zombie*)

You know things have changed when Disney releases a PG-13 cannibal-zombie comedy. The nation's mainstream critics nearly had a collective heart attack reviewing it. A nice, shy, suburban teen (Andrew Lowery) is shot and returns as a rotting zombie who wants to take Traci Lind to the prom. His body parts fall off, he resorts to cannibalism, he's almost lynched, and finally he's judged in a heavenly court. It's pretty lame, but the leads are appealing and the cast is filled with familiar faces: Paul Dooley and Ed (*Texas Chainsaw*) Neal as local yokels, Bob Dishy as a helpful gravekeeper, Mary Beth Hurt and Edward Herrmann (confused parents), Austin Pendleton as an evil doctor, and Cloris Leachman. The end theme by the Sextants is excellent. Balaban also made *Parents*, a more disturbing cannibal comedy.

MY BREAKFAST WITH BLASSIE

(Rhino, 1983) **D/S/P/E:** Johnny Legend, Linda Lautrec

Andy Kaufman talks with wrestling manager Freddie Blassie over breakfast in this hour-long takeoff on *My Dinner with André* (1981) set in a Sambo's restaurant. This was the first Rhino video release. The late conceptual comic Kaufman (a regular in the TV series *Taxi*) can also be seen in *Heartbeeps* and in several performance videos.

MY BROTHER HAS BAD DREAMS

(VCI, 1972) **D/S/P:** Bob Emery

A disturbed Norman Bates clone named Carl lives with his virgin older sister. He masturbates while spying on her undressing and talks to (and sleeps with) his "mother" (a mannequin). Carl, always in underwear or cutoffs, sweats, cries, and groans a lot. His nightmares reveal that their alcoholic father killed their crippled mother. One day he swims naked with a Nam-vet biker and then brings him home for dinner. After several murders and more disturbing nightmares Carl rides off on the motorcycle with the mannequin strapped on the back. This unique wonder from Florida used to play on NYC's Channel 9 (with the nudity cut). Did I mention the sharks?

MY BROTHER'S WIFE

(SW, 1966) **D/S/P:** Doris Wishman

After a long fight in a billiard hall over a woman who killed herself, Frankie (who loses) remembers, "The first time I saw Mary I knew there'd be trouble," and we're in a feature-length flashback. Bob, a balding wrestling fan who wears a black shirt and white tie, is married to Mary. When his no-good brother visits their NYC apartment and stays, Mary (June Roberts) thinks, "He's so exciting!" The characters think a lot, since the sound was all dubbed in later. Frankie starts having sex with his sister-in-law, then with his ex-girlfriend, Zena, and they both love the bastard. Most of the sex is offscreen (or in shadows), but the women wear negligées and Zena takes a shower to harpsichord music. There's an arty lesbian scene, a black woman doing funky dancing at a party, and lots of closeups of feet whenever anybody goes someplace. One clever shot shows a woman sitting on the camera for a chair point of view. This is a pretty typical mid-period b/w Wishman drama.

Sex was her master! Lust was her destiny!

JURI PRODUCTIONS INC., presents

MY BROTHER'S WIFE

ADULTS ONLY

one sheet

starring JUNE ROBERTS and SAM STEWART with BOB ORAN DARLENE BENNETT S. STEWART JONI ROBERTS D. SWANSON

produced and directed by Doris Wishman

Distributed by JER PICTURES INC.

MY CHAUFFEUR

(Vestron, 1985) **D/S:** David Beaird **P:** Marilyn J. Tenser

Deborah Foreman becomes the first female chauffeur for an LA company. Sam J. Jones (*Flash Gordon*) costars, with Howard Hesseman, E. G. Marshall, Penn and Teller, and Cindy Beal. This film, which copies *My Tutor*, is from Crown International.

MY DAUGHTER'S KEEPER

(Live, 1991) **D/S:** Heinrich Dahms **S:** Richard Deynoms **P:** Paul Raleigh   S. Africa (*Au Pair*)

An American author in England (Nicholas Guest) takes his family and their beautiful new Portuguese nanny (Ana Padrao) to Mozambique (actually South Africa) while his red-haired wife (Jocelyn Broderick), a reporter, is away on assignment. He has an affair with the nanny, and she (surprise!) turns out to be a jealous psycho who kidnaps his daughter. This derivative feature was picked up by Miramax.

MY DEGENERATION: THE MOVIE

(CD, 1984) **D/S:** Jon Moritsugu
S: Daryl Chin

In the grand tradition of *Beyond the Valley of the Dolls* and *Desperate Teenage Love Dolls,* this is the story of a female rock trio. The 70-minute film shows how the group Bunny Love becomes the hit-making Fetish by promoting the meat industry. Amanda Jones (Loryn Sotsky), the blond bass player, narrates, has visions of cottage cheese and canned peach halves, and falls in love with a (real) pig's head that thinks out loud. The group hits with "beef rock" and the LP *Meat Is Love* (on liver-colored vinyl). They appear on talk shows and star in a comic book, and bootlegs from Japan and Australia appear. The music (by Vomit Lunch, Government Issue, and others) is great. The experimental techniques (dialogue loops, scratched film stock,

negative scenes, crude animation) are effective, and the humor is very on-target, but it's sometimes hard to tell whether or not out-of-focus scenes and tape jumps are deliberate.

MY DEMON LOVER

(RCA, 1987) **D:** Charles Loventhal
S: Leslie Ray **P:** Robert Shaye
M: David Newman

Scott Valentine (from the TV series *Family Ties*) is a lovable homeless street musician who becomes a demon when aroused. Women are killed by "the Mangler," but this is a romantic horror comedy with a fantasy ending. Michelle Little costars, and Arnold Johnson and Larry "Bud" Melman appear. New Line made this PG-13 mess in NYC. The score is on Varèse Sarabande.

MY FAVORITE BUTLER: *See* WHAT THE SWEDISH BUTLER SAW

MY FRIENDS NEED KILLING

(1976) **D/S/P/E:** Paul Leder

Greg Mullavey (from the TV series *Mary Hartman, Mary Hartman*) stars as a Nam vet who rants, flips out, kills his Nam buddies, or makes them kill themselves. Meredith MacRae (from *Petticoat Junction*) is his wife. Both showed up in more strange, obscure movies by Paul Leder, and were married in real life.

MY GRANDPA IS A VAMPIRE

(Republic, 1991) **D:** David Blyth **S:** Michael Heath
P: Murray Newey   New Zealand (*Moonrise; Grampire*)

Al Lewis, from the TV series *The Munsters* (who used to advertise his NYC restaurant on cable-TV sex shows), stars as a cheerful, senile, and weak 18th-century vampire in modern-day New Zealand. His American grandson and a friend help him survive. They buy him raw hamburgers at McDonald's. This fairly boring kids' movie has Steven Spielberg–style floating-in-the-air scenes. David Blyth also made *Red Blooded American Girl.*

MYLÈNE FARMER

(VSOM, 1986–93) **D:** Laurent Boutonnat

Mylène Farmer, who is very popular throughout Europe and in Japan, sings romantic French songs, usually about death, pain, and suffering. This subtitled and letterboxed tape compiles 10 videos. Sometimes she plays a fighting rebel and/or a liberator in historical settings. Several of the videos are amazing, beautifully done little epics set in various times and countries and with dialogue in various languages. "Libertine" and its sequel look like some reels from Kubrick's *Barry Lyndon.* "Allan" (as in Poe), is based on *The Tomb of Ligeia.* She's burned at the stake in one and is Snow White in another. Several have sex and nudity

(usually during instrumental passages, so that they can be cut for various markets), and a few are smaller in scale and surreal. Dead characters from previous videos show up in others. You'd think some American cable network would show this stuff. Video Search also offers *Mylène Farmer in Concert.*

MY LOVELY BURNT BROTHER AND HIS SQUASHED BRAIN

(1987) **D/S/A:** "Jay Jay Hard"/Giovanni Arduino

This amateur gore movie features a killer in a KKK hood who reads *Fangoria,* lots of blood, H-bomb footage, drugs, comic sound effects, bad dubbing, and very sick humor. The 60s-type garage band is pretty good. Some fanzines claim it's from Italy, but I doubt it.

MY LOVELY MONSTER

(1990) **D/S/P:** Michel Bergmann   Germany

A silent-film character (Silvio Francesco) who looks like Lon Chaney in *London After Midnight* is stuck in a German theater and wants to return to his film. This horror-movie spoof features Forrest J. Ackerman as "the Master" (he wrote additional dialogue), Ferdy Mayne, Bobbie Bresee, and Sara Karloff (daughter of Boris). It's dubbed into German and has English subtitles.

MY MOM'S A WEREWOLF

(Prism, 1988) **D:** Michael Fischa
S: Mark Pirro **P:** Steven J. Wolfe

Susan Blakely is bitten on the toe by a pet-shop owner (John Saxon), a werewolf who eats mice. This PG horror comedy features Katrina Caspary as her daughter, Ruth Buzzi as a fortune-teller, John Schuck, Marilyn McCoo, and Forry Ackerman. Crown International released it. It's by the director of *Death Spa* and *Crack House.*

MY NAME IS NOBODY

(VSOM, 1973) **D:** Tonino Valeri **S:** Ernesto
Gastaldi **P:** Sergio Leone **M:** Ennio Morricone
Italy/France/W. Germany (*Il Mio Nome E Nessuno*)

Henry Fonda and Terence Hill star as gunmen, in this western spoof. Fonda is the older one who wants to retire. This big Panavision production, originally running 130 minutes, was filmed in Spain and America. Many think that Sergio Leone directed parts of it. Fonda had been in Leone's classic *Once Upon a Time in the West* (1968), and Hill had just been in the popular Trinity movies. With Jean Martin, Leo Gordon, R. G. Armstrong, Geoffrey Lewis, and Steve Kanaly. The video runs 116 minutes.

MY NEW GUN

(Columbia, 1993) **D/S:** Stacy Cochran **P:** Michael Flynn

A suburban housewife (Diane Lane) is given a loaded .38 by a neighbor (James LeGros). This comedy by a first-time director features Tess Harper, Stephen Collins, and Bruce Altman. From IRS.

MY SCIENCE PROJECT

(Touchstone, 1985) **D/S:** Jonathan Beteul
P: Jonathan Taplin

Some students reactivate a time-warp machine found in a fallout shelter and battle post-nuke mutants, gladiators, and dinosaurs in the future. The FX are by Rick Baker. John Stockwell stars, with Danielle von Zerneck and Fisher Stevens. Dennis Hopper (in his first role after he bottomed out in 1983) is their science teacher. With Richard Masur, Raphael Sbarge, Michael Berryman, Barry Corbin, Ann Wedgeworth, and Pamela Springsteen. It's from Disney.

MY SISTER, MY LOVE: *See* THE CAGE

MY SOUL IS SLASHED

(VSOM, 1990) **D:** Sunsake Kaneko
S: Saka Kawamura   Japan

A businessman (Ken Ogaka) is killed in an arranged "accident" and is blamed for a business scandal. A year later he returns to his family, naked and confused, thanks to a tranfusion of Dracula's blood. A vampire-expert doctor (Narumi Yasuda) teaches him to float, and he becomes a white-haired "Japanese version of a full-fledged Dracula" and seeks revenge. Hikari Ishida is his daughter, and Eisi Aramoto (*King Kong Escapes*) is the doctor's servant. The theme song is by Mylène Farmer. This subtitled horror comedy from Toho is by the director of *Last Frankenstein*.

MY STEPMOTHER IS AN ALIEN

(RCA, 1988) **D:** Richard Benjamin **S:** Jerico Weingrod, Herschel Weingrod, Timothy Harris, Jonathan Reynolds
P: Ronald Parker, Franklyn R. Levy

An alien cyclops/snake (with an NYC accent) and Kim Basinger land in a flying saucer. She watches porno movies to learn how to make love to Dan Aykroyd (in the same hit-filled year as *Caddyshack II, The Couch Trip,* and *The Great Outdoors*), and they get married. The film opens with a *Barbarella* copy (a floating woman). Also featured are Jon Lovitz and the voice of Harry Shearer. John Dykstra (*Star Wars*) did the FX. It was the sixth feature film directed by Richard Benjamin. President Bush attended the premiere because he was a friend of executive producer Jerry Weintraub. It was a box-office flop.

MYSTERIES FROM BEYOND THE TRIANGLE

(1976) **D/P:** William F. Miller, Laurence P. Crawley

Parapsychology scientists (played by actors) sail a schooner into the Devil's Triangle. They take Kirilian photos, have out-of-body experiences, discuss UFOs and Atlantis, get lost, run out of water and fuel, and sing "The Sloop John B."

THE MYSTERIOUS DR. FU MANCHU

(Starlite, 1929) **D:** Rowland V. Lee
S: Florence Ryerson, Lloyd Corrigan

This was the first of three stylish Paramount features with Warner Oland as Sax Rohmer's famous villain. It introduces Fu during the Boxer Rebellion. After "foreign devils" kill his wife and child he vows to kill the British officers he holds responsible. With Jean Arthur as the adopted daughter he hypnotizes, O. P. Heggie as Sir Nayland Smith, Neil Hamilton, Tully Marshall, and Noble Johnson. The Swedish-born Oland played Fu again in *The Return of Dr. Fu Manchu* (1930), with the same cast, and *Daughter of the Dragon* (1931), starring Anna May Wong. In 1931 he starred in the first of his seven Charlie Chan films. Boris Karloff played Fu in *The Mask of Fu Manchu* (1932).

MYSTERIOUS DR. SATAN

(Republic, 1941) **D:** William Witney, John English **S:** Franklyn Adreon, Ronald Davidson

Robert Wilcox is Bob Wayne, aka the masked hero Copperhead, in this 15-chapter Republic serial. Eduardo Ciannelli is Dr. Satan, who uses the same old clunky Republic robots. With Ella Neal and C. Montague Shaw. Dave Sharp and Tom Steele are the main stuntmen. The 1966 feature version is *Dr. Satan's Robot.*

MYSTERIOUS ISLAND

(1929) **D/S:** Lucien Hubbard **D:** Maurice Tourneur, Benjamin Christensen **P:** J. Ernest Williamson

This recommended rarity, based on a Jules Verne novel (a sequel to *Twenty Thousand Leagues Under the Sea*), was in production for more than two years as directors were replaced and scenes were reshot. It has very odd partial sound. All of a sudden one character will say a line. Then it's back to intertitles. Lots of great miniatures are used, and the pretty amazing ending features thousands of little underwater creatures played by dwarves in suits (they look kind of like Howard the Duck), a real alligator with attached horns and fins, and a giant octopus. Lionel Barrymore stars as Count Dakkar (Captain Nemo in the novel), and Montague Love is the villain, Falon (with a fur hat). Also with Jane Daly and Lloyd Hughes. It's been shown on TNT.

MYSTERIOUS ISLAND

(Stokey, 1949) **D:** Spencer Gordon Bennet **S:** Lewis Clay, Royal K. Cole, George H. Plympton **P:** Sam Katzman

Dennis Hopper in *My Science Project.*

Richard Crane is Captain Harding and Leonard Penn is Captain Nemo, in this 15-chapter Columbia serial. The plot (about Civil War castaways) is similar to the 1961 Ray Harryhausen version, but Nemo can walk through walls, and aliens from Mercury show up with ray guns. With Karen Randle, Marshall Reed, Gene Roth, and Bernie Hamilton. Crane went on to play Rocky Jones on TV. Penn played more villains in the serials *King of the Congo* (1952) and *The Lost Planet* (1953). Another version of Jules Verne's novel was made in Europe in 1972, starring Omar Sharif.

THE MYSTERIOUS MAGICIAN

(Sinister, 1964) **D:** Alfred Vohrer **S:** Herbert Reinecker   W. Germany (*Der Hexer*)

A killer called "the Wizard" seems to return from the dead. Edgar Wallace's novel *The Ringer* had been filmed five times previously. Joachim Fuchsberger stars, with Heinz Drache, Sophie Hardy, and Eddi Arent.

MYSTERIOUS MR. M

(Stokey, 1946) **D:** Lewis D. Collins, Vernon Keays **S:** Joseph F. Poland, Paul Huston

Richard Martin stars as federal investigator Grant Farrell, in the very last of Universal's 69 sound serials. It's 13 chapters of fights and chases. Pamela Moore costars, with Jane Randolph, Byron Foulger, and Jack Ingram. Mr. M uses a drug called "hypnotrene" to help steal submarine equipment. Columbia and Republic kept making serials until the mid-50s.

MYSTERIOUS TWO

(1982) **D/S:** Gary Sherman **P:** Alan Landsburg

Evangelists John Forsythe and Priscilla Pointer are really aliens, brainwashing earthlings so that they can take over! Only James Stephens knows what's going on. This NBC-TV series pilot by the director of *Raw Meat* features Vic Tayback, Noah Berry Jr., and Robert Englund.

MYSTERY DATE

(1991) **D:** Jonathan Wacks **S:** Parker Bennett, Terry Runte **P:** Cathleen Summers   Canada

Shy Ethan Hawke, on an arranged date with Teri Polo, discovers a pair of bodies in his trunk. He's pursued by cops and Chinese gangsters (led by Broadway star B. D. Wong). With Fisher Stevens, James Hong, Victor Wong, and (in a surprise appearance) Gwar. This PG-13 Orion release was filmed in Vancouver by the director of *Powwow Highway*.

MYSTERY LINER

(Sinister, 1934) **D:** William Nigh **S:** Wellyn Totman **P:** Paul Malvern

Noah Berry Jr., Gustav von Seyffertitz, and Astrid Allyn star in this 62-minute Monogram movie about murder on board an ocean liner. There's a mad lab, a secret weapon, and an apparition of a dead captain. It's based on "The Ghost of John Holling," a story by Edgar Wallace published in the *Saturday Evening Post*.

THE MYSTERY OF EDWIN DROOD

(1993) **D/S:** Timothy Forder **P:** Keith Hayley   UK

Robert Powell stars as Jasper, an opium-smoking choirmaster, in this version of Charles Dickens' last, unfinished novel, a murder mystery. It was first filmed in 1935 by Universal with Claude Rains. Michelle Evans costars, with Jonathan Phillips, Nanette Newman, and Freddie Jones.

MYSTERY TRAIN

(Orion, 1988) **D/S:** Jim Jarmusch **P:** Jim Stark

A series of three intertwining stories centering on a night in a run-down Memphis hotel make up this slow but engrossing and often funny movie, which features Elvis everything. Some parts are subtitled. Youki Kudoh and Masatoshi Naguse are a pair of young Japanese tourists. Nicoletta Braschi (*Down by Law*) is a widow who hears a ghost story from Tom Noonan. Screamin' Jay Hawkins is great as the desk clerk. With Joe Strummer as a British Elvis, Steve Buscemi, Rick Aviles, Sy Richardson, Elizabeth Bracco, Rockets Redglare, and Tom Waits as the voice of radio DJ Rufus Thomas. Elvis' "Blue Moon" is heard several times, and *Lost in Space* is discussed. *Night on Earth* (1992) was the Ohio-born director's next film.

MY SWEET SATAN

(Film Threat, 1992) **D/S/A:** Jim Van Beeber

The Ohio-based maker of *Deadbeat at Dawn* did some amazing short films while hoping to complete his feature-length *Charlie's Family* (about Manson). This is about believable, directionless, drug-addled young people in Dayton involved with a cult murder. It's extreme, disturbing, violent, and so well made that it's easy to forget that Van Beeber and his friends are talented actors. The gory *Roadkill* (about a killer cannibal) and *Doper*, a drug documentary, are also on this compilation tape.

MY TALE IS HOT!

(SW, 1964) **D/S/P:** "Seymour Tokus"/Dan Sonney

Lucifer (a guy in a cheap Devil suit) emerges from the ground in a suburban garden (a set) and tries to tempt Ben (very short burlesque comedian Little Jack Little) with a series of naked women. Many women take it all off in various settings and some are viewed on a "sinnervision" set. Some frolic in a wading pool. The joke is that faithful husband Ben turns out to have his own harem, and at the end all his naked wives do the twist. This fun and revealing (for the time) color nudie comedy from Sonney Amusements also features a Hell set and the Devil's wife. Top-billed stripper (and notorious stag-reel star) Candy Barr dances and strips down to pasties on a stage set in what looks like a short added as a publicity-grabbing afterthought. The tape is a David F. Friedman presentation. The next year Sonney and Friedman teamed up for *The Defilers,* and Little was in Arch Hall's *Deadwood 76* and *The Nasty Rabbit.*

MY THIRD WIFE GEORGE

(SW, 1969) **D/P:** Harry Kerwin **S:** Wayne Rafferty **P:** Leroy Griffith

Ralph (Bill Kirwin, aka Thomas Wood, who narrates) is a voyeur who lives with his mother in a mansion. After watching the oriental maid undress he relates three flashbacks at a bar. He takes an LSD sugar cube and has sex (still in his underwear) with three "virginal flower children" in their "kooky pad." The other stories involve a guy in a gorilla suit and pictures taken for a divorce. B/W features were a rarity by 1969. This one was made in Florida. With Jeri Winters and Doug Hobart in drag.

MY TRUE STORY

(1951) **D:** Mickey Rooney **S:** Howard J. Green, Brown Holmes **P:** Milton Freedman

Mickey Rooney was 31 when he directed this Columbia movie about a jewel thief (Helen Walker). With Willard Parker and a very young Aldo Da Re (Ray).

MY TUTOR

(MCA, 1983) **D:** George Bowers **S:** Joe Roberts **P:** Marilyn Tenser

Teen Matt Lattanzi (he was married to Olivia Newton-John and was later in the TV series *Paradise Beach*) wants to get laid. His rich father (Kevin McCarthy) hires a blond tutor (Caren Kaye) who swims nude at night and gives him French lessons. With Kitten Natividad as a hooker, Crispin Glover (in an early role), Clark Brandon, Katt Shea, and Jewel Shepard. It's a Crown International release by the director of *The Hearse* and *Private Resort*.

NADJA

(Evergreen, 1994) **D/S:** Michael Almereyda
P: Mary Sweeney, Amy Hobby

Elina Lowensohn is the sexy daughter of Dracula in downtown Manhattan in a b/w feature partially shot in Pixelvision. With Jared Harris as the vampire's twin brother, Suzy Amis as a private nurse, Peter Fonda as Dr. Van Helsing (!), Martin Donovan, and Galaxy Craze as Lucy. It's a David Lynch presentation, and he appears as a morgue guard. Lowensohn was also in the director's *Another Girl, Another Planet*, and Amis was in his *Twister*. The soundtrack features My Bloody Valentine, Verve, and Portishead.

NAIL GUN MASSACRE

(Magnum, 1985) **D/S/P:** Terry Loftin **D:** Bill Leslie

Here's some more dumb sex and violence from Texas. A rural killer in combat gear uses a nail gun with a big yellow power pack and talks with a deep, echoing voice, spouting corny Freddy Krueger-style lines. We're set up to think that the killer is a woman who works at a lumberyard, on a vengeance spree after an (offscreen) gang rape. It turns out to be her brother, Bubba, even though the killer has a female body. Lots of people are killed and found with nails sticking out of their bodies. The sheriff figures, "Some guy went plumb loco with a hammer and a box of nails!" After a bunch of young people working on an old house are slaughtered the rest of them *still* stay there. A couple have sex against a tree, and the guy is shot during orgasm. One guy cuts off his own hand with a chainsaw after being nailed. Some editing would have helped a lot. Acting teacher Adam Roarke is thanked at the end.

NAILS

(1992) **D:** John Flynn **S:** Larry Ferguson, Roderick Taylor **P:** George W. Perkins

Dennis Hopper is a crazed above-the-law cop who's after drug dealers, in a feature planned for theaters but released to cable TV. Anne Archer (who used a body double) costars, with Tomas Milian, Keith David, Charles Hallahan, and Cliff De Young. Flynn returned with *Scam* with Christopher Walken.

NAKED AFRICA

(1957) **D/P:** Cedric Worth

Quentin Reynolds narrates this color documentary on the Xhosa tribe of Cape Nguni. It played on an AIP double bill with *White Huntress*.

(NAKED) AS NATURE INTENDED

(SW, 1961) **D/S/P/A:** Harrison Marks   UK

This is the best-looking nudist movie I've seen. It's a historical travelogue in excellent color that takes us on a narrated tour of Southwest England, including Somerset, Lands End, the ancient fishing village of Clavelly, and even Stonehenge, and shows gorgeous, platinum-blond Pamela Green naked (as nature . . .). After three city women on vacation meet up with two blond gas-station workers who are nudists all five are soon frolicking and swimming naked on various beaches and visiting the Sun Club in Cornwall. Marks appears as a number of characters they meet on the way. Pamela Green seems to have been sort of the Betty Page of England. In this film she plays Ping-Pong, relaxes on a hammock, takes a shower, and swings on a swing, always naked (as nature . . .). The only real disappointment is that Marks missed the opportunity to have his stars naked at Stonehenge. Tony Tenser was the executive producer. It was released in America by Crown International.

THE NAKED CAGE

(Media, 1985) **D/S:** "Paul Nicholas"/ Lutz Shaarwachter **P:** Chris D. Nebe

Shari Shattuck is Misty, a nice, innocent country girl set up by Christina Whitaker and sent up for a bank robbery. Nearly everyone in the prison, including the lesbian warden (Angel Tompkins), goes out of their way to make Misty miserable. With Lucinda Crosby, John Terlesky, Nick Benedict (from the soap opera *All My Children*), and Lisa London. By the director of *Chained Heat* (1982). The Fabulous Thunderbirds are on the soundtrack, and most of the inmates in the cage do get naked. From Cannon.

NAKED COMPLEX

(CH 13, 1963) **D/S:** Ron Mart

If you've never seen a nudist-colony movie here's a good one to start with. An offscreen narrator informs us, "This is Miami Beach." The film's title is written in the sand, and a cool, crude surf theme plays. Roy Savage stars as Johnny. He narrates too, since whenever people actually talk their voices are badly postdubbed. Johnny is seriously nervous around women, so he goes to see a doctor about his "malady." The doctor takes him to the Café des Artistes in Miami, where they watch a sexy dancer. A pretty awkward four-piece band in suits and white socks plays that theme song some more, and then they try "Harlem Nocturne," bad notes and all, while Esmeralda dances with two snakes. The next morning a photo of Johnny (a famous race-car driver) is on the cover of a newspaper with the headline "HE FAINTS AFTER A KISS!" Totally humiliated, he writes a long goodbye letter noting his pluses: "I'm an expert at judo, water skiing, golf, tennis, scuba diving." We see Johnny excelling at everything. Then he gets into a private plane and bales out over the ocean. He parachutes into a tree, weakly yells, "Help, help, help" about 20 times, and passes out. Now comes the reason for this wonderfully dated color movie: The Carribean island he ends up on (actually the Sun Beach Club in Tampa) is a nudist retreat for seven women (and a few monkeys), all naked and working out on the beach. One of them is bench-pressing bricks. They discover Johnny and go running in different directions for a ladder, a rope, an axe, and a bucket of water. The women are shot from many angles, often from the ground up, and all look pretty fine, but pubic hair was still too much for adults-only audiences in the great year of 1963. The leader is red-haired Dolores Carlos, also the film's executive producer. Carlos was also in *Nature Camp Confidential*, Herschell Gordon Lewis' *A Taste of Blood*, and others. She says, "You never can tell what monster lies in a man!" so they tie him up, then take his clothes off (except for his underwear). Johnny, who is afraid to look at the naked women, escapes and is recaptured. The women lounge around, go swimming, and pretty much ignore him. Finally Johnny is cured, takes off his underwear, and runs to join the women in a pond. A happy ending.

The Naked Cage

THE NAKED EDGE

(1961) **D:** Michael Anderson **S:** Joseph Stefano
P: Walter Seltzer, George Glass   UK

Gary Cooper (in his last feature) plays a businessman in London who's accused of murder and gets involved with blackmail. Peter Cushing is the prosecutor in the courtroom scenes. Deborah Kerr costars, with Diane Cilento, Eric Portman, Hermione Gingold, Ronald Howard, and Michael Wilding. When UA released this b/w film the publicity compared it to *Psycho* (which Joseph Stefano had also written).

THE NAKED FLAME

(Sinister, 1963) **D/P:** Lawrence Matlansky **S:** Al Everett Dennis   Canada (*Deadline for Murder*)

Female members of a Russian pagan sect in a small Canadian town chant and sing, burn their own buildings, and take their clothes off so that "God will see their anguish." Incredibly, this color exploitation movie is based on reality. A surreal sequence with naked women (who look like nudie-movie models) standing in front of flaming buildings is not easily forgotten. In other scenes the older women leave their underwear on. Dennis O'Keefe stars as a lawyer for mine owners, sent to his hometown, where he encounters soap-opera-style situations and obscure battles between "Orthodox Freedomites" and "Dukhobors" (actual sects). A laughing, bearded blackmailer (*Battlestar Galactica's* John Colicos) rapes and kills the girlfriend of the mine owner's son (Barton Heyman), and it all ends up in a courtroom. It was made in Calgary, Alberta, and not released in America until 1970 (several years after O'Keefe had died), by Headliner. This would make a great Canadian double bill with *Playgirl Killer*.

THE NAKED GUN: FROM THE FILES OF POLICE SQUAD!

(Paramount, 1988) **D/S/P:** David Zucker
S/P: Jerry Zucker, Jim Abrahams **S:** Pat Proft

It's rare for a hit movie to be based on a short-lived flop TV series, but this PG-13 comedy is based on the 1982 series *Police Squad* (which is also on video). Leslie Nielsen stars as the oblivious Lieutenant Frank Drebin, with George Kennedy and Priscilla Presley. It's full of the puns and sight gags that the makers of *Airplane!* were known for, and it ends at a baseball game. Ricardo Montalban is a South American drug dealer who plans to have hypnotized assassins kill the queen of England (Queen Elizabeth lookalike Jeannette Charles). With O. J. Simpson, Weird Al Yankovic, Dr. Joyce Brothers, Lawrence Tierney, and Brinke Stevens (an extra).

THE NAKED GUN 2 1/2

(Paramount, 1991) **D/S:** David Zucker
S: Pat Proft **P:** Robert Kweiss

The original creative team had split up by the time this sequel was made, but it was a much bigger box-office hit than the original. Nielsen, Presley, Kennedy, and Simpson (in a bigger role) all return. Lieutenant Drebin goes to Washington, DC, Robert Goulet is the main villain, and there's lots of topical humor about the environment, pollution, and atomic energy. This PG-13 comedy includes a *Ghost* gag, and somebody portrays President and Mrs. Bush. With Lloyd Bochner, Gina Mastrogiacomo, and Zsa Zsa Gabor and Mel Torme as themselves.

NAKED GUN 33 1/3: THE FINAL INSULT

(Paramount, 1994) **D:** Peter Segal **S:** Pat Proft, David Zuckerman, Robert LoCash **P:** Robert K. Weiss

Lieutenant Drebin (Nielsen), now married to Jane (Priscilla Presley), is after terrorists. This PG-13 comedy sequel is packed with spoofs of other movies (including *Thelma and Louise, Jurassic Park*, and *The Crying Game*) but will be remembered as the last major pre-arrest role for O. J. Simpson, who played Detective Norberg for the third time. It all ends at an Oscar ceremony. With Fred Ward, Kathleen Freeman, and model Anna Nicole Smith as the terrorists, Ellen Greene, Julie Strain, and guest stars Raquel Welch, Pia Zadora, Vanna White, and Weird Al Yankovic.

NAKED INSTINCT

(Dementia, 1993) **D:** "Ellen Cabot"/David DeCoteau **S:** Eric Black **P:** Ian Icarian

Michelle Bauer tells her shrink about the affairs that she and her friend (blond DeAnne Power)

have had with a series of "hunky" younger men. The naked men are featured as much as or more than the women.

NAKED KILLER

(Worldwide, 1992) **D:** Clarence Fok Yiu Leung
S/P: Jing Wong   Hong Kong (*Chiklo Gouyeung*)

This cartoonish sex/action comedy copies *La Femme Nikita* and *Basic Instinct* but also has rapists chained up in a cellar, castration, and lesbian sex in a pool of blood. Kitty (Chingmy Yau, a former Miss Hong Kong) is trained by Sister Cindy (Kelly Yao) to become a man-hating professional assassin. A Hong Kong cop (Simon Yam) and the evil princess (Carrie Ng) both fall for Kitty. *Naked Killer II* (1993) is a follow-up without most of the first movie's female characters.

NAKED LUNCH

(Fox, 1991) **D/S:** David Cronenberg
P: Jeremy Thomas   Canada/UK

You don't have to be familiar with William Burroughs' writings to enjoy this bizarre drug-fantasy movie. It's about what might have been in Burroughs's mind while he was writing his famous 1959 novel. Peter Weller stars as William Lee (a Burroughs pseudonym), a NYC writer working as an exterminator. His wife, Joan (Judy Davis), injects bug powder. Her accidental death is what puts Lee into "Interzone"/Tangier (all atmospheric sets). Chris Walas created special-effects creatures like the disturbing roach/typewriters that talk though their assholes and the alien-look mugwumps (maybe they should have been left out). Davis also plays another (fantasy) woman. Weller does a good Burroughs voice, Davis (in *Barton Fink* the same year) is excellent, and the (often gay) sex is offscreen (which angered some Burroughs fans). With Ian Holm, Julian Sands, Roy Scheider, and Nicholas Campbell. Ornette Coleman is featured on the Milan soundtrack by Howard Shore. There was also a British documentary, *Naked Making Lunch* (1992), by Chris Rodley (who also made *Long Live the New Flesh*, about David Cronenberg).

NAKED MASSACRE

(Questar, 1975) **D/S:** Denis Heroux   Canada/W. Germany/France/Italy (*Die Hinrichtung; Born for Hell*)

A returning Nam vet (Matthieu Carrière) kills eight nurses in Ireland. Kind of like the Richard Speck story set in Belfast, it was shot in Germany

David Cronenberg and Peter Weller promoting *Naked Lunch*.

by the Canadian director of *The Uncanny* with an international cast, including Eva Mattes, Debby Berger, and Carol Laure (after *Sweet Movie*).

NAKED OBSESSION

(Vestron, 1991) **D:** Dan Golden
S: Robert Dodson **P:** Ron Zwano

This sex/horror movie is ridiculous, but at least it tries to be different. A California city councilman (William Katt) checks out the Yin Yang club in the "Dante's Square" area. He's tempted by a philosophical young homeless thief (Rick Dean) who seems to be the Devil himself! Katt starts going home with strippers and is blamed for a series of murders. His first stripper (Maria Ford) teaches him about oxygen-deprivation sex. During b/w nightmares he's elected mayor and assassinated. With Elena Sahagun, Wendy MacDonald, Madison Stone, and Fred Olen Ray as the club MC. Some of the strip acts are pretty imaginative. This Concorde release is available in R and unrated versions.

NAKED PREY

(Paramount, 1966) **D/P/A:** Cornel Wilde
S: Clint Johnson

Cornel Wilde went all out for this excellent survival movie, shot on location in Africa and set in the 19th century. Because of a stupid, arrogant safari leader who plans to take slaves, the members of an ivory-hunting party are captured and tortured. One man is covered in clay and baked. Another has to act like a bird and is put in a ring with a deadly cobra. A nameless hunter (Wilde) who understands the local language and customs is set free (with only a loincloth) and given a chance to live while being hunted down by warriors (led by Ken Gampu). Incredibly, the sick, starving man survives by eating raw snakes. He also fights vicious Arab slavers and befriends a kid who escapes from them. Most of the movie is in native languages. It features nudity and surprising mondo scenes of natives drinking goat's blood and climbing inside a huge elephant carcass. Wilde made *Beach Red* next.

NAKED PURSUIT

(SW, 1968) **D:** Toshio Okuwaki
S: Shunichi Naho   Japan (*Kufun*)

This arty, subtitled b/w exploitation movie told in flashbacks has almost no dialogue. It does have several (soft-core) rape scenes and long scenes of a naked woman (Maki Oaki) running over sand dunes. There's also footage of student riots and very strange music. The tape is letterboxed. When it was released in theaters by Boxoffice International there was a color sequence.

NAKED UNDER LEATHER

(1968) **D:** Jack Cardiff **S:** Ronald Duncan **P:** William Sassoon
UK/France (*Girl on a Motorcycle*)

Rebecca (Marianne Faithfull), married only two months and bored with her schoolteacher husband,

Marianne Faithfull is *Naked Under Leather*.

takes off on her Harley (a wedding present from her ex-lover Alain Delon), wearing only her black-leather jumpsuit. On the way to meet Delon in Heidelberg she flashes back to their soft-focus lovemaking with rose petals (and thorns), and eventually she ends up with her head smashed through a car windshield. Audiences usually crack up laughing during this nice-looking attempt at "erotic symbolism" directed by the same cinematographer who made *Mutations*. With Marius Goring and Catherine Jourdan. Rebecca says, "Skin me!" It was rated X in America. The soundtrack, *Girl on a Motorcycle,* was issued by Bill Cosby's company, Tetragrammaton.

NAKED VENGEANCE

(Lightning, 1985) **D/P:** Cirio H. Santiago **S:** Reilly Askew **P:** Anthony Marharaj   (*Satin Vengeance*)

A woman (Deborah Tranelli) is gang-raped, and her family is killed. Her revenge includes men being set on fire, shot in the head, and castrated. With Don Gordon. This Roger Corman/New World production is available in R and unrated videos.

NAKED VENUS

(Dark Dreams, 1958) **D/P:** Gaston Hakim

A young American artist and his French wife, Yvonne, an artists' model, live in France with their kid. They visit America, but his horrible, meddling mother hires a detective to prove that Yvonne is an unfit mother. It seems that she once posed for a painting of a naked Venus. The wife hires a lady lawyer who argues in divorce court that "art is *never* morally objectionable." Luckily for us, Yvonne is also a nudist, so she takes her daughter (and her poodle) to the Royal Palms seaside nudist camp, where we see a nude wedding and silent footage of typical nudist sports. Nudist footage is also projected in court and used as flashbacks. Even the men are full-frontally naked in this b/w feature.

NAKED WARRIORS = THE ARENA

THE NAKED WITCH

(Sinister, 1960) **D/S/E:** Larry Buchanan
P: Claude Alexander

Larry Buchanan's first feature is a real find. A stake is pulled out of "the widow witch" (Libby Hall) in the old-fashioned German village of Luchenbach, Texas. She returns (after some bad time-lapse changes) to kill descendants of the townspeople (seen in a flashback) with an axe. She has wild eyebrows and is naked walking through a graveyard, but she's optically censored! In other scenes she wears a see-thru negligée, dances in a cave to bongo music, and takes a nude swim. With Robert Short as a meddling student (who also narrates), Jo Maryman, and Der Sängerbund Children's Choir. Buchanan said that he made this for "$8,000 in 16mm and color." A very long intro is read (by Gary Owens, from the TV show *Laugh-In*) over close-ups of Hieronymus Bosch paintings. The sound is by S. F. Brownrigg. The video (which is b/w) is jumpy in spots but has some choice trailers at the beginning.

THE NAKED WITCH

(1964) **D:** Andy Milligan **S:** Clay Guss
P: Claude Alexander   (*Naked Temptress*)

A college student on the Atlantic coast digs up the grave of a woman executed as a witch in the 1800s. She returns as a vampire. He falls for a village girl with a deaf-mute hunchback friend. Everybody thinks it's strange that Larry Buchanan and Andy Milligan both made movies with the same title and nearly the same plot, but that's exploitation. William Mishkin released this one in 1967.

NAKED WORLD

(1968) **D:** Francesco De Feo, Albert T. Viola
S: Giuseppe Marotta, Giancarlo Fusco
Italy (*Mondo Nudo*)

This documentary features a visit to Hiroshima, nude sunbathers in Denmark, the Mexican "Day of the Dead," a gay fashion show in the Philippines, hypnotism, and "free love" among prisoners on a Pacific island. New footage was added to the 1963 film for the American release.

THE NAKED WORLD OF HARRISON MARKS

(1967) **D/S/P/A:** George Harrison
Marks **S:** Terry Maher, Jim McDonald

Marks plays himself (a photographer) and has a series of comic dreams, all with naked ladies. He appears as Dracula, James Bond, and other characters. Blond Pamela Green (his real-life wife) is the main attraction. The film is narrated by Valentine Dyall.

NAKED ZOO

(NPY, 1969) **D/P:** William Grefe
D: Barry Mahon **S:** Roy Preston
(*The Hallucinators; The Grove*)

Miami-based William Grefe was the president of the Ivan Tors studios

(producers of the *Flipper* and *Gentle Ben* TV shows). He also directed about a dozen cheap, crazed movies like *The Death Curse of Tartu*. This mean-spirited, embarrassing rarity (from a story by Grefe) stars Steven Oliver (*Motor Psycho*) as Terry, a crazy, sadistic playboy writer gigolo with sideburns. Rita Hayworth (who later died of Alzheimer's) plays the wealthy Mrs. Golden. Terry gives her LSD, then scares her to death, disguised as her wheelchair-bound husband (whom he killed earlier). Fay Spain has the most demeaning part, as a middle-aged woman in a wig trying to be hip while being humiliated and drugged at a pot party where Canned Heat plays (!). They do "One Kind Favor," a good cut from their second album. Bob "the Bear" Hite sings, and "Blind Owl" Wilson plays a guitar solo. The ironic lyrics go, "Did you ever hear that coffin sound?" In an incredible scene Terry has one puff of grass, screams in pain, imitates a hellfire preacher, and convinces everybody at a friend's party to start a fire on the floor and throw the furniture into it! "Special guest star" Joe E. Ross, former burlesque comic and *Car 54* star, has a short scene talking on a phone. Steve Alaimo, the worst artist ever on Chess records, is heard singing horrible ballads. To spice up the movie, nudie specialist Barry Mahon was hired to shoot sex scenes. A girl with a vibrator is edited in during the party sequence. There's a lesbian character and a "spade-chick" girlfriend ("We can miscegenate!"), and one of the dumb cops at the end is Herschell Gordon Lewis star William Kerwin!

NAM ANGELS

(Media, 1989) **D:** Cirio H. Santiago **S:** Dan Gagliasso **P:** Christopher R. Santiago

The Hell's Angels are hired to liberate some POWs in Vietnam. This bad copy of *The Losers* stars Brad Johnson (who was the Marlboro man) and Vernon Wells. The Hell's Angels sued Concorde over their depiction. They had also sued Corman more than 20 years earlier over *The Wild Angels*.

A NAME FOR EVIL

(Paragon, 1970) **D/S:** Bernard Girard
P: Reed Sherman   Canada (*The Grove*)

An evil ghost of Robert Culp's ancestor makes him kill his wife in his haunted Southern mansion. Or is it all a dream? Samantha Eggar costars, with Sheila Sullivan (also in Culp's *Hickey and Boggs*).

ACTUALLY FILMED IN A NATURE COLONY

The Naked Venus

NAKED VENGEANCE

Sex scenes with full frontal nudity (including Culp) were featured in Playboy. The music is by Dominic Frontière and Billy Joe Royal. Cinerama released this film in 1973.

THE NAME OF THE ROSE

(Nelson, 1986) **D:** Jean-Jacques Annaud
S: Andrew Birkin, Gerard Brach, Howard Franklin, Alain Godard **P:** Bernd Eichinger
Germany/Italy/France

This murder mystery set in a 13th century abbey was based on Umberto Eco's bestseller. Sean Connery is William of Baskerville, a Franciscan brother who's an early Holmes-style detective, and Christian Slater is his assistant. It features gore, torture, lots of scary, ugly, perverted monks, gargoyles, and great M. C. Escher–style labyrinths. With Valentina Vargas in a memorable sex scene, F. Murray Abraham, William Hickey, Michael Lonsdale, and Ron Perlman as a hunchback. It's by the director of *Quest for Fire*.

NARCOTICS STORY

(SW, 1958) **D/P:** Robert W. Larson
S: Roger Garris   (*The Dread Persuasion*)

The ultimate anti-drug movie is a stark, color, semi-documentary "Police Science Production" made by (and originally for) police. Users and dealers in a small California town are discussed and examined. The local dealer runs the malt shop. We're shown (in great detail) how to score, roll, inhale, price, and sell marijuana, then how to prepare heroin to sell or to shoot. If you want to become a cop this will show you how to search rooms and how to properly bust a teen "tea party" in a car. Future dealers can gain foolproof tips on how to lure young girls into using junk. The very serious narration is by Art Gilmore, and there's a flashback. Today's viewers may find a few cheap laughs, but this is mostly too realistic for ridicule. Publicity claimed that the cast was made up of "dope addicts, narcotics investigators, and dope pushers." I don't know about that, but the characters and unknown faces are great, and some are very convincing. This was released with an exploitation campaign in 1958 and again in 1962. It played drive-ins for years.

NASHVILLE

(Paramount, 1975) **D/P:** Robert Altman
S: Joan Tewkesbury

This 2-hour drama about the country-music business received a number of Oscar nominations. It's here because of Karen Black as Connie White and Keith Carradine as Tom Frank (and because it's good). They both sing, and Carradine even had a real world hit ("I'm Easy," which won an Oscar). Some others in the interesting cast are Ned Beatty, Ronee Blakley, Geraldine Chaplin, Shelley Duvall, Henry Gibson, Michael Murphy, Scott Glenn, Keenan Wynn, Robert DoQui, Elliott Gould, Gwen Welles, and Jeff Goldblum.

NASHVILLE GIRL

(1976) **D:** Gus Trikonis **S/P:** Peter J. Oppenheimer
(*Country Music Daughter; New Girl in Town*)

New World put this into drive-ins the year after *Nashville*. Monica Gayle leaves the farm for the big city (Nashville). With Glenn Corbett and country star Johnny Rodriguez (in his acting debut).

NATION AFLAME!

(Sinister, 1937) **D/P:** Victor Halperin
P: Edward Halperin

The KKK is the topic of this exploitation movie from the makers of *White Zombie*. The cast includes Lila Lee (*The Unholy Three*), Noel Madison, and Snub Pollard. The racist, anti-foreigner group in the film, created by a con man who wants control of a state, is called the Avenging Angels. This has been on video with *Probation* (which features a 16-year-old Betty Grable).

NATIONAL LAMPOON'S ANIMAL HOUSE

(MCA, 1978) **D:** John Landis **S:** Harold Ramis, Douglas Kennedy, Chris Miller
P: Matty Simmons, Ivan Reitman

The ultimate frat-house comedy was a huge hit and is still being imitated. Any movie with "Louie Louie" in it is OK with me. It takes place in 1962. John Belushi is Blutarsky, and the other defiant rejects are Tim Matheson, Tom Hulce, Stephen Furst, Kevin Bacon, Peter Riegert, and Bruce McGill. With Karen Allen, John Vernon as Dean Wormer, Verna Bloom as his wife, Donald Sutherland as a pot-smoking professor, Mary Louise Weller, and *Playboy* Playmate Martha Smith. Vernon, Furst, and McGill were also in *Delta House*, one of three short-lived 1979 TV series based on this movie. The soundtrack features Otis Williams and the Knights, an Isley Brothers type group. MCA also released the Elmer Bernstein score.

NATIONAL LAMPOON'S CLASS REUNION

(Vestron, 1981) **D:** Michael Miller
S: John Hughes **P:** Matty Simmons

A mad killer attacks members of the class of '72. This horror spoof was the second major flop with the Lampoon name on it. With Gerrit Graham, Michael Lerner, Stephen Furst, Zane Busby, Anne Ramsey, and Misty Rowe. Michael Miller went on to direct *Silent Rage*. Scriptwriter John Hughes (who shows up in a dress with a paper bag over his head) later became a big-deal director.

NATIONAL LAMPOON'S LOADED WEAPON I

(New Line, 1993) **D/S:** Gene Quintano
S: Don Holley **P:** Suzanne Todd, David Willis

Emilio Estevez and Samuel L. Jackson star in this spoof of the Lethal Weapon series done in *Naked Gun* style by the director of *Honeymoon Academy*. William Shatner and Tim Curry are the main villains. Kathy Ireland is featured in a *Basic Instinct* takeoff, and specific scenes from all three *Lethal Weapon* movies are parodied. With Denise Richards, Jon Lovitz as the Joe Pesci character, and guest stars Whoopi Goldberg, F. Murray Abraham, Bill Nunn, Dr. Joyce Brothers (who's also in *The Naked Gun*), James Doohan, Richard Moll, Charlie Sheen, Phil Hartman, J. T. Walsh, Charles Napier, Bruce Willis, Erik Estrada, and Corey Feldman. It's

PG-13. *National Lampoon's Last Resort* (Vidmark, 1994) and *National Lampoon's Attack of the 5'2" Women* (Paramount, 1995) were the next unrelated franchise comedies.

NATIONAL LAMPOON'S MOVIE MADNESS

(MGM, 1981) **D:** Bob Giraldi, Henry Jaglom
S: Tod Carroll, Shary Flenniken, Pat Mephitis, Gerald Sussman, Ellis Weiner **P:** Matty Simmons
(*National Lampoon Goes to the Movies*)

A producer of *Animal House* returned with this barely released movie spoof made up of three segments (a disaster-movie segment by Henry Jaglom was removed). The themes are a "personal growth" film, a soap opera, and a police movie. The cast includes Peter Riegert, Diane Lane, and Candy Clark in the first segment, Robert Culp, Joe Spinell, Mary Woronov, Dick Miller, and Fred Willard in the second, and Richard Widmark, Christopher Lloyd, Elisha Cook Jr., Henny Youngman, and Harry Reems in the third. Also featured are Robby Benson, Julie Kavner, Olympia Dukakis, Bobby DiCicco, Margaret Whitton, and a theme song by Dr. John. Bob Giraldi later made the "Beat It" video. What were they thinking when they hired Jaglom?

NATURAL BORN CRAZIES

(1992) **D/S/P/E:** George Baluzy, Mike Baluzy   (*Memoirs of a Madman*)

During a Christmas party four inmates escape from a state asylum and take a doctor with them. Brad Bechard is pretty convincing as the extremely psychotic white-trash leader, Butch. One inmate is a cartoonish geek, a pathetic one in drag has a French accent, and James (Richard Craven) is a good-looking one on medication. Sometimes we hear their thoughts. The almost constant narration (by a guy with a very affected British voice) is both irritating and funny ("Oh, how they begin to resemble wild beasts"). There's a heavy-metal band, a (male) shower scene, rape, murder, and suicide (nothing graphic). Taylor Mead and Quentin Crisp appear briefly. Most of it was shot in fields and woods in upstate New York.

NATURAL BORN KILLERS

(Warner, 1994) **D:** Oliver Stone **S:** David Veloz, Richard Rutowski **P:** Jane Hamsher

Stone threw in every underground-movie technique (now common in TV commercials and rock videos) for his cartoonish, frantic, self-indulgent, over-the-top 2-hour-long parody of serial killers and modern media. It features parts shot in Super 8, on video, and in b/w; Japanese-style animation (by Mike Smith); peyote-eating Indians and hallucinations; and scenes from newsreels, *Captain Sinbad*, *Night of the Lepus* (giant bunnies) and many other horror movies. The quick flashes of demon faces are very effective. Many hated it, but if nothing else it was the best drug-experience movie in years. Juliette Lewis and Woody Harrelson star as the young killers Mickey and Mallory Knox. Robert Downey Jr. is the New Zealand–accented tabloid-TV star reporter Wayne Gale, Tommy Lee Jones is pretty hilarious as the prison warden, Tom Sizemore is a famous author/cop (and a psycho killer himself), and Rodney

Dangerfield is Mallory's abusive father in TV-sitcom flashbacks. Also with Russell Means, Balthazar Getty, Edie McClurg, Ashley Judd, Denis Leary, Steven Wright, and Arliss Howard. A real Chicago prison and inmates were used. Stone shot two endings, and several scenes were cut for an R rating. It was based on an original screenplay by Quentin Tarantino, who had hoped to direct it himself. The bestselling soundtrack, produced by Trent Reznor (from Nine Inch Nails), includes older tracks by Patti Smith, Duane Eddy, Patsy Cline, L7, and Ministry, and a great new Leonard Cohen theme song.

NATURAL ENEMIES

(1979) **D/S/E:** Jeff Kanew **P:** John E. Quill

Hal Holbrook stars as a successful publisher who decides to kill his entire family. First he hires a group of hookers for a private orgy. Don't expect lots of sex and violence, though. It's mostly talk. With José Ferrer, Louise Fletcher as the wife, Elizabeth Berridge as the daughter, and Viveca Lindfors. Kanew later made *Revenge of the Nerds*.

THE NATURE GIRL AND THE SLAVER

(1957) **D:** Hermann Leitner
P: Helmut Volmer   W. Germany
(*Liane, die Weisse Sklavin*)

Marian Michael stars in this sequel to *Liane*. She's back in the jungle and has more topless scenes. With Adrian Hoven and Saro Urzi.

NATURE'S PARADISE

(1955) **D:** Charles Saunders **S:** Leslie Bell, Dennis Kaye **P:** Frank Bevis   UK (*Nudist Paradise*)

An American art student in England falls for a nudist and joins her at a camp. This movie features Anita Love and Katy Cashfield. It was filmed in Cinemascope and Eastmancolor. Fanfare released it in 1960.

NATURE'S PLAYMATES

(Video Dimensions, 1962) **D:** Herschell Gordon Lewis **S/P:** David F. Friedman
S: Bentley Williams **P:** Thomas J. Dowd

A cheery blond private eye (Vicki Miles) and her male partner (who resembles Keenan Wynn) pose as a brother and sister and go to nudist camps searching for a missing husband with a navy tattoo. Miles (aka Allison Louise Downe) went on to star in *Goldilocks and the Three Bares, Boin-n-g*, and others by Friedman and Lewis, then switched to production jobs and wrote the screenplays for *The Gruesome Twosome* and *She Devils on Wheels*! In this one she wears lots of makeup and high heels while going "natural." The nude highlights are women bouncing on a trampoline and a twist contest. The video of this color movie is in b/w.

NAUGHTY DALLAS

(SW, 1964) **D/S:** Larry Buchanan
(*Mondo Exotica; Naughty Cuties*)

The action is narrated by some guy, then Toni (Toni Shannon), a small town girl in Dallas, then a theatrical agent, then a burly club owner. She thinks, "What a lucky break! I'm in show business!", chickens out during an amateur stripper night, but becomes a hit after some private lessons. Most of the movie (filmed as early as 1959) is vintage real strip acts, with some unfunny comics (one in drag), and Bill Peck and his Peckers band. Some strippers leave pasties on. My faves were the two "maids," Jada (who gets a pie in the face), and the woman on the tiger skin rug. In glorious faded color. It was shot in several Dallas burlesque houses but, despite the false publicity, *not* in Jack Ruby's Carousel club.

NAUGHTY NYMPHS: *See* DON'T TELL DADDY

NAUGHTY STEWARDESSES

(Super, 1973) **D/P:** Al Adamson **S:** Sam Sherman

Connie Hoffman, Donna Desmond, Tracy King, and Regina Carrol star in a movie that copies the hit *The Stewardesses*. Former cowboy-movie star Robert Livingston is also in it. From Independent International. *Blazing Stewardesses* was a more comical sequel.

NAVAJO JOE

(MGM, 1966) **D:** Sergio Corbucci **S:** Mario Pierotti, Fernando Di Leo **P:** Ermanno Donati, Luigi Carpentieri **M:** Ennio Morricone   Italy/Spain (*Un Dollaro a Testa*)

An Indian warrior (Burt Reynolds) is hired by a town to stop Also Sambrell, an evil bounty hunter who kills and scalps Indians, causing revenge attacks. Fernando Rey is a priest. Ruggero Deodato was the assistant director.

NAVAJO RUN

(1964) **D/P/A:** Johnny Seven **S:** Jo Heims

A rancher saves a Navajo half-breed from death by snakebite, but it's part of a revenge plot. Warren Kemmerling and Virginia Vincent are also in this obscure AIP western.

THE NAVIGATOR: A MEDIEVAL ODYSSEY

(1988) **D/S:** Vincent Ward **S:** Kelly Lyons, Geoff Chapple **P:** John Maynard, Gary Hannam   New Zealand/Australia

In 1348 a young Welsh psychic (Hamish McFarlane) dreams of a way to save his village from the black plague. He leads four others through a tunnel, and they emerge in present-day New Zealand (where people are dying of AIDS). This acclaimed PG film was shot in b/w and color on a very low budget.

NAZARÍN

(1959) **D/S:** Luis Buñuel **S:** Julio Alejandro
P: Manuel Barbachano Ponce

Francisco Rabal stars as a priest who tries to follow the teachings of Christ in turn-of-the-century Mexico. The Church defrocks him after he shelters a prostitute (Rita Macedo). He goes on the road, followed by her, another woman (Marga López), and a dwarf (Jesús Fernández). Some consider him a saint, but his efforts to do good land him in jail. Luis Buñuel returned to the same theme with *Simon of the Desert* (1965).

NAZI LOVE CAMP NO. 27: *See* LOVE CAMP 27

NEAR DARK

(HBO, 1987) **D:** Kathryn Bigelow **S:** Eric Red **P:** Steven-Charles Jaffe **M:** Tangerine Dream

The first vampire/road movie is a unique classic, although it borrows ideas from Anne Rice's book *Interview with the Vampire*. Lance Henriksen leads a "family" group of vicious, unrelenting vampires in search of victims. They travel in a car with blacked-out windows and stay in motels. Since vampires are ageless some of them are kids. Henriksen (still wearing his Civil War uniform), Bill Paxton, and Jenette Goldstein are the main vampires (they were in *Aliens* too). An Oklahoma farm boy (Adrian Pasdar) is seduced by Jenny Wright and becomes one of them but still won't kill. With Joshua Miller and Tim Thomerson. The score is on Varèse Sarabande. The Cramps are heard on a jukebox doing "Fever," which is fitting since Paxton is made up to resemble Cramps singer Lux Interior.

THE NEBRASKAN

(1953) **D:** Fred F. Sears **S:** David Lang, Martin Berkeley **P:** Wallace MacDonald

Phil Carey is an army scout in this 3-D color Columbia feature about an Indian uprising, with Roberta Haynes, Jay Silverheels, Wallace Ford, Lee Van Cleef, Regis Toomey, and Dennis Weaver.

NECROMANCER

(Forum, 1987) **D:** Dusty Nelson **S:** Will Naud **P:** Roy McAree   (*Satan's Servant*)

An acting student (Elizabeth Kaitan) is gang-raped. She contacts a necromancer (who advertises in the newspaper) for help in getting revenge. While possessed she seduces the attackers and kills (and castrates) them. We see a claw, glowing eyes, and a (very bad) monster face. Russ Tamblyn is a Shakespeare-spouting acting teacher who casts her in *The Taming of the Shrew*.

NECROMANIA

(SW, 1971) **D/S:** Edward D. Wood Jr.

Wood's last feature as a director, a soft-core sex movie, is only for completists. Real-life couple Rene Bond and Ric Lutz star. They're at the home of a "witch" so that he can be cured of impotence. Based on Wood's novel *The Only House*, it's a series of sex scenes (about half of them are lesbian), an odd and brief look at damned souls, plus a woman getting off with help from a fake skull. The gag ending is Lutz forced to join "Madame Heles" in a coffin. Dialogue includes "Bet your sweet bippy!" and "We shall return to the *red room*." (Did Stanley Kubrick see this?) Frank Henenlotter introduces the video and returns at the end to talk to Rudolph Grey about it. Since this version runs only 43 minutes, an edited version of *Love Feast*, starring Wood, follows.

NECROMANIAC = GRAVEYARD OF HORROR

NECRONOMICON

(1993) **D/P:** Brian Yuzna **D:** Christopher Gans, Shu Kaneko **S:** Brent V. Friedman **P:** Samuel Hadida

This horror trilogy based on H. P. Lovecraft features Jeffrey Combs as Lovecraft in wraparound segments. In "The Drowned" (by Christopher Gans, from France) Richard Lynch stars as a man who inherits a remote New England hotel from his uncle, who made a pact with the Devil. The cast also includes Bruce Payne, Maria Ford, and Belinda Bauer. Bess Meyer tells a story to a Boston reporter (Gary Graham) in "The Cold" (by Shu Kaneko, from Japan). With David Warner as a mad scientist and Millie Perkins. Signy Coleman is a futuristic Philadelphia cop in "Whispers" (by Brian Yuzna). Don Calfa and Judith Drake costar. Tom Rainone supervised the many name FX experts, and Tom Savini was an adviser. The US release was delayed.

NECROPOLIS: CITY OF THE DEAD

(Lightning, 1986) **D/S:** Bruce Hickey **P:** Tim Kincaid, Cynthia De Paula

A blond Dutch witch (LeeAnne Baker) is reincarnated as a punk biker in NYC. She sacrifices virgins and sucks souls through victims' foreheads. She also grows four extra breasts to feed some followers with. Joel von Ornsteiner is also in the cast. Ed French did the FX.

NED KELLY

(1970) **D/S:** Tony Richardson **S:** Ian Jones **P:** Neil Hartley   Australia

Mick Jagger with a beard stars as a young 19th-century Irish outlaw who fights corrupt British Protestant colonists in Australia. The real Ned Kelly is a famous historical figure down under. He's arrested for stealing pigs, serves time, then is framed by a policeman. In some scenes he and his gang wear homemade armor. While this was being filmed in 1969 Brian Jones was buried. Marianne Faithfull showed up to costar but ended up in the hospital from a drug overdose and was replaced by Diane Craig. When it was released Jagger called the movie "a load of shit." It's not that bad. The UA soundtrack features Waylon Jennings, Kris Kristofferson, and one accustic Jagger cut. *Mad Dog Morgan*, with Dennis Hopper, is similar, and *Reckless Kelly* (1993) is a modern-day takeoff. *Freejack, Ned Kelly,* and *Performance* are the only feature films starring Jagger. *Performance* was made first (in 1968) but released second.

NEEDFUL THINGS

(New Line, 1993) **D:** Fraser Heston **S:** W. D. Richter **P:** Jack Cummins

Max von Sydow is Leland Gaunt (the Devil), who opens an antique shop in Castle Rock, Maine, and plays people against each other. Eventually there's fighting in the streets and the town is on fire. This adaptation of Stephen King's 1991 novel has some good acting (especially Ed Harris as the sheriff), but it has too many subplots and makes little sense. As in other King-based movies, animals are mutilated. With J. T. Walsh as a corrupt local poli-

tician, Bonnie Bedelia, Amanda Plummer, Duncan Fraser, Valri Bromfield, and Lisa Blount (mostly cut out). This overlong (120-minute) Columbia release was shot in British Columbia.

NEGATIVES

(1968) **D:** Peter Medak **S:** Peter Everett, Roger Lowry **P:** Judd Bernard

Theo (Peter McEnery) and Vivien (Glenda Jackson) live together above an antique shop. They dress up and pretend to be the famous murderer Dr. Crippen and his mistress, Ethel La Neve. A German photographer (Diane Cilento) rents a room and throws their routine off balance by convincing Theo to "become" WWI flying ace Baron von Richtofen. He even has a plane on the roof. Jackson had been in only one film (*Marat/Sade*). Maurice Denham and Norman Rossington are also in this black comedy.

THE NEIGHBOR

(Academy, 1993) **D:** Rodney Gibbons **S:** Kurt Wimmer **P:** Tom Berry   Canada

Rod Steiger is Myron Hatch, a creepy, balding retired obstetrician who's renting his old house to a pregnant woman (Linda Kozlowski from *Crocodile Dundee*). Myron becomes her doctor, and she has bloody nightmares. He's always around, is creepy as he stares at (and drugs) her, and cries while he kills. Too bad Steiger sounds like he's playing W. C. Fields again! Flashbacks reveal that as a kid Myron was a psycho ventriloquist and baby killer. Ron Lea is the dimwit husband. This disturbing but absurd film was made in Quebec. The executive producer was Pierre David.

NEIGHBORS

(RCA/Columbia, 1981) **D:** John G. Avildsen **S:** Larry Gelbart **P:** Richard D. Zanuck, David Brown

Vic and Ramona (Dan Aykroyd and Cathy Moriarty) are the out-of-control new neighbors who torment bourgeois suburbanites John Belushi and Kathryn Walker. This was a big flop. Belushi died, and Moriarty (*Raging Bull*) didn't work for years afterward. The movie was based on Thomas Berger's novel.

NEKROMANTIK

(Film Threat, 1987) **D/S:** Jorge Buttgereit **S:** Franz Rodenkirchen **P:** Manfred O. Jelinski   W. Germany

Rob (Daktari Lorenz) works for Joe's street-cleaning agency, cleaning up after accidents on the Autobahn. He starts taking body parts home, then a whole rotten corpse. His girlfriend, Betty (Beatrice M.), bathes in blood and gets into it so much that she leaves with the corpse, her new lover. Rob loses his job and goes to a gore movie at the Xenon (a very old West Berlin revival theater where the young director was a projectionist). He tries to make it with a hooker in a cemetery but kills her (and the caretaker). This 71-minute film has a great ending, but despite its gross-out cult reputation it doesn't have good enough FX.

NEKROMANTIK II: DIE RÜCKER DER LIEBEN TOTEN

(Film Threat, 1989) **D/S:** Jorge Buttgereit **S:** Franz Rodenkirchen **P:** Manfred O. Jelinski   Germany

Monika M. stars as a blond necro who digs up stiffs while in her high heels. When the corpses rot too much she cuts them up for disposal but keeps the penises in the fridge. She also dates the live Mark Reedek and works doing voiceovers for porno movies. The budget was slightly higher this time, and there's even a dream sequence. In 1992 a Berlin court ruled that the negative and all promotional materials had to be destroyed (!) because the film "propagates violence." The episodic *Der Todskind* (1990) and a behind-the-scenes documentary called *Corpse Fucking Art* (1992) are also available.

NEMESIS

(Imperial, 1992) **D:** Albert Pyun **S:** Rebecca Charles **P:** Ash R. Shaw, Eric Karson, Tom Karnowski

Olivier Gruner (*Angel Town*) stars as a futuristic part-cyborg fighting cop with an identity crisis in a dismal post-nuke 2020. He's drugged, a bomb is planted in his heart, then he's forced (by Brion James and Tim Thomerson) to go to Baja, Rio, and Java. Later lots of time is spent on gun battles (often with female terrorists), and Deborah Shelton has a nude sex-then-fight scene. Thomerson becomes an animated metal skeleton. A female narrator tries to make sense of it all. With Merle Kennedy as a petite fighter, Cary-Hiroyuki Tagawa, Nicholas Guest, and Jackie Earle Haley. This theatrical release copies *Blade Runner, Terminator, Robocop,* etc. It has Bernard Herrmann–inspired music and was filmed in Hawaii (where the director is from). Sequels (also by Pyun) followed.

NEMO

(1984) **D/S:** Arnaud de Selignac **S:** Jean-Pierre Esquenazi, Telshe Boorman **P:** John Boorman, Claude Nedjar   France/UK

An adolescent Nemo (Jason Connery) in NYC takes an elevator that contunues to the center of the earth, then into outer space. He finds the *Nautilus* in a dream world and rescues a princess (Mathilda May) from the masked villain, Mr. Legend (Harvey Keitel!). This fantasy, based on Jules Verne's *Twenty Thousand Leagues Under the Sea*, is by a 26-year-old first-time director. The cast also includes Nipsey Russell (in two roles), Carole Bouquet, Katrine Boorman, and Charley Boorman. Columbia was going to release it in America (as *Dream One*) but didn't.

NEON CITY

(Vidmark, 1991) **D/S/A:** Monte Markham **S:** Buck Finch, Jeff Negun **P:** Wolf Schmidt

In the bleak, snow-covered wasteland of 2053, Stark (Michael Ironside) takes a "red star" (Vanity) to Neon City for "credits." The perilous trip in an old truck (driven by Lyle Alzado) takes a group of various desperate characters through dangerous territory where people with burned faces wait to die. Richard Sanders (from the TV series *WKRP*) sells poison to people for quick suicides. Basically a remake of *Stagecoach*, this is worth watching but is one of the bleakest post-nuke movies around. It's a relief when the expected action/chase scene finally takes place and when they arrive in the economical "city." With Valerie Wildman, Nick Klar, and Juliet Landau. It was filmed at the same Salt Lake City locations as *Carnival of Souls*.

Lyle Alzado, Vanity, and Michael Ironside in *Neon City*.

NEON MANIACS

(Lightning, 1985) **D:** Joseph Mangine
S: Mark Patrick Carducci **P:** Steven Mackler, Chris Arnold

Armed, rubbery "monsters" (biker, samurai, soldier, etc.) from under the Golden Gate Bridge kill high-school students in San Francisco. Water pistols kill them. The cast includes Marta Kober and Allan Hayes. The soundtrack, featuring various artists, is on Easy Street.

NERDS OF A FEATHER

(1992) **D/S/A:** Mario Romeo Milano **D:** Gary Graver

A couple (Mario Romeo Milano and Kathleen Kichta) working as nursing-home orderlies in Venice, California, become involved with a mad professor and midget Russian spies who are after a secret formula. This dumb comedy features Anya Karin, Pat McCormick, Charles Pierce as Grandma, and Charles Dierkop as a biker. Troma released it.

NERO

(VSOM, 1992) **D/S:** Giancarlo Soldi **S:** Tiziano Sclavi **P:** Giovanna Romagnoli   Italy

This offbeat gore comedy with surreal touches was written by the author of the Italian comic strip *Dylan Dog*. Sergio Castellitto thinks his girlfriend (Chiara Caselli, from *My Own Private Idaho*) is a murderess. Claudio Argento was the executive producer. The music is by Mau Mau.

THE NEST

(MGM/UA, 1988) **D:** Terence H. Winkless
S: Robert King **P:** Julie Corman

A resort town on a Washington State island is threatened by giant cannibal roaches. They evolve and become what they eat, so we get a cat/roach, a man/roach, etc. Corrupt mayor Robert Lansing becomes a man/roach and attacks his daughter (Lisa Langlois). With Franc Luz and Terri Treas. Parts of this copy *The Fly* and other 80s movies, but it would make a good double bill with *Bug* (1975).

DAS NET

(1976) **D/S:** Manfred Purzer **P:** Luggi Waldleitner   W. Germany

Mel Ferrer stars in this movie about a psycho killer and an aging writer, with Klaus Kinski, Elke Sommer, Heinz Bennent, and Andrea Rau. It was filmed in English.

NETHERWORLD

(Paramount, 1991)
D/A: David Schmoeller **S:** Billy Chicago **P:** Thomas Bradford

Michael Bendetti (from *21 Jump Street*) arrives at his late father's old southern mansion, run by a housekeeper (Anjanette Comer, from *The Baby*) who has an underage blond daughter. People warn him about the local roadhouse, where the hookers are really witches (and Edgar Winter is in the house band!). In a scene copied directly from the Phantasm movies, a statue hand comes to life, zooms through the air, and embeds itself in (obvious dummy) heads. Most of it is silly, confusing, or boring, but you can tell it's by David Schmoeller (*Tourist Trap, Crawlspace,* etc.). The movie is bird-obsessed, the "tonk" is atmospheric, and the grounds of the mansion are beautiful. I'd like to live there. Moonstone released the soundtrack by David Byran (of Bon Jovi). At the time Full Moon threatened to release one tape a month (!), and unfortunately they did.

NEVADA HEAT : *See* FAKE-OUT

THE NEVERENDING STORY

(Warner, 1984) **D/S:** Wolfgang Petersen
S: Herman Weigel **P:** Bernd Eichmon, Dieter Geissler   W. Germany/UK

A young boy (Barret Oliver) becomes part of the book he's reading. In the empire of Fantasia a disease makes people forget hopes and dreams, and lots of furry creatures, flying dogs, talking rocks and other (childish-looking) special effects appear. The director of *Das Boot* filmed this PG kids' movie in Canada and in Munich studios, but it's set in an American town. It cost a record (outside the US and the USSR) $27 million and has ILM FX. With Moses Gunn and Gerald McRaney. Michael Ende, whose novel the film is based on, had his name removed. Sequels followed.

NEVERENDING STORY II: THE NEXT CHAPTER

(Paramount, 1990) **D:** George Miller **S:** Karin Howard **P:** Dieter Geissler   US/Germany

This PG fantasy about saving a child empress has a different cast but the same creatures as the first film. Jonathan Brandis stars as the same kid. It was filmed in Munich studios, Canada, Argentina, France, and Italy. Mark Damon was the executive producer. *Neverending Story III* followed (1994).

NEVER ON TUESDAY

(Paramount, 1987) **D/S:** Adam Rifkin
P: Brad Wyman, Lionel Wigram

Claudia Christian is in a car crash with some guys in another car (Andrew Lauer and Peter Berg). They're all stranded, and she tells them she's a lesbian. Gilbert Gottfried, Charlie Sheen, Emilio Estevez, and Judd Nelson play in small roles. The director later made *The Dark Backwards*.

NEVER PICK UP A STRANGER

(IVE, 1979) **D:** Joseph Bigwood **S:** Robert Jahn
P: Joseph Zito, Alan A. Braverman   (*Blood Rage*)

A shy voyeur psycho (Ian Scott) narrates while he kills hookers in NYC. Lawrence Tierney plays a cop.

NEVER SAY NEVER AGAIN

(Warner, 1983) **D:** Irvin Kershner **S:** Lorenzo Semple Jr. **P:** Jack Schwartzman

In 1983 there were two Bonds to choose from. Sean Connery returned after 12 years in this *Thunderball* remake. It was a lot better than *Octopussy* but not up to the 60s features. Klaus Maria Brandauer is a high point as Largo, who steals two nuclear-armed cruise missiles. Barbara Carrera is Fatima Blush, and Kim Basinger is Largo's mistress, Domino. The role (and her *Playboy* layout) took her from obscurity to stardom. With Max von Sydow, Bernie Casey as Felix Leitner, and Edward Fox as M. It was a Taliafilm (backed by Talia Shire) and unfortunately lost money. Roger Moore (who is three years older than Connery, by the way) played the role only once more (in *A View to a Kill*).

NEVER TAKE CANDY FROM A STRANGER

(Sinister, 1960) **D:** Cyril Frankel **S:** John Hunter
P: Anthony Hinds   UK (*The Molester; Never Take Sweets from a Stranger*)

Hammer made this b/w drama about a wealthy, senile psycho (Felix Aylmer) in a Canadian town. He's been in a mental hospital for molesting young girls, but his actions are covered up by his son. A new high-school principal (Patrick Allen) presses charges because of what his daughter tells him. With Niall MacGinnis and Gwen Watford. The tape is letterboxed.

NEVER THE TWAIN

(1974) **D:** Frank M. "Brad" Grinter **S:** Manny Dietz
P: George M. Souter, Herbert R. Benton

Ed Trostle (in real life a Mark Twain impersonator) claims that the spirit of Twain has taken him over while he's been doing his stage show at a nudist colony. His wife (Kathy Weldon) calls in Richard Webb (star of the *Captain Midnight* TV show) to battle the spirit. This rare R-rated film is basically a filmed stage play. It's by the maker of *Blood Freak*.

NEVER TOO LATE TO MEND

(Sinister, 1937) **D:** David MacDonald **P:** George King   UK (*It's Never Too Late to Mend*)

Squire Meadows (Tod Slaughter) runs a prison. He frames Jack Livesey so that he can have his fiancée (Marjorie Taylor). The prisoners, his "children," are tortured, whipped, and thrown into "the black hole" by the mad squire. This melodrama had been filmed twice before as silent features.

NEVER TOO YOUNG TO DIE

(Charter, 1986) **D/S:** Gil Bettman **S/P:** Steven Paul **S:** Lorenzo Semple Jr., Anton Fritz

John Stamos is the son of a James Bond–type secret agent (George Lazenby) who is killed. The high-school gymnast teams with a spy (Vanity) to save Los Angeles. Gene Simmons is Velvet Von Ragner, a psychotic hermaphrodite who's trying to poison the LA water supply. He sings too. This spoof borrows from *Road Warrior, The Rocky Horror Picture Show*, and other films. With Peter Kwong, Robert Englund, and Tara Buckman.

THE NEW ADVENTURES OF PIPPI LONGSTOCKING

(RCA, 1988) **D/S/P:** Ken Annakin **P:** Gary Mehlman, Walter Moshay

Astrid Lindgren's books have been favorites of girls for years. Tami Erin stars as the anarchistic tomboy with pigtails who has fantastic adventures, in this G-rated adaptation with music. With Eileen Brennan, George DiCenzo, and Dick Van Patten. Fans should search for the four Swedish/German Pippi movies produced in 1969, which played early-70s American kiddie matinees. Inger Nilsson starred in them.

NEW ADVENTURES OF TARZAN

(Video Dimensions, Sinister, 1935) **D:** Edward Kull, Wilbur McGaugh **S:** Charles F. Royal **P:** George W. Stout, Ben S. Cohen, Ashton Dearholt, Edgar Rice Burroughs

Edgar Rice Burroughs personally supervised this 12-chapter serial backed by his own company. It was the first Tarzan movie filmed on location (under nearly impossible conditions in Guatemala). Olympic decathalon champ Herman Brix (later Bruce Bennett) stars as Tarzan, who speaks perfect English (just as he does in the books). Ula Holt costars, with Jiggs the chimp. Tarzan goes to South America, finds a lost city (real Maya ruins) ruled by "the green goddess," and fights spies. It was released by Republic as a serial and as two features (*Tarzan's New Adventure* and *Tarzan and the Green Goddess*). Feature versions are also available on video.

THE NEW BARBARIANS: *See* WARRIORS OF THE WASTELAND

NEW EDEN

(MCA, 1994) **D:** Alan Metzger **S:** Dan Gordon **P:** Harvey Frand

Stephen Baldwin (who says, "I'm not much of an entertainer") is an engineer who is left on a post-nuke planet. He becomes a slave for a while, trains with a warrior (Tobin Bell), and falls for a "Scav" (Lisa Bonet) with a "cute" kid. He helps her peaceful tribe irrigate and purify the desert. Another prisoner (Michael Bowen) joins the bad sand pirates. Since each tribe has one black female, the bad one (Janet Hubert Whitten, who has a whip), and the good one (Bonet) end up fighting with swords. Nicholas Worth is in one scene. It's rated R but looks like a PG.

THE NEW GLADIATORS

(Media, 1983) **D/S/A:** Lucio Fulci **S:** Elisa Briganti, Dardano Sacchetti, Cesare Frugoni   Italy (*Rome 2072; The New Gladiators; 2020 New Barbarians*)

A futuristic human (actually a computer) runs rival TV networks that air violent gladiatorial death-games starring prisoners. Broadcasts are shown on giant outdoor screens. Jared Martin, Fred Williamson, Al Cliver, and Haruiko Yamanouchi are on the same team. The plot is nearly the same as *The Running Man*, which came out later (1987).

THE NEW INVISIBLE MAN

(Sinister, 1957) **D/S:** Alfredo Crevenna **P:** Guillermo Calderón Stell   Mexico (*El Hombre Que Logro Ser Invisible*)

The plot of this is the same as *The Invisible Man Returns* (1940). Arturo de Cordova is framed for a murder, becomes invisible in jail, and escapes, seeking revenge. He goes mad in the end and threatens to poison the city's water supply. With Ana Luisa Peluffo and Augusto Benedico.

NEW JACK CITY

(Warner, 1991) **D/A:** Mario Van Peebles **S:** Thomas Lee Wright **P:** Doug McHenry, George Jackson

Exactly 20 years after *Sweet Sweetback's Baadasssss Song*, its director's son made the highest-grossing black-cast film ever (up to that time). The story starts in 1986 and looks at drug dealing as a profitable business. Wesley Snipes stars as a drug lord (partially copied from the real-life Nicky Barnes) who has a whole factory/fortress for his lucrative NYC crack business. Ice T (very good in a serious role) and Judd Nelson are cops who report to Detective Stone (Mario Van Peebles). With Chris Rock, Russell Wong, Bill Nunn, John Aprea, Tracy Camilla Johns (*She's Gotta Have It*), the other Vanessa Williams, Thalmus Rasulala (in his last feature), and Eeek-a-Mouse. It was filmed in Harlem and the Bronx and makes good use of Marvin Gaye's "Inner City Blues." There's a *Sweet Sweetback* film clip. The movie sparked a predictable controversy over theater violence.

THE NEW KIDS

(RCA/Columbia, 1984) **D/P:** Sean S. Cunningham **S:** Stephen Gyllenhaal **P:** Andrew Fogelson

Lori Loughlin and Shannon Presby star as an orphaned sister and brother at Santa Funland, their uncle's run-down Florida amusement park. They're terrorized by a gang, and characters die by electrocution, decapitation, and falling off the ferris wheel. Novelist Harry Crews reportedly contributed "the authentic swamp-trash dialogue." With James Spader as the main bully and Eric Stoltz (who both went on to much bigger features) and John Philbin. This PG film was shot in Florida.

THE NEWLYDEADS

(City Lights, 1987) **D/S/P:** Josepeh Merhi **S:** Sean Dash **P:** Richard Pepin

A lakeside-resort motel owner kills a transvestite. The spirit of "the cross-dress killer" returns 15 years later and murders honeymoon couples. There are decapitations and an exorcism. With Jim Williams, Jay Richardson, Roxanne Michaels, and Captain Mike.

NEW YORK NIGHTS

(VSOM, 1980) **D:** Simon Nuchtern **S/P:** Romano Vanderbes

This exploitation version of the much-filmed play *La Ronde* is told in nine interlocking segments. It was good for some laughs on 42nd Street. Corinne Alphen (Wahl) is top billed, with Marcia McBroom (*Beyond the Valley of the Dolls*) and Willem Dafoe as "the punk boyfriend." Rod Stewart's "Passion" is on the soundtrack. The director also made *Silent Madness* in NYC.

NEW YORK NIGHTS

(York, 1994) **D:** Ernest G. Saver **S:** Mike McDonald **P:** Gary P. Connor

A trio of women from various places end up sharing the same luxury apartment in NYC while looking for rich men. Marilyn Chambers stars in this sex comedy, with Julia (claims to be Dolly's cousin) Parton and *Penthouse* Pet Susan Napoli. It's available unrated or in the R-rated version I fast-forwarded through. This and other lame Chambers features (*Party Incorporated, Breakfast in Bed, The Marilyn Diaries,* etc.) frequently show up on cable.

NEW YORK RIPPER

(Vidmark, 1982) **D/S:** Lucio Fulci **S:** Gianfranco Clerici, Dardano Sacchetti, Vincenzo Mannino **P:** Abrizio De Angeli   Italy (*Lo Squartatore di New York*)

A detective (Jack Hedley) is after a slasher who kills "loose" women in NYC and talks with a Donald Duck voice. This gory feature with scenes in a sex club was cut in America. With Alexandra Delli Colli and Andrea Occhipinti.

NEXT DOOR

(1994) **D:** Tony Bill **S:** Barney Cohen **P:** Jay Benson

It's a cultured college professor (James Woods) and his teacher wife (Kate Capshaw) and son vs. their new suburban neighbors, a beer drinking butcher (Randy Quaid), his wife (Lucinda Dickey), and son. The feud in this black comedy involves killing dogs and torture. The music is by Van Dyke Parks. A Showtime debut.

THE NEXT KARATE KID

(Columbia, 1994) **D:** Christopher Cain
S: Mark Lee **P:** Jerry Weintraub

John Avildsen made three *Karate Kid* movies in the 80s, all with Ralph Maccio as the kid and Pat Morita as his karate instructor, Mr. Miyagi. This time Morita teaches a teen orphan (Hilary Swank) to defend herself at her Boston high school. Michael Ironside is her evil gym teacher, Chris Conrad is her boyfriend, Constance Towers (from 60s Sam Fuller movies) is her grandmother, and there's a group of fun-loving monks. It's rated PG.

NEXT OF KIN

(Media, 1982) **D/S:** Tony Williams **S:** Michael Heath
P: Robert Letet   Australia/New Zealand

Linda (Jackie Kern, who looks sorta like Nastassja Kinski) inherits her mother's retirement home, which seems to be haunted. Her mother's diary describes "the evil in this house." Lots of characters are killed, and in one of the dream sequences a (very real-looking) dead old man shows up floating outside a window! There's an effective Klaus Schulze score, excellent cinematography, and an action-packed, explosive ending. Although slow and moody (parts resemble *The Shining*), it includes an eyeball stabbing, a head blown off, and other suprises. This little-known scary movie was filmed in New Zealand and New South Wales.

NEXT OF KIN

(Warner, 1988) **D:** John Irvin **S:** Michael Jenning **P:** Les Alexander **M:** Jack Nitzsche

Patrick Swayze (with a ponytail) stars as a Chicago cop named Truman Gates. A Mafia hitman (Adam Baldwin) working in the juke-box racket kills his brother (Bill Paxton). Another brother (Liam Neeson), a deer hunter, arrives from Kentucky seeking vengeance, and eventually the whole clan battles the gangsters using crossbows, hatchets, and snakes! The climactic action sequence takes place in a cemetery. With Helen Hunt, Michael J. Pollard, Ted Levine, Andreas Katsulas, Ben Stiller, and Del Close.

THE NEXT ONE

(Vestron, 1981) **D/S:** Nico Mastorakis   US/Greece

Adrienne Barbeau lives on a Greek island with her son (Jeremy Licht). She falls for a Christlike stranger (Keir Dullea) from the future. Mastorakis coproduced *The Greek Tycoon* (1978), about Aristotle Onassis.

NEXT VICTIM

(Thriller, 1974) **D:** James Ormerod
S: Brian Clemens **P:** Ian Fordyce

Wheelchair-bound Carroll Baker lives alone in an apartment in a nearly deserted building. She lets a repairman in. He turns out to be a psycho strangler. This BBC-TV movie was videotaped. It has music by Laurie Johnson.

THE NEXT VICTIM (1970): *See* BLADE OF THE RIPPER

NICE GIRLS DON'T EXPLODE

(Starmaker, 1987) **D:** Chuck Martinez
S: Paul Harris **P:** Doug Curtis, John Wells

Michelle Meyrink stars as a telekinetic teen who starts fires when she gets aroused. Barbara Harris is her mom, who has the same power. With William O'Leary and Wallace Shawn. This comedy from New World was shot in Lawrence, Kansas.

NICK KNIGHT

(CBS, 1989) **D:** Farhad Mann **S:** James D. Parriot **P:** S. Michael Formica

New World produced this CBS-TV series pilot. Rick Springfield is a good-guy vampire who's a cop in San Francisco. Michael Nader is a killer vampire. They both fly around and fight, and "Papa Oom Mow Mow" is heard on the soundtrack. With Laura Johnson, Cec Verrell, and Irene Miracle. It's on video in Europe as *Midnight Cop*. The idea was later reused for the CBS (later USA Network) series *Forever Knight*, with a different cast.

NIGHT ANGEL

(Fries, 1989) **D:** Dominique Othenin-Girard
S: Walter Josten **S/P:** Joe Augustyn

A lot of things about this movie are painfully dumb, but it's still one of the best recent erotic horror movies, and many of the scenes and effects are excellent and surprising. Isa Anderson stars as Lilith, a winged female demon who rises from the earth and goes about killing off the male staff of a hip fashion magazine *Siren*. In her sexy human form she has black hair, nails, and (sometimes) lips. Karen Black as Rita, an editor who is seduced into worshipping the demon, mainly seems to want to be a cover girl. The gorgeous Debra Feuer is Kristie, Rita's sister from Milwaukee. There's a great Hell sequence, an old black lady (Helen Martin) in a yellow cab who's a Van Helsing type ("She is Satan's whore!"), Cronenberg-inspired sex zombies in the office (turned on by photos!), hearts ripped out, photos that come to life, good dreams, and plenty of nudity and sex. Some of the music is by Barrence Whitfield and the Savages, and there's a great new song by Screamin' Jay Hawkins, "Siren's Burning." Roscoe Lee Browne is the narrator. With Susie Sparks and Gary Hudson. The Swiss-born director also made *After Darkness* (1985), with Julian Sands, and *Halloween 5*.

NIGHT BEAST

(Paragon, 1982) **D/S/P/E:** Don Dohler

An alien with a laser weapon decapitates and tears up locals in backwoods Maryland. The low-budget alien (played by two people in a suit) is pretty scary-looking, and there's some nudity and gore. Tom Griffith as a sheriff, George Stover as a doctor, and Don Liefert are in this movie, which was later picked up by Troma.

NIGHTBREAKER

(1989) **D:** Peter Markle **S:** T. S. Cook **P:** William R. Greenblatt

Emilio Estevez plays an army psychiatrist stationed in Nevada during the 50s, when the US government exposed soldiers to atomic tests. Martin Sheen (an executive producer) plays the same character today. With Lea Thompson, Melinda Dillon, Nicholas Pryor, Joe Pantoliano, and James Marshall. This is an adaptation of Howard Rosenberg's novel *Atomic Soldiers*, which is based on real events. Screenwriter T. S. Cook also wrote *The China Syndrome*. This was made for TNT.

NIGHT BREED

(Media, 1990) **D/S:** Clive Barker **P:** Gabriella Martinelli **M:** Danny Elfman

Craig Sheffer is a Canadian teen who's accused of being a serial killer. He's under the care of a doctor (David Cronenberg) who is the real killer. Cronenberg has a great mask, but he should stick to directing. The confused young hero escapes to the secret, underground world of Midian, below a cemetery, where good monsters dwell. Lots of interesting monsters were created (people in makeup), but the movie, based on Clive Barker's

Isa Anderson as the *Night Angel*.

novel *Cabal,* just doesn't work. It was cut for an R rating, and Suzi Quatro was cut out altogether. With Anne Bobby, Charles Haid, Catherine Chevalier, Doug Bradley, and John Agar as the gas-station owner. The score is on MCA.

THE NIGHT BRINGS CHARLIE

(Quest Entertainment, 1990) **D:** Tom Logan
S: Bruce Carson **P:** Wally Parks, Paul Stubenrach

This one's a dumb, small-town-slasher movie filled with false scares and inane plot twists (and a nude shower scene). After a number of unsolved gore murders local girls plan a slumber party. Charlie is a big, mute Nam vet with a limp, goggles, and power tools. Maybe it's a comedy. It was filmed in Orlando.

NIGHT CALL NURSES

(VGB, 1972) **D:** Jonathan Kaplan **D/S:** George Armitage **P:** Julie Corman   (*Young LA Nurses II*)

Alana Collins (Stewart) stars as a blond nurse who falls for a speed-freak truck driver. Mittie Lawrence is a nurse who becomes a black activist after she finds out what goes on in "the suicide ward." Patti Byrne falls for a hippie encounter-group leader. With Dixie Lee Peabody (star of *Bury Me an Angel*), Lynne Guthrie, and Dick Miller. It was the first by the NYC student director and was part of New World's nurse series.

NIGHT CHASE

(1970) **D:** Jack Starrett **S:** Marvin A. Gluck **P:** Collier Young

David Janssen is a rich man who flees to Mexico in a cab driven by Yaphet Kotto after his wife is murdered. With Victoria Vetri, Elisha Cook Jr., and Richard Romanus. This CBS-TV movie was made the same year as Jack Starrett's *The Losers.*

NIGHT CHILDREN

(Vidmark, 1989) **D/S/P:** Norbert Meisel

David Carradine is Max, a uniformed Hollywood cop who loves a probation officer (Nancy Kwan). It's interesting that both of them made martial-arts instructional tapes and hawked them on TV after this movie was made, but anyway, this is about horrible, cop-killing punks (including Griffin O'Neal and Tawny Fere) with "anarchy" painted on their jackets. They kill at least four cops and steal a police car. No big deal. Kwan gets punched after kneeing a bad punk in the crotch. At one point they tie up Carradine, put a pig sign around his neck, and make him play Russian roulette. It's pretty ridiculous.

NIGHT CRIES

(VCL, 1978) **D:** Richard Lang
S: Brian Tagert **P:** David Manson

Susan St. James receives messages from her dead baby. This ABC-TV movie features Michael Parks as her husband, William Conrad, Cathleen Nesbitt, and Dolores Dorn.

NIGHT EYES

(Prism, 1989) **D:** Jag Mundhra **P:** Ashok Amritraj

Andrew Stevens stars as a surveillance expert hired to spy on Tanya Roberts, who runs an art gallery and is married to an obnoxious, long-haired has-been rock star. It's all some kind of set-up. This *Body Heat* copy features some videotaped sex. Roberts drips candle wax onto Stevens, and then they have (near-X) sex in the shower. A cut TV version is called *Hidden View.* R and unrated tapes are available.

NIGHT EYES II

(Prism, 1991) **D:** Rodney McDonald
S: Simon Louis Ward **P:** Ashok Amritraj

Andrew Stevens returns as a security guard who gets involved with another set-up, another married woman (Shannon Tweed), and more videotaped sex. Her husband is a wealthy South American diplomat. The most explicit sex scene features Stevens' black partner (Tim Russ), who later (surprise!) is killed. Stevens also wrote the story and was the supervising producer. It's available R or unrated but is pretty boring either way.

NIGHT EYES III

(Prism, 1993) **D/S/A:** Andrew Stevens
S: Michael Potts **P:** Ashok Amritraj

It's Andrew Stevens as Will again, and Shannon Tweed again as a different character. This time she's the star of a TV cop series whom he's protecting between sex scenes. Shannon's real-life sister Tracy Tweed costars and has nude scenes too. Also with Monique Parent. It's available in R and unrated versions.

NIGHTFALL

(1957) **D:** Jacques Tourneur **S:** Sterling Silliphant **P:** Ted Richmond

Aldo Ray stars as a man framed for a murder and pursued by the real killers, in this adaptation of a David Goodis novel. Ray relates his flashbacks. Brian Keith and Anne Bancroft costar, with James Gregory, Jocelyn Brando, and Frank Albertson. The director's next film was the classic *Curse of the Demon.*

NIGHTFALL

(MGM/UA, 1988) **D/S:** Paul Mayersberg
P: Julie Corman

Nightfall occurs only every 1000 years on a world with three suns. Paul Mayersberg, who wrote the script of *The Man Who Fell to Earth,* made this talky, slow, PG-13 adaptation of Isaac Asimov's short story. David Birney stars, with Sarah Douglas, Starr Andreeff, Andra Millian, and Alexis Kanner. It was filmed in Arizona. From Concorde.

NIGHTFIRE

(Triboro, 1994) **D/P:** Mike Sedan
S: Catherine Tavel, Helen Haxton

Shannon Tweed is a businesswoman who is unhappily married to John Laughlin. They live on a remote ranch. He hires a swinging couple (Rochelle Swanson and Martin Hewitt) to turn her on, but they have sadistic ideas. It's available in R and unrated versions.

NIGHTFLYERS

(IVE, 1987) **D:** "T. C. Blake"/Robert Collector
S/P: Robert Jaffe **M:** Doug Timm

An evil brain in a smoky old rented spaceship tries to kill scientists, and a laser decapitates people. This film is based on a George R. R. Martin book but copies *Alien.* With Catherine Mary Stewart, Michael Praed, Lisa Blount, and Michael Des Barres. It's by the director of *Red Heat.* The soundtrack is on Varèse Sarabande.

NIGHTFORCE

(Lightning, 1986) **D/S:** Lawrence D. Foldes
P: Victoria Paige Meyerink

The stars of *Roller Boogie* return! Linda Blair and her frat buddies go to Central America to rescue a friend kept in a bamboo cage by terrorists. James Van Patten costars, and Richard Lynch is a helpful, flute-playing Nam vet with a pet monkey. With Cameron Mitchell as a senator, Chad McQueen (son of Steve McQueen), and Kathleen Kinmont. Claudia Udy is the one who is kidnapped and has the nude scenes. It's by the director of *Nightstalker* (1979).

NIGHT FRIGHT

(Sinister, 1967) **D:** James A. Sullivan **P:** Wallace Clyde Jr.

The monster in this movie must be related to *Robot Monster.* It's a gorilla with three-toed footprints and an alien head. We don't see much of it, but we do see a lot of John Agar as Clint Crawford, sheriff of Holliston, Texas. Overage sorority girls are being killed in Satan's Hollow, but he gets angry at them: "Look, punk. Don't ever call me fuzz!" The monster is the result of a NASA experiment gone wrong. The Wildcats provide cool instrumental music, and the kids wear V-neck sweaters and white boots. It was directed (near Dallas) by Larry Buchanan's assistant director on *Zontar* and *Curse of the Swamp Creature* (both with Agar), and it's a remake (!) of the obscure Russ Marker movie *The Demon from Devil's Lake* (1964). Marker is even in it, and Bill Thurman is the deputy. It's called *The Extraterrestrial Nasty* (!) in England and doesn't seem to have been released anywhere until video came along.

NIGHT GAME

(HBO, 1989) **D:** Peter Masterson **S:** Spencer Eastman, Anthony Palmer **P:** George Litto **M:** Pino Donaggio

In Galveston, Texas, a police detective (Roy Scheider) tracks a psycho who kills blondes with a hook. A Houston Astros pitcher is the main suspect. It was advertised as a slasher movie, and there's a death in a house-of-mirrors sequence, but nothing much is shown. With Karen Young as the cop's reporter girlfriend, Paul Gleason, and Lane Smith. It's from TWE.

NIGHT GAMES

(VSOM, 1980) **D:** Roger Vadim **S:** Anton Diether, Clarke Reynolds **P:** André Morgan, Roger Lewis

Cindy Pickett has erotic fantasies and nightmares (due to a childhood rape). She has sex with a man in a bird suit. Pickett and Joanna Cassidy have nude scenes, but nobody bothered to see this sex fantasy when it was first released. Raymond Chow was the executive producer. Golden Harvest, a Hong Kong production company, made it in the US. With Gene Davis, Paul Jenkins, and Barry Primus. The Avco Embassy release was the last feature for Roger Vadim until he remade his own 1956 film *And God Created Woman* in 1987.

THE NIGHT HAS EYES

(Sinister, 1942) **D/S:** Leslie Arliss
S/P: John Argyle   UK (*Terror House*)

A shell-shocked composer (James Mason) living in a Scottish mansion thinks he's a werewolf killing on the moors during the full moon. It's all a frame-up (just like the one in the later *Daughter of Dr. Jekyll*). With Joyce Howard as a schoolteacher who loves him, Tucker McGuire as her friend, Wilfred Lawson, and Mary Clare.

NIGHTHAWKS

(MCA, 1981) **D:** Bruce Malmuth
S: David Shabeer **P:** Martin Poll

Sylvester Stallone stars in one of his best movies as a NYC cop. His partner is played by Billy Dee Williams. They're assigned to stop a terrorist named Wulfar (Rutger Hauer, in his first American film) who has had plastic surgery to disguise his face. Scenes take place on the subway, in a disco, and in the cable car to Roosevelt Island. With Lindsay Wagner, Persis Khambatta, Nigel Davenport, Joe Spinell (as a police lieutenant), Catherine Mary Stewart, and Jamie Gillis. Dick Smith did the makeup. MCA released the soundtrack by Keith Emerson. Some of the original rock songs by the Rolling Stones were replaced on the reissue tape.

A NIGHT IN PARADISE

(1946) **D:** Arthur Lubin **S:** Ernest Pascal **P:** Walter Wanger

Universal made this expensive comic adventure in Technicolor about the legendary storyteller Aesop (Turhan Bey). Merle Oberon stars as Princess Delarai, who's promised to the evil Croesus, ruler of the kingdom of Lydia (Thomas Gomez). Gail Sondergaard is Queen Attossa, a sorceress. With Ray Collins, George Dolenz, John Litel, Ernest Truex, Douglas Dumbrille, Marvin Miller, Jerome Cowan, and Julie London. Characters use modern-day (40s) slang. Universal's earlier costume adventures had starred Maria Montez.

NIGHT LIFE

(RCA/Columbia, 1989) **D:** David Acomba
S: Keith Critchlow **P:** Charles Lippincott

Scott Grimes (from the Critters movies) is Archie, a red-haired teen mortician working for his strict uncle (John Astin). Other kids harass him and call him things like "little corpse-fucker," but he has one friend, a beautiful tomboy mechanic named Charlie (Cheryl Pollak). When Archie and his uncle prepare a corpse and drain the blood, it's like watching a mondo movie. After a long time some of the hateful school jocks die in a car crash and somehow come back as zombies (who still enjoy sex), and this becomes a pretty exciting horror/action movie. Phil Proctor (from Firesign Theatre) is in a sitcom-style comic scene, and Anthony Geary shows up for a drunk scene. The FX are by Craig Reardon.

NIGHTLIFE

(MCA, 1989) **D/S:** Daniel Taplitz
S: Anne Beatts **P:** Robert T. Skodis

Maryam D'Abo and Ben Cross are vampires in modern day Mexico City. Keith Szarabajka, a doctor who owns the blood clinic she's haunting, falls in love with her. This horror comedy also features Glenn Shadix. It was shot in Mexico City and debuted on the USA Network.

NIGHT LIFE OF THE GODS

(1935) **D:** Lowell Sherman **S:** Barry Trivers **P:** Carl Laemmle Jr.

Alan Mowbray stars as an eccentric scientist who discovers how to turn people into statues (and vice versa) with a ray from a ring. Statues of eight Greek gods and goddesses are brought to life at the Metropolitan Museum of Art. With Florine McKinney, Peggy Shannon, Douglas Fowley, William Stage Boyd, and Irene Ware. The film is said to have excellent special effects by John P. Fulton and makeup by Jack Pierce. It's based on a novel by Thorne Smith, whose *Turnabout, Topper,* and *I Married a Witch* were also filmed. This "lost" Universal film exists in the UCLA archives.

NIGHTMARE

(1942) **D:** Tom Whelan **S:** Dwight Taylor

An American gambler (Brian Donlevy) breaks into the home of an English couple and discovers the body of the husband (Henry Daniell). He and the wife (Diana Barrymore) run from the police and from Nazi spies. Also with Gavin Muir, Hans Conried, and Arthur Shields. Universal released this as part of the original *Shock Theater* TV package.

NIGHTMARE

(1973) **D:** Kevin Billington **S:** George Kirgo
S/P: Robert Enders   UK (*Voices*)

David Hemmings is a writer, and Gayle Hunnicutt is his wife (in real life they were married at the time). She goes crazy after their son drowns and is in and out of an asylum. They go to an isolated country mansion, where she hallucinates and ghosts appear in a surprise *Carnival of Souls*–type of ending. It's based on a play by Richard Lortz.

NIGHTMARE

(New Horizons, 1992) **D:** John Pasquin
S: John Robert Bensink, Rick Husky
P: Graham Cottle   (*Don't Touch My Daughter*)

This PG-13 made-for-TV movie copies parts of *Cape Fear*. Jonathan Banks is a relentless, disgusting suspected child molester who threatens a divorced mom who teaches math (star Victoria Principal, who was also an executive producer). He had briefly kidnapped her 11-year old (Danielle Harris, from the Halloween sequels). A police lieutenant (Paul Sorvino) tries to help, but the system fails again, and mom confronts the psycho on her own. Also with Greg Henry and Christine Healey.

NIGHTMARE ASYLUM

(Cinema Home, 1992) **D/S/P/E/M/A:** Todd Sheets

A girl (Lori Hassel) finds herself trapped in a building (an actual amusement-park type of "haunted house" with horror props) where hyper psychos yell, fight, dance, sing, and dismember people. A mummy, a wolf man, and zombies show up, and there's lots of gore. There's no story, the acting is terrible, and nearly everyone has long bad haircuts, but at least something is always happening. One part is a re-creation of a *Texas Chainsaw Massacre* scene starring 6'4" Todd Sheets as the loud, talkative butcher. I liked the zombie in a giant rat trap. David DeCoteau was the executive producer.

NIGHTMARE AT 43 HILLCREST

(USA, 1974) **D/P:** Dan Curtis

Jim Hutton stars in this 68-minute videotaped TV movie, with Mariette Hartley and Peter Mark Richman, about a family whose home is mistakenly raided by the police. Dan Curtis was making lots of horror and suspense shows at the time.

NIGHTMARE AT NOON

(Republic, 1986) **D/S/P:** Nico Mastorakis
S: Kirk Ellis   (*Death Street USA*)

Residents of a small southwestern town start bleeding green and killing each other after drinking water contaminated by toxic chemicals used by albino scientist Brion James. This horror western stars Wings Hauser (just passing through) and Bo Hopkins (a hitchhiker) as the heroes who drink beer. With George Kennedy as the sheriff and Kimberly Beck.

NIGHTMARE CIRCUS = BARN OF THE NAKED DEAD

NIGHTMARE HOUSE = SCREAM, BABY, SCREAM

NIGHTMARE IN RED CHINA

(SW, 194?)   India

An American distributor took an Indian movie (filmed in English) about the civil war in China and spiced it up with some new scenes. After A-bomb explosion footage and some narration about the end of WWII we meet a friendly, heroic Indian doctor who is sent to China to aid the (anti-Communist) guerrillas there. His assistant turns out to be a woman in disguise, and they fall in love. Since it's an Indian feature, the story stops for traditional musical and dance sequences! Ambitious sets and miniatures are used, along with impressive location work. Most of the Chinese characters are unconvincingly played by Indian actors (American movies were cast the same way). It's all pretty interesting on many levels, even without the crude added "flashbacks" of Russian Commie doctors doing germ-warfare experiments and soldiers raping a nurse and bayonetting a priest!

NIGHTMARE IN THE SUN

(Ace, 1964) **D/P:** Marc Lawrence **S:** Ted Thomas, Fanya Lawrence **D/A:** John Derek

Ursula Andress picks up a hitchhiker (John Derek). They have an affair, which leads to murder and blackmail. Arthur O'Connell is her rich ranchowner husband, Aldo Ray is the devious sheriff, and Sammy Davis Jr. is a truck driver. With Keenan Wynn, John Marley, and Richard Jaeckel and Robert Duvall as motorcyclists. The same year Andress was in *Once Before I Die*, directed by and starring Derek, her husband at the time.

THE NIGHTMARE NEVER ENDS: *See* CATACLYSM

NIGHTMARE OF TERROR = DEMONS OF THE MIND

A NIGHTMARE ON ELM STREET

(Video Treasures, 1984) **D/S:** Wes Craven
P: Robert Shaye, Sarah Risher

Wes Craven created one of the most effective horror movies of the 80s (and the most popular character). Unlike in most of the sequels, the scarred, supernatural dream killer Freddy Krueger (Robert Englund) is mysterious and scary, and he doesn't wear out his welcome. The story centers on suburban schoolgirl Nancy Thompson (Heather Langenkamp), who's trying to stay awake to avoid the horrors in her dreams after a friend (Amanda Wyss) is killed. Her cop father (John Saxon) doesn't believe her, her divorced mother (Ronee Blakley) drinks, and her neighbor and would-be boyfriend (Johnny Depp) fails to protect her. The terrified girl (whose hair is turning gray) decides to stand up for herself and defeat Freddy. Craven used some great, clever shock ideas and effects (often borrowed from other films, including his own), and the teenagers are much more likable and convincing than usual. Parts of the production were rushed, and it suffers from a dumb ending, but it's no surprise that it caught on so fast and is still being copied. A scene from *The Evil Dead* is glimpsed on TV. The Charles Bernstein soundtrack is on Varèse Sarabande. New Line released the film.

A NIGHTMARE ON ELM STREET PART 2: FREDDY'S REVENGE

(Video Treasures, 1985) **D:** Jack Sholder
S: David Chaskin **P:** Robert Shaye, Sarah Risher **M:** Christopher Young

In the first sequel Jesse (Mark Patton), a boy living in the same house five years later is possessed by Freddy Krueger (Robert Englund). The concepts and ideas that worked in the first movie are thrown away here as the dream killer shows up at any time and makes wisecracks. The terrifying child killer quickly became a comic teen killer. The only thing that makes Part 2 memorable is the surprising gay theme concerning a gym coach (Marshall Bell) and an S&M bar. Meryl Streep lookalike Kim Myers is the girlfriend, and Clu Gulager and Hope Lange are the parents. Some of the FX are fun, but an exploding killer parakeet and an obvious toy-bus scene are awful. The soundtrack is on Varèse Sarabande. Jack Sholder made *Alone in the Dark* and *The Hidden*, also from New Line.

A NIGHTMARE ON ELM STREET 3: DREAM WARRIORS

(Video Treasures, 1987) **D/S:** Chuck Russell **S:** Wes Craven, Bruce Wagner, Frank Darabont **P:** Robert Shaye, Sarah Risher **M:** Angelo Badalamenti

Wes Craven returned to cowrite this sequel, which pretends part 2 didn't exist. It made more money than the first two movies and made more entries a sure thing. A more grown-up Nancy (Heather Langenkamp) returns as the therapist of seven troubled teens in the psycho ward of a mental hospital. Freddy Krueger (Robert Englund) makes kids kill themselves, and Nancy teaches them how to defend themselves. John Saxon also returns as her cop dad. It's got lots of surprising effects and even some stop-motion animation. Krueger is revealed to be "the bastard son of a thousand maniacs" (!?). With Craig Wasson, Patricia Arquette, Priscilla Pointer, Bradley Gregg, Laurence (Larry) Fishburne, Jennifer Rubin, and Brooke Bundy. Dick Cavett and Zsa Zsa Gabor play themselves on TV. The tape includes a tie-in video by Dokken. The soundtrack is on Varèse Sarabande. The director also made the remake of *The Blob*.

A NIGHTMARE ON ELM STREET 4: THE DREAM MASTER

(Video Treasures, 1988) **D:** Renny Harlin **S:** Brian Helgeland, Scott Pierce **P:** Robert Shaye, Rachel Talalay

By this time these movies just tried to top the previous entries with more gags and special effects. Each made more money than the previous one, and this was the biggest box-office hit of them all. Lisa Wilcox stars as Alice, working at an old-fashioned soda fountain, and three surviving teens from the third movie are killed off. Screaming Mad George and Steve Johnson created many of the imaginative but silly FX. Also with Andras Jones, Rodney Eastman, Ken Sagoes, Brooke Bundy, Hope Marie Carlton, Robert Shaye, and Linnea Quigley as a lost soul on Freddy's chest. One nightmare sequence is repeated (a good idea), and clips from *Kronos* and *Reefer Madness* are shown. The Freddy "rap" end theme by the Fat Boys and music by various other artists are on the Chrysalis soundtrack album, and a "making of" video is available. Freddy mania continued with more tie-in products, ripoffs, porno spoofs, and obsessive horror-magazine coverage.

A NIGHTMARE ON ELM STREET 5: THE DREAM CHILD

(Video Treasures, 1989) **D:** Stephen Hopkins **S:** Leslie Bohem **P:** Robert Shaye, Rupert Harvey

Freddy overkill helped make this the least profitable entry in the entire series. Why pay for a mediocre movie when you could see the same concept and main character on TV for free? Lisa Wilcox returns as Alice. She tries to prevent Krueger (Robert Englund) from entering the dreams of her unborn child. In this pro-life horror

Freddy invades Dick Cavett's talk show in *A Nightmare on Elm Street 3*. Zsa Zsa Gabor is the guest.

fantasy Freddy wants to be reborn. The spirit of Freddy's nun mother (the victim of "a hundred rapes") helps Lisa. A 10-year-old dream child appears. Krueger isn't onscreen as much as in the earlier movies. Some of the drug-like dream sequences are pretty interesting (one character dreams in b/w), but some of the FX are (again) too silly. One guy becomes a motorcycle, and a girl is stuffed to death. The M. C. Escher–inspired nightmare sequence idea had already been used in *Hellbound* (1988). With Danny Hassel and Erika Anderson. The movie ends with another Freddy rap song. The soundtrack (on Jive) is by Jay Ferguson, with tracks by various artists. R and unrated videos are available. The director also made *Predator 2*. The next entry was *Freddy's Dead*.

NIGHTMARE ON THE 13TH FLOOR

(Paramount, 1990) **D/P:** Walter Grauman **S:** J. D. Feigelson, Dan Di Stefano

A travel reporter (Michele Greene) goes to a Victorian hotel in LA with a 13th floor sealed off since 1901, when a Satanist doctor (James Brolin) killed 16 people with an axe. Now the murders start again. With John Karlen, Louise Fletcher, and Terri Treas. It debuted on the USA Network.

NIGHTMARES

(MCA, 1983) **D:** Joseph Sargent **S:** Jeffrey Bloom **S/P:** Christopher Crowe

This 4-part horror anthology borrows most of its ideas from other films. A chain-smoking housewife (Cristina Raines) is threatened by an escaped psycho. With William Sanderson. Emilio Estevez (with blond hair) plays video games and ends up in a game. Some real punk music is used, and Moon Zappa appears. Lance Henriksen is a priest facing an evil car. Richard Masur and Veronica Cartwright battle a giant rat. Also with James Tolkan. It was made for TV but released in theaters.

NIGHTMARE SISTERS

(TWE, 1986) **D/P:** David DeCoteau **S:** Kenneth J. Hall   (*Sorority Sisters*)

Linnea Quigley, Brinke Stevens, and Michelle Bauer are "plain" sorority girls who become sexy (and evil) with magic from a genie. They develop fangs and have sex with men (who disintegrate). It all takes place in a house and features lots of nudity. The TV version has tamer alternate scenes. With Richard Gabai and Sandy Brooke. The music is by Haunted Garage. Hall also wrote *Evil Spawn*.

NIGHTMARE WEEKEND

(Lightning, 1985) **D:** Henry Sala **S:** George Faget-Bernard **P:** Bachoo Sen

Three bimbos in a Florida house encounter a scientist conducting mind-change experiments. There's senseless gore, nudity, and a puppet creature. Debbie Laster and Dale Midkiff are in this Troma release, which includes new footage added to an already incomprehensible movie.

NIGHT OF A THOUSAND CATS

(Laser Leasing, 1972) **D/S:** Rene Cardona **S:** Mario Marzac **P:** Mario Z. Zacharias Mexico (*Blood Feast; La Noche de los Mil Gatos*)

Hugo (Hugo Stigliz) keeps heads in glass cases and has a huge cage full of howling, hungry cats in his old stone monastery. He throws fistfuls of raw meat to them. He strangles his sexy blond wife, then courts a married woman (Anjanette Comer). Gorgo, a mute butler with a limp, plays chess. A lot of time is spent showing nice Acapulco scenery from Hugo's helicopter as he looks for new victims. There's some (PG) sex, a slow-motion flashback, and lots of zoom-lens work. It's almost up there with Rene Cardona's *Night of the Bloody Apes* (1968).

NIGHT OF BLOODY HORROR

(Paragon, 1968) **D/S/P:** Joy N. Houck Jr. **S:** Robert A. Weaver

Dan Quayle's favorite TV show was *Major Dad*, starring Gerald McRaney. The vice president was even a guest. Wonder if he saw McRaney's first movie? The sensitive Wesley (McRaney) complains of a headache, and we see a psychedelic swirl. The

woman he was attempting to have sex with goes to church to confess, but the preacher stabs her in the eye! Years later Wes, who still lives with his domineering mother, broods and drinks. He has bad headaches and childhood flashbacks. In a nightmare the woman in bed with him becomes his mother. A nurse takes him home after he's been beaten and robbed, but she ends up with an axe in her chest, and he's arrested. The cops call him nuts, a fruit, and a fag, but they release him on bail. He goes to see a crude, noisy band (the Bored), and the film switches to negative while they sing about "plastic fantastic dreams." Another victim spurts blood when his hand is cut off. I won't reveal the ending of this low-budget, 16mm, *Psycho*-inspired movie shot in New Orleans, but you should know that it was filmed in "Violent Vision" and that the families of theater patrons were offered $1000 if their relatives died while watching it. Most of the music was borrowed from *The Phantom Planet* (1964). It was made by the great Howco company (run by Joy N. Houck Sr.), known for 50s hits like *The Brain from Planet Arous* and *Carnival Rock*. McRaney's next film was *Women and Bloody Terror* (!), also by Houck.

NIGHT OF EVIL

(Sinister, 1962) **D/P:** Richard Galbreath **S:** Louis Perino **P:** Lou Perry

Lisa Gaye stars as a high-school cheerleader with foster parents who is raped (offscreen) and sent to a girls' camp. She later becomes Miss Colorado, helps hold up a liquor store, marries a hoodlum (William Campbell), and ends up on skid row. At least I think so (the end of the video was missing). There's lots of narration of flashbacks. Earl Wilson narrates this obscure Astor release (filmed in Fort Wayne, Indiana) and claims that it's all true. Gaye was also in *Face of Terror* and *Castle of Evil*.

NIGHT OF HORROR

(1981) **D/S:** Tony Malanowski

The ghosts of Confederate soldiers appear in this very homemade local movie (filmed in Maryland). It's padded with Civil War battle reenactments, and Don Dohler is thanked at the end.

NIGHT OF TERROR

(1986) **D:** Felix Gerard **S/P/A:** Rene Harmon

The producer and star of *Lady Street Fighter* and other low-budget wonders made this shot-on-video movie about vengeance, set in an asylum.

NIGHT OF THE BLOODSUCKERS = VAMPIRE HOOKERS

NIGHT OF THE BLOODY TRANSPLANT

(United, 1970) **D/P:** David W. Hanson (*The Transplant*)

A doctor performs an illegal heart transplant, but his drunken brother ruins it. This amateur film from Flint, Michigan, stars Dick Grimm and Cal Seeley. It features footage of open-heart surgery, body painting, and performance art.

NIGHT OF THE COMET

(CBS/Fox, 1984) **D/S:** Thom Eberhardt **P:** Andrew Lane, Wayne Crawford

A comet wipes out most of the population. Valley-girl sisters Catherine Mary Stewart and Kelli Maroney go shopping in empty LA stores, fight over Robert Beltran, and face zombies. Some scientists (Mary Woronov and Geoffrey Lewis) want the girls for experiments. Sharon Farrell and Michael Bowen are also in this amusing PG-13 film. The soundtrack, featuring various artists, is on Macola. Woronov and Beltran were both in *Eating Raoul*.

NIGHT OF THE CREEPS

(HBO, 1986) **D/S:** Fred Dekker **P:** Charles Gordon

An alien experiment in the late 50s results in zombie teens on campus years later. This horror comedy is a lot better than it sounds and is full of surprises, scares, and some laughs. Some frat brothers break into a medical lab and steal a body containing alien slugs that enter victims' mouths and breed in the brain. Soon jock zombies are everywhere, and Jason Lively, Jill Whitlow (*Porky's*), and a paraplegic friend (Steve Marshall) have to fight them. Tom Atkins is great as a seasoned police detective. A *Plan 9* clip is seen on the TV, and lots of in-joke names are used. With Suzanne Snyder, Dick Miller, Kenneth Tobey, and Bruce Solomon. The version shown on cable TV has a completely different ending.

NIGHT OF THE CRUEL SACRIFICE

(VSOM, 1980) **D/S:** Jean Rollin France (*La Nuit de Traquees*)

Elizabeth (Brigitte Lahaie), a woman with amnesia, goes to Paris and has sex with a man who has helped her. Then a doctor and his assistant

Gerald McRaney is an axe murderer in *Night of Bloody Horror*.

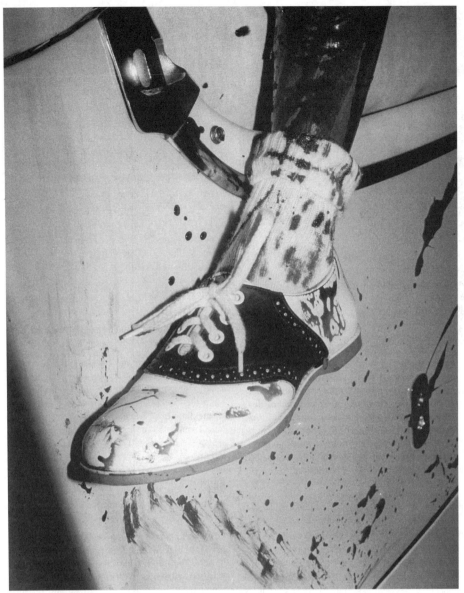

Night of the Creeps

NIGHT OF THE DEMONS

(Republic, 1987) **D:** Kevin S. Tenney
S/P: Joe Augustyn   (*Halloween Party*)

A bunch of obnoxious and hateful teens go to a former funeral parlor for a Halloween party. They're trapped inside, unleash Angela, a floating demon (Mimi Kinkade), and are killed off. Special-effect scenes (by Steve Johnson) include Linnea Quigley poking out a guy's eyeballs and pushing a lipstick tube into her nipple. There's also sex in a coffin, and Quigley has a nude scene. With Cathy Podewell (*Dallas*) and Jill Terashita. It was heavily cut in theaters but is available R or unrated (uncut) on video. It's by the director of *Witchboard*.

NIGHT OF THE DEMONS 2

(Republic, 1994) **D:** Brian Trenchard-Smith
S: Joe Augustyn **P:** Walter Josten

This more imaginative and outrageous sequel to Kevin S. Tenney's original movie features troubled Catholic-school girls going to the same Hell house, still haunted by Angela (Amelia Kinkade). A nun (Jennifer Rhodes) saves the day with holy water in a squirt-gun Uzi. There's some nudity, crotch gags, gory decapitations, breasts becoming arms, and an impressive snake monster. Steve Johnson did the FX again. Cristi Harris is top-billed as Bibi. With Merle Kennedy as Mouse, who has nightmares about her possessed sister Angela, and Bobby Jacoby. Jehovah's Witnesses will not like the opening scene.

NIGHT OF THE DEVILS

(VSOM, 1972) **D:** Giorgio Ferroni **S:** Romano Migliorini **P:** Luigi Mariani   Italy (*La Notte dei Diavoli*)

Remember the Boris Karloff "Wurdalak" segment of Mario Bava's *Black Sabbath*? This is the same story, with a peasant family in the woods becoming vampires. John Garo and Augustina Belli star. The ending suggests that it all might have been a dream.

THE NIGHT OF THE FOLLOWING DAY

(MCA, 1969) **D/S/P:** Hubert Cornfield
S: Robert Phippeny

Outside of Paris, Bud the chauffeur (Marlon Brando) and "the Leer" (Richard Boone) kidnap a nameless girl (Pamela Franklin). They take her to a drug-addicted stewardess (Rita Moreno) at a beach house and hold her for ransom. Several characters die, including "the girl," who wakes up at the end as the whole ordeal begins again (!). Annie Ross is on the soundtrack. Brando, who had just been in *Candy*, was considered box-office poison (in America) when he made this in France. Universal released this rough, R-rated movie to zero business, and it later showed up (cut) on TV. The 95-minute video is uncut. Brando became a desirable star again in 1972.

NIGHT OF THE GHOULS

(Rhino, 1958) **D/S/P/A:** Edward D. Wood Jr.
(*Revenge of the Dead*)

Wood's first movie after *Plan 9 From Outer Space* (completed in 1956 but released in 1959) wasn't

---

arrive and take her away to "the black tower," which must be inspired by early David Cronenberg movies. She and her "roommate" (who can't use her hands) both forget whatever they've heard or learned almost instantly but want to escape. There's a bald rapist, and bodies are burned in an oven. A nuclear attack is blamed. Jean Rollin's movies are an acquired taste. They're uniquely odd, with simple plots and always some horror and some sex, but they're in a class by themselves, sort of elegant exploitation. It's subtitled in English.

NIGHT OF THE DAY OF THE DAWN OF THE SON OF THE BRIDE OF THE RETURN OF THE TERROR: THE REVENGE OF THE TERROR OF THE ATTACK OF THE EVIL, MUTANT, HELLBOUND, FLESH-EATING, SUBHUMANOID LIVING DEAD, PART 2

(Jyvass, 1991) **D/S/P:** Lowell Mason

They took George Romero's (supposedly public-domain) original and added new sound effects, music, and dumb/offensive/juvenile comic dia-

logue. Duane Jones now uses jive talk. Men do the female voices too. Characters talk about what will happen next. There's also new irritating filler material and a (very good) female-led art-rock band doing a song, for some reason. This has been condemned by some critics and fans, but it made me laugh a few times. It was distributed by the Palmer Video chain.

NIGHT OF THE DEATH CULT = NIGHT OF THE SEAGULLS

NIGHT OF THE DEMON

(Lettuce, VCI, 1979) **D:** James C. Watson
S: Mike Williams **P:** Jim L. Ball

A professor and his students encounter a rapist Bigfoot-type monster in a very long flashback (and in flashbacks inside that flashback). The ridiculous-looking monster kills Girl Scouts, rips its victims' guts out, and tears a biker's dick off. Michael J. Cutt is the professor, and Shane Dixon is the monster (names to remember).

Night of the Living Dead (1990)

seen by the public until the video release in 1984 (!) and is a sequel to his *Bride of the Monster* (1955). Much misinformation has been printed about this movie, but for Wood fans it was worth the wait to see it. A séance with bodies, a head, and floating trumpets is priceless. Kenne Duncan (*The Sinister Urge*) is phony spiritualist Dr. Acula, Tor Johnson is Lobo, and Criswell narrates from his coffin. Valda Hansen is "the white ghost," and Jeannie Stevens is "the black ghost." Duke Moore is Lieutenant Bradford, and Paul Marco is Kelton the cop. A scene with Wood fighting with Conrad Brooks was shot in 1956 for an unfinished film to be called *Rock and Roll Hell*. It also shows up in Wood's *The Sinister Urge* (1961). Some other scenes are from a short 1957 pilot film called "The Final Curtain." The executive producer was a retired Marine major. It's 69 minutes long and has cinematography by William C. Thompson. Elvira hosts the Rhino version.

THE NIGHT OF THE HUNTER

(1991) **D:** David Greene **S:** Edmond Stevens

This is a TV remake of the 1955 classic, which was directed by Charles Laughton. Richard Chamberlain stars as the preacher, with Diana Scarwid, Amy Bebout, and Burgess Meredith. Look for the original (from MGM/UA).

NIGHT OF THE KICKFIGHTERS

(AIP, 1990) **D/P:** Buddy Reyes
S: Ron Schultz   (*Night Rangers*)

Andy Bauman (a real kickboxing champ but no actor) stars as Cady, hired to return the kidnapped daughter of Adam West, a rich businessman who has a new computerized laser weapon. Cady assembles a rescue team with a black fighter, a hippie electronics expert (with Nunchuck guns), and a stage magician (with an inflatable ninja). Marcia

Karr is the cartoonish, laughing, Spanish-speaking villainess who has a pet cobra and makes deals with evil Arabs. Her assistant is Carel (Lurch) Struycken, who looks cool but is not convincing as a fighter. After lots of fighting, shooting, and dune-buggy chases an obvious model of the secret headquarters blows up. It was filmed in Arizona.

NIGHT OF THE LIVING DEAD

(RCA/Columbia, 1990) **D:** Tom Savini **S:** George A. Romero **P:** John A. Russo, Russ Steiner

The original b/w horror classic (1968) had already spawned two official sequels by George A. Romero, two sanctioned *Return of the Living Dead* spoofs, and countless (mostly Italian) copies. Other movies ripped off every possible element from the Romero movies. Romero never made any money from his movie, though, so he served as executive producer of this color remake and let his frequent special-effects makeup expert direct. It's actually less gory than the original and is pretty good. Patricia Tallman (who was in Romero's *Knight Riders*) is the tough female lead with short red hair and glasses. She takes charge, dresses for action, and kills zombies. The other characters trapped in the remote house act the same and say many of the same lines as in the original, but the famous ending is changed (ruined). Tony Todd is Ben, and Tom Towles is the scowling, loud, bug-eyed dad. It's from 21st Century.

NOTLD: 25TH ANNIVERSARY

(Tempe, 1994) **D:** Thomas Brown

FIlm clips and interviews with director George A. Romero, writer John Russo, the original actors, and some "famous fans" (Sam Raimi, Wes Craven, Tobe Hooper, Fred Olen Ray, David DeCoteau, and others) make up this documentary. The original 1968 film has been colorized and released as a cheap, washed-out public-domain title,

and footage has been lifted for use in other films. There were cash-in trading cards and books, and Varèse Sarabande even released the original soundtrack, consisting of "library music" stolen from 50s science-fiction films. A deluxe, special Elite Entertainment edition laserdisc version was released in 1994 with audio commentary and a supplementary disc. It was remastered by THX, a division of Lucasfilm, because George Lucas is a fan.

NIGHT OF THE SHARKS

(Edde, 1987) **D:** "Anthony Richmond"/
Tonio Ricci **S:** Tino Carpi **P:** Fulvio
Lucisano   Italy (*La Notte degli Squali*)

In Mexico, John Steiner hires Janet Agren to obtain some incriminating evidence from her ex-husband (Treat Williams). Cyclops, a one-eyed killer shark, attacks them. Antonio Fargas and Chris Connelly are also in this PG-13 movie. Agren had also been in *The Shark's Cave* (1978).

NIGHT OF THE STRANGLER

(1972) **D:** Joy N. Houck Jr. **S:** J. J. Milane **P:** Al Salzer

A New Orleans man has his sister and her black lover killed. The man's brother, a priest from NYC, seeks revenge. Micky Dolenz, the former Monkee (!), is the local priest. This movie, shot on location by the director of *Night of Bloody Horror*, has violence, nudity, and an awkward subplot about racism. With James Ralston and Susan McCullough.

NIGHT OF THE WARRIOR

(Vidmark, 1991) **D:** Rafal Zielinski
S/P: Thomas Ian Griffith **P:** Mike Erwin

Lorenzo Lamas stars as a kickboxer in East LA. His real-life wife (Kathleen Kinmont) and mother (Arlene Dahl, in her first film in 20 years) costar. Anthony Geary as a sleazy promoter and Ken Foree are the villains. With choreographed dance sequences, a big fight with a Korean martial artist (Daniel Kamekona), and Willie Dixon.

NIGHT OF THE ZOMBIES

(Vestron, 1980) **D:** "Vincent Dawn"/ Bruno Mattei
S: Claudio Fragasso, José Mariá Cunilles **P:** Sergio
Cortona   Italy/Spain (*Virus; L'Inferno dei Morti-Viventi;
Apocalipsis Canibal; Zombie Creeping Flesh*)

Toxic chemicals create cannibal zombies (with mediocre makeup) in New Guinea, and a SWAT team fights them. Margit Evelyn Newton stars as an Italian journalist who spends part of the movie topless and in native makeup. Lots of stock animal and mondo footage is used, and the Goblin soundtrack from *Dawn of the Dead* is reused. With maggots, vomiting, and a rat emerging from a stomach. Victor Israel costars. It was released in America unrated.

NIGHT OF THE ZOMBIES II

(Prism, 1981) **D/S/A:** Joel M. Reed **P:** Lorin E.
Price   (*Gamma 693; Night of the Zombies*)

The II was added to the title of this video to make renters think that maybe it was a sequel to the Italian *Night of the Zombies*. At least that movie had some action and blood. This one is talky, too dark, and much too long. In fact, it's terrible in every way. It starts with a Hitler speech, then introduces campers in the Bavarian Alps looking for the remains of WWII American soldiers. Nazi zombies shoot them. Porno star Jamie Gillis shows up as a spy smoking a pipe and looking for WWII deserters (?!). He goes to Munich (actually NYC most of the time) and talks to people about a youth drug. A telling quote is "Why do I have to sit and listen to this insipid repartee?" Director Joel M. Reed, known to some for his *Bloodsucking Freaks*, costars as the man behind the "plot."

NIGHT ON EARTH

(New Line, 1992) **D/S/P:** Jim Jarmusch

In five cities cabdrivers pick up passengers at the same time. Winona Ryder drives Gena Rowlands in LA, Armin Mueller-Stahl picks up Giancarlo Esposito and Rosie Perez in NYC, an immigrant from the Ivory Coast (Isaach de Bankolé) drives a blind woman (Beatrice Dalle) who talks about her sex life in Paris, Roberto Benigni (Paolo Bonacelli) confesses his outrageous sex life to a priest in Rome, and a Helsinki driver (Matti Pellonpaa) picks up drunks. It's 128 minutes long.

NIGHT OWL

(E. I. Video, 1990–93) **D/S/P/E:** Jeffrey Arsenault

A guy (James Rafferty) squatting in an East Village apartment picks up women in bars, drinks their blood during sex, and cuts up the bodies (offscreen). Meanwhile, Angel (John Leguizamo before he was well known) looks for his missing sister. The story stops cold for some rapping (by Screamin' Rachel), performance art at the Mudd Club, and a long (and very good) interview on TV with Caroline Munro talking about the vampire movies she was in. With Karen Wexler (*The Re-*

frigerator) as the sister, Lisa Napoli, Holly Woodlawn in a bar scene, and Michael Musto as an MC. Work on this b/w movie (which has very good music) took three years.

NIGHT OWL

(1993) **D:** Matthew Patrick
S: Rose Schacht **P:** Julian Marks

A speach therapist (Jennifer Beals) and a musician (James Wilder) are a couple with marital problems. Meanwhile, the voice of a mysterious late-night DJ drives men crazy and lures them to their death. Jackie Burroughs is an occult specialist. Gil Melle wrote the score. This 120-minute Lifetime TV movie was filmed in Toronto.

NIGHT PATROL

(Starmaker, 1985) **D/S/P/E:** Jackie Kong
S: Murray Langston, William Levey
S/P: William Osco

This is a very stupid *Police Academy* ripoff with lots of fart jokes. Murray Langston, a cop who wants to be a comic with a bag on his head ("the Unknown Comic") is accused of murder. With Linda Blair, Pat Paulsen, Jaye P. Morgan, Billy Barty as the police captain, Pat Morita, Jack Riley, Lori Sutton, and Kitten Natividad. It's from New World.

NIGHT RHYTHMS

(Imperial, 1992) **D:** Gregory Hippolyte
S/P: Andrew Garoni

Martin Hewitt is the host of a late-night radio talk show who is framed for murdering Tracy Tweed (after having sex with her on the console). This "erotic thriller" features women masturbating while on the phone and some major lesbian scenes with the station engineer (Delia Sheppard). With Deborah Driggs, Julie Strain, Kristine Rose, Erika

Nann, Sam Jones as a detective, and David Carradine as a strip-club owner. R and unrated videos are available.

THE NIGHT RUNNER

(1957) **D:** Abner Biberman **S:** Gene
Leavitt **P:** Albert J. Cohen

Ray Danton is a psycho killer who's paroled from a mental hospital and seems normal. When his girlfriend's father calls him crazy he kills him. With Colleen Miller and Merry Anders. From Universal.

NIGHT SCENES: PROJECT SHADOWCHASER II

(New Line, 1995) **D/P:** John Eyres
S: Nick Davis **P:** Gregory Vanger

Frank Zangarino returns from *Project Shadowchaser* as a blond terrorist android who takes over a nuke plant during Christmas with a team of killers and threatens to nuke Washington, D. C. Bryan Genesse (from *Street Justice*) is a kickboxer janitor who teams up with a scientist (Beth Toussaint) and her son.

NIGHT SCREAMS

(Prism, 1987) **D:** Allen Plone
S/P: Dillis L. Hart II **S:** Mitch Brian

High-school grads are killed off by escaped cons at a party in a remote house. This movie from Wichita includes soft-core sex footage with porno stars Seka, John Holmes, and Honey Wilder. Herbert L. Strock (director of *The Crawling Hand*) was the editor, and Courtney Joyner was a script consultant. A band called the Dogs does a Prince song.

NIGHT SHIFT

(Warner, 1982) **D:** Ron Howard **S:** Lowell
Ganz, Babaloo Mandel **P:** Brian Grazer

Michael Keaton (real name Michael Douglas), in his film debut, is a fast-talking morgue attendant. He convinces mild-mannered coworker Henry Winkler (the star) that they should become "love brokers," so they set up a nighttime whorehouse at the morgue. Shelley Long is the hooker neighbor who helps Winkler. With Bobby DiCicco, Nita Talbot, Joe Spinell, Ashley Cox, Ola Ray, Dawn Dunlap, Monique Gabrielle, K. C. Winkler, and Kevin Costner as a frat boy. This surprising comedy was Ron Howard's second theatrical feature as a director (after *Grand Theft Auto* in 1977).

NIGHT SLASHER: *See* HE KILLS NIGHT AFTER NIGHT

THE NIGHT STALKER: TWO TALES OF TERROR

(MCA, 1974) **D:** Rudolph Borchert, David Chase

This video consists of two episodes from the TV series *Kolchak: The Night Stalker*. Darren McGavin stars, with Simon Oakland. Mickey Gilbert and Roberta Collins are in "Jack the Ripper." "The Vampire" features Susanne Charney, Kathleen Nolan, Larry Storch, Milt Kamen, and Jan Murray. The series pilot is also available from CBS/Fox. *The Night Strangler* is a sequel.

Micky Dolenz stars in *Night of the Strangler.*

NIGHT STALKER (1979): *See* DON'T GO NEAR THE PARK

NIGHT STALKER

(Lightning, 1985) **D:** Max Kleven **S/A:** John Goff **S/P:** Don Edmunds   (*Painted Dolls; Striker*)

Prostitutes are being killed, and Chinese characters are painted on their bodies. Robert Z'Dar is the indestructible killer who steals their souls. Charles Napier stars as an alcoholic LA cop, Sergeant Striker. It's great to have Napier in a starring role, but the movie isn't very good. With Gary Crosby, Buck Flower, and Lydie Denier. Joan Chen (from the TV series *Twin Peaks*), Ola Ray (from the *Thriller* video), and Tally Chanel are hookers.

NIGHTSTICK

(1987) **D:** Joseph L. Scanlan **S:** James L. Docherty **P:** Martin Walters   Canada

Bruce Fairbairn is a cop who tries to prevent extortionists from blowing up NYC with nitro. This Sandy Howard production features John Vernon, Robert Vaughn, Isaac Hayes, and Leslie Nielsen. It was made in Toronto.

THE NIGHT THEY KILLED RASPUTIN

(SW, 1960) **D/S:** Pierre Chenal **S:** André Tabet, Ugo Libertore **P:** Vincent Fotre France/Italy (*L'Ultimo Czar*)

Edmund Purdom is Rasputin, Gianna Maria Canale is Czarina Alexandra, and John Drew Barrymore (Drew Barrymore's dad) is Prince Yousoupoff. Christopher Lee played the role next in *Rasputin, the Mad Monk* (1966).

A NIGHT TO DISMEMBER

(VSOM, 1979) **D/P:** Doris Wishman **S:** Judith J. Kushner

This is Doris Wishman's last-known film to date and definitely the most incoherent. It was filmed mostly in 1979 and advertised in *Variety* in 1983. A detective who narrates tries in vain to explain what's going on with some cursed family. A typical newspaper headline screams, VICKI KENT RELEASED FROM STATE ASYLUM! A dubbed-in voice tries to help by saying, "So it was Billy who chased her through the woods!" The movie features stock footage, library music, Wishman's famous walking-feet closeups, nudity, an arty solarized sex scene, and a dream sequence in negative. It also features something new for the director: gore, lots of it. It's got decapitations, a blood-spurting torso, fingers cut off, guts pulled out, heads and bodies all over the place. It's a disastrous meeting of Wishman and H. G. Lewis. This very bad (but rare) video "stars" porno star Samantha Fox! It's 70 minutes long.

NIGHT TRAIN TO TERROR

(Prism, 1985) **D/P:** Jay Schlossberg-Cohen **D:** John Carr, Philip Marshak, Tom McGowan, Greg Tallas

Somebody got hold of three horror movies, edited them down, added new footage, and actually re-leased this mind-boggling movie in theaters. In an attempt to copy *Dr. Terror's House of Horrors* (1964), where death foretold the future of doomed people on a train, "Mr. Satan" and God argue over the fates of three people while taking a ride on "the Devil's cannonball." God is played by Ferdy Mayne (*The Fearless Vampire Killers*). A new-wave band provides idiotic MTV-style filler before and after each story, and even breakdance. Their song goes "Everybody's got something to do, everybody but you!" (a mean message to viewers of this tape). *Cataclysm* and *Death Wish Club* are also available on tape complete, under various titles. *Cataclysm*, a pretty good serious horror movie, here becomes a partial comedy, with several crudely animated stop-motion monsters throwing dolls of cast members around! The third tale here is a badly edited-down (unfinished) film (*Scream Your Head Off*) by John Carr. It stars John Phillip Law as Harry Billings. He's given shock therapy in an asylum and forced to drug women and bring them to mad doctors who sell their body parts. Naked women are tied down, handcuffed, gagged, and tormented by Otto (Richard Moll, also in *Cataclysm*) before they're dismembered. There's plenty of blood and nudity, a gory decapitation, and some unintentional laughs. Jars of decapitated heads are labeled with the victims' names. After three nearly incomprehensible tales we get to see a model train crash. The band dies, but God (who earlier had defended rock music!) intervenes, and the train is seen ascending to Heaven! What other video gives you so much? Don't miss it!

NIGHT VISION

(Prism, 1987) **D/S:** Michael Krueger **S:** Nancy Gallanis **P:** Sarah Liles-Olson, Douglas Liles-Olson

A would-be writer (Ellie Martins) goes to the big city and works in a video store, where she's possessed by a Satanic video. This was made in Denver.

NIGHT VISIONS

(1990) **D/S:** Wes Craven **S/P:** Thomas Braun **P:** Nick Nathanson, Marianna Madelena

A cop (James Remar) is teamed with a psychic (Lori Locklin) to pursue a serial killer, in this NBC-TV series pilot. With Penny Johnson, Jon Tenney, Mitch Pileggi, and Timothy Leary as a New Age minister (Pileggi and Leary were also in Craven's *Shocker*).

NIGHT VISITOR

(MGM/UA, 1989) **P:** Rupert Hitzig **S:** Randall Viscovich **P:** Alain Silver   (*Never Cry Devil*)

A boy (Derek Rydall) sees his teacher (Allen Garfield) slaughter a hooker (Teri Weigel), but nobody believes him. The plot (which borrows from *Fright Night*) concerns Devil worship and voyeurism. With Elliott Gould as a detective, Michael J. Pollard as a Satanist brother, Richard Roundtree, Henry Gibson, Shannon Tweed, and Brooke Bundy. Weigel was a *Playboy* centerfold who lived with Fred Lincoln and did many hard-core movies.

NIGHT WARS

(AIP, 1987) **D/S:** David A. Prior **P:** Fritz Matthews

Nam vets Brian O'Connor and Cameron Smith have the same nightmares. They wake with real wounds and arm themselves. Dan Haggerty is a shrink. Haggerty had been through a coke bust (1984), three months in jail (1985), income-tax charges, and a motorcycle accident before he started specializing in direct-to-video junk.

NIGHTWISH

(Vidmark, 1988) **D/S:** Bruce R. Cook **P:** Keith Walley

Jack Starrett stars as a crazed psychiatry professor who takes students to the old Valley of Fear ranch.

Vic Morrow in *1990: The Bronx Warriors*.

He uses them as guinea pigs for deep-sleep experiments. They have a séance and see fake ghosts, then real ghosts. It's dream-vs.-reality stuff with gore and alien monsters. With Robert Tessier as a bald mutant, Clayton Rohner, Alisha Das, Elizabeth Kaitan, and Brian Thompson. Tessier and Starrett both died shortly after acting in this. Available in R and unrated versions.

9 AGES OF NAKEDNESS
(Media, 1969) **D/S/P/A:** Harrison Marks   UK

British photographer Harrison Marks, in the tradition of Peter Sellers (and Jerry Lewis), made comedies in which he played many characters. In his first feature, *The World of Harrison Marks* (1967), he played seven famous characters, including James Bond and Count Dracula. His movies exist, though, to show naked women, so his corny burlesque characters get real tiresome. He's like a less talented Benny Hill with the women showing more skin. Marks, playing himself (a nudie photographer with beard, glasses, and long hair), tells an unseen shrink about his family history to illustrate his problems with women. There's plenty of nudity and simulated sex. A cave-man scene is influenced by *The Flintstones* and an Egyptian sequence features lesbians. We go to Greece, to China, and back to the UK, where The Great Marko shows his living statues. In the strangest sequence topless women with robot servants at a moonship control center in the future whip cave men: "Take them to the extermination center!" A pair of all-silver alien women visit and watch a couple have sex through a hole in a mirror. There's a *Blowup*-tennis-ball gag and narration by actor Charles Gray.

9 1/2 WEEKS
(MGM, 1986) **D:** Adrian Lyne **S:** Patricia Knop **P:** Anthony Rufus, Zalman King

This is the nearly plotless movie that pretty much started the "erotic thriller" craze, which resulted in hundreds of R and unrated videos. Mickey Rourke stars as a Manhattan broker who pursues an art-gallery owner (Kim Basinger). They have sex in various places and use ice cubes, food, and masks. With Margaret Whitton, Karen Young, Christine Baranski, and David Margulies. A longer version played in Europe, where the film was very influential. It's from Mark Damon's Vision International. Lyne returned with the bigger hit *Fatal Attraction* (1987). Zalman King ran with the "erotic" concept and made *Two-Moon Junction* (1988), *Wild Orchid* (1989, also with Rourke), and *The Red Shoe Diaries* TV series (1992–).

NINE DEATHS OF THE NINJA
(Media, 1985) **D/S:** Emmett Alston **P:** Ashok Amritraj

Sho Kosugi and his kids Shane and Kane are in number four in a "series" that started with *Enter the Ninja*. This is the funniest. Sho and Brent Huff are anti-terrorists who free a bus full of American hostages in the Philippines from a clichéd Nazi type. There are also bad Arabs, a lesbian guerrilla, lady terrorists in shorts, drugs, and fighting dwarfs. Alston also made *Demonwarp*. Menahem Golan and Yoram Globus were the executive producers of this Cannon release.

THE NINE LIVES OF FRITZ THE CAT
(1974) **D/S:** Robert Taylor **S:** Fred Halliday, Eric Monte **P:** Steve Krantz **M:** Tom Scott

AIP released this R-rated sequel, made without the participation of R. Crumb, who had created the character, or Ralph Bakshi, who had made the original animated film, *Fritz the Cat*. It's filled with flashbacks to other times, including the Depression in the US and the Hitler era in Germany, and there's a flashforward to a separate black state in the future. The voices include those of Louisa Moritz and Pat Harrington Jr.

976-EVIL
(RCA/Columbia, 1988) **D:** Robert Englund **S:** Rhet Topham, Brian Helgland **P:** Lisa M. Hansen

A nerd named Hoax (the irritating Stephen Geoffreys) is jealous of his cool, motorcycle-riding cousin and lives with a religious nut aunt (Sandy Dennis). He calls a phone number and obtains supernatural revenge powers. It rains fish, Hell opens up, and the mutated teen makes Freddy Krueger–type wisecracks, no surprise since it was directed by Freddy himself. Parts were reshot by another director, and it's still too confusing. The cast also includes Jim Metzler and Patrick O'Bryan.

976-EVIL 2: THE ASTRAL FACTOR
(Vestron, 1992) **D:** Jim Wynorski **S:** Eric Anjou **P:** Paul Herzberg

This sequel has a good, mock-spaghetti-western theme and an inspired, out-of-left-field *Night of the Living Dead* crossed with *It's a Wonderful Life* (!) scene. Otherwise it's awful. Brigitte Nielsen, featured on the box, is in one scene. Patrick O'Bryan (from the original, which was pretty bad itself) arrives in a small college town on his motorcycle. The dean turns out to be a rotting killer ghost. With blond Debbie James, Rene Assa, Karen Mayo Chandler, Monique Gabrielle, and Buck Flower.

1984
(IVE, 1984) **D/S:** Michael Radford **S:** Jonathan Gems **P:** Simon Perry   UK

John Hurt stars as Winston Smith, a government employee in a totalitarian state called Oceania. George Orwell's novel had been filmed in 1955, but this much more expensive, R-rated, color version is more grim and horrifying. Suzanna Hamilton is the women Smith loves, and Richard Burton (in his last role) is the party official who puts rats on the faces of nonconformists. With Phyllis Logan and Cyril Cusack. The Eurythmics music was released on an album but dropped from the US release. The director also made *Van Morrison in Ireland* (1981).

1941
(MCA, 1979) **D:** Steven Spielberg **S:** Robert Zemeckis, Bob Gale **P:** Buzz Feitshans

This big, long (118-minute), too expensive, PG-rated star-filled WWII comedy flop was made by Steven Spielberg after *Close Encounters of the Third Kind*. It does have its moments, of course, like Christopher Lee and Toshiro Mifune as Axis

officers in a submarine off the coast of California with Slim Pickens as their prisoner. Eddie Deezen is more memorable than the *Saturday Night Live* stars, and Murray Hamilton and Lorraine Gary return from *Jaws*. Also with Ned Beatty, Tim Matheson, Warren Oates, Robert Stack, Treat Williams, Patti LuPone, Nancy Allen, and John Candy. Watch for Elisha Cook Jr., Lionel Stander, Samuel Fuller, Dick Miller, John Landis, Lucinda Dooling, Audrey Landers, and Mickey Rourke. John Milius was the executive producer and cowrote the story. An extra 26 minutes were put back into the TV version.

1991: THE YEAR PUNK BROKE
(Geffen, 1992) **D/C/E:** David Markey

American bands toured Europe in 1991 and appeared before the biggest crowds most of them had ever played for up until then. This16mm documentary spends the most time on Sonic Youth (they do eight songs), but Nirvana (with Kurt Cobain) will now be the main attraction. They do five songs (including "Smells Like Teen Spirit"), and Cobain smashes his equipment onstage. The camera follows members of Sonic Youth to a German carnival, where they act goofy and sarcastic. Also with Dinosaur Jr., Babes in Toyland, Gumball, and (briefly) the Ramones. If you don't already like these groups this movie won't make you a convert, since none of them are seen (or heard) to their best advantage. It's by the director of *Desperate Teenage Lovedolls*.

1990: THE BRONX WARRIORS
(Media, 1982) **D/A:** Enzo G. Castellari **S:** Dardano Sachetti **P:** Fabrizio De Angelis
Italy (*I Guerrieri del Bronx*)

Hammer (Vic Morrow) is after the kidnapped daughter of a millionaire in the post-nuke Bronx. Mark Gregory as Trash and Fred Williamson as the Ogre join forces to fight Morrow and other gangs. This violent movie has hippie bikers, Indian punks, a roller-skating gang called the Zombies, and impaled people. With Christopher Connelly and George Eastman. Some parts were shot in Brooklyn. UFD released this after Morrow (who was from the Bronx) died. The sequel is *Escape from the Bronx*.

92 IN THE SHADE
(Key, 1975) **D/S:** Thomas McGuane **P:** George Pappas

Peter Fonda and Warren Oates are rival Florida Keys fishing-boat owners. Many bizarre and funny characters are in this odd movie featuring William Hickey, Margot Kidder, Burgess Meredith, Harry Dean Stanton, Sylvia Miles, Joe Spinell, and William Roerick. The original (death) ending was changed when it was rereleased.

NINJA III: THE DOMINATION
(MGM/UA, 1984) **D:** Sam Firstenberg **S:** James R. Silke **P:** Menahem Golan, Yoram Globus

After *Enter the Ninja* and *Revenge of the Ninja* Cannon made this exorcism/martial arts movie. It's pretty wild and hilarious. Lucinda Dickey stars as an Arizona electrical worker who takes aerobics classes and is possessed by a fire-breathing ninja.

Her boyfriend is amazed. You will be too! Sho Kosugi is a good ninja who has to defeat her. With James Hong and Andy Bauman. Lots of cops are killed.

THE NINTH CONFIGURATION

(Starmaker, 1979) **D/S/P:** William Peter Blatty
(*Twinkle, Twinkle, Killer Kane*)

Blatty made this unique existential movie based on his novel. Stacy Keach is Marine Colonel Kane, the new head psychiatrist at a government "study center"/asylum in a castle full of Nam vets. The cast includes Scott Wilson, Jason Miller, Neville Brand, Moses Gunn, Robert Loggia, Joe Spinnell, Tom Atkins, Ed Flanders, Alejandro Rey, and George DiCenzo. You won't believe Richard Lynch and Steve Sandor as bikers in a violent bar-fight scene. The Warners release was 140 minutes, 118 minutes, or 99 minutes, depending on when and where you saw it.

THE NINTH GUEST

(1934) **D:** Roy William Neill **S:** Garnett Weston

During a party eight guests are killed off by a madman. Donald Cook stars in this 65-minute Columbia release. It received an H (horrific) certificate in the UK. With Genevieve Tobin and Hardie Albright.

NOCTURNA

(Media, 1978) **D/S:** "Harry Tampa"/
Harry Hurwitz **P:** Vernon Becker

Nai Bonet was the executive producer and star of *Nocturna*. A dancer in movies since 1964, she played her first major role in *Devil's Angels*. Here she's "the granddaughter of Dracula" (John Carradine), who's upset because she's in love with a blond hunk with a British accent. Carradine seems to be having a good time with the role, but his hands, badly disfigured from arthritis, are distracting (in his other later movies his hands are usually offscreen). It's worth it to see him at a disco with Yvonne De Carlo and joining her in a double coffin. They follow Nai to Manhattan, where a group of vampires has secret meetings, then all turn into cartoon bats (a fun special effect). Brother Theodore is Theodore, a desk clerk/werewolf (he never transforms) at the Transylvania Hotel. He declares, "As long as there is death there's hope!" Sy Richardson is a pimp/drug dealer vampire with vampire hookers. Hit-makers Gloria Gaynor and Vicki Sue Robinson are heard on the soundtrack, and the Moment of Truth, a disco group with wide, flaring pants, do two whole songs. The always smiling Bonet has lots of brightly lit closeups and a hard-to-place accent, and she dances a lot. She wears a see-through red gown, strips, then takes a long standing bath and oils herself while a hidden Theodore watches. It's like a much sexier version of George Hamilton's hit *Love at First Bite*. Bonet also starred in her production of *Hoodlums*.

NO ESCAPE

(HBO, 1994) **D:** Martin Campbell **S:** Michael Gaylin **P:** Gale Anne Hurd **M:** Graeme Revell

In 2022 a fearless loner and former Marine (Ray Liotta) is taken to an island prison, escapes, and stays at a fort with a group of peaceful colonists led by Lance Henriksen. The men barely survive attacks by a primitive jungle group led by the sarcastic Marek (Stuart Wilson). Everyone is monitored by the sadistic warden (Michael Lerner). An expensive box-office flop, this is pretty good for what's basically a *Road Warrior* retread without the chases. It does have some good acting, (off-screen) cannibalism, and decapitations. The all-male cast includes Kevin Dillon, Ernie Hudson, Kevin J. O'Connor, and a dwarf. Based on the novel *The Penal Colony*, by Richard Herley, it was filmed in New South Wales, Australia. The director is from New Zealand.

NO ESCAPE, NO RETURN

(PM, 1993) **D/S:** Charles T. Kanagis
P: Joseph Merhi, Richard Pepin

LA cops Maxwell Caulfield, Dustin Nguyen (from the TV series *21 Jump Street*) and Denise Loveday go underground to infiltrate a drug ring. Michael Nouri is a corrupt DEA agent, and John Saxon is the top cop.

NO HOLDS BARRED

(RCA, 1989) **D:** Thomas J. Wright
S: Dennis Hackin **P:** Michael Rachmil

Hulk Hogan is Rip, the World Wrestling Federation champ. An evil network-TV executive (Kurt Fuller) wants him to throw a fight. With Joan Severance, Tom "Tiny" Lister (formerly Eddie Murphy's bodyguard), Jesse "the Body" Ventura, and Mean Gene Okerlund. The executive producers of this PG-13 film were Hogan and Vince McMahon. The original *No Holds Barred* was a Bowery Boys wrestling movie. Hogan was in *Suburban Commando* next.

NO JUSTICE

(1989) **D/S/P:** Richard Wayne Martin **D:** Fred Dresch

The plot of this made-in-Tennessee movie is a lot like *Dixie Dynamite* or a lot of other 70s drive-in car-chase movies. Bob Orwig is a sadistic, dumb, small-town deputy sheriff appointed by his corrupt, alcoholic uncle, "the major" (Cameron Mitchell), who deals in "mari-wani" and bootleg liquor on the side. The bad guys want to take the land of some "half-breeds." Steve Murphy, another nephew and deputy, is the hero. With Camille Keaton (*I Spit on Your Grave*), Lisa Case, and Donald Farmer as a reporter. It was released in Europe on video.

NOMADS

(Paramount, 1986) **D/S:** John McTiernan
P: George Pappas, Cassian Elwes

Pierce Brosnan is a French anthropologist who battles mythic spirits disguised as LA punks in a van. When he dies he passes on his memories to an emergency-room doctor (Lesley-Ann Down) who tried to save him. All of a sudden weird punks, junkies, and whores go after her. Adam Ant is "Number One." With Mary Woronov and Nina Foch. The director went on to bigger things like *Die Hard* and *The Hunt for Red October*.

NOMADS OF THE NORTH

(Kino, 1920) **D/S:** David M. Hartford
S: James Oliver Curwood

Lon Chaney is a Canadian who returns home to his unfaithful wife. Betty Blythe and Lewis Stone are also in the cast of this 109-minute First National release, which has a musical score.

NON-STOP NEW YORK

(Sinister, 1937) **D:** Robert Stevenson
S: Roland Pertwee   UK

A futuristic luxury airliner goes from London to NYC in this Hitchcock-type thriller with a murder plot. Anna Lee stars with John Loder, Francis L. Sullivan, Frank Cellier, and Desmond Tester.

NO PLACE TO HIDE

(Video Treasures, 1981) **D:** John Llewellyn Moxey
S: Jimmy Sangster **P:** Jay Daniel, S. Byron Hickox

Kathleen Beller is an art student being stalked by a masked killer. With Mariette Hartley as her stepmother, Keir Dullea as a shrink, and Arlen Dean Snyder. This CBS-TV movie copies *Dressed to Kill*.

NO PLACE TO HIDE

(Cannon, 1993) **D/S:** Richard Danus **P:** Alan Amiel

Drew Barrymore is good as a bratty, slang-talking 14-year-old whose life is in danger after her topless-dancer sister is killed during a rehearsal of Swan Lake. She's put under the protection of a depressed LA detective (Kris Kristofferson). Drew narrates from her diary. Kristofferson flashes back to when his family died and weeps. The murder turns out to be part of a far-reaching conspiracy. With Martin Landau as a police captain, O. J. Simpson as a wheelchair-bound former football star, Dey Young as Kristofferson's partner, Bruce Weitz as an asshole cop, Lydie Denier, and Kane Holder.

NO RETREAT, NO SURRENDER

(Starmaker, 1985) **D:** "Corey Yuen"/Yuen Kwei
S: Keith W. Strandberg **P:** Ng See Yuen

Kurt McKinney stars a kid who gets beaten up a lot until he's helped by the ghost of Bruce Lee (!). Jean-Claude Van Damme (in his first American film) is a bad Russian kickboxer. It was made in Seattle (where Lee lived).

NO RETREAT, NO SURRENDER II

(1987) **D:** "Corey Yuen"/Yuen Kwei
S/P: Roy Haran **S:** Keith W. Strandberg

In this *Rambo*-style Vietnam adventure that has nothing to do with the first movie, a young American kickboxer (Loren Avedon) fights Khmer Rouge guerrillas to rescue his fiancée. With Matthias Hues, Max Thayer, Dale Jacoby, and Cynthia Rothrock. From SGE.

NORMA

(American Video, 1970) **D/A:** William Rotsler
S: Norman Stevens **P:** William Christian

Norma (Maddy Maguire) bravely goes to Dr. Bradley, a shrink (Chris Warfield), and explains, "I suffer from an emotional disorder known as nymphomania." During frequent visits she tells him about her sex adventures ("Old, young, handsome, ugly, it didn't matter") and a disturbing vision of a mystery man that "appears every time I'm about to climax." She goes to an orgy (which includes Uschi Digart) with a guy in drag (who freaks out), goes home with a tough, abusive biker but leaves him sulking in the corner, and makes it with a female carhop in a bathtub. In the most erotic and imaginative scene she goes to a movie theater (playing *Fanny Hill* and *Erotic Mushroom*). After closing time she seduces the manager onstage while psychedelic sex scenes are projected on them and bongo music plays. The manager is played by director William Rostler, and the clips are from his earlier films. Finally the doc hypnotizes her, and she remembers how her childhood boyfriend was killed with a pitchfork while they were making out after riding horses. Just then her mother shows up at the doc's office. She's a man in drag, the killer! The mother is played by Buck Flower. This has better-than-usual acting, pretty realistic (simulated) sex, and lots of cheesy organ lounge music. Despite the ridiculous ending it's one of the better adults-only movies of the time. American Video Corporation has put out a whole series of rare, vintage 60s/early 70s adult movies in deceptive, ripoff boxes, making them look like recent porno videos.

NORMAN'S AWESOME EXPERIENCE

(Southgate, 1987) **D/S/P:** Paul Donovan
Canada (*A Switch in Time*)

A young lab assistant (Tom McCamus) goes back in time to ancient Rome with a model (Laurie Paton) and her Italian photographer. They fight barbarians. It was filmed in Argentina, and then parts were reshot by another director. Ray Sager was the supervising producer.

THE NORSEMAN

(1979) **D/S/P:** Charles B. Pierce

Lee Majors is an 11th-century Viking prince who sails to North America to find his father (Mel Ferrer), who has been captured by Indians (!). AIP released this PG adventure. It also features Cornel Wilde, Jack Elam, Chris Connelly, and Kathleen Freeman.

NORTH BY NORTHWEST

(MCA, 1959) **D/P:** Alfred Hitchcock
S: Ernest Lehman **M:** Bernard Herrmann

This was the last of four Hitchcock movies with Cary Grant and the last Hitchock movie before the shock of *Psycho*. It was expensive ($4 milion) and was a major hit. MGM wanted to cut it, but it remained 136 minutes long. Grant is Roger O. Thornhill, a NYC ad man mistaken for a double agent. Memorable scenes take place at the UN, on a train, in a desolate field, and on Mount Rushmore. Eva Marie Saint costars, with James Mason, Leo G. Carroll (in his fifth Hitchcock film), Jessie Royce Landis, Martin Landau, Edward Platt, and Les Tremayne. The director is seen running for a bus. The title comes from *Hamlet*. The complete soundtrack wasn't released until the 70s, on Varèse Sarabande.

NORTHSTAR

(1986) **D:** Peter Levin **S/P:** Howard Lakin
(*The Einstein Man*)

An astronuat (Greg Evigan) returns from space as a superman hero who's sensitive to sunlight. Mitchell Ryan is his boss. This ABC-TV series pilot also features Mason Adams, Sonny Landham, and Ken Foree.

NORTHVILLE CEMETERY MASSACRE

(Paragon, 1974) **D/S/P:** William Dear, Thomas L. Dyke **M:** Michael Nesmith (*Harley's Angels*)

This came out a little late for the biker-movie craze, but it's pretty good. If you're tired of psycho bikers in movies, this time the Spirits, bikers accused of a rape in a local town, are innocent. The local rednecks and police are the bad guys. There's a wild shootout in a cemetery that leads to a downbeat ending. David Hyry and Carson Jackson star. It was made in Detroit and features members of the real Scorpions motorcycle club. It was released by Cannon. William Dear also directed Nesmith's *Elephant Parts*.

NO SAFE HAVEN

(Virgin, 1987) **D:** Ronnie Rondell **S/A:** Wings Hauser, Nancy Locke **P:** Gary Paul

A Nam vet and former CIA agent (Wings Hauser) and big, bald, tattooed Robert Tessier are US spies after gangsters at home then go after more gangsters and drug lords in a fortress in Honduras. Hauser's football hero brother was murdered, so he wants revenge. With Marina Rice, Branscombe Richmond, and Hauser's (at the time) wife Nancy as a Peace Corps worker.

NOSFERATU

(Kino, Video Yesteryear, Republic, 1921)
D: F. W. Murnau **S:** Henrik Galeen Germany
(*Nosferatu: Eine Symphonie des Grauens*)

Max Schreck stars as Count Orloc in this amazing first film version of Bram Stoker's novel *Dracula*. Orloc looks scary just standing there and is very creepy when he floats. Nina (Greta Schröder), not Dr. Van Helsing, destroys the frightening, phantom-like vampire. Stoker's heirs won a lawsuit in England, and the negative was ordered destroyed there. By the time the 95-minute film was released in America in 1929 it had been cut and altered. The Kino version is 84 minutes and has new inter-titles. The Image laserdisc (also 84 minutes) uses the original tints and has an alternate soundtrack commentary by Lokke Heiss. The Video Yesteryear version is longer because it's at a slower speed. Other videos run only 63 minutes. Various versions have different musical scores too. *The Last Laugh* (1925) and *Faust* (1926) by Murnau are also on video. Werner Herzog's 1979 version copied many scenes exactly.

NOSTALGIA

(1983) **D/S:** Andrei Tarkovsky **S:** Tonino Guerra **P:** Francesco Casati Italy/USSR

Erland Josephson stars as a Soviet musicologist in Italy. A man who warns of a nuclear holocaust immolates himself on a statue. This color and b/w film runs 2 hours. The cast also includes Domiziana Giordano and Oleg Jankovskij.

NOSTRADAMUS

(Orion, 1994) **D:** Roger Christian **S:** Knut Boeser, Piers Ashworth **P:** Edward Simons, Harold Reichebner

Tcheky Karyo is the medieval scholar and prophet Michel de Nostradame (1503–66), who lived during the time of the Inquisition and plague. This historical epic is nearly two hours long. Directed by the art director of *Alien*, it includes flash-forwards showing wars and leaders (Hitler and JFK) he predicted. The cast includes Rutger Hauer as a crazed monk, F. Murray Abraham, Michael Gough, Amanda Plummer, and Julia Ormond. It was filmed in Romania, France, and England.

NOT FOR PUBLICATION

(HBO, 1984) **D/S/A:** Paul Bartel
S: John Meyer **P:** Anne Kimmel

Nancy Allen is a reporter for a *National Enquirer* type of paper who also works in the reelection campaign of a NYC mayor (Laurence Luckenbill). This old fashioned "screwball comedy" costars David Naughton and Alice Ghostley.

NOTHING BUT TROUBLE

(Warner, 1991) **D/S/A:** Dan Aykroyd
P: Robert K. Weiss

When are the ex–*Saturday Night Live* people going to leave us alone!? Chevy Chase and Demi Moore leave New York and drive through New Jersey. They're stopped for speeding and trapped in a bizarre fantasy town run by Dan Aykroyd (with tons of makeup) as an old judge. They try to escape. It's not funny, and the blobby monsters are stupid. With John Candy. Warner released the soundtrack.

NOTHING LASTS FOREVER

(1984) **D/S:** Tom Schiller **P:** Lorne Michaels

Zach Galligan is a NYC artist in the future. He takes a trip to the moon. This PG comedy by *Saturday Night Live* people, shot partially in b/w, features Apollonia Van Ravenstein, Dan Aykroyd, Buck Henry, Imogene Coca, Anita Ellis, Sam Jaffe, and Mort Sahl.

NOTHING PERSONAL

(1980) **D:** George Bloomfield **S:** Robert Kaufman **P:** David M. Perlmutter US/Canada

Donald Sutherland is a lawyer trying to stop baby seals from being killed. This romantic comedy was released by AIP the year it became Filmways. Suzanne Somers costars, with Roscoe Lee Browne, Dabney Coleman, and Catherine O'Hara.

NOTHING UNDERNEATH

(Sony, 1985) **D/S:** Carlo Vanzina **S:** Enrico Vanzina, Franco Ferrini **P:** Achille Manzotti **M:** Pino Donaggio   Italy (*Sotto il Vestito Niente*)

A Yellowstone Park forest ranger (Tom Schanley) with psychic powers is drawn to Italy to prevent his twin sister's murder. There's a psycho killer, lots of Euro models, and a surprise ending. A beautiful lesbian artist kills her short-haired blond model lover and keeps her body in the studio. Donald Pleasence is a cop. There's impressive Argento-look photography. The hit song "One Night in Bangkok" is heard. The sequel is *Too Beautiful to Die* (1988).

NO TIME TO KILL

(1958) **D/S/P:** Tom Younger   UK/Sweden/W. Germany (*Med Mord i Bagaget*)

John Ireland is released from prison, where he served time for arson, and goes to Sweden to find the man who framed him. This b/w drama was a Jerry Warren presentation in 1963.

NOT OF THIS EARTH

(MGM/UA, 1988) **D/S/P:** Jim Wynorski **S:** R. J. Robinson **P:** Murray Miller

This cheap (of course) remake opens with lots of great but completely unrelated scenes from New World movies like *Piranha, Humanoids from the Deep*, and *Galaxy of Terror*, and even *The Terror* (from AIP) and goes on to incorporate cost-cutting scenes from other movies during the story, which is exactly the same as the 1956 version. Except for Corman fans, not many people would have cared about this video if it weren't for Traci Lords, from Steubenville, Ohio. Dozens of porno tapes she was in were recalled in 1986, the year when she (supposedly) turned 18. She then starred in *Traci, I Love You* (1987), her last, only legal (and of course best-selling), X-rated video, attended Actor's Studio classes, was a guest on *Wiseguy*, accepted an MTV award for Guns 'N' Roses, and starred in this. She's the nurse working for an alien vampire (Arthur Roberts) and has one major nude scene after a bath. But in every other (long) shot high heels appear on her feet. The director substituted hookers for bums to put into the matter transformer, made the alien in a closet a hippie, and added a female alien in punk clothes. Otherwise it's the same characters and story. With Ava Cadell, Monique Gabrielle, Roxanne Kernohan, Becky LeBeau, Taaffe O'Connell, Rebecca Perle, Kelly Marooney, and Cynthia Ann Thompson. A third version debuted on Showtime in 1996.

NOT OF THIS WORLD

(1991) **D:** Jon Daniel Hess **S:** Robert Glass **P:** Jonathan Brauer

A seldom-seen shape-shifting creature (designed by Carlo Rambaldi) feeds on energy. This CBS-TV movie features Lisa Hartman, Pat Hingle, Tracey Walter, Cary Hiroyuki-Tagawa, Tim Choate, and A Martinez. Hess also directed *Watchers* and *Alligator II*.

NOTORIOUS

(Fox, 1946) **D/P:** Alfred Hitchcock **S:** Ben Hecht

Devlin (Cary Grant) is an American agent. Alicia Huberman (Ingrid Bergman) is the sexy daughter of a convicted spy who marries a rich Nazi (Claude Rains) to help the Americans. This romantic spy thriller is set in post-WWII Rio de Janeiro. Leopoldine Konstantin is Rains' mother, and Louis Calhern is Grant's boss, and Ivan Triesault and Reinhold Schünzel are Nazis. The FBI was concerned at the time about the uranium 235 in wine bottles (the film was made a year before the A bomb was announced). The score, by Roy Webb, was conducted by Constantin Bakaleinikoff.

NOTORIOUS

(1992) **D:** Colin Bucksey **S:** Douglas Lloyd McIntosh **P:** Ilene Amy Berg

John Shea stars as a CIA agent in France. Jenny Robertson, as the daughter of a Soviet spy, marries an arms dealer. With Marisa Berenson and Jean-Pierre Cassel. This remake debuted on Lifetime.

THE NOTORIOUS CLEOPATRA

(SW, 1970) **D/P:** Peter Stootsberry **S:** Jim Macher

This Boxoffice International release has one notable (and rare) difference, a black star (Sondra) as a sexy and usually naked Cleopatra. Most of this nudie movie is a series of soft-core orgies, and there's a "virgin sacrifice." The soundtrack includes comical sound FX and some psychedelic rock. With blond Dixie Donovan (who has sex with Cleopatra and later with a giant in a prison), Johnny Rocco as Marc Antony, and Christopher Stone (all were also in *The Joys of Jezebel*). I wonder whether Sondra was in anything else.

NOTORIOUS CONCUBINES

(SW, 1969) **D:** Koji Wakamatsu   Japan

If you want to see ancient Chinese history, a Japanese exploitation movie isn't the place to look. The confused story (supposedly based on *The Golden Lotus*) is told with flashbacks inside of flashbacks. It's about a woman who seduces and poisons her way to the top, and it shows nudity, women being tied up and whipped, and an ear being cut off. Some scenes are optically censored. It was released (dubbed) by Boxoffice International. The video is letterboxed. The director made *The Love Robots* (1965), also released in America.

THE NOTORIOUS DAUGHTER OF FANNY HILL

(SW, 1966) **D/P:** Peter Stootsberry **P:** Bradford Hallworthy **C:** Laszlo Kovacs

Stacy Walker stars in this nudie period film. Characters include "the orgy master" and the marquis de Sade. Sonney Amusements released it, and David F. Friedman was a producer. The star (real name Barbra Jean Moore) was a college dropout from Texas making her film debut. She returned in *A Smell of Honey, a Taste of Brine*. The first issue of *Adam Film Quarterly* was entirely devoted to this movie. The issue cost $1.

NOT TONIGHT, HENRY

(SW, 1958) **D/C:** Merle Connell **S/P:** Ted Paramour, Bob Heidrich

This color comedy was made right after the success of Russ Meyer's *The Immoral Mr. Teas*. Hank Henry, a burlesque comic (who resembles Rodney Dangerfield), is a henpecked husband who dreams that he's in a series of historical situations. He meets Cleopatra, Lucrezia Borgia, and Pocahontas. It's very much like sketches from the Benny Hill show. There's even a short comic sidekick (Little Jack Little). The only scene with skin features topless Indian women. A strange dinosaur is lifted from a Jungle Jim movie. The makeup is by Harry Thomas, known for creating monsters in many low-budget horror movies.

NO WAY BACK

(Unicorn, 1976) **D/S/P/A:** Fred Williamson

Fred Williamson is LA detective Jesse Crowder. He goes to San Francisco, where he's hired to find a missing man and some money. With Charles Woolf, Tracy Reed, Virginia Gregg, Mike Henry, and Don Cornelius. It was the first of Williamson's many Po Boy productions and was accused of being violent and sexist. He returned as the same character in *Death Journey*.

NO WAY TO TREAT A LADY

(Paramount, 1968) **D:** Jack Smight **S:** John Gay **P:** Sol C. Siegel

You've got to like Rod Steiger to enjoy this psycho "lipstick murderer" movie. He's the owner of a NYC theater who uses various disguises and accents as he strangles women and calls to taunt the police. George Segal is a detective on the case, and his new girlfriend (Lee Remick) is an intended victim. With Eileen Heckart, Murray Hamilton, and Michael Dunn as Mr. Kupperman, who claims he's the killer. It's based on a novel by William Goldman. The American Breed is heard on the soundtrack of this Paramount release.

NOWHERE TO RUN

(MGM/UA, 1989) **D:** Carl Franklin, Jack Canson **P:** Julie Corman   (*Temptation Blues; Caddo Lake; A Hero Stands Alone*)

In 1960 in Caddo, Texas, Kieran Mulroney (who narrates) works at a bait house owned by a local crime boss (David Carradine). Carradine is also an escaped killer, and the kid sees things he shouldn't and goes on the run. With Jillian McWhirter and Henry Jones as a judge. This Corman/Concorde release is based on real events.

NOWHERE TO RUN

(Columbia, 1992) **D:** Robert Harmon **S:** Joe Eszterhas, Leslie Boehm, Randy Feldman **P:** Craig Baumgarten

Jean-Claude Van Damme (in a "serious" career move) stars as an escaped convict (from Quebec) who helps a poor farm widow (Rosanna Arquette, who has nude scenes) and her kids (Kieran Culkin and Tiffany Taubman) battle evil land developers led by Joss Ackland. With Ted Levine. It copies *Shane* and features horse and motorcycle chases. The director made *The Hitcher*. The story was by Joe Eszterhas and the late Richard Marquand.

NUCLEAR RUN

(Sen Sei, 1980) **D/S:** Ian Barry **D:** George Miller
P: David Elfick   Australia (*Chain Reaction*)

Ross Thompson is exposed to a lethal dose of radiation during an accident at the nuke plant he works at. With Steve Bisley and Mel Gibson (he is *not* the star, despite what a video box might claim), who were both in *Mad Max*. George Miller was also an associate producer.

NUDE IN HIS POCKET

(1957) **D:** Pierre Gast **S:** France
Roche France (*Amour de Poche*)

Jean Marais is a professor experimenting with suspended animation. He accidentally shrinks a dog. His assistant (Agnes Laurent) drinks some of the liquid and becomes a 3" statue, which Marais keeps in his pocket. Salt water restores her to normal. Laurent is sometimes naked in this fantasy/comedy, so it was an adults-only art-house release in America. It was based on a story in *Astounding Science Fiction*.

NUDE ON THE MOON

(VCI, Sleaziest, 1960) **D/S/P:** "Anthony Brooks"/ Doris Wishman

This full-color science-fiction/nudist-colony oddity is one of Wishman's earliest features. The credits are all fake, but Doris pretty much did it all, at the Coral Castles in Homestead, Florida. Ralph Young (of Sandler and Young) sings "I'm Mooning Over You," backed by Doc Severinsen and his band. Then we find out how handsome young rocket scientist Jeff (who has inherited $3 million) and the older Dr. Huntley manage to secretly blast off to the moon. The rocket is a toy in closeups, and stock footage shows it taking off. The men talk into hand mikes to communicate even though they're sitting next to each other, and they sleep through the landing. On the moon they wear funny-colored tights, boots with silver stars, and helmets. The moon people wear only low-slung bathing-suit bottoms (and have antennae). It should have been called *Topless on the Moon*. The playful moon women dance, toss a plastic ball, and lounge around like the Eloi in *The Time Machine* (1960). The muscular men have slicked-back hair, and even the little kids have to wear bathing suits. The telepathic queen (Marietta) likes Jeff, but the doc says, "You're acting like a schoolboy. Don't forget we're rocket scientists!" Another memorable song is "Moon Doll." Watch for the theater marquee with Wishman's *Hideout in the Sun*.

NUDES ON TIGER REEF

(SW, 1965) **D/P/C:** Barry Mahon **S:** Clelle Mahon

Sande, a "Broadway director" (Sande Johnsen), goes to a Florida nudist camp on an island. He's "both shocked and amused" to find that his star, Nadja (Nadja Swensen in a blond wig), is there too and decides to make an (8mm) movie. The main models on display are young and cute, and both of them smoke. There's topless scuba diving, nude card playing, baseball, showering, exercising, and running. For variation they leave their bathing suits on for volleyball. It's in color and 64 minutes long.

NUDIST COLONY OF THE DEAD

(Artistic License, 1991) **D/S:** Mark Pirro
P: Mark Headley

Nudists commit suicide and vow revenge against the religious group who closed down their camp. They return five years later as zombies and attack people at a church summer camp. This Super-8 musical comedy has choreographed numbers and exaggerated gore FX. The zombies are not completely naked, though. With Deborah Lynn and Rachel Latt. Forry Ackerman guest-stars as a judge.

NUDITY REQUIRED

(Raedon, 1988) **D:** John Bowen **S:** Danny King
P: Ted Sirota, Frank Rubin, J.T. Bown, Ron Lavery

Surfers pose as film producers in Julie Newmar's Beverly Hills mansion. This sex comedy features Troy Donahue, Edy Williams, Becky LeBeau, Heidi Payne, Windsor Taylor Randolph, and porno stars Misty Regan and Debbie Diamond. Newmar (58 at the time) plays a Russian and has a nude shower scene. The director of this unrated feature is aka porno director "John T. Bone."

NUMBERED DAYS: *See* SAVAGE ABDUCTION

NUMBER ONE WITH A BULLET

(MGM, 1987) **D:** Jack Smight **S:** Gail Morgan Hickman **P:** Golan/Globus

In a movie much like the same year's *Lethal Weapon*, Robert Carradine and Billy Dee Williams are cops who go after drug boss Barry Sattels. With Valerie Bertinelli, Peter Graves, and Bobby Di Cicco.

NUMBER 17

(Republic, 1932) **D/S:** Alfred Hitchcock
P: John Maxwell   UK

A detective story starts in a spooky old house and ends with a cross-country bus-and-train chase. Leon M. Lion stars as a tramp who discovers the hideout of some jewel thieves. Ann Grey, John Stuart, Barry Jones, and Donald Calthrop costar in this 63-minute film based on a novel and play by Jefferson Farjeon.

NURSES FOR SALE

(1971) **D:** Al Adamson **D/S:** Rolf Olson   W. Germany
(*Kapitän Rauhbein aus St. Pauli; Captain Typhoon*)

Curt Jurgens stars as a German sea captain who saves some nurses from bandits and fights drug smugglers. It was filmed in Puerto Rico. Independent International added 20 minutes of new (more exploitative) footage for the American release.

NUTTY, NAUGHTY CHATEAU

(1963) **D/S:** Roger Vadim **S:** Claude Choulbier
France/Italy (*Château en Suède*)

In an isolated Swedish castle, Hugo (Curt Jurgens) lives with his young wife (Monica Vitti), her brother (Jean-Claude Brialy), and his older sister. They dress up in 18th-century costumes. Hugo's crazy first wife, Ophelie (Françoise Hardy), shows up as a "ghost." Everybody has affairs, and characters are killed. With Sylvie as the senile grandmother, Jean-Claude Trintignant, and Daniel Emilfork as the weird butler. It's based on a play by Françoise Sagan and was filmed in northern Sweden.

A NYMPHOID BARBARIAN IN DINOSAUR HELL

(1990) **D/S/P:** Brett Piper **P:** Alex Pirnie, Lloyd Kaufman, Michael Hertz   (*Dark Fortress*)

Linda Corwin (in an animal-skin loincloth) is the last woman on Earth after a nuclear war. Green lizard men, a sea serpent, and mutants all want to mate with her. She's held captive in a castle by a skull-headed medicine man. This was made in New Hampshire for a reported $5000. Piper, who also did the FX (including some animation), directed *They Bite* next. Nymphoid debuted on the USA Network.

NYOKA AND THE TIGERMEN

(Republic, 1942) **D:** William Witney **S:** Ronald Davidson, Norman S. Hall, William Lively
(*The Perils of Nyoka*)

This 15-chapter Republic serial is a sequel to *Jungle Girl* (1940). Kay Aldridge (taking over the role of Nyoka) is hunting for her father and living with a tribe of North African Bedouins. Clayton Moore shows up looking for "the lost tablet of Hippocrates" (which can cure cancer) in "the tomb of the moon god." With William Benedict (from the Bowery Boys), Lorna Gray as Vultura, leader of a group of Arab killers, Charles Middleton as Cassib, Tristram Coffin, and Satan the gorilla. *Nyoka and the Tigermen*, the name of the feature version, is now being used for the entire serial on video.

OASIS OF THE ZOMBIES

(Wizard, 1981) **D:** "A. M. Frank"/Marius Le Soeur
S: A. L. Mariaux **P:** Daniel Le Soeur   France
(*Tombs of the Living Dead; Bloodsucking Nazi Freaks*)

Some German teens search for gold hidden by Field Marshal Erwin Rommel in North Africa. They're killed by Nazi zombies (with mediocre makeup). Manuel Gelin stars, and Jesús Franco plays a zombie. There's a time-wasting WWII battle sequence. This is not to be confused with the similar *Zombie Lake*, made around the same time.

OBLIVION

(Paramount, 1994) **D:** Sam Irvin **S:** Peter David **P:** Vlad Paunescu, Ileana Paunescu   (*Welcome to Oblivion*)

Richard Joseph Paul stars as the pacifist son of a murdered sheriff. This science-fiction/comedy/western has slo-mo battles, bad gags, bad acting, and *Gunsmoke* and *Star Trek* references. The high points are a scorpion monster (animated by David Allen) and Carel Struycken as an undertaker. Andrew Divoff is a lizard-faced alien outlaw bad
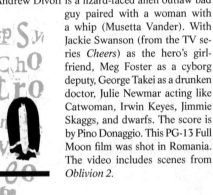
guy paired with a woman with a whip (Musetta Vander). With Jackie Swanson (from the TV series *Cheers*) as the hero's girlfriend, Meg Foster as a cyborg deputy, George Takei as a drunken doctor, Julie Newmar acting like Catwoman, Irwin Keyes, Jimmie Skaggs, and dwarfs. The score is by Pino Donaggio. This PG-13 Full Moon film was shot in Romania. The video includes scenes from *Oblivion 2*.

OBSESSION: A TASTE FOR FEAR

(Imperial, 1988) **D/S:** Piccio Raffanini
S: Lidia Ravera **P:** Jacques L. Goyard
Italy (*Pathos*)

In the near future a bisexual erotic photographer (Virginia Hey, from *Road Warrior*) and a macho detective track down a psycho who has been killing models. Most of the models (including a bald black woman) have nude scenes. So does Hey, who is also tied up. This offbeat, stylish film also features Kid Creole (of the Coconuts), Eva Grimaldi, and bodybuilder Teagan.

O.C. AND STIGGS

(MGM, 1983) **D/P:** Robert Altman **S:** Donald Cantrell, Ted Mann **P:** Peter Newman

Daniel H. Jenkins and Neill Barry are O.C. and Stiggs, a couple of clever teens who think up funny ways to disrupt the lives of their neighbors and parents one summer. It's based on a *National Lampoon* story by Todd Carroll and Ted Mann. With Paul Dooley as the rich insurance man they target, Dennis Hopper as a drug-dealing Nam vet, Sterling Hayden in his last feature, Tina Louise, Melvin Van Peebles, Jane Curtin, Jon Cryer, Ray Walston, Louis Nye, Martin Mull, Nina Van Pallandt, Cynthia Nixon, Rebecca Ferratti, and King Sunny Ade and His African Beats. MGM shelved this for several years, but it has some very funny sequences.

THE OCCULT EXPERIENCE

(RCA, 1969) **D/C:** R. L. Frost **D/E:** Luigi Scattini
Italy (*Witchcraft '80; Angeli Bianchi; Angeli Neri*)

It's hard for me to tell whether some of these scenes are real or not, but the Louisiana segments with snake handlers and a "mass hysteria" voodoo-dance ceremony are convincing and pretty incredible. The British nude black mass (with some scratched-out faces) and the naked American hippie cult in the woods are pretty suspect, and we're constantly being told that various scenes are secret "8mm home movies." Men in Bali stab themselves, a faith healer works in Stockholm, a woman in Italy contacts car-crash victims, Carnival witches are shown in Brazil, and Anton Levay is seen conducting a Church of Satan wedding. A nonstop-talking California cop really slows things down. Frost added more scenes for the AIP/TransAmerica release, which was rated X in 1970, then rerated R years later. It all ends at the Spahn ranch. British actor Edmund Purdom narrates. Frost had also produced *Mondo Bizarro* and *Mondo Freudo*. Other post-Manson occult/sex documentaries released in 1970 are *Sex Rituals of the Occult* (including sex in a coffin) and *Sex and Astrology*.

THE OCCULTIST

(Unicorn, 1987) **D/S:** Tim Kincaid **P:** Cynthia DePaula   (*Maximum Thrust; Waldo Warren, Private Dick Without a Brain*)

Rick Gianasi stars as a cyborg private eye hired to protect a Caribbean president in NYC. The leader's daughter (Jennifer Kanter) supports the revolutionaries who are out to assassinate him. Voodoo is involved. With Matt Mitler. By the director of *She's Back*.

THE OCTAGON

(Media, 1980) **D:** Eric Karson **S:** Leigh Chapman **P:** Joel Freeman

Chuck Norris has to fight off evil ninjas when he's hired to be a bodyguard for a woman named Justice (Karen Carlson). A mercenary soldier (Lee Van Cleef) and a tough woman (Carol Bagdasarian) team up with Norris, who has a good fight scene in an arena with Kyo the ninja. With Tadashi Yamashita, Art Hindle, Kim Lankford, Tracey Walter, Jack Carter, Richard Norton, and Mike Norris as Chuck's father in a flashback.

OCTOPUSSY

(CBS/Fox, 1983) **D:** John Glen **S:** George MacDonald Fraser, Richard Maibaum, Michael G. Wilson **P:** Albert R. Broccoli **M:** John Barry

This was the official number 13 Bond film. Roger Moore starred in it the same year that Sean Connery returned in *Never Say Never Again*. *Octopussy* was one of the biggest-grossing Bond movies, so Moore won at the box office, but it's pretty bad. Anonymous stuntmen costar, with Steven Berkoff as an evil Russian, Louis Jourdan, Maud Adams (*The Man with the Golden Gun*) as Octopussy, Kabir Bedi, and series regulars Lois Maxwell and Desmond Llewelyn. The soundtrack

(with a theme by Rita Coolidge) is on A&M. Liberty also released the *13 Original James Bond Themes* compilation album in 1983.

ODE TO BILLY JOE

(Warner, 1976) **D/P:** Max Baer Jr.
S: Herman Raucher **P:** Roger Camras

The second of three country movies directed by Jethro from *The Beverly Hillbillies* is this dramatic PG hit based on what might have happened in Bobby Gentry's 1967 hit song. Robby Benson is the suicidal Billy Joe McAllister, and Glynnis O'Connor is Bobby Lee. James Best plays a character who turns out to be a homosexual. It was filmed in Mississippi. The soundtrack is on Warner.

OFF BEAT

(Touchstone, 1986) **D:** Michael Dinner
S: Mark Medoff **P:** Joe Roth, Harry Ufland

A librarian (Judge Reinhold) impersonates a NYC cop to impress a real cop (Meg Tilly). This PG comedy has a surprising supporting cast, including Harvey Keitel as a bank robber, Joe Mantegna, Amy Wright, Anthony Zerbe, James Tolkan, John Turturro, Fred Gywnne, Bill Sadler, and Penn Jillette.

OFFERINGS

(South Gate, 1988) **D/S/P:** Christopher Reynolds

I never thought I'd see horror movies from Oklahoma, but there were several in the 80s. My grandfather, who moved there not long after the territory became a state, would not be amused. This one is a *Halloween* copy. Johnny, a traumatized kid who won't talk, is badgered by his ugly, scary mom in curlers: "You're sick!" Then, taunted by other kids, he falls into a well. "Ten years later" he's sedated in a sanitarium, kills a nurse with a syringe, and escapes to become a cannibalistic serial killer, cutting up victims (offscreen) and leaving body parts for the one girl who was his childhood friend. Characters watching TV say, "This show is boring" and "It's stupid," dialogue that applies to this video. A dumb sheriff wondering about a bloody ear or a nose found inside a newspaper just doesn't have the same effect as *Blue Velvet*. I loved the authentic local version of Valley talk, though.

OFFICE LOVE-IN, WHITE-COLLAR STYLE

(Rhino, 1968) **D/P:** "A. C. Stevens"/Stephen Apostoloff **S:** T. J. Casey   (*Swinging Secretary*)

People working at the Date-a-Mate computer service have after-hours affairs. Kathy Williams (one of the best-looking women in nudie movies) stars as a swinging secretary who unknowingly becomes involved with her boss, his wife (Marsha Jordan), and both of his sons. People try to duplicate what they see in an 8mm stag movie at a party, and a gay guy at the office tries on women's underwear. With Foreman Shane. It's on *Saturday-Night Sleazies, Volume III*.

OFFICIAL DENIAL

(Paramount, 1993) **D:** Brian Trenchard-Smith
S: Bryce Zabel   Australia

Parker Stevenson is kidnapped by aliens but befriends an alien named DOS. The US government has it all hushed up. Erin Gray is his wife, Chad Everett is a general, and Dirk Benedict is a security specialist. Michael Pate and his son Christopher play Indians. It debuted on The Sci-Fi Channel.

THE OFFSPRING

(IVE, 1986) **D/S:** Jeff Burr **S/P:** Darin Scott **S:** C. Courtney Joiner **P:** William Burr
(From a Whisper to a Scream)

In a small Tennessee town a historian (Vincent Price) relates four horror stories to a reporter (Susan Tyrrell). All of them have southern settings and are more shocking than the stories in more childish horror anthologies. Clu Gulager stars in a creepy tale of necrophilia, Rosalind Cash and Angelo Rossitto are in a story about a carny glass eater and voodoo, Cameron Mitchell faces Confederate cannibals, and the fourth tale is about a 200-year-old Bayou man. Martine Beswick and Lawrence Tierney are in a connecting segment about an electrocution. The director was in his 20s.

OF MICE AND MEN

(1939) **D:** Lewis Milestone
S: Eugene Solow **P:** Hal Roach

Burgess Meredith is George, and Lon Chaney Jr. is the half-wit Lenny, who doesn't know his own strength, in this classic version of John Steinbeck's 1937 tale about depression-era migrant workers. The Hays code insisted that the murderer must be punished (unlike in the novel). With Leigh Whipper as a bitter black man, Charles Bickford, Bob Steele, Betty Field, and Noah Beery Jr. The music is by Aaron Copeland. Producer Hal Roach also cast Chaney in *One Million BC* (1940). Then Chaney became famous in Universal horror movies. He later spoofed the Lenny role many times: "Tell me about the rabbits, George!" From U. A. There was a TV remake in 1981 with Robert Blake and Randy Quaid (from Prism). John Malkovich starred in Gary Sinise's 1992 version (from MGM video).

OF UNKNOWN ORIGIN

(Warner, 1983) **D:** George Pan Cosmatos
S: Brian Taggert **P:** Claude Heroux   Canada

A NYC yuppie (Peter Weller) battles a very large, seemingly indestructible, intelligent rat in his brownstone. He becomes obsessed with killing the creature to the point of tearing his home apart. It's based on a novel, *The Visitor,* by Chauncey G. Parker III, and is better than you'd expect. With Shannon Tweed as the wife, Jennifer Dale, and Maury Chaykin. It was filmed in Montreal by the director of several Stallone movies.

THE OGRE

(Videotec, 1987) **D/S:** Lamberto Bava   Italy

A little girl in Portland, Oregon, who saw something growing in the basement, grows up to be a horror writer (Virginia Bryant). On vacation in an Italian castle with her husband and son, she finds her childhood teddy bear and the drooling monster of her dreams. It was called *Demons III* in England.

OH, GOD!

(Warner, 1977) **D:** Carl Reiner
S: Larry Gelbart **P:** Jerry Weintraub

George Burns stars as a cigar-smoking God in this light PG fantasy/comedy. It costars John Denver but was a hit anyway. With Teri Garr, Donald Pleasence, Ralph Bellamy, William Daniels, Barnard Hughes, Barry Sullivan, Jeff Corey, Paul Sorvino as an evangelist, and Dinah Shore as herself. Burns returned in two sequels by other directors, also from Warner, made in the 80s.

OILY MANIAC

(1977) **D:** Ho Meng-Hua **P:** Raymond Shaw, Run-Run Shaw   Hong Kong

A cripple uses a magic talisman to become the title character and fight some evil brothers. Based on a late-50s TV series, it's by the inspired director of *Goliathon* and *Inframan.*

OLD IRONSIDES

(Paramount, 1926) **D:** James Cruze **S:** Walter Woods, Dorothy Arzner, Harry Carr **P:** B. P. Schulberg

Charles Farrell and Wallace Beery are 19th-century merchant seamen in the Mediterranean who fight Barbary pirates, including Boris Karloff. Esther Ralston and George Bancroft costar in this major Paramount production based on Oliver Wendell Holmes' 1830 poem. This 111-minute-long silent movie includes music. James Cruze later directed *The Great Gabbo* (1929).

OLD MOTHER RILEY'S GHOSTS

(Sinister, 1941) **D/P:** John Baxter **S:** Con West, Geoffrey Orme, Arthur Lucan   UK

An Irish charwoman, Mother Riley (Arthur Lucan), helps the black-sheep son of the owner of an old castle. Fake ghosts are created in order to steal a new motor. With Kitty Shane (the star's real-life wife) and John Stuart. Lucan starred in a series of 14 Mother Riley comedies, always in drag. *My Son, the Vampire* (1952) was the last one (it costars Bela Lugosi).

OLGA'S HOUSE OF SHAME

(SW,1964) **D:** Joseph P. Mawra **P:** George Weiss

Audrey Campbell (a beautiful model from Cincinnati) starred as Olga in a series of short (70-minute), b/w adults-only movies, the likely inspiration for the 70s Ilsa series. In this one (the third), she runs a "school of torture" in upstate New York and trains her female captives to be hookers and drug dealers. *White Slaves of Chinatown* (SW) was first and *Olga's Girls* (Audubon)

was second. All three were released in 1964. *Mme. Olga's Massage Parlor* (1965) starred Alice Linville as Olga. Weiss is the same man who backed Ed Wood's *Glen or Glenda* and Mawra (aka José Priete) later made *Shanty Tramp* and *Fireball Jungle.*

OLIVER TWIST

(Kino, 1922) **D/S:** Frank Lloyd **S:** Harry Weil

Jackie Coogan (who had costarred in Charlie Chaplin's *The Kid* in 1921) was the main attraction when this silent version of Charles Dickens' novel was made. Lon Chaney (who devised his own makeup as usual) plays Fagin in this First National release. Other versions are available, including the first with sound (1933).

LOS OLIVIDADOS

(1950) **D/S:** Luis Buñuel **S:** Luis Alcoriza
P: Oscar Dancigers   Mexico
(The Young and the Damned)

Although Luis Buñuel had directed three famous shorts in Europe this was only his third feature-length film. At a time when only a few American films had dealt seriously with juvenile delinquents this must have left audiences speechless. It still does. The Mexico City slum kids rob anyone (including a legless beggar) and kill. A blind beggar is also a rapist. The script is based on actual events, and many viewers thought that the nonprofessional actors were real street kids. Alfonso Mejia stars as Pedro, who has an incredible dream sequence. Buñuel made 20 films in Mexico (1947–61).

O LUCKY MAN!

(Warner, 1973) **D/P/A:** Lindsay Anderson **S:** David Sherwin **P/A:** Michael Medwin **M:** Alan Price

In a semi-sequel to Lindsay Anderson's *If* (1968) Malcolm McDowell (whose previous film was *A Clockwork Orange*) plays Mick, a coffee salesman who works his way to the top. This 186-minute-long film is a brilliant and bizarre satire of society. With Ralph Richardson, Rachel Roberts, Helen Mirren, Mona Washbourne, Arthur Lowe, and Edward Judd. Many of them play more than one role, and the director also appears. The excellent soundtrack is on Warner and Price (the original Animals keyboardist) also appears as himself, performing his songs. Anderson's *Britannia Hospital* (1982) also features McDowell in a small role.

OMAR KHAYYAM

(Paramount, 1957) **D:** William Dieterle
S: Barre Lyndon **P:** Y. Frank Freeman Jr.

Cornel Wilde stars as the poetic Persian astrologer, and Debra Paget is the fourth wife of the shah (Raymond Massey). This Technicolor and Vistavision film includes a drug scene, severed heads, and the phenomenal singing of Yma Sumac. With John Derek as a prince, Sebastian Cabot, Michael Rennie, Edward Platt, and Perry Lopez.

OMEGA COP

(Southgate, 1990) **D:** Paul Kyriazi **S:** Salli McQuaid **P/A:** Ron Marchini **P:** Garrick Huey

A post-nuke cop named John Travis (fighting champ Ron Marchini) protects three women while traveling across the wasteland. This *Road Warrior* copy features Adam West, Troy Donahue, and Stuart Whitman. *Karate Cop* was a sequel.

OMEGA SYNDROME

(Starmaker, 1987) **D:** Joseph Manduke **S:** John Sharkey **P:** Luigi G. Cingolani

Journalist Ken Wahl enlists some Nam-vet buddies to go after tattooed neo-Nazi kidnappers who have his daughter (Nicole Eggert). With George DiCenzo, and Doug McClure as a cop. It's from New World.

OMEN IV: THE AWAKENING

(Fox, 1991) **D:** Jorge Montesi, Dominique Othenin-Girard **S:** Brian Taggert **P:** Harvey Bernhard   Canada

Faye Grant and Michael Woods adopt a devil girl (Asia Vieira) from an orphanage. She has a black dog as a companion and a deadly snake, burns some hippies and causes many deaths at her Catholic school and at a psychic fair. Michael Lerner is a detective. The European theatrical version is longer than what debuted on Fox-TV. The Varèse Sarabande soundtrack reuses the original Jerry Goldsmith score. Director Othenin-Girard quit halfway through and was replaced. The original *The Omen* (1976), a big-budget major-studio horror movie with big stars and gore FX, was followed by *Damien: Omen II* (1978) and *The Final Conflict* (1981), all produced by Harvey Bernhard and all on Fox video. This one was shot in Vancouver.

OMOO OMOO, THE SHARK GOD

(Sinister, 1949) **D/S:** Leo Leonard **S:** George D. Green **P:** George S. Picker

A captain returning some cursed black pearls stolen from an idol in the South Seas is murdered and his daughter (Devera Burton) becomes cursed. With Ron Randell, George Meeker, and Pedro De Cordova. Part of the title (but none of the plot) is from Herman Melville's 1847 novel *Omoo*. The Screen Guild (later Lippert) release is only 58 minutes long.

ON BORROWED TIME

(MGM, 1939) **D:** Harold S. Bucquet **S:** Alice Duer Miller, Frank O'Neill, Claudine West **P:** Sidney Franklin

An old man (Lionel Barrymore) doesn't want to die yet, so he and his grandson (Bobs Watson) trap Death (Cedric Hardwicke) in a tree. This fantasy/drama, based on a play, features Beulah Bondi, Una Merkel, and Ian Wolfe. Franz Waxman scored this MGM release. The director made some of the films in the Dr. Kildare series (also with Barrymore). This was given an H (horrific) certificate in England.

ONCE

(1973) **D/S/P/C:** Morton Helig **P:** Marianne Helig

Have you ever wandered what else Marta Kristen (Judy Robinson in the TV series *Lost in Space*) did? She costars with Chris Mitchum in this obscure, arty allegory about creation. There's no dialogue, and Marta spends the whole film topless! Mitchum is a man who just appears on a beach one day. Another man shows up in a loincloth, and he creates things (including Marta). Marta (from Norway) was also in *Terminal Island* (1973) and *Gemini Affair* (1974).

ONCE A THIEF

(VSOM, 1965) **D:** Ralph Nelson **S/A:** Zekial Marko   US/France

An ex-thief (Alain Delon) and his wife (Ann-Margret) move to San Francisco. A cop (Van Heflin) harasses and arrests him. Delon's brother (Jack Palance!) talks him into helping with a million-dollar robbery. This b/w MGM release features Jeff Corey, Tony Musante, and John Davis Chandler.

ONCE A THIEF

(1991) **D/S:** John Woo **S:** Clifton Ko, Janet Chun **P:** Linda Kuk, Terence Chang Hong Kong (*Zongheng Sihai*)

Art thieves (Chow Young Fat, Leslie Cheung, and Cherie Chung) who were childhood friends are betrayed by their boss and seek revenge. It's more romantic and comic than the director's more violent hits and borrows from Hitchcock's *To Catch a Thief*, but it still has lots of stunt work and shooting. Nearly half the action takes place in France. A sequel, *Once a Thief 2* (1991), also by Woo, included the same stars except for Chow.

ONCE BEFORE I DIE

(1964) **D/P/A:** John Derek **S/A:** Vance Skarstedt   US/Philippines

Derek is a WWII major in the Philippines, and Ursula Andress (Derek's wife at the time) is his Swiss fiancée, Alex. He's killed during a Japanese attack, and she has sex with a virgin soldier before a massacre occurs. With Richard Jaeckel as a bloodthirsty lieutenant named Custer, Rod Lauren, and Ron Ely. It was filmed on location. Andress was in her husband's *Nightmare in the Sun* the same year.

ONCE BITTEN

(Vestron, 1985) **D:** Howard Storm **S:** David Hines, Jeffrey Hause **P:** Dimitri Villard, Robby Wald, Frank E. Hildebrand

Jim Carrey stars as a virgin student who becomes the victim of a modern-day vampire countess (Lauren Hutton). Cleavon Little is her gay vampire assistant. The soundtrack of this not-very-funny PG-13 comedy, featuring various artists, is on MCA . The Canadian-born Carrey became a major comedy-movie star nearly 10 years later.

ONCE UPON A FRIGHTMARE = FRIGHTMARE

ONCE UPON A KNIGHT

(SW, 1961) **D/S/P:** Bob Cresse

An insurance investigator (Frank James) searching for a stolen painting in Venice, California, is allergic to naked women. He sees lots of them in a steam bath. Virginia Gordon, *Playboy*'s Miss January 1959, is the main attraction in this color nudie movie from Olympic International. It was the first of her many 60s film appearances.

ONCE UPON A TIME

(1943) **D:** Alexander Hall **S:** Lewis Meltzer, Oscar Saul **P:** Louis F. Edelman

Cary Grant stars as a Broadway producer who plans to exploit an (offscreen) dancing caterpillar that belongs to a little boy (Ted Donaldson). This flop comedy/fantasy is based on a story and a radio play. Janet Blair costars as the kid's older sister, with William Demarest, Kirk Alyn, and Lloyd Bridges. Alexander Hall had directed the hit *Here Comes Mr. Jordan* (1941). Donaldson also starred in the Rusty the Horse series, also from Columbia.

ONCE UPON A TIME IN CHINA

(Festival, 1991) **D/S/P:** Tsui Hark Hong Kong (*Wong Fei Hong*)

Jet Li stars as the acrobatic, kung-fu-fighting Cantonese folk hero Dr. Wong Fei Hong. This very popular (in Asia) widescreen, 140-minute, historical kung-fu epic set in the 1870s is superior in every way to most of the 70s Chinese period action movies. Foreigners with guns and a local gang are the villains. With Rosamund Kwan as the westernized Aunt Yee, Yuen Baio as the hero's comic sidekick Fu, and Jacky Cheung. The ladder-duel scene is a standout. Sequels followed. Raymond Chow was the executive producer of this Golden Harvest series.

ONCE UPON A TIME IN CHINA 2

(Long Shong, 1992) **D/S/P:** Tsui Hark **S:** Hanson Chan, Cheung Tan **P:** Ng See Yuen   Hong Kong (*Wong Fei Hong 2*)

Jet Li and Rosamund Kwan return as Wong Fei Hong and Aunt Yee. They travel to Canton in 1895 for a medical convention. Many think that this sequel is even better than the first movie, although it has more comedy. It features bumbling British and the fanatical anti-foreigner White Lotus sect. The real-life revolutionary leader Sun Yat-sen is a character. With Mok Siu Chung as Fu and David Chiang.

ONCE UPON A TIME IN CHINA 3: DANCE OF THE LION KING

(Long Shong, 1993) **D/S/P:** Tsui Hark **P:** Ng See Yuen   Hong Kong (*Wong Fei Hong 3*)

This sequel concerns a martial-arts tournament planned by the dowager empress and the first movie camera in China, which exposes a Russian conspiracy. Jet Li, Rosamund Kwan (now Wong Fei Hong's fiancée), and Mok Siu Chung all return. It was filmed in mainland China. Parts 4 (without Jet Li) and 5 followed immediately.

ONCE UPON A TIME IN THE WEST

(Paramount, 1967) **D/S:** Sergio Leone **S:** Bernardo Bertolucci, Dario Argento **P:** Fulvio Morsella **M:** Ennio Morricone   US/Italy   (C'era una Volta il West)

This remains the ultimate western of all time. Although the complex screenplay borrows from earlier movies, everything about this long, widescreen, very emotional and political epic has been copied and parodied, from the extreme closeups, to the Ennio Morricone score, to the dusters the gunmen wear. The equally important leads (all excellent) are Henry Fonda as the gunman-for-hire Frank, Charles Bronson as the mysterious Mexican Harmonica, Jason Robards as Cheyenne, and Claudia Cardinale as Jill. The supporting cast includes Lionel Stander, Keenan Wynn, Frank Wolff, and, in the famous opening, Woody Strode and Jack Elam. It was shot in Spain, Arizona, and Utah. A major hit around the world, it was almost ignored when first released (cut by Paramount) in America. A 4-hour version exists somewhere, but you can enjoy a panned and scanned or letterboxed widescreen 165-minute version on laserdisc. RCA released the soundtrack. Leone later made the equally fascinating historical epic *Once upon a Time in America* (1984) and planned to direct *Once upon a Time in Russia,* but he died in 1989.

ONCE YOU KISS A STRANGER

(1969) **D:** Robert Sparr **S:** Frank Tarloff, Norman Katkov **P:** Harold A. Goldstein

In this remake of *Strangers on a Train* Carol Lynley seduces a professional golfer (Paul Burke) and offers to kill his opponent (Phil Carey). He is supposed to kill her psychiatrist (Whit Bissell), who wants her committed. She clubs Carey to death and blackmails Burke. With Stephen McNally as a detective, Martha Hyer, Peter Lind Hayes, and George Fenneman (Groucho Marx's TV sidekick). The Warner release was rated M. Would-be Hitchcock Sparr also directed *More Dead than Alive* (1969).

ON DEADLY GROUND

(Warner, 1994) **D/P/A:** Steven Seagal **S:** Ed Horowitz, Robin U. Russin **P:** Julius R. Nasso, A. Kitman Ho

Seagal tries to be the Billy Jack of the 90s in this one. He's a nonviolent former CIA terminator in Alaska who (in a dream sequence) is convinced to stop being nonviolent and battle an evil oil-company head (Michael Caine). He even makes an ecology speech. The local natives consider him a spirit warrior, and an Inuit woman (Joan Chen) becomes his partner. The cast also includes John C. McGinley, R. Lee Ermey, Mike Starr, and Shari Shattuck. This was the Seagal's first box-office flop.

ON DRESS PARADE

(1939) **D:** William Clemens, Noel Smith **S:** Tom Reed, Charles Belden **P:** Bryan Foy

This was the last (and the least interesting and shortest, at 62 minutes) of the Warner Brothers Dead End Kids movies. Billy Halop, Leo Gorcey, Bobby Jordan, Huntz Hall, Gabriel Dell, and Bernard Punsley were all together for the seventh time

but had to play military cadets. The next stop for most of the gang was Monogram, where some of them stayed (as the Bowery Boys) until 1958!

ONE DARK NIGHT

(HBO, 1983) **D/S:** Tom McLoughlin **S:** Michael Hawes **P:** Michael Schroeder   (Rest in Peace)

Nice Meg Tilly is forced to spend the night in a mausoleum as her initiation into a club called the Sisters. This PG teen horror movie features the "psychic vampire" Raymar, a dead man with telekinetic powers who drains the energy of the girls. With Robin Evans, Adam West, Leo Gorcey Jr., and Kevin Peter Hall. The FX are by Tom Burman.

ONE DEADLY OWNER

(Thriller, 1973) **D:** Ian Fordyce **S:** Brian Clemens   UK

Donna Mills is a model who buys a haunted Rolls-Royce. This made-for-TV movie costars Jeremy Brett and Robert Morris.

ONE DOWN, TWO TO GO

(Media, 1982) **D/P/A:** Fred Williamson **S:** Jeff Williamson

Richard Roundtree is the promoter of a New Jersey martial-arts tournament. His three tough-guy friends come to the rescue when he's cheated out of the receipts by a crooked fight promoter and gangster (Joe Spinell). Fred Williamson, Jim Brown ("I may not know kung fu, but I'm an expert in gun fu"), and Jim Kelly (who all had been in *Three the Hard Way*) are the fighting friends. Kelly, in his last-known film, spends much of the time in a coma, though. Lots of white guys are shot. With Paula Sills and Laura Loftus.

ONE FALSE MOVE

(Columbia, 1992) **D:** Carl Franklin **S:** Tom Epperson, Billy Bob Thornton **P:** Jesse Beaton, Ben Myron

After a bloody shootout over coke money in LA the ex-con killers head for Star City, Arkansas. An addicted, long-haired biker (cowriter Billy Bob Thornton), his girlfriend, Fantasia (Cynda Williams), and a psycho (Michael Beach) are the deadly trio. Bill Paxton has one of the best roles of his career as Hurricane Dixon, a local cop with secrets in his past. None of the characters are clichés (Williams, Beach, and the director are black), and this movie has a rare combination of action, humor, and serious issues. Jim Metzler and Earl Billings are LA detectives. Because of good reviews this violent thriller from IRS received a theatrical release. Carl Franklin was an actor (often in the TV series *The A-Team*) who had directed three movies for Roger Corman.

ONE FLEW OVER THE CUCKOO'S NEST

(Warner, 1975) **D:** Milos Forman **S:** Lawrence Hauben, Bo Goldman **P:** Michael Douglas, Saul Zaentz **M:** Jack Nitzsche

The adaptation of Ken Kesey's 1962 novel, the first movie since 1934 to win all five top Oscars, is one of the great anti-conformist features. Jack Nicholson is McMurphy, a patient in a 60s mental institution (it was shot in an actual Oregon state

hospital). Most of the supporting cast went on to fame (mostly in exploitation movies reviewed in this book). Louise Fletcher got most of the attention (and an Oscar) at the time, but check out the performances of Brad Dourif as Billy Bibbitt, Will Sampson as Chief Bromden, William Redfield, Scatman Crothers, Danny DeVito, Sydney Lassick, Christopher Lloyd, Michael Berryman, Vincent Schiavelli, and Louisa Moritz. Many of them were making their film debuts. The soundtrack is on Fantasy. This United Artists release was the most successful Nicholson film (until *Batman*).

ONE FRIGHTENED NIGHT

(Sinister, 1935) **D:** Christie Cabanne **S:** Wellyn Totman **P:** Nat Levine

Charley Grapewin is an elderly millionaire who summons his relatives to his old house, in this 67-minute Mascot chiller. The identity of the masked killer is a mystery, and the thunderstorm never lets up. Wallace Ford costars as a wisecracking vaudeville magician, with Mary Carlisle, Regis Toomey, Hedda Hopper, Lucien Littlefield, and Rafaella Ottiani. It's available on *Matinee at the Bijou, Volume III*.

100 RIFLES

(Fox, 1969) **D/S:** Tom Gries **S:** Clair Huffaker **P:** Marvin Schwartz

This western (shot in Spain) stars Jim Brown as an American sheriff, Raquel Welch as Sarita, an Indian revolutionary, and Burt Reynolds as Yaqui Joe, a half-breed Indian bank robber. Brown falls for Welch, and they all battle Fernando Lamas, Dan O'Herlihy, and Eric Braeden in Mexico. With Soledad Miranda. It was released by 20th Century–Fox.

ONE MAGIC CHRISTMAS

(Disney, 1985) **D:** Philip Borsos **S:** Thomas Meehan **P:** Peter O'Brian   US/Canada

Mary Steenburgen is a poor (and suicidal) mom in this G-rated Disney fantasy. A guardian angel (Harry Dean Stanton!) and Santa Claus (Jan Rubes) get together and help out. With Elisabeth Harnois, Gary Basaraba, Arthur Hill, and Elias Koteas.

ONE MAN FORCE

(Academy, 1989) **D/S/P:** Dale Trevillion

Former Oakland Raiders star John Matuszak is suspended LA detective Jake Swan. He's after the drug dealers who killed his partner (Sam Jones, from *Flash Gordon*), and a rock star called Blueberry is kidnapped. Richard Lynch and Robert Tessier are henchmen of Charles Napier. Also with Ronny Cox, Sharon Farrell, George "Buck" Flower, Maria Celedonio, and Stacey Q. It's from SGE.

ONE MAN JURY

(VCI, 1977) **D/S:** Charles Martin **P:** Theodore Bodnar, Steve Bond **C:** Gary Graver

Jack Palance stars as a *Dirty Harry*–style vigilante cop. Chris Mitchum costars, with Pamela Shoop, Angel Tompkins, Cara Williams, Joe Spinell, Royal Dano, and Mike Mazursky.

ONE MILLION AC/DC

(Even Steven, 1969) **D/P:** Ed DePriest
S: "Akdon Telmig"/Edward D. Wood Jr.

This is one of Ed Wood's lesser-known credits, a ridiculous soft-core sex fantasy. In what must be a tribute to *Robot Monster* a man in a gorilla suit kidnaps a woman and takes her to Bronson Canyon! All kinds of dinosaurs appear: a small lizard made to appear huge, men in horrible-looking suits, toys, and that old standby, tinted b/w footage from *One Million Years BC*. The ancient people speak modern English. There's a pig-out food scene, a girl fight, a lesbian scene leading to a "virgin sacrifice," and other sex scenes. The most worthwhile segment is a long, nude outdoor run worthy of Russ Meyer (Gary Graver shot it). One of the photographers was Michael Weldon. R. L. Frost and Bob Cresse were credited as "historical consultants." The (video) insert title is *Attack of the Cave Babes*.

ONE NIGHT STAND

(1984) **D/S:** John Duigan **P:** Dara Murphy   Australia

Two teen couples are trapped in the empty Sydney Opera House on New Year's Eve when a nuclear war breaks out. The band Midnight Oil performs.

ONE ON TOP OF THE OTHER

(1969) **D/S:** Lucio Fulci **S:** Roberto Gianviti   Italy (*Una Sull'altra*)

Jean Sorel is a doctor suspected of killing his wife (Marisa Mell). His mistress (Elsa Martinelli) tries to help prove his innocence. Also with Americans John Ireland as a detective and Faith Domergue. It was filmed in San Francisco and in the actual San Quentin gas chamber.

1+1 (EXPLORING THE KINSEY REPORT)

(Sinister, 1961) **D/S/P:** Arch Oboler   Canada

A professor (Leo G. Carroll) introduces four talk-filled episodes, in this dated movie based on a radio play by Arch Oboler. Each time the camera zooms in on a person who remembers tales of affairs. One episode is humorous, and the last one (which would have been a selling point in the early 60s) deals with abortion and includes an onscreen debate. Also with Kate Reid. It was made in Toronto. Oboler's next film, *The Bubble* (1967), is more interesting.

ONE SHOCKING MOMENT

(SW, 1965) **D/S/P/C/E:** Ted V. Mikels

Cliff and his giggling wife, Mindy, move to a new apartment in LA. One of their female neighbors, Tanya (Verne Martine), is a bisexual belly-dancing club owner (and bouncer) who makes money on the side from S&M sessions. Cliff says, "This is my kind of a joint, a real hep place." Tanya ties up her slave and whips and kicks him while a loud clock ticks away. Mindy sings at a bongos-and-drinking party that almost becomes an orgy, but the couple "overcome those temptations," according to the narrator. This b/w adult feature runs 71 minutes. It has brief nudity and too much talking. Ted V. Mikels's next was *The Black Klansman*.

ONE STEP BEYOND

(Video Specials, 1959–61) **D:** John Newland
P: Collier Young

This half-hour ABC-TV series was once a rival to *The Twilight Zone* (which debuted the same year). But these stories are all (supposedly) based on real occurrences. Some are pretty chilling, and the casting was always great. Christopher Lee, Patrick Macnee, Patty McCormack, William Shatner, Donald Pleasence, Anton Diffring, Robert Lansing, and Warren Beatty are some of the many actors. Director Newland is the host. Harry Lubin's familiar, creepy music was released by Decca (later Varèse Sarabande). *The Next Step Beyond* was a short-lived syndicated color revival of the show.

ONE STEP TO HELL

(1968) **D/S/P:** Sandy Howard **S:** Jack De Witt, Robert L. Joseph   US/Italy/Spain

In 1905 a South African cop (American Ty Hardin) chases three sadistic killers who have escaped from jail and are after gold. Pier Angeli costars, with Rossano Brazzi, Tab Hunter, George Sanders, Jorge Rigaud, Helga Line, and Alan Collins. It was filmed in Spain and South Africa. Sandy Howard produced *A Man Called Horse* (1970) next.

1000 CONVICTS AND A WOMAN!

(1971) **D:** Ray Austin **S:** Oscar Brodney **P:** Philip N. Krasne   UK

Alexandra Hay is Angel, the nympho daughter of a British prison governor. She seduces guards and inmates, and Sandor Eles and Harry Baird decide to blackmail her. AIP released it. Austin later made TV movies.

ONE TOO MANY

(Sinister, 1950) **D:** Erle C. Kenton
S: Malcolm Stuart Boylan **P:** Kroger Babb   (*Mixed-Up Women*)

Lots of familiar character actors are in this pro–Alcoholics Anonymous Hallmark road-show movie about an alcoholic former concert pianist who's now a housewife. Ruth Warrick (*Citizen Kane* and later the TV soap opera *All My Children*) stars. Richard Travis (*Mesa of Lost Women*) is her reporter husband. Sullivan (Rhys Williams), a friendly AA-member bartender, helps her recover, but first she has a "blur-o-vision" dream and goes to the "psycho ward" in a straitjacket. It all ends happily with a benefit show. Also with Onslow Stevens and Victor Kilian (later in the TV series *Mary Hartman, Mary Hartman*). When it was rereleased, the ads claimed that Lyle Talbot (who is in one scene!) was the star. Kroger Babb wrote the story. This is the last film by Erle C. Kenton, whose career ranged from the incomparable *Island of Lost Souls* (1933) to the birth-of-a-baby movie *Bob and Sally* (1948), also for Hallmark.

ONE TOUCH OF VENUS

(Republic, 1948) **D:** William A. Seiter **S:** Harry Kurnitz, Frank Tashlin **P:** Lester Cowan

Ava Gardner stars as a statue of the Greek goddess of love, Venus. Robert Walker is the window dresser who kisses her and brings her to life. With Dick Haymes, Eve Arden, Tom Conway, Olga San Juan, and Arthur O'Connell. This b/w Universal romantic fantasy is based on a Broadway musical and is similar to the previous year's *Down to Earth* with Rita Hayworth. The score by Kurt Weill, with lyrics by Ogden Nash, has been released several times. The same concept was later used for *Mannequin* and its sequel.

ONE-TRICK PONY

(Warner, 1980) **D:** Robert M. Young **S/A/M:** Paul Simon **P:** Michael Yannen, Michael Hausman

Singer Paul Simon, in his only starring role, is a troubled, washed-up pop star on the road with marriage and money problems. One place he plays is the Cleveland Agora, and the B-52's, Sam and Dave, and the Lovin' Spoonful also perform. With Blair Brown, Rip Torn, Joan Hackett, Allen Garfield, Mare Winningham, Harry Shearer, Lou Reed as a record producer, Daniel Stern, and Tiny Tim. Warner released the soundtrack, but Simon's theme song made it only to number 40.

ONE-WAY WAHINE

(1965) **D/P:** William O. Brown **S:** Rod Larsen

Anthony Eisley convinces some runaway teens (Joy Harmon and Adele Claire) in Hawaii to help him drug and rob a pair of bank robbers. With Alvy Moore, Harold Fong, and Edgar Bergen as a beach bum. Ray Peterson sings the songs, including "Wahine Does the Bird." This comedy was filmed on location and was from United Artists.

ONE WISH TOO MANY

(Sinister, 1954) **D:** John Durst **S:** John Eldridge **P:** Basil Wright   UK

A marble grants wishes to a boy, until he asks for a giant steamroller and it overruns London. This fantasy stars Anthony Richmond and Rosalind Gourgey. It's only 56 minutes long.

ON HER BED OF ROSES

(SW, 1966) **D/S:** Albert Zugsmith **P:** Robert Caramico   (*Psychopathia Sexualis*)

The start of this interesting psycho movie is a lot like *Targets* (1968). A troubled young guy named Stephen (Ronald Warren) kills himself after picking off passengers on a highway with a rifle. His blond fiancée, Lisa (Sandra Lynn), explains why she blames herself in flashbacks told to a psychiatrist. The parents are really to blame. One of her dream sequences is like one in *Daughter of Horror* (1953). There's too much talking, but we also get topless dancers and every psychological cliché in the book. Lynn looks great and is great in the part. She was also in Zugsmith's *Movie Star American Style, or LSD, I Hate You!* the same year. Caramico also produced *Orgy of the Dead,* and Pat Barringer, from that hit, appears here as a topless dancer. The cool experimental music by Joe Green (who made records with his Little Green Men) was released by Mira.

ONIBABA

(Conoisseur, 1964) **D/S:** Kaneto Shindo **P:** Kindai Eiga Kyokai, Tokyo Eiga   Japan   (*The Demon*)

A mother and her daughter-in-law survive during a medieval civil war by ambushing soldiers, killing them, and selling the armor. The devious and jealous older woman (Nobuko Otawa) tries to scare away a farmer by wearing a demon mask. The cursed mask tightens and disfigures her face. This b/w movie is very grim and scary. The video is letterboxed and subtitled. Shindo also made another excellent samurai/ghost movie, *Kuroneko* (1968). Masaki Kobayashi's *Kwaidan* is another Japanese horror movie from the same year that you should look for (from Sinister). William Friedkin says that he was inspired by the scary faces in *Onibaba* to do *The Exorcist.*

ONLY THE STRONG

(1993) **D/S:** Sheldon Lettich **S:** Luis Esteban **P:** Samuel Hadida

Mark Dacascos stars as a master of "capoeira," a (real) Brazilian martial arts style that looks like a combination of kung fu and lambada dancing (?!). A former teacher (Geoffrey Lewis) in Miami has him battle drug dealers. Stacy Travis costars. This PG-13 20th Century–Fox movie features Brazilian music and was made by a frequent director of movies starring Jean-Claude Van Damme.

ON THE AIR

(1992) **P:** David Lynch, Mark Frost

Ian Buchanan (from the TV series *Twin Peaks*) stars in this short-lived comedy series about a live TV program being produced in 1957 Manhattan. Each episode shows the rehearsal, then how the show really turns out, mistakes and all. Only three episodes of this half-hour series were aired by ABC-TV. The entire series (seven episodes, directed and written by various people) was issued on a Japanese laserdisc. The book *Bad TV* called this "the worst show in the history of television." It

features Miguel Ferrer, Nancye Ferguson, David L. Lander, Tracey Walter, Sydney Lassick, Chuck McCann, and Kim McGuire (*Cry-Baby*).

ON THE EDGE

(Vestron, 1985) **D/S/P:** Rob Nilsson **P:** Jeffrey Hayes

Bruce Dern stars as a middle-aged runner determined to win a long-distance race in California. Pam Grier is an aerobics instructor, in a romantic subplot. About 10 minutes of footage with some Grier nudity and sex were cut from the R version, after some people at sneak previews objected, but were restored on the unrated video version.

ON THE LINE

(Nelson, 1984) **D/S/P:** José Luis Boaru **S:** Barbara P. Solomon **P:** Stephen Kovacs   Spain

Scott Wilson is a border guard. David Carradine smuggles Mexicans over the border. With Victoria Abril (later in *Tie Me Up! Tie Me Down!*), Jesse Vint, and Sam Jaffe. It was shot on the Texas-Mexico border.

ON THE TRAIL OF ED WOOD

(Videosonic Arts, 1990) **D:** Michael Copner **P:** Buddy Barnett

Actor Conrad Brooks, who was in *Glen or Glenda* and *Plan 9 from Outer Space,* is the friendly star of this hour-long video, remembering Ed Wood and taking us on a tour of where Wood lived and worked in Hollywood. He shows some rare photos and says that Tor Johnson was a piano mover in NYC (!) and wrestled in Hong Kong. The video includes trailers for *Plan 9* and *Jail Bait.*

OPEN HOUSE

(Prism, 1987) **D:** Jag Mundhra **P:** Sandy Cobe **S:** David Mickey Evans

Joseph Bottoms plays a radio psychologist whose girlfriend (Adrienne Barbeau) sells real estate. A serial killer who keeps slaughtering people in new, empty houses (and then calls the radio show) turns out to be a homeless maniac who kills because houses are too expensive (!). This movie covers all the exploitation bases. The killer (a big guy wearing a duster) slices women up with razorblades on a stick. Barbeau has another topless scene, a woman goes for a nude swim before being decapitated, and there's a dumb comic S&M scene. It's one of those movies where characters keep acting as if nothing has happened even after several coworkers have been killed. With Tiffany Bolling and Mary Stavin. The prolific director, Jag Mundhra, made many more soft-core sex movies with name stars.

OPERATION CAMEL

(1960) **D:** Sven Methling Jr. **S:** Bob Ramsing, Preben Kass **P:** Henrik Sandberg   Denmark

Nora Hayden (*Angry Red Planet*) stars as a French dancer rescued by Danish UN soldiers in Gaza. This color comedy was released in b/w by AIP. It's part of a series of Danish soldier movies. The red-haired Hayden wrote the bestseller *How to Satisfy a Woman Every Time* in 1983.

OPERATION DELILAH

(1967) **D/S:** Luis de los Arcos
S/P: Sidney Pink   US/Spain

Rory Calhoun and Gia Scala star in this comedy about a coup on a Caribbean island. They try to depose a bearded Castro-type leader. With Marvin Kaplan.

OPERATION GANYMEDE

(Marathon, 1977) **D/S/P:** Rainer Erler   W. Germany

When five astronauts, led by Dieter Laser, crash-land near Mexico, they find a desolate Earth after five years in space. They try to survive, fight each other, and hallucinate, and one becomes a cannibal. This very serious, and dark 2-hour film was made for TV and features Horst Frank as the mission commander and Jurgen Prochnow. The video is a shortened version.

OPERATION GOLDEN PHOENIX

(MCA, 1994) **D/P/A:** Jalal Merhi

Merhi is a kickboxing security specialist protecting half of a valuable medallion. He has to battle Loren Avedon (*King of the Kickboxers*) and an evil warlord (James Hong). With Karen Shepard and Al Waxman.

OPERATION 'NAM

(On Line, 1985) **D:** "Larry Ludman"/
Fabrizio De Angelis **S:** Edwin C. Dietrich
Italy/W. Germany (*Cinque Uomini Contro Tutti;
Operation Overthrow; Power Play; A State of Shock*)

Here's another movie about Nam vets going back to rescue their leader from a POW camp. Donald Pleasence is top-billed, but you'll see more of John Ethan Wayne (one of the Duke's lesser-known sons), Christopher Connelly, John Steiner, Alan Collins, Oliver Tobias, and Gordon Mitchell.

OPERATION SNAFU

(1961) **D:** Cyril Frankel **S:** Harold
Buchman **P:** S. Benjamin Fisz   UK
(*On the Fiddle; Operation Warhead*)

AIP released this b/w WWII comedy starring Sean Connery in 1965 after he became famous as James Bond. Connery is Pedlar Pascoe, a Gypsy who teams up with a Royal Air Force conman (Alfred Lynch) for various swindles. They end up as war heroes in France. With Cecil Parker, Stanley Holloway, and Wilfrid Hyde-White. It opened in Cleveland.

OPERATION THUNDERBOLT

(MGM/UA, 1977) **D/S:** Menahem Golan
S: Clark Reynolds **P:** Yoram Globus   Israel

This is the best of several raid-on-Entebbe movies about Israeli commandos rescuing hijacked plane passengers in Uganda. Yehoram Gaon and Klaus Kinski star, with Sybil Danning, Assaf Dayan, and a mostly Israeli cast. It's PG and runs more than 2 hours.

OPERATION WAR ZONE

(AIP, 1989) **D/S:** David A. Prior **P/A:** Fritz Matthews

An honest soldier (Matthews) battles a corrupt arms dealer. Joe Spinell costars. This is one of his last roles. The others are in Prior's *Rapid Fire* and *The Undertaker* (which was never released).

THE OPIUM CONNECTION

(Bingo, 1966) **D:** Terence Young **S:** Jo Eisinger
P: Euan Lloyd   (*The Poppy Is Also a Flower*)

Nobody seemed to like this international drug deal movie when it debuted on NBC-TV. It's based on an Ian Fleming story, is by the director of three vintage Bond films, was backed by the United Nations (!), and has an incredible cast. It's confusing, but you won't regret watching it. Trevor Howard and E. G. Marshall travel around the world trying to break up a dope ring. Rita Hayworth is an addict married to a rich dealer (Gilbert Roland). With Angie Dickinson, Yul Brynner, Eli Wallach, Hugh Griffith, Marcello Mastroianni, Stephen Boyd, Omar Sharif, Barry Sullivan, Jack Hawkins, Senta Berger, Anthony Quayle, Howard Vernon, Harold Sakata, and Trini Lopez. The video is the full 100 minutes.

OPPOSING FORCE

(HBO, 1986) **D:** Eric Karson
S: Gil Cowan   (*Hell Camp*)

Lisa Eichhorn and Tom Skerritt are part of a military-training mission on an isolated tropical island. The commander (Anthony Zerbe) goes nuts and uses psychological torture. With Richard Roundtree and John Considine. Eichhorn has nude scenes, and there's lots of sex and violence.

THE ORACLE

(USA, 1984) **D:** Roberta Findlay
S: R. Allen Leider **P:** Walter E. Sear

Spirits from the beyond (a glowing magic box) are in a NYC apartment. A murdered businessman possesses a woman. The killer turns out to be a fat woman in male drag. It's similar to *Witchboard* (made later).

THE ORBITRONS

(Ghost Limb Films, 1990) **D/S/A:** Christopher C. Frieri
C: Nathan Schiff

Who would have expected a good, dirty, low-down, and (very) low-budget, b/w science-fiction/horror spoof from Newark? It's not for everybody, of course, but it's a unique gross-out surprise that proudly borrows from *Plan 9 from Outer Space, Frankenstein Meets the Space Monsters, Night of the Living Dead,* and probably John Waters. Kubash (Christopher C. Frieri) is a greasy biker who rides around to newly recorded versions of "Cities on Flame with Rock and Roll" and "White Room." He's badly beaten by dumb, doughnut-eating cops, then encounters aliens and cannibal zombies in a graveyard where he's gone to jack off (for old times' sake). His big biker friend says, "That's one fucking be-zar story!" The alien queen wears Frederick's of Hollywood–type clothes and is good spouting lots of dialogue but stumbles on the word "erection." One zombie pukes on Kubash (for a long time), and the queen whips him and puts a needle in his dick. These and other effects are not exactly realistic. The original music is by I Love You and the Drills.

ORDER OF DEATH: *See* CORRUPT

ORDER OF THE BLACK EAGLE

(1985) **D:** Worth Keeter **S:** Phil Behrens
P: Betty J. Stephens, Robert P. Eaton

A secret agent (Ian Hunter) and Boon the baboon (in a tuxedo) save the world. There's a plot to revive Hitler. This sequel to *Unmasking the Idol* was filmed in Shelby, North Carolina, by a director who worked for Earl Owensby.

ORDER OF THE EAGLE

(AIP, 1989) **D:** Thomas Baldwin **S/P/A:** William Zipp

ORMONDS

The Ormond Organization was Ron Ormond, an Italian-American former stage magician, his wife June, a former vaudeville comedy dancer and, later on, their son Tim. Ormond had directed "a dozen" Lash LaRue westerns, some musicals, and several early 50s movies with Jackie Coogan (including *Mesa of Lost Women*). After a break, when the Ormonds, among other things, took The Three Stooges on tour, they turned to exploitation movies like *Untamed Mistress*, about a woman's relationship with a gorilla. They made three 60s country movies in Nashville—*The Girl with Tobacco Road, Forty Acre Feud,* and the musical *White Lightning Road*. Many of their movies include the same simple repetitive flamenco guitar music (also used in Ed Wood's *Jail Bait*) and disorienting harmonica duets. By the 70s, (after Ron had been born again) they made amazing Baptist religious movies like *The Burning Hell* and *The Grim Reaper* (featuring Dr. Jerry Falwell!). Ron died in 1981, but his grown-up son Tim made *The Second Coming.*

Frank Stallone and his industrial hitmen go after an Eagle Scout who has accidentally discovered the plans for the Star Wars defense system.

ORGY AT LIL'S PLACE

(1963) **D/P:** J. Nehemiah **S:** Allan Naidob

Kari Knudsen (*Playboy*'s Miss February 1962) and June Ashley are sisters in Manhattan who become involved with nude modeling for artists. One of them is almost tricked into prostitution. This is a b/w nudie movie with color sequences. William Mishkin distributed it. Del Tenny was the assistant director.

ORGY OF THE DEAD

(Rhino, 1965) **D/P:** "A. C. Stevens"/Stephen C. Apostoloff **S:** Edward D. Wood Jr.

Orgy of the Dead is one of the greatest movies ever made. There's nothing like it (and it's in Astravision and Sexicolor). The undead Criswell rises from his coffin and rants about "monsters to be pitied, monsters to be despised," a line lifted from Ed Wood's earlier *Night of the Ghouls*. A horror novelist and his red-haired girlfriend (Pat Barrington) drive and have a typically awkward autobiographical Wood conversation. Outside it changes from day to night to day. After the car crashes they find themselves captives of Criswell, "the black ghoul" (Fawn Silver), a mummy, and a howling werewolf. They're forced to watch a series of eternally damned women (all pro strippers) dancing and stripping on the graveyard set. Each has her own bizarre musical theme. They are, in order: the Indian ("She died in flames"), the Streetwalker, Gold Girl (also Barrington, who dances to Martin Denny–type music until two men in skirts dip her in molten gold), Cat Woman (she dances in a leopard costume with holes cut out for her breasts and is whipped), the Slave (she rolls around on the ground in a G-string), the Mexican (she kisses a skull), the Hawaiian (does a bump and grind to bongo music), the Skeleton (a woman does the swim and the jerk to rock music in front of her husband's skeleton), and the Zombie (a very slow dance). Some say this is too long at 90 minutes, but I'm hoping for a longer director's cut. Ted V. Mikels was the assistant director. Cinematographer Robert Caramico later directed *Sex Rituals of the Occult* and shot the *Falcon Crest* TV series. Wood's photo novel (with an introduction by Forrest J. Ackerman) was published by Greenleaf (it sold for 75 cents). I got my copy at the late, great Kay's Books in Cleveland. It was one of many now collectible Wood books. Wood later wrote early-70s nudie movies for Stephen C. Apostoloff.

ORIGINAL INTENT

(Paramount, 1989) **D/S/P:** Robert Marcarelli **S:** Joyce Marcarelli

Candy Clark and Jay Richardson star as a professional couple. He's talked into doing legal work for the homeless. Vince Edwards is the industrialist villain. This PG attempt to copy Frank Capra's films has many guest stars, including Robert DoQui, Kris Kristofferson, Joseph Campanella, Cindy Pickett, Martin Sheen, and Bruce Jenner. It was released (on video) three years after it was produced.

ORLAK: THE HELL OF FRANKENSTEIN

(Sinister, 1960) **D/P:** Raphael Baledón **S:** Alfredo Ruanova, Carlos E. Taboada   Mexico

A scientist goes to jail for stealing bodies but escapes. In his castle he brings a body back to life by putting a metal box over the head and creates a superstrong monster. This was originally made as four half-hour TV shows. It's in Spanish only.

ORLOFF AND THE INVISIBLE MAN: *See* THE INVISIBLE DEAD

ORPHAN = FRIDAY THE 13TH: THE ORPHAN

ORPHEUS

(Sinister, 1949) **D/S:** Jean Cocteau **P:** André Paulvé   France (*Orphée*)

Jean Marais stars as Orpheus, a poet who meets his own death and travels to a phantom zone through a mirror. If anything in this cinema classic looks familiar it's because many of the brilliant effects have been copied in science-fiction and horror movies and in rock videos over the years. Jean Cocteau later made *The Testament of Orpheus* (1959). *Black Orpheus* (1959) is an excellent retelling of the same legend set during the carnival in Rio de Janeiro. Jacques Demy made a version called *Parking*.

ORSON WELLES' GHOST STORY

(MPI, 1953) **D/S/P/A:** Hilton Edwards **P/A:** Micheal MacLiammoir   Ireland (*Return to Glenascaul*)

On the set of Orson Welles's *Othello*, the cast breaks for lunch, and he introduces and narrates a flashback story about a hitchhiker and a ghost, featuring Michael Lawrence. This 23-minute b/w film was nominated for an Oscar as best short. There's a new color intro with Peter Bogdanovich. It's presented by Richard Gordon and was first released on video in 1994.

OSA

(HBO, 1985) **D/S:** Oleg Egorov **P:** Constantin Alexandrov

This *Road Warrior* copy has female stars. It's another movie about post-nuke battles for radiation-free water. With Kelly Lynch and Daniel Grimm.

THE OSTERMAN WEEKEND

(HBO, 1983) **D:** Sam Peckinpah **S:** Alan Sharp, Ian Masters **P:** Peter S. Davis, William N. Panzer **M:** Lalo Schifrin

Peckinpah's last feature is a bizarre thriller based on a Robert Ludlum novel. CIA man John Hurt convinces a TV-news director (Rutger Hauer) that his friends are Soviet agents. Sex videos, lots of cocaine use, and guns and crossbows are involved. With Craig T. Nelson as Osterman, Meg Foster, Dennis Hopper, Chris Sarandon, Burt Lancaster, Helen Shaver, Merete Van Kamp, and Cassie Yates. Peckinpah, who had been using coke him-

self since 1973, directed two Julian Lennon videos before he died. Varèse Sarabande released the soundtrack.

THE OTHER HELL

(Vestron, 1980) **D:** "Stefan Oblowsky"/Bruno Mattei **S:** Claudio Fragasso   Italy (*L'Altro Inferno; Guardian of Hell*)

A priest investigates some convent murders. With mutilations, strange violence, crazed nuns, and an exorcism. A nun gives birth to a demon too. It copies Dario Argento's *Inferno* and Ken Russell's *The Devils*. The music is by Goblin.

THE OTHER WOMAN

(Imperial, 1992) **D:** Jag Mundhra **S:** Georges Des Esseintes **P:** Andrew Garroni

Lee Anne Beaman is an investigative newpaper reporter married to a famous writer/psychiatrist (Adrian Zmed). She's working to expose a corrupt, violent businessman (Sam Jones) and ends up falling in love with a black model/hooker (*Penthouse* Pet Jenna Persaud). With Melissa Moore. This "erotic thriller" is available in R and unrated versions.

OUR MAN FLINT: DEAD ON TARGET

(1976) **D:** Joseph Scanlon **S:** Norman Klenman **P:** R. H. Anderson

Unfortunately, James Coburn never did make a third Flint spy movie, but ABC-TV showed this pilot starring Ray Danton as the superspy. Sharon Acker costars. Of course it did not become a series, and Danton retired from acting to concentrate on directing.

OUR WINNING SEASON

(1978) **D:** Joseph Ruben **S:** Nick Niciphor **P:** Joe Roth

High-school student Scott Jacoby tries to win a race so that he can win a scholarship (and a draft deferment). This PG-rated AIP release was inspired by *American Graffiti*. With Deborah Benson, Dennis Quaid, P. J. Soles, Joe Penny, and Joanna Cassidy. The music is by Dave Loggins. Writer Nick Niciphor directed *Death Sport*.

OUTBACK

(1971) **D:** Ted Kotcheff **S:** Evan Jones **P:** George Willoughby   US/Australia (*Wake in Fright*)

A sensitive young teacher (Gary Bond) can't deal with the rough, hard-drinking characters who hunt kangaroos in a remote outback village. With Donald Pleasence as a doctor, Sylvia Kay, Chips Rafferty, and Jack Thompson. The original version runs 114 minutes.

OUTBREAK

(Warner, 1995) **D:** Wolfgang Peterson **S:** Laurence Dworet, Robert Roy Pool **P:** Arnold Kopelson **C:** Michael Balhaus

Dustin Hoffman is an Army medical researcher who literally has to save the world (or at least one small California town) from a deadly virus, usually while wearing a yellow work suit. He's reunited with his estranged wife Rene Russo (just like in *The Abyss*). Yes, it's another expensive version of the kind of B sci-fi movies that were made in the 50s, but it's a very impressive one with good acting, suspense, action, and some gore FX and is very believable and scary. It even has a movie theater scene that should remind you of *The Tingler* (or *The Blob*). Donald Sutherland (in the same year he appeared in *Robert A. Heinlein's The Puppet Masters*) is the military bad guy who plans to nuke the town to cover his ass. Also with Cuba Gooding Jr. (who teams with Hoffman for surprising James Bond–style action scenes), Morgan Freeman, Kevin Spacey, Patrick Dempsey, and Zakes Mokae. The script was inspired by "Crisis in the Hot Zone," an article in *The New Yorker*. Major scenes were filmed in Hawaii (subbing for Africa) and Ferndale, California. The Warner release is not too long at 127 minutes.

OUTCASTS

(1982) **D/S:** Robert Wynne-Simmons
P: Tony Dollard   UK

In 1810 in Ireland a widower's daughter is accused of witchcraft. She's saved by a magical fiddler. The cast includes Mary Ryan, Mick Lally, and Cyril Cusack.

OUT COLD

(HBO, 1988) **D:** Malcolm Mowbray **S:** Howard Glasser, George Malko **P:** George C. Braunstein   (*Stiffs*)

A butcher (John Lithgow) and his wife (Teri Garr) try to hide a body. This black comedy also features Randy Quaid as a private eye, Lisa Blount, Bruce McGill, and Debra Lamb.

THE OUTER LIMITS

(MGM/UA series, 1963–65)

All 48 episodes of this amazing show are available on tape (or six-per-laserdisc boxed sets). One of the first episodes ("Architects of Fear") was censored in Cleveland because the local ABC affiliate thought that the mutant gelatine-look monster was too scary. The publicity made it a big deal, and every kid *had* to watch it to see the monster. I would have watched it anyway. The series was thought-provoking and scary, had good guest stars and a great b/w look, and was often pretty damned disturbing. Tapes are 52 minutes each. "The Inheritors" (with Robert Duvall) is a two-part episode. Joseph Stephano and Leslie Stevens were the producers. Frequent directors were Stevens, Byron Haskin, Gerd Oswald, and Laslo Benedek. The soundtrack album (on GNP Crescendo) is by Dominic Frontiere. A new *Outer Limits* series debuted on Showtime in 1995.

THE OUTER LIMITS: SAND KINGS

(MGM, 1995) **D:** Stuart Gillard
S: Melinda M. Snodgrass   Canada

Beau Bridges stars as a scientist studying soil from Mars at home. Scorpionlike aliens hatch from eggs in the feature pilot for the Showtime revival of the 60s series. It's based on "Sandkings" by George R. R. Martin. With Helen Shaver as his wife and Dylan Bridges as their son, Lloyd Bridges as the grandfather, and Kim Coates. Craig Nicotero and Walter Klasen created the aliens.

THE OUTFIT

(1974) **D/S:** John Flynn **P:** Carter DeHaven

Robert Duvall stars as an ex-con who declares war on the mob after his brother is killed. Karen Black and Joe Don Baker help him rob the crooks. Robert Ryan is the bank owner and syndicate boss. The great cast includes Elisha Cook Jr., Marie Windsor, and Timothy Carey (all from *The Killing*), Sheree North, Richard Jaeckel, Jane Greer, Henry Jones, and Anita O'Day as herself. It's based on a novel by Donald E. Westlake.

THE OUTFIT

(MCA, 1993) **D/S/P/A:** J. Christian Ingvordsen
S: Whitney Ransick **S/P/C:** Steve Kaman

Lance Henriksen (also in the director's *Comrades in Arms*) stars as gangster Dutch Schultz, Billy Drago is Lucky Luciano, and John Mosby is Legs Diamond. John Christian (the director) is the FBI-man hero. Also with Martin Kove and Rick Washburne.

OUT FOR BLOOD

(PM, 1992) **D:** Richard W. Munchkin
S: David S. Green, Paul Muslak, Neva Friedenn **P:** Joseph Merhi, Richard Pepin

Don "the Dragon" Wilson is a lawyer whose family is killed by drug smugglers. He awakens from a coma with only a partial memory but trains with Aki Aleong and becomes a mysterious vigilante known as "the karate man." With Shari Shattuck, Ken McLeod as Blade, Todd Curtis, and many real martial-arts fighters. This is the seventh of many quickly made features starring Wilson.

OUT FOR JUSTICE

(Warner, 1991) **D:** John Flynn **S/P:** Steven Seagal
S: David Lee Henry **P:** Arnold Kopelson

Steven Seagal stars as Gino, an Italian-American cop in Brooklyn (complete with awkward accent) who's after a crazed Mafia killer and crack addict (William Forsythe). With Jerry Orbach, Jo Champa, Julie Strain, Shareen Mitchell, Gina Gershon, Shannon Whirry (in her feature debut), and John Leguizamo.

THE OUTING

(IVE, 1985) **D:** Tom Daley **S/P:** Warren Chaney   (*The Lamp*)

Some teens spend the night in a museum run by one girl's father. A huge, green, Iraqi killer genie is released, and the daughter wishes her father were dead. With Deborah Winters (wife of the director) as a teacher. There's some gore and nudity.

OUTLAW BIKERS = THE HELLCATS

OUTLAW BLUES

(Warner, 1977) **D:** Richard T. Heffron
S: B. W. L. Norton **P:** Steve Tisch

Peter Fonda is an ex-con who becomes a country-singing star, in a movie that borrows ideas from Elvis' *Loving You* and *Jailhouse Rock*. Susan Saint James is a backup singer who promotes his career. James Callahan is a singer who steals the hit song he wrote in prison. The couple have to go on the run to get it back. With Michael Lerner, Matt Clark, and John Crawford. It was the last hit movie for Fonda. Capitol released the Hoyt Axton soundtrack, and a picture-sleeve 45 of Fonda singing was issued.

OUTLAW FORCE

(TWE, 1988) **D/S/P/A:** David Heavener
P: Ronnie Hadar

Racist rednecks rape and kill the Nam-vet country-singer hero's wife and kidnap and sell his daughter for porno-movie work. He becomes (surprise!) a vigilante. With Paul Smith and Frank Stallone as LA cops, Warren Berlinger, and Devin Dunsworth.

OUTLAW OF GOR

(Warner, 1987) **D:** John Bud Cardos
S: Richard Marx **P:** Avi Lerner, Harry
Alan Towers   S. Africa

Urbano Barberini stars as a Conan-like hero trying to defeat an evil queen. This sequel to *Gor* features Rebecca Ferratti (from *Playboy*) and Jack Palance as Xenos. It's been shown on *Mystery Science Theater 3000*.

OUTLAW WOMEN

(Monterey, 1951) **D:** Sam Newfield **D/P:** Ron Ormond **S:** Orville H. Hampton   (*Boot Hill Mamas*)

A narrator says, "Men are men, but I bet you'd never guess that women are women too!" The action takes place in Los Mujeres, a western town run by women, specifically Iron Mae McCloud (Marie Windsor). Female card sharks and gamblers work in Mae's saloon, and (male) bandits work for her on the side. Jackie Coogan (!) plays a bearded gunslinger with bushy eyebrows called Peyote Bill. The future Uncle Fester experiments with a new "scientific" draw. A pair of sisters have a cat fight over a handsome doctor (Allan Nixon of *Mesa of Lost Women*). Comic Billy House is a snake-oil salesman and bartender, and Tom Tyler has a role. June Carr (later Mrs. Ormond) was the associate producer. She wrote the song "C-c-crazy Over You" ("I'm crazy as a daisy"). Other Ormond family touches include the use of comic sound effects, a big newspaper headline (BANDITS ON THE LOOSE!), and a barbershop quartet (the Four Dandies). At the end the judge (Lyle Talbot) announces the first federal election. Only male citizens can vote, so they take over. All the women get married except for one cigar-smoking holdout who smiles at the camera. This ridiculous comedy/western, shot in economical Cinecolor, looks pretty good considering the low budget it had. The script (by the same guy who wrote *The Alligator People*) predates *Johnny Guitar* by two years and

Roger Corman's western-women movies by five. This is the last of 22 movies that Ormond produced and/or directed for the Lippert company (from 1948 to 1952). Codirector Sam Newfield directed more than 140 (!) features (most for PRC).

OUT OF BOUNDS

(RCA, 1986) **D:** Richard Tuggle **S:** Tony Kayden **P:** Charles Fries, Mike Rosenfeld

Anthony Michael Hall (who had been in John Hughes teen hits) stars as an Iowa farm boy in LA who ends up blamed for a murder and holding a bag of heroin. Killer dealers go after him. Jenny Wright costars, with Jeff Kober, Glynn Turman, Meat Loaf, and Raymond J. Barry. The IRS soundtrack features the Cult, Siouxsie and the Banshees, and others.

OUT OF CONTENTION

(Eagle Crest, 1972) **D:** Herschel Daugherty **S:** Merwin Gerard **P:** William Frye   (*The Victim*)

Elizabeth Montgomery stars as a rich woman terrorized by a mystery killer in a remote house during a storm. This ABC-TV movie is a remake of an episode from the TV series *Thriller* (called "The Storm"). With George Maharis, Eileen Heckart, and Sue Ane Langdon.

OUT OF CONTROL

(Starmaker, 1984) **D:** Allan Holzman **S:** Sandra Weintraub Roland, Vicangelo Bullock **P:** Fred Weintraub, Daniel Grodnick

After the prom a rich high-school senior (Martin Hewitt) takes his girlfriend (Betsy Russell) and six other kids to his parents' island. The plane crashes, they all get drunk, and play sex games, and then drug smugglers attack. This action/sex "comedy" is narrated by Hewitt and features a theme song by the Brothers Johnson. Also with Claudia Udy and Sherilyn Fenn. It was shot in Yugoslavia and released by New World.

OUT OF SIGHT, OUT OF MIND

(Prism, 1989) **D:** Greydon Clark **S:** John Platt, Roy Langsdon **P:** Richard L. Albert   (*Sight Unseen*)

A woman (Susan Blakely) is haunted by her dead daughter. There's also a serial killer on the loose and a religious cult. With Lynn-Holly Johnson, Edward Albert, Richard Masur, and Jessica Player. Wings Hauser is a guest star.

OUT OF THE BLUE

(Media, 1980) **D/A:** Dennis Hopper **S/P:** Leonard Yakir **S:** Gary Jules Jouvenat, Brenda Nielson Canada   (*No Looking Back*)

Hopper's first feature as a director after *The Last Movie* is a disturbing look at people on the edge. At 15, CeBe (Linda Manz) considers herself a punk and idolizes Elvis and Johnny Rotten. Her father (Hopper), an ex-biker and ex-con, was responsible for plowing a truck into and killing a whole busful of school kids. Sharon Farrell is his

junkie wife and Don Gordon is his hard-drinking friend. When they get wasted anything goes. Raymond Burr has a scene as a guidance counselor. "My My Hey Hey" by Neil Young is put to good use on the soundtrack. Hopper replaced the original director. It was shot in Vancouver.

OUT OF THE BODY

(SVS, 1988) **D:** Brian Trenchard-Smith **S:** Kenneth G. Ross **P:** David Hannay   Australia

Mark Hembrow is a musician in Sydney. He dreams of a killer who gouges eyes out. With Tessa Humphries and Shane Briant.

OUT OF THE DARK

(RCA, 1988) **D:** Michael Schroeder **S/P:** Zane W. Levitt **S:** J. Greg De Felice

Cameron Dye is a photographer suspected of being a psycho killer who dresses as Bobo the clown. The victims all work for a phone-sex service run by Karen Black. Some good character actors, lots of pretty women, some humor, and interesting plot twists make this above average. Plus, it features Divine (in his last film) as a police detective! With Bud Cort, Tracey Walter as a detective, Starr Andreef, Karen Witter, and Karen Mayo-Chandler. Also with Paul Bartel (an executive producer), Geoffrey Lewis, Tab Hunter, and Lainie Kazan. All of them (and Divine) are also in *Lust in the Dust*. It's from New Line

OUT OF THE DARKNESS

(1985) **D/S:** John Krish **P:** Gordon L. T. Scott   UK

Some Derbyshire children see the ghost of a 17th-century boy who was lynched during a plague because the townspeople thought he was contagious. With Gary Halliday and Michael Flower.

OUT OF TIME

(1988) **D:** Robert Butler **S/P:** Kerry Lenhart, John J. Sakmer **S:** Brian Alan Lane **P:** David Latt

A cop from the future (Bruce Abbott) travels back in time to LA and teams up with his grandfather to pursue a notorious criminal (Adam Ant). With Leo Rossi and Rebecca Schaeffer. A pilot that aired on NBC-TV, this is on tape in Europe.

OUT OF TIME

(1989) **D/P:** Anwar Kawadri **S:** Jesse Graham   UK/Egypt

Jeff Fahey is an archaeologist competing with villains to find a treasure. Camilla More and Michael Gothard costar.

OUT ON A LIMB

(Prism, 1986) **D:** Robert Butler **S/A:** Shirley MacLaine **S:** Colin Higgins **P:** Stan Margulies

Shirley MacLaine turned her best-selling autobiographical book into an ABC-TV miniseries. She has an affair with a British politician (Charles Dance), but she also gets into her past lives and her "outer being" with John Heard (complete with

special effects) in Peru. It's unusual to see these things treated (very) seriously on TV, but (if you don't believe it) this is good for some laughs. With Anne Jackson as Bella Abzug, Jerry Orbach, and several real psychics as themselves. A 160-minute tape and a 234-minute "collector's edition" (including two of MacLaine's books in paperback) are available.

OUT ON BAIL

(TWE, 1989) **D:** Gordon Hessler **S:** Michael D. Sonye, Jason Booth, Tom Badel **P:** Alam Amiel   S. Africa

In a Tennessee town Robert Ginty is blackmailed by corrupt politicians who want him to assassinate a reform candidate for mayor. With Kathy Shower and Sydney Lassick. The South African supporting players are not convincing as Americans.

OUTRAGE!

(1985) **D:** Robert T. Heffron **S:** William Wood **P:** Irwin Allen   (*One Angry Man*)

Robert Culp wages a one-man war against teen punks in a suburb. This CBS-TV movie features Marilyn Mason, Beah Richards, Scott Colomby, and Gary Clarke. Movies like this (from CBS) improve with age.

OUTSIDE CHANCE

(1978) **D/S:** Michael Miller **S:** Ralph Gaby Wilson **P:** Roger Corman

Jackson County Jail did so well that Corman had the same director do a remake/remodel for CBS-TV. Yvette Mimieux stars again as the businesswoman who is abused in a southern jail. She escapes with Royce D. Applegate (in the Tommy Lee Jones role). This time they become involved with hillbillies selling illegal bearskin rugs. Frederic Cook, Severn Darden, and Betty Thomas return from the original. Footage with Robert Carradine and Howard Hesseman is simply reused.

THE OUTSIDERS

(Warner, 1983) **D:** Francis Ford Coppola **S:** Kathleen Knutsen Rowell **P:** Fred Roos **M:** Carmine Coppola

Coppola made this romantic feature based on a novel by S. E. Hinton, then made the radically different *Rumble Fish* with many of the same actors. They're both set in Tulsa in the mid-60s. This nice-looking would-be epic benefits from Dean Tavoularis' production design. The story of rich-kid "socs" vs. poor greasers was a launching pad for many teen actors. C. Thomas Howell stars (as Ponyboy), and Patrick Swayze and Rob Lowe (as Sodapop) are his brothers. With Matt Dillon, Ralph Macchio, Emilio Estevez, Tom Cruise, Leif Garrett, Diane Lane as Cherry Valance, Michelle Meyrink, and William Smith as a store clerk. Hinton wrote *The Outsiders* when she was only 17.

OUTSIDE THE LAW

(Kino, 1921) **D/S/P:** Tod Browning **S:** Lucian Hubbard

Lon Chaney plays two roles, Black Mike Sylva and Ah Wang, in this early gangster movie. Top-billed Priscilla Dean is jewel thief Silky Moll and Wheeler

Oakman (her real-life husband) is her partner. Sylva is a gangster, and Wang is a disciple of Confucius who helps them go straight. This Universal silent film was remade in 1930 with Edward G. Robinson.

OUTSIDE THE LAW

(1956) **D:** Jack Arnold **S:** Danny Arnold **P:** Albert J. Cohen

Ray Danton is an ex-con who goes overseas to revenge the death of a GI friend and to infiltrate and bust up a gang of international criminals. Leigh Snowden and Grant Williams are counterfeiters in this Universal release. With Onslow Stevens and Jack Kruschen. Williams returned the next year in Jack Arnold's *The Incredible Shrinking Man*.

OUTTAKES

(1984) **D/S/P/A/C/E:** Jack M. Sell **S/P:** Adrienne Richmond **S:** Jim Fay

The late Forrest Tucker is the host in-between segments of this *Tunnelvision*-style sex spoof of TV shows. With a Donahue spoof, a slasher Santa, late night news reports, and more. It was started in 1983, and released in 1987.

OUTWARD BOUND

(1930) **D:** Robert Milton **S:** J. Grubb Alexander **P:** Jack L. Warner

Douglas Fairbanks Jr. and Helen Chandler (soon to be in *Dracula*) are lovers who committed suicide and find themselves on a ghostly ocean liner with no captain. Leslie Howard stars as the first passenger to catch on. An examiner judges them, sending them to Heaven or Hell. With Beryl Mercer, Alison Skipworth, Alec B. Francis, and Montague Love. This serious Warner Brothers release, based on a play by Sutton Vane, was remade as *Between Two Worlds* (1944).

OVERDRAWN AT THE MEMORY BANK

(Starmaker, 1983) **D:** Douglas Williams **S:** Corinne Jacker **S:** Robert Landis

In the future five corporations rule everything. Raul Julia stars (in two roles), with Linda Griffiths.

OVER-EXPOSED

(1956) **D:** Lewis Seiler **S:** James Gunn, Gil Orlovitz **P:** Lewis J. Rachmil

Blond Cleo Moore has "camera, curves, and no conscience!" This story about blackmail photos costars Richard Crenna. The Columbia release was one of the last films for Moore, who had been in *Women's Prison* (1955) by Lewis Seiler and seven (!) Hugo Haas features.

OVEREXPOSED

(MGM/UA, 1990) **D/S/A:** Larry Brand **S:** Rebecca Reynolds **P:** Roger Corman

A horror movie with a soap-opera setting isn't a bad idea, and this isn't a bad movie. Catherine Oxenberg is the daytime-soap star who starts having blackouts and dreams/flashbacks about a horrible birthday party. Is somebody trying to drive her crazy? David Naughton is her useless boyfriend, but the standout acting here is by Karen Black. She has a scary and inspired scene as a deranged suspect who rants in TV clichés ("The Devil's box! It spoke the truth!") and is punched in the face by a cop. An actor dies from acid cold cream, there's a strange Doors reference, and Jennifer Edwards (daughter of Julie Andrews and Blake Edwards) makes her horror debut. Oxenberg has a sex scene but used a double.

OVERKILL

(Vista, 1986) **D/S/P:** Ulli Lommel **S:** David Scott Kroes

An LA detective (Steve Rally) teams up with the brother of a yakuza (John Nishio) to battle Japanese mobsters. Michelle Bauer has a small role.

OVERKILL: THE AILEEN WUORNOS STORY

(1992) **D:** Peter Levin

Jean Smart stars as the real-life serial killer Aileen Wuornos, a lesbian prostitute in her late 20s who admitted to killing seven men she picked up on Florida highways. With Park Overall and Brion James. *Aileen Wuornos: The Selling of a Serial Killer* (Fox Lorber) is a documentary by Nick Broomfield.

OVERLAND MAIL

(Stokey, 1942) **D:** Ford Beebe, John Rawlins **S:** Paul Huston

Lon Chaney Jr. stars in this 15-chapter Universal western serial. It was the last serial by Ford Beebe, who had started at Mascot in 1931. Helen Parrish costars.

OVER THE EDGE

(Orion, 1979) **D:** Jonathan Kaplan **S:** Charlie Hass, Tim Hunter **P:** George Litto

Few saw this great look at modern, bored American teenagers when it was new. The kids exist in a "perfect," new, sterile community called New Granada. After a cop kills one of them they lock all of the parents in a gym during an emergency meeting to discuss what to do about the violence, and then they smash up cars. It's based on what actually happened in Foster City, California. Michael Kramer stars, with 14-year-old-Matt Dillon (his first film), Vincent Spano, and Pamela Ludwig. Andy Romano and Ellen Geer are parents. The Warner soundtrack features the Ramones ("Lobotomy"), the Cars, Cheap Trick, and others. Planned as the first feature by Orion, this was released (barely) by Warner. It was directed by a Corman protegé who had just been fired from *Great Rock and Roll Swindle*. Screenwriter Tim Hunter went on to direct another realistic teen classic, *River's Edge*.

OZONE

(Tempe, 1993) **D/P/A/C/E:** J. R. Bookwalter **S:** David Wagner

Eddie Bone (James Black, who they say played for the Cleveland Browns) is a cop who is stuck with a syringe by a drug dealer. It seems like nearly everyone is becoming some kind of zombie led by a pig-faced creature. Eddie and a woman mutate and produce a baby monster. The most ridiculous scene has the hero forced to battle another black man in gladiator style. Unlike most of the 27-year-old director's efforts this is imaginative (if not exactly coherent), and the FX are more science-fiction than gore. There's also some minimal morphing in a nightmare sequence. The creators of *The Killer Nerd* also appear as mutants. It was filmed around Akron.

OZONE: ATTACK OF THE REDNECK MUTANTS

(Muther, 1988) **D/P:** "Max Devlen"/Bret McCormick **S:** Brad Redd **P:** Max Raven

We probably didn't need another low-budget, comic redneck/zombie movie, but this one's actually pretty good. Blue Thompson stars as a tough (part-Oriental), ecology-minded young woman, and Scott Davis is a rich jerk. They encounter green-slime-drooling, neck-biting, bloody-faced zombies out in the sticks. There are lots of good insults and corny accents, decapitations, a bizarre talent contest at the general store, and some John Waters touches along the way. If you can get past the guy puking and a loud comic "mom" interrupting the story you might like *Ozone* too. It was shot on Super 8.

PACIFIC HEIGHTS

(Fox, 1990) **D:** John Schlesinger **S:** Daniel Pyne **P:** Scott Rudlin, William Sackheim

One of the best of the many yuppie-couple almost-horror movies features Michael Keaton as a clever, psycho tenant who won't go away. Melanie Griffith and Matthew Modine buy a great Victorian apartment house in San Francisco and have to resort to drastic measures to stay together and safe. With Beverly D'Angelo, Mako, Nobu McCarthy, Laurie Metcalf, Luca Bercovici, Dan Hedaya, Nicholas Pryor, and Tippi Hedren (Griffith's real-life mother). When cockroaches invade, Tracey Walter is the exterminator. It's much scarier than Schlesinger's zombie movie *The Believers*.

PACIFIC INFERNO

(VCL, Virgin, 1977) **D/S:** Rolf Bayer **S:** Roland S. Jefferson **P:** Spencer Jourdain, Cassius V. Weathersby   US/Philippines

Jim Brown, who costarred in *The Dirty Dozen*, was the executive producer and star of this *Dirty Dozen* copy. He leads a team of navy divers forced by the Japanese to recover a fortune in Filipino silver pesos dumped into the Manila Bay harbor by General Douglas MacArthur. With Richard Jaeckel (*The Dirty Dozen*), Tim Brown, Rik Van Nutter, and Vic Diaz. It wasn't released until 1985.

PACIFIC VIBRATIONS

(1970) **D/S/P/C:** John Severson

AIP released this 16mm surfing movie backed by *Surfer* magazine. It was filmed in Hawaii and California and includes a warning about pollution and industrial waste. Jock Sutherland stars. Some of the music is by Paul Beaver and Bernie Kraus, Ry Cooder, Leo Kottke, Little Walter, Steve Miller, and Cream.

THE PACK

(Warner, 1977) **D/S:** Robert Clouse **P:** Fred Weintraub, Paul Heller
(*The Long, Dark Night*)

In one of the best of many 70s killer-dogs movies, two families on a resort island are threatened by abandoned canines. This PG feature stars Joe Don Baker as the hero, with Hope Alexander-Willis, Bibi Besch, R. G. Armstrong, and Richard B. Shull. It's based on a novel by David Fisher.

THE PACKAGE

(Orion, 1989) **D:** Andrew Davis **S:** John Bishop **P:** Beverly J. Camhe

Gene Hackman is a navy officer who has to transport a psycho assassin (Tommy Lee Jones) from East Berlin to America. With Joanna Cassidy, John Heard, Dennis Franz, Pam Grier, and Thalmus Rasulala. Grier had also been in Davis's *Above the Law* (1988).

PACTO DIABÓLICO: *See* JEKYLL AND HYDE: PACT WITH THE DEVIL

PAGANINI

(VSOM, 1989) **D/S/A:** Klaus Kinski **S:** Massimo Lentini **P:** Augusto Caminito   Italy

The notorious Italian violinist and composer Niccolò Paganini (1782–1840) is called "a vampire with a violin" by a female narrator. Klaus Kinski's movie has great period detail and lots of frenzied violin-playing, but it's largely made up of back-and-forth memory fragments, too much slow motion, and very little dialogue. The long-haired Paganini/Kinski looks great as he literally plays himself to death after fucking just about any woman (no matter how young) in sight. With Debra (Kinski) Caprioglio as his neglected young wife, Dallia Di Lazzaro, Eva Grimaldi, Bernard Blier, Nicolai Kinski, and Marcel Marceau (!). The film's producers (Scenta) called it "close to porno" (the only graphic sex scene stars horses) and sued Kinski. The same year his scandalous autobiography, *All I Need Is Love*, was recalled by Random House. Kinski never acted again and died in 1992. This rare (subtitled) film is a must for Kinski fans. The first *Paganini* (1923) stars Conrad Veidt. *Paganini Horror* (1988) is a present-day rock/horror version.

PAGAN ISLAND

(SW, 1960) **D/P:** Barry Mahon **S:** Clelle Mahon

The survivor of a shipwreck relates his story to a sailing-ship captain with an eye patch and a scar. The queen of an all-female tropical island says, "White man no good" (in a European accent), but the only black natives are some men who are killed. The women wear leis and dance in front of a pretty funny-looking sea-god/monster statue. Our hero falls for and marries a princess (Nani Maka) who says, "He say I built like small brick house." Bunny Yeager cast the "30 beautiful girls." This early b/w Barry Mahon movie runs 67 minutes. The video is hosted by Johnny Legend.

THE PAGANS

(1952) **D:** Ferruccio Cerio **S:** Alessandro Ferrau, Giuseppe Mangione   Italy (*Il Sacco di Roma*)

The walled city of Rome is invaded by the Spaniards in 1527. Pierre Cressoy stars, with Hélène Ramy and Anna Maria Bugliari (a former Miss Italy). Allied Artists released this b/w epic in 1957, and it was considered exploitable enough for Hemisphere to rerelease it in 1964 as *The Barbarians*.

THE PAGEMASATER

(Fox, 1994) **D:** Joe Johnston, Maurice Hunt **S:** David Casci, Ernie Contreras **S/P:** David Kirschner **P:** Paul Gertz, Michael R. Joyce

A librarian (Christopher Lloyd) sends an outcast kid (Macaulay Culkin) into a cartoon world of literary classics (including *Frankenstein* and *Treasure Island*). This G-rated pro-reading fantasy features the voices of Patrick Stewart, Leonard Nimoy, Whoopi Goldberg, and Phil Hartman. Ed Begley Jr. and Mel Harris play the parents. James Horner provided the score. The live footage was shot in 1992 when Culkin was 12. A Christmas release with lots of tie-ins and promotion, it was produced by 20th Century–Fox and Turner Pictures.

PAID

(1930) **D:** Sam Wood **S:** Lucien Hubbard, Charles MacArthur

Yes, even Joan Crawford starred in a women-in-prison movie. She's a shopgirl wrongly convicted of a crime. After three years of menial work in prison she's released and takes revenge by marrying the son of the employer who framed her. With Robert Armstrong and Marie Prevost. This MGM release was based on a play that had been filmed in 1917 and 1923 and was filmed again as *Within the Law* (1939).

PAID TO KILL

(1954) **D:** Montgomery Tully **S:** Paul Tabori **P:** Anthony Hinds UK (*Five Days*)

Lippert released this Hammer thriller. A failing businessman (Dane Clark) hires a hood (Paul Carpenter) to kill him so that his wife (Thea Gregory) can collect his life insurance. Then he changes his mind.

PAINT IT BLACK

(Vestron, 1989) **D:** Tim Hunter, Roger Holzberg **S:** Michael Drexler, Tim Harris, Herschel Weingrod **P:** Anne Kimmel, Mark Forstater

Rick Rossovich stars as a sculptor accused of murder. A psycho killer (Doug Savant) covers bodies with clay. With Sally Kirkland as an art dealer, Martin Landau, Julie Carmen, and Monique Van de Ven. Some of Bernard Herrmann's unused score for Alfred Hitchcock's *Torn Curtain* is used. The cliffhanger ending is pretty good. Tim Hunter (*River's Edge*) replaced the original director. It went directly to video in America.

PALE BLOOD

(Triumph, 1989) **D/S:** V. V. Dachin Hsu **S:** Takashi Matsuda **P:** Omar Raczinarczyk, Michael J. Leighter

George Chakiris is Michael Fury, a grim, quiet vampire in LA. Wealthy Wings Hauser is busy making a video documentary and we eventually discover that he's the real villain, a nut who kills to lure and capture a vampire. He even has a blood-draining machine. There's also a young woman (Pamela Ludwig) obsessed by vampires and a new innovation, a portable canvas coffin with a zipper. Too much time is spent on generic footage of the city and on Agent Orange, a band that plays on three occasions. The director is a woman from Hong Kong who previously made documentaries and commercials. There's a film clip from the silent version of *Nosferatu*.

PALE RIDER

(Warner, 1985) **D/P/A:** Clint Eastwood
S: Michael Butler, Dennis Shryack

Eastwood returns as Preacher, a stranger in a small California gold-rush town during a war between prospectors and a mining company. This mythical western features Michael Moriarty, Carrie Snodgress, Christopher Penn, Richard Dysart, Richard Kiel, and John Russell as a hired killer. Eastwood's next western was the hit *Unforgiven* (1992).

PALISADES HIGH

(MCM, 1976) **D/S/P:** Joseph Ruben   (*Pom Pom Girls*)

Rival California high-school kids hang out, have sex, get in trouble, and have a deadly "chickie run." Robert Carradine and Bill Adler star, with Jennifer Ashley, Lisa Reeves, and Cheryl "Rainbeaux" Smith. This Crown International release was a big drive-in hit. Joseph Ruben went on to make *Sleeping with the Enemy* and *The Stepfather*.

PALM SPRINGS WEEKEND

(Warner, 1963) **D:** Norman Taurog
S: Earl Hamner Jr. **P:** Michael A. Hoey

Connie Stevens is a high-school girl who pretends to be a rich college student. Troy Donahue is a college basketball captain. They meet during spring vacation, and both of them sing. This was the third and final Troy-and-Connie movie (after *Parrish* and *Susan Slade*) and was by the director of eight Elvis movies. The rest of the cast members are better known for TV roles: Ty Hardin, Stefanie Powers, Robert Conrad as the rich-guy villain, Andrew Duggan as the police chief, Jack Weston, Jerry Van Dyke, and Billy Mumy. Warner released the soundtrack.

PANAMA RED

(1976) **D/S:** Robert C. Chinn

A man (Jim Wingert, who also provides the songs) with a pregnant wife begins dealing pot in shoe boxes. Everybody smokes a lot, black militants rip him off, and cops go after him. It's a comedy, made by a porno director known for making John Holmes movies.

PANDEMONIUM

(MGM, 1981) **D:** Alfred Sole **S:** Richard Whitley, Jamie Klein **P:** Doug Chapin   (*Thursday the 12th*)

Tom Smothers stars as a Mountie, and Paul Reubens (later Pee-wee Herman) is his deputy. This PG-rated slasher spoof from United Artists features Carol Kane as a *Carrie*-like killer/psychic teen at a cheerleader school. The impressive cast also includes Tab Hunter as the killer, Eve Arden (in her last role), Donald O'Connor, Phil Hartman, Pat Ast, Miles Chapin, Marc McClure, Debralee Scott, Richard Romanus, Kaye Ballard, Sydney Lassick, Edie McClurg, Eileen Brennan, a blond Judge Reinhold, David L. Lander, and Godzilla. The director also gave us the classic, serious horror movie *Alice, Sweet Alice* and the sexy fantasy *Tanya's Island.*

PANDEMONIUM

(1987) **D/S/P:** Hayden Keenan **S:** Peter Gailey **P:** Alex Cutler   Australia

This comic horror movie is set in a haunted film studio in Sydney. Ghosts, vampires, and an aboriginal Holy Ghost appear. David Argue and Amanda Dole play "dingos."

The Pom Pom Girls, aka *Palisades High*

PANDORA AND THE FLYING DUTCHMAN

(Kino, 1950) **D/S/P:** Albert Lewin
P: Joseph Kaufman   UK

James Mason is the Dutch sailor who is cursed to sail forever but is saved by the love of a modern-day American woman (Ava Gardner). With Nigel Patrick, Sheila Sim, and Abraham Sofaer. MGM released the 122-minute color romantic fantasy. Jack Cardiff was the cinematographer. Other versions were made in 1923 and 1965 (an opera) in Germany.

PANDORA'S BOX

(Public Media, 1928) **D/S:** G. W. Pabst
S: Ladislaus Vadja **P:** George C. Hosetzky
Germany (*Die Büchse der Pandora; Lulu*)

Louise Brooks (from Kansas) is Lulu, one of the most fascinating female characters ever on the screen. Adapted from two plays by Frank Wedekind, this look at decadence and corruption in Berlin and London was criticized, cut, and censored over the years. Fritz Kortner costars, with Franz (later Francis) Lederer, Alice Roberts as a lesbian countess, and Gustav Diessl as Jack the Ripper. Originally 131 minutes long, it was restored, with new intertitles and a symphonic score, in 1983 and now runs 110 minutes. G.W. Pabst also made the great original version of *The Threepenny Opera* (1931). Walerian Borowczyk remade *Pandora's Box* as *Lulu* (1979), which is also the title of a 1962 Austrian version. Earlier silent versions were made in Germany in 1919 and 1923.

PANIC IN THE CITY

(1968) **D/S:** Eddie Davis
S: Charles E. Savage **P:** Earl Lyon

Howard Duff is a government agent who teams up with a radiologist (Linda Cristal) to find out how and why a scientist was killed. Nehemiah Persoff and Anne Jeffries plan to start WWIII by detonating an A bomb in Los Angeles! At the end radiation poisoning kills some people, and Duff sacrifices himself with the bomb over the ocean. The cast also includes Dennis Hopper as Goff, John Hoyt, Stephen McNally, Stanley Clements, and Mike Farrell. It was released by the short-lived Commonwealth United.

PANIC IN THE STREETS

(Fox, 1950) **D:** Elia Kazan **S:** Richard Murphy **P:** Sol C. Siegel

Richard Widmark stars as a New Orleans health inspector in this excellent documentary-style drama. He tries to find a gangster who killed an illegal alien and carries pneumonic plague. Everything was shot on location, on docks, in diners, and in slums, and includes many very real down-and-out local residents. Walter (later Jack) Palance, in his first role, is the man on the run, and Zero Mostel is his partner. With Barbara Bel Geddes, Paul Douglas as a cop, and Tommy Rettig. It's from 20th Century–Fox.

PANTHER GIRL OF THE CONGO

(Republic, 1955) **D:** Franklin Adreon
S: Ronald Davison

Phyllis Coates stars in one of the last (and cheapest) 12-chapter Republic serials. Most of the jungle-girl footage is from *Jungle Girl* (1941) and Myron Healey has to rescue her most of the time. With Arthur Space, Gene Roth, ridiculous-looking natives, a man in a gorilla suit, and a giant crayfish. The feature version is called *The Claw Monsters*. Republic's next (and last) serial, also by Adreon, was *King of the Carnival* (1955).

PANTHER SQUAD

(Vestron, 1984) **D:** Peter Knight **S:** George Freedland **P:** Daniel Lesoeur   France/Belgium

Sybil Danning stars as a mercenary named Ilona, with a team of female commandos, in this Bond-type spy story. She was also an associate producer of this confused, spliced-together movie. With Karin Schubert (who was also in porno movies like *The Devil in Mr. Holmes*), Shirley Knight (an Oscar nominee in 1960 and 1962 whose career later took a terrible dive), Donald O'Brien, and Jack Taylor.

THE PAPERBOY

(Republic, 1994) **D:** Douglas Jackson **S:** David Peckinpah **P:** Tom Berry   Canada

Johnny (Marc Marut) is a 12-year-old suburban-Ohio paperboy who wants a local divorcée (Alexandra Paul) to be his mother. He kills people who get too close to her. With Brigid Tierney as her little daughter, William Katt, Frances Bay, Krista Errickson, and Peaches the dog. It was shot outside Montreal. The screenwriter is Sam Peckinpah's nephew.

PAPERHOUSE

(Vestron, 1988) **D:** Bernard Rose **S:** Matthew Jacobs **P:** Sarah Radclyffe   UK

An imaginative 11-year-old girl (Charlotte Burke) lies a lot. When she's bedridden her drawings become real during her fever dreams and affect the life of a dying boy her doctor has told her about. She adds new details to his barren house, but when she crumples up and throws away the drawing the house is in ruins. Ben Cross shows up in scary scenes as her alcoholic father, and Glenne Headly is her mother. The soundtrack (on RCA) is by Hans Zimmer and Stanley Myers. This fascinating PG-13 fantasy is based on the novel *Marianne Dreams*, by Catherine Storr. It was the feature-film debut of a rock-video director who later came to America and made *Candy Man*. The video opens with a Joyce Jillson astrology ad.

PAPER MASK

(Academy, 1991) **D:** Christopher Morahan **S:** John Collee **P:** Christopher Morohan, Sue Austin   UK

A medical aide (Paul McGann) assumes the identity of a dead doctor. A nurse (Amanda Donohoe) becomes his lover, and he tries to cover up the death of one of his patients. With Barbara Leigh-Hunt, Frederick Treves, and Tom Wilkinson.

THE PARADINE CASE

(Fox, 1947) **D:** Alfred Hitchcock **S:** Alma Reville **P:** David O. Selznick **M:** Franz Waxman

David O. Selznick has been blamed more than Alfred Hitchcock for this expensive (more than $3 million), long (132-minute), talk-filled box-office flop. It's still worth seeing, though. A happily married lawyer (Gregory Peck) defends and falls for a woman accused of killing her wealthy, crippled husband. Alida Valli (making her US debut) co-stars. This courtroom drama, set in England, features Ann Todd, Charles Laughton, Ethel Barrymore, Charles Coburn, Louis Jourdan, and Leo G. Carroll. Alma Reville (Hitchcock's wife and frequent collaborator) wrote the screenplay, based on a novel by Robert Hichens. The score was later released on an LP with music from *Spellbound*. The director is seen carrying a cello case. The United Artists release was cut several times, eventually to 116 minutes. A TV remake was presented in 1962 with Richard Basehart, Viveca Lindfors, and Boris Karloff.

PARADISE

(Nelson, 1981) **D/S:** Stuart Gillard **P:** Robert Lantos, Stephan J. Roth

Young Phoebe Cates and Willie Aames are alone in the desert, in this ripoff of the previous year's *The Blue Lagoon* (Columbia sued). They have sex after they see a chimp masturbate. Underwater cameras show Cates swiming naked, but an obvious body double was used for the sex scenes. Cates sang the theme song, which was a hit in Europe. Her

father, Joseph Cates, directed *Who Killed Teddy Bear?* (1965), starring Sal Mineo, and *The Fat Spy* (1966), with Jayne Mansfield.

PARADISIO

(Starmaker, 1961) **S/P:** Jacques Henrici **S:** Lawrence Zeitlin, Henri Haile   UK

When Professor Sims (Arthur Howard, the less-famous older brother of Leslie Howard) puts on his special glasses that make clothes disappear we put on red-and-blue 3-D glasses (hope you have a pair; everybody should) and see color segments with naked ladies filmed all over Europe. A smiling, naked girl tends her sheep in a pasture. In a nightclub the professor is happy just to stare at the naked cigarette girl and photographer, but when he accidentally spots a male waiter he quickly looks away and goes, "Owww!" He also gets drunk and faints after seeing a woman with three breasts. Lots of women are viewed around a pool, on the Riviera, and, in my favorite scene, boarding a bus. Eventually Sims is chased all around some ruins in Berlin by spies. The sparse dialogue is dubbed in, but no expense was spared filming on location in Paris, Munich, Venice, and other cities. This is a real time-capsule item, the best of several similar films (including Russ Meyer's *The Immoral Mr. Teas*), and it seems more friendly and innocent than most of today's leering, cynical TV situation comedies. It was released by Joe Solomon and Fanfare.

PARALYZED

(MPI, 1972) **D/S:** Aldo Lado **P:** Dieter Geissler **M:** Ennio Morricone   Italy/W. Germany/Yugoslavia (*La Corte Notte delle Bambole di Vetro*)

Jean Sorel is a comatose journalist in Prague trying to remember what happened to him. A mad scientist conducts brainwashing experiments, bodies are frozen, and there's a Devil cult of old people who sacrifice naked women. Ingrid Thulin, Barbara Bach, and Mario Adorf costar.

PARANOIA

(NTA, 1968) **D/S:** Umberto Lenzi **S:** Ugo Moretti   Italy/France (*Orgasmo*)

Carroll Baker is Katherine West, an alcoholic, rich former NYC artist who arrives at her late Italian husband's villa. A sarcastic hustler (Lou Castel) worms his way into her life and home. They have sex in the shower, on the lawn, by the pool. He brings his sexy, short-haired "sister" (Colette Descombs) along. They both have sex with the confused widow and with each other, drive away the servants, drug her, tie her up, blackmail her with photos, and torture her by playing the same bad rock-and-roll song over and over. At that point she's suicidal: "When I think of myself I want to vomit!" Like most 60s Italian exploitation movies this one has jerky camera work, with lots of fast zooms, and funny music with female voices merrily going "da da dee dee." Director Umberto Lenzi throws in thunder and lightning, some psychedelic sequences, a discotheque scene, and Baker being served a toad by her captors. She starred in two back-to-back films by Lenzi. The other, *A Quiet Place to Kill*, was also known as *Paranoia*, causing

a lot of filmography confusion. This was rated X in America when released by Fanfare.

PARENTS

(Vestron, 1988) **D:** Bob Balaban **S:** Christopher Hawthorne **P:** Bonnie Palef   Canada

Terrified 6-year-old Michael (Bryan Madorsky) has nightmares and starts spying on his cheerful but odd 50s suburban parents. Randy Quaid and Mary Beth Hurt are the Laemmles, who turn out to be killer cannibals. Dad works at a nuke plant. Also in the cast are Sandy Dennis as a school shrink, Graham Jarvis, and Kathryn Grody. This black comedy doesn't really work all the way though, but parts of it are pretty disturbing and it all looks very colorful. It was shot in Toronto. The first-time director acted in *Altered States, Close Encounters of the Third Kind,* and *2010*.

PARIS TROUT

(Media, 1991) **S:** Stephen Gyllenhaal **S:** Pete Dexter **P:** Frank Konigsberg, Larry Sanitsky

Dennis Hopper is Paris Trout, a racist storekeeper in 1949 Georgia who kills a black man. Barbara Hershey is his wife, and Ed Harris is his attorney. It's based on a novel by Pete Dexter. Made for theaters, this serious and violent film debuted on cable TV. *A Killing in a Small Town* is another superior movie by Stephen Gyllenhall that went straight to TV.

PARTY CAMP

(Vestron, 1986) **D/C:** Gary Graver **S:** Paul L. Brown **P:** Mark Borde

Andrew Ross becomes a camp counselor. This sex comedy features Kerry Brennan, Jewel Shepard, and April Wayne. Most of Graver's many films made around this time were porno.

PARTY INC.

(Starmaker, 1989) **D/P:** Chuck Vincent **S:** Craig Horall, Edd Rockis   (*Party Girls Incorporated*)

Marilyn Chambers (playing Marilyn) invites a camera crew to her mansion to film a documentary about her porno-star life so that she can pay off her husband's tax debt. She sings several times in this boring, R-rated sex "comedy," which features a guy in a chicken suit, Ruth Collins, and Christina Veronica. Chambers returned in *Breakfast in Bed* (1990).

PARTY LINE

(SVS, 1988) **D/P:** William Webb **S:** Bernard Brandes **P:** Tom Byrnes, Kurt Anderson

Former teen idol Leif Garrett and Greta Blackburn star as a rich brother and sister who are psycho killers. She lures men into her bed, and he slashes their throats. In one scene he puts on his mother's wedding dress and masturbates. With Richard Hatch as a cop, Richard Roundtree, former Miss Universe Shawn Weatherly, and Karen Mayo-Chandler.

THE PARTY'S OVER

(1962) **D:** Guy Hamilton **S:** Marc Behm **P:** Anthony Perry

Oliver Reed stars in his first non-Hammer film as Moise, the leader of "the Pack," a group of "depraved beatniks." An American industrialist (Eddie Albert) is upset because his daughter has joined them. Allied Artists released this b/w film in America in 1966. The release was delayed (here and in England) because of censorship problems concerning a sex-with-a-corpse scene. Actor Jack Hawkins was an executive producer, and Annie Ross (later in the sequels to *Basket Case*) sings the title song. Hamilton directed *Goldfinger* next.

THE PASSAGE

(1978) **D:** J. Lee Thompson **S:** Bruce Nicholayson **P:** John Quested   UK/France

A Basque (Anthony Quinn) helps a Jewish chemist (James Mason) and his family (Patricia Neal, Kay Lenz, and *The Beast Within* star Paul Clemens) escape over the Pyrenees. An out-of-control Malcolm McDowell as the evil Nazi Captain von Berkow makes you forget the other actors, though. He rants and glares, chops off a partisan's fingers, and sets a Gypsy (Christopher Lee) on fire. McDowell starred in *Caligula* the same intense year. Also with Michael Lonsdale.

THE PASSENGER

(Warner, 1975) **D/S:** Michelangelo Antonioni **S:** Mark Peloe, Pater Wollen **P:** Carlo Ponti   Italy

Most Americans didn't bother with this vague, noncommercial movie set in North Africa. Jack Nicholson is a TV reporter who changes identities with a dead businessman who turns out to have been a gunrunner. With Maria Schneider (*Last Tango in Paris*), Jenny Runacre, Ian Hendry, Steven Berkoff, and James Campbell as a witch doctor. From MGM. It was the director's first film after *Zabriskie Point*. Nicholson's next appearance was in *Tommy*.

PASSENGER 57

(Warner, 1992) **D:** Kevin Hooks **S:** David Loughery, Dan Gordon **P:** Lee Rich

Wesley Snipes (*New Jack City*) is Cutter, an action-hero airline-security expert, in this violent, *Die Hard*–inspired hostage movie set on a hijacked jet (and later at a country fair). Bruce Payne is a psycho Euro-terrorist. With Tom Sizemore, Alex Datcher, Robert Hooks as an FBI agent, Ernie Lively, and Elizabeth Hurley. Director Kevin Hooks starred in *Aaron Loves Angela* (1975), and his father, Robert, was the hero of *Trouble Man* (1972). The score is by Stanley Clark.

THE PASSING OF EVIL

(Warner, 1970) **D:** Jerry Paris **S/P:** Jerry Belson, Garry Marshall   (*The Grasshopper*)

A teen chorus dancer from Canada (Jacqueline Bisset) falls for a former football star (Jim Brown, playing a nice guy) in Las Vegas. He's murdered. She goes to work for an escort service and becomes a hooker and drug addict. After her life is ruined she's arrested for hiring a skywriter to write FUCK in the air. Also with Joseph Cotten and Corbett Monica. The soundtrack (on National General) features the Brooklyn Bridge and Vicki Lawrence. Paris usually directed comedies.

THE PASSING OF THE THIRD FLOOR BACK

(Sinister, 1935) **D:** Berthold Viertel **S:** Michael Hogan, Alma Reville   UK

A Christ-like man (Conrad Veidt) suddenly appears and helps the miserable tenants of an evil slumlord (Frank Cellier). With Anna Lee, Cathleen Nesbitt, Jack Livesey, and Sara Allgood. This allegorical play by Jerome K. Jerome had also been filmed in 1918. Reville was Hitchcock's wife.

PASSION AND VALOR

(Magnum, 1983) **D/S/P:** Hall Bartlett (*Love Is Forever; Comeback*)

Here's a chance to see Little Joe Cartwright meet Emanuelle. Michael Landon (the executive producer) plays real-life Australian journalist John Everingham, who rescued his Laotian girlfriend in Communist Laos. She's played by "black Emanuelle" series star Laura Gemser (aka Moira Chen). Also with Priscilla Presley, Jurgen Prochnow, Edward Woodward, and Gemser's real-life husband, Gabrielle Tinti. Laura Branigan sings the title song. It had a brief theatrical release but debuted on NBC-TV later the same year (at 180 minutes) and was later cut.

PASSIONATE STRANGERS

(1968) **D/S:** Eddie Romero **P:** M. J. Parsons   Philippines

An American (Michael Parsons) who runs a sugar mill accidentally kills a union organizer, and anti-American demonstrations result. With Valora Noland and Vic Diaz. Romero made this b/w drama the same year as his *Brides of Blood*.

PASSION IN PARADISE

(A-Pix, 1989) **D:** Harvey Hart **S:** Andrew Laskos **P:** Michael Custance   Canada

Armand Assante becomes a murder suspect when the millionaire father of his lover (Catherine Mary Stewart) is killed. Voodoo and sexual rites are involved. With Mariette Hartley, Kevin McCarthy, Michael Sarrazin, Wayne Rogers, and Rod Steiger. It was released (on tape) in 1994.

PASSION IN THE SUN

(SW, 1964) **D/P/A:** Dale Berry (*The Girl and the Geek*)

A pleasantly plump stripper (Josette Valague) is kidnapped by two killers, escapes, stops for a nude swim, takes a nap, and dreams (about her own burlesque act!). Meanwhile a howling carny geek (!) complete with a fright wig shows up in the woods and chases her (she's still naked) for a long time. She finally stops to dress and is driven away by a truck, but the geek jumps on top. They end up at a carnival on the wild-mouse ride! The action is interrupted by strip acts at the club she was on her way to perform at and is explained by a narrator. In one scene a dead woman breathes. This recently discovered wonder was made in Texas. *The Weird Ones* (1962) was the first of many by director Dale Berry(stein).

THE PASSION OF BEATRICE

(Virgin Vision, 1987) **D/S:** Bertrand Tavernier France (*Beatrice*)

Medieval witch-burning and all types of debauchery occur in this nightmarish movie. Julie Delpy stars as an innocent girl tortured by a priest (Bernard Pierre Donnadieu). It's subtitled, runs 128 minutes, and features lots of nudity. The second-unit director was horror specialist Ricardo Freda.

PASSION PLAY: *See* LOVE LETTERS

A PASSION TO KILL

(A-Pix, 1994) **D:** Rick King **S:** William Delligan **P:** Bruce Cohn Curtis

Scott Bakula is another of those idiot movie shrinks. He falls for the obviously deranged wife (Chelsea Field) of his best friend (John Getz). Her former husband (Rex Smith) tries to warn people that she's a psycho using a fake identity. This soap-opera/slasher movie takes place in beach houses and features Field and Bakula in a car sex scene. Sheila Kelly is a jealous and foolish assistant DA, France Nuyen is a wise shrink, and Eddie Velez is a cop.

THE PASSOVER PLOT

(Warner, 1976) **D:** Michael Campus **S:** Millard Cohen, Patricia Knop **P:** Menahem Golan   US/Israel

Forget about *The Last Temptation of Christ*. This movie was first. It shows Christ (Zalman King) as a false messiah. He fakes miracles, hallucinates, and plans his own crucifixion and resurrection. With Harry Andrews, Hugh Griffith, Donald Pleasence as Pontius Pilate, Scott Wilson as Judas, Robert Walker Jr., and Dan Hedaya. It's based on a book by Hugh J. Schonfeld.

PASSPORT TO CHINA

(1960) **D/P:** Michael Carreras **S:** Gordon Bentley   UK (*Visa to Canton*)

Richard Basehart stars as a pilot who goes to China to rescue an American (Lisa Gastoni) and ends up helping refugees. This color Hammer film features Eric Pohlmann and Burt Kwouk. Parts were filmed in Hong Kong. Columbia released it in b/w in America.

PAST MIDNIGHT

(Columbia, 1991) **D:** Jan Eliasberg **S:** Frank Norwood **P:** Lisa M. Hansen

Rutger Hauer stars as a convicted killer on parole in Washington State after serving 15 years for killing his wife. Natasha Richardson, a social worker living in a remote house, believes he's innocent. She falls in love with him, but after she does some research she thinks that maybe he did do it. A b/w

8mm snuff film proves who the killer is. There's good acting, a bloody arm, and a reference to David Goodis novels. Clancy Brown and Guy Boyd costar. It was written by a former social worker, but Quentin Tarantino (an associate producer) probably wrote the screenplay using a pseudonym.

PAST TENSE

(Republic, 1994) **D:** Graeme Clifford **S:** Scott Frost, Miguel Tejada-Flores **P:** Stephen Brown

Scott Glenn stars as a craggy novelist and cop. Lara Flynn Boyle is a friendly neighbor who is killed. The authorities claim that she never existed. There are flashbacks. With Anthony LaPaglia.

PAT GARRETT AND BILLY THE KID

(MGM, 1973) **D:** Sam Peckinpah **S/A:** Rudy Wurlitzer **P:** Gordon Carroll

Sheriff Pat Garrett (James Coburn) tracks down and kills Billy the Kid (Kris Kristofferson). MGM drastically cut and reedited this unique, rambling western, adding an opening scene with Garrett as an old man. Another version was created for TV, with violence and nudity cut and new scenes added. The full 122-minute version was finally made available on video in the early 90s. Sam Peckinpah directed this after the success of *The Wild Bunch* and *Straw Dogs,* but it was developed by Rudy Wurlitzer and Monte Hellman (who was at one time supposed to direct). Bob Dylan plays Alias, wrote the instrumental music, and provided the famous song "Knockin' on Heaven's Door" (on the Columbia soundtrack LP). The cast also includes Jason Robards as the governor, Richard Jaeckel, Katy Jurado, and the ultimate collection of desert-scum character actors: Chill Wills, Slim Pickens, R.G. Armstrong, Matt Clark, Jack Elam, L.Q. Jones, Dub Taylor, Harry Dean Stanton, and Luke Askew. Also with Rita Coolidge, Charles Martin Smith, Rutanya Alda, Elisha Cook Jr., Gene Evans, John Beck, Paul Fix, and Barry Sullivan (TV version only).

PATRICK 2

(VSOM, 1980) **D:** Mario Landi **S:** Piero Regnoli **P:** Gabriele Cristani   Italy (*Patrick Vive Ancora*)

Patrick is a 1978 Australian movie about a comatose young telekinetic killer. This gorier "sequel" has Patrick (Gianni Dei) in a new clinic. People are decapitated, boiled alive, and torn apart by dogs. Carmen Russo costars.

THE PATRIOT

(Vestron, 1986) **D/C:** Frank Harris **S:** Andy Ruben, Katt Shea Ruben **P:** Michael Bennett

Gregg Henry is after terrorists who are intercepting government nuclear weapons. Most of the action takes place underwater. The cast also includes Simone Griffeth, Michael J. Pollard, Jeff Conaway, and Leslie Nielsen. It's from Crown International.

PATRIOT GAMES

(Paramount, 1992) **D:** Phillip Noyce **S:** Peter Iliff, Donald Stewart **P:** Mace Neufeld, Robert Rehme

A grim Harrison Ford takes over as former CIA agent Jack Ryan in this follow-up to *The Hunt for Red October.* Irish terrorists (Sean Bean and Patrick Bergin) are the problem, and there's a boatchase climax. With Anne Archer as his wife, Thora Birch as his daughter, Richard Harris, Samuel L. Jackson, James Fox, and James Earl Jones. *Clear and Present Danger* (1994), also starring Ford and directed by Phillip Noyce, followed. All are based on Tom Clancy novels. Ford, who once had to give up his film-acting career and work as a carpenter, has so far starred in three incredibly popular series.

PATTY

(1975) **D/S/P:** Robert L. Roberts **S:** Joyce Richards

The director of *Sweet Savior* (about Charles Manson) returned with this X-rated exploitation movie about Patty Hearst. "Real" experts and doctors sit around and discuss what happened, and Sarah Nicholson (a porno actress) plays Hearst in the sex and conditioning scenes. Also with Renay Granville, Lenny Montana (*The Godfather*), and Jamie Gillis. The Stang records soundtrack features music by the Moments, the Rimshots, and Chuck Jackson. *The Abduction* (1975), *Tanya* (1976), and *Patty Hearst* (1988) are also "about" Hearst. The real Patty showed up in John Waters's *Cry-Baby* and *Serial Mom.*

PAYBACK

(Republic, 1990) **D:** Russell Solberg **S/A:** Corey Michael Eubanks **P:** Bob Eubanks

An escaped con (Corey Michael Eubanks) goes after a drug-dealer and killer (Don Swayze). The stunt-specialist star is the son of the host of *The Newlywed Game* (who produced this). With Michael Ironside, Teresa Blake as a sheriff's daughter, and Vince Van Patten. The same people made *Forced to Kill.*

PAYBACK

(Vidmark, 1994) **D:** Anthony Hickox **S/P:** Sam Bernard **P:** Nathan Zahavi

After 13 years in jail C. Thomas Howell (with a droopy mustache) stays with a couple at their remote oceanside café in order to kill the former owner, a sadistic prison guard (Marshall Bell), now blind, and locate a hidden treasure. Meanwhile he's seduced by the wife (Joan Severance). A deputy sheriff and a black ex-con cause problems as the ludicrous plot twists add up. The selling point, though, is sex scenes. One copies the remake of *The Postman Always Rings Twice* closely, but the good one features Severance and Howell naked on top of a car. The funniest scene has Howell as a cartoonish-look "punk" holdup man, and the most surprising scene has him totally naked and filthy in solitary confinement. This is the R version, but an unrated one is also available. R. G. Armstrong is an old convict. Howell and Severance were also paired in *Dangerous Indiscretion* the same year.

PAYMENT IN BLOOD

(1967) **D/S:** Enzo Girolami **S:** Tito Carpi   Italy (*7 Winchester per un Massacro; Renegade Riders*)

Edd "Kookie" Byrnes stars as a bounty hunter who pretends to join a group of former Confederate soldiers who are after a fortune in gold. Guy Madison and Louise Barrett costar. Byrnes was also in *Any Gun Can Play* the same year.

PAYOFF

(Media, 1991) **D:** Stuart Cooper **S:** David Weisberg **P:** Andrew Sugarman, William Stuart

An ex-cop (Keith Carradine) seeks revenge for the death of his parents. There's also a casino robbery plot at Lake Tahoe. With Kim Griest, Harry Dean Stanton, John Saxon as a Mafia boss, and Jeff Corey. It debuted on Showtime.

PCU

(Fox, 1994) **D:** Hart Bochner **S:** Adam Leff, Zak Penn **P:** Paul Schiff

In what tries to be an *Animal House* for the 90s, Jeremy Piven leads a coed gang who live in a dorm called the Pit and clash with politically correct groups at Port Chester University. Chris Young and David Spade costar, with Sarah Trigger, Megan Ward, and Jessica Walter as the school president. George Clinton and Parliament play. This PG-13 feature was made by the original screenwriters of *Last Action Hero.*

THE PEACE KILLERS

(Starmaker, 1971) **D/C/E:** Douglas Schwartz **S:** Michael Berk

Violent bikers terrorize a peaceful commune. They tie the Christ-look leader to a giant peace symbol, and in one scene guys on motorcycles chase a woman on horseback. With Michael Ontkean, Clint Ritchie, and Albert Popwell. New World released it.

PEACEMAKER

(Fries, 1990) **D/S:** Kevin S. Tenney **P:** Andrew Lane

A humanoid alien cop (Robert Forster) fights a killer humanoid alien (Lance Edwards) on Earth. Both are violent and indestructible, and both claim to be the good guy, which keeps things interesting for a while. Also with Hilary Shepard as an LA-police medical examiner who is kidnapped, Robert Davi as a cop, and Bert Remsen.

THE PEANUT BUTTER SOLUTION

(Starmaker, 1985) **D/S:** Michael Rubbo **P:** Rock Demers, Nicole Robert   Canada

When 11-year-old Mathew Mackay visits a haunted house he loses his hair. Then friendly ghosts put a concoction on his head that makes his hair grow back extremely fast. He's kidnapped, and his hair is used to make paint brushes. It's a Cineplex Odeon production.

LA PEAU DE TORPEDO

(1969) **D/S:** Jean Delannoy **S:** Jean Cau   France/Italy/W. Germany

A Parisian woman (Stéphane Audran) shoots her art-dealer husband and blames a spy ring. Klaus Kinski and Lilli Palmer costar.

Paul Reubens in *Pee-wee's Big Adventure*.

PEEK-A-BOO

(SW, 1953) **D:** Lillian Hunt

Strippers alternate with three comedians in this filmed burlesque show, which opens with a carny barker who raps about the sideshow. The strippers go as far as pasties, G-strings, and high heels and always bow when done. The final name-value stripper is Venus. In a ball-toss comedy routine "I killed a colored boy yesterday" is a joke. William C. Thompson of Ed Wood movie fame was the cinematographer. The b/w print is excellent. A short (*Bust-a-Rama*) with three strippers is also on the video, presented by David F. Friedman.

PEEK-A-BOO

(1954) **D:** Jean Loubignac **S/A:** Robert Dhéry **P:** Edgar Bacquet   France (*Ah! Les Belles Bacchantes*)

A small-town police inspector (Louis de Funès) checks out a variety show with strippers. This color nudie comedy includes several staged numbers with naked women. Fanfare released a cut version in 1961.

THE PEEK SNATCHERS

(SW, 1965) **D:** Joseph P. Mawra **P:** George Weiss

Watching a "tel-star machine" (a TV), two burlesque comics see various burlesque routines and more comics. Women dance and strip down to pasties and G-strings, and one puts snakes into her mouth. Princess Ming Chu is the headliner. This 50s-style b/w adult movie might get a PG-13 today.

PEER GYNT

(1941) **D/S/P/C:** David Bradley **S:** Thomas A Blair

As a student at Northwestern University, 18-year-old Charlton Heston starred in this silent, b/w, 16mm, amateur version of the Henrik Ibsen fantasy play. It was filmed in Illinois and Wisconsin, near where Heston grew up. The director later filmed other classics, including Shakespeare's *Julius Caesar* (1949), also with Heston. In 1964 he directed *They Saved Hitler's Brain*! In 1965 new footage was added to *Peer Gynt*, narration was added (by Francis X. Bushman), and it played in some theaters, opening at the same time as Heston was starring in *The War Lord*. I wonder how many viewers paid to see it, thinking it was a new (real) movie! And why isn't this on video?

PEE-WEE'S BIG ADVENTURE

(Warner, 1985) **D:** Tim Burton **S:** Phil Hartman, Michael Varhol **S/A:** Paul Reubens **P:** Robert Shapiro, Richard Gilbert Abramson **M:** Danny Elfman

Pee-wee Herman (Paul Reubens) searches for his bicycle. This PG comedy/fantasy hit was the first feature by 25-year-old former animator Tim Burton, and it's a riot. Pee-wee visits the Alamo, dances to "Tequila," and meets Large Marge (!). With Elizabeth Daily, Diane Salinger, Ed Herlihy, Cassandra Peterson, Josh Brolin, Morgan Fairchild, Milton Berle, Tony Bill, Twisted Sister, dinosaurs, and Ghidrah. The Pee-wee character was first seen in a 1982 TV special on HBO, then in the (toned-down) TV series (released on Media Video).

PEGGY SUE GOT MARRIED

(Fox, 1986) **D/P:** Francis Ford Coppola
S: Jerry Leichtling, Arlene Sarner
P: Paul R. Gurian **M:** John Barry

Coppola made this PG-13 Capra-style fantasy because he needed money, and the movie got him out of debt. It was supposed to be directed by Penny Marshall and star Debra Winger. Kathleen Turner passes out during her 25th class reunion, goes back in time, and relives high school. Some of the acting is excellent, it's a lot more thought-provoking than *Back to the Future* and its sequels, and John Carradine has his last role in a real feature. With Nicolas Cage, Barry Miller, Catherine Hicks, Kevin J. O'Connor, Barbara Harris, Don Murray, Maureen O'Sullivan, Marshall Crenshaw, Leon Ames, Jim Carrey, and Helen Hunt.

PEKING OPERA BLUES

(Rainbow, 1986) **D/P:** Tsui Hark
S: To Kwok Wai   Hong Kong

In the early 1900s three women from different backgrounds help expose a government conspiracy. This movie has great action, politics, and comedy. Sally Yeh is a singer and thief, Lin Ching Hsia is a revolutionary who is the daughter of a corrupt general, and Cherie Chung is an aspiring actress whose father runs the opera (which employs men in female roles).

THE PENALTY

(Fright, 1920) **D:** Wallace Woolsey
S: Charles Kenyon, Philip Lonergan
P: Samuel Goldwyn

You won't believe this incredible Lon Chaney movie. He's Blizzard, a scary, sadistic, sneering, manipulative, romantic, piano-playing "master of the underworld" on San Francisco's Barbary Coast. He's also a vengeance-seeking "cripple from Hell" because his legs were (needlessly) amputated when he was a child. The acrobatic, legless Chaney is simply amazing, using slides, ramps, trapdoors, and poles to get around, conveying every emotion in the book (often several at once), and posing for a bust of Satan! This 76-year-old movie has flashbacks, flashforwards, and mob riot scenes (shot on location). It also has a drug addict, a naked model, slave-girl hat makers, and an undercover female cop. It was reissued by MGM in 1926. The print is excellent. There is no soundtrack. Recommended!

PENITENTIARY

(Tempe, 1979) **D/S/P:** Jamaa Fanaka

Leon Isaac Kennedy (from Cleveland) is Martel "Too Sweet" Gordone, a boxer who's sent to prison for killing a biker. He's put into a cell with a boxing trainer and competes in fights, eventually winning his freedom. Nearly everybody in this pretty realistic prison movie has names like Seldom Seen, Hi-Fi, and Half Dead. With Floyd Chatham, Tommy Pollard, and Hazel Spears. It was released by Jerry Gross.

PENITENTIARY II

(MGM, 1982) **D/S/P:** Jamaa Fanaka

Leon Isaac Kennedy returns as Too Sweet, now on parole and working as a messenger on skates. Half Dead (Ernie Hudson) escapes from prison and kills his girlfriend, and Too Sweet ends up back in prison because of a big (fixed) fight. This sequel is more exploitative than the original, with more outrageous stuff about hookers, a midget, and Mr. T. as himself. Also with Rudy Ray Moore, Glynn Turman, and Peggy Blow. MGM released this one, so more people saw it.

Leon Isaac Kennedy and Kessler Raymond in *Penitentiary III*.

PENITENTIARY III

(Warner, 1987) **D/S/P:** Jamaa Fanaka
P/A: Leon Isaac Kennedy

Leon Isaac Kennedy (this time with a little pony-tail) is back in jail for killing a man (it was another setup). *General Hospital* star Anthony Geary is Serengeti, a rich prisoner with spiky white hair and ear studs who never speaks above a whisper. He has a French chef and enjoys manicures from his companion in drag (Jim Bailey). Guards in protective suits and helmets are seen leading what sounds like a ferocious lion down the prison corridor. It's the Midnight Thud, who turns out to be a killer martial-arts-fighting midget! Raymond Kessler (aka the Haiti Kid) is the Thud. After howling and beating our hero with a lead pipe, he's returned to a rat-infested dungeon where he smokes crack and watches 16mm films! Then Too Sweet is given shock treatments and becomes incoherent. He's scheduled to fight Big Hugo but needs training. Suddenly the crazed Thud cleans up his act and dresses and acts normal. He gives a lecture (with his Jamaican accent) about the soul of man, trains the proud Too Sweet (in slow motion), and proves that "it's amazing what a little self-respect can do for a man!" It's amazing what Jamaa Fanaka can do with a sequel. Forget all those clichéd prison/horror movies. This is the one. It's from Cannon. RCA released the various artists soundtrack.

PENN AND TELLER GET KILLED

(Warner, 1989) **D/P:** Arthur Penn
S/A: Penn Jillette, Teller

The famous comic magicians play "themselves." On a TV show Penn suggests that a viewer try and kill him. The movie features magic, murder, blood, gore, tumor surgery, suicide jokes, and eyeball-plucking reality. It also has Trump Tower and Diet Coke plugs. With Caitlin Clarke, Jon Cryer, Christopher Durang, and Eddie Goredetsky. Some Velvet Underground music is heard, and Teller talks. Also look for *Penn and Teller's Cruel Tricks for Dear Friends.*

THE PENTHOUSE

(VSOM, 1967) **D/S:** Peter Collinson
P: Harry Fine   UK

People who call themselves Tom, Dick, and Harry terrorize an adulterous couple (Suzy Kendall and Terence Morgan) in a penthouse apartment. This color movie, although not graphic, features sex, drugs, bondage, and rape that still shock viewers. Martine Beswicke, who plays Harry, is one of the main attractions. From Paramount. United Artists issued the soundtrack, with dialogue.

THE PENTHOUSE

(Turner, 1989) **D:** David Greene **S:** William Wood,
Frank DeFelita **P:** Harold Tichenor   Canada

Robin Givens is the star, but David Hewlett (*Pin* and *Scanners II*) is the reason to watch this. He's convincing as an obsessed, childish, suicidal killer psycho who escapes from a mental hospital and decides to hold the rich daughter (Givens) of a record exec (Robert Guillaume) hostage in her penthouse. He also booby-traps the building with

dynamite. It was filmed in Vancouver. The video is "rated" M. Givens was better in *A Rage in Harlem.* A 1967 British film has the same title (see above), and there's a 1933 film called *Penthouse.*

PENTHOUSE LOVE STORIES

(Penthouse, 1986)

Scream-queen fans will want to check out this softcore sex anthology with Michelle Bauer, Monique Gabrielle, Julie Parton, Barbara Peckinpah, Shauna Grant/Coleen Applegate, Raven, and Xaviera Hollander as herself. *Penthouse on the Wild Side* (1989) features most of same cast.

THE PEOPLE NEXT DOOR

(1970) **D:** David Greene **S:** J. P. Miller
P: Herbert Brodkin **M:** Don Sebesky

Maxie (Deborah Winters), a suburban teen, takes LSD, and her parents (Eli Wallach and Julie Harris) freak out. They blame their son (Stephen McHattie) and throw him out. Later on they find out that the supplier is their next-door neighbor (Don Scardino, from *Squirm*), whose parents are Hal Holbrook and Cloris Leachman. Also with Rue McClanahan, Nehemiah Persoff, and the Bead Game as themselves playing at a party (where Maxie tries STP). Avco Embassy released the movie and the soundtrack. It's based on a 1968 TV play.

THE PEOPLE UNDER THE STAIRS

(MCA, 1991) **D/S:** Wes Craven
P: Marianne Maddelena, Stuart M. Besser

This is a bizarre, cartoonish horror comedy with a social and political message. Brandon Adams stars as a bright little ghetto kid called Fool. He goes along with a man (Ving Rhames, from *Pulp Fiction*) to break into a big old house. The landlords are an insane, depraved, hyped-up brother and sister who keep pathetic, zombie-like, captive cannibals (whose tongues have been cut out) in the many secret passages of the house and abuse a captive teen girl (A. J. Langer). They also own the decaying ghetto apartment Fool lives in and have so much money that they just throw it all into the basement. Everett McGill and Wendy Robie (then known for playing a couple in the TV series *Twin Peaks*) have a killer Rottweiler, shotguns, and rubber suits. Too bad the set is so cramped and everything is so dark. The soundtrack was released by Bay Cities. After this Craven created *Nightmare Café*, a short-lived TV series with Robert Englund.

PERCY

(1971) **D:** Ralph Thomas **S:** Hugh
Leonard **P:** Betty Box   UK

A young man (the very dull Hywel Bennett) who has had a penis transplant wants to find out who the late, anonymous donor was, so he visits recent widows. Denholm Elliott is a professor who uses endless double entendres. With Janet Key as a cheating wife, Tracy Crisp (seen in bondage gear), and Sue Lloyd. Britt Ekland and Elke Sommer have topless scenes as girlfriends of the donor. There's footage of the Rolling Stones at Hyde Park and a man in a gorilla suit. Thomas had directed the *Doc-*

tor in the House movies. The soundtrack (which features a couple of excellent Kinks ballads, including "The Way Love Used to Be") was released only in England. The sequel is called *It's Not the Size That Counts* in America.

THE PERFECT BRIDE

(Fox, 1990) **D:** Terrence O'Hara **S:** Claire Montgomery, Monte Montgomery **P:** Pierre David

Sammi Davis-Voss stars as Stephanie, a British "nurse," in this (very good) ripoff of *The Stepfather.* In America (probably Canada, actually) she kills her fiancé with a syringe, then moves on to another one and stays with his family. Anybody who suspects something is wrong dies, except for the unsuspecting guy's sister (Kelly Preston), who tries to save her family from the cute but devious psycho. Davis-Voss is pretty amazing when she loses her cool (which is pretty often), and John Agar has his best and largest role in years. He's a senile but cheerful grandfather who could have been comedy relief but isn't. The feature debuted on the USA Network.

PERFECT STRANGERS

(Nelson, 1984) **D/S:** Larry Cohen
P: Paul Kurta   (*Blind Alley*)

Anne Carlisle (*Liquid Sky*) is a single mom whose 3-year-old son (Matthew Stockley) witnesses a mob hit in an alley. The kid can't really talk yet, but the killer (Brad Rijn, from *Smithereens*) thinks that he can identify him, so he starts a romance with the mom. With Steven Lack (*Scanners*) as a detective and Ann Magnuson. The scenes of the killer going after the kid are especially good. *Witness* (1985) used the same idea, and *Dangerous Affection* (1987), a TV movie, was a close copy. Cohen also filmed in Katz's deli years before *When Harry Met Sally . . .* did. Cohen made this and *Special Effects* quickly, back to back. He hired a cast of mostly NYC "underground" actors and shot on location in the Village.

PERFECT VICTIMS

(Academy, 1988) **D/S:** Shuki Levy **S:** Joe Hailey,
Bob Barron **P:** Jonathan Braun   (*Hidden Rage*)

In this tasteful exploitation movie an AIDS-infected killer rapes two models. Deborah Shelton stars as the head of a model agency. With Lyman Ward, Clarence Williams III, John Agar, and Jackie Swanson.

THE PERFECT WEAPON

(Paramount, 1990) **D/P:** Mark DiSalle
S: David Campbell Wilson **P:** Pierre David

Jeff Speakman (a real black belt) stars as a kenpo karate-fighting hero who battles the Korean Mafia in LA's Koreatown. James Hong is a mob lord with a superstrong yakuza bodyguard (Professor Tanaka). With Mako, Cary-Hiroyuki Tagawa, and Mariska Hargitay. Some of the fight scenes are pretty good, but most of it is about as exciting as a *Karate Kid* movie. It's by the director of *Kickboxer.* The hit "The Power" is from this movie. Speakman returned in *Street Knight.*

THE PERFECT WOMAN

(1981) **D/P:** Robert Emenegger

An alien king sends two idiots to Earth to find him a queen, in this very stupid comedy made for Gold Key syndicated TV. Cameron Mitchell, who co-stars, did half a dozen films for the company. With Fred Willard, Rudy Vallee, Marie Windsor, Peter Kastner, and Barry Gordon.

THE PERILS OF GWENDOLINE (IN THE LAND OF YIK YAK)

(Vestron, 1983) **D/S:** Just Jaeckin **P:** Jean-Claude Fleury France (*The Perils of Gwendoline in the Land of the Yik-Yak*)

The director of the original *Emmanuelle* made this fantasy/adventure based on John Willie's 1940s erotic comic strip. Tawny Kitaen is Gwendoline, who's searching for her father in the Far East. Brent Huff is a soldier of fortune who helps her, and Bernadette Lafont is an evil queen. It copies *Barbarella* and the *Raiders* movies and features sexy costumes, some cartoonish violence and S&M, lots of topless Amazon women in a kingdom under the desert, and cannibals. The American Kitaen (later a regular in the TV series *Hercules*, and then briefly in the spotlight as a girlfriend of O. J. Simpson) has several nude scenes. With Zabou and Jean Rougerie.

THE PERILS OF NYOKA: *See* NYOKA AND THE TIGERMEN

THE PERILS OF PAULINE

(Stokey, 1934) **D:** Ray Taylor **S:** Ella O'Neill, Basil Dickey, George H. Plympton

This 12-chapter Universal serial is a remake of the famous 1914 Pathé serial. Blond Evelyn Knapp stars as the daughter of a scientist, with Robert Allen and James Durkin. The plot concerns an ancient civilization and an evil doctor who's after a formula for a deadly gas on an ivory disc. Some chapters are "The Mummy Walks" and "Pursued by Savages." The 1947 *The Perils of Pauline* is supposed to be about Pearl White (star of the original), and the 1967 film is the pilot for a TV series.

THE PERILS OF P.K.

(1986) **D:** Joseph Green **S/A/M/E:** Nora Hayden **P/A:** Sheila McCrea

Nora Hayden (*The Angry Red Planet*) stars as a has-been actress now doing strip shows. She goes to a shrink (Dick Shawn), and we see her fantasies and flashbacks. The oddball comic cast includes Kaye Ballard, Heather MacRae, Larry (and Norman) Storch, Sammy Davis Jr. (and his wife, Altovese), Louise Lasser, Professor Irwin Corey, Jackie Mason, Joey Heatherton, Anne Meara, and Virginia Graham! Hayden later became a health-book writer. It's by the director of *The Brain That Wouldn't Die*.

PERILS OF THE JUNGLE

(1953) **D:** George Blair **S:** Frank Art Taussig, Robert T. Smith **P:** Robert White Jr.

This 63-minute Lippert cheapie was the end of the jungle trail for 30s star Clyde Beatty. He searches for rare lions. Phyllis Coates, TV's first Lois Lane, costars, with John Doucette.

PERSONA

(MGM, 1966) **D/S/P:** Ingmar Bergman **C:** Sven Nykvist Sweden

Liv Ullmann stars as a famous stage actress who has a nervous breakdown. Bibi Andersson is a nurse assigned to care for her at a seaside cottage in this b/w film. The identity-switch idea was later copied in *Performance*, and other films borrowed the experimental cinematic techniques. It was a Lopert release. It was followed by Ingmar Bergman's *Hour of the Wolf* and *Shame,* completing a fantasy trilogy for patient viewers.

PERSONAL CHOICE

(1989) **D/S:** David Saperstein **P:** Joseph Perez

An ex-astronaut (Martin Sheen) suffers from fatal radiation poisoning due to his 70s moon walk. The barely released, talky film costars Christian Slater, Robert Foxworth, Sharon Stone, Olivia D'Abo, and F. Murray Abraham.

THE PERSONALS

(1981) **D/S/C:** Peter Markle **P:** Patrick Wells

A recently divorced man (Bill Schoppert) places a personal ad and falls for a married woman (Karen Landry). New World released this PG independent comedy made in Minneapolis.

THE PERVERSE COUNTESS

(VSOM, 1973) **D/S:** "Clifford Brown"/Jess Franco France (*La Comtesse Perverse*)

Howard Vernon and Alice Arno are the flesh-eating Count and Countess Zaroff in a movie that copies *The Most Dangerous Game.* Lina Romay is tricked by Robert Woods into spending time with him on their island. Eventually Arno (naked but with a bow and arrows) chases Romay (also naked) through the woods. This dubbed version contains some hard-core sex footage from an alternative European version.

PERVERSE PREACHERS, FASCIST FUNDAMENTALISTS, AND KRISTIAN KIDDIE KOOKS

(Zontar Home Video, 1991)

Zontar magazine editor Jan Johnson slaved over countless hours of cable and local TV religious broadcasting to compile this brilliant, two-hour compilation video. It's the ultimate mondo movie. See the worst of self-serving preachers, like Pat Robertson, Jim and Tammy Faye Bakker, Jerry Falwell, Oral Roberts, Jimmy Swaggart, and Dr. Jack Van Impe! Hear about how Communism, 666, and heavy-metal music will result in Armageddon! Any day now! See Captain Hook, "the Christian pirate" (with singing puppets and a ventriloquist's dummy who raps), make sinning children walk the plank!

And if you think that's bad there's a segment on New Age shows and commercials that will leave you speechless.

PETER CUSHING: A ONE-WAY TICKET TO HOLLYWOOD

(Blood Times, 1988) **D:** Alan Bell **P:** Gillian Harrow UK

Peter Cushing proves to be very funny (and romantic) in this British TV documentary about his life and films. He talks about being directed by James Whale in Hollywood in 1939 and meeting his wife in Montreal. Cushing was known at one time as a TV star, so rare scenes from the BBC version of *1984,* the Morecambe and Wise comedy show, and a Pils commercial are shown. Cushing sings, rides a bike, and imitates Christopher Lee's voice. The reason there is less about Hammer films than you'd expect is that this was produced by rival Tyburn, which also frequently hired Cushing (who died in 1994).

PETEY WHEATSTRAW

(Active, 1977) **D/S:** Cliff Roquette **P:** Theodore Tony (*The Devil's Son-in-Law*)

More people should see this outrageous fantasy/comedy. Petey Wheatstraw, or "Mr. Excitement" (Rudy Ray Moore), is a legendary comedian and club owner who makes a deal with the Devil in Hell after rival club owners Skillet and Leroy have his friends machine-gunned at a funeral. Petey has sex with a whole room full of women and fights caped, horned devils in tights. There are fast-motion chases, slow-motion deaths, a scene shown backwards, watermelon jokes, kung-fu fighting, and a guy scared shitless. Don't miss the incredible rhyming intro and the birth of Petey Wheatstraw. With Ebony Wright as the Devil's daughter and Sy Richardson. The soundtrack was released by Magic Disk. Moore, Skillet and Leroy, and costars Jimmy Lynch, Wildman Steve, and Lady Reed all recorded for Laff records. Record Rendezvous in Cleveland used to stock them all.

PETS

(Imperial, 1973) **D/P:** Raphael Nussbaum **S:** Richard Reich

Candice Rialson stars as Bonnie, a hitchhiker. She seduces an older man while another woman throws his poodle off a cliff. She encounters a lesbian artist played by Joan Blackman (who was in two Elvis movies). Then she becomes the captive of a rich art collector with a bullwhip (Ed Bishop, from the TV series *UFO*), who keeps women (one is black) in cages in his castle. The captives appear topless and in collars and chains and are whipped. With K. T. Stevens. It was released by Mardi Rustam.

PET SEMATARY

(Paramount, 1989) **D:** Mary Lambert **S/A:** Stephen King **P:** Richard R. Rubenstein **M:** Elliot Goldenthal

A magical Indian burial ground in rural Maine revives a cat, so a dense father whose kid walked into the path of a speeding truck thinks, "Why not my dead baby?" A killer zombie baby results. This very serious and grim horror movie was cut for an R rating. It still has some gory scenes, plus dream sequences and a helpful ghost. Dale Midkiff and Denise Crosby star. Fred Gwynne (with an overdone accent) costars. I hated it, but for some reason it was the most successful Stephen King adaptation (after *Misery* and *The Shining*) up to that time. King has a bit as a minister. The Ramones do the end theme. Varèse Sarabande released the soundtrack.

PET SEMATARY II

(Paramount, 1992) **D:** Mary Lambert
S: Richard Outten **P:** Ralph S. Singleton

Here's another sequel that's even worse than the first movie. It has false scares, nightmares, gore, rape, and topless scenes. Lots of animals (not real) are killed. A vet (a balding Anthony Edwards) and his son (Edward Furlong) move near the magical graveyard in Maine. Furlong and a new friend revive a dead dog. Then the asshole local sheriff (Clancy Brown) is revived (why??), followed by the dead actress mom (Darlanne Fluegel). Also with Jared Rushton and Sarah Trigger. Stephen King had nothing to do with this one, which was filmed in Georgia. Steve Johnson did the convincing FX. The rock soundtrack includes Traci Lords singing and the Ramones' "Poison Heart" as an end theme.

PETRIFIED BEAST FROM THE FROZEN ZONE

(Dark Dreams, 1990) **D/S/A/M/E:** Fred Hopkins

Many directors use stock footage, but Fred Hopkins has gone too far! Most of this movie consists of b/w abominable-snowman-movie footage from *Half Human*, *The Snow Creature*, and *Man Beast*, with the bizarre (color) nightclub sequence from *Fireball Jungle* thrown in, plus some more science-fiction-movie footage. The rest is Hopkins (as Fred Vortex) ranting (with his unsynced voice) in an office, a guy in a bear mask, and some (very good) local Seattle bands playing live.

PHANTASM II

(MCA, 1988) **D/S:** Don Coscarelli
P: Roberto A. Quezada

A better-known actor (James LeGros) stars as Mike this time. He and a girl share dreams. Angus Scrimm returns as the mysterious "tall man" at the mausoleum. The floating killer spheres are improved, and there's a big fight with flamethrowers and a chainsaw. It's more like a more morbid remake of the 1979 movie (a personal fave) than a sequel, but it has its moments (and some flashbacks to the original). With Reggie Bannister (returning from the original), Paula Irving, Samantha Phillips, and Stacy Travis. Silver Screen released a soundtrack recording with music from both films by Fred Myrow and Malcolm Seagrave.

PHANTASM 3

(MCA, 1994) **D/S/P:** Don Coscarelli

Reggie (star Reggie Bannister) and Mike (Michael Baldwin, returning from the first *Phantasm*) continue trying to find and destroy "the tall man"

(Angus Scrimm). They're joined by a tough black female army vet with nunchucks named Rocky (Gloria Lynn Henry) and a kid (Kevin Connors) with a killer Frisbie. Rocky says, "This kickin' zombie ass just ain't my thing" but sticks around long enough for a cat fight in a mausoleum and a topless sex scene. This sequel has laughing zombies, various spheres, flashbacks, nightmares, and a very irritating nonending. A very impressive real, large, old mausoleum was used. The cast also includes Bill Thornbury (returning from the first movie) as the spirit of Mike's brother and John David Chandler (star of the 1961 movie *Mad Dog Coll*). This Universal release is padded with scenes from the first two movies.

THE PHANTOM

(Stokey, 1943) **D:** B. Reeves Eason **S:** Morgan B. Cox, Victor McLeod, Sherman Lowe **P:** Rudolph C. Flothow

Tom Tyler stars as the costumed jungle hero based on a comic strip by Lee Falk and Ray Moore. The "ageless" character (who also appears as Godfrey Prescott) lasts forever because whenever he dies a son always takes over. This 15-chapter Columbia serial features Jeanne Bates, Kenneth R. MacDonald, Frank Shannon, and Ace the dog.

THE PHANTOM CHARIOT

(Redemption, 1920) **D/S/A:** Victor Sjöström
Sweden (*Körkarlen*; *The Stroke of Midnight*; *The Phantom Carriage*; *Thy Soul Shall Bear Witness*)

A drunken failure (Victor Sjöström) dies, but his spirit is doomed to collect the spirits of the dead and take them to the land of the dead. This flashback-filled film is partially tinted. It's based on a novel by Selma Lagerlöf. It was remade in France as *La Charrette Fantôme* (1939) by Julian Duvivier and in Sweden as *Körkarlen* (1958) by Arne Mattson. Sjöström directed American movies in the 20s (including several with Lon Chaney) as Victor Seastrom. He made his last screen appearance as the star of Ingmar Bergman's *Wild Strawberries* (1957).

THE PHANTOM CREEPS

(Stokey, 1939) **D:** Ford Beebe, Saul A. Goodkind **S:** George Plympton, Basil Dickey, Mildred Barish

Bela Lugosi stars as Dr. Zorka in this fun 12-chapter Universal serial. Zorka has a giant, always snarling robot (!), an invisibility belt, a death ray, and a mechanical spider, and he can cause suspended animation. With all that he still resorts to dropping little bombs out of a biplane. Chapter 12 is "To Destroy the World." Robert Kent is the hero, Captain West, but Lugosi (with his robot) is the reason to watch. With Dorothy Arnold, Regis Toomey, Roy Barcroft, and Edward Van Sloan. Some chapters are also on the video series *Saturday Night Serials* (Rhino) with three other serials. There was also a short feature version.

PHANTOM EMPIRE

(Rhino, Sinister, 1935) **D:** Otto Brower, B. Reeves Eason **S:** John Rathmell **S/P:** Armand Schaefer

This 12-chapter Mascot serial is pretty great and has similarities to *Flash Gordon* (which wasn't released until the next year). It's easy to find and has been released by at least five video companies. Gene Autry stars as himself (the singing-cowboy star of the *Radio Ranch* radio show). He falls into a hole and discovers the futuristic, subterranean city of Murania underneath his ranch! (The funny-looking robots with flamethrower hands and metal top hats had first been used in the 1933 musical *Dancing Lady*, with Joan Crawford.) Dorothy Christy is the evil Queen Yika, and Wheeler Oakman is the high chancellor. With Frankie Darro as Frankie, Betsy King Ross as Betsy, and Smiley Burnette. Feature versions are called *Men with Steel Faces* and *Radio Ranch*. It's also on the video series *Saturday Night Serials* (Rhino) with three other serials.

THE PHANTOM EMPIRE

(Prism, 1986) **D/S/P:** Fred Olen Ray **S:** T. L. Lankford

A monster that looks like it escaped from a Larry Buchanan movie rips a guy's head off. Then Susan Stokey hires the hard-drinking, wisecracking team of Ross Hagen and Dawn Wildsmith to lead an expedition underground to find some jewels. First they visit a survivor of a previous party (Russ Tamblyn). Mineral experts Jeffrey Combs and Robert Quarry join them as they enter Bronson Canyon. Cast members chase each other, running endlessly through the cave (like in *The Flintstones*). Cannibals attempt to roast Stokey on a spit, and animated dinosaur footage (from *Planet of the Dinosaurs*) threatens them. Sybil Danning shows up on a space tank leading a female tribe, and a mute Michelle Bauer runs around topless. With Fox Harris and Robby the Robot (with a new head). A few ideas from the old serial are used, but this effort, filmed in six days, is not a remake.

THE PHANTOM OF CRESTWOOD

(1932) **D:** J. Walter Ruben **S:** Bartlett Cormack

A scheming woman (Karen Morley) invites the men in her life to an old mansion and threatens to

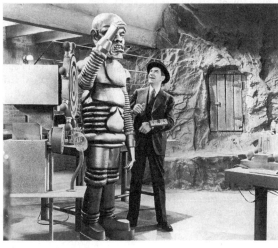
Bela Lugosi stars in *The Phantom Creeps*.

blackmail all of them. She's killed by someone in a glowing death mask. Ricardo Cortez stars as a gangster who tries to solve the mystery before the cops arrive. This RKO release (the executive producer was Merian C. Cooper) was a gimmick film in its day. NBC presented a six-week radio mystery of the same name. To find out the identity of the killer you had to see the movie. With Anita Louise, Pauline Frederick, Skeets Gallagher, H. B. Warner, and George E. Stone.

PHANTOM OF DEATH

(Vidmark, 1987) **D:** Ruggero Deodato
S: G. Clerici, V. Mannino, G Battaglini
Italy (*La Casa di Viarubens; Off Balance*)

A pianist (Michael York) has progeria, a rare disease that causes premature aging. He kills people but ages so fast that nobody recognizes him. Edwige Fenech is his girlfriend, and Donald Pleasence is the police detective who's determined to capture the killer. This unrated horror movie was shot in Venice and features Argento-style slow-motion bloody deaths. The music is by Pino Donnaggio.

THE PHANTOM OF 42ND STREET

(Sinister, 1944) **D/P:** Albert Herman
S: Milton Raison **P:** Martin Mooney

A theater critic (Dave O'Brien) tries to discover who murdered an actor during a play. Kay Aldridge, Frank Jenks, and Alan Mowbray are also in the cast of this 58-minute PRC mystery. Albert Herman made *The Missing Corpse* and *Rogues' Gallery* the same year, ending a career that went back to the silents.

THE PHANTOM OF LIBERTY

(Cinematheque, 1974) **D/S:** Luis Buñuel
S: Jean-Claude Carrière **P:** Serge Silberman
France (*Le Fantôme de la Liberté*)

There is no plot in this brilliant, fascinating, funny, and very disorienting film. It's the ultimate dream movie. After each incident or scene the camera follows a seemingly unimportant character to another one. It deals with death, religion, history, pornography, police, and politics. A sniper signs autographs, monks encourage people to whip each other, and people at a dinner party eat in the bathroom and sit on toilet seats around the table. With Jean-Claude Brialy, Monica Vitti, and Michael Lonsdale. 20th Century–Fox released it, subtitled. Luis Buñuel made only one more film, *That Obscure Object of Desire*.

THE PHANTOM OF PARIS

(1931) **D:** John S. Robertson
S: Bess Meredyth, John Meehan

A magician (John Gilbert) is accused of killing the father (C. Aubrey Smith) of his girlfriend (Leila Hyams, from *Island of Lost Souls*). The complex plot involves plastic surgery. With Ian Keith, Lewis Stone, Jean Hersholt, and Alfred Hickman. This MGM release was based on a novel by Gaston Leroux, author of *The Phantom of the Opera*.

PHANTOM OF THE AIR

(Stokey, 1933) **D:** Ray Taylor **S:** Ella O'Niell, Basil Dickey, George H. Plympton

Tom Tyler stars as ace flyer Bob Raymond, who has a remote-controlled "phantom" plane. In this 12-chapter Universal serial characters are after an antigravity device called a "Contragrav." The cast also includes Leroy Mason as Mort Crome, Walter Brennan as Skid, Gloria Shea, and William Desmond.

PHANTOM OF THE MALL: ERIC'S REVENGE

(Fries, 1988) **D:** Richard Friedman **S:** Scott J. Schneid, Tony Michelman, Robert King **P:** Tom Fries

Eric (Derek Rydall), a disfigured young phantom, hides in airshafts and catacombs beneath a shopping mall. Characters die by snake bite, flamethrower, crossbow, and escalator. Kari Whitman (Kennell) (from *Playboy*) is his former girlfriend, a waitress. Morgan Fairchild is the evil mayor (she's impaled). With Ken Foree (from another mall movie, *Dawn of the Dead*), Pauly Shore, and Brinke Stevens. Incredibly, a "making of" documentary was made about this.

THE PHANTOM OF THE OPERA

(Video Yesteryear, Sinister, 1925)
D: Rupert Julian, Edward Sedgwick
D/A: Lon Chaney **S:** Elliot J. Clawson
P: Carl Laemmle

One of the most famous horror movies of all time was a troubled production. The original director, Rupert Julian, was replaced by Edward Sedgwick (who specialized in westerns and comedies), and Lon Chaney himself helped to direct some scenes. In 1929 Universal re-released it with more new sequences and added sound. This is the version that used to be shown on TV. Everybody knows the story, based on Gaston Leroux's novel. The phantom's makeup is scarier than any later movie monster's, and the great sets were created by Maurice Tourneur. The story is set in Paris and has many wonderful and ma-cabre moments. Some parts are just like an old serial. With Mary Philbin, Norman Kerry, Gibson Gowland, and Arthur Edmond Carewe. Another new version added dialogue (but not for the phantom). Video versions are various lengths. A restored version was released in 1991, with the original musical score and the hand-tinted color ballroom (*bal masque*) sequence. The Image laserdisc includes the 114-minute 1925 version and the tinted 77-minute 1929 version, complete with a 2-color Technicolor sequence and a new score by Gaylord Carter. The Lunavision laserdisc includes a new score by Korla Pandit. The next adaptations (both in color) were made in Hollywood in 1943 with Claude Rains (MCA Video), and in England by Hammer in 1962, with Herbert Lom (RCA Video).

THE PHANTOM OF THE OPERA

(1983) **D:** Robert Markowitz **S:** Sherman Yellin **P:** Robert Halmi Sr.

Maximilian Schell stars as a phantom named Sándor in a version of the famous story set in Hungary and filmed in Budapest. Stan Winston created the phantom's makeup. With Jane Seymour, Michael York, Diana Quick, and Jeremy Kemp. It debuted on CBS-TV.

THE PHANTOM OF THE OPERA: THE MOTION PICTURE

(RCA/Columbia, 1989) **D:** Dwight H. Little
S: Duke Sandefur **P:** Harry Alan Towers

This version, the goriest so far, was made to cash in on the popular and long-running Broadway musical. Jill Schoelen (*The Stepfather*) is hit on the head in NYC and transported back to 19th-century London for the familiar story. Robert Englund is better than you might expect as the phantom. He cuts the faces off his victims and stitches them onto himself. Characters are beheaded and impaled. Menahem Golan was the executive producer. It was shot in Budapest (like the 1983 version). The cast also includes Stephanie Lawrence and Alex Hyde-White. *Danse Macabre* was sort of a sequel.

Lon Chaney stars in the original version of *The Phantom of the Opera.*

THE PHANTOM OF THE OPERA

(1990) **D:** Tony Richardson **S:** Arthur Kopit **P:** Ross Miloy, Edgar J. Scherick

The second TV version (an NBC 2-part miniseries) stars Charles Dance as a romantic phantom. It was made in Europe and features a lot of opera. Arthur Kopit adapted his 1983 play. Burt Lancaster co-stars as the phantom's father, with Teri Polo, Ian Richardson, Andrea Ferreol, and Jean-Pierre Cassel. Another 1990 version is a filmed play starring David Staller.

THE PHANTOM OF THE RED HOUSE

(Sinister, 1954) **D:** Miguel M. Delgado
S: María Cristina Lesser   Mexico
(*El Fantasmo de la Casa Roja*)

A masked killer knocks off some heirs who are fighting each other and looking for gold in an old mansion. Alma Rosa Aguirre inherits the house and a club called El Infierno (Hell). This horror film includes musical numbers and comedy relief. AIP released it to TV.

PHANTOM OF THE RITZ

(Prism, 1988) **D:** Allan Plone **S:** Tom Dempsey **P:** Carol Marcus Plone

Peter Bergman (from Firesign Theater) buys an old, boarded-up movie theater and puts on a 50s rock show. "Accidents" kill people. Deborah Van Valkenburgh costars. Joshua Sussman is the fat phantom. The Coasters (or what was left of them) perform at the show, and there's an Elvis impersonator. This horror comedy was made in Florida. Allan Plone also made *Night Screams* (1986).

THE PHANTOM SPEAKS

(1944) **D:** John English **S:** John K. Butler **P:** Armand Schaefer

Stanley Ridges (in *Black Friday*) is a scientist who wants to communicate with the dead. A recently electrocuted gangster (Tom Powers) takes over his body and seeks revenge. Richard Arlen is the reporter hero, and Lynn Roberts is the scientist's daughter. With Jonathan Hale. This 69-minute movie by the director of Republic's *Dick Tracy* serial was released on a double bill with *The Vampire's Ghost.*

THE PHANTOM TOLLBOOTH

(MGM, 1970) **D:** David Monahan, Abe Levitow **D/S/P:** Chuck Jones **S:** Sam Rosen

A bored kid named Milo (Butch Patrick, from *The Munsters*) receives a magic toolbooth and a car, and he heads for the "kingdom of Wisdom," where he and everything else become animated cartoons. This G-rated fantasy stresses learning and imagination. Mel Blanc, Daws Butler, Hans Conried, Cliff Norton, and Les Tremayne provide the voices.

THE PHARAOH'S WOMAN

(1960) **D:** Giorgio Rivalta, Wenceslav Tourjansky **S:** Ugo Liberatore, Remigio Del Grosso **P:** Giorgio Venturini   Italy (*La Donna del Faraone*)

Sabaku (John Drew Barrymore) and Ramisis (Armando Francioli) are rival princes and cousins in ancient Egypt. They both want Alis (Linda Cristal), and Sabaku starts a civil war when Ramisis is made pharaoh.

THE PHENIX CITY STORY

(1955) **D:** Phil Karlson **S:** Crane Wilbur, Daniel Mainwaring **P:** Samuel Bischoff, David Diamond

Richard Kiley stars as a Korean War vet who returns to his corrupt hometown to practice law. This hard-hitting documentary-style film is based on real events that happened in an Alabama town. Kathryn Grant costars, with John McIntire and Edward Andrews, plus Meg Myles (*Satan in High Heels*) as a saloon singer. Karlson used the same idea nearly 20 years later for the hit *Walking Tall*. The 13-minute prologue is sometimes missing.

THE PHILADELPHIA EXPERIMENT

(Starmaker, 1985) **D:** Stewart Raffill **S:** William Gray, Michael Janover **P:** Douglas Curtis, Joel B. Michaels **M:** Ken Wannberd

An American battleship disappears in 1943, and a sailor goes through a time warp to 1984. The whole world is threatened by a "time tornado." Michael Paré and Nancy Allen (a couple at the time) star, with Bobby DiCicco. A clip from *Humanoids from the Deep* is seen on a TV. Executive producer John Carpenter wrote the story for this New World release and was once set to direct it. So were Joe Dante, Jonathan Kaplan, and Harley Cokliss. The plot is the reverse of *The Final Countdown* (1980). The score is on Rhino.

THE PHILADELPHIA EXPERIMENT II

(Trimark, 1993) **D:** Stephen Cornwell **S:** Kevin Rock, Nick Payne **P:** Mark Levinson, Douglas Curtis

If you can follow a story that goes from 1984 (the setting of the original movie) to 1993, then to a fascist USA in the alternate 1993 (if the Nazis had won WWII thanks to a Stealth bomber that went back in time) and back to Germany in 1943, then this PG-13 sequel is OK science fiction and has some merit. Brad Johnson stars as the time-traveling character (played before by Michael Paré). Gerrit Graham is good as both a Nazi scientist (and his grim son) and Marjean Holden is a futuristic freedom fighter. There are b/w 50s government film clips, hallucination scenes, and dull slow-motion battle scenes.

PHOENIX THE WARRIOR

(Sony, 1987) **D/S:** Robert Hayes **S:** Dan Rotblatt **P:** Peter Yuval

Kathleen Kinmont is the heroine who has to battle sexy post-nuke Amazon women with guns. Only one male (James Emery) is left, and they try to restart the population with a sperm bank. With Persis Khambatta as Cobalt, Peggy Sands, Roxanne Kernohan, and Sheila Howard.

PHOTOS OF JOY

(VSOM, 1987) **D:** Lamberto Bava **S:** Gianfranco Clerici **M:** Simon Boswell   Italy (*Le Foto di Gioia*)

Serena Grandi (a very large-breasted woman) stars as Gioia, a model for *Pussycat* magazine. She inherits the men's magazine and becomes the publisher and editor, but models are being killed in various ways (death by bees, pitchfork, etc.). With Daria Nicolodi, George Eastman, and Capucine.

PICASSO TRIGGER

(Warner, 1988) **D/S:** Andy Sidaris **P:** Arlene Sidaris

Like most Sidaris movies, this is a slickly made, senseless spy adventure with lots of nice scenery in various countries and Hawaii, women with big breasts, and guys with big muscles. It's perfect for late-night cable TV. The centerfold cast includes Hope Marie Carlton and Dona Speir as federal agents, Cynthia Brimhall, Patty Duffek, Liv Lindeland, and Roberta Vasquez. Steve Bond is topbilled, and John Aprea (the title character) and Bruce Penhall are bad guys.

THE PICKLE

(Columbia, 1993) **D/S/P/A:** Paul Mazursky

Critics hated this box-office flop because it's pretentious, egotistical, and embarrassing (all true), but some parts are funny, and I liked it anyway. Danny Aiello stars as Harry Stone, a depressed famous director of serious films who's in NYC for the preview of his sellout teen science-fiction movie. The movie within the movie is about a flying pickle/spaceship from the planet Cleveland, where Little Richard is president. We see b/w flashbacks to the director's Coney Island childhood. With Clotilde Courau (his teen girlfriend), Dyan Cannon (his exwife), Shelley Winters (his mother), Barry Miller (a *Psychotronic* reader, as a studio exec), Jerry Stiller (his agent), and Chris Penn (his son). Ally Sheedy, Griffin Dunne, Isabella Rossellini, and Dudley Moore are in the sci-fi movie. Also with Donald Trump, Stephen Tobolowsky, and Spaulding Gray. Paul Mazursky also made the somewhat similar *Alex in Wonderland* (1970).

THE PICK-UP

(1968) **D/S:** R. L. Frost **S/P/A:** Wesdon Bishop

A pair of mob couriers pick up two women who seduce and rob them. This b/w adult drama (with nudity) received an X rating. The actors include John Alderman, David F. Friedman, and R. W. Cresse.

PICKUP ON SOUTH STREET

(Fox, 1953) **D/S:** Samuel Fuller **P:** Jules Schermer

Richard Widmark stars as Skip, a small-time pickpocket who lives in a riverfront shack. He accidentally steals microfilm with atomic secrets from a Soviet courier on a NYC subway. The Commies and the feds are after him. This *film noir* classic features Jean Peters as a former hooker, Richard Kiley, Milburn Stone, and Thelma Ritter as Moe, an informer. It's from Twentieth Century–Fox.

PICNIC AT HANGING ROCK

(Vestron, 1975) **D:** Peter Weir **S:** Cliff Green **P:** Hal McElroy, Jim McElroy   Australia

A teacher (Rachel Roberts) and three schoolgirls mysteriously disappear during a picnic in turn-of-the-

EXPOSED IN LIFE, LOOK and SAT. EVE. POST!
NOW The Year's Greatest SCREEN SENSATION!
THE PHENIX CITY STORY
Released thru ALLIED ARTISTS
THE ALABAMA PULITZER PRIZE EXPOSE
won by the Columbus Ledger
STARRING
JOHN McINTIRE
RICHARD KILEY
KATHRYN GRANT
EDWARD ANDREWS
FILMED IN ALABAMA'S SIN CITY!
Produced by SAMUEL BISCHOFF and DAVID DIAMOND · Directed by PHIL KARLSON · Screenplay by CRANE WILBUR and DANIEL MAINWARIN

century Victoria. The cast also includes Helen Morse and Dominic Guard. It's based on the novel by Joan Lindsey. This soft-focus, misty film deals with sexual repression and fantasy. Nothing is explained. It's rated PG.

PIECES

(Edde, 1981) **D:** Juan Piquer Simón **S/P:** Dick Randall **S:** John Shadow, Jack Taylor **P:** Steve Minasian   Italy/Spain   (*Mil Gridos Tiene la Noche*)

A kid making a puzzle of a naked woman kills his mom. Years later on a Boston college campus a professor (Edmund Purdom) kills women and collects body parts to reassemble his human puzzle. This gory movie is a laugh riot, filled with continuity errors and ridiculous dialogue as cops find arms and legs. Also with Christopher George as a cop, Lynda Day George, Paul Smith, Gerard Tichy, and Jack Taylor.

THE PIED PIPER OF HAMELIN

(Media, 1957) **D:** Bretaigne Windust **S:** Irving Taylor **S/P:** Hal Stanley

This "Colorscope" musical version of the famous legend was made for TV, then was released to theaters in 1961 by K. Gordon Murray. Van Johnson stars as the piper who leads the rats, then the children from the town of Hamelin. All the characters speak in rhyme. With Claude Rains as the mayor, Lori Nelson, Jim Backus, Kay Starr, and Doodles Weaver. The "Peer Gynt Suite" is used on the soundtrack which was released by RCA. A darker version was made by Jacques Demy in 1972, and there's a Faerie Tale Theatre version (Fox) from the early 80s.

THE PIG KEEPER'S DAUGHTER

(SW, 1970) **D/S:** Bethel Buckalew **P:** Harry Novak

This traveling-salesman/hillbilly movie is filled with outdoor sex scenes featuring some pretty (and pretty young-looking) women. One, a virgin, masturbates on a rooftop while watching a couple go at it in many positions in a pigpen. Other scenes are in a hayloft and in a bathtub in the yard. There are brief hard-core segments (which probably were the talk of the drive-ins) and (offscreen) comic-relief gay sex. Terry Gibson and Patty Smith star.

PIGS: *See* DADDY'S DEADLY DARLINGS

PIN: A PLASTIC NIGHTMARE

(Starmaker, 1988) **D/S:** Sandor Stern **P:** René Malo   Canada

This creepy psycho movie, based on a novel by Andrew Neiderman, is one of the best in years. Dr. Linden (Terry O'Quinn, from *The Stepfather*) is a brilliant small-town doctor and ventriloquist who is very strict with his two kids. He convinces them that Pin, an anatomically correct medical display, is real, and he uses it to teach them lessons about life and sex. David Hewlett (*Scanners II*) grows up to be a paranoid schizophrenic who still believes in Pin and thinks that his sister (Cyndy Preston) should too. Some of it sounds unlikely, but the acting is good enough to convince, and the movie is

filled with nice, surprising touches and has a nasty edge to it. Bronwen Mantel is their neatness-freak mom.

PIN DOWN GIRL

(Sinister, 1950) **D:** Robert C. Dertano **P:** George Weiss   (*Blonde Pickup, Wrestling Racket Girls*)

Timothy Farrell stars as Scali: drug dealer, pimp, bookie, and manager of wrestling women. The road show movie features real wrestlers, real fight footage (nine fights), and lots of training. Rival gangsters cause trouble and there's a court hearing. With the top-billed Peaches Page, Clara Mortensen, and Rita Martinez from Mexico. The cinematography is by William C. Thompson, who also filmed Ed Wood movies. Farrell returned as Scali in *Dance Hall Racket* (1954).

THE PINK ANGELS

(Prism, 1971) **D/S:** Lawrence Brown

Bikers called the Cupcakes wear typical biker-movie things (Nazi helmets, Confederate flags), but they drink champagne by candlelight at a picnic, ignore naked women, and go in drag to a transvestite ball. When "normal" bikers show up they put rouge and hair ribbons on them when they're asleep. This comedy has a surprise shock ending, as all the bikers are hung from trees!? With John Alderman, Tom Basham, Michael Pataki, Bruce Kemp, and Dan Haggerty. This Crown International release used to play on drive-in triple bills. The director also made *Psychopath* (1973), starring Basham.

THE PINK CHIQUITAS

(Starmaker, 1986) **D/S:** Anthony Currie **S/P:** Nicholas Stiliadas   Canada

A pink meteor turns on small-town women. Frank Stallone (in his first starring role) is a private eye who tries to stop them. The voice of the meteor is Eartha Kitt's. Also with Elizabeth Edwards and Claudia Udy. *Zombie Beach Party III* is playing at a drive-in. Stallone (a Scientologist) wrote the music for this dumb comedy. He recorded four LPs (collect 'em all!).

PINK FLAMINGOS

(Lightning, 1972) **D/S/P:** John Waters

David Hewlett and Cyndy Preston in *Pin: A Plastic Nightmare.*

Bob Geldof stars in *Pink Floyd: The Wall.*

John Waters's first color feature cost "$12 thousand," ran for 10 years as a midnight cult hit, and made "over $12 million in worldwide rentals." It was billed as "an exercise in poor taste," and, in the tradition of old road-show hits, people were dared to see it. Babs Johnson (Divine) strives to be the filthiest person in the world. She lives in a trailer in Baltimore with Eddie the egg lady (the incredible Edith Massey, in a crib). The Marbles (Mink Stole and David Lochary) are Babs' rivals. With Mary Vivian Pearce, Danny Miles, and Cookie Mueller. The best possible screen use is made of a Link Wray instrumental. The cast all returned in *Female Trouble* (1974). Unfortunately, nearly every cast member listed here was dead by 1990. Mink Stole has continued to appear in Waters' films. *Trash Trio* (1988) is a book of Waters' original scripts, including this and the still unfilmed sequel *Flamingos Forever.*

PINK FLOYD: THE WALL

(MGM/UA, 1982) **D:** Alan Parker **S:** Roger Waters **P:** Alan Marshall   UK

Bob Geldof stars as Pink, who grows up during WWII and becomes a confused, miserable, rich rock star. Based on Pink Floyd's double 1979 album, this is a depressing but incredible-looking movie with many fantasy and nightmare images (with monsters and blood). With Christine Hargreaves, Bob Hoskins as the manager, and Jenny Wright and Nell Campbell as groupies. "Another Brick in the Wall" had been a number 1 hit, and the album had been staged by the group. The animated sequences are by Gerald Scarfe. *The Wall: Live in Berlin* (Polygram, 1990) is Pink Floyd performing the album at the Potsdamerplatz in Berlin just after the Berlin Wall was opened in 1990.

PINK MOTEL

(Thorn EMI, 1982) **D:** Mike MacFarland **S/P:** James Kouf **P:** Ed Elbert

Phyllis Diller and Slim Pickens (in his last role) run a sleazy motel. Various couples show up for sex dramas. This strange, episodic, R-rated comedy/drama is more depressing than sexy or funny. It's similar to an earlier adults-only movie, *Motel Confidential.*

PIRANHA II: THE SPAWNING

(Nelson, 1981) **D:** James Cameron **S:** H. A. Hilton
P: Chako Van Leuwen US/Italy (*The Spawning*)

In this "sequel" to Joe Dante's 1978 movie, flying piranhas attack a Caribbean resort. With Lance Henriksen as a cop, Leslie Graves (a former *Sesame Street* regular), Tricia O'Neil, and Steve Marachuk. One fish bursts from a chest. It was shot in Jamaica. Nobody could have predicted from this that James Cameron (who was fired before the film's completion) would make *Terminator* next and later become one of the highest-paid directors in the world. The executive producer was Ovidio G. Assonitis.

THE PIRATE AND THE SLAVE GIRL

(1960) **D:** Piero Pierotti **S:** Luciano Martino, Bruno Rasia France/Italy (*La Scimitarra del Sareceno*)

Lex Barker stars as Dragut, a 15th-century pirate who kidnaps women for an evil slave trader, Miriam (the gorgeous Chelo Alonso). A love triangle develops with Dragut, Miriam, and a sea captain.

THE PIRATE OF THE BLACK HAWK

(1959) **D/S:** Sergio Grieco **S:** Enzo Alfonsi **P:** Giorgio Pescino France/Italy (*Il Pirata dello Sparviere Nero*)

Minjanou Bardot (Brigitte's sister) stars as a 16th-century duke's daughter captured by Manfred, a usurper of the throne. This was a Filmgroup/AIP color release.

PIRATES

(Avid, 1986) **D/S:** Roman Polanski **S:** Gérard Brach **P:** Tarak Ben Ammar US/Tunisia

Walter Matthau is pretty good as Captain Red in this large-scale, widescreen pirate comedy. Cris Campion is the young protegé of the crusty, disgusting, back-stabbing pirate. With 15-year-old Charlotte Lewis, Ferdy Mayne, Roy Kinnear, Daniel Emilfork, Anthony Peck, Ian Dury, and Anthony Dawson. The movie cost $31 million and made $.07 million in North America. The full-scale replica of a Spanish galleon broke records for prop costs and was made in Malta by 2,000 shipbuilders. It's PG-13 and runs 124 minutes.

THE PIT

(Prism, 1980) **D:** Lew Lehman **S:** Ian A. Stuart **P:** Bennett Fode (*Teddy*)

Jamie (Sammy Snyder), a difficult, lonely, voyeuristic 12-year-old boy, talks to his teddy bear and visits furry cannibal "trolls" with shiny eyes that live in a hole in the ground. He feeds them raw meat until his bear tells him to feed them humans, including a blind old lady in a wheelchair. Soon everyone who was ever mean to him has disappeared. This New World release has a strange topless scene and some gore. It was shot in Beaver Dam, Wisconsin.

THE PIT AND THE PENDULUM

(Paramount, 1990) **D:** Stuart Gordon **S:** Dennis Paoli **P:** Albert Band **M:** Richard Band

Gordon shows us the horrors of the 15th-century Spanish Inquisition, in his best film since *From Beyond*. Star Lance Henriksen is perfect as the grand

Phyllis Diller and Slim Pickens in *Pink Motel.*

inquisitor. He kneels on broken glass and has himself flogged, but he still has fevered visions of the young Mariá (Rona De Ricci), whom he has accused of being a witch. An old woman eats gunpowder before they burn her. A little boy is whipped while his mother is strangled. Oliver Reed shows up as a sensible Italian cardinal, Jeffrey Combs is here, and Tom Towles (*Henry*) is pretty ridiculous as a soldier. There's some intentional humor along with all the suffering and torturing. A dried-up corpse gets 20 lashes, and then the bones are ground up. Peter O'Toole was originally supposed to star. The script has nothing to do with the Roger Corman film of the same name but does have the famous pit at the end. It was filmed in Italy. The soundtrack is on Moonstone.

PIT STOP

(Johnny Legend, 1967) **D/S/E:** Jack Hill **P:** Lee Strosnider

Dick Davalos (*East of Eden*) stars as Rick, a cynical loner who becomes a driver in deadly figure-8 races (lots of real crashes are featured). His main rival is Hawk (Sid Haig), who says, "You gotta be dingy. I'm the dingiest there is!" Hawk also does the jerk and the swim and takes an axe to Rick's car (while Beverly Washburn is in it!). Brian Donlevy is fine as the man who sponsors the disposable drivers, and Ellen Burstyn seems like a potential star as the wife of a top driver. Also with George Barris as himself and Titus Moody. A nice bonus in this rare feature is the lead-guitar heavy psychedelic instrumental music by the Daily Flash, a group from Seattle that was based in California. Like *Spider Baby*, this was shelved for several years and was considered too dated (it's b/w) when finally released. Roger Corman was the executive producer. Johnny Legend interviews Jack Hill at the end of this welcome video release.

A PLACE CALLED GLORY

(VSOM, 1966) **D:** Sheldon Reynolds **S:** Edward Di Lorenzo **P:** Bruce Balaban Spain/W. Germany (*Amati*)

In a variation on their Old Shatterhand films, Lex Barker and Pierre Brice are western gunmen who become friends but are forced to stage a shootout in the town of Glory. With Marianne Koch and Jorge Rigaud.

A PLACE CALLED TODAY

(Monterey, 1972) **D:** Don Schain (*City in Fear*)

A black lawyer (J. Herbert Kerr Jr.) decides to run for mayor. A political activist (Lana Wood) helps him win with a scheme to encourage black militants to cause trouble, run an anti-violence campaign, and "scare" white people into voting for him (!?). Cheri Caffaro (not playing Ginger for a change) costars as the current mayor's daughter who is kidnapped. Both actresses are naked a lot. This Avco Embassy release originally received an X but was later rated R.

A PLACE OF ONE'S OWN

(1944) **D/P:** Bernard Knowles **S:** Brock Williams, Osbert Sitwell **P:** Maurice Ostrer UK

The young companion (Margaret Lockwood) of an older couple (James Mason and Helen Haye) is possessed by the ghost of a murdered woman. Also in the cast are Dennis Price and Ernest Thesiger. This Eagle Lion release is based on a novel by Osbert Sitwell. Mason (who was only 36 at the time he played this role) was later in *Lady Possessed* (1951), which has a similar theme. Producer Maurice Ostrer was the father of Mason's first wife, Pamela.

PLANET BURG

(Sinister, 1962) **D/S:** Pavel Klushantsev **S:** Alexander Kazantsev USSR

This is the movie that Roger Corman bought and used footage from for *Voyage to the Prehistoric Planet* (1965), *Queen of Blood* (1966) and *Voyage to the Planet of Prehistoric Women* (1968). Now that Russia is our friend we can see this entire science-fiction movie with English subtitles. It features a robot and lizard men.

PLANET OF INCREDIBLE CREATURES: *See* FANTASTIC PLANET

PLAN TEN FROM OUTER SPACE

(1994) **D/S:** Trent Harris **P:** Walter Hart

This musical sci-fi comedy spoofs Mormons and was filmed in Salt Lake City. It stars Karen Black as an alien queen (who sings). Lawsuits by the current owners of *Plan 9 from Outer Space* threatened to prevent its release.

PLATOON LEADER

(Media, 1988) **D:** Aaron Norris **S/P:** Harry Alan Towers **S:** Rick Marx, Andrew Deutsch S. Africa

Michael Dudikoff stars as a West Point Lieutenant fighting Commies in Vietnam. With Paul Smith, William Smith, and Robert F. Lyons. It's from Cannon. Aaron Norris usually directs his brother Chuck.

PLAY DEAD

(Academy, 1981) **D:** Peter Wittman **S:** Lothrop W. Jordan **P:** Francine C. Rudine

Rich Aunt Hester (Yvonne De Carlo) uses magic and a Rottweiler dog to kill her relatives off. It's all because her late sister married the love of her life. This was made the same year as Earl Owensby's *Dogs of Hell* by a Texas husband-and-wife team who also made *Ellie*. Troma released it in 1985.

THE PLAYER

(Columbia, 1992) **D:** Robert Altman **S/P:** Michael Tolkin **P:** David Brown, Nick Wechsler **M:** Thomas Newman

Tim Robbins kills a screenwriter (Vincent D'Onofrio) and gets away with it, in a Hollywood satire/murder mystery that was created to irritate. Greta Scacchi costars, with Peter Gallagher, Fred Ward, Whoopi Goldberg (as a Columbo-type detective teamed with Lyle Lovett), Dean Stockwell and Richard T. Grant as screenwriters, and screen slime Brion James. In a film within the film Julia Roberts is strapped into an electric chair by Steve James. Like many earlier Robert Altman movies this reportedly has 65 bit parts and walk-ons. Some are played by Karen Black, Gary Busey, Robert Carradine, James Coburn, Cher, Peter Falk, Louise Fletcher, Scott Glenn, Buck Henry, Sally Kirkland, Malcolm McDowell, Martin Mull, Jill St. John, Rod Steiger, and Ray Walston. It's from Fine Line (a division of New Line). The film was originally 123 minutes. The video includes scenes that were cut and an interview with the director. The Voyager laserdisc includes different interviews, more cut scenes, and a guide to the star cameos. The soundtrack is on Varèse Sarabande.

PLAYGIRL

(1954) **D:** Joseph Pevney **S:** Robert Blee **P:** Albert J. Cohen

Colleen Miller arrives in New York from Nebraska and makes the mistake of rooming with a singer (Shelley Winters, in her last blond-bombshell role). Shelley kills her publisher boyfriend (Barry Sullivan), and Miller ends up involved with gangsters. With Gregg Palmer, Richard Long, and Kent Taylor. From Universal. The next year, Winters was in more serious films like *I Am a Camera, The Night of the Hunter,* and *The Big Knife.*

PLAYGIRLS INTERNATIONAL

(1963) **D/P:** Doris Wishman **S:** Cy Eichman

Someone narrates this international "documentary" showing sexy dancers in various countries. After visiting Europe, Japan, Hawaii, and Mexico, Louie Prima's twist show features Sam Butera and the Witnesses in Las Vegas. The end segments are the payoff, though, as nudists in Florida do the Twist, the Hula, and "an Apache war dance."

PLAY IT COOL

(1962) **D:** Michael Winner **S:** Jack Henry **P:** David Deutsch   UK

Singer Billy Fury stars as singer Billy Universe, on tour in Europe with his group, the Satellites. There isn't much plot in this musical comedy, but Billy sings and so do Shane Fenton and the Fentones, Bobby Vee, Helen Shapiro, and others. Also with Dennis Price. Allied Artists released it in America, where Fury was (and still is) unknown.

PLAYMATES

(1973) **D/S/P:** "Pierre La France"/Stephen Gibson

Some good Deep Vision 3-D effects are used in this adult movie, which was released in three versions (with more or less sex). There are also scenes from other films. With Donna Michelle and Rene Bond.

PLAY MISTY FOR ME

(MCA, 1971) **D/A:** Clint Eastwood **S:** Jo Heims, Dean Reisner **P:** Robert Daly **M:** Roberta Flack

You can't accuse Clint Eastwood of not trying to change his image. His first film as a director was made after *Paint Your Wagon* (1969; Clint sings), *Two Mules for Sister Sara* (1970; he's fooled by a woman), and *The Beguiled* (1971; he's trapped and killed by women). He's a Monterey DJ menaced by a jealous, psychotic woman (Jessica Walter) who uses a butcher knife to attack. *Fatal Attraction* copied a few ideas from this one. With Donna Mills, Jack Ging, and Don Siegel as a bartender. The Cannonball Adderley Quintet plays, and the Johnny Otis show does "Hand Jive" too. It was rereleased on a good double bill with Alfred Hitchcock's *Frenzy.*

PLAYROOM

(Republic, 1989) **D:** Manny Coto **S:** Keaton Jones **P:** Luigi Cingolani   (*Schizo*)

Archaeologist Christopher McDonald has nightmares about his family being killed in a Yugoslav monastery when he was a kid. He goes back and encounters the sadistic ghost of a boy prince and a Devil worshipper. A monster at the end makes stupid Freddy Krueger–type wisecracks in perfect English. With Jamie Rose as his girlfriend and Vincent Schiavelli. This laughable horror fantasy was made in Belgrade. Manny Coto, who was just out of the American Film Institute, also made *Dr. Giggles.*

PLEASE DON'T EAT MY MOTHER

(Video Dimensions, 1971) **D/S/P:** "Jack Beckett"/Carl Monson (*Hungry Pets; Sexpot Swingers*)

With all the attention paid to the musical remake of Roger Corman's film *The Little Shop of Horrors* nobody seemed to remember that it had already been remade as a nudie movie. Henry Fudd (Buck Kartalian) buys a talking plant (with a sexy female voice) from a gay florist. Henry lives with his nagging, nosy mother, who drinks Coors and gossips on the phone. The plant (and its pot) grows extremely fast and demands food (insects, frogs, dogs, and finally, of course, people). The major difference is that Henry is a *Playboy*-reading voyeur. He watches a couple having sex in a car, leaves, and returns home four times, and they're still at it! Another couple having sex in a park are forced at gunpoint to become plant food. Adult-movie star Rene Bond has sex with her boyfriend, argues with him, and kills him. Henry, watching at the window, offers to hide the body. Although this is a silly comedy, parts of some of the sex scenes are no-faking hard-core. As late as 1982 (!) this Boxoffice International release was playing at drive-ins. Buck Kartalian was in *The Devil's Angels, Planet of the Apes,* and *Stay Away Joe* (with Elvis) and was the wolf man in the late-70s Saturday-morning kids' show *The Monster Squad* (!).

PLEASE DON'T TOUCH ME!

(Ormond, 1959) **D/S/P:** "Vittorio Di Nardo"/ Ron Ormond **S/A:** Ormond McGill

The most outrageous Ormond-family movie (after *The Exotic Ones,* maybe) is this full-color, made-in-Hollywood exploitation classic. It was the only Ormond movie to play Times Square and was also known as *Teenage Bride.* You won't believe it! The plot is about why newlywed Vicki (gorgeous, red-headed Ruth Blair in plunging necklines) cannot have sex with her husband (Al "Lash" la Rue). Her concerned mom says, "Most men are brutes anyhow," and he has a *Glen or Glenda*–style dream with his mother-in-law holding back his seductive wife. A doctor tries to help with his "Electro-Cyclometer" (it has a pleasure-and-pain meter), and a hypnotist (played by stage hypnotist Ormond McGill) uses his spinning "Hypno-Box." This alone would be entertaining enough, but a long, narrated, "historical," part-mondo prologue features the director as a mesmerist, real open-heart surgery, real flagellant footage, a needle going through skin, a drawing of a giant scrotal tumor, a Borneo fakir, and a bit of nudity. You're also en-

EGYPTIAN WOMEN HAD THE SAME PROBLEM

Ron Ormond's *Please Don't Touch Me!*

couraged to "try and hypnotize yourself" with a "Hypno-Disc." The soundtrack features the same maddening flamenco guitar and piano music used in *Mesa of Lost Women* and Ed Wood's *Jailbait* and the usual Ormond harmonica music.

THE PLEASURE GIRLS

(1965) **D/S:** Gerry O'Hara **P:** Harry Fine   UK

Francesca Annis is a new model in London who falls for a photographer (Ian McShane). Her roommates also have relationships and problems, and one gets pregnant. With Klaus Kinski as Nikko and Suzanna Leigh. It's presented by Tony Tenser.

PLEASURE UNLIMITED

(Private Screenings, 1972) **D/S/P:** "A.C. Stevens"/ Stephen C. Apostoloff **S:** Edward D. Wood Jr. (*Dropout Wife; Sensuous Wife*)

"Women's lib or women's fib?" asked the original ads for this soft-core adult movie. Ed Wood wrote lines for characters to say like "If we put chastity belts on under our panties and we threw away the key, you can damn well be sure that every male in the world would be on their knees begging us to let him out of the toilet." With Angela Canon, Terry Johnson, Foreman Shane, Rene Bond, Ric Lutze, and Rick Cassidy.

PLEDGE NIGHT

(Imperial, 1990) **D/E:** Paul Ziller **S/P:** Joyce Snider   (*A Hazing in Hell*)

Former porno filmmakers filmed this frat-house horror movie at Rutgers University. A student dumped in acid 20 years earlier becomes a monster and kills another student. It was cut for an R rating. It has a dumb ending and various ridiculous ways to die. Joey Belladonna (*Anthrax*) is in it.

PLUCKED

(1967) **D/S:** Giulio Questi **S:** Franco Arcalli **P:** Franco Marras   France/Italy (*La Morte ha Fatto l'Uovo; Death Laid an Egg*)

In one of the stranger European movies to reach these shores a couple (Gina Lollobrigida and Jean-Louis Trintignant) run a modern, high-tech chicken-breeding ranch. The husband (who is a mass murderer) and sexy Ewa Aulin (*Candy*) plot to kill his wife. A group called "the Association" conducts genetic experiments on the chickens, resulting in mutant all-white-meat chickens without heads.

THE PLUMBER

(Media, 1978) **D/S:** Peter Weir **P:** Matt Carroll Australia (*The Mad Plumber*)

A crazed plumber (Ivar Kants) claims that he has to make repairs in the apartment of an academic couple (Judy Morris and Robert Coleby). He tears up the bathroom and engages in a battle of wits with the wife. Peter Weir made this black comedy for TV after *The Last Wave*.

PLUTONIUM BABY

(TWE, 1986) **D/P:** Ray Hirschman **S:** Wayne Behar

A kid whose mother died from radiation exposure after working in a nuke plant lives in the woods with his grandfather. Their home looks like an outhouse. Mom, who was dumped in a drum of nuclear waste and became a monster, attacks and kills some teen campers (offscreen) and government-agent villains. A rat puppet also attacks, and in the best scene the son gulps down a whole fish. After a while you'll think the movie is over, but no such luck. The story picks up in NYC "10 years later" with a long (under-covers) sex scene followed by a long aerobics-workout scene, and just when you think you can't stand any more a government agent turned monster fights the now grown-up fish-eating boy in the ridiculous climax.

THE PLUTONIUM INCIDENT

(1980) **D:** Richard Michaels **S:** Dalene Young **P:** David Susskind

CBS-TV gave us this cut-rate *Silkwood* in our living rooms three years before that film. Janet Margolin stars as the nuclear-plant worker whose life is in danger after she dares to point out unsafe conditions. Also with Bo Hopkins, Joseph Campanella, Powers Boothe, Bibi Besch, and Nicholas Pryor.

POINT BLANK

(MGM, 1967) **D:** John Boorman **S:** Alexander Jacobs, David Newhouse **P:** Judd Bernard, Robert Chartoff

Lee Marvin stars as Walker, a man driven by revenge. This color, Panavision *film noir* classic is almost a psychedelic crime movie. Angie Dickinson and John Vernon (he's thrown out of a window) are the main targets. Some of the best scenes were filmed in the federal penitentiary at Alcatraz. The cast also includes Keenan Wynn, Carroll O'Connor, Lloyd Bochner, James B. Sikking, and Sid Haig. It's based on the novel *The Hunter*, by Richard Stark (Donald E. Westlake). It was John Boorman's second film (after *Having a Wild Weekend*, starring the Dave Clark Five). The letterboxed laserdisc includes interviews, the trailer, and "The Rock," a short about the making of the film.

POINT BREAK

(Fox, 1991) **D:** Kathryn Bigelow **S:** W. Peter Iliff **P:** Peter Abrams, Robert L. Levy

Keanu Reeves is a young FBI agent named Johnny Utah who goes undercover in Southern California to infiltrate a gang of bank robbers who wear masks of presidents' faces. Patrick Swayze is Bodhi, the cosmic leader of the gang, Gary Busey is Reeves's seasoned FBI partner, and Lori Petty is his girlfriend, who is kidnapped. Also with James LeGros, John McGinley, John Philbin, Michael Kopelow, Julie Michaels, and Debra Lamb. This violent (if silly) movie has some excellent surfing and free-fall-skydiving scenes. Kath-

ryn Bigelow's then-husband, James Cameron, was the executive producer of this Twentieth Century–Fox release.

POINT OF IMPACT

(Vidmark, 1993) **D:** Bob Misiorowski **S:** David Zito, Les Weldon, George Fernandez   S. Africa (*Spanish Rose*)

Michael Paré is a former customs agent in Miami who's hired by a sadistic, rich Cuban gun smuggler (Michael Ironsides) to protect Barbara Carrera. This is all (surprise!) a setup, and there are plenty of explosions, crashes, and chases, but if you want to check out how great Carrera still looks in her 40s, this is the place. She swims topless, and she and Paré fuck all over a large home. It was filmed in Natal. R and unrated versions are available.

POINT OF NO RETURN

(Warner, 1993) **D:** John Badham **S:** Robert Getchell, Alexandra Seros **P:** Art Linson

Bridget Fonda stars in an Americanized remake of *La Femme Nikita*. Gabriel Byrne is the guy who trains her, and Anne Bancroft is the woman who teaches her manners. After her black hair is dyed strawberry blond and she's gotten all that conditioning, she kills her first victims in a Washington, DC, restaurant. In Venice, California, she falls for a photographer (Dermot Mulroney). She also assassinates a woman during the Mardi Gras in New Orleans. A "cleaner" (Harvey Keitel) shows up after a killing, a part he later parodied in *Pulp Fiction*. Also with Miguel Ferrer, Olivia D'Abo, Richard Romanus, Calvin Levels, and Geoffrey Lewis. The Beatles' "Something" is on the soundtrack, along with songs by Nina Simone, L7, and Buckwheat Zydeco.

Lee Marvin, Guy Way, and Carroll O'Connor in *Point Blank*.

Bridget Fonda stars in *Point of No Return*.

POINT ZERO: *See* THE SKI BUM

POISON

(Fox Lorber, 1991) **D/S:** Todd Haynes
P: Christian Vachon

The maker of the Barbie Doll–cast short *Superstar: The Karen Carpenter Story* (1989) made this trilogy of stories inspired by the writings of Jean Genet. A suburban kid murders his father in the documentary-style "Hero." A 50s scientist isolates the sex drive but becomes a murdering mutant in the b/w "Horror." A 40s French prison is the setting of "Homo," the part that caused controversy because of some (post-production) funding by the National Endowment for the Arts. The video is available in NC-17, unrated, and R (no male nudity) versions.

POISON IVY

(New Line, 1992) **D/S:** Katt Shea Ruben
S/P: Andy Ruben

A seductive blond teen with a nose ring and a tattoo on her thigh (Drew Barrymore) moves in with a wealthy Hollywood family, disrupts their already fucked-up lives, and even becomes a killer. Sara Gilbert is the withdrawn daughter, who narrates (and hallucinates). Tom Skerritt is the horny, recovering-alky dad. Cheryl Ladd is the suicidal mom. The publicity stressed the hints of lesbianism, and Barrymore posed naked in *Interview* to help promote the film. Only Skerritt is seen naked in the movie, though (Barrymore used a body double). The director's first feature that wasn't for producer Roger Corman is pretty slow going.

POLICE ACADEMY: MISSION TO MOSCOW

(Warner, 1994) **D:** Alan Metter
S: Randolph Davis, Michele S. Chodos **P:** Paul Maslansky

Number 7 (!) in a stupid series went directly to video. This time the comic cops fight the Moscow Mafia, and Christopher Lee is a top Moscow cop. With series regulars George Gaynes, Michael Winslow (he's in all seven), Leslie Easterbrook, and David Graf. Ron Perlman is the main Russian gangster, who's plotting world domination through computers.

POLICE CONNECTION = THE MAD BOMBER

POLICE FORCE

(Rainbow, 1985) **D/A:** Jackie Chan **S:** Edward Tang **P:** Leonard Ho   Hong Kong (*Police Story*; *Jackie Chan's Police Force*)

Jackie Chan stars as a cop assigned to protect a reluctant key witness (Li Hsing Chia) for a gangland trial. This action comedy features amazing stunts and slapstick and the complete destruction of a large squatters' camp. The most incredible scene of action and inventive destruction, though, takes place in a shopping mall. Maggie Cheung is the detective's girlfriend. This was screened at the 1987 NYC Film Festival and became one of the first Chan films to receive much mainstream attention in America. *Police Story II* is the first sequel.

POLICE SQUAD! HELP WANTED!

(Paramount, 1982) **D/S:** too numerous to list
P: Jim Abrahams, David Zucker, Jerry Zucker

The creators of *Airplane!* did this ABC-TV series instead of *Airplane II*. Leslie Nielsen is the bumbling Detective Frank Drebin. Directors like Joe Dante did episodes, and even the opening and end credits are hilarious. This anarchistic comedy series didn't catch on, but they later turned the concept into the hit *Naked Gun* and two sequels. This and *More! Police Squad!* have 3 episodes each on 75-minute videos.

POLICE STORY II

(1988) **D/S/A:** Jackie Chan **P:** Raymond Chow

This was a much bigger hit in Asia than the original. It has less humor (and plot) and even more amazing stunts. Jackie Chan is put on an extortion case involving dynamite smugglers. It starts with scenes from *Police Force* and ends with outtakes. Maggie Cheung returns from the original. She's also in *Police Story III* (1992), also called *Super Cop*. *Police Story IV* (1993) is also called *Crime Story*.

POLICEWOMAN

(VCI, 1974) **D/S:** Lee Frost **P:** Wes Bishop   (*The Insiders*)

Jackie Chan in his *Police Story III*.

Heather O'Rourke and Julian Beck in *Poltergeist II.*

Sondra Currie (*Class of '74*) is a lady cop called Lucy Bond who goes undercover in an all-female gang. This Crown International drive-in release costars Jeanne Bell and Laurie Rose as prison escapees and William Smith in a small role as a karate instructor. It features lots of all-female fighting.

A POLISH VAMPIRE IN BURBANK
(Edde, 1983) D/S/P/A: Mark Pirro

Mark Pirro is a virgin vampire, Lori Sutton is his vampire sister, and Eddie Deezen is his dead brother in flashbacks. The original star, Deezen, quit, so Pirro dubbed his voice. A movie called *Enema Vampires* is being produced in this comedy. With Myra Grant and Conrad Brooks as a bartender. It was the first Super 8 feature aired on national cable TV (it was cut) and is said to have cost less than three thousand dollars. Pirro also made *Deathrow Gameshow* and *Curse of the Queerwolf.*

POLTERGEIST II: THE OTHER SIDE
(MGM/UA, 1986) D: Brian Gibson S/P: Mark Victor, Michael Grais M: Jerry Goldsmith

"They're back," in this bad PG-13 sequel to the 1982 hit. It takes place just months later. JoBeth Williams, Craig T. Nelson (who throws up a giant tequila worm), Heather O'Rourke as Carol Ann, and Zelda Rubinstein all return. The older sister is missing because actress Dominique Dunne was murdered after the first movie. The floating-family fantasy scenes are too dumb for words. With Will Sampson (who died in 1987) and Julian Beck (from the Living Theater) as Kane, making the frequent and unsettling statement "You're going to die!" He knew that he was going to die in real life (this was released after his death in 1985). Geral-

dine Fitzgerald is the grandma, who dies. Steve Johnson worked on the FX. The score is on Intrada.

POLTERGEIST III
(MGM/UA, 1988) D/S: Gary Sherman S: Brian Taggert P: Barry Bernardi M: Joe Renzetti

This senseless second sequel, even worse than the first, moves the action to a haunted Chicago high-rise. Tom Skerritt and Nancy Allen are the aunt and uncle whom the troubled Carol Ann (Heather O'Rourke) comes to live with. O'Rourke died (at 12) before the movie's release, and the ads featuring her seemed especially tasteless. Nathan Davis impersonates the late Julian Beck, and Zelda Rubinstein is back again. With Lara Flynn Boyle and Kip Wentz. Dick Smith did the makeup FX. The score is on Varèse Sarabande. It's PG-13.

POOR PRETTY EDDIE: *See* HEARTBREAK MOTEL

POOR WHITE TRASH
(Monterey, 1957) D: Harold Daniels S: Edward L. Femler P: M. A. Ripps   (*Bayou*)

This was shot on location at about the same time as Roger Corman's *Swamp Woman.* Both feature Corman regulars Jonathan Haze and Ed Nelson. It was directed by Harold Daniels, who had co-directed the famous road show hit *The Prince of Peace.* In 1961 producer M. A. Ripps, based in Mobile, Alabama, bought back his film from United Artists, added some new sex and shock se-

quences and a great new pre-credits banjo theme-song/intro, and gave it the new title *Poor White Trash.* Often unconvincing doubles were used for the stars. When northerner Peter Graves and sexy Lita Milan finally start to make love in a cabin the scene continues with bare legs, caresses, closeups of eyes, and the storm outside. But what everybody remembered was the long scene, shocking at the time, when the Cajun bully Ulysses (Timothy Carey) attacks Milan. In the new footage Carey's shirtless double chases Milan's double though the woods, ripping away her clothes as they run. Eventually she's running naked, then crawling in the mud screaming. More new footage shows her praying in church. Even Carey's death scene was spiced up with a bloody axe-in-the-back insert. Carey's standout bit, though, is doing an incredible, uninhibited dance to accordion music. He hops into the air, does rubber-leg moves, caresses himself, and scratches like he has fleas while a storm brews. The dance is so good that it's edited in several times. Because of the new scenes and a brilliant exploitation advertising campaign (radio and newspaper teasers) this adults-only movie was still playing in theaters as late as 1971 (!) and grossed an estimated $10 million (!). Its success helped to spawn other country shockers, like *Common-Law Wife* (from Ripps), *Girl on a Chain Gang, Shotgun Wedding,* and several each from Russ Meyer and Herschell Gordon Lewis.

POOR WHITE TRASH, PART 2
(Magnum, 1974) D/P: S. F. Brownrigg S: Mary Davis   (*Scum of the Earth*)

After her new husband is killed with an axe a woman (Nora Moore) flees and ends up trapped with an unbalanced backwoods family. Otis (Gene Ross), a gross drunk, has sex with his grown daughter Sara (Carmilla Carr), abuses his pregnant wife, Emmy (Ann Stafford), and berates his idiot son, Bo (Charlie Dell). This movie has several bloody mur-

Timothy Carey swings at Peter Graves in *Poor White Trash.*

ders and a rape but was filmed like a play and is more concerned with acting than action or shocks. Most of the actors (especially Carr) are excellent. An insane killer Nam vet shows up for the (surprise) ending. The ballad theme is "Death Is a Family Affair." S. F. Brownrigg made this drive-in movie in East Texas after his *Don't Look in the Basement*. Dimension released it. Then M. A. Ripps acquired and retitled it, advertised it as a sequel, and made lots of money.

POPCORN: AN AUDIO-VISUAL THING

(1969) **D:** Peter Clifton **P:** Peter Ryan   US/Australia

There's some good rock footage in this thrown-together documentary, but you have to get through some awful filler footage to see it, and some of the advertised groups are just on the soundtrack. It was a ripoff when it was new, but it's an okay period piece now. Highlights are the Rolling Stones, Jimi Hendrix, Otis Redding, and Traffic. There's also Twiggy, surfing, and other teen-appeal stuff. A lot of this footage later showed up in other compilations too. It was released by Sherpix.

POPCORN

(RCA/Columbia, 1989) **D:** Mark Herrier **D/S:** Alan Ormsby (uncredited) **S:** Bob Clark (uncredited) **P:** Torben Johnke, Gary Goch, Ashok Amritraj

This contrived plot concerns a haunted film featuring a Satanist, a phantom in an old movie theater who can impersonate his victims, and a science-fiction marathon put on by film students. But Alan Ormsby's re-creations of old movies are inspired and convincing. Bruce Glover in the b/w *Attack of the Amazing Electrified Man* (with wired audience seats) is my favorite. Other William Castle–inspired gimmicks are used, and there's a fun giant-bug minimovie too. Jill Schoelen and Tom Villard star, with Dee Wallace Stone, Ray Walston, Tony Roberts, and Karen Witter. It was filmed in Kingston, Jamaica, which explains the reggae band. Mark Herrier (costar of *Porky's* and its sequels) replaced Ormsby after three weeks. Bob Clark (who had worked with Ormsby as far back as *Children Shouldn't Play with Dead Things*) also supervised the production but had his name removed from the credits.

THE POPE MUST DIE

(Fox, 1991) **D/S/A:** Peter Richardson **S:** Pete Richens **P:** Stephen Wooley   UK

A priest (Robbie Coltrane, from *Nuns on the Run*) is mistakenly elected pope. He rids the Vatican of crooked cardinals and banking corruption (also a theme in *The Godfather III*). Herbert Lom is a mobster, Paul Bartel is a monsignor, Alex Rocco is an outrageous cardinal, and Beverly D'Angelo is the mother of Joe Don Dante (Balthazar Getty), a heavy-metal singer. This comedy was filmed in Yugoslavia. Miramax's ads were refused by many papers, so in some areas the title was changed to *The Pope* or *The Pope Must Diet* (!)

POPEYE

(Paramount, 1980) **D:** Robert Altman
S: Jules Feiffer **P:** Robert Evans

Everybody was too familiar with the Max Fleischer cartoons for this PG musical fantasy based on E. C. Segar's characters to catch on, but the casting is inspired and kids seem to love it. Robin Williams is the mumbling sailor, Shelley Duvall is Olive Oyl, Ray Walston is Pappy, Paul L. Smith is Bluto, and Paul Dooley is Wimpy. Music by Van Dyke Parks and singing by Harry Nilsson are on the Boardwalk soundtrack. Paramount and Disney produced it.

PORKY'S

(CBS/Fox, 1982) **D/S/P:** Bob Clark
P: Don Carmody   US/Canada

This famous bad-taste teen comedy, which made $54 million, is supposedly set in Florida in the early 50s. It's a classic of its kind, but they all have the wrong haircuts. Porky's is a gambling club/whorehouse in the next county. Dan Monahan stars as Pee Wee, with Wyatt Knight, Mark Herrier, Tony Ganios, Scott Colomby, and Kaki Hunter. All of them appeared in the sequels too. With Nancy Parsons (*Motel Hell*) as Ballbreaker the gym teacher, Susan Clark as hooker Cherry Forever, Alex Karras as the sheriff, Kim Cattrall, Jill Whitlow, and Chuck Mitchell as Porky. It's a 20th Century–Fox release.

PORKY'S II: THE NEXT DAY

(Fox, 1983) **D/S/P:** Bob Clark **S:** Roger E. Swaybill, Alan Ormsby **P:** Don Carmody   US/Canada

Most of the same cast returns in this very inferior sequel. There's no Porky, but a fundamentalist preacher tries to stop a school Shakespeare festival. Corrupt politicians have to be taught a lesson,

and the KKK harasses Seminole Indians. The director shows his horror-movie roots in a graveyard scene with fake zombies. With Nancy Parsons, Kim Cattrall, Susan Clark and Alex Karras (married in real life and both from the TV series *Webster*), and Jill Whitlow.

PORKY'S REVENGE

(Fox, 1985) **D:** James Komack **S:** Ziggy Steinberg **P:** Robert L. Rosen

Porky returns, now running operations on a riverboat. The plot is about a basketball game. Most of the same cast members return, with Kim Evenson (from *Playboy*) and Nancy Valen. Some of the music (released by Columbia) is by Jeff Beck, Dave Edmonds, Robert Plant, and Phil Collins.

PORTRAIT IN TERROR

(SW, 1962) **D:** Rados Novakovic **S:** Vlastomir Radovanovic   US/Yugoslavia (*Operation Ticijan*)

This movie has haunted me since I saw it on late-night TV in Cleveland as a kid. It was filmed on location in old, picturesque Dubrovnik, Yugoslavia, on the Adriatic Sea. Patrick Magee, one of the greatest, most intense film actors ever, stars as a cultured, sadistic playboy, hitman, and art thief who wears dark sunglasses and white suits and is part of an involved plot about a stolen Titian painting. In the surprising opening scene he cuts the bikini top off an exotic dancer at an outdoor club, then beats up a sailor who tries to help her. Later on she goes to bed with him, explaining, "An interesting man always makes a woman curious." After murdering a deaf old man (and the man's dog!) with a silencer he says in his rich, distinctive voice, "The old gentleman had to go to sleep." William Campbell is an alcoholic assistant art curator and heir to the Sordi estate. He's obsessed with his infamous ancestor, a wife killer. His fiancée is understandably worried. They attend a historical play in an old castle and climb up steep stairs in a scene that might remind you of *8½* (filmed the same year). When a boy's body is dumped into the ocean it floats slowly to the bottom, as in Francis Ford Coppola's great *Dementia 13*. Coppola was the dialogue coach for this film. Right after it was made, Campbell and Magee were in *Dementia 13* (also with music by Ronald Stein), filmed in Ireland. In 1965 *Blood Bath*, directed by Jack Hill and Stephanie Rothman, starred Campbell and featured much of the best footage from *Portrait in Terror*, including the ending, with Magee dead and covered in wax, without any credit to the original filmmakers. *Track of the Vampire* (1966) is a different TV version. All of these films were AIP releases. Roger Corman is responsible for all of this confusion.

PORTRAIT OF A HITMAN

(Western World, 1977) **D:** Allan A. Buckhantz **S:** Yabo Yablonsky **P:** James Rokos, Andrej Krakowski   (*Jimbuck; Last Contract*)

Jack Palance stars as J.B., or Jimbuck, an artist and hitman hired by a gangster (Rod Steiger) to kill a brain surgeon (Bo Svenson!). The trouble is that Svenson is an old friend, and they're both in love with Ann Turkel. Also with Richard Roundtree, Philip Ahn, and Herb Jeffries. Flashbacks are used to explain things. Screenwriter Yabo Yablonsky directed *The Manipulator*.

PORTRAIT OF A SINNER

(1959) **D:** Robert Siodmak **S:** Audrey Erskine Lindop **P:** George Minter   UK (*The Rough and the Smooth*)

AIP released this "shockingly adult film!" about a blond German woman (Nadja Tiller) who seems to destroy everyone she becomes involved with. The cast also includes William Bendix, Tony Britton, Donald Wolfit, Joyce Carey, and Adrienne Corri.

PORTRAIT OF JENNIE

(Fox, 1948) **D:** William Dieterle **S:** Paul Osborn, Peter Berneis **P:** David O. Selznick **M:** Dimitri Tiomkin

Joseph Cotten is a poor NYC artist who meets the ghost of a little girl. As the ghost (played by Jennifer Jones) gets older he paints her. In the final (Technicolor) sequence, he dies so that he can be with her. This romantic (and very expensive) b/w United Artists release received an Oscar for special effects. It's based on a novel by Robert Nathan (as is the 1947 film *The Bishop's Wife*). With Ethel Barrymore, Lillian Gish, Cecil Kellaway, David Wayne, Henry Hull, and Anne Francis. Nancy Davis (Reagan) is an extra. William Dieterle also directed *The Hunchback of Notre Dame* (1939) and *All That Money Can Buy/The Devil and Daniel Webster* (1941).

POSED FOR MURDER

(Academy, 1988) **D:** Brian Thomas Jones **S:** John A. Gallagher, Chuck Dickerson **P:** Carl Fury, Jack Fox

Charlotte J. Helmkamp (from *Playboy*) poses naked for *Thrill* magazine and acts in *Meat Cleavers from Mars*. Her psycho bodybuilder boyfriend (Carl Fury) kills other men out of jealousy.

POSITIVE ID

(MCA, 1987) **D/S/P/E:** Andy Anderson

Stephanie Rascoe stars as a rape victim who assumes a new identity. Surprising plot twists occur in this clever, well-made independent film made in Dallas. Anderson, who teaches filmmaking at the University of Texas in Arlington, also made *Interface* (1984), about computer nerds causing campus killings.

POSSE

(Polygram, 1993) **D/A:** Mario Van Peebles **S:** Sy Richardson, Dario Scardapane **P:** Preston Holmes, Jim Steele   US/UK

A group of infantrymen from the Spanish-American War return as outlaws with a cache of gold. Their sullen leader (Mario Van Peebles) is after the men who lynched his father. He and his band travel from Cuba to New Orleans, then to Indian teritory, before arriving at an all-black town to settle scores. This is a good western with too many flashbacks. Big Daddy Kane as Father Time, Stephen Baldwin, Tiny Lister Jr., Tone Loc, and Charles Lane are in the posse. Billy Zane and

Richard Jordan are the racist white villains. The interesting supporting cast includes love interest Salli Richardson, Mario Van Peebles, Blair Underwood, Pam Grier, Isaac Hayes, Robert Hooks, Paul Bartel, and Nipsey Russell. The whole tale is related by an old cowboy (Woody Strode, a link to the westerns of John Ford and Sergio Leone). The A&M soundtrack by Michel Columbier features Tone Loc, Melvin Van Peebles, the Neville Brothers, and others.

THE POSSESSED

(Video Gems, 1974) **D/P:** Charles Nizet **S/A:** William Greer **S:** Deedy Peters   (*Help Me, I'm Possessed!*)

The dull Dr. Blackwood (William Greer), who claims, "Death is a fabrication of the mind," runs a sanitarium in his "castle" in the desert. His sadistic, hunchbacked servant whips women kept chained up in the basement and cuts the legs off bodies so that they'll fit in half-size caskets. A weird man named Zolak is decapitated by a guillotine, and a mutant monster is represented by a bunch of red hoses waved at the hand-held camera. More characters arrive for ridiculous plot complications, and they all have ugly haircuts and/or bushy sideburns. A dead character moves her leg, and the mind-numbing ending takes place in Bronson Canyon! It's pretty fascinating. This was released in 1984 and rated PG! Charles Nizet also directed the obscure *Voodoo Heartbeat* (1972) and *Slaves of Love*.

THE POSSESSED (1977) = DEMON WITCH CHILD

POSSESSED BY THE NIGHT

(Vision, 1994) **D/S:** Fred Olen Ray **S:** Mark Thomas McGee **P:** Alan Amiel

Shannon Tweed becomes a live-in typist for a horror novelist (Ted Prior) and his wife (Sandahl Bergman). A "cursed jar" from Chinatown possesses characters and causes nightmares, sex, and murder. In one scene Tweed forces the couple to fuck while she masturbates with a gun. This is followed by an (offscreen) threesome. A needless subplot involves Chad McQueen as a collector for Henry Silva ("I love bimbos!") and publishing espionage. The bizarre casting includes Frank Sivero (*Goodfellas*), who is pretty funny as Murray the agent, and the return of Turhan Bey (!). Kato Kaelin (of O. J. Simpson–trial fame) is a waiter working alongside the director.

POSSESSION

(Vestron, 1981) **D/S:** Andrzej Zulawski **P:** Marie-Laure Rayre   France/W. Germany

Isabelle Adjani was in her really weird period when she starred in this bloody and shocking broken-relationship horror movie, after *The Tenant* (1976) and *Nosferatu* (1978). Sam Neill is her ex-husband, who has a nervous breakdown. They yell a lot in an apartment next to the Berlin Wall and slash themselves with electric knives. She has a very messy miscarriage in a subway station and later gives birth to a tentacled monster (created by Carlo Rambaldi). The creature becomes her new lover and kills men. This was filmed in Berlin by a

Polish director. The uncut 127-minute version has been sold by mail order. The American-release video is only 80 minutes.

POSSESSION: UNTIL DEATH DO YOU PART

(Marathon, 1987) **D:** Michael Mazo **D/P:** Lloyd A. Simandl **S:** Lyne J. Grantham **P:** John A. Curtis   Canada

A psycho named Frankie (John R. Johnston) kidnaps women, kills them, and keeps the bodies in his closet. Later he kills his mom, puts on camouflage gear, and terrorizes campers at a lodge. This has lots of shower nudity and some male strippers. It was made in Vancouver.

POTS, PARENTS, AND POLICE

(SW, 1971) **D/S/P/A:** Phillip Pine **P:** Clark Johnson   (*The Cat Ate the Parakeet*)

TV watchers will recognize character actor Phillip Pine as the dad in this enjoyable, well-made movie aimed at kids but later marketed as an exploitation movie. Johnny (Robert Mantell), a loner kid, meets a friendly hippie couple who thoughtlessly get him high (and drunk), which leads to much confusion and trouble at home and police involvement. The hippie in a cocaine T-shirt with a pickup truck and a pretty blond girlfriend is a young Martin Margulies (aka Johnny Legend!). He eventually freaks out on mescaline ("I'm a bird! Free!") and falls down the stairs. This color film has split-screen camera work, flashbacks, and a nightmare sequence. The letterboxed video includes Legend interviewing Pine and talking about the film.

POWAQQATSI

(Imperial, 1988) **D/S/P:** Godfrey Reggio **S:** Ken Richards **P:** Mel Richards

After *Koyaanisqatsi* Godfrey Reggio made this, the second part of a planned trilogy. It's a beautifully made but horrifying look at how industrialization has nearly destroyed mostly Third World countries, including Brazil, Nepal, and Kenya. Haunting silent images show the faces of masses of hollow-eyed poor people working to strip their own lands. The Hopi Indian title means something like "bad witches who exploit others." The hypnotic music by Philip Glass was released by Nonesuch. Francis Ford Coppola and George Lucas presented this Cannon release.

P.O.W.: PRISONERS OF WAR: *See* THE SECRET OF BLOOD ISLAND

P.O.W.: THE ESCAPE

(Media, 1986) **D:** Gideon Amir **S:** Jeremy Lipp, James Bruner, Malcolm Barbour, John Langley **P:** Golan/Globus   (*Behind Enemy Lines*)

David Carradine is the highest-ranking prisoner of the Vietcong (led by Mako). He sings "Proud Mary" and helps many POWs escape, with sidekick Steve James, as Saigon falls. This was shot in the Philippines. From Cannon.

THE POWER

(Vestron, 1983) **D/S/P:** Jeff Obrow **D/S:** Stephen Carpenter **M:** Chris Young

After three students obtain a cursed 2-inch tall Aztec doll it possesses a guy, who becomes a monster with telekinetic powers. The score is on Cerberus.

POWER PLAY

(1978) **D/S:** Martyn Burke **P:** Christopher Dalton   UK/Canada (*Operation Overthrow*)

Peter O'Toole stars, with David Hemmings, Donald Pleasence, Barry Morse, and even Dick Cavett, in this film about a European military coup. Hemmings was also an executive producer.

THE POWER WITHIN

(1979) **D:** John Llewellyn Moxey **S:** Edward J. Lasko **P:** Alan Godfrey

Art Hindle stars in this ABC-TV pilot as a daredevil flyer who is struck by lightning and becomes superstrong. Secret agents go after him. With Edward Binns, Eric Braeden, David Hedison, and Dick Sargent.

PRANCER

(Orion, 1989) **D:** John Hancock **S:** Greg Taylor **P:** Raffaella De Laurentiis

A troubled little farm girl (Rebecca Harrell) meets a wounded talking reindeer, in this mix of *E.T.* and *Miracle on 34th Street*. This G-rated Christmas movie features Sam Elliott, Cloris Leachman, Rutanya Alda, Michael Constantine, and Abe Vigoda.

PRAYER OF THE ROLLERBOYS

(Academy, 1990) **D:** Rick King **S:** W. Peter Iliff **P:** Robert Mickelson   US/Japan

Corey Haim and Patricia Arquette go undercover to infiltrate a gang in the wasteland America of the future. The Rollerboys are LA drug-dealing fascist villains led by Christopher Collet. They sell a smoke-mist drug and look pretty ridiculous on their skates. With Devin Clark and Julius Harris.

PRAY FOR DEATH

(IVE, 1985) **D:** Gordon Hessler **S/A:** James Booth **P:** Don Van Atta

In a semi-remake of *Revenge of the Ninja* Sho Kosugi stars as a Japanese businessman in Houston. After he opens a new restaurant his family is attacked by gangsters, so he vows revenge. Throwing stars, arrows, samurai swords, axes, chains, and buzzsaws are used. It ends in a warehouse with naked mannequins. Typical dialogue is "I'm gonna rip your stinking guts out!" The main mobster is Michael Constantine (from the TV series *Room 222*). With Kosugi sons Kane and Shane Kosugi, Robert Ito, James Booth, and Donna Kei Benz. The violence was cut for an R rating for America.

PRAY FOR THE WILDCATS

(1974) **D:** Robert Michael Lewis **S:** Jack Turley **P:** Anthony Wilson

Andy Griffith, William Shatner, Marjoe Gortner, and Robert Reed (from the TV series *The Brady Bunch*) star as ad men who go on "a wild motorcycle trip into Hell!" Griffith is especially memorable as the drunken, lecherous, murderous boss. This ABC-TV movie costars Angie Dickinson, Janet Margolin, and Lorraine Gary.

PRAYING MANTIS

(1993) **D:** James Keach **S:** William Delligan, Duane Poole **P:** Robert Rolsky

Jane Seymour (an executive producer) stars as a psycho who has killed five husbands with cyanide. Wealthy new husband Barry Bostwick is her next victim. Frances Fisher is her suspicious sister-in-law, and Chad Allen is her new stepson. This Showtime movie was shot in Oregon.

PREACHERMAN

(Troma, 1971) **D/S/P/A:** Albert T. Viola **S:** Harvey Flaxman

Albert T. Viola, using the name Amos Huxley, stars (as "himself") in this southern comedy drive-in hit from North Carolina. Amos is a smooth-talking con-man and preacher who goes after blond hillbilly Mary Lou, who has "an unnatural hankerin' for menfolk." Preacherman's Angel Leroy con is very funny, and a guy named Farley (Pat Patterson) has sex with chickens (offscreen). The soundtrack is banjo music, the theme song is great, and there's a gospel-singing (one-armed) brother and sister who help sell moonshine ("God's nectar"). Patterson (*Dr. Gore*) was also the production manager. The video version seems to be cut, but it's still worth searching for. Viola went on to make movies for Roger Corman.

PREDATOR

(CBS/Fox, 1987) **D:** John McTiernan **S:** Jim Thomas, John Thomas **P:** Lawrence Gordon, Joel Silver, John Davis **M:** Alan Silvestri

Arnold Schwarzenegger and Carl Weathers star as Dutch and Dillon, part of an American S.W.A.T. team in South America. They're on a rescue mission but face a chameleon-like alien monster hunter (with "dreadlocks"). The sci-fi action movie actually copies the obscure film *Without Warning* (1980). With Jesse "the Body" Ventura, Bill Duke, Sonny Landham, R. G. Armstrong, and Kevin

Peter Hall. Kevin Peter Hall is the predator. Stan Winston, Steve Wang, Steve Johnson, and others provided some great FX. The soundtrack is on Varèse Sarabande.

PREDATOR 2

(CBS/Fox, 1990) **D:** Stephen Hopkins **S:** Jim Thomas, John Thomas **P:** Lawrence Gordon, Joel Silver, John Davis

This sequel has more action, more humor, and more blood. In the dismal LA of 1997 cops battle heavily armed South American drug dealers and deal with voodoo and hearts being cut out. Danny Glover as the hero cop also runs into the transparent alien hunter. Some action takes place on the LA subway (really the easy-to-recognize San Fransisco BART). With Ruben Blades, Maria Conchita Alonso, and Bill Paxton as cops, Gary Busey as a federal agent, Robert Davi, Adam Baldwin, Calvin Lockhart, Elpidia Carillo, Morton Downey Jr. as a reporter, and Teri Weigel. The 7-foot Kevin Peter Hall again plays the transparent monster. Glover even goes into the alien spaceship (full of skull trophies). The Stan Winston FX are excellent. The production design is by Lawrence G. Paull (*Blade Runner*). The Alan Silvestri soundtrack is on Varèse Sarabande. Some ads in large cities were aimed at Hispanics.

PREHYSTERIA!

(Paramount, 1992) **D/P:** Albert Band, Charles Band, **S:** Greg Sudeth, Mark Goldstein

In this PG-rated Full Moon release, eggs from South America hatch into six small (animated) dinosaurs in the home of an archaeologist (Brett Cullen). His Elvis-fan kid (Austin O'Brien, from *Last Action Hero*) and his blond older daughter have to help fight off the dumb comic-relief bad guys. The David Allen FX make this an okay light movie for kids. With Samantha Mills and Colleen Morris. The Bands also made two sequels with different casts.

PRELUDE TO A KISS

(1992) **D:** Norman Rene **S:** Craig Lucas **P:** Michael Gruskoff

Here's another body-switch movie. Alec Baldwin marries Meg Ryan, who seems to be someone else all of a sudden because she now has the soul of an old man. This PG-13 fantasy, based on a play (which also starred Baldwin), features Sydney Walker, Kathy Bates, Ned Beatty, Patty Duke, and Annie Golden.

PREMONITION

(1971) **D/S:** Alan Rudolph
P: Christopher R. Robertson

Red flowers cause three college students to have premonitions of death. With Carl Crow and Tim Ray. Alan Rudolph made *Barn of the Naked Dead* (1973), then went to work for Robert Altman.

THE PRESENCE

(Vidmark, 1992) **D:** Tommy Lee Wallace **S:** William Bleich **P:** Ted Swanson   (*Danger Island*)

A plane with nine adults and three kids crash-lands on an island where there's an empty house with a large research lab. One guy mutates into what looks like *The Monster from Piedras Blancas*, and Gary Graham (from *Alien Nation*) becomes a friendly monster. The stellar cast includes Kathy Ireland as a model, former TV Tarzan Joe Lara, June Lockhart (she narrates), Richard Beymer, and Eddie Velez. The FX are by Fantasy 2 and Gene Warren. This NBC-TV production (filmed in Hawaii) seems to be a series pilot film since the cast is still on the island at the end.

THE PRESIDENT'S PLANE IS MISSING

(1971) **D:** Daryl Duke **S/P:** Mark Carliner **S:** Ernest Kinoy

It's only a TV movie about the president's plane crashing and China threatening a nuclear attack, but it was held up for nearly three years because Nixon went to China in 1971 and ABC-TV didn't want to show a movie with Chinese bad guys! The all-star disaster cast, which makes it one to look for, includes Buddy Ebsen as the inept vice president (in charge) named Kermit, Peter Graves, Arthur Kennedy, Raymond Massey, Mercedes McCambridge, Rip Torn, Dabney Coleman, Joseph Campanella, John Amos, and Todd Andrews (*From Hell It Came*) as the president. It's based on a novel by Rod Serling's brother Robert.

PRESIDENT'S TARGET

(Hemdale, 1989) **D/S/P:** Yvan Chiffre

Stalker (John Coleman) is a CIA man in S. America who has Nam flashbacks. He hides out and trains in the home of an old man and his daughter (Brigitte Audrey). Somebody (could it be Nam vet Martin Kove or mercenary Bo Hopkins?) is behind the killing of some US officials. They all talk a lot and experience flashbacks.

THE PRESIDENT'S WOMAN

(1975) **D/E:** John G. Avildsen **S:** David Odell, Jack Richardson, Don Greenberg **P:** Carl Gurevich   (*Fore-Play*)

Zero Mostel is the president, and Estelle Parsons is the first lady. This barely released political/sex comedy features Pat Paulsen, Jerry Orbach, Paul Dooley, Professor Irwin Corey, and Louisa Moritz.

PRESSURE POINT

(MGM, 1962) **D/S:** Hubert Cornfield
P: Stanley Kramer

Sidney Poitier stars as a prison psychiatrist, in this serious and seriously strange movie about racism. Bobby Darin is a Nazi psycho with a troubled past who hallucinates that he's tiny and going down a drain. What he told Poitier during WWII is told in flashback to a young shrink (Peter Falk) in the present day. With Barry Gordon, Butch Patrick, Yvette Vickers as a drunk, and Richard Bakalyan as a juvenile delinquent. United Artists distributed this b/w film.

PRETTY BOY FLOYD

(1959) **D/S:** Herbert J. Leder **P:** Monroe Sachson

John Ericson is the young Pretty Boy Floyd, a real-life Depression-era outlaw, in one of several gangster bios that were probably inspired by the success of the TV series *The Untouchables*. Joan Harvey costars, with Barry Newman, Herb Evers (*The Brain That Wouldn't Die*), Peter Falk (also in *Murder, Inc.*, from the same year), and Al Lewis. It was shot in a studio in the Bronx and released by Continental. Audio Fidelity issued the jazz soundtrack. Fabian later played the same role in *A Bullet for Pretty Boy* (1971).

PRETTYKILL

(Lorimar, 1987) **D:** George Kaczender
S: Sandra K. Bailey **P:** John R. Bowey, Martin Walters   (*Tomorrow's a Killer*)

David Birney stars as an honest NYC cop, and Season Hubley (*Vice Squad*) is a high-class hooker. They search for a killer, and it turns out to be hooker Suzanne Snyder, a psycho who takes on her father's personality (and voice!). With Susannah York and Yaphet Kotto. It's a Sandy Howard presentation.

PRETTY MAIDS ALL IN A ROW

(1971) **D:** Roger Vadim **S/P:** Gene Roddenberry

Vadim's first American film was made after his hit *Barbarella*. It's a wonderfully dated black comedy with Rock Hudson as Tiger, a "hip" married high-school psychologist and football coach who advises a virginal kid (John David Carson, very good in a difficult role). Meanwhile, Tiger is fooling around with his female students, and some of them end up dead. Nobody expected this from the creator of *Star Trek*! Telly Savalas is a police captain, James "Scotty" Doohan is his partner, and Angie Dickinson is a substitute teacher who takes her clothes off. Also with Roddy McDowall, Keenan Wynn, William Campbell, and starlets Barbara Leigh, Joanna Cameron, Joy Bang, Brenda Sykes, Margaret Markov, June Fairchild, and Aimee Eccles. The lame title song is by the Osmonds. MGM released it.

THE PREY

(New World, 1980) **D/S:** Edwin Scott Brown
S/P: Summer Brown

"It's not human. And it's got an axe!" Teen campers in the Colorado Rockies stop to tell the famous

horror story "The Monkey's Paw" around a campfire. A tall Gypsy burn victim (Carel "Lurch" Struycken) kills them with his axe. Meanwhile we see lots of insects and reptiles. With Jackie Coogan and Steve Bond. It was released in 1984.

PREY OF THE CHAMELEON

(Prism, 1991) **D/S:** Fleming Fuller **S:** April Campbell Jones **P:** Pat Peach, Ron Rothstein

Daphne Zuniga is an escaped mental patient who's a serial killer. She befriends people in Texas, kills them, and assumes their identities. Then she falls for and kidnaps a cowboy hitchhiker (James Wilder). Alexandra Paul is his ex-fiancée, now a deputy sheriff. Also with Red West and Don Harvey. This debuted on Showtime.

PRICELESS BEAUTY

(Republic, 1989) **D/S:** Charles Finch
P: Nicole Sequin   Italy

Christopher Lambert is a guilt-stricken former pop star who discovers a genie (Diane Lane, his then real-life wife) on a Mediterranean island. She grants wishes and reunites him with his dead brother. With Francesco Quinn and J.C. Quinn. It was made (in English) by the son of actor Peter Finch.

PRIMAL IMPULSE

(Vestron, 1974) **D/S:** Luigi Bazzoni
C: Vittorio Storaro   Italy (*Le Orme*)

The moon and an abandoned astronaut somehow affect an interpreter (Florinda Bolkan) in Italy. She has dreams and identity problems. This arty science-fiction movie features Peter McEnery, Nicolette Elmi, Lila Kedrova, and Klaus Kinski in a small role as a scientist.

PRIMAL RAGE

(Warner, 1988) **D:** Vittorio Rambaldi **S:** Harry Kirkpatrick **P:** William J. Immerman   US/Italy

An experimental baboon in Florida bites people and infects them, making them kill. It all ends up at a Halloween party where infected killers spewing slime mix with kids in costumes. With Patrick Lowe, Cheryl Arutt, and Bo Svenson as a university scientist (with a ponytail). Carlo Rambaldi provided the FX.

PRIMAL SCREAM

(Magnum, 1988) **D/S:** William Murray
P: Howard Foulkrod

Kenneth J. McGregor is a futuristic private eye who investigates murders where only ashes are left. An energy catalyst is behind the killings. With Sharon Mason and Mickey Shaughnessy.

PRIME CUT

(Fox, 1972) **D:** Michael Ritchie
S: Robert Dillon **P:** Joe Wizan

Lee Marvin is a Chicago hitman sent to Kansas City to eliminate a gangster called Mary Ann (Gene Hackman). This is one of the early-70s new-cinema-freedom movies you have to see to believe. The mob uses a slaughterhouse to keep kidnapped slave women penned up. They also grind up their enemies into sausages. Sissy Spacek makes her acting debut alongside other naked girls in this National General release, with Angel Tompkins, Gregory Walcott, Janit Baldwin, and Eddie Egan.

PRIME EVIL

(Starmaker, 1988) **D/C:** Roberta Findlay **S:** Ed Kelleher, Harriette Vidal **P:** Walter E. Sear

Satanists in Manhattan sacrifice victims. There's an evil uncle, a struggle for power, and confusing time switches. Christine Moore stars, with William Beckwith, Amy Bretano, and Ruth Collins. Ed French did the FX. Crown International released it. Kelleher used to review drive-in movies for *Creem* magazine.

PRIME RISK

(Vestron, 1984) **D/S:** Michael Farkas **P:** Herman Grigsby

Lee Montgomery and Sam Bottoms figure out how to rip off automatic teller machines and discover a foreign conspiracy to sabotage the government. With Keenan Wynn, Clu Gulager, and Toni Hudson.

PRIME TARGET

(Hemdale, 1991) **D/S/P/A:** David Heavener

Multitalented (he thinks) David Heavener stars as a suspended small-town cop who has to transfer a gangster (Tony Curtis) to prison, in this bad Clint Eastwood copy (mostly *The Gauntlet*) with Eastwood movie costars, dialogue, and references. With Jenilee Harrison, Andrew Robinson as a corrupt police commissioner, Isaac Hayes as a police captain, Robert Reed, Don Stroud, and Michael Gregory. It was filmed in Bakersfield, California, and has a country-music soundtrack. Heavener also wrote the songs.

THE PRIME TIME

(SW, 1958) **D/P:** Herschell Gordon Lewis **S:** Robert Abel   (*Hellkitten*)

JoAnn LeCompte stars as Jean, a wild, tough 17-year-old who says, "I'm bored, bored, bored" and "I look at least 22!" She poses topless for an artist known as "the beard." He ties her up and drugs her, and her boyfriend, Tony, and the kids who hang out at Luigi's search for her. A sexy and bored-looking young Karen Black makes her film debut as a "live one" who poses for the artist on a bar stool. An impressive rockabilly band does "She's a Tiger" at the Golden Goose. There's a cat-fight flashback, an underwear swim scene, and some lame attempts at comic relief. This b/w movie was said to be the first feature filmed in Chicago "in 40 years." David F. Friedman was in charge of the "advertising, publicity, and exploitation" for Herschell Gordon Lewis' first effort. He later rereleased it and renamed it.

PRIME TIME MURDERS

(Imperial, 1993) **D:** Michael DeLuise **S/P:** Gary Skeen Hall

Anthony Finetti stars as a freelance journalist with a video camera who teams up with an ex-cop (Tim Thomerson) to track "the downtown skid-row slasher." With Laura Reed and Sally Kirkland as a TV news director.

THE PRINCE AND THE NATURE GIRL

(1965) **D/P:** Doris Wishman **S:** Andrew J. Kuehn

Leave it to Doris Wishman to make a nudist-colony movie about the leader of a mythical kingdom falling for a twin from Ohio. One twin fools him by wearing a wig, so the other twin finds herself a king. All of them are naked most of the time. It was filmed in Florida and New Jersey.

PRINCE JACK

(Vestron, 1984) **D/S/P:** Bert Lovitt **P:** Jim Milo

Probably the cheapest and least known of the Kennedy epics, this one stars TV actor Robert Hogan as JFK during the Cuban missile crisis, Kenneth Mars as LBJ, and Robert Guillaume as Martin Luther King Jr. Other stars (as more generic figures) are Dana Andrews (in his last-known role), Jim Backus, Cameron Mitchell, Theodore Bikel, Lloyd Nolan, and William Windom. It sounds like a TV movie but wasn't.

PRINCE OF DARKNESS

(MCA, 1987) **D/S/M:** John Carpenter **P:** Larry Franco

Most of this botched science-fiction story takes place in an abandoned church. People worry, argue, and run around because of a big green lava lamp. It's a dumb movie. With Donald Pleasence as a priest, Jameson Parker, Victor Wong, Lisa Blount, Dennis Dun, and Alice Cooper as one of the killer street people. John Carpenter wrote the script as Martin Quatermass. The soundtrack by Carpenter and Alan Howarth is on Varèse Sarabande.

PRINCE OF FOXES

(1949) **D:** Henry King **S:** Milton Krims **P:** Sol C. Siegel

Orson Welles plays the famous Renaissance villain Cesare Borgia in this b/w costume movie filmed in Italy. Tyrone Power stars as Orsini, with Everett Sloane, Wanda Hendrix, Marina Berti, and Katina Paxinou. Welles showed up in the next 20th Century–Fox movie starring Power, *The Black Rose,* too.

THE PRINCE OF PEACE

(1949) **D:** William Beaudine, Harold Daniels   (*The Lawton Story*)

"The Entire New Testament Story. Fifty-two New Testament Tableaux! 100 percent Nonsectarian!" The story concerns a little girl with a religious grandfather who convinces her mean, evil great-uncle to attend a Passion play (the last 20 minutes of the movie). A live Passion play presented annually in Lawton, Oklahoma, was filmed. The strong Oklahoma accents had to be redubbed. The star is little Ginger Price from Georgia. Kroger Babb

made this into a long-running road-show hit and even opened it in NYC, at the Criterion. A pitchman delivered a sermon before each screening and sold 8x10 pictures of Jesus and miniature Bibles. Joe Solomon also distributed this show-biz phenomenon.

THE PRINCESS ACADEMY

(1987) **D:** Bruce Block **S/P:** Sandra Weintraub   US/France/Yugoslavia

Eva Gabor is a countess running a Swiss finishing school for girls. This movie features hard-to-believe whore and shit humor. With Lar Park Lincoln and Lu Leonard.

THE PRINCESS BRIDE

(Nelson, 1987) **D/P:** Rob Reiner **S:** William Goldman **P:** Andrew Scheinman **M:** Mark Knopfler

A grandfather (Peter Falk) tells this PG-rated, comic, post-modern fairy tale to a little boy (Fred Savage). Cary Elwes is the hero who has to rescue a princess (Robin Wright). With good sword fights, some fantasy, and lots of funny characters, played by Mandy Patinkin, Chris Sarandon, Christopher Guest, Wallace Shawn, 7'4" wrestler André the Giant, Peter Cook, Carol Kane, Billy Crystal, and Mel Smith. The soundtrack is on Warner. An ad for Hershey's Kisses is on the video.

PRINCESS WARRIOR

(1990) **D:** Lindsay Norgard **S:** John Riley **P:** Philip Jones, James Holi

An alien women (Sharon Lee Jones) in LA is pursued by her evil sister and her female followers. This very low-budget effort features women in fist fights, a wet T-shirt contest, bad FX, joke names, and a pair of cops. It was shot on video.

THE PRINCIPAL

(RCA, 1987) **D:** Christopher Cain **S:** Frank Deese **P:** Thomas H. Brodek

James Belushi is a motorcycle-riding teacher ordered to become principal of the worst inner-city school around. Louis Gossett Jr. is a security officer and Rae Dawn Chong is a teacher helping him try to stop the drugs, violence, rape, arson, and murder. With Michael Wright, Esai Morales, and real members of an Oakland Chicano gang. Jelly-bean Benitez was the music producer. It's from Tri-Star.

PRISON

(Starmaker, 1988) **D:** Renny Harlin **S:** Courtney Joyner **P:** Irwin Yablans

A brutal guard (Lane Smith) is made warden of a reopened, rundown Wyoming prison closed for 20 years. The ghost of a wrongly executed man causes bizarre deaths. This smoky, dreary movie, which makes little sense, features Chelsea Field, Viggo Mortensen, Arlen Dean Snyder, Tom "Tiny" Lester, and Kane Hodder. It was directed at an actual (closed) Wyoming prison by the Finnish-born

Renny Harlin, making his first movie in America. Charles Band was the executive producer. John Beuchler provided the FX. The soundtrack by Richard Band and Christopher L. Stone is on Varèse Sarabande.

THE PRISONER
(MPI, 1967)

17 tapes running 50 minutes each make up this entire English cult TV series, starring and created by executive producer (and occasional director) Patrick McGoohan. He played #6, a former British secret agent trapped on a bizarre holiday island (actually in North Wales). The only other regular cast member was the little butler (Angelo Muscat) of whoever was #1 in that episode. Ahead of its time, the series was a follow-up to McGoohan's earlier series *Secret Agent* and is a timeless masterpiece of paranoia and surrealism, one of the best TV shows ever produced. The "lost episode" is an alternative version of "Chimes of Big Ben" (the second episode). There's also a "best of" video (30 minutes) and *The "Prisoner" Video Companion*(1990).

PRISONERS OF THE LOST UNIVERSE
(Virgin, 1983) **D/S:** Terry Marcel **S/P:** Harry Roberson

A TV journalist and a martial-arts champ are transported to a primitive world. Richard Hatch (*Battlestar: Galactica*) stars, with Kay Lenz and John Saxon as Kleel. This early Showtime cable movie was shot in South Africa by the director of *Hawk the Slayer*.

PRISON FARM
(1938) **D:** Luis King **S:** Eddie Welch, Robert Yost

A young woman (Shirley Ross) falls for an armed robber (Lloyd Nolan). She's arrested by a guard (J. Carroll Naish) at the Sunny Grove prison and ends up there doing laundry under the watchful eyes of mean matrons (Marjorie Main and Anna Q. Nilsson). With Mae Busch, John Howard, and Porter Hall as the warden. It's 69 minutes.

PRISON GIRL
(1942) **D:** William Beaudine **S:** Arthur St. Claire **P:** Lester Cutler

Rose Hobart (*Dr. Jekyll and Mr. Hyde*) stars as a doctor sent to prison on a mercy-killing charge, in this PRC movie with Sidney Blackmer and Claire Rochelle. She eventually escapes, is married, performs many heroic deeds, and is pardoned. William Beaudine made *The Living Ghost* and many more films the same year.

PRISON GIRLS
(1972) **D:** Thomas DeSimone **S/P:** Burton C. Gershfeld **S:** Lee Walters **P:** Nicholas J. Grippo

AIP released this women's-prison/sex movie in 3-D. Polaroid lenses were used. When six model prisoners are released for a weekend each has a separate segment involving sex, rape, a pimp, and, in one case, bikers. With Robert Whiting, Angie Monet,

Uschi Digart, Candy Samples, Jason Williams (*Flesh Gordon*), and Rick Lutz. Ronnie Ashcroft was the editor. DeSimone later made *The Concrete Jungle* and *Reform School Girls*.

PRISON HEAT
(1993) **D:** Joel Silberg **S:** David Alexander

Some American college friends (Rebecca Chambers, Lori Jo Hendrix, Kena Land, and Gilya Stern) drive a rented van to Turkey from Greece, and drugs are planted at the border. Toni Naples is a tattooed lesbian gang leader, and Avi Cohen is the warden.

PRISON PLANET
(Columbia, 1992) **D/S/P/E:** Armand Gazarian

James Phillips stars as a futuristic rebel with a sword who goes to a barren planet for some obscure reason and rescues a virgin (Deborah Thompson-Carlin, who was a coproducer) from rapists. Michael M. Foley (*The Divine Enforcer*) is awful as the Attila-like villain, but I liked the comic-relief guy in a suit. Some parts are unintentionally funny, and the sets and spaceships in this *Road Warrior*–inspired nonsense are the cheapest I've seen in a long time. It's from 21st Century.

PRISON STORIES: WOMEN ON THE INSIDE
(Prism, 1990) **D:** Penelope Spheeris, Donna Deitch, Joan Micklin Silver **S:** Julie Seabo, Martin Jones, Marlane Meyer **P:** Gerald T. Olson

These three stories about women in prison are pretty serious. Rae Dawn Chong is pregnant and deals coke to pay for day care. Annabella Sciorra is her cellmate. Rachel Ticotin and Talisa Soto are in a story about a drug dealer. Lolita Davidovich is a battered wife who killed her husband. It was made for HBO.

PRIVATE DUTY NURSES
(Charter, 1971) **D/S/P:** George Armitage
(*Young L.A. Nurses 2*)

Kathy Cannon (later in the TV series *Father Murphy*) stars, with Joyce Williams and Pegi Boucher,

in a story about nurses and waterbeds. The ads said things like "Honestly, doctor, I was only giving him a massage!" It's a follow-up to *The Student Nurses*. The director wrote Roger Corman's *Gas-s-s-s* and made *Miami Blues* years later. *Night Call Nurse* was next in this New World drive-in series.

THE PRIVATE EYES
(New World, 1980) **D/P:** Lang Elliott **S:** Tim Conway, John Myers **P:** Wanda Dell

Tim Conway and Don Knotts star as detectives in a haunted house. This PG comedy made more than $8 million and was one of New World's biggest hits. With Trisha Noble, Grace Zabriskie, Stan Ross, Irwin Keyes, Suzy Mandell, and Fred Stuthman (who had been LA TV horror host Jeepers Creepers) in the last of his many character roles. The same comedy team starred in *The Prize Fighter* (1979).

PRIVATE INVESTIGATIONS
(Fox, 1987) **D:** Nigel Dick **S:** John Dahl, David Warfield **P:** Steven Golin, Sigurjon Sighvatsson

Clayton Rohmer is an LA architect in trouble because a newspaper reporter (Anthony Zerbe) and gangsters led by Ray Sharkey think he has some hidden information. Also with Paul LeMat, Talia Balsam, Phil Morris, and Robert Ito.

PRIVATE LESSONS
(MCA, 1981) **D:** Alan Myerson **S:** Dan Greenburg **P:** Ben Efraim

A 15-year-old rich kid (Eric Brown) is seduced by the family maid (Sylvia Kristel), but she and the chauffeur (Howard Hesseman) are criminals. With Ed Begley Jr., Pamela Jean Bryant, and Crispin Glover. This comedy was a hit and inspired several copies, a sequel called *They're Playing with Fire* (1984), and *Private Lessons: Another Story* (Paramount, 1994), a late "sequel." MCA released the soundtrack. The director also made *Steelyard Blues* (1973).

PRIVATE RESORT

(RCA, 1985) **D:** George Bower **S:** Gordon Mitchell **P:** Ben Efraim, Don Enright

Rob Morrow and Johnny Depp star as teens trying to score at a Miami resort. Hector Elizondo is a jewel thief. Also with Emily Longstreth, Karyn O'Bryan, and Dodie Goodman. George Bower also made *My Tutor*.

PRIVATE SCHOOL

(MCA, 1983) **D:** Noel Black **S:** Dan Greenburg, Suzanne O'Malley **P:** Ben Efraim, Don Enright

This teen-sex comedy, a "sequel" to *Private Lessons*, is set at a girls' school. Phoebe Cates is a nice girl. Betsy Russell is a bad girl who rides a horse topless. With Matthew Modine, Sylvia Kristel (in a small part as Mrs. Copuletta), Martin Mull, Ray Walston, Kathleen Wilhoite, Lynda Wiesmeier, and Brinke Stevens (in the shower). MCA released the various artists soundtrack.

PRIVATE WARS

(PM, 1992) **D/S:** John Weidner **S:** Ken Lamplugh **P:** Richard Pepin, Joseph Merhi

This resembles a live-action cartoon complete with comic segments and a dumb rap song. Steve Railsback is Jack Manny, an alcoholic former LA cop who was set up and served eight years. A corrupt businessman (Stuart Whitman) and the police captain (Michael Champion), who's on his payroll, pay thugs and martial artists (led by James Lew) to terrorize the barrio with robbery, murder, and grenade launchers so that they can have the neighborhood torn down and redeveloped. He's finally convinced to help a citizens' group fight back, and he falls for Holly Floria (*Bikini Island*). A big, all-out street battle stops for one-on-one kickboxing. Seeing Railsback fighting in a drunken stupor almost makes it worthwhile, but unfortunately the character straightens out before long. There are bikers, a guy in drag, and a midget.

PROBABLE CAUSE

(1994) **D:** Paul Ziller **S:** Hal Salwen **P:** Richard Davis, Bruce Harvey   Canada

Michael Ironside is a police detective trying to catch a person who has been killing cops with steak knives. Kate Vernon is his sleepwalking new partner. With Craig T. Nelson, Michelle Miller, and James Downing. This flashback-filled feature was filmed in Edmonton, Alberta. It debuted on Showtime.

PROBLEM GIRLS

(1953) **D:** E. A. Dupont **S/P:** Aubrey Wisberg, Jack Pollexfen

Helen Walker, Susan Morrow, and Ross Elliott star in this women-in-prison movie. "Rich girls who go wrong," said the ads, which showed a red-haired woman hanging by her wrists and being hosed down by a prison matron. Columbia released it on a double bill with *One Girl's Confession*. The German-born director made *Variety* back in 1926.

He left directing and worked as an agent between 1940 and 1950. The same director, writer, and producer made *The Neanderthal Man* (1953).

THE PROFESSIONAL

(Columbia, 1994) **D/S:** Luc Besson **P:** Claude Besson   US/France (*Leon*)

Luc Besson followed his international hit *Le Femme Nikita* with this movie. Leon (Jean Reno), a tall, illiterate, milk-drinking, Sicilian loner who's a "cleaner" (hitman), is the hero. DEA cops in NYC, led by a manic Gary Oldman, are the villains. This is a very different, violent action movie. Leon reluctantly protects and trains Matilda (13-year-old Natalie Portman, from Long Island), the only survivor of a drug massacre, and she becomes a killer too. With Danny Aiello as an Italian gangster who never leaves his storefront social club, and Ellen Greene. This Columbia/Gaumont production was shot (in English) in the NYC neighborhoods of Spanish Harlem and Little Italy, but the interiors were done in France.

A PROFESSIONAL GUN

(Edde, 1968) **D/S:** Sergio Corbucci **S:** Luciano Vincenzoni, Sergio Spina **P:** Alberto Grimaldi **M:** Ennio Morricone   Italy/Spain
(*Il Mercenario; The Mercenary*)

Franco Nero stars as Kowalski, a mercenary with a machine gun fighting in the Mexican civil war. Jack Palance is a psychotic (and homosexual) mercenary named Curly working for the government, and Tony Musante is the revolutionary hero. This sometimes comic PG western ends in a *The Good, the Bad, and the Ugly*–inspired showdown in a bullfight arena. The United Artists ads said, "Life is cheap. Death isn't!"

THE PROFESSOR

(Sinister, 1958) **D/S:** Tom McCain

A local sheriff is killed with "maniacal fury," Commie spies meet in a library, and a missing scientist (Doug Hobart) turns out to be a howling werewolf. A balding professor who worked on a secret atomic project calls him "a soul crying in the miseries of Hell." Too many characters clutter the plot, and we don't see much of Hobart, but this fun, rare TV-pilot film was made by live-spook-show operators in Dayton, Ohio! The half-hour b/w film is on the same video as *Tales of Frankenstein* (intermission trailers are included).

PROGRAMMED TO KILL

(Media, 1986) **D/P:** Allan Holzman **S:** Robert Short **P:** Don Stern   (*Retaliator*)

Robert Ginty is a mercenary hired to stop a PLO terrorist (Sandahl Bergman). He kills her, but the villains implant a microcircuit in her brain and turn her into a "Barbie/Rambo killing machine" in a leather jumpsuit with frizzed-out hair. Then she turns against her creators. With James Booth.

PROJECT A

(1984) **D/S/A:** Jackie Chan **P:** Leonard K.C. Ho   Hong Kong

Jackie Chan is an early-1900s Coast Guard sailor, Yuen Biao is a cop, and Samo Hung is a gambler. They battle pirates with swords, chairs, bombs, and martial arts. This action comedy was a big hit in Asia, and *Project A, Part 2* (1987) followed, co-starring Maggie Cheung, Carina Lau, and Rosamund Kwan.

PROJECT ALIEN

(Vidmark, 1989) **D:** Frank Shields **S:** Anthony Able   UK/Australia/Yugoslavia (*Fatal Sky*)

This film is set in Norway and is about a UFO cover-up. Or is the military behind the animal mutilations and the deadly virus? It has American stars Michael Nouri as a newspaper reporter, Darlanne Fluegel as a pilot, Maxwell Caulfield as a TV reporter, and Charles Durning as a NATO chief, and it's very boring.

PROJECT ELIMINATOR

(Southgate, 1990) **D/S:** H. Kaye Dyal **P:** Morris Asgar

Frank Zagarino is John Slade, a quiet, muscular truckdriver with long blond hair. He stops a holdup by guys in Nixon and Reagan masks, is blamed by the local corrupt cops, and teams up with his old Nam buddy Ron (David Carradine), an ex-alcoholic restaurant owner who cooks, plays the piano, and sings. Ron's boss (Drew Snyder), who has created an "anti-personnel weapon" that looks like a small Buck Rogers spaceship, plans to get out of the weapons business to help the homeless (!) but is kidnapped by the bad guys before he can. Lots of gunfire, chases, and pointless explosions follow, all set to boring Tangerine Dream–type music. Also with Carradine's daughter Calista Carradine (but another actress plays his daughter), Hilary English, and Vivian Schilling (*Soultaker*). It was shot in New Mexico. Carradine and his wife, Gail, were the associate producers.

PROJECT GENESIS

(Prism, 1992) **D/S/P:** Philip Jackson **P:** Mark Terry   Canada (*Strange Horizons*)

Various characters (and a computer with a cartoon face) on a cargo spaceship (cramped sets) talk and talk. David Ferry stars, with Olga Prokhorova as a mute alien woman, Ken Lamaire as an older admiral, and Kyra Harper. There's narration, a brief topless scene, and very cheap FX. It was made for TV.

THE PROJECTIONIST

(Vestron, 1971) **D/S/P/E:** Harry Hurwitz

Chuck McCann is a NYC projectionist who daydreams that he's Captain Flash, a superhero. This PG comedy has some very serious moments (about Nazis and the end of the world). With Ina Balin and Rodney Dangerfield as the stingy theater manager.

PROJECT: KILL

(Paragon, 1976) **D:** William Girdler **S:** Donald G. Thompson **P:** David Shelton   (*Total Control*)

Leslie Nielsen stars as a defecting government agent pursued by drug-controlled assassins in the Philippines. Nielsen (before he became a comic actor) actually does some kung-fu fighting and falls for Nancy Kwan, who helps him through drug withdrawal. With Gary Lockwood. William Girdler went on to make *Grizzly*, *Day of the Animals* (also with Nielsen), and *The Manitou* before dying in a 1977 helicopter crash in the Philippines scouting locations for *The Overlords* (it was never made).

PROJECT: METALBEAST

(Prism, 1994) **D/S:** Alessandro De Gaetano
S: Timothy E. Sabo **P:** Frank Hildebrand

Here's another silly monster-in-a-building movie. In Budapest in 1974 an American secret agent injects himself with the blood of a werewolf. The laughable result looks like a man in a gorilla suit with a wolf's head. His body is put into suspended animation, then brought back 20 years later by a bad-guy colonel (Barry Bostwick). Bloody, painful plastic surgery with synthetic skin turns the "wereman" into what looks like the monster in *Predator*, and it eventually stalks two women (Kim Delaney and Musetta Vander) with a bazooka in scenes that copy *Alien*. John Carl Buechler created the FX, and Kane Hodder plays the monster.

PROJECT: SHADOWCHASER

(Prism, 1992) **D/P:** John Eyres **S:** Stephen
Lister **P:** George Griffiths

Martin Kove stars as a likable former football star kept frozen in a prison. He's thawed out and is forced to become a reluctant hero battling terrorists who have taken over a hospital. He also has to rescue the president's daughter (Meg Foster). This *Die Hard* copy has lots of stunts and one excellent flaming-man-falling-off-a-building scene. Frank Zagarino is a muscular blond android, Paul Koslo is an FBI agent, and Joss Ackland is the android's creator. It was filmed in British Columbia and at the Pinewood studios in England by the director of *Goodnight, God Bless*. *Night Siege: Project Shadowchaser 2* (1995) followed.

PROJECT VAMPIRE

(AIP, 1992) **D/S:** Peter Flynn
P: Darew Hicks, Simon Tams

An Austrian vampire leader and his blond partner have their cartoonish henchmen stick people in LA with syringes containing "superserum" as part of "Project Alpha." A Chinese computer-whiz doctor tries to help a runaway teen (Brian Knudson) and his new nurse-turned-vampire girlfriend (Mary-Louise Gemmick), and other vampires fight each other. This dull movie is padded with endless car and foot chases.

PROJECT X

(CBS/Fox, 1987) **D:** Jonathan Kaplan **S:** Stanley
Weiser, Lawrence Lasker **P:** Walter F. Parkes

Matthew Broderick works at the top-secret Strategic Weapons Research Center, where chimps are tested in flight simulations. Soon he takes a strong animal-rights stance. This PG film features Helen Hunt, Bill Sadler, Dick Miller, and many talented chimps.

PROM NIGHT III: THE LAST KISS

(IVE, 1988) **D/S:** Ron Oliver **D/P:** Peter
Simpson **P:** Ray Sager   Canada

Prom Night (1980) is a disco *Halloween* copy, with Jamie Lee Curtis, filmed in Canada. In 1987 some producers got the rights to the name and made *Hello, Mary Lou: Prom Night II*. In an attempt to create a female Freddy Krueger they also made this totally useless second sequel, a stupid teen/horror comedy with no gore and no nudity (except for one guy). Worst of all, after the dumb trailers on the tape, you have to sit through an anti-drug spot! Mary Lou (Courtney Taylor), whose face is partially mutilated (sometimes) from the 1957 fire she died in, escapes from Hell (filled with dancing girls in chains) with a nail file and terrorizes Hamilton High again. She has (offscreen) sex with a surprised student named Adam (Tim Conlon), helps him make a touchdown, kills teachers and a janitor, and makes the principal cut his finger off. Adam buries all of the bodies under the football field and tries to explain things to his girlfriend (Cyndy Preston). It was filmed in Toronto. *Prom Night IV* followed.

PROM NIGHT IV: DELIVER US FROM EVIL

(IVE, 1991) **D:** Clay Boris **S:** Richard
Beattie **P/A:** Ray Sager   Canada

A killer monk is kept in a monastery cell starting in 1957. In 1991 he escapes, looking the same but with a beard and ponytail. For some reason he terrorizes four teens in a remote house. Characters walk on glass barefoot and are crucified, and there's a shower-sex scene. This terrible sequel is by the director of *Quiet Cool*. Producer Ray Sager was an actor in Herschell Gordon Lewis movies and starred in *The Wizard of Gore*!

THE PROPHECY

(1994) **D/S:** Gregory Widen **P:** Joel Soisson

Christopher Walken is Gabriel, an angel who creates an army of damned souls, and Eric Stoltz is a good angel. With Adam Goldberg (*Dazed and Confused*), Elias Koteas, Virginia Madsen, Viggo Mortensen, and Amanda Plummer. Most of this fantasy was shot in Arizona. It was directed by the writer of *Backdraft* and *Highlander*.

PROSPERO'S BOOKS

(Video Treasures, 1991) **D/S:** Peter Greenaway
P: Kees Kanander   UK/Netherlands

John Gielgud is Prospero, a deposed duke on a desert island with his daughter, Miranda (Isabelle Pasco). This 128-minute anarchist fantasy is a version of Shakespeare's *The Tempest*. The title refers to the fact that Prospero owns 24 magic books. With Michael Clark, Michel Blanc, Tom Bell, Mark Rylance, and Erland Josephson. It features lots of nudity and was filmed in studios in Amsterdam.

PROSTITUTES PROTECTIVE SOCIETY

(SW, 1965) **D/S/P/C:** Barry Mahon   *(P.P.S.)*

Madame Sue narrates (with a strong European accent) and explains how many of her "Times Square" girls were stabbed, strangled, shot, and hanged by the Cosa Nostra just for being independent. She explains that "the local newspapers were having a tea party." When not being killed (offscreen) Sue's girls (one is black) take showers (alone or together), sunbathe naked, and play the piano topless. The main gangster goes on rides (alone) at the 1964 World's Fair and *Girl Happy* is on a marquee. The acting is awful, but the instrumental music by Vinnie Rogers and the Rockets is rockin' ("The Swim" is repeated over and over), the women look good, and the revenge ending is memorable. It's in b/w and only 62 minutes.

THE PROTECTOR

(Warner, 1985) **D/S:** James Glickenhaus
P: David Chan   US/Hong Kong

Jackie Chan, in his second US production, is a cop who battles punks in the South Bronx, then goes to Hong Kong on a case with Danny Aiello. There are some great action sequences and some funny parts. A villain falls down a neon sign (like in James Glickenhaus' *Shakedown*), there's a rotary-saw attack, and lots of naked women work in a drug factory. With Bill "Superfoot" Wallace. The soundtrack is on EAS.

PROTOTYPE

(King Bee, 1983) **D:** David Greene **S:** Richard
Levinson, William Link **P:** Robert A. Papazian

Christopher Plummer is a Nobel Prize scientist who steals his own humanoid creation (David Morse) from the Pentagon. This CBS-TV movie also features Frances Sternhagen and Arthur Hill.

PROTOTYPE X29A

(Vidmark, 1992) **D/S/P:** Phillip J. Roth
P: Gian-Carlo Scandiuzzi

Lots of this takes place on a computer screen (a gimmick that's getting way overused), but it's one of the better recent post-nuke movies. The setting is dreary, hopeless, and sweaty. A scientist (Brenda Swanson) convinces a guy in a wheelchair (Robert Tossberg) to be reborn as a very impressive (*Robocop*-copy) cyborg. A hooker (Lane Lenhart) who lives with her little "brother" (played by the producer's son) discovers that she's really "Omega." A tough guy with hair extensions and an Oriental sidekick snap people's necks. It doesn't make all that much sense, but it just looks impressive and has a nasty edge. Phillip J. Roth also made *Red Snow* (1991) and *Apex*.

PROVOKED

(Raedon, 1989) **D/P:** Rick Pamplin **S:** Steve Pake, Tara
Untiedt **P:** Anthony Bozanich, Dennis Donovan

A multiracial group of three guys escape from a road gang with a black "big mama" as their leader. They pick up another killer (Joel Van Ornsteiner), botch a holdup, and keep hostages in a building. Cindy Maranne (*Slash Dance*) tries to help but is arrested herself. There's slow-motion shooting, flashbacks, daydreams, rape, nudity, and a girl fight. At least the music is good.

PSYCHEDELIC FEVER: *See* MANTIS IN LACE

THE PSYCHIC

(SW, 1968) **D/S/P:** James F. Hurley **D:** Herschell Gordon Lewis   (*Copenhagen's Psychic Loves*)

Dan Thomas (Dick Genola), a suburban advertising executive, somehow acquires psychic powers (like in *The Dead Zone*). He starts a nightclub act with a blond dancer (Robin Guest) and is a guest on the Jerry Larsen TV talk show in NYC, where he "outs" people and eventually ruins his own life. Herschell Gordon Lewis was the cinematographer and added narrated sex flashbacks to liven up this talk-filled movie (it received an early X rating). Dan, with different sideburns, has sex with his sister-in-law while another woman sucks on a lollipop and a b/w lesbian couple are seen in action. There's a sappy theme song, a Mexican band, very bad-taste colors, and tacky 60s suburban-Chicago living rooms. It's by the guy who wrote Lewis' *Something Weird.*

THE PSYCHIC

(Vidmark, 1991) **D:** George Mihalka **S:** Miguel Tejada-Flores, Paul Korval **P:** Tom Berry   Canada

Zach Galligan is a college student who has psychic premonitions of serial murders. The cops arrest him instead of the real killer, a police psychiatrist (Michael Nouri). Catherine Mary Stewart is involved with both men and doesn't know what to think. This better-than-average serial-killer movie has good flashforwards and a few effective jolts. It all takes place around Christmastime and ends at a lodge in the snow. George Mihalka also directed the interesting *Eternal Evil*. It debuted on the USA Network.

PSYCHO II

(MCA, 1983) **D:** Richard Franklin **S:** Tom Holland **P:** Hilton A. Green

Norman (Anthony Perkins) is rehabilitated and released from the asylum after 22 years. He goes back to the Bates Motel, but he receives notes and calls from his mother, and people start to die again. Vera Miles returns as the sister from *Psycho,* and a homeless girl (Meg Tilly) stays at the motel. The killer is a surprise (maybe), the ending is full of plot twists that subvert the original story, and they resort to using clips from *Psycho.* Still, it's better than expected. With Robert Loggia as Norman's parole

Anthony Perkins in *Psycho IV.*

officer, Dennis Franz, and Hugh Gillin. The Jerry Goldsmith score (which uses Bernard Herrmann's original theme) is on MCA.

PSYCHO III

(MCA, 1986) **D/A:** Anthony Perkins **S:** Charles Edward Pogue **P:** Hilton A. Green

This time Norman is in love with a suicidal nun (Diana Scarwid) who sees visions. Anthony Perkins' movie is filled with in-jokes (and a *Vertigo*-influenced opening), and the studio added more blood. The cast also includes Jeff Fahey as a rock musician, future director Katt Shea as a victim, Juliette Cummins, and Hugh Gillin. Scarwid's body double was Brinke Stevens. There are flashbacks to the original. The Carter Burwell score is on MCA. In NYC the ceiling of the Murray Hill theater collapsed on the audience during a screening. After this sequel was released NBC-TV aired *Bates Motel* (1987), a feature-length pilot with Bud Cort as the new owner.

PSYCHO IV: THE BEGINNING

(MCA, 1990) **D:** Mick Garris **S:** Joseph Stephano **P:** George Zaloom, Les Mayfield

Norman (Anthony Perkins) is married, and his wife is expecting. He calls a radio talk show, and multiple flashbacks reveal his childhood days. Henry (*E.T.*) Thomas is the young Norman and Olivia Hussey is his sexy, demented mom. With Donna Mitchell, CCH Pounder, and John Landis in a cameo appearance. Joseph Stephano also scripted the Hitchcock original. Parts of the original Bernard Herrmann score are used. This debuted on Showtime.

PSYCHO COP

(Southgate, 1989) **D/S:** Wallace Potts **P:** Jessica Rains

After *Maniac Cop* came this obscurity about a wisecracking, devil-worshipping ex-cop called Officer Joe Vickers (Bobby Ray Shafer) who kills three teen couples at a mansion in the woods. With Jeff Quayle. It's presented by Cassian Elwes.

PSYCHO COP II

(Columbia, 1992) **D/A:** "Rif Coogan"/Adam Rifkin **S:** Dan Povenmire **P:** David M. Andriole

Bobby Ray Shafer returns, laughing and making jokes as he kills off a bunch of guys and the strippers they hired for an after-hours bachelor party at the office. It's pretty mindless, even with the scene that comments on the Rodney King beating. Barbara Lee Alexander costars as a beautiful blonde who is working late, with Miles David Dougal as a nervous guy and Julie Strain. It's by the director of *The Invisible Maniac* and (using his real name) *The Dark Backwards.* Cassian Elwes was the executive producer.

PSYCHO FROM TEXAS

(Paragon, 1974) **D/S/P:** Jim Feazall   (*The Butcher*)

John King III is Wheeler, a psycho killer who was abused as a child by his mom. He's involved in a kidnap scheme, and there's a long chase scene.

PSYCHOTRONIC HALL OF FAME

These important actors all died during the first few years of *Psychotronic Video* magazine. I wanted to run interviews with all of them.

1. John Carradine
2. Klaus Kinski
3. Vincent Price

4. Anthony Perkins
5. Peter Cushing
6. Cameron Mitchell
7. Donald Pleasence
8. Aldo Ray
9. Joseph Cotten
10. José Ferrer

Linnea Quigley is a barmaid who is forced to strip and dance. The video box features Charles Manson's eyes.

PSYCHO GIRLS

(MGM/UA, 1984) **D/S:** Gerard Ciccoritti
S/P: Michael Bockner   Canada

This is pretty warped. It's narrated by a would-be scriptwriter typing lines like "What is money anyway but paper with germs on it?" His story is about a woman who's been in an asylum since she was a child for killing her parents by putting rat poison in pancakes (!). She escapes to terrorize her sister, and in a shocking sequence she and two sadistic, laughing maniacs kill people during a dinner party. The sex and violence are off screen but still intense. The director shows up as a pizza-delivery boy. A character is shown reading *The Gore Gazette*. With Silvio Oliviero and Helen Papas. Cannon released the feature which was shot in Toronto. The director made *Graveyard Shift* next.

PSYCHOS IN LOVE

(Wizard, 1986) **D/S/P:** Gorman Bechard
S/A: Carmine Capobianco

A lot of people seem to hate this movie, probably because the stars talk to the camera, and it goes out of its way to remind you it's just a movie. Unlike some other features, revealing a microphone or the film crew is done on purpose. It was made in Waterbury, Connecticut, by a 27-year-old director for $75,000. It's about a bearded, balding strip-club owner (Carmine Capobianco) and a manicurist (Debi Thibeault, who sort of resembles Molly Ringwald). Both are likable serial killers who find happiness offing people and watching horror sequels together until a psychotic cannibal plumber shows up. Some ideas probably came from *The Hollywood Strangler Meets the Skid Row Slasher* (1979) and *Eating Raoul* (1982), but this is different. It's got flashbacks, b/w parts, narration, in-jokes, gore humor, a dumb comic love song, lots of blood, and lots of topless scenes (one features Ruth Collins). I liked it, but it's way too long. Bechard made *Galactic Gigolo* and *Cemetery High* after this.

PSYCHO SISTERS

(Prism, 1972) **D:** Reginald LeBorg **S:** Tony Crechales **P:** Sydney Chaplin, Robert J. Stone   (*The Sibling; So Evil My Sister*)

Millie (Faith Domergue) is a former mental patient living in a Monterey beach house. Her visiting sister, Brenda (Susan Strasberg), has embezzled her money and taken her supposedly dead husband (Sydney "son of Charlie" Chaplin). Brenda drugs Millie so that she'll have 60s-style nightmares and hallucinations featuring her husband in a death mask, rats, snakes, voodoo, and a goat-headed demon. The last film by the Austrian-born director has some great grade-Z-movie touches (like a retarded, clubfooted, axe-murdering handyman). Charles Knox Robinson is a cop who surfs, Kathleen Freeman is a maid, and John Howard is a doctor. William Tuttle did the FX. It was released (rated PG) by Joseph Brenner.

PSYCHOTIC: *See* THE DRIVER'S SEAT

PUBLIC DOMAIN

Any film that is not currently copyrighted is considered public domain. Thousands of pre-60s features have lapsed into public domain over the years and can be released on video by anybody. Some features from as recently as the 70s are public domain and many features made by major studios and by major directors (like Hitchcock for instance) fall into this legal category. A whole cottage industry exists selling copies of these movies.

PUCKER UP AND BARK LIKE A DOG

(Fries, 1986) **D:** Paul S. Parco **S:** Gary Larrimore, Mel Green, Jude Jansen **P:** Jeff Geoffrey   (*Tips*)

An LA artist (Jonathan Gries) falls for a waitress and aspiring actress (Lisa Zane), in this story about the film business. Many name actors have small roles. With Wendy O. Williams as a biker named Butch, Paul Bartel as a B-movie director making a women-in-prison movie, Nicholas Worth as a gay chef, Robert Culp as an art dealer, and Phyllis Diller.

PULP FICTION

(Buena Vista, 1994) **D/S/A:** Quentin Tarantino
P: Lawrence Bender

Tarantino's second film as a director is a prize-winning hit that amazes and impresses nearly everyone who sees it. It received even more attention when some audience members reportedly suffered heart attacks. It manages to mix some great acting, lots of drug use, violence (mostly off-screen), humor, rock and roll, surprise plot twists, and clever references to a number of classic older movies. Samuel L. Jackson and long-haired John Travolta star as hitmen who show up in several interwoven crime stories. Uma Thurman is the wife of their boss (Ving Rhames). Bruce Willis is a boxer with a French girlfriend (Maria De Medeiros). Tim Roth and Amanda Plummer hold up a coffee shop. Also with Harvey Keitel as Wolf, Eric Stoltz as a drug dealer, Rosanna Arquette, Steve Buscemi, Peter Greene, and Christopher Walken as a soldier in a flashback. The Jack Rabbit Slims restaurant is a set. The MCA soundtrack features great 60s surf instumentals, other choice oldies, and a hit remake of Neil Diamond's "Girl, You'll Be a Woman Soon" by Urge Overkill. It was nominated for seven Oscars but only won for screenwriting. From Miramax.

PULSE

(RCA/Columbia, 1988) **D/S:** Paul Golding
P: Patricia A. Stallone

Electricity in their house menaces a family. The son (Joey Lawrence) is the first to realize there's an alien force, and nobody believes him. Cliff De Young and Roxanne Hart are his parents. With Richard Romanus and Myron Healey.

THE PUMA MAN

(Parade, 1979) **D:** Alberto De Martino
S: Massimo De Rita, Luigi Angelo   Italy

A South American Indian (a descendant of aliens) instructs the American hero how to use a magic mask. Soon he wears a cape, can go through walls, and has "the power of a man-god." Walter George Alton stars, with Donald Pleasence as Coberus, a mesmerizing monk, and Sydne Rome (from Akron). It was filmed in English and has some of the worst FX (and costumes) in memory.

PUMPING IRON

(Rhino, 1977) **D/P:** George Butler
D/C: Robert Fiore **P:** Jeremy Gary

Arnold Schwarzenegger and Lou Ferrigno are the main attractions in this documentary about body-building, which also features Franco Columbo. Arnold, who is seen training for his sixth Mr. Olympia title, started his acting career in *Hercules in New York* (1970) and was in *The Long Goodbye* (1973) and *Stay Hungry* (1976). The year this was released he posed in *Cosmopolitan* magazine. George Butler made a sequel, *Pumping Iron II: The Women* (1985), and *In the Blood* (1989), about hunting.

PUMPKINHEAD

(MGM/UA, 1987) **D:** Stan Winston **S:** Mark Patrick Carducci, Gary Cerani **P:** Richard C. Weinman, Howard Smith

A backwoods dad (Lance Henriksen) goes to a witch woman and uses a curse after his son is killed by vacationing teens on motorcycles. A tall creature shows up, kills them, and begins to resemble the dad. This movie is dark, smoky, and dreary, but the creature (Tom Woodruff Jr. inside the suit he designed) is pretty great and resembles Ray Harryhausen's Ymir in *Twenty Million Miles to Earth*. Stan Winston is the FX expert responsible for the wonders in *The Thing, The Terminator,* and *Alien*. With Jeff East, John DiAquino, and George "Buck" Flower. *Pumpkinhead* was made for DEG and released several years late. A series of comic books and a sequel followed.

PUMPKINHEAD 2

(Live, 1993) **D:** Jeff Burr **S:** Steve Mitchell, Craig Van Sickle **P:** Brad Krevoy, Steve Staber   (*Blood Wing*)

In b/w flashback scenes a pathetic, deformed "feral boy" (the son of Pumpkinhead) is tortured and killed by Arkansas teens in 1958. Troublemaking modern-day teens bring back his spirit, and hateful older locals are killed (to country-music songs) in the Stephen King–like plot. Ami Dolenz stars as the daughter of the new sheriff (Andrew Robinson). With the return of Gloria Henry (*Live and Let Die*) as the coroner, Steve Kanaly as a corrupt judge, and Roger Clinton (Bill Clinton's brother) as Major Bubba: "This thing could put us on the map." Soleil Moon Frye is skewered, and Linnea Quigley has a major freak-out scene. KNB did the FX, including a gory decapitation. Kane Hodder (*Jason*) and R. A. Mihailoff (*Leatherface*) are the stuntmen. You know that our president had to watch this to check out his brother.

PUMP UP THE VOLUME

(RCA, 1990) **D/S:** Allan Moyle
P: Rupert Harvey, Sandy Stern

Christian Slater, a shy new student in Arizona, becomes a secret pirate DJ called Hard Harry. His out-of-it father is the new school superintendent. Harry plays music and takes calls from bored and suicidal kids. His uncensored basement broadcasts are the talk of the school, and the authorities try to shut him down. Samantha Mathis discovers who he is, they make out on the lawn, and a mild student revolution occurs. Ellen Greene is an understanding teacher, and Annie Ross is the horrible principal. With Scott Paulin, Cheryl Pollak, and Ahmet Zappa. The (old and current) music is good, but some of the songs are remakes. This and *Heathers* would make a good Slater double bill.

THE PUNISHER

(IVE, 1989) **D:** Mark Goldblatt **S:** Boaz
Yakin **P:** Robert Kamen   Australia

Dolph Lungren stars as ex-cop Frank Castle, in this Marvel-comics adaptation made in Sydney. Castle (thought to be dead) wages a nonstop one-man war against all gangsters and especially mob boss Jeroen Krabbe (*The Fourth Man*), who killed his family. The dark-haired, unshaven hero wears all black, rides a Harley, and meditates naked in his hidden sewer home. He kills by hanging, impalement, martial arts, shooting (with a giant machine gun), and general slaughter, but he has a soft spot for kids. Louis Gossett Jr. is pretty much wasted as his ex-partner. A yakuza gang led by the torturing dragon lady Lady Tanaka (Kim Miyori) kidnaps the kids of the Italian gangsters and sells them. The Australian locations don't really resemble America, and some of the local accents get in the way, but this relentless, violent action movie from New World deserved a theatrical release. The Japanese laserdisc is uncut.

THE PUNK ROCK MOVIE

(Rhino, 1978) **D/C:** Don Letts **P:** Peter Clifton   UK

This film consists of 8mm footage (mostly from the Roxy, a club in London) blown up to 35mm. It was released to some theaters (it played Cleveland!). The best bands here are (of course) the Sex Pistols (they do four songs), Johnny Thunders and the Heartbreakers ("Born to Lose" and "Chinese Rocks"), and Siouxsie and the Banshees ("Carcass"). We also get to see the Clash, X-Ray Spex (it's hard to see Poly), and Generation X. The singer for Eater smashes a pig's head onstage while

singing "You Got No Brains." I could have done without Slaughter and the Dogs and Jayne County. Some groups (Slits, Subway Sect) are just seen practicing. It's surprising how young and normal-looking most of the bands are. I wonder what Slaughter is doing these days. I found this for less than $3 at a Woolworth's going-out-of-business sale.

PUPPETMASTER

(Paramount, 1989) **D/S:** David Schmoeller
S: Joseph G. Collodi **P:** Hope Perello

André Toulan (William Hickey) kills himself in 1939 to keep his creations from the Nazis. Psychics at a Bodega Bay, California, hotel 50 years later are terrorized by five of his living puppets after Jimmie F. Scaggs brings them back to life. They're Pin Head, Tunneler, Jester, Blade (a skeleton with razor hands), and Leech Woman (a puppet with leeches that come out of her mouth). With Paul Le Mat, Irene Miracle, Kathryn O'Reilly, and Barbara Crampton. It's similar in some ways to *Dolls* (also from producer Charles Band). David Allen created the animated little killers for the entire series.

PUPPET MASTER II

(Paramount, 1990) **D:** David Allen **S:** David Fabian
P: David DeCoteau, John Schouweiler

When four more young psychic researchers arrive at the Bodega Bay hotel the same puppets attack, plus Torch, a new one. Steve Welles is Toulon (bandaged so that you can't tell it's a different actor), brought back by his creations, who need human brain fluid to live. The puppets are fun but are not really used well. With Elizabeth MacLellan, Collin Bernsen, Charlie Spradling, Nita Talbot, and George "Buck" Flower. At the end Charles Band promises more sequels, comic books, and merchandise tie-ins. The Moonstone soundtrack by Richard Band also features music from the first film in the series. David Allen did the FX.

PUPPET MASTER III: TOULON'S REVENGE

(Paramount, 1991) **D/P:** David DeCoteau
S: C. Courtney Joyner **P:** John Schouweiler

In this "prequel" Toulon (this time played by Guy Rolfe) is in Germany in the 30s. His wife is killed by the Gestapo, and Nazi scientists try to use his

Prince in Purple Rain.

secret formula to reanimate corpses to use as soldiers. He disguises himself as a blind man, hides out in an abandoned building with a helpful kid (Sean Ryan), and sends his five killer puppets (the 6-armed cowboy puppet is the silliest one) after the Nazis, led by Richard Lynch as Major Kraus. Old Universal sets were used for the town. Also with Ian Abercrombie, Sarah Douglas, Conrad Brooks, and Michelle Bauer in a brief sex scene.

PUPPET MASTER IV

(Paramount, 1993) **D:** Jeff Burr **S:** Todd Henschell, Steven E. Carr, Jo Duffy, Doug Arniokoski, Keith Payson **P:** Charles Band

Once kind of fun, the killer puppets are good guys now, and it took five people to write this useless sequel. A young scientist (Gordon Currie) who tests small robots invites three teens to a mansion. Meanwhile a glowing-eyed, skull-faced creature watches from the underworld. A new robot with changeable heads was left over from an unproduced Charles Band film (*Decapitron*). With Chandra West, Jason Adams, Teresa Hill, and the voice (and head) of Guy Rolfe. This was filmed back to back with V.

PUPPET MASTER V: THE FINAL CHAPTER

(Paramount, 1994) **D:** Jeff Burr **S:** Todd Henschell, Steven E. Carr **P:** Charles Band

The scientist (Gordon Currie) who controls the now good puppets and his girlfriend (Chandra West) return. Ian Ogilvy hires three young punks to go to a hotel to capture the puppets. There's an evil puppet, a long flashback, and a dream sequence. With Duane Whitaker, Clu Gulager, Teresa Hill, Nicholas Guest, Diane McBain, Kaz Garas, and the head of Guy Rolfe. The director (from Aurora, Ohio) became king of the sequels.

THE PUPPET MASTERS: *See* ROBERT A. HEINLEIN'S THE PUPPETMASTERS

PURGATORY

(New Star, 1989) **D/P:** Ami Artz **S:** Felix Kroll, Paul Aratow   South Africa

The ads said that this was about "the women's prison that's one step from hell!" Tanya Roberts stars as a Peace Corps worker in South America who's locked up on a phony drug charge. The female prisoners double as prostitutes. Her friend kills herself after being gang-raped. Tanya weeps, pukes, and finally leads a rebellion and escapes. Most of the sex and violence is offscreen.

THE PURPLE MONSTER STRIKES

(Republic, 1945) **D:** Spencer Gordon Bennet, Fred Brannon **S:** Royal Cole, Albert De Mond

Roy Barcroft as Mota and Mary Moore are medieval/futuristic-look Martians who land their spaceship on Earth, in this 15-chapter Republic serial. Mota becomes invisible and can take over the bodies of the Earthlings he kills, but he follows orders given by the emperor of Mars (John Davidson). Dennis Moore and Linda Stirling save the day. The condensed feature version is called *D-Day on Mars.*

PURPLE PEOPLE EATER

(Media, 1988) **D/S:** Linda Shayne **P:** Brad Krevoy

A kid (Neil Patrick "Doogie Hauser" Harris) plays Sheb Wooley's 1958 hit record and releases a very cheap and silly-looking friendly creature. Old folks (Ned Beatty and Shelley Winters) are being evicted (an idea copied from Steven Spielberg's *batteries not included*). With Peggy Lipton, Sheb Wooley, Chubby Checker as himself, and Little Richard as the mayor. This G-rated Concorde release was directed by the blonde actress from *Humanoids from the Deep, Screwballs,* and others. AJK released the mostly-oldies soundtrack.

PURPLE RAIN

(Warner, 1984) **D/S:** Albert Magnoli **S:** William Blinn **P:** Robert Cavaol, Joesph Ruffalo, Steven Fargnoli

The 24-year-old Prince (who had done the music for *J.D.'s Revenge* in 1976) is "the Kid." This semi-autobiographical hit movie, made in Minneapolis, has great songs and many stage-show segments. Apollonia (Patricia Kotero) costars, with Morris Day (who leads the rival band, the Time), Clarence Williams III as the alcoholic father, and Jerome Benton. Apollonia had posed for MPM ads for movies like *Satan's Playthings, Classroom Teasers,* and *Tricks of the Trade.*

THE PUSHER

(Shocktunes, 1958) **D:** Gene Milford **S:** Harold Robbins **P:** Gene Milford, Sidney Katz

This serious, b/w drug movie resembles the then-popular TV series *The Naked City.* It was shot in actual NYC locations, including Spanish Harlem and Central Park. A gum-chewing police detective (Robert Lansing) is investigating the hanging of a Puerto Rican junkie. He's engaged to the blond daughter (Kathy Caryse) of the lieutenant, and she turns out to be a junkie herself. She has a cold-turkey sequence: "Get me a fix!" The killer heroin pusher is named Gonzo. John Astin makes his film debut in one scene as a detective. United Artists released this in 1960.

PUSS BUCKET

(1991) **D/C:** Lisa Houle

Two long-haired brothers ("ignorant humanoids") are affected by a (toy) spaceship that hovers over their house. One brother dreams that he's Christ and goes out to kill "demons." A scientist dances and sings about UFOs. There's a cat fight (in the Scrap bar), a gorilla suit, and a Dianetics guy in drag. This fun but too-long science-fiction musical was shot in grainy b/w Super 8. The music is very good.

PUSS IN BOOTS

(Rhino, 1955) **D:** Herbert B. Fredersdorf **P:** Hubert Schonger   W. Germany (*Der Gestiefelter Kater*)

In this color film based on the famous fairy tale, three brothers (with weird hair) live in a mill. One inherits the mill, one gets the donkey, and the other gets a female cat who talks and sings. Of course the cat (a person in a suit who runs upright) helps battle an evil magician, and his owner becomes a duke and gets the princess. AIP released this West German feature (and a 1961 Mexican version of the same tale). Paul Tripp narrates. Young kids may enjoy it. Christopher Walken stars in *Puss in Boots* (1989), from *Faerie Tale Theatre,* with Ben Vereen and Gregory Hines.

PUTNEY SWOPE

(RCA, 1969) **D/S:** Robert Downey **P:** Ron Sullivan

A black man (Arnold Johnson) becomes chairman of an advertising agency and renames it "Truth and Soul." This satire (in color) includes great TV-ad spoofs in b/w. Also with Allen Garfield, Antonio Fargas, and Mel Brooks. A song in one ad says, "Eat flaming death, facist media pigs!" Robert Downey said that he looped the stars' lines.

THE PUZZLE OF THE RED ORCHID

(1961) **D:** Helmut Ashley **S:** Trygve Larsen W. Germany (*Das Rätsel der Roten Orchidee*)

Marisa Mell and Adrian Hoven star with Christopher Lee as Captain Allerman and Klaus Kinski in this prime Edgar Wallace mystery. Also with Fritz Rasp, once a regular in Fritz Lang films. You may have caught this on American TV as *The Secret of the Red Orchid.* The same story was remade in England as *The Verdict* (1964).

PYTHON WOLF

(Vidmark, 1988) **D:** William Friedkin **S:** Robert Ward **P:** David Salvern   (*C.A.T. Squad: Python Wolf*)

A private South African army makes an A-bomb. Joe Cortese stars as the leader of a government anti-terrorist unit. This NBC-TV series pilot is a sequel to a 1986 pilot, *Stalking Danger.* With Jack Youngblood, Steve James, Deborah Van Valkenburgh, and Miguel Ferrer.

QUADROPHENIA

(Rhino, 1979) **D/S:** Franc Roddam **S:** Dave Humphries, Martin Stellman **P:** Roy Baird   UK

Back in 1973 the Who recorded *Quadrophenia*, a much better "rock opera" than *Tommy* and possibly their greatest achievement. They should have broken up then and stayed that way, but at least that double album inspired this excellent 2-hour film starring Phil Daniels as James Michael, or Jimmy, the tortured and ill-fated 1964 "mod." His scooter, his clothes (and his speed) are as important to him as the great music, which is partly re-recorded versions of the original Who album plus choice original oldies (including "Green Onions," "Night Train," and "Louie Louie"). After he loses his job, his scooter, his girlfriend, and his home he heads for the seacoast town of Brighton. With Leslie Ash, Sting as Ace, Mark Wingett, Philip Davis, and Toyah Wilcox. The soundtrack is on Polydor.

THE QUAKE

(Concorde, 1992) **D:** Mike Elliot **S:** Markevan Schwartz **P:** Louis Morneau   (*Aftershock*)

The 1989 San Fransisco earthquake hits while *Attack of the Crab Monsters* is on TV. Erika Anderson is a defense attorney who is rescued by a photographer and surveillance expert (Steve Railsback) she knows from work. He turns out to be a scary, obsessed, voyeur and psycho killer who ties her up and keeps her captive. This is a pretty good, sick exploitation movie. Railsback makes a great psycho, and Anderson (*Zanda Lee*) has nude scenes. Roger Corman had some good footage of the actual quake, and that's mixed with some (very good) miniatures (from the Japanese *Tidal Wave*). With Eb Lottimer, Rick Dean, and Dick Miller as a store owner. It's by the director of *Fatal Games*.

QUANTUM LEAP

(MCA, 1989) **D:** David Hemmings **S:** Donald P. Bellisario **P:** Deborah Pratt, John Hill

Scott Bakula stars as Sam, a guy who enters the body of someone from a different era in each episode of this NBC-TV series, and sometimes alters (or fixes) history (shades of the early-80s TV series *Voyagers*). In this feature-length debut for the 1989–93 series he becomes a test pilot in 1956. With Jennifer Runyon and Bruce McGill. Series co-star Dean Stockwell is Al, a helpful hologram. The series was sometimes humorous science-fiction with a positive message but was often pretty silly. Bakula was in drag several times and once appeared as Lee Harvey Oswald! There are 48-minute videos of later episodes.

QUARANTINE

(Republic, 1989) **D/S/P:** Charles Wilkinson   Canada

In "the near future" a senator puts people with a deadly disease and those who have been caring for them into concentration camps. A supercomputer works to find a cure. With Beatrice Boepple and Garwin Sanford.

QUATERMASS AND THE PIT

(Sinister, 1958) **D:** Rudolph Carter **S:** Nigel Kneale   UK

This 6-part BBC-TV series (running 3 hours on 2 tapes) is the second appearance of Nigel Kneale's Professor Quatermass (the first was a 1953 series). It was very popular in England and led to the filming of Hammer's first international hit, *The Quatermass Experiment* (called *The Creeping Unknown* in the US; from Sinister), the same year. It was followed by *Quatermass II* (called *The Enemy Within* in the US; from Corinth). *Quatermass and the Pit* was itself redone as an excellent film in 1967 (called *Five Million Years to Earth* in the US). It all came full circle and went back to the telly in 1980 with *The Quatermass Conclusion* (HBO; available in a condensed form). This serious science-fiction series is crude-looking compared with the films, of course, but is a fascinating artifact. André Morell stars, with Cec Linder and Anthony Bushell.

QUEEN KONG

(1976) **D/S/P:** Frank Agrama **S:** Ron Dobrin **P:** André Genovese   UK/W. Germany/Italy/France

Yes, this is a real movie, made to cash in on the Dino De Laurentiis remake. He sued, though, and won. It's a comedy about a giant female gorilla who falls for an actor (Robin Askwith) and follows him back to London. With Rula Lenska and Valerie Leon.

THE QUEEN OF BLACK MAGIC

(Twilight Star, 1985) **D:** Lawrence Chen, L. Sudjio **S:** Iman Tamtowi **P:** Sabrin Kasdan   Hong Kong/Indonesia (*Black Magic Terror; Black Magic III*)

A big, traditional wedding ceremony starts off this black-magic/revenge story. The bride freaks out when she sees snakes and zombies. The corrupt husband accuses his ex-girlfriend, Mouri (Suzanna), of being a witch, burns her house, and throws her off a cliff. A magician catches her (!) and trains her. She does slow-motion somersaults in front of a full moon and says, "All men are devils!" She uses voodoo dolls and fireballs, makes heads explode, and sends bees to kill one villager. He sinks into a rice paddy while veins expand and burst and worms come out of his mouth. Characters say, "It's black magic!" every few minutes. Mouri kidnaps the couple's baby. A young Muslim from the city arrives ("This village has a curious aura of mystery!") and soon has everybody praying again. During a fight he pulls his own head off. The head floats through the air and bites people! A flashback provides a surprise ending. It was filmed in Jakarta, Indonesia.

QUEEN OF EVIL = SEIZURE

THE QUEEN OF SPADES

(1948) **D:** Thorold Dickinson **S:** Rodney Ackland, Arthur Boys **P:** Anatole De Grunwald   UK

Some people say that this movie, based on the story "Pique Dame" (or "The Queen of Spades"), by Alexander Pushkin, is the scariest they've ever seen. Too bad it's so hard to find. Anton Walbrook is a Russian officer in 1806 who's obsessed with winning at cards. The grandmother of the woman who loves him has sold her soul to the Devil for the secret of winning. The tale had been made into Russian silent films in 1911 and 1916, and Tchaikovsky's opera *Pique Dame* was filmed in the USSR in 1960. With Edith Evans, Ronald Howard, Mary Jerrold, Yvonne Mitchell, Miles Malleson, Anthony Dawson, and Valentine Dyall.

QUEEN OF THE AMAZONS

(Sinister, 1946) **D/P:** Edward Finney **S:** Roger Merton

Robert Lowery and Patricia Morison lead an expedition into the jungle and find another of those white jungle queens (Amira Moustafa). It's 61 minutes of nonsense from Screen Guild (later Lippert), released the same year as their mind-numbing Bela Lugosi movie *Scared to Death* and several all-black musicals.

QUEEN OF THE JUNGLE

(Sinister, 1935) **D:** Robert Hill **S:** J. Griffith Jay

Mary Kornman (Little Mary of the Little Rascals) stars as a jungle woman who can control leopards, in this 12-chapter serial from Screen Attractions. She starts out as a little girl accidentally cast off in a hot-air balloon. This very silly low-budget independent release uses lots of footage from the Selig serial *Jungle Goddess* (1922), including scenes of a giant stone idol with radium-beam eyes. With Reed Howes and Dickie Jones. There's a fish man and a strangling vine. A feature version is also available.

THE QUEST

(Nelson, 1986) **D:** Brian Trenchard-Smith **S:** Everett De Roche   Australia

Henry Thomas discovers a friendly Loch Ness type of monster in a lake near an Aboriginal burial ground. Thomas was known for being the main kid in *E.T.* and plays a similar role here. The director also made *Dead End Drive-In*.

QUEST FOR FIRE

(Fox, 1981) **D:** Jean-Jacques Annaud **S:** Gérard Brach **P:** John Kemeny, Denis Heroux   Canada/France

The prehistoric Ulam tribe is attacked by apes, cannibals, and wolves. They learn how to laugh and how to make fire, and also some new sexual positions. Novelist Anthony Burgess created the language for this ambitious film by the director of *The Name of the Rose*. It's based on a novel by J. H. Rosny. With Everett McGill, Rae Dawn Chong as a member of a more advanced tribe, Ron Perlman (later in the TV series *Beauty and the Beast*), and Joy Boushel. It was filmed in Canada, Scotland, Iceland, and Kenya. RCA released the soundtrack. The videodisc version is letterboxed. *Caveman*, released the same year, is a comedy on the same theme, with dinosaurs (and fiery farts).

QUEST FOR LOVE

(IVD, 1971) **D:** Ralph Thomas
S: Terence Feeney **P:** Peter Eton   UK

A man (Tom Bell) finds love in another, slightly different dimension where JFK is still alive and nobody has walked on the moon. He has the same name but is a famous playwright. He drinks and everybody thinks he's going crazy. He tries to win back his unfaithful wife (Joan Collins). This parallel-world science fiction movie is based on the story "Random Quest," by John Wyndham. With Denholm Elliott as a one-armed man, Laurence Naismith, and Simon Ward.

QUEST FOR THE LOST CITY

(AIP, 1988) **D/S:** T. Jardus Greidanus **S:** Christian Malcolm, Bruce Mitchell   Canada

A small-town kid (Bruce J. Mitchell) whose father had been killed finds a map to a lost civilization. Silly-looking bad guys with black hoods and machine guns go after him, and a huge UFO shows up at the end. This slow-moving nearly all-male movie is very serious. It's filled with chases and shootouts.

QUEST FOR THE MIGHTY SWORD

(RCA/Columbia, 1989) **D/S:** "David Hills"/ Aristide Massaccesi **P:** Carlo Mario Cardio Italy (*Ator III: The Hobgoblin*)

A big guy (Eric Allen Kramer) is the son of Ator. He's raised by Grindle, a devious dwarf (in a rubber mask) with magical powers who gives a potion to Ator's mother, making her wander aimlessly until somebody buys her. There's a Godzilla-like fire-breathing dragon, "frog men," lots of *Star Wars*–type alien faces, and a lovesick, wart-faced prince who makes sculptures like the ones by Walter Paisley in *A Bucket of Blood*. A pair of ineffective Siamese-twin robot warriors must have been inspired by *The Three Stooges Meet Hercules*. Laura Gemser, who was in the first Ator movie, shows up as an evil princess, and Melissa Mell

turns into a crow. This PG-13 movie has some good music and costumes, but the "action" scenes are laughable, and most of the acting is horrible. The same director also made the previous Ator movies.

QUICK

(Academy, 1993) **D:** Rick King **S:** Frederick Bailey **P:** David Lancaster

Teri Polo stars as Quick, a blond hitwoman in LA. She kills for her corrupt DEA-agent boyfriend (Jeff Fahey), who works for a mobster (Robert Davi) with an office behind a beauty shop. The plot concerns murder and double-crosses. Quick kidnaps a mob accountant (Martin Donovan, from Hal Hartley movies), then goes on the run with him. Tia Carrere is a good federal agent who gets to shoot some bad guys. Polo has a topless scene. The movie contains Kentucky Fried Chicken–eating. It's by the director of *Kickboxer III*.

THE QUICK AND THE DEAD

(MCA, 1995) **D:** Sam Raimi **S:** Simon Moore **P:** Joshua Donen, Allen Shapiro

This goofy western copies Sergio Leone shamelessly (especially *Once Upon a Time in the West*) and adds typical cartoonish Raimi-style violence (like giant bullet holes in heads). It's also extremely gun-obsessed, with many loving closeups of several late 1870s models. Sharon Stone stars as the vengeance-seeking Ellen. Herod (Gene Hackman) owns the corrupt town of Redemption where deadly annual shooting turnaments are held. Some parts of the movie are awkward, but Stone looks great and is fine, playing it very seriously. Russell Crowe (*Romper Stomper*) as the chained-up former gunfighter and Leonard DiCaprio as Hackman's teenage son (and, briefly, Stone's lover) are the best actors. Also with Lance Henrikson as an outrageous gunfighter, Tobin Bell, Roberts Blossom, Keith David, Kevin Conway, Pat Hingle, Gary Sinise, and the last appearance of Woody Strode. The score is by Alan Silvestri.

QUIET COOL

(RCA/Columbia, 1986) **D/S:** Clay Borris
S: Susan Vercellino **P:** Robert Shaye

James Remar is a NYC cop who goes to the Northwest to stop killer pot growers. Adam Coleman Howard, Jared Martin, and Nick Cassavetes are also in this bloody New Line release. The music is by Jay Ferguson of Spirit.

THE QUIET EARTH

(CBS/Fox, 1985) **D:** Geoff Murphy
S/P: Sam Pillsbury **S:** Bill Baer, Bruno Lawrence   New Zealand

The entire population of Earth has been transported to another world. Bruno Lawrence is a scientist who thinks that he's the last survivor on Earth but then meets a woman and a Maori man. It's based on a novel by Craig Harrison. In some ways it's like a better, R-rated version of *The World, the Flesh, and the Devil* (1959) or maybe Roger Corman's *The Last Woman on Earth* (1961).

A QUIET PLACE IN THE COUNTRY

(VSOM, 1968) **D/S:** Elio Petri
S: Luciano Vincenzoni **P:** Alberto Grimaldi   France/Italy (*Un Tranquillo Posto di Campagna*)

Leonardo, a popular artist (Franco Nero), and his mistress, Flavia (Vanessa Redgrave), go to a rented villa. Strange things happen, some of his paintings are damaged, and he decides to hire a medium to contact the ghost of a young woman. Then Leonardo loses his mind and claims to have killed Flavia and put her body in the refrigerator. Ennio Morricone wrote the score. Elio Petri also directed *The Tenth Victim* (1965).

A QUIET PLACE TO KILL

(Unicorn, 1969) **D:** Umberto Lenzi **S:** Marcello Coscia, Bruono De Geronimo   Italy/Spain (*Paranoia*)

Carroll Baker says that she was blacklisted by her studio (Paramount) from 1968 until the early 80s. She worked only in Europe, starring in some pretty sick movies, which she left out of her autobiography. In this one, which has a plot copied from *Diabolique*, she plays a woman who helps her ex-husband (Jean Sorel) cover up the murder of his rich new wife. Baker is a race-car driver who's in a coma at the beginning of the film. The US version of this *giallo* (the Italian word for "yellow," which also refers to a mystery or thriller) is typically cut. It should not be confused with *Paranoia/Orgasmo*, also starring Baker and by the same director, even though they both use the same song, "Just Tell Me."

Bruno Lawrence in *The Quiet Earth*.

RABID GRANNIES

(Media, 1988) **D/S:** Emmanuel Kervyn **P:** James Desert, Jonathan Rambert   Belgium/France

A Satanist turns two wealthy old aunts into *Evil Dead*–type monsters during their birthday party in a mansion. The partygoers are all greedy relatives who want to be in the will. The English accents are dubbed in. Troma released a very cut version of this gory movie for an R rating.

RACE FOR LIFE

(1954) **D:** Terence Fisher **S:** Richard Landau **P:** Mickey Delamar   UK (*Mask of Dust*)

Richard Conte stars as a stock-car racer trying to make a comeback in Europe. With George Coulouris and Mari Aldon. Lippert released a cut version of this Hammer studio drama.

RACQUET

(VCZ, 1979) **D/P:** David Winters **S:** Steve Michaels, Earl Doud **P:** Alan Roberts

Bert Convy stars as a tennis pro in this *Shampoo*-copy comedy with Edie Adams, Lynda Day George, Phil Silvers, Tanya Roberts, Susan Tyrrell, Bruce Kimmel, and Monte Rock III. Tennis pros Bobby Riggs and Bjorn Borg also appear. David Winters made this after he produced *Linda Lovelace for President* (1976).

RADAR MEN FROM THE MOON

(Republic, 1952) **D:** Fred C. Bannon **S:** Ronald Davidson **P:** Franklin Adreon

George Wallace stars as Commodore Cody, sky marshal of the universe, in this 12-chapter Republic serial. He has a cheap-looking rocket ship and a jet-propelled backpack to fly with. His enemy, Retik (Roy Barcroft), wants to take over Earth with his three-man army and atomic gun. The moon men rob Earth banks for funds. With Aline Towne, Clayton Moore, and the usual ace Republic stuntmen. The flying-man footage is from *King of the Rocket Men* (1949). The only thing that looked new at the time were some then modern spacesuits copied from *Destination Moon* (1951). A feature version is called *Retik, the Moon Menace*. A different actor played Cody in *Zombies of the Stratosphere* later the same year. Beware of the Goodtimes video version. It's at LP speed and is missing the last three chapters.

RADAR PATROL VS. SPY KING

(Stokey, 1949) **D:** Fred Brannon **S:** Royal K. Cole, William Lively, Sol Shor **P:** Franklin Adreon

Kirk Alyn (better known as Superman) stars as a federal agent trying to stop Baroda, the sinister "spy king" (John Merton). Baroda uses a mind-control serum and lots of nuclear gadgets. This 12-chapter Republic serial features Jean Dean, John Crawford, Eve Whitney, Eddie Parker, and Tristram Coffin.

RADIOACTIVE DREAMS

(Vestron, 1986) **D/S:** Albert Pyun **P:** Thomas Karnowski

Philip (John Stockwell) and Marlowe (Michael Dudikoff) spend 15 years in a post-nuke bomb shelter reading Raymond Chandler's novels. They emerge in 1996 and encounter disco-mutants, biker women, cannibals, midgets, and big rats. The land is divided into punk and video districts, and rival greaser and hippie groups fight over the keys to the last MX warhead. With Lisa Blount, George Kennedy, Don Murray, and Michelle Little.

RADIO FLYER

(RCA, 1992) **D:** Richard Donner **S:** David Mickey **P:** Lauren Shuler-Donner

Joseph Mazzello and Elijah Wood star as kids with an abusive stepfather. Mazzello flies away on a red wagon in the *E.T.*-type fantasy ending. Tom Hanks is one of the grown-up kids remembering his childhood. A clubhouse becomes a talking buffalo in a dream sequence. With John Heard, Lorraine Bracco, Adam Baldwin as the stepfather, and Ben Johnson. Michael Douglas, the executive producer of this Columbia box-office flop, fired and replaced the entire original cast and director.

RADIO ON

(1979) **D/S:** Chris Petit **S:** Heidi Adolph **P:** Keith Griffiths   UK/W. Germany

A disc jockey (David Beames) returns to his home in Bristol, England, to investigate his brother's death. Lisa Kreuzer costars. Wim Wenders was the associate producer of this angst-ridden road movie. Sting plays "Just Like Eddie," an in-joke that Wenders fans will get. Devo, David Bowie, Kraftwerk, and others are heard on the soundtrack.

RADIO PATROL

(Stokey, 1937) **D:** Ford Beebee, Cliff Smith **S:** Wyndham Gittens, Norman S. Hall, Ray Trampe **P:** Barney Sarecky, Ben Koenig

Grant Withers stars as hero Pat O'Hara in this 12-chapter Universal serial based on a comic strip. International criminals who use hypnotism kill the inventor of a new flexible bulletproof material and take his son. With Frank Lackteen as Thata, Catherine Hughes, Monte Montague, and C. Montague Shaw. Some chapters are "Hypnotic Eye," "Claws of Steel," and "Flaming Death."

RAGE

(1984) **D:** Tonino Ricci **S:** Jaime Comas Gil, Eugenio Benito **P:** Paola Ferrara   Italy/Spain

Musclebound Conrad Nichols returns as ex–Green Beret Rage, in this sequel to *Rush*. He battles an evil post-WWIII warlord named Slash.

RAGE AND HONOR

(Columbia, 1992) **D/S:** Terry S. Winkless **P:** Donald Paul Pemrick

Cynthia Rothrock is a high-school teacher and martial-arts instructor. She teams up with an Aus-

tralian undercover cop (Richard Norton) to battle killer drug dealers (Terri Treas and musclebound Brian Thompson, with long blond hair). Alex Datcher is the black leader of a cartoonish all-female kung-fu gang, Catherine Bach (from the TV series *The Dukes of Hazzard*) is the police chief, and Stephen Davies is a comic-relief junkie. Rothrock and Norton were associate producers of this IRS production.

RAGE AND HONOR II: HOSTILE TAKEOVER

(Columbia, 1992) **D:** Guy Norris **S:** Louis Sun, Steven Reich **P:** Donald Paul Pemrick, Keven Reidy

Cynthia Rothrock and Richard Norton return. This time they're after some corrupt Americans in Jakarta, Indonesia. Patrick Muldoon costars.

A RAGE IN HARLEM

(HBO, 1991) **D:** Bill Duke **S:** John Toles-Bey, Bobby Crawford **P:** Stephen Wooley, Kerry Boyle   UK/US

This crime movie set in 1954 is based on Chester Himes' (*Cotton Comes to Harlem*) novel. It wasn't a hit, but it's a pretty entertaining mixture of humor, sex, and violence. Forest Whitaker is a funeral home accountant involved with a sexy southern thief (Robin Givens) who's after some gold. Gregory Hines is a con man, Zakes Mokae (in drag) is the madam of a whorehouse, Danny Glover is a crime lord, Badja Djola is a crazed Mississippi gangster (he says "Pop goes the weasel" when he wants someone killed), and Screamin' Jay Hawkins shows up as himself, still looking the way he did in the 50s (!). Coffin Ed Johnson and Gravedigger Jones (stars of other Himes novels) are secondary characters. The Miramax release was filmed in Cincinnati. Elmer Bernstein wrote the score. Duke had directed *The Killing Floor* (1984) and *Johnny Gibson: FBI* (1988).

RAGE OF HONOR

(Media, 1987) **D:** Gordon Hessler **S:** Robert Short, Wallace Bennett **P:** Don Van Atta

Sho Kosugi is a US narcotics investigator stationed in Phoenix. He goes to Buenos Aires to avenge the death of his assistant and kills lots of villains, ninjas, and Indians in the jungle. Gordon Hessler also directed Kosugi in *Pray for Death* and other movies.

A RAGE TO KILL

(AIP, 1987) **D/S/P:** David Winters **S:** Ian Yule   S. Africa

James Ryan is Stryker, an American race-car driver in the Caribbean who is taken hostage. Cameron Mitchell is a CIA man, and Oliver Reed is a villainous general who has taken over the island. It's based on the Grenada invasion and features torture and shower scenes.

RAGIN' CAJUN

(AIP, 1987) **D/S/P:** William Byron Hillman **P:** Michelle Marshall   (*Loner*)

David Heavener stars as a kickboxer who has Nam flashbacks, in this martial-arts musical. Charlene

Tilton is his girlfriend, who is kidnapped. Both leads sing, and the multitalented Heavener wrote the songs. Also with Sam Bottoms, Samantha Eggar, Hector Elias, Tommy Roe, Rex Allen Jr., Billy Vera, and Benny "the Jet" Urquidez.

RAIDERS OF ATLANTIS
(Prism, 1983) **D:** "Roger Franklin"/Ruggero Deodato
S: Vincenzo Mannino, Dardano Sacchetti   Italy
(*I Predatori di Atlantide; Atlantis Interceptors*)

An atomic chain reaction causes Atlantis to reappear in the ocean, and its inhabitants kill people. Christopher Connelly and Tony King are mercenaries, and Marie Field is a scientist. With Ivan Rassimov and George Hilton. This confusing *Mad Max*–style movie was filmed in the Philippines and features a decapitation and some other novel deaths.

RAIDERS OF LEYTE GULF
(1963) **D/S/P:** Eddie Romero
S: Karl Kuntze   US/Philippines

Jennings Sturgeon stars as an American WWII intelligence officer captured and tortured by the Japanese in the Philippines. This b/w feature was released by Hemisphere, the company that later backed Romero's *Blood Island* horror movies.

RAIDERS OF THE LIVING DEAD
(1986) **D/S:** Brett Piper **D/S:** Sam Sherman **P:** Dan Q. Kennis

Robert Deveau stars as a newspaper reporter who goes to an island and discovers a mad doctor who creates zombies. With Donna Asali and Zita Johann (Boris Karloff's beloved in the original version of *The Mummy*) as a librarian. Scott Schwartz is the kid star. Brett Piper's movie *Dying Day* (he also did the F/X) was made in New Hampshire in 1983. Sherman bought it and later shot and added much new footage. This paste-up movie came out on video in Europe and made its American debut on Showtime. Tim Ferrante is credited with the music. John Donaldson was an editor.

RAINBOW BRIDGE
(Rhino, 1972) **D:** Chuck Wein **P:** Barry De Prendergast

Surfers, groupies, astrologers, and various New Age types talk about cosmic things at a Maui mansion owned by a man searching for the meaning of life. After 40 minutes Jimi Hendrix finally shows up for a July 30, 1970, concert played between two extinct volcanos. This PG film was made for Warner but released independently by its producers. Reprise released the soundtrack album.

THE RAINBOW THIEF
(Warner, 1990) **D:** Alexandro Jodorowsky
S/A: Berta Dominguez **P:** Vincent Winter   UK

Peter O'Toole is an eccentric prince who walks away from his inheritance and lives in (*Phantom of the Opera*–style) sewers. Omar Sharif is his servant, a thief. Christopher Lee has some great scenes as his equally eccentric rich uncle Rudolph, who prefers his Dalmatians to people, dances, sings (in French), and dies in a bed full of hookers. This was an attempt by Jodorowsky to make a more conventional feature after the success of *Santa Sangre*. It does have many typical Jodorowsky touches, including beautiful circus pipe music, period (1920s) detail, a midget, a giant, and a Gypsy in drag. Some parts were shot in Gdansk, Poland. Two different versions reportedly exist.

THE RAIN KILLER
(RCA/Columbia, 1990) **D:** Ken Stein
S: Ray Cunneff **P:** Rodman Flender

A serial killer (Woody Brown) blacks out and doesn't remember what he's done. He goes after women from a substance-abuse support group but kills only during rainstorms. Ray Sharkey is an LA cop who's after him. Maria Ford is a stripper who becomes one of the victims. This Concorde/Corman release has nudity and sex.

RAISING ARIZONA
(CBS/Fox, 1987) **D/S:** Joel Coen
S/P: Ethan Coen

A small-time holdup man called H. I. (Nicolas Cage, who narrates) and a police mug-shot photographer (Holly Hunter) marry. They want a baby so badly that they steal one, Nathan Arizona Jr., a quintuplet who they figure won't be missed. John Goodman and William Forsythe as ex-cons Gale and Evelle show up to complicate matters. With Trey Wilson, Frances McDormand (from the Coens' *Blood Simple*), Randall "Tex" Cobb as a biker "of the apocalypse," and M. Emmet Walsh in a bit part. The great, all-over-the-place cinematography is by Barry Sonnenfeld. The screenplay of this unique 20th Century–Fox comedy was published. Holly Hunter started out in a horror movie, *The Burning* (1981).

RAISING CAIN
(MCA, 1992) **D/S:** Brian De Palma
P: Gale Ann Hurd

You've really got to like John Lithgow to watch this, because he plays most of the roles. There's also a flashback inside a dream inside a dream and more viewer manipulation than many can handle. A child psychologist and his evil ex-con twin kidnap kids for their sadistic Norwegian psychiatrist father's experiments. They also kill parents and babysitters who get in the way. Lithgow plays both brothers, he's the father, and he "becomes" his own alter egos, a woman, and a kid. After the major flop *The Bonfire of the Vanities,* for which he "apologized," De Palma married producer Gale Ann Hurd (James Cameron's ex-wife) and made this derivative, over-the-top, showoff psycho movie, his first since *Body Double* (1984). There are impressive tracking shots, nightmare sequences, and plenty of *Peeping Tom, Psycho,* and even *Homicidal* cops. Lolita Davidovich and Steven Bauer costar, with Frances Sternhagen as a psychiatrist, Gregg Henry, Mel Harris, Teri Austin, and Barton Heyman. The Pino Donaggio soundtrack is on RCA.

LE RAISONS DE LA MORTE
(VSOM, 1978) **D/S/A:** Jean Rollin
S/A: Jean-Pierre Bouyxou, Christian Meunier **P:** Claude Guedj   France

A woman (Marie-George Pascal) takes a train ride. Her friend is killed by a crazed man, and she wanders into grape country, where people who drink wine become zombies and kill each other. A man kills his (topless) daughter with a pitchfork, and a (topless) woman is crucified and decapitated. I think some men die too. Zombies laugh, cry, and say, "Je t'aime" while killing. Brigitte Lahaie, who lives in the mayor's house and walks two big dogs, appears normal. A couple of guys who shoot zombies are all right because they drank beer! The bits of organ music sound pretty goofy.

Randall "Tex" Cobb in *Raising Arizona.*

RAMAR OF THE JUNGLE
(Video Resources, 1952)

Jon Hall stars as jungle doctor Ramar (or "white medicine man") in this syndicated, low-budget kids' TV series. Hollywood sets stood in for the Kenya jungle, and so much stock footage was used that the makers of *Congorilla* sued. The popular series was also criticized at the time for violence and racism. Three features were made up from episodes. Several of the (26 minute) episodes are on video. Hall, known for his 40s movies with Maria Montez at Universal, killed himself in 1979. His house later became Forrest J. Ackerman's "Ackermansion" museum.

aka *Ramar of the Jungle*

RAMBO: FIRST BLOOD II

(IVE, 1985) **D:** George Pan Cosmatos
S/A: Sylvester Stallone **S:** James Cameron
P: Buzz Feitshans **M:** Jerry Goldsmith

After the failures of *Staying Alive* and *Rhinestone* Sylvester Stallone made this action "prequel" to *First Blood*. It was released on the 10th anniversary of the end of the Vietnam War. President Reagan quoted it, and it made lots of money (much more than the original). It soon became one of the most copied movies of all time. Heavily armed John Rambo rescues America MIAs in Cambodia who have been ignored by their own government. This anti-Communist and anti "do nothing" America movie features lots of explosions and the popular leech torture by evil Russians. With Julia Nickson as a helpful Vietnamese woman, Richard Crenna (returning from *First Blood*), Steven Berkoff, Charles Napier, and Martin Kove. It was filmed in Mexico (where a special-effects man died working on it). This was the high point for Stallone, who was the second-highest-paid person in show business (after Bill Cosby) in 1987. The soundtrack (on Varèse Sarabande) includes Stallone's brother Frank.

RAMBO III

(IVE, 1988) **D:** Peter MacDonald **S/A:** Sylvester Stallone **P:** Buzz Feitshans **M:** Jerry Goldsmith

After the failure of *Cobra* and *Over the Top* Sylvester Stallone returned to what seemed like a sure thing. This time, after retiring to a Buddhist monastery Rambo goes to Afghanistan to rescue (on horseback) his mentor (Richard Crenna) from the evil Soviets. It cost a record $63 million, surpassing even *Superman* (1978). Rescuing American Nam vets was one thing, but most Americans didn't really give a shit about Afghanistan (or Crenna), and the Soviet Union was about to disband. With Marc De Jonge and Kurtwood Smith. There are lots of explosions and even-dumber-than-usual Stallone dialogue. It was filmed in Israel, Thailand, and Arizona. The soundtrack (on Scotti Brothers) includes Bill Medley.

RAMPAGE

(Paramount, 1987)
D/S/P: William Friedkin **P:** David Salven **M:** Ennio Morricone

Michael Biehn stars as a liberal district attorney who wants capital punishment for a suburban gas-station attendant and serial killer named Charlie Reece (Alex McArthur). Reece (who listens to "the Devil's station") killed an entire family (at Christmastime), drank their blood, and played with their guts. He later escapes and does more killing. There are flashbacks, flashforwards, fantasy scenes, and a long, dramatic courtroom silence to think about how long it took a victim to die. DEG produced this serious film, which argues against the insanity defense. When they went out of business it was unreleased for years. It came out on video in Europe first, and then Miramax released a revised version in America in 1992. Some horror-movie fans were disappointed after the big buildup. Deborah Van Valkenburgh is the district attorney's wife, Billy Green Bush is the judge, and Grace Zabriskie is the killer's psycho mom. Also with Nicholas Campbell, Art LaFleur, Whitby Hertford (the kid from *Nightmare on Elm Street V*), and Bert Convy (seen on TV). The score was released by Virgin. The film was originally 118 minutes, but the video is 97.

RAMPAGE AT APACHE WELLS

(VSOM, 1965) **D/S:** Harold Philipps
S: Fred Denger **P:** Horst Wendlandt
W. Germany/Yugoslavia (*Der Ölprinz*)

Stewart Granger is Old Surehand, and Pierre Brice is Winnetou. This western, part of a series based on Karl May's novels, is about a wagon train and bad guys who trick the Navajos into attacking. With Macha Meril, Harold Leipnitz, and Terence Hill. The English-born Granger made more than a dozen European adventure movies during the 60s. From Columbia.

RAMRODDER

(SW, 1969) **D/S:** Ed Forsythe, Van Guilder
P: David F. Friedman (*Savage Passion*)

Jim Gentry stars as a man who has an Indian-princess girlfriend (Kathy Williams) and is friendly with her tribe until he's framed for a rape/murder. The minimal plot of this adults-only movie has lots of naked "Indian" women swimming, a hot sex-in-the-water scene, a topless fight, some bondage, and an (offscreen) castration. Williams' "Dance of the Virgin" is a visual highlight. Marsha Jordan is an Indian, and Charles Manson follower Bobby Beausolie is a killer. Ed Forsythe (who later made *Chesty Anderson*) directed it, but Friedman had Van Guilder finish it.

RANA: THE LEGEND OF SHADOW LAKE

(Active, 1981) **D/P:** Bill Rebane

Rana is a (pathetic-looking) frog-man/monster. This movie (from Wisconsin) is told in flashback and has some gore. Troma picked it up and released it. Bill Rebane later made *Blood Harvest* (1986).

RANCHO NOTORIOUS

(Republic, 1952) **D:** Fritz Lang
S: Daniel Taradash **P:** Howard Welsh

Marlene Dietrich runs the Chuckaluck ranch, a hideout for outlaws. She falls for a man (Arthur Kennedy) who is after the men who raped and killed his fiancée. This tale of "hate, murder, and revenge" (in the words of the theme song, "Chuckaluck") is a classic color western from Howard Hughes' RKO. It was the last western by Fritz Lang and the last starring role for Dietrich. With Mel Ferrer, William Frawley, Jack Elam, Gloria Henry, and George Reeves (TV's Superman). An old folk song in the film, "Auralee," was later turned into the theme song of Elvis Presley's first movie, *Love Me Tender* (1956).

RAPID FIRE

(AIP, 1989) **D/S/P:** David A. Prior **S:** William Zipp

Joe Spinnell (in one of his last features) is a government man who hires a hero agent (star Ron Waldron) to hunt down an escaped terrorist. Michael Wayne is the main villain with a futuristic machine gun. It was filmed around Mobile, Alabama.

RAPID FIRE

(Fox, 1992) **D:** Dwight H. Little
S: Alan McElroy **P:** Robert Lawrence

Brandon Lee is a college student and sketch artist who teams with a single minded cop (Powers Boothe) who works out of a bowling alley. They break up a Chinese drug ring in Chicago. Lee's character is a "pacifist" who nonetheless turns to martial arts and violence pretty early in the feature. Kate Hodge is the hero's fighting girlfriend, and Nick Mancuso is a Mafia heroin dealer. The Tienanmen Square massacre is used as a plot point. An action highlight is a stick fight on an El track with Tzi Ma. This 20th Century–Fox release was Lee's first major starring role, nearly 20 years after his famous father's death.

RAPPIN'

(MGM, 1985) **D:** Joel Silberg **S:** Robert Litz, Adam Friedman **P:** Golan/Globus

Mario Van Peebles is an ex-con and breakdancer, in this action musical. His former girlfriend is now with a street-gang leader (Charles Flohe). He helps save a neighborhood from an evil developer (Harry Goz) and wins a rap contest (and a recording contract). With Kadeem Hardison, Tasia Valenza, Rutanya Alda, and Ice T. It was made by Cannon in Pittsburgh (a popular location after *Flashdance*). Atlantic released the soundtrack. Joel Silberg made this after *Breakin'* (1984).

THE RAPTURE
(New Line, 1991) **D/S:** Michael Tolkin
P: Nick Wechsler, Nancy Tenenbaum

Mimi Rogers is a bored LA telephone operator who is a swinger with a male partner (Patrick Bauchau). Eventually she's born again and joins a fundamentalist Christian group that believes in "the rapture" (the end of the world). Six years later, after her husband is shot, she goes to the desert to sacrifice her little girl. She ends up in jail having visions. New Line thought they might get publicity over the film being banned in the South, but a major theater chain explained that they had cancelled screenings because it was too boring. It is different, though, and Rogers has a nude shower scene and sex in a department store. With Will Patten, David Duchovny, and James LeGros. There are some Steve Johnson FX. It's by the screenwriter of *The Player* (1991), based on his novel. The Polydor soundtrack by Thomas Newman features some vintage tracks by Little Richard and the Velvet Underground.

RAQUEL!
(View, 1970)

This time-warp "silent majority" TV special (about 48 minutes) was executive-produced and staged by David Winters (later head of AIP video). It was shot on exotic locations all over the world. Raquel Welch can't sing but looks great doing "Aquarius" near some Mexican pyramids. The guests are Tom Jones (they do a Little Richard medley), Bob Hope (they do "Rocky Raccoon"!), and John Wayne (they visit an orphanage). View also offers time-warp TV shows like *Kenny Rogers and the First Edition: Rollin' on the River* (1971) and *The 5th Dimension Traveling Sunshine Show* (1971).

A RARE BREED
(MCA, 1981) **D:** David Nelson
S: Gardner Simmons **P:** Jack Cox

Tracy Vaccaro and her racehorse are kidnapped in Italy on the way to a race. This PG film was the third for David Nelson (Ricky's brother). Vaccaro later became a *Playboy* centerfold. With George Kennedy, Forrest Tucker, Tom Halick, and Don DeFore. From New World.

RASPUTIN
(1930) **D:** Adolf Trotz **S:** Ossip Dymov,
Adolf Lantz, Conrad Linzi   Germany
(*Rasputin, Dämon der Frauen*)

Conrad Veidt stars as the famous bearded Russian monk who used hypnotism and sex to gain influence in the court of Czar Nicholas II (Paul Otto). Earlier movies about Rasputin had been made in various countries. The next one was MGM's *Rasputin and the Empress* (1932), in America.

RASPUTIN AND THE EMPRESS
(MGM, 1932) **D:** Richard Boleslavsky
S: Charles MacArthur **P:** Irving Thalberg

This lavish MGM release was a major event in its day. It stars all three Barrymores, who are together for the only time on film. John Barrymore is (the fictional) Prince Chegodieff who kills Rasputin (Lionel Barrymore), and Ethel Barrymore is the czarina. For legal reasons a disclaimer was added saying that all the events shown were fictional, and for censorship reasons a rape scene was cut. With Ralph Morgan, Edward Arnold, Gustav von Seyffertitz, Mischa Auer, Lucien Littlefield, Diana Wynyard, Jean Parker, Charlotte Henry, Frank Shannon, and Frank Reicher. John Barrymore Jr. played the same role as his father in *The Night They Killed Rasputin* (1962). Many other Rasputin films have been made over the years, but Hammer's *Rasputin, the Mad Monk* (1965), with Christopher Lee, is probably the best known today. Other Rasputin movies were from the U.S.S.R. (1977), West Germany (1983), and an excellent cable TV version starring Alan Rickman (1996).

RATBOY
(Warner, 1986) **D/A:** Sondra Locke
S: Rob Thompson **P:** Fritz Manes

Locke, an Oscar nominee back in 1968, hadn't been in a theatrical feature without Clint Eastwood for over a decade when she directed for the first time. Backed by Eastwood's Malpaso Productions, this is an attempt at crossing a cynical, 30s-style screwball comedy with *The Elephant Man*. Locke plays an ambitious, harebrained Hollywood loser and schemer who tracks down and exploits a reclusive, pathetic, even suicidal "ratboy" (S. L. Baird, a female in convincing makeup designed by Rick Baker). Robert Townsend has the kind of clichéd role he ridiculed in his directorial debut, *Hollywood Shuffle*, as an irresponsible, jive-talking hustler. Also with Gerrit Graham, Christopher Hewitt (star of the TV series *Mr. Belvedere*), comedian Louie Anderson, Sydney Lassick, and Nina Blackwood. Put this one on the "hard to believe it got past the script stage" list. After her 1989 palimony suit against Eastwood Locke directed *Impulse*.

RATMAN
(ABC, 1987) **D:** "Anthony Ascot"/Giuliano Ascot
S: David Parker Jr. **P:** Maurice Matthew
Italy (*Quella Villa in Fondo al Parco*)

A genetic experiment results in a killer rat man that squeaks. The star is 27-inch-tall Nelson de la Rosa, from the Dominican Republic, who's in *The Guinness Book of World Records* as "the world's smallest man." He plays the unfortunate rat man with a hairy costume and fake teeth. The whole movie is too dark and of course very exploitative. With Italian-horror regulars Eva Grimaldi and Janet Agren as sisters and David Warbeck.

RATS
(Lightning, 1983) **D:** "Vincent Dawn"/Bruno Mattei
D/S: "Clyde Anderson"/Claudio Fragasso
S: Herve Piccini   Italy (*Ratti: Notte di Terrore*)

In a plot much like *Chosen Survivors* (a 1974 movie about bats) post-nuke survivors in 225 AB (after bomb) battle flesh-eating mutant rats. The rats eat their way out of bodies. With Richard Raymond as a biker-gang leader and Joanna Ryan.

RATTLERS
(VGB, 1976) **D/P:** John McCauley **S:** Jerry Golding

After two kids on vacation are killed by cobras after falling into a pit in the desert, a young LA college professor is called in to investigate. US Army germ warfare experiments buried in a mine shaft are to blame. Boxoffice International made this PG feature. I've tried three times and still haven't gotten to the end of it. With Sam Chew and Elizabeth Chauvet.

THE RAVAGER
(1970) **D/S:** Charles Nizet **P:** Dave Ackerman

Pierre Gastin stars as a demolition expert who is hospitalized for trauma and released back in America as a voyeur, rapist, and killer. He dynamites couples making love. Other Charles Nizet obscurities are *Slaves of Love* (1969), *Three-Way Split* (1970), *The Possessed!* and *Voodoo Heartbeat* (both 1974), and *Rescue Force* (1980).

THE RAVEN
(Sinister, 1915) **D/S:** Charles J. Brabin

Harry B. Walthall (the same year that he was in *The Birth of a Nation*) stars in this rare Essanay silent film based on a play about the life of Edgar Allan Poe. He has dreams, and there are fantasy segments. Charles J. Brabin directed *The Mask of Fu Manchu* (1932). Later movies using the same title all had completely different plots.

RAVEN
(1992) **D:** Craig R. Baxley **S:** Frank Lupo

Jeffrey Meek stars as Jonathan Raven, a kickboxer and former Green Beret who's searching for his lost son and seeking vengeance for the death of his Interpol-agent father. Lee Majors is his comic-relief friend, an irritating, alcoholic private eye. Meanwhile, the yakuza are after the daughter of the owner of the nightclub where Raven works as a bartender. With Clyde Kusatsu and Tamlyn Tomita. John Ashley was an executive producer of this CBS-TV pilot and the silly series that followed.

RAW COURAGE
(1984) **S/P:** Robert R. Rosen **S:** Mary Cox
P/A: Ronny Cox   (*Courage*)

In the New Mexico desert three marathon runners are captured by survivalists. Producer Ronny Cox stars, with Lois Chiles, Art Hindle, and M. Emmet Walsh.

RAW DEAL
(HBO, 1986) **D:** John Irvin **S:** Gary M. De Vore,
Norman Wexler **P:** Martha Schumacher

Arnold Schwarzenegger was really reaching in the acting department playing a small-town American sheriff (named Kaminski) who's thrown out of the

FBI. He goes undercover and infiltrates the Chicago mob. Lots of guns go off, there's lots of destruction, Arnold busts a drag bar, and he begins to throw out one-liners like "Who do I look like, Dirty Harry?" With Kathryn Harrold, Sam Wanamaker, Darren McGavin, Paul Shenar, Robert Davi, Steven Hill, Ed Lauter, and Robey. It's from DEG. Varèse Sarabande released the soundtrack.

RAW FORCE

(Media, 1981) **D/S:** Edward Murphy **P:** Frank Johnson   Philippines (*Shogun Island*)

Three karate-club members from Burbank, (led by Geoff Binney), become stranded on a mysterious island and fight kung-fu cannibal (!) monks who create zombies. Cameron Mitchell is the cruise-ship captain. This movie throws in a piranha attack, a Hitler lookalike, sex, drugs, nudity, decapitation, and gore. With Camille Keaton, Jillian Kesner as a SWAT-team member, Vic Diaz as a monk, Jennifer Holmes (also in *The Demon* with Mitchell), and Jewel Shepard. Lawrence Woolner (who had started New World with Roger Corman) was an executive producer.

RAWHEAD REX

(Vestron, 1986) **D:** George Pavlou
S: Clive Barker **P:** Kevin Attew   UK

A 9-foot pagan cannibal (Heinrich von Schellendorf) living in the Irish woods decapitates people. In one scene the scary-looking Rex pisses on his willing and evil assistant, a vicar (Ronan Wilmot). With David Dukes as an American historian and Kelly Piper. Barker adapted his story from his *Books of Blood*. The movie was filmed in Ireland and released by Empire. George Pavlou also directed *Transmutations* (1985), based on another Barker story.

RAW NERVE

(AIP, 1991) **D/S:** David A. Prior
S: Lawrence L. Simone **P:** Ruta K. Aras

Imagine a movie about a serial killer in which Traci Lords and big Randall "Tex" Cobb are the best actors. It's not too hard when Ted Prior (the director's brother) stars as a race-car driver who "sees" murders. Traci is his 18-year-old sister. Glenn Ford and Jan-Michael Vincent look and act weary and worn out as cops, and Sandahl Bergman is okay, I guess, in a throwaway role. Try to figure out the plot and the (surprise) suicide and incest angle. Traci wears red high heels and a striped tank top that vibrates for the camera. When a newspaper headline says, TWO GIRLS KILLED IN ROOM OF MIRRORS, you know you're in for quality entertainment. It was filmed in Mobile, Alabama.

THE RAY BRADBURY CHRONICLES: THE MARTIAN EPISODES

(Worldvision, 1985–86) **D:** John Lang, Eleanor Lindo, Anne Wheeler **S:** Ray Bradbury **P:** Jonathan Goodwill, Pamela Meekings-Stewart   Canada/New Zealand

This video consists of 5 episodes from the syndicated half-hour *Ray Bradbury Theater* series, first shown on the USA Network. The most interesting

has Paul Clemens claiming to be the dead son of John Vernon and his wife. When rejected he becomes somebody else's missing daughter. Some of the FX are pretty cheap-looking. Guest stars include Hal Linden, Ben Cross, David Carradine, and David Birney.

RAZORBACK

(Warner, 1984) **D:** Russell Mulcahy **S:** Everett De Roche **P:** Hal McElroy   Australia

American Gregory Harrison (from the TV series *Trapper John, MD*) stars as a man whose wife has been eaten by a giant wild boar in the outback. The boar kills many people and rips up cars and a house. Various crazed backwoods characters are after it. This was partially inspired by the same "Dingo baby case" as *A Cry in the Dark* (1988), with Meryl Streep, with a strong dose of *Jaws* thrown in. The director had done rock videos for Duran Duran and other groups. Dean Selmer, the cinematographer, also shot *Mad Max*.

REAL GENIUS

(RCA, 1985) **D:** Martha Coolidge
S: Neal Israel, Pat Proft, Peter Torokvei
P: Brian Grazer **C:** Vilmos Zsigmond

A college professor (William Atherton) secretly uses his brilliant young students to make a laser weapon for the CIA. Student Val Kilmer and his friends devise a plan to stop him. This comedy also features Michelle Meyrink, Jonathan Gries, Patti D'Arbanville, Severn Darden, Ed Lauter, Gabe Jarret, and Lynda Wiesmeier.

REALLY WEIRD TALES

(HBO, 1986) **D:** Paul Lynch, Don McBreaty, John Blanchard **S:** Joe Flaherty, David Flaherty, Catherine O'Hara, John McAndrew **P:** Seaton McClean, Pat Whitley   Canada

Host Joe Flaherty introduces 3 *Twilight Zone*–type tales in this spoof with a Second City cast. Martin Short is a lounge singer, John Candy is an albino alien, and Catherine O'Hara is a woman who loves people to death. With Olivia D'Abo.

REAL MEN

(CBS/Fox, 1987) **D/S:** Dennis Feldman
P: Martin Bregman

Jim Belushi is a renegade government agent who enlists John Ritter to help him contact aliens so that he can obtain the ultimate weapon. This barely released PG-13 spy spoof features Barbara Barrie and Iva Anderson.

RE-ANIMATOR

(Vestron, 1985) **D/S:** Stuart Gordon **S:** Dennis Paoli, William J. Norris **P:** Brian Yuzna

Seeing *Re-Animator* (released unrated) in a theater was one of the biggest shocks of the 80s. It's one of the most successful horror movies of the period (along with *The Evil Dead*). Stuart Gordon had been the director of Chicago's Organic Theater. This was his first feature, and he didn't play by the rules. Nobody going to see an H. P. Lovecraft

adaptation expected this strong mixture of over-the-top carnage, nudity, and humor. Jeffrey Combs stars as the egotistical young Herbert West, who knows how to revive the dead. With Bruce Abbott, Barbara Crampton as the dean's daughter, David Gale as Dr. Hill, and Tom Towles. The R-rated video version uses different scenes and runs 8 minutes longer but is missing the outrageous sex and gore scenes. Look for the unrated video to get the full impact. The Richard Band soundtrack (on Varèse Sarabande) is very good, but it copies Bernard Herrmann's score for *Psycho*. Robert A. Burns (*The Texas Chainsaw Massacre*) was the art director. Brian Yuzna directed the sequel, *Bride of Re-Animator*.

REAR WINDOW

(MCA, 1954) **D/P:** Alfred Hitchcock
S: John Michael Hayes

The ultimate voyeur movie. It's brilliant, fascinating, and one of Hitchcock's best. The script is based on the novella "It Had to Be Murder" by Cornell Woolrich. James Stewart is L. B. Jeffries, called Jeff, a much-traveled news photographer restricted by a broken leg to a wheelchair in his apartment on West 9th Street in Greenwich Village. Every window tells a story, and we see everything he does. Lars Thorwald (Raymond Burr!) has buried his wife's head in the garden and is about to discover Jeff's girlfriend, fashion model Lisa Fremont (Grace Kelly), snooping in his apartment. All we can do is watch along with Jeff. Thelma Ritter is a nurse, Wendell Corey is a cop, and Ross Bagdasarian is a composer whose piano music is heard throughout the film (he later created the Chipmunks). Franz Waxman wrote the score. The director is seen winding a clock. It was released the same year as *Dial M for Murder* and was nominated for four Oscars. Paramount re-released it to theaters in 1968 and (after it had been unseen for years) again in 1984.

REASON TO DIE

(Vidmark, 1989) **D:** Tim Spring **S:** Aubrey Rettan, Terry Ashbury **P:** Helena Spring   S. Africa

Wings Hauser stars as a bounty hunter in Africa who goes after a slasher killer. With Arnold Vosloo and Anneline Kriel.

REBECCA

(Fox, 1940) **D:** Alfred Hitchcock **S:** Robert E. Sherwood, Joan Harrison **P:** David O. Selznick

The first American film by Alfred Hitchcock was a big hit. It's based on Daphne Du Maurier's 1938 gothic novel. Laurence Olivier (a year after he was in *Wuthering Heights*) stars as a wealthy Englishman, Maxim De Winter. Joan Fontaine is his (nameless) second wife, and Judith Anderson is the sinister housekeeper, Mrs. Danvers, who's loyal to his dead first wife, Rebecca. With George Sanders, Nigel Bruce, Reginald Denny, Florence Bates, C. Aubrey Smith, Gladys Cooper, and Leo G. Carroll. At 130 minutes it was the longest feature by Hitchcock. (He's seen near a photo booth.) It was nominated for 11 Oscars and received them for best picture and best b/w cinematography. Franz Waxman wrote the score. The film was produced by Selznick International and released by United Artists. Fontaine returned the next year as another new wife in danger, in Hitchcock's *Suspicion.*

REBEL

(American, 1969) **D/S/P:** Robert Allen Schnitzer
S: Larry Beinhart **P:** David B. Appleton
(*No Place to Hide*)

Sylvester Stallone stars as Jerry Savage, a student and urban terrorist in a colorful poncho. This PG movie was filmed in NYC and upstate New York. It's also available (with new dialogue) as *A Man Called Rainbo.* This and *A Party at Kitty and Studs'* (later called *The Italian Stallion*) were the star's only featured roles until *The Lords of Flatbush* in 1974.

REBEL DREAMS: *See* VALLEY GIRL

REBEL LOVE

(1985) **D/S:** Milton Bagby Jr. **P:** John Quenelle

Jamie Rose stars as a Yankee widow from Indiana who finds a Confederate spy lover (Terence Knox). Troma released it.

REBEL VIXENS

(Luna, 1969) **D/A:** R. L. Frost
S/P/A: Bob Cresse   (*The Scavangers*)

Southerners still fight after the Civil War. Freed slaves battle the Confederates, and in the end the rebel leader is left for the vultures. This S&M sex western was released to black theaters because of the slave theme and to adult theaters in a more explicit version (*The Grabbers*). Incredibly, it played on 42nd Street as late as 1985. With Uschi Digart and Maria Lease, who later directed *Dolly Dearest.*

REBORN

(Ace, 1982) **D/S/P:** Bigas Luna **S:** R. Dunn   Spain

Director Bigas Luna is an original, and this movie starring Dennis Hopper as Reverend Tom Harley, a fake American healer, will be a surprise if you can find a copy. The reverend has a major televised moneymaking scam going. In one scene Michael Moriarty, who works for him, has sex with Maria (Antonella Murgia), a real healer from Italy. She goes into a trance, and he becomes stuck inside her. She later has a baby, and the Jesus parallels add up. With Francesco Rabal. Luna later made *Anguish.*

RECKLESS KELLY

(Warners, 1994) **D/S/P/A:** Yahoo Serious
P: Warwick Ross   Australia

Yahoo Serious plays a descendant of the famous outlaw (as seen in *Ned Kelly*) who's living on a happy private island (filled with every possible animal and symbol of Australia). Evil British bankers plot to take the island away, so he follows in the

family tradition and robs banks. He goes to America to rob one and somehow becomes the star of a movie called *A Christian Cowboy in Las Vegas.* With Melora Hardin and Kathleen Freeman. This goofy PG comedy features several remakes of classic 60s rock songs.

RECON GAME

(1974) **D:** Peter Collinson **S:** David Osborn **P:** José S. Vicuña   US/Spain/Switzerland (*Open Season*)

Peter Fonda, John Phillip Law, and Richard Lynch are Nam vets who kidnap and hunt humans. Cornelia Sharpe and Albert Mendoza are the victims, and William Holden has a cameo role. This Columbia release was filmed in Spain and around Detroit. The retitled tape is a cheap "sell through" item. Peter Collinson's next film was the third version of *Ten Little Indians.*

RECORD CITY

(1979) **D:** Dennis Steinmetz **S:** Ron Friedman **P:** James T. Aubrey

AIP released this plotless comedy set in a record store with Blondie and Cheap Trick posters on the wall. It was shot on video and copies the hit *Car Wash.* Leonard Barr stars with an amazing oddball cast, including Michael Callan, Ed Begley Jr., Sorrell Brooke, Jack Carter, Frank Gorshin, Larry Storch, Ruth Buzzi, Harold Sakata, Ted Lange, Alice Ghostley, Kinky Friedman, and Rick Dees. The soundtrack was released.

RED

(Film Threat, 1991) **D:** Christian Gore

The *Red* audiotapes have been sold on LP, cassette, and even CD (!), have been visualized by Drew Friedman, and have been copied in the TV series *The Simpsons* (without the swearing and the necrophilia references). In the 70s the owner of a New Jersey bar answers the phone and reacts angrily to the many comic crank calls. The anonymous, unseen caller repeatedly tricks him into calling out for "Al Koholic," "Pepe Roni," "Mike Hunt," and others, leading to incredible, raspy-voiced tirades from Red, then in his 80s. If you've never heard the audiotapes you'll be amazed by the creative swearing and insults. Christian Gore shot b/w stills of big, bald Lawrence Tierney as Red and used highlights from the original tape for this 35-minute short. To fill out the video a (live-action) section shows what might have happened to Red after he retired in Florida, and there's some unnecessary violence outside the bar. The audiotapes also inspired the later Jerky Boys records and movie (1995).

RED ALERT

(1977) **D:** William Hale **S:** Sandor Stern **P:** Barry Goldberg

An apparent accident in a nuke plant causes a computer to shut down and seal off the whole building. William Devane, Michael Brandon, Adrienne Barbeau, and M. Emmet Walsh are trapped

inside. It turns out to be the work of saboteurs. A CBS-TV movie with Warren Berlinger, Ralph Waite, David Hayward, and Wendell Burton.

RED BARRY

(1938) **D:** Ford Beebe, Alan James
S: Norman Hall, Ray Trampe

Buster Crabbe stars as another hero from the daily comics (just before playing Buck Rogers, then Flash Gordon again). He's a private detective in Chinatown searching for missing bonds. Frances Robinson costars in this 13-chapter Universal serial, with Edna Sedgwick as Natasha, Frank Lackteen as Quong Lee, Philip Ahn, Cyril Delevanti, and Wheeler Oakman.

RED BLOODED AMERICAN GIRL

(Prism, 1988) **D:** David Blyth **S/P:** Nicolas Stiliadis **S:** Allan Moyle   Canada

Dr. Alcor (Christopher Plummer) works at one of those modern research institutes (so common in post-Cronenberg Canadian films) developing an addictive vampire virus. He hires Andrew Stevens, who has created a "designer ecstasy" adrenaline spray and used it on himself. Blond Heather Thomas (from the TV series *The Fall Guy*) becomes infected after a bite and starts sucking her own blood. She ends up in a padded cell acting like Renfield in *Dracula*, then escapes and gets manic and trashy in stiletto heels and black leather clothes looking for nourishment. After Stevens shows up decked out like a ghost-buster and cures her with a blood transplant she reverts to normal (even her hair and makeup change!). With Kim Coates as a vampire assistant (in the scenes with the most sex and blood) and Lydie Denier. Director Blyth is from New Zealand. Scriptwriter Moyle directed *Pump Up the Volume.*

THE RED CIRCLE

(1959) **D:** Jürgen Roland **S:** Trygve Larsen, Wolfgang Menge   W. Germany (*Der Röte Kreis*)

Murder victims have circle marks on their necks, and Scotland Yard investigates. Karl Saebisch, Renate Ewert, and Fritz Rasp star. This Edgar Wallace story had already been filmed four times in England and Germany between 1922 and 1936.

RED DAWN

(MGM/UA, 1984) **D/S:** John Milius **S:** Kevin Reynolds
P: Buzz Feitshans, Barry Beckerman **M:** Basil Polidouris

This pro-NRA, anti-Communist movie is even more fun now that it's so dated, but unfortunately has become a top rental title for right-wing terrorists. It's like an expensive "prequel" to Jack Webb's *Red Nightmare.* Cuban and Soviet forces invade the US after major American cities are destroyed by "surgical" nuclear strikes. The invaders put people into camps and rape, pillage, and kill. Small- town teens become heroic guerrillas. Patrick Swayze stars, with C. Thomas Howell, Lea Thompson, Charlie Sheen, and Jennifer Grey. Ron O'Neal is a Cuban leader, and William Smith is a Russian. With grownups Powers Boothe, Ben Johnson, Lane Smith, and Harry Dean Stanton. The soundtrack is on Intrada.

C. Thomas Howell and Patrick Swayze discover that the Commies have taken over McDonald's, in *Red Dawn.*

RED DESERT PENITENTIARY

(Fox, 1986) **D/S:** George Sluizer   Netherlands

A Polish director (Giovanni Korporaal) is making a B movie in Texas based on the case of a man who was sent to prison for a crime he didn't commit. The convict (Will Rose) shows up on the set to complicate matters. James Michael Taylor is a Clint Eastwood type of star. Parts of this spoof were improvised, and long surreal flashbacks intrude. It's by the director of *The Vanishing.*

RED DRAGON

(Sinister, 1965) **D:** Ernst Hofbauer **S:** Hans-Karl Kubiak **P:** Gerö Wecker   Italy/W. Germany (*A-009: Missione Hong Kong*)

Stewart Granger is an FBI agent sent to Hong Kong to investigate murders and drug smuggling. Rosanna Schiaffino helps him. Harold Juhnke and Horst Frank are also in the cast. They use wrist watch radios. Woolner Brothers released it.

RED DWARF

(CBS/Fox, 1989–95) **D:** Andy De Emmony **S:** Rob Grant, Doug Naylor **P:** Justin Judd   UK

Episodes of this half-hour BBC science-fiction/comedy series about the mining spaceship Red Dwarf are available on 8 tapes. Chris Barrie and Craig Charles star. Aliens are featured.

RED HEAT

(Vestron, 1984) **D/S:** Robert Collector **S:** Gary Drucker **P:** Ernst R. Theumer US/Germany (*Röte Hitze*)

Linda Blair goes to prison (again). She visits her soldier fiancé (William Ostrander) in West Berlin and is kidnapped by Commies and put into an East German prison camp. Sylvia Kristel is a sadistic lesbian prisoner with orange hair and red underwear who does things for the warden. She claims that she killed her father because "he ate my pet snake!" There's a Kristel/Blair sex scene, and Blair leads a prison riot. The music is by Tangerine Dream (!). English-language and German-language versions were shot. It was released in 1988 in America. Despite its title *Chained Heat 2* is a remake.

RED HEAT

(IVE, 1988) **D/P:** Walter Hill **S:** Harry Kleiner **P:** Gordon Carroll

Walter Hill reworked his own hit, *48 Hours,* this time with Jim Belushi in the comic Eddie Murphy role. Arnold Schwarzenegger is a Soviet police officer, and Belushi is a Chicago cop. They have to team up to capture a Russian drug lord and psycho rapist. With Ed O'Ross, Peter Boyle, Laurence (Larry) Fishburne, and Gina Gershon. Some scenes of this violent, humorous action movie were shot in Moscow's Red Square (a first), but most of it was shot in Chicago. Virgin released the soundtrack. In 1988, Arnold was also in the comedy *Twins* and campaigned for George Bush.

THE RED HOUSE

(Sinister, 1947) **D/S:** Delmer Daves **P:** Sol Lesser

Edward G. Robinson stars as a kindly but deranged one-legged farmer living with his sister (Judith Anderson). His adopted daughter (Allene Roberts) realizes that she's in danger. A mysterious old red house in the forest holds the key to the past. This *"film noir* horror" from United Artists is based on a novel by George Agnew Chamberlain. Julie London is Tibby, a very seductive high-school student. With Rory Calhoun, Lon McCallister, Arthur Space, and Ona Munson. The Miklos Rozsa score, featuring a theremin, was released as a 10" LP with music from *Spellbound* on the other side.

RED LIGHT IN THE WHITE HOUSE

(VSOM, 197?) **D/S/P:** Paul Leder

Sushan Andrews (Karin Mary Shea) is running for the Senate, and a journalist (who narrates) is hired for the easy job of digging into her past. Various characters relate flashbacks (all featuring topless and brief sex scenes). It seems that she was raised in China and sold into marriage at 15. In America she had a lesbian affair with a teacher, became a hooker to help pay the debts of her black boxer boyfriend, and married a gay French actor who liked to watch her with other men. There's more, concerning suicide and even the president. Sushan is presented as a selfless, honest, strong, admirable, and capable person, as opposed to most politicians. The tape has Spanish subtitles. Video Search also has *The Education of Allison Tate* and *The Eleventh Commandment,* from the prolific Paul Leder.

THE RED MENACE

(Republic, 1949) **D:** R. G. Springsteen **P:** Herbert J. Yates

A WWII vet (Robert Rockwell) is duped by an American Commie group. This is low-key compared to some better-known anti-Communist movies of the period (there are no bombs or invasions) but touches all the bases. See how the Commies easily convert dissatisfied blacks, artists, and other minorities. With Hanne Axman and Barbara Fuller. R. G. Springsteen usually made B westerns.

REDNECK ZOMBIES

(TWE, 1987) **D/S/P:** Pericles Lewnes **P:** Ed Bishop, George Scott

Troma released this made-in-Maryland, shot-on-video gore video, yet another story of mutation caused by nuclear waste. Its humor is in the Troma tradition: piss, fart, fat-guy, and gay jokes. Some stupid redneck bootleggers use toxic waste for their new brew. There's an LSD sequence, some Three Stooges gags, and (the only thing this tape has going for it) lots of extreme gore, 6 minutes of which were cut for an R rating.

RED NIGHTMARE: *See* THE COMMIES ARE COMING!

RED NIGHTS

(TWE, 1988) **D:** Izhak Hanooka **S:** Phillip Ridley **P:** Domenic Anciano, Ray Burdis

Christoper Parker star as an East Coast kid who goes to Hollywood to try and make it. With William Smith and Jack Carter. The score is by the German synth group Tangerine Dream who did music for many increasingly cheap and obscure movies.

THE RED QUEEN KILLS SEVEN TIMES

(VSOM, 1972) **D/S:** Emilio P. Miraglia **S:** Fabio Pittorru Italy/W. Germany (*La Dama Rossa Uccide Sette Volte*)

Because of a curse in an old castle a little girl's sister is killed. The survivor grows up to become a successful fashion model, and other models start dying. Barbara Bouchet stars, with Marina Malfatti, Ugo Pagliai, and Sybil Danning as a prostitute. It's by the director of *The Night Evelyn Came out of Her Grave.*

RED RIDING HOOD

(1987) **D:** Adam Brooks **S:** Carole Lucia Satrina **P:** Golan/Globus

Craig T. Nelson is the evil ruler of a kingdom who turns his servant into a wolf and wants the wife (Isabella Rossellini) of his good twin. The characters all sing. This is part of Cannon's ill-fated fairy-tale series.

RED ROCK WEST

(Columbia, 1992) **D/S:** John Dahl **S:** Rick Dahl **P:** Sigunjon Sighvatsson, Steve Colin

Michael, a painfully honest ex-Marine (Nicolas Cage), is mistaken for a hired killer in a small Wyoming town. This leads to murder and many surprising (and sometimes funny) complications in a film so good that it opened in theaters after debuting on HBO and being released on video. Dennis Hopper as Lyle from Dallas and J. T. Walsh as the sheriff take the acting honors, and Cage is good too. Also with Lara Flynn Boyle, Dan Shor, and Dwight Yoakam (who also does the end theme). The Mercury soundtrack includes some Johnny Cash songs. The brothers from Montana who made this also did *Kill Me Again* and *The Last Seduction.*

Toshiro Mifune in *Red Sun*.

RED SCORPION

(SGE, 1989) **D:** Joseph Zito **S:** Arne Olsen
P: Jack Abramoff **M:** Jay Chattaway

A Soviet KGB agent (Dolph Lundgren) is sent to Africa to kill a black revolutionary. He turns against the Soviet and Cuban forces to help the oppressed locals. A witch doctor tattoos a red scorpion on his chest. Warner backed out of releasing this after negative publicity (it was shot in Swaziland by a South African producer), so SGE released it. It was unfair to single this movie out, since dozens of (usually mediocre action) movies released in America before the sanctions were lifted were filmed in South Africa. With M. Emmet Walsh and Brion James. Tom Savini provided the FX for the scene when Lundgren is tortured by Cubans.

RED SCORPION II

(MCA, 1994) **D:** Michael Kennedy **S:** Troy Bolotnik, Barry Victor **P:** Robert Malcolm   Canada

John Savage is a fascist businessman who uses skinheads to attack minorities. Michael Ironside is a government agent who assembles a *Dirty Dozen*–style team for battle. Matt McColm and Jennifer Rubin star in this unrelated "sequel" shot in Vancouver.

RED SHOE DIARIES

(Republic, 1992) **D:** David Saunders, Rafael Eisenman **D/P:** Zalman King **S:** Patricia Knop

A woman (Brigitte Bako) has affairs with a construction worker (Billy Wirth) and a shoe salesman, then kills herself. Her boyfriend (series regular David Duchovny) reads her diaries after she dies. With Anna Karina and Brenda Vaccaro. This 100-minute series pilot feature made for Showtime is available in R and unrated versions. A half-hour anthology series followed, and compilation tapes (each containing 3 episodes) and more features were released.

RED SONJA

(Fox, 1988) **D:** Richard Fleischer **S:** Clive Exton, George MacDonald **P:** Christian Ferry

After two *Conan* movies Arnold Schwarzenegger plays the very similar Kalidor. Brigitte Nielsen is Red Sonja, who survives a massacre. Sandahl

Bergman (also in *Conan the Barbarian*) is the evil queen. Big Paul Smith and little Ernie Reyes Jr. provide welcome intentional comic relief. Janet Agren (in a red wig) is Sonja's sister. This PG-13 film was based on Robert E. Howard's characters and was backed by Dino De Laurentiis. Varèse Sarabande released the Ennio Morricone score. Nielsen, from Copenhagen, had been in *Playboy*, was married to Sylvester Stallone (briefly), and was in *Rocky IV*.

RED SUN

(UAV, 1971) **D:** Terence Young
S: Laird Koenig, Denne Bart Petitclerc, William Roberts, Lawrence Roman **P:** Robert Dorfman
M: Maurice Jarre   France/Italy/Spain (*Soleil Rouge*)

Charles Bronson (in a leather jacket with fringes) is a gunfighter reluctantly teamed with a samurai (Toshiro Mifune) in this interesting international western based on a true incident involving a stolen samurai sword in 1860s Arizona. It was a big hit in Europe and just about everywhere but in America, and it's a lot better than the reviews would lead you to believe. With Alain Delon as the villain, Ursula Andress, and Capucine. It was filmed in Spain.

RED SURF

(Academy, 1990)
D: H. Gordon Boos **S:** Vincent Robert **P:** Richard C. Weinman

The drug dealers are heroes this time. They want to get out of the business, but a former partner turns on them. Dedee Pfeiffer is the pregnant girlfriend of a former surfing champ who's a drug runner (George Clooney). Doug Savant is his friend Attila, a biker. They deal with various LA crazies. One keeps wolves in the basement. Gene Simmons shows up as a Nam vet.

RED, WHITE, AND BLUE

(1970) **D/S/P/E/C:** Ferd and Beverly Sebastian

Sold as a serious documentary about President Nixon's Commission on Obscenity and Pornography, this movie is also about David F. Friedman (his Entertainment Ventures released it). He's seen testifying before the commission, and there's a behind-the-scenes segment about the making of his (soft-core) *Trader Hornee* and even a trailer for it. The rest features lots of naked women and interviews with sex-movie makers and actors. It's all narrated by attorney Robert Fitzpatrick.

RED WIND

(MCA, 1991) **D:** Alan Metzger **S/P:** Tom Noonan

Lisa Hartman stars as a psychotherapist interested in abusive relationships. A female patient acts out a fantasy by killing her husband. With Philip Casnoff as a detective, Christopher McDonald, and Deanna Lund. This cable-TV movie copies *Whispers in the Dark* and features death by tree shredder.

RED ZONE CUBA

(SW, 1966) **D/S/A:** Coleman Francis **P/A:** Tony Cardoza   (*Night Train to Mundo Fine*)

Yes, the determined people who made Tor Johnson's last movie, *The Beast of Yucca Flats* (1961), didn't stop there. *The Skydivers* (1963) and this marvel followed. John Carradine sings the theme song in his great bass voice, then appears as Mr. Wilson the train engineer and remembers how "he ran all the way to Hell" while setting up the feature-length flashback (filmed in 1961). A pair of escaped convicts and some migrant workers sign up to fight in the Bay of Pigs invasion of Cuba. They're captured, escape execution, steal a plane, and head for Arizona to claim somebody else's treasure. Big Coleman Francis stars as the brutal,

silent Griffin, who dumps an old man down a well and rapes a blind widow (offscreen) and ends up just like Tor in *The Beast of Yucca Flats*. The sound is bad, some of the music is comical-goofy, the dialogue was all (obviously) dubbed in later, and the image goes from light to very dark too often. It was originally from Hollywood Star Pictures, which also released *Free Grass* and early Ray Dennis Steckler movies.

REEFER MADNESS

(Media, Admit One, 1936) **D:** Louis Gasnier
S: Arthur Hoerl **P:** George A. Hirlman   (*The Burning Question; Tell Your Children; Dope Addict*)

One of the classic road-show anti-drug movies, this played for years (under various titles), had a second life as a "camp" midnight-movie hit (an early New Line acquisition), then found a new audience on video. Dave O'Brien (*The Devil Bat* and *Spooks Run Wild*) stars, with Dorothy Short and Lillian Miles. Jack Perry is the pusher. The scenes of wild-eyed characters frantically puffing on pot are unforgettable. Most of them end up dead, imprisoned, or ruined for life. The French-born Louis Gasnier had codirected the famous silent serial *The Perils of Pauline* (1914) and later made Spanish-language versions of Paramount films and worked at Monogram. *Reefer Madness* is a rerelease title. It's only 67 minutes but has been listed as running from 63 (Admit One) to 71 minutes.

REEFER MADNESS II: THE TRUE STORY

(1985) **D:** Kent Skov **S:** The LA Connection **P:** L. Randall Nogg

This is just the (public-domain) original with new comic dialogue (mostly sex jokes). It opens with a pair of reviewers arguing about the merits of the original, now told from the pusher's point of view. The high-school principal, Dr. Carroll, is now the head of the dope ring, and the dealer is an undercover cop.

THE REFLECTING SKIN

(Live, 1990) **D/S:** Philip Ridley   UK

To say that this disturbing, visually stunning, complex movie resembles Terence Malick's *Days of Heaven* if it had been directed by David Lynch doesn't really do it justice. A destructive young boy (Jeremy Cooper) living on the midwestern American prairie witnesses the world around him. His family is disintegrating, everybody is mean or crazy, and a pack of jd kidnappers seem to be killing his friends. His brother (Viggo Mortensen) returns from WWII with a photo of an A-bomb victim (this is where the title comes from), and the weird sheriff claims that a turtle got his hand. With all the real horrors and sickness around him he begins to think that a mummified baby is an angel and that an Englishwoman (Lindsay Duncan) who lives in an isolated house is a vampire. This British production was filmed in western Canada. The music is by the London Chamber Orchestra. It was made by the screenwriter of *The Krays* and was released by Miramax.

REFLECTIONS OF A CRIME

(1994) **D/S:** Jon Purdy **P:** Gwen Field

Sybil Danning and Pat Ast in *Reform School Girls*.

Mimi Rogers, convicted of killing her rich husband (John Terry), talks to a guard (Billy Zane) before her execution. Her various flashbacks tell the story. With Kurt Fuller. It's from Concorde.

REFORMATORY

(1938) **D:** Lewis D. Collins **S:** Gordon Rigby **P:** Larry Darmour

Frankie Darro is sent to the Garfield Reform School and tries to organize a breakout. Jack Holt, the new warden, has been improving conditions and trying to be fair. Inmate Bobby Jordan (from the Dead End Kids) likes the reforms and tries to stop the breakout. With Charlotte Wynters and Ward Bond. This Columbia release runs 59 minutes.

REFORM SCHOOL

(1939) **D:** Leo C. Popkin
S: Zelda Young **P:** Harry M. Popkin   (*Prison Bait*)

This all-black-cast production features Harlem's Tough Kids, a black version of the Dead End Kids (who had just been in *Crime School*). Louise Beavers (who in Hollywood movies played a maid working for white people) stars as a new warden who brings needed reforms to a state reform school. This Million Dollar Pictures release runs 58 minutes. Harlem's Tough Kids (led by Monty Hawley) returned in *Take My Life* (1941), in which the young troublemakers join the (segregated) US Army.

REFORM SCHOOL GIRL

(1995) **D:** Jonathan Kaplan **S:** Bruce Meade
P: Lou Arkoff, Walter Hill, Willie Kutner, David Giler

This movie, part of the Showtime series *Rebel Highway*, takes its name from a 1957 AIP release. Aimee Graham stars, with Elisa Pensler and Gabrielli and Leo Rossi. Kaplan, whose directing career had started at Roger Corman's New World in the 70s, made the theatrical-release-western *Bad Girls* (1994) before this.

REFORM SCHOOL GIRLS

(Starmaker, 1986) **D/S:** Tom De Simone **P:** Jack Cummins

The director of *The Concrete Jungle* made this misfire spoof of women-in-prison movies. Linda Carol is an innocent inmate. Wendy O. Williams (from the Plasmatics) rides on the top of a bus and is heard on the soundtrack. Pat Ast (from Andy Warhol movies) is the evil matron, and Sybil Danning is the Bible-quoting warden. The stars remain dressed, but Michelle Bauer, Linda Carol, Leslie Bremmer, and Sheri Stoner are in a shower scene. Stoner was later the model for the main characters in Disney's *The Little Mermaid* and *Beauty and the Beast*! It's from New World.

THE REFRIGERATOR

(Monarch, 1991) **D/S:** Nicholas Jacobs
P: Chris Oldcorn

A happy young couple (David Simonds and Julia McNeal) move from Chagrin Falls, Ohio, to a suspiciously cheap Manhattan apartment on Avenue D, in the East Village. The 60s Norge fridge is some kind of portal to Hell. She has childhood flashbacks and nightmares, and he dreams of little people in the fridge. The acting is fine, the dreams are great, and there's some gore and nice, unexpected humor. This 16mm production took four years to complete, and it was worth the wait. It's by Brown University grads from Cleveland. Kay Schuckhart (who designed the first *Psychotronic* calendars) was the set designer.

The Refrigerator

THE REGENERATED MAN

(Arrow, 1994) **D/S/P:** Ted Bohus **S:** Jack Smith

A scientist named Dr. Robert Clarke (Arthur Lundquist) is forced by thieves to drink his own potion. He occasionally becomes a monster-faced killer with a throbbing skull. His body opens up, and bone fragments impale victims. Gregory Sullivan costars as a detective, and George Stover appears. It was filmed in New Jersey by the producer of *Deadly Spawn* and *Metamorphosis*. There's some computer animation. *Vampire Vixens from Venus* was the next movie by Ted Bohus.

THE REJUVENATOR

(SVS, 1985) **D/S:** Brian Thomas Jones
S: Simon Nuchtern **P:** Steven Mackler
(The Rejuvenatrix)

It's the old plot of the *The Wasp Woman* again, with some ideas from *Sunset Boulevard*. A rich, aging, once-popular actress (Vivian Lanko) in a blond wig doesn't want to "rot away in this ugly carcass." A doctor, whose experiments she funds, uses serum from human brains to make her young, and she pretends she's her own actress niece. Her one-time love, Wilhelm, is the jealous butler. The problem is that sex makes her mutate. Ed French created several versions of her monster look. At first she loses hair, has a monster voice, and has balloon-like skin (like in the old Mexican movie *Braniac*). Later on her face gets worse, her head gets bigger, she grows big claws, her brain is exposed, and she decapitates people and eats their throbbing brains! It's good to see a movie like this that's pretty well done and not a spoof, although it gets pretty silly when coke-sniffing clubgoers in the ladies' room don't think that the monster/woman is anything special. There's also an all-girl heavy-metal group, a dancer in a see-through body stocking, and a rat puppet. It was made in NYC, but for a while I thought it was British because of its serious tone and some accents. Screenwriter Simon Nuchtern directed *New York Nights*.

RELATIVE FEAR

(1994) **D:** George Mihalka **S:** Kurt Wimmer **P:** Tom Berry   Canada

Darlanne Fluegel's new baby is somehow switched with the child of a psycho (Denise Crosby). Later the autistic 4-year-old boy (Matthew DuPris) seems to become a killer. This movie copies parts of *The Good Son*. Martin Neufeld is the father, M. Emmet Walsh is the grandfather, and James Brolin is a detective. Also with Linda Sorensen.

RELENTLESS

(RCA/Columbia, 1989) **D:** William Lustig **S:** "Jack T. D. Robinson"/Phil Alden Robinson **P:** Howard Smith

Judd Nelson must have gotten sick of reviewers making fun of him in teen movies. Here he's convincing and disturbing as the psycho sunset killer, who picks his victims from the phone book. Flashbacks reveal that he's the son of an abusive LA hero cop. Leo Rossi is a NYC cop teamed with LA cop Robert Loggia. Meg Foster is Rossi's ex-wife. With Angel Tompkins and George "Buck" Flower. Nelson and Rossi are very good. Like most William Lustig movies this is violent and has some good chase scenes. The screenwriter directed *Field of Dreams*. The music is by Jay Chattaway. Nelson got even farther out in *The Dark Backwards*.

RELENTLESS II: DEAD ON

(RCA, 1991) **D:** Michael Schroeder
S: Mark Levi **P:** Lisa M. Hansen

Leo Rossi returns as the NYC cop in LA. Miles O'Keeffe is the silent, busy serial killer who uses disguises (including appearing in drag), bathes naked in ice cubes, and smears symbols on walls in blood. Ray Sharkey is an irritating FBI agent, Meg

Foster returns as the ex-wife, and Judd Nelson is seen in flashbacks as the psycho from the superior original movie. The cinematography is excellent, but this is not much of a sequel. Also with Perry Lang and Shelby Chong. It's by the director of *Cyborg II*. More sequels followed.

RELENTLESS 3

(New Line, 1993) **D/S:** James Lemmo
P: Paul Hertzberg, Lisa M. Hansen

Leo Rossi (looking more like Regis Philbin all the time) is after yet another serial killer. This time it's creepy William Forsythe ("I am the fucking star!") as a necromaniac who somehow charms waitresses, then kills and mutilates them. The cheapness shows in the minimal cast and script, but it's a lot sicker than the second movie. Forsythe mails tattooed pieces of skin, shows up in drag, and scalps several cops. It had to be cut for an R rating. A girlfriend (Signy Coleman) is put into peril, then simply forgotten. The ending is awful. It's by the director of *Tripwire*.

RELENTLESS 4: ASHES TO ASHES

(New Line, 1994) **D:** Joel Soisson
S: Mark Sevi **P:** Russell D. Markowitz

Leo Rossi is Sam Dietz, and Colleen Coffey (from *Lawnmower Man*) is his partner. A deformed psycho who uses religious death rituals is on the loose, Famke Janssen (before her Bond-girl fame) is a shrink whose patients are being killed, and Christopher Pettiet is the cop's teen son.

THE REMARKABLE ANDREW

(1942) **D:** Stuart Heisler **S:** Dalton Trumbo **P:** Richard Blumenthal

William Holden stars as a young small-town bookkeeper framed for embezzlement but helped by the ghosts of famous Americans from the past. This WWII-era fantasy/comedy features Brian Donlevy as Andrew Jackson, Rod Cameron as Jesse James, and Montague Love as George Washington. Also with Ellen Drew (also in the director's *The Monster and the Girl*, from the same year) as the fiancée, Richard Webb, Porter Hall, and Frances Gifford. It's from Paramount. Dalton Trumbo's other WWII ghost movie was *A Guy Named Joe* (1943).

REMEMBER MY NAME

(1978) **D/S:** Alan Rudolph **P:** Robert Altman

Geraldine Chaplin, just released from prison, is after married construction worker Anthony Perkins. She disrupts his life and terrorizes his (real-life) wife Berry Berenson. With Moses Gunn, Tim Thomerson, Alfre Woodward, and Jeff Goldblum as a nerd. Columbia released the Alberta Hunter blues soundtrack.

REMOTE CONTROL

(IVE, 1987) **D/S/P:** Jeff Lieberman **P:** Scott Rosenfelt

A b/w video tape called *Remote Control* features strange-looking, 50s-type, futuristic aliens. Watch-

ing the video makes viewers kill. Kevin Dillon stars as a guy working in a video store. He and Deborah Goodrich realize what's going on and try to stop the killing. Nobody noticed this when it was released (directly to video), but it's pretty fun and worth watching just for the video segments with the bizarre aliens. With Jennifer Tilly and Bert Remsen.

REMO WILLIAMS: THE ADVENTURE BEGINS

(HBO, 1985) **D:** Guy Hamilton
S: Christopher Wood **P:** Larry Spiegel

A James Bond director and writer made this movie, based on the Destroyer novels. It was planned as the first of a series. Fred Ward stars as a NYC cop recruited and trained by a mystical Korean martial-arts master (Joel Grey in some amazing makeup). A fight on the Statue of Liberty and a killer-dog attack are some action highlights. With Kate Mulgrew, Wilford Brimley, Michael Pataki, and William Hickey. Dick Clark was one of the producers of this PG-13 feature. There was no sequel.

RENALDO AND CLARA

(1978) **D/S/A/E:** Bob Dylan **S/A:** Sam Shepard **P:** Mel Howard, Jack Baron

Parts of Dylan's ambitious all-star 1975–76 Rolling Thunder Review tour were filmed. The footage was edited down, and interviews and fantasy segments were added to make this uncommercial autobiographical epic. Dylan is Renaldo, and his wife at the time, Sara, is Clara. Actors sing and singers act. Ronnie Hawkins plays Dylan, and Ronee Blakley is his wife. Also with Sam Shepard (in his film debut), Joan Baez, Ramblin' Jack Elliott, Harry Dean Stanton, Allen Ginsberg, Arlo Guthrie, Joni Mitchell, Roger McGuinn, Mick Ronson, and David Blue (who died while jogging). It played some theaters at 292 minutes and was later reedited (by Dylan) to 112. Few have seen it at any length.

RENEGADE RIDERS: *See* PAYMENT IN BLOOD

RENEGADES

(MCA, 1989) **D:** Jack Sholder
S: David Rich **P:** David Madden

How about a teen version of *Red Sun*? This time modern-day teens out West are after a sacred Indian spear, and they have chases in cars instead of on horseback. Lou Diamond Phillips is a Lakota Sioux who teams up with East Coast cop Kiefer Sutherland. Jami Gertz and Rob Knepper costar.

RENTED LIPS

(IVE, 1988) **D:** Robert Downey **S/A:** Martin Mull **P:** Mort Engelberg **M:** Van Dyke Parks

A naive industrial-film director (Martin Mull) and his cameraman (Dick Shawn) are hired to finish a porno movie (with a Nazi theme) after the original director dies. Mull, who lives with his mother, falls

Repo Man

for actress Jennifer Tilly. Robert Downey Jr. and Edy Williams star in the movie that's being shot. It's not very funny, but a lot of name guests show up, including Kenneth Mars as an evangelist, Eileen Brennan, James Coco, Shelley Berman, June Lockhart, Mel Welles, Pat McCormick, and Jack Reilly. There's also a dwarf. Shawn died (onstage) after making this.

REPO MAN

(MCA, 1984) **D/S:** Alex Cox **P:** Jonathan Wacks

Repo Man received horrible reviews when released (on video before its theatrical run), but it's excellent. It's the only good movie starring Emilio Estevez. He's Bud, a novice car-repo man in L.A., learning the trade from Otto (Harry Dean Stanton). The incredible comic science-fiction plot concerns UFOs, aliens, and punks, and features a great nod to *Kiss Me Deadly*. Fox Harris is a nuclear physicist with an alien corpse in his '64 Chevy Malibu. With Tracey Walter, Sy Richardson, Olivia Barash, Vonetta McGee, Angelique Pettyjohn, and the Circle Jerks. The cinematography is by Wim Wenders regular Robby Muller. The MCA soundtrack features a good Iggy Pop theme and some great songs by Black Flag, Suicidal Tendencies, the Plugz, and others. The screenplay was published. Alex Cox also prepared the cut TV version. The executive producer of this Universal release was ex-Monkee Michael Nesmith!

REPOSSESSED

(Live, 1990) **D/S:** Bob Logan **P:** Steven Wizan

This silly spoof beat *Exorcist III* to theaters (or at least to video stores). Linda Blair stars, and Leslie Nielsen is the exorcist, so there's lots of sub–*Airplane/Naked Gun* humor. Ned Beatty plays a Jim Bakker type who broadcasts grown-up Linda's repossession. Besides the obvious gags, jokes are made about Oliver North, Ted Kennedy, and Sean Penn, and the pope shows up in his "popemobile." I guess the highlight is Nielsen singing "Devil with a Blue Dress On" while imitating Billy Idol, Michael Jackson, and Elton John. For the record, some guest bits are by Wally George, Jack LaLanne, Jesse "the Body" Ventura, and Mean Gene Okerlund. Melissa Moore has a topless scene. Bob Logan also directed Blair in *Up Your Alley* (1988).

THE RESCUE

(Touchstone, 1988) **D:** Ferdinand Fairfax **S:** Jim Thomas, John Thomas **P:** Laura Ziskin

Kevin Dillon and his teen friends take matters into their own hands after their navy dads are captured by North Koreans. This anti-Communist PG-rated Disney movie features Charles Haid and Edward Albert.

RESCUE ME

(Warner, 1993) **D:** Arthur Alan Seidelman **S:** Mike Snyder **P:** Richard Alfieri

Stephen Dorff stars as a naive Nebraska high-school photographer in love with class queen Ami Dolenz. When she's kidnapped he teams up with a grizzled Nam vet (Michael Dudikoff) on a motorcycle for a cross-country rescue. With Peter DeLuise as a stupid kidnapper and Dee Wallace Stone. This Cannon movie is rated PG.

RESERVOIR DOGS

(Live, 1992) **D/S/A:** Quentin Tarantino **P:** Lawrence Bender

This intricate, flashback-filled movie about a botched LA heist started the much-publicized directing career of Quentin Tarantino, then still in his 20s. Lawrence Tierney and his son (Chris Penn) recruit six pros, give them color names, and have them rob a jewelry store. Harvey Keitel (who was a coproducer) stars as Mr. White, and Tim Roth is Mr. Orange. Steve Buscemi, Michael Madsen, Kirk Baltz, and Tarantino are the others. It was controversial because of the violence, but not that much is actually shown. There are nods to Kubrick, Scorsese, Leone westerns, and various French and Hong Kong crime movies. The all-70s soundtrack starts with the great "Little Green Bag" by the George Baker Selection but includes many irritating hits. During production Tierney was arrested for shooting holes in an apartment. Monte Hellman, who had wanted to direct it, was an executive producer. The Pioneer laserdisc has interviews and behind-the-scenes footage.

THE RESIDENTS: TWENTY TWISTED QUESTIONS

(Voyager, 1992)

Along with Devo, the San Francisco–based cult band the Residents pioneered modern rock videos in the late 70s. Some of their bizarre and surreal videos are b/w and use stop motion. A cover of "Land of a Thousand Dances" is one of my faves. All of the Residents' videos plus brief concert sequences are on this hour-long laserdisc. Penn Gillette narrates one segment.

REST IN PIECES

(IVE, 1987) **D:** "Joseph Braunstein"/José Larraz **S:** Santiago Moncada **P:** José Frade US/Spain/UK

A woman (Lorin Jean Vail) inherits a haunted suburban house from her aunt (Dorothy Malone), who killed herself (her death is preserved on video). This very confused movie features Nazis, killer priests, topless scenes, and psycho ghosts who slaughter a string quartet. With Scott Thompson Baker, Jack Taylor, Patty Shepard, and Fernando Bilbao.

THE RESTLESS YEARS

(1958) **D:** Helmut Kautner **S:** Edward Anhalt **P:** Ross Hunter

Universal's ads called this a story about "two decent youngsters in love and a town with a dirty mind!" John Saxon and Sandra Dee star, with James Whitmore, Teresa Wright, Luana Patton, Virginia Grey, Jody McCrea, and Margaret Lindsay. Teen star Saxon had already been in *Running Wild, The Unguarded Moment, Rock, Pretty Baby,* and *Summer Love* and was about to graduate from teen roles. He was still very active in the 90s.

THE RESURRECTED

(Live, 1992) **D:** Dan O'Bannon **S:** Brent Friedman **P:** Ken Raich, Mark Borde **M:** Richard Band Canada

H. P. Lovecraft's "The Case of Charles Dexter Ward" is the basis for this (as well as for 1963's *The Haunted Palace*). It's a slow-moving version, narrated by a private eye (John Terry) in Providence, Rhode Island, with a record number of flashbacks (and flashbacks inside of flashbacks). But if you're patient you'll see some pretty great shocking mutants and a surprising ending. A living, mutilated half-body is a disgusting highlight. Chris Sarandon stars both as a modern cosmetics-firm engineer who acts real strange and as his 18th-century sorceror ancestor. Jane Sibbett is his wife, who hires the detective. With Jewel Shepard. It was filmed near Vancouver by the director of *Return of the Living Dead* and the producers of *Hollywood Hot Tubs* and its sequel.

Steve Buscemi and Harvey Keitel in *Reservoir Dogs.*

RETRIBUTION

(Virgin, 1987) **D/S/P/A/E:** Guy Magar
S: Lee Wasserman

A misfit LA artist (Dennis Lipscomb) commits suicide on Halloween. His body is possessed by a killer gangster with the same birthday who died at the same time. The formerly meek man commits vengeance murders. This looks more like a drug-effects movie (the photography is excellent) than a horror movie, and the artist's poor, eccentric hotel neighbors are all treated sympathetically. Leslie Wing costars as a shrink, with Suzanne Snyder, Jeff Pomeranz, and Hoyt Axton. Alan Howarth composed the score. It had to be cut for an R rating, and a longer version was released overseas.

RETURN

(Academy, 1984) **D/S:** Andrew Silver **P:** Philip Spinelli

A girl (Karlene Crockett) tries to locate the spirit of her grandfather using hypnosis. With John Walcutt, Anne Lloyd Francis, Lisa Richards, and Frederic Forrest. It's based on a Donald Harrington novel.

THE RETURNING

(Imperial, 1983) **D:** Joel Bender
S: Patrick Nash   (*Witch Doctor*)

Susan Strasberg and Gabriel Walsh star in this slow-moving tale of reincarnation and possession. A cursed stone causes it all. It's by the director of *Gas Pump Girls*.

THE RETURNING

(1991) **D/S:** John Day **S:** Arthur
Baysting **P:** Trishia Downie   NZ

Philip Gordon stars in this "erotic fantasy" as a young lawyer who hides out in an old mansion and is seduced by a 100-year-old female ghost. Alison Routledge costars.

THE RETURN OF A MAN CALLED HORSE

(1976) **D:** Irvin Kershner **S:** Jack De Witt
P: Terry Morse Jr. **M:** Laurence Rosenthal

Richard Harris (from the original 1970 hit) is an honorary member of the Yellow Hand tribe. He returns from England to help fight off some evil fur trappers. There's a 17-minute pre-title sequence and a 20-minute "sun vow ritual," this time with a dozen Indian braves hanging from their flesh. One Indian slashes his own eyes. Somehow this was rated PG. With Gale Sondergaard, Geoffrey Lewis, and Claudio Brook. It was filmed in Mexico. The soundtrack is on UA. *The Triumphs of a Man Called Horse* is another sequel.

THE RETURN OF CAPTAIN INVINCIBLE

(Magnum, 1982) **D:** Philippe Mora
S: Steven E. De Souza **P:** Andrew Gaza
Australia (*Legend in Leotards*)

Alan Arkin is a retired, drunken, costumed superhero called back to battle the evil Mr. Midnight (Christopher Lee). Michael Pate is the US president. There's a US spy base in Australia, and characters sing. This comedy/fantasy/musical uses footage from *The Day the Earth Stood Still.*

THE RETURN OF CHANDU

(Rhino, Sinister, 1934) **D:** Ray Taylor
S: Barry Barringer **P:** Sol Lesser

Bela Lugosi was in the feature *Chandu the Magician* (1932) as the villain. In this 12-chapter Principal serial he's the magician hero! The Egyptian Ubasto cult wants Princess Nadji (Maria Alba) as a human sacrifice. The giant-wall set from *King Kong* was reused. With silent-film star Clara Kimball Young. This was originally released as a serial, as a feature plus 8 episodes, and also as 2 features. The second feature was called *Chandu on Magic Island*. A 61-minute condensed version is also on video.

THE RETURN OF DR. FU MANCHU

(Startime, 1930) **D:** Rowland V. Lee
S: Florence Ryerson, Lloyd Corrigan

Fu (Warner Oland) escapes from a coffin at the start of the immediate sequel to *The Mysterious Dr. Fu Manchu* (1929). He intends to kill off the British family of the fiancé of his adopted daughter (Jean Arthur). With Neil Hamilton, O. P. Heggie (the blind hermit in *Bride of Frankenstein*) as Sir Nayland Smith, William Austin, and Tetsu Komai. This Paramount release was also filmed in a German-language version. Oland returned in *Daughter of the Dragon* (1931).

THE RETURN OF MICKEY SPILLANE'S MIKE HAMMER

(1986) **D:** Ray Danton **S:** Larry Brody, Janis
Hendler, James M. Miller **P:** Gary Frederickson

Stacy Keach returned to his CBS-TV series after his 1985 British drug bust. In the feature-length first show Hammer goes to Hollywood to find the kidnapped daughter of a movie star (Lauren Hutton). Lindsay Bloom and Don Stroud return too. With Vince Edwards, Mickey Rooney, John Karlen, Dabney Coleman, and Dionne Warwick. The revived series lasted only a few months.

THE RETURN OF SABATA

(VSOM, 1971) **D/S:** "Frank Kramer"/Gianfranco
Parolini **S:** Renato Izzo **P:** Alberto Grimaldi
Italy/Spain (*Il Ritorno di Sabata*)

Lee Van Cleef stars in a sequel to *Sabata* (1969), with Reiner Schone and Annabelle Incontrera. He works in a Wild West show and is after some crooks who stole his loot. United Artists released it with a PG rating.

THE RETURN OF SPINAL TAP

(MPI, 1992) **D:** "Jim DiBergi" **S:** Christopher
Guest, Michael McKean, Harry Shearer

Christopher Guest, Michael McKean, and Harry Shearer return as Spinal Tap (and their acoustic opening group, the Folksmen) in this direct-to-video sequel. A concert at the Royal Albert Hall is featured, plus interview segments and cameos by *This Is Spinal Tap* director Rob Reiner (as Marty DiBergi), Paul Shaffer, Fred Willard, June Chadwick, Bob Geldof, Graham Nash, Jamie Lee Curtis, Richard Lewis, Martha Quinn, Jeff Beck, Martin Short, Paul Anka, Mel Torme (who sings "Big Bottom Girls"!), and others.

THE RETURN OF SUPERFLY

(Vidmark, 1990) **D/P:** Sig Shore **S/P:** Anthony Wisdom

Nathan Purdee stars as Priest (played by Ron O'Neal in *Superfly* and *Superfly TNT*). He infiltrates his old gang. This anti-drug, pro-cop sequel features a reworked Curtis Mayfield score with rap music. It was released near the time Mayfield was struck by lightning and paralyzed. With Margaret Avery (*The Color Purple*) and Tone Loc.

RETURN OF THE ALIEN'S DEADLY SPAWN

(Arrow, 1982) **D/S:** Doug McKeown, Tim
Sullivan **P:** Ted Bohus   (*Deadly Spawn*)

This marvel of imaginative, low-budget (16mm) filmmaking features some teens in a house with alien tadpole monsters in the basement. The creatures (with rows of sharp teeth) multiply and grow until some of them are bigger than the house. A kid who's a horror-movie fan becomes the hero. Watching this movie (made in New Jersey) at a theater on 42nd Street was a high point of my Manhattan moviegoing days. Charles George Hildebrandt stars with Tom De Franco and Jean Tafler. A soundtrack was issued on Deadly records. *Metamorphosis* was a later "sequel."

RETURN OF THE DRAGON

(CBS/Fox, 1973) **D/S/A:** Bruce Lee

Bruce Lee's third starring feature and the only one he had control of, was made after *Fists of Fury* and *The Chinese Connection*. It was promoted in America as being a "sequel" to *Enter the Dragon* but was actually made before it. Lee plays Tang Lung, a country boy who goes to Italy to help out in a Chinese restaurant and has to fight gangsters. In one of Lee's great fight scenes (he did the choreography) he goes up against Chuck Norris at the Colosseum in Rome. It was all shot in Hong Kong, though. Norris and Lee had also appeared in the Matt Helm movie *The Wrecking Crew* (1969).

RETURN OF THE EVIL DEAD = RETURN OF THE BLIND DEAD

RETURN OF THE FAMILY MAN

(Raedon, 1989) **D/S:** John Murlowski **S:** John Fox
P: Johann Van Rooyen, Karl Johnson   S. Africa

An escaped mass murderer (Ron Smerczak) in the American Pacific Southwest is called the "family man" by the press. The man, who has a mansion with the bodies of his first victims (his family) in the basement, had devised the Star Wars Defense system (!). With Liam Cundill and Terence Reis.

RETURN OF THE INCREDIBLE HULK

(1977) **D:** Alan J. Levi **S/P:** Kenneth Johnson

This was the second pilot film for the TV series (1978–82) starring Bill Bixby turning into the Hulk (Lou Ferrigno). With Laurie Prange, William Daniels, and Gerald McRaney. It's not to be confused with *The Incredible Hulk Returns* (1988).

RETURN OF THE JEDI

(CBS/Fox, 1983) **D:** Richard Marquand
S: Lawrence Kasdan, George Lucas
P: Howard Kazanjian **M:** John Williams

This is now one of the highest-grossing films of all time, so you've probably seen it, cute teddy bears and all. Mark Hamill, Harrison Ford, Carrie Fisher, and Billy Dee Williams all return from *The Empire Strikes Back*, and Frank Oz is Yoda. Also featured are Alec Guinness, the voice of James Earl Jones, Anthony Davis, Kenny Baker, David Prowse, and the usual crew. Another bestselling soundtrack was released (on RSO) as well as two behind-the-scenes videos (Playhouse). The *Star Wars* concept went to TV next with Ewok movies and became a Disneyland tour. The four main series stars went into extreme career (and real-life) dives after this, with only Ford surviving as a major actor. The entire trilogy is available on laserdisc as a deluxe boxed set from Fox. A Star Wars Trilogy box CD set (20th Century) is also available.

RETURN OF THE KILLER TOMATOES: THE SEQUEL

(New World, 1988) **D/S/A:** John DeBello
S: Stephen F. Andrich, Constantine Dillon
P: J. Stephen Peace, Lowell D. Blank

This includes flashbacks from the 1977 cult comedy, but otherwise it has little to do with the original. Somebody noticed how many video units had been sold, so a "sequel" was ordered. John Astin is Professor Gangrene, who plans to take over the

John Astin in *Return of the Killer Tomatoes*.

world with tomato warriors. Steve Lundquist is his assistant, Igor. This PG comedy, which led to more sequels and a TV cartoon series, also features Anthony Starke, George Clooney, and future porno star Teri Weigel.

RETURN OF THE LIVING DEAD

(HBO, 1985) **D/S:** Dan O'Bannon
P: Tom Fox, Graham Henderson

This horror comedy was released the same year as George Romero's *Day of the Dead*. The original script was by John Russo, who cowrote *Night of the Living Dead*. There was a legal battle with George Romero over the title, but many fans liked this movie better than the official sequel. I like them both a lot. Clu Gulager and James Karen (both great in their roles) run Uneeda Medical Supplies in Louisville. Talking cannibal zombies are released, yelling "Brains!" and "More brains!" and a group of punk kids show up to party. A living half-dog and a half-human corpse are visual highlights in a movie that manages to be scary, surprising, and funny. The whole state of Kentucky is nuked by the military at the end! With Thom Mathews, Linnea Quigley, Jewel Shepard, Don Calfa, and Brian Peck. The good various artist rock soundtrack (on Enigma) features the Cramps, the Damned, and Roky Erikson. Tobe Hooper was once slated to direct it (in 3-D).

RETURN OF THE LIVING DEAD, PART II

(Lorimar, 1987) **D/S:** Ken Wiederhorn **P:** Tom Fox

James Karen and Thom Mathews return in a terrible sequel that plays like a teen-comedy remake of what was already an unofficial comedy sequel. With Michael Kenworthy, Dana Ashbrook, and Forry Ackerman as a zombie. A various artists soundtrack (Julian Cope, Anthrax, Zodiac Mindwarp) is on IRS. The video contains a merchandising ad. The director did *Meatballs II*.

RETURN OF THE LIVING DEAD 3

(Vidmark, 1993) **D/P:** Brian Yuzna
S: John Penny **P:** Gary Schmoeller
M: Barry Goldberg

This unrelenting, serious horror movie would have done better without the sequel title. It has more in common with *Re-Animator* and the original *Hellraiser* than with the other *Return of the Living Dead* movies. A teen army brat (J. Trevor Edmond) uses Trioxen to bring his dead girlfriend (Mindy Clarke) back to life after a motorcycle accident.

Return of the Living Dead.

She becomes a sympathetic cannibal zombie with an incredible punk S&M look with self-pierced body parts, but he still loves her. Multi-racial gang members become zombies in the LA sewer system, and Basil Wallace is a homeless hero. It mixes extreme horror and shooting FX with the tragic true-love theme. With Kent McCord (from *Adam-12*) as Edmond's military father, Sarah Douglas as a Pentagon colonel working on turning the dead into soldiers, Fabio Urena, Pia Reyes, and Anthony Hickox. Tom Raimone was the second-unit director and was in charge of the FX, created by a record five shops. It had to be cut for an R.

RETURN OF THE MAN FROM U.N.C.L.E.

(TWE, 1983) **D:** Ray Austin
S: Michael Sloane **P:** Nigel Watts

Robert Vaughn and David McCallum returned as Napoleon Solo and Ilya Kuryakin in this CBS-TV series pilot film, this time working for new U.N.C.L.E. boss Patrick Macnee. They're called out of retirement to stop Anthony Zerbe as a T.H.R.U.S.H. villain who has stolen a nuclear bomb. With Gayle Hunnicutt, Geoffrey Lewis, Keenan Wynn, and George Lazenby as "JB." Ray Austin was a stunt director, then director of *The Avengers* series. The original *The Man from U.N.C.L.E.* series ran from 1964 to 1968. A revived series never happened. Just as well.

RETURN OF THE MUSKETEERS

(MCA, 1989) **D:** Richard Lester **S:** George MacDonald Fraser **P:** Michelle De Broca, Pierre Spangler   UK/France/Spain

This sequel, set 20 years later than the hits *The Three Musketeers* (1974) and *The Four Musket-*

eers (1975), is based on the Alexandre Dumas novel *Twenty Years After*. Richard Lester directed again, and many of the original stars returned, but nobody cared, so this PG film went directly to cable TV in the USA. With Michael York, Oliver Reed, Frank Finlay, Geraldine Chaplin, Christopher Lee, Richard Chamberlain, and Billy Connolly. Roy Kinnear died in a horseback-riding accident during production, and a double had to be used for some scenes. New characters are played by Philippe Noiret as Cardinal Mazarin, C. Thomas Howell as the adopted son of Athos, and Kim Cattrall as the evil daughter of Milady De Winter. It was filmed in Spain.

THE RETURN OF THE SIX MILLION DOLLAR MAN AND THE BIONIC WOMAN

(1987) **D:** Ray Austin **S/P:** Michael Sloane

People everywhere were greatly relieved that this attempt to create a new series about the bionic son (Lee Majors II) of Steve Austin (Lee Majors) failed. Lindsay Wagner and Richard Anderson return from those lame 70s science-fiction/action shows, and Martin Landau plays the villain. With Gary Lockwood. Another NBC-TV pilot attempt was called *Bionic Showdown* (1989).

RETURN OF THE SWAMP THING

(RCA/Columbia, 1989) **D:** Jim Wynorski **S:** Derek Spencer, Grant Morris **P:** Ben Melniker

This PG-13 sequel to Wes Craven's 1982 film was followed by a syndicated TV series. Dick Durock (also in the series) is "the swamp thing," and Louis Jourdan returns as Dr. Arcane, who's busy creating bizarre mutants. Heather Locklear is a relative who comes to stay, and Sarah Douglas is the doctor's assistant, but the real stars are a pair of little kids. Monique Gabrielle and Ace Mask are also featured. CCR's "Born on the Bayou" is on the soundtrack.

RETURN OF THE TEXAS CHAINSAW MASSACRE

(1994) **D/S:** Kim Henkel **P:** Robert Kuhn

This indy movie (made after sequels from Cannon and New Line) was filmed near Austin. Director Kim Henkel (who cowrote the original 1974 classic *The Texas Chainsaw Massacre*) claimed that this was the real sequel although it didn't feature any of the original cast; it's actually a remake with added subplots and characters. Renee Zellenger stars, with Toni Perensky, Matthew McConaughey (*Dazed and Confused*), and Robert Jacks as Leatherface.

RETURN OF THE ZOMBIES: *See* THE HANGING WOMAN

RETURN TO FANTASY ISLAND

(1978) **D:** George McGowan **S:** Marc Brandel **P:** Michael Fisher

This is the second ABC-TV pilot film for the mind-rotting series that ran from 1978 all the way to 1984. Ricardo Montalban and Hervé Villechaize

star, and the guest cast is superb, as usual: Joseph Cotten, Cameron Mitchell, two Georges (Chakiris and Maharis), France Nuyen, Adrienne Barbeau, Horst Buchholz, Joseph Campanella, and perky Karen Valentine. Who wasn't in this show? It was a Spelling/Goldberg production.

RETURN TO HORROR HIGH

(Starmaker, 1987) **D/S:** Bill Froelich **S/P:** Mark Lisson **S:** Dana Escalante

A surviving screenwriter (Philip McKeon) relates this horror-movie spoof about filming at a haunted school. Nightmare sequences mixed with flashbacks add to the confusion. A white-masked killer hides in the basement. Alex Rocco plays the producer, and Scott Jacoby is the director. With Andy Romano, Maureen McCormick (from the TV series *The Brady Bunch*) as a cop, Lori Lethin and Brendan Hughes as the top-billed actors in the film within a film, and Darcy Demoss. In one scene Vince Edwards is nailed to the floor. From New World.

RETURN TO MACON COUNTY

(Vestron, 1975) **D/S:** Richard Compton **P:** Elliot Schick

AIP released the sequel to *Macon County Line* (1974), by the same director but with none of the same characters. Don Johnson (the same year as *A Boy and His Dog*) stars with a young Nick Nolte (in his movie debut) as two late-50s Georgia guys who want to go to California to enter a drag race. Robin Mattson, as an on-the-edge waitress who wants to be an actress, joins them and causes problems. The plot concerns sex and murder. With Robert Viharo and Eugene Daniels. The very good vintage-oldies soundtrack is on United Artists.

RETURN TO OZ

(Disney, 1985) **D/S:** Walter Murch **S:** Gil Dennis **P:** Paul Maslansky

I guess too many people have the original 1939 *The Wizard of Oz* permanently imbedded in their minds to appreciate this PG sequel based on a different L. Frank Baum novel. I caught it on late-night TV and thought it was great. Fairuza Balk stars as Dorothy. She's put into a sanitarium and given electroshock treatments (!) after she tells Auntie Em (Piper Laurie) and Uncle Henry (Matt Clark) about her adventures in Oz. Dorothy ends up back in Oz, now in ruins, and faces the evil Nome King (Nicol Williamson) and Princess Mombi (Jean Marsh). Her companions this time are a talking chicken, Pumpkinhead, and Tik-Tok the robot. George Lucas and Steven Spielberg both helped with this darker commercial flop PG version from Disney and Will Vinton's Claymation is used for the rock faces. Sonic Atmospheres released the soundtrack.

A RETURN TO 'SALEM'S LOT

(Warner, 1987) **D/S:** Larry Cohen **S:** James Dixon **P:** Paul Kurta

Michael Moriarty (from *Q*) stars as a tough anthropologist (and mondo filmmaker) who is hired by

the residents of a small Maine town to write their local history and discovers that everyone there is a vampire. The locals are also old-fashioned, drug-free, flag-waving small-town Americans who are afraid of AIDS. He takes along his estranged pre-teen son (Ricky Addison Reed), and they're joined by a clever old cigar-chomping Dr. Van Helsing type (wonderfully played by director Samuel Fuller). There are sights like little-kid vampires getting married and killing, and old ladies lapping up a victim's blood. It's not really a sequel to the 1979 Stephen King TV movie and is obviously a rushed production (with some mediocre FX) but is still one of Larry Cohen's best. With Andrew Duggan as the judge, 40s stars June Havoc and Evelyn Keyes, Katya Crosby, Jill Gatsby, Brad Rijn, and Ronee Blakley. It was shot in Vermont.

RETURN TO TWO MOON JUNCTION

(Vidmark, 1993) **D:** Farhad Mann **P:** Zalman King

Melinda Clarke (*Return of the Living Dead* 3) is a model who returns to her Georgia home and has an affair with a sculptor (John Clayton Schafer). With Yorgo Constantine, Louise Fletcher (from the original), and Matt Frewer in drag.

REVENGE

(United, 1986) **D/S:** Christopher Lewis **P:** Linda Lewis

Patrick Wayne, who would do only PG-rated films when his father was alive, stars in this shot-on-video sequel to *Blood Cult*. John Carradine is the head of a small-town cult that worships the dog god Caninus. "They wag their tales and tear out our hearts!" said the ads, which claimed that this was Carradine's "500th" movie (nonsense). The video includes bad takes. The Oklahoma filmmakers also gave us *The Ripper*.

REVENGE IN THE HOUSE OF USHER

(Wizard, 1979) **D/S/P/C:** "J. P. Johnson"/ Jesús Franco   Spain (*El Hundimiento de la Casa Usher; The Sinister Dr. Orloff; Nervosus*)

Dr. Usher, "the son of Dr. Orloff" (Howard Vernon), uses his ugly brother Morpho to kidnap naked women so that he can restore his daughter's beauty. Blood transfusions help keep Usher alive. The many b/w flashbacks are from Jesús Franco's 1962 movie *The Awful Dr. Orloff* (also with Vernon), of which this is basically another remake. With Lina Romay and Robert Forster.

THE REVENGE OF BILLY THE KID

(VSOM, 1991) **D/S:** Jim Groom **S/P:** Tim Denison **S:** Richard Mathews   UK

This crude horror comedy is set on a remote island farm. After farmer McDonald (Michael Balfour) fucks a goat, a goat man is born (a dwarf with a goat's head), and he kills it. It doesn't really die but grows to giant size and kills off the cast, which includes Jackie D. Broad as Ma and Hammer regular Michael Ripper.

REVENGE OF DRACULA = DRACULA VS. FRANKENSTEIN

REVENGE OF DR. X

(Regal, 1970) **D:** ????? **S:** Ed Wood Jr.
Japan (*The Double Garden*)

Wood wrote a script called *Venus Fly Trap*, which ended up being filmed in Japan by Toei. The video box lists the wrong cast and credits (they're for the 1969 Filipino movie *The Mad Doctor of Blood Island*). The star is American James Craig, MGM's "replacement" for Clark Gable during WWII. He also was in *Bigfoot* (1969), so you can see how well his career was going. The full-color action starts at Cape Kennedy (NASA stock footage is used). Dr. Bragan (Craig with his usual pencil-thin mustache) yells a lot during a delayed launch and collapses. A Japanese colleague suggests a rest in his homeland, but first Bragan has car trouble in Wilmington, North Carolina, on the way to the airport (!?). The local garage mechanic is also a snake handler. When he disembarks from his plane in Tokyo all he carries is a box containing his precious, hungry venus fly-trap plant. The hunchbacked servant at a run-down old hotel near a volcano plays clichéd Western horror-movie music at the organ (and has his own theme music). Bragan is alternately mean and grouchy or cheerful to Noriko, his able new female assistant. Obsessed with the plant ("You will become the most powerful thing in the universe!"), he hopes to combine it with another plant ("I refuse the word impossible!"). He and Noriko travel to the seaside and hire a group of topless diving girls to find a rare, giant underwater plant, which they place in a clear glass box. Back at the hotel the movie becomes *Frankenplant 1970*. On a typical mad-lab set the plants are raised on an operating table so that lightning can bring life. The resulting monster is incredible!! It's a 50s-style creature with a long tail, fly-trap hands, and fly-trap feet. It gets stronger by eating a puppy. Bragan yells, "Your mother was the earth! The rain your blood! The lightning your power! Ah ha ha ha!!!" He feeds it mice and promises a human heart. At a local hospital he takes the blood from a pregnant woman. The creature emits a sleeping gas. It escapes, walking through the nearby village. The screen turns red when it kills. The angry villagers gather with torches. Bragan brings it a baby goat to eat, but he and his creation fall into an active volcano (just like the end of *The Manster*)!! Amazing!

REVENGE OF JOHNNY FIRECLOUD:
See JOHNNY FIRECLOUD

REVENGE OF THE CHEERLEADERS

(VGB, 1976) **D/P:** Richard Lerner **S:** Ted Greenwald, Ace Bandage, Nathaniel Dorsky **P:** Nathaniel Dorsky

This forgotten drive-in movie stars Patrice Rohmer, Jeri Woods (*Switchblade Sisters*), who has the most nude scenes, and Cheryl "Rainbeaux" Smith. Watch it if you want to see David Hasselhoff naked (as Boner) and magician and actor Carl Ballantine (from the TV series *McHale's Navy*), who keeps his clothes on.

REVENGE OF THE DEAD

(Lightning, 1983) **D/S:** Pupi Avanti
S/P: Antonio Avanti **S:** Maurizio Costanzo
Italy (*Zeder; Voice from the Darkness*)

A novelist (Gabriele Lava) in Bologna travels to investigate messages on his wife's typewriter ribbon. He visits graveyards and crypts, going through layers of history, and discovers a French research group (in a former nudist colony) tring to revive a dead priest who shows up laughing on TV screens. People are stabbed and decapitated, and it all involves a magical "K zone" and a pet cemetery. MPM released this in America.

REVENGE OF THE LIVING ZOMBIES

(Magnum, 1989) **D/S/P/A/E:** Bill Hinzman
S: Bill Randolph   (*Flesh Eater*)

Even zombie actors made uncredited remakes of *Night of the Living Dead*! The very first onscreen zombie in *NOTLD* (he appears when Johnny says "They're coming to get you, Barbara!") was Bill Hinzman. This is a teen-zombie movie but copies a lot from the original and is very non-Hollywood (people drink Iron City Beer). College students on a Halloween hayride 20 years later spend the night in the woods smoking pot, drinking, and making out. The famous Hinzman zombie kills a farmer, and more people become walking dead as the kids try to warn the unbelieving local authorities. A cop says, "These kids are not human!" It's gory (axe in head, pitchfork in chest, bitten-off nose) and has nudity (naked, bloody zombies and a long shower scene). An angelic-looking little-girl zombie kills her mother. They wait until dad comes home and have him for dinner. Hinzman even gets to thrust his arm right through a naked girl. There's the boarded-up house surrounded by zombies, local TV reports, and a twist on the original surprise ending. Some of the effects are good, but there's at least one obvious dummy head, and the acting is pretty horrible. All in all it's pretty entertaining.

REVENGE OF THE NERDS

(Fox, 1984) **D:** Jeff Kanew **S:** Steve Zacharias
P: Ted Field, Peter Samuelson

Robert Carradine is Lewis and Anthony Edwards is Gilbert, new college "nerds." They start their own fraternity with various other social misfits and fight back against macho jocks and bitchy coeds. This surprise comedy hit is better than average for a teen comedy. With Julia Montgomery, Curtis Armstrong (funny as Booger), Timothy Busfield, Michelle Meyrink, Courtney Thorne-Smith, Matt Salinger, Ted McGinley, Bernie Casey, and John Goodman as a coach. This 20th Century–Fox release is rated R. Scotti Brothers released the various artists soundtrack.

REVENGE OF THE NERDS II: NERDS IN PARADISE

(Fox, 1987) **D:** Joe Roth **S:** Dan Guntzelman, Steve Marshall **P:** Ted Field, Robert Gort, Peter Bart

This time the nerds go to Fort Lauderdale, the music is by Devo, and the rating is PG-13. Robert Carradine returns with Curtis Armstrong and Timothy Busfield, and Anthony Edwards makes a token appearance. Ed Lauter and James Hong are also in the cast.

REVENGE OF THE NERDS III: THE NEXT GENERATION

(Fox, 1992) **D:** Roland Mesa **S:** Steve Zacharias

Robert Carradine returns to help younger college nerds when Morton Downey Jr. and Ted McGinley conspire to bring the jocks back to power at Adams College. Curtis Armstrong, Julia Montgomery, Bernie Casey, and other cast members return from the first movie. It debuted on cable TV.

REVENGE OF THE NERDS IV: NERDS IN LOVE

(Fox, 1994) **D/S:** Steve Zacharias
S: Jeff Buhai **P:** Ooty Moorehead

Booger (Curtis Armstrong) plans to marry the daughter (Corinne Bohrer) of wealthy Joseph Bologna. Nerds arrive from all over for the wedding. Robert Carradine (one of the executive producers) and Julia Montgomery are now married. Christina Pickles and Jessica Tuck are featured, and there are bit roles for Bernie Casey, Ted McGinley, and Marvin Kaplan. It debuted on Fox-TV with some pretty bogus gimmicks: a scratch-and-sniff segment and a 3-D segment. Cards were available from 7-Eleven.

REVENGE OF THE NINJA

(MGM/UA, 1983) **D:** Sam Firstenberg
S: James R. Silke **P:** Golan/Globus

Sho Kosugi's family is slaughtered, so he runs a doll shop with his surviving son (his real-life son Kane). This "sequel" to *Enter the Ninja* (1981) features heroin in dolls and lots of action. It was remade in 1985 as *Pray for Death* (also with Kosugi). Arthur Roberts, Virgil Frye, Ashley Ferrare, and John Lamotta are featured. The same title was used for a Malaysian horror movie in 1988. *Ninja III* was next for Kosugi.

REVENGE OF THE RADIOACTIVE REPORTER

(Magnum, 1988) **D/S/P:** Craig Pryce
S: David Wiechorek   Canada

In this really stupid Troma-inspired comedy a reporter named Mike (Dave Scammell) is pushed into nuclear waste and becomes a phantom killer with a bandaged face and the touch of death. He rips some heads off, kills a woman by pissing in her bathtub, and has a b/w dream of a mutant baby. A cop says, "Sounds like you've been watching too many bad horror movies."

REVENGE OF THE RED BARON

(New Horizons, 1994) **D:** Robert Gordon
S: Michael J. McDonald **P:** Mike Elliot

This "sequel" to Roger Corman's *Von Richthofen and Brown* (1971) stars a kid (Toby Maguire). Baron Ferdinand von Richthofen magically comes to life in a toy plane (?!) and starts killing with tiny bullets from a toy machine gun while making wisecracks. Mickey Rooney is the kid's grandfather, who shot down the baron during WWI. Laraine Newman and Cliff De Young are the parents.

REVENGE OF THE SHOGUN WOMEN

(1977) **D:** Mei Chung Chang **S:** Lorenz Soma
P: Frank Wong   Hong Kong (*13 Nuns;
Shogun Women; Revenge of the 13*)

Women in 18th-century China are raped by bandits. Years later they're ready for revenge, with their short hair and martial-arts skills. With lots of impressive 3-D effects, bloody sword and axe fights, and nudity. Shisuen Leong, Han Tsiang-Chin, and Pai Ying star. This was released in America in 1981 in 3-D by 21st Century and is fondly remembered by those who saw it.

REVENGE OF THE VIRGINS

(Video Dimensions, 1959) **D/P:** Peter Perry Jr.
S: Peter La Roche

A narrator (Ed Wood regular Kenne Duncan) informs us about a Stone Age tribe of California Indians, "amazons of the West." These female warriors lurk in the background shooting arrows, and, oh yeah, they're all topless. This boring, talk-filled movie is full of clichéd gold prospectors and bad guys, and the 53-minute print is too dark. It's for topless-western completists only. It was re-released in 1966.

REVENGE OF THE WILD BUNCH

(CNH, 1970) **D/S:** Paul Hunt **S/P/C/E:** Ronald V.
Garcia **P:** Harry Novak, Phil Yankowitz
(*Machismo; 40 Graves for 40 Guns*)

This violent western (obviously inspired by the previous year's *The Wild Bunch*) is pro-Hispanic and anti-Gringo, making it unique. Robert Padilla stars as a Mexican bandit promised a pardon if he and his men bring back some killer American gold thieves who have crossed the border. Mexicans are called greaseballs and worse by small-town drunks and cowards. The climactic battle/massacre is very bloody and gory. The slow-motion love scenes and out-of-focus sex scenes are ridiculous. With Leslie York, Stanley Adams, Sue Bernard, Bruce Gordon, Nancy Caroline, and Royal Dano as a grizzled racist. Boxoffice International released it.

REVENGE OF THE ZOMBIE:
See KISS DADDY GOODNIGHT

REVENGER

(AIP, 1989) **D:** Cedric Sundstrom **S:** John Cianetti
P: Jonathan Vanger, Gregory Vanger   S. Africa

Michael (Frank Zagarino), a young sax player "in LA", is set up and sent to prison for three years. He moves in with his girlfriend after being paroled, but the bad guys think he knows where some loot is, so they kidnap her. The hero teams up with his one-eyed, one-legged Nam-vet buddy for the big rescue. Jack (big Oliver Reed with a gray mustache) snorts coke, smokes crack, and makes a woman watch porno (and snuff) movies (which he financed) before raping her. When his addicted, bisexual girlfriend is killed he yells, "I'm going to cut his balls off!" It all ends in a shootout copied from *Who'll Stop the Rain* (1978). There's an amusement-park

fight, the hero in a shower, a kung-fu cop, and a (fairly graphic for an R video) look at Jack's porno production.

REVOLT OF THE SLAVES

(VSOM, 1961) **D:** Nunzio Malasomma **P:** Paola Moffa
Italy/Spain, W. Germany (*La Rivolta degli Schiavi*)

Rhonda Fleming falls for slave Lang Jeffries. They become Christians and are sent into the arena. Fleming and Jeffries were married for a while in real life. It was one of the last leading roles for the red-haired 50s star, who had been in four movies opposite Ronald Reagan. She later campaigned for him (and George Bush).

REVOLT OF THE ZOMBIES

(Hal Roach, 1936) **D/S:** Victor Halperin **S:** Howard
Higgin, Rollo Lloyd **P:** Edward Halperin

This one (from Academy Pictures) is pretty bad but very entertaining. It opens with a lineup of indestructible Cambodian zombie soldiers helping the French fight Nazis in Europe. The story moves to Cambodia, where an international expedition tries to find the ancient zombie formula and destroy it. Characters act in front of rear-projection photos of the Angkor Wat ruins. A woman does a very awkward "exotic" dance, and a troublemaking blonde creates a love triangle. The jilted, lovesick man (Dean Jagger) turns his servant into a zombie by heating the secret potion (like crack) and blowing the smoke into his face. Jagger broods, laughs, cries, and says things like "Bunha, we're learning to be ruthless!" The Halperins didn't have Bela Lugosi again, so they used his superimposed glowing eyes from their hit *White Zombie* (1932) all through this movie, and a bad guy is dressed to resemble Lugosi. Jagger turns the whole cast into zombies, and yes, they do revolt.

RHINO'S GUIDE TO SAFE SEX

(Rhino, 1987)

Johnny Legend put together this 60-minute compilation of clips dealing with sex, dating, and diseases from movies going back to the 20s. Choice scenes are from *Tomorrow's Children, Ship of Shame,* and other government films warning servicemen about VD. One features TV Superman George Reeves. *Dating Dos and Don'ts* (directed by Ed Wood Jr!) is the best-known short. Trailers from some Ed Wood and H. G. Lewis movies are here. Some silent shorts feature nudity. A 50s teen actor, Kenny Miller, sued Rhino for putting his picture on the cover of the video box.

WEIRDEST STORY IN 2,000 YEARS

"REVOLT OF THE ZOMBIES"

with
**DEAN JAGGER
DOROTHY STONE**
DISTRIBUTED BY FAVORITE FILMS CORP.

THE RIBALD TALES OF ROBIN HOOD

(Impact, 1969) **D/S:** Richard Kanter
P: Edward Paramore, John Harvey

All the usual Sherwood Forest characters appear, but the women have heavy eye makeup and take their clothes off. Blond-haired Robin Hood has a lot of sex but usually keeps his tights on. It's all pretty dull except for a scene that could have been in a Jesús Franco movie: the naked evil princess has the naked Maid Marian chained up and hung over a bed of nails, then forces her to lick her body. David F. Friedman did the original publicity, and Bambi Allen is in it. When rereleased in 1991 it was rerated NC-17.

RICH AND STRANGE

(Republic, 1932) **D:** Alfred Hitchcock **S:** Alma Reville,
Val Valentine **P:** John Maxwell   UK (*East of Shanghai*)

Freddy and Emily Hill (Henry Kendall and Joan Barry) are a couple with inherited money who travel around the world on a ship. They each have affairs and are shipwrecked. They're rescued by a Chinese junk and get back together. It was a sound film without much dialogue.

RICH GIRL

(HBO, 1991) **D:** Joel Bender **S:** Robert Elliot
P: Michael B. London **M:** Jay Chattaway

Jill Schoelen (*The Stepfather*) stars as a Beverly Hills girl who's working as a waitress and falls for a rock singer (Don Michael Paul). With Cherie Currie, Bentley Mitchum, and blues great Willie Dixon as himself.

RICOCHET

(Columbia, 1991) **D:** Russell Mulcahy
S: Steven E. de Souza **P:** Joel Silver

Denzel Washington stars as Nick Styles, a cop who becomes an assistant DA after he catches Earl Blake (John Lithgow), a violent, sadistic, devious, foul-mouthed killer. When Blake escapes from prison he ruins Styles' life by cleverly convincing people that the honest, crusading public servant is really a womanizing drug addict whose corruption led his best friend, a transvestite and child molester, to commit suicide. This often shocking movie deals with media manipulation at its worst and shows how homemade videotapes can make or break a career. It all ends in a one-on-one fight atop the Los Angeles Tower. The stars are both excellent in their roles, but it's hard to accept Lithgow as a killer so tough that he can easily make all the other prisoners (including white supremacists) cower. Ice-T is the major crack dealer brother who actually comes to the rescue, and Josh Evans is Blake's jailhouse-punk assistant. Also with Kevin Pollak, Mary Ellen Trainor, Lindsay Wagner, John Amos, Sarah Suzanne Brown, Jesse Ventura in a gladiator-fight scene, and the voice of Ernie Anderson. Fred Dekker cowrote the story. A clip of James Cagney in *White Heat* is used.

RIDE HARD, RIDE WILD

(SW, 1970) **D:** Elou Peterssens
S: Lennart Nielsen **P:** B.T. Kobenhaven

Karl, a sadistic voyeur who's a professional bike racer, has nightmares of the crash that scarred his face. He gets revenge on Leif, a guy on vacation in a van, by taking his blond girlfriend, Annelise (Brigit Kroter). Much of this movie is made up of long dirt-race sequences and straight, lesbian, group, and forced sex accompanied by slow jazz (and pot and amyl nitrate). Said to be Danish, this was apparently made in Hollywood with fake credits and a 50s Danish pop song added. The (awful) "dubbing" was supervised by Lee Frost, and the color is faded.

RIDE IN THE WHIRLWIND

(VidAmerica, 1965) **D/P:** Monte Hellman
S/P/A: Jack Nicholson

Roger Corman received no credit but backed this effective "existential" western shot in Utah. Cameron Mitchell and Jack Nicholson are cowboys who are mistaken for outlaws and pursued by vigilantes. Millie Perkins and Harry Dean Stanton are featured. Nicholson did four movies with Monte Hellman. This was made back to back with *The Shooting* (also with Nicholson and Perkins). Few Americans saw either until they were released on video.

RIDER ON THE RAIN

(1970) **D:** René Clement **S:** Sebastian Japrisot,
Lorenzo Ventavoli **P:** Serge Silberman
France/Italy (*Le Passager de la Pluie*)

Charles Bronson stars in a Hitchcock-type murder mystery as an American in the South of France who's after an escaped sex maniac. It was a big hit in France and was released here by Avco Embassy. With Marlene Jobert, Jill Ireland, and Gabriele Tinti. Capitol released the Francis Lai soundtrack.

RIDERS OF THE STORM

(Nelson, 1985) **D:** Maurice Phillips **S:** Scott Roberts
P: Laurie Keller, Paul Cowan   UK (*The American Way*)

Some pot-smoking Nam vets in an old B-29 that never leaves the sky jam right-wing TV broadcasts. Dennis Hopper is the captain, and Michael J. Pollard is on board. This misfire political satire includes a religious-TV parody, clips from old movies (including *The Devil's Bride* and *Captain Blood*), and clips of Jimi Hendrix and the Kinks. The new rock songs are mediocre. The right-wing female presidential candidate is played by a man (Nigel Pegram). The American version is 15 minutes shorter than the British, which is probably a good thing.

RINGO AND HIS GOLDEN PISTOL

(VSOM, 1966) **D:** Sergio Corbucci **S:** Adriano Bolzoni,
Franco Rozzetti **P:** Joseph Fryd   Italy (*Johnny Oro*)

Mark Damon (*The House of Usher*) stars as a bounty hunter with lots of dynamite, in this western featuring Valeria Fabrizi and Franco De Rosa. Damon was in many European movies directed by

Mario Bava, Jesús Franco, Umberto Lenzi, Riccardo Freda, and others before becoming a successful producer.

RING OF FEAR

(1954) **D:** James Edward Grant
S: Paul Fix **P:** Robert M. Fellows

In this odd Warner Cinemascope feature, famous lion tamer Clyde Beatty (playing himself) hires famous writer Mickey Spillane (playing himself) to solve a murder mystery. Sean McClory is the Irish psycho killer. Also featured are Pat O'Brien, Marian Carr, Kenneth Tobey, and John Bromfield. The Clyde Beatty Circus footage is all real. It was produced by John Wayne's company, Batjac Productions, and directed by a screenwriter of several Wayne hits. Spillane also starred (as Mike Hammer) in *The Girl Hunters* (1963).

RING OF FIRE

(Imperial, 1991) **D:** Richard W. Munchkin
S: Steve Tymon **P:** Joseph Merhi, Richard Pepin

Don "the Dragon" Wilson stars as mild-mannered Dr. Johnny Wu in Venice. He falls for Maria Ford and is forced to seek revenge using martial arts. With Gary Daniels, Ian Jacklin, Vince Murdocco, and Lisa Saxton. Wilson was also in *Out for Blood*, by the same producers.

RING OF FIRE II: BLOOD AND STEEL

(PM, 1992) **D:** Richard W. Munchkin
S: Steve Tymon **P:** Joseph Merhi, Richard Pepin

Don "the Dragon" Wilson returns as Dr. Johnny Wu, who is forced to fight after his fiancée (Maria Ford) is kidnapped and taken to a secret tunnel city underneath LA. The plot copies *Escape from New York* and various post-nuke-look movies. With Sy Richardson as a Nam vet, Ian Jacklin, Dale Jacoby, and Evan Lurie.

RING OF FIRE III: LION STRIKE

(PM, 1995) **D:** Rick Jacobson
P: Joseph Merhi, Richard Pepin

Dr. Johnny Wu (Don "the Dragon" Wilson again) is on vacation with his son (his real-life son Jonathan Wilson). He meets a forest ranger (Bobbie Philips, from *TC2000*) and has to battle Mafia assassins who work for Robert Costanza and are after a computer disk.

RING OF STEEL

(MCA, 1994) **D:** David Frost **S/A:** Robert
Chapin **P:** David Speaker, Alan M. Solomon

Richard Chapin stars as a fencing champ with long blond hair. Joe Don Baker (in all-black clothes) runs an illegal underground nightclub. Gary Kasper and Carol Alt are featured.

RIOT

(Paramount, 1969) **D:** Buzz Kulik
S: James Poe **P:** William Castle

Jim Brown and Gene Hackman are prisoners who take some guards hostage. Hackman convinces

everybody that he wants to improve prison conditions, but he's just trying to escape, alone. Brown enjoys a dream sequence, and the prison has a transvestite "queens' row." It was filmed at the Arizona State Penitentiary with the real governor, warden, and inmates. With Ben Carruthers and Mike Kellin. Alan Rudolph was the assistant director. William Castle also produced *Rosemary's Baby* at Paramount. Brown returned to prison in *The Slams* (1973).

RIOT IN CELL BLOCK 11

(Republic, 1953) **D:** Don Siegel
S: Richard Collins **P:** Walter Wanger

One of the great prison movies stars Neville Brand and a psychotic Leo Gordon (an ex-con in real life) as leaders of the riot. Producer Walter Wanger had served a short sentence for shooting the agent of his wife, actress Joan Bennett, not long before he backed this movie. The all-male cast includes Emile Meyer as the warden, Robert Osterloh, Frank Faylen, Alvy Moore, and Jonathan Hale. Paul Frees and Whit Bissell are guards held hostage. Allied Artists announced that it would be shot in 3-D, but it wasn't. It was filmed at the real Folsom Prison, though.

RIOT ON 42ND ST.

(1987) **D/S:** Tim Kincaide **P:** Cynthia De Paula

Jeff Fahey (soon to go on to bigger projects), Frances Raines, Kate Collins, and Ron Van Cleef are all in this barely released exploitation movie by the director of *Breeders* and *Bad Girls Dormitory*. Raines was in all of them.

RIPLEY'S BELIEVE IT OR NOT

(1982–86)

Jack Palance was a good choice to host this TV series. While introducing strange but real stories he often acted out scenes in such an out-of-control, hysterical way that he seemed just a few steps from the loony bin. He got to travel around the world for location shoots, and for two years his own daughter Holly was the cohost. For the last season the cohost was Marie Osmond! There are 6 volumes running 23 minutes each. Ripley himself had hosted a 1949 version but died during production. *Ripley's Believe It or Not* (Turner, 1994) is a very interesting feature-length documentary on Ripley with an actor (Richard Portnow) playing the eccentric, rich, and very famous Ripley looking back on his own unusual life. It includes many vintage clips.

THE RIP-OFF

(Worldvision, 1975) **D:** "Anthony M. Dawson"/
Antonio Margheriti **S:** Giovanni Simonelli, Mark Princi,
Paul Costello   US/ Italy (*The Big Rip-Off; The Squeeze*)

Lee Van Cleef stars in this crime movie about a diamond heist partially shot in NYC. He plans one last job. Edward Albert, Lionel Stander, Robert Alda, and Karen Black costar.

THE RIPPER

(United, 1985) **D:** Christopher Lewis
S: Bill Groves **P:** Linda Lewis

It was shot on video in Tulsa, it's gory, and Tom Savini acts for several minutes. A film professor teaching a course on famous criminals is possessed by Jack the Ripper. There's a plug for *Blood Cult*, from the same Oklahoma filmmakers.

THE RISE AND FALL OF LEGS DIAMOND

(1960) **D:** Budd Boetticher **S:** Joseph Landon **P:** Milton Sperling

Ray Danton stars as Depression-era gangster Jack "Legs" Diamond, in one of many early-60s b/w gangster movies inspired by the TV series *The Untouchables*. With Karen Steele, Elaine Stewart, Jesse White, Simon Oakland, and Robert Lowery as Arnold Rothstein, and look for Warren Oates and Dyan Cannon. Danton played the role again in *Portrait of a Mobster* (1961). This was released by Warner.

RISING STORM

(1988) **D:** Francis Schaeffer **S:** Gary Rosen, William Fray **P:** Jay Davidson, James Buchfuehrer (*Rebel Waves*)

In 2009 the US is run by a fascist, anti-rock-and-roll TV evangelist. Zach Galligan and Wayne Crawford join freedom fighters June Chadwick and Elizabeth Keifer on the run from sadistic John Rhys-Davies. William Katt is also featured. This post-nuke spoof was filmed in South Africa.

RISING SUN

(Fox, 1993) **D/S:** Philip Kaufman **S:** Michael Crichton, Michael Backes **P:** Peter Kaufman

A police detective (Wesley Snipes) and a zen master (Sean Connery) investigate the death of a hooker in a Japanese-owned skyscraper in LA. This controversial hit based on Michael Crichton's bestseller shows the dirty business tactics and customs of Japanese businessmen in America but condemns Americans a lot more. Both stars are in kung-fu fight scenes, and there's some good high-tech stuff about altering reality with video, a crowd-pleasing barrio-attack scene, and some nudity. Tia Carrere is a half-Japanese computer technician, Cary-Hiroyuki Tagawa is a playboy suspect, Harvey Keitel is a corrupt LA cop, and Ray Wise is a corrupt senator. Mako, Steve Buscemi, and Clyde Kusatsu are also featured. The production design is by Dean Tavoularis. It's from 20th Century-Fox.

THE RISK

(1959) **D:** John Boulting, Roy Boulting **S:** Nigel Balchin   UK (*Suspect*)

Spies are after Professor Sewell (Peter Cushing), who has developed a germ that can end bubonic plague. The government is afraid that the discovery will be used for germ warfare. Tony Britton stars in this b/w movie, with Virginia Maskell, Ian Bannen as a one-armed traitor, Thorley Walters, Donald Pleasence, and Spike Milligan. Cushing was in *The Mummy* and *Mania* (with Pleasence) the same year.

THE RITES OF DRACULA: *See* THE SATANIC RITES OF DRACULA

RITUAL OF DEATH

(Complete, 1990) **D:** Fauzi Mansur **S:** Filipe Grecco, Anthony Roark **P:** J. Davila   Brazil

It's loaded with sex, gore, goo, flashbacks, flash-forwards, and hallucinations. It would get an X here if rated and shows the influence of Dario Argento and Brazilian horror director and star Marins. There's even a Satanic character (he resembles Marins) who writes a horror play and has bloody sex in a bathtub with a woman and a goat's head. The stage-actor hero becomes possessed because of some hairy book. He eats raw meat, and frogs appear (!?). He acquires a giant zit, mutates, and kills the other actors, while a black cop investigates. The soundtrack is filled with loud screams, and it all ends with a basement full of screaming, moaning bodies. It's very strange and was mostly filmed in some very interesting locations.

RITUALS

(Embassy, 1978) **D:** Peter Carter **S:** Ian Sutherland **P/A:** Lawrence Dane   Canada (*The Creeper*)

On a wilderness vacation five doctors face death by bear trap, fire, hornets, and decapitation. Some disfigured killers are to blame. Hal Holbrook and Lawrence Dane star in this *Deliverance* copy.

RIVER OF DEATH

(Warner, 1989) **D:** Steve Carver **S:** Andrew Deutsch, Edward Sampson **P:** Harry Alan Towers, Avi Lerner   S. Africa

Michael Dudikoff is an American tour guide searching for a captured girl in the Amazon jungle. The plot of this movie, based on an Alistair MacLean novel, concerns Nazis developing a deadly virus. The victims have boils and lots of pus. The filmmakers also throw in mercenaries, Israeli Nazi hunters, cannibals, boxing dwarfs, and a lost city. Robert Vaughn, Donald Pleasence, Herbert Lom, and L.Q. Jones all costar with Sarah Maur-Thorp.

RIVER OF DIAMONDS

(Turner, 1989) **D:** Robert J. Shawley **S/P:** Hans Kuhle **S:** Ian Yule   Germany/S. Africa

This ripoff of the Indiana Jones movies is about a search for diamonds in the 60s. Dack Rambo and Ferdy Mayne star with Angela O'Neill.

RIVER'S EDGE

(Embassy, 1986) **D:** Tim Hunter **S:** Neal Jimenez **P:** Sarah Pillsbury, Midge Sanford

Some bored and alienated kids live in a small town in Oregon. One of them kills a girl. Based on a real incident, this is one of the great 80s teen movies. Crispin Glover is the main scene-stealer as Layne, and Dennis Hopper is Feck, a one-legged ex-biker with a plastic sex doll. Keanu Reeves and Ione Skye Leitch (who was 14) are the only ones who think something should be done. Daniel Roebuck is the killer, who says it doesn't matter that he killed somebody. Joshua Miller (who was 11), Roxana Zal, and Leo Rossi are also featured. Sarah Pillsbury produced *Desperately Seeking Susan*. Tim Hunter went on to direct some *Twin Peaks* episodes and *Paint It Black*. This is an Island production. The Enigma soundtrack includes tracks by Slayer, Agent Orange, and Burning Spear.

THE RIVER WILD

(MCA, 1994) **D:** Curtis Hanson **S:** Denis O'Neill **P:** David Foster, Lawrence Turman

A family is taken hostage by killer thieves (Kevin Bacon and John C. Reilly) during a rafting vacation in the Pacific Northwest. Meryl Streep (then 45 years old) stars as the Boston history teacher who used to be a river guide. David Straithairn is her architect husband, Joseph Mazzello (*Jurassic Park*) is their son, and Buffy is their dog. This expensive ($45 million) PG-13 *Deliverance*-type Universal release was shot in Montana and Oregon (subbing for Idaho). Jerry Goldsmith wrote the score.

ROAD HOUSE

(CBS, 1948) **D:** Jean Negulesco **S/P:** Edward Chodorov

Richard Widmark is the psychotic Jefty, owner of a backwoods road house managed by Cornel Wilde. Ida Lupino is hired to sing there, and Jefty decides that he owns her. This 20th Century-Fox release also features Celeste Holm, O.Z. Whitehead, and Robert Karnes. It's Widmark's third movie, after *Kiss of Death* (1947) and *The Street with No Name* (1948).

ROAD HOUSE

(MGM, 1989) **D:** Rowdy Harrington **S:** David Lee Henry, Hilary Henkin **P:** Joel Silver

Patrick Swayze stars as a college-educated bouncer who uses martial arts to keep the peace in a honky-tonk Kansas City bar. Kelly Lynch becomes his girlfriend, and grizzled Sam Elliott shows up to help. Ben Gazzara is a sadistic local gangster who sends his goons around to cause more trouble. The movie has violent brawls and lots of *Playboy* centerfold models as waitresses and topless dancers. The Jeff Healey Band has to play behind chicken wire.

Crispin Glover and Dennis Hopper in *River's Edge*.

With John Doe (from the rock group X), Kathleen Wilhoite, Kim Herrin, Terri Lynn Doss, Kym Malin, Laura Albert, Christina Veronica, Heidi Payne, Julie Michaels, and Jasae. Arista released the soundtrack. It's by the director of *Jack's Back.*

ROADHOUSE 66

(Key, 1984) **D:** John Mark Robinson **S:** Galen Lee, George Simpson **P:** Scott M. Rosenfelt, Mark Levinson

Willem Dafoe hitchhikes and is picked up by Judge Reinhold in a '55 T-Bird. The car breaks down in an Arizona town, and they stay for the racing and the girls (Kate Vernon and Kaaren Lee).

ROAD HUSTLERS

(1968) **D:** Larry E. Jackson **S:** Robert Baron **P:** Robert M. Newson

A man (Jim Davis) and his three sons run an illegal liquor business and have to battle the sheriff (Andy Devine) and local gangsters led by Scott Brady. Robert Dix is one of the sons, and Victoria Carroll is Nadine, a "playgirl." Also featured are Sue Rainey and John Cardos. All of the main actors (except for Devine) were also in Al Adamson movies around the same time. This AIP release was filmed in the Carolinas.

ROADIE

(Woos Knapp, 1980) **D:** Alan Rudolph **S:** Big Boy Medlin **P:** Carolyn Pfeiffer

Meat Loaf stars as a Texas mechanic who becomes a roadie. He and Kaki Hunter (from *Porky's* and its sequels) want to meet Alice Cooper. This comedy with rock music costars Art Carney, and the cast also includes Sonny Carl Davis, Don Cornelius as a rock-show producer, Joe Spano, Debbie Harry and Blondie, Roy Orbison, and Hank Williams Jr. A double soundtrack was issued by Warner. Zalman King was the executive producer of this United Artists release.

ROADKILL

(1989) **D/P/A:** Bruce McDonald **S/A:** Don McKellar **P:** Colin Brunton   Canada

This is a good b/w cosmic road/journey movie in the Jim Jarmusch vein. The naive Ramona (Valerie Buhagiar, who narrates) is sent by her boss in Toronto to "terminate" the tour of the Children of Paradise, a rock band. Her journey involves a pot-smoking cabdriver, a would-be serial killer, a drive-in theater, an underage boy, a hot-dog vendor who has taken a vow of silence, and a van full of documentary filmmakers who want her to star in their film and who make her drive despite the dead muskrats on the road: "If you wanna drive, you gotta kill." She goes all the way north to Thunder Bay, where everything comes together. The Ramones, Cowboy Junkies, and the Paupers are heard, Nash the Slash plays and burns his violin, and Joey Ramone appears as himself. The video and soundtrack are available in Canada.

THE ROAD KILLERS

(Live, 1993) **D:** Deren Serafian **S:** Tedi Serafian

Roadshows

Back in the 20s and up through the 50s, any movie that did not have the U.S. government's censor approval was not allowed in regular respectable theaters. The rules and the themes changed over the years, but a whole industry existed that showed Americans what they weren't supposed to see and/or ripped them off with misleading ad campaigns. Kroger Babb from Ohio was the king of these features. The distributors drove from town to town with prints (often ripped off from their competitors) and used carny advertising techniques to pack the house. Some shows were segregated by sex. Birth-of-baby movies were big draws for years, as were many features about drugs, alcohol abuse, and sex, the biggest draw of them all. *Freaks,* made by MGM, was a roadshow hit for years. Many of these wonders of another age are now on tape.

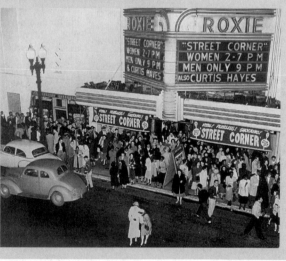

In what's practically a remake of *Hot Rods to Hell* (1967), Craig Sheffer leads a group of young Southwestern psychos who terrorize motorists in the desert and kidnap a teen girl. Christopher Lambert has the Dana Andrews avenging-dad role and Adrienne Shelly has the Mimsy Farmer role. With David Arquette, Michelle Forbes, Christopher McDonald (also in *Kalifornia*), plus the director's father, Richard Serafian (who directed *Vanishing Point* back in '71). Miramax declined to release this theatrically, but when it came out on tape in 1995 it fit right in with countless other serial killer/road movies. Serafian followed with *Gunmen* (1994) and *Terminal Velocity* (1995).

ROAD-KILL U.S.A.

(AIP, 1993) **D/S/P:** Tony Ellwood **S:** Mark Kimray **P:** Tony Locklear

For a change the hitchhiker character, Josh (Sean Bridges), is a nice, fairly naive college student, and Clint and Marla (Andrew Porter and Deanna Perry), the couple who pick him up, turn out to be psycho killers. Everybody talks a lot, lots of people die (including a clown), and a cheap-motel owner and rapist has his mouth and nose sealed with Crazy Glue. There's some good, disturbing instrumental music, and some of the songs are by Hillbilly Frankenstein. It's by the North Carolina makers of *The Killer*.

"ROAD LAWYERS" AND OTHER BRIEFS

(AIP, 1990) **D/S/P:** David Lipmann, Robert Rhine **D/S/A:** Tim Doyle

This video has three comic student shorts. "Road Lawyers" (1987), which features some stop/motion animation, is about lawyers. In "Escape from Heaven" (1989), made at USC, a nun goes to Purgatory for a venial sin. "Hairline" (1982) has bald men in a freak show. Also included is *Radar Men from the Moon* (1952), edited down and with new comic dialogue. A prologue was added in 1990.

ROAD RACERS

(1958) **D:** Arthur Swerdloff **S/P:** Stanley Kallis **S:** Ed Lasko

The gung-ho father of Rob, a Monterey race-car driver (Joel Lawrence), blames him for a death and sponsors a rival racer. Rob drinks, and a love triangle develops, in the soap-opera-style plot. Sally Fraser (*The Spider* and *War of the Colossal Beast*) is Rob's sister, and Marian Collier is a singer in a bar. Skip Ward is also featured. The best parts of this b/w AIP teen-appeal movie are the excellent pre-psychedelic race scenes using stills, negative images, and repeated dialogue. The director made documentaries. The theme song is "Leadfoot." RCA planned to release this on video but didn't.

ROADRACERS

(1994) **D/S/E:** Robert Rodriguez **S:** Tommy Nix **P:** Debra Hill, Lou Arkoff

David Arquette, who wants to play the guitar like Link Wray, dates Salma Hayek. He's in trouble with a gang led by Jason Wiles and a sadistic sheriff (William Sadler). Lance LeGault and Helen Shaver are her parents. Also featured are Kevin McCarthy, John Hawkes, and Johnny Reno (who scored the rock music) as the bandleader. There's a skating-rink action scene, the original *Invasion of the Body Snatchers* is showing at a theater, and vintage Wray instrumentals are heard. This first aired as part of a series (*Rebel Highway*) of 10 Showtime movies using the names and some plot elements of AIP 50s jd movies. It's by the accomplished young director of *El Mariachi*. The A&M series soundtrack is new cover versions of 50s hits by people like Hasil Atkins and Charlie Sexton.

ROADSIDE PROPHETS

(New Line, 1992) **D/S:** Abbe Wool **P:** Peter McCarthy

John Doe (from the rock group X) takes his motorcycle from LA to the El Dorado casino in Nevada carrying the ashes of a guy who was zapped by a video machine. Adam Horovitz (from the Beastie Boys) keeps showing up and tries to imitate him. Doe is low-key, and Horovitz almost does Jerry Lewis. They run into various (60s-

based) characters, and *Easy Rider* references abound. David Carradine singing, smoking a bong, and telling a story is the acting highlight. With Ellie Raab as an exotic dancer, Barton Heyman, Stephen Tobolowsky, Timothy Leary, Arlo Guthrie, and John Cusack eating a lot. The soundtrack includes cuts by the Beastie Boys, Harry Dean Stanton, and others. The director wrote Alex Cox's best movies, but this is no *Repo Man*, and the "straight" characters are too cartoonish.

ROAD TO HONG KONG

(MCA, 1962) **D/S:** Norman Panama **S/P:** Melvin Frank   UK

In the last movie in the popular comedy series a mad scientist tries to rule the world from the moon. Bob Hope and Bing Crosby, plus guest star Dorothy Lamour as herself, end up on the planet Plutonium, where they meet Frank Sinatra and Dean Martin at the end. With Joan Collins as a spy, Robert Morley, and bits by Peter Sellers, David Niven, and Jerry Colonna. Lippert issued the soundtrack of this United Artists release. Hope, Crosby, and Lamour's first had been *Road to Singapore*, 22 years earlier. It and three others in the series are also on video (MCA).

THE ROAD TO MANDALAY

(Fright, 1926) **D:** Tod Browning **S:** Eliot Clawson

Lon Chaney (with great dead-eyes makeup) is the ugly Singapore Joe, a tough criminal ("I ought to slit your tongue!") in Southeast Asia with a dwarf assistant. Rosemary (17-year-old Lois Moran) is a shop owner who doesn't know that she's his daughter. He tries to prevent her from marrying a smuggler (Owen Moore) by having him shanghaied and sent "back where he belongs, with the yellows, blacks, and browns." Sojin is the smiling, knife-throwing Charlie Wing, and Henry B. Walthall is a reverend. The story that was the basis of the script of this MGM release was written by Tod Browning and Herman Mankiewicz. The video has a musical score, but the visual quality is poor. You can't see the next Browning/Chaney movie (*London After Midnight*) at all, so this video release is welcome.

THE ROAD TO RUIN

(Sinister, 1933) **D/S/P:** Mrs. Wallace Reid **D:** Melville Shyer

Girls smoke pot, drink, play strip crap games, and swim naked. "Sex delinquent" Ann (Helen Foster)

gets pregnant, has an abortion, and dies. Grant Withers is also featured. This is a 57-minute remake of a 45-minute silent movie from 1928. Actor Wallace Reid's wife, actress Dorothy Davenport, made this adults-only warning because of his death from a drug overdose in 1923. She had also been in the similar *Human Wreckage* (1923). The daughter of silent-film comedienne Alice Davenport and character actor Harry Davenport, she acted from 1909 to 1926, then went on to produce, direct, and write until the 50s, using the name Dorothy Reid.

ROAD TO SALINA

(Charter, 1971) **D/S:** Georges Lautner **S:** Pascal Jardin, Jack Miller **P:** Joseph E. Levine   France/Italy (*Sur le Route de Salina*)

Rita Hayworth runs a roadside gas station and café. She thinks that a drifter (Robert Walker Jr.) is her lost son. Her blond daughter (Mimsy Farmer) has an affair with him. This movie has drugs, sex, and nudity. Even the cut version on local TV is one of the most surprising things I've ever seen. Unlike *The Naked Zoo* (also with Hayworth), which is sleazy exploitation, this is actually a good, very underrated movie. Also with Ed Begley (in his last role), who does the frug with Hayworth, and Sophie Hardy. It was a widescreen Avco Embassy release.

ROAR!

(1981) **D/S/P/A:** Noel Marshall

This family home movie reportedly took 11 years and $17 million to finish! The production was stopped by floods, fires, and injuries. Tippi Hedren's husband directs, and they both star. She plays a woman who takes her kids (her real-life sons John and Jerry Marshall and daughter Melanie Griffith) to Africa (really the couple's Soledad, California, animal preserve) to visit their father, an eccentric scientist they haven't seen in years. This comedy/adventure is very pro-wildlife. Griffith was mauled by a lion during filming in 1977 and had to have plastic surgery.

ROBBERS OF THE SACRED MOUNTAIN

(Prism, 1982) **D:** Bob Schulz **S:** Olaf Pooley **P:** Keith Rothman   Canada (*Falcon's Gold*)

John Marley stars as an archaeologist who goes to Mexico to investigate a statue of a fertility goddess. This *Raiders of the Lost Ark* copy features Simon MacCorkindale and debuted on Showtime.

THE ROBE

(Fox, 1953) **D:** Henry Kostner **S:** Philip Dunne **P:** Frank Ross

Richard Burton is a Roman tribune who wins Christ's Crucifixion garment in a dice game, then begins to think that it's cursed. This 20th Century–Fox hit was the first Cinemascope feature. Jean Simmons costars, with Victor Mature as Demetrius, Michael Rennie as Peter, and Jay Robinson, memorable

David Carradine, John Doe, and Adam Horovitz in *Roadside Prophets*.

as the crazed Caligula. Also featured are Jeff Morrow, Dean Jagger, Torin Thatcher, Richard Boone, Betta St. John, Ernest Thesiger, Dawn Addams, Michael Ansara, and Frank De Kova. It's based on the best-selling novel by Lloyd C. Douglas and received five Oscar nominations. Mature returned in *Demetrius and the Gladiators,* a sequel.

ROBERT A. HEINLEIN'S THE PUPPETMASTERS

(Buena Vista, 1994) **D:** Stuart Orme **S:** Ted Elliot, Terry Rossio, David S. Goyer **P:** Ralph Winter   (*The Puppet Masters*)

Alien parasites take over humans in an adaptation of Robert Heinlein's 1951 novel serialized in *Galaxy* magazine. It's much better than the somewhat similar *Body Snatchers* remake (also 1994) and uses simple, old-fashioned FX. Eric Thal stars as the son of Donald Sutherland, both with the Office of Scientific Intelligence. Everything takes place in Iowa (Des Moines locations were used) and Washington D.C. With Julie Warner as a scientist, Keith David, Will Patton, Richard Belzer, Yaphet Kotto, Marshall Bell, and Andy Robinson. It was the first feature by a British director of rock videos and TV movies. A Buena Vista Hollywood release. *The Brain Eaters* (1958) was based on the same novel.

ROBIN HOOD

(Fox, 1991) **D:** John Irvin **S:** Mark Allan Smith, John McGrath **P:** Sarah Radclyffe

Patrick Bergin stars as Robin Hood, with Uma Thurman as Maid Marian, Edward Fox as Prince John, Jurgen Prochnow, and Jeroen Krabbe. This version of the familiar tale debuted on TV before the Kevin Costner movie *Robin Hood: Prince of Thieves* (1991) and originally ran 150 minutes. It played theatrically in Europe. Bergin also starred in *Frankenstein* (1992), which debuted on TV before *Mary Shelley's "Frankenstein"* was released.

ROBIN HOOD: MEN IN TIGHTS

(Fox, 1993) **D/S/P/A:** Mel Brooks **S:** J. David Shapiro, Evan Chandler

Cary Elwes stars in this PG-13 spoof of *Robin Hood: Prince of Thieves* (and various older movies), which also copies Mel Brooks' own short-lived TV series *When Things Were Rotten* (1975). Brooks was a lot funnier in the 70s. Richard Lewis is the evil Prince John, Roger Rees is the sheriff of Nottingham, and Amy Yasbeck is Maid Marian. With Isaac Hayes, Tracey Ullman, Mark Blankfield, Dom DeLuise, Chuck McCann, Clive Revill, Dick Van Patten, Patrick Stewart as King Richard, and Brooks as Rabbi Tuchman.

ROBIN HOOD: PRINCE OF THIEVES

(Warner, 1991) **D:** Kevin Reynolds **S/P:** John Watson, Pen Densham

Kevin Costner stars in the biggest and (at 141 minutes) the longest Robin Hood movie of all time. Mary Elizabeth Mastrantonio is Maid Marian, Morgan Freeman is the Moor Azeem, and Alan Rickman stands out as the evil sheriff of Nottingham. Also featured are Christian Slater, guest star Sean Connery as King Richard, Geraldine McEwan, and Brian

Blessed. From Warner. Earlier versions star Douglas Fairbanks (1922), Errol Flynn (1938), Russell Hicks (1946), Jon Hall (1948), Robert Clarke (1951), Richard Todd (1952), Richard Greene (1960), Sean Connery (1976), and many others.

ROBINSON CRUSOE OF CLIPPER ISLAND

(VY, Sinister, 1936) **D:** Mack J. Wright, Ray Taylor **S:** Morgan Cox, Barry Shipman, Maurice Geraghty

Mala, a real native of the South Seas, stars as Mala, in this 13-chapter Republic serial. A machine makes a volcano erupt and various bad guys and spies disrupt an island paradise. With Rex and Buck as Rex and Buck, Mamo Clark as Princess Melani, Herbert Rawlinson, and Selmer Jackson. A condensed version is called *Manhunt on Mystery Island*. Mala is also in the serial *Hawk of the Wilderness* (1938) as an Indian.

ROBO C.H.I.C.: *See* CYBER C.H.I.C.

ROBOCOP

(Orion, 1987) **D:** Paul Verhoeven **S:** Edward Neumeier, Michael Miner **P:** Arne Schmidt **M:** Basil Poledouris

The first Hollywood film by the biggest director in Holland is a classic. Few movies have so successfully combined all-out action, science fiction, and very pointed political satire. Seeing it in a large, packed Times Square theater was a special experience. The whole audience was excited all the way through. Peter Weller is Murphy, a Detroit cop in the near future who is brought back from near death as a crime-fighting robot (created by Rob Bottin). Ed 209, another fantastic (animated) robot, malfunctions violently during a board-room meeting. Daniel O'Herlihy and Ronnie Cox are corporate villains, and Kurtwood Smith is excellent as a gang leader. Some of the TV commercials that frequently interrupt the action are classics in themselves. With Nancy Allen, Miguel Ferrer, Robert DoQui, Ray Wise, and Leeza Gibbons. It was filmed in Dallas and had to be cut for an R rating. The soundtrack is on Varèse Sarabande. *The Making of Robocop* (UAV) was also released. Sequels, a cartoon series, and a TV series followed. The director did *Total Recall* next.

ROBOCOP 2

(Orion, 1990) **D:** Irvin Kershner **S:** Frank Miller, Walon Green **P:** Jon Davison **M:** Leonard Rosenman

It cost a reported $28 million (twice the original) and brought back the major stars, but this sequel totally missed the point. It's more violent and nasty, but the humor is gone. Peter Weller returns, with Nancy Allen and Daniel O'Herlihy. The animation during the end battle with two robots is excellent. With Tom Noonan (spreading a drug called Nuke), Gabriel Damon as a 12-year-old gangster, Belinda Bauer, Patricia Charbonneau, Fabiane Udewid, and John Glover (in a bit part). It was the first movie in

many years by the director of *The Empire Strikes Back*. The soundtrack is on Varèse Sarabande. A real-life psycho who killed six people claimed that he copied a slashing in this movie.

ROBOCOP 3

(Orion, 1991) **D/S:** Fred Dekker **S:** Frank Miller **P:** Patrick Crowley

Robocop (Robert Burke, from *Dust Devil*) eventually switches sides and fights for the rebel underground (just like in *Demolition Man*). He also teams with a computer-whiz orphan girl (Remy Ryan) and a scientist (Jill Hennessy). An evil Japanese corporation led by Mako (on a TV screen) joins with Omni Consumer Products (led by Rip Torn), and they use silly-looking "splatter punks" to drive out Detroit residents. This sequel has more comedy and (with a PG-13 rating) less violence. Robocop can fly with a jet pack and fights a cyborg samurai in one scene. With CCH Pounder as the leader of the freedom fighters, Nancy Allen, Felton Perry, and Robert DoQui from the previous movies, and James Lorinz in a small role. There are brief flashbacks from the previous movies. It played overseas first, then was finally released here in 1993.

Nancy Allen and Peter Weller in *Robocop*.

ROBOCOP: THE SERIES—THE FUTURE OF LAW ENFORCEMENT

(Orion, 1994) **D:** Paul Lynch **S:** Edward Neumeier **P:** J. Miles Dale   Canada

This expensive syndicated series pilot stars Richard Eden as Robocop and Yvette Nipar as his partner, Lisa. Cliff De Young is the recurring villain, Dr. Malardo, a scientist working for Omni Consumer Products. Andrea Roth and David Garber are also featured. The short-lived series returned to the fun TV commercials from the first movie, but was pretty toned down compared to any of the movies and had more cartoonish characters and laughs than action or violence. Other (one-hour) episodes are also on tape.

ROBOFORCE

(VSOM, 1988) **D:** Chung Chi Man **D/S/P/A:** Tsui Hark **S:** Yuen Kai Chi **P/A:** John Sham   Hong Kong
(*I Love Maria*)

In this nonstop comedy/action/science-fiction movie Sally Yeh plays the villainess, Maria, and her robot double, who joins the good guys. Tsui Hark is an alcoholic petty criminal working with a comic cop. A giant, clunky, noisy robot fights a sleek, pretty one. Tony Yeung costars in this Golden Harvest release. Another Hong Kong movie (with more sex) is called *Robotrix* (Star, 1991).

ROBO MAN = WHO?

ROBOT HOLOCAUST

(Lightning, 1986) **D/S:** Tim Kincaid **P:** Cynthia De Paula

This was the first then-recent movie deemed bad enough to be shown on Comedy Central's *Mystery Science Theater 3000*. In the future, after the robots have rebelled, hand-puppet worm monsters appear. Norris Culf stars, with Angelika Jager as the villainess, Jennifer Delora, Joel Von Ornsteiner, and Amy Bretano. It was made in NYC and uses Ed French FX.

ROBOT JOX

(RCA/Columbia, 1987) **D:** Stuart Gordon **S:** Joe Haldeman **P:** Albert Band (*Robojox*)

In post-nuke Siberia televised "games" are played by heroes inside giant transformer-type robots. The losers are crushed. After 300 spectators are killed when the "good" robot falls on them Achilles (Gary Graham), the hero inside, quits. Athena, a determined synthetic black woman "tubie" (Anne-Marie Johnson), tries to replace him, but sabotage causes more problems. Paul Koslo is the Russian villain. This PG-rated adventure filmed in Italy has great David Allen robots but is not what anyone would expect from the director of *Re-Animator*. Also featured are Carolyn Purdy-Gordon, Robert Sampson, and Jeffrey Combs in a bit part. Characters say, "Crash and burn," the name of Albert Band's other then-recent robot movie, which uses leftover FX scenes from this one. Characters also say, "Robojox," the original title, changed for legal reasons after the makers of *Robocop* movies objected. *Robot Wars* is sort of a sequel.

ROBOT NINJA

(Cinema Home, 1989) **D/S/P/M:** J. R. Bookwalter

A scientist (Michael Todd) helps a comic-book artist become his own creation to track down a killer-rapist gang in a small town. This cheap gore comedy with *Batman* gags has "special appearances" by Burt Ward and Linnea Quigley, and Scott Spiegel is in there too. It was made in Ohio by the director of *The Dead Next Door*. David De-Coteau was the executive producer.

ROBOT WARS

(Paramount, 1993) **D:** Albert Band **S:** Jackson Barr **P:** Charles Band

In this forgettable sort of sequel to *Robot Jox* and *Crash and Burn,* Don Michael Paul is a smart-mouthed captain with a comic sidekick named Stumpy (James Staley). Barbara Crampton as a scientist is the love interest. A giant, scorpion-like passenger robot is attacked, and a conspiracy is

discovered involving evil Japanese and toxic waste. Part of the "action" economically takes place in "a 1940s ghost town." David Allen did the FX.

ROCK AND ROLL MOBSTER GIRLS

(Phoenix, 1988) **D/S/E:** Rick Werner **P/A:** Fred Hopkins

Up in Seattle, "back in the early 80s," the five-member Doll Squad, led by Linx Lapaz, can't find work and have to get food from restaurant dumpsters. They decide to sign with a notorious local promoter, psycho Bruno Multrock, played convincingly by producer Fred Hopkins. Filmed in "Perform-Vision," in semi-documentary style, local rock stars are interviewed and bands play in clubs in between plot segments. Scott McCaughey (from the Young Fresh Fellows) and Jeff Simmons (who did the Straight Label soundtrack for *The Naked Angels*) are interview highlights. One band plays The Arrows' "Blue's Theme." Cheesy MOR organ music is usually heard in the background. An effective dream sequence uses old home movies and crude animation, and long, narrated scenes of cars on a highway seem to be a nod to *Glen or Glenda*. Bruno has people butchered and talks to his brother's head, and at the end his decapitated body still makes the rounds of clubs. The Doll Squad does one entire song, "Psycho Girls." At one point some people are stuck listening to a mutant landlord rant for what seems like an hour. Then a title says "15 minutes later," and he continues. Funny idea, but what this tape desperately needed was an editor. Even if you were part of the Seattle scene yourself you'll wish it were half as long.

ROCK AND RULE

(MGM, 1983) **D:** Clive A. Smith **S:** Peter Sauder, John Halfpenny **P:** Patrick Loubert, Michael Hersch

This PG animated post-nuke movie is about mutants and a rock star's search for immortality. *Heavy Metal* is better. The main voices are by Don Franks, Susan Roman, Paul Le Mat, Sam Langevin, and Catherine O'Hara. The songs are by Iggy Pop, Debbie Harry, Lou Reed, Cheap Trick, and others.

ROCK 'N' ROLL HIGH SCHOOL FOREVER

(Live, 1990) **D/S:** Deborah Brock **P:** Jed Horovitz

In this pointless sequel to the Roger Corman–produced 1979 cult hit *Rock 'n' Roll High School* Corey Feldman (with a ponytail) has a band, sings, and dances. Mary Woronov (from the original) is Dr. Vadar, the dominatrix principal of Ronald Reagan High School, who has a metal hand with a whip attached. With Larry Linville (from the TV series *M*A*S*H*) as the principal, Mojo Nixon, food fights, and pranks with video cameras and cellular phones. The school blows up like in the original, and oldies are on the SBK soundtrack. Worth Keeter was the second-unit director.

ROCK 'N' ROLL NIGHTMARE

(Academy, 1987) **D:** John Fasano **S/P/A:** Jon-Mikl Thor Canada (*The Edge of Hell*)

Members of a heavy-metal band practicing in a barn studio are killed. Band singer Jon-Mikl Thor is really the archangel Triton, and he has to battle

a skeleton Satan while wearing a jeweled loin-cloth, heavy eye makeup, and teased blond hair. This has lots of music and puppet monsters. It's rated PG-13. Thor also stars in *Zombie Nightmare*. You might want to experience a double bill.

ROCK AROUND THE WORLD

(1957) **D:** Gerard Bryant **S:** Norman Hinds **P:** Nat Cohen, Stuart Levy UK (*The Tommy Steele Story*)

Nobody in America cared when AIP released this nearly plotless musical about the blond early British rocker Tommy Steele, but in his homeland he was a big deal before Cliff Richard came along, with hits from 1956 to 1961. The songs here include "Elevator Rock" and "Doomsday Rock." Nancy Whiskey costars. Steele returned in *The Duke Wore Jeans* (1958) and *Tommy the Toreador* (1959).

THE ROCKETEER

(Disney, 1991) **D:** Joe Johnston **S:** Danny Bilson, Paul De Meo **P:** Lawrence Golden, Charles Gordon, Lloyd Levin

It's too bad this did so badly, because it's a fun nod to science-fiction adventure movies of the past. It's based on Dave Stevens's 1981 graphic novel, which itself was largely based on Republic's *King of the Rocket Men* (and other serials). Bill Campbell stars as the young hero with a rocket backpack in LA of 1938. Alan Arkin costars. Timothy Dalton is an Errol Flynn type of character who's a Nazi. Jennifer Connelly's character was originally based on Betty Page but was changed for this PG movie. Tiny Ron as Lothar, a character made up by Rick Baker to resemble deformed 40s actor Rondo Hatton, fights on top of a zeppelin. With Paul Sorvino, Terry O'Quinn as Howard Hughes, Ed Lauter, and Clint Howard. This $40 million movie has ILM FX. A stuntman died during production. Joe Johnston was an ILM art director and also made the hit *Honey, I Shrunk the Kids*.

ROCK HUDSON'S HOME MOVIES

(Bear, 1992) **D/S:** Mark Rappaport

This is a 63-minute compilation film with the dead Rock Hudson (actually an actor who looks more like Christian Slater) commenting on scenes from his movies. The narration is ironic (and out of context). Lots of clips (of varying quality) are used, especially from movies directed by Douglas Sirk and other ones with Doris Day. Many scenes concern diseases and death (*Seconds* works well here). It was backed by Ohio State University.

ROCKIN' THE BLUES

(Norton, 1956) **D:** Arthur Rosenblum **P:** Fritz Pollard

DJ Hal Jackson is the all-rhyming onstage host of this all-black musical. He shows us "a rock 'n' roll revue, not on wax but in person!" Most of the many acts are priceless, but I like Connie Carroll, who sings "Everybody's Going Mad, Rock 'n' Roll Is the Latest Fad" and "I'm a Fast-Movin' Mama," and Pearl Woods, who does "He's Too Lazy" on a kitchen set with a slow-motion dancing husband. Meanwhile the comedy team of Mantan Moreland and F. E. Miller do vaudeville skits and try to sneak in and hang out with the sexy showgirls backstage. One of them calls Mantan (who also appears in drag) Birmingham. Others play, dance, and sing, and scenes of an all-white audience are edited in. Not too many adult whites were ready for songs like "My Love Comes Oozing Down" (the Wanderers) in 1956, though. I wonder what show they were really watching. Also featured are the Hurricanes and the Afro-Cuban Dancers.

ROCKTOBER BLOOD

(Vestron, 1984) **D/S/P:** Beverly Sebastian **S/P/C/E:** Ferd Sebastian

A killer rock star from a Kiss-type band is executed, a female rock star (Donna Scoggins) is stalked, and the murdering continues. Kiss were in only one movie (*Kiss Meets the Phantom*), but the theatrical band inspired many (bad) low-budget horror movies like this.

ROCKULA

(Cannon, 1989) **D:** Luca Bercovici **S/P:** Jeffrey Levy **S:** Christopher Verwiel

Dean Cameron is a teenage vampire and Tawny Fere is a reincarnated rock singer in this PG-13 misfire. It's almost worth it to see Bo Diddley and Susan Tyrrell in a band. Also featured are Toni Basil as an Elvira-type mom, Thomas Dolby, and Tamara DeTreaux (who played ET) as Bat Dork.

ROCKY

(MGM, 1976) **D:** John G. Avildsen **S/A:** Sylvester Stallone **P:** Irwin Winkler, Robert Chartoff **M:** Bill Conti

Sylvester Stallone wrote this in four days. He had played supporting roles in *Death Race 2000, Cannonball,* and *Capone* (all Roger Corman productions) and wanted to be a star. This PG hit from United Artists was nominated for 10 Oscars (!) and received awards for best picture, direction, and editing. Stallone was the first person after Charlie Chaplin and Orson Welles (!) to be nominated for best screenwriter and actor in the same movie. Talia Shire costars, with Burt Young, Burgess Meredith as Mickey, Carl Weathers as champ Apollo Creed, Joe Spinell, Frank Stallone (who sings), Thayer David (from the TV series *Dark Shadows*), and Joe Frazier. The soundtrack (on UA) includes "Gonna Fly Now," a number 1 hit. Troma's Lloyd Kaufman was a production assistant and appears as a drunk. John G. Avildsen, who had done obscure adults-only movies, didn't have another hit until he reworked the same formula in *The Karate Kid* and its sequels.

ROCKY II

(MGM, 1979) **D/S/A:** Sylvester Stallone **P:** Irwin Winkler, Robert Chartoff **M:** Bill Conti

After the failure of *FIST* and *Paradise Alley* Sylvester Stallone directed himself as Rocky, back for "one last fight," a rematch. This sequel uses the same basic cast and the same theme song, and Rocky jogs up the Philadelphia Museum of Art steps again. The UA soundtrack features hit songs by brother Frank Stallone.

ROCKY III

(MGM, 1982) **D/S/A:** Sylvester Stallone **P:** Irwin Winkler, Robert Chartoff **M:** Bill Conti

After the box-office failure of *Nighthawks* and *Victory* (both 1981) this was announced as the last movie in a trilogy. It's the second-highest-grossing in the series, and it's pretty funny. Apollo Creed (Carl Weathers) becomes Rocky's trainer after Mickey (Burgess Meredith) leaves (then he dies). Rocky makes a comeback at 34, and a statue is dedicated to him. Talia Shire is his pregnant wife, and Burt Young is a racist. There's a good 3-round fight with the big-mouthed Clubber Lane (Mr. T) at the end. Also featured are huge wrestler Hulk Hogan (who went on to his own acting career), Thunderlips, and Dennis James. The soundtrack (on Liberty) includes the inescapable number 1 hit "Eye of the Tiger" by Survivor and more by Frank Stallone.

ROCKY IV

(MGM, 1985) **D/S/A:** Sylvester Stallone **P:** Irwin Winkler, Robert Chartoff

Sylvester Stallone is by far the most successful actor and director of all time, with his five Rocky movies. This was the highest-grossing of the whole series and cost 40 (!) times what the first one did. It's also the most absurd of the series, and for that reason it's highly recommended! It was released the same year as Stallone's *Rambo: First Blood II,* and both are mid-Reagan-era anti-Communist movies. Sly literally wraps himself in the American flag. Dolph Lundgren is the steroid-filled Soviet fighter Ivan Drago. Brigitte Nielsen is his wife and trainer, Ludmilla. She and Sly were married for less than two years and were also in *Cobra* together. Michael Pataki is Nikolai Koloff, and series stars Carl Weathers (Apollo is killed!), Burt Young, and Talia Shire return. James Brown sings his last hit, "Livin' in America," which caused a brief career boost. The Scotti Brothers soundtrack features various artists.

ROCKY V

(MGM, 1990) **D:** John G. Avildsen **S/A:** Sylvester Stallone **P:** Irwin Winkler, Robert Chartoff

The original director returned, and Sylvester Stallone wrote himself a simpler story, but this was a flop. The brain-damaged Rocky returns to his Philly roots. Stallone received a record $27.5 million plus 34 percent of the gross. Sage Stallone costars as Rocky Jr., with Delia Sheppard, Tommy Morrison, Lloyd Kaufman, and the usual cast, plus the returning Burgess Meredith.

ROCKY JONES, SPACE RANGER

(Video Yesteryear, 1954–55) **P:** Roland Reed

This early syndicated kids' series stars Richard Crane as Rocky Jones, wearing a cap and T-shirt in his ship the Orbit Jet, with Sally Mansfield as Verna Ray, Scotty Becket (from the Our Gang shorts) as Winky, Maurice Cass as Professor Newton, and

various villains. It's a nostalgic favorite for people who grew up watching it, but for anybody who didn't it's hysterical. If you think TV shows look cheap today wait till you see these. They were filmed at the Hal Roach studios. Video Yesteryear has 78-minute tapes with three shows per tape. Sinister offers 7 of the 14 *Rocky Jones* "features," made up of episodes that were shown theatrically overseas.

ROCK, YOU SINNERS

(Dark Dreams, 1957) **D:** Dennis Kavanaugh **P:** B. C. Fancy   UK

Joan Collins' sister, Jackie Collins, now a famous trash novelist, costars in this early rock-and-roll movie. All the songs have bad, clichéd lyrics about rock and roll, but the music (by Art Baxter and His Rockin' Sinners, Tony Crumbie and His Rockets, and others you never heard of) is pretty swingin', sax-driven, and Bill Haley–inspired. The plot is about a radio DJ and his hip writer friend planning a rock TV show. Jackie works at a record shop where the first Haley LP hangs on the wall. There's a sappy dream sequence, a calypso club called Brazil Expresso, and a great documentary-style look at what a giant old British dance hall was like.

Brigitte Nielsen, Dolph Lundgren, and Michael Pataki in *Rocky IV.*

ROGER & ME

(Warner, 1989) **D/S/P/A:** Michael Moore

The most successful non-music feature-length documentary of all time was made by an unemployed writer from Flint, Michigan. In 1991 General Motors announced massive layoffs and plant closings. This movie centers on Michael Moore's efforts to interview GM chairman Roger Smith. It includes lots of TV news footage featuring Ronald Reagan, GM spokesman Pat Boone, Anita Bryant, the Reverend Robert Schuller, Bob Eubanks (who tells dirty jokes), and Miss America. We see Auto World (!) and hear the Barking Dogs and the Beach Boys on the soundtrack. The makers of *The Atomic Café* helped Moore get started. Rick Prelinger provided archive footage. A 24-minute 1992 update is called *Pets or Meat: The Return to Flint.*

ROGER CORMAN: HOLLYWOOD'S WILD ANGEL

(MPI, 1978) **D:** Christian Blackwood

This excellent hour-long documentary concentrates on Roger Corman's New World (which he later sold). It includes choice clips from his New World

A returning Nam-vet POW (William Devane) returns to his East Texas town and is given a thousand silver coins (one for each day he was a captive). He becomes extremely alienated, his wife and kids are killed, his valuable coin collection is stolen, and his arm is shoved into a garbage disposal by low-life thieves led by James Best. Devane spends the rest of this excellent revenge movie with a hook hand as he and a vet friend (Tommy Lee Jones) track the redneck killers to a Mexican whorehouse. This 123-minute AIP release also features Luke Askew, Dabney Coleman, Cassie Yates, and Linda Haynes (*Human Experiments*).

(and AIP) productions and interviews with a typically on-the-edge Martin Scorsese, Paul Bartel, Jonathan Demme, Joe Dante, Allan Arkush, Jonathan Kaplan, Ron Howard, David Carradine, Peter Fonda, and other directors and actors whose careers got started (or restarted) by producer and director Corman. Corman himself proudly explains how he brought movies by Federico Fellini and Ingmar Bergman to their largest American audiences.

RO GO PAG

(Kino, 1962) **D/S:** Roberto Rossellini, Jean-Luc Godard, Pier Paolo Pasolini, Ugo Gregoretti **P:** Alfredo Bini   Italy/France

This 4-part anthology was banned in Italy because of Pier Paolo Pasolini's segment, starring Orson Welles as a director shooting a crucifixion scene in which the actor actually dies. Jean-Luc Godard's segment, shot in Paris, is about the day after an atomic explosion. The title is made up from the first letters of the directors' last names.

ROGUES' TAVERN

(Sinister, 1936) **D:** Bob Hill **S:** Al Martin

A detective (Wallace Ford) and his fiancée (Barbara Pepper) go to an old hotel to be married, but the guests there are being killed, apparently by a wolf dog. With Joan Woodbury and Clara Kimball Young. This 65-minutes independently produced mystery was directed by the man who wrote the screenplay for the original version of *The Cat and the Canary* (1927).

ROLLER BLADE

(New World, 1986) **D/S/P/C:** Donald Jackson **S:** Randall Frakes

Futuristic roller-derby amazon nuns called the Bod Sisters use Shakespearean English, worship a glowing happy face, and fight fascists on wheels. Secret ceremonies are held, and there's some nude skating, but bikini babes on skates take up most of the time. Suzanne Solari stars as Sister Sharon Cross, with Shaun Michelle, Michelle Bauer, and Barbara Peckinpaugh. The director of *Demon Lover* shot footage using credit cards, and then New World put more money into it for a direct-to-video release. Incredibly, there were sequels.

THE ROLLERBLADE SEVEN

(York, 1992) **D/S/P/C:** Donald Jackson **S/P/A/M/E:** Scott Shaw

The extremly pretentious, laughable, awkward, overlong, slow-moving fantasy might entertain you if you use enough powerful drugs first. Hawk (Scott Shaw, a guy with long blond hair who resembles Johnny Winter and can't act) roams the beach and the desert with a sword, fighting punk ninjas and samurai on rollerskates and meeting various out-of-control guest stars and topless lady skaters (including porno star Jade East). Don Stroud (wearing a tophat and swimsuit) sends him on a rescue mission. William Smith talks endlessly (and cries) in a wheelchair. Karen Black gives Hawk mushrooms, leading to an *Easy Rider* graveyard-trip scene. The non-famous Allison Chase costars, and Frank Stallone, Joe Estevez, and Rhonda Shear also appear. Supposedly this was two sequels (partially shot in Mexico) edited into a single movie by executive producer Tanya York. It's been on cable TV as *Return of the Roller Blade Seven*.

ROLLERBLADE WARRIORS: TAKEN BY FORCE

(Raedon, 1988) **D:** Donald Jackson **S:** "Lloyd Strathern"/Randall Frakes **P:** Jonathan S. Kaplan

Kathleen Kinmont stars as Sister Sharon Cross, a skater with samurai swords who tries to rescue a seer (Elizabeth Kaitan) from being sacrificed. With Rory Calhoun, Lisa Toothman, Suzanne Solari (returning from *Roller Blade*), and Abby Dalton (Kinmont's real-life mom). This unrated sequel went directly to cable in America.

ROLLER BOOGIE

(1979) **D:** Mark L. Lester **S:** Barry Schneider **P:** Bruce Cohn Curtis

The mob tries to close down the roller disco, but kids stop them. Linda Blair and Jim Bray star in this PG time-warp movie from United Artists, with Mark Goddard (from the TV series *Lost in Space*) as the main bad guy, Kimberly Beck, Beverly Garland, and Jimmy Van Patten. Casablanca released a various artists double soundtrack. This was the first non-*Exorcist* starring role in a theatrical release for Blair, who returned in *Hell Night* (1981).

ROLLING THUNDER

(Vestron, 1977) **D:** John Flynn **S:** Paul Schrader, Heywood Gould **P:** Norman T. Herman

ROLLING VENGEANCE

(Charter, 1987) **D/P:** Steven S. Stern **S:** Michael Montgomery   Canada

A young Ohio truckdriver (Don Michael Paul) creates a monster, 8-ton, fire-spitting vehicle in his yard. Then he uses it for revenge against the hicks who killed his family and raped his girlfriend. Villain Ned Beatty owns a topless bar and has a gang of violent, dimwitted sons.

THE ROLY POLY MAN

(1994) **D:** Bill Young **S:** Kym Goldsworthy **P:** Peter Green   Australia

Paul Chub stars as a pudgy, bumbling private eye who narrates a tale of exploding heads and strange medical experiments. Susan Lyons and Les Foxcroft costar in this comic science-fiction/horror movie.

ROMEO IS BLEEDING

(Polygram, 1993) **D:** Peter Medak **S/P:** Hilary Henkin **P:** Paul Webster

Gary Oldman stars as a corrupt NYC police sergeant (who narrates) on the take from the mob. He has to guard Mona Demarkov (Lena Olin), a sexy killer from a Russian crime family. She cuts her arm off and wears a robotic arm with an S&M-look black leather brace. This attempt to update *film noir* includes some funny dialogue and over-the-top violence and characters. With Annabelle Sciorra (wife), Juliette Lewis (blond mistress), Roy Scheider (gangster), Will Patton, and Ron Perlman.

Linda Blair and Jim Bray in *Roller Boogie.*

ROMPER STOMPER

(Academy, 1992) **D/S:** Geoffrey Wright
P: Daniel Scharf, Ian Pringle   Australia

A neo-Nazi skinhead gang living in a Melbourne warehouse terrorizes Asian immigrants. This disturbing, downbeat movie borrows from *A Clockwork Orange* but has a teen love triangle. Things get worse when Vietnamese "gooks" (who are subtitled) buy the skinheads' favorite bar and everybody loses. Russell Crowe (a very good actor who started working in Hollywood after this) stars as the *Mein Kampf*–reading leader, with Daniel Pollock and Jacqueline McKenzie as the blond epileptic and drug addict who comes between them. With racist punk songs. Some sex scenes resulted in an NC-17 rating. Wright made *Metal Skin* (1994) next. One of the producers is now in jail for an art theft in America.

ROOFTOPS

(IVE, 1989) **D:** Robert Wise **S:** Terrence Brennan **P:** Howard Koch Jr.

Robert Wise returned to the themes of his *West Side Story* for this teen musical/drama set in NYC. Jason Gedrick stars as a martial-arts-fighting and dancing good guy, with Tisha Campbell as his Hispanic girlfriend, Troy Beyer, and Eddie Velez as a crack dealer. It was Wise's first movie since *Star Trek* (1979) and remains his last to date. Capitol released the soundtrack.

THE ROOKIE

(Warner, 1990) **D/A:** Clint Eastwood **S:** Boaz Yakin, Scott Spiegel **P:** Howard G. Kazenjian

Clint Eastwood is paired with a spoiled rich-kid cop (Charlie Sheen) as they investigate a car-theft ring. This box-office flop was a low point for Eastwood. Sonia Braga and Raul Julia play the German (?!) villains. There are lots of car chases. Also featured are Tom Skerritt, Lara Flynn Boyle, and Mara Corday (from Eastwood's early days at Universal).

ROOM 43

(Video Dimensions, 1958) **D:** Alvin Rakoff **S:** Patrick Alexander **P:** John Klein   UK

Here's a dream-cast B movie. Evil, vain gangster Nick (Herbert Lom) and his mistress trick and blackmail women into working at his large, profitable whorehouse. American-born Eddie Constantine (*Alphaville*) plays a Canadian taxi driver who marries Malou (Odile Versois), a French waitress, so that she can stay in the country. They fall in love, but she's sent to the dreaded Room 43, and hooker Diana Dors takes her out onto the streets. Dors wants revenge because her sister killed herself after having acid thrown in her face. All three female leads are bleached blondes. After Malou is given a drugged cigarette she has a wonderful, surreal hooker-Hell dream where she's thrown into a vat of men. Constantine, a great every-

man hero, gets beaten up several times. It all ends in a big fire and a brawl with all the taxi drivers. In Germany, where Constantine was a big star (as he was in France), this was called *Eddie, Tod, und Teufel*. In England it was *Passport to Shame*. Alvin Rakoff also directed *Hot Money Girl* (1959), with Constantine and Christopher Lee.

ROOM TO LET

(Sinister, 1949) **D/S:** Godfrey Grayson **S:** John Gilling **P:** Anthony Hinds   UK

This interesting early Hammer mystery (based on a BBC play) stars Valentine Dyall (*The Queen of Spades, Horror Hotel, The Haunting*) as Dr. Fell, a mysterious and nosy early-20th-century bearded lodger in a tophat and cape who might be Jack the Ripper. A reporter called Curley (Jimmy Hanley) relates the story in flashback. The doctor, who escaped an asylum fire, orders around the house's crippled owner, Mrs. Musgrove, and her daughter (Constance Smith, a beautiful actress who returned in another Jack the Ripper movie, *Man in the Attic*, in 1953). Curley solves the case. Or does he? Godfrey Grayson also directed the Dick Barton movies for Hammer. John Gilling directed many features, including *The Gamma People* (1955) and *The Flesh and the Fiends/Mania* (1960).

ROOTS OF EVIL

(Cannon, 1991) **D:** Gary Graver **S:** Adam Berg **P:** Sidney Niekerk

Alex Cord and Jillian Kesner star as LA detectives who are after a serial killer who preys on strippers and hookers, in this "erotic thriller" with Deanna Lund as a lesbian who has her husband killed, Charles Dierkop as a killer, Delia Sheppard, Daphne Cheung, Jasae, and Brinke Stevens as a scream queen. R and unrated versions are available.

ROPE

(MCA, 1948) **D/P:** Alfred Hitchcock **S:** Arthur Laurents **P:** Sidney Bernstein

Alfred Hitchcock's first Technicolor film uses some innovative techniques. It was filmed entirely on a single set, a NYC apartment, in ten-minute takes.

Diana Dors in *Room 43*.

It's an adaptation of a 1929 play by Patrick Hamilton (who also wrote *Gaslight*), which was based on "the crime of the century," the Leopold/Loeb case (also the basis of the 1959 film *Compulsion*). James Stewart stars as Professor Rupert Cadell. Farley Granger and John Dall are rich (possibly homosexual) college students who have killed a friend and hidden his body in an antique chest just for the intellectual thrill of it. Cedric Hardwicke, Constance Cummings, and Joan Chandler are among the guests at a cocktail party in the same room as the chest. The phony skyline seen through the large windows is distracting, but the play/film is disturbing. It was produced by Transatlantic Pictures and distributed by Warner Brothers. The director is seen crossing a street. It was rereleased in 1984.

THE ROSE AND THE SWORD: *See* FLESH + BLOOD

THE ROSEBUD BEACH HOTEL

(1984) **D/P:** Harry Hurwitz **S:** Harry Narunsky, Thomas Randolph **S/P:** Irving Schwartz

Peter Scolari tries running an old hotel to impress his girlfriend, Colleen Camp. Christopher Lee tries to blow the hotel up. This comedy also features Eddie Deezen as an alien, Fran Drescher (of *The Nanny*), Cherie Currie and her twin sister, Marie Currie, Monique Gabrielle, Julie Parton, Chuck McCann, and Hamilton Camp. The female bellhops undress a lot. Lee was also in *Safari 3000*, by Hurwitz.

ROSELAND

(SW, 1970) **D/S/P:** Fredric Hobbs

A likable, bearded man called Adam (E. Kerrigan Prescott, probably the director himself) talks to his shrink about the art of Hieronymus Bosch in this unique hippie-era sex "fable." We see his b/w dream sequences: topless women in bondage gear tie him up, and lots of naked people are seen dancing, frolicking, and fondling outdoors around a giant penis. During a bizarre dance number (supposedly on the Ed Sullivan show!) Adam sings with a strong operatic voice. Meanwhile a funny fat man and Bosch himself (a black man) make comments. Adam is put into a mental hospital (where he has sex with two nurses) but is eventually seen in Bosch's painting *The Garden of Earthly Delights*. With members of the Magic Theater and the rock group Loading Zone. This is not a typical Boxoffice International "raincoat-crowd" movie but is a very ambitious (if dated) counterculture movie that was reviewed in underground papers when released. It has a free-form jazz soundtrack. Fredric Hobbs also made *Troika* (1969) and *Alabama's Ghost* (1972).

ROSEMARY'S DISCIPLES = NECROMANCY

ROSWELL: THE U.F.O. COVER-UP

(Republic, 1994) **D/S/P:** Jeremy Kagan **S:** Arthur Kopit **P:** Ilene Kahn

UFO remains and alien bodies are found in New Mexico in 1947. Kyle MacLachlan is an army-intelligence major who investigated, then was ridiculed. In 1977 he interviews survivors and exposes the cover-up. Kim Greist as his wife, Doug Wert as his son, Dwight Yoakum as a rancher, Peter MacNichol, Charles Martin Smith, J. D. Daniels, and Martin Sheen are featured. This is based on a 1991 book about the claims of a real major. Steve Johnson created the alien FX. This PG-13 movie debuted on Showtime. *UFO Secret: The Roswell Crash* (Republic) is a documentary about the same events.

R.O.T.O.R.

(Imperial, 1987) **D/P:** Cullen Baline
S/P: Budd Lewis **P/A:** Richard Gesswein

Richard Gesswein stars in this low-budget *Terminator* and *Robocop* copy from Dallas.

ROUGE

(1987) **D:** Stanley Kwan **S:** Lee Berk
Wahl **P:** Jackie Chan, Leonard K. C. Ho
Hong Kong (*The Legend of Flower*)

Look for this excellent romantic ghost story, which takes place in two time periods. In the 1830s Leslie Cheung backs out of an opium-induced suicide pact, but his lover, a singer and high-class prostitute named Flower (Anita Mui), dies. She returns in modern times as a ghost and a young journalist and his girlfriend help her search for her lover. There are scenes of the making of a ghost movie. It's from Golden Harvest.

ROUGH RIDERS = ANGELS' WILD WOMEN

ROUND TRIP TO HEAVEN

(Prism, 1992) **D:** Alan Roberts **S:** Shuki
Levy, Winston Richard **P:** Ronnie Hadar

Corey Feldman and Zach Galligan star as a couple of guys searching for a dream girl (Rowanne Brewer) in Palm Springs. Stoneface (Ray Sharkey) is after them for the money in their trunk. With Julie McCullough, Pat Harrington, Kristine Rose, Tara Buckman, and Cyndi Pass.

ROYCE

(Paramount, 1993) **D:** Rod Holcomb
S: Paul Bernbaum **P:** J. Boyce Harman Jr.

James Belushi stars as a CIA agent, with Chelsea Field as his ex-wife, Miguel Ferrer, and Peter Boyle. This action movie about stolen nuclear warheads was made for Showtime.

R.P.M.

(1970) **D/P:** Stanley Kramer **S:** Erich Segal

Anthony Quinn stars as "hip" professor Paco Perez, who's asked to be acting president during a student sit-in. Ann-Margret is his grad-student girlfriend. It ends with a riot and cops busting heads and has ridiculous dialogue and songs by Melanie. Gary Lockwood, Paul Winfield, Graham Jarvis, and Teda Bracci are featured. Bell released the soundtrack.

R.S.V.P.

(Vestron, 1984) **D:** Lem Amero
S: La Rue Watts **P:** John Amero

A dead body is found in the pool at a Hollywood party. Adam Mills stars, with Katt Shea, Lynda Weismeier (from *Playboy*), Jane Hamilton/Veronica Hart, and *Deep Throat* star Harry Reems as a writer. Chuck Vincent was the executive producer and it debuted on Playboy TV.

RUBIN AND ED

(Columbia, 1991) **D/S:** Trent Harris **P:** Paul Webster

Crispin Glover is long-haired recluse Rubin Farr. He wears exaggerated 70s clothes and keeps a dead, cross-eyed cat in his freezer. Real-estate agent Ed Tuttle (Howard Hesseman) drives him to the desert to bury the cat. This odd road movie from IRS was filmed in Utah. Karen Black also appears in it.

RUBY

(Columbia, 1991) **D:** John MacKenzie **S:** Stephen Davis **P:** Sigurjoh Sighvatsson, Steve Golin

Although ignored after the controversial *JFK* (which was released first), this what-if movie with Danny Aiello as Oswald killer Jack Ruby is pretty interesting. He's sent to Cuba to be a hitman for the mob, works for the FBI, and runs his Dallas Carousel club. Sherilyn Fenn is the (fictional) stripper Candy Cane. Another stripper has an affair with Kennedy, and this movie manages to place the president, Ruby, Oswald and a Sinatra character all in the same nightclub at the same time. Arliss Howard, Tobin Bell, David Duchovny, Joe Cortese, and Marc Lawrence are also featured.

RUCKUS

(Paragon, 1980) **D/S:** Max Kleven
P: Paul Maslansky (*The Loner*)

Dirk Benedict is a Nam vet who escapes from a military hospital's psychiatric ward in a southern town. This is basically a comedy version of *First Blood*. He sleeps in trees. Linda Blair costars, with Ben Johnson, Richard Farnsworth, and Matt Clark. The country music is by Willie Nelson, Janie Fricke, and others. It's a New World release.

RUDE AWAKENING

(Thriller, 1980) **D:** Peter Sasdy
S: Gerald Savory UK

Denholm Elliott stars as a hen-pecked real-estate agent who lives in a dream world. Pat Heywood co-stars. Elvira hosts this hour-long Hammer TV drama.

RUDE AWAKENING

(HBO, 1989) **D/P/A:** Aaron Russo
D: David Greenwalt **S:** Neil Levy,
Richard La Gravenese

Cheech Marin and Eric Roberts star as hippies who return to NYC after 20 years in a commune. They know a secret CIA plan and tell their old friend (Julie Hagerty), now a neurotic designer, and Robert Carradine. Cliff De Young is a psycho government agent who's after them. With Buck Henry, Louise Lasser, Cindy Williams, Andrea Martin, Timothy Leary, Jerry Rubin, Bobby Seale, David Peel, and a talking fish. Scenes on St. Mark's Place were shot in a reconstructed 60s store. The original director was replaced. The Elektra soundtrack features some Jefferson Airplane and Grateful Dead but is mostly 80s rock.

RUDE BOY

(SMV, 1980) **D/S/P:** Jack Hazan,
David Mingay **S/A:** Ray Gange UK

Ray Gange, a poor Clash fan who works in a sex shop, becomes a roadie for the Clash. His only friend is a little skinhead. The band practices ("Gar-age Land") and plays at clubs, rallies, and concerts. It's all mixed with National Front demonstrations, Margaret Thatcher's speeches, and political discussions. Jimmy Pursey helps sing "White Riot." In a subplot, a black kid is arrested. The band doesn't sound very good most of the time (the records were great, though), and this is a pretty dreary docudrama look at England. The one great musical moment is when they do "Complete Control." I saw this on opening night in NYC. It was also the only time I saw Andy Warhol in person. He walked out.

RUE MORGUE MASSACRE = HUNCHBACK OF THE MORGUE

THE RULING CLASS

(Nelson, 1972) **D:** Peter Medak **S:** Peter Barnes
P: Jules Buck, Jack Hawkins **M:** John Cameron UK

Peter O'Toole (who is excellent) stars as the fourteenth earl of Gurney, a relative of the royal family who at various times thinks he's Jack the Ripper, Jesus Christ, and God. His family wants him committed. He sees the House of Lords as a gallery of corpses and imagines other incredible sights. This hilarious satire/fantasy is based on a play by Peter Barnes. With Alastair Sim, Arthur Lowe, Harry Andrews, Coral Browne, and Nigel Green (who died in 1972 from sleeping pills). It's 154 minutes long. The soundtrack (on Avco Embassy) includes dialogue.

Peter O'Toole in *The Ruling Class.*

RUMBLE FISH

(MCA, 1983) **D/S:** Francis Ford Coppola
S: S. E. Hinton **P:** Fred Roos, Doug
Claybourne **M:** Stewart Copeland

The incredible, dreamlike look of this movie, one
of the overlooked classics of the 80s, has been very
influential. It's b/w with one part tinted, and the
production design is by Dean Tavoularis. S. E.
Hinton's teen novels set in Tulsa, Oklahoma, have
been made into four films, three starring Matt Dillon. This time he's Rusty James, and Mickey
Rourke is his idol and older brother, Motorcycle
Boy. They drink, have *West Side Story*–inspired
rumbles, and try to deal with their drunken father
(Dennis Hopper). Diane Lane is Rusty's schoolgirl
girlfriend, and Diana Scarwid is a junkie. With
Vincent Spano, Nicolas Cage, Christopher Penn,
Lawrence (Larry) Fishburne, J. P. Ryan, Tom
Waits, Tracey Walter, and William Smith as the
local heat. The excellent instrumental soundtrack
(on A&M) features an end theme by Stan Ridge-
way. There's a scene from *Murder by Television*.

RUMPELSTILTSKIN

(1955) **D:** Herbert B. Fredersdorf **P:** Hubert
Schonger   W. Germany (*Rumpelstilzchen*)

This color fairy tale (released here by K. Gordon
Murray) is worth watching for the tiny little
bearded dwarf who levitates things and helps the
miller's pigtailed daughter when she has to spin
gold for the king. If he's in other movies I want to
see them. This one's narrated by a woman.

RUMPELSTILTSKIN

(Media, 1987) **D/S:** David Irving
P: Golan/Globus

Billy Barty stars as the rhyming and singing dwarf
who demands a baby in exchange for his help in
spinning gold. Amy Irving (sister of the director)
stars, with Priscilla Pointer (mom of the director),
Clive Revill, and John Moulder-Brown. This Cannon production was shot in Israel. Also look for
the early 80s *Faerie Tale Theatre* version (Fox).

RUNAWAY

(RCA/Columbia, 1984) **D/S:** Michael Crichton
P: Michael Rachmil **M:** Jerry Goldsmith

Tom Selleck stars as a robotics expert. He and a
policewoman (Cynthia Rhodes) are assigned to
track down short-circuited killer robots in a big
city. Televised mind control is used by bad guy
Gene Simmons. Kirstie Alley and Cec Verrell are
also in this PG movie. Like all of the movies starring the born-again TV star Selleck, this was a
box-office flop. The soundtrack is on Varèse Sarabande.

RUNAWAY DAUGHTERS

(1994) **D:** Joe Dante **S:** Charlie
Haas **P:** Lou Arkoff, Debra Hill

Holly Fields, Julie Bowen, and Jenny Lewis are
teens who steal a car and go cross-country after the
guy who got one of them pregnant and joined the
navy. Like Joe Dante's *Matinee* this is filled with
Cold War references. With Roger Corman, Dick

William Smith, Matt Dillon, and Mickey Rourke in *Rumble Fish*.

Miller, John Astin, Fabian, and a clip from *I Was a
Teenage Werewolf*. Part of the Showtime *Rebel
Highway* series, this uses the title of the 1956 Alex
Gordon AIP movie but not the plot or characters.

RUNAWAY GIRL

(SW, 1962 and 1966) **D/P:** Hamill Petroff
S: Stewart Cohn

Stripper Lili St. Cyr (then in her forties and looking great) stars in her last film as Louise, a sweet,
friendly stripper (the "hottest personality in the
whole word"). She hides out, working at a vineyard, to get away from it all, and falls for the owner
(Jock Mahoney). The adopted son of Italians, he
has a jealous girlfriend (Laurie Mitchell) and a
troublemaking half brother (Ron Hagerty, acting
like Elisha Cook Jr.). Nothing is revealed during
the lone tame strip show flashback, so when this
b/w feature was rereleased (at only 62 minutes),
three new scenes were added to spice things up.
Naked women spray shaving cream at each other
during an outdoor shower and later swim underwater and there's another on-stage stripper scene.
Robert Shayne plays Louise's manager. Mahoney
was also in Petroff's *California* (1963).

RUNAWAY NIGHTMARE

(All Seasons, 1982) **D/S/A:** Michael Cartel
P: Eldon Short

Female beauties kidnap worm ranchers in Death
Valley and steal plutonium from the Mafia. There's
a wolf man and a vampire woman in this very
cheap effort.

RUNAWAY TRAIN

(MGM, 1985) **D/S:** Andrei Konchalovsky **S:** Djordje
Milicevic, Paul Zindel **P:** Golan/Globus

Jon Voight is a convict in an Alaska prison who escapes through a sewer with Eric Roberts. They
hop on a train, the engineer has a heart attack,

and the out-of-control train continues to go full
speed ahead. The screenplay of this exciting movie
is a re-worked version of a screenplay by Japanese
director Akira Kurosawa. Rebecca De Mornay
works on the train, and John P. Ryan is the sadistic warden. T. K. Carter and John Bloom are also
featured. Both stars received Oscar nominations,
but Voight didn't work again until the awful *Eternity* (1990), and Roberts went on to commercial
flops and direct-to-video movies.

THE RUNESTONE

(IVE, 1990) **D/S:** Willard Carroll **P:** Harry E. Gould Jr.,
Thomas L. Wilhoite **M:** David Newman

Peter Riegert is a sarcastic Italian-American NYC
cop. He's after a vicious killer who turns out to be
a 6th-century Norse demon from another dimension, freed from a mine in Pennsylvania. His ex-
girlfriend (Joan Severance) is an artist. William
Hickey is an expert on the Norse legend of "Ragna-
rokk" and Alexander Godunov is a mysterious
clockmaker who aids the monster. It's just a man-
in-a-suit monster, but this ambitious movie has a
lot of atmosphere and builds a sense of dread. A
police detective (Lawrence Tierney) says, "It's a big
guy in a bulletproof dog suit." The plot is pretty involved, and there are a lot of characters. I liked the
scene where the monster attacks a pretentious
performance-art show and the nightmare within a
nightmare. Although set mostly in Manhattan, it
was filmed in LA. It's based on a novella by Mark
E. Rogers.

RUN FOR THE SUN

(1956) **D/S:** Roy Boulting **S:** Dudley
Nichols **P:** Harry Tatelman

Richard Widmark and Jane Greer are forced to
land a plane in a jungle in a Technicolor and
Superscope updated version of *The Most Dangerous Game* (1932), based on a short story by Richard Connell. Trevor Howard is a British traitor in

the jungle with Nazis like Peter Van Eyck as an assistant. This United Artists release was shot in Mexico. *The Game of Death* (1946) is another version, and there have been countless other uncredited versions and rip-offs.

RUN IF YOU CAN!

(Today, 1987) **D/P:** Virginia Lively Stone
S/P: J. A. S. McCombie

Before his Oscar nomination for *Tucker*, Martin Landau was so desperate that he costarred in this movie (and in *Death Blow*) with Jerry Van Dyke (from the TV series *My Mother the Car*). They play cops in this nutty movie about snuff films. Van Dyke's eyeglass lens keeps falling out to make his character more lovable. A student (Yvette Nipar) house-sitting in Beverly Hills is watching an old Leslie Howard movie on TV. All of a sudden a color porno movie is on. The guy kills the woman and puts her into a plastic bag. The bright student thinks that she's still watching the same movie! More women are killed, and naked bodies in bags are found in garbage cans all over town. The cops hang around watching her TV for clues and try to protect her. It's all got something to do with a satellite company that sells snuff tapes. This dumb movie could win a contest for having the most false leads and false scares. It also has a very long and dark ending, and I still don't know what the hell was going on.

RUNNING AGAINST TIME

(MCA, 1990) **D:** Bruce Seth Green **S:** Stanley Shapiro, Robert Glass **P:** Pat Finnegan, Sheldon Pinchuk

Robert Hays uses a time machine invented by Sam Wanamaker to try to prevent the assassination of JFK. Catherine Hicks costars, and James DiStefano is Oswald. The cable TV movie, based on Stanley Shapiro's novel *A Time to Remember*, aired before Oliver Stone's *JFK* came out.

RUNNING COOL

(Paramount, 1993) **D/S/P:** Ferd Sebastian, Beverly Sebastian

Good-guy, tattooed, Harley-riding bikers try to save a swamp in South Carolina. Andrew Divoff stars as Bone, who falls for a crippled waitress (Dedee Pfeiffer). Paul Gleason is a greedy developer backed by violent rednecks. The bikers stage a wet-T-shirt contest and a greased-pig-chase show. Also featured are Tracy Sebastian, Arlen Dean Snyder, Bubba Baker as Bear, James Gammon as Ironbutt, and a reported 900 real bikers. It was filmed in Florida and features a country-music soundtrack.

RUNNING DELILAH

(Signet, 1992) **D:** Richard Franklin
S: Ron Koslow **P:** Mel Efros   UK

Kim Cattrall is shot while undercover to catch arms dealers. Reconstructed (only her head and an arm are real), she trains and then uses her new powers. Billy Zane costars as her partner, with François Guetary and Yorgo Voyagis. Diana Rigg

("It's mind-boggling") hits a career low point as her boss, usually behind a desk. This boring PG-13 TV movie (another rip-off of *La Femme Nikita*) is set in France.

RUNNING HOT

(Vestron, 1984) **D/S/P:** Mark Griffiths **P:** David Calloway, Zachary Feur   (*Lucky 13; Highway to Hell*)

Eric Stoltz is a 17-year-old wrongly convicted and sentenced to death for killing his father. He escapes and hides out with an older hooker (Monica Carrico, featured in topless scenes) in a vintage Cadillac convertible. This road movie with murders costars Stuart Margolin, Juliette Cummins, and Virgil Frye. New Line released it.

THE RUNNING MAN

(Vestron, 1987) **D:** Paul Michael Glaser
S: Stephen E. de Souza **P:** Tim Zimmerman

Arnold Schwarzenegger stars as a cop framed as "the butcher of Bakersfield" in 2019 and sent to prison, where he has to participate in death games. It's based on a Stephen King story (written under the name Richard Bachman) but is very similar to a 1983 French film, *The Prize of Peril*, and also copies *Rollerball*. Characters wear ugly jumpsuit costumes. Richard Dawson costars as the host of the games, with Maria Conchita Alonso, Yaphet Kotto, Jim Brown as Fireball, Jesse "the Body" Ventura, Erland Van Lidth, Professor Tanaka, Mick Fleetwood, and Dweezil Zappa. Paul Michael Glaser, who replaced director Andrew Davis, also directed *Band of the Hand*. Varèse Sarabande released the soundtrack.

RUNNING OUT OF LUCK

(Fox, 1986) **D/S:** Julian Temple   UK

There's a very loose plot in this 88-minute release built around nine videos from Mick Jagger's "She's the Boss" solo LP. Jagger stars (of course) as himself, with Jerry Hall, Rae Dawn Chong as a slave girl, and Dennis Hopper as a video director. It's by the director of *The Great Rock 'n' Roll Swindle*.

RUSH

(USA, 1984) **D:** "Anthony Richmond"/
Tonino Ricci **S:** Tito Carpi   Italy /Spain

Musclebound post-nuke hero Conrad Nichols is Rush, and Gordon Mitchell is "the Ruler." Laura Trotter is featured. Sybil Danning hosts the video. The sequel is called *Rage*.

RUSH

(MGM, 1991) **D:** Lili Fini Zanuck **S:** Peter Dexter **P:** Richard D. Zanuck **M:** Eric Clapton

Jason Patric is a bearded narc in Beaumont, Texas, in the early 70s, and Jennifer Jason Leigh is a rookie cop. They buy from redneck dealers, and soon they become lovers, then addicts using needles and suffering from withdrawal. With William Sadler, Sam Elliott, Max Perlich (*Drugstore Cowboy*), and Gregg Allman as a club owner. It's based on a semi-autobiographical novel by Kim Wozencraft, a mystery writer who was once a narcotics cop.

RUSH WEEK

(RCA/Columbia, 1988) **D:** Bob Bravler
S/P: Michael V. Leighton **S:** Russell V. Manzatt

This is another stupid, boring teen/horror movie, but at least the Dickies show up and play two songs. Toni (Pamela Ludwig), a college reporter, investigates the disappearance of several coeds. Kathleen Kinmont, posing topless with a (fake) corpse (for $100), is killed by someone with a medieval axe. Some of the fun frat guys charge $10 a head to watch a couple have sex but substitute a (real) male corpse as a gag. The frightened girl runs away and becomes victim number two. Roy Thinnes is the college dean. Gregg Allman (!) has a bit part as Cosmo Kinkaid, seen showing off his tattoos and meditating with a topless woman. The movie is complete with an axe battle, decapitations, a tarantula, gay jokes, and a very stupid ending. A typical bad line is "Wake up! This is real life, not some stupid horror movie!" Allman returned in the unrelated *Rush* (1991). With Dean Hamilton and Laura Burkett.

RUSSKIES

(1987) **D:** Rick Rosenthal **S:** Alan Jay Glueckman
P: Mark Levinson, Scott Rosenfelt

Some American kids (Whip Hubley, Leaf Phoenix, and Peter Billingsley) think that WWIII has started after a Soviet sailor washes ashore in Florida, but he falls in love, and everybody likes him. This PG movie copies *The Russians Are Coming! The Russians Are Coming!* (1966).

RUST NEVER SLEEPS

(Vestron, 1979) **D/A:** "Bernard Shakey"/
Neil Young **P:** Elliot Rabinowitz

Neil Young performs 16 songs in concert, sometimes backed by Crazy Horse and going all the way back to his Buffalo Springfield days. The music is what you hear on the *Live Rust* LP. A bunch of space dwarfs appear, and there's a short 3-D sequence. It's a Warner release. "Bernard Shakey" also used Devo in his *Human Highway* (1982).

THE RUTHLESS FOUR

(Paragon, 1967) **D:** "George Holloway"/Giorgio Capitani **S:** Augusto Caminito, Fernando Di Leo   Italy/W. Germany (*Ognuno per Se*)

Van Heflin strikes gold, but his helpers plot to take it. This western costars Gilbert Roland, Klaus Kinski as "the Blond," and George Hilton.

SABATA

(VSOM, 1969) **D/S:** "Frank Kramer"/Gianfranco Parolini **S:** Renato Izzo **P:** Alberto Grimaldi
Italy (Echi, Amico, c'e Sabata ... Hai Chiuso!)

Lee Van Cleef stars as a stranger who rides into town, kills some bank robbers, and blackmails the businessmen who had hired them. A Mexican, an Indian acrobat, and a guy with a gun in his banjo (William Berger) help him. With Franco Ressel, Linda Veras, and Pedro Sanchez. UA released the PG western and *Return of Sabata* (1972), also with Van Cleef. *Adios Sabata* (1970) with Yul Brynner was an unrelated, retitled movie.

SABOTAGE

(Budget, Sinister, 1936) **D:** Alfred Hitchcock
S: Charles Bennett **P:** Michael Balcon,
Ivor Montagu UK (*A Woman Alone*)

This early Hitchcock classic was based on *The Secret Agent* by Joseph Conrad. A woman (star Sylvia Sidney) lives with her immigrant husband, Verloc (Oscar Homolka), above his cinema. He's actually an anarchist who sends her young brother out with a bomb. The kid and a whole busload of people are killed. With John Loder as a detective posing as a vegetable salesman, Torin Thatcher, and a very clever use of Disney's "Who Killed Cock Robin" cartoon.

SABOTEUR

(MCA, 1942) **D:** Alfred Hitchcock
S: Peter Viertel, Joan Harrison,
Dorothy Parker **P:** Frank Lloyd,
Jack H. Skirball

Robert Cummings is a WWII munitions factory mechanic falsely accused of espionage. He goes on the run across America handcuffed to Priscilla Lane. Parts are similar to *The 39 Steps* and the later *North by Northwest.* Watch for a scene in a circus with Siamese twins, a bearded lady, and Billy Curtis. There's also a Radio City Music Hall shootout and a great ending on the Statue of Liberty. With Otto Kruger, Ian Wolfe, Norman Lloyd as the saboteur, and the director, seen at a newsstand. From Universal.

THE SACRIFICE

(Pacific Arts, 1986) **D/S/E:** Andrei Tarkovsky
Sweden/France

Erland Josephson stars as an intellectual actor celebrating his birthday with five other people at a remote estate. A newscast announces that a nuclear war has begun. Sven Nykvist was cinematographer for the very serious (and subtitled) 145 minute feature. The Swedish Film Institute backed the Russian director's seventh and last film. He died in Paris in 1986.

SADDLE TRAMPS

(High Desert, 1973) **D:** Maurizio Lucidi
S: Rafael Azcona **P:** Alfonso Sansone Italy/Spain
(*Si Puo Fare ... Amigo; It Can Be Done Amigo*)

The Saint

The Saint was created by Leslie Charteris in 1928. He's Simon Templar, a very cool Londoner who steals only from criminals and is wanted by Scotland Yard. *The Saint in New York* was the first film (from RKO in 1938). Louis Hayward starred. RKO then made five more (1938–41) with George Sanders and *The Saint's Vacation* (1941) with Hugh Sinclair. *The Saint Strikes Back* (1938) is on tape from Turner. Republic made *The Saint Meets the Tiger* (1943) starring Hugh Sinclair and Hayward returned for *The Saint's Girl Friday* (1954) for RKO. The last three were filmed in England, where Roger Moore became the Saint on TV (1967–69). *Vendetta for the Saint* (1969) with Moore, is a feature-length episode and 7 volumes of the series (2 shows each) are available from IVE. Ian Ogilvy took the role on TV in 1978. Several attempts have been made since to revive the TV series. And a movie is in the works.

Bud Spencer stars as a con artist/horse thief who helps a kid defend his ranch from bad guys. The comedy western costars Jack Palance as a bounty hunter and Dany Saval.

SADISMO

(1967) **D/P:** Salvatore Bilitteri **S:** Philip Marx Italy

This mondo movie explores bizarre customs around the world and shows animal and human torture, various cults, body painting, and Japanese Devil masks. They even threw in a birth-of-a-baby scene and some Nazi concentration camp footage. Some of the stronger footage was cut shortly after the American release by Trans American (an AIP offshoot). Burt Topper narrates and the music is by Les Baxter.

SADISTEROTIC

(Redemption, 1967) **D/S:** Jesús Franco
S: Louis Revenga **P:** Jose Lopez Moreno
W. Ger./Spain (*Rote Lippen—Sadisterotica*)

Janine Reynauld and Rosanna Yanni star as the Red Lips, detectives trying to find missing models and dancers. Adrian Hoven is the killer pop artist Klaus Thriller who uses the werewolf-like Morpho (Michel Lemoine) to kidnap victims. The spy spoof has the same main cast as Franco's *Kiss Me Monster* from the same year.

SAFARI 3000

(MGM, 1980) **D:** Harry Hurwitz
S: Michael Harreschou **P:** Arthur
Gardner, Jules V. Levy S. Africa

David Carradine is a Hollywood stuntman race car driver in a trans-Africa race. He's forced to take along a *Playboy* photographer (Stockard Channing). The PG-rated comedy action movie includes Christopher Lee as Count Borgia and Hamilton Camp. Carradine had already been in *Death Race 2000* and *Cannonball,* also both about cross-country races.

A SAFE PLACE

(1971) **D/S:** Henry Jaglom **P:** Bert Schneider

Tuesday Weld stars as a young hippie who relives her life in her mind, and becomes stuck in time. Orson Welles is a (real?) magician who wants to make animals in the Central Park Zoo disappear. Jack Nicholson costars in the seldom seen, largely improvised experimental New York City feature with Philip Proctor and Gwen Welles. Weld, Welles, and Nicholson smoke pot. Welles' last film (*Someone to Love,* 1987) was also by Jaglom. The GP-rated Columbia release was backed by BBS, who had also done *Easy Rider* and *The Last Movie.*

SAGA OF THE DRACULAS: *See* DRACULA— THE BLOODLINE CONTINUES

SAHARA

(MGM, 1983) **D:** Andrew V. McLaglen
S: James R. Silke **P:** Golan/Globus

In 1927, Brooke Shields disguises herself as a boy in order to enter a cross-country car race in the Sahara desert. She falls for Sheik Jaffar (Lambert Wilson), who kidnaps her. With John Rhys-Davies as a bad Arab, Horst Buchholz, Perry Lang, Ronald Lacey, Sir John Mills, and Steve Forrest. Cannon made the PG flop, Brooke's last theatrical release as a star (unless you count *Brenda Starr*).

SAIGON COMMANDOS

(Media, 1988) **D:** Clark Henderson
S: Thomas McKelvey Cleaver **P:** John
Schouweiler, Isabel Sumayao

Richard Young stars as Sgt. Stryker, and P. J. Soles is a reporter who discovers corrupt politicians are behind drug-related murders in South Vietnam. From Concorde.

SAINT JACK

(Vestron, 1979) **D/A:** Peter Bogdanovich
S: Howard Sackler, Paul Theroux **P:** Roger Corman

Ben Gazzara stars as Jack Flowers, an American pimp in early 70s Singapore. The New World release is based on a novel by Paul Theroux. Robby Muller shot it on location and Hugh Hefner was an executive producer. With Denholm Elliot, Joss Ackland, George Lazenby, and a mostly Asian support cast. Bogdanovich started out as Corman's assistant director on *The Wild Angels* (1966).

THE SAINT'S GIRL FRIDAY

(1954) **D:** Seymour Friedman **S:** Allan Mackinnon **P:** Anthony Hinds   UK (*The Saint Returns*)

Louis Hayward stars as the Saint in a mystery from Hammer films. He goes after the killers of his ex-girlfriend. With Naomi Chanes and Diana Dors. Hayward had been the first actor to play the Saint in *The Saint in New York* (back in 1938). RKO released his second go-round in America.

THE SALAMANDER

(Charter, 1980) **D:** Peter Zimmer **S:** Robert Katz **P:** Paul Maslansky   US/Italy/UK

A colonel (Franco Nero) tries to stop a modern-day fascist plot to take over Italy. It's based on a novel by Morris L. West. With an all-star cast including Anthony Quinn, Martin Balsam, Eli Wallach, Christopher Lee, Sybil Danning, Paul Smith, and Claudia Cardinale.

SALO, OR THE 120 DAYS OF SODOM

(Water Bearer, 1975) **D/S:** Pier Paolo Pasolini   Italy

Pasolini updated a novel by the Marquis de Sade and set it in a villa in the fascist Salo Republic in Italy during the end of WWII. Scenes of the torture of naked teenagers—including shit eating (it was really chocolate), piss drinking, and rape (all faked)—helped make it one of the most controversial features of all time. U.A., which had distributed Pasolini's previous features in America, passed on this one. John Waters has called it "beautiful" and praised the sets and sound. The director was bludgeoned to death by a teenage boy while this, his last feature, was being edited. *Salo* was originally nearly two hours long and is subtitled. Criterion offers it on laser disc (at about 112 minutes). It made news in 1994 when videos sold in a (gay) bookstore were seized by police in Cincinnati.

SALT IN THE WOUND

(Interglobal, 1969) **D/S:** Theodoro Ricci **S:** Piero Regnoli   Italy (*Il Dito Nella Piaga*)

Klaus Kinski, George Hilton, and Ray Saunders are in a WWII battle movie set in Italy. The stars are American soldiers, one black, one white.

SALVATION! HAVE YOU SAID YOUR PRAYERS TODAY?

(Vista, 1987) **D/S/P:** Beth B. **S:** Tom Robinson **P:** Michael H. Shomberg

Beth B. codirected underground films in New York City (*Vortex* was the last), then made some rock videos. Her background shows in this professional satire. It has scary, believable lower-class unemployed Americans. Exene (from the group X) becomes a popular, rich, born-again, heavy metal Christian TV crusader after getting to know the famous Jimmy Swaggart–type Rev. Randall (played by Steven McHattie). *Salvation* has comedy, violence, erotic sex, a good modern rock soundtrack by groups I thought I didn't like (Cabaret Voltaire,

New Order), and unpredictable plot moves. Also with the very sexy Dominique Davalos and Rockets Redglare.

SAMSON AND DELILAH

(Paramount, 1949) **D/P:** Cecil B. DeMille **S:** Jesse Lasky Jr., Frederick M. Frank

Victor Mature is Samson and Hedy Lamarr cuts his hair. The ending, where Samson, whose eyes have been burned out, brings down the Philistine temple, was a big crowd pleaser, and the 128-minute Technicolor Biblical epic from Paramount was a smash hit. Lines like "Your tongue will dig your grave" help too. George Sanders costars as the Saran of Gaza. With Angela (*Murder, She Wrote*) Lansbury, Henry Wilcoxon, Fritz Leiber, Frank Reicher, George Reeves, Mike Mazurki, Tom Tyler, and Rusty Tamblyn as the young King Saul. DeMille only made two more epics, *The Greatest Show on Earth* (1952) and a remake of his own *The Ten Commandments* (1956), two of the biggest-grossing features of the 50s. Mature was also in a 1984 Samson TV remake (available from Prism) as Samson's father.

SAMSON AND HIS MIGHTY CHALLENGE

(Sinister, 1964) **D:** Giorgio Capitani **S:** Sandro Continenza, Roberto Gianvitu   Italy

Alan Steel (Sergio Ciani) stars as Samson in an adventure featuring Hercules, Maciste, and Ursus too.

SAMURAI

(SW, 1944) **D/S:** Raymond Cannon **P:** Ben Mindenberg

This has to be one of the most outrageous (and cheapest looking) American WWII propaganda movies. A Samurai priest in California grooms Ken, a young Japanese orphan, to serve "His Satanic Majesty." Eventually Ken (Paul Fung) smuggles secret plans in his paintings, kills his English school friend, helps doctor news photos in Shanghai, kills his own adoptive parents, prepares for the invasion of California, and becomes governor! The priest commits hari-kari and is decapitated at the end. Chinese actors play Japanese characters, and newsreel footage of wartime misery in China is used. It was released by Calvacade Pictures in 1945, too late to make much impact at the box office.

SAMURAI (1974): *See* SHOOT FIRST

SAMURAI

(1979) **D:** Lee H. Katzin **S:** Jerry Ludwig **P:** Allan Balter, Ronald Jacobs

Joe Penny stars as a "half Asian" San Francisco D.A. who becomes a hero Samurai at night and battles a villain with an earthquake machine. The ridiculous pilot film was aired by NBC. With James Shigeta, Geoffrey Lewis, and Michael Pataki. Danny Thomas was an executive producer.

SANDCASTLES

(1972) **D:** Ted Post **S:** Stephen & Elinor Karpf, James M. Miller **P:** Gerald I. Isenberg

Bonnie Bedelia falls in love with the ghost of a long-haired young man (Jan-Michael Vincent) who was killed in a car crash. With Herschel Bernardi, Mariette Hartley, and Gary Crosby. The CBS-TV movie was videotaped on the coast of Malibu.

SANDERS OF THE RIVER

(1963) **D/S:** Lawrence Huntington **S/P:** Harry Alan Towers **S:** Nicholas Roeg, Kevin Kavanaugh   UK/W. Germany (*Death Drums Along the River*)

Richard Todd stars as a police inspector in Africa in a remake of Edgar Wallace's novel. It had been filmed as a Paul Robeson movie in 1935 (available from Nelson). With Albert Lieven, Walter Rilla, and Marianne Koch. Towers followed it with a sequel, *Coast of Skeletons* (1965).

SANDRA, THE MAKING OF A WOMAN

(SW, 1970) **D/S/C/E:** Gary Graver **S:** Robert Aiken   (*I Am Sandra*)

Monica Gayle, a vet of many nudie movies, stars as an unhappy dyed blonde living with a drunken slob father in a small town. The cinematography is very arty and some of the editing is pretty amazing. During one confusing flashback (to when her father caught her mother with another man), he drives a car over a cliff—she climaxes—then the car blows up! When Sandra hitches to San Francisco, she rents an apartment from Uschi Digart, who mentions the "wacancy." She has encounters with a lingerie salesman and a biker before falling for her new boss, a shrink. The print is very jumpy and a lesbian scene with Uschi is missing, as is another scene with Eric Stern (*The Love Butcher*) in drag. Graver shoots most of Fred Olen Ray's movies, and he still directs, too.

SANDS OF BEERSHEBA

(1965) **D/S/P:** Alexander Ramati   US/Israel (*Mordei ha'or*)

During the Palestinian War of 1948, an American (Diane Baker) falls in love with her late fiancé's friend, an Israeli gunrunner. AIP released the b/w movie in America.

SANDY THE RELUCTANT NATURE GIRL

(1963) **D:** Stanley Pelc **S:** S.M.C. Mitchell **P:** Michael Deeley   (*The Reluctant Nudist*)

David, a nudist, lies to his girlfriend Sandy about where he goes on weekends. She (Annette Briand) hires a detective to follow him, then hides in the trunk of his car. Of course she joins the camp at the end of the Eastmancolor feature.

SANGAREE

(1953) **D:** Edward Ludwig **S:** David Duncan **P:** William H. Pine

Fernando Lamas is an indentured servant who rises to power in 1780s colonial Georgia. Arlene Dahl co-stars in the 3-D and Technicolor Paramount release, based on a novel by Frank Slaughter. With Patricia Medina and Tom Drake.

SANTA AND THE ICE CREAM BUNNY

(United, 1972) **D:** Barry Mahon, R. Winer

A narrator informs us that Santa Claus (he's skinny and too young) is "stuck in the sand, way down in Florida." Santa just sits there, sweating and thinking, then lip synchs a song. Some kids (one has a "Keep on Truckin'" T-shirt) try to help by bringing various real animals (and a gorilla) to try and pull the sleigh. Santa decides to tell them a story and we see Mahon's 1970 color feature *Thumbelina*, complete with original credits ("Pirates World Presents . . ."). It's really not bad for a kids' matinee movie. Shay Gardner is the appealing singing star. She encounters giant props, a scary forest with talking spiders and frogs, and an old mole man who wants to marry her. Shay also plays a teen girl in a miniskirt listening to the story (which is narrated by a lady mole). Then Santa is rescued by a man in a rabbit suit to justify the stupid title.

SANTA CLAUS

(Silver Screen, 1959) **D/S:** Rene Cardona, **S:** Adolfo Portillo **P:** William Calderon   Mexico

A narrator tells us about the kids from all nations and races who visit Santa. Santa plays the organ in a *long* opening segment in which cute kids, dressed in their native costumes, sing in their own languages. The kids are from all over S. America, Asia, America, and "even Russia," and the kids from Africa wear loincloths and have bones on their heads. Devils (with tails and pitchforks) dance in a fiery cave and one (Pip) is sent to Earth, where he uses three bad little boys (in leather jackets) to help him sabotage Christmas. Some rich kids have everything but aren't loved and poor little Lupita just wants a doll. They all have dream sequences. Merlin helps save the day and all the kids are happy. This hard-to-believe color Mexican movie was a 60s Christmastime matinee staple for years in America thanks to K. Gordon Murray. Maybe you (or your parents) saw it and it made your holiday season bright. Some video versions cut out the African kids.

SANTA CLAUS DEFEATS THE ALIENS = SANTA CLAUS CONQUERS THE MARTIANS

Santa Claus—Mexican style.

SANTA CLAUS: THE MOVIE

(Media, 1985) **D:** Jeannot Szwarc **S:** David Newman **P:** Ilya Salkind, Pierre Spengler

David Huddleston is Santa, Dudley Moore is Patch the elf, and John Lithgow is B.Z. the evil toy manufacturer in a "heartwarming" PG fantasy with the "biggest budget of all time—$50 million." The surefire Christmas release was a box office disaster and that record amount was doubled a few years later by *Terminator II*. With Burgess Meredith as an ancient elf and Judy Cornwall. Szwarc had also directed the big-budget flop fantasy *Supergirl*. Bad Santa movie fans should also check out *Santa Claus Conquers the Martians* (1964). May your next Christmas season be really jolly.

SANTA SANGRE

(Rep., 1989) **D/S:** Alexander Jodorowsky **S/P:** Claudio Argento **S:** Roberto Leoni   Italy

Santa Sangre is beautiful, moving, shocking, disgusting, and fascinating throughout. It's partially based on a real Mexican serial killer, partially based on the director's own life, and is packed with symbolism, tattoos, hookers, elephants, blood (lots of blood), and tributes to Luis Buñuel, James Whale, and Tod Browning (especially *The Unknown*). The director's son, Axel Jodorowsky, stars as a very traumatized young man who has grown up in the circus (as the director himself had). He becomes part of a bizarre mime act with his mother (Blanca Guerra), the leader of a religious cult. With Guy Stockwell and three other Jodorowsky kids. It was produced by Dario Argento's brother (he also backed *Deep Red* and *Suspiria*) and Rene Cardona Jr. in Mexico. Argento also brought along excellent music by Simon Boswell (of Goblin) which was released on a soundtrack (not in America, though). *Santa Sangre* was released in a shorter R version and the uncut (123 minute) NC-17 version, but there's no reason not to see it all. This was Jodorowsky's first released feature since *The Holy Mountain* (1974). He followed it with the more mainstream *Rainbow Thief* (1990).

SANTA VISITS THE LAND OF MOTHER GOOSE

(Sinister, 1967) **D/C:** Herschell Gordon Lewis **P:** J. Edwin Baker (*The Magic Land of Mother Goose*)

This whole (color) movie is a filmed amateur stage play with canned music added. If you've ever seen those great silent fantasy shorts by George Méliès, this looks like an incredibly long, very bad imitation of one of them. There's some (intentional) humor in the wrap-

Axel Jodorowsky stars in Santa Sangre.

around segments, added for a timely Christmas release. A skinny Santa talks ("Heh Heh Heh!") until he falls asleep in the intro and becomes hysterical and loses it at the end ("Ho Ho! . . . He He! . . . Ha Ha! . . ."). Kinda scary. King Cole talks to everybody, he talks to us, and he talks to a balloon. A witch shows up and yells, "I Hate everybody! . . . None of you will be happy!" and freezes everyone. "Merlin the Magician's" long boring stage magic show uses some optical tricks to help it along. He (Roy Huston) levitates Sleeping Beauty and puts swords through a life-size Raggedy Ann doll (with a death's-head face!). A mention of the (copywritten character) Casper the Ghost was electronically altered to avoid lawsuits. This is the worst Lewis film I've seen (so far). I dare you to sit through it.

SARAH T.—PORTRAIT OF A TEENAGE ALCOHOLIC

(1975) **D:** Richard Donner **S:** Richard A. and Esther Shapiro **P:** David Levinson

Linda Blair is 15-year-old Sarah Travis, teenage alcoholic. Mark Hamill co-stars. It's one of those 70s movies you have to hope to catch on some local TV station. Various adults are played by Larry Hagman, Verna Bloom, William Daniels, Michael Lerner, and M. Emmet Walsh. The NBC-TV movie followed Linda's notorious and highly rated *Born Innocent*.

SARTANA

(Domovideo, 1968) **D/S:** "Frank Kramer"/ Gianfranco Parolini **S:** Renato Izzo W. Germany/Italy (*Sartana, Bete Um Deinen Tod*)

William Berger stars in a story about a battle for a trunk of gold. John Garko, Klaus Kinski, Sydney Chaplin, and Fernando Sancho costar. It's on tape in Italian only. Several Sartana westerns (with different stars) were made. Kinski was also in *Sono Sartana, Il Vestro Becchino* (1969).

SASSY SUE

(SW, 1972) **D/S:** Bethel Buchalew

Sharon Kelly (aka Colleen Brennan) is the main attraction in this outdoor sex comedy, especially when she runs through the woods naked. Some of the sex scenes are nearly hard-core. A woman moos, characters enjoy threesomes, and there's a whipping scene. It ends with a couple outside in an old bathtub. The overpowering hillbilly humor is pretty low. Ma gets stuck in the outhouse and Sassy Sue is a cow that Junior has sex with (no, it's not shown). Harvey Forman co-stars.

SATANIC ATTRACTION

(Complete, 1990) **D/S:** Fauzi Mansur
S: Filipe Grecco **P:** J. Davila   Brazil

It starts with black people dancing by a waterfall, then shows blond kids (a brother and sister) participating in a blood ceremony. "Fourteen years later" at Sun Coast, a guy stabs a woman on the beach, cuts off her foot, and feeds her remains to a lion. He collects her blood in a bucket and pours it on his sister's grave. More killings occur (a hatchet to a head . . .) and Fernanda, a local DJ, has the whole town talking about her on-the-air horror stories which always seem to come true. During a nightmare scene involving a corpse, the film itself was scratched for a weird cheap effect. This didn't make all that much sense to me and the dubbing is sometimes awkward or laughable, but I liked the fact that people ate mangoes after a sex scene.

(THE SATANIC) RITES OF DRACULA

(Liberty/ABC, 1973) **D:** Alan Gibson
S: Don Houghton **P:** Roy Skeggs
UK (*Count Dracula and His Vampire Bride*)

A satanic cult made up of rich influential men gets hold of a deadly plague bacteria. The cult seems to be run by an Oriental woman (Barbara Yu-Ling) with a dragon jacket, who commands a group of biker thug snipers in fur vests! A nude blonde on a sacrificial altar becomes a vampire. More female vampires are kept chained in the basement. Dracula (Christopher Lee), the real villain, disguised as a Howard Hughes–type tycoon, wants the "supreme blasphemy"—armageddon! Unfortunately, most of the movie's deaths are by guns. Peter Cushing shows up as Van Helsing again and Joanna Lumley (later on the *Absolutely Fabulous* series) is his daughter. A government agent (Michael Coles) who didn't even believe in vampires instantly knows how to kill them with a stake. Lee's European accent comes and goes, and after the promise of a great conspiracy theme movie, his last on-screen vampire death is caused by a thorn bush! With Freddie Jones and William Franklin. In America, the last Hammer Dracula film starring Lee was shelved by Warner Brothers, announced to be released by AIP, then over five years later was badly released by the independent Dynamite company, cut for an R rating.

SATAN IN HIGH HEELS

(SW, 1962) **D:** Jerald Intrator **S:** John T. Chapman **P:** Leonard M. Burton

Stacey Kane (Meg Myles), a carny burlesque dancer, robs her junkie ex-husband, goes to NYC, and gets a job at a high-class club. She becomes the mistress of the wealthy owner, seduces his piano-playing son (assistant director Del Tenney), and causes a murder. In a stand-out scene, Stacey, with leather clothes and a riding crop, sings "More Deadly Than the Male." With Grayson Hall and Sabrina (as herself), who sings. It was filmed (in b/w) at La Martinique club. Myles's nude swim scene was cut to PG status in this U.S. version. A jazz soundtrack (from Parker Records) was released and a paperback novelization was published! Meg Myles went on to soap opera roles (*All My Children*), Hall was a regular on *Dark Shadows,* and Tenney made *Horror of Party Beach*!

THE SATAN KILLER

(AIP, 1993) **D:** Stephan Calamari
S: Edward Benton, James Brandauer
P: Joel Silverman, Ross Borden   (*Death Penalty*)

A grizzled alcoholic widower detective (Steve Sayre) who kills anybody in his way goes after a tall, laughing, mass-killer biker (Billy Franklin) who rides a Harley. The cop joins a tough impressive old P.I., who grabs people by their eyeballs and says things like "Scum suckin', mother fuckin', ball bitin' death machine." The hero has a nightmare starring his dead wife and the biker has flashbacks of his sexy abusive mother. With a haunted house and sex with a TV reporter (Belinda Borden). The sound is bad and the soft rock is boring, but this is the kind of out-there local movie I can enjoy. Filmed in Virginia Beach and Norfolk, Virginia.

SATAN'S BED

(SW, 1965) **D:** Marshall Smith, Tamijian
P: Jerry Burke, Roger Wilson

It's Yoko Ono's film debut—in a sleazy adults-only S&M drug movie, partially made by Roberta and Michael Findlay (*Snuff*). Michael was the photographer and editor and Roberta acted and did the lighting. *Satan's Bed* is really an earlier "unfinished" feature called *Judas City* by "Tamijian" with new footage and characters edited in. Yoko (in a kimono) shows up in New York to marry Paulie, who wants out of the drug business. She can't speak English and he's preoccupied, so she's taken to a filthy cheap hotel room. A gangster (in the concrete business) rapes her on the floor (offscreen). He take her to his penthouse and rapes her again. Interwoven with this footage is the sick tale of Snake, Dip, and Angel, addicts in black clothes, who look like part of Andy Warhol's Exploding Plastic Inevitable show. The first line heard is

"I'd like to take his needle and shove it in his greedy mouth." They roam around tying up women (Angel helps), and raping them. Finally a Long Island housewife with a gun escapes from the hopped-up trio and footage of Yoko escaping is intercut. *Satan's Bed* was released about the same time as *Help!*

SATAN'S BLACK WEDDING

(World, 1974) **D/S:** "Phillip Miller"/
Steve Millard **P:** Tamara Brown

This is *bad.* Everything about it is bad except maybe the enticing video box. Mark (Greg Braddock) comes to Monterey for his sister's funeral. He wants to know why she killed herself. She returns as a vampire (with *big* teeth) and bites some relatives. Shots of rats are badly edited in. Flashbacks show her working on a book with another woman. A drooling priest (Ray Miles) talks about Satan and a wedding but we never see either. The ending was either never shot or is missing and the tape only runs about an hour. A solo piano and/or synthesizer plays constantly. By the director of *Criminally Insane* (1973)!

SATAN'S BLADE

(Starmaker, 1984) **D:** L. Scott Castillo Jr. **S:** Thomas Cue

In a *Friday the 13th* copy, a local guy is possessed by the ghost of a mountain man. He kills at a ski lodge where lesbian bank robbers are hiding out.

SATAN'S BLOOD

(All American/Mogul, 1977) **D:** Carlos Puento
S: Eva Del Castillo **P:** Francisco Ariza   Spain
(*Escalofríos; Don't Panic*)

This opens with a priest kissing and squeezing the breasts of a naked woman on a sacrificial altar. He has sex with her, then stabs her. What looks like a satanic (almost) porno movie is a good example of the liberalization in Spanish cinema after Franco died (in 1975). It's kind of like early 70s American movies made right after the old censorship system ended. All of a sudden movies packed in as much depravity and nudity as possible. After the credits (all in Spanish), a couple is lured to a castle by a mystery couple who claim to know them. There's a Ouija board séance, lots of thunder and lightning, and nightmare sequences. Their dog is killed and discovered hanging on a butcher hook. Cast members caress each other in the shower, enjoy three-

EXPOSED! At Last! As Never Before on the Screen. The Story of Angry Youths Who Terrorize Young Innocents. They Stalked the City's Streets, Making Them by Day -- HELL -- and by Night . . . . .

SATAN'S BED

somes and group gropes, and scream loud during orgasms. The host growls like a dog. The hostess (Angel Arand) talks in several voices. They both eat like dogs. A porcelain doll comes to life. People are killed or commit suicide, then return, and a twist ending borrows some ideas from *Rosemary's Baby*. Executive producer Juan Piquer Simon later directed *Pieces* and *Slugs*.

SATAN'S DAUGHTERS = VAMPYRES

SATAN'S PRINCESS

(Paramount, 1989) **D/P:** Bert I. Gordon
S: Stephan Katz

Gordon, remembered for his 50s giant monster science fiction movies, also made witch movies. This came after *The Witching* (1971) and *The Coming* (1980). In a prologue, set in 1654 Barcelona, comedian Jack Carter (!) plays a priest and a diseased monk paints "the Malediction" (also the shooting title). Robert Forster is Lou, the cliché tough, heavy-drinking, divorced ex–LA cop who walks with a cane and has a retarded son, Joey, and a nice girlfriend he treats badly. Nicole (Lydie Denier), the French-Canadian head of a model agency, owns the cursed painting and is really a demon. She takes nude swims and has a lesbian scene with one of her young girl model/victims. She even takes over Joey, who has demon eyes and stabs his surprised father with an ice pick. Lou simply pulls it out, no blood, no pain. He takes Joey to a psychic (Ellen Geer), who jumps out her window. Lou says, "This is worse than a fucking nightmare!" When Nicole transforms in the end she rips her own face off and looks like a woman in a wet suit with a dreadlocks wig. Lou says, "Burn, you fucker!" as he gets out his flamethrower. This movie features more suicides, dream sex sequences, pimps, a man being blown by another man in drag, a topless fire eater, a voyeur's head shoved in a toilet, a naked man slashed with fingernails in a gym, and a *Popeye* cartoon. With Debra Lamb, Marilyn Joi, Caren Kaye, and Leslie Huntly.

SATAN'S STORYBOOK

(Even Steven, 1989) **D:** Michael Rider
P/A: Steven K. Arthur

"Star" Ginger Lynn appears on the video box cover and in intro segments for two stories, shot on video. A serial killer picks victims from the phone book and a clown kills himself and goes to hell.

SATAN'S SUPPER: *See* CATACLYSM

SATISFACTION

(Fox, 1988) **D:** Joan Freeman
S: Charles Purpura **P:** Aaron Spelling,
Alan Greisman   (*The Girls of Summer*)

Justine Bateman leads a four-girl (and one-guy) band in a mindless PG-13 teen movie. They break into Liam Neeson's beach house because he owns a beach resort. Julia Roberts is the "slut" bassist. Also with Trini Alvarado and Debbie Harry. It's the worst movie (so far) to use a Rolling Stones song for its title. From 20th Century.

SATURDAY NIGHT FEVER

(Paramount, 1977) **D:** John Badham
S: Norman Wexler **P:** Robert Stigwood

One of the best-known movies of the 70s, this was responsible for making disco music a hundred times more popular than it already was, made John Travolta (who received an Oscar nomination) a major star, and revived the Bee Gees' singing career. Young modern-day audiences seem fascinated by it, and it even became a midnight hit in LA in 1993. Based on a story by Nik Cohn, it's about young working-class people in Bay Ridge whose lives center around a disco. "You know what I'm talkin'?" Karen Lynn Gorney and Barry Miller costar. With Donna Pescow, Denny Dillon, Fran Drescher, and Monti Rock III as the disco DJ. Screenwriter Wexler also wrote *Joe* and *Mandingo*. Lloyd Kaufman (from Troma) was location director. The double RSO soundtrack (now in Goodwills everywhere) was the best-selling movie soundtrack of all time. *Staying Alive* (1983) was a flop sequel. Available in R and PG-13 versions.

SATURDAY NIGHT SERIALS

(Rhino series)

This was a novel way to break up long serials (and hopefully sell a lot of video tapes). Each 60-minute tape includes one chapter from four different serials made in the 30s (*The Phantom Creeps, Phantom Empire, Junior G-Men,* and *Undersea Kingdom*). All four are also available complete and separately.

SATURDAY NIGHT SHOCKERS

(Rhino series)

These double bills also include great movie trailers, old cartoons, and refreshment stand commercials. #1 is *The Creeping Terror* (1964) and *Chained for Life* (1950). #2 is *Man Beast* (1955) and *The Human Gorilla* (1948). #3 is a Tod Slaughter double bill of *Murder in the Red Barn* (1935) and *The Face at the Window* (1939) and #4 is *The Monster of Piedra Blancas* (1958) and *Mesa of Lost Women* (1952).

SATURDAY NIGHT SLEAZIES

(Rhino series)

All of these 60s adults-only movies were made by A. C. Stevens (Stephen C. Apostoloff). #1 is *College Girl Confidential* and *Suburban Confidential,* #2 is *Lady Godiva Meets Tom Jones* and *Bachelor's Dream,* and #3 is *Motel Confidential* and *Office Confidential.* All are reviewed elsewhere in this book.

SATURDAY THE 14TH STRIKES BACK

(MGM, 1988) **D/S:** Howard R. Cohen **P:** Julie Corman

A house is built on an entrance to Hell and monsters (a female vampire, a werewolf . . .) attack a kid (Jason Presson) on his birthday. Footage from earlier Corman movies shows up in this cheap PG sequel from Concorde, and vampire women sing and dance. With Ray Walston as Gramps, Avery Schreiber and Patty McCormack as the parents,

Leo Gordon, and Michael Berryman as a mummy. Cohen also directed *Saturday the 14th* (Embassy, 1981) from Corman's New World.

THE SAUCY AUSSIE

(1963) **D/P:** Walter Bowley   (*The Obscene Couch*)

An Australian tourist in San Francisco is given some headache pills that make him hallucinate. All of a sudden, he can see through women's clothes. The 65-minute color nudie feature is in the tradition of *The Immoral Mr. Teas* and *Paradisio*.

SAVAGE!

(1973) **D/P:** Cirio H. Santiago
S: Ed Medard   Philippines (*Black Valor*)

Ex–Pittsburgh Pirates player James Inglehart (also in *Bamboo Gods . . .*) stars as "the Savage" in South America. He's arrested by rebels and eventually joins them and fights the authorities with the help of a female task force. With Carol Speed (*Abby*) and Lada Edmund Jr. From New World.

SAVAGE ABDUCTION

(Genesis, 1973) **D/S/P:** John Lawrence
(*Numbered Days, Cycle Psycho*)

A lawyer (Stanley Kubrick regular Joseph Turkel) hires a necrophiliac psycho to kill his wife. The man then blackmails him and he seeks revenge. The cast includes Tom Drake and Stafford Repp (from the *Batman* TV series). With female bikers, machetes, hacksaws, and knives as weapons. Johnny Legend worked on the Cinemation release.

SAVAGE ATTRACTION

(1983) **D/S:** Frank Shields **S:** John Lind
W. Germany/Australia (*Hostage:
The Christine Maresch Story*)

An Australian woman (Kerry Mack) is held captive and forced to help rob banks by her new husband, a psychotic German neo-Nazi (Ralph Schicha). It's based on an actual early 70s case.

SAVAGE BEACH

(RCA, 1989) **D/S:** Andy Sidaris **P:** Arlene Sidaris

A lone Japanese WWII soldier still guarding some gold on an island helps some stranded women. Dona Speir and Hope Marie Carlton star for the third (and last) time as government drug enforcers in Hawaii. The action-and-sex movie features Communists, four *Playboy* centerfolds, and one *Playgirl* centerfold. With John Aprea and Bruce Penhall as naval officers, Teri Weigel, Patty Duffek, Al Leong, Rodrigo Obregon, and Gary Hertz.

SAVAGE DAWN

(Bingo, 1984) **D:** Simon Nuchtern **S:** William P. Milling, Max Bloom **P:** Gregory Earls

Bikers led by William Forsythe terrorize a small western town in a *Mad Max* copy with comedic touches. Lance Henriksen is Stryker, the blond hero. Karen Black is kidnapped, yells, screams, and is in a cat fight. George Kennedy sits in a mototorized wheelchair with a flamethrower and a rocket launcher. Also with Richard Lynch as a weak and horny preacher, Leo Gordon as the sheriff, Elizabeth Kaitan, Claudia Udy, and a dwarf. Henriksen and Forsythe were later in a better biker movie, *Stone Cold*.

SAVAGE DAWN (1983): *See* STRYKER

SAVAGE GRINGO

(1965) **D:** Mario Bava, Jesus Navarro **D/S:** Antonio Romano   Italy/Spain (*Ringo del Nebraska*)

Ken Clark and Yvonne Bastien star in a western released in America by AIP TV. It was credited to Romano, but is said to be the work of Bava. On tape in Germany it's called *Nebraska Jim*.

THE SAVAGE GUNS

(1962) **D:** Michael Carreras **S:** Edmund Morris **P:** Jimmy Sangster   UK

Richard Basehart is a wounded gunman hiding out in Mexico in a western filmed in Spain by Hammer studio regulars. With Don Taylor, Alex Nicol, Paquita Rico, and Fernando Rey. An MGM color release.

SAVAGE HARVEST

(1981) **D:** Robert Collins **S:** Robert Blees **P:** Ralph Helfer, Sandy Howard

Lions attack a family in Africa. Tom Skerritt and Michelle Phillips are the parents in the PG feature.

SAVAGE INMATES

(TZ, 1976) **D:** Hubert Frank **S:** Jean-Lacques Duval   Germany/France (*Island of 1000 Delights*)

There's lots of nudity, S&M, and violence in this tale of slavery and casino gambling. Olivia Pascal co-stars. This has played (heavily cut) on Showtime.

THE SAVAGE INNOCENTS

(1959) **D/S:** Nicholas Ray **P:** Maleno Malenotti   France/UK/Italy (*Les Dents du Diable*)

Anthony Quinn stars as Inuk the Eskimo in this underrated documentary-style feature. He marries Asiak (Toko Tani) and they travel to an outpost and witness how crazy white men have corrupted others with drink and music. "Sexy Rock" plays on the jukebox. Back at the igloo, Inuk accidentally kills a missionary who refuses to sleep with his wife and is arrested by Canadian troopers. With Peter O'Toole (who was dubbed) and Anna May Wong. Producer Malenotti co-directed *Slave Trade in the World Today,* and this movie has some very "mondo" moments. It inspired Dylan to write the hit "The Mighty Quinn."

SAVAGE INSTINCT

(AIP, 1989) **D/S/P:** Patrick G. Donahue   (*Edge of Fear; They Call Me Macho Woman*)

Debra Sweaney is a young big-city widow who witnesses a backwoods drug smuggling operation. Mongo (Brian Oldfield, an Olympic winner) and his gang try to wipe her out with hatchets, ankle blades, and throwing nails. Mongo has a spike on

his head for ramming people. She escapes, hides in the woods, and later attacks back with axes and spikes. Men are impaled, stabbed, and whipped. Ads said, "Born to Shop—I Learned to Kill!" Troma released it.

SAVAGE INTRUDER

(Unicorn, 1968) **D/S/P:** Donald Wolfe   (*The Comeback; Hollywood Horror House*)

Thirties star Miriam Hopkins (in her last role) plays a *Sunset Boulevard*–type former star living in a mansion (actually the Norma Talmadge estate) managed by Gale Sondergaard. John David Garfield (the lookalike son of the late John Garfield) plays the pushy, sarcastic new live-in personal attendant—with an attaché case full of weapons. Garfield has frequent disturbing and grotesque psychedelic flashbacks, the Oriental female cook is decapitated, and a midget offers coke and acid at a hippie party. Hopkins imagines (?) herself "Queen of the Christmas parade" and (in her late 60s) has a nearly topless scene. Some effects are good for the time, like when a bloody hand is chopped off. Others are terrible, like when an obvious mannequin stands in for a "dismembered body." And former Stooge Joe Besser plays a tour bus driver. What more could you want?

SAVAGE ISLAND

(Force, 1984) **D:** Edward Muller **D/S:** Nicholas Beardsley **S:** Michelle Tomski **P:** Robert Amante, Mark Alabiso

Linda Blair "stars" in some footage (by Beardsley) added to the Italian movie *Escape from Hell*. The tropical women-in-prison movie stars the black American/Brazilian Ajita Wilson and Anthony Steffen. Wilson, who died in 1987, was a major sex star in Europe. This movie has lots of nudity and violence. Charles Band and his Empire company was responsible for the rip-off theatrical release. The original Blairless version is also available as *Hellfire on Ice II*.

THE SAVAGE IS LOOSE

(VCI, 1974) **D/S/P/A:** George C. Scott   (*Savage*)

A shipwrecked family at the turn of the century are stuck on an island for many years. When the father (Scott) dies, an incestuous relationship develops between the mother (Scott's real-life wife Trish Van Devere) and their son (John David Carson). With Lee Montgomery. Scott, who had turned down his Oscar for playing Patton (1970), also distributed his movie himself. His other movie as director/star was *Rage* (1972).

SAVAGE JUSTICE

(1988) **D:** Joey Romero **S:** David Howard, Parker Bratel **P:** Lope V. Juban, Rod M. Confesor   Philippines

An American ambassador's daughter gets involved in a revolution. The revenge story features Buddhist monk martial arts fighters and a midget landlord. The director is probably the son of director Eddie Romero.

SAVAGE LUST

(AIP, 1989) **D/S:** Joseph Laraz **P:** Brian Smedley-Aston, Angel Somolinos   (*Deadly Manor*)

Six young people on vacation pick up a fugitive hitchhiker and go to an old abandoned house. A gloved mystery killer picks them off and a flashback eventually explains who and why. There are nude photos and a sex nightmare, but the visual highlight is a Big Boy statue. With William Russell and Jenifer DeLora. It was made (by people who used to make movies in England) in Suffern, N.Y., near Bear Mountain.

SAVAGE PASSION: *See* RAMRODDER

SAVAGES FROM HELL

(SW, 1968) **D/S:** Joseph Prieto **S:** Reuben Guberman   (*Big Enough and Old Enough*)

This one concerns racism and revenge in Florida. The good guys are poor Hispanic migrant workers (called "beanheads" by the locals) and a black gas station owner (played by Cyril Poitier!). Bobbie Byers co-stars and Viola Lloyd is the naive teenage Teresa. The bad bikers are led by a guy named Hi Test (William P. Kelley). The R-rated color feature has instrumental rock music, a beach party, lots of wigs, body painting, a cat fight, and a kidnaping. It all ends in the swamp. The Naples, Florida, customized swamp buggy race on a flooded track is almost worth the price of the tape. The director (and most of the crew) were Cuban exiles.

SAVAGE SISTERS

(VSOM, 1974) **D/P:** Eddie Romero **S:** H. Franco Moon, Harry Corner **P/A:** John Ashley   Philippines

Gloria Hendry is an interrogation officer at an island prison camp who saves two female thieves played by Rosanna Ortiz and Cheri Caffaro (from the *Ginger* movies). Soon, you've got a black, a white, and an Oriental woman, running around in cut-offs with machine guns—a perfect drive-in movie situation. John Ashley co-stars as a playboy. Villains Sid Haig and Vic Diaz are buried up to their necks in the sand at the end and drown. Ashley retired from acting after co-starring in this AIP release, *Black Mamba* (never released in America), and *Black Mama, White Mama.*

SAVAGES OF THE SEAS

(Video Specialists, 1925) **D:** Bruce Mitchell

Frank Merrill (who went on to play Tarzan twice) stars in this rediscovered indy silent adventure (from Hercules Films). Most of it takes place on a sailing ship and there's a fairly involved plot with a mutiny and the hero falling for his own sister (who turns out to have been adopted) and battling a corrupt rich man (who turns out to be his father). Merrill has a lot of fight scenes. The silliest part is the wide paved (LA) streets supposedly on a South Sea Island. With music and tinted scenes.

SAVAGE STREETS

(Vestron, 1984) **D:** Danny Steinmann
S: Norman Yonemoto **P:** John C. Strong III

Linda Blair stars in one of her most popular exploitation hits as a nice girl turned LA vigilante with a crossbow. She leads the all-female Satins in fights against the male Scars for revenge after her deaf-mute sister (Linnea Quigley) is raped in the high school. Blair has a nude bathtub scene. With John Vernon (*Chained Heat*) as the principal, Debra Blee, Suzanne Slater, and Kristi Somers. It was rated X, then rerated R.

SAVAGE VENGANCE

(Magnum, 1992) **D/S/A:** Donald Farmer
P: Barney Griner

Camille Keaton (billed as "Linda Lehl") more or less re-creates her famous *I Spit on Your Grave* revenge role, 14 years later. Director Farmer plays a goofy psycho and gives himself frequent freeze frame close-ups. His rapist buddy has Elvis hair. The rapists (and their victims) keep their pants on and there's lots of walking and running through the woods in this lowly Southern shot-on-tape exploitation release. Melissa Moore sings with a band in a club scene. The tape has some bad sound dubbing problems and the title is *not* our typo. It's part of a bogus "I Will Dance on Your Grave" series.

SAVAGE WEEKEND

(Paragon, 1976) **D/S/P:** David Paulson
P: John Mason Kirby   (*The Upstate Murders; The Killer Behind the Mask*)

Two families on vacation in the woods are killed off by a masked killer who at one point uses a chainsaw. It's not good, but it was made before *Friday the 13th* and has a few name actors (Christopher Allport, David Gale, and William Sanderson) and nudity. Cannon released it in 1981. Paulson also directed *Schizoid* (1980), a Cannon film with Klaus Kinski.

SAVAGE WILD

(1970) **D/S/P/A:** Gordon Eastman

A cameraman below the Arctic Circle raises three timber wolves. Bounty hunters in a plane try to kill them. The G-rated AIP feature was filmed in the Yukon territory.

SAVE ME

(Columbia, 1993) **D:** Alan Roberts
S: Neil Ronco **P:** Alan Amiel

This unrated "erotic thriller" has a very minimal cliché plot and lots of sex scenes featuring Lysette Anthony from *Dark Shadows* (the 1991 version) and Harry Hamlin. The sex-by-a-fire and the sex-while-watching-a-naked-woman-through-a-two-way-mirror scenes are pretty good, but the rest is a bore. Also with a wasted support cast: Michael Ironside as her doctor who runs a clinic, Bill Nunn (with fake gray hair) as a cop, Steve Railsback, Olivia Hussey, and Joseph Campanella. By the director of *The Happy Hooker Goes to Hollywood* (with help from Fred Olen Ray). An R version is also available.

SCALPS

(Marquee, 1982) **D/S:** Fred Olen Ray **P:** T. L. Langford

Ray's first movie that got distribution was filmed in 16mm and was inspired by William Grefe's *Death Curse of Tartu* (1967). Students unleash an Indian spirit and die by decapitation, scalping, and an arrow in the eye. *Scalps* makes *Tartu* look good. With bit parts by Kirk (*Superman*) Alyn, Carroll Borland (*Mark of the Vampire*), and Forrest J. Ackerman. The final credits announce a sequel that never appeared. This was on a double tape with *Slayer*.

SCANNER COP

(Republic, 1993) **D/P:** Pierre David
S: George Saunders, John Bryant   Canada

Daniel Quinn (also in *Dead Bang*) stars as a good guy scanner, the adopted son of a late LA cop. Richard Lynch is a cop-killer villain, whose injections cause hallucinations. Hilary Shepard is his sexy fortune-teller assistant and Darlanne Fluegel is a blond police shrink. Ephemerol is the drug that can control scanners. With some good hallucination scenes, nightmares, flashbacks, and one exploding head (John Carl Buechler did the FX). Luca Bercovici is in it and there are small roles by Brion James and Cydi Pass. Rene Malo was executive producer. *Scanners—The Showdown* was a sequel.

SCANNERS—THE SHOWDOWN

(Republic, 1994) **D:** Steve Barnett
S: Mark Sevi **P:** Pierre David
Canada (*Scanner Cop II: Volkin's Revenge*)

In what could have been called *Scanners 5*, Daniel Quinn returns as Sam, the LA scanner cop who wants to find out who his mother was. This time Patrick Kilpatrick is basically a serial killer scanner/vampire who saps the power from other scanners. A new kind of Ephemerol has been developed without side effects. Sam has a research center girlfriend (Khrystyne Haje), also a scanner, and he has many b/w flashbacks. With Stephen Mendel, Robert Forster, and Jewel Shepard in a bit part. John Carl Buechler handled the FX again. Bladder FX are used for death scenes, and one head explodes. The entire series is better than average.

SCANNERS II: THE NEW ORDER

(Media, 1990) **D:** Christian Duguay
S: B. J. Nelson **P:** Rene Malo   Canada

The cinematography, special effects, and action sequences are excellent in this sequel to David Cronenberg's 1981 hit and yes, more heads blow up real good. David Hewlett plays David, a nice vet student who doesn't know he's the son of the character Cameron Vale (and is a scanner). Deborah Raffin is his sister. An evil police chief (Yvan Ponton) uses junkie-like scanners at the Neurological Institute for his "new order" law enforcement plans. A scary long-haired scanner (Raoul Trujillo) causes chaos at a video arcade and eventually has it out with the good scanners. Filmed in Montreal. Several versions were shot for different markets, and it was shot back to back with *Scanners III*.

SCANNERS III: THE TAKEOVER

(Republic, 1991) **D:** Christian Duguay **S:** B. J. Nelson, Julie Richard, David Preston **P:** Rene Malo

Liliana Komorowska (a Polish actress) stars as a bad ambitious scanner who takes over a pharmaceutical corporation. Her scanner brother (Steve Parrish) goes to Thailand to meditate and learn to control his powers. *Scanners III* has an awesome exploding head scene, guns, kung fu, kickboxing, some good stunts, and Komorowska makes a good villainess (and does nudity). There's more comedy this time, though, and the wisecracks, gags, and some real dumb parts bring it down a few notches. Also with Valerie Valois and Daniel Pilon. It was shot in Montreal by the director of *Scanners II*. *Scanner Cop* followed.

THE SCARECROW

(1981) **D/S:** Sam Pillsbury **S:** Michael Heath
P: Rob Whitehouse   New Zealand
(*Klynham Summer*)

A small-town boy in the 1940s has problems with a bully, and a sleazy psycho killer (John Carradine!) shows up. The PG feature is based on a novel by Ronald Hugh Morrieson. Jonathan Smith and Daniel McLaren star.

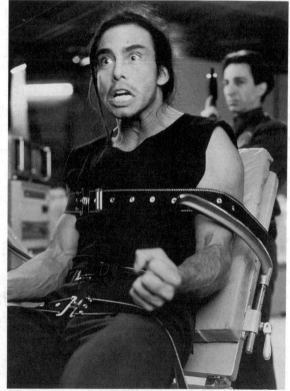

Raoul Trujillo in *Scanners II.*

SCARECROWS

(Forum, 1988) **D/S/P/E:** William Wesley
S: Richard Jeffries **P:** Cami Winikoff

Some military guys steal $3 million, kidnap a pilot and his daughter, and hijack their plane. They all parachute into a graveyard near a southern California farm where three possessed scarecrows attack with pitchforks. The victims become zombies. Ted Vernon and Michael Sims star. It was filmed in Florida and is pretty slow, dark, and dreary. Available in R or bloodier unrated tapes.

SCARED STIFF

(1945) **D:** Frank McDonald **S:** Geoffrey Homes **P:** William Pine, William Thomas

Jack Haley (the Tin Woodsman from *The Wizard of Oz*) stars as the nervous chess editor at a newspaper who accidentally ends up in a tavern run by two weird brothers (both are Lucien Littlefield) where murders occur. Ann Savage (from *Detour*) co-stars with Barton MacLane as a gangster after gold chess pieces, Veda Ann Borg as a detective, and Roger Pryor. The forgotten Paramount comedy release was based on the play *The Ghost Breakers*, which had been filmed already in 1914, 1922, and the best known version in 1940 with Bob Hope. It was remade yet again (as *Scared Stiff*) in 1953 starring Dean Martin and Jerry Lewis. At least the other sound versions had zombies. Haley also starred in the horror comedy *One Body Too Many* (1939).

SCARED STIFF

(Republic, 1986) **D/S:** Richard Friedman
S: Mark Frost **P:** Daniel F. Bacaner

An ex–mental patient and her son move into a haunted Southern house that 19th-century slaves had cursed. It has gore, flashbacks, nightmare scenes, and time travel, and is pretty dumb. Screenwriter Frost went on to create *Twin Peaks* with David Lynch. With Andrew Stevens (who becomes possessed) and Mary Page Keller.

SCARED TO DEATH

(Video Treasures, 1980) **D/S:** William Malone
P: Rand Marlis, Gil Shelton

Genetic experiments result in a tall (*Alien*-type) monster called Syngenor in the sewers of LA. The monster sucks out human spinal fluid with its needle tongue, and an ex-cop and a black detective investigate the murders. Malone was the chief designer at the famous Don Post mask studios. This movie wasn't released until 1984. An unofficial sequel was called *Syngenor* (1990).

SCARE THEIR PANTS OFF!

(SW, 1968) **D/S/E:** John Maddox **P:** Ronald Sullin

This cheap-looking b/w adult sex comedy is like a bad, filmed play. A man with a mutant face covered by a metal mask narrates with a mechanical voice. Some women in a room with peepholes are drugged and briefly seen topless. Some guys attempt to torture them. The music is strange and characters talk a lot. The director was also a cameraman for *Monterey Pop*.

SCARFACE

(MCA, 1983) **D:** Brian DePalma **S:** Oliver Stone
P: Martin Bregman, Peter Saphier **M:** Georgio Moroder

Scarface is one of the ultimate trash classics. It lost money at the box office but is the best movie De-Palma ever made, all 170 minutes of it. The advance publicity for a "shocking" chainsaw killing was nonsense (nothing is shown) but *Scarface* did break a swearing record (fuck is said "206" times) and shows more cocaine than any other feature in memory. It was based on Ben Hecht's script for the 1932 original (look for it on MCA), but having the gangsters be unwanted Cubans brought into America by a deal President Carter made and throwing in more vicious Colombians made it even better. Al Pacino stars as Tony Montana with Steven Bauer (a.k.a. Esteban Rocky Echevarría) making his film debut as his partner in crime. With Michelle Pfeiffer, Mary Elizabeth Mastrantonio as Tony's sister, Robert Loggia, F. Murray Abraham, Paul Shenar, and Harris Yulin. Katt Shea, Angela Aames, and Lana Clarkson all show up at the Babylon. The score is on MCA.

SCARLET STREET

(Video Yesterday, 1945) **D/P:** Fritz Lang
S: Dudley Nichols

Edward G. Robinson is Criss Cross, the henpecked New York City bookkeeper and amateur artist whose life is ruined when he meets Kitty (Joan Bennett) and her pimp (Dan Duryea). She becomes a famous artist passing off his paintings as her own. He ends up sleeping on park benches. The ice pick stabbing scene was considered very shocking at the time. It's a remake of Renoir's *La Chine* (1931) and has been colorized. The three stars had also been in Lang's *Woman in the Window* (1944).

SCARY MOVIE

(Generic, 1991) **D/S/P:** Daniel Erickson **S:** David Lane Smith, Mark Voges **P:** Keith Brunson

Warren (John Hawkes) is a sweaty nervous nerd character who acts like a psychotic Don Knotts, but this is no comedy. He's so scared that he somehow gets lost in a spook house on Halloween, while an escaped maniac is rumored to be in the area. One attraction is a chainsaw room. The music, cinematography (and the spook house itself) are all impressive, and the ending is clever, but it's slow going and nothing much happens. Roky Erickson and the Butthole Surfers are on the soundtrack. It was made in Driftwood, Texas (near Austin), and an unrecognizable Butch Patrick is in it. Hawkes was also in *Futurekill* and *From Dusk to Dawn*.

SCAVENGER HUNT

(Fox, 1979) **D:** Michael Schultz
S/P: Stephen A. Vail **S:** Henry Harper

If you want to see a lot of name stars make fools of themselves, look for this comedy. In the opening scene Vincent Price is a millionaire who dies in bed while recording his will. Robert Morley reads the will, and various relatives have to collect "100 items" to qualify. Richard Benjamin stars with (among others) Richard Mulligan, Arnold Schwarzenegger, James Coco, Scatman Crothers, Ruth Gordon, Cloris Leachman, Cleavon Little, Tony Randall, Roddy McDowell, Dirk Benedict, Meat Loaf, and Carol Wayne. From 20th Century. Schultz had also directed the all-star *Sgt. Pepper* movie (1978).

SCENES FROM THE CLASS STRUGGLE IN BEVERLY HILLS

(Virgin, 1989) **D/A:** Paul Bartel
S: Bruce Wagner **P:** James C. Katz

The stars of *Eating Raoul* were reunited for this R-rated sex comedy about servants Ray Sharkey (playing a bisexual) and Robert Beltran making a bet about who can have sex with their female bosses first. A TV star (Jacqueline Bisset) and her neighbor (Mary Woronov) are the targets. With Ed Begley Jr., Wallace Shawn, Arnetia Walker (in the best sex scene), and Paul Mazursky (as a ghost of a husband). Rebecca Schaeffer was murdered in real life shortly after playing Bisset's daughter. Screenwriter Wagner later created the *Wild Palms* comic strip.

SCENES FROM A MURDER

(Lightning, 1972) **D:** Alberto de Martino
S: Vincenzo Mannino   Italy (*L'assassino … E Al Telefono; The Final Curtain*)

Anne Heywood is a famous theater actress whose lover has been murdered. She suspects a hitman named Ranko (Telly Savalas) and tries to convince others that's she's right. With Rossella Falk.

SCENES FROM THE GOLDMINE

(Charter, 1987) **D/S:** Marc Rocco
S: John Norvet **P:** Danny Eisenberg

Catherine Mary Stewart and Cameron Dye are in a rock group managed by Steve Railsback, but a record company exec (Joe Pantoliano) tries to break up the group and make her a star. With Jewel Shepard, Lee Ving, Alex Rocco, Pamela Springsteen, and Lesley-Anne Down. John Ford Coley and Timothy B. Schmit are also in the band. The director (in his early 20s at the time) is the son of actor Alex Rocco. He also made *Where the Day Takes You* (1992) and others.

SCHIZOID

(Nightmare, 1971) **D/S:** Lucio Fulci **S:** Roberto Gianviti, Jose Luis Martinez Molla **M:** Ennio Morricone   Italy (*Una Lucertola Con A Pelle Di Donna; Lizard in a Woman's Skin*)

Florinda Bolkan stars as a woman who tells her psychiatrist about her dreams of murdering somebody. Carlo Rambaldi designed a disturbing dream sequence with a red-haired hippie, eyeless corpses, swarms of bats, and dogs with their stomachs cut open. The director had to go to court in Italy to prove that the dogs were mechanical. This movie demonstrates how LSD and lesbianism lead to death. With Stanley Baker as a detective, Jean Sorel, Anita Strinberg, and Leo Genn. AIP released it (cut) in America.

SCHOOL FOR UNCLAIMED GIRLS

(1969) **D:** Robert Hartford-Davis **S:** John Peacock
P: Peter Newbrook   UK *(The Smashing Bird I
Used to Know; The House of Unclaimed Women)*

Madeline Hinde is sent to a woman's prison for
murder. With Dennis Waterman, Maureen Lipman, and a teenage Lesley-Anne Down in one of
her first roles. AIP released it.

SCHOOLGIRL KILLER

(AIP, 1967) **D/S:** "Anthony Dawson"/
Antonio Margheriti **S:** Franco Bottari
P: Lawrence Woolner   Italy *(Sette Vergini
Per Il Diavolo; The Young, the Evil, and the Savage)*

AIP released this murder mystery set at St. Hilda's,
a girl's finishing school. Michael Rennie stars as an
inspector with Sally Smith, Mark Damon, Eleonora
Brown, and Allan Collins (a.k.a. Luciano Pigozzi).
The (cross-dressing) killer is a surprise (of course).
Mario Bava wrote the story and was originally set
to direct the Woolner Brothers production.

SCHOOLGIRLS IN CHAINS

(World Premiere, 1973) **D/S/P:** Don Jones
C: Ron Garcia   *(Let's Play Dead)*

Two brothers (the results of incest) live in a secluded house. One is a retarded voyeur in farmer
clothes who kidnaps women in an old Packard and
chains them in the root cellar. Sometimes he puts a
leash on one of "the pets" and makes them play
childish games. Some try to escape, but don't get
far. His impotent brother Frankie (Gary Kent) sits
and broods. Their mama (seen in character-
building flashbacks) sits in a chair *(Psycho* style).
With Tom Kelly (the star of *Targets*) and Merrie
Lynn Ross. Kent acted frequently for Richard
Rush, Al Adamson, *and* Ray Dennis Steckler. Jones
also directed *The Love Butcher* (1975) and *The
Forest* (1981).

SCHOOL SPIRIT

(Media, 1985) **D:** Alan Holleb
S: Geoffrey Baere **P:** Jeff Begun

A rebellious college student named Billy Batson
(Tom Nolan) dies in a car crash but his ghost uncle
arranges for him to have an extra day on earth. The
(invisible) guy spies on naked girls in an *Animal
House*–influenced comedy. With Elizabeth Foxx,
Roberta Collins as the drunken wife of the college
president (Larry Linville from *M*A*S*H*), Beach
Dickerson, Leslie Bremmer, Linda Carol, Julie
Gray, Becky LeBeau, and Marlene Janssen (from
Playboy). The Roger Corman release was shot at
UCLA. It features music by the Gleaming Spires
and others.

THE SCHOOL THAT COULDN'T SCREAM

(Sinister, 1971) **D/S:** Massimo Dallamano
S: Bruno Di Geronimo **P:** Leonard Pescardo,
Fulvio Lucisano **C:** Aristide Massaccesi **M:** Ennio
Morricone   Italy *(Cosa Avete Fatto a Solange?)*

Enrico (Fabio Testi), a married Italian professor in
London, is accused of a series of brutal murders of
St. Mary's school girls after having an affair with
one of the victims (Karin Baal). This is a very good
giallo mystery, based on an Edgar Wallace novel
(which had also been filmed in 1929 and 1961 in
England). It features nightmares, flashbacks, a
lineup of priests, and full nudity in shower room
scenes. With Joachim Fuchsberger as a Scotland
Yard inspector, Christine Galbo as Enrico's blond
German wife, and Camille Keaton in a small but
very important role. The tape is letterboxed and
dubbed.

SCIENCE CRAZED

(Interamerican, 1989) **D/S:** Ron Switzer
P: Donna Switzer

In this amateur comedy, a mad scientist gives injections to a woman who gives birth to a full-grown
man/monster.

SCISSORS

(Paramount, 1990) **D/S:** Frank De Felitta **P:** Mel Pearl

Sharon Stone is a lonely virgin obsessed with the
antique dolls she collects and restores. While staying in a giant model loft, she talks to a pig puppet,
hears a raven talk, and has nightmares, but it's all
a plot to drive her crazy. Steve Railsback has two
roles, as a soap opera actor neighbor and his crippled brother. With Michelle Phillips, Vicki Frederick, Albert Popwell, and Ronny Cox as the
shrink. Directed by the writer of *The Entity* and
Audrey Rose.

SCOOP

(1987) **D:** Gavin Millar **S:** William
Boyd **P:** Sue Birtwistle   UK

Michael Maloney stars as a nature column writer,
accidentally assigned to cover the war in Ethiopia
in 1935. It's a satire based on Evelyn Waugh with
a support cast including Donald Pleasence, Herbert Lom, Denholm Elliott, Rene Soutendijk, and
Michael Hordern. Filmed in England and Morocco.

SCORCHY

(Vestron, 1976) **D/S/P:** Hikmet Avedis

This was the last lead role for Connie Stevens (real
name: Concetta Rosalie Ann Ingolia), and it was
an outrageous, violent role for the 60s star. She's
an undercover cop in Seattle after drug dealers
(and has nude scenes). With William Smith, Cesare Danova, Marlene Schmidt, and Greg Evigan.
The video release of the AIP movie was rescored.

SCORE

(Magnum, 1973) **D:** Radley Metzger **S:** Jerry
Douglas **P:** Ava Leighton   US/Yugoslavia

This atypical erotic movie, set in a coastal European town, is about a swinging couple (Clair Wilbur and Calvin Culver) initiating a visiting couple
(Lynn Lowry and Gerald Grant) into lesbian and
gay sex. They all use pot and amyl nitrate. Like
other Metzger movies, it's very well made and is
surprisingly light, with comical narration. Apparently a partial hard-core version played in NYC.

Lowry, who plays the naive Catholic Betsy, went on
to act for George Romero, David Cronenberg, and
Jonathan Demme, and Culver became gay porn
star Casey Donovan. Sylvester Stallone had been in
the off-Broadway play version (not as a bisexual).
Shot in Zagreb, it was Metzger's last feature before
making successful hard X movies (as Harry Paris).

SCORNED

(Prism, 1993) **D/A:** Andrew Stevens
S: Barry Avrich **P:** Damian Lee

A widow (Shannon Tweed) seeks vengeance after
her husband (who had lent her out to other men to
get a promotion) kills himself. Stevens is the one
who got the corporate job, so she becomes a live-
in tutor for his son (Michael D. Arenz). She seduces the son and drugs and seduces the wife (Kim
Morgan Green). Tweed also commits murder and
even kills their pet bird. In one scene she's
punched and thrown out of a window but walks
away fine. It's more R or unrated sex from the stars
of the *Night Eyes* movies. Ashrok Amritraj was
executive producer.

SCORPION

(RCA, 1986) **D/S/P:** William Reed

Tonny Tulleners stars as a martial arts expert who
fights terrorists. With Don Murray, Robert Logan,
and Ross Elliot. A Crown International release.

SCORPION WITH TWO TAILS

(Cinema Shares, 1982) **D:** "Christian Plummer"/
Sergio Martino **S:** Ernesto Gastaldi, Maria Chianetta
Italy *(Assassino Al Cimitero Etrusco)*

John Saxon is an archeologist who intrudes upon
an Etruscan tomb. He's killed off pretty soon in a
drug smuggling mystery that was a TV miniseries
in Italy. Van Johnson uses artifacts to smuggle heroin into America. Elvire Audray is a magical descendant of the Etruscan queen, who has visions of
maggots.

SCOTT OF THE ANTARCTIC

(Sinister, 1948) **D:** Charles Frend **S:** Walter Meade,
Ivor Montagu **P:** Sir Michael Balcon   UK

John Mills stars as the Arctic explorer, and a young
Christopher Lee has a small role as part of the expedition. With James Robertson Justice and Kenneth More.

SCRATCH HARRY

(1969) **D:** Alex Matter **S:** Stephen R. Winstein
P: Christopher C. Dewey   *(The Erotic Three)*

A man finds his wife and mistress in bed together
so he kills his mistress. Later, he and his wife kill
each other and both fall into an open grave. It's
all a drug-induced hallucination, caused by the
"Shadow," who appears as a 1950s jazz musician.
Cannon released it.

SCREAM

(Vestron, 1981) **D/S:** Bryan Quisenberry
P: Clara Huff, Hal Buchanan   *(The Outing)*

486

A psycho kills campers (offscreen) near a western ghost town. John Wayne's son John Ethan Wayne stars, and Alvy Moore and Hank Worden are killed off very early on. With Greg Palmer and Woody Strode (the surprise hero). It's frequently too dark and is very slow going. The director was a stuntman.

SCREAM AND DIE

(Vestron, 1973) **D:** Joseph Laraz **S:** Derek Ford **P:** Diana Daubeney   Spain (*Psycho Sex Fiend*)

A model witnesses a murder in this slow, dark, unpleasant movie. Her roommate is raped and killed. Her new neighbor who seems like he must be the killer (but of course isn't) wears black gloves and has a room full of pigeons. Another character is a young guy who has sex with his much older aunt. Laraz also made the ultimate erotic vampire movie, *Vampyres* (1974).

SCREAM AND DIE (1974) = THE HOUSE THAT VANISHED

SCREAM BABY SCREAM

(Regal, 1969) **D/P:** Joseph Adler **S:** Lawrence Robert Cohen   (*Nightmare House*)

This hippie-era horror movie has a great chaotic structure—you know, flashbacks inside of flashbacks. You can tell it was barely finished by the mismatched film stock. Four art students leave class, take acid (in coffee), hop on motorbikes, and race off to "see what's shakin' in the outer limits!" One of them, Chris Martel (from *The Gruesome Twosome*!) is in a rock band (the Odyssey). The substandard trip sequence takes place at a zoo. The class's nude model had been kidnapped by funny-looking zombies and held by Charles Butler, "Master of the Macabre," an artist famous for painting mutated faces, who creates real-life mutant models. Their faces are like something from an underground comic. You won't believe them. I still can't. It was re-released by Troma and was directed by a guy whose only previous film was *Sex and the College Girl* (1964). Filmed in Miami.

SCREAM DREAM

(Lettuce, 1989) **D/S:** Donald Farmer **P:** Bob Allison, Barney Griner

A girl (really a witch) is fired from her rock band and possesses her replacement (Melissa Moore). The 69-minute tape was shot on video in Tennessee.

SCREAM FOR HELP

(Lorimar, 1984) **D/P:** Michael Winner **S:** Tom Holland

A killer stepfather is after a family fortune and nobody believes the teen daughter (Rachel Kelly). The plot is similar to the later (and better) *The Stepfather*. With David Brooks and Corey Parker. It's set in New York state but was filmed in England. The score, by John Paul Jones from Led Zeppelin, was on Atlantic.

SCREAM FREE: *See* FREE GRASS

SCREAM GREATS VOL. 1

(Paramount, 1986) **D:** Damon Santostephano

Starlog and *Fangoria* magazines released this one-hour look at Tom Savini and his gory special effects for movies like *Friday the 13th* and *Dawn of the Dead*. *Scream Greats Vol. 2* (Paramount, 1986) is a documentary about satanism and witchcraft.

THE SCREAMING DEAD

(Wizard, 1972) **D/S:** Jesús Franco **S:** Paul d'Ales **P:** Robert de Nesle, Luis Lasala   Spain/France/Portugal/Liechtenstein (*Dracula, Contra Frankenstein*)

Dr. Frankenstein (Dennis Price) sends out the Frankenstein monster to kidnap a red-haired cabaret singer and uses her blood to revive a green-faced Dracula (Howard Vernon). The doc has a hunchback servant called Morpho and a werewolf fights the monster. The camera zooms a lot, the makeup is terrible, the bats are rubbery, and the time period is extremely confused. The soundtrack is zither music and there's almost no dialogue. With Britt Nichols and Anne Libert. Some fans view this as an intentional comedy. This American video release is missing some sex scenes. Franco's more serious followup (with most of the same cast) was *The Erotic Rites of Frankenstein*.

SCREAM OF STONE

(VSOM, 1991) **D:** Werner Herzog **S/P:** Walter Saxer **S:** Robert Geoffrion **P:** Richard Sadler, Henry Lange   France/Germany/Canada

Donald Sutherland co-stars as a TV announcer and narrates this story about high-stakes mountain-climbing in Patagonia, Argentina. A young upstart challenges a master climber (Ultorro Mezzo Giorno) and claims he made it to a snow-capped mountain peak (while his partner falls to his death). He upsets the world of climbing, becomes a media celebrity, and even takes away the man's girlfriend (Mathilda May). It's kinda slow going, but Brad Dourif is great as an eccentric "crazy" climber who gets the punchline. Also with Al Waxman as a crass TV producer and the director in a bit part. It's in English.

SCREAM OF THE BUTTERFLY

(SW, 1965) **D:** Eber Lobato **S:** Alan J. Smith **P:** Howard Veit **C:** Ray Dennis Steckler

Much of this b/w adult movie is flashbacks showing what led to the murder of blond Marla (Nelida Lobato). She marries an extremely dumb rich guy with a butch haircut, has an affair, and plots her husband's death. Her lover turns out to be a bisexual con man. Marla is seen in a bikini, dancing on a table, in a bubble bath (twice), and in long slow-motion topless scenes. Meanwhile the D.A. and his assistant have some great cynical dialogue. I don't think Eber and Nelida Lobato ever made another movie but they should be remembered for this one. It was shot in Las Vegas. The tape (a great print) is introduced by Johnny Legend.

SCREAMPLAY

(1983) **D/S/A/E:** Rufus Butler Seder **S:** Ed Greenberg **P:** Dennis M. Pianna

The director stars as Edgar Allen, a screenwriter in Hollywood. Murders in his new script occur in real life and a midget cop investigates. The experimental b/w psycho killer movie parody includes some gore and was made in Boston on sets painted like in a silent German expressionist feature. With Katy Bolger and George Kuchar as an apartment super. Troma released it.

SCREAM QUEEN HOT TUB PARTY

(Wyn Ray, 1992) **D/P:** Jim Wynorski, Fred Olen Ray

Actresses who usually took their clothes off in direct-to-video releases became major attractions at fan conventions by the late 80s. "Scream Queen" books, magazines, and trading cards were available, and more tapes were produced to cash in. This horror comedy (made up mostly of clips from earlier movies) features Brinke Stevens, Michelle Bauer, Monique Gabrielle, Kelli Maroney, and Rozanne Kernohan. Some others from the same period were *Scream Queen Swimsuit Sensations* (JTC), with Melissa Moore, Veronica Carothers, and Jasae, directed by John Russo, and *Scream Queen Bloopers and Outtakes* (with Linnea Quigley, Moore, Mary Woronov, and others).

SCREAM STREET

(CNH, 1971) **D/P:** Carl Monsoon **S:** Eric Norden **P:** Harry Novak   (*Scream in the Streets*)

This softcore sex-and-violence Box Office International release concerns plainclothes LA cops (a married man and Stryker, the tough bachelor) after a rapist. The perpetrator is a guy in drag with a curly blond wig who laughs hysterically. A pot-smoking voyeur watches lesbian housewives (in a scene cut from some versions). A man goes to a masssage parlor, smashes the owner in the face with a beer bottle, then whips a woman with his belt. With slow-motion death scenes, wah-wah-pedal rock music, cops harassing innocent black men, a split-screen end, and future porn star Sharon Kelly in one of the better (near-porn) sex scenes. It was first released on tape with *Axe*.

SCREAMTIME

(Vestron, 1983) **D/P:** "Al Beresford"   UK

Some guys steal horror videos from a Times Square store and watch them. The American framing scenes were added to three British shorts about killer puppets, a haunted house, and some ghouls. Michael Armstrong (*Mark of the Devil*) made one of them (called *Scream House*).

SCREEN SCARIES: *See* DRIVE-IN MADNESS!

SCREEN TEST

(RCA, 1985) **D/S/P:** Sam Auster **S/P:** Laura Auster

Four students pretend to be porno producers to meet girls. There's an original idea. Monique Gabrielle, Michelle Bauer, and Tracey Adams take their clothes off.

SCREWBALL ACADEMY

(TWE, 1983) **D:** "Reuben Rose"/John Blanchard **S/P:** David Mitchell **S:** Charles Dennis, Michael Pasedrvek **P:** Damien Lee Canada (*Loose Ends*)

A movie crew in a small beach town has problems with wacky locals. The comedy features Colleen Camp and Ken Welsh.

SCREWBALLS

(Warner, 1983) **D:** Rafael Zielinski **S/A:** Linda Shayne **S:** Jim Wynorski **P:** Maurice Smith   Canada

A bowling ball gets stuck on a guy's dick in this stupid *Porky's* rip-off set in the 60s. The plot is about trying to seduce a virgin. Blond Shayne is Bootsy Goodhead. With Raven De La Croix as Anna Tomical and Jim Coburn. It was from Corman's Concorde. *Loose Screws* was a sequel.

SCROOGE

(Video Yesterday, 1935) **D:** Henry Edwards **S:** Seymour Hicks, H. Fowler Mear **P:** Julius Hicks, Hans Brahm   UK

The first sound feature-length version of Dickens's famous short fantasy story *A Christmas Carol* stars Seymour Hicks (who had also written and starred in a 1913 version) as Scrooge. With Donald Calthrop, Robert Cochran, and Mary Glynne. Future director John Brahm was the editor. The next version, *A Christmas Carol* (1938), was American.

SCROOGE

(Fox, 1970) **D:** Ronald Neame **S:** Leslie Bricusse **P:** Robert H. Solo   UK

Albert Finney stars in a lavish musical version of Dickens's familiar tale, meets the usual ghosts, and even goes to Hell. Alec Guinness, Edith Evans, and Kenneth More are ghosts and the cast includes Roy Kinnear, Kay Walsh, and Laurence Naismith. National General released it in America. Director Neame made *The Poseidon Adventure* (1972) next.

SCROOGED

(Paramount, 1988) **D/P:** Richard Donner **S:** Michael Glazer, Michael O'Donoghue **P:** Art Linson **M:** Danny Elfman

Donner made this modernized PG-13-rated Dickens adaptation in between *Lethal Weapon* movies. Bill Murray stars as a Scrooge-like network TV chief in New York, putting on yet another production of *A Christmas Carol*, while firing people. Carol Kane is the ghost of Christmas present, David Johansen is the cabdriver ghost of the past, and the future death figure was created by the Tom Burman studios. With Karen Allen, John Glover, John Forsythe, Bobcat Goldthwait, Robert Mitchum, Michael J. Pollard, Alfre Woodard, and Jamie Farr. Buddy Hackett, John Houseman, Robert Goulet, Mary Lou Retton, and Lee Majors appear as themselves, and other guest stars appear.

SCUM OF THE EARTH

(SW, 1963) **D/S:** Herschell Gordon Lewis **P:** David F. Friedman

Scum of the Earth is surprisingly similar to Ed Wood's *The Sinister Urge* (1961). Thomas Sweetwood/William Kerwin (with weird part-gray hair and a beard) stars as Harmon, a weary, guilt-ridden nudie photographer. He works for the horrible, cigar-chomping Mr. Lang, who likes to play with wind-up toys. Larry (Mal Arnold from *Blood Feast*!) is the sadistic "distributor," selling the dirty pictures to eager high school students. Harmon is forced to use Ajax, a goon rapist, as his assistant—"Keep that ape away from me!" All kinds of horrible unspeakable things are implied, but not shown. Sandra, an older model, is forced to "recruit new fresh talent." Kim (top-billed Vicki Miles) is the innocent new swimsuit model trying to make money for college, who finds herself blackmailed into doing topless shots (no nudity is shown) and worse. The incredible ending has death by baseball bat and a tiny gun and a ridiculously long chase scene on foot. The highlight is Lang's over-the-top lecture to Kim—"All you kids make me sick, you're damaged merchandise . . . dirty! Dirty! . . ." The camera closes in on his face, then his mouth, as he spits out the words. This b/w drama has pretty bad acting (no surprise) and was made in Florida the same year as the famous *Blood Feast*. Producer Friedman also did the sound. Before it opened, four-page *Scum of the Earth* comic books were given out in theaters to entice patrons to return and see it.

SEABO

(1977) **D:** Jimmy Huston **S:** Tom McIntyre **P/A:** Earl Owensby

Owensby stars in another of his North Carolina drive-in movies, with singer David Allan Coe plus Don Barry, Ed Parker, and Sunset Carson. Coe was also in Owensby's *Lady Grey*. Huston also made the horror movies *Final Exam* (1981) and *My Best Friend Is a Vampire* (1986).

THE SEA HOUND

(Stokey, 1944) **D:** Walter B. Eason, Mack Wright **S:** George Plympton, Lewis Clay, Arthur Hoerl **P:** Sam Katzman

Buster Crabbe stars as Captain Silver in a 15-chapter sea adventure Columbia serial. His character is based on a short-lived radio show and comic book. Pamela Blake, James Lloyd, and Ralph Hodges costar, and there's a man-eating plant on an island.

SÉANCE ON A WET AFTERNOON

(Public Media, 1964) **D/P:** Bryan Forbes **P/A:** Richard Attenborough   UK

Kim Stanley is a professional medium who makes her husband (Attenborough) kidnap a child so she can gain fame and ransom money by finding it. She thinks she can contact beings in the other world through her (stillborn) son. With Nanette Newman and Patrick Magee. It's a very creepy b/w feature. The director is still a best-selling spy novelist.

SEAQUEST DSV

(1993–95) **D:** Irvin Kershner **S:** Rockne S. O'Bannon, Tommy Thompson **P:** Gregg D. Fienberg

Remember the *Voyage to the Bottom of the Sea* show? Well, nearly 30 years after it debuted, the concept returned to TV with a (much) bigger budget, a high-tech look, talking dolphins, and holograms. Roy Scheider stars as the 21st-century supersub captain. Guest star Shelley Hack is the vengeful renegade skipper who attacks with her own sub. With series regulars Stephanie Beacham, John D'Aquino, Jonathan Brandis (computer whiz kid), Stacy Haiduk, and Darwin the dolphin. Also with Ted Raimi and Eric Da Rae. The NBC feature pilot was executive produced by Steven Spielberg (and the screenwriters). The rating were low, so the series got sillier as it went along, and Scheider was eventually replaced by Michael Ironside and the show was retitled *Seaquest 2032*.

These Men Are—*Scum of the Earth.*

SEA RAIDERS

(UAV, 1941) **D:** Ford Beebe, John Rawlins **S:** Clarence Upson Young, Paul Huston

It's the second of three WWII-themed 12-chapter Universal serials starring members of the Dead End Kids. They were Billy Halop (Billy), Huntz Hall (Toby), Gabriel Dell (Bilge), and Bernard Punsley (Butch). This time they were after the "Sea Raider" who had been sinking Allied ships.

SEARCH AND DESTROY

(1978) **D:** William Fruet **S:** Don Enright **P:** James Margellos Canada (*Striking Back*)

A Nam vet (Don Stroud) fights a Vietnamese official (Park Jong Soo) who comes to America after the war to seek revenge for being left behind. Perry King is another ex-G.I. whose life is in danger. The PG-rated feature by the director of *House by the Lake* ends at Niagara Falls. With Tisa Farrow and George Kennedy.

SEARCH FOR DIANA

(1992) **D/S/P:** Milad Bessada **S:** Maissa Bessada Patton Canada

Dancer Diana Calenti stars as a Toronto choreographer who believes she's the reincarnation of an Egyptian high priestess. In Egypt, an archeologist friend (Brett Halsey) plans to sacrifice her to the gods.

SEARCH FOR THE EVIL ONE: *See* HE LIVES

THE SEA SERPENT

(Lightning, 1984) **D:** "Gregory Greens"/ Amando Ossorio **S:** Gordona Osburn **P:** Joseph Frada Spain (*La Serpiente del Mar*)

Timothy Bottoms is an (Ahab-inspired) sea captain searching for a sea monster awakened by A-bomb tests. The serpent is an obvious puppet, similar to the ones in *The Giant Claw* and *Reptilicus*. With Taryn Power, Jared Martin, Jack Taylor, Ray Milland (in his last role), Victor Israel as a drunken watchman, and Leon Klimovsky as a lawyer. It was shot in Spain and Portugal.

SEASIDE SWINGERS

(Nelson, 1965) **D:** James Hill **S:** Anthony Mariott **P:** Ronald J. Kahn **C:** Nicolas Roeg UK (*Every Day's a Holiday*)

After the Beatles, the Dave Clark Five, and Herman's Hermits had all starred in movies, someone had the bright idea to put Freddie and the Dreamers in one. They star with John Leyton (a singer unknown in America) in a teen movie about a televised talent contest at a seaside resort. With Michael Sarne, Liz Fraser, Ron Moody, Michael Ripper, and the Mojos. A soundtrack album was issued by Mercury. Freddie, the laughing king of silly rock at the time, was also in *Out of Sight* and *Disk–O Tek Holiday*.

SEASON OF FEAR

(Fox, 1989) **D/S:** Doug Campbell **P:** Ryan J. Carroll

In a *Body Heat*–type movie, Michael Bowen becomes involved with his inventor father's new wife (Clara Wren). With Ray Wise, Clancy Brown, and Michael J. Pollard. By the director of *Zapped Again!*

SEASONS IN THE SUN

(1973) **D:** Ian Soodor **P/A/M:** Terry Jacks Canada

Singer Terry Jacks (playing himself) collapses at a show at Madison Square Garden and has life-after-death experiences. He hallucinates, discovers he has a terminal disease, and quits showbiz to fish. John Ireland is a Communist spy, whose daughter Kathryn Witt is a CIA agent. It was filmed on the Mystic Isles of British Columbia. Jacks' theme song made it to #1 in America in 1974. He and his wife also had hits as The Poppy Family.

SECOND CHANCE

(1953) **D:** Rudolph Maté **S:** Oscar Millare, Sidney Boehme **P:** Sam Weisenthal

RKO's ads said: "For the First Time! 3-Dimension with IMPORTANT Stars!" Robert Mitchum is a has-been boxer and Linda Darnell is an ex–gun moll. Jack Palance is Cappy, the villain, and it all ends up in the air with a cable-car accident filmed in Mexico. With Milburn Stone and Dan Seymour. It was a Howard Hughes presentation.

SECOND COMING OF SUZANNE

(American, 1974) **D/S:** Michael Barry **P:** Ralph Burris (*Suzanne*)

Sondra Locke is Suzanne, who portrays a female Christ figure who is crucified in a movie within this movie. The experimental feature was inspired by Leonard Cohen's song. Jared Martin is a Manson-type filmmaker in 1969 San Francisco, and Richard Dreyfuss and Paul Sand co-star. Gene Barry was executive producer for his young son's feature and appears as a TV commentator. Locke was in *Death Game* the same year.

SECOND SIGHT

(Warner, 1989) **D:** Joel Zwick **S:** Tom Schulman, Patricia Resnick **P:** Mark Tarlov

Bronson Pinchot becomes a psychic detective and is exploited by John Larroquette. This dumb PG comedy features Stuart Pankin, Bess Armstrong as a nun, William Prince, James Tolkan, and Cornelia Guest.

SECOND TIME LUCKY

(1984) **D:** Michael Anderson **S:** Ross Dimsey, David Sigmund **P:** Anthony I. Ginnane Australia/NZ

The Devil makes a bet with God (Robert Morley) that if Earth started over again Adam (Roger Wilson) and Eve (Diane Franklin) would make the same mistake. Franklin (*Amityville II*) also appears as Cleopatra and Mata Hari and has nude scenes.

SECRET AGENT

(MPI series, 1965–66) UK

Patrick McGoohan played secret agent John Drake on *Danger Man* (1960), then this (1965–66) serious b/w spy series, shown in America on CBS. Executive producer Ralph Smart also wrote many of the 45 episodes. It was considered pretty violent at the time and is a real contrast to the more comic spy shows (and movies) that were so popular at the time. The excellent hit theme song (American version only) is by Johnny Rivers, and Drake's clothes are pretty gear. The same character later showed up in McGoohan's classic cult series *The Prisoner*. Eight 50-minute tapes are available as well as a 1966 color double episode ("Koroshi") set in Japan, which has also been around on tape.

SECRET AGENT 00 = OPERATION KID BROTHER

SECRET AGENT FIREBALL

(1965) **D:** "Mario Donen"/Luciano Martino **S:** Sergio Martino **P:** Mino Loy Italy (*Killers Are Challenged; Lie Spie Uccidone A Beirut*)

Richard Harrison stars as a CIA agent after some microfilm containing the formula for an H-bomb. Spies torture people and Dominique Boschero co-stars. AIP released the feature, which was filmed all over Europe.

THE SECRETARY

(Republic, 1995) **D/S:** Graham Flashner **S:** Randy Kornfield **P:** Pierre David

Sheila Kelly is a psycho office worker who blackmails and murders. Mel Harris is her new boss. With Barry Bostwick, James Russo, Mimi Craven, and Sondra Curry. Not to be confused with *The Temp*. Andrew Lane was executive producer.

SECRET BEYOND THE DOOR

(NTA, 1948) **D/P:** Fritz Lang **S:** Sylvia Richards **M:** Miklos Rozsa

Joan Bennett stars in her fourth, last, and least-known Lang feature. Her husband Walter Wanger was executive producer. She's an heiress on vacation in Mexico who meets and marries Michael Redgrave. They go to his mansion and, in a plot similar to *Suspicion*, she thinks he may have murdered his first wife. He has rooms that are exact re-creations of rooms where famous murders were committed. The stylish Universal feature was based on a novel by Rufus King. It includes a dream sequence, was shot by Stanley Cortez, and a score with some music that was played and recorded backwards (!). With Anne Revere and Natalie Schafer.

THE SECRET CINEMA

(Rhino, 1966) **D/S:** Paul Bartel

A New York City woman (Amy Vane) is constantly being filmed secretly and episodes of her life are shown to crowds at a local theater. It's a very clever b/w "underground" classic. Bartel's remake of this short was on the *Amazing Stories* TV series. The tape also includes Bartel's color short *Naughty Nurses*, about a dominatrix, and is 37 minutes total. Bartel's first feature was *Private Parts* (1972), also recommended.

Joan Bennett in *Secret Beyond the Door*.

magazine. Nan, who looks good in heart-shaped sunglasses and a bikini, hires Max. Her mysterious faceless boss (who only communicates by tape recorder), turns out to be "the conscience of Hollywood," who editorializes against scandal magazines on TV. Clarke's character disappears for the whole middle of the film. Some movie execs go into a projection room and watch a very long scene from their new crime feature, and you can see the mike in the film-within-a-film too! They keep talking about rock star "Zippy Daniels," but they never show him! From Crown International.

THE SECRET FOUR

(Sinister, 1939) **D:** Walter Forde
S: Roland Pertree   UK (*Four Just Men*)

This mystery, involving murder and the Suez canal, is a version of an Edgar Wallace novel that had also been filmed in 1921. With Hugh Sinclair, Anna Lee, and Alan Napier, who later gained fame as Alfred on the *Batman* TV show.

SECRET GAMES 3

(Academy, 1994) **D:** Alexander Gregory Hippolyte
S: Don Simmons, Tucker Johnson **P:** Andrew Garroni

Diana (the large-breasted Rochelle Swanson) is a wealthy wife who is led astray by a new blond neighbor, Gwen (Mary Karasun), and becomes a high-class hooker in a mansion with closed-circuit TV cameras. Gwen has a sex scene, then Diana has five of them (taking up most of the tape). One rich John (Woody Brown) turns out to be a contract killer who blackmails her, and after all the soft-core sex, the tape becomes a psycho movie. Also with Branda Swanson. *Secret Games* (Imperial, 1991) had exactly the same plot with Michelle Brin being harassed by Martin Hewitt. Delia Sheppard and Catya Sassoon costarred. Hewitt returned in *Secret Games 2* (1993) with Sara Suzanne Brown and Amy-Rochelle Weiss. All three are available in R or unrated versions.

THE SECRET LIFE—JEFFREY DAHMER

(Magnum, 1993) **D/P/M:** David R. Bowen
S/P/A: Carl Crew

Here's a suprisingly well done, serious look at one of America's worst and most horrifying serial killers. We see how the soft-spoken young Dahmer starts killing in Bath Township, Ohio, then later gets better at it in Milwaukee. He lures males to his apartment, offering money to pose for Polaroid pictures, drugs them, kills them, and dismembers the bodies. The victims are black, white, gay, and straight. Dahmer, who goes on probation for sex with a minor, conducts horrifying "zombie experiments," fondles skulls, and feeds human meatloaf to some victims. This all unfolds in a series of flashbacks. Dahmer is seen wearing a *She Devils on Wheels* T-shirt. It was made in California. Dah-

mer, convicted of killing 17 people, was murdered in jail in December of 1994. This is a strong indictment against the Milwaukee police department and would make a great double bill with *Comrade X*.

SECRET OF BLOOD ISLAND

(1965) **D:** Quentin Lawrence
S: John Gilling **P:** Anthony Nelson-Keyes
UK (*P.O.W.: Prisoner of War*)

The Hammer studio was making nearly all horror movies when they did this Eastmancolor WWII drama set in a Japanese prisoner-of-war camp in Malaya. It features torture sequences and was considered very gory when released. Barbara Shelley (who had also been in *Camp on Blood Island*) stars as Elaine, a secret agent, also with Jack Hedley, Patrick Wymark, Michael Ripper, and Bill Owen.

SECRET OF THE BLACK TRUNK

(Sinister, 1962) **D:** Werner Klinger
S: Percy Allan   UK/W. Germany
(*Das Geheimnes der Schwarzen Koffer*)

People are killed in a famous hotel in this Edgar Wallace mystery filmed in England. Senta Berger and Horst Jansen star.

SECRET OF THE CHATEAU

(1934) **D:** Richard Thorpe
S: Albert Demond, Harry Behn

Universal released this mystery whodunit as if it were an outright horror movie. Characters in Paris kill for possession of a Gutenberg Bible. Claire Dodd stars with Clark Williams, Jack LaRue, and Osgood Perkins (the father of Tony) as the butler.

SECRET OF THE INCAS

(1954) **D:** Jerry Hopper **S:** Ronald McDougall, Sydney Boehm **P:** Mel Epstein

Charlton Heston stars as an adventurer with a treasure map, but Yma Sumac is the main reason to watch. VCR alert: the mysterious multi-range singer (who was recording for Capitol at the time) appears in the mountains for one incredible song. With Robert Young, Thomas Mitchell, and Glenda Farrell. It makes a good Heston double bill with *The Naked Jungle* from the same year. Also look for *Yma Sumac: Hollywood's Inca Princess* (1992), a feature-length German documentary.

THE SECRET OF THE LOCH

(Sinister, 1934) **D:** Milton Rosmer **S:** Billie Bristow, Charles Bennett **P:** Bray Wyndham   UK

Seymour Hicks stars as a professor who believes in the Loch Ness Monster. After some comedy and drama, a reporter does finally locate the ancient monster hatched from an egg. Director Ken Russell later said the monster scene scared him as a kid, and claimed the monster was really a live plucked chicken! Others say it was an iguana. David Lean was the editor.

THE SECRET CODE

(Stokey, 1942) **D:** Spencer C. Bennet **S:** Basil Dickey, Leighton Brill, Robert Beche **P:** Larry Darmour

Paul Kelly stars as the Black Commando in a 15-chapter Columbia WWII serial. He battles German spies who use explosive gas and artificial lightning. With Anne Nagel.

THE SECRET DIARY OF SIGMUND FREUD

(Fox, 1984) **D:** Danford B. Greene **S:** Roberto Mitrotti, Linsa Howard **P:** Wendy Hyland, Peer J. Oppenheimer

Bud Cort stars as the young Freud. He learns about sex with his mother (Carroll Baker) and hypnotizes his assistant (Carol Kane) to make her fall in love with him. He also experiments with drugs. With Klaus Kinski as Uncle Max, Marisa Berenson, Ferdinand Mayne, and Dick Shawn as "the ultimate patient." The comedy is 129 minutes long.

SECRET FILE HOLLYWOOD

(Loonic, 1961) **D:** Ralph Cushman
S: Jack Lewis **P:** Rudolph Cusumano

This absurd b/w movie looks like it was made in the 40s at PRC. I don't remember *ever* seeing a movie with so many shots of painfully visible boom microphones (the cameraman was Ray Dennis Steckler!). Robert Clarke (*The Hideous Sun Demon*) stars as Maxwell Carter, private eye. During a fight in a beatnik joint, his gun goes off and kills an innocent bystander. The morning papers announce: HOLLYWOOD PRIVATE EYE IN BEATNIK SHOOTOUT! He loses his license, drinks, and piles up gambling debts. Francine York (*Curse of the Swamp Creature*) plays Nan Tor, the beautiful, corrupt blackmailing editor of *Secret File Hollywood*

SECRET OF THE RED ORCHID

(1961) **D:** Helmut Ashley **S:** Trygve Larsen W. Germany (*Das Ratsel der Roten Orchidee*)

Rival American gangster families show up in London and blackmail rich men. Adrian Hoven stars (as the inspector) with Marissa Mell, Christopher Lee (as Captain Allerman), Klaus Kinski, and Fritz Rasp. It went direct to TV in America. The Edgar Wallace mystery was remade in England as *The Verdict* (1964).

SECRET OF TREASURE ISLAND

(Stokey, 1938) **D/S:** Elmer Clifton **S:** George Resener, George M. Merrick **P:** Louis Weiss

Don Terry stars in a 15-chapter Columbia serial about the hunt for a pirate treasure on a Mexican island. Hobart Boswell is Dr. X, a skull-faced ghost. With Gwen Gaze, Grant Withers, and Yakima Canutt.

SECRETS BEYOND THE DOOR = THE FOLKS AT RED WOLF INN

SECRET SERVICE IN DARKEST AFRICA

(Stokey, 1943) **D:** Spencer Gordon Bennet **S:** Royal Cole, Basil Dickey, Jesse Duffy

Rod Cameron is Rex Bennett, the hero in a 15-chapter Republic serial. The final chapter is "Nazi Treachery Unmasked," and there's a death ray and suspended animation drugs. With Lionel Royce in two roles, Joan Marsh, Duncan Renaldo, Kurt Katch, and Jack LaRue. *The Baron's African War* was a 60s condensed feature version.

SECRET SEX LIVES OF ROMEO AND JULIET

(SW, 1969) **D/P:** Peeter Stootsberry **S:** Jim Shumacher

Shakespeare's play is performed at the Globe Theatre to a drunken male audience. Forman Shane and Dicora Carse star in the Box Office International sex comedy. Stuart Lancaster is Capulet. It was rerated NC-17 in 1990.

SECRETS OF THE FRENCH POLICE

(1932) **D:** Edward Sutherland **S:** Samuel Ornitz, Robert Tasker

Gregory Ratoff is a master spy and hypnotist who tortures victims and covers them in wax in his mad lab. Frank Morgan stars with Gwili Andre and Rochelle Hudson. RKO released the forgotten 55-minute feature that managed to copy *Mystery of the Wax Museum* before it was released. With a Max Steiner score.

SECRET YEARNINGS: *See* THE SHAMING

THE SEDUCERS

(SW, 1970) **D:** Ottavio Alessi   Italy/W. Germany (*Top Sensation; Sklavin Ihrer Triebe*)

An oil-rich woman hires a decadent couple and another woman on a Mediterranean cruise on a private yacht. She hopes one of the women (Euro beauties Rosalba Neri and Edwige Fenech) will se-

duce her pyromaniac teen son Tony. After opium smoking, sex, and dynamiting fish, the "jet setters" abuse a Greek shepherdess (Ewa Thulin).

THE SEDUCTION

(Video Treasures, 1982) **D/S:** David Schmoeller **P:** Irwin Yablans, Bruce Cohn Curtis **M:** Lalo Schifrin

An LA TV reporter (Morgan Fairchild) is stalked by a crazed photographer fan (Andrew Stevens). TV star Fairchild has a nude scene and spends a lot of time in her pool, jacuzzi, and bath in her first theatrical feature since *A Bullet for Pretty Boy* (1970). With Michael Sarrazin, Vince Edwards, and Colleen Camp. This and *The Fan* (1981) wouldn't have existed without the Lennon and Reagan shootings. Schmoeller made it in between *Tourist Trap* and *Crawlspace*.

SEDUCTION: THREE TALES FROM THE INNER SANCTUM

(1992) **D:** Michael Ray Rhodes **S:** Barry Brown, Robert Glass, Steven Whitney **P:** Carroll Newman

Executive producer Victoria Principal and John Terry star in all three stories of this ABC-TV movie based on the old *Inner Sanctum* radio show. (Several 40s Lon Chaney Jr. movies were also based on it.) Two stories are period pieces, set in the 40s and 50s, and they all have surprise endings.

SEED PEOPLE

(Paramount, 1992) **D:** Peter Manoogian **S:** Jackson Barr **P:** Anne Kelly

It's *Critters* meets *Invasion of the Body Snatchers* (they wish!) as a man in a hospital (Sam Hennings) narrates his boring flashback. A plant spews out *lots* of white goo on a man, and a monster (a half-man in a suit, walking on his hands) emerges. Comet Valley locals are brainwashed and more creatures roll like tumbleweeds. By the director of *Arena* and other Charles Band releases.

SELF DEFENSE

(Media, 1982) **D:** Paul Donovan, Maura O'Connell   Canada (*Siege*)

Right-wing fanatics in Halifax take over and kill most of the patrons in a gay bar during a police strike. One guy escapes and teams with tenants of an apartment building (some are gay, blind, or retarded) who fight with makeshift weapons. Donovan later made *Defcon 4* and O'Connell also made *Norman's Awesome Experience*.

SELL OUT

(Edde, 1976) **D:** Peter Collinson **S:** Murray Smith, Judson Kinberg **P:** Josef Shaftel   (*The Set Up*)

Oliver Reed stars as a double agent who the Americans and Soviets want to eliminate. With Richard Widmark as a retired CIA agent, Sam Wanamaker, and Gayle Hunnicut. The PG feature was made in Israel.

SENIOR PROM

(1958) **D:** David Lowell Rich **S:** Hal Hackady **P:** Harry Romm

Columbia made this high school love musical starring Jill Corey and Paul Hampton. Watch it for singing guest stars Louis Prima and Keely Smith. Also with Tom Laughlin, Ed Sullivan, Bob Crosby, Freddy Martin, Frieda Inescort, and Selene Walters.

THE SENIORS

(Edde, 1978) **D:** Rod Amateau **S/P:** Stanley Shapiro

Some college guys open a sex clinic so they can meet girls, and it becomes a booming business. Dennis Quaid and Priscilla Barnes are in the cast of the comedy by the director of *Drive-In* (1976). With Edward Andrews and Robert Emhardt.

SENIOR WEEK

(Vestron, 1987) **D:** Stuart Goldman **S:** Jan Kubicki **P:** Ken Schwenker, Matt Ferro

The Palisades Park, N.J., Junior-Senior High School was rented for a week (for $1,500) as a location. When the movie was released, it made national news and caused the suspension of the principal. Michael St. Gerard (*Hairspray*) walks into a classroom filled with girls wearing only underwear. The teacher walks up to him and opens her blouse. Several girls remove their bras. His failing report card is delivered and the girls chant "You're a failure, Everett!" and laugh at him. The sexy dream sequence was done after the rest of the film, against the director's wishes. Ironically, it's the most memorable part of the movie. The rest follows a typical teen comedy group of dumb unlikable guys on a drive to Daytona Beach, Florida, with a kidnapped brainy nerd forced to work on a term paper. Everett's girlfriend and his English teacher (inspired by *Ferris Bueller*'s principal), a headache-inducing woman overacting in a neck brace, follow them all the way there. The soundtrack includes music by the Bongo Teens, Sam the Sham and the Pharaohs, Beat Rodeo, and others.

SENSATION

(Columbia, 1994) **D:** Briant Grant **S:** Doug Wallace **P:** John Morrissey

Former MTV VJ Kari Wuhrer (who seems to have had breast implants) stars as a college art student with psychic senses who becomes a willing and paid paranormal experiment subject for a doctor (Eric Roberts). She moves into a murdered woman's apartment (Polanski's *The Tenant* is mentioned) in his building, falls for him, and has frequent sex scene flashes. Everyone in the cast is a murder suspect. It's a better-than-average "erotic thriller" with arty cinematography. Claire Stansfield is featured in sex scenes, Ron Perlman is a morbid cop, Tracy Needham is the student best friend, Paul Le Mat is a voyeur landlord, and Ed Begley Jr. shows up as a masher in a bar.

THE SENSUOUS NURSE

(Fox, 1975) **D:** Nella Rossati **S:** Paola Vidali, Claudia Floro   Italy (*L'Infirmiera*)

Ursula Andress is a night nurse hired to help love a man to death so his nephews can inherit his fortune. Jack Palance as an American gangster and Lucianna Paluzzi are also in the unfunny sex comedy.

SENSUOUS TABOO

(Private Screenings, 1966) **D:** R. Lee Frost
P: R. W. Cresse   (*Mondo Freudo*)

"Hidden cameras" record sexual practices around the world in an adult mondo movie. Various (mostly staged) sequences show strippers in Tijuana, a Mexican slave market, a black mass in New York City, body painting, and mud wrestling.

THE SENSUOUS WIFE

(Private Screenings, 1970) **D/S/P:** Joseph F. Robertson
(*Mrs. Stone's Thing*)

The man who had produced *The Crawling Hand* and *The Slime People* (!) made this unique, hard-to-believe, equal-opportunity sex comedy featuring Ed Wood Jr. (!). Most of the movie is a plotless look at a Hollywood swingers party held at "the McMahons'." Some of the themes explored (as listed by the American Film Institute) are "sado-masochism, autoeroticism, homosexuality, lesbianism, tranvestism (this is where Wood comes in), bisexuality, flagellation, bestiality" and yes, even "body painting." Characters with sideburns and wigs smoke pot or drink, run around naked, and have sex indoors or out by the pool. One couple is so big that they need two pool tables to lie on. Wood, who acts shy about wearing women's clothes, is referred to as having "published 28 books." This tape can be found in video chain stores that don't carry X-rated videos. Wood also wrote *Love Feast* (1969) for Robertson and appeared in drag again in his own *Take It Out in Trade* (1970).

SEPARATE WAYS

(Vestron, 1979) **D/P:** Hikmet Avedis **S:** Leah Appet

An unhappy housewife (Karen Black) has an affair with art student David Naughton (in his feature debut). Her race car driver husband (Tony LoBianco) is having an affair too, and she leaves to become a waitress. This Crown International release also features Sybil Danning, Sharon Farrell, Jack Carter, William Windom, Robert Fuller, Arlene Golonka, and Pamela Jean Bryant. It's by the director of *They're Playing with Fire*.

SEPTEMBER STORM

(1960) **D:** Byron Haskin **S:** W. R. Burnett
P: Edward L. Alperson

Joanne Dru and Mark Stevens star in a 3-D story about sunken gold. With a 3-D hurricane, and shark and jellyfish attacks. This 20th Century release was filmed in Spain. 3-D movies were not common in 1960.

SEPTEMBER 30, 1955

(MCA, 1977) **D/S:** James Bridges **P:** Jerry Weintraub   (*9/30/55; 24 Hours of the Rebel*)

Richard Thomas is a young James Dean fan named Jimmy in Arkansas who loses it when Dean dies. With Lisa Blount, Tom Hulce, and Susan Tyrrell as Jimmy's white trash mother. Dennis Quaid and Dennis Christopher also have small roles. It's rated PG. The MCA soundtrack is by Leonard Roseman (who had also scored *East of Eden* and *Rebel Without a Cause*).

SERIAL

(Paramount, 1980) **D:** Bill Persky **S:** Rich Eustis, Michael Elias **P:** Sidney Beckerman

Martin Mull stars in this satire about modern life in Marin County, California, based on the novel by Cyra McFadden. His wife (Tuesday Weld) has an affair with a poodle groomer, and his daughter joins a religious cult. Christopher Lee, as a business tycoon (patterned after Malcolm Forbes?), is also the leader of a gay biker gang ("Born to Be Wild" is heard again when they ride). Also with Sally Kellerman (who appears topless), Stacy Nelkin, Nita Talbot, Bill Macy, Pamela Bellwood, Peter Bonerz, and Tom Smothers.

SERIAL MOM

(HBO, 1993) **D/S:** John Waters
P: Pat Moran **M:** Basil Poledouris

Kathleen Turner is perfect as Beverly Sutphin, a cheerful Baltimore mom who becomes a famous celebrity serial killer. Suzanne Somers wants to play Beverly in the TV movie. She only kills when somebody crosses members of her family: Sam Waterston (dentist husband), Ricki Lake (after she

lost 120 lbs. and became a TV talk-show hostess), and Matt Lillard (the gore-movie-fan son who works at a video store). *Serial Mom* has many good video store gags. Justin Whalin (Jimmy Olsen on the *Lois and Clark* TV series) masturbates to a video of Chesty Morgan in *Double Agent 73*. With Mink Stole, Mary Vivian Pearce, Traci Lords, and Patty Hearst, who had all acted for Waters before, plus Brigid Berlin, Joan Rivers, and the punk group L7. After two PG-rated features, this one (from Savoy) was rated R. It even features clips from H. G. Lewis's *Blood Feast*.

THE SERPENT AND THE RAINBOW

(MCA, 1988) **D:** Wes Craven **S:** Richard Maxwell, A.R. Simoun **P:** David Ladd, Doug Claybourne **M:** Brad Fiedel

A Harvard anthropologist (Bill Pullman) goes to Haiti to search for drugs that create zombies. The story mixes fantasy with horrible reality (Duvalier's Ton Ton Macoutes . . .). Cathy Tyson (daughter of Cicely) is a psychiatrist and love interest, and Zakes Mokae is pretty scary as a torturing secret police officer. With Paul Winfield, Michael Gough, Badja Djola, and Dey Young. Pullman is buried alive with a tarantula and finds zombies. It was "inspired by" Wade Davis's acclaimed nonfiction book and was filmed in Haiti. The soundtrack is on Varèse Sarabande.

SERPENT OF THE NILE

(Budget, 1953) **D:** William Castle
S: Robert E. Kent **P:** Sam Katzman

Columbia let Castle and Katzman use the sets from the bigger-budgeted *Salome* to make this Technicolor costume drama. Rhonda Fleming is Cleopatra, Raymond Burr is Mark Antony, and William Lundigan is the romantic lead. With Michael Ansara and Julie Newmeyer (Newmar) as a "golden girl."

THE SERPENT'S EGG

(Vestron, 1976) **D/S:** Ingmar Bergman **P:** Dino De Laurentiis **C:** Sven Nyquist   W. Germany/U.S.

David Carradine stars as a Jewish-American trapeze artist living in Germany just before WWII breaks out. The dark, nightmarish feature has strong horror-movie overtones and even has Gert Frobe as the police commissioner. With Liv Ullmann and James Whitmore. It was shot in Munich. After the box-office failure of this (and *Bound for Glory*), Carradine was usually found in less serious movies.

SERPENT WARRIORS

(1983) **D:** John Howard/Niels Rasmussen
S: Martin Wise   US/UK (*The Golden Viper*)

Clint Walker and Chris Mitchum star in a fantasy adventure. With Eartha Kitt as the snake priestess and Anne Lockhart.

SERVANTS OF TWILIGHT

(Vidmark, 1991) **D/S/P:** Jeff Obrow
S: Stephen Carpenter **P:** Venetia Stevenson

Serials

Screen serials or chapter plays were first produced by the Edison Company (1912's *What Happened to Mary*). The most famous and successful silent serial, *The Perils of Pauline*, was released in 1914. Of over 270 silent serials produced in America, less than 20 (!) survive today. Many of the 162 American sound serials (made from 1929–56, when TV killed them off forever) are available on tape. For many years the only way to see an entire serial (unless you owned the reels and a projector) was to see one of the pathetic feature versions edited down for TV. Now you can see all 10 to 15 chapters of a serial whenever you want. See individual entries for Dick Tracy, Superman, Batman, Flash Gordon, Tarzan, and others. Many serials (not reviewed here) were westerns. John Wayne and Rin-Tin-Tin were major serial stars, and there were even series about Canadian Mounties and Boy Scouts.

A frazzled young private eye in an asylum (Bruce Greenwood) tells the story to his shrink. Belinda Bauer has a big-eyed 6-year-old son named Joey (Jarrett Lennon). "Mother Grace" (Grace Zabriskie) shows up and says, "He's got to die!" Grace and her widespread religious cult think Joey is the anti-Christ and will do anything to destroy him. Greenwood is hired to protect him. Carel (Lurch) Struycken is cult enforcer. It has good action, a bat attack, bleeding palms, and a decapitated dog. The acting (especially Greenwood and Bauer) is excellent and the ending is a stunner. It's based on a Dean R. Koontz book (*Twilight*). The producer was in *Horror Hotel*! William Sachs, Wayne Crawford, and Andrew Lane were also producers. With Kelli Maroney and Jillian McWhirter. It debuted on Showtime.

THE SET UP: *See* THE SELL OUT

SEVEN

(IVE, 1979) **D/P:** Andy Sidaris
S: William Driskill, Robert Baird

William Smith hires seven hitmen to kill seven mobsters in Hawaii. The funny and violent movie is better than anything Sidaris made later. With Elvis's bodyguard Ed Parker as himself, Reggie Nalder as an assassin, John Alderman, Martin Kove, Barbara Leigh, Art Metrano, Susan Lynn Kiger (from *Playboy*), and Lenny Montana. The AIP release was the director's first after *Stacey*. Sybil Danning provides an intro for the tape. Leigh, the sister of Tanya Roberts, was married to Timothy Leary.

SEVEN DEAD IN A CAT'S EYE

(Prism, 1972) **D/S:** Antonio Margheriti
S: Gioliano Simmonelli **P:** Luigi Nannerim
Italy/France/W. Germany
(*La Morte Negli Occhi Del Gatto*)

Jane Birkin arrives at her aunt's old house in Scotland and people start to die. Anton Diffring is a doctor and the late Serge Gainsbourg (Birkin's real-life husband) is a detective. It's too dark, dumb, and boring. It also has a killer cat and a guy in a gorilla suit. With Hiram Keller and Alan Collins. The music was recycled from the director's much better *Castle of Blood* (1964).

SEVEN DOORS OF DEATH

(Thriller, 1981) **D:** "Louis Fuller"/ Lucio Fulci
S: Giorgio Mariuzzo, Dardano Sacchetti
P: Fabrizio de Angelis   Italy (*L'aldila; The Beyond*)

Katherine MacColl inherits a remote, old, and cursed New Orleans hotel with a door to Hell in the basement. The gory horror fave has zombies, tarantulas, and scenes of Hell. With David Warbeck as a doctor and Sarah Keller. It was partially filmed on location in Louisiana. 10 minutes were cut from the Aquarius release in 1983, and the credits were "Americanized."

SEVEN DWARVES TO THE RESCUE

(VSOM, 1950) **D/S/P:** Paolo W. Tamburella
Italy (*Sette Nani Alla Riscossa*)

Rosanna Podesta (*Hercules, Horror Castle . . .*) stars as Snow White. The seven dwarves save Snow and her husband Prince Charming from the Prince Of Darkness. The laughable Childhood production was released in America in 1965, then AIP released it to TV.

SEVEN HOURS TO JUDGMENT

(Media, 1988) **D/A:** Beau Bridges **S:** Walter Davis, Elliot Stephens **P:** Mort Abrahams

Bridges stars as a judge who has to release the punks who killed the wife of Ron Leibman. A crazed Leibman gives him seven hours to produce evidence to convict them or he'll have his wife (ex–Mrs. Springsteen Julianne Phillips) killed. With Al Freeman Jr. and ex–UCLA basketball star "Tiny" Ron Taylor.

SEVEN KEYS TO BALDPATE

(1917) **D:** Hugh Ford **S/A:** George M. Cohan

Cohan had written a 1913 Broadway version of this rare old-dark-house mystery based on a novel by Earl Derr Biggers. He starred in this first film version with the Swedish Anna Q. Nilsson and Hedda Hopper. Paramount made this and a 1925 remake. The music was added in 1973. Three other versions (all from RKO) came out in the 30s. The most recent version was called *House of the Long Shadows*.

THE SEVEN MAGNIFICENT GLADIATORS

(MGM, 1984) **D/E:** Bruno Mattei **S:** Claudio Fragasso
P: Golan/Globus   Italy (*I Sette Magnifici Gladiatori*)

The *Seven Samurai* plot was used again for this PG muscleman movie. Lou Ferrigno stars as Gan with Sybil Danning (both had also been in *Hercules*). With Brad Harris and Don Vadis from 60s muscleman movies and Mandy Rice-Davies.

SEVEN REVENGES

(1960) **D/S:** Primo Zeglio **S:** Sergio Leone,
Sabatino Ciuffini   Italy (*Le Sette Sfide*)

Rival Mongol chiefs have to prove themselves with challenges. Ed Fury stars with Elaine Stewart and Bella Cortez.

THE SEVENTH COMMANDMENT

(Dark Dreams, 1960) **D/S/P:** Irvin Berwick
S: Jack Kevan

Jonathan Kidd, an actor who seems like Don Knotts impersonating Humphrey Bogart, stars as a San Francisco man who develops amnesia after a car crash. A friendly tent preacher (with a truck called Noah's Ark) puts him on the right path, and seven years later, he's the Rev. Tad Morgan, busy curing people at revival meetings. "PRAISE THE LORD!" Meanwhile, the girlfriend he had left behind in the car crash (Lyn Statten) has become an ex-con blond floozy living with a lowlife crook in a crummy apartment. They see Morgan as their "meal ticket" and proceed to ruin his life with booze, sex, and blackmail. It all ends in a graveyard where the Lord's Prayer is evoked and a Bible stops a bullet. My favorite line is, "I want you to meet the epitome of pulchritude!" The sound mixer was future director S. F. Brownrigg. A crippled kid is played by Charles Herbert (*The Fly* and *13 Ghosts*). At Universal during the 50s, Berwick was a dialogue director (he worked on 11 Jack Arnold movies) and Kevan was a major talent in the makeup department. They formed Van Wick (later Irvmar) productions together and made the incredible *Monster of Piedras Blancas* (1959), this one from Crown International, and *The Street Is My Beat* (1966). Berwick went on to produce and/or direct *Hitchhike to Hell*, Larry Buchanan's *Loch Ness Monster*, and others. His son Wayne (who acted in his films) directed *Microwave Massacre* (!).

THE SEVENTH CURSE

(VSOM, 1986) **D:** Lan Dei Tsa
P: Raymond Chow   Hong Kong

Explorers in Thailand encounter worm tribe ceremonies and *Alien*-inspired creatures in the jungle. It's one of the more outrageous Asian horror

---

The 70s used to seem like a stupid, wasted decade to many. Now that we can look back on life in the 80s, the 70s look pretty fascinating and so do an awful lot of the movies. It was the decade of black action movies, kung fu, all-star disaster movies, and porno features. We got the last biker movies and spaghetti westerns and enjoyed the last flourishing days of drive-ins. A record number of horror and exploitation movies were produced around the world. Because American directors had just recently been given freedom from censorship, many 70s movies are about returning Nam vets, junkies, hookers, pimps, student radicals, and various dysfunctional psychos, and pushed the limits with nudity, swearing, gore, drugs, and politics.

Eventually, the modern "blockbuster" event movie appeared and after a while Lucas and Spielberg ruled at the boxoffice. The first features to break the hundred million mark were *Star Wars, The Empire Strikes Back,* and *Jaws*. Some others making over $40 million were *The Exorcist, Superman, Close Encounters, National Lampoon's Animal House, Star Trek, American Graffiti, Jaws II, Heaven Can Wait, Towering Inferno, The Poseidon Adventure, Airplane,* and *Alien*.

movies, featuring gore, nudity, sex, kung fu, a walking skeleton, lots of worms, and slimy bugs. A spell uses the blood of children from a rival tribe and a mutating man is cured when a woman cuts off her nipple and feeds it to him. With Chow Yung-Fat (*The Killer*) as the rich hero, Chin Suit Ho, and Ti Wei. Based on a novel by Ni Kuang and from Golden Harvest.

THE SEVENTH SIGN

(RCA/Columbia, 1988) **D:** Carl Schultz
S: Clifford and Ellen Green **P:** Ted Field

The world will end if Demi Moore has a baby with no soul. God's messenger (Jurgen Prochnow) rents a room over the garage. The confusing movie shows Biblical disasters and has flashbacks to ancient Rome, but the only memorable image is a suicidal Demi Moore pregnant and naked in a bathtub (her stomach was a very convincing prosthetic device). Michael Biehn is her lawyer husband and John Heard has a standout bit as a minister. Also with Richard Devon. From Tristar. Moore was also in the 3-D horror movie *Parasite* (1982).

THE SEVENTH VEIL

(VidAmerica, 1945) **D:** Compton Bennett
S/P: Sidney Box **S:** Muriel Box **UK**

Ann Todd is a concert pianist who has a mental breakdown and becomes mute and suicidal. Her psychiatrist (Herbert Lom) hypnotizes her, revealing her romantic problems with three men in narrated flashbacks and dream sequences. James Mason is her relative guardian.

THE SEVERED ARM

(Video Gems, 1973) **D/S:** Thomas S. Alderman
S: Darryl Presnell, Larry Alexander, Marc B. Rand
P: Gary Adelman

Some people trapped in a cave draw lots, and the loser's arm is cut off and eaten. After being rescued, they're killed off one by one in their homes. Former AIP starlet Deborah Walley has her last known role in this bizarre low-budget exploitation movie. With Marvin Kaplan as "Mad Man Herman," John Crawford, and Paul Carr.

SEVERED TIES

(Columbia, 1991) **D:** Damon Santostefano
S: John Nystrom, Henry Dominic
P: Christopher Webster *(Army)*

Fangoria magazine backed this grotesque horror comedy that refuses to be funny or scary. A Nazi scientist (Oliver Reed) helps a horrible woman (Elke Sommer) force her son (Billy Morrissette) to continue with her late husband's genetic experiments. He creates a living arm that kills, then hides out with clichéd silent homeless people in a new secret lab assembled from junk. With narration and flashbacks inside of flashbacks. Garrett Morris costars, and Johnny Legend has a good role as a crazed preacher ("Testify!") who gets his face ripped off. It was shot in Wisconsin.

SEX AND BUTTERED POPCORN

(Central Park, 1989) **D/S/P:** Sam Harrison

Exploitation movies from the silent days through the early 50s are covered in this amazing feature-length historical documentary. The on-screen host is overworked actor Ned Beatty (in a bow tie), but the knowledgeable guest star experts, David F. Friedman and Dan Sonney, actually distributed these roadshow classics to the "skid row scratch houses" of America. This tape includes choice clips from dozens of the old (mostly) b/w adults-only drug/sex movies like *Reefer Madness, Child Bride of the Ozarks, Wild Weed,* and *Maniac.* Some highlights are a nude baseball game from *Elysia* (1933), naked women in chains from *Forbidden Daughters* (1927), and Lenny Bruce in *Dance Hall Racket* (1955). To illustrate how alternate versions were available, a scene with women talking is intercut with the same "hot" underwear version. Friedman tells how old nitrate prints were routinely dumped into the ocean, and what "square up reels" were. The 70-minute documentary was originally shown on cable TV as *For Adults Only.*

SEX AND THE ANIMALS

(Video City, 1969) **D/S:** "Hal Dwain"/
Harold Hoffman **P/E:** Larry Buchanan

It opens with turkeys mating to Ravi Shankar music. This "adult" documentary is nothing but footage of wild animals mating. In the early 90s, it and other similar features were being shown in European discos as background for dancers! Hoffman (*The Black Cat,* 1966) was the producer of several early Buchanan features and wrote others.

SEX AND THE COLLEGE GIRL

(Strand VCI, 1964) **D/S:** Joseph Adler
S: William A. Bairn, Warren Spector
P: Robert N. Langworthy, Ben Parker
(The Fun Lovers)

This mild drama was shot (in color) in Puerto Rico by Floyd Crosby and retitled and released in 1970. It concerns a no-good, rich, gambling, drinking, playboy piano player. Charles Grodin, in his first role, is the shy, glum, drag of a best friend. He acts just like Grodin does now only not as well. Richard Arlen and Luana Anders are better. There's a party scene copied from *La Dolce Vita* and some twist dancing, but mostly just relationship problems and *talk.* Director Adler later made the much more interesting *Scream Baby Scream.*

SEXBOMB

(1989) **D:** Jeff Broadstreet
S: Robert Benson **P:** Rick Eye

In another spoof about low-budget filmmaking, a producer (Robert Quarry) makes "I Rip Your Flesh With Pliers" and "Werewolves in Heat." Delia Sheppard stars as Candy, the wife who wants him murdered. With Linnea Quigley as a horror movie actress, Spice Williams, and lots of topless scenes. Fred Olen Ray was an executive producer. High on scream queen fan want lists, this movie has never been on tape.

SEXCALIBUR

(Essex, 1983) **D:** Dinin Dicimino

The Mask (1961), from Canada, was the inspiration for many later movies including this 3-D X-rated porno video. Maria Tortuga dreams of her previous life as a sorceress after she puts on a mask. She has sex with a knight and other characters. With Drea, Lee Carol, and Ken Starbuck. Tapes came with glasses.

SEX IS CRAZY

(VSOM, 1979) **D/S:** Jesse (Jesús) Franco
Spain (*El Sexo Está Loco*)

Lina Romay (in a blond wig) stars as a Brazilian hooker who is impregnated by Martians in a bizarre episodic horror sex comedy. She's also sacrificed by naked people in masks, and is the girlfriend of a gambler. Most of the movie seems to be in her imagination. Franco is seen filming and even enters the scene to correct the actors. With subtitles.

THE SEX KILLER

(SW, 1967) **D/P:** Barry Mahon (*The Girl Killer*)

Tony, a doomed, loner voyeur who works at a mannequin factory, buys a set of binoculars in Times Square. He watches topless sunbathers on rooftops. We see them through a lens-shaped cutout. He takes a mannequin head to a bar (where a man makes a face into the camera) and on the BMT. A blond hooker wants too much, so he pays her $10 to just strip. Soon, he's strangling women. Some of the nude scenes are top notch in every way, especially the nurse and the black sunbathers. The Manhattan locations are also great. Tony goes to the Cafe Bizarre on 9th St. and a marquee advertises *Love Hunger* (1965). The music is a repeated rock instrumental. Presented by Frank Henenlotter. The b/w adult movie runs 55 minutes.

SEX KITTENS GO TO COLLEGE

(1960) **D/P:** Albert Zugsmith **S:** Robert Hill

You may be familiar with this silly b/w all-star slapstick comedy with Mamie Van Doren as a sexy new college professor, but wait until you see the uncut version! Thinko, the large clunky robot, dreams that four strippers do routines for him. They get down to G-strings and one humps against him. The extraordinary sequence includes the chimp and the midget too. For the record, the cast also includes Marty Milner, Louis Nye, Maila "Vampira" Nurmi as his assistant, John Carradine (he jitterbugs with Mamie), Conway Twitty (he sings about Mamie), and Jackie Coogan. Tuesday Weld and Mijanou Bardot are in a love triangle with an idiot football star (Woo Woo Grabowski) and Mamie says, "I'm so far out already, I'm on another planet." This rare longer print played the Z Channel in LA in the 80s and was bootlegged, but is still hard to find. It may have played theatrically in Europe. Zugsmith later made adults-only movies like *On Her Bed of Roses.*

SEX, LIES AND RENAISSANCE: *See* FANNY HILL

1. *The Abominable Dr. Phibes* (1971)
2. *Alice Sweet Alice* (1976)
3. *Apocalypse Now* (1979)
4. *Deep Red* (1976)
5. *Eaten Alive* (1977)
6. *Eraserhead* (1978)
7. *God Told Me To* (1976)
8. *The Hills Have Eyes* (1977)
9. *Martin* (1978)
10. *Phantasm* (1979)
11. *Pink Flamingos* (1972)
12. *The Shining* (1980)
13. *Squirm* (1976)
14. *Suspiria* (1978)
15. *Switchblade Sisters* (1976)
16. *Taxi Driver* (1976)
17. *The Tenant* (1976)
18. *Texas Chainsaw Massacre* (1975)
19. *They Came from Within* (1977)
20. *UP!* (1976)

SEX ON THE RUN

(Slightly Blue, 1976) **D/P:** Franz Antel **S:** Joshua Sinclair, Tom Priman   Germany/France/Italy
(*Casanova and Co.; Some Like It Cool*)

Tony Curtis stars as Casanova and as Giacomino, a guy who looks like him. A number of international beauties and lots of nudity help assure that this period sex comedy will stay in release for a long time (under various titles). With Marisa Berenson, Britt Ekland, Sylva Koscina, Marisa Mell, Olivia Pascal, Lillian Muller, and Jeanne Bell (as a slave girl). Also with Hugh Griffith and Victor Spinetti. It was filmed in Venice. Curtis returned in *The Manitou* and *Sextette* (the next year).

THE SEXORCIST

(Arrow, 197?) **D:** "Sven Hellstrom"/ Ray Dennis Steckler **S:** Arnold Blatt **P:** Hans Leek   (*Sexorcist Devil*)

This is one of many bad hardcore porno movies by the man who directed *The Incredibly Strange Creatures . . .* and other 60s cult movies. A female reporter for an occult magazine narrates and a hooded man with an echo voice kills people. Meanwhile, a roommate talks about drug addict hookers, lots of amateur horror art is shown, there are several sex scenes (one in a pool) and lots of BJs. Lilly Lamara and Kelly Guthrie star and Steckler's former wife and one-time star Carolyn Brandt is seen sitting at a typewriter.

SEX PERILS OF PAULETTE

(1965) **D/P:** Doris Wishman

A woman from Ohio goes to New York City but can't pay her rent. She fails as a waitress, and tries to avoid becoming a hooker. She becomes one anyway, a man wants to marry her, but she says she's not fit. The "adult" drama features the debut of actor Tony LoBianco (*The Honeymoon Killers*). Wishman also narrates.

SEXPOT

(Academy, 1988) **D/P:** Chuck Vincent **S:** Craig Horrall

Ruth Collins stars as Mrs. Barrington, who marries wealthy men and arranges their "accidental" deaths. It's an R-rated remake of Vincent's porno movie *Mrs. Barrington* (1974), and characters speak into the camera. With Jane Hamilton, Jennifer DeLora, Christina Veronica, and name guest stars Troy Donahue and Jack Carter.

SEX RITUALS OF THE OCCULT

(SW, 1970) **D:** Robert Caramico

It's an adults-only "documentary" with lots of nudity and sex. The director was the cameraman for *Orgy of the Dead* (!) and later worked on *Falcon Crest*! Dogs and goats join in the orgy scenes. Vincent Stephens narrates.

THE SEX SYMBOL

(1976) **D:** David Lowell Rich **S:** Alvah Bessie **P:** Douglas S. Cramer

Connie Stevens stars as a thinly disguised Marilyn Monroe in an ABC-TV movie that was shown theatrically overseas with additional nude scenes. With Shelley Winters as a gossip columnist, Don Murray as a Kennedy character, and William Smith as the Joe DiMaggio character. Also with William Castle as a director, Jack Carter, James Olson, Nehemiah Persoff, and Joseph Turkel.

SEXTETTE

(Media, 1977) **D:** Ken Hughes **S:** Herb Baker **P:** Daniel Briggs, Robert Sullivan

Everyone figured that *Myra Breckinridge* would be the last feature for Mae West, but the 85-year-old (!) sex star returned for one last embarrassment. Her ex-husbands show up on her latest honeymoon and she remembers her past. It's all based on her play. With George Hamilton as a gangster, Timothy Dalton as her latest husband (who turns out to be a secret agent), Ringo Starr as a director, Tony Curtis, Dom DeLuise, Alice Cooper, Keith Moon, George Raft, Walter Pidgeon (it was his last film), Regis Philbin, Rona Barrett, and lots of bodybuilders. From Crown International.

SEX THROUGH A WINDOW

(Vestron, 1973) **D:** Jeannot Szwarc **S:** Michael Crichton **P:** Paul N. Lazarus
(*Extreme Closeup*)

James McMullan stars as a voyeur Hollywood TV newscaster in a movie about surveillance equipment. Szwarc made this before Coppola's *The Conversation*. He made *Bug* next. The National General release features Kate Woodville and James A. Watson.

SEXTON BLAKE AND THE HOODED TERROR

(Sinister, 1938) **D/P:** George King
UK (*The Hooded Terror*)

Tod Slaughter, who usually was the only star of his movies, shares billing this time with George Curzon as Baker St. detective Blake. It was the third in a series of Blake movies. Slaughter is an industrialist stamp collector, secretly the head of a secret society of hooded killers. He has a futuristic TV set and a torture chamber full of snakes.

SEXUAL MALICE

(A-Pix, 1993) **D:** Jag Mundhra **S:** Carl Austin **P:** Andrew Garroni

Diana Barton (also in *Body of Influence*) stars as a businesswoman with a sullen, smirking, uncaring husband (the sullen, smirking Edward Albert). She has an affair with a male stripper (Douglas Jeffrey). After sex in a dressing room and sex under a pier, she's photographed having sex with a black woman. Blackmail and murder result. With Jack Laughlin as an ex-boyfriend cop, Samantha Phillips as the girlfriend, Chad McQueen as the brother, Don Swayze as a cop, and Kathy Shower in a minor role. The best part is seeing Jerry "The Beaver" Mathers as a desk sergeant! The tape I saw is unrated but seems more like an R. Gregory Hippolyte is the executive producer.

SEXUAL OUTLAWS

(Monarch, 1994) **D/S:** Edwin Brown **S:** Summer Brown **P:** Gregory Hippolyte

The married publisher (Erika West) of a sex fantasy magazine answers letters from, and becomes involved with, a mute drifter ex-con (former Olympic star Mitch Gaylord). Much of the running time is taken up by sex (including several lesbian scenes) and a hooker is murdered. With Mike McCollow as the husband, Nicole Grey, Monique Parent, Kimberly Dawson, and X star Devon Shire. Available R or unrated.

SEXUAL RESPONSE

(Columbia, 1992) **D:** Yaky Yosha **S:** Brent Morris **P:** Ashok Amritraj

Michael Madsen and Shannon Tweed star in another "erotic thriller." It's available R or unrated and features Catherine Oxenberg and Vernon Wells.

SEX WITH A SMILE

(VSOM, 1975) **D/S:** Sergio Martino **S:** Tonio Guerra **P:** Luciano Martino
Italy (*Gradia All'Ombra Del Lenzuolo*)

This comic anthology movie with Barbara Bouchet, Sydne Rome, Dayle Haddon, and Marty Feldman played America in drive-ins. I saw it at one, but oddly enough can only remember Feldman. *Sex with a Smile 2* (1976) featured Bouchet and Ursula Andress.

SEXY MAGICO

(1963) **D:** Mino Loy, Luigi Scattini
P: Enrico C. Putatto   Italy

Scenes showing sexual rites and dances around the world are contrasted with cabaret shows at places like the Crazy Horse Saloon. AIP released the mondo documentary in 1967.

SEXY PROBITISSIMO

(SW, 1963) **D:** Marcello Martinelli
P: Gino Mordini   Italy

"18" strippers are featured in this comic, narrated b/w "documentary" showing women through the ages, cavewomen to space women. My fave sequences show a woman who strips for the executioner in France during the Revolution and a "spider woman" with a web. There's a vampire scene and a Frankenstein monster scene (the nurse strips). Topless is as far as they go. Some scenes seem to be lifted from other movies (or vice versa), like the lesbian nightclub act, also in *The Wild, Wild World of Jayne Mansfield*. One of Frank Henenlotter's Sexy Shockers, it's only 63 minutes long and is partially letterboxed.

S.F.W.

(Polygram, 1994) **D:** Dale Pollack **D/S:** Jefery Levy

Four terrorists hold Cliff Spab (Stephen Dorff), a guy from a trailer park, hostage in a convenience store for 36 days, along with an upper-class girl (Reese Witherspoon). It's all videotaped and broadcast on network TV and Cliff briefly becomes a teen hero. With Jake Busey, Joey Lauren Adams, Pamela Gidley, and Jack Noseworthy. The same actor (John Roarke) plays all the major TV news and talk show personalities. The title means "So Fucking What." Based on a book by Andrew Wellman. Levy was also director of *Inside Monkey Zetterland*. The A&M soundtrack includes songs by Gwar, Hole, Babes in Toyland, Soundgarden, and others.

SGT. KABUKIMAN N.Y.P.D.

(Troma, 1991) **D/S/P:** Lloyd Kaufman **D/P:** Michael Herz **S:** Andrew Osborne, Jeffrey W. Sass

New York Cop Rick Gianasi is possessed by a Japanese spirit. He becomes a costumed hero with a painted face, who has visible wires when flying. Susan Byun is the niece of the original Kabukiman and the villain (Bill Weeden) becomes a dragon at the end. The much publicized PG-13 Troma comedy was co-produced by two Japanese firms.

SGT. PEPPER'S LONELY HEARTS CLUB BAND

(MCA, 1978) **D:** Michael Schultz
S: Henry Edwards **P:** Robert Stigwood

Making an (American) rock musical out of the Beatles' most famous album was a stupid idea (at

least *Tommy* had a storyline). Peter Frampton stars as Billy Shears (in Heartland, USA) in the PG-rated disaster. The double RSO soundtrack album of cover versions landed in many cut-out bins. The Bee Gees costar with comedian Frankie Howerd, Donald Pleasence, George Burns, and Steve Martin (making his film debut). Aerosmith play the bad guys. With Alice Cooper, Earth Wind and Fire, Billy Preston, Jim Dandy of Black Oak Arkansas, Leif Garrett, Mark Lindsay, Del Shannon, Tina Turner, Kim Miyori, and so many more. At the awful end, "All You Need Is Love" is sung by Donovan, Monti Rock III, Frankie Valli, Helen Reddy. . . . Jack Nicholson was once considered to direct this!

SHACK OUT ON 101

(Republic, 1955) **D/S:** Edward Dein
S: Mildred Dein **P:** Mort Millman

One of the oddest movies of the fifties takes place all on one set. Lee Marvin stars as "Slob," a short order cook at a greasy spoon diner owned by George (Keenan Wynn). Slob says things like "Life's 90 percent slop," and he is really a Communist agent, trying to get government secrets from scientist Frank Lovejoy, who has his eyes on the waitress (Terry Moore). It has amazing dialogue, sax music, and skin diver suits. With Whit Bissell and Frank DeKova. Lovejoy had been the hero in *I Was a Communist for the FBI* (1952). Dein ended his film career with *The Leech Woman* (1960). From Allied Artists.

SHADEY

(1987) **D:** Philip Saville **S:** Snoo Wilson
P: Otto Plaschkes   UK

An auto mechanic (Anthony Sher) can transmit his visions to film. A secret agent (Billie Whitelaw) wants him to use his power to locate Soviet submarine plans. He wants to earn money so he can afford a sex change. The comedy fantasy also stars Patrick Macnee and Katherine Helmond.

THE SHADOW

(1940) **D:** James Horne **S:** Joseph Poland, Ned Dandy, Joseph O'Donnell
P: Larry Darmour

Victor Jory stars in a 14-chapter Columbia serial, and Veda Ann Borg is Margo Lane. It's been called one of "the best" serials and Jory looks like "a pulp cover come to life." As in the 90s version, the Shadow appears as Lamont Cranston and as Lin Chang. The Black Tiger is the villain, who can become invisible. The Shadow was created by Walter B. Gibson (as Maxwell Grant) in pulps, was a popular radio show from the late 20s until 1954, and was also in comics. *The Shadow Strikes* (Imperial, 1937) was the first film. *The Shadow Returns* was in 1946.

THE SHADOW

(MCA, 1994) **D:** Russell Mulcahy **S:** David Koepp
P: Martin Bregman, Will Baer

Alec Baldwin is a Chinese warlord in Tibet who becomes playboy Lamont Cranston in 1920s NYC. Cranston becomes the Shadow and can "cloud men's minds" (and laughs while doing it). Villain Shiwan Khan (John Lone) has the same powers and threatens the city with an atom bomb. With Penelope Ann Miller as the psychic Margo Lane, Sir Ian McKellen as her scientist father, Peter Boyle as a cab driver/secret agent, Tim Curry, and Jonathan Winters as the police commissioner. The script is by the writer of *Jurassic Park*. The "$45 million" movie has a great art Deco look, lotsa FX, and a nice invisible building on Houston Street, but it was a box-office flop. Jerry Goldsmith did the score and Jellybean Benitez was music supervisor. The PG-13 Universal release runs 119 minutes. Available as a letterboxed laser disc.

SHADOW HUNTER

(Republic, 1992) **D/S:** J. S. Cardone
P: Carol Kottenbrook, Scott Einbinder

A Navajo Indian named Two Bear (Benjamin Bratt) is a mystical "Skin Walker" who kills and eats his victims for power and can disappear at will. A depressed Phoenix cop (Scott Glenn), who had Two Bear in custody, teams up with (and eventually falls for) an Indian lady tracker (Angela Alvarado) during the dangerous manhunt on horseback. With Robert Beltran as a reservation cop. The above-average cable TV movie by the di-

rector of *Shadowzone* (1989) includes a flashback, a nightmare, and some violent visions. It was filmed in Arizona.

SHADOW OF A DOUBT
(MCA, 1942) **D:** Alfred Hitchcock **S:** Thorton Wilder, Alma Reville, Sally Benson **P:** Jack H. Skirball

Joseph Cotten is perfect as Uncle Charlie, a "lonely hearts" killer visiting unsuspecting relatives in Santa Rosa. Theresa Wright is his adoring niece Charlie, who learns the truth. With Wallace Ford and Macdonald Carey as detectives and Hume Cronyn. The classic American psycho movie was filmed on location and was a personal favorite of the director (who is seen on a train). From Universal. *Step Down to Terror* (1959) was the first remake.

SHADOW OF A DOUBT
(1991) **D:** Karen Arthur **S:** John Gay

Mark Harmon takes the Uncle Charlie role in this TV remake by the director of *Lady Beware*. The time is changed to the early 50s and nods to other Hitchcock features are included. With Margaret Webb as the niece and Diane Ladd, Shirley Knight, and Tippi Hedren.

THE SHADOW OF CHIKARA
(Starmaker, 1977) **D/S:** Earl E. Smith   (*The Curse of Demon Mountain; Thunder Mountain; Demon Mountain; Wishbone Cutter; The Ballad of Virgil Cane*)

Joe Don Baker stars in a post–Civil War movie with fantasy elements. Sondra Locke (in her last theatrical feature without Clint Eastwood until 1986) costars with Joy Houck Jr. and Slim Pickens. The made-in-Arkansas New World PG feature is on tape under many titles.

SHADOW OF CHINATOWN
(Stokey, 1936) **D:** Robert F. Hill **S:** W. Buchanan, Isadore Bernstein, Basil Dickey **P:** Sam Katzman

Bela Lugosi is Victor Poten, a mad scientist in a 15-chapter Victory studios serial. He plots to drive West Coast Chinese businessmen out of business and at one point disguises himself as a Chinese man. He also uses a long-distance hypnotism machine. It's the cheapest looking of Lugosi's five sound serials. Katzman later produced all of Lugosi's Monogram features. Herman Brix/Bruce Bennett is the hero and Luanna Walters is Lugosi's assistant. A feature version was called *Yellow Phantom* and is also on tape.

SHADOW OF THE EAGLE
(Rhino, 1932) **D/S:** Ford Beebee **S:** C. Clark, Wyndham Gittens

John Wayne stars as a carnival skywriter hero in a 12-chapter Mascot serial. A death ray is one of the problems he faces. Dorothy Gulliver co-stars with Roy D'Arcy and Yakima Canutt.

SHADOW PLAY
(Starmaker, 1986) **D/S/P:** Susan Shadburne **P:** Dan Biggs, Will Vinton

Dee Wallace Stone stars as a New York playwright on an island, haunted by a dead fiancé who had killed himself. Cloris Leachman and Ron Kuhlman are also in the New World supernatural release.

THE SHADOW RETURNS
(1946) **D:** Phil Rosen **S:** George Callahan **P:** Joe Kaufman

The Shadow (Kane Richmond) arrives at a mansion after jewels are stolen from a grave. Barbara Reed is Margo and George Chandler is Shrevie the taxi driver. With Tom Dugan. It's the first of three approx. 1-hour-long movies from Monogram, all from 1946 and all by Rosen. *Behind the Mask* and *The Missing Lady* followed with the same stars. Richmond also starred in serials as *Spy Smasher* and *Brick Bradford.* The next Shadow movie was *The Invisible Avenger* (Imperial, 1958).

SHADOWS
(Sinister, 1922) **D:** Tom Forman **S:** Eve Undsell, Hope Loring

Dying Chinese laundryman Yen Sin (Lon Chaney Sr.) converts to Christianity to prevent a friend from being blackmailed. Chaney's makeup was the main attraction. With the original Harrison Ford. The 70-minute drama is from Preferred Pictures.

SHADOWS AND FOG
(Orion, 1992) **D/S/A:** Woody Allen **P:** Jack Rollins, Charles H. Joffe

Allen plays Kleinman, a nervous clerk (and amateur magician), in a b/w tribute to German expressionism. Only the shadow of a killer is seen, and Allen becomes the Kafka-style prime suspect. It's fun to see Donald Pleasence as a scientist performing autopsies and Kenneth Mars is a drunken magician. Mia Farrow costars and the cast is filled with celeb bits. Lily Tomlin, Jodie Foster, and Kathy Bates are hookers. With John Cusack, John Malkovich, Madonna, Kate Nelligan, Fred Gwynne, Julie Kavner, Kurtwood Smith, and Wallace Shawn. Some of Kurt Weill and Bertolt Brecht's *Threepenny Opera* songs are heard in the PG-13 feature, which was filmed in Astoria, Queens, studios. It was Allen's last release before the Soon-yi scandal broke.

SHADOWS IN THE CITY
(1990) **D/S:** Ari Roussimoff **P:** Jim Grib

A suicidal former carnival barker (Craig Smith) returns to New York City. He hangs out with tattooed bikers but ends up in a netherworld populated by pasty faced (*Carnival of Souls*–inspired) zombies. The underground feature includes appearances by Nick Zedd, Brinke Stevens as a fortune teller, Taylor Mead, Joe Coleman, and Annie Sprinkle. Filmmakers Jack Smith (as the spirit of Death) and Emile De Antonio both died shortly after appearing in it. Roussimoff had

wanted the late Joe Spinnell to star. *Shadows . . .* was shot over a five-year period using various b/w and color film stocks.

SHADOWS RUN BLACK
(Vestron, 1981) **D:** Howard Heard **S:** Craig Kusaba, Duke Howard **P:** Eric Louzil

Sixth-billed Kevin Costner is a suspect in this movie about a vigilante serial killer called "the Black Angel" who goes after coeds. With William Kulzer as the cop star and Barbara Peckinpaugh and Terry Congie for topless or nude scenes. It was released in 1986 by Troma. *Sizzle Beach* was another movie with Costner, rereleased to cash in on his later fame.

THE SHADOW STRIKES
(Sinister, 1937) **D:** Lynn Shores **S:** Al Martin **P:** Max and Arthur Alexander

Rod LaRocque stars as Lamont "Granston," The Shadow, who solves a murder in an old house. Lynn Anders and Norman Ainsley co-star in the 61-minute mystery based on the popular radio show. It and a sequel, *International Crime* (1938) were from the short-lived Grand National company. The next Shadow was Victor Jory in the 1940 serial.

SHADOWZONE
(Paramount, 1989) **D/S:** J. S. Cardone **P:** Charles Band

NASA dream research in an underground lab unleashes a shapeshifting monster from another dimension. David Beecroft stars as an investigator and James Hong is the European scientist who experiments on naked people in a glass sleep chamber. The creature becomes a monkey and a giant rat. With Louise Fletcher, Shawn Weatherly, Lu Leonard, and Robbie Reves. By the director of *Slayer.*

SHAFT
(MGM, 1971) **D:** Gordon Parks Sr. **S:** Ernest Tidyman, John D. F. Black **P:** Joel Freeman

This followed *Sweet Sweetback* and started off the 70s black action craze. *Shaft,* the first major Hollywood "blaxploitation" movie, made over $7 million. Richard Roundtree is a detective who has an

Richard Roundtree is *Shaft.*

office in Times Square and a bachelor pad in Greenwich Village. He's hired by a gangster named Bumpy (Moses Gunn) to help find his daughter, who has been kidnapped by the mob. It's based on Ernest Tidyman's novel. Roundtree had been a stage actor and model in *Ebony* magazine. With Gwenn Mitchell and Antonio Fargas. The famous bestselling double soundtrack (originally on Enterprise) is by Isaac Hayes ("Shut your mouth!") and started a long-lasting trend of using wah-wah guitar for soundtracks. Hayes received an Oscar.

SHAFT IN AFRICA

(MGM, 1973) **D:** John Guillermin
S: Sterling Silliphant **P:** Roger Lewis

Shaft (Richard Roundtree for the third time) is hired by some African diplomats. He goes to Africa and eventually wipes out a Paris-based slavery ring run by Frank Finlay. This outrageous international sequel has lots about African customs, torture scenes in a former Nazi prison, and James Bond references. The parts about tricking Third World workers into slavery are actually very believable and fact-based. Vonetta McGee co-stars as the virgin daughter of an emir, but Neda Arneric has the major sex and nude scenes. Actually Roundtree is naked a lot himself. It was filmed in Ethiopia, Spain, and NYC. The Four Tops do the theme song (it was on the ABC soundtrack). Roundtree also starred in a short-lived (1973–74) and of course very watered-down *Shaft* CBS-TV series.

SHAFT'S BIG SCORE!

(MGM, 1972) **D/M:** Gordon Parks Sr.
S/P: Ernest Tidyman **P:** Roger Lewis

Richard Roundtree and Moses Gunn returned in the immediate sequel to the hit *Shaft,* based on another Tidyman novel. Shaft's a bit more like James Bond this time, instead of a 40s-style detective. He's hired to retrieve a quarter of a million dollars (for a Harlem child welfare fund) stolen by a gangster, and avenges a friend's murder. The action ends at a New York harbor. With Kathy Imrie and Julius W. Harris. O. C. Smith is on the MGM soundtrack.

THE SHAGGY DOG

(1994) **D:** Dennis Dugan **S:** Tim Doyle
P: George Zaloom, Les Mayfield

Ed Begley Jr. stars in the Fred MacMurray dad role in a remake of the 1959 fantasy comedy. Scott Weinger is the teen who becomes a sheepdog. With Sarah Lassez as the girlfriend and Natasha Gregson Wagner. It includes a scene from *Curse of the Werewolf.* It debuted on ABC-TV and was followed by more remakes of other old-style Disney movies. The original, which has been colorized (badly), was followed by *The Shaggy D.A.* (1976) and *The Return of the Shaggy Dog,* a 1987 TV movie.

SHAKA LULU: *See* MARK OF THE HAWK

SHAKA ZULU

(Starmaker, 1986) **D:** William C. Faure   S. Africa

The story of Shaka, the early-19th-century king of the Zulus (Henry Cole), was a popular syndicated TV mini-series running 300 minutes. The video adds more violence and nudity. The British cast includes Christopher Lee, Edward Fox, Robert Powell, Gordon Jackson, and Fiona Fullerton.

SHAKEDOWN

(MCA, 1988) **D/S:** James Glickenhaus
P: J. Boyce Harman Jr.

A New York City public defense attorney (Peter Weller) teams with a worn-out undercover cop (Sam Elliott) to expose high-level corruption. The action sequences are excellent, especially when a Coney Island rollercoaster leaves the tracks. The famous 42nd St. New Amsterdam theater (which had closed in the early 80s) is used as a scary crack den. With Patricia Charbonneau, Antonio Fargas, Shawn Weatherly (a former Miss Universe), Paul Bartel, Shirley Stoller, and Tom Waits. Glickenhaus's *The Soldier* (1982) is seen playing in a theater.

SHAKE, RATTLE AND ROLL

(1994) **D:** Allan Arkush
P: Lou Arkoff, Debra Hill

Teens Renee Zellweger (*Love and a .45*) and Latanyia Baldwin start a band, open a nightclub, and encounter opposition from anti-rock community members. With Howie Mandel as a DJ. The Showtime Rebel Highway feature is not a remake of the 1957 AIP movie, available from RCA. Arkush had directed *Rock 'n' Roll High School* (1979).

SHAKER RUN

(1985) **D:** Bruce Morrison **S:** James Kauf Jr.
P: Larry Parr, Igo Kantor New Zealand

Cliff Robertson and Leif Garrett are out-of-work American stunt drivers hired to transport a stolen deadly viral culture from New Zealand to America. Terrorists are after them in the car chase movie. With Lisa Harrow and Shane Briant.

SHAKES THE CLOWN

(Columbia, 1992) **D/S/A:** Bobcat Goldthwait
P: Ann Luly, Paul Colichman

Shakes (Goldthwait) is an alcoholic (and acrobatic) party clown in "Palookaville, USA." Clowns are everywhere (especially drinking in the bar), but not everyone is a clown. Clowns hate mimes, tough rodeo clowns beat up other clowns, and clowns fight each other for better jobs. Shakes is blamed for the murder of his boss (Paul Dooley) and his friends try to get him to stop drinking. Julie Brown is Shakes's (non-clown) waitress girlfriend, Tom Kenny is his sadistic rival Binky, and Adam Sandler and Blake Clark are his best friends. Some reviewers thought this movie was in *bad taste.* What knuckleheads! And what a great way for Goldthwait to start (and most likely end) a directing

career! With funny bits by Florence Henderson as a drunken clown groupie, LaWanda Page (!), Tom Villard, Sidney Lassick, and Robin Williams. From I.R.S.

SHAKMA

(Quest, 1990) **D:** Tom Logan
D/P: Hugh Parks **S:** Roger Engle

Shakma is a killer baboon (played by "Typhoon") trapped in a research building. Teens are killed while acting out a Dungeons and Dragons–type game. Roddy McDowall is the scientist who causes it all. With Christopher Atkins, Amanda Wyss, and Ari Meyers. It was filmed at the Universal Florida studios.

SHALLOW GRAVE

(Prism, 1987) **D:** Richard Styles **S:** George E. Fernandez **P:** Barry H. Waldman

Four Catholic co-eds on the way to Fort Lauderdale see a Georgia sheriff murder a woman. Two of them are killed and two others are arrested. The sheriff puts all three dead women in one grave.

SHALLOW GRAVE

(Polygram, 1995) **D:** Danny Boyle
S: John Hodges   Scotland

Three young professionals rooming in an Edinburgh flat fight over drug money from a new fourth roomate after he ODs. The body is dismembered and gangsters want the stolen money. The violent black-humor script was written by a doctor. Ewan McGregor, Kerry Fox, and Christopher Eccleston star.

SHAME

(Republic, 1988) **D:** Steve Jodrell **S:** Beverly Blankenship **P:** Damien Parer, Paul D. Barron   Australia

A lawyer (Deborra-Lee Furness) who rides a Suzuki on her vacation has to stay in an outback town for repairs. She discovers many local women have been gang raped. No one will bring charges, so she teaches them to fight back. The feminist action movie is very good. A huge *Shame* billboard was in Times Square for many months after the brief theatrical run. It was later remade for American TV.

Shakes the Clown (Bobcat Goldthwait) and Julie Brown.

SHAME

(Prism, 1992) **D:** Dan Lerner **S:** Rebecca Soladay **P:** Michele Maxwell MacLaren   Canada

This pretty good USA cable remake is set in Oregon. Amanda Donohoe (with short blond hair and in leather) stars as an L.A. attorney who just wanted to get away for a while on her motorcycle. She ends up fighting local jocks, the sheriff, and the town's main employers. With Dean Stockwell as the mechanic father of a scared rape victim (Fairuza Balk).

THE SHAMELESS

(1962) **D/P:** Jay Martin **S:** William L. Rose
(*The Barest Heiress*)

A detective visits nudist camps around the world looking for a woman's sister so she can inherit her father's legacy. Dori Davis and Sheila Gilliam star. It was filmed in America, Denmark, Germany, and France.

SHAMELESS SHORTS

(SW)

This color tape includes a dozen nudie "featurettes," often shown before adult movies in the 60s. Most feature dancing, modeling, and sunbathing. The one with "Instant Orgy" punch shows topless women dancing to a surf instrumental. Barry Mahon's *Censored* (this one is part of a feature) shows some pretty great "nudist" scenes. A scene with a black woman and a blonde helping each other look over, then under, a fence is pretty memorable. An incredible short (from Italy?) shows a wild-eyed blonde writhing in a bamboo cage to some great music. It ends with her shooting up (!). David Friedman's 1966 short stars Stacy Walker (*A Taste of Honey . . .*) and a wisecracking agent attending a nudist camp beauty contest. This one manages to be sexy and funny (on purpose), a major accomplishment.

THE SHAMING

(Roach, 1979) **D:** Marvin J. Chomsky **S:** Polly Platt **P:** Raymond Stross   (*Good Luck, Miss Wyckoff; Secret Yearnings; The Sin*)

Anne Heywood stars as a schoolteacher who has an affair with a (black) janitor (John LaFayette) after he rapes her. The drama, based on a William Inge novel, has been retitled many times and sold as an exploitation tape. With Donald Pleasence, Robert Vaughn, Carolyn Jones (it was her last theatrical feature), Dorothy Malone, Ronee Blakely, Earl Holliman, Joycelyn Brando, and R. G. Armstrong.

SHANGHAI BLUES

(VSOM, 1984) **D/P:** Tsui Hark   Hong Kong

In an excellent romantic comedy, a nightclub dancer (Sylvia Chang from the *Mad Mission* movies) briefly meets a musician (Kenny Bee) in 1930s Shanghai, then under Japanese bombardment. They're separated by war and don't recognize each other ten years later, after the war, even when living in the same building. Comedian Sally Yeh co-

stars. It was a remake of a Chinese feature called *Street Angel* (1930), itself a remake of the 1928 American film of the same name. Hark followed with *Peking Opera Blues*.

SHANGHAI JOE: *See* MANCHURIAN AVENGER

SHANGHAI SURPRISE

(Live, 1986) **D:** Jim Goddard
S/P: John Kohn **S:** Robert Bently

Madonna was in some flop movies, but this adventure co-starring her then-husband Sean Penn is probably the worst. She's a missionary in 1937 China who hires him to track a shipment of opium. It was backed by George Harrison's Handmade Films and helped sink the company. With Paul Freeman, Richard Griffiths, Kay Tong Lim, Clyde Kusatsu, and Victor Wong, and a cameo by Harrison. From MGM.

SHANGRI-LA

(SW, 1961) **S:** E. S. Seeley **P:** Dick Randall

If you've ever seen *Bela Lugosi Meets a Brooklyn Gorilla* (1951) you know that it starred Duke Mitchell and Sammy Petrillo, a team of Martin and Lewis imitators. Petrillo was sued by Jerry Lewis for copying him and the team broke up. Here Sammy is Sammy, a zookeeper who plays cards with Pinky the gorilla in a cage and tells his British friend about his unusual vacation. In flashbacks, he follows two beautiful women to the National Historical Wax Museum in D.C. (where he talks to wax figures), a snake farm in Florida (where he water skis and we see gator wrestling), and last and best of all, to a nudist camp. Sammy watches unseen, but finally joins in and gets to do a standup show and imitates Jerry Lewis and Dean Martin. The puns and jokes are awful, but I like when he refers to himself as "a stringless Howdy Doody." Weegee (later played by Joe Pesci) was the "trick photographer" and most scenes were shot on actual locations. Women swim naked, ride horses topless, and hold towels in front when walking. Jackie Miller (a well-known model) and Pamela Perry co-star. Exploitation producer George Weiss appears as a beauty contest judge. *Shangri-La* is 63 minutes long. It was reviewed as being in color but the tape is not.

SHANTY TRAMP

(Sinister, 1967) **D:** Joseph Prieto **S:** Reuben Guberman **P:** K. Gordon Murray

Lee Holland stars as Emily, a sexy, dangerous, trouble-making young white trash sharecropper's daughter in this b/w exploitation classic from Florida. She messes with bikers and causes the death of a black man by crying rape. The acting, editing, and sound are all good and the movie really delivers with action, blood, and surprising nudity (although they use "friggin'" for swearing). There's also a great theme song ("I'm gonna love love love you baby . . .") heard on a jukebox. Bill Rogers (star of *A Taste of Blood*) is a lecherous revival tent preacher. The assistant director was Bob (*Porky's*) Clark. Murray is the same guy known for his imported kiddie matinee releases. Kroger Babb also

released this for a while, and Jerry Gross and his Cinemation rereleased it in the 70s. The underrated Prieto also made *Fireball Jungle*.

SHARK!

(Genesis, 1969) **D:** Raphael Portillo **D/S:** Sam Fuller **S:** John Kingsbridge **P:** Skip Steloff   US/Mexico
(*Un Arma de los Filos; Man Eater*)

Burt Reynolds stars as a wiseguy illegal arms dealer on the run in the Sudan. He escapes on the boat owned by Silvia Pinal and Barry Sullivan. Reynolds tries to cheat them out of some gold from a sunken ship and sharks attack and kill. Arthur Kennedy plays an alcoholic. A stunt diver was actually killed by a shark, and Fuller disowned the feature.

SHARK'S CAVE

(1978) **D:** "Anthony Richmond"/Tonino Ricci **S:** Fernando Galiana, Manrico Melchiorre **P:** Nino Segurini   Italy/Spain/Venezuela
(*La Fossa Naledetta*)

Villain Arthur Kennedy hires a diver to locate an airplane which had crashed in the Bermuda triangle. Janet Angren (from Sweden) helps the diver. Killer sharks guard a lost undersea city (which we never see).

SHARKS' TREASURE

(MGM, 1974) **D/S/P/A:** Cornel Wilde

Wilde owns a small boat being used by a group of treasure hunters. They bring up a fortune in gold from a wreck but are held captive by an escaped con (Cliff Osmond, who whips his partner). In one sequence, real sharks attack. Sixty-year-old Wilde does one-handed push-ups. With Yaphet Kotto, John Neilson, David Canary, and Caesar Cordova. U.A. released the PG adventure after *Jaws*, but it was made first (as *The Treasure*). Wilde's last as director was filmed in the Dutch West Indies.

SHARKY'S MACHINE

(Warner, 1981) **D/A:** Burt Reynolds
S: Gerald Di Pego **P:** Hank Moonjean

Burt stars as an undercover vice squad leader who falls for an expensive hooker named Domino (Rachel Ward). She works for Atlanta drug king Vittorio Gassman. With Brian Keith, Henry Silva, Charles Durning, Bernie Casey, Daryl Hickman, and Earl Holliman. John Boorman was originally going to direct. The violent feature was filmed in Atlanta and uses ideas from *Laura*.

SHATTER DEAD

(Tempe, 1993) **D/S:** Scooter McCrea

A weary woman named Susan ("Stark Raven") passes through a small (upstate N.Y.) town populated by pitiful-seeming living dead. She goes to a house where one suicidal long-haired guy (Daniel Johnson) and a lot of females stay. There's a lot of talk (especially from the bald Preacherman) about the "new breed," but there are also blood-splattered deaths, bizarre dream sequences (sucking off a gun in a graveyard, naked angels . . .), some sex, and quite a bit of surprising matter-of-fact nudity. A scene where one of the two naked women standing in a shower turns out to be some kind of slowly rotting corpse is unique. The Betacam production seems to be inspired by *The Last Man on Earth* with a touch of *Carnival of Souls* added. The credits are mostly fake names but Pericles Lewnes (*Redneck Zombies*) did the FX.

SHATTERED

(Media, 1972) **D/S:** Alastair Reid **P:** Michael Klinger   UK (*Something to Hide*)

Peter Finch is a businessman married to an overbearing Shelley Winters (who leaves after about ten minutes). He picks up a (pregnant) hitchhiker (Linda Hayden) who manipulates him, and violence and murder result. With Colin Blakeley. Winters was in *The Poseidon Adventure* the same year.

SHATTERED

(MGM, 1991) **D/S/P:** Wolfgang Petersen **P:** John Davis, David Korda

Wealthy San Francisco architect Tom Berenger has extensive plastic surgery after a car crash but loses his memory. He has violent and erotic flashbacks, though. Bob Hoskins is an eccentric private detective (and pet shop owner) trying to help him figure out his past. The first American film by the director of *Das Boot* was based on *The Plastic Nightmare* by Richard Neely. It was shot along the Pacific coast by Laszlo Kovacs. "Nights in White Satin" is heard on the soundtrack while waves are intercut with a sex scene. With Greta Scacchi as his wife, Joanne Whalley-Kilmer, Corbin Bernsen, and Theodore Bikel.

SHATTERED SILENCE = WHEN MICHAEL CALLS

THE SHAWSHANK REDEMPTION

(Columbia, 1994) **D/S:** Frank Darabont **P:** Nikki Marvin

Tim Robbins stars as a Maine banker falsely accused of killing his wife and her lover in the late 40s. How he deals with his brutal life in prison until the 60s is the basic story. Morgan Freeman (who narrates) is Red, the lifetime prisoner who helps him out. The Castle Rock production is based on a short story from Stephen King's *Different Seasons* collection (so was *Stand by Me*). It was not promoted as a King film, it's long (142 minutes), and people couldn't pronounce or remember the title. Still it received an incredible seven Oscar nominations. It was shot in a real 19th-century Mansfield, Ohio, prison. With William Sadler, James Whitmore, David Proval, Clancy Brown as the corrupt guard, and Bob Gunton as the warden. Darabont had directed a King short (available on *Night Shift*) and *Buried Alive* and scripted several features (including *Mary Shelley's Frankenstein*). Another non-horror King adaptation with an awkward name (*Dolores Claiborne*) followed in 1995.

SHE

(Sinister, 1925) **D:** Leander De Cordova **S:** Walter Summers **P:** George Berthold Samuelson   UK

Betty Blythe stars as the ageless She (who must be obeyed) in the last of many silent versions of the famous H. Rider Haggard fantasy. Some versions of

Michael Shayne

A Miami private eye created by novelist and pulp writer Brett Halliday, Mike Shayne was the hero of a dozen features. Lloyd Nolan starred in a quality 20th Century series of seven (1941–42). *The Man Who Wouldn't Die* is an old dark house mystery with a magician murder victim. PRC made five more features (1946–47) starring a pre–*Leave It to Beaver* Hugh Beaumont. Four of them were directed by Samuel Newfeld and the last was by William Beaudine. In 1960 Richard Denning starred in a TV series version.

the 98-minute feature run only 57 minutes. With a music score. The next versions were in 1935, from RKO (the best), then the 1965 Ursula Andress version from Hammer. Sinister also offers an earlier Thanhouser studio version from 1911. The very first version was made by Thomas Edison in 1908.

S*H*E*

(Prism, 1980) **D:** Robert Michael Lewis **S:** Richard Maibaum **P:** Martin Bregman

Cornelia Sharpe is Lavinia Kean, international spy, in this CBS-TV pilot made in Italy that was also released to some theaters. Omar Sharif is the playboy villain and the cast includes Robert Lansing, Anita Ekberg, and Fabio Testi. Maibaum was known for writing James Bond scripts.

SHE

(Lightning, 1982) **D/S:** Avi Nesher **P:** Renato Dandi **M:** Rick Wakeman   Italy

Sandahl Bergman (who had just been in *Conan*) bathes nude in a spring to stay young. The comic book action story is set in the future and is loaded with in jokes, dumb gags, and TV and movie references. It has heroes in armor, vampires, mutants, and a robot. Characters are named Tom, Dick, and Harri, and a comedian who clones himself sings "Popeye, the Sailor Man." With Harrison Muller, Tom Goss and Gordon Mitchell as the ugly leader of the bad guys. Motörhead is on the soundtrack. With singing by Justin Hayward and Maggie Bell. The Sarlui production bears little resemblance to the H. Rider Haggard novel.

SHEBA BABY

(Orion, 1975) **D/S:** William Girdler **P:** David Sheldon

Pam Grier stars as Chicago private investigator Sheba Shayne. She returns home to Louisville, Kentucky, to help her father battle black mobsters. There's a wild party on a yacht and a chase through a fun house. The PG-rated AIP release was a letdown after Grier's more outrageous R-rated Jack Hill features. With Austin Stoker as her new boyfriend, D'Urville Martin, and Charles Kissinger. The Buddah soundtrack features Barbara Mason.

SHE CAME INTO THE VALLEY

(Media, 1979) **D:** "Albert Band"/Alfredo Antonini **S:** Frank Ray Perilli   (*Texas in Flames*)

Singer Freddy Fender stars in a story about a poor family during the Mexican Revolution. The cast includes Scott Glenn, Ronee Blakley, and Dean Stockwell. It was made in Texas. Band's first western was *The Young Guns* (1956).

SHE CAME ON THE BUS

(SW, 1969) **D:** Harry Vincent **P:** Peter Jackson

A gang attacks a suburban woman, then takes over a bus and kills the driver. This low budget adults-only sex shocker was filmed silent in 16mm with voiceovers.

SHE DEVIL

(Sinister, 1940) **D:** Arthur Hoerl **P/E:** Louis Weiss   (*Drums O'Voodoo; Louisiana*)

Sack Amusements made this very-low-budget all-black feature about Amos, an ex-con preacher who uses a voodoo woman known as Aunt Hagar (Laura Bowman) to get rid of "Tom Cat, spawn of the Devil." Tom, who owns a "Louisiana jook," is blackmailing him. Aunt Hagar says spells in rhyme and says things like: "Creepy, crawlin', lizard eatin' black cat," "You stinkin' skunk," and "I'm gwyna blind ya!" There's lots of high-energy preaching and singing ("Don't Let Nobody Turn You Round," "Good News," . . .) plus drumbeat voodoo ceremonies. Modern viewers might be surprised at characters calling each other "nigger." Director Hoerl usually worked for Monogram as a writer. The print is jumpy.

SHE DEVILS IN CHAINS: *See* EBONY, IVORY AND JADE

SHE DEVILS IN CHAINS: *See* SWEET SUGAR

SHE DEVILS OF THE SS: *See* THE CUTTHROATS

SHEENA

(RCA/Columbia, 1984) **D:** John Guillermin **S:** David Newman, Lorenzo Semple Jr. **P:** Paul Aratow

Blond Tanya Roberts rides a zebra (an obvious painted horse) and saves the day with animals. *Sheena*, based on the old jungle-woman comic books, has lots of nudity for a PG feature and some unintentional laughs, but it's pretty dull. The natives use better English than she does. With Ted Wass, Elizabeth Toro, and Donovan Scott. It was shot on location in Kenya by the director of *Shaft in Africa*. It lost millions for Columbia.

SHEENA IN WONDERLAND
(Three Hearts, 1987) **D/P:** "Edward Dinero"

Here's a tape with a very misleading box. It strongly implies that this is a "Roger Rabbit"–style sex movie, mixing blond part-Oriental porn star Sheena Horne with cartoon characters. She says, "Hi. I'm Little Miss Muppet, official hostess of this adult cartoon show," introducing the unidentified, already shown in American theaters, 1973 Italian/French cartoon feature *King Dick*. Some people might enjoy this harmless silly story about star "Little Dick," the impotent king "Master Limpcock," and the witch "Nymphomania," but you shouldn't have to be tricked into enduring it. Once in a while Sheena is cut in to make dumb Elvira-style comments, and in-between cartoon segments near the end, does typical hard-core porno things with two different guys on the cheap kid show set. The grass rug moves and you can hear the director's voice (not uncommon in today's direct-to-video porn tapes). If you wanted to see a Sheena Horne porno tape, there are plenty to choose from. If you want to see a European sex cartoon, this one is also available in its original form.

SHEENA, QUEEN OF THE JUNGLE
(Moviecraft, 1955–56)

This silly Saturday morning kids' jungle show, based on a comic book, was pretty hot stuff at the time because of sexy star Irish McCalla, a men's magazine model. Sheena's friends are Chim the chimp and Trader Bob. 26 episodes were filmed in Mexico. McCalla was also in *She Demons* (1958) and several other features. She was still appearing at fan conventions in the 90s. Six video tapes are available containing 2 episodes each.

SHELF LIFE
(1992) **D/A:** Paul Bartel **S/A:** O-Lan Jones, Andrea Stein, Jim Turner **P:** Bradley Laven **M:** Andy Paley

A 60s suburban family in Anaheim retreats to their concrete-lined bomb shelter when Kennedy is shot and stay there. The parents die from botulism but their three kids grow up in the shelter. Thirty years later the still sheltered trio have a JFK shrine and keep their parents' skeletons around. The feature, based on a play by the stars, was filmed all on one set designed by Dean Tavoularis.

SHELL SHOCK
(1964) **D/S:** John Hayes **S:** Randy Fields **P/A:** Beech Dickerson

Roger Corman stock company regular Dickerson stars as a sergeant in Italy in a b/w WWII movie. He thinks that Carl Crow is faking shell shock and plots against him. With Pamela Grey and Frank Leo.

SHE MAN
(SW, 1967) **D:** Bob Clark **S/A:** Jeff Gillen

A "doctor" behind a desk who can't seem to get his lines right introduces the first feature by the then 24-year-old Clark. Albert Rose (Leslie Marlow), a wealthy Korean war vet, is blackmailed by Dominita (Dorian Wayne), a blonde with a riding crop. Rose has to become Rosey and be a personal maid for a year ("Yes, Dominita" . . .). So instead of the expected sex-change movie, you get two men in drag (Wayne is more convincing). Dominita has a house full of victims and a bald mute bodyguard. Her assistant (who has a flashback) falls for Rosey and they plot an escape and revenge. The music is all vibes. The executive producer of the b/w Miami Beach movie was David P. Puttnam (*Cottonpickin' Chickenpickers*).

SHE MOB
(SW, 1968) **S:** Diana Paschal **P:** Maurice Levy

This is one of the odder adults-only movies to come from Texas. With outrageous hair, makeup, costumes, heavy regional accents, and women who are not exactly beauty queens, it's very much in John Waters territory. The wealthy Brenda supports her gigolo lover Tony. Big Shim, "the bitchiest dyke in the world," who wears black leather and a very pointy leather bra, lives with four lesbian prison escapees. They tie up Tony and hold him for ransom so Brenda hires Sweetie East (Monique Duvall), a lady detective (patterned after TV spy Honey West) with a pet jaguar. Characters play poker and drink beer, Tony is strung up and whipped while in drag, and Sweetie and Shim have a big fight. For some reason, Marni Castle plays both Brenda and Shim! There is no director credited. The b/w feature is from Sack Amusements.

THE SHERIFF WAS A LADY
(1964) **D:** Sobey Martin **S:** Gustav Kampendonk W. Germany (*Freddy Und Das Lied Der Prairie*)

Freddie Quinn (born Manfred Petz in Vienna) is the singing Black Bill and Mamie Van Doren is the saloon girl who pretends to be the sheriff and helps him avenge the death of his parents. With Rik Battaglia and Beba Loncar. Quinn, the closest thing Germany had to Elvis, was also in the musical *Heimweh Nach St. Pauli* (1963) with Jayne Mansfield.

SHERLOCK HOLMES
(Foothill, 1954) UK (*Adventures of Sherlock Holmes*)

30 half-hour episodes were produced of this early TV series starring Ronald Howard as Holmes and H. Marion Crawford as Dr. Watson. The series was filmed in France and syndicated in America. Howard is a son of the more famous Leslie Howard. 17 volumes with 2 shows each are available.

SHERLOCK HOLMES
(Paramount, MPI, 1985) UK (*Adventures of Sherlock Holmes; The Casebook of Sherlock Holmes*)

These atmospheric, high quality, 50-minute English Granada TV shows were first aired in the U.S. on the PBS *Mystery* program (originally hosted by Vincent Price). Jeremy Brett became the definitive Holmes for many viewers and David Burke (later replaced by Edward Hardwicke) played Watson. Hardwicke is the son of the late Sir Cedric Hardwicke. At least 21 episodes are on tape.

SHERLOCK HOLMES AND THE CRUCIFER OF BLOOD
(Turner, 1991) **D/S/P:** Fraser C. Heston UK (*The Crucifer of Blood*)

Charlton Heston stars as Sherlock Holmes in a TNT cable TV movie based on the stage play of "The Sign of Four." With Richard Johnson as Watson, Susannah Harker, and Edward Fox. Heston's son Fraser also directed *Treasure Island* for TNT.

SHERLOCK HOLMES AND THE INCIDENT AT VICTORIA FALLS
(Vestron, 1991) **D:** Bill Corcoran **S:** Bob Shayne UK

Sherlock Holmes, the Golden Years, was a rival series to the Jeremy Brett Granada series. Christopher Lee seems totally bored as an older Holmes and Patrick Macnee is just wrong as Watson. This one is a mystery involving Thugees and Indians in South Africa. With Jenny Seagrove and Richard Todd. The Zimbabwe locations are nice and historical characters including Teddy Roosevelt show up, but it's pretty slow going. It was shown in 2 parts on TV.

Sherlock Holmes

Before the famous Basil Rathbone Holmes movies (1939–46), which are all easy to find on tape, there were many silent films from various countries based on Sir Arthur Conan Doyle's famous detective. The first sound Holmes feature was *The Return of Sherlock Holmes*, starring Clive Brook, who was also in *Sherlock Holmes* (1932). In England, there was *The Speckled Band* (1931) with Raymond Massey and *The Hound of the Baskervilles* (1931) with Robert Rendel. Back in Hollywood, Reginald Owen starred in *A Study in Scarlet* (1933) and Arthur Wontner starred in the first sound Holmes series, five features (from 1937–39). Many of these rare 30s Holmes features are available on Foothill Video and several are from Sinister Video.

SHERLOCK HOLMES AND THE LEADING LADY

(Vestron, 1990) **D:** Peter Sasdy **S:** Bob Shayne,
H.R.F. Keating **P:** Frank Agrama, Alessandro Tasca   UK

The first feature from *Sherlock Holmes, the Golden Years* stars Christopher Lee and Patrick Macnee with Morgan Fairchild as an opera singer. Actors play Freud, Elliot Ness, and Emperor Franz Joseph. It's set in Vienna but was filmed in Luxumbourg and concerns Bosnian rebels in 1920. Harry Alan Towers was the executive producer of the four-hour mini series. With Engelbert Humperdinck.

SHERLOCK HOLMES AND THE PRINCE OF CRIME

(1990) **D:** Stuart Orme **S:** Charles Edward Pogue
P: Norman Foster   (*Hands of a Murderer*)

Edward Woodward is Holmes and John Hillerman is Watson in a TV movie with Anthony Andrews as Moriarty. Also with Kim Thompson and Peter Jeffrey.

SHE'S BACK

(Vestron, 1988) **D:** Tim Kincaid **S:** Buddy Giovinazzo
P: Cynthia DePaula   (*Dead and Married*)

In her book *Postcards from the Edge,* Carrie Fisher said that she had problems with cocaine, Percodan pills, and LSD. You have to wonder which ones she was on when she starred in this disaster. It was her first featured role in an American movie after *Hollywood Vice Squad.* Kincaid had just directed *Breeders, Robot Holocaust,* and *Mutant Hunt,* so she couldn't have expected much. The scriptwriter had directed (the incredible) *Combat Shock.* Anyway, she's a Queens wife, killed by a gang of over-acting thugs, who returns to haunt her confused, nice-guy husband (Robert Joy). She shows up at all hours (sometimes on the TV) demanding revenge. She nags and whines in her forced accent, talks about being dead, and makes him kill. A comic sewage plant worker helps. With an *It's a Wonderful Life* clip, Sam Coppola, and Bobby DiCicco. Watch the walls of the house set move.

SHE'S DRESSED TO KILL

(USA, 1979) **D:** Gus Trikonis **S:** George
Lefferts **P:** Barry Weitz, Merrill Grant
(*Someone's Killing The World's Greatest Models*)

Eleanor Parker is an alcoholic fashion designer who gives a private showing at her mansion. The screenwriter must have seen Mario Bava's *Blood and Black Lace,* since a mystery psycho kills off the models. With Jessica Walter, Connie Sellecca, Joanna Cassidy, Corinne Calvet, John Rubenstein, Clive Revill, and Peter Horton. An NBC-TV movie.

SHE SHOULDA SAID NO: *See* WILD WEED

SHE WOLF = LEGEND OF THE WOLF WOMAN

SHINE

(Warner, 1977) **D:** Gus Trikonis **S:** Herbert
Smith, Daniel Ansley **P:** Ed Carlin
(*Moonshine County Express*)

Three daughters of a murdered moonshiner continue with his business. John Saxon is top-billed with William Conrad as the main bad guy. With Claudia Jennings, Candice Rialson, Jeff Corey, Dub Taylor, Morgan Woodward, and Maurine McCormick (from *The Brady Bunch*). New World released the PG feature.

THE SHINING BLOOD

(Thrill Entertainment, 1993)
D/S/P/A: Stash Klossowski **S:** Patrick Longo

Machel Penn is a woman on the run in Arizona who teams up with a farm boy and a kung fu–fighting old Polish man (Klossowski). They visit the palace of an Oriental nobleman (also Klossowski) which is run by John Phillip Law. Also with Nina Huang, Lisa Compshaw (featured in a sex scene), and Jonathan Gill. The creator of this oddball low-budget letterboxed vanity video feature is Prince Stanislas Klossowski, a London socialite who was a best friend of Brian Jones and hung out with the Beatles and the Stones. As far as I know, he never acted or directed before this. With topless dancers, bar brawls, gila monsters, and Indian spirits.

SHIP OF THE MONSTERS

(SW, 1960) **D:** Rogelio A. Gonzales
S: Fredo Varela Jr. **P:** Jesus Sotamajor
Mexico (*La Nave de los Monstruos*)

One of the most entertaining Mexican science fiction comedy movies, this is very much like the later American *Invasion of the Star Creatures* (1962). Two very sexy space women with a robot land their spaceship on earth. They encounter bumbling earthlings and unleash lots of hard-to-believe monsters. Lalo Gonzales stars with Lorena Valeques and Ana Bertha Lupe. It's not dubbed into English. Gonzales made the even wilder *Conquest of the Moon* the same year.

SHOCK

(Sinister, 1923) **D:** Lambert Hillyer **S:** Charles Kenyon

A criminal gang sends a cripple (Lon Chaney Sr.) to San Francisco to expose a banker they've been extorting. He falls for the banker's daughter. The Universal release ends with a San Francisco earthquake. Hillyer later made *Dracula's Daughter* and *The Invisible Ray.*

SHOCK CINEMA VOL. I

(Cinema Home, 1990) **D/C:** Bob Haynes
P: Brinke Stevens

Actress Stevens (whose former husband Dave created the *Rocketeer* comics) introduces this hour-long series of interviews with 11 young low-budget filmmakers. It can be hard to tell who's who sometimes, and unless you're fascinated by what these guys have to say, some of them might put you to sleep. Most of them cite Corman, Sam Raimi, and *Fangoria* as influences and encourage would-be directors to just "do it." Director Jeff Burr says, "New Line has utter contempt for the genre," and Fred Olen Ray says, "I'm just a working schmo," mocks some of Corman's claims, and says, "Naked women are the cheapest special effects." With Charles

Band, Scott Spiegel, C. Courtney Joyner, Ernest D. Farino, J. R. Bookwalter, Mark McGhee, and the tape's executive producer David DeCoteau.

SHOCK CINEMA VOL. 2

(Cinema Home, 1991) **D/C:** Bob Haynes
P: Brinke Stevens

More behind-the-scenes people (and some actors) are interviewed, including Forry Ackerman, Robert Quarry, Deanna Lund, Melissa Moore, Gary Graver, Steve Neill, and Ted Newsom. Stevens hosted still more one-hour tapes in the series. *Vol. 3* (Cinema Home, 1991) features bloopers and trailers from direct to video movies, mostly by David DeCoteau. With Linnea Quigley. *Vol. 4* covers the makeup used in the same low-budget movies covered in *Vol. 3.*

SHOCKED: *See* MESMERIZED

SHOCK 'EM DEAD

(Academy, 1990) **D/S:** Mark Freed
S: Andrew Cross **P:** Eric Louzil

We didn't need another heavy metal horror movie, but this one got some attention because Traci Lords is top-billed. As the manager of the band she doesn't have a whole lot to do. Stephan Quadros is the real star, playing an embarrassing nerd guitarist who sells his soul to a black voodoo woman to become Angel, superstar. He obtains instant teased hair, a closet full of leather clothes, a hot tub with live-in groupies/zombies led by Karen Russell, and takes over a Spinal Tap–like band with a junkie singer. Angel and his girls have to kill to survive. During a concert he plays a silly double-neck guitar and makes points by puking on the audience. Troy Donahue shows up as A&R head of Casualty Records and Aldo Ray (in his last role) runs the pizza stand that Angel used to sweat for. The FX (especially a dream sequence) are pretty mediocre. With Suzanne Ager.

SHOCKER

(MCA, 1989) **D/S:** Wes Craven **P:** Marianne
Maddalena, Barin Kumar **M:** William Goldsmith

After Craven's involvement with the *Nightmare on Elm Street* series ended, he tried to develop another supernatural killer who could star in a series. A TV repairman and mass killer named Horace Pinker (Mitch Pileggi) is executed. His spirit lives in TV sets and he can change bodies. In a scene that had the Times Square audience howling with laughter, he possesses a little girl, who drives a bulldozer. Peter Berg (*The Last Seduction*) is the teen hero and Michael Murphy is his cop/father. With Cami Cooper and bits by Heather Langenkamp (as a victim), Theodore Raimi, Timothy Leary (as a TV evangelist), Eugene Chadbourne, John Tesh (the "new age" musician from *Entertainment Tonight*), and Craven himself. They even threw in a *Leave It to Beaver* scene. Despite all this, *Shocker,* which was cut for an R, just doesn't work. The score is on Varèse Sarabande and includes Megadeth's remake of Alice Cooper's "No More Mr. Nice Guy."

SHOCKING AFRICA

(Hurricane, 1982) **D/P:** Angelo and Alfredo Castiglioni **S:** Guglielmo Guariglia Italy (*The Last Savage II; Faces of Pain*)

This ripoff video "borrowed" scenes from *Africa Blood and Guts* and other mondo movies. It features animal mutilation and human circumcision scenes.

SHOCKING ASIA

(Magnum, 1974) **D:** Emerson Fox **P:** Wolfgang Von Schiber   W. Germany/Hong Kong

A very graphic sex-change operation in Singapore is the most memorable part of this mondo movie, a hit on 42nd St. It also concentrates on Japanese sexual obsessions and shows a "sex museum." With midget and female wrestling and cremation in India. Different scenes were added for different markets because of local censorship.

SHOCKING ASIA II

(Magnum, 1974) **D:** Emerson Fox **P:** Wolfgang Von Schiber   W. Germany/Hong Kong

This sequel features real (and faked) footage concentrating on prostitutes and strippers in various countries. Also with a real Thai leper colony and psychic surgery in the Philippines. The narration is partially read by a woman this time.

SHOCKING CANNIBALS

(1974) **D/P:** Alfredo, Angelo Castiglioni **S:** Alberto Moravia   Italy (*Naked Magic*)

No cannibals are in this mondo documentary, but it does show various African tribes, psychosurgery, and animals being killed. Alberto Grimaldi was the executive producer. It played 42nd St. in 1985.

SHOCK! SHOCK! SHOCK!

(Rhino, 1987) **D/S:** Todd Rutt, Arn McConnell

Most horror or sci-fi spoofs are made by people with dollar signs in their eyes who should be selling used cars. This short b/w tape, made in Brooklyn, starts like a splatter movie and shifts to a superhero adventure somewhere along the way (sort of like some of Ray Dennis Steckler's 60s features). Some of you might notice similarities to scenes from Argento's *Deep Red,* and Japanese *Starman* movies. The evil Stigmatons are after the mystic Star of Bartos, and a parent killer (Brian Isaac) escapes from an asylum. There's a trip sequence ("Your mind will be ripped open!"), great death rays from an alien with Ping-Pong ball eyes, lots of flashbacks, nice animated titles, a crudely animated monster, blood, maggots, you name it. The cinematography and music (by Bruce Gordon and the Cyphers) are great, and these guys love the movies they parody and have a unique sense of humor. Alan Rickman (whose acting career later took off in a big way) is Zont-El. It was made with a budget that couldn't buy Spielberg's dinner. The talented director team is from Grand Junction, Colorado.

A SHOCK TO THE SYSTEM

(HBO, 1990) **D:** Jan Egleson **S:** Andrew Klavan **P:** Patrick Egleson

Michael Caine stars as an NYC ad executive who kills his way to the top with "magic" powers. Caine, who also narrates, uses electricity, gravity, etc. in the black comedy. With Elizabeth McGovern, Swoosie Kurtz, Peter Riegert, Will Patton, Jenny Wright, and Samuel L. Jackson. It's based on a novel by Simon Brett.

SHOCK TREATMENT

(CBS/Fox, 1981) **D/S:** Jim Sharman **S/A:** Richard O'Brien **S:** Brian Thompson **P:** John Goldstone

Jessica Harper and Cliff De Young are the singing Janet and Brad, trapped as contestants on the *Marriage Maze* TV show. The PG-rated *Rocky Horror Picture Show* followup was by the same director and includes some of the same cast members (like Richard O'Brien and Charles Gray). The original continued to play midnight shows for many years and was a big deal when finally released on tape, while this was a flop. Rhino released a soundtrack.

THE SHOES OF THE FISHERMAN

(MGM, 1968) **D:** Michael Anderson **S:** John Patrick, James Kennaway **P:** George Englund

Anthony Quinn stars as a Russian archbishop who had been a prisoner in Siberia. He's released and becomes a cardinal, then Pope Kiril I. He tries to prevent a nuclear war and mass starvation in China and gives away the church's wealth to the poor. The unlikely story was based on the novel by Morris L. West. With David Janssen as a reporter, Oskar Werner, Vittorio De Sica, Laurence Olivier, John Gielgud, Leo McKern, Frank Finlay, Burt Kwouk, and Clive Revill. It's 160 minutes long (152 on tape) and was shown in 70mm at some original screenings. By the maker of *Orca*.

SHOOTERS

(AIP, 1990) **D/P:** Peter Yuvall **S:** Jeff Mandel, Michael Bogart Yuvall

It's a war games comedy with Aldo Ray (in one of his last roles) as the commanding officer. Benjamin Schick stars, and his group fights against the Red Vipers and an all-female group.

SHOOTFIGHTER: FIGHT TO THE DEATH

(Columbia, 1992) **D:** Patrick Allen **S:** Larry Feliz Jr., Judd B. Lynn, Peter Shaner **P:** Alan Amiel

Bolo Yeung (usually a villain in Hong Kong movies) stars as Master Shingo, an LA-based martial arts teacher. Two of his students (Billy Zabka and US karate champ Michael Bernardo) are tricked into entering illegal shootfighting death matches in an arena in Tijuana. With Maryam D'Abo and James Pax, Edward Albert, and Martin Kove as bad guys. Available unrated (with gory fight scenes) or R.

SHOOT FIRST

(High Desert, 1974) **D/S/P:** Sergio Corbucci **S:** Mario Amendola, Santiago Moncada Italy/Spain/France (*Il Bianco, Il Giallo, E Il Nero; Shoot First, Ask Questions Later; Samurai; Samurai Kid*)

In Europe, this western with Eli Wallach, Giuliano Gemma, and Tomas Milian had a title that copied *The Good, the Bad and the Ugly.* It was one of several early-70s westerns that added martial arts and was the last western for Wallach.

THE SHOOTING

(Continental, 1965) **D:** Monte Hellman **S:** Carol Eastman **P/A:** Jack Nicholson

Millie Perkins hires bounty hunter Warren Oates for an unspecified job in this "existential" cult western. Nicholson as Spear, a psychotic killer, co-stars with Will Hutchins. The incredible ending made some think it was a reference to the JFK assassination. Roger Corman was a producer but received no credit. Nicholson took *The Shooting* (and *Ride in the Whirlwind,* which was made the same year) to Cannes in 1966. The company that bought them went bankrupt, and *The Shooting* finally opened in Paris in 1969, where it played for a year nonstop. Eastman (who used the name "Adrien Joyce") later wrote the screenplay for *Five Easy Pieces.*

SHOOT IT BLACK, SHOOT IT BLUE

(HBO, 1974) **D/S:** Dennis McGuire

A black student (Eric Laneuville, later a *St. Elsewhere* regular) films a corrupt and racist cop (Michael Moriarty) killing someone, then follows him around filming more of his escapades. The indy feature was made in Kansas City and also stars Paul Sorvino. Levitt Pickman released it when it was 10 years old.

SHOOT LOUD, LOUDER... I DON'T UNDERSTAND

(Nelson, 1966) **D/S:** Eduardo De Filippo **S:** Suso Cecchi D'Amico **P:** Pietro Notarianni **M:** Nino Rota Italy (*Spara Forte, Più Forte, Non Capisco*)

Marcello Mastroianni stars as an artist who doesn't know when he's dreaming. He sees a murder and his poet uncle Nico communicates only with fireworks. Raquel Welch is also in the odd comedy. Joesph E. Levine was executive producer of the Avco Embassy release.

SHOOT THE LIVING, PRAY FOR THE DEAD

(All Seasons, 1970) **D:** "Joseph Warren"/ Giuseppe Vari **S:** Mark Salter   Italy (*Prega Il Morto E Amazza Il Vivo*)

Dean Stratford, Victoria Zuny, and Klaus Kinski star in a revenge western about a gang of bank robbers.

SHOOT TWICE: *See* AND GOD SAID TO CAIN

SHORT CIRCUIT

(Fox, 1986) **D:** John Badham **S:** S.S. Wilson,
Brent Maddock **P:** David Foster, Lawrence Turman

The ultimate weapon becomes a peaceful comic
talking robot called Number 5. Ally Sheedy thinks
it's an alien in the PG-rated *E.T.* copy. Steve Guttenberg and a comic Indian scientist (Fisher Stevens) search for the clunky looking missing robot.

SHORT CIRCUIT 2

(RCA, 1988) **D:** Kenneth Johnson **S:** S. S. Wilson,
Brent Maddock **P:** David Foster, Laurence Turman

Fisher Stevens returns in a sequel with the robot
"Johnny 5" in the big city. Michael McKean and
bad guy Jack Weston go into the toy business and
try and exploit and merchandise the robot. With
Cynthia Gibb. It was filmed in Toronto.

SHORT EYES

(Vestron, 1977) **D:** Robert M.Young **S/A:** Miguel
Pinero **P:** Lewis Harris   (*Slammer*)

The very grim prison story is based on Miguel
Pinero's 1974 play (which was based on real incidents). The slang-filled movie was a 42nd St. hit.
Bruce Davison is a child molester, hated by the
black and Puerto Rican inmates in New York's
"Tombs," where it was actually shot. With Jose
Perez, Nathan George. Singers Curtis Mayfield and
(real ex-con) Freddy Fender play inmates. Both sing
in the movie and are on the Curtom soundtrack.

SHORT FUSE

(Vidmark, 1986) **D/S:** Blaine Novak
P: Doug Dilge, Sean Ferrer   (*Good to Go*)

Art Garfunkel (in his first role since *Bad Timing*)
stars as a journalist framed for rape and murder.
The Washington, DC, go-go music scene is the
backdrop, so watch it for Trouble Funk, Chuck
Brown and the Soul Searchers, and others. With
Robert Doqui and Harris Yulin.

A SHOT IN THE DARK

(MGM, 1964) **D/S/P:** Blake Edwards
S: William Peter Blatty

This is the best of the Pink Panther detective comedies. It's the sequel that introduced the Dreyfuss
(Herbert Lom) and Kato (Burt Kwouk) characters
who returned in the 70s sequels (and rip-offs).
Peter Sellers stars as Inspector Jacques Clouseau
with Elke Sommer. The nudist camp scene was inspired by the many nudist movies playing at the
time. With George Sanders and Tracy Reed.

THE SHOUT

(Vid American, 1978) **D/S:** Jerzy Skolimowski
S: Michael Austin   UK

A mentally disturbed man (Alan Bates) tells a bizarre story to a musician (John Hurt) at an asylum
during a cricket match. In the flashback (or hallucination), he wanders to his house and takes over
his wife (Susannah York). He claims to be able to
kill by shouting. It's based on a story by Robert

Cary-Hiroyuki Tagawa tortures Brandon Lee in *Showdown in Little Tokyo.*

Graves. With Tim Curry and a surprising York
nude scene. The music is by Tony Banks and Mike
Rutherford of Genesis.

SHOUT AT THE DEVIL

(Vestron, 1974) **D:** Peter Hunt
S: Wilbur Smith **P:** Michael Klinger   UK

AIP released a cut version of this WWII action
movie set in Mozambique. Lee Marvin and Roger
Moore star as men who try to blow up a German
battleship. With Barbara Parkins and Ian Holm.

THE SHOW

(Fright, 1927) **D:** Tod Browning **S:** Waldemar Young

For years, this MGM release was considered a lost
feature. The print is jumpy and a little blurry, but it
was exciting to see after only seeing tantalizing
photos in *Famous Monsters* for years. It's almost as
strange as some of Browning's Lon Chaney Sr.
movies and has obvious similarities to *Freaks*. John
Gilbert stars as Cock Robin, a womanizing con
man at the Palace of Illusions sideshow in Budapest. There's a melodramatic murder plot, but the
background, filled with stage illusions and (fake)
freaks, is more important. A living hand takes the
tickets. There's a mermaid, a half woman, and a
Salome show with a talking decapitated head. The
most bizarre element is a poisonous iguana that
leaps into the audience (!) and bites a man. A title
reads: "God, but you're a real dame, right straight
to the core!" Renee Adoree costars with Lionel
Barrymore as "the Greek." It's based on the 1910
novel *The Day of the Souls* by Charles Tenny Jackson. Adoree died in 1933 from TB, and Gilbert
died only three years later.

SHOWDOWN: *See* THE TRAMPLERS

SHOWDOWN

(AIP, 1991) **D/S/P/A:** Leo Fong

Parts of the print are faded and the camera goes out
of focus once, but this homegrown kung fu movie
is a riot. Richard Lynch is the "Commander" of a
small town, owned by seemingly helpless retired

opera-fan mobsters (!?). He calls on
his martial arts instructor/special
agent/Nam vet friend (Fong) to battle invading bikers (played by real
long-haired bikers) led by a big ugly
blond psycho (Werner Hoetzinger).
This movie has loud kung fu sound
FX, female martial arts fighters,
sex, totally out-of-place strippers, a
good hard rock soundtrack (by Riot
House) and bazooka battles. With
Michelle McCormick (*Fatal Pulse*)
and Troy Donahue (also in the Fong
movie *Low Blow*) in one scene.
Made in Nevada.

SHOWDOWN

(Imperial, 1993) **D:** Robert Radler
S: Stuart Gibbs **P:** Ash R. Shaw

Ken Scott is a school kid who is
trained by the martial arts janitor (!)
(Billy Blanks) so he can fight off a bully (Ken Mc-
Cleod). With Christine Taylor, Patrick Kilpatrick,
Nick Hill, and Brion James as the principal. R or
PG-13 versions of the action feature by the direc-
tor of the *Best of the Best* movies are available.

SHOWDOWN IN LITTLE TOKYO

(Warner, 1991) **D/P:** Mark L. Lester **S:** Stephen
Glantz, Caliope Brattlestreet **P:** Martin E. Caan

Dolph Lundgren and Brandon Lee star as cop partners after Yakuza in LA. Dolph's character was
raised in Japan, speaks Japanese, and is very serious. Lee is very American. Tia Carrere (from
Wayne's World) is a singer in a gangster nightclub.
She has sex with Dolph (but used a body double).
It's a violent action-packed movie with some scenes
designed to drive an audience wild. Too bad nobody saw it in theaters. Dolph jumps over cars and
beats up five guys at once. It all ends with a sword
fight during a street parade. The main bad guy
(Cary-Hiroyuki Tagawa) starts having sex with a
topless blonde while she smokes ice and he decapitates her. A biker's hand is cut off. Dolph wears
tiny shorts a lot and Lee at one point says, "You
have the biggest dick I've ever seen on a man" (!?).
With Simon Rhee.

SHRECK

(Tempe, 1990) **D/A:** Don Adams, James Picardi

Horror fan teens resurrect a Nazi killer (in a gas
mask) during a séance. It was shot on video by 26-
year-old directors from Wisconsin, who also made
the horror anthology *Red Eyes*.

SHREDDER ORPHEUS

(AIP, 1990) **D/S/A:** Robert McGinley **P:** Lisanne Dutton

A futuristic skateboard hero named Orpheus
(McGinley) goes to hell with some friends to stop
TV signals that are brainwashing America and killing viewers. Don't expect Cocteau, but this is a
clever and unique feature made in Seattle over four
years' time. With Megan Murphy, Jesse Bernstein,
Gian-Carlo Scandiuzzi, and Linda Severt. The rock
music is by Roland Barker and the Shredders.

A SHRIEK IN THE NIGHT

(Video Yesteryear, Sinister, 1933) **D:** Albert Ray **S:** Francis Hyland **P:** M. H. Hoffman

Ginger Rogers and Lyle Talbot star as rival reporters. She takes an undercover job for a rich man in a skyline penthouse and a mystery killer uses poison gas to eliminate cast members. The 66-minute feature includes comedy about stealing news stories. The stars had already been teamed in *The Thirteenth Guest* (1932).

THE SHRIEKING = HEX

SHRUNKEN HEADS

(Paramount, 1994) **D:** Richard Elfman **S:** Matthew Bright **P:** Charles Band

It was announced as "Full Moon's first theatrical release." It's by the director of *Forbidden Zone* and the writer of *Guncrazy* (the Drew Barrymore one). I guess uniquely awful is the best description. Three kids on a vacant cliché–New York street set are killed by young hoodlums and are brought back as floating, spinning, glowing zombie-like heads by a former Haitian Ton Ton Macoute cop (Julius Harris). A scene with video store owners perishing in a bus crash is inspired, but the rest is nearly unwatchable. Aeryck Egan stars as Tommy, with Becky Herbst as the cute girl who falls for him, and Meg Foster as a dyke gangster with a bimbo girlfriend. With music by Richard Band and a theme by Danny Elfman.

SH! THE OCTOPUS

(1937) **D:** William H. McGann **S:** George Brickner **P:** Bryan Foy

Two bumbling detectives (Allen Jenkins and Hugh Herbert) investigate a deserted lighthouse. A master criminal who lives there is after a death ray and has a giant mechanical octopus. The odd Warner comedy mystery (with the great name) was based on a play. With Marcia Ralston.

THE SIBLING: *See* PSYCHO SISTERS

SID AND NANCY

(Nelson, 1986) **D/S:** Alex Cox **S:** Abbe Wool **P:** Eric Fellner

It opens with the body of Sex Pistols bassist Sid Vicious and flashbacks show his brief life as a "star" in London and New York. Gary Oldman stars and Chloe Webb is Nancy Spungen, the Long Island girlfriend he was accused of murdering in a drug haze. This is the best "punk rock" movie, and it has the best Thanksgiving dinner scene since *Eraserhead*. Actors play Malcolm McLaren (David Hayman) and Johnny Rotten (Drew Schofield) and the other members of the Pistols. Parts were shot at Manhattan's famous Chelsea Hotel. With Sy Richardson, Fox Harris, Sandy Barron, Iggy Pop, and future rock star Courtney Love as a groupie. The MCA soundtrack features the Pogues and Joe Strummer.

SIDEKICKS

(Columbia, 1993) **D:** Aaron Norris **S:** Don Thompson, Lou Illar **P:** Don Carmody **M:** Alan Silvestri

Jonathan Brandis (*The NeverEnding Story II*) stars as an asthmatic Texas kid tormented by bullies who has fantasies about Chuck Norris movies. His father (Beau Bridges) is a useless computer programmer, so he takes martial arts lessons from Mako. In the fantasy sequences (with Norris as himself), the kid takes on dozens of ninjas with ease. With Julia Nickson-Soul as a teacher, Joe Piscopo as a karate instructor, Danica McKellar, Richard Moll, and scenes from earlier Norris movies (*Lone Wolf McQuaid*, *The Hitman*, *Missing in Action*). The PG-rated Triumph release was shot in Houston and financed by Jim "Mattress Mack" McIngvale, known for his local TV commercials.

THE SIEGE OF FIREBASE GLORIA

(Fries, 1989) **D:** Brian Trenchard-Smith **S:** William Nagle, Tony Johnston **P:** Howard Grigsby, Rudolpho S. M. Confessor   Australia

Viet Cong slaughter Americans during the 1968 Christmas ceasefire. Wings Hauser stars as a sadistic Marine during the Tet offensive. With R. Lee Ermey (just after *Full Metal Jacket*) and Albert Popwell. Filmed in the Philippines.

SIEGE OF SYRACUSE

(VSOM, 1960) **D/S:** Pietro Francisci **S:** Giorgio Graziosi **P:** Enzo Merolle   France/Italy (*L'assedio di Siracusa*)

Rossano Brazzi creates a giant reflecting glass that burns up the enemy ships at the end of this historical drama. Tina Louise, as Diana, loses her memory after being attacked by Roman soldiers. With Sylva Koscina.

SIEGFRIED

(Kino, 1923) **D:** Fritz Lang **S:** Thea Von Harbou **P:** Erich Pommer   Germany (*Siegfrieds Tod, Kriemhilds Rasche*)

After the popular 2-part *Dr. Mabuse*, Lang made *Die Nibelungen*, a 2-part fantasy epic. It was the biggest German film at the time and has been copied in many ways over the years (*Flash Gordon* serials, *Star Wars* . . .). The huge sets and costumes are incredible and the (mechanical) dragon was pretty advanced for the time. Siegfried uses an invisibility cloak, meets a troll king, and becomes invincible by slaying the dragon and bathing in its blood. Paul Richter stars as Siegfried. Margarete Schon is Kriemhild (star of the second part) and Rudolf Klein-Rogge is King of the Huns. The first sound on film score by Hugo Rioesenfeld was prepared for the New York debut in 1925. Both parts are available remastered on tape. The Kino tapes run the longest (186 minutes total) and have an organ score. *Siegfried* is tinted. Lang's next project was *Metropolis*. A 2-part W. German *Siegfried* remake appeared in 1966.

SIESTA

(Lorimar, 1987) **D:** Mary Lambert **S:** Patricia Louisianna Knop **P:** Gary Kurfirst   US/UK

Ellen Barkin is a daredevil skydiver who awakes with partial amnesia in Spain. The arty feature uses flashbacks and time jumps and borrows some ideas from *Carnival of Souls*. Gabriel Byrne (who married Barkin in real life) costars as her trapeze-artist lover. With Julian Sands, Isabella Rossellini, Martin Sheen, Grace Jones (with a rat on her shoulder), and Jodie Foster. Barkin has a nude scene and the original rating was X. Miles Davis provided the score. It was filmed in Spain by the director of some Madonna videos and the *Pet Sematary* movies. Zalman King was executive producer.

THE SIGN OF FOUR

(Paramount, 1983) **D:** Desmond Davis **S:** Charles Pogue **P:** Otto Plaschkes   UK

Ian Richardson and David Healy star as Sherlock Holmes and Watson in a TV movie. An ex-con wants revenge on an Army major who took a treasure and left him in a penal colony. With Cherie Lunghi, Joe Melia, John Pedrick as a cannibal dwarf, and Thorley Walters. Richardson returned as Holmes in *The Hound of the Baskervilles* the same year. Only two of a planned series were produced.

SIGN OF THE CROSS

(MCA, 1932) **D/P:** Cecil B. DeMille **S:** Waldemar Young, Sidney Buchman

It's another of those throw-the-Christians-to-the-lions epics, but DeMille, one of Hollywood's great showmen, added a gorilla, dwarves, and scenes of torture and horror. Fredric March stars as Marcus with Claudette Colbert as the evil Poppaea, who bathes in milk. An outrageous Charles Laughton is her emperor husband Nero. With Elissa Landi, Ian Keith, William V. Mong, Joe Bonomo, Charles Middleton, and John Carradine. It was a remake of a 1914 feature. Paramount reissued it in 1944 with a new WWII-themed prologue but minus nearly 20 minutes (!) of the best sex and violence. It was restored at UCLA in 1990. You have to see the original 124-minute version for the full impact.

SIGN OF THE GLADIATOR

(SW, 1959) **D:** Vittorio Musy Glori **S:** G. Mangione, Sergio Leone **P:** Guido Brigone   France/Italy/Yugoslavia (*The Sign of Rome*)

AIP released this to cash in on the then-current Hercules craze. There is no gladiator in the plot but there sure was in the posters. Romans are the heroes in the African desert. Anita Ekberg stars as Queen Zenoba, and the beautiful Cuban-born Chelo Alonso is the virgin Bathsheba. Georges Marchal is the hero. Riccardo Freda directed the battle scenes. Available prints (in color and Royal-score) are blurry.

SILENCE OF THE HAMS

(Cabin Fever, 1993) **D/S/P/A:** Ezio Greggio **P:** Julie Corman

Despite the title, this is a very silly but sometimes funny take-off of *Psycho*, complete with Martin Balsam (reprising his detective role), and with Dom DeLuise added as the Hannibal Lecter character. Italian comic Ezio Greggio is the Norman

Bates character, who narrates after his death. Shelley Winters is his mother and Joanna Pacula and Charlene Tilton are the sisters. Billy Zane has more screen time as an FBI agent, but you'll want to see it for the guest stars including Larry Storch and Stuart Pankin (FBI agents), Phyllis Diller and Bubba Smith (real estate workers), John Astin, Rip Taylor, Eddie Deezen, Erwin Keyes plus Mel Brooks, John Landis, Joe Dante, John Carpenter, and I think some I missed. Also with Cleveland jokes, George Bush and Hillary Clinton lookalikes, and a black dwarf.

THE SILENCE OF THE LAMBS

(Orion, 1991) **D:** Jonathan Demme **S:** Ted Tally
P: Edward Saxon, Kenneth Utt, Ron Bozman

This horror movie became the *Psycho* of the early 90s. It received lots of attention, money, and Oscars for best movie, director, and both stars (there were seven nominations). The fact that a movie where the main character is an intelligent cannibal who skins people achieved so much set the stage for more major-release serial killer and psycho killer features. *Lambs* is based on Thomas Harris's bestseller (and was partially based on the real-life killer Gary Heidnik). Jodie Foster stars as Clarice Starling, the FBI trainee, with Anthony Hopkins as Dr. Hannibal Lecter, locked in a very old maximum-security prison. With Scott Glenn as an FBI man and Ted Levine as serial killer "Buffalo Bill." Also with Charles Napier as the cop who gets gutted and hung up in a cage, Diane Baker (in her first theatrical feature in ten years) as the senator mother of kidnapped girl Tracey Walter, Chris Isaak, and Roger Corman. Although most of the horrible deeds aren't shown, there's a mangled dead body worthy of a *Fangoria* spread and graphic police photos. The 118-minute-long hit was filmed in Pittsburgh (note George Romero appearance). The Howard Shore soundtrack is on MCA. This was once set to be directed by Gene Hackman! Lecter was also a character in *Manhunter*. The widescreen Criterion laserdisc has seven extra scenes, commentary by Demme, Hopkins, Foster, actual FBI agents, and Pauline Kael, plus production stills and storyboards.

THE SILENCER

(Academy, 1992) **D/S:** Amy Goldstein
S: Scott Kraft **P:** Brian J. Smith

Lynette Walden stars as Angel, a female assassin who seduces men in a boring Crown International production set in L.A. She usually wears all black and shows off her silicone work in a sex-in-the-tub scene. In a safe-sex scene she says, "No glove, no love." Chris Mulkey (from *Twin Peaks*) watches it all on a video screen and provides the sleep-inducing voiceover narration. With Paul Ganus and Morton Downey Jr.

SILENT ASSASSINS

(Forum, 1987) **D:** Lee Doo-Yong, Scott Thomas
S: Will Gates, Ada Lin **P/A:** Jun Chong, Phillip Rhee

Sam Jones is an LA cop fighting against a former CIA man turned criminal. Linda Blair is his girlfriend. The villain kidnaps a research scientist to get a biological warfare formula. There's a gang

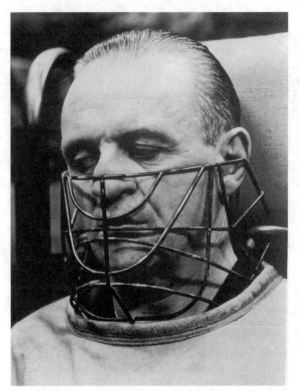

Hannibal Lecter (Anthony Hopkins) in *The Silence of the Lambs*.

fight with axes. With fighting producers Chong and Rhee, Mako, Rebecca Ferratti, Gustav Vintas, Bill Irwin, Bill "Superfoot" Wallace, Simon Rhee, and Karen Witter.

SILENT HUNTER

(New Line, 1994) **D/A:** Fred Williamson
S: Errol Dasilva, Bud Fleisher, Richard Loncar **P:** Claudio Castravelli

Miles O'Keeffe stars as a burned-out Miami Beach cop who battles the gang of armed killers who murdered his family high in the snowy mountains with a crossbow. The psycho brothers (Peter Colvey and Jason Cavalier) have a lesbian sister (Lynne Adams). Williamson (not the star of his own movie for a change) is the sheriff.

SILENT MADNESS

(Media, 1983) **D/P:** Simon Nuchtern
S/P: William P. Milling **S:** Robert Zimmerman (!)

A psycho (Solly Marx) is accidentally released to kill again at a small-town sorority house. Belinda Montgomery stars as a New York City psychiatrist who poses as a sorority girl in this 3-D release. With Viveca Lindfors, Sydney Lassick as the sheriff, and Elizabeth Kaitan. People in the audience laughed when a cartoony hatchet was thrown at the camera. It had the same cinematographer as the 3-D *Friday the 13th Part 3*.

SILENT NIGHT, DEADLY NIGHT

(IVE, 1984) **D:** Charles Sellier Jr. **S:** Michael Hickey **P:** Ira Richard Barmak   (*Slayride*)

This movie received a lot of publicity when released just before Christmas by Tristar. Some citizens pro-

tested (especially in Chicago) and Siskel and Ebert read the credits on TV, saying shame, shame on the filmmakers. It was pulled from release then dropped and picked up by an indy distributor. It wasn't the first, best, or last movie with a killer Santa. It's just the best known. Billy, a young psycho whose parents were beaten and killed by a man (Charles Dierkop) dressed as Santa, is mistreated at an orphanage. He (Robert Brian Wilson) grows up and at 18, plays Santa at a department store. He goes on a Christmas killing spree with an ax, bow and arrow, and even Christmas lights. With Tara Buckman, Toni Nero, and Linnea Quigley, who is impaled by moose antlers while topless.

SILENT NIGHT, DEADLY NIGHT PART II

(IVE, 1987) **D/S/E:** Lee Harry **S:** Joseph H. Earle **P:** Lawrence Applebaum

Watch this for a lesson in exploitation. Because enough people remembered the name of the original, this "sequel" got away with re-using 40 (!) minutes from the first feature. This time Billy's brother Ricky (muscular Eric Freeman) is in an orphanage remembering what happened. He loses it when he sees red and emerges to kill. He impales a mobster with an umbrella (which he then opens) and decapitates a nun. In one scene Ricky goes to a movie with Elizabeth Kaitan and more footage from *Silent Night* is shown! This pathetic movie includes Dierkop, Quigley, Buckman, and Nero (all in repeat footage).

SILENT NIGHT, DEADLY NIGHT III: BETTER WATCH OUT!

(IVE, 1989) **D:** Monte Hellman
S: Carlos Laslo **P:** Arthur H. Gorshon

Ricky (from part II) is grown up and in a coma. He escapes on Christmas Eve, kills an asshole playing Santa, and successfully hitchikes even though he's in a hospital gown and his brain is exposed (!). Ricky (played by Bill Moseley from *Chainsaw II*) then terrorizes a blind psychic (Samantha Scully) at a remote house, as an angry cop (Robert Culp) and a wacky doctor (Richard Beymer) try to find him. With Eric Da Re, Laura Herring, and Charles Dierkop (seen in flashbacks). This was the first American film directed by Monte Hellman since *Cockfighter* (1974). It's full of plot holes, but is pretty interesting and has some strange dialogue. It also includes a direct *Carnival of Souls* "tribute," two *Twin Peaks* stars, a scene from the first *Silent Night*, and several scenes of Boris Karloff and Jack Nicholson in *The Terror* (which Hellman co-directed).

SILENT NIGHT, DEADLY NIGHT IV: INITIATION

(IVE, 1990) **D:** Brian Yuzna
S: Woody Keith **P:** Richard N. Gladstein

Instead of bringing back Ricky again, this is a "sequel" in name only. It has enough sex, violence, and weird special effects to keep things interesting, though. The plot borrows from *Rosemary's Baby* and *Invasion of the Bee Girls* (1973). A bookstore owner named Fema (Maud Adams) leads a group of occult women and chooses an LA newspaper writer (Neith Hunter) to give birth to some kind of creature. Clint Howard (as a very strange guy named Ricky) eats bugs and does evil things for Fema. Lots of cockroaches of all sizes were created by Screaming Mad George. With Reggie Bannister from the *Phantasm* films, Jeanne Bates (star of *Mom*), and Allyce Beasley. The 2nd-unit director and special effects co-ordinator was Tom Rainone and there are several shots of an issue of *Psychotronic* magazine!

SILENT NIGHT, DEADLY NIGHT V: THE TOYMAKER

(IVE, 1991) **D/S:** Martin Kitrosser
S/P: Brian Yuzna **P:** Richard N. Gladstein

Several cast members return from *IV*, but this is no sequel. A sad-looking Mickey Rooney stars as "Joe Petto," the modern-day toymaker and shop owner. He makes a spaced-out-looking android robot named Pino (Brian Bremer) become his substitute son. Characters are killed in various ways and a bad android turns out to be responsible. In one scene, toys attack a couple in bed. With Jane Higginson and Neith Hunter. With more (but not better) Screaming Mad George FX. The 2nd unit director and special effects coordinator was Tom Rainone.

SILENT PARTNER

(1978) **D:** Daryl Duke **S:** Curtis Hanson
P: Joel B. Michaels   Canada

Christopher Plummer is a psychotic bank robber and Elliott Gould is a meek bank teller who knows too much. The very good violent movie has some gruesome murders. Plummer first appears as a maniac Santa. With Susannah York and John Candy. Hanson's next filmed script was *White Dog*.

SILENT RAGE

(Columbia, 1982) **D:** Michael Miller
S: Joseph Fraley **P:** Anthony B. Unger

Chuck Norris is a karate expert Texas sheriff after an indestructible killer zombie, the results of a genetic breeding and a secret formula. It has more sex and violence than a typical Norris movie. With Toni Kalem, Ron Silver, Stephen Furst (as the comic deputy) and William Finley as a research scientist. Aaron Norris was associate producer of the Columbia picture.

SILENT SCREAM

(Thriller, 1980) **D:** Alan Gibson **S:** Francis Essex   UK

Peter Cushing is a pet shop owner (and former Nazi) who conducts behavior-control experiments on his animals. A prison parolee and his wife become his new subjects. Elvira also appears during

a break and at the end to tell you how bad she thinks it is. With Brian Cox. A one-hour Hammer TV presentation.

SILENT TONGUE

(Vidmark, 1992) **D/S:** Sam Shepard
P: Carolyn Pfeiffer, Ludi Boeken

An Irish man (Alan Bates) who runs a traveling Indian medicine show in the old West sells one of his half-Indian daughters to Richard Harris. She's given to Harris' son (River Phoenix, in his last completed role). She (Sheila Tousey) dies but returns as a ghost. Phoenix goes mad and Harris kidnaps the other man's daughter. Bates and his son (Dermot Mulroney) go after her. The French-produced feature was shot in New Mexico.

SILHOUETTE

(MCA, 1990) **D:** Carl Schenkel **S:** Jay Wolf,
Victor Buell **P:** Chris Chesser, Alan Beattie

Faye Dunaway is an architect who witnesses a murder from her window at a New Mexico hotel. She has to stay in town as a witness in a mystery with Hitchcock movie references. With David Rasche, Talisa Soto, and Nancy Parsons. Dunaway was also an executive producer.

SILK

(MGM/UA, 1986) **D/P:** Cirio H. Santiago
S/A: Fred Bailey

Cec Verrell stars as the eponymous Honolulu cop whose parents were killed on a case in this Concorde release that was shot in Hawaii. It's very much like Santiago's earlier *TNT Jackson* or *Firecracker* movies.

SILK 2

(MGM/UA, 1989) **D:** Cirio H. Santiago
S: Robert King **P:** Christopher R. Santiago

Monique Gabrielle (from the pages of *Penthouse*) takes over the role of brunette Honolulu cop Silk in a plot about missing Japanese scrolls. She has a topless martial arts fight (just like in Santiago's

TNT Jackson). With Jan Merlin as the leader of an art forgery scam, Ken Metcalf, and Peter Nelson. It was shot in the Philippines. From Concorde.

SILK DEGREES

(Imperial, 1994) **D:** Armand Garabidian **S:** Stuart Gibbs, Douglas J. Sloan **P:** Alan B. Burnsteen

Federal agents Marc Singer and Mark Hamill try to protect a sexy TV star (Deborah Shelton) who has witnessed a murder. They go to a remote country lodge run by Adrienne Barbeau. It's pretty boring and features tame R sex, a catfight, and a few ridiculous plot twists. With blonde Katherine Armstrong, Michael Des Barres as a terrorist killer who has a sex/murder scene with big-breasted India Allen, Charles Napier as a cop, and Gilbert Gottfried in a one-scene bit as a director. This movie's director went to UCLA.

SILVER BULLET

(Paramount, 1985) **D:** Dan Attias **S:** Stephen King
P: Martha Schumacher **M:** Jay Chattaway
(*Stephen King's Silver Bullet*)

At first, only a small town kid in a motorized wheelchair (Corey Haim) knows that there's a werewolf in town. Later on, his sister (Megan Follows, who narrates) and their often drunk uncle (Gary Busey) help track the reverend/werewolf (Everett McGill), who is being hunted by vigilantes. With Terry O'Quinn as the sheriff and Lawrence Tierney as the local bartender. It's based on the novelette "Cycle of the Werewolf" and was made in North Carolina. Dino De Laurentiis backed it and Carlo Rambaldi created the monster. The soundtrack is on Varèse Sarabande.

THE SILVER CHALICE

(Warner, 1954) **D/P:** Victor Saville **S:** Lesser Samuels

A Greek silversmith named Basil (Paul Newman) makes the chalice for the last supper. Newman, who was making his screen debut, took out an ad apologizing for being in this movie. What more reason do you need to want to see it? With Virginia Mayo, Pier Angeli, Jack Palance, Joseph Wiseman, Michael Pate, Natalie Wood, E. G. Marshall, Robert Middleton, Ian Wolfe, Albert Dekker, and Lorne Greene, in his screen debut. The Warner release is in scope and color and runs 144 minutes (the tape is 135).

Silents

No longer only names in film-history books, many silent features are now available on tape. Watching silent movies is an acquired habit, but I suggest trying some classics. Many are reviewed in this volume. If you don't like the rinky piano or melodramatic organ soundtracks some of them use, just turn it off. So many early films have been lost forever that it's exciting to be able to see rediscovered features. Of the 14 top money makers of the silent era, two were biblical epics (*Ben-Hur* (1926) and *The Ten Commandments* (1923)), one was a fantasy (1924's *Thief of Bagdad*), and one was a documentary (*Paul J. Rainey's African Hunt*). D. W. Griffith's *The Birth of a Nation* (1915) was the highest-grossing feature of the era ($10 million in domestic grosses).

SILVER NEEDLE IN THE SKY: *See* ROCKY JONES

SIMON

(Orion, 1980) **D/S:** Marshall Brickman
P: Martin Bregman

A group of college geniuses convince a professor (Alan Arkin) that he's an alien, and he becomes a TV messiah. The satire features Austin Pendleton, William Finley, Wallace Shawn, Fred Gwynne, and Madeline Kahn.

SIMON OF THE DESERT

(Hens Tooth, 1965) **D/S:** Luis Buñuel **P:** Gustavo Alatriste   Mexico (*Simón del Desierto*)

Simon/Christ (Claudio Brook) communes with God on top of a tall pillar. He restores the severed hands of a thief and talks with a dwarf shepherd who has sex with goats. Simon is tempted by the Devil (Silvia Pinal) who appears in different forms. In the brilliant ending, Simon ends up dancing the "Radioactive Flesh" in a New York disco while a very cool rock band plays. The (subtitled) b/w feature is only 42 minutes long and was the director's last feature in Mexico. Buñuel made *Belle de Jour* (1966) in France next and became one of the world's most honored directors.

SIMPLE JUSTICE

(1989) **D:** Deborah Del Prete
S: T. Jay O'Brien **P:** Gigi Pritzker

A multiracial group of robbers kill a newlywed woman during a robbery. They're arrested, released, and go after her husband and grandparents (Cesar Romero and Doris Roberts). It was made in Pittsburgh.

SINBAD OF THE SEVEN SEAS

(Warner, 1986) **D/S:** Enzo Castellari, Luigi Cozzi **S:** Tito Cari **P:** John Thompson   Italy

Lou Ferrigno stars as a curly-haired Sinbad who has to find five magic gems. He fights Amazon women, ghost warriors, and eventually his own double. With Teagan Clive and John Steiner as an evil wizard. Daria Nicolodi tells the whole silly tale to her daughter. The story is said to be based on Poe. It was made by Cannon for TV, shelved, then reworked by Cozzi in 1989 with added FX scenes.

SINBAD THE SAILOR

(Turner, 1947) **D:** Richard Wallace
S: John Twist **P:** Stephen Ames

Douglas Fairbanks Jr. stars in a comic Technicolor adventure movie with Maureen O'Hara. It's all told in flashback by Sinbad. Anthony Quinn is the evil Emir. With Walter Slezak, Jane Greer, Sheldon Leonard, Alan Napier, Mike Mazurki, and Glenn Strange. From RKO.

SINDERELLA AND THE GOLDEN BRA

(SW, 1965) **D:** Loel Minardi
S: Frank Squires **P:** Paul Mart

This (faded) color nudie musical (!) version of the old story substitutes a bra for the slipper. Suzanne

Sybele stars and sings with a French accent. Sidney Lassick (later a well-known character actor) is the drunken fairy godfather who sings, dances, cries, and appears in drag. With puppets, dream sequences, and topless dancers. Pretty bad.

THE SINFUL DWARF

(SW, 1973) **D:** Vidal Raski **S:** William Mayo
P: Nicolas Poole   Denmark/US (*Dvaergen*)

This resembles *The Gruesome Twosome* (1968) or a John Waters movie without the humor. A leering, laughing, ugly, childish, piano-playing dwarf with a thick accent named Olaf (Torben) lures young women for his alcoholic, scarfaced, dancer mother Lila Lash's creepy former-nightclub boarding house. Naked women are kept drugged with heroin in a secret room where men come and pay for (pretty graphic) sex with them. Drugs smuggled in toys, rape, bondage, whipping, and voyeurism are offset slightly by Lila doing her Carmen Miranda routine and the Olaf dummy thrown off a roof. The adults-only feature was released by Box Office International.

SINGLES

(Warner, 1992) **D/S/P/A:** Cameron Crowe
P: Richard Hashimoto

It's the lives of young people in a Seattle apartment building as told by one of them (Kyra Sedgwick). The PG-13 teen movie is by the author of *Fast Times at Ridgemont High,* but it comes off more like a modern version of *Love, American Style.* It's hard to believe a movie about Seattle rock bands where drugs are never even mentioned. Bridget Fonda stars with Campbell Scott (son of George C.), Sheila Kelley, long-haired Matt Dillon (who sings with a band called Citizen Dick, played by members of not-yet-famous Pearl Jam), and Bill Pullman. Actors in bit parts include Tom Skerritt as the mayor, Eric Stoltz as a mime, James Le Gros, Tim Burton, Gus Van Sant, and many locals. *Singles* benefited by the then-newsworthy Seattle rock scene and has an Epic soundtrack by Paul Westerberg (Replacements) with cuts by Pearl Jam, Mudhoney, Alice in Chains, Screaming Trees, and others. The tape has additional scenes.

SINGLE WHITE FEMALE

(Columbia, 1992) **D/P:** Barbet
Schroeder **S:** Don Roos

Red-haired Bridget Fonda advertises for a roommate for her large Upper West Side rent-controlled NYC apartment (in the old Ansonia building). Jennifer Jason Leigh moves in, befriends her, imitates her hair and clothes, and later snaps and starts killing off her friends. There's death by high heels and a catfight in an elevator. The two stars and the director are all more talented than the plot might suggest, and this is one of the best of the many early-90s big-budget psycho movies. With Steven Weber, Stephen Tobolowsky, Peter Friedman, Kenneth Tobey,

Rene Estevez, and Gloria Grahame (seen on TV). It's based on a novel by John Lutz. The Columbia release was Schroeder's third American feature (after *Barfly* and *Reversal of Fortune*).

SIN IN THE SUBURBS

(SW, 1964) **D/S:** Joe Sarno **P:** Burton Bradley

Some bored suburbanites organize a swinging club where members wear exotic masks. The b/w adult movie plays like a serious soap opera with lots of close-ups of faces and some nudity. The jazzy music is similar to the original *Little Shop of Horrors* score. Husbands are seen commuting to work and everybody does the twist. Audrey Campbell (from the *Olga* series) stars with Alice Linville (from *Olga's Massage Parlor*) as her daughter. Future *Ilsa* series star Dyanne Thorne is also in the cast. It was based on an article Sarno wrote for *Coronet* magazine. Something Weird offers a dozen of Sarno's many 60s nudie movies.

SINISTER INVASION : *See* ALIEN TERROR

SINNER'S BLOOD

(Saturn, 1970) **D:** Neil Douglas **S:** Lee Stone

In this low-budget obscurity, two sisters whose parents have died move in with their white trash uncle who has a voyeur son and a lesbian daughter. One of the girls has an affair with a local biker, but when she catches him having sex with someone else, she spikes his drink with LSD, which leads to death and a revenge plot.

SINNERS IN PARADISE

(Sinister, 1938) **D:** James Whale **S:** Lester Cole,
Harold Buckly **P:** Ken Goldsmith   (*Secrets of a Sinner*)

Survivors of a plane crash are stranded on a jungle island where a mysterious man (John Boles) lives. With Bruce Cabot, Dwight Frye, Madge Evans, and Gene Lockhart. Boles and Frye had both been in the director's *Frankenstein*. From Universal.

SINS OF DESIRE

(Columbia, 1992) **D:** Jim Wynorski
S: Mark Thomas McGhee **P:** Linda Borgeson

Bridget Fonda and Jennifer Jason Leigh in *Single White Female.*

Tanya Roberts, in another "erotic thriller," tries to find out who killed her sister by going undercover at a sex therapy clinic. Nick Cassavettes is an insurance investigator and Delia Sheppard and Jay Richardson run the clinic. Also with Jan-Michael Vincent, Roberta Vasquez, Becky LeBeau, Monique Parent, Gayle Robyn Harris, and a nightmare sequence. Tanya and Delia have a lesbian scene. R or unrated tapes are available.

THE SINS OF DORIAN GRAY

(Playhouse, 1983) **D:** Tony Maylam **S:** Ken Auhust, Peter Lawrence **P:** Jules Bass

Belinda Bauer is Dorian Gray, an ageless New York model working with an evil fashion world starmaker (Anthony Perkins). She only ages in her Hollywood screen-test footage. It was made for theaters but debuted on ABC-TV. Also with Joseph Bottoms and Michael Ironside. Producer Bass usually made cartoons, and coproduced the Christmas kiddie classics *Frosty the Snowman* and *Rudolph, the Red-nosed Reindeer*.

SINS OF JEZEBEL

(1953) **D:** Reginald LeBorg **S:** Richard Landau **P:** Sigmund Neufeld

Paulette Goddard is Jezebel and George Nader is her man. The low-budget color costume drama features John Hoyt as the prophet Elijah (who creates a rainstorm), Eduard Franz, and Joe Besser! From Lippert, the studio that LeBorg made *Bad Blonde* for the same year.

SINS OF ROME

(Sinister, 1954) **D:** Riccardo Freda **S:** Mari Bori, Jean Ferry   Italy (*Spartaco*)

Massimo Girotti and ballet star Ludmilla Tcherina star in an epic version of the Spartacus story, made six years before Kubrick's version. With Gianna Maria Canale. From RKO. Freda soon started the Italian horror movie business with his *Devil's Commandment* (1956).

SINS OF THE FLESHAPOIDS

(1965) **D/P/C/M:** Mike Kuchar

This 16mm 50-minute color underground parody was inspired by *Creation of the Humanoids*. Bob Cowan stars as Mister Robot with Donna Kernes as the "voluptuous Princess" and George Kuchar as the evil Prince. It was filmed in the Bronx, with sets by director Kuchar.

SINS OF THE NIGHT

(Academy, 1992) **D:** "Gregory Hippolyte" **S:** Russell Lavelle **P:** Andrew Garoni

Nick Cassavettes stars as Jack Nietzsche (really), an ex-con insurance scam investigator who narrates a series of sex flashbacks, flashbacks inside of flashbacks, and dream sequences inside of flashbacks. He's always either secretly photographing sex or enjoying it himself. The women are usually on top. Deborah Shelton (once a regular on *Dallas*) plays Roxie, the woman with the biggest breasts. She has the two main fuck scenes and

says, "I like a man with scotch on his breath." Michelle Moffett (*Wild Cactus*) is the visual highlight, in my opinion. She, Laura Brin, and Miles O'Keeffe (as a gangster with a ponytail) are also in sex scenes. With Lee Anne Beaman and Richard Roundtree as a bartender.

SIN SYNDICATE

(SW, 1965) **D/C:** Michael Findlay **P:** Joseph Brenner   (*Zero Girls*; *Jazz Me Baby*)

This is the story (in b/w) of what happened to four very bitter young women who became "Zero girls" in New York. Their stories are being told during Senate crime hearings. It's a pretty crudely made feature with bad sound and a lot of jumps, but has some priceless dialogue. Yolanda Moreno stars as the "Chinese/Spanish" Dolores. Strip acts take up a lot of the time, there are flashbacks inside of flashbacks, and news footage about Castro and WWII battle footage is used to stretch the running time even more.

SINTHIA: THE DEVIL'S DOLL

(SW, 1968) **D/C:** "Sven Christian"/ Ray Dennis Steckler **S/A:** Herb Robbins

Sinthia is a plotless sex "trip" movie about a woman (Shula Roan) in analysis because she killed her parents while they were doing it. Endless cries of "Mommy," then "Daddy," and repeated sex scenes with psychedelic colors and editing are pretty hard to enjoy. A witches' coven is led by Lucifer (Herb Robbins). Other stars are Diane Webber, a famous nude model and *Playboy* Playmate, and Gary Kent. With lesbian scenes and strange seashore walks and chases, Steckler trademarks. Some of you might enjoy *Sinthia* more than I did. Drugs might help. Maybe not.

SIN, YOU SINNERS!

(Sinister, 1961) **D/S:** "Anthony Farrar"/ Joe Sarno

A suburban hypnotist fortune teller stripper uses a magical Haitian medallion to keep young. She makes a club owner kill, and characters plot to take her powers away. There's no nudity but lots of talking in the b/w adult feature, one of the first of many for Sarno.

SIR DRONE

(Provisional, 1989) **D/S/P/A:** Raymond Pettibon

Dwayne and Jinx are two guys in a crummy apartment who want to start a punk band in (I think) the late 70s. They tattoo each other, think up band names, and audition for a singer and drummer. Jinx reluctantly has his long hair cut. The minimal movie is short (57 minutes) and pretty funny if you were around the 70s punk scene at all. The Ramones are heard in the background.

SIREN OF BAGDAD

(1953) **D:** Richard Quine **S:** Robert E. Kent **P:** Sam Katzman

Paul Henreid and Patricia Medina star in a color comedy fantasy adventure. Hans Conried is a ma-

gician with a magic box who becomes a woman for a disguise. With Laurette Luez from *Prehistoric Women* (1950). Medina had similar roles in *Aladdin and His Lamp* and *The Magic Carpet* (both 1951).

SIRENS

(Miramax, 1994) **D/S/A:** John Duigan **P:** Sue Milliken

Sam Neill is an eccentric bohemian Australian painter in the 1930s on a mountain paradise with models who like to bathe in a river. Hugh Grant is an Anglican priest sent to convince him to remove an offensive (nude) painting from an exibit. His wife (Tara Fitzgerald) is tempted by a blind naked man. The couple can't seem to leave and they both renew their sex life. Elle Macpherson (prominently featured in the publicity), Kate Fischer, and Portia de Rossi are the main attractions. The upscale erotic movie (it played in theaters) is by the director of *Wide Sargasso Sea*.

SIR HENRY AT RAWLINSON END

(1980) **D:** Steve Roberts **S/A/M:** Vivian Stanshall **P:** Tony Stratton Smith   UK

The drunken, crazy Sir Henry (Trevor Howard) lives in a mansion with ghosts. He tries to exorcise the ghost of his brother (Vivian Stanshall), some German WWII POW's, and his mother's body. Parts are in tinted b/w. It was based on a Bonzo Dog Band song that became a radio serial and an album by Stanshall. With Patrick Magee as the reverend. A soundtrack album was on Charisma.

THE SISTERHOOD

(Media, 1985) **D/P:** Cirio H. Santiago **S:** Thomas McKelvey Cleaver   Philippines

Rebecca Holden and Barbara Hooper, leaders of the Sisterhood, have special powers in one of Santiago's many *Mad Max* copies. They discover modern weapons (guns) and go through mutant territory to rescue their (topless) sisters in the city. Lynn-Holly Johnson communicates with her hawk. With Chuck Wagner. A Concorde release.

SISTERS IN LEATHER

(SW, 1969) **D/P:** Zoltan G. Spencer

A man (who resembles Liam Neeson) is blackmailed by female bikers after he has sex in a convertible with a "teenage sexpot." Butch, Dolly, and Billie then take his wife Mary (Kathy Williams) on a picnic and enjoy some nude motorcycle riding and outdoor lovemaking. The husband finds some male bikers and they try and save Mary from "becoming a dyke." It's no *Faster Pussycat! Kill! Kill!*, but the b/w adults-only movie is pretty outrageous and delivers with the nudity. Pat Barrington costars. The music is a trio doing jazz and some psychedelic music.

SISTER, SISTER

(Starmaker, 1987) **D/S:** Bill Condon **S:** Joel Cohen, Ginny Cerrella **P:** Walter Coblenz

Sisters Jennifer Jason Leigh and Judith Ivey have turned the family mansion in the bayou into a guest house. Leigh is an artist who has been in a

The 60s

The decade with the most obvious chaos in America was also the time when monster mania peaked. It was largely nostalgia for the old horror movies mixed with new hits from Hammer, Toho, and AIP. The late 60s saw the end of censorship (and the end of b/w movies). The 28 features making over $20 million during the decade include *Thunderball, 2001: A Space Odyssey,* and *Goldfinger.* In the epoch of turmoil, change and rebellion, the top-grossing feature was *The Sound of Music* (it made nearly $80 million), followed by two Disney animated features and *Love Story.*

mental hospital. A "Congressional aide" (Eric Stoltz) arrives and disrupts their lives. The plot involves deep secrets, ghosts, nightmares, dog killing, murder, and sex. Some character names were borrowed from *Hush, Hush, Sweet Charlotte* (1965) and it was filmed in Louisiana. With Dennis Lipscomb as the sheriff. Condon also wrote *Strange Behavior* and *Strange Invaders.* From New World.

SISTERS OF DEATH

(VCI, 1972) **D:** Joseph Mazzuca **S:** Peter Arnold, Edwyn Richards   (*Death Trap*)

During an all-girl secret society initiation, one new member is killed playing Russian roulette. Years later, the survivors are all invited to a reunion at a remote Spanish-style house with a pool and an electric fence. It's owned by the grumpy father (Arthur Franz) of the dead girl. He lurks in the walls watching them, makes bullets—and plays the flute (!). After the first girl dies, the rest still wait around. Claudia Jennings (with pigtails) is the only reason to watch this PG-rated obscurity which wasn't released until 1978. The credits are blurry and the boom mike shows several times. Also with Paul Carr.

SISTERS OF SATAN

(Academy, 1975) **D/S:** Juan López Moctezuma **S:** Yolanda L. Moctezuma, Alexis T. Arroyo **P:** Eduardo Moreno, Max Guefen   Mexico (*Alucarda; La Hija de las Tinieblas; Mark of the Devil, Part 3*)

This is the strongest, most imaginative, and visual witch movie since Ken Russell's *The Devils* (1971), and shouldn't be confused with any of the many European 70s ripoff lesbian nun movies. It has more blood, loud screaming, and nudity (male and female) than just about any horror movie I can think of. Justine (Susana Kamini) is sent to live with nuns. She meets the strange Alucarda who wears all black. Soon the nuns' clothes disappear, a hunchback cuts their breasts, and they drink each other's blood while they cry and it rains blood outside. In another scene, Justine rises naked and screaming from a coffin of blood, attacking nuns and biting their necks, while blood spurts everywhere. A nun who levitates and sweats blood can kill witches. There's an exorcism and a crucifixion. The church seems more brutal than the devil worshipers when they whip their

own bodies ("foul receptacles of sin!") to beat out the devil. Claudio Brook (*The Exterminating Angel*) plays a goat-headed demon who leads an orgy, the hunchback, and Dr. Oszek who protects the witches. Although it seems to be in English, the accents are very strange, and some of the actors are (obviously) from the stage. It's available on tape under several titles. Moctezuma produced *El Topo* (1971), and directed the surreal *Dr. Tarr's Torture Dungeon* (1972).

SIX AGAINST THE ROCK

(1987) **D:** Paul Wendkos **S:** John Gay **P:** Terry Carr

David Carradine plans to take hostages and break out of Alcatraz in 1946 with five others. Howard Hesseman costars in the NBC-TV movie with David Morse, Charles Haid, Jan-Michael Vincent, Richard Dysart, and Dennis Farina.

SIX FIVE SPECIAL

(SW, 1958) **D:** Alfred Shaughnessy **S:** Norman Hudis **P:** Herbert Smith

This musical is based on the BBC-TV show of the same name which was produced by Jack (*Shindig*) Good. An amateur singer (Diane Todd) and her girlfriend take a train to the taping of the program. Musicians playing on the train will make you think of *A Hard Day's Night.* Highlights are Jim Dale (later a Broadway star) doing "The Train Kept a Rollin'" (later done by the Yardbirds) and Lonnie Donnegan, who is incredible here doing a rocking climactic "Jack o' Diamonds" (later done by Fairport Convention). Also with the John Barry Seven (sounding like the Bonzo Dog Band), Petula Clark

Flip Wilson in *Skatetown U.S.A.*

doing a dumb teen love song, and Cleo Laine. A lot of the other music here is jazz, pop, and a little R&B by relative unknowns, but it's all fun to watch. The music stops for a serious talk with the famous old actor Finlay Currie. After the movie, Johnny Legend interviews the very knowledgeable Ian Whitcomb, who says that Donnegan is the one who influenced the Beatles the most and that Jack Good is a monk these days. The print is excellent.

SIX HOURS TO LIVE

(1932) **D:** William Dieterle **S:** Bradley King

Warner Baxter is murdered but is brought back to life for six hours by a ray. It gives him just enough time to catch his killer. With Irene Ware and John Boles. From Fox. Dieterle soon graduated to major, expensive movies like *A Midsummer Night's Dream* (1935) and *The Hunchback of Notre Dame* (1939).

SIZZLE BEACH USA

(Startmaker, 1974) **D:** Richard Brander **S:** Craig Kusaba **P:** Erix Louzil   (*Malibu Hot Summer*)

Troma re-released this in 1987 because a very young Kevin Costner plays a horse ranch owner. He's also featured on the misleading video cover. With a crippled midget, lots of nudity, and bad folk music. Star Terry Congie and Costner were also both in *Shadows Run Black,* made the same year.

SKATEBOARD

(Vista, 1978) **D/P:** George Gage **S:** Richard A. Wolf **P:** Harry N. Blum

Allen Garfield is Manny Bloom, a small-time agent who backs the LA Wheels skateboard team to get out of debt. The PG movie features Leif Garrett, Kathleen Lloyd, Anthony Carbone, and Sondra Theodore from *Playboy.* Dr. John and members of Jefferson Starship sing. A soundtrack was on RCA. *Roller Boogie* and *Skatetown, U.S.A* were also released around the same time to cash in on the roller disco fad.

SKATETOWN, U.S.A.

(1978) **D/P:** William A. Levey **S:** Nick Castle **P:** Lorin Dreyfuss

This PG comedy is set in a giant roller palace (owned by Flip Wilson). Patrick Swayze (making his debut) is the bad-guy skater. With Greg Bradford, Scott Baio, Ron Palillo, Ruth Buzzi, Maureen McCormick, Dorothy Stratten, Billy Barty, David Landsberg, Murray Langston, Gary Mule Deer, plus Dave Mason, who acts and sings. The Columbia soundtrack included the hit "Born to Be Alive" by Patrick Hernandez, plus tunes by the Jacksons, Earth Wind and Fire, Mason, and others. By the director of *Blackenstein* and *The Happy Hooker Goes to Washington,* so you know it's excellent entertainment.

510   **SISTERS OF DEATH**

SKEETER

(New Line, 1993) **D/S:** Clark Brandon
S: Lanny Horn **P:** James Glenn Dudelson

Toxic waste in a southwestern mine creates giant killer mosquitoes. Tracy Griffith stars with Jim Youngs as her deputy boyfriend. This movie has mosquito POV shots, *Birds*-style swarm attacks, some sex, and lots of plot and characters. With Michael J. Pollard as a local nut who talks in rhyme, Charles Napier as the corrupt sheriff, Jay Robinson as a creepy land developer, and William Sanderson as a geologist. George "Buck" Flower relates an out-of-place flashback. Also with Sarah Douglas, Richard Herd, and John Goff. Don (*Ilsa*) Edmunds was the executive in charge of production.

SKELETON COAST

(Nelson, 1988) **D:** John (Bud) Cardos **S:** Nadia
Calliou **P:** Harry Alan Towers   South Africa

Ernest Borgnine hires seven mercenaries to rescue his CIA agent son in Angola. The bad guys, led by evil East German Robert Vaughn, include Cubans. With Oliver Reed as an evil diamond security chief, Nancy Mulford, Herbert Lom, and Leon Isaac Kennedy. It was shot in Namibia. Towers, an international con artist who likes to recycle ideas, also produced *Coast of Skeletons* (1965).

SKETCH ARTIST

(MGM, 1992) **D:** Phedon Papamichael
S: Michael Angeli **P:** Brad Krevoy

Jeff Fahey stars as an LA police sketch artist. A witness (Drew Barrymore, whose character doesn't last too long) describes a murder suspect that looks just like his interior designer wife (Sean Young). He tries to cover for his wife with disastrous results. With Tcheky Karyo, James Tolkan, Charlotte Lewis, and Stacy Haiduk. It debuted on Showtime. Fahey returned in a sequel.

SKETCH ARTIST II: HANDS THAT SEE

(MGM, 1995) **D:** Jack Sholder
S: Michael Angeli **P:** Brad Krevoy

A blind woman (Courteney Cox) describes a rapist/murderer to a police sketch artist (Jeff Fahey) in a Showtime cable sequel. With Brion James as the captured criminal's defense attorney, Michael Beach, James Tolkan, and Jonathan Silverman.

SKETCHES OF A STRANGLER

(Fox Hill, 1978) **D/S/P:** Paul Leder **P:** Tom Spalding

Allen Garfield stars as a sweaty religious nut art student who kills hookers in Hollywood. Meredith MacRae is a sister of a victim, who goes undercover as a hooker to trap the killer. It was made by the prolific director of *I Dismember Mama*.

THE SKI BUM

(Nelson, 1971) **D:** Bruce Clark
P: David R. Dawdy   (*Point Zero*)

Zalman King is a ski bum in Colorado who is used by a woman (Charlotte Rampling) and the Mafia.

He's suspected of being a drug informer after cops raid a pot party. The long (136-minute) underground feature was made by a 26-year-old UCLA student and was based on a Romain Gary novel. The script is uncredited. Avco Embassy released it. The video release is cut.

SKIN ART

(Fox, 1994) **D/S:** W. Blake Herron
P: Ron Mcghee, Jonathan Jardine

Kirk Baltz (*Reservoir Dogs*) stars as an obsessed lower-Manhattan tattoo artist and former Nam POW (even though he's obviously too young) who works on Asian hookers. Ariane, Nora Ariffin, and Jake Weber co-star. The movie includes *Peeping Tom* references.

SKINHEADS: THE SECOND COMING OF HATE

(New Star, 1988) **D/S/P:** Greydon Clarke
S: David Reskin

A group of students (including Jason Culp and Liz Sagal) on the way to California are chased by vicious killer skinheads (led by Brian Brophy) in the mountains outside Reno. Chuck Connors (in a small role as a WWII vet) comes to the rescue with his rifle. It has bad dubbing, bad lighting, and a dumb script. With Barbara Bain plus some music by Elvis Hitler.

SKINNED ALIVE

(Cinema Home Video, 1990) **D/S/E:** Jon Killough
P/A/M: J. R. Bookwalter

This is a very low budget (around $20,000) 16mm first-time-director effort filmed in Mogadore, Ohio (a suburb of Akron). Three crazed killers in a van move in on a family and slaughter them. Crawdaddy, the big killer mom, has an eye patch and is in a wheelchair. Her daughter is a seductive blonde and her ponytailed son Phink (Scott Spiegel) wears a suit and granny glasses. A divorced, alcoholic, patriotic, ex-cop neighbor tries to be the hero. A lot of the humor is intentional (including comic sound effects), there's plenty of swearing (funny insults like "fuckwad," "dingleberry," and "shit-for-

brains"), and some gore. The best effect is an ax going all the way through a fat man. Others are just dumb, and the whole movie moves too slowly and gets real boring after a while. The executive producer was David DeCoteau.

SKINNER

(A-Pix, 1993) **D:** Ivan Nagy **S:** Paul Hart-Wilden
P: Brad Wyman, Jeff Pollon

This is one of the most extreme, tasteless, and disturbing movies I've seen in many years. It's also very well done. Dennis, a smiling psycho (Ted Raimi), moves into a spare room in an old house owned by Carey (Ricki Lake) and her usually absent truck driver husband (David Warshofsky). Dennis, who works as a janitor, kills hookers and cuts off and wears their skin and hair. Traci Lords (in her most memorable non-porn role to date) is Heidi, a depressed, deformed morphine addict out to kill Dennis. She has a withered arm and leg and half her face is scarred. She spends time in a sleazy crumbling hotel room being watched by a voyeur neighbor while shooting up and sobbing. In one detailed FX scene, Dennis skins a naked woman's corpse. In the most over-the-top part, he skins a black man (offscreen) and then walks around in the bloody skin talking in exaggerated black slang. *Skinner* has very knowing visual references to *Psycho, Eyes Without a Face, Circus of Horrors, The Naked Kiss, The Texas Chainsaw Massacre,* and other horror classics. The music is by Contagion. The incredible, convincing FX are by the KNB group. The director (who was born in Hungary) had mostly done minor TV movies. He became newsworthy as a boyfriend of the notorious Hollywood madam Heidi Fleiss. *Skinner* was released in 1995. The publicity centered on Lake, now a TV talk-show hostess.

SKI SCHOOL

(HBO, 1990) **S/P:** Damian Lee **S:** David Mitchell

If you liked *Hot Dog*, here's another teen ski sex comedy. Dean Cameron stars with Mark Thomas Miller as the bad guy, Darlene Vogel, Charlie Spradling, and Ava Fabian. It even has lambada gags. *Ski School 2* (Monarch, 1995) followed, also with Cameron.

SKULL: A NIGHT OF TERROR

(Academy, 1989) **D/S/P:** Robert Bergman **S:** Gerard Ciccoritti Canada (*Don't Turn Out the Light*)

Skull, a bald escaped con with an eye patch, and his buddies take a woman hostage in a farmhouse. The man of the house is a cop (Robert Bideman), troubled after having killed an innocent girl. They torment his wife and kill his mistress.

SKY BANDITS

(Sinister, 1940) **D:** Ralph Staub **S:** Edward Halperin **P:** Phil Goldstone

Dwight Frye is the mad inventor of a death ray. Criminals use it to blast planes out of the sky. Hero Mounties save the day in an indy feature that was distributed by Monogram. With James Newill and Dave O'Brien. Frye, typecast as a maniac after his famous roles in *Dracula* and *Frankenstein,* died young in 1943.

SKYJACKED

(1972) **D:** John Guillerman **S:** Stanley R. Greenberg **P:** Walter Seltzer (*Sky Terror*)

Charlton Heston (later in *Airport 1975*) is the pilot in a PG-rated *Airport* copy. James Brolin is the deranged Nam vet bomber. The plane is taken to the USSR but they won't let it land. Mariette Hartley has a baby and Rosey Grier gets drunk and plays a cello like a guitar. With Susan Dey, Walter Pidgeon, Yvette Mimieux, Claude Akins, Jeanne Crain, Leslie Uggams, John Hillerman, Ross Elliot, Mike Henry, Nicholas Hammond, and Ken Swofford (from *Common Law Cabin*).

SLACKER

(Orion, 1991) **D/S/P/A:** Richard Linklater

This movie follows people doing nothing during 24 hours in Austin—talking about political conspiracies, selling Madonna's pap smear, or the usual "same old same old." *Slacker* has no structure at all but is filled with great and funny moments. It's an end-of-the-world movie that shows America as a big asylum. It was financed for $23,000 and shot in 8mm and 16 plus some pixelvision video. Orion Classics blew it up to 35mm, released it, and had a critical low-budget hit. With references to Charles Whitman, Uncle Fester, and the Smurfs. Linklater went on to make more commercial features starting with *Dazed and Confused.* A *Slacker* book was also published.

SLAMDANCE

(Fox, 1987) **D:** Wayne Wang **S/P/A:** Don Opper **P:** Rupert Harvey, Barry Opper

Tom Hulce is an LA cartoonist blamed for the murder of a hooker (Virginia Madsen). With Mary Elizabeth Mastrantonio, Harry Dean Stanton, Millie Perkins, Don Opper as a hitman, Adam Ant, Rosalind Chao, and Lisa Niemi. There is no slamdancing but there are some nude scenes. By the director of *Chan Is Missing.*

SLAMMER GIRLS

(Vestron, 1985) **D/S/P:** Chuck Vincent **S:** Craig Horrall

Devon Jenkin is the new innocent inmate in a dumb women's prison spoof. One man goes undercover as a woman (with mustache). The cast includes porn director Henri Pachard, Veronica Hart (not bad as a sadistic matron), Tally Chanel, Tally Brittany, Sharon Kane, Samantha Fox, Sharon Kelly/Colleen Brennan, Sherri St. Claire, and Captain Haggerty.

THE SLAMS

(1973) **D:** Jonathan Kaplan **S:** Richard L. Adams **P:** Gene Corman

Curtis Hook (Jim Brown) is put in prison after hiding some mob money. The mob wants him killed and the FBI wants him to talk. Girlfriend Judy Pace and Paul E. Harris help him plan an escape. The violent MGM release also features Frank de Kova, Ted Cassidy as a con, and Dick Miller as a cab driver. Brown was in *I Escaped From Devil's Island* the same year (1973). Kaplan had been directing at New World and did *Truck Turner* (1974) next.

SLAPSTICK (OF ANOTHER KIND)

(1984) **D/S/P/A:** Steven Paul

Jerry Lewis and Madeline Kahn star as ugly twin aliens and their parents in a comedy based on Kurt Vonnegut's novel. The twins are sent to earth and kidnapped by Chinese midgets. They're super intelligent only when they're together. With Marty Feldman, Jim Backus as the U.S. president, Sam Fuller as a military school colonel, Merv Griffin, Pat Morita, John Abbott as Dr. Frankenstein, Virginia Graham, and the voice of Orson Welles. It was the first effort by the teenage (!) director of *Falling in Love Again. Slapstick* never opened theatrically in America, but a different version debuted in West Germany.

SLASHDANCE

(Impulse, 1989) **D/S:** James Shyman **P:** Andrew Maissner

A female Hollywood cop (played by "Americana") goes undercover as a dancer in an old theater to capture an unknown hooded maniac with a saw who has been killing women auditioning for a musical. Americana was a star of G.L.O.W. (*Gorgeous Ladies of Wrestling,* a hard-to-believe popular TV show). This ridiculous, boring, modern *Phantom of the Opera* rip-off features seemingly endless scenes of dancers practicing, repeated over and over with the same irritating repetitious music. There's a comic flasher, 6' 4" "Queen Kong" (another G.L.O.W. star), offscreen sex and violence,

pointless Hollywood street scenes, and Jay Richardson as a comic police captain. Joel Von Ornsteiner, a veteran of David DeCoteau, Roberta Findlay, and Troma (!) films, plays the producer's brother, the main suspect, who proves how crazy he is by eating a goldfish. Shoe fans should know that this movie includes a death-by-high-heel scene.

SLASHED DREAMS

(Academy, 1974) **D/S/P:** James Polakoff (*Sunburst*)

James Keach is a psycho killer in the forest. Kathy Baumann (a Miss America finalist from Ohio) costars (and takes her clothes off). With Peter Brown, Anne Lockhart, Peter Hooten, Rudy Vallee (!), and Robert Englund as a hermit.

THE SLASHER

(1952) **D/S:** Lewis Gilbert **S:** Vernon Harris **P:** Daniel M. Angel UK (*Cosh Boy*)

In England it was advertised as being "Wild . . . Wayward . . . Hellbent!" It's all about a London juvenile delinquent with a razor. James Kenny stars with Joan Collins and Hermione Gingold. Lippert released it in America.

SLAUGHTER

(Fox, 1972) **D:** Jack Starrett **S:** Mark Hanna, Don Williams **P:** Monroe Sachson

Jim Brown had his first solo starring role as Slaughter, after being famous for playing for the Cleveland Browns and acting in films since 1964. He's a violent ex–Green Beret whose parents in Cleveland are killed by the mob. He ends up in Mexico seeking revenge—and he gets the girl (Stella Stevens, who appears topless). Rip Torn, after his "underground" period (*Coming Apart, Tropic of Cancer,* and two by Norman Mailer) costars as a racist gangster. With Don Gordon as Slaughter's helper, Cameron Mitchell, and Marlene Clark. Billy Preston is on the soundtrack. The AIP release was shot in Mexico City,

SLAUGHTER

(21st Genesis, 1976) **D:** Burt Brinkerhoff **S:** O'Brian Tomalin **P:** Allan F. Bodoh, Bruce Cohn (*Dogs*)

David McCallum is a college professor who helps to scientifically create killer dogs (all kinds from Dobermans to poodles). The dogs kill students but they are not scary. With Linda Gray, who has a *Psycho* shower scene. Years later, *Man's Best Friend?* used the same idea.

SLAUGHTERDAY

(Genesis, 1976) **D/S:** Peter Patzak **S:** Walter Kinder, Ossi Bronner **P:** Gunter Kopt Italy

Rita Tushingham is a medical student and there's a violent bank robbery. William Berger and Gordon Mitchell are in the action drama.

Slaughterhouse

SLAUGHTER HIGH

(Vestron, 1986) **D:** George Dugdale, Mark Ezra, Peter Litten **P:** Steve Miniasian, Dick Randall UK (*April Fool's Day*)

It was billed as "From the Makers of *Friday the 13th.*" That was a lie, but the music is by Henry Manfredi who scored *Friday* movies. Students pull mean tricks on a nerd (Simon Scuddamore), who dies after nitric acid is thrown at him. Five years later a man in a clown outfit commits gore murders during a school reunion. Caroline Munro is the top-billed victim. R and unrated versions are available.

SLAUGHTERHOUSE

(Charter, 1987) **D/S:** Rick Roessler **P:** Ron Matonak

Backwoods Lester Bacon and his fat son Buddy (who snorts) kill to save the farm in a *Texas Chainsaw Massacre* copy. They also kill off some teens (led by Sherry Bendorf) making a horror video. It's pretty gory and opens with a montage of (real) hogs being slaughtered with funny music.

SLAUGHTERHOUSE ROCK

(Sony, 1987) **D:** Dimitri Logothetis **S:** Ted Landon **P:** Louis George

Nicholas Celozzi (the son of the executive producer) visits Alcatraz prison after dreaming about the dead there. A cannibal demon possesses his brother (Tom Reilly), and the ghost of a heavy metal singer (Toni Basil) who was killed along with her band (called Bodybag) tries to help battle the supernatural killer. Hope Marie Carlton is raped by a monster. This one has dreams, flashbacks, zombies, lots of FX, and some music by Devo.

SLAUGHTER IN SAN FRANCISCO

(Rhino, 1973) **D/S:** William Lowe **P:** Leonard K. C. Ho (*Karate Cop*)

Don Wong stars as a Chinese American cop out for revenge. With Sylvia Channing and a young Chuck Norris (before he shaved his back) as a drug-dealing villain. It was re-released many times to capitalize on Norris's later fame as a movie hero.

SLAUGHTER OF THE INNOCENTS

(MCA, 1993) **D/S:** James Glickenhaus **P:** Frank K. Isaac

Scott Glenn is an FBI man stationed in Cleveland who goes to Utah to track a maniac who kills (and sodomizes) kids. Thankfully we don't see the bearded religious nut (Zitto Kazann) killer at work, but he does tie up a little girl. He thinks he's Noah and has a huge ark in a cave that's filled with rotting corpses and skeletons (kind of like in *Texas Chainsaw Massacre*). The agent's crime-solving computer expert kid is played by Jesse Cameron-Glickenhaus—the director's son. He's a little too smart to believe, but is the real star of the movie. With Sheila Tousey, Darlanne Fluegel, and Zake Moakes as a janitor. Gabe Bartalos provided gore FX for the above-average HBO movie, filmed in Utah (and downtown Clevo). The MCA laser disc includes deleted footage and commentary by the director.

SLAUGHTER'S BIG RIP-OFF

(Fox, 1973) **D:** Gordon Douglas **S:** Charles Johnson **P:** Monroe Sachs

Jim Brown returns for more revenge after his friend is killed at the LA airport, and he fights martial arts experts. Ed McMahon plays a mob boss! With Brock Peters as a detective, Don Stroud as a hitman, and Gloria Hendry and Judy Brown as Slaughter's girlfriends. Also with Art Metrano, Scatman Crothers, and Valda Hansen. A new substitute score was done for the video release. You'll have to search out the old Polydor LP for the real music (James Brown and Lynn Collins!). From AIP.

SLAVE GIRL

(1947) **D:** Charles Lamont **S/P:** Michael Fessier, Ernest Pagano

Ed McMahon as a pimp in *Slaughter's Big Rip-Off.*

Yvonne De Carlo stars in a Universal color comedy desert drama narrated by a talking camel. With George Brent, Broderick Crawford, Albert Dekker, Andy Devine, Arthur Treacher, and Lois Collier. The Canadian De Carlo was in *Song of Scheherezade* the same year.

SLAVE GIRLS FROM BEYOND INFINITY

(Tempe, 1987) **D/S/P:** Ken Dixon **P:** John Eng, Mark Wolf

This slow, talky science fiction adventure version of *The Most Dangerous Game* is about blond slaves in bikinis who escape in a rocket ship and wake up on an island. The villain, wearing all black, has a castle, a laser crossbow, and twin robots that decapitate people. John Buechler provided special effects. The women (Cindy Beal, Elizabeth Kaitan, and Brinke Stevens) go topless once in a while to try and relieve the boredom. "Fate sure weaves a curious tapestry!"

SLAVERS

(New Pacific, 1976) **D/P/A:** Jurgen Goslar **S:** Henry Morrison W. Germany

Trevor Howard is top-billed in an exploitation movie about the slave trade in Africa. With former Tarzan Ron Ely, Britt Ekland, Ray Milland, Ken Gampu, and Cameron Mitchell. It was released in America the same year as the *Roots* miniseries. Akira Fitton did the US posters and ad mats. Goslar also made *Albino*.

SLAVES

(1969) **D/S:** Herbert J. Biberman **S:** John O. Killens **P:** Philip Langer

Ossie Davis is the hero Kentucky slave who incites a rebellion at the end. Stephen Boyd co-stars as an evil Mississippi plantation owner and Dionne Warwick is Cassy his mistress. This is a much more serious attempt than the later *Mandingo* and it predated the *Roots* mini-series. With Shepperd Strudwick, Julius Harris, and David Huddleston. Also with Gale Sondergaard in her first role since 1949. She and her director husband Biberman (*Salt of the Earth*) had been blacklisted. Bobby Scott and Dionne Warwick songs are on the Skye soundtrack.

SLAVES IN BONDAGE

(Sinister, 1937) **D:** Elmer Clifton **S:** Robert A. Dilon **P:** J. Kendis

Donna Lee (Lona Andre) is the manicurist girlfriend of an unemployed reporter (Donald Reed). He says, "You're making me a sissy with all these manicures." Wheeler Oakman is the main sleazeball con man behind an illegal roadhouse and a nightclub. Donna is saved just in time from a life of sin. Much of this old roadshow hit is taken up by comic acrobats, a lady contortionist, an Oriental fan dancer, and large newspaper headlines. There's also a catfight. By the director of *Gambling* with *Souls* (1936) and *Assassin of Youth* (1937). Scenes from the Jay-Dee-Kay Production were later re-used in *Teen Age.*

SLAVES OF BABYLON

(1953) **D:** William Castle
S: DeVallon Scott **P:** Sam Katzman

Richard Conte is the Israelite hero in a Technicolor biblical tale. With Maurice Schwartz as Daniel, Linda Christian, Michael Ansara, and Julie Newmar as a dancer. The Columbia release was one of many period films by Castle. Ansara and Newmar were also in Castle's *Serpent of the Nile* from the same year.

SLAVES OF LOVE

(Media, 1969) **D/S:** Charles Nizet **P:** David Ackerman

Amazon women (led by Tina Brown) with machine guns wear minidresses and boots on an island. The women use a magnetic force to force down planes. They enslave two detectives and make the men have sex with them in their underground headquarters. They also dance and go swimming naked. Narrated flashbacks tells us what's going on. By the uniquely talented and unfairly obscure director of *Possessed.*

SLAVE TRADE IN THE WORLD TODAY

(Shockwave, 1964) **D:** Roberto Malenotti, Folco
Quilici **S:** Baccio Bandini, Gianfranco Calderoni
France/Italy (*Le Schiave Esistono Ancora*)

Lord Robert Maugham blames America and England for looking the other way while oil-rich Arabs continue to deal in human beings. "Hidden cameras" offer proof. With b/w footage of young captive British hookers. The exposé was filmed in Africa, the Middle East, and India. In one scene, giant crabs drag skeletons of escaped slaves across the sand. There was a London label soundtrack.

THE SLAYER

(Continental, 1981) **D/P:** J. S. Cardone
S/P: William R. Ewing   (*Nightmare Island*)

A female artist on vacation dreams of a monster. Her friends and relatives die when she sleeps. It's a gory movie with decapitations and fishhooks in faces. Filmed on Tybee Island, Georgia, this was on a double tape with *Scalps.*

SLAYGROUND

(HBO, 1983) **D:** Terry Bedford **S:** Trevor
Preston **P:** John Dark, Gower Frost   UK

It was advertised in America as a horror movie, but is actually a crime movie set partially in upstate New York. Peter Coyote goes to a British amusement park to avenge the killing of his daughter. With Mel Smith and Billie Whitelaw. Based on the "Richard Stark"/Donald E. Westlake novel.

SLEAZEMANIA

(Rhino, 1984)

A lot of people got into weird and obscure movies by watching this 60-minute tape created and compiled by Johnny Legend. The first volume is the best and is packed with scenes and trailers from horror and exploitation wonders like *The Pin Down Girls* and *The Smut Peddler.* There's a promo reel for *Star Slammer,* plus some old color stripper shorts.

SLEAZEMANIA ON PARADE

(SW, 1994)

Johnny Legend comments on the smiling celebrities (Angie Dickinson, Gene Autry, Steve Allen, Mr. T, Doug McClure . . .) passing by in a Hollywood Christmas parade, interspersed with trailers or scenes from their movies. Then lots of rare trailers are shown (*No Morals, I Passed for White, Swamp Girl* . . .). *The Naked Zoo, Incredible Sex Revolution, Curse of the Teenage Nazi,* and *Door to Door Maniac* trailers are my faves. Next Hollywood stars represented on the sidewalk are shown with more appropriate trailers and the parade ends with an appearance by the Aztec Mummy. Tom Rainone shot the original Hollywood footage. Part of this tape were previously on a tape called *Mondo Legend* (1991).

SLEAZEMANIA STRIKES BACK

(Rhino, 1985)

This volume shows you why you need to know more about Ed Wood Jr., H. G. Lewis, A. C. Stevens, and others. When this compilation came out with scenes from Fred Olen Ray's *Beach Blanket Bloodbath,* few knew the (unfinished) movie had been written by Ed Wood Jr. This even features Johnny Legend's own *Teenage Cruisers. Sleazemania III: The Good, the Bad and the Sleazy* (Rhino, 1989) followed, featuring the notorious (and long) *Smut Peddler* trailer, then there was *Sleazemania: The Special Edition* (Rhino), a shorter (18-minute), "clean" best-of tape for viewers who couldn't take the sex and violence.

SLEDGEHAMMER

(World, 1983) **D/S:** David A. Prior **P:** Nicholas Imaz

A young boy kills his mom and her lover with a hammer. Ten years later (yeah it's another one of those), he kills teens spending a vacation weekend. It was shot on video for $40,000. With Ted Prior.

SLEEPAWAY CAMP

(Media, 1983) **D/S:** Robert Hiltzik
P: Michele Tatosian, Jerry Silva

In a nasty *Friday the 13th* rip-off that's better than most, campers are killed in upstate New York. Melissa Rose is the shy murderous Angela, and there's a *Homicidal*-style sex switch involved. Ed French created the grisly FX. With Mike Kellin and Robert Earl Jones.

SLEEPAWAY CAMP II: UNHAPPY CAMPERS

(Nelson, 1988) **D/P:** Michael A. Simpson
S: Fritz Gordon **P:** Jerry Silva

The original did well on video, so two sequels were made back to back. Bruce Springsteen's grinning sister (!) Pamela Springsteen plays the boy who became the psycho killer Angela. She returns to the summer camp, this time as a singing counselor, and kills "bad" people. This sequel has more novel ways of dying, gore, and nudity, and Springsteen even sings. With Renee Estevez as the token virgin, Valerie Hartman, and Susan Marie Snyder. It was filmed in Georgia.

SLEEPAWAY CAMP III: TEENAGE WASTELAND

(Nelson, 1988) **D/P:** Michael A. Simpson
S: Fritz Gordon **P:** Jerry Silva

Pamela Springsteen is back killing off the entire unsuspecting cast of irritating multi-ethnic kids and their stupid counselors in this stupid, goreless, tasteless, horror comedy with flashbacks to Part II and the usual topless scenes. The overworked Michael J. Pollard acts even weirder than usual as a horny, goofy, always-mugging counselor. Springsteen kills by decapitation, an M-80 in a nose, a garbage truck, and a spike through a head. With Tracy Griffith (also in *Fast Food,* along with Springsteen and Pollard), Jill Terashita, and in-joke character names. *Sleepaway Camp IV* was also announced.

SLEEPING BEAUTY

(UAV, 1955) **D/S/P/A:** Fritz Genschow **S/A:** Renee
Stotbrawa   W. Germany (*Dornröschen*)

Sleeping Beauty movies were being made as early as 1902 (in France). This was the first feature-length live-action sound version and is in color. The director himself stars as Prince Charming. New songs and narration by Paul Tripp were added for the American release by AIP. The next version of the famous tale collected by the Brothers Grimm was the 1959 animated classic from Disney. Bernadette Peters stars in the 60-minute *Faerie Tale Theatre* version (Fox, 1983). An earlier TV version, hosted by Shirley Temple, is available from Wood Knap.

SLEEPING BEAUTY

(Warner, 1987) **D:** David Irving
S: Michael Berz **P:** Golan/Globus

Tahnee Welch (Raquel's daughter) stars with Morgan Fairchild as the queen. Also with Sylvia Miles as the red fairy, Kenny Baker as an elf, and Jane Weidlin (from the Go-Go's) as the white fairy. It was made in Israel.

THE SLEEPING CAR

(Vidmark, 1989) **D/P:** Douglas Curtis **S:** Greg O'Neil

David Naughton is Jason, a divorced, wisecracking student who rents half of a haunted train car, even after he sees a body in his bed! He plays heavy metal music on a reel-to-reel tape recorder and everybody makes jokes about how old he is. He acquires a very forward girlfriend (Judie Aronson from *Friday the 13th IV*). Her jealous ex breaks into the car and is killed by couch springs (!). More characters are crushed in the couch bed or killed by the springs. Kevin McCarthy, who lives in the other half of the car, believes in white magic and listens to sitar music. Jeff Conaway is a rebellious journalism teacher who tells a Dan Quayle joke. After sex and a lot of fast editing and strobe lights, Aronson becomes possessed. It's all because of the landlady's transparent ghost husband. Also with Nicole Hansen. John Carl Buechler provided the FX credit and acts. The ending stinks.

SLEEPING DOGS

(1977) **D/P:** Roger Donaldson **S:** Ian Mune, Arthur Baysting   New Zealand

This was the first New Zealand feature to open in America and was the debut for the director and star. In the near future, Sam Neill is a loner who joins a violent resistance movement to overthrow the fascist government. With Warren Oates and Ian Mune.

SLEEPING WITH THE ENEMY

(Fox, 1991) **D:** Joseph Ruben **S:** Ronald Bass **P:** Leonard Goldberg **M:** Jerry Goldsmith

Julia Roberts fakes her own drowning death to escape life with her rich neat-freak psycho husband (Patrick Bergin). She calls herself Sarah and settles in an old-fashioned small Iowa town. She eventually falls for an acting teacher (Kevin Anderson) but her husband kills her mother and tracks her down. Ruben's followup feature to *The Stepfather* got more attention simply because of Roberts, and it has similar psycho-husband themes. The score is on Varèse Sarabande. From 20th Century–Fox.

SLEEP OF DEATH

(Prism, 1978) **D/S/P:** Calvin Floyd **S:** Yvonne Floyd   Sweden/Ireland
(*Ondskans Vardshus; Inn of the Flying Dragon*)

A young inexperienced man (Per Oscarsson) goes to France in the early 1900s. His new traveling companion is a marquis (Patrick Magee) and he falls for a mysterious countess (Marilu Tolo). It's a vampire story based on a J. Sheridan Le Fanu novel. The period detail is excellent but the "vampires" are part of a conspiracy and are not real. With Curt Jurgens as the count. By the director of *In Search of Dracula* (1972).

SLEEPOVER MASSACRE

(W.A.V.E., 1989) **D:** Gary Whitson

This feature-length vampire tape is as obscure as you can get. It's from W.A.V.E. Productions, a Centerton, New Jersey, company that will videotape your script for money. Their productions resemble backwoods high school film student projects from Hell. This one features girl fights, long flashbacks, lots of talk, gore, shower scenes, cardboard walls that move, and a synth score that will drive you up a wall. I'm not really sure if it's an example of what some person actually paid them to tape or an enticement for people to send scripts and money.

SLEEPWALK

(Nelson, 1986) **D/S/P:** Sara Driver **S:** Kathleen Brennan

A woman (Suzanne Fletcher) who works as a computer operator translates an ancient Chinese manuscript. It magically affects her life. The underground movie features Ann Magnuson, Steve Buscemi, and Tony Todd, who all went on to bigger projects. Jim Jarmusch was a cinematographer.

SLEEPWALKERS

(Columbia, 1992) **D:** Mick Garris **S:** Stephen King **P:** Mark Victor, Mark Grais

It's another bad Stephen King adaptation, and he wrote it himself. In an Indiana town, new student Brian Krause and his sexy mom Alice Krige are vampire-like "sleepwalker" cat people with some confusing powers and absurd weaknesses (normal cats). Madchen Amick is the virgin girl in danger. *Sleepwalkers* is full of stupid comic relief, Freddy Krueger-type wisecracks, death by pencil and an ear of corn, and typical first victims (gay and black characters). The transformation FX are minimal, the street set is too obvious, and John Landis, Joe Dante, Tobe Hooper, King himself, and Clive Barker show up for useless guest bits. With Cindy Pickett, Glen Shadix, Ron Perlman, and Mark Hamill. The Columbia release was cut for an R. Milan issued a soundtrack (by Nicholas Pike) featuring Santo and Johnny's title instrumental from 1959. My favorite part was the excellent end theme.

SLIDERS

(1995) **D:** Andy Tennant **S:** Tracy Torme, Robert K. Weiss **P:** Steven Ecclestine

The X-Files TV series did so well that Fox started another sci-fi series with lots of FX. This was the pilot feature. Jerry O'Connell (the fat kid from *Stand by Me*) stars as a genius physics student who can visit other times and alternate reality worlds through the Gateway. Sabrina Lloyd and John Rhys-Davies are other members of the Sliders team. The series was shot in Vancouver. John Landis is an executive producer.

SLIME CITY

(Camp, 1987) **D/S/P:** Gregory Lamberson **P:** Peter Clark, Marc Makowski

A New York City art student moves into a tenement building. Green wine from some odd neighbors turns him into a slime killer with a bandaged face. The gory local first effort was made for "$50,000." With an early appearance by Alan Rickman.

SLIPPING INTO DARKNESS (1974) = CRAZE

SLIPPING INTO DARKNESS

(Virgin, 1988) **D/S:** Eleanor Gaver **P:** Jonathan D. Krane

Three co-eds in a small town Nebraska boarding house are blamed for a retarded kid's death. The older brother (John DiAquino) and his biker friends go after and kidnap them. One of the girls dies and a psycho tenant keeps her body. Parts are influenced by *River's Edge*, and there are black humor and bondage scenes. Michelle Johnson stars with Neill Barry and Adam Roarke. It was filmed in Fremont, Nebraska.

SLIPSTREAM

(Virgin, 1988) **D:** Steven Lisberger **S:** Tony Kayden **P:** Gary Kurtz **M:** Elmer Bernstein   UK

In the bleak future, Mark Hamill is a mean, bearded airborne bounty hunter. Another bounty hunter (Bill Paxton) takes his captive away. Kitty Aldridge co-stars with Bob Peck as a robot. Ben Kingsley, F. Murray Abraham, and Robbie Coltrane all have small roles. The PG-13 ecological science fiction movie is by the director of *Tron* and

the producer of *Star Wars*. It was shot in Turkey and on the British moors and went straight to tape in America.

SLIVER

(Paramount, 1993) **D:** Phillip Noyce **S:** Joe Eszterhas **P:** Robert Evans **C:** Vilmos Zsigmond **M:** Howard Shore

Sharon Stone (after the huge hit *Basic Instinct*) stars as a Manhattan book editor with an extremely expensive new apartment (in the real Morgan Court building). William Baldwin is Zeke, the rich, young computer whiz voyeur owner of the building where murders occur. The script, based on the Ira Levin novel, borrows from *The Tenant, Rear Window, Peeping Tom,* and others. With Tom Berenger as an alcoholic writer, Colleen Camp, Keene Curtis, Martin Landau, Polly Walker, Nina Foch, Nicholas Pryor, CCH Pounder, and Shannon Whirry. It was cut for an R, and an irritating alternate ending was used. *Sliver,* producer Evans's first project after *The Cotton Club* (1984), was a hit overseas (with additional sex footage) and on tape. The soundtrack (Virgin) includes UB40, Neneh Cherry, Heaven 17, and others.

SLOW BURN

(Xenon, 1989) **D:** John E. Eyres **S:** Steven Lister **P:** Geoff Griffiths   Canada

Anthony James stars in a New York Chinese gang vs. Mafia movie. William Smith is a Mafia don. It was filmed in Vancouver.

SLUGS

(Starmaker, 1987) **D/P:** Juan Piquer Simon **S:** Ron Gantman **P:** José A. Escriva, Francesca De Laurentiis   Spain

The plot is about toxic waste causing killer slugs and some of the scenes are copied from *Squirm* (1976). The sarcastic hero is a health inspector in a small town, with a schoolteacher wife. Big black slugs breed in the sewer and come out of sinks and toilets. Most deaths are offscreen, but the bloody standout scene here is when a naked teen couple in bed are surprised by slugs and the girl, trying to escape, is covered with them. Some parts were filmed in Lyons, NY, but most scenes were done in Madrid. The accents are real weird. Some actors speak *Twilight Zone* English, others are dubbed. They all seem obsessed with drinking, or talking about drinking. The music is by the Royal Philharmonic Orchestra. From New World.

SLUMBER PARTY '57

(MGM, 1977) **D:** William A. Levey **S:** Frank Farmer **P:** John Ireland Jr.

In 1957, six underage high school girls relate R-rated sex flashbacks at a mansion. The all–Mercury label soundtrack includes good real oldies, but many of them are from the 60s! A drive-in shows a trailer for *Cauldron of Blood* (the U.S. release was 1971!) and there are some very 70s haircuts. Debra Winger from Cleveland (who should have been about 21 at the time) eats a banana suggestively and appears topless for her film debut. The girls all are photographed underwater in (or out of) their underwear. Will Hutchins (TV's *Sugarfoot*) is a drunken older man in bed with a naked girl, but her father (Bill Thurman from Larry Buchanan movies) interrupts and spanks her over his knee. One segment concerns making a man-in-the-pot cannibal movie. With Janet Wood, Cheryl "Rainbeaux" Smith, Rafael Campos as a "dope fiend," astrologer Joyce Jillson as a car hop, and Joe E. Ross (driving Car 54). From Cannon.

SLUMBER PARTY MASSACRE II

(Nelson, 1987) **D/S/P:** Deborah Brock **P:** Don Daniel

The first sequel to Amy Jones's 1982 film (available on Embassy Video) takes place five years later and features an all-girl band in a condo on a gulf course. Crystal Bernard (later to star in the *Wings* series) is the now-grown-up little sister from the original. She has flashbacks and nightmares of a killer black leather rock guitarist with a drill guitar. With music segments, a hand in a hamburger bun, a zit spurting green pus, and in-joke names. The cast includes *Playboy* centerfold Kimberly McArthur, Patrick Lowe, Juliette Cummins, Heidi Kozak, and Maria Ford. The Roger Corman Concorde release also has a *Rock 'n' Roll High School* clip on TV.

SLUMBER PARTY MASSACRE III

(New Horizons, 1990) **D:** Sally Mattison **S/P:** Catherine Cyran

Roger Corman has assigned females to make all of these slumber movies. They keep getting worse, but that's the sequel business. This one has less gore and skin but is filled with ridiculous suspects (a "weirdo" with dark glasses and a goatee, a tall voyeuristic hippie, horny guys in monster masks . . .) and lots of palm trees. Other exploitation clichés include bathtub death by electric (?!) vibrator (it's usually a radio or heater, so I guess they tried to be different), idiotic victims who can't even figure out how to leave a house, and a lone black guy (the first to die) who is not missed by the rest of the cast. And the killer is impotent. Keely Christian stars, but the only familiar cast members are Maria Ford and Hope Marie Carlton.

SMALL KILL

(VCI, 1992) **D:** Rob Fresco, Gary Burghoff **S/P/A:** Fred Carpenter **S:** James McTernan **P:** Tom Poster

Gary Burghoff (Radar from *M*A*S*H*) finally gets to show his real dramatic talents as Fleck, a psychotic drug dealer and kidnapper in Nassau County, Long Island. He also appears in a (very unconvincing) drag disguise as an old lady fortuneteller (!) and—he directed all his own scenes! *Small Kill* starts with some surprising extreme gore FX as hands and heads are blown off. Burghoff slashes people with a straight razor, shoots people in the face, is in bed with a naked boy, and has sex in a chair with a woman with huge breasts before killing her. There's a naked suicidal man and topless dancers to relieve the boredom while you wait for Radar to reappear. Jason Miller is very convincing as a pathetic drunken informer and Rebecca Ferratti (from *Playboy*) is the wife of the

bearded hero cop (Carpenter). With Donnie Kerr. The producer was an editor at the New York *Daily News*.

A SMALL TOWN IN TEXAS

(Vestron, 1976) **D:** Jack Starrett **S:** William Norton **P:** Joe Soloman

Crooked sheriff Bo Hopkins frames ex-con Timothy Bottoms in a drug bust and takes his woman (Susan George). The PG-rated AIP revenge movie features Morgan Woodward, Art Hindle, and John Karlen. Norton also wrote *Big Bad Mama* and *I Dismember Mama*.

SMART ALEC

(1986) **D/S/P:** Jim Wilson **S:** Rob Sullivan (*The Movie Maker; Hollywood Dreaming*)

Ben Glass stars as a would-be filmmaker who tries to finance his first movie. The comedy features Orson Bean, David Hedison, Antony Alda, Lucinda Crosby, and Zsa Zsa Gabor. The name is from a famous old porno reel.

A SMELL OF HONEY, A TASTE OF BRINE!

(SW, 1966) **D:** B. "Ron Elliot"/ Byron Mabe **S/P/A:** David F. Freidman **C:** "Art Radford"/Laszlo Kovacs

Stacy Walker stars as a sexy office worker who teases men and sends one to jail on false date-rape charges. She takes a lot of baths and also teases her lesbian roommate, then laughs, "I may be a bitch, but I'll never be butch!" One guy dreams about tying her up but the dream goes wrong when she castrates him! The great-sounding, simple garage band music was by "et cetera," a real Beatle-hair group (they appear in a bar scene) that got to split $100 for their efforts. Walker (real name: Barbara Jean Moore), who also starred in *The Notorious Daughter of Fanny Hill*, really carries the movie, doing nude scenes and really acting. She was a Texas dropout who returned to Houston after her two features. Friedman is fun to spot in two roles. The 71-minute b/w adult release was the last release from Sonney Amusements.

THE SMILING GHOST

(1941) **D:** Lewis Seiler **S:** Kenneth Gamet **P:** Bryan Foy

Wayne Morris is a chemist who pretends to be engaged to Elinor Bentley Fairchild (Alexis Smith) because her grandmother promises him money. It turns out that Elinor is known as "The Kiss of Death Girl" because her previous men have died violent deaths. Relatives gather at a spooky old mansion where the ghost of a suicide victim is supposed to be. The 71-minute Warner comedy mystery includes Brenda Marshall as a reporter, Willie Best from *Ghost Breakers* (1940) as the scared servant, Alan Hale as the butler, Lee Patrick, and David Bruce.

SMITHEREENS

(First Run, 1982) **D/P:** Susan Seidelman **S:** Ron Nyswaner, Peter Askin

Susan Berman is Wren, a girl who wants badly to make it in the Manhattan downtown scene. She

starts a "Who is this?" self-promotion and tries to become a band manager, with pathetic results. It's a good period piece and was the first American indy feature to compete at Cannes. With Brad Rijn, Richard Hell, and music by the Feelies. Seidelman made *Desperately Seeking Susan* next.

SMOKE AND FLESH

(SW, 1968) **D/S/C:** Joe Mangine

A woman narrates this arty soft-core b/w drug movie made in NYC. An impotent bald voyeur (who has bulging head veins) and his wife hold a party to "research" his sex book. Young people smoke "dynamite grass" in paper-towel-roll bongs. Characters get the munchies and eat ice cream, which leads to a black woman being covered with whipped cream. Others talk about the fish in a tank or have sex (seen through the fish tank). The fun is disrupted when some bikers crash the party and their drinks are spiked with LSD. The freakout scenes include on/off negative visions and bikers crying. The music is raga rock jams. Mangine was also a cinematographer for others.

SMOKE IN THE WIND

(1971) **D:** Joseph Kane, Andy Brennan **P:** Billy, Whitey Hughes

John Ashley stars with John Russell, and Walter Brennan (whose son co-directed) narrates and appears in one of his last roles. This Southern appeal drama was backed by money from Arkansas turkey ranchers and probably played in the Oklahoma drive-ins owned by Ashley. It was the final credit for Kane, who had directed Gene Autry and Roy Rogers westerns.

SMOKEY BITES THE DUST

(Charter, 1981) **D:** Charles B. Griffith **S:** Max Apple **P:** Roger Corman, Gale Ann Hurd

Jimmy McNichol stars as a small-town delinquent who steals cars and smashes them with the homecoming queen at his side. It's a super-low-budget follow-up to *Eat My Dust!* (1976) and *Grand Theft Auto* (1977) and uses the car chase and crash scenes from those and other Corman-produced movies. With William Forsythe and Janet Julian. McNichol, the brother of Kristy, was also in the bizarre psycho movie *Night Warning* (1982).

SMOOTH TALKER

(Academy, 1990) **D:** Tom E. Milo **S:** Darrah Whitaker **P:** Eduardo Montes, Craig Shapiro

A divorced cop (Joe Guzaldo) tracks a serial killer who goes after phone-sex women. With a cast including Susan Ager, Stuart Whitman, Burt Ward, and Sydney Lassick and such an original plot, how could you lose?

THE SMUT PEDDLER

(1965) **D:** Warner Rose **P:** Herbert Lannard

It can't possibly live up to what's promised in the incredible (and long) coming attraction trailer (included on *Sleazemania*), but this b/w title is one of the most sought-after nudie movies. D. G. (Degenerate) Rawlins, the publisher of *Dream Girl* magazine, seduces the models and so does his lesbian feature editor. A Broadway columnist writes about him and the magazine is closed down. Rose and Lannard returned the next year with *Professor Lust.*

SNAKE EATER

(Media, 1989) **D:** George Erschbamer **S/P:** John Dunning **S:** Michael Paseornek   Canada

"Soldier," a tattooed Nam vet and ex-cop (Lorenzo Lamas), gets on his Harley and goes after the psycho hillbillies in the swamp who killed his parents and kidnapped his sister. The action movie with gore and humor has a scene where a woman swallows a whole snake. Lamas' character is sort of like Mel Gibson in *Lethal Weapon.* Also with a killer in bear suit and an aqua cycle. With Josie Bell, Robert Scott, Ron Palillo, and rockabilly legend Ronnie Hawkins as a friendly biker. The title is the name of the hero's Marine squad. A sequel was filmed at the same time.

SNAKE EATER II: THE DRUG BUSTER

(Paramount, 1990) **D:** George Erschbamer **S/P:** John Dunning **S:** Don Carmody, Michael Paseornek   Canada

Vigilante ex-cop Soldier (Lorenzo Lamas) is sent to a mental hospital by the authorities. He escapes to fight some drug dealer bikers who sell real bad stuff. Michelle Scarabelli costars and Lamas's then-wife Kathleen Kinmont plays another cop. It was filmed in Montreal.

SNAKE EATER III: HIS LAW

(Paramount, 1992) **D:** George Erschbamer **S/P:** John Dunning **P:** Irene Litinsky

All of these violent, cartoonish action movies (by the same director and producer) have lots of fights and killing, a little sex, and some bad taste scenes. Soldier (Lorenzo Lamas) is hired to find members of The Hell's Fury, a real scummy biker gang who kidnapped a girl and made her a nympho zombie. Wrestler Scott "Bam Bam" Bigelow gives a standout performance as a big dumb biker with a tattooed head. With Minor Mustain as Soldier's cowboy P.I. sidekick, Tracy Cook as his girlfriend, and Holly Chester as a stripper. Like the others, it was filmed around Montreal (note accents).

THE SNAKE PIT

(Fox, 1948) **D/P:** Anatole Litvak **S:** Frank Partos, Millen Brand **P:** Robert Bassler **M:** Alfren Newman

Olivia De Havilland stars in this famous women's mental hospital movie, based on the novel by Mary Jane Ward. She's a new bride who is committed, goes through shock therapy, and is given truth serum (triggering flashbacks). It was considered pretty shocking in its day and is still pretty interesting. Watch for one surreal shot looking down into the "pit" of Ward 33, later copied in *Nightmare on Elm Street III.* With Mark Stevens, Leo Genn, Celeste Holm, Glenn Langan, Leif Erickson, Lee Patrick, and Natalie Schafer. A 20th Century release.

SNAKES: *See* FANGS

THE SNAKE WOMAN

(Cinemacabre, 1960) **D:** Sidney J. Furie **S:** Orville H. Hampton **P:** George Fowler   UK

In 1890, in Northern England, a doctor shoots up his wife with snake venom to "cure her sick mind." She gives birth to "the Devil's baby" and villagers burn the house down. The baby girl is raised by a flute-playing shepherd and twenty years later a Scotland Yard agent arrives to investigate deaths by snakebite. It's one of the cheapest-looking British horror movies from the period, and the sound dubbing is pretty bad, but a few scenes are good. Susan Travers (also in *Peeping Tom*) stars. Furie was from Toronto. This and *Dr. Blood's Coffin* were his first features made in England and played on a double bill. This 66-minute version has some bad jumps, and new credits were added.

SNAPDRAGON

(Prism, 1993) **D:** Worth Keeter **S:** Gene Church **P:** Ashrok Amritraj

Pamela Anderson (Lee) is Felicity, a blonde with amnesia who may have the clue to a series of murders. An LA police shrink (Steven Bauer) dreams he has sex with her, almost has sex with her (his undercover cop girlfriend Chelsea Field interrupts), then—finally—has sex with her. Plotwise, it seems that Felicity had been raised by white slavers in the evil Orient where she learned to slit men's throats during sex with a razor in her mouth and is a schizo (or something much more ridiculous). Anderson, from *Baywatch,* obviously had some silicone body improvement to prepare for tapes like this. With Matt McCoy and Rance Howard. Terri Treas co-wrote the convoluted story. By the director of *Rottweiler/Dogs of Hell.*

THE SNIPER

(1952) **D:** Edward Dmytryk **S:** Harry Brown **P:** Stanley Kramer **M:** George Antheil

Susan Travers is *The Snake Woman.*

Arthur Franz stars as an ex-con in San Francisco who is driven to kill brunettes with a high-powered rifle. Adolphe Menjou is Lieutenant Kafka in the excellent documentary-style thriller. With Marie Windsor as a victim, Gerald Mohr, and Frank Faylen. The Columbia release was the first American feature in five years for Dmytryk, a director who had been blacklisted. *The Sniper* on tape (Arena, 1975) is really *The Deadly Tower,* with Kurt Russell as 1966 Austin sniper Charles Whitman.

SNIPER

(Columbia, 1993) **D:** Luis Llosa **S:** Michael Frost Beckner, Crash Leyland **P:** Mark Johnson, Walon Green, Patrick Wachsberger

Tom Berenger stars as a Marine assassin on assignment in Panama with a young Washington bureaucrat marksman (Billy Zane). They argue, act macho, and fight during action scenes, and bullets are seen in closeup going through the air. With J. T. Walsh and Aden Young. The Tristar release was shot in Queensland, Australia, by a frequent Roger Corman director who was born in Peru.

SNO-LINE

(American, 1985) **D:** Douglas F. O'Neons **S:** Robert Hilliard **P:** Robert Burge

Vince Edwards is a New York City DA with a Texas-based cocaine and gambling ring on the side. The mob tries to muscle in. With June Wilkinson as his girlfriend, Paul Smith, and Phil Foster.

SNOW BUNNIES

(Nite Flight, 1970) **D/P:** "A. C. Stevens"/ Stephen Apostoloff **S:** Ed Wood Jr.

It's a "Blizzard of Fun, an Avalanche of Action!" It's also another unbelievable softcore sex movie written by Ed Wood Jr. With the once-popular sex team of René Bond and Rick Lutz, Marsha Jordan, Sandi Carey, and Terri Johnson. It was made back to back with *Cocktail Hostess.*

SNOW KILL

(1990) **D:** Thomas J. Wright **S/P:** Raymond Hartung **S:** Harv Zimmel

Escaped cons (led by David Dukes) go after a coke stash and terrorize office workers staying in a cabin. The USA cable movie features some bloody killings. With Terence Knox, Patti D'Arbanville, Jon Cypher, and Joey Travolta.

SNOW WHITE

(UAV, 1955) **D:** Erich Kobler **S:** Konrad Lustig, Walter Oehmichen W. Germany (*Schneewitten und die Sieben Zwerge*)

This was the first live-action sound version of the Grimm Brothers' fairy tale. Childhood productions released it in 1965 with new songs and narration by Paul Tripp, then it was an AIP TV package title. The same treatment was given to the sequel,

Snow White and Rose Red (*Schneeweisschen und Rosenrot*), which starred two little girls, a dancing bear (actually a cursed prince), and an evil bearded dwarf. Both titles are on tape.

SNOW WHITE

(1987) **D/S:** Michael Berz **P:** Golan/Globus

This was a low point for *Avengers* star Diana Rigg, who is the best part as the evil Queen. Billy Barty (also in *Rumpelstiltskin,* also from Cannon) is Iddy. It's a musical version. *The Faerie Tale Theatre* TV version (Fox, 1983) features Vincent Price in the mirror of the witch (Vanessa Redgrave).

SOCIETY

(Republic, 1989) **D:** Brian Yuzna
S: Woody Keith, Rick Fry **P:** Keith Walley

Yuzna made this before his *Bride of the Reanimator.* It's very anti-establishment, deals with conspiracies, and has some plot similarities to the same year's *Parents.* Billy Warlock (from *Baywatch* and *Days of Our Lives*) stars as Beverly Hills teen William Whitney. A friend has a tape of his rich parents talking about orgies with his sister at her coming out party. He becomes paranoid (with good reason) and gives the tape to his shrink. Screaming Mad George created the FX for the surreal and disturbing (also silly and awkward) cannibal orgy scenes in which a person is pulled inside out. *Society* doesn't really work that well (neither did *Parents*), but they'll be revived some day as examples of attempts to warn Reagan-era viewers. With Devin De Vasquez (from *Playboy*) as girlfriend Clarissa, Patrice Jennings as the sister, Evan Richards, Ben Meyerson, Heidi Kozak, Jason Williams, and Tom Rainone. Five minutes were cut out for America. The Japanese laser disc is 100 minutes long and uncut.

SODOM AND GOMORRAH

(Fox, 1961) **D:** Robert Aldrich, Sergio Leone
S: Hugo Butler, Giorgio Prosperi **M:** Miklos Rozsa
US/France/Italy (*Sodome et Gomorra*)

At the end of this Book of Genesis biblical spectacle, Lot (Stewart Granger) is freed by angels and his wife Ildith (Pier Angeli) is struck by lightning and turned into a pillar of salt. Then the earth splits apart and both cities burn. It's 154 minutes long and from 20th Century. A 171-minute version exists somewhere. Leone directed the battle sequences. With Anouk Aimee, Stanley Baker, Rossana Podesta, Giacomo Rossi-Stuart, and Gabriele Tinti. The score was issued by RCA. A silent version (1922) was directed by Michael Curtiz. Leone, who certainly deserved more credit, also shot the massive "cast of thousands" action scenes for *Quo Vadis, Helen of Troy,* and *Ben-Hur.* Aldrich's next project was *What Ever Happened to Baby Jane?*

SO I MARRIED AN AXE MURDERER

(Columbia, 1993) **D:** Thomas Schlamme **S:** Neil
Mullarkey **P:** Robert N. Fried, Cary Woods

This is the movie that Mike Myers got to star in after the success of *Wayne's World.* He's a nice San Francisco part-time beat poet who marries a butcher (Nancy Travis), then suspects that she's a husband-killer. Myers also plays his own Scottish father. The PG-13 comedy partially copies Hitchcock's *Suspicion* and has a number of guest stars. With Anthony LaPaglia as a cop, Amanda Plummer, Alan Arkin, Michael Richards, Brenda Fricker, Phil Hartman, Steven Wright, Charles Grodin, and Debi Mazar. It was shot in San Francisco.

SOLARBABIES

(MGM, 1986) **D:** Alan Johnson **S:** Walon
Green **P:** Irene Walzer, Jack Frost Sanders

A magical sphere appears in a superstrict futuristic orphanage and helps kid roller skaters gain control of the world's water supply. The PG-13 box office flop (Mel) Brooksfilm is teen sci-fi, set in the year 2025. Jami Gertz stars with Jason Patric, Lukas Haas, Peter DeLuise, James Le Gros, and Adrian Pasdar. Richard Jordan is the mean cop Grock. The other adults are Sarah Douglas and Charles Durning. With an octopus robot and FX by Steve Johnson. Green also wrote *The Wild Bunch.*

SOLAR CRISIS

(Vidmark, 1990) **D:** "Alan Smithee"/Richard C.
Sarafian **S:** Joe Gannon, Ted Sarafian **P:** Tsuneyuki
Morishima **M:** Maurice Jarre   (*Star Fire*)

A mission to prevent the sun from frying Earth in 2050 is the theme of this episodic, slow-moving, clichéd, all-star science fiction adventure. Tim Matheson stars as the ship captain with a bearded Charlton Heston as his Navy admiral father. There's a subplot (which is never resolved) about Heston searching for his grandson (*The Stand*'s Corin Nemec) in the Nevada desert. Annabel Schofield is a British cyborg who is reprogrammed by a bad guy (and has a nude scene and a flashback). Peter Boyle is a corporate villain and Jack Palance rides a motorcycle in the desert and sings. Also with Tetsuya Bessho, Paul Koslo, Dan Shor, Brenda Bakke, Michael Berryman, and Paul Williams as the voice of "Freddie the bomb." It was based on a Japanese novel and was made (in English) in America. The "$35 million" production was a moderate hit in Japan.

THE SOLDIER

(Neslon, 1982) **D/S/P:** James Glickenhaus
M: Tangerine Dream

Soviet terrorists hold the world ransom with a stolen plutonium bomb in a Saudi Arabian oil field. Ken Wahl is the mercenary hero. With William Prince as the US president, Klaus Kinski as Dracha, Steve James, Alberta Watson, and Peter Hooten.

SOLDIER BLUE

(Nelson, 1970) **D/A:** Ralph Nelson
S: John Gay **P:** Gabriel Katzka, Harold Loeb

Candice Bergen and Peter Stauss are survivors of a Cheyenne Indian massacre. At the end of this "just like Nam" movie, the cavalry fights back with a large-scale bloody massacre. They were "Stained with the Blood of the Innocent!" as the ads claimed.

With Donald Pleasence, Jorge Rivero, and John Anderson. Buffy Ste. Marie sings. The Avco Embassy release was shot mostly in Mexico. Bergen was in another violent box-office flop next, *The Hunting Party.*

SOLDIERS OF FORTUNE

(Edde, 1970) **D:** Peter Collinson **S/A:** Leo V. Gordon
P: Gene Corman   (*You Can't Win 'Em All*)

Charles Bronson and Tony Curtis star as soldiers of fortune in the Turkish civil war of 1922. Considered an all-around international flop, the comic PG adventure was originally planned to be directed by Howard Hawks. Screenwriter Gordon (who also acts) is a character actor who was often in Roger Corman features. With Michele Mercier, Patrick Magee, and Horst Jansen. A Columbia release.

SOLDIERS OF FORTUNE

(Republic, 1990) **D:** Arthur N. Mele **S/P:** Jeffrey C.
Hogue **S:** Charles Douglas Lemay **P:** Michael Biber

A rich California high school cheerleader is kidnapped by masked terrorists, so soldier of fortune Gil Gerard, her mom's ex, goes to the rescue. His all-vet team includes a knife-throwing ex-con (Dan Haggerty), a tough woman who has to prove herself (Janus Blythe), a bar owner (George "Buck" Flower), and a blind black blues musician. With flashbacks of evil revolutionaries in Central America. Also with P. J. Soles, Charles Napier as a kidnapper, and a Chucky doll. It's based on a story by Hogue and Fred Olen Ray and is an OK timewaster.

SOLE SURVIVOR

(Vestron, 1982) **D/S:** Thom Eberhardt
P: Don Barkemeyer

Ad executive Anita Skinner is the only survivor from a plane crash. Her friends at home become walking corpses. Brinke Stevens is a teenager at a party. Yes, it's another *Carnival of Souls* copy. The director made *Night of the Comet* next.

SOL MADRID

(1968) **D:** Brian G. Hutton
S: David Karp **P:** Hall Bartlett

David McCallum stars as an undercover narc after heroin dealers in Mexico led by Telly Savalas. Stella Stevens is kidnapped, shot up, and has a psychedelic trip sequence. With Ricardo Montalban, Rip Torn, Pat Hingle, Michael Ansara, Paul Lukas, Perry Lopez, and Michael Conrad. The MGM release, filmed in Acapulco, was McCallum's first post–*Man from U.N.C.L.E.* feature.

SOME LIKE IT COOL

(1961) **D/S:** Michael Winner **P:** Adrienne Fancey   UK

Star Julie Wilson convinces her new husband to join her at a nudist colony by honeymooning near a camp. The color adult movie was backed by producer Edwin J. Fancey, as were all of Winner's early features.

SOME LIKE IT COOL (1976): *See* SEX ON THE RUN

SOME LIKE IT VIOLENT

(Alpha Blue, 1968) **D/P:** Kemal Horulu

This adults-only movie is pretty hilarious, and the acting is some of the worst I've seen. Johnny Skaro is a New York gangster with a James Cagney voice who takes over a computerized dating service to use for hookers. Meanwhile his men talk a lot, women wearing panties talk, and a blonde who goes undercover for a cop lies around naked for a while. The only memorable scene is when Skaro cuts up some mannequins with a machete! Frankie, a guy with a very fake mustache, says, "The sight of fuzz bugs me to no end." Barry Mahon was executive producer.

SOME OF MY BEST FRIENDS ARE

(1971) **D/S:** Mervyn Nelson
P: Marty Richards, John Lauricella

The year after *The Boys in the Band*, AIP released this forgotten R-rated gay-themed feature. The cast includes future *Buck Rogers* series star Gil Gerard, Gary Sandy (from *WKRP*), and Dick O'Neill (who was in *Gammera*). Also with comedienne/author Fannie Flagg, Sylvia Syms, Candy Darling (from Warhol movies), and Rue McClanahan (*The Golden Girls*).

SOMEONE BEHIND THE DOOR

(UAV, 1971) **D/S:** Nicholas Gessner **S:** Jacques Robert, Marc Behm **P:** Raymond Danon
France (*Quelqu'un Derrier la Porte*)

Charles Bronson is a stranger with amnesia under the care of a neuro-psychiatrist (Anthony Perkins) in France. Since he's Anthony Perkins, he discovers that Bronson is a killer and uses mind control and plots to use him to kill the lover of his wife (Jill Ireland).

SOME PEOPLE

(1962) **D:** Clive Donner **S:** John Eldridge **P:** James Archibald   UK

Ray Brooks, David Andrews, and David Hemmings (as Bert) are factory workers with motorcycles. They're thrown out of a youth club when the vicar catches them playing rock and roll in the church. They're good lads though, so their rock band plays at the church hall to raise money for motorcycle licenses. Proceeds from this color movie went to a charity set up by the Duke of Edinburgh. AIP released it (a bit late) in America in 1964. With Kenneth More and Annika Wills. Hemmings was also in movies like *Live It Up/Sing and Swing* (about another band) and *Be My Guest*.

SOMETHING IS OUT THERE

(1988) **D:** Richard Colla **S/P:** Frank Lupo

This four-hour NBC-TV miniseries was a pilot for a very short-lived (9 episodes) series. An LA undercover cop (Joe Cortese) is teamed with Ta'ra (Maryam D'Abo) an alien woman in a jumpsuit who can get drunk from coffee. They find an alien shapeshifter beetle. It's a lot like *The Hidden*

(1987) and features makeup by Rick Baker and FX by John Dykstra. With George Dzundza, Gregory Sierra, Kim Delaney, and Robert Webber. John Ashley was the executive producer. The pilot was released on tape in Europe.

SOMETHING OF MINE

(Terran, 1991) **D/S:** Keith Randall Duncan **S/P:** Todd Camp **S:** Kevin Schmidt **M/A:** Michael Price

Satanists conjure up a demon that shows up at a campus Halloween "Castle of Fear" spook show. The rotted ghoul cuts ears, eyes, a nose . . . off its victims and puts them on himself and makes Freddy Krueger–type wisecracks. The best gore effect is cutting off lips with scissors. Tom Rainone plays a cigar-chomping detective in what seems to be a tribute to Orson Welles in *Touch of Evil*. A police switchboard operator is a guy in drag and the students, busy with hazing pranks, piss a lot. Flashbacks to 1882 show how it all started. It's only 50 minutes long and from the Dallas/Fort Worth area.

SOMETHING'S HAPPENING

(SW, 1967) **D:** Edgar Beatty **P:** Art Lieberman   (*The Hippie Revolt*)

Many voice-overs are heard and some people are shown talking in this look at what was going on in LA and Haight-Ashbury at the time. See actual love-ins, an acid test, body painting, pot smoking, dancing to strobe lights, and a nude beach plus footage of the "Moonfire Funeral" and a huge antiwar rally (with Muhammad Ali). The #1 topic, though, is drugs. The music is by the Love Generation. From Headliner (*The Sinister Urge, The Naked Flame* . . .).

SOMETHING SPECIAL

(Magnum, 1986) **D:** Paul Schneider **S:** Walter Carbone, Carla Rueben **P:** M. David Chilewich, Fred Berner   (*Willy/Milly; I Was a Teenage Boy*)

A young teen girl (Pamela Segall) becomes a boy during a solar eclipse. With Patty Duke and John Glover. The PG-13 Concorde comedy was shot in Atlanta. It predated the onslaught of late-80s body-switch movies if nothing else.

SOMETHING WICKED THIS WAY COMES

(Disney, 1983) **D:** Jack Clayton **S:** Ray Bradbury **P:** Peter Vincent Douglas

Bradbury's excellent fantasy novel was announced to be filmed many times over the years, to be directed by Gene Kelly (1958), Sam Peckinpah (!) (1971), and Steven Spielberg (1972). It ended up at Disney, and despite some good scenes (and Stan Winston FX), is a big disappointment. In the early 1900s, two smalltown Illinois boys have to face Mr. Dark (Jonathan Pryce) when his sinister traveling Pandemonium carnival comes to town. Everything is seen from the kids' point of view. With Jason Robards as the hero librarian dad, Diane Ladd, Pam Grier as the Dust Witch, Royal Dano, and Angelo Rossitto.

SOMETHING WILD

(HBO, 1986) **D/P:** Jonathan Demme
S: E. Max Frye **P:** Kenneth Utt

Jeff Daniels, in an *After Hours*–type Manhattan yuppie role, is a sorry guy whose wife and family have left him. He meets Lulu/Audrey (Melanie Griffith in black wig) and the adventure of his life begins. It starts out funny, becomes a violent, scary road movie, then gets happy at the end. Ray Liotta takes acting honors as the hyped-up psycho ex-con husband of Audrey. With Margaret Colin, Tracy Walter, Charles Napier, John Sayles, and John Waters as a used car salesman. The Feelies play at a high school reunion. John Cale, David Byrne, Laurie Anderson, and others are on the hip 80s soundtrack. From Orion.

SOMETIMES AUNT MARTHA DOES DREADFUL THINGS

(Active, 1971) **D/S/P:** Thomas Casey

Look for a copy of this Miami psycho movie obscurity. It's surefire cult movie material! Scott Lawrence (aka Wayne Crawford) is Stanley, a coke-snorting young guy with a painted hippie van who is wanted for murder back home in Baltimore (was Casey a John Waters fan!?). Stanley is overprotected by his jealous aunt Martha who is really his friend Paul (Abe Zwick) (seen in various stages of drag throughout the movie) stay in a suburban house and argue a lot but sleep together ("Come on, Aunt Martha, let's ball!"). If you can picture a drugged Jonathan Richmond as Stanley and Andy Kaufman as Martha you'll have an idea of how these guys look. An older junkie from Baltimore moves in ("Destiny and the Zodiac brought me") and blackmails them and, oh yeah, somebody kills women (who all seem attracted to Stanley). With flashbacks in negative, a good jazzy score, and a visible microphone. A Who's Who of Florida exploitation worked on this sick but very funny bizarro movie. Harry Kerwin was production manager, the assistant director was Chris Martel (*Flesh Feast*), and Thomas Wood aka William Kerwin (*Blood Feast*) and Brad Grinter (*Blood Freak*) play cops. Recommended!

SOMETIMES THEY COME BACK

(Vidmark, 1991) **D:** Tom McLoughlin
S: Lawrence Konner, Mark Rosenthal
P: Michael S. Murphy

Tim Matheson (who narrates) is a high school teacher who returns to his home town. Students are killed off and are "replaced" by the same guys who had killed his brother, then were hit by a train 27 years earlier. His brother's ghost helps him fight the juvenile delinquents from Hell. The CBS-TV movie is sentimental horror based on a Stephen King *Night Shift* short story. With Brooke Adams as his wife, Robert Rusler, William Sanderson, and Bentley Mitchum. With flashbacks, nightmares, clips of Soupy Sales and Dino De Laurentiis's *King Kong*. Dino presented it and it was co-produced by Milton Subotsky in Missouri, Kansas, and LA. More scenes were added to the tape so it could qualify for an R rating.

SONG OF INDIA

(1949) **D/P:** Albert S. Rogell
S: Art Arthur, Kenneth Perkins

Sabu can control wild animals in India (just like he had done in *Elephant Boy,* a dozen years earlier). The Columbia release was filmed in sepia tones. With Gail Russell, Turhan Bey, Anthony Caruso, Fritz Leiber, and Jay Silverheels.

THE SONG REMAINS THE SAME

(Warner, 1976) **D/S:** Peter Clifton
S: Joe Massot **P:** Peter Grant

Led Zeppelin had recorded five hit albums when their 1973 Madison Square Garden concert was filmed for this, the last great drug/concert movie. Besides the live footage, Robert Plant, Jimmy Page, and John Paul Jones each has his own fantasy segment, and the late drummer John Bonham is seen racing cars and enjoying his home life. One segment shows gangsters (including manager Peter Grant) at a table being decapitated and colored blood spurting out of their necks. The 136-minute movie was a hit and made nearly six million dollars in North American rentals alone. The double Swan Song soundtrack made it to #2 on the charts.

SONNY BOY

(Media, 1987) **D:** Robert Martin Carroll
S: Graeme Whifler **P:** Olividio G. Assonitis

If you're looking for something really different, rent *Sonny Boy.* It's a warped tale about a baby kidnapped by a criminal "family" in New Mexico. As he grows up, the boy's tongue is cut out and he's treated like an undesirable dog in a wire cage. He devolves into a pathetic innocent teenage "animal man" killer (Michael Griffin) who narrates his life story. The casting director deserves credit for putting together big Paul L. Smith as "Papa," the leader, David Carradine in drag (always) as his wife (!) Pearl, Brad Dourif as the manic long-haired Weasel, sniveling Sidney Lassick, and Conrad Janis (as a discredited doctor who sews a monkey tongue in Sonny Boy's mouth). Also with Savina Gersak. All of the actors are excellent. Not just a sick exploitation movie, *Sonny Boy* has many inspired, funny, and surprising moments. Even the simple desert set is great and could have been inspired by old *Krazy Kat* comics. There's a trailer in a junkyard with a guard tower and a pyramid filled with stolen goods. Papa is also a surreal artist and enjoys blowing up cops with a cannon. Carradine also sings the title song. Screenwriter Whifler also made Residents videos.

SON OF ALI BABA

(MCA, 1952) **D:** Kurt Neumann **S:** Gerald
Drayson Adams **P:** Leonard Goldstein

Tony Curtis is Ali Baba's son Kashma, and Piper Laurie is the Princess Azura. The adventures concern the Forty Thieves, the treasure, and of course, characters say "Open Sesame." With Susan Cabot, Hugh O'Brian as the evil Hussein, Victor Jory, Gerald Mohr, and Morris Ankrum. It was a color followup to *The Prince Who Was a Thief,* also with Curtis and Laurie, who were just doing what Universal ordered.

SON OF DARKNESS: TO DIE FOR II

(Vidmark, 1991) **D:** David F. Price
S: Leslie King **P:** Richard Weinman

The same good/bad vampire brothers from *To Die For* return, this time in a northern California resort town. Michael Praed stars as a romantic, long-haired Romanian emergency room doctor (with a British accent) who calls himself "Max Schreck." He falls for a single mother (Rosalind Allen) with a baby (usually a very obvious doll) that cries a lot. Amanda Wyss and Steve Bond (the evil brother) return as vampires and Vince Edwards is a grim police lieutenant. It's a pretty boring sequel, but a *NY Post* article in 1992 claimed that a man in Milwaukee watched this movie on New Year's Eve and cut his girlfriend and tried to suck her blood. One World issued a soundtrack (by Mark McKenzie). Part 3 has been announced.

SON OF DRACULA

(VSOM, 1974) **D:** Freddie Francis **S:** Jay
Fairbanks **P/A:** Ringo Starr *(Count Downe)*

The late Harry Nilsson proved that he was no actor by starring in this horror musical comedy as Dracula in modern times. He sings in a club, fights a wolfman, becomes a (cartoon) bat, falls in love (with Suzanna Leigh), and wants to become human. Freddie Jones is Dr. Frankenstein and Dennis Price is Van Helsing. Ringo (looking like he did in *Magical Mystery Tour*) is Merlin and he has a horror museum. Rock fans will want to see the band consisting of Peter Frampton, Keith Moon, John Bonham, and Klaus Voorman. Also with Shakira Baksh, Jenny Runacre, the dwarf (Skip Martin) from *Masque of the Red Death,* and a *Nosferatu*-look vampire. The Apple production was (barely) released in America by Jerry Gross's Cinemation. Apple released the soundtrack, featuring "Jump Into the Fire" and "Without You."

SON OF THE PINK PANTHER

(MGM, 1993) **D/S:** Blake Edwards **S:** Madeline
and Steve Sunshine **P:** Tony Adams

Italian comedian Roberto Benigni stars as the illegitimate gendarme son of Inspector Clouseau in the eighth in the "series." With Debrah Farentino as a missing princess, Jennifer Edwards, and Robert Davi. Herbert Lom, Burt Kwouk, and Claudia Cardinale also return in the PG-rated MGM misfire slapstick movie.

SONS OF SATAN

(1968) **D/S:** Duccio Tessari **S:** Ennio
Di Concini, Mario De Nardo **P:** Turi
Vasile   W. Germany/Italy/France
(I Bastardi)

Rita Hayworth is the alcoholic mother of two criminal brothers (Klaus Kinski and Giuliani Gemma) who plan a jewelry store robbery in Arizona. They double-cross each other and it all ends in an earthquake. With Margaret Lee and Claudine Auger. Filmed in Madrid, Rome, and in America. Hayworth's next was *The Naked Zoo.*

SONS OF STEEL

(1988) **D/S:** Gary L. Keady
P: James Michael Vernon   Australia

A rock singer called Black Alice (Bob Hartley) is the main character in the futuristic story of a race to stop a nuclear accident. It takes place in tunnels under "Oceana." With intentional humor and heavy metal music.

SORCERER

(MCA, 1977) **D/P:** William Friedkin
S: Walon Green **M:** Tangerine Dream

Few people went to see this expensive and long (122 minutes) 70mm remake of Clouzot's 1952 *The Wages of Fear.* It's not what they expected from *The Exorcist*'s director, but it's a greatlooking movie. The misleading title is the name of the truck, and the audience gets to see lots of in-your-face close-ups of its working parts. Roy Scheider stars with Bruno Cremer and Francisco Rabal. It was filmed in Mexico, Paris, Israel, and America and was released by Universal and Paramount together. The score on MCA also features some Charlie Parker.

SORCERESS

(Thorn EMI, 1982) **D/S/P:** "Brian Stewart"/Jack Hill

Twins Lynette and Leigh Anne Harris, disguised as men, go after the evil wizard who killed their parents. A muscleman, a Viking, and a satyr with horns help them. The twins bathe naked and experience each other's orgasms. This movie, which was made in Mexico, has silly-looking fighting gorillas, zombies, a winged lion, and other cheap wonders. The story was written by Jim Wynorski. The music is from *Battle Beyond the Stars.* It was one of Corman's last New World releases. He had it recut and Hill's name was removed and replaced by the first names of Corman's kids! The Harris twins (also in *I, the Jury*) were later indicted for income tax evasion involving the estate of their 87-year-old "sugar daddy." They were acquitted in 1991.

SORCERESS

(Triboro, 1994) **D:** Jim Wynorski **S:** Mark
Thomas McGhee **P:** Fred Olen Ray

In this senseless erotic horror movie, a lawyer (Larry Poindexter) accidentally kills his wife (Julie Strain, who overdid it with the silicone), a witch.

Lynette and Leigh Anne Harris in *Sorceress.*

Meanwhile, Linda Blair (also a witch) helps her crippled lawyer husband (a zombie-like Edward Albert) and seeks revenge. She makes a woman named Carol (Rochelle Swanson) imagine herself in a lesbian three-way. Swanson is the real star and the main attraction in several hot sex scenes. This is typically filled with flashbacks, nightmares, dreams inside of dreams, and a shower scene. Also with Tony Naples, Kristina DuCati, Michael Parks (gardener), and William Marshall (runs law firm). R or unrated. Wynorski also wrote the unrelated 1982 movie of the same name.

SORORITY BABES IN THE SLIMEBALL BOWL-O-RAMA

(Tempe, 1987) **D/P:** David DeCoteau **S:** Sergei Hasenecz **P:** John Schouweiler   *(The Imp)*

The "Imp," an awful rubbery puppet (with a clichéd soul voice inspired by the *Little Shop of Horrors* remake) escapes from a bowling trophy during a sorority initiation rite in a shopping mall. *Day of the Dead*–inspired events occur as three girls become killers (a dominatrix, a zombie, and a *Bride of Frankenstein*–like monster). A tough biker girl named Spider (Linnea Quigley) saves the day. The horror comedy with nude scenes also features Andras Jones, Michelle Bauer, Brinke Stevens, and George (Buck) Flower. The much cheaper *Sorority Babes in the Dance-A-Thon of Death* (Video Outlaw, 1992) claims to be a sequel.

SORORITY GIRLS AND THE CREATURE FROM HELL

(Complete, 1990) **D/S/P:** John McBrearty

Topless women and a 50s-look monster are featured in this 8mm horror comedy with Deborah Dutch, Len Lesser, Dori Courtney, and Vicki Darnell.

SORORITY HOUSE MASSACRE

(Warner, 1986) **D/S:** Carol Frank **P:** Ron Diamond

After Corman's *Slumber Party Massacre*, his Concorde presented more girls (and their boyfriends) being killed, this time copied directly from *Halloween*. Angela O'Neill stars as the co-ed with bad dreams and John C. Russell is her escaped psycho killer brother. With topless scenes, and lots of flashbacks and hallucinations to keep things interesting.

SORORITY HOUSE MASSACRE II

(New Horizons, 1990) **D/P:** "Arch Stanton"/Jim Wynorski **S:** J. B. Rogers, Bob Sheridan **P:** "Shelly Stoker"/Julie Corman   *(Nightie Nightmare)*

A black-hooded killer with a hook stalks five girls trapped in a house. They (tall blonde Melissa Moore, the British Robin Harris, Bridget Carney, Stacia Zhivago, and Dana Bentley) take showers, dance topless, and scream. Moore becomes possessed. Cops who hang out at a strip club eventually show up, and Peter Spellos plays big menacing Orville Ketchum. Also with the late porn star Savannah dancing. The ridiculous Roger Corman/Concorde release features a long flashback from *Slumber Party Massacre*. The music is imitation Morricone ("Stanton" was the name on the tombstone in *The Good, the Bad, and the Ugly*). This

was filmed back-to-back with *Hard to Die*. They both have the same basic plot, some of the same girls, the same flashbacks, the same cops, and Orville.

THE SORROWS OF SATAN

(Fright, 1926) **D/P:** D. W. Griffith **S:** Forrest Halsey

A writer in a boarding house (Ricardo Cortez) says, "I'd sell my soul for money," so Prince Lucio/Lucifer (Adolphe Menjou, in formal wear and top hat) arrives (while lightning flashes) to oblige. The slow-going silent has several worthwhile scenes. It opens with winged angels cast down to become black demons. The shadow of Lucio becoming a giant winged demon is very impressive. There's also an elaborate stage show with frolicking maidens and horned men. With Carol Dempster (in her last role) as the woman who loves the writer and Lya de Putti as the sexy Russian exile temptress Olga. The Paramount release (originally planned for Cecil B. DeMille) was filmed at studios in Astoria, Long Island. It's based on a novel by Marie Corelli that had already been filmed twice, in England and Denmark (by Carl Dreyer). *Sorrows* was not a hit and was considered "too gruesome" by critics of the day. The print is excellent and has a musical score.

SORRY, WRONG NUMBER

(Paramount, 1948) **D/P:** Anatole Litvak **S:** Lucille Fletcher **P:** Hal Wallis **M:** Frank Waxman

Barbara Stanwyck stars as a frantic (and unlikable) rich bedridden lady in her mansion, who accidentally overhears plans to kill her on the phone. Stanwyck was nominated for an Oscar in the suspense classic. Burt Lancaster is the husband who wants her money. With Wendell Corey, Ann Richards, Ed Begley, Leif Erickson, and William Conrad. The Paramount release is based on a radio drama by Fletcher that had starred Agnes Moorehead. The director's next was *The Snake Pit*. A USA cable TV remake (Paramount, 1989) starred Loni Anderson (who is no Barbara Stanwyck).

S.O.S. COAST GUARD

(Sinister, 1937) **D:** William Whitney, Alan James **S:** Morgan Cox, Ronald Davidson

Ralph Byrd is the hero in this 12-chapter Republic serial and Bela Lugosi is Boroff, a crazed munitions inventor. Boroff develops a disintegration gas and plans to sell it to a foreign power. With Richard Alexander and Maxine Doyle. It was also released as a feature (also available from Sinister).

SOUL HUSTLER

(Monterey, 1973) **D/S/P:** Burt Topper   *(The Day the Lord Got Busted)*

Fabian stars as a guy with sideburns living in a van who smokes pot, takes reds, uses hookers, and shoots up. A tent preacher helps turn him into Matthew, "Son of Jesus," a singing evangelist who appeals to kids and soon has a hit record. After his Nam vet helper ODs, he hides out with Nai Bonet (from *Nocturna*). Also with a curly-haired Casey Kasem, Tony Russell, and Larry Bishop. Fabian sings at a large "Matthew" concert at the LA

Forum. Collectors' warning: The Harley Hatcher soundtrack was released on MGM. Topper also directed the former teen idol in *Fireball 500* (1966) and *The Devil's Eight* (1967), both for AIP.

SOUL MAN

(Starmaker, 1986) **D:** Steve Miner **S:** Carol Black **P:** Steve Tisch

C. Thomas Howell passes for black to earn a Harvard Law School scholarship in a comedy. He falls for Rae Dawn Chong (they later were married in real life for a while). James Earl Jones, Leslie Nielsen, Jeff Altman, James B. Sikking. and Julia Louis-Dreyfus are also in the silly comedy along with the president's son Ron Reagan Jr. A PG-13 New World release by the director of *House* and *Warlock*.

THE SOUL OF A MONSTER

(Sinister, 1944) **D:** Will Jason **S:** Edward Dein **P:** Ted Richmond

A woman prays for her dying doctor husband (George Macready). A mysterious devil worshiper hypnotist (Rose Hobart) saves him, then controls his life and uses him to kill. It's a great title for a mediocre Columbia release that copies Val Lewton's productions and runs about an hour.

THE SOUL OF NIGGER CHARLEY

(1973) **D/S/P:** Larry Spangler **S:** Harold Stone

In a sequel to *The Legend of Nigger Charley*, some ex-Confederates in Mexico hold former slaves captive. Fred Williamson returns with D'Urville Martin as Toby. They team with a Mexican bandit (Pedro Armendariz) to free them. With Denise Nicholas (*Room 222*), Nai Bonet, and Richard Farnsworth. By the director of *The Life and Times of Xaviera Hollander*. Lou Rawls is featured on the MGM soundtrack.

SOUL OF THE DEMON

(Far West, 1992) **D/S/P:** Charles Lang

Two teens dig up a gargoyle statue and unleash a demon during a séance just before a Halloween party. It has some good FX and gore and was made by a Las Vegas TV commercial director.

SOUL PATROL

(1980) **D:** Christopher Rowley **P:** Martin Wraggle **S.** Africa   *(Black Trash)*

Nigel Davenport is a cop who teams with a black newspaper reporter (Ken Gampu) to investigate the deaths of several drug dealers. Peter Dyneley is also in the badly edited action movie.

SOUL SOLDIER

(New Pacific, 1970) **D:** John "Bud" Cardos **S:** Marlene Weed **P:** James M. Northern   *(Red, White and Black)*

10th Calvary soldiers Robert DoQui and Rafer Johnson fight off Indians in Texas. They also fight over Janee Michelle. It was called the "first" black western but there were others in the 30s and 40s. With Cesar Romero and Barbara Hale as a couple at the fort and Robert Dix. It's a PG feature from Joe Solomon's Fanfare.

SOULTAKER

(AIP, 1990) **D:** Michael Rissi **S/A:** Vivian Schilling **P:** Eric Parkinson, Connie Kingrey

Martin Sheen's brother Joe Estevez plays the love-sick mystical title character in a long black coat. He can vanish at will and works for "the angel of death" (Robert Z'Dar with long hair). The sight of the cartoonish pair, both with heavy eye shadow, was too much for me. They resemble a moody rat man hanging out with Rondo Hatton's professional wrestler son. Anyway, the movie is about two teens, the mayor's daughter Natalie (writer Schilling), and her ex-boyfriend (Gregg Thomsen) who hangs out with a coke dealer. They die in a car crash, but continue to exist in a sort of half life. They have to get back to their bodies in time and the Soultaker wants to spend eternity with Natalie. Some interesting things happen, but this is a tame sort of romantic movie (when someone swears they say "frickin'"). Bullets can't kill Estevez, but he can be knocked out. One character exclaims: "Led Zeppelin was wrong, man! There is no stairway to Heaven!" Filmed in Mobile, Alabama.

SOULTANGLER

(1987) **D/S/C:** Pat Bishow **S:** Lance Laurie, John Bishow **P:** Paula Vlodkowsky

A long-haired mad doctor (Pierre Devaux) at "Whitewood Institute" narrates, then a lady reporter (Jane Kinser) narrates, then somebody else narrates. Yes, it's a very confusing movie, but it does have ambitious and effective FX. There's a living brain with eyes, a convincing bloody decapitation, a talking dummy, hallucinations, and running zombies. A hooded killer with a hammer kidnaps women for bloody experiments. The title song is by the Hypnolovewheel and the film clip is from *Witchcraft Through the Ages*. This was made in Commack, New York.

SOUL TO SOUL

(Videotakes, 1971) **D:** Dennis Sanders **P:** Richard Bock, Tom Mosk

American groups and singers travel to Africa and play at an all-night concert honoring the 14th anniversary of the independence of Ghana. With Wilson Pickett doing "Land of 1,000 Dances," Ike and Tina Turner, Santana, The Staple Singers, Les McCann, The Voices of East Harlem, and others. From Cinerama. Sanders made *Invasion of the Bee Girls* next.

SOUL VENGEANCE

(Xenon, 1975) **D/S/P/M/E:** Jamaa Fanaka
(*Welcome Home Brother Charles*)

Some people don't think this movie really exists. Here's proof. It starts with bizarre industrial music over the credits. Charles (Marlo Monte), a former drug dealer/pimp, is spending three years in the

"slams." The plot is *very* confusing, but flashbacks, nightmares, and flashbacks inside of flashbacks try to explain things. One nightmare features hysterical laughter, banging pianos, and lots of photos of men in prison. A hateful corrupt white LA cop (who had caught his wife with a black man) sets up Charles, beats him in the police car, and attempts to castrate him with a razor. After he's released, a black woman works as a waitress to support him while he seduces, then kills, the wives of the people who had put him away. This sick, crazy time piece has platform shoes, afros, red jump suits, the Watts Tower, people shooting up, and topless dancers, all typical 70s elements, but there's more. Thanks to a mystical cellmate, Charles can mesmerize women with his magic growing dick. A doctor explains, "His penis had grown to frightening limits!" In the scene that will make viewers doubt their sanity, you see it grow and strangle somebody. Crown International, a name to remember, was the original releasing company. Fanaka (the black Ed Wood Jr.?) went on to make the only slightly less warped *Penitentiary* films.

SOUTH BEACH

(Prism, 1992) **D/P/A:** Fred Williamson
S: Michael Montgomery

Williamson assembled his most impressive cast for this one. He's Mac Derringer, a Miami P.I. (and ex-football star) who is teamed with either Gary Busey (partner) or a ponytailed Peter Fonda (bar owner friend). It's almost comical the way the action shifts from Busey to Fonda and how they almost, but never quite appear in the same scene together. It was strange to see Busey in this the same week as *The Firm* and nice to see Fonda doing something. The rambling plot concerns a masked killer and black-mail with porno pictures. Vanity has little to do as Mac's ex, a phone sex worker. All the women want the cigar-smoking star (of course), but his one breast-kissing sex scene is with an unknown (white) woman. Also with Robert Forster as a cop friend, Henry Silva (one scene) as a gangster, Stella Stevens, and Isabel Sanford (*The Jeffersons*) as Fred's mom! The ending is awful and there's a rapper informant.

SOUTH BRONX HEROES

(Dura Vision, 1985) **D/S/P:** William Szarka **S:** Don Schiffrin
(*The Runaways*)

Mario Van Peebles is released from a Mexican jail and moves in with his teacher sister (Megan Van Peebles) in the Bronx. They help some white kids, victims of child abuse and porno. With Brendan Ward.

SOUTHERN COMFORT

(Goldwyn, 1981) **D/S:** Walter Hill
S/P: David Giler **S:** Michael Kane

In the early 70s, National guard troops on maneuvers become stranded in Louisiana Cajun terri-

tory swamps. Some Cajun trappers that they had made fun of kill off the disorganized and unprepared men in a violent and horrifying Vietnam allegory. Keith Carradine and Powers Boothe stars with Fred Ward, Peter Coyote, T. K. Carter, and Lewis Smith. Brion James is memorable as a one-armed trapper and the Ry Cooder music is excellent.

THE SOUTHERN STAR

(1968) **D:** Sidney Hayers **S:** David Purcell, John Seddon **P:** Roger Duchet   France/UK (*L'Etoile du Sud*)

This comic adventure about a diamond is set in 1912. It's based on a Jules Verne story and was filmed in Senegal. George Segal stars with Johnny Seka, Orson Welles as an alcoholic trader villain, and Ursula Andress as the daughter of a local dictator (Harry Andrews) with a pet ostrich. Also with Ian Hendry and Michel Constantin. French and English versions were filmed.

SOUTHWEST PASSAGE

(1954) **D:** Ray Nazarro **S:** Harry Essex, Geoffrey Homes **P:** Edward Small

Joanne Dru and Rod Cameron star in a 3-D Pathecolor story of bank robbers and when the U.S. Calvary used camels in the desert. The Indians think the camels are Gods. With whips and a 3-D decapitation scene! The cast includes John Dehner, Daryl Hickman, and Morris Ankrum. From United Artists. Essex also wrote the 3-D hits *Creature from the Black Lagoon* and *It Came From Outer Space*.

SO YOUNG, SO BAD

(1950) **D/S:** Bernard Vorhaus **S:** Jean Rouverol **P:** Edward and Harry Danziger

Paul Henreid is the new understanding psychiatrist at a girls' school with sadistic matrons. One

a.k.a. *Soul Vengeance*

girl is driven to suicide and the corrupt authorities try to have him discredited. It's a good early jd movie, complete with cat fights, and three of the four young female stars went on to greater fame. Anne Jackson, Anne Francis (as a young mother), Rita Moreno, and Enid Pulver are the main female jds. UA released it the same year as Warner's *Caged*.

SPACEBALLS

(MGM, 1987) **D/S/P/A:** Mel Brooks
S: Thomas Meehan, Ronny Graham

Brooks's movie parody is an obvious *Star Wars* spoof about the "power of the Schwartz." Daphne Zuniga stars as Princess Vespa and Bill Pullman is Lone Star. Brooks himself plays the President and Yugurt. With John Candy as a dog/man, Rick Moranis as Dark Helmet, Dick Van Patten, Michael Winslow, John Hurt (as himself), Deanna Booher, and the voice of Joan Rivers (as a robot). This PG feature and *History of the World—Part I* (1981) were the only movies Brooks directed in the 80s, but he executive produced others.

SPACECAMP

(Vestron, 1986) **D:** Harry Winer **S:** W.W. Wicket, Casey T. Mitchell **P:** Patrick Bailey

In an "uplifting" PG-rated teen science fiction movie, astronaut Kate Capshaw is showing a spaceship to some kids. It accidentally blasts off and they end up in outer space. With Lea Thompson (the same year as *Howard the Duck*), Kelly Preston, Leaf Phoenix, Tate Donovan, Tom Skerritt, Barry Primus, and Terry O'Quinn. From 20th Century.

SPACED INVADERS

(Touchstone, 1990) **D/S:** Patrick Read Johnson **S:** Scott Lawrence Alexander
P: Luigi Cingolani   (*Martians!*)

Five short comic aliens land on Halloween in a midwest town after hearing a rebroadcast of Orson Welles's *War of the Worlds* radio show on its 50th anniversary. One alien has a Jack Nicholson voice. The PG-rated Disney movie also features Douglas Barr and Royal Dano.

SPACED OUT

(Thorn EMI, 1979) **D:** Norman J. Warren **S:** Andrew Payne **P:** David Speechley   UK (*Outer Touch*)

Alien women discover sex in a science fiction parody. With Glory Annen and Barry Stokes (both also in the director's *Alien Prey*) and Ava Cadell. Comic New York City voices were dubbed for the computer and jukebox for the Miramax US release. They also added some extra nudity.

SPACEFLIGHT

(1965) **D:** Bernard Knowles **S:** Harry Spalding **P:** Robert L. Lippert   UK

In 2015, a spaceship with a full crew travels through space on the way to a colony. A woman kills herself and there's a mutiny. With Bill Williams as the maniacal captain and Kathleen Breck. The forgotten b/w feature from Lippert/20th Century is by the director of *Frozen Alive* (1964).

SPACEHUNTER: ADVENTURES IN THE FORBIDDEN ZONE

(Goodtimes, 1983) **D:** Lamont Johnson
S: David Preston, Edith Rey, Dan Goldberg, Len Blum **P:** Don Carmody, Andre Link, John Dunning   Canada

Captain Wolff (Peter Strauss) is stuck with a bratty tomboy named Nikki (Molly Ringwald) on a plague-ridden planet. He's searching for three women kidnapped by Overdog (Michael Ironside), a mutant cyborg. The PG Columbia movie was one of several early 80s 3-D science fiction releases. With Ernie Hudson and Andrea Marcovicci. Elmer Bernstein wrote the scrore. Ivan Reitman was the executive producer. The original director, Jean LaFleur (*Ilsa, the Tigress of Siberia*), was replaced. Partially filmed in Canada and Utah.

SPACE IS THE PLACE

(Rhapsody, 1974) **D:** John Coney
S: Joshua Smith **P:** Jim Newman

Sun Ra (in his ancient-Egyptian-look clothes) lands in a spaceship in Oakland to "plan for the salvation of the black race." The "black youth of planet Earth" laugh at him, but soon realize that "the dude's got a tight rap." This high quality 63-minute movie is serious, surreal, funny (on purpose), and partially autobiographical. Ra/Sonny Ray is seen in 1943 at a club in Chicago, where he causes a riot (!) by playing discordant notes on the piano. Singer June Tyson is featured chanting in musical segments. It was made at a time when Ra was on the cover of *Rolling Stone* and had a new LP out on Blue Thumb (both are shown) and has excellent editing and color. Repeat: "It's the end of the world. Don't you know that?"

SPACEMAN IN KING ARTHUR'S COURT

(1979) **D:** Russ Mayberry **S:** Don Tait
P: Ron Miller   (*Unidentified Flying Oddball*)

A scientist astronaut (Dennis Dugan) and his look-alike robot go through a time warp and end up in sixth-century England. With Jim Dale, Ron Moody, and Kenneth More. The Mark Twain *Connecticut Yankee . . .* update is from Disney.

SPACE MUTINY

(AIP, 1987) **D/P:** David Winters **S:** Maria Dante

A musclebound hero called Ryder (Reb Brown) helps spaceship commander Cameron Mitchell (in a bushy white beard!) and his blond miniskirted daughter (Cissy Cameron). A mutiny is led by the security force (John Phillip Law and James Ryan). Law laughs and rides around in vehicles that resemble modified golf carts. Ryan is a crippled killer. If the disco scene (with hula hoops) or the telepathic alien women dancing in bathing suits don't have you laughing, just concentrate on Cissy, Mitchell's real-life daughter. She's not only too old for the role, her acting makes everyone else in the cast seem like surefire Oscar material! The familiar-looking space footage is all from *Battlestar Galactica* and the interiors look just like a warehouse. It was shot in South Africa.

SPACE: 1999

(J2 series, 1975–77)
S/P: Gerry and Sylvia Anderson   UK

This was the second live-action series (after *UFO*) by the creators of Super Marionation. Martin Landau and (his then wife) Barbara Bain star on Moonbase Alpha. It was the most expensive sci-fi series ever produced at the time and Rudi Gernreich designed the unisex uniforms. Four one hour-episodes of the 48-episode series are available. Guests on the tapes include Richard Johnson and Christopher Lee. Barry Morse and Catherine Schell as an alien woman are other regulars. A feature-length episode *Space: 1999—Journey Through the Black Sun* (IVE) is hosted by Sybil Danning. Gerry Anderson later created the *Space Precinct* show (1994).

SPACE PATROL

(Rhino series, 1951–55)

This crude early kids' science fiction show (originally on ABC) is set in the 30th century. Ed Kemmer stars as Commander Buzz Corey, Lyn Osborn is Cadet Happy, and Virginia Hewitt is Carol. Also with Bela Kovacs as Prince Baccarratti and Marvin Miller as the evil Proteus. Rhino has three 90-minute volumes of 3 episodes each and Sinister offers 15 volumes, each with 2 episodes and original commercials. One live episode was reportedly shot in 3-D.

SPACE RAGE

(Vestron, 1985) **D:** Conrad E. Palmisano
S: Jim Lenahan **P:** Morton Reed

John Laughlin is a bounty hunter and Michael Paré is the villain Grange in a futuristic sci-fi western prison planet movie. With Richard Farnworth as an ex-LA cop hero on another planet, Lee Purcell, and William Windom. It has a rock soundtrack.

SPACE RAIDERS

(Warner, 1983) **D/S:** Howard R. Cohen
P: Roger Corman   (*Star Child*)

A 10-year-old child is a stowaway and there's an alien on a space ship. Vince Edwards is the name star. Also with Luca Bercovici and Dick Miller as Crazy Mel. Concorde released the PG feature that uses footage and music from *Battle Beyond the Stars*.

SPACE RANGERS

(Cabin Fever, 1993)

There are 3 100-minute tapes available of this CBS series, which tried to compete with several *Star Trek* series. Jeff Kaake stars as the leader of futuristic space troubleshooters. With an alien side-kick (Cary-Hiroyuki Tagawa), Linda Hunt, Marjorie Monaghan, Jack McGhee, and Clint Howard.

SPACE PARTS

(Vidmark, 1983) **D/S/P:** Rainer Erler
W. Germany (*Flesh*)

A woman (Jutta Speidel) investigates when her husband is kidnapped by an ambulance. The *Coma*-type black market organ plot is set in New York and New Mexico. It's based on a novel by the director and sounds similar to the later movie *The Ambulance*.

SPACE THING

(SW, 1968) **D/P:** "B. Ron Elliott"/Byron Mabe
S: "Cosmo Politan" **P:** David F. Friedman

A guy who ignores his wife and reads science fiction magazines in bed dreams he's a space hero (with a goatee) in the future. He takes invisibility pills and narrates ("The male Terranean was kissing and licking . . ."). After several sex scenes (one with lesbians and whips), the ship lands and he keeps his gold lamé pants on during sex in the desert (outside Bronson Canyon). He blows up the ship at the end. The cheapest possible effects are used (toy spaceship, bar stools for seats), microphone shadows are visible, and the makeup is incredible. The lady captain of the Terraneans looks great. The (fake) credits are on nude body parts. Elliott also directed *The Acid Eaters* and other David F. Friedman productions.

SPACE VAMPIRES = ASTRO ZOMBIES

SPARROWS

(Sinister, 1926) **D:** William Beaudine
S: C. Gardner Sullivan

Gustav Von Seyffertitz is the evil farmer Grimes who uses orphan kids for slave labor. Ten of them, led by the oldest (Mary Pickford), escape through the quicksand and an alligator-filled Louisiana swamp. The tape runs 84 minutes and has a music score. It's considered the classic in the long career of Beaudine, who directed so many B movies (all the way up until the mid 60s). From UA.

SPASMO

(VSOM, 1974) **D/S:** Umberto Lenzi
S: Massimo Franciosa, Luisa Montagnana
P: Ugo Tucci **M:** Ennio Morricone   Italy

This confusing mystery set in a deserted chateau concerns an assassin in a drive-a-brother-insane scheme. Suzy Kendall, Robert Hoffman, and Ivan Rassimov star. It's rumored that George Romero shot ten minutes of additional (violence) footage for the US release.

SPASMS

(HBO, 1981) **D:** William Fruet **S:** Don Enright **P:** John G. Pozhke, Maurice Smith
M: Tangerine Dream   Canada (*Death Bite*)

Oliver Reed is a big game hunter who has a telepathic link to a snake. The devil snake grows to giant size and its bite causes victims in a college town to puff up and die. Peter Fonda is a parapsychologist and Al Waxman is the villain. It has some good death scenes, thanks to makeup by Dick Smith, and a mechanical snake. Based on a novel by Michael Maryk and Brent Monahan.

SPEAK OF THE DEVIL

(AIP, 1991) **D/S/P:** Raphael Nussbaum **S:** Bob Craft

A corrupt southern evangelist couple (Robert Elarton and Jean Miller) are run out of town. They flee to Hollywood, move into a haunted house with a devil inside, and become satanists. The exorcist is a rabbi. With George "Buck" Flower.

SPECIAL BULLETIN

(Lorimar, 1983) **D/P:** Edward Zwick
S/P: Marshall Herskovitz

Protesters threaten to destroy Charleston, SC unless the nuclear warheads stored there are deactivated. It's all presented as if being reported on a real newscast. When first shown on NBC, this taped feature was accompanied by disclaimers so viewers wouldn't think it was really happening (like when Orson Welles broadcast his *War of the Worlds*). With Ed Flanders, Kathryn Walker, Roxanne Hart, Christopher Allport, and Rosalind Cash.

SPECIAL DELIVERY

(Vestron, 1976) **D:** Paul Wendkos
S: Don Gazzaniga **P:** Richard Berg

Bo Svenson is a Nam vet and Cybill Shepherd is an artist in a comic bank robbery movie. With Tom Atkins, Gerrit Graham, Jeff Goldblum, Sorrell Brooke, Robert Ito, and Vic Tayback. The PG-rated AIP release was a Bing Crosby production.

SPECIAL EFFECTS

(Nelson, 1984) **D/S:** Larry Cohen **P:** Paul Kurta

Eric Bogosian (*Talk Radio*), in his first major role, is a famous New York director whose last feature was a flop. He films himself actually killing a would-be actress (Zoe Tamerlis) and arranges to have her husband (Brad Rijn) from Oklahoma blamed for the killing, and acts in his docudrama about the case. His new feature will center on the real "snuff" footage. *Special Effects* borrows from *Peeping Tom, Paris, Texas,* and *Vertigo* (Tamerlis, from *Ms. 45*, plays two roles). The director, a conspiracy fanatic (as is Cohen) is seen watching the Zapruder footage over and over. Also with Kevin O'Connor and Bill Oland. Rijn was also in Cohen's *Perfect Strangers*. Both low-budget features are among Cohen's best.

THE SPECIALIST

(Vid America, 1975) **D:** Hikmet Avedis
S/P/A: Marlene Schmidt

Ahna Capri (from *Enter the Dragon*) stars as a killer for hire. She also has topless scenes in the R-rated Crown International release. With John An-

derson, Adam West as a lawyer, and Alvy Moore. The director and producer were married. They made *Dr. Minx* the same year.

THE SPECIALIST

(Warners, 1994) **D:** Luis Llosa **S:** Alexander Seros **P:** Jerry Weintraub **M:** John Barry

After *Speed* and *Blown Away*, we got more bombs in this adaptation of novels by John Shirley. Sylvester Stallone is mumbling ex-CIA assassin and explosives expert Ray Quick. Sharon Stone wants to hire him to kill gangsters who killed her family (seen in flashbacks). James Woods is the former CIA partner gone bad. Scenes were cut and some were reshot so Stallone's role would be more important. With overacting Rod Steiger and Eric Roberts as father and son Cuban drug runners in Miami.

THE SPECKLED BAND

(Foothill, 1931) **D:** Jack Raymond
S: W. P. Lipscomb **P:** Herbert Wilcox   UK

Raymond Massey (making his screen debut) stars as a modern-day Sherlock Holmes in a version of a story that had been a popular London play concerning poisonous snake bites. Holmes uses intercoms and an automated filing system. With Athole Stewart as Watson. It was the second sound Holmes movie, after *The Return of Sherlock Holmes* (1929). The Canadian Massey was in *The Old Dark House* the next year.

SPECTERS

(Lightning, 1987) **D/S:** Marcello Avallone
S/P: Maurizio Tedesco, Andrea Purgatori, Dardano Sarchetti   Italy (*Spettri*)

With a plot inspired by the excellent *Quatermass and the Pit,* archeologists (led by Donald Pleasence) dig in an ancient vault in Rome. Work on a subway interferes and a monster (shown for about two seconds) is unleashed. There's a *Nightmare on Elm Street* bed scene rip-off, and one good part in an otherwise boring movie (that was made for TV). Filmmakers are shown making a remake of *Creature from the Black Lagoon*.

SPEED

(Fox, 1994) **D:** Jan DeBont
S: Graham Yost **P:** Mark Gordon

In a very exciting nonstop 115-minute-long summer action hit, three disasters occur: in a highrise on an elevator, on a Santa Monica bus wired to explode, and on the then-new LA subway. Keanu Reeves stars as LA SWAT team hero cop Jack Traven, and Dennis Hopper is a crazed ex-cop terrorist (who gets decapitated). Sandra Bullock drives the speeding bus, and Jeff Daniels is the cop partner. Also with Joe Morton. The Dutch director was the cinematographer of Paul Verhoeven movies, *Die Hard,* and *Lethal Weapon 3*. The Fox soundtrack features songs about vehicles including Gary Numan's "Cars." I'm not one to blame any real-life events on movies, but within a year of this, *Blown Away,* and *The Specialist,* all major 1994 releases about terrorist bombings, Oklahoma City happened. A sequel is planned.

THE SPEED LOVERS

(SW, 1968) **D/S/P/A:** William McGaha
S: Elaine Wilkerson, Fred Tuch

This stock-car-racing drama, filmed at various real tracks around the country, includes dream sequences and split-screen scenes. Racing champ Fred Lorenzen plays himself and the title theme is by rockabilly singer Billy Lee Riley. Johnny Legend presents the video release. McGaha also made a nudie comedy, *Bad Girls for the Boys* (1966).

SPEED ZONE!

(Media, 1989) **D:** Jim Drake **S:** Michael
Short **P:** Murray Shostak US/Canada

It's actually *Cannonball Run III,* but the name was changed. It's a sad thing to see former SCTV stars in a dumb illegal race comedy that spoofs dumb illegal race comedies. John Candy stars with Joe Flaherty and Eugene Levy, and Peter Boyle is the sheriff. Also with Donna Dixon, Brooke Shields, Melody Anderson, Shari Belafonte, Tim Matheson, the Smothers Brothers, Jamie Farr (from the other *Cannonball* movies), Lee Van Cleef (wasted in his last role), Art Hindle, Carl Lewis, Matt Frewer, and Michael Spinks. The Raymond Chow presentation was one of the most expensive movies ever made in Canada.

SPELLBINDER

(Fox, 1988) **D:** Janet Greek **S:** Trace
Torme **P:** Joe Wizan, Brian Russell

Timothy Daly stars as an LA lawyer whose new girlfriend (Kelly Preston) is a witch. She's trying to escape from an occult group led by Anthony Crivello that wants to use her for a sacrifice. The MGM release reuses some *Fatal Attraction* ideas. With Rick Rossovich and Cary-Hiroyuki Tagawa.

SPELLBOUND

(Sinister, 1940) **D:** John Harlow
S: Miles Matheson **P:** R. Murray-Leslie
UK (*Spell of Amy Nugent; Passing Clouds*)

A spiritualist materializes a man's dead fiancé (Diana King). Apparitions are seen, and a woman is possessed. Derek Farr stars with Vera Lindsay and Hay Petrie. PRC released the 63-minute feature in America in 1945.

SPELLBOUND

(Key, 1945) **D:** Alfred Hitchcock **S:** Ben Hecht, Angus
MacPhail **P:** David O. Selznick **M:** Miklos Rozsa

Gregory Peck is an amnesiac doctor who has spells whenever he sees dark lines against a white background. Ingrid Bergman is his psychiatrist in the Freudian murder mystery, based on a novel by Francis Beeding. It was nominated for many Oscars. This has the famous Salvador Dalí dream sequence, and a gunblast is seen in red Technicolor for two frames, a startling near-subliminal effect. The soundtrack (originally released on a 10-inch record) includes a theremin, another innovation.

With Rhonda Fleming, John Emery, Leo G. Carroll, Michael Chekhov, Wallace Ford, and Regis Toomey. Hitchcock gets off an elevator in a hotel.

SPELLCASTER

(Columbia, 1986) **D:** Rafal Zielinski **S:** Dennis
Paoli, Charles Bogel **P:** Roberto Besi

When it was released (in 1993), the box said "the *Rocky Horror* of the 90s!" There really should be a law. Some kids win a contest and get to go on a treasure hunt in a castle outside Rome. It's hosted by an obnoxious, alcoholic singing star. Adam Ant shows up as Diablo and Tracy Lin is in the cast. There's a killer chair, a zombie attack, and for humor, a guy called "Fatso" turns into a pizza and there's an anti-Cleveland joke. From a story by Ed Naha and with more mediocre John Buechler FX. Made in Italy by the director of *Screwballs* and *Valet Girls.*

THE SPHINX

(Sinister, 1933) **D:** Phil Rosen **S:** Robert E. DeMond

Lionel Atwill stars as a killer who is put on trial, but is acquitted because he proves he's a deaf-mute (a witness had heard the killer speak). The trick is, he's really two twin brothers. With Sheila Terry, Theodore Newton as a New York City newspaper man, plus comic relief from a dumb detective and a janitor. Monogram also remade the just over one-hour-long feature as *The Phantom Killer* (1942).

THE SPIDERS

(Kino Int., 1919) **D/S:** Fritz Lang **P:** Erich
Pommer Germany (*Die Spinnen*)

This is the earliest surviving Lang feature and was once thought to be lost. A serial with 4 feature-length parts was planned, but only 2 were filmed ("The Golden Sea" and "The Diamond Ship"). Carl de Vogt stars as Kay Hoog, an American sportsman in the Andes. Ressel Orla is Lio Sha, leader of the Spiders gang, after an Inca treasure, and Lil Dagover is a priestess. It features Chinese villains on the Falkland Islands, pre-*Mabuse* gangsters, lost civilizations, and human sacrifices. A restored (but not complete) 137-minute version with an organ score and color tinting was shown in America in 1979 and is on tape.

SPIDERS VENOM = THE LEGEND OF BLOOD FOREST

SPIES

(Kino, 1928) **D:** Fritz Lang **S:** Thea Von Harbou
P: Erich Pommer Germany (*Spione*)

Lang's first feature after the epic *Metropolis* stars Rudolf Klein-Rogge as the wheelchair-bound international spymaster Haghai. His plot against England includes Japanese and Russian agents. Sonja (Gerda Maurus) and government agent #326 (Willy Fritsch) are teamed to defeat him. Haghai ends his life on stage as Nemo the clown. MGM released it in America with a music score. The 88-

minute Kino version has an organ score by Gaylord Carter. This historical feature once ran as long as 130 minutes. The same stars (minus Klein-Rogge) returned in *Woman in the Moon* (1929). Both films were produced by Lang's own company.

SPIES LIKE US

(Warner, 1985) **D:** John Landis
S: Dan Aykroyd, Lowell Ganz, Babaloo
Mandel **P:** Brian Grazer, George Folsey

Chevy Chase and Dan Aykroyd are comic CIA recruits in a flop comedy patterned after Bob Hope (who appears here) and Bing Crosby road movies. With Steve Forrest, Donna Dixon, Bruce Davison, Bernie Casey, William Prince, and Vanessa Angel. Lots of directors and behind-the-scenes talents show up for bit parts, including Terry Gilliam, Sam Raimi, Ray Harryhausen, Joel Coen, Frank Oz, and Michael Apted.

SPIKE OF BENSONHURST

(Virgin, 1987) **D/S:** Paul Morrissey **S:** Alan
Bowne **P:** David Weisman, Nelson Lyon

Sasha Mitchell (later a martial arts movie regular) is a Brooklyn mobster's son who wants to be a boxer in this Mafia comedy. With Ernest Borgnine as a mobster who sells drugs and runs bootleg video stores, Rick Aviles, Talisa Soto, and Sylvia Miles. The music is by Coati Mundi of Kid Creole and the Coconuts.

SPIRITISM

(Sinister, 1961) **D:** Benito Alazraki **S:** Raphael Garcia
Travesi **P:** Guillermo Calderon Mexico (*Espiritismo*)

A mother (Carmen Gonzalez) gets three wishes in a *Monkey's Paw*–derived horror movie. Satan helps with her mortgage but she also wishes her son were still alive. K. Gordon Murray imported it. AIP released it to TV.

SPIRIT OF '76

(RCA, 1990) **D/S:** Lucas Reiner **P:** Susie Landau

David Cassidy, Olivia D'Abo, and Geoff Hoyle enter a time machine in 2176 planning to return to 1776 and find out what the American Constitution was. They end up in 1976 instead. This simple but great idea lets the director throw in every lame 70s fad and cliché, and the results are often hilarious. Jeff and Steve McDonald (of the group Red Kross and *Desperate Teenage Love Dolls*) become the guides for the confused visitors from the future. Eight-track tapes, Grand Funk, disco, gas lines, smile buttons, and Constitution shirts all have to be explained. With Leif Garrett as "Eddie Trojan, the Bone Master," the Kipper Kids as comic CIA men, Iron Eyes Cody, Tommy Chong, Julie Brown, and Moon Zappa. *Spirit* was a real family affair. Director Lucas Reiner is the son of Rob (who plays a self-help seminar leader) and the grandson of Carl (who plays a sick old man visited by members of Devo in the prologue). Producer Landau is the daughter of Barbara Bain, who is also in *Spirit of '76.* Roman Coppola was the executive producer. Lots of 70s music is on the soundtrack along with some new music by Red Kross and the Dickies.

SPIRIT OF THE BEEHIVE

(C.D., 1973) **D/S:** Victor Erice **P:** Elias Querejeta
Spain (*El Espíritu de la Colmena*)

A lonely little girl (Teresa Gimpera) sees the 1931 *Frankenstein* in a Spanish village in 1943. She and her sister decide the character is real and search for the monster (actually a police fugitive). With subtitles.

SPIRITS

(Vidmark, 1990) **D:** Fred Olen Ray
S: Jeff Falls, R. V. King **P:** Lee Lankford

A team of investigators (led by Robert Quarry) go to a house once owned by a French occultist. A psychic (Brinke Stevens) hears distorted groans, and cartoonish-sounding voices of kids having sex. Eventually she becomes possessed, her eyes go white, and she pounds a nail into her hand. Meanwhile in a church, a priest (Erik Estrada) talks to an understanding nun (Carol Lynley) and worries about his lack of faith. Michelle Bauer (with a demon voice) seduces him in a dream and a guy in the house has succubus sex. A ghoul says, "Fuck you, father," but Estrada saves the day. Here are some other signs of a haunted house: a plywood door breaks, a hole in the basement changes dimensions, and a microphone shadow "mysteriously" appears.

SPIRITS OF THE DEAD = THE ASPHYX

SPLASH

(Touchstone, 1984) **D:** Ron Howard **S:** Lowell Ganz, Babaloo Mandel, Bruce Jay Friedman **P:** Brian Grazer

A mermaid (Daryl Hannah) surfaces at the Statue of Liberty one day. A flashback shows how she had saved a kid (played by Tom Hanks as a grownup) from drowning. The likable fantasy comedy was the first big (PG) hit for Disney's Touchstone Pictures. With John Candy as Hanks's brother, Eugene Levy as a scientist, Dody Goodman, Howard Morris, Shecky Greene, and Bobby DiCicco. *Splash, Too* (1988) was a Disney TV movie with only Goodman returning.

SPLATTER: ARCHITECTS OF FEAR

(North America, 1986) **D:** Peter Rowe
S: Janet Schacter   Canada

It's a documentary behind-the-scenes look at the filming of an unreleased zombie wrestling-woman movie called *Amazon Queens Versus the Mutants*. It was shot on video and includes some sex and gore.

SPLATTER FARM

(Donna Michelle, 1987) **D:** P. Alan **P:** J. K. Farlew

You won't believe this regional shot-on-video obscurity. Teen twins (John and Mark Polonia) are sent to stay with their weird aunt (Marion Costly). Her young handyman Jeremy (Todd Rimatti) chops up people and keeps their body parts in the barn. There's lots of extreme amateur gore FX (using obvious dummies), but this has some male nudity, pissing, a sick nightmare toilet scene, and

incest. The music is harpsichords and pianos. The twins resemble two young Robby Bensons and the aunt reminded me of Edith Massey (her acting is that good too). Mark Polonia (of Wellsboro, PA) also made *Saurians,* a super-8 feature with claymation dinosaurs in the mid-90s. Brother John stars.

SPLATTER UNIVERSITY

(Vestron, 1982) **D/S/P/E:** Richard Haines
S/P: John Michaels **S:** Michael Cunningham

This awful Troma release, set at a Catholic college, was filmed in 16mm by an NYU film school grad. R and unrated videos are available. Haines also made *Class of Nuke 'Em High*, which at least had a few dumb laughs.

THE SPLIT

(1968) **D:** Gordon Flemyng **S:** Robert Sabaroff
P: Irwin Winkler, Robert Chartoff

Jim Brown stars as McCain, a thief who plans to rob the LA Coliseum during a Rams football game. Julie Harris helps plan the job and Diahann Carroll is his ex-wife. It's similar to Kubrick's classic *The Killing* but is based on Donald E. (*Point Blank*) Westlake's novel. With Gene Hackman as a corrupt cop, Ernest Borgnine (the muscles), Jack Klugman (the driver), Warren Oates (the safecracker), and Donald Sutherland (the killer). Also with James Whitmore as the psycho killer landlord, who takes the loot, and Jackie Joseph.

SPLIT

(AIP, 1987) **D/S/A/C/M/E:** Chris Shaw
P/A: Barbara Horscraft

This odd science fiction movie is not a typical AIP video release. It has arty cinematography, computer graphics, and some excellent FX. A "stalker" (Timothy Dwight) who appears in various disguises is being monitored by evil men who believe he could become a Christ figure. It doesn't make a whole lot of sense and parts are downright irritating, but it has acid flashes, hallucination scenes, nightmares, some nudity, some Keystone Kops footage, and burning Pop Tarts. The title sequence is especially good.

SPLIT IMAGE

(Embassy, 1982) **D/P:** Ted Kotcheff
S: Scott Spencer   Canada (*Captured*)

Michael O'Keefe is lured into a Moonie-like cult by a "home lander" (Karen Allen). James Woods is incredible as an obnoxious, manic deprogrammer, and Peter Fonda is the blissful cult leader. Elizabeth Ashley and Brian Dennehy are the concerned parents. Also with Lee Harcourt Montgomery and Michael Sacks. The Filmways/Orion release was filmed around Dallas. The director made *First Blood* next. *Ticket to Heaven* told a similar tale.

SPLIT SECOND

(RKO, 1953) **D:** Dick Powell **S:** William Bowers, Irving Wallace **P:** Edmund Garinger

Gangsters who have broken out of prison hold hostages in a Nevada atomic test area ghost town.

At the end, people are trying to flee while the countdown occurs, an A-bomb blast literally tears the town apart, then they all walk away OK!!! Alexis Smith stars with Jan Sterling, Keith Andes, Arthur Hunnicut, and Richard Egan. The escaped cons are Stephen McNally, Frank DeKova, and Paul Kelly. Powell directed *The Conqueror* next, a movie with real-life atomic problems.

SPLIT SECOND

(HBO, 1991) **D:** Tony Maylam, Ian Sharpe
S: Gary Scott Thompson **P:** Laura Gregory   UK

This boring, dull, misty science fiction movie is set in a flooded London in 2008. Rutger Hauer is Harley Stone, a disgusted cop who says fuck a lot, drinks coffee, smokes cigars, and is attuned to a serial killer creature. Neil Duncan is his new Oxford grad partner. The briefly-seen Chris Walas–created reptile monster rips out hearts and writes messages in blood. With Kim Cattrall in a nothing role, Michael J. Pollard as a rat catcher, and Ian Dury as a doorman. Sharpe directed the tube station climax. Cab Calloway and the Moody Blues ("Nights in White Satin") are on the soundtrack (which was issued by Milan). Maylam also made *The Burning* (1981).

SPONTANEOUS COMBUSTION

(Media, 1989) **D/S:** Tobe Hooper **S:** Howard Goldberg **P:** Jim Rogers, Jerrold W. Lambert

A nice couple is used in a 1955 H-bomb experiment. A baby is conceived after the blast. Years later, the troubled, grown up, and divorced son is Brad Dourif. On his 35th birthday, people start to die because of his out-of-control mental powers. A German lady scientist tries to help. This movie has an intriguing start and some great fire FX, but the conspiracy plot makes very little sense. Fire comes over a phone, from mouths, and from a hole in an arm. With Jon Cypher, Cynthia Bain, William Prince, Melinda Dillon, Dey Young, Dick Butkus, John Landis as a burn victim at a radio station, and the voice of George "Buck" Flower.

SPOOKIES

(Sony, 1986) **D/S/P:** Eugenie Joseph **D/S:** Thomas Doran, Brendan Faulkner **P:** Frank M. Farel

Twisted Souls (1984) was an unreleased horror comedy filmed in upstate New York by Doran and Faulkner. Others added new framing scenes to make this confusing but fun feature. It has lots of FX, some very impressive and some pretty mediocre. A German sorcerer in an old mansion wants to revive his bride and his geek assistant thinks he's a cat. There's a possessed kid, an Ouija board, monsters, zombies, and the Grim Reaper. Jimmy Muro operated the steadicam.

SPOOKS A-POPPIN

(Cinemanure, 1992) **D/S/P:** Jim Ridenouer

This unique historical tape features many rare vintage spook show trailers and film clips, interviews with Don Davison, Dr. Houston, Phillip Morris (later owner of a very successful mask/costume business), and (a very old) Raymond showing his collection in his trailer. The brother of spook show king Jack Baker is seen on stage doing a show, and the A-Bones provide the instrumental theme. The editing and the interview camerawork are amateur at best, and the many wonderful rare posters are hard to see, but this is a labor-of-love project and is a must for fans of live Spook Shows, which flourished in this country from the depression through the 50s and lingered on until the early 70s. The *Vampire's Coffin/Robot vs. the Aztec Mummy* trailer in "Hypnoscope" is a personal fave.

THE SPOOK WHO SAT BY THE DOOR

(Video City, 1973) **D/P:** Ivan Dixon **S/P:** Sam Greenlee **S:** Marvin Clay **M:** Herbie Hancock

The only black CIA agent (Lawrence Cook) has enough of being treated badly, so he organizes teens and leads a full-scale revolution against the government! Riots occur around the country and the president declares a state of emergency. Paula Kelly costars. The United Artists release is based on a novel by Greenlee. Dixon, formerly of *Hogan's Heroes* and one of the few black directors of 70s black action movies, also made *Trouble Man* (1972).

THE SPORTING CLUB

(Nelson, 1971) **D:** Larry Peerce **S:** Lorenzo Semple Jr. **P:** Lee M. Rich

This much hated (by critics) movie has young members of a hunting club in Michigan going on a violent rampage. They use drugs and go after rich women. It's based on a novel by Thomas McGuane. Robert Fields stars with Nicholas Coster, Jack Warden, William Roerick, Logan Ramsey and his wife Anne Ramsey, and a young pre-*Exorcist* Linda Blair. Avco Embassy cut out an orgy scene. The Buddah soundtrack featured cuts by Jerry Lee Lewis and others.

SPRING BREAK

(RCA, 1983) **D/P:** Sean S. Cunningham **S:** David Smilow

Teens go to Fort Lauderdale again. With Perry Lang, Corinne Alphen (Wahl), the 1982 *Penthouse* Pet of the Year, who leads an all female band, Richard B. Shull, Sheila Kennedy (also from *Penthouse*), and David Knell. With lots of wet T-shirts and Miller beer plugs. It was Cunningham's first after *A Stranger Is Watching*. From Columbia.

SPY MAKER: THE SECRET LIFE OF IAN FLEMING

(Turner, 1990) **D:** Ferdinand Fairfax **S:** Robert Aurech **P:** Aida Young   UK (*The Secret Life of Ian Fleming*)

Sean Connery's son Jason Connery stars as James Bond creator Ian Fleming. He's seen as a reporter and a WWII spy. Most of it isn't based on fact, and it's filled with Bond in-jokes. With Kristin Scott Thomas, David Warner, Joss Ackland, Fiona Fullerton, and Richard Johnson. The tape is longer than the TNT cable TV version.

SPY SMASHER

(Stokey, 1942) **D:** William Witney **S:** Ronald Davidson, Norman S. Hall, William Lively

Kane Richmond stars as a costumed WWII hero in a 12-chapter Republic serial. It's based on the character in *Whiz Comics*. He has a bat plane and a TV for spying. With Hans Schumm as "The Mask," Marguerite Chapman, Sam Flint, and Tristram Coffin. *Spy Smasher Returns* was an edited 60s feature version.

THE SQUEAKER

(Sinister, 1937) **D:** William K. Howard **S:** Bryan Edgar Wallace, Edward O. Berkman UK (*Murder on Diamond Row*)

Edmund Lowe stars as a disgraced inspector, out to catch a jewel thief called the Squeaker. With Ann Todd, Alastair Sim, and Robert Newton. It's a high-class Korda production with music by Miklos Rozsa. Edgar Wallace's novel *The Squeaker* had already been filmed twice—in England (1930) and Germany (1931). A fourth version was made in 1963.

THE SQUEAKER

(Sinister, 1963) **D:** Alfred Vohrer **S:** H. B. Peterson   W. Germany (*Der Zinker*)

Heinz Drache stars as Inspector Elford in a mystery about diamond robberies. With Barbara Rutting and Klaus Kinski as Tierpfleger Krischna. It's one of the many sixties Edgar Wallace/Scotland Yard mysteries that used to show up late nights on American TV.

THE SQUEEZE: *See* THE RIP OFF

SQUEEZE PLAY!

(1979) **D/P:** Michael Herz, "Samuel Weil"/Lloyd Kaufman

The first Troma hit is a suburban sex and baseball comedy with low humor. With Jennifer Hetrick, Al Corley (later on *Dynasty*), and Jim Metzger. Elizabeth Kaitan is the model on the poster. The small New York company made *Waitress!* next.

S.S. EXPERIMENT (LOVE CAMP)

(Wizard, 1976) **D/S:** Sergio Garrone **S:** Vinicio Marinucci **P:** Mario Caporall Italy (*Lager SSadis Kastrat Kommandantur; Captive Women II*)

A number of sleazy Italian movies like this were released to cash in on the success of the first *Ilsa* movie. Garone made several. This one is a flashback-filled feature with the castration of a Nazi prison officer, who then has a penis transplant. Sex and torture scenes make up much of the time. An uncut version has Spanish subtitles.

S.S. EXPERIMENTS, PART II: *See* S.S. HELL CAMP

S.S. GIRLS

(Media, 1976) **D/S:** "Jordan B. Mathews"/Bruno Mattei **S:** Giacinto Bonacquisti   Italy (*Casa Privata Per Le SS*)

More of the dregs of the exploitation business. It's about a Nazi whorehouse at the end of the war and has the usual nudity and violence. With Alan Collins. Mattei also made *S.S. Extermination Camp* (1977).

S.S. HELL CAMP

(Video City, 1976) **D:** "Ivan Katansky"/Paolo Solvay   Italy (*The Beast in Heat; Nazi Holocaust; S.S. Experiments II*)

Scientists create a Neanderthal man/rapist (played by Ook from *Frankenstein's Castle of Freaks*). This one has lots of nudity, torture, sickness, and an *Ilsa*-type torturer. It's all mixed with war footage about the Italian underground. With Brad Harris as an Italian partisan and Brigette Skay (*Bay of Blood*). By the director of *Devil's Wedding Night* and *Desert Tigers*.

STACEY!

(Video Gems, 1971) **D/S:** Andy Sidaris **S:** Leon Mirell   (*Stacey and Her Gangbusters*)

Sidaris was a director for ABC sports who made *The Racing Scene* (1970), a documentary, then this, his first fictional feature. *Playboy* centerfold Anne Randall stars as a sexy private eye investigating a Moonie-type cult. With Anitra Ford, Christina Raines (aka Tina Herazo), James Westmoreland, Miki Garcia (also from *Playboy*), and John Alderman. New World released the sex and violence movie in 1973. Sidaris made *Seven* next. *Malibu Express* was his remake of *Stacey!*

STAGE FRIGHT

(Warner, 1949) **D/P:** Alfred Hitchcock **S:** Whitfield Cook   UK

A Royal Academy drama student (Jane Wyman) helps a man (Richard Todd) who has been accused of murdering the husband of a musical stage star (Marlene Dietrich). Michael Wilding is a Scotland Yard detective. It was filmed in England with a cast including Alastair Sim, Dame Sybil Thorndike, Kay Walsh, and Patricia Hitchcock. The Warner release is based on characters created by Selwyn

Anne Randall is *Stacey!*

Jepson. The director is seen staring at Wyman on the street. It was released the year she divorced Ronald Reagan.

STAGE FRIGHT

(Vid America, 1982) **D/P:** John Lamond
S/P: Colin Eggleston   Australia (*Nightmares*)

A stage actress (Jenny Neumann from *Mistress of the Apes*) had caused the death of her mother 20 years earlier. The killing resumes during production of an arty play as actors are slashed with glass. With nudity and blood.

STAGEFRIGHT

(Imperial, 1987) **D:** Michele Soavi **S:** Luigi Montefiore **P:** Aristede Massaccesi **M:** Simon Boswell   Italy (*Deliria; Bloody Bird*)

An owl-masked actor from an asylum kills off the cast members of an arty murder musical. The cast is locked in for the night. The killer uses a drill, a chainsaw, an ax, and knives, and most of the characters are very mean. With David Brandon, Barbara Cupisti, and John Morghen. The screenwriter is actor "George Eastman." Aquarius released it in America. This movie seems to be a rival to Dario Argento's very similar (but much better) *Terror at the Opera* from the same year.

STAGE TO THUNDER ROCK

(1964) **D:** William F. Claxton
S: Charles A. Wallace **P:** A. C. Lyles

Barry Sullivan stars as a sheriff who has to fight another officer for the reward money for a robber prisoner. With Marilyn Maxwell, Scott Brady, Keenan Wynn, John Agar, Lon Chaney Jr., Wanda Hendrix, and Robert Lowry. All of the westerns from producer Lyles had great B movie casts and cliché plots. From Paramount.

STAKEOUT!

(1962) **D/S:** James Landis **P:** Robert and William Hughes, Joe R. Gentile

An ex-con (Bing Russell) and his son (Billy Hughes) can't find work, so they kidnap a boy for ransom money. The b/w drama was filmed in Texas. Landis made his classic, *The Sadist*, next. From Crown International.

STALKER

(Fox Lorber, 1979) **D/S:** Andrei Tarkovsky
USSR/W. Germany

A man (Alexander Kaidanovsky) guides two others through "the zone." The long (140-minute) very serious science fiction feature is part b/w and part color. Tarkovsky made it after *Solaris*. Afterwards, he defected and made *Nostalghia* in Italy (1983).

STALKING DANGER

(Starmaker, 1986) **D:** William Friedkin
P: David Salvern **M:** Ennio Morricone

Joe Cortese, Jack Youngblood, and Steve W. James are a government counter-terrorist squad with fu-

turistic weapons. It was a TV pilot for a projected series called *C.A.T. Squad*. With Patricia Charbonneau and Barry Corbin. The second pilot is on tape as *Python Wolf*.

THE STAND

(Republic, 1994) **D:** Mick Garris **S:** Stephen King **P:** Marshall Galin **M:** "Snuffy" Waldon (*Stephen King's The Stand*)

After a devastating virus escapes from a military installation, survivors either follow good (Ruby Dee as old Mother Abigail, who lives in a mystical cornfield) or evil (Jamey Sheridan as Flagg, who morphs into the devil). Eventually, the hand of God (!) appears in Las Vegas. Gary Sinise (as a Texan) and Adam Storke (as an NYC rock singer) are the hero stars. Miguel Ferrer, Matt Frewer, Laura San Giacomo, Corin Nemec, and Shawnee Smith are the main bad humans. Other good ones include Rob Lowe as a mute, Bill Fagerbakke as a retarded man, Ray Walston, Molly Ringwald, and Ossie Davis. Also with Ed Harris, Diane Ladd, Moses Gunn, and Joe Bob Briggs, plus cameos by Kareem Abdul-Jabbar, Kathy Bates, Tom Savini, and directors Sam Raimi and John Landis. King (also the executive producer) appears as a trucker. Most of it was shot in Salt Lake City. The incredible opening sequence is set to Blue Öyster Cult's "Don't Fear the Reaper." Waldon wrote the theme music to *Roseanne*. The Steve Johnson team handled the FX. Originally lasting 8(!) hours (with ads), the $25 million 4-part ABC ratings winner miniseries is based on King's 1978 novel. The double tape (6 hours) includes *The Making of The Stand* short. *The Stand* was once to be a theatrical feature directed by George Romero, then by John Boorman.

STAND ALONE

(Starmaker, 1984) **D:** Alan Beattie
S: Roy Carlson **P:** Leon Williams

A hero WWII vet (Charles Durning) does a *Rambo* in LA and fights bad Mexicans and drug dealers. With Pam Grier as a lawyer, James Keach as a cop, and Bert Remsen. A New World release by the director of *The House Where Death Lives*.

STAND BY ME

(RCA, 1986) **D:** Rob Reiner **S/P:** Bruce A. Evans, Raynold Gideon **P:** Andrew Scheinman

Some kids in Castle Rock, Oregon, in 1959 find a dead body. This was a big hit and it deserved to be. It's one of the best movies about being an innocent kid and the real and imagined horrors of growing up. And the tall-tale pie-eating scene is a gross-out classic. Wil Wheaton stars as the Stephen King substitute character and Richard Dreyfuss (as the grown-up writer) narrates. With River Phoenix, Corey Feldman, Jerry O'Connell, Kiefer Sutherland, Casey Siemaszko, Bradley Gregg, and Marshall Bell. It's based on and would have been known as "The Body," but because of a brilliant last-minute title change it's named after an unrelated song. Ben E. King's (1961) title song (only two years off) became a hit again and was used to sell many products. *Stand by Me* (from Columbia)

started an irritating trend of naming movies after name-value old hits. Reiner went on to direct another superior King adaptation, *Misery*.

STAR CRYSTAL

(Starmaker, 1985) **D/S:** Lance Lindsay **P:** Eric Woster

In this dull *Alien* copy, a tentacled alien on board a space shuttle in the year 2032 kills crew members (ugly woman, black guy, blond bimbo—in that order). Characters spend a lot of time crawling on their hands and knees through tunnels. Eventually a sad-eyed E.T.-like alien befriends the surviving couple. It was a New World release.

STARDUST

(1974) **D:** Michael Apted **S:** Ray Connolly
P: David Puttnam, Sandy Lieberson   UK

David Essex returns as Jim MacLaine in the hit sequel to *That'll Be the Day*. He and his (Beatletype) sixties group, The Stray Cats, become hitmakers. Later, he becomes a solo star, has drug problems, and dies. With Adam Faith, Larry Hagman, Keith Moon, Dave Edmunds, and Edd Byrnes. In America, 16 minutes were cut out. The double Arista soundtrack contains 40 "original hits."

STAR 80

(Warner, 1983) **D/S:** Bob Fosse
P: Wolfgang Glattes, Kenneth Utt

Mariel Hemingway is the Canadian *Playboy* Playmate turned actress Dorothy Stratten (née Hoogstratten) and Eric Roberts (in a classic irritating psycho role) is Paul Snider, the small-time hustler who married, then murdered her in 1980. With Cliff Robertson as Hugh Hefner, Carroll Baker as her mom, Josh Mostel, Jordan Christopher, and Keenan Ivory Wayans. Hemingway actually had her breasts enlarged for the role. Sven Nykvist was the cinematographer. *Death of a Centerfold* was an earlier TV movie based on the same events.

STARFIGHTERS

(1964) **D/S/P:** Will Zens

This low-budget color adventure about Air Force pilots stars Robert Dornan (a conservative US Congressman in the 90s) as Lt. Witkowski. In the plot he becomes lost in a storm and tries to live up to the reputation of his father, a WWII fighter pilot, now a Congressman. Zens also made the Vietnam war movie *To the Shores of Hell* (1966) and *Hell on Wheels* (1967), both also with Dornan; country music movies; and the minimalist anti-Communist *Capture That Capsule!* (1961). Somebody should release these movies. Maybe someday we'll have a Dornan–Sonny Bono presidential ticket.

STARFLIGHT ONE

(Vestron, 1983) **D:** Jerry Jameson
S: Robert Malcom Young **P:** Arnold Orgolini, Peter Nelson   (*Starflight*)

The world's fastest (hydrogen-powered) plane accidentally ends up in outer space. Lee Majors is the captain. With a typical all-star disaster movie cast including Lauren Hutton, Ray Milland, Tess Harper, Robert Webber, Jocelyn Brando, Robert Englund, and Kirk Cameron. When first shown on ABC it was called *Starflight: The Plane That Couldn't Land,* and it was shown theatrically overseas as *Starflight One.* John Dykstra created the special effects and Henry "The Fonz" Winkler was the executive producer of the *Airport* copy.

STARGATE

(Live, 1994) **D/S:** Roland Emmerich **S/P:** Dean Devlin, Oliver Eberle **P:** Joel B. Michaels

In this epic sci-fi movie, a gate to another world is discovered in Egypt. It seems that aliens were behind the building of the pyramids and they still live on a parallel desert planet with a large slave population living in a village and building more pyramids. James Spader is the Egyptologist who figures out how the huge circular stargate portal works and Kurt Russell is the quiet, suicidal military-man expedition leader. With Jaye Davidson (from *The Crying Game*) as the stony-faced alien leader Ra, Alexis Cruz, John Diehl, Viveca Lindfors as the scientist in opening segments, and Leon Rippy. The aliens are subtitled. The PG-13 hit cost as much as $70 million and was shot in Arizona. It was backed by French Canal Plus and distributed by MGM. The soundtrack is from Milan Records.

STAR IN THE DUST

(1956) **D:** Charles Haas **S:** Oscar Brodny **P:** Albert Zugsmith

Richard Boone stars as a hired gun about to be hanged in a Universal Technicolor western. Watch it for the great team of John Agar as the sheriff and Mamie Van Doren as his fiancée. Also with Leif Erickson, Coleen Gray, James Gleason, Paul Fix, Henry Morgan, Kermit Maynard, and an unbilled Clint Eastwood. Clint had also been in *Revenge of the Creature* and *Tarantula,* which both starred Agar.

STARK

(Fox, 1985) **D:** Rod Holcolmb **S:** Ernest Tidyman **P:** David B. Balkan

Nicolas Surovy stars as a Wichita cop who takes on the mob while searching for his chorus girl sister in Las Vegas. The CBS-TV pilot film features Marilu Henner and Dennis Hopper, in his first American project in years, as Stark's partner. Also with Pat Corley and Denise Crosby. *Stark: Mirror Image* (1986) was a second pilot, also with Surovy, Hopper, and Corley.

STARK FEAR

(Sinister, 1961) **D/P:** Ned Hockman **S/P:** Dwight V. Swain **P:** Joe E. Burke

Beverly Garland stars as a woman in Oklahoma City who discovers that her sneering, abusive husband (Skip Homeier) is also a mother-obsessed liar from a horrible small Oklahoma town. This b/w movie (shot in Norman and Lexington, OK) is

filled with hateful, neurotic, scary, lecherous, drunken men. In one shocking scene, the husband watches while she's raped on his mother's grave. Meanwhile oblivious, poverty-stricken Indians dance nearby. She eventually triumphs and falls for her widower oilman boss (Kenneth Tobey), the only really decent male character. The stars of this dreary soap opera with horror movie touches are all good and probably enjoyed playing more serious roles than they usually were offered.

STARK MAD

(1929) **D:** Lloyd Bacon **S:** Harvey Gates

Some people on a Central American yachting expedition search for a missing son. The captain turns out to be a madman and there's a killer gorilla. H. B. Warner stars with comedienne Louise Frazenda, Irene Rich, and Lionel Belmore. The Warner movie was released in silent and sound versions.

STAR KNIGHT

(Vidmark, 1985) **D/S/P:** Fernando Colomo **S:** Andeu Martin, Miguel Angel Nieto Spain (*El Caballero del Dragón*)

Klaus Kinski (with his *Aguirre* hair) is a good guy necromancer and alchemist. He befriends an alien in a medieval village. The sad, silent, telepathic alien has hair like Vanilla Ice's and wears all black. Harvey Keitel is a foolish clumsy knight with wings on his helmet, out to slay the dragon (actually a spaceship) and rescue the princess (Marie Lamour), who falls for the alien. Fernando Rey is the priest who encourages Keitel and plots against the Count. In one in-joke scene, Keitel asks "Are you talking to me?" in his familiar accent (!). The odd feature uses an impressive real castle and has some funny moments, but the effects are mediocre and the stars are wasted. Kinski's voice was dubbed by another.

STARK RAVING MAD

(1976) **D:** George F. Hood **P:** Tiger Warren, Don Gronquist (*Execution*)

Several movies have been based on Charles Starkweather (including *The Sadist* and *Badlands*), but this is the least known and the closest to the facts. Russell Fast stars as "Richard Stark," a short former Nebraska garbage man who smokes Luckies. He relates his famous 1958 multi-state murder spree story to a prison guard after his head is shaved. Marcie Severson plays his 14-year-old girlfriend.

STARLET!

(Private Screenings, 1969) **D:** Richard Kanter **S/P/A:** David F. Friedman **P:** William A. Castleman

Starlet! is a softcore behind-the-scenes look at the making of a nudie movie called "Youth in Babylon." Stuart Lancaster (best known for Russ Meyer movies) and John Alderman are the filmmakers. Shari

Mann stars as Carol, who sleeps her way to the top and becomes "Starliss Knight." One funny scene shows the making of a biker movie, "Heaven's Devils," on a set, and a nudie actress considers a role in an Italian western a step down. There's blackmail with a stag reel, the obligatory lesbian, spanking, and rape scenes, and an actress is electrocuted. Kanter also directed *The Ribald Tales of Robin Hood.* Friedman remade this in 1984 as *Matinee Idol,* a hardcore version and Friedman's last feature.

THE STARLETS

(1976) **D:** Daniel L. Symmes, Joseph Tebber

This obscure X-rated 3-D movie was advertised as being a Marilyn Monroe bio in "4-D." It isn't. With Dorothy Newkirk, John Leslie, and Candida Royalle, later a talk show regular, promoting her "Femme" line of porn for women.

STARMAN

(RCA/Columbia, 1984) **D:** John Carpenter **S:** Bruce A. Evans, Raynold Gideon **P:** Michael Douglas, Larry J. Franco

An alien (Jeff Bridges) lands in Wisconsin and takes the form of the late husband of Karen Allen in this romantic science fiction road movie. Richard Jaeckel (a government agent) and Charles Martin Smith (a scientist) are after him. It was executive produced by Michael Douglas and was once planned to be directed by Adrian Lyne, John Badham, or Tony Scott (among others). *Starman* features FX by ILM, Stan Winston, Rick Baker, and Dick Smith (a very impressive lineup). The PG Columbia release also became a short-lived 1986 ABC-TV series starring Robert Hays.

STARSHIP

(Cinema Group, 1985) **D/S:** Roger Christian **S:** Mathew Jacobs   UK (*Lorca and the Outlaws*)

This *Star Wars*–derived movie was filmed in Australia. It features 21st-century robots and human slaves owned by android bosses on the mining planet Odessa. John Tarrant stars with a cute robot. Christian had worked on *Alien, Star Wars,* and other blockbuster hits.

David F. Friedman's *Starlet.*

STAR SLAMMER

(Vidmark, 1984) **D/P:** Fred Olen Ray
S: Michael D. Sonye **P:** Jack H. Harris
(Prison Ship; The Adventures of Tara Part I)

Sandy Brooke (who has one topless scene) is Taura, sent to prison for destroying the hand of Ross Hagen. The silly comic adventure is a mixture of *Alien*, a little *Star Wars*, and women's prison movies. The torture and bondage scenes seem to be inspired by the *Flash Gordon* remake. Aldo Ray (with a half-mutated face) seems to have a good time torturing an Oriental woman wearing a Vampirella uniform. John Carradine appears for about three seconds in what looks like an outtake from *Frankenstein's Island*. Johnny Legend is a wandering priest who gets zapped, and Mayra Gant wears an eyepatch as a warden. I liked the hologram of a kid in a Mexican wrestling mask, but they didn't do a very good job re-using the monster from *Deadly Spawn, Return of the Aliens* and that rat puppet was pretty pathetic. The time is padded out with endless running through passageways in Roger Corman's familiar, rented spaceship set. With Bobbi Bresee, Susan Stokey, Dawn Wildsmith, Eric Caidin, and some *Dark Star* footage. It sat on a shelf for a while, then was presented by Jack Harris.

STAR TIME

(Monarch, 1992) **D/S/P:** Alexander Cassini

Michael St. Gerard stars as a nervous, confused misfit who becomes suicidal when his favorite TV show is canceled. An agent named Sam Bones (John P. Ryan) promises to make him a TV star if he kills people, so he becomes the "Baby Mask Killer." Maureen Teefy (*Fame*) is a social worker. It was a first effort by an AFI grad and includes an *It's a Wonderful Life* clip. There are a few good visual images, but I found it irritating, vague, and boring.

STAR TREK

(Paramount series, 1966–69)

The NBC-TV show that won't go away only lasted three seasons, but Gene Roddenberry's ideas and characters created an industry that will probably outlive this century. So far there have been seven features, four TV series, and enough fans and merchandise to ensure endless conventions and revenue. All 79 tapes of the original NBC series are available, running 51 minutes each. As dated and often cheap-looking as they are, they're still more fun to watch than any of the big-budget movies. *Menagerie* (#16), from 1966, is the only two-part feature length tape. A series of soundtracks are on GNP. Paramount also released the book *William Shatner's Star Trek Memories* (1995).

STAR TREK III: THE SEARCH FOR SPOCK

(Paramount, 1984) **D/A:** Leonard Nimoy
S/P: Harve Bennett **M:** James Horner

In a direct sequel to *Star Trek II: The Wrath of Khan* (1982), Kirk (William Shatner) and his crew shanghai the Enterprise to save Spock (Leonard Nimoy), and the Klingons (led by Christopher Lloyd) attack. The usual crew (DeForest Kelley,

James Doohan, George Takei, Walter Koenig, and Nichelle Nichols) return, plus the late Merritt Butrick (he died from AIDS in 1989) as Kirk's son and Dame Judith Anderson as a Vulcan priestess. The ILM FX are impressive. Also with Robin Curtis, John Larroquette, Miguel Ferrer, and Robert Hooks. Spock is reborn at the end. It's based on Nimoy's story. The soundtrack is on GNP.

STAR TREK IV: THE VOYAGE HOME

(Paramount, 1986) **D/A:** Leonard Nimoy
S: Steve Meerson, Peter Krikes, Nicholas Meyer **P:** Harve Bennett

Nimoy's second feature as director was the highest-grossing of the whole series. With the usual crew plus Jane Wyatt, Catherine Hicks, Mark Lenard, Brock Peters, Michael Berryman, and Jane Weidlin. They time-travel to 20th century San Francisco in a junker ship to attend a trial. The crew saves two humpback whales (real footage of whales being killed is used) and there's lots of comedy and joking around and ILM FX. Spock, still not himself, is considered an "acid casualty." The real U.S.S. *Enterprise* ship was used. The Paramount director's series edition is widescreen with outtakes, a Nimoy interview, and a making-of segment. After Sylvester Stallone, Nimoy is the most successful director/actor ever with his two *Trek* movies.

STAR TREK V: THE FINAL FRONTIER

(Paramount, 1989) **D/A:** William Shatner **S:** David Loughery **P/A:** Harve Bennett **M:** Jerry Goldsmith

After Nimoy directed two *Trek* movies, the producers let Shatner cowrite the story and direct this one. The results are often laughable and attendance dropped drastically. The usual crew goes on a mission to rescue ambassadors being held hostage on a distant planet. With David Warner, Laurence Luckinbill (as Spock's Vulcan half-brother), bodybuilder Spice Williams as a Klingon, and the director's daughter, Melanie Shatner. The cast sings "Row row row your boat" and the ending copies *The Wizard of Oz*. The first five *Trek* movies were offered in a boxed set for the 25th anniversary in 1991.

STAR TREK VI: THE UNDISCOVERED COUNTRY

(Paramount, 1991) **D/S:** Nicholas Meyer
S: Denny Martin Flinn **P:** Ralph Winter

The director of *Star Trek II: The Wrath of Khan* (1982) returned to guide the usual crew. It's an end-of-the-cold-war parallel story. A Chernobyl-type disaster leads to the Klingons offering peace, but their leader (David Warner) is assassinated. George Takei is now a Federation captain with his own ship. Shatner and Nimoy were 60, and Kelley (who has an important role this time) and the very large Doohan were 71 at the time. Also with Christopher Plummer as a Shakespeare-quoting bald Klingon, Brock Peters, Kim Cattrall, Kurtwood Smith, Somali model Iman as a shapeshifter, Rene Auberjonois, and Christian Slater in a bit part. Actors from various *Trek* TV shows are there too (Michael Dorn, Mark Lenard, and even Grace Lee Whitney). The story is by executive producer Nimoy. ILM FX were used as usual. Series creator Gene Roddenberry died during production. It was

the lowest-grossing of the series. *The Starfleet Collection* (Paramount) was a limited package of six features in widescreen. A *Star Trek 25th Anniversary Special* (Paramount) with members of both TV series (and Vice President Dan Quayle) is also on tape.

STAR TREK: DEEP SPACE NINE

(Paramount, 1992) **D:** David Carson
S: Michael Piller **M:** Dennis McCarthy

The pilot (*Emissary*) for the third, darker (syndicated) *Trek* series borrows from *Slaughterhouse Five* and is set in the 24th century. Avery Brooks is the bitter Sisko, with a run-down space station. Nana Visitor is an alien first officer, Rene Auberjonois is a shape-shifting security officer, and Armin Shimerman is a scheming Ferengi (called anti-Semitic by some critics). Also with Terry Farrell (from *Hellraiser III*). Patrick Stewart showed up in the premiere, as well as various characters from other *Trek* series later. The soundtrack is on GNP. A rival TV series debuting the same year was *Babylon 5*.

STAR TREK: GENERATIONS

(Paramount, 1994) **D:** David Carson
S: Ronald D. Moore, Brandon Braga
P: Rick Berman **M:** Dennis McCarthy

Star Trek feature #7 was the first *Next Generation* movie and most likely the last with any of the originals. Patrick Stewart stars with the entire main *Star Trek: The Next Generation* TV cast (including Whoopi Goldberg) plus (thanks to a time warp) William Shatner and (briefly) Walter Koenig and James Doohan. Malcolm McDowell is the alien villain Dr. Soran and Alan Ruck is the current *Enterprise* commander. Data getting an emotion chip implant is part of the plot. It's rated PG. The British Carson also directed episodes of *The Next Generation* and the *Deep Space Nine* pilot. With cinematography by John Alonzo. The soundtrack is on GNP. Paramount (surprise!) plans more *Trek* features.

STAR TREK: THE CAGE

(Paramount, 1965) **D:** Marc Daniels

This once-rare, part-color, 73-minute episode is a real oddity and worth seeing. It's the original pilot that was later re-edited and used as flashbacks for the two-part "Menagerie" episode. Jeffrey Hunter stars as Captain Pike, Leonard Nimoy is Spock (with different makeup), and Majel Barrett is the first officer. The other crew members are all different. Pike is held captive by big-brain telepathic aliens (played by slender women in elaborate makeup). Also with Susan Oliver, John Hoyt as Dr. Boyce, and Julie Parrish. Also available on *Star Trek: The Beginnings*, along with *Where No Man Has Gone Before* and the pilots of *The Next Generation* and *Deep Space Nine*.

STAR TREK: THE NEXT GENERATION

(Paramount series, 1987–94)

The second *Trek* series has much higher production values, better acting, and lasted longer than the original. Episodes cost a record $1.2 to

$1.4 million each. The British Patrick Stewart is excellent as Picard, but he did too many TV commercial voiceovers after his newfound fame. Series regulars Denise Crosby and Wil Wheaton dropped out and Whoopi Goldberg later joined. Leonard Nimoy, Mark Lenard, and James Doohan even made appearances on the series. Episodes were available on tape in Europe first, then Paramount released episodes in America. There were 178 episodes total plus a 2-hour 1994 wrap-up finale followed by the theatrical feature, *Star Trek: Generations* and the documentary tape *Journey's End: The Saga of Star Trek: The Next Generation*. A series of GNP soundtrack albums is available.

STAR TREK: THE NEXT GENERATION: ENCOUNTER AT FARPOINT

(1987) **D:** Corey Allen **S:** D. C. Fontana **P:** Robert H. Justman

The pilot feature for the second *Trek* series is set 80 years further in the future and uses ILM FX. Patrick Stewart stars with series regulars Jonathan Frakes, LeVar Burton, Denise Crosby, Michael Dorn, Marina Sirtis, and Wil Wheaton. With John de Lancie as Q, the main recurring villain, DeForest Kelley from the old series in a bit role, and Cary-Hiroyuki Tagawa. Available as part of *Star Trek: Beginnings* (Paramount).

STAR TREK: VOYAGER

(Paramount, 1995) **D:** Winrich Kolbe **S/P:** Michael Piller, Jeri Taylor **P:** Rick Berman **M:** Jay Chattaway

By the time of this 4th (!) *Trek* series the word "overkill" wasn't enough. It was the first series on the new United Paramount Network. This $23 million pilot feature (*The Caretaker*) does have impressive FX. A Federation Starfleet crew is lost in space and time. Kate Mulgrew stars as the first female captain and Robert (*Eating Raoul*) Beltran is leader of the enemy Maquis. The two groups join forces. With Roxann Biggs-Dawson as a half-Klingon chief engineer, Tim Russ as the Vulcan security oficer, Robert Picardo as a holographic doctor, Robert Duncan McNeill, Jennifer Lien, Garrett Wang, and Ethan Phillips as a comic alien cook.

STATELINE MOTEL

(1973) **D:** Maurizio Lucidi **S:** Franco Enna **P:** Nicholas Demetroules **M:** Ennio Morricone   Italy
(*L'Ultima Chance; Last Chance for a Born Loser*)

Fabio Testi steals Ursula Andress from her husband (Massimo Girotti) in a crime thriller with a motel settting. With Eli Wallach and Barbara Bach. It was shot in Canada.

THE STATE OF THINGS

(Pacific Arts, 1982) **D/S:** Wim Wenders **S:** Robert Kramer **P:** Chris Sievernich
W. Germany (*Der Stand der Dinge*)

Wenders was making *Hammett* in America when production was put on hold. In the meantime, he made this more typical Wenders feature. In it, characters are making "The Most Dangerous Man on Earth" (a remake of Roger Corman's *The Day the World Ended*!) in Portugal. The company is stranded by the Hollywood backers without funds. It's two b/w hours with subtitles. With Patrick Bauchau, Rebecca Pauley, Isabelle Weingarten, Sam Fuller as a cameraman, Paul Getty III as a writer, Allen Garfield as the broke producer (who sings), Viva, and Roger Corman himself as a lawyer.

STATIC

(IEI, 1985) **D/S:** Mark Romanek **S/A:** Keith Gordon **P:** Amy Ness

Gordon stars as an orphan electronics whiz who works at a crucifix factory. He invents a TV that receives pictures from Heaven. Bob Gunton is the evangelist cousin waiting for the "big one." Amanda Plummer and Barton Heyman are also in the comedy drama. The soundtrack features Elvis, Eno, and others. Gordon also directed *The Chocolate War*.

THE STAY AWAKE

(Nelson, 1987) **D/S:** John Bernard **P:** Thys Reyns, Paul Raleigh   S.Africa

This stupid, irritating teen horror movie starts in America in 1968 as a ponytailed mass murderer goes to the gas chamber ("I'm the angel of darkness!"). Twenty years later at the St. Mary's School for Girls in "Europe" students have an all night "stay awake" to raise money. They're put through a strenuous aerobics class, watch horror videos on the gym floor, all pretend to be dead (as a joke), fool around with boys who sneak in, and are killed off by a mystery monster. This movie is filled with false scares and we see lots of it through the growling unseen monster POV camera shots. The 50s-style green monster with tentacles makes baby noises, burps, is afraid of crosses, and possesses a girl ("You dirty stinking slut! I'll see you back in the hell where you belong!"). Maybe it's supposed to be funny. With Macdonald Carey's daughter Michelle.

STAY TUNED

(Warner, 1992) **D/C:** Peter Hyams **S:** Tom S. Parker, Jim Jennewein **P:** James C. Robertson

A Seattle couple is trapped inside their TV for 24 hours in a PG fantasy comedy full of TV-show spoofs. John Ritter is the TV-addict husband and Pam Dawber is his wife. Jeffrey Jones is the Satan figure who offers them a new satellite dish system. They show up in commercials, in a cat and mouse cartoon (directed by Chuck Jones), and shows like "Meet the Mansons" and "Three Men and Rosemary's Baby." With Eugene Levy, Bob Dishy, Fred Blassie, and the voice of Ernie Anderson.

STEALTH HUNTERS

(VCII, 1991) **D/P:** Matt Trotter **S:** Tom Anthony

Super zombie-like warriors created by a businessman kill off a platoon of soldiers in a low-budget Texas horror movie. The one survivor and a group of teen campers try and fight off the killers.

STEEL

(Vestron, 1980) **D:** Steve Carver **S:** Leigh Chapman **P:** Peter S. Davis   (*Men of Steel; Look Down and Die*)

Lee Majors stars in a movie about the dangers of putting up a skyscraper in record time. Jennifer O'Neill is the daughter of contruction boss George Kennedy. With Richard Lynch, R. G. Armstrong, Robert Tessier, Albert Salmi, Art Carney, Harris Yulin, and Carol Malory. It was filmed in Lexington, Kentucky.

STEEL AND LACE

(Fries, 1990) **D:** Ernest Farino **S:** Joseph Dougherty **P:** David DeCoteau

Bruce Davison (nominated for an Oscar the year this was made) is the moody, gray-haired scientist brother of a pianist (Clare Wren) who has killed herself after being raped. For revenge, he reconstructs her as a cyborg and sends her off to destroy the guilty, now wealthy young gangster businessmen. Disguised as different women, she seduces, then kills, them in incredible ways. Big drills emerge from her chest and go right through one, she pulls the head off another, and castrates a third during sex. That last death isn't exactly shown, but the ones that are use excellent and shocking FX. Stacy Haiduk (*Luthor the Geek*) is a courtroom artist who investigates with the reluctant help of her former boyfriend, cop David Naughton. With William Prince and David ("Squiggy") Lander as the coroner. Farino (from Texas) has done effects work for many films and used to animate the Pillsbury Doughboy!

STEEL ARENA

(Vestron, 1973) **D/S/P:** Mark L. Lester **P:** Peter S. Traynor

Demolition derby champ and daredevil driver Dusty Russell plays himself in this partial documentary about his "Circus of Death" show. It was made years before the Evel Knievel movies. With lots of crashes, real stuntmen, and a man who blows himself up in a coffin. Lester, from Cleveland, made *Truck Stop Women* next.

STEEL BAYONET

(1957) **D/P:** Michael Carreras **S:** Howard Clewes   UK

Soldiers defend a deserted farmhouse in Africa during WWII. United Artists released the Hammer film in America. Leo Genn stars with Kieron Moore, Michael Medwin, and Michael Ripper, and Michael Caine as a German soldier.

THE STEEL CAGE

(1954) **D/P:** Walter Doniger **P:** Berman Swartz

UA had released *Duffy of San Quentin* in 1954. They decided to produce a TV series based on the film, but when it didn't sell, they packaged three episodes as this trilogy feature. Three stories about San Quentin prisoners feature Walter Slezak, John Ireland, Lawrence Tierney, Kenneth Tobey, Lyle Talbot, and Arthur Franz. Paul Kelly is the warden and Maureen O'Sullivan is his wife, repeating their characters from *Duffy*.

STEEL DAWN

(Vestron, 1987) **D/P:** Lance Hool
S: Doug Lefler **P:** Conrad Hool

Patrick Swayze stars in a post-nuke battle-for-scarce-water movie that copies *Shane, High Noon,* and (of course) *Road Warrior.* It has some good sword fight scenes. With Swayze's real-life wife Lisa Niemi, Christopher Neane, Brion James, and Anthony Zerbe as the main bad guy. It was filmed in the Namibian desert in Africa. By the director of *Missing in Action II.*

STEELE JUSTICE

(Paramount, 1987) **D/S:** Robert Boris **P:** John Strong

Martin Kove stars as a Nam vet in LA out for revenge. A former South Vietnam general (Soon-Tech Oh), now running drugs, is responsible for the slaughter of his best friend and his whole family. With Sela Ward, Ronny Cox, Bernie Casey, Joseph Campanella, Sarah Douglas, Shannon Tweed, and Mark Dacascos. Chris Hillman and the Desert Band play, and the choreography is by Jeff Kutash.

STEELE'S LAW

(Academy, 1992) **D/S/P:** Fred Williamson
S: Charles Eric Johnson **P:** Marvin Towns

Chicago detective John Steele (Williamson) is sent to Dallas to stop Keno (Doran Inghram) a psycho assassin with a long gray ponytail. Keno uses a sword and likes rough sex. Steele is paired with a pathetic tubby partner, but when things get tough, the police captain (Bo Svenson) helps kick ass. Some of the martial arts fights are pretty good. Typically, Steele's new girlfriend (Phyllis Cicero) is raped (offscreen) and dies, shortly after the lone sex scene. A head arrives in a box. There's talk about "the war" and lines like "I'd nuke the towel-head bastards!" Keno is speared by an American flag (!) at the end. Notice the poster on the Chicago police headquarters wall for *Tabloid,* a movie by Brett McCormick, the assistant to the producer. It was filmed in the "Deep Ellum" area of Dallas (the same time as *JFK*).

THE STEPFATHER

(Columbia, 1987) **D:** Joseph Ruben
S: Donald E. Westlake **P:** Jay Benson

It wasn't a big theatrical hit or anything, but *The Stepfather* is one of the great horror movies of the 80s. Terry O'Quinn is excellent as Jerry Blake, a pleasant-seeming man whom most people take to right away. All he wants is an ideal American family. When his wife and kids don't measure up to his expectations, he simply kills them and tries again. He moves to a new town, becomes a real-estate agent, and marries Shelley Hack. Jill Schoelen (his new stepdaughter) realizes that something is very wrong, and meanwhile his previous brother-in-law is after him. Jerry also whistles "Camptown Races." *The Stepfather* has some scenes that really hit home for many viewers. It also has some Hitchcock references, if you look for them.

STEPFATHER II: MAKE ROOM FOR DADDY

(HBO, 1989) **D:** Jeff Burr **S:** John Auerbach
P: William Burr, Darin Scott

It starts with scenes from #1, then the serial killer dad (Terry O'Quinn) wakes in a Washington state mental institution. He kills a therapist and assumes the man's identity. Soon he's running suburban neighborhood group therapy lessons! Meg Foster is his new choice for a wife. The highlight is a chaotic marriage ceremony (with gore FX by Michelle Burke). O'Quinn is good (again) but this doesn't come close to the original, and the jokey dialogue ("Make room for daddy!") ruins it. With Caroline Williams and Jonathan Brandis. Miramax cut the film, then added gore scenes without consulting the director.

STEPFATHER III: FATHER'S DAY

(Vidmark, 1991) **D/S/P:** Guy Magar
S: Marc Ray **P:** Paul Moen

In a b/w opening, the psycho stepfather goes to a sleazy surgeon for (gory) plastic surgery. He (Robert Wightman this time) emerges not only with a new face, but younger (!?) and with more hair. He goes to a California town where he becomes a gardener and plans to marry Priscilla Barnes. When he decides things aren't perfect enough, he starts an affair with another single mom (*Escape from New York*'s Season Hubley). The hero is Barnes's computer whiz kid in a wheelchair (David Tom). The stepfather character is no longer calculating and is reduced to making Freddy Krueger-style re-

Terry O'Quinn is *The Stepfather.*

marks when he kills. The sequel (from ITC) isn't bad for TV horror (it debuted on HBO) but is full of plot holes. By the director of *Retribution.*

THE STEPFORD CHILDREN

(1987) **D:** Alan J. Levi **P:** Edgar J. Scherick

After *The Stepford Wives* (1975), there was a TV sequel, *Revenge of the Stepford Wives* (1980). Bankable concepts die hard, so this third one was another TV movie. Two NYC teens move to the "perfect" suburb with their family. With Barbara Eden, Don Murray, James Coco, Richard Anderson, Ken Swofford, Pat Corley, and Dick Butkus. It was released on tape in Europe. The director also made sequel TV movies featuring The Incredible Hulk and The Six Million Dollar Man. There was also *The Stepford Husbands* (1996)!

STEPHEN KING'S NIGHT SHIFT COLLECTION

(Karl, 1983–7) **D:** John Woodward, Jack Garrett

"Disciple of the Crow" is an early short version of *Children of the Corn,* set in Oklahoma in 1971. It manages to tell the story much more effectively than the 1984 feature. "The Night Waiter" concerns ghosts in an old hotel. The two stories together run 40 minutes. *Stephen King's Night Shift Collection 2* (Simitar) followed with "The Bogeyman" by Jeff Shiro and "The Woman in the Room" by Frank Darabont. To look up other features that are sometimes titled *Stephen King's . . . whatever,* see the real titles!

STEPMONSTER

(New Horizon, 1993) **D:** Jeremy Stanford **S:** Mark Thomas McGhee, Craig J. Nevius **P:** Steve Rabiner

A comic book fan kid (Bill Corben) realizes that his stepmom (Robin Riker) is really a shapeshifting lizard monster with a bat puppet sidekick. It's a PG-13 horror comedy from executive producer Roger Corman that copies the bigger budget box office flop *My Stepmother Is an Alien.* Fred Olen Ray is credited with the story. With Ami Dolenz as the babysitter, Alan Thicke as the father, Eddie McClurg, John Astin as a priest, and Corey Feldman as Phlegm.

THE STEPMOTHER

(Academy, 1973) **D:** "Howard"/Hikmet Avedis **S/P/A:** Marlene Schmidt

Alejandro Rey stars with John Garfield Jr. in a murder mystery. A woman forced to seduce her husband's son is part of the plot. With John Anderson, Katherine Justice, Larry Linville, and Claudia Jennings in a small role (naked). The Crown International release was the first by Avedis, who returned with *The Teacher* and *The Specialist.*

STEPPENWOLF

(Vidmark, 1974) **D/S:** Fred Haines **P:** Melvin Fishman, Richard Herland   US/Switzerland

It's an inner "trip" movie based on Hermann Hesse's novel, which was very popular with students at the time. Max von Sydow stars as Harry Haller, a man who plans to kill himself at 50. He smokes pot, goes crazy, and experiences a lot of things that are shown with video images and animation. Dominique Sanda and Pierre Clementi co-star. The PG feature was shot in Switzerland.

STEPSISTERS

(Regal, 1974) **D/S:** Perry Tong   (*Texas Hill Killing*)

There's a backwoods *Diabolique* plot, as a man and his sister-in-law plot to kill his wife. The cinematography is arty and it was made in Texas by the director of the *Scuba World* cable TV program.

STEREO

(Nightmare, 1969) **D/S/P/C/E:** David Cronenberg   Canada

The now-famous director made this 63-minute b/w film for "$3500" when he was 26 years old. It's an *Alphaville*-like look at the future and concerns telepathic surgery at the "Canadian Academy for Erotic Inquiry." A voiceover explains what's going on. It's on tape with Cronenberg's *Crimes of the Future*.

STEWARDESS SCHOOL

(RCA, 1986) **D/S:** Ken Blancato **P:** Phil Feldman

Two guys enroll in an all-female training school in this bad *Police Academy* copy. Donny (*Happy Days*) Most stars. With Vicki Frederick, Sandahl Bergman, Judy Landers, Corinne Bohrer, Lillian Muller, Sherman Hemsley, and Brooke Bundy. From Columbia.

THE STEWARDESSES

(Video Dimensions, 1968) **D/S/P:** "Allan Silliphant"/ Alf Silliman Jr.

This Stereovision 3-D softcore sex hit made nearly $7 million after Sherpix released it in 1970. It was considered *hot* stuff at the time and played for years. A blonde says, "I've got the whole place to myself . . . I'll take some acid!" She takes it (with low-fat milk) and during her trip sequence has sex with a stone head with a lamp attached. An ad exec beats a would-be actress during sex so she kills him then jumps out her window. The best 3-D part is a carnival ride in the dark with a devil, skulls, and a decapitated head. There's a Nam vet, Indian music, a rock band with Beatle hair, strobe light dancing, sex in a nightclub, a drunken lesbian scene, and pool cues, feet, and a coat rack jabbing into the camera. Christina Hart stars. Adult film regular Monica Gayle and Donna Stanley were both also in Ed Wood Jr.'s *Take It Out in Trade* (1970). It was rated X, then cut for an R. A much shorter version with hardcore inserts (added years later) also exists with an onscreen disclaimer ("Without original cast"). There were many rip-offs, copies, and "sequels" including *Swinging Stewardesses* (1971) from Germany.

THE STEWARDESSES II: *See* INTERNATIONAL STEWARDESSES

STICK IT IN YOUR EAR

(SW, 1970) **D:** Charles Morgan   (*Vortex*)

This very obscure, arty, and mostly silent b/w hippie movie with fancy editing and in-jokes seems to be influenced by *Carnival of Souls* and was filmed in Boston. An unshaven guy wakes in the ruins of a church with amnesia and wanders around trying to find anybody who knows him. Characters say "groovy" and "heavy" at a pot party and some pretty wild guitar feedback is heard. With some sex and nudity, flashbacks, drug sequences, and important Vietnam war references. Whan a man on the street asks, "Want to buy some dirty pictures?" our confused hero says, "No thanks, I'm in one." A Hare Krishna chant becomes "Kurosawa, Kurosawa." Pretty cool actually and full of surprises. H. G. Lewis picked this up and double-billed it with with his own very different *The Gore Gore Girls*.

STIGMA

(Vista, 1972) **D/S:** David E. Durston **P:** Charles B. Moss Jr.

Philip Michael Thomas, later famous as Tubbs on *Miami Vice,* claimed to have made "11 major movies" before hitting TV stardom. Some of them remain mysteries, but this well-made oddity was apparently his first. Director Durston is known to exploitation fans for *I Drink Your Blood* (1971), a strong, upsetting rabid-hippie movie. This equally queasy follow-up stars Thomas (with mustache) as a doctor who goes to a fishing village on a remote island where he encounters racism, murder, and, eventually, a VD epidemic. A grim, real 16mm film-within-the-movie features New York disc jockey "Cousin Brucie" Morrow showing slides of advanced syphilis victims with collapsed noses and horrible chancre sores. Thomas is actually quite good in a difficult role and the script poses some challenging moral questions about sex, the law, and covering up the truth, but *Stigma* is exploitation in the tradition of *Sex Madness.* It was released by Jerry Gross.

STILL LIFE

(Prism, 1990) **D:** Graeme Campell **P:** Nicolas Stiliadis   Canada   (*A. K. Art Killer*)

A psycho artist in NYC (really Toronto) kills homeless people, makes sculptures out of them, and sells them as art. Suspect Jason Gedrick is in a performance art group. With Jessica Steen and Stephen Shellan. The PG-13 feature is another one inspired by Roger Corman's *Bucket of Blood.*

STILL OF THE NIGHT

(MGM, 1982) **D/S:** Robert Benton **P:** Arlene Donovan

Meryl Streep and Roy Scheider star in a murder mystery that was filmed as *Stab* (too bad they didn't keep the title). He's a psychiatrist who wanted to be a baseball star and she might have killed one of his patients. With Jessica Tandy and Sara Botsford. The MGM release borrows from Hitchcock's *Spellbound,* complete with a dream sequence.

STILL SMOKIN'

(Paramount, 1983) **D/S/A:** Thomas Chong **S/A:** Cheech Marin **P:** Peter MacGregor-Scott

Cheech and Chong go to Amsterdam and hold a "dope-a-thon" to raise money for a film festival. The box-office flop comedy features a Dutch cast and ends with 20 minutes of comedy concert footage. With Carla Van Amstel as Queen Beatrix, and Linnea Quigley.

STINGRAY

(Nelson, 1978) **D/S:** Richard Taylor **P:** Donald Ham, Bill Bruce

Christopher Mitchum and Les Lannom buy a cool '62 Chevy Stingray but don't know about a stash of heroin in the trunk. Gangsters want it back. Sherry Jackson is the violent leader of the drug ring. With chases, crashes, and motorcycles, and Sondra Theodore from *Playboy.* The music is by Byron Berline, John Hartford, and others. It was filmed in St. Louis.

STONE AGE WARRIORS

(VSOM, 1991) **D/P:** Stanley Tong   Hong Kong

In the jungles of New Guinea, two kung-fu fighting women face natives, mercenaries, lizards, scorpions, and a komodo dragon and discover a secret drug factory. With lots of action and gore. Elaine Lui from the *Angel* movies and Li Chi star.

STONE COLD

(RCA, 1991) **D:** Craig R. Baxley **S:** Walter Doninger **P:** Ben Ami

Ex-football linebacker Brian "Boz" Bosworth stars as a big sneering blond cop with an earring working for the FBI. He infiltrates a Mississippi motorcycle gang that has been killing local politicians. Lance Henriksen is the ambitious and psychotic biker leader Chains and William Forsythe plays Ice. There's a wild biker funeral, a violent, major action shootout at the end, and a great motorcycle and helicopter stunt. With Arabella Holzbog, Paulo Tocha, and Laura Albert. By the director of *I Come in Peace* and *Action Jackson.* It was filmed in Arkansas and had to be cut from an NC-17. From Columbia.

STONED AGE

(Vidmark, 1993) **D/S:** James Melkonian **S:** Rich Wilkes **P:** Neal Moriz, David Heyman

This is like a cruder, ruder *Dazed and Confused* with more about trying to get high and laid than alienation and character development. It's pretty damned funny, though. Joe (Michael Kopelow), a guy with long red hair, hangs out with his violent, asshole friend Hubs (Bradford Tatum) as they cruise, cop, and crash a party at a California beach home. China Kantner (daughter of Grace Slick) and Renee Allman are the female stars. All four leads are good and the all–70s soundtrack is great. Black Sabbath's "Paranoid" is the theme song and Blue Öyster Cult's "Don't Fear the Reaper" is important to the plot. BOC even appears in a concert flashback and an after-the-credits gag scene. With a *2001* parody, some Screaming Mad George FX, and Frankie Avalon.

STONER
(VSOM, 1976) **D:** Huang Feng **S:** No Kuan
P: Raymond Chow   Hong Kong/Australia

One-time James Bond actor George Lazenby is an Australian cop who is teamed with a Chinese policewoman (kung fu movie goddess Angela Mao) in a spy and martial arts movie. A religious cult in Australia develops a killer aphrodisiac heroin mixture and their "Happy Pills" are discovered in Hong Kong. With Samo Hung and blond Romano-lee Rose in sex scenes (cut for US TV).

STONES OF DEATH
(Sony, 1988) **D:** James Bogle **S:** Ian Coughlan
P: David Hannay   Australia

A new housing developement built on sacred Aborigine burial grounds is the setting for a *Poltergeist*-inspired horror movie with teen stars. Characters die in various bloody ways. Zoe Carides stars as the girl who has nightmares. With Tom Jennings and Eric Oldfield.

STOOGEMANIA
(Paramount, 1985) **D/S/P:** Chuck Workman
S: Jim Geoghan **P:** James Ruxin

Back in 1960, when the Three Stooges became popular again, somebody threw together *Stop! Look! and Laugh!*, a mixture of new non-Stooge footage and old Stooges film clips. 25 years later the Stooges reached new heights of popularity. "The Curly Shuffle" was on the radio and this Stoogesploitation comedy was released. Josh Mostel stars as a guy obsessed with the long-dead comedians. Stooge clips (some are colorized) mostly feature Shemp. With Melanie Chartoff, Sid Caesar, hopeless real Three Stooges fanatics, Stooge imitators, and "sons."

STOP
(1970) **D/S:** Bill Gunn **P:** Paul M. Heller

A writer (Edward Bell) and his wife (Linda Marsh), in the midst of breaking up, go to Puerto Rico to stay at an inherited mansion where a suicide/murder had taken place. He has nightmare visions of what happened. A friend shows up with his (black) wife (Marlene Clark) and they swap wives. It received an X and was shelved by Warner Brothers and was first reviewed 20 years later. The cinematography is by Owen Roizman, who later filmed *The Exorcist*. Ry Cooder is on the soundtrack. Gunn (who died in 1989) also made the unique vampire movie *Ganja and Hess* (1973), available under many titles on tape.

STOP ME BEFORE I KILL!
(1961) **D/S/P:** Val Guest   UK (*The Full Treatment*)

A race car driver (Claude Dauphin) marries Diane Cilento. He finds himself strangling her on their honeymoon and soon believes he's killed her. It's all because his psychiatrist wants her, and has been messing with his patient's mind, using drugs and hypnotism. It takes place in France and London. Columbia released it in America. Guest made *The Day the Earth Caught Fire* next.

STORMQUEST
(Media, 1987) **D:** Alax Sessa **S:** Charles Saunders **P:** Hector Olivera

Women rule the kingdom of Kimba and hero Brent Huff is a male liberationist. With Kai Baker, Christina Whitaker, and huge Linda Lutz as the evil "Stormqueen." It was filmed in Argentina.

STORM RIDER: *See* THE GRAND DUEL

STORM SWEPT
(Marsh Entertainment, 1994) **D/S/E:** David Marsh
S/P: Svetlana Marsh

An actress (Julie Hughes) invites filmmaker friends over to her new haunted mansion. They're trapped during a storm and experience sex fantasies. With Kathleen Kinmont living in the basement, Melissa Anne Moore, and Justin Carroll.

STORY OF A JUNKIE
(Media, 1985) **D/P:** Lech Kowalski   (*Gringo*)

The director of the punk documentary *D.O.A.* made this grim documentary look at a young, real-life New York City junkie with dyed blond hair and an eye patch, called John Spacely. The camera follows him everywhere. He died sometime after the movie was done. Troma rereleased it with the new "Junkie" title. A mural of Spacely, painted when this was new, was still on St. Marks Place a decade later. Maybe it's still there.

THE STORY OF O
(C.D., 1975) **D:** Just Jaeckin **S:** Sebastian Japisot   France   (*Histoire d'O*)

Jaeckin made this glossy S&M sex hit set in the 1930s after his *Emmanuelle*. Allied Artists released it and it made $700,000 in North American rentals alone. Ken Russell almost directed it and probably wished he had. O (Corinne Clery) is whipped, pierced, and passed around by wealthy jaded men. Udo Kier is René and Anthony Steele is Sir Stephen his stepbrother. *The Story of Joanna*, an American porno copy, made a reported $4 million itself. *The Journey of O* was another X-rated copy, and there was a 10-chapter early-90s Euro remake. Kier was in *Spermula* next.

THE STORY OF O PART II
(Republic, 1980) **D/S:** Shuji Terayama
P: Anatole Bauman, Hiroku Govaers   France/Japan
(*Fruits of Passion; The Story of O Continues*)

Klaus Kinski stars as Sir Stephen, a kinky Brit in early 1900s Hong Kong. His lovers are O (Isabelle Illiers) and Arielle Dombasle. It's an impressive-looking but slow-moving adaptation of Pauline Réage's O sequel, *Return to the Chateau*.

STRAIGHT TO HELL
(Key, 1987) **D/S:** Alex Cox
S/A: Dick Rude **P:** Eric Fellner

After *Sid and Nancy*, Cox took a bunch of friends and scenemakers to Spain and made this aimless, boring spaghetti western spoof. Characters drink coffee and talk about how boring things are. With Sy Richardson, Joe Strummer, and Dick Rude as outlaws. Also with Dennis Hopper, Grace Jones, Elvis Costello, Jim Jarmusch, and Ellen Barkin in a bit part. The music is by the Pogues, who also appear.

STRAIT JACKET: *See* DARK SANITY

STRANDED
(RCA, 1987) **D:** Tex Fuller **S:** Alan Castle
P: Scott Rosenfelt, Mark Levinson

Long-haired, pale aliens take Ione Skye and her grandmother (Maureen O'Sullivan) hostage from a farmhouse. Joe Morton (star of *The Brother from Another Planet*) is the sheriff, who has problems with local rednecks. With Cameron Dye, Brendan Hughes, Spice Williams, and Flea from the Red Hot Chili Peppers. There's a lizard woman too. New Line released the PG-13 movie.

STRANGE ADVENTURE
(Sinister, 1932) **D:** Phil Whitman **S:** Lee Chadwick
P: I. E. Chadwick   (*Wayne Murder Case*)

Regis Toomey stars as a police lieutenant and June Clyde is a reporter in a one-hour Monogram mystery. There's a hooded killer in an old dark house. With Dwight Frye, William V. Mong, Jason Robards Sr., and Eddie "Snowflake" Toones for typical black comic relief.

STRANGE BREW
(MGM, 1983) **D/S/A:** Dave Thomas,
Rick Moranis **S:** Steve DeJarnatt   Canada

The Bob and Doug McKenzie "Great White North" show was a popular segment on SCTV. Thomas and Moranis play the same dimwit beer drinkers in this comedy, based on *Hamlet*. It starts with an angry audience chasing them after sitting through their first movie. Max von Sydow is a mad brewmeister who plots to take over the world. He gives drugged beers to hockey-player mental patients in his remote castle. With Paul Dooley and the voice of Mel Blanc. Shot in "Hoserama."

THE STRANGE CASE OF DR. JEKYLL AND MR. HYDE
(Cannon, 1989) **D:** Michael Lindsay-Hogg
S: J. Michael Straczynski **P:** Bridget Terry

Anthony Andrews stars as the famous doctor in one of the most filmed stories of all time. With Laura Dern, Nicholas Guest, Rue McClanahan, Lisa Langois, and Elizabeth Gracen. The 60-minute Nightmare Classics presentation debuted on USA cable.

STRANGE COMPULSION
(1964) **D/P:** Irv Berwick **S:** Jason Johnson

Preston Sturges Jr. stars as a young medical student who goes to a shrink to cure his compulsive voyeurism. The b/w obscurity is by the makers of *Monster of Piedras Blancas*.

THE STRANGE COUNTESS

(Sinister, 1961) **D:** Josef von Baky **S:** Robert A. Stemmle, Curt Hanno Gutbrod W. Germany

Lil Dagover (from *The Cabinet of Dr. Caligari*) is the countess in an Edgar Wallace mystery about killers after money. Joachim Fuchsberger stars with Brigitte Grothum, Klaus Kinski (as Stuart Bresset), and Fritz Rasp. It went direct to TV in America.

STRANGE FETISHES

(1967) **D/P:** Enrico Blancocoello

Sammy Arena stars as a missing TV horror host. The station manager had killed him (with acid) in a fight, but the body disappears. A scarfaced phantom begins killing people (including some go-go dancers) around the station. It's another obscure b/w movie that would be interesting to see released on tape.

STRANGE HOLIDAY

(1940) **D/S:** Arch Oboler **P:** A. W. Hackel, Edward Finney

Claude Rains is a businessman who returns to America from a vacation and discovers that the Constitution has been suspended and a new fascist dictatorship is in control. It's all a dream at the end. It was based on Oboler's radio play and was made for employees of General Motors! The corporation backed off from showing it and MGM bought it. They shelved it too. PRC finally released the 61-minute feature but not until 1946, after the war had ended. With Martin Kosleck, Helen Mack, Barbara Bates, Milton Kibbee, and Gloria Holden. Oboler was usually ahead of his time. He also made the first 3-D feature (*Bwana Devil*) in 1952.

STRANGE HORIZON

(1992) **D/S/P:** Philip Jackson Canada

David Ferry is a 23rd-century spaceship pilot who crashes on a remote planet. Olga Prokhorova is an alien woman who uses illegal drugs. The talky sci-fi movie was shot in Toronto.

STRANGE ILLUSION

(Sinister, 1945) **D:** Edgar G. Ulmer **S:** Adele Commandini **P:** Leon Fromkess

A boy (James Lydon) dreams that his father is killed and his mother is a victim of con men. It all comes true and he pretends to be insane to catch the killer, his mother's suitor (Warren William). The PRC release was loosely based on *Hamlet*. With Sally Eilers and Regis Toomey.

STRANGE INVADERS

(Vestron, 1983) **D/S:** Michael Laughlin **S:** William Condon **P:** Walter Coblenz

After *Strange Behavior* (RCA, 1981), Laughlin scored again with this science fiction spoof. Aliens

in human form who took over a small midwestern town in the 50s plan to leave after 25 years. They need the help of the daughter of Paul Le Mat, a divorced college profesor. A tabloid reporter (Nancy Allen) helps him investigate. Part of the joke is that the aliens still live like Norman Rockwell–picture Americans. With Diana Scarwid as his alien ex-wife, Michael Lerner, Caroline Munro, Louise Fletcher, Wallace Shawn, Fiona Lewis, Kenneth Tobey, and June Lockhart. From Orion.

THE STRANGENESS

(TWE, 1980) **D/P/M:** David Michael Hillman **P/A:** Mark Sawicki, Chris Huntley

An expedition for gold uncovers an animated, tentacled Indian-lore monster in a mine. The amateur feature has Ernest Farino stop-motion FX.

THE STRANGER

(RCA, 1986) **D:** Adolpho Aristarain **S:** Dan Gurskis **P:** Hugo Lamonica US/Argentina

Bonnie Bedelia sees three murders, then ends up in a hospital with amnesia. The killers go after her. With Peter Riegert as a doctor and Barry Primus. It was filmed in Buenos Aires but is set in a California town. With b/w flashbacks.

THE STRANGER

(Ghost Limb, 1994) **D/S/C:** Christopher Frieri

A cynical tattooed loser (Mark Fucille, also in *I Was a Teenage Mummy* and the *Toxic Avenger* sequels) narrates with his heavy New Jersey accent. He gets a job as a janitor in a bar run by a cigar-smoking dwarf and in one scene, gets up and sobs the Bee Gees' "I Started a Joke" dressed like Elvis while a blonde fondles her breasts. He also rides subway cars, has nightmares, takes a lot of LSD, yells at his pregnant girlfriend, and kills people. The image that sticks in my mind is the chimp wandering through a graveyard. The mostly b/w feature uses some found footage and very disorienting music (plus some rock by the A-Bones). The end credits are spoken. This was Frieri's third feature.

STRANGE RAMPAGE

(SW, 1967) **D:** Ignatz Volpe **S:** Mel Carto **P:** Harry "Niwreck"/Kerwin

A narrator talks a lot, then a "sex doctor" discusses three of his cases. We see a schoolteacher and a secretary dancing topless to a Bo Diddley instrumental followed by a drugged orgy (in shadows). Ann (Ann Howe—love that name!) is an exhibitionist who becomes a stripper and Sally (Bunny Ware from *Mundo Depravados*) strips and takes a mannequin to bed. This light, just-over-an-hour-long b/w nudie movie was made in Florida. With Linda Miller, who later went to Japan and acted in *King Kong Escapes* and *The Green Slime*!

THE STRANGER AND THE GUNFIGHTER

(RCA, 1974) **D/S:** "Anthony Dawson"/ Antonio Margheriti **S:** Giovani Simonelli **P:** Carlo Ponti Italy/Spain/Hong Kong (*La Dove non Batte il Sole; Blood Money*)

Dakota (Lee Van Cleef), a hard-drinking gun-fighter, teams up with a martial arts expert (Lo Lieh), in a comedy kung fu western set in China. They're after a treasure, and parts of the map are tattooed on ladies' asses. With Patty Shepard, Erica Blanc, Femi Benussi, and Karen Yeh. Lieh had already been in "50" features including *Five Fingers of Death* and the Italian *Three Supermen Against the Orient* (1973). Run Run Shaw was executive producer.

STRANGER BY NIGHT

(A-Pix, 1994) **D:** Gregory H. Brown **S:** Daryl Haney, Richard Filon **P:** Andrew Garroni

Steven Bauer stars as a tough LA police detective after a serial killer. He has alcoholic blackouts and b/w nightmares and becomes a suspect in the deaths of several hookers. With Jennifer Rubin as his shrink, William Katt as his obnoxious partner, Michael Parks, Michelle Greene, J. J. Johnson, and Luca Bercovici. Director Brown is a.k.a. Gregory Hippolyte.

STRANGER IN TOWN

(1966) **D:** Luigi Vanza **S:** Giuseppi Mangione **P:** Carlo Infascelli Italy/US (*Un Dollar Tra i Denti*)

Tony Anthony stars as a bounty killer known as the Stranger, who makes wisecracks as he kills. He's in Mexico after a bandit leader (Frank Wolf) who cheated him. Anthony returned in *The Stranger Returns* (1967) and *The Stranger in Japan* (1969) which was held up for legal reasons and not released until 1977. All three were backed by New York lawyer Allen Klein, who worked for the Beatles and the Rolling Stones. The first two movies were major releases in America from MGM. Series star Anthony, an American whose western career mirrored Clint Eastwood's, also played the stranger role in *Get Mean* (1975). Other Italian westerns with "stranger" titles were unrelated.

STRANGERS

(1990) **D/P:** Craig Lahill **S:** John Emery **P:** Wayne Gross Australia

A man (James Healy) going through a divorce has a one-night stand with a possessive woman (Anne Looby), who decides to kill off his family.

STRANGERS IN PARADISE

(1983) **D/S/P/A:** Ulli Lommel **S:** Susanna Love

The German Lommel made some strange movies, but this was his ultimate vanity production. He plays a stage mentalist who is frozen in 1940. He's revived in modern-day California and starts a right-wing group against rock and roll. With lots of music and repeated scenes. Lommel also plays Hitler (in the prologue). The music is by a Cleveland-area Doors copy band called Moonlight Drive!

STRANGERS ON A TRAIN

(Warner, 1951) **D/P:** Alfred Hitchcock **S:** Raymond Chandler, Czenzi Ormonde

This broke Hitchcock's box-office losing streak (*Notorious* in 1946 had been his last hit). The famous story is based on a Patricia Highsmith novel.

Robert Walker is a deranged playboy killer who devises a murder exchange with tennis champ Farley Granger. With Ruth Roman, Leo G. Carroll, and Patricia Hitchcock. The famous end takes place on a merry-go-round. The director carries a bass on the train. Walker died the year of the Warner release. The "director's cut" is actually the British version, running two more minutes, with some alternate dialogue and a different ending. *Once You Kiss a Stranger* (1969) was a remake, *Throw Mama from the Train* (1987) was a comedy copy, and other features have borrowed from the plot.

THE STRANGER WITHIN

(1990) **D:** Tom Holland **S:** John Pielmeier **P:** Paulette Breen

Teen psycho Rick(y) Schroder shows up on Halloween claiming to be Kate Jackson's long-lost son. Chris Sarandon is her boyfriend. Former child star Schroder is pretty creepy. New World made it for CBS.

THE STRANGER WORE A GUN

(1953) **D:** Andre de Toth **S:** Kenneth Gamer **P:** Harry Joe Brown

Randolph Scott stars as a spy with Quantrill's Raiders in a 3-D western from Columbia. It has more dangerous objects hurled at the audience than most and one character spits tobacco juice at you! With Joan Weldon (from *Them*), Claire Trevor, George Macready, Lee Marvin, Ernest Borgnine (as Bull), and Roscoe Ates. De Toth also directed *House of Wax* in 3-D.

STRANGE SHADOWS IN AN EMPTY ROOM

(Vestron, 1977) **D:** "Martin Herbert"/Alberto De Martino **S:** Vincent Mann, Frank Clark **P:** Almondo Amati   Italy/Canada (*Una Magnum Speciale Per Tony Saitta; Blazing Magnums*)

A sadistic police detective searches for his sister's killer in Montreal. The all-star cast includes Stuart Whitman, John Saxon, Tisa Farrow, Gayle Hunnicut, Martin Landau, and Carole Laure. The violent AIP release has a great car chase.

STRANGE TALES: RAY BRADBURY THEATRE VOL. 1

(HBO, 1986) **D:** Don McGrearty, Bruce Pittman, Douglas Jackson **S:** Ray Bradbury **P:** Seaton McLean

Three Poe-influenced tales from the HBO anthology series make up this tape, hosted by Bradbury. Jeff Goldblum stars in "The Town Where No One Got Off," Drew Barrymore is in "The Screaming Woman," and Peter O'Toole plays a director in Ireland (based on John Huston) in "Banshee." Also with Charles Martin Smith. *Ray Bradbury Theatre Vol. 2* and *Ray Bradbury Chronicles: The Martian Episodes* are also available.

THE STRANGE WOMAN

(Hens Tooth, 1945) **D:** Edgar G. Ulmer **S:** Herb Meadows **P:** Jack Chertock

Hedy Lamarr stars as an early-19th-century woman in a Maine lumber town. She marries a rich man (Gene Lockhart), seduces his son (George Sanders), and works her way to the top by arranging murders. Louis Hayward is the man she really wants and it all ends tragically. With Hillary Brooke and Alan Napier.

THE STRANGE WORLD OF COFFIN JOE

(SW, 1968) **D/P/A/M:** Jose Mojica Marins **S:** Rubens F. Luccetti **P:** George Michel Serkeis (*O Estraho Mundo De Ze De Caixo*)

Marins introduces his b/w horror trilogy, asking questions about life and death and saying "Horror is you!" "The Dollmaker" is a revenge tale with decapitation, eyes removed, rape, and characters twisting. The sick (and silent) "Obsession" has a necro hunchback balloon seller stalking a new bride, lightning, rats, and spiders. The last, best, and by far the most shocking and outrageous ("Theory"), stars Marins as a professor who appears on a TV program, then puts the TV host and his wife in cages at his home. It features snakes, frogs, blood drinking, torture, whipping, acid in a face, a burlesque show, orgies, a crucifixion, cannibalism, and gore. Filmed in São Paulo, Brazil. Subtitled, but I wonder about translations like "major league babes."

THE STRANGLER

(Key, 1964) **D:** Burt Topper **S:** Bill S. Ballinger **P:** Samuel Bischoff

Victor Buono, an underrated 300-lb. character actor who went on to play King Tut on *Batman*, only starred in two movies, this and the Italian *The Mad Butcher* (1972). He's pretty disturbing as Leo Kroll, a mama's-boy hospital lab technician who murders women after winning dolls at a ring toss game at the Fun Palace. He keeps a drawer full of dolls at home, and sweats and shakes as he undresses them. A doctor tries to explain his fetish. His nagging mother (Ellen Corby) dies, and he violently smashes up his room. There isn't much more plotwise—the cops interrogate him, stupidly let him leave to commit even more murders, then finally catch him. The cinematography in this low-budget b/w psycho film is often excellent. The opening shot of a nurse undressing, seen from inside a large eyeball, is great. Otherwise it looks like an old TV show shot on sterile Hollywood sets. Director Topper went on to narrate *Mondo Teeno* and *Sadismo*.

STRANGLER OF BLACKMOOR CASTLE

(Sinister, 1963) **D:** Harold Reinl **S:** Gustav Kampendank, Ladislas Fodor   W. Germany (*Der Wurger Von Schloss Blackmoor*)

A hooded nine-fingered strangler carves the letter M in his victims' foreheads and a decapitated head arrives in the mail. It's based on a novel by Bryan Edgar Wallace. With Karin Dor and Ingmar Zeisberg. Reinl directed many interesting features including *The Return of Dr. Mabuse* (1961), and *Blood Demon* (1967).

STRANGLER OF THE SWAMP

(Sony, 1945) **D/S:** Frank Wisbar (Franz Wysbar) **S:** Harold Erickson **P:** Raoul Pagel

Director Wisbar fled Germany in the 30s and came to America, where he made six impossibly cheap movies at PRC and Screen Guild. This is a remake of his *Fahrmann Maria* (1936). Rosemary La Planche (Miss America 1941), who was also in Wisbar's *Devil Bat's Daughter* (1946), stars as Maria in this spooky, atmospheric ghost story set in a lonely swamp. After her grandfather, the ferryman, is killed, she takes his job, pulling a small wooden platform with passengers across the swamp. The blurry, floating ghost of an innocent man who was hanged for murder is played by Charles Middleton, best known as Ming in *Flash Gordon* serials. The locals are terrified of the cursed noose, still hanging from a tree. "Run 'til your heart bursts!" Future director Blake Edwards plays the love interest. Shot mostly on one simple set (which must have inspired Tobe Hooper for his *Eaten Alive*), *Strangler* is only one hour long and is a must for anybody interested in good early horror.

STRAWBERRIES NEED RAIN

(1970) **D/S/P/E:** Larry Buchanan

Death (Les Tremayne) sits on a grave with a scythe on his shoulder and narrates this overlong flashback-filled color adult drama. It's supposed to take place somewhere in Europe, but nearly everyone has Southern accents! Monica Gayle stars as Erica, a poor girl who has various sexual encounters before Les finally takes her away. A farm boy can't do it, a playboy biker beats her, and she falls for a poetry-reading teacher. Parts are very tedious, parts are unintentionally funny, and parts are pretty sexy (Gayle is naked in a river, in a field, climbing a ladder . . .). Buchanan claims his Bergman copy played in Texas theaters—as a Bergman film—and nobody knew the difference! Gayle went on to many Hollywood nudie movies.

THE STRAWBERRY STATEMENT

(MGM, 1970) **D:** Stuart Hagmann **S/A:** Israel Horovitz **P:** Irwin Winkler

Bruce Davison stars as a guy who only cares about girls and boat races. Kim Darby and the arrival of National Guardsmen who crack some skulls make him become political. The Columbia University student riot comedy was made the same year as Kent State. With Bud Cort, Bob Balaban, Michael Margotta, James Coco, and Erica Gavin. The double Reprise soundtrack includes cuts by CSNY, Thunderclap Newman's "Something in the Air" (also in *The Magic Christian* the same year), Buffy Ste. Marie, and Neil Young.

STRAW DOGS

(Fox, 1971) **D/S:** Sam Peckinpah **S:** David Zelag Goodman **P:** Daniel Melnik

It's the revenge movie that others try to be. Dustin Hoffman stars as the pacifist mathematician in an English country home who finally fights back. With Susan George as his British wife, Peter Vaughan, David Warner, and Chloe Franks. When Cinerama went backrupt, AIP (then Filmways) took over distribution of the controversial R-rated hit. It made over $9 million. The running time was 118 minutes when first released.

STRAYS

(MCA, 1991) **D:** John McPherson
S: Shaun Cassidy **P:** Nikki Marvin

Kathleen Quinlan, Timothy Busfield, and their little girl are in their new remote country house. Killer cats with glowing eyes attack them. The cats are mechanical and the script copies *Eye of the Cat.* The USA-TV movie has too many routine cat-POV shots. With Claudia Christian as a visiting sister and William Boyett. Check out who wrote it.

STREET ASYLUM

(Magnum, 1988) **D:** Gregory Brown
S: John Powers **P:** Walter Gernet

An out-of-control LA cop (Wings Hauser) discovers that he has a control device on his back. Other cops, including his partners, become psychotic. G. Gordon Liddy, a right-wing candidate for mayor, is behind the confused plot. He hires a dominatrix, then kills her because she doesn't cause enough pain. With Sy Richardson as Hauser's new partner, Brion James as a TV preacher, Alex Cord, and Roberta Vasquez (from *Playboy*). R or unrated tapes are available. Hauser was also in *Dead Man Walking*, also made by Brown of the "Dark Brothers," of porno fame.

STREET DRUGS

(Majestic, 1969) **D:** Bill Brame **S/P:** John Lawrence
S: James Gordon White, Gerald Wilson
C: Austin McKinny   *(Free Grass)*

Some idiots ruined this 60s drug movie (in 1989) by adding lots of solarization and senseless nude shots, slowing down scenes, and dubbing in irritating disco-synth music. They also changed the title and claim that Casey Kasem is the star, but that's OK. Russ Tamblyn, with wild curly hair and the same hat he wore in *Satan's Sadists,* does a great job as Link, a hippie speed freak (he injects) working for a gangster (Kasem). Richard Beymer falls in love with Lana Wood at a nightclub (where the Boston Tea Party play). Her first line is "I'm Snow White, would you like to trip with me?" Link says, "She looks juicy!" Nice guy Beymer wants to take her to Dayton, Ohio, but accepts a Mexican border drug-running job first. Things go seriously wrong after Kasem and his partner execute two agents (Jody McCrea and Lindsay Crosby) by shooting them in the head. Russ does lots of crazy and sick things (his stand-out manic scene is ruined in this altered version), Lana is tied up (twice), and Richard has a lengthy (very well done) LSD freakout scene. Cinematographer McKinny also shot *The Thrill Killers, Spider Baby,* and other 60s faves.

STREETFIGHT

(1975) **D/S:** Ralph Bakshi
P: Albert S. Ruddy   *(Coonskin)*

Bakshi's third feature is an R-rated mixture of live action and animation that parodies Disney's *Song of the South.* Scatman Crothers tells the tale of a southern rabbit, a bear, and a fox who go to Harlem and have adventures. With Barry White, Charles Grodone, and Philip Michael Thomas.

William A. Fraker was the cinematographer, and music is by Chico Hamilton. Bryanston distributed after some critics called it racist and Paramount backed off. Bakshi's animated *Hey Good Lookin'* (Warner, 1975) which is set in the 50s, wasn't released until 1980.

THE STREETFIGHTER

(New Line, 1974) **D:** Shighiro Ozawa
S: Koji Takoda, Steve Autres   Japan

Sonny Chiba stars as Terry Tsuguri, a vicious, bitter (flashbacks reveal why) half-breed killer-for-hire in this notorious action feature which was the first movie rated X for violence when released (cut) by New Line (with a new title sequence by Jack Sholder). Tsuguri beats a man and throws him out a window, then sells his sister. We see blood spurting, vomit, a dagger in an eye, skulls smashed, and a throat being ripped out during a big battle in the rain. With Doris Nakajima as the oil heiress Tsuguri is hired to kidnap and Gerard Yamada as the comic relief trainer and cook Ratnose. The music is Ennio Morricone–style with 70s "wacka wacka" guitar. Scenes from this movie were later used in *True Romance.* Quentin Tarantino, a major fan, arranged the uncut video release of this, *Streetfighter II: Return of the Streetfighter* (1975), *Sister Streetfighter* (1976), starring Etsuko Shiomi, and *Streetfighter's Last Revenge* (1979). There was also a *Streetfighter 4.* Chiba (aka Chiba Shinichi) is a cult star. He starred in Toho features as early as 1961 (*Invasion of the Neptune Men*) and was also in *The Executioner* (1976), *The Bodyguard* (1976), *Karate Killer* (1981), and many others.

STREET FIGHTER

(MCA, 1995) **D/S:** Steven de Souza
P: Edward Pressman

Jean-Claude Van Damme stars as Guile, a red-haired career colonel in SE Asia in an action movie based on a video game. Raul Julia (who died in 1994) is the psychotic Nazi-look dictator who has kidnapped 63 relief workers and who feuds with an arms-dealing warlord (Wes Studi from *Last of the Mohicans*). With Ming-Na Wen (*The Joy Luck Club*) as a fighting TV reporter, Kylie Minogue, Damien Chapa, Roshan Seth, giant spiders, and dragons. The DJ heard throughtout the movie is the guy that *Good Morning, Vietnam* was based on. The PG-13 Universal release was the directorial debut of the writer of the *Die Hard* movies. It was shot (by William A. Fraker) in Australia and Bangkok. The Priority soundtrack has rap music.

STREET HITZ

(AIP, 1988) **D/S/P/C/E:** Joseph P. Vasquez

Junior (Angelo Lopez), a son of a barber, is unhappy living with his new wife on East 138th St. in the Bronx. He's a hothead with black best friends who likes to fight. His smarter brother goes to college and seems to have a future. Gangsters and the realities of ghetto life result in many senseless deaths and a depressing end. There's too much talking (or yelling) and soul-searching but it's a well-made first-effort low-budget 16mm feature,

and the salsa music helps things along. Vasquez, who was black/Puerto Rican, was in his mid-20s when he made it (he died in 1996).

STREET HUNTER

(RCA, 1990) **D/S:** John A. Gallagher
S/A: Steve James **P:** David Gil

After co-starring in lots of ninja movies, the late New Yorker Steve James stepped out for his only starring role. As Logan Blade, bounty hunter and ex-cop, James lives in a van with a Doberman, eats beef jerky, has a singer girlfriend, and dresses like a character from a Leone western. Big blond Reb Brown plays a Nam vet mercenary fighter who quotes Nietzsche. A drug-dealing Hispanic gang led by a young scene-stealing John Leguizamo hires him to wipe out Italian mobsters, and he ends up in an impressive martial arts battle with Blade in an abandoned church. *Street Hunter* has lots of shooting, death, and action scenes. The Manhattan locations include a coffin store, 42nd Street, and the Variety Photoplays theater. Singer Richie Havens (!) plays a nightclub owner. With Sam Coppola and Susan Napoli (from *Penthouse*). From 21st Century.

STREET KNIGHT

(Warner, 1993) **D:** Albert Magnoli
S: Richard Friedman **P:** Mark DiSalle

Jeff Speakman (*Perfect Weapon*) plays an ex-cop running a garage in LA, who becomes involved in a violent black vs. Latino gang war. Christopher Neame is the racist Shakespeare-quoting villain behind all the trouble. With Jennifer Gatti, Bernie Casey, Richard Allen, and Ramon Franco. Magnoli also made *Purple Rain.* From Cannon.

STREET OF A THOUSAND PLEASURES

(SW, 1970) **D/S/P:** William Rotsler
S: Sam Dakota **P:** Merrill Dakota

A long-haired LA geologist goes to North Africa. He foils an assassin, so as a reward is taken to a secret slave market. He checks out all the ("71") naked women (some chained or tied up) while the camera shows closeups of their nipples. They laugh, smile, and dance and he says things like "Nice buttocks." Eventually he has sex with one white one, then one black one. The End. Rotsler said some of the (16mm) footage had been shot in his own yard years earlier, including the first nude footage of Uschi Digart.

STREET OF NO RETURN

(VSOM, 1989) **D/S/A:** Sam Fuller
S/P: Jacques Bral   France/Portugal

Keith Carradine stars as a pop star named Michael, who fools around with the wrong woman in Europe and has his throat slashed. He becomes a long-haired alcoholic bum with a falsetto voice, is arrested for the murder of a cop, and escapes during a riot. It's based on a David Goodis novel. With Valentina Vargas, Bill Duke, and Andrea Ferreol.

STREET PEOPLE

(Vestron, 1974) **D:** Maurizio Lucidi
S: Ernest Tidyman, Randall Kleiser
P: Manolo Bolognini, Luigi Borghese   Italy

The nephew (Roger Moore) of a San Francisco
Mafia don searches for a fortune in stolen heroin
with his race car-driving friend Stacy Keach. AIP
released the action drama.

STREETS

(MGM, 1990) **D/S:** Katt Shea Ruben **S/P:** Andy Ruben

Christina Applegate (from the long-running *Married . . . with Children* show) stars as Dawn, a Venice, California, teen junkie prostitute. She leads a
grim unglamorous life, living with other homeless
kids. If things weren't bad enough, a psycho killer
cop (Eb Lottimer) goes after her. With Starr Andreef and Kay Lenz in a bit part. Roger Corman
was the exective producer for his Concorde.

STREET SISTERS

(New Pacific, 1972) **D/S:** Arthur Roberson
P/C/E: Joseph Holsen

Here's a depressing black cast movie based on the
director's play. It's set in the rural 30s (but looks
like the 70s) and shows how a little girl raised by
her grandmother grows up to be a young woman
(Durey Masen) and faces racism, hate, and savage
pimps. There's a lot of talk about God and sin, and
gospel and blues music is heard.

STREET SMART

(Media, 1987) **D:** Jerry Schatzberg **S:** David
Friedman **P:** Golan/Globus **M:** Miles Davis

Christopher Reeve stars as a New York magazine
reporter assigned to do a story about a pimp. He
makes it all up, but the D.A. thinks it's based on a
pimp called Fass Black, played by Morgan Freeman, who steals the movie. With Kathy Baker
as a hooker, Mimi Rogers as Reeve's girlfriend,
and Andre Gregory. Reeve got the role in the surprisingly good movie because he agreed to star in
Superman IV. It was shot in Montreal.

STREETS OF DEATH

(Argosy, 1987) **D/S:** Jeff Hathcock **P:** John Tom Linson

R. L. Ryan and Jane Arakawa in *Street Trash*.

Two psychos, disguised as student filmmakers in a
van, "start a whole new trend in snuff video,"
torture and kill hookers (off screen) and sell
the tapes. They also eat Froot Loops. The quality
of this shot-on-video obscurity is extremely low, although the cameraman tries to make things interesting. For all the hookers around, the only nudity
is an old man. CELEBRITY ALERT: A heavy-set, balding Tommy Kirk (who also worked for Larry
Buchanan and Al Adamson) plays an alcoholic ex-
cop who gives a long serious speech about getting
his dignity back and breaks down and cries before
attempting to track down the killers on his own.
Filmed in Los Alamitos.

STREETS OF FIRE

(MCA, 1984) **D/S:** Walter Hill **S:** Larry
Gross **P:** Lawrence Gordon, Joel Silver

This "rock and roll fable" is an attempt to do a live-
action *Heavy Metal* comics–type movie. It has
a set-bound look and takes place during some
past/future time period. Michael Paré stars, and
rock singer Ellen Aim (Diane Lane, whose singing
is dubbed) is kidnapped by the Bombers gang. The
sledgehammer fight is a highlight. With Rick Moranis for comic relief, Amy Madigan as a tough
dyke, Willem Dafoe, Lee Ving, Deborah Van Valkenburgh (*The Warriors*), Bill Paxton, Robert
Townsend, and Ed Begley Jr. Also with Lee Allen
and the Blasters playing in a club while an erotic
dancer (Marine Jahan, who did the dancing in
Flashdance) shakes it up. The MCA Ry Cooder
soundtrack features "I Can Dream About You" by
Dan Hartman.

STREETS OF RAGE

(Monarch, 1994) **D:** "Aristide Sumatra"/
Richard Elfman **S/P/A:** Mimi Lesseos

Martial arts champ Mimi Lesseos stars as a special
forces commando turned LA reporter with romantic and crime complications. With Oliver Page as
the leader of a child prostitution ring, and Christopher Cass.

STREET TRASH

(Lightning, 1986) **D:** Jim Muro
S/P: Roy Frunkes

This basically plotless feature about winos drinking
contaminated Tenafly Viper booze goes out of its
way to be offensive and was released unrated. If the
production values and special effects
weren't so good, it would resemble a
Troma release (Troma regular big
guy R. L. Ryan is even in it), but it
has effective sick humor. The Nam
flashbacks were some of the most
disturbing I've seen, and the comic
doorman character (James Lorinz)
working for the mob is hilarious. Vic
Noto, who plays the Nam vet, really
was one, and the cop is an ex-cop.
The real Brooklyn Wrecking Company (owned by the then-20-year-
old director's father) makes an
excellent set. It's hard to make necrophilia, castration, and (offscreen)
gang rape funny, and these guys

haven't always succeeded, but *Street Trash* is an unforgettable experience. If you're looking for something shocking, grim, and surprising, with some
extreme gore (FX by Jennifer Aspinal), this is it.
The complete version runs 100 minutes (the tape
is 90). Muro's original *Street Trash* (1984) was a
10-minute, 16mm short. He went on to operate his
steadicam for *Terminator II* and *JFK*.

STREETWALKIN'

(Vestron, 1985) **D/S:** Joan Freeman **S/P:** Robert Alden

Concorde's first release stars Melissa Leo (from *All
My Children*) as a runaway hooker called Cookie.
Dale Midkiff is the relentless, sadistic pimp Duke,
and Julie Newmar is Queen Bee. With Antonio
Fargas, Annie Golden, and Samantha Fox as a
topless dancer. It was made by a husband/wife
team who had made documentaries. R and unrated tapes are available. Corman had it remade as
Uncaged (1991).

STREET WARRIORS

(All Seasons, 1971) **D/S:** José Antonio
De La Loma   Spain

JDs get away with everything in a violent movie featuring a castration scene. Christa Leem and Nadia
Windell star. *Street Warriors II* (All Seasons, 1974),
also by De La Loma, is said to be more violent.

STREET WARS

(Triboro, 1992) **D/S/P:** James Fanaka
P: Bryan O'Dell, Ben Caldwell

Allan Joseph (who narrates) stars as "Sugarpop,"
a motorcycle-riding aviation cadet whose older
brother Frank (Bryan O'Dell) is a suburban LA
crack-dealing "gangster" with a Muslim-style
"roundtable" of followers. Frank is assassinated
and after a joyful gospel music and dance funeral,
Sugarpop takes over. He trains gang members to
fly glider planes with machine guns, gets revenge,
and eventually closes the "rock house." In his
stand-out scene, controversial Nation of Islam
spokesman Khalid Muhammad talks about "behavior learned from the devil" (white people). With a
dance called the Rooster, a sex-change character,
and a rap end theme.

STREETWISE

(New World, 1985) **D:** Martin Bell
S/P: Cheryl McCall **S:** Mary Ellen Mark

Two homeless kids in Seattle are the main "stars"
of this acclaimed documentary. It shows how runaways barely stay alive by begging and by selling
drugs or their bodies and is a stark contrast to the
many fictional movies about the same topic.

STRIKE COMMANDO

(IVE, 1986) **D/E:** "Vincent Dawn"/Bruno Mattei
S: Claudio Fragaso **P:** Franco Gaudenzi   Italy

Reb Brown, Christopher Connelly (who died in
1988), and Alan Collins star in a *Rambo* rip-off
with Russian villains and lots of big guns. Collins
returned in *Strike Commando II* (1987) by the
same director.

STRIKE ME DEADLY

(SW, 1963) **D/S/P:** Ted V. Mikels **S/A:** Stephan Ihnat

This clever b/w drama has a good script (by Ihnat, who acted in *In Like Flint*) and excellent cinematography by Basil C. Bradbury, also the associate producer. Gary Clarke (*Dragstrip Riot*) is Jimmy, a forest ranger who witnesses a murder. He and his pretty wife (Jeannine Riley, later on *Petticoat Junction* and *Hee Haw*) end up being held captive by the killer in a remote cabin. Jimmy has a long (but useful) flashback to when they were playful newlyweds and encountered the same man in a nightclub. One visual highlight is a long chase scene through the woods, filmed without any cuts. Mikels made *Dr. Sex* next.

STRIKER

(AIP, 1987) **D:** "Stephen M. Andrews"/ Enzo G. Castarelli **S:** Tito Carpi, Umberto Lenzi **P:** George Salvioni   Italy (*Combat Force*)

Frank Zagarino stars as Jack Slade, forced to rescue a war hero journalist (John Phillip Law) in Nicaragua. The plot concerns evil Sandinistas and lots of machine guns. Both sides are revealed to consist of corrupt drug dealers. Zagarino is tortured with electricity and Law watches a cockfight. The female lead, Melanie Rogers, is black, and John Steiner is in this feature, which was made around Miami.

STRIKING DISTANCE

(Columbia, 1993) **D/S:** Rowdy Herrington **S:** Martin Kaplan **P:** Aron Michan, Tony Thomopoulos

Bruce Willis stars in another action movie, this time as an alcoholic former Pittsburgh cop working for the River Rescue squad. He's after a serial killer, who he insists is a cop. With boat action on the Ohio River and flashbacks to try and explain the plot. Sarah Jessica Parker costars as his partner, with Dennis Farina (cop uncle), Brion James (detective), Robert Pastorelli (ex-partner), John Mahoney (his chief of detectives father), and Tom Sizemore. Brad Fiedel did the soundtrack and "Little Red Riding Hood" by Sam the Sham and the Pharaohs is heard several times.

STRIPORAMA

(Video Dimensions, 1953) **D:** anonymous **P:** Martin Lewis

Lili St. Cyr is top-billed in the plotless, color, famous-stripper revue movie from Venus Films. With Virginia ("Ding Dong") Bell, Scarlet Knight, and Rosita and her trained pigeons. Betty Page takes a "Most Daring" bubble bath and appears in a scene with burlesque comics. Lili and Betty both returned in *Varietease* (1954).

STRIPPED TO KILL

(MGM, 1986) **D/S:** Katt Shea Ruben **S/P/A:** Andy Ruben **P:** Mark Byers, Matt Leipzig

Katt Shea started out acting in cheap movies for Chuck Vincent (*Preppies*) and Roger Corman (*The Devastator*). Corman, in his typical fashion, gave her the first chance to direct. Kay Lenz stars as an undercover LA cop working at a topless dance club owned by Norman Fell. She's there to catch a serial killer, but she likes her work. With Greg Evigan (*B.J. and the Bear*) as her partner, Debra Lamb, and Karen Mayo Chandler. It made money on video (especially in France), so she got to direct a sequel too. Corman later had it remade as *Dance with Death* (1992) and made many other movies set in strip clubs.

STRIPPED TO KILL II

(MGM, 1989) **D/S:** Katt Shea Ruben **P:** Andy Ruben

A stripper (Maria Ford) with ESP has dreams of razor slasher murders, and other dancers at the Paragon club die. Like in the first movie, a lot of time is spent showing the strippers doing their acts. With Eb Lottimer, Karen Mayo Chandler, Virginia Peters, and Debra Lamb. From Corman's Concorde.

STRIP TEASE BABY DOLLS FROM CLEVELAND MEET THE UNKILLABLES

(197?) **D/A:** Raymund L. Gunn

A Walter Winchell imitator narrates this silly gangster comedy, which features scenes on W. 25th St., in the billiard hall beneath the old Hippodrome theater on Euclid, and a shootout at a rapid transit station. The "plot" is frequently interrupted by commercial spoofs and a doctored TV interview with Richard Widmark (with a *Kiss of Death* clip). Choice sound FX were borrowed from the Little Rascals and some music is from *Psycho* and disco records. It ends with strippers at a club.

STRIPTEASE COLLEGE GIRLS

(Channel 13, 194?) **D/S:** Lawrence Rainmond

In this silly old adult comedy, women at Striptease College wear bikinis, play leapfrog, take fencing lessons, and exercise. They sleep in stripper costumes and one dreams of being on stage in her pasties. One goes for a walk in the woods in high heels and a bikini. "Risqué" dialogue includes jokes about bananas and pussies. Cheyenne stars as Dora Dare and Charlie Craft is a comic European-accented professor.

THE STRIPTEASE MURDER CASE

(SW, 1950) **D/S:** Hugh Prince **P:** Arthur Jarwood, Chauncey Olman

An offsceen narrator tells us all about 42nd St., "Sin Street" in NYC, then we see a series of strippers in a cabaret-type club with couples at tables and a jazzy band. The show includes a comedian, a crooner, and a belly dancer. Every once in a while we see bits of a minimal plot about Johnny the club owner being accused of killing a pencil-thin-mustached blackmailer over the star singer. The narrator says, "Johnny is what ya might call your leading man in this drama." Tall stripper Denise Darnell is the main attraction. The tame strip scenes could be PG today and the print is worn.

STRYKER

(Starmaker, 1983) **D/P:** Cirio H. Santiago **S:** Howard R. Cohen   Philippines (*Savage Dawn*)

A gang of bald guys battle women with crossbows on motorcycles over a water supply in the future. The *Road Warrior* copy stars Steve Sandor with a cowboy hat as Stryker, William Ostrander, Julie Gray, Ken Metcalf, and Monique St. Pierre (who is gang raped). A man is buried up to his neck in the sand, and a midget army is a visual high point. From New World.

STUCK ON YOU

(Troma, 1982) **D/S/P:** Michael Herz, "Samuel Weil"/ Lloyd Kaufman **S:** nine of them!

Troma made this divorce-theme comedy with Prof. Irwin Corey as an angel sent to earth to bring a couple back together.

THE STUD

(Thorn EMI, 1978) **D:** Quentin Masters **S:** Jackie Collins   UK

Rich and married Joan Collins becomes the lover of a young disco manager (Oliver Tobias), who sleeps his way to the top. With Sue Lloyd and Chris Jagger. This sex- and disco-music-filled followup to *The Bitch* was also based on a trashy novel by Joan's sister Jackie. Joan's third husband produced them both. Soon she was to make record money on *Dynasty* in America. The soundtrack includes tracks by Roxy Music, 10cc, Hot Chocolate, plus many disco hits. Released in America by Trans America/AIP.

STUDENT AFFAIRS

(Vestron, 1987) **D/S/P:** Chuck Vincent **S:** Craig Horall

There's a (50s teen movie) film-within-a-film in this sex comedy. Louie Bonanno stars with porn stars like Traci Adams and Veronica Hart using other names.

THE STUDENT BODY

(Continental, 1975) **D:** Gus Trikonis **S:** Hubert Smith **P:** Ed Carlin

It's the story of three coeds. With Warren Stevens, June Fairchild, Peter Hooten, and the acting debut of Jillian Kessner. This is the movie showing in a drive-in in the documentary *The Thin Blue Line*. It was on tape with *Jailbait Babysitter*.

STUDENT CONFIDENTIAL

(Media, 1987) **D/S/P/A/M/E:** Richard Horian

Doing it all guarantees obsessive, off-the-wall filmmaking. To introduce the characters, the camera swoops all over the place showing us the home lives of four Midvale high school students. Johnny (Kirk Douglas's youngest son Eric, also in *Tomboy*) is the working-class kid whose slob father yells, "You're gonna be a CPA!" Joseph (Michael Jackson's brother Marlon) is a computer whiz living with his mother. Elaine is a seductive would-be actress, and Susan (*Playboy* centerfold Susan Scott) is a gorgeous but shy blonde with a bad facial scar. Director Horian plays Mr. Drake, a serious, bearded workaholic millionaire who drops out of the business world to become the school's new guidance counselor. His ungrateful wife is having an affair and he has nightmares with an old lady strangling him. Horian/Drake, in what has to be an at least partly autobiographical role, talks endlessly, giving himself lots of stilted dialogue. When things get slow, he adds nude scenes of his wife and Susan. Ronee Blakley is his admiring secretary. I would guess that Horian is a fan of the old *Naked City* series and maybe caught a few choice Afterschool Specials before making *Student Confidential*. The kids' problems inspire him—he encourages them, shocks them, yells at them, forces them to face their faults, and manages to put all the troubled students on the right path. He pays for the shy, friendless blonde to have a new hair style, which awkwardly covers her scar, and all of a sudden everybody wants to know her. Elaine and Susan flee some phony producers who try to start an orgy. A severely depressed Mr. Drake is attacked by a street gang. "I want to go out fighting! I want you to kill me!!" All four kids miraculously converge in the same bad neighborhood, help their benefactor home, then stop him from commiting suicide! You've never seen a movie quite like this. It took a company like Troma to release it to theaters, but now it can be used to enrich your life at home.

THE STUDENT OF PRAGUE

(1912) **D:** Stellan Rye **S:** Hanns Heinz Ewers
P/A: Paul Wegener   Germany (*A Bargain with Satan*)

A student (Wegener) receives a fortune in exchange for his reflection, which takes on an evil life of its own. The video runs 45 minutes. With German titles. The same Doppelgänger story was told by Poe as "William Wilson," filmed by Louis Malle as a segment of *Spirits of the Dead* (1967).

THE STUDENT OF PRAGUE

(LSVideo, 1926) **D/S:** Henrik Galeen
S: Hanns Heinz Ewers   Germany
(*Der Student Von Prague; The Man Who Cheated Life*)

Conrad Veidt stars as Balduin, the 1820s student who sells his reflection to Scapinelli the Devil (Werner Krauss). The director had also written *Nosferatu*. This is considered the classic version of Poe's "William Wilson." A 1935 version starred Anton Walbrook.

STUDENT TEACHERS

(1973) **D:** Jonathan Kaplan **S:** Danny Opatoshu **P:** Julie Corman

An alternative learning center at Valley High School is the setting for this drive-in sex drama with a clown-masked killer. Susan Damante stars with Brooke Mills. With Charles Dierkop, Don Steele, Dick Miller, and Chuck Norris (!). Kaplan had also directed *Night Call Nurses* (1972). This was followed by *Summer School Teachers*. All were from New World.

STUDS LONIGAN

(MGM, 1961) **D:** Irving Lerner **S/P:** Philip Yordan

Christopher Knight (not the one from *The Brady Bunch*) stars as Studs in a pretty downbeat film based on James T. Farrell's 30s trilogy about directionless overaged juvenile delinquents in 1920s Chicago. Frank Gorshin, Jack Nicholson, and Rob-

ert Caspar co-star. They mostly hang out at a pool room and drink. There's a tacked-on happy ending. Nicholson was in *The Wild Ride* and *Little Shop of Horrors* around the same time. With Venetia Stevenson, Dick Foran, Jay C. Flippen, and Titus Moody. From UA. There was also a 1979 TV miniseries based on the same books.

A STUDY IN SCARLET

(Foothill, 1933) **D:** Edward L. Marin **S:** Robert Florey

This Sherlock Holmes movie has little to do with the novel it's named after. The plot is close to *Ten Little Indians* (which hadn't been written yet). Reginald Owen isn't the greatest Holmes, but it's worth seeing for costar Anna May Wong. With Warburton Gamble as Watson, Alan Mowbray, and Tetsu Komali. It was a one-shot indy production distributed by Fox.

THE STUFF

(Starmaker, 1985) **D/S:** Larry Cohen **P:** Paul Kurta

Americans are eating an addictive junk food that comes out of the earth. The stuff turns people into consumer zombies and eventually eats them from the inside. Michael Moriarty stars as an industrial spy who goes to upstate New York and discovers the conspiracy. It's not one of Cohen's most coherent movies. With Andrea Marcovicci, Garrett Morris as a Famous Amos cookie maker clone, and Paul Sorvino as an anti-Communist survivalist. Also in small roles or walk-ons: Danny Aiello, Brooke Adams, Abe Vigoda, Patrick O'Neal, Tammy Grimes, and Clara Peller. FX are by David Allen, Jim Danforth, and Ed French. It was filmed in Kingston, New York. New World released the science fiction comedy.

STUFF STEPHANIE IN THE INCINERATOR

(Media, 1989) **D/S/P:** Don Nardo **S:** Peter Jones

Troma released this PG-13 movie with a misleading title. Bored rich people act out murders and kidnappings. With M. R. Murphy and Catherine Dee as Stephanie.

THE STUNT MAN

(Fox, 1978) **D/P:** Richard Rush **S:** Lawrence B. Marcus

Nam vet Steve Railsback, on the run from police, is blackmailed by crazed director Eli Cross (Peter

Dick Miller in *The Student Teachers*.

O'Toole) into becoming the replacement for a stuntman who was killed. He drifts in and out of reality on the hectic outdoor anti-war movie set. The excellent black comedy was shelved for several years, then 20th Century barely released it, but O'Toole was nominated for an Oscar. The script, based on Paul Brodeur's existential novel, was first written (by Rush) in 1970. With Barbara Hershey, Allen Garfield, Alec Rocco, Sharon Farrell, and Adam Roarke. It's 129 minutes long and has a score by Dominic Frontiere. Rush didn't direct again until *Color of Night* (1994).

STUNTS

(Edde, 1977) **D:** Mark L. Lester **S:** Dennis Johnson, Barney Cohen **P:** Raymond Lofaro, William Panzer (*Who Is Killing the Stuntmen?*)

Robert Forster takes the place of his late stuntman brother on a film set and investigates his accidental death. A maniac is killing people busy working on a cop movie by the ocean. With Fiona Lewis as a journalist, Joanna Cassidy, Richard Lynch (and his actual chest scars), Bruce Glover, Ray Sharkey, and Candice Rialson as the movie star. The PG New Line release has an early Michael Kamen score.

SUBSPECIES

(Paramount, 1991) **D:** Ted Nicolau
S: Jackson Burr **P:** Ion Ioneson

Two beautiful coeds (Laura Tate and Michelle McBride) visit a former classmate in Romania. They stay at an ancient castle and become vampires. Anders Hove is the main long-haired teen vampire. Michael Watson is the hero good vampire brother. With Angus Scrimm in a silly wig as King Vladislav (in one scene) and a waste of good David Allen stop-motion FX. He provided the little demon monsters. Some *Nosferatu* scenes are copied. The Full Moon, Charles Band production was shot on location in Transylvania, Romania. The Moonstone soundtrack is by Stuart Brotman (from Kaleidoscope) and the Aman Folk Orchestra. Nicolau shot two sequels back to back. The first was *Bloodstone*.

SUBSTITUTE

(Paramount, 1993) **D:** Martin Donovan
S: David S. Goyer

Amanda Donohoe stars as a midwest teacher who discovers that her husband has been having an affair with a student. She kills them, fakes her death, and reappears in another state as a substitute who kills blackmailers. With Dalton James as a student she has an affair with, Natasha Gregson Wagner (the daughter of Natalie Wood), and rapper Marky Mark (Wahlberg). The USA Network movie was filmed in Vancouver. The director also made *Apartment Zero*.

SUBURBAN COMMANDO

(New Line, 1991) **D:** Burt Kennedy
S: Frank Cappello **P:** Howard Gottfried

Hulk Hogan (also the executive producer) stars in a PG science fiction comedy as an alien warrior stranded on earth with a magic power suit. He stays with a suburban couple (architect Christopher Lloyd and wife Shelley Duvall) and fights an alien. The script was written for Arnold Schwarzenegger. Larry Miller, Jack Elam, and Christopher Neame are also in it. With comic nods to *Star Wars* and other hits. Steve Johnson worked on the FX. Hogan was accused of using steroids about the time it was released. He was also in *No Holds Barred,* also from New Line.

SUBURBAN CONFIDENTIAL!

(Rhino, 1966) **D/P:** "A. C. Stevens"/
Stephen C. Apostoloff **S:** Jason Underwood
(*Suburban Roulette*)

Stevens's first project after *Orgy of the Dead* opens with a "Dr. Legrand" discussing the private lives of various female patients. Housewives have sex with a TV repairman, a salesman, a bellboy, and a milkman. There's a lesbian scene, a little bondage, and a transvestite scene. The episodic black and white video is missing the segment about a Korean war bride. *Motel Confidential* followed.

SUBURBAN ROULETTE

(Sleaziest, VCI, 1967) **D:** Herschell Gordon Lewis
S: James Thomas **P:** David Chudnow

A couple move into a new suburban house and become involved in wife swapping with the neighbors. They have parties by the pool and in living rooms and at one point use a roulette wheel to choose partners. Arguments and fistfights result and they go back to good family values at the end. Elizabeth Wilkinson and Ben Morre star with Vicki Miles and William Kerwin. Joe Bob Briggs introduces one version of the color tape (which has no nudity).

SUBURBIA

(Vestron, 1984) **D/S:** Penelope Spheeris
P: Bert Dragin   (*The Wild Side*)

No-future punk kids live in an abandoned, run-down communal house. Outraged locals try and have them thrown out. Some of the music is by T.S.O.L. and the Vandals. With Flea from the Red Hot Chili Peppers. Spheeris made this after her *The Decline of Western Civilization* (1981). She followed it with more modern American teens-in-trouble movies: *The Boys Next Door* (1985) and *Dudes* (1987). From Roger Corman's New Horizons.

SUBWAY

(Fox, 1985) **D/S/P:** Luc Besson **S:** Pierre
Jolivet **P:** Francois Ruggieri   France

Christopher Lambert (with blond hair) is a thief who lives (along with many others) in the Paris Métro system. Isabelle Adjani costars in the silly but very stylish movie which was dubbed in America. Besson, who had already directed *Le Dernier Combat,* is better known (in America) for his *La Femme Nikita.*

SUBWAY RIDERS

(1981) **D/S/P/A:** Amos Poe **P:** Johanna Heer

Robbie Coltrane stars as a cop in this New York city "underground" feature. With John Lurie as a street saxophonist who kills a listener, Cookie Mueller, Susan Tyrrell, and Bill Rice. Poe also made *Alphabet City.*

SUCCABARE

(VCR, 1981)   Hong Kong

The Mayo tribe in Northwest China is ruled by four princesses with colorful costumes and braids, who can never leave their land. They practice snake-poison magic. An offscreen narrator tells us this fictional film was made with "the reluctant participation of the people. The producers have endeavored to replace their native language with English wording(!)." A playboy outsider gets one of the princesses pregnant and leaves, so he's cursed. He becomes a white-faced "vampire." During an exorcism attempt his stomach is opened and bloody snakes wriggle out. Somebody else pukes green worms. Although it's presented as a horror/fantasy, *Succabare* has some unsettling real mondo moments. Every once in a while, a man is shown eating a live snake, toad, lizard, mouse, . . . and real bulls are skinned. With some martial arts fighting, a moondance, and a partial synthesizer score. One actor, Carter Wong, later showed up in John Carpenter's *Big Trouble in Little China.*

SUCCUBUS

(VGB, 1967) **D:** Jesús Franco **S:** Pier A. Caminneci
P: Adrian Hoven   W. Germany
(*Necronomicon—Getraumte Sunden*)

Succubus has a dream-vs.-reality plot, so anything goes. Michel Lemoine, a French actor with glowing eyes, narrates: "She had done well . . . a disciple . . . a devil on earth." She (Janine Reynaud) is part of an S&M nightclub act, teasing a tied-up couple, then stabbing the man. She lives in a castle, dreams about sex and killing men, and wanders around Lisbon in a red robe. Franco regular Howard Vernon plays a word association game with her: "Justine." "Love." "Religion." "Gomorrah." "Goethe." "Kafka. . ." There's a lot of pretentious Godard-inspired dialogue. In a discussion about what's antiquated, the Rolling Stones are deemed "not bad, but antiquated." Sugar cubes are passed out at a party (complete with a dwarf and a guy in drag) and people bark on their hands and knees. She tells her shrink that horror films are her weakness and the camera scans over all the old Aurora monster models (!). There's also a long sex scene shot through a fish tank (the tank is in focus), a lesbian scene, mannequins that come to life, an eyeball stabbing, a jazz soundtrack, and a scenic drive through West Berlin. What more could you ask for? This was a 1969 X-rated Trans-American release, one of the few Franco movies to receive a theatrical release in America. Unfortunately this print is worn and has pretty bad sound.

SUCCUBUS = THE DEVIL'S NIGHTMARE

SUCKER MONEY

(Sinister, 1933) **D:** Dorothy Reid,
Melville Shyer **S/P:** Willis Kent

Mischa Auer is a phony swami who tricks people out of money with fake spiritualists. Mae Busch (*The Unholy Three*) costars in the rare indy drama, distributed by Hollywood Films.

THE SUCKLING

(J.D.R., 1989) **D/S/P/E:** Francis Teri **P:** Michael Helman

In 1973, a tentacled, mutant monster (Michael Gingold, later a *Fangoria* editor) terrorizes and kills off everybody trapped in a rickety old Brooklyn whorehouse run by "Big Mama," a part-time illegal abortion doctor. The monster was a baby, exposed to toxic waste after being flushed down the toilet. The monster's mother has a flashback of what happened while drugged in a hospital. The various pimps, hookers, and johns argue, bitch, and fight while they die one by one. Frank Reeves stands out as Axel, a crazed, wired human killer (sort of like Harvey Keitel would have been in *Night of the Living Dead*). This very tasteless low-budget horror movie by film students has some good camera work, a dream within a dream, a crawling hand, decapitations, animation, sex, blood, gore, humor, violence, *Halloween*-type music, and one of the strangest comic S&M scenes ever filmed. It's not boring.

SUDDEN DEATH

(Media, 1975) **D:** Eddie Romero
P/A: John Ashley   Philippines

Robert Conrad (in between TV series) and Felton Perry go to the Philippines to capture the killer of the president of a corporation. Don Stroud is the assassin sent to kill Conrad. With some martial arts, John Ashley, Larry Manetti, and Vic Diaz. Bryanston released it. Ashley also starred in Romero's *Black Mamba,* about a snake woman, around the same time.

SUDDEN DEATH

(Vestron, 1985) **D/S:** Sig Shore
P: Steven Shore, David Greene

A New York City executive (Denise Coward James) becomes a rape victim then turns into a *Ms. 45*–type avenger and guns down men. The star was Miss Australia 1978. Shore backed the *Superfly* movies.

SUDDEN IMPACT

(Warner, 1983) **D/P/A:** Clint Eastwood
S: Joseph C. Stinson

Clint Eastwood is Dirty Harry for the fourth time. It was the worst of the bunch, but President Reagan got a lot of use out of "Go ahead, make my day." Sondra Locke (in the last of six movies with Clint) is the man-killer who has been raped. Cocks are blown off, a farting bulldog provides comic relief, and Clint beats up a lesbian. With Pat Hingle, Bradford Dillman, Albert Popwell, Nancy Parsons, and Lisa London (*The Naked Cage*). It was shot in Carmel, the California town that made the star its mayor. Charles B. Pierce (*Boggy Creek*) co-wrote the story.

SUDDENLY

(Hal Roach, Sinister, 1954) **D:** Lewis Allen **S:** Richard Sale **P:** Robert Bassler

Frank Sinatra stars as a cold-blooded war vet killer waiting in a small California town (called Suddenly) to assassinate the president (who is never seen). He and two others take over a home and keep a woman, her kid, and her father-in-law hostage. With Sterling Hayden as the sheriff, James Gleason, and Nancy Gates. Paul Frees and Christopher Dark are Sinatra's associates. Rumors later claimed that Oswald saw this before the JFK assassination. Sinatra (who also starred in *The Manchurian Candidate*) later tried to have all prints destroyed. Now it's common on tape; the United Artists release has even been colorized. Even without the bizarre real-life parallels, it's a good movie.

SUDDEN TERROR

(1971) **D:** John Hough **S:** Ronald Hardwood **P:** Paul Maslansky   UK (*Eyewitness*)

Mark Lester stars in a pretty tense PG "Boy Who Cried Wolf" story set on scenic Malta. He sees the assassination of a visiting black statesman during a public celebration. Nobody believes him, but the killers show up at the lighthouse where he lives with Lionel Jeffries and Susan George. Peter Vaughn is the main assassin.

SUDDEN THUNDER

(AIP, 1990) **D/P:** David Hunt **S:** Steve Rogers

Andrea Lamatsch (who has a heavy Zsa Zsa accent) stars as an undercover Miami cop. Armed men set her small-Southern-town sheriff father on fire. Four of her big city cop friends join her there for revenge. Most of the time is taken up by chases and shooting but she takes the time for a nude swim. With another corrupt sheriff, a helpful black moonshiner, and South American drug dealers.

SUGAR COOKIES

(Troma, 1972) **D/S:** Theodore Gershuny **S/A:** Lloyd Kaufman **P:** Ami Artzi

Mary Woronov and Lynn Lowry (in two roles) star in this rare NYC feature about sex, mind games, murder, and making movies. It's similar in some ways to *Performance* and is a lot more interesting than most of today's "erotic thrillers." Woronov and Lowry have nude scenes together and the haunting "Sally Go Round the Roses" by the Jaynettes, always rumored to be a lesbian theme, is on the soundtrack. Also with Warhol stars Ondine and Monique Van Vooren and porn star Jennifer Welles. A 42nd St. marquee announces *See No Evil* and *Die, Die My Darling*. Troma president Kaufman (also the executive producer) plays a lawyer. *Cookies* was given an

X, but was later recut for an R. Gershuny made *Silent Night, Bloody Night* next (also with Woronov). Then they were divorced and Woronov was in *Seizure* by Oliver Stone—who was also the associate producer of *Sugar Cookies*!

SUGAR HILL

(Fox, 1993) **D:** Leon Ichaso **S:** Barry Michael Cooper **P:** Rudy Langois, Gregory Brown

Wesley Snipes and Michael Wright star as Harlem brothers who have become rich drug dealers after white mobsters (led by Abe Vigoda) kill their junkie father (Clarence Williams III) and their mother ODs. Snipes wants out and he wants nice girl Theresa Randle. The moody, flashback-filled movie includes Ernie Hudson as a rival dealer and Joe Dallesandro. By the director of *Crossover Dreams* and written by the scripter of *New Jack City*. The 123-minute-long, indy feature has a jazz score. The laser version has extra scenes. Not to be confused with *Sugar Hill* (1974), the black voodoo and gangster movie or the late 80s *Sugar Hill* video series (from Active Video) with Ashley Eastwood as detective Yolanda Hill.

THE SUICIDE CLUB

(Academy, 1987) **D/P:** James Bruce **S:** Matthew Gaddis **P:** Steve Crisman

Bored rich kids play a card game where the winner has to drink poison in this slow adaptation of a Robert Louis Stevenson story. Mariel Hemingway stars with Robert Joy, Madeleine Potter, Michael O'Donoghue, and Anne Carlisle. The director was an assistant to Louis Malle. The story had been filmed twice in England and as a 1973 TV movie.

SUICIDE CULT

(Continental, 1977) **D:** Jim Glickenhaus **P/A:** Mark Buntzman   (*Astrologer*)

There's too much talk in this obscure horror story about the virgin birth of a demigod. It was the first by Glickenhaus, who later made better movies (like *Shakedown*) and formed SGE.

Lynn Lowry stars in *Sugar Cookies*.

SUMMER CAMP

(1979) **D:** Chuck Vincent **S:** Avrumie Schnitzer **P:** Mark Borde

Teens return for a ten-year camp reunion in a stupid sex comedy. Linnea Quigley has a small role.

SUMMER CAMP NIGHTMARE

(Nelson, 1985) **D/S:** Bert Dragin **S:** Penelope Spheeris **P:** Robert T. Crow, Emilia Lesniak-Crow

A camp counselor (Charles Stratton) leads a rebellion. He locks up all the adults and takes over. It leads to violence and death. This starts like a typical dumb teen comedy but a *Lord of the Flies* plot takes over. Chuck Connors is the new overstrict, religious butterfly-collecting camp counselor. The PG-13 Concorde release is based on *The Butterfly Revolution* by William Butler. Dragin (from Cleveland) also produced *Suburbia*.

SUMMER DREAMS

(A-Pix, 1990) **D:** Michael Switzer **S:** Charles Rosin **P:** Joel Fields   (*The Story of the Beach Boys*)

This is one of the better rock bio films. Bruce Greenwood is excellent, starring in what should have been called "The Story of Dennis Wilson." The drummer and only surfing Beach Boy drowned in 1983 after marriage, drinking, and drug problems. Many of the facts here are questionable, but it's pretty interesting to see actors playing the various band members, their father, Murray, and, yes, even Charles Manson. With Greg Kean as Brian Wilson and Casey Sander as Mike Love, Arlen Dean Snyder, and Bo Foxworth. The familiar hits were rerecorded by others. The ABC-TV movie was based on *Heroes and Villains* by Steven Gaines. The R-rated tape had some additional topless scenes.

SUMMER HOLIDAY

(1963) **D:** Peter Yates **S:** Peter Myers, Ronald Cass **P:** Kenneth Harper

Cliff Richard and three other young mechanics use a double-decker bus for a travel service in France and Greece. They take along some girl singers and an American girl singer (Lauri Peters) disguised as a boy. The Shadows do "Stranger in Town" and other instumental greats. With Ron Moody. AIP opened the Cinemascope feature in Oklahoma City. Richard had also been in *Expresso Bongo* (1959).

SUMMER OF FEAR = STRANGER IN OUR HOUSE

SUMMER OF SECRETS

(VidAmerica, 1976) **D:** Jim Sharman **S:** John Aitken **P:** Michael Thornhill   Australia

A mad doctor on an island tries to revive his dead wife. Others watch home movies. With Arthur Dignam, Kate Fitzpatrick, and Nell Campbell. It's by the director of *The Rocky Horror Picture Show*.

SUMMER SCHOOL

(Paramount, 1987) **D/A:** Carl Reiner **S:** Jeff Franklin **P:** George Shapiro, Howard West

This is a PG-13 teen comedy starring Mark Harmon as a teacher, but some of the kids are pretty outrageous and parts of it become a gore comedy (with superior FX by Rick Baker). With Kirstie Alley, Robin Thomas, Patrick Laborteaux, Fabiana Udenio, and Dean Cameron as "Chainsaw."

SUMMER SCHOOL TEACHERS

(GWN, 1977) **D:** Barbara Peeters **P:** Julie Corman

In a followup to *Student Teachers,* some teachers upset the school administration by making students think for themselves. Candice Rialson stars with Pat Anderson and Rhonda Leigh Hopkins. Dick Miller is a macho coach. The music is by J. J. Jackson, later an original MTV VJ. From New World. Peeters had already directed *Bury Me an Angel.*

THE SUN BUNNIES

(Night Flite, 1976) **D/S/P:** "A. C. Stevens"/Stephen Apostoloff **S:** Ed Wood Jr. (*The Beach Bunnies*)

A scandal magazine writer stays at a beach hotel with her girlfriends. She tries to get the facts about movie star Rock Sanders, rumored to have had a sex change. Rock's gay agent tries to keep her away and everybody has sex on boats or on the beach. The filmmakers show their sensitive side by having a woman raped on the beach at night by three men, then telling her friends how much she enjoyed it. Wendy Cavanaugh stars with Brenda Fogerty, Foreman Shane, and Rick Cassidy. It was one of several features Ed Wood wrote for Stevens before Wood died, an alcoholic, in 1978.

SUNDOWN: THE VAMPIRE IN RETREAT

(Vestron, 1989) **D/S:** Anthony Hickox **S:** John Burgess **P:** Jef Richard **M:** Richard Stone

A family arrives in Purgatory, a town of vampires with a plasma plant. The good in-control vampires face off against the old-fashioned bloodthirsty vam-

pires in a fun comedy horror movie. Bruce Campbell is the comic Van Helsing character and David Carradine is good as Count Mardulak, owner of the town. One scene features a demonic animated bat/ man. John Ireland leads the renegade vampires. M. Emmet Walsh is part of a funny ZZ Top–inspired trio of old vampires. With Jim Metzler, Morgan Brittany, Maxwell Caulfield, Deborah Foreman, Dana Ashbrook, and Buck Flower. It was shot in Utah and was dedicated to director Douglas Hickox (*Theatre of Blood*), who died in 1988. Silva issued a soundtrack.

SUNNYSIDE

(1979) **D/S:** Timothy Galfas **P:** Robert L. Schaffel

Joey (not John) Travolta stars in this AIP movie as a street kid who wants to stop all the fighting. With John Lansing, Talia Balsam, and Joan Darling.

SUNSET BOULEVARD

(Paramount, 1950) **D/S:** Billy Wilder **S/P:** Charles Brackett **S:** D. M. Marshall Jr.

One of the greatest movies about Hollywood and fame is told in flashback by Joe Gillis (William Holden), a dead man floating in a pool. The brilliant black comedy received three Oscars. Gloria Swanson is silent star Norma Desmond, writer Holden is her new gigolo, and Erich von Stroheim is Max the butler, who holds a funeral for a monkey. With Jack Webb, Fred Clark, Cecil B. DeMille, Hedda Hopper, Buster Keaton, H. B. Warner, and Yvette Vickers. The music is by Franz Waxman. A 1993 London then 1994 Broadway musical was based on this Paramount classic.

SUNSET GRILL

(New Line, 1993) **D:** Kevin Connor **S:** Marcus Wright, Faruque Ahmed

Peter Weller stars as a drunken, old-fashioned LA private eye whose wife (Alexandra Paul) has been killed. He and Lori Singer discover that Mexicans are being killed and sold for their body parts. With Stacy Keach as a sadistic gangland killer, Sandra Wild, and John Rhys-Davies. The R or unrated tape is set in LA and Mexico.

SUNSET HEAT

(New Line, 1992) **D:** John Nicolella **S:** Max Strom, John Allen Nelson

Michael Paré stars as a reformed drug dealer (now a photojournalist) in Malibu accused of ripping off an-

other dealer (Dennis Hopper trying to copy his own *Blue Velvet* role). With Daphne Ashbrook as his ex, Tracy Tweed, Julie Strain, and Traci Dali (most are featured in the many sex scenes), Adam Ant as a crook, and Little Richard. The "erotic thriller" is available in R or unrated versions.

SUNSET STRIP

(Vestron, 1985) **D/S/P:** William Webb **S:** Brad Munson

Tom Eplin is hunted by the LA police while looking for the killers of his friend, a strip club owner played by British blues legend John Mayall (!).

SUNSET STRIP

(PM, 1992) **D:** Paul G. Volk **S:** Nick Stone **P:** Nancee Borgnine

Michelle Foreman is a topless stripper in a *Flashdance* copy. Old (Helen Costa) and young (Cameron) strippers help train her and other strippers are murdered in the "erotic thriller." Protective Jeff Conaway owns the bar. With Lori Jo Hendrix and Shelley Michelle (the *Pretty Woman* body double).

SUPERCHICK

(Prism, 1973) **D:** Ed Forsyth **S/P:** John Burrows

Future astrologer Joyce Jillson stars as Tara B. True, a pot-smoking blond stewardess and kung fu fighter with lovers in many major US cities. Jillson used a body double for nude scenes. With John Carradine as an ex-actor surgeon who likes S&M, Uschi Digart, Candy Samples, and Dan Haggerty as a biker. From Crown International.

Visitors at the "Art of Hollywood" exhibit in London (1980) stare at the "corpse of William Holden" from *Sunset Boulevard*.

SUPER COP: POLICE STORY III

(VSOM, 1992) **D:** Tong Kwei Lai **S/P:** Tang King-Sung
S: Ma Mei-Ping, Lee Wei-Yee **P:** Willie Chan

In his most expensive feature (at the time), Jackie Chan plays a Hong Kong cop who goes to the mainland (then Malaysia and Thailand) while undercover to help bust a drug ring. With action scenes involving a train, helicopters, and motorcycles, and comedy scenes. Michelle Yeoh/Kahn is his Cantonese partner posing as his sister and Lo Lieh is an arms dealer. The director was a stunt coordinator. Funny and/or dangerous outtakes are shown at the end. A sequel, *Supercop II* or *Project S* (1993) starred Yeoh, with Chan in a cameo.

SUPERFLY

(Warner, 1973) **D:** Gordon Parks Jr.
S: Phillip Fenty **P/A:** Sig Shore

Shaft was the only black cast movie that outgrossed this landmark action hit in the 70s. Ron O'Neal is Youngblood Priest, a cool-looking, longhaired Harlem coke pusher trying to make that one last big deal. The NAACP asked Warner Brothers to have him die at the end. With Sheila Frazier, Carl Lee, Julius Harris, and Curtis Mayfield. The great Mayfield score was on Curtom. Parks Jr. is the son of the director of *Shaft*. He also directed *Three the Hard Way* and *The Education of Sonny Carson* (both 1974).

SUPERFLY T.N.T.

(Western, 1973) **D/A:** Ron O'Neal
S: Alex Haley **P:** Sig Shore

Ron O'Neal returns, directing himself in this sequel made in Europe, Rome, and Africa (the same year as *Shaft in Africa*). The ex-drug dealer helps an African official on a gun-running mission. With Roscoe Lee Browne, Sheila Frazier, and Robert Guillaume. The Buddah soundtrack is by Osibissa. Shore later presented *Return of Superfly*, a flop 1990 rehash.

SUPER FORCE

(MCA, 1990) **D:** Richard Compton **S:** Janis Hendler, Larry Brody **P:** Michael Attanasio

This is two episodes of a syndicated TV kid show (running a long 92 minutes). Ken Olandt stars as a 21st-century NASA astronaut turned martial-arts-fighting LA cop, with a super cycle and a *Robocop* suit developed by his black scientist friend (Larry B. Scott). The slo-mo gun battles, cheap FX, and barren sets make for maximum boredom. With regulars Lisa Niemi and Patrick Macnee's voice and scrambled face as the late Mr. H, plus guest villains G. Gordon Liddy and Marshall Teague.

SUPER FUZZ

(Embassy, 1981) **D/S:** Sergio Corbucci
S: Sabatino Ciuffini **P:** Maximilian Wolkoff
Italy (*Miami Supercop, Trinity; Good Guys, Bad Guys; Supersnooper*)

Terence Hill stars as Dave Speed, a Miami cop exposed to radiation from an atom bomb test. He becomes an awkward comic hero with superpowers and goes after mobsters led by Marc Lawrence.

His cop partner Ernest Borgnine looks surprised a lot. With Joanne Dru and Julie Gordon. It was filmed in Miami. I saw it in San Francisco on a triple bill at the Standard.

SUPERGIRL

(Avid, 1984) **D:** Jeannot Szwarc
S: David Odell **P:** Timothy Burrill

Helen Slater (in her film debut) stars as Kara, Superman's blond cousin. Faye Dunaway is the evil—but comic—Selena who hides out at a small-town carnival spook house. The plot is mostly about which woman gets Hart Bochner. It's pretty stupid, but at least Slater is more fun to watch flying than Christopher Reeve. Peter O'Toole is Supergirl's friend and mentor, Peter Cook and Brenda Vaccaro are the other villains, and Mia Farrow (in her only non–Woody Allen movie for many years) and Simon Ward are Supergirl's parents. Also with Marc McClure (returning from the *Superman* movies as Jimmy Olsen) and Matt Frewer. The video was released in Japan (with an extra 20 minutes) before the PG feature opened in America. USA video also released *The Making of Supergirl*, but nobody cared.

THE SUPERGRASS

(Nelson, 1987) **D/S:** Peter Richardson
S: Pete Richens **P:** Elaine Taylor   UK

It's a comedy thriller from the Comic Strip Group, about waiting for a drug shipment by the sea. Adrian Edmondson stars as a police informer with Jennifer Saunders and Robbie Coltrane. Richardson went on to *Eat the Rich* and *The Pope Must Die*.

SUPERMAN III

(Warner, 1983) **D:** Richard Lester
S: David Newman **P:** Pierre Spangler

After two enjoyable *Superman* movies, this bad comedy came out. Superman (Christopher Reeve) again returns to a Smallville reunion where he sees Lana Lang (Annette O'Toole). Meanwhile Robert Vaughn and Annie Ross hire a comic computer wizard (Richard Pryor) to make synthetic kryptonite. With Pamela Stephenson (Lee) as Lorelei. Jackie Cooper, Margot Kidder, and Marc McClure all return in smaller roles than before. It's a very long 123 minutes and the network TV version is 19 minutes longer! The Salkinds sold the film rights to Cannon after making this (and *Supergirl*). And see *The Adventures of Superman, Atom Man vs. Superman*, and TV's *Greatest Adventures of Superman* for earlier versions of the comic book legend.

SUPERMAN IV: THE QUEST FOR PEACE

(Warner, 1987) **D:** Sidney J. Furie **S:** Lawrence Konner, Mark Rosenthal **P:** Golan/Globus

Christopher Reeve himself co-wrote the anti-nuke story that helped kill off the once-promising series. He rescues a Russian astronaut, addresses the U.N., and intercepts missiles. Lex Luthor (Gene Hackman, back from *Superman II*) creates an evil

a.k.a. Super Soul Brother

Superman double called Nuclear Man and the super-opponents fight at the Great Wall of China. With Jon Cryer, Sam Wanamaker, and Mariel Hemingway, who wants Clark Kent. Jackie Cooper, Marc McClure, and Margot Kidder (in a very small role) all return again. The voice of Susannah York is also heard, and there's a score by Alexander Courage that was credited to John Williams. Each feature made much less than the previous one. This was followed by the *Superboy* syndicated TV series (1988–92), then the *Lois and Clark* network series (beginning in 1993). The Salkinds bought back the rights and promised a *Superman V* (with a new star).

SUPERMAN: THE SERIAL: *See* THE ADVENTURES OF SUPERMAN

SUPER MARIO BROS.

(Hollywood, 1993) **D:** Rocky Morton, Annabel Jankel **S:** Parker Bennett, Terry Runte, Ed Solomon **P:** Jake Eberts, Roland Joffe

Buena Vista figured this would be a sure thing for the many kids who know the Nintendo video game. They were wrong. Bob Hoskins and John Leguizamo star as Brooklyn Italian plummers who go to Dinohattan, a cheap-looking *Blade Runner* copy (sets by David L. Snyder) parallel universe. Dennis Hopper is the lizard king Koopa (look for the Koopa dolls!) who devolves people that get in his way. Fiona Shaw is his evil partner and Samantha Mathis (*Pump Up the Volume*) is the princess in peril. With Fisher Stevens and Richard Edson (who become stupid, comic-relief, lizard-head henchmen), Mojo Nixon, Lance Henriksen, and some small dinosaurs. The creators of *Max Headroom* directed the $50 million PG flop, partially in an old factory in North Carolina. It didn't stop more movies based on video games. The Capitol soundtrack includes George Clinton, Megadeth, and the Divinyls.

THE SUPERNATURALS

(Embassy, 1985) **D:** Armand Mastroianni
S/P: Michael S. Murphy, Joel Soisson

Confederate zombies seeking revenge attack young National Guard trainees in the Alabama woods. The Mark Shostrom–made-up zombies are good, but the movie is kind of dull, and sad ghosts show up. Nichelle Nichols (in her only non–*Star Trek*

544

film since *Truck Turner*) is the sergeant. With Maxwell Caulfield, Talia Balsam (daughter of Martin), LeVar Burton, Scott Jacoby, and Bobby DiCicco. Some will want to see it for the past and present *Star Trek* actors.

SUPERSONIC MAN
(United, 1978) **D/S:** Juan Piquer
S: Sebastian Moi   Spain/Italy

Michael Coby is the super hero from another galaxy. Dr. Gluck (Cameron Mitchell) has a robot-controlled army. See some of the worst flying scenes in history. It was made the same year as *Superman*.

SUPERSONIC SAUCER
(Sinister, 1956) **D:** S. G. Ferguson **S/P:** Frank Wells   UK

A baby alien from Venus (a puppet) can turn into an (animated) flying saucer. Some crooks kidnap it, but kids come to the rescue. It's only 50 minutes long.

SUPER SOUL BROTHER
(Xenon, 1978) **D/S/E:** Rene Martinez
S: Laura S. Diaz   *(Six Thousand Dollar Nigger)*

Wildman Steve was a "party album" comedian (who worked on stage with Rudy Ray Moore). He starred in this grainy-looking comedy as a wino who is made bulletproof by some gangsters so he can commit robberies for them. In his new luxury surroundings, he eats beans and rice, gets high, and seduces a pretty nurse. He also tells lots of jokes, gives a pro-marijuana speech, and goes back to the ghetto and beats up the bums who used to harass him. The serum was discovered by Dr. Zippy, a white dwarf with a bad Euro accent who can't remember his lines and dances with a topless blonde in one scene. A sequel (!) is announced at the end.

SUPER SPOOK
(1975) **D/S:** Anthony Major **S/P:** Ed Dessisso
S/A: Leonard Jackson, Bill Jay, Tony King

This very-low-budget *Shaft* parody was made in New York City. It's real. I've seen the trailer.

SUPERSTAR: THE LIFE OF ANDY WARHOL
(Vestron, 1990) **D/S/P/E:** Chuck Workman

Many interviews, both new and old, fill up most of the time in this interesting documentary about one of the least-known and most-famous people of the postwar art (and movie) world. Some of the most revealing scenes are in (Warhol's) Pennsylvania hometown. It also covers the 1968 assassination attempt and his suspicious death in a hospital in 1987. With Lou Reed, Viva, Ultra Violet, Holly Woodlawn, Candy Darling, Dennis Hopper, Taylor Mead, Sally Kirkland, Shelley Winters, Sylvia Miles, Grace Jones, and many more.

SUPERSTITION
(Lightning, 1981) **D:** James W. Roberson
S: Donald G. Thompson **P:** Ed Carlin   *(The Witch)*

Andy Warhol as seen in *Superstar*.

A centuries-old haunted house in Vermont is the scene of gory murders. An alcoholic reverend (James Houghton) and his family move in and people are drowned, decapitated, cut in half, and cooked in the microwave. The reverend eventually kills the witch responsible. With Albert Salmi as an inspector, Jacqueline Hyde, Larry Pennell, Stacy Keach Sr., Lynn Carlin, and John Alderman.

SUPER STOOGES VS. THE WONDER WOMEN
(1973) **D/S:** "Al Bradley"/Alfonso Brescia
S: Aldo Crudo **P:** Ovidio Assonitis
Italy/Hong Kong *(Three Fantastic Supermen)*

This wacky period fantasy comedy adventure stars three heroes with fighting specialties. The multi-racial stars are Nick Jordan as the Darma, Yueh Hua as a kung fu master, and Mark Hannibal as the black strongman. They fight (and fall in love with) Amazon women, and there's a magician. With Karen Yeh and Melissa Longo. Did anybody out there catch this on an AIP PG-rated double bill with the Vincent Price movie *Madhouse*?

SUPERVAN
(Cinema Home, 1977) **D:** Lamar Card
S: Neva Friedenn, Robert Easter
P: Sal A. Capra, Sandy Cohen

A customized van contest is the topic of this PG teen movie from New World and the director of *The Clones*. With Morgan Woodward.

SUPERVIXENS
(RM, 1975) **D/S/P/A/C:** Russ Meyer

This was Meyer's first 70s hit (after several career setbacks). It's his most violent and cartoon-like movie and was rated X. Many actors and characters from previous Meyer movies show up. Shari Eubank is SuperAngel/SuperVixen, Charles Napier is the sneering impotent psycho cop Harry Sledge, and Uschi Digart is SuperSoul. Also with Charles Pitts, Henry Howland (as Martin Bormann), Sharon Kelly, John LaZar, Stuart Lancaster, Richard Pryor's one-time wife Deborah McQuire (as Super-Eula), Ann Marie, and Haji. *Supervixens* was shot

The Super Stooges vs. the Wonder Women

in Arizona and New Mexico. It made $4 million in North American rentals and "over $17 million" worldwide. *Up!* was next.

SURF II

(Media, 1982) **D/S:** Randall Badat
P: George G. Braunstein, Ron Hamady

A mad geek teen scientist (Eddie Deezen) turns surfers into zombies with his "Buzz Cola," and teens eat garbage, in a spoof of teen drive-in movies. It's full of sub-*Porky's*-type humor. There was no *Surf I.* The cast includes Eric Stoltz (who probably leaves it off his résumé), Morgan Paul, Cleavon Little, Lyle Waggoner, Ruth Buzzi, Carol Wayne (who drowned in 1984), Ron Palillo, Corinne Bohrer, Linda Kerridge, Britt Helfer, and Brinke Stevens (an extra). The music is oldies and New Wave.

SURFER GIRLS

(1978) **D/S/P:** "Allan Silliphant"/Alf Silliman Jr.
P: Chris J. Condon   (*Kahuna*)

It's more 3-D sex from the makers of *The Stewardesses.* Filmed in Hawaii and California.

SURF NAZIS MUST DIE

(Media, 1987) **D:** Peter George
S: Jon Ayre **P:** Robert Tinnell

Some people wanted to see this Troma movie because of its name, but don't be fooled. "Samurai Surfers" and "Surf Nazis" fight for control of a post-earthquake California beach in a comedy with lots of surfing scenes. With Dawn Wildsmith, Bobbi Bresee as a mom, and a black lady heroine on a motorcycle.

SURF NINJAS

(IEI, 1993) **D/A:** Neal Israel
S/P: Don Gordon **S:** Sara Risher

Surf kids (Ernie Reyes Jr. and Nicolas Cowan) discover that they're the lost princes of an island na-

tion. With Leslie Nielsen as the evil dictator with a half mask, Tone Loc as a helpful cop, and Kelly Hu. Ernie Reyes Sr. was martial arts choreographer and also acts. New Line released the PG comedy.

THE SURROGATE

(1984) **D/S/P:** Don Carmody
S: Robert Geoffrion **P:** John Dunning   Canada

Art Hindle and Shannon Tweed seek help from sex therapist Carol Laure. Soon their friends start to die. The murder mystery with erotic scenes features Michael Ironside, female impersonator Jim Bailey as Eric, and Jackie Burroughs. Tweed was busy making similar movies more than 10 years later.

SURVIVAL GAME

(Media, 1987) **D/S:** Herb Freed
S: Susannah de Nimes **P:** Gideon Amir

Gangsters are after a manufacturer of LSD, recently released from jail. Mike Norris falls for the man's daughter (Deborah Goodman) who is kidnapped. He uses martial arts, and psychedelic 60s songs (including "Psychotic Reaction") are heard. With Seymour Cassel and Arlene Golonka. Freed, also the director of *Haunts* and *Graduation Day,* is from Youngstown, Ohio.

THE SURVIVALIST

(TWE, 1987) **D/P:** Sig Shore **S:** John V. Kraft **P:** Steven Shore, David Greene

The USSR blames the USA for a nuke explosion in Siberia. Martial law is declared in America and bikers and rapists take over in Texas. Steve Railsback is the hero and Marjoe Gortner is an evil National Guardsman. With Jason Healy, Cliff De-Young, Susan Blakely, and David Wayne. It was filmed in the Moab desert.

SURVIVAL QUEST

(Fox, 1986) **D/S:** Don Coscarelli **P:** Roberto Quezada

Good guy and bad guy leaders run survival courses in the Rockies and the groups eventually clash. It's from the maker of the *Phantasm* movies. With Lance Henriksen, Mark Rolston, Traci Lin, Dermot Mulroney, Reggie Bannister, and Brooke Bundy. Long on the shelf, it was the 30,000th film rated by the MPAA when released in 1989. It received an R.

SURVIVAL RESEARCH LABORATORIES: VIRTUES OF NEGATIVE FASCINATION

(SRL, 1986) **D/P/E:** Jonathan Reiss, Joe Rees

This 80-minute tape contains highlights of five controversial performances by the obsessive Survival Research Laboratories (SRL) in San Francisco, LA, Seattle, and New York. The Frisco-based group (Mark Pauline, Matt Heckert, and Eric Werner) create amazing, frightening remote

control-operated destruction (and self-destruction) machines and robots. During a live performance, which is something like a demolition derby presented as a "happening," ear-piercing sirens go off, a cannon fires, and various machines attack each other, smoke, burn, and explode. What might appear as chaos is actually very well planned. What most viewers find most upsetting is the mixture of metal and meat. Real (dead) animals are sometimes ripped in half (a pig) or reanimated (a rabbit). Most of the shows use huge metal machines and were presented to large audiences watching from bleachers, but the smaller-scale New York show was in a corner of a club, where the audience itself was (harmlessly) assaulted by a machine squirting water. Pauline also talks between segments ("I'm a parasite . . ."). Most of the music heard is "pre-Muzak Muzak" (Les Baxter, The Harmonicats . . .). There's also an excellent b/w dream sequence featuring a doomed crawling machine with a human head being attacked, which tops most anything in commercial horror movies. Reiss later made disturbing videos for Nine Inch Nails.

SURVIVAL ZONE

(Prism, 1983) **D/S/P:** Percival Rubens **S:** Eric Brown

A post-nuke rancher family is doing OK until a cannibal motorcycle gang that has killed off a group of nuns shows up. Gary Lockwood stars with Morgan Stevens and Camilla Sparv.

SURVIVAL ZONE

(AIP, 1992) **D:** Chris Jones **S:** Mark Talbot-Butler   (*The Runner*)

TV war correspondents (Raymond Johnson, Paris Jefferson, and Terence Ford) take a WWIII preparation course. Meanwhile, an insane Marine (Ivan Rogers) kills.

SURVIVING THE GAME

(New Line, 1994) **D:** Ernest Dickerson
S: Eric Bernt **P:** David Permut

It's *The Most Dangerous Game* plot yet again with Ice-T as a homeless derelict with dreadlocks hired by hunters to help with an expedition in the Northwest woods who discovers that he is their prey. Former CIA member killers with high-powered rifles, cycles, and tanks include Rutger Hauer (with a goatee), Gary Busey as a shrink, Charles S. Dutton, John C. McGinley, and F. Murray Abraham. Also with Jeff Corey. Stewart Copeland provided the score. By Spike Lee's cinematographer, who also directed *Juice.*

SURVIVOR

(Vestron, 1987) **D:** Michael Shackleton
S: Bima Stagg **P:** Martin Wragge   S. Africa

Chip Mayer stars as a post-nuke NASA astronaut who returns to Earth and wanders through the wastelands. Villain Richard Moll runs an underground Russian power station containing all the best-looking women left for repopulation. With Sue Kiel as "the woman."

SUSANA

(Media, 1951) **D:** Luis Buñuel **S:** Jamie Salvador
P: Oscar Dancigers   Mexico (*Demonia y Carne*)

A seductive girl (Rosita Quintana) escapes from prison after praying and hides out with a family on a plantation. She brings bad weather and tragedy to the family that helps her.

SUSPICION

(Turner, RKO, 1941) **D:** Alfred Hitchcock
S: Samson Raphaelson, Alma Reville

Cary Grant is great in a different role (for him) as Johnny, a charming liar and possible killer. Joan Fontaine received an Oscar for playing his new wife and probable victim. It's set in England and has an excellent support cast including Sir Cedric Hardwicke, Nigel Bruce as Beaky, Dame May Whitty, and Leo G. Carroll. The original ending (she's pregnant, he poisons her, and she dies) was changed by RKO under orders of the Production Code. Now it's all in her mind. It's loosely based on *Before the Fact* by Anthony Berkeley. A colorized version is available from Turner.

SUSPICION

(Fox Hills, 1987) **D:** Andrew Greieve
S/P: Barry Levinson **S/A:** Jonathan Lynn   UK

Anthony Andrews and Jane Curtin star in a remake of Hitchcock's 40s hit. With Betsy Blair and Michael Hordern. *Masquerade* (1988) with Rob Lowe and Meg Tilly from the same year was also a *Suspicion* remake.

SVENGALI

(IVE, 1983) **D:** Anthony Harvey
S: Frank Cucci **P:** Robert Halmi Sr.

Peter O'Toole is Anton Bosnyak, a modern-day Svengali singing teacher in New York City. His rock-singer Trilby is Jodie Foster. With Elizabeth Ashley and Holly Hunter. The CBS-TV movie has music by John Barry. Other versions of George du Maurier's tale were in 1927 (starring Paul Wegener), 1931 (John Barrymore), and 1954 (Donald Wolfit). The last two are available from Sinister.

SWAMP COUNTRY

(Paragon, 1966) **D/P:** Robert Patrick
S/A: David DaLie **P:** Jerome Sandy

When a blonde in a red dress staying at a motel is killed, a big guy from California (DaLie) is blamed and escapes into the Okefenokee Swamp. Since he happens to be a survivalist/hunter, he survives attacks by gators, bears, snakes, and a mountain lion and rescues a little girl. The wildlife footage is excellent, and so are some of the songs sung by Baker Knight, featured in love triangle and bootlegger subplots. He does the great title theme ("land of the tremblin' earth . . .") and some talking blues numbers with his Johnny Cash–type voice. Former singing cowboy Rex Allen is the sheriff and Lyle Waggoner is the deputy. The color Southern drive-in title also features Carol Gilbert (*Bigfoot*), Vincent Barbi (*Astro-Zombies*) as a gangster, and some stereotypical wide-eyed blacks. It was filmed on lo-

cation in the Okefenokee Swamp in Georgia. Patrick also produced *Road to Nashville* the same year.

SWAMP DIAMONDS: *See* SWAMP WOMEN

SWAMP GIRL

(SW, 1971) **D/P:** Don Davis
S/P: Jay Kulp **P:** Jack Vaughn

Simone Griffith (*Death Race 2000*) stars as an innocent young "ghost girl" with long blond hair who was raised in the Bayou. Country singer Ferlin Husky is a friendly Okefenokee Swamp ranger with an air boat who helps her after her "pa" (who turns out to be a black man) is killed by an escaped female con and her boyfriend. The PG-rated feature has flashbacks about a drunken abortion doctor who sold babies and includes a girl/girl mud fight and death by quicksand, axe, and snakes. The music score (not country) is excellent. Filmed in Waycross, Georgia, and Orlando, Florida. The print is very good. The same director made several Marsha Jordan sex movies.

SWAMP OF THE LOST MONSTERS

(Genesis, 1958) **D:** Raphael Baledon
S: Ramon Obon **P:** Alfred Ripstein Jr.
Mexico (*El Pantano de las Animas*)

In this musical western comedy horror movie, a big human rodent that looks like "Swamp Man" turns out to be fake. Gaston Santos stars with his horse Moonlight, a comic sidekick, and Manola Saavera. K. Gordon Murray released a dubbed version in America and AIP released it to TV.

SWAMP OF THE RAVENS

(VSOM, 1973) **D/P:** "Michael Cannon"/Manuel Cano
S: Santiago Moncada   Spain/US

A mad scientist called Dr. Frosta experiments on humans in the swamp. The dismembered limbs he throws away come to life, and hands kill people. With Raymond Oliver and Fernando Sancho. The R-rated feature includes some actual autopsy footage. It was filmed in Miami by the director of *Voodoo Black Exorcist* and *King of the Jungle*. The video has Greek subtitles.

SWAMP VIRGIN

(SW, 1947) **D/P:** Ewing Scott **S:** Taylor Caven,
Paul Gerard Smith   (*Untamed Fury*)

An old man (Leigh Whipper) tells a story to a writer in flashback. Mikel Conrad (star of *The Flying Saucer*) is the bitter backwoods Gator, working as a guide for a city woman. Jeff (Gaylord Pendleton), now a big city engineer, returns home to the bayou and a love triangle/battle develops. Lots of underwater photography fills the one-hour running time, and a young E. G. Marshall does the calls at a barn dance. The plot of the PRC movie, based on the story *Gator Bait*, is very much like *Poor White Trash/Bayou* (1957). The tape is jumpy.

SWAMP WOMAN

(1941) **D:** Elmer Clifton **S:** Arthur G. Durlam
P: George M. Merrick, Max Alexander

Burlesque star Ann Corio made her film debut as a honkytonk dancer who returns to her Florida swamp home. She discovers that her ex-lover (Jack LaRue) is engaged to her niece and solves a murder. From PRC.

SWAMP WOMEN

(Sinister, 1956) **D:** Roger Corman **S:** David Stern
P: Bernard Woolner   (*Swamp Diamonds*)

Marie Windsor is Josie, a policewoman who goes undercover in prison to infiltrate the all-female Nardo gang run by the sadistic red-haired Vera (Beverly Garland). The film opens with typical Corman arty titles and jazz music. Silent Mardi Gras footage with dubbed-in crowd noises fills up time and establishes that we're in New Orleans. Jonathan Haze plays a pickpocket and Ed Nelson is a cop. The women escape by jumping out the window. They steal a boat and take rich oilman Mike "Touch" Connors and his whimpering blond girlfriend hostage in the swamp while they search for stolen diamonds. The women (including Carole Mathews as Lee) drink booze, turn their prison jeans into sexy cutoffs, argue, fight, kill people, and tie Touch to a tree. He says, "Red, you talk too much!" Vera doesn't trust Josie ("That dame gripes me! I'll kill that dame!"). Vera has a big punch-out fight with Lee, then double-crosses everybody and hides in a tree using Touch as bait. Most of this movie was shot on location in the Louisiana bayou. It's not one of Corman's best, but is a worthwhile 50s bad-girl movie. An important scene with a snake is missing in the Sinister version. This was Corman's only film for the Woolner Brothers (*The Human Duplicators, Hillbillys in a Haunted House . . .*), but Bernard Woolner later helped him form New World.

THE SWAP

(Vestron, 1969/83) **D/S:** "Jordan Leondopoulos"/
John C. Broderick, John Shade
P: Christopher C. Dewey   (*Line of Fire*)

Cannon took *Sam's Song*, an obscure, slow-moving, and arty 1969 movie starring Robert De Niro, and released the two-hour-long feature in 1980 to cash in on De Niro's fame. De Niro plays a film editor spending a weekend on Long Island. This version was a theatrical flop but played on local TV stations. The (1983) video is a 90-minute-long, totally reworked version with added (R-rated) scenes with Anthony Charnotta as Sam's ex-con brother Vito, and De Niro footage used for complex flashbacks. The (new) plot about Vito looking for Sam's killer involves a political cover-up, murders, drugs, blackmail, and porno movies. Also with Sybil Danning, James Brown (the actor), and Lisa Blount in new footage and Jennifer Warren (a *Smothers Brothers Show* regular) and Viva in the old footage. Danning and Warren play the same character.

SWEDEN HEAVEN AND HELL

(1968) **D/S:** Lyigi Scattini **P:** Mario Bregi
Italy (*Svenzia, Inferno e Paradiso*)

Edmund Purdom narrates a mondo documentary about Sweden. It shows contraceptives for teen girls, lesbian nightclubs, wife swapping, porno movies, biker gangs, and Walpurgis Night celebrations. It also examines Swedish drug, drinking, and suicide problems. Avco Embassy released it. The soundtrack (on Ariel) featured the classic nonsense song "Ma-Na-Ma-Na," later used on the *Sesame Street* show.

SWEDISH FLY GIRLS

(1971) **D/S/P:** Jack O'Connell   Denmark (*Christa*)

Birte Toove stars as a stewardess who has sex in various cities, but the father of her son threatens to kill himself. In English and with Daniel Gelin. AIP released it. The music is by the British group Manfred Mann (also in *Venus in Furs*). By the maker of *Revolution* (1969).

SWEET AND SAVAGE

(1981) **D:** Antonio Climati, Mario Morra **P:** Alessandro Fracassi   Italy

This mondo movie was a hit in Tokyo. The producer was sued by the government of Iran in 1987 over a "phony" sequence showing Iranian soldiers tearing arms off of Iraqi POWs. Also with religious sects, animal sex, and animals (including dolphins) being killed.

SWEET BEAT

(SW, 1958) **D:** Ronnie Albert **S:** Ron Ahran **P:** Jeffrey S. Kruger   UK

Julie Amber is Bonnie Martin, a "holiday princess" (beauty contest winner) from Exeter. After one contest, she says, "I feel like a joint of meat in a butcher shop window!" Bonnie sings "Thanks" and wins a recording session at Miracle Records. In just a few hours, her test pressing is on the radio, and she hangs out at Al Burnette's Stork Room in London, an instant star. Soon, a sleazy, slick (and married) American promoter takes her to New York, where he puts the moves on her at the Hotel Astor: "Come on, this is New York, not old fashioned Boston or London!" After a kiss and

a hard slap, he says, "Alright, I'm a heel! You dumb broad!" This movie looks even cheaper than its American counterparts. The frequently mismatched reaction shots, bad acting, camerawork, and editing add to the overall hilarity. Most viewers will watch this just for the musical segments. Highlights are Billy Myles singing his 1957 hit "The Joker" and the Five Satins doing their great "In the Still of the Night" ("I remember, I remember, I remember . . . "). Most of the others acts are British and do tunes like "Your Careless Caresses." *The Amorous Sex* (also on tape from SW) was an "adult" version presented by William Mishkin with added scenes of strippers with pasties and a brief topless scene.

SWEET BIRD OF AQUARIUS

(SW, 1970) **D:** Harry Kerwin **S:** "Edmund Niwrek" **P/C:** Earl Wainwright

This scratchy color nudist colony/swinger movie uses some (stolen) music from *Tommy* by the Who and Dr. John's *Gris Gris* album! William Kerwin stars as a Florida TV news studio cameraman with a new, frigid blond wife (Suzanne Robinson). They go to a party where swingers try to "corrupt them," but find happiness by visiting a nudist colony. Unlike more modest nudist movies of the earlier 60s, this one shows everything, women and men—but they still play volleyball. Director Harry is the brother of William, who was also assistant director.

SWEET CANDY: *See* CANDY STRIPE NURSES

SWEET GEORGIA

(Video Dimensions, 1972) **D/P:** Edward Boles

Marsha Jordan stars as the new wife of a fat, violent, dumb, drunken hillbilly in this minimal one-hour-long nudie movie, but Barbara Caron (later in *The Stewardesses* and *Sinthia*), who plays her stepdaughter, has the most memorable scene. Caron

rides a horse naked and it's so memorable, it's shown twice. With a lesbian scene in a cave, a character stomped by a horse, a pitchfork through a chest, and incest. The print is jumpy.

SWEET HOSTAGE

(1975) **D:** Lee Philips **S:** Edward Hume **P:** Richard E. Lyons, Sidney D. Balkin

Linda Blair is Doris Mae, an illiterate farm girl who is kidnapped by an escaped mental patient (Martin Sheen). He takes her to a remote cabin and they develop a love relationship. It's based on *Welcome to Xanadu* by Nathaniel Benchley. With Bert Remsen and Jeanne Cooper. The ABC-TV movie was filmed in Taos, New Mexico. Linda's next was *Exorcist II* and Martin's was *The Little Girl Who Lives Down the Lane*.

SWEET JAMES, PREACHER MAN

(1973) **D:** John Hayes **S:** John Cerullo **P:** Daniel B. Cady   (*Sweet Jesus, Preacher Man*)

Roger E. Mosley stars as a hit man who works for white mobsters (including William Smith). He goes undercover in an LA ghetto church as a Baptist preacher and tries to take over the local action while seducing women. With Michael Pataki as a senator. The MGM release is by the director of *Black Bunch, Black Alley Cats,* and other bottom-of-the-barrel black action movies.

SWEET JUSTICE

(Triboro, 1991) **D/S:** Allen Plone **S:** Jim Tabilio **P:** Carol Marcus Plone

Finn Carter (also in *Tremors*) stars as Sunny Justice, a short-haired lady boxer who reunites her all-female "special forces" team to battle a small-town gangster played by Frank Gorshin (who cries in one scene). The fighters (all tall beauties except for Carter) include Catherine Hickland, Kathleen Kinmont, and red-haired Patricia Talman from *Night of the Living Dead* (take 2). The black one (Marjean Holden) has the lone notable nude scene. They train, ride motorcycles, and use kung fu and machine guns to waste a lot of men. The main battle takes place in what looks like a western ghost town set. Marc Singer is the sheriff and Mickey Rooney shows up briefly as a grizzly fat store owner who gets punched out. By the director of *Phantom of the Ritz*.

SWEET KILLING

(Paramount, 1992) **D/S:** Eddy Matalon **P:** Suzanne Girard   France/UK/Canada

Adam (Anthony Higgins), a bank officer, kills his comically irritating wife (Andrea Ferreol) and uses Eva (Leslie Hope) for an alibi. A cop (Michael Ironside) is determined to prove that Adam is guilty while F. Murray Abraham, who claims to be a fictional character, blackmails him. The pretty dull mystery has some odd b/w fantasy segments and a non-ending. It's based on a novel by Angus Hall. Too many American flags tip you off that it wasn't made here. By the director of *Cathy's Curse*.

That's Troy Donahue as a Manson-type killer in *Sweet Savior*.

SWEET MOVIE

(VSOM, 1973) **D/S:** Dusan Makavejev
France/Canada/W. Germany

This bizarre satire is guaranteed to shock and confuse just about everyone. Set in the future (1984), little boys are seduced and killed, there's sex in sugar, death in chocolate, WWII footage of corpses, images of Stalin, nudity, puke, piss, and shit. Carole Laure is a virginal beauty contest winner who is shipped to Europe in a suitcase and is seen sucking on nipples. Laure (later a top singer in Quebec) walked off the set, then sued in a French court to stop screenings. John Vernon plays a clichéd Texan billionaire with a solid gold penis. Also with Pierre Clementi. The director, from Belgrade, Yugoslavia, went on to make the more conventional *Monte-negro* (1980) and *The Coca Cola Kid* (1984).

SWEET MURDER

(Vidmark, 1990) **D/S:** Percival Rubens
P: Paul Raleigh   S. Africa

What seems to be a copy of *Single White Female* was actually made first. That doesn't make it good, though. A mousy, unemployed, shy American girl from Kentucky (Canadian actress Helene Udy) discovers that her new tall, pretty roommate (Embeth Davidtz, later in *Schindler's List*) has become an heiress, so she decides to make herself look sexy and starts seducing and/or killing off people. There's some nudity (both stars), but everything happens off screen and the stupid ending will make you want to smash the tape. Rubens also made *The Demon* (1981) and *Survival Zone* (1983).

SWEET POISON

(MCA, 1991) **D:** Brian Grant **S:** Wally Klenhard

Steven Bauer stars as an escaped con who kidnaps a couple on the way to a funeral. Edward Herrmann is the wimpy husband who eventually gets tough, and Patricia Healy is his trashy young wife Charlene. The made-for-cable movie borrows from several Peckinpah features. Grant had directed innovative videos for Peter Gabriel, Donna Summer, and others.

SWEET REVENGE

(Media, 1986) **D:** Mark Sobel **S:** Steve
Krauzer, Tim McCoy **P:** Steve Stabler

Nancy Allen stars as an LA TV reporter investigating a Far East slavery ring led by Martin Landau. She and three models are kidnapped, but she goes "Rambo" and saves them. With Ted Shackleford, Stacey Adams, Gina Gershon, and Michelle Little. From Corman's Concorde.

SWEET SAVIOR: *See* THE LOVE THRILL MURDER

THE SWEET SCENT OF DEATH

(1984) **D:** Peter Sasdy **S:** Brian Clemens   UK

Bitter days...Sweet nights

Her machete isn't her only weapon

Their world... a plantation

Their battleground... a tropical inferno

Sweet Sugar

Dean Stockwell stars as an American diplomat in London. While staying at a secluded country house, someone tries to drive his attorney wife (Shirley Knight) insane and their new guard dog is killed. Michael Gotthard is also in the Hammer Studios TV movie.

SWEET 16

(Vestron, 1982) **D/P:** Jim Sotos/
Dimitri Sotirakis **S:** Erwin Goldman

Friends of a Texas girl (Aleisa Shirley) who just turned 16 are killed. Local Indians are blamed by sheriff Bo Hopkins. It's a pretty dull movie, but it does have a very interesting cast (and Shirley has nude scenes). With Susan Strasberg as the mom, Patrick Macnee, Don Stroud, Sharon Farrell, Michael Pataki, Henry Wilcoxon, and Larry Storch. There was actually a soundtrack too, by Ray Ellis, on Regency.

SWEET SUGAR

(Continental, 1972) **D:** Michel Levesque
S: Stephanie Rothman, Don Spencer
P: Charles S. Swartz   (*Hellfire on Ice; She Devils in Chains; Captive Women III; Chaingang Girls*)

Phyllis Davis (from *Terminal Island*) is Sugar, a hooker framed in Costa Rica for marijuana possession. She's arrested and put in a jail where inmates cut sugar cane and are used for sex and experimented on by a sadistic doctor. Voodoo rituals are held and there's rape, torture, cannibalism, and even a burning at the stake. Sugar eventually leads a revolt and escapes. Obviously this is one of the best women-in-a-tropical-prison movies. With Ella Edwards, Timothy Brown, Pamela Collins, James Whitworth, and Cliff Osmond. The director of the Dimension release (made in Costa Rica) had been an editor for Russ Meyer. This was first on tape with *Escape from Women's Prison,* but has been reissued under several titles.

SWEET SWEETBACK'S BAADASSSSS SONG

(Magnum, 1971) **D/S/P/A/M/E:** Melvin Van Peebles

It was "Rated X by an all-white jury," stars "the black community," made over $4 million, and started the black action movie trend (along with *Shaft*). It starts with the 12-year-old Sweetback enjoying sex with a hooker. Later, he does live sex shows in a California whorehouse and is arrested for a crime he didn't commit. He kills a cop after seeing him beat a black revolutionary. Biker John Amos (later on the *Good Times* show) helps out. Most of this overlong movie is Sweetback (played by the director) running towards the border while funky instumentals by Earth Wind and Fire are heard. Van Peebles uses "underground" techniques (freeze frames, solarization, split screen . . .) and the nudity and violence probably would have resulted in an R rating if it was a white-cast movie. Cinemation opened it (in Detroit) and Roger Corman's New World re-released it in 1974. With Van Peebles' kids Mario and Megan. Stax released the soundtrack. The director had already made *Story of a Three Day Pass* (1967) and *Watermelon Man* (1970). He became a trader on the stock exchange in the 80s. In 1995, his son Mario directed his screenplay *Panther,* returning to the themes of *Sweetback.*

THE SWINGER

(1966) **D/P:** George Sidney **S:** Lawrence Roman

Ann-Margret wants to be a writer, so she fakes a biographical story, "The Swinger," for "Girl Lure" magazine. To prove that she didn't make it up, she pretends to be an alcoholic nympho and becomes a human paintbrush at a party/orgy. She rides a motorcycle, sings, and dances, but this dated comedy is a lot like a TV sitcom. Her dance scenes make it worthwhile, though. With Tony Franciosa as the editor, Yvonne Romain as his jealous girlfriend, Robert Coote, Horace McMahon, Barbara Nichols, and Bert Freed. Some of the many bikini extras were Phyllis Davis and China Lee. The costumes are by Edith Head, and Andre Previn wrote songs. The Paramount release is by the director of *Viva Las Vegas.*

SWINGER'S MASSACRE

(Even Steven, 1975) **D/P:** Ronald V. Garcia **S:** Helen Arthur

Charlie (Eastman Price from *Suburban Confidential*), a lawyer in "the Valley," tells his wife Amy (Jan Mitchell) that he wants them to join a swing club. She replies, "No! They're sick. You're sick. I'm sick!" After he demonstrates his premature ejaculation problem, she says "OK." First they go to a club where a long-haired band do "Filthy McNasty's," also the name of the place. They meet some people and go to a private party where everybody talks: "Did you get to ball Supercock!?" . . . Charlie goes to a room with a woman but can't "do it." Then he lies in bed next to his wife and another guy who can. Charlie gets mean and drinks, other guys make fun of him, and we hear a song, "Inside Amy" (the original title). Now the "massacre" starts. The crazed would-be swinger gases two guys

from the party in a car, shoots one, drugs somebody's drink, strangles one man and hangs his wife, then kills his own wife. The End. The video version is too dark, and despite the plot (and sex star cast) has no nudity. With Renee Bond, Marsha Jordan, Uschi Digart, Gary Kent, and Ann Perry, who later directed *Sweet Savage* (1979), a porno western with Aldo Ray.

SWINGERS' PARADISE

(1964) **D:** Sidney J. Furie **S:** Peter Myers, Ronald Cass **P:** Kenneth Harper   UK (*Wonderful Life*)

Cliff Richard stars as Johnnie, with his group, the Shadows. They play on an ocean liner, but are thrown off and end up on the Canary Islands. Johnnie becomes a stuntman for a movie being shot there, finds love, and manages to become the leading man and director. With Walter Slezak and Susan Hampshire. AIP released it in America. Cliff and the Shadows returned in *Finders Keepers.*

THE SWINGING BARMAIDS

(1975) **D:** Gus Trikonis **S:** Charles B. Griffith **P:** Ed Carlin   (*Eager Beavers*)

William Smith is a cop after a psycho who kills cocktail waitresses (including Dyanne Thorne) and uses disguises. With Bruce Watson. The busy Trikonis made *Super Cock* and *Nashville Girl* around the same time.

THE SWINGING CHEERLEADERS

(Monterey, 1974) **D/P:** Jack Hill **S:** Jane Witherspoon, Betty Conkey   (*H.O.T.S. 2*)

Before making the incredible *Switchblade Sisters*, Hill made this one for the same producer and company (Centaur). It has a lot of politics and feminism to go along with the action. A reporter for a student underground newspaper (Jo Johnson) infiltrates the school's cheerleaders for an article. She

leaves the radical editor (with a Nixon dartboard), who turns out to be an egotistical, misogynistic jerk, and falls for a football jock. The school establishment is totally corrupt. The football coach, a black teacher (who used to run numbers), and a sporting goods store owner rig the games. Rosanne Katon, who plays the cheerleader who has an affair with the teacher, was later one of the few black *Playboy* centerfolds (September 1978). The stuck-up rich blond cheerleader is Colleen Camp. She's the only one of the three leads without a nude scene. If you can overlook the silly slapstick end fight, this is definitely one of the best of the countless 70s movies about three sexy women who are nurses, teachers, inmates, stewardesses, track runners. . . . Scenes later showed up in *The Thin Blue Line* (1987).

SWITCH

(Warner, 1991) **D/S:** Blake Edwards **P:** Tony Adams

Ellen Barkin stars in a copy of *Goodbye Charlie* (1964). Perry King is murdered by three old girlfriends (JoBeth Williams, Lysette Anthony, and Victoria Mahoney), goes to purgatory, and has to return in a woman's body (Barkin). A baby saves a soul in the pro-life ending. ILM FX were used for the comic changes. With Lorraine Bracco as a lesbian, Tony Roberts, and Jimmy Smits.

SWITCHBLADE SISTERS

(Monterey, 1975) **D/S:** Jack Hill **P:** John Prizier   (*Playgirl Gang*)

A lot of 70s drive-in movies were predictable formula time-wasters, nothing but tease and filler. This gem is a wild, amazing, anything-goes tale of how the Dagger Debs—tough female followers of The Silver Daggers gang—wise up, break away, and become the Jezebels. I don't know where Hill found his young actresses, but they're all good, and star Robbie Lee (*Big Bad Mama*) gives her all

Jean-Luc Godard greets Bill Wyman while filming *Sympathy for the Devil.*

as the confused, vicious, but tender Lace (wearing all black leather), often hysterical, and cursing through clenched teeth. The plot contains lots of jealousy, revenge, mixed allegiances, manipulation, and cartoon politics. The Silver Daggers sell drugs (and women) at the high school. A rival gang (who dress like members of Slade) sell drugs through a phony rehabilitation clinic. You get to see women prison scenes (complete with a big lesbian guard), a massacre at a roller rink, and after the Jezebels join up with a black female revolutionary group, a street battle with machine guns and tanks! Joanne Nail is Maggie, the new gang member. Monica Gayle is Patch, a devious behind-the-scenes troublemaker wearing an eye patch, and Marlene Clark, star of several good black horror movies, is the leader of militant new comrades. Lenny Bruce's daughter Kitty plays Donut, the gang member who has to squeal like a pig. This is one of the best female jd movies ever, and, unfortunately was the last (credited) film work that Hill did.

SWORDKILL

(1984) **D:** J. Larry Carroll **S:** Tim Curnan
P: Charles Band   (*Ghost Warrior*)

Hiroshi Fujioka is a samurai warrior frozen in ice for 300 years who is thawed out in the modern-day USA. With Janet Julian.

SWORD OF HEAVEN

(TWE, 1984) **D:** Byron Meyers
P/A: Joseph P. Randazzo

Tadashi Yamashita is a Japanese cop in LA who uses a magic 400-year-old sword to battle killers with an extortion ring. The star barely speaks English and does a stake-out scene in drag. Randazzo pushes a nun in a wheelchair over a cliff. With Gerry Gibson and Bill "Superfoot" Wallace.

SWORD OF THE BARBARIANS

(1983) **D:** "Michael E. Lemick" **S:** Pietro Regnoli
P: Pino Buricchi   Italy (*Barbarian Master*)

Peter MacCoy (real name: Pietro Torisi) stars as Sangral, the "son of Ator." With Sabrina Siani as the Golden goddess, and hunchback priests who sacrifice women.

SWORD OF THE CONQUEROR

(1961) **D:** Carlo Campogalliani **S:** Paola Barbara,
Primo Zeglio   Italy (*Rosmunda e Alboino*)

Jack Palance is Alboino, the Lombard king in 566 A.D. He wants Eleanora Rossi-Drago but she's in love with a warrior (Guy Madison). United Artists released the Cinemascope feature.

SWORD OF THE VALIANT

(MGM, 1982) **D:** Stephen Weeks
S: Philip M. Breen **P:** Golan/Globus

Miles O'Keeffe (who is dubbed) stars as Gawain, a knight on a quest for the court of King Arthur (Trevor Howard). He decapitates the magical Green Knight (guest star Sean Connery), who then replaces his head. Peter Cushing, Ronald Lacey, and Douglas Wilmer are the villains, and Emma Sutton is an evil sorceress. With Cyrielle Claire, Lila Kedrova, John Rhys-Davies, and Wilfrid Brambell (in his last role). The music is by Ron Geesin. The PG Cannon feature was filmed in Ireland. It's a remake of *Gawain and the Green Knight* (1972) by the same director. The original starred Murray Head and Nigel Green.

SWORDSMAN

(1990) **D:** King Hu **S:** Louis Cha
P: Tsui Hark   Hong Kong

Characters are after a sacred scroll in a Ming Dynasty black magic movie. With lots of bloody decapitations, gravity-defying sword battles, and fantasy. Sam Hui and Jacky Cheung star, and Brigitte Lin is the villain, Asia the Invincible. Six directors worked on this very expensive (for Hong Kong) movie. *Swordsman II* (1992) and *Swordsman III: The East Is Red* (1993) followed, also produced by Hark but both with different casts.

THE SWORDSMAN

(Republic, 1992) **D/S:** Michael Kennedy
P: Nicolas Stiliadis   Canada

A dull Lorenzo Lamas stars as a psychic detective with long hair and tattoos who is troubled by frequent violent b/w flashbacks and visions. A white-haired warrior (Michael Champion) from a fencing club is after the sword of Alexander the Great. They're both reincarnations and eventually have battles in misty blue light. The talk-filled, often senseless *Highlander* copy from Toronto also features Claire Stansfield as an archeologist and Raoul Trujillo as Jo Jo. With music by one-time James Gang guitarist Domenic Troiano.

SWORDS OF THE SPACE ARK

(Celebrity, 1978) **D/S/P:** Bunker Stevens
D: Minoru Yamada   Japan

After the *Star Wars*–inspired Japanese/American movie *Message from Space*, a TV series of the same name ran in Japan, using footage from the feature. This is an edited, Americanized version of the series.

SYMPATHY FOR THE DEVIL

(Abkco, 1970) **D/S:** Jean-Luc Godard **P:** Michael
Pearson, Ian Quarrier   UK (*One Plus One*)

Black revolutionaries in a junkyard execute some white women. Eve Democracy (Anne Wiazemsky) is interviewed and creates political graffiti messages. All this is edited in with the Rolling Stones creating and rehearsing their song "Sympathy for the Devil" in 1968. The producer changed the name (against the director's wishes, of course), shortened it, and added the finished version of the song at the end. New Line released it. With the late Brian Jones (looking pretty out of it most of the time) and the late Nicky Hopkins.

SYMPTOMS

(1974) **D/S:** Jose Larraz **S:** Stanley Miller
P: Jean Dupuis   UK (*Blood Virgin*)

Angela Pleasence (Donald's daughter) stars as a repressed lesbian in an old haunted British country house. She kills her girlfriend, the gardener, and others. The *Repulsion* copy is by the director of the bloodier *Vampyres* (1974).

SYNANON

(1965) **D/P:** Richard Quine **S:** Ian Bernard

Alex Cord is Zankie Albo, a junkie who hides out at a Santa Monica beachfront rehabilitation center. Stella Stevens falls for him. Edmond O'Brien is the reformed alcoholic who runs the house. With Chuck Connors, Richard Conte, Eartha Kitt, Alejandro Rey, Bernie Hamilton (later in *Walk the Walk*), and many real junkies. Columbia released the grim b/w movie. The Neal Hefti soundtrack is on Liberty.

SYNDICATE SADISTS

(Super, 1975) **D:** Umberto Lenzi **S:** Vincenzo
Mannino Italy   (*Rambo Sfida la Città*)

This is a crime thriller with Tomas Milian as Rambo, the hero biker, and Joseph Cotten as a blind mobster. Femi Benussi is also in the Independent International release.

SYNGENOR

(South Gate, 1990) **D:** George Elanjian Jr.
S: Brent V. Friedman **P:** Jack F. Murphy

The creature from *Scared to Death* (1980) returns in this unofficial sequel. This time there are "at least 20" monsters in an office building. David Gale has another over-the-top role as a crazed cartoonish drug-addicted corporate head who plans to unleash robot warriors to fight for America in the Middle East (!). Starr Andreeff tries to expose the plan and stop her late uncle's (nearly) indestructible creations with help from a reporter. The scaly man-in-a-suit monsters are pretty good, but the lack of security is ridiculous, and the monster attacks should have had more action and scares. Also with William Shatner's daughter Melanie as a comic receptionist, and Lewis Arquette.

TABLOID

(Tapeworm, 1985) **D/S:** Bret McCormick, Matt Shafton, Glen Coburn

Aliens invade an aerobics class before the credits roll in this three-story spoof illustrating outrageous stories that might be found in a tabloid newspaper. A backwoods guy in a pickup truck buys some bad pot and decides to kill the dealer. There's a lot of hillbilly humor and shootin', then a baby is born with a beard. An old man emerges from a graveyard and goes to his son's house. He invites other (dead) couples over for a barbecue. In the last (overly long) segment, a weatherman predicts tornadoes and a killer vacuum cleaner destroys a town. The highlight is a whoopee cushion scene. Filmed in Fort Worth.

TABOOS AROUND THE WORLD

(GWN, 1963) **D/S:** Romolo Marcellini **S:** Ugo Guerra   Italy (*I Tabu*; *Taboos of the World*)

Mondo scenes in this feature include public bathing, tattoos, blood drinking, childbirth, drug addiction, prostitution, child selling, and atom bomb victims. Also with a look at the customs of Buddhists and Muslims. When AIP released the documentary in 1965, narration by Vincent Price was added. The video release has a different narration, though.

TAG: THE ASSASSINATION GAME

(Embassy, 1982) **D/S:** Nick Castle **P:** Peter Rosten, Dan Rosenthal

Robert Carradine stars as a college newspaper reporter looking into the assassination-game phenomenon. Rubber bullets are used in dart guns, but one contestant (Bruce Abbott) cracks under the pressure after losing for the first time and starts really killing students. Carradine becomes involved with a determined player (Linda Hamilton). It's probably the best of several features with the same theme. With Kristine De Bell, Perry Lang, Forest Whitaker, and Michael Winslow. New World released the PG feature.

T&A ACADEMY: *See* H.O.T.S.

T&A ACADEMY 2: *See* GIMME AN F

TAINTED

(Southgate, 1984) **D/S/P:** Orestes Matacena **P:** Phyllis Redden (*Body Passion*)

Blonde Shari Shattuck (*The Naked Cage*) stars as a small-town elementary school teacher. Her mortician husband (who has a necro assistant) kills a young thief, then dies of a heart attack. She buries the thief in the yard and makes it seem like the husband died while driving. Later she starts losing her mind and has nightmares. *Tainted* borrows from *Diabolique, Repulsion,* and *Blood Simple* and has some logic problems, but it's pretty good—and Shattuck has a sex scene, a shower scene, and a

bath scene. It was filmed in Hendersonville, North Carolina, and has music by the Symphony Orchestra of London. With Park Overall and singer Joe Ely. It was released by Cannon in 1988.

TAINTED BLOOD

(Paramount, 1993) **D:** Matthew Patrick **S:** Kathleen Rowell **P:** Jonathan Furie

Raquel Welch stars as a well-known writer and investigative reporter looking for the twin of a teen psycho killer. Joan Van Ark, Kerri Green, and Natasha Wagner are also in the cable TV movie.

THE TAKE

(1974) **D:** Robert Hartford-Davis **S:** Del Reisman **P:** Howard Brandy

Billy Dee Williams and Albert Salmi are crooked cops taking bribe money from a gangland leader (Vic Morrow). Eddie Albert is the police chief. With Frankie Avalon (!) as a stool pigeon, Sorrell Brooke, and Tracy Reed. The Columbia release was shot in New Mexico.

TAKE A GIANT STEP

(1959) **D:** Philip Leacock **S/P:** Julius J. Epstein **S:** Louis S. Peterson

Johnny Nash stars in a serious juvenile delinquent feature set in a middle-class white community. With Estelle Hemsley, Ruby Dee, Frederick O'Neal, and Ellen Holly. Burt Lancaster was the executive producer of the United Artists release, which was based on a play. He also backed *The Young Savages* (1961). Nash returned in *Key Witness* (1960), but had more success as a singer. His biggest hit was "I Can See Clearly Now."

TAKE A HARD RIDE

(Fox, 1975) **D:** "Anthony Dawson"/Antonio Margheriti **S:** Eric Bercovici **P:** Harry Bernen, Leon Chooluck **M:** Jerry Goldsmith   Italy/US (*La Parola Di Un Fuorilegge … E Legge!*)

In a western (filmed in the Canary Islands), a cowboy (Jim Brown) is teamed with a cool card shark (Fred Williamson) and a silent Indian (Jim Kelly). The black action trio had been in *Three the Hard Way* the year before. A dying cattleman (Dana Andrews) hires Brown to transport some money to Mexico. With Lee Van Cleef as a bounty hunter, Catherine Spaak, Barry Sullivan, and Harry Carey Jr. A PG Twentieth Century release.

TAKE IT OUT IN TRADE— THE OUTTAKES

(SW, 1970) **D/S/A/E:** Ed Wood Jr. **P:** Richard Gonzalez, Edward Ashdown

The demand for Ed Wood product is so great that people actually pay to see this one-hour tape of silent scenes! The whole movie (with sound) will be released eventually. A private eye searches for a

wealthy man's daughter. He finds her working at "Madame Penny's Thrill Establishment." The soft-core sex feature has slapstick humor and psychedelic and horror touches. Lots of red items are everywhere, and naked women appear on a red staircase. Wood plays Alecia in a blonde wig. With Donna Stanley, Michael Donovan O'Donnell, and Monica Gayle. After this Wood directed and wrote *Necromania* (1971). He also wrote scripts for soft-core Stephen Apostoloff movies.

THE TAKING OF BEVERLY HILLS

(Nelson, 1991) **D:** Sidney J. Furie **S:** Rick Natkin, David Fuller **P:** Graham Henderson

Ken Wahl is a playboy ex-football star who teams with a corrupt cop (Matt Frewer) to battle an evil billionaire (Robert Davi). Harley Jane Kozak costars with Lee Ving James and Tony Ganois. Lots of things explode. It was filmed in a Mexico City stadium made to resemble Beverly Hills streets. From Columbia.

TAKIN' IT ALL OFF

(Vestron, 1987) **D/S:** Ed Hansen **P:** Robert T. Gervasoni

Candie Evans and Becky LeBeau star in a sex-tease comedy sequel to *Takin' It Off* with George (Buck) Flower as a preacher. It features flashbacks from the first movie including Kitten Natividad. *Party Favors* (Vestron, 1989) was another sequel with Evans, Flower, and Blondie Bee. Hansen later made *Takin' It Off Out West!* (1995).

TAKIN' IT OFF

(Vestron, 1984) **D/S:** Ed Hansen **P:** Robert T. Gervasoni

Kitten Natividad stars as "Betty Bigones" in a sex comedy that resembles a nudie from the 60s. If you want to see Kitten naked, this is a good tape. With Angelique Pettyjohn, Becky LeBeau, and Ashley St. John. Hansen also made Natividad's "exercise" tape, *Eroticise,* and *Takin' It Off* sequels.

TALE OF A VAMPIRE

(Vidmark, 1992) **D/S:** Shimako Sato **S:** Jane Corbett **P:** Simon Johnson   UK

Jim Brown and Fred Williamson in *Take a Hard Ride.*

Alex (Julian Sands), a modern-day junkie-like vampire in London, thinks a librarian (Suzanna Hamilton) is the reincarnation of his 18th-century lover. Her lover has been killed by a bomb. Everything has a Victorian look in a minimal-cast feature that's romantic, very bloody, and has too much talking. Alex has flashbacks and visions and the Van Helsing figure (Kenneth Cranham) seems to be Edgar Allan Poe. The director is a Japanese woman who lives in London.

A TALE OF TWO CITIES

(1980) **D:** Jim Goddard **S:** John Gay
P: Norman Rosemont   UK

Chris Sarandon stars in a double role in this version of Dickens's novel. Peter Cushing is second-billed as Dr. Manette. With Flora Robson (in her last role), Barry Morse, Billie Whitelaw, Kenneth More, and Alice Krige. It played theaters in Europe but debuted on CBS in America. Some earlier versions available on tape are the first sound version (MGM, 1935), including Basil Rathbone, and another British one (Vestron, 1958) with a cast including Christopher Lee and Donald Pleasence.

TALE OF TWO SISTERS

(Raedon, 1989) **D:** Adam Rifkin
P: Lawrence Bender, Randolph Turrow

Claudia Christian and Valerie Breiman are sisters who have a reunion after five years and remember their childhood and mutual resentments. It's an experimental feature with an improvised script and b/w flashbacks. By the director of *The Dark Backward*. With Sidney Lassick, Jeff Conaway, and Dee Coppola. Charlie Sheen narrates.

TALES FROM THE CRYPT

(HBO, 1988) **D:** Richard Donner, Robert Zemeckis, Walter Hill **P:** Joel Silver, David Giler, William Teiter

The three directors of this pilot trilogy were also the executive producers of the HBO cable series (1988–95). The stories were all based on "material published by William M. Gaines," from his various early-50s E.C. horror comics. Some of the stories had already been filmed in British Amicus studio 70s horror anthologies, but this time violence and gore and sometimes nudity was added. The grinning skull-face host the Crypt Keeper is a special effects creation with a high-pitched laugh. Danny Elfman wrote the theme music. Hill also wrote his "The Man Who Was Death," the best episode, starring Bill Sadler as an executioner, with effective Ry Cooder music. Fred Dekker wrote the killer-Santa story "And All Through the House" by Zemeckis. Mary Ellen Trainor stars. Terry Black wrote "Dig That Cat, He's Real Gone" directed by Zemeckis. With Joe Panoliano as a circus performer with nine lives, and Robert Wuhl. Each new season opened with a feature-length trilogy. More compilation volumes were released by HBO. In England *Tales from the Crypt* tape compilations were called *Vault of Horror*. Directors included William Friedkin, John Frankenheimer, Jodie Foster, Mary Lambert, Tobe Hooper, Tom Savini, Ted Gershuny, Tom

Hanks, Michael J. Fox, and Arnold Schwarzenegger. The 6th season (1994–95) ended with the 80th episode. The entire series was then syndicated in alternate (tamer) versions and the producers started making *Tales from the Crypt* movies. ABC also ran a *Tales from the Crypt-keeper* Saturday morning cartoon show.

TALES FROM THE CRYPT PRESENTS DEMON KNIGHT

(MCA, 1995) **D:** Ernest Dickerson
S: Ethan Reiff, Cyrus Voris, Mark Bishop **P:** Gilbert Adler

After a too long and involved comedy intro with the Crypt Keeper, Billy Zane stars as the supernatural Collector in a horror story, set on an unrealistic boarding house set, that features invading demons. It's pretty senseless, dumb, irritating, and has gratuitous silicone topless scenes. William Sadler is the war vet with the magical key filled with the blood of Christ that can keep the demons out. They look like the one on the airplane wing in *Twilight Zone—The Movie* and are on screen too long. With Jada Pinkett as a tough ex-con, Brenda Bakke as a hooker, CCH Pounder (who is slowed down when her arm is ripped off), Dick Miller (in one of his biggest roles since the 50s) as a drunk, and John Larroquette. The ending was reshot and the release was delayed. Dickerson also directed *Juice* and *Surviving the Game*. The FX are by Todd Masters. The heavy metal Atlantic soundtrack includes loud tunes by Ministry, Henry Rollins, Biohazard, and Machine Head. More *Tales* features followed.

TALES FROM THE CRYPT PART II = VAULT OF HORROR

TALES FROM THE DARKSIDE

(IVE series, 1984–88)

George Romero created this syndicated series after making the feature *Creepshow* (1982). The quickly made, low-budget half-hour episodes were shot on both coasts. 7 volumes, running 78 minutes, include 3 episodes each. Some of the directors were Bob Balaban, Frank DePalma, Armand Mastroianni, Jodie Foster, Tom Savini, Ted Gershuny, and Michael Gornick. There was also *Tales from the Darkside: The Movie,* and a companion show, *Monsters* was made by the same production team. Both shows had some good ones, but many tales were very silly and/or had weak scripts. The show's success inspired the production of the *Tales from the Crypt* show, which had the advantage of existing stories, lots more money, and bigger name directors and stars to work with, although many directors and actors worked on both programs. At least 6 volumes (each with 5 tales) were released by Worldvision, and more will likely follow.

The Cryptkeeper presents *Demon Knight.*

TALES FROM THE DARKSIDE: THE MOVIE

(Paramount, 1990) **D:** John Harrison
S: Michael McDowell, George Romero
P: Richard Rubenstein, Mitchell Galin

Although this feature looks a lot better than the series, most people thought twice about paying to see what they could get for free on TV. Harrison, the director, had done eight episodes of the TV show. Two of the scripts are by *Beetlejuice* writer McDowell. The tales are told by a kid to a witch (Deborah Harry) so she won't put him in an oven. Christian Slater and Steve Buscemi are in "Lot 249," about a mummy (based on a story by Sir Arthur Conan Doyle). David Johansen and William Hickey star in "Cat From Hell" (based on a Stephen King story). The final tale ("Lover's Vow") has the most impressive FX but the story was ripped off from part of the Japanese movie *Kwaidan*. With James Remar, Rae Dawn Chong, and Robert Klein.

TALES FROM THE GIMLI HOSPITAL

(Kino, 1987) **D/S/C/E:** Guy Maddin   Canada

Two rival doctors named Einar and Gunnar work in a hospital in 1920s Manitoba during a smallpox epidemic. The surreal, dark comic feature is told in flashbacks, stories ("based on ancient Icelandic myths") and nightmares. Part of the 72-minute b/w, 16mm feature are tinted. The director was 31 and the cost was "$22,000." It's been compared to *Eraserhead* for lack of anything else to compare it to. The tape includes Maddin's 1986 short *The Dead Father*. He also made *Archangel* (1990) and *Careful* (1993).

TALES FROM THE QUADEAD ZONE

(BC, 1987) **D/S/P/M/E:** Chester N. Turner

Tales from the Hood (1995) wasn't the first black cast horror anthology after all. The mother (Shirley L. Jones) of an invisible ghost kid reads three bizarre stories to him. It's another homemade obscurity from the director of *Black Devil Doll*. Unlike that all-black feature, this has an integrated cast and leaves out the sex and nudity.

TALES OF FRANKENSTEIN

(Sinister, 1958) **D:** Curt Siodmak **S:** Catherine and Henry Kuttner **P:** Michael Carreras

It was great to see this Hammer Studios pilot after hearing about it for so long. Too bad it never became a series. I guess the determined Baron (Anton Diffring) would have returned each week to steal more brains, break more laws, and make more creatures. Don Megowan is the Karloff-look monster, but Helen Wescott has a more important role. This impressive short opens with scenes lifted from Universal's *Inner Sanctum* series and *Dracula*.

TALES OF HOFFMAN

(Criterion, 1951) **D/S/P:** Michael Powell, Emeric Pressburger   UK

Unhappy German composer Ernest Amadeus Hoffman (Robert Rounseville) drinks heavily while telling three tales in which he is featured. One features a robot ballerina (Moira Shearer), and one features an evil woman (Ludmilla Tcherina) after his reflection. The last has a singer (Ann Ayars) under the care of a vampiric doctor. Pamela Brown and several other actors appear in all three tales, based on the 1881 opera. Lippert released the Technicolor 138-minute-long feature in America. The Voyager laser version features commentary by Martin Scorsese, who also arranged the re-release of Powell's *Peeping Tom* (1959).

TALES OF ORDINARY MADNESS

(Vestron, 1983) **D/S:** Marco Ferreri **S:** Sergei Amidei **P:** Jacqueline Ferreri   Italy (*Storie di Ordinaria Follia*)

Charles Bukowski said he hated it, but this was based on his stories years before *Barfly*. Ben Gazzara stars as "Charles Sirking," an alcoholic LA writer/poet searching for the essence of love through drinking, sex, and self-destruction. He rapes Susan Tyrrell, and a hooker (Ornella Muti) puts a big safety pin through her cheek. With Katya Berger. Tyrrell was also in *The Killer*, an underground feature with Bukowski.

TALES OF THE DEAN'S WIFE

(VCR, 1970) **D:** Benjamin Onivas **S/P:** L. K. Farbella   (*The Dean's Wife*)

Some swinger students invade the country house of the college dean and his nympho wife (Christine Murray). This results in lots of sex, nudity, LSD taking, whippings, and tragedy. Jim Gentry, who plays the dean, was later the star of *The Love Butcher!* Murray was in many nudies including *The Joys of Jezebel, Miss Nymphets Zap In*, and *Trader Hornee*. The Twin Peaks Production was shot by Henning Schellerup. The video box shows porn stars not in this movie.

TALES OF THE THIRD DIMENSION

(1985) **D/S:** Tom McIntyre, Worth Keeter, Todd Durham **D/P:** Earl Owensby

Three 3-D comedy horror tales are introduced by a mechanical "Igor," similar to the host of the later *Tales from the Crypt* series. The first tale features a vampire couple who have a werewolf kid. The others concern grave robbers and a killer grandmother. Made in North Carolina.

TALES OF TOMORROW

(Rhino, Fox Hills, 1951–53)

Various 30-minute episodes of the early-50s ABC anthology series are on tape from several video companies. "Frankenstein" stars Lon Chaney Jr. as the monster with John Newland as the doctor. James Dean and Rod Steiger are in "The Evil Within," Henry Jones stars in "The Spider's Web," and Boris Karloff and Paul Newman are in one episode.

TALES OF THE UNEXPECTED

(Prism, 1981) **D:** Gordon Hessler, Norman Lloyd, Paul Annett, Ray Danton   UK

This tape includes four episodes from the syndicated *Roald Dahl's Tales of the Unexpected* TV series. Don Johnson, Samantha Eggar, and Arthur Hill are in the first tale and Tom Smothers and Sharon Gless are in the second. Frank Converse and Sondra Locke are in the last, about a winged monster. Two are based on stories by John Collier.

TALES OF THE UNKNOWN

(AIP, 1990) **D:** John Kim, Greg Beeman, Todd Marks, Roger Nygard

Three USC shorts are followed by a strange out-of-place one from Minnesota. They were made from 1983–1989. The first (by Kim) is about a corporate cheat who meets death in an elevator and has to kill a female co-worker. The second (by Beeman) is the best. It's about a huge nightmarish garage in the desert where customers are trapped for eternity. The everyman hero tries to escape and is attacked by German mechanics. The third, nearly silent, short (by Marks) is about a guy whose every move is being watched on TV screens (Paul Bartel did it better with his *The Secret Cinema*). The last short (by Nygard) is called *Warped* and it is. A crazy old farm lady (who had been raped as a young girl) chases her female cousin with a pitch-fork and ties her up in bed. A sheriff, so big he can barely fit through the door, takes a long time to die, even after a big chunk of him has been hacked out.

TALKING WALLS

(Starmaker, 1983) **D/S:** Stephen Verona (*Motel Vacancy*)

Stephen Shellen stars as a student who secretly videotapes people in a Hollywood sex fantasy hotel. It's a comedy and features Sally Kirkland, Sybil Danning, Barry Primus, Judy Baldwin, and June Wilkinson (still doing topless scenes after all these years). By the director of *The Lords of Flatbush* and *Pipe Dreams*.

TALL, DARK AND DEADLY

(1995) **D:** Kenneth Fink **S:** Mary Anne Kasica, Michael Scheff **P:** Bob Roe

Kim Delaney stars in this USA TV movie as a woman who falls for a guy (Jack Scalia) she meets in a bar. He's a devious killer who eventually chains her to a sink. With Todd Allen, Gina Mastrogiacomo, and Ely Pouget. It was shot in Houston.

TALL, TAN AND TERRIFIC

(Hollywood Select, 1946) **D/P:** Bud Pollard **S:** John E. Gordon

Dancers, singers and comedians perform at the Harlem Golden Slipper club. Top-billed Mantan Moreland plays himself, a Hollywood star, throws out some hilarious lines, does a comic dance, and talk/sings a number. In the mimimal plot, Handsome Harry, the debt-ridden gambling club owner (Monte Hawley, once called the black Clark Gable) is arrested for murder. *Tall, Tan and Terrific* is a singing act. With The Two Fat Men, The Gorgeous Astor Debutantes, and an all-female orchestra. Only 40 minutes The same year Pollard also directed *Beware* starring Louis Jordan. Mantan was also in *The Dreamer* (1948). All of them were Astor Pictures.

THE TALL WOMEN

(1966) **D/P:** Sidney Pink **S:** Mino Roli, Jim Henaghen   Austria/Italy/Spain (*Las Siete Magníficas*)

Apaches attack a wagon train in the 1870s. The only survivors are seven women—led by Anne Baxter—who have to cross the desert on foot. With Gutav Rojo, Maria Perschy, Christa Linder, and European extras as savage American Indians. From Allied Artists.

TALONS OF THE EAGLE

(MCA, 1992) **D:** Michael Kennedy **S:** J. Stephen Maunder **P/A:** Jalal Merhi   Canada

Producer Merhi (with a ponytail) and muscular Billy Blanks (a former US karate champion) are martial arts expert cops in Toronto after a major drug king (James Hong). With Priscilla Barnes as an undercover agent posing as the villain's woman, Matthias Hues, Pan Quing Fu, and plenty of skin and fighting. From SGE.

TAMING SUTTON'S GAL

(1957) **D:** Lesley Selander **S:** Thames Williamson, Frederic Louis Fox **P:** William O'Sullivan

Gloria Talbott is "Seventeen and lonesome," and she falls for John Lupton. The teen drama co-stars Jack Kelly and May Wynn. It played on a Republic double bill with *Wayward Girl* by the same director. The teen appeal movies were advertised as being in "Naturama."

TAMMY AND THE T REX

(Image, 1994) **D/S:** Stewart Raffill **S:** Gary Brockette **P:** Diane Raffill

A mad scientist (Terry Kiser) puts the brain of a dying teen (John Franklin) into a mechanical dinosaur that goes out for revenge. Tammy, the girlfriend (Denise Richards), rides the dinosaur. With Ellen Dubin as the doctor's assistant, Paul Walker as the homosexual son of the sheriff, and George

"Buck" Flower. By the director of *Ice Pirates* and *The Philadelphia Experiment*. The PG-13 movie was aimed at young *Jurassic Park* fans.

TAMPOPO
(Republic, 1986) **D/S:** Juzo Itami   Japan

A truck driver (Tsutomu Yamazaki) and a friend (Koji Yakusho) help a widow named Tampopo (Nobuko Miyamoto), who runs a noodle shop. This odd cult movie is filed with strange things about food (and food and sex) and clever spoofs of gangster movies and spaghetti westerns.

TANGO AND CASH
(Warner, 1989) **D:** Andrei Konchalovsky
S: Randy Feldman **P:** Jon Peters, Peter Guber

Sylvester Stallone and Kurt Russell are rival cops forced to team up as LA narcotics officers in a cartoonish action movie. At least there's a good cast of villains (Jack Palance, Brion James, and James Hong). The stars run into Robert Z'Dar and Clint Howard in a scary prison. They also both show their butts, and Russell appears in drag. Teri Hatcher is Stallone's sister, and Michael J. Pollard makes a super van for them. With Roxanne Kernohan, Billy Blanks, and Shabba-Doo. After years of increasingly mediocre American features, Konchalovsky returned to Russia after this.

TANK GIRL
(MGM/UA, 1995) **D:** Rachel Talalay
S: Ted Sarafian **P:** Richard B. Lewis

Lori Petty stars as the futuristic (but late-70s punk look) Rachel Buck (a.k.a Tank Girl), heroine of a comic book that was created by Alan Martin and Jamie Hewlett. Naomi Watts is Jet Girl, Malcolm McDowell is the evil industrialist ruler of a desert planet, and Jeff Kober is a Ripper (kangaroo man). The cast includes Ice-T, Don Harvey, and Scott Coffey. By the time this came out it seemed like every other theatrical release was based on a comic book, a video game, some virtual reality nonsense, or an old TV show, and this one was lost in the shuffle. With lots of FX and a song and dance production number. The soundtrack by Graeme Revell includes tracks by female rock groups and singers: Belly, Bush, Bjork, Hole, L7, Veruca Salt, and Joan Jett, plus Ice-T and Devo. From MGM.

TANYA
(SW, 1976) **D/P:** Nate Rodgers **S:** Charles Townsend   (*Sex Queen of the SLA*)

Several 70s movies were based on the famous Patty Hearst kidnapping, but this one is probably the funniest (and has the most sex). "Charlotte Kane" (Marie Andrews) is kidnapped by the "Symphonic Liberation Army." During one of her many enthusiastic (soft-core) sex scenes (in an abandoned church) she thinks "I feel capable of maintaining my cool." A female SLA member tells one of the men, "You're no different than the insect swine of the ruling class." A black woman with large breasts and a big afro is featured in several of the lesbian scenes. A picture of Marx hangs on the wall and there's an unlikely long-haired TV news reporter in b/w segments. The print of the Box Office International release is scratchy.

TAPEHEADS
(Pacific Arts, 1987) **D/S:** Bill Fishman
S/P: Peter McCarthy

John Cusack and Tim Robbins, years before both of them graduated to bigger things, are security guard friends who lose their jobs. They enter the independent music video production business and acquire a tape that could damage the career of a politician (Clu Gulager). It's full of conflicts about selling out, music biz gags, and celeb cameos, and it became dated real fast. With Katy Boyer, Doug McClure, Connie Stevens, Mary Crosby, Lyle Alzado, Susan Tyrrell, Jessica Walter, Sy Richardson, and Ted Nugent. Junior Walker and Sam Moore do a great song together, and *Soul Train*'s Don Cornelius is good in a serious role. With music by Fishbone. Executive producer Michael Nesmith also backed *Repo Man* and has a cameo role.

TARGET … EARTH?
(VCI, 1980) **D/P:** Joost Van Rees

Victor Buono (in his last role) is "Homer the Archivist." He and some lady aliens (wearing see-through plastic suits) watch disaster footage and interviews about the end of the world. Homer introduces an old Universal newsreel about a 1908 Siberian meteorite explosion and shows interviews with Russian scientists. Various theories are explored, and Isaac Asimov and Carl Sagan are interviewed. Film research was done by Pierce Rafferty (*Atomic Cafe*). This ill-conceived documentary has been known to confuse and bewilder unprepared late-night TV viewers.

TARGET: EMBASSY
(Ace, 1972) **D:** Gordon Hessler **S:** William Fairchild **P:** Mel Ferrer   UK (*Embassy*)

Richard Roundtree is an American spy who has to go to the Mideast and bring back a defector (Max von Sydow). Chuck Connors is a KGB agent. Also with Ray Milland and Broderick Crawford. The *Shaft* star also made *Charley One Eye* in England.

THE TARTARS
(1960) **D:** Richard Thorpe **S:** Sabatino Ciuffini, Gaiao Fratini **P:** Richard Gualino   Italy (*I Tartari*)

Victor Mature is Oleg the Viking chieftain and Orson Welles is Tartar leader Burundai in a Technicolor epic shot in Yugoslavia. With Folco Lulli, Bela Cortez, and Liana Orfei. An MGM release.

TARZANA, THE WILD GIRL
(Sinister, 1969) **D:** "James Reed"/Guido Malatesta **S:** Philip Shaw **P:** Glen Hart
Italy (*Tarzana; Sesso Selvaggio*)

Jack Palance and James Hong in *Tango and Cash.*

Femi Benussi (from Yugoslavia) rides elephants and has a chimp buddy as the jungle woman (actually an heiress) in Nairobi. The female Tarzan movie is in the tradition of *Liane*. Glen, the blonde hero (Ken Clark), leads the expedition to find her. Benussi spends the whole movie topless, natives (including the black British sex movie star Beryl Cunningham) dance topless, and a blonde (Franca Polerello) on the safari takes it all off several times to bathe or shower. It was a followup to the same director's *Samoa, Queen of the Jungle,* which starred Edwich Fenich and had Benussi in a smaller role. The tape is letterboxed, but is from a very worn print.

TARZAN IN MANHATTAN
(1989) **D:** Michael Schultz **S:** Anna Sandor, William Gough **P:** Charles Hairstone

Using some ideas from *Tarzan's New York Adventure* (1942), this CBS pilot feature has Tarzan (Joe Lara) saving Cheetah from vivisectionists in the city. Kim Crosby is Jane, a cab driver. With Tony Curtis and Jan-Michael Vincent. A short-lived series followed (1991–92) and Lara went on to other minor musclebound action roles.

TARZAN OF THE APES
(Video Yesterday, 1918) **D:** Scott Sidney
S: Fred Miller, Lois Weber **P:** Bill Parsons

Elmo Lincoln (real name: Otto Elmo Linkenhelt) stars in the basic story of how Tarzan grew up in the jungle and met Jane (Enid Markey). Lincoln looks like a big-chested wrestler and wears an over-the-shoulder fur and a headband. It was the very first Tarzan movie and it was made in Louisiana by the National Film Corporation. In one scene the actor actually killed a lion that had attacked him. Actors play the bizarre-looking apes and monkeys. 61 minutes long and with music. It was a hit, so Lincoln returned in an immediate sequel, *The Romance of Tarzan,* and later starred in a serial, *The Adventures of Tarzan* (1928). In later years he appeared at circuses as "the original Tarzan."

TARZAN'S GREATEST CHALLENGE

(VSOM, 1969) **D/P:** Manuel Cano **S:** Santiago Mioncada, J. R. Hernandez   Spain/Italy
(*Tarzan en la Gruta del Oro; King of the Jungle*)

Steve Hawkes (from *Blood Freak!*) stars as "Zan" in this illegal Tarzan movie which was shot in Surinam and Miami by the maker of *Voodoo Black Exorcist.* The Elvis-look Zan (who swims a lot) saves the (white) daughter of a queen and at one point is trapped in an underwater cave by a man in a gorilla suit! A prospector with a talking parakeet searches for gold. Kitty Swan co-stars, and Fernando Sanchez plays three comic roles. This dubbed version played American theaters. It's pretty entertaining. Apparently there was another Zan movie with Hawkes too.

TARZAN THE TIGER

(Stokey, 1929) **D:** Henry McRae
S: Ian McClosky Heath

Silent and part-sound versions were released of this rare Universal serial. Only 10 of the 15 chapters are available on tape, though. Tarzan (Frank Merrill) has amnesia during most chapters. He wears a leopard skin and a fur headband, swings from vines, and was the first Tarzan you could hear yell. The lost city of Opar is ruled by the spellcasting Queen La. Natalie Kingston is Jane, and the serial includes ugly beastmen, slavers, jewel thieves, and men in gorilla suits. It's based on ERB's novel *Tarzan and the Jewels of Opar* and was a sequel to *Tarzan the Mighty* (1928). The next and most famous Tarzan was Johnny Weissmuller.

A TASTE FOR KILLING

(MCA, 1992) **D:** Lou Antonio **S:** Dan Bronson **P:** Michael S. Murphy

Jason Bateman and Justin Henry star as college grads working on an offshore Texas oil rig during the summer. A con man coworker (Michael Biehn) offers to help them kill their crew boss in a minimal-cast *Strangers on a Train*–derived plot. Helen Cates is also in the cable-TV movie.

A TASTE OF BLOOD

(SW, 1967) **D/P:** Herschell Gordon Lewis
S: Donald Stanford

Lewis's 2-hour, filmed-in-Miami, Eastmancolor, modern-day vampire movie was released the same year as Roman Polanski's nearly 2-hour *The Fearless Vampire Killers.* Polanski's is now considered a classic. This is considered an H. G. Lewis movie. A box marked "gravest urgency" arrives from London at the office of John Stone (Bill Rogers from *Shanty Tramp*). Stone has a corny deep voice, a

THE MOST ACTION-PACKED BATTLE... EVER FILMED!!!

HALF CORPSE...ALL KILLER HE LED A HANDFUL OF GUERRILLAS AGAINST AN ENTIRE ARMY ...ON A DOOMED MISSION OF REVENGE!

HARRY NOVAK presents

A TASTE OF HELL

THE EXPLOSIVE STORY THAT COULDN'T BE TOLD UNTIL...NOW!!
Color

PG PARENTAL GUIDANCE SUGGESTED

starring JOHN GARWOOD · WILLIAM SMITH · A BOXOFFICE INTERNATIONAL PICTURES RELEASE

maid, and a chatty wiseass secretary. He practices his putting in his luxurious living room and spends time on the course with his best friend Dr. Hank Tyson (William Kerwin), a nice guy who happens to be in love with Stone's blond wife. The box contains brandy that makes him an irritable insomniac. He takes a ship to a very foggy London, where the papers announce a murder.

Back home, he uses a big ugly ring to hypnotize his wife, then goes to Strip City, where he picks up Vivacious Vivian (!). After he bites her neck, he leaves the blood smeared all over his face. He sneaks off to Houston, where he stabs a woman in a bathing suit with a huge knife. When he becomes a vampire, a blue light shines on his face and wolves are heard howling. A bald Dr. Howard Helsing (with no accent) arrives from Hamburg University. Dr. Tyson says, "Vampirism? Voodoo? It's all mumbo jumbo! This is the space age!" but the two doctors follow Stone. "If you're trying to scare me to death, Helsing, you just did!" Last-minute intentional comedy relief is provided by a weird guy and his dog, before the expected stake-in-the-heart climax. Lewis himself appears as a British seaman. You've got to appreciate the dialogue (there's a lot of it) to enjoy this movie. The music (partly jazz) is very good. The video is letterboxed.

A TASTE OF FLESH

(SW, 1967) **D/S/P:** "Louis Silverman"/Doris Wishman

In this typically mind-boggling Wishman nudie movie, two assassins who claim to be plumbers arrive at the home of three female roommates and plan to kill the prime minister of "Netia." Characters look out of windows a lot, strip, takes showers, and enjoy lesbian lovemaking. Some are also whipped, beaten, raped, and even killed. One woman has a long bizarre drag dream sequence that's worth the price of admision. In b/w and with voiceover narration. Wishman returned with *Love Toy* (1968) and *Passion Fever* (1969).

A TASTE OF HELL

(Starmaker, 1973) **D/S:** Neil Yarema
P/A: John Garwood   Philippines

Garwood stars as a WWII American soldier in the Philippines. Japanese soldiers kill his men and leave him horribly disfigured. William Smith, a soldier behind enemy lines, joins the Filipino guerrillas and falls in love with a local girl. At the end Garwood decapitates the Japanese officer. With Vic Diaz. The PG-rated feature is from Box Office International.

TASTE OF SIN

(VC2, 1981) **D/S/P/A:** Ulli Lommel
S: John P. Marsh, Ron Norman   (*Olivia*)

Suzanna Love stars as Olivia, a woman who has witnessed the murder of her hooker mom as a child. Her mother's voice tells her to kill and she dresses as a hooker and goes to the London Bridge (now in Arizona). With Robert Walker, Jeff Winchester, and Lommel as a detective. Walker was also in Lommel's *Devonsville Terror.*

THE TATTOO CONNECTION

(Embassy, 1978) **D:** Lee Tso-Nam
S: Luk Pak Sang **P:** H. Wong   Hong Kong

Jim Kelly stars as an American kung fu insurance agent in Hong Kong. He fights a gangster played by big Bolo Yung. Both were cast because they had been in *Enter the Dragon* with Bruce Lee. With Chen Sing and Tan Tao Liang.

TAXI DANCERS

(AIP, 1993) **D/S/P:** Norman Thaddeus Vane

Brittany McCrena stars as the new blonde ("Don't call me a bimbo!") who goes to work at the LA Shark dance club. Diamond Jim (Sonny Landham), a "high roller from Texas," wants her, but so does a long-haired biker musician. Meanwhile, the Yellow Dragon gang extorts money and weary, doomed characters emote. Robert Miano is the Nam vet club owner who uses cameras to spy on everybody. With Mirage Micheaux as Mercedes, Josie Byrd as a crack addict, Michelle Hess, and (porn star) Raven as Svetlana. It was backed by German producers. Vane also made the similar *Club Life* (1985), which had name stars.

TAXI DRIVER

(RCA/Columbia, 1976) **D/A:** Martin Scorsese
S: Paul Schrader **P:** Michael and Julia Phillips
C: Michael Chapman **M:** Bernard Herrmann

It took years of living in Manhattan for this controversial, one-of-a-kind shocker to really make sense. Robert De Niro stars as Nam vet Travis Bickle. Joe Spinell hires him to drive a cab. Young hooker Iris (Jodie Foster) works for Sport (Harvey Keitel). With Peter Boyle, Cybill Shepherd, Albert Brooks, Diahnne Abbott, and Scorsese himself. De Niro, Foster, and the film were nominated for Oscars. The Columbia release was drastically cut for network TV showings, which is where many first saw it. The cinematography is excellent, and the still-shocking FX are by Dick Smith. The classic soundtrack on Arista includes some choice De Niro dialogue. The screenplay was published in 1990. A widescreen Voyager laser disc is available.

TAZA, SON OF COCHISE

(1954) **D:** Douglas Sirk **S:** George Zuckerman **P:** Ross Hunter

See Rock Hudson in 3-D playing Indian Chief Taza and Barbara Rush as Oona. With Gregg Palmer, Joe Sawyer, Rex Reason, Morris Ankrum, and Jeff Chandler as Cochise, repeating his role from *Broken Arrow* and *Battle at Apache Pass*. The Universal release was filmed in Arches National Park.

TC 2000

(MCA, 1992) **D/S:** T. J. Scott **P/A:** Jalal Merhi   Canada

Billy Blanks, with his square-top hair and shaved sides, stars and narrates as a futuristic tracker. His beautiful blond female partner Zoe (Bobbie Philips) is killed, so the "controller" turns her into an impressive cyber killer machine. Bolo Yeung helps Blanks (who says things like "Don't screw with me, you sack of shit!") train. The "Surfaceworld" bad guys have terrible makeup, but the fighting stars are good as they kick, punch, and shoot each other in a factory. Matthias Hues is the main villain, and Merhi plays Micky Picasso. Shot in Toronto. Most of the cast were also in *Talons of the Eagle*.

THE TEACHER

(Vid America, 1974) **D/S/P:** Hikmet Avedis

A student (Jay North, formerly *Dennis the Menace*!) learns about sex from a sexy teacher (Angel Tompkins) who lives next door. Angel is topless a lot while sunbathing. Meanwhile, a voyeur psycho Nam vet killer (Anthony James) watches and threatens. With Marlene Schmidt (the associate producer) and Sivi Aberg. Avedis made several R drive-in features for Crown International.

TEASERAMA

(SW, 1955) **D/P:** Irving Klaw

Redhaired stripper Tempest Storm stars in a color feature that imitates a live burlesque show. It features Klaw's cult discovery Betty Page dancing and introducing other dance sequences. Comedians

Peter Boyle, Joe Spinell, and Robert De Niro in *Taxi Driver*.

(including Joe E. Ross of *Car 54, Where Are You?*) and various strippers (who usually leave pasties on) do their acts and it's all "SPICY! TORRID!" Also with Trudy Wayne, Honey Baer, Cherry Knight, and female impersonator Vickie Lynn. Klaw also made the similar *Varietease* (1954).

TED AND VENUS

(Columbia, 1991) **D/S/A:** Bud Cort **S:** Paul Ciotti **P:** Randolph Turrow, William Talmadge

Nearly 20 years after *Harold and Maude*, grown-up Cort stars as Ted, an overaged hippie/poet on disability on Venice Beach in 1974. He thinks a beautiful community service worker (Kim Adams) has emerged from the sea. He falls for her and becomes an irritating pest, then a deranged threat. With Carol Kane as twins and Jim Brolin. Many name actors have bit parts including Woody Harrelson, Timothy Leary, Andrea Martin, Martin Mull, Tracy Reiner, Vincent Schiavelli, Gena Rowlands, Rhea Perlman, Cassandra Peterson, and Pat Ast.

TEEN AGE

(Sinister, 1943) **D:** "Dick L'Estrange"/ Gunther Von Strensch **S:** Elmer Clifton **P:** J. D. Kendis   (*Teenage Jungle*)

Although it bears a 1959 copyright, most of this less-than-one-hour-long WWII-era release (from Continental Pictures) was filmed in the 30s (!), and has nothing at all to do with teenagers! The D.A. (top-billed Herbert Heyes) gets us started with a series of ridiculous comic flashbacks of acrobatic sisters, jalopies, and jitterbugging. In flashback #3, some guys and gals steal cars—then all of a sudden we see a blonde in a (30s) gambling club, gangsters, and an Oriental fan dancer show. Actor Wheeler Oakman is in the 30s footage (bad guy) *and* the 40s footage (now a reformed ex-con telling a flashback to his wayward son). He says that he "pulled a boner." More flashbacks appear in flashbacks. *Teen Age* was billed as "A Dramatic Thunderbolt of Modern Youth." Try and imagine going to a theater in 1959 to see what you thought was a new jd movie and seeing this. INCREDIBLE! The older footage is from *Slaves in Bondage* and *Gambling in Souls*, earlier Kendis roadshow hits.

TEENAGE BONNIE AND KLEPTO CLYDE

(Vidmark, 1993) **D/S:** John Shepphird **S:** Steve Janowski **P:** Menahem Golan

Maureen Flannigan (from the *Out of This World* TV series) stars as the police chief's very cute blond daughter. She and her boyfriend (Scott Richard Wolf) are small-town Catholic high school students who go on a (sometimes comic) crime spree. They even die in slow motion at the end in a movie that copies the Beatty movie a lot. With Bentley Mitchum, Don Novello as a cop, and Tom Bower. The 21st Century release was shot in Utah.

TEENAGE CATGIRLS IN HEAT

(1995) **D/S:** Scott Perry **S:** Grace Smith

A Sphinx statue causes cats to kill themselves, and they return as meowing and purring women who have sex with men, then kill them. The catgirls also run around topless a lot. The silly low-budget movie from Austin was picked up by Troma. With Esmereldas Huffhines, Carrie Vanston, and Helen Griffiths.

TEENAGE CONFIDENTIAL

(Rhino)

This tape of shorts and scenes going back to the 40s was compiled by Johnny Legend. Trailers for *Teenage Crime Wave, Curfew Breakers,* Ed Wood's *The Violent Years,* and others are shown, along with rare scenes from government shorts (with psychiatrists or the church providing direction) and rare features. In "Satan Was a Teenager," the parents blame themselves for teen trouble, Tab Hunter does a mental illness spot, and some of the best scenes are included from *Rock Baby Rock It, Carnival Rock, Teenage Devil Dolls* and others (all Rhino tapes, of course). Actually it makes a good commercial for the rest of Rhino's Teenage Theatre series, hosted by Mamie Van Doren. If you've seen the 7 features in the series (you should!) you will have seen about half of this hour-long tape already. The box shows Jack Elam from the movie *Girl in Lovers Lane* (1960).

TEENAGE CRUISERS

(PVX, 1977) **D:** Tom Denucci **D/S/P/A/M/E:** Martin Margulies   (*Young, Hot 'n' Nasty Teenage Cruisers*)

This *American Graffiti*–inspired, plotless sex/rock comedy was mostly shot in 1975 (judging from the *Dog Day Afternoon* marquee). Margulies (a.k.a. Johnny Legend) is radio D.J. Mambo Remus who smokes pot and does fast raps over the air, intercut with unrelated segments. The "nuthouse nympho" escapes and has (hardcore) sex scenes with a bound and gagged guy and some animated dildos. "Guest star" John Holmes (the late Ohio-born porn legend) does it with two girls in and out of a pool. Enthusiastic star Serena drives around with her girlfriend, masturbates, and ends up in a van with a bored hippie who comes so much he floods the street. Some parts are actually funny. The sex scenes are a mixture of porn loops and more comical softcore segments. The music's great, but you have to wonder who the audience was for this off-the-wall concoction. The soundtrack album (originally on Rollin' Rock) is also on Rhino. It features the Blasters, Billy Zoom of X, Ray Campi, Charlie Feathers, and rockabilly singer/wrestling manager Legend.

TEENAGE DEVIL DOLLS

(Rhino, 1952) **D:** Bramlett L. Price, Barbara Marks, Robert A. Sherry …   (*One Way Ticket to Hell*)

Cassandra joins a gang and becomes a drug addict in a 58-minute anti-drug pseudo-documentary that was made by UCLA students. It's narrated. Mamie Van Doren is the hostess of the tape (one of a series of 8).

TEENAGE EXORCIST

(AIP, 1990) **D/P:** Grant Austin Waldman
S/A: Brinke Stevens

Brinke Stevens buys a house (the usual Fred Olen Ray movie house) and becomes possessed. For a while she's a "queen of Hell" in a dog collar and a leather bikini and boots. A comic pizza-delivery boy (Eddie Deezen) shows up, and corny jokes and dumb situations abound. In one odd scene, rats are played by minks. Elena Sahagun takes a shower, Jay Richardson walks around in a dress, Robert Quarry is a priest, and zombies and a horned demon show up. Michael Berryman was around long enough to have his picture taken for the video box. Ray was a producer and wrote the original story.

TEENAGE GANG DEBS

(SW, 1966) **D:** Sande S. Johnsen
S: Hy Cahl **P:** Jerry Denby

"Cool it." "Don't bug me, man." "It's a drag." "I'm hip." These are just a few of phrases used in this great b/w gang movie. Terry (Diane Conti) from Manhattan's Golden Falcons gang takes over Johnny and his Brooklyn Rebels. One long hand-held camera sequence with no dialogue shows the Aliens (bikers from Queens with WWII helmets) in a violent deadly rumble. With a cat fight, a switchblade fight, an offscreen gang bang ("line up"), dancing, and lots of mindless violence and senseless deaths. The female Rebels get revenge at the end. The music is mostly jazz or light instrumental rock and Lee Dowell sings "Black Belt," a karate dance number! New York movies from the mid-60s are almost always much more realistic and interesting than anything from Hollywood. Some of you might think the 50s elements are out of place in a mid-60s movie, but a lot of people still looked and talked like that then. Many still do. Johnsen also made *The Beautiful, the Bloody and the Bare*. The tape includes a wraparound with Johnny Legend and trailers. Dig it?

TEENAGE MOTHER

(Sinister, 1966) **D/S/P:** Jerry Gross

Arlene Farber stars as Arlene, a school girl with serious piled-up hair plus leather skirts and boots designed by Betsey Johnson (!). Miss Erika Peterson (Julie Ange) from Sweden is the new high school health teacher. Erika is nearly raped by pot-selling students ("$10 a load"), a dealer tries to blackmail her, and she's blamed when Arlene says she's pregnant. Everything is cleared up at an emergency town meeting where a birth-of-a-baby short is screened. Comedian Fred Willard makes his film debut as a coach, Arlene's boyfriend races cars and there's some great go-go dancing with music by the Young Set. The actual East Rockaway High School on Long Island was used. Ange and Farber were also both in Gross's *Girl on a Chain Gang*, advertised here on a drive-in marquee. Both classic exploitation movies played for years.

TEENAGE MUTANT NINJA TURTLES

(IVE, 1990) **D:** Steve Barron **S:** Todd W. Langen,
Bobby Herbeck **P:** Kim Dawson, Simon Fields,
David Chan, R. Chow

Every kid in America must have lined up to see this PG-rated adaptation of Kevin Eastman and Peter Laird's comic books (created in 1984). It was a huge hit for New Line and broke the record (previously held by Avco Embassy's *The Graduate*, then AIP's *The Amityville Horror*) as the most successful indy feature of all time. A TV cartoon show, Turtle toys, cereal, and video games all came first. A live stage presentation and feature sequels followed, and kids picked up turtle slang. There was a lawsuit over the phrase "Cowabunga!" (first used on the *Howdy Doody* TV show). The same fight choreographer (Pat Johnson) as the Karate Kid movies was used, and the turtles are from the Jim Henson workshop. Elias Koteas and Judith Hoag star, and Corey Feldman provided one of the voices (as he did for the sequels). The movie is filed with fast-food plugs directed at all the young consumers. Hong Kong's Golden Harvest backed the New Line release (and the sequels).

TEENAGE MUTANT NINJA TURTLES II: SECRET OF THE OOZE

(RCA, 1991) **D:** Michael Pressman
S: Todd W. Langen **P:** Thomas K. Gray

The more expensive immediate sequel suffered from turtle overkill and was a flop in comparison with the original. Paige Turco returns as a NYC newscaster, Ernie Reyes Jr. is a martial arts expert pizza delivery boy, and David Warner plays a professor. New monsters are introduced, and Vanilla Ice is featured in a rap/dance sequence. The movie is dedicated to Jim Henson, whose Creature Shop provided the "animatronics."

TEENAGE MUTANT NINJA TURTLES III

(Columbia, 1993) **D/S:** Stuart Gillard
P: Thomas K. Gray, Kim Sawson, David Chan

The four turtles time-travel to 17th-century Japan to rescue a modern-day NYC reporter (Paige Turco) while two warlords battle each other and British villains who want to sell arms interfere. With Elias Koteas, Vivian Wu as a resistance fighter, and Sab Shimono. It was shot in Oregon. Soon the lucrative turtles craze died out and kids turned to the Mighty Morphin Power Rangers on TV and then in the movies.

TEENAGER

(New World, 1974) **D:** Gerald Seth Sindell
S: Reginald Thumb, Earl Jay **P:** Allan Zinn
Hodshire   (*The Real Thing*)

Somebody must have seen Dennis Hopper's *The Last Movie* and decided to make a simpler variation on the same theme. Billy, an egotistical low-budget director (he looks a bit like Roger Corman), convinces the young stars of his new biker movie to invade a small town for real while he films the realistic action. The locals get real riled up and death results ("This isn't a movie anymore!"). A scene in a church copies *The Wild Angels*. Meanwhile, a local girl (the teenager of the misleading title) and the lead actor fall in love. With Sue Bernard from *Faster, Pussycat! Kill! Kill!*, and John Holmes as a cop! It was presented

by Jack Harris, who always picked up interesting features (*The Blob, Equinox . . .*). Sindell later made *H.O.T.S.* (1979).

TEENAGE REBEL

(1956) **D:** Edmund Goulding **S/P:** Charles
Brackett **S:** Walter Reisch

Betty Lou Keim is a daughter in trouble. Ginger Rogers is her divorced mom. The 20th Century Cinemascope release was based on a play called "A Roomful of Roses." With Michael Rennie as the new stepfather, Mildred Natwick, Louise Beavers, Warren Berlinger, and Diane Jergens. Goulding, who had directed classics like *Grand Hotel* (1932) and *Nightmare Alley* (1947), ended his career with *Mardi Gras* (1958), a Pat Boone movie.

TEENAGE REBELLION

(SW, 1967) **D/S/P:** Norman J. Herman   (*Mondo Mod*)

I had the Sidewalk label soundtrack (produced by Mike Curb) for this b/w AIP/TransAmerica documentary for years (it set me back 50¢) and it was great to see the movie finally. It deals with teenagers around the world, but the tone of Burt Topper's narration seems aimed at parents and has a major moral message at the end to reassure them. There's some great mid-60s footage here of the Sunset Strip, Carnaby St., and of protests and riots in Paris, Rome, and Vienna. Many scenes are from Sweden and Japan. With bikers (and Davie Allan music), a demolition derby, mud wrestling, tattooing, some excellent surfing scenes, and lots of dancing. The segments on LSD, unwed mothers (with their faces blocked out), and homosexuals in Rome are pretty memorable. Parts are obviously staged and some real scenes are made dubious by faked voiceovers.

TEENAGE U.F.O. ROCK 'N' ROLL MONSTER SHOW

(SW, 1994)

This two-hour comp features around 40 trailers for teen and rock movies plus two shorts. Some of my faves are *The T.A.M.I. Show* (featuring rare Beach Boys footage cut from the actual feature), *Disc O Tek Holiday* (great Freddy Cannon scene), *The Proper Time* (Tom McLaughlin), *Key Witness* (Dennis Hopper), *The Thrill Killers* and *Psychout*. *Hallucination Generation* and *Sting of Death* are just two of the many trailers from Florida movies. *Teenage Crusade* is a promo film for a series of religious family films. *Twist Craze* (produced by Bill Rebane) is a great/hilarious 1961 short from Chicago that originally played with the Louis Prima movie *Twist All Night*. Enthusiastic dancers twist to a surf instrumental group in a high-class club, then everybody joins in! Johnny Legend is the host.

TEENAGE SCHLOCK CLASSICS

(Sinister)

This entertaining grab bag of more than two dozen trailers covers all types of teen movies . . . from juvenile delinquents and controversial themes (*Too Soon to Love* is about abortion) to *Gidget* and all six AIP beach party movies. Some highlights include Vic Morrow in *Blackboard Jungle*, Jack Nicholson in *Cry Baby Killer*, Corman's *Sorority Girl*, and great trailers for *The Beatniks* and *Teenage Tramp*.

Sally Kellerman gets stabbed in *Reform School Girl*, Mamie Van Doren sings in *Born Reckless,* and you won't believe the singers in *Senior Prom*! Also with celebs like Louis Prima and Keely Smith, Zohra Lampert, Molly Bee, Dick Clark, James Brown, Edd "Kookie" Byrnes and Robert Vaughn.

TEENAGE STRANGLER

(SW, 1964) **D:** "Bill Posner"/ Ben Parker **S/P:** Clark Davis

I love obscure early-60s regional movies like this! A mystery "lipstick" killer is strangling schoolgirls with stockings in the Huntington, West Virginia, area (where this marvel was filmed). Some of the characters are straight out of *Rebel Without a Cause*, but with Southern accents. Jimmy—a member of the Fastbacks, a pretty harmless "gang" (they wear black jackets with bulldogs on the backs)—is a suspect. He stands up for a guy everybody calls Runt, and has a girlfriend named Betty Jean. His family had to relocate because of his police record. Jimmy even has a drag race with Curley, the gang's tough guy. Kids do the twist and drink pop at Marty's where Betty Gay (not Betty Jean) announces, "Fellow citizens and lovers of good music—for those of you that pledge allegiance to Peter, Paul and Mary . . . the Beatles . . . the Teen Queens . . . Paul Anka, and the Chad Mitchell Trio . . ." and a guy (from the Huntington Astronauts) sings "Yipes Stripes." Despite Betty Gay's horrifying list, the instrumental rock on the soundtrack (by Danny Dean and the Daredevils) is fine. Meanwhile more girls are strangled. One is killed in a shower while we see a shadow of somebody with a ducktail haircut. This is a classic cheat scene, since we later discover that Mr. Wilson, the demented school janitor ("I hate every one of you!!") is the killer. In 1967, the color *Teenage Strangler* played around the country with *A Taste of Blood*. Try and imagine being at the drive-in for that double bill! The b/w release in 1990 and the write-up in *Psychotronic* resulted in local screenings, newspaper articles, and cast reunions!

TEENAGE WOLFPACK

(Sinister, 1956) **D/S:** Georg Tressler **S:** Will Tremper **P:** Wenzel Ludecke   W. Germany (*Halbstarken*)

"Nothing like him has hit the screen since James Dean!" He is "Henry Bookholt" (Horst Buchholz) who stars as Freddie. He works at an Esso station, wears black leather pants, and has a 15-year-old girlfriend named Sissy (Karin Baal). He also buys a gun, steals a car, and leads his small gang on a botched mail truck robbery with tragic results. Based on a "true story." The dubbing is pretty good and the theme is jazz. D.C.A. released it here on a bill with the British *Teenage Bad Girl*. Also look for Buchholz in *Tiger Bay* (1959) and Billy Wilder's *One, Two, Three* (1961).

TEEN ALIEN

(Prism, 1988) **D/S/P:** Peter Semelka **S:** James Crofts

A killer alien disguised as a student kills at a Halloween spook show at an abandoned mill. It's rated PG.

TEEN VAMP

(Starmaker, 1988) **D/S:** Samuel Bradford **P:** Jim McCullough

A nerd (Beau Bishop) is bitten by a hooker at a roadhouse. He becomes a cool 50s jd-look vampire. With Clu Gulager as a minister, Karen Carlson, and Mike Lane. The New World horror comedy was shot in Shreveport, LA. A good rule is to avoid 80s movies with "Teen" in the title.

TEEN WITCH

(Media, 1989) **D:** Dorian Walker **S:** Vernon Zimmerman **P:** Alana Lambros

Robin Lively stars as an uncool schoolgirl. Fortuneteller Zelda Rubinstein tells her she'll become a witch before she turns 16, and she does. It's a comedy fantasy with music and dancing. With Joshua Miller, Dick Sargent (from *Bewitched*), and Shelley Berman. Notice all the product placements (for Coke, Ford . . .). TWE released the PG-13 feature.

TEEN WOLF

(Paramount, 1985) **D:** Rod Daniel **S:** Joseph Loeb III, Matthew Weissman **P:** Mark Levinson, Scott Rosenberg

The only reason this was a hit was because star Michael J. Fox was starring on the popular *Family Ties* show and was in *Back to the Future* the same year. The PG teen horror comedy is like a terrible version of one of those Disney movies like *Son of Flubber*, and like that movie, *Teen Wolf* is about school sports. With Susan Ursitti. A various artists soundtrack is on Southern Cross. *Teen Wolf* became an animated cartoon series, and there was a sequel.

TEEN WOLF TOO

(Paramount, 1987) **D:** Christopher Leitch **S:** R. Thomas Kring **P:** Kent Bateman

Jason Bateman, a college freshman who becomes a comic werewolf, is a cousin of the original. With Kim Darby as a professor, John Astin as the college dean, Paul Sand as a coach, Kathleen Freeman, and Michael Worth. The PG feature has bad makeup. This wolf lip-synchs "Twist and Shout" and wins a school boxing match. A various artists soundtrack, put together by Mike Curb, is on CBS. A third Teen Wolf movie was announced.

TEKWAR: THE ORIGINAL MOVIE

(MCA, 1994) **D/A:** William Shatner **S:** Alfonse Ruggiero Jr., Westbrook Claridge **P:** Jamie Paul Rock, Stephan Roloff (*William Shatner's Tekwar*)

Greg Evigan (*B.J. and the Bear*) stars as a futuristic cop taken out of his cryogenic freeze in 2044 to stop the flow of a dangerous virtual-reality drug (called Tek). It's based on executive producer Shatner's novels, and Shatner plays the boss of the Cosmos detective agency. With Eugene Clark, Torri Higginson, Barry Morse, and Sheena Easton. This rather dull syndicated TV feature led to a USA cable series in 1995. The hour shows are much better and have some fun FX. All were shot in Toronto.

TELEFON

(MGM/UA, 1977) **D:** Don Siegel **S:** Peter Hyams, Sterling Silliphant **P:** James B. Harris **M:** Lalo Schifrin

Charles Bronson fans didn't know what to think about this one, but it's good. He plays a Russian KGB agent who is also the hero. He's sent to try to stop human time bombs that were programmed in the 50s to destroy America. It was based on Walter Wager's novel. With Lee Remick, Donald Pleasence as the Stalinist villain, Patrick Magee, Tyne Daly, Sheree North, John Mitchum, and newscaster John Hambrick. Director Hyams was replaced by Siegel. The score includes a repeated loud player-piano tune. It was partially filmed in Finland. Bronson was in the ridiculous De Laurentiis production *The White Buffalo* the same year.

THE TELL-TALE HEART

(SW, 1963) **D:** Ernest Morris **S:** Brian Clemens, Elden Howard **P:** Edward J. and Harry Lee Danzinger   UK

A good gimmick intro warns the audience to close your eyes when you hear heartbeats. Lawrence Payne stars as Edgar, a shy man ("a decent sort") who goes home to look at "French postcards" after being intimidated by bar girls. He watches a new neighbor (Adrienne Cori) across the street (the Rue Morgue) undress, then meets and awkwardly courts her. When his friend becomes her lover, Edgar flips. Although it looks more like a 40s film, *Heart* features some pretty modern blood, nightmares, and flashbacks and very effective freakout scenes when the killer (and we) hear a loud beating heart (which he had cut out and buried). The print is jumpy and scratchy, though. It was re-released in America as *Hidden Room of 1,000 Horrors.*

THE TEMP

(Paramount, 1993) **D:** Tom Holland **S:** Kevin Falls **P:** Tom Engleman

Timothy Hutton stars as a troubled and divorced marketing manager for a successful baking goods company in Portland run by Mrs. Appleby (Faye Dunaway). Lara Flynn Boyle is the temporary secretary who seduces him and seems to be behind a series of murders. Office workers die by bee sting, hanging, cookies with ground glass, and one guy's hand goes into a paper shredder (Steve Johnson FX are used). The Paramount release is by the director of *Child's Play*. Several endings were filmed but few viewers liked the double surprise one that was used. With Dwight Schultz and Oliver Platt.

TENAFLY

(1973) **D:** Richard Colla **S/P:** Richard Levinson, William Link

Shaft became a short-lived CBS series in 1973, so NBC countered with this pilot film developed by the people behind *Columbo*. It starred James McEachin as Tenafly, a married suburban LA detective. With Ed Nelson (who is murdered), Mel Ferrer as a lawyer, John Ericson, Anne Seymour, and series regulars David Huddleston and Lillian Lehman. It lasted one season as a series.

TEN DAYS' WONDER

(Connoisseur, 1972) **D:** Claude Chabrol **S:** Paul Gegauff, Paul Gardner, Eugene Archer **P:** Andre Genovese   France (La Decade Prodigieuse)

Charles Van Horn (Anthony Perkins) is the adopted son of rich and powerful Orson Welles and his young red-haired wife (Marlene Jobert). He falls for his stepmother, wakes with blood on his hands, and develops amnesia. The stepfather wants everything to be as it was in 1925. The confusing mystery, based on an Ellery Queen novel, features a fever dream with an octopus, nightmares, and flashbacks. Also with Michel Piccoli. Welles had directed Perkins in The Trial.

TENDER DRACULA

(Blood Times, 1974) **D/S:** Pierre Grunstein **S:** Justin Lenoir **P:** Jerome Kanapa   France (La Grande Trouile)

Peter Cushing is excellent in this atmospheric romantic horror/sex comedy musical. He plays MacGregor, an eccentric horror star who lives at a great-looking remote old castle on an island with his loving witchlike wife Heloise (Valli). The usually restrained Cushing (sometimes made up as a scary vampire) yells and laughs a lot and is very funny. His producer sends two scriptwriters and two sexy starlets to try to bring him out of retirement. One writer is Bernard Menez (also in the Christopher Lee French vampire comedy Dracula and Son). Boris, the Russian one, is also a makeup artist. Statues cry, people are killed or cut in half, the servant accidentally cuts off his own body parts with an ax, and the whole movie is filled with is-it-real-or-is-it-a-dream? sequences. One of the starlets is Miou-Miou (a well-known star in France) in a curly wig. She and her friend both run around naked a lot and sing silly songs ("I'm scared, I swear . . ."). Cushing even gets to waltz, spank Miou-Miou (in an electric chair), and play his own gravedigger father in a flashback. This could never have been made anywhere but France.

TENDER LOVING CARE

(1973) **D/S/P:** Don Edmunds **P:** Chako Van Leeuween

Donna Desmond stars in a New World nurse movie. She investigates the death of a boxer (John Daniels) and her roommate is blackmailed by a male nurse for stealing drugs for an addicted doctor.

TENDERNESS OF WOLVES

(VSOM, 1973) **D:** Ulli Lommel **S/A:** Kurt Raab **P/A:** Rainer Werner Fassbinder   W. Germany (Zaerlichkeit Der Wolfe)

A bald vampire-like homosexual killer preys on young boys in post-WWI Hanover. This is based on the crimes of the real-life Fritz Haarman (as was Lang's M). The feature is bloody (for the time) and includes nudity and nods to Nosferatu. Jeff Roden co-stars as the police inspector with Raab, Ingrid Caven, and others from the Fassbinder acting community. Lommel moved to America in the late 70s.

TENEMENT

(IVE, 1985) **D/C:** Roberta Findlay **S:** Joel Bender, Rick Marx **P:** Walter E. Sear   (Game of Survival)

A gang of crack smokers hang out in the basement of an isolated South Bronx apartment building. When a gang member is arrested, the others seek revenge and battle the tenants. Already sad and tragic characters are raped, murdered, and impaled, and one black man reluctantly becomes a hero. Frequent titles tell us what time it is and what floor the action is occurring on. It's well made but pretty grim. With Karen Russell and a rap theme song. Findlay made it after Shauna, Every Man's Fantasy (1985).

TEN LITTLE INDIANS

(Warner, 1989) **D:** Alan Birkinshaw **S:** Jackson Hunsicker, Gerry O'Hara **P:** Harry Alan Towers   South Africa (Death on Safari)

This third version of Agatha Christie's murder mystery made by Towers is set in Africa in the 30s. Characters staying in tents are killed off, and there's a ridiculous triple surprise ending. With Herbert Lom (also in the 1975 version), Donald Pleasence, Paul L. Smith, Sarah Maur (from Edge of Sanity), Brenda Vaccaro, Frank Stallone, and Warren Berlinger (looking a lot like Orson Welles in the 1975 version). Gregory Dark was the assistant director. From Cannon. Part of the same cast was in Towers's stupid Masque of the Red Death remake too. His first Ten Little Indians was released in 1965.

THE TENNIS COURT

(1984) **D:** Cyril Frankel **S:** Andrew Sinclair   UK

A woman is possessed on the grounds of a house she's inherited. The haunted-tennis-court movie features death by tennis net and WWII-era flashbacks. Peter Graves stars with Hannah Gordon and Isla Blair. A Hammer TV presentation.

10 RILLINGTON PLACE

(RCA, 1970) **D:** Richard Fleischer **S:** Clive Exton **P:** Martin Ransohoff, Leslie Linder   UK

Richard Attenborough stars as John Reginald Christie, the real-life tea-drinking English landlord and killer who buried his eight female victims in his yard. He drugged, raped, and murdered women in the late 1940s. John Hurt plays Timothy Evans, the dim-witted boarder who was wrongly convicted and hanged for one of Christie's murders, an event that led to the banishment of capital punishment in England. With Judy Geeson, Bernard Lee, and Andre Morell. Fleischer also made Compulsion and The Boston Strangler.

TEN SECONDS TO MURDER

(CNH, 1970) **D/S:** Wayne Avery **S:** P.A. Hedberg **P:** Harry Novak   (Booby Trap)

I can't think of another movie about a hysterical Nam vet in an RV, planning to blow up a rock music festival. He never makes it to the festival, but he does blow up some people with his stolen arsenal and talks a lot ("Too many people. The world is full of freaks!"). Scarfo (Buck Kartalian) runs a Hollywood strip club where the madman's ex-wife works. Scarfo is thrown off a rooftop, but walks away O.K. In a scene typical for an "adult" movie of the period, there's a gay character who gets beat up. The strangest thing about this sad little movie from Box Office International is that some of the music sounds a lot like the German group Can!

10 TO MIDNIGHT

(MGM/UA, 1983) **D:** J. Lee Thompson **S:** William Roberts **P:** Pancho Kohner, Lance Hool

Bronson stars as a tough LA cop ("I hate quiche") after a serial killer/rapist (Eugene Davis) who runs around naked. Bronson is thrown off the force, but stays on the case. Andrew Stevens is his by-the-book partner and Lisa Eilbacher is his daughter in peril. With Geoffrey Lewis, Wilfred Brimley, Kelly Preston, and Jeana Tomasino and Ola Ray (both from Playboy).

TEN VIOLENT WOMEN

(World, 1978) **D/S/P/A/E:** Ted V. Mikels **S:** James Gordon White

Some women work in a gold mine. It explodes, so they go to Vegas for a jewel heist and end up in jail. They take showers in their underwear and are victimized by the sadistic warden during the women's prison part, then escape. Leo the fence (director Mikels) is killed by a high heel through his heart, and the women use kung fu. Sherri Vernon and Dixie Lauren star with Georgia Morgan as the lesbian Miss Terry. It was released in 1982 and played 42nd St. Mikels' next was Warcat (1987).

TEOREMA

(Connoisseur, 1968) **D/S:** Pier Paolo Pasolini **P:** Franco Rossellini, Manolo Bolognini **M:** Ennio Morricone   Italy

Terence Stamp stars as a mysterious stranger who arrives in Milan at the household of a very rich family. After he leaves, they all change (including the servants). The son becomes an artist but pisses on his paintings. The maid levitates and is considered a saint. The father gives his factory to the workers and wanders off naked. The religious allegory was banned in Italy when first released but has been copied by other filmmakers since. Silvana Mangano is the mother and Massimo Girotti is the father. Letterboxed with English subtitles.

TERESA'S TATTOO

(1994) **D:** Julie Cypher **S:** Georgie Huntington **P:** Lisa M. Hansen

A dumb girl (Adrienne Shelly) with a dragon tattoo is taken hostage by C. Thomas Howell because she has space secrets in her hologram earrings. She dies, so a college math whiz lookalike (also Shelly) is kidnapped, drugged, and tattooed for an extortion scheme. The comedy with chase scenes includes music by Melissa Etheridge. With Lou Diamond Phillips as an FBI agent, Jonathan Silverman, Nancy McKeon, Casey Siemaszko, and bits by Majel Barrett, Nanette Fabray, Tippi Hedren, k. d. lang, Mary Kay Place, Joe Pantoliano, Mare Winningham, and Kiefer Sutherland.

TERMINAL CHOICE

(Vestron, 1982) **D:** Sheldon Larry **S:** Neal Bell
P: Gary Magder   Canada (*Critical List; Deathbed*)

Patients die at a computer-run clinic. Joe Spano is the hero and David McCallum and Robert Joy are doctors. With Nicholas Campbell, Diane Venora, Teri Austin, and Ellen Barkin as a coroner who throws up. It was shot in Montreal and includes some real autopsy footage.

TERMINAL CITY RICOCHET

(1990) **D:** Zale Dalen **S/P:** John Conti
S: Bill Mullen, Phil Savath   Canada

Peter Breck runs for mayor in a futuristic city. Space junk is all around, and the police shoot looters. With Jello Biafra and the group D.O.A. Made in Vancouver.

TERMINAL ENTRY

(Celebrity, 1987) **D:** John Kincade **S:** David Mickey Evans, Mark Sobel **P:** Sharon Reis Cobe

Some computer hacker kids battle terrorists (led by Kabir Bedi) trying to destroy the USA and kill the president. With Eddie Albert as a military captain, Yaphet Kotto, and Paul Smith. Jill Terashita, Barbara Edwards (from *Playboy*), and Tracy Brooks Swope show up for some R-rated nudity in the *War Games*–inspired movie.

TERMINAL EXPOSURE

(Vestron, 1988) **D/S/P:** Nico Mastorakis
S: Kirk Ellis   (*Double Exposure*)

Some Venice Beach guys busy taking pics of women's asses accidentally photograph a murder. John Vernon and Joe Phelan costar. The R-rated mystery comedy has many beauties, mostly from the pages of *Playboy* (Luann Lee, Hope Marie Carlton, Ava Fabian, and Tara Buckman).

TERMINAL FORCE

(Starmaker, 1987) **D/P:** Fred Olen Ray
S/A: Ernest D. Farino **P:** Grant Austin

Eurostar Richard Harrison is a suspended cop who has to protect a mob squealer, and a mobster's daughter is kidnapped by Jay Richardson. With Troy Donahue, Dawn Wildsmith, Fox Harris, Michelle Bauer, and Robin Shurtz. New World released it.

TERMINAL USA

(1994) **D/S/A:** Jon Moritsugu **P:** Andrea Sperling

Comic sex, gore, and drug-taking are featured in a 54-minute long 16mm film about a suburban San Francisco Japanese-American family. With the director as twin sons, Sharon Omi, Ken Narasaki, and Jenny Woo. Morotsugu followed with *Mind Fuck Explosion*.

TERMINAL VELOCITY

(Hollywood, 1994) **D:** Deran Sarafian **S:** David Twohy **P:** Scott Kroopf, Tom Engleman

Charlie Sheen stars as a reckless skydiving instructor named Ditch who is blamed for the death of a student (Nastassja Kinski). She's actually a former KGB spy who only pretended to die, and the ridiculous plot concerns Russian spies after a gold shipment. The most outrageous of the many action sequences has both stars trapped in a sports car while it free-falls from an airplane. James Gandolfini (acting like Gene Hackman) is the spy pretending to be working for the local D.A. With Christopher MacDonald as a blond killer and Melvin Van Peebles. It was a comeback for Kinski, who had divorced her Egyptian husband and moved to America with Quincy Jones. The PG-13 feature cost $50 million and was a big money loser until its video release. A soundtrack is from Varèse Sarabande.

THE TERMINATOR

(HBO, 1984) **D/S:** James Cameron
S/P: Gale Ann Hurd **S:** William Wisher

Although it copied episodes of *The Outer Limits* and/or *Cyborg 2097* (1966), *The Terminator* did it all right and was the exciting hit that made Arnold Schwarzenegger a real star. Writer Harlan Ellison gets a superimposed credit at the end, as ordered by the court after he sued. The violent nonstop action science fiction hit from Hemdale has itself been copied many times since. Linda Hamilton costars as Sarah Connor, the woman that the Terminator from the future has been sent to kill. Arnold kills street punks, lots of cops at a police station, and several wrong women. With Michael Biehn, Paul Winfield, Lance Henriksen, Bill Paxton, Rick Rossovich, Brian Thompson, and Dick Miller as a gun shop owner. The FX are by Stan Winston and the robot animation is by Ernie Farino. The Brad Fiedel soundtrack is on Enigma. The laser disc is letterboxed and includes a making-of short. In Europe there was an Italian ripoff called *Terminator II* (1989) directed by Bruno Mattei, but the real *Terminator 2* wasn't until 1991.

TERMINATOR 2: JUDGMENT DAY

(Live, 1991) **D/S/P:** James Cameron **S:** William Wisher **P:** Gale Ann Hurd, M. Kassar

Allthough this sequel cost "$100 million" (!!), it made lots of money and was the biggest (and at 135 minutes, the longest) hit of the year. The state-of-the-art FX by ILM and Stan Winston are excellent. The typical loud Times Square crowd was shocked into complete silence (a unique and rare experience) during the scene where LA is nuked. This will remain the ultimate apocalypse scene for years to come. Arnold Schwarzenegger returns as a different terminator, and he promises not to kill people. Linda Hamilton is a muscular and crazed Sarah Connor, and her kid (Edward Furlong) orders Arnold around. Robert Patrick is T-1000, a bad terminator, disguised as a cop. The liquid metal–look transformation scenes are also outstanding. With Joe Morton (also in *The Brother from Another Planet*, a movie that stole ideas from the same places as *Terminator*), Jenette Goldstein, and a record number of bullets, guns, and car crashes. Jim Muro was a steadicam operator. The Brad Fiedel soundtrack is on Varèse Sarabande,

and Guns N' Roses had a hit from it. The Pioneer "Special Edition" laserdisc contains about 16 minutes of extra footage, including a scene with Michael Biehn. It's available letterboxed or "pan and scanned." A *Terminator Box* contained both features, a making-of short, interviews, a booklet, and a 3-D cover. A deluxe illustrated screenplay book was also published. The even more expensive next Arnold movie (*Last Action Hero*) tried to top this and failed.

TERMINATOR WOMAN

(Vidmark, 1992) **D/A:** Michel Qissi
S: John S. Soet **S/P:** Jeanette Francesca Qissi

Karen Shepard and Jerry Trimble are cops protecting a government witness. The action movie costars Ashley Hayden and kickboxer Qissi (*Bloodsport*).

TERMINUS

(VSOM, 1986) **D/S:** Pierre William **S:** Patrice Duvic **P:** Anne François   W. Germany/France

French singing star Johnny Hallyday, American Karen Allen, and German Jurgen Prochnow star in a computerized truck race movie that copies *Road Warrior*.

TERRA COTTA WARRIOR

(VSOM, 1988) **D:** Ching Siu-Yung **S:** Li Pik Wah
P: Chu Mu, Hon Pou Chu   Hong Kong/China

The personal swordsman of the first emperor of China is encased in clay for having a love affair with a concubine (Gong Li). She's burned to death for sorcery. He's revived in the 20th century (thanks to an elixir) and she is reincarnated as an actress. A gang plans to rob the ancient tombs. Parts of the impressive romantic action fantasy (shot in mainland China) are pretty silly, and scenes are copied from the *Raiders . . .* films. Star Zhang Yimou has a stony Buster Keaton face and is very good, though. He also directed the quality serious features *Red Sorghum* (1987) and *Ju Dou* (1989), both with Gong Li. *Terra* is by the director of *Chinese Ghost Story*, and the FX are by Tsui Hark.

THE TERRIBLE PEOPLE

(Sinister, 1960) **D:** Harald Reinl **S:** J. Joachim Bartsch, Wolfgang Schnitzler   W. Germany
(*Hand of the Gallows; Die Bande Des Schreckens*)

A condemned crook (Otto Colin) promises to return for revenge for death by hanging. The Edgar Wallace mystery had also been filmed as a Pathé serial in 1928. With Joachim Fuchsberger, Karin Dor (who was married to the director), Eddi Arent, and Fritz Rasp.

THE TERROR

(Sinister, 1938) **D:** Richard Bird
S: William Freshman   UK

The old dark house mystery based on an Edgar Wallace novel (and play) had been filmed as *The Terror* (1928) and *Return of the Terror* (1934) in America. Wilfred Lawson stars in this version with Arthur Wontner, Bernard Lee, and Alastair Sim.

TERROR ABROAD

(1933) **D:** Paul Sloane **S:** Harvey Thew, Manuel Seff **P:** William Le Baron

Everyone is found dead on an ocean liner. Flashbacks introduce the passengers and show how they were killed. One is hung on a hook in the freezer and blood is seen. Critics considered the Paramount release in very bad taste at the time. John Halliday is the ship's captain and killer. Neil Hamilton (the hero) and Shirley Grey costar with Charlie Ruggles for comedy relief, Jack LaRue, and Verree Teasdale. Ruggles returned the same year in a similar role in Paramount's *Murder in the Zoo*.

TERROR AT LONDON BRIDGE

(Fries, 1985) **D:** E. W. Swackhamer **S:** William F. Nolan **P:** Jack Michon, Richard Maynard (*Bridge Across Time; Arizona Ripper*)

The spirit of Jack the Ripper follows the London Bridge to Arizona and kills again. With David Hasselhoff as a detective, Adrienne Barbeau, Lindsay Bloom, Lane Smith, Clu Gulager, and Rose Marie. The NBC-TV movie used the same idea as Ulli Lommel's earlier *A Taste of Sin* (1983).

TERROR AT ORGY CASTLE

(SW, 1971) **D:** Zoltan G. Spencer

Tourists Bill and Lisa arrive at a castle owned by the countess Dominova, who at one point turns into a count and has sex with two women. There's a dinner table orgy, a black mass featuring Lisa and men in goat heads, and two succubi who entertain Bill. Everyone is naked a lot and the frequent sex scenes are pretty explicit. Everything is narrated (some of the dialogue is missing). The music starts with spooky organ, gets bluesy for sex scenes, then becomes psychedelic. You'd swear this soft-core sex movie was European, but it's from California. The impressive sets are the same ones that were used in *Blood of Dracula's Castle* and *Gallery of Horror* (both featuring John Carradine)! *Terror* was made back-to-back with Spencer's *The Hand of Pleasure*. A Frank Henenlotter Sexy Shocker release.

TERROR AT TENKILLER

(United, 1986) **D/P:** Ken Meyer **S:** Claudia Meyer

Some girls at a lakeside resort are killed. It was shot on tape, by the Oklahoma-based makers of *The Ripper* and *Copperhead*.

TERROR AT THE OPERA

(Southgate, 1987) **D/S:** Dario Argento **S:** Franco Ferrini **P:** Mario and Vittorio Cecchi Gori (*Opera*)

Ian Charleson (from *Chariots of Fire*) is a horror movie director, presenting a staged avant-garde production of Verdi's opera Macbeth (Argento planned to do the same in real life). The play includes guns, crashed airplanes, and real ravens swooping into the audience. After the play's star is hit by a car, a crazed fan kills off friends of the Lady Macbeth understudy (Christina Marsillach). This is Argento at his stylish, horrifying best. He manages to make a cliché story seem brand new. The star is forced to watch killings, and her eyes

are taped open while her lover is killed. Ravens peck a face apart. Her agent (Daria Nicolodi) is killed as the camera follows the bullet through the gun and into her brain. There's also an incredible ending in the mountains. Michelle Soavi was the second unit director. The music is by Claudio Simonetti with cuts by Brian and Roger Eno and Bill Wyman. R and unrated tapes are available, but the original end scene is missing from the US video. Charleson later died of AIDS.

TERROR BEACH = NIGHT OF THE SEAGULLS

TERROR CIRCUS: *See* BARN OF THE NAKED DEAD

TERROR EYES

(AIP, 1988) **D:** Steve Sommers, Michael Rissi **D/S/P:** Eric Parkinson **S/P/A:** Vivian Schilling

Parkinson and Schilling took two USC shorts, filmed one of their own, and added framing scenes. The odd and pretty senseless new scenes feature a white trash couple who receive a deadly "book of life." They wake (it was all her dream) and go camping, where the other tales are told. Sommers's interesting short is about a small-time crook in a time warp and Rissi's is about a female chess player who is thrown in a maze by an evil maker of violent games. With Dan Roebuck (in two roles) and Fox Harris. Parkinson and Schilling returned with *Soultaker*.

TERRORGRAM

(Monarch, 1988) **D/P:** Stephen M. Kienzle

Three people receive packages from a delivery man, leading to three horror tales. These shorts have a very strong moral attitude. The director is more concerned with getting across (often very confused) messages than being scary. The first has a mean (gay?) director of what looks like a Troma movie trapped in a (junk-induced) nightmare version of his own movie. Women take the abusive roles and female bikers keep men in chains. The second is about a TV anchorwoman who uses a hit-and-run death she was responsible for to further her career. She imagines a talking corpse and, of course, pays for her deeds. The last is about an abusive drinker and wife beater who had been responsible for a student being drafted back in 1968. He ends up trapped in a Nam battle, is tortured, and is practically talked to death by a walking corpse. The makeup is excellent and the first two stories feature some nudity. James Earl Jones reads an introduction that is so long and overly serious that it must be a joke.

TERROR HOSPITAL = NURSE SHERRI

TERROR IN BEVERLY HILLS

(AIP, 1988) **D/S:** John Myhers **P:** Ron Lavery, Pierre Mzadeh

Hero Hack Stone (Frank Stallone) runs a martial arts school and Palestinian terrorists kidnap the president's daughter. With Cameron Mitchell and William Smith (who is dubbed) as the president.

TERROR IN THE AISLES

(MCA, 1983) **D/P:** Andrew Kuehn **S:** Margaret Doppelt **P:** Stephen Netburn

This compilation of scenes from "75" (mostly horror) movies from the 40s to the early 80s actually played in theaters. Donald Pleasence and Nancy Allen sit in a theater and narrate. They try to sound serious and worried and wear out their welcome pretty fast. Watching all the scenes can be overwhelming even for a longtime horror fan, but some of them are pretty great. It had to be cut for an R rating even though none of the movies covered was rated anything stronger than an R. Some titles covered are *The Exorcist, The Thing, Scanners, Alien, Nighthawks, The Seduction,* and *Vice Squad*.

TERROR IN THE JUNGLE

(1968) **D:** Tom De Simone, Andy Janzack, Alexander Grattan **S/P:** Enrique Torres

A blond boy (Jimmy Angle) survives a plane crash in the Amazon and is treated as a god by Jivaro Indians. The chief plans to sacrifice him, though, and his parents arrive in Peru for a rescue mission. Crown International released the Pathecolor feature, filmed on location in Peru. With Robert Burns and Fawn Silver (from *Orgy of the Dead*). Music by Les Baxter and the Hypnotics.

TERROR IN THE SWAMP (1976) = CREATURE FROM BLACK LAKE

TERROR IN THE SWAMP

(Starmaker, 1983) **D:** Joseph L. Catalanotto **S/A:** Billy Holiday **P:** Martin Folse (*Nutriaman: The Copasaw Creature*)

Two scientists inject a nutria (a kind of rodent) and create a barely seen Sasquatch-type monster that escapes in the Louisiana Bayou. New World released the regional PG feature.

TERROR IN TOYLAND: *See* CHRISTMAS EVIL

TERROR OF DR. HITCHCOCK = THE HORRIBLE DR. HITCHCOCK

TERROR OF MECHA-GODZILLA = TERROR OF GODZILLA

TERROR OF THE BLOODHUNTERS

(Sinister, 1962) **D/P:** Jerry Warren **S:** Jacques LeCotier

Here's a mindless hour that only seems like it lasts four. Narrated flashbacks take us to Devil's Island where Duvaal, an artist prisoner (Robert Clarke) tries to escape with the commander's daughter (Dorothy Laney) and some other guy. They mostly stand around in the dark and talk while we see lots of badly edited stock footage of a leopard and natives dancing. Repeating one short loop of native dialogue over and over is pretty disorienting. So are the topless black women edited into scenes of white natives. This played with Warren's *Invasion of the Animal People*.

TERROR OF THE DOLL

(MPI, 1975) **D/P:** Dan Curtis **S:** Richard Matheson

This is the famous killer-doll segment (with Karen Black) of the *Trilogy of Terror* TV movie. It's 30 minutes long.

TERROR OF THE SHE WOLF = LEGEND OF THE WOLF MAN

THE TERROR OF TINY TOWN

(Video Yesteryear, Admit One, 1938) **D:** Sam Newfield **S:** Fred Myton, Clarence Marks **P:** Jan Buell

This all-little-people western comedy opens with two midgets arguing over who is the star. Little Billy is the villain and Billy Curtis is the hero. They both ride ponies. In one barroom scene "Diamond Dolly" sits on an old man's lap and sings "Hey, Look Out! (I Want to Make Love to You)." With a cast of 60 (average height 3' 8"). It's only 63 minutes long and was released (by Principle) shortly before *The Wizard of Oz.* Newfield also directed the black-cast western *Harlem on the Prairie* (1939). Also see *Even Dwarfs Started Small, Little Cigars, Under the Rainbow,* and *Willow.*

THE TERROR ON ALCATRAZ

(TWE, 1986) **D:** Phillip Marcus **S:** Donald Lewis **P:** Marvin G. Lipschultz

Some teenagers on a tour are locked in Alcatraz overnight. A former prisoner shows up looking for some money he hid and starts killing them off. With Aldo Ray, Sandy Brook, and Alisa Wilson.

TERROR ON TAPE

(Continental, 1985) **D:** Robert A. Worms III **S:** Philip L. Clarke

Cameron Mitchell runs the "Shoppe of Horrors" video store. He horrifies two customers by showing them gory scenes from "20" movies that used to be available from Continental Video like *Scalps, Nightmare,* and *Return of the Aliens: Deadly Spawn.* Others are *Vampire Hookers, Madhouse Mansion,* and *City of the Walking Dead.* He shows some H. G. Lewis clips to a third customer (Michelle Bauer) to try and shock her.

TERROR ON THE MENU = THE FOLKS AT RED WOLF INN

TERROR ON TOUR

(Media, 1980) **D:** Don Edmunds **S:** Dell Lekus **P:** Sandy Cobe

While a Kiss-type band called the Clowns play, groupies are being killed by a psycho dressed as a band member. With nudity and gore. By the director of Ilsa movies.

TERROR SQUAD

(Forum, 1987) **D/P:** Peter Maris **S:** Chuck Rose

Libyan terrorists invade Kokomo, Indiana, take over a nuclear plant, and take teen hostages. Chuck Connors is the police chief in a Brooklyn Dodgers jacket. The *Red Dawn* ripoff features lots of explosions. With Greer Brodie, Ken Foree, and actual citizens of Kokomo.

TERRORVISION

(Lightning, 1985) **D/S:** Ted Nicolaou **P:** Albert Band

In a dumb science fiction comedy, an alien enters a swinger's house through a satellite dish. Gerrit Graham and Mary Woronov are the parents, but they don't last very long. With Diane Franklin, Chad Allan, Alejandro Rey, Jennifer Richards as an Elvira-type TV hostess, and Bert Remsen (as grandpa). Clips from *Earth vs. the Flying Saucers, Robot Monster,* and *The Giant Claw* are thrown in, and there are lots of in jokes. The Richard Band soundtrack is on Enigma. The Empire release was filmed in a studio in Italy.

THE TERROR WITHIN

(MGM/UA, 1989) **D:** Thierry Notz **S:** Thomas M. Cleaver **P:** Roger Corman

Roger Corman made *Alien* copies in space, under water, and this one, under the desert. It's set on Earth in an underground lab after a worldwide plague. A woman the scientists rescue gives birth to a mutant creature that becomes a man-in-a-suit monster. There's a chest burster scene, and a dog whistle (!) stops the creature. With George Kennedy, Andrew Stevens, Starr Andreeff, and Terry Treas. Notz is from Switzerland.

THE TERROR WITHIN II

(Vestron, 1991) **D/S/A:** Andrew Stevens **S:** Lee Lankford **P:** Mike Elliot

Stevens roams the post-plague desert with his dog. He runs into a group of cave people (living in Bronson Canyon!) led by an evil black woman. Stevens cuts off his ZZ Top beard, his dog is killed, and his new girlfriend (Clare Hoak) is raped doggie-style by a mutant. Another monster attacks the underground lab sanctuary. Andrew and his real-life mom Stella Stevens deliver a killer mutant baby. R. Lee Ermey yells. The best part is a slimy red (man-in-a-suit) monster with a big lump on its head. With Chick Vennera. Roger Corman was the executive producer.

TESS

(RCA, 1979) **D/S:** Roman Polanski **S:** Gerard Brach **P:** Claude Berri   France/England

After being arrested in Hollywood in 1977 and serving 42 days in prison, Polanski had to cancel several planned American features. Instead he made this lush and long (170-minute) period film based on Thomas Hardy's novel. Natassja Kinski stars as a peasant girl seduced and abandoned by nobleman Alec D'Urberville (Leigh Lawson). Her baby dies, and she has to work on a farm. Angel Clare (Peter Firth) marries her but leaves on their wedding night, ashamed of her past. It all ends with more tragedy. With Suzanna Hamilton and Arielle Dombasle. A 1924 American version is considered a lost film.

TESTAMENT

(Paramount, 1983) **D/P:** Lynne Littman **S:** John Sacret Young **P:** Jonathan Bernstein

The same year as *The Day After,* this smaller film covers similar territory in less time. The Wetherly family in Hamlin, CA, are nuke survivors. Jane Alexander (who was Oscar nominated) stars with William Devane, Lukas Haas, Philip Anglim, Rebecca De Mornay, Kevin Costner, and Mako. It was made for the PBS *American Playhouse,* then was released in theaters, prompting SAG to sue.

THE TESTAMENT OF DR. MABUSE

(Nelson, Sinister, 1932) **D/P:** Fritz Lang **S:** Thea von Harbou   Germany (*Das Testament des Dr. Mabuse; The Crimes of Dr. Mabuse*)

Rudolf Klein-Rogge returned in the sound sequel to Lang's silent *Dr. Mabuse* (1922). He controls a criminal organization from his asylum cell and when he dies, is reincarnated in the body of the director of the asylum (Oskar Beregi). Inspector Lohmann (Otto Wernicke) uncovers the master criminal in the end. It was to premiere in Berlin in 1933 but was banned by the Nazi government, and Lang fled the country, saying that his film denounced fascism. His screenwriter wife von Harbou chose to stay. *Testament . . .* wasn't screened in Germany until after the war. A French-language version was shot at the same time with a partially different cast. Originally 122 minutes long. TV prints and the (subtitled) video are only 75 minutes. It was remade in West Germany in 1962.

THE TESTAMENT OF ORPHEUS

(Home Vision, 1959) **D/S/A:** Jean Cocteau **P:** Jean Thuillier   France (*Le testament d'Orphée*)

Cocteau returned to the themes of his classic *Orpheus* (1950) and stars as an 18th-century poet who dies and rises from the dead. He enters the 20th century "age of reason" and meets characters from *Orpheus* (including Jean Marais). It's b/w with color sequences and the American version is narrated. With Yul Brynner, Jean-Pierre Leaud, Daniel Gelin, Claudine Auger, Pablo Picasso and his wife, Charles Aznavour, Roger Vadim, and Brigitte Bardot. Cocteau died in 1963.

TEST TUBE BABIES

(SW, 1948) **D:** W. Merle Connell **P:** George Weiss   (*Sins of Love*)

Timothy Farrell (with glasses and no mustache, for a change) made his film debut as Dr. Wright, a friendly, patient gynecologist in a once-scandalous movie about artificial insemination. A married couple is happy but the husband is sterile, so they become a happy family with help from the doc. Stuff about their "wolf" friend and footage of a drunk at a party and a cat fight help fill up the time. The Screen Classics feature was re-released in 1967 (!) with new footage as *The Pill.* Farrell also played Dr. Weiss in *Hometown Girl/Secret Scandal,* made around the same time. With trailers for *Pin Down Girls* and *Dance Hall Racket,* which were also once available from (the now-defunct) Hollywood Confidential company.

TEST TUBE TEENS FROM THE YEAR 2000

(Paramount, 1993) **D:** "Ellen Cabot"/David DeCoteau
S: Kenneth J. Hall **P:** Karen L. Spencer   (*Virgin Hunters*)

Two guys from the future take a time machine to a present-day girls' school run by Morgan Fairchild (has she ever been in a good movie?). This shamelessly copies a good movie (*Spirit of '76*) plus all those awful teen comedies with guys in drag just to be around school babes. With shower and sex scenes and a comic *Terminator* clone. Sara Suzanne Brown (*Mirror Images II*) and Michele Matheson (*Howling IV*) are the main attractions. A "Torchlight" productions from Full Moon.

TETSUO: THE IRON MAN

(Fox Lorber, 1990) **D/S/A/C/E:** Shinya Tsukamoto
Japan (*Tetsuo*)

This amazing 66-minute 16mm b/w film was an underground, midnight hit in Tokyo and could be described as a "cyberpunk *Eraserhead*." It's fast-paced, shocking, scary (and funny!) and features time-lapse action photography, surprising FX, monsters, a mutant cat, flashback sex, and lots of sweat, pain, spurting blood, maggots, mutating, and loud screams. It was done on an obvious low budget, but you can tell that the filmmakers spent a long time getting everything just right. I think it's a warning to "Salaryman." The "industrial" music (by Tadashi Ishikawa) is also excellent. The MPAA would probably give it an NC-17 for "general tone." The subtitled tape includes *Drumstruck* (1991), a very good 25-minute b/w short by Greg Nickson made in Chicago.

TETSUO II: THE BODY HAMMER

(1991) **D/S/A/C/E:** Shinya Tsukamoto   Japan

The best part of the color sequel to the original cult film is a long hidden-camera b/w flashback of bizarre experiments to turn people into weapons. Otherwise, the more expensive feature makes less sense (to me anyway) and just doesn't have the same kind of impact. Tomoroh Taguchi (from *Tetsuo*) stars. Subtitled copies are around.

TEX

(Disney, 1982) **D/S:** Tim Hunter
S: Charlie Haas **P:** Tim Zimmerman

Matt Dillon and Jim Metzler star as brothers living by themselves in rural Oklahoma. The PG Disney feature was the first to be based on a novel by S. E. Hinton (she appears as a teacher). With Meg Tilly, Ben Johnson, Emilio Estevez, and Zeljko Ivanek. Pino Donaggio wrote the score. Hunter also made *River's Edge*. Dillon went on to more Hinton adaptations: *The Outsiders* and *Rumblefish*.

TEXAS CHAINSAW MASSACRE PART 2

(HBO, 1986) **D/M:** Tobe Hooper
S: L. M. Kit Carson **P:** Golan/Globus

The original 1974 classic made millions for somebody, but not Hooper, so Cannon made a deal with him. He made the *Invaders from Mars* remake and this sequel for them. It's a parody written by the

TETSUO

same guy who had just written the *Breathless* "remake." The production was rushed. It was still shooting in July and was released in August! It tales place 14 years after the events in the original. Dennis Hopper is the grim Lt. Lefty Enright. He (and his obvious double) team up (sort of) with Caroline Williams (a great screamer) as a DJ called "Stretch." Hopper dresses like a modern cowboy and is armed with a chainsaw and two small ones in holsters. Bill Moseley is Chop Top ("Nam Flashback!") and Bill Johnson is Leatherface. They have trash culture references (an idea copied from *Mother's Day*) and there's a *Dr. Strangelove* in-joke. Jim Siedow (the only returning cast member) is Cook, now in the Dallas area running a catering business out of an enormous bone-filed complex underneath the abandoned Texas Battle amusement park. Tom Savini really delivers in the FX department (it was released unrated), but the main plot line is Leatherface in love. A various artists soundtrack is on IRS. *Leatherface*, an unrelated sequel, followed.

THE TEXAS CHAINSAW MASSACRE: A FAMILY PORTRAIT

(MTI, 1988) **D/S/P:** Brad Shellady

Chicago-based filmmakers traveled from Maine to Michigan to Texas and California to interview stars Gunnar Hansen, Edwin Neal, and Jim Siedow plus Forry Ackerman and Charles Balun. The 64-minute documentary about the original horror classic was from 32 hours of videotape.

THE TEXAS COMEDY MASSACRE

(1988) **D/S/P/A/E:** Marcus Van Bavel

Van Bavel filmed this over a period of five years and plays "46" roles. It's a series of TV parodies including "Star Dreck" and "The Mild Kingdom."

TEXAS DETOUR

(1978) **D/S/P:** Hikmet Avedis

Patrick Wayne stars as a stunt driver. With Priscilla Barnes (who appears topless), R. G. Armstrong, Cameron Mitchell, and Lindsay Bloom.

TEXAS IN FLAMES: *See* SHE CAME INTO THE VALLEY

TEXAS LAYOVER: *See* BLAZING STEW-ARDESSES

TEXAS LIGHTNING

(Media, 1980) **D/S:** Gary Graver
P: Jim Sotos

Cameron Mitchell and his son Channing Mitchell star as father and son truck drivers who go on a hunting trip. They hang out at a honky tonk bar and the son gets involved with a waitress. With Maureen McCormick (from *The Brady Bunch*) and porn star Lisa Deleuw. The director was on a break from making nonstop X features.

T-FORCE

(PM, 1994) **D/P:** Richard Pepin
S: Jaconson Hart **P:** Joseph Merhi

In a sci-fi action movie set in LA of 2007, Jack Scalia is a detective who has to work with violent cyborgs led by Evan Lurie. Bobby Johnson is the cyborg partner. With Erin Gray (from the *Buck Rogers* TV series) as the mayor and Vernon Wells as a terrorist.

THANK GOD IT'S FRIDAY

(RCA, 1978) **D:** Richard Klane **S:** Barry
Armyan Bernstein **P:** Rob Cohen

It's one night at the Zoo, a Hollywood disco. Valerie Landsburg stars in the hit musical with Terri Nunn, Chick Vennera, and Donna Summer. Jeff Goldblum owns the disco and Debra Winger is there too. Like other disco movies, it will be rediscovered and reevaluated in the future. The Commodores are on the nonstop double Casablanca soundtrack which features Summer's "Last Dance." Neil Bogart was executive producer. From Columbia.

THAR SHE BLOWS!

(VCR, 1969) **D/S:** Richard Kantner
S/P/A: David F. Friedman

John Alderman (as Phil Latio) and Stuart Lancaster charter a yacht and bring starlets along. A gruesome flashback shows how the impotent Captain Frigate (Vincent Stevens) was gouged in the groin with a hook. Shari Mann is his sister, who likes to walk around naked. The adults-only movie features sex, showers, spanking, lesbian scenes, masturbation, and suicide. Friedman shows up as the bartender.

THAT COLD DAY IN THE PARK

(Republic, 1969) **D:** Robert Altman **S:** Gillian Freeman **P:** Donald Factor **C:** Lazslo Kovacs   US/Canada

Sandy Dennis is a wealthy spinster in Vancouver who invites a boy (Michael Burns) home for dinner. He returns and gives her marijuana brownies. She hires a hooker (Luana Anders) for him to try to keep him around, but he snaps and kills her and others. With Susanne Benton, John Garfield Jr., and Altman regular Michael Murphy.

THAT'LL BE THE DAY

(1973) **D:** Claude Whatham **S:** Ray Connolly **P:** David Puttnam, Sandy Lieberson   UK

David Essex plays a lower-class working husband and father in 1958, who finally decides to leave it all behind and be a rock singer. His rise to stardom came in the sequel, *Stardust*. With an oldies soundtrack put together by Neil Aspinall and Keith Moon, who also acts. With Billy Fury and Ringo Starr. The hit "Rock On" by Essex is the end theme.

THAT MAN BOLT

(1973) **D:** Henry Levin, David Lowell Rich **S:** Quentin Werty, Charles Johnson **P:** Bernard Schwartz

Fred Williamson is Jefferson Bolt, a James Bond–type agent with a black belt who is hired to transport a fortune and battles Japanese villains. Teresa Graves (a former regular on *Laugh-In*) is his singer girlfriend. The action shifts from Hong Kong to LA to Vegas to Mexico City. With Miko Mayama, Ken Kazama as Spider, Jack Ging, and Paul Mantee. Original director Levin became ill after filming the Hong Kong sequences and was replaced. From Universal.

THAT MAN IN ISTANBUL

(1965) **D/S/P:** "Anthony Isasi"/Antonio Isasmendi **S:** George Simonelli, Nat Wachsberger Spain/France/Italy (*L'Homme d'Istanbul*)

A playboy spy (Horst Buchholz) and an FBI agent posing as a stripper (Sylva Koscina) search for a missing atomic scientist. Terrorists led by Klaus Kinski are making him build an H-bomb. Columbia released it and there was a Mainstream soundtrack.

THAT OBSCURE OBJECT OF DESIRE

(Nelson, 1977) **D/S:** Luis Buñuel **P:** Serge Silberman   France/Spain

Buñuel was called a traitor, an anarchist, an atheist, a pervert, and worse. His last feature was a version of a novel by Pierre Louys. It had also been filmed by Joseph von Sternberg as *The Devil Is a Woman* in 1935. Fernando Rey is the rich old man who suffers for his young maid. The maid is played in various scenes by either Carole Bouquet or Angela Molina. Rey's voice was dubbed by Michel Piccoli. Available subtitled or dubbed. Look for Buñuel's autobiography, *My Last Sigh*. He died in 1983.

THAT'S ACTION

(AIP, 1990) **D/S:** David A. Prior **P:** Kimberley Casey

Robert Culp's career had fallen a long way when he hosted this 77-minute-long commercial for cheap films from Action International Pictures. Scenes are divided into categories like "high speed chases and crashes," "fight scenes," and "body burns."

THAT'S ADEQUATE

(Southgate, 1985) **D/S/P:** Harry Hurwitz **P:** Irving Schwartz

Tony Randall narrates the history of an old (fictional) B studio in this faked documentary spoof. James Coco is the studio head who started in the circus and is interviewed on *The Joe Franklin Show*. His studio copied everybody else and turned out features like *Sluts in the South* and *Young Hitler* (starring Robert Vaughn) and created imitation Ritz Brothers and Three Stooges. With Stiller and Meara, Ina Balin, Prof. Irwin Corey, Susan Dey, Robert Downey Jr., Richard Lewis, Chuck McCann, Peter Riegert, Brother Theodore, Robert Townsend, Renee Taylor, Martha Coolidge, Marshall Brickman, and even Bruce Willis. With dubbed *Hoppity Goes to Town* animated footage and dubbed Republic serial scenes.

THAT'S THE SPIRIT

(1945) **D:** Charles Lamont **S/P:** Michel Fessier, Ernest Pagano

A vaudeville dancer (Jack Oakie) wishes he could die instead of his newborn baby, so a silent lady grim reaper (Karen Randle) takes him instead. He's allowed to return to Earth 18 years later (in 1916) as a friendly ghost with a magic flute. He helps his daughter (Peggy Ryan), a singing dancer. He can walk through walls and cars pass through him. The flute makes people act childish. The Universal musical comedy fantasy featured FX by John Fulton. Also with June Vincent, Gene Lockhart, Andy Devine, Arthur Treacher as a butler, Irene (Granny Clampett) Ryan as a maid, and Buster Keaton as the head of the complaint department in Heaven.

THAT'S THE WAY OF THE WORLD

(Abackus, 1975) **D/P:** Sig Shore **S:** Robert Lipsyte   (*Shining Star*)

Harvey Keitel is a record producer with mob problems. He's working with Earth Wind and Fire. The group appears and their leader Maurice White acts. With Bert Parks as a child molester (!), Ed Nelson, Murray the K, and Jimmy Boyd as a junkie. From U.A. and the producer/director of *Superfly*. The Columbia soundtrack went to #1, but not that many people saw the movie.

THAT TENDER TOUCH

(1969) **D/S/P:** Russell Vincent

Sue Bernard (from *Faster, Pussycat! Kill! Kill!*) stars as a traumatized orphan who has a brief lesbian affair. Later she marries, and the former lover, failing to win her back, kills herself. The flashback-

filled movie that explores "The wall between two kinds of love!" was rated R and features an actress named Phae Dera.

THAT TENNESSEE BEAT

(1966) **D/P:** Richard Brill **S:** Paul Schneider

Jim Birdsell (Earl Richards from *The Girl from Tobacco Row*) is a country singer who steals to get ahead in Nashville. He gets in more trouble but is saved by Opal (Sharon De Bord) and a lady preacher (Minnie Pearl) who hires him as a handyman. With Dolores Faith, Merle Travis (who sings the title song), the Statler Brothers, Boots Randolph, Pete Drake, and the Stony Mountain Cloggers. When this color movie was released by 20th Century, "country music" still meant hillbilly music.

Earl "Snake" Richards sings to Sharon De Bord in *That Tennessee Beat.*

THAT WAS ROCK

(Media) **S:** Steve Binder, Larry Peerce

In the 80s somebody edited down the great all-live music features *The T.A.M.I. Show* (1964) and *The Big T.N.T. Show* (1966 but filmed in 1965) into one 90-minute video and added new color intros by Chuck Berry. The two movies (originally released by AIP) should both be available, but until they are, this (now out of print) video is all there is on tape and is well worth searching for. Highlights include great performances by Bo Diddley (with the Duchess), Ike and Tina Turner, and the Ronettes (all from *TNT*) and James Brown, the Rolling Stones, and Motown acts Marvin Gaye, the Miracles, and the Supremes (all from *T.A.M.I.*). You might not miss some of the British invasion, pop, and folk acts that were omitted, but the fact that James Brown's dynamite set was cut down is a terrible thing. Jack Nitzsche was musical director of *T.A.M.I.* and David Winters was the choreographer (the frantic dancers, some in bikinis, are an important part of the experience). Phil Spector was producer and musical director of *TNT*.

THAT WAS THEN ... THIS IS NOW

(Paramount, 1985) **D:** Christopher Cain **S/A:** Emilio Estevez **P:** Gary R. Lindberg, John M. Ondov

Estevez (also in *Tex*) adapted another S. E. Hinton novel and stars as the drug-dealing, car-stealing half-brother of Craig Sheffer. With Kim Delaney, Jill Schoelen, Barbara Babcock, and Morgan Freeman. The music is by Keith Olson.

THELMA AND LOUISE
(MGM, 1991) **D/P:** Ridley Scott **S:** Callie Khouri **P:** Mimi Polk

A Bakersfield waitress (Susan Sarandon) and her naive housewife friend (Geena Davis) go on a vacation together in a convertible, encounter drunks who won't take no for an answer, and end up as fugitives wanted for murder, headed for the Moab desert. Some compared it to *Easy Rider,* some thought it was a feminist classic (Khouri's screenplay received an Oscar), and a lot of us just thought it was cool road movie in the tradition of many drive-in classics from the 70s. The cosmic ending is even like the ending of *Vanishing Point* (1971). With Harvey Keitel as an understanding FBI man, Brad Pitt, Michael Madsen, Stephen Tobolowsky, and Christopher McDonald. It's 128 minutes long.

THEMROC
(1973) **D/S:** Claude Faraldo **P:** Hlena Vager   France

Themroc (the always excellent Michel Piccoli) quits his job, has sex with his sister (Beatrice Romano), barricades himself in a cavelike room, and kills cops and cooks them on a spit for dinner. In this wild comic anarchist movie, Themroc talks with a made-up language and eventually just screams. With Marilu Tolo.

THEN CAME BRONSON
(1969) **D:** William A. Graham **S:** D. B. Petticlerc **P:** Robert H. Justman

Michael Parks quits his newspaper writing job and takes off on a motorcycle to find himself. Bonnie Bedelia costars as a runaway bride. With Akim Tamiroff (in one of his last roles), Gary Merrill, Sheree North, and Martin Sheen. It was the pilot for a CBS TV series that only lasted one year. The *Easy Rider* influence reached suburban homes pretty fast.

THERE GOES MY BABY
(Orion, 1991) **D/S:** Floyd Mutrux **P:** Robert Shapiro   (*The Last Days of Paradise*)

Eight California high school grads are seen during two nights in the summer of 1965 when anti-war protests and the Watts riots occurred. The *American Graffiti*–type movie includes the expected great oldies. With Dermot Mulroney, Rick Shroeder as a surfer, Kelli Williams, Jill Shoelen, Noah Wyle, Seymour Cassell, Andrew Robinson, and narration by Anne Archer. William Fraker was the cinematographer, as he had been for the director's *American Hot Wax* and *Hollywood Knights.* The feature was shelved when Orion went bankrupt and was finally released in 1994.

THERE GOES THE BRIDE
(1979) **D:** Terence Marcel **S/P:** Ray Cooney **P:** Martin Schute   UK

Tom Smothers is the father of the bride-to-be at a wedding party. He romances the ghost of a 1920s model (Twiggy) that only he can see. The comedy, based on a play, features Martin Balsam, Jim Backus, Sylvia Syms, Broderick Crawford, and Phil Silvers. Marcel also made *Jane and the Lost City.* Smothers also starred in the equally obscure movies *Get To Know Your Rabbit* (1970) and *Pandemonium* (1981).

THERESE AND ISABEL
(1968) **D/P:** Radley Metzger **S:** Jesse Vogel

Therese (Essy Persson) remembers her boarding school days in flashback. The lonely girl had befriended Isabelle (Anna Gael) and they had a brief affair. It was filmed in France in b/w and released by Audubon Films. Persson was known for the hit *I, a Woman,* which Metzger had "Americanized." Metzger made *Camille 2000* next.

THERE IS NO 13
(1973) **D/S/P:** William Sachs

Mark Damon is a Nam vet who speaks to the camera as flashbacks and flashforwards unfold. The title refers to the number of affairs he had. With Margaret Markov (from *Naked Warriors* and *The Hot Box*) and Harvey Lembeck from the *Beach Party* movies. By the director of *The Incredible Melting Man.*

THERE'S NOTHING OUT THERE
(Prism, 1990) **D/S:** Rolfe Kanefsky **P:** Wolf Kanefsky

After a good nightmare sequence in a video store, this becomes a very knowing takeoff of teens-in-a-cabin horror movies. The sarcastic odd-man-out horror film fan Mike (Craig Peck) keeps warning everyone what is bound to happen, but the others only care about sex. Nearly every female cast member has topless or nude scenes, and one wears an excellent swimsuit. One is possessed and there's a (briefly seen) slimy green monster and a decapitation. The New York area feature, made for "$300,000," played some midnight shows. It has very good cinematography, music, and acting, and some funny lines. The producer, the then-20-year-old director's father, owns an editing facility.

THEY: *See* INVASION FROM INNER EARTH

THEY BITE
(1989) **D/S:** Brett Piper **P:** William J. Links

A group of people staying at a Florida seaside hotel are trying to film "Invasion of the Fish Fuckers." A female fish specialist (Donna Frotscher) is staying in the next room. Ron Jeremy is one of the filmmakers and Christina Veronica is the porn movie star. Despite the porno connections, it's a fun science fiction spoof without much sex or nudity and features some pretty good (alien) fishmen who attack a bar during a wet T-shirt contest. A dream sequence is also a b/w movie trailer. A nightmare features Susie Owens (from *Playboy*), with a castrating vagina with teeth. Also with Blake Picket. Piper, who also did the FX, also made *Raiders of the Living Dead, Nymphoid Barbarian Women,* and several other features that were released only in Europe.

THEY CALL HER ONE EYE
(1974) **D/S:** Alex Fridolinski **P:** Bo A. Vibenius Sweden (*Thriller-en Grym Film*)

Christina Lindberg is sold, beaten, and raped by a slaver. He cuts her eye out when she tries to escape. Later, she wears different colored eye patches (and minis) while she seeks revenge. The villain ends up buried up to his neck in the ground. A rope around his neck is tied to a hungry horse trying to reach a bucket of food. AIP released it in America.

THEY CALL ME BRUCE?
(United, 1982) **D/S/P:** Elliot Hong **S:** David Randolph, Johnny Yune, Tim Clawson   (*A Fistful of Chopsticks*)

Korean comedian Johnny Yune stars as a chef working for the Mafia. He's given cocaine disguised as flour to deliver and is mistaken for Bruce Lee. With Margaux Hemingway and K. C. Winkler. *They Still Call Me Bruce* was the sequel.

THEY CALL ME TRINITY
(MVD, 1970) **D/S:** Enzo Barboni **P:** Italo Zingarelli   Italy (*Lo Chiamavano Trinità*)

Terence Hill and big Bud Spencer play half brothers who help some Mormons battle the henchmen of an evil cattle baron (Farley Granger) in a hit slapstick comedy western. Trinity is lazy and eats beans a lot. The spaghetti western made Hill and Spencer international stars and is filled with comic fight scenes (and even some karate). It was so popular that the stars returned in sequels, there were copies, and some unrelated movies that Hill and Spencer appeared in were given Trinity titles. *Trinity Is Still My Name* followed.

THEY CAME TO ROB LAS VEGAS
(1967) **D/S:** Antonio Isasmendi **S:** Luis Comeron, Jorge Illa   France/Italy/Spain/W. Germany

Gary Lockwood is a Vegas casino dealer who plans an armored truck robbery. Elke Sommer helps. Lee J. Cobb is a mobster and Jack Palance is a federal agent. With Jean Servais and Gerard Tichy. Lockwood plays two roles. Warner released a shorter version of the 130-minute feature in America.

THEY DRIVE BY NIGHT
(Sinister, 1938) **D:** Arthur Woods **S:** Derek Twist **P:** Jerome Jackson   UK

A small-time crook called Shorty (Emlyn Williams) is released from prison, goes to see his old girl-friend, and discovers she's been strangled. He hitches rides from trucks then hides out in an old dark house. The killer (Ernest Thesiger) poses as a detective. Thesiger (who had already been so good in *Bride of Frankenstein* and *The Old Dark House*) uses silk stockings to kill, likes cats, and keeps a scrapbook of his murders. It's based on a novel by James Curtis. Warner used the title for a Bogart movie, and this was not released in America. The director died in the war.

THEY EAT SCUM
(Penetration, 198?) **D/S/C/E:** Nick Zedd

This anything-goes, no-budget 8mm underground comedy feature was filmed in Brooklyn and NYC. The image sometimes flickers and jumps or is out of focus, but all that sort of fits with the rambling plot about Susie Putrid, a junkie punk singer who tells pogoing fans at CBGB to "Kill! Kill! Kill your entire family!" Cannibal punks eat people, make a girl eat a rat, and dismember her with a chainsaw. A guy is castrated, Susie's brother has sex with a rabid poodle, and a band plays a whole song at Max's Kansas City. After Susie is killed on stage (by her father), her twin sister emerges from a mental hospital, kills the entire population of Manhattan, proclaims herself queen, and is killed by a lobster man during a mutant attack. There's even a bit of crude animation. The found music includes bits of the Beach Boys, the Village People, and Mr. Rogers.

THEY LIVE!

(MCA, 1988) **D/S/M:** John Carpenter **P:** Larry Franco

Carpenter's great anti–Republican/George Bush science fiction movie was released on the eve of the November 1988 presidential election. *They Live* didn't do very much business and we all know how the election turned out. Aliens secretly rule America as more people are forced to live on the streets. Characters put on special sunglasses that reveal subliminal messages (everywhere) like "Obey," "Stay Asleep," and "No Independent Thoughts." The glasses also reveal scary skeleton-like alien faces. The b/w glimpses of "reality" are great. Roddy Piper stars as Nada, an unemployed everyman with a flannel shirt in LA, who becomes the hero. With Keith David, Meg Foster, George "Buck" Flower, Sy Richardson, and Raymond St. Jacques. It was based on a short story by Ray Faraday Nelson. The score by Carpenter and Alan Howarth is on Enigma.

THEY MADE ME A CRIMINAL

(1939) **D:** Busby Berkeley **S:** Sig Herzig **P:** Hal B. Wallis

One of four Warner Brothers "Dead End Kids" movies released in 1939, this was a remake of *The Life of Jimmy Dolan* (1933) starring Douglas Fairbanks Jr., John Garfield, Claude Rains (as a detective), Ward Bond, Ann Sheridan, and Gloria Dickson are the adult stars. The real stars (Billy Halop, Bobby Jordan, Leo Gorcey, Huntz Hall, Gabriel Dell, and Bernard Punsley) all have the same character names they had in *Dead End* (1937).

THEY'RE COMING TO GET YOU

(Super, 1972) **D:** Sergio Martino **S:** Santiago Moncada, Ernesto Gastaldi Spain/Italy (*Todos Los Colores de la Oscuridad; Day of the Maniac; Demons of the Dead*)

A mentally unbalanced woman in London (Edwige Fenech) has nightmares and starts going to a psychiatrist. The *Rosemary's Baby*–inspired plot concerns a black magic cult. She drinks dogs' blood during a black mass ceremony where cult members resemble zombies. With George Hilton, Jorge Rigaud, and Ivan Rassimov. Independent International released it as being in "Chillo-Rama."

THEY'RE PLAYING WITH FIRE

(HBO, 1984) **D/S/P:** Hikmet Avedis
S/P: Marlene Schmidt

A sexy lady professor (Sybil Danning) seduces a student (Eric Brown, returning from *Private Lessons*). She wants him to help cheat an old lady out of her money and to kill her husband (Andrew Prine). Meanwhile, a masked psycho kills people. With Paul Clemens and Alvy Moore. Danning (who has three major nude scenes) was also in *Separate Ways* by Avedis. From New World.

THEY STILL CALL ME BRUCE

(Starmaker, 1987) **D/S/P/A:** Johnny Yune
D/S/P: James Orr

In this comedy sequel, Yune comes to America to find the G.I. who saved his life during the Korean War. Yune is an inept karate expert with a magic sock, and he fights villains. It doesn't have much to do with *They Call Me Bruce,* it's just dumber. With Robert Guillaume, Pat Paulsen, and Joey Travolta. From New World.

THEY WATCH

(Columbia, 1993) **D:** John Korty
S: Edith Swensen **P:** Bridget Terry

Patrick Bergin is an architect haunted by his daughter (Nancy Moore Atchinson) who died in a car crash. He searches for an old North Carolina mansion in his daughter's drawing where a blind mystic (Vanessa Redgrave) tells of "lost souls" in the woods. The PG-13 fantasy, based on a Kipling story, debuted on Showtime. With Valerie Mahaffey.

THEY WEAR NO CLOTHES

(Video Dimensions, 1941)

A very friendly-sounding man narrates a series of (b/w) scenes and tells corny jokes while light music plays. We see fan dancers, models posing outdoors, strippers, and sunbathers. Hula dancers are being watched by men in blackface with spears! So far it's what you'd expect for a 40s adult movie (nothing is really shown). The next sequences provide the payoff, though. "Modern day Eves" (one is black, very surprising for the time) are seen by a pool, then two naked women ride horses. These revealing sequences are topped by elaborate scenes of seven more smiling and laughing naked beauties posing outdoors and swimming. Then some people play croquet at a nudist camp. It's only 52 minutes long and seems to be made up

of many short films or scenes, some probably from years earlier. Whoever released this probably retired comfortably from the profits.

THIEF OF BAGHDAD

(Republic, HBO, Budget, 1924) **D:** Raoul Walsh
S/P/A: Douglas Fairbanks **S:** Lotte Woods

A record big budget ($2 million) was spent on this classic fantasy hit and it made $3 million at the box office. Fairbanks stars as Ahmed the thief and Julanne Johnston is the princess. Sixteen-year-old Anna May Wong plays a Mongol slave and the cast includes Sojin, Noble Johnson, and Brandon Hurst. With a flying carpet, a winged horse, a giant spider, a cloak of invisibility, and various monsters. William Cameron Menzies was the set designer of the U.A. feature, and the sets are amazing. It ran 155 minutes when new, but videos run 140. The HBO version is tinted. Remakes were British (1940 and 1978) and Italian (1960).

THINGS

(IAE, 1989) **D/S/P/A:** "Barry J. Gillis"/
Andrew Jordan Canada

This senseless amateur Toronto gore movie opens with an H-bomb blast. A woman in a devil mask strips (a dream). Some guys with Great White North accents in a house somehow manage to conjure up monsters with a Satanic book they find in the fridge. Meanwhile they drink beer, talk, tell stories, and watch TV, laughing at a cheap b/w slasher film. One of them puts a bug in a sandwich for a joke. The wife of the owner of the house gives birth to a monster that kills them both. The two surviving brothers run out of beer, start drinking hard liquor, and wander around the house smashed while insect monsters breed in the basement. Every once in a while American porn star Amber Lynn and some guy awkwardly read cue cards and give comic in-joke newscasts on TV. They make jokes about George Romero and Traci Lords. They comment about the stranded brothers ("Don and Fred may still be alive after 14 days"). A doctor shows up near the end and says "This is ghastly, brutal, horrible—insane!" The special effects and sound dubbing are awful. There's some original synth and punk music on the soundtrack. Amber Lynn was in movies like *Amber Pays the Rent* and *Friday the 13th: A Nude Beginning,* but you couldn't tell what a bad actress she was in those.

Aliens disguised as American riot cops in *They Live!*

THINGS ARE TOUGH ALL OVER

(1982) **D:** Thomas K. Avildsen
S/A: Cheech Marin, Tommy Chong
P: Harold Brown

At one point, Cheech and Chong decided to stop doing drug humor (a bad idea). In this post-drug-humor flop, they play comic chauffeurs driving a limo packed with money to Las Vegas. They also play rich Arab brothers and appear in drag. With Evelyn Guerrero and both of the stars' real-life wives. From Columbia.

THINGS HAPPEN AT NIGHT

(Sinister, 1948) **D:** Francis Searle **S:** St. John L. Clowes
P: A. R. Shipman, James Carter   UK

A girl is possessed by a poltergeist and there's a psychic maid. With Gordon Harker, Alfred Drayton, and Gweneth Vaughn. Based on the play *Poltergeist* by Frank Harvey.

THINK BIG

(Media, 1990) **D/S:** Jon Turtletaub **S:** Edward Kovach, David Tausik **P:** Brad Krevoy, Steven Stabler

Peter and David Paul (a.k.a. the Barbarian Brothers) are dumb truckers hauling atomic waste. With Ari Meyers (from the *Kate and Allie* show), Martin Mull as the villain, and David Carradine as a repo man. Also with Claudia Christian, Richard Kiel, Richard Moll, Michael Winslow, Peter Lupus (from *Mission: Impossible*), Tiny Lester Jr., and other wrestlers. Jim Wynorski cowrote the story for the PG-13 comedy from Corman's Concorde. Note the Coca-Cola plugs.

THINKIN' BIG

(Starmaker, 1986) **D/S:** S. F. Browrigg **S:** Robert Joseph Sterling, Loretta Yearin **P:** Jim C. Harris

The teen sex comedy was filmed on the Texas shore by the maker of *Don't Look in the Basement.* Everybody thinks "Wong" (Randy Jandt) has a cock as big as Long Dong Silver so all the girls want him. Maybe they should have called it "Don't Look in the Pants."

THE THIRD SEX

(SW, 1957) **D:** Veit Harlan **S:** Dr. Felix Lutzkenorf
P: Helmut Volmer   W. Germany
(*Anders Als Du und Ich*)

This movie about the gay subculture of Berlin was directed by the same man who made *Jud Süss* (1940) and *Kolberg* (1945) for the Nazis. 16-year-old Klaus rides a scooter and paints. His banker dad doesn't understand him and wishes he'd stop hanging around with Manfred, his blond best friend. Dr. Winkler, an art dealer ("Just call me Boris") has the boys over to look at Asian art and listen to "musique concrète" that he plays on an "electron" keyboard. This spooky science fiction music is heard whenever something homosexual seems to be going on. One night at Boris's, two boys in underpants wrestle (while the camera tilts at odd angles) for entertainment. Klaus's angry dad ends up in a drag club, and his worried mom encourages Gerte, a beautiful young girl, to make it with her wayward son. After sex (on the lawn), Klaus is in love and can't get enough. Manfred gets jealous and mom goes to jail for procuring! Like *Lianne,* from the same producer, *The Third Sex* has some nudity and would have been strictly adults-only in the American 50s. With Paula Wesley, Paul Dahlke, and Christian Wolfe.

THE THIRTEENTH CHAIR

(1929) **D:** Tod Browning **S:** Elliot Clawson

Everything I ever read about this prepared me for the worst. The print I saw looked awful but it was well worth watching. It's a murder mystery set in a British mansion in Calcutta. Bela Lugosi has a good major role (and lots of dialogue) as the clever Inspector Del Sante who arrives, takes charge, and manipulates the characters into revealing the real killer. Margaret Wycherly (a later Oscar nominee) is the real star, however, as Madame LaGrange, a funny, sarcastic, complex Irish character brought in to conduct a spooky séance. Much is made of the price of the British class system. Nothing has much to do with India, but killer Thugee cults are discussed. Conrad Nagel (*London After Midnight*) and Leila Hyams (*Island of Lost Souls*) are the leads, and Holmes Herbert is Sir Crosby. The MGM feature was Browning's first non-Chaney film since 1925. A silent version was also released, and it was remade in 1937.

THE 13TH FLOOR

(Paramount, 1989) **D/S:** Chris Roach
P: David Hannay, Charles Hannah   Australia

A woman (Lisa Hensley) camps out on the abandoned haunted floor of an office building. The ghost is friendly though and protects her from killers. He had been electrocuted by her evil politician father twenty years earlier.

THE THIRTEENTH REUNION

(Thriller, 1980) **D:** Peter Sasdy
S: Jeremy Burnham   UK

Julia Foster is a reporter who discovers cannibals at a weight-loss clinic. Elvira hosts this one-hour Hammer TV movie. With Dinah Sheridan.

THIRTEEN WOMEN

(1932) **D:** George Archainbaud
S: Bartlett Cormack, Samuel Ornitz

Myrna Loy is a Eurasian woman (wearing some wild clothes) who plots to kill a dozen of her former sorority sisters for revenge. A swami (C. Henry Gordon) helps. Ricardo Cortez is a detective who shows up after the movie is half over. Irene Dunne is top billed and the cast includes Jill Esmond, Mary

---

30s Faves Top 10
(ALPHABETICAL)

1. *Bride of Frankenstein* (MCA, 1935)
2. *Dr. Jekyll and Mr. Hyde* (MGM/UA, 1931)
   The tape is restored with 12 of the 17 minutes cut from the theatrical reissue.
3. *Flash Gordon* (1936)
4. *Freaks* (MGM/UA, 1932)
   The tape restores the happy end footage with the rich Hans reunited with Frieda.
5. *Hunchback of Notre Dame* (Turner, 1939)
6. *Island of Lost Souls* (MCA, 1932)
7. *King Kong* (Turner, 1932)
   Several violent scenes were restored in the 80s. A 60th anniversary (1992) package comes with *It Was Beauty Killed the Beast*, a 24-minute documentary. *Kong* has also been colorized.
8. *M* (Admit One, 1931)
9. *Mad Love* (MGM, 1935)
10. *Things to Come* (Sinister, 1936)

Johnny Eck and Angelo Rossitto in *Freaks*.

The 30s

More excellent quality features were made in the thirties then in any other decade. Any horror movie from the period is worth watching, and the best serials were made. The top-grossing features of the decade include *The Wizard of Oz, King Kong, Lost Horizon, The Hurricane,* and Hitchcock's *Rebecca. Gone With the Wind* was by far the biggest money-maker of the decade (nearly $89 million) and later became the highest-rated movie on TV. It was followed by three Disney cartoon features. A few notable restored 30s features are *Tarzan and His Mate* (1934) with Maureen O'Sullivan's nude swim scene and the restored *Lost Horizon* (1937).

Duncan, and Peg Entwhistle (who in real life jumped to her death from the Hollywood sign after acting in this). The RKO release is only one hour long and has a Max Steiner score.

THE 39 STEPS

(Media, Sinister, 1935) **D:** Alfred Hitchcock
S: Charles Bennett, Alma Reville **P:** Michael Balcon UK

Spies and killers are after a visiting Canadian (Robert Donat). He flees to Scotland and is handcuffed to Madeleine Carroll by fake police. Great entertainment, and it's still being copied. With Godfrey Tearle as Professor Jordan, Wifrid Brambell, and Helen Hayes. The best character is Mr. Memory (Wylie Watson). Based on John Buchan's 1915 novel. The director is seen on the street. It was Hitchcock's followup to his hit *The Man Who Knew Too Much* (1934). The first (and last) time I attended a film class, the teacher announced that we would see Hitchcock's *The 39 Steps*. He received a print of the 1959 remake with Kenneth More by mistake. Nobody else cared or even noticed, and he showed the remake anyway.

THE 39 STEPS

(1978) **D:** Don Sharp **S:** Michael Robson **P:** Greg Smith UK

Robert Powell stars in the second remake of Hitchcock's classic spy thriller. It adds a WWI plot and a climax at Big Ben. With David Warner, Karen Dotrice, Eric Porter, John Mills, Andrew Kier, and Robert Flemyng.

THIS IS A HIJACK

(1973) **D:** Barry Pollack **P:** Paul Lewis

Adam Roarke hijacks a plane filled with passengers owned by Jay Robinson for ransom. It was a rare lead role for Roarke, who had been a regular in 60s AIP movies. Neville Brand, Lynn Borden, Milt Kamen, John Alderman, and Dub Taylor are in the Fanfare release, executive produced by Joe Soloman.

THIS IS ELVIS

(Warner, 1981) **D/S/P:** Malcolm Leo, Andrew Solt

This bizarre mixture of real and faked footage, fantasy and fact should appeal to Elvis fans, Elvis haters, and mondo movie fans. I saw it with Sally Eckhoff and Lester Bangs in Times Square. Lester (who died not long afterward) took it very seriously. Great music clips from films, TV appearances, and interviews are used. Three different actors appear as Elvis, and Elvis (the voice of Ral Donner) narrates his life (from the grave!). It ends with the horrifying, bloated, out-of-it real Elvis on stage. With Larry Raspberry as Dewey Philips. Colonel Tom Parker had final say in what was in this post-death feature. A double RCA soundtrack was released. Solt also directed *Imagine: John Lennon* and codirected *It Came from Hollywood* and *25∞5: The Rolling Stones.*

THIS IS SPINAL TAP

(Columbia, 1983) **D/S/A/M:** Rob Reiner
S/A/M: Christopher Guest, Michael McKean, Harry Shearer **P:** Michael Murphy

Reiner's fake rock documentary is a brilliant, right-on-target, must-see comedy. The band is like Black Sabbath (or maybe Status Quo). David St. Hubbins (McKean), Nigel Tufnel (Guest), and Derek Smalls (Shearer) tell Reiner about the long history of Spinal Tap while on an American tour. Various drummers die, the group visits Elvis's grave, and at one point they are reduced to opening for a puppet show. With Tony Hendra, Fran Drescher, Paul Shaffer, June Chadwick, Joyce Hyser, Patrick Macnee, Billy Crystal, Fred Willard, Ed Begley Jr., Zane Busby, Howard Hesseman, Anjelica Huston, and Brinke Stevens. The group promoted their *Smell the Glove* LP on Joe Franklin after the movie came out. They "reunited" in 1992 and an updated "remastered" version of the tape was released along with *Return of Spinal Tap* (MPI). In 1994, a Criterion laser version was released with three audio tracks, a 20-minute demo reel, and an hour of outtakes. Also on CD ROM (from Voyager). More exciting was the discovery of (bootleg) copies of the uncut, uncensored original, running five hours and containing more drugs, groupies, music, and stupidity. Supposedly 50 hours of footage was shot!

THIS NIGHT, I'LL POSSESS YOUR CORPSE

(SW, 1966) **D/S/A:** Jose Mojica Marins Brazil
(*Esta Noite Encarnarei No Teu Cadaver*)

This sequel is Marins's ultimate movie. It begins with the end sequence of *At Midnight I Will Take Your Soul.* All the credits are animated, quivering and mutating over a quick-change collage of shocking and unbelievable scenes from the feature you're about to see (and a few scenes that must have been cut). Ze do Caixao (or Coffin Joe) searches in vain for "the perfect woman." His assistant is a badly scarred hunchback. In one scene a whole room full of kidnapped women sleep in see-through negligees. The hunchback lets dozens of huge (real) tarantulas in and they crawl all over the screaming captives. One woman somehow manages to stay calm and just brushes them off. While he's undressing her, a trapdoor next to the bed opens and she's forced to see more women in a pit being killed by big snakes. A man gets an axe in his head, a woman is killed by acid, and a (real) mouse is crushed by a rock. You never know what sick thing to expect next. Ze is tortured by vivid nightmares. One night an eerie phantom (that looks like a human skeleton from a sideshow in dance tights and a hood) literally drags him to hell. The hell sequence is in full color (!). Ze's hell has old-fashioned devils with pitchforks poking the damned, but it's freezing, not hot, with a steady snowfall. The ice cave walls have Cocteau-like body parts. Screaming heads hang down from above, and arms, legs, breasts, asses, etc., protrude from every angle. The damned all scream loudly, and constantly, while more disturbed experimental music plays on the soundtrack. Ze has to face the devil, played by (who else?) Jose Mojica Marins. Although the budget was low, Marins must have hired the best technical people available. Many of the effects are excellent and the cinematography is often stunning. I was lucky enough to see this in a movie theater in São Paulo, an unforgettable experience. Now it's subtitled in English and available on tape.

THIS NUDE WORLD

(1935) **D:** Mich Mindlin

One of the earliest nudist movies, this historical document features nonstop narration and classical music. First "we pass the new George Washington Bridge" and go to upstate New York where nudists are seen from the back. The French segment features topless nightclubs but people on an island wear bathing suits. To spice things up, a scene of a completely naked woman (probably shot in Hollywood) is spliced in. The last third of this movie is the impressive part, though. At the world's largest nudist camp (in Germany) crowds of naked people exercise, hundreds of naked people run through the woods, and some of them follow each other on their hands and knees. I imagine this incredible footage was shot earlier, during the days of the Weimar Republic. With the founder of the German (and French) nudist movement, Adolph Koch. I saw this thanks to *Trashola* magazine.

THIS STUFF'LL KILL YA!

(SW, 1970) **D/S/P/M:** Herschell Gordon Lewis

Jeffrey Allen (also memorable in *2,000 Maniacs*) is always the center of attention as the Bible-quoting con man and moonshiner Rev. Boone. He's almost like Foghorn Leghorn come to life. He even sings "I Love That White Lightning." A new bride is raped (offscreen), a woman is stoned, and two others are crucified. The goriest scene is when a head is blown off. It doesn't make much sense, parts are real boring, actors flub lines, and the soundtrack is damaged, but "One More Swig Of Moonshine" is a good song, and how many extremely tasteless hillbilly gore comedies are there, anyway? With Ray Sager, *Dr. Giggles* star Larry Drake, and Tim Holt (from *Treasure of the Sierra Madre*) playing it straight, in his last role, as a revenuer.

THOMASINE AND BUSHROD

(1974) **D:** Gordon Parks Jr. **S/P/A:** Max Julian

Max Julian (from *Psych-Out* and *The Mack*) and his real-life girlfriend Vonetta McGee become bank robbers in black cowboy clothes in 1911 Texas. They're considered heroes by Indians and blacks. The black Bonnie and Clyde variation was shot in New Mexico. Also with Glynn Turman.

THOSE REDHEADS FROM SEATTLE

(1953) **D/S:** Lewis R. Foster **S:** Geoffrey Homes **P:** William H. Pine, William C. Foster

The first 3-D musical stars Rhonda Fleming and Gene Barry. Agnes Moorehead and her four daughters journey to the Klondike during the gold rush. With Teresa Brewer, Guy Mitchell, and Roscoe Ates. From Paramount.

THOU SHALT NOT KILL...EXCEPT

(Starmaker, 1985) **D/C/E:** Josh Becker **S/P:** Scott Spiegel (*Stryker's War*)

The fiancée (Cheryl Hansen) of Sgt. Stryker (Brian Schulz), a loner Nam vet with a bad leg, is kidnapped by a demented ("I am Christ!") cult leader (Sam Raimi) who has taken lots of hostages who are kept tied up in the woods. Three vet friends help Stryker in the harrowing rescue attempt. Not much of a plot, but it's a pretty great action movie with lots of impalements, Nam flashbacks, and grisly surprises. The year (1969) is represented by references to *Rosemary's Baby*, Manson, and the death of Karloff. The 16mm feature was made near (and shown theatrically only in) Detroit. Bruce Campbell also worked on the script. Becker later made *Lunatics* starring Ted Raimi (who also acts here).

A THOUSAND PLEASURES

(SW, 1968) **D/P:** "Julian Marsh"/Michael Findlay **P/A/C:** "Anna Riva"/Roberta Findlay

Here's proof that the Manhattan-based Findlays made the most twisted softcore adult movies of them all. It's hard to believe this was released. Two guys with a body in the trunk of their station wagon pick up two women then go home with them. The women drug them, ridicule them, and have sex with them while a man with a goatee watches. One guy says, "I had the feeling that I was going to be smothered by all that flesh" and calls one woman "Boobarella." The women are part-time lesbians who want a child by artificial insemination but meanwhile they have "Baby," a naked (adult) blonde in a playpen who masturbates with a candle. One woman breast-feeds her while the other one whips her. The b/w movie with full nudity has ridiculous narration and classical music.

THRASHIN'

(AIP, 1986) **D:** David Winters **S:** Paul Brown **P:** Alan Sachs

Skateboard gangs fight each other. It was one of the first releases from AIP Video, formed by Winters and David A. Prior. Winters had been a dancer in *West Side Story* (which is where this story was copied from). Josh Brolin stars with Sherilyn Fenn, Pamela Gidley, and Chuck McCann.

THREADS

(New World, 1984) **D/P:** Mick Jackson **S:** Barry Hines   UK/Australia

After *The Day After, Testament,* and *Special Bulletin* in the USA, the BBC backed this serious postnuke feature. Characters suffer slow, painful deaths in Sheffield. With Karen Meagher, Rita May, and David Brierly. It's 125 minutes long.

THREE BAD SISTERS

(1955) **D:** Gilbert L. Kay **S:** Gerald Dryson **P:** Howard Koch

Kathleen Hughes beats sister Marla English with a whip (!) in part of a plot to gain their father's estate. Sara Shane is the third sister and John Bromfield is the pilot who falls for and marries her. Madge Kennedy is their psycho aunt. From U.A. English returned as *The She Creature*.

THREE CASES OF MURDER

(1954) **D:** Wendy Toye, David Eady, George More O'Ferrall **S/P:** Ian Dalrymple **S:** Donald Wilson, Sidney Carroll **P:** Hugh Perceval   UK

Welsh actor Alan Badel appears in three different murder stories. People enter a painting in a museum in one ghost story called "In the Picture" and a man with amnesia might be a killer in another. The third tale, based on a W. Somerset Maugham story, stars Orson Welles (who sings and dances) as a British Foreign Secretary who has nightmares about a rival (Badel) he has mocked. Andre Morell is a doctor.

THREE DAYS TO A KILL

(HBO, 1991) **D/S/A:** Fred Williamson **S:** Charles Eric Johnson, Steven Iyama

Williamson and a robber out on parole (Bo Svenson) are paired (for the umpteenth time) in this dull feature. Kim Dakour as the ex of Colombian crime boss Henry Silva helps them rescue an ambassador who was kidnapped. Sonny Landham (with 70s Elvis hair) works for Silva. Chuck Connors and Van Johnson, playing Navy brass, sit in a car and talk, but I'll bet their scenes were shot at different times. With chases, exploding cars, strippers, and an obese black hooker for comic relief. From 21st Century.

THREE DIMENSIONS OF GRETA

(1972) **D/P:** Peter Walker **S:** Murray Smith UK (*The Four Dimensions of Greta*)

Four 3-D segments make up this sex comedy. With Tristan Rogers, Karen Boyes, and Robert Askwith (also in the director's *Cool It Carol*). Dimension released it in America. Walker made the part-3-D *Flesh and Blood Show* next.

THREE FANTASTIC SUPERMEN

(VSOM, 1967) **D/S:** Frank Kramer **S:** Marcello Coscia Italy/W. Germany (*Die Drei Supermanner Raumen Auf*)

Tony Kendall, Brad Harris, and Nick Jordan wear bulletproof suits as they battle a mad scientist, spies, and assassins. The adventure features martial arts fighting. It was followed by *Three Supermen in the Jungle* (also with Kendall and Harris) and *Three Supermen Against the Orient* (1973) with Lo Lieh and Shih Szu as two of the costumed superheroes.

3:15—THE MOMENT OF TRUTH

(1984) **D:** Larry Gross **S:** Sam Bernard, Michael Jacobs **P:** Dennis Brody, Robert Kenner

Teen school gangs fight each other. Adam Baldwin and Deborah Foreman star with Ed Lauter, Rene Auberjonois, and Mario Van Peebles. Wings Hauser and his wife play Foreman's parents.

THREE IN THE ATTIC

(1968) **S/P:** Richard Wilson **S:** Stephen Yafa

This R-rated comedy was one of AIP's top-grossing releases. *Wild in the Streets* star Christopher Jones is Paxton Quigley. After fooling around with and lying to three girls at once, they keep him captive in an attic then try to wear him out with sex for punishment. Yvette Mimieux, Judy Pace, and Maggie Thrett costar. With John Beck and Richard Derr. The rare soundtrack was on Sidewalk and features Chad Stuart and Jeremy Clyde. It was filmed in North Carolina. A "sequel," *Three in the Cellar,* followed.

THREE IN THE CELLAR

(HBO, 1970) **D/S:** Theodore J. Flicker **P:** Samuel Z. Arkoff, James H. Nicholson   (*Up in the Cellar*)

A poet (Wes Stern) plans to kill himself after losing a scholarship. Instead, for revenge he seduces the wife, mistress, and secretary of the college president (Larry Hagman). With Joan Collins, Judy Pace (also in *Three in the Attic*) and folksinger Hamilton Camp. It was made by the director of *The President's Analyst* and was retitled by AIP. Two soundtracks were issued by AIP records, one under each title. Filmed in New Mexico.

THREE KINDS OF HEAT

(Warner, 1987) **D/S:** Leslie Stevens **P:** Michael J. Kagan   (*Fireworks*)

Robert Ginty, Victoria Barrett, and Shakti star as Interpol kung fu fighters in New York City. They fight the evil Oriental Black Lion organization. The Cannon release was filmed in London and was directed by the producer of *The Outer Limits.*

THE THREE MUSKETEERS

(Disney, 1993) **D:** Stephen Herek **S:** David Loughery **P:** Joe Roth, Roger Birnbaum

In the tradition of the *Young Guns* movies and *Mobsters,* this is a teen-cast version of an overfamiliar story. Kiefer Sutherland, Charlie Sheen, Oliver Platt (as the comic Porthos), and Chris O'Donnell star. With Rebecca De Mornay as Milady, Tim Curry as Cardinal Richelieu, Michael Wincott as the evil count with an eye patch, Gabrielle Anwar as the queen, and Julie Delpy. It was filmed in Austria and was cut for a PG rating. The score is by Michael Kamen. By the director of *Bill and Ted.* Earlier versions are from 1916 (Video Yesteryear), 1921 (Grapevine) with Douglas Fairbanks, 1935 (RKO) with Walter Abel, 1939 (Fox) with Don Ameche and the Ritz Brothers, and 1948 (MGM) with Gene Kelly. See also *Return of the Musketeers.*

THREE O'CLOCK HIGH

(Lorimar, 1987) **D:** Phil Joanou **S:** Richard Christian Matheson, Thomas Szollosi **P:** David E. Vogel

Casey Siemaszko stars as a student journalist with many problems. He's challenged to fight a large and dangerous bully (Richard Tyson) at three in the schoolyard. With Anne Ryan, Jeffrey Tambor, and John P. Ryan. It features fancy camera work and a Tangerine Dream soundtrack.

THREE STOPS TO MURDER

(Sinister, 1953) **D:** Terence Fisher **S:** Jan Reed **P:** Michael Carreras   UK (*Blood Orange*)

Tom Conway stars in a mystery with Mila Parely and Naomi Chance. Astor released the Hammer film in America.

THREE THE HARD WAY

(Xenon, 1974) **D:** Gordon Parks Jr. **S:** Eric Bercovici, Jerry Ludwig **P:** Harry Bersen

In one of the most outrageous black action movies, an LA record promoter (Jim Brown) teams with his Chicago friend (Fred Williamson) and a Manhattan karate expert called Mr. Keyes (Jim Kelly). They have to stop a neo-Nazi madman (Jay Robinson) from putting a serum in America's water systems that kills only black people. Three black beauties wearing only black leather pants help by torturing bad guys expecting a good time. The Allied Artists hit was by the director of *Superfly.* With Sheila Frazier (from the *Superfly* movies), Alex Rocco, Corbin Bernsen, Irene Tsu, Roberta Collins, and Jeanne Bell. The (post–Curtis Mayfield) Impressions were on the Curtom soundtrack (look for a copy) and appear in the film. The three leads were teamed again in *Take a Hard Ride* (1975) and *One Down Two To Go* (1982).

THREE TOUGH GUYS

(1974) **D:** Duccio Tessari **S:** Luciano Vincenzoni, Nicola Badalucco **P:** Dino De Laurentiis   US/Italy

An ex-cop (Isaac Hayes) and an ex-con priest (Lino Ventura) are after killer Joe Snake (Fred Williamson) in Chicago. It was a rare bad guy role for Williamson. With Paula Kelly, William Berger, and Juliano Salce. Hayes, who was acting for the first time, also provided the soundtrack (released on Enterprise as just *Tough Guys*). From Paramount.

THRILLED TO DEATH

(Republic, 1988) **D/P:** Chuck Vincent **S:** Craig Horall

A mystery writer and his wife (Blake Bahner and Krista Lane) become victims of a swinger couple (Christine Moore and Rick Savage). Drugs, sex, and murder are involved. With Christina Veronica, Sheri St. Claire, and Jacqueline Lorians. The stars of the R-rated movie are mostly porn regulars, and Gloria Leonard and Al Goldstein play themselves.

THRILLER

(MCA series, 1960–62)

This is an underrated TV show that scared me a lot as a kid. 6 volumes of episodes were released in 1994, including 3 starring host Boris Karloff: "Incredible Dr. Markesan," directed by Robert Florey, "The Predication," directed by John Brahm, and "The Premature Burial," directed by Douglas Heyes. The others are "Grim Reaper" with William Shatner, "Terror in Teakwood" with Guy Rolph and Hazel Court, and "Masquerade," a comic tale with Tom Poston and John Carradine. Available as a 3-disc box set with all 6. 67 episodes of the NBC series were produced. The theme music is by Jerry Goldsmith.

THE THRILL KILLERS

(Sinister, 1965) **D/S/A:** Ray Dennis Steckler **S:** Gene Pollack **P:** George J. Morgan   (*Monsters Are Loose*)

I love Steckler's *Incredibly Strange Creatures . . .* (1964), but in some ways this b/w followup is even better. It definitely exists in its own twisted reality but "the events are true." Mort Click ("Cash Flagg," a.k.a. director Steckler) is a serial killer who says "People ain't no good!" Meanwhile three psychos (Herb Robbins, Gary Kent, and Keith O'Brien) escape from the loony bin. Characters are shot and decapitated. Liz (Liz Renay, later a stripper, author, and cult star) is an actress turned artist whose husband ("Brick Bardo," a.k.a. rockabilly singer Ron Haydock) is a broke dreamer. With Carolyn Brandt, Atlas King, and Titus Moody. Morgan (the producer) and Arch Hall Sr. play themselves at a party. At least some of this was shot as early as 1963 (note the *Cleopatra* sign). The tape includes the amazing full-color introduction in which the Amazing Ormond hypnotizes us with a swirling disc ("You will actually seem to hallucinate!"). At some screenings ushers disguised as the killers would run through the theater with cardboard axes. Robbins, Kent, and Moody all went on to make their own movies.

THRONE OF BLOOD

(Voyager, 1957) **D/S/P:** Akira Kurosawa **S:** Hideo Oguni, Shinobu Hashimoto   Japan

After Orson Welles and before Roman Polanski made their versions of Shakespeare's *Macbeth,* Kurosawa turned it into a classic samurai movie. An impressive full-size castle was created for the film. Toshiro Mifune stars. Available subtitled and on laserdisc.

THRONE OF FIRE

(1982) **D:** Franco Prosperi **S:** Nino Marino **P:** Ettore Spagnuolo   Italy

Sabrina Siani, who was in a half-dozen similar ridiculous features made the same year, is a princess. Peter McCoy (real name: Pietro Torrisi) is the hero Siegfried, and Harrison Muller (*2020 Texas Gladiators*) is Belial (and his son).

THROUGH THE MAGIC PYRAMID

(1981) **D/P:** Ron Howard **S:** Rance Howard, Herbert J. Wright   (*Tut and Tuttle*)

A magic toy pyramid transports a boy to ancient Egypt where he helps out young King Tut. Ron Howard's actor dad Rance helped out with this kid fantasy pilot film, originally aired on NBC in two parts. With Hans Conried, Vic Tayback, Jo Ann Worley, and Elaine Giftos (from Ron's New World days).

THUMB TRIPPING

(VSOM, 1970) **D:** Quentin Masters **S:** Don Mitchell **P:** Irwin Winkler, Robert Chartoff

Young Meg Foster and Michael Burns (*That Cold Day in the Park*) encounter various characters on their aimless way while hitchhiking together in California. It's one of those counterculture movies nobody went to see. A (brief) high point is when a laughing Bruce Dern with a switchblade threatens to turn the movie into *Last House on the Left.* Another is when Marianna Hill, as a wild and drunken sexy blond white-trash wife, runs into a bar in her bikini and dances on the bar. Joyce Van Patten is an obnoxious mom, and a trucker (Mike Conrad) pays Meg for sex. Foster and Hill both have topless scenes. The music by the Friends of Distinction is pretty sappy. From Avco Embassy and the producers of the *Rocky* movies.

THUNDER ALLEY

(1985) **D/S:** J. S. Cardone **P:** William R. Ewing

Scott McGinnis leads a young rock band. They start to make it but he gets hooked on drugs. With Jill Schoelen, Leif Garrett as the singer, and Clancy Brown as Weasel. From Cannon.

THUNDER AND LIGHTNING

(Key, 1977) **D:** Corey Allen **S:** William Hjortsberg **P:** Roger Corman

David Carradine stars as a bootleg liquor hauler in this modern *Thunder Road*–type movie filled with car crashes. Kate Jackson (on *Charlie's Angels* at the time) costars. With Roger C. Carmel, Sterling Holloway, and Charles Napier as Jim Bob. Lewis Teague was second unit director of the PG Fox release.

THUNDERBIRDS ARE GO (1966) and THUNDERBIRD 6 (1968)

(MGM) **D:** Barry Lane **S:** Gerry Anderson **S/P:** Sylvia Anderson   UK

Both of these Supermarionation theatrical features are available letterboxed on a double laserdisc. They were spinoffs from the TV series set in the 21st century. Peter Dyneley (star of *The Manster*) is the voice of International Rescue hero Jeff Tracy, whose sons are all named after American astronauts. Lady Penelope and Brains are the other main characters. In *Thunderbirds Are Go,* puppets of Cliff Richard and the Shadows play in a dream sequence. The tapes *Thunderbirds in Outer Space* and *Thunderbirds: Countdown to Disaster* are re-edited from the show. 32 of the 50-minute TV episodes are available in Japan on disc. Fox TV showed severely cut versions of the TV epsiodes in 1994.

THUNDER COUNTY

(Prism, 1974) **D/A:** Chris Robinson **P:** K. Gordon Murray   (*Women's Prison Escape; Convict Women; Swamp Fever; Cell Block Girls*)

This starts out as a prison movie (complete with a lesbian warden), but four women escape and end up in the swamp with the filthy lecherous Beau and his pet gator. Meanwhile an undercover agent (Robinson, the star of *Stanley*) and a three-man heroin smuggling gang led by Ted "Lurch" Cassidy show up after spending a lot of time in an air boat. Cassidy is pretty cool in a serious role as Cambini, a killer always in shades. Carol Lawson and "Onya Mark" (the then-wife of Alan Ormsby) costar. Top billed Mickey Rooney shows up for a few minutes as a slob store owner. Joseph Brenner released the PG-rated feature from Florida. It's a lot like Corman's *Swamp Women.*

THUNDERCRACK!

(VSOM, 1975) **D/C/E:** Curt McDowell **S/A:** George Kuchar **P:** John Thomas, Charles Thomas

In this long (150-minute) b/w underground sex/horror comedy, characters talk to themselves and argue with each other in an old dark house during a storm. They also have sex (straight, gay, and solo) which is hardcore, making this a unique curiosity item if nothing else. Also with many flashbacks, a gorilla, overdone theatrical makeup, and enough thunder, lightning, and rain for five other movies. Marlon Eaton stars with Melinda McDowell and George Kuchar (from the Bronx), a well-known underground filmmaker himself. *Thundercrack!* had some limited success as a midnight movie.

THUNDER IN PARADISE

(Vidmark, 1993) **D:** Douglas Schwartz **S:** Michael Berk **P:** Paul Cajero, James Pergola

This PG-13 syndicated TV pilot feature stars Hulk Hogan as a daredevil with a special boat in Florida. He and Chris Lemmon are commandos for hire. With series regular Carol Alt plus Patrick Macnee, Felicity Waterman, Sam Jones, Charlotte Rae, and Robin Weisman. Hogan (real name: Terry Bollea) was in the PG *Mr. Nanny* the same year. *Thunder in Paradise II* and *III* followed (also from Vidmark, 1995) with the same main cast.

THUNDER ISLAND

(1963) **D/P:** Jack Leewood **S:** Jack Nicholson, Don Devlin

Nicholson wrote his first screenplay for this 65-minute b/w 20th Century Cinemascope release filmed in Puerto Rico the same year he was in the Roger Corman movies *The Raven* and *The Terror.* Gene Nelson stars as a sadistic mercenary (and health food nut) in South America. The feature got some good reviews which praised the complex and cynical political plot elements. With Fay Spain (also in *Flight to Fury* with Nicholson) and Brian Kelly.

THUNDER MOUNTAIN: *See* SHADOW OF THE CHIKIRA

THUNDER RUN

(Media, 1985) **D:** Gary Hudson **S:** Charles Davis, Carol Heyer **P:** Carol Lynch   Australia

A US government representative (John Ireland) asks an old army buddy (Forrest Tucker) to drive plutonium through the Arizona desert in a heavily armed supertruck. Tucker takes his grandson along and Palestinian terrorists attack. With Cheryl Lynn, Jill Whitlow, and Elizabeth Kaitan. Rated PG-13.

THUNDER WARRIOR

(TWE, 1983) **D/S/P:** "Larry Ludman"/Fabrizio De Angelis **S:** David Parker Jr.   Italy (*Thunder*)

Mark Gregory stars as an Indian who becomes a Rambo-type warrior fighting the white men who cheated his people. Bo Svenson is the sheriff. It was filmed in Arizona.

THUNDER WARRIOR II

(TWE, 1987) **D:** David Parker Jr. **D/S/P:** "Larry Ludman"/Fabrizio De Angelis

Mark Gregory returns, is pardoned from jail, and teams up with sheriff Svenson to battle drug traffickers in Monument Valley. A part III followed (also on TWE) also with Gregory but not Svenson.

THE TICKET OF LEAVE MAN

(Sinister, 1937) **D/P:** George King **S:** H. F. Matby, A. R. Rawlinson   UK

British horror star Tod Slaughter is in this adaptation of a Victorian play that had introduced the first private eye (named Hawkshaw). Slaughter is "Tiger" Dalton, who helps reformed ex-cons but really heads a crime sydicate.

TICKET TO HEAVEN

(MGM/UA, 1981) **D/S:** Ralph L. Thomas **S:** Anne Cameron **P:** Vivienne Leesbosh   Canada

Canadian Nick Mancuso loses his girlfriend, so he goes to San Francisco and is seduced by Meg Foster. Before he realizes what he's gotten into, he's a member of the Moonie-like "Heavenly Children" cult. They have to eat treated vegetarian food and chant a lot. His best friend (Saul Rubinek) arrives to try and deprogram him. Based on the book *Moonwebs.* With Kim Cattrall and Jennifer Dale. The effective and scary feature was made before the better known *Split Image* (1982).

TICKS

(Republic, 1993) **D:** Toney Randel **S:** Brent V. Friedman **P:** Jack F. Murphy   (*Infested*)

Tyler (Seth Green) is sent to a camp for troubled kids. Fertilizers used by redneck marijuana farmers cause blood-sucking ticks. Their bite numbs the victim and causes hallucinations. They also enter bodies and cause mutations. With Rosalind Allen, Ami Dolenz as a rich bitch, Alfonso Ribeiro (from *The Fresh Prince of Bel Air* series), and Peter (*Bosom Buddies*) Scolari. Clint Howard is a pot grower who mutates, and his father Rance Howard plays the sheriff. Doug Beswick created the (mechanical and stop-motion) bug FX and Brian Yuzna was the executive producer. It was planned for a theatrical release, but was (wisely) sent direct to video. Not to be confused with similar movies (*Skeeter* and *Mosquito*) from around the same time.

TIDES OF WAR

(Arrow, 1994) **D:** Neil Rossati **S/A:** David Soul **S:** Andrej Karakowski

David Soul stars as a German naval officer on a remote British island who turns against the Nazis during WWII. With Yvette Heyden as the British love interest, Bo Svenson as an SS officer, and guest star Ernest Borgnine as a missionary doctor.

TIGER BAY

(Paramount, 1959) **D:** J. Lee Thompson **S:** John Hawkesworth, Shelly Smith   UK

12-year-old Hayley Mills is excellent in her film debut as Gillie, a lonely orphan tomboy who sings in a church choir. She witnesses a murder of passion and lies to the police so she can keep the gun she found. She also likes the Polish seaman (Horst Buchholz) who has killed his girlfriend (Yvonne Mitchell). John Mills is the police chief.

TIGER CLAWS

(MCA, 1991) **D:** Kelly Makin **S:** J. Stephen Maunder **P/A:** Jalal Merhi   Canada

High-kicking Cynthia Rothrock and Jalal Merhi star as martial-arts-fighing New York cops in Chinatown. They're after the "Death Dealer" (Bolo Yeung), who leaves claw marks on kung fu masters. The DEG release was shot in Toronto.

TIGER FANGS

(Sinister, 1943) **D:** Sam Newfield
S: Arthur St. Claire **P:** Arthur Schwartz

Real-life big-game hunter Frank Buck goes to Brazil to fight Nazis involved in the rubber industry. The PRC WWII-theme feature runs 59 minutes and was one of 23 (!) 1943 features directed by Newfield.

TIGER MAN

(1978) **D/S:** "Matt Cimber"/Matteo Ottaviano **P:** George Roberts   (*Fist*)

A Bruce Lee fan battles Tong gangsters. The 3-D feature was filmed in "the far East" and Hollywood. Terrence Young shot additional scenes. Cecil Peoples and Don Wong star. Gene Corman was an executive producer.

THE TIGERWOMAN: *See* NYOKA

TIGERS IN LIPSTICK

(Monterey, 1978) **D:** Luigi Zampa **S:** Tonino Guerra, Georgio Salvioni   Italy (*Letti Selvaggi; Wild Beds*)

An impressive lineup of four sexy European stars (Ursula Andress, Laura Antonelli, Sylvia Kristel, and Monica Vitti) act in seven short comedy segments about aggressive women. With Roberto Benigni.

TIGHTROPE

(Warner, 1984) **D/S:** Richard Tuggle
P/A: Clint Eastwood

Clint Eastwood stars as a New Orleans cop raising his two daughters alone. He searches for a psycho who kills prostitutes, the same ones he goes to. In this dark and very different Eastwood movie, he could be the killer himself (maybe it should have been billed with *Angel Heart*). Genevieve Bujold costars with Dan Hedaya, Jamie Rose, Randi Brooks, and Alison Eastwood. Local director Joy N. Houck Jr. plays a massage parlor owner.

THE TIGRESS: *See* ILSA, TIGRESS OF SIBERIA

THE TIGRESS

(Vidmark, 1992) **D/S:** Karin Howard
P: Dieter Geissler   Germany

Valentina Vargas stars as a dancer in 1920s Berlin who schemes with an American (James Remar) to cheat a Texas oilman (George Peppard). With Hannes Jaenicke as the gangster boyfriend, Ferdinand Mayne as an Austrian count, and Belinda Mayne. Vargas has nude scenes in the R or unrated release, based on a novel by Walter Serner.

TIJUANA STORY

(1957) **D:** Leslie Kardos **S:** Lou Morheim **P:** Sam Katzman

Rudolfo Acosta and James Darren star in a movie about gangs, drug dealing, and addiction in Tijuana. With Jean Willes, George E. Stone, and Robert Blake. The Columbia release was filmed on location.

TIL DAWN DO US PART = STRAIGHT ON TILL MORNING

TIL DEATH DO US PART

(Vestron, 1972) **D/S:** Timothy Bond **S:** Peter Jobin **P:** James Shavik, Lawrence Hertzog   Canada

Dr. Sigmund Freed (director Claude Jutra) invites feuding couples to his booby trapped estate. The husbands die one by one. James Keach stars in the made-for-TV movie. Not to be confused with *Till Death* (1978), about resurrecting a dead woman.

TIL DEATH DO US PART (1974) = THE BLOOD SPATTERED BRIDE

TIL DEATH DO US PART

(Triboro, 1991) **D:** Yves Simoneau **S:** Philip Rosenberg

In 1966 a devious ex-cop (Treat Williams) marries then kills women to get their insurance money. Arliss Howard plays real-life LA D.A. Vincent Bugli-

Genevieve Bujold in *Tightrope*.

osi (who later prosecuted Charles Manson). The topnotch TV movie is based on Bugliosi's book. With Jennifer Runyon, Embeth Davidtz, Rebecca Jenkins, and John Schuck. The video release adds a topless scene.

TIL DEATH DO US SCARE

(1982) **D:** Lau Kar-Wing **S:** Raymond Wong, Ko Chi-Sum **P:** Mai Jia, Dean Shek
Hong Kong (*Xiaosheng Papa*)

It's a horror comedy with three ghosts who play cupids for the woman they were all married to in life. Tom Savini was flown over to provide some gore FX. Alan Tam stars.

TILT

(Continental, 1979) **D/S/P:** Rudy Durand
S: Donald Cammell

A country rock singer (Ken Marshall) cons a 14-year-old pinball wiz (Brooke Shields) and they travel cross country to challenge the pinball champion (Charles Durning). With Johnny Crawford, Geoffrey Lewis, Gregory Walcott, and Fred Ward. A soundtrack for the flop PG-rated Warner feature was issued on ABC. Shields starred in three movies released in 1979.

THE TIMBER TRAPS

(1975) **D:** Tay Garnett
D/S: Chuck D. Keen   (*The Big Push*)

A major oldtimers cast was assembled for this obscure Howco adventure filmed in Alaska. With Leon Ames, Joseph Cotten, Cesar Romero, Rosey Grier, Stanley Clemens, and Claude Akins.

TIM BURTON'S THE NIGHTMARE BEFORE CHRISTMAS

(Touchstone, 1993) **D:** Henry Selick
S: Caroline Thompson **P:** Tim Burton

The idea of a feature-length stop-motion Christmas musical sounded like torture to me, but I ended up liking this a lot. The PG-rated hit resembles a $22 million version of George Pal's old Puppetoons and it's more of an *Addams Family*–influenced horror fantasy than a Christmas movie. Released in theaters in time for Halloween, it was still running during Christmas. Jack Skellington from Halloweentown visits Christmastown. Chris Sarandon provides the voice and Danny Elfman (who wrote the score) is the singing voice. Also with the voices of Catherine O'Hara, William Hickey (the evil scientist), Glen Shadix (the mayor), and Paul Reubens. It was based on a poem Burton wrote while working for Disney (Touchstone) in the early 80s. The running time is a sensible 75 minutes. A deluxe laser disc box set is available with commentary, a making-of documentary, deleted scenes, a book, plus shorts by Burton (*Frankenweenie* and *Vincent*) and director Selick.

TIME BOMB

(1984) **D:** Paul Krasny **S:** Westbrook
Claridge **P:** Barry Weitz

A female terrorist (Morgan Fairchild) and a group of hijackers try to capture a cargo of plutonium for bomb making. Billy Dee Williams, Joseph Bottoms, and Merlin Olsen costar in the NBC feature.

TIMEBOMB

(MGM, 1990) **D/S:** Avi Nesher
P: Raffaella De Laurentiis   (*Nameless*)

Michael Biehn stars as Eddie, a watchmaker who is also a programmed killer. Richard Jordan, who was head of an experimental program during the war, tries to terminate him by sending a team of assassins. With Patsy Kensit as a psychiatrist on the run with Eddie, Raymond St. Jacques and Robert Culp as cops, Tracy Scoggins, Billy Blanks, and Ray Mancini. Eddie has nightmares and frequent (near-X) sex dreams featuring Kate Mitchell. There's also a shoot-out in an old LA porno theater. A huge, unused, dusty research lab in Arizona still works perfectly, and plot holes are common. The director is an Israeli army war vet, who also made *She* (1982).

TIME BURST—THE FINAL ALLIANCE

(AIP, 1989) **D/S/P:** Peter Yuval **S:** Michael Bogert

Characters are after ancient Japanese tablets that contain the secret of immortality. Samurai battles take place in a California forest and a 300-year-old man (Scott David King) has amnesia. With Michiko and Jay Richardson.

TIME COP

(MCA, 1994) **D/C:** Peter Hyams **S:** Mark Verheiden
P: Moshe Damant, Robert Tapert, Sam Raimi

Criminals go through time to plunder the past (during the Civil War and the Depression). Max Walker (Jean-Claude Van Damme) is a special government agent who pursues the criminals. Van Damme gets to play his character in two time periods (2004 and 1994) and pursues corrupt senator Ron Silver (who also confronts himself). Mia Sara is the wife who is is killed in 1994, and Gloria Reuben is Max's partner. Also with Bruce McGill. Based on a Dark Horse comic, it was filmed in Vancouver. The end theme is a remake of the Outsiders' "Time Won't Let Me." It was Van Damme's biggest hit to date and better than you might expect.

A TIME FOR KILLING

(1967) **D:** Phil Karlson **D/P:** Roger Corman
S: Halsted Welles **P:** Harry Brown
(*The Long Ride Home*)

Roger Corman took over direction of this Civil War drama even though Karlson received the credit. Glenn Ford stars as a Union captain, and George Hamilton is a Confederate major who kidnaps his wife. Inger Stevens (just after the run of her *Farmer's Daughter* series) is the wife. With Paul Peterson (from *The Donna Reed Show*), Max Baer, Timothy Carey (as Billy Cat), Kenneth Tobey, Dick Miller, Harry Dean Stanton, and a young Harrison Ford. Monte Hellman was the editor and Daniel

Haller was the art director. This was made the same year as Corman's *The Trip* and *The St. Valentine's Day Massacre*.

THE TIME GUARDIAN

(New Line, 1987) **D/S:** Brian Hannant
S: John Baxter **P:** Norman Wilkinson   Australia

Tom Burlinson stars as the 24th-century warrior Time Guardian in a movie that copies *Star Wars* and *Road Warrior*. He travels in a spaceship to the present-day Australian outback with Carrie Fisher. Also with Nikki Coghill, Dean Stockwell as the "boss," and some killer cyborgs.

TIME OF THE APES

(Celebrity, 1975) **D:** Atsuo Okunaka,
Kiyo Sumi Fukazawa   Japan (*Saru No Gudan*)

Many cable viewers saw this on *Mystery Science Theater 3000*. It's a hilarious feature version of a cheap-looking Japanese TV series that copied the Planet of the Apes movies. Some kids trapped in an earthquake wake up in the future where humans are run by apes. The masks and makeup are the worst.

TIMERIDER: THE ADVENTURES OF LYLE SWAN

(Pacific Arts, 1983) **D/S/A:** William Dear
S/M: Michael Nesmith **P:** Harry Gittes

Mike Nesmith wrote the script and the music and was executive producer of this science fiction comedy biker western. A bike racer (Fred Ward) is accidentally zapped back to 1877. With Belinda Bauer, Peter Coyote, Tracy Walter, Ed Lauter, L. Q. Jones, Richard Masur, and the voice of Nick Nolte. Dear also directed Nesmith's *Elephant Parts* video tape and *Northville Cemetery Massacre* (which had Nesmith music).

TIME RUNNER

(New Line, 1992) **D/S:** Michael Mazo **S/P:** John A. Curtis **S:** Chris Hyde **P:** Lloyd Simandl

Mark Hamill (fire your agent!) goes back in time 30 years in a space pod and teams up with a scientist (Rae Dawn Chong) for car chases and shoot-outs in present-day Washington State as an evil guy with white hair tries to kill him. Brion James is the President of the future. The dull movie borrows several ideas from *The Terminator*. It was shot in Vancouver and took four screenwriters to create. The screener has an ad for *The Player* in the middle (!) of the tape.

TIME SLIP

(VSOM, 1981) **D:** Kosei Saito **S:** Toshida Kaneda
P: Haruki Kadokawa   Japan (*Sengoku Jietal*)

Sonny Chiba leads a defense force that's magically time warped back to feudal times. An ancient warrior shows up in modern times too. It's from the Toei company. Chiba was also in the sci-fi movies *Message from Space* (1978) and *Virus* (1980).

TIMES SQUARE

(HBO, 1980) **D:** Alan Moyle
S: Jacob Brackman **P:** Robert Stigwood

A homeless punk fan (Robin Johnson) and a runaway rich girl (Trini Alvarado) run around a fantasy Times Square. One becomes a stripper and forms a band called the Sleaze Sisters. They play on top of the marquee of the Times Square theater on 42nd St., an unlikely but memorable sight. With Elizabeth Pena, Tim Curry, and David Johansen. RSO released a double new-wave hits soundtrack that features the Ramones, Patti Smith, Roxy Music, Lou Reed, and others.

TIMESTALKERS

(Fries, 1987) **D:** Michael Schultz
S: Brian Clemens, Ray Brown

Scientists from the year 2586 travel back to the Old West. At least they did it before *Back to the Future Part III*. Klaus Kinski is Dr. Joseph Cole. With William Devane, Lauren Hutton, Forrest Tucker (in his last role), Tracey Walter, and John Considine. A CBS-TV movie.

A TIME TO DIE

(Media, 1979) **D/S:** "Matt Cimber"/Matteo
Ottaviano **S:** John Goff, William Russell
P: Charles Lee   (*Seven Graves for Rogan*)

Associate producer/star Edward Albert Jr. is an American spy who goes after ex-Nazis. He wants to avenge the wartime death of his wife. It's based on a book by Mario Puzo and was filmed in Europe. With Rex Harrison (guest villain), Rod Taylor, and Raf Vallone. Ennio Morricone provided "additional" music. Cimber went on to make Pia Zadora movies.

A TIME TO DIE

(PM, 1992) **D:** Charles Kanganis **P:** Joseph
Merhi, Richard Pepin, Charla Driver

Traci Lords stars as a divorced photographer mom. Her ex-husband got the kid and she's on probation after being set up by a cop. Now she has incriminating negatives of that same drug-snorting psycho cop killing somebody and he's after her and anybody else in the way. Jeff Conaway is another cop and Richard Roundtree is her parole officer. It has too many slow-motion scenes but some good plot twists and is one of Lords's best. She shows a lot of different emotions and is good in a serious role (unlike, say, Madonna).

A TIME TO LOVE AND A TIME TO DIE

(Kartes, 1958) **S:** Douglas Sirk
S: Orin Jannings **P:** Robert Arthur

John Gavin stars in a romantic anti-war WWII story about a German soldier on furlough who marries Liselotte Pulver, then returns to the Russian front. With Jock Mahoney, Keenan Wynn, Thayer David, Jim Hutton (his debut), and Klaus Kinski. The long (133-minute) Universal Cinemascope and Eastmancolor release was based on a novel by Erich Maria Remarque.

TIME TROOPERS

(Prism, 1986) **D:** L. E. Neiman **S:** James
Wagner, James Becket   Australia

Androids control human breeding in the future. Albert Fortrell and Hannelore Eisner star. The flashback-filled story copies *Logan's Run*.

TIME TRACKERS
(MGM, 1989) **D/S:** Howard R. Cohen
P: Roger Corman

Scientists from the year 2033 come back to the present to stop an evil scientist named Zandor (Lee Bergere) from changing history. They also travel to medieval England. With Ned Beatty as a cop, Wil Shriner, Kathleen Beller, Robert Cornthwaite (from *The Thing*), and Alex Hyde-White. The PG-rated comedy is from Concorde.

TIME WALKER
(Charter, 1982) **D:** Tom Kennedy **S:** Karen Levitt, Tom Friedman **P:** Dimitri Villard, Jason Williams

An alien mummy with the touch of death appears in California after jewels are stolen from the sarcophagus. With Ben Murphy, Nina Axelrod, James Karen, Shari Belafonte-Harper, Melissa Prophet, Greta Blackburn, and Jason Williams. Rated PG and from New World.

TIME WARP = JOURNEY TO THE CENTER OF TIME

TIN MAN
(1983) **D/P:** John G. Thomas
S: Bishop Holiday

A deaf and dumb auto mechanic (Timothy Bottoms) invents a computer that speaks and hears for him. With John Phillip Law and Troy Donahue.

THE TITAN FIEND: *See* CREATURE

T.N.T. JACKSON
(Charter, 1974) **D/P:** Cirio H. Santiago
S/A: Dick Miller, Ken Metcalf   Philippines

"She'll Put You in Traction" said the New World ads. Because her brother is missing, T.N.T. Jackson from Harlem (beautiful Jeanne Bell from *Playboy*) goes undercover as a hooker in Hong Kong, and battles the Chinese Mafia. With a topless kung fu fight. Pat Anderson and Stan Shaw costar. Metcalf, who cowrote the screenplay and was the martial arts fight coordinator, had been in *The Beast of the Yellow Night*, *The Twilight People*, and *The Womanhunt*. Santiago's *Firecracker* (1981) and *Angel Fist* (1992) reused the same story.

TO ALL A GOODNIGHT
(Media, 1980) **D/A:** David Hess
S: Alex Rebar **P:** Jay Rasumy

A slasher in a Santa suit kills at a female sorority house two years after a pledge was accidentally killed. Characters are decapitated and there's a *Psycho* shower scene. With Jennifer Runyon and Buck West. The writer starred in *The Incredible Melting Man* and the director was in *Last House on the Left*.

TO BE THE BEST
(PM, 1993) **D/P:** Joseph Merhi
S: Michael January **P:** Richard Pepin

Michael Worth stars as an American kickboxer being blackmailed in a movie that copies *Best of the Best*. Alex Cord is the Las Vegas gambler who rigs the world championship. With Martin Kove as the father, Brittney Powell, and Stephen Vincent Leigh.

TOBRUK
(1967) **D:** Arthur Hiller **S/A:** Leo V. Gordon
P: Gene Corman

Rock Hudson stars as a British officer in a WWII adventure set in North Africa (but filmed in Arizona). George Peppard leads a group of Palestinian Jews who pose as Nazi soldiers in part of a plan to defeat Rommel in Libya. With Nigel Green, Guy Stockwell, and Peter Coe. It's one of several movies written by Gordon, also an actor in Roger Corman movies.

TO CATCH A THIEF
(Paramount, 1955) **D/P:** Alfred Hitchcock
S: John Michael Hayes

Hitchcock made a more romantic feature after *Dial M For Murder* and *Rear Window* (both 1954). It was his third in a row with future Princess of Monaco Grace Kelly and the third with Cary Grant. He's "The Cat," an ex–jewel thief accused of crimes on the Riviera, and she's an American heiress. With John Williams and Jessie Royce Landis. Based on a novel by David Dodge. Hitchcock appears on a bus. Paramount released it the same year that *Alfred Hitchcock Presents* debuted on TV and the first issue of the (still published) *Alfred Hitchcock's Mystery Magazine* was printed. 1955 was the year the director became a star.

THE TODD KILLINGS
(Warner, 1971) **D/P:** Barry Shear **S:** Dennis Murphy, Joel Oliansky   (*A Dangerous Friend*)

Robert F. Lyons is Skipper Todd, a young psycho killer who uses drugs and preys on teenage girls. It's based on a real case and is surprisingly sleazy. With Richard Thomas (just before *The Waltons* series) as a kid from the reformatory, Belinda Montgomery,

Jeanne Bell is *T.N.T. Jackson*.

Barbara Bel Geddes (in her last film) as Todd's mother, Edward Asner, James Broderick, Holly Near, Fay Spain, Gloria Grahame, and Michael Conrad. From National General. Shear also directed *Wild in the Streets*.

DER TODSKING
(1989) **D/S/A:** Jörg Buttgereit
P: Manfred Jelinsky   Germany

Five short vignettes are connected by a man who mails chain letters before he kills himself. Each person who receives a letter is involved in death or murder. Buttgereit appears as a concentration camp victim in a video rented by one of the characters. It was originally to be called *Seven Suicides,* but the producer had two of them cut out. This was made in between the notorious *Nekromantik* films.

TO DIE FOR
(Academy, 1989) **D:** Deran Sarafian
S: Leslie King **P:** Barin Kumar

Brendan Hughes is the immortal young-looking Vlad who buys a "castle" in LA complete with hot tub. He's the good romantic vampire. The bad one (who wears granny sunglasses and smokes little cigars) is jealous and out for revenge. In one scene he's a lumpy-faced monster who breaks the back of a coke snorter and drains his blood. Amanda Wyss becomes a vampire and almost has her head cut off. There's some slow-motion sex, and the two growling vampires fight while floating in the air. A few scenes are botched, but this is a very entertaining modern vampire movie with excellent cinematography. It was also a comic book. The late Duane Jones from *Night of the Living Dead* had a bit part in a real estate office. With Sydney Walsh, Steve Bond, Scott Jacoby, Ava Fabian, and John Buechler FX. The sequel was *Son of Darkness: To Die For II.*

TOGETHER BROTHERS
(1974) **D:** William A. Graham
S: Jack De Witt **P:** Robert L. Rosen

In a variation of "The Boy Who Cried Wolf," five black kids look for the psychotic killer of a popular cop in the ghetto of Galveston, Texas. Ahmad Nurradin stars as a gang leader, with Anthony Wilson as the little kid who saw the murder and was scared speechless. Their search takes them to pool halls and bars and leads to a drag queen protecting the killer. With Glynn Turman and Richard Yniguez. The 20th Century soundtrack by Barry White and his Love Unlimited Orchestra is more famous than the movie.

TO HEX WITH SEX
(1969) **D/S/P:** Simon Nuchtern
S: Arthur Littman

A shy man (Stefan Peters) makes a three-wish deal with a female devil (Paula Shaw) he meets in the boiler room of his apartment building. One of his wishes is to make sex movies. The sex comedy is by Nuchtern, who made other adults-only features and later made *Silent Madness* and *Savage Dawn*.

TO KILL A CLOWN

(Media, 1970) **D/S:** George Bloomfield **P:** Teddy B. Sills

Alan Alda stars as a deranged Nam vet who terrorizes a feuding couple with his killer Dobermans. It's set on a New England island. With Blythe Danner and Heath Lamberts. Alda played several psycho roles before *M*A*S*H* changed his image forever.

TO KILL A STRANGER

(Virgin, 1982) **D:** Juan Lopez Moctezuma **S:** Emerich Oross, Rafael Buñuel **P:** Raul Vale Mexico

In South America, a killer rapist military hero (Donald Pleasence) kills women in a house during a storm. Angela Maria eventually kills him, and she and her husband become victims of the military government. With Aldo Ray and Dean Stockwell.

TOKYO DECADENCE

(Triboro, 1993) **D/S/P:** Ryu Murakami **M:** Ryuichi Sakamoto Japan

A 22-year-old hooker (Miho Nikaido) makes big money and does many strange and degrading things to earn it. She also works at an orphanage for deaf kids. She becomes obsessed with a married client, and an older woman introduces her to opium and heroin. The director of this serious NC-17 feature is a best-selling novelist in Japan.

TO LIVE AND DIE IN L.A.

(Vestron, 1985) **D/S:** William Friedkin **S:** Gerald Petievich **P:** Irving H. Levin

William L. Petersen is a Secret Service man after a ruthless counterfeiter (Willem Dafoe). The movie is very violent and has nudity and a great car chase. It was shot by Robby Muller. With John Pankow, Debra Feuer, John Turturro, Darlanne Fluegel, Dean Stockwell, Steve James, and Robert Downey Jr. The music is by Wang Chung, who were popular for a few months.

TOLLBOOTH

(1994) **D/S:** Salome Brezinger **P:** Steven J. Wolfe

A tollbooth collector (Lenny Von Dohlen) in the Florida Keys thinks that a blonde (Fairuza Balk) who pumps gas would be the perfect woman for him, but she's with a bait salesman (Will Patton). The love triangle movie involves a dysfunctional family and murder. With Louise Fletcher and Seymour Cassell as her parents, James Wilder, and William Katt.

THE TOMB

(TWE, 1986) **D/P:** Fred Olen Ray **S:** Kenneth J. Hall, T. L. Langford **P:** Ronnie Hadar

The Egyptian princess Nefratis (Michelle Bauer) rips out hearts and tears off heads in modern-day

LA. This was filmed very quickly, partially on left-over sets from a TV commercial, and was partially based on an H.P. Lovecraft story. With Cameron Mitchell, John Carradine, Sybil Danning, and Dawn Wildsmith as a lesbian. The scene with Kitten Natividad as a stripper was cut from the TV print, along with the blood and gore. Bauer was also in *Café Flesh*.

TOMBOY

(Vestron, 1985) **D:** Herb Freed **S:** Ben Zelig **P:** Marilyn J. Tenser, Michael D. Castle

Betsy Russell (*Avenging Angel*) stars as a mechanic who becomes a stunt driver. With Kristi Somers, Eric Douglas (a son of Kirk), Cynthia Ann Thompson, and Michelle Bauer. The Crown International release features topless and S&M scenes. By the director of *Haunts* and *Graduation Day*.

TOMB OF THE UNDEAD = GARDEN OF THE DEAD

TOMCAT

(Republic, 1993) **D/S:** Paul Donovan **P:** William Vince, Robert Vince Canada (*Dangerous Desires*)

Scientists operate on the brain of long-haired Richard Grieco using cat genes. He becomes the first of a "new species," can jump from high buildings unharmed, kills people, and seems to be irresistible to the female cast members including Natalie Radford (with very short platinum blond hair) and Brit scientist Maryam D'Abo. The minimal plot feature has no sex scenes, but there's a disco *Swan Lake* rock video scene and a "Feline Sex Club" set. I think it's aimed at the teen-girl following the star once had. Some of the various locations are interesting. It was made in Vancouver by the director of *Defcon 4*.

TOM JONES MEETS LADY GODIVA

(Rhino, 1969) **D/P/A:** "A. C. Stevens"/ Stephen Apostoloff (*Lady Godiva Rides*)

In England, Lady Godiva (Marsha Jordan, not bothering with any accent) is accused of murder, sentenced to hang, and escapes to America on a ship. On board, women lounge around naked and take showers on deck. The nudie movie becomes a western when the exiles become dance hall girls in Tombstone. With mud wrestling, spanking, whipping, and Tootsie O'Hara, a large man in drag who dances and sings. The ship is a toy, the sound is bad, and mike shadows are visible. Forman Shane is Tom Jones and Liz Renay has a small role. Also available on the *Saturday Night Sleazies Vol. II* tape.

THE TOMMYKNOCKERS

(Vidmark, 1993) **D:** John Power **S:** Lawrence D. Cohen **P:** Jayne Bieber, Jane Scott

Stephen King's variation of *Invasion of the Body Snatchers* stars Marg Helgenberger as a writer who discovers a glowing buried monolith in the woods that transforms her and other locals into intelligent zombies with a mission. Her boyfriend, an alco-

holic poet (Jimmy Smits), is the only unaffected person, because of a metal plate in his head. He eventually saves everyone from the aliens in an underground spaceship. The two-part ABC miniseries, based on King's 1987 novel, is too long and makes little sense. With Joanna Cassidy as a sheriff, E. G. Marshall, Traci Lords (!) as the local postmaster, Robert Carradine, Cliff DeYoung, and Allyce Beasley. The "Maine" village was really in New Zealand. The tape runs 125 minutes (it was originally 192).

TOMORROW NEVER COMES

(Unicorn, 1978) **D:** Peter Collinson **S:** David Pursall, Jack Seddon, Sidney Banks **P:** Julian Melzack, Michael Klinger UK/Canada

Stephen McHattie loses his girlfriend (Susan George) and goes on a shooting spree. Oliver Reed is a police lieutenant who returns to his small town and is put in control. With Raymond Burr, John Ireland, Donald Pleasence, and Paul Koslo.

TOMORROW'S CHILDREN

(Video Yesteryear, Sinister, 1934) **D:** Crane Wilbur **P:** Bryan Foy

An exploitation hit about forced sterilization from the 1930s? Yes, and it's still a shocker. A judge orders a young woman to be sterilized because of her family history. A doctor calls the family "a house full of idiots and cripples." The judge eventually backs off because it turns out the woman was adopted! With Diana Sinclair and Sterling Holloway. It's only 55 minutes long. Producer Foy (of the "Seven Little Foys" vaudeville act) went on to produce hits like *House of Wax* and *Women's Prison*.

TONGS: AN AMERICAN NIGHTMARE

(Academy, 1988) **D:** Philip Chan **S:** Stacy Asip **P:** Jimmy Yang

Simon Yam and Tan (just one name) star as refugee brothers in a *Scarface*-type gangster story set in NYC's Chinatown. One brother wants to go to school, the other sells drugs. The original script (which includes references to the Chinese Cultural Revolution and corrupt NYC cops) was by a former member of the Last Poets. Locations include Washington Square Park, where the story stops for a performance artist, and there's a gang fight outside the Essex theater. With subtitles.

TONIGHT FOR SURE

(Video Yesteryear, 1961) **D/S/P:** Francis Ford Coppola

Coppola, then a 22-year-old UCLA film student, made a nudie short called *The Peeper*, inspired by Russ Meyer's *The Immoral Mr. Teas*. He then combined it with a nudie western (filmed by others) and added some more footage that Jack Hill photographed. The resulting 66-minute feature uses flashbacks and hallucinations to justify the mismatched footage. It was first known as *Wide Open Spaces*. Two prudes blow up a burlesque house at the end. With Virginia Gordon (from *Playboy*). The music is by Carmine Coppola. Coppola and Hill also shot new scenes for the nudie feature *Playgirls and the Bellboy*, then made the horror classic *Dementia 13* for Roger Corman.

TONIGHT LET'S ALL MAKE LOVE IN LONDON

(1968) **D/S/P/C/E:** Peter Whitehead   UK

Swinging London in 1967 is the topic of this documentary which contains seven "movements." Allen Ginsberg comments and Pink Floyd plays. The Animals, the Rolling Stones, and the Small Faces are heard. Other celebs in sight are Michael Caine, Vanessa Redgrave, Julie Christie, David Hockney, and Lee Marvin. The rare soundtrack was reissued in the 90s.

TOO HOT TO HANDLE

(GMI, 1959) **D:** Terence Young **S:** Herbert Kretzner **P:** Phil C. Samuel   UK (*Playgirl After Dark*)

Jayne Mansfield got to play sexy but tough characters with brains in her English movies. This one has a great cast and is set in the Pink Flamingo strip club in Soho, where the motif is large cocktail glasses. Leo Genn is owner Johnny Solo with gangster problems, and Christopher Lee (with a pimp mustache) is Novak, his sleazy club manager (and emcee). Midnight Franklin (Jayne) is the star attraction and is in charge of all the other girls. Subplots involve German actor Karlheinz Boehm (just before *Peeping Tom*) as a French (!) writer, an intellectual Austrian stripper (Kai Fischer) and an underage stripper called Ponytail (Barbara Windsor). A lot of time is devoted to elaborate fantasy numbers (steam bath, a calypso number, and a staged monsoon, complete with rain) with almost naked women. Jayne sings and wears her then-scandalous sequined dress. The theme song (heard twice) is priceless. In America, this film was cut and released as *Playgirl After Dark*. Director Young's next feature was *Dr. No*.

TOO HOT TO HANDLE

(1975) **D:** Don Schain **S:** J. Michael Sherman **P:** Ralph T. Desiderio

Cheri Caffaro (who usually played Ginger) stars as Samantha Fox, a bounty hunter hired to stop black market merchants. Caffaro dresses as a dominatrix to seduce and kill a man and fantasizes during a cockfight. The New World release also features former football star Tim Brown and Corinne Calvet. The Samantha Fox character name was soon being used by an NYC-area porno star and later by a British pop singer.

TOO MUCH

(1987) **D/S:** Eric Rochat **S:** Joan Laine **P:** Golan/Globus

Bridgette Andersen is a little girl with a robot friend named "TM" for Too Much (Masato Fukazama) in Japan. An evil scientist threatens them. It's a PG movie for kids.

TOO MUCH FEAR

(VSOM, 1975) **D/S:** Paola Cavara **S:** Bernardino Zapponi   Italy (*E Tanta Paura*)

People at a sex party are killed by a black-gloved psycho. A cop (Michele Placido) and a bisexual hooker (Corinne Clery) whose life is at stake team

up and look for the killer. Eli Wallach, Tom Skerritt, and John Steiner costar, and there's nudity and gore.

TOO MUCH TOO OFTEN!

(SW, 1968) **D/S/P:** "Louis Silverman"/Doris Wishman

A man whips and abuses people, works as a pimp, and blackmails a masochistic NYC ad exec into giving him a job. Buck Star and Sharon Kent star in the b/w adults-only feature. Ads said "Whip Me! Whip Me!" It was probably filmed several years before its release date.

TOO SCARED TO SCREAM

(Vestron, 1982) **D:** Tony Lo Bianco **S:** Neal Barbera, Glenn Leopold **P/A:** Mike Connors   (*The Doorman*)

An NYC police detective (Mike Connors) and an undercover cop (Anne Archer) investigate murders in a high rise. Ian McShane (later star of the British *Lovejoy* TV series) is the Shakespearean doorman suspect living with his invalid mother (Maureen O'Sullivan). With John Heard, Leon Isaac Kennedy, Murray Hamilton (in his last role), Victoria Bass, and Val Avery. The theme song is by Charles Aznavour. The first-time director is the star of *The Honeymoon Killers*.

TOO SOON TO LOVE

(1960) **D/S/P:** Richard Rush **S:** Lazlo Gorog **P:** Mark Lipsky

After starring in *Cry Baby Killer* (1958) and doing his bit in *Little Shop of Horrors* (1960), Jack Nicholson appeared in this juvenile delinquent movie, the first by Rush. Richard Evans and Jennifer West are top-billed as young lovers who "go too far." He turns to robbery to pay for her abortion, but they get married and have a kid at the end. The parents are to blame for the kids' problems in the Universal release. "Buddy" (Nicholson) is in a fight scene. Rush later directed him in the better-known *Hell's Angels on Wheels* and *Psych-Out*.

TOPAZ

(MCA, 1969) **D/P:** Alfred Hitchcock **S:** Samuel Taylor

Hitch's expensive at the time ($4 million) "M" rated political thriller, based on the novel by Leon Uris, was shot partially on location in Paris, Copenhagen, and New York. It lacked major (American) stars and did badly at the box office. Frederick Stafford stars as a French agent working for America, trying to find out what Russia is up to in Cuba in 1962. John Vernon is the Castro character visiting New York (based on the real visit). With Dany Robin, Karin Dor, Michel Piccoli, Philippe Noiret, Roscoe Lee Browne, and John Forsythe. The director is seen in a wheelchair at the airport. Several endings were filmed for the 125-minute Universal feature. In America, it ends in the suicide of Piccoli (an ending not shot by Hitchcock, who wanted to use a duel-in-a-stadium ending). A new "feel good" ending (also not by Hitchcock) was substituted for Europe. The laserdisc has both endings. After all those hits, even Hitchcock's films could be tampered with. He did the nastier *Frenzy* (1972) next, followed by his last feature, the light *Family Plot* (1976).

TOP BANANA

(1954) **D:** Alfred E. Green **D/P:** Albert Zugsmith **S:** Gene Towne

This vaudeville movie was filmed in color and 3-D but U.A. released it flat and now it's only available in b/w. Phil Silvers stars with Rose Marie, Jack Albertson, and Flash the singing dog. The movie didn't do much business, but Silvers became Sgt. Bilko on TV the next year.

EL TOPO

(1969) **D/S/P/A/M/E:** Alexandro Jodorowsky   Mexico

In this indescribable but fascinating zen western, a man (Jodorowsky) must kill four master gunfighters. The highest-grossing film from Mexico in the U.S. at the time, it debuted at the Museum of Modern Art. Seeing this years later, it's incredible how bloody, uncompromising, and meaningful it all is. I'm sure viewers who saw it in theaters in the 70s (it was a midnight hit) will never forget it. The Mexican sets were left over from the Glenn Ford western *Day of the Evil Gun* (1968). Allen Kleir and his Abkco company (using Beatles money) backed it, and it was said to be a favorite of John Lennon. Klein owns the rights and kept it (and Jodorowsky's *The Holy Mountain*) out of circulation for many years. Originally 135 minutes long, it was trimmed to 123 when released in 1971. The rare soundtrack is on Apple.

TOP OF THE HEAP

(Unicorn, 1972) **D/S/P/A:** Christopher St. John

One of the stars of *Shaft* made this Fanfare release and stars as a troubled Washington, D.C., family man and cop. He escapes reality by dreaming of going to the moon or having an affair with a blond nurse. With Paula Kelly as his mistress, Allen Garfield, Tiger Joe Marsh, and Richard M. Dixon as President Nixon.

TOP SECRET!

(Paramount, 1984) **D/S:** Jim Abrahams, David Zucker, Jerry Zucker **S:** Martyn Burke **P:** Jon Davidson, Hunt Lowry

Val Kilmer (in his feature debut) stars as Nick Rivers, an Elvis-type singer on tour in East Germany. The comedy from the *Airplane* team has a spy plot about trying to reunite Germany! Lucy Gutteridge costars with Jeremy Kemp, Omar Sharif, and Michael Gough. Peter Cushing is featured in a stand-out scene—speaking backwards. Kilmer, who later played Jim Morrison in *The Doors* (1991), also sings. The director team later split up and made less funny "anything goes" comedies.

TORCHLIGHT

(Embassy, 1985) **D:** Tom Wright **S/A:** Pamela Sue Martin **S:** Eliza Moorman **P:** Joel Douglas, Michael Schoeder

Pamela Sue Martin, who played Nancy Drew before she became a regular on *Dynasty*, stars as an artist who marries a wealthy man (Steve Railsback). An art dealer (Ian McShane) introduces them to freebasing cocaine. One of many 80s anti-coke movies, it was released by FilmVentures.

TORMENT

(Nelson, 1985) **D/S/P:** John Hopkins, Samson Aslanian

William Witt is a San Francisco detective after a maniac who kills women. The killer snaps after a woman rejects him, hides in a house, and terrorizes the detective's girlfriend (Taylor Gilbert) and her invalid mom. From New World.

THE TORMENTOR

(Wizard, 1973) **D/A:** "Robert Hoffman"/ Maurizio Pradeaux **S:** Arpad De Riso
Italy (*Passi di Danza Su Una Lama di Rasoio*)

Susan Scott witnesses a murder while on vacation with her fiancé (played by the director). The psycho killer wears all black and uses a cane and a razor. More people are killed (including artists and ballerinas) and many characters are suspects. With George Martin as a cop.

THE TORMENTORS

(TWE, 1971) **D/P:** "David B. Eagle"/ David L. Hewitt **S/P/A:** James Gordon White (*Terminators*)

Bank-robbing, motorcycle-riding American Nazis in Monterey kill a woman. Her fiancé (William Dooley) goes undercover to get evidence but he falls for one of their women. The "Fourth Reich" plans to kill a hippie leader, known as "The Messiah," to gain the support of "the young people," which leads to a ridiculous hippie vs. Nazi brawl. There's a love-in (with live band) and a dream sequence. It's pretty awful and has way too many badly dubbed long conversations in small rooms. Some scenes were added years later and it was first released in 1986 (!). James Craig (*Revenge of Dr. X*) is a behind-the-scenes leader and Anthony Eisley is a cop. Also with Chris Noel and Bruce Kemp. The rock music is by Rudy and the Love Slaves.

TORN CURTAIN

(MCA, 1966) **D/P:** Alfred Hitchcock **S:** Brian Moore

Hitchcock's 50th feature is a Cold War espionage drama set in East Germany, Copenhagen, and Sweden (but was filmed in Hollywood). It seemed pretty mainstream after *The Birds* and *Marnie* and is remembered mostly for the long, difficult death scene in a farmhouse. Paul Newman stars as a nuclear scientist who fakes a defection to East Berlin; with Julie Andrews and Lila Kedrova. The director is seen in a lobby with a baby on his lap. The Universal release runs 128 minutes. The John Addison soundtrack is on Decca. The original soundtrack by Bernard Herrmann was rejected by the studio (but itself was later released).

THE TORTURE CHAMBER: *See* THE TORTURE ZONE

THE TORTURE CHAMBER OF BARON BLOOD: *See* BARON BLOOD

TORTURE SHIP

(1939) **D:** Victor Halperin
S: George Sayre **P:** Sig Neufeld

The Halperin brothers made 10 wacked-out features—from *Party Girl* (1930) to *Girls' Town* (1942). This obscure (and absurd) release (from Producers Pictures) was "based on" a Jack London story. A mad doctor (Irving Pichel) arranges for a group of headline-making killers to sail on a boat with him at midnight. The passengers include a bomber, a wife killer, a strangler, and "Poison Mary." A newspaper headline says HARRY THE CARVER—MACHINE GUN SLAYER IS MISSING! Pichel operates on their endocrine glands in a misguided rehabilitation attempt, but they die, so he chooses a "normal" victim, Bob, the ship's captain, who is his nephew. Bob, who becomes a violent zombie, is played by Lyle Talbot, looking like Curly Howard with hair and suspenders. He leads a revolt. With Jacqueline Wells (from *The Black Cat*), a comic Swedish servant and lines like, "Get more wine or I'll cut your ears off!"

THE TORTURE ZONE

(MPI, Unicorn, 1968) **D:** Juan Ibanez **D/S:** Jack Hill **S/P:** Louis Enrico Vergara   US/Mexico (*La Cámara del Terror; The Fear Chamber*)

This is undoubtedly the low point of Boris Karloff's long career and is badly put together, but still fascinating. Boris is the good Dr. Mantel. His daughter (Julissa) and her boyfriend (Carlos East) discover a living rock in a cave. Then—a woman goes to bed and a dwarf (Santanon) sneaks in her bedroom. The entire room turns around to reveal a big scary cavern full of snakes, bones, and spiders. Some bizarre, hard-to-see stop-motion changes occur. Men in hooded black robes grab the terrified woman and take her to a torture chamber. She sees them put another woman on hot coals who, after a thumbs down from Dr. Mantel, is stabbed to death. Mantel tells the first woman, "You must be punished for your sins!" and she gets the same treatment, but is suddenly wheeled into an operating room, where the torturers turn out to be doctors extracting something or other from terrified people. Dr. Mantel's daughter and her boyfriend go on vacation, and the weak doctor ends up in bed, leaving his sadistic, voyeuristic assistant Helga (Isela Vega) in charge. She plots with Roland, a lobotomized hunchback (Yerye Beirute), a cliché-sinister East Indian, and the dwarf. The living rock grows tentacles and kills women. Helga and Roland watch a stripper do a long topless dance. The rock watches too before grabbing her. Helga whips a bloody blonde in chains. Roland keeps saying "I'm gonna be king of the world!" Boris has a bad dream, but recovers and saves the world with his computer. Karloff's last line is "I can only pray we've stopped it before it could transmit the information it gathered to others like it!" and Roland runs around in a cave yelling "I'm the king of the world!" The Spanish-language video release doesn't even mention Boris's name on the box. You won't believe it.

TO SLEEP WITH A VAMPIRE

(New Horizons, 1992) **D:** Adam Friedman
S: Patricia Harrington **P:** Mike Elliot

Roger Corman ordered up this pointless remake of his *Dance of the Damned* (from way back in 1988), using much of the same dialogue. This time Scott Valentine is the vampire who wants to get to know a suicidal stripper (Charlie Spradling). It's filled with homeless people, arty touches, and lots of dialogue. They argue ("Stop staring at my neck!"), he cries, paints, and finally makes her a vampire, after sex on the strip club runway. *Shadows in the Dark* (1989), a porno tape, was an earlier "remake" of the same story.

TOTAL CONTROL: *See* PROJECT: KILL

TOTAL RECALL

(LIVE, 1990) **D:** Paul Verhoeven **S/P:** Ronald Schusett **S:** Dan O'Bannon, Gary Goldman **P:** Buzz Feitshans **M:** Jerry Goldsmith

Arnold Schwarzenegger is a puzzled construction worker who pays Rekall Inc. so he can imagine (or does he?) that he's a hero on a colonized Mars in 2084. Based on Philip K. Dick's "We Can Remember It for You Wholesale," this was once to be produced by Dino De Laurentiis and directed by Cronenberg (in 1984), then by Bruce Beresford (in 1987). It ended up costing a then-record $70 million and wasn't really a box-office hit. It had to be cut for an R rating but still has some extreme, eye-popping ILM FX and "110 acts of violence an hour." Arnold rips an arm off and shoots his own wife (Sharon Stone). Also with a record 55 product placements. Rachel Ticotin costars, with Ronny Cox (also in Verhoeven's *Robocop*) and Michael Ironside as villains and Marshall Bell as the underground leader. An Oscar went to Rob Bottin for FX including the mutants at a futuristic whorehouse. It was filmed in the Mexico City Churubusco studios. A remastered letterboxed laser version is available. The score is on Varèse Sarabande. *Terminator 2* topped *Total Recall*'s budget and *Hook* equaled it. Verhoeven's next was *Basic Instinct* (also with Stone).

TO THE SHORES OF HELL

(1966) **D/S/P:** Will Zens **S:** Robert McFarland

Years before *Rambo*, a Marine major (Marshall Thompson) takes a group through the Vietnamese jungle to try to rescue his doctor brother (Robert Dornan) from the Viet Cong. Dornan later became a very conservative Republican Congressman and presidential candidate. He was also in *The Starfighters* (1964) and *Hell On Wheels* (1967), both also by Will Zens (*Capture That Capsule!*, 1961). Thompson also made and starred in *A Yank in Viet-Nam* (1964). Crown International released this color feature.

THE TOUCHABLES

(SW, 1961) **D/S:** Monte Mann **D/P:** Jay Sheridan

During Prohibition, a cowardly bookkeeper hides out from gangsters at the "Fat Chance Rejuvenation Center." The gangsters and the star all end up running around in drag in silent-comedy-style chase scenes. Boxoffice International kept this *Some Like It Hot*–inspired adult comedy in circulation for years, using different ad campaigns. At one time, it featured naked women, but in this version they all wear polka dot bikinis (popular in the

Tower of Screaming Virgins

30s, I'm sure). Claire Brennan, who later starred in *She Freak* (!), is top billed. The AFI catalog says the short (about an hour) color feature was also called *Nude Heatwave* and may have had 3-D sequences at one time.

THE TOUCHABLES

(1968) **D:** Robert Freeman
S: Ian La Fresnais **P:** John Bryan   UK

This sex comedy was a rival to the somewhat similar *Three in the Attic* (also 1968). Judy Huxtable and three other mod London women dressed as nuns kidnap a pop singer (David Anthony) and keep him in their huge plastic "pleasure" dome (with a revolving bed) by the seaside. The singer's manager and a black gangster search for him. Ads called the 20th Century release "Love in the Fifth Dimension!" The British group Nirvana does the theme song. There was a soundtrack album.

TOUCH AND DIE

(Vestron, 1991) **D/S:** Pier Nico Solinas
S: John Howlett   Italy

Martin Sheen stars as an alcoholic US journalist in Rome who investigates grisly murders concerning a nuke conspiracy where workers' hands are cut off. Renée Estevez (Sheen's daughter) plays his daughter. Also with Franco Nero and David Birney.

A TOUCH OF HER FLESH

(1967) **D/P/E:** "Julian Marsh"/Michael Findlay
P/C: "Anna Riva"/Roberta Findlay

Richard Jennings (Robert West) sees his wife with another man, runs away, and is hit by a car. He loses one eye and his legs are temporarily paralyzed. He drinks Old Crow and kills strippers (and his wife) in various ways using darts, a crossbow, a poison rose, and even a buzzsaw. Meanwhile we see various memorable strip acts at a go-go club and hear instrumental rock, some classical music, and a good soul song called "Right Kind of Lovin'." The outrageous b/w adult feature was shot in many real NYC locations and features a look at some long-gone theaters and restaurants in the Lower East Side, a black stripper, and an (offscreen) decapitation. It was part of a sick trilogy by the future makers of *Snuff*. *Curse of Her Flesh* and *The Kiss of Her Flesh* followed.

TOUCH OF THE SUN

(1978) **D/S:** Peter Curran **S:** George Fowler **P:** Elizabeth Curran

The local emperor Sumooba (Edwin Manda) holds an American space capsule for ransom after it lands in Central Africa. Peter Cushing is a comical commissioner who doesn't know that WWII ended, and Oliver Reed, Keenan Wynn, and Bruce Boa are officials sent after the capsule. Also with a Tarzan-type character. The first international feature filmed in Zambia, the adventure comedy was never released in Europe or America.

TOUGHER THAN LEATHER

(RCA, 1988) **D/S/A:** Rick Rubin
S: Ric Menello **P:** Vincent Giordano

The rap group Run-DMC (Joseph Simmons and Darryl McDaniels) star as themselves in a music business exploitation movie by record producer Rubin. The white record producers are also drug dealers. There's a revenge plot, Mafia killers, sleazy Jewish record executives, and rednecks. With the Beastie Boys, Slick Rick, Jenny Lumet, Richard Edson (*Stranger Than Paradise*) and porn star Lois Ayers in a dog collar. From New Line. Run-DMC were also in *Krush Groove*.

TOUGH GUNS

(Abacus, 1972) **D:** "Godfrey Daniels"/Stuart Segall
S: Don Edmunds   (*Two Rode with Death*)

The director of *Drive-In Massacre* made this sex western. Flashbacks reveal a revenge plot concerning bounty hunters (one is black). With John Alderman as the main villain and Rene Bond.

TOUGH GUY

(1994) **D/S:** James Merendino **S:** Megan Heath
P: Rustam Branaman, Danny Kuchuck

A Los Angeles woman (Heather Graham) is terrorized by various men in her apartment after her husband kills her lover then kills himself. Her role is a lot like Deneuve's in Polanski's *Repulsion*. The director had previously made *The Upstairs Neighbor*, which was a lot like Polanski's *The Tenant*. Lisa Zane is her friend and Paul Herman is the guy of the title. Also with Max Perlich, Balthazar Getty, Don Calfa, and Richard Lynch.

TOUGH GUYS DON'T DANCE

(Media, 1987) **D/S:** Norman Mailer **P:** Golan/Globus

Mailer made one of those typical Cannon studios multipicture deals. He appeared in Jean-Luc Godard's *King Lear* and got to direct this surprising adaptation of his own twisted crime novel. Ryan O'Neal tells an incredible story to his helpful father (Lawrence Tierney, in one of his best roles). Flashbacks inside of flashbacks and flashforwards reveal how the son had bottomed out and might have

killed an ex-porno star. He can't remember. *Screw* magazine ads are important to the plot, and two severed heads end up in garbage bags. Wings Hauser stands out as a crazed, pot-smoking Nam vet police chief. With Isabella Rossellini, Frances Fisher, Clarence Williams III, Debra Sandlund, and Penn Jillette. Filmed in Provincetown, Mass.

TOWER OF SCREAMING VIRGINS

(Video Dimensions, 1968) **D:** François Legrand
S: Kurt Nachmann **P:** Wolf C. Hartwig   Germany, France, Italy (*Der Turm Der Verbotenen Liebe*)

The masked, red-haired "witch of the tower" has blindfolded men brought to her by a hunchback. She and her two companions enjoy sex with them, then she has them killed. Plot twists worthy of Alexandre Dumas (whose story it's based on) reveal that she is really the Queen, a one-time lover of the always smiling "rascal" swordsman hero, and unknowingly has had sex with their son. It's a pretty lavish-looking color adventure with some wild costumes, nudity, and very out-of-place jazz and bongo music! The tape is letterboxed. Terry Torday and Uschi Glas star.

TOWER OF TERROR

(Sinister, 1941) **D:** Lawrence Huntington
S/P: John Argyle **S:** John Reinhart   UK

A mad lighthouse keeper (Wilfred Lawson) in Germany terrorizes people in a house. His wife is buried in the basement and he thinks a woman (Movita) who escaped from a concentration camp is her reincarnation. Michael Rennie stars as a British spy. The one-hour-long Monogram release is borderline horror and includes a killer with a hook hand.

A TOWN CALLED HELL

(1971) **D:** Robert Parrish **S/P:** Benjamin Fisz   UK/Spain
(*Una Ciudad Llamada Bastard; A Town Called Bastard*)

Martin Landau is a bounty hunter after a priest (Robert Shaw) who is a Mexican revolutionary. The great cast of this Euro western includes Telly Savalas as a Mexican bandit who controls a town, Stella Stevens as a mystery woman with a coffin, and Fernando Rey. Parrish, from Georgia, was based in England, where he also directed *Journey to the Far Side of the Sun* (1969).

THE TOXIC AVENGER

(Troma, 1984) **D/P:** Michael Herz,
Lloyd Kaufman **S:** Joe Ritter

This was the first bad-taste, gross-out horror comedy hit from New York's Troma after years of teen comedies. A nerd janitor, Marvin (Mitchell Cohen), falls into toxic waste and becomes a good guy monster who battles local corruption and has a blind girlfriend. With Pat Ryan Jr. as the mayor and Marisa Tomei (an extra). The "cult hit" was shot in Boonton, New Jersey. R or unrated versions are available. Sequels followed.

The Toxic Avenger doing publicity in Germany.

THE TOXIC AVENGER, PART II

(Warner, 1989) **D/S/P:** Lloyd Kaufman
D/P: Michael Herz **S:** Gay Partington Terry

Apocalypse Inc. plans to take over Tromaville and "Toxie" (played by Ron Fazio and John Altamura) battles Satan himself. Parts of this sequel were shot in Tokyo, and Japanese actors appear. With Phoebe Legere as the "beautiful blind buxom bimbo," Lisa Gaye, and lots of dumb jokes. This was shot back to back with Part III. The Japanese version is longer.

THE TOXIC AVENGER, PART III: THE LAST TEMPTATION OF TOXIE

(Vestron, 1989) **D/P:** Lloyd Kaufman,
Michael Herz **S:** Gay Partington Terry

Toxie goes to work for a corporation run by the Devil (Rick Collins) so he can afford to cure his girlfriend's (Phoebe Legere) blindness. It has the same cast as Part II minus the Japanese actors. Available R or unrated. Marvel Comics started a short-lived syndicated *Toxic Crusaders* TV cartoon series (1991) and toys were offered, but few cared.

THE TOXIC MONSTER: *See* MONSTER

TOXIC SPAWN = ALIEN CONTAMINATION

TOXIC ZOMBIES = BLOOD EATERS

THE TOY BOX

(SW, 1970) **D/S:** Ron Garcia

Here's another weird one from Boxoffice International. Donna, a blonde (who narrates), remembers her "uncle's" parties. The fat, bearded, telepathic man with no eyes is from another planet (I think). He holds strange sex parties with women in togas in his mansion during thunderstorms while spooky music plays. Women dance naked, some are chained and whipped, others just talk endlessly. A decapitated head appears. Guests receive a "reward" from the "toy box" (one of those hand-grabs-a-coin things) for doing "tricks for uncle." In one outdoor scene, a guy in a mask scares a woman during sex, so she kills him with a pitchfork. Most of it's too dark to see well and it

sure doesn't make much sense. Marsha Jordan is in it. Garcia was later cinematographer for the *Twin Peaks* movie.

TOYS

(Fox, 1992) **D/S/P:** Barry Levinson
S: Valerie Curtin **P:** Mark Johnson

Michael Gambon is a general who inherits a toy factory and starts manufacturing only war toys. Robin Williams and Joan Cusack (a robot) are his childlike nephew and niece. It's a long (over 2 hours) anti-war fantasy satire that resembles *Willy Wonka* and was a boxoffice flop. It does have some impressive (Oscar-nominated) sets and good FX by Rob Bottin. With Robin Wright, Jack Warden, Debi Mazar, LL Cool J, and Donald O'Connor. Not to be confused with the equally bad *The Toy* from ten years earlier. Rated PG-13.

TOY SOLDIERS

(Starmaker, 1983) **D/S:** David Fisher
S: Walter Fox **P:** Darrell Hallenbeck

Some Beverly Hills kids are taken captive during a Central American cruise. They escape, join up with a mercenary, and Jason Miller and Cleavon Little lead a hostage rescue mission. With Tracy Scoggins, Tim Robbins, and Terri Garber. From New World.

TOY SOLDIERS

(RCA, 1991) **D/S:** Daniel Petrie
S: David Koepp **P:** Jack E. Freedman

Some brutal, heavily armed South American terrorists take over a Virginia prep school and hold students hostage. The leader (Andrew Divoff) wants his father released from prison. Sean Astin and Keith Coogan are the main problem kids who fight back, and the FBI, Army, and Mafia become involved. It's all pretty entertaining, and there's a good cast and good music. Also with Wil Wheaton, Louis Gossett Jr. as the dean, Denholm Elliott as the headmaster, Mason Adams (FBI), R. Lee Ermey (Army), and Jerry Orbach (Mafia). Made in Virginia, it was based on a novel by William Kennedy.

TRACKS

(Paramount, 1976) **D/S:** Henry Jaglom
P: Howard Zucker, Irving Cohen, Ted Shapiro

In a very serious post-Nam movie, a soldier (Dennis Hopper) escorts the body of a friend home on a train. He hallucinates, imagines Taryn Power is gang raped, and at one point, runs through the train naked. With Dean Stockwell, Michael Emil, Zack Norman, Sally Kirkland, and Alfred Ryder.

TRACK 29

(Warner, 1988) **D:** Nicolas Roeg
S: Dennis Potter **P:** Rick McCallum   UK

A bored Texas housewife (Theresa Russell) imagines that hitchhiker Gary Oldman is her lost baby, now grown up. Her crazed doctor husband (Christopher Lloyd) is obsessed by his entire floor of

computerized toy trains. With Colleen Camp, Sandra Bernhard, and Seymour Cassel. George Harrison was an executive producer for his Handmade Films. It was filmed in North Carolina.

TRADER HORN

(1931) **D:** W. S. Van Dyke **P:** Irving Thalberg

Harry Carey is a jungle dealer and Edwina Booth is the white goddess in this jungle classic. It was shot on location during seven months in Africa in 1929. Booth got sick from the heat, sued MGM, retired from acting the next year, and went to work at a Mormon temple. Much of the footage was judged unusable, and the rest was reshot in Mexico. It was a hit though and influenced many poverty row and roadshow jungle movies featuring gorillas and white jungle queens. With Duncan Renaldo and C. Aubrey Smith. Van Dyke went on to direct *Tarzan the Ape Man* (1931), which used footage leftover from *Trader Horn*, and *The Thin Man* (1934), starting off two very popular MGM series.

TRADER HORN

(1973) **D:** Reza Badiyi **S:** William
Norton, Edward Harper

This PG-rated MGM remake uses lots of stock footage and adds German and British soldiers to the plot. Rod Taylor stars with Anne Heywood, Jean Sorel, and Don Knight. It's interesting that this was produced after the original was spoofed in *Trader Hornee* (1970).

TRADER HORNEE

(SW, 1970) **D:** "Don Tsanusdi"/
Jonathan Lucas **S/P:** David F. Friedman

Deborah Stills stars as Algona "the white goddess" in this adults-only jungle-cliché comedy, filled with in-jokes, soft core sex, and nudity. Buddy Pantsati is private detective Hornee and Elisabeth Monica is Jane his assistant. The natives use jive talk and the white gorilla turns out to be an escaped Nazi. Also with John Alderman. An impressive production for a movie aimed at the adults-only market, it played drive-ins and also some midnight shows. Lucas also directed the Dean Martin TV show.

TRAIL OF THE PINK PANTHER

(1982) **D/S/P:** Blake Edwards **S:** Frank Waldman,
Tom Waldman, Geoffrey Edwards

Peter Sellers, who played Inspector Clouseau in five Pink Panther movies (all directed by Edwards), died in 1980. This sequel, in the grand tradition of *Plan 9 from Outer Space* and *The Game of Death*, features old scenes and a double for the star. Joanna Lumley is a reporter who interviews David Niven, Capucine, Burt Kwouk, Robert Loggia and Richard Mulligan, who all "remember" scenes and outtakes from the previous films. The double for Sellers has his head covered in bandages. Also with Harvey Korman and footage of Herbert Lom (who was in all five original features). It was bad enough, but at the same time Edwards threw together *The Curse of the Pink Panther* (1983) too. Sellers's last wife, actress Lynn Frederick (*Schizo*), sued and won a $1,687,000 award from United Artists.

TRAIN RIDE TO HOLLYWOOD

(1973) **D:** Charles Rondeau
S: Dan Gordon **P:** Gordon Webb

The soul group Bloodstone star as a group called the Sinceres in a fantasy comedy. The singer dreams that the group is on a train going to heaven filled with famous cliché late-golden-era Hollywood stars (played by impressionists) plus Dracula, Brando, and a gorilla. With Jay Robinson and Roberta Collins. Incredibly, the G-rated Billy Jack Production was released by Tom Laughlin!

TRAITOR'S GATE

(1964) **D:** Freddie Francis **S:** "John Sansom"/ Jimmy Sangster W. Germany/England (*Der Verratertor*)

Albert Lieven is a London businessman who plots to steal the crown jewels from the Tower of London. With Gary Raymond, Margot Trooger, Catherina von Schell, and Klaus Kinski as Kinski (!). The Edgar Wallace story had also been filmed as *The Yellow Mask* in England in 1930. Freddie Francis is a famous, award-winning British cinematographer (*The Innocents, The Elephant Man)* but he also directed lots of (mostly horror) movies. He made several in Germany including *The Brain* (1962), a *Donovan's Brain* remake, and *The Vampire Happening*. Two versions (German and English) were shot.

TRAMPLERS

(Nelson, 1966) **D/S/P:** Albert Band **S:** Ugo Liberatore **P:** Alvaro Mancori Italy (*Gli Uomini dal Passo Pesante; Showdown*)

Joseph Cotten is an ex–Confederate general who organizes a private army to protect his Texas cattle empire from Yankees in a post–Civil War western.

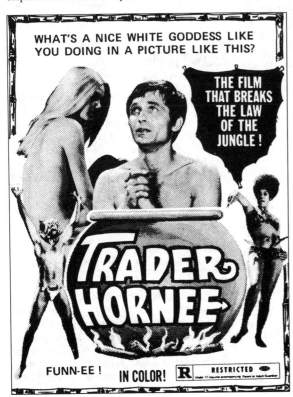

WHAT'S A NICE WHITE GODDESS LIKE YOU DOING IN A PICTURE LIKE THIS?

THE FILM THAT BREAKS THE LAW OF THE JUNGLE!

TRADER HORNEE

FUNN-EE! IN COLOR! **R** RESTRICTED

His sons (Gordon Scott and James Mitchum) set up a rival ranch. With Franco Nero. Joseph E. Levine and Embassy released it.

TRANCE

(N.P.Y., 1981) **D/S:** Eckhart Schmidt **P:** Barbra Moorse, Martin Moskowicz W. Germany (*Der Fan*)

Simone (Desiree Nosbusch) is a schoolgirl seriously obsessed with a Gary Numan–type pop singer (Bodo Staiger). She meets him (after fainting) at a Munich TV studio and they have sex. The surprise part (which I have to give away to get anybody interested) is what makes this well-made movie special. When he treats her like a cast-off groupie, she kills him, cuts him up with an electric knife, freezes the body parts, then cooks and eats him! Also with Joachim Fuchsberger. Nosbusch later became a TV star and was Boris Becker's girlfriend. Schmidt has directed many teen and drug movies since the 60s. In English and seen on a Canadian video.

TRANCERS

(Vestron, 1985) **D/P:** Charles Band **S:** Danny Bilson, Paul DeMeo (*Future Cop*)

Tim Thomerson (who was a stand-up comic) is Jack Deth, a future detective who goes back 300 years to mid-80s LA to stop a Manson-type villain with psychic powers who creates "trancer" slaves. With Helen Hunt, Art La Fleur, Anne Seymour, and Richard Erdman. Rated PG-13. Thomerson returned in *Trancers II.*

TRANCERS II: THE RETURN OF JACK DETH

(Paramount, 1991) **D/P:** Charles Band
S: Jackson Barr **P:** David DeCoteau

Thomerson returns from the future and becomes stuck in 1990, where he protects the life of an ex–baseball star. The evil Richard Lynch turns homeless people into zombies, and Helen Hunt and Megan Ward appear as Deth's past and present wives. With Martine Beswick, Jeffrey Combs, Barbara Crampton, Sonny Carl Davis, and Art La Fleur. This script was originally filmed as a segment of the unreleased anthology *Pulse Pounders,* then was remade as this feature.

TRANCERS III: DETH LIVES

(Paramount, 1992) **D/S:** C. Courtney Joyner **P:** Albert Band

A big alien called Shark takes detective Deth (Thomerson) to LA of the future and back again in this confusing sequel. "Col. Muther" (Andrew Robinson) is behind an out-of-control trancer soldier plot, and there are some fighting women to relieve the boredom. With Melanie Smith, Stephen Macht plus Megan Ward and a token "special appearance" by Helen Hunt (by then a major TV star). *Trancers IV* followed.

TRANCERS IV: JACK OF SWORDS

(Paramount, 1994) **D:** David Nutter **S:** Peter David **P:** Vlad Paunescu, Oana Paunescu

In this pretty awful sequel, Jack Deth (Thomerson yet again) ends up in medieval times where noblemen are vampires who consider commoners "meat." Characters talk a lot and there are a few (intentional) laughs. With Stacie Randall, Ty Miller, and Stephen Macht. It was filmed in Romania back-to-back with *Trancers V: Sudden Deth*, the "last" sequel.

TRANS EUROPE EXPRESS

(1967) **D/S/A:** Alain Robbe-Grillet
P: Samy Halfon France

Filmmakers on a train imagine a dope smuggling plot starring a fellow passenger (Jean-Louis Trintignant as himself). With Marie-France Pisier and Daniel Emilfork. Trans America, an AIP offshoot, released the b/w feature in America, making it the only one of Robbe-Grillet's movies as director to have much exposure in America. The cult author's first screen credit was as screenwriter of *Last Year At Marienbad* (1961).

TRANSFORMATIONS

(Starmaker, 1988) **D:** Jay Kamen
S: Mitch Brown **P:** Bob Wynn

Rex Smith (who had one hit single back in 1979), stars as Wolf, an astronaut, in this terrible man-in-a-monster-suit-on-a-spaceship movie. The prison-mining-colony setting predated *Alien 3* by several years, though. That, and some gore, nudity, and (near-X) sex might make it worth seeing. Lisa Langlois is the nurse who loves Rex, even though sex makes him mutate. With Patrick Macnee as a priest, Christopher Neame, Pamela Prati, and Cec Verrell. Made (in Italy) by Band's Empire company and not released until 1991.

TRANSGRESSION

(Chiaroscuro, 1993) **D/S/P:** Michael P. DiPaolo **P:** Thomas Kalamar, Susan Skoog

A woman (Molly Jackson) on death row narrates on/off flashbacks. She had been a TV news reporter doing a story about a serial killer working in the meat packing district. He (Marc St. Camille) wears a bloody bondage mask and makes others watch as he ties up victims. He even has his own childhood trauma flashback. Despite the topic, this is slow moving, with soft music and characters who quote Baudelaire and Nietzsche. The director spent nine years videotaping confessions for the Brooklyn D.A. This was shot (16mm) in NYC and upstate New York in 12 days.

TRANSMUTATIONS

(Vestron, 1986) **D:** George Pavlou
S: Clive Barker, James Caplin **P:** Keven Attew, Don Hawkins (*Underworld*)

Motherskill (Steven Berkoff), a gangster, wants his mistress back from subterranean mutant junkies living in tunnels under London. A mad scientist

(Denholm Elliott) has created the ultimate addictive drug, called "white man." It's a pretty slow movie, with a stylish whorehouse set and rock video segments. With Miranda Richardson and Ingrid Pitt. Pavlou made Barker's *Rawhead Rex* too.

TRANSYLVANIA 6-5000

(Starmaker, 1985) **D/S:** Rudy DeLuca **P:** Mace Neufield, Thomas H. Brodek **M:** Lee Holdridge

Jeff Goldblum and Ed Begley Jr. star as tabloid newspaper reporters in a horror comedy. Geena Davis looks real sexy dressed like Vampirella and Joseph Bologna is the mad doctor. With Jeffrey Jones as an innkeeper, Carol Kane and John Byner as servants, Michael Richards, Norman Fell, and the Frankenstein monster, a wolfman, and a mummy. The director had cowritten Mel Brooks movies. The PG-rated "New World/Dow Chemical Co. Picture" (!) was filmed in Yugoslavia. The soundtrack is on Varèse Sarabande.

TRANSYLVANIA TWIST

(MGM/UA, 1989) **D:** Jim Wynorski **S:** R. J. Robertson **P:** Alida Camp

Any horror fan could find something to like in this in-joke–filled PG-13 horror spoof. Robert Vaughn stars as Byron Orlok, a vampire. Teri Copley (who had just been in *Playboy* and gets to sing two songs here) is his visiting niece. Boris Karloff is shown in outtakes from Roger Corman's *The Terror* (edited in with new footage), and Angus Scrimm has the Dick Miller role. Lots of old Corman-produced footage is used, along with plenty of wacky *Airplane*-style gags. There's a nice re-creation of a scene from *Horror of Dracula*, a *Honeymooners* spoof (Why? The only answer is, Why not?), and a surprising gag scene with Jason, Freddy, Leatherface, and Pinhead. There are also nods to *The Exorcist, Phantasm, It Conquered the World,* Elvis, and even "Papa-Oom-Mow-Mow." Also with Steve Franken, Howard Morris, Jay Robinson, Brinke Stevens, Deanna Lund, Monique Gabrielle, Toni Naples, Kelly Mulrooney, and Forrest J. Ackerman.

THE TRAP

(Sinister, 1922) **D:** Robert Thornby **S:** George C. Hull

Gaspar (Lon Chaney) steals the son of the man he had sent to prison on false charges. Chaney also cowrote the revenge story (with Irving Thalberg). With Alan Hale and Irene Rich. From Universal.

TRAPPED ALIVE

(AIP, 1988) **D/S:** Leszek Burzynski **S:** Julian Weaver **P:** Christopher Webster   (*Forever Mine*)

Some prisoners who escape at Christmas, two female hostages, and a deputy somehow all fall down a mine shaft where a barely-shown cannibal with long white hair grabs victims with giant tongs. The deputy and a local woman have (PG-13) sex, the youngest escapee falls in love with top-billed Sullivan Hester (who swims in her underwear), and her friend has a topless scene in the cave. Meanwhile Cameron Mitchell plays the worried father of one of the women and has an emotional solo scene on the telephone. It was made in Eagle River, Wisconsin.

TRAPPER COUNTY WAR

(Republic, 1989) **D:** Worth Keeter **S:** Russel V. Manzatt **P:** Michael W. Leighton

Robert Estes and Noah Black star as New Jersey musicans in a small North Carolina town who meet a waitress (Betsy Russell). She wants to sing, but her demented backwoods relatives (Don Swayze and R. G. Armstrong) object. Violence results. With Bo Hopkins as the sheriff and Ernie Hudson.

TRAP THEM AND KILL THEM

(Twilight, 1977) **D/S/C:** "Joe Damato"/ Aristide Massacessi **S:** Romano Scandariato **P:** Gianfranco Couyoumdjian   Italy (*Emmanuelle e Gli Ultimi Cannibali*)

Laura Gemser is Emanuelle, a reporter for the "New York Evening Post." While working undercover in an NYC hospital (and hiding a camera in a doll), a crazy female inmate who has been raised by cannibals eats a nurse's breast. After watching a graphic cannibal film together and having sex on an NYC dock, Emanuelle and an anthropologist (Gabrielle Tinti) are sent to the Amazon. She convinces the cannibals that she's a goddess in order to save Tinti. The softcore sex movie features lots of voyeurism and female masturbation, rape, decapitation, castration, and a man torn in half. It was made before the tamer but somewhat similar *Slave of the Cannibal God* (1978) with Ursula Andress.

TRASH

(Paramount, 1970) **D/S/C:** Paul Morrissey **P:** Andy Warhol   (*Andy Warhol's Trash*)

Joe Dallesandro is an impotent junkie thief in this sympathetic, sad and funny look at outcasts. He lives in a lower East Side basement with a roommate (Holly Woodlawn, immortalized in "Walk on the Wild Side") who collects trash, goes to the Fillmore East, and wants to go on welfare. With Jane Forth as a wealthy acidhead wife (with a Pink Floyd LP visible in her apartment), Michael Sklar as the welfare inspector, and Geri Miller as the go-go dancer. This 16mm underground feature shocked people with its scenes of shooting up and of Holly masturbating. Morrissey was the editor of *Interview* magazine at the time. Sissy Spacek was an extra (and she did music for *Lonesome Cowboys*!). *Heat* was next.

TRAUMA

(Wizard, 1978) **D/S:** Alberto Negrin **S:** Marcello Coscia, Massimo Dallamano Italy (*Virgin Terror; Enigma Rosso*)

Wealthy schoolgirls involved in a sex party operation are being killed (with a dildo). Fabio Testi stars as a cop and there's nudity and blood. With Christine Kaufmann, Ivan Desny, Jack Taylor, and Helga Line.

TRAUMA

(Worldvision, 1993) **D/S/P:** Dario Argento **S:** T. E. D. Klein **M:** Pino Donaggio

Asia Argento is an anorexic teen who escapes from a clinic and is rescued from a suicide attempt by an ex–drug addict TV station worker (Christopher Rydell). They try to discover who is the "Head Hunter," a local killer who decapitates people with a specially built mechanical noose. With Frederic Forrest as Dr. Judd, Laura Johnson, James Russo as a cop, and Brad Dourif. Piper Laurie is the medium mother who runs the mysterious clinic. It was shot in Minneapolis/St. Paul and was Argento's first feature made entirely in America. Although it lacks some of the flourishes of some of his earlier films, *Trauma* manages to be scary and disturbing. With FX by Tom Savini (lots of decapitated heads). The laser version is unrated.

THE TRAVELING EXECUTIONER

(1970) **D/P:** Jack Smight **S:** Garrie Bateson

Stacy Keach is Jonas Candide, an executioner in 1918. He drives from prison to prison in a truck with his own electric chair and a mortician assisant (Bud Cort). He charges $100 per death. A warden (M. Emmet Walsh) hires him to execute a brother and sister. He falls for the sister (Marianna Hill—real name Schwarzkoff) and fakes her death, with tragic/comic results. With Graham Jarvis, Logan Ramsey, and Val Avery. Alan Rudolph was the assistant director. The MGM release was shot in a real Alabama prison.

TREASURE ISLAND

(Jet, 1971) **D:** John Hough **S/A:** "O. W. Jeeves"/ Orson Welles **S:** Antonio Margheriti, Wolf Mankowitz **P:** Harry Alan Towers   UK/France/W. Germany/Spain

Orson Welles is the one-legged Long John Silver in a feature he had once planned to direct himself. His script was credited to a W. C. Fields–type pseudonym. With Kim Burfield as Jim Hawkins, Lionel Stander, and Walter Slezak. Some earlier adaptations of Robert Louis Stevenson's pirate tale were the famous MGM version (1934) and a Disney version (1950).

TREASURE ISLAND

(1986) **D/S:** Raul Ruiz   France/US

A kid watches TV and imagines himself in a version of *Treasure Island* which features in-jokes, stories inside of stories, and characters who step out of character. With Vic Tayback as Long John Silver, Martin Landau, Lou Castell, Anna Karina, and Pedro Armendariz Jr. Jean-Pierre Leaud (who also acts) narrates and tries to make some sense of the (unfinished) scenes. The Cannon movie was shot in Portugal.

TREASURE ISLAND

(Turner, 1989) **D:** Fraser Heston **P/A:** Charlton Heston

Christian Bale (from *Empire of the Sun*) is Jim Hawkins and Charlton Heston is Long John Silver in a lavish version of Stevenson's tale that debuted on TNT cable. It was filmed on the same ship used for the 1962 *Mutiny on the Bounty* and features a score by the Chieftains. The support cast includes Oliver Reed, Christopher Lee, and Richard Johnson. The next remake was *Muppet Treasure Island* (1996), with Tim Curry.

TREASURE ISLAND IN SPACE

(VSOM, 1987) **D:** Antonio Margheriti
S: Renato Castelani, Licia De Cara Italy
(*Isola del Tesoro; Space Pirates*)

This is a feature version of a TV miniseries. A kid in outer space encounters the usual pirate characters. With David Warbeck, Anthony Quinn, Ernest Borgnine, and John Morghen. The full version runs 8 hours.

TREASURE OF MAKUBA

(1966) **D:** Joe Lacy **S:** Manuel M. Remis **P:** Sidney Pink US/Spain (*El Tesoro de Makuba*)

Cameron Mitchell searches for stolen pearls in the jungle of a Polynesian island. He and a native girl (Mara Cruz) are sentenced to death by natives.

THE TREASURE OF THE AMAZON

(Vestron, 1983) **D/S:** Rene Cardona Jr.
Mexico (*El Tesoro Del Amazonés*)

It's "based on a true story" set in the 50s and concerns diamonds, headhunting cannibals, crocodiles, topless natives, a piranha attack, giant snakes, and leeches. The international cast includes Stuart Whitman, Donald Pleasence, Bradford Dillman, John Ireland, and Hugo Stiglitz. By the director of *Guyana: Cult of the Damned* (1980) with much of the same cast.

TREASURE OF THE FOUR CROWNS

(MGM/UA, 1982) **D:** Ferdinando Balbi
S/P/A: Tony Anthony **S:** Lloyd Battista,
Jin Bryce, Jerry Lazarus Spain/US
(*El Tesoro de las Cuatro Coronas*)

In a PG-rated 3-D *Raiders* . . . copy made after Baldi's more successful *Comin' at Ya!* (1981), characters try to steal jewels from an evil cult. There's very little dialogue, but lots of FX thrust at the audience (skeletons, fireballs, a spinning head) and impressive sets including a haunted castle. Tony Anthony stars as J. T. Stryker, with Gene Quintano, Marshall Lupo, Roger Petitto, and Francisco Rabal. From Cannon.

TREASURE OF THE MOON GODDESS

(Vidmark, 1988) **D:** Joseph Louis Agraz **S/A:** Asher Brauner **S:** Eric Weston **P:** Gerald Green

In this *Raiders* . . . ripoff, Don Calfa dictates a story to his secretary. He had taken a singer named Lu De Belle (Linnea Quigley) to a town in South America where she was mistaken for the reincarnation of a goddess. The confused movie was shot over several years first in Manila in 1984, then in Mexico.

TREASURE OF THE YANKEE ZEPHYR

(Vestron, 1983) **D/P:** David Hemmings
S: Everett de Roche **P:** Anthony I. Ginnane,
John Barnett NZ (*Race for the Yankee Zephyr*)

Ken Wahl, Donald Pleasence, and Lesley Ann Warren search in New Zealand for a downed plane that contains $50 million. With Bruno Lawrence.

Fred Ward and Finn Carter in *Tremors*.

THE TREASURE SEEKERS

(MGM, 1971) **D:** Henry Levin **S/A:** Rod Taylor
P: Sam Manners UK (*Jamaica Gold*)

Jeremy Kemp and Rod Taylor (soon to be in a *Trader Horn* remake) star in this adventure movie with Stuart Whitman, Elke Sommer, and Keenan Wynn. Levin had directed Matt Helm movies.

TREMORS

(MGM, 1989) **D:** Ron Underwood
S/P: S. S. Wilson, Brent Maddock

It's like an updated 50s sci-fi movie, like maybe, *Attack of the Killer Shrew,* set in the desert and with a light tone. Four giant worms (similar to the ones in *Dune*) attack characters in a diner. Kevin Bacon and Fred Ward star as handymen with singer Reba McEntire (in her acting debut) and Michael Gross as survivalists, Finn Carter, Victor Wong, Charlotte Stewart, Bobby Jacoby, and Bibi Besch. The San Francisco opening was canceled because of the title and the recent earthquake. Gale Anne Hurd was executive producer of the PG-13 feature. *Tremors 2* (MCA, 1996) went direct to video.

TRESPASS

(MCA, 1992) **D:** Walter Hill **S:** Bob
Gale, Robert Zemeckis **P:** Neil Canton

Bill Paxton and William Sadler are Arkansas firemen who go to an abandoned East St. Louis factory to search for a buried stash of gold. They witness a black gangland killing and become marked men, having to fight against ghetto crime lords played by rappers-turned-actors Ice-T and Ice Cube. The action hit copies parts of *Treasure of the Sierra Madre.* A character called Video constantly tapes the action. With Bruce A. Young, Tiny Lester, Art Evans, and Stoney Jackson. Sire released two soundtrack albums, one by Ry Cooder and one by various rap artists. It was filmed in Atlanta and Memphis. The Universal release was to be called *Looters,* but the name was changed (and the release delayed) because of the 1992 LA riots.

THE TRIAL

(Orion, 1992) **D:** David Jones
S: Harold Pinter **P:** Louis Marks UK

This BBC production, filmed in Prague, is based on Kafka's frightening 1913 novel set in the Austro-Hungarian Empire. It was produced after the movie *Kafka.* Kyle MacLachlan stars as Joseph K. with Jason Robards as the Lawyer, Alfred Molina, Jean Stapleton, Juliet Stevenson, Polly Walker, and Anthony Hopkins as the Priest. Anthony Perkins had starred in Orson Welles's 1961 version.

THE TRIAL OF BILLY JACK

(1974) **D/S/A:** Tom Laughlin **P:** Joe Cramer

Delores Taylor narrates this very 70s tale of the Freedom School massacre from her hospital bed. The Freedom School has its own TV station and helicopters, but a government conspiracy leads to occupation by the National Guard. Billy Jack (Tom Laughlin) has Nam flashbacks inside of his wife's flashbacks. Out of jail after five years, he has a spiritual drug trip with Indians in the desert and has important visions. Master Bong Soo Han helps Billy battle rednecks with Hapkido fighting. The movie includes references to Kent State and actual Indian land swindle cases. A kid plays guitar with his hook hand. With Teresa Laughlin, Teda Bracci (*Centerfold Girls*), Sacheen Littlefeather, William Wellman Jr., Diane Webber (from *Playboy*), and Cathy Cronkite (Walter's daughter). The Elmer Bernstein soundtrack was on ABC. Credited director Frank Laughlin was the star's 19-year-old son. The sequel (which started out as an AIP feature) was a hit

Ice Cube and Ice-T in *Trespass*.

583

during a saturation release by U.A. *Billy Jack Goes to Washington* was the fourth and last Billy Jack movie.

TRICK BABY

(1973) **D/S:** Larry Yust **P:** Marshall Backlar   (*Double Con*)

Kiel Martin (later on *Hill Street Blues*) stars as "White Folks," a con man in Philadelphia who has gangsters and cops after him in a story based on a novel by Iceberg Slim. Mel Stewart (another familiar TV actor) is his partner. With *Love Boat* regular Ted Lange as a pimp. Yust also directed *Homebodies* (1974).

TRICK OR TREAT

(Lorimar, 1986) **D/A:** Charles Martin Smith **S/P:** Michael S. Murphy, Joel Soisson **S:** Rhet Topham

Marc Price (*Killer Tomatoes Eat France*) is a nerd teen who uses satanic messages found on a record and conjures up the mangled ghost of a dead Kiss-type heavy metal rock star (Tony Fields) who kills with electricity. The comic teen horror movie from DEG features Lisa Orgolini, Gene Simmons as Nuke, Ozzy Osbourne as a reverend, and Smith, the first-time director, as a teacher. "Lunch of the Dead" is playing at a movie theater. The music by Fast Eddie Clarke and Fastway was released on Columbia.

TRICK OR TREATS

(Vestron, 1982) **D/S/P/C/E:** Gary Graver

On Halloween somebody (Peter Jason) is killing people in a house. Star Jackelyn Giroux is the babysitter whose husband had been committed. Chris Graver (the director's son) is the trick-playing son of Carrie Snodgress. Also with Paul Bartel as a wino, John Blythe Barrymore, Jillian Kessner, and surprise bits by David Carradine as a boyfriend and Steve Railsback. Orson Welles, for whom Graver had worked as a cinematographer, is listed as a consultant.

TRINITY IS STILL MY NAME!

(New Pacific, 1971) **D/S:** "E. B. Clucher"/ Enzo Barboni **P:** Italo Zingarelli   Italy (*Continuavano A Chiamarlo Trinità*)

Terence Hill and Bud Spencer return in the sequel to *They Call Me Trinity*. The backwoods brothers become good guy bandits, fight gunrunners, and save a monastery's fortune. With Harry Carey Jr. and Jessica Dublin as Pa and Ma and Yanni Somer. The slapstick western was rated G when released by Embassy.

TRINITY: GOOD GUYS, BAD GUYS: *See* SUPERFUZZ

TRIPODS

(Sony, 1984–85) **D:** Graham Theakston, Christopher Barry **P:** Richard Bates   UK

Aliens take over, people are controlled by metal caps, and a teen underground emerges. 25 half-

hour episodes, based on books by John Christopher, were filmed by the BBC, but a planned third season never happened. Episodes were shown on PBS.

TRIPWIRE

(RCA, 1988) **D:** James Lemmo **S:** B. J. Goldman **P:** Lisa M. Hansen

When the son of a terrorist (David Warner) is killed, he kills the wife (Meg Foster) and kidnaps the son of an FBI man (star Terence Knox). Isabella Hoffmann helps Knox. With Charlotte Lewis, Sy Richardson, Yaphet Kotto, and Tommy Chong. The first-time director had been a cinematographer for movies by William Lustig and Abel Ferrara. From New Line.

TRIP WITH THE TEACHER

(1974) **D/S/P:** Earl Barton

Two psycho biker brothers (Zalman King and Robert Porter) discover a small group of female students and their teacher (Brenda Fogerty) in a broken-down bus in the desert, then terrorize them at an abandoned shack. King's acting is totally out of control as he rants, snickers, kills, whips, and rapes. The females are pretty slow about the escape possibilities and a nice guy who had been with the brothers eventually arrives for a (violent) rescue. King later gained fame and fortune producing and directing erotic movies and cable TV shows. The drive-in movie is from Crown International.

TRISTANA

(Hens Tooth, 1970) **D/S:** Luis Buñuel **S:** Julio Alejandro   France/Italy/Spain

Catherine Deneuve stars as a woman in 1929 who goes to live with her guardian Don Lupe (Fernando Rey). She falls for an artist (Franco Nero), loses her leg, and eventually returns to the aging Don, who has found religion. It was filmed in Toledo, Spain, and received a PG rating. Deneuve had also been in Buñuel's *Belle du Jour* (1967).

TRIUMPH OF SHERLOCK HOLMES

(Foothill, 1935) **D:** Leslie S. Hiscott **S:** H. Fowler Mear, Cyril Twyford **P:** Julius Hagan   UK

Arthur Wontner stars in the fourth (and reportedly, the most faithful and best) of his five Sherlock Holmes films, based on the novel *The Valley of Fear*. Ian Fleming is Dr. Watson and Lyn Harding is Professor Moriarty. Harding also played Moriarty in the last of the series, *Silver Blaze/Murder at the Baskervilles* (1937).

TRIUMPHS OF A MAN CALLED HORSE

(1984) **D:** John Hough **S:** Ken Blackwell, Carlos Aured **P:** Derek Gibson   US/Mexico

Michael Beck stars as the half-breed son of the Richard Harris character from *A Man Called Horse* and *Return of a Man Called Horse*. He has

to save his people from prospectors. The too-late PG-rated sequel features Anne Seymour, Buck Taylor, and an appearance by Harris.

TROLL

(Vestron, 1986) **D:** John Carl Buechler **S:** Ed Naha **P:** Albert Band

Michael Moriarty and his wife (Shelley Hack) move into an old SF apartment building with doors to other dimensions, and their daughter is possessed by a troll (dwarf actor Phil Fondacaro). The ridiculous fantasy comedy also features Sonny Bono (he mutates into a tree), June Lockhart (a good witch), and her daughter Anne Lockhart, plus Gary Sandy, Brad Hall, and Julia Louis-Dreyfuss (from *Saturday Night Live* and *Seinfeld*). It was a low point for the career of Moriarty, but he gets to lip-synch to a Blue Cheer record. Buechler also did FX. The Empire feature was made in Italy. The Richard Band soundtrack is on Enigma.

Zalman King stars in *Trip with the Teacher*.

TROLL 2

(Columbia, 1987) **D/S:** "Drago Floyd"/ Aristide Massaccesi   Italy

Troll was terrible, but at least it had a fun cast. This "sequel" shot in Utah is stupid, laughable, and has some of the worst acting ever. With cannibal goblins (midgets in rubber masks), irritating teens, a dead grandfather, and an anti-meat sermon. It stars a kid, who at one point pisses on the dinner table to stop his family from eating green food. George Hardy, who plays the father, was a local dentist making his acting debut. The costumes are by Laura Gemser. *Troll III* was released as *Crawlers*.

TROMA'S WAR

(Troma, 1988) **D/S/P:** Lloyd Kaufman **D/P:** Michael Herz **S:** Mitchell Dana, Eric Hattler, Thomas Martinek   (*War*)

Tourists on a Caribbean island stop a terrorist invasion of America. The terrorists plan to infect Americans with AIDS. This headache-inducing mess features exhausting action, bad taste gags, and some twisted political humor. Available in R or a ten-minute-longer unrated versions.

TRON

(Disney, 1982) **D/S:** Steven Lisberger **P:** Donald Kushner **M:** Wendy Carlos

Jeff Bridges is a video game designer who is transported into his own game. The ahead-of-its-time first feature-length computer-animated movie was a technical breakthrough at the time and was shot in 65 mm. The G-rated plot is your basic good vs. evil (David Warner). He, Bruce Boxleitner, Cindy Morgan, and Barnard Hughes all play two roles. Also with Dan Shor.

TROPICAL HEAT

(Prism, 1993) **D:** Jag Mundhra
S: Michael W. Potts **P/E:** Ashok Amritraj

Rick Rossovich, working for an American insurance company, goes to India to investigate the death of a millionaire maharajah who was stomped by an elephant. Three woman are featured in sex scenes with the "hero." I saw the unrated version, but there's also an R. Maryam D'Abo is the "American" widow (sex in a river) and Lee Anne Beaman is a fake blonde (sex in and around a pool). Asha Siewkumar, a dark-skinned young Indian woman, has the best sex scenes (and body) in the movie. This is a pretty subversive movie by the Indian-born filmmakers, who usually made their features

(*Night Eyes, Last Call . . .*) in America. Parts are laughable (D'Abo's acting), but the Indian locations and buildings are beautiful and I don't mind revealing that the western women turn out to be lesbian killers and that elephants (!) save the day!

TROPICAL SNOW

(Paramount, 1986) **D/S:** Ciro Duran **P:** J. D. Leof

Madeleine Stowe (early in her acting career) and Nick Corri star as a Colombian couple who want to go to New York. Oskar the drug lord (David Carradine) offers them passage but forces them to swallow and transport cocaine packets. The fairly depressing movie features nudity. It was filmed in Colombia.

TROUBLE BOUND

(Fox, 1992) **D:** Jeff Reiner **S:** Darrell Fetty, Francis Delia **P:** Tom Kuhn, Fred Weintraub

In a comic Southern road-chase crime movie, Michael Madsen is an ex-con who doesn't know he has a body in his trunk of the Cadillac he won in a

card game. He picks up Patricia Arquette, the lying granddaughter of a mobster. With Seymour Cassell as a mobster, Florence Stanley as an old lady gang leader, and Ginger Lynn Allen (on TV). Parts are like *Detour*. By the director of *Blood and Concrete*.

TROUBLE IN MIND

(Charter, 1985) **D/S:** Alan Rudolph
P: Carolyn Pfeiffer, David Blocker

In the near future an ex-detective (Kris Kristofferson) is released from prison after killing a mobster. Genevieve Bujold is his former lover running a diner. Keith Carradine is a crook living in a trailer with Lori Singer, and Divine (very good as a man for a change) is a gangster. Carradine's character gets stranger and stranger in this very strange movie filmed in Seattle. With Joe Morton, George Kirby, and John Considine. Marianne Faithfull sings the title song. Bujold was also in *Choose Me* (1984) and *The Moderns* (1988) by Rudolph.

TROUBLE IN THE SKY

(1960) **D:** Charles Frend **S:** Robert Westerly
P: Aubry Baring   UK (*Cone of Silence*)

A military captain (Michael Craig) tries to help clear the name of a pilot (Bernard Lee) whose jet had gone down in India. With Peter Cushing as Captain Judd, George Sanders, Elizabeth Seal, Andre Morell, and Gordon Jackson. Universal released a cut version of the b/w British Lion feature here.

TROUBLE MAN

(1972) **D:** Ivan Dixon **S:** John
D. F. Black **P:** Joel D. Freeman

The producer and screenwriter of *Shaft* did the same duties for this private eye movie, the first directed by actor Dixon, a former *Hogan's Heroes* regular. Many have called it the worst "blaxploitation" movie, but obviously those critics missed a lot of the others. Robert Hooks stars as "Mr. T." Gangster Chalky Price (Paul Winfield) frames him for a murder. With Ralph Waite as Chalky's white partner, Paula Kelly, William Smith as a police captain, Julius W. Harris, Tracy Reed, and real pool player James Earl "Texas Blood" Brown. It includes one of those *Lady from Shanghai* house of mirrors shootouts. The music by Marvin Gaye was on a Tamla LP. From 20th Century. Dixon directed *The Spook Who Sat By The Door* (1973) next.

THE TROUBLE WITH HARRY

(MCA, 1955) **D/P:** Alfred Hitchcock
S: John Michael Hayes

Various characters think they killed a man in beautiful rural Vermont and try to hide the body. The Technicolor Vistavision black comedy is one of Hitchcock's lesser-known gems. His unique dark sense of humor didn't appeal to many Americans in the 50s, but *Harry* is similar to some of Hitchcock's TV programs. It's based on a story by John Trevor. Shirley MacLaine made her film debut as the wife of Harry. John Forsythe costars with Edmund Gwenn, Mildred Natwick, and Royal Dano. Jerry Mathers finds the dead Harry in the woods.

Keith Carradine in *Trouble in Mind*.

The music is by Bernard Herrmann (his first score for the director). Hitchcock walks by an outdoor art exhibition. From Paramount. Hitch did his remake of *The Man Who Knew Too Much* (1956) next. Both were re-released to theaters in 1984.

TRUCK STOP WOMEN
(Bingo, 1974) **D/S/P:** Mark Lester **S:** Paul Deason

Anna (Lieux Dressler) runs a truck stop whorehouse in New Mexico. Her daughter Rose (Claudia Jennings) drives an 18-wheeler. When the Mafia tries to take over their racket they fight back and rob trucks. Plenty of violence and nudity plus a shocking ending helped make this a drive-in favorite. With Uschi Digart. Lester had previously directed the underground *Tricia's Wedding* (featuring the Cockettes) and *Steel Arena* (1973). *Truckstop Women 2* (VGB) was a retitled unrelated movie.

TRUCK TURNER
(Orion, 1974) **D:** Jonathan Kaplan **S:** S: Leigh Chapman **P:** Fred Weintraub, Paul Heller *(Black Bullet)*

Isaac Hayes stars as a violent bounty hunter who goes after pimps and pushers in an AIP hit. He also provided the score, released on Enterprise as a double album. *Truck Turner* includes a pimp funeral and a big hospital shootout massacre. Alan Weeks is Truck's partner and Annazette Chase is his shoplifter girlfriend. Nichelle Nichols from *Star Trek* (in her only 70s feature) is a mean, foul-mouthed whorehouse madam. With Yaphet Kotto as a gangster, Scatman Crothers, Dick Miller, Matthew "Stymie" Beard, Annik Borel, and Don Megowan.

TRUE BLOOD
(Fries, 1989) **D/S:** Frank Kerr **P:** Peter Maris

Jeff Fahey and Chad Lowe star as the Trueblood brothers in NYC. Fahey returns from years of Marine service to find his brother involved with a gang led by Spider (Billy Drago), a scarred, cop-killing gangster with a switchblade and spider earrings. With Sherilyn Fenn, and James Tolkan and Ken Foree as cops after Fahey, who had been falsely accused of killing a cop.

TRUE LIES
(Fox, 1994) **D/S/P:** James Cameron **P:** Stephanie Austin **M:** Brad Feidel

Arnold Schwarzenegger stars as Harry Tasker, a married computer salesman dad who moonlights as a spy chasing nuclear terrorists. Cameron and Schwarzenegger both had to try and top their previous features, so this action hit is bigger and dumber than any of them, and cost a record $120 million. It copies a lot from Bond movies but is a loose remake of French action comedy *La Totale!* (1991). In order to top *Terminator 2,* it features another Cameron nuke blast (in the Florida Keys), but this time it's treated as a harmless joke. Some of the FX are incredible. Jamie Lee Curtis costars as his unsuspecting wife, who eventually joins in the mayhem, and Tom Arnold is his (funny) spy partner. With Bill Paxton as a con-man car salesman, Tia Carrere as a sexy villainess, Art Malik as the main Arab terrorist (with four nuclear weapons), Eliza Dushku as the daughter, and Charlton Heston. The 20th Fox release runs 141 minutes. Letterboxed laser discs are available (of course). I wonder how James and Arnold will top this one?

TRUE ROMANCE
(Warner, 1993) **D:** Tony Scott **S:** Quentin Tarantino **P:** Bill Unger

A call girl who calls herself Alabama (Patricia Arquette) marries Clarence (Christian Slater), a Detroit comic book store clerk. He becomes a heroic killer holding a stash of coke and they drive to LA in a purple Cadillac. It's based on Tarantino's first script and in many ways is the ultimate film/comic book nerd fantasy movie. It's filled with memorable characters, surprising violence, and some good laughs. One great scene stars Dennis Hopper as the ex-cop father and Christopher Walken as a mobster. Gary Oldman is a scary pimp with dreadlocks, Brad Pitt is a guy who is always happily stoned, and Val Kilmer (his face obscured) is the helpful ghost of Elvis. With Saul Rubinek, Michael Rapaport, Bronson Pinchot, Christopher Penn, Tom Sizemore, and Samuel L. Jackson. Sonny Chiba and John Woo movie scenes are also used. It was originally to be a small movie directed by William Lustig. The Warner release is available in 121 minute unrated versions, an R version (two minutes shorter) and on a widescreen disc. Jackson and Walken were also in Tarantino's *Pulp Fiction* and Penn was in his *Reservoir Dogs.*

TRULY, MADLY, DEEPLY
(Thorn EMI, 1991) **D/S:** Anthony Minghella **P:** Robert Cooper UK

Juliet Stevenson (*Drowning by Numbers*) is the grieving lover of Alan Rickman, whose ghost returns in the romantic ghost story. It was released by the Samuel Goldwyn Co.

TRUNK TO CAIRO
(1966) **D/P:** Menahem Golan **S:** Marc Behm, Alexander Ramati   Israel/W. Germany

American WWII hero Audie Murphy stars as an Israeli agent in Cairo. He falls for the daughter (Marianne Koch) of a German scientist (George Sanders) who has developed a nuclear-powered moon rocket. It was filmed in Italy and Israel. The first Golan-directed feature to play in America was released by AIP.

TRUST
(Republic, 1990) **D/S/P:** Hal Hartley

In Hartley's second Long Island movie, Adrienne Shelly is Maria, a pregnant high school dropout who meets an anti-social mechanical genius (Martin Donovan) who carries hand grenades, insults and punches out people, and hates TV sets. Her mother (who blames Maria for her father's death) kicks her out, and there's a fight in an abortion clinic. Believe it or not, this movie, which is played very seriously, is funny. Hartley's *Surviving Desire* (1991), also with Donovan, *Simple Men* (1992), and *Amateur* (1995) followed.

THE TRUST
(1993) **D:** Neil Havers **D/S:** J. Douglas Killgore **P:** Gary Chasen

This turn-of-the-century mystery is about the murder of (the real) Texas philanthropist William Marsh Rice. Sam Bottoms is the man's attorney and Karen Black is a widow. The 2-hour-long indy feature is based on a play by Killgore (an industrial filmaker) and was filmed in Houston.

TRUST ME
(Virgin, 1989) **D/S:** Bobby Houston **S:** Gary Rigdon **P:** George Edwards

In an artwork satire by a star of *The Hills Have Eyes,* Adam Ant is a British gallery owner who has clients killed to raise prices ("Dead means bread"). He tries to kill off young artist David Packer. With Talia Balsam and her real-life mother, Joyce Van

Patten, and Barbara Bain. Real art by Andy Warhol, Jean-Michel Basquiat, and Keith Haring (who all died shortly after this movie was released) is seen.

TRUTH OR DARE?

(Peerless, 1986) **D/S/P:** Tim Ritter

Here's one to make you think you've lost your mind. Who makes these senseless things, and who puts up the money!?! A guy finds his wife cheating on him and hides in the woods. A red-haired woman (the devil?) appears and dares him to cut his finger off, then rip his chest open. He does, she rips her eyes out, then disappears. He ends up in the nuthouse where he continues to play "truth or dare" with other inmates. One guy puts a hand grenade in his mouth and pulls the pin out. After more (imagined?) mutilation, he gets out, puts on a gold metal mask, runs over a baby, and kills a kid with a chainsaw. A seemingly retarded cop tries to catch him. At one point the tape becomes a comedy (at least that's what I think). With Mary Fanaro. Some of the fast editing is really good, but the theme song ballad ("Critical Madness") is the worst. It was shot (in 16mm) in Palm Beach. Madonna copied the title! *Wicked Games* (1993) was Ritter's mail-order-only sequel.

THE TRYGON FACTOR

(1966) **D:** Cyril Frankel **S:** Derry Quinn, Stanley Munro **P:** Brian Taylor   UK/W. Germany

Cathleen Nesbitt and her daughter (Susan Hampshire) operate a crime syndicate from a mansion where (fake) nuns live. Star Stewart Granger is Inspector Smith. With Sophie Hardy, Eddi Arent, Robert Morley, James Robertson Justice, and Terry-Thomas. The Edgar Wallace mystery was filmed in two versions (English and German). Warner released it in America.

TRYST

(Suma, 1994) **D/S:** Peter Foldy
P: Lawrence Applebaum, Jackelyn Giroux

The formerly-lost son (star Johnny La Spada) of a maid (Louise Fletcher) shows up and ends up moving in with the rich dysfunctional couple she works for. He also has an affair with the lady of the house (Barbara Carrera) who plans to have her corrupt detective lover (Steve Bond) kill her cold husband (David Warner, who spends most of the movie in a coma). There's also a jealous girlfriend (Jamie Luner) staying at a motel run by a voyeur photographer Desert Storm vet. It's your basic direct-to-video erotic film noir attempt. The sex scenes all seem to be cut (it's rated R), and it's way too long at 101 minutes.

TRY THIS ON FOR SIZE

(1989) **D/S:** Guy Hamilton **S/P:** Sergio Gobbi **S:** Alec Medieff   France

Michael Brandon stars as a James Bond–like insurance investigator, and David Carradine is the villain who steals a rare Russian icon. With Guy Marchand as a French cop and Arielle Dombasle. It was based on James Hadley Chase's novel and was part of a planned series.

TUFF TURF

(Starmaker, 1985) **D:** Fritz Kiersch
S: "Jette Rinck" **P:** Donald P. Borchers

James Spader is the new kid in a rough LA neighborhood and Paul Mones is the local gang leader. It's an awkward mix of violence and dancing. With Robert Downey Jr., Kim Richards, Matt Clark, Olivia Barash, Lene Lovich, and Catya Sassoon. Southside Johnny and Jim Carroll are on the soundtrack of the New World release.

TUNNELVISION

(MPI, 1976) **D:** Brad Swirnoff **D/S:** Neal Israel **S:** Michael Mislove **P:** Joe Roth

A Congressional hearing on television is the framing device for a series of TV show and commercial spoofs. This comedy features many familiar faces (and voices). With Phil Proctor, Howard Hesseman, Chevy Chase (also in *The Groove Tube*), Laraine Newman, Franken and Davis, Ernie Anderson and his wife Edwina, Betty Thomas, Gerrit Graham, Ron Silver, Joe Flaherty, and William Schallert. Israel made *Americathon* next.

THE TURN OF THE SCREW

(Cannon, 1989) **D:** Graeme Clifford **S:** Robert Hutchinson, James Miller **P:** Bridget Terry

Amy Irving stars and narrates another version of Henry James's ghost novel. David Hemmings costars with Bathazar Getty. It was one of the 60-minute Shelley Duvall Nightmare Classics. Lynn Redgrave starred in a 1974 TV version (released by Thriller Video). Forget both and search for the great version, *The Innocents* (1961).

THE TURN OF THE SCREW

(Live, 1992) **D/S:** Rusty Lemorande
P: Staffan Ahrenberg, Nicole Sequin
UK/France/Luxembourg

Patsy Kensit stars as Jenny the new governess in this version of the Henry James novel, set (for some reason) in the mid-60s. Stephane Audran costars, and Julian Sands (in a small role) is the guardian. Too much narration (by Kensit and Marianne Faithfull), too many false scares, dream sequences, and nightmares help ruin the story. Faithfull is seen in a b/w intro and a there's a nice (*Road Warrior*–inspired!) ending. It was filmed on a gorgeous estate in Surrey and has Simon Boswell music.

THE TURN ON

(New Horizons, 1985/93) **D:** Steve Barnett
D/S: Jean Louis Richard **P:** Milo Manera
France (*Le Delic; Click*)

A researcher in New Orleans discovers a remote device that controls sexual behavior. His chauffeur (Jean-Pierre Kalfon) steals the device and uses it on a young woman (Florence Guerin) who had rejected him. She strips in public places and offers herself to strangers. It's based on erotic French adult comics by Milo Manera that are very popular in Europe. Guerin looks great, but while the comics are clever erotic fantasies, the movie concentrates on awkward embarrassment. Roger Corman

hired Steve Barnett to Americanize this and shoot new scenes of women stripping in public and some comedy (he did the same with *Emmanuelle 5*). A beach sex scene was also cut. The new scenes feature Maria Ford, Debra Lamb, Toni Naples, and George "Buck" Flower. Video Search of Miami offers the original with subtitles.

TURN ON TO LOVE

(1969) **D/C/E:** John Avildsen **P:** Leonard Kirkman

Sharon Kent (also in several Doris Wishman movies) is a bored housewife who goes to the East Village for pot orgies and has an affair with a married Italian filmmaker. Avildsen followed this b/w drama, from a porn producer, with *Guess What We Learned in School Today?* (1970).

TURN ON, TUNE IN, DROP OUT

(1967) **D:** Robin Clark **P:** Henry G. Saperstein

Timothy Leary is seen lecturing on stage in New York, Indian music is heard, and there's an animated LSD segment. The Mercury soundtrack album includes dialogue. Producer Saperstein also imported some Toho giant monster movies and backed Woody Allen's *What's Up Tiger Lily?* Leary's only other 60s film appearance was in *Diaries, Notes and Sketches* (1969) by Jonas Mekas.

TUSK

(VSOM, 1980) **D/S:** Alexandro Jodorowsky
S: Nick Niciphor, Jeffrey O'Kelly   France

A little girl and an elephant are born at the same time in turn-of-the-century India. She (Cyrielle Clair) grows up, develops a psychic link with "Tusk," and is kidnapped by bad guys. With Anton Diffring as her father and Christopher Mitchum. The barely released 119-minute feature, based on a novel, was filmed in English. It was the last feature by Jodorowsky until *Santa Sangre* (1989), which also features elephants.

TUSKS

(Magnum, 1985) **D/S:** Tara Moore
S/A: John Rhys-Davies **P:** Keith C. Jones

Lucy Gutteridge stars as an artist in Africa. She and Julian Glover look into the illegal poaching of elephants. With John Rhys-Davies as the villain, Andrew Stevens, and James Coburn Jr. Simon Nuchtern was a film doctor for this feature, which took five years to release. It was filmed in Zimbabwe.

TV'S GREATEST ADVENTURES OF SUPERMAN

(Warner series, 1951–57)

George Reeves (who either shot himself or was killed in 1959) is faster than a bullet in these all-time-favorite early TV episodes. Phyllis Kirk was Lois Lane (also in *Superman and the Mole Men*) for the first episodes (made in 1951) but was replaced by Noel Neill. The other regulars are Jack Larson as Jimmy Olson, John Hamilton as Perry White ("Great Caesar's Ghost!"), and Robert Shayne as Inspector Henderson. These shows have been and will continue to be repeated over and over on TV. The very-low-budget production values and fun guest villains make them irresistible even though they were aimed at young kids. Tapes each containing 2 episodes of the famous syndicated series run 52 minutes each. B/W episodes are sometimes paired with color ones (which were very unusual for the 50s). Many were directed by Thomas Carr, who had codirected *The Adventures of Superman* serial in 1948.

12:01

(New Line, 1993) **D:** Jack Sholder **S:** Philip Morton **P:** Robert J. Degus, Cindy Hoftnickle

I like movies where characters bounce back and forth in time. This was based on a student film (by Morton) which itself was copied by *Groundhog Day.* Jonathan Silverman stars as an office worker at the Utrel Corp. who is trapped repeating the same work day over and over and trying to save the life of a scientist (Helen Slater) and win her love. Anyone who has worked in an office will appreciate the funny scenes of the hero playing around with the fact that he knows exactly what everyone there is going to say and do. With Martin Landau and Jeremy Piven (from *The Larry Sanders Show*). The PG-13 release, based on a story by Richard A. Lupoff, debuted on cable.

12 + 1

(1970) **D/S:** Nicholas Gessner **P:** Claude Giroux Italy (*Una Su Tredici; The Thirteen Chairs*)

This is the same story as Mel Brooks's *The Twelve Chairs* from the same year (both are based on a Russian novel). Sharon Tate (in her last role) is topbilled with Orson Welles as a theater manager busy presenting *Dr. Jekyll and Mr. Hyde.* Vittorio De-Sica, and Terry-Thomas. Tate and Vittorio Gassman hunt for the 12 chairs, after discovering a fortune is in one of them.

24 HOUR LOVER

(1968) **D/S:** Marran Gosov **P:** Rob Houwer W. Germany (*Crunch; Bengelchen Liebt Kreuz Und Quer*)

A Munich wine salesman is a bachelor who fools around and upsets his family. Harold Leipnitz stars with Brigitte Skay. AIP released the R-rated comedy.

25 ∞5: THE CONTINUING ADVENTURES OF THE ROLLING STONES

(GMV, 1990) **D:** Nigel Finch **P:** Andrew Solt

You're probably sick of hearing about the Rolling Stones. Maybe you wish they had broken up years ago. If you ever loved this band, though, don't miss this 2-hours-plus chronological documentary tape with interviews (new and old, with lots of choice quotes), news clips, and TV and concert footage. It covers the hits, the hype, the censorship, deaths and drugs, marriages and the Maharishi. There's enough great material here from the Brian Jones, London/Decca days to make it worthwhile. Don't expect many whole songs, but unless you're a fanatic collector, you've never seen many of these rare clips, going back to 1964. Early highlights are Brian playing slide guitar on "Little Red Rooster," a real rock riot in The Hague, and Brian introducing Howlin' Wolf on *Shindig.* There's part of the amazing "2000 Light Years from Home" video,

but unfortunately, the music from their underappreciated "psychedelic" period gets passed over too quickly.

Things get spotty after *Exile on Main St.,* but the arena years go by faster and are still fascinating to look back on. They do embarrassments like "Angie" and "Star Star" (a.k.a. "StarFucker") but also play "I'm a Man" with Muddy Waters, and Keith sings "Happy." The Stones doing the entire "You Can't Always Get What You Want" on the never-aired *Rock and Roll Circus* TV special, Jagger doing "Memo from Turner" from *Performance,* and gray-haired Charlie Watts talking are still more reasons to see this tape. By the way, "Stew and Brian formed the band," says Bill Wyman in an old interview. The Stones' theatrical releases were *Gimme Shelter* (1969), the never officially released *Cocksucker Blues* (1972), *Ladies and Gentlemen, The Rolling Stones* (1974), *Let's Spend the Night Together* (1982), and *Rolling Stones at the Max* (1992).

20,000 LEAGUES UNDER THE SEA

(1916) **D/S:** Stuart Paton **P:** Carl Laemmle

The plot of this Universal silent is partially based on Jules Verne's *The Mysterious Island.* Union Army men drift in a balloon to an island (just like in the well-known 1960 version). The dark Captain Nemo (Allen Holubar) has flashbacks of battles when he was an Indian rajah and there's a "Nature Girl" (June Gail) who wears a leopard skin and sleeps in a tree. Scenes were shot in the Bahamas. J. Ernest Williamson and his brother George, who handled the underwater FX, also worked on the 1929 *Mysterious Island.* Prints run 105 minutes. It's been shown on the Sci-Fi Channel with new titles and music.

2020 TEXAS GLADIATORS

(Media, 1982) **D:** "Kevin Mancusco"/Aristede Massaccessi **S:** Alex Carver **P:** Helen Handris   Italy

Neo-nazis and bikers kill and rape in a *Mad Max*–style post-nuke western with nuns, cowboys, and Indians. The civilized Al Cliver is killed and his wife (Sabrina Siani) is saved from the bad guys by a trio of good guys (Harrison Muller, Peter Hooten, and Al Yamanouchi). A Sarlui production.

William Shatner and Pat Breslin on *The Twilight Zone.*

TWICE BITTEN = VAMPIRE HOOKERS

TWICE DEAD

(Nelson, 1988) **D/S:** Bert Dragin
S/P: Robert McDonnell **P:** Guy J. Louthan

A poor family moves into a run-down haunted LA mansion, the parents leave, and the kids fight off a punk gang. They try to scare them with homemade horror FX, then the real ghost of an actor (Jonathan Chapin) helps, causing deaths by various ways. Tom Breznahan and Jill Whitlow are the kid stars. With Brooke Bundy, Charlie Spradling, and Todd Bridges (the *Diff'rent Strokes* star who was arrested for attempted murder). From Concorde.

TWILIGHT OF THE COCKROACHES

(Streamline, 1987) **D/S/P:** Hiroki Yashida
P: Carl Macek (English version) Japan

Live action is mixed with cute animated insects. The action is seen from the roach POV. A very neat woman (Setsuko Karamsumarau) moves in with a man and the life of the roaches is threatened by cleaning and toxic sprays. There's also a talking turd and a post-nuke ending.

TWILIGHT'S LAST GLEAMING

(Fox, 1977) **D:** Robert Aldrich
S: Ronald M. Cohen **P:** Merv Adelson

Burt Lancaster is an ex–Air Force general who with the help of a (largely black) renegade group takes over an ICBM silo and demands that America admit its secret Vietnam policies or the missiles will be launched. Richard Widmark costars with Melvyn Douglas, Gerald O'Loughlin, and Charles Durning (as the President). Also with Paul Winfield, Burt Young, Roscoe Lee Browne, Richard Jaeckel, Vera Miles, William Marshall, Leif Erickson, Charles McGraw, and William Smith. The Allied Artists/Lorimar release was too political and too long (146 minutes) for some, but is one of Aldrich's finest. It was partially shot in Bavaria. Jerry Goldsmith provided the score. I wonder if Robert McNamara saw this.

THE TWILIGHT ZONE

(CBS/Fox, 1959–64)

36 episodes of Rod Serling's classic series are available in 18 volumes running 50 minutes each. Titles were released four at a time. Some are thematic double bills. The double cassette *Treasures from the Twilight Zone* (Fox, 1992) includes "An Occurrence at Owl Creek Bridge," "The Encounter," "Where Is Everybody" (the premiere episode), plus three other episodes, a Rod Serling sales pitch short, and an interview. *Twilight Zone: The Creative Vision* (Vol. 1 and 2) are Fox 4 laser disc box sets with 15 episodes each plus an early 70s TV special with Serling talking about writing (on Vol. 1). *The Best of the Twilight Zone CD* (Varèse Sarabande) includes music by Bernard Herrmann and others. There was also a "new" *Twilight Zone* TV series (1985–89), but don't bother looking for those.

THE TWILIGHT ZONE: ROD SERLING'S LOST CLASSICS

(1994) **D:** Robert Markowitz **S:** Richard Matheson, Rod Serling **P:** S. Bryan Hickox

The title of this CBS TV feature is misleading. Two unfilmed scripts (not intended for *The Twilight Zone*) were discovered by Rod Serling's widow Carol and filmed. The half-hour short "The Theatre" with Amy Irving, Gary Cole, and Priscilla Pointer concerns hallucinations and real people replacing the actors on a movie screen. The 90-minute "Where Dead Is Dead" is more of a horror story set in the 19th century with Patrick Bergin as a surgeon visiting Jack Palance on an island. James Earl Jones hosts. It was made in North Carolina.

TWILIGHT ZONE—THE MOVIE

(Warner, 1983) **D:** Steven Spielberg, Joe Dante, George Miller **D/S:** John Landis **S:** George Clayton Johnson, Richard Matheson, Josh Ragan

Three old *Twilight Zone* episodes were remade plus a new story and wraparound segments. It's worth seeing for the Dante and Miller episodes, which are both great and improve on the originals. Spielberg did "Kick the Can," the "nice" one with Scatman Crothers. Dante did "It's a *Good* Life" with Jeremy Licht as Anthony, the kid who controls everthing around him, Kathleen Quinlan, Kevin McCarthy, William Schallert, Dick Miller, and Billy Mumy (who starred in the original episode). The fun FX are by Rob Bottin. Miller did "Nightmare at 20,000 Feet" starring John Lithgow, with Abbe Lane and Donna Dixon. Landis did the one not based on the TV show, a convoluted tale of racism partially set in Vietnam. Unfortunately, star Vic Morrow and two kid extras were killed in 1982 while acting in a scene with a helicopter. Landis was indicted for involuntary manslaughter on the day the movie was released. A trial started in 1986 and he was acquitted. The book *Outrageous Conduct* was about the case. The Jerry Goldsmith score is on Warner Bros. Dan Aykroyd and Albert Brooks are in the intro.

TWIN DRAGONS

(1991) **D:** Tsui Hark, Ringo Lam Hong Kong

Jackie Chan stars as twins in an action comedy that copies ideas from *Double Impact*. One grew up in America and is a wealthy concert pianist, the other is a street hoodlum. Both become involved in gangster trouble and end up fighting in a Mitsubishi plant. Maggie Chung costars with Nina Li and Teddy Robin Kwan. Since this was made to benefit the Hong Kong Directors Guild, directors Hark, Lam, John Woo, and others make cameo appearances.

TWIN PEAKS

(Warner, 1990) **D/P:** David Lynch **S:** Mark Frost **P:** David J. Latt **C:** Ron Garcia

When this unique ABC pilot spoof was aired, many viewers were mesmerized and looked forward to the series. Kyle MacLachlan stars as agent Dale Cooper investigating a brutal murder in the Pacific Northwest. The primetime soap opera murder mystery surprised viewers with the disturbing oppressive misery and corruption, the bizarre characters, plus comic and fantasy touches. Sheryl Lee is the murdered Laura Palmer (and later her own cousin) and Ray Wise is her father Leland. The cast includes Michael Ontkean, Joan Chen, Piper Laurie, Grace Zabriskie, Sherilyn Fenn, Lara Flynn Boyle, Dana Ashbrook, James Marshall, Madchen Amick, Richard Beymer, Everett McGill, Wendy Robie, Russ Tamblyn, Robert Davenport, Peggy Lipton, Kimmy Robertson, and Eric DaRe. Jack Nance and Catherine E. Coulson had both been in Lynch's *Eraserhead*. It was filmed in Snoqualmie, Washington, where tourists later visited. Warner Brothers released the soundtrack, with the voice of Julee Cruise and haunting music by Angelo Badalamenti. The video was released in Europe before it debuted on US TV and has 15 additional minutes at the end (featuring Bob). The American 1992 video release is a "director's cut."

TWIN PEAKS

(World Vision series 1990–92)

What started as probably the most extreme and surreal program ever on network TV eventually got too boring, meandering, silly, and confusing to care about. For a while obsessed viewers formed clubs and the show was the talk of the town, but several schedule changes and the fact that people wanted to know who the killer was caused the rating to drop. In addition to the many cast regulars from the pilot, the series featured a giant (Carel Struycken), a dwarf (Michael Anderson), Miguel Ferrer, Frank Silva, Michael Parks, Royal Dano, David Warner, Dan O'Herlihy, Billy Zane, and Lynch himself. Episode directors included Diane Keaton, Tina Rathbone, Tim Hunter, and Caleb Deschanel. The series was a hit in Japan in 1992. *Twin Peaks: Special Collectors Edition* is all 29 hour-long episodes on 6 tapes. Also on laser discs from Image.

TWIN PEAKS—FIRE WALK WITH ME

(New Line, 1992) **D/S/A:** David Lynch
S: Robert Engels **P:** Gregg Fienberg

It was a hit in Japan months before the US release, but the long (135 minutes) theatrical prequel to Lynch's TV series was a big flop here. It's very serious and weird with scenes that couldn't have been shown on network TV. In fact this is one of the strangest movies ever to receive a major release. Sheryl Lee stars as the depressed, coke-sniffing incest victim Laura Palmer during the last week of her life. She works in a sex club just over the Canadian border. Parts are related as flashbacks, nightmares, dreams, and visions, some characters need subtitles, and an angel appears. Moira Kelly (replacing TV series regular Lara Flynn Boyle) is her best friend Donna, and James Marshall is the good biker who loves her. Many of the TV regulars are missing but the cast includes Ray Wise as Leland, Laura's father, Grace Zabriskie as her mother, and Frank Silva as Bob. Kyle MacLachlan as agent Dale Cooper and Chris Isaak as another FBI agent show up, and Miguel Ferrer, Kiefer Sutherland, and David Bowie are other briefly seen agents. Also with Michael Anderson, Dana Ashbrook, Pamela Gidley, Jurgen Prochnow and cameos by Peggy Lipton, Madchen Amick,

Julee Cruise, and Harry Dean Stanton. Cinematographer Ron Garcia is a veteran of exploitation and adults-only movies. The strange but excellent score is by Angelo Badalamenti.

TWINSANITY = GOODBYE GEMINI

TWIN SISTERS

(Vidmark, 1992) **D/P:** Tom Berry
S: David Preston **P:** Franco Battista

Stepfanie Kramer (from the *Hunter* series) stars as a Beverly Hills housewife who goes to Montreal to visit her twin sister, now a missing high-price hooker. She goes undercover as a hooker. With Frederic Forrest as a police detective, James Brolin, and Susan Almgren.

TWIST

(New Line, 1992) **D/P:** Ron Mann   Canada

The Lindy Hop (1953), the Itch (1954), the Jitterbug (1955), the Bop (1956), the Stroll (1957), and the Madison (1959) are all seen as leading up to the "vulgar" international dance craze that Marshall McLuhan called "cool and unsexy." This entertaining historical documentary shows how the twist became big business and includes good interviews with Hank Ballard, Chubby Checker, and Joey Dee. It features excellent TV and movie clips of dancers on *American Bandstand* and *The T.A.M.I. Show*, The Flamingos (from *Go, Johnny, Go*) and Louis Prima and June Wilkinson (*Twist All Night*). Mann also made *Comic Book Confidential*.

TWISTED

(Hemdale, 1985) **D:** Adam Holender
S: Glenn Kershaw **S/P:** Bruce Graham

Christian Slater (who was on the *Ryan's Hope* soap opera at the time) stars as an evil kid in a feature made in Danbury, Connecticut. He kills kittens, burns a cat, dissects other animals, and has a secret sound system (like in *Ferris Bueller's Day Off*). He torments his babysitter (Lois Smith) with loud Nazi march music and Hitler speeches and even kills a local jock who had humiliated him. It's full of false scares and has a very stupid ending, but it's interesting to see Slater as a psycho kid. It wasn't released until 1992. With Tandy Cronyn and Dina Merrill.

TWISTED FATE

(1994) **D/S:** Donald Jackson
S: Randall Frakes **P:** Eric Warren

Three women on vacation in a cabin are terrorized by a pair of psychos. It's seen through the lens of one of the women's video cameras. With Julie Nine, Nancy Jury, and Suzanne Solari (from Jackson's *Rollerblade* movies).

TWISTED ISSUES

(1988) **D/S/A/C:** Charles Pinion
S: Steve Antczak Hawk

Described as "a psycho-punk splatter comedy," this underground, self-distributed tape was made in Gainesville, Florida. The sort-of hero is a young nonviolent, short-haired skateboarder who doesn't smoke or drink. Violent drunk bad guys (and girls) start a fight with him, then run him over. A pot-smoking doctor brings him back to life as a mutant wearing a sieve on his mangled face. He drills through his foot and bolts on his skateboard. Meanwhile Charles watches TV. He sees the mutant skateboard monster killing people, scenes from movies (like *Psych-Out*), actual commercials and anti-drug spots, and some pretty funny new TV footage created for this tape. Other found footage edited in (like in Oliver Stone's *Natural Born Killers*) features H-bombs, Hitler, the Pope, Reagan, Thatcher, and a slaughterhouse. Lots of local bands (Doldrums, Hell Witch, Mutley Chix . . .) provide the soundtrack music, and one all-female band plays live at a crowded house party. My favorite song was "I'm Feelin' Very Ugly." Somebody gets an axe in the chest and a head is cut off with hedge clippers, but there was no effects budget so there's pretty cheap gore. I thought it was kind of slow and too long, but it's great to see an equal opportunity regional horror movie with punk sensibilities, and any readers who are into skateboards and punk groups would probably love it. Pinion later made *Red Spirit Lake*.

TWISTED JUSTICE

(Arena, 1990) **D/S/P/A:** David Heavener

Star David Heavener is renegade cop in LA 2020, where regular guns are outlawed and stinger tranquilizer guns are used. He battles a superpowerful "turbo-charged fruit loop" on drugs who kills women. The stellar support cast includes Erik Estrada, Tanya Roberts, Karen Black, Shannon Tweed, Jim Brown, Don Stroud as a psycho, James Van Patten, Julie Austin, and Bonnie Payne.

TWISTED NIGHTMARE

(TWE, 1982) **D/S:** Paul Hunt **P:** Sandy Horowitz

Teen couples who won a free camping trip are killed in the woods (built over an Indian burial ground) in this senseless and too dark *Friday the 13th* copy. A retarded guy who had been burned is the big growling creature. He slashes, decapitates, and mutilates in slow motion to rock music. Meanwhile four females have nude scenes, characters have dreams and flashbacks, and the guys all look like body builders. With Rhonda Gray and Robert Padilla. It was released in 1987.

TWISTER

(Vestron, 1989) **D/S:** Michael Almereyda
P: Wieland Schulz-Keil

The Cleveland family, led by a retired soda pop tycoon (Harry Dean Stanton), live in a mansion in Kansas. Suzy Amis and Crispin Glover are sister and brother and a tornado threatens. The strange comedy is based on the novel *Oh!* by Mary Robison. With Dylan McDermott, Jenny Wright, Lois Chiles, William Burroughs, and Tim Robbins. By the screenwriter of of Wim Wenders's *Until the End of the World*, who also made a Dennis Hopper short called *A Hero in Our Time* (1987) and *Another Girl, Another Planet* (1992) filmed with a Pixelvision camera. Not to be confused with the 1996 blockbuster starring Helen Hunt.

TWO EVIL EYES

(Fox, 1990) **D/S/P:** Dario Argento **D/S:** George A. Romero **S:** Franco Ferrini **P:** Achille Manzotti
Italy/US (*Due Occhi Diabolici*)

Originally planned to be four modernized Poe stories, this should have been either a trilogy or one complete Argento movie. It opens with Poe's actual house and tombstone. Adrienne Barbeau and E. G. Marshall are in *The Facts in the Case of M. Valdemar* directed by Romero. The story had previously been filmed by Roger Corman in his *Tales of Terror* trilogy. This version is pretty weak. Also with Tom Akins and Christina Romero. The second story is *The Black Cat* by Argento. It's one of Argento's best and benefits from having Harvey Keitel as Roderick Usher, a hard-drinking photographer who specializes in real-life horror photos. *The Black Cat* contains an effective nightmare sequence, some extreme gore, and lots of Poe in-jokes and references. With Madeleine Potter as his wife Annabel, John Amos as a cop, Martin Balsam, Kim Hunter, Sally Kirkland, and Tom Savini (who also did the FX). Luigi Cozzi was the second unit director of *The Black Cat*. The score is by Pino Donaggio. Both stories were filmed in Pittsburgh. The US theatrical version was cut to 95 minutes but the tape runs 115 minutes.

TWO FACES OF EVIL

(Thriller, 1980) **D:** Alan Gibson
S: Ronald Graham   UK

Elvira hosts this hour-long Hammer TV episode with a plot about replacing a family on vacation with doubles. Anna Calder-Marshall and Gary Raymond star.

TWO GIRLS FOR A MADMAN

(SW, 1968) **D/S:** Stanley H. Brasloff **S:** Dustin Williams **P/C:** Victor Petrashevic

An aggressive young NYC ballet student named Toni goes on a date with a "producer." Frank (played by "Lucky Kargo") is a giggling, armed psycho killer/rapist who meets them at a folk music club and takes them to an orgy in the back room. Toni dances in her underwear, others smoke pot, strip, and wear creepy clear masks. Frank later attacks Toni (she likes it) in a car, then goes after her roomate Sonja (who has a shower scene). It all ends with a headline in the *Daily News*. With locker-room nudity and lines like "I've heard of all kinds of happenings in the past, but this is ridiculous." The b/w adult movie is from Distribpix.

TWO GUN LADY

(1956) **D/P:** Richard H. Bartlett **S:** Norman Jolley

Blonde Peggie Castle "had other weapons besides guns—and she used them!" She teams up with William Talman to fight Marie Windsor in this indy western. With Robert Lowry and Joe Besser (!). From Associated Film Releasing. Castle was also in Corman's *Oklahoma Woman* the same year.

200 MOTELS

(MGM/UA, 1971) **D:** Tony Palmer **D/S/A:** Frank Zappa **P:** Jerry Good, Herb Cohen   UK

This was the first feature shot on video and transferred to film. I saw it when it was new and hated it, but it seems pretty interesting now. The Mothers of Invention are on the road in "Centerville, U.S.A.," which was created by Cal Schenkel. Concert footage is mixed with computer graphics, dental hygiene animation, and solarized footage. Mark Volman and Howard Kaylan appear with Theodore Bikel, Ringo Starr (as Zappa), Keith Moon (as a nun) and the Royal Philharmonic Orchestra. The U.A. album of the same name is not exactly the soundtrack to this U.A. release feature. *The True Story of 200 Motels* (MPI) is a Dutch TV program. *Uncle Meat* (MPI) is another Zappa tape not based on the album of the same name.

THE TWO JAKES

(Paramount, 1989) **D/A:** Jack Nicholson
S: Robert Towne **P:** Robert Evans, Harold Schneider

15 years after *Chinatown*, Nicholson finally got to make his sequel and like every other feature he directed it's pretty interesting but with a lot of problems. Years and (a reported $3.5 million!) were lost on developing the project before this was shot. Its release was held up by Paramount and it was a flop at the box office. The confusing plot takes place in postwar LA. Harvey Keitel is the other Jake and Meg Tilly is his wife. Some memorable parts take place in a gay bar, and there's an unlikly explosion scene that seems to have been copied in *Die Hard II*. With Madeleine Stowe, Eli Wallach, Ruben Blades, Frederic Forrest, David Keith, Richard Farnsworth, Tracey Walter, and Tom Waits. The only returning characters besides J. J. Gittes (Nicholson) are played by James Hong and Perry Lopez.

TWO LANE BLACKTOP

(VSOM, 1971) **D/E:** Monte Hellman **S:** Rudy
Wurlitzer, Will Cory **P:** Michael S. Laughlin

"The Driver" (James Taylor) and "the Mechanic" (Beach Boys drummer Dennis Wilson) drive through the Southwest in their '55 Chevy and challenge GTO, an older drifter with a yellow Pontiac GTO, to a cross-country race. They also pick up "the Girl" (Laurie Bird). GTO (Warren Oates, the only real actor among the leads) says "If I'm not grounded pretty soon I'm gonna go into orbit." The existential road movie ends with the film getting stuck, breaking and burning. Also with Alan Vint, Rudy Wurlitzer, Jim Mitchum, and Harry Dean Stanton. *Two Lane* was backed by BBS (*The Last Movie, Drive, He Said . . .*) and Gary Kurtz was associate producer. Before Universal released it, the entire screenplay was published in *Esquire*, then it flopped badly at the box office and has been hard to see ever since. TV prints are censored. Wilson drowned and Bird died from a drug overdose (when she was engaged to Art Garfunkel).

TWO MINUTE WARNING

(MCA, 1976) **D:** Larry Peerce **S:** Edward
Hume **P:** Edward S. Feldman

This is a great movie for football haters, and it would make a good double bill with *Black Sunday*

(1977). A sniper is ready to start killing in the LA Memorial Coliseum during a game; meanwhile, a SWAT team is deployed and various characters (about to be killed) deal with their personal problems. Charlton Heston stars with John Cassavetes, Martin Balsam, Beau Bridges, David Janssen, Jack Klugman, Gena Rowlands, Walter Pidgeon, Brock Peters, Robert Ginty, Pamela Bellwood, Andy Sidaris as the TV director, and Merv Griffin singing the National Anthem. From Filmways. The network TV version has an additional 40 minutes of new footage that tried to explain/justify the assassin.

TWO MOON JUNCTION

(RCA/Columbia, 1988) **D/S:** Zalman King
P: Donald P. Borchers

Sherilyn Fenn is a wealthy engaged blonde Alabama girl who has an affair with a muscular carnival worker (Richard Tyson). Fenn has several major nude scenes and her character cries a lot. With Louise Fletcher as her grandma, Kristy McNichol as a bisexual, Burl Ives, Martin Hewitt, Millie Perkins, Milla Janovich, Screamin' Jay Hawkins, and Herve Villechaize. Fenn is the niece of Detroit rocker Suzi Quatro. *Return to Two Moon Junction* followed.

TWO OF A KIND

(Fox, 1983) **D/S:** John Herzfeld **P:** Roger M. Rothstein

The stars of *Grease* returned in this fantasy flop. John Travolta is Zack Mellon, a small-time bank robber, and Olivia Newton-John is the bank teller who ran off with the loot. They must perform great sacrifices for each other or God will flood the earth. Both sing (off camera). Four angels (Charles Durning, Beatrice Straight, Scatman Crothers, Castulo Guerra) picked them for the responsibility. With Ernie Hudson, Oliver Reed as Beazley (the devil), and Gene Hackman as the voice of God!

TWO ROSES AND A GOLDEN ROD

(SW, 1969) **D/S:** Albert Zugsmith
P: Hal Senter   (*Ménage à Trois*)

A screenwriter (John Alderman) has a British actress wife (Lisa Grant) with short hair and an exhibitionist virgin stepdaughter. All three think out loud, he types, and some of his sex scenes are illustrated. We also see a comic story about an angel watching sin on earth. Meanwhile, the jealous wife invites her lesbian friend to move in for revenge. Most of the dialogue is pretty hateful, but lines like "For one so round, you're awful square" stand out. There's a lot of psychological agonizing plus nudity and sex. Zugsmith made more adult movies than most realize. *The Outrageous Unbelievable Mechanical Love Machine* and *Violated!* followed. Grant was also in *Trader Hornee* and *Wilbur and the Baby Factory*.

TWO SMALL BODIES

(1994) **D/S:** Beth B. **S:** Neal Bell

Fred Ward is a cop on a child abduction case and Suzy Amis is a divorced mother who works at a

strip bar. Also with Viggo Mortensen. The feature, based on a play by Bell, was funded by German TV. B. also made *Salvation.*

2010

(MGM/UA, 1984) **D/S/P/C:** Peter Hyams

America and the USSR join together to recover a spaceship threatening to crash on Jupiter. The black monolith from *2001* is still a mystery and a global war threatens. Roy Scheider stars with John Lithgow, Helen Mirren, Madolyn Smith, and Bob Balaban. Keir Dullea (returning as Dave) claims "Something wonderful will happen," but most viewers diagreed when they saw this unwise PG sequel to Kubrick's 1968 classic, which was based on Arthur C. Clarke's novel.

2000 YEARS LATER

(1966) **D/S/P:** Bert Tenzer

Terry-Thomas and Edward Everett Horton host the "International Culture Hour" TV show. John Abbott is Gregorius, a mute ancient Roman sent to modern Hollywood. He's exploited by the comedy team on TV as they launch a Roman fad. With Pat Harrington, Monti Rock III, Casey Kasem, Rudi Gernreich, and Milton Parsons. The R-rated Warner fantasy comedy was shelved for three years.

TWO TICKETS TO PARIS

(1962) **D:** Greg Garrison **S:** Hal
Hackady **P:** Harry Romm

On the way to Paris on a boat to sing, Joey Dee has problems when his fiancé (Kay Medford) flirts with another singer (Gary Crosby). All of them sing a lot in the forgotten Columbia musical twist comedy and Dee's Starlighters play. Some tunes are "Teenage Vamp," "The Lady Wants to Twist," and the unforgettable "Twistin' on a Liner."

TWO TO TANGO

(Virgin, 1988) **D:** Hector Olivera **S:** Yolande Finch,
Jose Feinman **P:** Roger Corman   US/Argentina

Don Stroud is a hitman who wants out of the business but falls for his next target, a dancer (Adrienne Sachs). There's a Nazi subplot. It's a remake of *Last Days of the Victim* (1982), which Olivera produced. A Concorde release.

UFO

(Today Home series, 1972–73) **D:** David Lane, Ken Turner **P:** Gerry and Sylvia Anderson UK

The Andersons had created great 60s science fiction puppet series like *Thunderbirds* and *Captain Scarlet and the Mysterians*. This was their first with live actors, but the actors are made to resemble and even act like marionettes! Bizarre to say the least. Ed Bishop stars as the alien fighting Commander Styker of SHADO. Jean Marsh guest-stars on one of the four episodes on two video volumes. The spaced-out couple's next project was *Space: 1999*.

UFO—EXCLUSIVE

(1978) **D/P:** Wheeler Dixon

A boring mixture of amateur home movies, NASA stock footage, stills, and narration. It's all designed to convince you that aliens are out there in spaceships. From Gold Key, a company that made countless 70s documentaries and features for TV syndication.

UFO JOURNALS

(1978) **D/P:** Richard Martin **P:** Herbert L. Strock

Here's more speculation in a documentary with NASA footage and stills. It was produced by the man who directed *The Crawling Hand*.

UFOria

(MCA, 1980) **D/S:** John Binder **P:** Gordon Wolf, Susan Spinks

Cindy Williams is a born-again Christian grocery store clerk waiting for her salvation in a flying saucer. Her truck driver boyfriend (Fred Ward) works for the phony tent preacher Brother Bud (Harry Dean Stanton). With Harry Carey Jr. Universal shelved it for several years, but the unique comic feature with Jesus freaks, con artists, New Agers, and just plain folk was worth waiting for.

UFOS ARE REAL

(1979) **D:** Ed Hunt **P:** Marianne Chase

A documentary with interviews and UFO footage. Betty Hill, whose UFO abduction was the basis for the TV movie *The UFO Incident* (1975), is interviewed. From Gold Key and the director of *Starship Invasions* (1977), which was about an alien suicide ray.

UFOS: IT HAS BEGUN

(1979) **D:** Ray Rivas **S:** Robert Emenegger **P:** Allan Sadler

Rod Serling, Jose Ferrer, and Burgess Meredith all provide narration for a documentary with lectures and the usual NASA footage. From Gold Key.

UFO SYNDROME

(1980) **D/P:** Richard Martin **S/P:** Herbert L. Strock

More from the makers of *UFO Journals*. Anthony Eisley (*The Mighty Gorga*) narrates the mixture of stock footage, stills, and artwork. A man "becomes" an alien when under a trance, and the mysteries of Stonehenge are explored. From Gold Key.

THE UGLY DUCKLING

(1959) **D:** Lance Comfort **S:** Sid Colin, Jack Davies UK

Bernard Bresslaw is a modern-day descendant of Dr. Jekyll (and Mr. Hyde) in a comic version of the famous story. This Hyde goes to dance halls and steals jewelry. With Jon Pertwee. Columbia released the Hammer film in America. The next year, Hammer made a serious version (called *House of Fright* in America).

UHF

(Orion, 1989) **D/S:** Jay Levey **S/A:** Al Yankovic **P:** Gene Kirkwood, John Hyde

Weird Al Yankovic (known for his rock video parodies) inherits the tiny failing TV channel 62. A janitor (scene-stealing Michael Richards) turned kiddie host becomes the star attraction. It's a *Tunnelvision*-type feature with spoofs of Spielberg hits, TV commercials, and music videos. Some programs are "Leave It to Bigfoot" and "Bestiality Today." With Victoria Jackson, Kevin McCarthy, Trinidad Silva, Gedde Watanabe, Billy Barty, Sue Ane Langdon, Fran Drescher, Emo Philips, the Kipper Kids, David Bowie, and Dr. Demento. Anthony Geary becomes a bug-eyed monster. Rated PG-13. Fans of Al can also look for *The Compleat Weird Al Yankovic* video collection.

ULTIMATE DEGENERATE

(SW, 1969) **D/A:** Michael Findlay

Maria answers an ad in a sex paper, goes to Coney Island, then hallucinates at an upstate New York country house with lesbians and go-go dancers. Michael Findlay plays a cripple who photographs and tortures women after shooting them up with aphrodisiacs. His wife, Roberta Findlay, is the cinematographer. It's b/w and only 70 minutes long. *All Night Rider* and *Closer to the Bone* were other adults-only Findlay movies from around the same time.

ULTIMATE DESIRES

(Prism, 1991) **D/P:** Lloyd A. Simandl **S:** Ted Hubert **P:** John A. Curtis Canada (*Beyond the Silhouette*)

Tracy Scoggins stars as a lawyer who goes undercover as a call girl after a prostitute she was representing is killed. Brion James is Wolf, a hit man with a blond ponytail and a German accent. He's a bad guy, but he helps a 13-year-old girl about to be sold by a coked-up nightclub owner. The "erotic thriller" takes place during "the new Cold War" and involves a secret brotherhood plotting to assassinate the President. Tracy has sex scenes with Marc Singer, whose character is not what he

Weird Al Yankovic meets the Kipper Kids in *UHF*.

seems. He helps explain the plot when he says, "It's a bit of a long story that you don't really need to hear."

ULTRAFLESH

(VBM, 1980) **D/P:** Svetlana

In this porno science fiction movie, Seka is an alien who saves the Earth by curing earth men of impotence. With Jamie Gillis, Serena, Lisa De Leeuw, Candida Royale, Little Oral Annie, and dwarf Louis De Jesus. It's cheap-looking and pretty stupid with some "special" effects like lightning zaps, but there's plenty of sex.

ULTRA VIOLET

(New Horizons, 1992) **D:** Mark Griffiths **S:** Gordon Cassidy **P:** Catherine Cryan

Esai Morales is a psycho after a woman in a trailer home (Patricia Healy, who has topless scenes) in Death Valley. Stephen Meadows is her husband. By the director of the *Hardbodies* movies.

ULTRA WARRIOR

(New Horizons, 1993) **D:** Augustin Tamayo, Kevin Tent **S:** Len Jenkins, Dan Kleinman **P:** Luis Llosa

After an H-bomb opening, we learn that Kansas City in 2058 is called "Oblivion." Most of this flashback-filled post-nuke tape is footage from older Corman productions. Several characters narrate ("I remember it well . . ."). George Peppard can be seen in space battle scenes, and Corman himself shows up as the President. The doubles in the several R sex scenes have different color hair than the leads and their faces are obscured. Dack Rambo "stars" with Clare Beresford (who looks and sounds like a British model) and Meshach Taylor (from *Designing Women*) as a crazy black guy. Their parts are from the Corman release *Welcome to Oblivion* (1990), filmed in Peru. Pathetic for sure, but still entertaining if you don't feel too ripped off.

UNASHAMED

(Moore, 1937) **D:** Allen Stuart

Doctors recommend that a businessman go to a nudist camp. His secretary shows up there, too. This rare early nudist-colony movie (one of several from the 30s) played the roadshow circuit for years. The same "plot" was later used several times in the 60s. It's 67 minutes long.

THE UNBELIEVABLE TRUTH

(Vidmark, 1989) **D/S/P/E:** Hal Hartley

Robert Burke (later in *Dust Devil*) is an ex-con who might also be a serial killer. He's hired as a mechanic on Long Island and falls for the boss's daughter (Adrienne Shelly) who is working as a model. The unique first feature by the then 34-year-old Long Islander Hartley was made for $75,000. Shelly returned in his *Trust*.

THE UNBORN

(RCA, 1991) **D/P:** Rodman Flender **S:** Henry Dominic

Brooke Adams stars as a children's book author who want to have a baby in this monster-baby exploitation movie. She goes to a New Age doctor (James Karen) for artificial insemination, then a birthing class run by lesbians. It turns out that Karen is a mad doctor planning a new master race of super babies. After one genius baby kills her brother, and another pregnant woman stabs herself in the stomach, Adams has an illegal back-alley abortion, but the mutant baby (a Chucky doll–like model) crawls out of the garbage. The baby stabs Adams's husband (who was never around when she needed him) in the eye, and she decides to raise him after all. The most memorable scene shows the lesbians killing each other. Adams is good as usual. The music is by Gary Numan (!).

THE UNBORN II

(New Horizons, 1994) **D:** Rick Jacobson **S:** Mike Even Schwartz, Daniela Percell **P:** Mike Elliot

Michelle Greene is single mom in a suburban home who writes children's books. Her killer kid Joey (a moving doll like in the first movie) eats

meat and bites necks. Meanwhile an assassin (Robin Curtis) goes around shooting babies who were the result of experiments in *Unborn*, and Scott Valentine is a neighbor who protects them. Brittny Powell is the sexy neighbor babysitter, whose nosy parents provide irritating comedy relief. Pretty bad.

UNCAGED

(RCA/Columbia, 1991) **D:** "William Duprey"/ Lisa Hunt **S:** Catherine Cyran **P:** Mike Elliot (*Angels in Red*)

Ideas must have been pretty scarce around Roger Corman's Concorde by the early 90s. This is a remake of an earlier Concorde release, *Streetwalkin'* (1985). The cast is less known, but the story is the same: Basically, a psycho pimp (Jeffrey Morgan) abuses and even kills prostitutes in LA. Some of the women fight back. It's well made and has enough nudity and action. Leslie Bega stars with Elena Sahagun, Daryl Haney, and Monique Gabrielle.

UNCLE SILAS

(1947) **D:** Charles Frank **S:** Ben Travers   UK (*The Inheritance*)

An uncle (Derrick De Marney) and his governess (Katina Paxinou) plot to kill their heiress niece (Jean Simmons). It's based on a J. Sheridan Le Fanu novel and features thunder and lightning in an old dark house. With Esmond Knight and Guy Rolfe. Simmons had just been in *Great Expectations* and played Ophelia in *Hamlet*.

UNCLE TOM'S CABIN

(Xenon, 1965) **D:** Al Adamson **D/S:** Geza von Radvanyi **S:** Fred Denger **P:** Aldo Von Pinelli Germany/France/Italy/Yugoslavia (*Onkel Tom's Hutte*)

Master showman Kroger Babb bought the rights to a big-budget, 170-minute, 70mm Eastmancolor

version of Harriet Beecher Stowe's famous pre–Civil War tale. He opened it (in Savannah, GA) in 1969. Somewhere along the line, Al Adamson shot some new scenes and Independent International rereleased it (in 1977) as *White Trash Woman* (!). The story was old-fashioned even when it was filmed (several times) in the silent days (a 1928 version from Universal had also been a roadshow hit). The music (issued by Philips) includes spirituals and is excellent (it sounds like Ennio Morricone). Herbert Lom is the evil Simon Legree with a big scar and a black mistress and John Kitzmiller (from *Dr. No*) is Uncle Tom. Out-of-place elements include a slapstick bar fight, monks, some modern jazz, and a western shootout ending. With O. W. Fischer as the good St. Claire, Mylene Demongeot, Juliette Greco, Eleonora Rossi-Drago, and Eartha Kitt, who sings. The scratchy tape is dubbed and runs 118 minutes.

THE UNDERACHIEVERS

(Lightning, 1987) **D/S/P:** Jackie Kong **S:** Tony Rosato, Gary Thompson   (*Night School*)

A group of rejects attend night school in a comedy patterned after the *Police Academy* series. Some might want to see it for Jewel Shepard (who strips off her *Star Trek* uniform) or Becky LeBeau (naked in a pool with a plastic alligator). Or maybe you want to see the name stars including Barbara Carrera, Susan Tyrrell, Michael Pataki, Edward Albert Jr., Mark Blankfield, Garrett Morris, and Vic Tayback.

UNDER AGE

(1941) **D:** Edward Dmytryk **S:** Robert D. Andrews **P:** Ralph Cohn

Blonde Nan Grey and her friends are released from a detention home. Tom Neal asks them to help trap gangsters so they go undercover in a vice ring to find the killer of Nan's sister. With Alan Baxter, Mary Anderson, and Don Beddoe. The short (59 minutes) exploitation feature followed other similar titles from Columbia (*Girls Under 21, Girls of the Road,* and *Glamour for Sale*). The director was later one of the "Hollywood Ten."

UNDER AGE

(1963) **D/S:** Larry Buchanan **S/P:** Harold Hoffman

Here's more proof that Buchanan was a pretty good director before making those AIP remakes (like *Zontar, the Thing From Venus*) that's he's known for. Like *Free, White and 21*, this is a well-made Dallas-based federal district courtroom drama with dramatic flashbacks from all major characters, and we the audience are the jury. Anne MacAdams (*Common Law Wife*) plays the mother, accused of "aiding and encouraging" the "carnal knowledge" between her then-13-year-old daughter Linda (Judy Adler) and a boy (George Gomez) from "Little Mexico." The Alpine Trio do "Boil Them Cabbage Down" at a hootenanny. The copy I saw was (badly) shot off of a screen. Adler went on to *Satan's Bed, Zero Girls, Mondo Freudo,* and other adult movies.

Herbert Lom in *Uncle Tom's Cabin*.

UNDER CAPRICORN

(Vid America, 1949) **D/P:** Alfred Hitchcock
S: James Bridie **P:** Sidney Bernstein   UK

Hitchcock returned to England to make this Technicolor 19th-century costume drama, which was a box-office flop. Ingrid Bergman stars as an Irish woman who elopes with her father's groom (Joseph Cotten). She kills her brother and ends up at an Australian penal colony where a maid (Margaret Leighton) terrorizes her with shrunken heads. With Michael Wilding. The Warner release is the only feature where Hitchcock himself appears twice. Part of the reason it did bad business in America probably had to do with Bergman's then-newsworthy and scandalous romance with director Roberto Rossellini. Hitchcock remained in England to make *Stage Fright* (1950).

UNDERGROUND ACES

(Vestron, 1981) **D:** Robert Butler
S: Jim Carabatsos **P:** Jay Weston

Parking lot attendants wreck cars on purpose and enjoy sex on the job. Dirk Benedict stars with Melanie Griffith, Jerry Orbach, Frank Gorshin, Sid Haig, T. K. Carter, and Audrey Landers. The Filmways release was by a former Disney director.

UNDERGROUND TERROR

(SVS, 1988) **D:** James McCalmont
S: Robert Zimmerman, Brian O'Hara
P: Steven Mackler   (*Underground*)

A murdering gang led by "Boris" lives in the NYC subway. The director also made *Escape from Safehaven*.

UNDERGROUND U.S.A.

(1980) **D/S/P/A:** Eric Mitchell **P:** Erdner Rauschalle

Mitchell works his way into the life of a has-been movie star (Patti Astor). The New York City movie is full of one-time Andy Warhol (or John Waters) associates. With Jackie Curtis, Cookie Mueller, Taylor Mead, and Mudd Club owner Steve Mass. Many of the early 80s underground features (and shorts) from Manhattan seem to have disappeared.

UNDER HOT LEATHER: *See* THE JESUS TRIP

UNDER INVESTIGATION

(Columbia, 1994) **D/S:** Kevin Meyer
P: Bruce Cohn Curtis, Ronnie Hadar

Harry Hamlin is a down-and-out LA detective after a psycho killer, and Joanna Pacula is his lover and prime suspect. The "erotic thriller" also features Lydie Denier, Ed Lauter, and Richard Beymer.

THE UNDERSEA KINGDOM

(Republic, 1936) **D:** B. Reeves Eason, Joseph Kane
S: John Rathmell, Maurice Gerachty **P:** Nat Levine

Republic's answer to Mascot's *The Phantom Empire* and Universal's *Flash Gordon* is 12 entertaining chapters of characters running around in Roman gladiator costumes. They ride horses but have robots and spiked tanks. People from the Earth's surface take a rocket-powered submarine to the domed lost city of Atlantis. Ray "Crash" Corrigan plays Navy officer Crash Corrigan, whose friends are a newspaper reporter (Lois Wilde), a scientist (C. Montague Shaw), and his son. The bad guys are the evil Ming-like Khan (Monte Blue) and Hakur (Lon Chaney Jr.), captain of the guards. Also with William Farnum as Sharad and Smiley Burnette. A condensed TV version was *Sharad of Atlantis*. Also on *Saturday Night Serials* (Rhino) with three other serial chapters.

UNDER SIEGE

(Warner, 1992) **D:** Andrew Davis **S:** J. F. Lawton
S/P: Steven Seagal **P:** Arnon Michan, Steven Reuther

Seagal is a cook (actually a Navy Seal) who saves the USS *Missouri*, a nuclear battleship, when it's hijacked by psycho military experts. Tommy Lee Jones (in black leather) is an ex-CIA agent and Gary Busey (who has a drag scene) are the main bad guys. They plan to steal the Tomahawk missiles on board and attack Hawaii. The *Die Hard*–inspired action hit from Warner features *Playboy* Playmate Erika Eleniak popping out of a cake, Patrick O'Neal as the captain, Nick Mancuso, and Andy Romano. It was shot around Mobile, Alabama. Davis returned with *The Fugitive* (1993), an even bigger hit, also with Jones, and *Under Siege II* (Warner, 1995) followed.

THE UNDERSTUDY: GRAVEYARD SHIFT II

(Virgin, 1988) **D/S:** Gerald Ciccoritti
P: Stephen R. Flaks, Arnold H. Bruck   Canada

In an arty sequel to *Graveyard Shift*, Silvio Oliviero is a vampire who replaces an actor starring in a vampire film called "Blood Lover" (being directed by a woman). Wendy Gazelle is the actress who becomes a real vampire too. He bites hands, not necks, and is a pool hustler in the movie-within-the-movie. The plot is confusing and it's hard to tell if scenes are from the movie being shot, dreams, or "reality."

THE UNDERTAKER

(AIP, 1988) **D:** Franco Steffanino
S: William James Kennedy
P: Steve Bono

Joe Spinell stars in his last movie as Uncle Roscoe, an undertaker in a religious cult. He kills people (usually women) to stay immortal and buries the bodies for profit. His nephew tries to stop him. Spinell, one of the busiest movie tough guys since appearing in *The Godfather* (1972), made this, *Operation War Zone*, and *Rapid Fire* before he died in 1989.

UNDER THE BOARDWALK

(Starwalk, 1988) **D:** Fritz Kiersch
S: Robert King **P:** Steven H. Chanin,
Gregory S. Blackwell   (*Wipeout*)

The plot of this teen romance surfing movie (narrated by a character 20 years in the future) is straight out of *West Side Story*. With Keith (grandson of Jackie) Coogan, Danielle Von Zerneck, Dick Miller, Sonny Bono, Tracey Walter, and Elizabeth Kaitan. From New World.

UNDER THE CHERRY MOON

(Warner, 1986) **D/A:** Prince
S: Becky Johnson **P:** Robert Cavallo

Prince unwisely fired original director Mary Lambert and directed himself in a forgettable PG-13 b/w romantic fairy tale. He's an American entertainer gigolo in France. With Kristin Scott-Thomas, Jerome Benton, Steve Berkoff, Alexandra Stewart, Victor Spinetti, and Francesca Annis. Prince also directed his concert feature, *Sign "O" The Times* (1987).

UNDER THE GUN

(Magnum, 1988) **D:** James Sbardellati
S: Almer John Davis **P:** Warren Stein

Dethroned Miss America Vanessa Williams had been in *The Pickup Artist* (1987) but made her starring acting debut as a lawyer who teams with an LA cop (Sam Jones) to catch a plutonium thief (John Russell) in this one. With Nick Cassavetes and Sharon Williams.

UNDER THE RAINBOW

(Warner, 1981) **D:** Steve Rash **S:** Pat
McCormick, Harry Hurwitz, Martin
Smith, Pat Bradley **S/P:** Fred Bauer

Many viewers still can't believe this one was made. It's based on the concept that the midget actors in *The Wizard of Oz* were out-of-control wild drunks off screen. They smash up a hotel while German spies lurk. Chevy Chase and Carrie Fisher star with Billy Barty, Eve Arden, Mako, Adam Arkin, Pat McCormick, and Zelda Rubinstein. The PG-rated comedy had the largest cast of little people since

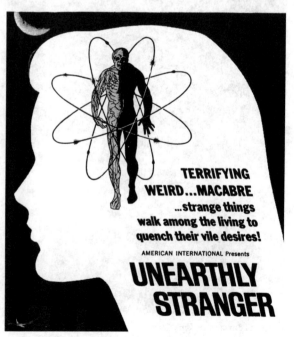

TERRIFYING
WEIRD...MACABRE
...strange things
walk among the living to
quench their vile desires!

AMERICAN INTERNATIONAL Presents

UNEARTHLY STRANGER

Even Dwarves Started Small (1968) or *The Little Cigars* (1973). Maybe if Chevy Chase wasn't the star it would have been a hit.

UNDERWATER!

(Turner, 1955) **D:** John Sturges
S: Walter Newman **P:** Harry Tatleman

Jane Russell stars in a tale of Caribbean sunken treasure with Richard Egan, Gilbert Roland, Lori Nelson, and some sharks. RKO announced it as a 3-D movie but shot it in "Superscope" instead. 200 journalists were flown to Florida to attend the underwater premiere, and Jayne Mansfield, who is not in the film, showed up and distracted photographers. The song "Cherry Pink and Apple Blossom White" made the pop charts in two versions.

UNDERWORLD U.S.A.

(Columbia, 1961) **D/S/P:** Sam Fuller

Tolly Devlin (Cliff Robertson) has a lifetime obsession since seeing his father murdered in an alley as a child. He grows up and works for gangsters as part of a revenge scheme. This hard-hitting, brutal feature points out how easily businessmen, police, and government officials can be bought. It's essential viewing along with Fuller's other increasingly bizarre modern-day 60s features, *Shock Corridor* (1964) and *The Naked Kiss* (1966). With Dolores Hart as Cuddles, Beatrice Kay, Robert Emhardt, and Richard Rust. From Columbia.

THE UNDYING BRAIN = BRAIN OF BLOOD

THE UNEARTHLING

(Prism, 1993) **D/S/P:** Wyre Martin   (*Aswang*)

This horror movie is about the Null family, wealthy vampires in a lakefront estate who spin webs around victims and have extremely long red tentacle/tongues. A pregnant girl (Tina Ona Paukstelis) is paid to impersonate Null's wife so her child will become the heir, but she's chained up in a decrepit shack. A crazed sister attacks with a chainsaw and an absurd highlight is the crippled mother hanging from her own tongue. Several of the actors aren't too great, but the music is good and the FX are shocking and original, even after being cut for the video release. Norman Moses is Null and Mildred Nierras is the Filipino maid. Made by former film students in Wisconsin.

UNEARTHLY STRANGER

(1963) **D:** John Krish **S:** Rex Carlton
P: Albert Fennell   UK

A British scientist (John Neville) working on a secret project marries a woman (Gabrielle Licudi) who can't blink her eyes and has no pulse. When a coworker discovers that she's an alien, he's killed. More alien women arrive and kill her (only her clothes remain) because she had fallen in love with her intended victim. With Jean Marsh. It was made by some of the people behind *The Avengers* series. AIP released the cult favorite in America.

UNHINGED

(Lighthouse, 1982) **D/S/P:** Don Gronquist
S: Reagan Ramsey

Three college girls smash up their car then go to an old mansion run by a hateful woman in a wheelchair who lives with a handyman and her daughter (who turns out to be a boy). It's 70 minutes long with nudity, gory ax murders, and in-joke names. Available in R or unrated versions.

THE UNHOLY

(Vestron, 1988) **D:** Camilo Vila
S: Philip Yordan, Fernando Fonseca
P: Mathew Hayden

A red-haired demon (Nicole Fortier) seduces priests at Easter time in New Orleans. She becomes a slimy monster in a church and splits into two monster midgets at the end. The silly ending was reportedly added by the studio, but it's the only memorable part. Somebody actually says "Get thee behind me, Satan!" Ben Cross stars as a priest who survives falling off a building and has to save the world somehow. With Hal Holbrook, Trevor Howard (who died in 1988), Ned Beatty, and Jill Carroll. Some good New Orleans locations were used.

THE UNHOLY FOUR

(1954) **D:** Terence Fisher
S/P: Michael Carreras   UK
(*A Stranger Came Home*)

Paulette Goddard stars in a Hammer Studios mystery. Her husband (William Sylvester) returns to their country home after three years. He can't remember anything, but is suspected of murder. With Patrick Holt. Lippert released it in America.

THE UNHOLY NIGHT

(1929) **D:** Lionel Barrymore
S: Edwin Justice Mayer

Roland Young, Ernest Torrence, and Dorothy Sebastian star in a old-darkhouse movie based on a story by Ben Hecht. Veterans of a war in India are killed off in a London mansion. With Sojin (who holds a séance), Boris Karloff, Lionel Belmore, and John Loder. Barrymore directed several early talkies. The MGM release has been shown on TNT.

UNHOLY ROLLERS

(HBO, 1972) **D:** Vernon Zimmerman
S: Howard R. Cohen **P:** John Prizer

AIP made this copy of the Raquel Welch movie *Kansas City Bomber* from the same year. Claudia Jennings stars in one of her best roles as vicious roller derby queen Karen Walker. It covers the rise and fall of the LA Avengers team and features typical show biz corruption. Martin Scorsese was the

supervising editor. With Roberta Collins, Betty Anne Rees, Candice Roman, and Charlene Jones as other skaters, Alan Vint, and Kathleen Freeman. By the director of *Fade to Black*. The video has a new music score.

THE UNHOLY THREE

(Cinemacabre, 1925) **D/P:** Tod Browning
S: Waldemar Young

Lon Chaney, "The Man of a Thousand Faces," is Professor Echo, a sideshow ventriloquist who dresses up like an old Granny O'Grady and commits jewel robberies with help from Tweedledee, a pretty hostile and scary midget (Harry Earles) who can pass as a baby, and Hercules the strong man (Victor McLaglen). Chaney runs a pet shop as a front and uses ventriloquism to provide voices for "talking" birds (with title cards of course). A pickpocket (Mae Busch) and a gorilla also help. The whole setup falls apart because of jealousies. It's based on a story by Tod Robbins, as was Browning's *Freaks* (also with Earles and also from MGM). The tale is introduced by a carny barker (as was *Freaks*). In 1925 Chaney, America's first horror star, was also in *The Phantom of the Opera, The Monster,* and *Tower of Lies.*

Harry Earles and Lon Chaney in *The Unholy Three* (1925).

THE UNHOLY THREE

(MGM, 1930) **D:** Jack Conway
S/A: Elliott Nugent **S:** J.C. Nugent

For his first (and as it turned out, last) talkie, the great Lon Chaney repeated his crook-in-drag ventriloquist role and Earles returned as Tweedledee the scary cigar-smoking midget disguised as a baby. Ivan Linow is the strong man and Lila Lee (from the original *Blood and Sand*) is the pickpocket. They left out the man in a gorilla suit, and the ending was changed so that Chaney slips up in court by using his regular voice while appearing as the kindly old lady. On August 26, about a month after *The Unholy Three* was released, Chaney was dead. Two years later, Lon Chaney Jr. made his film debut (in a bit part). For years, the silent version was easier to find. I didn't see Chaney's last movie until somebody showed it to me in Sweden. It was worth the trip. It also explained the inspiration for an Our Gang short called *Free Eats* (1930) that I

had seen many times on TV as a kid. It had jewel thieves disguised as a couple with "fidget" babies. *The Unholy Three* is on laser disc with *West of Zanzibar.*

THE UNHOLY WIFE

(1957) **D/P:** John Farrow **S:** Jonathan Latimer

British sex symbol Diana Dors was billed as "Half-Angel . . . Half-Devil" in her American debut. Posters also told us that "She Made Him Half-A-Man!" He is Rod Steiger as the grape-grower husband whose life in in danger, and Tom Tryon is the guy she has an affair with. With Marie Windsor and Arthur Franz. RKO released the Technicolor movie.

THE UNINVITED

(New Star, 1987)
D/S/P/A: Greydon Clark

A cat who escaped from a lab in Fort Lauderdale is taken on a yacht run by gangsters. Three vacationing guys and two cliché bikini bimbos end up on board and the fun (?) begins. The cute cat has a mutant devil cat that comes out of its mouth. Clu Gulager is an alcoholic hit man. George Kennedy has his ankle shredded. Alex Cord is the corrupt businessman/killer star. Except for Kennedy's ankle, the FX stink and nothing is delivered. The atomic cat story has a PG-13 rating. With Shari Shattuck.

UNION CITY

(Columbia, 1980) **D/S:** Mark Reichert
P: Graham Reichert

Dennis Lipscomb is obsessed with catching a milk-bottle thief while his wife (Deborah Harry) has murder in mind. It's based on the Cornell Woolrich story "The Corpse Next Door" and has music by Chris Stein from Blondie. Lipscomb (*Eyes of Fire, Retribution . . .*) is good, but it's a slow-going movie. With Pat Benatar and Taylor Mead in brief roles. It was filmed in Union City, New Jersey.

UNIVERSAL SOLDIER

(Live, 1992) **D:** Roland Emmerich **S:** Dean Devlin, Richard Rothstein, Christopher Leitch
P: Craig Baumgarten, Allen Shapiro

Two action stars for the price of one battle in an action science fiction zombie movie. Jean-Claude Van Damme and Dolph Lundgren are soldiers in a 1969 massacre in Vietnam. They kill each other, but 23 years later, they're revived by the defense department as super-strong emotionless warriors. They're supposed to fight terrorists, but Van Damme meets a wisecracking blonde reporter (Ally Walker) and starts to remember. Both become out of control and go after each other. Van Damme beats up everybody in a diner and Lundgren collects his victims' ears. Some action takes place at the Hoover Dam

and the Grand Canyon. With Jerry Orbach as the scientist who revives them, Ed O'Ross, Simon Rhee, Ralph Moeller, and Leon Rippy. The TriStar release was the first American feature for the German director (who replaced Andrew Davis).

THE UNKNOWN

(Fright, 1927) **D:** Tod Browning **S:** Waldemar Young

The Unknown is one of the most fascinating collaborations between Browning and Lon Chaney. Chaney is Alonzo the armless wonder, star of a Gypsy circus based in Madrid. During his act, he shoots clothes off Estrelita, a young horse rider, with his feet while both are on a spinning platform. He falls for Estrelita (Joan Crawford!), who can't bear to be touched. It sounds like a perfect arrangement except that the strong man (Norman Kerry) wants her too and Chaney is really a fugitive thief and murderer *with* arms (and two giant thumbs on one hand). He decides to have his arms amputated for her! He plans for the strong man to be torn in half by horses on stage! He also has a cigar-smoking hunchback dwarf assistant named Cujo who wears a devil costume. Scenes of Alonzo smoking and playing guitar with his feet will remind you of *Freaks.* Scenes of Alonzo and little Cujo walking with similar hats and capes were later copied in movies with Lugosi and Angelo Rossitto. Joan Crawford (in her second year in films) yells, "Hands! Men's hands! How I hate them!" Alexandro Jodorowsky's great *Santa Sangre* is a tribute to this MGM movie. And there's more, all in 61 minutes. Waldemar Young, who wrote the brilliant tale, wrote many features for Browning and yes (it makes perfect sense), *Island of Lost Souls*! In 1927, Chaney was also in Browning's famous lost vampire feature, *London After Midnight.*

UNKNOWN POWERS

(Video Gems, 1978) **D/S/P:** Don Como
S: Richard Croy, Brad Steiger

This PG-rated New Age/mondo documentary from Gold Key has four on-screen celebrity hosts and covers a lot of territory. Most events seem real, some scenes are (admitted) reenactments. Jack Palance in a black suit and turtleneck is the first host. A few years later he became host of the syndicated *Ripley's Believe It or Not* series, but despite his familiar deep breathing and lengthy pauses, he's a little more subdued here. His segments concern Korean martial arts masters, Kirilian photographs, channeling, a couple who sleep under a pyramid, a Dutch man who puts needles through his arms without spilling blood, and a Russian woman who moves objects with willpower. Samantha Eggar shows the wartime use of astrologers by Hitler and the Allies, a woman who talks to animals, a psychic who solves an LA mutilation murder, and a man whose hands bleed near undiscovered oil wells. Will Geer, known to millions as Grandpa Walton, hosted the beyond-death segments, walking around in a cemetery, shortly before he died in real life. He shows some amazing ghost and ectoplasm photos. Roscoe Lee Browne hosts the longest segment, concerning psychic surgery (with real footage), the late Katherine Kuhlman, faith healer, and the Reverend Jim Jones (who made this movie topical). You get to see San Francisco People's Temple services with Jones practicing faith healing, watched by a hysterical crowd. A note informs us of the Guyana deaths.

UNLAWFUL ENTRY
(Fox, 1992) **D:** Jonathan Kaplan **S:** Lewis Colick
P: Charles Gordon **M:** James Horner

A robber breaks into the expensive home of an LA couple (Kurt Russell and Madeleine Stowe). Cops save the day, but one of them (Ray Liotta) is a relentless brutal psycho who wants the schoolteacher wife for himself. He destroys Russell's credit rating and arranges for him to go to jail. When not beating suspects or having sex with hookers, he gives a friendly traffic safety talk at a school assembly. This movie makes the strong point that America's drug laws can easily be used against anybody. Liotta is great as a scary killer (see *Something Wild* for more). With Roger E. Mosley, Andy Romano, Sherrie Rose, and Dick Miller. A 20th Century release.

UNMASKED: PART 25
(Academy, 1988) **D:** Anders Palm
S/P: Mark Curforth   UK

Gregory Cox and Fiona Evans star in a *Friday the 13th* parody with a killer and a blind girl. Available R or unrated. By the director of *Dead Certain* (1990).

THE UNNAMABLE
(Starmaker, 1987) **D/S/P:** Jean-Paul Ouellette
P: Dean Ramsel

This H. P. Lovecraft adaptation was made after the success of *Reanimator*. Carter (Mark Kinsey Stephenson), a self-assured horror writer from Miskatonic University (he looks like Eddie Haskell from *Leave It to Beaver*), tells some other guys about an old house, sealed years ago by a priest. Howard is the always incredulous, worried, lovesick, nerd character. Eventually they end up trapped in the house along with two jocks and their beautiful dates (one is Laura Albert). Despite lots of irritating false scares, loud screams that nobody ever hears, unconvincing killer tree branches, and characters running endlessly through a small house (like in *Flintstones* cartoons when Fred runs past a dozen windows in a one-room stone home), this movie has enough good points to make it fun. It's got some interesting eccentric characters, blood, decapitations, a topless starlet, and flashbacks. A pretty amazing female monster with hooves, wings, horns, and long white hair shows up near the end. The love song at the end was a bad idea. The director also made *Chinatown Connection* (1988) and videos for Penthouse.

THE UNNAMEABLE II:
THE STATEMENT OF RANDOLPH CARTER
(Prism, 1992) **D/S/P:** Jean-Paul Ouellette

Mark Kinsey Stephenson returns as Carter in a more expensive sequel that picks up the story the next day. Maria Ford is Alida, a 300-year-old possessed girl found in a tunnel. She's featured in *Splash*-inspired can't-relate-to-the-modern-world scenes and has a standout gratuitous nude scene on her hands and knees. Love conquers all and eventually a winged monster (Julie Strain) appears and turns into a chair (!?). The three surviving characters are the same actors from the first movie, but name stars are added. John Rhys-Davies is a professor, Peter Breck is a cop, and David Warner is a school chancellor who sits behind a desk.

UNNATURAL
(Sinister, 1952) **D:** Arthur Maria Rabenalt
S: Fritz Rotter   W. Germany (*Alraune*)

Erich von Stroheim uses artificial insemination to create a "perfect" woman (Hildegarde Neff) who has no soul. With Karlheinz Bohm. DCA released it in America in 1957, the year von Stroheim died in Paris. It was based on a novel by Hans Heinz Ewars, and had been filmed five times previously. A silent Hungarian version was by Michael Curtiz and the first sound version (1934) was by Richard Oswald.

UNSANE
(Fox Hills, 1982) **D/S:** Dario Argento **S:** George Kemp **P:** Claudio Argento   Italy (*Tenebrae*)

A horror writer (Tony Franciosa) in Rome becomes a suspect when murders based on his new novel (called "Tenebrae") are committed. Characters are killed by razor or an axe in broad daylight, and pages of the book are stuffed in the victims' mouths. It's pretty fascinating (and a bit confusing). When a woman's arm is cut off, her stump sprays blood all over a white wall, and there's a surprising and disturbing flashback scene. With

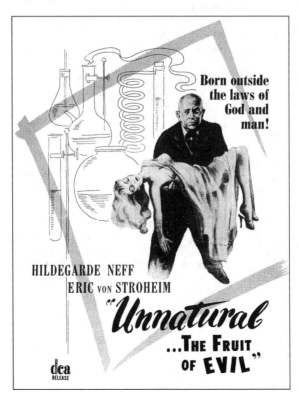

Born outside the laws of God and man!

HILDEGARDE NEFF
ERIC VON STROHEIM
"*Unnatural*
...THE FRUIT OF EVIL"

dca RELEASE

John Saxon as the literary agent, Daria Nicolodi (who was dubbed by Theresa Russell), Giuliano Gemma, and John Steiner. Lamberto Bava and Michele Soavi were the assistant directors. The music is by Simonetti Pignatelli. After the popular *Suspiria* (1977), Argento's *Inferno* (1980) and this one were not released in America until years after the fact and then cut, on tape. The American tape release is missing 10 minutes (it was 100 minutes long), but it's complete on the Japanese laser disc.

UNTIL THE END OF THE WORLD
(Warner, 1991) **D/S:** Wim Wenders
S: Peter Carey **P:** Jonathan Taplin
C: Robby Muller   Germany/France/Australia

After the magnificent *Wings of Desire,* Wenders made this romantic science fiction road epic which was filmed in 15 cities in eight countries on four continents. Subtitles are used for various languages. He said it was inspired by Stanley Kramer's *On the Beach* (1959). A nuclear satellite is about to crash on Earth in 1999, a time when new technology (including video phones) is common. After a chase around the world, the main characters end up in Australia, where an invention allows the blind to see and can "suck our dreams and turn them into television." Solveig Dommartin (from *Wings of Desire*) and William Hurt star, and Sam Neill plays her boyfriend and narrates. With Max von Sydow and Jeanne Moreau as his parents, Rudiger Vogler as a detective, Allen Garfield, Lois Chiles, and David Gulpilil. Many new rock songs were written and performed for the film. The U2 theme song is especially good, and other tracks are by Can, Nick Cave, Peter Gabriel, R.E.M., and Elvis Costello (doing a Kinks song). The original feature ran 8 (!) hours, but America, typically, got a shorter version (157 minutes).

UP!
(RM, 1976) **D/S/P/A/C/E:** Russ Meyer
(*Russ Meyer's Up!*)

Meyer outdid himself with this outrageous, mind-boggling hyperdrive barrage of fast-edited sex, violence, and comedy with a self-imposed X. Raven De La Croix breaks a man's back after he rapes her and is arrested by the sheriff (Monte Bane). He gets her a job at Alice's Restaurant. This movie has the best outdoor sex scenes ever and a chainsaw battle. Too much goes on to describe, but naked Kitten Natividad runs around the woods and helps us understand as the "Greek Chorus" (with a dubbed-in voice). With Mary Gavin, Robert McLane, Edward Scaaf (as Adolph), Candy Samples, Elaine Collins, Su Ling, and Janet Wood. It has the look of a sign-off last feature. The last image is of Meyer, alone, trudging up the hills with his camera equipment. He completed one more film, though, *Beneath the Valley of the Ultravixens.*

UP AGAINST THE WALL

(1991) **D/S/A:** Ron O'Neal
P: Chuck Colbert, Zuindl Colbert

A teen track star is tempted by drug deals. The PG-13 feature with a Christian message was made by the star of *Superfly*. With Marla Gibbs and Stoney Jackson.

UPHILL ALL THE WAY

(Starmaker, 1984) **D/S:** Frank Q. Dobbs
P: Burr Smidt, David L. Ford

Singers Roy Clark and Mel Tillis star in a comedy about out-of-work good ol' boys mistaken for bank robbers. With Burl Ives as the sheriff, Glen Campbell, Sheb ("Purple People Eater") Wooley, Frank Gorshin, Trish Van Devere, and an appearance by the king of this kind of country-appeal action comedies, Burt Reynolds. From New World.

UP IN SMOKE

(MCA, 1978) **D/P:** Lou Adler **S/A:** Cheech Marin, Tommy Chong **P:** Lou Lombardo

The first and best of the Cheech and Chong dope comedies stole its name from a (1957) Bowery Boys movie, which is fitting. It was made by the president of Ode Records. Pedro and Man smoke a lot of pot, take LSD, and drive a van made of marijuana across the Mexican border. Stacy Keach is a cop who uses confiscated stash and who starts becoming a lizard with a long tongue (!). Tom Skerritt is a crazed Nam vet having flashbacks. The interesting support cast includes Edie Adams, Strother Martin, Zane Busby, Louisa Moritz, David Nelson, June Fairchild, Rainbeaux Smith, and Rodney Bingenheimer. The punk concert finale at the Roxy club includes the Dils and the Whores. The Warner soundtrack album (the team's seventh) includes dialogue.

UP LIKE A SHOT: *See* BLAZING STEWARDESSES

UPON A FRIGHTMARE: *See* FRIGHTMARE

UP THE ACADEMY

(Warner, 1980) **D:** Robert Downey **S:** Tom Patchett, Jay Tarses **P:** Marvin Worth, Danton Rissner

Mad magazine (possibly the most important publication of this century) backed, then disowned, this dumb military school comedy. Alfred E. Neuman appeared on the ads, though. Star Ron Leibman had his name removed, too. Watch it and you'll see why. With Ralph Macchio (making his film debut), Tom Poston, Ian Wolfe, Stacey Nelkin, and Barbara Bach. The "new wave" Capitol Soundtrack featured Blondie, Jonathan Richman ("Road Runner"), and others.

UP THE CREEK

(Vestron, 1984) **D:** Robert Butler **S:** Jim Kouf **P:** Michael L. Metzer, Fred Baum

It's "Animal House on vacation" with crude college losers in a raft race against military cadets and col-lege jocks. With Tim Matheson, Jennifer Runyon, Stephen Furst, Dan Monahan (*Porky's* star), Tom Nolan, Jeff East, Romy Windsor, Lori Sutton, and *Playboy* centerfold Jeana Tomasino. John Hillerman is the Dean, and the theme song is by Cheap Trick. Samuel Arkoff and his son Louis were the executive producers of the Orion release, directed by a Disney vet.

UP THE DOWN STAIRCASE

(1967) **D:** Robert Mulligan
S: Tad Mosel **P:** Alan J. Pakula

In sort of an updated *Blackboard Jungle*, Sandy Dennis is an idealistic young New York public school teacher faced with juvenile delinquents and bureaucracy. With Patrick Bedford, Ellen O'Mara, Eileen Heckart, and Jean Stapleton. The lighter British *To Sir with Love* from the same year was more popular. This one's long (124 minutes). There was a UA Soundtrack.

UP YOUR ALLEY

(IVE, 1988) **D/S:** Bob Logan **S/P/A:** Murray Langston

Linda Blair stars as an LA undercover reporter in tale of homeless people writen by "the Unknown Comic." It's a comedy, but a psycho kills bums. Blair falls for Langston. With Ruth Buzzi, Johnny Dark, Bob Zany, and Jack Hanrahan. Mike Curb was an executive producer. Blair was also in *Repossessed* by the same director.

URGH! A MUSIC WAR

(Fox, 1981) **D:** Derek Burbidge **P:** Michael White   UK

33 post-punk or "new wave" acts were filmed live in various cities for this sampler movie which, surprisingly, was released in theaters by Filmways/Orion. The Cramps ("Tear It Up"), Devo, Pere Ubu, Gang of Four, Wall of Voodoo, Gary Numan, Joan Jett, Klaus Nomi and others perform one cut each. Only the Police (then the best-selling rock artists on A&M) do more. The A&M soundtrack was a double set.

URSUS IN THE VALLEY OF THE LIONS

(Sinister, 1961) **D:** Carlo Ludovico Braglia
S: Alessandro Continenza **P:** Giuseppe Fatigati
Italy (*Ursus Nella Valle dei Leoni*)

Ed Fury (from *The Wild Women of Wongo*) is raised by lions and holds back a team of elephants in the arena climax. With Moira Orfei as the evil Diar and Alberto Lupo. The American Fury returned in *The Mighty Ursus* (1961) and *Ursus in the Land of Fire* (1963). Other Ursus movies were *The Rebel Gladiators* (1963), with Don Vadis, *Tartar Invasion* (1963), with Joe Robertson, *The Invincible Three* (1964) with Alan Steel, *Hercules, Prisoner of Evil* (1964), with Reg Park, and *Samson and the Mighty Challenge* (1964) with Yann Larvor.

USED CARS

(Columbia, 1980) **D/S:** Robert Zemeckis
S/P: Bob Gale

Kurt Russell is funny as a fast-talking used-car salesman working for Jack Warden. Warden also plays his own brother, the hated used-car-selling rival. The competitors stop at nothing to drum up more business. With Gerrit Graham, Andrew Duggan, and Betty Thomas, plus David L. Lander and Michael McKean (a.k.a. Lenny and Squiggy from the *Laverne and Shirley* show.) Al Lewis (Grandpa Munster) is in it too. Spielberg was the executive producer. 15 years later Zemeckis was on top with his *Forrest Gump*.

USS VD: SHIP OF SHAME

(Video Yesteryear, 1942)

The notorious 40-minute WWII documentary was made for and shown to servicemen. The scenes of what can result from fooling around when overseas are still pretty strong, but they weren't very effective, were they? The Budget video version also includes *Red Nightmare*.

U.S. VICE: *See* MURDER GANG

UTOPIA

(Video Yesterday, 1950) **D/S:** Leo Joannon **P:** R. Eger
France/Italy (*Atoll K, Robinson Crusoeland*)

After an island appears in the ocean, people move there and attempt to create a perfect society. Things start to go wrong when uranium is discovered and everybody gets greedy. The island sinks back into the sea. It was a good idea for a political fable, but aging stars Stan Laurel and a huge Oliver Hardy (the team had retired from films in 1945) are misused and kind of hard to watch. It was released (partially dubbed) in America in 1955.

V

(1983) **D/S:** Kenneth Johnson **P:** Chuck Bowman

Marc Singer is a TV news reporter and Faye Grant is a scientist who lead a group of freedom fighters against evil invading lizard aliens. This once-popular NBC miniseries cost a record $14 million. The "Visitors," disguised as humans, have convinced most people that they're peaceful. It was supposed to be an allegory of how the Nazis took over Germany, but the selling point was good scary makeup. The 2-part presentation was 4½ hours long. With Jane Badler as the alien leader, Even C. Kim, Andrew Prine, Jennifer Cooke, Rafael Campos, Robert Englund, and Myron Healey.

THE VAGRANT

(MGM, 1992) **D:** Chris Walas **S:** Richard Jeffries **P:** Gillian Richardson

A low-key Bill Paxton stars as a junior executive who loses his mind in a new home. He has nightmares about the long-haired vagrant (Marshall Bell, from *Total Recall*) living in an abandoned lot across the street. After many irritating and strange things happen, he fortifies the house. The paranoia comedy includes some severed body parts, but is not really a horror movie. It costars Michael Ironside as a police detective, Mitzi Kapture, Mark McClure, and Colleen Camp as the real estate lady. The MGM release was made in Phoenix, Arizona by the director of *The Fly II*. Both are Brooksfilms (backed by Mel Brooks).

VALET GIRLS

(Vestron, 1986) **D:** Rafael Zielinski **S:** Clark Carlton **P:** Dennis Murray

Grace Jones in *Vamp*.

Three Hollywood female parking attendants party a lot in a dumb comedy by the director of *Spellcaster* and *Screwballs*. With April Stewart, Richard Erdman, John Terlesky, and Ron Jeremy. From Empire.

VALLEY GIRL

(Vestron, 1983) **D:** Martha Coolidge **S/P:** Wayne Crawford, Andrew Lane   (*Rebel Dreams*)

Deborah Foreman falls for the wrong guy (Nicolas Cage), a Hollywood punk. It's a fun movie that capitalized on the "Valspeak" fad, and it was good to see a "punk" character who wasn't a psycho gang member for a change. Colleen Camp and Frederic Forrest are Foreman's former hippie parents. With Cameron Dye, Lee Purcell, Michelle Meyrink, and Joyce Hyser. The limited-release soundtrack (featuring the Psychedelic Furs, Sparks, and others) was reissued by Rhino in 1994.

THE VALLEY (OBSCURED BY CLOUDS)

(Warner, 1971) **D/S:** Barbet Schroeder **S:** Paul Gegauff **P:** M. Chanderli, Stephane Tchalgadjieff **C:** Nestor Almendros   France (*La Vallée*)

Jean-Pierre Kalfon (*Weekend*), Bulle Ogier (*Maitresse*), and Michael Gothard (*The Devils*) are Europeans in Papua New Guinea searching for a magic feather. They eventually go native, joining the primitive mud people. The feature was shot on location. Real natives and mondo touches help make it memorable. Because of Pink Floyd's soundtrack (on Harvest), *The Valley* played some midnight shows in America. The group also did the music for Schroeder's *More* (also shot by Almendros).

THE VALS

(Vestron, 1982) **D/S/P:** James Polakof **S:** Deborah Amelon

Some girls try to con money from drug dealers to save an orphanage. Jill Carroll stars with Tiffany Bolling, Chuck Connors, Sue Ane Langdon, and guest stars John Carradine and Sonny Bono as a "spaced-out guest."

VAMP

(Starmaker, 1986) **D/S:** Richard Wenk **P:** Donald P. Borchers **M:** Jonathan Elias

Two college kids (Chris Makepeace and Robert Rusler) try to hire a stripper for a frat party. They take along "wild and crazy" Gedde Watanabe because he owns a car. Most of the movie takes place in the mysterious "After Dark" strip club. The silent vampire Katrina (Grace Jones) does an arty strip show. Her interesting set and white body paint were designed by the late Keith Haring. Everything is bathed in colored neon (it was the *Miami Vice* influence) and the vampires are inconsistent. Some are albinos, some have rotten

teeth, and the makeup changes. With Dedee Pfeiffer, Billy Drago, and Sandy Baron as the Renfield-like manager. From New World. The soundtrack is on Varèse Sarabande.

VAMPIRE AT MIDNIGHT

(Key, 1987) **D:** Gregory McClatchy **S:** Dulany Russ Clements **P/A:** Jason Williams **P:** Tom Friedman

Dr. Radcoff (Gustav Vintas) is a rich, balding, New Age hypno-therapist with a growing following, who makes people kill. His tall female assistant slashes a cop's throat with a razor and drinks his blood. Jason Williams (the star of *Flesh Gordon*) is a plainclothes hero LA cop. This one's a bit better than you'd expect, but when the hero's hand is bitten, his arm is bandaged in the next scene. With Esther Alise, Leslie Milne, and Christina Whitaker.

VAMPIRE COP

(Panorama, 1988) **D/S/A:** Donald Farmer **P:** Max and Faye Chesney

The only reason you might want to see this 16mm release is *Blood Feast* star Mal Arnold as a cop who gets killed by a chainsaw. This tape has more slow-motion scenes than most viewers will be able to handle, and other scenes are repeated in slow motion. It's also got too many fang closeups and the usual elements: hookers, pimps, and big breasts. Melissa Moore looks good as the TV reporter, though. With William Lucas as the big blond hunk vampire cop and Robin Schurtz. Filmed in Atlanta and Pensacola, Florida.

THE VAMPIRE HAPPENING

(United, 1970) **D:** Freddie Francis **S:** August Rieger **P:** Pier A. Caminneci W. Germany (*Gebissen Wird Nur Rachts*)

This vampire/sex comedy was inspired by Polanski's *The Fearless Vampire Killers*, complete with an all-vampire costume party and Ferdy Mayne as Dracula. Pia Dagermark (the producer's real-life wife) plays Betty Williams, the blond Hollywood movie star (also a baroness) who inherits a castle next to an all-girls school run by monks. Her great-grandmother is a revived witch. Dagermark plays both characters, so there's all the expected role-switching and confusion. A monk becomes a vampire and lives in an open grave. In dreams, a naked woman is put on the rack in the castle torture chamber and a topless woman runs through a forest of skeletons (not as good as it sounds). It's all pretty dated and silly. Dracula arrives in a "bat copter."

VAMPIRE IN VENICE

(Vestron International, 1987) **D/P:** Augostino Caminito **S:** Corto Alberto Alfieni, Leandro Lucchetti   Italy (*Nosferatu in Venice*)

Klaus Kinski returns in a "sequel" to Herzog's *Nosferatu* remake. Kinski refused to wear the same makeup again, but looks impressive with big teeth and long hair. Too bad the movie is so . . . boring. Nosferatu is revived by Gypsies then pushes an old lady out of a window onto spikes. With Christopher Plummer as a professor who tries to kill him, Barbara De Rossi (nude in sex scenes) as a princess, and Donald Pleasence as an ineffectual priest. Kinski disagreed with Caminito and directed himself for a while, then "film doctor" Luigi Cozzi was called in to finish. The score is "based on" a Vangelis LP and the dialogue is in English. Caminito also produced *King of New York*.

VAMPIRES AND OTHER STEREOTYPES

(Brimstone, 1992) **D/S/P/E:** Kevin J. Lindenmuth

Three girls and a guy headed for a downtown Manhattan party, two cops and a crooked businessman all find themselves in a loft that's actually—HELL! Corpses hang upside down, monsters try to get in, a crawling hand talks, and there's a giant rat and a whole wall of laughing, taunting heads. One character says "Reanimated heads really piss me off!" Cast members are possessed or decapitated, and Elvis and Jim Morrison make an appearance (bad idea). This very silly, unrated, low-budget Manhattan feature borrows from *The Evil Dead* but resembles an episode of the *Monsters* TV show. The FX range from mediocre to pretty imaginative and it only uses vampires as a punchline, but it's pretty funny once you get into it. With blond Wendy Bednarz (also in *There's Nothing Out There*), Mick McCleery, William White, and Rick Poli. The music is by the Krypt. Lindenmuth also made *Twisted Tales*.

VAMPIRE'S EMBRACE

(1991) **D/S/P:** Glen Andreiev
P: Nicholas Furris, Michael Minock

Some kids are killed by a ghoul. Later on, a guy's wife fools around too much and he meets a blonde named Angela after leaving a horror movie. Eventualu he leaves his wife and marries Angela, but when he goes to the Historical Society where she works, they claim they never heard of her. Seems like she's a vampire lured back into her old ways by her blond vampire "sister" Cassandra. A flashback to 200 years ago explains how she got that way, and her husband accepts her as she is. In one scene kids find a victim's hand during an Easter egg hunt in a cemetery (!?) and a vampire is killed in a way I've never seen before. This one's from Westport, Long Island. It has some decent FX.

VAMPIRE'S KISS

(HBO, 1989) **D:** Robert Bierman
S: Joseph Minion **P:** Barry Shils

A yuppie NYC literary editor (Nicolas Cage) takes Jennifer Beals to his apartment for a one-night stand. After sex, she flies out the window and he decides that he's become a vampire. He doesn't have any powers and nobody believes him. He makes a bloody mess biting victims with fake teeth and eats (a real) live cockroach. Cage has never been so over the top and out of control. You'd think the director was asleep during some of his scenes. With Maria Conchita Alonso as his abused

secretary, Elizabeth Ashley as his shrink, and Kasi Lemmons. By the writer of Scorsese's *After Hours*. It was shot on locations in and around NYC.

VAMPIRE TRAILER PARK

(Cinemondo, 1991) **D/P:** Steve Latshaw
S/A: Patrick Moran

A drinking detective (Robert Shurtz) and a psychic (Cathy Moran) investigate a Florida trailer park slasher. The owner of the Twin Palms park hires a sexy girl (Blake Pickett) and her boyfriend, who stage holdups to kill off his elderly tenants. Meanwhile an 18th-century vampire (Patrick Moran) moves in with his lady assistant. He hypnotizes victims with a TV set and pukes up (lots of) blood every time he feeds. It's a clever comedy with funny bad taste ideas and good characters, but the puke sounds can get pretty irritating and the *Magnum P.I.* narration gets a little old after a while. Latshaw even put a copy of *Psychotronic* magazine in his movie. Moran looks perfect as the young-looking creepy aristocrat vampire, and I liked the big turtle.

VAMPIRE VIXENS FROM VENUS

(Shanachie, 1994) **D/S/P:** Ted A. Bohus

Three ugly alien drug smugglers become sexy Earth women (Theresa Lynn, J. J. North, and *Penthouse* Pet of the Year Leslie Glass) and drain the essence from men. The comic sci-fi movie borrows ideas from *Lifeforce* and stars Peter Grimes as a detective. With Michelle Bauer, Joseph Pallister (from *Playgirl*), Charlie Callas, and Fred Olen Ray. It was made in Ft. Lee, New Jersey.

VAMPYRE

(Raedon, 1990) **D/S/P/A/E:** Bruce Hallenbeck
P: Antonio Paneta

Vampyre was shot on video in Eastfield Village, New Jersey for only "$20,000" and was inspired by the famous avant garde 1932 feature of the almost same name (*Vampyr*). A character named David Gray narrates and is first seen as a kid with a huge cross around his neck. I'm impressed by the impossibly low budget, but I still didn't understand why a period film with horses and candlelight has characters wearing jeans and modern ties walking around to music with a rock beat. Slow-paced mov-

ies can be great, but except for one topless vampire woman and a scene where some legs are cut off, there wasn't much going on to keep my interest. Writer John McCarty plays a victim. *The Vampyr* (CBS, 1993) is a modernized version of an 1827 opera.

VAMPYROS LESBOS

(VSOM, 1970) **D/S:** Jesús Franco
S: Jaime Chavarri **P:** Artur Brauner
Spain/W. Germany

Franco's semi-sequel to his *Count Dracula* (1969) is loosely based on a Bram Stoker short story. Basically, it's a very strange and sexy lesbian vampire movie with Lucy (Eva Stromberg), an American in Istanbul, having dreams of a stripper, actually the vampire Countess Nadine (Soledad Miranda), who has her own island. Other characters are Dr. Seward (Dennis Price), with a mute assistant named Morpho, a shrink (Paul Muller), and a boyfriend (Viktor Feldman). The Spanish/Portuguese Miranda (also in Franco sex films as Susan Korda) died in a car accident before the movie was released. Different versions were made for various countries in Europe. The video is letterboxed and subtitled.

THE VANISHING

(Fox Lorber, 1986) **D/S/E:** George Sluizer
S: Tim Krabbe **P:** Anne Gordon
Holland/France (*Spoorloos*)

This unnerving Hitchcock-type psychological movie takes place over a three-year period. The wife (Johanna Ter Steege) disappears while a couple is on vacation in France. The husband (Gene Bervoets) and the family man (Bernard-Pierre Donnadieu) who kidnapped her are the main characters. The woman had been buried alive. Originally two hours long, it's based on "The Golden Egg" by screenwriter Krabbe. It was released in the US in 1991 at 101 minutes, then was remade.

THE VANISHING

(Fox, 1992) **D:** George Sluizer
S: Todd Graff **M:** Jerry Goldsmith

20th Century-Fox brought over the original director to make this Americanized remake, but softened the effect by changing the ending. The

PHILO VANCE

Vance, a detective created by S. S. Van Dine, is a young aristocrat and amateur detective (who reads Nietzsche). Dick Powell was the first-seen Vance in *The Canary Murder Case* from Paramount (1929). It was a silent with sound added, and Louise Brooks costarred. Powell returned in three more films. The last, *The Kennel Murder Case* (1933), directed by Michael Curtiz, was at War-

ners. Meanwhile Basil Rathbone was Vance in *The Bishop Murder Case* (1930) at MGM. There were 11 more Vance movies, with various actors at various studios. Some stars were Warren William, Paul Lukas, Wilfrid Hyde-White, and Grant Richards. The last three released by PRC in 1947 were the closest thing to a series. One of the radio Vances was José Ferrer.

characters are very different too. Jeff Bridges stars as the twisted family man (with a Dutch accent) and kidnapper. Kiefer Sutherland is the Seattle man whose girlfriend (Sandra Bullock) disappears near Mount St. Helens and Nancy Travis (in a larger role than in the original) is his new girlfriend. With Park Overall and Lisa Eichhorn.

THE VANISHING SHADOW

(1934) **D/E:** Lewis Friedlander **S:** Het Manheim, Basil Dickey, George Morgan

Onslow Stevens uses a destroying ray, a big robot, and an invisibility vest to get revenge for the death of his father. The 12-chapter Universal serial also stars Ada Ince, Walter Miller, William Desmond, and Monte Montague. The director (as Lew Landers) went on to make features like *The Raven* (1935) and *The Return of the Vampire* (1943), both with Bela Lugosi.

VAN NUYS BOULEVARD

(Starmaker, 1979) **D/S:** William Sachs **P:** Newton P. Jacobs

Bobby (Bill Adler) is a small town boy who drives to Van Nuys for drag racing and disco dancing. He also gets thrown in jail and encounters a biker party with topless dancing. A Crown International release with Susan Severeid, Cyndi Wood (from *Playboy*), and Melissa Prophet. The soundtrack was on Mercury. The director made *Galaxina* next.

VARIETEASE

(SW, 1954) **D:** Irving Klaw

The Manhattan-based Klaw, famous for making and marketing b/w mail order shorts featuring Betty Page and other models, also made two 35mm, color burlesque review features. This was his first and it stars Lili St. Cyr with Christine Rogers, Betty Page, who dances dressed as a harem girl, plus comics and a female impersonator. It's 70 minutes long. Klaw made *Teaserama* (1955) next.

VARIETY

(HBO, 1984) **D:** Bette Gordon **S:** Kathy Acker **P:** Renee Schafransky

Sandy McLeod is a ticket taker at the (real) X-rated Variety Photoplays theater in New York near Union Square. She becomes fascinated with the male patrons and follows one around. With Will Patton, music by John Lurie, and some good location work. Before being closed down by the health department during the AIDS scare, the Variety Photoplays theater, built during the silent days, was a porno theater that showed unusual exploitation and horror double bills on some days. Seeing this nonexploitive feature at its debut in the Variety surrounded by people who had probably never been there before was a strange experience. The theater was later renovated and plays were presented there.

VEGAS IN SPACE

(Troma, 1992) **D/S:** Philip R. Ford **S/A:** Miss X, Doris Fish

Male astronauts are disguised as Vegas showgirls on an all-female planet called Clitoris in the future. "Doris Fish" stars as Capt. Dan Tracy in the very low budget sci-fi musical drag comedy. The San Francisco production took several years to complete. Fish died in 1991. Troma picked up the rights to the movie.

VEGAS VICE

(1994) **D/S/P:** Joey Travolta **S:** Rich Dillon

Sam Jones and Shannon Tweed are Vegas cops after a serial killer in a movie directed by the actor brother of John Travolta. With James Gammon, Miguel Nunez, and Rebecca Ferratti.

VELVET

(1984) **D/P:** Richard Lang **S:** Ned Wynn

Four female secret agents posing as aerobics instructors rescue a laser scientist who can make nuclear weapons useless. The *Charlie's Angels*–type ABC-TV pilot film stars Shari Belafonte-Harper, Leah Ayres, Mary Margaret Humes, and Sheree J. Wilson. With Polly Bergen, Leigh McCloskey, Bruce Abbott, Andrea Marcovicci, William Windom, and Clyde Kusatsu. Lang also directed feature-length episodes of *Vega$, Kung Fu,* and *Fantasy Island*.

VELVET SMOOTH

(Paragon, 1976) **D/P:** Michael Fink **S:** Leonard Michaels, Jan Weber **P:** Marvin Schild, Joel Schild

Johnnie Hill plays Velvet Smooth, a karate-kicking black female private detective with an all-lady staff who is hired by a drug dealer. Most of the very-low-budget movie is three women kicking and karate-chopping men. Owen Wat-son plays the ghetto gang leader and also was the martial arts coordinator.

VENDETTA

(Vestron, 1985) **D:** Bruce Logan **S:** Emil Farkas, Simon Maskell **P:** Jeff Begun   (*Angels Behind Bars*)

A Hollywood stuntwoman (Karen Chase) who uses Bushido fighting techniques goes undercover in prison to catch her sister's killer. The butch prison gang leader (Sandy Martin) deals in drugs and prostitution. A woman does a Prince imitation and a punk country band plays at a party. With Michelle Newkirk and Roberta Collins. From Concorde.

VENGEANCE

(1964) **D:** Dene Hilyard **S:** Alex Sharp **P/A:** William Thourlby

Crown released this b/w post–Civil War revenge western. With Melora Conway and Tiger Joe Marsh. Thourlby had been in the infamous *The Creeping Terror*.

VENGEANCE IS MINE

(Video Treasures, 1975) **D/S:** John Trent **S:** Robert Maxwell **P:** David Perlmutter *Canada/UK (Sunday in the Country; Blood for Blood)*

Ernest Borgnine is a farmer and grandfather who fights back when murdering crooks, led by Michael J. Pollard, attack. Borgnine shoots, hangs, or sics dogs on them. With Hollis McLaren and Al Waxman. AIP released the *Straw Dogs*–inspired feature.

VENGEANCE OF THE ZOMBIES

(All Seasons, 1972) **D:** Leon Klimovsky **S/A:** "Paul Naschy"/Jacinto Molina **P:** Jose Antonio Perez Giner   Spain/Italy (*La Rebellión de las Muertas*)

A British woman in 19th-century India whose family has been cursed becomes involved with a Krishna cult and zombies. Naschy plays two roles in a feature similar to Hammer films like *Plague of the Zombies* (1966).

VENGEFUL DEAD: *See* KISS DADDY GOODBYE

VENUS

(1984) **D:** Peter Hollison **S:** Jean Jabely **S/P:** Pierre Benicheu   France/US

Odele Michel stars as Venus in an erotic feature shot in 3-D.

VENUS FLYTRAP

(Legacy, 1988) **D/S:** T. Michael **S/P:** Marvin Jones **P:** Kevin M. Glover, Steve Malis

In a shot-on-video feature, punk rockers hold up a store, crash a party, play strip darts and Russian roulette, have sex, then end up victims of a man-eating plant.

VENUS IN FURS

(SW, 1967) **D/S/A:** Joe Marzano **P:** Lou Campa

This 65-minute b/w Box Office International release claims to be based on the 1870 novel by Sacher-Masoch and was released near the time of first Velvet Underground album (with a song of the same name). A NYC shoe salesman reads *Venus*. He goes home with a rich suburban woman and witnesses a party with various fantasy rooms. His drink is drugged and he ends up tied to a tree while two women make love. But it was all a dream, which starts up again after he wakes. The dialogue (there's a lot) is very stilted. The only nudity is when a woman takes a milk bath, then crawls around like a cat. Shep Wild stars with "Elinore," Pat Barnett, and Bhob Stewart. The music is by Vito and the Vikings. Two Euro movies with the same name (by Dallamano and Franco) were released shortly after this one, and a Dutch version was released in 1994.

VERMILION EYES

(1987) **D/S/P/E . . . :** Nathan Schiff

Schiff had made short films since 1979, but this is a *long* 98 minutes. A guy who reads and collects issues of *True Detective* keeps a radiation suit in his trunk for when he just happens to discover dead women (death by car crash, train runs over . . .). He also goes out and kills hookers (or dreams that he does) and eventually he starts killing children

James Stewart surrounded by Kim Novak in *Vertigo*.

and chases his sister through a graveyard (thinking philosophical thoughts all the while). This disturbing feature has some imaginative camera shots and hallucination scenes, but is mostly one gory death after another with some decapitations and sex with a silicone blonde thrown in for variation.

VERTIGO
(MCA, 1958) **D/P:** Alfred Hitchcock **S:** Alec Coppel, Samuel Taylor **M:** Bernard Herrmann

James Stewart stars as Scottie the acrophobic San Francisco cop in Hitchcock's obsessive and disturbing necrophilia/"ghost" movie. It's the favorite of many of the director's fans and was based on *Sueur Froid* by Pierre Boileau and Thomas Narcejac (who also wrote the book *Diabolique* was based on). Kim Novak is Madeline *and* Judy. With Barbara Bel Geddes, Tom Helmore, Henry Jones, and Ellen Corby. It was the last of Stewart's four Hitchcock movies. The John Fulton FX and the soundtrack (released on Mercury) are top grade. The 128-minute Paramount feature was rereleased in theaters in 1984. You've seen every plot twist and idea copied in many inferior movies, but if you haven't seen *Vertigo*, what are you waiting for?

THE VERY FRIENDLY NEIGHBORS
(1969) **D:** Albert Zugsmith **P:** Donald E. Lion

This obscure sex film about Hollywood wife-swapping, group sex, and hypnotism was one of the last by the man who once produced Orson Welles and Douglas Sirk movies.

VIBES
(RCA, 1988) **D:** Ken Kwapis **S:** Lowell Ganz, Babaloo Mandel **P:** Deborah Blum, Tony Ganz

Psychics Cyndi Lauper (a beautician who specializes in astral projection) and Jeff Goldblum fall in love in Ecuador. They discover a lost civilization and encounter gangsters. With Julian Sands, Peter Falk, Elizabeth Pena, Michael Lerner, and Steve Buscemi. Ron Howard was executive producer of this PG flop from Columbia. It was the only starring vehicle for singer Lauper ("Girls Just Wanna Have Fun").

VICE ACADEMY
(Prism, 1988) **D/S/P/E:** Rick Sloane

If you thought the *Police Academy* series was stupid, wait till you suffer through the *Vice Academy* series. Shawnee (Karen Russell) and Didi (Linnea Quigley) are new vice cops who infiltrate a porno racket and bust a movie shoot. With Ginger Lynn Allen as Holly, the police chief's daughter, and Viper, a tattooed porn star.

VICE ACADEMY PART 2
(Prism, 1990) **D/S/P/E:** Rick Sloane

Ginger Lynn Allen and Linnea Quigley return with Jay Richardson as a cop, Melissa Moore, and bodybuilder Teagan Clive as "Bimbicop." This time some evil woman puts Spanish fly in the city water supply.

VICE ACADEMY PART 3
(Prism, 1991) **D/S/P:** Rick Sloane

Ginger Lynn Allen (in all entries in this lame comedy series) is Holly, an undercover cop in prison. Julia Parton becomes a green-haired mutant holdup woman after a toxic accident. She commits crimes with her punk boyfriend and her ex-con girlfriends. With Elizabeth Kaitan (who has a topless scene), Darcy DeMoss, and Jay Richardson playing a cop. There's also *B-Movie Queens Revealed: The Making of Vice Academy* (1993) with scenes from all three.

VICE SQUAD
(Nelson, 1982) **D:** Gary A. Sherman **S:** Sandy Howard, Kenneth Peters, Robert Vincent O'Neil **P:** Brian Frankish

An LA cop is after a sadistic pimp played by Gerald Dwight "Wings" Hauser (known at the time for *The Young and the Restless* soap opera). He's called Ramrod and sings the song "Neon Slime"! The violent feature helped launch Hauser's long exploitation movie career. He's after a hooker (Season Hubley) who gave evidence against him, and Nina Blackwood (an original MTV vj) is beaten with a coat hanger. A softer TV version was also filmed. With Jonathan Hayes and Cheryl "Rainbeaux" Smith. By the director of *Raw Meat* and *Dead and Buried*.

VICE VERSA
(RCA/Columbia, 1988) **D:** Brian Gilbert **S/P:** Dick Clements, Ian La Frenais

A Chicago executive (Judge Reinhold) changes places with his 12-year-old son (Fred Savage), thanks to a magic skull from Bangkok. With Swoosie Kurtz and William Prince. It was the best of many body-switch films released in the late 80s, probably because it's basically a remake of a 1948 British feature of the same name directed by Peter Ustinov.

VICE WARS: *See* COCAINE WARS

VICIOUS
(Sony, 1988) **D/S:** Karl Zwicky **S:** Paul J. Hogan **P:** David Hannay, Charles Hannah   Australia

This unrated violent movie features a bored suburban Sydney teen (Tamblyn Lord) who joins a trio of poverty-stricken teen psycho burglars. They kill a couple, kidnap the daughter, and continue to rape, torture, and kill. With Craig Pearce. It was not written by the *Crocodile Dundee* star (with the same name).

VICIOUS VIRGINS
(Cinema 2000, 1973) **D:** Henning Schellerup (*The Black Bunch*)

In Africa, villagers are massacred by mercenaries. Four (usually topless) native women join a rescue team searching for the son of Michael Pataki and seek revenge. The director made *Black Alleycats* for the same company. The (Canadian) video release is cut.

The Video Dead

VICTORIAN FANTASIES: *See* THE GROOVE ROOM

THE VIDEO DEAD

(Embassy, 1986) **D/S/P:** Robert Scott

A teenage brother and sister are in the new family house before their parents arrive. They find a haunted TV set showing *Zombie Blood Nightmare*. The guy smokes pot and watches TV. A blonde comes out of the set and strips for him. "The garbage man" also shows up on the screen. Eventually, zombies emerge from the set and a guy from Texas arrives at the door to help defeat them. One scene is copied from *Phantasm*, the girl dreams she's being eaten alive, and the zombies (who laugh) eat each other at the end. This is a silly, low-budget first effort with some gore, but I liked the characters and seeing people hunt zombies with arrows. The oddest part features the brother hanging from a tree with a chainsaw waiting for the living dead to attack.

VIDEODROME

(MCA, 1983) **D/S:** David Cronenberg
P: Claude Heroux   Canada

Cronenberg was at his outrageous, challenging, ahead-of-his-time best when he made this one. James Woods stars as Toronto cable Channel 83 TV pirate Max Renn. He discovers a snuff broadcast (from Pittsburgh) that causes (incredible) hallucinations. Scenes of a breathing videocassette and Woods extracting a gun from his stomach are not easily forgotten. Cronenberg was inspired by Toronto's real City TV, known for showing "baby blues" (Swedish sex movies). Deborah Harry is the hostess of the "Emotional Rescue" radio show and Jack Creley is Prof. Brian O'Blivion ("Television is reality. Reality is less than television"). With Sonja Smits and Bob Clark. The excellent FX are by Rick Baker and Steve Johnson. It was cut for the theatrical release and rated R, but the video release is uncut. An alternative version missing nudity and blood but with interesting previously unseen foot-

age has been on A&E cable TV and also was sold through the mail on tape. The Howard Shore soundtrack is on Varèse Sarabande. "Long live the new flesh!"

VIDEO MURDERS

(TWE, 1987) **D/S/P:** Jim McCullough Jr.
P: Jim McCullough Sr.

A traveling psycho (Eric Brown from *Private Lessons*) kills Shreveport, Louisiana, hookers in his hotel room and makes snuff tapes. He keeps one woman chained up. With disco and cemetery scenes but little on-screen sex or violence. It's a 16mm effort by the father/son makers of *Mountaintop Massacre*.

VIDEO VIOLENCE: WHEN RENTING IS NOT ENOUGH!

(Camp, 1986) **D/S/E:** Gary Cohen **P:** Ray Clark

A couple open a video store. The customers are psycho killers who rent only horror tapes. It was shot on tape, is bad, and features bad FX, but *Video Violence II: The Exploitation* (Camp, 1988) followed with the same couple.

VIETNAM, TEXAS

(TWE, 1990) **D/P/A:** Robert Ginty
S: C. Courtney Joyner **P:** Mark Damon

Ginty stars as a kung-fu-fighting Nam-vet priest in Houston. He had fathered a Nam kid, whose mom is now married to a Vietnamese Mafia boss. Haing S. Ngor (*The Killing Fields*) also costars; he was shot down outside his home in 1996. Ginty also directed *The Bounty Hunter*.

A VIEW TO A KILL

(MGM/UA, 1985) **D:** John Glen **S:** Richard Maibaum
P: Albert Broccoli, Michael G. Watson

This was the last (finally!) of the Roger Moore Bond movies. At least the villains are interesting.

Grace Jones is May Day, the killer mistress of global industrialist villain Max Zorn (Christopher Walken). May Day and Zorn are both results of an ex-Nazi's genetic experiments. With Tanya Roberts, Patric Macnee, Fiona Fullerton, and Dolph Lundgren in a small role (his first). The climax takes place at the Golden Gate bridge. The John Barry soundtrack was on Capitol and the hit theme was by Duran Duran. During its original release it made less than its $30 million cost. Moore and Sean Connery each played Bond seven times. Timothy Dalton took the role next, in *The Living Daylights* (1987).

VIGILANTE

(Vestron, 1983) **D/P:** William Lustig **S:** Richard Vetere **P:** Andrew Garroni   (*Street Gang*)

Robert Forster is a good New York family man and factory worker who joins coworker Fred Williamson's vigilante group after his family is attacked and his kid is killed. He's put on trial and goes to jail for assaulting the judge, but gets out for more revenge in a gritty, violent movie. With Carol Lynley as the Queens D.A., Joe Spinell as an attorney, Willie Colon, Rutanya Alda, Woody Strode, and Steve James. Jay Chattaway wrote the score. By the director of *Maniac* (1980) and *The Violation of Claudia* (1977).

VIGILANTE FORCE

(1976) **D/S:** George Armitage **P:** Gene Corman

A Nam vet (Kris Kristofferson) is hired to fight off oilfield workers in a California town. With Jan-Michael Vincent, Victoria Principal (her last theatrical role), Bernadette Peters, Andrew Stevens, Brad Dexter, David Doyle, Anthony Carbone, Yvette Vickers, Richard Rust, and Dick Miller. The PG-rated U.A. release was a flop, and Armitage didn't direct again until *Miami Blues* (1990).

VIKING MASSACRE

(Mega, 1967) **D/S:** "John Hold"/Mario Bava
S: Alberto Liberati, George Simonelli **P:** P. Tagliaferri
Italy (*I Coltelli del Vendicatore; Knives of the Avenger*)

One of Cameron Mitchell's last movies before playing Buck on *The High Chaparral* (1967–71), this was his third for director Bava. An old lady fortune teller on a beach warns a woman and her young son to "Beware of Og!" A flashback reveals the time when the warrior Ogden interrupted a royal wedding by showing off decapitated heads and was cursed by the king. Rurik (Mitchell with blond hair) is the bitter mystery man who shows up to protect the fatherless family. His flashback, complete with narration, reveals more plot complications and shows him raping and pillaging in a black metal mask. Later, during a knife fight, Rurik proclaims, "I could split your liver, I could quarter you, but I want your heart!" At the end of this tale of vengeance, Rurik rides off alone, just like in an Italian western, which this could have been with just a few costume changes and some guns. Of course, Bava, known for his horror movies, also directed westerns, and Mitchell had acted in an early Italian western (*Minnesota Clay*, 1964).

James Woods and Deborah Harry in *Videodrome*.

THE VILLAIN

(Columbia,1979) **D:** Hal Needham **S:** Robert G. Kane
P: Paul Maslansky   (*Cactus Jack*)

This PG slapstick comedy western was inspired by Road Runner cartoons with Kirk Douglas as Wile E. Coyote. He uses lots of explosives, is dragged by horses, and boulders fall on him. Sped up photography and old Warner Brothers cartoon music themes are added. Arnold Schwarzenegger (!) is "the handsome stranger," the bodyguard for Ann-Margret. With Paul Lynde as an Indian chief, Foster Brooks, Ruth Buzzi, Jack Elam, Strother Martin, R. G. Armstrong, Robert Tessier, and Mel Tillis. It was made during Douglas's most ridiculous acting period (*Holocaust 2000, Saturn 3 . . .*)

VINDICATOR

(Key, 1984) **D:** Jean Claude Lord **S:** Edith Rey, David Reston **P:** Don Carmody, John Dunning Canada (*Frankenstein '88*)

A scientist is killed and brought back to life as a robot/mummy monster (a Stan Winston FX creation). Pam Grier is the bounty hunter (named "Hunter") hired to kill it and Terri Austin is the wife. Some ideas are lifted from *The Terminator*, and there's some sex and violence.

THE VINEYARD

(Starmaker, 1988) **D/S/A:** James Hong **D:** William Rice **S:** Douglas Condo, James Marlowe **P:** Harry Mok

Hong (in old-age makeup) stars as Dr. Po, a scientist on an island in search of immortality. The evil Po says things like "Castrate him! Kill the eunuch!" and plants zombie men in the yard (like in *Motel Hell*). He also keeps semi-nude women chained up in the basement. He fertilizes his vineyard with human blood and markets rejuvenating wine. With Karen Witter (from *One Life to Live*) as an actress who shows up hoping for a film role and Cheryl Larson (who throws up spiders). The New World release tries to be like some of the wilder 80s Asian horror movies and includes martial arts.

VIOLATED

(Sinister, 1954) **D/S/P:** Kurt Neumann **S:** Felix Leutzkenforf   W. Germany (*Mannequins für Rio*; *Party Girls for Sale*; *They Were So Young*)

A man relates a flashback about Madame Zenoba and her Rio model agency, actually a slavery operation with captive European women. Johanna Matz is Eva, a German girl who is eventually exiled to a riverboat hell patronized by drunken coffee workers, and Scott Brady is the American engineer hero. A Dutch girl who runs away is beaten and drugged. The man behind it all is a respectable tycoon named Hieme Colla (Raymond Burr!). With Ingrid Stenn, Kurt Meisel, and Gert Frobe as the captain. Lippert released the exploitable feature. This retitled rerelease print is jumpy. Neumann, from Nuremberg, made *Carnival Story* in Germany around the same time.

VIOLATED

(Vestron, 1984) **D/S:** Richard Cannistraro **S:** Bennet Sims

A New York City actress fights back against gangsters who use and abuse party girls. April Daisy White stars with J. C. Quinn as a cop. Viewers were surprised to see John Heard (giving another good performance in a brief role) in this lowly exploitation movie with rape and nude scenes. Also with Elizabeth Kaitan and Samantha Fox.

THE VIOLATERS

(1957) **D:** John Newland **S:** Ernest Pendrell **P:** Himan Brown

Nancy Malone stars as a teenager "On Parole! Too Young To Know Better . . . Too Hard To Care!" It's not as exploitive as it sounds. Arthur O'Connell plays her dad and Fred Beir is her boyfriend. The director later created and hosted the *One Step Beyond* series. From Universal.

THE VIOLATION OF CLAUDIA

(VSOM, 1972) **D/S:** Claudio Guerin Hill **S:** Giovanni Simonelli   Spain/Italy (*La Violación*)

Ornella Muti stars as a 17-year-old having an affair with a man at a villa filled with pigeons. When he returns to her mother (Lucia Bose), the girl loses it. Hill made the bizarre *A Bell From Hell* (1973) next, before dying on location.

VIOLENT PLAYGROUND

(1957) **D:** Basil Dearden **S:** James Kennaway **P:** Michael Relph   UK

David McCallum is incredible as Johnny, a dangerous psycho teen pyro who holds a classroom full of little kids hostage at gunpoint. It was one of the first roles for the blond actor, who later moved to America to costar on *The Man From U.N.C.L.E.* Stanley Baker is top-billed as a cop, Anne Heywood is Johnny's sister, and Peter Cushing, just before becoming a horror star, is an ineffectual priest. U.A. released the b/w Rank feature in America.

VIOLENT ROAD

(1958) **D:** Howard W. Koch **S:** Richard Landau **P:** Aubrey Schenck

The Wages of Fear plot was borrowed for this Universal release about some men driving a truckload of explosives over a bumpy road. Brian Keith stars with Dick Foran, Efrem Zimbalist Jr., Merry Anders, and Ann Doran. Koch made *Frankenstein 1970* the same year.

VIOLENT SHIT

(Tempe, 1988) **D/S/P:** Andreas Schnaas W. Germany (*Violent Trash*)

Mass murderer Karl the Butcher escapes and kills. The cheap and gory movie from Hamburg is on video letterboxed and subtitled. It's 75 minutes long. Schnaas also made *Zombie 90: Extreme Pestilence* (1990) and *Violent Shit II: Mother Hold My Hand* (1992).

VIOLENT WOMEN

(1959) **D/P:** Barry Mahon

Here is minimal filmmaking at its finest. Five female prisoners kill a snitch and escape through a drainpipe. They emerge on the streets of New York. It's only an hour long in b/w from Exploit Films. With Jennifer Slater and Jo Ann Kelly. Mahon had already made *Cuban Rebel Girls* with Errol Flynn and went on to make many entertaining adults-only movies.

VIPER

(Fries, 1988) **D/P:** Peter Maris **S:** Frank Kerr

CIA agents kill university administration members and take over a university building in Indiana. They blame Mideast terrorists in order to start a war. Linda Purl, now a widow, investigates and becomes a female Rambo. With James Tolkan, Ken Foree, and Chris Robinson. By the director of *Terror Squad.*

VIPER

(1994) **D/S/P:** Danny Bilson **S/P:** Paul DeMeo

A real-souped-up Chrysler Viper sports car stars with James McCaffrey as the scientist hero in California of the near future. The car can shoot missiles and change colors. The NBC pilot features series regulars Dorian Harewood and Joe Nipote plus Sydney Walsh.

A VIRGIN AMONG THE LIVING DEAD: *See* ZOMBIE 4

VIRGIN HIGH

(RCA/Columbia, 1990) **D/P/A:** Richard Gabai **S:** Jeff Neill

Late-night cable was the place for this stupid Catholic girls' school comedy. Burt Ward is the dad of star Tracy Dali, and the director plays her boyfriend disguised as a priest. With Linnea Quigley, Michelle Bauer, and an Elvis impersonator.

THE VIRGIN OF NUREMBERG = HORROR CASTLE

THE VIRGIN PRESIDENT

(1968) **D/S/C:** Graeme Ferguson **S/P/A:** Severn Darden

In the near future, the President of the USA (Darden) is succeeded by his naive son Fillard Millmore (also Darden), and advisors to the new President plot to nuke Manhattan and blame the Chinese. With Richard Neuweiler, Peter Boyle, and Louis Waldron. Darden was in *The President's Analyst* and *Fearless Frank* around the same time. New Line released the underground satire.

THE VIRGIN QUEEN OF ST. FRANCIS HIGH

(1987) **D/S:** Francesco Lucente

A bet about if a guy can score with a virgin high school beauty is the plot of this PG-rated Crown International release. Stacy Christensen and Joseph R. Straface star.

Erica Gavin and Vincene Wallace in *Vixen!*

THE VIRGIN WITCH

(Prism, 1970) **D:** Ray Austin **S:** Klaus
Vogel **P:** Ralph Solomans UK

Christine (Anne Michelle, also in *The Haunted*), a miniskirted model who has premonitions, goes to the country for a job and brings along her sister Betty (real-life sister Vicki Michelle from *Psychomania*). Sybill (Patricia Haines), who is in charge, turns out to be a (lesbian) high priestess who uses black magic and wants the virgin sister for a ceremony. Much of this "adult" movie is naked dancing (to bongo music) and hard-to-see orgies, but the Michelle sisters are worth a look. Joseph Brenner released the Tigon film in America in 1978 on a double bill with *Devil's Rain*. Austin later directed episodes of *Space: 1999* and *The New Avengers*.

VIRIDIANA

(Hens Teeth, 1961) **D/S:** Luis Buñuel **S:** Julio Alejandro
P: Ricardo Muñoz Suay Spain/Mexico

The wealthy Don Jaime (Fernando Rey) hangs himself after he drugs his niece Viridiana (Silvia Pinal), who is studying to become a nun. She and the man's son (Francisco Rabal) inherit the estate. She invites beggars into the house, but they have a drunken orgy and in one famous scene, re-create the last supper. *Viridiana* was an international hit, and Buñuel soon returned to Europe to direct. It was partially filmed in Spain but was banned there for years. Authorities tried to have all prints confiscated.

THE VISION

(SVS, 1987) **D:** Norman Sloane **S:** William
Nicholson **P:** David M. Thompson UK

A "people's channel" subverts the viewing audience. Lee Remick and Dirk Bogarde star in the BBC TV movie. With Helena Bonham Carter and Eileen Atkins.

VISIONS OF EVIL = SO SAD ABOUT GLORIA

VISITANTS

(TWE, 1985) **D/S/P:** Rick Sloane

Some aliens chase a teen who stole one of their ray guns. Another bad one by the director of the *Vice Academy* series.

VISITING HOURS

(Fox, 1981) **D:** Jean Claude Lord **S:** Brian
Taggert **P:** Claude Heroux Canada

Killer Michael Ironside (then known for *Scanners*) goes after a feminist TV newscaster (Lee Grant) in a hospital. William Shatner is her ex-boyfriend. Also with Linda Purl and Lenore Zann. The director also made *The Vindicator*.

THE VISITORS

(Vidmark, 1988) **D/S:** Joakim Ersgard **S:** Patrick
Ersgard **P:** Hakan Ersgard Sweden

An American ad man and his family move into a remote house in Sweden. He loses his job, everybody fights, and they suspect something supernatural is going on. An expert arrives with heavy electrical equipment and the family sleeps while all kinds of loud yelling and noise goes on. Eventually we see a bloody spirit monster from the attic. It's all very slow-moving and would have made a good comedy. Keith Berkeley and Lena Endre star.

VISITOR FROM THE GRAVE

(Thriller, 1980) **D:** Peter Sasdy **S:** Anthony Hinds UK

An intruder is shot and buried but seems to return to life. Simon MacCorkindale and Kathryn Leigh Scott are the couple living in a country home. Elvira hosts this hour-long Hammer House of Horror TV program.

VIVA KNIEVEL!

(Warner, 1977) **D:** Gordon Douglas
S: Antonio Santillan, Norman Katkov
P: Stan Hough **M:** Charles Bernstein

Real-life stunt driver Evel Knievel plays himself in a ridiculous PG-rated fictional adventure movie. Some drug dealers in Mexico try to kill him for his truck and he inspires miracles at an orphanage. The hero also jumps over burning oil and lions. The support cast includes Marjoe Gortner, Lauren Hutton, Gene Kelly, Leslie Nielsen, Red Buttons, Cameron Mitchell, Albert Salmi, and Frank Gifford. *Evel Knievel* (1971) had starred George Hamilton as the self-promoting daredevil. Warner had high expectations for this movie. It was the last movie directed by Douglas, who had done everything from *General Spanky* (1936) to *Them!*

VIXEN!

(RM, 1968) **D/P/A/C/E:** Russ Meyer
S: Robert Rudelson

Erica Gavin is married to a Canadian bush pilot (Garth Pillsbury) who flies up people for fishing and hunting. She enjoys sex with her brother (Jon Evans), and her black draft-dodger lover (Harrison Page) wants to go to Cuba, but rejects communism in the end. In one scene Gavin puts a big fish down her blouse and in her mouth. The 71-minute-long feature was a big hit for Meyer. Vic Perrin narrated

Viridiana

and Peter Carpenter is in the cast. A soundtrack was issued by Beverly Hills Records. Rudelson also wrote the Jason Robards movie *Fools* (1970).

VOICES: *See* NIGHTMARE

VOICES FROM BEYOND

(Nightmare, 1991) **D/S:** Lucio Fulci
S: Piero Regnoli   Italy

In a "gothic thriller," the spirit of a dead man (Duilio Del Prete) looks for his killer. His daughter helps.

VOODOO BLACK EXORCIST

(Dura Vision, 1974) **D:** M. Cano **S:** S. Monkada
Spain (*Vudú Sangriento*)

Here's a crazy mummy movie you might have missed, a Madrid/ Miami production with some scenes shot in Haiti, Jamaica, and the Dominican Republic. On a tropical island two natives (Spanish actors in blackface) fight over Kenya (Tanyeka Stadler). During a voodoo ceremony—complete with frenzied topless black dancers—Kenya is decapitated and her (very fake-looking) head is passed around. The titles show up over NASA stock footage. A *Love Boat*–type cruiser contains the casket of a mummy (Aldo Sambrel), who can change, wolfman-style, into a "normal" scary bald man with a magic ring. He makes a shipworker his servant and pursues Kenya's reincarnation. He decapitates a man and puts the head in bed with her. In Kingston he has a man run over by a steamroller, and is interviewed on TV: "Three centuries in museums. I've learned many things!" In Port-au-Prince somebody fights the mummy with a water hose. He kidnaps his lost love and takes her to a huge cave. His obvious double goes down in flames at the end. The music ranges from sitars to Davie Allan–style guitar soundtrack rock. This movie has lots of talk and flashbacks and a fire-eating belly dancer. In my favorite scene, the mummy man is seen in a mirror, slapping a dancer around. The cameraman is clearly seen in the mirror, too. Director Cano also made *King of the Jungle*.

VOODOO DAWN

(Academy, 1989) **D:** Steven Fierberg **S:** John Russo, Jeffrey Delman, Thomas Rendon **P:** Steven Mackler

Gina Gershon has the main role as Tina, a migrant worker whose lover is hacked to death. The boyfriend's NYU buddies show up and Madame Daslay (Theresa Merritt) instructs them in zombie protection. One of them stops to rollerskate around an empty mansion. Raymond St. Jacques gets to battle the tall zombie Makoute (Tony Todd from the *Candyman* movies) and explain that the killer was "head of the Haitian secret police" and is "looking for body parts," but doesn't explain what he's doing in America. This movie is slow and boring, the killing is offscreen or too dark to see, and the end is confusing. It was filmed around Charleston, South Carolina.

VOODOO DOLLS

(1989) **D:** Andre Pelletier **S:** Ed Kelleher, Harriette Vidal **P:** Roger Racine   Canada

A drama professor at a private girls' college in Louisiana becomes possessed while putting on a play called *White Darkness,* written by a killer. It was made in Montreal along with the movie *Madonna* and is by the same American screenwriters.

VORTEX

(1982) **D/S/M/E:** Scott and Beth B.

Lydia Lunch is a detective exposing corrupt government defense policies. The New York City "underground" feature has a strange cast including James Russo, Richard France (from Romero's *The Crazies*), Bill Rice, Ann Magnuson, Haoui Montaug, and Bill Landis. With music by Lunch and Adele Bertei. The "B.'s" had also directed *The Black Box* (1978), *The Offenders* (1979) and *The Trap Door* (1980). Beth B. made features on her own after this one.

VOYAGE OF THE ROCK ALIENS

(Vestron, 1984) **D:** James Fargo, Bob Giraldi **S:** James Guidotti, Edward Gold **P:** Michaelle H. Keller, Brian Russell

Pia Zadora is Dee Dee in a frat comedy musical sci-fi *Beach Party* retread with lots of costumes and dance routines. With Tom Nolan as an alien with a rock band and a guitar-shaped spaceship, Ruth Gordon as the sheriff, Michael Berryman as Chainsaw, and Craig Sheffer. Pia and Jermaine Jackson sing a duet which somehow made it to #54 on the charts in 1985. This barely released feature was the fourth and last of Pia's star vehicles. Mike Curb was an executive producer. After this she had a kid with her millionaire husband and recorded her *Pia and Phil* LP.

V—THE FINAL BATTLE

(Warner, 1984) **D:** Richard T. Heffron
S: Brian Taggert, Peggy Goldman, Diane Frolov, Faustus Buck **P:** Dean O'Brien, Patrick Boyriven

Marc Singer, Faye Grant, Jane Badler, Andrew Prine and other cast members return in an even longer (6-hour) but not better followup miniseries about lizard aliens. Also with Richard Herd, Michael Ironside, Sarah Douglas, Greta Blackburn, and Dick Miller (as a drunk). A regular weekly series followed, but only lasted one year. Singer was one of the most overworked actors in direct-to-video releases by the early 90s.

VULTURES

(Prism, 1983) **D/S/P:** Paul Leder

Members of a Mexican-American family gather around a dying old man and are killed off. Stuart Whitman is the main suspect and Yvonne De-Carlo says "I can't fuck and think at the same time!" Everyone seems to have lovers half their age. Greg Mullavey is a cop and Meredith MacRae is a doctor. With Whitman's son Kipp (from *Bummer!*), Spanish horror star Maria Perschy (as a movie star), and Aldo Ray (killed in the first scene). Oh yeah, the real (surprise!) star is female impersonator Jim Bailey who plays *six roles!* In one scene he plays three people—but two are dead! He also does Streisand! Leder directed a whole series of brain-numbing movies featuring Mullavey (from *Mary Hartman . . .*) and his wife MacRae (from *Petticoat Junction*).

THIS DUDE MEANS BUSINESS
SO WATCH OUT WHEN YOUR NERVES *START TO SHATTER!*

EASTMAN
COLOR

WARNING
WE ARE NOT RESPONSIBLE TO ANY PERSON THAT THIS FILM MAY DISTURB. EITHER PHYSICALLY OR MENTALLY.
SEE IT AT YOUR OWN RISK

VOODOO BLACK EXORCIST
TERRIFYING STUPEFYING

WACKO

(Vestron, 1981) **D/P:** Greydon Clark
S: Dana Olsen, Michael Spound

In a slasher parody with *Airplane*-type gags, a cop (Joe Don Baker making fun of *Walking Tall*) searches for the pumpkin-headed "Lawnmower Killer." Stella Stevens, George Kennedy, and Julia Duffy are the Grave family. With Charles Napier, Jeff Altman, Scott McGinnis, and Andrew Dice Clay. Baker was also in *Joysticks* and *Final Justice* by Clark around the same time.

THE WAGES OF FEAR

(Home Vision, 1952) **D/S/P:** Henri-Georges Clouzot **S:** Jerome Geronimi   France/Italy

An international group of four men in a Central American oil town volunteer to drive two trucks full of nitro needed to put out an oil fire for reward money. The all-time suspense classic is by the director of the original *Diabolique* (also available from Home Vision) and is based on a novel by Georges Arnaud. At one time Hitchcock tried to obtain the rights and direct it. Yves Montand stars with Charles Vanel, Peter Van Eyck, Folco Lulli, and Vera Clouzot. The 156-minute feature was filmed in France. 34 minutes were cut out of the original American version because of politics (Third World countries being raped by US businesses) and some homosexual implications. The uncut version wasn't shown in American theaters until 1991 and is now available (subtitled) on tape. It was copied by *The Violent Road* (1958) and remade as *Sorcerer* (1977).

WAITRESS!

(Troma, 1981) **D/P:** Michael Herz, Lloyd Kaufman
S: Michael Stone, Charles Kaufman

Three women work as New York waitresses in a badly run restaurant. The early Troma comedy features Anthony Denison (*Crime Story*) and Larry "Bud" Melman.

WAIT UNTIL DARK

(Warner, 1967) **D:** Terence Young
S: Robert Carrington, Jane-Howard Carrington **P:** Mel Ferrer

Audrey Hepburn stars as Suzy Hendrix, a blind woman in a New York home who has to outsmart a psycho criminal (Alan Arkin) who uses disguises. He's after a doll with heroin inside. Richard Crenna and Jack Weston are Arkin's accomplices, and Efrem Zimbalist Jr. is the absent husband. Robby Benson was an extra. Based on a hit Broadway play by Frederick Knott (as was *Dial M for Murder*), it was copied many times in later years. Hepburn was nominated for an Oscar. Ferrer, her husband at the time, produced a number of features before returning to acting.

WALKABOUT

(1971) **D/C:** Nicholas Roeg **S:** Edward Bond
P: Si Litvinoff, Max L. Rabb   UK/Australia

Two kids lost in the Australian outback are befriended by an aborigine (David Gulpilil). 16-year-old Jenny Agutter and Lucien John (the director's son) are the stars of the complex culture-clash feature. John Barry wrote the music. Roeg worked on *Deadly Honeymoon* (1972), but was replaced, then made *Don't Look Now* (1973). Agutter had been in films since she was a little girl, and Gulpilil went on to a long acting career. From 20th Century–Fox.

WALKER: A TRUE STORY

(MCA, 1987) **D:** Alex Cox **S:** Rudy Wurlitzer **P:** Lorenzo O'Brien

Ed Harris stars as the (real) William Walker, an American soldier of fortune who declared himself president of Nicaragua in 1855. Cornelius Vanderbilt (Peter Boyle) backs him. 20th-century anachronisms (tape recorders, cars . . .) were thrown in to remind viewers of America's then-topical role in the country. People die in slow motion. The total box-office failure of this very political movie and Cox's *Straight to Hell* ended the British director's American career. He moved to Mexico and made *Highway Patrolman*. With Richard Masur, René Auberjonois, Keith Szarabajka, John Diehl, Marlee Matlin, Sy Richardson, Pedro Armendariz Jr., and Gerrit Graham. The music is by Joe Strummer from the Clash.

WALKER: TEXAS RANGER

(1993) **D:** Virgil W. Vogel **S:** Louise McCarn
P: Nancy Bond   (*One Riot, One Ranger*)

The CBS pilot starring Chuck Norris as a half-Indian Texas Ranger who'd rather kick than shoot

Joe Don Baker as Buford Pusser in *Walking Tall*.

led to a series. With Sheree J. Wilson and Clarence Gilyard. *Walker: Texas Ranger: Deadly Reunion* (Warner) is another feature-length episode. They were shot in Texas.

WALKING AFTER MIDNIGHT

(1988) **D/P:** Jonathan Kay   Canada

The Dalai Lama of Tibet is in this star-studded documentary about reincarnation. Martin Sheen, James Coburn, Willie Nelson, k. d. lang, Helen Shaver, Donovan, Rae Dawn Chong, and Dennis Weaver all appear too. It was narrated by Ringo Starr (who checked into an alky clinic the year it was released) and was backed by the National Film Board of Canada.

WALKING TALL

(Vestron, 1973) **D:** Phil Karlson **S/P:** Mort Briskin

Bing Crosby, of all people, put the money behind this drive-in classic. Joe Don Baker stars as real-life Tennessee sheriff Buford Pusser, who uses a "pacifier" club to beat local gangsters and killers. Elizabeth Hartman costars with Gene Evans, Noah Beery Jr., Bruce Glover, Logan Ramsey, and Kenneth Tobey. Pusser himself was hired as an advisor. Johnny Mathis (!) sings the title song. Karlson had just directed the hit *Ben*. Cinerama made and released both, then went bankrupt. AIP took over distribution of *Walking Tall*, then made the sequels (with Bo Svenson).

WALKING TALL, PART 2

(Vestron, 1975) **D:** Earl Bellamy
S: Howard B. Kreitsek **P:** Charles A. Pratt   (*Part 2—Walking Tall*)

Bo Svenson replaced original star Joe Don Baker as the legendary Tennessee sheriff and he whups some more bad guys. Buford Pusser was going to play himself, but died in a car crash. With Luke Askew, John Chandler, Robert DoQui, Richard Jaeckel, Angel Tompkins, and Leif Garrett. Noah Beery Jr., Bruce Glover, Logan Ramsey, and Lurene Tuttle all return from the first film (although not all as the same characters). The Bing Crosby production was AIP's biggest hit of the year.

WALKING TALL: THE FINAL CHAPTER

(Vestron, 1977) **D:** Jack Starrett **S:** Howard B. Kreitsek
P: Charles A. Pratt   (*Final Chapter—Walking Tall*)

Bo Svenson returned in this "final" chapter about the Tennessee sheriff Buford Pusser. With Forrest Tucker, Margaret Blye, Morgan Woodward, and H. B. Haggerty. Bruce Glover, Lurene Tuttle, Leif Garrett, and Logan Ramsey also returned from Part 2. A Bing Crosby Production released by AIP, it was the company's biggest hit of 1977. *A Real American Hero* (1978), aka *Hard Stick* (on Mntex Video), starring Brian Dennehy, was a Pusser TV movie, and Svenson returned in a very short-lived NBC-TV series in 1981.

WALKING THE EDGE

(Vestron, 1983) **D:** Norbert Meisel **S:** Curt Allen
P: Sergei Goncharoff **M:** Jay Chattaway

Robert Forster stars as an LA cab driver who helps Nancy Kwan. She wants vengeance after her husband and son are killed. Joe Spinell is the main torturing gangster. From Empire.

WALK LIKE A MAN

(MGM, 1987) **D:** Melvin Frank
S: Robert Klane **P:** Leonard Kroll

Bobo (Howie Mandel) is raised by wolves, then reunited with his real family in a PG comedy. With Christopher Lloyd, Cloris Leachman, Colleen Camp, and George DiCenzo.

WALK OF THE DEAD=VENGEANCE OF THE ZOMBIES

WALK THE WALK

(1970) **D/S/P:** Jac Zacha

This R-rated anti-drug movie was the the last from the famous road-show king, Kroger Babb. Bernie Hamilton stars as a black theological student hooked on heroin and booze. He eventually manages to straighten out, but after an injury, a doctor gives him sedatives. He returns to drugs and hangs himself. The depressing tale was advertised with lines like: "Hear six new songs! See a hippy wedding!" With Honor Lawrence as a female pusher and Eric Weston. It opened in the summer, just after *The Cross and the Switchblade*. Hamilton had also been in *Let No Man Write My Epitaph* (1960) and *Synanon* (1965), both also about hard drug addiction.

WALLS IN THE CITY

(Provisional, 1994) **D/S/P/C/E:** Jim Sikora
S: Chris Sims **P:** Tamara Willis

One woman (Paula Killen) is featured in 3 interlocking stories of down-and-out, on-the-edge characters in Chicago. Most of them drink a lot, and the sex scene is the kind that features the guy's hairy butt. It's 70 minutes long, and includes scenes from *Point Blank*. The Castaways' "Liar Liar" and Johnny Cash's "Home of the Blues" are on the soundtrack (on Skin Graft Records). Tom Fitzpatrick and Bill Cusack costar. The middle part (based on Charles Bukowski) is also on the *Small Gauge Shotgun* compilation tape.

WANDA NEVADA

(Warner, 1979) **D/A:** Peter Fonda
S: Dennis Hackin **P:** Neal Dobrofsky

Peter Fonda (as a gambler in 1950) wins Brooke Shields in a poker game. They find gold in the Grand Canyon and meet a series of strange characters. With Fiona Lewis, Luke Askew, Severn Darden, and Henry Fonda in a fake-looking beard. The PG feature was Peter Fonda's last as director.

WANDA, THE SADISTIC HYPNOTIST

(SW, 1969) **D/S/P:** Greg Corarito **E:** Gary Graver

Walk the Walk from Kroger Babb.

A man is kidnapped by Wanda (Katharine Shubeck), a tall woman with a fashion-model body, heavy eye makeup, and a riding crop. Women swim naked in her LA pool; people are whipped (not realistically). She hypnotizes a saleslady and makes her dance, and a laughing escaped maniac breaks in. He and the first man smoke pot and pass around LSD pills, followed by a trip sequence. All the while, this silly (narrated) movie is being watched by one lone guy in a grindhouse theater (who started out by imagining nudes in a shop window then watching a nudist short). The garage rock music is by the Masochists, and there's a cosmic ending. The sound dubbing is as bad as possible. Richard Compton was the assistant director.

THE WANDERERS

(Warner, 1979) **D/S:** Philip Kaufman
S: Rose Kaufman **P:** Martin Ransohoff

In 1963, a Bronx gang fights the "Baldies" (who are tricked into joining the Marines) and the "Ducky Boys." Ken Wahl stars with Karen Allen, Linda Manz (as PeeWee), Erland Van Lidth de Jeude, Val Avery, and Olympia Dukakis. The Kennedy assassination is on TV, and at the end Wahl follows a girl into a folk club where "The Times They Are A-Changin'" is being performed by Bob Dylan (not shown). It was based on the novel by Richard Price. A good oldies soundtrack is on Warner Brothers. *The Wanderers* was released the same year as the more fantastic gang movie *The Warriors*, which got all the attention.

WANTED : DEAD OR ALIVE

(Starmaker, 1986) **D/S:** Gary Sherman
S: Michael Patrick Sherman, Brian Taggert
P: Robert C. Peters

Rutger Hauer is a former CIA agent turned bounty hunter in LA. He's supposed to be the "great-grandson" of the Steve McQueen character from the western TV show of the same name (1958–61). Of course most of the potential mid-80s audience members never heard of the series. Hauer becomes a victim of a government conspiracy. Gene Simmons is an Arab terrorist who blows up a theater showing *Rambo*. With Mel Harris and Robert Guillaume. From New World.

WAR AND REMEMBRANCE

(MPI, 1989) **D/S:** Dan Curtis
S: Earl W. Wallace, Herman
Wouk **P/A:** Barbara Steele

Cult horror star Barbara Steele has a brief role in an early episode of this sequel to Curtis's *The Winds of War* (1983). The ABC miniseries was a very long 14 hours. The story covers 1941–45 (Pearl Harbor to Hiroshima). Robert Mitchum (looking too old) stars, with a cast of hundreds. Sharp-eyed viewers can spot many American and European character actors well known from exploitation movies. Sharon Stone has a role. It's all on 2 volumes of tapes (13 cassettes). When I visited Vienna, a beautiful old city with countless historical sights, I was shown *War and Remembrance* locations.

WARBIRDS

(Starmaker, 1989) **D/S:** Ulli Lommel **S/P:** Susanna
Love **S:** Clifford B. Wellman **P:** Kurt Eggert

US flyers stop an Arab uprising in a very cheap *Iron Eagle* (or *Top Gun*) copy. With Cully Holland, Jim Eldert, and Timothy Hicks.

WAR BUS COMMANDO

(Trylon, 1989) **D:** Frank Valenti **S:** David Parker Jr. Italy

A soldier named Johnny Hondo (Mark Gregory) is sent by John Vernon to Afghanistan on a suicide mission. With Savina Gersak.

WARCAT

(TWE, 1987) **D/M/E:** Ted V. Mikels **S:** Gary Thompson
P/A: Jeffrey C. Hogue (*Angel of Vengeance*)

This was the first released movie directed by Mikels (Theodore Vincent Mikacevich) since *10 Violent Women* back in 1978. An athletic female writer (Jannina Poynter) arrives in a small town. She catches fish with a sharp stick, runs a lot, and sings "Blowin' in the Wind" (!). A camouflaged military survivalist group in the desert, led by "the Major," easily wipes out a group of partying dirtbikers but spares one female, whom they lock in a cage for sex. A stupid construction worker kidnaps the nature-loving writer and is whipped by the Major. She's tied up, raped (offscreen), and escapes. During an endless chase, she kills off the men by cutting throats, stabbing eyes, and using snakes, traps, and dynamite. (Mikels also did the FX.) Original director Ray Dennis Steckler's touch is evident during "meanwhile" scenes where two goons (like the ones in *The Thrill Killers*) rob and kill couples. They meet up with the victorious killer heroine at the end.

THE WAR GAME

(Nelson, Sinister, 1965) **D/S/P:** Peter Watkins UK

If you want to see what a city under nuclear attack might look like (without known actors to distract you), look for this extraordinary documentary-style 48-minute b/w film. It was made for, then banned by, the BBC. They finally aired it in 1985! I saw it in high school. It shows food riots, firestorms, and people with radiation sickness. The Nelson tape release also includes Watkin's *Culloden*. Watkins made *Privilege* next. He also made *The Journey* (1987), a 14¹/₂-hour anti-nuke documentary.

WAR GAMES

(MGM, 1983) **D:** John Badham **S:** Lawrence Lasker, Walter F. Parkes **P:** Harold Schneider

Matthew Broderick taps into a Pentagon computer and nearly starts a "global thermonuclear" WWIII. The hit PG adventure/comedy with a message ending costars Ally Sheedy, with Dabney Coleman as a computer defense specialist. With Barry Corbin, John Wood, Dennis Lipscomb, James Tolkan, Eddie Deezen, and Michael Madsen. Original director Martin Brest was fired. Badham made *Blue Thunder* the same year.

WAR GODDESS

(SW, 1972) **D:** Terence Young **S:** S. Richard Aubrey **P:** Nino Krisman   Italy (*Le Guerrière del Sno Nuda; The Amazons*)

This outrageous R-rated period adventure (by the director of the first James Bond movies) had a high budget for this kind of thing. Stars Alean Johnston and Sabine Sun have a nude catfight, and topless Amazon warriors ride horses. Luciana Paluzzi and Malisso Longo are also in the AIP release. Young's next was *The Klansman* (1974).

WAR ITALIAN STYLE

(1967) **D:** Luigi Scattini **S:** Franco Castellano **P:** Fulvio Luciasano   Italy (*Due Marines e un Generale; The Amazons*)

AIP backed this WWII comedy about a German lady spy, two American soldiers, and some missing plans. With the comedy team of Franco Franchi and Ciccio Ingrossia (from *Dr. Goldfoot and the Girl Bombs*), Buster Keaton (in his last released feature), Martha Hyer, and Fred Clark.

WARLOCK

(Vidmark, 1988) **D/P:** Steve Miner **S:** David Twohy **M:** Jerry Goldsmith

Julian Sands is the blond warlock dressed in black who escapes into the future after a nice beginning in 1691, in Massachusetts Bay Colony. Richard E. Grant (*Withnail and I*) follows him in an attempt to prevent the "uncreation," and the movie turns into a *Terminator*-in-reverse plot set in modern times. Sands flies on wires (like Peter Pan) and needs to boil virgin boys' fat (!) to achieve his goal. He also occasionally cuts off fingers and plucks out eyeballs, and he puts a fast-aging curse on Lori Singer. *Warlock* has some good fantasy ideas and a few shocking scenes, but parts are laughable. The final battle is on a very fake Boston graveyard set. With Mary Woronov as a medium. The New World production finally was released to American theaters by Trimark in 1991, and a sequel followed. The soundtrack is on Intrada. By the director of *Friday the 13th Part 2* and *Part 3*.

WARLOCK: THE ARMAGEDDON

(Vidmark, 1993) **D/A:** Anthony Hickox **S:** Kevin Rock, Sam Bernard **P:** Peter Abrahm

There are some good FX (including morphing) and more gore than in the original, but the story is even sillier, and it's set in a boring western set town. Julian Sands (returning as the floating warlock) emerges full grown, bloody, and naked from a woman who had become instantly pregnant. Paula Marshall (*Hellraiser III*) and Chris Young are the teen stars who try to defeat him. With a zombie, voodoo, scalping, a crucifixion, and Micha the dwarf in drag. Also with R. G. Armstrong as one of the Druid guardians, Joanna Pacula (a victim in a bizarre fashion show scene), Bruce Glover, and in bit parts, Ferdinand Mayne, George "Buck" Flower, and Zach Galligan.

WARLORDS

(Vidmark, 1988) **D:** Fred Olen Ray **S:** Scott Ressler **P:** Harel Goldstein

David Carradine tries to rescue his wife (Brinke Stevens) in the post-nuke future desert. A female Rambo type (Dawn Wildsmith) and a ridiculous puppet head in a box help, and mutants threaten. With Sid Haig as a warlord villain, Ross Hagen, Fox Harris, and Robert Quarry. Stevens is seen topless and chained to a cross and Victoria Sellers (daughter of Peter), Michelle Bauer, and Debra Lamb also have topless scenes. For a while Stevens replaced Wildsmith in the director's life (and movies).

WARLORDS FROM HELL

(Warner, 1987) **D:** Clark Henderson **S:** James Mitchell Belkin, Tom Campbell

Two brothers on dirt bikes accidentally find a Mexican marijuana plantation run by sadistic bikers (led by Robert Patrick). With Brad Henson and Jeffrey Rice. It's a pretty bad one.

WARLORDS OF THE 21ST CENTURY

(Embassy, 1981) **D/S:** Harley Cokliss **S:** Irving Austin, John Beech **P:** Lloyd Phillips, Rob Whitehouse **C:** Chris Menges   US/New Zealand (*Battletruck*)

In the future, during a fuel shortage, James Wainwright runs an outlaw army with a giant supertruck in this PG New World release. Hero Michael Beck (from *Xanadu*) is Hunter. With Annie McEnroe and Bruno Lawrence.

WARNING SHADOWS

(Video Yesterday, 1922) **D/S:** Arthur Robinson **S:** Rudolph Schneider **C:** Fritz Otto Wager Germany (*Shatten*)

This influential drama includes disorienting camera tricks with distorted faces, scary shadows, and odd lighting. A traveling magician hypnotizes characters in a house at night. Cinematographer Wager also shot *Nosferatu* and early Fritz Lang movies. American director Robinson also made *The Student of Prague* (1935) in Germany. Originally 93 minutes, the tape (with German and English titles) only runs 60.

WARNING SIGN

(Fox, 1985) **D/S:** Hal Barwood **S:** Matthew Robbins **P:** Jim Bloom **M:** Craig Safan   (*Biohazard*)

Workers become violent toxic zombies during germ warfare research in Utah. The government tries to cover it up. An antitoxin is found in pregnant women. Sam Waterston stars with Kathleen Quinlan, Yaphet Kotto, Jeffrey DeMunn, Richard Dysart, and Rick Rossovich. The soundtrack is on Southern Cross.

WAR OF THE WIZARDS

(VSOM, 1978) **D:** Sadamasa Arikawa, Richard Caan **S:** F. Kenneth Lin **P:** Frank Wong   Taiwan (*The Phoenix*)

Big Richard Kiel is the mute Grasshopper in this period fantasy adventure. The hero is a Thai fisherman who encounters an evil fox and a giant bird that battles a rock monster. Parts are similar to Toho giant monster movies, but not as good.

WARP SPEED

(1975) **D/P:** Allan Sandler **P:** Robert Emenegger

A spaceship takes a psychic to see what has happened to a missing crew. Adam West and Camille Mitchell are in the Gold Key direct-to-TV movie.

WARREN OATES: ACROSS THE BORDER

(1992) **D/P:** Tom Thurman

"For some of us, Warren Oates is the only human being in pictures." That's how this excellent look at the late Kentucky-born actor with "the meaningful squint" begins. Many choice film clips (*The Shooting, Cockfighter, 92 in the Shade, Bring Me the Head of Alfredo Garcia,* in which he "played" director Sam Peckinpah . . .) are shown, and some of the people interviewed are Monte Hellman, Peter Fonda, Stacy Keach, Robert Culp, and Harry Dean Stanton. Ned Beatty (also from Kentucky) narrates.

THE WARRIOR AND THE SORCERESS

(Vestron, 1984) **D/S/P:** John Broderick **P:** Frank K. Isaac Jr.

It's an outer space post-nuke Samurai western with David Carradine as Kain, "the Dark One." It's also an uncredited *Yojimbo* remake with tentacled monsters. Naja (Maria Socas) is topless throughout the entire movie, and one woman has four breasts. Luke Askew is Zeg. From Corman's New Horizons.

WARRIOR OF THE LOST WORLD

(HBO, 1983) **D/S:** David Worth **P:** Roberto Bessi, Frank E. Hildebrand

In another post-nuke adventure, the hero "Warrior" (Robert Ginty) and his talking computer motorcycle try to rescue Persis Khambatta and her father (Harrison Muller). Fred Williamson is "Henchman," who works for the evil leader Prosser (Donald Pleasence). The Sarlui production includes martial arts, trucks, and Amazons. It was later ridiculed on the *Mystery Science Theater 3000* program.

WARRIOR QUEEN

(Vestron, 1985) **D:** Chuck Vincent
S: Rick Marx **P:** Harry Alan Towers,
Aristede Masacessi   US/Italy (*Pompeii*)

Towers and Vincent were a match made in hell, and this embarrassment features orgies and slave auctions. Sybil Danning is the mistress of the Roman emperor Claudius (Donald Pleasence, in probably his worst role ever). She travels to rescue a slave (Tally Chanel aka Britanny). With Josephine Jacqueline Jones, David Gaughton, Richard Hill, and porn star Samantha Fox (in two roles). The volcano eruption footage is from *Last Days of Pompeii* (1960). The unrated tape has more sex scenes and runs 79 minutes. The R version is ten minutes shorter.

THE WARRIORS

(Paramount, 1979) **D/S:** Walter Hill
S: David Shaber **P:** Lawrence Golden
C: Andrew Laszlo

A Clockwork Orange–inspired gang with makeup and baseball bats, among others, chase a more normal-looking gang from the Bronx all the way to their home turf (Coney Island) on the subway. This got (good) negative publicity because of real gangs fighting in theaters. It's a pretty good action movie and for me has improved with age. What happens in New York City isn't realistic (not quite yet), but lots of real locations were used. A major fight scene takes place in a subway restroom. With Michael Beck, James Remar (his debut), David Patrick Kelly, Deborah Van Valkenburgh, Mercedes Ruehl (her debut) as a cop, and Steve James. Based on a novel by Sol Yurick. The A&M soundtrack features "Nowhere To Run" and Joe Walsh's "In the City," the end theme.

The Warriors

WARRIORS

(Republic, 1994) **D/P:** Shimon Dotan
S: Alexander Epstein, Benjamin Gold
P: Shimon Arama   Canada/Israel

Gary Busey and Michael Paré star as government-trained mercenaries who battle and chase each other. Wendi Fulford is a hooker.

WARRIORS 5

(1960) **D/S:** Leopoldo Savona **S:** Dino
De Santis, Ugo Pirro **P:** Fulvio Lucisano
Italy/France (*La Guera Continua*)

An American paratrooper is helped by Italian guerrillas in 1943. Jack Palance and Giovanna Ralli star in the AIP release.

WARRIORS OF THE APOCALYPSE

(Vestron, 1985) **D/P:** Bobby A. Suarez
S/A: Ken Metcalf   Philippines
(*Searchers of the Voodoo Mountain*)

In a post-nuke adventure, a hero named Trapper (Michael James) fights Indians in the jungle. He

discovers the sexy queen (Deborah Moore) of Voo-doo Mountain, who has mutant slaves in a nuke plant.

WARRIORS OF THE WASTELAND

(Thorn EMI, 1982) **D/S/A:** Enzo Castellari
S: Tito Carpi **P:** Fabrizio De Angelis   Italy
(*The New Barbarians; I Nuovi Barbari*)

In another *Road Warrior* copy, Timothy Brent (as Skorpion) teams with Fred Williamson (as Nadir!). They battle a post-nuke gang of raping homosexual Templars led by George Eastman. Nadir has a crossbow and exploding arrows. With some silly-looking customized old cars and a decapitation vehicle. It was cut for an R when released by New Line.

WARRIORS OF THE WIND

(Starmaker, 1984) **D/S:** Hayao Miyazaki
P: Isao Takahata   Japan
(*Naussica in the Valley of the Wind*)

Princess Zandra and her flying wing encounter giant bugs and an army run by Queen Salena. The animated post-nuke fantasy was cut for America when released by New World.

WATCHERS

(IVE, 1988) **D:** Jon Hess **S/P:** Damien
Lee **S:** Bill Freed   Canada

Corey Haim and his mom (Barbara Williams) find a superintelligent golden retriever named Einstein. The government creates an "Oxcom" (a hairy orange monster) that bites heads off and wants to kill the dog, and a superhuman killer (Michael Ironside) is disguised as a government agent. It was based on (part of) Dean R. Koontz's novel. With Christopher Carey, Duncan Fraser, and Lala the dog. Roger Corman was executive producer of the Concorde feature.

WATCHERS 2

(IVE, 1990) **D:** Thierry Notz **S:** Henry Dominic
P: Roger Corman, Rodman Flender   Canada

This is better than the first Dean R. Koontz *Watchers* adaptation, but it's not really a sequel. The super dog and "the Outsider" (a man in a lizard suit) both escape from the secret government lab. Marc Singer is the war-hero vet who teams with the dog to fight off the monster. With Irene Miracle, Tracy Scoggins, Mary Woronov, and Dakai the dog. Roger Corman was executive producer of the Concorde feature.

WATCHERS 3

(New Horizons, 1993) **D:** Jeremy Stanford
S: Michael Palmer **P:** Luis Llosa

Dean R. Koontz sued executive producer Corman over the use of his name on this sequel, which rips off *Predator* and the original *Watchers*. Wings Hauser leads a squad of ex-military convicts in South America to investigate mysterious deaths. They encounter the decapitating Outsider monster, and Einstein the dog helps. With Gregory Scott Cummins and Daryl Roach.

WATCH ME WHEN I KILL

(HBO, 1977) **D/S:** Antonio Bido
S: Vittorio Schiraldi   Italy
(*Il Gatto Dagli Occhi di Giada*)

People are being murdered in Rome and a detective (Corrado Pani) is on the case. The victims turn out to have been Nazi collaborators during the war, being killed for revenge. It was distributed by Herman Cohen.

THE WATER ENGINE

(Turner, 1992) **D:** Steven Schacter
S/A: David Mamet **P:** Donald P. Borchers

In 1934 Chicago, a man (William H. Macy) invents an engine that runs on water. An attorney (Joe Mantegna) plans to kill him off for the valuable invention. With John Mahoney, Patti LuPone, Joanna Miles, Treat Williams, Andrea Marcovicci, Charles Durning, and the voice of Martin Sheen. Spielberg's Amblin Entertainment backed the serious TNT cable feature.

WATERFRONT

(Sinister, 1944) **D:** Steve Sekely
S: Martin Mooney **P:** Arthur Alexander

John Carradine is a Nazi spy in San Francisco, posing as an optometrist. He and J. Carrol Naish kill to obtain a stolen codebook. The 68-minute PRC feature costars Maris Wrixon and Terry Frost.

WATTSTAX

(1973) **D/P:** Mel Stuart **P:** Larry Shaw

Stax Records and Wolper Productions collaborated on this concert feature (from several 1972 shows at the LA Coliseum). The main acts are the Dramatics, the Staple Singers, Albert King, the Bar-Kays, Little Milton, Carla and Rufus Thomas, and Isaac Hayes. Richard Pryor (in top comic form) is the host, the Rev. Jesse Jackson appears, and Melvin Van Peebles staged the concerts, which were sponsored by Schlitz Beer. From Columbia. MGM sued over the use of songs from *Shaft*, so Hayes did some other songs that were edited in.

WAVELENGTH

(Nelson, 1983) **D/S:** Mike Gray **P:** James Rosenfield **M:** Tangerine Dream

Robert Carradine is a folk singer, and Cherie Currie (from the Runaways) can communicate with aliens. Three of the tiny bald-headed aliens (played by babies) are kept underground in Hollywood. Military scientists freeze them and plan to perform autopsies. With Keenan Wynn as a prospector. Gray also wrote *The China Syndrome*.

WAX, OR THE DISCOVERY OF TELEVISION AMONG THE BEES

(1991) **D/S/P/A:** David Blair

A deadpan voice narrates this mesmerizing, complex, unique, and well-made science fiction "documentary" video. It involves bees, spirit photography, the Trinity bomb, and the Tower of Babel. The *2001*-influenced FX and editing are top-notch, and lots of computer graphics and old film clips are used. Blair also narrates. It was made on location at Carlsbad Caverns and the Trinity site, with a NYSCA grant and backing from the AFI. It took six years to complete. William S. Burroughs also appears.

WAXWORK

(Vestron, 1988) **D/S/A:** Anthony Hickox **P:** Staffan Ahrenberg

A group of obnoxious chain-smoking college students visit a wax museum that appears overnight on a suburban street. They become victims of wax scenes that temporarily come to life. The faithful-looking b/w *Night of the Living Dead* scene is very well done, and the cannibal vampire segment with Miles O'Keeffe (as Dracula) is extremely gory. The cinematography and FX are mostly top-notch, but the "wax" figures move when they shouldn't. While most scenes involve well-known old movie monsters, one features token virgin Deborah Foreman having her first orgasm while being whipped by the Marquis de Sade (the director). David Warner owns the museum, with famous circus midget Michu as his assistant. Patrick Macnee is the wheelchair-bound savior of the world, and John Rhys-Davies becomes a werewolf. Zach Galligan, Michelle Johnson, and Dana Ashbrook are the other main kids. Hickox is the son of the director of *Theatre of Blood* and the great-grandson of J. Arthur Rank. R and unrated tapes are available.

WAXWORK II: LOST IN TIME

(LIVE, 1991) **D/S:** Anthony Hickox **P:** Nancy Paloian

The original had its moments, but this dumb, dull, comic sequel is a senseless mess. Zach Galligan returns with a new girlfriend (model Monika Schnarre). They enter a time portal mirror and show up in uninspired misfire spoofs of old movies (or just characters) wearing bad wigs. Alexander Godunov and John Ireland are in the (too long) segment about medieval black magic. Bruce Campbell is in a gory b/w "tribute" to *The Haunting*. Other spoofs are of *Frankenstein, Dawn of the Dead, Aliens,* and *Nosferatu*. Also with Buck Flower and a living hand. You'll have to look hard

for Marina Sirtis, Michael Des Barres, Sophie Ward, David Carradine, Juliet Mills, and even Drew Barrymore. Patrick Macnee shows up to give advice, and David Warner appears in a flashback. It ends with a rap song.

WAXWORKS

(Sinister, 1924) **D:** Paul Leni **S:** Henrik Galeen Germany (*Das Wachsfigurenkabinett; Three Wax Men; Weird Tales*)

Three strange tales involving historical figures star major actors of the day and feature expressionist sets. Emil Jannings is Haroun Al-Raschid in Asia. Conrad Veidt is Ivan the Terrible (with a torture chamber), and Werner Krauss is Jack the Ripper. The stories are told by a writer (future director William Dieterle) to the owner of the fairground waxworks and his daughter. The video runs 63 minutes, but the original running time was 84 minutes. Leni went to California and made *The Cat and the Canary* (1927). Some earlier German horror anthologies were *Tales of Hoffmann* (1915), also with Werner Krauss, and *Tales of the Uncanny* (1919), with Conrad Veidt as Death.

WAYNE'S WORLD

(Paramount, 1992) **D:** Penelope Spheeris **S/A:** Mike Myers **P:** Lorne Michaels

Another movie based on *Saturday Night Live* skits sounded like a bad idea, but this is pretty funny and was a hit. It was also the biggest hit ever directed by a woman, by the way. Heavy metal fans Wayne (Mike Myers) and Garth (Dana Carvey) host a public-access TV show in a basement in suburban Aurora, Illinois. The bare gag-filled plot has the likable Wayne falling for a "mega-babe" Oriental singer named Cassandra (Tia Carrere). A media sleazeball (Rob Lowe) convinces the guys to sell out. The music is strictly late 60s and early 70s. It doesn't even matter that the two stars are twice the age of the characters they play and wear obvious long-hair wigs. With Lara Flynn Boyle, Brian Doyle-Murray, Colleen Camp, Alice Cooper (as himself), Ed O'Neill, Robert Patrick, Ione Skye, Donna Dixon, and Meat Loaf. Tia sings "Ballroom Blitz," there's a *Laverne and Shirley* spoof, and several alternative endings. Rated PG-13. The soundtrack brought Queen back to the charts, just after singer Freddie Mercury had died.

WAYNE'S WORLD 2

(Paramount, 1993) **D:** Stephen Surjik **S:** Mike Myers, Bonnie and Terry Turner **P:** Lorne Michaels

Imagine a PG-13 sequel to a movie based on *Saturday Night Live* characters that's actually clever and funny. I know it's hard, but there are exceptions to every rule. Wayne and Garth have a new warehouse studio (and apartment) for their public-access show. Jim Morrison and an Indian (in dream sequences copied from *The Doors*) tell Wayne to put on Waynestock (this was just before the actual 25th anniversary Woodstock concert). Meanwhile Cassandra (Tia Carrere) records for an evil A and R man (Christopher Walken). Other gag scenes parody *Thelma and Louise, The Graduate*, and a martial arts movie. With James Hong (subtitled), Kim Basinger, Charlton Heston, Drew Barrymore,

Harry Shearer, Jay Leno, Rip Taylor, Chris Farley, Kevin Pollak, Olivia D'Abo, and Ed O'Neill. The Reprise soundtrack features vintage (60s/70s) cuts by Golden Earring, the Village People, Joan Jett, and Robert Plant doing "Louie Louie," plus songs by newer artists. Despite her role, Carrere doesn't sing this time, but Aerosmith plays. The director was from the Canadian *Kids in the Hall* show.

WE ARE GOING TO EAT YOU

(VSOM, 1980) **D:** Tsui Hark **P:** Ng See Yuen Hong Kong (*Diyu Wu Men*)

A government agent goes to a village to search for a bandit. He encounters cannibals with skin masks, and men are sawed in half. Hark's second movie features sex humor, a female impersonator, and blood and gore. With Tsui Siu-Chang and Cheung Mu-Lian.

WEBB WILDER'S CORN FLICKS

(Praxis, 1992) **D/S/P:** Stephen Mims **P:** R. S. Field

Wilder is a Nashville rock singer who stars in two short films on this tape. The best (and longest one at 49 minutes) is "Horror Hayride" (1991). He's a laid-back detective who goes to Nashville to investigate the making of a driver's-ed film for the governor. He has a recurring dream with flying saucers and aliens, and after being slipped a drugged drink, does a killer version of "I Had Too Much to Dream (Last Night)" (the only part in color). The songs, instrumentals, and cinematography are all excellent, and the dialogue and situations are funny. It was filmed in Austin. In the earlier and cruder "Private Eye" (1984), he's a J. C. Penney security guard. "Aunt Halle" is a very clever non-Wilder short, also by Mims. They were filmed in Mississippi.

WEDDING IN WHITE

(1973) **D/S:** William Fruet **P:** John Vidette   Canada

Carol Kane stars as a teenager who becomes pregnant by a drunken soldier friend of the family during WWII. Donald Pleasence is the outraged father. It was the first starring role for Kane and the first feature by Fruet, who later specialized in horror movies.

WEDDING NIGHT

(1969) **D:** Piers Haggard **S:** Robert I. Holt, Lee Dunne **P:** Phillip N. Krasne   Ireland (*I Can't, I Can't*)

AIP released this drama about a new bride (Teresa Wyatt) in Dublin who won't let her husband (Denis Waterman) touch her. It deals with the Catholic church and its opposition to birth control. The director made *Blood on Satan's Claw* (1970) next.

THE WEDDING PARTY

(VidAmerica, 1963) **D/S/P/E:** Cynthia Munroe, Brian De Palma, Wilford Leach

This talk-filled comedy about fear of marriage was the first director credit for De Palma. Jill Clayburgh stars with Charles Pfluger. It's not very good, but it was also the film debut for Clayburgh and Robert De Niro (whose name is spelled DeNero, and who is not impressive here at all) and costars Jennifer

Bill Paxton and Ilan Mitchell-Smith in *Weird Science*.

Salt (also in later De Palma features). It was filmed on Shelter Island, New York, and was first released in 1969. It was later picked up by Troma.

WEDLOCK
(1991) **D:** Lewis Teague **S:** Broderick Miller
P: Frederick S. Pierce, Michael Jaffe

Joan Chen and James Remar betray star Rutger Hauer after a diamond heist. He goes to a special prison where inmates wear collars that explode if they try to escape. An exploding head scene (like in *Scanners*) is the FX highlight. Hauer and Mimi Rogers escape (with their collars) and are tracked by authorities. Hauer spends a lot of this movie being beaten and is punished in a sensory deprivation tank when he won't reveal where the diamonds are. It debuted on HBO.

WEEKEND
(New Yorker, 1967) **D/S:** Jean-Luc Godard
France/Italy

If you just see one Godard feature, this should be it. If you have the patience, it's a fascinating, apocalyptic vision with bloody accidents, mutilated cars, and bodies everywhere. An alienated couple (Jean Yanne and Mireille Darc) leave Paris by car and encounter the world's longest traffic jam (seen during an eight-minute tracking shot). With typical Godard word play, hippies and anarchists, and a cannibalism ending. My favorite image is the drummer playing in the woods. With Jean-Pierre Leaud. 105 minutes with subtitles. A version without subtitles is also on tape.

WEEKEND AT BERNIE'S II
(Columbia, 1993) **D/S:** Robert Klane
P: Victor Drai, Joseph Perez

Andrew McCarthy and Jonathan Silverman return as the young businessmen hustlers from *Weekend at Bernie's* (1989) and go to the Virgin Islands seeking the money embezzled by their late boss Bernie (Terry Kiser). Meanwhile Bernie is reanimated by two voodoo practitioners (Steve James and Tom Wright). The unlikely PG-rated corpse comedy also features Barry Bostwick.

WEEKEND PASS
(Vestron, 1984) **D/S:** Lawrence Bassoff
P: Marilyn J. Tenser, Michael D. Castle

Crown International released this sex comedy about four sailors on leave in Los Angeles who meet strippers. With D. W. Brown, Patrick Hauser, Hilary Shepard, and Ashley St. John.

WEEKEND WARRIORS
(Vestron, 1986) **D:** Bert Convy
S: Bruce Belland, Roy M. Rogosin
P: Hannah Hempstead

Some Hollywood actors and singers join the National Guard to avoid the draft. The comedy stars Chris Lemmon, Tom Villard, Vic Tayback as a sergeant, Lloyd Bridges as a colonel, and Graham Jarvis as a congressman. Also with Monique Gabrielle and Brenda Strong. The director was a member of the 50s group The Cheers and was later known as a TV game show host.

WEEKEND WITH LULU
(1961) **D:** John Paddy Carstairs **S/P:** Ted Lloyd   UK

A guy (Bob Monkhouse) who wants to get away with his girlfriend (Shirley Eaton) somehow ends up in France driving an ice cream truck with her mother along for the ride. The Hammer Studios comedy was released by Columbia. With Sidney James and Kenneth Connor.

WEIRDO, THE BEGINNING
(Raedon, 1986) **D/S/C:** Andy Milligan
P: Kenneth Haker, Neva Friedenn

Milligan fans will enjoy his usual bickering miserable characters, but this talky West Coast movie tries to be artistic (lots of blackouts), sensitive, and sensational. Donny (Steve Burlington) lives in a shed behind an old lady's house, does errands for her, and collects junk. Long-haired locals torment him, beat him up, and make him crawl like a dog. Donny seems like a fairly normal, shy, young voyeur but people talk about him like he's a monster. He makes friends with a lonely, short, nice girl in a leg brace who has been raped. His horrible mother calls him stupid, beats him with a belt, and says his father was her brother. She cuts an angel food cake with a meat cleaver. There's a (very phony) decapitated head, a cross thrust through a woman's chest, electrocution by Xmas lights, a pitchfork through a neck, hands cut off, and puking, but nothing is really shown happening. One of the brief topless scenes features porno

star Gina Carrera (I think). At the end Donny's girlfriend asks, "Why can't people be nice to one another?" Original *Psychotronic* contributor Charlie Beesley worked on this.

WEIRD SCIENCE
(MCA, 1985) **D/S:** John Hughes **P:** Joel Silver

Hughes wrote the script for this PG-13 fantasy comedy in "two days" after making the hits *Sixteen Candles* and *The Breakfast Club*. Two nerdy computer whiz kids (Anthony Michael Hall and Ilan Mitchell-Smith) somehow create the "ideal" woman (Kelly LeBrock). They also turn an obnoxious older brother (Bill Paxton) into a toad. A wild party taking place while the parents are away is invaded by bikers, including Michael Berryman (who is funny) and Vernon Wells reprising his *Road Warrior* role. With Robert Downey Jr., Steve James, Jill Whitlow, Kym Malin (from *Playboy*), and Judie Aronson. A colorized *Bride of Frankenstein* clip is used, and *The Munsters* are seen on TV. A USA cable TV series based on this movie debuted in 1994.

WEIRD TALES: *See* WAXWORKS

THE WEIRD WORLD OF LSD
(SW, 1967) **D:** Robert Ground **P:** George B. Roberts

A clip of a cartoon chicken hallucination from this bizarre—but extremely unhip—narrated b/w anti-drug "exposé" was on one of the *Sleazemania* tapes. Now you can experience it all and see how various middle-aged types react to LSD. A bored salesman in a strange town runs around crazed. A lonely "350-pound" art dealer eats an entire turkey. The best sequences feature FX. A hand is cut off and faces mutate (rubber monster masks are used). Strip-show scenes (without nudity) were probably lifted from another movie, and there's a catfight. The music is lite jazz. A newspaper headline says: LSD USER SUICIDE! Doug Hobart devised an outlandish advertising campaign and managed to get the feature booked on college campuses.

WELCOME TO 18
(IVE, 1986) **D/S:** Terry Carr **S:** Judith Sherman Wolin **P:** David C. Thomas

Mariska Hargitay (the daughter of Jayne Mansfield and Mickey Hargitay) stars in a PG-13 comedy about three girls working at a dude ranch. Hargitay (who has a shower scene) was in *Jocks* the same year.

WELCOME TO OBLIVION
(1990) **D:** Augusto Tamayo **S:** Len Jenkin **P:** Luis Llosa

Dack Rambo stars as a post-WWIII Mad Max–type hero. There's a mutant woman and gladiators to fight. The Concorde theatrical release (filmed in Peru) was later cut up for the tape *Ultra Warrior* (1993).

WELCOME TO SPRING BREAK
(IVE, 1988) **D/S:** "Harry Kirkpatrick"/Umberto Lenzi **P:** William J. Immerman **M:** Claudio Simonetti   Italy
(*La Spiaggia Del Terrore; Nightmare Beach*)

Chuck Connors in *Werewolf*.

Gory murders are committed at a Florida resort after Diablo, a biker from the Demons gang, is executed. Suspects include an alcoholic doctor (Michael Parks) and a kinky sheriff (John Saxon). The FX are by Alex Rambaldi (whose father did *E.T.*). It was filmed in Fort Lauderdale.

WEREWOLF

(1987) **D:** David Hemmings

A teen werewolf (makeup by Rick Baker) has to track down the guy who bit him. John S. York stars with Lance LeGault as a bounty hunter and Michelle Johnson. Captain Janos Skorzeny (Chuck Connors) is the "source of the bloodline." The executive producer was John Ashley. The Fox-TV pilot was released on tape in Europe. It became a short-lived series. Hemmings also directed pilot features for *In the Heat of the Night* (1988), *Quantum Leap* (1989), and others.

WEREWOLF OF WOODSTOCK

(1975) **D:** John Moffit

When I saw this ABC-TV movie (which debuted late at night), I couldn't belive that a major network would make and air such a ridiculous, shoddy, shot-on-tape project. An electric charge at the site of the Woodstock rock festival turns a farmer into a killer wolfman. Tige Andrews stars with Meredith MacRae and Michael Parks. Bad movie fans should demand a video release. Call executive producer Dick Clark.

WES CRAVEN'S NEW NIGHTMARE

(New Line, 1994) **D/S/A:** Wes Craven
P: Marianne Maddalena

New Line lied (see *Freddy's Dead*) and brought Freddy Krueger back again (it was #7 in the series). This is fantasy intruding into the real world during the making of a new Elm Street movie ten years after the original. Craven's concept was a good idea, but the results are pretty ponderous and boring. Heather Langenkamp stars as herself and she and her son, Dylan (Miko Hughes), find themselves in peril and her FX expert husband (David Newsom) is killed. It all takes place during California earthquakes. Robert Englund appears as himself and Freddy Krueger. John Saxon and Craven himself also play themselves, along with New Line head Robert Shaye and other behind-the-scenes people. Milan released the soundtrack. The next likely step for the horror character will be to meet Jason from the Friday the 13th movies.

WEST OF ZANZIBAR

(MGM, 1928) **D:** Tod Browning
S: Elliot Clawson **P:** Irving Thalberg

A skeleton in a coffin is the first thing you see in this MGM Lon Chaney movie, and director Browning never lets up. The convoluted plot is about Phroso the illusionist and magician and how he becomes the sadistic, vengeance-seeking "Dead Legs" in the African jungle. Chaney is incredible. He's very convincing as a pathetic cripple crawling like a baby in a church or dragging himself across a filthy floor, he's scary with his mean leer and bald head, and he acts up a storm, sometimes laughing and crying in the same scene. He eats fire and breathes smoke! Browning includes several mind-boggling sequences like the quick "evolution" scene showing insects and spiders, followed by alligators, then men. Most of the movie takes place in an atmospheric jungle and involves voodoo, cannibals, death ceremonies, dancing native women (giving Chaney a private show), prostitution, and a great "monster" with two heads and lots of skulls. The excellent cast includes Lionel Barrymore, Warner Baxter as alcohol-soaked "Doc," and Mary Nolan as the bitter, fallen woman. A lot happens in only 63 minutes (6 minutes were removed by some jerk decades ago). It's available on a high-quality double laserdisc with *The Unholy Three* (1930). *Kongo* was a 1932 remake with Walter Huston.

WEST SIDE STORY

(MGM, 1961) **D:** Robert Wise,
Jerome Robbins **S:** Ernest Lehman

It's the Jets vs. the Sharks in one of the most enjoyable musicals ever made. UA released the Technicolor Super Panavision 70mm hit, based on the 1957 Broadway musical. Some call it a romantic *Romeo and Juliet* retread (true), but don't miss an opportunity to see it on a big screen. *West Side Story* won 10 Oscars and was a big influence on Coppola's *Rumble Fish*, Alice Cooper (check out the *Easy Action*

and *School's Out* albums), and other movies and groups. In England, the Nice even made the charts with their version of "America." Marni Nixon (*Daughter of Horror*) is the singing voice of Natalie Wood. Richard Beymer costars with Rita Moreno, George Chakiris, Russ Tamblyn as Riff, Simon Oakland, and John Astin. Future schlock moviemakers Gus Trikonis and David Winters are in there too. The West 64th St. locations are now the site of Lincoln Center. With Leonard Bernstein music and Stephen Sondheim lyrics. The soundtrack is on Columbia.

WET GOLD

(IVE, 1985) **D:** Dick Lowry **S:** David Sherman, Otis Jones **P:** Bill Cokel

Brooke Shields stars as a waitress in a sunken-treasure-hunt TV movie that's a reworking of *The Treasure of the Sierra Madre* plot. Burgess Meredith costars as an old drunk. With Brian Kerwin. It was a theatrical release in Europe. Lowry also made *The Jayne Mansfield Story* and *The Hank Williams Jr. Story*.

WHAM BAM THANK YOU SPACE MAN

(SW, 1972) **D/P:** William A. Levey **S:** Shomo D. Weinstein (*Erotic Encounters of the Fourth Kind*)

Two alien men go to a Hollywood whorehouse to "impregnate earth women." They watch some sex while in a semi-transparent state, then transport women back to their tinfoil ship. This awful, unfunny comedy includes nudity, a lesbian scene, rape, masturbation, a jive-talking black guy, gay jokes, and a penis with an eye. With Dyanne Thorne (with a very high voice), Valda Hansen (*Night of the Ghouls*) and "guest star" John Ireland Jr. *Wham* plugs other Boxoffice International features. Levey also made the unbelievable *Blackenstein* and *Slumber Party '57*.

WHAT!

(1963) **D:** Mario Bava **S:** "Julian Berry"/ Ernesto Gastaldi, Ugo Guerra, Luciano Martino **P:** Elio Scardamaglia   Italy (*La Frusta E il Corpo; Night Is the Phantom*)

Considered a bit too strong for most viewers in the mid 60s, *What!* is excellent and should be as well known as Bava's *Black Sunday*. It's not only at-

Russ Tamblyn confronts Simon Oakland in *West Side Story*.

mospheric as hell and scary, but yes—romantic, and those camera zooms can be pretty effective. Christopher Lee is in top form as the hateful, sadistic Kurt Menliff (always in a black cape) who returns to the family castle by the sea. His dying father says, "You're not my son, you're a serpent!" Kurt whips the newlywed Nevenka, is found dead, then returns from the crypt (or does he?). Daliah Lavi, a former Miss Israel, looking a lot like Barbara Steele in some scenes, is Nevenka. With Tony Kendall as her husband, and Harriet White Medin. It was filmed in France. Scriptwriter Gastaldi also wrote *The Horrible Dr. Hitchcock* and other prime Italian horror movies.

WHAT DO YOU SAY TO A NAKED LADY?

(Key, 1970) **D/S/P:** Allen Funt

Despite the X rating, this hidden-camera "comedy" was the highest-grossing non-performance documentary of its time. Funt's much-copied *Candid Camera* show (on and off TV since 1948) was a show I was fascinated and appalled by at the same time as a kid. Same goes for this movie—and then some. Funt and his candid camera cashed in on the new cinema freedom by making this series of scenes showing how everyday people react to (hired) naked people (usually women) in public. With a pre-*Shaft* Richard Roundtree. A soundtrack was on UA. It was later rerated R. *Money Talks* (1972), also from UA, was Funt's less successful follow-up feature about greed.

WHAT EVER HAPPENED TO BABY JANE

(Atlantic, 1991) **D:** David Greene
S: Brian Taggert **P:** Barry Bernardi

Vanessa Redgrave and her overacting sister Lynn play sisters Jane and Blanche Hudson. The novelty of seeing one actress known for her political causes and the other known for her diet food ads playing has-been actresses tormenting each other does have a certain appeal. William Aldrich, the son of Robert Aldrich (who directed the classic 1962 Joan Crawford and Bette Davis original), was an executive producer of this ABC-TV remake. With John Glover in the Victor Buono role and Amy Steel.

WHATEVER IT TAKES

(1993) **D:** Mike Quarles

All those old nudie movies unearthed by Something Weird had an effect on some indy filmmakers. This is exactly like a plotless 60s adult movie. A southern guy (Roger Moore, who narrates) seeks help finding models for his nudie movie and we see 10 dance and/or strip segments, all professionally shot with good-looking models. Highlights are a stripping hitchhiker, a woman sneaking into a whirlpool bath, and a "cowgirl" (Wynoka Prather) who smiles and laughs as she strips and gets into a tiny tub of water. The Georgia-based Quarles also wrote *Down and Dirty: Hollywood's Exploitation Filmmakers* (McFarland).

WHAT HAVE THEY DONE TO SOLANGE?

(Nightmare, 1971) **D/S:** Massimo Dallamano
S: Bruno Di Geronimo **P:** Leonardo Pescarolo
Italy/Germany (*Das Geheimnis der Grunen Stecknadel; The School That Couldn't Scream; Terror in the Woods*)

It's based on an Edgar Wallace novel previously filmed twice in England as *The Clue of the New Pin* (1929 and 1961). This version is a violent slasher movie more in the spirit of Dario Argento's movies of the period. A killer in black stabs women at a girls' school, a female teacher sees psychic images of the murders, and Scotland Yard investigates. Joachim Fuchsberger is Commissioner Barth, and the cast includes Fabio Testi, Christine Galbo, Karin Baal, and Camille Keaton (*I Spit on Your Grave*) as Solange. The music is by Ennio Morricone and the cinematographer later directed as "Joe D'Amato." AIP/Newport released it in America in 1976 (as *Terror in the Woods*). Dallamano returned with *What Have They Done to Your Daughters?* (1972).

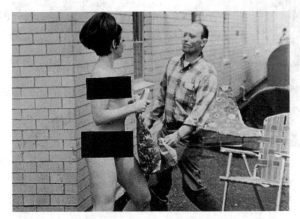

Allen Funt's *What Do You Say to a Naked Lady?*

WHAT'S LOVE GOT TO DO WITH IT

(Touchstone, 1993) **D:** Brian Gibson
S: Kate Lanier **P:** Doug Chapin, Barry Krost

Angela Bassett and Laurence Fishburne star as Anna Mae Bullock/Tina Turner and Ike Turner in a movie based on Tina's autobiography (written with Kurt Loder). Both were nominated for Oscars. It starts in St. Louis in the late 50s and shows three decades of fashion and soul and rock music changes along with the celebrity wife-abuse story. With Jenifer Lewis as Tina's mother and Vanessa Bell Calloway. The real Turner is heard singing and is seen singing at the end. Other music is by Stanley Clarke. By the director of *The Josephine Baker Story.*

WHAT'S UP, HIDEOUS SUN DEMON

(1989) **D/S:** Craig Mitchell **P:** Greg Brown, Jeff Montgomery, Hadi Salem

New comic voices were added to Robert Clarke's 1959 feature. As a fan of the original, which was made for $50,000 during weekends, I don't really see the point. Clarke later regretted helping to trash his own movie, and few people saw the results. Jay Leno dubs Clarke's man-into-monster character and Susan Tyrrell does singer Patricia Manning. The comedy is mostly sex and drugs. Some new scenes were also added along with a color intro. It's a Wade Williams production.

WHAT'S WRONG WITH THE NEIGHBOR'S SON?

(AFT, 1986) **D:** Daniel Benjamin M.D. **D/E:** Trent Meeks **P:** Ron Cerasuolo (*The Disturbance*)

I guess this short (about an hour) low-budget "docudrama" made in Miami was intended as a serious look at schizophrenia to be shown to help people, but anybody who liked *Repulsion* or 60s drug movies could enjoy it as a good no-frills shocker. A (real?) doctor introduces the case ("over two million Americans suffer from hallucinations" . . .) and a different doctor (reading cue cards) summarizes what we've seen at the end. The synthesizer score (in Dolby stereo) is very spooky, and the cinematography is great. It looks like it was shot with Super 8 or 16mm film. 27-year-old Clay lives with his always-arguing parents in the suburbs and walks to his job as a dishwasher. He's on medication, but has lost his girlfriend, then loses his job after dropping a pile of dishes that were covered by (imagined) giant cockroaches. He hears kids mocking him, and at home alone he sees eyeballs in the bathtub. The mirror cracks when he looks at it, his hand disintegrates, he freaks out and kills the family cat, and ends up chained in a medieval jail.

WHAT THE SWEDISH BUTLER SAW: *See* THE GROOVE ROOM

WHAT WAITS BELOW

(Lightning, 1983) **D:** Don Sharp
P: Sandy Howard (*The Secrets of the Phantom Cavern*)

Scientists go under the earth in South America and discover mutant underwater albino aliens. The old-fashioned PG fantasy stars Robert Powell with Lisa Blount, Timothy Bottoms, Richard Johnson, and Anne Heywood. It was shot in Alabama and Tennessee.

WHEELS OF FIRE

(Vestron, 1984) **D/P:** Cirio H. Santiago
S: Frederick Bailey US/Philippines
(*Desert Warrior; Vindicator*)

Gary Watkins stars as a muscular bounty hunter with a nuclear car in another *Road Warrior* copy. With Laura Banks, Lynda Wiesmeier, Linda Grovenor, Dennis Cole, and Don Gordon as "Robot." From Concorde.

WHEELS OF TERROR

(USA, 1990) **D:** Christopher Cain
S: Alan B. McElroy **P:** Richard Lerrman

Don't bother with this senseless, slow, and boring rip-off of 70s movies like *Dune, Crash,* and *The Car* from the director of *Young Guns.* Joanna Cassidy stars as the bus driver mom whose daughter is kidnapped by a supernatural car responsible for killing (and raping) little girls. The part where she endangers a whole bus full of terrified kids during a chase is especially ridiculous. Filmed in Arizona for USA cable.

WHEELS ON MEALS

(1984) **D/A:** Samo Hung **P:** Raymund Chow

Jackie Chan and Yuen Baio run a fast-food business in Spain. They save the life of a hooker (Lola Firner) whose father (Herb Edelman) is an evil count. A detective (director Hung) joins the heroes in kung fu fights. The modern-day action comedy features lots of stunts, bikers, and skateboarding.

WHEN A STRANGER CALLS BACK

(MCA, 1992) **D/S:** Fred Walton **P:** Tom Rowe

Some kids disappear while staying with a babysitter. "Five years later," a babysitter (Jill Schoelen) who attends college is tormented by a mysterious psycho mime. Carol Kane, now the head of a women's crisis center, and Charles Durning as a retired cop return from the original *When a Stranger Calls* by the same director. The Showtime sequel to the 1979 feature (available from RCA) was shot in Vancouver.

WHEN NATURE CALLS

(IEI, 1982) **D/S/P:** Charles Kaufman **S:** Straw Weisman **P:** Frank Vitale   (*The Outdoorsman*)

The director of *Mother's Day* made this Troma comedy release, a parody of outdoorsman movies. A family is on vacation in the woods, and many guest stars appear. With G. Gordon Liddy, Willie Mays, John Cameron Swayze, Myron Cohen, Fred Blassie, and Morey Amsterdam. The daughter rapes a bear in one scene. Watergate felon Liddy later acted in *Street Asylum, Super Force,* and *Adventures in Spying,* but was better known as the right-wing radio-talk-show host who told listeners to shoot Federal agents in the head.

WHEN THE BOUGH BREAKS

(Prism, 1994) **D/S:** Michael Cohn **P:** Barbara Javitz

A flash flood uncovers a bag of severed hands of children with numbers tattooed on them. The evidence is sent to the Houston police and a forensic expert (Ally Walker) goes to a mental hospital to try and communicate with a mute telepathic kid with mental links to the serial killer. With Ron Perlman and Martin Sheen as the chief of police.

WHEN THE WIND BLOWS

(IVE, 1988) **D:** Jimmy Murakami
S: Raymond Briggs **P:** Joan Coates   UK

A nice retired British couple living in the countryside keep their blind faith in everything the government says, even as a nuclear war rages around them. The animated feature is very effective and well done. The voices of Dame Peggy Ashcroft and Sir John Mills help immensely. David Bowie did the theme song. Murakami also made the live-action *Battle Beyond the Stars* (1980), a Corman production.

WHEN WOMEN LOST THEIR TAILS

(Simitar, 1971) **D:** Pasquale Festa Campanile
S: Ottavio Jemma, Marcello Coscia, Jana Tiastri
P: Silvio Clementelli   Italy/W. Germany
(*Quando le Donne Persero*)

Senta Berger returns in a sequel to *When Women Had Tails* (Sinister, 1970). The caveman comedy

costars Frank Wolff and has an Ennio Morricone score. The prehistoric series was popular in Europe. *When Women Played Ding Dong* (1971) was yet another sequel.

WHERE ARE THE CHILDREN?

(RCA/Columbia, 1985) **D:** Bruce Malmuth
S: Jack Sholder **P:** Zev Braun

The kids of Jill Clayburgh are kidnapped by her psycho ex-husband (Frederic Forrest). The script is based on a Mary Higgins Clark novel and was once to be directed by Brian De Palma. With Harley Cross, Max Gail, Barnard Hughes, and Clifton James.

WHERE ARE YOUR CHILDREN?

(1944) **D:** William Nigh **S:** Hilary Lynn,
George Wallace Sayre **P:** Jeffrey Bernerd

Gale Storm (later a TV and recording star) is accused of murdering a gas station operator in a Monogram juvenile delinquent movie. Jackie Cooper costars with Patricia Morison and John Litel.

WHERE DO WE GO FROM HERE?

(1945) **D:** Gregory Ratoff
S: Morrie Ryskind **P:** Sam Katzman

Fred MacMurray finds a magic lamp in a WWII-era fantasy from 20th Century–Fox. He asks the genie (Gene Sheldon) to get him into the army and he ends up serving General Washington in the Revolutionary War. With Joan Leslie, June Haver, and Anthony Quinn.

WHERE EAST IS EAST

(Cinemacabre, 1929) **D:** Tod Browning
S: Richard Schayer

Lon Chaney stars as Tiger Haynes, an animal trapper whose face has been clawed by tigers. His wife (Estelle Taylor) tries to seduce the fiancé of their daughter Toyo (Lupe Velez), so Tiger lets his killer ape loose. It was the last of several bizarre Browning/Chaney features and was based on Browning's story. From MGM.

WHERE IS PARSIFAL?

(1983) **D:** Terence Young
S: Berta Dominguez **P:** Daniel Carrilo

Tony Curtis stars in a flop movie about a miraculous skywriting machine (it writes with color 3-D letters). He wants to use it to get rich, but his wife wants to use it to help spread peace in the world. Orson Welles (in his second-to-last role, as the Gypsy king) and Erik Estrada (!) also bid for the contraption. With Donald Pleasence, Peter Lawford (in his last role), Ron Moody, and Anthony Dawson.

WHERE SLEEPING DOGS LIE

(Columbia, 1991) **D:** Charles Finch
S: Yolande Turner **P:** Mario Sotela

Bruce (Dylan McDermott), an unsuccessful Hollywood writer working as a real estate agent, moves into an abandoned mansion (where a family had been murdered). While working on a script about a serial killer, he rents a room to a nervous tenant (Tom Sizemore) who actually is a serial killer. With Sharon Stone and Mary Woronov in small roles. Finch is the son of the late actor Peter Finch, and screenwriter Turner is his mother. From New Line.

WHERE THE BOYS ARE

(MGM, 1960) **D:** Henry Levin
S: George Wells **P:** Joe Pasternak

Four midwestern college girls go to Ft. Lauderdale during Easter vacation in the hit comedy from MGM. It's better than most of the big studio "nice" teen movies from the period. Dolores Hart stars with Yvette Mimieux, Paula Prentiss (making her debut as the "kooky" one) and Connie Francis (who sings). With Jim Hutton as a toned-down beatnik character, George Hamilton, Frank Gorshin, Barbara Nichols, and Chill Wills. The theme song by Francis went to #4. MGM put Hutton and Prentiss together in three more features.

WHERE THE BOYS ARE '84

(Fox, 1984) **D:** Hy Averback **S:** Stu
Krieger, Jeff Burkhart **P:** Allan Carr

After nobody wanted to see Carr's *Grease* sequel, he returned with this updated and R-rated remake from TriStar, and it was a big box-office flop too. Both feature Lorna Luft, Judy Garland's forgotten daughter. Lisa Hartman stars with Wendy Schaal, Lynn-Holly Johnson, and Alana Stewart.

WHERE THE BUFFALO ROAM

(MCA, 1980) **D/P:** Art Linson **S:** John Kaye

Bill Murray plays the partying "gonzo" journalist Hunter S. Thompson in a comedy partially based on Thompson's books *Fear and Loathing in Las Vegas* and *Fear and Loathing on the Campaign Trail '72.* With Peter Boyle, Bruno Kirby, René Auberjonois, R. G. Armstrong, Craig T. Nelson, and Rafael Campos. The music is by Neil Young and others. This and the 1984 remake of *The Razor's Edge* were both movies starring Murray in unusual roles for him. Audiences stayed away in droves.

WHERE THE DAY TAKES YOU

(New Line, 1992) **D/S:** Marc Rocco **S:** Michael
Hitchcock, Kurt Voss **P:** Paul Hertzberg

Dermot Mulroney (with goatee and tattoos) and Lara Flynn Boyle star as transient teen runaways living on the streets of LA. Their story is related to a social worker (Laura San Giacomo). With Sean Astin as a speed freak and Balthazar Getty, James Le Gros, and Ricki Lake as various runaways, busy stealing and selling drugs and themselves. Also with Kyle MacLachlan as a dealer, Peter Dobson, Will Smith, Stephen Tobolowsky, Adam Baldwin, Nancy McKeon, Alyssa Milano, Rachel Ticotin, and Christian Slater in small roles. The soundtrack by Melissa Etheridge includes a remake of "For What It's Worth."

WHERE THE EAGLE FLIES

(1972) **D:** John Florea **S:** Anthony Blake
P: Christian Whitaker   *(Pickup on 101)*

Lesley Ann Warren is a coed who hitchhikes with a rock musician and a bum in a PG-rated drama from AIP. Martin Sheen costars with Michael Ontkean and Jack Albertson. Warren, formerly a Disney star, has a topless scene.

WHERE THE GREEN ANTS DREAM

(Cinematique, 1984) **D/S/P:** Werner Herzog
S: Bob Ellis **P:** Lucki Stipetic   W. Germany/Australia

A group of Aborigines oppose the bulldozing of their sacred land by a uranium mining company. Dreaming of the ants there prophesies the end of the world. Bruce Spence (from *Road Warrior*) stars with Wandjuk Marika and Roy Marika.

WHILE I LIVE

(Sinister, 1947) **D/S:** John Harlow
S: Doreen Montgomery   UK *(Dream of Olwen)*

A girl thinks her sister's reincarnated, and ghosts appear. With Tom Walls and Clifford Evans. Harlow also directed supernatural-themed *The Spell of Amy Nugent* (1940) and *Dark Tower* (1943).

WHIRLPOOL

(1949) **D/P:** Otto Preminger **S:** Ben Hecht,
Andrew Solt **M:** Andrew Newman

Gene Tierney stars as a kleptomaniac married to a rich psychiatrist (Richard Conte). Young Jose Ferrer (in his second feature) is the real star, though. He's a hypnotist who rescues her from being prosecuted by a department store and proceeds to blackmail her and cleverly avoid a murder rap. *Whirlpool* is worth watching just for the hospital-room ending, which would have fit in a 30s horror movie. It's based on a novel by Guy Endore. With Charles Bickford and Eduard Franz. From 20th Century–Fox.

WHIRLPOOL

(1970) **D/S:** José R. Larraz **P:** Sam Lomerg
Denmark *(She Died with Her Boots On)*

A London fashion model (Pia Anderson) and her "nephew" (Karl Lanchbury) lure a young Danish model (Vivian Neves—who was a model) home. She has sex with both of them, but discovers that they had killed the last model they brought home. Jerry Gross and Cinemation released this X-rated sex, drugs, and murder feature by a Spanish director known for his horror movies. It was advertised as being "More Shocking Than *Psycho*!, More Sensual Than *Repulsion*!, More Nerve-Ripping Than *Baby Jane*!"

WHISPERING SHADOW

(Stokey, 1933) **D:** Albert Herman, Colbert
Clark **S:** George Morgan, Wydham Gittens

Mascot made this 12-chapter serial, the first with Bela Lugosi. He plays the mysterious Dr. Adam Strang, who runs a wax museum. The villain (not Bela as it finally turns out) can project his shadow. Bela gets to play with a lot of electric gadgets. This serial has no music. Viva Tattersall and Malcolm McGregor star with Henry B. Walthal and Roy D'Arcy. Bela was in *The Return of Chandu* the next year.

WHISPERS

(LIVE, 1989) **D:** Donald Jackson **S:** Anita
Doohan **P:** Don Carmody   Canada

Victoria Tennant is a novelist who kills a serial killer (Jean LeClerc), but the man keeps returning. It's based on the Dean R. Koontz novel and has a lot of interesting convoluted plot twists and a clever surprise ending. Chris Sarandon plays a cop. A necrophilia scene shows a morgue attendant having sex with a girl who puts on makeup and pretends to be dead. *Whispers* also includes cockroaches, Satanism, drugs, incest, nudity, and Joe Blasco FX.

WHISPERS IN THE DARK

(Paramount, 1992) **D/S:** Christopher Crowe
P: Martin Bregman

Annabella Sciorra (*The Hand That Rocks the Cradle*) stars as a meek New York City psychiatrist who gets turned on by the confessions of a patient named Eve (Deborah Unger) and has out-of-focus sex dreams. She falls for a test pilot (Jamey Sheridan), the same guy Eve had described. Eve is found hanged and naked and many characters are suspects. Sciorra also treats a disturbed artist (John Leguizamo), and Alan Alda and Jill Clayburgh are her professional friends. The slick psycho thriller has dreams and flashbacks and despite the tired ideas is worth it for the surprise ending. With Anthony LaPaglia as a detective, and Anthony Heald.

A WHISPER TO A SCREAM

(Virgin, 1989) **D/S/P:** Robert Bergman
S/P: Gerard Ciccoritti   Canada

Nadia Capone stars as an actress working as a phone sex girl. Her psycho boss strangles strippers and records their dying voices. With Yaphet Kotto as a police detective and Silvio Oliviero.

WHISTLING IN THE DARK

(MGM, 1941) **D:** S. Sylvan Simon
S: Albert Mannheimer, Robert
MacGunigle **P:** George Haight

Wally Benton (Red Skelton) stars as The Fox, a radio detective who becomes involved in a real-life murder plot. Conrad Veidt is the lead villain, a smooth-talking leader of a phony religious sect. The cast includes Eve Arden, Ann Rutherford, Virginia Grey, Reed Hadley, and Rags Ragland. The popular mystery comedy was based on a Broadway play, which had also been filmed by MGM in 1932. Skelton returned as the same character in the sequels *Whistling in Dixie* (1942) and *Whistling in Brooklyn* (MGM, 1943) also with Rutherford.

WHITE ANGEL

(1993) **D/S:** Chris Jones **S/P:** Genevieve Jolliffe   UK

A mild-mannered London dentist (Peter Firth) is also a psycho who kills blondes who wear white. He meets a pulp writer (Harriet Robinson) who has killed her husband. With Don Henderson as a cop.

WHITE CANNIBAL QUEEN

(Video City, 1980) **D/A:** Jesús Franco **S:** A. L. Mariaux
P: Franco Prosperi   Italy *(Mondo Cannibale)*

Al Cliver returns to an island ten years after his arm had been eaten by cannibals there and tries to rescue his blond daughter (Sabrina Siani). The tribe have adopted her and made her a goddess. The natives (badly made up Caucasians) enjoy slow-motion cannibal feasts. With Lina Romay, and Franco himself as an American "parasite" businessman. In some countries it was titled to make people think it was a sequel to earlier cannibal movies.

WHITE COMANCHE

(United, 1967) **D:** "Gilbert Kay"/Jose Briz
S: Robert L. Holt, Frank Gruber **P:** Sam White
Spain *(Commanche Blanco; Rio Hondo)*

For the William Shatner fan who has everything, here's a movie where that great space hero plays two Indians! He's Notah Moon, a wild, drug-crazed, bare-chested blond half-breed in war paint who kills white men and rapes white women. He's also Johnny Moon, the depressed, innocent brother who's always being mistaken for Notah and is almost lynched. Johnny tells Notah, "Eat the peyote, drug of the Devil! Dream your dream of hate! One of us must die!" After a lot of double-crosses, misunderstandings, and killings and a long Notah speech to his people, the Indians and the townspeople are all at funerals and the two opposing Shatners face each other in a battle to the death! This ultra-cheap spaghetti western filmed in Spain has some Leone-style face close-ups, jazz music, and Joseph Cotten as the sheriff. You might know

William Shatner is the *White Comanche.*

costar Rossana Yanni from Paul Naschy horror movies. The print is so washed out that the sky (and Shatner's pants) are usually purple.

WHITE FIRE

(TWE, 1983) **D/S/P:** Jean-Marie Pallardy
P: Tony Edwards   France/UK/Turkey

Robert Ginty is a jewel thief in Istanbul who misses his sister, and so he has another woman (Belinda Mayne) turned into an exact copy of her with plastic surgery. He falls for the sister clone and they try to break into a mine and have to fight Fred Williamson as a hitman villain. With Gordon Mitchell.

WHITEFORCE

(New Star, 1989) **D:** Eddie Romero **S:** Henry Tefay
P: Lope V. Juban, Marilyn G. Ong   Philippines/Australia

Flash Gordon movie star Sam Jones is accused of killing his partner (Ken Metcalf), so he has to expose the real druglord villain. With Vic Diaz.

WHITE GHOST

(TWE, 1988) **D:** B. J. Davis
S: Gary Thompson **P:** Jay Davidson

William Katt is an American Green Beret still fighting in Vietnam (on the Cambodian border) in Kabuki makeup. A band of mercenaries is sent in to find him. With Rosalind Chao, Martin Hewitt, Wayne Crawford, and Reb Brown. Filmed in Zimbabwe.

WHITE HOT

(Academy, 1988) **D/A:** Robby Benson
S: Robert Madero **P:** Fred Berner, Jubran Jubran
M: Nile Rodgers   (*Crack in the Mirror*)

If *Clean and Sober* and *The Boost* were two of your fave 80s features, here's Robby Benson as a yuppie who turns to coke and crack dealing. He and Tawny Kitaen become addicted and have a long slow-motion sex scene. Robby gives himself nude scenes. With Danny Aiello, Sally Kirkland, and Judy Tenuta. It was the second feature shot on HDTV.

WHITE HUNTER

(1965) **D/S/P/A:** George Michael

Herts Lion, the company that brought us *Carnival of Souls* and *Dungeon of Harrow,* released this Eastman Color "semi-documentary" filmed in Africa. It's about a big game hunter played by the director.

WHITE HUNTRESS

(Sinister, 1957) **D:** George Breakston **S:** Dermot Quin **P:** John Croydon, Peter Crane

In the 1890s, a blonde (Susan Stephen) encounters hostile natives, a giant python, and other perils. It played on an AIP double bill with *Naked Africa.* With John Bentley. Breakson also codirected *The Manster.*

WHITE LIGHT

(Academy, 1990) **D:** Al Waxman **S:** Ron Base **P:** Anthony Kramreither   Canada

Martin Kove stars as a cop killed by gangsters. He's revived and a female doctor gives him experimental drugs to help him relive experiences. He searches for the woman he was with when he died. The director and the star were regulars on the *Cagney and Lacey* show.

WHITE LIGHTNING ROAD

(SW, 1965) **D/S/P/A/E:** Ron Ormond **P:** June Ormond

Snake (Earle "Snake" Richards) is a low-down cheating rural stock-car race driver who works for Slick (Ron Ormond) and makes life hell for his rival Joe. Arlene Hunter is Ruby, a beautiful blond hill-billy Marilyn Monroe type. In fact, Hunter, a *Play-boy* centerfold back in 1954, had been passed off as Monroe in a famous stag film. Other characters are Tim (Tim Ormond), an orphan fan of Joe, Gimpy (seen putting on his wooden leg), and the bearded killer Ace. Also with a catfight (two blondes) and moonshining. The country-appeal color movie uses some jazzy music plus the familiar guitar sounds that Ormond had used in several other features. Actual race scenes were filmed in Atlanta. The Ormonds, the South's first family of exploitation movies, returned with *The Exotic Ones.*

WHITE LINE FEVER

(RCA, 1975) **D/S:** Jonathan Kaplan
S: Ken Friedman **P:** John Kemeny

Jan-Michael Vincent stars as an Air Force vet turned diesel truck driver who refuses to haul stolen goods for gangster bosses. With lots of car crashes and a good support cast. Kay Lenz costars with Slim Pickens, L. Q. Jones, R. G. Armstrong, Don Porter, Martin Kove, and Dick Miller. From Columbia. Kaplan's previous feature was *Truck Turner.*

WHITE OF THE EYE

(Paramount, 1987) **D/S:** Donald Cammell **S:** China Cammell **P:** Cassian Elwes, Brad Wyman   UK

The camera is everywhere in this violent psychedelic psycho-killer movie set in a small Arizona town. We know right away who the killer is. It's David Keith, a car and stereo repairman who makes house calls. Cathy Moriarty is his wife from New York City. Lots of flashbacks, the mind-blowing camera work of Larry McConkey, and music by Nick Mason of Pink Floyd help make it a unique experience. Don't miss the explosive ending. With Alan Rosenberg and Art Evans as a cop. Cammell's other credits are *Performance* and *Demon Seed.* Too bad so few people bothered to see *White of the Eye* in theaters.

THE WHITE ORCHID

(Sinister, 1954) **D/S/P:** Reginald Le Borg
S: David Duncan

William Lundigan and Peggy Castle star in a color movie about a mysterious tribe of natives in Mexico. A guide (Armando Silvestre) takes them through the jungle, and the tribe sentences them to death.

WHITE PHANTOM: ENEMY OF DARKNESS

(Vidmark, 1987) **D:** Dusty Nelson **S:** David Hamilton, Chris Gallagher **P:** Roy McAree, K. L. Kim

Modern ninja wars erupt and a plutonium weapon is at stake. Jay Roberts Jr. stars with Page Leong and Bo Svenson as a colonel.

WHITE SHADOWS OF THE SOUTH SEAS

(1928) **D:** W. S. Van Dyke, Robert Flaherty
S: Jack Cunningham, John Colton

MGM's first sound film was a "docudrama" featuring topless native women. It was shot on location on the Marquesas Islands by Flaherty (who quit), and synchronized sound effects and music were added in New Jersey. Monte Blue plays a drunken doctor involved with a native girl (Raquel Torres). Van Dyke made more exotic MGM hits including *Trader Horn* and *Tarzan.*

WHITE SLAVE

(Force, 1984) **D:** "Roy Garrett"/Mario Gariazzo **S:** Franco Prosperi   Italy
(*Amazonia—The Catherine Mills Story*)

The man who wrote *Mondo Cane* came up with this one too. A blond English housewife (Elvire Audray) becomes a member of a (friendly) Amazon tribe after her parents are decapitated and eaten. She falls in love with a tribesman, and is later tried for murder, relating her story in flashbacks. She uses blowguns to kill the real guilty parties in London. Partially shot in South America.

WHITE SLAVE SHIP

(1962) **D:** Silvio Amadio **S:** Sandro Continenza
P: Giorgio Agliani, Rodolphe Somsen
Italy/France (*L'ammutinamentos*)

Women prisoners take over a ship headed for the colonies in the 18th century. Pier Angeli stars with Edmund Purdom and Ivan Desny. AIP released it and added Les Baxter music. It's in color and "Totalscope."

WHODUNIT

(Vestron, 1981) **D/S/P:** Bill Naud **P:** Tom Spalding, Sally Todd   (*Island of Blood*)

Kids go to a California island to be in a slasher movie. Gore killings happen as described in some rock songs.

WHO FRAMED ROGER RABBIT

(Disney, 1988) **D:** Robert Zemeckis
S: Jeffrey Price, Peter S. Seaman **P:** Robert Watts

Steven Spielberg was an executive producer of the most expensive movie made until *Terminator 2* (1991). The combination of animation and live action cost "$70M," but it was a hit, and the FX and animation are pretty great. This is the only feature with appearances by Donald Duck (from Disney), Daffy Duck (from Warner), and Betty Boop (from a company engulfed by Disney). The 1940s big business conspiracy subplot is kind of hard to take, considering. Too bad the whimpering cartoon rabbit star isn't a better character. Bob Hoskins stars with Christopher Lloyd as Judge Doom, Joanna Cassidy, and Stubby Kaye. Kathleen Turner is the speaking voice of Jessica Rabbit, and Amy Irving (who divorced Spielberg in 1989) does her singing. Lots of other past cartoon characters make appearances too. Richard Williams was the director of animation. A record number of names were listed in the credits (743). When the laserdisc version was released in 1994 there was a "scandal" when some people realized you could freeze-frame to see what's under Jessica's skirt. "Roller Coaster Rabbit" (also with ILM FX) was a special opening short.

WHO'LL STOP THE RAIN

(MGM, 1978) **D:** Karel Reisz **S:** Judith Roscoe, Robert Stone **P:** Herb Jaffe, Gabriel Katzka   (*Dog Soldiers*)

A box-office flop, this now looks like one of the best of the 1970s. Nick Nolte is Ray Hicks, a Nietzsche-reading Nam vet merchant seaman. When war correspondent Michael Moriarty has him deliver a package of heroin to his pill-popping wife (Tuesday Weld), corrupt CIA agents enter the picture. It all ends in a violent siege at a remote summer home. With Anthony Zerbe, Ray Sharkey, Richard Masur, Charles Haid, and Connie Strickland. It's based on Stone's novel *Dog Soldiers*. The Creedence Clearwater Revival title song is on the soundtrack. From UA.

WHOLLY MOSES

(RCA, 1980) **D:** Gary Weis
S: Guy Thomas **P:** Freddie Fields

Herschell (Dudley Moore) believes that he was chosen to lead the Israelites out of Egypt. It's a failed attempt at making a Mel Brooks–type comedy, with John Houseman as the Archangel, Madeline Kahn as a sorceress, Richard Pryor as Pharaoh, and John Ritter as the Devil. Also with Laraine Newman, Paul Sand, Jack Gilford, Dom DeLuise, James Coco, David L. Lander, and Tanya Boyd.

WHOOPS! APOCALYPSE

(Pacific Arts, 1981) **D:** John Readon
S: Andrew Marshall, David Renwick
P: Humphrey Barclay   UK

An American nuclear bomb is stolen in a comedy centering on the news coverage leading up to WWIII. With John Barron, John Cleese, Rik Mayall, and Barry Morse as the president. It was a British TV series and the tape runs 137 minutes.

WHOOPS! APOCALYPSE

(MGM, 1986) **D:** Tom Bussman **S:** Andrew Marshall, David Renwick **P:** Brian Eastman   UK

In the feature based on the TV series, a nuclear strike against a Soviet base in the Caribbean leads to the end of the world. Loretta Swit is the president. Some of the stars are Peter Cook, Rik Mayall

(also in the original), Ian Richardson, Herbert Lom as General Mosquera, Murray Hamilton, and Clifton James.

WHORE

(Vestron, 1991) **D/S/A:** Ken Russell **S:** Deborah Dalton **P:** Dan Ireland, Ronaldo Vasconcellos
(*If You Can't Say It, Just See It*)

Many papers wouldn't print the title of this downbeat look at the life of a hooker (Theresa Russell). She explains her life and talks to the camera. At the time it was considered a realistic alternative to the mega-popular *Pretty Woman*. The cast includes Benjamin Mouton as her pimp, Antonio Fargas, John Diehl, Jack Nance, Tom Villard, and Ginger Lynn Allen. Four (!) video versions were released: unrated, NC-17, and R (under both titles). Ken Russell himself appears as a waiter. *Whore 2* (Vidmark, 1995) was, of course, completely unrelated.

WHOSE CHILD AM I?

(EVI, 1974) **D:** Lawrence Britten
S: James Stevens **P:** Basil Appelby   UK

This arty test-tube-baby movie features lots of softcore sex. A lesbian couple want a child. A criminal doctor gives a black man's sperm to a pothead woman. Kate O'Mara (from *The Vampire Lovers*), Paul Freeman, and Edward Judd star.

WHO'S GUILTY?

(Stockey, 1945) **D:** Howard Bretherton, Wallace Grissell **S:** Ande Lamb, George Plympton **P:** Sam Katzman

This 15-chapter Columbia serial takes place in an old dark house full of secret panels and passageways. Robert Kent stars with Amelita Ward, Tim Ryan, Charles Middleton, Wheeler Oakman, and Milton Kibbee. Kent was also in *The Phantom Creeps* (1939).

WHO'S THAT KNOCKING AT MY DOOR?

(Warner, 1968) **D/S:** Martin Scorsese   (*J.R.*)

Harvey Keitel stars as J.R., a guy with religious hang-ups who doesn't have a clue how to keep his WASP girlfriend (Zina Bethune). It was shot on weekends in the winter, and started in 1965 as an NYU student film. The feature was done in 1967, then an additional nude scene (backed by the Doors' "The End") was shot in Amsterdam in 1968 at the request of Joseph Brenner, who first released it. The excellent soundtrack of old singles, including the doo-wop title song by the Genies, is similar to the soundtracks Scorsese put together for *Mean Streets* (also starring Keitel) and *GoodFellas*. Characters discuss John Wayne and Charlie Chan movies, and Catherine and Martin Scorsese also appear.

THE WICKED

(Hemdale, 1987) **D/S:** Colin Eggleston
S: David R. Young **P:** Jan Tyrell, James Michael Vernon
Australia (*Outback Vampire; Tomorrow's News*)

This vampire movie with comedy has good parts but gets progressively sillier. Bizarre characters in

a fort-like town provide victims for a vampire family in the "slaughterhoose" on a hill. Two guys and a girl become stranded there and try to escape. The sexy vampire daughter can float, others walk on walls, and one vampire becomes a giant. A rock band (Perfect Strangers) appears for no reason, and too many blue filters were used on the cameras. The accents are very thick.

THE WICKED CITY

(Long Shore, 1992) **D:** Mak Tai Kit
P: Tsui Hark, Raymond Lee   Hong Kong

This FX-filled live-action fantasy adventure is based on an illustrated adult novel (anime) by Hideyuki Kikuchi. An animated version was also made in Japan. Leon Lai and Jacky Cheung star as special agents who hunt down "Raptures" (alien criminals that can cross dimensions). With some nudity and a woman changing into a pinball machine during sex. Michele Li and Tatsuya Nakadai costar. The director was born in Vietnam.

WICKED STEPMOTHER

(MGM, 1989) **D/S:** Larry Cohen **P:** Robert Litman

Bette Davis, the very old and frail-looking star, left the set of this PG-13 comedy fantasy after two weeks of shooting, saying she needed dental work. Quick rewrites were done and Barbara Carrera was hired to play the Davis character, magically transformed into her witch "daughter." More (not very) special comic effects were added. Davis's scenes (her last film appearance) look like outtakes, and her slurred diatribes are painful to watch. She's Miranda, an insulting, chain-smoking, meat-eating new mother-in-law who terrorizes suburban vegetarian yuppies Colleen Camp and David Rasche. Lionel Stander is her new husband. With Tom Bosley, Richard Moll, Evelyn Keyes, Seymour Cassel, and Laurene Landon (in a bit role). A sequel, announced at the end, never happened.

WICKED WOMAN

(1954) **D:** Russell Rouse **P:** Clarence Greene

Blond Beverly Michaels, one of the great 50s "B" girls, is a waitress who lures a bar owner (Richard Egan) away from his alcoholic wife in a California town. "She's nothing but trouble . . . Every voluptuous inch of her!" With Percy Helton. Michaels had already been in two Hugo Haas movies (*Pickup* and *The Girl on the Bridge*). She married director Rouse (*D.O.A.*) in real life. From UA.

WILBUR AND THE BABY FACTORY

(SW, 1969) **D/S:** Tom Wolfe **P:** Alec McCombie   (*The Loving Machine*)

Wilbur (Tom Shea, who looks kinda like Glen Campbell) is a quiet USC student and anti-war protest leader who lives in a tent. After he receives his draft notice he volunteers to be the subject for an experimental program in an isolated house. He has to run every day, his every move is monitored, and eventually a series of nameless women undress and join him in bed. It's more of an attempt at social and political comedy (there isn't much onscreen sex) than the usual adults-only Boxoffice

International release. Stuart Lancaster plays a cranky, crippled millionaire and Ronee Blakley sings. The music is rambling rock instrumentals.

THE WILD AND THE NAKED

(SW, 1962) **D:** Stan Roberts **P/C:** Carlos Martinez

Colette (the beautiful Tanya French) is a French model in America. After a trip to the zoo, some posing at a studio, and dancing in a bikini to a Latin band, she hitchhikes to a beach. The driver ("He was a fresh one") chases her (she's in her bikini bottom) on the beach, then she swims naked and sunbathes. A bearded madman shows up and chases her. She runs naked through the woods, through fields, crawls on her hands and knees in the mud, then is tied up. The two men fight but a handsome third man rescues her. Then a man in a monkey suit (!) chases both of them. If that wasn't enough, topless native women swim, then dance to a rock and roll instrumental. Eventually Colette wakes up. Brilliant! The b/w feature was "filmed in Latin America" (actually Texas). Martinez also produced *Passion in the Sun*, which had similar naked running scenes.

WILD AT HEART

(Media, 1990) **D/S:** David Lynch **P:** Monty Montgomery **M:** Angelo Badalamenti

Nicolas Cage stars as Sailor, a redneck Elvis fanatic. After two years in jail for smashing in a man's skull (the opening scene), he and Lula (Laura Dern, who is excellent) head for New Orleans in a convertible. The unique, violent comic road movie/love story (based on a novel by Barry Gifford) is packed with inspired performances, disturbing moments, flashbacks, voodoo, gangsters, and lots of Elvis and *Wizard of Oz* references. Dern's real-life mother, Diane Ladd, plays her horrible mom. Willem Dafoe is the very creepy Bobby Peru, Harry Dean Stanton is scary when watching extreme mondo movies, and Crispin Glover puts cockroaches down his pants. With blond Isabella Rossellini, Grace Zabriskie, Calvin Lockhart, Freddie Jones, Marvin Kaplin, John Lurie, Jack Nance (as "O O Spool"), Koko Taylor, Sherilyn Fenn in a car crash, and Sheryl Lee as the good witch. Also with Charlie Spradling, Mia M. Ruiz, Debra Lamb, and Lisa Ann Cabasa for various topless scenes. A (very well done) decapitation scene was cut, but I still wonder how this got an R rating. It was released while Lynch's *Twin Peaks* series was still running and features several stars from the series. It's 127 minutes long.

THE WILD BEASTS

(Lightning, 1983) **D/S/P:** Franco E. Prosperi
Italy (*Savage Beasts*)

PCP accidentally put in the water supply of a German zoo makes animals attack and kill. In one scene, an elephant crushes a woman's head and lots of cars crash too. By the maker of *Mondo Pazzo*.

THE WILD BUNCH

(Warner, 1969) **D/S:** Sam Peckinpah **S:** Walon Green **P:** Phil Feldman **C:** Lucien Ballard

Laura Dern and Nicholas Cage in *Wild At Heart*.

The "*Citizen Kane* of the Vietnam generation" surpassed *Bonnie and Clyde* (1967) with its realistic violence. William Holden, Ernest Borgnine, Warren Oates, Ben Johnson, Edmond O'Brien, and Jaime Sanchez are doomed outlaws attempting one last train robbery on the Tex-Mex border in 1913. Robert Ryan is a bounty hunter after Holden, and Emilio Fernandez is the Mexican general who wants the stolen American weapons. The great cast also includes Strother Martin, L. Q. Jones, Albert Dekker, Bo Hopkins, Dub Taylor, and Alfonso Arau (later the director of *Like Water for Chocolate*). When a "director's cut" with ten minutes of additional footage (flashbacks) was released in 1994, the MPAA ordered that the feature (originally an R) be rated NC-17, then backed off. A 70mm version was a theatrical rerelease in 1995. Screenwriter Green was later executive producer of the *NYPD Blue* and *Law and Order* 90s TV shows.

WILD CACTUS

(IEI, 1992) **D:** Jag Mundhra **S:** Carl Austin **P:** Alan B. Burnstein

A young wife (India Allen) living in a desert home is held hostage by an escaped con (Gary Hudson) and his girlfriend (Michelle Mofett). As far as silly direct-to-video erotic thrillers go, this one isn't bad and Allen, a *Playboy* centerfold, has many nude scenes. David Naughton is the husband, Kathy Shower (also from *Playboy*) is killed in her trailer, and the cast includes Anna Karin, Robert Z'Dar, and Wendy McDonald. It's available R or unrated.

WILDCATS = THE DOLL SQUAD

WILDCAT WOMEN

(1976) **D/P:** Stephen Gibson

This 3-D sex movie was released in three versions, each having more sex than the last. Serena is in it, and the trailer is on the *Mad Ron's Previews from Hell* tape.

WILDER NAPALM

(Columbia, 1993) **D:** Glenn Gordon Caron **S:** Vince Gilligan **P:** Mark Johnson, Stuart Cornfeld

Two rival brothers can make objects burst into flame. Wallace (Dennis Quaid) works for the circus and wants to be famous as "Dr. Napalm." He also wants the wife (Debra Winger) of his strait-laced brother Wilder (Arliss Howard), a volunteer fireman. She's a pyromaniac arsonist under house arrest. There's a fiery duel, and in the cartoonish FX scenes things melt, boil, and blow up. With Jim Varney, M. Emmet Walsh, and the Mighty Echoes as doo-wop singing firemen. The music is by Michael Kamen. Barry Levinson was a coproducer of the odd TriStar PG-13 comedy, which spent time "on the shelf." *Spontaneous Combustion* (1989) and *Pyrates* (1991), also critical and commercial flops, were about the same topic.

WILDEST DREAMS

(Vestron, 1987) **D/P:** Chuck Vincent **S:** Craig Horall   (*Bikini Genie*)

James Davies runs a Greenwich Village antique shop. A "bikini genie" (Heidi Payne) grants him three wishes. The sex comedy features Ruth Collins, Veronica Hart, and Tracey Adams.

WILD EYE

(1967) **D/S:** Paola Cavada **S:** Tonio Guerra **P:** Georges Marci   Italy (*L'Occhio Selvaggio*)

Philippe Leroy stars as a very amoral mondo filmmaker faking scenes and abusing people in Third World countries. It was filmed on location in Africa, Asia, and North and South Vietnam. The same premise was later used for gory cannibal movies. With Delia Boccardo and Gabrielle Tinti. AIP released it. A soundtrack was on RCA.

WILDFIRE

(MCA, 1988) **D/S:** Zalman King **S:** Mathew Bright **P:** Jerry Tokofsky

Steven Bauer and Linda Fiorentino run away from an orpanage and rob a bank. After eight years in prison he gets out and she leaves her husband for him. With Marshall Bell and Will Patton. It was released in 1992.

WILD, FREE AND HUNGRY

(SW, 1970) **D:** "H. P. Edwards"/Paul Hunt **P/A:** Graver

Graver, also a cinematographer and director, stars as a motorboat racer who rides a motorcycle and faces opposition from gangsters. The adults-only plot also involves a carnival and love affairs. With Barbara Caron and Monica Gayle (both also in *The Stewardesses*) and Jane Tsentas (*Wilbur and the Baby Factory*). From Boxoffice International.

WILD GALS OF THE NAKED WEST!

(RM, 1961) **D/S/P/C/E:** Russ Meyer
(*The Immoral West—and How It Was
Lost; Naked Gals of the Golden West*)

An old prospector tells the story of this gag-filled
nudie western. Julie Williams stars with Sammy
Gilbert, Jack Moran, Frank Bolger, and "the To-
panga Gulch Players." The next year, Francis Ford
Coppola's nudie western, *Tonight for Sure,* was released. The 65-minute early Meyer feature played
drive-ins as late as 1976 on all-Meyer triple bills. It
was released on tape in 1992.

WILD HORSE HANK

(Vestron, 1978) **D:** Eric Till **S:** James Lee Barrett
P: Bill Marshall, Henk Van Der Kolk   Canada

Linda Blair, in one of her rare non-exploitation
roles, is a horse lover trying to stop a family that
stampedes wild horses. With Richard Crenna and
Al Waxman. Blair competed in horse shows in real
life.

WILDING: THE CHILDREN OF VIOLENCE

(AIP, 1990) **D/S/P:** Eric Louzil **P:** Lillian
Balteanu   (*Night of the Wilding*)

Some LA teens go on the rampage in a movie "inspired" by a (then) famous Central Park incident.
Wings Hauser and Joey Travolta star as cop partners. With Catlyn Day and Karen Russell.

WILD LIFE

(MCA, 1984) **D/S:** Art Linson **S/P:** Cameron Crowe

Christopher Penn (acting like his brother Sean)
stars in the less successful "sequel" to *Fast Times
at Ridgemont High,* set in a singles apartment. The
teen comedy costars Eric Stoltz as a high school
grad new to the "swinging" scene. With Randy
Quaid, Lea Thompson, Jenny Wright, Hart Bochner, Ilan Mitchell-Smith, Rick Moranis, Sherilyn
Fenn, and director Leo Penn playing his real son's
father. Also with Lee Ving, plus Kitten Natividad
and Ashley St. John/Angelique Pettijohn as strippers. With music by Eddie Van Halen.

WILDMAN

(Celebrity, 1988) **D/A:** Fred Lincoln
S: Marc Jonathon **P:** Alan Nadohl

A Vegas casino owner (Don Scribner) works for
the government. He uses a magic ring, becomes
invulnerable and fights a drug lord. With Ginger
Lynn and Michelle Bauer. Lincoln, a *Last House
on the Left* star, is best known for directing porno
movies.

THE WILD McCULLOCHS

(1975) **D/S/P/A:** Max Baer Jr.   (*The McCullochs*)

After the success of *Macon County Line,* Baer did
it all in this tale of a tough self-made Texas millionaire (Forrest Tucker) and his sons. AIP released

the PG movie featuring two *My Three Sons* regulars. With Julie Adams, Don Grady, and William
Demarest.

WILD ONES ON WHEELS

(Sinister, 1962) **D/P:** Rudolph Cusumano
S: Eugene Pollack **C/A:** Ray Dennis Steckler
(*Drivers to Hell*)

Duke is released from jail (old prison movie stock
footage is used here) and heads for a remote diner
and motel to reclaim his loot and girlfriend Hazel
(Francine York). Hazel runs the place with her
"gimpy" brother. Meanwhile a gang led by King
Tut (Edmund Tontini) shows up in three jeeps and
a convertible driven by Preacher (Steckler). This
movie is pretty dull despite Steckler talking jive
and York seen topless (from the back). Characters
talk a lot, fight, have a deadly chickie run, and one
is "tortured" with a small lizard. The b/w feature
wasn't released until 1967. York also starred in
the even cheaper *Secret File Hollywood* by the
same producer.

WILD ORCHID

(RCA, 1990) **D/S:** Zalman King **P:** Tony Anthony

Revlon girl Carré Otis stars as a New York lawyer
who goes to Rio during Carnival to work for Jacqueline Bisset. She encounters Mickey Rourke as
a brooding Harley-riding millionaire voyeur. The
pretentious lush sex fantasy was made after *9¹/₂
Weeks* (also with Rourke). Typical publicity ("they
really did it") surrounded the Otis/Rourke sex
scenes. It was cut for an R in America and is available in R or uncut versions on tape. The cable TV
hit was executive produced by Mark Damon. He,
producer Anthony, and director King are all former
movie actors. King later used footage from this for
his *Boca* (1994).

WILD ORCHID 2: TWO SHADES OF BLUE

(Columbia, 1991) **D/S:** Zalman King **P:** David
Saunders, Rafael Eisenman   (*Blue Movie Blue*)

Nina Siemaszko stars as Blue, a California teen in
the late 50s who becomes a wig-wearing hooker
at a house run by a madam (Wendy Hughes) and
appears in a porno movie. She leaves and attends
school as a "normal" teen, falls in love with Brent
Fraser, and is blackmailed. Tom Skerritt is her
heroin-addict jazz musician father. With Robert
Davi, Joe Dallesandro, and Lydie Denier. Mark
Damon was executive producer of this (in name
only) sequel. It was followed by King's *Red Shoe
Diaries* series.

THE WILD PACK

(1971) **D/S/P:** Hall Barlett
(*The Sandpit Generals; The Defiant*)

Black and white orphans in Brazil survive by stealing. The AIP release won the Grand Prize at the
Moscow Film Festival. With Kent Lane, Tisha Sterling, Butch Patrick, and Mark de Vries. Bartlett
also made *Jonathan Livingston Seagull.*

THE WILD PAIR

(Media, 1987) **D/A:** Beau Bridges **S:** Joseph Gunn
P: Paul Mason, Randall Torno   (*Devil's Odds*)

A cop (Beau) and an FBI man (Bubba Smith) team
up and battle a private army led by a racist drug
dealer (Lloyd Bridges). With Gary Lockwood,
Raymond St. Jacques, and Ellen Geer.

WILD PALMS

(ABC, 1993) **D:** Keith Gordon, Phil Joanou,
Kathryn Bigelow, Peter Hewitt
S: Bruce Wagner **P:** Michael Rauch

This limited-run TV series, based on Bruce Wagner's comic strip in *Details* magazine, is pretty bizarre for network TV. Unlike *Twin Peaks,* it's very
political and didn't really get that much attention.
Set in LA in 2007, it features corrupt politics, conspiracies, addictive virtual-reality drugs, hologram
TV shows, a computer-graphic monster, and surreal dreams and nightmares. *Wild Palms* also has
many clever references and in-jokes, and believable cultural-reference slang. James Belushi stars
as a patent attorney who goes to work for Senator Kreutzer (Robert Loggia), the leader of the
(Dianetics-style) Synthiotics religion. Kreutzer
is also secretly leader of the fascist Fathers and
he helps the attorney's son (Ben Savage) become a
TV messiah. Many characters are involved, including Angie Dickinson as Kreutzer's evil sister
(she pushes an artist's eyes out) and David Warner
as the leader of the underground group Friends.
Dana Delaney and Kim Cattrall are the female
leads, and Brad Dourif has a memorable role. Also
with Ernie Hudson, Nick Mancuso, Robert Morse,
Robert Cornwaithe, sci-fi writer William Gibson,
Bebe Neuwirth, and William Schallert. Executive
producer Oliver Stone appears as himself on TV.
The score by Ryuichi Sakamoto plus some choice
60s oldies (including "Gimme Shelter" . . .) is on
Capitol. The two features plus the two hour episodes are all available on a two-tape set or a three-
disc box set.

THE WILD PARTY

(Embassy, 1975) **D:** James Ivory
S: Walter Marks **P:** Ishmail Merchant

AIP released this Merchant/Ivory feature loosely
based on the famous Fatty Arbuckle scandal.
James Coco is the silent-era comedian who throws
a big Hollywood party where a girl dies. Raquel
Welch costars with Perry King, Tiffany Bolling,
Royal Dano, and David Dukes. The 107-minute
feature was cut to 95 minutes by AIP. *Day of the
Locust* from the same year is better.

WILD RAPTURE

(Video Dimension, 1950)

This exploitation hit documentary (with jokey narration) was filmed in the Congo region of central
Africa. It shows members of the "Ubangi" tribe
with lips stretched with wooden disks and pygmies hunting a gorilla. The scenes of the gorilla
hunt (and kill) were once sold as an 8mm short by
Castle Films under the title *Killer Gorilla.* Native

children eat huge caterpillars and the pygmies butcher an elephant carcass. The video box features ad art from another film, *Mau Mau*.

A WILD RIDE

(Applause, 1969) **D:** "Revilo Ekard"/Oliver Drake
S/P: William and Rachel Edwards   (*Ride a Wild Stud*)

Quantrill and his men rape women and run a whorehouse in a sex western. Josie Kirk is kidnapped and Hale Williams is the cowboy hero. Drake had directed many B westerns at Monogram and PRC. He sure picked a hard-to-guess pseudonym.

WILD RIDERS

(Academy, 1971) **D/S:** Richard Kanter
P: John Burrows   (*Angels for Kicks*)

Two slimy crazed bikers (Alex Rocco and Arell Blanton) grab two rich women. Stick (Rocco) wears plastic sunglasses, eats garbage, and freaks out. From Crown International. Rocco, who was really on an exploitation roll, went on immediately to *Stanley, Detroit 900,* and *Three the Hard Way.* Kanter made *The Ribald Tales of Robin Hood.*

WILD SCENE

(SW, 1970) **D:** William Rowland **S:** Michael Karike, William Keys **P:** Sam Jacobs

A psychiatrist (Alberta Nelson) relates real-life episodes from her planned book to her publisher. A rich girl with a horrible mother has sex with her father (offscreen). Three girls become hookers and are given (fake) birth control pills. A man (Barry Kroeger from *Nightmare in Wax*) has to beg his lesbian mistress for sex, and a girl dies at a drug party. Every once in a while the shrink tells about how her own rebellious daughter (Anita Eubank) fell for a campus radical. He says, "These demonstrations pay off like slot machines" and gives her VD. The cast of this grim, very anti-hippie adults-only movie includes Ida Lupino's sister Rita and Nancy Czar from *Wild Guitar.*

WILD SEED

(1965) **D:** Brian G. Hutton
S: Les Pine **P:** Albert S. Ruddy

Daffy (Celia Kaye) runs away from a foster home in New York, rides a train with a young bum (Michael Parks), and looks for her father in California. With Ross Elliott. It was the second feature for Parks, considered a James Dean type at the time. Marlon Brando Sr. was an executive producer for the Universal release.

WILD STYLE

(World, 1982) **D/S/P:** Charlie Ahearn

Few thought rap music would last as long as it has (when will it end?!). This was the first feature about rap (and the graffiti art scene) and is more realistic than the cash-in movies that followed. It was filmed semi-documentary style in New York City. Lee George Quinones stars as a graffiti artist from the ghetto trying to deal with the high-society art world. It all ends in a great rap show at a

Lila Leeds discovers the results of pot smoking—*Wild Weed.*

park bandshell. With Patti Astor, Fab 5 Freddy, and Busy Bee. Chris Stein from Blondie was in charge of the music. The soundtrack is on Animal Records.

WILD THING

(Paramount, 1987) **D:** Max Reid
S: John Sayles   US/Canada

Robert Knepper stars as a Tarzan-type orphan brought up in "The Zone" (tenements) of Quebec. He becomes the protector of some locals against drug dealers and bad cops. Kathleen Quinlan costars with Robert Davi, Betty Buckley, and Maury Chaykin. The theme song for the PG-13 feature is the Troggs' song of the same name.

WILD WEED

(Sinister, 1949) **D:** Sam Newfeld
S: Richard H. Landau **P:** Richard Kay
(*The Devil's Weed; She Shoulda Said No!*)

This is the story of "tea" or "tomatoes" and is the best-looking and most entertaining of the old drug-scare movies. Newsworthy star Lila Leeds (as blond dancer Ann Lester) was cast because she had been busted along with Robert Mitchum and served six months for possession. Alan Baxter (acting a lot like Robert Ryan) plays the ambitious, heartless pusher Markey. Whenever a joint (kept in Aztec Tomato cans) is present, spooky theremin music is heard. *Weed* includes a guy who can only play "Chopsticks" imagining himself performing a piano concerto at Hollywood Bowl, suicide, a scare tour of an asylum and morgue, and an excellent time-lapse freak-out scene where Ann sees herself aging in a mirror. Other notable stars are Lyle Talbot as a narcotics chief, young Jack Elam as a killer hood, and Leo Gorcey's brother David. Art director Eugene Lourie (*Gorgo, The Giant Behe-*

moth . . .) added greatly to the classy look of this "adults-only" drug horror classic. Director Newfeld had already directed over 180 features, including *The Terror of Tiny Town, Beast of Berlin,* and *I Accuse My Parents.* A Hallmark Roadshow attraction from Kroger Babb.

WILD WILD WORLD

(1965) **D:** Bob Sokoler **P:** Alessandro Jacovoni   Italy

Forties star Eddie Bracken narrates the English-language version of this mondo movie. It shows opium smoking, prostitution, stag films, bullfighting, strippers, cock fights, and Vince Taylor and the Playboys. Taylor was a British rocker in black leather who became a big star in France. People eat monkey brains, dogs, insects, and live mice. It was presented by Dick Randall.

THE WILD, WILD WORLD OF JAYNE MANSFIELD

(Good Times, 1968) **D:** Arthur Knight **S:** Charles Ross

If you haven't seen this brilliant, fascinating fake documentary masterpiece yet, it's about time! Jayne conducts a mondo tour including strip clubs, a nudist colony, and a drag fashion show. The tour footage was filmed (from 1964–66) in Rome, Paris, Cannes, New York, and Hollywood. Since she was already dead by 1968, "Jayne's" breathy narration was done by a woman who dubbed countless Italian movies. Sometimes a Jayne stand-in is used for scenes. Sometimes Jayne "remembers" scenes from some of her movies. The editor deserved an Oscar. With Rocky Roberts and the Airdales (doing "The Bird Is the Word") while Jayne dances, and a topless rock band (the Ladybirds). It all ends with tasteless footage of Mansfield's body and her grieving husband Mickey Hargitay. With clips of Jayne in *The Loves of Hercules* (1960) (letterboxed!), *Spree* (1963), nude scenes from *Promises Promises* (1963), and *Primitive Love* (1964). Most video versions are cut and are missing essential segments (including the topless band!). You need the Good Times or out-of-print Video Home version. Presented by exploitation genius Dick Randall.

WILD WOMEN

(Sinister, 1951) **D:** Norman Dawn

A small safari is captured by the (white) female Ulama tribe. The movie features lots of old narrated stock footage including brief (real native women) nudity as flashbacks, and claims to be shot in Africa. With women in tiger skins dancing for their high priestess, wrestling, and a man in a gorilla suit. The just-over-an-hour feature is similar to *Prehistoric Women* (1950) or *Untamed Women* (1952) but even cheaper and worse.

WILLIE DYNAMITE

(1973) **D:** Gilbert Moses III **S:** Ron Cutler
P: Richard D. Zanuck, David Brown

Roscoe Orman (later a regular on *Sesame Street*!) is Willie Dynamite, a New York pimp who reforms at the end thanks to a social worker (Diana Sands, who died before the release). With Roger Robinson as an outrageous gay rival pimp, Thalmus Rasulala, Juanita Brown, and Marcia McBroom. Martha Reeves is on the MCA soundtrack. By the director of *The Fish That Saved Pittsburgh.*

THE WILLIES

(Prism, 1990) **D/S:** Brian Peck
P: Gary Depew, Brad Southwick

Scary stories are told around a campfire in a PG-13 horror anthology. Giant flies and a stop-motion monster appear. Sean Astin, Joshua Miller, and James Karen are in the framing segments. Also with Kathleen Freeman, Clu Gulager, Kirk Cameron, Dana Ashbrook, and Kimmy Robertson.

WILLOW

(RCA, 1988) **D:** Ron Howard
S: Bob Dolman **P:** Nigel Wooll

After *Splash* and *Cocoon* hit, Howard made this PG-rated fantasy adventure. Warwick Davis stars as the dwarf Willow, who has to rescue a baby from a magic queen (Jean Marsh). Val Kilmer is a mercenary fighter and Joanne Whalley is the nice daughter of the evil Queen. With Billy Barty and a whole village of little people, Gavin O'Herlihy, and David Steinberg. Some of the ILM FX are excellent (this was the first feature to use morphing, now used everywhere), and it's a good kid movie. The $30 million feature was not a hit, and the merchandising products didn't sell. It was based on a story by executive producer George Lucas.

WIMPS

(Lightning, 1984) **D/S/P:** Chuck Vincent **S:** Craig Horall

A college nerd (Louis Bonanno) is forced to help an awkward jock court Tracey Adams by writing love letters for him. The porno star cast includes Veronica Hart and Annie Sprinkle. Like most Vincent movies, it's very stupid and plays cable TV a lot.

THE WIND

(Lightning, 1986) **D/S/P:** Nico Mastorakis
S: Fred C. Perry

Meg Foster is a mystery writer stranded on a Greek island in a mansion. Wings Hauser is an unshaven alcoholic psycho killer handyman. With Steve Railsback, David McCallum, and Robert Morley as the landlord. *The Next One,* by the same director, had the same Greek setting.

THE WINDOW

(1949) **D:** Ted Tetzlaff **S:** Mel
Dinelli **P:** Frederic Ullman Jr.

Cornell Woolrich wrote the story that this excellent thriller from RKO was based on. Bobby Driscoll stars as a New York City tenement kid who witnesses a murder from the fire escape. Nobody believes him and the killers (Paul Stewart and Ruth Roman) chase after him. Arthur Kennedy and Barbara Hale are the parents. Driscoll, who was also in Disney films, received a special Oscar. He died in 1968 after spending time as a drug addict. *The Window* has some similarities with *Rear Window* (1954), also based on Woolrich. It would make a great kids-in-peril double bill with *Invaders from Mars* (1953). It was remade as *The Boy Cried Murder* (1966) in England and also as *Cloak and Dagger* (1984).

WINDOWS

(Vid-America, 1979) **D:** Gordon Willis
S: Barry Siegel **P:** Michael Lobell

Elizabeth Ashley is a lesbian psycho killer after Talia Shire. She even hires a man to rape her to turn her against men. She also puts her cat in the freezer. The director is the famous cinematographer (*The Godfather* . . .). With Joe Cortese as a cop. It's pretty dreary. With an Ennio Morricone score. It was shot in Brooklyn Heights about the same time that *Cruising* was filming in Manhattan. From UA.

THE WINDS OF WAR

(Paramount, 1983) **D/P:** Dan Curtis **S:** Herman Wouk

If you want to learn about WWII and don't want to read about it, I recommend *The World at War* video series from HBO. If you want to see the war as brought to you by the creator of *Dark Shadows,* you should at least know who to look for because it's an international goldmine for spotting B actors. Let's try some alphabetically: Ralph Bellamy (as FDR again), Scott Brady, Anton Diffring, David Dukes, Lisa Eilbacher, Leo V. Gordon, Peter Graves, John Houseman, Ferdy Mayne, Ali McGraw, Robert Mitchum (the star), Barry Morse, Wolfgang Preiss, Edmund Purdom, Logan Ramsey, Barbara Steele (she was the associate producer and has a small role in an early segment), Victoria Tennant, Jan-Michael Vincent, Deborah Winters, and many, many more. *Winds* leads up to Pearl Harbor.

It cost $40 million. Originally 18 hours long, it's available uncut on 7 cassettes. *War and Remembrance* was the even bigger sequel.

WINGS OF DANGER

(1952) **D:** Terence Fisher **S:** John
Gilling **P:** Anthony Hinds   UK

Zachary Scott stars as an airline pilot who discovers a smuggling ring. With Kay Kendall and Diane Cilento. Lippert released the Hammer film in America.

WINGS OF DESIRE

(Orion, 1987) **D/S/P:** Wim Wenders **S:** Peter Handke
P: Anatole Dauman   (*Der Himmel über Berlin*)

Don't miss this pre-reunification Berlin fantasy with two angels (Bruno Ganz and Otto Sander) wandering effortlessly from the West to the East listening to people's thoughts. It's nothing like the countless angel movies you've probably seen. Damien (Ganz) falls for a circus acrobat (Solveig Dommartin) and eventually chooses to become human again. With Peter Falk as himself, Curt Bois (in films since 1909), and Nick Cave and the Bad Seeds. The subtitled PG-13 feature is part b/w (the way angels see things) and runs 130 minutes. *Faraway, So Close* was the sequel.

WINGS OF THE HAWK

(1953) **D:** Oscar "Budd" Boetticher
S: James E. Moser **P:** Aaron Rosenberg

Van Heflin and Julia Adams (just after *The Creature from the Black Lagoon*) star in a 3-D Universal movie about the Mexican revolution. With Abbe Lane, Noah Beery Jr., Pedro Gonzales-Gonzales, and George Dolenz (Micky's dad).

WIN, PLACE OR STEAL

(Vestron, 1975) **D/S:** Richard Bailey **S:** Anthony
Monaco **P:** Thomas C. Cooney   (*The Big Payoff;
Three for the Money; Just Another Day at the Races*)

Dean Stockwell, Russ Tamblyn, and Alex Karras star in a racetrack comedy. With Harry Dean Stanton and McLean Stevenson. Before it was made, Tamblyn had been unemployed and living in a trailer.

WINTERBEAST

(Tempe, 1986) **D/S:** Christopher Thies
P/E: Mark Frizzell

Forest rangers deal with legendary creatures in a local movie filmed in Newbury, Mass. Most of the animation (tree monster, lizard creature . . .) is pathetic, but I like it anyway. A creepy character named Sheldon looks kinda like Malcolm McDowell. He prances around a room while an entire old record ("Oh, Dear, What Can the Matter Be") plays. I still can't get that damn song out of my head! A hooded demon (good makeup) makes an appearance, there's some gore, and one topless scene. The screams are from the old Disney "Chilling, Thrilling Sounds of the Haunted House" album (!).

WINTERHAWK

(1976) **D/S/P:** Charles B. Pierce

Michael Dante stars as a Blackfoot Indian who kidnaps two kids after white men attack him for no reason. The PG Howco movie features Leif Erickson, Woody Strode, Denver Pyle, L. Q. Jones, Elisha Cook Jr., Arthur Hunnicutt, Dawn Wells, and Sacheen Littlefeather.

WINTER KILLS

(Columbia, 1979) **D/S:** William Richert **P:** Fred Caruso **C:** Vilmos Zsigmond **M:** Maurice Jarre

This black comedy is all about the Kennedy assassination, with names and places changed. Jeff Bridges stars as the brother of the late president "Kegan," who learns of a second rifle that was used. With John Huston as the Joseph Kennedy figure, Anthony Perkins (*WUSA*) as a computer genius, Sterling Hayden (*Suddenly*), Dorothy Malone, Eli Wallach, Ralph Meeker, Toshiro Mifune, Richard Boone, Thomas Milan, Brad Dexter, Belinda Bauer, Tisa Farrow, Candice Rialson, and Elizabeth Taylor. The Avco Embassy release was reedited and rereleased in 1983.

WIRED

(IVE, 1989) **D:** Larry Peerce **S:** Earl Mac Rauch **P:** Edward S. Feldman

Nobody liked this anti-drug comedy based on Bob Woodward's book. Michael Chiklis stars as the late comedian John Belushi. He's dead at the start of the movie, and his guardian angel (Ray Sharkey) takes him on a time trip through his life. With J. T. Walsh, Patti D'Arbanville, Alex Rocco, Billy Preston (as himself), and an Elvis impersonator. It was backed by the Lion Breweries of New Zealand. Peerce also made *Elvis and Me*.

WIRED TO KILL

(Lightning, 1986) **D/S:** Franky Schaeffer **P:** Jim Buchfueher   (*Booby Trap*)

This *Mad Max* copy is set in 1998 after the plague. People ride in garbage trucks and mutant gangs attack. Devin Hoelscher goes on a revenge spree in his wheelchair and a remote-control robot helps. The Shakespearean gang leader (Merritt Butrick) uses various bizarre ways to kill. The Yellowjackets provided the theme music. It was cut for an R.

WISE BLOOD

(MCA, 1979) **D/A:** John Huston **S:** Benedict Fitzgerald   US/W. Germany

One of Huston's least known features is one of his best. It's based on a Flannery O'Connor story. Brad Dourif is religious fanatic Hazel Motes, who returns from the war and starts "The Church of Truth Without Christ" in a southern town. Daniel Shor steals a mummy and another preacher (Harry Dean Stanton) lives in a hotel room with Amy Wright. With Ned Beatty, William Hickey, and Huston as Hazel's hellfire-and-brimstone grandfather. New Line released it.

WISE GUYS

(MGM, 1986) **D:** Brian De Palma **S:** George Gallo **P:** Aaron Russo

Danny DeVito and Joe Piscopo hide out from their mobster bosses in a gangster comedy. Whoever decided to team these two actors deserves some kind of severe punishment. Harvey Keitel plays an Atlantic City mobster casino manager. With Ray Sharkey, Dan Hedaya, Patti Lupone, Captain Lou Albano as Frank "the Fixer," and Martin Scorsese's parents. It includes nods to *Taxi Driver* and other Scorsese features.

WISHFUL THINKING

(Hemdale, 1992) **D/S/P/A:** Murray Langston

A screenwriter (Langston) rescues a gnome (Billy Barty); his dreams are fulfilled and Michelle Johnson is his prize. With Ruth Buzzi and Ray "Boom Boom" Mancini. Director Langston, aka "The Unknown Comic," was also in *Two Top Bananas* (1982), *Night Patrol* (1985), and *Up Your Alley* (1988).

WISHMAN

(Monarch, 1991) **D/S:** Michael Marvin **P:** Lon D. Tinney

A bald Geoffrey Lewis (father of Juliette) is a genie (with an on-and-off Irish accent) whose magic bottle is missing. A nice Beverly Hills junk collector (Paul Le Mat) and a funny Nam vet from Texas (Brion James) try to help, and Le Mat falls for a childlike blond heiress (Quin Kessler) being held captive by Nancy (*Porky's*) Parsons and Paul Gleason. Lewis, Le Mat, and James make an interesting and fun team, but why does this tape, which seems aimed at kids, have subplots about impregnating the girl with an idiot's sperm, a Roman orgy, and porno star Gloria Leonard (!) as a fortune teller? Also with Liz Sheridan, Rance Howard, and Savage Steve Holland. The Mike Curb–backed tape is by the director of *The Wraith*.

THE WITCH

(Sinister, 1966) **D/S:** Damiano Damiani **P:** Alfredo Bini **S:** Ugo Liberatore   Italy (*La Strega in Amore*)

An older Mexican woman living in a big old house hires no-good playboy Richard Johnson (*The Haunting*) to translate a library of erotic memoirs written by her husband (embalmed in a glass case). Gian Maria Volante (*A Fistful of Dollars*) is the unhinged previous librarian ("I'm in a living hell and I love it!"). They both have to be around the sexy young daughter, Auro (Rosanna Schiaffino), who keeps disappearing. Johnson says, "She's my ideal girl, a liar and corrupt!" Mind games, madness, murder, drugs, and other surprises should keep you interested. It's all based on a Mexican novel by Carlos Fuentes. Damiani returned to horror with *Amityville II: The Possession*.

WITCHBOARD

(Magnum, 1986) **D/S:** Kevin S. Tenney **P:** Gerald Geoffray

A Ouija board summons up a dead little boy during a teen party. Then the spirit of a mass murderer possesses star Tawny Kitaen. With Todd Allen, Kathleen Wilhoite as the medium, and Rose Marie in a bit part. With an exorcism, dream sequences, Tawny in the shower, and too many false scares. It was shot around San Francisco by a first-time director from USC.

WITCHBOARD 2: THE DEVIL'S DOORWAY

(Republic, 1993) **D/S:** Kevin S. Tenney **P:** Walter Josten

Blond Ami Dolenz stars as an artist/accountant who moves into a furnished loft building. She falls under the spell of a Ouija board and the spirit of "Susan" (Julie Michaels). With false scares, flying killer tools, a possessed car, and an automatic writer. John Gatins costars with Timothy Gibb, Laraine Newman as an ex-hippie landlady, and Marvin Kaplan as a "Jewish occultist." *Witchboard: The Possession* (Republic, 1995) followed.

WITCHCRAFT

(Academy, 1988) **D:** Robert Spera **S:** Jody Savan **P:** Megan Barnett, Yoran Barzilai

This one has some ideas from *Rosemary's Baby* and opens with scenes of a woman giving birth, intercut with a witch burning. A new "Polish" mother (Anat Topol Barzilai) reluctantly joins her husband and moves in with her mother-in-law after their house mysteriously burns down. The house includes a mute zombie-like butler, weird visiting old people and *Dark Shadows*–style lightning outside the windows. The grandmother keeps taking the baby away, and in a dream, eats a dog. A visiting Catholic father has a burning vision and pukes. This slow-moving movie filmed in California has a decapitation, suicide, and lots of ridiculous false scares.

WITCHCRAFT II: THE TEMPTRESS

(Academy, 1989) **D:** Mark Woods **S:** Sal Manna, Jim Hanson **P:** Megan Barnett, Reza Mizban

This one is a teen movie, complete with rock music, a rock video scene, and teenagers who look like they're in their late 30s. Delia Sheppard is Taurus, the big-breasted blond temptress with a British accent who paints a house while wearing a body stocking, high heels, and dark sunglasses. Will (Charles Solomon) is a boring adopted student. His (virgin) girlfriend (Mia Ruiz), the daughter of a preacher, is attacked by her pillow and has sex with Will's best friend in a dream. Will is really "the supreme warlock," or something, and he's destined to have a son who will rule the world. Meanwhile, his friends are being killed. With Jay Richardson. Flashbacks from *Witchcraft* are used.

WITCHCRAFT III: THE KISS OF DEATH

(Academy, 1991) **D:** R. L. Tillman **S:** Gerry Daly **P:** Holly MacConkey

Charles Solomon (*Witchcraft II*) returns as a young lawyer who doesn't realize he's the son of a warlock. He has to battle a devious stud vampire. This entry in the series has several cliché black characters and some very R-rated sex. The only memorable scenes involve Lena Hall and Lisa Toothman naked.

WITCHCRAFT IV: VIRGIN HEART

(Academy, 1991) **D/S:** James Merendino
S: Michael Paul Gerard **P:** Holly MacConkey

Charles Solomon returns again as an attorney with magical powers. Rock musicians are selling their souls to the Devil, an evil Brit named Santara. Belladonna, a stripper (six-foot *Penthouse* Pet of 1992 Julie Strain) is featured in some of the sex scenes.

WITCHCRAFT V: DANCE WITH THE DEVIL

(Academy, 1993) **D:** Talun Hsu **S:** Steve Tymon,
James Merenoino **P:** Drew Peloso, Michael Feifer

All the featured women are fake blondes in this stupid, cheap-looking, and very confusing sex movie. An irritating, pretentious long-haired "Collector" (David Huffman) takes over a rock club and does a hypnotism act. He makes his new, big-breasted dumb-blond assistant (Nicole Sassaman) seduce "William" (Marklen Kennedy), the guy who doesn't know he's a white witch, to make him help capture souls. Sassaman has several sex scenes (usually on top), and a possessed preacher gets it on with his assistant. Carolyn Taye-Loren has the standout featured sex-in-many-positions-in-the-shower scene (in the unrated version anyway). There are also two girl/girl fights. None of this is suggested on the video cover, which sells it as a horror sequel.

WITCHCRAFT VI

(Academy, 1994) **D/S:** Julie Davis
S: Peter Fleming **P:** Michael Feifer

Some Hollywood cops are after a serial killer, and a ponytailed Satanist with a night club sends a temptress (Debra Beatty) after divorce lawyer and occult specialist Will Spanner (Jerry Spicer this time). Interviews with psychics provide out-of-place comedy, blond virgins are drugged, and Beatty is featured (on top) in the major bathtub fuck scene. One cops says, "This is a big fucking waste of time." My thoughts exactly. Still more pathetic sequels followed.

WITCHCRAFT 70: *See* THE OCCULT EXPERIENCE

WITCHCRAFT THROUGH THE AGES

(MPI, NY Film Annex, 1921) **D/S/A:** Benjamin
Christiansen **P:** Ernest Mattson Sweden (*Haxen*)

Everyone should see this brilliant silent movie about witchcraft. It's a history lesson that at times looks like a Hieronymus Bosch painting come to life. It re-creates 15th- and 16th-century trials and shows how some of the fears persisted into the early 20th century. Scenes of people being tried and tortured are mixed with fantasy scenes (and some comedy). Witches kissing a devil's ass is one memorable vision. The religious themes and some nudity caused the film to be banned in various places over the years. The director (who appears as the big scary Devil) was Danish. He later worked in Germany, America (*Seven Footprints to Satan*), and Denmark. In 1969, Anthony Balch released a reedited version with Jean-Luc Ponty music and

William Burroughs narrating. The narration is priceless, and this is the version people used to see at midnight movie shows. Versions range from a full 128 minutes to only 82 minutes long.

WITCH DOCTOR: *See* THE RETURNING

WITCHERY

(Vidmark, 1988) **D:** "Martin Newlin"/
Fabrizio Laurenti Italy (*La Casa 4*)

David Hasselhoff is a photographer staying in an abandoned hotel on an island with a writer (Catherine Hickland, Hasselhoff's then-wife) who is determined to stay a virgin. Pregnant Linda Blair has nightmares. Her whole family shows up with a real estate guy and a lady assessor to buy the island, and they all end up stranded there, victims of a German-speaking witch (Hildegarde Knef). Lots of bloody and disturbing deaths occur. Annie Ross plays Linda's mom. Her mouth is stitched up, she's hung upside down in a fireplace and burned, and nobody misses (or smells) her! The virgin is raped by a grotesque guy with a bloody mouth, but nobody hears her screams. Witches eat a dead baby and a man is crucified. Despite all that (and a *Sesame Street* tape recorder) this Italian production is still boring. It was filmed in Massachusetts and was called *Ghosthouse II* in England. *Baywatch* TV star Hasselhoff also became a singing star in Germany in the early 90s.

THE WITCHES

(1965) **D:** Luchino Visconti, Mauro Bolognini,
Pier Paolo Pasolini, Franco Rossi, Vittorio De Sica
P: Dino De Laurentiis Italy/France (*La Streghe*)

In between starring in "man with no name" westerns, Clint Eastwood played Silvana Mangano's boring husband in one of the five episodes in this fantasy anthology. Mangano stars in all five. In the De Sica episode, she imagines Eastwood fighting comic book characters (Flash Gordon, Mandrake, Diabolik, and Batman)! Also with Annie Girardot, Alberto Sordi, and Toto. UA released it in America in 1967.

THE WITCHES

(Warner, 1989) **D:** Nicholas Roeg
S: Allan Scott **P:** Mark Shivas UK

A witch plans to give poisoned chocolate to British kids on holiday at a seaside resort and turn them all into mice. The PG-rated fantasy based on Roald Dahl's book is a great children's movie for adults. Anjelica Huston is the Grand High Witch. Two mice kids are the heroes and Mai Zetterling is the helpful grandmother. With Rowan Atkinson (star of the *Black Adder* series). It was shot in Norway. Executive producer Jim Henson and novelist Dahl (who didn't like it) both died just after completion. The US version has a tacked-on happy ending.

WITCHES' BREW

(Embassy, 1978) **D/S:** Richard Shorr
D/E: Herbert L. Strock **P:** Dana Ashbrook

This is an uncredited comedy remake of *Weird Woman* (1944) and the British *Burn Witch Burn*

(1962), which were both based on the novel *Conjure Wife* by Fritz Leiber. Teri Garr stars as the wife of a college professor (Richard Benjamin). She and her friends use spells to help their husbands advance at work. With Lana Turner (in her last role) as a witch and a stop-motion Devil by David Allen. Strock directed additional scenes. The PG feature debuted on HBO after being shelved.

THE WITCHES OF EASTWICK

(Warner, 1987) **D:** George Miller **S:** Michael Cristofer
P: Neil Canton, Peter Guber, Jon Peters
C: William Zsigmond **M:** John Williams

Jack Nicholson is Daryl Van Horne, a sometimes charming Devil with a ponytail in a war-of-the-sexes fantasy comedy based on John Updike's novel. It's not what you'd expect from the director of *Road Warrior*. Cher, Susan Sarandon, and Michelle Pfeiffer are bored women in a New England town (it was shot outside of Boston) who somehow conjure up Van Horne as their ultimate lover. Nicholson becomes a giant, and Veronica Cartwright vomits cherry pits. With Carel Struycken as Omar, Richard Jenkins, and Harriet White Medin. The FX by Rob Bottin and the ILM group are top-notch. The score is on Warner Brothers.

WITCHFIRE

(Lightning, 1985) **D/S:** Vincent J. Privitera
S/P: James Orr

Shelley Winters (who was also the executive producer) is a mental patient who escapes with two friends from an asylum in Texas. She traps a hunter looking for his son and performs witchcraft ceremonies. An ad said: "Not since *Cuckoo's Nest* has insanity been so fun!" With Vanessa Blanchard.

WITCH HUNT

(HBO, 1994) **D:** Paul Schrader **S:** Joseph Dougherty
P: Michael Joyce, David Gale, Betsy Beers
M: Angelo Badalamenti

Dennis Hopper is detective Harry Lovecraft in a sequel to *Cast a Deadly Spell*. Both films are fantasy mystery comedies set in a fictional past where real magic is commonplace, but this one adds politics. This time Lovecraft (who doesn't use magic) is hired by an actress (Penelope Ann Miller) in 1953 Hollywood. Bizarre characters and FX (by Gene Warren) are mixed with a spoof of the McCarthy hearings. Eric Bogosian is an evil senator, Julian Sands is a warlock, and Sheryl Lee Ralph is the good witch landlady. With Alan Rosenberg, Debi Mazar, and drag queen Lypsinka. The HBO movie uses a real Frank Lloyd Wright house for a brothel, and scenes from *The Big Combo*. Gale Ann Hurd was the executive producer.

THE WITCHING

(AEI, 1971) **D/S:** Bert I. Gordon **S/P:** Gail
March **P:** Sidney L. Caplan (*Necromancy*)

Pamela Franklin (whose British accent comes and goes) and her husband (Michael Ontkean) move to a small town that turns out to be full of witches (all under 30) led by Mr. Cato (Orson Welles). Cato plans to use her in an attempt to resurrect his dead son. Welles (with a fake nose) is good despite the half-assed script filled with flashbacks and nightmares. Lee Purcell, Sue Bernard (*Faster Pussycat . . .*), and Harvey Jason costar. Also with a naked man whipped by topless women, a naked woman burned at the stake, and a bizarre time-lapse skeleton scene. Franklin had been in *The Innocents* (1961), *The Nanny* (1965) and *Night of the Following Day* (1968) in England. This 1983 version includes added scenes of full-frontal nudity during a coven (the original was rated PG). The new scenes include Brinke Stevens.

THE WITCHING

(Tempe, 1993) **D/S:** Eric Black **P:** Todd Sheets

A refrigerator becomes a gateway to Hell and a family battles a (black) witch. The very-low-budget horror tape includes some morphing FX. It was made in Kansas City and Ohio.

WITCHING TIME

(Thriller, 1980) **D:** Don Leaver **S:** Anthony Read   UK

Elvira hosts this (censored) one-hour Hammer TV drama starring Jon Finch as a composer and Patricia Quinn as a 17th-century witch in modern day London.

WITCH KILL = THE WITCHMAKER

WITCHMASTER = THE WITCHMAKER

WITCHTRAP

(Magnum, 1989) **D/S/P/A:** Kevin S. Tenney
P: Dan Duncan

Members of a paranormal crew are killed off in a haunted house. A ghost uncle with a missing heart is responsible. Linnea Quigley is a victim, and there's a part-Chinese hero. This movie has terrible acting and some of the worst dialogue in years. By the director of *Witchboard*.

THE WITCH WHO CAME FROM THE SEA

(Unicorn, 1976) **D/P:** "Matt Cimber"/
Matteo Ottaviano **S:** Robert Thom

It's no wonder this didn't play around much. It's very bizarre, pretty graphic and shocking, but star Millie Perkins is so good it rises above most exploitation movies. She's Aunt Molly, a very troubled barmaid who has sex with various men, then castrates them with a razor. We discover why in disturbing flashbacks of her childhood. In one scene she has a mermaid tattooed on her chest by a completely tattooed man called Jack Dracula, played by Stan Ross (*Beyond the Valley of the Dolls*). It's a shock to see Perkins (*Diary of Anne Frank*) running around naked and bloody (years before *Blue Velvet*). In one scene she gets high, ties up two musclebound football stars in her bed, then uses her razor until their blood spurts all over. With Vanessa Brown, Lonny Chapman, George "Buck" Flower, Roberta Collins, and porno star Serena in a party scene. Perkins was in *Wild in the Streets*, also written by her scriptwriter-husband Thom (who died in 1979). She retired from the screen for many years after *Witch* was made.

WITHOUT A CLUE

(Orion, 1988) **D:** Thom Eberhardt
S: Larry Strawther, Gary Murphy
P: Marc Stirdivant   UK (*Sherlock and Me*)

Michael Caine is an actor hired to impersonate Sherlock Holmes, and Ben Kingsley is a brilliant Watson. The comedy features Jeffrey Jones as Lestrade, Lysette Anthony (also in *Jack the Ripper* with Caine), Peter Cook, and Nigel Davenport.

THE WIZ

(MCA, 1978) **D:** Sidney Lumet
S: Joel Schumacher **P:** Rob Cohen

Motown Records backed this big budget G-rated flop disco Oz musical based on the 1975 Broadway musical. Casting 34-year-old Diana Ross as Dorothy was a bad idea. With Michael Jackson as the Scarecrow, Nipsey Russell as the Tin Man, Ted Ross as the Lion, Lena Horne as the Glinda the Good, and Richard Pryor as the politician Wizard. The FX are by Stan Winston. MCA released the double soundtrack.

THE WIZARD OF BAGHDAD

(1960) **D:** George Sherman **S:** Jesse L.
Lasky Jr., Pat Silver **P:** Sam Katzman

A genie (Dick Shawn) temporarily loses his magical powers. Diane Baker costars as the princess. The 20th Century–Fox release features a flying carpet and a magic horse. With Barry Coe. This was released the same year as MGM's *Thief of Baghdad* remake.

THE WIZARD OF OZ

(Video Yesterday, 1925) **D/S/A:** Larry Semon
S: L. Frank Baum Jr., Leon Lee

Chadwick Pictures made this strange version with Oliver Hardy as the Tin Woodsman (and as an evil prince) and Semon as the hero Scarecrow. There isn't much of a story but the characters fight a lot. The Cowardly Lion is a scared black servant in a lion suit. Dorothy Dwan is Dorothy. The once popular comic Semon died bankrupt in 1928. The tape has a jazz score. There were many (now probably lost) silent Oz movies before this, but it was the last version until the famous 1939 one.

THE WIZARD OF SPEED AND TIME

(Southgate, 1988) **D/S/A/E:** Mike Jittlov
P: Richard Kaye, Deven Chierighino

Somebody bets a young FX expert that he can't finish a feature. The PG comedy about making movies was expanded from a short film and includes slapstick gags and animation FX. With Paige Moore as his girlfriend, his real mother as his mother, and Arnetia Walker. Guest stars include Steve Brodie, Angelique Pettyjohn, Philip Michael Thomas, Forry Ackerman, Page Leong, Frank Laloggia, and Jim Danforth. Jittlov did the FX.

WIZARDS

(Fox, 1977) **D/S/P:** Ralph Bakshi

In the post-nuke future everyone is either dwarves and goblins or elves and fairies. Bob Holt is the voice of Avatar. It was Bakshi's fifth feature and was released by 20th Century–Fox. The animator returned with *Lord of the Rings,* another PG-rated fantasy.

WIZARDS OF THE DEMON SWORD

(Troma, 1990) **D/P:** Fred Olen Ray
S: Dan Gordon, Ernest Farino **P:** Grant
Austin Waldman   (*Demon Sword*)

Heidi Payne and Blake Bahner are the stars in a comic fantasy adventure. Lyle Waggoner as the evil Lord Khoura says things like "My dear, I *am* eternal damnation" and captures the "keeper of the blade" (Russ Tamblyn). Lawrence Tierney is a slaver. With Dawn Wildsmith, Jay Richardson, Hoke Howell, and Michael Berryman. Also with stock footage, many lame jokes, and bad stop-motion dinosaurs. It was made in six days on castle sets borrowed from Roger Corman and took three years for someone to release it.

WIZARDS OF THE LOST KINGDOM

(Media, 1983) **D:** Hector Olivera
S: Tom Edwards **P:** Frank Isaac

Bo Svenson stars as the warrior swordsman Kor who helps a boy magician battle monsters. Vidal Peterson and Maria Socas costar in the PG Concorde movie, filmed in Argentina. It also features mermaids. The magician returned in a sequel.

WIZARDS OF THE LOST KINGDOM II

(Media, 1988) **D/S:** Charles B. Griffith
S: Lance Smith **P:** Reid Shane

That boy magician is back trying to save the three kingdoms. The PG sequel features David Carradine as "Dark One," Lana Clarkson, Sid Haig, Mel Welles as a wizard, and plenty of scenes lifted from executive producer Roger Corman's earlier Concorde productions.

WOLF

(Columbia, 1994) **D:** Mike Nichols **S:** Jim Harrison,
Wesley Strick **P:** Douglas Wick **M:** Ennio Morricone

Nicholson was better as a wolf man than De Niro was as the Frankenstein monster, but this glossy major release is better as a publishing-world story than as horror and is more like Cronenberg's *The Fly* than other werewolf movies. The action scenes are all in slow motion, typical of a director who doesn't like action scenes. Jack Nicholson loses his job as an NYC book editor, seeks revenge, and finds love with Michelle Pfeiffer, daughter of the billionaire publishing tycoon (Christopher Plummer) who let him go. James Spader is the weasel assistant who gets the job and the wife (Kate Nelligan). Rick Baker (*American Werewolf in London*) did the FX, but there are no transformation scenes. Elaine May did script rewrites. The publishing house is (obviously) in the Bradbury Building in LA. The 125-minute Columbia release failed to make back its $70-million-plus budget at the box office. A widescreen laserdisc version is available.

"The Woman Who Wouldn't Die" is the story of a girl who twice came back from the grave.

WOLFMAN CHRONICLES

(Rhino, 1991) **D/S:** Ted Newsom

Wolfman, part of a Rhino series of narrated one-hour monster movie trailer compilations, is padded with background on both of the Chaneys and on Dr. Jekyll movies, but is pretty complete in compiling nearly every werewolf trailer up through the 50s. Long scenes are also used from the Mexican *Face of the Screaming Werewolf* and the *Route 66* Halloween special (both featuring Chaney Jr.). Interesting 40s trailers I had never seen include *She Wolf of London* and *The Undying Monster*.

THE WOLVES OF WILLOUGHBY CHASE

(1988) **D:** Stuart Orme **S:** William M. Akers **P:** Mark Forstater   UK

Some girls are in the care of an evil governess (Stephanie Beacham) who commands a pack of wolves and plans to take over an estate. Mel Smith is also in the Victorian fantasy.

WOMAN HUNT

(Charter, 1972) **D/P:** Eddie Romero **P/A:** John Ashley   Philippines (*The Highest Bidder*)

A millionaire (Sid Haig) hunts and kills women in a *Most Dangerous Game* copy. John Ashley, in one of his many Philippines features, is the hero. With Pat Woodell, Charlene Jones, and Lisa Todd as a lesbian wearing all-black clothes. From New World.

A WOMAN IN LOVE

(SW, 1968) **D/S:** Albert T. Viola **S/P/E:** Mathias Sebald **S:** Jerold Brody, Joseph Sutherin

It's hard to figure who the target audience was for this talky, arty b/w drama about psychosexual problems made in New York State. It's pretty confusing and has no nudity to speak of. Some of the cinematography is excellent, though. A man

(Phillip R. Allen) goes to a house in the woods and reads a letter, which leads to a narrated flashback with a fantasy sequence in it. More flashbacks show a little boy with a stick hitting a couple having sex, and it all has a cosmic ending. It features Audrey Campbell (star of the *Olga* movies). Viola later made *The Hot Box* and *Angels Hard As They Come* with Jonathan Demme.

THE WOMAN INSIDE

(Simitar, 1979) **D/S:** Joseph Van Winkle **P:** Sidney H. Levine   Canada

Gloria Manon stars as Holly/Hollis, a transsexual Nam vet, who goes from male to female. The star had a sex change in real life too. The low-budget exploitation feature from 20th Century–Fox was the last for 30s star Joan Blondell (she died in 1979), who plays Manon's wisecracking aunt. Also with Dane Clark as the doctor, and comedians Jackie Vernon and Joe E. Ross. Doris Wishman's much sleazier and more graphic *Let Me Die a Woman* is from the same year.

WOMAN IN THE MOON

(Video Yesteryear, 1929) **D/P:** Fritz Lang **S:** Thea Von Harbou   Germany (*By Rocket to the Moon; Girl in the Moon*)

Lang's last silent feature is historically important for several reasons, but not that great to watch really. International financiers back a trip to the moon. Five plus a young stowaway go, and they fight over gold on the moon. Lang consulted with Willy Ley and Prof. Hermann Oberth for then up-to-date rocket designs. It was made after Lang's *Spies* (1928) with most of the same cast. With Gerda Maurus, Willy Fritsch, and Fritz Rasp. The "complete" version runs 156 minutes. Lang made *M* next.

WOMAN IN THE WINDOW

(1944) **D:** Fritz Lang **S/P:** Nunnally Johnson

Edward G. Robinson is a New York psychology professor who meets Joan Bennett, a woman he saw in a painting. He ends up helping to investigate a murder that he committed himself, drives around with a corpse sitting in the back seat of his car, and is blackmailed by the victim's sleazy bodyguard (Dan Duryea). With Raymond Massey as the DA, and young Robert Blake. The ending might be a surprise in more ways than one. From RKO. The main cast (minus Massey) returned in Lang's *Scarlet Street* (1945).

A WOMAN OBSESSED: *See* **BAD BLOOD**

WOMAN OF DESIRE

(Vidmark, 1993) **D/S:** Robert Ginty **P:** Danny Learner

Jeff Fahey is arrested for murder on a Caribbean island (with lots of American flags). His on/off flashbacks reveal that he was captain of a yacht owned by the millionaire Asby twins (both played by Steven Bauer) and had an affair with the wife of one of them. She (Bo Derek) is "one of America's top models." Robert Mitchum (pretty good, considering) is his defense attorney. In court, Bo (who has one good sex scene on a Harley) has her own flashbacks. Her voice-over tries to explain it all at the end. With a ridiculous scene featuring clowns and mimes. The R or unrated tape was shot around Johannesburg.

THE WOMAN WHO CAME BACK

(SVS, 1945) **D:** Walter Colmes **S:** Dennis Cooper, Lee Willis

A woman (Nancy Kelly) in modern-day New England survives a bus accident and thinks she's a 300-year-old witch. John Loder and Otto Kruger costar in the Republic picture.

THE WOMAN WHO WOULDN'T DIE

(1964) **D:** Gordon Hessler **S:** Daniel Mainwaring **P:** Neil McCallum, Jack Parsons   US/UK (*Catacombs*)

An American man (Gary Merrill) in England kills his rich crippled British wife (Georgina Cookson) and plans an easy life with his mistress (Jane Merrow). A woman is hired to impersonate the wife but the body disappears. The Warner release is

EXPLOITATION

based on a novel by Jay Bennett. Screenwriter and novelist Mainwaring also wrote *Invasion of the Body Snatchers* (1956), based on Jack Finney's novel. With Neil McCallum and Rachel Thomas.

WOMEN IN CAGES
(Charter, 1971) **D:** Gerry De Leon **P:** Cirio H. Santiago   Philippines (*Women's Penitentiary III*)

Judy Brown, Roberta Collins, and Jennifer Gan star in a New World women-in-prison movie. Pam Grier is memorable as Alabama, the whip-cracking, drug-smoking lesbian warden. The women do field work, take showers, are sent to the torture chamber, and eventually escape. It's more sadistic, but lacks the humor and politics in Jack Hill's *Big Doll House* and *Big Bird Cage,* which had some of the same stars.

WOMEN IN CELL BLOCK 7
(USA, 1977) **D/S:** Rino Di Silvestro
Italy (*Love and Death in a Women's Prison*)

Anita Strindberg stars as a mobster's daughter who goes undercover in a prison to clear her father's name. Sybil Danning is the video host. Silvestro also made *Legend of the Wolfwoman* and *SS Special Section Women.*

WOMEN IN PRISON
(1938) **D:** Lambert Hillyer **S:** Saul Elkins

Wyn Cahoon is framed on a drunk-driving manslaughter charge and sent to prison. It happened because her mother, the prison superintendent, refused to pardon a gang member inmate (Mayo Methot). With Ann Doran, Margaret Armstrong, and Bess Flowers. The Columbia release is only 59 minutes long.

WOMEN OF SAN QUENTIN
(1983) **D:** William A. Graham **S:** Mark Rodgers **P:** Stephen Cragg, R. W. Goodwin

Stella Stevens stars in a movie about female guards at San Quentin. A riot takes place on Black History Day. With Debbie Allen, Amy Steel, Hector Elizondo, Yaphet Kotto, Rockne Tarkington, and William Sanderson. Stevens played a similar role in *Chained Heat* the same year. Larry Cohen co-wrote the story for the NBC-TV movie. Some of it was filmed on location.

WOMEN OF THE WORLD
(SW, 1963) **D/S/E:** Gualtiero Jacopetti
S: Paolo Cavara, Franco Prosperi   Italy
(*La Donna del Mondo*)

The makers of *Mondo Cane* made this dated (and overlong) b/w documentary, partially with leftover footage from that international hit. It features the Reeperbahn in Hamburg, Hong Kong hookers, hired mourners in Sardinia, female Israeli soldiers, topless young Tahitian dancers, topless Japanese sea divers, nudists, lesbians (and gays), eye surgery, and breast injections. After all the lighter scenes (complete with comical music), the ending is a real downer. Thalidomide kids are shown, followed by a gory plastic surgery operation. Peter Ustinov provides the often sarcastic narration. It was released by Joseph E. Levine's Embassy and a soundtrack was issued by Decca.

WOMEN'S PENITENTIARY: *See* THE BIG DOLL HOUSE

WOMEN'S PENITENTIARY II: *See* THE BIG BIRD CAGE

WOMEN'S PENITENTIARY III: *See* WOMEN IN CAGES

WOMEN'S PENITENTIARY IV: *See* CAGED WOMEN

WOMEN'S PENITENTIARY VII: *See* ISLAND WOMEN

WOMEN'S PENITENTIARY VIII: *See* FUGITIVE GIRLS

WOMEN'S PENITENTIARY X: *See* WOMEN'S PRISON MASSACRE

WOMEN'S PRISON MASSACRE
(Vestron, 1983) **D:** "Gilbert Roussel"/Bruno Mattei
S: Claudio Fragasso, Oliver Lefait **P:** Jan Lefait
Italy/France (*Blade Violent; Emmanuelle's Escape from Hell; Women's Penitentiary X*)

Laura Gemser stars as a reporter who is framed and sent to prison in a companion feature to *Caged Woman.* Some escaped male convicts take female prisoners hostage. It's a pretty violent, sick movie. Gemser keeps her clothes on this time, though. With Lorraine De Selle and Gemser's husband Gabriele Tinti.

WOMEN WITHOUT NAMES
(1940) **D:** Robert Florey **S:** William R. Lipman **P:** Eugene Zucker

A recently married woman (Ellen Drew) is sent to jail and her new husband is put on death row for killing a cop. Both were innocent. With Robert Paige, Fay Helm, Mae Busch, Louise Beavers, and Kitty Kelly. The Paramount release is 62 minutes long. Florey returned with *The Face Behind the Mask* (1941).

THE WONDERFUL LAND OF OZ
(1969) **D/S/P:** Barry Mahon

Mahon, known for his many adults-only features, made this Oz kids movie starring his son Channy Mahon. It includes musical numbers and miniskirted female soldiers. The characters are the same ones later seen in *Return to Oz* (1985). Both were based on L. Frank Baum's *The Marvelous Land of Oz,* a 1904 sequel book. Mahon made five more pictures for "Childhood Films."

WONDERGUY
(1992) **D/S/P/A:** Murad Gumen

Darnel (director Gumen), a short, often humiliated secretary, becomes a superstrong and superfast costumed hero after being given a serum. Thomas Groves is a nervous, inept, theatrical, vampire-like Warlock who leads a coven of red-robed witches, takes over the local mob, and conjures up a man-in-a-suit monster. This charming fantasy comedy has a cartoon opening (with a theme song), a funny b/w nightmare, a Tor Johnson–look wrestler, and an animated Devil. Ann Osmond costars as a witch. Todd Rutt was the art director, and *Wonderguy* has much of the same triumph-over-low-budget fun as his movie (*Shock! Shock! Shock!*)—and the same effective film stock scratch death rays. It was shot in Queens (and Brooklyn). There's a comic book version too.

WONDERWALL
(Studio, 1968) **D:** Joe Massot **S:** Guillermo Cabrera Infante **P:** Andrew Braunsberg   UK

Jack MacGowran (best known as the Professor in Polanski's *The Fearless Vampire Killers*) stars as an absent-minded professor, disturbed by the music from the apartment next door. This very 60s movie is about literally breaking down the walls. The professor becomes obsessed with the wild things happening next door, calls in sick, and starts staring through a hole in the wall. Soon he's removing bricks, tearing a hole in the ceiling, and imagining that the wall is glass. He sees models posing, bubbles, people smoking bongs and having sex, then some negative results (unwanted pregnancy, an OD). He also sees The Fool, a fashion-conscious group sponsored by the Beatles, and Jane Birkin as a mermaid under a microscope. Mounted (cartoon) butterflies escape. The director tries to be surreal, but *Wonderwall* is a mixture of slapstick comedy and boredom. I guess it's good for the "swinging London" fashions and the music. Most Americans only know of this movie because of the George Harrison Apple-label soundtrack, the very first

Bruce Dern in *World Gone Wild*.

"solo" album by one of the Beatles. The music is piano and mellotron, droning sitar music, and some uncredited guitar from Eric Clapton.

WOODCHIPPER MASSACRE

(Donna Michelle, 1988) **D/S/P/A:** Jon McBride

This amateur Connecticut feature was shot with a VHS camcorder and was inspired by a real local murder. Kids kill an aunt and her son (the wood chipper).

THE WORKING GIRLS

(Charter, 1974) **D/S:** Stephanie Rothman
P: Charles Swartz

Sarah Kennedy stars as Honey, the new dancer at a strip club. Cassandra (Elvira) Peterson is a friendly topless dancer called Katya who gives her advice. With Mary Beth Hughes, Laurie Rose, Solomon Sturges (son of director Preston Sturges), and Lynne Guthrie. The Dimension release was Rothman's first after *Terminal Island*.

WORK IS A FOUR LETTER WORD

(1968) **D:** Peter Hall **S:** Jeremy
Brooks **P:** Thomas Clyde   UK

David Warner stars in a science fiction counterculture comedy. In a fully automated future, all he wants to do is grow mushrooms. He obtains a job at a power station and grows giant psychedelic mushrooms there. The movie ends with all the characters eating them and destroying the plant. Cilla Black plays his wife and sings the title song. Universal released it.

WORLD APARTMENT HORROR

(VSOM, 1991) **D/S:** Katsuhiro Otomo
S: Keiko Nobumoto **P:** Hiro Osaki   Japan

Otomo, who had directed the popular animated *Akira*, made this live-action horror/gangster comedy with a strong message of racial tolerance. Hiro Tanaka stars as a young gangster working for the Yakuza. When he's ordered to evict an apartment of (foreign) Asian immigrants, he faces resistance, hallucinations, and even a monster. The tape is letterboxed and subtitled.

WORLD BY NIGHT

(1960) **D:** Luigi Vanzi **P:** Francesco
Mazzei   Italy (*Il Mondo di Notte*)

Gualtiero Jacopetti narrates a 2-hour-long documentary look at famous nightspots and amusement centers of the world. It was another good way to show some skin. The Crazy Horse Saloon (Paris), the Sands Hotel (Vegas), and the Queen Bee Cabaret (Tokyo) are all represented. Six additional directors are credited for various countries. With Wee Willie Harris, the Chinese Opera Co., Bob Williams and his dog "Louis," and, of course, strippers. It was released by Warner Brothers. *Mondo di Notte Number 2* and *Number 3* were purchased by David Friedman and Dan Sonney. Bob Cresse combined them into one American feature (*Ecco*) and AIP released it.

WORLD GONE WILD

(Media, 1988) **D:** Lee H. Katzin **S:** Jorge
Zamacona **P:** Robert L. Rosen

In 2087, Bruce Dern is a hippie magician who recruits a group to defend a peaceful desert post-nuke community from a crazed religious cult leader, Derek (Adam Ant). Derek's killer followers wear white choir robes and use a Charles Manson book as their bible. The *Seven Samurai*–style fighters include a comic cannibal, a black muscleman, a biker, and an alcoholic gunslinger. People

eat mushrooms and there's a trip sequence and nudity. With Catherine Mary Stewart as a teacher and Michael Paré. It was shot in Arizona.

THE WORLD OF ACID

(VCR, 1967) **D:** Edgar Beatty **P:** Art Lieberman
(*The Hippie Revolt; Something's Happening*)

It's a documentary "written and told by the hippies themselves," and is all actual footage of California alternative lifestyles in 1967. People talking about what's going on and how they feel are heard over scenes of be-ins, love-ins, a "moonfire funeral," and life around Haight-Ashbury. Watching this might make you think the world ended over twenty years ago (see *The Day the Earth Caught Fire* (1961) for some similar scenes) and also points out what normal-looking (short-haired) kids most of these "hippies" were. Not really about drugs at all, this sometimes boring tape leads up to scenes of massive anti-war demonstrations in Los Angeles. Made by a former TV commercial director, it's an interesting artifact and a treasure trove of historical footage.

WORST OF HOLLYWOOD = MANIAC *and* PROTECT YOUR DAUGHTERS

WORST OF HOLLYWOOD VOL. 2 = CRIME OF DR. CRESPI *and* FUGITIVE ROAD

THE WORST WITCH

(Prism, 1986) **D:** Robert Young **S:** Mary
Pleshette Willis **P:** Colin Shindler

Fairuza Balk (from *Return to Oz* and later in *The Craft*) stars in an adaptation of a children's fantasy book (by Jim Murphy) about a school for witches. With Diana Rigg, Tim Curry, and Charlotte Rae. The G-rated movie was made for cable.

WOYZECK

(New Yorker, 1978) **D/S/P:** Werner Herzog
W. Germany

Klaus Kinski stars in the least commercial of his features by Herzog. It's based on the play by Georg Buchner. Woyzeck is a soldier who is abused and kicked around until he cracks and murders people. With Eva Mattes. Kinski mostly worked in France after this. He starred in *Zoo Zero* (1978), *La Chanson de Roland* (1978), *Haine* (1979) and *La Femme-Enfant* (1980), all hard to find in America.

THE WRAITH

(Vestron, 1986) **D/S:** Mike Marvin **P:** John Kemeny

Here's a dumb PG-13 teen/science-fiction/action movie, featuring actor relatives. Nick Cassavetes plays Packard, a sadistic psycho in a cartoonish punk/geek gang of Arizona car thieves, with names like Skank, Gutterboy, and Craterhead. Charlie Sheen is the mysterious hero, who gets to wear a black spacesuit and drive a black Dodge

Turbo Interceptor that can disappear. Clint Howard has an Eraserhead haircut and explains the movie's title (it means a vengeful ghost). Griffin O'Neal gets to say lines like "I'll rip your head off and piss down your throat!," and Randy Quaid plays the local law officer. Quaid was probably cast because he's 6' 5" and is one of the only actors who could seem threatening to Cassavetes (who is 6' 6"). Also with Sherilyn Fenn. You know right away that this is strictly a teen-appeal project, because the characters call each other "dude" or "bro," and keep saying "no problem" and "far out." Every once in a while you also get to hear part of a rock song by Billy Idol, Ozzy Osbourne, Robert Palmer, and others. If we could hear the songs whole and as they were intended, instead of in the background, they might actually make the endless scenes of car races, car crashes, and explosions in the desert seem more exciting. A stuntman died making it. Marvin wrote *Hot Dog* and directed *Hamburger*. The various-artists soundtrack is on Scotti Brothers.

WRESTLING RACKET GIRLS: *See* PIN DOWN GIRL

WRITE TO KILL
(RCA, 1990) **D/P:** Ruben Preuss
S: Miguel Tejada-Flores **P:** Bonnie Sugar

Scott Valentine is framed for a murder and ends up teamed with a lying, swearing Joan Severance as they flee from a bald gangster and his men. There's one minor sex scene, chases, and Valentine, looking extremely ridiculous, "disguised" in leather and studs. With two *Twin Peaks* actors (Ray Wise and Chris Mulkey).

WRONG IS RIGHT
(RCA, 1982) **D/S/P:** Richard Brooks
(*The Man with the Deadly Lens*)

Few people wanted to see this apocalyptic comedy starring Sean Connery as a global TV commen- tator who discovers that the world is being run by the CIA. It's very anti-CIA, -FBI, and -USA and has a very entertaining cast. With Robert Conrad, Katharine Ross, John Saxon, Henry Silva, Leslie Nielsen, Robert Webber, Rosalind Cash, Hardy Kruger, G. D. Spradlin, Dean Stockwell, Jennifer Jason Leigh, Ron Moody, and George Grizzard. From Columbia.

THE WRONG MAN
(Warner, 1956) **D/P:** Alfred Hitchcock
S: Maxwell Anderson, Angus McPhail

This is Hitchcock at his darkest. It's a semi- documentary-style real-life nightmare that was shot on location. Henry Fonda stars as Manny, a New York jazz musician accused of an armed holdup in Queens. Vera Miles is his wife, who cracks under the pressure after he goes to jail. It was based on a real incident. With Anthony Quayle, Harold J. Stone, Nehemiah Persoff, and an unbilled Harry Dean Stanton. Hitch was obsessed with Vera Miles at the time, but dropped her as a star when she got pregnant. He also narrates. From Warner.

THE WRONG MAN
(Republic, 1993) **D:** Jim McBride **S:** Michael Thomas **P:** Chris Chesser, Alan Beatty

Rosanna Arquette is Missy and John Lithgow is her drunken husband. The dangerous and crazed white trash couple are in Mexico when they meet up with a ship hand (Kevin Anderson) who is on the run and is wanted for murder. The excellent sound- track is by Los Lobos. R or unrated videos are available. McBride made *Blood Ties* the same year.

WUSA
(1970) **D:** Stuart Rosenberg **S:** Robert Stone
P/A: Paul Newman **P:** John Foreman

Paul Newman stars as a drunken drifter in New Orleans who obtains a job reading editorials on a right-wing radio station. The station sponsors a big political rally and Tony Perkins plans to assassi- nate a candidate there. The very political movie has a tragic ending. With Laurence Harvey (from *The Manchurian Candidate*), Joanne Woodward, Pat Hingle, Cloris Leachman, Don Gordon, Moses Gunn, Bruce Cabot, Lou Gossett Jr., Robert Quarry, Wayne Rogers, and Diane Ladd. Neil Dia- mond is on the soundtrack. From Paramount.

WUTHERING HEIGHTS
(Nelson, 1939) **D:** William Wyler **S:** Ben Hecht, Charles MacArthur **P:** Samuel Goldwyn

It's the most famous, biggest, and most Hollywood version of Emily Brontë's gothic novel set on the Yorkshire moors. Laurence Olivier stars as Heath- cliff and Merle Oberon is Cathy (and her ghost). With David Niven, Cecil Kellaway, Leo G. Carroll, Donald Crisp, Flora Robson, and Geraldine Fitz- gerald (an Oscar nominee for her role). Greg Tol- and received an Oscar for the photography. Goldwyn had a new ending added with doubles for the actors. From UA.

WUTHERING HEIGHTS
(Cinematique, 1953) **D/S:** Luis Buñuel
S: Arduino Maiuri **P:** Oscar Dancigers
Mexico (*Abismos de Pasión*)

Buñuel's version of Emily Brontë's gothic novel is very different from the more familiar 1939 hit, but well worth seeing. Irasema Dilian stars as Katy the servant girl and Jorge Mistral is Alejandro. A sub- titled version played America in 1983.

WUTHERING HEIGHTS
(HBO, 1970) **D:** Robert Fuest **S:** Patrick Tilley
P: Samuel Z. Arkoff, James H. Nicholson
M: Michael Legrand   UK

AIP released this stylish version by the director of the Dr. Phibes movies. Timothy Dalton and Anna Calder-Marshall star with Harry Andrews, Hugh Griffith, Ian Ogilvy, and Judy Cornwell. The sound- track was issued on AIP records.

WUTHERING HEIGHTS
(1992) **D:** Peter Kosminsky **S:** Anne Devlin
P: Mary Selway **M:** Ryuichi Sakamoto   UK

This version covers the entire novel, told in flash- back. It shows Heathcliff as an orphan brought into a wealthy family. French actress Juliette Binoche stars as Catherine/Cathy and Ralph Fiennes (before *Schindler's List*) is the long-haired Heathcliff. It was partially shot on location in Yorkshire. With Sophie Ward and Simon Ward. TNT aired it in America in 1994.

Nick Cassavetes threatens Griffin O'Neal in *The Wraith.*

XANADU

(MCA, 1980) **D:** Robert Greenwald
S: Richard Christian Danus, Marc Reid
Rubel **P:** Lawrence Golden

This remake of the Rita Hayworth movie *Down to Earth* (1947) stars Olivia Newton-John as a goddess sent to help roller-skating Michael Beck. Gene Kelly costars in the unpopular misfire. With Sandahl Bergman, "Fee" Waybill of the Tubes, Matt Lattanzi, the voice of Wilfred Hyde-White, and some Don Bluth animation. More people bought the MCA soundtrack, which included three Olivia hits (one with ELO, one with Cliff Richard, and "Magic," which I used to enjoy on the radio), than paid to see the movie.

X–15

(1961) **D:** Richard Donner
S: Tony Lazzarino **P:** Henry Sanicola

Charles Bronson stars as an X–15 test pilot in a Technicolor and Panavision feature from UA. David McLean and Ralph Taeger are the other pilots. Only one of them ends up going to outer space at the end. Lizabeth Hush, Mary Tyler Moore (just before *The Dick Van Dyke Show*), and Patricia Owens are the worried wives and girlfriends. Also with Brad Dexter, James Gregory, Kenneth Tobey, and Stanley Livingston. The patriotic JFK-era feature is narrated by James Stewart. It debuted in Washington, DC. It also was the first of four movie roles for future Congressman Robert Dornan (*Starfighters* was his next).

THE X-FILES

(20th Century–Fox series, 1993–   )
D/P: Bob Bowman **S:** Chris Carter

David Duchovny (also in *Twin Peaks*) and Gillian Anderson star as deadpan FBI special agents who track paranormal activity in a Fox-TV series. The series was created by executive producer and screenwriter Chris Carter and is shot in Vancouver. It borrowed ideas from *Kolchak, the Night Stalker* and added in conspiracy theories. *The X-Files* soon had fan clubs and even conventions. The success of this series led Fox to add the sci-fi shows *VR.5* and *Sliders* to their schedule in 1995.

XTRO

(HBO, 1982) **D:** Harry Bromley Davenport
S: Iain Cassie, Robert Smith **P:** Mark Forstater   UK

A father is abducted by aliens. An upside-down alien monster lands on earth and rapes a woman, who then gives birth to a full-grown man. The dad (Philip Sayer) is "reborn" and goes to retrieve his son. Some of the kids' toys come to life and attack people. The awkward "adult" science fiction movie is in pretty bad taste (which could be a plus), but most of it just doesn't make any sense. With Bernice Stegers and Maryam D'Abo. From New Line.

XTRO II: THE SECOND ENCOUNTER

(New Line, 1990) **D:** Harry Bromley Davenport
S/P: John A. Curtis, Lloyd A. Simandl   Canada

Scientists send three humans to a parallel world in a dull *Alien* copy. Jan-Michael Vincent, a survivor from an earlier attempt, is the only one who can maybe save them. A lot of time is spent on a love triangle and characters arguing, and a lot of machine guns are fired. The stomping monster has a tail and screams, and there's a chest-burster scene. I don't know what it has to do with *Xtro*. With Paul Koslo and Tara Buckman. Filmed in Vancouver. *Xtro 3* followed.

THE YAKUZA

(Warner, 1975) **D/P:** Sydney Pollack **S:** Paul Schrader, Robert Towne   (*Brotherhood of the Yakuza*)

An army vet (Robert Mitchum) returns to Japan to try and rescue the kidnapped daughter of his businessman friend (Brian Keith). He ends up fighting Japanese organized crime members. With Takakura Ken, Richard Jordan, James Shigeta, and Herb Edelman. This was the first feature credit for Schrader, who followed by writing *Taxi Driver* and De Palma's *Obsession*. Towne started out by writing *The Last Woman on Earth* for Roger Corman.

YARDBIRDS

(Delilah, 1992) **D:** Martin Baker

I was happy to find this one-hour authorized documentary full of vintage clips and interviews with all surviving Yardbirds members. Some of the live and TV clips from various countries are unfortunately partial, but they go back to 1964 (with Eric Clapton) and you get to see the group with Jeff Beck and Jimmy Page together. "I'm a Man" and "Heart Full of Soul" are high-energy high points, and where else can you see them do "Still I'm Sad" on Belgian TV? Giorgio Gomelsky, Mickie Most, and Peter Grant are also interviewed. Jeff Beck says Antonioni was a "pompous oaf," and Clapton (seen in a brief interview separate from the others) seems like he's one too. Delilah released a similar tape on Eric Burdon and the Animals.

YEAR OF THE CANNIBALS

(1971) **D/S:** Liliana Cavani **P:** Enzo Doris
M: Ennio Morricone   Italy (*I Cannibali*)

AIP released this controversial feature set in Milan after WWII, when the fascist government slaughtered rebels. Britt Ekland and Pierre Clementi star with Thomas Milan. It was "suggested" by the play *Antigone* by Sophocles. Cavani went on to direct *The Night Porter* (1974).

YEAR OF THE DRAGON

(MGM, 1985) **D/S:** Michael Cimino
S: Oliver Stone **P:** Dino De Laurentiis

Mickey Rourke stars as a grim (and not too believable) Nam vet police detective in New York's Chinatown who won't play by the rules. He also has

an affair with a rich Chinese-American TV newscaster (played by model Ariane). John Lone is the main international drug smuggler, and part of the story follows him to the Golden Triangle. You get a pretty insightful look at business as usual in New York City and how drugs end up here, along with some amazing action scenes. The impressive and convincing Chinatown scenes were all shot on sets in North Carolina. With Leonard Termo and James Pax. It was the first filmed Oliver Stone script after *Scarface*, and Cimino's first after *Heaven's Gate*. The 136-minute feature was remastered for the letterboxed laserdisc.

YEAR OF THE YAHOO!

(1972) **D/P:** H. G. Lewis **S:** Allen Kahn

Lewis' last hillbilly movie (after *Moonshine Mountain* and *This Stuff'll Kill Ya!*) was shot in and around San Antonio. Country singer Claude King stars as a southern country singer who is talked into running for senator by some sleazy media criminals from Washington. It was released in "Eye-Popping Color!" during a presidential election year. With Ronna Riddle, *Wizard of Gore* star Ray Sager (who later became a producer in Canada), and Dan Krogh (who wrote the first book about Lewis).

YELLOWBEARD

(Vestron, 1983) **D:** Mel Damski
S/A: Graham Chapman, Peter Cook
S: Bernard McKenna **P:** Carter De Haven

Chapman, from Monty Python, stars as a 17th-century pirate in an unpopular period comedy from Orion. Maybe they shouldn't have hired a director who had only done TV movie dramas. The cast is interesting, though: Peter Boyle, Cheech and Chong, Marty Feldman, Martin Hewitt, Michael Hordern, Eric Idle, Madeline Kahn, James Mason, John Cleese, Kenneth Mars, Spike Milligan, Susannah York, Stacy Nelkin, David Bowie, and Beryl Reid. It was the last feature with Chapman (who died in 1989) and Feldman (who died during production).

YELLOW HAIR AND THE FORTRESS OF GOLD

(Lightning, 1984) **D:** "Matt Cimber"/Matteo Ottaviano **S:** John Kershaw **P:** John Ghaffari, Diego Sempere   US/Spain

Laurene Landon stars as a blond half-breed heroine with a whip who was raised by Apaches in a copy of *Raiders of the Lost Ark* in the style of old cliffhanger westerns. It begins with a b/w sequence of kids at a movie theater and includes bad Mexicans and Aztecs. The Crown release was filmed in Spain, back-to-back with *Hundra* (also with Landon).

YELLOW SUBMARINE

(MGM, 1968) **D:** George Dunning **S/P:** Al Brodax
S: Lee Minof, Erich Segal, Jack Mendolsohn

The Beatles themselves had very little to do with this feature-length cartoon (others provide their voices), but 12 of their songs are used (4 of them were new), and they appear at the end. The then fresh and colorful looking animation borrowed a lot from Peter Max and is based on a Ringo song from the 1966 *Revolver* LP. The movie was a popular hit but the Beatles as fun, G-rated cartoon characters seemed pretty out of date in late 1968 after they had released songs like "Helter Skelter" and "Revolution #9" and John and Yoko had just posed naked on an album cover. The unrelated Saturday morning Beatles TV cartoon show was still running at the time too. UA released the Apple production in America. The next Apple feature (*Let It Be*, 1970) showed the group breaking up.

THE YESTERDAY MACHINE

(Video City, 1963) **D/S/P:** Russ Marker

A guy fixes a car while the radio blares rock and roll and his girl practices her baton twirling in a short skirt. She gets bored ("This is like lostville"), they go for a walk in the woods, the credits roll, two men shoot guns, more credits, cut to the *Daily Sentinel* where star reporter/playboy/hero Jim Crandale is ready for his vacation. But he has to go to a hospital to see the guy who was fixing the car who relates (in flashback) how they were shot at by Civil War soldiers(!), and his girlfriend disappeared. The convoluted, but fascinating, science fiction plot turns out to be about Prof. Ernest Von Hauser (Jack Herman) and his time machine. Herman gives an amazing performance, providing a long scientific explanation of time travel and a ranting pro-Hitler speech (he started his experiments during the war).

His laboratory, connected to a trapdoor in a graveyard, is guarded by two Nazi goons. The reporter teams up with the missing cheerleader's sister, Sandra De Mar, who sings in a nightclub ("Everybody twist!"), and they find themselves in the 18th century. Von Hauser's beautiful black Egyptian slave helps save the day as he attempts to send the baton twirler into the future. The time machine is a chair with a Nazi flag behind it and some flashing lights. Tim Holt, once a famous cowboy star, is police lieutenant Partane, who relates a concentration-camp story. With Larry Buchanan regular Bill Thurman. Maybe this movie was kept out of circulation because people considered it in bad taste. I've never seen anything quite like it and would love to see Marker's other feature, *The Demon from Devil's Lake* (1964), about a space capsule full of animals that mutate into one creature.

YOR, THE HUNTER FROM THE FUTURE

(RCA/Columbia, 1982) **D/S:** "Anthony Dawson"/ Antonio Margheriti   Italy/Turkey (*Il Mondo de Yor*)

Reb Brown stars in a loincloth as the hero Yor in this real silly futuristic action movie based on a comic book. It has spaceships, laser beams, ape men, dinosaurs, and a giant bat. With Corinne Clery (*The Story of O*), John Steiner, Alan Collins, and disco music on the soundtrack. It was filmed in Turkey and was originally a 4-part TV series in Italy.

YOU AND ME

(1938) **D/P:** Fritz Lang **S:** Virginia Van Upp

Lang's third American feature was also his third with Sylvia Sidney. George Raft and Sidney, both ex-cons, marry. Raft plans to rob the department store where he and other ex-cons are hired and trusted, but is discovered and let off. Sidney gives an anti-crime lecture to the gang. It's a unique comedy with Kurt Weill music and some rhyming dialogue. The Paramount cast includes Barton MacLane, Harry Carey, Roscoe Karns, Warren Hymer, and Robert Cummings.

YOU ARE WHAT YOU EAT

(1968) **D/P:** Barry Feinstein **P/A:** Peter Yarrow

One third of Peter, Paul and Mary backed this plotless documentary about be-ins, protests, and groovy Sunset Strip things. It features Tiny Tim singing "I Got You Babe," Barry McGuire ("the prophet of doom"), disc jockey Rosko, and lots of LA scenemakers and hippies. There was a Columbia soundtrack put together by John Simon featuring the Electric Flag, Paul Butterfield, Harper's Bizarre, and David Crosby.

YOU BETTER WATCH OUT: *See* CHRISTMAS EVIL

YOU NEVER CAN TELL

(1951) **D/S:** Lou Breslow **P:** Leonard Goldstein

A German shepherd who inherits a fortune is poisoned and returns to Earth as a man (Dick Powell) to seek revenge. Powell eats raw hamburgers and is attracted to fire hydrants in the fantasy comedy from Universal. With Peggy Dow, Charles Drake, and Joyce Holden, who becomes a horse.

YOUNG AMERICANS

(Live, 1992) **D/S:** Danny Cannon **S:** David Hilton **P:** Alison Owen, Paul Trybits   UK

Harvey Keitel stars as an LA DEA cop in London after some gangsters terrorizing nightclubs. The main one is an American drug dealer (Viggo Mortensen). Craig Kelly costars as the son of a murdered man who goes undercover.

YOUNG AND INNOCENT

(Budget, 1937) **D:** Alfred Hitchcock **S:** Charles Bennett, Alma Reville **P:** Edward Black   UK (*The Girl Was Young*)

Derrick De Marney is accused of the murder of a woman and goes on the run in the Cornish countryside with Nova Pilbeam. She helps him and solves the mystery. This is similar in some ways to Hitchcock's earlier *The 39 Steps* and was based on a novel by Josephine Tey. The memorable ending features the real killer discovered in a ballroom. The director can be spotted as a photographer outside a courtroom. Ten minutes were cut from the 80-minute feature for its US release.

YOUNGBLOOD

(1978) **D:** Noel Nosseck **S:** Paul Carter Harrison **P:** Nick Grillo, Alan Richie

AIP released this anti-drug ghetto movie with Lawrence Hilton-Jacobs as a Nam vet back home in LA. Bryan O'Dell is Youngblood, a member of the Kingsmen gang. It's no relation to the 1986 Rob Lowe hockey film of the same name. The UA soundtrack was by War. Nosseck also directed *Las Vegas Lady* (1976).

YOUNG DILLINGER

(1964) **D:** Terry O. Morse **S:** Danolad Zimbalist, Arthur Hoerl **P:** Alfred Zimbalist

Nick Adams stars as John Dillinger, who goes to jail and meets Baby Face Nelson (John Ashley), Pretty Boy Floyd (Robert Conrad), and Homer

Yor (Reb Brown) and Corinne Clery.

The Young Nurses

Van Meter (Dan Terranova). They escape and form a gang. The b/w Allied Artists feature also stars "the brilliant new star" Mary Ann Mobley, Victor Buono, John Hoyt, Reed Hadley, Anthony Caruso, Gene Roth, Ted Knight, and Beverly Hills. The music is by Shorty Rogers. Adams's next movie was *Die, Monster, Die!*

YOUNG EINSTEIN

(Warner, 1989) **D/S/P/A:** "Yahoo Serious"/ Greg Pead   Australia

This wacky musical comedy was a big hit Down Under, where "Serious" is well known, but a bomb in the US when Warner released it. The spike-haired star plays Einstein, a Tasmanian farm boy. He develops carbonated beer while splitting the atom and invents rock and roll to impress Marie Curie (played by the real-life "Mrs. Serious", Odile Le Clezio). Other historical figures and events are mixed up in a nice-looking movie with a few laughs. It was first screened in 1986, then reedited with a whole hour of new footage. Serious was an editor and documentary filmmaker.

YOUNG GOODMAN BROWN

(1993) **D/S:** Peter George **P:** Robert Tinnell

Tom Shell is Goodman Brown in an adaptation of the Nathaniel Hawthorne story about 17th-century witchcraft. John P. Ryan is the Devil, and Mindy Clarke and Judy Geeson costar. By the makers of *Surf Nazis Must Die.*

THE YOUNG GUNS

(1956) **D:** "Albert Band"/Alfredo Antonini **S:** Louis Garfinkle **P:** Richard Heermance

Russ Tamblyn stars as the peaceful son of a famous gunman who is forced to fight. Gloria Talbott costars with Perry Lopez and Scott Marlowe. Guy Mitchell sings the theme song. The teen-appeal western from AA was the first feature by Albert Band. He made *I Bury the Living* (1958) and *Face of Fire* (1959) next, and much later formed the Media, Empire, and Full Moon video companies with his son Charles.

YOUNG GUNS

(Vestron, 1988) **D/P:** Christopher Cain **S:** John Fusco **P:** Joe Roth

Emilio Estevez stars as Billy the Kid in a popular teen-appeal western. Terence Stamp is a British rancher who hires a group of young men to battle an evil cattle baron (Jack Palance). Kiefer Sutherland, Lou Diamond Phillips, Charlie Sheen, Dermot Mulroney, and Casey Siemaszko costar. Also with Terry O'Quinn, Brian Keith, Patrick Wayne, Cody Palance, and Pat Lee. From 20th Century–Fox.

YOUNG GUNS II

(Fox, 1990) **D:** Geoff Murphy **S:** John Fusco **P:** Irby Smith, Paul Schiff

Emilio Estevez returns in this western sequel, along with Kiefer Sutherland and Lou Diamond Phillips. The sequel (this time rated PG-13) also stars Christian Slater, Balthazar Getty, and Alan Ruck as the other young gunfighters on the run in Mexico. With William L. Peterson as Pat Garrett, James Coburn, Jennifer Wright, Viggo Mortensen, Tracy Walter, Tom Dove, and Ginger Lynn Allen. By the director of *Freejack* (also starring Estevez).

YOUNG INDIANA JONES AND THE CURSE OF THE JACKAL

(1992) **D:** Carl Schultz, Jim O'Brien **S:** Jonathan Hales **P:** Rick McCallum

After three blockbuster Raiders features, executive producer George Lucas took his concept to ABC-TV as *Young Indiana Jones*. A very old Jones (George Hall) remembers when he was a globe-trotting kid (Corey Carrier, then replaced by series regular Sean Patrick Flannery). The pilot feature concerns the Mexican Revolution and a jackal headpiece stolen from an Egyptian mummy. The very expensive show was shot on location. Actors play real historical figures and history lessons aimed at kids are included. Varèse Sarabande released a soundtrack LP. The low-rated series was canceled in 1993 by ABC after they aired 28 of the 32 hour episodes that had been shot, so Lucas moved to The Family Channel. *Young Indiana Jones and the Hollywood Follies* (1994) was the first of the cable TV movies. Sean Patrick Flannery starred.

YOUNG LADY CHATTERLEY

(Lightning, 1976) **D/P:** Alan Roberts **S:** Steve Michaels, David Winters

Harlee MacBride stars as a descendant of the original Lady Chatterley. This originally had a self-applied X and is now available in R and unrated versions. With Ann Michelle and Brett Clark. The director also made *Zodiac Couples* (1970) and *Panorama Blue* (1974).

YOUNG LADY CHATTERLEY II

(Lightning, 1984) **D/S:** Alan Roberts **S:** Anthony Williams **P:** Stanton Korey   (*Private Property*)

Harlee MacBride returns in a story about developers who want to build a nuke plant on the

Chatterley estate. With Sybil Danning, Monique Gabrielle, Alexandra Day, and Adam West (for some ridiculous comic relief). There's lots of sex and nudity in the R and unrated versions. Playboy backed the Concorde release.

YOUNG L.A. NURSES = STUDENT NURSES

YOUNG L.A. NURSES II: *See* PRIVATE DUTY NURSES

THE YOUNG MASTER

(1980) **D/A:** Jackie Chan **P:** Raymund Chow   Hong Kong

In his second feature as director, Chan is an orphaned kung fu student who has to battle his bad brother (Wei Pei). It's a period action comedy with Yuen Biao, Shih Kieh (*Enter the Dragon*), and Wang Ing Sik (*Return of the Dragon*). The Golden Harvest feature was a major hit in Asia. The US TV version has Chan singing the theme song in English but removes the original soundtrack (Holst's Planets Suite).

THE YOUNG NURSES

(Charter, 1973) **D:** Clint Kimbrough **P:** Julie Corman

It's another New World drive-in nurse movie, this time concerning a drug ring. Sam Fuller (!) is a villain, though. The cast includes Jack LaRue Jr., Dick Miller, Sally Kirkland, Allan Arbus, and Mantan Moreland (in his last feature). The black nurse (Angela Gibbs) is involved in a drug orgy on a yacht. The other nurses are Jean Manson and Ashley Porter. Tim Kincaid was production designer.

YOUNG NURSES IN LOVE

(Vestron, 1986) **D/S/P:** Chuck Vincent **S:** Craig Horall

Russians raid the US sperm bank for the sperm of Edison and Einstein in a sex comedy. The all porno star cast includes "Jane Hamilton," Jamie Gillis, Jennifer DeLora, and Annie Sprinkle.

THE YOUNG ONE

(1960) **D/S:** Luis Buñuel **S:** Hugo Butler **P:** George P. Werker   Mexico (*La Joven; Island of Shame*)

A black American jazz musician (Bernie Hamilton) flees a southern town after being accused of rape and goes to an island. A racist game warden (Zachary Scott) lives there with the innocent pre-teen daughter (Key Meersman) of his late handyman. With Claudio Brook as a preacher. Based on "Travelin' Man" by Peter Matthiessen, it was the director's only feature in English and one of his last before returning to Europe. In 1962, it played the southern exploitation circuit as *White Trash* (!). Ads claimed it was "filmed where it happened—in coastal Carolina."

YOUNG RUNAWAYS

(1968) **D:** Arthur Dreifuss **S:** Orville H. Hampton **P:** Sam Katzman

Three teen runaways (Brooke Bundy, Kevin Coughlin, and *Bad Seed* star Patty McCormack) go to Chicago. The ads claimed it was "Torn from today's headlines!" Richard Dreyfuss plays a shifty draft dodger. It all ends with pregnancy, death, and tragedy and has a message that Jack Webb would have liked. With Lloyd Bochner, Lynn Bari, Norman Fell, Army Archerd as himself, and the Gordion Knott. From MGM. The next Katzman/Driefuss look at the counterculture was *Angel, Angel, Down We Go* (1969).

THE YOUNG SAVAGES

(Fang, 1961) **D:** John Frankenheimer **S:** Edward Anhalt **P:** Pat Duggan, Harold Hecht **M:** David Amram

Burt Lancaster is an honest, hard-working assistant DA who tries to find the facts about the killing of a blind boy. The pretty grim b/w movie about New York Italian and Puerto Rican teen gangs was based on Evan Hunter's novel *A Matter of Conviction*. It was released the same year as the romantic and colorful *West Side Story*. Dina Merrill costars with Shelley Winters, Telly Savalas (making his debut as a cop), Edward Andrews, Jody Fair, John Davis Chandler, and Chris Robinson. Lancaster returned in four more Frankenheimer feaures. Filmed on location in New York and released by UA. The soundtrack was on Columbia.

YOUNG SHERLOCK HOLMES

(Paramount, 1985) **D:** Barry Levinson **S:** Chris Columbus **P:** Mark Johnson *(Pyramid of Fear)*

Nicholas Rowe and Alan Cox are Holmes and Watson as kids in an English prep school. They investigate a series of deaths caused by a religious cult. The victims die from hallucinogenic drugs. The excellent FX include a computerized glass knight and animated food. Steven Spielberg was executive producer for the PG-13 Paramount release. With Sophie Ward, Anthony Higgins, Freddie Jones, Michael Horden, and Maurice Denham.

THE YOUNG STRANGER

(1957) **D:** John Frankenheimer
S: Robert Dozier **P:** Stuart Miller

James MacArthur stars as a teenager who is neglected by his rich father and gets involved with crime. It had been done as a TV program by the same star and director in 1955 and was the first feature for both. With Kim Hunter, James Daly, James Gregory, and Whit Bissell. Frankenheimer returned with a look at inner city juvenile delinquents in *The Young Savages* (1961). From RKO.

YOUNG WARRIORS

(MGM/UA, 1983) **D/S:** Lawrence D. Foldes
S: Russell W. Colgin **P:** Victoria Page Meyerink
US/Canada *(The Graduates of Malibu High)*

What seems to be a sex comedy becomes a violent vigilante movie after Lynda Day George is gang-raped and four frat house guys seek revenge. Ernest Borgnine is her cop dad. With Richard

Roundtree, James and Nels Van Patten, Anne Lockhart, Mike Norris (Chuck's son), Dick Shawn, Linnea Quigley, and an animation sequence. The director and producer of the Cannon sequel to *Malibu High* (1979) were both in their early 20s.

YOU ONLY LIVE ONCE

(1937) **D:** Fritz Lang **S:** Graham Baker, Gene Towne **P:** Walter Wanger

The first movie (partially) inspired by Bonnie and Clyde was Lang's second in America. Henry Fonda stars as an ex-con trying to go straight and Sylvia Sidney is his new wife. Both are victims of the Depression society. He's wrongly convicted of a murder, sentenced to die, and put in a scary cell in the middle of a dark room (like in *The Silence of the Lambs*). He kills the prison chaplain and escapes. The classic feature from UA looks great. It was shot by Oscar-winner Leon Shamroy. With Barton MacLane, Ward Bond, Margaret Hamilton, William Gargon, Jonathan Hale, Jerome Cowan, and Jack Carson.

YOU'RE A BIG BOY NOW

(Warner, 1966) **D/S:** Francis Ford Coppola
P: Phil Feldman

For his first major studio feature as director (after several years working for Roger Corman), Coppola made a fun offbeat coming-of-age nightmare comedy. Peter Kastner is the very awkward Bernard working (on roller skates) at the New York Public Library. He tries to get away from his overbearing parents (Geraldine Page and Rip Torn). Bernard ignores the nice girl who loves him (Karen Black) and falls for a crazy man-hating go-go-dancer actress named Barbara Darling (Elizabeth Hartman) who lives with her "biographer" (Michael Dunn). With Julie Harris as Miss Thing, Tony Bill, and Dolph Sweet. Most of the film was shot

on location, and there's a good look at what 42nd St. peepshows were like in the 60s. Doris Wishman's *My Brother's Wife* is on a marquee. The Lovin' Spoonful recorded the soundtrack (released by Kama Sutra) which includes "Darling Be Home Soon" and the title song.

YOUTH RUNS WILD

(1944) **D:** Mark Robson **S:** John Fante **P:** Val Lewton

Glen Vernon and Tessa Brind (later called Vanessa Brown) star as small-town teens who start to go bad while their parents are too busy with the war effort. With Bonita Granville, Kent Smith, Lawrence Tierney, Arthur Shields, Dickie Moore, and Elizabeth Russell. The 67-minute early jd feature was "inspired by" the even earlier RKO movie *Are These Our Children?* (1931). Lewton wanted his name removed after the studio made extensive cuts (including an important scene where a boy kills his sadistic father after too many beatings). It was controversial (and popular) at the time anyway. Some immediate and cheaper imitations were *Where Are My Children?* from Monogram and *I Accuse My Parents* from PRC. Lewton produced *Curse of the Cat People* the same year.

YOU'VE GOT TO WALK IT LIKE YOU TALK IT OR YOU'LL LOSE THAT BEAT

(1968) **D/S/P:** Peter Locke **E:** Wes Craven

Zalman King stars as a young New Yorker failing in marriage, in his Madison Ave. job, and in his search for sex, in a forgotten bad-taste counterculture comedy. With Richard Pryor, Allen Garfield, Robert Downey Sr., Liz Torres, and Roz Kelly. The soundtrack by Steely Dan was issued on an LP years later. The movie was released in 1971, but few people saw it.

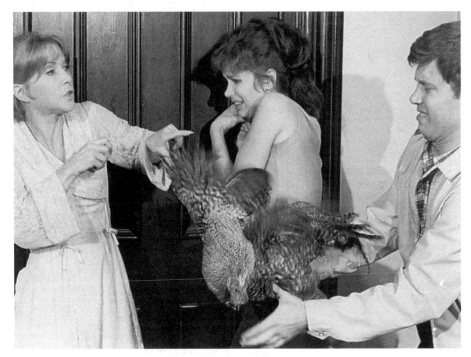

Julie Harris, Karen Black, and Peter Kastner in *You're a Big Boy Now*.

ZABRISKIE POINT

(MGM/UA, 1970) **D/S:** Michelangelo Antonioni **S:** Fred Gardner, Sam Shepard, Tonino Guerra, Clare Peploe **P:** Carlo Ponti

Mark Frechette stars as a college radical on the run from the police who steals an airplane. He ends up with a secretary (Daria Halprin) in Death Valley where they (and many other imagined people) make love in the dunes. It's worth seeing just for the classic slow-motion explosion ending with Pink Floyd's "Careful with That Axe, Eugene" playing and symbols of commercialization floating through the air. The production design was by Dean Tavoularis. With Rod Taylor, G. D. Spradlin, Paul Fix, Severn Darden, and Harrison Ford. The American movie was a commercial flop and a big setback for the director's career. Pink Floyd scored the entire feature, but Antonioni decided to only use three tracks. They're on the MGM soundtrack along with the Grateful Dead and others. The young, non-actor stars lived in a Boston commune together for a while, then Halprin was briefly married to Dennis Hopper. Frechette went to prison for robbing a bank (for political reasons, he claimed) and died in a 1975 prison "accident." From MGM.

ZACHARIAH

(Fox, 1971) **D/P:** George Englund **S:** Joe Massot, The Firesign Theatre

John Rubenstein, Pat Quinn, and Don Johnson star in a GP-rated hippie rock western. The Firesign Theatre, who cowrote it, hated it and disowned it. With members of Country Joe and the Fish and the James Gang (with Joe Walsh), Doug Kershaw, and Elvin Jones. The New York Rock Ensemble (with Michael Kamen) do the closest they ever had to a hit, "Gravedigger." The soundtrack was on Dunhill. Also with Dick Van Patten.

ZADAR! COW FROM HELL

(1988) **D/P:** Robert C. Hughes **S:** Merle Kessler

A movie is being made about a radioactive cow in this comedy made in Iowa by the Duck's Breath Mystery Theater comedy troupe.

ZAMBA (THE GORILLA)

(1948) **D:** William Berke **S:** Barbra Worth **P:** Maurice H. Conn

Eagle Lion made this story of a six-year-old boy (Beau Bridges!) who parachutes out of a burning plane in Africa and is raised by a gorilla. He remembers his real mother in time to save her life in the end. With Jon Hall and June Vincent. It was tinted sepia. Berke was making around a half-dozen movies a year at the time, including many in the Jungle Jim series.

ZANDALEE

(IVE, 1990) **D:** Sam Pillsbury **S:** Mari Kornhauser **P:** William Baylock

Erika Anderson (who looks great and is naked a lot) is torn between a ridiculous, pretentious artist (Nicolas Cage) and her poet husband (Judge Reinhold). The erotic soap opera is even more pretentious than Zalman King movies and is set in New Orleans. With Viveca Lindfors, Marisa Tomei, Zach Galligan, Aaron Neville, and Joe Pantoliano. Available R or unrated.

ZAPPED!

(Nelson, 1982) **D/S:** Robert Rosenthal **S:** Bruce Joel Rubin **P:** Jeffrey D. Apple

Telekinetic teen Scott Baio uses his powers to humiliate his school enemies and see some girls naked in a lame *Carrie* spoof. With Corinne Bohrer, Heather Thomas, Willie Aames (*Paradise*), Scatman Crothers, Sue Ane Langdon, Rosanne Katon, and Jewel Shepard.

ZAPPED AGAIN!

(Nelson, 1989) **D:** Doug Campbell **S:** Bruce Joel Rubin **P:** Jeff D. Apple, Robert Rosenthal

A new kid (Todd Eric Andrews) has the zap powers in this comedy sequel with Linda Blair, Karen Black (in a small role), Sue Ane Langdon returning from the first one, and Lyle Alzado. Rubin (*Ghost*) had his name removed to try and avoid further embarrassment.

ZEBRA FORCE

(Media, 1976) **D/S/P:** Joe Tornatore

White Nam vets wearing masks, and thought to be black, rip off money and drugs from the Mafia. A racial gang war results. The leader of the vets is their one-armed, scar-faced platoon leader who talks with a voice box. Mike Lane, Richard X. Slattery, and Rockne Tarkington star. With some early Rick Baker FX and slo-mo shootouts. *Code Name: Zebra* was a 1987 sequel. The director later made ridiculous horror movies like *Grotesque* and *Demon Keeper*.

A ZED AND TWO NOUGHTS

(Pacific Arts, 1985) **D/S:** Peter Greenaway **P:** Kees Kasander UK/Netherlands (*Zoo*)

Twin brother zoo-curator doctors (Brian and Eric Deacon) are the main characters in a bizarre feature that's similar in some ways to David Cronenberg's later *Dead Ringers*. One brother becomes obsessed with using time-lapse photography to film (real) rotting animals. The other watches documentaries and chews glass. Both of their wives are killed in car accidents and the driver (Andrea Ferreol) loses her leg. They both have sex with her so she has twins. She has her other leg amputated, goes off with a double amputee, and the dads commit double suicide.

ZERAM

(Fox Lorber, 1991) **D/S:** Keita Amemiya **S:** Hajime Matsumoto **P:** Yoshinori Chiba, Kouichi Sugisawa Japan (*Zeiram*)

An alien woman bounty hunter (Yuko Moriyama) with a talking computer tries to recapture Zeram, a big faceless death figure (kind of like the one in

Brazil). Zeram has a small red-eyed female face on its forehead that emerges like a snake (a great special effect). Meanwhile, two comical phone company workers (obviously patterned after the Super Mario Brothers) show up and get involved in the battle in a vacant town. With kickboxing, a small rubbery monster, and an animated skeleton and monster. It's letterboxed and dubbed. *Zeram 2* (1994) followed.

ZERO BOYS

(Vestron, 1986) **D/S/P:** Nico Mastorakis **S:** Fred C. Perry

Teen survivalists holding war games go camping at an empty cabin. They find snuff videos and get killed off in the woods by psycho hunters. With Daniel Hirsch, Kelli Maroney, and Joe Phelan as the killer.

ZERO IN AND SCREAM

(SW, 1970) **D/P/C:** "Les Emerson"/Lee Frost **S:** Howard Edding

A conservative loner (Michael Stearns) becomes a sniper and picks off rich Hollywood hills lovers. He also falls for a stripper at the Classic Cat club. He kills many at a pool orgy, and sex scenes are seen through his rifle sight.

ZETA ONE

(Sinister, 1969) **D:** Michael Cort **S:** Christopher Neame UK (*The Love Factor*)

A secret agent (who talks a lot) narrates a senseless story about Zeta (Dawn Addams), the alien queen having Earth women kidnapped. But first he plays strip poker with blond Yutte Stensgaard. A stripper is talked into infiltrating the alien women, who wear white knee boots, red clothes, and black hats. Tony Tenser was executive producer.

ZIPPERFACE

(AIP, 1991) **D/P:** "Mansour Pourmand"/Vernon Becker **S:** Barbara Bishop

Someone in a serious studded leather outfit kills hookers. The first female detective in a California town (cute Dona Adams) eventually goes undercover. Everyone is a suspect in the who-is-the-killer plot. There's a little bit of sex, some whipping, lots of kicks to the killer's crotch, and one of the worst decapitation scenes in memory. Becker also made the 3-D sex comedy *What the Swedish Butler Saw* (1977), also available under many other titles.

THE ZODIAC KILLER

(Academy, 1971) **D/P:** Tom Hanson **S:** Manny Cordoza, Sam Cantrell

An intro claims this feature is "based on real facts" and takes place in San Francisco in 1969. A narrator warns us that "Somebody sitting next to you or behind you has killed!" We're introduced to a man who could be the famous Zodiac killer. Grover is a balding truck driver who brags about scoring, and sells dope on the side. At night he puts on an outrageous toupee and pretends to be a rich businessman at a bar. Jerry (Hal Reed) is a mailman who raises rabbits. He talks to them and when one dies he cries. He's a nice, handsome, friendly mass murderer. He shoots a couple and kills a waitress (she was serving rabbit stew). He puts on a black hood, ties up a sunbather, and stabs her repeatedly. He kills an old woman with a tire, shoots a cab driver, stabs a man and cuts off his ear, and shuts a car hood on a woman and jumps up and down on it. Jerry kills a *lot* of people (while jazz drums are heard), calls the police, and leaves obvious clues everywhere. Voices speak to him and he rants at home—"Atlantis shall rise again! I am the super zodiac!" In Australia this rare feature was shown as part of a "turkey" series. There are some bad reaction shots, a microphone shadow is visible, and there's a funny scene with a man in a wheelchair rolling down a hill, but *The Zodiac Killer* is actually pretty disturbing and effective. The anti-female dialogue is very hateful. Even comedian Doodles Weaver (!) delivers a woman-hating speech, ending with. "I like them plump and juicy and dumb!" The people behind this movie also made *The Hellcats* back in 1968.

ZOLTAN, HOUND OF DRACULA = DRACULA'S DOG

ZOMBIE 2: THE DEAD AMONG US = ZOMBIE

ZOMBIE 3

(Midnight, 1987) **D:** Bruno Mattei, Lucio Fulci **S:** Claudio Fragasso, Rossella Drudi   Italy (*Zombi 3*)

People (and animals) in a Philippines town are affected by an escaped virus and become zombies. Soldiers and tourists fight for their lives. With Deran Sarafian. This gory movie was started by Lucio Fulci, who had a stroke. He was replaced, but was credited, even though only about "15" minutes of the feature are his. Romero's *Dawn of the Dead* (1979) was called *Zombie* in Europe. The Italian *Zombie 2* (1980) was called *Zombie* in American theaters, then *Zombie 2* on tape. Got that?

ZOMBIE 4

(Edde, 1971) **D/S/A:** Jesús Franco **P:** Karl Heinz Mannchen   France/Italy/Liechtenstein (*Christina; Princess of Eroticism; A Virgin Among the Living Dead*)

A woman (Christina Von Blanc) arrives for the reading of her uncle's will and discovers dead zombie relatives. A scene of the uncle (Howard Vernon) floating through a forest is memorable, but 37 minutes of sex and gore were cut for the American Wizard (then Edde) video release, making it senseless. With Anne Lipert, Britt Nichols as the aunt, Franco himself as the mute servant, and Paul Muller. An alternate softcore sex version was released in France. Video Search of Miami created an ultimate composite version, with scenes from the Spanish, Italian, and both (!) French video releases. The dream sequence with attacking ghouls was shot by Jean Rollin. *Zombie 4: After Death* (Midnight, 1988) is another unrelated Italian feature.

ZOMBIE ARMY

(Tempe, 1991) **D/A:** Betty Stapleford **S:** Roger Scearce **P:** John Kalinowski

An "idiot savant" has flashbacks to 1989, when the Army took over a former asylum. Pot-smoking soldiers discover two people still in solitary confinement and become killer zombies. Shock therapy makes a head blow up. The female sergeant in command says, "This shit makes My Lai look like a salad bar!" The zombie makeup and guitar feedback music is good but all the guts and intestines look ridiculous. It was shot on video in Delaware and Pennsylvania.

ZOMBIE BLOODBATH

(Asylum, 1993) **D/S/P:** Todd Sheets

This gore video features girl-gang street fights, heavy metal music, a *NOTLD*-styled attack on a house, melting people, gut puking, gut munching in a video store, and "850" locals as slow-moving zombies shuffling through Kansas City. A WWII vet and three kids fight to survive in a closed nuke plant, and as one says, "This sounds like a trashy zombie flick to me, not reality!" Lots of local publicity was generated, and there was a theatrical (!) premiere in Independence, Missouri. The 25-year-old Sheets lived in a mobile home with his mother at the time. *Zombie Bloodbath 2* followed.

ZOMBIE CHILD: *See* THE CHILD

ZOMBIE HIGH

(Cinema Group, 1987) **D:** Ron Link **S:** Tom Doyle, Elizabeth Passerelli **P:** Marc Toberoff

The first female students at a formerly all-male boarding school find all the boys very dull. It's because some mad professors have been lobotomizing students to prolong their own lives. The USC film school backed the mediocre horror movie with social satire. With Virginia Madsen, Sherilyn Fenn as her roommate, and singer Paul Williams.

ZOMBIE ISLAND MASSACRE

(Fox Hills, 1982) **D:** John N. Carter **S:** Logan O'Neill, William Stoddard **P/A:** David Broadnax (*The Last Picnic*)

Everybody picks on this movie because Abscam scandal celebrity Rita Jenrette takes too many showers (and sings). I liked it OK while watching it on 42nd St. Some Caribbean tourists in a bus are stranded, people are decapitated, and voodoo ceremonies take place. There are no real zombies, just drug dealer killers. The Troma release features reggae on the soundtrack.

ZOMBIE LAKE

(Wizard, 1980) **D/A:** Jean Rollin **S:** Al Mariaux **P:** David Lasoeur France (*Le Lac des Mortes Vivants*)

Nazis drowned during WWII rise from a lake and terrorize a lot of naked lady bathers. Locals blow up the green zombies in a barn. It was intended to be a Jesús Franco feature, and his regular star Howard Vernon plays the mayor. Director Rollin has a cameo. The American *Shock Waves* (1977) did a better job with the same underwater Nazi zombie theme.

ZOMBIE NIGHTMARE

(Starmaker, 1987) **D:** Jack Bravman **S:** David Wellington **P:** Pierre Grise   Canada

This old-fashioned (minimal sex and blood) horror movie looks like it's from the early 70s. Muscular singer Jon-Mikl Thor stars as a good samaritan killed by hit-and-run would-be rapist teens. He returns from the grave as a green-faced instrument of revenge and kills one guy with a baseball bat through the stomach. Tia Carrere costars and Manuska Rigaud is pretty offbeat as a Haitian voodoo priestess. Adam "Batman" West is a police captain who figures in the bizarre (surprise!) ending. The soundtrack is heavy metal, and the filmmakers had the right idea using Motörhead's "Ace of Spades" for the opening theme. From New World. Thor also starred in *Rock and Roll Nightmare*.

ZOMBIE PARTY

(Plush Pup, 1989) **D/P:** Rodd Matsui, Scott Tanaga, Samuel Oldham

Zombie Party features blood and gore, rap, and blond bimbos who sing (for a long time). The zombies are eventually killed by Budweiser beer. The joke-filled shot-on-video California horror comedy was made for "a few thousand dollars" on weekends. Matsui did the makeup for *Dark Romances* and worked on *Nightmare on Elm Street VI*.

ZOMBIES = I EAT YOUR SKIN

ZOMBIES OF THE STRATOSPHERE

(Republic, 1952) **D:** Fred C. Bannon **S:** Ronald Davidson

Judd Holdren (who also played Captain Video in serials) took over the role of Commando Cody in this sequel to *Radar Men from the Moon* (1951). Aline Towne costars, and an unimpressive Leonard Nimoy plays Nareb, one of the three Martians in funny costumes who hang around in caves with Earth gangsters. Nearly everything about this serial was old, leftover, and overly familiar when released. The jet-pack flying footage is from *King of the Rocketmen* (1949) and the spaceships and robots had been used and reused since the 30s. The 12-chapter serial is on two cassettes. Republic Video also released a colorized version of the condensed feature (*Satan's Satellites*) which shows on TV. Holdren and Towne returned again in a Commando Cody TV series (1953), which was also released in theaters.

ZOMBIE'S RAGE = THE GRIM REAPER

ZOMBIETHON

(Wizard, 1986) **D/P:** Ken Dixon

Some might see this tape as a rip-off, but if you're a zombie fan, it's a painless sampler. Ken Dixon, who later directed *Slave Girls from Beyond Infinity*, filmed the linking segments for this plotless compilation featuring scenes from four Jesús Franco movies, two other Euro zombie movies, and a token American feature. The new arty slow-

Commando Cody (Judd Holdren) in *Zombies of the Stratosphere*.

motion scenes always end up in a movie theater with an all-zombie audience. They're not bad and sort of fun to watch. Most of the old scenes feature nudity, some are gory, and some are pretty funny. The most effective gore scenes are from Lucio Fulci's *Zombie* (1980). The oldest scenes are from Ted V. Mikels's *The Astro-Zombies* (1968). *Fear* (1980) by Ricardo Freda features Laura Gemser, but no zombies. Other scenes are from *Zombie Lake* (1980), *Oasis of the Zombies* (1981), and Franco's *The Invisible Dead* (1970) and *Zombie 4* (1971). All seven titles are (or were) available on their own if you're a completist.

THE ZOMBIE WALKS
(1968) **D:** Alfred Vohrer **S:** Ladislav Fodor
W. Germany (*Im Banne des Unheimlichen*)

It's an Edgar Wallace adaptation with Inspector Higgens (Joachim Fuchsberger) returning to crack the case of "the Laughing Corpse" (a man with a skull and skeleton hands). He kills with a poison scorpion ring. With a theme song called "Feel My Heartbeat" and a gravedigger named Romero. With Pinkas Braun and Siv Mattson. Watch for it on syndicated TV.

ZONE TROOPERS
(Lightning, 1985) **D/S:** Danny Bilson
S/P: Paul De Meo **M:** Richard Band   Italy

How's this for a plot? Some mutant aliens help a group of cliché WWII GIs in Italy fight the Nazis. Tim Thomerson stars with Timothy Van Patten and Art La Fleur. John Buechler provided the cheesy FX, and a lot of machine guns are fired. From Empire.

THE ZOO GANG
(Starmaker, 1985) **D/S:** John Watson **S/P:** Pen Densham

New World released this PG-13 rated movie about teenagers who want to open their own nightclub but have gangster problems. With Jason Gedrick and Ben Vereen.

ZUMA BEACH
(1978) **D:** Lee H. Katzin **S:** William A. Schwartz, John Carpenter **P:** Bruce Cohn Curtis, Brian Grazer

A fading rock star (Suzanne Somers) goes to the beach to get away from it all and becomes involved with a group of teens. With Kimberly Beck, Perry Lang, Michael Biehn, Rosanna Arquette, Steve Franken, P. J. Soles, Tanya Roberts, Timothy Hutton, and Janus Blythe. Carpenter's *Halloween* (also with Soles) was released the year this aired on NBC-TV.

ZU: WARRIORS OF THE MAGIC MOUNTAIN
(1981) **D:** Tsui Hark **P:** Raymund Chow   Hong Kong

This amazing martial arts fantasy was ahead of its time and is recommended. It features non-stop fantasy FX (by American technicians who had worked on movies like *Star Wars*) and was mostly made in a gigantic studio. Yuen Biao stars as the warrior hero, with Cheng Siu Tsou, Lin Ching Hsia, Samo Hung, and Moon Lee. Hark, who had already directed *The Butterfly Murders* (1979) and *We Are Going to Eat You* (1980), gained notice in America a few years later with more realistic movies like *Peking Opera Blues* (1986).

Bibliography

I've referred to way too many books, magazines and fanzines over the years to list but I'd like to mention the many invaluable film reference books from McFarland (especially ones by Harris M. Lenz), Walt Lee's *Reference Guide to Fantastic Films*, *The American Film Institute Catalog*, Crown's books on major studios, the Citadel "films of" series, *Screen World* annuals, Jerry Osborne's *Official Price Guide to Soundtracks*, and *The Bare Facts Video Guide* by Craig Hosoda.

Publications (some defunct) include: *Alternative Cinema, Asian Trash Cinema, Celebrity Sleuth, Cineraider, Confessions of a Trash Fiend, Critical Condition, Dreadful Pleasures, Ecco, Entertainment Weekly, European Trash Cinema, Exploitation Journal, Exploitation Retrospective, Famous Monsters of Filmland, Fangoria, Fatal Visions* (Australia), *Femme Fatales, Film Threat, The Gore Gazette, The Joe Bob Report, Killbaby* (Canada), *M.A.M.A., Monster, The Phantom of the Movies' Videoscope, She* (Canada), *Shock Express* (U.K.), *Sleazoid Express, Spaghetti Cinema, Subhuman, Sub-Terrenea* (Canada), *Trashola, Video Business, Video Confidential, Video Watchdog, Weekly Variety, Westerns All' Italiana,* and many other monster movie magazines and fanzines of the past.

Video Sources

These are just a few of the mail order video companies that offer the widest variety of VHS titles. Write for ordering info and catalogs. See issues of *Psychotronic® Video* for many other reliable companies.

CAPE COPY CENTER 631 Main Street, Hyannis, MA 12601. A good source for rare, out of print, factory boxed horror, exploitation, and sex tapes. Lots of seventies rarities.

MOVIES UNLIMITED 6736 Castor Avenue, Philadelphia, PA 19149. Sells every possible tape of every kind currently in print in America. Their catalog is huge.

SCORCHED EARTH P.O. Box 101083, Denver, CO 80250. Specializes in horror, sci-fi, and exploitation from the thirties through the sixties.

SINISTER Box 4369. Medford, OR 97051. Specializes in horror, sci-fi, and mysteries from the thirties through the sixties.

SOMETHING WEIRD (SW) Box 33664, Seattle, WA 98133. Lots of horror and exploitation rarities but what makes SW unique are the countless soft-core sex and adults-only titles.

VIDEO SEARCH OF MIAMI (VSOM) Box 16-1917, Miami, FL 33116. This is the first place to look for rare and uncut foreign horror, explotation, sex, and music videos. VSOM has subtitled many tapes in English for the first time.

Photo Credits

This page constitutes an extension of the copyright page.

Permission to use photos and illustrations is gratefully acknowledged:

[redacted] Frontispiece photo by Nigel Dickson. *Abby* © American International. *The Adventures of Buckaroo Banzai* © 1984 Sherwood Productions, Inc. *After Hours* © 1985 The Geffen Film Company. *Aguirre: The Wrath of God* © 1977 New Yorker Films. *AIP* © American-International Pictures. *Akira Kurosawa's Dreams* © 1990 Warner Bros., Inc. *Alias the Champ* © Republic Pictures Corp. *Alice Cooper: Welcome to My Nightmare* © 1975 Key Pictures, Inc. *Aliens* © 1986 Twentieth Century Fox Film Corp. *Alone in the Dark* © 1982 New Line Cinema Corp. *Amazon Women on the Moon* © 1987 Universal City Studios, Inc. *American Graffiti* © Universal City Studios, Inc. *American Hot Wax* © 1978 Paramount Pictures Corp. *Amin: The Rise and Fall* © 1981 Intermedia Productions. *Android* © 1982. Photo by M. J. Elliott. *Angel Heart* © 1987 TriStar Pictures, Inc. Photo by George Kontaxis. *Angels* © 1971 New World Pictures, Inc. *Anguish* © 1987 Spectrafilm. *Another Day, Another Man* © Juri Productions. *Apocalypse Now* © 1979 United Artists. *Backbeat* © 1994 Gramercy Pictures. *Bad Girls Go to Hell* © Sam Lake Enterprises, Inc. *Bang, Bang, You're Dead* © 1966 American International Pictures. *Basket Case 2* © 1989 Shapiro Glickenhaus Entertainment Corp. *The Bat Whispers* © 1930 United Artists. *Beetlejuice* © 1988 The Geffen Film Co. *Beyond and Back* © 1977 Sun Classic Pictures, Inc. *Big House, U.S.A.* © 1955 United Artists Corp. *Big Trouble in Little China* © 1986 Twentieth Century Fox Corp. Photo by John Shannon. *Bill & Ted's Excellent Adventure* © 1989 by Orion Pictures Corp. Photo by Phil Caruso. *Billy Jack* © 1971 Warner Bros. Corp. *Black Belt Jones* © Warner Bros. Inc. *Black Caesar* © American International. *Black Samson* © Warner Bros. Inc. *The Blob* © 1988 TriStar Pictures, Inc. *The Blood of Heroes* © 1990 Kings Road Entertainment. Photo by Robert Macfarlane. *Blue Velvet* © 1986 De Laurentiis Entertainment Group. *Boccaccio '70* © 1962 Embassy Picture Corp. *Brazil* © 1985 Universal City Studios. *A Bullet for Pretty Boy* © 1970 American International Pictures. *Boxcar Bertha* © 1972 American International Pictures. *Candy Stripe Nurses* © National Screen Service Corporation. *Cape Fear* © 1962 Universal Pictures Company, Inc. *Cape Fear* © 1992 Universal City Studios. *Captain Gallant of the Foreign Legion* © Television Programs of America, Inc. *Carny* © 1980 by Lorimar Productions, Inc. *The Cars That Eat People* © New Line Cinema. *Cheech & Chong's Nice Dreams* © 1981 Columbia Pictures Industries, Inc. *Cherry, Harry & Raquel* © 1969 Eve Productions Inc. *Chinatown* © 1974 Long Road Productions. *The Christine Jorgensen Story* © 1970 United Artists, Transamerica Corp. *Circuitry Man* © 1989 I.R.S. Media, Inc. *Cleopatra Jones* © 1973 Warner Bros. Inc. *Codename: Wildgeese* © New World Pictures. *Code of Silence* © 1985 Orion Pictures Corp. Photo by James Zenk. *Coffy* © 1973 American International Pictures. *Conan the Destroyer* © 1984 Universal City Studios, Inc. *The Cool Ones* © 1967 Warner Bros. Pictures Inc. *Crawlspace* © 1986 Empire Pictures. *Creepers* © 1985 New Line Cinema Corp. *Crimson Ghost* © 1946 Republic Pictures Corp. *Cry-Baby* © 1989 Universal City Studios Inc. Photo by Henny Garfunkel. *Cul-De-Sac* © 1967 Filmways/Sigma III. *Dark Intruder* © 1965 Universal Pictures Co., Inc. *Darkman* © 1990 Universal City Studios Inc. Photo by Melinda Sue Gordon. *Darktown Strutters* © New World Pictures. *Daughter of the Dragon* © Paramount Pictures. *Daughter of the Sun!* © LPE Inc. *Daughter of the Sun God* © 1963 Hert-Lion International Corp. *Day of the Dead* © 1985 Dead Films, Inc. *Day of Anger* © 1969 National General Pictures Corp. *Dead Ringers* © The Rank Organisation. *Deathstalker* © Concorde Pictures. *Def by Temptation* © Orpheus Pictures. *The Delta Force* © 1985 Cannon Productions N.V. *Demons* © New World Video. *Deranged* © Platinum Pictures, Inc. *De Sade* © 1969 American International Pictures Export Corp. *Desperate Living* © New Line Cinema. *Dick Tracy* © Touchstone Pictures. Photo by Peter Sorel. *Dick Tracy vs. Phantom Empire* © Republic Pictures Corp. *Dillinger* © 1973 American International Pictures. *Dirty Harry* © Warner Bros. Inc. *D.O.A.* © United Artists. *Do or Die* © 1991 Andy Sidaris/Malibu Bay Films. *Dracula* © 1992 Universal City Studios Inc. *Dragon* © 1993 Universal City Studios Inc. *Disaster* © 1976 Columbia Pictures Industries, Inc. *Dune* © 1984 Universal City Studios Inc. and Dino De Laurentiis. *Ebony, Ivory & Jade* © 1976 Dimension Pictures Inc. *Edge of Sanity* © 1988 Allied Vision Ltd. *Edward Scissorhands* © 1990 Twentieth Century Fox Film Corp. Photo by Zade Rosenthal. *Elvira, Mistress of the Dark* © New World Pictures Inc. *Encounter at Raven's Gate* © 1989 Helmdale Releasing Corp. *Enter the Dragon* © 1973 Warner Bros. Inc. *Exorcist III* © 1990 Morgan Creek Film Partners. *Fast Times at Ridgemont High* © 1982 Universal City Studios, Inc. *The Female Bunch* © Dalia Productions, Inc. *Female Jungle* © 1956 American Releasing Corp. *La Femme Nikita* © 1990 Gaumont-Gaumont Production-Cecchi Gori Group Tiger Cinemtagrafica. *A Fistful of Dynamite* © 1971 United Artists Corporation. *Five Fingers of Death* © Warner Bros. *Flesh + Blood* © 1985 Orion Pictures Corp. *The Fly* © 20th Century Fox. *The Fool Killer* © 1967 American International Television Inc. *Force: Five* © 1981 American Communications Industries Inc. *The Fourth Man* © 1984 International Spectrafilm Distribution Inc. *Foxy Brown* © 1974 American International Pictures Inc. *Frankenhooker* © 1989 Shapiro Glickenhaus Entertainment Corp. *Freaky Friday* © Walt Disney Productions. *Friday Foster* © 1975 American International Pictures. *Fright Night* © 1985 Columbia Pictures Industries, Inc. *Full Metal Jacket* © 1987 Warner Bros., Inc. *Get Crazy* © 1983 Rosebud Films. *Ginger* © 1971 Derio Productions, Inc. *The Girl in Black Stockings* © Bel Air Productions. *The Glove* © 1979 Key Pictures Inc. *Godzilla 1985* © 1985 New World Pictures. *Grand Theft Auto* © New World Pictures. *The Greed of William Hart/Horror Maniacs* and *Gremlins 2: The New Batch* © 1990 Warner Bros., Inc. *Guilty as Charged* © 1991 I.R.S. Media, Inc. *Gun Crazy* © United Artists. *Half Human* © Gross Krasne Productions. *The Happy Hooker Goes to Washington* © Cannon Releasing Corp. *The Harder They Come* © 1973 New World Pictures Inc. *Hardware* © 1990 Millimeter Films. Photo by Chris Clunn. *Hello Mary Lou: Prom Night II* © 1987 The Samuel Goldwyn Company. *Highway to Hell* © 1992 Hemdale Film Corp. *The Hitcher* © 1986 TriStar Pictures, Inc. *The Hitchhikers* © 1972 Entertainment Ventures, Inc. *The H-Man* © 1958 Columbia Pictures. *The Hoodlum* © 1951 United Artists Corp. *The Hot Box* © New World Pictures Inc. *H.O.T.S.* © Derio Productions, Inc. *The House Where Death Lives* © New American Films. *The Human Tornado* © 1976 U.T.A. *Inga and Greta* © Independent-International Pictures. *Invasion U.S.A.* © 1985 Cannon Films, Inc. *I was a Communist for the F.B.I.* © Warner Bros. Pictures. *Jackson County Jail* © TBC Productions-I. *Jaws 3-D* © 1983 Universal City Studios, Inc. *Joe* © The Cannon Releasing Corp. *Jungle Holocaust/The Last Survivor* © United Producers. *Just for the Hell of It* © Unusual Pictures International. *Kickboxer 2* © 1991 Trimark Pictures. *The Killer* © 1990 Circle Releasing Corp. *Kill Squad* © Summa Vista Pictures. *The Last Movie* © Universal Pictures. *Li'l Abner* © 1959 Paramount Pictures Corp. and Triad Productions. *Liquid Sky* © 1982 Z-Films. *Lolita* © 1961 A. A. Productions Ltd. *The Mack* © 1986 Charter Entertainment. *Mad Max Beyond Thunderdome* © 1985 Warner Bros. Inc. *Mahogany* © 1975 Jobete Film Corp. *A Man Called Horse* © 1970 Cinema Center Films. *To Trap a Spy* © MGM Entertainment Co. *Manson* © 1973 American International Pictures Inc. *Mardi Gras Massacre* © Omni Capital Releasing. *Master Gunfighter* © 1975 Avondale Productions, Inc. *Matinee* © 1993 Universal City Studios, Inc. *Mondo Cane/Mondo Cane 2* © Cinemation Industries. *Mondo New York* © 1988 4th and Broadway Films. Photo by Daniel Root. *The Mongols* © 1962 Colorama Features Inc. *The Monster Squad* © Taft Entertainment Pictures/Keith Barish Productions. *Mudhoney* © Delta Films, Inc. *Murphy's Law* © 1986 Cannon Films, Inc. *My Brother's Wife* © Jer Pictures Inc. *My Science Project* © 1985 Touchstone Films. *The Naked Cage* © 1985 The Cannon Group, Inc. *Naked Lunch* © 1991 Twentieth Century–Fox. Photo by Attila Dory. *Naked under Leather* © Claridge Pictures. *The Naked Venus* © Howco International. *Neon City* © 1992 Vidmark Entertainment. *Night Angel* © 1989 Night Angel Partners. *A Nightmare on Elm Street 3: Dream Warriors* © 1987 New Line Cinema Corp. *Night of Bloody Horror* © 1969 Taste of Blood Corp. *Night of the Living Dead* © 1990 Columbia Pictures Industries, Inc. *Night of the Strangler* © 1973 Howco Pictures. *1990: The Bronx Warriors* © United Film Distribution Co. *1,000 Convicts and a Woman* © American International. *Palisades High* © Crown International Pictures. *Pee-wee's Big Adventure* © 1985 Warner Bros. Inc. *Penitentiary 3* © 1987 Cannon Films, Inc. *The Phantom of the Opera* courtesy of the Academy of Motion Picture Arts and Sciences. *The Phenix City Story* © Allied Artists. *Pink Floyd—The Wall* © 1982 MGM/UA Entertainment Co. *Pink Motel* © 1982 New Image Releasing. *Please Don't Touch Me!* © Ron Ormond Enterprises. *Point Blank* © 1967 Metro-Goldwyn-Mayer, Inc. *Point of No Return* © 1993 Warner Bros. *Poltergeist II* © 1986 MGM Entertainment Co. *Poor White Trash* © 1957 United Artists Corp. *Purple Rain* © 1984 Warner Bros., Inc. *The Quiet Earth* © 1985 Mr. Yellowbeard Productions Ltd. *Raising Arizona* © 1987 Circle Films Inc. Photo by Melinda Sue Gordon. *Ramar of the Jungle* © Arrow Pictures Inc. *Red Dawn* © 1984 United Artists Corp. *Red Sun* © 1972 National General Pictures. *Reefer Madness* © 1972 New Line Cinema Corp. *Reform School Girls* © 1986 New World Pictures. *Repo Man* © 1984 Universal City Studios Inc. *Reservoir Dogs* © 1992 Miramax Films. *Return of the Killer Tomatoes* © New World Video. *Return of the Living Dead* © 1985 Orion Pictures Corp. Photo by Rory Flynn. *River's Edge* © 1987 Island Pictures. *Street Corner* © Wilshire Pictures. *Roadside Prophets* © Fine Line Features. Photo by Merrick Morton. *Robocop* © 1987 Orion Pictures Corp. Photo by S. Karin Epstein. *Rocky IV* © 1985 United Artists Corp. *Roller Boogie* © 1979 United Artists Corp. *The Ruling Class* © 1972 United Artists Corp. *Santa Claus* © 1970 K. Gordon Murray Productions. *Satan's Bed* © Prometheus Ventures. *Scanners II* © 1991 Triton Pictures. *Scum of the Earth* © Box Office Spectaculars, Inc. *The Silence of the Lambs* © 1990 Orion Pictures Corp. *Single White Female* © 1992 Columbia Pictures Industries, Inc. *Shaft* © 1972 Metro-Goldwyn-Mayer, Inc. *Shakes the Clown* © 1991 I.R.S. Media Inc. *Showdown In Little Tokyo* © 1991 Warner Bros. Inc. *Skatetown U.S.A.* © 1978 Columbia Pictures Industries, Inc. *Slaughter* © American International. *Slaughter's Big Rip Off* © 1973 American International. *Slaughterhouse* © 1988 Charter Entertainment. *The Snake Woman* © 1961 United Artists Corp. *Soul Vengeance* © Crown International Pictures. *Starlet* © 1969 Entertainment Ventures, Inc. *Stacey!* © 1973 New World Pictures. *The Stepfather* © 1986 ITC Productions. *Street Trash* © 1987 Lightning Pictures. *Student Teachers* © 1973 New World Pictures. *Sugar Cookies* © 1972 General Film Corp. *Summer School Teachers* © New World Pictures. *Super Soul Brother* © Mirror Releasing. *The Super Stooges* © 1976 21st Century Distribution. *Superstar* © 1990 Aries Film. *Sweet Savior* © Trans-World Attractions, Corp. *Take A Hard Ride* © 1975 20th Century–Fox Film Corp. *Tales from the Crypt* © Universal City Studios Inc. *Tango and Cash* © 1989 Warner Bros. Inc. *A Taste of Hell* © Boxoffice International. *Taxi Driver* © 1976 Columbia Pictures Industries, Inc. *That Tennessee Beat* © 1966 20th Century–Fox Film Corp. *They Live* © 1988 Universal City Studios Inc. *Three Dimensions of Greta* © Dimension General. *Freaks* © 1932 MGM. *Tightrope* © 1984 Warner Bros. Inc. *TNT Jackson* © New World Pictures. *Tower of the Screaming Virgins* © Maron Films Ltd. *Toxic Avenger* © Troma Films. *Trader Hornee* courtesy of Central Park Media *Tremors* © MCA/Universal. *Trespass* © 1993 Universal City Studios. Photo by Sam Emerson. *Trip with the Teacher* © 1974 Crown International. *Truck Turner* © American International. *UHF* © 1989 Orion Pictures Corp. *Uncle Tom's Cabin* © 1969 KBA. *Unearthly Stranger* © 1964 American International Pictures. *Unholy Rollers* © American International. *The Unholy Three* © 1925 MGM. *Unnatural* © DCA. *Vamp* © 1986 New World Pictures. Photo by Douglas Kirkland. *Vertigo* © 1958 Paramount Pictures Corp. *The Video Dead* © 1987 Embassy Home Entertainment. *Videodrome* © 1983 Universal City Studios. *Viridiana* © Kingsley International. *Vixen!* © 1968 Eve Productions, Inc. *Voodoo Black Exorcist* Donald L. Velde Inc. *Walking Tall* © 1974 American International Pictures. *Walk the Walk* © 1970 Hallmark Attraction. *The Warriors* © 1979 Paramount Pictures Corp. *Weird Science* © 1984 Universal City Studios. *Werewolf* © 1987 Fox Broadcasting Company. *West Side Story* © 1961 United Artists. *What Do You Say to a Naked Lady?* © 1970 United Artists. *Wild At Heart* © 1990 PolyGram Filmproduktion GmbH. *The Woman Who Wouldn't Die* © Warner Bros. *Women in Cages* © New World Pictures. *World Gone Wild* © 1987 Apollo Pictures Inc. *The Wraith* © 1986 Turbo Productions, Inc. *Yor* © 1983 Columbia Pictures Industries, Inc. *The Young Nurses* © 1973 New World Pictures Inc. *You're a Big Boy Now* © 1966 Seven Artists Associated Corp. *Zombies of the Stratosphere* © 1952 Republic Pictures Corp.

Stills and illustrations are from the author's own collection, from Tom Rainone, or from Hollywood Book and Poster.

INDEX

643

644